# FASCISM: A READER'S GUIDE

104

# FASCISM
## A READER'S GUIDE

Analyses, Interpretations, Bibliography

Edited by Walter Laqueur

WILDWOOD HOUSE

First published in 1976 by Wildwood House Limited
First published in paperback in 1978 by Penguin Books Limited

Reprinted in 1988 by
Wildwood House Limited
Gower House
Croft Road
Aldershot
Hants GU11 3HR
England


ISBN 0 7045 0190 2

Printed in Great Britain at the
University Press, Cambridge

# Contents

# Preface

Despite the three decades that have passed since the end of the second world war, fascism remains a subject of much heated argument. In daily usage it is hurled as an invective against political enemies. It is frequently invoked in the media; in the universities it attracts more students of history and political science than almost any other subject; and on the loftiest level, it has become the topic of metaphysical speculation. It also continues to be a subject of controversy, partly because it collides with so many preconceived ideological notions, partly because generalizations are made difficult by the fact that there was not one fascism but several fascisms. While these fascisms have certain features in common, the differences between them are not negligible. It would be surprising if there were unanimity on such issues as the relevance of ideology to the understanding of fascism, its social character, the importance of the leader, to name but a few aspects; many issues more distant in history remain unresolved to this day.

If much remains to be explored and agreed upon, much has been achieved and the present volume aims at presenting an interim balance sheet of fifty years of the study of fascism. One book cannot replace libraries, but it can at the very least distil some of the accumulated wisdom and point to areas of particular importance. The contributors to this volume discuss the work that has been done in the field, thus providing a guide to further study and reflection. The essays point to the main issues that have emerged, the arguments and counter-arguments that have been voiced, and they try, whenever possible, to take the interpretation of various aspects of fascism a few steps further. It provides a synopsis of the work in the field done hitherto, discusses the important studies published since the 1920s, including the most up-to-date work, and at the same time identifies the main problems that have arisen and have led to discussion among students of twentieth-century history. Thus it provides on the one hand a reference work summarizing previous research in the field and at the same time it is an original work of synthesis and new interpretation. Lastly, it indicates lines of future research. It is one of the first works on fascism to look at many aspects of the phenomenon. Among the contributors are historians, political scientists, sociologists, economists, and a psychoanalyst. The contributors are recognized as leading authorities in their field.

This project was organized and supported by the *Institute of Contemporary History and Wiener Library*. Our thanks are also due to *Stiftung Volkswagenwerk* for its generous financial assistance.

W. L.

# Notes on Contributors

KARL DIETRICH BRACHER is Professor of Political Science and Contemporary History at the University of Bonn. His publications include *Die Auflösung der Weimarer Republik* (1971), *Die nationalsozialistische Machtergreifung* (1962), *Deutschland zwischen Demokratie und Diktatur* (1964), *The German Dictatorship* (1970), *The German Dilemma* (1975) and *The Crisis of Europe* (forthcoming).

FRANCIS L. CARSTEN is Masaryk Professor of Central European History at the University of London. He is the author of *Reichswehr und Politik 1918-1933* (1964), *The Rise of Fascism* (1967) and *Revolution in Central Europe 1918-1919* (1972).

WILLIAM CARR is a Fellow of the Royal Historical Society and Reader in Modern History at the University of Sheffield. He is the author of *A History of Germany 1815-1945* (1969) and other studies.

ALISTAIR HENNESSY is Professor of History and Chairman of the Joint School of Comparative American Studies at the University of Warwick. His publications include *The Federal Republic of Spain, 1868-74* and *Modern Spain*.

JUAN J. LINZ is Professor of Sociology and Political Science at Yale University. He is Chairman of the Committee on Political Sociology, Research Committee of the International Sociological Association and the International Political Science Association.

ADRIAN LYTTELTON is Senior Research Fellow at St. Antony's College, Oxford. His publications include *The Seizure of Power: Fascism in Italy 1919-1929* (1973).

ALAN S. MILWARD is Professor of European Studies at the University of Manchester Institute of Science and Technology and is the author of *The German Economy at War* and other books.

HANS MOMMSEN is Professor of Modern History at the Ruhr-Universitaet Bochum. His publications include *Die Sozialdemokratie und die Nationalitaetenfragen im Habsburgischen Vielvoelkerstaat* (1963) and *Beamtentum im Dritten Reich* (1966).

STANLEY G. PAYNE is Professor of History at the University of Wisconsin and the author of *Falange: A History of Spanish Fascism* (1961), *Politics and the Military in Modern Spain* (1967) and other studies.

ZEEV STERNHELL is Senior Lecturer in Political Theory at the Hebrew University, Jerusalem and the author of *Maurice Barrès et le Nationalisme français* (1972).

BELA VAGO is Professor of General History at the University of Haifa and is the author of several books on the political and social problems of Central and East European countries.

EUGEN WEBER is Professor of History at UCLA and is the author of *Action Française, Varieties of Fascism*, with Hans Rogger, *The European Right*, and *Peasants into Frenchmen. The Modernization of Rural France 1870-1914*.

# PART I

# 1

# Some Notes Toward a Comparative Study of Fascism in Sociological Historical Perspective

JUAN J. LINZ

## INTRODUCTION

When Lipset and Rokkan published their *Party Systems and Voter Alignments,* they made little effort to place the fascist movement in their comprehensive model of social cleavages and the emergence of the European party system.[1] It could be argued that there was no need to do so since fascist parties have not survived with any significant strength in post-second world war Europe, and they were unable to conquer permanently any distinctive social base comparable to those of socialist, communist, Christian Democratic, conservative and north European farmer parties. They rightly emphasize that at some point in the twenties there was a freezing of the major party alternatives in the wake of the extension of suffrage and the mobilization of major reservoirs of new potential supporters. Even further, the party systems of the 1960s reflect with few but significant exceptions the cleavage structures of the 1920s. 'A crucial characteristic of Western competitive politics in the age "of high mass consumption" [is that] the party alternatives, and in remarkably many cases the party organizations, are older than the majorities of the national electorates. To most of the citizens of the west the currently active parties have been part of the political landscape since their childhood or at least since they were first faced with the choice between alternative "packages" on election day.'[2] Certainly, there have been important shifts between the old socialist bases and the strengthened communist parties after the second world war, and from many conservative and liberal bourgeois parties to the strengthened Christian Democratic parties. However, between 1918 and 1945, the party system that had started to crystallize in the first elections after the first world war, if not earlier, was confronted by the more or less successful competition of fascist movements. Many of their supporters had been voters and even members of other parties and after the defeat of fascism would again turn to other banners. Does this mean that fascism did not have, in contrast to other parties, a distinctive social base? Was it only

a conjunctural phenomenon, perhaps attracting supporters from a heterogeneous social base largely on the basis of generational cleavages rather
than on account of structural characteristics? This might be the clue why a
strictly sociological analysis of fascism fails when compared to other political movements. Obviously, it could also be argued that fascism was displaced from the political scene, not only by its failure to satisfy the expectations of many of its supporters but by the monstrosity of its rule, particularly in the case of nazism, and ultimately by its involvement in the war and
its defeat in 1945. Certainly, fascism did not experience a slow and continuous growth in opposition and power, in competition with other
political forces but, by its own nature, aimed at gaining power revolu-
tionarily or by coup d'état and thereby losing its character of 'a party
among other parties,' attempting instead to be a representation of the
whole national community rather than of particular social strata. As an
official party, either ruling totalitarianally or as part of an authoritarian
regime and, in many cases, linked with a foreign occupier, such parties
could not build up a distinctive social base.

## Fascism, a latecomer on the political scene

For an understanding of fascist movements it is essential to note that they
were latecomers on the political scene, at a time when, in most countries,
the party system had already crystallized. The different sectors of society
had identified with particular political options and with the organizations
of different parties, trade unions, and associated interest groups had penetrated the social structure. This meant that irrespective of the intentions of
their leadership, their ideological and programmatic appeals, and their
ambition to represent particular social strata, their success was largely pre-
empted. Contemporary political sociology has shown how strong party
loyalty is despite changes in the political outlook of parties, changes in the
social structure, and even policy reversals and failures. In our view, it is
essential to remember that fascist parties, more often than not, could not
gain the support of the social groups to which they directed their appeal
and that, therefore, they were often forced to appeal, integrate, and represent social forces with which, in terms of the initial ideological commitments, we might not have expected them to become strongly identified.[3] It
also meant that in many countries they remained minority movements with
little or no electoral appeal. In many cases only the strength of the commitment of their minority following, the new forms of political organization
and tactics that gave them an advantage in the struggle for power by violent means rather than ballots, made them successful contenders for
power. Moreover, in several cases only the vagaries of war and foreign help
gave their leaders an opportunity to play their tragic role on the political
scene.

The fact that fascism is a latecomer helps to explain, in part, the essential anti-character of its ideology and appeal. Undoubtedly, fascism was much more than an anti-this or anti-that movement (a point to which we shall turn later). Its distinctiveness lies in its style and in its confused vision of the future which it in many respects incorporated, transforming elements present in other ideologies and movements. The various 'antis' of fascism served to define its identity in contrast to other parties and to appeal to the supporters of one or another on the basis of being more militantly against others. It is paradoxical that for each rejection there was also an incorporation of elements of what they rejected. This largely accounts for the heterogeneous following in the initial group of fascists, and the fact that many of its initial cadres were recruited among men who had been active in other parties and even gained pre-eminence in their leadership (the Nazis were an exception in this). It also meant that those men, when they failed in their efforts to carry along support from the constituencies in which they had risen, turned to other social strata and became bitterly hostile not only to their former comrades but also to the social forces that continued following them. In this perspective, the turn toward middle and upper classes, the willingness to enter into collusion or coalition with conservative, bourgeois, and capitalist interests is not so much a reflection of the ideological initial commitment and goals of the leaders but of their failure to gain working class and sometimes any support. So it becomes understandable that leaders with a relatively similar ideology and style should have found echoes in terms of party membership and electoral support in quite different social strata in the various countries. As a latecomer with a large number of 'anti' appeals and an ideological hope to integrate the whole nation, overcoming the cleavages created in modern society and expressed through modern parties, their social bases and relative success would depend more than any other type of political movement on the particular historical constellation of social and political forces in each country. This would be particularly true when we go beyond the initial founding nucleus, when they became mass organizations, in their electoral bases and the kind of alliances they were able to make in the effort to take power. This accounts for the often quite different social compositions of the initial founding nucleus, the activists particularly in the paramilitary organizations, the electorate, and finally the support for the parties in power or the coalition in which they participated under authoritarian rule.

Fascist movements, in their ideological and pragmatic eclecticism and their effort to appeal to all strata, were a prefiguration of the post-second world war catch-all party described by Otto Kirchheimer.[4] Perhaps the greater rigidity of the social structure inherited from the nineteenth century, the greater faith in ideology in the twenties, and the fixation on the urban proletariat as the class of the future among most Marxists made such an attempt appear unprincipled and unviable and only possible in an authoritarian framework. With different points of gravity in institutional bases, Christian democracy and social democratic parties have now become such parties of broad integration — *Volksparteien* — electorally, if not in their membership. Even communists have learned from the fascist experience the importance of appealing to various lower-middle-class sectors, including even the old middle class which had no future in the nineteenth-century Marxian view of social evolution. A more fluid social structure, the exhaustion of ideological passion, the needs of national reconstruction in post-fascist Europe made programmatically eclectic heterogeneous parties possible and successful.

Any comparative study of fascist movements has to focus on the unique historical constellation of forces in each country at the time of the founding of the party and in the course of its struggle for support and power. This is true for any party but more so for fascism, due to its nationalistic character and to its being a latecomer. Other parties emerged from the cleavages and tensions basically common with varying intensities to all western societies or particular groups of western societies. There is no question that in most countries the basic parties emerged to some extent independently but in close succession, even when the ideological formulations that acquired particular clarity and success in some of them rapidly diffused in others. Liberalism had appeared in the wake of the French Revolution with the emergence and strengthening of the bourgeoisie in many countries, linking more or less explicitly with the traditions of the Enlightenment, Jacobinism, and English constitutionalism. In response to it with varying strength, conservative ideologies and parties, even reactionary movements made their appearance, often linking with feudal agrarian and precapitalist social structures.

Undoubtedly there were important national variations in the degree to which the religious and secularizing sentiments became identified with conservatism and liberalism, and contributed to the factional splits within those parties. There were also differences in the degree to which the national identity, the nation-building forces, became identified with conservatives or liberals and in some cases with the bourgeois left. Industrialization in all countries led to the organization of trade unions or workingmen's associations, which in some cases could link with the left wings of the liberal bourgeoisie but in most countries soon led to the emergence of proletarian parties with one or another socialist ideology. Only in a few cases was the working-class protest led into anarchist and later anarcho-syndicalist movements. The threat of a more or less secularizing liberalism and an anti-clerical and even anti-religious working class revolutionary movement, Marxist or anarchist, in Catholic countries, soon produced a reaction in the form of Catholic conservative or Christian Democratic parties. They very often emerged without the blessing of the hierarchy of the

Church which was still linked to the state and the monarchical establishment. But the response of the Papacy to those two threats in the encyclicals, particularly of Leo XIII's *Rerum Novarum*, and the creation of a Catholic lay movement gave to those parties a common orientation. The peasant and farmers' parties in the less industrialized countries (in which, in addition a state church did not mobilize the peasant masses as did the Catholic church) responded to a greater extent to unique national constellations of forces. Even so, soon an international of peasant parties appeared in eastern and southeastern Europe. Only the regional nationalist parties on the peripheries of unintegrated states rather than nations, empires rather than modern nation-states, did not have a distinct and comparable social base nor in many cases an ideology shared across the borders, and this accounts for the fact that they could be conservative, clerical, republican Jacobin, peasantist, and even incipiently socialist. It is no accident that some of the peripheral nationalisms would develop considerable affinity with fascism; that in Eastern Europe integral nationalism would often be fascist or quasi-fascist.[5] The party system on the eve of or in the first election after the first world war responded to common structural characteristics of European societies and based its appeal on ideologies diffused across borders from a few centres of ideological creativity.

Fascism was the novel response to the crisis — profound or temporary — of the pre-war social structure and party system and to the emergence of new institutional arrangements as a result of war and post-war dislocations. It would be particularly acute in defeated nations, in those which were divided about entry into the war and disappointed with the fruits of victory, such as Italy, and those countries where the crisis led to unsuccessful revolutionary attempts. Fascism would be a counter-revolutionary response led by a revolutionary elite. To paraphrase Borkenau's characterization of the Communist party[6] as a party of revolutionaries linked with the proletariat, we could define fascism as a party of revolutionaries linked with the middle classes of city and/or countryside.

When fascism appeared on the scene first in Italy, it had to attempt to find its place within this already largely pre-empted political space. It was a unique response to the particular Italian situation and for some time fascists themselves and scholars studying the movement attempted to understand it from that distinctive Italian perspective.[7] However, similar strains existed in other European societies and led to the emergence in the early twenties of similar movements which in their nationalism attempted to emphasize their links with the historical past of their country and with the unique problems faced by their states and societies in a post-Versailles world. Soon, however, like other parties before them, they turned to the most successful of them, Italian fascism, and later to the even more successful National Socialists for inspiration and guidance. In this way, paradoxically, fascism that was ultra-nationalist turned also into an international movement, like those whose internationalism the fascists rejected.[8] However, in contrast to those other parties, which reflected some of the common social structure characteristics of European societies, fascists in their goal of representing the whole national community, integrating all classes, overcoming class conflict, and appealing to former supporters of old parties on account of common national interests in conflict with other societies or with groups defined as alien such as the Jews, would be ultimately less comparable in their social support. Their success would range widely from a mass electorate in Germany to almost insignificant groups in many countries.

The Christian Democrats, another relative latecomer, did not emerge in some countries and achieved very different degrees of mobilization of the potential Catholic electorate. They also encountered difficulty in gaining the support of the working class and the peasantry to which ideologically much of their effort was directed, depending on the earlier success of the socialist labour movement and of different conservative, liberal, and left liberal parties. In the case of Christian Democracy too, the mass electoral support did not depend exclusively on the ideological appeal or the social composition of the initial leadership nucleus. Both were often very similar in societies where the parties had quite different electoral social bases.

The same is true for the communists, another latecomer of the twenties, whose success depended on their capacity to split the socialist parties and to appeal to the followers of the socialist labour movement. Even when the strength of communism in the inter-war years and after the second world war varies very much from country to country, from mass parties like the Italian or the French and small minorities in Scandinavia and the Low Countries, the distance between the successful and the least successful never was as great as between insignificant and mass fascist parties. The opportunity to build on the pre-war and particularly wartime tensions within the socialist party gave the communists in most countries an initially organized basis of support to start with.

## Unity and heterogeneity of fascism

Different national conditions account for the different opportunities to emerge, the very different space still to be occupied in the political arena, and the very different and contradictory social basis available to the initially comparable leadership nucleus. While fascism more than any other western political movement did not appeal to a particular constituency defined in terms of socio-economic interest, religious institutional loyalty, or ethnic national identity except in irredenta border areas or nations that had not gained statehood, fascist ideologies responded to distinct political historical and social situations and their relative success can therefore be understood by a comparative sociological historical analysis. Undoubtedly, personal characteristics of the leadership group, demagogic and organizational skills account for some of the national differences, but the fact that some of the parties never got off the ground cannot be attributed to the quality of leadership.[9]

We need to keep quite distinct the conditions for the emergence of the fascist movement in each national context and not just by diffusion and imitation, and those leading to varying degrees of success.

To answer those questions, we have to start with a definition of fascism, or at least a description of an ideal type which with some deviations would fit the variety of movements around the world. To do so is far from easy since the success of Italian fascism and National Socialism in Germany led many movements and parties, particularly single parties created from above by royal and military bureaucratic dictatorships, to incorporate fascist elements in their ideology, their style, and their organization, attempting to capitalize on the appeal of fascism.[10] In our view, it is necessary to use a narrow definition of fascism, even when the analysis of semi-fascist, pseudo-fascist, and proto-fascist movements and ideologies can contribute to our better understanding of the phenomenon. Such a narrow definition excludes proto-fascist movements like nineteenth-century Bonapartism, Boulangism, and even Action Française.[11] It also excludes the typical official single dominant or privileged parties of the royal military-bureaucratic-oligarchic dictatorships in Hungary, Rumania, Yugoslavia, the Unión Patriótica of Primo de Rivera, the União Nacional of Portugal, the Vaterländische Front created by Dollfuss, the Camp of National Unity (OZON) in Poland, the Imperial Rule Assistance Association in Japan, and even the Movimiento Nacional in the later years of the Franco regime despite their incorporation of fascist elements. They were parties created from above rather than parties that conquered power for their leaders and supporters. We would exclude them not only for their ideological syncretism and flexibility but above all for their recruitment of leaders and members through cooptation of leaders of pre-existing parties, of higher civil servants, officers, successful professionals, and many opportunists who otherwise might have remained apolitical; men, sociologically and psychologically very different from the activists of the fascist movements before taking power. All imitations of fascism and its style could not hide the essentially different spirit. Our narrow definition also excludes the authoritarian, nationalist monarchical parties like the Deutschnationale Volkspartei (DNVP) and Renovación Española despite their extreme right and anti-democratic authoritarianism. Neither would it include those Catholic parties that turned toward authoritarian corporativist positions in the thirties.

It is, however, not as narrow as it would be if we were to accept the distinction between fascism and National Socialism suggested by Eugen Weber and Stanley Payne.[12] It would cover those distinguished by Wolfgang Sauer as western, central, and east European types of movements and those that Henry Turner is inclined to distinguish as more anti-modernist and modernizing.

The movements and their appeal cannot be understood from the perspective of an analysis of fascist parties in power, as it would be difficult to understand the attraction of communism to workers and peasants in many countries in terms of the policies of parties in power in the Soviet Union or Eastern Europe, even when the successes of parties in power in both cases contributed to their attraction in other countries, particularly to certain types of intellectuals. Undoubtedly, fascism in power in Italy and Hitler in Germany and their successers contributed to the emergence of other fascist movements and their appeal but, like Stalinism in the Soviet Union, also to the strong rejection by many who otherwise might have found fascist ideas and national fascist parties attractive. Our focus, therefore, will be on the emergence of the parties and their appeal before coming to power, since take-over of the state or participation as coalition partners in authoritarian regimes without being obliged to compete with other parties for social support creates quite different conditions for the building of a distinct social constituency.[13]

The question we have to raise is, to what extent did different fascist parties not in power attract to the initial nucleus, to their cadres, and to their electorate similar or different social groups, and what kind of explanation can we offer for those differences? Our basic hypothesis is that while ideological differences between those movements account for some of the variations, the most important ones are due to the particular historical national situation in which they were born, the political space already occupied before the arrival of those latecomers, and some distinctive social structural problems of the different societies.

We obviously start from the assumption that there is such a phenomenon as fascism, making its appearance in many countries, not only in Europe,[14] with sufficiently common characteristics to be studied as a distinctive sociopolitical-historical phenomenon. While there are pre-fascist ideological currents and small movements that can be considered as antecedents, fascism only makes its appearance after the first world war. After the second world war it is merely a survival of the past even when many political tendencies in the world today incorporate consciously or unconsciously elements which we would call fascist. The Movimento Sociale Italiano (MSI), the small German neo-Nazi groups, the Nationaldemokratische Partei Deutschlands (NPD), and other such parties[15] are only historical survivals, as Spanish Carlism is a reminder of the struggle between counterrevolution and liberalism in the first half of the nineteenth century, of protest parties with characteristics recalling fascism. Only Peronism occupies a special position as a movement emerging at the end of the fascist era with some links with the fascist past but without many of its distinctive characteristics. It is highly debatable but it can be argued that it is the last successful survivor of that era. The same is true to a limited extent for the Spanish Movimiento in which the fascist components have been mixed and transformed in thirty years of Franco rule, but not of the small radical neofascist groups appearing in Spain today. In fact their emergence is an indicator that they do not feel at home in what was supposed to be their party. Fascism like anarchism has had its great historical moment and, like it, has left a heritage that in very different ways will resurface in other movements, often undetected except by observers very familiar with it. It could be argued that only a few of the fascist movements were original in their ideology and that the leadership of many of them was more oriented toward Rome or Berlin than to the problems and traditions of their own country. But we guess that the same could be said about some of the least successful and more derivative communist parties, particularly in the Stalinist era.

Once we have denied that fascism was a uniquely Italian phenomenon not for export, we still have to face the question, was German National Socialism a fascist movement or something different? Certainly, Hitler and his followers did not perceive their movement as derivative from the Italian but, with some exceptions, even before taking power and the creation of the Axis alliance, even when their interests were in conflict with Italy, felt the affinity and recognized the early achievement of Mussolini.[16] Despite many criticisms of their German comrades and the distaste of Mussolini and many fascists — before the later thirties — for Nazi racism, Italian fascists saw nazism as a kindred movement even when distrusting German power. Conflicts between fascist powers, different emphases in their ideology and policies are not an argument against the use of a broader category of fascism as the divergences between the Russian leadership, Mao, and even Tito do not prevent us from speaking of communism. However, many of the distinctive features of National Socialism, mostly derived from the cultural ideological heritage of Germany and Austria in the nineteenth century, the elements that might be described by the term *völkisch* and biological racism, make nazism a distinctive branch grafted on the fascist tree. The success and power of Hitler's Germany gave the Nazi ideology a particular strength which exercised its attraction even on a few Italian fascists and contributed to the introduction of alien elements into its ideology — such as racism[17] — and should the war not have destroyed both, might have led some of its leaders even to challenge the authority of the Duce. Certainly National Socialism was in the thirties already a different pole of ideological attraction and influence for fascist parties that might be distinguished as being in the Italian or the German sphere of ideological influence. National Socialism under the leadership of Hitler carried some of the implications of the fascist conception of politics to a monstrous extreme. But it would be a mistake to interpret the fascist phenomenon from the perspective provided by Hitler's rule, as it would be to analyze communism only in the light of Stalinism.

How can we define fascism? Any definition of this latecomer movement has to emphasize the things against which it stood; we noted earlier its anti-dimension but we should also consider its new appeal and its conception of man and society. In addition to those ideological elements, no definition can ignore the importance of its distinctive style, its rhetoric and its symbolism, its chants, ceremonies, and shirts that attracted so many young people in the years between the two wars. But neither ideology nor style, given its electoral weakness, except in Germany, would have made it a decisive factor in the political life of many societies without the new forms of organization and political action. The discovery of the paramilitary political organization ready to use violence against its opponents, rather than electioneering or conspiring, was a tragic innovation that made even minor fascist parties a significant factor in the crisis of many European democracies. The appeal of fascism was not only its ideology but its style and the new forms of political action it developed. Other movements would imitate one or another of those aspects but they would not synthesize them and link them so perfectly. In addition, the combination of electoral politics with the politics of violence in the streets, of legalism, and the readiness to enter coalitions with the use of violence, assured its road to power in a way previously unknown. Obviously, after its success in Italy and Germany, the formula became more difficult to apply; both democratic and authoritarian regimes denied fascist movements the opportunity and the freedom to build up their strength,[18] and fewer of the old parties were ready to enter into coalition with the fascists in the hope of co-opting them or would act disunitedly in the face of the fascist threat. This has to be taken into account in attempting to understand the relative strength of early and late fascist parties.

We shall use a multi-dimensional typological definition of fascism in our analysis, a definition which in our view covers all the movements discussed here even when some dimensions might be more central to one or another of them. We define fascism as a hypernationalist, often pan-nationalist, anti-parliamentary, anti-liberal, anti-communist, populist and therefore anti-proletarian, partly anti-capitalist and anti-bourgeois, anti-clerical, or at least, non-clerical movement, with the aim of national social integration through a single party and corporative representation not always equally emphasised; with a distinctive style and rhetoric, it relied on activist cadres ready for violent action combined with electoral participation to gain power with totalitarian goals by a combination of legal and violent tactics. The ideology and above all the rhetoric appeals for the incorporation of a national cultural tradition selectively in the new synthesis in response to new social classes, new social and economic problems, and with new organizational conceptions of mobilization and participation, differentiate them from conservative parties. The appeal based on emotion, myth, idealism, and action on the basis of a vitalistic philosophy is initially directed at those least integrated into the class structure — youth, students, demobilized officers — to constitute a self-appointed elite and later to all those disadvantageously affected by social change and political and economic crisis against the political system. In a plesbicitarian mobilization of the masses, the fascist appeal is based on an inflation of national solidarity and the rejection of the institutionalization of conflict and cleavages in modern societies and therefore a destruction and/or demobilization of the parties that organize those cleavages, particularly working class but also clerical parties. Hyper-nationalism is reflected in a deep-seated hostility to all organizations and movements that can be conceived as international in character — that is communism, even socialism, international finance capitalism, the Catholic church or at least the Vatican, Freemasonry, the League of Nations, pacifism, and the Jews, even in those movements that are not initially anti-Semitic and even less racist.

A proof that this definition is not far from the self-image of the fascists can be found in the following definition of the fascist attitude by the founder of the Spanish Juntas de Ofensiva Nacional Sindicalista (JONS), Ramiro Ledesma Ramos.

> Deep national idea. Opposition to demo-bourgeois institutions, to the liberal parliamentary state. Unmasking of the true feudalistic powers of present society. National economy and people's economy against the great financial and monopolistic capitalism. Sense of authority, discipline and violence. Hostility to the anti-national and anti-human solution that proletarian classism offers to solve the obvious problems and injustices of the capitalist system.[19]

Contrary to those who would argue that fascist ideology is of little interest in understanding its appeal, success and, particularly, policies when in power, on account of the opportunism of the leaders on the road to power, and the betrayal of their ideology and their followers with their policies, we shall argue that the ideology accounts for much of the success or failure in any particular country of the movement. Certainly, the initial nucleus of followers that provided fascism with the cadres in its struggle for power and much of the elite once in the saddle was attracted by that ideology. Without a sufficient number of people susceptible to it, fascist movements would not have got going even when their later success in becoming a mass movement depended on the capacity of that initial nucleus to seize opportunities created by social crises, to appeal on more pragmatic grounds to particular social strata and to make compromises with the Establishment, to gain access to power. The inconsistency between policies of fascists in power, particularly in a period of consolidation of their control and later in war time, does not make the ideology irrelevant. The fact that the life of fascist regimes, particularly National Socialism, was cut short by defeat should not be forgotten in the analysis of those compromises. Let us imagine that Lenin had disappeared from the political scene after the NEP period in order to suggest how dangerous it would be to ignore the potentialities for practical implementation of even the most out-of-the-way ideas of fascist leaders. The readiness to enter into coalitions, compromises with the Establishment and vested interests, and institutions of the pre-fascist society has to be seen in the light of the fact that none of the societies in which they attempted to come to power was fully disorganized by war, defeat, civil war, or foreign dependency. Despite the crises in the states in which the fascists aspired to gain power, the Establishment forces retained considerable strength, and fascists were intelligent enough to realize that a revolutionary take-over was impossible. That is why they turned to 'legal revolution,' as they called it, and the tactic of neutralizing by ideological deflection and often by real concessions, potential opponents like the churches, the army, the monarchy, and big business, as well as appealing to their fears of an apparently revolutionary working class. Only keeping in mind that these latecomers on the political scene appeared in societies not fully disorganized can we understand that despite their ideological and often personally deep-seated hostility against the Establishment, they would use other elements in their ideological conception and particularly the fear of communism and the class-conscious working class to gain access to power. The ambiguities and contradictions in the ideology and even more in the policies leading to power can also be better understood when we consider the failure of the initial leadership nucleus in making any inroads among the well-organized working-class parties, trade unions, and cooperatives. The negative integration achieved by the social democratic, and in some cases, communist working-class subculture, isolated the fascist activists from a constituency which, ideologically, they were often strongly committed to gain. Their goal of integrating the working class into a national community of producers, a national socialism or national syndicalism on the basis of a common struggle of all classes against one form or another of foreign dependence or for a larger share of the so called proletarian nations in the wealth of the world was largely unsuccessful. In fact it could be argued that hostility toward the proletariat is in many cases the result of an unrequited love. As we shall see in a few cases in Hungary and to some extent in Rumania, semi-authoritarian rule had prevented the integration of popular strata into Marxist movements, and their availability allowed the Arrow Cross[20] and Iron Guard[21] to gain the support of the masses—workers in one case and peasants in another—against the Establishment which turned against them, brutally suppressing them as in the case of Rumania. In analyzing ideology we have to keep in mind that not all movements can get the support of the social groups to which they direct their appeal and that all movements gain support among unlikely classes, often with the consequence of adding to their ideology apparently incongruous elements, or redefining it (the position of the Italian Communist party toward the so called *ceti medi produttivi* is a good example).

Fascism is above all a nationalist movement and therefore wherever the nation and the state are strongly identified it also exalts the authority of the state, and its supremacy over all social groups and conflicting interests. In those countries where the nation is not yet a state, it sometimes becomes difficult to say if the movement is just an extremist nationalist one or a fascist movement. In some cases, as in Slovakia, a movement that is not originally fascist becomes increasingly fascist in the struggle for national independence. For complex historical reasons, nationalism occupied a very different place in the minds of people in different societies and this probably accounts for the relative strength of fascism more than any other variable. It is no accident that Nolte should consider the integral nationalism of the Action Française as an immediate predecessor of fascism. The Action Française, after all, was born in the climate created in the France of the turn of the century in the aftermath of the defeat of 1870. The defeated nations or those like Italy which considered themselves cheated by the victorious powers were those where fascism made its greatest gains and emerged earliest: Italy, Germany, Hungary, Austria. Nationalism in less extreme forms was shared by many political movements, particularly by conservatives and liberals including Jacobin liberalism. Fascism in addition to exacerbating nationalist sentiments combined them with its distinctive anti-positions which all had an implicit or latent anti-international component. Many fascist movements were also characterized by pan-nationalist ideas which represented a challenge to the existing states and account for much of their aggressive expansionist foreign policy.

## The 'anti' character of fascism

Fascism is an anti-movement; it defines itself by the things against which it stands but this antithesis in the minds of the ideologists should lead to a new synthesis integrating elements from the political creeds they so violently attack. This is one of the roots of the basic ambivalence and ambiguity of the fascist appeal and is not only a pragmatic opportunism in the struggle for power but also is understandable in terms of its being a latecomer that could not ignore the interests and sentiments appealed to by its competitors. The basic anti-dimensions of fascism can be summarized as follows: it is anti-Marxist, anti-communist, anti-proletarian, but also anti-liberal, anti-parlimentarian, and in a very special sense, anti-conservative, and anti-bourgeois. Anti-clericalism, perhaps with the exception of the Iron Guard, the Ustacha, and Brazilian Integralismo, is a more or less central component which in some cases drifts into hostility to established religion. Anti-individualism and anti-democratic authoritarianism and elitism are combined with a strong populist appeal. Anti-Semitism is not originally characteristic of all fascist movements but central to many of them. Anti-urbanism, or at least anti-metropolitanism, is not found in all fascist movements but is often an important element.[22] A distinctive type of anti-capitalism is originally present in many fascist movements. Sometimes anti-feminism appears. Those anti-positions have been summarized as anti-modernism, but that interpretation seems dubious in many cases.

A number of these anti positions can be best understood by considering them anti-international and anti-cosmopolitan positions. Thus anti-Marxism, anti-communism and hostility to the socialist party is originally directed to their ideological internationalism. Let us not forget that Mussolini's break with his old party was due to his turn toward interventionism in 1919 and the rejection of the neutralist position of the Italian socialists. The conception of the proletarian nation substitutes for the conflict between proletariat and bourgeoisie *within* each society a class conflict *between* societies, rich and poor. This formulation served both to reject the Marxist view of modern industrial society and to build bridges across class cleavages within each society. It is no accident that fascists should look with sympathy upon national communism and that the boundaries between left fascism and national communism were sometimes grey.[23] It also accounts for an understanding by some fascists of Stalinism as another national revolution of the same type as they were pursuing, in an attempt to make a distinction between Russian national communism and international communism.[24]

Anti-Marxism is a common characteristic but responds in different countries to a variety of roots. In all of them it serves to challenge the dominance of the social-democratic and communist parties among the working-class electorate, and to rally the support of all those classes who felt threatened by those parties. In some cases it is linked explicitly with the Jewish leadership of many socialist movements and the Jewishness of Marx. In others it is more closely tied to the rejection of the militant secularism, if not atheism of Marxist movements. Elsewhere, the internationalism, anti-militarism, anti-imperialism of the Marxists serves as a rallying cry that appeals to army officers, civil servants, veterans, and what Salvatorelli has called 'the humanistic bourgeoisie'[25] inspired by a sense of national mission, including overseas expansion of the fatherland. On a deeper level fascist ideologists reject the economic and determinist view of the social process, substituting for it a basically political and voluntaristic view of social change and nation building. The fixation of Marxist conceptions on the role of the proletariat, the industrial working class and its theoretical identification of the dependent white-collar middle classes with the proletariat, ignoring the status and cultural differences between them and the blue-collar workers, offers fascists a new opportunity with the growth, through downward and upward mobility, of those classes in modernizing societies, particularly Germany. The lack of understanding of traditional Marxist theory and especially Central European social democracy for the plight of the peasant and pre-industrial strata, like the artisans and small independent businessmen,[26] allows fascists to oppose their populism to the idealization of the proletariat. The broader category of 'producer,' of 'workers of brow and fist' (*Stirn und Faust*) allows left fascists to combine anti-capitalism with the rejection of proletarian Marxism.[27] It is significant that the Italian communists after the experience of fascism have been very careful to include in their post second world war appeal those strata that in a strictly Marxist view would be inevitably reactionary and condemned to disappear in the process of social economic change. Let us note that the antiproletarian affect was not incompatible with socialist and welfare state programmatic commitments. The failure in most countries to draw any widespread support among the working class already deeply integrated into a class community — a socialist sub-culture — was compensated by success among a peasantry with strong anti-urban working-class interests and affects, and among a variety of middle-class groups. The bitter hatred against the working-class parties, from which fascist leaders had often broken away, led them to fight the working-class organization and, in countries where the capitalist entrepreneurial classes had been threatened, led that group to look upon the fascist squads as a defence of their interests. However, this was the case only in certain countries where the state-bureaucratic-military apparat did not provide them with an adequate defence, and where they had experienced a serious revolutionary threat from the anarchist, communist, or maximalist-socialist working class.

As Theodor Geiger's[28] analysis of the social basis of the NSDAP has shown and the electoral map of Germany makes clearly apparent, the Nazis found support among Protestants in the same strata in which the Catholic Zentrum was able to hold on to most of its electorate. The same has been shown for Austria by Walter Simon.[29] Catholic parties and the organizational network of Catholic sub-culture in many countries, particularly Germany, Belgium, the Netherlands, Austria, and the Czech territories of the Republic, had integrated many of the social groups to which fascists wanted to appeal and succeeded in gaining in other societies. This competition accounts for the strong hostilities between them and the clerical and Christian Democratic parties. The fact that in Italy the *Partito Populare Italiano* (PPI) of Sturzo and in Spain the CEDA of Gil Robles

appeared on the political scene almost at the same time as the fascist movements made their competition particularly bitter, especially in the northern Italian countryside. In the case of Germany, the Nazis exploited much
of the latent distrust against the Catholics of the northern German Protestant bourgeoisie identified with the Bismarckian Reich that had not forgotten the *Kulturkampf*, something that might account for their success
among some segments of the Protestant clergy, school teachers, and students. Certainly, fascist anti-communism, anti-Marxism, and in some
cases, anti-liberalism and even anti-Semitism could be linked with the
defence of the Christian tradition using ambiguous phrases like 'positive
Christianity' and identifying the national cultural tradition with the Christian heritage. That combination was obviously particularly feasible in the
case of Rumania where a traditional national Greek Orthodox Church
rooted in the peasantry was challenged by cosmopolitan influences coming
from Bucharest, a secularized bourgeoisie and an important Jewish community. It is no accident that the only religiously oriented fascist movement with considerable appeal to the local clergy and the sons of
clergymen should have been the Iron Guard that called itself symbolically
the Legion of the Archangel Saint Michael. The nationalism of the fascists,
however, excluded any identification with the churches and religions, since
they were strongly aware that large segments of their societies were already
secularized and that an effort of national integration, particularly of the
working class, on a religious basis was already impossible.[30] The authoritarian emphasis on the role of the state also made them advocate separation of church and state. Fascist anti-clericalism often underlines the international character of the Church and the interference of Vatican politics
in national political life. Even anti-Semitism is often formulated as anti-
Zionism in the countries in which there is no large non-integrated Jewish
population. Zionism is then defined as a competing loyalty with that of the
nation for the Jewry of their country. Cosmopolitan cultural styles are
another argument against the Jewish intelligentsia, the leftist cultural
bohemians, and have an important impact on the cultural policies of
fascist regimes.

Paradoxically, the more or less explicit anti-clericalism was combined in
many cases with an historicist identification with the religious national
heritage. The positivist use of the Catholic tradition for political purposes
by Maurras, in this as in other respects, set an example for many fascists.
Only in those countries like Germany, where it was possible to link with the
mythical pre-Christian tradition along the lines of völkisch Germanic
thought, an explicit anti-Christian component entered into the ideology.[31]
The anti-Marxism, and in some cases anti-liberalism, the hatred of Freemasonry, and the pseudo-conservative return to a national tradition
endeared fascism to some churchmen unaware of the neo-pagan compo-

nent of fascism. On the other hand, the success of fascist movements among youth, the appeal of their style, the exaltation of preindustrial social groups, the use of corporatism to overcome class cleavages also found a certain echo in Catholic parties which felt that they could that way better compete with the fascists. This phenomenon found expression in movements and regimes that have been labeled 'clerico-fascist' which were looked upon with special scorn by the true fascists. Those later movements therefore encountered many more difficulties in penetrating the social strata under the influence of the Church, something that accounts for the failure of Belgian and particularly Spanish fascism.

These ambiguities in the position of fascist parties toward religion and the churches obviously initially limited their appeal to traditional conservative sectors of the society; but at a later stage also allowed them adroitly to neutralize some of the hostility they encountered in the established church, and to appeal at the same time to those segments of the intelligentsia that rejected clericalism in politics and the church monopoly of the national cultural heritage.

The bourgeois and capitalist revolution had succeeded very unevenly in different European countries. In many of them its achievements had been limited and many sectors of society were critical of those representing it. The individualism, the moral justification of selfishness, the high evaluation of economic compared to other activities had not been accepted by many sectors of society. Those same sectors, however, were hostile to the political ambitions of the organized working class and felt their status to be threatened. Fascist ideologies and propagandists could combine an ambiguous anti-bourgeois and anti-capitalist appeal with the commitment to respect for private property and the middle-class status order. Certainly, the peasantry—often squeezed between rising industrial prices and lower agricultural prices and the demands of the urban population for cheaper food, affected by overseas imports of foodstuffs, sometimes favoured by urban oriented governments, resentful of the credit givers and tax collectors—offered a sympathetic ear to such appeals. The same was true in some cases for a self-conscious artisan stratum, the German *Handwerk*. Sometimes the public sector with fixed incomes which compared unfavourably with the profits of business, hurt by inflation and disturbed by the demands and actions of a militant working class, could identify with the critique of a plutocratic bourgeoisie, particularly war profiteers and sometimes Jewish and foreign businessmen. The stereotype of the self-contented, selfish, and hedonistic bourgeoisie could become a negative symbol for those returning from the front lines of the first world war, for the youth not yet integrated into bourgeois society, for certain intellectuals, and for the students. A romantic youth protest against bourgeois society was captured by the fascists, often recruiting the sons of the bourgeoisie themselves, who resented the style of life and values of their parents. The distinctions made between financial, banking, international capitalism, and the individual entrepreneur appears in many fascist movements, particularly those of the fascist left, and among their intellectual spokesmen. Once the movements failed to gain an important working-class basis and access to power required economic resources, those ideological elements were tuned down to reappear later when economic interests challenged the policies of some of the fascist regimes. The emphasis on style, on symbolic expression, allowed fascism to challenge the bourgeois style of life and bourgeois conventions, without threatening its immediate economic interests.

The bourgeoisie is often perceived as uprooted compared to the peasants, the artisans, 'the people.' Frequently anti-capitalism is centred on finance capitalism, the banks and the stock exchange, whose international links make them suspicious. The strong anti-bourgeois character of some fascist movements is, particularly in Eastern Europe, linked with the cosmopolitan orientation of the national bourgeoisie, its cultural dependency on foreign centres setting their life style.

In some cases, the economic backwardness of their countries is interpreted by fascists as a result of their dependency. Much of the hostility toward the great democratic powers of the time, England and France, is linked with their internationally dominant position after the first world war. They are described as the plutocratic democracies that are behind the League of Nations, another preferred target not only in the countries which were negatively affected by the Versailles settlement but even in places as far off from Geneva politics as Spain.[32] Democracy is often hated because it provides a political arena in which these various anational influences and the movements linked with them can express themselves freely. In some cases, particularly Germany, democracy is also perceived as a political form influenced by foreign models whose installation was made possible and fostered by foreign defeat. To understand better the appeal of these various internally oriented anti-international responses, we have only to look at many third world countries today. Let us not forget that fascism was particularly successful in a number of new states in central and eastern Europe.

The hostility against the existing parties, against parliamentarism, and against the professional politicians and notables in political life was obviously appealing to those young people with political ambitions but without the social status, the economic position, the local influence, the professional standing to be successful in the old parties of notables. They also found it difficult to accept the discipline and the atmosphere of working-class parties, and were too secularized to make their political career in religious parties where access was largely through religious organizations of laymen under the indirect leadership of the clergy. There were in the lower middle and middle class many men in that situation, particularly in some countries where there was considerable professional unemployment of semi-intellectuals. The more acute consciousness of national problems of politics created by the first world war and its aftermath of semi-revolutionary situations plus the interrupted careers due to the economic crises created a pool of men eager to enter politics through a different and faster channel than the old parties. They could despise parliamentary politics, notables, and party bureaucrats, and demand power on account of their share in the war effort, of their commitment to the ideals of a better national community rather than the representation of specific narrow interests. They would be a new political elite, justified by their devotion to the cause and the leadership that would leave the more prosaic aspects of interest politics to corporative representation.

While fascists would have accepted our emphasis on the various anti-positions we have described, they would not necessarily have accepted the label of 'anti-democratic.' In fact, many of them argued that they were fighting for a purer and more genuine democracy in which the participation of the individual in politics would not be mediated by professional politicians, clerical influences, the availability of the mass media, but through personal, almost full-time involvement in a political movement and through identification with the leader who would represent the feelings and sentiments of the whole people. Elections for them corrupted the opportunity for the expression of the genuine interest of all the people. Democracy reduced to voting occasionally and secretly represented a low level of political involvement in the fate of the nation. The anti-democratic position of fascism was certainly not that of the old fashioned conservative. The elite was not based on adscriptive characteristics or on high social educational or economic status but on those dedicated to the cause, open to all those, irrespective of social origin, willing to devote their energies to the movement. The authoritarianly led fascist parties were to be genuinely democratic in their recruitment and the opportunities of access to power they were to offer. The new movements, representing the whole society rather than a particular class, occupational group, religious community (and not recruiting their leadership from organized groups like trade unions, religious associations of laymen, masonic orders, economic interest groups, or rural notables) would be more democratic. To them the old parties in which very often the highest positions were only accessible after a slow *cursus honorum* appeared as oligarchical, and the new movement open to the young and those without adscribed status or even achieved status appeared as more democratic. The elitism and the authoritarianism of the parties appeared to the initial nucleus of activists compatible with a claim to be democratic on account of their populism. Their success would later establish the most oligarchic rule of a small revolutionary group. The leadership principle — *Führerprinzip* — was not always there initially, but soon became characteristic and a source of many difficulties in the growth and development of the movement. It was congruent with many elements in the ideology, organization, and initial social basis, but we would argue that it was not essential.

Movements with this type of programme and ideology in societies that had not experienced a serious social dislocation by war and failed revolutions, depression and inflation could find an important nucleus of activists, but generally failed in creating a mass membership and even more in gaining the support of a mass electorate. The frantic and single-minded effort to gain power by the use of violence and the readiness to enter coalitions with the Establishment, the putschist mentality, the *hic et nunc* activist voluntaristic time perspective, are very congruent, both with the ideology and the difficulties encountered within the framework of democratic mass politics of these latecomers.

One of the great paradoxes of fascism is that, from its inception, being a nationalistic movement, responding to the particular problems of each society, it would become one of the most international European political movements with strong affinities between the leaders in different countries, mutual support in the struggle for power, extreme dependency of the minor parties on the stronger ones, and often a betrayal of national self-interests for the solidarity of the movement. In a sense, fascism underwent the opposite development from communism, which started with a strong international orientation, and recognizing the leadership of the first socialist country, moved toward a polycentric and sometimes quite nationally oriented group of parties. Some of the fascists were aware of this contradiction and refused to attend meetings like that of Montreux. Obviously, the Germans often betrayed kindred political movements for the sake of their power interests. In addition to ideological affinities, certainly the fact of having common enemies contributed much to the sense of solidarity between fascist movements in the same way as anti-fascism was temporarily able to unite quite different political forces.[33] This internal contradiction, however, was another important obstacle, particularly in view of the national egoism of the German Nazis and even the Italians for the success of particular fascist movements.

Even if fascism had not been radical and extremist in its tactics, in its violence, and in its demagogy, this accumulation of anti-positions and its lack of overt links with established structures of society, as well as the comparative youthfulness of its leadership, made its radical character unavoidable. Fascism in many countries was unable to make a revolution but, as one ex-fascist put it very well, the fascists, even when they were only making punitive expeditions against working-class organizations, serving the stability of the old order, behaved emotionally and subjectively, as if they were living through a real revolution.[34]

The anti-positions of fascism on their own are not sufficient to define the phenomenon. They certainly were decisive in its capacity to attract a following but they probably would have been almost as much an obstacle as an advantage if they had not been combined with other characteristics to which we shall turn later. It is important to stress that many other movements would have emphasized one or another of the anti-characteristics but that would not allow us to define them as fascist. Anti-parliamentarism and the dream of a corporative system of representation as a substitute for parliaments was widely shared by Catholics, conservatives, and even some liberals.[35] Conservatives criticized democracy, liberalism, and party politics as much as the fascists but they would not have shared their populism, their anti-capitalism, and probably would have been reluctant to take the same position towards the Church. We could go on noting how elements of the fascist creed could be found in other movements, more in some than in others, who because of that would be more likely to be initial allies but also often deeply resented as competitors by the fascists. The fact that these programmatic positions were, so to speak, in the air at the time is an obvious sign that they could be appealing. The question in each country would be to what extent the particular combination of these elements offered with varying emphasis by the fascist movement could attract a large enough following and to what extent the defence of those different positions could attract from existing parties and movements a sufficient number of followers for the new combination. The greater or lesser success in attracting followers from competing movements with common political goals would depend on the particular historical, social, and political constellation in each country and on the leadership and organizational capabilities of the fascists.

### Pre-conditions for the success of fascist anti-appeals

Only a few countries provided the conditions which made the emergence of a fascist party possible, and in even fewer were there the necessary conditions for achieving mass support for these movements. In the following pages the different 'anti-appeals' of fascism are analysed and the extent to which different European societies were susceptible to such an appeal are explored.

### The basis of anti-parliamentarism and anti-'democracy'

The opposition to parliamentarism and political parties, directed against oligarchical landed interests and professional politicians controlling them, by the educated classes and intellectuals did not exist in all countries. In the well-established democracies that had emerged slowly out of an estate society by a progressive democratization of suffrage in which the protective elites retained considerable prestige and in which a relatively democratic and autonomous local government linked the elites with the people, the negative image of parliamentarism that we find in other countries did not develop. Nor could opposition to parliament have the same strength in societies in which parties and their elites were strongly integrated with a complex network of secondary groups like trade unions, co-operatives, farmers' organizations, local chambers of commerce, and religious associations, particularly when those religious associations were also linked with functional groups. When those interest groups were not identified with particular parties, but wanted to be above party strife, they were particularly susceptible to fascist infiltration. Such criticism would acquire a special strength in those countries in which a relatively widespread suffrage was introduced before the art of association of which Tocqueville wrote had developed—countries with large rural populations, economically dependent on noble and particularly bourgeois landowners, societies with a large illiterate rural population, and in which, in addition, the centralized bureaucratic Napoleonic type of state made local government dependent on the decisions of the central administration and the prefects. In such societies, a corrupt form of semi-liberal, semi-democratic politics with manipulated elections producing deputies heavily dependent on the government that had made possible their election, could easily be criticized. The post-Risorgimento Italy particularly in the south, the Italy of the *transformismo*, the Spain of the Restoration with its *caciquismo*, the even more politically backward Portugal, and the independent states of eastern Europe, like Hungary and Rumania, could certainly not arouse enthusiasm for parliamentary liberal democracy. It is no accident that some of the critics of that type of system, Pareto, Mosca, and many other Italian writers,[36] Joaquín Costa[37] and others in Spain, would contribute to a critical climate of opinion that would later be linked with fascism. Certainly such criticism was not absent in France, even when the links between parliamentary representation and local and departmental government probably made French deputies more genuinely representative of their communities than was usual. It seems doubtful that the same kind of criticism of parliamentary representation would be valid for northern Europe, Belgium, and the Netherlands, and even less so for the United Kingdom. In the latter country the respect for the Constitution that Bagehot emphasized and the traditional legitimacy of aristocratic elites and the elites produced by the educational system, combined with the success of the state in the world, prevented any such bitter criticism. The hostility toward parliamentarism in the case of Germany is, however, more difficult to explain, except in terms of the fragmentation of political parties, their relative lack of responsibility due to their dependency on interest groups, and the contrast of the political instability of the Weimar Republic with an idealized image of the Imperial past. Certainly scandals and corruption contributed in critical moments to the success of the extreme right groups in France in the thirties and the initial appeal of Rex in Belgium.

*Sources of hostility to socialism and the proletariat, and the appeal of fascism*

Unfortunately, we do not have an accurate account of the reaction of different groups in European societies to the labour movement. To a greater or lesser degree, certainly those most directly affected, employers in city and countryside, were hostile to the emerging trade union movement and to political parties representing the working class. Undoubtedly in countries without an agricultural proletariat and particularly a large unemployed or under-employed rural working class, the class conflict did not extend to the countryside to the same extent as, for example, in Italy, and in the thirties in Spain, and potentially in Eastern Europe. It should not be forgotten that the most violent activist fascist *squadrismo* developed in the agricultural regions of the Po Valley where the peasants had only recently acquired their land and were forced to submit to the pressures of poorer farm labourers and peasants.[38] What is more difficult to explain is the response to the socialist labour movement of those segments of society not directly involved in the economic class struggle. Here certainly there is a difference between those countries which are involved in international political conflicts in which the internal social conflicts appear as a threat to the national goals, particularly in the case of latecomers to the overseas colonial expansion where they could not rely on foreign auxiliaries in that expansion. Certainly, the conflict between the nationalists and the labour movement in Italy was exacerbated by the African wars of colonial expansion.[39] The same is true when foreign policy goals, such as the recovery of the irredenta on the Austrian and Dalmatian border, encounter the lack of support for intervention on the part of the Italian socialist party. In France, nationalism also created tensions between those not directly involved in the economic conflicts and the labour movement but the nationalist turn of the latter assisted by the Jacobin tradition, the historical hostility to Germany, and the identification of imperial Germany with reaction, facilitated the integration of labour in a way that was not possible in other major powers. In Germany had it not been for defeat and the yearning for peace that coincided with tensions created by delayed democratization, the patriotic behaviour of the social democratic leadership, with some notable exceptions at the beginning of the war, would have facilitated a similar process of integration.[40] These problems were not present in the case of the smaller European democracies except for Finland and the

Baltic countries, where there were ambivalences created by the Russian Revolution and the combination of struggle for national independence and conservative political reaction. It is obviously difficult to prove, but it seems as if the hostility of a large part of the establishment of army officers, civil servants, professionals, and intellectuals to the labour movement cannot be explained in terms of the economic class conflict but rather in their dislike of the position of social-democracy — at least on the ideological level — and later the Communist parties in relation to the national political aims particularly strongly held by those groups.[41] Another major difference between countries is obviously the degree to which the working classes, or segments of them, were ready to respond to the revolutionary opportunities provided by social and economic crisis at the end of the first world war and the response to the Russian Revolution in different countries. While it is historically false that communist revolutions were defeated by fascism, it is true that fascism was more successful in those societies in which the bourgeoisie had been deeply scared by revolutionary attempts, however unsuccessful, and where the labour movement held on to a maximalist revolutionary rhetoric, even when it was unable to mobilize for revolution. The Räterepublik and the Spartakist attempts in Germany, the occupation of factories and the Red domination of the countryside in the Po Valley in Italy, the Bela Kun regime in Hungary, the revolutionary attempts of the working class in Finland, certainly left such an heritage. The same would be true in Spain with the 1934 October Revolution and the endemic anarcho-syndicalist violence. In some of these cases international links with the Russian Revolution, real or imaginary, contributed to the desire to srengthen the state against such threats or to overthrow a state whose weakness had led it to make compromises with demands perceived as revolutionary. Unsuccessful revolutions, as the Linz programme of the Austro-Marxists emphasized, contributed much to the authoritarian responses, both conservative and fascist. In those cases where Jews played prominent roles among the leadership of the labour movement, this became an additional stimulus for the fascist response, rationalizing their anti-Semitism.

### Secularization, religion and fascism

It has been noted already how the Christian democratic parties and before them, the Catholic conservative parties developed as a response to the strains of modern society in the process of liberal democratization and the secularizing policies of liberals and socialists. Wherever that response incorporated a large part of the population, particularly pre-industrial sectors such as peasants, artisans, independent middle classes, civil servants, and even white-collar employees, and in a few cases large segments of the working class, fascist hostility to liberalism and Marxist socialism encountered a serious competitor that had pre-empted much of its political space. This certainly was true in the Netherlands where the verzuilingen both by Catholic and Calvinist parties never allowed its National Socialist party to make much progress. Thus in Belgium a semi-fascist movement like Rex and Flemish nationalist groups, when faced with the overt hostility of the Church hierarchy and the Catholic subculture, found it difficult to make progress, even when not overtly attacking the Church. In spite of the many factors favouring a fascist response in Austria, neither the native semi-fascist Heimwehr movement nor the Nazis gained a strength comparable to their comrades in non-Catholic Germany. Despite the rapid success of the Partito Populare Italiano in the first postwar elections in Italy, the delayed entry of the Catholics into public life (due to the Roman question that had imposed on Catholics for so many years the 'non-expedit,' and limited the development of their lay-organizations) together with the strong element of anti-clericalism remaining from the unification struggles, left significant sectors of Italian society open to competition from the fascists. It is no accident that the most secularized parts of Italy, formerly part of the Papal States, would become a stronghold of fascism in the countryside and small towns. In Spain in the thirties the success of a Catholic defensive movement against the laicist left bourgeois policies mobilized behind Gil Robles and the CEDA a large part of peasant and provincial middle-class Spain, which on other grounds would have been a potential basis for the Falange. In fact, the disintegration of the CEDA probably allowed many of its supporters to turn to the Falangist banners during the Civil War. The availability of secularized or at least anti-clerical middle classes with strong nationalistic sentiments, hostile to a revolutionary or maximalist labour movement, represented a limit to Catholic and Christian democratic parties which they would overcome successfully only after the second world war with the defeat of fascism and disillusionment with nationalism. It is our impression that the latent hostility of much of the Protestant bourgeoisie and educated classes against the *Kaplanokratie* of the Zentrum and the memories of the *Kulturkampf* of the Bismarckian empire with the Church contributed to the hostility to the Weimar coalition. After all the new regime had brought together in the government the Zentrum and the Social Democrats, the two main opponents of Bismarck. The regional strength of the Nazis in areas like Franconia, the Protestant enclave in Bavaria, might be linked to this historical heritage. The same is true for the areas traditionally supporting 'liberal Germanism' rather than the Catholic party in Austria. In Spain the recent disestablishment of the Church with the coming of the Republic, the illusion still tying the secularized middle classes to the leadership of the left Republicans like Azaña, and in the case of Catalonia the left bourgeois nationalist radicalism of Esquerra, deprived Spanish fascists of another potential social base. It is perhaps no accident that some of the founding nucleus of the first Spanish fascist group, *La Conquista del Estado*, should have moved toward Azaña, and that an early admirer of Italian fascism like Giménez Caballero should also have been an admirer of the left bourgeois leader for whom José Antonio had more respect than for Gil Robles. Unfortunately we do not know how much of the support of the Belgian Rex came from ex-liberals, but there is evidence that the Dutch fascists encountered more difficulty in making gains among voters of the religious parties than among voters of the secular bourgeois parties. We should not forget that Germany was one of the few countries in which there was a tradition of conservative bourgeois in addition to working-class criticism of religion in politics, and a sufficiently important minority of religiously confused fringe groups in the völkisch milieu. The traditions of the Lutheran state church in a militaristic nationalist country provided another fertile ground for the strange combination that Hitler would offer under the confused label of positive Christianity, anti-Marxism, and nationalistic reconstruction of the national community.

We have obviously ignored in this discussion the eastern European cases, partly because we know too little about the religious base of movements like the Arrow Cross in Hungary and because the Rumanian situation is radically different. In Croatia and Slovakia the integral nationalism, given the links between nationality and religion, also creates a unique situation, even when in Slovakia the different degrees of integration into the Church might have distinguished the more fascist nationalists from those closer to a Catholic nationalist party. It should be stressed, to avoid any misunderstanding, that to some extent the successful competition of Catholic parties with the fascists, particularly in Spain in the thirties for the youth of the universities, and in Austria, was made possible by the incorporation of some semi-fascist positions like anti-liberalism, anti-parliamentarism, corporativism, and in some cases the assimilation of a pseudo-fascist style. There is in this a certain parallelism to the success of the Austro Marxists compared to the German social democrats in their competition with the communists.

## Rural-urban conflict and fascism

We have noted how certain ideological positions and the constellation of political social forces favoured the success of fascism among the independent peasantry in a number of countries, particularly so in Germany and Rumania. In this context it is especially important to stress that in countries in which agrarian and peasant parties had built a strong organizational base, reinforced in some cases by successful agrarian reforms as in Finland and the Baltic countries, the fascists encountered an insurmountable obstacle. This was not the case in Germany where the independent peasantry of northern and western Protestant regions had been slowly aban-

doning the liberal urban-based parties or the great agrarian-oriented conservative party dominated by East Elbian landlords whose interests did not
coincide with theirs. The peasantry of those areas moved through a variety
of political changes from local or small agrarian interest-group-based parties, and finally, in the 1928 election and afterwards, massively toward the
National Socialists. Something similar started to occur in Austria. In
eastern Europe the peasant parties also offered an obstacle, but their lack
of success, given the constraints of the oligarchic authoritarian regimes and
the difficulties caused by the relationship of dependent agricultural
nations with industrial central European countries, and the disintegration
of peasant parties offered new opportunities to the populist fascists. Sten
Nilson,[42] in an analysis of the success of nazism compared with Scandinavian fascism, has emphasized the very different response of the social
democrats in both areas to the plight of the peasantry during the depression, and particularly the possibility and the willingness to make a social
democratic-farmer party alliance. The studies of German Protestant rural
communities show clearly the isolation in which the few social democrats
found themselves in those areas.[43] Given the traditional position of the
social democratic party after the failure of David's revisionism to make an
effort to penetrate the countryside and the late formulation of an agrarian
programme at the Kiel Congress, the Nazi strength in the countryside is
not surprising. In France, despite the attempts by demagogues like
Agricola in Brittany to capitalize on rural discontent and the later success
of Poujade, parties of the left had sufficient roots in provincial rural
France, including the socialists and even the communists, to leave little
room for the later emerging fascist groups.

*Conditions for extreme nationalism and fascism*

Nationalism was the central appeal of fascist movements and certainly
countries where the national boundaries had been historically fixed long
ago such as Spain, Portugal, the United Kingdom, Netherlands,
Scandinavia (with the exception of Denmark), and Switzerland offered
little opportunity for appeals based on irredentism and the struggle of
ethnic communities in mixed border areas. In this context it should never
be forgotten that the initial style of fascist movements, many of their symbols, shouts, parades, banners and even programmatic positions were invented by D'Annunzio in the struggle for Fiume, and that the areas that
most disproportionately gave their support in terms of membership to the
PNF were the areas bordering on the old Austro-Hungarian Empire.[44]
Even today neo-fascism has some of its strongholds in this part of Italy. The
historical antecedents of National Socialism also were born in the ethnic
border struggle in the Sudeten and in the context of the struggle between a
German and Czech working class for occupational opportunities. Border

conflicts contributed decisively to the emergence of the irregular armed
forces of Heimwehren and Freikorps. In Germany they would contribute
many of the initial cadres of the National Socialist movement and the same
is true for Carinthia in Austria. Balkan fascisms would also draw much of
their strength from border area ethnic cultural conflicts. Finnish
right-wing nationalism, particularly of the Karelia Society students and
some of the support of the *Lapua* movement, would be linked with the
existence of an irredenta of great symbolic value across the border with the
Soviet Union and the existence of a communist Finnish regime on the other
side of the border that justified the view of the communist movement as not
only a socio-economic threat but a national threat. In the western nations
only Belgium with its unsettled identity of Flemish and Walloons, with the
possibility of a Flemish nationalism or a Dietsch larger unit with the
Netherlands offered opportunities for a radical nationalism of a semifascist
or fascist character.[45] Interestingly enough, Spanish fascism made much of
the problem of the identity of the Spanish state and its historical mission
when confronted with the threat of regional peripheral linguistic cultural
nationalism. It is perhaps no accident that Valladolid, a city identified
with a liberal party hostile to Catalan regionalism under the Monarchy,
should also be one of the initial nuclei of Spanish fascism. It is often forgotten that in Catalonia Dr Dencàs created a semi-fascist movement of
Catalan separatists, *Estat Català*, that apparently also had Italian support
and combined extreme nationalism with some of the external trappings of
fascism.[46] Sociologically, the Basque Country would have been fertile
ground for the kind of nationalistic fascism that we find in the eastern
European periphery with its peasant small entrepreneur and skilled
working class, resentful both of a capitalist oligarchy oriented toward
Spain and a Marxist socialist labour movement. In this case, however, the
dominant role of the Church in the regional community oriented the
Basque Nationalist Party, the PNV, in a Christian Democratic direction.

### Democratic and authoritarian regimes and the growth of fascism

This analysis of the space available in the social and political map of
Europe for fascist movements indicates the limits in which their appeal
would find a response and helps to explain the early or late appearance of
such movements. However, the reader might ask why fascism had so little
success in some of the eastern European and Balkan countries, where even
an impressionistic view would suggest there was such fertile ground for it.
Here an additional variable needs to be introduced. Fascism, to become a
mass movement and even to organize successfully its nucleus of militant
activists, required a minimum degree of political freedom, and a number
of countries in this part of the world were under royal bureaucratic military dictatorships which in their more liberal phases allowed relatively

tamed parties to compete unequally with the official government sponsored or created authoritarian national party, ready to co-opt them or corrupt them, if not suppress them. Under these circumstances, fascist movements could not gain sufficient strength. In a number of those countries,
particularly in the Baltic area, when fascist movements or semi-fascist parties made their appearance, leaders of the established parties moved
toward authoritarian rule to prevent their growth. In addition, a number
of eastern European countries had not reached the level of economic,
social, cultural, and political development that would have made the more
complex ideological response to the historical social situation possible and
necessary. The oligarchies of those countries were ready to turn to other,
simpler solutions. In addition, the urban classes that could have provided
the ideological leadership for fascist type movements were as state bourgeoisies too closely tied to the bureaucratic military professional and commercial establishment exploiting the countryside. In other cases, such as
Macedonia, the nationalist movement facing suppression from different
states covering the area had no choice but to turn to conspiratorial terrorist
revolutionary politics rather than to the creation of a mass movement of
the fascist type. In addition, too little is known about the minor fascist
movements and parties emerging in this area and their chequered history,
moving between suppression and co-optation by pragmatic authoritarian
rulers. Even so, in Rumania we find one of the most interesting fascist
movements of the inter-war years: the Iron Guard whose leaders felt an
affinity with their comrades in other countries and whose history belies the
typical Marxist interpretation of the fascist phenomenon. The same is
largely true for the Arrow Cross in Hungary. Unfortunately, except for the
excellent study by Eugene Weber of the Iron Guard and the work of Lackó
on the Arrow Cross, we have little sociological analysis of the basis of support or leadership of the Balkan and East European fascist movements.

The different historical fate of various nationalities contributes to
account for the success or failure of fascism in that part of the world. Certainly the dominant Serbian state building nationality had little interest in
the fascist extremists since their military bureaucratic bourgeois elites were
ruling the country. The same is largely true for the Polish supporters of the
authoritarian regime of Pilsudski who could identify with a nationalistic
army guaranteeing the newly won statehood. In the Czech territory of
Czechoslovakia, the veterans of the legions that had struggled for the independence of the country could identify with the new democratic regime of
Benes and Masaryk that had founded the state and could also identify with
them in their anti-fascism. In those three countries only fringe groups
seems to have supported minor fascist-type parties or organizations.[47]

The case of Slovakia exemplifies the interaction of the different variables
accounting for the emergence and strength of fascism. The marginal
national society, mostly composed of peasants and small-town dwellers, a

magyarized upper class, a Jewish community occupying a dominant position in the business life, with a left largely dominated by the communist
party, hostile to the Czechs dominant in the new state, would lead one to
expect a strong fascist movement.[48] In addition, the identification of
Prague with cosmopolitanism, free thinking, and Freemasonry would reinforce such a predisposition. However, until the thirties the nationalist
movement, which included pseudo-fascist elements, was led by the priests,
Hlinka and later Tiso, who in moderate terms, stood for regional autonomy. Later, the younger generation in the movement emerged from the
paramilitary organization, the Hlinka Guard, under the leadership of new
men like Tuka, Mach, and Durčansky who, advocating separatism, an
authoritarian state, and violent anti-Semitism, were ready to follow the
lead of Germany and the National Socialists. As Nolte formulates it,
Catholicism was the 'father of fascism.' It led initially only to a pseudo-
fascist Catholic populist movement, but the second generation turned to
real fascism. The common commitment to nationalism, however, led Tiso
and the older generation to protect the younger competitors against outside opponents. Moreover, one of the barriers to the success of these movements was the strength of the peasant party in the area.

### Crises situations as an opportunity, stabilization as an obstacle

It has been stressed how fascism as a latecomer, with its 'anti-positions' and
its ambiguous reformulation of the things it stood against, in a form that it
thought was a new synthesis dominated by nationalism, inevitably found it
difficult to build mass support, particularly in relatively stable societies
that had not experienced defeat, failed or pseudo-revolutions, and had
weathered the depression relatively well. Certainly in some countries
nationalism, which was advocated by other parties too, against a non-
national state, provided them with a unique opportunity, but one which
pushed their distinctively fascist aims into the background. The compromises and alliances that Italian fascism and later Hitler had to make, or
appear to make, with conservative and Establishment interests gave anti-
fascists an excellent opportunity to reject the ideology as insincere and to
isolate the masses from its appeal. In this respect, as in many others, the
Spanish Civil War was decisive in defining fascism as socially conservative.
Moreover, in most countries, after an initial revolutionary shock in the
immediate post-world war period, it was realized that there were safer ways
of protecting the established socio-economic order and that the threat of
revolution was not as immediate as had been feared. For the sake of democracy and their own freedom, the social democratic parties gave up some of
their revolutionary rhetoric and were able to cooperate with other parties
in the defence of democracy. All this seriously limited the success of the
fascist parties founded in the thirties. Even the successes of the Axis powers

could not serve for a mass attraction to those parties, as similarly the success of the Soviet Union after the second world war was not able to boost the appeal of communist parties that had not achieved a mass basis before the war. The contradiction between a nationalistic programme and appeal and the internationalism of the fascist movement, that is, the leadership of Italy and particularly Germany, in fact lowered their chances even among their potential constituencies in a number of societies. One of the great paradoxes in the history of fascism is that in the last years of the second world war, with the struggle against the Soviet Union and communism and the emergence of the United States as a major power in the war and an ally of the Soviet Union, many fascist leaders also shifted, with more or less sincerity, to a new theme: the defence of Europe. At that point the international solidarity of fascist European nations in a new order became one of their slogans, which paradoxically is reflected in the fact that post-war fascism has as one of its organs of expression a magazine and a movement labelled 'Young Europe.' In this new form, it attempted to appeal to a new young generation but defeat and the ability of other political forces, particularly the post-war Christian democrats, to integrate into their appeal the European idea plus the terrible legacy of Nazi terror meant the end of fascism as it was known in the inter-war years.

*Fascism: a generational revolt*

While the social structure, the historical and political situation of different countries, and the inherent ambiguities of the fascist appeal that became particularly explicit in the case of those movements founded late account for their failure to gain a mass base, and even more, a mass electorate, it still has to be explained why in so many countries they could recruit a small but devoted following of activists, and how men who had achieved positions of influence in other parties in the thirties broke with them and felt moved to create new fascist movements. To understand this success of fascism we have to look less to structural variables than to the analysis of their success or failure in building a mass base. In that context we have to pay infinitely more attention to the positive appeal rather than the 'anti-themes' of fascism, the ideological, intellectual, and emotional needs it satisfied. Here the poetry, the symbolism, the rhetoric, the new forms of participation offered by fascism became central. Here, too, the worst aspects of the fascist phenomenon, its opportunity for activists' violence and the sublimated expression of criminal impulses also become relevant. Social scientists have devoted much attention to the psychological interpretations of extremist movements, particularly fascism, and even more, nazism, as in the literature on the authoritarian personality and some analysis of national character. In our view, those efforts are not particularly fruitful in explaining mass electoral support or even mass membership, but may help our understanding of individual activists. Similarly, a study of communist supporters using psychological variables seems to be fruitful in understanding the appeal of communism in the United Kingdom and the United States, but off the mark for French or Italian communism. A psychological approach might be important to understand why some people joined the British Union of Fascists or the variety of fascist parties under the occupation in France but the same would not be true for the PNF after 1921, the NSDAP in the early thirties, or the Iron Guard. This does not mean that the activists, even of those parties, would not have distinctive psychological characteristics, but the fact that men of those characteristics would join those parties rather than other movements is more easily explained by social structural and historical factors. Without denying the importance of psychological factors, the positive appeals of fascism can also be used to explain the success of the movements among particular social groups, like students, veterans, officers, certain segments of the old elites, even some types of intellectuals, and for the different attractions of fascism to those groups in different societies. To do so, however, we have to describe something that is far from easy, the image that fascism created, the appeals it offered, that were significant for such groups. It is difficult to describe them because they were more a matter of style, or rhetoric, of action than of ideas, and today it is difficult to convey the emotional tone created at the time without extensive quotes and ideally unavailable audio-visual documentation. Autobiographical material from fascists is perhaps our best source for grasping the emotional appeal of fascism.[49] However, from this distance in time and with an unsympathetic attitude inevitable after the fact, it is difficult to understand today that experience of conversion to fascism of a significant segment of the inter-war generations.

Fascist movements in their style and organization offered those generations a particular appeal that cannot be understood simply in terms of their ideology or their programmatic positions, and even less in terms of the policies pursued by their leaders when about to take power and after the takeover. It is those appeals that explain the composition of the initial nucleus of many fascist parties, rather than their mass membership and even less their mass electorates, wherever they succeeded in gaining them. Those elements of style combine in a contradictory and paradoxical way the best and the worst of fascism. Ignoring national variants, fascism offered from its beginnings, inspired by D'Annunzio and his Fiume adventure, a new style in politics; new symbols, new rhetoric, new forms of action, new patterns of social relations that satisfied certain basic yearnings of young people and that were particularly congruent with a sector of post-war generations.[50] Fascism had a strong romantic component — an appeal to emotion and sentiment, to the love of adventure and heroism, the belief in action rather than words, the exultation of violence and even death — elements that had not been alien to the romantic nationalist movement of the nineteenth century and anarchism, and that in the past had attracted students and the bohemian intelligentsia. However, those elements were combined in a new way with the search for community and discipline. The desire for community rather than individualism was symbolically expressed in the love for uniforms. The discovery of shirts of different colours as a way of rejecting the individualized bourgeois business suit, at the same time symbolized the rejection of the grey everyday life, the deviance from conventionality and the vicarious identification with the lower classes against the bourgeoisie.[51] The uniform was also a link with the recent military experience of the generation and offered the younger ones the vicarious experience of being in uniform that their age had not allowed them to satisfy during World War I. The new style of political activity, the marches, the rallies, the songs, the burials of dead comrades, the salute, represented something essentially different from the style of political activity of their parents: the occasional electioneering, the clubhouses, the formal banquets of the notables, the hypocrisy imposed by parliamentary procedures at party meetings, the deals of city-hall politics, etc. This new style found particularly fertile ground in Germany, where the youth movement had for similar reasons emotionally rejected the style of politics and public life of the rising bourgeoisie of the *Gründerjahre* and the stiff status structures of the aristocracy.[52] It allowed people to be close to each other, cutting across status barriers, breaking away from traditional bourgeois and aristocratic conventions, sharing an adventurous and sometimes dangerous experience. In the autobiographies of Nazis collected by Abel and analyzed by Merkl, the war experience and that of the Free Corps[53] in breaking the rigid conventions of German status-ridden society appears over and over, and is empirical evidence that the *Volksgemeinschaft*, breaking class and status barriers, overcoming the class conflict that divided the nation, was again possible, as it had been in the trenches in the face of the common enemy. Fascism in its actions satisfied both the desire for the heroic deed of romantic individualism and the desire to submerge in a collective enterprise, in a group, for a bourgeois youth that had been socialized in a culture based on conventionality and whose mentors proposed to them goals of individual, private success. Obviously, those motives became mixed with those we know from the gang of adolescents beating up those of another gang, the cravings for self aggrandizement and abuse of authority, and sometimes the basest motives of aggression, brutality, and sadism. Those impulses, sometimes unleashed by the experience of war, could find an ideologically legitimized channel in the punitive expeditions of the fascist squads in the brawls with opponents for the sake of a higher cause. The resentments against a militant working class which, with its increase of consciousness, with its access to political power, and its organization, had crossed the boundaries of subordination to its betters, could also find expression in the new style of radical violent politics. The new movement also contrasted with the traditional style of religious organizations, the meetings of Catholic youth under the leadership of priests with their devotions, their formalism, their repression of sexuality and violence that made those participating in them look effeminate. Fascism appealed to a confused sense of manliness. The new style equated frankness, spontaneity, lack of manners, public use of insult and ridicule with honesty, sincerity, and a break with bourgeois hypocrisy and conventionality. Passion was to be a substitute for reason, readiness to fight a substitute for useless sophistic arguments. Let us not forget that fascist movements directed their appeal mostly to young men and that apparently even the electorate remained disproportionately male, a point on which they were distinct from the Christian Democratic parties which competed for the same social strata but had a distinctive success among the women.[54] It is hard to judge to what extent the war experience — in which young men spent years together in close comradeship, the years of university studies again in a male community, in societies in which the interaction between the sexes was still controlled, among the bourgeoisie particularly by conventionality, and ultimately the risk of committing oneself to marriage, at that time economically difficult for this generation — might have made this male political community attractive. The romanticization of the male community with its homosexual undertones in the German youth movement has not escaped attention, and it might not have been an accident that in the SA such tendencies were not absent. The idealization of leadership, of loyalty to leaders, also satisfied certain needs in an atomized society and was particularly congruent with the generation that had before it the worship of military leadership and heroism.

*Veterans and officers.*

The new style politics obviously was particularly attractive to certain social groups that were salient among the founding nucleus of fascist parties. Prominent among them we find the war veterans, those who had volunteered and often succeeded on account probably of their better education and personal qualities of heroism in becoming reserve officers, but who would find it difficult either to return seriously to their studies or to a relatively grey existence in unexciting jobs. It is perhaps no accident that among the initial fascist leadership we should find a disproportionate number of war pilots, and the pilot was a romantic figure at the time.[55] Young army officers who after demobilization would find their careers interrupted or reduced to dull garrison duty, would certainly find fascist activism attractive. University students unwilling to commit themselves fully to the goals of a successful professional career sometimes with uncertain prospects for the future, undecided vocations, would constitute another group. In societies where border conflicts or semi-revolutionary situations after the war had mobilized otherwise stable segments of the society into civic guards, volunteer services, to maintain order and fight external or internal enemies, would in the process have discovered a new 'camaraderie' and a new style of politics. Returning veterans and young students were obviously less integrated into the existing class and status structures of society and therefore more prone to accept the fascist view of the national community, of politics as a collective endeavour rather than a conflict of interests. Nationalism could have for them a special appeal beyond class and religion — the two main bases of politics in Europe. Academic unemployment, the impact of the economic crisis of inflation and depression, the number of those who pursued studies in view of the difficulties of entering the labour market, the initial easing of education requirements for those returning from the war, for example in Italy, must all have contributed to increase the size of this group. The frustrations of downward and upward mobility, the tensions created by a change from a society of individual entrepreneurship and professionalism to a more bureaucratic society must have made escapism into political activism, even if only at weekends, highly attractive. The new camaraderie would also offer to those who had come from rural or small town backgrounds an opportunity for social integration in the new metropolis. Demographic changes must have contributed to this emergence of the generational politics of youth, including the demand for positions of authority for those under thirty-five and the caricature of the Establishment and elites as fat old men. Certainly, a longer life in societies with a relatively stagnant economy must in contrast with the period after the second world war have limited the career horizons and the choices of occupational mobility for those generations. The evident failures of the older generation to solve the problems of their societies inevitably justified the demands for power of the new movements and the new men leading them. Soon their elders, who would disagree with the methods, the violence and the strife, but who shared many of the same nationalistic values, the same resentment against international structures they did not understand, the same anti-clericalism, in some countries the same anti-Semitism, the same resentment against a disrespectful if not unruly working class, would ambivalently sympathize with their youngsters. They would give them economic support, join the party but not the squad, and increasingly become important as experts and respectable leaders, particularly when the new movements came closer to power. Certainly, fascism initially was a generational movement, but if the age composition of the initial nucleus and of the later joiners is studied, a slow and continuous change becomes apparent. The core of fascism generally came from a generational revolt, but the beneficiaries and the later leadership would be found in a wider age spectrum. The generational experience of World War I seems to have been unique and not repeated in the second world war and therefore hard for us to understand. Reading the biographies of leaders and rank and file

members, not only German, the *Fronterlebnis* and even the vicarious participation of those too young to fight, it is clear that the war experience
strongly marked a segment of that generation. Certainly other segments
would draw other political conclusions and those different ways of experi-
encing an historical event would contribute to the bitterness of other, particularly social economic, conflicts.[56] Let us not forget that the basic
stimulus for Italian fascism noted by Salvemini and many other observers
and well documented for the Nazis in the Abel data and Merkl's analysis
was the culture shock after returning home and particularly the real or
pseudo-revolutionary situations, the lack of deference to uniforms, medals,
and wounds by an anti-militarist, pacifist working class, and in some cases
the complacent living of the rear-guard bourgeois. That deep sense of crisis
based on the contrast between discipline and class solidarity in the trenches
was heightened by politically organized class conflict in the defeated countries. This crisis was made more acute in Germany, Austria, and Hungary
by threats on their borders of irredentist nationalist uprisings, and further
exacerbated by military occupation, particularly the occupation of the
Ruhr by the French,[57] and for Hungarians the loss of a large part of their
territory. These external events coinciding with attempted revolutions at
home provided the necessary ingredients for the growth of fascism. The
immediate post-independence struggle on the Finnish and Baltic borders
had a similar impact.

It would seem useful to speculate briefly why the participants in World
War II do not seem to have felt the same way about their war service, particularly after fascism had in the inter-war years given ideological expression to such ultra-nationalistic heroic values. The difference between the
two wars might have been that the first one followed more than forty years
of peace, decades in which the educational systems from primary school to
university built up the feeling of national identity and romanticized the
struggles that had contributed to nation building. Most participants perceived the war as either defensive, or as necessary for the achievement of
national goals. Life in the trenches and life at home were two different
worlds—so unlike World War II where bombing, total mobilization,
rationing, and war service reduced the inequities so visible in 1918. The
rigid status structures of pre-World War I society in which the aristocracy
still occupied a distinct position particularly among the professional officers, in which educational differences defined social position, could be
contrasted with the reality of social equality in front of the enemy, the
opportunities for promotion for valour to non-commissioned and even officer status, that represented a new experience of solidarity. The return to
civilian life with its lower-class hostility and upper-class snobbism and a
basically unchanged status structure of society shocked many veterans.
Against these experiences, how welcome then was the appeal of a national
community free of class conflict that the fascists offered as an alternative to

the heightened self-confidence of the proletariat. To this we have to add the lack of planning for the demobilization and incorporation into civilian life of those returning from the front, compared to the end of the second war. This time the assumption of full authority by the victors prevented revolutionary or pseudo-revolutionary bids for power. Nor did it allow the emergence of the complex world of *Heimatwehren*, civic and white guards, free corps, legionaires of Fiume, volunteers fighting the Russian revolution in the east, and so forth, that allowed so many of the war generation and the youth of the early twenties to enter a heroic life of violence and romanticism rather than grey everyday jobs in civilian society, to which many never returned. Obviously, the economic and social impact of unemployment caused by demobilization,[58] loss of positions in the bureaucracy in Vienna or Budapest with the emergence of new independent nations, economic insecurity caused by inflation and depression, growth of the intellectual proletariat with expansion of education without a change in expectations and the structure of occupations, heightened the frustrations of these generations, the hostility to the present social political order, the longing for many aspects of the pre-war society without, however, ignoring the impossibility of returning to the status and class structure of the past. World War I not only produced an unexpected and deep dislocation of the bourgeois-aristocratic class and status order and the identity of political units but also, reacting to these crises, an emergent group that perceived the war and these changes in an unique way. Unfortunately, it is not possible to trace the impact of that generational experience systematically in the available data, except perhaps for the Nazi activists, and if the research were to be done probably for the core of the fascist leadership in Italy. There can be no question, however, that the size and commitment of the initial nucleus of fascists in the different countries of Europe is clearly related to the importance and the character of those generational experiences in each country.

In this context it is no accident that the fascist leaders, militants, and members would be disproportionately war veterans and that the number of those with a distinguished war record, those with wartime promotions, and with a favourable memory of those days, would be over-represented among them. The exaltation of military virtues, the anti-pacifism, in addition to the nationalism, made those parties attractive to professional officers, particularly junior officers. Obviously the restraint on political activity of officers in many cases limited or prevented public adherence, and in countries with bureaucratic military authoritarian regimes the attraction of the revolutionary fascist movements might have been weaker than in liberal democracies. The attraction was probably higher for retired rather than active officers. It is likely that quite similar personality types among officers would be attracted to fascists and the left, for example in the milieu of the *tenentes* in Brazil and even in Spain in the thirties, while the bulk of the officer corps remained attached to the army as a national institution above parties and regimes, ready to play the role of the moderating power and to fill the vacuum left by civilian authority in crisis-ridden societies. Officers might have looked with sympathy upon some of the goals of the fascists, the mentality and ideology of the armed forces might have assimilated fascist conceptions, but other themes of the new movements must have cooled their enthusiasm. In the Abel sample, for example, we find only 6 career officers among 581 respondents. In Italy, the proportion might have been higher, and the highest we know from the limited data we have seems to be found among the Brazilian Integralists. [59]

*Intellectuals and fascism.*

It is beyond the scope of our analysis to explore the role of intellectuals, academics, writers, and artists in fascist movements. The anti-intellectualism, or more specifically, the anti-rationalism of fascism and particularly the petit bourgeois tastes imposed by Hitler should not obscure the attraction of fascist movements and ideas for many intellectuals. However, few among them would commit themselves to the organized parties and accept the party discipline, and many would only pass through the movement or flirt with it. In a number of cases like early Italian fascism, some of the French fascist groupuscules, the initial support of Mosley, Falange, the Brazilian Integralists, the movement had a particular attraction for some intellectuals. They probably never played a role in fascist parties as politically important as in liberal democratic parties and socialist parties, and the fascist leadership never would find equally successful ways of linking them with the movement, as the communists did through their various front organizations in the era of anti-fascism of the late thirties. Even though it is perhaps a risky generalization, it seems that western, rather than central and northern European, and eastern Balkan fascism found an answering echo among the intellectuals. A reading of Alastair Hamilton's *The Appeal of Fascism*[60] suggests that it was more an aesthetic literary type of intellectual rather than members of the academic establishment, the social scientists, and above all, the natural scientists who were attracted, often passingly, by the new politics: poets, playwrights, and critics rather than professors, who when they were on the right supported more conservative authoritarian alternatives, like the Nationalists in Italy, Renovación Española in Spain, conservative Catholicism in Austria, and authoritarian bureaucratic regimes in eastern Europe.

*The mass basis and social crisis.*

It cannot be emphasized enough how difficult it is to generalize about the membership of parties ranging from small sectarian groups to a mass membership party like the NSDAP. We probably will never have the data to trace the changing social composition of parties expanding rapidly in a crisis situation and on the road to power, and therefore, will be unable to account in terms of changes in social composition for the shift in ideological and policy emphasis over time. Similarly for the comparison between small sectarian communist parties in, let us say, the United Kingdom and the United States, and mass electoral parties as in France, Italy, and Finland, different explanations will be more fruitful for one or another type.[61] The smaller parties are likely to be understood more in terms of a particular generational experience of personal crisis preventing the integration into the existing party system, or leading to a break with other parties, as well as in psychological variables. Mass parties are more susceptible to a sociological explanation in terms of interests not finding adequate representation through other parties, like northern central Protestant German farmers shifting from one party to another after finding the representation of their interests through the conservatives dominated by eastern agrarian interest groups inadequate, and finally finding a home in the national-socialist mass movement. Given the short period of participation of fascist parties in democratic political competition and their growth coinciding with national, political, and economic crises like the depression, it is hard to say if they would without gaining full power have retained over decades the support of the strata to which they appealed. It cannot be excluded that through a network of organized interests identified with the movement representing in the opposition and in coalition governments interests neglected by other parties, they could have become a permanent component of democratic multi-party systems. In that case, they would have retained a much smaller proportion of the support they mobilized as the result of a particularly deep crisis, with an appeal based on a total critique of the system which allowed them not to offer specific solutions that would alienate one group or another. The appeal on the basis of a principled critique and charismatic leadership would have had to be replaced by specific programmatic policies. In this respect the persistent re-emergence of neo-Nazi parties in certain rural and provincial areas of Germany in recent decades without direct continuity with the symbols and the leadership of the past indicate that they could serve as a vehicle for certain structural strains of European societies. This however might have meant splits in the movement between a more national socialist and a more petit bourgeois party. In the case of Germany the latter probably would have been more anti-Semitic and the National Socialists would have had, probably, to disavow the emerging charismatic leadership of Hitler. In the process they would have become parties of negative integration of groups marginal to the major integrative cleavages of class and religion that had appeared before World War I. However, the destiny of fascism and the inherent dynamics of its activist core pushed in another direction and the particular historical crisis of liberal democracy in Italy, compounded in Germany with the economic crisis, gave it a unique chance to gain power. In understanding that process, clues should not be searched for in the social composition but in the organizational capacity, the impact of activism, the combination of violence with the capacity to penetrate a complex network of interest groups loosely linked with existing party structures whose members were ideologically predisposed to some but not all the themes of the movement, and which exercised enormous influence over their members and the community networks of rural and small-town Germany. The works of Heberle, Stoltenberg, Wulf, Noakes, Allen, Mierendorff, Winkler, and the theoretical analysis of Lepsius suggest that the sociological explanation should not focus on the individual joining or voting for the party, but on the process by which the intermediary structure was taken over by the Nazis.[62] Contrary to the theorists of mass society,[63] their success was not due to the attraction of isolated mass men, but to the gaining of control by devoted activists of a complex pre-existing set of networks. It was the absence of such networks, their resistance to being infiltrated, their close ties with the Church and in some countries with interest-oriented parties, like the farmers' parties in northern Europe, that constituted the most serious obstacle to the growth of fascism, even in countries undergoing serious crisis. In this context it would be particularly important to study the process of take-over of northern Italian and Po Valley society by the fascists before the March on Rome, the link established between the activists and the agrarian interest groups and even some labour organizations, rather than to focus, as much of the historiographic material does, on the process of destruction of the socialist networks of organization and power at the local level. It is probably no accident that the fascists would succeed in the most developed and commercially viable agricultural region and make almost no progress in the socially much more disintegrated atomistic or clientelistic south. Rural and provincial Spain, except those regions where the Church or nationalistic anti-centralist movements had created social networks, was more similar to southern Italy and this must have, until almost before taking power or even after, limited the success of Falangism. In this context it should be emphasized that the failure of the neo-fascist movement, particularly in Germany but also in Italy, after World War II has been largely due to their incapacity to penetrate into interest groups and to co-opt their leadership, even when their appeals and programmatic positions would seem congruent with the dissatisfactions of their members. The fact that pragmatic catch-all parties like the Christian Democrats, once they had abandoned a dominant religious and clerical orientation and even the parties of the left, once they had abandoned ideological *ouvrierisme*, were able to retain the loyalty of such organizations, placed an insuperable limit to the expansion of neo-fascism.

## FASCIST LEADERSHIP

In parties that assigned to the leader a unique authority and historical mission, rejecting democratic election and revalidation of his authority (initially found in party statutes) for a *Führerprinzip*, the study of who the leaders were is particularly important. Soon the lieutenants, the *ras* and *Gauleiter* would claim similar authority over their subordinates. Unfortunately only the Nazi,[64] and to a lesser extent, the Italian fascist[65] and Brazilian Integralist[66] leadership have been studied, and few data seem available on other fascist movements.[67]

In addition, it is risky to interpret the information available without systematic comparisons with other parties in the same societies, since we suspect that politically active elites in many of them are likely to be recruited from similar backgrounds. Given the very partial information, the analyst is tempted to generalize from the leadership of the NSDAP which in some respects seems to be atypical due to the unique crisis in post-World War I German society. A collective portrait of the founding leaders of other parties would point to some salient differences.[68] Perhaps the most important is that many of the founders of other parties and movements had considerably more political experience, even successful careers, outside of fascist political groups. A significant number of them had been leaders in other parties; starting with Mussolini, a leading figure in Italian socialist politics, we find a number of important leaders of the left like the communist Doriot, the socialist Déat who had become minister in a Third Republic government, Mosley the promising Labour party leader, Quisling a Farmers' party cabinet member, Plinio Salgado who had been a deputy of another party, and so on. Other founders were not as socially marginal as the lower middle-class teachers, white-collar employees, minor civil servants, small businessmen, farmers, born in rural and provincial Germany who became *Gauleiter* and political leaders of the NSDAP. Some other parties would have a socially and intellectually more respectable leadership. Few data are as revealing about the Nazi top echelon as the fact that in the German *Who's Who* published in the spring of 1928, including 15,000 names, none of those of the top Nazis, including Adolf Hitler, appeared. Nothing could symbolize more the sudden rise to power of a new elite, most of whose members it would be hard to imagine as successful in German society in more stable times.

### Fascists—a young elite

After World War I, new elites would challenge the old conservative and bourgeois liberal social order. The expansion of suffrage and the mobilization of the masses facilitated by the war and economic crisis would bring into parliaments and governments socialist leaders, and in some countries like Germany and Italy, those of political Catholicism; with the fascists and communists in the opposition in the streets and in parliament until the fascists took power. If we focus our attention on the men who were leading actors on the political scene of these four movements challenging the old conservative liberal order of the nineteenth century, we discover some very interesting differences in their age structure, which naturally correlate with certain generational historical experiences. Those age differences with some of their psychological correlates, and those very different generational experiences contribute to the explanation of the deep crisis of the interwar years, particularly in Europe (see table 1).

The most striking finding is that the age structure of fascist and communist elites is quite parallel, except for a few older socialist leaders who moved to the new party. More than half of the fascist leadership was born between 1890 and 1910, and consequently participated in World War I or the national liberation and border struggles in eastern Europe, or lived them vicariously as adolescents. In contrast, the socialist leadership that had to face the threat of fascism was born between 1860 and 1880, and therefore at the time of World War I were already mature men, after dedicating at least a decade or two to the building of the labour movement and its organizations and having faced the *fin de siècle* conservative reaction. Not having been in the cohorts called to front duty, they would not share in the enthusiasms and despairs created by that experience. In spite of ups and downs in the fate of the labour movement, they had seen its continuous progress and partial victories and could therefore entertain an evolutionary view of social processes. In contrast, the secessionist communist leadership was appreciably younger, and close to one-half was in the age group that had personally experienced the holocaust of war, which in many cases must have led them to pacifist responses, suffering discrimination for their socialist ideas in the armed forces, and often led them to join the revolutionary councils of soldiers and workers in 1918. Over 60 per cent of the socialist leadership was born before 1880, while over 60 per cent of the communist leaders were born after that date, as was the case with the fascists. The leadership of Catholic and Christian Democratic parties including that of minor Protestant parties was generally born between 1870 and 1890. Their entry into politics must have been largely a response to the renewal in the Church initiated by Leo XIII, the Rerum Novarum encyclical, and the response to the Marxist challenge. Many of those leaders began their political life in organizing Christian trade unions to challenge the socialist monopoly of the representation of labour and in the variety of interest groups, like farmers' organizations, to implement Catholic social doctrine. Many of them in the universities confronted a liberal secular science-oriented culture, and became active in Catholic student groups. Given their age most of them had already embarked on a stable

## TABLE 1

Decade of Birth of Top Leadership of Fascist, Christian, Socialist, and Communist Parties in the Inter-War Years (with special attention to the Italian and German parties)

(in percentages)

| Decade of birth | Fascist | Christian | Socialist | Communist | PNF | PPI | PSI | PCI | NSDAP top | NSDAP second level | Zentrum CSVD | SDP | KPD |
|---|---|---|---|---|---|---|---|---|---|---|---|---|---|
| 1850 or before | 1 | 2 | 15 | 1 | - | - | 14 | - | - | - | - | - | 5 |
| 1860s | 4 | 14 | 20 | 3 | 7 | 10 | 14 | 8 | 5 | 3 | 14 | 13 | - |
| 1870s | 9 | 38 | 33 | 13 | 15 | 50 | 29 | 23 | - | 11 | 21 | 13 | 20 |
| 1880s | 25 | 20 | 20 | 21 | 40 | 30 | 14 | 8 | 25 | 25 | 36 | 60 | 45 |
| 1890s | 33 | 18 | 7 | 34 | 26 | 10 | 29 | 46 | 55 | 42 | 22 | 7 | 20 |
| 1900 | 20 | 4 | 2 | 13 | 7 | - | - | 8 | 15 | 17 | 7 | 7 | 10 |
| 1910 | 2 | - | - | 5 | - | - | - | - | - | 3 | - | - | - |
| No inf. | 6 | 4 | 4 | 10 | 4 | - | - | 8 | - | - | - | - | - |
|  | (110) | (50) | (55) | (101) | (27) | (10) | (7) | (13) | (20) | (36)* | (15) | (14) | (20) |

* Reichsleiter and stable important Gauleiters, not included in top group. They have not been included in the total of fascists in the first column in the table.

professional career and a political *cursus honorum* through various levels of government before the guns of August disturbed the normal course of life of many middle-class youths, not too dissimilar in social background from those who would become the leaders of fascism. As relative late-comers compared to the socialists, one of their formative experiences would be the struggle with Marxists and their rejection of a liberal bourgeois secularizing culture that in some cases would appear associated with an emerging Jewish intelligentsia. In some cases their generational experience, particularly of those involved in the labour movement and in some cases the local government of larger cities, led them to respect moderate socialist leaders. But there would remain a latent distrust of Marxism that would often make a common front against the emerging youthful fascists and communists difficult. In some cases their experience would not facilitate a strong identification either with the liberal democratic elites still in power, that had placed the issues of separation of church and state on the agenda of European governments before the turn of the century. They certainly would not sympathize with the youthful excesses of the fascists. But many of them could share some of the themes of hostility to the liberal democratic bourgeois order of the nineteenth century as well as a resentment against the dominance of a more or less anti-clerical labour movement, particularly after its ideological revival under the impact of the Russian Revolution.

This basic pattern is reproduced with some interesting variations in Italy and Germany where these four ideological camps would face each other most dramatically. The top leadership of the Populari was quite heterogeneous in its age composition, something that might contribute to explaining some of the difficulties of integrating different tendencies in the new party founded in 1919. Only two months later Mussolini would found the fascist movement. But while around 60 per cent of the top Populari leadership was born before 1880 a similar proportion of the followers of Mussolini would have been born after that date and therefore ready to volunteer or serve in the war. It is no accident that the Populari should be against intervention and the fascists rise under the banner of intervention. The Italian communist leadership was even more youthful than the fascist, a fact that contributes to account for a considerable continuity at the top of the party after World War II. Bordiga, Gramsci, and Togliatti were all born in 1889 while two intellectual fathers of fascism, Corradini and D'Annunzio, were born in 1865, Marinetti in 1876, and Mussolini himself in 1883. It is the rhetoric and the ideas of those men that mobilized the younger generation of fascist leaders, the Farinacci's, Bottai's, and the even less distinguished *ras* of *squadrismo*.

In Germany the generational conflict was in many respects even more accentuated. Three-quarters of the top Nazi leadership was born after 1890 and Hitler himself in 1889. A large number of them could not have embarked on a normal professional career, and given their age and middle-class background when the war started, they could not have become involved in the day-to-day efforts of organization of trade unions and interest groups, nor, being Protestants or non-believers, integrated into the organizational network of the Catholic sub-culture. Their discovery of politics would be made in the war, and particularly in the free corps and nationalistic and anti-Semitic sects of the post-war. For them, like many of the communists, politics would not be an avocation, but a full-time calling that accounts for the primacy of politics for fascists over all other endeavours and values. More than in Italy, the socialists, during the Weimar Republic, would be led by men well into their forties, and only an insignificant minority would be of the same generation as the Nazi leadership. The founders of German communism, however, seem to have been older than their Italian colleagues, and this combined with the many factional splits, the Stalinization of the party, and the toll of Hitler's persecution and Stalin's purges, contributes to the absence of an imaginative leadership after fascism in a party that had among its founders distinguished names like Rosa Luxemburg. The Zentrum, almost to fit its own name, stands in between the aging leadership of the SPD and the youthful radicals of the NSDAP. The heterogeneity in its age composition and the presence of the relatively significant number of young leaders in addition to its socio-economic heterogeneity, might account for its capacity to hold the loyalty of the Catholic population during the onslaught of the Nazis.

West European fascists, particularly the French and the Spaniards, would be even more youthful and not have shared the experience of World War I, but largely respond to the success of Italian fascism and later of Nazism. Their response would, in many respects, be more intellectual and less a result of a generational personal experience. This might account for the greater ideological heterogeneity, the greater difficulties in finding mass support in the absence of a generation of men having undergone the same experiences, and the often more critical attitude towards some of the manifestations of the two leading fascist powers: the social conservatism and betrayal of the original ideological ambitions by Mussolini and the irrationalities of Hitlerian racism.

*Education*

All parties in relatively stable societies tend to be led by men with considerable educational achievements, generally with university educations and, until recently, predominantly by men with legal backgrounds which were particularly adequate to the task of legislating. Certainly, in recent years other backgrounds have become important, particularly training in economics. In the time period we are considering, in addition to law, journalism, based on skills acquired in a humanistic education or by apprenticeship in party publications, was another prominent channel of entry into politics. Even in the labour parties, as Robert Michels already pointed out, the intellectuals occupied a pre-eminent position, especially in Italy and other Latin countries (see table 2).

The fascist leadership, before co-opting many conservative civil servants and experts to govern, is characterized by a low proportion having completed a university education to which we can add a significant minority that had started but not completed university studies. In the case of fascists, war and later full-time involvement in politics must have prevented university graduation, as it must have done for a significant portion of communists who started at the universities. Congruent with the relatively small proportion of fascists of working-class background, like those who made their careers in trade unions, socialist city governments and the party press, with only primary education, we find few fascists with less than secondary education. Around one-fifth of the socialists and somewhat less of the communist leadership had only attended primary school. The relatively small proportion of communists having completed university studies contrasts with the half of the socialist leadership with university degrees. Except for the large minority with military education among the fascists, and a similarly large one with only primary education among the communists, both extremist parties are more similar in terms of educational background, than they are to their closest competitors in the centre.

Among the leaders of Catholic and Christian Democratic parties and social democracy we find a fairly similar proportion of university educated. Among Christian parties in this period, and at a time in which the Church hierarchy still took a very active interest in guiding the laity, we find a significant minority of clergymen in the leadership. In contrast to the fascists, among the Christian parties we find some men with only primary education who made their career through the trade-union movement, a group which constitutes at least one-fifth of the social democratic leadership.

The most striking thing about the fascist leadership is the relatively large number of men with different types of secondary education, particularly lower technical or professional, commerce, normal schools for teachers, and others. This is a group that is found also among communist leaders but is relatively underrepresented among Christian Democrats and socialists. Much has been written about second choice occupations; the status frustrations of those unable to attend the university but eager to obtain an education, which did not provide them with positions commensurate with their ambitions. More striking is the fact that among fascists there are a larger proportion with a technical education, as engineers, agronomists, veterinarians, and so forth, than in the other movements. In terms of education, fascists again are characterized by their heterogeneity compared to the two pillars of social democratic parties: men with a university educa-

TABLE 2

Education of Fascist, Christian, Socialist, and Communist
Top Leaders in the Inter-War Years
(in percentages)

|  | Fascists | Christian | Socialists | Communists |
|---|---|---|---|---|
| *Education* | | | | |
| Primary | 2 | 6 | 18 | 17 |
| Secondary | 6 | - | 6 | 6 |
| Lower technical commerce | 6 | - | 2 | 6 |
| Teachers college | 4 | 4 | 2 | 7 |
| University not completed | 7 | 2 | 2 | 10 |
| University | 31 | 48 | 51 | 20 |
| Higher technical (Technische Hochschule) | 7 | 2 | - | 1 |
| "Grand Ecole" | 2 | 2 | - | - |
| Military | 14 | 2 | 2 | 3 |
| Ecclesiastical | 1 | 12 | - | - |
| No information | 23 | 22 | 20 | 32 |
|  | (111) | (50) | (55) | (100) |

In this and some of the following tables percentages can add up to more than 100 due to multiple coding.

tion and workers who in late nineteenth-century Europe had no access to any education beyond grade school. The interruption of education by war and later by political activism accounts for the number in both communist and fascist elites that started at university but did not graduate.

Paradoxically, from the point of view of those who interpret on the bases of certain ideological pronouncements and particularly the Nazi romantic anti-urbanism, and so on, fascism as an anti-modern movement, we find a significant minority of men with higher technical education among its top leadership. Except for the already noted presence of clergymen in the Christian Democratic parties and of trade-union leaders with little formal education among socialists, both parties in the centre of the scene look more alike than they do the extremists on their side of the spectrum. By contrast, the fascists and the communists, except for the presence of the military educated among the first and the workers with only primary education among the second, look more like each other than they do to the Christian and social democratic parties on the centre of the democratic stage.

### The birthplace of fascist leaders and those of other parties

The birthplace can serve as an indicator of the milieux from which elites come. Obviously, it is an imperfect indicator since someone might be born in one place and have spent his formative years in another. In fact, all leaders with a higher education are likely to have spent late adolescence and early manhood in either a large city or at least a university town. Even so, the place of birth indicates, with the above mentioned margin of error, the milieu in which the family of the leader moves (see table 3).

Our data show some striking differences between the leadership of the major inter-war-year parties. Not unexpectedly, the top fascist leadership does not differ too much from its closest competitor for the same social base, the Christian parties, except perhaps for a somewhat larger representation of important cities congruent with the higher professional status of many Christian Democratic leaders. In contrast, the top leadership of the socialist parties was fundamentally urban in background, with a heavy proportion coming from the national capitals. Few of the socialists come from smaller provincial cities and rural areas. The important role of the industrial working class in the founding group of socialist parties and in some countries of academics obviously correlates with that urban background. What is more surprising is that the national capitals and other large cities are weakly represented among the top communist leaders. We did not expect such a large proportion of them to have been born in rural areas, 37 per cent compared to 18 per cent of the social democrats.

One-half of the top leadership of the NSDAP was born in the rural context although in relatively important villages. Among the second rank

## TABLE 3

### Character of Birthplace of Fascist, Christian, Socialist, and Communist Leaders
(in percentages)

| | Fascist | Christian | Socialist | Communist | Top NSDAP | Gauleiter & Reichs-leiter | Z CSVD | PNF | PPI |
|---|---|---|---|---|---|---|---|---|---|
| National capital | 7 | 8 | 33 | 5 | – | 3 | – | 4 | – |
| Other large city | 10 | 22 | 24 | 22 | 25 | 20 | 21 | 15 | 30 |
| Provincial city | 19 | 18 | 16 | 16 | 25 | 25 | 21 | 22 | 20 |
| Important village | 15 | 20 | 4 | 6 | 35 | 6 | 21 | 22 | 40 |
| Small village | 26 | 24 | 18 | 37 | 15 | 47 | 36 | 33 | 10 |
| No inform. | 23 | 8 | 5 | 14 | – | – | – | 4 | – |
| *Total* | (110) | (50) | (55) | (100) | (20) | (36) | (14) | (27) | (10) |

The data are only indicative of trends since no exact information on the size of communities at the time of birth has been used but the inclusion in *The Oxford Atlas* and the relative importance in the urban ranking in each country.

Nazis, important Gauleiter and Reichsleiter of lesser prominence than the twenty we consider the top leadership of the party, the proportion of those born in smaller rural communities seems to be even greater. The comparison with the leadership of the Zentrum and Christlich-Soziale-Volksdienst, the small Protestant party, shows a striking parallelism with the Nazi elite. In the top Christian leadership, Berlin, a Protestant city with no tradition of deeply religious and socially progressive Protestantism, obviously is not represented. But even the second level cities of Germany did not contribute to the leadership of the Zentrum in any significant proportion. The point so strongly emphasized by Theodor Geiger of the parallelism in the social bases of the Zentrum and the NSDAP can also be found in this background characteristic, quite in contrast to others like the generational experiences of both leadership groups.

The differences in type of community of birth between the PNP and the Populari are also minor, even though a somewhat larger number of fascists were born in the small communities of rural Italy, like Mussolini himself.

*Occupational background of the fascist leadership in comparison to that of other parties*

It is obviously far from easy to define the occupational background of politicians, particularly since many of them enter politics at a young age and never practise the profession for which they studied or the occupation for which they were trained. In other cases, the occupation pursued is not the one from which they live, since income derived from property might allow them to live for politics rather than from politics. Many politicians pursue careers in organizations closely linked with political parties, like trade unions, farmers' organizations and, above all, the party press. In those cases the occupational background in terms of education and training tells us little about the milieu in which the leader moves, the interests with which he might identify, the influences to which he might be subject. Revolutionary parties, particularly the communist party, but also some of the fascist parties, like the Iron Guard, were founded by young men who had just completed their studies or got involved in radical activities in their student years without completing their education, spending years in jail or exile. Such men, like those who early in their lives joined the staff of a party newspaper, a pattern very frequently found among the socialist leaders, not only lived for politics but very often from politics, without pursuing any stable occupation in civil society.

In our analysis of occupational background of leaders we have made an effort to take into account any information about a gainful occupation pursued even for a short period before engaging almost full time in politics or related activities (see table 4). Not surprisingly it is among the leaders of Christian parties that we find a smaller proportion living off politics while

## TABLE 4

### Occupational Background of Inter-War Political Leaders
(in percentages)

| | Fascist | Christian | Socialist | Communist | Top NSDAP | Gauleiter & Reichs- leiter | Z CSVD | PNF | PPI |
|---|---|---|---|---|---|---|---|---|---|
| Peasant & agricult. entrepren. | 1 | — | — | — | 5 | 3 | — | — | — |
| Large landowner | 1 | 2 | — | — | — | — | — | — | — |
| White collar: | | | | | | | | | |
| lower | — | — | 4 | 2 | — | 24 | — | — | — |
| upper & middle | 1 | 2 | 7 | 1 | 5 | — | 7 | — | — |
| Civil servant: | | | | | | | | | |
| lower | 2 | — | — | — | 5 | 11 | — | — | — |
| middle | 1 | 2 | 2 | — | — | 3 | — | — | — |
| higher | 4 | 6 | 2 | — | 10 | 3 | 21 | 4 | — |
| Military: | | | | | | | | | |
| non com. | — | — | — | — | — | 3 | — | — | — |
| below col. | 6 | — | — | — | 5 | 3 | — | 4 | — |
| above col. | 2 | — | — | — | — | 3 | — | — | — |
| officer n.i. | 9 | 2 | 2 | 3 | 10 | 8 | — | 4 | — |
| Teacher: | | | | | | | | | |
| primary | 4 | 4 | 2 | 9 | 10 | 8 | 14 | — | — |
| secondary | 4 | 8 | 2 | 2 | — | 3 | 14 | 4 | 10 |
| university | 5 | 4 | 18 | 1 | — | — | — | 15 | — |
| Priest or pastor | 1 | 12 | — | 1 | — | — | 14 | — | 10 |

TABLE 4 (Continued)

| | Fascist | Christian | Socialist | Communist | Top NSDAP | Gauleiter & Reichs-leiter | Z CSVD | PNF | PPI |
|---|---|---|---|---|---|---|---|---|---|
| Lawyer | 14 | 36 | 20 | 5 | — | 3 | 7 | 22 | 40 |
| Other liberal professions | 9 | 2 | 9 | 5 | 20 | 6 | — | 4 | — |
| Writer | 9 | — | — | — | 10 | — | — | 11 | — |
| Business: small | 1 | — | — | — | — | 8 | — | — | — |
| medium and large | 4 | — | — | — | — | 3 | — | — | — |
| Artisan and skill work: | 1 | 4 | 13 | 15 | 5 | — | 14 | — | — |
| Unskill work. | 2 | — | 9 | 11 | — | 6 | — | — | — |
| Journalist | 21 | 14 | 24 | 15 | 10 | 6 | 14 | 33 | 20 |
| Trade union leader | 3 | 6 | 2 | 1 | — | — | 7 | 11 | 20 |
| Professional politician (no other occupat.) | 5 | — | 2 | 14 | 10 | 6 | — | 7 | — |
| No inf. | 3 | 6 | — | 16 | — | — | — | 4 | 10 |
| Total | (110) | (50) | (55) | (100) | (20) | (36) | (14) | (27) | (10) |

In a number of cases more than one occupation has been coded, so that percentages can add up to more than 100%. Preference has been given to any occupation of a non-political character recorded.

that proportion is highest among the communists, which after all were conceived by Lenin as a party of professional revolutionaries, and whose conspiratorial activities very often prevented their integration into civil society with a stable occupational career.

In the first half of the century it was not exceptional that even top leaders of Christian parties should be clergymen. Let us only mention the names of Sturzo, Kaas, Seipel, among others, and given the anti-clerical position of Marxist and socialist parties we do not find clergymen among their top leaders. The same is true for the fascists, among whom we might have misclassified Monsignor Tiso. In fact a large number of leading fascists were religiously non-practising, and quite a few religiously heterodox, playing with confused philosophical religious ideas they opposed to Christianity. There is a great congruence between the exaltation of heroic virtues, the love for direct action and even violence, the hyper-patriotism, and the decisive role of World War I in the generational experience of fascist leaders, and the large number, 19 per cent, of them with a military career background. Let us emphasize that this figure does not include those who gained reserve officer promotion for their participation in the war. In contrast, practically none of the leaders of other parties had a military career background — one respectively among Christian and socialist leaders and three among the communists.

Both fascists and Christian democrats are characterized by the relatively small number of manual workers among their leaders, in contrast to both socialists and communists, even though the presence of trade union leaders and a small number of skilled workers among the Christian democrats reflects their appeal to the Catholic working class. Even the PNF with its attraction to interventionist syndicalists had fewer trade union leaders in its top echelon than the Populari.

None of the parties recruited its leaders among rural society. None of the communists or socialists was a farmer or peasant. In spite of the success of the Nazis and some other fascist parties among the peasantry only two of the leaders were agricultural entrepreneurs or large landowners, even though a number of them had ties with rural society as agronomists, veterinarians, and professionals in a rural setting. The same is true for the Christian parties despite their success among the peasantry.

The top leaders of conservative and particularly liberal bourgeois parties were often lawyers and other free professionals. In contrast the new mass parties, particularly radical activist parties, do not allow their leaders to devote their time to a professional practice, and therefore, very few of the communists and somewhat more among the fascists were professionals. The contrast between 10 per cent of professionals among the communists with 29 per cent among the socialists tells us a great deal about both parties. Similarly, the contrast between 36 per cent of the Christian democrats leadership who were lawyers compared to 14 per cent among the fascists is quite congruent with the different attitude toward the law of both parties. This contrast can be found both in Germany and Italy, particularly in Germany where among the top Nazis none was a lawyer while 7 per cent of the Christian leaders pursued that profession. Other liberal professions, particularly technical and those linked with the agrarian world, felt a certain attraction to the fascists. Perhaps the biologistic thinking of some fascist movements had something to do with this.

The teaching professions tend to be over-represented in the leadership of all political parties in relationship to their number in the population. Obviously, few communists in this period were university professors, or even secondary school teachers, while primary school teachers constituted an important minority with 9 per cent. The different position in society of the socialist leadership is reflected in the significant number of university professors, 18 per cent, among their leaders. The plebeian character of the Nazi party even among fascist parties is reflected in the significant number of primary school teachers and the absence of the professoriate, compared to the PNF which soon could attract a significant minority of university professors. In contrast we find among the fascist leaders and founders 9 per cent of writers and litterateurs, particularly in France and Italy. It would seem as if the academic intelligentsia would be attracted to the social democrats and the literary intelligentsia to the fascists. Certainly the emphasis on rhetoric, style, romanticism, cultural critique of modern society of the fascists had its attraction for this type of intelligentsia.

None of the parties we are discussing had a strong attraction for civil servants and they were often incompatible with remaining in the service. Their number among the bourgeois parties, fascist and Christian, was somewhat larger, particularly among the Christian democrats of higher civil service. Let us not forget that they were at this time still largely opposition parties. The literature has put much emphasis on the role of the lower-white-collar employees in German society and their status dissatisfactions caused by inflation and depression in the success of the Nazi movement. However, neither among the Nazis nor among the other fascist movements were upper- or lower-white-collar employees overrepresented in the very top leadership. Once we turn to the second echelon of the Nazi leadership, however, we find that almost one-fourth had been one type or another of lower white collar employees. That figure and the larger number of lower civil servants and primary school teachers confirms the image of the party as an expression of the resentments of the lower middle class rejecting an identification with the proletariat. This pattern, however, is not confirmed in the case of the PNF, nor should we forget the important proportion of socialist leaders with such a background (see tables 5, 6, and 6a).

Businessmen are absent from the top leadership of the anti-capitalist parties, but also from that of the Christian democratic parties. They are present among the top fascist leaders, but their number compared to the

# TABLE 5

### Occupational Background of Deputies of the PNF and MSI, Candidates of Rex and Deputies of the Arrow Cross, and Comparison with other Parties

| Party / Occupation | Italy Deputies PNF 1924 | % | Italy Deputies PPI 1921 | % | Italy Deputies MSI % | Belgium Candidates Rex elections leg. & prov. 1936 % | Belgium Candidates Rex elections munic. 1938 % | Hungary Candidates 1939 Arrow Cross & other nat. socialists % | Hungary Candidates 1939 Hungarian Life government party % |
|---|---|---|---|---|---|---|---|---|---|
| Landowners | 11 ⎫ | ⎫ | 4 ⎫ | ⎫ | ⎫ | 27 | | 12 | 22.3 |
| Tenants | 1 ⎬ 13 | ⎬ 4.0 | 2 ⎬ 8 | ⎬ 6.5 | ⎬ — | | | — | — |
| Peasants | 1 ⎭ | ⎭ | 2 ⎭ | ⎭ | ⎭ | | | 16 | — |
| Industrialists & Financiers | 20 | 5.4 | 4 | 3.4 | 2.3 | 33 | 17 | 16 ⎫ | 5.8 ⎫ |
| Shopkeepers | | | | | | 57 | 58 | ⎬ | ⎬ |
| Artisans, indep. workers | | | | | | | | ⎭ | ⎭ |
| White collar | 3 | .8 | 3 | 2.4 | | 17 | 8 | | 51.6 ⎫ |
| Civil Servants | 8 | 2.3 | 3 | 2.4 | | 28 | 31 | 4 | ⎬ |
| Officers | 24 | 6.4 | 10 | 8.2 | 7.0 | 12 | 17 | 12 | ⎭ |
| University professors | 22 | 5.9 | 12 | 9.8 | 2.3 | | | | |
| Teachers | 8 | 2.1 | 2 | 1.6 | 7.0 | | | | |

## TABLE 5 (Continued)

| | Italy Deputies | | | | | Belgium Candidates — Rex elections | | | | Hungary Candidates (1939) | |
|---|---|---|---|---|---|---|---|---|---|---|---|
| | PNF (1924) | | PPI (1921) | | MSI | leg. & prov. 1936 | leg. & prov. 1938 | munic. 1936 | munic. 1938 | Arrow Cross & other nat. socialists | Hungarian Life government party |
| **Party / Occupation** | n | % | n | % | % | % | % | % | % | % | % |
| Lawyers | 137 | 36.7 | 57 | 46.3 | 39.5 { | 27 | 12 | 33 | 18 | 32 { | 20.3 { |
| Other liberal professionals | 36 | 9.6 | 7 | 5.7 | 4.6 { | 25 | 11 | 8 | 4 { | | |
| Cadres superieurs | 41 { | | 6 { | | 4.6 { | | | | | | |
| Journalists | { | | { | | 16.3 | | | | | | |
| Politicians | 8 { | 13.4 | 2 | 8.9 | 16.3 | | | | | | |
| Union Leaders | 1 | | 3 { | | | | | | | | — |
| Workers | | | | | | 13 | 6 | 24 | 13 | 8 | |
| Other | | | | | | 6 | 3 | 6 | 3 | | |
| No information | 52 | 13.9 | 6 | 4.8 | 4.6 | | | | | | (?) |
| (N) | | (373) | | (123) | (43) | (233) | | (187) | | (75) | |
| Aristocracy | | | | | | | | | | 12 | 38.5 |

The data are from Paolo Farneti, 'The Italian Elite' to be published in forthcoming book on elites edited by M. Dogan and J. Linz. Those for the MSI from Giovanni Sartori, ed., *Il Parlamento Italiano* (Naples, 1963). For Belgium, Jean-Michel Etienne, *Le Mouvement Rexiste Jusqu'en 1940* (Paris, 1968). For Hungary, Andrew C. Janos, 'The One-Party State and Social Mobilization: East Europe Between the Wars,' in S. P. Huntington and C. H. Moore, eds. *Authoritarian Politics in Modern Society: The Dynamics of Established One-Party Systems* (New York, 1970).

professional civil servants and above all the military careers is far from significant. Certainly, fascist parties might have been successful in gaining support from small businesses and financial contributions from more important businesses, but practically none of their leaders had a background in business. In fact they had only two per cent more than did labourers or trade union leaders.

The interesting differences between the twenty top leaders of the NSDAP and the thirty-six leading Gauleiter or Reichsleiter not included in those twenty suggest the interest of further comparison of the different levels of leadership within the parties. Obviously a more refined coding of some of the career lines, particularly of those engaged full time im politics or politically related activities like trade union leaders and party journalists, would further illuminate the biography of the leadership groups of parties in the inter-war years. Certainly, more of the fascist leaders than those of the Christian parties were full-time politicians or party journalists, as a contrast between the NSDAP and the Zentrum and even more that of the PNF leaders with those of the PPI shows. In this respect the top leadership and the founders of fascist and communist parties tend to be more similar.

## THE MEMBERSHIP OF FASCIST PARTIES

There are many difficulties and pitfalls in the sociological analysis of the membership of the fascist movements. Certainly, there are obvious motives for joining the party in power when other parties are outlawed and membership implies important advantages expressed in the famous Italian transcription of the initials of the PNF (Partito Nazionale Fascista) as 'per necessita familiare' (out of family need). The comparison of fascist membership before taking power and after, particularly when we can take into account the date of joining the party, could also tell us much about the party's penetration into the society as well as about the disillusionment of certain of the old fighters dropping out. The high turnover, with policy shifts and leadership crises of parties not anchored in pre-existing social structures, such as a church and its lay organizations, or well-organized interest groups, such as trade unions, cooperatives, farmers organizations, and others, is particularly striking. To give just one example of the 191 participants in the Milan founding meeting at San Sepolcro, 103 were still members in March 1932 while 19 had died and 67 were no longer members of the party.[69] Probably in smaller and less successful fascist parties the turnover of membership would be even greater. Consequently, it is very important to take into account the date to which the data refer (see table 5).

It is unlikely that the social composition of Italian fascism in May 1920 when it claimed 27,430 members and 3,700 student vanguard members was the same as that in May 1922 with 322,210 members. Certainly the 118 *fasci* in 1920 were located in very different social contexts to the 2,124 in May 1922.[70] This must be even truer for the 1,672 NSDAP members before the beer hall putsch in November 1923, compared to the 129,563 members in September 1930 and 719,446 affiliated with the party on 30 January 1933 at the time of the *Machtübernahme*.[71] If we consider that by 1932 the party had given out 1,414,975 party cards, we realize the extreme fluctuation in membership, both by rapid growth but also by enormous losses of one-time members. Certainly the analysis of membership characteristics of parties having grown slowly over long periods of time and retaining a stable membership over decades has a different significance. If we add in the case of the PNF that in north central Italy many farm labourers, farmers, and even workers might have been forced to join the party and its organizations, particularly its trade unions under duress in areas dominated by fascist squads, the validity of the analysis becomes even more dubious.

It would be interesting to follow closely the changing composition with the shifts in political orientation of the parties. Already in August 1921 Gramsci called attention to the existence of 'two fascisms': one of them 'urban' personified by Mussolini, *piccolo borghese*, ready for collaboration, and another 'agrarian,' tied to rural capitalism, full of intransigence.[72] To give just one example, in March 1921 the borderline nationalist fascists of Trieste still constituted 18 per cent of the membership and only two months later their share had been reduced to 8 per cent. Certainly the motives for joining the party in Trieste must have been very different from those of 21.9 per cent members from the Emilia-Romagna with its bitter social conflicts. One thing is certain: Italian fascism found most of its membership before the march on Rome, and, in contrast with today's neofascism, in northern and northern central Italy, in highly industrial regions like Lombardy, and in the Po valley, with its modern capitalist agriculture, rather than in the underdeveloped south and in the islands. Italian fascism in a short period of time had become a mass party, comparable in membership strength even if not in electoral support to the socialist party that at the time of the 1921 Leghorn congress had 216,327 members in 4,367 sections. With that growth the social composition must have changed radically several times.

*Occupational composition*

The data on the occupation of fascist party members are scant, only available for a few dates, not always reliable; the occupational classification used in the official party publications and by the scholars is far from satisfactory and unbiased for a comparative sociological analysis. We have attempted to bring together the available information using fairly detailed classifications (occasionally combined in brackets for comparison) for the

## TABLE 6

### Occupation of Fascist Party Members and Leaders and Members of the DC and Socialist Parties*

| | PNF | | | | | DC | | Socialist |
|---|---|---|---|---|---|---|---|---|
| | Members | % | Top leaders | 1924 Deputies | % | Membership % 1955 | Membership % 1961 | Membership % Dec. 1903 |
| Landowners and peasants (incl. tenants) | 18,084 | 12.0 | — | 13 | 3.5 | 14.8 | 12.4 | small owners 4.9 / tenants 6.1 |
| White collar employees (lower & upper) | 14,988 | 9.8 | — | 8 | 2.3 | | 9.2 | 3.3 |
| Civil servants state & municipal | 7,209 | 4.8 | 4 | 6.4 | | 9.4 | 9.2 | |
| Military | | | 8 | | | | | |
| Teaching secondary | 1,680 | 1.1 | 4 | 8 | 2.1 | | | |
| university | | | 15 | 22 | 5.9 | | | |
| Liberal prof. | 9,981 | 6.6 | | | | 4.8 | 5.3 | 2.7 |
| Lawyers | | | 22 | 137 | 36.7 | | | |
| Other | | | 4 | 36 | 9.6 | | | |
| Writers | | | 11 | | | | | |
| Journalists | | | 33 | 41 | 11.7 | | | |

*Data of membership of the Fascist party reported by U. Pasella in *Il Popolo d'Italia*, 8 November 1921 on the occasion of the Rome Congress, based on 151,644 of the 217,072 members reported on 31 October 1921. Quoted in Renzo De Felice *Mussolini il fascista. La Conquista del potere 1921-1925* (Torino, 1966), 6-7.

TABLE 6 (Continued)

| | | | | | | | |
|---|---|---|---|---|---|---|---|
| Industrialists businessmen | 4,269 | 2.8 | — | 20 | | 5.4 | — |
| Merchants and artisans | 13,878 | 9.2 | 3 | | 11.3 | 9.2 | 14.9 |
| Industrial workers | 23,418 | 15.4 | — | — | 19.4 | 21.2 | 42.3 |
| Maritime activities | 1,507 | 1.1 | — | — | | | |
| Sharecropper | | | | | 2.2 | 2.0 | |
| Agricultural workers | 36,847 | 24.3 | — | | 6.0 | 5.0 | 14.0 |
| Students | 19,783 | 13.0 | — | | 2.5 | 2.5 | 1.1 |
| Trade union leaders | | | 11 | 1 | 0.3 | — | — |
| Professional poli. | | | 7 | 8 | 2.1 | — | — |
| Retired | | | | | 2.9 | 4.5 | |
| Housewives | | | | | 24.0 | 25.5 | |
| No information | 2,007 | 4 | 52 | 13.9 | 2.7 | 2.5 | 9.6 |
| *Total* | 151,644 | (27) | 373 | 100 | 100 | 100 | (33,686) |

Data on top leadership collected by us.

Data on 1924 deputies of the PNF from Paolo Farneti, 'The Italian elite,' forthcoming.

Data on membership of the Democristian party, from Giorgio Galli and Alfonso Prandi, *Patterns of Political Participation in Italy* (New Haven, 1970), 123. The data for 1961 do not include members from Bergamo, Brescia, Avellino and Agrigento.

Data for the Socialist party in December 1903 based on 803 sections and 33,686 members. Apparently, according to Michels, 14,256 did not respond to the survey. From Arturo Zambianchi, *Relazione della Direzione del Partito* (Imola, 1904); quoted by Robert Michels, *Sozialismus in Italien* (Munich, 1925), 192-93.

PNF, the NSDAP on several dates, the Brazilian Integralists, the Norwegian *Nasjonal Samling* and scattered data on other parties, and to make some comparison between them and between members and leaders.

The secretariat of the *Partito Nazionale Fascista* in November 1921 provided information about somewhat less than half of the membership.[73] At that time it was claimed that of the 151,644 members 87,182 were veterans, something that tells us a great deal about the generational and age composition of the party. The figures on occupational composition deserve some comment (see table 5). Certainly the rural element, 24.3 per cent farm labourers and 12 per cent farmers from large landowners to tenants adds up to 36.3 per cent indicating the importance of agrarian fascism both voluntary and probably in part coerced or opportunistic. Even so, considering the importance of the rural sector in Italian society, these figures would make the membership of the PNF less agrarian than that of the NSDAP which had from 1930 on a higher proportion of peasants than the proportion for the population as a whole and whose local leadership, the Ortsgruppenleiter in 1935, were one-quarter peasants.[74] It might seem strange that in 1921 the PNF was more working class in its composition than the NSDAP, but only thanks to the large share of farm labourers. Industrialists, merchants, and independent artisans adding up to 12 per cent constituted an important part of the membership, but particularly considering the occupational structure of Italy, the number of white-collar employees, state and municipal civil servants, professionals and those engaged in teaching, adding up to 21.7 per cent, is striking. This figure certainly agrees with the interpretation of fascism as the expression of the *piccola borghesia umanistica*, emphasized by Luigi Salvatorelli[75] with its susceptibility to rhetoric. The importance of the romantic nationalist appeal is underscored by the thirteen per cent members who were students. Students, free professionals, and teachers contributed two out of every ten members of the party. We should not forget either that the educated, the intellectual proletariat, was particularly numerous in Italy and that as Michels[76] had noted in his studies of the socialist party membership and elites in Italy, these groups were also heavily over-represented, particularly in comparison to the much more working-class German social democracy.

It would have been interesting to compare the occupational background of the fascists with that of the members of the Populari and the socialist party of the time. But we have not been able to locate data to do so. A comparison with the Democrazia Cristiana, the post-war successor to the PPI, membership for 1955 shows considerable similarities in the social base, as we would have expected. One difference is the smaller number of farm labourers and share croppers in the DC, probably explained by the successful pressure of the PNF in the Po Valley and to intervening changes in the social structure of Italy. Another is the significantly larger number of workers among the DC which confirms the more middle-class character of the PNF than probably the PPI, whose working-class base the DC

TABLE 6a

Occupation of Members of the German Reichstag (MdR) 1919-1932 by Party

| | NSDAP | | | | DNVP | Z | BVP |
|---|---|---|---|---|---|---|---|
| | Elected before July 1932 | July and Nov. 1932 | Total legislators | Gauleiter* | | | |
| Farmers*[1] | | | | | | | |
| small | 2.3 | 15.9 | 9.3 | – | 16.3 | 10.4 | 22.7 |
| middle | 3.8 | 4.3 | 3.7 | 1.4 | 10.9 | 3.9 | 4.6 |
| entrepreneur | 3.0 | 5.1 | 4.5 | – | 4.9 | – | – |
| White collar employees | | | | | | | |
| lower | 6.8 | 4.3 | 5.2 | 5.5 | – | | |
| middle | 5.3 | 4.3 | 4.8 | | 3.5 | 1.1 | 4.5 |
| Civil servants | | | | | | | |
| lower | 0.8 | 2.2 | 1.5 | 9.6 | – | 0.5 | – |
| middle | 4.5 | 1.4 | 3.0 | | 3.5 | 3.3 | 2.3 |
| upper | 6.0 | 2.2 | 4.1 | 1.3 | 14.3 | 11.0 | 9.1 |

Data on occupation from the biographies in Max Schwarz, *MdR. Biographisches Handbuch der Reichstage* (Hannover, 1965), 607-795. The data refer to individuals ever holding a seat representing the party before the Machtergreifung. As a result, some are counted under more than one party, for example, NSDAP and DNVP members, since they changed parties. Obviously many MdR's were elected repeatedly so that the 270 NSDAP MdR's held 591 incumbencies; the 202 DNVP (Deutschnationale Volkspartei—German National People's Party) members held 510 incumbencies; the 182 Zentrum MdR's 480; and the 44 BVP (Bayerische Volkspartei—Bavarian People's Party) 129. (Disregarded in counting incumbencies were the 90 seats held by the Christliche Volkspartei that preceded the Z and BVP in the Constituent Assembly of 1919.) Since the information available is quite imprecise, the figures should be considered indicative rather than definitive.

*The data on Gauleiters (1925-1932-33) are from Albrecht Tyrell, ed., *Führer Befiehl . . . Selbstzeugnisse aus der 'Kampfzeit' der NSDAP Dokumentation und Analyse* (Düsseldorf, 1969).

1. Those who give as occupation Landwirt, Gärtner, et al., have been considered 'small' farmers even when they are likely to be also medium. As 'medium and large,' we have considered the Gutsbesitzer, Rittergutsbesitzer, and some similar categories. Under entrepreneur, we have classified a variety of agricultural activities not easy to fit into the previous classifications.

## TABLE 6a (Continued)

| | NSDAP | | | | DNVP | Z | BVP |
|---|---|---|---|---|---|---|---|
| | Elected before July 1932 | July and Nov. 1932 | Total legislators | Gauleiter* | | | |
| Military[2] | | | | | | | |
| below colonel | 9.9 | 6.5 | 8.2 | 4.1 | 3.0 | 0.5 | — |
| colonel or above | 1.3 | 2.2 | 1.8 | | 2.0 | — | — |
| soldier | | | | 1.4 | | | |
| Teaching | | | | | | | |
| primary | 6.8 | 2.2 | 4.1 | 17.8 | 1.5 | 4.4 | 2.3 |
| secondary | 5.3 | 1.4 | 3.3 | | 3.0 | 6.3 | 2.3 |
| university | 0.8 | 0.7 | 0.7 | — | 3.0 | 1.7 | 2.3 |
| Priests, pastors[3] | 1.3 | — | 0.7 | — | 3.9 | 8.2 | 4.5 |
| lawyers | 3.0 | 1.4 | 2.2 | | 2.0 | 6.6 | 4.5 |
| other free professionals | 7.6 | 15.9 | 12.2 | 12.3 | 4.5 | 3.3 | 6.8 |
| writers, artists | 3.0 | 1.4 | 2.2 | — | 3.5 | 0.5 | — |
| journalists | 0.8 | 1.4 | 1.1 | 4.1 | 1.5 | 6.6 | 4.5 |
| Business | | | | | | | |
| small | 10.6 | 7.3 | 8.9 | 15.1 | 1.0 | 3.8 | 2.3 |
| middle | 1.3 | 3.1 | 2.2 | | 7.4 | 5.5 | 4.5 |

2. The officers are 'a.D.' ('ausser Dienst'), that is, retired. It is not always clear if they were professionals or reserve officers. Those giving another occupation have not been counted as military except one MdR of the Zentrum, making even more striking the difference with the NSDAP and DNVP.
3. The clerical members of the Z and BVP are Catholic priests; those of the NSDAP and DNVP Protestants.

## TABLE 6a (Continued)

| | NSDAP | | | | DNVP | Z | BVP |
|---|---|---|---|---|---|---|---|
| | Elected before July 1932 | July and Nov. 1932 | Total legislators | Gauleiter* | | | |
| Workers | | | | | | | |
| skilled and artisans | 9.8 | 10.8 | 10.4 | 4.1 | 3.5 | 7.1 | 6.8 |
| unskilled | 2.3 | 1.4 | 1.8 | – | – | – | – |
| farm | 2.3 | 1.4 | 1.8 | – | 0.5 | – | – |
| Trade union leaders[4] | – | – | – | – | 2.5 | 16.5 | 11.4 |
| Organization officials | – | – | – | – | 2.5 | 6.6 | 4.6 |
| Professional politicians[5] | – | – | – | – | – | 1.1 | – |
| Students | | | | 4.1 | | | |
| Housewives | – | – | – | – | 0.5 | 2.2 | – |
| No information | 0.8 | 3.6 | 2.2 | – | 1.0 | 1.1 | – |
| | (132) | (138) | (270) | (73) | (202) | (182) | (44) |

4. In the case of trade union leaders or officials, we have given preference to their union role rather than to their occupation as workers or employees, a fact to be taken into account in the comparisons.

5. Obviously, many of those coded under other occupations particularly in the NSDAP are also professional politicians. This is only a residual category of those not giving any other occupation and in top leadership positions.

inherited. The fascists, however, seem to have done better among the professionals and probably the public servants. A comparison with the socialist party membership in the first decade of the century shows the different social basis, particularly the relatively small contribution of the non-rural working class to the PNF. In the middle class the main difference is the fascist success among students, professionals, civil servants, the military, and white collar employees, while the difference between socialist and fascist in the proportions of artisans and small businessmen seems to be less marked. At least before the war Italian socialists had gained considerable strength among those groups which they apparently did not have in Germany, where they would become so important for the Nazi movement.

We unfortunately do not know how many of the 19,783 students affiliated with the party were university students or in other fields, or still in secondary schools. We can, however assume that a large proportion must have been at the universities. Therefore, we can put that figure into perspective by noting that between 1919 and 1922 the average number of students in higher education was 50,651; even assuming that only half of the party members would be university students, that would mean close to one out of every five. A number of factors must have contributed to this wave of fascist enthusiasm among students, one of them being the increase in the number of students in higher education from an average for the period 1904 to 1913 of 26,691 and even 35,256 from 1914 to 1918 to the figure we mentioned, which must have affected, together with the economic crisis, the expectations of employment. Another factor must have been the presence on the campuses of veterans of the war, many of them reserve officers, some of them still serving in the army but stationed in university towns and with leaves to pursue their studies. Special legislation provided for access to education of war participants.

Students, as we know from scattered data on other fascist parties, particularly Rumania, Spain, France, Norway, and Latvia, constituted an important element in all fascist parties, In spite of the success of the Nazis in academic elections,[77] students constituted a much smaller proportion of the party membership. Even in 1920 there were only 7 per cent and in 1933 1.2 per cent, and it would seem that the free professionals were not heavily represented in the ranks of the NSDAP compared to the economic old middle classes of the *Handwerk* (artisans) and the shopkeepers. In fact, one of the striking data on the NSDAP is that in its Führerkorps (the political leadership) free professionals numbered only 2.1 per cent.[78] The comparison between the membership of the PNF in 1921 and the NSDAP in 1930, at relatively comparable moments in the growth of the parties, suggests that Italian fascism probably similarly to other Latin countries like France and Spain, and semi-developed countries, particularly some Balkan countries, was less a movement of social-economic groups affected by the economic crisis — the victims of changes in advanced industrial societies, old

independent owning classes — than was national-socialism. This would also
account for a much less radical break with the cultural traditions, an initially much greater sensitivity for new cultural phenomena like futurism,
and modern art, a much greater attraction for many intellectuals, and for
Mussolini compared with Hitler, a greater capacity to co-opt capable professionals to implement fascist policies. Italian war veterans, the young
*arditi* must have been in many respects different in social position from the
members of the Freikorps and the small town plebeians mobilized by the
Nazis.

One point that might deserve further investigation is the relatively small
proportion of *insegnanti* (teachers) in the PNF, 1.1 per cent compared to
1.7 per cent among the NSDAP in 1930, and their disproportionate presence among the leadership and even the top leadership of the NSDAP.
Franz Neumann[79] has analyzed very well the sociological conditions linked
with national-liberalism and the *Kulturkampf* traditions that made German teachers particularly susceptible to nazism, for reasons that paradoxically are not too different from those attracting them to radical-socialism
and the left in the third republic in France. Perhaps in Italy they were loyal
on the one side to the church and on the other to the left. One interesting
finding is that at the time of the first congress of syndical corporations in
June 1922, 8,200 *dirigenti tecnici* and 5,000 members of the *corporazione
nazionale teatro*,[80] again support the Salvatorelli thesis.

What might be called the intellectual bourgeoisie in contrast to the economic bourgeoisie also seemed to play a dominant role in Brazilian *Integralismo*.[81] Among its 24 national leaders, 21 came from liberal professions
— professors, journalists, students, and higher civil servants. Among 61
regional leaders, 41 came from this stratum, and none in either group from
the business, industrial, or landowning bourgeoisie. In the *Chamber of
Forty*, the economic bourgeoisie held 7 seats compared to 24 of the middle
intellectual bourgeoisie, and in that of the 400, 136 were doctors and lawyers, compared to 63 from the economic bourgeoisie and 23 small businessmen, small industrialists, and small landowners. Among 525 national and
regional leaders of the AIB (Brasilian Integralist Action), 304 came from
the middle intellectual bourgeoisie (see table 7). Unfortunately we have no
comparable data for the Spanish Falange and the JONS, but the reading of
the biographies of the leaders and the history of the party would suggest
that its composition would not be too different. Obviously, the rank and
file membership in Brazil included a much larger proportion of the small
bourgeoisie in the cities and small landowners, 54 per cent compared to 24
per cent from the intellectual bourgeoisie. The few data given by Eugen
Weber[82] on the occupational background of 251 Rumanian legionnaires
who had taken refuge in Germany after the rising in 1941 and were
interned in Buchenwald, most likely to reflect the leadership of the Iron
Guard in Bucharest and a few other centres, is not too different. Students,

## TABLE 7

### Social Composition of the Ação Integralista Brasileira

| | National leaders | Regional leaders | Chamber of 40 | Chamber of 400 | Total leaders | % | Sample of local militants and leaders | Image of social composition 1st place |
|---|---|---|---|---|---|---|---|---|
| Industrialists, merchants and landowners | 0 | 0 | 7 | 63 | 70 | 13.3 | 0 | 0 |
| Liberal professionals, writers, journalists, professors, students higher civil servants | 21 | 41 | 24 | 218 | 304 | 57.9 | 20 | |
| Higher military officers | 2 | 9 | 9 | 26 | 46 | 8.8 | 4 | 0 Md. cl. 5 |
| Small businessmen and landowners | | | | 23 | 23 | 4.4 | 16 | 30 |
| Public and private white collar | | | 44 | 44 | 8.4 | 38 | 35 |
| Workers, farm labourers | | | | 14 | 14 | 2.7 | 22 | 29 |
| No information | 1 | 11 | — | 12 | 24 | 4.6 | | 1 |
| | (24) | (61) | (40) | (400) | (525) | 100 | (100) | |

Data from Helgio H. Casses Trindade, *Integralismo (O facismo brasileiro na decada de 30)*, 140-41, 143, 145.

professors, school teachers, lawyers, doctors, engineers, and journalists numbered 147 of the 231 for which we have information on occupations. In fact 26 per cent were students. Among 76 legionnaires executed in concentration camps as reprisals for the murder of the prime minister in 1939, 35 were university or high school students. In France, among 736 delegates participating in the first national congress in November 1936 of Doriot's Parti Populaire Français (PPF) the students seem less prominent, but 195 were free professionals, journalists, technicians, or civil servants compared to 56 businessmen, merchants or managers of enterprises, and 63 white collar employees.[83] The PPF, claiming to be a populist party led by a former prominent communist leader who initially carried support in his working-class constituency and among some former communists, is stated according to this data to have 422 workers and peasants among its delegates (see table 8). In summary, there is some evidence that a number of fascist parties were more successful than the Nazis among students and professionals and perhaps among emerging technicians than among independent artisans, small businessmen, and industrialists.

The success of fascist parties among civil servants seems to vary appreciably from country to country and might be linked with the different response of the government to membership in extremist organizations. Even in Germany, Mierendorff[84] has emphasized how important the distinction between higher civil servants (*Hoheitsbeamte*) and lower civil servants, particularly those who have only an employee rather than civil service status, was for the relative attraction of the party. It has been said in Germany that the employees of public services like the post offices, the railways, and urban transportation were particularly susceptible to national socialist appeals, especially in Austria. The strength of the fascist *corporazioni* of local public services and transport, respectively 10,700 and 43,000 compared to industrial trade unions 72,000, would be similar, even when we have to take into account the early influence of a pro-D'Annunzio leadership among merchant seamen and harbour workers.[35] Perhaps this lower civil-service group was particularly sensitive to relative status deprivations with the rising power and income of the working class.

A variety of sources allow us to follow through time the social composition of the Nazi movement: from the participants in the founding meeting of the Deutsche Arbeiterpartei on 12 September 1919, the first membership list of January 1920, the members just before the November 1923 beerhall putsch, 1930-1933, to the party in power in 1935. Those data summarized in table 9 show how the party expanded from its urban base, in which skilled workers and artisans together with soldiers joined with lower white-collar employees and small businessmen, to include a number of farmers larger than their proportion in the population. With the passing of time it would seem as if the proportion of white collar employees — that is the new middle class — would have grown more rapidly

## TABLE 8

Social Composition of the Leadership of Action Française
and Doriot's Parti Populaire Français

| | Action Française 1933 League officials | | PPF 1936 delegates |
|---|---|---|---|
| Free professionals | | | |
| Lawyers | 11.4 | | |
| Doctors | 23.2 } 35.0 | | } 10.6 |
| Other | 1.4 | | |
| Technicians | | | 11.1 |
| Civil servants | 3.3 | | 2.2 |
| Military officers | 15.2 | | |
| White collar employees | 3.7 | | 8.6 |
| Businessmen | | | |
| Shopkeepers | } 21.8 | 28.8 | } 7.6 |
| Industrialists | 8.0 | | |
| Farmers and landowners | 12.3 | | |
| Peasants | | | } 57.3 |
| Workers | | | |
| Students | | | 2.6 |
| | (212)* | | (736)** |

*With information on occupation among 873 listed in the 1933 Almanach, quoted by Eugen Weber, *Action Française. Royalism and Reaction in the 20th Century* (Stanford, 1962), 267.

**Among 736 responding to a party questionnaire. See Dieter Wolf, *Die Doriot-Bewegung* (Stuttgart, 1967) 139-41.

TABLE 9

Social Composition of Membership of the Nazi Movement 1919-1935 (in percentages)

| | DAP founding meeting 9/12/1919 | DAP membership list 1/1920 | Sept./Nov. 1923 | Gordon sample 1923 | Members 1930 | | 1/30/33 | 1/1/35 | Active population 1935 |
|---|---|---|---|---|---|---|---|---|---|
| Peasants | — | — | 10.4 | 2.0 | 13.2 | 14.0 | 12.5 | 10.2 | 10.0 |
| White collar | 2 | | | | 24.0 | 25.6 | 20.6 | | 12.4 |
|   Sales | | ← 14 → | low 11.1 | 10.8 | | | | 11.5 | |
|     up. | | | up. 1.8 | | | | | | |
|   Technical | | | | 2.4 | | | | 3.5 | |
|   Other | | | | 10.8 | | | | 4.4 | |
| Civil servant | — | | | 10.6 | 7.7 | 6.6 | ← 6.5 → | 9.0 | 3.9 |
| Teaching | — | | low 6.2  up. 0.4 | 2.4  1.8 | | 1.7 | | 3.4 | 0.9 |
| Free professionals | 6 | 14.5 | 1.7 | 8.4 | ← 18.9 → | 20.7 | ← 17.3 → | 3.2 | 1.0 |
| Artists | — | — | 1.4 | 3.6 | | | | | |
| Small business | 4 | 16 | 16.2 | 3.5 | | | | 7.5 | 3.9 |
| Artisans | 4 | ← 33 → | 20.0 | | | | | 8.3 | 4.7 |
| Apprentices | | | 1.5 | 1.9 | | | | — | |
| Skill. workers | 12 | ← 2.5 → | 8.5 | 21.5 | 26.3 | 28.1 | 32.5 | 19.2 | 46.3 |
| Unskill. work. servants | — | | 9.5  1.7 | 4.5 | | | | 6.5 | |
| Mining | — | | | | | | | 0.8 | |

TABLE 9 (Continued)

| | | | | | | | | |
|---|---|---|---|---|---|---|---|---|
| Farm labourers | — | | — | | | | | 3.8 |
| Officers and soldiers | 6 | 13 | 0.6 | | | | | |
| Students | 5 | 7 | 4.2 | 10.7 | | | 1.2 | 1.4 |
| Pensioners | | | — | 1.7 | | | 1.6 | 1.5 |
| Housewives | | | 3.8 | 2.8 | | | 4.1 | 2.6 |
| Other | | | 1.5 | 9.9 | 3.3 | 16.9 | 3.7 | 3.2 |
| No information | 6 | | — | | | | | |
| Total | 45 | (190) | (4726) | (1126) | 100* | 100** | 100 | 100 |

Data on the participants on the 12 September 1919 meeting of the DAP, from George Franz-Willing, *Die Hitlerbewegung. Der Ursprung 1919-1922* (Hamburg, 1962) 126.

Data on those listed in the oldest membership list, January 1920, ibid., p. 130.

Data on 4,726 members of the NSDAP in November 1923, from Michael H. Kater, 'Zur Soziographie der Frühen NSDAP.' *Vierteljahrshefte für Zeitgeschichte*, 19, 2 (April 1971), 124-59. See table 2, 139. This article contains a detailed analysis of the data file and tabulations by region, size of town, sex, age, and cross tabulations by these variations.

The sample of party members—1,126 persons—for whom occupational data were available is described by Harold J. Gordon, Jr. *Hitler and the Beer Hall Putsch* (Princeton, 1972), 80-83, and appendix, 622-26. Of those coded by other occupations, 20 were regular officers before the war, 39 were reserve officers, and 103 were of unknown status, probably mostly in the reserves. Only 19 majors or above.

Data for members in 1930, 1933, and 1935 are from the *NSDAP Partei-Statistik. Stand: 1935.* Published by Der Reichsorganisationsleiter der NSDAP as a confidential publication in 3 volumes. The information in Volume I has been used by Wolfgang Schäfer, *NSDAP. Entwicklung und Struktur der Staatspartei des Dritten Reiches* (Hannover, 1957), 38, and David Schoenbaum, *Hitler's Social Revolution: Class and Status in Nazi Germany 1933-1939* (Garden City, N. Y., 1967), p. 28 and 67.

*Data in Schoenbaum, p. 28.

**Data in Schäfer, p. 17.

than that of the old middle class of small businessmen and shop owners. The proportion of manual workers, contrary to what might have been expected in the 1923 NSDAP, was not larger than in 1930 and 1933, even when apparently among them the unskilled constituted the larger proportion to be replaced, particularly after taking power, by a large number of skilled workers and a significant number of farm labourers. In the thirties, when around 46 per cent of the population could be classified as manual workers, between 28 and 32 per cent of the membership of the NSDAP were workers. Quite congruently with the analysis of Geiger pointing to the disillusionment of the white-collar employees affiliated with the nationalist's trade union movement sympathetic to the Nazis in the early thirties with a conservative tendency in social policy matters of Hitler, the share of that group in the total membership in January 1933 reached a low. The impact of the taking of power and the appeal of the party to civil servants and teachers is reflected in their increasing presence in its ranks, probably also the result of the lifting of some of the restrictions imposed by government on membership of those groups. In 1930 teachers constituted 1.7 per cent of the membership and in 1935, 3.4 per cent.

The data for Protestant and largely rural Lower Saxony districts show the importance of the peasantry for the party compared to its insignificance in the initial Bavarian nucleus. Those for the Gau of Treveris, a Catholic area, on the other hand, show the resistance of the Catholic peasantry. Small and not fully representative information on militants involved in one way or another in violence leading to action by the authorities in Austria do not differ appreciably from those for Germany. In the mid-1920's, however, mainly in Vienna, students constituted an important group among these activists, 14 per cent, together with skilled workers and *Angestellte*. Apparently, the self-employed became more important later. The Austrian data also allow a comparison between the SA and the SS showing the more proletarian character of the former and the more middle-class character of the latter (see table 10).

The comparison between pre-1933 members, the *Alte Kämpfer*, and the newcomers between the *Machterfreifung* and 1935, both for the Reich and for the Gau of Treveris, a district in which most of the members had joined in that period, shows how dangerous it is to make inferences on the composition of the fascist party before taking power from data on its composition when it is the state party (see tables 11 and 12). Before 1933 civil servants and teachers constituted little less than 7 per cent of the membership, but they would be over 15 per cent of the newcomers. In the total membership in 1935, civil servants and teachers who had joined before 1933 would be 2.3 per cent and those who joined after Hitler became Chancellor would be 10.1 per cent of the total membership. This dramatic increase has to be taken into account when one reads

## TABLE 10

### Occupational Composition of Austrian NSDAP Militants*

| | Militants** | | | 1923 - 1933 | | | |
| | 1923-25 mainly in Vienna | Whole of Austria | Vienna only | All Nazi militants | Party members | SA | SS since 1932 |
|---|---|---|---|---|---|---|---|
| | | 1929-1932 | | | | | |
| Farmers | — | — | — | — | — | — | — |
| White collar | 32 | 26 | 28 | — | — | — | — |
| Commerce | | | | 13 | 5 | 14 | 26 |
| Other | | | | 13 | 9 | 15 | 13 |
| Civil servants and public employees | 8 | 12 | 9 | 9 | 9 | 10 | 18 |
| Professionals | — | 6 | — | 2 | 5 | — | — |
| Self employed | 5 | 12 | 27 | 8 | 16 | 3 | — |
| Workers | | | | | | | |
| Skilled | 32 | 29 | } 27 | 32 | 29 | 43 | 30 |
| Unskilled | 1 | 6 | | 4 | 5 | 3 | 9 |
| Apprentice pupils | 4 | 6 | 9 | 8 | 15 | 6 | — |
| Students | 14 | 3 | — | 9 | 7 | 5 | 4 |
| Other | 4 | — | — | 2 | — | 3 | — |
| | (73) | (34) | (11) | (167) | (49) | (37) | (23) |

*Data from a paper by Gerhard Botz, 'Aspects of the Social Structure of the Austrian Nazi Party 1922-1940,' presented at the Bergen Conference on Comparative European Nazism and Fascism, Bergen, 19-21 June 1974.

**Participants in political deeds of violence as perpetrators, injured, casualties, and witnesses.

## TABLE 11

### Occupation and NSDAP Membership in the Reich on 1 January 1935

| | Alte Kämpfer* | | Newcomers | | Total | % of members | % party members of occupation | Active population |
|---|---|---|---|---|---|---|---|---|
| Peasants | 4.3 | 12.6 | 5.9 | 8.9 | 10.10 | 10.7 | 7.7 | 10.0 |
| White collar employees | 7.2 | 21.1 | 12.2 | 18.5 | 19.50 | 20.6 | 12.0 | 12.4 |
| Civil servants | 2.3 | 6.8 | 10.1 | 15.3 | 12.40 | 9.4 | 18.4 | 3.7 |
| Teaching | | | | | | 3.6 | 30.0 | 0.9 |
| Business & self empl. | 6.0 | 17.6 | 13.0 | 19.8 | 19.00 | 20.2 | 15.2 | 9.6 |
| Workers | 11.0 | 31.4 | 19.6 | 29.7 | 30.30 | 32.1 | 5.1 | 46.3 |
| Other | 1.3 | 3.7 | 2.0 | 1.5 | 3.23 | 3.4 | 1.5 | 16.9 |
| Students | .4 | 1.2 | 1.0 | 1.4 | 1.35 | — | — | — |
| Rentiers & pensioners | .6 | 1.6 | 1.0 | 1.5 | 1.52 | — | — | — |
| Housewives | 1.4 | 4.0 | 1.2 | 1.9 | 2.60 | — | — | — |
| *Total* | 34.5 | 100.00 | 66.0 | 98.5†† | 100.00 | 100.00** | 7.3 | 100.00† |

Data calculated on the basis of information in Franz J. Heyen, *Nationalsozialismus im Alltag*, 330-31, and from Wolfgang Schäfer, *NSDAP Entwicklung und Struktur der Staatspartei des Dritten Reiches*, 38.

*Those who had joined before the Machtergreifung.

**Based on 2,357,884 members, equal to 94.5% of membership.

†Based on active population equal to 49.5% of the population; % equal 32, 306,074.

††Rather than 100% due to rounding out of figures.

TABLE 12

Occupation and NSDAP Membership in the
Gau of Treveris,* 1 January 1935

| | Alte Kämpfer | | Newcomers | | Total |
|---|---|---|---|---|---|
| Peasants | 2.3 | 12.4 | 9.4 | 11.5 | 11.7 |
| White collar employees | 3.1 | 16.9 | 10.1 | 12.4 | 13.2 |
| Civil servants incl. teaching | 1.1 | 5.8 | 14.0 | 17.1 | 15.0 |
| Business & self. empl. | 3.2 | 17.6 | 12.9 | 15.8 | 16.1 |
| Workers | 7.1 | 39.1 | 31.3 | 38.2 | 38.4 |
| Other | .5 | 2.9 | 1.6 | 1.9 | 2.09 |
| Students | .1 | | .8 | .8 | .92 |
| Rentiers & pensioners | .3 | 1.8 | 1.2 | 1.4 | 1.51 |
| Housewives | .1 | 2.9 | .8 | .7 | 1.08 |
| Total | 17.8 | 100.0 | 82.1 | 99.9 | |

Data calculated on the basis of information in Franz J. Heyen, *Nationalsozialismus im Alltag*, 330-31.
*Gau of Treveris is a Catholic district with low NSDAP vote.

an analysis showing that 18.4 per cent of all civil servants and 30 per cent of all teachers were members of the party. They certainly were in 1935 but that does not mean that the same proportions would have joined or sympathized with the party if it had not come to power. On the other hand, by 1933 the party seems to have exhausted its capacity to make sizeable inroads into a number of social groups, increasing its share in absolute numbers between 1933 and 1935 but with no disproportionate new gains among workers, peasants and white-collar employees. The data for the Gau of Treveris once more show the same patterns in a microcosm despite the fact that here 82 per cent of the party members were new-comers compared to 66 per cent in the Reich. In Treveris there was no major change except the disproportionate number of civil servants and teachers among the late joiners and the levelling off of the attraction to white-collar employees, independent business, and the peasants.

Using official party records in the Berlin Document Center, Henry Turner has studied the membership in the NSDAP of 92 big business executives mentioned in the literature as linked with the Nazi party or tried after the war in Nuremberg. Among them 47 per cent had no record of party affiliation and among the members only 12 per cent had joined before the *Machtergreifung* and another 37 per cent before 1 May 1933, some of them thanks to the backdating of their affiliation by the officials. Considering the biased character of this sample, there is little evidence that a significant number of big business executives would have joined the party, and even many of those who joined did so only after 1936.

The decision of the Norwegian government after World War II to make all the members of the Nasjonal Samling (Quisling's party) during the War subject to prosecution has allowed Norwegian social scientists to undertake a major sociological study of 54,651 members after 9 April 1940, making possible comparisons by date of joining, region, age and, particularly, occupation (see table 13). Given the high turnover in membership, we cannot be certain that those who joined before the war and stayed in the party would be representative of all those who joined in the thirties. They certainly would be the core of the party. A comparison between them and the late joiners, especially those who did so in response to the military success of the German armies, that correlates with membership increases as a result of the pressures of the occupation authorities and the Norwegian collaborators, is particularly interesting. That comparison should certainly serve as a caution to those who would be tempted to derive conclusions about the social composition of fascist, or any parties, before taking power from membership after gaining it. And even more in the case of parties collaborating with the occupier. This unique body of data confirms some of the patterns we have found for membership in other countries. Among the Nasjonal Samling members before 1939, we find that one-third were under thirty years old and that more than 60 per cent were

## TABLE 13

Occupation of Members of the Nasjonal Samling in Norway
Automatically Prosecuted for Membership after the German
Invasion. Data from Jan Petter Myklebust[*]

| | Joined before April 1940 | Joined April 1940 or later in war | Total members (incl. no information on date of joining) |
|---|---|---|---|
| Farmers | 9.0 | 10.9 | 10.5 |
| Lower white collar employees | 15.3 | 11.2 | 11.1 |
| Lower and middle public servants | 3.3 ⎫ | 2.7 ⎫ | 3.0 ⎫ |
| Police | 1.4 ⎬ 6.9 | 4.0 ⎬ 8.0 | 3.8 ⎬ 8.1 |
| Civil servants | 2.2 ⎭ | 1.3 ⎭ | 1.3 ⎭ |
| Teachers | 1.4 | 1.7 | 1.6 |
| Technicians and engineers | 3.3 ⎫ | 1.2 ⎫ | 1.3 ⎫ |
| Free professionals | 2.9 ⎬ 7.4 | 1.1 ⎬ 3.1 | 1.2 ⎬ 3.3 |
| Artists | 1.2 ⎭ | 0.8 ⎭ | 0.8 ⎭ |
| Managing private | 8.1 ⎫ 11.6 | 3.6 ⎫ 5.8 | 3.7 ⎫ 5.9 |
| Businessmen | 3.5 ⎭ | 2.2 ⎭ | 2.2 ⎭ |
| Skilled workers | 7.6 ⎫ | 8.5 ⎫ | 8.2 ⎫ |
| Unskilled workers | 8.9 ⎬ 16.9 | 18.2 ⎬ 30.4 | 17.3 ⎬ 28.0 |
| Servants | 0.4 ⎭ | 3.7 ⎭ | 2.5 ⎭ |
| Students | 4.6 | 3.7 | 3.6 |
| Pensioners | 0.4 | 0.8 | 0.8 |
| Housewives | 13.5 | 18.6 | 17.8 |
| No information | 12.9 | 6.8 | 9.2 |
| *Total* | (2,691) | (49,437) | (54,651) |

(*)From a paper on the sociography of the Nasjonal Samling presented at the Bergen conference on Comparative European Nazism and Fascism, Bergen, 19-21 June 1974. See also the paper by Stein Ugelvik Larsen presented at the same conference on the recruitment to the NS in Norway.

under forty-one. Even without the crisis created by war, defeat, failed revolutionary attempts, and the consequent disruption in the life of several generations, Norwegian fascism had its main appeal to the young. Occupationally, 2,691 pre-war members out of some 15,000 claimed by the party in 1935, were a heterogeneous group. They were certainly disproportionately middle class, but it would be a mistake to ignore a not insignificant number of unskilled workers in addition to the skilled and artisans — some 18 per cent. They would represent a more sizeable proportion among the later joiners. The farmers, to whom Quisling made a special appeal — let us not forget that he himself had been identified with the Agrarian party and that the Depression had seriously affected certain rural areas — constituted an important group that would increase during the war, despite the fact that it was probably the least affected by pressures from the authorities to join. As in other central European fascist parties, white-collar employees, both lower and managing, constituted an important source of members to which we might add the engineers and technicians whose presence in the leadership of fascist parties we had already noted. This presence contrasts with the relatively weak support of other professionals: 3.3 per cent engineers compared to 2.9 in the other liberal professions, a figure that is high even in comparison with business directors and owners of private enterprises (3.5 per cent). Except for the peasants, it would seem that the employed, rather than the self-employed, middle-class was attracted by these minor fascist parties. The important contingent of peasants fits well with the image of fascism as the romantic, *völkisch*, neo-traditionalist, and to some extent anti-modern movement. But the presence of the employed middle classes and, particularly, the engineers and technicians also shows the attractiveness of some of its emphasis on production and planning, in contrast with the irrationalities of the free market and the economic crisis resulting from capitalist business cycles. However, these more respectable middle-class groups that joined in the earlier period of the party represented a lower proportion among the late joiners. The relative share of the top status groups diminished drastically in the course of the war years in which opportunists, responsive to pressure to join particularly in the public sector, and probably in response to the ideology of the peasants, became more significant. Since there are also data on withdrawals from the party it is interesting to note that farmers were less likely to drop membership than professionals, teachers, and managers. Significantly, the social groups of lower status were more likely to join in the more peripheral regions of the country.

The documentation on the members of the NS also allowed some analysis of the heterogeneous motives and particularly the pragmatic reasons for joining during the war: the impact of unemployment, of social pressures from family and friends, but also from ideological appeals among which, surprisingly, anti-communism did not play an important role.

Interviews with samples of ex-members would make the Nasjonal Samling probably the best studied of the minor fascist parties.

*Age*

The evidence on age composition of the membership is more clear-cut and similar than that on occupation. There can be no doubt about the youthfulness of the membership in Italy, particularly in the early period of the party, Rumania, Germany, France, Spain, and probably other countries. For 994 of the 1,672 members of the NSDAP before November 1923 for which we have information, 610 were under 31 years of age, and 1935, 21 or less.[86] In September 1930, 36.8 per cent of the membership and 26.2 per cent of the leadership was 30 or younger, and respectively 31.8 per cent and 34.7 per cent, 41 years or over. The average age of the Rumanian legionnaires mentioned above was 27.4 years in 1940 and that of the delegates to the Parti Populaire Français (PPF) congress in 1938 was 34 years.[87] In 1933 the majority of the leaders and militants of Brazilian Integralism was under 25 years and three-quarters under 30. Among 25 top national and regional leaders only five were above 30.[88] This youthfulness accounts for some of the difficulties in attempting to understand the fascist phenomenon in socio-economic terms. Too many of the fascist activists and leaders had not achieved a well-defined position in the social class system, had no well-defined interests, and very often their involvement in extremist politics left them no time to pursue a normal career. Obviously, their family background provided them with a location in the social structure, but one that oriented them more toward the general abstract view of the right kind of social order rather than the defence of particular interests. It is this free-floating social position that allowed them their activism, their rejection of existing parties, including those of their fathers representing particular interests, and the mixture of idealism and irresponsibility that characterizes their action. It is no accident that the programme of the JONS should demand that the political position of highest responsibility should be turned over to youth, to the Spaniards of less than 45 years of age.

*Religion*

We have practically no information about the religiosity of members of fascist parties, particularly when compared with what we know about some of the top leaders, and on their voters from ecological analyses. There are some scattered data for Nazi activists and a more thorough analysis of the *Partei-Statistik* would allow some ecological inferences. While the NSDAP originated in southern Germany—a Catholic area— even there it had a strong appeal in Protestant Franconia and soon gained its main strength in Protestant northern and eastern Germany. In Italy fascists, like most Italians, were Catholic by birth, but we do not know how far they were practising Catholics or anti-clerical Catholics in the *Risorgimento* tradition. Certainly those who came from sindicalism or the left interventionism, like Mussolini himself, were anti-clerical and agnostic. Our ecological analysis would show that party membership was highest in areas where integration into a Catholic sub-culture was weakest.[89]

Using the data provided by De Felice on the affiliation to the Italian Fascist party for 71 territorial units of 30 April 1921 and the returns for the parliamentary election of 15 May 1921 (see table 14), we have explored the impact of the strength or weakness of the Partito Populare Italiano (PPI) on the affiliation rate per thousand males over 21 at the time, assuming that most of the members of the PNF would be males, even when many were probably below that age. The analysis uses party affiliation rather than election returns as in Germany, because the PNF before taking power did not compete alone in any election before 1924 and therefore it is difficult to estimate its electoral strength before the March on Rome. Nor was it possible to classify the 71 units for which we have membership data by their religiosity, since it would be difficult to make their limits comparable with those of the dioceses for which we had data on affiliation to Catholic Action and other indicators of religiosity. Even when many practising Catholics would not support the PPI, its supporters were certainly among the most religious in all sectors of the population, including the working people and particularly the peasants, but also the urban middle classes. Since in 1921 neither the PPI nor the PNF had made strong inroads in the electorate south of Rome, including the capital where the PNF was still weak, we have limited our analysis to the 18 electoral districts north of Rome. In the 13 districts where the Populari obtained more votes than their national average of 20.6 per cent, the affiliation to the fascists was 7.2 per thousand, while in the ten districts where the PPI poll was below average, the fascists' affiliation rate was 15.8. Since, however, the rate in Venezia Giulia, Trieste, and the Yugoslav border area was disproportionately high—57.1—it is fair to make the comparison excluding that hotbed of extremist nationalism; but even so the rate of 11.7 is appreciably higher. One might suspect that those figures reflect the differences between the more religious Veneto and the Alpine valleys of Piedmont, and particularly, Lombardy, in contrast to the more de-Christianized Po Valley, the stronghold of agrarian fascism. We decided to separate the north from the centre. In the north, the 11 districts in which the Populari were strong, differ from the 3 in which they were weak with affiliation rates of 6.6 and 11.6 per thousand. Even in central Italy, that is, Emilia, Romagna, Tuscany, Marche, and Umbria, the fascist appeal was weaker in the 2 districts in which the

TABLE 14

Fascist Party Membership by Region and Electoral Districts Above or Below Average
Vote for the Populari and Socialists in the 15 May 1921 Election

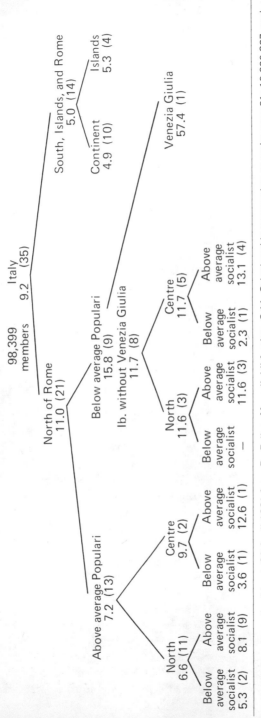

Fascist Party membership on 30 April 1921 from De Felice, *Mussolini il fascista*, 8-11. Calculated in proportion to males over 21: 10 690 327, and expressed in per thousand. The population figure from: Instituto Centrale di Statistica e Ministero per la Costituente, *Compendio delle Statistiche Elettorali italiane dal 1848 al 1934*, 1 (Roma, 1946), 64-65. The election returns by district from Ugo Giusti, *Le correnti politiche italiane attraverso due riforme elettorali dal 1909 al 1921* (Florence, Unione Statistica delle Citta Italiane, 1922), 80-88. The district of Bolzano has been left out of the analysis since there is no information on fascist membership. The average vote for the Populari was 20.6 and for the socialist, 25.1. These figures have been used as cutting points.

Populari were strong, 9.7, than in the 8 where they were weak, 11.7. There can be little doubt in view of this data that both parties must have competed for some of the same social groups and that success of one limited the chances of the other. On the other hand, we know that fascism was largely a response to socialism and the maximalist domination of northern Italy and the political economic and social power of socialist organization in the Po Valley agricultural areas after the war. In fact, Albert Szymanski,[90] using fascist violence (which in turn correlated 0.87 with affiliation) found a correlation with socialist vote in 1919 of 0.55, a correlation that was particularly strong when he controlled for industrialization 0.60, given a slightly negative correlation between industrialization and fascism. In view of this, we wanted to see if the presence of the Populari continued reducing the appeal of the fascists in areas of above average socialist strength in the 1921 election, that is, about 25.1 per cent. The analysis shows that north of Rome the fascist appeal was weakest in the two districts in which the Populari were strong and the socialists below average, 5.3 fascists per thousand, and strongest for central Italian districts in which the Populari were weak and the socialists were strong, 13.1 per thousand. In fact, in one of those districts, Bologna, Ferrara, Ravenna, Forli, they reached 29.1 per thousand. Only one year later they would reach the same level in Tuscany. For our analysis, however, it is more interesting to note that in the north Italian districts in which both the PPI and the socialists had strength above average, the fascists were still weaker than in the three in which the PPI was weak and the socialists strong, the rate being respectively 8.1 and 11.6 per thousand.

These data, which show a pattern not too dissimilar from the one found in Germany between the strength of the Zentrum and the NSDAP, suggest that the competition between Christian parties and fascists was of decisive importance and largely for the same type of electorate. De-Christianization and secularization (let us not forget that the German Protestants were appreciably more secularized than German Catholics) was one of the pre-conditions for the fascist success. The Italian data which we have calculated are particularly interesting, since the PNF, while having an anti-clerical tradition (let us not forget the youthful Mussolini writing an anti-clerical novel) was far less incompatible with the Church than the neo-pagan racism of many Nazis. Certainly, the Italian Church had not taken a militant anti-fascist position like the German anti-Nazi before the *Machtergreifung*. In Italy the competition for a similar clientele must have played a greater role or perhaps in Germany the resistance of the Zentrum electorate to the Nazi appeal was due more to the Catholic organizational network than the ideological conflict. In this context, the later decision of Vatican circles to disengage from the PPI and its leader Dom Sturzo, and years later the pressures on the Zentrum under the leadership of Kaas to find a *modus vivendi* with the Nazis for the sake of the interests of the Church acquired special importance.

The bitter conflict between the Catholic sub-culture and the Nazis before the *Machtergreifung* and the pronouncements of the hierarchy against them is well known. It is therefore no surprise that the autobiographical data collected by Abel and analyzed by Merkl[91] reflect a high level of secularization, since over 50 per cent of the biographies make no mention of religion, with an absolute majority of those living in Protestant areas. Only one in ten has a Catholic background to which one might add 7 per cent not mentioning religion, but born in Catholic areas, compared to one-quarter of the Abel sample which was clearly Protestant. The injunctions of the Catholic Church against the party before taking power and the social pressures applied to Catholics joining the party must have limited its appeal to them, but not to Protestants and particularly not to secularized Protestants. The detailed data offered by Schäfer[92] on the NSDAP membership in relationship to population, the proportions of late versus early joiners, and the proportion of non-party officials in local government after takeover in different regions confirmed the weakness of the party among Catholics so clearly shown by the electoral data.

The hostility of the Belgian and Dutch[93] hierarchies, the latter followed soon by Protestant leaders, must have been a serious obstacle to the growth of the fascist movement in the Low Countries. There can be little doubt that the *verzuilingen* of the Dutch electorate by the religious parties against which the followers of Mussert directed their attacks, the joint efforts of Christian social and socialist parties in Belgium when faced with the competition of the Rex, and even the strength of the more authoritarian and fascisticized clerical party in Austria, represented a serious barrier for the fascist movement in those countries where the social structure and, to some extent, the impact of the depression would have led us to expect that they would have a greater success.

There are no systematic data on other fascist movements that would allow us to know the level and type of religiosity of their members. In Spain, after the Civil War, we find a certain inverse relationship between the areas of highest affiliation to women's Catholic Action and the women's section of Falange, despite the incorporation of religious activities in the party.[94] The situation must have been quite different in Rumania where a populist religiosity became part of the Iron Guard appeal. This is even more true in the case of Slovakia and Croatia where the national identity was closely linked with religious identity. In the case of Brazil we find however a relatively high level of church membership among the Integralistas including the presence of seven priests in the chamber of 400 and the sympathy of some bishops.[95] Perhaps the secular character of the Brazilian state made this extremist opposition movement appealing to Catholics, even when there was a significant minority of Protestants among its members. The nationalistic cultural reaffirmation, the search for a new sense of community in this case was compatible with religion.

### Fascist Jews

Obviously racist fascist movements would have no Jewish members, and it is unlikely that even the non-anti-Semitic movements after Hitler's rise to power could have attracted Jews. However, Italian fascism had at least five Jews among the 191 participants in the founding act in 1919, and three among the martyrs of the revolution, and of nine Jewish deputies in 1921, one was fascist. In Ferrara, a city with a large well-to-do Jewish community, the squads of Italo Balbo found supporters among them.[96] The application of the racial laws in 1938 have provided data indicating that 10,125 Italian Jews over 21 were party members, 739 of them fascists or nationalists before 28 October 1922 compared to 22,161 non-members. Given the position in Italian society of the Jews, the membership in the party is not surprising and we should not forget the prominent role played by many of them in the socialist parties and in the anti-fascist opposition, particularly among intellectuals. In fact, very early on, a number of Zionist leaders felt uneasy about the fascist rise to power; the identification of many Jews in Italy, and particularly abroad, with anti-fascism would over the years make Jewishness incompatible with fascism and lead Mussolini to adopt a racist policy. Certainly Italian Jews responded to the political appeals of the first post-war years in the same way as other Italians (51 of them participated in the Fiume expedition), in terms of Italian nationalism, the defence of their class interests supporting fascism, as a larger number of them for other sociological reasons responded to the appeals of anti-fascist parties. For them the later racism, despite the provisions exempting them from some of the measures of the racial laws initially, must have been a double tragedy.

### Other Characteristics

One aspect in the study of the membership of fascist parties that has received attention only in the case of nazism, particularly in the book by Merkl, is a systematic comparison between the membership of the party and the paramilitary organizations like the SA and later the SS, or in Italy the *squadrismo* activists compared to just dues-paying members. The books honouring the dead of the movement, the local histories of the party, the work of Ciurco, and the numerous histories of the struggle between fascists and anti-fascists and their respective victims that have recently appeared, should allow a more systematic analysis of the social composition of the activist core. Let us not forget that fascist parties conceive of themselves as composed of a front line and a second line of reserves in contrast to other mass parties. A very neglected aspect is the study of the social composition of the functional groups of fascist parties: the youth organizations, the women's organizations, and particularly the trade-union or workplace organizations like the NSBO and, in the case of the Nazis, the very successful and important professional associations of lawyers, teachers, and others.[97] The parties attracted little electoral support from women, generally more identified with the religious parties; they exalted masculinity and could in many ways be characterized as anti-feminist. Among the top leaders with political and ideological influence we find no women, unlike the position in the socialist and communist movements. However, paradoxically, fascist parties in power contributed to the political mobilization of women in traditional societies and women activists often gave strong emotional support to their menfolk. The welfare state with ideology and voluntary participation that contributed to the appeal of fascist regimes was in large measure supported by women committed to the movement.

## THE ELECTORAL BASIS OF FASCISM

A basic source for the sociological study of political movements has been the analysis of electorates,[98] initially by more or less sophisticated analysis of electoral statistics, and particularly since World War II by extensive analysis of public opinion surveys. The second source does not exist for the pre-World War II fascist movements, and even the electorate of the neo-fascist parties, except in Germany, has not been the subject of intensive study by survey techniques. The analysis of electoral data is based on inferences on ecological correlations. That analysis presupposes the accumulation of information over a number of elections and is most feasible when parties have highly visible strongholds in particular districts of distinctive social characteristics, specifically class and religious parties, preferably in two-party systems. Let us not forget that in highly fractionalised multi-party systems most ecological analyses are based on a dichotomy between working-class and bourgeois parties, or clerical and anti-clerical or like parties, without shedding much light on the internal differentiations within those blocs. The fact that fascist parties were generally minority parties and participated in fewer elections, except in Germany, makes ecological analysis difficult.

Certainly much research remains to be done on the electoral basis of minor fascist parties even though the elections in which they participated in some eastern European countries generally do not satisfy the requirement of having been free and honestly counted elections. Electoral sociology can give us little information on a number of fascist parties that made their appearance under authoritarian regimes moving from tolerance, co-optation to repression, as in Hungary and for most of the time in Rumania. In Brazil the growing fascist movement would soon be outlawed by the authoritarian regime of Vargas.

The Portuguese national syndicalists would not have a chance to compete in elections under the military bureaucratic dictatorships that preceded Salazar. Nor would the variety of fascist movements in Vichy France have a chance to test their strength in elections and the same would be true in some of the Baltic countries. Only in Belgium, the Netherlands, Scandinavia, and Finland did fascist parties have a chance to compete in free elections and only in Belgium was their electoral strength sufficient even to attempt a fruitful ecological analysis. In Spain the late founding of fascism, the size of the constituencies, the incertitude about electoral data, which makes ecological analysis even of the major parties difficult, does not leave room for a study of the social basis of Falange. In Italy the fact that the fascists participated under their own label only in one election and later mostly within a broad and heterogeneous coalition of the national blocs, again limits the possibilities of electoral research. In Austria we can study the electoral strength of the native semi-fascist, semi-conservative parties, but not of national-socialism whose success coincides with the period of only regional and municipal elections, and an authoritarian regime outlawing the party. Even so, the scattered data for a number of countries and the massive information on German elections provides some insight into the electoral appeal of the parties[99] (see table 15).

The ecological analysis of German and to some extent Austrian elections seems to confirm the following main trends: a disproportionate Nazi strength among Protestants and a weakness among Catholics which is only slowly overcome; a disproportionate strength in rural peasant communities, particularly of northern and north-western Germany, apparently greater in those areas with a more homogeneous class structure and particularly those affected by market fluctuations and the economic crisis; and a greater strength in small towns than in metropolitan centres, probably even if the occupational structure were not different, as it certainly was.

Nico Passchier[100] has calculated the average Nazi vote in 1930 to 1933 for different areas of Germany using 68 relatively homogeneous units to show the impact of religious and rural urban differences. While the average Nazi vote in Germany was 33.1 per cent, that vote in Catholic Germany was 28.6 compared to 36.3 in Protestant Germany. Among both Catholics and Protestants, the areas that were predominantly agricultural in their occupational structure voted more for the Nazis, particularly in Protestant Germany (respectively 29.8 and 40.6 per cent). The non-agricultural districts gave fewer votes to the NSDAP and among

## TABLE 15

Electoral Strength and Parliamentary Representation of Fascist and Some Semi-Fascist Parties in Free or Relatively Free Elections

| Country, party, year of election | Votes no. | % | no. | Seats % | total |
|---|---|---|---|---|---|
| *Germany* | | | | | |
| Deutschvölkische Freiheitsbewegung | | | | | |
| 1924 May | 1,918,310 | 6.5 | 32 | 6.8 | (472) |
| Nationalsozialistiche Freiheitsbewegung | | | | | |
| 1924 December | 906,946 | 3.0 | 14 | 2.8 | (493) |
| NSDAP | | | | | |
| 1928 | 809,771 | 2.6 | 12 | 2.4 | (491) |
| 1930 | 6,406,924 | 18.3 | 107 | 18.5 | (577) |
| Presidential election (Hitler vote) | | | | | |
| 1932 March 13 | 11,339,446 | 30.1 | | | |
| 1932 April 10 | 13,418,547 | 36.8 | | | |
| 1932 July | 13,779,111 | 37.4 | 230 | 37.8 | (608) |
| 1932 November | 11,737,391 | 33.1 | 196 | 33.6 | (584) |
| 1933 March | 17,277,200 | 43.9 | 288 | 44.5 | (647) |
| *Italy* | | | | | |
| PNF | | | | | |
| 1921 | 29,549 | 0.5 | 2 | .4 | (535) |
| National Bloc | | | | | |
| 1921 | 1.260,007 | 19.1 | 105 | 19.6 (31 fascist) | |
| PNF | | | | | |
| 1924 | 4,671,550 | 65.3 | 375 | 70.1 | (535) |
| MSI | | | | | |
| 1953 | 1,582,567 | 5.8 | 29 | 4.9 | (590) |
| *Rumania* | | | | | |
| Iron Guard | | | | | |
| 1927 | 10,761 | 0.4 | — | — | (387) |
| 1928 | — | — | — | — | (387) |
| 1931 June | 30,783 | 1.1 | — | — | (387) |
| 1932 July | 70,674 | 2.4 | 5 | 1.3 | (387) |
| 1933 December | — | — | — | — | — |
| 1937 December | 478,378 | 15.6 | 66 | 17.1 | (387) |
| LANC (Cuza) | | | | | |
| 1926 | 124,778 | 4.8 | 10 | 2.6 | (387) |
| 1927 | 52,481 | 1.9 | — | — | (387) |
| 1928 | 32,273 | 1.1 | — | — | (387) |
| 1931 | 113,863 | 3.0 | 8 | 2.1 | (387) |
| 1932 | 159,071 | 5.2 | 11 | 2.9 | (387) |
| 1933 | 133,205 | 4.5 | 9 | 2.3 | (387) |

TABLE 15 (Continued)

| Country, party, year of election | Votes no. | % | Seats no. | % | total |
|---|---|---|---|---|---|
| *Hungary* | | | | | |
| Fascist groups 1935 | 68,040 | 2.9 | 19 | 5.3 | (245) |
| Nyilaskeresztes (Arrow Cross) 1939 | | 25.0 | 31 | 11 | (283) |
| Other minor Nemzetissozialista | | | 18 | 7 | (283) |
| *Belgium* | | | | | |
| Rex 1936 | 271,491 | 11.49 | 21 | 10.4 | (202) |
| Bruxelles by election 1937 | | 18.50 | | | |
| 1939 | 103,821 | 4.43 | 4 | 2.0 | (202) |
| *Austria* | | | | | |
| NSDAP 1927 | 779 | | | | |
| Völkisch-Soziale Block 1930 | 111,843 | 3.0 | | | (165) |
| Heimatblock (Austro-Fascist) 1930 | 227,197 | 6.2 | 8 | 4.8 | (165) |
| NSDAP 1932 (No national elections only Landtag and municipal in selected districts) | | 20.0 | | | |
| Vienna 1932 April | 200,00 | 17.4 | | | |
| *Netherlands* | | | | | |
| NSB (Mussert) 1935 April (Den Haag) (Amsterdam) | 294,596 | 7.94 12.02 10.80 | | | |
| 1937 (Den Haag) (Amsterdam) | 171,137 | 4.22 5.93 6.16 | 4 | 4.0 | (100) |
| *Norway* | | | | | |
| Nasjonal Samling (Quisling) 1933 | 27,850 | 2.2 | | | |
| 1936 | 26,577 | 1.8 | | | |
| *Denmark* | | | | | |
| NSAP 1932 November | 757 | 0.1 | | | |
| 1935 October | 16,257 | 1.0 | | | |
| 1939 April | 31,032 | 1.8 | 3 | 2.0 | (148) |
| 1943 March | 43,309 | 2.1 | 3 | 2.0 | (148) |

## TABLE 15 (Continued)

| Country, party, year of election | no. | % | no. | Seats % | total |
|---|---|---|---|---|---|
| **Sweden** | | | | | |
| Sveriges Nationalsocialistika Parti | | | | | |
| 1932 | 15,170 | 0.6 | | | |
| 1934 (Landsting) | 8,170 | 0.5 | | | |
| 1934 (Municipalities) | 15,645 | 0.9 | | | |
| 1936 | 20,508 | 0.7 | | | |
| 1938 (Landsting) | 9,925 | 0.5 | | | |
| 1944 | 4,204 | | | | |
| **Spain** | | | | | |
| Falange Española | | | | | |
| 1936 | 44,971 | 0.7 | – | – | (470) |
| Valladolid Maximum | 8,228 | 4.9 | | | |
| **United Kingdom** | | | | | |
| 1931 October | 36,377 | 0.2 | – | – | |
| (% when opposed candidate) (No national elections until after WW II) | | 3.9 | | | |
| **Switzerland** | | | | | |
| Nationale Front parties | | | | | |
| 1935 National Council | 13,740 | 1.50 | | | |
| Zürich | | | | | |
| 1933 city | 6,085 | 7.7 | 10 | 8.0 | (125) |
| 1935 city | | 8.9 | | | |
| 1935 canton | 9,211 | 6.2 | 6 | 3.3 | (180) |
| 1938 city | 1,913 | 2.4 | | | |
| **Czechoslovakia** | | | | | |
| Different fascist groups | | | | | |
| 1935 | 167,433 | 2.0 | 6 | 2.0 | |
| Sudeten German party | | | | | |
| 1935 (K. Henlein) | 1,249,530 | 15.2 | 44 | 15.2 | |
| In Slovakia Hlinka party | 489,641[*] | 10.1 | 22 | 6.9 | (330) |
| (*including Polish and Ruthene minority vote) | | | | | |
| **Latin America** | | | | | |
| **Bolivia** | | | | | |
| Falange Socialista Boliviana | | | | | |
| 1956 Presidential elec. | 130,669 | 13.6 | | | |
| 1958 Congressional | 56,948 | 12.1 | | | |
| 1960 Presidential | 139,713 | 14.1 | | | |
| 1962 Congressional | 74,734 | 7.0 | | | |
| **Chile** | | | | | |
| Movimiento Nacional Socialista | | | | | |
| 1937 Congressional | 14,564 | 3.5 | 3 | | |

Electoral data from: Stein Rokkan and Jean Meyriat, *International Guide to Electoral Statistics,* Vol. I, 'National Elections in Western Europe' (The Hague, 1969). Dolf Sternberger and Bernhard Vogel, eds., with the collaboration of Dieter Nohlen, *Die Wahl der Parlamente und anderer Staatsorgane, Band I Europa,* in 2 parts (Berlin, 1969).

them those whose population was predominantly Catholic considerably less than the Protestant ones (respectively 27.2 and 32.5 per cent of their votes). These data provide systematic confirmation for the point already made by Geiger and previous ecological analyses. Post-war survey data on the impact on the family of the respondent of the de-Nazification process and on attitudes towards the Third Reich confirmed those different responses to the Nazi appeal of Catholics and Protestants, whatever their occupational position.

They have a special strength in areas with a tradition of regional peripheral hostility to centralistic policies in which regional parties often had considerable strength under the empire and in previous elections, like Lower Saxony where the Nazis seem to have absorbed much of the electorate of the old Guelph party, in Schleswig-Holstein, and apparently in Franconia, which resented the dominance of Munich in the Bavarian state. Insofar as there were Protestant and rural border regions in the east of Germany they also gave disproportionate support to the NSDAP.[101] More complex is the issue of the relationship between Nazi strength and the success of the communist party among the workers. But there are some indications of a positive correlation between the two anti-democratic forces in the Weimar Republic. Some scattered data on separate voting on men and women suggest that at least in the early elections the NSDAP was mainly a male party.[102] The ecological data however tell us much less about the internal composition in terms of social strata of the composition of the Nazi electorate within those broad categories. What kind of Protestants — small town dwellers, anti-centralists, regionalists, border area residents — voted for the NSDAP? The more refined ecological analyses are still to be done for many part of Germany, but some of the existing studies allow some preliminary conclusions.

Before turning to those findings, we might note that some of the patterns revealed by the German data are confirmed in other countries. In Belgium the border districts in the Ardennes also gave disproportionate support to the Rex. Italian fascism had, and the neo-fascists still have, their main strongholds in the ethnic border areas recovered from Austria, in which Italian nationalism clashed with the Germans and Yugoslavs. In Italy, too, the strongholds of Italian Catholicism, the areas of highest affiliation with Catholic Action would remain loyal to the Populari even in the 1924 half-free election, while the de-Christianized Po Valley and Romagna would be early strongholds of fascism. Both genuine Austrian fascism of the Heimatschutz and the Heimwehr and the Austrian branch of the Nazis would have their greatest success in border areas, like Carinthia and Styria and the border with Germany. Here again, rural areas would provide considerable support to both movements, and the more strongly Catholic areas would resist the appeal of the Nazis, which would absorb votes from the pockets of Protestant peasantry. The factor of rural class homogeneity, communalism, noted by Heberle for Schleswig-Holstein, would also characterize, as Eugen Weber has shown, some of the areas of greatest strength of the Rumanian Iron Guard.

The ecological analysis, however, tells us much less about which sectors of the urban small-town and metropolitan middle and upper classes turned to Nazism and why and when. Much of the analysis has been based on the shift between the different bourgeois and conservative parties and in Austria of 'Germanic liberalism,' and the NSDAP. But without survey data such inferences are risky, since they cannot take into account changes within the composition of the electorate of those parties. The analysis is further complicated by the important changes in turn-out between 1928 and 1930, and the drop in voters in 1932. Ecological analysis can also tell us very little about the relative importance of the nationalistic foreign policy appeals, the impact of unemployment, particularly on the academic professions and white-collar employees, the different economic impact of the depression on various types of business and on artisans and the response to the crisis of the party system, of parliamentary and authoritarian presidential governments. Recent research has shown the importance of the process of taking over from the grassroots by activists of interest groups, the defeat or neutralization of their former leadership and the manipulative use of the grievances of different social groups. The support by the masses, therefore, rather than the response of atomized isolated individuals of mass society alleged by certain theoretical interpretations, was the response of men integrated into organizations and groups that came under Nazi influence. While previous ideological and cultural positions — the status consciousness of the German *Mittelstand*, the affinities of certain conceptions of society of the German *Handwerk* and the Nazis, the penetration of the ideas of the *völkisch* tradition through the educational system — all explain the susceptibility of those strata to the Nazi appeal, the impact of the depression in Germany, that has no parallel in Europe, cannot be stressed enough. Repeated inconclusive elections, called by governments unable to cope with the crisis, provided the Nazi activists with a unique opportunity to mobilize the frustrations of the society on the basis of messianic hopes for change by a new leadership. I would not go as far as Wolfgang Sauer when he defines fascism as a revolt of those who lost, directly or indirectly, temporarily or permanently, by industrialization, in their search to return to the earlier natural ways of life. Not all those who voted for the Nazis were losers, even though many of the activists, the crisis strata that were uprooted, would fit such a characterization. Already in the thirties Marxist sociologists provided many insights into some of the responses of middle-class groups to the crisis, particularly Theodore Geiger with his analysis of different mentalities, his use of the distinction between old and new middle classes, and the role of positionally inadequate (*Standort*) and time inadequate (*Zeit*) responses to that social position during the crisis. The biographical data in Abel's study on Nazi motivation suggests that we have to distinguish carefully between the hostility to the working class, particularly the socialist organized working class, as a reason to turn to fascism, and the hostility to the privileged who contributed to the creation of a society divided by class conflict. In that context Wolfgang Sauer is right in noting the resentments caused in German society by the differentiation based on *Bildung* (education) rather than *Besitz* (property): those privileged with a humanistic education, that opened unique career opportunities, and those with a *Realschule* education, which seems to be reflected in some of the data on the different strength of the Nazis in elections in the *Technische Hochschulen* and the universities, and in the importance of engineers, agronomists, and veterinarians, in the Nazi leadership. Some of the attitude data of the first elections after World War II suggest that different educational levels have considerable importance in the formation of political attitudes in Germany. Even more complex is the question of the impact of upward and downward mobility on the political attitudes of these middle-class sectors, particularly in the white-collar (*Angestellten*) group, recruited both from the sons and daughters of the working class and from déclassé upper and upper-middle classes. The different response of the upper bourgeoisie in different parts of Germany, the resistance of the *Bürgertum* in certain areas with a liberal tradition, is undoubtedly linked with some of these differences in status consciousness. Another factor that has been pointed out but never exhaustively studied, is the internal differentiation within Protestantism, particularly between the Lutheran tradition and those areas with a Calvinist tradition linking politically even with the Netherlands that resisted the turn toward extreme nationalist authoritarianism by supporting the Christlich-Soziale Volksdienst. Geiger pointed out that the support for the Nazis in those fateful elections probably changed, particularly in view of the withdrawal of some of the support by the Deutschnationaler-Handelsgehilfenverband (DHV), in response to the more economically conservative and anti-trade-union turn of the Hitler movement. One thing is certain: while among the activists of the movement a lower middle-class or middle middle-class recruitment was decisive, the size of its electoral support in the thirties suggests that it must have been broader based, including upper-middle-class groups.

A problem that deserves further research is that of the inroads of the national-socialists into the socialist and communist electorate. The literature is full of loose and propagandistic statements on the interchanges between the communists and the SA, particularly among the younger generation. But more interesting is the fact that the added strength of the Marxist parties, both nationally and in many districts of quite different social composition, changes appreciably in the rapidly succeeding elec-

tions in the early thirties. In view of the changing rate of electoral participation, the analysis cannot be based only on the percentage of votes
cast, but has to take into account the absolute figures, since a drop in the
percentage of votes might largely be the result of an increase in the number of voters, either former non-voters or young first voters, without a
change in the support of old Marxist voters. Even assuming that the
socialist and communist voters continued loyal to their parties, this would
imply that the Nazis made inroads among the new young voters that in
terms of their class position should have supported those parties. Even so,
Milatz[103] has shown that the SPD lost votes that did not go to the communists, and that in industrial areas of the west, the northern Rhineland,
and Hessen-Nassau, the two socialist parties lost votes in April 1932. Some
of these voters must have gone to the Zentrum, but others must have
supported the NSDAP. For example, in Düsseldorf Regierungsbezirk,
the SPD lost 44,000 of its 289,000 voters in 1930, and the communists
74,000 of their 496,000.

Milatz[104] summarizes these trends by noting that in April 1932 in contrast with 1930, in five *Länder* the socialist parties lost 820,000 votes with
the Catholic parties gaining only 300,000. The NSDAP gained 4,900,000
while the number of valid new voters was some 500,000. Even assuming
that all those votes would have gone to the NSDAP, in addition to the
3,900,000 coming from the bourgeois parties, he calculates that some
500,000 must have still come from the parties of the left. He suggests that
in the second round of the presidential election, after the disappointing
result of the Thälmann candidacy, they might have been attracted by the
active Nazi campaign to the other radical candidate. The same would be
true for the inroads into the support of the Austrian socialist party, even
after discounting the shifts to the communists, particularly in areas like
Salzburg, Vorarlberg, and Innsbruck, where the Marxist parties had
never been very strong.[105] These data pose the question of whether there
was a working-class Nazi vote in those depression years. It obviously could
be argued that those leftist votes moving to the NSDAP would come from
the non-working class electorate of those parties, and that multiple shifts
might have been involved. Once more white-collar and lower-middle-class
SPD voters moving to the Nazis but being replaced by communist workers
rejoining the SPD with a resulting greater class homogeneity of both socialist parties might be suggested as an explanation. While the efforts of the
NSDAP to appeal to the worker have been the object of an interesting
monograph, their success in terms of membership in the party, the SA, the
NSBP, and the electorate remains to be investigated. Let us not forget that
the NSDAP was in its own self-conception a catch-all party rather than a
class party, and that in a crisis situation like the depression with rapidly
succeeding elections, it cannot be excluded that a party calling itself
National Socialist Workers' Party should have gained working class votes.

The question remains: what kind of workers? Often the easy way out is found by talking about a *Lumpenproletariat*, those who had never been employed, the young workers to whom some of the socialist sociologists of the time refer, workers in the public services who had some of the status consciousness of the civil servant, and the self-employed and the workers at home working on an out-put (*Verlag*) system. Data on the social composition of the Nazi party, the SA, and, interestingly enough, the Hitler Youth movement suggests that while the representation of the working class was considerably below its share in the population it certainly was far from negligible. The problem is of significance not only in explaining the rise to power of the NSDAP but also in accounting for the relatively passive acceptance of the new rulers after the *Machtergreifung* and the rapid dismantling of the working-class trade unions and the incorporation of the German masses in the DAF, the Labour Front.

Geiger and other German sociologists of the time analyzed in detail the economic mentalities and interest cleavages within the non-working-class sector of the society, and raised the question to what extent the Nazi effort to unite them within a single party could have a success comparable to the Zentrum in which the *ständisch* ideological elements and the trade union interests of the white-collar employees and even of the Catholic workers were bridged by the long standing identification with the church and its organizations. In his view the nationalist and particularly the racist component of the ideology would not prove strong enough. Certainly these sociological questions were and are central to an understanding of the viability of a secular nationalist catch-all party. They continue to be relevant for Peronism today, perhaps even more acutely in view of its working-class basis.

*Economic crisis and the Nazi upsurge*

The sudden upsurge in NSDAP voting and membership in the early thirties is unique among fascist parties. Only the sudden rise in membership of the PNF in northern Italy and the rapid 'conversion' of the south to support the new party in power in typically *transformismo* fashion can be compared with it. Perhaps the 1939 electoral success of the Arrow Cross as an opposition party to the government party in Hungary might be comparable. Possibly, the Iron Guard, under less hostile conditions without the loss of its charismatic leader and in a Rumania with greater civil liberties, might have had a more spectacular success than the 15.6 per cent of the vote it obtained in 1937, considering the crisis in the Rumanian economy and society.

While the relationship between social economic changes in Germany and the rise of the Nazi and communist strength have been studied systematically, there is no comparable monograph correlating the various crisis indicators in Italy from the war to the consolidation of Mussolini in power, even when the data for such an analysis are available. To give some example, we might recall that in April 1921 the party had 471 sections with 98,399 members. By December of that same year they would be, respectively, 1,333 and 218,453. In the same period of time the number of unemployed rose from 250,000 to 541,000 and we should not forget that in the second half of 1920 the figure had oscillated around 100,000. Contrary to the generally observed pattern of fewer strikes in the time of economic recession and unemployment, the heightened political consciousness in the post-war years is reflected in the strike mobilization achieved by the left. The highest figure of industrial strikers before the war was reached in 1913 with 384,000 and the highest in agriculture in 1907 with 254,000. In 1919 the number of industrial strikers would rise to 1,049,438 and that of agricultural workers to 505,128, and in the following year to 1,267,953 in industry and 1,045,732 in agriculture. In 1921, with the rising presence of the fascists, the split of the socialist party, the industrial strikers would be reduced to 644,564, still a respectable figure, but in the countryside the number would be reduced dramatically to 79,298. Simultaneously, the price index of consumer goods for working-class and white-collar-employee families changed from 1,000 in 1914 to 2,681 in 1919, up to 4,168 in 1921. We already noted how the number of students in higher education had risen from an average of 26,000 in 1904 to 1913 to 50,000 for the period 1919 to 1922 and that of secondary students from 144,000 to 384,000. In addition this period saw a rapid demobilization of the armed forces. Between January and July 1919, 100,000 officers and over two million non-commissioned officers and soldiers were sent back home and before the end of the year 3,260,000 were licensed from the army. To these figures we might add the important changes in the property structure in north-central Italy that allowed many tenants and share tenants to become smallholders and therefore take a very different position toward the imposed employment of labour from the trade unions. [106]

These massive changes in the social economic position of Italians particularly in the north, caused by war, unemployment, labour unrest, inflation, and political mobilization go far in accounting for the rapid success of the fascists, who in May 1921 would have 322,000 members.

A systematic quantitative analysis of the rates of change on these different indicators for different regions and even provinces or cities would be one of the most interesting contributions to the study of crisis politics.

The Nazi electoral swell in the early thirties was unique among fascist parties and even among mass movements in general. It requires specific explanations. An obvious one, although not a sufficient one, is the impact of the economic crises on German society. The Nazi support among its middle classes and peasants was brought to its peak by the uniqueness of the German depression, particularly coming after previous economic crises. Kaltefleiter[107] has shown the parallelism between the unemployment curve and the growth of the Nazi vote. An economic interpretation of the phenomenon imposes itself, and one has to emphasize the hostility to the organized working class it largely reflects. However, it would be a mistake to consider that upsurge structurally determined by capitalism, per se. The particular German social economic structure, the co-existence of some of the most modern forms of capitalism with the persistence of pre-capitalist institutions and values, particularly large scale inefficient agricultural units in the east, whose owners justified their privileged position on status and political grounds as Max Weber had already stressed, would be a more correct explanation. Even so, the economic and social strains caused by these class structures would not have had the same political consequences without the presence of other non-economic variables. The strains of the economic crisis became so politically decisive because they combined with and added to: (1) an initial and continuous conservative opposition to the new state created at Weimar after defeat and by political-social forces never fully integrated into the Reich in the imperial period — the socialists, the Catholics, and the left liberals; (2) the possibility of linking the bitter economic and political dependency on the war victors of Versailles through the question of the war reparations. The perception of that link, even if for different reasons, was largely shared by governments and opposition. The government, for example Brüning, was attempting to use the crisis as an argument to revise the agreements. The opposition used the link between the economic situation and the reparations question to find a common issue and to mobilize the population against the regime at the time of the Young Plan referendum; (3) the ineffectiveness of the governments in dealing with the crisis that led many voters to support the opposition irrespective of particular policies, disagreeing with many of its programmatic positions to 'get over with the mess'; (4) the possibility for a party with devoted young activists to penetrate from the grassroots a variety of interest groups and use them to communicate, even when contradictory, its demagogic message to different constituencies; (5) the mobilization on the streets and marching grounds made possible by the involvement of available unemployed contributing to the atmosphere of polarization and tension requiring a resolution; (6) last, but certainly not least, the charismatic appeal of Hitler, his ability to overcome internal crises in his party and to neutralize the fears of many initially suspicious of one or another aspect of his party's programme: socialism, anti-Semitism, radicalism and violence, and anti-Christianity, by pragmatically tuning them down but allowing loyal sub-leaders to continue exploiting their appeal.

   The additional mobilization — with the depression — of potentially democratic voters and the radicalization of those initially uprooted from the established party's loyalties by the shift to ineffective interest group, peasant and regionalist parties, gave Hitler a margin of votes over previous anti-Weimar forces on the right; together with the KPD it immobilized the forces supporting the regime and planted the idea that his party had to be included in a government coalition to ensure stable government. The loss of power, the power vacuum, and abdication of power of the democratic parties, made possible and reinforced by constitutional provisions like Article 48 and the presidential powers, and further the unfortunate repeated calling of elections in the middle of the crisis made necessary by these factors, combined with the 'court politics' at the top around Hindenburg led to Hitler's chancellorship.

Even so, in 1933 already in power in the last semi-free election,[108] Hitler and the NSDAP were not able to unite behind them, in a party presumably representing the whole *Volk* in a new and unique national revolutionary integration, more than 43.9 per cent of the vote and 44.5 per cent of the seats, less than the SPD in 1919 and the CDU after 1953. Only with the support of the DNVP-led right with 8 per cent could it claim a majority, in a no longer fully free election. Paradoxically the *listone* offered by Mussolini in 1924, in an election that was probably less free than the 1933 one in Germany, obtained 66.3 per cent, more than the 56 per cent the fascists expected; perhaps because the PNF-led candidacy included many men of the old political class.

The fascist plesbiscitarian dream of overcoming the class and religious cultural cleavages of unintegrated German and Italian societies failed because of the opposition of the working class left and the Catholics. In Germany the 1933 share of the vote of the SPD was 18.2 per cent versus 20.7 per cent in November 1932, the KPD 12.2 per cent versus 16.9 per cent, the Zentrum and the Bavarian party 14.1 per cent versus 15 per cent. In 1924 in Italy the socialists obtained 10.9 per cent versus 25.3 per cent in 1921, the PCI 3.7 per cent versus 4.6 per cent in 1921, and the Populari 9.1 per cent versus 20.4 per cent. Apparently the Catholic subcommunity in Germany was more integrated and resistant than the just created Christian Democratic party in Italy, a fact that contributes to the explanation of the bitter hostility of Hitler toward the Catholic church and the eagerness of Mussolini to reach a compromise with the church. In those elections the participation, sincere or coerced, increased in Germany from 79.9 in November 1932 to 88 per cent and in Italy from 58.4 in 1921 to 63.8 in 1924. If we were to calculate the support for fascist rule in those already purely symbolic elections in proportion to those eligible to vote, the figures would not fit the image the new regimes wanted to convey of a massive majority supporting them. The fascist dream of a monopoly of the political elite devoted to the common good rather than to sectional interests with an enthusiastically supporting united people was only possible by force, but not by free choice. The ideal of peoples' parties freely supported by majorities would be reserved in a few societies to those expanding their appeal on the basis of the by-now established and institutionalized class and/or religious cleavages beyond their confines; by social democrats and Christian democrats. Only a coalition of interests like those behind American parties or the post-independence unity behind the Congress party in India would achieve something comparable. The fascist dream could only be realized by violence by a violent generation in unique circumstances and was justly defeated. But we should not forget the illusions, legitimate grievances, and fears that led so many to support it at a particular juncture in history and in one of the deepest economic crises in the western world. It is the task of democratic leadership to prevent the constellation that led to it, and the task of intellectuals to be suspicious of simple ideas promising a society without conflict and a powerful nation capable of solving its problems alone.

## PASSING WAVE, OR STABLE NEW FORCE?

Any analysis of the electoral strength of the NSDAP, and the same is true for Italian fascism, faces the difficult question of how much the support for those parties could have been consolidated over time in successive free elections, after the economic or political crisis that suddenly mobilized their support would have passed its peak. In the case of Germany the question remains: to what extent a drop in unemployment and other signs of economic and social crisis would have led to a return of many NSDAP voters to more moderate bourgeois parties and would the same be true for a consolidation of authority of the Giolittian state in Italy against both the *squadristi* and the working-class organizations? Would the predictions of the impossibility of retaining the loyalty of the heterogeneous following of the fascist parties made by many analysts of the time have proven true? Would the factional tendencies within those parties, in the case of Italy between the agrarian reactionary fascism of the Po Valley and the more urban petit-bourgeois idealistic and even revolutionary fascism have led to a split? Would the northern nazism of Strasser or Goebbels with its more socialist orientation and the more conservative Hitler wing of the party based in the south, the interest group based electorate, and the radical activists of the SA have split the party? Would there have been different competing or antagonistic fascist parties like those we find among Rumanian extremists between the romantic Iron Guardists and the more socially and culturally conservative anti-Semitic followers of Cuza and the LANC, to say nothing of the different tendencies within French wartime fascism? The answer to those questions depends in part on the weight we are ready to assign to the sociological, economic, and conjunctural determinates of the strength of those parties, and to the new type of charismatic emotional identification with the movement and its leader. In the case of Italy, the crisis in the party at the time of the pacification pact and the subsequent resignation of Mussolini indicates that perhaps the momentum of the party and its unity would not have been assured by a relatively questionable personal charismatic leadership on the part of Mussolini. All the evidence, however, in the case of Hitler, indicates that his hold over the party activists and probably a large part of the Nazi electorate was such that none of the other leaders could have carried along any significant share of the party and even less of the electorate. This would suggest that there are serious limits to a conventional sociological approach to the study of the social bases of fascist parties. These uncertainties, together with a power vacuum created by the indecisions and ambivalences of the democratic leadership and the attitude of the communists and even large parties of the socialist movements toward a bourgeois democratic parliamentary regime, contributed to the frantic effort to conquer power by the fascists. The adroit combination of violence in the streets and subtle bargaining with the Establishment together with the novelty of the fascist phenomenon led to the overthrow of democratic politics. The March on Rome and the *Machtergreifung* make the questions we have raised idle speculation and leave them without an answer.

The experience in other democratic countries does not provide one either. In Austria, Rumania, the Baltic countries and Brazil with Vargas outlawing the *Integralistas*, the anti-fascists on the right opted for an authoritarian response to the fascist threat and the possibility of civil war. Only in a few smaller European democracies with relatively weak fascist parties were they allowed to compete in successive free elections into the late thirties. The data for Belgium, the Netherlands, Switzerland, Denmark, Norway, Sweden, and the United Kingdom show that in stable democracies the initially growing fascist parties were unable to retain their momentum. However, it should not be forgotten that none of those countries had the structural and historical conditions necessary for a successful fascist movement. We have noted before that in none was there a sufficient crisis stratum to build a large core of activists and that in several of them the movements acquired a very derivative character. In practically all of them the working class had not supported revolutionary Marxist movements, either communist or maximalist-socialist. In those countries, also, fascism was a late-latecomer and therefore from the beginning it encountered a widespread effective hostility or suspicion on the basis of the historical record of Italy and Germany. The case of Belgium exemplifies, in the Brussels by-election, how far democratic parties were ready to overcome their divergences to put a stop to the fascist threat. In other cases, particularly Spain, non-fascist parties were able to incorporate fascist appeals, becoming semi- or pseudo-fascist, particularly in the youth organizations, to compete successfully with them; and establishment interests were more cagey about entering an unequal alliance with the new revolutionaries of the centre or the right. Late-latecoming fascism found itself even more isolated than the early movements. There can be no question that many of the actions, particularly of the Nazis like the 'night of the long knives' and the 'crystal-night,' the uncivilized anti-Semitism, the aggressive German nationalism, must have alienated many potential supporters of fascist parties in those countries. The drop in fascist votes in free elections in the late thirties must be attributed to those factors at least as much as to the change in economic conditions. There is some similarity in this drop in fascist support at the high point of its success in Italy and Germany with the drop in the communist vote in those same countries after the initial post-war rise in the aftermath of the Prague coup in 1948. Sociological analysis cannot ignore, particularly in the case of small parties resulting from diffusion of ideology from other centres, the reaction to the policies of governments dominated by fraternal parties. In addition, whatever appeal the welfare-state policies and their emotional propagandistic build-up in fascist countries could have for an alienated bourgeois youth desiring to carry out a similar national integrating anti-Marxist policy, the class character of the Spanish Civil War must have contributed to disillusion them as it did many younger Italian fascists. In addition as Sten Nilson[109] has rightly underlined, the less doctrinaire position of northern European socialist parties toward the peasantry and willingness to work with the farmers' parties limited the opportunities of the native fascists to penetrate the rural electorate, which for other reasons might have been susceptible to their appeal.

## FASCISM AND THE THIRD WORLD

Fortunately many third world countries for which the fascist ideological package might have been attractive in the thirties did not have democratic political institutions or had not even achieved independence. Only in some of the more developed Latin American countries was there room for fascist movements. Therefore, it is particularly unfortunate that we have, with the exception of Brazil, no serious studies of the impact on Latin American political life of fascism.[110] The confused concept of fascism used by many scholars lumping together conservative authoritarian military bureaucratic rule with fascism has contributed to this neglect. In this context a more thorough study of the initial nucleus of Peronism would be particularly interesting, as would fascist influences in Bolivia and Peru. It is significant that Ramiro Ledesma Ramos saw in the Mexican PRI what we might call a functional alternative to fascism. The same could probably be said about the Turkish republican party of Ataturk, so often mentioned in the fascist literature as a kind of precursor movement which, however, had not freed itself of liberal democratic pre-World War I ideological elements. Fascism had its resonance in the Arab world, particularly in opposition to the upsurge of Zionism, but the size of the social

groups susceptible to it and necessary to create the core of a fascist movement and the possibilities of mobilization under colonial or authoritarian
rule were too insignificant. In this context the problem of Japanese fascism acquires particular theoretical interest. There can be no question
that there was an intellectual ferment that can be clearly described as fascist, that there was a multitude of groups comparable to the ultra-
nationalists and radical non-Marxist groups in Europe, but there was no
mass fascist party. A complex combination of repression and co-optation
by the Establishment, the central role of the army and the bureaucracy,
the persistence of elements of traditional legitimacy in the emperor system, the political use of Shinto national religion, and the creation of a
syncretic official party — the Imperial Rule Assistance Association, under
a bureaucratic military oligarchical authoritarian regime — ultimately
dwarfed the possibilities of a mass-based fascist movement. This despite
the fact that many social structural conditions would have seemed favourable to its emergence. A widespread nationalist sentiment transmitted
through the educational system, considerable economic and educational
modernization, but a relatively low standard of living, large-scale peasant
discontent, hostility to political parties that could be seen as alien to the
national tradition, distrust of western liberal democracies, the League of
Nations perceived as an obstacle to national greatness, hostility to communism and to the labour movement combined with considerable splits
within the political left, a pan-nationalism of Asia for the Asians, criticism of the power of big business and the corruption of politicians, a
romanticization of pre-modern cultural values of community, family,
paternalism, and heroic virtues, a radicalized junior officer corps — all
were certainly fertile ground for a fascist movement. Ideologists and small
groups seized on those themes of the society as an extended family, the
agrarianism and the anti-urban affect, an anti-liberal conception of production and an Asian ultra-nationalism, but no movement appeared that
would mobilize those who in the 1936 and 1937 elections were ready to
withdraw support by non-participation from the existing party system.
Perhaps the number of pseudo-intellectuals and particularly of students
ready to give support to such a movement was small. The fact that until
1925 teachers in elementary schools, priests, and religious teachers had
been proscribed from political participation in parties, as students had
been too, might have been a factor limiting the extremist mobilization of
these key sectors. However, Masao Maruyama offers the most fruitful
explanation when he writes, comparing Japanese and European developments, that the strength of the democratic movement prior to the fascist
structure determines the extent of democratic trappings within fascism.[111]
The leaders of Japanese fascism (we would say anti-democratic and anti-
working-class authoritarianism) were not obliged to manipulate or
counter any strong proletarian movement and in the absence of the bour-

geois democratic background they were able to effect a comparatively small consolidation of state power from above by amalgamating supporting groups that were already in existence. The result was the Imperial Rule Assistance Association, of which the leader of one of the radical nationalist groups would say that 'it lacks a soul, because it is an attempt to collect opportunists and bureaucrats with neither faith nor ideals and to launch them all on a spiritual venture with government money.'[112] This is another example comparable to some southeastern and eastern European cases of an official single party incorporating fascist elements but lacking the soul and romanticism, the activism, and the mass participation of fascism.

Neo-fascism lacks many, if not most, elements that made fascism attractive between the two wars. While fascism as a distinctive political movement is dead, many of its ideological formulations, appeals, and occasionally its rhetoric, can be found in many contemporary movements and regimes, sometimes where we would least expect it. The combination of nationalism with social revolutionary or populist appeals, the affirmation of authority and collective ends against competitive democracy, individualism and capitalism, the ethnocentric populism of disadvantaged nations against the successful Western nation-states, and the new voluntarism against pragmatic reformism are found almost everywhere. The affinity of those positions with basic fascism is undeniable. It has been the merit of A. James Gregor[113] to stress these affinities in third world nationalisms, national-communism, the Cuban revolution, and the ideology of the New Left, and obviously in South African Apartheid ideology. Few claim the fascist heritage, but fascist ideas are—unfortunately—far from dead and are operating under other guises.

Authoritarian regimes, new, established, post-totalitarian, some with single parties, are found all over the world, but genuine fascism with its mobilization of youthful enthusiasms, its activist fervour and sense of participation, its myths and dramatic performances, but also its principled amoral commitment to violence, war, and destruction of its enemies, is dead. A great dream for a few aging men and a nightmare for others, a phenomenon difficult to understand for scholars, a distorted, unknown, and largely incomprehensible symbol of evil—we hope—for generations that did not live through it. Let us hope that routine politics 'everyday' democracy even with its failings, and even pragmatic authoritarian rule, will not be challenged again by youthful enthusiasm and irate protest, but that the energies mobilized by the fascist dreams will find other less destructive channels.

# NOTES

The research for this paper was made possible by my stay at the Institute for Advanced Study, Princeton, supported by a grant from the National Science Foundation number CS-31730X2 to the Institute. The collection of data, particularly those on the leadership of different parties, has been supported by the Concilium on International and Area Studies of Yale University.

I want to thank my wife, Rocío de Terán, for her collaboration and analysis of data used in the paper. Rainer M. Lepsius offered useful criticism of an early version.

1. Seymour M. Lipset and Stein Rokkan, *Party Systems and Voter Alignments Cross-National Perspectives*, (New York, 1967). Introduction 1-64.

2. Ibid.

3. The problem of availability of support rather than search for support is well stated by Ramiro Ledesma Ramos, *Fascismo en España? Discurso a-las juventudes de España* (Barcelona, 1968), 294, when accounting for the limited social change accomplished by Italian fascism, the persistence of the 'old anti-historical powers representing the great bourgeoisie and the reactionary spirit' among possible explanations, who writes: 'One of them is that every regime needs as broad a basis of support as possible, and if fascism arriving at victory after a struggle with a marxist oriented working class found itself deprived of the due support and collaboration of large proletarian nuclei, had to lean more than it is convenient on a different constellation.'

4. Otto Kirchheimer, 'Germany: The Vanishing Opposition,' *in* Robert A. Dahl, ed., *Political Oppositions in Western Democracies* (New Haven, 1966), 237-59.

5. John Armstrong, 'Collaborationism in World War II: The Integral Nationalist variant in Eastern Europe,' in *Journal of Modern History*, 40, 3 (September, 1968), 396-410.

6. Franz Borkenau, *The Communist International* (London, 1938), 374.

7. Let us emphasize that an explanation of fascism on the basis of the distinctive Italian historical, social, intellectual context is not incompatible with interpretations of fascism based on some common characteristics of certain European societies present to a heightened degree in Italy. Perhaps without the additional distinctively Italian factors, the first fascist movement would not have become so powerful, would not have developed some of its more appealing features, its unique style, and without success in a west European society, there would not have been a paradigmatic model to serve as a source of legitimation and ideas for weaker tendencies of similar character and for extremist nationalists in less advanced and 'central' societies. Methodologically the problem has some similarity with that of the origins of capitalism in the Weberian tradition. Without an unique constellation of circumstances, the first capitalism might not have emerged when and as it did; but once it did, it was easier in other societies with functionally equivalent or alternative conditions, to grow.

We cannot summarize here the interesting early Italian contributions to an interpretation of fascism as an Italian phenomenon. See Ernst Nolte, *Theorien über den Faschismus* (Cologne, 1967), 18-34, for a review of the writings of Zibordi, Nanni, Labriola, Gobetti, Salvatorelli, Croce, and among the Germans Hermann Heller, to which we would add the Italo-German Robert Michels. Three Italian works, Renzo de Felice, *Il Fascismo. Le interpretazioni dei contemporanei e degli storici* (Bari, 1970); and Renzo de Felice, ed., *Il Fascismo e i partiti politici italiani. Testimonianze del 1921-1923* (Rocca San Casciano, 1966), reprint essays by contemporary figures and analysts ranging over the whole political spectrum, but all written before 1923; and Constanzo Casucci, ed., *Il Fascismo. Antologia di scritti critici* (Bologna, 1961) are indispensable.

Robert Michels, *Sozialismus und Faschismus als politische Strömungen in Italien. Historische Studien* (Munich, 1925), particularly vol. 2, *Sozialismus und Faschismus in Italien,*

provides an excellent background with particular emphasis on the early fusion of the socialists and nationalists and the revolutionary romantic heritage, and the social structure facilitating those developments. Let us not forget, to give one example, that the Garibaldi red-
shirts were the first shirts that became a political symbol. His analysis of the links between
the demographic pressures and the birth of imperialism represented by Nationalism and the
thought of Corradini is particularly interesting.

The early Italian interpretations emphasizing the economic under-development, the
weakness of the capitalist bourgeoisie, the dual economy, the lack of social integration of
the recently unified state, the peculiar position of sectors of the intelligentsia and the educated, the weakness of the state, the problems of resistance of a new working class to industrial discipline, etc., are obviously relevant to understand an authoritarian, partly fascist
response to their problems in semi-developed countries in the so-called third world today.

The analysis of Arthur Rosenberg, a Marxist scholar in 'Der Faschismus als Massenbewegung, Sein Aufstieg und seine Zersetzung,' reprinted in Wolfgang Abendroth, ed., *Faschismus und Kapitalismus* (Frankfurt a. M., 1968), 93-114, in his specific analysis but not in his
general theoretical position, summarizes well that Italian development.

8. Michael Arthur Ledeen, *Universal Fascism. The Theory and Practice of the Fascist
International, 1928-1936* (New York, 1972).

9. To give some examples: while it would be possible to attribute the failure of the British
Union of Fascists, despite the personality of its leader Mosley, to the blatantly imitative
character of the movement, the same would not be true for the Spanish fascists who despite
a capable leadership could not rally even an effective nucleus of party cadres and sympathizers and even less, an electoral support.

10. Andrew C. Janos, 'The One-Party State and Social Mobilization: East Europe between the Wars,' 204-36, and Juan J. Linz, 'From Falange to Movimiento-Organización:
The Spanish Single Party and the Franco Regime, 1936-1968,' in Samuel P. Huntington
and Clement H. Moore, eds., *Authoritarian Politics in Modern Society* (New York, 1970),
128-203. Let us note that this distinction between fascism and authoritarian regimes and
military dictatorships was made by early Marxist analysts, like Clara Zetkin (1923) and
Ignazio Silone (1934). See E. Nolte, *Theorien über den Faschismus*, 23, 55, and 88-89.

11. Action Française poses a special problem. It is certainly not a typical fascist movement, but it also has affinities with fascism rightly stressed by Ernst Nolte in *Three Faces of
Fascism. Action Française, Italian Fascism, National Socialism* (New York 1969, first published in German, Munich, 1964). It is, however, distinct, by the central place given initially to royalism, while other fascist movements were in principle republican, even when
they, like Mussolini, ended accepting the monarchy. This combined with the anti-democratic social elitism, the original identification with Catholicism, the support among traditional sectors of society, particularly the nobility, distinguishes it from the basically more
plebeian and generally more secular fascist movements. However, the activism of the Came-
lots du Roi, the anti-capitalist national socialist ideas inherited from Barrès, the willingness
to risk a conflict with the Church, even its anti-Semitism, its romantic appeal to intellectuals, its relatively limited support for big business, the efforts of a Georges Valois to woo
the workers, bring it closer to fascism than other conservative or reactionary parties, like the
Deutschnationale Volkspartei (DNVP) or Renovación Española, that ideologically was
strongly influenced by Action Française. In our view, it occupies even in time an intermediary position like the Italian Nationalism of Enrico Corradini that fused with fascism. We
would consider Action Française, the Italian Nationalists and, perhaps, the German Alldeutscher Verband as proto-fascist movements. Their organization and in many respects their
style, and above all their social bases were, however, quite distinct from fascist parties.

It is natural that Nolte, emphasizing rightly but perhaps excessively the ideological dimension of fascism, should include the Action Française in his purview. Since the movement led
by Charles Maurras was an ideological movement that did not succeed to the same extent, let

us say, as the DNVP or even Renovación Española to link with organized interest groups, it was closer to the primacy of politics, the 'politique d'abord' of fascism that so often conceived politics 'like a religion.' The same is largely true for the Italian Nationalists. In addition, in terms of ideology, Drumond and Barrès were in many respects closer to the fascists than the more intellectual Maurras.

12. Stanley G. Payne, 'Spanish Fascism in Comparative Perspective,' in *Iberian Studies*, II, 1 (Spring 1973), 3-12.

13. We certainly would not compare the social composition of the communist party of the USSR with that of the Italian or French communist party. In the same way it makes little sense to compare the social basis of the NSDAP or the PNF in power with fascist parties before taking power. On the contrary, it would make a lot of sense to compare those parties while in power and before the *Machtergreifung* and perhaps also with communist parties in power, since in both cases the fact that the party is the government party with major tasks assigned to it in the state is likely to attract significant membership from similar groups: civil servants, teachers, officers, the younger generation emerging out of the Konsomol or Hitler-Jugend, etc.

14. It should be noted that this essay does not attempt to review the ideological, sociological, and socio-psychological interpretations of fascism — latu sensu — a task already performed. See Ernst Nolte, *Theorien über den Faschismus*, in his introductory essay, 12-75; Renzo de Felice, *Le Interpretazioni del Fascismo*, (Bari, 1969), with particular emphasis on the Italian analyses. See also A. James Gregor, *Interpretations of Fascism* (Morristown, N.J., 1974). The work of Nolte, *Three Faces of Fascism*, has provoked a lively discussion which he reviews in: *Die Krise des liberalen Systems und die faschistischen Bewegungen* (Munich, 1968), 432-58. A recent contribution to the debate is the collection 'Faschismus Theorien' first published in *Das Argument*, and translated in *International Journal of Politics* (Winter 1972-73). The collection of papers by Otto Bauer, Herbert Marcuse, Arthur Rosenberg, August Thalheimer, and Angelo Tasca, edited by Wolfgang Abendroth, *Faschismus und Kapitalismus* is useful for the more sophisticated Marxist interpretations. A good analysis with reference to empirical data from this perspective is Eike Henning, *Thesen zur deutschen Sozial- und Wirtschaftsgeschichte 1933 bis 1938* (Frankfurt a.M., 1973).

15. The German neo-Nazis have attracted considerable attention. See John David Nagle, *The National Democratic Party. Right Radicalism in the Federal Republic of Germany* (Berkeley and Los Angeles, 1970); E. K. Scheuch and H. D. Klingemann have written a number of detailed reports on the sociology of the NPD vote published in mimeograph form by the Köln Institut für Vergleichende Sozialforschung, Zentralarchiv für empirische Sozialforschung, 1967, 1969, and later the Forschungsinstitut der Konrad-Adenauer Stiftung. For detailed references, see Erwin K. Scheuch, *Politischer Extremismus in der Bundesrepublik*, forthcoming. Reinhard Kühnl, Rainer Rilling, Christine Sager, *Die NPD Struktur, Ideologie und Funktion einer neofaschistischen Partei* (Frankfurt a.M., 1969); Peter von Oertzen, *Soziologische und Psychologische Struktur der Wähler und Mitgliedschaft der NPD* (Hannover, 1967). For an earlier neo-Nazi party see Otto Busch and Peter Furth, *Rechtsradikalismus im Nachkriegsdeutschland* (Berlin, 1957). In contrast, the much more politically important Movimento Sociale Italiano has been neglected by scholarship. Frank L. Casale, University of Kentucky, is preparing a monograph on the MSI.

16. Ernst Nolte 'Nationalsozialismus im Urteil Mussolinis und Hitlers' in *Faschismus-Nationalsozialismus. Ergebnisse und Referate der sechsten italienisch-deutschen Historiker Tagung in Trier, 1963* (Braunschweig, 1964), 60-72. Klaus-Peter Hoepke, *Die deutsche Rechte und der italienische Faschismus* (Düsseldorf, 1968), 125-240. See also on fascism and Nazi racism Renzo de Felice, *Storia degli ebrei italiani sotto il fascismo* (Turin, 1961); Joseph Goebbels, *Der Faschismus und seine praktischen Ergebnisse* (Schriften der Deutschen Hochschule für Politik, Heft 1) (Berlin, 1934); George Mosse, *The Crisis of German Ideol-*

*ogy. Intellectual Origins of the Third Reich* (New York, 1964), 312-17, offers important insights into the profound differences between National Socialism and other fascisms, and the criticism by other fascists of the German variant. In that context the confused work by Otto Strasser, *Der Faschismus, Geschichte und Gefahr* (Munich, 1965), 71-82, on 'Faschismus und Nationalsozialismus' which interprets Hitlerism as fascism but attempts to save a distinct national-socialist tradition he links with Masaryk, emphasizing the socially progressive versus the conservative tendencies, should also be mentioned.

17. Renzo de Felice, *Storia degli ebrei italiani*, the major study on the problem.

18. Let us not forget that the Rumanian Iron Guard, the Hungarian Arrow Cross, the Estonian Vabadussõ jalaste Liit, the Latvian *Ugunkrust* (which changed its name to *Perkondrust*), the Ação Integralista Brasileira, and other minor parties, were persecuted or outlawed by authoritarian regimes. Democracies also imposed restrictions on fascist parties, for example: several of the top leaders of the Falange, including José Antonio Primo de Rivera and Onésimo Redondo, were in jail in March 1936 and party headquarters were closed.

19. Ramiro Ledesma Ramos, *Fascismo en España? Discurso a las juventudes de España*, 53, 55.

20. Lackó Miklós, *Nyilasok Nemzetiszicialisták 1935-1944* (Budapest, 1966), and idem., *Arrow-Cross Men. National Socialists 1935-1944* (Budapest, 1969).

21. Nicholas M. Nagy-Talavera, *The Green Shirts and the Others. A History of Fascism in Hungary and Rumania* (Stanford, 1970); Eugen Weber, 'The Men of the Archangel,' *in* Walter Laqueur and George L. Mosse, eds., *International Fascism, 1920-1945,* (New York, 1966), 101-26.

22. The question of anti-modernism and fascism is a moot one and deserves more research. There can be no doubt that a number of fascist movements romanticized pre-industrial social structures, the peasant, the artisan, the soldier, and rejected urban, industrial, commercial values and styles of life. In their rejection of cosmopolitanism, commercialism, consumerism, and their appeal for a return to nature, they coincided with the peasantist ideologists, with certain brands of populism and powerful intellectual currents at the turn of the century. They were particularly articulate in Germany, as Klaus Bergmann has shown in his *Agrarromantik und Grosstadtfeindlichkeit* (Meisenheim am Glan, 1970). See particularly 277 to 366. It would seem that, with some exceptions like Onésimo Redondo in the provincial Castilian city of Valladolid, that this ruralist outlook was more characteristic of German, Nordic, and east European fascism than of its western manifestations. It certainly would not be true for British fascism, Ramiro Ledesma Ramos, Rex, and particularly Mussolini. Let us not forget that Franz Borkenau linked fascism with the requirements for industrialization of less developed countries, an interpretation that led him to reject the possibility of Hitler coming to power in an article that appeared days after the *Machtergreifung*. In this context the work by Juan Velarde Fuertes, *El Nacionalsindicalismo cuarenta años después (análisis crítico)* (Madrid, 1972), deserves to be mentioned as an analysis of the economic thought of Spanish fascism. We should not forget that the nationalism, the concern with dependency from the plutocratic capitalist democracies, the expansionism and the committment to military preparedness, the concern for planning for collective purposes, inevitably pushed fascists towards industrialization policy. It is no accident that Mihail Manoilescu, an engineer- economist, sympathizer with the Iron Guard, author of one of the most interesting books on the single parties of the thirties, should also have been one of the first formulators of a theory about the unequal relationship between agrarian societies and the advanced industrial countries. Finally, we cannot ignore the futurist passion for technology, shared by Mussolini, and following him by other fascist leaders. In view of all this, we would not include 'anti-modernism' to our definition of fascism. On this question see Henry Ashby Turner, Jr., 'Fascism and Modernization,' *World Politics*, 24 (4 July 1972), 547-64, the critique by A. James Gregor, 'Fascism and Modernization: Some Addenda,' *World Politics*, 26, 3 (April 1974), 370-84, and Turner's response 'Fascism and Modernization: A Few Corrections,' in the same journal (forthcoming).

23. For a better understanding of the ideological commitments of fascism and the impossibility of overcoming sociological obstacles that it faced, it is particularly interesting to study the numerous groupuscules attempting to combine nationalism against Versailles and the western plutocratic democracies with genuine social revolutionary aspirations, and the left dissidents from Hitler-dominated national socialism. On these groups, see Otto Ernst Schüddekopf, *Linke Leute von rechts. Die nationalrevolutionären Minderheiten und der Kommunismus in der Weimarer Republik* (Stuttgart, 1969), and Karl O. Paetel, *Versuchung oder Chance? Zur Geschichte des deutschen Nationalbolschewismus 1918/1932* (Göttingen, 1965). Unfortunately, due to the small size of those groups, their lack of electoral presence, and their later fate, the information on their efforts to gain a social base and the social composition of their following in contrast to their ideological disputes have been little studied. The fact that they were late-latecomers to a scene dominated by the KPD and the NSDAP in addition to the democratic parties made their efforts quite futile, but tells us much about the failure of left fascism, and national communism, in advanced societies with electoral and organizational mass politics.

There is a parallelism in the sympathy of some other dissident national socialists with the national Bolshevists, in the comments of Ramiro Ledesma Ramos in *Fascismo en España*, 66-67, about Joaquín Maurin, a leader of dissident communism in Catalonia and later of the POUM, (Partido Obrero de Unificación Marxista), under the heading 'Un nacionalismo obrero español?.' Tragically for those men, fascism as a party of national integration confronted with an already organized working class and with a more articulate Marxist ideological heritage, could be nothing but a radicalism of the centre often condemned to be co-opted by the right. It is important to note how the fascist left in Germany, for example, Otto Strasser and Ledesma Ramos, increasingly reject the label fascist to avoid being confused with Italian fascism whose conservative social character they perceived and criticized.

24. See for example Ramiro Ledesma Ramos, *Fascismo en España*, 62: 'In our epoch, in our own days, national revolutions develop with unbelievable success. See these names that represent them: Mussolini, Kemal, Hitler, and — why not — Stalin,' and 288-91 on 'Bolshevism, Russian Nationalist Revolution.' Similar statements can be found among the left of nazism which favoured an eastern orientation in German foreign policy and a Bund of the oppressed nations, including the USSR; see Reinhard Kühnl, *Die nationalsozialistische Linke, 1925-1930* (Meisenheim am Glan, 1966), 38, 118-26. In Italy, James Gregor, 'On understanding Fascism: A Review of Some Contemporary Literature,' *American Political Science Review*, 67, 4 (1973), 1332-47, n. 36, quotes the following articles: Agostino Nasti, 'L'Italia, il bolcevismo, la Russia,' *Critica Fascista* (15 March 1937), 162-63; Tomaso Napolitano, 'Il fascismo di Stalin ovvero l'URSS e noi,' *Critica Fascista* (15 October 1937), 396-98; Berto Ricci, 'Il fascismo di Stalin,' *Critica Fascista* (15 July 1937), 317-19.

25. Luigi Salvatorelli, *Nazionalfascismo* (Turin, 1923), selection reprinted in de Felice, *Il Fascismo. Le interpretazioni. . .*, 54-63, see also 59-61.

26. Theodor Geiger, 'Die Mittelschichten und die Sozialdemokratie,' *Die Arbeit*, 8 (1931), 617-35.

27. Max H. Kele, *Nazis and Workers. National Socialist Appeals to German Labor, 1919-1933* (Chapel Hill, N. C., 1972); Joseph Nyomarkay, *Charisma and Factionalism in the Nazi Party* (Minneapolis, 1967), 74-135, provides evidence on the orientation toward working class of the 'Working Association of the North and West' and the later shift toward other constituencies; Dietrich Orlow, *The History of the Nazi Party: 1919-1933*, 2 vols. (Pittsburgh, 1969 and 1973), I, 1917-1933, chap. 4, 1926-1928, 'The Failure of the Urban Plan,' 76-127, and chap. 5, 1928-1930, 'Socialism: That is really an unfortunate word,' 128-85, is a good history of the internal evolution of the party and its changing orientation. The failure to gain the support of the working class is well reflected in the membership figures for the NSBO despite their growth from approximately 3,000 in January 1931 to 294,042 in December 1932 when we compare them with the membership of the trade unions (167 vs. 163-66) and the lack of success in work council elections even after being in

power (126-29), in Hans-Gerd Schumann, *Nationalsozialismus und Gewerkschaftsbewegung* (Hannover, 1958). On 1935 industrial elections, see also Theodor Eschenburg, 'Streiflichter zur Geschichte der Wahlen im Dritten Reich,' *Vierteljahreshefte für Zeitgeschichte* (3 July 1955), 311-16.

28. Theodor Geiger, *Die soziale Schichtung des deutschen Volkes. Soziographischer Versuch auf statistischer Grundlage* (Stuttgart, 1932). On Geiger's work see Paolo Farneti, *Theodor Geiger e la coscienza della societa industriale* (Turin, 1966).

29. Walter B. Simon, 'The Political Parties of Austria,' (Ph.D. diss., Columbia University, 1957).

30. Ramiro Ledesma Ramos, *Fascismo en España*, 238-40, 260-63.

31. Not only many Nazis played with pseudo religious or non-Christian conceptions as the cases of Szálasi in Hungary, Celmiņš in Latvia and Quisling in Norway show.

32. Ramiro Ledesma Ramos, *Fascismo en España*, 283-87: 'Geneva reactionary trench, Geneva metropolitan capital of French Imperialism.'

33. It would be important to analyze how the anti-fascism of liberals, the socialist left, manipulated and simplified by the communists and, after the rise to power of Hitler, by Jewish groups, particularly at the time of the Spanish Civil War, contributed to create a greater sense of common identity and affinity of fascist movements, to overcome serious conflicts of national interest and differences in ideology, particularly on the issue of racial anti-Semitism and to bring Mussolini closer to Hitler. In this there is some similarity with the identification of communists with Stalinist communism rather than a polycentrism in the years of cold-war anti-communism.

In addition the readiness of the left to prevent fascist propaganda by all means contributed to re-enforce the proclivity for violence of fascists, even where the leaders did not particularly glory in it.

34. Dionisio Ridruejo, *Escrito en España* (Buenos Aires, 1962), 79, quoted in Juan J. Linz, 'From Falange to Movimiento Organización...,' 136.

35. See the excellent analysis of the variety of *corporativisms* in Philippe Schmitter, 'Still the Century of Corporatism?,' *Review of Politics* (January 1974), 85-131.

36. William Salomone, *Italian Democracy in the Making. The Political Scene in the Giolittian Era 1900-1914* (Philadelphia, 1945), and the extensive literature on Mosca, Pareto, Sorel, Michels, and their influence.

37. Enrique Tierno Galván, 'Costa y el regeneracionismo,' *Escritos 1950-1960* (Madrid, 1971), 369-539. A comparative historico-sociological study of intellectual critiques of liberal-democracy-parliamentarism at the turn of the century in different countries would be an important contribution to intellectual and political history.

38. The history of how the urban-intellectual-youthful-interventionist and in many aspects still radical fascism linked with the agrarian reaction to socialist trade union and party dominance in the Po Valley remains to be written. Mario Missiroli, 'Il Fascismo e la crisi italiana' (1921), 293-357, in Renzo de Felice, ed., *Il Fascismo e i partiti politici italiàni*, provides many insights into that socio-economic-political context. The many local histories of fascism and its heroes, and the recent works on the popular struggle of the left against fascism, provide a wealth of information that could be linked with data on property, tenancy, wages, changes in economic relations, over time, elections, etc., in those areas. See Albert Szymanski, 'Fascism, Industrialism and Socialism: The Case of Italy,' *Comparative Studies in Society and History*, XV, 4 (October 1973), 395-404, for an excellent ecological analysis of fascist violence in relation to rural socialist strength. Manfredo de Simone, ed., *PNF. Pagine Eroiche della Rivoluzione Fascista* (Milano, 1925) for accounts of incidents and biographical sketches of dead fascists. Friedrich Vöchting, *Die Romagna. Eine Studie über Halbpacht und Landarbeiterwesen in Italien* (Karlsruhe, 1927), an excellent study of social relations in the area, the historical background, the political alignments, etc. Frank M. Snowden, 'On the Social Origins of Agrarian Fascism in Italy,' *European Journal of Sociology*, 13, 2 (1972),

268-295, is an excellent study of rural social conflicts and their political consequences with references to numerous recent Italian monographic and local studies. See also Luigi Preti, *Lotte Agrarie nella Valle Padana* (Torino: Einaudi, 1955) 371-477; Walter Zanotti, 'Lotte Agrarie nel Primo Dopoguerra nella Provincia di Forli e le Origini del Fascismo,' 'Ilva Vaccari, Il Sorgere del Fascismo nel Modenese,' and Bruno Casonato, 'Agli Inizi del Fascismo Parmense,' all three in Luciano Casali, ed., *Movimento Operaio e Fascismo nell'Emilia Romagna* (Roma, 1973); Alessandro Roveri, *Dal Sindacalismo Rivoluzionario al Fascismo. Capitalismo Agrario e Socialismo nel Ferrarese. (1870-1920)*, 297 ff.; A. Roveri, 'Il Fascismo Ferrarese nel 1919-1920,' *Annali* (Milano, 1972), 106-154; Mario Vaini, *Le Origini del Fascismo a Mantova* (Roma, 1961), 54-154; Renato Zangheri, ed., *Le Campagne Emiliane nell'Epoca Moderna* (Milano, 1957), 273 ff. Dora Marucco, 'Note sulla Mezzadria all'Avvento del Fascismo,' *Rivista di Storia Contemporanea*, 3 (1974), 377-388; Emilio Sereni, 'L'Agricultura Toscana e la mezzadrina nel Regime Fascista e l'Opera di Arrigo Serpieri,' in the collective volume, *La Toscana nel Regime Fascista*, 2 vols. (Firenze, 1971), II, 316 ff.; Rodolfo Cavandoli, *Le Origini del Fascismo a Reggio Emilia* (Roma, 1972), passim; Simona Colarizi, *Dopoguerra e Fascismo in Puglia (1919-1926)* (Bari, Laterza, 1971), passim.

39. The link between nationalism, imperialism, and the discovery by Corradini of the idea of the proletarian nation, with the problems of emigration of a country without colonies, was first emphasized by Robert Michels, *L'Imperialismo italiano, Studi politico demografici* (Milan, 1914; first published in German, 1912). The importance of protest against the African adventures in the radicalization of Italian and Spanish labour, and perhaps in France too, have never been studied. William Sheridan Allen, 'The Appeal of Fascism and the Problem of National Disintegration,' in Henry A. Turner, Jr., ed., *Reappraisals of Fascism* (New York, 1975), has emphasized the role of incomplete national integration, becoming visible with World War I and the conflict over interventionism in Italy and the war goals in Germany, in the emergence of fascism.

40. This point is highly debated among historians, see Guenther Roth, *The Social Democrats in Imperial Germany* (Totowa, N.J., 1963).

41. Heinrich August Winkler, *Mittelstand, Demokratie und Nationalsozialismus, Die Politische Entwicklung von Handwerk und Kleinhandel in der Weimarer Republik* (Cologne, 1972), chap. 8, 'Mittelstand und Nationalsozialismus,' 157-82 has noted how the Marxist interpretation linking capitalism and fascism is insufficient, how the radicalization of certain middle-class property owners requires additional explanation. In that context he writes: 'the lack of a successful bourgeois revolution that would have overcome the institutional and ideological elements of pre-industrial society would be one. Formulated positively, fascist movements had special opportunities for success where pre-industrial power holders, mainly the nobility, the military, the bureaucracy, the Church, could save their privileges beyond the industrial revolution and gain a determining influence on other social groups. Schumpeter, who seriously failed to understand imperialism as a general phenomenon when he defined it as the objective predisposition of a state to forceful expansion without definable limits, with that analysis hit on fascism, *malgré lui*, much better. He called attention to the decisive role of pre-industrial feudal elements in the attempts of quasi-objectless expansion.' (P. 162) Winkler's interpretation differs from ours, but is in part complementary.

42. Sten S. Nilson, 'Wahlsoziologische Probleme des Nationalsozialismus,' *Zeitschrift fur die gesamten Staatswissenschaften*, 110, Bd. 2 (1954), 279-311.

43. Juan J. Linz, 'The Social Bases of West German Politics' (Ph.D. diss., Columbia University, 1959), 772, shows how farmers supporting the SPD in 1953 were more socially isolated in terms of their number of acquaintances. Chap. 24, 753-90 on post-second world war German farmers' politics analyzes some of the social and political attitudes of farmers that must have facilitated their susceptibility to the Nazi appeal or the persistence of attitudes acquired in the thirties.

44. For an example of border nationalism-fascism, see Elio Apih, *Italia, Fascismo e Anti-fascismo nella Venezia Giulia (1918-1943), Ricerche Storiche* (Bari, 1966), passim. For example in Trieste the list including the fascists received 45.3 per cent of the votes, with 8.8 per cent going to Slavic candidates, 20.0 per cent communists, 25.9 per cent for other Italian parties. In Istria the proportions were respectively 56.9 per cent, 19.4 per cent, 7.3 per cent, 16.3 per cent (see 162). This pattern has a continuity in the electoral strength of the MSI in the 1944 municipal elections in Trieste with 10,170 votes, 9.4 per cent among 106,872 votes for Italian parties. See François Duprat, *L'Ascension du M.S.I.* (Paris, 1972), 43. Another example of nationalistic-border area fascism was the Styrian Heimatschutz, see Bruce Frederick Pauley, 'Hahnenschwanz and Swastika: The Styrian Heimatschutz and Austrian National Socialism 1918-1934' (Ph.D. diss., University of Rochester, 1967). The Styrian Heimatschutz was the largest single segment of the entire Austrian Heimwehr—the native non-Nazi fascist organization—whose leaders and members later would fuse with the Austrian NSDAP. It was also the area of greatest Hitler-Jugend strength. In Carinthia, Styria and Salzburg—three border regions—the Korneuburg declaration, with its fascist ideology, was received most favourably, in contrast to the response of the Upper Austrian leadership. For an ecological analysis of Carinthian and Styrian border area support for nazism, see Walter B. Simon, 'Political Parties of Austria.' The appeal of Doriot's PPF to the colons in Algeria shows the success of the combination of nationalism with social reform to those self-made upward mobile immigrants in a cultural border position, particularly in Oran where many of the colons were assimilated Spanish immigrants. In addition the colons felt threatened by communist anti-colonialism (see Dieter Wolf, *Die Doriot-Bewegung* [Stuttgart, 1967], 135-36). The Mussert led Nazi party also found considerable support among Dutch residents in Indonesia (2,000 of 29,000 members, 1940), and one of the most important leaders, van Tonningens, was born there as son of an officer; see Konrad Kwiet, 'Zur Geschichte der Mussert Bewegung,' *Vierteljahreshefte für Zeitgeschichte*, 18 (1970), 164-95.

45. Jean Stengers, 'Belgium,' *in* Hans Rogger and Eugen Weber, eds., *The European Right. A Historical Profile* (Berkeley and Los Angeles, 1966), 128-67. R. Baes, *Joris van Severen. Une Ame* (Zulte, 1965), for a sympathetic biography of the leader of Verdinaso. Jean-Michel Etienne, *Le Mouvement Rexiste jusqu'en 1940* (Paris, 1968).

46. Ricardo de la Cierva, *Historia de la Guerra Civil española. Antecedentes, Monarquía y República, 1898-1936* (Madrid, 1969), 284-91.

47. Jan Havránek, 'Fascism in Czechoslovakia,' 47-55 and Joseph F. Zacek, 'Czechoslovak Fascisms,' 52-62, *in* Peter F. Sugar, ed., *Native Fascism in the Successor States 1918-1945* (Santa Barbara, Calif., 1971). The same dominant position of the Serbs and Poles in their victor states account for their resistance to the appeal of fascism or fascisticized nationalism.

48. The literature on Slovak nationalism and the politics of independent Slovakia is highly partisan and provides practically no information on the social bases of parties and the fascist wing emerging in the nationalist movement. Yeshayahu Andrew Jelinek, 'Hlinka's Slovak People'a Party, 1939-1945,' (Ph.D. diss., Indiana University, 1966), is a competent review of the history and the factional fights.

49. Theodor Abel, *The Nazi Movement* (New York, 1965), (first published 1938 as *Why Hitler came to power*). For a unique socio-psychological analysis see Peter H. Merkl, *Political Violence under the Swastika: 581 Early Nazis* (Princeton, 1975).

50. The appeal to youth is central to Ledesma Ramos, *Discurso a las juventudes de España*, 269-77. Let us not forget that the Italian Fascist anthem was Giovinezza (youth).

51. The symbolic significance of uniforms is discussed by ibid., 332-34. A systematic and comparative study of fascist symbolism still remains to be written.

52. On the German youth movement, its ideology and style as well as the partial affinity with fascism, see Walter Z. Laqueur, *Young Germany. A History of the German Youth Movement* (London, 1962); George L. Mosse, *The Crisis of German Ideology,* chap. 9, 171-89; Peter H. Merkl on the youth movement background of Nazis in the Abel collection

of biographies (forthcoming); Peter Loewenberg, 'The Psycho-Historical Origins of the Nazi Youth Cohort,' *American Historical Review*, 76 (1971), 1457-1502, is an interesting, even when sometimes highly speculative, attempt to link the historico-socio-economic experiences of different German age cohorts with their political expressions introducing psychological intervening variables.

The average age of the NSDAP members in 1923, studied by Michael H. Kater, 'Zur Soziographie der frühen NSDAP,' *Vierteljahreshefte für Zeitgeschichte*, 19 (1971), 159, ranged for different occupational groups around the mean of 28 years, from 25 for the white-collar employees (*Angestellte*), 26-27 for workers and *Handwerker*, to 33 for businessmen, 35 for army officers, 39 for the higher civil servants and *leitende Angestellte* (upper white collar), a good indication of the youthfulness even of those in slower career lines. Only the welfare recipients were an older group, with an average of 44 years. Apparently, they were somewhat younger than the founding nucleus studied by Franz-Willing for 1920 whose age was 30 to 32, indicating that new members were younger and shaped by the *Fronterlebnis*. The 48 per cent male members 23 years or younger certainly could not have been integrated in the parties of pre-war. The north German members, particularly the rural supporters were even younger, while the Munich contingent was older (67 per cent over 23) which might contribute to explain its 'old-fashioned' anti-Semitic character and the more anti-class Gemeinschaft radicalism of the northern wing. Between 1930 and 1933 the youthful component seems to have increased.

53. Ernst Posse, *Die politischen Kampfbünde Deutschlands* (Berlin, 1931), and Robert G. L. Waite, *Vanguard of Nazism. The Free Corps Movement in Postwar Germany 1918-1923* (Cambridge, Mass., 1952).

54. On the differential appeal of National Socialists and the Zentrum to women, see Herbert Tingsten, *Political Behavior. Studies in Election Statistics* (London, 1937), 41-71.

55. The names of D'Annunzio, Balbo, Bono, Goering, Mosley, Ruiz de Alda, come to mind.

56. The biographies of the founders of communist parties also suggest a generational basis for the split of the socialist movement and that the war experience, opposition to war, participation in soldiers' protests and councils, must have contributed to the radicalization of the left. See the data on age composition of the KPD leadership and biographies in Hermann Weber, *Die Wandlung des deutschen Kommunismus. Die Stalinisierung der KPD in der Weimarer Republik*, 2 vols. (Frankfurt a.M., 1969).

57. The impact of the Ruhr occupation is well documented in the Merkl monograph. It was that experience that led Karl Radek to his famous Schlageter speech and, incidentally, to his more sophisticated analysis of the fascist phenomenon.

58. On the demobilization process with all its economic and indirectly political implications, see Giorgio Rochat, *L'Esercito Italiano da Vittorio Veneto a Mussolini (1919-1925)* (Bari, 1967), 26-27, 170-83. In June 1919 there were 85,891 reserve officers—*officiali di complemento*—of whom 59,732 were discharged by March 1920, leaving some 26,000, many garrisoned in cities, to be able to engage in private activities or with two to four months' leave to take university examinations. By summer 1922 they would be some 4,000. The border tensions particularly with Yugoslavia retained many men under arms, in an area where they could be politicized. In addition the number of professional officers fluctuated from 14,509 in 1910 to 21,926 in December 1918 to 1,500 foreseen in the *ordinamento* of 1920 (see chap. VII, 'I rapporti tra Fascismo e Esercito,' in 185, in ibid.).

59. Hélgio Henrique Casses Trindade, *Integralismo (O fascismo brasileiro na década de 30)* (Sao Paulo, 1974). Available in French as *L'Action Intégraliste Brésilienne. Un Mouvement de type fasciste des années 30,* Thèse pour le Doctorat de Recherches, Fondation Nationale des Sciences Politiques, Cycle Supérieur d'Etudes Politiques (Paris 1971).

60. Alastair Hamilton, *The Appeal of Fascism. A Study of Intellectuals and Fascism 1919-1945* (New York, 1971).

61. Gabriel Almond, *The Appeals of Communism* (Princeton, 1954).

62. Rudolf Heberle, *Landbevölkerung und Nationalsozialismus. Eine soziologische Unter-*
*suchung der politischen Willensbildung in Schleswig-Holstein 1918-1932* (Stuttgart, 1963).
Horst Gies, 'NSDAP und landwirtschaftliche Organisationen in der Endphase der Weimarer
Republik,' *Vierteljahreshefte für Zeitgeschichte*, XV (October 1967), 341-76; Jeremy Noakes,
*The Nazi Party in Lower Saxony 1921-1933* (Oxford, 1971); Peter Wulf, *Die politische*
*Haltung des schleswigholsteinischen Handwerks 1928-1932* (Cologne, 1969), 56-57, 96-99.

For a theoretical analysis, see Rainer Lepsius, 'The Collapse of an Intermediary Power
Structure: Germany 1933-1934,' *International Journal of Comparative Sociology*, IX, 3-4
(September-December 1968), 289-301. For an excellent account of events in a north German town, William Sheridan Allen, *The Nazi Seizure of Power. The Experience of a Single*
*German Town 1930-1935* (Chicago, 1965); Heinrich August Winkler, *Mittelstand, Demo-*
*kratie und Nationalsozialismus. Die politische Entwicklung von Handwerk und Kleinhandel*
*in der Weimarer Republik* (Cologne, 1972), chap. 8, 156-82, provides an analysis of the
pre- *Machtergreifung Gleichschaltung* through local and regional grassroots pressure of
national interest groups.

63. The classic formulation is William Kornhauser, *The Politics of Mass Society*
(Glencoe, Ill., 1959), who reviews the theoretical literature and empirical evidence relevant
to it.

64. A useful, even though partisan and selective source is *Das Deutsche Führerlexikon*
*1934/1935* (Berlin, 1934) (It was published in May, but corrected in August to take into
account a 'series of political events' by covering with a piece of paper the names of those
purged and leaving blank spaces where their biographies would have appeared). In addition
to party leaders it includes other prominent men in the Third Reich and German society. A
monograph based on it is by Daniel Lerner, with the collaboration of Ithiel de Sola Pool
and George K. Schueller, *The Nazi Elite* (Hoover Institute Studies, 1951; reprinted in
Harold D. Lasswell and D. Lerner, *World Revolutionary Elites, Studies in Coercive Ideo-*
*logical Movements* [Cambridge, Mass., 1966], 194-318). However, the study deals not only
with party leaders but with government and military officials of the regime. The same data
could be analyzed focussing more specifically on the party elite. Erich Stockhorst, *Fünf-*
*tausend Köpfe. Wer war was im Dritten Reich* (Volbert, 1967), is much less useful. Peter
Huttenberger, *Die Gauleiter, Studie zum Wandel des Machtgefüges in der NSDAP* (Stuttgart, 1969), is a useful monograph with brief biographical sketches we have used as data for
tables. Wolfgang Schäfer, *NSDAP. Entwicklung und Struktur der Staatspartei des Dritten*
*Reiches* (Hannover, 1957), passim, provides data on the social background of the Führerkorps of the party and particularly differences in the proportion of old fighters in different
types of positions and regions. Karl Astel and Erna Weber, *Die Kinderzahl der 29000 poli-*
*tischen Leiter des Gaues Thüringen der NSDAP und die Ursachen der ermittelten Fort-*
*pflanzungshäufigkeit* (Berlin, 1943) (only for internal use in the party, not for sale). This
Nazi study gives data on the occupational background at different levels of party leadership
from Blockwart — the smallest neighbourhood unit — to the Land level. The studies on German elites by Wolfgang Zapf, the role of the nobility by Preradovich, the diplomatic service,
etc., contribute to our understanding of the Third Reich but are not focussed on the role of
the party per se. The very important work by Dietrich Orlow, *The History of the Nazi*
*Party*, I, 1917-1933; II, 1933-1945, does not focus on a sociological analysis of the leadership, membership, or electorate of the NSDAP, but provides an excellent background on
the organization, factional struggles, the leadership of Hitler, and the changing appeal of
the party. See however Vol. I, table 4 for the birth year, occupation, and education of
Gauleiter, data on occupation and education of Reichsleitung, Gauleiters, district, and
local leaders from a 1929 police report, tables 6a and 6b, 172. Albrecht Tyrell, *Führer*
*befiehl. . . Selbstzeugnisse aus der 'Kampfzeit' der NSDAP* (Düsseldorf, 1969), presents an
excellent table with basic biographical data on Gauleiters and Reichsleiters.

65. On the Italian elite in power in the thirties prior to the Ethiopian War, see Harold D.
Lasswell and Renzo Sereno, 'The Fascists: The Changing Italian Elite,' *in* Harold D. Lass-

well and Daniel Lerner, eds., *World Revolutionary Elites*, 179-93, based on biographies in Edoardo Savinio, *La Nazione Operante* (Milan, 1934). This study did not deal only with party elites and obviously would not be fully representative of the leadership before the March on Rome, nor does it distinguish fascists and nationalists before that date. The data on the PNF and Populari legislators in table 5 are from a study of Italian political elite from the *Risorgimento* to our time by Paolo Farneti, to be published in a volume on political elites edited by M. Dogan and J. Linz.

66. Trindade, *Integralismo*, passim.

67. There are obviously biographies and memoirs of the top fascist leaders, some of them important scholarly works, others just hagiographic efforts of dubious value. For the Nazi references see in Orlow, *The History of the Nazi Party*, II, 508-13, 516-17. Except for Mussolini and a few others there are fewer materials on Italian leaders. O. Mosley has written recently an autobiography that despite its apologetic character reveals much about him and the period. The biography of José Antonio Primo de Rivera is hagiographic but relatively adequate, as is that of Ramiro Ledesma Ramos (see Stanley Payne in this volume). Quisling has also been the object of one by Paul M. Hayes, *The Career and Political Ideas of Vidkun Quisling, 1887-1945* (Newton Abbot, 1971). The Dieter Wolf study of Doriot is an important contribution even when not strictly a biography. None of the other French fascists and their movements have been the object of a comparable study. The biographical material on the fascists of the Low Countries is seriously inadequate. Even more regrettable given the personalities involved is the lack of a good biography of Codreanu and Szálasi. Ernst Nolte, *Der Faschismus von Mussolini zu Hitler. Texte, Bilder und Dokumente* (Munich, 1968), 388-93, has included capsule biographies of top fascists. With the sources quoted and a variety of *Who's Who's*, encyclopaedias, publications such as *Current Biography*, we have attempted to collect data for a 'collective portrait' of fascist leadership.

A collective portrait of the British fascist leadership with interesting information on travels and foreign contacts, particularly in the Empire, in addition to standard biographical data is W. F. Mandle, 'The Leadership of the British Union of Fascists,' *Australian Journal of Politics and History*, XII, 3 (1966), 360-83. This study shows the social heterogeneity, the varied political background, the youthfulness, and relatively high education of BUF leaders. A source I was unable to consult is K. Brix and E. Hansen, *Dansk Nazism under Besaettelsen* (Copenhagen, 1948), based on the files of the party.

68. The biographical data for the collective portrait of fascist leaders and the comparisons with those of Christian democratic, socialist, and communist parties have been taken from a variety of sources too long to list here. The main sources and method used in defining those to be included will be described in another paper in progress.

For the fascists basically we have included the top founder and top leader of every party—including a few parties that might not be strictly fascist like Action Française, the Slovak People's Party, Lapua, but does not include men like Salazar, Franco, and Horthy. The basic list was taken from Ernst Nolte, *Der Faschismus von Mussolini zu Hitler*, 'Kurzbiographien,' 388-93, excluding those authoritarian rulers that co-opted fascist parties. To that list we added leaders from other minor fascist parties, Latin American parties and subleaders in proportion to the importance of the movement, particularly in Germany and Italy, with an important role in the movement (rather than the regime), e.g., the key members of the Gran Consiglio, the Pentarchia, Gauleiter, and Reichsleiter. We also included some of the dissident fascists and Nazis.

For purposes of comparison we selected the Christian democracy party leaders for the period 1919-1945. Their number is smaller due to the absence of such parties in a number of countries, particularly in that period, and the stability of the leadership. The importance of the Zentrum, the Austrian party, and the Italian Populari is reflected in the data that are therefore particularly comparable to our sample of fascists. The list has been compiled using a number of party histories and Joseph N. Moody, *Church and Society. Catholic Social and Political Thought and Movements 1789-1950* (New York, 1953). The Zentrum biographies can be found in Rudolf Morsey, ed., *Zeitgeschichte in Lebensbildern. Aus dem deutschen Katholizismus des 20. Jahrhunderts* (Mainz, 1973) (21 biographies, including Erzberger, Fehrenbach, H. Brauns, Wirth, W. Marx, Stegerwald, Held, Joos, Brüning, Kass), with detailed bibliography and reference to sources.

The names of the socialist leaders for the period 1919-1940s before take-over of power by fascist — and therefore excluding exile and resistance — in the countries with fascist movements, have been taken basically from Helga Grebing and Günther Dill, *Der Sozialismus vom Klassenkampf zum Wohlfahrtsstaat. Texte, Bilder und Dokumente* (Munich, 1963), 'Kurzbiographien,' 413-33, and the most frequently indexed names in Julius Braunthal, *History of the International, 1914-1943*, II (London, 1967) (translated from the German). For Germany we added the names of chancellors and Reich cabinet members, and in other countries, factional leaders and leaders of independent socialist parties. The communists included have been taken from Iring Fetscher and Günther Dill, eds., *Der Kommunismus von Marx bis Mao Tse-tung. Texte, Bilder und Dokumente* (Munich, 1969), 'Kurzbiographien,' 370-78, and the indexes of Franz Borkenau, *The Communist International*; Paolo Spriano, *Storia del Partito comunista italiano. I: Da Bordiga a Gramsci* (Turin, 1967) (those leaders before 1925, receiving more than four lines); Hermann Weber, *Die Wandlung des deutschen Kommunismus* (those in the index receiving more than five lines), and Annie Kriegel, *Les communistes français. Essai d'ethnographie politique* (Paris, 1968) (those receiving more than two lines) for the PCF between wars. We also used for the French socialist leadership her *Le Congrès de Tours (1920). Naissance du Parti communiste français* (Paris, 1964). In some cases, e.g., Doriot, the same person appears in more than one sample.

Obviously, the Russians constitute a large part of the communist sample. The factional fights and instability of leadership accounts for the somewhat larger sample.

The data presented here could be refined and have a considerable margin of error. The conclusions based on them should be considered suggestive rather than definitive.

69. Renzo de Felice, *Mussolini il fascista, L'Organizzazione dello Stato fascista 1925-1929* (Turin, 1968), n. 68.

70. De Felice, *Mussolini il fascista. La conquista del potere 1921-1925* (Turin, 1966), 5-11, particularly the detailed tables for 71 geographic units covering the country giving number of sections and members for ten different dates, from March to December 1921 and April to May 1922.

71. Harold J. Gordon, *Hitler and the Beer Hall Putsch* (Princeton, 1972), analyzes data for those 1,672 in a file of members; W. Schäfer, *NSDAP, Entwicklung und Struktur der Staatspartei des Dritten Reiches*; see also Hans Buchheim, 'Mitgliedschaft bei der NSDAP,' in Paul Kluke, ed., *Gutachten des Instituts für Zeitgeschichte* (Munich, 1958) that provides information on membership policies of the party. Data on the social composition of membership for Lower Saxony are found in Jeremy Noakes, *The Nazi Party in Lower Saxony*, and Franz Josef Heyen, *Nationalsozialismus im Alltag. Quellen zur Geschichte des Nationalsozialismus vornehmlich im Raum Mainz-Koblenz-Trier* (Boppard a.R., 1967), 330-31. See also Eberhart Schön, *Die Entstehung des Nationalsozialismus in Hessen* (Meisenheim am Glan, 1972) who gives biographical information on 83 Ortsgruppenführer in 1930.

72. R. de Felice, *Mussolini il fascista. La conquista...*, 115 on the 'localism' of the party, and on the dualism in the party see 12-13, quoting A. Gramsci ('I due fascismi,' *Il Ordine Novo*, 22 August 1921). Sigmund Neumann, *Die Parteien der Weimarer Republik* (Stuttgart, 1965, first published 1932), 73-87, 130-35, was among the first to emphasize the need to distinguish regional differences within the NSDAP. The data of Schäfer show the very different degree and date of penetration of the party in different regions.

73. These 1921 November Congress data have been used in all the literature on fascism. See de Felice, *Mussolini il fascista. La conquista...*, 6-7. Palmiro Togliatti, *Lezioni sul Fascismo* (Rome, 1972), 44-45, also comments on them and so did A. Tasca and I. Silone in their works on fascism.

74. W. Schäfer, *NSDAP*..., 47.

75. Luigi Salvatorelli, *Nazionalfascismo*, selection reprinted in de Felice, *Il Fascismo. Le interpretazioni*..., 54-63, see also 59-61.

76. See Robert Michels, *Sozialismus in Italien. Intellektuelle Strömungen* (Munich, 1925), Chap. III, on the social composition of the parliamentary, provincial, and municipal elite of the party, its candidates, and party membership (with comparisons with Germany), 162-206, and on the role of students, professors and free professionals in the party and Italian society, 209-48.

77. Data in Bracher, *Die Auflösung der Weimarer Republik*, 147-49; Hans Peter Bleuel and Ernst Klinnert, *Deutsche Studenten auf dem Weg ins Dritte Reich. Ideologien-Programme-Aktionen, 1918-1935* (Gütersloh, 1967); Wolfgang Kreutzberger, *Studenten und Politik, 1918-1933. Der Fall Freiburg im Breisgau* (Göttingen, 1972); Wolfgang Zorn, 'Student Politics in the Weimar Republic,' *Journal of Contemporary History*, 5 (1970), 128-43. For the appeal of anti-Semitic Swedish fascism to students, see Eric Warenstam, *Fascismen och Nazismen i Sverige 1920-1940* (Stockholm, 1970), 102-03. For Spain, Stanley Payne in this volume, for Rumania, Eugen Weber, 'The Men of the Archangel,' 101-26. Even in stable and democratic Switzerland at the Eidgenössische Technische Hochschule of Zurich the Nationale Front was the largest student organization (1933) and its activities mobilized political interest at the university. However, the Frontists at the university soon lost strength and dissolved in 1937. Walter Wolf, *Faschismus in der Schweiz. Die Geschichte der Frontenbewegungen in der deutschen Schweiz, 1930-1945* (Zurich, 1969), 122-23.

An interesting study is Risto Alapuro, 'Students and National Politics: A comparative study of the Finnish student movement in the interwar period,' *Scandinavian Political Studies*, VIII (1973), 113-40, comparing the Akademic Karelian Society with the Legion of the Archangel Michael.

78. W. Schäfer, *NSDAP*..., 19, table 4; 47, table 32. It is striking that free professionals should be 3.2 per cent of the membership and only 2.1 of the Führerkorps, compared to respectively 20.0 per cent and 22.6 per cent that were white collar employees (*Angestellte*) or respectively 7.5 per cent and 7.3 per cent small businessmen (*Kaufleute*). The already quoted study by K. Astel and E. Weber, *Politische Leiter in Thüringen in 1939*, shows this pattern even more clearly.

79. Franz Neumann, *Behemoth. The Structure and Practice of National Socialism 1933-1944* (New York, 1963; first published 1942, 1944), 378-79. See also George L. Mosse, *The Crisis of German Ideology*, chap. 8, 'Education comes to the aid,' 149-70, on the diffusion of *völkisch* ideas among educators.

80. De Felice, *Mussolini il fascista. La conquista...*, 249 (data for June 1922).

81. Trindade, *Integralismo*, 137 ff.

82. Eugen Weber, 'The Men of the Archangel,' 108-09.

83. Dieter Wolf, *Die Doriot-Bewegung*, 141 (there is a French translation).

84. Carlo Mierendorff, 'Gesicht und Charakter der nationalsozialistischen Bewegung,' *Die Gesellschaft* (8 June 1930).

85. De Felice, *Mussolini il fascista. La conquista...*, 249.

86. Michael H. Kater, 'Zur Soziographie der frühen NSDAP,' 124-59. Harold J. Gordon, Jr., *Hitler and the Beer Hall Putsch*, see 'Social Composition and Attitudes,' 68-87; Appendix, 622-28, age and occupation of members before the Putsch and of local NSDAP and SA leaders.

87. Eugen Weber, 'The Men of the Archangel,' 108.

88. Trindade, *Integralismo*.

89. Data on PNF party membership calculated from de Felice, *Mussolini il fascista. La conquista...*, 8-12, for 31 March 1921 and 30 April 1922, and a comparison with the strength of the Partito Populare Italiano (PPI) in the 1919 and 1921 elections, and the map of Catholic Action membership in 1951, in Jean-Paul Chassériaud, *Le Parti Démocrate*

*Chrétien en Italie* (Paris, 1965), 150-51, 171, 373-76. Post-war Movimento Sociale Italiano deputies report no membership in religious associations in contrast to 10.9 per cent of the Monarchists and obviously 85.2 per cent of the Christian Democrats. In this they are similar to the liberals and Republicans. Surprisingly small percentages of socialists and communists report having been members. See S. Somogyi 'Costituente Deputati 1946-1958,' *in* Giovanni Sartori, *Il Parlamento Italiano 1946-1963* (Naples, 1963), 104.

90. Albert Szymanski, 'Fascism, Industrialism and Socialism: The Case of Italy,' 15, 395-404.

91. Merkl, *Political Violence under the Swastika*, statistical analysis of the Abel data collection.

92. Schäfer, *NSDAP*, tables 8, 9, 10, 16-17.

93. On the explicit condemnation at the time of the 1937 election, see Jean-Michel Etienne, *Le Mouvement Rexiste jusqu'en 1940*, 136-37. Konrad Kwiet, 'Zur Geschichte der Mussert-Bewegung,' 164-95.

94. See Juan J. Linz, 'La realidad asociativa de los españoles,' in *Sociología Española de los Años Setenta* (Madrid, 1971), 307-48, see also 327-30.

95. Trindade, *Integralismo*.

96. See the outstanding monograph by de Felice, *Storia degli ebrei italiani*, 73-75 and passim.

97. On the important role of such groups in the final expansion of the party, see Dietrich Orlow, *The History of the Nazi Party 1919-1933*, 193-200.

98. The best review of the social bases of fascist parties is Seymour M. Lipset, 'Fascism-Left, Right and Center,' in *Political Man. The Social Bases of Politics* (Garden City, N.Y., 1960), 131-76. Lipset makes an extremely interesting effort to distinguish fascist radicalism as that of the middle distinct from those of the established right and left. In S. J. Woolf, ed., *The Nature of Fascism* (London, 1968), Gino Germani, 'Fascism and Class' (65-96), with less reference to electoral and membership data presents a stimulating theoretical analysis. In the same volume, S. L. Andreski, 'Some sociological considerations on fascism and class' (97-102) notes that sociological analysis of recruitment might not, in and by itself, be a key to the fascist attitude toward the existing class order; see also the discussion of both papers (104-15). A recent article reviewing the books by Keele, Noakes, and Winkler among others, 'The coming of the Nazis,' *Times Literary Supplement*, 1 February 1974, should also be mentioned here.

99. As basic sources for the electoral sociology of Nazism in Germany and Austria on which our analysis is based, we can mention: the important review for different parties and periods with excellent maps by Alfred Milatz, *Wähler und Wahlen in der Weimarer Republik* (Bonn, 1965), see mainly 110-13; on elections 1929-1933, 123-50. In English, see James K. Pollock, 'An Areal Study of the German Electorate, 1930-1933,' *American Political Science Review*, 38 (1944), and the study of the 1930 election by Samuel Pratt, 'The Social Basis of Nazism and Communism in Urban Germany,' (M.A. thesis, Michigan State University, 1948). See also Ernst August Roloff, 'Wer wählte Hitler? Thesen zur Sozial- und Wirtschaftsgeschichte der Weimarer Republik,' *Politische Studien*, 15 (1964), 293 ff. Hans Fenske, *Wahlrecht und Parteiensystem. Ein Beitrag zur deutschen Parteien-geschichte* (Frankfurt a.M., 1972), focusses on the complex question of the role of the electoral system and rise of Nazism first posed by Ferdinand A. Hermes in 1933. His book includes detailed discussions on the areas of right radical strength in different Länder (chaps. 6-8). A study with particular emphasis on Bavaria is Meinrad Hagman, *Der Weg ins Verhängnis. Reichstagswahlergebnisse 1919 bis 1933, besonders aus Bayern* (Munich, 1946). There are a number of regional studies, in addition to the well-known study by R. Heberle (From Democracy to Nazism) of Schleswig-Holstein, and others of agrarian areas, among which Bernhard Vogel and Peter Haungs, *Wahlkampf und Wählertradition. Eine Studie zur Bundestagswahl von 1961* (Cologne, 1965), covers the religiously mixed area of Baden and Heidelberg. Richard Hamilton of McGill Uni-

versity, Montreal, has undertaken a detailed ecological analysis of the urban electoral support of the NSDAP as well as the vote of the vacationing letter voters (*Briefwähler*). Preliminary findings show a larger upper- and upper-middle-class support for the party in the early thirties than most of the literature assumes. Among the few studies of urban voting, we can mention H. Anschütz, 'Die NSDAP in Hamburg. Ihre Anfänge bis zur Reichstagswahl vom 14. September 1930,' Ph.D. diss. Hamburg 1956), we could not consult. See also Andreas Alther, 'Die örtliche Verteilung der Wähler grosser Parteien in Städtekomplex Hamburg aufgrund der Reichstagswahlen vom 14. September 1930,' *Hamburgs Verwaltungs- und Wirtschaft-Monatschrift des Statistischen Landesamtes*, 8, 6 (1931). Herbert Kühr, *Parteien und Wahlen im Stadt- und Landkreis Essen in der Zeit der Weimarer Republik* (Düsseldorf, 1973), shows the resistance of the Catholic Zentrum electorate, particularly the working class, to the NSDAP appeal, as well as that of the working-class voters of the KPD and SPD, compared to the rural and middle class, particularly Protestant electorate. Dietrich Thränhardt, *Wahlen und politische Strukturen in Bayern 1848-1953* (Düsseldorf, 1973), 134-137, 152-188, documents those patterns for Bavaria. The best ecological study of Austrian elections in the first republic is Walter B. Simon, 'The Political Parties of Austria,' (Ph.D. diss. Columbia University, 1957). He shows how the German oriented anti-clerical middle class that in 1930 still supported the Nationaler Wirtschaftsblock und Landbund, Führung Dr. Schober, in provincial elections in 1931 and 1933, shifted to the Nazis (except the Jewish middle-class voters of the ticket).

100. Nico Passchier, 'Regional Differences in the Rise of German Nazism, 1930-1933. Their Extent and their Relevance for further Studies,' paper presented at the Bergen Conference on Comparative European Nazism and Fascism (June 1974).

101. The rural support for Nazism after 1928 is well documented by electoral and institutional analysis. It is obviously difficult to judge the extent to which that support was an expression of protest of farmers against government policies, foreclosures for taxes and mortgages, price squeezes, discontent with the leadership of agricultural interest groups linked to other parties (particularly the DNVP), or a response to the Nazi anti-urban *völkisch*-romantic ideology. Certainly, the alienation from the Weimar system had already expressed itself in the support for local and minor farmers' parties, protest movements, and the beginning swing to the NSDAP in 1928 came as a surprise to the leadership that had tried to gain an urban base, but afterwards directed its efforts to the peasants. Certainly the religious loyalties of Catholic farmers integrated into a network of interest groups linked to the Zentrum and under the influence of the Church stresses the importance of cultural variables, but the comparison of communities of similar characteristics also show the importance of economic factors in the depression (see Werner Kaltefleiter, *Wirtschaft und Politik in Deutschland. Konjunktur als Bestimmungsfaktor des Parteiensystems* [Cologne, 1968], 41-46). On the rural vote see Carl J. Friedrich, 'The Agricultural Basis of Emotional Nationalism,' *Public Opinion Quarterly*, I, 1 (1937), 55; Charles P. Loomis and J. Allen Beegle, 'The Spread of German Nazism in Rural Areas,' *American Sociological Review*, II, 6 (1946). The outstanding monograph of Rudolf Heberle, *From Democracy to Nazism. A Regional Case Study on Political Parties in Germany* (Baton Rouge, 1945). A Nazi regional analysis, Eugen Schmahl, *Entwicklung der völkischen Bewegung* (Giessen, 1933), shows the shift of voters from the Landbund in Hessen to the NSDAP. M. Hagmann, *Der Weg ins Verhängnis*, 27-28, shows how the Bayerische Bauern- und Mittelstandsbund, a regional agrarian-middle class party, apparently lost its votes predominantly to the Nazis. Hans Beyer, 'Die Agrarkrise und das Ende der Weimarer Republik,' *Zeitschrift für Agrargeschichte und Agrarsoziologie*, 13 (1965), 62 ff. Horst Gied, 'NSDAP und landwirtschaftliche Organisationen in der Endphase der Weimarer Republik,' *Vierteljahreshefte für Zeitgeschichte*, 15 (1967), focusses on the rural interest groups. The importance of rural support and leadership for the NSDAP finds a parallel in another Nordic fascist movement — Quisling's *Nasjonal Samling*. In the 1933 elections 71 per cent of its candidates were farmers or forest owners. In

1944 when the party had 42,975 members, 17.3 per cent were farmers or forest owners, to which the party directed its appeal, exploiting the crisis created by the depression.

The question of the extent to which the voters in rural areas and small towns moved between 1928 and 1930 toward the NSDAP in response to the economic crisis rather than the party appealing to them effectively and the influence of activist nuclei— Ortsgruppen and Stützpunkte—would deserve more research. As Heinrich Bennecke, Wirtschaftliche Depression und politischer Radikalismus 1918-1938 (Munich, 1970), 94, notes in 1930 the party had 4,964 local organizations, while the Reich had 63,500 municipalities; that means one party unit for every 13 municipalities. In East Prussia for 7,084 municipalities there were 218 local organizations, but the party managed to increase its vote from 8,114 to 236,000 of the 1,392,000 eligible voters. Bennecke suggests that initially the organizational strength was the result of the electoral success, even when in turn it contributed to strengthen the party. The relative contribution of the loosening of ties with the large parties in 1928, the impact of the economic crisis and organizational presence of the party, as contributing factors, should be systematically investigated, allowance being made for the religious variable.

102. On the weakness of female support for the NSDAP—like other extremist and antireligious parties—see Herbert Tingsten, Political Behavior, chap. 1: 'Women and Politics,' see tables on 43, 48, 51-58 (for Germany); 68-69, for Austria; see also chap. 2, 'Age groups in politics,' 111-12 for Sweden and Gabriele Bremme, Die politische Rolle der Frau in Deutschland (Göttingen, 1956), 74-77, 111, 243-52.

103. Alfred Milatz, Wähler und Wahlen.

104. Milatz, 'Das Ende der Parteien im Spiegel der Wahlen 1930 bis 1933,' in Erich Matthias and Rudolf Morsey, eds., Das Ende der Parteien 1933 (Düsseldorf, 1960), 769-70. See also pages 140-41.

105. Walter B. Simon, 'Political Parties of Austria,' passim.

106. The data for this analysis are from a variety of sources: de Felice, Storia degli ebrei italiani. . . , for party membership; Istituto Centrale di Statistica (Italy) Sommario di Statistiche Storiche Italiane 1861-1955 (Rome, 1958) for strikers, unemployment, price index for consumer goods, and students in higher education; Giorgio Rochat, L'Esercito Italiano da Vittorio Veneto a Mussolini (1919-1925), for demobilization.

107. The close connection between the rise of nazism and the economic depression and its impact on the social structure and politics is analyzed in M. Rainer Lepsius, 'The Breakdown of the Weimar Republic 1930-1933,' in J. Linz and A. Stepan, eds., Breakdown and Crises of Democracies (forthcoming). For a graph of the rise in unemployment and NSDAP vote, see Werner Kaltefleiter, Wirtschaft und Politik in Deutschland, 37. Kaltefleiter provides an excellent analysis of the elections of the period in this context. Heinrich Bennecke, Wirtschaftliche Depression und politischer Radikalismus, analyzes the impact of the depression on political stability in Austria. He also notes how the massive shift of Sudeten German voters from the socialist and Catholic German parties to the nazified Sudetendeutsche Partei was not only due to heightened nationalism, the appeal of a powerful Germany led by Hitler, but to the particularly strong impact of the depression on their economic condition. On the impact of the depression on electoral behaviour, see R. I. McKibbin, 'The Myth of the unemployed: Who did vote for the Nazis?' The Australian Journal of Politics and History, XV, 2 (August 1969), 25-69. For a fascist's awareness of this relationship, see this summary of a point made by Bardèche, 'that fascism is a doctrine which lacks a natural clientele among the electorate; only during times of crisis does it find one among the petty bourgeoisie, a class which feeling threatened from above and below responds emotionally to "heroic" leadership. Consequently, when there are no occasions for heroism, fascism declines.' Robert Soucy in 'The Nature of Fascism in France,' Walter Laqueur and George Mosse, eds., International Fascism 1920-1945, 31.

108. The March 1933 election tends to be neglected in the analysis of Nazism on account of

the limitation of the freedom of parties to campaign, and the fact that almost all the KPD leadership and a large part of that of the SPD were under arrest or persecuted and, therefore, the election can be considered only semi-free. However, by showing the hard-core resistance to the NSDAP appeal, it is evidence of the ultimate limits to its expansion. See the detailed analysis of the Gemeinden which gave 60 per cent or more of their votes to the opposition, in Karl Dietrich Bracher, Wolfgang Sauer, Gerhard Schulz, *Die nationalsozialistische Machtergreifung. Studien zur Errichtung des totalitären Herrschaftssystems in Deutschland 1933/ 1934* (Cologne, 1960), 88-136. The awareness of that persistence of the social basis of opposition is reflected in a file ordered by the NSDAP in November 1937 for each local unit Ortsgruppe giving the degree of Nazi organization of the population, date of founding of the party unit, membership by 14 September 1930 and 30 January 1933, and reporting on the climate of opinion and those shaping it, such as the clergy, etc. These interesting data have been published for the NSDAP Kreis Trier-Land West in Franz Josef Heyen, *Nationalsozialismus im Alltag*, 328-51. They provide real insight into the difficulties encountered even by a totalitarian party to penetrate the society.

109. Sten S. Nilson, 'Wahlsoziologische Probleme des Nationalsozialismus.'

110. Robert J. Alexander, *Latin American Political Parties* (New York, 1973), chap. 22, 428-38 deals briefly with Açāo Integralista Brasileira, Partido Nacista de Chile, Falange Socialista Boliviana, Unión Nacional Sinarquista; and Mario Rolón Anaya, *Política y Partidos en Bolivia* (La Paz, 1966), on the Falange Socialista Boliviana (FSB), and the Movimiento Nacionalista Revolucionario (MNR), 243-308. For a recent monograph see Michael Potashnik, '"Nacismo": National Socialism in Chile, 1932-1938' (Ph.D. diss. University of California at Los Angeles, 1974).

111. Masao Maruyama, *Thought and Behaviour in Modern Japanese Politics*, Ivan Morris ed. (London, 1963), 33-39. And the general discussion by George Macklin Wilson, 'A New Look at the Problem of "Japanese Fascism,"' *Comparative Studies in Society and History*, X, 4 (1968), 401-12 (also in Henry A. Turner, *Reappraisals of Fascism*, 199-214).

112. M. Maruyama, *Thought and Behaviour*.

113. A. James Gregor, *The Fascist Persuasion in Radical Politics.* (Princeton, 1974). This work came to our attention too late to be referred to more often in this paper. Another basic source is Tein Ugelvik Larsen, Bernt Hagtvet and Jan Petter Myklebust, *Who were the Fascists? Social Roots of European Fascism* (forthcoming) with chapters on a large number of countries.

# PART II
## Italy and Germany

# 2

# Italian Fascism

ADRIAN LYTTELTON

A guide to the literature on Italian fascism must start with the works of two men, Gaetano Salvemini and Angelo Tasca. Both had been deeply involved in politics before fascism forced them into exile. Both had previously been militants; Salvemini had left the socialist party to become an independent democrat, while Tasca had seceded from the communist party. They were each possessed of an unusual degree of intellectual independence and courage. Here the resemblance ends. Salvemini was a polemicist and moralist of passionate temperament; Tasca had a more prosaic and analytical mind. This contrast should not, however, be overdrawn. It is always necessary when reading Salvemini's works on fascism to remember their purpose. He saw himself as a front-line combatant in the war against the lies of fascist propagandists and the half-truths of their apologists. In his anxiety to prove that fascism was irrational and absurd, he perhaps comes close at times to making it incomprehensible in historical terms. For instance, his anxiety to prove that fascism did not save Italy from revolution arguably led him to underrate the gravity of the postwar crisis. He was prescient in his warnings that Mussolini's rhetoric about expansion and war must be taken seriously, because in the end he would be forced by the momentum of his own creation to try to translate words into action. But in Salvemini's work on Mussolini's foreign policy his determination to show Mussolini's irresponsibility and ignorance on every occasion is excessive.[1] In saying this, however, one is dealing with only one side of Salvemini. He was no mere polemicist, but a historian by vocation, with an enormous appetite for facts and great intellectual energy. The overriding lesson to be learnt from both Salvemini and Tasca is that it is the historian's duty to be concrete. They both insisted that there were no short-cuts to the understanding of fascism, in Italy or in general. Tasca warned his readers against the temptation of simple and abstract formulae: there were already, he wrote, too many conflicting 'definitions' of fascism, and he had no intention of adding to their number—'For us, to define fascism is above all to write its history.'[2] Fascism was not static, but continually changing; and it was not an entity in itself but 'the resultant of a whole situation from which it cannot be separated.' Tasca's warning against the mania for definitions, which had particularly afflicted Marxists, should not however be read as an unqualified commitment to pure narrative history, or as a condemnation of the general concept of 'fascism.' Tasca recognises clearly that, if we speak of fascism in general, and not just Italian fascism, we must use the comparative method 'to indicate a certain number of common characteristics susceptible of being incorporated into a general definition of fascism.'[3]

Salvemini's knowledge of Britain and America made him conscious of a different kind of danger. In the older and wealthier democracies there was a tendency, even among intellectuals, to regard fascism simply as a manifestation of 'racial instinct' or 'national character.' This, Salvemini said, was a mark of the 'lazy mind'; instead, 'if one wants to understand why democratic institutions collapsed in Italy or in France and are in jeopardy everywhere, one has to set aside a priori schemes and empty slogans and must ascertain why and how the fascist movement arose in a given country, what social groups contributed to it, why and how the struggle between fascists and anti-fascists developed, and why and how the fascists overcame their foes.'[4]

## FASCISM AND LIBERALISM: THE PROBLEM OF CONTINUITY

One of the problems most often debated has been that of the continuity between the liberal and the fascist regime. Did fascism represent a break with the past, or did it merely accentuate trends already evident? Was it a 'parenthesis,' or a 'revelation' of the national past? The clarity of these alternatives is deceptive. They originate in slogans which their own authors did not perhaps believe wholeheartedly. Thus Piero Gobetti, the young theorist of the 'liberal revolution,' who described fascism as the 'autobiography of the nation,' seems also to have been the first to describe fascism as a 'parenthesis.'[5] The problem of fascism is still a live one in Italy, and so the problem of continuity has two aspects, that of the continuity between liberal Italy and fascism, and that of the continuity between fascism and the Republic of today. The attitude of historians to the past is inevitably coloured by the present, and there is a tendency to identify these two different aspects of the question; but they are to some degree distinct.

How did the fascists themselves see this problem of continuity? The two most distinguished intellectuals of the regime, the philosopher Gentile and the historian Volpe, gave distinct but similar answers. Neither Gentile nor Volpe, it should be noted, had been fascists before Mussolini came to power in October 1922. As representatives of a broader tradition of conservative nationalism, they were particularly concerned with the problem of how to relate fascism to the Italian past. For Gentile, fascism

represented the return to the heroic ideals of the Risorgimento.[6] It was
the continuation of a struggle between the 'two souls' of Italy, the idealist
spirit of Mazzini and the materialist scepticism of the liberal statesman
Giovanni Giolitti, who had ruled Italy for most of the decade before the
war. Both Gentile and Volpe saw 1915, when Italy intervened in the war,
as a first decisive break, in which the forces of 'idealism,' 'action,' or
'will,' had successfully revolted against the spirit of compromise. This element in the fascist interpretation of fascism does, I think, offer one
valuable clue. The 'break' in Italian history took place as much in 1915,
with the intervention crisis, as in 1922 with the March on Rome. The second common feature in the interpretations of Gentile and Volpe was the
attempt to present fascism as the successor to socialism. They recognized,
that is to say, that socialism and the rise of the masses had undermined
the old liberal oligarchy. The fascist regime was a new synthesis, in which
the new force of the masses would be finally identified with the patriotic
ideal, which in the Risorgimento had been the belief only of minorities.

No anti-fascist could agree with Gentile or Volpe that Italian fascism
fulfilled the kind of aspirations aroused by socialism. Words like justice
and equality were not part of the basic fascist vocabulary. But nonetheless Italian fascism did aspire to incorporate the masses in a new political
structure. The communist leader Togliatti described fascism as a reactionary regime with mass support.[7] Insofar as this description is correct, it
can be argued that such a regime did represent a break with the past. If
one had to provide an equally synthetic definition of the regime which
governed Italy until 1913-14 one could suggest that it was a 'progressive
oligarchy.' But at this point the reader will probably already have remembered the warning of Tasca which I quoted at the beginning of this essay.
Simple definitions do violence to the reality of history.

The problem of continuity needs to be seen in a comparative perspective. The deficiencies of the Italian political system before 1914, though
real enough, sometimes look less remarkable when compared with the
experience of other countries. The existence of a limited electorate until
1912 is one example. The obvious comparisons are with Germany on the
one hand and with England and France on the other. Why did Italy and
Germany go fascist while England and France remained democratic? A
whole line of Marxist interpretations of Italian history has followed
Lenin's hypothesis that one can distinguish a 'Prussian way' to capitalism,
marked by the persistence of feudal residues and the alliance between
aristocracy and bourgeoisie in a single power bloc, from an 'English way,'
in which the capitalist bourgeoisie at a decisive stage of its development
attacks the aristocracy, destroys its feudal character, and eventually
forces it into a subordinate position. Gramsci applied Lenin's theory to
Italy, and his interpretation has served as the basis for more recent works
by Marxist scholars. Particularly worthy of note are E. Sereni's works on

agrarian history, and an article by G. Procacci.[8] More recently a young
Marxist historian N. Tranfaglia has re-examined the question, arguing
that the Italian way to capitalism essentially resembled the German and
differed from the French and English. One may not feel entirely convinced by the traditional arguments put forward to prove this point. One
might argue equally well that Italy was like France in that the bourgeoisie
and middle classes really had replaced the aristocracy as the ruling class,
whereas in England as in Germany there was a condominium. In fact,
Tranfaglia notes that 'the Giolittian experiment in the first ten years of
the century appears as the reflection of the greater relative force of the
Italian bourgeoisie compared to the German.'[9] However, the case can
perhaps be made out in a modified form. It is rather striking that the
three Axis nations—Germany, Italy and Japan—were all faced with similar problems in the second half of the nineteenth century. They were latecomers both in industrial and in national development; that is to say that
they had to achieve industrialization and full national independence
simultaneously. Each of these achievements was a condition of the other:
for in an industrial age non-industrial states were client states, while
industry could not develop without a large and protected market. The
specifically economic reasons for the accentuated role of the state in the
economic development of the 'latecomers' have been explained in a
classic work by Gerschenkron (*Economic Backwardness in Historical Perspective*)—which makes full proviso for individual variations from the
pattern. But in addition, when dealing with the political consequences of
industrialization, one ought to emphasize the importance of the association between these two processes of institutional unification and industrialization. One can see this most clearly if one compares the Italian
nationalist movement with the Action Française. The Italian nationalists
were convinced that national self-assertion and industrial power were part
of the same package; for the French the connection was less obvious, and
therefore the thought of the Action Française remained traditionalist.
The resemblance between Italy and Germany in this respect was latent
until the war; it only became striking when in both countries the reaction
to industrialization, in the shape of a powerful working-class movement,
seemed to pose a decisive challenge to the ideals and structures of the unitary national state. Hence the rigidity of the ruling classes and the violence of the 'patriots' when faced with this dual threat.[10]

I am not sure how far the recognition of this similarity in Italian and
German development implies, as some authors seem to think, an acceptance of the continuity thesis. Tranfaglia, for example, treats the Giolittian period, rather than fascism, as a 'parenthesis.' The intervention crisis
marked a break with the Giolittian 'experiment,' but this, he argues,
merely signified a reversion to the dominance of the old power bloc. But
was this really the case? The success of the interventionist movement was

vitally dependent on the participation of new social forces, still overtly democratic or revolutionary in ideology. When the prime minister Salandra, the representative of the old power bloc par excellence, tried to ignore this reality, he fell from power. For Procacci, on the other hand, in the essay cited, the state of the wartime period 'marks a profound break with the liberal state.'[11] The concentration of industry, the increasingly close co-ordination between industry and the state, and the emancipation of the government and bureaucracy from all effective control by parliament — all foreshadowed the structures of the fascist regime. Of course the wartime regime was intended to be temporary; but the return to peacetime conditions was prevented by what R. Vivarelli has called 'the psychological reality of the war,'[12] as well as by the weight of the new vested interests that it constituted.

## THE CLASS STRUGGLE

The success of fascism in Italy was the consequence of a period of acute class struggle. This raises a number of problems. Why did the class struggle become so acute at this particular time? Why did various forms of mediation not succeed? And why were the fascists rather than their opponents victorious? Beyond these questions there is the problem of the weakness of the Italian state.

The origins of the accentuated class tension in Italy go back to the period between the Libyan and the Great War. Although there are a number of useful histories of Italian socialism,[13] there has as yet been no real study of the social base of the *massimalisti*, as the revolutionary wing of the Italian socialists were known. The only studies which really succeed in showing the relationship between the politics of the working-class movement and its social base are those of Procacci, but these only deal with the first years of the century. However, a good history of the trade union movement has appeared recently.[14] L. Lotti's book on the 'Red Week' of June 1914 (*La settimana rossa*) shows the success of Mussolini's new tactics and style of oratory in mobilizing the disorganized, and the doubts which other socialists had about this process. The classic judgements of Tasca and Nenni on the failings of the socialist leadership in the postwar period have not been, and perhaps cannot be, refuted; but there have been a number of attempts to rehabilitate the leader of the socialist party, Serrati, and Gramsci's ultra-left antagonist in the communist party, Bordiga.[15] The best argument that can be made out for the leaders of Italian socialism is that they faithfully reflected the moods and attitudes of their followers. Popular discontent expressed itself spontaneously and the leaders were often powerless to restrain it; while the democratic traditions of the party precluded the acceptance without question of any unitary strategy imposed from above. Moreover, though the *massimalisti* had conquered the majority in the party, the reformists were still strong in the parliamentary group, in the communes, and above all in the unions. The expulsion of the reformists, as demanded by the Third International, would inevitably have led to a temporary weakening of the party. Nevertheless, to accept Lenin's revolutionary aims while rejecting his strategy of separation from the reformists was a logical contradiction, which was bound to condemn the socialist party to impotence.[16] One of the most important weaknesses of the working-class movement was its provincialism. It was a provincialism of structure rather than attitude; the Italian workers and peasants often showed themselves willing to give generous support to national and international causes. However, the most characteristic and effective organizations of Italian socialism were the provincial *Camere del Lavoro*[17] and the *fasci* were in many respects their mirror-image. The *Camere del Lavoro* were broad, local alliances of the working classes; the fasci were broad, local alliances of the middle classes. Both, with the aid of a certain initial imprecision of aim, succeeded in forming a united bloc out of somewhat disparate interests. However, while the members of the *Camere del Lavoro* shared at least a large degree of common socialist and democratic aims, the fasci were much more heterogeneous still.

It is at least arguable that the class struggle in industry could have been contained by the structures of the liberal state. The decline of working-class militancy was in part the result of the 1921-22 recession and some industrialists seem to have thought that the assistance of the fascists had not been truly decisive and was, in any case, of only temporary utility. Where the mediating function of the state really broke down completely was in the countryside. The fascist movement 'took off' in the regions of capitalist agriculture of the Po Valley, as well as in the sharecropping regions of Tuscany and Umbria. It is interesting to note that there is some apparent discordance between this fact and the well-known theses of Barrington Moore,[18] who has suggested that capitalist commercial agriculture based on wage labour has been favourable to democratic development. However, whereas in England the rise of industry absorbed surplus population, this did not take place in Italy. Consequently rural capitalism in Italy did not drive the workers off the land, or even lead to the disappearance of peasant family farms. An alternative explanation stresses the incomplete nature of this capitalist development and the persistence of 'feudal residues.' Certainly, in some areas, the landowners, alarmed by the growth of rural socialism, deliberately tried to reverse the trend towards wage labour in favour of sharecropping or tenancy. An interesting general approach to the problem of fascism and the agrarian structure of Italy has been formulated by Frank Snowden, along lines suggested by Barrington Moore.[19]

## THE POSTWAR CRISIS AND THE RISE OF FASCISM

For an understanding of the postwar crisis, the classic work of Tasca remains indispensable. Until 1956, no work appeared which had much to add in the way of serious research. In the last eighteen years, however, there have been a wealth of serious and well-documented studies. One of the most important conditions for the progress of research has been the opening of the state archives to scholars. The most notable contributions to the interpretation of the rise of fascism have been those of Valeri, de Felice, and Vivarelli.[20] Valeri's study is highly selective and concentrates on two problems; the significance of d'Annunzio's new style of politics, and the relationship between fascism and liberalism. The literary elegance and psychological insight of Valeri's work are in a class by themselves. No one else has explained with such brilliance the extraordinary change in cultural climate which d'Annunzio helped to bring about. Valeri's archive researches enabled him to shed much new light on Mussolini's strategy in the period of the March on Rome, and particularly on his complicated intrigues with the liberal statesmen. One may have some reservations about his thesis that the prime minister Facta betrayed his political mentor, Giolitti. A. Repaci has defended Facta against this charge with perhaps excessive zeal in his work on the March on Rome.[21] Repaci in his two volumes has assembled an impressive amount of information gathered from newspapers, personal interviews, and private archives. Repaci's work is of great assistance in reconstructing the narrative of events: his revelations on the obscure but crucial subject of the attitude of the king, Victor Emmanuel III, are of particular interest. He is less successful in his depiction of the general context of the March, and I do not find his analysis of the role of the army or of Mussolini's strategy ultimately convincing. The mobilization of the fascist para-military forces, though not a true 'revolution' as the fascists claimed, was nonetheless a necessary element in the process which brought Mussolini to power. I have argued in my own book, *The Seizure of Power*, that 'the military and political planes of action were not separate but complementary.'[22]

De Felice's massive biography of Mussolini touches on every aspect of Italian history between 1911 and 1929. It is perhaps to be read with more profit as a general history of the period than as a study of Mussolini's personality, although of course the two cannot be separated. It is the first volume of de Felice's work, *Mussolini il rivoluzionario*, which has created the greatest controversy. His interpretation of the nature of Mussolini's early socialism and of his conversion from internationalism to patriotism in 1914 has been questioned by Valiani and others.[23] Even more serious doubts have been expressed about de Felice's interpretation of the next phase in Mussolini's career (1915-1919). According to Vivarelli, de Felice

has in the first place failed to distinguish between the 'revolutionary interventionism' of Mussolini and his friends, whose inherently contradictory
nature explains its convergence with imperialist nationalism, and the
'democratic interventionism' of men like Bissolati and Salvemini, who
were fighting for a new 'Europe of the peoples' based on self-determina-
tion.[24] Italy's annexationist ambitions in the Adriatic were the crucial
issue which divided nationalists from democrats in 1918-19, and Mussolini sided without hesitation with the latter. De Felice shows that Mussolini was receiving large subsidies from armament firms from 1918 on, and
that he had many contacts with military and nationalist circles; yet he
still describes him as a 'revolutionary' in 1919. Even if one accepts that
any movement whether of right or left which is directed to the overthrow
of the existing political structure is 'revolutionary,' there is still reason to
question this description of Mussolini in 1919, on the evidence which de
Felice himself adduces. For in fact Mussolini was so concerned with the
threat of a thoroughgoing Bolshevist revolution, that he gave only hesitant and partial support to the efforts of d'Annunzio to launch a 'national
revolution' after his seizure of Fiume in September 1919. If this kind of
'revolution' is meant, then Mussolini was more of a revolutionary in
1921-22 than in 1919.

Perhaps the clearest explanation of Mussolini's stance in 1919 remains
that of Tasca. He describes Mussolini not as a 'revolutionary' but as an
'adventurer.'[25] He agrees that in 1919 Mussolini made overtures to the
unions and other left-wing groups, and that he still gave support to strikes
and punitive taxation of profits; but this did not in any way mean that he
had returned to socialism. He was simply trying to gain time, to acquire a
following, and to divide the opposition. It is highly significant that other
groups of apparently similar aims such as the republicans came to show a
marked distrust of the fasci after even their first few months of life.
Vivarelli shows that from the outset the fasci were above all anti-socialist
in character, and that there was much in common between them and
other anti-Bolshevik associations. This does not mean that one should go
to the other extreme and ignore the differences between the fasci and the
old right, even including the nationalists. The fascist movement was novel
in its violent activism and its demagogic use of propaganda motifs derived
from the revolutionary left. The origins of the new phenomenon of
'national syndicalism' or 'subversive nationalism' have been well investigated by E. Santarelli,[26] although more work needs to be done, especially
on the various patriotic organizations of the 'home front' from 1915
through 1918.

During 1921 fascism became a mass movement. It ceased to be an
organization exclusively of displaced or 'marginal' men and professional
adventurers, and attracted a huge influx of recruits. The study of this

process of expansion has been until recently comparatively neglected. The reader who wants a broad, impressionistic picture of the sources of fascist support will still find it worthwhile to consult the series of essays edited by R. Mondolfo between 1921 and 1923 under the title, *Il Fascismo e i partiti politici*; Mondolfo invited representatives of all the major political parties to contribute. The series has recently been republished in a single volume edited by de Felice.[27] The contributors revealed a fair measure of agreement on the nature and origins of the new movement. They agreed that fascism was a movement of the middle classes, the petty bourgeoisie, and the *déclassés*, in which particular importance attached to the role of the young demobilised ex-officers and the students. They also agreed, though with considerable differences of emphasis, that the movement had become a tool in the hands of agrarians and industrialists who had used it to destroy the power of working-class organizations in the countryside and the factories. Both middle-class participation and the employers' support could be explained by the heightened level of class conflict which resulted from the war, and by the fear of a 'bolshevist' revolution. However, several writers noted that the fascist attack on the working class only really got under way when the danger of revolution had already passed. The anarchist Luigi Fabbri termed fascism a *preventive counter-revolution*; but in his essay he makes the important point that the employers, particularly in agriculture, were not so much moved by fear of a general revolution as by the erosion of their own authority and property rights which had already taken place locally; 'The bosses felt they were no longer bosses.'[28] An article by Gramsci in 1921 already distinguished between 'two fascisms,' urban and agrarian.[29] At this time, it looked as if the fascist movement might split into two parts over the question of the 'pact of pacification' with the socialists. Very approximately, the division over this question coincided with the social divide between middle-class urban fascists, who supported Mussolini and pacification, and the agrarians, who refused to relax the terror. The recent analyses of the movement by de Felice and by myself have tended to confirm the validity of this interpretation.

The chief way in which knowledge of the fascist movement has advanced recently is through local studies. There have been several good studies of agrarian fascism, notably that of M. Vaini on Mantua and S. Colarizi on Apulia.[30] Vaini's study gives valuable details about the protests of urban fascists against the reactionary policy of the agrarians. This theme is also stressed by P. Corner in his excellent study of Ferrara.[31] Corner also provides very important evidence on the success of fascist propaganda in winning over sectors of the peasantry by grants to individual cultivators, in contrast to the Socialist policy of collectivisation. Emilia, the region of the first fascist breakthrough, has naturally been the object of the most research. The success of agrarian fascism in other regions of Italy, such as the Veneto, Piedmont, and Tuscany, has not as yet been examined in sufficient detail.

The peculiarities of fascism in southern Italy have received more attention. Aside from the work of Colarizi, already mentioned, there is an excellent study of Sardinia by S. Sechi, and the rise of fascism in Naples has been described by R. Colapietra.[32] In the south, the fascist movement was soon caught up in the factional struggles between local political cliques. Many of the latter joined the nationalist association to provide a counterweight to the fascists. Another important theme which emerges from these studies is that of the relationship between fascism and the official ex-servicemen's organization. During 1919-1920 the majority of the ex-combatant organizations favoured a democratic policy and were suspicious of the extreme nationalism of the fasci. This was particularly true in the south where the combatant movement achieved its greatest successes. In both Apulia and Sardinia in 1919, the movement succeeded in organizing large masses of peasant ex-combatants under the leadership of their former officers. But there the resemblance ends. In Sardinia, peculiar factors gave the ex-combatant movement a cohesion which it did not have elsewhere, and it served as the basis for the foundation of a regionalist party, the Partito Sardo d'Azione. This was at first a barrier to the progress of fascism in the island; the story of how it was overcome during 1922-1923 is a particularly intriguing example of Mussolini's tactical flexibility. Whereas elsewhere he favoured an agreement with the old liberal clientèles, in Sardinia he gave credit to the illusion of a 'pure' and revolutionary fascism in order to divide the leadership of the Sardinian combatants and to absorb their following.

The growth of fascism in urban and industrial areas is still a neglected field of research. The case of Trieste is an exception. Trieste, annexed by Italy in 1918, presented a particularly favourable atmosphere for the growth of fascism, thanks to the national tension between the Italians and the Slavs. The movement took hold there even before its expansion in Emilia. There is a good general study of the area by E. Apih which pays particular attention to economic factors and more recently C. Silvestri has published a most illuminating study of the origins of the movement.[33] Silvestri shows how the superficial radicalism of the fascists and their successful exploitation of syndicalist slogans enabled them to acquire a mass following, which comprised not only the middle classes but large numbers of workers. This success enabled the fascist movement to assert its leadership over the old bourgeois parties who had tried to control it. However, if fascism triumphed over the bourgeois politicians, it soon proved subservient to the interests of the industrialists and ship owners. The radical elements in fascism, indispensable during the period of growth, were rapidly purged or reduced to insignificance once success had been achieved.

Trieste, though important, was certainly not a typical city. To understand more about urban fascism and the mood of the middle classes, we
need studies of fascism in the big cities such as Milan, Turin, or Genoa.

However, the most serious deficiencies in the study of the growth of fascism are not geographical in nature. What we really need above all to
increase our understanding of the problems is to know more about Italian
society. The middle classes, it is commonly agreed, were the backbone of
fascism. Until we have studied their structure, their income levels and the
effect of inflation, and their previous political allegiances, the analysis of
fascism will lack an important dimension. The study of particular occupational groups and their professional organizations (artisans, shopkeepers,
bank clerks, urban landowners) might also be revealing.

Another, more surprising, gap is that there is no good history of the
fascist party. The relationship between the party and the state during the
period 1922-26 has been examined in considerable detail by de Felice and
by myself; but the internal organization of the party, the effect of the
various purges on membership, and so forth, still require further study.
The failure of the party to create an efficient, centralised machine, spe-
cialised according to functions, was part and parcel of its eventual decline
as an effective political force. A study of this failure cannot be separated
from a study of the shortcomings of fascism as an operative ideology. An
attempt was made to create a kind of parallel bureaucracy within the fascist movement in the shape of the so-called groups of competence. Their
inglorious history is examined in an article by Aquarone.[34]

## FASCISM AND THE ITALIAN STATE

The problem of continuity is inextricably involved with the problem of
the relationship between fascism and the administrative and judicial
apparatus of the state. Recent studies have shown that fascism did not
make a clean break with the previous legal order, at least in formal
terms. It is certainly important to draw attention to the width of discretion allowed to the police under Italian law, and to the corresponding
insecurity of the rights of the citizen, to the lack of independence of the
magistracy from the executive, and to the all-important political function
of the prefects, who were members of the bureaucracy strictly dependent
on the minister of the interior. A study by G. Neppi Modona has shown
the limitations imposed on the right to strike throughout the liberal
period, and also the constant response by the magistracy to the directions
of the government of the day.[35] All these features of the Italian state
made the transition to fascism smoother. However, even these continuities
may be seen as not truly decisive compared with the change represented
by the effective suppression of almost all possibility of protest against
administrative injustice, and the creation of parallel organizations (the

fascist party and the unions) which brought the formerly free associative life of society under the control of the state. Finally, one should note here the importance of the problem of the persistence of fascist legislation in postwar Italy.

The best general study of the fascist state is Aquarone's *L'organiz-zazione dello stato totalitario*.[36] This study deals with institutions and laws rather than decisions and policies, although it is often revealing even in the latter sphere. The title is a little misleading, as Aquarone does not in fact conclude that fascism was a true totalitarian state. Several independent centres of power survived, which did not depend on the will of the dictator or on the fascist movement, notably the king and the army, the Church and big business. The slogan of the 'totalitarian state' itself was interpreted to mean that the fascist party must be subordinate to the organs of government. In general, it seems well established that Mussolini from 1926 onwards consolidated his dictatorship by strengthening the old administrative apparatus, rather than by destroying it and creating something new. The studies of Neppi Modona on the magistracy, already mentioned, suggests that the fascist regime for the most part needed only to intensify the traditional methods of pressure which the government had always exerted in order to bring the magistrates into line with its policies. G. Rochat's studies on the army[37] have shown how the fascist government bought the army's support by abandoning plans for reform and allowing the generals to run things as they wanted, under Mussolini's nominal control. The surrender of fascism to the military was to have fatal consequences for the regime; the fascist state exalted preparation for war as the highest priority, and yet Mussolini's co-ordination of the armed forces was only nominal.

In what, then, did the novelty of the fascist state consist? I would suggest that the beginning of a solution to the contradictions both in the thesis of 'continuity' and in the thesis of the 'break' is to be found in the observation that the structures of the Italian state evolved more slowly than those of Italian society. An important qualification must at once be added; the evolution of Italian society was highly uneven, indeed dualistic, so that most of the south, together with some other rural areas, shared and supported the state's slow tempo. Nonetheless, the general trend between 1870 and 1920 was towards the growth of parties, unions, associations, and a free press; the administrative state remained, and the mechanism of parliamentary control over its operations was imperfect in the extreme. But against and in spite of it, this autonomous growth of social institutions did take place. The war accentuated this contradiction: (1) It greatly reinforced the power of the administrative state; (2) it produced a serious schism inside the ruling class (between interventionists and neutralists), which affected even the institutions of the state; and (3) in the reaction to the war the authority of the state was radically challenged. Fascism continued the trend described in (1) but reversed both (2) and (3): the ruling class, reinforced by new elements, was unified by a system of hierarchical controls, and new *social* institutions were devised (party, corporations, etc.) to take the place of the old free associations. These new institutions, however, were both authoritarian in their internal structure and formally subordinated to the administrative state.

Even this fairly complicated schema expresses the theory rather than the reality of the fascist state. It is a description of the fascist state as envisaged by the nationalist legislator Alfredo Rocco, rather than of the actual practice of the regime as guided by Mussolini. Mussolini deliberately fostered untidiness and illogicality in the structure of government. Like other dictators, he saw in instability and the conflict between different authorities with overlapping fields of authority a guarantee for his personal power.

Historians have only recently begun to turn their attention to the 1930's, and there is still much that we do not know about the working of the regime in those years. Of the earlier works on fascism, the book by H. Finer, *Mussolini's Italy*, is still useful, in spite of a rather uncritical view of the Duce's genius.[38] His description of the fascist party as 'a species of civil service for the manufacture of obedience' is apt. Finer's work is also interesting because it was written during the period 1933-35, at a time when the prestige of the regime was at its maximum, both abroad and at home. Both Aquarone and Deakin[39] have examined the problem of the decline of fascism with much insight. The principal reasons for the fall of fascism were, of course, military and foreign policy failures; but it is still necessary to explain why Mussolini was overthrown with such ease in 1943. What were the flaws in the apparently imposing structure of the so-called totalitarian state? Both Aquarone and Deakin have pointed to the vital importance of the problem of the succession. By leaving the question of his successor open, and by deliberately encouraging the fragmentation of the fascist governing class, Mussolini weakened his own regime. Many leading fascists were convinced that if Mussolini should die the monarchy and the army would be the decisive force, and therefore developed a dual loyalty, to the king as well as the Duce. This was the foundation for the later anti-German and monarchist 'fronde' which brought about Mussolini's fall from power in July 1943.

The contrast between the appearance and the reality of fascist institutions was striking. The most remarkable example is that of the corporations. Held up as fascism's most imposing creation, they in fact performed no serious function, except, during the period of autarchy, that of serving as a front for the control of raw material allocations and investment decisions by groups of leading industrialists. In the case of the fascist party itself the façade of strength was deceptive. Admittedly, we do not yet have a satisfactory study of the party during this period. Germino's book takes fascist claims to totalitarian control at their face value.[40] The studies of Aquarone and Deakin show, however, the degeneration of the party's capacity for real leadership, and the consequent decline in its morale. The secretariat of Giuriati (1930-31) was a critical period in this process. His fall marked the decisive defeat of the attempt to make the party into an active and functional elite, and to free it from corruption. The failure of Giuriati was determined by Mussolini's own attitude. Under the secretariat of Starace, the huge growth in numbers of the party was not a sign of strength but the effect of new criteria, which made membership in the party obligatory for those seeking office in the state or local administration. In these circumstances membership in the party ceased to be truly voluntary and became a simple badge of good conduct. However, in a recent essay E. Ragionieri has suggested that the change in the nature of the party under Starace did not signify the end of its functions. 'If, it is true, the type of fascist party that had tried to dispute the direction of Italian life with the traditional organs of the State came to an end, a type of party which organized the Italian population in its various components and social strata in support of the fascist state was fully realised.'[41] The activity of the fascist party needs to be studied both locally, especially in the major cities, and nationally. How did the party (and the Militia) respond (a) to the great slump of 1929-33? (b) to the Ethiopian and Spanish wars, or (c) to the world war itself? We do not know the answer to these questions and until we do our knowledge of the regime's political evolution will be imperfect.

Another field which needs more detailed study is that of the relationship between fascism and the Church. There has been a relative neglect of this theme after a promising beginning. With the exception of a brief but interesting anthology of texts edited by P. Scoppola, the most authoritative works are still those of Jemolo, Binchy, and Webster.[42] Jemolo's insight, which derives from a passionate commitment to the lost cause of liberal Catholicism, makes his work a classic. It is one of the books which will always be worth reading, even if some of his conclusions are disputed. Webster gives a valuable analysis of the activities of various Catholic groups, both pro- and anti-fascist, under the regime. Binchy's book, written from a more orthodox standpoint, gives a subtle if somewhat apologetic picture of the relationship between Pius XI and Mussolini. One crucial episode in the history of the relationship between Church and fascism is the conflict over Catholic Action in 1931. We can expect that the next volume of de Felice's biography will throw new light on this question. There is a stimulating essay by Mario G. Rossi in the volume *La Toscana nel regime fascista*; he points out that the Church and Catholic Action saw the alliance with fascism not merely as a means of maintaining their position, but as a way of restoring their power in society. 'The crucifix in the schools, religious teaching, the recognition of the

Catholic university, the banning of freemasonry were immediately seen not as final concessions but as the first steps towards the return of the Catholics in society, towards a reconquest that would annul the effects of a sixty years' absence.'[43] How successful was this restoration of the power of the Church? The question needs more investigation, and given the diversity of traditions, further regional studies will make an important contribution.

## FASCISM AND CAPITALISM

Was fascism characteristic of a particular phase of the development of capitalism? If so, why did it appear in Italy before it did elsewhere? Such questions have clearly been of central importance to Marxist writers. Recently the a priori solutions to these problems imposed during the Stalinist period have been questioned, and the relationship between the regime and economic forces, particularly industry, has become the object of empirical research.

Fascism claimed to have reconciled capital and labour within the framework of the so-called corporate state. In the 1930's these .claims were subjected to meticulous examination by a French scholar, L. Rosenstock-Franck. He demonstrated the fraudulent nature of the 'representation' allowed to labour, and the subjection of the whole system to government directives.[44] Salvemini came to the same conclusions in his work, *Under the Axe of Fascism!* Salvemini stresses throughout that the state usually acted in the interests of the great capitalist enterprises; but in his conclusion he nonetheless rejected the idea that fascism was a 'capitalist dictatorship.' Instead, Mussolini's personal dictatorship rested on a process of mediation between several powerful interest groups; the influence of the capitalists was contested by the officials of the party, the civil administration, and the army. The fascist party with its satellite organizations no longer depended on the subsidies of big business and was therefore 'no longer an organization of mercenaries in the service of capitalism ...but an independent force.'[45] Tasca, in his epilogue, came to conclusions very similar to Salvemini's. The policy of autarchy adopted after 1936 was certainly leading to an even greater concentration of capital and to the ruin of the small producers, both urban and rural; but not all the middle classes had been sacrificed to capital. On the contrary, the fascist petty and middle bourgeoisie had penetrated the regime en masse, 'contributing to the formation of the immense fascist bureaucracy which is today the political ruling class of the nation.' Moreover, Tasca argues, to claim that fascism is the dictatorship of capital involves an even more fundamental misunderstanding. 'The sphere of fascism is that of *power* and not that of *profit*.'[46] The fascist economy was planned for war, and in this sense the political objectives of fascism determined the limits even of the 'sphere of profit.' Vice versa, the capitalists could not determine the political objectives of fascism; they could influence them, not as an independent class but only through their participation in the political and administrative apparatus of the new state.

The first studies after the war which were specifically devoted to the theme of capitalism and the fascist state rejected the reservations of Salvemini and Tasca. The Marxist P. Grifone and the Salveminian radical Ernesto Rossi were much more unilateral in their view of the dominance of big business. Rossi stated bluntly that 'the will of the great industrialists has been a determining factor in the political and legal order...because the great industrialists had a lot of cash at their disposal.' Politicians, in his view, were merely puppets who declaimed on the stage, while the industrialists pulled the strings.[47] Rossi's book belongs to the tradition of the Italian free-trade propagandists, who ever since the introduction of tariff protection in 1887 had denounced the collusion of the state with industry at the expense of the consumer. Rossi's assumption that the great industrialists controlled the fortunes of the early fascist movement has been attacked by P. Melograni and by de Felice. De Felice discovered that the administrative secretary of the fascist movement, Marinelli, had kept detailed records of donations; on the basis of these records he argued that the role of ordinary members and above all of the agrarians in financing fascism had been more significant than that of industry.[48] Another article by de Felice on the revaluation of the lira in 1926-27 showed that Mussolini's decision to fix the exchange rate at 'quota 90' (to the £) was criticized by the dominant groups in finance and industry, on the grounds that it would damage exports and produce a recession. From this, de Felice drew the conclusion that the main motives of Mussolini's decision had been a desire for prestige and the deliberate intention to show his independence from the capitalists.[49] In favour of this last thesis one can also cite the fact of the industrialists' opposition to the establishment of obligatory arbitration in labour relations in the preceding period. Mussolini during 1925-26 had achieved a *modus vivendi* with industry and finance; but he wished to make clear that the responsibility for major decisions rested with him. Subsequent articles, especially those by R. Sarti and G. G. Migone, have shed more light on the problem of 'quota 90.'[50] They have tended rather to play down the importance of the disagreement between Mussolini and the industrialists, and to emphasize that a moderate revaluation was actively desired by industry, as well as by the inflation-haunted middle classes. Sarti shows how the industrialists rapidly recovered from 'quota 90' and in fact used it to aid their efforts towards rationalization. Migone's research, in a field hitherto unexplored, that of the economic relations between Italy and the United States, has shown the importance of the international context for an understanding of Mussolini's economic policy. His most striking discovery is that the unification of the banks of issue, hitherto attributed to the fascist drive towards centralization, was in fact suggested by the great house of J. P. Morgan. He argues also that de Felice does not sufficiently stress the social objectives of Mussolini's revaluation policy designed to placate the discontent of the petty bourgeoisie and middle classes, who formed the mass base of the fascist party.

Was the fascist movement manipulated from the beginning by the interests of industry, or was it instead a relatively autonomous reaction of the agrarians and the middle classes, which only later received the support, more grudging than wholehearted, of industry? The works of P. Melograni and M. Abrate have argued in favour of this latter thesis. Melograni showed that the Italian Confederation of Industry had not supported the idea of the March on Rome, and would have preferred a conservative government under Salandra or Giolitti (though with fascist participation) to one headed by Mussolini.[51] Abrate, in a long and closely documented book based on the records of the *Lega industriale* of Turin, paid particular attention to the attitude and policies of the secretary of the confederation, Gino Olivetti.[52] Even after 1922 Olivetti continued to distrust· fascism, above all because he feared that the party and the government might intervene in industry in support of the fascist trade unions. In general, recent studies have shown that although industry often turned even the new forms of state intervention to good account, the traditional free-enterprise ideology retained its hold over most industrialists. The extension of state power over industry was seen as a potential if not always an actual threat.

The revisionist interpretations of de Felice, Melograni, and Abrate have not gone unchallenged. Sarti strikes a judicious balance between the de Felice-Melograni line and the older interpretation.[53] He is perhaps nearer the former, insofar as he regards the dominant process as being that of the expansion of private power. The so-called corporative state in essence merely gave legal sanction and confirmation to the power of the Confederation of Industry, which in real terms retained a very large degree of autonomy in the economic sphere. On the other hand, Sarti stresses that the industrialists' influence operated within strict limits. They recognized that 'politics,' which meant above all foreign policy, was exclusively Mussolini's responsibility. But this neat division between the political and the economic sphere became increasingly impracticable during the 1930's, when the growth of state intervention was inextricably linked to the demands made by an aggressive foreign policy. The 1930's were marked, in fact, by a growing confusion between the roles of private enterprise and the state. The result was a mixed economy, whose direction was not in the main determined either by central planning or by market forces, but by agreement between powerful oligopolistic groups, some of them under public control. Sarti's book has the great merit of clarity. Its chief (though deliberate) limitation seems to me to be the author's refusal to examine the objectives of the leading industrial sectors, or of great 'captains of industry,' like Agnelli or Pirelli. This robs his analysis of a necessary dimension. The Confederation of Industry, though powerful, was not dictatorial, and had to mediate between the desires of different industrial groups.

The huge biography of the founder of Fiat, Agnelli, by V. Castronovo helps us to see further into this question.[54] In particular, he shows the conflict in 1932 between the Keynesian views of Agnelli and the deflationary policy favoured by the Edison and Montecatini combines and the later, even more significant, clash of 1936-37 between the 'German' strategy of Volpi and the 'American' strategy of Agnelli. Castronovo is in some respects close to the traditional interpretation. Although he agrees that the agrarians may have been more wholehearted in their support of fascism, the alliance of the latter with the industrialists was nonetheless, he argues, decisive. He has amply documented the growing control exerted by the large industrialists over the Italian press, both before and under fascism. However, the picture that emerges both of Agnelli and of the other industrialists in relationship to fascism is still notably different from that of Rossi or Grifone. In substance he agrees with Sarti and even Abrate in substituting for the image of an united group of industrial magnates pursuing a single-minded strategy that of a divided class which adapted to the changing political situation, and which in general allowed short-term and partial gains to obscure the long-term economic and social issues posed by fascist policy.

The only recent book which deals with fascist economic policy as a whole is that of S. La Francesca.[55] The older book by R. Romeo, *Breve storia della grande industria*[56] is still extremely useful for the period in question. However, a number of recent articles show that an active attempt is also being made here to question traditional interpretations. An attack has been mounted, this time from the left, on the assumption made by the first generation of anti-fascist historians that the regime had pursued an archaic and irrational economic policy, resulting in stagnation. The observation that the Italian economy grew more slowly under fascism than during comparable periods either before 1914 or after 1945, though true, is certainly not in itself conclusive, since this fact primarily reflects the general slow-down of the European economy due to the great recession of 1929-33. A recent article by D. Preti points out, moreover, the crucial importance of the American restrictions on emigration for the Italian balance of payments.[57] In this light, the fascist policy of 'ruralism,' which in real terms signified the restraint of internal emigration from the countryside to the city, appears less as an arbitrary ideological decision, and more as a response to changed economic conditions. However, the ideological and political explanation of 'ruralism' cannot be altogether discarded, since the associated decision to launch a 'demographic campaign' to check the decline in the birth rate must be regarded as quite irrational from an economic point of view. It remains true, I believe, that the policy of 'ruralism' was directed primarily towards ensuring the regime a stable social base and to appeasing agrarian interests.

There is an urgent need for a new study of the period of autarchy (1936-40). E. Fano Damascelli, in a recent article, argues that the high degree of industrial concentration during the 1930's marked a qualitative leap forward of the industrial economy.[58] As in the case of the dispute between the theses of 'continuity' and 'break,' the issue of whether the fascist period was one of 'stagnation' or 'development' cannot easily be resolved in absolute terms. It is not a question of black or white, but of less or more; and in the economic field the answers can and should be quantified. It is necessary, I believe, to question the assumption that concentration necessarily implies rationalization from a productive point of view. This is almost as doubtful in the Italian case as the old belief in the virtues of free enterprise and the small firm. G. Mori, for instance, has recalled that the period 1936-38 was marked by a growth in industrial concentration, but also by a fall in productivity.[59] It would seem justified to conclude that the compression of wages and of internal consumption under fascism served to maintain rather than accelerate industrial development. The essential contradiction of fascist economic policy was that between the tendency towards a closed economy (which was only in part deliberate, but in large measure, particularly after 1929, the result of a general international trend), and the impoverishment of the home market produced by the regime's inegalitarian social policies. This contradiction could only be overcome by a return to a policy of heavy state expenditure on armaments and war. From an economic point of view, Keynesian policies would have been an alternative; but, like the land reclamation programme, they ran up against obstacles of a social nature. There is a constant risk of underestimating the autonomy of foreign policy. Few capitalists showed much enthusiasm for imperialist expansion during the 1920's, and in 1938-39 leading circles in industry were markedly unenthusiastic about German alliance. But given the nature of the regime, empire and rearmament were the only way out of the impasse in which the fascist economy found itself after the slump, and once this policy had been chosen, it became increasingly hard both in political and economic terms to reverse it.

## FASCISM AND CULTURE

The study of culture under fascism has still a long way to go. It is understandable, but hardly helpful, that a number of historians have taken the line that there can, a priori, be no connection between fascism and culture. The reduction of all manifestations of support for the regime to 'opportunism' is not valid. It does not make sense either to assume that the intellectuals who supported fascism were all deluded about its nature and aims. It is true that a number of intellectuals, especially among the younger generation in the 1930's, were inspired by the illusion that fascism was a revolutionary and anti-capitalist force. Their state of mind has been described in a well-known book by R. Zangrandi, the most valuable part of which is autobiographical.[60] The ideology of the 'fascist left' in literature and its precedents has been studied with great acumen, if sometimes questionable conclusions, by A. Asor Rosa.[61] The ideology of Ugo Spirito and the idea of the 'proprietary corporation,' have been critically examined in a recent article.[62] The propaganda in favour of the universality of fascism is the subject of a book by M. Ledeen.[63] This centres on the activities of a curious organization, the CAUR (Comitati d'Azione per l'universalità di Roma). There is a certain danger in taking too seriously the importance of the activities of such groups, who operated on the margins of official policy. To form a serious estimate of the directives and effect of fascist propaganda abroad, it would be necessary to make a serious study of the organization of the *Fasci all'estero*, as well as the consular service and such bodies as the Dante Alighieri Society. Some interesting information about this is to be found in the important work of J. P. Diggins on American reactions to fascism.[64]

The archives of the Ministry of Popular Culture have now been made available for scholars. They contain an abundance of material on all aspects of fascist propaganda and also on the relationship of intellectuals to the regime. An American scholar, P. V. Cannistraro, is expected to publish a general study based on his research in these archives. Cannistraro has already published several articles from which interesting conclusions emerge. In the first place, his studies seem to confirm the impression that the inconsistency and uncertainty of aim of fascist propaganda were a serious hindrance to its effectiveness, in spite of the great expansion of the propaganda *apparat* from 1934 onwards. However, this expansion was nonetheless, as Cannistraro points out, the symptom of a new phase in the development of the 'totalitarian ambitions' of fascism, in great part stimulated by the example of Nazi Germany.[15] The hesitant beginnings of fascist cultural policy during the 1920's have also received some attention. In these years intellectuals were still drawn to fascism either out of spontaneous conviction or in the hope of securing patronage. Overt censorship was comparatively rare, and in the artistic and literary fields both modernists and traditionalists could claim in good faith to be in harmony with the spirit of fascism. Gentile was prepared to overlook the anti-fascist political attitudes of contributors to the Italian encyclopedia, in spite of opposition from the party.[66] The main threat to the intellectual independence of the enterprise came from the Church. Other institutions, such as the Italian Academy (created by Mussolini), the universities, and the Venice Biennale, would repay study. The policy of fascism towards education and the organization of youth is another important field in which much remains to be done. There is a useful book by T. Tomasi on education, while the general problem of fascist attempts to indoctrinate youth has been posed with lucidity in an article by G. Germani.[67] In general, one might say that so far the higher forms of culture have received disproportionate attention compared with those which were addressed to a wider audience. Both the postcard and the comic strip have been the subject of recent works. But we still do not have a comprehensive study of school textbooks or of the regime's leisure-time organization, the *Dopolavoro*, whose importance was rightly emphasized by Togliatti in his lectures on fascism.[68]

## FASCISM AND FOREIGN POLICY

The study of fascist foreign policy has been influenced by the progress of studies in other fields. Several historians have shown their discontent with the methods of traditional diplomatic history and have attempted to relate internal to external policy. They have before them a magnificent example: the work of F. Chabod on the 'premises' of Italian foreign policy after unification.[69] Chabod wished to demonstrate the difference between the moral atmosphere of the Risorgimento and that of fascism. His analyses of the cult of Rome, of hero-worship, and of the modifications in the idea of the nation, are all obligatory reading for anyone who wants to understand the success of Mussolini's appeal.

It has been suggested that Mussolini conceived of foreign policy as an adjunct of propaganda. This assertion does not however by itself tell us much. It raises important further questions: how far did Mussolini sacrifice long-term objectives for short-term popularity? And what was really new about his methods? Recent studies, particularly of the 1920's, have tended to show a greater constancy in Mussolini's policy than Salvemini was willing to concede. At the same time, they have not confirmed the conservative and apologetic view of Mussolini's 'decade of good conduct' before the rise of Hitler and the Ethiopian adventure. The studies of Rumi, Di Nolfo, and Carocci[70] all show the early origin and continuing importance of Mussolini's 'revisionism,' or desire to change the Versailles settlement. Alan Cassels has drawn particular attention to Mussolini's contacts with the German right, and to the importance of anti-fascist exiles and public opinion as factors influencing his policy.[71] At the same time, Carocci's study, the most thorough yet to have appeared, though limited to the years 1925-28, shows that friendship with England was still a cornerstone of Mussolini's policy. One factor which Carocci's otherwise comprehensive approach overlooks is that of financial relations with the United States. The dependence of Italian industry on American capital was arguably an important restraining influence on Mussolini's adventurism. After 1929 this influence was removed, at the same time as the rise of Hitler shifted the balance of forces in Mussolini's favour. A lucid analysis by a young German historian suggests that Mussolini was aware that the success of Hitler gave him an advantage, which would be, however, only temporary.[72] The fear of German revival and rearmament would keep France occupied and make her anxious for an agreement with Italy; but if and when Germany really recovered freedom of action, then Italy herself would be menaced and her bargaining power would thus be reduced. It was determination to exploit the uniquely favourable circumstances of the transition period which, Peterson argues, determined the timing of the Ethiopian adventure. The alternative explanation, favoured by G. Rochat and G. W. Baer,[73] puts more emphasis on the regime's internal difficulties. If it is true that by 1935 the Italian economy was well on the way to recovery, it must be remembered that planning for the attack had begun as early as November 1932, when the economic crisis was at its most grave.

There would seem to be a particular need to integrate the study of home and foreign policy in the years 1936-40. The policy of autarchy, and the attempts of Mussolini to achieve a new 'totalitarian breakthrough' in internal affairs (which signified among other things, reducing if not abolishing the residual power of the monarchy), interacted powerfully with the course of foreign policy. Economic weakness seriously handicapped Mussolini's attempts to preserve a degree of independence from Hitler and to retain a sphere of influence in the Balkans. On the other hand, it was an important and for a time decisive argument in favour of neutrality. For the moment, the best guides to the policy of these years are still old works such as E. Wiskemann's *Axis*, and, of course, Ciano's *Diaries*.[74] In general, anyone who wants to understand the decline and fall of fascism should begin by reading the *Diaries*. They throw as much light on the men and institutions of fascism as they do on the conduct of fascist diplomacy. Their fascination—all the greater because of Ciano's superficiality—has of course always been recognised.

## CONCLUSION: FASCISM AND MUSSOLINI

Fascism cannot be reduced to an expression of Mussolini's personality, nor can Mussolini's personality be identified entirely with fascism. But certainly one cannot conceive of the fascist regime in Italy without Mussolini, and the relationship of personality to history is a theme which his career imposes upon our attention. How can we explain his success, his policies, the acceptance of the myth of his infallibility? D. Cantimori, in his introduction to de Felice's biography, lays emphasis upon the representative character of Mussolini's career, and de Felice himself speaks of

Mussolini as a 'symbol of crisis.'[75] His complex and contradictory personality, and his instability of aim allowed a variety of different groups to project their hopes upon him. On the other hand, de Felice, like Deakin and others, sees Mussolini as far less of a 'leader' than might appear from his myth. He had little capacity for long-range planning, and for all his brilliance as a political tactician in the really serious crises of his political career, he often proved himself hesitant and vacillating. At the outset, he possessed at least a keen perception of political realities; but as de Felice points out in his third volume, from 1927 to 1928 onwards his natural tendency to suspicion and scepticism aggravated the isolation which tends to afflict dictators. Here de Felice shows very well the interaction between personality and situation.[76]

The more weaknesses we find in Mussolini, the more inexplicable at first sight does his myth become. Of course, one can argue that any dictator can achieve a reputation for infallibility with the aid of such a massive deployment of propaganda as Mussolini put into action during the 1930's. But is this true? Mussolini did to some extent make his own myth, and we can perhaps still find out more about how he did it. It is through a study of his technique and particularly of his language that we may be able to go beyond the obvious, and identify, at least in part, the source of the fascination which he exerted over the Italians, and not only Italians. Secondly, it may be profitable to trace the emergence in Mussolini's thought and actions of a more universal characteristic of modern dictators. This is the need to claim that they have a special understanding of history, whether derived from doctrine or intuition; it is the secular equivalent of the special relationship with the divine which formerly constituted charisma. The need to appear as a 'historic' figure was all the greater in Mussolini's case because of the compromises on which his rule in fact rested; he could not claim to represent tradition in the face of the Church and the crown. He needed a new principle; and that only fascism could provide. There was a certain necessity about Mussolini's megalomania.

## NOTES

1. See G. Salvemini, *Prelude to World War II* (London, 1953), passim.

2. A. Tasca, *Nascita e avvento del fascismo* (Bari, 1965), 2, 553.

3. Ibid., 2, 554, N.B. the *Epilogue* from which these quotations are taken is not included in the English edition which Tasca published under the pseudonym of A. Rossi— *The Rise of Italian Fascism* (London, 1938).

4. G. Salvemini, *The Origins of Fascism in Italy*, trans. with introd. by R. Vivarelli (New York and London, 1973). This is the text of the lectures which Salvemini gave at Harvard in 1942. The volume contains a good short bibliography.

5. P. Gobetti, *Scritti politici*, ed. P. Spriano (Turin, 1960), 1065. See also the comments of C. Pavone, 'Italy: trends and problems,' *Journal of Contemporary History*, II, 1 (January 1967), 65.

6. G. Gentile, *Origini e dottrina del fascismo,* in *Il fascismo, antologia di scritti critici,* ed. C. Casucci (Bologna, 1961), 15-50.

7. P. Togliatti, *Lezioni sul fascismo,* 9-10. Togliatti had, of course, formally to subscribe to the empty definition laid down by the Comintern. (Ibid., 3.)

8. E. Sereni, *La questione agraria nella rinascita nazionale italiana* (Rome, 1946). *Il capitalismo nelle campagne 1860-1900,* 2d ed. (Turin, 1971); idem, *Capitalismo e mercato nazionale in Italia* (Rome, 1966); G. Procacci, 'Crisi dello stato liberale e origini del fascismo,' *Studi storici* 1965, 221-37. For the analysis of fascism by Gramsci and Togliatti, the so-called Lyons theses, prepared for the 3d congress of the Italian Communist party, are the fundamental document. They can now be consulted in A. Gramsci, *La costruzione del partito comunista 1923-1926* (Turin, 1971), 488-513.

9. N. Tranfaglia, *Dallo stato liberale al regime fascista* (Milan, 1973), 27.

10. Several attempts at a systematic comparison between the origins and nature of German national socialism and Italian fascism have been made by Marxists outside Italy; see D. Guerin, *Fascisme et grand capital* (Paris, 1945); N. Poulantzas, *Fascisme et dictature: à la IIIème internationale face au fascisme* (Paris, 1970); R. Kühnl (Ital. trans.) *Due forme di dominio borghese: liberalismo e fascismo* (Milan, 1973).

11. Procacci, 'Crisi dello stato liberale,' 233.

12. R. Vivarelli, *Il dopoguerra in Italia e l'avvento del fascismo (1918-1922),* I, *Dalla fine della guerra all'impresa di Fiume* (Naples, 1967), 100.

13. G. Arfe, *Storia del socialismo italiano 1892-1926* (Turin, 1965); L. Cortesi, *Il Socialismo italiano tra riforme e rivoluzione* (Bari, 1969) represent respectively the reformist and the revolutionary viewpoint.

14. G. Procacci, *La lotta di classe in Italia agli inizi del secolo XX* (Rome, 1972); I. Barbadoro, *Storia del sindacalismo italiano,* 2 vols. (Florence, 1973).

15. See R. de Felice, *Serrati, Bordiga, Gramsci e il problema della rivoluzione in Italia 1919-1920* (Bari, 1971); A. de Clementi, *Amadeo Bordiga* (Turin, 1971).

16. Vivarelli, *Il dopoguerra in Italia,* 72.

17. Procacci, *Lotta di classe,* 62-63.

18. Barrington Moore Jr., *The Social Origins of Dictatorship and Democracy: Lord and Peasant in the Modern World* (London, 1967). For the employment problem in the countryside and the rise of fascism, see Barbadoro, *Storia del sindacalismo italiano,* I, 236-53.

19. F. M. Snowden, *European Journal of Sociology,* XIII, 2 (1972), 268-95.

20. N. Valeri, *Da Giolitti a Mussolini: momenti della crisi del liberalismo* (Florence, 1956); R. de Felice, *Mussolini il rivoluzionario (1883-1920)* (Turin, 1965); idem, *Mussolini il fascista;* vol. 1, *La conquista del potere (1921-25)* (Turin, 1966); vol. 2, *L'organizzazione dello stato fascista (1925-29)* (Turin, 1968); Vivarelli, *Il dopoguerra in Italia.* N.B. also the important work by G. De Rosa, *Storia del movimento cattolico,* vol. 2, *Il partito popolare* (Bari, 1966).

21. A. Repaci, *La marcia su Roma,* 2 vols. (Rome, 1963).

22. A. Lyttelton, *The Seizure of Power* (London, 1973), 90.

23. See L. Valiani, 'Le origini della guerra del 1914 e dell'intervento italiano nelle ricerche e nelle pubblicazioni dell'ultimo ventennio,' *Rivista storica italiana* (1966), 3, 609.

24. R. Vivarelli, 'Benito Mussolini dal socialismo al fascismo,' *Rivista storica italiana* (1967), 2, 428-58.

25. A. Tasca, *Nascita e avvento del fascismo,* 549-53.

26. E. Santarelli, *Origini del fascismo* (Urbino, 1963).

27. R. de Felice, ed., *Il Fascismo e i partiti politici italiani* (Bologna, 1966).

28. L. Fabbri, 'La controrivoluzione preventiva,' ibid., 178 ff.

29. A. Gramsci, *Socialismo e fascismo, L'Ordine Nuovo 1921-1922* (Turin, 1966), 297-302.

30. M. Vaini, *Le origini del fascismo a Mantova* (Rome, 1961); S. Colarizi, *Dopoguerra e fascismo in Puglia (1919-1926)* (Bari, 1971).

31. P. Corner, *Fascism in Ferrara 1915-1925* (Oxford, 1974).

32. S. Sechi, *Dopoguerra e fascismo in Sardegna* (Turin, 1971); R. Colapietra, *Napoli tra dopoguerra e fascismo* (Milan, 1962).

33. E. Apih, *Italia, fascismo e antifascismo nella Venezia Giulia, 1918-1943* (Bari, 1966); C. Silvestri, 'Storia del fascio di Trieste dalle origini alla conquista del potere (1919-1922),' in *Fascismo, guerra, resistenza; lotte politiche e sociali nel Friuli-Venezia Giulia 1918-1943* (Trieste, 1969).

34. A. Aquarone 'Aspirazioni tecnocratiche del primo fascismo,' *Nord e Sud*, XI, n.s., 52 (April, 1964), 109-28.

35. G. Neppi Modona, *Sciopero, potere politico e magistratura, 1870-1920* (Bari, 1969). See also idem 'La magistratura e il fascismo,' in *Fascismo e società italiana*, ed. G. Quazza (Turin, 1965), 127-81.

36. A. Aquarone, *L'organizzazione dello stato totalitario* (Turin, 1965).

37. G. Rochat, *L'esercito italiano da Vittorio Veneto a Mussolini* (Bari, 1967); idem., *Militari e politici nella preparazione della campagna d'Etiopia (1932-1936)* (Milan, 1971); idem., 'L'esercito e il fascismo,' in *Fascismo e società*, 125-81.

38. H. Finer, *Mussolini's Italy*, 2d ed. (London, 1964).

39. F. W. Deakin, *The Brutal Friendship: Mussolini, Hitler and the Fall of Italian Fascism* (London, 1962).

40. D. Germino, *The Italian Fascist Party in Power: a study in totalitarian rule* (Minneapolis, 1959).

41. E. Ragionieri, 'Il partito fascista,' in *La Toscana nel regime fascista (1922-1939)*, 80.

42. P. Scoppola, *La chiesa e il fascismo: documenti e interpretazioni* (Bari, 1971); A.C. Jemolo, *Chiesa e stato in Italia negli ultimi cento anni* (Turin, 1948), transl. [incomplete] D. Moore, *Church and State in Italy 1850-1960* (Oxford, 1960); D.A. Binchy, *Church and State in Fascist Italy*, 2d ed. (Oxford, 1970); R.A. Webster, *Christian Democracy in Italy 1860-1960* (London, 1961).

43. Mario G. Rossi, 'La chiesa e le organizzazioni religiose,' in *La Toscana*, 360.

44. L. Rosenstock-Franck, *L'économie corporative fasciste en doctrine et en fait* (Paris, 1934).

45. G. Salvemini, *Under the Axe of Fascism* (London, 1936), 420.

46. A. Tasca, *Nascita e avvento*, 2, 568.

47. E. Rossi, *Padroni del vapore e fascismo*, 2d ed. (Bari, 1966), 9; P. Grifone, *Il capitale finanziario in Italia*, 2d ed. with introd. by V. Foa (Turin, 1971). Grifone had worked for a time as an official of the Confindustria; his book was written during his confinement as a political prisoner on the island of Ventotene.

48. R. de Felice, 'Primi elementi sul finanziamento del fascismo dalle origini al 1924,' *Revista Storica del Socialismo* 22 (August, 1964), 224 ff.; P. Melograni, 'Confindustria e fascismo tra il 1919 e il 1925,' *Il Nuovo Osservatore* VI (November, 1965), 834-73.

49. R. de Felice, 'I lineamenti politici della "quota 90" attraverso i documenti di Mussolini e di Volpi,' *Il Nuovo Osservatore* VII (May, 1966), 370-95.

50. R. Sarti, 'Mussolini and the industrial leadership in the battle of the lira 1925-1927,' *Past and Present* (May, 1970), 97-112; G.G. Migone, 'La stabilizzazione della lira: la finanza americana e Mussolini,' *Rivista di storia contemporanea* (1973), 2. See also idem., *Problemi di storia nei rapporti tra Italia e Stati Uniti* (Turin, n.d.), 64-5.

51. Melograni, 'Confindustria e fascismo,' 842-44.

52. M. Abrate, *La lotta sindacale nella industrializzazione in Italia 1906-26* (Turin, 1967).

53. R. Sarti, *Fascism and the Industrial Leadership in Italy, 1919-1940* (Berkeley, Los Angeles, London, 1971).

54. V. Castronovo, *Giovanni Agnelli* (Turin, 1971).

55. S. La Francesca, *La politica economica del fascismo* (Bari, 1972).

56. R. Romeo, *Breve storia della grande industria*, 2d ed. (Bologna, 1961).

150                                                                          ADRIAN LYTTELTON

57. D. Preti, 'La politica agraria del fascismo: note introduttive,' *Studi storici* XIV, 4 (1973), 802-69.

58. E. Fano Damascelli, 'La "restaurazione antifascista liberista": ristagno e sviluppo economico durante il fascismo,' *Movimento di liberazione in Italia*, XXIII (1971), 104.

59. G. Mori, 'Per una storia dell'industria italiana durante il fascismo,' *Studi storici* XIII (1971), 13-14.

60. R. Zagrandi, *Il lungo viaggio attraverso il fascismo* (Milan, 1962).

61. A. Asor Rosa, *Scrittori e popolo: il populismo nella letteratura italiana contemporanea*, 2 vols. 2d ed. (Rome, 1966).

62. G. Santomassimo, 'U. Spirito e il corporativismo,' *Studi storici*, XIV, 1 (1973), 61-113.

63. M. Ledeen, *Universal Fascism: the theory and practice of the Fascist International, 1928-1936* (New York, 1972).

64. J. P. Diggins, *Mussolini and Fascism: the view from America* (Princeton, 1972).

65. P. V. Cannistraro, 'Burocrazia e politica culturale nello stato fascista: il ministero della cultura popolare,' *Storia contemporanea*, I, 2 (1970), 273-98. See now, idem., *La fabbrica del consenso. Fascismo e mass media* (Bari, 1975).

66. See G. Turi, 'Il progetto dell'Enciclopedia Italiana: l'organizzazione del consenso fra gli intellettuali,' 93-152.

67. T. Tomasi, *Idealismo e fascismo nella scuola italiana* (Florence, 1969); G. Germani, 'Political socialization of youth in Fascist regimes: Italy and Spain,' in *Authoritarian Politics in Modern Society*, ed. S. P. Huntington and C. H. Moore (New York, 1970).

68. P. Togliatti, *Lezioni sul fascismo*, 97-116: C. Carabba, *Il fascismo a fumetti* (Florence, 1973).

69. F. Chabod, *Storia della politica estera italiana dal 1870 al 1896: le premesse*, 2d ed. (Bari, 1962).

70. G. Rumi, *Alle origini della politica estera fascista (1918-1923)* (Bari, 1968); E. Di Nolfo, *Mussolini e la politica estera italiana (1919-1933)* (Padua, 1960); G. Carocci, *La politica estera dell'Italia fascista 1925-1928* (Bari, 1969).

71. A. Cassels, *Mussolini's early diplomacy* (Princeton, 1970), 146-74, 354-55, 365-76.

72. J. Petersen, 'La politica estera del fascismo come problema storiografico,' in R. de Felice, ed., *L'Italia fra tedeschi e alleati: la politica estera fascista e la seconda guerra mondiale* (Bologna, 1973), 11-55.

73. Rochat, *Militari e politici*, G. W. Baer, *The Coming of the Italian-Ethiopian War* (Cambridge, Mass., 1967).

74. E. Wiskemann, *The Rome-Berlin Axis* (New York, 1949); A. Mayer, ed., *The Ciano Diaries 1937-1938* (London, 1952); H. Gibson, ed., *The Ciano Diaries 1939-1943* (New York, 1946). See also M. Muggeridge, ed., *Ciano's Diplomatic Papers* (London, 1948).

75. de Felice, *Mussolini il rivoluzionario*, IX-X; de Felice, *Mussolini il fascisti*, 1, 460 ff.

76. de Felice, *Mussolini il fascista*, 2, 357; see also ibid., 1, 464-65.

Note: The last volume of Professor de Felice's biography, *Mussolini il duce: I. Gli anni del consenso, 1929-1936* (Turin, 1974) appeared after the completion of this survey.

# 3

# National Socialism: Foreign Policy and Wehrmacht

## WILLIAM CARR

In the years immediately following the collapse of Hitler's Reich, as the full horror of Nazi brutality was revealed in all its grisly detail in concentration camps overrun by allied armies, and later in testimony given at the Nuremberg Trials, objective writing on Nazi Germany was virtually impossible. The all-embracing nature of modern war, in particular the mobilisation of popular passion and prejudice which is an essential ingredient of it, does not leave historians unmoved. Nowhere is this more poignantly recorded for posterity than in A. J. P. Taylor's *The Course of German History* (London, 1945), a period piece bristling with anti-German sentiment which reflected fairly accurately the prevailing mood of public opinion in Britain when it appeared in 1945. At a more sophisticated level Sir Lewis Namier, turning from the minutiae of politics in the reign of George III to the study of international politics in the 1930s, was not one whit less vehement in his denunciation of Nazi leaders and appeasement-minded politicians alike in a series of highly readable works: *Diplomatic Prelude 1938-1939* (London, 1948), *Europe in Decay: a study of disintegration 1936-1940* (London, 1950), and *In the Nazi Era* (London, 1952). A robust and avowed Germanophobe, Namier never doubted for one moment that Hitler was an unspeakably evil man who established his barbaric empire by force of arms in accordance with a premeditated plan of aggression precisely formulated in November 1937; the annexation of Austria, the seizure of Czechoslovakia, and the attack on Poland were not disconnected episodes but calculated steps on the road to eastern expansion. Writing with great panache, a bitterly sardonic wit, and an unrivalled command of the available source material, Namier expressed a point of view held by a whole generation of historians. Sir John Wheeler-Bennett, the first historian of the German army; Alan Bullock, author of a still unsurpassed biography of Hitler; Professor Hugh Trevor-Roper, whose *The Last Days of Hitler* (London, 1947) remains the classic account of Hitler's miserable end in the Berlin bunker; and the Swiss historian Walter Hofer, whose study of the last days of peace *Die Entfesselung des zweiten Weltkrieges* (Stuttgart, 1954) was quickly translated into English under the significant title of *War Premeditated* — all were in complete agreement with Namier. In *The Gathering Storm* (London, 1948), the first volume of his history of the war, Sir Winston Churchill set his imprimatur on this interpretation of the origins of the war. And as late as 1960 the gospel according to Sir Lewis was being preached as confidently as ever by the American journalist William L. Shirer in *The Rise and Fall of the Third Reich* (London, 1960), a massive anti-German compilation which enjoyed immense success in Britain and in the United States.

Much of the archival material used by these historians was published as a direct result of the decision of the allied governments to place the political and military leaders of Nazi Germany on trial for crimes against peace and humanity. Immediately after the German surrender, investigating teams ransacked the captured German archives and assembled a formidable mass of documentation on various aspects of the Third Reich. *The Trial of the Major War Criminals before the Nuremberg Military Tribunal*, 42 vols. (Nuremberg, 1946-49) and additional documentation in *Nazi Conspiracy and Aggression*, 8 vols. (Washington, 1951-53) supplied historians with valuable material on German foreign policy drawn principally from foreign office and military archives. Though the authenticity of this documentation has not, by and large, been called into question, it was assembled very hurriedly and in a highly selective manner by prosecution lawyers whose brief was to prove the guilt of the accused, not to place the events of the 1930s in any kind of historical perspective. The contributory blunders and miscalculations of the victorious powers were passed over in silence for only the fact not the circumstances of German aggression mattered to the tribunal. And as the defence counsels were allowed only extremely limited access to the captured archives, the balance of the documentation is weighted very heavily on the side of the prosecution. If a better case could have been made out for the defendants in answer to the charge of planning wars of aggression, it was certainly not possible to make it in these emotionally charged circumstances.

To remove any lingering doubt that war had been forced on the reluctant and blameless democracies by the calculated wickedness of Hitler, the allied governments decided to publish with all speed a selection of documents from the captured German foreign office archives. The nineteen volumes of *Documents on German Foreign Policy 1919-1945* covering the period 1933 to 1941 offer as comprehensive a picture as is possible on the basis of foreign office material (an important qualification) thanks to the enlightened editorial policy of including some military directives from the OKW and minutes from the ministry of economics and the Führer's chancellery as well as official dispatches to and from the Wilhelmstrasse. Because of the sheer volume of material it was decided not to proceed beyond 1941 nor to publish material before 1933. The German archives were, however, extensively microfilmed to facilitate the task of the editors, and these records—which include material from the naval high command and from party offices—are available for research in the National Archives

Washington and in the Public Records Office in London.[1] A Quadri-partite Commission established in 1960 has started to publish documents from 1918 to 1932 and from 1941 to 1945.[2]

The inevitable spate of memoirs appeared in the immediate post-war years from diplomats, statesmen, and soldiers. On the German side they were mostly written to defend the actions of individuals and made little attempt to see the Nazi era in any kind of historical perspective. There is little of value in the reminiscences of Ribbentrop, Papen, Weizsäcker (the permanent head of the foreign office), or Meissner (the secretary of state). Exceptions are B. Dahlerus, whose *The Last Attempt* (London, 1947) is an important source on the unofficial contacts between British and German officials on the eve of war; P. Schmidt, *Statist auf diplomatischer Bühne 1923-1945* (Bonn, 1949), Hitler's chief interpreter who attended many important conferences; and *Inside the Third Reich* (London, 1970), the long-awaited memoirs of Albert Speer full of fascinating material on Hitler and Nazi Germany though thin on foreign policy where he was clearly an outsider.

Towards the close of the 1950s an Irish historian had already expressed serious reservations about Namier's tidy and uncomplicated explanation of the outbreak of the war.[3] Shortly afterwards in 1961, a major attack was launched on it by A. J. P. Taylor in *The Origins of the Second World War*, a lively and provocative book which precipitated a fierce controversy about the nature of German policy still smouldering a decade later.

Claiming to be doing no more than looking afresh at the documents, Taylor arrived at characteristically iconoclastic conclusions. For the thesis of premeditated war he could find no shred of evidence. He brushed aside Hitler's much publicised 'declaration of intent' in *Mein Kampf* as idle chatter, having no long term significance. Taylor saw Hitler not as a man of ideas or a planner but as a feckless coffee-house dreamer, a vaguely Chaplinesque figure who wanted, like all German leaders before him, to make Germany master of Europe but had no clear idea how to achieve this. By bluff and intrigue he had clawed his way to power and by the same means he hoped to win success abroad. Micawber-like, he hung around for something to turn up and his enemies obliged him. It was Schuschnigg who forced him to seize Austria when he threatened to allow the Austrian peo-ple to decide their own destiny by plebiscite; and it was Chamberlain who took the initiative over the Sudetenland and created a crisis where none had existed. With such accommodating opponents on his side, Hitler bluffed his way with impunity from the Rhineland to Czechoslovakia. Is it altogether surprising that he attempted similar tactics over Poland and by error stumbled over the precipice? 'He became involved in war through launching on 29 August a diplomatic manoeuvre which he ought to have launched on 28 August,' says Taylor.[4] Thus he concludes that 'the war of 1939, far from being premeditated, was a mistake, the result on both sides of diplomatic blunders,' and that Hitler 'was no more wicked and unscrupulous than many other contemporary statesmen' even if 'in wickedness he outdid them all.'[5] Not surprisingly, neo-Nazi circles in West Germany hailed the book with glee, seeing in it a complete vindication of Hitler's policy which was certainly not Taylor's intention. In the other corner some critics, greatly incensed that a professional historian could bring himself to transform the ogre of Berchtesgaden into a rational statesman and equate him with his democratic opponents, vehemently denounced the book as a mischievous, irresponsible, and deliberately perverse exercise by the Puck of the historical fraternity.

Admittedly the book suffers from several defects. It is not free from ambiguities and contradictions about Hitler's objectives; in several instances Taylor ignores evidence in conflict with his thesis; and most serious of all, he has allowed his love of paradox to cloud his historical sense. To suggest that Schuschnigg, Chamberlain, and Hacha made the running while Hitler stumbled after them willy-nilly is to stand the truth on its head as those who lived through the period — including Taylor, as staunch an opponent of Hitler as any — were well aware. Finally, the book illustrates the weakness of diplomatic history too narrowly conceived. Taylor relies almost exclusively on diplomatic records and memoirs. In fact, these tell us relatively little about Hitler (who preferred to operate independently) but much about the Wilhelmstrasse personnel, who, like Taylor, regarded international affairs as a perpetual quadrille conducted by the Great Powers in defence of their national interests. Far too little attention is paid by Taylor to socio-economic pressures inside Germany and to the dynamic ideology of the Nazi movement, both factors of some importance in any analysis of Nazi policy, as T. W. Mason pointed out in a perceptive review.[6]

For these reasons Taylor's book has not transformed the study of the origins of the second world war in the way Fritz Fischer's *Griff nach der Weltmacht* (Düsseldorf, 1961) altered quite fundamentally historical interpretation of the first world war. Nevertheless, by challenging accepted wisdom in forthright and provocative terms Taylor did historians a great service; he has liberated them at long last from Namier's seductive literary spell and has encouraged a more objective and less emotive approach to the subject. If most historians — especially German — still believe that Hitler had far-reaching aims which he pursued with some degree of consistency to the point of war, no one would now subscribe to the belief that there was a detailed blueprint for aggression, or deny that in evaluating Hitler's intentions we are dealing with a balance of probability not with verifiable certainties; this change of attitude is due in no small measure to Taylor's perceptive book.

Curiously enough, Namier's generation, though ready to believe that Hitler was fanatically bent on having his own way to the point of war, paid scant attention to the nature of these fanatical beliefs. For practically thirty years it was fashionable to regard him as an unscrupulous opportunist and committed power-seeker, completely without firm ideological convictions, though able, chameleon-like, to assume the correct colouration to suit the immediate occasion. Lack of principle seemed the obvious explanation of a man who protested his love of peace one minute and practised blatant aggression the next, and who, after preaching hatred of communism all his political life, sent Ribbentrop posthaste to negotiate with Stalin in 1939. This picture of Hitler as 'the supreme opportunist' we owe very largely to Hermann Rauschning, a former associate of Hitler's and one-time Gauleiter of Danzig, who eventually broke with nazism and published in 1939 *Hitler speaks*, an account of conversations with Hitler in the mid-1930s which, despite all the doubts expressed by several historians about its reliability, still remains an important source for that period.[6a] Hugh Trevor-Roper questioned the validity of Rauschning's opportunistic thesis in the preface to *The Table Talk of Adolf Hitler 1941-1944* (London, 1953), where he argued forcefully that however repulsive, shallow and unoriginal Hitler's ideas seem to civilised people, they were the expression of a powerful intellect and as such merited more serious consideration than they had hitherto received.

Surprisingly enough, despite further signs of dissatisfaction with Rauschning in the course of the 1960s, no systematic analysis of Hitler's ideology appeared until Eberhard Jäckel's important study *Hitlers Weltanschauung. Entwurf einer Herrschaft* in 1969.[7] Jäckel probably overstates the degree of rationality and consistency in Hitler, but he succeeded in demonstrating that Hitler had a coherent philosophy of life. The evolution of his ideas was much more complex than Hitler pretended in *Mein Kampf*, and was not complete until the late 1920s by which time he had forged a coherent programme of action for the Nazi party out of three major concepts: anti-Semitism, the Social Darwinian belief that struggle was the basis of all human existence, and a new-found conviction that Germany's destiny lay in the east. Destruction of Jewry at home coupled with the conquest of 'Jewish-Bolshevik' Russia became the dominant theme of the Nazi programme. Despite all the tactical twists and turns along the road, a fanatical sense of mission and a dedication to first principles kept Hitler on course to the bitter end, or so Jäckel argues. It is, therefore, no accident that what Hitler did coincided more or less with what he promised to do in *Mein Kampf*. The exact relationship between tactical necessity and ideological commitment must remain a matter for conjecture but it is fair to say that historians now agree that Hitler's ideology has been seriously undervalued, and that his opportunistic policy must be seen within the framework of a firmly held *Weltanschauung*.[8]

One important consequence has been to enhance the significance of Hitler's writings and sayings. If what he believed did matter after all, then *Mein Kampf*, the bible of the movement published in 1925-26 in Munich, and the so-called *Secret Book*, a treatise on foreign affairs written in 1928 but only published in 1961 in New York, become important sources on Hitler's foreign policy. By the same token his speeches cannot be neglected either (especially the ones delivered at intimate gatherings); the most comprehensive and useful collections are N. H. Baynes, *The Speeches of Adolf Hitler 1922-39*, 2 vols. (London, 1942) and M. Domarus, *Hitler: Reden und Proklamationen*, 2 vols. (Würzburg, 1962-63).[9] References to foreign policy appear in *Hitlers Tischgespräche im Führerhauptquartier 1941-42* (Stuttgart, 1951; new edition 1963), Hitler's rambling disquisitions in the Wolfsschanze,[10] and in A. Hillgruber, editor, *Staatsmänner und Diplomaten bei Hitler. Vertrauliche Aufzeichnungen über Unterredungen mit Vertretern des Auslandes*, 2 vols., (Frankfurt a.M., 1967-70), a most valuable source on Hitler's wartime meetings with foreign statesmen and diplomats. Finally, *The Testament of Adolf Hitler: the Hitler-Bormann Documents February-April 1945* (London, 1961) contains interesting retrospective comment but must be used with caution as long as the owner of the letters will not permit their examination by scholars.

As long as historians believed in the monolithic unity of Nazi Germany where all power was concentrated in the hands of the dictator, it was a natural corollary to credit Hitler with sole responsibility for foreign policy. After the war ex-Nazis were swift to pounce upon this inviting alibi and absolve themselves from all blame for what had gone wrong. However, recent research has shown that behind a facade of unity the Third Reich was in reality a battleground for powerful quasi-feudal interest groups all struggling for dominant influence while Hitler deftly played off one against the other to maintain his own authority. Inevitably, this raises the question whether one can continue to equate German policy with Hitler. Even if we accept — as we must in the present state of research — that he played a major role in the formulation and direction of foreign policy, one must not overlook the part played by institutions and organisations — the armed forces, party organisations, and economic pressure groups as well as the foreign office — and also by individuals such as Goebbels and Himmler who were often blamed in post-war memoirs for the radicalisation of foreign policy after 1937.[11]

About the role of the Foreign Office much is already known thanks to the documentary publications referred to above. P. Seabury examined the role of the foreign office in *Die Wilhelmstrasse. A study of German diplomats under the Nazi regime* (Berkeley and Los Angeles, 1954). There are two useful essays in *The Diplomats 1919-1939* (Princeton, 1953) edited by G. Craig and F. Gilbert; Gordon Craig describes the German foreign office from Neurath to Ribbentrop, that is, to 1938, and Carl E. Schorske discusses the diplomats Dirksen and Schulenburg.

By far the most important study on the structure of foreign policy to appear in recent years is H.-A. Jacobsen's massive *Nationalsozialistische*

*Aussenpolitik 1933-1938* (Frankfurt a.M., 1968). Jacobsen emphasises the basic duality at the heart of German foreign policy after 1933. Nominally the conduct of foreign affairs remained in the hands of the Wilhelmstrasse for, despite Hitler's contempt for foreign office officials and diplomats, whom he consulted less and less with the passage of time, he recognised that peaceful revision of the Versailles Treaty—a policy in which the foreign office genuinely believed—was a convenient smokescreen until such time as the army was ready for a more adventurous policy. Simultaneously and behind the scenes Hitler's real revolutionary aims, in particular the dream of establishing a new racial order in Europe, were being assiduously promoted by a number of party organisations, all fighting tooth and claw for the Führer's favour. Rosenberg's *Aussenpolitisches Amt* was busily working out the implications of Hitler's anti-communism and planning the break-up of Soviet Russia, while the *Volksdeutsche Mittelstelle* had the more practical task of turning the German minorities in central and eastern Europe into obedient instruments for the disruption of neighbouring states, a device of which Hitler made full use in 1938-39. Possibly most influential of all was the *Dienststelle Ribbentrop*; when Ribbentrop became foreign minister in 1938 the last vestiges of independence were snuffed out and the foreign office was brought completely under Nazi control. It is clear from Jacobsen's pioneer study (regrettably it does not go beyond 1938) that while Hitler made the vital decisions on foreign policy, party agencies were still able to exert some influence, though probably not quite as much as Jacobsen imagines. One thing is certain; we need further studies of this calibre before we can disentangle the web of internecine rivalry and personal feuding round the person of Hitler and are able to assess objectively the influence of pressure groups and of individuals on foreign policy.[12]

Subversion and armed might were not the only weapons Hitler used to achieve his objectives. In the initial stages, at least, he attached very great importance to the adoption of what he considered to be the 'correct' diplomatic strategy. This, like the 'grand design' itself, only crystallised in the mid-1920s as Günther Schubert demonstrated in a well-documented analysis of the origins of Hitler's policy: *Anfänge einer nationalsozialistischen Aussenpolitik* (Köln, 1963). When Hitler entered politics in 1919 he was indistinguishable from any run-of-the-mill nationalist agitator; his enemies were Britain and France, his aim the destruction of the Versailles '*Diktat,*' the recovery of the lost colonies (to solve the overpopulation problem), and the general restoration of Germany's greatness possibly with Italy as an ally. Towards Russia, the traditional ally of conservatives, he remained ambivalent. Though staunchly anti-communist, he showed a shrewd awareness of her potential value as an ally against the west always provided that she could shake off bolshevism. By 1924 his ideas had undergone a profound metamorphosis. France remained the arch enemy; but Russia now joined her as a major foe — at whose expense Germany would expand — while Britain was bracketed with Italy as a potential ally. To win Italian friendship Hitler abandoned the Germans in the South Tyrol (much to the discomfiture of his nationalist friends), and to secure British support he wrote off the former colonies. Once assured of British and Italian support, he calculated that Germany would be able to defeat France and then turn eastwards to smash Russia.

There is no doubt about Hitler's change of direction but the reasons for it remain a matter for conjecture. In a recent contribution to the argument, *Hitlers aussenpolitisches Programm* (Stuttgart, 1970), Axel Kuhn seeks to demonstrate, somewhat unconvincingly, that neither Pan-German nor geopolitical considerations turned Hitler against Russia but a simple realisation in 1923 during the Ruhr crisis that Britain had become a potential ally against France; and that the logical alternative to the abandonment of colonial claims against Britain was a commitment to expand eastwards in order to solve the overpopulation problem. The influence of individuals such as Ludecke, Rosenberg, and Scheubner-Richter on Hitler in this seminal period is still obscure. It is touched upon most fully in W. Laqueur, *Russia and Germany. A century of conflict* (London, 1965). On Rosenberg there is much interesting material in R. Cecil's biography *The Myth of the Master Race. Rosenberg and Nazi ideology* (London, 1972).

Turning to the sequence of events in the 1930s, the most reliable general account is G. Weinberg, *The foreign policy of Hitler's Germany. Diplomatic Revolution in Europe 1933-1936* (Chicago, 1970). This, the first of a two-volume study of the pre-war years, is a model of meticulous scholarship based on an exceptionally wide knowledge of the sources. Though primarily diplomatic history, Weinberg pays some attention to domestic developments, though without establishing very positive connections between internal and external affairs.

In the first two years of power Hitler went out of his way to reassure the world of his pacific intentions, being well aware that a forward policy was excluded until the armed forces were ready for action (whether to fight or intimidate opponents is another question). Only when the risks were minimal did he take unilateral action, withdrawing from the Disarmament Conference and the League of Nations in 1933 and re-introducing conscription in 1935. A clear account of the early years, especially good on the Great Powers' initial reactions to the Hitler regime, is C. Bloch, *Hitler und die europäischen Machte 1933/4 Kontinuität oder Bruch?* (Frankfurt a.M., 1966) which suggests it was a mixture of both. So on the whole does the most recent work by Gunter Wollstein, *Vom Weimarer Revisionismus zu Hitler* (Bonn, 1973). Another valuable analysis of the first two years is K. D. Bracher, 'Das Anfangsstadium der Hitlerschen Aussenpolitik,' *Vierteljahrshefte für Zeitgeschichte* (Stuttgart, 1957) which argued—

before the 'primacy of internal policy' was a fashionable doctrine — that the key to Hitler's policy was the internal consolidation of the regime.

Germany remained isolated at the beginning of 1935 (the Polish Pact apart). Hitler's conciliatory gestures had not allayed suspicion aroused by his clumsy interference in Austria nor diminished the revulsion Nazi treatment of the Jews had aroused abroad. Then in mid-summer Germany's diplomatic position suddenly improved with the signing of the Anglo-German naval treaty, an agreement which a delighted Hitler confidently expected would lead to a formal alliance.[13]

The whole issue of Anglo-German relations is of central importance between 1933 and 1941 because the failure to obtain the British alliance obviously upset Hitler's strategy for the conquest of Europe and possibly of the world as well — a point to be taken up later. The story of the deteriorating relationship has been traced most recently and with great clarity by Axel Kuhn in the second part of *Hitlers aussenpolitisches Programm*. At first Hitler tried to pressurise Britain into active co-operation with Germany, Italy, and Japan in a new Holy Alliance, the so-called Anti-Comintern Pact. By the end of 1937 an increasingly impatient Führer had virtually abandoned hope of securing the alliance and simply hoped that the solidarity of the Anti-Comintern powers would frighten Britain into a neutral posture whilst Germany expanded in Europe. Finally, British intervention over Czechoslovakia and the guarantee to Poland appear to have convinced him that the anti-British Ribbentrop was right to anticipate war with Britain at some point before Germany completed her conquest of Europe. It might well be argued that the *Mein Kampf* strategy now lay in ruins; for by attacking Poland without British acquiescence, he plunged into a general war which it had not been his intention to wage or certainly not in 1939. On British policy towards Germany the standard work is likely to be O. Hauser, *England und das dritte Reich*, the first volume (Stuttgart, 1972) covering the years 1933 to 1936. Using cabinet papers, committee proceedings, and foreign office records, Hauser confirms the utter unreality of Hitler's hopes of a British alliance. Also important for the economic background to appeasement is B.-J. Wendt, *Economic appeasement. Handel und Finanz in der britischen Deutschlandpolitik 1933-1939* (Düsseldorf, 1971).[14]

Attempts to establish cordial relations with Italy fared much better after a temporary setback in 1934 when Mussolini, alarmed by events in Austria, dispatched troops to the Brenner frontier. On the partnership with the Italian dictator there are two general works of quality: Elizabeth Wiskemann, *The Rome-Berlin Axis* (London, 1949 and 1966) and F. W. Deakin, *The brutal friendship. Hitler, Mussolini and the decline of Italian fascism* (London, 1962). The dictators were brought together more by the dynamics of power politics than by any affinity of ideology as M. Funke demonstrates convincingly in a careful analysis of the diplomacy of the mid-1930s: *Sanktionen und Kanonen. Hitler, Mussolini und der nationale Abessinienkonflikt 1934-1936* (Düsseldorf, 1970). The Italian attack on Abyssinia and the imposition of sanctions by the League of Nations helped pave the way for an eventual understanding, though it certainly did not lead to an immediate *rapprochement*. Both dictators played unashamed power politics. Despite Hitler's benevolent neutrality towards Italy, he simultaneously supplied arms to the Negus hoping that prolonged Italian involvement in Ethiopia would give the Germans the free hand they wanted in Central Europe. With Britain, France, and Italy at loggerheads, Hitler seized his chance in March 1936 and re-occupied the Rhineland, a real turning-point in the interwar years which marked the beginning of a shift in the balance of power away from Paris and back to Berlin. The most reliable account of this event is M. Braubach, *Der Einmarsch deutscher Truppen in die entmilitarisierte Zone am Rhein im März 1936* (Köln, 1956). Incidentally, it used to be thought that had the French called Hitler's bluff, he would have withdrawn his three battalions at once and suffered a humiliating defeat. D. C. Watt suggested recently that it would have been a fighting withdrawal, which, if true, is a significant comment on the growing confidence of the regime.[15]

What really brought Germany and Italy together was Spain. The outbreak of the Spanish Civil War repeated the Abyssinian syndrome; the Italians were tied down this time in the Iberian peninsula and increasingly dependent on the Germans. In the autumn the Axis came into being, dividing Europe into armed camps, once more, though the dictators were very far from a complete meeting of minds on all subjects. Hitler's own motives in agreeing to send limited assistance to Spanish fascists are still obscure; ideology, *Machtpolitik*, and economic considerations (the pressing need for raw materials) probably all played a part.[16]

The few fragmentary records we possess of Hitler's secret conferences in the 1930s are a valuable source for the evolution of his policy. One of the most controversial of these gatherings took place in November 1937 in the Reichs chancellery when Hitler addressed a group of top Nazi leaders on the future pattern of German foreign policy. In a long monologue—his 'political testament' as he called it (though Goering denied that the phrase was ever used)—Hitler insisted that Germany's economic problems had to be solved at the latest by 1943-45 and by force if necessary. He discussed the possibility of seizing Austria and Czechoslovakia even before that date if favourable circumstances arose. In 1945 a copy of a summary of the speech drawn up by Colonel Hossbach, one of Hitler's adjutants, came into American hands. The Nuremberg Tribunal accepted the prosecution submission that this, the so-called Hossbach Protocol, was proof positive of Nazi intent to wage wars of aggression. Doubts have been cast on the authenticity of the document, but there seems no reason to believe that it is not a fair summary of what Hitler said.[17]

It is not, in fact, the authenticity of the Hossback Protocol which is in question so much as the interpretation placed on it. Alan Taylor was the first to argue in *The Origins of the Second World War* that the importance of the meeting had been grossly exaggerated. Basically, Taylor maintains that Hitler frequently rambled on alarmingly for effect and that close associates, well aware of the Führer's weakness, discounted most of his private diatribes. A more likely explanation of the speech was Hitler's desire to isolate Schacht and pressurise Fritsch into further rearmament; and had it not been for Nuremberg no one would have given a second thought to the speech. A good deal can be said for this re-interpretation. All the same, even if one accepts that this was no blueprint for aggression, the consensus of opinion still favours the view that Hitler was serving notice on Blomberg and Fritsch that a more adventurous (and dangerous) phase in foreign policy was imminent. Set against the background of Hitler's other pronouncements in the autumn of 1937, the Hossbach speech assumes its real significance; at Augsburg on 21 November he referred to Germany's shortage of *Lebensraum* and emphasised the need to accomplish 'the tasks set before us'; and three days later he repeated these arguments to political cadets at Sonthofen. This points to a hardening of attitude and to a determination to run greater risks whatever the reasons. Another relevant factor, rather neglected in the past, was Hitler's conviction that he was mortally ill and had to act while there was still time.[18] But the most compelling evidence for taking the speech of 5 November seriously is the fact that in December Hitler's threat to attack Austria and Czechoslovakia in the near future was incorporated in the annual army directive. Hitler may have refused to read Hossbach's protocol (which Taylor regards as proof that it signified little) but he did not hesitate to sign the amended directive, surely proof that he meant what he said in broad terms at least.

Military strategy in the 1930s has been examined in three important books. G. Meinck in *Hitler und die deutsche Aufrüstung 1933-1937* (1959) relates the progress of rearmament to foreign policy with some reference to economic affairs. He shows that military planning was at first purely defensive, being based on the not unreasonable assumption that Germany might be attacked by a combination of France, Russia and Czechoslovakia. It seems likely, though Meinck is not of this opinion, that aggressive intent was implicit in the 1937 army directive in the passage where Blomberg (probably in consultation with Hitler) declared that the army must exploit favourable political situations as and when they arose. The transition to open aggression clearly dates from December 1937 when the amended directive gave the highest priority to a preventive strike at Czechoslovakia in time of peace.

The second work, *Hitler's pre-war policy and military plans 1933-1939* (1963) by E. M. Robertson, also examines the connection between foreign policy and military planning. This book has, in fact, been quoted with approval by revisionists and Namierites alike in defence of their respective positions. Robertson is clearly a traditionalist insofar as he believes that Hitler's objective was the conquest of *Lebensraum*; that he fully intended to seize the Sudetenland by force; and that he was not bluffing over Poland. On the other hand, Robertson implies that Hitler, whom he thinks seldom saw more than one step ahead, had been blown off course by 1937. Mounting hostility to Britain superseded the traditional anti-Russian policy, a change of direction for which Mussolini was more responsible than previously supposed, in Robertson's opinion. Military planning took the form of improvisations to meet a rapidly changing situation; thus Hitler talked in May 1938 of seizing Czechoslovakia, not as a step on the road to eastward expansion, but rather as an essential precaution to secure Germany's rear during war with the west. Robertson concludes that Hitler was swept along by events outside his control and ended up fighting a general war against the west which had not been expected for another three or four years (if then, and for which Germany was militarily unprepared. Finally, W. Bernhardt in a most illuminating study *Die deutsche Aufrüstung 1934-39. Militärische und politische Konzeptionen und ihre Einschätzung durch die Allierten* (1969) examines the politico-military assumptions behind German strategy and draws attention to the considerable element of bluff in Hitler's programme which the western powers failed to understand.

Whatever the reasons, there is no doubt that German policy accelerated in pace in 1938. The first quarter of the year was dominated by the Austrian problem. The best general account of this is Jürgen Gehl, *Austria, Germany and the Anschluss 1931-1939* (London, 1963). The first crisis in Austrian affairs, when Austrian Nazis staged an abortive putsch in Vienna and murdered Dollfuss, is examined in detail by Dieter Ross in *Hitler und Dollfuss. Die deutsche Österreichpolitik 1933-1934* (Hamburg, 1966) and by G. Brook-Shepherd *Dollfuss* (London, 1961). What still remains uncertain is Hitler's role in the putsch. It is generally thought that he had no prior knowledge of it, though Weinberg feels this is scarcely credible given Hitler's dominant position in Germany by 1934. On the other hand, there is no conclusive proof of his involvement. One thing is certain. German policy changed abruptly; the bullying tactics of open subversion were abandoned in favour of the restrained, but equally subversive tactics of von Papen, the newly appointed special envoy in Vienna.

The second crisis occurred in the spring of 1938. At a meeting with Schuschnigg in February, Hitler succeeded in tightening his grip over Austria to such an extent that peaceful absorption seemed only a matter of time. No doubt Hitler was taken aback early in March when Schuschnigg announced the holding of a plebiscite. In that sense the crisis was of Schuschnigg's making as Alan Taylor argues. What this overlooks, of course, is the elementary fact that the threat of a plebiscite forced Hitler to invade and annex Austria only because he had designs on that country and dared not allow its people to decide their own future if the decision was likely to go against union with the Reich.

Hardly was the Austrian crisis over before Czechoslovakia erupted on the international scene. In the events of the next six months leading to the controversial decision to surrender the Sudetenland at the Munich Conference, Britain played a leading role. After the war — which seemed to many critics the inevitable consequence of the Chamberlain appeasement policy — British historians made determined efforts to lay the ghost of Munich. The first account of the origins of the Czech crisis *Munich: Prologue to Tragedy* (London, 1948; unrevised edition, 1962) by John Wheeler-Bennett depicted Chamberlain as the culpable dupe of a Hitler bent on having his way with Czechoslovakia by war if necessary and only headed off at the last moment by a combination of fortuitous circumstances. The same line is taken in the *Survey of International Affairs for 1938*, Vol. II: *The crisis over Czechoslovakia* (London, 1951) and Vol. III (London, 1952) by R. G. D. Laffan. On the German side there is B. Celovsky, *Das Münchener Abkommen von 1938* (Stuttgart, 1958), a diplomatic history written by a Sudeten German also hostile to Chamberlain and loyal to Benes. To date the most detailed and reliable study is Helmuth K. G. Rönnefarth, *Die Sudetenkrise in der internationalen Politik. Entstehung-Verlauf-Auswirkung* (Wiesbaden, 1961).

Without guidance and support from Hitler's Germany, the Sudeten Germans could not have disrupted the Czech state in 1938. That is not to say that the form the crisis took was entirely predetermined. Both E. M. Robertson and G. K. Robbins in *Munich 1938* (London, 1968) feel that Konrad Henlein's Sudeten German party was not the completely passive and subservient instrument of Berlin it is usually depicted as being. For example, when Hitler revealed his aggressive intentions towards Czechoslovakia on 5 November 1937 could it not have been because the serious disturbances at Teplitz Schönau in October had drawn Nazi attention forcibly to the smouldering fire on the frontiers of the Reich? Is it inconceivable that on meeting Henlein in March 1938 Hitler, far from encouraging the impatient Sudeten German leader as is usually supposed, was really anxious not 'to drive things to the limit?' Even the September crisis may have taken Hitler by surprise; the Sudeten Germans broke off negotiations with the Czechs on their own initiative and staged an uprising which Hitler certainly approved but had not planned and which occurred before his military preparations were complete. This is an interesting interpretation which calls for further examination in depth. At the same time, it must not be carried too far, for we know that since November 1937 Hen-

lein was totally committed to the incorporation of Bohemia in the Reich
and not to dominion status inside Czechoslovakia for which most of his followers would probably have settled.

Did Hitler seriously intend to go to war in the autumn of 1938? Or was
he, as Taylor and Robbins maintain, bluffing from start to finish, rattling
the sabre because he believed Britain and France had written off
Czechoslovakia and felt instinctively that sustained pressure would break
up the Czech state? No one can know what went on in Hitler's mind. All
one can say is that the evidence we possess suggests very strongly that the
threat to Czechoslovakia was a very real one. It is scarcely credible that elaborate military preparations for a Blitzkrieg would have been made — with
Hitler's eager participation — had armed intervention not been seriously
contemplated. And if it was deception, then Hitler was so accomplished an
actor that he took in his closest associates as well. Probably Alan Bullock
comes nearest to solving the riddle when he suggests that Hitler kept the
options of war or peace open to the very last moment. War was the preferred solution for putting the upstart Czechs in their place *ceteris paribus*.
But should the western powers threaten, unexpectedly, to intervene, then a
negotiated settlement was never excluded from his calculations. And by
late September this 'partial solution' became virtually unavoidable because
of the embarrassing eagerness of Britain and France to accommodate him.
Either way he stood to gain, evading a peaceful solution when it suited him
as at Bad Godesberg, only to agree to it at Munich.[19]

Characteristically, Hitler was quickly disgruntled at the peaceful outcome and almost at once set about the complete destruction of Czechoslovakia. Taylor's view that the occupation of Prague in March 1939 was
'without design' is quite untenable. As J. K. Hoensch demonstrates in an
indispensable study *Die Slowakei und Hitlers Ostpolitik* (Köln, 1965), the
Nazis undermined Czechoslovakia assiduously in the winter of 1938-39,
having discovered in the Slovaks a willing Trojan horse, tailor-made to
their requirements. Only the exact timing of the final operation is still
obscure. Hoensch thinks that Hitler decided as early as December 1938 to
occupy Prague in the spring while other writers favour the end of January
or the end of February 1939.[20] It seems likely that Hacha's last despairing
effort to preserve the Czech state from complete disruption in March preceded German action by only a few days.

The six months between the Munich Agreement and the British guarantee to Poland are probably the most decisive in the history of the 1930s and
deserve much closer attention than they have hitherto received. For it
seems likely that Hitler lost his bearings temporarily and was genuinely
uncertain where to turn next. With Poland delicate negotiations were
under way to take her into a junior partnership. Had Hitler succeeded in
this operation — as well he might — he would then have had a clear choice:

either to thrust eastwards into the Ukraine with active Polish support or to turn westwards against Britain and France, a not impossible course of action in view of his endorsement of Ribbentrop's argument that war with Britain was probably inevitable even before Germany was master of Europe. So much hung in the balance that winter, when history might easily have taken a dramatically different turn, that an investigation in depth of the various possibilities facing Hitler and of his reactions to them would be a valuable exercise if only to dispel the lingering illusion that he moved with the 'assurance of a sleepwalker' from Czechoslovakia to Poland.[21]

The breakdown of the negotiations with Poland and the British guarantee to that country ended Hitler's indecision. The course was set to the east. The diplomacy of the next six months has been thoroughly examined by Namier and Hofer in the works mentioned earlier, and also by Hans Roos, *Polen und Europa. Studien zur polnischen Aussenpolitik 1931-1939* (Tübingen, 1957). As over Czechoslovakia, it is impossible to divine Hitler's intentions with mathematical precision. Did he hope for a Polish 'Munich' as Taylor believes? That is always possible but on balance hardly credible in view of the elaborate military preparations. Furthermore, as Bullock remarks in his British Academy lecture, Hitler knew that his room for manoeuvre was diminishing rapidly and that the temporary balance of military advantage in Germany's favour would decline as her opponents grew in strength. It is even more difficult to decide whether he was reconciled to the inevitability of (possibly token) intervention by the west. Certainly, the Russo-German Non-Aggression Pact was designed to scare off the western powers, an effect which, much to Hitler's surprise, it failed to have. On the origins of the pact and on Russo-German relations generally G. Weinberg, *Germany and the Soviet Union 1939-1941* (Leiden, 1954) is now somewhat outdated. A more recent but unexciting account is J. E. McSherry, *Stalin, Hitler and Europe 1939-1941*, 2 vols. (Cleveland, Ohio, 1970).

In recent years work has begun in earnest on the economic history of the Third Reich. Recent research in this field has, indirectly, thrown a good deal of light on German foreign policy. Even before Taylor delivered his broadside at the Namierites, Burton Klein had paved the way for a revision of orthodoxy with his *Germany's economic preparations for war* (Cambridge, Mass., 1959). Using the voluminous reports of the United States Strategic Bombing Survey, Klein came to the conclusion that, contrary to popular belief, Germany was not armed to the teeth and fully prepared for war in 1939. Though Klein went too far in the opposite direction, seriously underestimating the extent to which Germany was actually geared to war by 1939, he did succeed in demonstrating that she lacked the resources for waging major wars; at most, she could afford a series of small wars executed with lightning speed to ensure success. It is no accident that Taylor relied heavily on Klein's work, interpreting his findings, however, as proof that Hitler never intended war at all.

In the 1960s two important books appeared. First, and quite outstanding was Alan Milward's *The German economy at war* (London, 1965) which analyses in depth the work of Todt and Speer in the total war situation after 1942. In a brilliant first chapter Milward pinpoints the political and economic realities underlying the Blitzkrieg strategy and Germany's preference for rearmament in breadth not in depth. Hitler's instinctive fear that a concentration of economic power in a few hands and a depression of living standards (both likely consequences of total war preparations) would undermine the regime emerge as the decisive factors; whatever the irrepressible Goering said, the Germans had guns *and* butter up to 1942. Bernice Carroll confirms Milward's thesis in her lucidly written *Design for Total War, Arms and Economics in the Third Reich* (The Hague, 1968). She shows that one may speak of a 'war economy' only after 1938 when 17 per cent of the GNP was spent on rearmament (compared with 8 per cent in Britain), and not until 1942 was the economy totally geared to war. To some extent the findings of economic historians strengthen the revisionist case. It clearly made sound economic, as well as political sense, for Hitler to try and obtain as much as possible by bluff—though this is not necessarily conclusive proof that he was averse to war as 'the supreme arbiter.'

By way of contrast the work of historians in the German Democratic Republic points back towards the Namierite interpretation, if for very different reasons. Rigidly committed to an inflexible Marxism-Leninism, East German historians maintain that an unholy alliance of landowners and monopoly capitalists put Hitler in power with the express intention of breaking the power of the organised working class and of launching Germany on an imperialist war of aggression. Their summary dismissal of Hitler as a shadowy puppet of capitalism is so much at variance with all that we know of his very real influence on policy that there is a danger of underestimating the importance of their investigations into the role of powerful pressure groups, in particular of the autarky lobby led by I. G. Farben. D. Eichholtz in *Geschichte der deutschen Kriegswirtschaft 1939-1945*, Vol. I (East Berlin, 1969) and in *Anatomie des Krieges. Neue Dokumente über die Rolle des deutschen Monopolkapitals bei der Vorbereitung und Durchführung des zweiten Weltkrieges*, Vol. I (East Berlin, 1969) with W. Schumann—especially important for the war years—shows that I. G. Farben directors such as Carl Krauch were in the corridors of power from the beginning. Thus the Four Year Plan of 1936 'the weapon of monopoly capitalism for expansion' was based on a Krauch memorandum; in the shadow of the Czech crisis Krauch urged that the production of gunpowder, explosives, and vital chemicals be accelerated to reach a maximum—significantly enough—in the autumn of 1939; and in his report to the Four Year Plan Council in April 1939 he referred openly to the imminence of war and to the need for a great economic empire capable of exploiting the wealth of the Ukraine.

What is much more difficult to sustain is the thesis that monopoly capitalism was the driving force behind Hitler's foreign policy. On the evidence we possess, a more likely explanation is that monopoly capitalists, like other pressure groups, followed in Hitler's wake seizing opportunities to secure positions of power and profit without necessarily determining the course of policy.[22] A modest attempt to examine the relationships between economic pressures, rearmament, and foreign policy is made by W. Carr in *Arms, Autarky and Aggression. A study in German foreign policy 1933-1939* (London, 1972). Carr does not deny the importance of socio-economic factors — he believes that Hitler imposed priorities on the economy which in turn created tensions confirming him in his expansionist diagnosis — but he thinks military considerations were probably of paramount importance in 1939. There is a need for much solid work on the mass of archival material still largely untouched before definitive conclusions can be arrived at — if then. For, very probably, as in the parallel case of the origins of the first world war on which Fritz Fischer assembled much impressive material relating to the socio-economic structure of pre-war Germany, documentary proof of a direct causal relationship between the economic substructure and the foreign policy superstructure will continue to elude historians. This raises the more fundamental question of whether one should expect such an exacting degree of proof in this area of investigation? On the face of it, it does seem highly probable that the existence of a common cultural heritage and of a broad identity of interest between the Nazis and their supporters on social and economic matters would have exerted some influence on foreign policy. The problem facing the historian is that influences of this kind are not ordinarily expressed in documentary form but in those subtle nuances, unspoken assumptions, and delicate undertones which the tools presently at the disposal of political historians are too insensitive to detect.

Since the appearance of Fischer's seminal work, West German historians have also begun to re-interpret the nineteenth and twentieth centuries in less rigidly political terms. At times it almost seems as if Ranke's 'primacy of foreign policy' has been superseded by a no less dogmatically held belief in the 'primacy of domestic policy.' H. Böhme, U. Wehler, and M. Stürmer have already shown how intimately foreign and domestic policy were interwoven in the days of Bismarck and William II. More recently, Klaus Hildebrand, in a stimulating essay now translated as *The foreign policy of the Third Reich* (London, 1972), has performed a similar function for the Nazi era, placing it squarely in the mainstream of German history since 1871. He argues that the essential social function of foreign policy was to divert the attention of the masses from the inequitable distribution of wealth and power at home. In William II's Germany a jingoistic *Welt-politik* had sufficed to rally the masses round the throne but by 1930 the increasing polarisation of propertied classes on the one hand, and the proletariat on the other, necessitated much more radical expedients—anti-bolshevism, anti-Semitism, and a stronger dose of Bonapartism in the shape of Hitler—to preserve the status quo. Far from being unique, Hitler's programme merely integrated 'all the political demands, economic requirements and sociopolitical expectations prevailing in German society since the days of Bismarck.'[23] That it finally failed is attributed to the predominance in the equation of racial fanaticism which plunged Germany into war and eventually destroyed the very social order the dictatorship was designed to preserve.

Re-interpretations which depend on the validity of parallels between autocratic empire and popular dictatorship obviously raise the related question of continuity in German history. In their day the Nazis, for propaganda purposes, emphasised the element of continuity between their Reich and previous political forms. On the other side Angle-Saxon hack-writers during the war cheerfully traced Hitler's pedigree back to Luther, Frederick the Great, and Bismarck with a complete disregard for historical accuracy. After the war German historians not unnaturally reacted strongly against accusations of 'collective guilt' and treated the Nazi era as an aberration, qualitatively different from all that had preceded it, a view advanced as late as 1969 in H.-A. Jacobsen's *Nationalsozialistische Aussenpolitik*.

However, Fischer's contention that Germany was as responsible for the outbreak of the first world war as she was universally held to be for the second—two acts in a single drama—sparked off anew the old controversy. The case for continuity has been developed most vigorously by A. Hillgruber in *Deutschlands Rolle in der Vorgeschichte der beiden Weltkriege* (Göttingen, 1967) and *Kontinuität und Diskontinuität in der deutschen Aussenpolitik von Bismarck bis Hitler* (Düsseldorf, 1969). There is much to be said on both sides. The appalling  brutality of the Nazis taken in conjunction with Hitler's plans for a biologically pure master race to rule Europe are still weighty arguments for regarding 1933 as a cesura. Yet at least as powerful a case can be made on the other side. Eastward expansion and Weltpolitik were both well-established themes deeply embedded in the socio-economic structure of Germany between 1871 and 1945; as Hillgruber has shown, Hitler's *Lebensraum* plans bear a striking resemblance to Ludendorff's annexationist wartime plans; and from Bismarck to Hitler it is notorious that Germans have used the same bullying tactics to intimidate opponents and have never hesitated, on occasion, to go to war in order to impose their will on the rest of Europe.

The arguments in favour of continuity have been further strengthened by current research into Hitler's alleged plans for world domination. For long it was assumed by historians that Hitler's ambitions were exclusively continental in nature; he understood Czechs and Poles but, unlike William II, had no interest whatsoever in the wider world outside Europe. Doubts were first expressed by G. Moltmann who inferred from an analysis of what Hitler said in *Mein Kampf* and in the *Second Book* that world domination was indeed the logical consequence of the Nazi belief in Aryan racial superiority, as well as forming a counterblast to the 'Jewish plan for world mastery.'[24] Andreas Hillgruber in *Hitlers Strategie. Kriegführung und Politik 1940-1941* (Frankfurt a.M., 1965) was the first to argue, in broad terms, that Hitler thought, in fact, in terms of a two-phase strategy, that is, he envisaged a second phase — long after his day — when Europe, dominated by Germany from the Atlantic to the Urals, would have to fight the United States (and possibly Britain) for world supremacy. Thus Hillgruber regards Hitler's revival of Germany's colonial demands in 1936 not as a tactical manoeuvre to force Britain's hand, but as a serious preparation for the second phase of expansion. Obviously Hillgruber's thesis implies that the British alliance, far from being the sheet-anchor of Hitler's policy, was a temporary agreement likely to be dissolved once Germany was master of Europe.

Klaus Hildebrand has elaborated on this theme in a major study of the somewhat neglected colonial question *Vom Reich zum Weltreich. Hitler, NSDAP und koloniale Frage 1919-1945* (Munchen, 1969). He shows that Britain's refusal to consider a German alliance seriously upset the timing of the two-phase strategy. By 1937 Hitler began to suspect that the struggle for world mastery would not be delayed until some distant future but would, in all probability, occur in the late 1940s; that explains the new emphasis after 1937 on naval re-armament, particularly the adoption of the Z Plan in 1939. Though the swift victory in the west in 1940 temporarily reawakened hopes that Britain might still come to terms, it is significant that Hitler now toyed with the idea of acquiring colonial bases in preparation for the second round against the United States. But with the attack on Russia all prospect of moving on to the second phase quickly receded into the distant future once again.

Hillgruber and Hildebrand have fathered a flourishing school of research into various aspects of Hitler's *Weltpolitik*. Several important studies have already appeared. On naval policy M. Salewski, *Die deutsche Seekriegsleitung 1935-1945*, Vol. I, *1935-1939* (1970) and J. Dülfer, *Weimar, Hitler und die Marine. Reichspolitik und Flottenbau* (Düsseldorf, 1971); and on Anglo-German relations J. Henke *England in Hitlers politischem Kalkul 1935-1939* (Boppard am Rhein, 1972). At this stage it would be premature to attempt any final evaluation of the Hillgruber-Hildebrand thesis. But it is already becoming apparent that we will have to modify considerably the old view of Hitler as interested exclusively in Europe and indifferent to the rest of the world.

Prussian militarism has always been an emotive phrase in the Anglo-Saxon world where Mirabeau's celebrated comment: 'La Prusse n'est pas un pays qui a une armée: c'est une armée qui a un pays' has never been quite forgotten. During the second' world war 'Prussian generals' were blamed as much as Ruhr industrialists and East Prussian landowners for putting Hitler in power in the first place and giving him unflagging support since 1933.

The anti-militaristic mood of 1945 is faithfully mirrored in what is still one of the most widely read (and informative) studies of the German army, J. W. Wheeler-Bennett, *The nemesis of power. The German army in politics 1918-1945* (London, 1953). Germany's military leaders emerge from the book as shabby and sinister figures who contributed substantially to the rise of Hitler (if only because they failed to act against him), and who dishonoured the army through shameful complicity in the purge of 1934 when they could have overthrown the regime 'with a nod.' Wheeler-Bennett is equally scathing about the German opposition to Hitler; it was not primarily moral revulsion at Nazi excesses which turned many officers into active opponents of Hitler by 1943 but fear of a humiliating military defeat if they remained inactive. Furthermore, while conceding that the 1944 conspirators were honourable men, he argues that even if the conspiracy had succeeded, negotiation with a government of reactionaries would have constituted a betrayal of all the allied powers were fighting for; far better unconditional surrender and the complete destruction of militarism. The arrangements for a German contribution to the defence of Europe being worked out in the early 1950s prompted Wheeler-Bennett to wonder whether this was '..."where we came in" in the repetitive history of the German army in politics.'[25] An equally unsympathetic view was taken by the American historian Gordon Craig in *The politics of the Prussian army 1640-1945* (Oxford, 1955). As the Federal Republic began to recover some of its old power at the close of the 1950s, there were signs of dissatisfaction with this blanket condemnation of the German military. For example, in 1957 Gerhard Ritter, the doyen of the German historical fraternity, then engaged on his monumental work on German militarism, attempted to exonerate the German generals from at least some of the blame by drawing attention to the fact that massive popular support rather than the machinations of the military put Hitler in power in 1933.[26]

In more recent years, with West Germany re-established as a powerful — and peaceful — member of the European Community, the old fears of militarism have largely subsided. A less emotive and more objective treatment of the Wehrmacht is at last possible as, for example, in R. O'Neill's important study: *The German army and the Nazi Party 1933-1939* (London, 1966). Whilst not attempting to exculpate the army from all responsibility for the German catastrophe, the author, who is a soldier by profession, shows considerable sympathy for the predicament of the German officer class. Though a few influential officers, notably von Blomberg and von Reichenau, played a conscious political game, the vast majority were 'rudderless ships amidst swift currents,'[27] quite out of their depth in a complex situation, slow to appreciate the criminal nature of the regime, and ultimately trapped into acquiescence by their instinctive habit of obedience.

New studies on the army by German historians also emphasise the complexity of the relationship with the Nazis. In the most detailed and recent account *Das Heer und Hitler. Armee und nationalsozialistisches Regime 1933-1940* (Stuttgart, 1969). K. J. Müller reminds us that the attitude of individual officers ranged from unrestrained enthusiasm through lukewarm approval to outright rejection. On the other hand, both Müller and K. D. Bracher in *The German Dictatorship* (London, 1970) — a good general account of the Nazi era — are much less inclined than O'Neill to give the army leaders the benefit of the doubt. Great blame rightly attaches, in their view, to men who were generally well disposed to the Third Reich because it approximated more closely to their authoritarian ideas than the Weimar Republic had done. Rapid expansion, Hitler's repeated assurances that army and party were 'the twin pillars of the state,' as well as the general euphoria generated by the 'national revolution' symbolised by the continued presence of Hindenburg at the head of affairs — all encouraged the military leaders to believe that they could exert great influence on the regime and even restore the old intimacy between officer corps and state which had characterised William II's Germany, another example, *en passant*, of continuity in modern German history from Bismarck to Hitler. Disagreements among the leading generals were, so Müller argues, purely tactical in nature. Whereas enthusiastic Nazis such as von Blomberg, the minister of war, and von Reichenau, his cool calculating assistant, were convinced that the army must embrace the Nazi movement if it was to exert effective influence, other officers such as von Fritsch, the commander-in-chief of the army, and Beck, his chief of staff, hoped to achieve exactly the same end by keeping the party at arm's length.

That the 'alliance' with the Nazis failed to preserve the army's independence is a matter of history. Recent writing strongly suggests that the explanation is not to be found in Wheeler-Bennett's sinister 'nemesis of power' but in sheer political ineptitude. Blomberg and Fritsch failed completely to appreciate that totalitarianism in the state was incompatible with genuine independence in the army. Only politically naive men could have congratulated themselves in 1934 on the removal of a dangerous rival in the SA without appreciating the ugly implications of Hitler's ruthless methods. And only men who had woefully misread Hitler's character could have supposed that an oath of personal allegiance would bind the Führer more closely to the army, turn it into the main pillar of the regime, and put the party in its place. Because Hitler refrained from interference in military matters before 1938, army leaders were encouraged in their fond belief that he respected them. In fact, Hitler resented their social exclusiveness, despised their caution, and tolerated them only because he desperately required their expertise to create a powerful army.

The illusions were rudely shattered in 1938 with the controversial dismissal of Blomberg and Fritsch.[28] It has been argued that Hitler had planned their removal ever since their criticism of his schemes at the Hossbach meeting. This seems unlikely in Blomberg's case as Hitler owed much to the minister of war's smooth handling of the army. On the other hand, the *mésalliance* with Erna Gruhn forced his hand and may well have genuinely shocked him. The distasteful prospect of having the cautious Fritsch as his next minister of war fully explains Hitler's ready acceptance of the trumped-up Gestapo charges against the commander-in-chief. What is not in dispute are the epoch-making consequences of the structural changes in the high command. With Hitler as commander-in-chief of the Wehrmacht, the OKW reduced to a personal planning staff under the subservient Keitel, and with the pliable Brauchitsch as commander-in-chief of the army, the conservative-aristocratic dream of an autonomous army was destroyed forever. On Keitel, Jodl, and Brauchitsch, Hitler could rely absolutely; these were technocrats of a new breed, dazzled by the Führer, ready to subordinate professional scruples to his intuition and content to follow him slavishly to the bitter end.

Resentment at this dramatic shift of power probably played some part in the emergence of opposition to Hitler during the Czech crisis. Opinions differ about the motives which prompted this small group of officers and civilians, led by Beck and Goerdeler, to plan the removal of Hitler.[29] Some historians, for example Harold Deutsch, emphasise the moral revulsion older officers and civil servants felt towards the inhuman (and vulgar) Nazis; others, such as K. J. Müller, tend to see the major causes in the conspirators' realisation that Germany was too weak to face a major war, and in their chagrin at Hitler's contemptuous dismissal of their weighty objections to his plans. Revealing on the political and social objectives of the conspirators are essays by H. Graml and H. Mommsen in *The German Resistance to Hitler* (London, 1970). The chances of the conspiracy succeeding were, in fact, extremely slight, and after Hitler's triumph at Munich resistance melted away overnight. During the Polish crisis there was virtually no opposition to Hitler, partly because he had removed many unreliable officers after Munich and abolished the long-established right of chiefs of staff to share in strategic decisions, but also because this was a popular war against a hated foe.

With the outbreak of war, Hitler, unlike William II in 1914, quickly emerged as the dominant figure in the Wehrmacht. Until fairly recently it was customary to dismiss Hitler as a bungling amateur in military matters, the opinionated corporal of the First World War, who brought ruin on

Germany through his insane conduct of the war. This interpretation owed much to the memoirs of generals, particularly Halder, Guderian, and Manstein, who were quick to blame Hitler for the defeats while claiming the credit for operations that went well.[30]

Some re-appraisal of Hitler as a military leader has been long overdue and is possible now that so much important archival material has been returned to Germany. Especially important publications based on this material are the official war diary of the high command: *Kriegstagebuch des Oberkommandos der Wehrmacht 1940-1945*, 7 vols. (1961-65) edited by P. Schramm; the private diary of F. Halder, *Kriegstagebuch 1939-1942*, 3 vols. (Stuttgart, 1962-64); W. Hubatsch, ed. *Hitlers Weisungen fur die Kriegsführung 1939-1945 Dokumente des OKW* (Frankfurt a.M., 1962); and H. Heiber, ed. *Hitlers Lagebesprechungen. Die Protokollfragmente seiner militärischen Konferenzen 1942-1945* (Stuttgart, 1962), 900 pages of the stenographic reports of the Fuhrer's daily war conferences. This material has not, as yet, been properly assimilated in an authoritative study of the war leader. There is a useful preliminary essay 'The Military Leader' by Percy Schramm in *Hitler the man and the military leader* (London, 1972). Werner Maser, one of the many Hitler biographers, pays particular attention to this somewhat neglected aspect in his *Hitler* (trans., München, 1973) though the attempt to correlate the progression of Hitler's illness with Germany's decline after 1941 is unconvincing. It is already quite clear that we can no longer accept the folk myth of a carpet-biting maniac utterly immune to all rational argument. The truth is that he did possess at least some of the qualities expected of a military leader: a flair for strategy; an understanding of tactics, and a knowledge of weaponry which astonished general staff officers and enabled him to hold his own with experts; and a quite amazing will power and determination to achieve his objectives.

Early in the war Hitler served notice on the army that he intended to take charge personally of strategic planning. After the Polish campaign, Hitler's generals were perfectly content to remain on the defensive in the west and even inclined to a negotiated peace, when to their utter consternation Hitler ordered an attack before the winter. The story of their opposition and the abortive plot in November to remove Hitler is told in minute detail by Harold Deutsch in *The conspiracy against Hitler in the twilight war* (Minneapolis, 1968). For the controversial origins of the strategic plan of 1940, H. A. Jacobsen, *Fall Gelb: Der Kampf um den deutschen Operationsplan zur Westoffensive* (Wiesbaden, 1957) is indispensable. It would appear that several factors conspired together to produce *Sichelschnitt*: army dissatisfaction with Halder's Schlieffen-style plan; unavoidable delays which allowed time for second thoughts; Manstein's genius; and, not least, Hitler's instinct for the unconventional. Characteristically, he claimed full credit for the victory in the west though it is clear from the campaign that the Germans enjoyed much good fortune in what a leading military expert described as 'a lucky series of long-odds chances.'[31] After the fall of France few generals went as far as the sycophantic Keitel who triumphantly proclaimed Hitler 'the greatest strategist of all time.' Yet, with Germany virtually master of all Europe, grudging admiration for the Fuhrer's 'genius' overcame much of the real apprehension aroused by his personal intervention in the Norwegian and Western campaigns. In this context it should also be remembered that lack of co-ordination between the three services greatly assisted Hitler in assuming overall direction of the war.

In the light of recent research, the six months which elapsed after the fall of France while an increasingly perplexed Hitler waited in vain for Britain to capitulate, emerge as a period of central importance for the subsequent course of the war. From June to December 1940 Hitler wrestled with the problem of how to end the unwelcome war with Britain. Invasion—to which he turned reluctantly in July—was abandoned for sound military reasons in September. For a time he toyed with a 'peripheral' strategy of attacking British bases in the Mediterranean and Atlantic.[32] He also looked with apparent favour on Ribbentrop's scheme for a huge continental block stretching from Madrid to Tokyo which might pressurise Britain into surrender and secure a Central African empire for Germany into the bargain. This should not be interpreted as a sign that Hitler was seriously committed to the traditional anti-British strategy of foreign office and naval command. More likely it was stop-gap improvisation on the road to war in the east, as Andreas Hillgruber argues in an authoritative study of the complex period, *Hitlers Strategie. Politik und Kriegführung 1940-1941* (Frankfurt a.M., 1965). However, when Hitler finally opted in December 1940 for war in the east he contrived to combine the anti-British and anti-Russian strategies in a 'world Blitzkrieg' strategy designed to solve his problems 'at a stroke.' The attack on Russia not only represented a life's ambition but would have far-reaching strategic consequences; Japan would be encouraged to expand in Asia; this, in turn, would prevent American intervention in Europe—and Hitler was acutely aware of deepening bonds between Britain and America throughout 1940—so that, finally, Britain, without allies, would have to capitulate. Germany would then be master of Europe and in a position to make a bid for world power. That Hitler was seriously contemplating this is suggested by the order in July 1940 for the resumption of work on the Z Plan suspended at the outbreak of war; and while the Russian campaign was going well in July 1941 Hitler discussed with the Japanese ambassador a joint operation against the United States.

When the Blitzkrieg came to a halt before the gates of Moscow in December 1941, Hitler's gamble had failed and final defeat was inescapable, as he was one of the first to realise. Good comprehensive accounts of the Russian campaign are A. Clark, *Barbarossa* (London, 1965) and A. Seaton, *The Russo-German War 1941-1945* (London, 1971). Barry A. Leach throws light on the origins of the plan of attack in *German strategy against Russia 1939-1941* (Oxford, 1973). Until recently it was fashionable to lay the blame for the German failure on Hitler's reckless disregard of the lessons of history. Leach rightly points out that army command was as committed to the attack as Hitler; it was every bit as optimistic about the outcome and underestimated the Russians as grossly as he did. Indeed, it might well be argued that during the first six months of the campaign Hitler often showed more perception than his military advisers; and in the critical month of December it was only Hitler's determination to stand fast which prevented a disastrous German retreat.

On the other hand, as the tide turned against Germany after 1942, Hitler, now his own commander-in-chief, revealed very serious defects of character: a frightful obstinacy about matters of detail; a paranoid mistrust of many staff officers; a growing belief, as dream and reality ceased to coincide, that fanatical determination and will power were the real keys to victory; stubbornness in withdrawing units until it was often too late to save more than a remnant; and a habit of interfering in operations which cramped initiative by subordinates. The inability to appreciate the proper relationship between operational goals and available resources, which lay at the root of his troubles, may have been accentuated by illness, for example, during the Kursk offensive of July 1943, but in the main it was attributable to a deep-seated repugnance for the harsh realities of failure coupled with the conviction that he had no alternative but to resist until the bitter end.

After the Stalingrad debacle — for which Hitler must bear major responsibility — the army's faith in the Führer began to falter, and opposition to the regime grew rapidly both in military and civilian circles. The attempts to remove Hitler by assassination culminating in the abortive Bomb Plot of July 1944 are described in E. Zeller, *The flame of freedom* (London, 1968) and R. Manvell and H. Fraenkel, *The July Plot* (London, 1964). This was the end of the road for the army. Hitler's pent-up resentment of the officer corps burst forth in a savage repression of the July plotters; hundreds of officers were arrested and many executed; the Nazi salute was at last made compulsory in the army; and for the last few months of the Third Reich the SS was in the ascendancy with Himmler as commander-in-chief of the replacement army.

By this time the allied invasion of Europe, the liberation of France and Belgium, and the mounting devastation caused by allied bombardment of German cities had brought Germany near to the point of collapse. Indeed, had it not been for disagreements in the allied camp, Germany would have been overrun in the autumn. As it was, the allied advance came to a halt, enabling the Reich to hold out through the winter of 1944-45. Hitler made use of this unexpected breathing space to launch one last offensive in the Ardennes where the great victory of 1940 was forged. The standard work on this campaign will probably be *Die Ardennenoffen-*

*sive 1944/5. Ein Beispiel für die Kriegsführung Hitlers* (Göttingen, 1971) by H. Jung who treats it as a classic example of the strengths and weakness of Hitler's military leadership. Whether he genuinely thought there was still hope for Germany remains uncertain. Some evidence suggests he expected disagreements with Russia to disrupt the grand alliance, and hoped that the Ardennes offensive would surprise the allies and make them amenable to a compromise peace, in itself an indication of the unreal atmosphere he lived in, oscillating between wild hope and deep despair. Ends and means were hopelessly out of joint; there was no hope of seizing Liège (the army's objective) let alone Antwerp (Hitler's aim).

The Ardennes offensive was decisive in one sense. The eastern front was so weakened by this last effort that when the Russians launched their last great offensive in the spring of 1945 and the Anglo-Americans crossed the Rhine, Germany was utterly without resources and forced to surrender unconditionally. In the midst of the great catastrophe which now engulfed Germany and destroyed the old Europe forever, the suicide of the Führer in the chancellery bunker on 30 April was an almost irrelevant comment on the margin of events which left the Wehrmacht and the German people largely unmoved.

## NOTES

1. G. O. Kent, ed., *A catalogue of files and microfilms of the German Foreign Ministry archives 1920-45*, 3 vols. (Stanford, 1962-66).

2. Other major collections containing material on German foreign policy are: *Documents on British Foreign Policy 1919-1939: Documents diplomatiques français 1932-1939* (see especially the perceptive reports of François-Poncet, French ambassador in Berlin 1931-38); *I documenti diplomatici italiani* (so far only material from March 1939 to July 1940); *Foreign Relations of the United States* for 1931-41; and *Documents and Materials relating to the eve of the Second World War*, 2 vols., the second volume being the papers of Dirksen, German ambassador in London 1938-39.

3. T. Desmond Williams, 'The historiography of World War II,' *in* E. M. Robertson, ed., *The Origins of the Second World War. Historical Interpretations* (London, 1971).

4. A. J. P. Taylor, *The Origins of the Second World War* (London, 1961), 278.

5. Ibid., 79.

6. T. W. Mason, 'Some Origins of the Second World War' *Past and Present* (Oxford, 1964).

6a. For a careful evaluation, see T. Schieder, *Hermann Rauschnings Gespräche mit Hitler* (Opladen, 1972).

7. Eberhard Jäckel, *Hitlers Weltanschauung. Entwurf einer Herrschaft* in 1969 (Tübingen, 1969); recently translated as *Hitler's Weltanschauung: A Blueprint for Power* (Middletown, Conn., 1972).

8. N. Rich in *Hitler's War Aims. Ideology, the Nazi State, and the Course of Expansion* (London, 1973), the first of a two-volume study tracing the development of Hitler's policy to 1941 against the background of his ideas, favours a much higher degree of consistency than most historians would now be inclined to accept.

9. A comprehensive collection of Hitler speeches, memoranda, and letters to 1925 is being

published by the Institut für Zeitgeschichte and the Historisches Institut, University of Stuttgart.

10. The English version: *The Table Talk of Adolf Hitler 1941-1944*, ed., Hugh Trevor-Roper (London, 1953) is based on Bormann's notes. It has been treated with reserve by many historians because Bormann undoubtedly formulated Hitler's views more sharply for party ends. For a dissenting opinion see N. Rich, *Hitler's War Aims*, 269-70.

11. A study of the role of Ribbentrop and Goering in foreign affairs would be particularly useful; we do not know how far Hitler's disillusionment with Britain was due to Ribbentrop nor why Goering, a powerful figure in the hierarchy in 1939, was unable to do more to restrain Hitler from war.

12. In *Vom Reich zum Weltreich* (München, 1969) K. Hildebrand shows that the colonial movement exerted some influence on Hitler without changing the direction of his policy.

13. The best treatment of the agreement is D. C. Watt, 'The Anglo-German naval agreement of 1935: an interim judgment,' *Journal of Modern History* (Chicago, 1956) written, however, before the publication of the German documents. On the German side W. Malonowski, 'Das deutsch-englische Flottenabkommen vom 18 Juni 1935 als Ausgangspunkt fur Hitlers doktrinäre Bundnispolitik', *Wehrwissenschaftliche Rundschau* (1958).

14. See also C. A. MacDonald, 'Economic appeasement and the German "moderates" 1937-1939. An introductory essay,' *Past and Present* (Oxford, 1972).

15. D. C. Watt, 'German plans for the reoccupation of the Rhineland: a note,' *Journal of Contemporary History* (London, 1966).

16. On economic aspects see G. T. Harper, *German economic policy in Spain during the Spanish Civil War* (The Hague, 1967) and M. Einhorn, *Die ökonomischen Hintergründe der faschistischen deutschen Intervention in Spanien 1936-1939* (Berlin, 1962).

17. H. W. Koch, 'Hitler and the origins of the Second World War: second thoughts on the status of some of the documents,' *Historical Journal* (London, 1968) expresses reservations. The essay is reprinted in E. M. Robertson, ed., *The Origins of the Second World War. Historical Interpretations*. See W. Bussmann, 'Zur Entstehung und Überlieferung der Hossbach Niederschrift,' *Vierteljahrshefte für Zeitgeschichte* (München, 1968) for a convincing defence.

18. The salient facts about Hitler's health are in W. Maser, *Hitler* (1973), though the interpretation placed on them is questionable.

19. Alan Bullock, 'Hitler and the Origins of the Second World War,' *Proceedings of the British Academy*, L, III (1967).

20. L. Hill, 'Three crises 1938-39,' *Journal of Contemporary History* (London, 1968); W. H. C. Frend, 'Hitler and his foreign ministry 1937-1939,' *History* (London, 1957).

21. D. C. Watt's forthcoming study of the year war came may cast some light on Hitler's options in the early months of 1939.

22. This is substantially the thesis of A. Schweitzer, *Big Business in the Third Reich* (London, 1964) who argues that industry, army, and party worked together harmoniously from 1933 to 1936, each deriving benefit from the general expansion of the economy. After 1936, when the economy switched to war preparations, industry and army found themselves subordinate partners in a party-dominated state. Schweitzer's thesis is strongly criticised by the East German historian D. Eichholtz in *Jahrbuch für Wirtschaftsgeschichte*, III (Berlin, 1971).

23. K. Hildebrand, *The foreign policy of the Third Reich*, 146.

24. G. Moltmann, 'Weltherrschaftsideen Hitlers,' in *Europa und Übersee: Festschrift fur E. Zechlin* (Hamburg, 1961).

25. J. M. Wheeler-Bennett, *The nemesis of power*, 702.

26. Gerhard Ritter, 'The military and politics in Germany,' *Journal of Central European Affairs* (Boulder, Colo., 1957).

27. R. O'Neill, *The German army and the Nazi party 1933-1939*, 172.

28. The latest study is Harold Deutsch, *Hitler and his generals. January-June 1938* (1974).

29. On Beck see W. Foerster, *Ein General kämpft gegen den Krieg: aus nachgelassenen Papieren des Generalstabschefs Ludwig Beck* (München, 1949). N. E. Reynolds of Trinity College, Oxford, is preparing a study of him based on new material. On Goerdeler the standard work by G. Ritter is *Carl Goerdeler und die deutsche Widerstandsbewegung* (Stuttgart, 1954; trans., London, 1958).

30. F. Halder, *Hitler as Warlord* (London, 1950); H. Guderian, *Panzer Leader* (London, 1952); Erich von Manstein, *Lost Victories* (London, 1958).

31. B. H. Liddell-Hart, *History of the Second World War* (London, 1970), 66.

32. M. van Creveld, *Hitler's Strategy 1940-1941. The Balkan Clue* (London, 1973) argues that Hitler attached greater importance to the peripheral strategy than is usually believed.

# 4

# National Socialism: Continuity and Change

HANS MOMMSEN

I

Explanations of the national socialist variety of fascism have so far fallen into two categories; one starting from a consideration of the fascist mass movement, the other interpreting the specific features of the National Socialist governmental system. Particularly during the immediate aftermath of World War II, stress was laid on the ideological forebears of national socialism[1] and on attempts, starting in the late thirties, to provide a sociological explanation, which paid especial attention to the radicalization of the lower middle classes during the Weimar Republic.[2] This line of research belongs to the first type of interpretation and usually assumes that the mobilization of people to the fascist cause during the pre-1933 campaign decisively shaped the policies of the National Socialist regime. As against this, almost all Marxist and neo-Marxist theories of fascism start from the realities of fascist dictatorship, conceived, with variations, as the reign of 'finance capitalism.'[3] To a greater or lesser degree, these theories fail, like the original Comintern theory of fascism, in that they take insufficient account of the social causes and the specific manifestations of fascist mass parties.[4] This is also true of the totalitarian dictatorship theory[5] that evolved as early as the war years and was disseminated mainly by German refugees, deriving some indirect support from attempted interpretations by conservative teachers of constitutional law within the Third Reich.[6] Its various forms[7] are pre-eminently based on the national socialist regime, stressing its monolithic and terrorist aspects.[8] Elsewhere a mirror-image reverse of the Comintern theory of fascism, it shares with it the presupposition of a rationally structured government apparatus and of an effective centre of political decision.

Initially, the concept of totalitarian dictatorship served a useful purpose. By replacing the earlier, mainly ideological derivation of National Socialism, it provided a starting point for a comparative study of fascist movements[9] and systems, despite the drawback that parallels drawn (more markedly under the influence of the Cold War) between fascist and bolshevist regimes tended to obscure the specific elements of fascist policies and government. Historical researchers have in consequence largely abandoned this concept as a hindrance to the understanding of the National Socialist regime's antagonistic power structure.[10] Quite apart from this aspect, however, the weakness of such a theoretical starting point was that it gave a somewhat inadequate answer to the question as to which factors were instrumental in the NSDAP's success as a mass movement. The concept of totalitarianism as a definite rational government by a single party was reduced to an ideological syndrome, by which it was assumed that the chief attraction of National Socialist propaganda was essentially to be found in the authoritarian and totalitarian disposition of the population groups to whom it was addressed.[11]

Special emphasis was, however, laid on the plebiscitary and charismatic elements of Hitler's leadership; the 'leadership principle' and the part played by the centralized party structure were made to appear as the trademarks of National Socialist policy. This theory does, it is true, overcome the difficulty that National Socialist *Weltanschauung* was neither consistent nor particularly original: rather it was an eclectic conglomeration of *völkisch* concepts indistinguishable from the programmes of out-and-out nationalist organizations and parties of the imperialist period, or from the ideas of right-wing bourgeois parties during the Weimar era. The interpretation of National Socialism as a Machiavellian technique, tailored to Hitler's personality, for seizing and exercising power may have lent credibility to conservative apologists who have presented National Socialism essentially as 'Hitlerism,' characterized partly by its ruthlessness in the choice and application of political methods and partly by Hitler's own destructive fanaticism.[12]

The totalitarian dictatorship theory may indirectly have taken over a function similar to that of the Comintern analysis of fascism, which started from the premise that the National Socialist regime relied on the effective suppression of the greatest possible number of the people and should therefore be regarded as a specific manifestation of domination by a capitalist elite. Such a view also served to strengthen the hypothesis of a growing resistance among the mass of the people under the leadership of the Communist party.[13] The KPD's obstinate attachment to the slogan of 'social fascism' and its continued struggle against the SPD as the main enemy, even after Hitler's seizure of power, was thereby quietly relegated to the background.[14] At the same time, the totalitarianism theory, with its emphasis on the Machiavellian and demagogic nature of the Hitler regime, favoured the conspiracy of silence about the conservative's share of responsibility in the eventual victory of National Socialism.[15]

Moreover, the totalitarian theory, by equating bolshevism and National Socialism, has stood in the way of a proper understanding of the structural features peculiar to fascist parties. It is undoubtedly true that both Mussolini and Hitler, in developing their own movements, took socialist party movements for their model; the Austrian Christlich-Soziale Partei, too, served Hitler as a pattern. Attempts were also made by the National Socialists to take over some structural elements of the Communist party, such as the system of blocks and cells. The main difference between the NSDAP and the existing parliamentary parties consisted in the substitution of the Leadership Principle for the principle of democratic procedure within the party. At the same time, however, its organizational structure differed widely from the communist principle of democratic centralism which, by preventing the formation of splinter groups among the lower echelons and insisting on their commitment to party decisions, ensured strict obedience to the central leadership. In Communist parties, elections and internal discussions about central issues nevertheless continued to exist at all party levels, including, despite the cult of Stalin, collective decisions as to leadership.

The form of the NSDAP, which evolved in the later twenties under the influence of the central Munich leadership, presented a completely new type of party, fundamentally different both from the Communist and from the traditional democratic parliamentary parties. Simulating, with increasing success, the pattern of nineteenth-century socialist party movements, it deliberately moulded itself into a 'negative' people's party. It neither saw itself as a traditional parliamentary party which would give its followers some kind of share in directing the party's own ideological development, nor did it see its function as the fighting of electoral campaigns, despite its ever-increasing success in this field after 1926. The NSDAP was in essence a political propaganda organization. Party officials and members limited their efforts to making propaganda, to obtaining the means for propaganda, and to representing the party in public, if only by sporting its badge. Since the party's policies were in all essentials established by the central office and the party press, and since any discussion of party matters was regarded as obsolete and a lapse into the despised 'parliamentarianism,' the NSDAP was, as it were, held together from outside, by its own propaganda and, more and more, by a systematically built up Führer cult.[16] Similarly, the aestheticization of politics, a characteristic of fascist movements, served the purpose of externalizing the party; as by the cult of uniforms, the adoption of the völkisch salute, the observance of rituals such as consecration of banners and standards, the hoisting of flags at party rallies and meetings, the development of a peculiar and intentionally spectacular ceremonial, and the predilection for paramilitary demonstrations.[17]

A significant feature of the organizational structure of the NSDAP is the virtual absence of any internal mechanism of integration. Hitler's first accession to power in 1920, with the fusion of the DAP and the NSDAP, was accomplished by means of propaganda meetings rather than by the intervention of the official party leadership; the executive committee was faced with his ultimatum, sanctioned by the acclaim of party audiences at public meetings, as a fait accompli. The leadership principle which replaced the statutory executive was not exclusive to the NSDAP; it took its model from the Alldeutscher Verband and völkisch groups such as the Deutschvölkischer Schutz- und Trutzbund. In the NSDAP, however, it reached an acme of refinement, dispensing with all responsible, even merely advisory, bodies. More and more, NSDAP party rallies lost any other function than to cheer the leader. Whereas at first, some motion or another might have been introduced at local or regional level or sporadic political discussion might have taken place, the party rally eventually became no more than a propaganda platform, a medium for the acclamation of the Führer: even in internal party committees, exchange of political views dwindled. Leadership conferences, which had still retained some importance in the latter half of the twenties, either vanished altogether or were transformed into demonstrations or gatherings whose sole purpose was to receive orders from above. When, in 1928, Hermann Dinter demanded an advisory council for Hitler, party headquarters in Munich saw to it that the motion was unanimously rejected. The Senate Hall in the Brown House was never put to its proper use. Despite honest endeavours by the Reichs Chancellery,[18] Hitler's often-repeated promise to institute a senate or some similar body to elect a leader was never kept.

The intensification of the leadership principle resulted in the absence of any institutional means available to the NSDAP for dealing with conflicts of interest within the party. Such conflicts were, however, inherent in the principle of imposing on party officials a duplicated control — as to their function and by means of discipline — and were further aggravated by the fact that, apart from occasional interference by instructors from head-quarters, there was no effective supervision of section leaders, who were usually appointed from above. Obviously, such a mass organization, bolstered up by an ever-growing bureaucracy and engaged almost exclusively in progaganda activities,[19] was totally unable to cope with the exercise of control and guidance urgently needed after the National Socialist seizure of power.

It follows that the NSDAP, as a political mass organization within the National Socialist regime, became almost devoid of political function and restricted to welfare and training activities; the party as a whole never achieved the role of a central control agency, effectively overseeing both administration and social institutions and directing their policies. Such a theoretical presupposition of totalitarian dictatorship was in line with the Third Reich's self-image rather than with its reality. On the other hand, the political style evolved in the Movement phase and the specific organizational pattern of a dynamic party exclusively devoted to propaganda activities decisively influenced both the process of political decision-making and the internal structure of the National Socialist regime. To this extent, the tension between the elements surviving from the Movement phase and the political requirements of the System phase of National Socialism is of basic importance to any adequate description of the political process within the Third Reich. In consequence, modern comparative fascism theory has introduced an essential criterion in differentiating between the Movement phase and the System phase.[20]

In the main, the model of totalitarian dictatorship evolved from the attempt to explain the relative stability and effectiveness of fascist governments. In the case of the Third Reich, as opposed, say, to the Spanish Falange, successfully subdued by authoritarian groups led by General Franco, the question why the Nazi regime could not curb its plethora of objectives and so achieve lasting stability of the system is at least of equal importance. Surely, Hitler's personal charisma and the role of Nazi ideology can hardly suffice as the sole explanation. The process of cumulative radicalization, hampering any creative reform by the regime, exposing it to early disintegration and eventually to inevitable dissolution from within, cannot simply be ascribed to the effect of ideological factors. The latter may rather be correlated with the regime's specific inability to adjust itself to interim priorities and to find constructive solutions for existing social and political conflicts of interest.[21]

The explanation of the National Socialist regime's relative stability is that, during the Seizure of Power phase, Hitler had been obliged to make far-reaching concessions to the conservative elite controlling the army, economy, and administration, thereby frustrating those elements in the Nazi movement who pressed for total seizure of all social and political institutions. Although indirectly annulled as time went by, these concessions acted as a brake, enabling the regime to consolidate itself with remarkable success before the movement's destructive forces, geared to disintegrate the system of government, could bring about a final overstretching and overtaxing of available resources and the economic bases of power. The root of these forces lay in the movement's own apolitical and millennial dynamics and also in the antagonistic interests among the various groups in the National Socialist leadership. Nevertheless, it was this structure which allowed an unprecedented short-term mobilization of all available political energies to achieve particular political ends, especially in foreign and military policy areas, although the price paid was an epidemic of split political responsibility, an unbounded and increasing antagonism between all power groups and institutions having any say in the political process, and a growing irrationality in political decision-making, which was completely subordinated to the rivalries among the National Socialist leadership elite.[22] In this respect the regime failed to overcome the shortcomings of the Movement phase; the relative stabilization, achieved in 1933-34 with the dismantling of the National Socialist 'revolution,' was in fact nullified by the customary quarrels and conflicts which, exacerbated by the second world war, again broke out within the National

Socialist movement. The leadership rivalries during the last weeks of the Third Reich were a characteristic expression of this development, arising from the inner logic of fascist policies.[23]

## II

Central to contemporary historical research is the elucidation of the social and political causes of the NSDAP's breakthrough as a mass movement. Marxist interpretations tend to underrate the fact that substantial big business support for the NSDAP, if indeed there was any, occurred only after the September 1930 elections,[24] when it had managed to become the second largest parliamentary party with 18.3 per cent of the vote. Consequently, tentative 'agent' theories miss the point of the problem. Contrary to current belief, the NSDAP's rise was by no means uninterrupted. Anton Drexler's Deutsche Arbeiterpartei, set up with the support of the völkisch organizations and the Bavarian Reichswehr, had at first been an insignificant splinter group; it achieved regional importance after the early twenties as the NSDAP under Hitler's leadership. The rise of the party was linked with the nationalist restoration countermovement following the defeat of the Munich Soviet Republic, within the counterrevolutionary climate of the Bavarian capital, marked by the illegal activities of the subsequently disbanded Freikorps and Heimwehr organizations.[25]

In the crisis year of 1923 the NSDAP, absorbing the nationalist völkisch groups in Munich and some parts of Bavaria, was able to enlist 55,000 more members and to extend its organizational activities to Württemberg, Baden, and northern Germany. As it became involved in plots to overthrow the government, engineered by authoritarian Bavarian groups associated with Captain Ehrhardt and Erich Ludendorff, Hitler attempted to enforce his leadership by staging the Beer Hall Putsch. Following the failure of the march on the Feldherrenhalle, Hitler's arrest and sentence, and the proscription of the party, NSDAP membership suffered a sharp decline.[26] The North German NSDAP and surrogate organizations, such as Alfred Rosenberg's Grossdeutsche Volksgemeinschaft and Julius Streicher's Franconian Deutsche Arbeiterpartei, ensured continuity of the organization, although competition arose from von Graefe's Deutschvölkische Freiheitspartei, which was for a time joined by part of the successor organizations to form the Nationalsozialistische Freiheitspartei.[27] Hitler's adroit move in re-establishing the NSDAP and driving Ludendorff into political isolation by supporting his hopeless candidature for the Reich presidency in 1925, enabled him to assume unquestioned leadership of the party. In this he was assisted by the Führer mythology, built up to a peak of elaboration, particularly by Hermann Essler, during Hitler's imprisonment in Landsberg Fortress. To obtain control, Hitler had to grant independence for a time to a federation of Gauleiters in northwest Germany who, however, never managed to dislodge the power monopoly of the Munich branch and, although they deprecated the opportunism of the Munich leadership, lacked the ideological consistency to prevail against it.[28]

Despite continued legal harassment, the NSDAP made remarkable strides during the 1925 through 1928 phase, membership rising from 27,000 to 108,000. Electoral success, however, did not keep pace: during the May 1928 Reichstag elections, the NSDAP suffered a crushing defeat, obtaining only 2.6 per cent of the vote. For a time the party was proscribed and, in Prussia, Hitler was forbidden to speak until 1928; that these prohibitions were lifted must be taken in conjunction with the general opinion that the party had lost all parliamentary influence. The contradiction between a flourishing of the organization and a lack of electoral success during the decisive phase of consolidation is explicable by the absorption into the party at that time of the potential adherents of their former competitors, the völkisch associations and especially the Deutsch-Völkische Freiheitspartei.[29] Extreme racial anti-Semitism, with its implied resentment of capitalism, and the uncompromising anti-parliamentarianism of National Socialist propaganda ensured a monopoly for the NSDAP within the völkisch movement. No genuine mass basis, however, could be gained in this way; what was needed was the penetration of large sectors of the bourgeois-conservative electorate.[30]

From the end of 1928 onward, however, that is, even before the devastating effects of the world economic crisis had been felt in Germany, the NSDAP enjoyed rapid growth, culminating in considerable success in the local elections of 1929 and thereafter in the breakthrough of September 1930. Evidently this turning-point was not preceded by any basic change in National Socialist propaganda, as Dietrich Orlow has suggested, but thereafter National Socialist propaganda was intensified in rural areas and middle-sized towns. This does not mean a deliberate break with an alleged 'urban plan.'[31] NSDAP invasion of the bourgeois centre and right-wing parties—the Zentrum alone was almost totally immune to fascist infiltration—presupposes the beginnings of doubt among bourgeois middle-of-the-road voters as to the efficiency of their political representation, particularly in relation to the protection of middle-class and agrarian interests. One indication of this process is the growing importance of parties, such as the Wirtschaftspartei, standing for bourgeois middle-class interests; this led to splinter groups, particularly among the conservative organizations, and to a multiplication of parties in general. The political undermining of the centre and right-wing parties must be seen in the light of increasing anti-parliamentarian tendencies during the phase of bourgeois party coalition governments.

Recent publications, including Jeremy Noakes's excellent study,[32] point out that during this phase, the NSDAP, here and there allied to the DNVP and DVP, succeeded in invading the political infrastructure of the bourgeois parties at the local level (the Zentrum again excepted), at the same time obtaining a decisive influence over bourgeois and agrarian pressure groups. This applied to every kind of middle-class organization, as well as to the Reichslandbund. With the memory of November 1918 in mind, Walther Darré's 'agrarian political apparatus' had originally been set up to forestall a possible agricultural boycott and the ensuing collapse of food supplies in the event of a revolutionary take-over by the NSDAP. By this strategic move, coupled with preliminary 'packing' of local groups followed by propaganda pressure on their central leadership, the agrarian organizations were successfully subverted.[33]

Through their growing influence in bourgeois and agrarian bodies and local tie-ups with the DNVP, the National Socialists were assured not only of increasingly favourable treatment by the right-wing nationalist press but also of a measure of respect from bourgeois groups, previously repelled by the political rowdiness of the party and particularly the SA. Hitler's about-turn after Landsberg towards strict legality, in the formal sense, and his far-reaching concessions to capitalist notions, did not mean that party propaganda ceased at the same time to use pseudo-socialist slogans to win over marginal groups from the SPD. Under the pretext that a united front was needed to combat the 'Marxist' parties, strenuous efforts were later made to secure all vital key positions for NSDAP officials. The consequent mobilization of voters, especially of agrarian groups, ensured the NSDAP's tactical error in giving it a share in the agitation for a plebiscite against the Young Plan.

The conquest of the bourgeois infrastructure, at the end of the National Socialist phase of consolidation, simultaneously linked with the perfecting of both the National Socialist propaganda machine and the vast local and regional bureaucratic organization of the party, was one of the most important social preconditions for its seemingly irresistible momentum up to mid-1932.

Moreover, the NSDAP's undoubted attraction for younger people was an important socio-psychological factor.[34] At that time, Ludwig Kaas was appointed leader of the Zentrum, the DNVP's chairmanship passed from Westarp to Hugenberg, opposition to Stresemann's policies was increasing on the DVP right wing, and later on the DDP was transformed into the Deutsche Staatspartei. In this way, all the bourgeois parties were displaying a tendency towards the strengthening of traditional ideological alignments, whereas attempts at revision in the intermediate parties — Volkskonservative, Jungdeutscher Orden, and Christlich-Sozialer Volksdienst — met with no success. The rift between the generations was thereby widened: the high-level political leadership of the Weimar Republic, including the Social Democrats, were striving to regain their respective pre-war political positions; while the younger generation in all political camps, to whom the Kaiser's era and the world war meant only post-war privations and inflation, endeavoured to create new political styles and structures. Young people were thirsting for a new political perspective, offering something more than a return to 1913: the desire for a new German future was, however, systematically and with growing success exploited by the NSDAP to recruit young members and voters. The unfavourable age structure of the SPD and the bourgeois parties (except the Zentrum, which drew its support from the broad spectrum of Catholic organizations) clearly showed their lack of political attraction for the younger generation,[35] whereas the age structure of the NSDAP, and to some extent that of the KPD, showed a decided tendency towards a decreasing age level. Whilst the traditional bourgeois youth movement had already become outdated,[36] the NSDAP profited from the need of large sectors of bourgeois youth for political integration and commitment to forward-looking policies.

Up to the summer of 1932, the NSDAP drew roughly a third of its gains in voting strength from former DNVP and DVP voters, another third from young voters, and the remainder from those who had previously abstained.[37] Nevertheless, its influence on working-class youth was limited; possibly it was only effective on young trainees, unable to begin their working life because of mass unemployment, and therefore never having been exposed to trade union influence, whether independent or Christian. Although the NSDAP had succeeded in transforming itself into a mass movement, it could not achieve an overall landslide; both Catholic areas and urban centres displayed a marked immunity to National Socialist propaganda.[38] The consequences of the world economic crisis exacerbated the situation. Not only mass unemployment but also the social disorientation of middle-class groups, aggravated by the crisis and the lowering of wages and incomes, particularly affected employees, minor officials, and small traders. The comparatively passive acceptance by Social Democrats and the Zentrum of Brüning's deflationary policies reinforced these socio-psychological effects and the desire for a fundamental change of direction in German politics. At the same time, the anti-Marxist propaganda by right-wing parties, clearly shown by William Sheridan Allen,[39] coupled with the growing polarization among the parties and the increase in communist voting strength, acted in favour of the NSDAP, which, for instance, now attacked the von Papen government's capitalism and the SPD's passive, and therefore pro-capitalist, attitude during the crisis. By this means it was to a large extent able to mobilize in its own favour the resentment among non-socialists against capitalism, revived by the economic crisis, and at the same time gain the sympathies of part of the army and a number of industrial magnates. These men, fearing a serious threat to the capitalist structure from recently intensified left-wing demands for nationalization, intended to use the NSDAP as auxiliaries on this particular front, even though in other respects they had strong reservations about it and fully supported von Papen's idea of a 'new state.'

Impressed by its extraordinarily rapid growth after 1928, the public viewed the NSDAP as an irresistible force. Propaganda manoeuvres deliberately stressed this aspect; incessant skirmishing kept all party members constantly on the move and the NSDAP seemed to be everywhere at once.[40] By innumerable individual actions, meetings, rallies, and also by systematic provocation of terrorist incidents, the party leadership achieved an approximate imitation of traditional Socialist party movements. Even during the Regime phase, mass rallies, processions, and well-rehearsed public appearances by the Führer were used to give an impression of a party based on mass support, an impression confirmed by the plebiscites of 12 November 1933 and 19 August 1934.[41] As a consequence, the mass-movement nature of the NSDAP and the plebiscitary foundation of Hitler's rule have been greatly over-estimated, even up to the present day.

Closer analysis of the membership and voting patterns, however, puts a different complexion on the matter. Prior to 30 January 1933, sharp fluctuations in membership occurred; this to a lesser extent was also true of the KPD. Out of 239,000 members joining before 14 September 1930, only 44 per cent were still in the party by early 1935; at that time, the membership was 2,494,000, but another 1,506,000 had already left the party.[42] Even though the statistical data available permit no absolutely precise deductions to be made, it is virtually certain that the NSDAP could not permanently assimilate its mass following to any significant extent, apart from a small, predominately middle-class hard core. From this it is reasonable to conclude that the mass-movement aspect of the NSDAP was a transient phenomenon, for the millionfold membership of the Regime phase can scarcely be ascribed to actual political mobilization, but rather to the need to conform. What is known of the violent fluctuations within the corps of political leaders,[43] too, suggests that the organization's mass character was preserved only by the petrifaction of the largely depoliticized party apparatus and by massive political pressure.

Researches so far carried out, especially Heberle's and Stoltenberg's studies of Schleswig-Holstein,[44] throw some doubt upon Seymour Martin Lipset's argument that in the main National Socialism represented a revolt by formerly liberal sectors of the middle class.[45] Rather, the NSDAP succeeded in penetrating various fields of voting potential, without, however, effecting more than a temporary capture. Agrarian voters, the mainstay of the party's electoral success in September 1930, had for the greater part already defected by the November 1932 elections. The false impression of a popular movement was given by the fact that various social and professional groups — not industrial workers nor the stalwarts among the Zentrum voters — joined the NSDAP for a time, only to fall off again fairly rapidly. Confirmation for this may be seen in the NSDAP's internal crisis at the end of 1932, especially in the decreasing commitment among members.[46] Under the influence of the economic crisis, a simultaneous bandwagon effect masked this tendency, and is sufficient, quite apart from exploitation of anti-Communist tendencies and political pressure, to explain, if not diminish, the electoral success of 5 March 1933.

In view of the NSDAP's internal inconsistency and its inability to mobilize little more than a third of the electorate, Hitler's appointment (as a result of von Papen's intrigues against Schleicher) as Chancellor of a Cabinet of National Concentration, assumed major importance. Whereas Gregor Strasser had urged the adoption of a constructive policy, Hitler's obstinacy in demanding vital key positions in a presidential government now reaped its political reward. Whether Hitler sensed that, in view of the cracks within the National Socialist movement, a partial success would be tantamount to defeat is a matter which might repay closer investigation. In any event, it should be emphasized that the National Socialist share in the governments of Brunswick and Thuringia had led to disillusion among the electors and a fall in voting strength.[47] To that extent, Brüning's tactics of allowing the NSDAP to fritter away its strength in various *Länder* coalitions are shown to have been correct in principle, however problematical a Zentrum-NSDAP coalition might have been.[48] Apart from this, however, the NSDAP — as has been repeatedly stressed — would have suffered considerable losses in any further electoral campaign. Goebbels was quite aware that the party's success depended on the maintenance of its propaganda dynamic: his sceptical feeling that the NSDAP would, in electoral terms, 'kill itself with winning,'[49] since no outward success in the form of any responsible share of government was forthcoming, throws some light on the critical situation before the turning point engineered by von Papen came at the end of December 1932.

## III

Seldom has any party been so unprepared for political power as was the NSDAP on 30 January 1933.[50] Basically, their objectives did not go beyond a political power monopoly. Some sporadic groundwork, it is true, had been carried out at central and Gau headquarters as a preliminary to a possible achievement of power. It had not progressed very far and was primarily concerned with measures to safeguard power once it had been obtained. Draft legislation for a prospective National Socialist government, such as there was, had been produced by outsiders.[51] In addition, the Nazi leadership had envisaged the setting up of a comprehensive indoctrination machinery, which was to be realized only imperfectly in the Ministry for Public Enlightenment and Propaganda.[52] No model for the construction of a state was contained in the Boxheim documents, they merely sketched extensive measures for eliminating political adversaries and dealt with a transition period before National Socialist rule should have become stable. The institutional form of such rule was visualized in contradictory terms. Opinions were united on the necessity of removing the parliamentary system; middle-class tradesmen and skilled workers in particular welcomed endeavours at that time to replace parliamentarianism by corporate order. Nowhere, however, not even in the leadership circles closest to Hitler, were there any clear ideas as to the nature of a National Socialist state. Hitler had referred in *Mein Kampf* to the transfer of the National Socialist party organization to the state, but without going into details.[53] How this could be put into practice remained to be seen. The party, almost exclusively bent on propaganda, had adopted a political style in which all options remained open and decisions were dealt with ad hoc.

Moreover, the quasi-legal seizure of power, achieved on 30 January 1933, had come as a complete surprise. The party as a whole had always believed that its accession to power would in some way be linked with the suppression of a communist rising and would therefore be revolutionary. Presidential government politics had offered the alternative of a pseudo-legal seizure of power through the existing constitution and by strategic use of the parliamentary system for the party's own purposes. A majority within the party regarded the formation of a Cabinet of National Concentration and the elimination of the Reichstag by means of the Enabling Act as preliminaries to the achievement of total power. They expected complete revolutionary change, analogous to the November Revolution of 1918, without, however, any clear idea of its eventual form and aims. When Goebbels called the formation of the government on 30 January 1933 a 'national' and later a 'National Socialist' *revolution*, it was not simply a stroke of propaganda to justify the NSDAP's immediate usurpation of power positions supposedly under constitutional safeguard; its aim was also to appease the mass following of the movement. Goebbels remarked that it was extremely difficult to lead the movement out of its previous frenzy into the legality of the National Socialist state.[54] He interpreted the process of *Gleichschaltung*, accelerated after March 1933, as a revolutionary act and maintained that 'the German revolution had been carried out from below and not from above.'[55] To the same end, Hitler and Frick repeatedly vowed in the summer of 1933 that the National Socialist revolution had been completed, adding the assurance that complete Gleichschaltung of state and society would be introduced by legal means.

Party supporters, however, regarded the seizure of power and the marriage with the apparatus of state—Goebbels spoke of it as the 'last stage of a revolutionary act'[56]—as a further stage in the progress of a revolutionary act and not at all as its termination. Hitler's alliance with the traditional army, civil service, and economic elites seemed to them a tactically motivated transition state, beyond which lay the party's undivided mastery.

Corroboration for this view was provided by the agreement made prior to the seizure of power that National Socialist holders of government appointments should also retain their party appointments.[57] Party veterans (*Alte Kämpfer*) and active members of the SA, in particular, still clung to their expectations of revolution and readiness to fight in its cause; they dreamt of the day when the NSDAP and the SA would comprise virtually the whole of the population and replace the existing social order.[58] In fact, the evolving National Socialist system of government was necessarily rather tentative and temporary in nature, characterized as it was by the tension between the old institutions and the superimposed areas of government by party elites. In some National Socialist cadres, there still survived the utopian idea of a future more radical new order, although without any definite programme for this; the conviction that a truly National Socialist state would yet be built was once again revived during World War II. At first, local party organizations imagined that they were carrying out the wishes of the leadership by arbitrary action on their own account: they needed no sophisticated combination of revolutionary measures from below and sanctioning legislation from above, even though, during the process of seizing power, such tactics might have proved highly effective.[59] Except for the SA under Ernst Roehm, the party acquiesced in national disciplinary measures, though sometimes with reluctance.

Only against the background of the myth of the National Socialist movement's final victory can the reality of the Third Reich be interpreted. The party, as an organization of the whole people, became more and more politically expendable, to the same degree as its membership rose to several million, before the May 1933 clampdown on new enrolments. It was, as it were, fixed in its Movement phase structure; in consequence, clashes intensified between the divergent regional, social, and economic interests represented in the NSDAP and its affiliated organizations, nor was there any apparent possibility of reconciling these interests. Conflicts first appeared in the field of social Gleichschaltung, although this was a continuation of party policy prior to 30 January. Predictably, party officials at all levels sought compensation for the party's dwindling influence on central decisions and were at pains to build up subsidiary power positions.

In Spring 1933 the need for a renewed electoral campaign mounted with vast expenditure of effort, masked the party's atrophy of function. In Prussia, Gleichschaltung had been well prepared and anticipated the total seizure of power elsewhere. This sparked off Gleichschaltung within the Länder, even before the March 1933 elections, and to the party it predominantly appeared as a tactical manoeuvre to facilitate the intended suppression of left-wing parties by means of controlling the police. Moreover, the Reichstag fire gave the National Socialists a chance to anticipate the Enabling Act by declaring a state of civil emergency; the emergency decrees of 28 February, despite the qualifications of Goering's[60] imple-

menting ordinance, amounted in effect to such a declaration.[61] While the
original strategy had foreseen the act as the starting point for the acquisi-
tion of total power and the elimination of conservative competition, it
would now set the seal of legality on National Socialist rule. In fact, the
aura of legitimacy conferred by the election results had already been used
by the government to initiate a mounting stream of ever harsher elimination measures.

Yet again, and for the last time, were the energies of the movement
committed to the actions by which first the SPD and the trade unions, and
then the bourgeois parties and associations (including the Stahlhelm) were
eliminated, and which must be considered as a continuation of an electoral
campaign rife with repression and propaganda.[62] For the radical elements
of the NSDAP, this heightened activity carried with it the vague hope of a
'second revolution.' Disappointment at the absence of a decisive change
and at the waning of NSDAP influence in local and regional sectors was
expressed in a growing irritation with governmental bureaucracy. An outlet was, however, provided by the exercise of patronage in official appointments, particularly in local government posts. For the SA, with its growing
numbers and insufficient funds, there was on the whole no such outlet,
since Roehm, for tactical reasons, strongly objected to simultaneous tenure
of party and government positions. Small wonder then that the SA,
although its social composition differed little from that of the NSDAP, was
the focus of discontent manifesting itself in the call for a 'second revolution.' Under pressure from Goering and Frick, it had been obliged to surrender its function as an auxiliary police force and to a large extent
abandon the Commissar system.[63] Apart from the rancorous Bavarians,[64]
the SA had no place in the evolving power structure of the regime; Hitler,
believing an alliance with the Reichswehr leaders to be essential, was determined to curb Roehm's military ambitions, whose aim was to make the
Reichswehr equal or subordinate to the projected SA People's Army. Once
Gleichschaltung was complete, the SA lost all function in power politics.
On 30 June 1934, as a result of intrigues by Himmler and Goering and
from fear of a counter-coup by the conservatives, the final blow was delivered, precipitately and at grave risk to the prestige of the regime.[65] In the
eyes of the public, the SA's fall opened the way for a stable form of
government.

Measures to supplant Länder autonomy and to institute structural
reform of the Reich were introduced by the Ministry of the Interior, at first
in emulation of Prussia. Though initially ambiguous,[66] their purpose was
to end or at least control the overlaps in areas of competence, particularly
the usurpation of official positions, which stemmed from the ideology of
the Movement phase. At local government level, this was achieved by the
introduction of the *Deutsche Gemeindeordnung* (German Local Government Order) of 1935, with its far-reaching concessions, counterbalanced

however by a tightening of the state's supervisory powers. It is common knowledge that no such success was forthcoming at the level of the controversial 'intermediate government' because of opposition among the Gauleiters, who either favoured particularism or were anxious to protect their personal authority. This is not the place for an account of the often-quoted defeat — foreseeable at an early stage and finally brought about in 1942 — of the Ministry of the Interior's attempts to build up some kind of rational state structure.[67] Frick's endeavours are known to have foundered not least because of Hitler himself and his characteristic rejection, partly influenced by legal considerations, of the suggestion that a Reichs Constitution should replace the Enabling Act. Further, Hitler prevented any attempt to assist him by introducing a legislative senate, or even a senate whose sole function would be to elect the Führer, although this would have been a source of political unification, after the cabinet as an integrating influence had lost all power and fallen into desuetude.[68] The question here is rather how far a perpetuation of specific elements of the Movement phase was responsible for the National Socialist regime's metamorphosis, so often described, into an antagonistic and chaotic rivalry of individual power blocs, which it would be an oversimplification to call a dualism of party and state.

For a true internal stabilization of the regime, fundamental reorganization of the NSDAP was a prerequisite, and Hitler was neither ready nor in a position to carry this out. He saw the NSDAP as a driving force on which to rely should the state apparatus fail or oppose him. At one time, the Ministry of the Interior debated whether the party should again become an elite body entrusted with the selection of political leaders. The position of the Gauleiters, answerable only to the Führer, made this impossible.. The Law to Safeguard Unity of State and Party (December 1933) granted wide autonomy to the party but deprived it of all real political function. Even before this, Hitler as Chancellor had largely neglected the duties of the party leader; the appointment of Rudolf Hess as Deputy Führer intensified the incessant rivalry among the NSDAP's top rank. Hess proved quite inadequate as de facto head of the party, which promptly split into myriad widely-separated power blocs and competing organizations.[69]

While the SS managed to take over a number of functions within the state and so gradually to acquire an all-important position of power in the regime, ultimately monopolizing political control,[70] the NSDAP itself was confined more and more to non-political social work. Significantly, its highest ambition was to supplant the local priest. Consequently, leading party members idealized the institution of the Catholic Church.[71] Propaganda duties, hitherto the main task of the party, were now taken over by the Reichs Propaganda Ministry which, in a typical fusion of state and party machinery, assumed direct control over the NSDAP propaganda sections. Political indoctrination work was still left to the party, but even here it was faced with competition from Alfred Rosenberg and the Deutsche

Arbeitsfront.[72] As a result, the party organization per se became more and more depoliticized and incapable of integrating divergent community interests. Languishing behind the lines, it might well regret the gradual loss of its vaunted 'common touch' and its growing inability to bridge the gaps—Hess deplored the 'vacuum' between leadership and grass roots.[73]

To curb the prevalent opportunism and increasing bureaucratic inflexibility, the NSDAP would have needed to absorb the independently administered positions of political power as they stood. Instead, the principle of simultaneous tenure of state and party office led to an ever-tightening grip on the party by officialdom, the loss of many party functionaries who preferred state to party employment, and indirectly to progressive depoliticization. Many foreign observers, impressed by well-organized mass rallies and plebiscitary support for the system, took it for granted that the NSDAP as a political mass organization exerted an authoritative radicalizing influence on decision-making; yet, in fact, it was increasingly condemned to political sterility.[74]

Political importance resided not in the party but rather in high-ranking party officials who used their position as a steppingstone to the usurpation of public office and functions of state. Only the personal drive of the men concerned determined how far they were able to interfere in local or regional affairs; significantly, party influence at local level varied to a remarkable degree with the political forces involved.[75] Even in the Third Reich, effective political ascendancy depended on holding public office. Party officials, unless they took on some additional state assignment, remained more or less impotent. Notably, Martin Bormann's growing preeminence was due far less to his immensely strong personal position within the party than to his success, through the office of Deputy Führer and later through the Party Chancellery, in ensuring for himself a monopoly of control over the legislation, although total mastery of the Gauleiter group eluded him. The function of the Party Chancellery as a co-ordinating ministry in competition with the Reichs Chancellery gave him a further chance to dominate subsidiary party apparatus—often over the heads of the Gauleiters; despite this, he never quite managed to turn the party into a true channel of executive power.[76]

Similarly, Himmler's power stemmed from the fusion of the offices of Reichsführer SS and Chief of German Police, although in the latter position he was nominally subordinate to Frick. As Reichs Commissar for the consolidation of the German *Volkstum*, he was able to neutralize the authority of the Ministry of the Interior in the annexed and occupied territories up to 1943, when he himself became head of the ministry and could further erode its jurisdiction for the benefit of the Reichssicherheitshauptamt.[77] Again, Robert Ley's influence as head of the NSDAP Reichs Organization was reinforced by his simultaneous leadership of the Deutsche

Arbeitsfront, numerically and financially far and away the strongest mass organization in the Third Reich.

The much-discussed enmity between different offices in the Third Reich arose largely because the party organization, while not troubling itself to integrate them politically, lent a veneer of legality to the usurpation of public office by National Socialist party officials, a practice which Frick had only temporarily been able to hold in check. Moreover, the party itself exemplified the progressive fragmentation of political competence and responsibility which finally led to the loss of political rationality and the disintegration of the regime. Whilst the NSDAP as a mass organization declined into political sterility, party officials, first and foremost the Gauleiters, persistently created spheres of influence for themselves, so establishing a system of patronage and cliques. The strictly personal concept of politics, absence of respect for institutions, pretensions to the guardianship of the movement's true interests, the party's susceptibility to corruption—these were the contributory causes for the transformation of the national socialist government system into a tangle of personal interdependence, clashing governmental machinery, disputed claims to fields of competence and the unbridled arbitrary rule of each man for himself among the Nazi elite.

IV

Leadership rivalries, internal power struggles, and the eventual self-disintegration of the regime have been ascribed to Hitler's basic Social Darwinist ideas, coupled with his multiplication of areas of competence in order to consolidate his own position as supreme arbiter and at the same time to bring his own ends nearer to achievement. Hitler was undeniably motivated by Social Darwinism; nevertheless, the question remains how far he himself felt obliged to make his position, by that time incontestable, even more secure by putting this mechanism into action. Tim Mason has pointed out Hitler's continual uncertainty as to popular reactions, particularly those of the workers, and Alan Milward has shown that fear of unpopularity induced him to relegate measures for the prosecution of total war to the background. [78] Nevertheless, he certainly did not see his position threatened by any organization, however powerful. Hitler never impeded the ascendancy of the SS; on the contrary, he emphatically supported it, evidenced by his appointment of Thierack as Reichs Minister of Justice. [79] Furthermore, apart from interference with the judiciary, Hitler usually intervened only if potentates of the regime had put pressure on him. Peterson makes the down-to-earth comment that Hitler's disinclination to determine priorities often arose more from a sense of inadequacy and a truly characteristic hesitancy, than from simple lack of interest. [80] Accordingly,

his escape into Social Darwinism when faced with the need to resolve conflicts can hardly be called a rational pattern of decision on the lines of
*divide et impera.*

Throughout his reign, Hitler was fearful of institution-backed power; he
certainly never displayed the slightest understanding of any attempts
towards setting it up. His aversion from any institutional restriction may
indeed be explained by the circumstances of his life; in some respects an
element of personal insecurity seems to be involved. His call for assent by
plebiscite to his union of the Chancellorship and Presidency may have been
due in part to some similar over-caution in domestic politics; in the main,
however, the plebiscite was held for reasons of foreign policy and therefore
of propaganda, in order to strengthen the government. In this it was undoubtedly successful. Hitler resigned as party leader but transferred his
accustomed style of political leadership to the affairs of state. This meant
concentration on matters of current priority, combined with utter neglect
not only of routine business but also of all long-term problems. In February
1933 he told Sefton Delmer that there was nothing at all to the business of
governing.[81]

Instead of acting as a balancing element in the government, Hitler disrupted the conduct of affairs, partly by continually acting on sudden
impulses, each one different, and partly by delaying decisions on current
matters. His totally unbureaucratic type of leadership, nothing being dealt
with in writing, his frequent absences from Berlin, his utter lack of contact
with departmental ministers, his dependence on advice from outsiders
(often given by chance-comers and usually incompetent), and his dismissal
of officialdom as too unwieldy to carry out political necessities — all this
gave his government an aura of instability and sometimes of self-contradic-
tion. As party leader, he had always avoided early intervention in quarrels
within the party, not wishing to put the loyalties of lower-rank leaders at
risk. By deliberately remaining impartial in the policy dispute between the
party leaders in Munich and the Gauleiters of northwest Germany, and
restricting himself to tactical measures, he preserved the many facets of the
party programme, opening the way for the bandwagon of the early thirties.
Not only that, he also stabilized his position of leadership as a unifying
force and the symbolic representative of the whole movement.

And all this was not merely the outcome of Machiavellian deliberation,
but rather of Hitler's experience as a propagandist. As Chancellor and
President of the Reich — significantly, he refrained from using the latter
title — he had no real need to consolidate his power by such means. He
avoided all measures which might have been considered inconsistent or an
admission of earlier mistakes. He balked at breaking with men who had
held leading positions in the movement or the state; he appointed Baron
von Neurath President of the Privy Council, he delayed dealing with Frick's
resignation. To part from Gauleiters cost him a severe inner struggle; and

it was only after a virtual ultimatum from Goering and Himmler that he assented to Roehm being shot. Creation of double and triple competencies was the inevitable consequence. 'The principle of letting things take their course until the stronger man has won the day,'[82] which the Gauleiter of Weser-Ems called the 'secret of the movement's astounding development and achievement,' in short that Social Darwinism so often attributed to Hitler, hardly ever brought about the absolute elimination of the loser. The alleged logic of the Social Darwinist style of leadership, therefore, failed to achieve its full effect, since victor and vanquished might still change places. Karl Dietrich Bracher sees this aspect of the Third Reich as intentional: 'The antagonism between rival agencies was resolved only in the omnipotent key position of the Führer. But precisely herein and not in the functioning of the state as such lay the profound purpose of an "integration" that was by no means complete. For the key position of the dictator derived precisely from the complex coexistence and opposition of the power groups and from conflicting ties.'[83] Unquestionably, this was the case. Increasingly relieved from the actual duties of leadership, particularly during the last months of the Third Reich, Hitler remained throughout the point of reference for all the rival power blocs. The question is, however, whether a personalized interpretation, hinging on Hitler's attempts to consolidate his absolute leadership, can suffice; a Machiavellian enjoyment of power would seem to imply rough handling of subordinate leaders, but, on the contrary, Hitler exerted himself to win them over by forceful oratory and personal appeals, with marked success. The ruthless action demanded from his subordinates, which he himself practised by arbitrary interference in jurisdiction and elsewhere, contrasts somewhat with his extremely careful manipulations whenever he felt his personal prestige to be at risk. The common denominator of these two attitudes was his reliance on propaganda. No quarter towards political adversaries had long been one of Hitler's propaganda maxims, qualified by the characteristic proviso never to get involved with a superior enemy: on matters of prestige, however, he advocated the greatest flexibility.

As Chancellor, therefore, Hitler personified the specific political style which had ensured the movement's success. One aspect of this was the postponement of decisions on political priorities, for the sake of tactical flexibility: even after 1933, Hitler did his utmost to avoid hard-and-fast political rulings wherever possible. A side effect of this tendency was to obscure the real intentions of the National Socialist leadership, however often they might be displayed in all their ambiguity. As dictator, Hitler still obeyed the maxims of the successful publicity man: to concentrate on the aims of the moment, to profess unshakable determination to achieve them, and to use parallel strategies, heedless of the political consequences resulting from the inevitable inter-institutional friction entailed. When he spoke, time and again, of the need to inspire the masses with a close-knit ideology and a fanatical will to fight, it was from a genuine belief in the superiority of a publicity campaign to a totalitarian, and hence necessarily pragmatic, organization. His insuperable dislike for any form of bureaucracy must be seen in this context, as must his emphasis on a principle of 'leadership of men,' which caused him to despise all administrative activity, and which led to the fiction of a 'government without administration.'[84] Playing off rival power blocs against one another was not so much a matter of securing his own omnipotence, but rather for the satisfaction of an instinctive need to reward all and any fanatical pursuit of an end, no matter whether institutionally fixed competencies were ignored or whether, an advantage having been gained, its bureaucratic safeguards were sacrificed to overt dynamics.

Such an attitude had, in the days of campaigning, allowed total mobilization of the movement; once a full-scale dictatorship had been established, however, it engendered substantial losses as a result of friction, as well as a lack of objective efficiency. Overall meddling and unbureaucratic 'leadership of men,' coupled with a chronic underrating of professional skill, led to an uncontrolled hegemony of personal patronage at all levels, to the spread of corruption and denunciations, and to total fragmentation of political decision-making. The cabinet soon lost all importance and did not meet after 1938; party leader meetings were sporadic and little more than a claque; the nominal Reichs leadership of the NSDAP was an uncoordinated bureaucratic apparatus devoid of real power. In short, no formal mechanism leading to integration was in existence. In its absence, clashes of interest within the party were of necessity settled by intrigue and horse-trading, so that all conflicts inevitably sank to the personal level. Significantly, the National Socialist leadership evolved the naive premise that, by picking the right men, the ubiquitous petty frictions could be obviated, although in fact the clashes were structurally inherent. For the system to function, the Führer would have had to fix the political guidelines and give his casting vote on matters of principle; this, however, was the exception rather than the rule and when it did occur, it was always too late. An atmosphere of personal distrust among the leaders of the Third Reich was unavoidable.

Researchers into this period frequently assert that, in the last instance, Hitler was the invariable driving force pushing the regime into a progressive radicalization of its aims and thereby overtaxing its strength.[85] The point is repeatedly made that, despite some tactical flexibility now and then, he pursued and achieved the fixed objectives already set out in *Mein Kampf*.[86] Such an interpretation, based solely on ideology, is necessarily open to considerable objections. Schoenbaum has demonstrated that, precisely in the field of domestic policies, National Socialist achievements were, in many cases, the exact opposite of the original intentions.[87] It is questionable, too, whether National Socialist foreign policy can be considered as an unchanging pursuit of established priorities. Hitler's foreign policy aims, purely dynamic in nature, knew no bounds; Joseph Schumpeter's reference to 'expansion without object' is entirely justified.[88] For this very reason, to interpret their implementation as in any way consistent or logical is highly problematic.

One question above all others remains open: how was it possible that remote and fantastic aims should suddenly be brought within easy reach? In reality, the regime's foreign policy ambitions were many and varied, without any clear aims and only linked by the ultimate goal: hindsight alone gives them some air of consistency.[89] In domestic politics, the question is more easily answered. The specific style of leadership, largely based on postponement of decisions and delay in defining fundamental priorities necessarily led to a diminishing sense of reality. The leadership's one-sided attitude was reflected in highly coloured reports and hand-picked information; but impressionistic reportages could never replace hard news as an ingredient in the formation of public opinion.[90] Increasing blindness to reality was the result. Political decision-making was more and more influenced by personal ambitions and official corruption, and took on the irrational guise of non-institutional power struggles between the clients of state and party patronage. In place of the civil service, there was an overt system of competitive ruling cliques which, while using existing institutions to bolster up their own power, were at the same time parasitically eroding them. The merry-go-round of changing potentials for influence revolved about the dictator, who in his turn followed a policy of balance between divergent political interests, not so much by pragmatic compromise as by reference either to objectives in the far distant future or to those which were immediate and short-term. In this way, any vestige of political stability was dissipated as soon as it was achieved. In this context, Martin Broszat has referred to the 'negative selection of some elements of *Weltanschauung*' activated by this system.[91]

Wherever massive interests of the various power blocs conflicted, no viable solution was to be found. Any initial attempts towards positive reorganization were sacrificed to an unbridled clash of social interests, clearly to be seen in rival party mechanisms no less than in society at large. Political motive forces, such as the desire on the part of the power blocs to prove themselves politically and so to extend and secure their position, had to take the line of least resistance. This state of affairs was evident in, for example, the treatment of the 'Jewish question.' In each individual case, the common denominator of the competing power blocs was not a midstream compromise, but whatever in any given circumstances was the most radical solution, previously considered as beyond the realms of possibility. To avoid surrendering its overall authority on the Jewish question, the Ministry of the Interior consented to drastic discriminatory measures which once and for all showed that the 'rule of law' had been nothing but a painstakingly maintained facade. To prevent Jewish property falling into the hands of the Gau organizations as a result of wild-cat 'aryanization,' Goering, following the November Pogrom (of which he, like Heydrich, disapproved), gave orders for aryanization by the state; the departments involved hastily busied themselves with supporting legislation, even if only to retain their share of responsibility. The impossible situation created by the material and social dispossession of the Jews caused individual Gauleiters to resort to deportations, regardless of consequences, a move bitterly resisted by the departments concerned. However, the result was not the replacement of deportation by a politically 'acceptable' solution but, on the contrary, the systematic mass murder of the Jews, which no one had previously imagined possible—the most radical solution, and incidentally one which coincided with Hitler's own wishes.[92]

Typical of fascist politics and also of the Movement phase is the use of propaganda slogans, such as *Volksgemeinschaft* (community of the people), to cover up actual social conflicts and to replace political compromise and choice of priorities. While the Movement as such was steadily declining in importance within the regime and no longer initiated any policies, its principle of 'solutions without conflict' was carried over into the sphere of government, now divested of much of its authority. This tendency led to a cumulative radicalization, so that extravagant objectives, far away at first, came nearer to immediate realization. In this way, it provided the possibility of anticipating some of the millennial aims of the Third Reich, such as annihilation of the Jews, eradication of Eastern European elites, Himmler's chimerical plans for resettlement, and the breeding of a Greater German elite. These efforts were choked by a torrent of crime, blood, and mediocrity, and stood revealed in all their inadequacy; nevertheless, they were still impelled by the inhuman consistency of machinery running on, without the slightest relevance to actual political interests and realities. Ample evidence shows that Hitler drew back whenever he met public resistance, such as on euthanasia[93] and the Church question.[94] Early in his reign, too, he tended to listen more to the representations of Schacht and civil servants at the Ministry of the Interior than to the radical promptings of his party colleagues. It is not enough, therefore, to cast Hitler as the fanatical instigator. Even the 'Final Solution of the Jewish Question' came to pass only in the uncertain light of the dictator's fanatical propaganda utterances, eagerly seized upon as orders for action by men wishing to prove their diligence, the efficiency of their machinery, and their political indispensability. Characteristically, Goering took it upon himself to give the word of command for the Final Solution, although, as in other cases, he gladly left it to others (in this case Himmler) to put it into practice.

In this regard, the search for the elements of continuity and change after the Movement phase must be taken up anew. National Socialist dictatorship was based, not on the movement's popular plebiscitary victory but on an alliance of interests between the conservative elites and the fascist party. This equilibrium rapidly gave way to the total exercise of fascist power, but was still propped up by the more or less undisturbed apparatus of government, including the overwhelmingly conservative nationalist civil service, staffed in the main by the same men as before.[95] Initially, too, the autonomy and weapon monopoly of the armed forces was maintained, and the capitalist structure of the economy was kept in being, though politically subordinated. At the same time, the economic sector was rewarded for political good behaviour, by such means as elimination of organized labour and by an armaments boom, enthusiastically welcomed, at least in its beginnings.[96] Fusion of the party and its associated groups (the SA excluded) with the government apparatus seemed at first to ensure internal and external stabilization of the regime. Material assistance in this respect was contributed by the restraining power of the ministerial civil service which was initially able to prevent calamitous errors of judgement in foreign and domestic affairs: but this presented a bitter paradox. The civil service largely succeeded in curbing the plebiscitary role of the mass party and in giving the dictatorship an independent standing as the Führer State[97] by means of subsidiary methods of legitimization. However, its ability to control Hitler and moderate his actions diminished with time. His tendency to pile office on office continually reduced his involvement in individual decisions; proportionately, however, the unbridled forces of the Movement phase, now transformed into uncontrollable and uninhibited power conflicts between independent factions, established a type of cumulative radicalization which annulled the temporary stabilization. The result was an erosion of the apparatus of government and the independence of the army, and increasing inroads into the monopoly of capitalist economy, so that the conservative social foundations of the system itself were threatened even though they had undergone no marked change. A similar process occurred in the field of foreign policy, where excessive and overtaxing demands drove the Reich into a hopeless military situation.

V

By delaying the revelation of the insoluble contradictions within the regime, the war provided it with some stability, at the same time, however, presenting a threat for the not too distant future. The regime's internal ambiguity, the restlessness caused by constant innovation, and the impossibility of pinpointing responsibility prevented consolidation of oppositional forces, both within and outside the party. The people's grievances concerning the regime's many abuses were never moulded into a nationwide criticism of the whole system. As a mythical figure inspiring unity, Hitler could be loyally accepted even by those who utterly despised the rule of party bosses. The confusing co-existence and antagonisms of rival mechanisms and power blocs nurtured the fiction of one rational entity high above the turmoil — the dictator, that is, in the role of Providence — whilst abuses were laid at the door of subordinate leaders. In such a diffuse atmosphere of conflicting power structures, the resistance movement of 20 July could develop without coming to the Gestapo's notice at an early stage. Nevertheless, it too was fatally hampered by the feverishness and instability of the National Socialist leadership.[98] The failure of Operation Walküre meant the senseless prolongation of the war in just those last few months of terrible losses. Hitler's order to apply the 'scorched earth' policy to Germany, effectively countermanded by Albert Speer, his curse on the German nation as unworthy of survival, and his injunction on posterity to continue the annihilation of the Jews — all this throws light on the falsehood at the core of a gangster regime which had destroyed traditional social and political structures only to proliferate corruption, petty-bourgeois mediocrity, and a band of criminals of historical proportions, regarded as heroes by shallow moralists. How far the National Socialist state had disintegrated from within is reflected in the internecine struggles during the last weeks of the regime: the deposing of Himmler and Goering, the awarding of the Reichs Presidency to the politically colourless Grand Admiral Doenitz, and the turning over of the Chancellorship to Goebbels, who evaded the absurd prospect by suicide, while somewhere in Schleswig-Holstein, Doenitz was forming an impotent rump government.[99]

In fascist Italy, the conservative elites had maintained some measure of independence from the fascist government and were able to protect Italy from total destruction and political paralysis by a successful rebellion. Hitler, on the other hand, managed to wield his fatal influence to the last: the National Socialist leadership cliques, burdened with guilt, could not free themselves from their traumatic dependence on the dictator, now verging on physical and mental collapse and encapsulated from the outside world within the Führer bunker.[100] Was this the result of the integrating force of the Führer myth, or was that myth only the lie at the heart of a regime now reeling towards total bankruptcy? The Führer myth and the leadership rivalries were interdependent. In combination, they formed an atavistic principle of political rule, entirely consonant with propaganda objectives and allowing maximum tactical flexibility, yet condemned to failure under the conditions of a great modern industrialized state, even when allied to up-to-date forms of bureaucratic rule within the emergent patterns of power competing with the traditional apparatus of government. The destructive dynamics of atavistic leadership rivalries gained extraordinary strength by the total exploitation of the technical and bureaucratic efficiency of rapidly established commissions and organizations. Initially held in check by foreign policy considerations and by the restraining power of a hide-bound civil service, the emergent National

Socialist leadership groups lost all sense of reality and proportion in the chase after loosely connected aims.

Ever more embroiled in the feverish and confused process of decision-making, the traditional leading elites in the apparatus of government, in the army and the economy, were forced either to join in the cumulative radicalization of the regime or to decline into political oblivion. What ensued was that political decision-making was altogether lowered to the personal level and became progressively more irrational; the unified administrative system was destroyed; communication between divergent leadership factions, and from them to their subordinates, was lost; and feedback mechanism, which might have allowed effective supervision of the increasingly independent power groups, was non-existent. From this stemmed a sense of insecurity as to the success of the regime's domestic policies.

Political energy was, by the same token, dissipated in endless and increasingly obdurate personal squabbles, as well as in actions of dubious value in terms of practical politics, squandering the regime's strength. Such actions included the fateful destruction of European Jewry and of a large proportion of the elite of Eastern Europe, Himmler's fanciful resettlement plans, and his concept of a 'Greater German Empire of the German Nation,' whose end result was envisaged as overlordship by a Germanic elite at some future time. In the same category, too, were Speer's misconceived plans for armaments, with their laborious, but belated, amendments, and the systematic theft of art treasures throughout Europe by Goering and Rosenberg—a mixture of hubris and dilettantism.

The Nazi regime could unleash gigantic energies for short-term priorities. Total mobilization of available resources occurred only at a late stage, and even then only in the face of Hitler's delaying manoeuvres, resulting from his anxiety to avoid an internal political situation like that of late autumn 1918.[101] As in the Movement phase, the existence of the regime depended on the people never being allowed to settle. Certainly this was not consciously intended. The dynamic force of precipitate and overlapping actions, cutting across all previous planning, was quite in keeping with the fascist leaders' way of life and with Hitler's mentality; the irrationality of political decision-making also bore an equal part in the general restlessness. Undoubtedly Hitler welcomed the flurry of activity brought about by leadership rivalries. It exactly reproduced the pre-1933 NSDAP style of politics and propaganda, and glossed over the lack of internal political integration and thoughtful future planning. Paradoxically, this confused political opponents to the same extent that it kept the people in suspense and neutralized political resistance.

The regime knew well how to perpetuate the crisis atmosphere which had given it birth and how to transmute policies into a series of emergency measures before which internal political differences had to give way. It was incapable of stabilization or of any progress beyond a parasitic erosion of traditional political structures. Hence the chameleon character of the National Socialist system; hope of a return to normality persisted, and side by side with the 'prerogative state,' the 'normative state,' however insignificantly, continued to exist.[102] The inner contradictions of the system — a magnified reflection of the contradictions in the National Socialist programme — necessarily led to its internal and external disintegration, while preventing early destruction from within.

Glossing over social tensions, unchanged if not intensified, was a well-tried NSDAP propaganda technique. Terrorist pressure exerted by an ever more bureaucratic police force for an outward show of compliance with the crumbling letter of the law gave the lie to the tenet, stoutly maintained by the inner circle of National Socialist leaders, that planned indoctrination would achieve their desired aim: ideological unity and the 'fanatical closing of the ranks,' called for by Hitler again and again. Significantly, Hitler's subordinate leaders increasingly began to dream of the Kampfzeit, when 'genuine idealism' still existed and positive tasks had been assigned to them. Bormann hoped to revive the party, at least after the war, as a self-contained political fighting unit. But the movement was dead; only its elements remained — corruption, rivalry, and the supplanting of policy by propaganda. The myth of the 'thousand-year Reich' faded among the ruins of German cities and defeated German armies; political power lay almost entirely in the hands of Himmler and his henchmen, and the Gauleiters as Reichs Defence Commissaries. The goal of total domination over state and society had been attained; the NSDAP had transferred its 'revolutionary legality' to the state; but as the relics of traditional government structures disappeared, so vanished the basis of National Socialist dictatorship. In all its ghastly inhumanity, it was now revealed as a gigantic farce upon the stage of world history.

## NOTES

1. For the study of German self-assessment after 1945, Friedrich Meinecke, *The German Catastrophe* (Cambridge, Mass., 1950) is of fundamental importance. For the conventional interpretation, see William L. Shirer, *The Rise and Fall of the Third Reich* (New York, 1960) and A. J. P. Taylor, *The Course of German History* (London, 1945). Ideological critical analyses are: Martin Broszat, *German National Socialism 1919-1945* (Santa Barbara, Calif., 1966), George L. Mosse, *The Crisis of German Ideology* (New York, 1964), Fritz Stern, *The Politics of Cultural Despair* (New York, 1961), Kurt Sontheimer, *Antidemokratisches Denken in der Weimarer Republik* (Munich, 1962). A good summary is to be found in Karl Dietrich Bracher, *The German Dictatorship*, 4th ed., (New York, 1973).

2. Seymour Martin Lipset, 'Der "Faschismus," die Linke, die Rechte und die Mitte,' in *Kölner Zeitschrift für Soziologie und Sozialpsychologie*, XI (1959); Talcott Parsons, 'Some Sociological Aspects of the Fascist Movements 1942,' in *Essays in Sociological Theory* (Glencoe, Ill., 1964); Theodor Geiger, *Die soziale Schichtung des deutschen Volkes* (Stutt-

gart, 1932; new ed. Darmstadt, 1967); Ernst Nolte, *Die faschistische Bewegung*, (Munich, 1966); Michael Kater, 'Zur Soziographie der frühen NSDAP,' in *Vierteljahrshefte für Zeitgeschichte*, XIX (Munich, 1971) (hereafter cited as *VfZ*); also Heinrich-August Winkler, *Mittelstand, Demokratie und Nationalsozialismus* (Cologne, 1972).

3. Cf. Iring Fetscher, 'Faschismus und Nationalsozialismus: Zur Kritik des sowjet-marxistischen Faschismusbegriffs,' in *Politische Vierteljahresschrift*, III (Cologne, 1962) (hereafter cited as *PVS*); Theodor Pirker, ed., *Komintern und Faschismus 1920-1940* (Stuttgart, 1965); also my 'Antifascism,' article in *Marxism, Communism and Western Society*, I (New York, 1972), 134-41 (hereafter cited as *MCWS*); Wolfgang Abendroth, ed., *Faschismus und Kapitalismus* (Frankfurt, 1967); E. Nolte, ed., *Theorien über den Faschismus*, 2d ed. (Cologne, 1970).

4. Cf. my article on 'National Socialism,' in *MCWS*, VI (New York, 1973); D. Eichholtz, 'Probleme einer Wirtschaftsgeschichte des Faschismus in Deutschland,' in *Jahrbuch für Wirtschaftsgeschichte 1963*, pt. 3.

5. From the now enormous literature on the subject, the following are the most important: Hans Kohn, 'Communist and Fascist Dictatorship: A Comparative Study,' in *Dictatorship in the Modern World* (Minneapolis, 1935); Franz L. Neumann, *Behemoth: The Structure and Practice of National Socialism 1933-1944*, 2d ed. (New York, 1944); Franz L. Neumann, *The Democratic and the Authoritarian State*, ed. H. Marcuse (Glencoe, Ill., 1957); Sigmund Neumann, *Permanent Revolution*, ed. Hans Kohn, 2d ed. (New York, 1965); C. J. Friedrich and Z. K. Brzezinski, *Totalitarian Dictatorship and Autocracy*, 2d ed. (Cambridge, Mass.). A survey by Bruno Seidel and Siegfried Jenkner, 'Wege der Totalitarismus-Forschung,' in *Wege der Forschung* CXL (Darmstadt, 1968); M. Greiffenhagen et al., *Totalitarismus: Zur Problematik eines politischen Begriffs* (Munich, 1972).

6. Above all, Carl Schmitt, 'Die Wendung zum totalen Staat 1931,' in *Positionen und Begriffe* (Hamburg, 1940); Ernst Forsthoff, *Der totale Staat* (Hamburg, 1933); Ulrich Scheuner, 'Die nationale Revolution: Eine staatsrechtliche Untersuchung,' in *Archiv des öffentlichen Rechts*, new series XXIV (1933-34); and cf. Gerhard Schulz, 'Der Begriff des Totalitarismus und des Nationalsozialismus,' in Seidel and Jenkner, op. cit., 438 ff.

7. It should be remembered here that Hannah Arendt, *Origins of Totalitarianism* (New York, 1951) starts from a different premise in dealing with the ideological and social origins of National Socialism, and therefore refers only to a 'so-called totalitarian state.' For more recent discussion, see K. Hildebrand, 'Stufen der Totalitarismus-Forschung,' in *PVS*, IX (1968); M. Greiffenhagen, 'Der Totalitarismus-Begriff in der Regimenlehre,' ibid.; Howard D. Mehlinger, *The Study of Totalitarianism: An Inductive Approach* (Washington, D.C. 1965); Tim Mason, 'Das Unwesen der Totalitarismustheorien,' in *Der Politologe*, VII (1966).

8. Apart from Franz Neumann's *Behemoth*, which is still relevant, Ernst Fraenkel's analysis, *The Dual State* (New York, 1941) is of basic importance and, with Sigmund Neumann, influenced the earlier writings of K. D. Bracher, particularly in Bracher et al., *Die nationalsozialistische Machtergreifung*, 2d ed. (Cologne, 1962).

9. The initiative for the comparative study of fascism arose from E. Nolte's fundamental study, *Der Faschismus in seiner Epoche* (Munich, 1963), English title, *The Three Faces of Fascism* (New York, 1966). For the present state of the discussion, see Wolfgang Schieder 'Faschismus und kein Ende?' in *Neue Politische Literatur*, XV (1970), Heft 2.

10. David Schoenbaum, *Hitler's Social Revolution*, 2d ed. (Garden City, N.Y., 1967) xiii. A survey of recent tendencies and research problems is to be found in Hans Mommsen et al., 'Faschistische Diktatur in Deutschland,' in *Politische Bildung*, V (Stuttgart, 1972), Heft 1, and in Wolfgang Sauer, 'National Socialism: Totalitarianism or Fascism?,' in *American Historical Review*, LXXIII (1967).

11. For socio-political analyses of 'totalitarian' mass movements, see first and foremost Theodor W. Adorno et al., *The Authoritarian Personality* (New York, 1950); Eric Fromm, *Escape from Freedom* (New York, 1941). The wealth of differing versions precludes a sum-

mary survey of the psychological and sociological attempts to explain the 'totalitarian' susceptibility of the German middle classes. Besides the linking of socialist and liberal attitudes
stemming from the atomization and depoliticization of German society under the influence of
a capitalist national state (H. Arendt), there is the widely held conviction that totalitarianism
was a pathological extension of radical democracy (J. L. Talmon, *The Origins of Totalitarian
Democracy* [New York, 1961]). However, the theory of F. Neumann and S. Neumann, postu-
lating that National Socialism destroyed the existing social structure and intentionally kept
the mass of the people in a state of constant tension and permanent revolution has had an
even more lasting influence on subsequent research, by stressing that these were the specific
totalitarian intentions of Hitler's policies. But National Socialism, notwithstanding its
dynamic social power, did not effectively level out social differences and structures (except in
the anti-aristocrat campaign following 20 July 1944). Instead, it camouflaged them by its
community ideologies (see Schoenbaum, op. cit., 275 ff.).

12. Cf. Hans Buchheim, *Das Dritte Reich* (Munich, 1958) and idem., *Totalitäre Herrschaft* (Munich, 1962). See also Robert C. Tucker, 'Towards a Comparative Politics of Move-
ment-Regimes,' in *The American Political Science Review*, LV (1961), who points out that
the party's tendency to abandon sociological and plebiscitary fundamentals in favour of the
psycho-pathological character of the Führer was a characteristic of fascist mass movement
rule; he considers 'Hitlerism' to be the appropriate term for this development.

13. See Günther Plum's article, 'Resistance Movements,' in *MCWS*, VII (New York, 1973).

14. On KPD policy see Siegfried Bahne, in Erich Matthias and Rudolf Morsey, eds., *Das
Ende der Parteien 1933* (Düsseldorf, 1960).

15. One of K. D. Bracher's great merits is that, in *Die Auflösung der Weimarer Republik*,
4th ed. (Villingen, 1964), he brings out the continuity between the presidential cabinets and
the Third Reich, and contradicts the widely held belief that January 1933 represented a
major break with the past.

16. See in particular Wolfgang Horn, *Führerideologie und Parteiorganisation in der
NSDAP 1919-1933* (Düsseldorf, 1972), and also J. Nyomarkay, *Charisma and Factionalism in
the Nazi Party* (Minneapolis, 1967). Central to the latter's research is the connection between
the Führer cult and the party's forming itself into sub-groups.

17. Deliberate fostering of aestheticizing elements as a means of integration distinguishes
fascist from imperialist movements; see S. J. Woolf, ed., *European Fascism* (New York, 1969)
and W. Laqueur and G. Mosse, eds., *International Fascism 1920-1945* (London, 1969).

18. Cf. the Reichs Chancellery draft for the establishment of a senate to elect the leader,
June 1941 (Bundesarchiv Coblenz, R. 43 II, 1213a); and M. Broszat, *Der Staat Hitlers:
Grundlegung und Entwicklung seiner inneren Verfassung* (Munich, 1969), 360 f.

19. See in particular Jeremy Noakes, *The Nazi Party in Lower Saxony 1921-1933* (Oxford,
1971), 156 ff., 164 f. Cf. also Geoffrey Pridham, *Hitler's Rise to Power, The Nazi Movement
in Bavaria* (New York, London, 1974).

20. Wolfgang Schieder, 'Fascism,' in *MCWS*, III (New York, 1972), 282 ff.

21. See the authoritative essay by M. Broszat, 'Soziale Motivation und Führerbindung des
Nationalsozialismus,' in *VjfZ*, XVIII (1970), as distinct from the overemphasis on biographical elements in interpretative models relating to Hitler, found in Eberhard Jäckel, *Hitler's
Weltanschauung: A Blueprint for Power* (Middletown, Conn., 1972; German ed. (Tübingen,
1969), and the earlier tendency, reintroduced recently by Joachim C. Fest, *Adolf Hitler*
(Berlin, 1973), to exaggerate Hitler's role in political decision-making. For criticism of this
method, see Edward N. Peterson, *The Limits of Hitler's Power* (Princeton, 1969), 11 ff.

22. This is the unanimous conclusion of many recent monographs: A. S. Milward, *The
German Economy at War* (London, 1965); Reinhard Bollmus, *Das Amt Rosenberg und seine
Gegner* (Stuttgart, 1970); Heinz Höhne, *The Order of the Death's Head: The Story of Hitler's
SS* (London, 1969); see also my study, *Beamtentum im Dritten Reich* (Stuttgart, 1969); and

the earlier comments by Robert Koehl, 'Feudal Aspects of National Socialism,' in *American Political Science Review*, LIV (1960).

23. Hugh Trevor-Roper, *The Last Days of Hitler* (London, 1949); Reimer Hansen, *Das Ende des Dritten Reiches* (Stuttgart, 1966).

24. See Henry A. Turner, 'Big Business and the Rise of Hitler,' in *American Historical Review*, LXXV (1969), and ibid., *Faschismus und Kapitalismus in Deutschland* (Göttingen, 1972); on the role of industry see also H. Mommsen et al., eds., *Industrielle Entwicklung und politisches System in der Weimarer Republik* (Düsseldorf, 1964).

25. Werner Maser, *Die Frühgeschichte der NSDAP* (Frankfurt, 1965); Georg Franz-Willing, *Die Hitlerbewegung* (Hamburg, 1962).

26. Henry J. Gordon, *Hitler and the Beer Hall Putsch*, 2d ed. (Oxford, 1973); Ernst Deuerlein, *Der Hitler-Putsch* (Stuttgart, 1962).

27. See in particular W. Horn, op. cit. and Dietrich Orlow, *The History of the Nazi Party 1919-1933* (Pittsburgh, 1969).

28. For the National Socialist left, see W. Horn, op. cit., as well as an earlier study by Reinhard Kühnl, *Die nationalsozialistische Linke 1925-1930* (Meisenheim, 1966) and Noakes, op. cit., 72 ff. Max H. Kele's theory, in *Nazis and Workers* (Pittsburgh, 1973) that Goebbels remained true to his socialist beliefs whereas Gregor Strasser conformed to Hitler's ideas, is without precedent.

29. See Uwe Lohalm, *Völkischer Radikalismus: Die Geschichte des Deutschvölkischen Schutz- und Trutzbundes 1919-1933* (Hamburg, 1970).

30. For the part played by anti-Semitism in the political power struggle during the last stages of the Weimar Republic, see the detailed analyses in Werner E. Mosse, ed., *Entscheidungsjahr 1932* (Tübingen, 1965).

31. Orlow, op. cit., 89 ff., 95 ff., 140 ff.; cf. Noakes, op. cit., 106.

32. Noakes, op. cit., 121 ff.

33. Ibid., 129 ff., Horst Gies, 'NSDAP and landwirtschaftliche Organisationen in der Endphase der Weimarer Republik,' in *VjfZ*, XV (1967).

34. See Niethammer in Mommsen et al., *Politische Bildung*, op. cit.

35. See Richard N. Hunt, *German Social Democracy 1918-1933* (New York, 1964); and my essay 'Sozialdemokratie in der Defensive,' in H. Mommsen, ed., *Sozialdemokratie zwischen Klassenbewegung und Volkspartei* (Frankfurt, 1974).

36. Walter Z. Laqueur, *Young Germany* (New York, 1962).

37. See Attila Chanady, 'The Disintegration of the German People's Party 1924-1930,' in *Journal of Modern History*, XXXIX (1967), 65 ff.; Karl O'Lessker, 'Who Voted for Hitler?,' in *American Journal of Sociology*, LXXIV (1968-69), 63-69.

38. See voting analyses in Alfred Milatz, *Wähler und Wahlen in der Weimarer Republik* (Bonn, 1965), 141 ff.

39. William Sheridan Allen, *The Nazi Seizure of Power* (Chicago, 1965).

40. See Z. A. B. Zeman, *Nazi Propaganda*, 2d ed. (London, 1973).

41. Cf. Bracher et al., *Die nationalsozialistische Machtergreifung*, 95 ff., 350 ff., and also Bracher, *The German Dictatorship*, 29.

42. Reichsorganisationsleiter der NSDAP, ed., *Parteistatistik* (*Als Manuskript gedruckt*: Munich, 1935), 26; Reichsführer SS, ed., *Der Weg der NSDAP* (Berlin, 1934), 91; cf. Niethammer, op. cit., 29.

43. On this, see above all Wolfgang Schaefer, *NSDAP* (Frankfurt, 1956) and Hans Gerth, 'The Nazi Party: Its Leadership and Social Composition,' in *American Journal of Sociology*, XLV (1940), 517 ff.

44. Rudolf Heberle, *Landbevölkerung und Nationalsozialismus* (Stuttgart, 1963); Gerhard Stoltenberg, *Politische Strömungen im schleswig-holsteinische Landvolk* (Düsseldorf, 1962).

45. Cf. also Heinrich-August Winkler, op. cit.

46. Cf. particularly Noakes, op. cit., 233 f.

47. Ibid. 230 f.

48. See Josef Becker, 'Brüning, Prälat Kaas und das Problem einer Regierungsbeteiligung der NSDAP 1930-1932,' in *Historische Zeitschrift*, CXCVI (1963), 74 ff., and also Detlef Junker, *Die Deutsche Zentrumspartei und Hitler 1932/33* (Stuttgart, 1969), 86 ff.

49. Joseph Goebbels, *Vom Kaiserhof zur Reichskanzlei* (Berlin, 1934), 87, 143.

50. See Peter Diehl-Thiele, *Partei und Staat im Dritten Reich* (Munich, 1969), 33.

51. Above all Helmut Nicolai, Ernst von Heydebrand und der Lasa, as well as Hans Pfundtner: cf. H. Mommsen, *Beamtentum im Dritten Reich*, op. cit., 28 f; Diehl-Thiele, op. cit., 32 n. 90.

52. Joseph Goebbels, op. cit., 140, 158; cf. Helmut Heiber, *Joseph Goebbels* (New York, 1972).

53. Adolf Hitler, *Mein Kampf*, 67th ed. (Munich, 1933), 503.

54. Goebbels, op. cit., 294.

55. Joseph Goebbels, *Idee und Gestalt des Nationalsozialismus* (Berlin, 1935).

56. Ibid.

57. Joseph Goebbels, *Vom Kaiserhof zur Reichskanzlei*, op. cit., 261.

58. Cf. Heinrich Bennecke, *Hitler und die SA* (Munich, 1962), and also W. Sauer in Bracher et al., *Die nationalsozialistische Machtergreifung*, 880 ff., 927 ff.

59. Cf. K. D. Bracher, 'Stages of Totalitarian "Integration,"' in Hajo Holborn, ed., *Republic to Reich: The Making of the Nazi Revolution* (New York, 1972), 115; and K. D. Bracher, *The German Dictatorship*, op. cit., 206.

60. See M. Broszat, *Der Staat Hitlers*, 103 f.

61. See my 'The Political Effects of the Reichstag Fire,' in H. A. Turner, ed., *Nazism and the Third Reich* (New York, 1972), 134 f.

62. K. D. Bracher's strongly intentionalistic interpretation, in *Stages of Totalitarian 'Integration,'* in my view overrates the degree of central direction involved in spontaneous actions by the SA and party groups.

63. Bracher et al., *Die nationalsozialistische Machtergreifung*, 460 ff.

64. See Diehl-Thiele, op. cit., 86 ff., and Broszat, *Der Staat Hitlers*, 137 ff.; Peterson, op. cit., 166 ff.

65. See mainly Heinrich Bennecke, *Die Reichswehr und der 'Roehmputsch'* (Munich, 1964). The number of victims is usually overestimated in the relevant literature; there were 88.

66. The *Reichsstatthaltergesetz* (7 April 1933), the *Neuaufbaugesetz* (30 January 1934), and the measures preceding them were quite inadequately co-ordinated. Cf. Broszat, *Der Staat Hitlers*, 151 ff.; Diehl-Thiele, op. cit., 40 ff. and 61; also Walter Baum, 'Reichsreform im Dritten Reich,' in *VjfZ*, III (1955).

67. Cf. Diehl-Thiele, op. cit., 195 ff.; Mommsen, *Beamtentum*, 117 ff.

68. See n. 18 above.

69. See Dietrich Orlow, *History of the Nazi Party 1933-1945* (Pittsburgh, 1973), 102 ff., 139 ff.; Diehl-Thiele, op. cit., 34.

70. See above all H. Höhne, op. cit.; Hans Buchheim et al., *Anatomy of the SS-State* (London, 1970).

71. See memorandum of the Gauleiter Weser-Ems (1942) National Archives Microcopy No. T-81, Roll No. R-71, *NSDAP-Parteikanzlei*, 14591 f.; Orlow, op. cit., 352 f., proves that the memorandum cannot have originated with Röver, but was probably written by his successor, Paul Wegener, and hence reflects the opinions of the Party Chancellery.

72. Orlow, op. cit., 84 ff.; Orlow, 'Die Adolf Hitler Schulen,' in *VjfZ*, XIII (1965); R. Bollmus, op. cit.

73. Speech by Rudolf Hess to the Leader Corps of the NSDAP at the Reichsparteitag in Nuremberg, 16 September 1935 (Bundesarchiv Coblenz NS 25/vorl. 1183; abstracted in *Faschistische Diktatur in Deutschland* op. cit., M 20 ff.).

74. Cf. Sigmund Neumann, op. cit., 115 ff.; Franz L. Neumann, *The Democratic and the Authoritarian State*, 249.

75. Apart from W. S. Allen and E. N. Peterson (chaps. 4-8), see H.-P. Görgen's study, *Düsseldorf und der Nationalsozialismus* (Cologne, 1968). Horst Matzerath, *Nationalsozialismus und kommunale Selbstverwaltung* (Stuttgart, 1970) has great merits, but limits itself to headquarters level. That regional studies are necessary and fruitful is shown by Jeremy Noakes' book, already mentioned on several occasions.

76. Cf. Orlow, *History of the Nazi Party 1933-1945*, 77 ff., 139 ff., 339 ff., and Diehl-Thiele, op. cit., 216 ff.; see also the informative research by Peter Hüttenberger, *Die Gauleiter* (Stuttgart, 1969).

77. Diehl-Thiele, op. cit., 197 ff.

78. A. S. Milward, op. cit., 11 f.; Tim Mason, 'The Legacy of 1918 for National Socialism,' in Anthony Nicholls and Erich Matthias, eds., *German Democracy and the Triumph of Hitler* (London, 1971), 220 ff., 238 f.

79. Cf. Broszat, *Der Staat Hitlers*, 421.

80. Peterson, op. cit., 4 ff., 15 f.

81. Sefton Delmer, *Trail Sinister* (London, 1961), I, 181.

82. Memorandum of the Gauleiter Weser-Ems (cf. n. 18 above), 14517.

83. Bracher, *Stages of Totalitarian 'Synchronisation,'* 127 f.

84. Jane Caplan, *The Civil Service in the Third Reich* (Ph.D. diss., Oxford, 1973).

85. Cf. H.-J. Fest, op. cit., 1028; Bracher, *German Dictatorship*, 348; Broszat, *Der Staat Hitlers*, 436 ff.

86. Cf. E. Jäckel, op. cit.; Hans-Adolf Jacobsen, *Nationalsozialistische Aussenpolitik* (Frankfurt, 1968), 16 f.

87. D. Schoenbaum, op. cit., above all 285 f.

88. Cf. Joseph Schumpeter, 'Zur Soziologie der Imperialismen,' in *Archiv für Sozialwissenschaft und Sozialpolitik*, XLVI (1918-19).

89. Cf. Klaus Hildebrand, *The Foreign Policy of the Third Reich* (English ed.; Berkeley, 1973); Andreas Hillgruber, *Kontinuität und Diskontinuität in der deutschen Aussenpolitik von Bismarck bis Hitler*, 3d ed. (Düsseldorf, 1971).

90. On the problem of the 'mood' in the Third Reich, see, apart from Heinz Boberach, *Meldungen aus dem Reich: Auswahl aus den geheimen Lageberichten des Sicherheitsdienstes der SS 1939-1944* (Neuwied, 1965), the investigation by Marlies G. Steinert, *Hitlers Krieg und die Deutschen: Stimmung und Haltung der deutschen Bevölkerung im 2. Weltkrieg* (Düsseldorf, 1970).

91. M. Broszat, *Soziale Motivation und Fuhrer-Bindung des Nationalsozialismus*, 405.

92. On National Socialist persecution of the Jews, see, as well as the description of the Final Solution policy by Raul Hilberg, *The Destruction of the European Jews* (Chicago, 1961), the researches by Uwe D. Adam, *Judenpolitik im Dritten Reich* (Düsseldorf, 1972), and Karl A. Schleunes, *The Twisted Road to Auschwitz: Nazi Policy toward German Jews 1933-1939* (Urbana, Ill., 1970).

93. On euthanasia, see Klaus Dörner, 'Nationalsozialismus und Lebensvernichtung,' in *VjfZ*, XV (1967), 121-152.

94. See, above all, John S. Conway, *The Nazi Persecution of the Churches* (New York, 1968); Günther Lewy, *The Catholic Church and Nazi Germany* (London, 1954).

95. On the role of the civil service, as well as the works by J. Caplan, E. N. Peterson, and H. Mommsen already quoted above, see D. Schoenbaum, op. cit., 193 ff.

96. Tim W. Mason, 'Labour in the Third Reich 1933-1939,' in *Past and Present*, XXXIII (1966), 112-141; Hans-Gerd Schumann, *Nationalsozialismus und Gewerkschaftsbewegung* (Frankfurt, 1958); A. Schweitzer, *Big Business in the Third Reich* (London, 1964).

97. Typical of this is the commentary by Ernst Rudolf Huber, *Verfassungsrecht des Grossdeutschen Reiches* (Hamburg, 1939); cf. Diehl-Thiele, op. cit., 29, and also Helmut Krausnick et al., *Anatomy of the SS-State* (New York, 1968), 129, 133.

98. On the Resistance movement, see above all Hermann Graml et al., *German Resistance to Hitler* (London, 1970).

99. Cf. R. Hansen, op. cit.

100. See the impressive and still valid report by H. Trevor-Roper, *The Last Days of Hitler*, 1st ed. (London, 1947).

101. Cf. T. Mason, *The Legacy of 1918 for National Socialism*, 227.

102. Cf. Fraenkel, op. cit., and Buchheim, op. cit., 133 f.

# 5
# The Role of Hitler:
# Perspectives of Interpretation

KARL DIETRICH BRACHER

I

For more than half a century National Socialism and its leader have been the object of countless reports and polemics, and of extensive research and interpretation. Since the days when fifty years ago the frustrated ex-soldier and self-styled demagogue Adolf Hitler made his attempted putsch in Munich, which was intended to instigate a march on Berlin following the model of Mussolini's legendary march on Rome, the literature on both Hitler and National Socialism has been growing abundantly, with no evidence of a foreseeable slowdown.[1] On the contrary, looking back at the dramatic postwar developments—the cold war and Stalinism, Hungary and Suez, the crisis of colonialism and the Near East, Czechoslovakia and Vietnam, with all their shocking consequences—we realize that they have all contributed to a continuing interest in the phenomenon of nazism. Personified by Hitler, the Nazi period somehow seems to be in the background of most of these contemporary and revolutionary events. The second world war, which was foremost Hitler's war, has indeed changed the world, or at least has made it ripe for change, perhaps more profoundly than in any preceding period of history.

This cannot, however, be the only reason for the recurring waves of interest and for what has been called the Hitler-boom during the past few years, with the resultant mass of publications—books, pamphlets, films, cartoons, and so forth, appearing on both sides of the Atlantic. It seems strange that this should happen in face of the much more real and pressing issues of the day, when important political changes are taking place and the long process of stabilization of the European and German status quo in the aftermath of Hitler has been achieved, marking the definitive end of the post-second world war period. We now acknowledge that the worldwide best-seller written by one of Hitler's closest collaborators, Albert Speer, in 1969-70 is the symbolic counterpart to the equally successful *Rise and Fall of the Third Reich*, written ten years earlier in 1960 by William Shirer and expressing opposite points of view. The appearance of extensive studies such as that of Werner Maser in 1971[2] and the largest and most recent biography of Hitler by Joachim Fest are also notable.

All this points to a set of motives which extends far beyond the historico-political interest. Of course, there is the inevitable and continuing sensational aspect caused by the excessive features of Hitlerism, which can be taken as a kind of modern Ghengis Khanism or an example of that combination of cruel efficiency and superhuman will-power which frequently is identified as typically German, to be horrified or admired, or both simultaneously. It is indeed the function of a prototype beyond the historical phenomenon that makes for the lasting importance of Hitler and National Socialism.

This seems equally true with respect to very diverse types and groups of interests from the scholarly and academic and the political and literary 'user' of the Hitler topic, to the masses of spectators observing the monumental horrors and catastrophes of history, who primarily expect it to be translated into stories and pictures of human interest.

Yet at the same time we are confronted with the fact that this preoccupation concentrates on a man who seems to be much less than a great individual, even the evil Renaissance-Borgia type. He does not appear as one of the great personalities of history. There is little to arouse one's interest in the man himself, indeed he is almost totally submerged in the history of his political movement and the Third Reich. Aside from the relatively few incidents we know of his childhood and youth in Linz and Vienna, and of his experiences in the first world war and afterwards, there is very little to constitute a personal biography—his life being identical to, and often disappearing behind, the life of National Socialism. It is only at the end of his life, in the Führerbunker in Berlin in 1945, that it becomes more visible again. How difficult is it then to understand and explain the rise of a man from so narrow and parochial an existence to a formidable figure on whom depended a development of such universally historical dimensions and consequences.

But this is the precise core of the Hitler phenomenon, marking the basic features of its appearance and effect, and hinting at the most important problem of nazism: its fundamental underestimation by (1) political groupings and parties of both the right and left within Germany, thus enabling Hitler to come to power, and (2) externally on the international scene, facilitating his march to war and quest for European domination.

The problem of adequate estimation and interpretation has become even more complicated today, as the immediate experience of both nazism and Stalinism disappears into distant history. As a consequence, it has again become fashionable among intellectuals to deny any possible comparison between right- and left-wing extremism, fascism, and communist dictatorship, or between Hitler and Stalin—in short to attack and abolish the notion of totalitarianism as it was used in postwar discussion and research.[3]

At the same time, the names of Hitler or fascism are used to denounce anti-communist politics in general and in the present, with comparisons (e.g., of Vietnam to Nazi crimes) that amount to a gigantic misinterpretation of both, thus minimizing nazism.

One important argument for such misleading comparisons and distinctions is the apparent difference in ideological substance and direction between communism and fascism. This leads to the assumption that fascist or Nazi movements, by their very nature and by their lesser emphasis on, and the poorer intellectual quality of their ideology, if compared to socialist or communist Marxism, are not to be taken seriously as independent political movements in their own right, but only as a part or instrument of reactionary and capitalistic power agencies. This so-called agent theory seems to be proved not only by the poor and trivial intellectual substance of fascist movements, but also by the mediocre human and ideological stature of most of their leaders and followers.

But it is exactly at this point that illusions and fictions occurred that led to the fatal underestimation of Hitler and his movement. They were never taken seriously intellectually because its proclaimed 'national socialism' lacked the sort of coherent doctrine which was evident in Marxist socialism, although it was in fact the eclectic nature of fascist and Nazi ideology that proved to be a source of strength and paved the way for the formation of mass movements and for the politics of fanaticism.

In view of this problem of achieving a realistic assessment of nazism, it is noticeable even today that the large number of publications on the subject contrasts sharply with the small quantity of substantial contributions they make. Most publications are dedicated to the collection and display of details that satisfy private curiosity, whilst only very few have something to say on the question of Hitler's historical role and weight with respect to the great currents of our time.

This applies also to the fundamental problem of any discussion about Hitler: how is the place of the individual within the historico-political process to be defined under modern conditions? What are the possibilities and the limits of a rational explanation of a movement like National Socialism? And to what degree do we have to perceive its shape and success in terms of the demonic force of a specific individual? Here the problem of Hitler's personality remains crucial indeed. It is, of course, true that we have to be made fully aware of the dangers of a demonological interpretation of National Socialism (as well as of communism). This danger was felt acutely in Germany immediately after 1945 when many commentators tried to hide German responsibility behind the back of the superhuman and all-responsible demon Hitler. Such views represented a reversion to the leader cult, suitable to and often used for the purpose of conservative and nationalistic apologies or mystifications. They even influenced respected older historians like Gerhard Ritter in for example his contribution to the UNESCO volume of 1955, *The Third Reich*.

In view of these problems, we are still faced as before with two basic questions which are central to all serious books on Hitler from the pioneer work of Konrad Heiden in 1936 to the classic by Alan Bullock in 1952: to what degree *does* a biography of the 'Leader' disclose the nature and essence of National Socialism, or could and should we simply speak of Hitlerism? Or conversely, is it possible at all to get a true personal biography of the man whose life appears almost as nothing apart from the complete identification with the history of National Socialism? Is it not true that he lacks the stature of other great personalities of world history? And yet his career manifested a power to move men and events almost unequalled in history.

Indeed, the categories of historical greatness as discussed by Jacob Burckhard and other 'classical' historians and philosophers are not to apply to him, and it becomes clear that in our age of mass society, of totalitarian movements in democratic disguise, of pseudo-religious ideologies, the concept of historical greatness is no longer valid nor are the measures of eighteenth- and nineteenth-century humanism, culture, and statecraft that may have been applied to figures like Napoleon, Bismarck, Lincoln, and maybe even Lenin. Hitler and, in his way, Stalin represent a new type of the great movement and party leader combining the qualities of fanatical ideological fixation and virtuoso mass demagogy, and replacing the traditional statesman and warrior as the great type of historical figure.

It may be better not to use the renaissance and romantic idea of the great man and political greatness any longer when basic conditions of political leadership have changed so drastically. But this does not mean that the role of the individual has become less important. The fashionable tendency to dissolve all historical developments into structural and collective processes represents an understandable reaction to the crude concept of *Männer machen Geschichte* — history is made by great men. It is true that this concept of history as the history of great men was propagated not only by fascism and nazism, corresponding as it did to their very nature as dictatorships with a sole leader, but also by communist regimes where, although quite contrary to their dogma of collectivism, it was in keeping with the psychology of mass mobilization by charismatic leadership. The great examples of this cult of leadership and pseudo-religious veneration and adoration are Lenin and Stalin and at present Mao and the North Korean demigod Kim Il Sung.

But if we critically analyse the ideological character of the cult of leadership, we have to recognize the impact it makes on the structure of the regime and at the same time what part the leader plays in the totalitarian systems of the twentieth century. Leonard Shapiro and Robert Tucker have also stressed this point with respect to Russian and Chinese totalitarianism.[4] The integral role of the great man, often denied in communist theory, was, of course, always underlined in fascism and National Socialism. But while in the case of Mussolini the totalitarian role of the Duce was never wholly realized, and fascism may therefore be defined beyond and apart from a Mussolinism, in the case of Hitler there was never any question of a *fronde* against the leader, and one of the significant features of both National Socialism and the Third Reich is the fact that from the beginning to the very end it stood and fell with this man, with his decisions, his ideological fixations, his purely political way of life, and his need for the grandiose alternative of victory or catastrophe. This indicates a passion for extreme solutions and for ultimate consequences that have been seen as the transplantation, onto the stage of history, of the theatrical pathos of Richard Wagner's operas, in which Hitler had been immersed since his youth in Linz and Vienna. It influenced not only the ideological goals of the movement but even more the organization of mass meetings displaying overwhelming power and leader-worship. For these reasons, National Socialism can indeed be called Hitlerism. This man and his intentions and actions will always be in the very centre of nazi history. But at the same time, Hitler himself is to be understood and analysed in terms of the German and European traditions which formed the framework and feeding ground of a National Socialist movement that existed well before Hitler.

The question of the role of the individual may thus be answered simultaneously in two ways. First, Hitler was the most radical expressor and the most effective propagator of a set of ideas and emotions forming the nucleus of extreme German nationalism, that is, anti-democratism, imperialism, racism. Without his activity and success, German and European history including the second world war would have followed a totally different course. Second, the real and long term consequences of Hitler's politics have produced results almost diametrically opposite to those he intended. But if seen as an actor or agent of world history in the terms of Hegel's *List der Vernunft*, Hitler has brought about or left behind him revolutionary changes that cannot be grasped within the clichés of the counter-revolutionary role of fascism. One may have reservations against the thesis of Ralf Dahrendorf,[5] that Hitler and National Socialism have decisively influenced (or even brought about) modernization in Germany. At any rate, the experience of the Hitler regime has deeply changed the German elite, German attitudes and behaviour, and facilitated the more stable experiment of the second German democracy.

## II

If one goes beyond the general discussion of the role of the individual in history and tries to define Hitler's place in his epoch and after, one can then concentrate on a set of questions which seems central to any discussion of the problem:

1. What is the nature and the relevance of the changes, short and long term brought about by Hitler's politics? Did they not only profoundly alter history but amount to a revolution (as proclaimed in another sense also by Nazi propaganda)? Or is the verdict of most contemporary critics that they were basically a reactionary counter-revolution still correct?

2. What is the consequence of such definitions with regard to the important problems posed by a generalization of the Hitler phenomenon, that is, Hitler as a type or symbol, and the quest for a general theory of fascism? Is Hitler, with his movement and regime, primarily a form (if most extreme) of *the* fascist in general, as for example the studies of Ernst Nolte have stated and many new general books on fascism maintain?[6] And, moreover, is fascism, in the Marxist definition, nothing but the form, the system, and the instrument of monopoly capitalism exposing its most aggressive nature and potential in all bourgeois democracies, which, of course, means that there is no clear cut borderline between western democracies and fascism?

All these formulas imply that nazism and the Hitler phenomenon should no longer be studied and explained as a specifically German problem, but rather in terms of its European and twentieth-century reference.

Against this background, there is a tendency among younger historians and social scientists to seriously question the main findings and conclusions of research during the fifties and the sixties. Although this of course seems quite natural, there has in the meantime been more research into detail so that interest is shifting from a strongly German to a more general focus of explanation and interpretation. Moreover, the moral and liberal set of values which originally determined the interpretation of Nazism, is being questioned by a sceptical relativism; the standards of western democracy seem no longer to be a reliable yardstick against which to measure the man and the system. Nothing less than a so-called normalizing of the debate on Nazi history is demanded.

Such criticism was expressed for instance in a series of reviews by Geoffrey Barraclough in the *New York Review of Books* (October/November 1972). This rather unqualified attack made more noise than was justified by its conclusions and neglects or misrepresents our research positions. It is, of course, true that the interpretation of history depends on the political age and problems of the historians themselves, and these have altered since the days of clear-cut fronts against totalitarianism in the era of Hitler and Stalin.

Seen in the light of current interpretations, what then is the nature and relevance of the Hitler phenomenon—reaction or revolution? There can first of all be no doubt that, quite contrary to both the Nazi and the Marxist interpretation, Hitler's road to power was never inevitable, since rarely in history has there been such a close inter-dependence of general and personal factors and the indispensable role of the individual as in the crucial period between 1919 and 1945, from Hitler's entry into politics to his exit.

This applies, in particular, to the decisive period of the seizure of power around 1933. The key role played by a small camarilla around President Hindenburg is as obvious as the impact of Hitler's tactics of legal revolution, which represents the key concept of the Nazi take-over. Neither the German parties, from centre to communist, nor the social groups and organizations had any determining influence in the decisions which were made, so that in the final analysis the process of definitive power seizure, *Machtergreifung*, between February and March 1933, corresponds almost exactly to the legality concept which Hitler developed from his experience of the abortive putsch of 1923.[7]

From such analysis it becomes clear that the nature of the Nazi revolution cannot be defined in terms of a capitalist manoeuvre nor of Hitler being the servant and slave of reactionary forces. It was exactly this misunderstanding of Hitler's 'legal revolution' that kept conservatives as well as socialists and communists from a realistic judgment. They were all paralysed and reacted ineffectively not least because they failed to recognize the revolutionary character of the process: the conservatives when they believed they would be able to tame Hitler, and the left when they expected (and even feared) the reactionary right around Hindenburg, Papen, and Hugenberg to be the real masters of the situation and the real enemies of the left. But instead of the anticipated counter-revolution, be it in the form of the restoration of monarchy or a military dictatorship, Hitler's total take-over on his own became complete within a few months, being much faster and more radical than that of Mussolini ten years before. Furthermore the Duce had to respect the condominium of powerful rivals like the monarchy, the aristocracy, the church, and the army.

Here again, a basic difference between fascism and National Socialism becomes apparent. But it is even more evident with respect to the political aims and the ideological fixations lurking behind them. It was indeed Hitler's *Weltanschauung* and nothing else that mattered in the end, as is seen from the terrible consequences of his racist anti-Semitism in the planned murder of the Jews.

A general theory of fascism will always remain questionable when confronted with this problem. It is, of course, possible to find and define similarities in the realm of ideas between nationalist dictatorships in various countries. But not only was Hitler's background deeply different from that of Mussolini, the same applies also to the leading ideology. While fascism centered around the quest for the strong state, *stato totalitario* as the basis of a renewed *impero Romano*, Hitler's basic notion was the primary role of the race, the racist foundation of a future empire, to which the organization of a strong state was no more than instrumental—never an end in itself. The modish use of the general catchword *fascist* explains little and produces many clichés. What is more, it means minimizing the insane ideas and terrible reality of Hitlerism if we throw it into one and the same category with fascism. Surely, it is wrong for this term to be used as indiscriminately as it is today not only in political polemics but also in the writings of many historians and social scientists. Should they not primarily be interested in coming to grips with reality by *distinguishing* the phenomena instead of lumping them together under the slogan of fascism, not to speak of the current pseudo-Marxist practice of calling all non-'socialist' systems (and even social-democrats) potentially fascist, as was done in the early thirties with the fatal consequence that the communists were fighting against the Weimar Republic and even entered into an unholy alliance with the National Socialists at times.

This problem also belongs to the crucial chapter of underestimation. Quoting Hitler and the Nazi example today, with application to contemporary tendencies and events, and referring to them as fascist lends itself to manifold manipulations, both in revitalizing the Nazi atrocities and in defaming present political enemies. Comparisons can be justified only on the grounds of a sober analysis of the matter in question, and it should be understood primarily in the sense of actualizing the terrible experience of the past in its full dimensions. One should be wary of introducing, for daily use, terms emanating from and applied to the Nazi extermination policy. As Peter Gay rightly criticizes people to whom Hitler's dictatorship is mere history, 'in their indiscriminate indictment of modern society, [they] tend to treat the Nazi crimes as no less reprehensible, certainly, but also as no more reprehensible than the bombing of Dresden or the war in Vietnam.'[8]

In this context we also have to look critically at the revisionism of historians like Geoffrey Barraclough (in his article in the *New York Review of Books* already mentioned), who think that we have now arrived at a period of complete detachment where the historian should no longer, as we supposedly did, magnify the Nazi experience. Against such criticism of the liberal historiography of the past thirty years, which goes so far as to deny the fact that 1945 was a chasm in German history (and in European and world history, for that matter), I should like to stress the moral and intellectual obligation of the responsible historian who upholds the Nazi experience, 'terrible and oppressive as it was, as the tragic but indispensable counterpoint of a saner, humane view of the world and even of our time' (P. Gay).

### III

Coming back to the historical case one has to stress the degree to which Mussolini and Hitler acted from basically diverging points, and this can also be found quite distinctly in each of the other later so-called fascist systems, from the Balkans through Austria to Spain, Portugal, and Peronism: indeed it makes little sense to insist on *the* idea or *the* theory of fascism. Indeed, the formation and translation of Hitler's ideology remains the central problem of any analysis, and the question of the revolutionary role of Hitler and his politics can be answered only in this context.

The most important lesson to be learnt with respect to a theory of revolution is that of the successful technique of legal revolution as demonstrated by both Mussolini and Hitler to represent the twentieth-century type of take-over. We have to adapt the term of revolution to such phenomena instead of trying to keep to the romantic nineteenth-century idea of the 'good' revolution as against evil counter-revolutions.

The myth of the good revolution is, of course, still part of our political reality in so far as it is used for manipulating public opinion in favour of take-overs by leftist minorities while similar manoeuvres by the right are disqualified: the misjudgment of Hitler's revolution in being incomparable to a socialist revolution (and no revolution at all) continues in the allegation that revolution is possible only from the left.

It seems necessary also for this politico-practical reason that a re-evaluation of the revolutionary aspect of Hitlerism takes place with respect to its specific features of take-over and power structure as well as to its general perspectives. *Revolution from the Right* [1931] was the title of a widely read book by the German sociologist and Nazi sympathizer, Hans Freyer. The slogan should be taken more seriously than it was and is by the ideologists of the so-called true revolution. The reality of our times is, of course, communist dictatorship. But equally important remains the possibility of revolutionary regimes led by nationalists with socialist claims and with the broad consent of the masses, driven and mobilized by way of articulation and mystification by the great fear of socio-economic technological and political threats, and manipulated by plebiscites, anticapitalist slogans, the old *panem et circenses*, and a charismatic leader.

It is true that the degree of social and economic change accompanying Hitler's political revolution is still a topic of controversy both among contemporaries of Hitler and historians. And it is of course also true that in the end Hitler failed utterly in all his aims. But not only were the human costs and the political consequences of this failure immensely high and far reaching, they amounted to a truly revolutionary acceleration of processes of historical dimensions: in Germany, division and modernization; in Western Europe, close cooperation; and in the world, decolonization, shifting of power, and the rise of the Soviet Union.

It was a paradoxical revolution — paradoxical in the way in 1933 it posed simultaneously as legal and revolutionary. But it may also be called a 'blind' revolution, with a course and with results far from, and even opposed to, the intended goals of Hitler and nazism. Think, for instance, of the Hitler-Stalin Pact of 1939, gravely contrary to the whole of Hitler's deeply fixed ideology, with the equally momentous consequence of opening Central Europe to Stalin. But, of course, there are many more examples of this, including the communist revolutions that diverge so deeply from the prognosis and expectations of Marx and Engels, and, in part, even Lenin. This interpretation of the paradoxical and even self-contradictory character of revolution is also plausible because the very nature of Hitler's thought and action is clearly ambivalent: romantic-irrationalist *whilst* technocratic-modernizing, backward and future oriented elements are closely combined and even intertwined in the Weltanschauung as in the political practice of National Socialism.

I would, however, be reluctant to positively identify it with modernization, even if unintentional. Such a thesis is expounded by Ralf Dahrendorf and also by scholars like David Schoenbaum, who in his *Hitler's Social Revolution*, speaks of a 'double revolution . . . at the same time a revolution of means and ends.'[9] The modernization thesis tends to move too far away from the concrete phenomenon of National Socialism and particularly Hitler to be of much real help in the interpretation of such a movement and system, and such political figures. It is true that in his way Hitler was modern and an admirer of modern techniques and a rationally organized industrial state, which he needed for a realization of his war and his goals of domination. The same is true of some of his closest cooperators like Goebbels, the virtuoso promoter of mass communications, and Albert Speer and other technicians of power.

But I would prefer more cautious interpretations like that of Henry Ashby Turner who tries to do full justice to the ambivalence and intentional structure of nazism (in its connections with capitalism).[10] It remains essential that the very manner of the Nazi revolution is characterized by this ambiguity and by the fact that it was brought about and performed largely and emphatically in the name of a glorified past, of a pre- and post-industrial age, and with a set of antimodernistic values (e.g., agrarian society against urbanisation, corporative state against parliamentary democracy). It was exactly this revolt against modernism that found a strong backing and echo within the middle-class population which formed the main following of Hitler. And we have to be aware of the fact that among the elements and motives for neo-fascist and related movements in our time antimodernist arguments and emotions still rank high.

If there remain doubts about the revolutionary 'quality' of National Socialism, surely Hitler the ideologist and the politician, the sovereign manipulator of the means and ends of this movement was a revolutionary man. When he came to power as a pseudo-democratically legalized dictator, many contemporaries were deceived by his disguise. Today we know that not for one moment in his career did he waver in his unbending intention of encompassing and realizing the visions of forceful change and domination. He not only represented the essential tendencies of his time; he was, in the words of Hugh Trevor-Roper, 'the Rousseau, the Mirabeau, the Robespierre, and the Napoleon of his revolution, he was its Marx, its Lenin, its Trotsky, and its Stalin. By his character and nature he may have been inferior to most of them, yet he succeeded, as none before him, in controlling his revolution in each phase, even in the moment of defeat. This speaks for a considerable understanding of the forces he has brought about.'[11]

And we may add that he effected cataclysms like few before — for example, Lenin, Napoleon, the French revolutionaries. His concept of a racist world empire, his conviction of a Social Darwinism determining all life, his cult of force and power, and his ideal of the artist of genius as the true master of the world — all this points to strong contemporary currents of thought and behaviour. But he outdid all other exponents of such ideas in his mental rigidity and in the practical consequences that followed. He was indeed that extremely rare exception — an intellectual with a practical sense of power. If a revolutionary is defined by his ability to combine a radical concept of change with the capacity to mobilize the necessary forces, then Hitler can even be called the prototype of a revolutionary, and some of the actual interest in Hitler, despite his failure, may be caused by the incredible interplay of ideological fixation and ability to introduce it into the realm of politics.

## IV

Many attempts have been made to trace not only the historical framework and the intellectual and socio-economic conditions that made National Socialism possible but to explain also the psychological roots and meaning of the Hitler phenomenon. Most recently this gave rise to the new school of psychohistory, whose efforts have been widely publicized especially in the American discussion. In 1973 this event led to the founding of a new periodical, *The History of Childhood Quarterly*, covering 'cases' as different as Bismarck, Hitler and, most recently, Henry Kissinger.[12] To date the new method has not been particularly rewarding; there are more hypothetical guesses than established facts. We shall have to wait for the announced Hitler books by the declared psychohistorians Rudolph Binion and Robert G. L. Waite, among others. There is a danger of even more speculations around the Hitler phenomenon, mystifying rather than enlightening the real connections, as it has already been the case for many years with the discussion about alleged Jewish ancestors of Hitler, which I think was and is pointless.[13]

There are of course arguments pro and contra psychohistory. On the positive side, a new emphasis on the dimension of persons and their complicated role in history is to be welcomed, as against a mainly structural view of history stressing the collective and predetermined elements. On the other hand, the question of reliable sources with respect to a verification of the various psychological theories seems in most cases quite insoluble, and especially in the case of Hitler. The lack of reliable sources on his childhood furthers the tendency of psychohistorical reconstructions derived from theories supplanting evidence. Indeed, psychohistory must be founded 'on hard factual evidence to support psychological interpretations,' and not the other way round.[14] As to the psychoanalytical approach in particular, it would be quite misleading to concentrate the research for causes and motives almost exclusively on childhood: in the case of Hitler, the age from 20 to 35, that is, the years 1909-1924, contain the real crucial process of personal and political formation. After all, he was a political man, and his way into politics is what really matters. There may be thousands of people with similar childhood history, including close relationship to the mother and a mother trauma (as stressed by Binion) or sexual perversion (as maintained by Waite), yet with quite different or no political consequences at all, at least as far as our scarce knowledge of Hitler's childhood allows any comparisons.

And thus the real historical problems remain — with or without a hypothetical childhood analysis — namely, how the formative coincidence of personal and political conditions came about. It is foremost the process of political transformation that has to be studied from the manner and the utterances of the man before and after November 1918, when Hitler had his much-stressed hysterical shock at the end of the war. And such a comprehensive analysis is certainly to be continued up to 1933, when he attained the final crucial experience of gaining absolute power by means of a pseudolegal revolution: an experience he repeated during the following years in expanding his foreign policy, by means of peace talk and threats simultaneously.

For all these reasons it is certainly not enough to call Hitler a criminal of super-dimensions and to stamp his accomplices as mere caricatures of butchers and murderers, as the cartoons like to do — another underestimation of the Nazi phenomenon. Hitler's strength of will and his fascination for a fanatical following was based on a perverted moral energy, to which the most terrible acts of suppression and extermination were special proof of his highest values: unfeeling rigour against himself as justification for the rigour practiced against others; and the readiness to kill for the regime and its superhuman Weltanschauung was praised by Hitler and his chief executioner, Himmler, as heroic moral virtue comprising and sublimating all the inner values of National Socialism, such as the respectable values of faith, sincerity, loyalty, rigidity, decency, and courage, but now reversed in a truly revolutionary fashion to serve the ideological terror system.

The real danger of this perverted political and oral justification of the crime can be seen from the easy functioning of the extermination apparatus of the SS, constantly driven and justified by such a mechanism of ideological moralism. It was based on the possible combination of primitive instincts and lust for cruelty with a fanatical conviction of the higher legitimacy of such crimes — a combination well known in all totalitarian systems. The contempt for bourgeois morality, *bürgerliche Moral*, expresses this ideological perversion which can be found on the extreme left as well as the right.

Hitler himself, with his ideological fixation and his sense of mission as saviour of a world doomed by racist decline, was the prototype of such a transvaluation, taking literally Nietzsche's vision of *Umwertung aller Werte* and transcending *bürgerliche Moral*.

This had been an obsession since his early days, when Hitler, the would-be artist of genius, declined to have the same concept of life and pleasure as the rest of the world, and when he got into the habit of posing as the man of special purity, of idealistic frugality, of readiness for sacrifice. He was always very careful to uphold this image and to hide his private life and emotions. In the end, he saw himself as the last person faithful to the idea and dying for its preservation, while the German people and even most of his closest collaborators received his final verdict of not having been strict enough with themselves, and, therefore, neither fit nor entitled to survive. He even reproached himself for not having been radical enough in his revolution and therefore failing to realize his idea fully. This was his only reaction to a war and a totalitarian regime that cost the lives of more than fifty million people.

The excesses accompanying the eclipse and decline of the Third Reich indeed illustrated the true character of a system which, contrary to the seductive theory of dictatorship, did not give its citizens political order and effective government or greater security and opportunities, but rather rested solely on organized despotism and pseudo-legal, ill-concealed crimes. Hitler had only one, egomaniacal answer: if the German people failed their historic test they thereby forfeited their national existence. He was obsessed with one idea to the end: that he would never capitulate, that what happened in November 1918 would never recur in German history. In his political testament written one day before his death he repeated the fixed ideas which had governed the rise and rule of National Socialism beginning with the ferocious hatred of 'international Jewry and its helpers,' who in Hitler's world were responsible for everything that was happening.

Ideas have to be taken seriously, even when they seem utterly abstruse and far from any possible realization. As the philosopher Hegel, himself a powerful generator of ideologies both of conservative etatism and of socialist Marxism, put it, 'the idea is not as powerless as to become only the ideal' It will always be a complex problem to recognize and explain the origin of ideas and their development into political strength and consequence. In the case of the man Adolf Hitler, the ideas of racist superiority, of living space, and of the uniqueness of a greater German nation found a carrier who was not a simple fascist agitator or dreamer, but a man with the radically fixed will to put his thoughts against reality. He aimed not simply at a traditional empire like Mussolini or the like, but in his very own way he oriented his politics totally, and with all the consequences of force and war and mass murder, on the theoretical construction of a racist empire in which finally reality was to match the idea completely.

In this respect, with his principles, rigorism, and perfectionism in following a deadly 'general' idea, he has been called very German and he indeed personified one among many different German traditions.[15] Thus he fulfilled the anxious prophecy of a German-Jewish poet writing one hundred years before Hitler's revolution. Heinrich Heine viewed with deep concern the sharp discrepancy between idea and reality, between intellectual radicalism and political backwardness in nineteenth-century Germany. This was the hotbed of Hitler's political thought, while corresponding political action became possible only under the conditions of the twentieth century, and in particular the first world war and its aftermath. In 1834 Heine wrote, as if to enlarge on Hegel's dictum of the idea always becoming more than an idea, 'The thought precedes the action like the lightning and the thunder. The German thunder though (to be sure) is also a German and not very flexible, and comes rolling somewhat slower; but it will come, and when you hear it roar one day as it has never roared in world history, you should know: the German thunder has finally reached its destination.'

Indeed, despite the worldwide repercussions, Hitler and National Socialism remain foremost a German — and Austrian — phenomenon. But it should be kept in mind and understood by all nations and politicians as transcending the national and historical conditionality and symbolizing a warning lesson never to be forgotten and never to be easily mistaken and misused. It is the lesson that extreme political concepts propagated as final solutions of all problems never serve humane ends but degrade people and their values into mere instruments of a destructive power mania and the regime of barbarism. That such extreme concepts would be doomed to ultimate failure is the hope to be drawn from the fall of Hitler.

## NOTES

1. Among the most recent interpretations of Hitler are two balanced articles by Klaus Hildebrand, 'Hitlers Ort in der Geschichte des preussisch-deutschen Nationalstaats,' in *Historische Zeitschrift*, no. 217 (1973), 584-632; 'Zwischen Mythos und Moderne: Hitler in seiner Zeit,' in *Das Historisch-politische Buch*, no. 22 (1974), 33-37. The comprehensive biography by Joachim Fest, *Hitler* (Frankfurt a.M., 1973), the best treatment since — and besides — Alan Bullock's classic work, has brought forth new discussions; cf. also K. D. Bracher, 'Hitler — die deutsche Revolution,' in *Die Zeit*, no. 42 (1973), 25.

2. See my critical remarks on Speer, in *Die deutsche Diktatur*, 545 ff; and on Maser, in *Encounter*, no. 39/3 (September 1972), 75 ff.

THE ROLE OF HITLER: PERSPECTIVES OF INTERPRETATION 225

3. For the arguments in favour of a modified but comprehensive concept of totalitarianism, cf. especially Leonard Shapiro *Totalitarianism* (London, 1972); also K. D. Bracher 'Totalitarianism,' in *Dictionary of the History of Ideas*, vol. 4 (New York, 1973).

4. Leonard Shapiro, 'The Role of the Monolithic Party under the Totalitarian Leader,' in J. W. Lewis, ed., *Party Leadership and Revolutionary Power in China* (Cambridge, 1970); Robert C. Tucker, 'The Dictator and Totalitarianism,' in *World Politics*, no. 17 (1965), 555 ff.

5. Ralf Dahrendorf, *Society and Democracy in Germany* (New York, 1967) with considerable influence on the international reinterpretation of Nazi Germany in the sense of a modernization process against the will.

6. Ernst Nolte's well-known books *Three Faces of Fascism* (London, 1965), *Theorien über den Faschismus* (Köln, 1967), and *Die faschistischen Bewegungen* (München, 1966) have been followed by a renaissance of 'general fascism,' from the traditional communist and the more elaborated Marxist versions to the liberal (English-American) use of the term.

7. Cf. Hajo Holborn, ed., *Republic to Reich, the Making of the Nazi Revolution* (New York, 1972); also *The Path to Dictatorship 1918-1933* (New York, 1966); K. D. Bracher, *Stufen der Machtergreifung* (Frankfurt, 1974). On the other hand there is the very competent book by Adrian Lyttelton, *The Seizure of Power, Fascism in Italy 1919-1929* (London, 1973), and Renzo de Felice's fundamental *Mussolini il rivoluzionario* (Torino, 1965), and *Mussolini il fascista* (Torino, 1966), 196 ff.

8. Peter Gay's introduction to *The German Dictatorship* (New York, 1970), vii.

9. David Schoenbaum, *Hitler's Social Revolution* (New York, 1966), xxii f. Since then a growing number of contemporary historians have followed those theses, which by no means are a specialty of conservative or rightist interpretation. From a more substantial point of view, the most recent interpretation by George Mosse is fundamental, *The Nationalization of the Masses* (New York, 1975); on the problem of a 'fascist revolution,' see his introduction to *International Fascism, 1920-1945* (London, 1965), 14 ff.

10. Henry A. Turner, *Faschismus und Kapitalismus in Deutschland* (Göttingen, 1972).

11. Hugh Trevor-Roper, *La testament politique de Hitler* (Paris, 1959), 13.

12. Cf. especially Rudolph Binion, 'Hitler's Concept of Lebensraum: The Psychological Basis,' in *History of Childhood Quarterly* 1 (1973), 187-258, with the important comments by George H. Stein, Bradley F. Smith, George L. Mosse, Andreas Dorpalen, and Dietrich Orlow, among others.

13. I have been criticized for this by psychohistorians; e.g., Peter Loewenberg, in *Central European History* 7 (1974), 262 ff. — a review in praise of Walter C. Langer, *The Mind of Adolf Hitler*, the wartime psychoanalysis (1943) whose reprint of 1972 served as exit point for the psychohistorical part of the Hitler wave. For a critical assessment, see especially the review article by Hans W. Gatzke, in *American Historical Review* 78 (1973), 394 ff. and 1155 ff. (discussion); cf. also L. Papeleux, 'Psychanalyse d'Adolf Hitler,' in *Revue d'histoire de la deuxième guerre mondiale* 24/96 (October 1974), 105-108.

14. The quotation is from G. H. Stein, op. cit., 216 ff. A typical example of the deductive, unhistorical treatment of disputable sources may be found in William L. Langer, op. cit., 17 (also quoted by Gatzke). He starts with a diagnosis (which fluctuates from hysteric psychopath to neurotic psychopath) and continues 'With this diagnosis as a point of orientation, we are able to evaluate the data in terms of probability. Those fragments that could most easily be fitted [!] into this general clinical category were tentatively regarded as possessing a higher degree of probability— as far as reliability and relevance was concerned — than those which seemed alien to the clinical picture.' The sources have to fit the picture — shouldn't it be the contrary?

15. Cf. J. Fest, op. cit., 513, 517 (German ed.).

# PART III
## Local Fascisms

# 6

# Fascism in Eastern Europe

BELA VAGO

Almost from the moment of its birth Italian fascism had its historians, some of whom were outstanding. Bonomi, Nitti, Sturzo, and Ferrero, Villari or Salvemini[1] published their works in the early twenties, some of them at a time when Mussolini had not yet seized complete control over Italy. Similarly, valuable documentary and analytical works on National Socialism had already appeared in Germany and elsewhere, before Hitler came to power.[2] By the end of the thirties the historical literature on nazism could already have filled entire libraries. East European fascism, however, unlike the Western fascist movements, received only secondary treatment. Not one single scholarly work about the East European fascist movements was published either in the countries involved or in the West until the first post-war years. Though their own 'court,' historians or their paid chroniclers did publish some writings about their movements during World War II, these were no more than official eulogies.[3] In the West too, during the war years, nothing important on this subject was published, as, understandably, Western historiography paid scant attention to East European fascism.

Naturally, immediately after the war National Socialism, and secondarily Italian fascism 'stole the show.' The lack of interest in East European fascism could also be attributed to the marked tendency to ascribe all that occurred on the extreme right in Eastern Europe to Hitler's and Mussolini's impact—a view that was not entirely in accord with reality. The external factor, that is, the German and Italian role in the fascist transformation of the area was given priority over the local struggles for power. Paradoxically enough, instead of stimulating scientific research into fascism, communist rule and Soviet control over Eastern Europe exerted a doubly discouraging influence upon such scholarly activities both in the East and in the West. The new regimes of the East European People's democracies in their early years were more interested in their struggle against social democracy and against bourgeois democratic and pro-Western forces on the ideological level, than in the struggle against fascism. At the same time the West was rather more concerned about the process of communization and contemporary Sovietization than about the recent fascist past. Decades had to elapse before the first noteworthy results of research into East European fascism appeared either in the West or the East.

At the outset it is necessary to indicate which movements are highlighted

[229]

in the present survey of East European fascism. To this end, without attempting to delimit the controversial and arbitrary borders between Central and Eastern Europe, or for that matter without going into the complex problem of defining the notions of East-Central Europe or South Eastern Europe, it is taken for granted that Eastern Europe covers the area east of Germany and Austria, overlooking the inner regional divisions.

Significant fascist movements did not spring up in all parts of Eastern Europe in the inter-war period and during World War II, and in only four countries (Romania, Hungary, and the two by-products of the liquidation of Czechoslovakia and of Yugoslavia, Slovakia and Croatia) did they actually seize power, and this only towards the end of the period and for a short span. Only two fascist movements played an important part for a relatively longer time, enjoying mass support: the Romanian Iron Guard and the Hungarian Arrow Cross. The bulk of this survey will be devoted to the historiography of these two movements. A rather more restricted scope will be allotted to the Slovakian Hlinka party, which can only be listed as a 'classical' fascist movement after the setting up of the Slovakian puppet state in 1939. Similarly, the Croatian Ustasha movement, which hardly had any history before April 1941 and whose programme and ideological foundation were little known among the Croatian masses, will only be given a brief treatment. Finally, some of the relatively few articles written about the insignificant Polish fascist organizations are noted. The scarce, fragmentary literature about Serbian, Bulgarian, or Baltic fascism, mostly published in their respective languages, does not merit inclusion in a short survey. The literature on East European fascism falls into three groups: (1) Post World War II local (communist) literature: (2) fascist emigré literature; and (3) works written in the west by non-involved historians. This survey will distinguish between the few general, synthesising works about East European fascism, published mainly in the West, and the great number of monographs about the main fascist movements, most of them published in Eastern Europe, or by fascist emigrés in the West. Because of the varieties of East European fascism and the chronological differences in the history of their appearance and disappearance, the relevant literature is treated on a regional basis.

As early as 1919 and in the twenties numerous fascist-type organizations, movements, and parties had sprung up in Romania, but only two of them had come to the forefront by the mid-thirties: Professor A. C. Cuza's and Octavian Goga's National Christian Party and Corneliu Zelea Codreanu's Iron Guard.

In 1923 Cuza founded the League of Christian National Defence, an extreme nationalistic and, par excellence, anti-Semitic organization, which gained only marginal votes in the parliamentary elections during the twenties and in the early thirties. The young student leader, Codreanu, left

Cuza's League in 1927, founded the Legion of Archangel Michael, set up the Iron Guard in 1930, as a complementary mass organization of the Legion, and after the Iron Guard was disbanded several times, he renamed the movement Totul pentru Țară (All for the Fatherland) party in 1934. The movement, known as the Iron Guard, and its followers, Legionaries or guardists, irrespective of their official designation, achieved a spectacular success in the 1937 elections, polling almost 16 per cent of the votes. However, it was again dissolved in February 1938 when all political parties were banned by King Carol's dictatorial regime, and its leaders were decimated during 1938 and 1939. It emerged anew in Autumn 1940 led by Horia Sima, in the wake of the dismemberment of Greater Romania, and acceded to power in a peculiar alliance with General Ion Antonescu's military clique. The so-called National Legionary State lasted barely five months. The armed rebellion of the Legionaries against Antonescu at the end of January 1941 and their crushing defeat put a violent end to their rule and to their activity in the country. Antonescu continued to rule without the Legionaries in the framework of a fascist-type military dictatorship until the coup d'état of August 1944, when Romania joined the Allies against Nazi Germany. However, a strong legionary emigration, supplemented by minor groups of emigrés of former Cuza, Goga, and Antonescu followers, continued to be active after the war in Western Europe and in the Americas, mainly engaged in polemics against communist Romania and amongst themselves.

The second important factor on the Romanian extreme right was the National Christian party, founded in 1935 after the merger of Cuza's League and Goga's rightist, ultra-nationalist agrarian party. This new party, which polled less than 10 per cent of the votes in the 1937 elections, came to power at the end of 1937 as a transitional solution to the internal crisis and actually served for 44 days until the inauguration of King Carol's dictatorship in February 1938. Although this survey concentrates on the Iron Guard, attention is also paid to the Goga-Cuza party, to the royalist dictatorship, and to the Antonescu regime.

In Hungary the emergence of fascist-type organizations and movements coincided with the counter-revolutionary organizing activity against Béla Kun's communist regime in 1919. A great many extreme right, extreme nationalist, racist, and later national socialist groupings emerged in the twenties and in the early thirties. The only movement which paralleled the role of the Iron Guard, and which actually came to power in October 1944 in the wake of the military debacle on the German-Hungarian front, and after Horthy's unsuccessful attempt to break with Nazi Germany, was Ferenc Szálasi's Arrow Cross. Although the arrow cross was the symbol of a number of national socialist parties and groups, it is only used here to refer to Szálasi's movement. Beside the Arrow Cross, Béla Imrédy's Party of Hungarian Revival will also be mentioned, as the second most important

extreme right party which played any role during World War II on the
Hungarian fascist scene.

Three periods can roughly be distinguished in the historiography of
fascism in Romania and Hungary in the course of the three decades that
have elapsed since World War II.

The works that appeared soon after the war in both countries — more in
Hungary, less in Romania — were mainly of a journalistic nature, with no
scientific pretensions. Around 1948-49, when the consolidation of the communist regimes had become an accomplished fact, and even later, in the
early fifties, fascism as a topic of research was kept under wraps. In neither
country did any noteworthy work appear on fascism in that period. The
cold war imposed anti-imperialist, anti-Western, and anti-cosmopolitan
slogans upon the satellite countries; the unmasking of local fascism was not
considered of topical interest. The defeated enemy was not dangerous any
longer and Moscow did not attribute any practical significance to research
into East European fascism. Another reason that may have accounted for
the lack of interest in this subject was probably the circumstance that in
both countries the new regimes were doing their utmost to 're-educate' and
win over the rank and file of the former fascist movements. The Romanian
communist leaders, including Ana Pauker, opened the gates of the Communist party to the masses of 'petty' legionaries who had been 'led astray,'
and Rákosi followed a similar policy towards the Hungarian *kisnyilasok*
(the little men of the Arrow Cross). It should also be noted that in the first
post-war years the documentary sources relating to local fascism counted as
classified security material. In this period discussion of fascism appeared
only in party literature and in the propaganda media. It was a term of
abuse and was used to describe most of the inter-war political parties and
regimes. It was only in the early sixties that the first works of a scientific
character appeared about the main fascist movements, yet even more years
were to elapse before the publication of any significant works dealing with
the subject — earlier in Hungary and later in Romania.

All in all, there are rather few works about the origins and the nature of
East European fascism. The literature explaining the role of ideas in the
life of the fascist movements is particularly poor, and few if any bibliographical reports of these movements have come out so far (none for the
Arrow Cross for instance). The ideological literature of the various movements is relatively scarce compared with Italian fascism or with German
National Socialism, while the published, or re-published basic material
appeared mostly in the local languages and even this source material is
hardly available.

There is a further difficulty. With the possible exception of a few non-
involved Western scholars, historians engaged in the research work are
extremely prejudiced, personally, politically, and in other ways. Even in

basic matters which seem to be beyond any controversy, precisely because they are based on facts (such as the resort to violence, terror, or anti-Semitic excesses), views are widely divergent, making it most difficult to present an impartial, unequivocal synthesis. Nor is there any consensus among historians of differing political backgrounds and attitudes in such *imponderabilia*, as for example the mass enthusiasm in the case of the Iron Guard or of the Arrow Cross.

Returning to the first stage of the historiography of East European fascism, the survey of the literature of the first post-war years begins with an exception. At the end of 1944, a few months after the anti-Nazi coup d'état in Romania, a book appeared in Bucharest by Lucreţiu Pătrăşcanu, *Sub trei dictaturi*[4] (*Under Three Dictatorships*), which analyses with amazing clarity the basic problems of Romanian fascism. Pătrăşcanu's early analysis is roughly valid to this day. The law graduate communist leader (the first communist minister of justice of post-war Romania and one of the first victims of Gheorghiu-Dej's purges), had elaborated his work as early as 1941. His book disappeared from the market in 1949 and only under Ceauşescu's nationalist rehabilitation campaign did a new edition appear in 1970. Pătrăşcanu's work essentially comprises those theses to which Romanian historiography has returned in recent years after a long and tortuous path, and which are partly shared by non-involved Western researchers as well. He emphasized the strong mass basis of Cuza's League and of the Iron Guard and believed that the reason for the relative successes achieved by these movements should be sought less in 'imports from abroad' than in the ability of Cuza and Codreanu to adapt fascism to the 'autochthonous' medium.[5] In the case of both movements Pătrăşcanu makes a point of stressing the incorporation of Christian Orthodoxy into political agitation both as to content and form.[6] To this day Pătrăşcanu's book is one of the very few attempts to analyse the social composition of the Iron Guard rank and file and of its élite. Naturally, he could only avail himself of very scarce documentary source material and he lacked the advantage of historical perspective; nevertheless, his analysis has hardly been surpassed to this day.

Pătrăşcanu does not deny the fact that the Iron Guard was essentially made up of the peasant and working class elements, but he attempts to lay special stress on the *Lumpen* elements in the midst of the Legionary masses, thus exonerating the conscious working class and the enlightened peasants from the charge of fascism. He even ventures into psychological interpretations by pointing out the significantly high rate of neurotics with inferiority complexes and even physically disabled people in the ranks of the Legion. Nevertheless, Pătrăşcanu does not minimize the decisive role of the young intellectuals in the Iron Guard, nor of the Orthodox clergy, for that matter. At the same time, however, he cannot help resorting to the Dimitrovian official Muscovite formulae, and he himself seems to believe

that the Romanian fascist movements essentially constituted 'a political
mass manoeuvre at the disposal of the ruling forces' against the democratic
parties and the workers' movements.[7]

For the official stand towards the problem of fascism in the early years of
the communist regime, there is the authoritative standard *History of the
Romanian Peoples' Republic*, edited in 1948 by Mihail Roller, the founder
of the post-war Romanian communist historical school.[8] The work
attributes the impetus of the fascist movements to the manoeuvrings of the
bourgeois and land-owner strata, while designating as fascist, without discrimination, the royalist dictatorship, the Legionary rule, as well as Antonescu's military dictatorship. There is no mention whatsoever of the social
structure of Romanian fascism and no attempt made towards an analysis
of its ideology.

Even in the spate of works on fascism in the early sixties, the researchers
dealt less with the character of Romanian fascism than with blown-up
descriptions of the anti-fascist struggle. A number of studies appeared in
the mid-sixties about the characteristics of the regimes between 1940 and
1944[9] and about the penetration of Nazi ideology,[10] but a bibliographical
essay published as late as 1965 did not yet mention any book on fascism.
Only in the late sixties and the first years of this decade was there a turning
point. The central event in this respect was the organization in Bucharest
of a symposium concerning the critical analysis and the unmasking of
fascism in Romania — in the words of the organizers — followed by the publication of the proceedings. In the same year the first book to be published
in communist Romania about the Iron Guard appeared, written by Mihail
Fătu and Ion Spălățeulu.[12] Characteristically, the main title of the symposium book is *Against Fascism*, denoting the militant tone and the principal
aim of the symposium: less analysis and more unmasking, bringing the
anti-fascist struggle to the fore. Nevertheless, most of the twenty-two
papers published in this volume represent the first scholarly contribution to
a Marxist analysis of fascism in Romania. A non-orthodox and non-dogmatic line pervades a number of essays (about the socio-economic foundation of fascism in Romania, the Iron Guard ideology, the 'Legionarism'
and literature, as well as the characterisation of the Antonescu Legionary
regime in 1940-41.[13] However, the symposium volume did not even try to
tackle such thorny problems as, for example, the mass support enjoyed by
the Iron Guard and even by Goga and Cuza in the ranks of the peasantry
and the working class, or the contradiction between the allegation on the
one hand of the support given by the National Liberal Party and by King
Carol to Codreanu, and on the other, the deadly blows administered by the
same two forces to the Iron Guard. In my opinion, regarding the
symposium and its book, it is essential, first and foremost, to keep in mind
the words of Valter Roman, who, surveying the blank areas of Romanian
historiography, pointed to the lack of works dealing with the theoretical

origins and the ideological aspects of Romanian fascism, and stated that there were still no basic works in Romanian about fascism in general and about Romanian fascism in particular. 'The history of Romanian fascism is only about to be written,' concluded Valter Roman in March 1971.[14]

Fătu's and Spălățelu's book about the Iron Guard has the great merit of using, for the first time, a rich archival material—that of the State Archives, of the Communist party and other collections usually hermetically closed to researchers. But the selection of the archival material is obviously biased and the work suffers from some grave shortcomings. One of the main aims of the authors seems to have been the emphasis on the alleged collusion between the ruling circles (the Camarilla, the National Liberal, and the National Peasant leaders) and the Iron Guard. The authors fail to convince the reader that such collusion existed, precisely because they overplayed this aspect. The polemical tone of the work and the outspoken aim of appealing to the widest possible public detracts considerably from the scholarly value of the book.

One major work dealing with the extreme right is Al. Gh. Savu's book about the royalist dictatorship (1938-40).[15] Although the work deals mainly with the political history of King Carol's dictatorship, laying stress upon its relations with Nazi Germany, the author devotes sufficient space to the analysis of the Goga-Cuza government (30 December 1937-10 February 1938), scrutinizes the political character of the royalist regime and examines it as the 'antechamber' of the fascist dictatorship inaugurated in September 1940. Unlike some Romanian historians Savu deems Cuza's movement to be fascist. In common with quite a few other historians he calls attention to the anti-Semitic agitation in the inter-war period, which —in his opinion too—proved itself a useful means of winning over a certain section of the population to fascism.[16] One of his assertions is particularly noteworthy, namely, that Romanian fascism was born in the guise of anti-Semitism.[17] Like other authors in contemporary Romania, Savu, too, contents himself with this assertion and does not devote much space to the problem of anti-Semitism. It is characteristic that the study of this most important component of Romanian nationalism and fascism should be completely absent from the works of Marxist authors. It seems that no study has yet been devoted in post-war Romanian historiography to the Jewish question or to the problem of anti-Semitism, not even in the context of research on fascism.

Among the essays published in Romania (in English, French, and also Russian), those that attempt to cast light upon the theoretical and ideological facets of the Iron Guard, and secondarily, of the Cuza movement should be singled out. Regarding the Iron Guard each work made a point of emphasizing its mysticism, irrationalism, cult of death and the dead, and its fanaticism. There is but one point which gives rise to diverging and even contradictory views: the racism of the Iron Guard. While it has gen-

erally been taken for granted that racism was not a characteristic feature of
the Iron Guard, some contemporary authors assert the contrary.[18] There
are some contradictions in the more recent literature about the relative
independence, originality, and autochthonous character of the two main
fascist movements. While more attention has lately been turned to the
local origins of Romanian fascism, the rigid view prevailing a quarter of a
century ago still persists, according to which Romanian fascism and primarily the Iron Guard were strengthened by foreign influence and foreign
support. The view still dominates contemporary works that the Iron Guard
essentially fulfilled the role of Nazi Germany's Fifth Column.[19] However,
there are still numerous studies that, in accordance with the original communist conception, consider the oligarchical and reactionary upper circles
as the main motive power behind the Iron Guard, the League of National
Christian Defence and other fascist formations.[20] On the other hand, quite
a number of recent studies draw a clear distinction between the different
extreme-right parties and regimes. While in the first post-war years the
Goga-Cuza government was equated with the Legionary period and with
Antonescu's regime, and even with King Carol's dictatorship—all of them
being qualified as fascist—some works published in recent years draw a
clear distinction between the royalist dictatorship and Antonescu's rule, for
example, denying the previous assertions about the fascist character of
King Carol's dictatorial regime.[21] Despite this positive symptom,
Romanian historiography has still a long way to go in defining the nature
of the different inter-war regimes and in renouncing the automatic use of
fascism when characterising rightist anti-marxist parties and regimes. It
seems probable that the lacunae found at the 1971 Bucharest symposium
will serve as stimulants for researchers to bring out some non-dogmatic
synthesizing works on Romanian fascism.

In the early post-war years the fascist Romanian emigrés, first of all the
Legionaries, and also some extreme right non-fascist emigrés (for example
among Antonescu's followers) produced a considerable number of works in
two categories. They re-edited and commented on the basic writings and
documents of the Iron Guard, and some former Legionaries and leading
figures of different dictatorial regimes embarked upon elaborating or re-
writing the history of the inter-war period.[22] The publications which had
come out in wartime Germany and in Italy before 1943 were invariably
crude propaganda, hardly acceptable as historical works.

The first post-war work which deserves attention is the voluminous history of the Iron Guard published by Ştefan Pălăghiţă in 1951.[23] The
author, an Orthodox priest belonging to the second-rank leadership of the
Iron Guard, wields his detailed description of the Legionary movement as
a polemical weapon in the factional struggle waged in the ranks of the Iron
Guard emigration. As a spokesman for the anti-Sima group, Pălăghiţă

accuses Horia Sima of terrorism and of common crimes, and of betraying the Iron Guard as an agent of King Carol and his Camarilla.[24] On the other hand, Pălăghiţă tried to embellish Codreanu's image in a most peculiar manner — by extolling his alleged non-violence and humanism. In the same year (1951) a senior official of the Antonescu administration, G. Barbul, published a eulogistic work in the defence of Ion Antonescu, the military dictator from January 1941 after the break with the Iron Guard, with which he had shared power from September 1940, acquitting him of the charges made by the Legionaries, communists, and democrats.[25] An authoritative book on Ion Antonescu appeared at about the same time (1952) written by General Ion Gheorghe, Antonescu's last minister in Berlin.[26] The general, a non-Legionary and a typical representative of the extreme-rightist and extreme-nationalist officer group which supported Antonescu's dictatorship, acquits the 'Conducator' of the crimes committed by the Iron Guard during the months of the common rule (September 1940-January 1941) and of the charge of having served as a nazi tool. He denies the fascist character of the Antonescu regime and asserts that after the abortive Legionary rebellion in January 1941, fascist ideas were extirpated from the political life of his country.

All these works mainly deal with the political development of Romania in the pre-war years and during the war, focussing attention on German-Romanian relations, but lacking any scientific analysis of the origins and ideas of local fascism.

In their writings published in the early post-war years, Pălăghiţă, Barbul, Gheorghe, and others in the forefront of the Legionary and Antonescu emigration, most conspicuously concealed or minimized the anti-Semitism of both the Iron Guard and of the Antonescu administration, although Gheorghe, for example, does not fail to emphasize the element of violence resorted to by the Iron Guard in the 'solution' of the Jewish question. Remarkably, however, at a later stage authors like Horia Sima became more outspoken about the extreme anti-Semitism of the Romanian nationalist camp.

Two major works on the Iron Guard have recently appeared by two senior survivors of the Legionary leadership: the memoirs of Prince Michel Sturdza,[27] Foreign Minister of the short-lived National-Legionary regime (September 1940-January 1941), and Horia Sima's history of the Legionary movement.[28]

Sturdza's non-scholarly work, largely devoted to foreign affairs, is a bitter attack not only against the anti-fascist opponents of the Iron Guard, but against Marshal Ion Antonescu too. In Sturdza's view Antonescu, whom he considers 'insane,' betrayed not only the Iron Guard but had earlier betrayed even Goga, and was one of those who brought about the collapse of the Goga-Cuza government. In the final analysis he shares

Horia Sima's conviction that Antonescu 'caused Rumania as much evil as
did Carol.'[29] The same Sturdza, who was wont to mention the 'Anonymous
Forces,' having in mind the 'Occult Forces,' an expression scattered
throughout Sima's writings, namely the 'Judeo-Marxist-Capitalist-Free-
mason' forces embodied in the Camarilla, is anxious to 'humanize' Codreanu's anti-Semitism. In his view, and contrary to reality, Codreanu had
always proclaimed that 'violence against Jews was a stupid mistake. He
[Codreanu] would have immediately expelled from the Movement any fool
who had so much as broken a window in a Jewish-owned shop.'[30]

Sima's history of the Legionary Movement (he has only published the
first part of the history of the Iron Guard, up to the December 1937 electoral success of Codreanu) is a very biased and passionate plea on behalf of
the Iron Guard, and a vehement attack against practically each and every
political force in inter-war Romania. Sima, unlike Pălăghiţă, Sturdza, and
others, devotes whole chapters to the doctrine and the ideology of the Iron
Guard. However, his pattern of the individual, the Nation, and God as the
three components of the axis round which the Legionary movement turns,
is not much of a contribution to the elucidation of the Legionary dogma.
According to the less analytical Pălăghiţă, the three main components of
the Legionary doctrine were Jesus Christ (i.e., religion), the Nation, and
the King, while Ion Gheorghe designated religious mysticism, anti-Semitism, and National Socialism as the three basic principles of the Iron
Guard.

As already pointed out, on the subject of the anti-Semitism of the Iron
Guard, Sima is more sincere and less cautious than his fellow chroniclers.
His work contains elaborate and strongly worded indictments against
Romanian Jewry, defending and justifying the extreme anti-Semitism of
the Legionaries. It seems likely that Sima's book ranks first among the most
vulgar anti-Semitic writings that saw the light after the submergence of
National Socialism, although he never fails to point out that the motivation of the Legionary anti-Semitism was neither racial nor religious but
social and economic. His history of the Legionary movement is a regression
compared to his *Destinée du nationalisme*,[31] a work about the fate of
post-war European nationalism, published in 1951, when he seemed to be
more reasonable and more restrained. After all, Sima's book, a passionate
plea for religious mysticism, irrationalism, fanaticism, and a glorification
of the 'Legionary spiritual revolution' is an eloquent example of the dis-
tortion of facts, which by no means contributes to the elucidation of the
controversies around the Iron Guard. Even worse is Carlo Sburlati's history
of the Iron Guard,[32] centred on Codreanu's biography. It is no more than a
thoroughly erroneous and naive eulogy of the Legionary movement.

Cuza and Goga are very scantily represented in the emigré literature.
Apart from short chapters and fleeting references in most of the emigré
publications, the only works devoted to Cuza and Goga appear to be a few

pamphlets written by Pamfil Şeicaru.[33] These short writings of the former leading rightist publicist fall far below anything that deserves to be considered as serious history.

Western historiography, including works by non-fascist Romanian scholars writing in the West, has so far produced only a few studies about Romanian fascism, and these came rather late, in the mid sixties. As with the previous two groups these historians also concentrate almost exclusively on the Iron Guard. Apart from some essays, not a single book has been published about the Legionary movement, excepting Nicholas Nagy-Talavera's comparative work about the Arrow Cross and the Iron Guard.[34] However, the few collections of studies about European fascism, which also include Eastern Europe, and those published about Eastern Europe show keen interest both in the Iron Guard and, as a matter of course, in the Arrow Cross. Western historians, more or less free from the prejudices and passions of the involved researchers and of the communist opponents of fascism, produced some valuable essays. It is not surprising that Western scholars should be interested primarily in those problems which, for some reason, rank second or even altogether elude the fascist and the Marxist researchers: the origins of Romanian fascism, its autochthonous characteristics, its degree of indebtedness to the Italian and German 'big brothers,' its links with orthodoxy, the real components of its doctrine, its anti-Semitism and, finally, the social composition of its mass following and its leadership.

First mention should be made of Eugen Weber, a pioneer researcher into the Legionary movement, for his three basic essays,[35] Zevedei Barbu, who published an excellent study from a philosophical and sociological point of view,[36] and Stephen Fischer-Galati, author of a number of interesting essays about nationalism and fascism in Romania.[37] Short chapters are devoted to East European fascism, including the Iron Guard and the Arrow Cross, in Ernst Nolte's *Die Faschistischen Bewegungen*[38] and in the *Rise of Fascism*[39] by F. L. Carsten. The Iron Guard is the subject of a number of essays published in recent years in Western specialized journals,[40] and is also dealt with in a number of general studies on East European fascism, as for examsple H. Seton-Watson's 'Fascism, Right and Left,' published in the *Journal of Contemporary History*.[41] The international symposium on Fascism and Europe, held in Prague in 1969, deserves mention as an attempt at reviewing the main characteristics of East European fascism in the framework of a synthesis. The paper presented by Miklós Lackó (from Hungary) about the characteristic features of South-East European fascism is noteworthy.[42] However, Romanian historians did not participate in this first event and among the twenty-five studies published in two volumes not a single one is devoted to Romania. I have mentioned the Prague symposium in this connection in order to point out the paucity of literature on Romanian fascism in the 'repertoire' of Western scholars and

the reluctance of Romanian scholars to cope with this complex of problems
at an international level.

The handful of Western historians who have published works on
Romanian fascism stress *populism* as a characteristic feature of the Legionaries, and almost all of them treat Codreanu's Legion as a *radical* movement. H. Seton-Watson writes about 'Romanian Fascist populism,' and
about the young Romanian *narodniki*, who were fascists.[43] Eugen Weber,
who tends somewhat to idealize Codreanu, emphasizes more than others
the populist character of the Iron Guard. In his view 'Far from being a
bourgeois or petty-bourgeois movement...the Legion was a popular and
populist movement, with a programme which the masses (in the Romanian
context of peasants and workers) recognized as radical enough for
them....'[44] He considers the Legion as a distinctly radical social force,
and mentions, even in the case of Cuza's League, the peasant support in the
poorest counties, thus crediting Cuza with a kind of social radicalism,
albeit only in the guise of anti-Semitism ('anti-Semitism could easily be
preached as a solution to economic and political problems in the midst of
the poor peasantry.')[46] Fischer-Galati also advocates the thesis of 'populist
fascism.' He attributes this characteristic not only to the Iron Guard but,
like Weber, even to Cuza's League (at least until 1927 when Codreanu
broke with Cuza — according to the author — precisely because of the
latter's non-radicalism in agrarian problems.'[47] As to the social composition of the Iron Guard, the merit of trying to tackle this little-documented
question belongs to Weber and to Barbu.

Nagy-Talavera, in his uneven work about the Arrow Cross and the Iron
Guard, differs from some previously mentioned Western historians in his
faith in the 'sincere devotion' of Codreanu (and of Szálasi) to social
justice.[48] He writes about the 'Archangelic Socialism of the Legion' and
about the class struggle waged by the radical fascist movements against
their own ruling classes.[49] He does not consider Cuza and Goga fascists but
on the contrary shares Codreanu's views about Cuza and Goga as 'the other
face of the Government,'[50] thus belonging to the non-fascist establishment.

Naturally, Western historians pay much more attention to the anti-
Semitism of Romanian fascism than historians publishing in Romania, or
even emigré writers, excepting perhaps Sima. But in none of their works is
a single chapter, let alone a separate study, allotted to fascist anti-Semitism
and to the Jewish policy of the fascist regimes.[51] In spite of the fact that
Codreanu himself, and later Sima, in common with most of the Legionaries saw their movement as an anti-communist (and of course anti-
Semitic) movement par excellence from its very inception, most Western
historians deny that communism played any significant part in the emergence of Romanian fascism (Z. Barbu for example),[52] and Weber points to
the circumstance that in under-developed and under-industrialized
Romania no working class parties could have threatened the vested

interests of the ruling classes.[53] Most Western scholars emphasize the independent development of Romanian fascism ('Ideological and financial
contacts between the Romanian fascists and their counterparts elsewhere
were surprisingly limited in the early thirties'),[54] and all dwell upon the
uniqueness of the Iron Guard on the European fascist map, even if they
differ in the degree of emphasis. In his chapter about Romania in *Die
Faschistischen Bewegungen* (a chapter unfortunately not without mis-
understandings and minor inaccuracies), Nolte sees the Iron Guard as one
of the most original political formations in inter-war Europe, and considers
it the most interesting and most complex fascist movement in Europe.[55]
Finally, there is a consensus among Western scholars that 'as far as primary
sources are concerned. . .most of the studies published so far, in Rumanian
or other languages, are on the whole under-documented'[56] (Z. Barbu).
Therefore it is not surprising that most of the Western studies should end
with unanswered questions[57] and the demand for more source material.

The numerous similarities, at least superficial, between the Iron Guard
and the Arrow Cross, the two main fascist movements of Eastern Europe,
tempt researchers to do comparative studies. Yet there are striking differences too, ideological, structural, and political, and the history of the two
movements shows diverging lines. The dissimilarities between the history of
the two countries and the fate of the two movements in the last years of the
war could not but affect the historiography of local fascism, bringing
about significant differences between the character and the quantity of the
relevant historical literature in the two countries.

Hungary suffered a traumatic shock in the last phase of World War II.
While Romania managed to get rid of the Iron Guard as early as January
1941 and in August 1944 was brought over to the Allied camp in the wake
of a successful coup d'état, Horthy's belated and amateurish attempt to
break with Hitler in October 1944 failed, and the country fell prey to
Arrow Cross terror. Szálasi seized power at a time when a fascist *Machtergreifung* had become a mere anachronism. A devastating war and a bloody
reign of savage, enraged *Lumpen*-elements marked the last months of
Hungary, before its complete liberation in April 1945. While the Iron
Guard emigration started in January 1941, and its former leaders could re-
emerge in the West after the war (among them Sima, the last head of the
movement, and a number of former Legionary ministers), the Arrow Cross
leadership did not survive the war. Szálasi and his friends were captured,
killed, or executed during the two post-war years. Not one front rank
Hungarist Arrow Cross leader has survived who could have written an
authoritative work about his movement. All those former Hungarian
fascists who turned up in the West after the war with pretensions of writing
history were in fact obscure publicists or politicians lacking any prestige—
like Ferenc Fiala, Lajos Marschalkó, and Pál Vágó—and their writings
amount to journalistic polemics.

In Hungary proper the shocking experience of Arrow Cross rule gave impetus to a rich anti-fascist literature, which was also outside the sphere of historical literature. As in Romania, historical research into fascism as such was not encouraged officially. Miklós Lackó, the best known Hungarian historian of local fascism, bluntly pointed to the lack of interest and will to tackle the fascist past. He found that the first post-war decades failed to produce a well-documented struggle against fascist ideologies, and he discerned a kind of 'pudency' towards fascist tradition, which in his view was hampering their complete extirpation. He also complains of the lack of sincere anti-fascist indignation among the large masses in post-war Hungary.[58] If tactical factors which influenced the officially guided research in the People's Democracies are added to all these circumstances, the scarcity of historical literature about local fascism in post-war Hungary is easily accounted for. The first thoroughly documented and scholarly works about Hungarian fascism came out in Hungary and abroad at about the same time as the first major scientific works about Romanian fascism, that is, as late as the mid-sixties. As mentioned earlier, only two fascist movements captured the attention of researchers: Szálasi's Arrow-Cross-Hungarist movement and Imrédy's Party of Hungarian Revival, though a few works also dealt with other groups and parties, such as the Scythe-Cross movements of Zoltán Böszörményi in the early thirties.

The first post-war book about Hungarian fascism was Jenö Lévai's *Horogkereszt, kaszáskereszt, nyilaskereszt*[59] (*Swastika, Scythe-Cross, Arrow-Cross*) published in 1945. The writer, a very prolific journalist, is the author of a number of useful works about the catastrophe of Hungarian Jewry. His book is essentially journalism rather than history. A similar book about fascism was published by Endre Sós,[60] also a publicist and belletrist. It contains only scanty data about Hungarian fascism.

The fifties produced the first seriously researched essays, mainly about the pre-fascist period, but they still suffer from party jargon and from cold-war militancy imposed on the researchers of that period. A pertinent example is a study by György Magos, 'The Role of the British and American Imperialists in the Stabilization of Horthy Fascism,'[61] published in the prestigious *Acta Historica*. The labelling of the Horthy regime as fascist should be noted here as a characteristic feature of the earlier interpretation when no demarcation line was drawn between the nature of the authoritarian but parliamentarian Horthy regime and the Szálasi dictatorship. Later, by the end of the fifties, a few studies came out about the Szálasi period, indicating that systematic research was in progress and that the time was ripe for the appearance of major scholarly writings about fascism in Hungary. And indeed, in the early sixties a few monographs were published about the Arrow Cross coup d'état and Szálasi's rule, as well as about the Scythe-Cross movement.[62]

A book deserving special mention in this context, although it does not fit into this group of works, is pertinent here because of its impact on Hungarian historiography. In 1957 C. A. Macartney published his monumental *October Fifteenth*.[63] In spite of the fact that the author prepared his work outside Hungary and did not use Hungarian archives, he draws on primary source material that was not available to researchers in Hungary itself. Macartney's work, which analyses Hungarian history between 1929 and 1945, is excellently documented about Szalasi's movement, and has been extensively used by Hungarian researchers, even when not quoted (as in the case of Agnes Rozsnyai). Macartney was obviously influenced by his numerous conservative-minded informants who stood close to the Horthy regime, and his not entirely negative views about Ferenc Szálasi are also controversial; nevertheless, his work remains to this day the most informative and most detailed history of wartime Hungary, the Arrow Cross included.

The aforementioned work of Miklós Lackó on the Arrow Cross and Hungarian National Socialists was published in 1966, marking the beginning of a more liberal and outspoken era in Hungarian historiography. Despite all the limitations imposed on the historian in an East European country, Lackó's work goes beyond political history and offers a scholarly insight into the social and ideological roots of Hungarian fascism, also tackling such delicate topics in a communist country as, for example, the social basis and the mass support of the Arrow Cross (although he overplays the role and the number of criminal and *Lumpen*-elements in the Arrow Cross following). Lackó is cautious in using the term *fascist* and does not consider Horthy a fascist nor any government preceding the German occupation of Hungary as such. His book stresses the autochthonous character of most of the Hungarian fascist movements without overestimating, for example, Szálasi's independence of Nazi Germany. The author's sphere of interest embraces the ideological-political components of fascism, which lend a *couleur locale* to Hungarian fascism, such as its specific nationalism, the agrarian and Christian idea, and Szálasi's peculiar peasant and worker policy. However, in the last analysis, Lackó tends to minimize the appeal of fascism among the peasantry and the working class, thus somehow losing in scientific objectivity.

Lackó's book is complemented by a scholarly work about Béla Imrédy and his Party of Hungarian Revival, written by Péter Sipos.[66] While Lackó deals with the 'popular' or 'plebeian' movements, Sipos concentrates on the 'gentleman' or upper class in the wide spectrum of Hungarian fascism. He juxtaposes Szálasi, who built his movement on the support of the petty bourgeoisie and the *Lumpenproletariat*, and Imrédy, a first-class financial expert, a former governor of the National Bank, and a former prime minister at the head of the rightist ruling party, who had gathered around him, from 1940, the extreme-right and fascist-minded elements of the mostly urban middle and upper classes. Sipos's work is an interesting research into the special problems of the fascist radicalization of different bourgeois, landowner, officer, clerical, and intellectual circles. However, his use and interpretation of 'total Fascism' in Imrédy's movement is somewhat vague and confusing. But even so, it is a valuable work which places in opposition radical fascism, that of the 'have-nots,' to the gentleman-type fascism of the 'haves,' in the early forties. This work, like Lackó's book, is more outspoken about anti-Semitism than most works on local fascism in Romania, for example. It should be emphasized that Hungarian historians largely agreed as to the strong racial basis of Hungarian anti-Semitism, a characteristic almost absent from the anti-Semitism of Romanian fascism.

A contribution by the Budapest historian, György Ránki to *Native Fascism*, is worth mentioning. The author of 'The Problem of Fascism in Hungary'[67] exemplifies the embarrassment of Marxist scholars working in Eastern Europe when they appear in western forums dealing with ideological problems deemed delicate in their own countries. His writing, on one hand, is an odd mixture of dogmatic remnants and of lip-service towards the communist authorities, and on the other hand, of tendencies to emancipation from the official dogmatic patterns. Ránki believes that the fascists did not attempt to approach the working class, which was considered to be Marxist and social democratic; he also asserts that the fascist movement was not able to free itself from the ideology of the Hungarian gentry.[68] Such doubtful assertions prove once more that in Eastern Europe there still exist limitations of a dogmatic nature that hinder historians in reaching independent conclusions in certain fields of research. Ránki, an influential figure in Hungarian intellectual life, took a courageous step forward in the direction of re-formulating the outdated Dimitrovian conception of fascism. While urging intensified research in order to elucidate the differences between 'classical' fascism (German and Italian) and special versions of fascism (including the Hungarian one), Ránki sounds a note of warning, hinting probably to his old-fashioned Marxist colleagues, or perhaps to the official ideologists of the regime, that considering fascism as simply a regressive mass movement, or a reactionary manifestation of big capital is a dangerous over-simplification.[69]

Western historians, excepting C. A. Macartney, did not enrich our factual knowledge about Hungarian fascism. Yet they asked questions which their colleagues in Hungary today would find difficult to raise, and they tried to provide answers to problems that were not clarified in the past. One of these questions concerns the fluctuation of some worker elements between the extreme left and the extreme-right. János Erös is among those researchers who discern such a fluctuation. ('In 1939 thousands of communist sympathisers must have voted for the Arrow Cross; in 1944 they showed their true colours.')[70] There seems to be general agreement over the issue of the preponderance of workers among Szálasi's henchmen. Erös asserts that the workers were indeed over-represented, but this following was recruited from among the unemployed, unskilled, or unorganized workers, whilst the workers in the big industries were as a rule anti-fascists.[71] István Deák asserts that 'for unskilled or unemployed workers, and for small artisans and their journeymen—the Arrow Cross was their first friend.... The Arrow Cross performed a function that the socialists were unable to fulfil.'[72] In George Mosse's view a further reason could account for the influx of worker elements into the ranks of the Arrow Cross: the chance offered by Szálasi (as by Codreanu in Romania) for the lower strata of the working classes to participate actively in the country's life as organic parts of the national community.[73] Though George Bárány attributes Szálasi's appeal to the masses to his social demagoguery and the ruthless methods advocated by the Arrow Cross, neither he nor any other Western researcher fails to stress the important role played by proletarian, or semi-proletarian elements in the Hungarian fascist movements. (It should be noted that some Western historians seem to exaggerate the worker participation in the Iron Guard, probably under the impact of the Arrow Cross analogy, just as they exaggerated the populist character of the Arrow Cross under the influence of the Iron Guard analogy.) Great interest is attached to the character of the Horthy regime itself. While for example Nagy-Talavera writes about the 'Szeged-Fascists,'[75] Erös makes a point of bringing out the dual character of the Horthy regime (divided between a fascist and a conservative wing, complemented by groups floating around the centre),[76] and Deák emphasizes the tolerant, non-fascist nature of the regime. For his part, although Bárány rejects the slogans about Horthy's 'counter-revolutionary fascist dictatorship,' he nevertheless holds to the view that 'the social premises for the fascisation [sic] of Hungarian life were taking shape well before the full impact of fascism could be felt,'[78] a suggestion which implies a gradual process of political life turning fascist long in advance of Szálasi's takeover.

Views about the Arrow Cross differ considerably among Western historians and one may ask what facts are there that can make such divergent interpretations and conclusions possible among non-involved and non-biased researchers. For some of them the Arrow Cross had been 'the only right-wing movement [in Hungary] seriously to bother with (and about) the workers' (Eugen Weber), and Ferenc Szálasi was 'the prophet of the new Hungary, able to impress many humble people' (F. L. Carsten). For others Hungarian fascism was backward and semi-feudal (J. Erös), while Szálasi was nothing but an insane demagogue. One can read about the most brutal anti-Semitism of the Arrow Cross, which ended up in the atrocities and massacres among Budapest Jewry in the autumn and end of 1944, but then at a symposium held in Jerusalem in 1969, Jenö Lévai, the Budapest Jewish researcher of the Jewish Holocaust, denied Szálasi's involvement in the anti-Jewish crimes and considerably diminished his

responsibility. The way leading out of the labyrinth of contradictory assertions can only be via the publication of the relevant source material and a
better knowledge of the multifarious aspects of modern Hungarian history.

As in Romanian and Hungarian fascism, Slovak fascism has its writers
among the post-war Marxist historians in Czechoslovakia, among fascist or
rightist emigrés in the West, and it also captured the interest of a handful
of 'non-involved' Western scholars. Little was written about inter-war Slovakia during the first two decades after the liberation of Czechoslovakia,
and particularly little about the Hlinka party.'[79] An essay about Slovak historiography by Ludovit Holotik[80] published in 1967 greatly contributes to
the survey of local research into fascism. It is remarkably outspoken about
the reasons for the apparent lack of interest in Slovak issues. Holotik
accuses the leadership in the Stalinist era in Czechoslovakia of hindering
any critical research into the national problems of Czechoslovakia, a situation that persisted up to the mid-sixties. It becomes evident from his review
that the few historians who treated the subject were more concerned with
the relations of the Slovak state with Nazi Germany, than with the analysis
of internal issues, local fascism included. This void has not been filled in
Czechoslovakia up to this day — at least not to my knowledge — and though
quite a number of essays in Slovakian do deal with some aspects of fascism
in Slovakia, there are no works available in other languages. As with
Romania, for example, attention has been centred mainly on the
anti-fascist struggle rather than on the history and nature of Fascism itself.

In Western literature the interpretations of Slovak fascism are quite controversial. Although the separatist and fascist (or Nazi) oriented wing of
Hlinka's People's Party gathered strength in the mid-thirties, there seems
to be no justification for labelling the party fascist prior to 1938. As to its
nature after 1938 and the characteristics of 'independent' Slovakia ruled by
the party leadership, there is no consensus as to the term *Clerical-Fascism*
(or *Clerico-Fascism*).[81] A vast Slovak rightist emigré literature denies the
fascist character of the Hlinka movement and even of the Tiso regime.[82] A
few Western historians also indulge in whitewashing the Tiso regime, and
especially Tiso himself.[83] Some impartial scholars tend to see the People's
party as conservative-nationalist or reactionary-nationalist rather than
Clerico-Fascist.[84] (Nolte does not consider either Hlinka or Tiso as
Fascists.)[85]

On the contrary, Slovak researchers, former opponents of the Hlinka-
Tiso party, or Marxist historians of the pre-Dubček era, regard the
People's party and Tiso's state as typically fascist and totalitarian.[86] Most
historians studying Slovak fascism — Marxists in Czechoslovakia, as well as
Western researchers — emphasize the extreme nationalism (mostly anti-
Czech and anti-Magyar, though some Slovak fascist leaders did not hesitate
to join hands with Horthy's Hungary), anti-communism, anti-Semitism,
and the clerical (Catholic) nature of the movement and of the regime. But

then, there are controversies about the originality of Slovak fascism and of the Tiso regime. Slovak fascism was a 'ludicrous imitation of the Reich model'[87] wrote one of the researchers recently, while others see an interwoven pattern of conservativism, clericalism, and fascism, typical only of Slovakia. One would suppose that the 1969 Prague Symposium about fascism was a good opportunity to elucidate some open questions concerning Slovak fascism. But among the twenty-five papers presented at this forum not a single one dealt with Slovakia (six were devoted to Czech subjects and one to the problem of fascism in the Sudetenland).

Among the types of fascism in the Danubian countries and the four fascist regimes in the area, the scantiest literature available is that on the Ustasha movement and the Croatian state of the Ustashi (1941-1945). There is no controversy about the fact that the Ustasha takeover in April 1941 was solely a German and Italian act and was not the outcome of a mass uprising in the wake of the military defeat and the dismemberment of Yugoslavia. However, the torrential influx of nationalistic masses to the Ustashi once Ante Pavelič had been installed in Zagreb, cannot be denied. In the typology of fascism the Ustasha movement belongs with the East European movements in spite of its long-standing links with Italian fascism. The main characteristics of the Ustashi are to be sought elsewhere than in its diffuse, nebulous ideology. They are rooted in the fanatical anti-Serbian ultra-nationalism, supplemented by anti-communist, anti-Semitic, and anti-democratic ideas, and by a *sui generis völkisch*-Christian (Catholic) anti-modernism. All the researchers make a point of stressing the savage terrorist nature of the Ustashi.

Anyone looking for sources and scholarly works about the Ustashi will be disappointed. Apart from the pamphlets published in Croatia after 1941 by Pavelič and his entourage (in both Italian and in German), and a few works published mainly in Italy and in Vienna during the thirties, no comprehensive or analytical work about the movement has yet appeared. Nor is the literature about the so-called independent Croatia much more informative. An exhaustive work on Yugoslav historiography[88] published in 1965 in Belgrade is ample evidence of the reluctance of historians in postwar Yugoslavia to tackle the Ustasha movement; there is little to be found about the subject in contemporary Yugoslav writings, except for a number of essays about the relationships of the movement with Nazi Germany and fascist Italy.

The relevant literature substantiates the assumption that the social make-up of the Ustashi was by no means similar to that of the Arrow Cross, or of the Iron Guard, for example. Workers and peasants were conspicuously under-represented, while the relatively high number of Catholic priests and of persons active in the secular organs and organizations of the Catholic Church, as well as the high percentage of officers, intellectuals, professionals, and mainly students, endowed the movement with a specific character, different from other fascist movements in the area. All these peculiarities leave some doubt about the justification of its being treated as a 'purely' fascist movement. The authors of a detailed scholarly work about the Croatian State — Andreas Hory and Martin Broszat — suggest the term *pre-fascist* or *semi-fascist* for the movement.[89] And in Nolte's view there is no certainty whatsoever that the Ustasha movement actually qualifies as fascist at all. Precisely the opposite thesis is expressed by Ivan Abakumovic who considers that the student of fascism in Yugoslavia 'is struck by the fact that the native fascists displayed repeatedly the same characteristics as fascists elsewhere in Europe.'[90] He also points out that the 'fascists had some working-class support, a fact that the communists will be the first to admit'[91] (contrary to Seton-Watson's view, who asserts that the working-class element was almost completely lacking in Croatia and in Slovakia).[92] Yugoslav Marxist historians (Dimitrije Djordjevič, for example) ascribe the growth of the Ustashi mainly to external factors — while not overlooking certain internal factors, among them some termed as 'unsettled national problems.'[93] Djordjevič concludes that fascism in Yugoslavia (Croatia included) was confined to extremist separatists — and it seems that he is representative of the 'official view' in Yugoslavia today — and its ideas 'never grew deep roots among the small, insignificant minority of youths and middle and upper middle class people.'[94]

For Poland it is sufficient to cite Janusz Żarnowski, a leading figure among contemporary Polish historians. There was no fascist mass party in Poland, nor was there a fascist and totalitarian regime, so that according to Żarnowski there are difficulties in discussing the characteristics of a Polish fascism.[95] There were merely fascist tendencies discernible in interwar Poland including a few extreme-right and extreme-nationalist *fascisant* groups, and even genuinely fascist organizations as the ONR-Falanga. But all these groups remained on the periphery, without gaining a mass following, and lacked any peasant or worker support. On the other hand, Pilsudski's or the colonels' rightist, ultra-nationalist and authoritarian regime could only be treated as fascist by communist party propagandists of the old school. Polish fascism 'operating on the margins of Poland's political life, was in many instances an artificial and imported product,' wrote a Western authority on Polish history.[96] One need not necessarily agree with these views (rejected, incidentally, by some Polish researchers). But all those who are not specifically engaged in researching this subject will have to wait for some convincing scholarly works in favour of another interpretation.

Miklós Lackó's paper about the characteristics of South-East European Fascism, presented in 1969, has already been noted. Now attention should be drawn to his essay about East-Central European Fascism, published in 1973 in Munich.[97] The point in mentioning the two studies is to stress the necessity felt by the author to delimit different areas of Eastern and Central Europe when tracing the development of fascist movements in this part of Europe. The few comparative studies and attempts at syntheses come up against obstacles inherent in the subject. The terminology 'East European Fascism' is used as opposed to the 'classic' Italian and German type of fascism. It would better fit reality if the term fascism *in* Eastern Europe were used or perhaps fascism*s* in Eastern Europe. Dissimilarities seem to prevail and when trying to outline the main common characteristics of the fascist movements one should first try to elucidate the specific local features and varieties, and join forces with those who are researching, for example, the problem of modern nationalism and anti-Semitism in the area, the interrelationship between the great powers and the small countries, and the specific socio-economic problems of under-developed, or belatedly and partially industrialized societies.

This short survey testifies to the fact that the available literature is by no means sufficient to provide satisfactory answers to the basic problems of the fascist movements in Eastern Europe.[98] The blank spots are particularly large on the map of problems with an ideological and social character. As to the doctrine and ideology of these movements, not a single monograph has seen the light of day in the west nor is there any satisfactory publication of sources of an ideological character. The social composition of most of the movements and of their elite is not sufficiently known nor can we reconstruct, even roughly, the make-up of those social forces that supported the fascist movements in the parliamentary elections. Similarly no work has yet appeared which sets itself the task of studying pre-fascist thought, or the belletristic literature that fostered the Iron Guard and the Arrow Cross ideas. Analyses of the relationship between these movements and religion and Church are also missing. Quite peculiarly, the rich literature of anti-Semitism lacks a systematic description and analysis of the anti-Jewish policy of the Arrow Cross or of the Iron Guard, for example.

Subjective reasons alone cannot account for these shortcomings. Apart from the scarcity of researchers who could have explored these problems, research has been considerably hampered to this day by a number of objective circumstances; for example, the availability of source material and other documentation. It is true, though, that there exists plenty of material in the West, which, unaccountably, has not been made use of by researchers. The periodical material lying about in Western libraries has remained unexploited for the most part. However, the source material freely available is insufficient to fill the gaps in our knowledge. A *sine qua non* for attaining the level of research equivalent to that into Italian fascism for example, would be the opening of the East European archives to Western scholars. It is only natural that the bulk of source material should be found in the respective countries. The record offices and the archives of the main ministries concerned (interior, education, etc.) must necessarily have in their possession a considerable amount of source-material which would be helpful in answering quite a number of puzzling questions. Yet these archives are practically closed to Western scholars and are accessible even to the local researchers in rare cases only, and then to a limited degree. Pending a radical change in this respect, scholars should consider the publication of the available source material and of monographs on the most neglected areas and about the most controversial problems.

## NOTES

1. G. Ferrero, *Four Years of Fascism* (New York, 1924); Luigi Villari, *The Fascist Experiment* (New York, 1925); Luigi Sturzo, *Italien und der Fascismus* (Köln, 1926), Francesco Nitti, *Bolschewismus, Fascismus und Demokratie* (Munchen, 1926).

2. E.g., Ernst Niekisch, *Hitler—ein deutsches Verhängnis* (Berlin, 1931); Otto Strasser, *Ministersessel oder Revolution?* (Berlin, 1930); Gregor Strasser, *Kampf um Deutschland* (München, 1932); Konrad Heiden, *Geschichte des Nationalsozialismus* (Berlin, 1932); Otto Dietrich, *With Hitler on the Road to Power* (London, 1934); F. L. Schuman, *The Nazi Dictatorship. A Study in Social Pathology and the Politics of Fascism* (New York, 1936); R. A. Brady, *The Spirit and Structure of German Fascism* (New York, 1937); Vilmos Böhm, *A nagy tragédia* (*The Great Tragedy*) (Wien,Leipzig, 1933).

3. E.g., Klaus Charlé, *Die Eiserne Garde* (Berlin, 1939); Alfonso Panini-Finotti, *La Guardia di Ferro* (Firenze, 1938); idem, *Da Codreanu a Antonescu. Romania di ieri e di oggi* (Verona, 1941); Harald Laeuen, *Marschall Antonescu* (Essen, 1943).

4. Lucrețiu Pătrășcanu, *Sub Trei Dictaturi* (*Under Three Dictatorships*) (București, 1944). (The 1970 edition of Pătrășcanu's work will be quoted.)

5. Ibid., 46.

6. Ibid., 52.

7. Ibid., 61.

8. *Istoria R.P.R.* (*The History of the Romanian Peoples' Republic*), ed. Mihail Roller (București, 1952).

9. Ion Popescu-Puțuri, 'Les principales caractéristiques du régime politique de Roumanie pendant la dictature militaire-fasciste et l'agression hitlérienne,' in *La Roumanie pendant la Deuxième Guerre Mondiale* (București, 1964), 9-36.

10. N. Copoiu, 'Sur la pénétration de l'idéologie nazie en Roumanie et l'attitude protestataire des intellectuels du pays (1940-1944),' in *La Roumanie pendant la Deuxième Guerre Mondiale*.

11. *Impotriva fascismului* (*Against Fascism*). Scientific session concerning the critical analysis and the unmasking of fascism in Romania, Bucharest, March 4-5, 1971 (București, 1971).

12. Mihai Fătu and Ion Spălățelu, *Garda de Fier. Organizație teroristă de tip fascist* (*The Iron Guard. A Fascist-type terrorist organization*) (București, 1971).

13. E.g., Constanța Bogdan about the social-economic foundation of fascism in Romania (29-43), Șerban Cioculescu about Legionarism and literature (118-23), and Gheorghe Zaharia about the nature of the regime set up in September 1940 (183-93).

14. Valter Roman, 'Condițiile apariției fascismului pe plan mondial si lupta poporului român impotriva fascismului international' ('The Conditions under which Fascism appeared on a world scale and the fight of the Romanian people against international Fascism'), in *Impotriva fascismului*, 11.

15. Al. Gh. Savu, *Dictatura regală* (*1938-1940*) (*The Royalist Dictatorship*) (București, 1970).

16. Ibid., 21.

17. Ibid., 16.

18. See for example Copoiu, op. cit., 131, 138.

19. Characteristic for this view is the title of an article by Titu Georgescu, 'Sur la cinquième colonne hitlérienne en Roumanie,' Revue d'Histoire de la Deuxième Guerre Mondiale, no. 18 (1968), 19-38. See also Ştefan Muşat, 'Coloana a V-a hitlerista in România ('The Hitlerist Fifth Column in Romania'), in Anale de Istorie, no. 6 (1970), and Florea Nedelcu, 'Etude concernant le role de l'Allemagne hitlerienne dans l'évolution des organisations fascistes de Roumanie dans la période 1933-1937,' in Revue roumaine d'histoire, no. 6 (1971), 991-1011.

20. E.G., Gh. I. Ioniţă, 'Sur l'histoire de la lutte antifasciste du peuple roumain,' in Etudes d'histoire contemporaine de la Roumanie (Bucureşti, 1971), II, 47-98. Popescu-Puţuri, op. cit., 12-14; and Florea Nedelcu, 'Carol al II-lea şi Garda de Fier — de la relaţii amicale la criza (1930-1937),' ('Carol II. and the Iron Guard — From Friendly Relations to Crisis'), in Studii, no. 5 (1971), 1009-28.

21. E.g., Savu, op. cit., 455-56.

22. See my two bibliographical notes: Rumania During the War. A Survey of Literature, in 'The Wiener Library Bulletin' (April 1963), and Rumanian Fascist Emigrés. A Survey of Their Literature, in 'The Wiener Library Bulletin' (July 1964).

23. Ştefan Pălăghiţă, Garda de Fer. Spre Reinvierea României (The Iron Guard. Towards Romania's Revival) (Buenos Aires, 1951).

24. Pălăghiţă considers Sima demented, as he does King Carol and Ion Antonescu. Ibid., 173.

25. G. Barbul, Memorial Antonescu: Le III-e Homme de l'Axe, Vol. I (Paris, 1951).

26. Ion Gheorghe, Rumäniens Weg zum Satellitenstaat (Heidelberg, 1952).

27. Michel Sturdza, The Suicide of Europe (Belmont, Mass., 1968).

28. Horia Sima, Histoire du mouvement légionnaire (Rio de Janeiro, 1972). Like almost every former Legionary, Sima too uses extensively the Mein Kampf of the Iron Guard, Corneliu Zelea Codreanu's Către Legionari (To the Legionaries) (Sibiu, 1936). Published in German as Eiserne Garde (Berlin, 1939).

29. Sturdza quotes Sima's writing Cazul Iorga-Madgearu (The Iorga-Madgearu Affair), op. cit., 165; see also 107, 165.

30. Ibid., 233.

31. Horia Sima, Destinée du Nationalisme (Paris, 1951).

32. Carlo Sburlati, Codreanu il capitano (Roma, 1970).

33. Pamfil Şeicaru, Octavian Goga and A. C. Cuza ('Carpaţii' Collection, Madrid).

34. Nicholas M. Nagy-Talavera, The Green Shirts and the Others. A History of Fascism in Hungary and Rumania (Stanford, 1970).

35. Eugen Weber, 'Romania,' in his Varieties of Fascism (Princeton, N.J., 1964), 96-105; 'Romania,' in The European Right. A Historical Profile, ed., Hans Rogger and Eugen Weber (London, 1965), 501-574; and 'The Men of the Archangel' in Journal of Contemporary History, no. 1 (1966), 101-26.

36. Z. Barbu, 'Rumania' in European Fascism, ed. S. J. Woolf (London, 1968), 146-66.

37. Stephen Fischer-Galati, 'Fascism in Romania,' in Native Fascism in the Successor States, 1918-1945, ed. Peter F. Sugar (Santa Barbara, Calif., 1971), 112-22. His contribution 'Romanian Nationalism,' in Nationalism in Eastern Europe, ed., Peter F. Sugar and Ivo J. Lederer (Seattle and London, 1969), 373-95, contains some valuable references to Romanian fascism too. Emanuel Turczynski published in Native Fascism a useful article titled 'The Background of Romanian Fascism,' 101-11.

38. Ernst Nolte, Die Faschistischen Bewegungen (Berlin, 1966). (I used the French edition of this work, Les mouvements fascistes [Paris, 1969]).

39. F. L. Carsten, The Rise of Fascism (Berkeley and Los Angeles; 2d printing 1969); the chapter about Romania: 'Anti-Semitism and Anti-Communism: the Iron Guard,' 181-93.

40. E.g. Theodor I. Armon, 'Fascismo Italiano e Guardia di Ferro' in *Storia contemporanea*, no. 3 (1972), 505-48.

41. H. Seton-Watson, 'Fascism, Right and Left,' in *Journal of Contemporary History*, no. 1 (1966), 183-97.

42. Miklós Lackó, 'Zur Frage der Besonderheiten des südosteuropäischen Faschismus,' in *Fascism and Europe* (Prague, 1970), II, 2-22, Mimeo.

43. Seton-Watson, op. cit., 193.

44. Weber, 'The Men of the Archangel,' op. cit., 117-18.

45. Ibid., 122.

46. Ibid., 107, 114.

47. Fischer-Galati, op. cit., 114, 116.

48. Nagy-Talavera, op. cit., 363.

49. Ibid., 357, 360-61, 374.

50. Ibid., 353.

51. My article about the Jewish policy of King Carol's dictatorship, published in Hebrew, is not available to a wide circle of readers, and anyhow is not relevant to the main Fascist movements. *Zion*, no. 1-2 (Jerusalem, 1964), 133-51.

52. Barbu, op. cit., 153.

53. Weber, 'The Men of the Archangel,' op. cit., 103.

54. Fischer-Galati, op. cit., 116. Cf. Weber, 'While Codreanu lived, the Legion was no conscious agent of Nazism.' (Weber, *The European Right*, op. cit., 554).

55. Nolte, op. cit., 243, 251.

56. Barbu, op. cit., 150.

57. For example Turczynski, op. cit., 111.

58. Miklós Lackó, *Nyilasok, Nemzetiszocialisták, 1935-1944* (*Men of the Arrow Cross, National Socialists*) (Budapest, 1966), 331-32. (An abridged version of this work was published in English under the same title in Budapest, 1969.)

59. Jenö Lévai, *Horogkereszt, kaszáskereszt, nyilaskereszt* (*Swastika, Scythe-Cross, Arrow-Cross*) (Budapest, 1945).

60. Endre Sós, *Európai fasizmus és antiszemitizmus* (*European Fascism and anti-Semitism*) (Budapest [s.a.]).

61. György Magos, 'The Role of the British and American Imperialists in the Stabilisation of Horthy Fascism' in *Acta Historica* (1954), II, 161-217.

62. At the end of the fifties and the beginning of the sixties, quite a number of studies about Hungarian fascism was published by Mihály Korom, Kálmán Szakács, Ágnes Rozsnyai, and Miklós Lackó. The first books appeared in the early sixties: Ágnes Rozsnyai, *A Szálasi puccs* (*The Szálasi Putsch*) (Budapest, 1962); Mihály Korom, *A fasizmus bukása Magyarországon. A népi demokratikus átalakulás feltételeinke létrejötte, 1943-1945* (*The Downfall of Fascism in Hungary. The Ripening of the People's Democratic Revolution* [sic]) (Budapest, 1961); Kálmán Szakács, *Kaszáskeresztesek* (*The Scythe-Cross-Men*) (Budapest, 1963).

63. C. A. Macartney, *October Fifteenth. A History of Modern Hungary, 1929-1945* (Edinburgh, 1957; 2d. ed., Edinburgh, 1961).

64. See n. 58.

65. Lackó, op. cit., 74-75, 117-36, 166-83.

66. Péter Sipos, *Imrédy Béla és a Magyar Megujulás Pártja* (*Béla Imrédy and the Party of Hungarian Revival*) (Budapest, 1970).

67. György Ránki, 'The Problem of Fascism in Hungary,' in *Native Fascism*, 65-72.

68. Ibid., 70.

69. Ibid., 71-72.

70. J. Erös, 'Hungary,' in *European Fascism*, 137.

71. Ibid.

72. István Deák, 'Hungary,' in *The European Right*, 397.

73. George Mosse, Introduction: 'The Genesis of Fascism,' *Journal of Contemporary History*, no. 1 (1966), 21.

74. George Bárány, 'The Dragons' Teeth: The Roots of Hungarian Fascism,' in *Native Fascism*, 78.

75. See his *Green Shirts and the Others*, 75.

76. Erös, op. cit., 111-12.

77. Deák, op. cit., 364-65.

78. Bárány, op. cit., 75.

79. For the relevant Slovak research see R. E. Lamberg, 'Father Hlinka's Separatists. New Slovak Publications,' in *The Wiener Library Bulletin*, no. 2 (April 1963).

80. Ludovit Holotik, 'Slowakische Geschichtschreibung der Gegenwart,' in *Historica Slovaca* (Bratislava, 1967), V, 255-86.

81. For the use of the expression *Clerical Fascism* see Yeshayahu Jelinek, 'Bohemia-Moravia, Slovakia and the Third Reich During the Second World War,' in *East European Quarterly*, no. 2 (1969), 236. About the character of the Hlinka Guard and of the Tiso regime see idem, 'Slovakia's Internal Policy and the Third Reich, August 1940-February 1941,' in *Central European History* (September 1971), 242-70, and 'Storm-troopers in Slovakia: the Rodobrana and the Hlinka-Guard,' in *Journal of Contemporary History*, no. 3 (1971), 97-120.

82. E.g., Joseph A. Mikus, *Slovakia. A Political History: 1918-1950* (Milwaukee, 1963); Milan Stanislao Durica, *La Slovacchia e le sue relazioni politiche con la Germania, 1938-1945, I-II* (Padova, 1964); and idem, *Die slowakische Politik im Lichte der Staatslehre Tisos* (Bonn, 1967).

83. E.g., Gilbert L. Oddo, *Slovakia and Its People* (New York, 1960).

84. Joseph F. Zacek, 'Czechoslovak Fascisms,' in *Native Fascism*, 59.

85. Nolte, op. cit., 277.

86. A view held by among others Jozef Lettrich, *History of Modern Slovakia* (New York, 1955).

87. Zacek, op. cit., 62.

88. *Historiographie Yougoslave 1955-1965*, ed. Jorjo Tadić (Beograd, 1965).

89. Ladislaus Hory and Martin Broszat, *Der kroatische Ustascha-Staat, 1941-1945* (Stuttgart, 1964), 177.

90. Ivan Avakumovic, 'Yugoslavia's Fascist Movements,' in *Native Fascism*, 140.

91. Ibid., 141.

92. Seton-Watson, op. cit., 193.

93. Dimitrije Djordjević, 'Fascism in Yugoslavia: 1918-1941,' in *Native Fascism*, 132.

94. Ibid., 133.

95. Janusz Żarnowski, 'Courants et tendences fascistes dans la Pologne des années, 1918-1939,' in *Fascism and Europe*, I, 158.

96. Piotr S. Wandycz, 'Fascism in Poland: 1918-1939,' in *Native Fascism*, 96.

97. Miklós Lackó, 'Ostmitteleuropäischer Faschismus,' in *Vierteljahrshefte für Zeitgeschichte*, no. 1 (1973), 39-51.

98. The proceedings of a Conference on Comparative European Nazism and Fascism held in Bergen in 1974 have not yet appeared in print; the typed material does not enable us to assess the contribution of these papers to the study of fascism in Eastern Europe.

# 7

# Fascism and Populism in Latin America

ALISTAIR HENNESSY

At first sight it is surprising that in spite of Latin America's turbulent history of dictatorship and authoritarianism, fascist movements did not take root there and that even regimes which have the trappings of fascism such as Vargas's Brazil and Perón's Argentina cannot easily be fitted into the fascist mould. In Europe fascism was a major expression of mass politics in the inter-war years and of the response to social and economic crisis: in Latin America the equivalent response is to be found in a wide range of mass nationalist movements which cannot easily be categorized in European terms and to which scholars have given the generic name 'populism.' Unsatisfactory though this term may be, as the Latin America usage differs broadly from usage elsewhere, it has now entered the political vocabulary and refers to a variety of reformist movements, such as Aprismo in Peru and its derivatives in Venezuela, Cuba, and Costa Rica, the MNR (Movimiento Nacionalista Revolucionario) in Bolivia, Getulismo in Brazil, Peronismo in Argentina, which are opposed to traditional parties narrowly based on conservative landowning elites. The heyday of these movements coincided with the period of import-substitute industrialization which lasted from the early 1930s and petered out in the mid-1960s.

There were also, in the 1930s, self-styled fascist movements but only the Brazilian Integralistas achieved a mass following sufficiently large to cause alarm; others such as the Mexican Dorados, the Chilean and Teuto-Brazilian Nazis and numerous Argentinian groups were limited in size if vocal in expression, but in no case did any fascist movement come to power and in every case where a fascist movement confronted a populist movement it suffered defeat and eclipse or was co-opted and absorbed. It might be argued that the conflict between Vargas and the Integralistas in Brazil was a struggle between rival fascisms or even that populism is a Latin American variant of European fascism, but to argue this is to transfer a European concept over which there is still a wide measure of disagreement in its application to Europe itself to a political, social, economic, and cultural situation where the use of the concept can only obfuscate although, as we will see later, there is a certain logic in the 'colonial fascist' thesis if one accepts Marxist premises.

Intellectuals flirted with fascist ideas in the 1930s as they did with every *nouvelle vague* emanating from Europe, but these ideas could not be easily reconciled with the imperatives of an aroused popular nationalism and were soon dropped. German and Italian diplomacy exerted great efforts to encourage and subsidize Nazi and fascist groups among the ill-assimilated sections of German and Italian minorities in Argentina and Brazil but their success was limited, as were the efforts of the Spanish government to strengthen ties with Spanish America by propagating the doctrine of *Hispanidad.*[1] The Spanish Civil War (the influence of which in Spanish America still awaits its historian) divided opinion, as Franco's propaganda convinced churchmen (many of whom were Spaniards) and the conservative elite that the Nationalists were fighting a religious crusade against atheistic communism which since the influential writings of Donoso Cortés in the mid-nineteenth century had been regarded by the Spanish church as a logical and inevitable consequence of liberty of conscience. The propaganda was aimed at those Latin Americans who avidly seize on anything which confirms their anti-United States, anti-Protestant, and anti-democratic prejudices. But even this influence was largely tempered by the Spaniards' assumption that they were the natural leaders of the Hispanic world and was limited to traditionalist elements among the clergy, landowners, and peasants. Hispanidad did not provide an inspiration for movements of the radical right. Hispanidad, in any case, had little appeal to immigrants of non-Spanish stock whilst German nazism with its assumptions of racial supremacy could have little influence in societies with a high proportion of mixed-bloods and where nativism was becoming an integral part of nationalist ideology. Thus one can largely discount the direct influence of European fascism. If there was to be a Latin American fascism it had to be of the home-grown variety.

Nevertheless, immediately after the second world war there was a widespread fear among the Allies (and this perhaps reflects their lack of knowledge of Latin American affairs) that fascism, defeated in Europe, would be rejuvenated in Latin America. This fear was encouraged by Perón's admiration for the Axis powers and his support for Franco's regime, by the fascist sympathies of Bolivia's revolutionary officers, by the corporatist trappings of Vargas's Estado Novo with its expressed admiration for Salazar's Portugal, and by the refuge given to fascist exiles. These exiles from Hitler's New Order eked out a precarious existence, haunted by the fear of retribution, but their influence seems to have been minimal, except possibly as a source for some virulent strains in Argentinian anti-Semitism, and as a stimulus to fiction writers. Fears of a phoenix-like revival of fascism were misplaced. Fascism, like other political movements inspired by the European example —liberalism, conservatism, socialism, and communism—failed to take root and was modified, under Latin American conditions, until the connections appeared tenuous and the similarities superficial. Part of the explanation for this must lie in the absence in Latin America of those conditioning factors which gave fascist movements in Europe their distinctive style. Six points are worth briefly considering:

1. Foremost is that in the twentieth century, Latin American countries have not experienced total war.[2] War has been a major factor in impelling social change: its absence deprives countries of the consequences of mass mobilization and of great collective effort; it removes an important impetus to the acceleration of social mobility and to the improvement of the position of women, minorities, and labour organizations, and it reduces the urgency for rationalizing productive processes and for strengthening state power. Most importantly, in the context of fascist movements, Latin America was spared the psychological legacies of war in such phenomena as veterans attempting to recapture the camaraderie of the trenches, and the psycho-social consequences of generational and sex imbalances caused by massive losses of men in their prime of life. Unlike the history of Europe, that of Latin America has not been conditioned by endemic warfare, and although the major impetus to change has occurred as a result of the economic impact of the two world wars together with that of the Great Depression, this was scarcely comparable to those factors described above. Nor have Latin American intellectuals been receptive to ideologies growing out of intra-national conflict. The social Darwinist assumptions of much fascist theorizing were confined in Latin America to explaining, in racial terms, the gap in social development between predominantly European and predominantly mestizo nations rather than to providing justification for inevitable conflict between them.

The most important political consequence stemming from absence of war in Latin America is that soldiers lack a military function, from which emerges a distinctive pattern of civil-military relations. In Europe, conservative officer corps had an ambivalent attitude towards fascist parties, distrusting upstart leaders with their stridency and radical aims but tolerating the rise of para-military militias which could counter-balance left-wing organizations, thus relieving the army of internal policing and releasing it for its proper function of national defence.[3] In Latin America, where there has been a tradition of military involvement in politics since the wars of independence of the early nineteenth century, and where there was little threat from the left and only an attenuated frontier defence function, the military have always looked askance at alternative sources of firepower which might compete with their own political ambitions. Even the habitual weakness and divisions of Latin American police forces reflect military distrust as well as indicate a willingness on the part of the military to undertake internal security tasks themselves. Thus the only road to success for fascist groups is to infiltrate the military as the Integralists tried to do with indifferent success in Brazil. Alternatively, the military itself might come under fascist influence independently of civilian parties, as happened in Bolivia after the Chaco war or in Argentina, but this is a very different

matter from having to co-exist and compete with an independently organized fascist movement drawing its strength from a mobilized and
politicized mass.

Militarism, whether as old-fashioned *caudillismo*, or under its institutionalized, bureaucratic form, reduces the area within which a fascist
movement can operate. The culture of violence has permeated Latin
American politics since the early nineteenth century. Where the use of violence has become a recognized means of changing power, that peculiar
élan offered by fascist movements has a lower resonance than in societies
where the use of violence for political ends invites moral opprobrium.
Fascist movements become irrelevant as their appeal to alienated, marginalized elements is offset by the clientilist and patronage techniques of the
populist politician. Nor can fascists claim to have the monopoly of the
ruthless use of violence, for if ruthlessness is necessary to purge the body
politic there is a tradition, sanctified by its longevity, of military intervention. The military, too, are able to exploit the symbols of nationality more
effectively than civilian politicians. Indeed, it is precisely at this point that
the military are able to fulfil the role ostensibly claimed by fascist parties of
clearing out the stables of an unheroic, stock-jobbing, materialist, parliamentary liberalism.

In Europe a restraint is placed on military intervention by professional
ethics. In Latin America, in contrast, the military's role as defender of constitutional government may be widely, if sometimes reluctantly, accepted.
Nor can the fascist cult of the superman have much to offer Latin Americans with the *macho* ways of generations of caudillos behind them. Finally,
one might point to the devaluation of the vocabulary of revolt in Latin
America habituated to an imagery of blood which might tend to reduce
the shock effect of fascism's appeal.[4] Given these pre-conditions, fascist
movements find it difficult to gain a mass response, and they end up as a
refuge for alienated intellectuals and those excluded from patronage
handouts.

2. An area where pre-conditions for fascism were unfavourable rises
from the ubiquity of Catholic culture. Catholicism's predominance
throughout society is shown both in the strength of the institutionalized
Church and in the pervasiveness of folk-Catholicism. Nor did the Church
feel itself threatened by alternative religious traditions or by a strong atheistic left, so thus did not need alliance with, or the protection of, fascist
groups. The Church in Latin America might give whole-hearted support
to conservative, traditional movements but adopted more caution towards
fascist groups, which, in Europe—even in Spain—were anti-clerical.

Where anti-clericalism took a militant form, as in Mexico in the 1920s,
the Church became a rallying point for a counter-revolutionary peasantry
akin, in some respects, to Spanish Carlism,[5] sharing a similar nativist outlook, reacting against the creeping influence of foreign and urban values.

Although a number of groups appeared in the 1930s calling themselves Falange these did not necessarily bear much relationship to the Spanish Falange. In the Colombian and Bolivian cases there were some parallels but in the case of Chile the Falange emerged as a liberal wing of the conservatives, and influenced by liberal Catholics like Maritain developed into the Christian Democrat party.

3. The absence of a strongly organized left removed an important incentive to the growth of fascist movements. The slow rate of industrialization was a brake on the growth of an urban proletariat and the predominance in some countries of a mining economy meant that the most militant workers were often far removed geographically from the centres of power. Where, as in the case of Buenos Aires, there was a large urban proletariat, much of the initiative for labour organization came from immigrants who brought with them conflicting socialist and anarchist traditions which fragmented the left. The foreign provenance of left-wing movements was a positive disadvantage in a period of rising nationalist feeling. Labour organizations were further weakened by cheap labour resulting from an ever-increasing flow of rural migrants driven off the land by an unreformed agrarian sector.

Urbanization without accompanying industrialization created a marginalized urban population susceptible to the appeal of the populist politician. In the absence of a strong left, Latin America might seem to approximate more closely to Eastern than Western Europe, but what is distinctive about Latin America was the skill with which populist politicians worked within a familiar patronage network which perpetuated, in an urban environment, the patron-dependent relationship of the countryside. Considerable attention has been focussed on 'clientilism' which many observers see as the key to explaining why, even under the twin processes of modernization and political mobilization, the consciousness of workers nevertheless remained frozen in a traditional mould of thought. The survival and strengthening of institutions like *compadrazgo* or the Brazilian *panelinha* are adduced as evidence of the ready acceptance of the mores of personalist politics in preference to impersonal bureaucratic norms. What weight should be given to these cultural factors has become a matter of dispute and we need many more studies of marginalism and of interest articulation before generalizations can be validated, but patriarchalism dies hard and the emphasis placed by radicals on 'raising the level of consciousness' and thereby breaking the crust of habitual deference and the expectation that benefits come from above, is indicative of the persistence of traditional behaviour patterns.[6]

4. The cultural crisis growing out of the first world war and the Great Depression, which drove many European intellectuals to adopt positions on the extreme left or extreme right, took a distinctive form in Latin America where the intelligentsia's reaction was anti-liberal, anti-European, and

anti-United States. This reaction took two forms: on one side a nativism, influenced by the Mexican revolution's vindication of Indians and which had a mass popular base, especially in Peru and Bolivia where large Indian populations underlined the relevance of the Mexican experience; on the other, there was a reappraisal of Hispanic traditions which had been largely repudiated after independence in favour of British and French models of constitutional liberalism. Here the social base was narrower and took the form of an assertion of traditional 'creole' values against radical immigrant influences, emphasizing the spiritual traditions of Hispanic Catholicism. This current was strengthened by ontological quests into 'national character' (paralleling a similar quest in Spain itself).[7] One consequence was to stimulate a revival of interest in Catholic social thought, with its corporatist assumptions, which, it was believed, was more 'natural' to peoples rooted in an Iberian and Mediterranean cultural ethos than the borrowed postulates of Lockean individualism. This became one inspiration of the Christian Democrat parties with their emphasis on communitarian democracy which began to appear in the 1930s. Fascist ideas were acceptable only insofar as these could be assimilated within this tradition, but running through most of the writings of the Latin American right is a repudiation of fascist *étatisme*.[8]

5. Another limitation on the adoption of the fascist model was its stress on economic autarchy. This originally was an attraction to nationalist groups, especially the Argentine military, but the pre-conditions of a fascist economy did not exist. No Latin American country was able to free itself from dependence on foreign trade. Sufficient capital could not be generated internally to finance heavy industry and there was a continuing need to maintain exports in order to purchase capital equipment from abroad. The fundamental weakness, however, lay in a restricted domestic market, which was insufficient to maintain a self-sustaining industrialization programme.

6. Fascist movements in Europe sustained much of their momentum from the support of student/youth movements. In Latin America, where students have a tradition of political involvement, their loyalties were already pre-empted by the University Reform movement dating from 1918 with its nationalist, Panlatinamerican, and radical ideology. In general, Latin American student movements are traditionally left of centre and the development of militant right-wing students is a comparatively recent growth dating from the late 1960s.

Given these pre-conditions the 1930s and 1940s saw the growth of populist parties — cross-class coalitions, a complex amalgam of nationalism, popular participation, social reform, and authoritarian centralism — rather than fascist parties. One of the first books to discuss the Janus-faced nature of these parties, which were reformist at the same time as they increased structural blockages, was C. Veliz, ed., *Obstacles to change in Latin*

*America* (Oxford, 1965). These essays by prominent Latin American academics, many of whom had practical experience in government, showed that the obstacles to reform were far more deep-seated than the optimistic planners of the Alliance for Progress in the early 1960s had assumed. They also showed the irrelevance of the historical experience of the advanced industrial countries for Latin America, and nowhere more clearly than in the role played by the middle classes. Unlike the European middle classes which had achieved economic power and then political power, those in Latin America had acquired political power first. They were essentially professional, bureaucratic sectors aspiring to landowner status, or to the security of government employment, rather than a national bourgeoisie generating its own scale of values, confident in its own economic power. Thus patronage and state paternalism became the fulcrum of the political system. Lacking autonomous power and lacking entrepreneurial drive, the state became the main promoter of industrialization at times hostile to and at others acting in concert with foreign capital.

These essays raised the question of whether mass populist parties could overcome these deficiencies and fulfil a reforming role. The one by Torcuato di Tella on 'Populism and reform in Latin America' was the first, and is still the most sophisticated analysis of the populist phenomenon and, with its five-fold typology, is the starting point for any serious analysis. His conclusion, guardedly optimistic, was that 'populism was the only force on the side of reform in Latin America.' Di Tella's trail-blazing essay has been followed up by few people. In his chapter in E. Gellner and G. Ionescu, *Populism: its meaning and national characteristics* (London, 1969), A. Hennessy is more pessimistic about populism's reform potential but he is more concerned with placing populism in a wider context and to draw the distinction between predominantly urban populist movements and movements which have a rural emphasis, such as Mexican *zapatismo* and *sinarquismo*, Acción Popular in Peru and even Castroism — those movements which seek national redemption through an uncorrupted peasantry and which are more akin to the Russian *narodnik* concept and to some (though not many) aspects of agrarian populism in the United States. H. Neira in 'Populismes ou césarismes populistes,' in the *Revue française de science politique*, Vol. 19, no. 3 (1969) is a very useful overview and he rightly questions the use of the word and wonders whether 'caesarism,' might not be more appropriate, although this is also open to objections.

General books on Latin American politics have brief analyses of populism such as Jacques Lambert in *Amérique Latine: structures sociales et institutions politiques* (Paris, 1963; English translation, Berkeley and Los Angeles, 1967). One full-length book is Von Niekerk, *Populism and political development in Latin America* (Rotterdam, 1974). The concept remains diffuse, and for an adequate detailed general treatment it would have to be based on a comprehensive theory of Latin American politics. An enormous literature is accumulating on this but until more empirical work has been done, a more fruitful approach would seem to be the analysis of specific examples of national populist parties. A key reference work for Latin American political parties generally is J. P. Bernard et al., *Guide to the political parties of Latin America* (London, 1973). One of the most controversial aspects of populism is the role played in it by the military. The crucial relationship between the middle classes and the military is explored by J. Nun in 'The middle class military coup' the most important essay in C. Veliz, ed., *The politics of conformity in Latin America* (Oxford, 1967).

If there have been few attempts to cover populism on a continental scale there have been none for fascism. It would be useful to have a descriptive book detailing the various self-styled fascist groups which have existed and, in some cases, still exist. The two countries, Brazil and Argentina, which have produced the most complex populist regimes as well as the greatest variety of fascist-style movements must now be examined in detail.

*Brazil:* The 1930 Revolution was a watershed in Brazilian history, overthrowing the Old Republic, ushering in the fifteen-year domination of Getulio Vargas, as well as the era of mass politics and the polarization of political forces between right and left on a scale which had no parallel in Latin America at that time. The most remarkable feature of the early 1930s in Brazil was the scale and speed of political mobilization—a reflection of urbanisation and the growth of the middle classes. Politics became nationalized; there was a swing against the decentralization of the Old Republic, enshrined in the 1891 Constitution, when politics consisted of conflicts between local state factions and between the most powerful states, São Paulo, Minas Gerais, and the capital Rio de Janeiro—the *politica dos governadores*. The death knell of the ephemeral state parties was sounded with the growth of national based parties, the most important of which were the Integralistas founded in 1932 and the Aliança Libertadora Nacional, the popular front party formed in 1935.

The Integralists, a fascist-style party, sprouted, flowered, and withered within the space of six years, crushed in 1938 after Vargas established his Estado Novo.[9] How were they able to expand so rapidly and why did they collapse so suddenly? The answer to the first question lies primarily in their originality in the context of Brazilian politics. They were sharply differentiated in both style and organization from preceding parties. The main thrust of their appeal lay originally in their anti-liberalism (this was to be replaced by anti-communism as the left grew in strength) and in their repudiation of the attendant *coronelismo* system and their desire to replace manipulative politics and narrow state loyalties by loyalty to a regenerated national state. Their visibility, their marches, salutes, rituals, songs, their press propaganda, educational and social organizations, and the deliberate externalization of their activities marked a total rejection of the hermetic style of traditional politics. Their leader Plinio Salgado's obsessional appeals to sentiment; his emotional and mystical rhetoric aimed at implanting in his readers and listeners a consciousness of *brasilidade*, made a direct appeal, as no other party had done, at a time of social and economic crisis when newly roused groups were seeking identity and reassurance. Those who joined the party entered a self-contained sub-culture. The Integralists had their own organizations for almost every aspect of social life.

They also benefitted from the groundswell of nationalist sentiment which had been growing since the early 1920s and which is covered in a short general survey of nationalism by E. B. Burns, *Nationalism in Brazil: an historical survey* (New York, 1968). The pessimistic self-questioning of the early years of the Old Republic had been giving way to a more positive evaluation of Brazilian potentialities. T. Skidmore analyses some of these intellectual currents in 'Brazil's search for identity in the Old Republic,' in R. S. Sayers, ed., *Portugal and Brazil in transition* (Minneapolis, 1968). Among the most important influences on nationalist thought in 1930 were the elitist, anti-democratic writings of Alberto Torres, especially *O problema nacional brasileiro*, published in 1914 and reprinted in 1933. His work is analysed in a useful article by W. D. McLain Jr., 'Alberto Torres ad hoc nationalist,' in *The Luso-Brazilian Review*, Vol. IV, no. 2 (December, 1967) and in a fuller study by Barbosa Lima Sobrinho. Torres's influence was particularly strong among the *tenentes* although his Jeffersonian agrarianism was not taken up as a prescription for Brazil's ills: the lure of industrialization was too strong. *Tenentismo* was the most significant expression of radical dissent during the 1920s and an early example of younger officers acting as a radical reforming force. Although their risings in 1922 and 1924 were crushed and they broke up as a coherent political force, after 1930 a considerable number became active in the communist and Integralist parties and during the Estado Novo. Their definitive history has yet to be written. In English a useful introduction is R. J. Alexander, 'Brazilian *Tenentismo*,' in the *Hispanic American Historical Review*, Vol. 36 (1956). Their role in 1930 is discussed in J. D. Wirth, '*Tenentismo* in the Brazilian Revolution of 1930,' *Hispanic American Historical Review*, vol. 44, no. 2 (May 1964). A further article by Alexander, 'The Brazilian *tenentes* after the Revolution of 1930,' in *Journal of Inter-American Studies*, vol. 15, no. 2 (May 1973) traces their subsequent career and influence up to and beyond 1964.

We still lack a comprehensive treatment of the 1930 revolution. J. Young, *The 1930 Revolution and its aftermath* (New Brunswick, N. J., 1967) provides one introduction. The Revolution is treated in the general histories of modern Brazil, the best of which in English is T. Skidmore, *Politics in Brazil, 1930-1964: an experiment in democracy* (New York,

1969). P. Flynn has a detailed examination of the proto-fascist groups between 1930 and 1932 in 'The Revolutionary Legions and the Brazilian Revolution of 1930,' in R. Carr, ed., *Latin American Affairs: St. Antony's Papers*, no. 2 (Oxford, 1970). This is an important article for understanding later developments. Based on Aranha's archives, it discusses the revolutionary programmes, some hitherto unpublished, of the various 'legions' which sprang up in a number of states during and after 1930. Flynn shows how the failure to create a national revolutionary party in the midst of an intensely personalist and localized political system created a vacuum which neither integralists nor communists were able to fill, leaving the army as the only vehicle for national political mobilization. Be that as it may, the programmes of the legions provide an interesting insight into the moralistic strain which was to be one of integralism's distinguishing features. Salgado himself held aloof from Vargas's revolution sensing, one suspects, that Vargas was changing the rules of the game rather than the game itself.

The standard work dealing with the middle thirties, the years of integralism's flowering, is R. Levine, *The Vargas regime: the critical years, 1934-1938* (New York, 1970), which has a comprehensive bibliography. The best short account of integralism is S. Hilton, '*Ação Integralista Brasileira:* fascism in Brazil, 1932-1938,' in *Luso-Brazilian Review*, Vol. IX, no. 2 (December 1972). An early book which gives a German view, reflecting the interest shown in integralism by the Teuto-Brazilian communities in Rio Grande do Sul is K. Hunsche, *Der brasilianische Integralismus* (Stuttgart, 1938). The most ambitious analysis of integralism is H. H. Trindade, *Integralismo: o fascismo brasileiro na decada de 30* (São Paulo, 1974). A full scale study of Plinio Salgado and integralism in English is E. R. Broxson, 'Plinio Salgado and Brazilian Integralism' (Ph.D. diss., Catholic University, 1973), available from University Microfilms. Researched from Salgado's own writings and the integralists' press, it is very useful for his early life and party organization, but has little on the party's social composition. Salgado may be studied from his writings, many of which have been reprinted, such as *O integralismo perante a nação* (Rio de Janeiro, 1955); *Discursos*, 2 vols. (São Paulo, 1948); *O integralismo na vida brasileira* (Rio de Janeiro, 1967); and two articles 'A marcha de integralismo,' in *Jornal do Brasil* (25 and 26 October 1970).

To trace Salgado's intellectual and spiritual odyssey it is necessary to study the influence of Catholic thinkers like Jackson Figueiredo and Cardinal Leme. There is a brief discussion of Jackson, as also of Farias Brito, another key influence, in J. Cruz Costa, *A History of ideas in Brazil*, trans. S. Macedo (Berkeley and Los Angeles, 1964). The relationship of the Catholic church to integralism is briefly discussed in T. C. Bruneau, *The Political transformation of the Brazilian Catholic Church* (Cambridge, 1973) and in M. T. Williams, 'Integralism and the Brazilian Catholic

Church,' *Hispanic American Historical Review*, vol. 53, no. 4 (August 1974). Salgado's ideas as well as the pre-1930 intellectual ambience is discussed in H. H. Trindade, 'Plinio Salgado e a revolução de 30: antecedentes da AIB,' in *Revista Brasileira de Estudos Politicos*, no. 38 (January 1974).

The anti-Semitic strain in integralism is touched on in R. Levine, 'Brazil's Jews during the Vargas regime and after,' *Luso-Brazilian Review*, Vol. V, no. 1 (June 1968). Although the integralists had a branch of their intelligence service devoted to monitoring Jewish activities, the small number of Brazilian Jewry—some 42,000 and internally divided—did not seem to pose a threat comparable to the much larger Jewish community in Argentina, numbering nearer half a million, where anti-Semitism took a more virulent form. Gustavo Barroso, the integralists' Jew-baiter, who wrote a number of anti-Semitic books, is an interesting example (like Salgado himself) of the type of marginal, auto-didact, provincial intellectual who is often attracted to fascist style movements, but he has not received the attentions of a biographer.[10]

The reason why integralism collapsed so easily lies partly in Salgado's tactical mistakes and in an overestimate of the party's strength. Hilton, in the article cited above, attributes their ultimate failure to lack of support in the army. The only hope for a fascist movement to succeed in Latin America, as mentioned earlier, lies in its ability to infiltrate the military. The integralists tried to do this (as the communists had tried to do before their disastrous coup in 1935), but although they gained some support among senior officers and NCOs, as well as acquiring a considerable following in the navy, for reasons which have not been satisfactorily explained, they were unable to wean influential officers away from Vargas. In a further article by Hilton, 'Military influence on Brazilian economic policy, 1930-1945: a different view,' *Hispanic American Historical Review*, vol. 53, no. 1 (February 1973) (in which he is primarily concerned to challenge J. Wirth's view of military influence on economic planning in *The Politics of Brazilian Development* [Stanford, 1970]) it is suggested that throughout the 1930s the military were obsessed by their weakness and lack of equipment—both in relation to the power of state militias (that of São Paulo had taken two months to subdue in 1932) and to Argentina's expanding military power, and hence were more interested in influencing Vargas's trade policies, by which arms purchases could be made from Germany, than in ambitious industrialization schemes to which they gave a lower priority. By playing off the United States against Germany, which is analyzed by S. Hilton, *Brazil and the Great Powers 1930-39: the politics of trade rivalry* (Austin, 1974), Vargas was able to acquire German arms and so satisfy the generals. What tied the military to Vargas rather than to the integralists was true also of civilians, as in the ultimate instance Vargas's success lay in his powers of patronage, which control of an expanded federal bureaucracy put at his disposal. With the federalization of taxes and the expansion of national enterprises, the individual state governments could no longer offer patronage plums, and although the integralists might retain the support of the quixotic and of certain sections of the professional classes (medical doctors, for example), they could offer few financial inducements to a job-hungry middle class. The integralists demanded financial self-sacrifices from their followers and although it has never been established how much money was contributed by big business interests there seems to have been no Brazilian Hugenberg. As the decade progressed and the economy picked up, Vargas was prepared to support coffee planters and industrialists so these possible sources of finance were not available, whilst during the early years of the Estado Novo, as Warren Dean shows in *The Industrialization of São Paulo, 1880-1945* (Austin, Texas, 1969), support for domestic industry and labour legislation, favouring employers, rallied them to Vargas. The much publicized subventions which the integralists were supposed to have received from foreign embassies seem to have added up to very little. An Italian subsidy paid for headquarters expenses, but the more considerable local expenses were met by subscription and dues.

The ways in which Vargas outmanoeuvered the integralists and crushed them, just at the moment they thought they would come into their own, is recounted in Levine and Broxson and in an article by F. D. McCann, 'Vargas and the destruction of the Brazilian *Integralista* and Nazi parties,' in *The Americas* (July 1969). The details of Vargas's conflicts with the German ambassador over Nazi infiltration among the Teuto-Brazilians are spelt out in McCann, *Brazilian-American Alliance, 1937-1945* (Princeton, 1973). Some unusual information and illustrations of Nazi activities in southern Brazil are provided by the regional police chief A. da Silva Py in *A 5a Coluna no Brasil* (Porto Alegre, 1942).

Vargas himself is not an immediately attractive figure for a biographer who is not prepared to become wholly immersed in the machinations of a political genius, exquisitely sensitive to changing political forces. It is still impossible to assess the magnitude and variety of his achievement, being a precursor of post-1964 authoritarianism and of the populist democracy of the 1945 to 1964 period and the creator, by his suicide in 1955, of a potent nationalist myth. Two biographies in English have been attempted. J. W. F. Dulles, *Vargas of Brazil: a political biography* (Austin, 1967) is strong on political narrative, weak on analysis. R. Bourne, *Getulio Vargas of Brazil, 1883-1955* (London, 1974) is the latest biography of possibly the most skilful politician Latin America has produced. There is an intimate portrait by his daughter, Alzira Vargas in Amaral Peixoto's *Getulio Vargas, meu pai* (Rio de Janeiro, 1960). Vargas's own pronouncements have been collected in *A nova politica do Brasil*, 11 vols. (Rio de Janeiro, 1933-1947). An informative but uncompleted history of the Vargas era is

H. Silva, *O ciclo de Vargas* (Rio de Janeiro, 1964). J. Love's, *Rio Grande do Sul and Brazilian regionalism 1882-1930* (Stanford, 1970) provides a masterly account of Vargas's home state and the political background of his early career. An old book, recently reprinted and still worth reading is K. Loewenstein, *Brazil under Vargas* (New York, 1942; reprint ed. 1973). His contemporary summing up of Vargas's regime was that it was:

> neither democratic nor a disciplined democracy: it is neither totalitarian nor fascist; it is an authoritarian dictatorship for which French constitutional theory has coined the apt term of *régime personnel*. It is one which exercises its theoretically unlimited power with the moderation demanded by the liberal democratic habitat of the Brazilian nation... If ever Brazil were to be converted into a genuinely fascist state...not a jot would have to be changed of the existing legislation, nor anything added to the statute book ... but fascist laws of the statute book alone do not make a state fascist in its entirety. [Pp. 372-373]

The reasons why Vargas established the Estado Novo can be explained by the support he gained from the middle classes which had failed to form viable national parties after 1930. A convincing hypothesis to explain Brazilian political development has been Helio Jaguaribe's Cartorial State model which he elaborated in *O nacionalismo na atualidade brasileira* (Rio de Janeiro, 1958), shorter accounts of which in English are his 'Dynamics of Brazilian nationalism,' in C. Veliz, ed., *Obstacles to change*, and in 'Political strategies of national development in Brazil,' in I. L. Horowitz, J. Gerassi, J. de Castro, eds., *Latin American radicalism: a documentary report on left and nationalist movements* (New York, 1969).

The Cartorial State is a polity in which superfluous jobs are exchanged for votes. The recipients are the middle classes, professional and bureaucratic groups, the product of urbanization without industrialization. Towards the end of the 1920s as urbanization increased, the middle classes had expanded beyond the capacity of the ruling coffee plantocracy to satisfy them. The final blow came when the collapse of the coffee economy in the Great Depression removed the source of funding the bureaucracy, creating a revolutionary situation in which the middle classes played a leading role. After the 1930 revolution, government by planters and export merchants was replaced by government by the middle classes, but the failure to organize a national reformist party created a stalemate which extremists of the left and right tried but failed to exploit. Fear that the broader suffrage of the 1934 constitution would enable the Old Republic elite to make a comeback, using their control of rural dependents to outvote the urban middle classes, gave Vargas the support of the latter when he abolished constitutional government and established the Estado Novo in 1937. An expanded civil and military bureaucracy was prepared to forego its liberal principles in return for the security which Vargas could offer.

Vargas was not prepared to press the conflict with the plantocracy and São Paulo industrialists; thus landowners were left undisturbed in control of their rural dependents at the same time as industrialists were given state support. In this manner the Estado Novo established a balance between conflicting forces.

With the left crushed, the middle classes bought off by posts in the expanded federal bureaucracy, and the landowners left with a free hand in the rural areas, there was no need for a fascist-style party and the integralists were expendable. Both left and right were now proscribed: Prestes, the communist leader was imprisoned and Salgado exiled. Jaguaribe writes:

> Vargas's Estado Novo was much nearer to Franco's Spanish Falangism or to Salazar's Portuguese Corporativism than to the German or even the Italian models. . . . The middle class was assured of its continued co-optation by the New State bureaucracy. It no longer had to barter jobs for votes. For the landowners the Estado Novo offered the advantage of not interfering in the agrarian economy of the country and of accepting them as official spokesmen for the countryside, thus keeping them in political control of their rural strongholds. . . . In terms of the interests of the urban bourgeoisie the Estado Novo repressed the socialist tendencies that were beginning to menace private appropriation of the means of production. It also offered the benefit of favouring the expansion of the internal market and protecting it with its right wing nationalism from foreign competition. . . . For the working class the Estado Novo, although repressing any attempt to create an independent political organization, adopted a strongly paternalist posture, introducing important new social legislation and assuring the protection of the workers rights. [P. 398]

Interpretations of the Estado Novo (1937-45) distinguish between the early years and the period 1942-45 when Vargas began to shift the basis of his support away from the bureaucratic middle class and rural notables to the new industrial bourgeoisie and urban working class created by the expansion of industry during the war. *Trabalhismo*, based on paternalist and corporatist labour organizations, made Vargas the spokesman for the mobilized urban masses. The revolutionary implications of this new alliance was one reason why the military deposed Vargas in 1945. The return of constitutional government now enabled the rural notables to reassert their political power but with the difference that now the newly formed parties had to incorporate a bigger electorate which had risen from 2.7 millions in 1934 to 7.4 millions in 1945.

A useful article discussing the ways in which the Brazilian electorate has expanded and comparing coronelismo with similar forms of vote manipulation elsewhere is J. Love, 'Political participation in Brazil, 1881-1969,' in *The Luso-Brazilian Review*, vol. 7, no. 2 (December 1970). The expectations of this new electorate went far beyond the limited patronage capacity of either the cartorial state or the Estado Novo. In this fluid situation the populist politician came into his own.

Populism presupposes the existence of a free vote and depends on the ability of the populist leader to satisfy the material and psychological needs of his followers. [11] It was the response to an open political system as distinct from the closed systems of either the Estado Novo or the predictable results of the coronelismo system of the Old Republic when landowners were able to manipulate the votes of their rural dependents. The mechanics of this new populism have been examined by F. Weffort, 'State and Mass in Brazil,' in I. L. Horowitz, ed., *Masses in Latin America* (New York, 1970); in 'Le populisme,' *Les Temps modernes* (October 1967); and in the *Revista civilazação brasileira*, I, 2 (May 1965). There is a full neo-Marxist study by O. Ianni, *Crisis in Brazil* (New York, 1970).

Andrew Pearse describes the setting within which populism operated in Rio de Janeiro in his chapter in P. Hauser, ed., *Urbanisation in Latin America* (Paris, 1961):

> ...populism is concerned with political power at the level of the municipality, the state and the Union, which is exercised directly and indirectly through the body of functionaries. It is supported by structures based on clientage in which benefits are handed down in return for votes and personal loyalties in manoeuvres. Most of these structures are informal and non-institutionalized and do not coincide with the formal structures of administration. Whilst the intermediary ranks receive benefits through the allocation of posts in the system of functionaries, jobs contracts, grants-in-aid of charitable, cultural and sports enterprises, etc., the masses receive them through defensive labour legislation and access to the services of medical assistance posts, sports clubs, religious and cult groups, etc., subsidized through the intervention of populist leaders at various levels, whose names are given due prominence. Populism does not favour the organization of common interest groups or co-operative groups, and power is usually delegated downwards rather than upwards. Representatives are appointed, but they are seldom elected from below. In its appeal to the masses populism uses symbols stressing the protective role of the great charismatic leaders, and the small scale operators use to the full the confidence of the populace in the great leaders: and even if confidence in the small-scale operator was lost, that in the great leader is apparently durable. [P. 202]

It can be readily seen from this that Brazilian populism is a variant of Boss Tweed's New York city politics and not of agrarian populism.

Vargas's response to these changing pressures was to organize urban workers in the PTB, the Brazilian Labour party, which provided him with mass support enabling him to be returned for the first time as a democratically elected president in 1950. The populist period continued for another nine years after Vargas's suicide in 1955 under a series of populist presidents, but the contradictions within the populist alliances became so acute that the cross-class coalitions began to break up into their constituent components. This polarization together with attempts to radicalize the rural areas alarmed conservatives and forced the military to intervene in 1964 as they had in 1889, 1930, and 1945. This time, however, they did not hand over to a civilian government but established an authoritarian military regime which has attracted considerable attention from foreign scholars, especially political scientists. Historians have fewer contributions to make. Skidmore's general study is crucial for the pre-1964 period whilst his contribution in Stepan's volume (see below) is a useful comparison of the Estado Novo with post-1964 authoritarianism. J. W. F. Dulles, *Unrest in Brazil: Civil military conflict, 1955-1964* (Austin, 1970), is a political chronicle rather than analysis whilst I. L. Horowitz, *Revolution in Brazil* (New York, 1964), collects a variety of viewpoints.

Ambitious attempts to explain Brazilian politics have been made in terms of systems analysis: prominent among these is R. M. Schneider, *The political system of Brazil: the emergence of a modernizing authoritarian regime* (New York, 1971). The second volume, in preparation, is to analyse the military's role since the end of the nineteenth century. This will supplement Alfred Stepan's fundamental *The military in politics: changing patterns in Brazil* (Princeton, 1971) which questions a number of long-held assumptions. Phillipe Schmitter's *Interest conflict and political change in Brazil* (Stanford, 1971) focusses on civilian interest groups and is one of the most significant contributions to the understanding of Brazilian politics to have appeared in any language. He has opened up an area of study which has equal relevance for Spanish American countries. Schmitter is one of a group of scholars in the United States to be discussed below, who are deriving new insights from comparisons with Iberian experience as may be seen from his essay, 'The Portugalization of Brazil,' in the important collection of essays edited by Stepan, *Authoritarian Brazil* (New Haven, 1973). Stepan's own essay attempts a comparison between the present Peruvian and Brazilian military regimes. Juan Linz's essay, 'The future of an authoritarian situation or the institutionalization of an authoritarian regime: the case of Brazil,' applies the model originally formulated in his 'An authoritarian regime: Spain,' in E. Allardt and V. Littunen, eds., *Cleavages, ideologies and party systems* (Helsinki, 1964) designed to explain why Franco Spain was difficult to fit into the fascist model. This article is indispensable for its insights into the nature of post-fascist authoritarianism.

An important essay in the Stepan collection is that by Fernando Henrique Cardoso, 'Associated-dependent development: theoretical and practical implications,' which introduces English readers to his analysis of the changing nature of dependency rising out of changes in the international economy. Cardoso criticizes models by other Brazilian theorists such as Celso Furtado, Candido Mendes, and Helio Jaguaribe's 'colonial fascist' hypothesis. This latter started from the assumption that 'fascism is a model for promoting economic development without changing the existing social order and that the adjustment of this model to dependence on foreign metropolitan centres transforms it into colonial fascism.' In this model the state is strengthened in order to preserve stability, the political and economic system is integrated into the Western system (the geo-political thinking of the military, their violent anti-communism and self-appointed role as defenders of the West in the South Atlantic has encouraged the United States to regard Brazil as the guardian of the West's interests in Latin America), and the economy remains, as far as possible, in private hands. Although Jaguaribe sees a trend to 'colonial fascism' after 1964, he does not believe it to be viable in the long run. Unlike Germany and Italy where the bourgeoisie allowed the middle class to take over political leadership in exchange for preserving the ownership of industry, in Brazil structural obstacles rising from dependence on foreign capital and markets would make such an arrangement unlikely and the polarization of political forces as a result of economic stagnation would eventually bring about the system's downfall. Jaguaribe argued that the metropolitan-colonial relationship was essentially undynamic, whereas in Cardoso's opinion, on the contrary, the relationship has become dynamic because of the changing role of the multi-national company.

He argues that the 1964 coup was not a simple restoration of authoritarian rule but a new departure coming as a response to changes in the international division of labour. Multi-national companies were now interested in establishing industries in peripheral states and thus had an interest in 'development,' but this development breaks up old alliances between the traditional, bureaucratic middle classes and backward agrarian sectors, replacing it by a new alliance between technocratic military and civilian bureaucracies together with the new industrialists and their workers in the new industries associated with multi-national companies. The growing class conflict of the declining populist system has now been replaced by clashes between those sectors of the middle classes who benefit from the new system and those who do not, as well as between a new labour aristocracy and workers in the purely national sector. The economy may be dynamic but the beneficiaries are limited, as the gap between the developing urban centres and under-developed rural areas — the 'internal colonies' the function of which is to provide cheap labour for the cities — grows wider. Meanwhile, foreign indebtedness grows as does social marginality: first, because the multi-national companies are more concerned with producing consumer durables for the growing urban middle class market than with producing basic necessities for the urban and rural poor, and second, because capital-intensive industrialization cannot provide employment for a rapidly increasing population. In this situation, authoritarian control becomes necessary to smother the opposition of the disadvantaged sectors of the middle classes, to dismantle dissident labour unions which had provided populist politicians with one of their power bases, and to ensure that the marginal sectors remain depoliticized. As to the future, Cardoso's conclusions, in common with Schmitter and Linz, are not optimistic. Although the regime may not be totalitarian, lacking both an ideology and an official party, there is no guarantee that it is simply a transitional phase in an inevitable progression towards a more broadly based participatory system.

*Argentina:* The origins of Peronism, the most baffling and least understood of all Latin American populisms, must be sought historically in the weaknesses of the political system as well as in the distortions caused by a semi-colonial economy. Analyses of these factors by contemporaries produced a counter-tradition of anti-liberal political thought and historiography which was to be an important pre-condition of Perón's rise to power.

Crucial to an understanding of Perón's success in the 1940s was the failure of Radicalism to bring about any substantial social changes and the blunting of their reforming drive when they were in power under Irigoyen between 1916 and 1930. Resulting from the introduction of universal male suffrage in 1912, Irigoyen's Radicals provide an early example of a populist movement based on the urban masses of Buenos Aires. D. Rock's article, which is amplified in his *Politics in Argentina 1890-1930: The rise and fall of Radicalism* (Cambridge, 1975), 'Machine politics in Buenos Aires and the Argentine Radical Party, 1912-1930' in the *Journal of Latin American Studies*, 4 (1972) is an important analysis of politics at the grass-roots level and of the mechanics of patronage which provides a model for much needed studies of other populist movements as well as for Peronism itself. Irigoyen is one of the most controversial figures in modern Argentinian history and biographies tend to be hagiography or defamation. He is an archetypical figure of the civilian caudillo; capable of inspiring fanatical devotion and incorruptible, he was nevertheless incapable of curbing the corruption of many of his followers. Radicalism's failure virtually closed the way to a reformist solution to Argentina's social and economic problems in the 1930s, as well as anticipating and foreshadowing many of the features of later populist movements.

The Perón period was preceded by a decade or more of ideological turbulence during which the cosmopolitanism of the Argentinian literary establishment and the economic and political assumptions of the ruling elite were called into question. This was a reflection of the general nationalist revival shared by all Latin American countries in the years following the first world war when peace brought the return of foreign economic interests, the re-establishment of pre-war patterns of economic activity, and the incursion of United States economic power. A major expression of the nationalism was the University Reform movement with its founding manifesto in the Argentinian city of Córdoba in 1918 which had repercussions throughout Latin America. Anti-European, anti-imperialist, and influenced by nativism and the Mexican Revolution, the Reform did not share the illiberalism of the right wing nationalists which developed during the late 1920s.

A useful analysis of this new nationalism, tracing the ideological roots of Peronism is J. Hernández Arreguí, *La formación de la conciencia nacional* (Buenos Aires, 1960). The best and most lucid detailed analysis of the myriad right wing groups in M. H. Gerassi, *Las nacionalistas* (Buenos Aires, 1968) which has a comprehensive bibliography. A. Ciria, *Partidos y poder en la Argentina moderna* (Buenos Aires, 1964) has a useful chapter on the right. The repudiation by right-wing intellectuals in the 1930s and 1940s of the established values of Argentinian culture and society had their roots in the growth of a cultural nationalism formulated in the writings of Ricardo Rojas earlier in the century, but although he was critical of the cosmopolitanism of Argentinian culture, he remained within the liberal tradition. Earl T. Glauert has written a useful introductory article, 'Ricardo Rojas and the emergence of Argentine cultural nationalism,' in *Hispanic American Historical Review*, 43, 3, (August 1963). Rojas's writings elaborate on an Argentinian Volksgeist and must be seen against the threat posed by the flood of immigrants in the years preceding the first world war. His career shows how difficult it was for a nationalist intellectual to remain a liberal. When he realized the use to which his ideas were being put by the right in the 1930s, he joined the Radicals, only to withdraw disillusioned. Other nationalist writers such as Manuel Galvez in his *El espíritu de la aristocracia* published in 1924 were unashamedly elitist.

The gap between Rojas's liberal nationalism and the increasingly strident nationalism of the right is best reflected in a new revisionist school of historiography which sought to rehabilitate the dictator Juan Manuel de Rosas who had dominated Argentina between 1829 and 1852. In liberal historiography, enshrined in school texts, the overthrow of Rosas ushered in the era of liberal enlightenment. The first salvo in the rehabilitation of Rosas was the publication of a biography by Carlos Ibarguren, the 'maestro de la juventud nacionalista' who had been a founder member of the nationalist La Nueva República in 1928 and who was the first person to try and organize an extreme right-wing party from among conservatives. In 1938 the new approach was institutionalised by the foundation of the Instituto Histórico Juan Manuel de Rosas. The literature of rehabilitation is summarized in C. B. Kroeber 'Rosas and the revision of Argentine history, 1880-1955,' in *Revista Interamericana de Bibliografía*, 11, 1 (1960). By the 1940s Rosas was ready for adoption by Peronist ideologues as a counter-hero to the heroes of liberal historiography.

Historical controversy also raged round the figure of General San Martín, the country's liberator during the Wars of Independence, who was now adopted as the symbol of the self-abnegation of the military patriot. Rojas felt compelled to write San Martín's biography to repudiate the militarist interpretation of his career. But this interpretation was symptomatic of a thread within both military and civilian nationalist thinking going back to the violent strike and street demonstrations of the Tragic Week in Buenos Aires in 1919. For Leopoldo Lugones, an erstwhile anarchist poet, on whom there is a useful study by N. Jitrik, *Leopoldo Lugones: mito nacional* (Buenos Aires, 1960), only the military could now save Argentina from anarchy. From the mid-1920s he argued that the *hora de espada* had come. Lugones was perhaps the most important single influence on the Argentinian right in the early 1930s. Federico Ibarguren, son of Carlos, in his *Orígines del nacionalismo argentina* (Buenos Aires, 1969) (a hotchpotch but useful source book) writes:

> We were all *lugonianos* which is very different from fascist. 'Fascism' as a theory was engendered in a laboratory of intellectuals, the socialist sperm — law and totalitarian — of the nineteenth century; in contrast Argentinian nationalism is nourished on the old Spanish cult of personality where the Catholic tradition germinates like a seed well ploughed in the earth. [P. 14]

Under Lugones eight pro-fascist groups were united in ADUNA (Afirmación de una Nueva Argentina) in 1933 but his own personal troubles and the fragmentation of these groups led to his suicide in 1938. Lugones, who exalted a life of action as compensation for a humdrum life as a school inspector, is well described by Gerassi as 'the Argentinian d'Annunzio who never knew his Fiume.' The military on whom Lugones set such store was slow to reciprocate his interest in it. The Germanophile General Uriburu, with a following among young officers, made his coup in 1930 with only minimal civilian support, breaking a seventy-year tradition of military non-involvement in politics and intending to establish a fascist-corporate style state. Most older officers, however, failed to respond, preferring to support General Justo in his understanding with liberals and conservatives in the *Concordancia* which lasted from 1932 to 1943. Thus the first attempt to establish a fascist-style regime failed, repudiated by the civilian oligarchy and the majority of the officer corps.

The romantic euphoria of civilian intellectuals was no substitute for the lack of a mass following, and they were not taken too seriously by the military nationalists. Strong German influence in the officer corps as shown in G. P. Atkins and L. V. Thompson, 'German military influence in Argen-

tina, 1921-40,' *Journal of Latin American Studies*, IV, 2 (1972), had bred
a spirit of exclusiveness but General Bautista Molina was attracted as well
by Hitler's political techniques and from 1937 to 1943 he was president of
the para-military Alianza de la Juventud Nacionalista. Facilities for week-
end training were available in army barracks which enabled the army to
retain some control.

The role of radical nationalism in the officers' lodges which is crucial to
understanding the military origins of Peronism can be studied in R. Potash's path-breaking book, *The army and politics in Argentina, 1928-45*
(Stanford, 1969). Potash was the first to use German Foreign Office files
and he has also made wide use of interviews. His book is the most detailed
study to date on any Latin American officer corps. He is at present engaged on a second volume to cover post-1945. Military politics are ably
analysed in less detail by M. Goldwert, *Democracy, militarism and nationalism in Argentina, 1930-66* (Austin, 1972) and in D. Canton, *La política
de los militares argentinos, 1900-1971* (Buenos Aires, 1971). The problem
of political control of the military once in power under Perón is discussed
by H. Rouquie, 'Adhesión militar y control del ejército en el régimen peronista (1946-1955),' *Aportes*, 19 (January 1971).

The dilemma of civilian nationalists was how to find a mass base. Re-
buffed by the left, hostile to the Radicals, they were ignored by the landowning elite, but the various strands of nationalist thought created a pool
of ideas from which could be fabricated a Peronist ideology, although
Peronism was a very different type of regime from that envisaged by
civilian nationalists. Like the integralists, the nationalists thought their
hour had struck when Perón came to power, but Perón was not exclusive in
his loyalties. For example, Raul Scalabrini Ortiz, the leading intellectual
of FORJA, the left wing of the Radicals, whose life and ideas are discussed
in M. Falcoff, 'Raul Scalabrini Ortiz, the making of an Argentinian nationalist,' *Hispanic American Historical Review*, 52, 1 (February 1972),
became one of Perón's confidants. It was the practical hard-headed nationalism of men like Scalabrini with his critical analysis of the British-owned
railways which could aid Perón's plans for autarchy and not the windy
rhetoric of Lugones's admirers.

The nationalist right either came to terms with Peronism because they
shared its anti-liberal, anti-imperialist stance or they degenerated into terrorist groups like the Tacuara, recruited from the psychopathic detritus of
big-city life and from right-wing Catholic students, many of whose fathers
were veterans of the Legión Cívica and other nationalist groups of the thirties. The Tacuara learnt its anti-Semitism from Mgr. Julio Meinvielle,
their spiritual assessor, who was the doyen of right-wing Catholics and
whose writings echoed the worst excesses of Hispanidad. The development
of Catholic thought is traced from independence by J. J. Kennedy, in
*Catholicism, nationalism and democracy* (Notre Dame, 1958) but he tends

to ignore the lunatic fringe of extremist Catholicism which became an integral component of right-wing nationalism.

In the same way as historians and political scientists have been drawn to study the past in order to explain post-1964 authoritarian Brazil, so also with Peronism, but with the difference that Peronism, unlike *getulismo*, is still *the* crucial issue in Argentinian politics. During the seventeen years of Perón's exile it was almost impossible for serious work to be done on Peronism because of its political overtones with the Peronists themselves proscribed from political activity. Two bibliographical articles which survey the early literature on the Perón period are F. Hoffman, 'Perón and After,' *Hispanic American Historical Review*, 36, 4 (November 1956), and 39, 2 (May 1959). Little scholarly work has been done in the immediate Perón period. One useful study which analyses conflicts within the meat industry and clarifies some of the labour union background is P. H. Smith, *Politics and Beef in Argentina: Patterns of Conflict and Change* (New York, 1969) to which may be added his article 'Social Mobilization, Political Participation and the Rise of Juan Perón,' in *Political Science Quarterly*, LXXXIV (March 1969). He has also written an important analysis of intra-elite conflict. A general study of the labour background is S. L. Baily, *Labor, Nationalism and Politics in Argentina* (New Brunswick, N. J., 1967). A broad study of United States-Argentinian relations which deals with the controversy over the 'Blue Book' is H. F. Peterson, *Argentina and the United States, 1810-1960* (New York, 1964).

The fallow period of Peronist studies is past and now we are being engulfed by a flood of exegetical literature. Most of this is by Argentinians and is characterized by strong disagreements over the nature of Peronism, swinging from those who regard it as an indigenous revolutionary movement, Castroism before Castro, aiming at making Argentina the leader of a 'justicialist' third force, neither capitalist nor communist, to those who condemn it as basically a conservative movement masquerading behind demogogic revolutionary slogans. Much of the analysis is committed and reflects not only deep differences within the Peronist movement but between Peronists and the non-Peronist left.

An interesting and provocative example of the new analysis is the review essay by E. Laclau, 'Argentina: Perón and the Revolution,' in *Latin America Review of Books* (London, 1973). Laclau divides the interpretations, most of which have appeared since 1969, under four headings: the liberal view, the 'third world' view, the national left, and the ultra-left. The liberal view, which is also that of the Argentine Communist party, saw Peronism as a peculiar form of Argentinian fascism. Few take this seriously now although most of the older books in English subscribe to this view, such as R. J. Alexander, *The Perón Era* (New York, 1951); G. I. Blanksten, *Perón's Argentina* (New York, 1953; reprint, 1967); and A. P. Whitaker,

*Argentina* (New York, 1964) whilst S. M. Lipset in *Political Man* (New York, 1969) characterized it as a 'fascism of the left.' Laclau rejects the description of fascism on the grounds that fascism's strategy is based on smashing the unions whereas Perón's power derived from the unions and that, so far from having the support of financial groups which is essential to fascism, Peronism's most determined enemies were landowners, traditional industrialists, and the commercial bourgeoisie. He is also rightly critical of the over-schematization and lack of historical awareness in the political science approach of J. Kirkpatrick, *Leader and vanguard in mass society: a study of Peronist Argentina* (Cambridge, Mass., 1971). Nor has he much time for work written under the influence of the 'sociology of modernization' and the 'politics of mass society' approaches, represented most notably by Gino Germani, in *Política y sociedad en una época de transición: de la sociedad tradicional a la sociedad de masas* (Buenos Aires, 1962) and also in a comparison with Italian fascism in S. J. Woolf, ed., *The nature of fascism* (London, 1968) where he analyses the four attempts to establish fascism in Argentina in 1930-33, 1943-45, 1955, and after 1966, in terms of primary and secondary mobilization. Germani explains Peronism in terms of the 'disposable mass' hypothesis whereby Perón's mass base was provided by uprooted rural migrants (of which an estimated one million moved into Buenos Aires in the course of ten years) who composed a lumpenproletariat — the *descamisados* — who could not be integrated into a stable democratic society and so were available for manipulation by a dictator. There is some substance in Laclau's criticism as electoral studies and more detailed studies of the mechanics of Peronist politics are made. Electoral analyses can throw light on Peronism because of the four national elections held in 1946, 1948, 1951, and 1954 during Perón's regime. Important electoral studies are P. H. Smith, 'The social base of Peronism,' *Hispanic American Historical Review,* 52, 1 (February 1072) and W. Little, 'Electoral aspects of Peronism, 1945-55,' *Journal of Inter-American Studies,* 53 (August 1973).

For Laclau the 'third world' interpretation consists of Marxists and non-Marxists, pro-Peronist communists and Peronists. Here Peronism is seen as the anti-oligarchic and anti-imperialist movement of a semi-colonial country. There is a prescriptive element in these groups in that they both argue that the fundamental contradiction in dependent countries is between imperialism and nationalism and not between bourgeoisie and proletariat.

The national left interpretation argues that although Peronism was initially the democratic-bourgeois stage of a semi-colonial country, the bourgeoisie is not strong enough to carry on the revolution, so that the working class must build its own organization independent of Peronism.

The final interpretation is the ultra-left view of Peronism as simply an inter-bourgeois struggle in which the working class has no motive for intervention. This view Laclau easily refutes by pointing out that it fails to distinguish between the agrarian and industrial bourgeoisie.

These interpretations tell us more about the prescriptions of their authors than about the historical origins and development of Peronism. In a different category are the essays in M. Murmis and J. C. Portantiero, *Estudios sobre les orígines del peronismo* (Buenos Aires, 1972). This sets out to explain the clash between cattle owners and industrialists in the 1930s and within the cattle interests themselves, as well as the internal conflict that developed among industrialists which caused an important sector to support Perón in 1943. The essays in this volume point the way to future research by exploring the complexities of inter-sectoral clashes rather than by talking in terms of undifferentiated classes.

Laclau's own general conclusion is that Peronism's originality lay in its policy of income redistribution in favour of wage earners rather than in its industrialization strategy: 'the working class always carried greater weight than the national bourgeoisie in the determination of the policies of the movement' (125); and 'it would be completely false to see in Peronism a kind of national bourgeois regime that made use of the working class as a tactical manoeuvre in its confrontation in the agrarian sector, but restricted the trade union movement to a secondary role within the alliance' (126). He argues that what enabled Peronism to survive the fall of Pérón, and what made it unique among populist movements, was that the working class constituted its social base in contrast with the more disparate alliances of other populist movements which fragmented under the influence of monopoly capitalism.

There is also a prescriptive element in Laclau's argument and his account of Peronism leaves many questions unposed. How is one to account for the bureaucratization of the labour unions and for those divisions between unions which the subsequent history of intra-Peronist conflict would suggest were as deep as those between sectors of the middle and upper classes? What form did participation take and how were labour leaders elected and once elected how responsive were they to their members? We need more studies like W. Little's 'La tendencia peronista en el sindicalismo argentino: el caso de los obreros de la carne,' in *Aportes*, 19 (January 1971) who also studies how the unions took the place of an official party in 'Party and State in Peronist Argentina,' *Hispanic American Historical Review*, 53, 4 (November 1973). How did the mechanism of Peronist control work at the grass-roots level? How revolutionary can a labour movement be which receives most of its benefits as handouts from the state? As with the Mexican labour movement, so in Perón's Argentina workers gained benefits by decree, and although it is true that unions acquired autonomy after Perón's fall (unlike those in Mexico which have never succeeded or wanted to escape from close state control), how autonomous were they during the Peronist period?

A cardinal feature of the Peronist regime which would seem to differentiate it from other populist movements in Latin America, as well as from fascist movements in Europe, was that it coincided in its initial phase with a period of unprecedented economic prosperity when huge financial reserves accumulated during the war could be redistributed in the form of higher wages and social benefits, thus enabling Perón to avoid a direct confrontation with the agrarian interests on which the wealth of the country continued to rest. If the influence of the workers in the Peronist alliance was as strong as Laclau stresses, and if they were as wedded to revolution as he suggests, why was the social structure virtually unaltered when Perón fell from power? As Little puts it, 'it is ironic that its [Peronism's] conservative tendencies were lost upon the conservative critics of the regime who saw only the illiberalism which accompanied it.'

Some light is thrown on this by an unpublished doctoral thesis by J. Taylor, 'Myth and Reality: the Case of Eva Perón,' (D. Phil. diss., Oxford University, 1973) where she uses a social anthropological approach to analyse the pervasive myths in Argentine culture showing how the attitudes of the landowning elite towards the populace have remained virtually unchanged since the days of Rosas through Irigoyen up to Perón. The rigidity of these attitudes has made it impossible for the elite to reach any objective evaluation of movements which involve participation by the Buenos Aires populace.

Two points connected with Peronism's loss of revolutionary impetus need elucidating. To what extent did the movement suffer from an influx of ex-Radicals whose job hunger dulled the edge of revolutionary fervour much as the Spanish Falange was swamped by office seekers during and after the civil war? And second, how crucial was Eva Perón to the sustaining of revolutionary purpose? Peronism was the first Latin American political movement to mobilize women and this was reflected in electoral support for Perón but how effective were they in contributing to the processes of mobilization? A scholarly assessment of the role of Eva is overdue. The current growth of 'Evitism' — the tendency to emphasize the figure of Eva more than Perón himself — takes us to the core of the tensions within the movement. The Peronist left, represented by its youth movement, disillusioned by Perón's conservatism on his return from exile, look back to Eva as the repository of revolutionary virtue as a counter to what they believe to have been the manipulative, opportunist, and demagogic characteristics of Perón. In this view Eva is seen as the spokeswoman of the *descamisados* and the intercessor with Perón on behalf of their interests. We know very little about the complex relationship between Perón and Eva, between Perón and the populace, and between Eva and the populace.

With the revival of Peronism as an active force in Argentinian politics, it is likely that the movement's history will become a battleground between rival factions as each group tries to appropriate the master's or the mistress's mantle. Out of these conflicts some light may be thrown on what promises to remain for many years a paradoxical and elusive phenomenon. Two useful British contributions are W. Little, 'The popular origins of Peronism,' and D. Rock, 'The survival and restoration of Peronism,' in Rock's *Argentina in the Twentieth Century* (London, 1975).

*Mexico:* Considering the volume of material which has been published on the Mexican political system, it is surprising that so little attention has been paid to the Mexican right. The resources and talents of the prestigious research centre at the Colegio de México have been concentrated on pre-revolutionary history or on the early years of the Revolution, although a new cooperative history of the post-1910 period is in process of being written. Research may have been deflected from more recent periods by the pervasiveness of an official revolutionary historiography and the ruling party's dislike of heterodox interpretations. For this reason most research on opposition movements has been done by foreigners who encounter difficulties in gaining access to private archival sources without the study of which (even supposing these exist) many questions must remain unanswered. Some progress has been made with oral history projects such as the pioneer work by J. W. Wilkie and E. Monzón de Wilkie, *México visto en el siglo XX* (Mexico, 1969).

A triumph over considerable difficulties is J. Meyer's superb study of the *cristeros, La Cristiada,* 3 vols. (Mexico, 1973), which reveals for the first time in a scholarly manner the massive scale of peasant mobilization in counter-revolutionary opposition to the Revolution's anti-clerical policies in the 1920s. An English version is to be published by Cambridge University Press. J. W. Wilkie, 'The meaning of the *cristero* religious war against the Mexican Revolution,' in *The Journal of Church and State*, VIII, 2 (1966), is concerned primarily with the political conflict.

Unfortunately, we lack any academic study of the *sinarquista* movement founded in 1936 and which claimed over half a million supporters at the height of its power in the early 1940s (although Meyer is at present studying this). Much of the movement's history is shrouded in mystery, as in the question of its precise relationship to the Base, a secret Catholic organization, aimed at penetrating all aspects of secular life somewhat in the manner of Opus Dei. M. Gill's, *El sinarquismo: su origen, su esencia, su misión,* 3d. ed. (Mexico, 1962) is undocumented and tells little about organization, source of funds, or social composition. A. Michaels's 'Fascism and *Sinarquismo*: popular nationalisms against the Mexican Revolution,' in *The Journal of Church and State*, VIII, 2 (1966) is a useful introduction, relying as do most writers on the sinarquista's press. Broader in scope is his article 'El nacionalismo conservador mexicano desde la revolución hasta 1940,' *Historia Mexicana*, XVI (October-December 1966). There is also H. G. Campbell, *The Radical Right in Mexico, 1929-49* (Ph.D. diss., University of California, Los Angeles, 1968). We need to know much more about the relationship between cristeros and sinarquistas: to what extent was there continuity and overlap? The cristero movement invites comparison with Spanish Carlism whereas sinarquismo is a more complex phenomenon, representing an attempt by Catholic intellectuals to canalise peasant discontent into counter-revolutionary channels in areas where the agrarian reform had little success and where administrative corruption seems to have been rife. It had strong ruralist, moralistic anti-foreign, and apolitical overtones. Like the cristero movement it was mainly a regional phenomenon and did not have much influence outside the western states and the Bajío. It had some of the characteristics of rural populism with middle-class students proselytising among the villages for a spiritual uprising against the godless communism of the Revolution but, unlike the cristeros, the sinarquistas lived more by a non-violent ethic which, in the context of Mexican politics and combined with their lack of grasp and even perhaps of interest in the realities of power and their absence of any economic programme, accounts for the gradual decline of their influence. The expansion of their numbers in the early 1940s may be explained by the widespread disillusionment with the latter years of the Cárdenas regime. This has been studied by A. Michaels in 'The crisis of Cardenismo,' in *Journal of Latin American Studies*, 2 (1970) whilst the inner contradictions of Cárdenas's regime have been analysed by David Raby in 'La contribución del cardenismo en el desarrollo de México,' in *Aportes*, no. 26 (October 1972), questioning some of the long-accepted assumptions about the nature of *cardenismo*.

Sinarquismo grew out of the *Centro anti-comunista* which had been founded in Guanajuato by a German professor at the university. But when the next year this group adopted the name Sinarquista (the antithesis to the anarchism which they felt was sweeping the country) the influence of foreign ideas, apart from Hispanidad, was minimal. The sinarquista equated nationalism with Catholicism in the tradition of nineteenth-century Mexican conservatives. Catholicism was regarded as the best bulwark against the insidious influence of the United States to which Mexico's backwardness was attributed. The anti-American current in sinarquista ideology was one reason why it enjoyed some following among Mexican-Americans, especially in the Los Angeles area where friction was acute after the 'zoot-suit' riots. Sinarquismo provided one way, albeit a minor one, by which chicanos expressed their resentment at their inferior position in United States society.

Part of the reason for the sinarquistas' decline in influence may be explained by the defection of middle-class supporters to the Acción

Nacional, the Catholic professional, business-oriented party which was
founded in 1939 and which was to become the major opposition party to
the PRI and which has been studied by Donald J. Mabry in *Mexico's
Acción Nacional: a Catholic alternative to revolution* (Syracuse, 1973)
(with an extensive bibliographical essay). However, this does not explain
the falling off in rural support: no one has shown, for example, that the
social conditions which gave rise to sinarquismo had been substantially improved. It may be that rural support fell away as the manipulative tendencies of the movement became apparent.

Specifically fascist groups had far less influence in Mexico although the
apparent increase in communist influence during Cárdenas's presidency
led to an increase in their number. The Acción Revolucionaria Mexicana
founded in 1933 as an anti-Semitic, anti-communist para-military organization, under an ex-villista general Nicolás Rodríguez and known as the
Dorados after their gold shirts and Villa's elite troops, conducted rowdy
meetings and held military parades until they were routed by the communists in street battles and proscribed by Cárdenas. They have not been
seriously studied and merit consideration in conjunction with other fascist
inspired groups such as the *Falange Español Tradicionalista*, formed by
Spanish merchants resident in Mexico to offset the consistent support given
by Cárdenas to the Republicans in the Spanish Civil War. Although the
Mexican Jewish community only numbered some 18,000 both the left and
the right shared anti-Semitic prejudices.

The Mexican revolution had a particular resonance in the Andean countries where the Mexicans' revindication of Indians influenced *indigenista*
theorizing. Large Indian populations, together with evidence of a great
historical past, gave nationalist theorists an alternative basis for a nationalist ideology to Hispanic Catholicism.

*Peru:* Peruvians took the lead in formulating an indigenista-based
ideology with Haya de la Torre's concept of Indo-America and Mariate-
gui's attempts to adapt Marxism to Peruvian conditions. Haya's ideology
was an amalgam of eclectic borrowings from Marxism, the British Labour
party, earlier Peruvian writers, and nazism and although ostensibly indian-
ist, the practical expression of the party's indianism was minimal. In its
hey-day it influenced other reformist parties like Acción Democrática in
Venezuela, Figueres's Social Democratic party in Costa Rica and the
Auténticos in Cuba, but unlike them Apra has never been in power,
mainly because of the army's hostility. Partly because of this, the party
changed its anti-imperialist and anti-capitalist stance and came to understandings with conservative politicians. With the subsequent erosion of its
student support much of the party's dynamism evaporated. Surprisingly,
there have been few studies of this, the most successful unsuccessful party
in Latin American politics, founded in 1926 and still under the same

leader. The key to the party's longevity does not seem to me to lie in its political aspirations so much as in the security which its sub-culture, touching all aspects of social life, offers to established as well as to socially mobile mestizos. Apra's opponents have always questioned its democratic pretensions, emphasizing the caudillo nature of Haya's domination of the party and what they sense to be its totalitarian tendencies. The *bufalos*, Apra strongarm squads, lend some credence to this view as did Haya's admiration for the Nazis' organizational efficiency. Ultimately, it is not ideology (which has been the most studied aspect of the party) but organization which has held it together. H. Kantor's, *The ideology and programme of the Aprista movement* (Berkeley, 1964) and R. J. Alexander's *Aprismo* (Kent, Ohio, 1973) which makes a wide selection of Haya's writings available in English for the first time, stress ideology. G. Hilliker, *The politics of reform in Peru: the aprista and other mass parties of Latin America* (Baltimore, 1971) concentrates on organization but he does not seem aware of the literature on populism. Apra is perceptively treated in F. Bourricaud, *Pouvoir et société dans le Pérou contemporain* (Paris, 1967; trans. London, 1971) and in F. B. Pike, *The modern history of Peru* (London, 1967). J. L. Payne *Labor and Politics in Peru* (New Haven, 1965) is an important contribution to the wider problem of 'structured violence' as well as throwing light on Apra which he regards with a critical eye.

Apra's failure to mobilize the Indian masses and its faded radicalism left the way open for the emergence of Fernando Belaúnde's Acción Popular party in 1956. This was a multi-class populist party with a strong narodnik-style ideology of regeneration via ancient Indian folkways matched with an emphasis on technocratic elitism. No serious study of Acción Popular has been attempted, although many of its ideas were taken up by the military reformists after 1968. Unlike Apra, Acción Popular succeeded in incorporating the military into the populist alliance, but because of divisions and corruption within the wide spectrum of its civilian support, the military overthrew Belaúnde in 1968 and introduced their own brand of technocratic nationalistic military reformism. Useful articles on 'military populism' are J. Cotler, 'Crisis popular y populismo militar en el Peru,' in *Estudios Internacionales*, no. 12 (January-March 1970) and on the corporative aspects of the present military regime J. Malloy's 'Authoritarianism, corporatism and mobilization in Peru,' in *The Review of Politics* (January 1974).

Peru is perhaps the most interesting country in Latin America for studying populist movements as, in addition to Apra and Acción Popular, General Odría's National Union had a strong populist appeal among the shanty-towns of Lima.

*Bolivia:* It is a unique case in Latin America, insofar as war provided the main impetus to the development of mass politics. Unexpected defeat in the Chaco war with Paraguay led to a period of national self-questioning in the course of which younger military officers, partly influenced by Nazi ideas, established a series of proto-revolutionary regimes which prepared the way for the revolution of 1952. The MNR was a multi-class coalition of militant miners and an aroused peasantry under mainly middle-class leadership, which faced more acutely than any other populist movement the dilemma of how to satisfy roused expectations at the same time as increasing productivity. An early standard account of the revolution is R. J. Alexander, *The Bolivian National Revolution* (New Brunswick, N. J., 1948) now partly superseded by J. M. Malloy, *Bolivia: the uncompleted Revolution* (Pittsburgh, 1970). The historical origins of the revolution have attracted few researchers except for the excellent study by H. Klein, *Parties and political change in Bolivia, 1880-1952* (Cambridge, 1969) whilst he discusses the military's reforming role in 'David Toro and the establishment of "Military Socialism" in Bolivia,' *Hispanic American Historical Review* 45, 1 (February 1965) and 'German Busch and the era of "Military Socialism" in Bolivia,' *Hispanic American Historical Review* 47, 2 (May 1967). Interesting light is thrown on United States attitudes to the early MNR and its allegedly Nazi sympathies by Cole Blaiser in 'The United States, Germany and the Bolivian revolutionaries, 1941-46,' *Hispanic American Historical Review* 52, 1 (February 1972). A more general discussion of the military's role is W. H. Brill, *Military Intervention in Bolivia; the overthrow of Paz Estenssoro and the MNR* (Washington, 1967).

There is no study of the Falange Socialista Boliviano which was founded by exiles in Chile in the late 1930s and became the main opposition to the MNR. It was recruited from dispossessed landowners and from the MNR's lower-middle- and middle-class supporters hit by the high inflation after 1952. It also has regional support in Santa Cruz. The Falange was inspired by the Spanish Falange and had fascist overtones, with its leader Unzaga de la Vega aspiring to become a führer style leader until his assassination in 1959. It has never succeeded in building up a mass following nor in acquiring political respectability by developing into a Christian Democrat style party in the manner of the Chilean Falange.

There is a larger literature on the post-1952 period than for any other Latin American country of comparable size. All that can be mentioned here is an important article by M. Burke and J. M. Malloy, 'Del populismo nacional al corporativismo nacional: el caso de Bolivia, 1952-1970,' *Aportes*, no. 26 (October 1972). Although the revolution of 1952 was regarded by Peronists as the first success of a Peronist-style revolution outside Argentina, no serious analysis of the links between the two has yet been attempted.

*Chile:* True to the Chileans' self-image of their Europeanism, the fascist versus popular front confrontation was acted out in the 1930s but with

curious consequences. A small Nazi-style party, the MNS (Movimiento
Nacional Socialista de Chile) was founded in 1932 by Jorge González von
Marées in the same year as the Partido Socialista, founded to fill the gap
left by the internecine rivalry between Stalinists and Trotskyites. It was not
limited, as its leader's name might imply, to Chile's sizable German community but appealed, as did its rival the Partido Socialista, to students and
young workers. The MNS has been described as the one recognizably
European-style Nazi group in Latin America, but F. B. Pike in *Chile and
the United States, 1880-1962* (Notre Dame, 1963) (which is far wider in
scope than the title indicates), denies it was simply imitative and stresses
the perceptiveness of its criticisms of Chilean society but suggests that it
failed to attract a larger membership because of the aristocracy's dislike of
its upstart leader and the party's stridency, and the threat which a potential mass party posed to the delicate balance on which Chilean politics
rested, as well as to the hitherto successful policy of co-optation by which
the landed elite had managed to assimilate a rising middle class. Significantly, too, it was distrusted by the army for its para-military pretensions.

In 1938 young *nacistas* captured in an unsuccessful coup against Ales-
sandri were assassinated in cold blood by the police. Ironically, this event
led ex-dictator Carlos Ibañez with whom the nacistas had an understanding, to throw the weight of his support behind the Popular Front candidate which thus came in partly with fascist support. Although the MNS
itself withered away, an extreme right tradition was revived when the
foundation of the MNCh. (Movimiento Nacionalista de Chile) in 1940
united ex-nacistas, and *ibañistas* on a corporatist programme. This group
may be traced through to the FNPL (Frente Nacionalista Patria y Liber-
tad) founded in 1970 to provide the shock troops of the anti-Allende opposition. An excellent analysis of the right is contained in H. E. Bicheno,
'Anti-parliamentary themes in Chilean history, 1920-1970,' *Government
and Opposition* no. 3 (1972). Bicheno is at present working on a Ph.D.
dissertation at Cambridge on the nacistas.

The Chilean army has not received the attention its behaviour warrants.
F. Nunn, *Chilean Politics, 1920-1931: the Honorable Mission of the
Armed Forces* (Albuquerque, 1970) is an introduction. The populist origins of the Socialist party are examined in P. Drake, 'The Chilean Socialist
party and coalition politics, 1936-46,' *Hispanic American Historical
Review*, 47, 1 (February 1973) where he concludes that 'by channelling the
populist drive of the lower sectors into a Marxist framework but also into
the existing system, the Chilean socialists may have given "mass politics"
the potential to be a more heady agent of change, however gradual and
limited, than in any Latin American country.' The influence of Perón's
justicialist doctrines in Chile have been studied by W. Bray, 'Peronism in
Chile,' *Hispanic American Historical Review*, 47, 1 (February 1967). We
need more analyses of the impact of Peronism on other countries as well.

The Chilean Falange had been founded in 1938 by a break-away group of young members of the Conservative party. Despite the name, they bore little relation to the Spanish Falange and were mostly influenced by the writings of liberal Catholics. In 1957 the group absorbed the bulk of another small Christian group and was reconstituted as the Christian Democrat party with populist and corporatist strains, emphasizing communitarianism. Their views are discussed, within the general context of Chilean politics, in J. Petras, *Politics and social forces in Chilean development* (Berkeley and Los Angeles, 1969). By populism, the Christian Democrats understood the active participation in decision-making by the poor, especially the marginal groups who had been largely overlooked by the secular left as an unreliable lumpenproletariat. The Christian Democrats were the first to recognize their electoral potential — especially the support they could get from women. Populism, in the Christian Democrats' sense, had a different emphasis, at least in theory, from the manipulative tendencies of Brazilian populism, although in practice the differences may not have been all that great. Some of the paradoxical features of Christian Democrat populism are discussed by E. de Kadt in 'Paternalists and populists: views on Catholicism in Latin America,' *Journal of Contemporary History*, 2 (November 1967).

Other Latin American countries have had their fringe fascist groups and their populist style movements, but they have not exercised much influence. In Ecuador, ARNE (Alianza Revolucionaria Nacionalista Ecuatoriana) was founded as a fascist-style group in 1948, but although it was prepared to support Velasco Ibarra it could not hope to compete against his old-style personalist, not to say populist appeal. In Colombia, where politics have traditionally revolved around the two historical parties, the Liberals and Conservatives, with their clientilist followings, there are no disposable masses for a fascist party to mobilize. Falangist ideas and Hispanidad exercised some influence on Laureano Gómez in the late 1930s and there was a Falangist group active in the early 1940s. Colombia produced in Jorge Eliecer Gaitán one of the most striking populist leaders of any Latin American country, but his assassination in 1948 cut short the development of any populist movement. Since then no one has been able to break the monopoly exercised by the two traditional parties although General Rojas Pinilla, influenced to some extent by Perón, tried to do so. A. Angell discusses populism in 'Populism and political change: the Colombian case,' in *Sociological Review Monograph*, no. 11 (February 1967). The military have still to receive full-length treatment although there is a brief analysis of its role in J. L. Payne's general book on Colombian politics, *Patterns of Conflict in Colombia* (New Haven, 1968) in R. H. Dix, *Colombia: the political dimensions of change* (New Haven, 1967), who also discusses populistic authoritarianism, and in V. L. Fluharty, *Dance of the Millions:*

*military rule and social revolution in Colombia, 1930-56* (Pittsburgh, 1957). Venezuelan political parties have not been analysed from the criterion of populism, although J. D. Martz, *Acción Democrática* (Princeton, 1966) is one of the fullest analyses of a Latin American political party we have. Venezuela produced in Valenilla Lanz's *Cesarismo democrático*, published in 1929, one of the only theoretical expositions of a military leader with a mass popular appeal, but mainly as an apologia for the rule of the dictator Juan Vicente Gómez, although it has also been taken as a prescription for successful government under prevailing Latin American conditions. It is an open question whether Batista in the 1930s or Castro in the early 1960s can be subsumed under the populist umbrella, although both their regimes had populist characteristics.

The serious study of Latin America's contemporary history and politics which has now become a major academic growth industry is of comparatively recent origin but, in spite of (or perhaps because of) the sophisticated techniques employed, many problems remain unsolved. During the key formative years of the 1930s and 1940s Latin American politics were virtually unstudied both abroad and in Latin America itself. Abroad, they were widely regarded as a corrupted strain of the liberal constitutionalism Latin America so avidly imitated, and the apparent inability to operate parliamentary government was adduced as evidence of congenital deficiencies and rarely attributed to structural problems. Latin Americans themselves contributed little to off-set widespread foreign misconceptions. Most political studies were cast in an arid juridico-legal mould and by taking the premises of their own political behaviour for granted they denied to foreigners insights which a native tradition of academic self-analysis might otherwise have provided.

It needed the jolt of the Cuban revolution to change attitudes and to give an impetus to serious academic study both within and outside Latin America, releasing a flood of money and endowing prestige to a field which had previously lacked serious recognition. Inevitably, much of the social science research done by United States scholars, who dominate the field, has tended to be of a predictive nature and policy-oriented. In the opening phase of this newly awakened interest, research was still culture-bound: few scholars were attuned to underlying cultural nuances and there was a tendency to apply uncritically techniques which had originally been devised for advanced industrial societies. However, there was a well-established tradition of social anthropological research which helped to provide the basis for a more realistic assessment once the advantages of an interdisciplinary approach were recognized.

Attention was directed primarily towards development problems and the process of modernization. Financial aid to Latin American countries was intended to serve a prophylactic function and neutralize the effects of the Cuban revolution. It was implicitly assumed that this aid would help the process of nation-building, establish social justice, increase the standard of living, bolster democracy, support agrarian reform, and stimulate industrialization. These aims were regarded as being both desirable and inevitable. All that was needed for their achievement was the injection of the much needed capital and technical assistance which Latin Americans lacked. In the early 1960s both official and academic circles in the United States were optimistic about the contribution which the Alliance for Progress would make towards modernization and democracy, which were regarded as being inseparable and mutually reinforcing. Latin America was not like Africa with its tribal complexities, or Asia with its impermeable culture and religious taboos: it was recognizably Western, a largely immigrant continent like the United States, an extension of Europe and hence obeying the laws of European social and historical development. Of all the areas of the Third World, Latin America seemed to be the furthest advanced along the traditional-modern continuum.

By the end of the 1960s, this reformist euphoria had evaporated, as the assumptions on which it had been based were shown to be false. It was true that the failure of countless guerrilla campaigns, climaxed in Guevara's failure in Bolivia in 1967, had revealed that Latin America was not ripe for revolution in the Cuban fashion but neither, it seemed, was it ripe for Western-style democracy. Instead a series of military coups initiated a new cycle of authoritarian government until by 1976 only a handful of Latin American states were under civilian rule. Even Uruguay, long regarded as a model of parliamentary probity, succumbed, and Chile which had prided itself on its European-style political stability showed that when it came to violence it could emulate its exemplars in that respect as well. Events in Brazil since the 'revolution' of 1964, and more particularly, events during and after the Allende regime in Chile, have re-introduced fascism into the vocabulary of Latin American political analysis as something more than a term of abuse. To the liberal democrat's question of what has gone wrong, Marxists might reply nothing, as given the pre-conditions of a capitalist system in crisis the trend to authoritarianism and 'colonial fascism' is inevitable and, from the standpoint of United States interests and those of multi-national companies, desirable as well, a view which is concisely expressed in books like Dick Parker's, *La nueva cara del fascismo* (Santiago, 1972). In this view, fascism is seen as the form of government arising in capitalist societies when contradictions develop between a technologically advanced industrial sector and a low-productivity traditional sector. In the face of working-class demands the fascist state attempts to defend the interests of proprietors in both sectors, supported by insecure elements of the lower-middle and middle classes. The private interests in the modern sector can be national or foreign. If the former, fascism takes the classic autarchic form. If the latter, 'colonial fascism' integrates the dependent country's economy, dominated by foreign capital, into the international capitalist economy.[13]

Whatever its validity, such an approach lies within an established tradition — not necessarily Marxist but often using Marxist insights — which exercises a wide influence throughout Latin American academic circles. It takes as its starting point the peripheral and dependent position of Latin America in the global economy and sets out to explain why, after 150 years of political independence, most Latin American countries remain primary producers, have monoproductive economies, and are still dependent on the advanced industrial powers, especially the United States, economically, politically, and culturally. This 'dependency theory,' a variant of general theories of imperialism, has been formulated mainly by Latin American scholars and marks an intellectual breakthrough, a decolonizing of the academic mind, as it looks at Latin American problems from a Latin American perspective.[14] Economists and sociologists have been in the forefront of this development with the United Nations Economic Commission for Latin America as its original forcing house. Historians have lagged behind for reasons related to inaccessibility of sources, the slower pace of historical research and, perhaps, through the conservative outlook of academic historians. Many of the hypotheses which have been formulated by social scientists are therefore often based on slender historical evidence although analysis of the 1930s and 1940s tends to be crucial to their arguments as one of the key problems is exactly why the industrialization process which accelerated from the early 1930s failed to break the pattern of dependence.

Problems of modernization, development and the impact of Western-based technologies, and the peasant responses to them have encouraged some historians to follow political scientists and sociologists into the field of comparative studies. Although the most ambitious of these, Barrington Moore's *The social origins of dictatorship and democracy* (New York, 1966) does not touch on Latin America, his model of fascism as a political system by which modernization is achieved without changing the social structure and his application of it to Japan has suggestive possibilities. From this viewpoint, Vargas's Estado Novo and Perón's Justicialismo could be classified as fascist. However, there is one element which is crucial to Moore's thesis which is absent in the Latin American case, and that concerns the peasantry. With the exception of sinarquismo, peasants do not become key figures in the elaboration of radical right ideologies, as was the case with the Nazis. The stress which Moore places on the role of peasants and the reasons why labour-repressive systems provide an important part of the institutional complex leading to fascism, contrasts markedly with the Latin American situation where peasants for the most part lacked economic independence and became enmeshed in clientilist arrangements with conservative or populist politicians and are not available for mobilization by the radical right, and indeed, proved difficult to organize even by the Castroite left which, unlike the radical right, had an interest in doing so.

Nor, in Latin America, was there the same anti-modern utopian strain which, it has been argued, was one key to the understanding of German Nazism (although not perhaps of Italian fascism). Industrialization was too desirable a goal as a means of achieving genuine independence to be rejected in favour of a peasant symbol of agrarian innocence. In any case, peasants who were often Indian, mestizo, black, or mulatto could not become carriers for an ideology of racial purity—at least on the right.[15]

It may be questioned whether the wide range of variables involved in cross-cultural analyses will produce fruitful results (except in the sense that comparative study can always pose new questions and open up new perspectives). Much more work needs to be done in comparative historical studies before convincing generalizations can be formulated. The difficulty —for historians at least—is that in trying to explain everything, one finishes by explaining nothing.

Historians may seem to have little to contribute to the on-going debate so long as many sociologists and political scientists are reluctant to give more weight to historical conditioning factors and reject the concept of political culture, but whatever advantages there may be in the fragmentation and specialization of disciplines in advanced industrial countries, these divisions constitute a major barrier to understanding developing areas. One field of study where this has been recognized and where the cross-fertilization of disciplines may throw new light on Latin American political processes is in the reviving interest in corporatism.

What might be regarded as the manifesto of this trend is the special edition of *The Review of politics* 36, 1 (January 1974) entitled 'The New Corporatism: Social and Political Structures in the Iberian World' and the book version published by Notre Dame University Press, 1974, edited by F. B. Pike. A further volume edited by H. Wiarda, *Politics and Social Change in Latin America: the Distinct Tradition* (1974), collects previously published articles including a major contribution by Richard M. Morse, the gadfly among United States Latin Americanists who has long been arguing for the recognition of the Thomistic roots of Latin American political behaviour and thought.

In *The New Corporatism* collection, J. Malloy explores corporatism as exemplified in the reformist military regime in contemporary Peru and argues that corporatism constitutes an empirically useful group theory of politics, at present reflected in three levels of analysis of Latin American politics: in the analysis of the institutional and cultural principles derived from the Hispanic tradition; in the analysis of group formation and interest articulation, which are inadequately grasped by liberal and Marxist group theories of politics; and in the analysis of how a political system has been organized and integrated, as in Mexico since 1917 and in contemporary Peru. Schmitter's seminal article suggests an operational definition of corporatism in terms of a distinctive modern system of interest representation, but he is concerned with wider implications and ramifications than the political culture arguments favoured by Wiarda's and Newton's articles which are confined to the Iberian world.

Ronald Newton, whose article 'On "Functional Groups," "Fragmentation" and "Pluralism" in Spanish American Political Society,' in *Hispanic American Historical Review* 50, 1 (1970) was an important and stylish first salvo in the current debate, presents the case for what he calls 'natural corporatism.' In contrast to corporatism in Europe between the wars which was adopted as an ideology and organizing principle once in power, 'natural corporatism' in Latin America

has evolved slowly, unacknowledged, within or parallel to the conventional and more or less constitutional processes of electoral civic paralysis, *golpes*. . . . Where European-derived corporatism has figured at all in the doctrinal writings and programmes of political activists, it has been the property of isolated sects and sectarians of the extreme right with few prospects of immediate access to power. [P. 39]

Newton refers to natural corporatism as 'an organizing hypothesis' used by scholars to explain socio-political phenomena which have not been elucidated in terms of the categories of conventional liberal-developmental scholarship in Latin America. Corporate ways of articulating group interests lie at the core of Hispanic politics, and both leftist and rightist regimes must take cognizance of this tradition if they wish to flourish. Corporate representation is not the monopoly of the left or right, but can be deployed both by populist regimes as a means of achieving participation and mobilization and by the authoritarian regimes which succeeded them, as a means of depoliticization and demobilization.

Wiarda's article amplifies an argument he had earlier presented in 'Towards a Framework for the Study of Political Change in the Ibero-Latin Tradition,' *World Politics*, 25, 2 (January 1973) for the recognition of a distinctive Ibero-American political tradition embedded in corporatism 'about the only one of the great "isms" that correspond to her historic and political culture.' He also distinguishes between corporatist regimes of the 1930s and 1940s, where corporatism was a system of authority, stressing functional representation and the integration of labour and capital into a hierarchically ordered system, and a historical tradition embedded in Ibero-Latin American history, embodying a dominant form of socio-political organization that is hierarchical elitist, authoritarian, bureaucratic, Catholic patrimonialist, and corporatist. While the discredited forms of corporatism associated with fascism were submerged and re-baptised under different names, the old corporatist tradition remained intact. Underneath democratic façades, the historic political culture of corpora- tist values was present all the time. Wiarda is a rare example of a political scientist taking historical influences seriously but one is bound to wonder if he is not doing his own cause and that of historians a disservice by overkill.

He also perhaps overestimates the influence of the United States in Latin America when he argues that because corporatist and integralist experi- ments had been discredited by European fascism the United States com- pelled Latin Americans to choose between false alternatives of communism and democracy by ruling out a middle way. The application of unilinear, ethnocentric development models deflected Latin Americans away from its real traditions and it is only now with the decline of United States cultural, economic, and political influence, and the discrediting of United States models, that Latin America, as in the 1930s, is searching for indigenous solutions.

The chapter by F. B. Pike (whose earlier book *Hispanismo, 1898-1936: Spanish Conservatives and Liberals and their relations with Spanish America* [Notre Dame, 1971] was a long overdue examination of mutual influences between Spain and Spanish America) suggests that in attempt- ing to carry out a bourgeois revolution from above the Latin American technocratic elite have chosen methods, including developmental nation- alism and paternalistic corporatism, designed to keep the lower classes in a dependent position and that corporatism now serves the security interests of the United States. Whatever criticisms may be brought against the cor- porate thesis generally or the various essays individually, this collection opens up a whole vista of possible approaches to the study of Latin Ameri- can political and social movements.

Finally, Wiarda insists that corporatism is not to be equated with fascism or nazism — parallels are only superficial: Ibero-Latin tradition is a distinct and separate type, fundamentally different from popular stereotypes. Authoritarian yes but fascist no. 'Fascism,' he concludes, 'and fascist can hardly be applied in an Ibero-Latin context with any accuracy. As an ade- quate analytic term fascism may have outlived its usefulness.'

It would be a relief to believe that the semantic hair-splitting to which definitional studies of fascism invariably descend is a thing of the past and that as far as Latin America is concerned we can forget such irrelevant criteria but with capitalism in the Western world in crisis, and with the example of Brazil and Chile and other Latin American states before us, optimism may be premature. Fascism is a blunt instrument for political science analysis but for the victims of authoritarian rule the fine distinc- tions of academics will seem irrelevant.

## NOTES

1. For German efforts, see A. Frye, *Nazi Germany and the American Hemisphere, 1933-41* (New Haven, 1967) with extensive bibliography and *Der Deutsche Faschismus in Lateinamerika 1933-1943* (Berlin, 1966). Hispanidad is discussed in B. W. Diffie, 'The ideology of Hispanidad,' in *Hispanic-American Historical Review*, 22 (August 1943).

2. The one exception is the Chaco war between Bolivia and Paraguay in the 1039s which in the former gave an impetus to fascist ideas but in the latter strengthened old-style caudillo rule. The siege mentality in Cuba since 1959 has produced results similar to those produced by actual warfare. The case of the Mexican civil war between 1913 and 1917 is not comparable as this created internal divisions.

3. The distrust is clear in the case of Germany and Spain but less clear in the case of Italy. See G. Rochat, *L'esercito italiano da Vittorio Veneto a Mussolini (1919-25)* (Bari, 1967). In Latin America scholars have virtually ignored police forces. It is a major research need and nowhere more than in Chile where the para-military *carabineros* held one of the keys to Allende's success or failure.

4. In a British context one has only to think of the shock impact of Powell's 'rivers of blood' speech.

5. The distinction between fascism and traditionalism in Spain is clearly made in R. M. Blinkhorn, *Carlism and Crisis in Spain, 1931-39* (Cambridge, 1975).

6. 'Concientização' became one of the key concepts of the 1960s, associated with the Brazilian educator Paolo Freire but after 1964 in Brazil it became discredited because of its political implications.

7. The key intellectual influence in Spain was Ramiro de Maeztu, a half-English, Anglophile liberal who believed before the Great War that Spain could be regenerated by liberal capitalism. Experience as a reporter on the Western Front cured him of illusions about the 'defence of civilization, and with the publication of *La Crisis del Humanismo* in 1916 he began a new career as spokesman for Hispanic values culminating in *Defensa de la Hispanidad* in 1934, the key text for Hispanic right wing movements.

8. Self-definition should be taken seriously in any analysis of fascist movements. Obviously structural factors are crucial in any definition but if people consistently reject the title, it is worth exploring the reasons why they do so.

9. They returned to active politics in 1950 and 1955 when Salgado polled 8% of the presidential vote.

10. We lack scholarly studies of anti-Semitism in Latin America. For Argentina there are two chapters in D. Eisenberg. *The Re-emergence of Fascism* (London, 1967). A useful discussion of the position of Jews in Latin America is the conference report, *Latin America and the future of its Jewish communities* (London, 1973).

11. The personalist element in Brazilian populism is well illustrated by its domestication of political leaders by using their Christian names—thus Getulio, Juscelino, Jangio etc., for Vargas, Kubitschek, Quadros—a contrast to the faceless military presidents after 1964. In Argentina the style was different. Perón distanced himself from the crowd and Eva's role was to act as intercessor. The Führerprinzip of nazism or Il Duce of fascism, or even El caudillo por la gracia de Dios of Franco is far removed from the Latin American populist style.

12. Ramiro de Maeztu had been Spanish ambassador in Buenos Aires in the late 1920s and had formed links with the Nueva República group. Another important Spanish influence justifying elite rule was Ortega y Gasset's *Rebelión de las Masas*, first published in 1926 but with very different underlying presuppositions to Maeztu.

13. In Parker's typology Italy, 1922-43 and Spain, 1940-49 are classic but stagnant fascisms: Germany, 1933-45 is classic but dynamic and Spain, 1960-? and Brazil, 1967-? are colonial fascist and dynamic.

14. A useful short analysis of dependence theory is P. O'Brien, *A critique of Latin Ameri-*

*can theories of dependency,* Glasgow University Institute of Latin American Studies, Occasional Papers, no. 12. A. G. Frank, *Capitalism and underdevelopment in Latin America* (New York, 1969), is a key text whilst the writings of Paul A. Baran were an important early influence.

15. There have been instances of attempts to formulate ideologies of racial purity—such as proving Mexicans were Aryans—but more usual have been ideologies of racial fusion: on this Integralists and Nazis clashed in Brazil. The Integralists' fanciful Indianism—their greeting was the Indian Tupi word *anauê*—was never taken seriously and they did not single out blacks for special consideration at a time when attempts were being made to organize them in the Frente Negra Brasileira. In 1933 Gilberto Freyre's *Masters and Slaves* was published which reversed the racial pessimism of Euclides da Cunha and those in the 1890s who were influenced by Gobineau and Gumplowicz. The influence of Freyre, who made a virtue out of racial necessity, was very great.

# 8
# Fascism in Western Europe

STANLEY G. PAYNE

Fascist and national socialist movements achieved comparatively little importance in western and northern Europe, with the single exception of Spain. Until recently they have drawn little historiographic attention. In the one case where there are major phenomena to study, the long duration of the Franco regime has inhibited scholarly investigation by Spaniards of its own origin and the inception of national syndicalism. Given the paucity of monographic works, the absence of broader analytical study is perhaps not surprising. There has thus been no real inquiry into whether there was such a thing as a unique 'west European' variant of fascism. The common assumption seems to be that the term *fascist* refers to all violent, authoritarian radical nationalist movements and that their differences are either unimportant or merely the inevitable result of national differences in nationalist movements.

The point of inception for fascistic ideas in the West has been a matter of debate. Miguel de Unamuno once said that the Spanish Carlists were the first fascists, but so simplistic a comparison cannot withstand analysis. Reactionary neo-traditionalist monarchism of the nineteenth century in both Spain and France lacked the distinctive characteristics and components of fascism, whether in terms of vitalistic, irrationalist culture, the development of a new state and system to cope with mass society and economics, or mass mobilization. This becomes clear from general works that deal in whole or in part with the monarchist ultra-right, such as Román Oyarzun's *Historia del carlismo* (Madrid, 1940, 1965), and René Rémond, *The Right Wing in France from 1815 to de Gaulle* (Philadelphia, 1969).

Though a major fascist movement at no time emerged in France, many of the specific ingredients of fascism appeared earlier there than anywhere else. This, of course, was also true of the notion of totalitarian democracy, communist ideas, and the modern revolutionary leftist dictatorship, simply because there was an earlier convergence of both the problems of modernization and the various aspects of modern development in France than in any other large country. Probably the first point at which specific pre-fascist ingredients can be identified is in the agitation of Paul Déroulède's 'League of Patriots' and the Boulangist movement in the 1880s. One of the classic motivations of fascism—status deprivation—weighed upon France rather than on Germany or Italy after 1871, and the French left,

still at that point ultra-nationalist, felt defrauded by the character of the
Third Republic just as did the nationalist left in central European countries a generation or more later. In Boulangism there was expressed a new
kind of nationalism that was at the same time authoritarian, contemptuous
of representative liberal democracy, and directed toward the masses. It
sought to harmonize the interests of diverse classes and appealed especially
toward small shopkeepers and the lower middle class. The central motif
was national vengeance, requiring a doctrine of neo-militarism and a mystique of discipline and death rooted in the national soil and the popular
culture.[1] Boulangism remained, however, rather more leftist than rightist
in inspiration, and could not exploit any genuine social crisis, which was
non-existent. In general European terms, it was premature, but when the
so-called fascist era later dawned in central Europe, French society was too
stable and mature for fascism.

The search for the roots of a French fascism has recently centered on the
figure of Maurice Barrès, which has been studied by Robert Soucy,
*Fascism in France: The Case of Maurice Barrès* (Berkeley, Los Angeles,
London, 1972), and Z. Sternhell, *Maurice Barrès et le nationalisme
français* (Paris, 1972), the latter, the richer work. Barrès was one of the
first to attempt to formulate the idea of a national socialism, and his mystique of *la terre et les morts* anticipated much of the mythos of the new
radical nationalism of the twentieth century. Sternhell and Soucy show
that Barrès combined the search for energy and vitalism with an emphasis
on national rootedness and a sort of Darwinian racism. He also propounded hero worship and charismatic leadership, but remained in many
ways basically conservative and failed in his efforts at broader mobilization.[2] Barrès later relapsed into traditionalism and a kind of fatalism that
differed considerably from the subsequent fascist cult of will.

The core of the modern French right was formed by the Action Française movement of Charles Maurras. Ernst Nolte has judged it one of the
three fundamental 'faces of fascism,'[3] not in the sense of a fully developed
fascism but rather as a seedbearer of ideas and tendencies more fully
developed in Italy and Germany. Yet even this seems to stretch the point,
for the Action Française altogether failed to meet the criteria of Nolte's
own 'fascist minimum' that he advanced in a later work.[4] Its reactionary
qualities were not so radical as to oppose all practical conservatism, and it
did not espouse the last principles included in Nolte's 'fascist minimum'—
a 'party-army' and the goal of totalitarianism. Cultural neo-classicism
clashed with vitalism and irrationalism, and the tactic of radical mobilization of the masses for violent or pseudo-revolutionary activity was lacking.
The Action Française was in fact the most sophisticated and modern movement of the elitist, semi-traditionalist right. Eugen Weber's *Action Française: Royalism and Reaction in Twentieth-Century France* (Stanford,
1962) is a masterful and comprehensive account that narrates the entire

history of the movement while analyzing its ideology and cultural influence, as well as its effect on the royalist right in other lands. Edward Tan-
nenbaum's *Action Française* (New York, 1962) is inferior in terms either of
perspective or comprehensiveness.

Between the 1920s and early 1940s France generated more small fascist,
semi-fascist, or pseudo-fascist movements of radical nationalism than any
other country, yet none assumed truly major proportions and most failed
to approximate the full model of the Italian movement. The largest of the
organized 'leagues,' as they were called in the 1930s, was the Croix de Feu
of Colonel de la Rocque, which at one point claimed, no doubt with exaggeration, to have more than 700,000 members. Yet the Croix de Feu
remained an amorphous veterans' association without clear-cut ideology or
goals. Rather than a French National Socialist party it was more nearly the
French version of the Stahlhelm. There is a fairly extensive if partisan
account by Philippe Rudaux, *Les Croix de Feu et le P.S.F.* (Paris, 1967).

The first of the new radical groups was the Faisceau band organized by
Georges Valois and a few other dissidents from Action Française in 1925.[5]
The source of its ideological inspiration was obvious, though the party
dwindled away to nothing in the stable and prosperous France of the
1920s. The only other French group to employ the term *fascist* semi-offici-
ally — at least on occasion — was the Francistes of Marcel Bucard,[6] who also
drew a subsidy from the Italian government[7] but were scarcely more successful than the Faisceau. The nearest thing to a serious fascist-type
movement in France was the Parti Populaire Français of Jacques Doriot,
organized by nationalistic ex-communists in 1936 and afterward along
lines that increasingly paralleled the earlier phases of the Italian model.
But even Doriot and the PPF long protested their non-fascist character.

Study of these groups has become extensive but rarely thorough. The
first attempt at a general treatment was J. Plumyene and R. Lasierra, *Les
Fascismes français 1923-63* (Paris, 1963), which served as an introduction
but lacked depth of true comprehensiveness. There are two general cata-
logues of fascist-type and collaborationist organizations in France. Henry
Coston, ed., *Partis, journaux et hommes politiques d'hier et d'aujourdhui*
(Paris, 1960), is the more extensive, a special number of *Lectures Fran-
çaises* edited by a sometime collaborationist. The second survey, also of
general utility, is given in David Littlejohn's *The Patriotic Traitors* (London, 1972), 185-290. The writers and aesthetes associated with the French
fascistic groups, especially the PPF, were the most able of their persuasion
in Western Europe and have been the subject of books by Paul Sérant,
Tarmo Kunnas, and Jacqueline Morand.[8] Important articles on French
fascism have been written by Eugen Weber,[9] Raoul Girardet,[10] and Robert
Soucy,[11] and a brief summary has also been given by Nolte in his *Krise des
liberalen Systems und die faschistischen Bewegungen*. Monographs on
individual groups and parties are much rarer, one exception being

Philippe Bourdrel's able study of the secret terrorist organization *La Cagoule* (Paris, 1970).

The major monographic study on French fascist movements is Dieter Wolf, *Die Doriot-Bewegung* (Stuttgart, 1967), an excellent account of Jacques Doriot and the Parti Populaire Français. It supersedes several unpublished dissertations[12] as well as all briefer accounts. An excellent piece of research, Wolf's book devotes considerable attention to Doriot's early communist years and his transition from revolutionary communism to semi-revolutionary national socialism. The analysis of the political background of the party's founders reveals that it was largely a convergence of elements of the extreme (communist) left and extreme right. Though there is no doubt that the PPF became the largest of hard-core fascist-type parties in France, Wolf reduces the membership figure of 295,000 officially claimed in January 1938 to a more realistic approximation of 50,000-60,000 regular members. The nationalisation of social radicalism and the revolutionary power lust proceeded through a series of stages, and *fascist* remained a dirty word for many members of the PPF. Only in the collaborationist phase after German occupation was the transition to full fascism completed, and the wartime quality of the PPF then more closely approximated German national socialism than southwest European fascism.

Distinctions of phase and of quality have to be drawn between the more or less spontaneous, native French fascistic movements of the 1930s, however much inspired by foreign models, and the collaborationist period from 1940 to 1944. Serious students have long appreciated that the Pétainist regime itself cannot be considered intrinsically fascist, but rather one of a large number of syncratic, conservative authoritarian regimes that proliferated mainly in the southern half of Europe and to some extent in Latin America from the 1920s on. The recent symposium on *Le Gouvernement de Vichy 1940-1942* (Paris, 1972) tends to stress elements of continuity in the policies of the Vichy regime. The best synthetic study of Vichy is Robert O. Paxton's *Vichy France* (New York, 1972), which supersedes Robert Aron's *Histoire de Vichy* (Paris, 1954) (trans. as *The Vichy Regime*). It analyzes the entire range of forces involved in Vichy, from reactionaries to moderate liberal modernizers, and finds that the genuine fascist elements had but minor roles in most sectors. Hard-line fascist and Nazi groups prospered much more in the German occupation zone of the north, but even then generated little independent strength. A complete catalogue of all collaborationist and fascistoid organizations in France under German occupation may be found in Littlejohn's book. J. Delperrie de Bayac, *Histoire de la Milice, 1918-1945* (Paris, 1969), is particularly useful with regard to Nazi influences.

Despite a broad variety of ideas, groups and personalities, French fascism added up to very little. This is not difficult to explain in view of the fact that almost none of the theoretical components advanced to account for the rise of fascism and nazism elsewhere were present in France. The country had not been defeated and was not suffering national status deprivation, at least prior to 1940, and after that date fascism remained identified with foreign oppressors. The French middle classes were severely buffeted by the depression but were not subjected to a genuine social crisis. However much criticised, the parliamentary system continued to sustain itself. The French left did not constitute a true revolutionary threat and there were no masses of unemployed veterans to mobilize. There was no crisis of modernization but rather a static equilibrium of moderate but not unreasonable development. Serious ethnic rivalry or concern was non-existent.

Thus when Maurice Bardèche looked back a generation later in his effort to redefine fascism, *Qu'est-ce que le fascisme?* (Paris, 1961), he found it hard to be specific. Rejecting either nazism on the one hand or the existing Franco regime on the other as synonymous with true fascism, he identified it instead as a spirit or an attitude — *la rêve fasciste* — the cultural mood of a time that sought physical and moral regeneration and the reconciliation of individualism and collective nationalism.

The situation in neighbouring Belgium was somewhat different, mainly because of the tensions resulting from the cleavage between Flemings and Walloons. The combined votes of the two chief Fleming and Walloon fascistic groups reached nearly 19 per cent in 1936, far and away the largest in western or northern Europe. The most important fascist party in the Low Countries was Rex, whose leader Léon Degrelle was probably the most flamboyant fascist chief in all of Western Europe. Rex began as a Catholic youth movement that emphasized radical national regeneration. It was based primarily on the middle classes of the Walloon provinces and only moved into a clearly fascist position after 1936. There is a careful study of the early Rexist movement by Jean-Michel Etienne, *Le Mouvement rexiste jusqu'en 1940* (Paris, 1968), and further work is now in progress. Degrelle himself is unique among major fascist leaders in that he survived the war — including many months of front-line combat on the eastern front — and has been loquacious in self-justification.[13] There are several chapters and articles that briefly summarize the world of Belgian fascism, dealing both with Rex and the Flemish-based Verdinaso and VNV parties,[14] and a recent booklet summarizes the several minor post-war expressions of the ultra-right and neo-fascism.[15]

Whereas Belgium harboured three different fascist movements of note, the only one of any consequence in Holland was Anton Mussert's Nationaal-Socialistische Beweging, which garnered 4 per cent of the Dutch vote in the 1937 elections. Aside from a few notes in general accounts,[16] it may best be approached through a brief treatment in Werner Warmbrunn's *The Dutch under German Occupation 1940-1945* (Stanford, 1963).

Adequate comparative study is lacking with regard to either the several varieties of French fascism or the various groups in the Low Countries. The only adequate monograph to treat a single party completely is that by Wolf. More thorough comparative study is required to sort out whatever differences may have existed in bases of recruitment and specific types of doctrine or ideological appeal. For example, some difference might be noted between the more conservative and corporatist fascist-type parties in the Low Countries (Verdinaso, the early Rexist movement and Mussert's NSB, originally not anti-Semitic) and the more radical, increasingly anti-Semitic Nazi-type groups (the VNV and the tiny National Socialist Dutch Workers Party, the latter a carbon copy of the NSDAP). While a healthy scepticism may be maintained about the validity of any very rigid categorization of fascistic groups, some degree of further sorting out is obviously in order. It might be added that German occupation and satellite status largely completed the nazification of nearly all these little groups, just as satellite status to some extent changed the direction of Italian fascism itself.

The minuscule fascist parties of Scandinavia were even weaker than those of France and Holland, with the temporary exception of the Lapua movement of Finland. The two would-be Swedish Nazi parties garnered 1.6 per cent of the popular vote in the 1936 elections, while their Norwegian counterparts of Vidkun Quisling's Nasjonal Samling (National Unification) group drew 2.16 per cent in 1933 and dropped to 1.84 per cent in 1936. The most important thing about Quisling has in a sense been the name, which became the symbol for political collaboration with Nazi occupation. The only reliable book on Quisling and his group in English is Paul M. Hayes, *Quisling* (London, 1971), accompanied by brief articles by Hayes[17] and T. K. Derry.[18] Ralph Hewings unsuccessfully attempted a revisionist biography entitled *Quisling: Prophet without Honour* (London, 1965), which is incomplete and poorly documented but nonetheless contains some interesting dissenting information. Hans-Dietrich Loock's *Quisling, Rosenberg und Terboven. Zur Vorgeschichte und Geschichte der national-sozialistischen Revolution in Norwegen* (Stuttgart, 1970) is a solid account of occupation policy that also includes considerable material on Quisling's political background. Discussion of the preconditions for a Norwegian nazism may be found in A. S. Milward's *The Fascist Economy in Norway* (Oxford, 1972), and there is further extensive literature in Norwegian.[19]

There is no systematic effort at studying the Scandinavian fascist or nazi parties as a whole or comparatively. The principal compilation is in Littlejohn, pages 1-82, and there is a brief review by Nolte.[20] Serious treatment of the nazi-type movements in Sweden and Denmark is confined to several works in the languages of those countries.[21]

If the weakness of fascism and nazism in most of Scandinavia would seem to require little explanation, the case of Finland was somewhat different. A small country but recently escaped from Russian domination, it had survived a revolutionary civil war that reversed for Finland the result obtaining in Russia. Nevertheless, the fear of Russian domination and hence of potential revolution remained. These might have provided powerful stimuli for fascism had it not been for the relatively stable structure of middle-class society in Finland and the influence of constitutional tradition. Despite genuine temptations that were much greater than in most of northern and western Europe, Finland did not succumb to fascism, and the decline of the fascist brand of anti-communism was in part responsible for Finland's ability to sustain its independence after 1945.

There is no adequate account of the Lapua movement and the temporary drift toward fascistic politics in Finland during the early 1930s. The most direct account in English is Marvin Rintala's *Three Generations: The Extreme Right in Finnish Politics* (Bloomington, Ind., 1962), but it is not altogether a well-balanced treatment. There are general articles by Rintala[22] and A. F. Upton,[23] and also a discussion of fascist tendencies and sympathies in Finland in C. Leonard Lundin's *Finland in the Second World War* (Bloomington, Ind., 1957). In Finnish there is more extensive treatment of individual aspects of radical nationalist and parafascist politics,[24] but no complete and integrated study.

There would seem to be one categorical difference between the movements in Scandinavia and those in southwestern Europe (Spain, France, Portugal, Belgium and, even to some extent, Holland). Those in Scandinavia tended to follow the Nazi model in their racism and mysticism, and often in their very choice of names. The Finnish Lapua movement placed emphasis on military expansion. By contrast, the southwestern movements were much more similar to the Italian fascist pattern in terms of their absence of racism and their frequent connection to Catholicism, their lack of equivalent emphasis on neo-militarism and their rather conservative-functional orientation to corporatism. The similarity in origin of the major French fascist group to that of the Italian prototype is striking. The idea-world and emulative pattern of National Socialism was extended primarily to east-central Europe, Scandinavia, and Holland, where German cultural influence was stronger. The Italian model exerted greater influence over southwestern Europe — and western Europe as a whole exclusive of Scandinavia — with some secondary influence in Austria, Hungary, and the Balkans. Only under the force of German occupation did Nazi influence and the desire to emulate Nazi practice become largely predominant.

All the factors that discouraged the growth of a strong and direct fascism in France were redoubled, as in Scandinavia, in the case of England, which produced only one insignificant group. Oswald Mosley's British Union of Fascists, founded in 1932, was indeed a clear-cut fascist group that did not shrink — like so many in western Europe — from the use of the label. It was partly modeled on Italian fascism, and followed the Mussolinian pattern insofar as its leader had only a year or two earlier been one of the most dominant younger leaders of the Labour party before becoming discouraged with personal and public prospects under the liberal democratic system. Anti-Semitism and Nazi influence soon became increasingly important, but the BUF was distinguished primarily by its impotence and could in no way be compared with some of the larger fascistic groups even in other liberal democracies such as France, Belgium, or Finland. Indeed, one of the best accounts of the group, Colin Cross's *The Fascists in Britain* (New York, 1963), tends possibly to exaggerate what importance it did have at its highwater mark around 1935-36. A later study by Robert Benewick, *Political Violence and Public Order. A Study of British Fascism* (London, 1969), is more solidly buttressed with a systematic scholarly apparatus and shows more concern to place the phenomenon in the broader setting of the British polity.[25] W. F. Mandle, *Anti-Semitism and the British Union of Fascists* (London, 1968), provides a short, balanced treatment of anti-Semitism.

Skeletal groups of British fascists have lingered long beyond the war years. A recent psychological study of communists and fascists in Britain has made an interesting analytic comparison and differentiation of the two types. Both communists and fascists were found to be more rigid, authoritarian, tough-minded, emphatic, and intolerant of ambiguity than the control group with which they were compared. Communists proved to be more overtly dominant and covertly aggressive, fascists more overtly aggressive and covertly dominant. Communists were the least ethnocentric group studied, fascists the most, and in general more conservative than communists.[26] These differences between small groups of British communists and fascists around 1970 were probably representative of counterpart elements in European radical politics as a whole during the inter-war generation.

If British fascism was extremely weak, the only group usually identified as an Irish fascist party, the National Guard or Blueshirt movement of Eoin O'Duffy, really was never a fascist organization at all. This is the conclusion of the only serious study, Maurice Manning's *The Blueshirts* (Dublin, 1970), which narrates the entire history of the group in convincing style and demonstrates that the patriotic conservativism and militia antics of the Blueshirts, coupled with a vague doctrinal interest in corporatism, amounted to no more than a kind of Celtic Croix de Feu. O'Duffy was not the stuff of which Duces and Caudillos are made, and resigned the leadership of his movement in 1934. His subsequent National Corporate Party scarcely got off the ground.

A different problem is presented by the case of Portugal, which lived under a right-wing authoritarian system from 1926 to 1974. Despite, or perhaps because of this there has been virtually no genuine fascism in Portugal. The New State of Dr. António de Oliveira Salazar was a conservative corporatist regime that shunned every kind of radicalism, including fascism. It lacked a genuine party or mobilized movement, for the National Union of the regime was merely an official front, not an autonomous movement of mass mobilization. The Salazar system rested on the military and bureaucracy, had no drastic new modern ambitions, and maintained rural Portuguese society as little changed as possible. The only genuine fascist movement under Salazar was the National Syndicalist group organized by Rolão Preto in 1932. It propounded a kind of fascist syndicalism under radical, modernizing dictatorship, and with considerable exaggeration soon claimed to have 50,000 members. After an abortive revolt in 1934 the movement was dissolved by the government. Salazar denounced it as having been 'inspired by certain foreign models' and singled out the National Syndicalist 'exaltation of youth, and the cult of force through direct action, the principle of the superiority of state political power in social life, [and] the propensity for organizing masses behind a single leader'[27] as fundamental differences between fascism and the conservative Catholic corporatism of the New State.

The most serious brief effort at analyzing the structure of Portuguese authoritarianism is an article by Herminio Martins,[28] but it fails to apply any rigorous definition of fascism and lumps the entire Salazar regime under that category. An historical grasp of the Portuguese system may best be obtained through A. H. de Oliveira Marques, *History of Portugal* (New York, 1972), vol. 2. The best biography of Salazar himself is Hugh Kay, *Salazar and Modern Portugal* (London, 1970), which strives for a degree of objectivity, while the most useful of the many laudatory accounts by rightists is Jacques Ploncard d'Assac, *Salazar* (Paris, 1967). On the Integralist movement of the monarchist right — the Portuguese equivalent of Action Française, whence it drew much inspiration — see Carlos Ferrão, *O Integralismo e a República*, 2 vols. (Lisbon, 1964-65), and Rivera Martins de Carvalho, *O Pensamento integralista perante o Estado Novo* (Lisbon, 1971). The legal structure of the Portuguese corporative system has been studied in the dissertation of Manuel de Lucena, 'L'Evolution du système corporatif portugais à travers des lois (1933-1971)' (Institut des Sciences Sociales du Travail, 1971).

The most important case among Western countries is that of Franquist Spain, whose political system, when all is said and done, has more nearly resembled that of fascist Italy than any other country. The analytical problem has been complicated by the need to define and interpret the significance of the fascist state party — in this case, Falange Española Tradicionalista — within the Spanish system. Once it was found in the 1950s that the Falange had no independence and virtually no autonomous significance within the Spanish system, it was judged by more and more observers that the Franquist system as a whole was not really fascist, and this conclusion was by any strict definition doubtless correct.

However, the existence of a strong, autonomous mass party cannot be made an independent variable in a strict definition of fascism, for after the late 1920s the Italian fascist party itself became largely a bureaucratic appendage of the state, deprived of any very significant element of autonomy. The fact that the Franquist system has gone through a series of distinct, sometimes almost contradictory, phases merely parallels the Italian experience, in which one may distinguish, for example, between (a) the radical fascist movement of 1919-22; (b) the Mussolini coalition regime of 1922-25; (c) the establishment of the pseudo-totalitarian fascist state system in 1925-28; (d) the conservative, pluralistic authoritarian regime of 1929-34; and (e) the imperialistic, increasingly radical, Nazi-influenced and emulatory policy of 1935-43. In the Spanish case, the Falange went through the first phase of radical but impotent fringe movement from 1931 to 1936, the Franco regime passed through the coalition phase, such as it was, in three months of civil war during 1936 rather than three years, and the regime then was increasingly influenced by the radical Nazi-fascist tide between late 1936 and early 1942. The weakness and marginality of Spain helped to save it from military involvement, and after the passing of the radical Nazi-fascist era in 1943-45, the Spanish regime finally settled into a 'normal,' peacetime structure of conservative, pluralistic authoritarianism and semi-corporative economics, in many ways similar to Italian fascism during its middle phase of relative normalcy. Two main differences are that Franco as absolute leader enjoyed the powers of head of state as well as head of government — something that Mussolini never possessed — and after 1945 the party bureaucracy of the regime had to be downgraded as a political entity considerably more than in the Italian experience. The post-fascist phase of the regime was finally made official in 1958 when the original Twenty-Six Points of fascistic Falangist ideology were quietly dropped, to be replaced by a set of anodyne 'Principles of the Movement' that merely exhorted to patriotism, unity, morality, and national well-being.

Spanish fascism proper thus refers essentially to the Falange, and more precisely to the Falangist movement in its historical and ideological heyday, from 1931 to 1937, and more tenuously to 1942. When all is said and done, Spanish fascism as an independent political manifestation was remarkably weak, as weak as fascistic movements in other western and northern European countries. In the climactic elections of 1936 — the last parliamentary contest in Spanish history — the Falange failed to elect a single candidate and garnered only 0.44 per cent of the vote. This performance was rivaled only by Mosley's group, was surpassed by Swedish and Norwegian Nazis (as well as Mussert's more equivocal Dutch group), and was greatly exceeded by the Belgian and French fascist organizations.

Falangism completely failed to mobilize support so long as Spain retained anything resembling a functional parliamentary political system. It only gained affiliates as the polity began to enter a phase of direct collapse in the spring of 1936, and finally achieved mass expansion under the impact of revolutionary civil war. Those very conditions, however, deprived it of independent organization and personality, since the counter-revolutionary forces were completely under the command of the military. Mass Falangism was thus immediately taken over and subordinated by a reorganized Spanish right. The situation was in that sense more similar to Horthy's Hungary and Antonescu's Rumania than to Italy and Germany.

The weakness of fascism in the regular Spanish polity was due above all to the remarkable absence of a militant, modern Spanish nationalism, which Falangism could not of itself incite. To this must be added the lagging secularization of the middle classes, which permitted the Catholic right virtually to monopolize the position of a new anti-left alternative on the one hand, and the vigour of the revolutionary left in Spain, on the other hand, which deprived radical Falangists of any hope of attracting non-rightists to an 'alternative revolution.'

Falangism and fascism in Spain should thus be studied in the broader context of the modern Spanish right, whose varied components participated in the creation of the semi-pluralist structure of the Franquist system. No broad over-arching study of the modern Spanish right exists. I have presented brief introductions in earlier articles,[29] and a survey of some of the preliminary ideological schema may be found in the sections on the Catholic right in Fredrick B. Pike, *Hispanismo, 1898-1936* (Notre Dame, 1971). The predecessor of Franquism was the Primo de Rivera dictatorship, but there is no adequate account of that, either. Dillwyn F. Ratcliff's *Prelude to Franco* (New York, 1957) is only the merest beginning. Equally useful is the semi-official apologium by Julián Pemartín, *Los valores historicos de la Dictadura* (Madrid, 1929). Juan Velarde Fuertes, *Politica economica de la Dictadura* (Madrid, 1968), is an able study of economic policy.

The fullest account of the Spanish right under the second Republic, whence issued the forces that later made up the Franco regime, will be found in Richard A. H. Robinson, *The Origins of Franco's Spain* (London, 1970), which may be supplemented with articles on Carlism by Martin Blinkhorn[30] and on Alfonsine right monarchism by Paul Preston.[31]

Ernesto Gimenez Caballero, the first exponent of fascist ideas in Spain, has recently been the subject of a dissertation by Douglas Foard, 'Ernesto Gimenez Caballero and the Revolt of the Esthetes' (Ph.D. diss., George Washington University, 1972). Tomás Borrás has published a lengthy apologetic biography of Spain's leading fascist intellectual of the thirties and the organizer of the first genuine fascist group, *Ramiro Ledesma Ramos* (Madrid, 1971), and Ledesma's own memoir-history of the early years of Falangism and pre-Falangism, *Fascismo en España?*, has been re-issued (Barcelona, 1970). It is a key source. A recent study of the thought of José Antonio Primo de Rivera, principal leader of the Falange — Adolfo Muñoz Alonso's *Un pensador para un pueblo* (Madrid, 1969) — discounts the fascistic values with which its subject was never at ease and emphasizes the individualist and humanist aspects of his thought. David Jato, *La rebelión de los estudiantes* (Madrid, 1967), deals with Falangism as student revolt. There are numerous memoir accounts in the form of regional histories or sketches of the pre-Civil War Falange, and new volumes continue to appear from time to time.

The first critical history of the Falange itself was my *Falange: A History of Spanish Fascism* (Stanford, 1961), which concentrated on the Falange as an independent political entity from 1931 to 1937, but also treated its later evolution to 1942, and closed with a brief account of the effort to revive the party as a strong political force in 1956. This was followed by another dissertation, Bernd Nellessen's *Die verbotene Revolution* (Hamburg, 1963), which is mainly restricted to the Republican period and concentrates on the ideology of the movement. The best brief account of early Falangism and its counterparts is the section on 'Los fascismos españoles,' in Ricardo de la Cierva's *Historia de la Guerra Civil española*, I, 507-75 (Madrid, 1969).

The appearance of my book provoked a desire for self-justification on the part of the last independent national chief of the Falange, Manuel Hedilla, who had been ousted by Franco in 1937. Hedilla, grown wealthy in his later years, hired the Falangist journalist and historian Maximiano García Venero to prepare a political biography of Hedilla and give the *hedillista* version of the climactic phase of independent Falangist politics in 1936-37. García Venero collected a valuable and extensive series of depositions, interviews, and memoranda from old-guard Falangists and prepared a lengthy volume, but when it was finished Hedilla submitted to pressure from the Spanish government and refused permission to publish the work.

Undeterred, García Venero made arrangements with the emigré Spanish left-wing press, Ruedo Ibérico, to publish the book through the latter's facilities in Paris, insisting that the rights to the manuscript pertained to him exclusively. The publication of a quasi-fascist apologia by an organ that declared itself of the revolutionary left posed a problem that was nominally resolved with the participation of the emigré leftist North American bibliographer and polemicist, Herbert R. Southworth. An apparently vague agreement was reached by which the publication of the book would be accompanied by bibliographical and critical notes prepared by Southworth. Ruedo Ibérico then brought out García Venero's full account of *La Falange en la guerra de España: la Unificación y Hedilla* (Paris, 1967), an extensive hedillista apologia that nonetheless contained important new information and documentation. It was accompanied simultaneously by a volume of Southworth's entitled *Antifalange: Estudio crítico de "Falange en la Guerra de España" de M. García Venero*, which subjected the preceding book to intense and hostile page-by-page criticism, as well as trying to elaborate a general theory of fascism based on the concept 'imperialism.' This situation infuriated both García Venero and Hedilla, the latter in the meantime having instituted a suit against the former, claiming that the manuscript was his property, not García Venero's, and trying to suppress publication in France.

Caught in a crossfire of acrimony between the hedillistas and the left, García Venero then tried to rectify his previous apologia by publishing in Spain a more critical account of the events of 1936-37 under the title *Historia de la unificación (Falange y Requeté en 1937)* (Madrid, 1970). Hedilla died that same year, and his heirs, holding Spanish title to the original manuscript, eventually published most of it in Spain, together with other justificatory material, as the *Testamento político de Manuel Hedilla* (Barcelona, 1972).

The best reconstruction of the climactic events of April 1937, when the Falange was taken over by Franco and transformed into a broader and more syncretic state party, has been made by Ricardo de la Cierva, 'La Trayectoria de la Falange hasta la unificación de 1937,' in *Aproximación historica a la guerra española (1936-1939)*, 205-40 (Madrid, 1970), and, in brief and general terms, in his *Historia ilustrada de la guerra civil española*, 2 vols. (Barcelona, 1971). There is an excellent account of the evolution of the Falangist organization from fascist party to subordinate state bureaucracy by Juan J. Linz, 'From Falange to Movimiento-Organización: The Spanish Single Party and the Franco Regime, 1936-1968,' in S. P. Huntington and C. H. Moore, eds., *Authoritarian Politics in Modern Society*, 128-203 (New York, 1970).

Only three Falangist leaders have published noteworthy memoirs or collections of writings. Franco's brother-in-law, Ramón Serrano Súner, who managed much of domestic politics during the first years of the regime before serving briefly as foreign minister during the central phase of World War II, soon afterward wrote an account of his political career from 1937 to 1942 entitled *Entre Hendaya y Gibraltar* (Madrid, 1947). Though totally apologetic, it is nonetheless a significant source. Serrano's close personal friend, Dioisio Ridruejo, was one of the regime's first propaganda chiefs. His post, his fervour, and his dark hair and short stature all combined to earn him the nickname of the 'Spanish Goebbels.' Years later he became the 'Spanish Djilas' after renouncing Franquism in favour of Western-style social democracy and drawing a brief prison term from the regime. His personal memoir, *Escrito en España* (Buenos Aires, 1962), is a key work, the only frank and searching memoir by anyone who has held important office within the Franco regime. Finally, the Falange's principal leader after the Serrano years, José Luis de Arrese, has issued a collection of his principal writings, *Treinta años de política* (Madrid, 1966), and announces plans for the publication of his political memoirs.

Several works may be recommended for the study of the evolution of the Franco regime. The classic political definition of the regime itself is Juan J. Linz's article, 'An Authoritarian Regime: Spain,' in E. Allardt and Y. Littunen, eds., *Cleavages, Ideologies and Party Systems*, 251-83 (Helsinki, 1964). The non-fascist source of Franco's main political inspiration has been analyzed by Richard A. H. Robinson, 'Genealogy and function of the Monarchist Myth of the Franco Regime,' *Iberian Studies*, 18-26 (Spring 1973). The best biography of Franco is J. W. D. Trythall's *El Caudillo* (New York, 1971). A milestone among apologetic biographies was reached, however, with the publication of the first volume of Ricardo de la Cierva's *Francisco Franco: Un siglo de España* (Madrid, 1973), which manages to be both laudatory and intellectually serious and contains much new information. Among contemporary analyses of the Franquist system, the best is Jacques Georgel, *Le Franquisme* (Paris, 1971). The transition from semi-fascistic autarchy to neo-liberalism in Spanish economic policy has been studied by Charles Anderson, *The Political Economy of Modern Spain* (Madison, Wisc., 1970).

The thinking of part of the minority of remaining neo-Falangist activists in the 1970s may be gauged by a recent collection of their responses to a political questionnaire by Miguel Veyrat and J. L. Navas-Migueloa, *Falange, hoy* (Madrid, 1972). The full history of Falangism and Franquism is, however, still to be written.

To summarize some of the consequences that may be drawn from the historiography of fascism and Nazism in Western Europe, considerably more study remains to be done in at least four areas. Though monographic investigation has accelerated in the past ten years, thorough individual case studies remain to be done in most instances. Only the Doriot and Mosley movements have been adequately investigated.

Second, systematic and comparative analysis of the social basis of the various movements and parties needs to be greatly expanded in order to gain a clear and complete picture of their places in West European political society.

Third, the notion that fascists had little or no coherent ideology needs to be corrected—or perhaps corroborated—by a careful and systematic analysis of differences and similarities in doctrinal content and precise goals of these groups.

Fourth, more attention is warranted to the question of sequences or phases in the evolution or metamorphosis of the fascistic parties. This will help to determine the extent to which different emphases were elicited prior to and during the several phases of the German diplomatic and military hegemony.

Such a programme of research would then facilitate the filling of what has already been called the principal interpretive vacuum — a comparative analysis and categorization of West European fascist groups, and a more appropriate answer to the question whether or not there really was a distinctive western or northern European brand of fascism.

## NOTES

1. See Zeev Sternhell, 'Paul Déroulède and the Origins of Modern French Nationalism,' *Journal of Contemporary History* (October 1971), 46-71.

2. For the early effort in France to mobilize a radical nationalist syndicalism, see George L. Mosse, 'The French Right and the Working Classes: Les Jaunes,' *Journal of Contemporary History* (July-October 1972), 185-208.

3. Ernst Nolte, *Three Faces of Fascism* (New York, 1966), 29-141.

4. Nolte, *Die Krise des liberalen Systems und die faschistischen Bewegungen* (Munich, 1968).

5. See Yves Guchet, 'Georges Valois ou l'illusion fasciste,' *Revue Française de Science Politique* (December 1965).

6. Later, under German occupation, the party broadsided its own brief *Sommaire du Francisme* (Paris, 1941) that read very much like a transcription of the Italian system but scarcely mentioned the term fascism.

7. This aspect of Italian fascism has been studied by Michael Ledeen, *Universal Fascism* (New York, 1972).

8. Paul Sérant, *Le Romantisme fasciste* (Paris, 1959); Tarmo Kunnas, *Drieu La Rochelle, Céline, Brasillach et la Tentation fasciste* (Paris, 1972); Jacqueline Morand, *Les Idées politiques de Louis-Ferdinand Céline* (Paris, 1972). Of the first two, Sérant's book is somewhat broader ranging, that of Kunnas more technical and systematic. A book of parallel usefulness is J.-L. Loubet del Bayle, *Les Non-conformistes des années 30* (Paris, 1969). Though it does not deal directly with fascism, it illuminates the mentality of restless young intellectuals seeking new alternatives.

9. Weber, *Varieties of Fascism* (New York, 1964), 130-39, and H. Rogger and E. Weber, eds., *The European Right* (Berkeley and Los Angeles, 1965), 71-127.

10. Girardet, 'Notes sur l'esprit d'un fascisme français, 1934-1939,' *Revue Française de Science Politique* (1955), 529-46.

11. Soucy, 'The Nature of Fascism in France,' *Journal of Contemporary History* (1966), 27-55; idem., 'French Fascism as Class Conciliation and Moral Regeneration,' *Societas* (Autumn 1971), 287-98.

12. The principal is G. D. Allardyce, 'The Political Transition of Jacques Doriot, 1926-1936' (Ph.D. diss., University of Iowa, 1966), of which a précis under the same title was published in the first number of the *Journal of Contemporary History*. Two other noteworthy dissertations on the movement toward national conciliation and corporatism among sectors of the French left are Stanley Grossman, 'Neo-Socialism: A Study in Political Metamorphosis' (Ph.D. diss., University of Wisconsin, 1969), and Martin Fine, 'Toward Corporatism: The Movement for Capital-Labor Collaboration in France, 1914-1936' (Ph.D. diss., University of Wisconsin, 1971).

13. Degrelle's two principal publications are *Die verlorene Legion* (Stuttgart, 1952), and *Hitler pour 1000 ans* (Paris, 1969), but see also Louise Narváez, *Degrelle m'a dit* (Paris, 1961).

14. Jean Stengers, 'Belgium,' in Rogger and Weber, 128-67; Nolte, *Die Krise*, 272-76; Littlejohn, *The Patriotic Traitors*, 131-84; and F. L. Carsten, *The Rise of Fascism* (Berkeley and Los Angeles, 1967), 204-18. R. Pfeiffer and J. Ladrière, *L'Aventure rexiste* (Brussels, 1966), is more of a denunciation than a study.

15. Michel Géoris-Reitshof, *Extrème droite et neo-fascisme en Belgique* (Brussels, 1962).

16. Littlejohn, *The Patriotic Traitors*, 83-130, and Nolte, *Die Krise*, 276-79.

17. Hayes, 'Quisling's Political Ideas,' *Journal of Contemporary History* (Autumn 1966), 145-57.

18. T. K. Derry, "Norway," in S. J. Woolf, ed., *European Fascism* (London, 1968), 217-30.

19. There is an account of the early years of the Nasjonal Samling by Hans Olof Brevig, *NS fra parti til sekt, 1933-1937* (Oslo, 1970); a general work by Hans Fredrik Dahl, *Hva er fascisme?* Et *essay om fascismens historie og sosiologie* (Oslo, 1972), that pays special attention to Norway; and a controversial psychohistorical study of Quisling by Sverre Hartman, *Forsvarsminister Quisling—hans bagrunn og vei inn i norsk politikk* (Oslo, 1970). (For these and succeeding references to works in Scandinavian languages I am indebted to my colleague Professor Pekka Hämäläinen.)

20. Nolte, *Die Krise*, 268-72.

21. The historian of Swedish Nazism is Eric Wärenstam, whose basic work is *Fascismen och nazismen i Sverige 1920-1940* (Stockholm, 1970). A subsequent somewhat popularized version, *Fascismen och nazismen i Sverige* (Stockholm, 1972), includes a chapter on the war years. An earlier study deals with radical right elements in the Swedish conservative youth movement, *Sveriges nationella ungdomsforbund och högern 1928-1934* (Stockholm, 1965). Some information on the influence of fascist and Nazi ideas on conservative and peasant groups in Sweden may be found in Rolf Torstendahl, *Mellan nykonservatismoch liberalism* (Uppsala, 1969). M. D. Shepard has written a dissertation on the leading figure of the non-Nazi radical right in Sweden, 'Adrian Molin, Study of a Swedish Right-wing Radical' (Ph.D. diss., Northwestern University, 1969).

Accounts of the Danish Nazis concentrate on the German occupation period, the only time in which they were of the slightest importance. The main work is Henning Poulsen, *Besaettelsesmagten og de danske nazister. Det politiske forhold mellem tyske myndigheder og nazistisken kredse i Danmark 1940-43* (Copenhagen, 1970), but there is also information in Erich Thomsen, *Deutsche Besatzungspolitik in Dänemark, 1940-1945* (Dusseldorf, 1971). Peter Gordy is currently completing a dissertation on Danish nazism at the University of Wisconsin.

22. Rintala, 'Finland,' in Rogger and Weber, *The European Right*, 408-22.

23. A. F. Upton, 'Finland,' in Woolf, *European Fascism*, 184-216.

24. To cite only the book-length studies: A three-volume work by N. V. Hersalo and Hannes Raikkala, *Suojeluskuntain Historia* (Vassa, 1962-66), deals with the Civic Guards, a rightist paramilitary force sympathetic to fascistic ideas; P. K. Hämäläinen, *Nationalitetskampen och sprakstriden i Finland 1917-1939* (Helsinki, 1969), deals with the language controversy and includes information on fascistic influences on both of Finland's linguistic groups; Lauri Hyvämäki, *Sinistä ja mustaa. Tutkielmia Suomen oikeistoradikalismista* (Helsinki, 1971), contains several articles on Lapua and the extreme right; and Risto Alapuro, *Akateeminen Karjala-Seura* (Helsinki, 1973), is a sociological study of the Academic Karelia Society, the radical nationalist student organization which developed strong fascistic sympathies.

25. Mention might also be made of James S. Barnes, *The Universal Aspects of Fascism* (London, 1928), probably the major English eulogy of Italian fascism, as an idealized expression of what English admirers thought worthy of emulation.

26. H. J. Eysenck and T. T. Coulter, 'The Personality and Attitudes of Working-Class British Communists and Fascists,' *Journal of Social Psychology* (June 1972), 59-73.

27. Jacques Ploncard d'Assac, *Salazar* (Paris, 1967), 107.

28. Martins, 'Portugal,' in Woolf, *European Fascism*, 302-36.

29. 'Spain,' in Rogger and Weber, *The European Right*, 168-207, and, on the problem of nationalism, 'Spanish Nationalism in the Twentieth Century,' *Review of Politics* (July 1964), 403-22.

30. 'Carlism and the Spanish Crisis of the 1930s,' *Journal of Contemporary History* (July-

October 1972), 65-88. Blinkhorn is the author of a dissertation on the politics of Carlism, 1931-36, which is current in press.

31. 'Alfonsist Monarchism and the Spanish Civil War,' *Journal of Contemporary History* (July-October 1972), 89-114.

# PART IV

# 9

# Fascist Ideology

ZEEV STERNHELL

While in our political vocabulary there are not many terms that have enjoyed such a considerable vogue as the word *fascism*, there are equally not many concepts in contemporary political terminology so notoriously blurred and imprecise in outline.

It would seem, in fact, that the study of fascism is still in its infancy, and that there are too few scholars anxious to avail themselves of a thorough understanding of this phenomenon. Such researches as are made are hampered, too, by the way fascism, which was supremely nationalistic and therefore above all exclusive, flourished in markedly different backgrounds —in the great industrial centres of Western Europe, as in the under-developed countries of Eastern Europe—and from its very beginnings appealed as much to the intellectual elite of the day as to unread peasants. Fascism has no sound and obvious footing in any particular social class, and its intellectual origins are in themselves confusing. In its most restricted sense the word *fascism* applies simply to the political regime in Italy in the period between the two world wars; at the other end of the scale, the 'fascist' epithet is used, and particularly by left wingers of various hue, as *the* term of abuse par excellence, conclusive and unanswerable.

The emotional content of this word has for a long time contributed to obscuring a political concept that was never in the first place very clear. When Mussolini and Léon Blum, Franklin D. Roosevelt, Franco and José Antonio, Codreanu, Pilsudski, Henri de Man, Joseph McCarthy, and Charles de Gaulle have each and all in their turn been labelled fascists, what then could fascism signify? And for as long as socialists were known as social fascists to the communists, while the Prussian Junkers, the Italian Conservatives, or the French Croix-de-Feu movement were designated as fascist by the very people whom Togliatti, Thorez, and Thälmann denounced as fascists, how could it be possible, even for the majority of politically sophisticated people, to discern what fascism really meant?

Though the 1960s[1] have seen a breakthrough, in that the first overall investigations of the subject have enabled us to block out the shape of fascism in a way which only a few years ago would not have been possible, yet it is clear that it is still no easy matter to pinpoint fascism precisely, and that there still exists no definition of fascism acceptable to all, or recognised as universally valid. We may with some justice feel more optimistic than Professor Hugh Seton-Watson, whose opinion it is that scientific precision is not at present obtainable and one may doubt whether it ever will be,[2] but we cannot for that reason overlook the difficulties.

I We should remember, however, that it is no easier to define democracy: the concepts are too broad for the words. It is highly probable that no single historical example can meet the exacting requirement of a carefully constructed 'model' of fascism or of democracy. That is what Professor N. Kogan may have had in mind when, after having carefully constructed a six-point model of fascism, and after drawing many of his examples of fascist thought and practice from the Italian regime, he concludes rather surprisingly that in actual practice 'Italy under fascism was not a fascist state.'[3] This is indeed true, if Kogan is suggesting that Italy under fascism was not an *ideal* fascist state, and the identical demonstration could be applied to democracy or to communism: what is the ideal model of democracy or of communism, what, exactly, are its component parts, and where is it put into practice? I

The task becomes more complex still when we narrow the field of inquiry to the ideology of fascism. For many years, after all, it was common form to see fascism either as completely wanting in ideological concepts or as having gotten itself up for the sake of the cause in a few rags of doctrine, which therefore need not be taken seriously, nor allowed even the minimal importance that is attached as a rule to the ideas professed by a political movement. This attitude was almost certainly bound up with a fundamental refusal to view fascism as anything other than a horrid *lapsus* in European history: in conceding to fascism a theoretical dimension one might have granted it a place and a significance in the history of our times, which many people, both of the right and of the left, and often for reasons that are at one and the same time similar and conflicting, were reluctant to do. I

Furthermore, the official Marxist interpretation of fascism, which conceives of it as the creature of monopoly or finance capitalism and its ideology—a crude rationalization of capitalist interests—has also helped to keep the study of fascist ideology at a standstill. There was a long period when the very suggestion that fascism could be a mass movement, sustained by an ideology well suited to the necessities of modern politics and of mass society, ran *contra bona mores*, and throughout the war years the man who took this line was suspected—sometimes with good reason—if not of collaborating with fascism or nazism, then at least of evincing toward them a favourable attitude.

I There were other interpretations of fascism which chose to argue, not that fascism or national socialism were lacking an ideology, but that the ideology was purely incidental and unimportant. They held that Mussolini and Hitler had come to power without stressing the nature of their doctrine, or once in power had not put doctrine into practice, and could therefore be characterized as nothing more than adventurers and opportunists with neither creed nor principle. It bears saying that this kind of reasoning is not often brought into play in the analysis of communism; and yet no one could pretend to discern in the October Revolution or in the seizure of power by other communist parties a meticulous putting into practice of the ideas propounded by Marx or Lenin, or any one of their disciples. It would be hard indeed to claim that the proceedings of the Soviet state are governed by an unfailing concern to see that policy conforms to the requirements of Marxist philosophy. Who would be capable, for that matter, of determining from day to day what those requirements were? and who would be recognised as competent to do so?

And yet, communist ideology is widely studied in order to obtain insights into communist behaviour; it is generally considered essential to our understanding of communism as a general system of social and political organisation. There is no reason why an identical method should not be applied to fascism. Moreover, as Professor Eugen Weber has pointed out, even when fascist or national-socialist manifestoes were not really carried out, or even if they had not been carried out at all, we could still learn a good deal by examining them, especially if we compare them to similar programmes or doctrines evolved in other countries, and perhaps in other circumstances. Politicians as well as political scientists know very well that platforms and ideologies are significant, partly because they do tell us something about what the candidate and his party think (would like to think, or would like the public to think they think), and partly because they reflect a public: the issues this public is likely to be affected by, to vote for, or in some way to support.[4]

This paper deals with fascism: it is confined to fascism and it deliberately omits nazism for reasons of space and division of labour between contributors, as well as for reasons of substance. A discussion of nazism would have widened its scope far beyond what can reasonably be contained within the framework of this volume, for nazism cannot, as I see it, be treated as a mere variant of fascism: its emphasis on biological determinism rules out all efforts to deal with it as such. The question is already a highly complicated one, and an examination of the specific characteristics of nazism, over and above what it has in common with fascism, would require not so much a study of fascism as a comparative analysis of fascism and nazism. This holds true even if one regards nazism as an exacerbated form of fascism: the exacerbation of a political phenomenon being in itself a new and different phenomenon. This is not to say that in certain strains of fascism there was no racialist factor: there was a school of fascism in France, for example, which in this respect resembled nazism more closely than it did Italian fascism. All in all, however, the evidence obliges us to concede that there comes a point when the degree of extremism in a political movement radically alters the very nature of that movement.

Furthermore, this article will confine itself to the study of fascist ideology. The term *ideology*, as Professor Martin Seliger has put it, is used to refer to a conceptual frame of reference which provides criteria for choice and decision by virtue of which the major activities of an organized community are governed. Therefore, the sets of ideas by which men explain and justify the ends and means of organized social action, with the aim of preserving or reconstructing a given reality, are ideologies. Two dimensions of ideological argumentation, however, can be observed in day-to-day politics. All action-oriented thought, from political philosophy down to party ideology, contains pragmatic considerations from the outset. For a party or movement holding power or engaged in the contest for power, the need inevitably arises for a more or less frank restatement of immediate goals. In shaping specific policies to deal with prevailing circumstances, no party has ever been able to avoid committing itself to lines of action which are irreconcilable with, or at least doubtfully related to, the basic principles and goals set out in its ideology. A conflict results not simply between ideology and action, but within ideology itself. The problem of preserving the movement's doctrinal purity exists in the parties of all political systems, and its existence attests to the fact of two-dimensional argumentation.[5]

Therefore the first crucial distinction in a discussion of fascist ideology is that between fascism in power and fascism in opposition, between movements and regimes, between origins and maturity. Fascism in power was something to which fascist parties made remarkably different contributions, depending on the country concerned. Every country where there was a fascist party had peculiarities duly reflected in its local political organizations; nevertheless, where a so-called fascist regime came into being, these national features usually became even more exaggerated. Thus movements have much more in common than regimes. They have indeed a great deal in common, and it is from this that a clear notion of what fascist ideology amounted to can be derived.[6]

Mussolini and the other fascist leaders were quite correct in arguing that the basic doctrinal postulates of fascist regimes had something of a universal character; but until the mid-sixties, strangely enough, the universalistic aspect of fascist doctrine was almost completely overlooked. And yet fascist ideologues never tired of announcing that fascism was, in the words of Sir Oswald Mosley, 'a worldwide creed. Each of the great political faiths in its turn has been a universal movement: conservatism, Liberalism and Socialism are common to nearly every country.... In this respect, fascism occupies precisely the same position.'[7] Mussolini had already argued that 'Fascism as an idea, a doctrine, a realisation, is universal,' because 'never before have the peoples thirsted for authority, direction, order, as they do now. If each age has its doctrine, the innumerable symptoms indicate that the doctrine of our age is the Fascist one.'[8]

The second distinction to be borne in mind is between what, like Seliger, we may call the fundamental and the operative dimensions of ideology: the fundamental principles determining the final goals, and the operative ideology whose purpose it is to justify the policies actually devised or executed by a party. Deviations from the fundamentals are a universal phenomenon:[9] fascist movements and fascist regimes cannot be considered more unprincipled than any other movement or regime, especially where these are revolutionary. Writing on this issue in *The Communist Party of the Soviet Union* (London, 1960), Leonard Shapiro points out that he has 'as yet not discovered a single instance in which the party was prepared to risk its own survival in power for considerations of doctrine.' This does not mean that the clash between theory and practice never caused serious difficulties, of the same kind indeed as occurred in Italy and Germany, or within any one of the other fascist parties. Much of fascist opportunism, its practice of legitimizing intermediate goals no matter how much they conflicted with fundamental principles, is inherent in the nature of every ideology called upon to shape a new society. There is no denying though that as the gap widens between the final objectives and the initial blueprint for the remodelling of society, the discrepancy between ideology and practice becomes more important and thus encourages the tendency to accuse the regime of opportunism, or to disregard completely the ideology on which it claims to rely.

The adaption of ideologies to changing conditions, be it falsely evaluated facts or unforeseen consequences of the realization of principles, is as general a phenomenon as the fact that no major piece of organization remains for long without ideological cover, even supposing it can come into existence without it in the first place.

In this respect therefore fascist ideology, far from being exceptional, rather proved the rule. Yet it is also true that here was an ideology which in fact aimed to be pragmatic as well as revolutionary and keep a firm grasp on everyday realities. Mussolini made it a political principle that fascist ideology be adaptable to the necessities of real life: ideology 'must not be a shirt of Nessus clinging to us for all eternity, for tomorrow is something mysterious and unforeseen.' Equally he was well aware that ideological argumentation existed on two different levels. Writing forty years ago, Mussolini anticipated some of the latest achievements of modern political science, and made a clear-cut division between 'the modest tables of our laws and programmes—the theoretical and practical guidance of fascism' and 'the fundamentals of doctrine,' commenting that the former 'should be revised, corrected, enlarged, developed, because already in places they have suffered injury at the hand of time.'[10]

In promulgating an ideology that would be closely linked to action, both by inspiring action and by reflecting it,[11] and in developing the theory of the unity of thought and action, Mussolini clearly enunciated, and took to himself, a principle which other ideologies might cry down, but which they yet were obliged to put into practice on their own account. The difference between fascists and socialists or communists came down to this: for the latter, as stern guardians of an unalterable doctrine, were compelled to endless rigmaroles and pretexts and a myriad of explanations to justify the process of development, which for the fascists was in the nature of things political, since they insisted not only on the continual adaptation of ideologies to meet practical necessities, and the constant evolution of ideology insofar as the realities changed, but also on the importance of supplying ideological cover to such sectors of political reality as were lacking in it.

Fascism in its various forms was confined in the main to the role of a political movement: only in two countries did it go on to the actual seizure of power — and in Germany, at that, in a particularly exacerbated form — so that the fascist era may be said to have been an era of political movements rather than of regimes. In any case where the history of ideas is concerned, it is the political movement which is of greater interest. It can be traced with advantage back to its origins, to the source which, being more pure, illustrates an outline as yet unmuddied. Fascist ideology in all its essentials is best perceived in its origins, and fascist movements can be seen for what they really are before they have acceded to power and been transformed by compromise and pressure into yet another governmental party. The true nature of doctrines, and the differences between them, are always more clearly seen in the shape of their aspirations than when put into practice.

## THE INTELLECTUAL CRISIS OF THE 1890s

In February 1936 the French review *Combat*, which was sympathetic to the fascists, published an article entitled *Fascisme 1913*,[12] by Pierre Andreu, one of the most faithful and authentic of George Sorel's disciples, in which he remarked on the curious synthesis of syndicalists and nationalists centered around the author of *Reflections on Violence*, and in nationalist circles connected with Action Française, immediately before the outbreak of the first world war. At about the same time, a similar comment came from Pierre Drieu La Rochelle, who a few months later — and in company with Bertrand de Jouvenel, a young economist of the left — became one of the leading intellectuals in the PPF, the largest of the French fascist parties. He observed that, 'looking back on that period, we can see how by 1913 certain elements of the fascist atmosphere had already come together in France, before they did in other countries. There were young men from all classes of society, fired by a love of heroism and violence, who dreamed of fighting what they termed the evil on two fronts — capitalism and parliamentary socialism — while culling from each what to them seemed good. Already the marriage between nationalism and socialism was on the cards.'[13]

The selfsame formula had already been used in 1925 by George Valois, the founder of the first non-Italian fascist movement, Le Faisceau, to define the idea in which the substance of the phenomenon was contained: 'Nationalism + socialism = fascism.'[14] Some ten years later Sir Oswald Mosley picked it up in his turn: 'If you love our country you are national, and if you love our people you are socialist.'[15] It was a powerfully clear and simple idea, possessing immense attraction, and by the time the former Labour minister came to found the British Union of Fascists it was already shared by all the European fascist movements.

The shock of the war and its immediate consequences no doubt precipitated the birth of fascism as a political movement, but its ideological roots in fact go back to the years 1880-1890, when an alliance sprang up between theories deriving from one or another type of socialism—whether non-Marxist, anti-Marxist, or indeed post-Marxist—and from nationalism. Those were the incubation years of fascism, as is attested to by Valois or Drieu, and equally by Gentile or by Mussolini. For on the eve of the first world war the essentials of fascist ideology were already well defined. The word did not exist yet, but the phenomenon it would eventually designate had its own autonomous existence, and thenceforward awaited only a favourable combination of circumstances in which to hatch into a political force. Fascist ideology is seen therefore as the immediate product of a crisis that had overtaken democracy and liberalism, and bourgeois society in all its fundamental values: the break-away was so disruptive as to take on the dimensions of a crisis in civilization itself.

Fascism was not a reflection of Marxism, nor did it come into existence simply as a reaction to organized Marxism; it had the same degree of autonomy that Marxism had, in that both were products of bourgeois society and reacted against that society, compared to which they each presented a radical alternative; both were agreed in that they put forward a new pattern of civilization. The growth of fascism therefore cannot be understood, or fully explained, unless it is seen in the intellectual, moral, and cultural context which prevailed in Europe at the end of the nineteenth century.

The changes that took place at this time, within the space of a single generation, were so profound that it would be no exaggeration to speak of them as constituting an intellectual revolution,[16] which in its themes and style was to pave the way for the mass politics of our own century. For the vast movement of thought of the 1890s was above all a movement of revolt: revolt against the world of matter and reason, against materialism and positivism, against the mediocrity of bourgeois society, and against the muddle of liberal democracy. To the *fin-de-siècle* mind, civilization was in crisis, and if a solution were possible it would have to be a total one.

The generation of 1890—which included among others, d'Annunzio and Corradini in Italy, Barrès, Drumont, and Sorel in France, Paul de Lagarde, Julius Langbehn and Arthur Moeller van den Bruck in Germany

—took as its point of departure not the individual, who as such had no importance in himself, but the social and political collectivity, which, moreover, was not to be thought of as the numerical sum of the individuals under its aegis. The 'new' intellectuals therefore inveighed violently against the rationalistic individualism of liberal society and against the dissolution of social links in bourgeois society. In identical terms sometimes, they one and all deplored the mediocrity and materialism of modern society, its instability and corruption. They decried the life of the great cities, which was dominated by routine with no room for heroism, and to the claims of the individual's powers of reason they preferred the merits of instinct, sometimes even of animality. Such is the soil to which Giovanni Gentile traces the root-origins of fascism, which he defines as a 'revolt against positivism'[17] and against the way of life fostered by industrial society, which revolt broke out at a time when the intellectual atmosphere was saturated with Darwinian biology and Wagnerian aesthetics, Gobineau's racialism, Le Bon's psychology, as well as the black prophecies of Nietzsche and Dostoyevsky, and, later, the philosophy of Bergson.

Of course neither Bergson's philosophy nor Nietzsche's are to be confused with the use to which they have been put at the hands of the 'dread simplificators' and other exponents, any more than we attribute to Darwin the social Darwinism touted by the generation that came after him. And yet, though philosophers and scientists cannot be held responsible for the uses made of their teachings, for the way they are interpreted and the meaning read into their thoughts, it was nevertheless their teachings which, when put into the hands of a thousand minor intellectuals who frequently had little aptitude for careful philosophical reasoning, shaped a new intellectual climate. In the aftermath of the dreadful shock of the war, the Soviet revolution, and the economic crisis, that intellectual climate allowed fascism to burgeon and grow into a powerful mass movement. For the masses were by then well conditioned to accept a new interpretation of the world and of human realities, and even a new morality, as the foundations of a new order.

The contributions made by scientists and pseudo-scientists to this new vision of the world were in point of fact legion. As the notion of social Darwinism gained widespread acceptance, it stripped the human personality of its sacramental dignity. It made no distinction between the physical life and the social life, and conceived of the human condition in terms of an unceasing struggle, whose natural outcome was the survival of the fittest. Positivism also felt the impact of social Darwinism, and underwent a profound change. In the latter half of the century its emphasis on deliberate and rational choice as the determining factor in human behaviour gave way to new notions of heredity, race, and environment.[18] Thus, social Darwinism played a large part in the evolution of nationalism and the growth of modern racialism. So too its influence is clearly to be seen in the interest taken by the generation of 1890 in the study of psychology and the discovery of the unconscious. For the new theories of social and political psychology rejected out of hand the traditional mechanistic concept of man, which asserted that human behaviour is governed by rational choice. Opinion now dictated that sentiment and feeling count for more in political questions than reasoning, and fostered contempt for democracy and its institutions and workings.

Throughout Europe the same fears and the same passions began to find expression at the same moment, and men from very different backgrounds, engaged in fields of study that were often quite unrelated to one another, each played their part in the formulation of the new ideology. The onslaught on bourgeois society went hand-in-hand with the wholesale condemnation of liberal democracy and parliamentary government, for one of the ideological tenets common to this whole vast protest movement was the reforming of all institutions in the authoritarian mould. The call for a leader, a saviour embodying all the virtues of the race, was to be heard throughout Europe, at the turn of the century. When the march of events gainsaid these theories, the setback was invariably blamed on a plot, and the instigators, also invariably, identified as Jews and Freemasons hand-in-glove with the international financiers. The men who at the turn of the century revolted against positivism, and also against liberalism and socialism which they regarded as a vague form of positivism to be treated in a similar manner, joined forces not merely to attack certain social structures or the nature of political institutions, but also to impeach Western civilization itself, which in their eyes was fundamentally corrupt. **✳**

It must be stressed too that these rebels were not men relegated to the fringes of contemporary opinion. Whatever the verdict of the historian of ideas on the intrinsic worth of their individual writings, it must be said that it is not the historians who fashion the sensibilities of a bygone generation. The men who put together the ingredients of fascist ideology, as it was on the eve of the Great War, were well-known interpreters, rendering into common language the work accomplished by the giants of their own or of the previous generation. They brought within reach of the general reader a system of ideas which was not easily understood, and which they themselves from time to time deformed or oversimplified. Such are the writers who in point of fact inform the everyday reader of newspapers and popular novels, the average university and high school student, and the people who in the counties and country towns make up a social elite, and who in their day enjoyed a tremendous success. Julius Langbehn was renowned from the year 1890, when he published *Rembrandt als Erzieher*, the book in which he denounced the intellectual and scientific bent of German civilization, and sang instead the praises of irrationalism. The two ensuing decades saw Arthur Moeller van den Bruck steadfastly renewing the attack on liberalism and democracy, until he came to fame in 1922 with *Das Dritte Reich*.[19]

The same is true of the Italian and French writers: d'Annunzio, Barrès, and Maurras ranked among the most important intellectuals of their generation, while Drumont's works went into more reprints than any other publication of the last century. Their thinking took root throughout the Latin- and French-oriented regions of Europe: they had an immense influence not only in Italy and France but in Spain, Switzerland, Belgium, and Eastern Europe, particularly in Romania. There was a professor at the Sorbonne, by the name of Jules Soury, who in 1902 published a book called *Campagne Nationaliste*—along the same lines as *Mein Kampf*—and was acclaimed as the equal of Bergson, while Gustave Le Bon was quoted at some length by the father of psychoanalysis and was sometimes seen as another Freud. Given the number of men writing on the subject, one may wonder if their prolific output does not account in some measure for the inattentive reception accorded to Hitler; for the author of *Mein Kampf* had nothing to say which had not already been said, and not by men of the lunatic fringe, but rather by the ranking intellectuals of the day.

In the years preceding the first world war Europe experienced an extraordinary revival of nationalism. Well before 1914 *Völkisch* ideology, the set of ideas which are crucial to the understanding of nazism, had found a widespread acceptance in German society, notwithstanding a remarkable flowering of the intellectual disciplines in that country, reminiscent of the classical period around 1800, over which Völkisch ideology nevertheless gained the upper hand. It must not be forgotten that, as Professor George Mosse has pointed out, the Nazis found their greatest support among respectable and educated people. Their ideas were eminently respectable in Germany after the first world war, and indeed had been current among large segments of the population even before the war. The essential element here is the linking of the human soul with its natural surroundings, with the 'essence' of nature, that the real and important truths are to be found beneath surface appearances. According to many Völkisch theorists, the nature of the soul of a Volk is determined by the nature of the landscape. Thus, the Jews, being a desert people, are regarded as shallow and dry people, devoid of profundity and totally lacking in creativity. Because of the barrenness of the desert landscape, the Jews are a spiritually barren people.[20]

The selfsame themes are to be met in the nationalist ideology of France: the Frenchman, nurtured by his soil and his dead, cannot escape the destiny shaped for him by past generations, by the landscapes of his childhood, the blood of his forebears. The nation is a living organism, and nationalism is therefore an ethic, comprising all the criteria of behaviour which the common interest calls for, and on which the will of the individual has no bearing. The duty both of the individual and of society is to find out what this ethic may be, yet only those can succeed who have a share in the 'national consciousness,' shaped over the course of the centuries: the Jews, as a foreign race, cannot enter upon this quest.[21]

In Italy, d'Annunzio and Corradini were the best-known spokesmen for a nationalist movement which reached far and deep, feeding on external defeat, as it had done in France in the aftermath of 1870. It was this movement indeed which by 1915 had brought Italy into the war, looking to war for glory. In France the young men of the coming generation were fired by patriotism, by a zeal for order, authority, and discipline, and were morally at the ready for war, many years before August 1914.

This resurgence of nationalism accounts, at least in part, for the failure of international socialism, and explains why the working class set off for war on a wave of patriotism, regardless of their long-standing tradition of anti-militarism and of countless resolutions adopted at each and every Socialist Congress. Throughout the years separating the two wars, the workers' movement did not recover, morally speaking, from this defeat, and it would weigh heavily in the balance when the fascist movements began to come to a head, and particularly, of course, in Italy.

## NATIONALISM, SOCIALISM, AND ANTI-LIBERALISM

During the nineteenth century, nationalism and liberalism had combined to become a force for liberation and emancipation; nationalism was deeply imbued with democratic and universalist values, and inherited from the French Revolution and from the philosophy of natural rights. But then when it came under pressure from new economic conditions and from the bitter competition these conditions provoked on the world market — as this competition pointed up the divergent interests of the great European powers; as it was seen how unity in Italy and Germany was born of fire and blood; and as the impact of social Darwinism, and then of Marxist and internationalist socialism, made itself felt — nationalism gradually changed its character.

In the shape it had acquired by the beginning of this century the nationalist movement, in France as in Italy, bore little resemblance to the nationalist aspirations of Michelet or of Mazzini; the nationalist spirit abroad in 1848 died out, for the French after Sedan, for the Italians after Adowa. The collapse of the Ethiopian campaign in 1896 was seen by Enrico Corradini, the spiritual and political leader of the Italian nationalists, as the collapse of the Italian democratic movement and its supporters on the extreme left. The French nationalists — Déroulède, Barrés, Maurras — opined that the defeat of 1870 had been inflicted on a country already undermined by a revolutionary ideology, by rationalism and individualism. The Republic's inability to avenge the country's humiliation and restore to France her lost provinces, or even simply to prepare for war, stemmed from the fundamental weakness of liberal democracy, its impotence and incoherence. So it was that the new European nationalism became first and foremost a movement of revolt against democracy and a violent critique of the regime in all its weakness, incoherence and impersonal character: it was a party to the general revolt against the values inherited from the French Revolution and the Enlightenment.

At the same time the new nationalism produced diatribes against the rich and against economic injustices; it denounced liberal democracy both as a pattern of government and as a socio-economic system, it demanded that the State take up authoritarian attitudes, and it attacked social injustices in the name of group solidarity. The nationalist movements sought to mobilise the most disadvantaged of the social classes, the people who were threatened by new techniques of industrial production and new forms of commercialization. This was the background that promoted the growth of a new variant of socialism—in France during the 1890s, in Italy or in Austria during the first decade of the twentieth century—which was not Marxist and not internationalist, but emphatically national. It was then that French nationalists first saw the possibilities of a synthesis of a certain type of socialism and of the nationalists' political authoritarianism, which went on to find acceptance in the Italian nationalist circles led by Corradini, and then among followers of Sorel and Mussolini, and finally gave birth to a fully structured fascist ideology.

Indeed in May 1898, during the period of violent unrest stirred up by the Dreyfus Affair, it was Maurice Barrès, while standing as the nationalist candidate for Nancy, who first coined the term 'Socialist Nationalism,'[22] which owes its origins to the idea that national cohesion would come about through the solution of the social question. Twenty years later, Enrico Corradini announced at the Nationalist Convention, 'First and foremost, since it is by definition national in politics, nationalism cannot be anything other than national in economics also, since the latter is the basis of the former.'[23] As for Maurras, he declared that there was a 'form of socialism which, when stripped of its democratic and cosmopolitan accretions, would fit in with nationalism just as a well-made glove fits a beautiful hand,'[24] and at his instigation Action Française made a considerable play for the support of the workers, from the moment it was realised how powerful was the disaffection of the proletariat from the liberal State.

A further experiment, which was nothing less than a trial run for fascism was the founding in 1903 of a National Socialist party, by a former socialist, Pierre Biétry. It was succeeded a year later by the Fédération Nationale des Jaunes de France. Yellow socialism—as opposed to Red socialism—preached national solidarity in lieu of the class struggle, and advocated the accession to property rather than expropriation, as well as workers' participation in company profits and a form of trade unionism in which workers' unions and management unions would exist side by side, which structure would be topped by a strong State, with an assembly of national and regional representatives sponsored by the trades and corporations. It goes without saying that the Yellow Movement was violently opposed to Marxism, while at the same time promoting the personality cult of the leader, who was in effect its mini-dictator; it was equally anti-Semitic. The Fédération des Jaunes de France, which has been described as 'obsessed with the idea of wresting the working-class out of its socialist rut,' was undoubtedly the first to try out the whole apparatus of fascist ideas in practical terms.[25] The French movement played the role of model for the Swiss and German yellow organizations with which it was closely connected. At the same time Austria produced the DAP (the German Workers' Party), founded the very year Biétry was launching his PSN.

National socialism was anti-Semitic, for anti-Semitism — social as well as racial — was the perfect tool for the integration of the proletariat within the national community and had the advantage of rallying the petty bourgeoisie in danger of proletarisation. Anti-Semitism gave the new radical right popular foundations and provided it with an instrument with which to appeal to the working classes and to arouse the masses: the anti-Jewish riots of the closing years of the century[26] bear a curious resemblance, by their violence and their scale, to the riots of the Nazis. The psychological determinism of someone like Jules Soury was no less influential than the racialism propagated by Houston Stewart Chamberlain or Alfred Rosenberg.[27] What early National-Socialism lacked was the social backdrop which would transform it into a political force: there were as yet no huge numbers of unemployed and frightened petty bourgeois, and no impoverished middle classes; it was fully possessed, however, of a framework of ideas no less developed than those of any other contemporary political movement.

Where all the European currents of nationalism were agreed of course was in their anti-parliamentarism. By the end of the 1880s nationalism and anti-parliamentarism had already coalesced in France. The synthesis of the two, when for the first time translated into political terms, evolved into *boulangisme*, the movement that launched on liberal democracy the first of the attacks to which henceforth it would be subjected. By the end of the decade a pattern of events had been established which thereafter became the classic gearing-in to fascism — namely, the shift from far left to far right of people with radical views on social problems and deeply opposed to liberal democracy. It had also become apparent how easily great sections of the working people could give their support to a party that took its social values from the left and its political values from the right, if by so doing they could make clear their dislike for liberal democracy or bourgeois society. This was where boulangisme broke new ground and opened the way to fascism.

Within two decades a very similar pattern of events took place in Italy:

Italian nationalism was profoundly averse to the democratic movement backed by the extreme left, and here too the nationalist movement turned to the workers and peasants. Enrico Corradini began to elaborate on topics that foreshadowed corporatism, complemented by an unambiguous preference for protectionism and other measures designed to appeal to the nation as a whole, such as the expansion of Italian industry and commerce abroad, and a colonial solution to the problems of population and emigration. A political programme relying on colonialism and protectionism and corporatism might perhaps have the right solution and seemed to hold out hope and the prospect of betterment to a whole bloc of society, while at the same time taking great pains not to exacerbate the class struggle.[28]

Corradini was vehemently anti-Marxist and yet considered his nationalist doctrine to be socialist: in December 1910, some twelve years after Barrès, he read a paper to the First Congress of Nationalists, held in Florence, in which he spoke of 'our national socialism.' Already, however, he gave the phrase a wider meaning, reflecting the latest ideas of the Italian school of political sociology: 'This is to say that just as socialism taught the proletariat the value of the class struggle, we must teach Italy the value of the international struggle.'[29] Italy was, in the material as in the moral sense, a proletarian nation[30] and could only survive by taking to heart a lesson already well known to the working classes, and putting into practice the doctrine of unremitting struggle. Corradini expressed a fulsome admiration for the results achieved by the proletariat of Europe, and the way in which the doctrine of class struggle had been put into practical operation to the benefit of the workers. It was on this very point that nationalism identified most closely with socialism and at the same time found itself in violent opposition to socialism. It identified with socialism insofar as 'the basic belief of our essentially dynamic doctrine is struggle, international struggle, even struggle at home, has produced similar effects.'[31] Socialism and nationalism both insisted on the heroic virtues and the warrior spirit, as they both despised democracy and abominated liberalism.[32] On the other hand, socialism sought to impugn the concept of the nation, and in its place preached internationalism: in this and this only it erred. The nationalist movement, however, by integrating the proletariat into the national community, and thereby wiping out the identification effected by democracy of the nation with its bourgeoisie, would restore to the national community its authenticity and integrity and wholeness. Socialism was transcended in National-Socialism.

It is important too to realize that nationalists such as Corradini or Barrès saw the troubles of their respective countries almost exclusively in political terms: if poverty and social injustice prevailed, if Italy suffered defeat in her colonies or showed signs of weakness on the international scene, it could all be laid at the door of a weak and ineffective government and a political philosophy which envisaged the State as an agent for private and sectarian interests, putting itself at the service of pressure groups and social groups that were inimical to one another. The country's ailments derived from the State's inability to recognise the nation's interests, and having indeed lost all national feeling. The reforming of the State along authoritarian lines was therefore an essential preliminary to any attempt at rehabilitating the economy or reforming society. The first enemy to be destroyed therefore was the liberal and bourgeois State, just as it was essential to eradicate the philosophy of natural rights.

It was in Italy that anti-parliamentarism acquired a solidly structured and systematic character, relying on an analysis which in its day was the last word in social sciences. As early as the 1880s, it had been thoroughly formulated in the works of Mosca and Pareto. It was rooted in an intensely elitist and anti-democratic view of society, which according to Pareto is made up of a minority of very gifted individuals and a huge majority of mediocrities, and which is therefore always organized in the shape of a great pyramid, with a governing elite at the top, supported by a passive majority at its base: the State merely embodied the organized control of the majority by the minority.[33] Pareto's elitism bears all the marks of the powerful influence of social Darwinism: he does not scruple to compare the social organism with a living organism nor to make out a parallel between natural selection as it takes place in nature, and what he claims is a process of natural selection occurring in human society.[34] His theory of the circular movement of elites, and of constant warfare between sundry aristocracies, by virtue of which they continually succeeded one another, is a clear pointer to the origins of his sociology, the more so when, in his *Systèmes Socialistes*, he refers explicitly to Ammon and Vacher de Lapouge while discussing the anthropological characteristics of these elites, stressing that history is made by the conflict between one aristocracy and another, and not, as is so often thought, by the struggle of the lower classes against the aristocracy: 'So far as these lower classes themselves are unarmed, they are incapable of ruling; ochlocracy has never resulted in anything save disaster.'[35]

It should be emphasized that this elitist sociology did not confine itself to an analysis of an actual state of affairs, but went on to postulate a universal law, which had governed human society from its beginnings and should therefore be recognised as a norm of behaviour, rooted in the natural order. Not only did this analysis of the structure of society and power play a very influential part in the formation of fascist ideology but also contributed heavily to the aura of respectability and seriousness and trustworthiness which anti-democratic and anti-liberal ideas so very quickly acquired.[36] From the years that had led up to the French Revolution until at least the middle of the nineteenth century, the ideology of egalitarianism had appeared to be based on science — on the natural sciences as well as on the humanities. It was in the name of science and reason that people had battered at the ancient ramparts of privilege and run up the flag of liberty. By the beginning of the twentieth century things were indeed changed, for now it was the new humanities themselves that challenged all the assumptions on which liberal democracy was based. An intellectual climate was thus created that undermined the self-confidence of democracy and did much to boost the ascendancy of fascism.

If anti-parliamentarism, in the form it assumed under the influence of Italian political sociology, was allied to nationalism and furnished it with new weapons, it also gave nurture to certain forms of socialism, and particularly to revolutionary syndicalism. For inasmuch as they were opposed to liberal democracy and to bourgeois society, syndicalists and nationalists were of one mind; they evaluated the mechanisms of bourgeois society in much the same terms, and both conceived of society as being dominated by a powerful minority, with the apparatus of State serving their will. When material conditions were no longer propitious to one particular minority, then another elite rose to the top, in accordance with a process of continuous rotation of elite groups, each of which stirred up the masses to its own purpose. Each minority advanced a sustaining myth, to act as a goad to rebellion during times of transition from the rule of an established elite to the rule of a contending elite, and as a legitimizing fiction once the contending elite had established its dominance. Behind the facade of representative institutions and parliamentary procedures, the bourgeois government was just such an established elite.[37]

This analysis of power made by modern political sociologists had a familiar ring for any Marxist, which explains how a revolutionary socialist, such as Roberto Michels, took it up and used it to show that the existence of a dominating social group is absolutely essential to political and social life.[38] At the beginning of the century this theory found increasing favour in the militant circles of socialism, among those who most violently denounced parliamentary and democratic socialism and advocated direct action. Over against the school of socialists who preached the conquest of power by means of universal suffrage and who thereby relegated the revolution to the unforeseeable future — to the year 3000, their enemies said — the radical wing of the movement insisted on the theory of the avant-garde of the workers who, as a conscious and activist minority, would lead the proletariat into revolution. Traditional socialism had allowed itself to be tamed and assimilated into the bourgeois order; it had been lured into ministerial drawing-rooms and had come to recognise the passwords and play to the rules established by liberal democracy: to all this, syndicalism preferred the revolutionary violence of a proletarian elite. Roberto Michels showed how elitist doctrine, which saw in the masses a source of energy who yet had no will to shape social evolution, in no way conflicted with the materialist interpretation of history or the concept of class struggle.[39] Michels belonged to the revolutionary wing of the German socialists, which came very close to the syndicalism of the French and Italians, and he was bitterly critical of the German Social-Democratic Party: it was passive and lacked the spirit of combat, it had a predilection for parliamentary practices, and it was possessed of a bureaucratic and hierarchical organization. which kept it in a state of paralysis and 'directed it out of the paths of manly striving, away from all acts of heroism.'[40] These were the words he used at a conference held in Paris in April 1907, on the subject of the relations between socialism and syndicalism, which he attended as the representative of the revolutionary wing among the German socialists, who most closely approximated the Italian and French syndicalists. Eventually Roberto Michels became a fascist.

At this same colloquy, Italy was represented by the great syndicalist leader Arturo Labriola, who stigmatized socialism as having become 'nothing more than a piece of parliamentary machinery, putting itself at the service of a handful of politicians.' He repeatedly castigated the official socialist movement for having accepted the rules of the game, for having become democratic and, in place of the class struggle, for preferring collaboration between the classes.[41] Some years later Labriola would discover the idea of the national entity, and end up by going over to militant nationalism.

France was represented by Hubert Lagardelle, the editor of *Le Mouvement Socialiste*, which was the doctrinal organ of orthodox Marxism in all its anti-parliamentary and anti-democratic aspects, fighting against all compromise and any deviation from the doctrine of class struggle. At socialist conferences Lagardelle was the very embodiment of doctrinal purity. In April 1907 he acclaimed 'the French workers' disaffection for the Republican State' as 'the culminating event in the history of these last years.'[42] The struggle against liberal democracy was the first and most important objective of socialism in the eyes of Hubert Lagardelle, who went on to become Marshall Pétain's Minister of Labour.

The leader of the CGT at this time was Victor Greffuelhes, and he, when debating the prospects for universal suffrage, concluded that, 'It seems clear to me that it should be relegated to the accessories shop,'[43] and proposed instead to implement the syndicalists' plans for direct action. According to yet another high-ranking syndicalist, Emile Pouget, direct action 'might proceed at a gentle and peaceable pace or, equally, by force and extreme violence.' Syndicalism and 'democratism' were irreconcilable principally because 'the latter, by means of universal suffrage, gives control into the hands of the ignorant and the *tardigrades*...and stifles the minorities who are the flag-bearers of the future.'[44] In this fashion, the extreme leftists in the socialist movement instilled in their sympathizers a contempt for democracy and parliamentarianism combined with the ardent desire for violent rebellion led by the minority of informed activists. Both France and Italy saw the same development of ideas among the far left syndicalists.

In 1909 these exact sentiments were being voiced by Angelo Olivetti and the Italian revolutionary syndicalists; socialism would come into its own only in consequence of action on the part of the working-class elite.[45]

Hence the strenuous efforts that were made to price the working class away from parliamentary democracy, and thus undo the work of the Dreyfus Affair, which had had an extremely important effect on the workers' movement throughout Europe. For during the Dreyfus Affair the French socialists had decided to come to the defence of the bourgeois Republic, and put their strength and organization at the disposal of liberal democracy, which was then threatened by a coalition of every possible party of the right, and by so doing they had set a precedent and a norm for every socialist party operating within a system of parliamentary government. This decision, instigated by Jaurès, no doubt saved the Republic but also had the immediate effect of dampening down the revolutionary zeal of the proletariat, which thereafter came to stand surety for the supremacy of the bourgeoisie. By giving support to government ministers and sharing in their counsels, the French socialists struck a heavy blow at the international solidarity of socialist parties. European socialists of the extreme left felt it in consequence essential to teach the proletariat to despise anything that smacked of bourgeois or liberal values, to hold in contempt bourgeois virtues and morals, and the bourgeois' respect for the law, for legal forms, for democratic government. The theorists of the syndicalist movement praised rather the warrior virtues, and violence, which begets morality, and the refining processes of social warfare; and in the writings of George Sorel syndicalism further discovered a rich seam of anti-intellectual and irrationalist argument.

George Sorel's work is well known today, and yet when in 1908 he published his *Reflections on Violence*, he was not saying anything that sounded unusual in syndicalists' ears. His books were quite simply a systematic reworking of the writings of socialist and syndicalist leaders far better known than Sorel himself. This was in fact how he acquired his importance and came to play such a large role, in Italy especially, in the conversion of certain syndicalist groups to the right. For Sorel and his associates contrived the synthesis of all the ideas and contemporary trends of thought which had in common the advocacy of revolt against a bourgeois society and all its moral and political values, revolt against the doctrine of natural rights, and revolt against liberalism and democracy. Revolutionary syndicalists and nationalists, as well as anti-democrats and anti-liberals of every colour, had now found common ground; the shift from revolutionary syndicalism to nationalism, or vice versa, had never in theory been beyond the bounds of possibility, and by the time the first world war loomed on the horizon it had taken on the appearance of inevitability.

In 1911-12, Sorel — the revolutionary syndicalist — put out a review called *L'Indépendance*, which was nationalist and anti-Semitic, at about the same time as two other publications were launched that rank among the more interesting and significant harbingers of fascism: *Les Cahiers du Cercle Proudhon* in France, and *La Lupa* in Italy. The Cercle Proudhon was founded in December 1911 and was presided over by Charles Maurras, with George Sorel as its moving spirit. It embraced both syndicalists and nationalists belonging to Action Française. A month later the first edition of *Les Cahiers du Cercle Proudhon* was published, and among its promoters two names stand out that are symbolic of the nature of the enterprise: George Valois, who belonged with the left wing of Action Française, who was the author of *La Monarchie et la Classe Ouvrière*, and who went on to found the Faisceau in 1925; and Edouard Berth, a disciple of Sorel's who in the 1920s shifted from the radical right to the extreme left. Nationalists and syndicalists alike were in agreement that 'democracy was the greatest mistake of the last century,' that it had allowed the most appalling exploitation of the workers, and had set up and then substituted 'the law of gold for the law of blood' within the capitalist system. It followed that 'if we wish to conserve and increase the moral, intellectual and material capital of civilization, it is absolutely imperative to destroy the institutions of democracy.'[46]

The convergence of revolutionary syndicalism and nationalism is best illustrated by the symptomatic development of Sergio Pannunzio, who later went on to expound the theories that shaped the institutional reforms implemented by the fascists. As a young man, Pannunzio was a syndicalist, but a syndicalist who from the first found himself in agreement with Mosca, and said as much; he combined Italian national themes with ideas borrowed from Sorel. He not only insisted that it was time to leave the outworn traditional liberal State behind but also favoured an assumption which other syndicalists had made before him, that the long-standing hostility between two antagonistic social sectors — bourgeoisie and proletariat — was in fact 'schematic.' He maintained that there existed rather two blocs, one of which was reactionary and conservative, and the other revolutionary. To the second, only militant syndicalists and anarchists belonged, and thus the new concept of anarcho-syndicalism, of conflict between the conservative bloc and the revolutionary bloc, began to gain the upper hand over the socialist concept of class struggle. Pannunzio ended up by advocating 'the politics of energy,' leading up to 'the decisive act' and the 'supreme daring' of Revolt — Revolt, and not Revolution, as Santarelli acutely remarks.[47]

As crisis succeeded crisis, first over Libya and then over interventionism, a number of syndicalist groups took up new stances which made a proven appeal to the nation and the people. More and more they leaned toward nationalism, and eventually infiltrated certain circles of traditional social-democracy. This regrouping of syndicalists and nationalists, which already amounted to fascism — though it as yet lacked the name — took place under the banner of *La Lupa*, a journal which first appeared the year before the Tripoli expedition. It was published in Florence and edited by Paolo Orano, a typical representative of the Italian school of syndicalists, whose goal it was to reconcile economic syndicalism and political nationalism. Among its contributors, *La Lupa* numbered Enrico Corradini, Arturo Labriola, and Roberto Michels, and could count on some help, albeit limited and not very concrete, from Sorel. The founder of modern Italian nationalism concentrated his endeavours on demonstrating that nationalism and socialism were well and truly identified with one another insofar as they both shared in the same specific 'virtuous substance.' 'For syndicalism the only moral imperative is to struggle. For nationalism the only moral imperative is . . . to wage war.'[48] They had a common adversary — the bourgeoisie.

In 1913 a new review was launched under the title *Lacerba*, by Giovanni Papini, who in 1904 had published *A Nationalist Programme*. *Lacerba* brought together Papini, Ardengo Soffici, and the Futurists, led by Marinetti. In a 1913 article, Papini called for 'a bloodbath': he saw war as the means for bringing about the internal regeneration of Italy and for destroying the false values of democracy. He and his colleagues combined nationalism with the subversion of established cultural and moral values.[49] In this we already see the influence of Marinetti and the Futurists: as early as 1909 the Futurists' Manifesto had set out the essentials of what subsequently became the moral ideals of fascism, to which the twenties and thirties made no new contribution:

1. We want to sing the love of danger, the habit of energy and rashness.

2. The essential elements of our poetry will be courage, audacity and revolt.

3. . . . we want to exalt movements of aggression, feverish sleeplessness, the forced march, the perilous leap, the slap and the blow with the fist. . . .

9. We want to glorify war — the only cure for the world — and militarism, patriotism, the destructive gesture of the anarchists, the beautiful ideas which kill, and contempt for women.

10. We want to demolish museums and libraries, fight morality, feminism and all opportunist and utilitarian cowardice.[50]

Marinetti remained faithful to fascism to the very end, and became an enthusiastic supporter of Salò Republic.

The shadow of war weighed more and more heavily over Europe, and against that backdrop the consciousness of each and every nation became gradually more susceptible to the influence of new trends. In the syndicalist and nationalist camp too, the wind of change was felt and shows particularly, for instance, in Roberto Michels's analysis of Italian neo-impe-

rialism in terms of 'an imperialism of the poor,' in which he enlarged on
ideas put forward by Corradini. The world was divided into wealthy
nations and proletarian nations, nations which already had a place in the
sun and nations whom it behoved to win such a place; and this concept too
would become one of the basic tenets of fascism. It entailed the transfer-
ence of the indispensable struggle from the theatre of the interior to the
exterior, and the elimination, in theory, of the problem of the proletariat,
which would be absorbed into the sphere of the war waged by the entire
nation: the future would be shaped by struggle, not between the proletarian and capitalist classes, but between the proletarian and plutocratic
nations. Instead of a class, it was the nation now that was going to set the
course of history, as the agent of progress and civilization; and this was the
change of ideas which made the shift from left to right so easy, for on every
other point the far left, composed of syndicalists and revolutionary socialists, and the radicals and nationalists of the new right, had already met
and agreed. Anti-liberalism, anti-parliamentarism, anti-Semitism (except
in Italy); the cult of the elite, of youth, of force and violence; the revolt
against the rationalism of the Enlightenment; the advocacy of political
authoritarianism — every one of the elements which went to make up fascism was by now in existence, and not merely in the shape of raw materials
for they already had been elaborated into a relatively coherent system. By
the time the old world crumbled away in August 1914 fascist ideology had
a past history going back to the 1880s. A few years later, with the numbers
of unemployed and terrified peasants and petty bourgeois growing to
immense proportions, the trauma of war and the permanent state of insecurity induced by the Versailles treaty, the shock of defeat for some, of victory for others, that resolved none of their difficulties, the success of the
Soviet revolution which had an effect — among others — of making people
believe that anything was possible — all combined to create the conditions
which allowed that ideology to become a true political force.

The collapse of the Socialist International on the eve of the war and the
inability of the working classes to prevent the clash, the haste and near
unanimity with which they ranged themselves, physically and morally,
behind the established order, and at one blow shattered the solidarity of
the proletariat, were tangible proof that the concept of class carried less
weight, as a factor of solidarity, than the concept of nation. Confronted by
the fervour which the idea of the nation aroused, the idea of class was
shown up in all its artificiality: the nation was a reality, which the International could never aspire to be. In the course of the war the socialists were a
legion who reached this same conclusion, particularly if they belonged
among the syndicalists and revolutionaries of the far left. Among the latter
there figured Gustave Hervé, one of the most popular and most vehemently
anti-militarist and anti-patriotic spokesmen for European socialism, who
altered the name of his newspaper from *La Guerre Sociale* to *La Victoire*

and who, having spent a lifetime preaching hatred of anything that smacked, however faintly, of nationalism or of collaboration with the bourgeois state, after the war turned fascist.

The most famous of these converts, however, is of course Mussolini. In 1910 he was a young socialist editing a publication called *La Lotta di Classe*, but by 1914 he was putting out a daily newspaper called *Il Popolo d'Italia*. Mussolini's change of tack cannot be said to be unique or particularly extreme, nor was he motivated by political opportunism. He could well have taken on such a role as was played by Léon Blum, Emile Vandervelde, Otto Bauer, or Ramsay McDonald, had he so wished. But for Mussolini it was not possible, since the socialism he professed was revolutionary and adhered strictly to the Marxist analysis of liberal democracy, its morals and laws, categorising these as the outward signs of the supremacy and self-interest of the bourgeoisie, and not as universal values. Like many others, however, Mussolini saw the notion of class disintegrate under the impact of war, and immediately became aware of the immense reservoir of energy contained in the idea of the nation: after half a century of socialism, national feeling emerged as the moving force of history, and the nation was found to embody the fundamental values of society. As soon as this change was seen to have working possibilities, while the fine flame of socialism was all but extinguished, the equation between revolution and socialism was left with its first term only, and reduced to the will to destroy democracy and liberalism and in their place set up a new order. So it was that nationalism became the functional myth of fascism, and from that moment the battle was engaged with Marxism.

Mussolini was far from being the only person to take this path. A quarter of a century later the same assessment of events was reworked by a number of men who were among the most dynamic figures in the European socialist movement, and who all had a long record of opposition to Mussolini's system. The most brilliant of these men was undoubtedly Sir Oswald Mosley, the youngest minister in McDonald's cabinet, followed by Marcel Déat, who was one of the few people still contributing to the theory of socialism in Europe in the period between the two wars, and a socialist minister in a government which had smoothed the way for the Front Populaire. Likewise, there was Jacques Doriot, a candidate to the General Secretariat of the French Communist party, who made the mistake of being in the right in advance of the times, and Henri de Man, the president of the Belgian Workers' party, and one of the most original socialist philosophers of the twentieth century, who in July 1940 welcomed 'the debacle of the parliamentary regime and the capitalist plutocracy in the so-called democracies' as the advent of a new era: 'For the working-classes and for socialism, this collapse of a decrepit world, far from being a disaster, is a deliverance.' For, 'the Socialist Order will be thereby realized, not at all as the thing of one class or of one party, but as the good of all, in the name of a national solidarity that will soon be continental, if not world-wide.'[51]

In September of the same year Marcel Déat summed up the essentials of fascism: 'All things considered, I think it comes down to this one observation: the driving force of Revolution has ceased to be class interest, and has become instead the general interest; we have moved on from the notion of class to that of the nation.' He then added a comment which is utterly characteristic of fascist thinking: 'I shall not try to weigh in the scales the parts played in this undertaking by what is national and by what is social, nor to discover whether it was a question of socializing the nation or of nationalising socialism. What I do know is that...this mixture is, in the best sense of the word, explosive: rich enough to set all the engine-forces of history backfiring.'[52]

## A NEW CIVILIZATION

In the period immediately after the first world war, as in the years preceding the second, the fascists clearly felt they were proclaiming the dawn of a new era, a 'fascist century' (Mussolini),[53] a 'new civilization' (Oswald Mosley).[54] And indeed, from its earliest beginnings, fascism presented itself as being nothing less than a counter-civilization, defining itself as a revolution of man, a 'total revolution,' a 'spiritual revolution,'[55] a 'revolution of morals,'[56] a 'revolution of souls.'[57] For its ideologists, fascism — to use Valois's expression — was fundamentally a conception of life, a total conception of national, political, economic and social life.[58] 'Total' was a word of which all fascist writers were extremely fond, and it was one of the key terms in their vocabulary: fascism was to be the first political system to call itself totalitarian precisely because it encompassed the whole range of human activity. It was totalitarian because it represented a way of life, because it would penetrate every sector of social and intellectual activity, because it meant to create at once a new type of society and a new type of man.

A movement of revolt, fascism drew its dynamism from its 'disruptive power,'[59] its total rejection of bourgeois society with its political and social structures and moral values. None of the elements that went to make up fascist ideology were new in themselves. What was new was the synthesis of these elements, a synthesis that only became possible in the aftermath of the war, and, of course, after the success of the Soviet revolution. In this sense, there is no doubt that fascism was the child of the post-war crisis: it was a politics of fear and crisis, inseparably bound up with the new difficulties liberal democracy was encountering.[60] But at the level of ideology, in its maturity, and even when, as in Italy and elsewhere, it had accumulated some years of experience, fascism still displayed essentially the same features that characterized the movement of revolt of the early years of the century.

In the minds of Gentile and Mussolini, Marcel Déat and Drieu La Rochelle, Jose Antonio and Codreanu, fascist ideology constituted a comprehensive alternative to liberal bourgeois civilization, its rationalism and individualism. After the nineteenth century, 'the century of the individual,' the fascist twentieth century would be the 'collective century, and therefore the century of the State.'[61] Everything sprang from this fundamental principle. Fascist ideology saw itself as a reaction against the 'materialistic positivism of the nineteenth century,'[62] which it sought to replace by a 'religious and idealistic manner of looking at life.'[63] It refused, in the words of José Antonio, 'to accept the materialistic interpretation of history,'[64] or, as Mussolini thought, 'the materialistic conception of happiness.... This means that fascism denies the equation: well-being = happiness, which sees in men mere animals, content when they can feed and fatten, thus reducing them to a vegetative existence pure and simple.'[65]

But it was a professional sociologist, Marcel Déat, who put his finger on a more specific cause of the malady: 'economic liberalism, which is bourgeois materialism, and its counterpart the working-class materialism of Marxism, both of which are incontestably the daughters of rationalism,' that 'straitjacketed and calamity-stricken' rationalism which was a 'denial of all aristocratism, a negation of hierarchy, a negation of the person, a negation of the State as an instrument of the community.'[66] This is the 'old eighteenth-century rationalism,' 'a philosophy now two hundred years past its prime,'[67] which still forms the basis of official liberal ideology today, and it was against this world of natural rights, individualism, matter, and reason, a world threatened by anarchy that fascism rebelled. 'We stand for a new principle in the world, we stand for sheer categorical definitive antithesis to the world of democracy, plutocracy, free-masonry, to the world which still abides by the fundamental principles laid down in 1789,' Mussolini said.[68]

In the minds of its leaders, fascism was very much a revolt of the younger generation: 'the present *Weltanschauung* of fascism may be summed up in one word — youth,' the English fascist James Barnes wrote.[69] The same sentiment was shared by Codreanu, José Antonio, Drieu La Rochelle, Oswald Mosley, and Georges Valois. For Léon Degrelle, the embodiment of the fascist revolt was a younger generation which 'would rather have blown everything up than start out on life following filthy paths, without even the smallest patch of clear sky in view.'[70] For Oswald Mosley 'the real political division of the past decade has not been one of parties, but a division of generations.'[71] And Adrien Marquet (a comrade of Déat's), the day neo-socialism was born, flabbergasted Léon Blum with his shout: 'No one gives their lives for thirty seats in the Chamber.'[72]

Fascism, young, new, and modern, was also a revolt against decadence, and here, too, it was echoing one of the main themes of the movement of revolt of the latter years of the nineteenth century. The thought of Drieu La Rochelle and Léon Degrelle, like that of Barrès before them, was the reaction of a younger generation to a Europe whose 'morals are in decay, whose faith is debased, and which is sick to the teeth of individualism, fanaticism and arrogance,'[73] a Europe 'slowly going to rack and ruin,' and expiring of manifold ills: country areas depopulated by the war, alcoholism, syphilis, the great industrial centres; towns full of 'cinemas and cafés, brothels, newspapers, stock exchanges, political parties and barracks'; a Paris that had become a centre of bohemian intellectuals, fast livers and homosexuals; drugs, music-halls, Catholic writers, Jews, Picasso's paintings....'[74] The fascists plumbed the depths of the sickness. *Gilles*, a novel which takes decomposition as its theme and is surely the most important work of fascist literature, abounds with images of death, annihilation and putrefaction. This world incapable of a virile and involuntary reaction, this rakish, self-satisfied world of heirs and descendants was, of course, the world of old bourgeois Europe, and the fascist rebelled against it. He would dig the grave of all the bourgeois virtues and of all the evils bourgeois power had spawned; he would be the herald of a new morality: 'To the financier, the oil-man and the pig-farmer who consider themselves the masters of the world and who want to run it according to the law of money, the needs of the automobile and the philosophy of pigs, and bend the peoples to the politics of the dividend,' George Valois said, fascism's answer was to 'raise the sword.' To the bourgeois 'brandishing his contracts and statistics:

— Two plus three makes...
— Nought, the Barbarian replies, smashing his head in.'[75]

The Barbarian, the fascist, thus saw himself as liberating the world from the bourgeois spirit and awakening a desire for reaction and regeneration that were simultaneously spiritual and physical, moral, social, and political. Fascism, for its ideologists, was a revolution of both the body and the mind, since for them the two were inseparable. This was where in the fascists' own view the originality of their movement lay: as an alternative to the economic man of liberal and Marxist materialism, they offered a brand of neo-idealism that put the spiritual above the material; in place of the liberal and pacific bourgeois and the city shop-keeper they offered the barbarian and the knight of the Middle Ages; as an alternative to the product of European rationalism they offered the cult of feeling, emotion, and violence; and in place of the degenerate man of a stay-at-home civilization to which physical effort had become repugnant, they offered the cult of the body, health, and the outdoor life.

The fascist rebellion thus took on the appeal of a new human adventure, for, in the words of Léon Degrelle, 'the great revolutions are not political or economic,...the true revolution...[is] the one that overhauls not the engine of the State, but the secret life of each soul.'[76] Fascism was a 'poetic movement' for José Antonio;[77] a 'state of mind,' 'something spiritual and mystical' for the Belgian Rexist José Streel.[78] For the fascist-type life, to quote Gentile, was a mission, and the militant was a crusader who had to be prepared to make any sacrifice.[79]

Within fascism, therefore, we find the cult of duty, sacrifice, and the heroic virtues. Mussolini, required to sum up fascism in a few words, said, 'We are against the easy life.' For the fascist, life meant 'duty, elevation, conquest,' it was 'serious, austere, religious.'[80] In the midst of the indescribable mediocrity that today surrounds us, Degrelle wrote, 'we represent fearlessness, initiative, self-sacrifice and discipline. . . .'[81] Life for the fascist 'is a continuous, ceaseless fight,' and his creed is 'a doctrine which is not merely political: it is evidence of a fighting spirit which accepts all risks.'[82] This is why the new type of human being, the fascist man, would be a man who 'liked taking risks, [had] self-confidence, group-sense and a taste for collective enthusiasm'; 'the politics of ink, saliva and ideology he will counter with the politics of soil, flesh and blood.'[83] Fascism meant strength, willingness to serve, obedience, authority, self-denial, and for Henri de Man, as much as for the killer Joseph Darnand, it meant a new world which would be built by 'an elite preferring a lively and dangerous life to a torpid and easy one.'[84] For the head of the Milice, the French version of the Gestapo, 'the bourgeois way of life is over': Fascism meant 'living dangerously';[85] it was, in Oswald Mosley's phrase, 'a great and hazardous adventure.'[86] This fascist adventure, adventure for adventure's sake, would produce the type of man who was always willing to 'try his luck,' who liked to go for 'all or nothing,'[87] and it did in fact ultimately produce the Mussolinian killer whose notorious motto, 'me ne frego,' epitomizes the spirit of fascism.[88]

Fascist ideology thus offered 'a new, vigorous, brutal explanation of the world, of the kind men have always needed and will always need.'[89] Incorporated in it was the cult of physical strength — Oswald Mosley wanted men 'to live like athletes' — and of life, health, and blood, combined with an obsession with virility and a contempt for intellectuals. None of these various manifestations of what amounted to an apologia of the instincts were original contributions on the part of the fascists and, in fact, apart from the experience of the war, it would be difficult to find in their thought a single idea not already developed by Barrès, Marinetti, d'Annunzio, Corradini, or Langbehn. What fascism represented was the full flowering of the movement of revolt of the end of the nineteenth century. The generation that had lived through the trenches brought only a further dimension to the nostalgia for the front and for danger: war was where men were put to the test, it brought out men's primal virtues and basic instincts. 'War is my fatherland,'[90] Gilles said, his words an echo not only of the 'glorification of war'[91] of the Futurist Manifesto, written at the turn of the century, but also of Jules Soury's claim that war was 'the source of all superior life, the cause of all progress.'[92]

The corollaries of the cult of war and physical danger were the cult of brutality, strength, and sexuality and, of course, contempt for anyone who believed in reasoned argument and the validity of statistics. In this connection, Drieu La Rochelle, attempting to define what divided the fascist from the traditionalist, established a distinction which is vital to a proper understanding of the deeper nature of fascism: 'A monarchist is never a true fascist . . . because a monarchist is never a modern: he has none of the brutality or the barbaric simplism of the modern.'[93] Here we have the essence of fascism, and Drieu's words also reveal what makes of fascism a true counter-civilization: rejecting the sophisticated rationalist humanism of Old Europe, fascism sets up as its ideal the primitive instincts and primal emotions of the barbarian. Had not Marinetti, in 1909, said his response to the high culture of Europe was to 'destroy the museums, libraries and all the academies' and 'free this country of the fetid gangrene of its professors, archeologists, cicerones and antiquaries'?[94]

Fascism was intent on changing man, but that was not all. Revolting against the big city and the great centres of industry, it wanted to alter man's environment and create for him a setting where he could lead a new life. The fascist revolution saw itself as a counter-revolution against an industrial revolution which had uprooted man from the open country and cooped him up in the city, and it proclaimed the superiority of the twentieth century, the country and the sports stadium over the nineteenth century, the urban hovel and the pub. In its desire to reconcile man with nature, save him from a lingering death and physical decrepitude and safeguard his primitive virtues and his natural environment, fascism was possibly the first environmentalist ideology of this century, combining the pursuit of technical progress and industrial growth with the protection of nature as the environment in which a civilization of leisure and sport could flourish.[95]

The 'great moral revolution' which was what Robert Brasillach understood by fascism, that revolution of the senses directed against the prevailing political philosophy, was to be a revolution of the body and of sexuality. Fascism would create a 'new life' of 'camping, sport, dancing, travel and communal hikes' which would sweep away the fusty world of 'aperitifs, smoky rooms, congresses and [bad] digestions.'[96] This world would be a virile world, and it is worth remembering in this context what a preference fascist satirists showed for sexual imagery and vocabulary. It was the virility of the fascist, his healthiness and bounding energy which finally distinguished him from the impotent bourgeois, liberals, and socialists.[97] But for all that fascism advocated a return to nature and the soil, it was not anti-modern. The fascist always showed a predilection for new industries and technical innovations, for aeroplanes and cars: d'Annunzio, Mussolini, and Hitler are familiar examples. 'We are the party of speed,' Drieu said.[98] Power, speed, vigour, toughness, solidity, and effectiveness are the essential fascist qualities, and they are also those of the modern motor, the car engine and sophisticated machinery. This taste extended to vocabulary. To convey the activist spirit of the fascist movement, Mussolini chose the phrase: 'Fascism is a dynamo.'

This movement which saw itself as one of new men was undoubtedly one of young men — those who had little vested interest in the established order, who felt strongly about the discrepancy between principles and practice, to whom rebellion came more naturally than to the rest of the population, and for whom ideology was something to be taken seriously. Belgian and Romanian fascisms both originated in student movements, and in France, Spain, Italy, and England, the young — the oldest of them had just returned from the trenches — predominated.

Both at the level of ideology and for purposes of recruitment, the fascists were able to use the fact that their movement was associated with the younger generation to present their ideology as the only twentieth century system of thought. Were not liberalism, socialism, communism, and nationalism all products of the preceding century? And had they not all aged very badly? This youthfulness of a movement whose leaders were still in their twenties and thirties when they achieved notoriety or came to power goes some way towards explaining its dynamic, activist and, ultimately, revolutionary character.

Since they regarded their ideology as an ideology of life and movement, all the various fascisms chose to describe themselves as 'movements' rather than 'parties.' They all considered themselves 'anti-parties,' because they challenged the inertia and dogmatism of the traditional political structures, declined to work out programmes or political manifestoes — refused, in other words, to play the game of traditional politics or accept its conventions.[99] They had, by contrast, an immense thirst for action, and not just action aimed at overthrowing the established order, but action for action's sake, since, in Mussolini's phrase, 'inactivity is death.'[100] The action the fascists glorified was not so much action with a specific end in view as action for its own sake: to act with blind passion, to think in terms of fist-fights and bursts of machine-gun fire was to rediscover the very principle of life itself. 'No man goes very far who knows where he is going'[101] was the principle Mosley adopted for himself, and Mussolini expressed the same sentiment in these terms. 'I am all for motion. I am one who marches on. . . .'[102] And for José Streel, 'you must come on board, let yourself be carried by the torrent; in other words, you must act. The rest will take care of itself.'[103]

The war, in which the great proportion of fascists had had direct experience, furnished them with a criterion of behaviour: the Bergsonian '*élan vital*,' reduced to the simple *élan* of the battlefield, was reinterpreted in terms of activism at home. Ex-servicemen played an extremely important part in the maturing of fascism. As depositaries of the national heritage and guardians of the nation's greatness, they considered themselves the bearers of a special mission—to see that their own sufferings and the sacrifice of their comrades had not been in vain, and to refashion society as a fighting unit, inculcating in it the fighting soldier's heroic virtues of discipline, sacrifice, self-denial, and brotherhood. The ex-servicemen wanted to convey their unique experience to society as a whole and reshape and transform it in the light of that experience; they had a profound sense of being 'outside and above preceding generations'[104] and placed themselves 'above party and class [as we were] during the war.'[105] Society, however, being a class society, and politics being party politics, a politics of factions and interest-groups, it is not difficult to see how the ex-serviceman became the enemy of the established order, of political pluralism and pacifist and humanitarian values. Since he wanted the salvation of his country and wished to regenerate the state and refashion the world in his own heroic image, the ex-serviceman 'wants the government of the country'[106] but was not prepared to work his way up in the traditional way through the committees and antechambers of democracy. Consequently, he became a rebel.

The ex-serviceman thus came to occupy a position alongside a multiplicity of maladjusted and dissatisfied elements who would see in fascism a promise of solutions that the traditional right and left were unable to offer. Fascist ideology was without doubt that best qualified to attract the malcontents who found no place in the world as it was, despised the conformism of left and right, and yet felt much closer to their enemies the communists—as the communists did to the rebels—than to the bourgeoisie which, however, at the critical moment, and under the pressure of events, was to become their ally.[107]

With their thirst for action for action's sake and struggle for struggle's sake, the fascists appeared to be the only authentically revolutionary political organizations, the only movements unconditionally opposed to the established order, the only people whose revolutionary credibility—unlike that of the parties of the left, including the communist parties—had not been damaged by compromise. After its accession to power, Italian fascism should certainly be regarded as a regime, and that it formed a regime makes it a special case, but it, too, goes to prove the rule: the generation of fascists of 1935 went into opposition against the regime, dreaming of a fascist utopia, a fascism purged, authenticated, renewed. However puerile this revolt may have been—and of its futility there can be no doubt—it nonetheless represented a rebellion against the compromises, betrayals, and abandoned ideals of an aging regime.[108] We may well wonder whether, had there been no war, similar difficulties would not have arisen in Germany. Certainly, in the cases of General Franco, Marshal Pétain,

and Admiral Horthy, no sooner had they come to power at the head of
what were fundamentally reactionary regimes, than they set about dis-
banding, muzzling, or neutralizing the fascist movements. Fascism did not
take kindly to reaction.

The fascist elite, those for whom life was sacrifice, devotion, and self-
denial, liked to imagine themselves as a kind of religious order, as *Croisés*,
'the handful of heroes and saints who will undertake the Reconquest.'[109]
Drieu rhapsodized about the age of epics, cathedrals, and crusades,[110] and
Marcel Déat proclaimed that 'Nietzsche's idea of the selection of "good
Europeans" is now being realized on the battlefield, by the LFV and the
Waffen SS. An aristocracy, a knighthood is being created by the war which
will be the hard, pure nucleus of the Europe of the future.'[111] But it was
Léon Degrelle, himself an SS officer back from the front, whose language
best conveys the character of that new man that the fascist revolution
would produce: 'The true elites are formed at the front, a chivalry is
created there, young leaders are born. That is where you find the true elite
of tomorrow...and there between us a complete fraternity grows up, for
since the war everything has changed. When we look to our own country
and see some fat, stupefied bourgeois, we do not feel this man to be a member of our race; but when we see a young revolutionary, from Germany or
elsewhere, we feel that he is one of ours, for we are one with revolution and
youth. We are political soldiers, the badge of the SS shows Europe where
political and social truth are to be found...we prepare the political cadres
of the postwar world. Tomorrow, Europe will have elites such as it has
never known. An army of young apostles, of young mystics, carried by a
faith that nothing can check, will emerge one day from the great seminary
of the front.'[112]

## THE INDIVIDUAL AND THE COMMUNITY

Fascist ideology was born of a political tradition that considered the individual a function of group life. The various currents of which fascism was
the confluence—nationalism, revolutionary syndicalism, anti-parliamentarism, and anti-liberalism of every hue—all shared a view of man as a
social animal. Even the nationalists of the latter years of the nineteenth
century had seen man as nothing more than the vehicle of forces generated
by the community, and their ethic was both unconditionally anti-individu-
alist and violently antagonistic to the theory of natural rights and the rights
of man. Fascist ideology thus appropriated to itself a view of man which in
its most recent form was already a good fifty years old, and which in its earliest form was as old as the fundamental ideas of anti-revolutionary
thought themselves. Such, then, is the genealogy of fascism's rejection of
the 'individualistic' or 'atomistic' conception of man central to the world
view of classical liberalism: the 'human individual is not an atom. Imma-

nent in the concept of an individual is the concept of society. . . . Man is, in an absolute sense, a political animal,' wrote Gentile.[113] According to him, the notion that man exists in perfect freedom anterior or exterior to society is simply a fiction. However much fascist thinkers may have differed on other questions, on this point they were all agreed. From José Streel, who asserted that 'the individual does not exist in the pure state'[114] to José Antonio in his polemic against Rousseau,[115] it was the 'mechanistic' view of society as nothing more than an aggregate of individuals that was attacked.

This view of man as an integral part of an organic whole is the basis of fascism's political philosophy. Fascism developed a conception of society which accorded moral privilege to the collectivity, its traditions, and particularly its juridical embodiment in the state, as against the empirical and transient individuals which constituted its membership at any particular time. According to Gregor, this was founded on the idea — most fully elaborated by Gentile — that insofar as man is outside the organization of society with its system of reciprocal rules and obligations, he has no significant freedom. Outside of society, man would be the subject of nature, not its master. He would be the enemy of all and friend of none. He would be threatened by persons and things alike. He would be in a state of abject dependence. There would be no freedom, no security, for each man would be exposed to the open wrongs of every enemy. There would be no assurance of life, much less of liberty. The freedom that man is supposed to barter away in part on entering society, in order to secure the remainder, has no real existence. It is, according to Gentile, an imaginary possession which then, by an imaginary transfer, is conveyed to society.

Man as a spiritual agent is an essentially social animal who finds freedom only in a rule-governed association with other men.[116] Ultimately, for Gentile, man has existence only insofar as he is sustained and determined by the community: 'for at the root of the "I" there is a "we".'[117] The Italian philosopher was here restating an argument that had been relatively common at the end of the nineteenth century, the main contention of which had been that the individual had no autonomy and only achieved the status of human being as a member of a community. In Mussolini's words: 'In the fascist conception of history, man is only man by virtue of the spiritual process to which he contributes as a member of the family, the social group, the nation, and in function of history to which all nations bring their contributions. Hence, the great value of tradition in records, in language, in customs, in the rules of social life. Outside history, man is a nonentity. Fascism is therefore opposed to all individualistic abstractions based on eighteenth century materialism.'[118]

In this sense, Mussolini, Gentile, and all the other fascist thinkers were traditionalist and conservative: man commences his rational and moral life as the denizen of a specific historical community. He rejects aspects of that community's prescriptions and proscriptions only when armed with sufficient reason. Man in the mythical state of nature, devoid of the rule-system governing human association, is a man devoid of human contacts, devoid of language, thought, and morality, devoid of humanity itself. [119]

Fascist thought did not stop there, however, but went on to develop a conception of liberty and an ideal of an organic society that went far beyond anything postulated by the first counter-revolution. Liberty, in Mussolini's terminology, was 'the liberty of the State and of the individual within the State.' This definition of liberty, which 'is to be the attribute of living men and not of abstract dummies invented by individualistic liberalism,' derived from one axiomatic tenet: 'the fascist view of life stresses the importance of the State and accepts the individual only insofar as his interests coincide with those of the State, which stands for the conscience and the universal will of man as an historic entity. . . .' Liberalism denied the State in the name of the individual, fascism reasserts the rights of the State as expressing the real essence of the individual.' [120] Mussolini's assertion is of fundamental importance for the understanding of fascism: this identification of the individual with the collective will was the very cornerstone of fascist social and political thought.

The individual was only seen in terms of the social function he fulfilled and his place in the community. For Gentile 'the only individual who can ever be found' is 'the individual who exists as a specialized productive force,' [121] and for Oswald Mosley 'real freedom' was 'economic freedom.' The English fascist leader defined freedom in language that is not unreminiscent of the language of a certain brand of popular Marxism: 'Real freedom means good wages, short hours, security in employment, good houses, opportunity for leisure and recreation with family and friends.' From this it followed that 'economic freedom cannot come until economic chaos ends; and it cannot end until a Government has power to act,' [122] until, in José Antonio's words, man's freedom was given 'a framework of authority, hierarchy and order.' [123]

In the fascist view, democracy, whose function was to guarantee and preserve the rights of the individual and which saw the individual as the supreme end of society, was to be replaced by a 'people acting organically on both the social and political planes,' [124] for nations and societies were living organic totalities which were an end in themselves and which possessed their own hierarchy and articulation. 'These totalities,' wrote Marcel Déat, 'both came before, and transcended, their parts—individuals and secondary groups.' This conception of nation and society of course went directly against the French rationalist view, according to which these totalities either came into being under the pressure of circumstances or were created through the artifice of a contract. It was from this fascist view of the individual and the society that the highly romantic notion of the *Volksgeist* arose. [125]

It was, then, in subordinating himself to the group that the individual found his *raison d'être*, and in integrating himself into the community that he found fulfilment. In the words of Mussolini's Minister of Justice: 'Instead of the liberal-democratic formula "society for the individual" we have "individuals for society." . . . For fascism, society is the end, individuals the means, and its whole life consists in using individuals as instruments for its social ends. . . . Individual rights are only recognized insofar as they are implied in the rights of the State.'[126] It was in this way, Gentile claimed, that fascism had resolved the famous 'paradox of liberty and authority. The authority of the State is absolute' and 'freedom can only exist within the State, and the State means authority.'[127] In the same vein, José Antonio maintained that 'to be really free is to be part of a strong and free nation.'[128]

In thus championing the state and the nation, 'this community of communities,'[129] fascism extolled the values of the group, of the collectivity, of the national community, producing a 'new conception of a living community, where abstract brotherhood is replaced by a relationship of the blood,'[130] and also providing a solution to alienation, to 'the frightening isolation of modern man, who, in the factory, the office and at home finds himself reduced to an orphan.'[131]

It was by way of such arguments that fascism arrived at that new man and new society so admirably characterized by Marcel Déat: 'the total man in the total society, with no clashes, no prostration, no anarchy.'[132] There can be no doubt that fascism's successes were in part due to man's longing to be merged with the collective soul and his exaltation at feeling, living, and acting in harmony with the whole. Fascism was a vision of a coherent and reunited people, and it was for this reason that it placed such great emphasis on march-pasts, parades, and uniforms—on a whole communal liturgy, in fact—and that it waged an implacable war against anything tending to divide or differentiate, or which stood for diversity or pluralism: liberalism, democracy, parliamentarism, multi-party system. This unity finds its most perfect expression in the quasi-sacred figure of the leader. The cult of a leader who embodied the spirit, will, and virtues of the people, and who was identified with the nation, was the keystone of the fascist liturgy.

For this romantic and mystic conception of life, fascism is a great adventure, an adventure one lives with all his being, a 'fever,' Robert Brasillach used to say. But long before him, d'Annunzio had written about the heightening of the meaning of life attained through sacred objects, the symbols of a secular religion: instruments of a cult around which human thought and imagination revolve, and which lift these to idealistic heights.[133] This new religion was a product of the change in the nature of politics which had taken place at the end of the nineteenth century.

Both fascist ideology and fascism's political style were obvious products of the new mass society: fascist politics were a reflection of the enormous difficulties which political structures that had been inherited from the nineteenth century would have to overcome if they were to survive into the twentieth. Eugen Weber has pointed out that the liberal politics of the nineteenth century were representative and parliamentary. But the representative system of which parliament is the symbol functioned adequately only in a deferential society, where distinction of achievement and wealth had replaced distinction of birth, but where the concept of distinction as such survived and the elector, who respected his representative, trusted him to serve his interests. The parliamentary representative system had been worked out by and for an elitist society not much more inclusive than the aristocratic society it replaced. In the mass society that took over at the end of the nineteenth century, with its democratic structure and its egalitarian ideology, parliament either did not, or was no longer felt to, work properly. Its shortcomings stood out, the bargains of everyday give-and-take became evidence of corruption, and compromise acquired a pejorative meaning, for mass society spoke in high-flown generalities and could not allow anything less than integral fulfilment.

The mass electorate might have been more tolerant had it felt better represented. But the petite bourgeoisie on the one hand, the newly significant industrial workers on the other, did not recognize either the pattern or the language of parliamentary politics as their own. The latter reflected the psychology of nineteenth-century elitist politics, which had been rationalistic and utilitarian: liberalism and Marxism both argued that, in the end, men will understand their interests and act in consequence. But the psychology of a mass electorate, as John Stuart Mill discovered before Gustave Le Bon, is irrationalistic, and politicians learned to appeal not to mind, but to emotion, seeking less to persuade than to manipulate.[134]

'Man is not only a rational being,' José Streel said, 'to make a people happy, it is not sufficient to bequeath it perfect laws: it also requires a climate.'[135] For Mussolini, who was frequently criticized by his peers for what they considered to be excessive rationalism, and even for Gentile, feeling 'was prior to thought and the basis of it.'[136] These appeals to feeling as opposed to the dry and grey argumentation of liberal politics were an essential part of great campaigns to conquer souls and hold them. Power had to be attained, national unity forged, the collective will asserted, by all available means. Essentially democratic, in its propaganda if not in its essence, fascism addressed itself to sentiments, deeply rooted prejudices, and intuitions—not to intellect. Rational appeals are accessible to few; they are also subject to criticism. Reasoning invites examination, speculation and disagreement. Feelings can be shared, arguments seldom, and then by few:[137] intellectual argument is by definition an agent of division, destruction, and moral death.

Fascism was clearly the spiritual heir to that nationalism of rebellion and adventure which since the end of the nineteenth century had been advocating the rejection of industrial society and liberal and bourgeois values. The malaise that led the generation of 1890 to rebel against the status quo reappears in near identical form with fascism, at least at the level of ideology. The violence of the earlier rebellion was modified to suit the changed conditions of an age of mass movements, and fascism was to be a mass ideology par excellence, belonging as it did to that current of thought which since the turn of the century had sought to replace the tentative and uncertain analytical procedures of the intellect by the infallible instinct of the masses. It propagated the cult of impulsive feeling and glorified both impatient instinct and emotion, which it considered superior to reason. In isolation, reason was doomed to sterility; too cultivated an inclination towards intellectual analysis debilitated the will, blunted vitality and stifled the voice of one's ancestors. Moreover, it enfeebled the individual's instinctive self-confidence and could lead him to doubt the truths of the nation. Intellectualism bred individualism, and frustrated man's primal impulses.[138]

Fascist ideology thus took on the character of an anti-intellectual reaction which pitted the powers of feeling and emotion, and irrational forces of every kind, against the rationality of democracy. It was the rediscovery of instinct, the cult of physical strength, violence, and brutality. This is, of course, what explains the attention paid to scenarios, the care lavished on décor, the great ceremonies, the parades — taken together, they made up a new liturgy where deliberation and discussion were supplanted by song, torches, and march-pasts. Viewed in this way, fascism appears as the direct descendant of the neo-romanticism of the 1880s and 1890s, only now the revolt had taken on dimensions commensurate with a mass society whose advent the fin-de-siècle generation had scarcely even foreseen.

This mystical, romantic, anti-rationalist fascism was as much a moral and aesthetic system as a political philosophy: it constituted a complete vision of man and the community. Usurping the place occupied by revealed religion, its aims were to create a world of fixed criteria, a world freed from doubt and purged of all foreign accretions; to give back their authenticity to man and the community; and reestablish the compromised unity of the nation. Once all this had been achieved, all the members of the national community, being of one body with it and existing through it alone, would react as one man and respond identically to the problems confronting it; and once this unanimity had been forged, political and social problems would be reduced to matters of detail. Moreover, the proletariat would now be an integral part of a nation which had become a community governed by a unified system of values, a purified and disciplined unit sufficiently well armed to compete with hostile communities in the struggle for existence. The nation's decline into decadence would be halted, action and heroism would become the respected virtues, and in consequence the vitality of the nation, which would now have a foundation of organic solidarity, would be free to flourish. In this sense, fascism represented a desire to transcend the banality of the bourgeois world, the materialism of industrial society, and the platitude of liberal democracy: behind it lay the desire to give life a new meaning. This is why, in the final analysis, fascism bore the character of a new religion which was complete with its own mysticism and which rejected in its totality the world as it was.

## A NEW 'SOCIALISM'

This mystical and irrational aspect of fascism, with its romanticism and emotionalism, was, however, only one side of the coin. The other was the fascism of 'planning'[139] — technocratic and managerial fascism, one might call it. Essentially socialist in origin, this fascism rejected Marxism, on the one hand, in the name of a modernized, national, and authoritarian socialism, and liberal democracy and bourgeois society on the other, in the first place in the name of social justice, but above all in the name of efficiency and technical and economic progress, which were the two aims that had to be given priority if the community was to survive the crisis that had come upon the world. For their realization these aims required first and foremost a powerful decision-making apparatus, in other words, a State free of the inherent weaknesses of the parliamentary system.

In this respect, this second fascism owes its origin far more directly to the great economic crisis of the twenties and the inability of traditional structure to adapt to new problems and new needs than does the other, romantic fascism. It was the defective functioning of the democratic institutions and the clumsy and futile efforts that were made to adjust institutions and doctrines created by and for the nineteenth century to quite different circumstances and situations which stimulated ideas about 'planning.' The failure of the Social Democratic and Labour Parties, and indeed of Marxist thought in general, in the period between the two wars, was a factor that greatly influenced the rise of fascism: the fascists' search for answers to the new problems and the solutions they recommended must be said to be an essential aspect of fascist thought. This form of fascism was, then, the result of a revision of Marxism and an expression of the attempt to adapt socialism to modern conditions on both the ideological and tactical planes. That this tendency should have manifested itself most clearly in the three industrial countries of Western Europe, and at a time when their respective working-class movements were either just reaching or had already passed the pinnacle of their power, was certainly no accident. There is clearly a close connection between Oswald Mosley's actions as a young Labour Minister and those of Henri de Man and Marcel Déat, and his thinking was the result of the same ideological shift and the same political analysis as theirs. Their development into fascists differed according to local circumstances: whereas Mosley was the first to burn his bridges and openly launch a fascist movement, claiming his kinship with Hitler and Mussolini as he did so, de Man and Déat would not identify themselves with the fascist revolution until the debacle of 1940. Nevertheless, from the middle thirties onwards, the new socialism they were promulgating bore the essential characteristics of fascism, although it must be added that this fact did not prevent them from exercising ministerial powers on behalf of socialist parties, nor hinder the one from becoming president of the Belgian Workers party or the other the leader of the Parti Socialiste de France when it was a member of the Front Populaire government. For at that time there were no clear ideological boundaries, since the phenomenon was a new one and nobody knew how to diagnose it.

The criticisms the 'planners' and neo-socialists levelled at Marxism revolved around two fundamental questions: the problems of the class struggle, and the recognition of *le fait national*, that is to say, the acknowledgement of the legitimacy of the national framework and the necessity of taking action within it. 'I believe, to sum up,' de Man wrote, 'that the socialism of the generation to come will be, under penalty of total collapse, as different from that of our fathers as [that] was from the socialism that preceded the communist manifesto.'[140]

According to Dodge, this new socialism took as its starting point, 'the entirely changed significance of the class struggle in the contemporary world.' Indeed, with regard to class structure, not only did it now appear that the proletariat would never constitute even the majority of the society, but social identification could not be predicted on the basis of an interest-analysis alone. Thus there was an ineluctable distinction between two social groups, the proletariat and the new middle classes, both of which shared essentially the same relationship — the exclusion from ownership — to the means of production.[141] Drawing his own conclusions from this, de Man proposed the formation of a 'Labour Front' which would include all those elements which found themselves at the mercy of finance capitalism. When, after 1930, Marcel Déat began suggesting that the socialists should head a vast 'anti-capitalist' alliance, he was in effect putting forward the very same idea, and one which, incidentally, implied the extinction of socialist specificity.[142] *Planisme* was consonant with, and an expression of, the more general socialist ideology developed by de Man, notably in that this ideology explicitly maintained that the removal of a given enterprise from the private sector of the economy was a decision to be taken on pragmatic grounds and not a question of doctrine. In the same way, de Man pointed out how unrealistic were the Marxist propositions on agriculture in countries where the small farmer flourished, and he also argued that direct socialization should only be applied to those sectors of the economy where the processes of manufacture had in themselves already in fact been collectivized, that is, large-scale industry.[143]

The Plan was a product of the crisis, an answer to the crisis, and, finally, a bid to rescue the middle classes, the stratum of society which the crisis had hit hardest. In the long term, the Plan was a substitute for the abandoned socialist aim of restructuring society: since the structures of the national economy remained untouched, it became in the event the life-belt of capitalism.

The true significance of the Plan and of Henri de Man's thought can be perceived most clearly in their political corallaries: the author of *Au-delà du Marxisme* was in fact advocating a far-reaching reform of the system. Dodge tells us that he spoke of the necessity of establishing a strong state capable of withstanding the attacks of the money powers: the classical division of powers would have to be reapportioned in favour of a division of functions by which the Legislative would be reduced to a supervisory role; and under benificent guidance the mixed economy of the nation would be organized to as large a degree as possible under corporatist inspiration. In a series of articles in *Le Peuple* entitled 'Corporatisme et Socialisme,' de Man undertook to demonstrate that it would be a mistake to let the Fascists monopolize the appeal of corporatism, which he defined as "... autonomous grouping and action in virtue of interests which derive from the practice of a trade or profession." On the contrary, such a principle of organization was exactly what was necessary if socialism were to avoid those evils of bureaucratization and centralization with which its opponents charged it.... A systematic corporatist organization of society would allow the peaceful resolution of conflict.[144]

In spite of the provocation his proposals represented and the opposition to him that had arisen within the Belgian Workers' party, on the death of Emil Vandervelde, Henri de Man became its President. It was in his capacity as leader of Belgian socialism that in June 1940 he announced the dissolution of his party as a gesture of welcome to the new world the Nazi victory had brought. In his view, the collapse of the parliamentary parties had cleared the way for the construction of a true and authoritarian socialism which, in its essential aspects, would be based on the Nazi model.[145]

The necessity of 'taking nationalism into account' and of rooting 'the national economy in the nation's soil'[146] constitute — along with the defence of the middle classes — one of the two pillars of neo-socialist ideology, which rapidly developed into a true fascist ideology. By moving 'onto the plane of a national reality,' by 'falling back into their national framework,' the peoples had abruptly created a totally new situation: 'they have forced us,' Marquet said, 'to follow them.'[147] In other words, just as they were on the point of leaving the SFIO to set up the Parti Socialiste de France, the neo-socialists arrived at conclusions which not only recapitulated those reached by Michels, Sorel, and Mussolini fifteen or twenty years earlier, but were, moreover, essentially the same as those reached by Barrès at the end of the preceding century, to wit: the allegiance of the masses could only be mobilized in the name of a more urgent and compelling reality —

the nation. The concept of the *nation* would be the key concept of political organization in the twentieth century.[148]

In essence what Déat and his companions were saying was that the traditional Marxist conception of class had lost its relevance: 'Marxism is the socialist answer to the capitalism of 1850.'[149] The middle classes were as gravely affected by the economic crisis as anyone, and since they were harder hit than the proletariat and were threatened with proletarianization, they had come out in revolt against the capitalist system and the liberal state. It was up to socialism to harness the revolutionary dynamism of this social stratum that had been crushed by the development of capitalism. It was up to socialism to harness the rebellion of the 'middle classes' who 'in their attempt to liberate themselves' were calling for 'the restoration of the State and the protection of the nation.'[150] Léon Blum was correct in speaking of a fascist contagion: in their efforts to combat fascism, his former companions were adopting fascist methods; as Blum realized, the primacy of the idea of the nation, the denial of the proletariat's special status and the denial of its revolutionary capability in a world in crisis could not but result in the denial of the very idea of class in the Marxist sense of the term.

This line of reasoning made it possible for Drieu La Rochelle to speak of 'bourgeois workers,' whom the 'Third Party' — the fascists — did not want to see destroyed but classed with the peasantry and the proletariat.[151] Mosley, José Antonio, and Belgian Rexism assessed the situation in very similar terms: the opposition was no longer between the proletariat and the bourgeoisie but between the 'workers of all classes' and 'banking capitalism, or hypercapitalism.'[152] This approach enabled economic parasitism and social exploitation to be eliminated without prejudicing the unity of the nation, which was compromised by the idea of the class struggle, and allowed the preservation of the realities of nation, family, and profession, which the artificial concept of class had threatened.[153] Twenty years earlier, it had been the abandonment of the idea of the class struggle, the pillar of his socialist doctrine, which had made Mussolini swing to fascism: with the socialist ministers de Man, Déat, and Mosley; with the communist leaders Doriot and Marion; and with the thousands of socialist and communist militants who committed themselves to fascism, we see the same process taking place. Thus this desire to bring socialism up to date and adapt it to the modern world ultimately resulted in fascism.

The national socialism of the end of the preceding century had taken the same path, its objective having been to unite the social and the national, incorporate both nationalism and socialism within one movement, and merge the right and the left. This legacy was inherited by that form of fascism that wished to be neither 'of the right nor of the left; because basically the right stands for the maintenance of an economic structure, albeit an unjust one, while the left stands for the attempt to subvert that economic structure, even though the subversion thereof would entail the destruction of much that was worthwhile. . . . Our movement will on no account tether its destiny to the vested interests of groups or classes which underlie the superficial division into right and left.'[154] This idea returns time and again, with only slight variation, in the writings of all fascist thinkers. Mussolini, for instance, six months after the Fasci di Combattimento was formed, indicated that it was 'a little difficult to define fascists. They are not republicans, socialists, democrats, conservatives, nor nationalists. They represent a synthesis of all the negations and all the affirmations. . . . While they renounce all the parties, they are their fulfilment.' In the minds of its promoters, fascism, being highly nationalistic and socially concerned, thus achieved a harmonious synthesis between the forces of the past and the demands of the future, between the weight of tradition on the one hand and revolutionary enthusiasm on the other. It borrowed from both the right and the left. In practice, of course, fascism's insistence on the cooperation of all social classes and their reconciliation within the corporative regime threw it irrevocably to the right.

Nationalism and socialism work to mutual advantage. Nationalism is to some extent fed from the social concern, and the social concern gains considerable impetus from the enhanced value acquired by all citizens in conditions of community euphoria. The desire to be a party above and far superior to all others is invariably there; very often much of the motive force behind it derives from a profound conviction that the society needs remaking from top to bottom. The nation must be renewed through idealistic energy largely generated from national solidarity.[155] Fascist ideology is part of attempts to cut out new political avenues, to forge doctrines fitted to the changing realities. The old right and the old left were not equal to the task because, according to Mosley, 'both are instruments for preventing things being done, and the first requisite of the modern age is that things should be done.'[156] 'We must dismantle the unwieldy machine of capitalism, which leads to social revolution, to Russian-style dictatorship,' José Antonio said; 'we must dismantle it, but with what will we replace it?'[157]

What was to take the place of the dictatorship of money, what middle road could be taken between 'hypercapitalism and state socialism'?[158] The answer was a controlled economy and corporative organization topped by a strong State, a powerful decision-making apparatus. It was a pragmatic system which did not set out to impose one property regime or another: however, it seemed to those fascist economists who came from the left that, as economic organization progressed, the active economic function of private capital would diminish until, its social utility extinguished, the significance and power of capital would disappear. De Man's Plan du Travail, which became the official policy of the Belgian Workers' party, envisaged a mixed economy in which 'political power would be used to create the economic conditions in which the country's productive and consumption capacities would be adapted to each other. This objective implies a double change in the doctrine of socialization: in the first place, the carrying into effect of a plan on the national plane is no longer subject to the international plane but takes precedence, which means that nationalization must be the present state of socialism; in the second place, the crux of nationalization is not the transfer of property but the transfer of authority — which means that the problem of management takes precedence over that of ownership.'[159]

These views were endorsed by official socialist bodies: by the Belgian Socialist party and by the French CGT. And it is not by accident that British fascism was born of well-founded reformist impatience among bona fide socialists: nevertheless, in their majority, European socialists did understand that these views came dangerously close to those expressed by corporatist economists, and which Italy and Germany were beginning to put into practice.

It was the Great Depression of 1929 that led socialists like Mosley, de Man, and Déat to take a public stand in favour of protectionism and national exclusivism. The economic crisis turned the socialists' gaze inwards towards the nation and towards the idea of a strong, powerful state, efficient and authoritarian, which would be capable of ensuring order and reconciling the divergent interests within the community; which would be 'the master of its money and capable of controlling the economy and finance'; and which would also, in the words of the neo-socialists themselves, be able to 'impose certain rules of conduct on the large capitalists' and 'prepare the ground for the controlled economy that is in the logic of things.' The present crisis, 'a crisis of democracy in general,' was a crisis of 'a State that is too weak.'[160] In de Man's case, the need to modernize the policy-making structures led to the idea of 'authoritarian democracy'[161] as a replacement for the old parliamentary democracy. For José Antonio, the new world would be one of authority, hierarchy, and order;[162] order, authority, and decision, according to Sir Oswald;[163] and order, authority, and the nation for the French neo-socialists.[164] Thus all three formulations contain the terms order and authority; the third varies in accordance with particular local circumstances. The reform of the relations of power and its structures, as we can see from these concerns, was the cornerstone of the fascist revolution.

## TOTALITARIANISM

'Ours will be a totalitarian state in the service of the fatherland's integrity,' said José Antonio, 'all Spaniards will play a part therein through the membership of families, municipalities and trade unions. None shall play a part

therein through a political party. The system of political parties will be resolutely abolished, together with all its corollaries: inorganic suffrage, representation by conflicting factions and the Cortes as we know it.'[165]

Innumerable passages in an identical vein are to be found throughout
fascist literature. Totalitarianism is the very essence of fascism, and fascism
is without question the purest example of a totalitarian ideology. Setting
out as it did to create a new civilization, a new type of human being and a
totally new way of life, fascism could not conceive of any sphere of human
activity remaining immune from intervention by the State. We are, in
other words, a state which controls all forces acting in nature. We control
political forces, we control moral forces, we control economic forces, . . .'
Mussolini wrote, 'everything in the State, nothing against the State,
nothing outside the State.'[166] For him, the fascist state was not only a living
being, an organism, but a spiritual and moral entity: 'The fascist state is
wide awake and has a will of its own. For this reason, it can be described as
"ethical."''[167] Not only does the existence of the State imply the denial of
the individual's rights — 'the individual exists only insofar as he is within the
State and subjected to the requirements of the State'— but the State asserts
the right to be 'a State which necessarily transforms the people even in their
physical aspect.'[168] Outside the State, 'no human or spiritual values can
exist, much less have value': 'no individuals or groups (political parties,
cultural associations, economic unions, social classes) outside the State.'[169]
The concrete consequences of such a conception of political power and the
physical and moral repression it would engender are not hard to imagine.
Here again we see how the communist and fascist totalitarianisms differ:
whereas the Stalinist dictatorship could never be described as an application of the Marxist theory of the State, fascist terror was doctrine put into
practice in the most methodical way. In fascism we have the perfect realization of the unity of thought and action.

Italian fascism took its glorification of the State so far as to identify it
with the nation. For Gentile, the State — and the nation — was not 'a datum
of nature' but a creation of the mind; for Mussolini 'it is not the nation
which generates the State; that is an antiquated naturalistic concept which
afforded a basis for nineteenth-century publicity in favour of national
governments. Rather it is the State which creates the nation, conferring
volition and therefore real life on a people made aware of their moral
unity.'[170] This view of the State is a perfect illustration of the difference
between the Italian — one is tempted to say Western — version of fascism
and nazism, which saw the State as the emanation of the Volk and the servant of the community and the race. It also explains why racialism was
originally alien to Italian fascism: 'Racism or the principle of racial self-
determination as it has been called in recent years,' the English fascist
Barnes wrote in a résumé of Mussolinian ideology, 'is a materialistic illusion, contrary to natural law and destructive of civilization. It is the *reduc-*

*tio ad absurdum* of Nationalism; any truly logical application of it is farci-
cal and impracticable.'[171] Only in Central and Eastern Europe did racialism form an integral part of fascist ideology; in Western Europe, it was
very often a foreign import, as the various fascisms developed in the late
thirties under the shadow of nazism and rapidly organized themselves on its
lines. Although the key-stone of Nazi doctrine, biological racialism cannot
therefore automatically be considered integral to fascism at all times and
in all places.

The fascist state, creator of all political and social life and of all spiritual
values, would of course be the undisputed master of the economy and
social relations. Political power was regarded as an instrument for reconciling and harmonizing the conflicting interests that existed within the
community. The State would, therefore, take control of the levers of the
economy, without however being obliged by this to mount an attack on
private property. Fascist supporters of left-wing persuasions saw this as the
weakness of the fascist case, since the retention of traditional economic
structures seemed scarcely compatible with the establishment of a new
social and human order. In the view of fascist thinkers, however, the primacy of the State and the subordination of economics to politics would be
sufficient guarantee against the return of the old order of things: the
novelty and originality of the system consisted in its making capitalism
serve the community. Fascism, while doing away with the most sordid
aspects of capitalism, would simultaneously benefit from its technical
achievements and from the deep-rooted psychological motivations that
underlay it. The pursuit of profit remained the moving force behind
economic activity, and on this point there was nothing to distinguish fascism from liberalism; what did distinguish it, radically, from both liberalism and socialism was its assertion of the primacy of politics. For Oswald
Mosley, 'capitalism is the system by which capital uses the nation for its
own purposes. Fascism is the system by which the nation uses capital for its
own purposes. Private enterprise is permitted and encouraged so long as it
coincides with the national interests. Private enterprise is not permitted
when it conflicts with national interests.'[172] And in Sir Oswald's view, 'This
implies that every interest, whether right or left, industrial, financial,
trade union banking, or banking system is subordinated to the welfare of
the community as a whole, and to the overriding authority of the organized
State. No state within the State can be admitted. "All within the state,
none outside the state, none against the state."'[173] Hence it was capitalism,
not private property, that the fascists attacked, and a clear distinction was
drawn between the two: 'property is the direct projection of the individual
on matter, it is a basic human attribute,' whilst capitalism, which 'has
gradually replaced this property of the individual with the property of
capital...ultimately...reduces bosses and workers, employees and
employers, to the selfsame state of anxiety, to the same subhuman condi-

tion of the man deprived of all his attributes, whose life is stripped of all meaning.'[174]

Just as the corporative system worked to the advantage not of the proletariat, but of the employers, so the capitalist system was not destroyed but rather perpetuated and, finally, saved by fascism. Even so, it cannot be denied that at the ideological level, the level of desiderata, fascism did aim to eliminate exploitation by bringing economic interests to heel. If an organic society is by nature inimical to political pluralism, it is no less antagonistic to the most flagrant forms of social injustice, and indeed this had to be so if the proletariat was to be integrated into the community and if social relations were to be fundamentally changed. For Mussolini, the very word 'corporation' was to be understood in its etymological sense of 'fashioning into a body,' a 'fashioning' which was the essential function of the State and the one that would insure its unity and its continued existence. If the community is an organic whole, deviation is corrupting and cannot be tolerated. All must act as one, shunning dissension as intrinsically harmful and seeking that unity which alone can save in the providential person of one man. It was this unitary life, the life of the nation, which led fascists to speak of an identity of interest uniting workers and employers. This organic view of the nation led naturally towards collectivism and to an emphasis on the most neglected and the most productive sections of the national community. Herein lay the socialism of national-socialism, the inspiration behind its anti-bourgeois and anti-capitalist orientation. If we remember the *embourgeoisement* and governmentalization of contemporary socialists during the twenties and thirties, it is easier to understand why fascists attacked them not only for dividing the nation but also for forgetting their revolutionary spirit.[175]

To be sure, once in power the fascists themselves proved singularly modest in their reformist ambitions; there was little of their revolutionary zeal to be seen in the way of structural reform. Admittedly, the only fascism not to come to power in war-time was the Italian, but in its case, too, the fascist revolution found itself caught up in a process to which those parties of the left which joined capitalist regimes fell victim: like the French and Belgian socialists, like the British Labour party, the fascists proved content to do no more than manage capitalism. It is also true that the fascists were to a large extent neutralized by the forces of reaction, whom they could not afford to ignore. But had Léon Blum's Front Populaire not come up against exactly the same problems? If fascism rejected Marxism and Bolshevism, it also rejected conservatism and the 'reactionary' label, and adopted a revolutionary ideology. On this all fascists were agreed: for some, fascism was the successor of the Jacobin dictatorship; for others, it had, in Italy, carried through a revolution as far-reaching as any, barring the French.[176] But if we leave aside for a moment its revolutionary aspirations, fascism is seen as representing a movement whose cardinal aim was to re-create that unity of the nation which had been ruptured by liberalism and individualism, and reintegrate into the nation the class most profoundly alienated from it — the proletariat. As the successor of national, anti-Marxist socialism, fascism constituted an extremely violent attempt to return to the social body its unity, integrity, and totality. And here we find the great internal contradiction which fascism was never able to escape: it wanted to be a movement of reunification, yet it became an agent of civil war. But, we may well ask, is that not the fate of any revolutionary movement?

Finally, thrown to the right by their hatred of class politics, which their organic nationalism rejected, the fascists found themselves, as a logical consequence of the conflicts with the left, driven into opportunist alliances which distorted their image, diluted their radicalism, and reinforced their anti-Marxism to the detriment of their nationalist collectivism. The revolutionary potential of the fascist movements was thus largely nullified by the workings of the left-right dichotomy in which they were trapped: at the critical moments, the only alliances open to them were with conservative and reactionary elements; ultimately, the fascists' greatest enemy was the left. Yet these alliances came about only where a left actually existed. As Eugen Weber has shown, in countries where there was no left, fascism was the revolutionary movement par excellence.[177]

Unlike those historians whose judgement seems rather to have been impaired than improved by 'detachment' and 'perspective,' the fascists and revolutionaries of Bucharest and London, Oslo and Madrid knew full well what divided them from the reactionary right, and they were not taken in by propagandist attempts to tar them with the same brush. Admiral Horthy, General Antonescu, Colonel Count de La Rocque, Marshal Pétain, General Franco, King Victor Emmanuel, and the Belgian and British Conservatives were well aware that it was only pressure of circumstances that had brought them into favour with the movements of Szálasi, Codreanu, Déat and Doriot, José Antonio and Mussolini, Degrelle and Oswald Mosley, and they discarded them as soon as they could.

The European conservatives, whether dictators or liberals — including reactionaries like Maurras — felt little sympathy with a movement which was essentially national socialist, in the fullest sense of that term, and which, while it attacked Marxism, itself wanted to put social relations on an entirely new footing and considered the established order the relic of an outdated world. In this sense, fascist ideology was a revolutionary ideology, since its principles represented a distinct threat to the old order of things. Dynamic, activist, and imbued with a spirit of rebellion that was visibly repugnant to the partisans of the established order, fascism practised a populist elitism which felt nothing but abhorrence for the old European aristocracy. Fascism promoted the cult of youth, brutality, and violence, and aimed to create both a new type of man and a new civilization in which a modern knighthood would have supremacy over the liberal bourgeois and the decadent, conservative aristocrat. Crowning all would be the totalitarian State, which in the hands of the leader would become the most perfect instrument ever conceived for the creation of a new order. These objectives were not ones to which the classic right could subscribe, nor indeed could such objectives, in the long term, serve its own interests.

It was where the right was too weak to hold its own ground that fascism achieved its most marked successes. In times of acute crisis, the right turned to the new revolutionary movement — the only one capable of confronting communism — for assistance, but never treated it with anything less than the deepest suspicion. By contrast, where the right was sufficiently confident to face the Marxist left itself, where its positions were not unduly threatened and it had a solid social base, it did everything in its power to prevent the fascist phenomenon getting out of hand. It concentrated above all on manipulating fascist troops and spending money to safeguard its own interests. Western Europe, Spain included, is a good case in point. It was not the strength of the right but its relative weakness, its fears, and its fits of panic, which created one of the essential conditions of fascist success.

## BIBLIOGRAPHY

This short bibliographical study does not, of course, claim to exhaust its subject. The books and articles discussed are ones that have a direct bearing on the specific questions dealt with in this paper.

Paradoxical as it may seem, until about ten years ago there were scarcely any scholarly studies of fascist ideology available. It was not until the beginning of the sixties that works of a general nature, comparative studies which tried to go beyond specifically national frameworks, began to appear. The first were Ernst Nolte, *Three Faces of Fascism: Action Française, Italian Fascism, National Socialism* (London, 1965) (the English translation of *Der Faschismus in Seiner Epoche* [Munich, 1963]) and Eugen Weber, *Varieties of Fascism* (New York, 1964). These were rapidly followed by Hans Rogger and Eugen Weber, eds., *The European Right: A Historical Profile* (Berkeley and Los Angeles, 1966), Walter Laqueur and George L. Mosse, eds., 'International Fascism 1920-1945,' *Journal of Contemporary History*, I, 1 (1966), Francis L. Carsten, *The Rise of Fascism* (London, 1967), John Weiss, *The Fascist Tradition* (New York, 1967), S. J. Woolf, ed., *European Fascism* (London, 1968), and *The Nature of Fascism* (London, 1968) and, finally, A. James Gregor, *The Ideology of Fascism: The Rationale of Totalitarianism* (New York, 1969). Most recently, we have Paul Hayes, *Fascism* (London, 1973), and Adrian Lyttelton's brilliant *Seizure of Power: Fascism in Italy 1919-1929* (London, 1973).

The sixties also saw the appearance of works which traced the immediate intellectual origins of fascism, thus enabling us to turn away at last from the search for possible 'ancestors' of fascism, from Plato to Fichte, and concentrate on the contemporary intellectual climate and cultural environment. In 1961 Fritz Stern's *The Politics of Cultural Despair: A Study in the Rise of the Germanic Ideology* (Berkeley and Los Angeles), appeared, and was an immediate success. This study of Paul Lagarde, Julius Langbehn, and Arthur Moeller van den Bruck is 'a study in the pathology of cultural criticism' (XI): it brings out clearly the nature of the revolt which rumbled beneath the surface of Germany from 1850 onwards: 'Their despair over the condition of Germany reflected and heightened the despair of their countrymen, and through these men we see the current of disaffection rising until it merged with the nihilistic tide of national-socialism. Above all, these men loathed liberalism...they attacked liberalism because it seemed to them the principal premise of modern society; everything they dreaded seemed to spring from it: the bourgeois life, Manchesterism, materialism, parliament and the parties, the lack of political leadership' (XII).

Professor Stern uses the term *conservative revolution* to denote the ideological attack on modernity, on the complex of ideas and institutions that characterize liberal, secular, industrial civilization: 'our liberal and industrial society leaves many people dissatisfied — spiritually and materially. The spiritually alienated have often turned to the ideology of the conservative revolution' (XVI).

Fritz Stern's work should be read together with George L. Mosse's *Crisis of German Ideology: Intellectual Origins of the Third Reich* (New York, 1964). Mosse shows how deeply the Nazi ideas were embedded in German history. They were current — indeed, eminently respectable — among several generations of Germans prior to Hitler's rise. Professor Mosse provides evidence of how these ideas became institutionalized in schools, youth movements, veterans' groups, and political parties. His work reveals the uniqueness of German fascism. Mosse is making a point of vital importance for the study and interpretation of fascism when he demonstrates that though fascism spread throughout Europe, the German variety came to be unique. 'It was unique not only in the way it managed to displace the revolutionary impetus, but also in the primacy of the ideology of the Volk, nature, and race. The revolutionary impetus produced an ideological reaction throughout the continent, but the German crisis was *sui generis*, besides being more deeply rooted in the national fabric. Nowhere else was the ideology planted so deep or for such a long time. Nowhere else was the fascist dynamic embedded in such an effective ideology. Deeply rooted as it was in a specific German heritage, it could hardly serve as an aid to the fascist movement in other countries' (315).

The same subject is studied from a different angle in Walter Z. Laqueur's *Young Germany—A History of the German Youth Movement* (London, 1962). Laqueur gives a clear picture of the strength, vitality, and depth of völkisch ideology, which was based on the overriding importance of the idea of race as opposed to those of nation or State. Laqueur provides further evidence of the uniqueness of the German experience. Nazism's biological racialism makes it a case apart, and that it does so forces us to the conclusion that, however much an ideology may retain elements that link it to a wider family of ideas, its degree of extremism will give it the status of a separate phenomenon. Such a conclusion would not seem to conflict with that reached by Eugen Weber at the end of a work which still remains the best introduction to a comparative study of fascism: 'Fascism is pragmatically activist, National-Socialism theoretically motivated, or at least expressed' ( *Varieties of Fascism*, 143). Although his whole book takes the form of a rigorous comparative analysis, Weber cautions his reader at the very outset against falling into a trap which nowadays is carefully avoided by students of socialism and communism. Which caution, however, does not prevent the author of the most recent of the works of synthesis (Paul Hayes, *Fascism*) from declaring at a very early stage in his book that 'the concept of racial superiority was a constituent part of fascist ideology' (20).

The success of nazism very often obscures the specific characters of the various fascisms. Even as shrewd an observer as H. R. Trevor-Roper has written that '"International fascism" is unthinkable without Germany' ('The Phenomenon of Fascism,' in S. J. Woolf, ed., *European Fascism*, 37). Trevor-Roper's over-emphasis on the Nazi experience is a direct consequence of his fundamental conception of fascism. For him, 'the public appearance of fascism as a dominant force in Europe is the phenomenon of a few years only. It can be precisely dated. It began in 1922-23. . . it came of age in the 1930s and it ended in 1945' ('Phenomenon of Fascism,' 18). Trevor-Roper is a representative of that school of modern scholarship which sees fascism as a phenomenon extremely limited in both time and place, and as the product of one unique historical situation. Ernst Nolte's monumental *Three Faces of Fascism* also inclines towards this school of thought. For Trevor-Roper, the precursors of fascism are no more than 'parochial figures' who 'in the public history of that time [before 1922] had no place and a historian writing in 1920 would probably not even have noticed them' (18). Is not Trevor-Roper yet one more illustrious victim of that much vaunted 'historical perspective'? Not only does the view of contemporaries frequently differ from ours; it may often be more accurate. Contemporaries knew perfectly well who were fascism's precursors, and they were quite able to identify pre-fascism. Here is what Julien Benda, writing in 1927, said in *La Trahison des Clercs* (Neuchatel, 1946), 234: 'About 1890, the men of letters, especially in France and Italy, realized with astonishing astuteness that the doctrines of arbitrary authority, discipline, tradition, contempt for the spirit of liberty, assertion of the morality of war and slavery, were opportunities for haughty and rigid poses infinitely more likely to strike the imagination of simple souls than the sentimentalities of liberalism and humanitarianism.' His entire book is nothing more nor less than an indictment, written after the first world war, of the fascist thinking that preceded political fascism by several decades. It is no accident that it has been the scholars who do not see fascism as a phenomenon limited to the period between the two wars who have paid the greatest attention to pre-fascism.

Weber's *Varieties of Fascism* is illuminating in this connection, since it shows how far fascist ideology had its roots in the European intellectual climate of the end of the nineteenth century; this is also the approach adopted by George L. Mosse, the last chapter of whose *Crisis of German Ideology* already anticipates the first of *International Fascism 1920-1945*. This short essay, in which Mosse depicts fascism not just in terms of a revolt but also in terms of the taming of that revolt, offers some important insights into the nature of fascism and pre-fascism. The same can be said of his study of d'Annunzio, *The Poet and the Exercise of Political Power* (Yearbook of Comparative and General Literature), no. 22 (1973), which is a study in the emergence of the fascist political style, the new political style which worked within the framework of myth, symbol, and public festivals. As a result of the rise of nationalism accompanied by the growth of a secular religion of the nation in the nineteenth century, and the changed nature of politics, politics became a drama, expressed through secular liturgical rites and symbols closely linked to concepts of beauty in which poetry felt at home (32-33). D'Annunzio excelled in this domain, and he did indeed create an entirely new political style. The romantic and mystical element represented by d'Annunzio was also present in futurism and its violent revolt, and in his *Intellectuals in Politics* (New York, 1960), James Joll gives an intellectual biography of Marinetti which is essential for an understanding of the intellectual climate from which fascism emerged. In two countries, Italy and France, a true literary avant-garde was involved in the development of fascist and pre-fascist ideology: besides d'Annunzio and Marinetti, there was Barrès, to whom two recent books have been devoted, Robert Soucy's *Fascism in France: the Case of Maurice Barrès* (Berkeley, Los Angeles, London, 1972) and my *Maurice Barrès et le Nationalisme Français* (Paris, 1972). In this context George Mosse's latest book will be extremely useful: *The Nationalization of the Masses: Political Symbolism and Mass Movements in Germany from the Napoleonic Wars through the Third Reich* (New York, 1975).

Studies of the socialist-national aspect of pre-fascism are rather restricted in number. The first to tackle the subject were Robert F. Byrnes, 'Morès the first national-socialist,' *The Review of Politics*, XII (July 1950), and Eugen Weber, 'Nationalism, Socialism and National-Socialism' *French Historical Studies* (Spring 1962). Three recent articles deal with the same subject: Enzo Santarelli, 'Le Socialisme national en Italie: Précédents et Origines,' *Le Mouvement Social* (janvier-mars 1965), my 'National-Socialism and Anti-Semitism: The Case of Maurice Barrès,' *Journal of Contemporary History*, 8, 4 (1973), and George L. Mosse, 'The French Right and the Working-Classes: *Les Jaunes*,' *Journal of Contemporary History*, 7, 3-4 (July-October 1972). For Austro-Hungary, one would do well to consult Andrew Whiteside, *Austrian National-Socialism before 1918* (The Hague, 1962). Pre-fascist ideology appears in these studies as a genuine mass ideology and the movements it inspired as mass movements. The fascist explosion is thus examined in depth, and it is explained as the result of a very profound wave of opinion.

A work of the same orientation is the highly controversial book by A. James Gregor, which in my view is the most thorough, lucid, and erudite study of Italian proto-fascism. As a parallel study of Italian syndicalism and the Italian school of political sociology on the one hand, and of the evolution of Mussolini's political thought on the other, it is, in my opinion, absolutely necessary.

Of the numerous studies of anti-Semitism at the end of the nineteenth century and the beginning of the twentieth, I consider the following to be indispensable: Robert F. Byrnes, *Anti-Semitism in Modern France* (New Brunswick, N.J., 1950); Michael R. Marrus, *The Politics of Assimilation: A Study of the French Jewish Community at the Time of the Dreyfus Affair* (Oxford, 1971); Norman Cohn, *Warrant for Genocide: The Myth of the Jewish World Conspiracy and the Protocols of the Elders of Zion* (London, 1967); Peter G. J. Pulzer is excellent on *The Rise of Political Anti-Semitism in Germany and Austria* (New York, 1964). The subject is also discussed in Hannah Arendt's famous book *The Origins of Totalitarianism*, where it is examined within the context of an analysis of the concept of totalitarianism. The intellectual origins of fascism and some basic trends in European history which made fascism possible are masterly examined by J. L. Talmon, *The Unique and the Universal* (London, 1965) and 'The Legacy of Georges Sorel,' *Encounter* (February 1970), 117-60. Indeed, the true dimensions of fascism can only be understood in the context of the intellectual revolution that took place at the end of the nineteenth century, and in this field the best works to consult are James Joll's brilliant *Europe Since 1870* (London, 1973), the most recent work to date; Peter Viereck, *Metapolitics: From the Romantics to Hitler* (New York, 1941); H. Stuart Hughes, *Consciousness and Society* (1961); John Weiss, ed., *The Origins of Modern Consciousness* (1965); Gerhard Masur, *Prophets of Yesterday* (1961), and W. Warren Wagar, ed., *European Intellectual History since Darwin and Marx* (1966). But to be properly understood, fascism must also be seen in its relation to the right, and here we come up against a crucial problem of interpretation: Was fascism a phenomenon of the right, essentially reactionary in character, or was it a far more complex phenomenon, as the fascists themselves believed? To obtain an impression of the ideological context of fascism and of its position vis-à-vis the right, one would do well to refer to *The European Right: A Historical Profile*. The value of this collection of essays lies in its attempt, taking the latter decades of the nineteenth century as its starting-point, to establish a distinction between the old and the new right. Admittedly, the contributors disagree about what kinds of groups are to be labelled 'right'—old or new. Also, they come up against objective difficulties inherent in comparative studies, which apply especially to a comparative study that ranges over eleven countries, from Finland to England and has as its subject movements of the extreme right, since these have none of the social homogeneity or doctrinal clarity of the extreme left, and variations from region to region are far more pronounced. It is, however, in the very fact that the book undertakes such a study, and shows what possibilities it holds, that its importance lies. The distinction between the traditionalist and modern 'rights,' between classical conservatism and 'right-wing radicalism' is, it must be said, not always made clear, and the standard of the contributions varies. Nevertheless, thanks in great part to the masterly General Introduction by Eugen Weber, which gives the whole work its meaning, and his two chapters on France and Romania, the book succeeds in throwing light on how the radicalism of the new right prepared the way for fascism, and thus provides a basis for establishing a clearer distinction between fascism and conservatism, fascism and reaction. From the viewpoint of the history of ideas, however, this volume has one serious defect: little attention is paid to the function of ideology in social agitation and politics.

A number of other works need to be consulted to help clarify the problem of distinguishing fascism from the 'right' and the factors that specifically characterize the fascist movements. *The Rise of Fascism*, by F. L. Carsten, is a very useful synthesis, and serves as a good introduction to a difficult subject. *The Nature of Fascism*, edited by S. J. Woolf, is quite different in character. It is the outcome of a conference held at the University of Reading in the spring of 1967, the purpose of which was to analyze fascism from the different standpoints of the historian and the social scientist. This comparative study is of considerable interest to the historian of ideas, even though the book contains only three papers on the problem of fascist ideology: N. Kogan's 'Fascism as a Political System,' and two contributions on 'Fascism and the Intellectuals' from George L. Mosse and P. Vita-Finzi. This multi-disciplinary undertaking follows an earlier collective volume edited by Stuart Woolf, also prepared at the University of Reading, *European Fascism* (1968), in the introductory chapter of which Professor Woolf offers some remarkable insights into what specific attributes distinguish fascism from the right.

This problem, of major importance to the study of fascism, and crucial to a thorough understanding of the fascist phenomenon, is further elucidated in a number of studies devoted to more specific subjects. Eugen

Weber's *Action Française* (1962), which is in fact an analysis of the whole of the French right, is indispensable for a deeper understanding of the general European thrust to the right. If we take Eugen Weber's book together with René Rémond's *The Right Wing in France from 1815 to De Gaulle*, expanded and revised in 1966, and Robert J. Soucy's 'The Nature of Fascism in France,' in *International Fascism*, we have three works which contain observations whose relevance transcends French politics. Stanley Hoffman's works on Vichy, 'Aspects du Régime de Vichy,' *Revue Française de Science Politique*, 1, 1 (janvier-mars 1956), and 'Collaborationism in France during World War II,' *Journal of Modern History*, 40, 3 (September 1968), are illuminating on what divides fascism from the right, and the observations, insights, and theoretical reflections contained in these articles make one look forward with impatience to the appearance of the forthcoming *Vichy 1940-1944: La Dernière Contre-Révolution Française.* The work done by Weber, Hoffman, and Rémond, to which should be added Raoul Girardet's 'Notes sur l'Esprit d'un Fascisme Français,' in *Revue Française de Science Politique*, V, 3 (1955), demonstrates clearly how misleading it is to identify fascism with the right. Further evidence for this is provided in a number of works devoted to other countries: Stanley Payne's *Falange: A History of Spanish Fascism* and Hugh Thomas's Introduction to José Antonio's *Selected Writings* for Spain; Weber's 'The Men of the Archangel,' in *International Fascism* and his chapter on Romania in *The European Right*; for Italy, Adrian Lyttelton's 'Fascism in Italy: The Second Wave,' in *International Fascism* and the chapters on Ideology and Culture in his *Seizure of Power*. Lyttelton's book, the most recent to be published on Italian fascism, is the best book on the subject, and is absolutely essential for any serious study of fascism.

In 'The Men of the Archangel,' in many respects a pioneering work, Weber strongly challenges the view that fascism was necessarily a reactionary middle-class movement. His argument constitutes the beginning of a comparative study of fascist sociology and fascist appeal, and at the same time takes issue with the view that fascism was the ideology of a declining bourgeois society. Weber draws our attention not only to the differences between Western and Eastern Europe—something Mosse and Woolf also do—but also to the general problem of underdeveloped countries, the role of fascism in non-Western societies where significant movements of the revolutionary left did not exist, where the working-classes were not organized, where the socialists were inaudible and the communists invisible. Here, fascism faced no radical competition, and the fascists' own radicalism was able to develop free of the need either to defend itself on the left or compromise too much with the forces of moderation (104-105).

Weber's conception of the nature of fascism is challenged in John Weiss' *Fascist Tradition* (1967), which is written in support of the view that fascism can unambiguously be classified as a right-wing conservative movement. John Weiss charges Eugen Weber with being too ready to take fascists' ideological statements at their face value. According to Weiss, Eugen Weber takes their 'leftism' far more seriously than he should (136).

To give such short shrift to a work as solidly documented as Weber's would require a book more solid, less hurried, and considerably more convincing than this. Moreover — though Weiss could not have known this — Max H. Kele, in his *Nazis and Workers* (1972), has implicitly confirmed what Weber said about fascist recruitment and fascism's appeal to workers. The book is a study of nazism, but has more general implications, since it throws serious doubt on the famous view of fascism as an 'extremism of the centre' which we find developed in Martin Seymour Lipset's *Political Man* (1960).

The criticisms that Weiss makes of Weber are also those Dante Germino makes of A. James Gregor. Germino, himself the author of a well-known work, *The Italian Fascist Party in Power*, and an important article, 'Italian Fascism in the History of Political Thought,' *Midwest Journal of Political Science*, VIII, 2 (May 1964), criticizes the author of *Ideology of Fascism* for taking literally some patently ridiculous and self-serving statements made by fascist propagandists, and for drawing a portrait of fascism which is unrecognizable because of the deep scars that have been omitted (*American Political Science Review*, no. 64 [June 1970], 165). The arguments put forward carry some weight: it is indeed difficult to subscribe to a definition of fascism as a 'humanism of labour,' or to agree that the fascist idea of the community should be defined in terms of the 'Kantian kingdom of ends' (20-21 of Gregor's work). Gregor's pursuit of scientific objectivity and intellectual detachment has led him a little too far. Nevertheless, his book cannot be fairly dismissed on the strength of this kind of shortcoming, since Gregor's scholarship is exemplary. His study of proto-fascism and of Mussolini's and Gentile's thought, and his analysis of Sorel, Pareto, Mosca, Michels and, of course, Gumplowicz, who is a veritable discovery on Gregor's part, are of an exceptionally high standard. Gregor gives a clear account of the genesis and maturation of fascist ideology, and his work is also invaluable in shedding light on the contribution of some minor intellectuals whom one can, if one wishes, treat as propagandists, but whose role in fascist Italy was considerable. Gregor deserves great credit for stressing that a Gini or a Papini are no less significant for an understanding of fascist ideology than a Gentile. These views, of course, place him in a totally opposed camp to such scholars as Ernst Nolte, for whom fascism can be summed up as Maurras, Mussolini, and Hitler, and yet it is the minor intellectuals who are read, and it is their thought that is most widely disseminated.

But Gregor's work is not solely a study of fascist ideology in Italy. It is the work of a social scientist who wishes not only to 'provide an historically accurate and objective account of the ideology of Mussolini's fascism,' but also 'to suggest a general typology of revolutionary mass movements that reflects contemporary thinking with respect to the description and analysis of totalitarian movements' (IX). This leads the author to consider fascism as 'a developmental dictatorship appropriate to partially developed or underdeveloped, and consequently status-deprived, national communities in a period of intense international competition for place and status' (XIII). What this approach finally leads to is not entirely unforeseeable: Leninism, Stalinism, the African socialisms, and Maoism are so many fascisms that are either unaware of, or do not acknowledge, their true names. The concluding part of the book should certainly be read with great circumspection, although the concept of 'developmental dictatorship' as a definition of fascism offers wide scope for future research. Nevertheless, it seems odd that Gregor should have thought an analysis of one model—the Italian—sufficient to justify the elaboration of such vast theories: surely, before tackling the underdeveloped countries and/or before presenting conclusions intended to be universal in their application, the author should have cast a brief glance in the direction of the other European fascisms. All in all, however, this highly controversial book, although written in a language at times far from transparent, is extremely stimulating and original and should be required reading for every student of fascism.

But it is Ernst Nolte who has set himself the most ambitious task. *Three Faces of Fascism* is an attempt to give a comprehensive explanation of fascism. The book is based on the most meticulous scholarship, the command of the material is impressive, and the methodological rigour is admirable. The work has been translated into English and French, and was acclaimed an immediate success. In reviews by, among others, Klaus Epstein, Hajo Holborn, James Joll, Walter Laqueur, George Mosse, Wolfgang Sauer, Fritz Stern, and Eugen Weber, this masterly work was hailed as a very great book.

Professor Nolte's work contains such a wealth of observations, information, insight, and throwaway ideas that are well worth keeping that inevitably one takes issue with some. First, his method. A philosopher by training, and of the school of Heidegger, Nolte is writing history within a philosophical framework. Thus it is that, having rejected the historical and typological approaches, he opts for the phenomenological approach, which he conceives as an attempt to return to Hegel's integration of philosophy and history (539-40). It is this method that permits Nolte to consider it legitimate to claim universal validity for his conclusions in spite of the fact that he limits his study to an analysis of the political ideas of three leaders—Maurras, Mussolini, and Hitler—and disregards not only their own movements and all the other European fascist movements, but also the socio-economic dimension of fascism. Nolte's analysis belongs strictly to the history of ideas, an approach perfectly legitimate in itself providing one is aware of the limitations and providing one reminds oneself that such broad generalizations as are found here cannot be put forward on the basis of such a narrow approach. Nolte is clearly floundering in problems of methodology, which explains how Action Française is elevated to the status of a fascism equivalent to nazism. The importance for Nolte of Action Française is clear: it provides him with the link he needs between the French and Soviet revolutions, testifies to the continuity of counterrevolutionary thought, and offers proof-positive of the very general character of that wave of revolt which swept nazism to power. In some ways, Ernst Nolte's approach recalls that of Gerhard Ritter and Friedrich Meinecke: Thomas More, for Ritter, Machiavelli, for Meinecke, and now Maurras, for Nolte, are so many proofs of the universality of evil, so many proofs that it was almost by accident, by a mere conjunction of political circumstances, that the Nazis arose in Germany.

This impression is considerably reinforced by the overriding importance Nolte attributes to the leaders of the movements, and by an observation he makes in this context which George Mosse, reviewing *Three Faces of Fascism* (*Journal of the History of Ideas*, 27 [1966], 624) has not failed to draw attention to. After the Führer's death, the Nazi leadership is said to have snapped back to its 'original position,' becoming once more 'a body of well-meaning and cultured Europeans.' This sort of statement casts doubt on Nolte's understanding of Nazi ideology as well as on his analysis of bourgeois society. Moreover, nazism is by implication reduced to something very minor: it arrives in this world, and disappears from it, with the Führer, and the concentration camp commandant quietly returns home to become again what he has never really ceased to be—an exemplary citizen and a lover of high culture. But if this is true, is nazism, as Nolte thinks, really dead? Surely it cannot be, if all it needs is the reappearance of a Hitler to turn a good, cultivated, and law-abiding European into a Nazi?

Nolte's definition of fascism has a dual aspect: fascism, in his view, is to be seen as a revolt against the universal process of secularization, democratization, and international integration in the modern era; in its final stage, fascism takes on the form of a resistance to 'transcendence.' 'That Maurras' whole thought represents a resistance to transcendence and unconditional defence of the autarkic-sovereign, martial, aristocratic state of the *ancien régime* as a paradigm for France for all time, can hardly be doubted' (530; all quotations from the 1969 Mentor edition). A page earlier, the argument reaches its conclusion: 'The power of "antinature" fills Hitler with dread: it is this "going beyond" in human nature which is capable of transforming the essence of human order and relations—transcendence. What Hitler—and not only Hitler—feels to be threatened are certain basic structures of social existence. He too—like Maurras—is afraid *of* man *for* man. But he did not only think, he acted. And in his actions, he carried his principle to its irrevocable end. Hence it is possible to define Hitler's

radical fascism, which called itself "National Socialism," as follows:
NATIONAL SOCIALISM WAS THE DEATH THROES OF THE SOVEREIGN, MARTIAL,
INWARDLY ANTAGONISTIC GROUP. IT WAS THE PRACTICAL AND VIOLENT RESIS-
TANCE TO TRANSCENDENCE' (529).

What Nolte does not tell us, as Wolfgang Sauer has already pointed out,
is why this revolt was most radical in Germany? If the modernization
process was universal, was fascist revolt also universal? If it was, why does
Nolte deal only with France, Italy, and Germany? If it was not, why did the
fascist revolt occur only in these (and some other) countries? (Wolfgang
Sauer, 'National Socialism: Totalitarianism or Fascism,' *American Historical Review*, LXXIII, 2 [December 1967], 413). Anyone familiar with
the fascist movements will find a large number of questions left unanswered, although it is true that these questions are easier to ask than to
answer. Nevertheless, it is impossible, when one has come to the end of this
exceptional work, not to be left with a feeling of unreality and to wonder
whether nazism has not been reduced to the level of an abstraction, an
intellectual exercise.

This feeling is not dispelled by the second aspect of Nolte's definition of
fascism, which he presents in terms of anti-Marxism: 'FASCISM IS
ANTI-MARXISM WHICH SEEKS TO DESTROY THE ENEMY BY THE EVOLVEMENT OF
A RADICALLY OPPOSED AND YET RELATED IDEOLOGY AND BY THE USE OF ALMOST
IDENTICAL, AND YET TYPICALLY MODIFIED, METHODS, ALWAYS, HOWEVER,
WITHIN THE UNYIELDING FRAMEWORK OF NATIONAL SELF-ASSERTION AND
AUTONOMY.' This definition implies that without Marxism, there is no
fascism, that fascism is at the same time closer to and further from communism than is liberal anti-communism... (40). This reads very much
like something from the good old totalitarian analysis, which is itself not
very new but dates back to the twenties and thirties: the Italian and French
fascists both spoke at length of the points of similarity between communism
and fascism. For Drieu La Rochelle, Stalinism was 'a red fascism' — which,
by the way, would not surprise Professor Gregor. Here again we have an
example of a contemporary arriving at an analysis which modern scientific
research hails as a revolutionary achievement.

Yet even those fascists who recognized the common ground between
themselves and the Marxists, while simultaneously fighting them to the
death — and this goes for Degrelle and d'Annunzio, Doriot and Valois —
always considered their real, natural enemy to be liberalism. This is particularly true as regards the origins of fascist thought. Nor does it seem to
be anti-Marxism that lies at the root of Hitler's thought: is it not rather
racialism and anti-Semitism? Was the enemy not the Jew, rather than the
Marxist? Is this not a point of dissimilarity between nazism and fascism
that simply cannot be ignored? Fascism was not, then, as Nolte would have
us believe, simply a shadow of Marxism. It was an entirely separate pheno-

menon and had a reality of its own which Nolte, transported into other realms by the phenomenological method, does not always perceive.

In sum, however, even when one cannot agree with Nolte on every point, indeed, even when one is unable to agree with him on the essential points, it is obvious that this book will serve as a landmark to scholars for many years to come.

## NOTES

I am deeply indebted to the Warden and Fellows of St. Antony's College, Oxford, for having elected me to a Wolfson Visiting Fellowship for the 1973-1974 academic year. It was here, in this true home of scholarship, that I was able to prepare this study, after the Yom Kippur War.

1. See the bibliographical part of this essay. As far as possible, the quotations refer to the English translations of the primary sources.

2. Hugh Seton-Watson, 'Fascism, Right and Left,' in *Journal of Contemporary History*, I, 1 (1966), 188.

3. N. Kogan, 'Fascism as a Political System,' in S. J. Woolf, ed., *The Nature of Fascism* (London, 1968), 16.

4. Eugen Weber, *Varieties of Fascism* (New York, 1964), 10-11.

5. Cf. ibid., 9-10; Martin Seliger, 'Fundamental and Operative Ideology: The Two Principal Dimensions of Political Argumentation,' *Policy Sciences*, I (1970), 325-27.

6. Cf. S. J. Woolf's Introduction in *European Fascism* (London, 1968), 9, and Michael Hurst, 'What is Fascism,' in *The Historical Journal*, XI, 1 (1968), 166 and 183.

7. Oswald Mosley, *The Greater Britain* (London, 1932), 14.

8. Benito Mussolini, 'Political and Social Doctrine,' in *Fascism: Doctrine and Institutions* (Rome, 1935), 31, 34, n. 2. Among other basic texts of fascist thought and legislation, this volume contains 'Fundamental Ideas' written for Mussolini by Gentile.

9. Seliger, op. cit., 327-28.

10. Mussolini, 'Political and Social Doctrine,' 33.

11. Ibid., 26: 'All doctrines aim at directing the activities of men towards a given objective; but these activities in their turn react on the doctrine, modifying and adjusting it to new needs, or outstripping it.'

12. *Combat*, 2 (February 1936).

13. Quoted in Michel Winock, 'Une parabole fasciste: Gilles de Drieu La Rochelle,' *Le Mouvement Social*, 80 (July 1972), 29.

14. Georges Valois, *Le Fascisme* (Paris 1927), 21.

15. Oswald Mosley, *Tomorrow we live* (London, 1938), 57.

16. Cf. the recent studies by H. Stuart Hughes, *Consciousness and Society: the Reorientation of European Social Thought 1890-1930* (New York, 1961); Gerhard Masur, *Prophets of Yesterday: Studies in European Culture 1890-1914* (New York, 1966); W. Warren Wagar, ed., *European Intellectual History since Darwin and Marx [Selected Essays]* (New York, 1966); John Weiss, ed., *The Origins of Modern Consciousness* (Detroit, 1965).

17. Giovanni Gentile, 'The Philosophic Basis of Fascism,' *Foreign Affairs*, VI (1927-28), 295-96.

18. H. Stuart Hughes, op. cit., 38-39. Cf. in particular Carlton J. H. Hayes, *A Generation of Materialism 1871-1900* (New York, 1963) and Jacques Barzun, *Race, a Study in Superstition* (New York, 1965), 162.

19. Fritz Stern's *The Politics of Cultural Despair* is the best treatment of Langbehn, Lagarde, and Moeller van den Bruck.

20. George L. Mosse, *The Crisis of German Ideology: Intellectual Origins of the Third Reich* (New York, 1964), 4-5.

21. Zeev Sternhell, *Maurice Barrès et le nationalism français* (Paris, 1972), 263-73.

22. Maurice Barrès, 'Que faut-il faire?,' *Le Courrier de l'Est,* (2ème série) (12 May 1898); idem., *Mes Cahiers,* 14 vols. (1929-57), II, 197; idem., 'Socialisme et Nationalisme,' *La Patrie* (27 February 1903).

23. Enrico Corradini, 'Nationalism and the Syndicates,' speech made at the Nationalist Convention, Rome, 16 March 1919, in Adrian Lyttelton's excellent anthology *Italian Fascisms from Pareto to Gentile* (London, 1973), 159.

24. Cf. the important article by Thierry Maulnier, 'Charles Maurras et le Socialisme,' *La Revue Universelle,* LXVIII, 19 (January 1937), 169. Maulnier is quoting from Maurras's *Dictionnaire Politique et Critique.*

25. Pierre Biétry, *Le Socialisme et les Jaunes* (Paris, 1906), and more particularly 99 and passim.

26. Cf. Stephen Wilson, 'The Antisemitic Riots of 1898 in France,' *The Historical Journal,* XVI, 4 (1973), 789-806.

27. Jules Soury, *Le Système Nerveux Central* (Paris, 1899), 1778; *Campagne Nationaliste (1894-1901)* (Paris, 1902), 65.

28. Enzo Santarelli, 'Le Socialisme National en Italie: Précédents et origines,' *Le Mouvement Social,* 50, (January-March 1965).

29. Corradini, 'The Principles of Nationalism,' in A. Lyttelton, op. cit., 147.

30. Cf. Corradini's 'The Proletarian Nations and Nationalism' (1911), in A. Lyttelton, op. cit., 149-51.

31. Corradini, 'Nationalism and Democracy' (political speech 1913), in A. Lyttelton, op. cit., 152.

32. Corradini, 'The Cult of the Warrior Morality' (December 1913), in A. Lyttelton, op. cit., 155-58.

33. A. James Gregor, *The Ideology of Fascism: the Rationale of Totalitarianism* (New York, 1969), 37-39.

34. Vilfredo Pareto, from *Les Systèmes Socialistes,* in A. Lyttelton, op. cit., 72-75.

35. Ibid., 78.

36. Gregor, op. cit., 78-80.

37. Ibid., 52.

38. Roberto Michels, *Political Parties* (London, n.d.), 395.

39. Ibid., 407. The whole of Chapter II of Part VI of this work is of considerable interest.

40. 'Le Syndicalisme et le Socialisme en Allemagne,' in *Syndicalisme et Socialisme* (Paris, 1908), 25. Speeches made at the conference held in Paris on 3 April 1907.

41. Arturo Labriola, 'Le Syndicalisme et le Socialisme en Italie,' in ibid., 11 and 9-13.

42. Hubert Lagardelle, 'Le Syndicalisme et le Socialisme en France,' in ibid., 36.

43. Victor Griffuelhes, *L'Action Syndicaliste* (Paris, 1908), 37.

44. Emile Pouget, *La Confédération Générale du Travail* (Paris, 1909), 35-36.

45. Michels, op. cit., 369.

46. 'Déclaration,' in *Cahiers du Cercle Proudhon,* I (January 1912), 1.

47. Santarelli, op. cit., 50.

48. Ibid., 52-53.

49. Lyttelton, op. cit., 98.

50. Ibid., 211-12.

51. Hendrik de Man, Manifesto to the Members of the POB, quoted in Peter Dodge, *Beyond Marxism: The Faith and Works of Hendrik de Man* (The Hague, 1966), 197.

52. Marcel Déat, 'L'Evolution du Socialisme,' in *L'Effort,* (25 September 1940).

53. Mussolini, 'Political and Social Doctrine,' 26.

54. Mosley, *Fascism: 100 Questions asked and answered* (London, 1936), Question 2.

55. 'What a Legionary believes,' Romanian Fascist Catechism, in Weber, op. cit., 169.

56. Paul Marion, *Programme du Parti Populaire Français* (Paris, 1938), 83.

57. Léon Degrelle, *Révolution des âmes* (Paris, 1938). The term counter-civilization is used in very much the same sense as Annie Kriegel uses the term counter-society in her well-known works on French communism; cf. particularly *Les Communistes Français: essais d'ethnographie politique* (Paris, 1970).

58. Georges Valois, *Fascisme* (Paris, 1927), 15-16.

59. Thierry Maulnier, *Mythes Socialistes* (Paris, 1936), 169-70.

60. Michael Hurst, 'What is Fascism,' 184, For the English fascist James Strachey Barnes, fascism was a result of the failure of 'liberal statecraft' (Barnes, *The Universal Aspects of Fascism* [London, 1928], 63.)

61. Mussolini, 'Political and Social Doctrine,' 26.

62. Mussolini, 'Fundamental Ideas,' 8.

63. Gentile, 'The Philosophic Basis of Fascism,' 293.

64. José Antonio Primo de Rivera, *Selected Writings*, ed. and intro. Hugh Thomas (London, 1972), 65.

65. Mussolini, 'Political and Social Doctrine,' 21.

66. Marcel Déat, *Pensée allemande et pensée française* (Paris, 1944), 63 and 99.

67. Pierre Drieu La Rochelle, *Chronique Politique 1934-1942* (Paris, 1943), 161. Twenty-five years earlier, in 1912, Barrès had said, 'The eighteenth century, which would like to go on living, is in its last throes. We have done with asking its advice on how to run our lives.' (Speeches in the Chamber, June 1912).

68. Mussolini, *Fascism*, Appendix, 40 (speech before the New National Directory of the Party, 7 April 1926).

69. James Strachey Barnes, *The Universal Aspects of Fascism* (London, 1928), 164.

70. Degrelle, op. cit., 145.

71. Mosley, *The Greater Britain*, 152.

72. Déat, Marquet, Montagnon, *Néo-Socialisme, Ordre, Autorité*, Nation (Paris, 1933), 43.

73. Degrelle, op. cit., 151.

74. Drieu La Rochelle, *Gilles*, 179, 340-42, 384, 455.

75. Georges Valois, *Révolution Nationale* (Paris, 1924), 97 and 151.

76. Degrelle, op. cit., 153-54.

77. Primo de Rivera, op. cit., 57.

78. José Streel, *Ce qu'il faut penser de Rex* (Brussells, n.d.), 106-108.

79. Gentile, 'The Philosophic Basis of Fascism,' 291-92.

80. Mussolini, *Fascism*, Appendix, 9, 19, 36. Cf. Primo de Rivera, op. cit., 137: 'Life is a militia and must be lived in a spirit purified by service and sacrifice.' Cf. also Degrelle, op. cit., 6: 'The easy life is the death of idealism. Nothing revives it better than the lash of the hard life.'

81. Degrelle, op. cit., 2-3.

82. Mussolini, *Fascism*, Appendix, 19 and 36.

83. Marion, op. cit., 99 and 104.

84. Hendrik de Man, 'Manifesto to the Members of the POB, July 1940,' in Dodge, op. cit., 197.

85. Quoted in Michèle Cotta, *La Collaboration 1940-1944* (Paris, 1964), 128.

86. Mosley, *The Greater Britain*, op. cit., 159.

87. Degrelle, op. cit., 3-4.

88. Mussolini, 'Political and Social Doctrine,' 19.

89. Drieu La Rochelle, *Chronique Politique*, 69.

90. Drieu La Rochelle, quoted in Winock, op. cit., 44.

91. 'The Futurist Manifesto,' in *Le Figaro*, February 1909.

92. Soury, *Campagne Nationaliste*, 185.

93. Drieu La Rochelle, 'Verra-t-on un Parti national et socialiste?' *La Lutte des Jeunes*, no. 2 (4 March 1934).

94. 'The Futurist Manifesto.'

95. Cf. Marion, op. cit., 85-95.

96. Ibid., 91-94.

97. Drieu La Rochelle, *Chronique Politique*, 69.

98. Drieu La Rochelle, *Avec Doriot* (Paris, 1937), 12.

99. Cf. for instance Primo de Rivera, op. cit., 52-54: 'We would be just another party if we were to formulate a programme of concrete solutions'; or Streel, op. cit., 105.

100. Mussolini, 'Fundamental Ideas,' in *Fascism*, 13.

101. Mosley, *The Greater Britain*, 159.

102. Mussolini, *Fascism*, Appendix, 38.

103. Streel, op. cit., 105.

104. Drieu La Rochelle, *Chronique Politique*, 15-16.

105. Valois, *Révolution Nationale*, 13.

106. Ibid.

107. Drieu's 'Gilles' never ceased to dream of a union of the 'valiant,' of all the rebels, of young bourgeois and young workers who together would overthrow the 'freemason dictatorship' (*Gilles*, 422). For Paul Marion, this alliance would be one of 'all those who have had enough, all those who want a change' (*Programme of the PPF*, 110).

108. Cf. Ruggero Zangrandi, *Le long voyage à travers le fascisme* (French trans. Paris, 1963). Cf. also George L. Mosse, 'The Genesis of Fascism,' in *Journal of Contemporary History*, I, 1 (1966), 17.

109. Degrelle, *Révolution des âmes*, 146.

110. Cf. Winock, op. cit., 40.

111. Déat, *Pensée allemande et pensée française*, 97-98.

112. Quoted in Weber, op. cit., 41-42.

113. Quoted in Gregor, op. cit. 213.

114. Streel, op. cit.

115. Primo de Rivera, op. cit., 49.

116. Gregor, op. cit., 212-13.

117. Ibid., 214.

118. Mussolini, 'Fundamental Ideas,' 9-10; cf. Marion, op. cit., 98: 'A man is not just a certain number of pounds of organic matter. He is someone who has a long ancestry, a long history, comes from a particular region, has a particular job.'

119. Gregor, op. cit., 220.

120. Mussolini, 'Fundamental Ideas,' 10-11, cf. also 39.

121. Gentile, 'The Philosophic Basis of Fascism,' 303.

122. Mosley, *Fascism: 100 Questions*, 9 and *The Greater Britain*, 22.

123. Primo de Rivera, op. cit., 55.

124. Streel, op. cit., 113.

125. Déat, *Pensée allemande et pensée française*, 84-85.

126. A. Rocco, 'The Political Doctrine of Fascism,' in C. Cohen, ed., *Communism, Fascism and Democracy* (New York, 1964), 341-42; cf. also Mussolini, 'Political and Social Doctrine,' 22-23.

127. Gentile, 'Philosophic Basis of Fascism,' 303-04.

128. Primo de Rivera, op. cit., 133.

129. Marion, op. cit., 94.

130. Déat, *Pensée allemande et pensée française*, 110.

131. Marion, op. cit., 93-94.

132. Déat, *Pensée allemande et pensée française*, 110. Cf. also René Rémond, *Introduction à l'histoire de notre temps: le XXème siècle de 1914 à nos jours* (Paris, 1974), 126-27.

133. George L. Mosse, 'The Poet and the Exercise of Political Power: Gabriele d'Annunzio,' *Yearbook of Comparative and General Literature*, 22 (1973), 32-33.

134. Eugen Weber, in Introduction to Hans Rogger and Eugen Weber, *The European Right: A Historical Profile* (Berkeley and Los Angeles, 1966), 17-18.

135. Streel, op. cit., 106.

136. Quoted in Gregor, op. cit., 225.

137. Cf. Weber, *Varieties of Fascism*, 37-38.

138. Cf. J. L. Talmon, *Destin d'Israel: l'Unique et l'Universel* (Paris, 1967), 75-81.

139. In 1933, Hendrick de Man's 'Plan du Travail' was adopted, on his recommendation, by an overwhelming majority of the Belgian Workers Party. The 'Planing' movement subsequently developed rapidly throughout Western Europe.

140. Hendrick de Man, 'Clarification,' in *Le Peuple*, 24 September 1933, quoted in Dodge, op. cit., 143.

141. Dodge, op. cit., 178.

142. Marcel Déat, *Perspectives Socialistes* (Paris, 1930) especially 43-85. Déat himself quotes Hendrick de Man, *Au-delà du Marxisme*, 45, 63.

143. Dodge, op. cit., 144.

144. Ibid., 160.

145. Cf. the address at Charleroi on May Day 1941 which served as the prototype of the speeches that he subsequently gave to various gatherings within the Labour Movement, *Travaille*, 6 May 1941, in Dodge, op. cit., 202.

146. Déat, *Néo-Socialisme*, 90.

147. Adrien Marquet, *Néo-Socialisme*, 57, 60. It was at this point in Marquet's speech, 'Are not the nations in the process of moving onto the plane of a new reality?' that Blum made his famous 'I can tell you, I am appalled.'

148. Gregor, op. cit., 89.

149. Déat, reply to an inquiry by the weekly *Monde*, 1 February 1930, 10.

150. Déat, *Néo-Socialisme*, 76, cf. 25-26 and 74 (Montagnon).

151. Drieu La Rochelle, 'Sous Doumergue,' in *La Lutte des Jeunes* (7 May 1934).

152. Streel, op. cit., 143.

153. Cf. Primo de Rivera, op. cit., 55, 62; Mosley, *Fascism: 100 Questions,* Question 8; Denis, *Principes Rexistes*, 17.

154. Primo de Rivera, op. cit., 53-64. At the same moment, at the other end of Europe, Codreanu was offering a doctrine which neither clashed with the nationalistic prejudices of workers and peasants nor aroused their suspicion of city slickers out to use and discard them (Eugen Weber, 'The Men of Archangel,' in *Journal of Contemporary History*, I, 1 [1966], 118-19).

155. Michael Hurst, 'What is Fascism,' 168-69.

156. Mosley, *The Greater Britain*, 18-19.

157. Primo de Rivera, op. cit., 180.

158. Denis, *Principes Rexistes,* 28.

159. Weber, *Varieties of Fascism*, 50-51.

160. Déat-Marquet-Montagnon, *Néo-Socialisme*, 23-24, 32-33, 53-54, 74, 95-98.

161. Dodge, op. cit., 180; cf. also 182-92.

162. Primo de Rivera, op. cit., 65.

163. Mosley, *The Greater Britain*, 20.

164. The title of *Néo-Socialisme: Ordre, Autorité, Nation.*

165. Primo de Rivera, op. cit., 133.

166. Mussolini, *Fascism*, Appendix, 40.

167. Mussolini, 'Political and Social Doctrine,' 27.

168. Mussolini, *Fascism*, Appendix, 38-39.

169. Mussolini, 'Fundamental Ideas,' 11.

170. Ibid., 12; Gentile, 'The Philosophic Basis of Fascism,' 302.

ZEEV STERNHELL

171. Barnes, op. cit., 59-60.

172. Mosley, *Fascism: 100 Questions*, Question 35.

173. Mosley, *The Greater Britain*, 27.

174. Primo de Rivera, op. cit., 178.

175. Weber, 'The Men of the Archangel,' 104.

176. Barnes, op. cit., 14-15; cf. also a characteristic passage by Robert Brasillach: '. . . We do not have much in common, in spite of appearances, Mr Conservative. We are defending a few truths in the way we think they ought to be defended, that is violently, passionately, disrespectfully, with our lives. At times, this has been of some value to us, Mr Conservative. It may be to you, one day. At moments when you think you can do without those compromising bodyguards, you prefer to talk of other things and look at them from a long way away. They are running their own risks, aren't they? That is their affair, not yours. It was you that said it, Mr Conservative. Their own risks. Not yours. We are not mercenaries. We are not the shock-troops of the *bien-pensants*. We are not the SA of conservatism.' (To a conservative, *Je suis partout*, 23 February 1940).

177. Eugen Weber, 'The Men of Archangel,' 124-25.

# PART V

# 10

# Fascism and the Economy

ALAN S. MILWARD

Attempts to formulate an accepted definition of fascism have never been wholly successful but there remains a measure of agreement that it is an apt, just, and convenient label for a particular set of political attitudes. There is less agreement about the question whether fascism constituted a set of political beliefs forming a separate political system, although it now seems quite usual to write of 'the fascist powers' in the inter-war period, emphasizing the essential similarities of the political systems of Italy and Germany. Did this similarity extend beyond the purely political sphere? Was there also a specific set of economic attitudes and policies which may equally aptly be labelled 'fascist'?

The confusion over whether fascism was a right-wing or a left-wing movement has in fact been largely due to the inability to fit the *economic* policies of fascism into these convenient mental pigeon-holes. The governments of Hitler and Mussolini ran the economy in each case through a battery of economic controls to which left-wing governments, outside the Soviet Union, could still only aspire, but the beneficiaries of their economic policies have usually been depicted as belonging to those social groups which would have usually supported more right-wing parties. If there were any consistent principles of economic thought and of economic action in fascism, how far did they represent the economic interests of those groups who supported fascist parties and governments? As soon as the feeble idea that fascism was solely a new label for personal and political opportunism is abandoned, the problem must be faced as to what forms of social discontent the movement fed on and what demands for social change it represented. For even if neither the political nor the economic ideas of fascism are accepted as constituting a consistent ideological view of the world, and even if both fascist economic and political programmes for action are interpreted as deliberate efforts to harness all discontents, however impossible to reconcile, it must still be accepted that support for fascist policies in German society was at least as strong as for any other policies and that this may also have been true of some periods in Italy. What did fascist movements see as the future of human society? Was there a distinct political economy of fascism? And how did it differ from that of other political groupings?

The more research that is published the less do existing theories of the political economy of fascism carry conviction. They are rapidly sinking to

[379]

the status of arguments cited only because they can be conveniently contradicted. There does not now seem any reason to linger over them here and
they will be described only briefly. Such brevity cannot do proper justice to
the complexity of some of these ideas, but the intention of the essay is to
suggest the conclusions to which current research is pointing rather than to
analyse or criticise these theoretical concepts. After some of the existing
theories have been reviewed, therefore, the extent to which the results of
recent research amplify and modify them will be considered. The essay
concludes with some suggestions which might help to formulate a more
acceptable theory of the political economy of fascism.

## THE EXISTING HYPOTHESES

When the experience of fascism in power was still confined to Italy, the
economic policy of fascism was often construed as an attempt to modernise
and develop the economy. This was the standpoint of what is still one of the
few works to try to deal in a comprehensive way with fascist economic
policy (W. G. Welk, *The Fascist Economic Policy* [Cambridge, Mass.,
1938]). Welk saw the main motive of fascist economic policy as the achievement of Italian national aspirations which had been long thwarted. In this
respect the popular movement for intervention in the first world war, he
argued, had shattered the old political framework and had produced a
coalition of political and economic interests which was able to force
through a strongly nationalistic economic programme. The normal workings of government were suspended and concentrated in a more centralised
and powerful state. The modernisation of the economy was one aspect of
the modernisation of the state, but this modernisation necessarily was an
intensely nationalistic one in which such goals as self-sufficiency and
rearmament received the highest economic priority. Rapid industrialisation and a high rate of investment in social overhead capital were an
integral part of the fascist experience.

The idea that rapid economic development might require a greater
degree of coercive power from the central government is frequently
expressed. But the German experience shows that this is a very insufficient
interpretation of fascism. Indeed any interpretation which depends on
showing that the Italian economy in the 1920s and the German economy in
the 1930s were in similar stages of development is not worth considering.
Whereas Italy in the 1920s was still in the throes of a rapid industrialisation
which had begun in the decade before the first world war, Germany's
economic problems were those of a highly developed economy in which the
comparable period of rapid industrialisation had been three quarters of a
century earlier. The proportional contribution to the GNP made by the
industrial sector of the Italian economy at the time of the March on Rome
had already been reached in Germany in the 1870s. In 1921 in Italy 24 per

cent of the economically active population was employed in the industrial sector; in Germany in 1925 the proportion was 42.2 per cent.

But the idea that particular types of government may be related to particular stages of economic development is a most persistent one. There have been several attempts to define the precise point of economic and social development at which fascism may occur in societies. Of these one of the more complex is that of Clemenz who, using the term on a wider front than here, suggests various points in political evolution, at stages of economic development certainly as widely apart as those of Italy in 1922 and Germany in 1933, at which a fascist 'counter-revolution' may emerge. Fascism, he argues, is inherent in capitalist society (M. Clemenz, *Gesellschaftliche Ursprünge des Faschismus* [Frankfurt a.M., 1972]).

In fact it was the German experience after 1933 which brought to the forefront this interpretation of fascism which had until then received less consideration. It laid the emphasis less on the nationalistic elements of fascist economic policy than on its anti-socialist and anti-communist aspects. The extreme form of this interpretation is the theory that the fascist state was the political tool of the major capital interests ('big business'). Once incorporated into Lenin's theory of imperialism, this view appeared as the statement that fascism was the last stage of imperialism. As profits declined 'monopoly capital' brought into power a government of despotic terror and brutality whose ultimate purpose was to unleash a war of conquest and thereby preserve imperialism and with it capitalism. This view is still maintained in publications in the Soviet Union and the German Democratic Republic. It is the theoretical basis of the work of Eichholtz where it is expressed in its most scholarly form backed by considerable research. 'The fascist state,' writes Eichholtz, 'was a state of monopolies, its policy the concentrated pressure of their economic relationships, that is to say of the conditions and needs of the ruling monopolies. The war was not an outburst of some kind of "demonic" power in and around Hitler; it was a war of monopolies for the control of Europe and the world. The fascist regime was entrusted with the function of preparing and carrying out such a war' (D. Eichholtz, *Geschichte der deutschen Kriegswirtschaft 1939-1945*, I, 1939-1941 [Berlin, 1969], 6).

The precise relationship between big business and fascism is perhaps the single aspect of the political economy of fascism which has come in for more attention than all others. The drive towards economic self-sufficiency and the high priority given to rearmament, together with the savage repression of socialist parties and labour movements, lent support to the idea that the fascist state was, in the economic sphere, a tool of 'business interests.' Without accepting the theoretical basis of the views of a writer like Eichholtz in their full rigour, many authors have proposed schematic explanations of fascism which link it closely to the pursuit of the economic interests of manufacturers and businessmen in general or to those of some particular section of the business community. The public divergences of interest between different industrial groups in Germany and Italy always suggested that any theory presupposing that the major capital interests were a monolithic bloc with a set of common goals would be some way from the truth. That there were different shades of support amongst different industries for fascist regimes is frequently suggested even by some who subscribe absolutely to the concept of fascism as the last stage of monopoly capitalism.

Kuczynski suggested that the business interests supporting fascism in Germany were those who benefitted most precisely from the pursuit of economic self-sufficiency whereas manufacturers of consumer goods or those who depended heavily on exports for their profits were altogether less enthusiastic (J. Kuczynski, *Darstellung der Lage der Arbeiter in Deutschland von 1933 bis 1945*, sect. 6, vol. 1 of *Die Geschichte der Lage der Arbeiter unter dem Kapitalismus*, [Berlin, 1964]). There have been several attempts to break down the real interests of big business in Germany along similar lines. Gossweiler attributes the birth of the fascist state to an internecine struggle among major capital interests which ultimately saw the victory of that group supporting nationalist 'German' policies over a similar group whose interests were more international (K. Gossweiler, *Grossbanken, Industriemonopole, Staat. Ökonomie und Politik des staatsmonopolistischen Kapitalismus in Deutschland, 1914-1932* [Berlin, 1971]). In a more sophisticated analysis Czichon divides the business world into those who wished to reinvigorate the economy after the crash of 1929 by orthodox Keynesian policies of reflation and those who preferred to effect the same thing by rearmament expenditure and who therefore gave their support to the NSDAP. An eventual split between the Keynesians over a policy of economic expansion in collaboration with the trade union movement shifted the decisive advantage to the Nazi side. (E. Czichon, *Wer verhalf Hitler zur Macht?* [Cologne, 1967]). These are all theories which relate specifically to the events in Germany but their starting point is to be found in earlier theoretical interpretations of the rise to power of the fascist party in Italy (E. Nolte, 'Zeitgenössische Theorien über den Faschismus,' in *Vierteljahrshefte für Zeitgeschichte*, no. 15 [1967]). The position that fascism was the final stage of the imperialism of monopoly capital was laid down by the Third International in 1935 and this basic framework has since been used to incorporate a wide variety of more complicated explanations of the relationship between major capital interests and fascism without altering the underlying assumptions. The capacity of this interpretation to absorb and turn to purpose the results of historical research may be seen by tracing the evolution of the simpler ideas of 1935 into more complicated positions as indisputable evidence about the more popular origins of fascism has been published. The two editions of Guérin's work reveal this development most neatly (D. Guérin, *Sur le fascisme; fascisme et grand capital* [Paris, 1936, 1965]).

The common ground between such interpretations is that they suggest a positive *intention* on the part of major capital interests to bring to power a despotic government pursuing economic policies advantageous to them. Kühnl, however, has proposed a different scenario in which major capital interests, suspicious of the revolutionary postures of fascism and cautious of the support for fascism from other sections of the community, turned to its support only when it was the last available means of preserving the capitalist system. As the National Socialist Party took over the votes and influence of right and centre-right parties in Germany after 1929, business interests gradually came to see it as their only defence against an even worse fate, he argues, and tried to manipulate it as best they could in their own interests. He suggests that in certain complex historical circumstances the inherent instability of liberal capitalism may give rise to the fascist state as the last possible defender of the capitalist order. More than that, fascist movements only came to power with the collusion of the very authorities whose duty it was to protect liberal democracy (R. Kühnl, *Formen bürger-licher Herrschaft; Liberalismus, Faschismus* [Reinbek bei Hamburg, 1971]). Although this thesis seems better to fit the facts that are so far known about the relationship between social forces and the NSDAP, it seems in one area to be on weak ground. Just how likely was the threat of a 'collapse of the capitalist system' in Germany in 1933 or in Italy in 1922?

One big stumbling block in making any theoretical connections along such lines between the fascist state and major capital interests is the anti-capitalist rhetoric of much fascist propaganda. There is also the fact that early fascist manifestoes everywhere, including Germany and Italy, proposed radical changes in taxation and landholding and controls on the use of capital. An avowedly 'anti-capitalist' element existed in fascist parties. By using the division of capital into different economic categories according to the schema of Max Weber, Schweitzer tried to come to grips with these troublesome facts. (A. Schweitzer, *Big Business in the Third Reich*, [Bloomington, Ind., 1964]). The attitude towards capitalism of many whose businesses would be better described as 'small' or 'medium,' he argued, was quite different from that of big business which they regarded more as enemy than ally. The apparent collapse of the capitalist economy in 1929 revived the strong anti-capitalist feeling among many lower-middle-class groups, and it was precisely in this area that the ideology of the NSDAP gained ground. Studies of voting behaviour have gone some way in confirming this generalisation. Thus what Schweitzer calls 'an economic program of counterrevolutionary anticapitalism' evolved side by side with the 'cherished goal of big business of employing the power of the state for the invigoration of capitalist institutions that had suffered during the Great Depression' (4). What emerged was a period of 'partial fascism' in which a far from monolithic state pursued these contradictory economic goals. It lasted until 1936, the beginning of the second Four Year Plan. The plan meant the victory of the Weberian category of 'political capitalism' over that of 'industrial capitalism' and the triumph of 'big business' over small, giving rise ultimately to what Schweitzer calls an 'organised capitalism,' in which major capital and military interests shaped the economic and foreign policies of the government. But in Schweitzer's exposition the stage of 'partial fascism' is a necessary one on the road to 'total fascism,' and a temporary and confused pursuit of anti-capitalist policies an essential prelude to the ultimate creation of a fascist capitalism. He does not seek to extend this interpretation to Italy but, superficially, it would not be hard to identify a period ending in 1926 or afterwards when the fascist state, in the economic sense, could be said to be 'partial' there.

Schweitzer's thesis marks the boundary between those interpretations which insist on the ultimate importance of the links between big business and fascism and a set of absolutely opposing interpretations which insist on the essentially anti-capitalist nature of fascism. Simplified greatly, the general standpoint of these is that fascism was a movement of those social groups threatened by the apparently inexorable trend of the capitalist economy towards increasing industrialisation and concentration of capital. It drew its support from handicraft workers, shopkeepers, white-collar workers, and workers in the agricultural sector. This new political alliance demanded an economic programme aimed at stability rather than growth, at preserving economic inefficiencies in the interests of social harmony rather than at an intensification of economic development. Just as it contradicted all the political tenets of liberalism so, it is argued, did fascism also overturn the liberal concept of 'economic man.' Rejecting the concept of man as a rational being, fascism rejected also the rational constructs of economics. The world of irrationality which it sought to create was essentially antagonistic to the aims of capitalist society. It sought an irrational and perhaps unobtainable social and economic harmony of interest, a world of military heroes, of a secure and stable bourgeoisie, and of a sturdy and equally stable peasantry, a return to an imaginary pre-capitalist Golden Age.

This particular range of interpretation naturally enough attributes a very low priority to the economic aspects of the fascist state. Indeed its exponents seldom venture into the economic field at all. They are, however, concerned to draw an important distinction between conservatism, or the 'traditional right' and fascism, which they regard as a radical and revolutionary (or counter-revolutionary) force. This distinction made in the field of political theory is so profound as to constitute also a powerful inference as to the political economy of fascism. The economic tendencies of fascist states within this interpretation would be more correctly described as anti-capitalist than as capitalist. They were an attempt to arrest the dynamic of economic development and the social changes which that dynamic brought with it, or to value other priorities so much higher as to make that dynamic irrelevant (E. Weber, *Varieties of Fascism* [New York, 1964]).

## THE SOCIAL BASIS OF FASCISM

The existing theories on the political economy of fascism cover virtually the full spectrum of possibilities, yet not one of them is entirely convincing. Some of the other essays published in this book show that historians, political scientists, and sociologists have, very belatedly, begun to find out something real rather than merely hypothetical about the membership of and support for fascist movements. Much of what is known about the answers to these vital questions will be published in the *Proceedings of the Bergen Conference on International Fascism* (to be published in 1976 by Norwegian Universities Press). Some further information is published in this book in the essay by Professor Juan Linz. Unfortunately there is one huge gap in this research — Italy. In formulating any hypothesis on the political economy of fascism the first considerations must be to discover which socio-economic groups joined, supported, and paid fascist movements, and then to decide which groups benefited from fascist government. It is now possible to provide reasonably accurate answers for Germany and most other countries. But most arguments about Italy are still only inferential, and there remains the possibility that inferences made about the nature of Italian fascism on the basis of our knowledge of other fascisms will not be correct. In the economic sphere this is a consideration of great weight, not just because of the different levels of economic development of the Italian and German economies, but because there are many easily observable differences of economic policy between the two countries. It will suffice to mention one: whereas the pursuit of the economic aims of the German central government led very quickly to an economy insulated as far as possible from the influence of the international economy, the Italian economy remained relatively open to such influences for most of the period of fascist government. We may not therefore come to any firm economic conclusions on the basis of the pragmatic research so far done. But what does this research suggest about the social and economic bases of fascist movements?

Fascism ought not to be analysed by too crudely a materialist technique, however much it may have ultimately depended on real social and economic interests. It may be argued that the propensity to join a fascist party was determined more by psychological considerations than by social class. And certainly it would appear likely that people of a certain psychological predisposition were readier to accept a politics of violent action, of conversion, and of total rejection of much of the political past. In part this accounts for the fact that in some countries fascist movements mobilised groups which had taken virtually no part in previous political life and that a certain portion of the fascist vote can often be identified as new voters rather than voters won from other political parties. Studies of the membership of some fascist movements have shown a comparative over-representation of those with criminal records. In the case of the Arrow Cross party in Hungary the high proportion of convicted criminals is particularly noticeable, even when all those whose convictions were for 'political' offences including street fighting and assault on the police are discounted. (M. Lackó, *Arrow-Cross Men, National Socialists, 1935-1944* [Budapest, 1969]). Out of a substantial sample of office-holders and party activists, 16 per cent had previous convictions for theft and over 7 per cent each for fraud and embezzlement. A further 16.7 per cent had convictions for a wide range of other non-political crimes.

It is probable that the mentality of fascist recruits was basically different from that of those who had taken an active part in earlier political movements. The political élites of the previous hundred years had moved in a world of rational and logical argument and had placed a low value on merely instinctual or emotional response. Insofar as there had been an appeal to groups outside the governing circles, it had been one of persuasion and education, not one of emotional conversion and manipulation. How little Quisling or Szalasi cared for what they thought of as these outmoded methods of political appeal may be seen from the incoherent nature of their final speeches in their own defence, when on trial for their lives. Fascist movements reached below the thin crust of rationality of liberal democratic politics to contact those who had only accepted the premises of a rational political world because they thought no alternative was respectable or because the only alternative had been some form of repressive absolutism. And in doing so they aroused a wealth of personal feelings which had had to be repressed because they had been for the most part resolutely ignored by the political establishment.

Nevertheless, certain social groups and political parties were very resistant to the psychological appeal of fascist movements whereas others proved very susceptible. Once the special psychological appeal of fascism is accepted the problem remains that, in spite of the insistence in fascist propaganda on the movement as a force for national unity, support for fascist parties did not come equally from all sections of the population. Although industrial workers were prominent in the foundation of fascist groups, if those groups developed from small sects to genuine mass movements they attracted very little further support on the way from organised labour. Socialist and communist parties, together with purely Roman Catholic parties like the German Zentrum, held on to their voters much better than other parties in the face of a mounting fascist vote.

In fact the most complicated problem for all fascist parties was to effect the transition from a small revolutionary (or counter-revolutionary) sect, with ideas fundamentally different from the society in which they existed, to becoming a mass political movement living in a real political world and mobilising a wide range of support in that world. The extraordinary difference between what could be thought and said in a small sect, such as the NSDAP until 1928, and the heavy responsibility attaching to every position taken up after that date is glaring. And nowhere did this apply with greater force than to economic questions. Because of the early connections of fascist thought with anarcho-syndicalism, both the membership and the social and economic ideas of fascist movements tended to be quite different in the stage of sect and in the stage of mass movement. So difficult was the transition between these stages and so great the differences made by it that there are two separate political economies of fascism to consider: (1) the political economy of the fascist sect, and (2) the political economy of the fascist movement.

For obvious reasons the first, although very interesting, is not very important. In fact in most European countries fascist sects remained sects, even in Norway where Nasjonal Samling by a series of political accidents was set up as a pseudo-government. The revolutionary anarcho-syndicalism of these sects appealed to organised workers as much as to any other group in society, as well it might, for its programme of political action depended on the existence of their organisations. The revolutionary syndicalists also provided the ideological basis of the Italian and German fascist parties and afterwards occupied important organising positions in the mass movements. But the dream of a working-class fascist revolution remained a dream. Even in the first elections in both countries in which fascism scored significant successes, it was relatively less successful in those areas where the proportion of industrial workers in the electorate was highest. The first manifestoes of the fascist party in Italy and the NSDAP in Germany represent the economic programme of fascism as a sect; they had little relevance in meeting the precise economic demands of those who subsequently supported fascist mass movements.

It is now clear that in all the societies of which we have an accurate enough knowledge significant fascist mass movements had two main social foundations. The first was urban, and either middle class or with middle-class attributes, shopkeepers, and shop-workers, minor bureaucrats and officials, professional people, students, unemployed personnel from the armed forces, and handicraft workers. The other was rural, peasant land-owners, sharecroppers and occasionally larger landowners. The actual mixture in each case differed with precise political circumstances; public officials for instance were often forbidden to join. But it was from an alliance of these groups that the fascist vote and much of the active support came, and these were the groups over-represented in fascist parties by comparison with their representation in other political parties.[1] That the urban middle-class group was moved towards fascism by socio-economic motives has been most cogently argued by H. A. Winkler in *Mittelstand, Demokratie und Nationalsozialismus* (Cologne, 1972).

One of the predominating reasons for the penetration of the NSDAP into these middle-class groups was their fear of economic evolution which seemed to leave them trapped and diminishing in political power between the two mighty and growing forces of 'big business' and organised labour. There were almost three million small enterprises, employing less than five people regularly, in the industrial and service sector of the economy. The opposition to many aspects of rapid economic development of opinion-forming circles, such as the Kathedersozialisten, in the second half of the nineteenth century had, by championing the cause of these independent middle-class groups, formed within them an attitude very different from the ferociously competitive individualism with which they are supposed to have behaved in countries which had industrialised earlier in periods when technology was less massive. Interpreting each cyclical crisis of the economy as evidence that they did not have the capital, the command over other resources, and the political power to compete, they increasingly pressed for an economic programme of protection, of restrictions on labour, on large firms, on department stores, and on cooperative movements. From this consciousness of a common conservative economic interest came also their consciousness of themselves as a limited group, the *Mittelstand*. Their predisposition to support a fascist party was turned decisively into commitment by the hyperinflation and then by the economic crash of 1929.

The economic motives of rural fascist voters have not been so well analysed. Heberle's study of Schleswig-Holstein shows how the long fall of agricultural prices and the feeling that all other parties had proved in their turn to offer no defence against this trend turned an agricultural region with a preponderance of small family farms into a pillar of the fascist movement (R. Heberle, *Landbevölkerung und Nationalsozialismus* [Stuttgart, 1963]). This electoral landslide, which happened to a lesser degree in two other areas where the structure of landholding was similar, Hesse and Baden, was not achieved without a conscious effort by the party to formulate an agricultural programme to win support of voters there, and to penetrate the social and economic organizations of the countryside. (H. Gies, 'NSDAP und landwirtschaftliche Organisationen in der Endphase der Weimarer Republik,' in *Vierteljahrshefte für Zeitgeschichte*, XV [1967]). 'The ideal-typical Nazi voter in 1932,' according to Seymour Lipset, 'was a middle-class self-employed Protestant who lived either on a farm or in a small community, and who had previously voted for a centrist or regionalist political party strongly opposed to the power and influence of big business and big labour' (S. Lipset, ed., *Political Man* [Berkeley and

Los Angeles, 1963], 149). In 1930 only 8.5 per cent of the membership of the NSDAP were workers employed in industry. Handicraft workers, shop-workers, officials, and the professionally employed, by contrast, were twice as numerous in relation to their proportion in the population as in other political parties. This political alliance lay also at the basis of the strong fascist movements in Austria, Hungary, and the Netherlands. There are seeming similarities with the socio-economic basis of Italian fascism where the headlong support of rural regions in northern and central Italy in 1921 affected the transition from sect to genuine political movement.

But what of 'big business'? Its importance for fascist parties has to be judged by counting neither heads nor votes but cash. Mussolini, but not the *fasci*, was receiving financial support from some Milan industrialists in 1919 and similar sources paid at that time for the publication of his news-paper *Il Popolo*. Important industrialists were prominent in the national list of the fascist party at its first contested elections and the businessmens' associations, Confindustria and the Associazione fra le Societa per Azioni levied their members to finance the fascist party at the election. But we do not know what proportion of the party's funds this accounted for. Neither is it known how much support was subsequently given and in what circum-stances. These questions have recently been illuminated for Germany for the period before 1933. (H. A. Turner, Jr., *Faschismus und Kapitalismus in Deutschland* [Göttingen, 1972]). Most of the representatives of German manufacturing industry gave their main support to the Brüning and after-wards to the Von Papen governments and only in December 1932 began to edge towards Hitler. Even then their motives were chiefly a distrust of Von Schleicher's interest in recovery in cooperation with the trade unions, and of the heavy public works expenditure. Most important industrialists still looked with deep suspicion on what they saw as Hitler's 'reactionary utopianism.' They thought only in terms of getting what immediate and contingent benefits they could out of a party which, while it might offer certain advantages, was also full of distant menace. Some of those, like Flick, who have long been known to have paid substantial sums to the NSDAP are now known to have paid even bigger sums to other non-socialist parties. And in other cases money was made available to leading figures of the NSDAP only to enable them to oppose the more anti-capitalist figures in their own party. This applied for example to the support from the firm which was subsequently to benefit most, I. G. Farben. It was limited, late, and mostly confined to the 'moderate' Funk.

None of this, however, seriously damages hypotheses such as those of Kühnl or Clemenz about the relationship of business and fascism, whatever it does to older and more rigid views. The question is still by no means completely answered as to what the relationship was between 'big business' and fascist parties, *once those parties were in power*. The brutally repres-sive policy towards organised labour meant that industrialists could forget entirely about interference from their work force. Interference from the government was another matter. In both Italy and Germany the objective of the industrialists' associations was to try to control their new masters and to effect the most favourable compromises possible with a party whose bedrock support did not seem particularly to favour pro-business policies. The ambiguities of the economic programme of the fascist movements in Germany and Italy contrasted with the clear and simple perceptions of the major industrialists of their own self-interest. In both countries the major capital interests were also well organised as pressure groups and in a good position to bring strong influence to bear on a new and insecure government. The subsequent evolution of this distrustful relationship is better considered in the wider framework of fascist economic policy in general.

It hardly seems likely that future research will change this picture of fascism as a broadly-based social movement drawing its support from disparate urban middle-class groups threatened by the process of economic change, and from small landowners and peasant farmers threatened by the same forces. Economically, its supporters had conflicting and very general aims such as guaranteed employment, safety from the pressures of organised labour and organised business, higher agricultural prices, security of land tenure, and a protection against inflation. From their stage as a revolutionary sect, however, fascist parties also inherited a revolutionary syndicalist anti-capitalist ideology and a small segment of 'working-class' support. On all this was superimposed the attempt by the business community to harness fascism to its own interests. What economic policies could possibly keep such an alliance together?

## COMMON ELEMENTS IN THE ECONOMIC POLICIES
## OF THE FASCIST STATES

Had economic considerations been as overriding in fascist propaganda as in that of the democratic parties, this new political alliance would have been more difficult to forge. But the fascist appeal to the people laid at least as much emphasis on the spiritual and emotional nature of man as on his material ambitions. Furthermore, the priority above all other matters of the political destiny of the nation and the *Volk* was a constantly emphasised theme. The transcendental nature of this theme was considered to lift it far above such issues as the distribution of economic rewards within society or the increase of material wealth. But National Socialism in spite of its exalted propaganda could no more emancipate itself *entirely* from the economic and social realities of society than the democratic parties. The low estimation which fascism accorded to the economic aspects of human existence did not eliminate the need for the formulation of an acceptable economic policy. In fact it was precisely in this area that the low esteem in which economics was held brought its own retribution. The pressure of the interests which supported the Nazi government was cushioned, not eliminated, by the autocracy of the regime. The supporters expected a different economic world, and the leaders themselves dreamed of a different and 'juster' system, a reactionary utopia. The movement never abandoned its erratic struggle towards the creation of a different society. The final justification of both the ideology and the revolution could only be the replacement of 'liberal man,' greedy, selfish, and isolated, with 'fascist man,' free from material desires, heroic, noble, and comradely. The other and more immediate political aims of the régimes did not exist to themselves alone, they were also judged against their value in the creation of that new society. Not only was the political upsurge of fascism based on vague but powerful demands for particular immediate economic and social changes but the ideology of the movement had helped it to a political breakthrough in some areas by expressing a most radical rejection of the social consequences of modern economic development. How far did fascist economic policy reflect the social composition of fascist movements? And how far did it try to implement the philosophical assumptions of the fascist ideology?

There is one obviously consistent aspect of fascist economic policy, so obvious that it need occupy little space here. For Germany, it has been most thoroughly analysed by T. Mason, *Arbeiterklasse und Volksgemeinschaft* (Cologne, 1975). Given the origins of the political support for the movement, such a policy involved little or no internal argument and no hesitations. This was the ruthless suppression of independent labour organisations and their supersession by organs of state control. It was easier for fascist governments to carry out policies hostile to the interests of industrial workers because they also initially gave a high priority to the reduction of unemployment. Registered unemployment in Italy fell from 541,700 at the end of 1921 to 122,200 four years later. The conquest of unemployment in Germany after 1933 absorbed enormous sums of public money. The effect of this in Germany was to initiate an increase in real earnings which was sustained until 1941. The upward movement of real wages, however, was relatively slight, partly because of agricultural protection and high food prices but also because the usual methods of political pressure on which workers had relied to increase wages no longer existed. The Reichs Labour Front was primarily an instrument of labour control and cultural propaganda. It did contribute to a certain improvement in working conditions as did its Italian counterpart, Dopolavoro. But the relentless pressure to hold down wages, even though it was repeatedly thwarted by the evasions of employers seeking labour, can be gauged from the fact that real weekly wages rose at an annual average of 2.8 per cent, for a longer working week, over the period 1933 through 1939 while the national income was increasing at an annual average rate of 8.2 per cent. In spite of an increase in net social product of 28 per cent between 1928-29 and 1937, the consumption of an average wage earner, as far as it can be calculated, seems to have improved very little over the same period. Less is known about the movement of real wages in Italy. The indications are that real wages and real earnings both moved downwards after 1926 during the attempt to stabilise the lira and as unemployment again increased. During the worst period of the depression, between 1929 and 1934, however, real wages in industry, for the employed, seem to have moved upwards once more whereas in the agricultural sector they began to fall. The steady upward pressure on prices after 1934 seems to have reversed this trend. Real wages may have fallen by as much as one-fifth by 1939, when they were well below their level in 1923. Were there any systematic comparative study of the question, it would probably show that those in regular employment, both in Germany and Italy, gained less in terms of material prosperity than their fellow workers in the liberal democracies, and that the distribution of income during the fascist period shifted in both countries significantly against the lower income groups. As a proportion of national income, in Germany wages fell from 57 per cent in 1929 to 52 per cent in 1938-39. Between 1933 and 1939 the proportional increase in the average income of the self-employed was almost one and a half times that of the average wage earner.

The attacks on unemployment by means of public investment in the provision of social overhead capital were not primarily motivated by considerations of welfare but by considerations of national strength. It was a common cliché of fascism that whereas all other political parties concentrated on the issue of the ownership of capital, fascism concerned itself only with whether capital was put to a socially productive use, regarding its ownership as a less important matter. Unemployed resources were seen simply as waste; there was no place in such an attitude for the hesitations which surrounded public relief schemes in liberal states. Petzina fairly describes the programmes of public investment in Germany as 'pre-liberal and mercantilistic' (D. Petzina, 'Grundriss der deutschen Wirtschaftsgeschichte 1918 bis 1945,' in Institut für Zeitgeschichte, *Deutsche Geschichte seit dem Ersten Weltkrieg* [Stuttgart, 1973], II, 757). The same terms describe the Italian government's direction of investment into hydroelectric schemes, railway improvement, construction of express highways, and land reclamation. Such programmes were not new. In Italy there was already a long history of investment of this type in the south and in Sicily and, since unification, there had been sporadic attempts to direct investment into land reclamation. In Germany the NSDAP, with no clear idea how to fulfil their promise to end unemployment, at first reaped the benefits of the employment-creation programme initiated by the Von Schleicher government. The 'Reinhardt Plan' for building express motor roads was inherited in its basic ideas from plans developed during the Weimar administration. The difference was not in the originality of fascist policy but in the much greater sums of public money made available for this type of investment. The total expenditure on land reclamation in Italy from 1870 to 1921-22 had amounted to 3,07 million 1927 gold lira; in the period 1921-22 to July 1936 it was 8,697 million. The Von Schleicher government had initiated the 'employment-creation' programme in Germany with an allocation of 600 million Reichsmarks; in the first financial year of the Nazi regime actual expenditure on employment-creation was ten times that of the previous financial year and the total sum allocated for this purpose between the *Machtübernahme* and the start of 1935 amounted to 3,800 million Reichsmarks. The ideology of the fascist state freed it from constraints which in the depressions of the inter-war period were not very useful ones. Nevertheless, the enormous public expenditure on such investment projects was one aspect of a financial profligacy which called for increasingly drastic controls on wages, prices, and profits and which widened the rift between the fascist economies and their main trading partners in the international economy.

Insofar as the unemployed benefitted from these projects, they did so inasmuch as their reemployment was an aspect of restoring national self-respect. In other areas of economic policy the relationship between the distribution of economic benefits and support for the movement was a much closer one. This was especially so in the agricultural sector. The main props of agricultural policy were a high protective tariff, an attempt to approach national self-sufficiency in food supply, which automatically brought a level of food prices well above prevailing prices on international markets, and an attempt to stabilise the land tenures and improve the conditions of the smaller farmers and tenants. The drive towards self-sufficiency also fitted in with the desire to be independent of strategic imports in a future war. Indeed it was not ultimately an achievable aim without a great expansion of the frontiers. But within the limitations of what was possible, the increase in national food production was consistently pursued. The 'battle of grain' in Italy concentrated on increasing wheat output. The average annual wheat harvest was increased to the point where after 1932, except in a bad harvest year like 1937, annual imports of wheat were about one-quarter their level over the period from 1925 to 1928. And this was not achieved merely by the expansion of the sown area but by a marked improvement in yields. The extension of agricultural education, the prizes and honours for efficient farmers, the subsidies for improved seed and for new equipment, all testified to the priority which the government gave to agriculture in a period of rapid industrialisation. In Germany the pursuit of self-sufficiency in food was carried out on a wider front. In spite of the tendency under bilateral trading agreements to pay higher guaranteed prices for foodstuffs, the net value of all food products imported into Germany in the period 1935 through 1938 was only one-third that of the period 1925 through 1928.

As in Italy, a high priority was given to improving the standard of agriculture and the budget of the Ministry of Agriculture rose, until the end of 1939, at a rate exceeded only by those of the Ministries of War, Aviation, Interior, and Justice. Eventually agriculture was included in the Four Year Plan as a strategic industry and state credits made available for machines, housing, and land rationalisation. But this expenditure brought less reward in Germany. Increases in output were only spasmodic and temporary. It has also of course to be remembered that the rise in per capita national income was not accompanied by a correspondingly large increase in food consumption. The steep increase in food prices served as one method of restraining the general level of consumption. This was the reality behind the statistical calculation that by 1938-39 83 per cent of Germany's food was domestically produced against 68 per cent in 1928. Yields of most crops did improve, but by comparison with most other West European countries they remained very low. Agricultural policy, highly favourable to the farming community, was in fact riddled with economic inconsistencies, which stemmed both from the electoral support of small farmers and the nature of the fascist ideology.

The material benefits to the farming community were great. They were rescued from the effects of the fall in world prices and their change of political allegiance after 1929 was rewarded also by the high esteem in which they were represented by NSDAP propaganda. Income from agricultural sales shrank less as a proportion of national income than wages, and the increase in self-employed farmers' earnings between 1933 and 1938 was over three times that of the increase in weekly wage rates. But the attempts at implementing fascist social ideas militated against the efficiency of farming methods. The attempt to create a secure hereditary class of yeomen farmers was summed up in the legislation to create the *Reichserbhöfe*, a new category of inalienable farm units. The size of these farms was set between 7.5 and 10 hectares, defined as 'that area of land necessary to support a family and maintain itself as a productive unit independent of the market and the general economic situation.' (D. Schoenbaum, *Hitler's Social Revolution: Class and Status in Nazi Germany 1933-1939* [New York, 1966], 157). That the new class of yeomen would be the source of an 'Aryan' regeneration of the population justified the revealing phrase 'independent of the market,' even of the guaranteed sellers' market created by the *Reichsnährstand*. In Italy fascism did not attempt to alter the structure of landholding but the number of cultivators, not all of whom were landowners, increased between 1918 and 1933 by 500,000 and continued to mount after that date. The annual mean percentage rate of growth of capital in the agricultural sector seems to have been higher over the period from 1920 to 1939 than at any time before the first world war or in the decade after 1945.

As the industrial recovery got under way in both countries, legislation was devised to keep the population on the land. In 1938 in Germany marriage loans were made available to farm labourers which could be written off if the labourer stayed put. New farm housing was exempt from taxation. In Italy legislation was designed specifically to prevent migration from the land to the towns in 1928 and 1929. These laws were a complete failure in both countries. Indeed in Italy this legislation was immediately followed by a widening of the gap between industrial and agricultural wages. The vision of a wholesome and stable rurality existed only in ideology and propaganda. It was strong enough, however, to prevent any reform of the severe structural problems which had bedevilled German agriculture in the 1920s. If any progress was made towards mending these structural weaknesses it came through the inexorable working of those economic forces which fascist legislation was struggling against. The percentage of labour employed in the agricultural sector in Germany fell from 28.8 per cent in 1933 to 25.9 per cent in 1939, whereas in the 1920s it had scarcely declined. The gap between rural and industrial wages was not narrowed. Rearmament in Germany and industrialisation in Italy, accelerated the decline of the very 'rurality' which fascist policy exalted. The number of new *Erbhöfe* created each year by the Reich fell, whereas the number of new farms created by the Weimar governments had grown every year. And the loss of labour from the land was in inverse proportion to the size of the farm because larger landowners were able, by manipulating tax benefits and subsidies, to retain their labour more successfully. The only apparent effect of these attempts to build a fascist society was to lower the efficiency of the agricultural sector.

Fascism's other main prop of support was a group with more conflicting and vaguer interests. The expansion of economic controls brought an expansion of public employment in the bureaucracy. The growth of employment in the tertiary sector of the economy in Germany in the 1930s was mainly in the public service area whereas in the preceding and succeding periods of growth it was mainly in trade and commerce. There can be no doubting the social and psychological rewards and the importance of the new status accruing to officialdom in Germany. These have been excellently described by Schoenbaum (op. cit.) and by H. Mommsen, in *Beamtentum in Dritten Reich* (Stuttgart, 1966). But there is no equivalent of the clear material improvement which accrued to the rural supporters. And the attempts to shelter handicraft workers and small businesses from the winds of economic change were no more successful than those to create a yeoman class or to retain labour on the land. Early legislation favoured the Mittelstand and specifically protected individual businesses. But recovery and rearmament alike favoured the bigger firms. The number of small firms fell faster than in the 1920s and handicraft workers shared in the decline.

The conflict between the defence of the Mittelstand and the régime's

final economic purposes was an insoluble one. The Four Year Plan determined the strategic priorities for public investment—synthetic fuels,
aluminium, synthetic rubber, explosives, basic chemicals, steel, and non-
ferrous metals. There was little room here for small firms and the Nazi
government became closely associated with a circle of large firms whose
production formed the manufacturing base of the war economy. Within
the space of eight years the construction of a large air force combined with
the government direction of investment to turn Germany into the world's
largest manufacturer of aluminium. Inevitably, companies in the non-
ferrous metals industry like Vereinigte Aluminiumwerke saw their directors intimately involved in government high finance and planning. Of the
big steel corporations much the same could be said. But the closest association was with the giant chemicals trust, I. G. Farben. The main weight of
investment in the Four Year Plan was in the chemical sector which was virtually the preserve of this one trust and the higher echelons of its personnel
became in many cases the responsible civil servants for deciding further
investment priorities in the sector (D. Petzina, *Autarkiepolitik im Dritten
Reich* [Stuttgart, 1968]).

A similar tendency could be observed in Italy. The state corporations
formed to increase and direct industrial investment seem to have bailed out
the bigger rather than the smaller firms, although a good study of their
activities still does not exist. The Istituto Mobiliare Italiano, created in
November 1931, was chiefly an attempt to protect firms against the effects
of the depression by providing capital against negotiable collateral. The
Societa Finanziaria Italiana was an intermediary institution to prevent
bank collapses in the same period. But the activities of the Istituto per la
Riconstruzione Industriale (IRI) were wider and it was seen by some industrialists as a government threat to their independence of action. It did
shore up the position of the banks by taking quantities of depreciated
industrial stocks off their hands. But this left it in some cases in control of
the firms. By the end of 1937 it operated a large shipping trust made up of
several of the biggest private shipping companies, whose finances had
never recovered from the 1929-33 slump, and also a substantial
steel-manufacturing trust. To this were then added important armaments,
engineering, and shipbuilding firms. IRI itself issued shares which were
subscribed to by the public. The Italian government had a controlling
interest through IRI in firms whose assets were equivalent to 17.8 per cent
of the capital investment in the country. These firms were often of special
technological importance, and the access which they thus acquired to
government sources of capital appears to have made capital much harder
to acquire for smaller firms outside the magic circle. Exactly the same situation was produced in Germany by less direct methods. The Ministry of
Economics had been empowered to declare vetoes on certain investments

in 1933 and from the start of 1937 every large investment project needed government approval. The volume of private capital issues had by that time shrunk to one-fifth its level of 1928. When the capital market was re-opened to a wider range of private transactions after 1937, it now served only as a supplemental source of supply to those firms to whom government capital was streaming out under the Four Year Plan. After March 1936 bank loans in Italy were restricted to short-term commercial credit.

Although we are still quite ignorant about Italy in the 1930s, the evidence does point to the fact that there, even more than in Germany, fascism did eventually produce a very different set of relationships between government and private capital. The fears of businessmen that fascist governments would intervene in a field in which they would for the most part have preferred a complete liberty of action seem to prove ultimately fully justified, although to what extent their control over business and industry was restricted will probably always remain a matter of interpretation. Guarneri's opinion, that in Italy the limits of government intervention were 'suggesting a few names for the various boards of directors' cannot be accepted because of the much greater control over every aspect of the economy which the fascist government exercised (F. Guarneri, *Battaglie economiche tra le due grandi guerre* [Milan, 1953], I, 317). Nor on the other hand has subsequent evidence borne out Rossi's argument that there were intimate connections between Italian manufacturing interests and the fascist government (E. Rossi, *Padroni del vapore e fascismo*, rev. ed. [Bari, 1966]). Fascist policy in Italy did in fact result in genuine limitations on the independence of action of industrialists but those limitations did not seriously endanger the things they most prized.

The formerly private associations of businessmen lost their independence by their integration into the administrative machinery of 'the corporate state.' Both in Italy and Germany they were transformed into instruments of economic control. But whereas in both countries the functions as well as the titles of these organisations changed, the personnel at the head of them usually did not. The threat to the independence of manufacturing interests came from the pressures which changed these businessmen into instruments of the state bureaucracy imposing a system of controls on their fellow businessmen. The line between government and business was blurred because the personnel became in many cases one and the same. The example of I. G. Farben had many parallels in Italy (L. Rosenstock Franck, *Les étapes de l'économie fasciste italienne; du corporatisme à l'économie de guerre* [Paris, 1939]). The first steps in this process were in fact taken in the period of exchange control and in Germany they went further than in Italy because the network of business committees subordinated to the party became the administrative channel through which permissible import quantities were assessed and import restrictions imposed. Even at this stage the manufacturers could easily thwart the more extreme policies of the Ministry of Economics since they were still basically assessing their own demand (J. S. Geer, *Der Markt der geschlossenen Nachfrage* [Berlin, 1961]). But the pressures of war were bound to weight the scales of power in favour of the government. The Italian invasion of Ethiopia and the League of Nations sanctions which it produced brought about a rapid deterioration in Italy's already dangerous foreign trading situation and produced the first serious clashes between the government and the business world which did not result in a compromise (R. Sarti, *Fascism and the Industrial Leadership in Italy, 1919-1940* [Berkeley, Los Angeles, London, 1971]). At this point the business world was coming into collision with the more fundamental principles of fascism. In Germany, with the advent after 1941 of more severe raw material shortages and with the extreme concentration of economic priorities which the war brought about, the Ministry of Armaments did eventually transform these committees into full-time organs of state administration.

One of the few major industrialists to commit himself wholeheartedly to the NSDAP before it came to power, the steel manufacturer Fritz Thyssen, was eventually driven into exile through his opposition to the government's determination to place the main weight of investment in the steel industry in a completely new works to use low-grade German iron ore at uneconomical prices. The Salzgitter works was in fact paid for almost entirely from the treasury and the opposition to it of the steel manufacturers meant that its management was closely controlled by party circles. Nothing could have more clearly demonstrated that, however sympathetic to the business world and however dependent on it, the Nazi government had its own interests which it was prepared to pursue. It was on the exact nature of these interests that the fears of the business world were chiefly concentrated. The assiduous and consistent pursuit of an aggressive foreign policy, and in Germany the callous racial exterminations brought a world of destruction and extermination which, well before May 1945, had nothing left in common with the advantages which the business world had hoped it might obtain from a fascist government. The decisive moment came in January 1944 when the Führer supported Sauckel's impossible plans to deport a further million workers from France during that year against the advice of Speer and the Ministry of War Production to organise more war production in the occupied territories. From that moment the position of the Ministry of War Production and of the businessmen who ran it became increasingly weaker than that of the more radically fascist parts of the administration. The business circles which had sought to control the movement in 1933 now had their most pessimistic fears fulfilled; they had themselves become the plaything of a political revolution (A. S. Milward, *The New Order and the French Economy* [Oxford, 1970]). The last act of the Italian fascist party during the war was the Republic of Salo whose economic policy reverted to the radicalism of the manifesto of 1919. The movement had returned to being only a sect.

Until that time, however, cases like that of Thyssen were exceptional. The new governments did not, contrary to Kühnl's hypothesis, 'preserve the capitalist system.' They changed the rules of the game so that a new system was emerging. But until the fascist régimes began to founder in defeat major capital interests were able to accommodate themselves to the new rules almost as comfortably as to the old. How far the 'system' was modified is a question still waiting for an answer, but it is unlikely, in the vocabulary of contemporary controversy (which fascist theorists would have regarded as meaningless), that 'fascism' will be shown to have made many dents in 'capitalism.' In Germany the undistributed profits of limited liability companies rose fourfold over the period 1928 to 1939. Alterations of the tax structure and income distribution did favour the Mittelstand but there was no alteration of basic economic structures in favour of the particular social groups which supported fascism. Nor were the more philosophical denunciations by fascist theorists of materialism and liberal greed, nor their insistence on a stable social order, translated into government action other than in minor and ineffectual ways. In Germany the fascist period was a period of rapid economic growth and social instability and change. The annual rate of growth of national income in Germany of 8.2 per cent in the period 1933-1939 was higher than in the period 1890-1913 and as high as in the so-called economic miracle of the post-war years. One aspect of this rapid growth was the 'rural exodus' from low-productivity agricultural employment to high-productivity industrial employment, so much lamented by fascist theorists. Italy's experience was a more mixed one: a rapid burst of growth over the period 1921-1925, slowing down in the crisis associated with the revaluation of the currency, a steadier growth until 1929, a deep depression until 1934, and then once more a resumption of rapid growth. In spite of the pause in the middle of the period, national income per capita at current prices in the period 1936-1940 was 16.5 per cent higher than in 1921-1925. Although as in Germany this represented a massive growth of public expenditure on armaments, it also reflected the continued industrialisation of the country. Agriculture contributed 34 per cent of GNP at constant prices in 1921 and 27 per cent in 1938; the comparable figures for industry are 24 per cent and 31 per cent. Economic growth was associated more with the fascist régimes in the inter-war period than with their liberal opponents.

Although economic growth satisfied some of the economic demands of those social groups which supported fascism, it threatened at the same time the very stability and freedom from the effects of economic evolution which they sought. It stemmed from and it furthered the nationalist aspirations of fascism. There was no necessary or implicit correspondence in the fascist state between growth and welfare. The growth of GNP was associated with quite different economic purposes—the exaltation of the nation and the ability to pursue an independent policy even to the extent of waging war. Given the promises of fascist ideology, war had an educative and re-integrative purpose in the fascist state and preparation for war was an important priority of fascist economic policy, in Germany after 1936 the first priority. 'Fascism,' wrote Mussolini, 'the more it considers and observes the future and the development of humanity quite apart from political considerations of the moment, believes neither in the possibility nor the utility of perpetual peace' (quoted by Welk, op. cit., 190). In both countries economic growth was partly a by-blow of an economic policy designed to promote territorial expansion.

This, although the most fundamental, was by no means the only contradiction to fascist economic policy. The tensions which arose came also from the contradictions between the radical-revolutionary view of the economic world expressed in the original fascist manifestoes and the retreat from this view which was imposed by having to satisfy the more conventional socio-economic demands of most fascist supporters. Not only was the fascist state committed at the same time to policies of reflation and stability, its further commitment to external aggression produced a volume of economic growth and social change which made the other goals of social and economic policy virtually unattainable. All these conflicting aims were the inescapable economic inheritance of fascist governments and all had to be pursued in the most unpromising international economic environment.

Indeed Mason has recently argued that the irreconcilable contradictions of economic policy in Germany were the cause of the war, which he sees as an escape into an irrational future, and also the chief determinant of the timing of the invasion of Poland (T. W. Mason, 'Innere Krise und Angriffskrieg 1938-1939,' in F. Forstmeier, ed., *Wirtschaft und Rüstung am Vorabend des zweiten Weltkrieges* [Düsseldorf, 1975]).

A profligate financial policy was no longer in Autumn 1939 able to achieve a satisfactory division of the national product between the conflicting claims of military and civil purposes. Increases in consumer purchasing power, acute shortages of labour, conflicting demands for materials, meant that the goal of war could no longer be pursued without a reversal of domestic economic policy. In these circumstances, he argues, the only political way out was to launch the war, because a war of annexation and looting was one solution to this impasse in economic policy. The war would permit effective restrictions on wages and consumer expenditure which would be otherwise politically impossible, and a ruthless policy of looting would ease the shortages. It is, however, rather a subjective judgement to suggest that the German economy was in a deeper crisis of policy in 1939 than at any time in the period 1936-44. Throughout all those years it pursued the same conflicting aims with the same vigour, and the staggering burden of public debt at the end dwarfed that of 1939.

## THE FASCIST ECONOMY AND EUROPE

There was, of course, nothing in the fascist state to dissuade it from war. But how implicit was the second world war in the political economy of fascism? Might it not be argued with equal cogency that the war was not merely, as Mason suggests, a short-term way out of a difficult situation, but also a necessary means to achieving the ultimate economic goals of the fascist state? In the act of war the inherent contradictions of fascist economic policy were less irreconcilable and preparation for war, no longer an additional contradiction in economic policy, might then become a vehicle for bringing nearer the completed fascist society. And since the completion of that society was more difficult within the frontiers of one or two countries, might not a war of territorial expansion have been an overriding objective both in Italy and Germany in creating a viable fascist society? Was the war in fact an attempt to create a fascist Europe and implicit from the outset in the fascist revolutions?

The magnitude of German plans, the consistency with which they were pursued, the extent to which they were central to the political ideology of the government, are all still much disputed. Two aspects of German policy, however, have always suggested that the Nazi government's economic aims were not just national ones but envisaged a socio-economic reconstruction of the whole continent. First, the theory of the economy of large areas (*Grossraumwirtschaft*) used to justify German trading policy after 1933 and economic policy during the occupations implied a specialisation of economic function over an area roughly corresponding to that of the continent of Europe. Second, the diligently pursued 'racial reconstruction' of the continent was justified as being a necessary aspect of this much greater degree of specialisation of economic function. Certain races had become in Nazi theory incapable of any but the most menial of these economic functions. How much light can be shed on those important questions by a consideration of the external economic policies of the German and Italian governments?

The origins of controls over foreign trade and exchanges in Germany and Italy were not expressive of fascist ideology; they were a pragmatic and unavoidable response to the collapse of international trade and to the actions of other powers. It was the Brüning government which introduced exchange controls in Germany to stop the outflow of capital and to control imports. As German trade continued to share in the decline of world trade over the next two years, the NSDAP never appears to have understood that the implementation of its own economic programme would certainly mean that trade and exchange controls would have to be retained at least until full employment was achieved. In fact it was the public works programme of the Von Schleicher government and the subsequent Reinhardt plan which first suggested that the exchange controls might not, as everywhere else, prove to be designed to meet a temporary emergency which was worse in Germany because of the devaluation of the pound sterling. When the expenditure on the *Autobahnen* was added to the cost of rearmament, of agricultural protection, and of the agricultural support programmes, it became clear that the government had given a higher priority to domestic recovery and the achievement of its longer term national aims than to reintegrating Germany into a reconstructed network of international trade and payments.

This was recognized by the 'New Plan' in 1934 which now gave the government the administrative capacity to regulate imports according to their political and economic desirability rather than merely to restrict their quantity. It was intended to reduce the import of manufactured goods over time and to alter the geographical pattern of German trade so that imports from developed countries would be replaced by imports of raw materials from the underdeveloped south-eastern European countries. In their turn German exports of manufactures would be diverted to underdeveloped countries. The mechanism chosen for this had already come into existence before the *Machtübernahme*, the bilateral trading treaty specifying the quantity and value of goods to be exchanged and an arbitrary exchange rate for the period of its validity. As the treaties proliferated all currency clearings were handled by a central clearing bank in Berlin. Germany thus developed a separate trading bloc in which she was the dominant power both politically and economically and which accounted for an increasing proportion of her international trade. National Socialist economists and publicists gave this bloc a specific fascist gloss in the theory of the economics of large areas. Germany was seen as the natural industrial heartland of Europe, the developed manufacturing core of the continent, while the peripheral states were seen as suppliers of foodstuffs and raw materials. This was a theory which had been popular in nationalist circles in the late nineteenth century, but it was transmuted into an overtly fascist concept by racial theorists in the NSDAP. It is possible in fact to identify two concepts of Grossraumwirtschaft in Nazi Germany. One is the specifically 'fascist' interpretation which saw German trading policy after 1934 as the first step in a reconstruction of Europe both racial and economic (for these two things were inseparable). The other is the older and vaguer idea of a politico-economic domination over eastern and south-eastern Europe.

The second and older concept had an obvious appeal to those German firms with specific plans and business interests in central and south-eastern Europe. In a period of very low international prices for food and raw materials, Germany was offering extraordinarily favourable terms to such exporters of primary produce as Bulgaria or Turkey. She was breaking her own policy of high agricultural protection to admit at high German prices guaranteed quantities of produce virtually unsaleable on the world market. In the situation of 1934 the underdeveloped European countries were being offered the only possibility open to them of economic development, guaranteed access to an increasingly prosperous market. The price for this was domination by the mark through the Berlin clearing, by German exports and by German business interests. In 1939 65.5 per cent of Bulgarian imports originated in Germany and the equivalent figure for Turkey was 51 per cent, for Hungary 48.4 per cent, for Yugoslavia 47.6 per cent and for Romania 39.2 per cent. The penetration of German capital and business interests into the economies of these countries proceeded so rapidly that before the first invasion and occupation of some of them certain German business groups, such as I. G. Farben and Karl Zeiss, had already submitted to the government detailed plans for furthering and extending their interests there after any occupation. Eichholtz has published some of this evidence in support of his hypothesis on the political economy of fascism (D. Eichholtz, op. cit.; D. Eichholtz and W. Schumann, *Anatomie des Krieges: neue Dokumente über die Rolle des deutschen Monopolkapitals bei der Vorbereitung und Durchführung des zweiten Weltkrieges* [Berlin, 1969]).

There can be no doubt that German trading policy was highly favourable to certain German business and industrial interests in this particular part of Europe. But the importance of the German trading bloc for German trade was still a limited one. Even by 1939 the six countries whose trade was most dominated by Germany took only 18.3 per cent of all German exports and supplied 18.5 per cent of all imports. It is sometimes argued that these imports were particularly important because of their strategic value, that Germany had an uninterrupted control over vital quantities of strategic raw materials. But this was not so at all. They were strategically important only in two areas, foodstuffs and bauxite. The success of German policy could be measured by the extent to which it encouraged alterations in the agriculture of these countries such that they did develop a genuine economic symbiosis with the German economy as exporters of those foodstuffs which were in genuine demand in Germany and which would be even more essential in the likely event of a European war and a British blockade of German food supply. This happened on only the most limited scale. In reality the construction of a German trading bloc was more a response to shortages of hard currencies than to long-term planning for a Grossraumwirtschaft. Any future Grossraum of the Nazi state would certainly include Poland and the Ukraine, but for political reasons German trade with Poland and the Soviet Union declined in the Nazi period. The Soviet Union had been one of the major trading partners of the Weimar state but between 1935 and 1940 German-Russian trade was quite insignificant. The Reichsmark trading bloc existed as an economic unit independently of wider political intentions and its existence did not foreshadow these intentions. It was not the result of an alliance between major capital interests and the fascist régime but one device among many which enabled that régime to pursue its own domestic economic priorities.

The price of pursuing these priorities was isolation from the international economy and, from the point of view of many German business interests, the advantages of this closed trading system were a poor substitute for what it had replaced. Over the last century the growth of exports from developed economies has been mainly due to access to markets in other developed economies. The capacity of central and south-eastern Europe to absorb imports of German manufacture had definite limits. Unless, therefore, the purpose of a reconstructed Europe was stability rather than growth the German trading bloc offered no satisfactory future. The percentage of German exports going to the United States, Britain, and France fell from 24 per cent in 1929 to 11.6 per cent in 1939, yet in the long run these were the markets on which the growth of German manufacturing capacity depended.

It is possible of course to resolve this paradox by arguing that the trading arrangements after 1934 were not thought of as permanent because the ultimate intention was to conquer Russia and to create an economic unit so large that there would ultimately be no need for any reintegration with the international economy. Within such far-flung frontiers and endowed with absolute command over so many resources, the difficulties attendant on pursuing the domestic economic priorities of fascism would be much less. Theoretically, the possibility always existed of an internal deflation and a devaluation of the Reichsmark. In reality the last date by which such a policy could have been adopted was 1936, but government expenditure continued to grow beyond that date. Expenditure on the armed forces rose from 18 per cent of total public expenditure in 1934 to 50 per cent in 1938. Between 1933 and the outbreak of war only about 80 per cent of this government expenditure was covered by normal treasury income, and the devices used to finance rearmament and the Four Year Plan increasingly shifted the burden onto the public debt. Even before the war, the need to make wage, price, and exchange controls more effective had already produced a completely separate price structure in Germany, and left no alternative to perseverance with exchange controls and bilateral trade. The increasing costs of rearmament might in fact be recouped from the proceeds of conquest. If this was the calculation it was no will o' the wisp; the financial payments alone from France to Germany in one year of the occupation were far greater than any possible calculation of the expenditure involved in conquering the country. The total contribution from the French economy to the German amounted to one-third of French national income in 1942, and almost one half in 1943 (A. S. Milward, *The New Order and the French Economy* [Oxford, 1970]). But the German public debt in its various forms continued to increase throughout the war leaving the Reich by 1944 in a situation where only the most draconian controls prevented a catastrophic inflation. And the continued existence of the Reich economy as a separate and insulated unit prevented any realisation of the widely discussed schemes for a 'New Economi Order' based on a wider customs union in Europe or a closer integration of the national economies.

German external economic policy before 1939 had little, therefore, in common with the theoretical justifications provided for it in the concept of Grossraumwirtschaft. Nor does it foreshadow any pan-European plans. But once the war was launched and territory occupied did not these theories become translatable into real economic terms and did not the New Economic Order become possible? It was in fact only at the height of success of the campaign in Russia in 1941 that there was space and time for discussion of what the New Economic Order might be. Once the blitzkrieg strategy failed in Russia in January 1942 and German domestic economic policy was forced to concentrate on mobilising all Germany's resources for war production, it was inevitable that the occupied territories should also come to be seen as part of 'the European war economy,' as Reichsminister Speer called it. But in the interval when most of Europe was conquered and the German domestic economy no more committed to military output than it had been at the end of 1938, there were clear indications that external economic policy was not concerned merely with short-term exploitation to assuage domestic economic difficulties but did have also long-term pan-continental objectives.

After the occupation of Norway, the German administration there embarked on an expensive programme of capital investment designed permanently to change the economic orientation of the Norwegian economy from its reliance on a wide network of international trade to a close integration with Germany. A long-term investment project was begun to utilise the cheap electric current in Norway for the production of aluminium, which would be wholly exported to German aircraft factories. Aluminium production was to be increased more than six times which would eventually have left Norway with a manufacturing capacity 60 per cent above that of the United States in 1939! In order to diminish the dependence on food imports, enormous projects for using the extensive Norwegian moorlands for sheep rearing and cattle farming were begun as well as smaller plans for extending market gardening. A start was made in providing capital for the fishing industry, especially in the form of freezing and canning plant, so that the value and quality of fish exports to Germany could be increased. Onto these expensive projects Hitler grafted his personal plans for main roads and railways to link Berlin to Trondheim in the first case and the Norwegian arctic in the second (A. S. Milward, *The Fascist Economy in Norway* [Oxford, 1972]). Such long-term planning was not limited to Norway nor entirely to the period before the first defeats in Russia. The plans for the Norwegian aluminium industry were based on a permanent control over the allocation of bauxite supplies from Hungary, Croatia, and France. Even in 1943 the plans for producing more consumer goods in France for Germany were based on a general agreement, not subsequently properly fulfilled, to undertake joint planning of distribution of raw materials within the German and French economies. The purpose of the war was neither just to avoid economic collapse at home nor just to loot the occupied territories. But until more is known about economic policy in the occupied eastern territories it is not possible to say exactly what weight these longer-term plans had in the direction of the German economy. It is as yet still only possible to guess at the extent to which German economic policy did entail a reorganisation of the continent, and therefore, also, at the economic goals of the war.

The Italian experience makes these matters no clearer. The concept of an Italian Grossraumwirtschaft and, after Germany's conquests, the concept of a joint Italo-German trade domination of the continent were both discussed in Italy. And during the worst period of the depression, and the Ethiopian war which followed afterwards, Italian trade controls seem to have aimed at creating a smaller version of the German trading bloc which would remove the pressure of external economic movements on Italian domestic economic policy. But how could such an ambition appear meaningful or realisable in the context of an economy like that of Italy? That it was even tried shows the inherent tendency of fascist economics towards the creation of an isolated economic system and the necessity of such isolation if the precarious balance of domestic economic policy was to be maintained. The recurrent deficits on commodity trade were the weakest point in the Italian economy in the inter-war period. After 1929 the weakness of the balance of payments was accentuated by the drop in remittances from emigrants. Not only was Italy's export capacity too low to emulate German policy but any attempt at creating a separate Italian trading bloc could only lead to a direct clash with German economic interests in the same area.

In fact, until 1928 the Italian economy remained relatively open, but as domestic economic policy struggled against the contrary international tides of falling output and mounting unemployment, trade and import controls increased until in April 1934 they were for the first time completely effective. From July 1935 the rearmament for the attack on Ethiopia could only be carried out by complete government control of the import of 'strategic' raw materials, including coal. The war itself brought economic sanctions imposed by the League of Nations and a system of rigid exchange controls in reply. No matter how unpromising the outcome, there seemed no alternative to abandoning the policy of the régime other than the creation of an Italian trading bloc controlled by a set of bilateral treaties on the German model. Persistence in a high level of public expenditure between 1930 and 1933 when normal treasury income was declining had already created a level of internal prices which made adherence to the trading methods of the 1920s even more difficult. The acceptance, indeed the usefulness and rightness, of war in the fascist state decided the issue. With the change in trading policy came also the attempt, as in Germany, to promote a higher degree of self-sufficiency, by developing high cost synthetic fuel and synthetic fibre industries. Mussolini spoke of such developments as the only way to preserve political autonomy. (F. Guarneri, *Autarkie und Aussenhandel* [Jena, 1941]).

The outcome was chastening. The only two significant European primary exporters for whom Italy was a major market were Hungary and Yugoslavia. In both countries German trade gained ground precisely at the expense of that of Italy, aided by the rigour with which Yugoslavia enforced the League of Nations sanctions. Only Albania was left as an Italian economic preserve. The failure and its dangers were soon apparent. When the gold bloc countries devalued in October 1936, the gold content of the lira was reduced to bring it back into parity with the standard of the most open of the world's trading systems. But the drive towards war by Germany and the growing strength of the political ties with that country made Germany itself the indispensable source of strategic imports. More than that, as Italian exports of primary produce to Germany increased in order to pay for the mounting imports, Italy itself became merely another subordinate member state of the German trading bloc. The weakness of the Italian economy compared with the German meant that the Italian government was in reality only able to pursue its own fascist economic policies *in exchange for* political autonomy.

Because of the circumstances outlined above, there is little point in trying to assess from Italian external policy what the ultimate implications of the fascist economic system were for the continent as a whole. Nor does the Italian experience do much to clarify the ambiguities of German economic policy. It was not possible in either country to pursue the economic policies which the political bases of the fascist movement demanded and to ally these policies to the original fascist ideology and at the same time to adhere to the multilateral trading system which had been so potent a factor in European economic growth. But to what degree was the external economic policy of fascist states an attempt to create a trading system designed to cater to priorities other than economic growth? To what extent were such far-reaching policies, involving countries which had not experienced a fascist take-over, inherently necessary to preserve the fascist system in Germany and Italy? Was a war of expansion a necessary consequence of the political economy of fascism? These are questions which historians and economists must still answer.

## TOWARDS A MORE VALID HYPOTHESIS

The argument presented above has travelled a long way from the hypotheses which were considered at the beginning of this paper. Not only are
the initial assumptions all simplifications of history but in varying degrees
they are inaccurate and misleading simplifications. The word *fascism*,
however, will not go away. How meaningful an economic label is it? The
historical evidence suggests that fascism emerged from a new combination
of social and political forces and that this combination was responsible for
an identifiably different set of economic attitudes and policies. It is not my
intention here to present yet another comprehensive theory of the nature of
this new combination of forces but, by extrapolating the present trend in
research, to indicate certain aspects of fascism that may well prove essential to any future and more valid hypothesis of its political economy.

First, the revolutionary (or counter-revolutionary) ideology of fascist
sects was not entirely submerged in the economic policies of fascist movements. It survived to play an economic role and has to be incorporated in
any useful hypothesis on the political economy of fascism. In this ideology
the Enlightenment, the French Revolution, and the evolution of the 'materialist' economic creeds of socialism and communism represented not progress but a deep and growing wound on human society. The assumptions
underlying most economic theory were therefore seen as incorrect, vicious,
and corrupting. The healing process could begin only with a small surviving unpolluted racial élite, uncorrupted by these assumptions. Mankind
was to be re-created and the fascist élite was the germ of the new society. In
Germany the SS saw itself as that new society coming to birth amongst the
debris of the old. Its economic empire was the only one to escape the
growing embrace of the Ministry of War Production after 1942 because it
was a permanent thing for the future whereas war production was but temporary. As support dropped away from fascist movements over the last
eighteen months of the war, they shrunk once again to the original sect, a
hard core of ideologists no longer needing to compromise nor to exist in a
real political world. The Republic of Salo tried to implement the original
fascist manifesto of 1919. And in the final unreality of the Berlin bunker
the first priority became the survival into the future of the unpolluted
Aryan élite in whose blood the instincts of fascism would still survive.

Second, this fascist ideology depended on the concept of an appeal to the
people; fascism was an élitist politics for a mass age. It offered to the
'people' the vain hope of an element of personal economic independence in
the face of apparently massive and impersonal economic forces. It
extended the delusion that the unorganised might yet defend themselves
against the inexorable economic pressures which they feared — 'big business,' 'organised labour,' inflation, and unemployment. Because of this
and its original anti-capitalist rhetoric, it penetrated into the popular revo-

lutionary socialist movements by way of anarchism and syndicalism. In Spain Ledesma actually chose the title 'national syndicalism' for his fascist movement. Fascist movements retained these revolutionary anti-capitalist ambitions and they were also not without influence on its economic policy. They formed, for instance, the intellectual background of Roberto Farinacci who rose to be Minister of Popular Culture in the Italian government and Fritz Sauckel who became Plenipotentiary General for Labour in Germany in 1942. Even at the height of his brutal labour 'recruitment' drives in Europe, Sauckel was still occupied, sometimes successfully, in trying to force 'the plutocrats' to improve working and living conditions.

Third, these early characteristics of fascism survived only as a guiding thread through the later experience of the movement. Fascism was mainly formed and shaped in the process of coming to power in Italy and Germany. In the course of acquiring in these two countries its essential mass support, it was quite transformed from its beginnings. It was in these two countries alone that fascism emerged from a small and violent sect to take power as the most important political movement. In the explanation of how this could occur the main roots of fascist economic policy may also be seen and understood.

The elements of a common national historical experience in these two countries must be stressed. They were the only two historically dominant nations in Europe to achieve their modern national unity late, in the face of opposition from the other European powers, and not to achieve it completely. It was this which encouraged an intellectual marriage between the deeply held traditional conservative sentiment of nationalism and the more rarefied and revolutionary ideas of fascism. Every political party had to account for its ideas against a nationalist alternative. The concept of a 'national socialism' came to the forefront in Italy during the first world war when the socialist party split on the question of whether to intervene in the war to pursue nationalist and democratic aims at the same time. In fact the nationalist party had already made inroads into the socialist party before 1914 and before Mussolini opted for intervention and formally split the party. (K. Priester, *Der italienische Faschismus, ökonomische und ideologische Grundlagen* [Cologne, 1972]). The theoretical Marxist basis of Italian (and Mussolini's) socialism was not very rigorous. In a country with a very small class of industrial workers the rural origins of some of the leaders and supporters of the party had favoured a socialism which was already heavily imbued with anarchist and syndicalist ideas. The offspring of this marriage of nationalism and socialism was a nationalism with a much deeper popular appeal and a socialism far distant from that of Marx. The great importance of national power and national development in the fascist economy was already established.

But Italy's situation in the first world war was unique; a popular politics overturned the alliance of the liberal élite with Germany and forced intervention on the democratic side. In Germany conditions were far less propitious. Even after the Versailles Treaty, most political support still went to the established parties whose opposition to the treaty was just as strong, although less violently expressed, than that of the fascist groups. The common elements in the national historical experience of the two countries are by no means enough to explain the transition from sect to movement in Germany.

All historians have rightly insisted on the importance of the collapse of the international economic order with which the Weimar republic was so closely integrated in putting a new and more vigorous wind into the sails of German fascism. There is no need to rehearse those events here. But there was a third force tending to promote a mass fascist movement in Germany which had been lacking, indeed had not been needed, in Italy. The marriage of syndicalism and traditional nationalism had supplanted older conceptions of nationalism by a new and virulent conception of racial purity. The fascist élite was not only an intellectual élite but an élite of the blood. The re-creation of European society depended on a mystical brotherhood of true blood, because it was in the blood and not the brain that ideas were borne. The worst threat to the healing of society came from the polluting presence of people of an alien race within the national frontiers. The commonly accepted idea that Italian fascism was not 'racial' and that these ideas constitute a fundamental difference between German national socialism and Italian fascism does not as yet rest on any profound examination of racial attitudes in the Italian fascist party. The question of purity of the blood, central to Nazi ideology, may have had very little use or relevance within Italy because it could drum up little support. The British Union of Fascists, who believed firmly in this set of racial ideas, also deliberately eschewed the use of them on the electoral platform at first because they were of no use as vote winners. Only in the decline of the party did they openly adopt, as a last desperate measure, an overtly anti-Jewish platform. (W. F. Mandle, *Anti-Semitism and the British Union of Fascists* [London, 1968]). Nasjonal Samling had to turn its anti-Jewish electoral stance into an attack on 'international Jews' because it was useless in a country with so homogeneous a population as Norway. In Italy, as in Britain and Norway, the conditions were unpropitious for the acceptance of the racial ideology of the fascist sect by the fascist movement. In Germany, however, they were such as to permit the NSDAP to turn its *Weltanschauung* into an electoral opportunity. The first world war and the rapid social change which followed had promoted a more virulent anti-Semitism, turning it from a defensive set of beliefs for defining 'Germandom' into an aggressive stance. For all nationalist parties to be against Weimar was also to be against 'Jews'; and the National Socialist Party was able to play on these important changes in attitude (W. E. Mosse, ed., *Deutsches Judentum im Krieg und Revolution, 1916-1923* [Tübingen, 1971]). The Jewish population was prominent in precisely those 'capitalist' occupations which the original ideology denounced, and it had also for obvious reasons supported 'liberal' causes. In these circumstances the fact of 'political anti-Semitism' was added to the racial fires. Those purifying fires were integral to economic policy. Auschwitz and German economic policy in Poland were as much the inescapable historical inheritance of Nazi economic policy as were the blast furnaces of Salzgitter. The campaign against the Jews of eastern Europe started at the same time as, and was an integral part of, the invasion of the Soviet Union. When in 1944 Germany faced extinction and labour had become a scarce economic factor, the concentration camps were allowed to use labour at risibly low levels of productivity while valuable resources were *increasingly* allocated to the slaughter of all who were deemed of the wrong race (J. Billig, *Les camps de concentration dans l'économie du troisième Reich* [Paris, 1973]).

But all electoral studies also show that this threefold explanation of the rise to power of fascism in two countries only is still incomplete. Something else was necessary—a period of extreme social mobility. The middle-class and rural support for fascism came from those who felt their economic and social status to be seriously threatened. In Italy this threat came from the onset of industrialisation after 1900, accelerated by the demands of the war. Social groups changed status with great rapidity in what had long been a static society. The concern of fascist economic policy with such concepts as 'stability' and 'rurality' reflects the preoccupations of its threatened supporters. In Germany this social mobility was provided by the hyperinflation, still lingering as a fearful memory to the middle classes when the depression of 1929 threw six million out of work in three years. Brought to power by social shocks of such magnitude, fascism sought inevitably to avoid further similar catastrophes, blamed on 'international plutocracy.' Beneath the massive government expenditure lurked, as Klein has shown, a constant fear of inflation which demanded ever stronger economic controls and an increased isolation of the German economy. (B. H. Klein, *Germany's Economic Preparations for War* [Cambridge, Mass., 1959]).

The circumstances, therefore, in which fascist movements attained political power were such as to saddle them with a cumbersome revolutionary ideology which flew in the face of the realities of modern economic development, an intense economic nationalism, an inherent racialism which had overriding economic aspects, and a widespread sentiment in favour of economic and social stability. All these elements have to be taken into account in formulating a hypothesis of the political economy of fascism. In this light even the most consistent of the hypotheses, those which equate fascism to a stage in capitalism or to the defensive reactions of major capital interests, are inadequate. There was in fact no way in which such disparate and contradictory elements could be fitted together into a logical and coherent economic whole, the more so as the acceptance of war as a necessary vehicle for the assertion of national power greatly strengthened the role of the major manufacturing interests in the state. The differences in priority given to these various elements accounts for many divergences between Italian and German economic policies in the fascist period and it may well be that these differences will be seen as more important and more interesting than the similarities. But most economic historians have so far adopted the convention of treating 'the fascist economies' as an entity in the inter-war period. The historical evidence partly justifies this convention. The new combination of social and political forces provided, at the least, the opportunity for a different range of economic policies; at the most it led to a revolutionary attempt at a socio-economic reconstruction of the continent. Which of these two views is nearer to the truth still remains to be decided, and that can only be done by further research.

## NOTE

1. Of particular relevance here are: W. S. Allen, *The Nazi Seizure of Power: The Experience of a Single Town* (Chicago, 1965); G. Botz, *Gewalt in der Politik* (to be published in 1975); H. S. Brevig, *NS - fra sekt til parti* (Oslo, 1970); A. A. de Jonge, *Het nationaalsocialisme in Nederland* (The Hague, 1968); G. A. Kooy, *Het echec van een 'volkse' Beweging* (Assen, 1964); J. Noakes, *The Nazi Party in Lower Saxony 1921-1933* (Oxford, 1973); K. O'Lessker, 'Who voted for Hitler?' in *American Journal of Sociology*, 74 (1968); N. Schäfer, *NSDAP: Entwicklung und Struktur der Staatspartei im dritten Reich* (Marburg, 1957); A. Szymanski, 'Fascism, Industrialism and Socialism: the Case of Italy,' in *Comparative Studies in Society and History*, XV, 4 (1973).

# PART VI
## Interpretations

# 11

# Interpretations of Fascism

FRANCIS L. CARSTEN

Eight years ago George L. Mosse, in the first issue of the *Journal of Contemporary History*, boldly stated: 'In our century, two revolutionary movements have made their mark upon Europe: that originally springing from Marxism, and fascist revolution... but fascism has been a neglected movement,' while many historians and political scientists had occupied themselves with the left-wing parties and revolutions.[1] Today fascism can no longer be called a neglected subject. Indeed, there is a large volume of books and articles, not only dealing with the fascist movements of individual countries but also many comparative studies, trying to establish the differences as well as the similarities between the various movements which have been called 'fascist.' This is partly due to the industry and devotion of Professor Ernst Nolte who in 1963 published one of the fundamental studies of the problem, a comparison of the Action Française, Italian fascism, and German National Socialism;[2] he has since then written several more books on the fascist movements[3] and has edited a volume of source material, assembling theories put forward by a large variety of writers on the subject of fascism during the past half-century.[4] His example has inspired many others, and the development of the New Left has provided another impetus to the study of fascism. No doubt some of the interest in the subject is purely political and polemical; but even on a more scholarly level the volume of recent publications seems to justify a survey of the theories, old and new, and a preliminary answer to the question to what extent they are new or merely restating older views, and what may be the most fruitful approaches to a further study of the problem. This paper does not pretend to be exhaustive but hopes to stimulate further discussion, by historians, political scientists, sociologists, and social psychologists, for the study of fascism invites a cooperative effort of several academic disciplines: a cooperative effort which is not always easy to achieve. This survey will largely neglect publications devoted to one country and concentrate above all on comparative and more general contributions to the subject.

One of the problems which from the outset occupied the attention of political analysts—and indeed remains one of the central issues of any analysis of fascism—was: where did the mass following of the fascist parties come from, and which social groups tended to support them? Clearly, it was not the industrial working class, which by and large followed the Marxist parties, nor was it the bourgeoisie proper which even numerically

could not have provided a mass following. Hence the answer given by
Italian critics of fascism as early as the early 1920s was that this mass support came from the *piccola borghesia*, the lower middle classes in town and
country. Thus Giovanni Zibordi wrote in 1922 that Italy was 'a country
which has a surplus of the lower middle classes, and it is they who, under
the influence of special circumstances and favoured by them, have made as
it were their own revolution, combining it with a counterrevolution of the
bourgeoisie.' Zibordi observed at the same time that, among the followers
of the fascists, 'those declassed by the war are particularly numerous: the
youngsters who went to the front before they were twenty years old and
came back at the age of 23 or 24, being neither able nor willing to return to
their studies or their places of work in a regular fashion; the petty
bourgeois from a very modest and inferior background who during the war
became officers or NCOs... and who today cannot get reconciled to go
back to their modest occupations.'[5] Zibordi's opinion was echoed in 1923
by Luigi Salvatorelli who stated 'that the petit-bourgeois element not only
predominates numerically, but in addition is the characteristic and
directing element.... Thus fascism represents the class struggle of the
lower middle class which exists between capitalism and proletariat as the
third [group] between two combatants.' But he added that the lower
middle class was not 'a true social class with its own strength and functions,
but a conglomerate living at the margin of the capitalist process of
production.'[6]

These views have since been echoed by numerous writers, Italian as well
as non-Italian. Thus Palmiro Togliatti, leader of the Italian Communist
party, wrote in 1928: 'The social basis of fascism consists of certain strata of
the petty bourgeoisie in town and country.... In the towns too fascism
leans above all on the lower middle classes: partly workmen (artisans),
specialists and traders, partly elements displaced on account of the war
(former officials, cripples, 'arditi,' volunteers).'[7] Another prominent
Italian left-winger, Angelo Tasca, stated a few years later: 'This petty and
middle bourgeoisie... formed the backbone of fascism in Italy and everywhere else. But the expression "middle class" must be given a wider meaning, to include the son of a family waiting for a job or for his inheritance to
*déclassés* of all kinds, temporary or permanent, from the half-pay officer to
the *lumpenproletarier*, from the strike-breaker to the jobless intellectual.'[8]
Similarly social psychologists like Erich Fromm and Wilhelm Reich wrote
during the second world war: 'Nazi ideology was enthusiastically welcomed
by the lower sections of the *Mittelstand*, small shopkeepers, artisans, white
collar workers and *Lumpenproletariet*'[9] and: 'The *Mittelstand* began to
move and, in the form of fascism, became a social force.'[10] More recently a
well-known American sociologist, Seymour Lipset, maintained: 'The thesis
that fascism is basically a middle-class movement representing a protest
against both capitalism *and* socialism, big business *and* big unions, is far

from original.... Data from a number of countries demonstrate that classic fascism is a movement of the propertied middle classes, who for the most part normally support liberalism.'[11]

At a conference in Reading some years ago, several speakers held that the lower middle classes were particularly prone to the fascist appeal. Thus Professor Kogan said: 'The lower-middle class, rejecting proletarian egalitarianism as socially degrading, while not having a secure position itself, would be most vulnerable to the fascist appeal.' And Dr. Solé-Thura: 'Fascist movements came about as an expression of discontent in the lower middle classes of both town and country.'[12] Professor Nolte, on the other hand, has tried to define more precisely what sections of the lower middle class belonged to the original fascists: 'the cadres of its shock-troops were not formed from "the" petty bourgeoisie, but from certain fringe sections of the petty bourgeoisie, the "mercenaries" and the academic youth with its irrational inclinations.'[13] A more recent German study of the origins of fascism emphasizes that it was above all the economic and social threat to the existence of the Mittelstand which made it susceptible to fascist propaganda; 'a precondition of fascism is the economic threat to one or several groups of the Mittelstand and the capitalist bourgeoisie. If capitalism were "harmonious," "free from crises"...there would be no need of fascism.'[14] Thus the view that certain sections of the middle classes — whether propertied or threatened, lower middle or middle, urban or rural — provided the first cadres and the mass following of fascism is widely held to the present day. It seems only a variant of this view if a well-known German historian, Martin Broszat, emphasizes that 'the fascist movements in all these countries (Germany, Italy, Hungary, and Rumania) discovered and used the national and political potential of the small peasants and agricultural labourers.... Often the small peasants above all voted for the fascists because the latter were the first national party whose propagandists came into the villages and identified themselves with the interests and the feelings of the peasants.'[15] Yet fascism practically everywhere was a movement that started in the towns and was later carried from the towns into the villages; that is true even of eastern Europe where the rural character of the fascist movements was more pronounced than in the more western countries, and where the neglect of the peasantry by the traditional political parties was proverbial.[16]

Apart from the peasants, who indeed were particularly prone to listen to fascist propaganda, two other social groups were extremely prominent among the earliest followers of fascist parties, and indeed provided them with their first semi-military squads or storm troops (and both were very largely of lower middle-class origin): former officers and soldiers, especially ex-servicemen of the first world war, and university students and young graduates; during the first years after 1918 these two groups overlapped. Again Zibordi was one of the first to make this point.[17] It has been repeated more recently by Stuart Woolf, who, discussing the effects of the first world war, has pointed out that it 'created vast masses of ex-combatants who were to form the most fertile seedbeds of nascent nationalistic and fascist movements.'[18] And on the other side of the Atlantic, Professor Sauer has found: 'It may even be said that a distinct interest group was formed within the fascist mixture by what might be called the military desperadoes, veterans of the First World War and the postwar struggles, who had not been reintegrated into either the civilian society or the armed forces.'[19] Similarly a German historian has recently stated: 'It was no accident that ex-servicemen who had not been socially reintegrated formed the nucleus of the fascist movements.'[20]

Perhaps the enthusiastic participation of university students in the fascist movements, above all in central and eastern Europe, has been stressed less often. Especially the Iron Guard started as an organisation of Rumanian students, and in Germany and Austria the universities became strongholds of National Socialism many years before the so-called 'seizure of power.' Here it was in the first instance bitter economic distress and the dismal prospects of ever obtaining a post, but even more so the fervent nationalism and anti-bolshevism of the post-war years that drove many thousands of students into the Free Corps and the para-military formations of the right, and then into the fascist camp. From Finland to Spain, from Flanders to Italy, students were among the most ardent and convinced fighters in the fascist cause. Indeed, at least one recent writer has gone further and finds in 'the mass rush into the fascist movements above all the signs of an aggressive and violent revolt of the young.'[21] This seems to be too wide and too vague a formulation, for we would still like to know from what sections of the population these youngsters came; and it takes too little account of the many older men among the leaders as well as among the followers of the fascist movements.

All the writers quoted so far seek the social basis of the fascist parties in the middle class or certain sections of it. Quite different is the interpretation of those who believe that these parties were able to attract followers from *all* sections of society, but especially the uprooted and declassed elements. Again this interpretation was formulated as early as the early 1920s and has been frequently restated since. Curiously enough, it apparently was first put forward by a well-known communist, Clara Zetkin — an interpretation which differs considerably from later communist pronouncements on the subject. 'The carrier of fascism,' she stated in 1923, 'is not a small caste, but broad social groups, large masses which reach far into the proletariat. . . . Masses of many thousands flocked to fascism. It became a refuge for those without a political home, for the socially uprooted, for those without an existence and the disappointed.'[22] And some years later a dissident communist theorist, August Thalheimer, wrote: 'Parasitic elements of all classes which are uprooted economically and socially, excluded from the direct process of production, are the natural elements, the natural tools of the "executive power which has made itself independent" ' —a definition which he applied to Bonapartism as well as to fascism.[23] This definition was then taken up and developed further by another Marxist writer with a similar intellectual background, Paul Sering (Richard Löwenthal), who found 'that this [fascist] party recruits itself from members of all classes, while within it certain groups are prevalent and form its nucleus, groups which have been called "middle groups" in a confusing terminology. The bourgeoisie is represented, but only the bourgeoisie which is in debt and needs support; the working class is represented, but only the workers who are chronically unemployed and unable to fight, living in distressed areas; the urban lower middle classes join, but only the ruined lower middle classes, the rentiers are included, but only the rentiers expropriated by the inflation; officers and intellectuals lead, but only ex-officers and bankrupt intellectuals. These groups form the nucleus of the movement—it has the character of a true community of bankruptcy—and this allows the movement to expand beyond its nucleus into all social classes parallel with the crisis because it is socially interlinked with all of them.'[24]

These views have been echoed more recently by several historians. Thus a German-American historian has stated: 'Historical evidence shows that support of fascism may not be confined to the classical elements of the lower middle class...but may extend to a wide variety of groups in the large field between the workers on the one hand and big business, the aristocracy, and the top levels of the bureaucracy on the other.'[25] Another American professor agrees: 'The component sectors of both fascism and nazism could not be reduced to lower middle classes and Lumpenproletariat; an assorted variety of social categories took an active part in fascist movements: war veterans, unemployed, young people, peasants. A common trait was recognized in all groups—their uprootedness.'[26] And a British survey concurs: 'Fascist parties, then, had a fairly uniform doctrine, but extremely varying social composition. From whatever class the support came, it was invariably made up of the chronically discontented.... Poor aristocrats and gentry, ex-service or junior officers, unemployed or underemployed university graduates and students, ambitious small businessmen and aspiring youths from the lower middle and working classes, all became prominent as the élite of the élitists.'[27] There can be little doubt that this analysis is basically correct, that the term 'lower middle class' is too general and too vague to explain the wide differences in social background of the fascist leaders and followers (and the participation of large numbers of the working class). The element of uprootedness, of social insecurity, of a position threatened and assailed, of loss of status, is of vital importance for the problem; and in this century the greatest uprooter, the greatest destroyer of security was the first world war with its aftermath of revolution and civil war. This would also explain why no mass fascist movements arose in the aftermath of the second world war, which was not followed by revolutions, civil war, and vast economic crises but by a great effort of economic reconstruction.

If violent opposition to socialist or proletarian revolution was one of the primary causes of the growth of fascism, it is also true that the fascist movements only developed *after* these revolutionary forces had been decisively defeated, when the threat had already disappeared.[28] In Italy the occupation of the factories by the workers ended in their evacuation and a signal defeat of the left, which was badly split and disunited. In Germany the left-wing risings of the early 1920s were defeated by the Free Corps and the army, and in the vast slump of the early 1930s the working-class movement was thrown onto the defensive and totally unable to act. In Hungary and Finland the fascist movements grew after the end of the civil war and decisive defeats of the local communists from which they were unable to recover. Again, the first to point this out, as far as Italy was concerned, was Zibordi who wrote in 1922: 'Fascism is...the instrument of a counter-revolution against a proletarian revolution which did exist only in the form of a programme and a threat.'[29] And after the Nazi victory in Germany, Otto Bauer pointed out: 'But in reality fascism did not triumph at the moment when the bourgeoisie was threatened by the proletarian revolution: it triumphed when the proletariat had long been weakened and forced onto the defensive, when the revolutionary flood had abated. The capitalists and the large landowners did not entrust the fascist hordes with the power of the state so as to protect themselves against a threatening proletarian revolution, but so as to depress the wages, to destroy the social gains of the working class, to eradicate the trade unions and the positions of power gained by the working class.'[30] Recently a young German left-wing analyst has once more emphasized this point: 'Fascism is preceded by an attempt at proletarian revolution which largely ended in failure or by revolution-like risings of the proletariat (as in Italy). These revolutionary attempts of the proletariat were supported by sections of the lower middle class and semi-proletarian groups.' Preconditions similar to these, he continues, also existed in Austria, Hungary, and Spain before the establishment of conservative dictatorships.[31]

Was the threat then purely imaginary, the fear of proletarian revolution unjustified — or to put it more crudely, was it deliberately exaggerated by an unscrupulous propaganda? This, on the whole, is not the opinion of the modern historians. Thus Professor Trevor-Roper has stated: 'For fascism, as an effective movement, was born of fear. It might have independent intellectual roots; it might owe its form, here and there, to independent national or personal freaks; but its force, its dynamism, sprang from the fear of a new, and this time "proletarian" revolution.'[32] And Renzo de Felice has spoken of a double fear: 'The winning fascist faction accepted a compromise with the existing order, because of the fear of revolution that haunted the ruling classes in Italy. But the basic motivation of this faction was also fear of revolution, a fear of the left-wing fascists mobilizing and taking power.'[33] A younger German writer of the New Left has made this point in much more general terms: 'The fact that capitalist industrial society cannot be overlooked and the experience of being without any power, of being the prisoner of anonymous forces produce a fear which then seeks a firm support.... In fascism there assembled above all the sections of the bourgeois middle classes which were declassed or immediately threatened with becoming déclassés. By their votes for fascism they protested against this threat.'[34] Yet relatively few historians have ventured into this field which they may feel belongs more properly to the social psychologists.

Indeed, social psychologists, social scientists, as well as historians have stressed much more the loss of prestige and of social security which affected the masses after the first world war. This point was made in its classical form by Erich Fromm in 1942 and has been repeated often ever since: 'The authority of the monarchy had been uncontested and, by leaning on it and identifying themselves with it, the members of the lower middle classes gained a feeling of security and of self-admiring, narcissistic pride.... There was the lost war and the overthrow of the monarchy. The state and the princes had been secure rocks on which—seen psychologically—the petit bourgeois had built his existence; their downfall and the defeat shook the foundation of his existence.... Not only the economic situation of the lower middle classes, but their social prestige too declined rapidly after the war. Before the war they could believe that they were something better than the worker. After the war the social prestige of the working class rose, and that of the lower middle class sank correspondingly. There was no one any longer on whom they could look down, a privilege which had always been one of the strongest positive factors in the life of the philistine.'[35] This interpretation has been restated by political scientists and others. Thus Professor Germani has told us: 'It is widely recognized that "disequilibration" had caused loss of status (in terms of prestige as well as in terms of power and wealth) for the urban middle class. Such loss had taken place both in relative and in absolute terms: decreasing distance because of the advance of the working class, absolute downward mobility in terms of unemployment, inflation, decreasing income, and decreasing political influence.... The advance of the working class was resented as an "invasion" or "usurpation" of status.'[36] And a German writer has spoken emphatically of the 'fear of decadence' and added: 'Blind fear of decline has been one of the most powerful roots of fascist tendencies, and not only in Germany.'[37] There can be no doubt that these fears were not imaginary but largely justified, that the middle and the lower middle classes, the 'little man,' had lost their stable place in society, their security and prosperity, that they felt helpless in the new order of things after the war, the victims of forces which they could not understand.

The social psychologists have pointed to other traits in the fascist make-up which had an important influence in attracting the masses. Thus Erich Fromm has enumerated the 'veneration of the strong' and the 'hatred of the weak,' 'the longing to submit, and the lust for power';[38] and Wilhelm Reich wrote at the same time: 'The fascist mentality is the mentality of the "little man," suppressed, longing for authority and at the same time rebellious.... The fascist is the sergeant in the vast army of our deeply ill civilization, the civilization of big industry.'[39] Reich also emphasized that the fascists strongly identified themselves with their Leader: 'every National Socialist felt himself, in spite of his dependence, like a "little Hitler." '[40] Fromm equally stressed another form of identification which worked strongly after the Nazi seizure of power: 'A further impetus to loyalty towards the Nazi regime became operative after Hitler had come into power: for many millions, the majority of the population, Hitler's government was identical with "Germany." As soon as he had formed the government, "to oppose him" meant no less than to exlude oneself from the community of the Germans.... Apparently nothing is more difficult for the average person to bear but the feeling not to be at one with a larger group. Even if German burghers were strongly opposed to the Nazi principles, as soon as they had to choose between standing alone and belonging to Germany the large majority chose the latter.'[41]

Such ideas have been fruitful in stimulating modern historians to accept terms and views imported from a different discipline. Thus Professor Mosse found: 'In under-developed countries, the stress upon the end to alienation, the belief in the organic community, brought dividends—for the exclusion of the workers and peasants from society had been so total that purely economic considerations could take second place.'[42] And the sociologist Dr. Barbu stated: 'One of the most fruitful approaches was to conceive of the party as a type of primary community, a corporate morality, which tried to reinforce the feeling of belonging to something, the primary emotional involvement of the individual.... In an industrializing society it might appeal to the lower middle class, in a transitional society to the people who became available through a primary mobilization process, the peasants who left the villages to come to the towns. But the problem remained the same all the time: the fascist movement appealed to people who needed strong bonds.... The fascist party offered a type of solidarity; it appealed to people who suffered from the disintegration of traditional or any kind of social solidarity.'[43] A young German historian wrote more recently of the 'salvation [found] in the submission to a strong authority. This can express itself in the identification either with a powerful collective—the state, the nation, the enterprise—or with the personality of the Leader: the "authoritarian-masochistic character" projects its ego-

ideal onto a Leader figure with which he identifies himself unconditionally.'[44] Indeed, there seems no reason why such a process should only
be at work 'in under-developed countries,' for in modern industrial
societies too the alienated might join a party with which they can totally
identify themselves, all the readier if that party stands in total opposition to
society and state and seeks to destroy them. This, of course, need not be a
fascist party, but under certain political and social conditions, and as far as
certain social groups are concerned, it would be a fascist party and Leader
with whom the masses could identify most easily, to whose promise of reintegration they would most readily listen. The 'people's community' (*Volksgemeinschaft*) promised by the leaders of the Third Reich did not
materialize, but millions were longing for it.

In the early stages of the rise of fascist movements, a very similar mechanism was operative on the local level. As Dr. Adrian Lyttelton has found
for Italy, 'The origins of many squads are to be found in a loose, informal
relationship between a group of adolescents, somewhat resembling that of
a youth gang.... Primary ties of kinship or friendship were important in
creating a feeling of camaraderie among the *squadristi*. The existence of
this "small group solidarity" served to protect the Fascist from the feelings
of impotence and ennui common among those in the grip of large, impersonal bureaucratic organizations; they seemed to allow the individual to
achieve both integration and independence. At the same time, of course,
the violence which was the essence of *squadrismo* allowed an outlet for
aggression.'[45] Exactly the same could be said of the 'gangs' of local
storm-troopers, or indeed of their predecessors, the Free Corps and
uniformed para-military associations in Germany.

There was another psychological factor, important for both Germany
and Italy (but not for some of the other countries where fascist movements
grew): the feeling of national shame which affected millions on account of
defeat and, what was in their eyes, an ignominious peace settlement. This
is most obvious for the countries defeated in 1918, Germany and Hungary;
but it is also true of Italy, where the crushing defeat of Caporetto caused
the same sense of shame, where the ultimate victory over the Austrians was
'mutilated' by the peace settlement, and where 'the war was won but the
peace lost.'[46] This feeling directly inspired the first fascist enterprises and
above all Gabriele D'Annunzio's expedition to Fiume, the dress rehearsal
for the march on Rome. Recently a younger German historian has drawn
our attention to 'the groups of enemies against which fascism directs the
wrath of the masses'; he believes that 'those social groups are especially
suited as objects of aggression which are distinguished from the large
majority by their looks or their behaviour and which therefore can easily be
recognized. Racial, national or religious minorities...thus function only
too often as objects of aggression. They have the additional advantage that
they are rather defenceless so that the mob can discharge its aggressions

without risk and punishment. Violence and murder...committed against members of the minorities are looked upon not only as permitted but even as an honourable national service.'[47] Admittedly, all these factors cannot be measured by statistics and defy a more precise definition, but they seem important in any assessment of the roots of fascism, and helpful in any attempt to answer the question why fascist movements were able to attract vast crowds and to perpetrate deeds which any normal society would classify as criminal. Here again the primary catalyst would seem to be the first world war which accustomed millions to the use of violence and elevated it to the rank of a patriotic duty.

This once more is not a new perception but it was recognized as early as 1928 by the Italian socialist Filippo Turati (who had been a pacifist during the war): 'The war... accustomed the youngsters as well as the grown ups to the daily use of usual and unusual weapons, ...it praised individual and collective murder, blackmail, arrest, the macabre joke, the torturing of prisoners, the "punitive expeditions," the summary executions, ...it created in general the atmosphere in which alone the fascist bacillus could grow and spread.'[48] Turati also thought that this spirit in particular affected the youngsters who, because of their age, had been unable to participate in the war but were all the more eager to win military laurels, especially in a situation where their lives were no longer at stake.[49] Because the Italian (and German) governments were notoriously weak and unable to cope with the ever-worsening economic crisis, there was 'a growing longing for a strong government,' a 'yearning for peace and order,' for 'a strong hand at the helm.'[50] The willingness of large masses to accept a Leader, who would overcome misery and strife and lead them to a glorious future, can partly be explained by the social and economic distress of the post-war period. As Professor Vierhaus has pointed out, 'sections of the population which politically and socially were without any orientation had a need of strong authority; they acclaimed the leaders in whom the masses not seldom put semi-religious hopes of salvation, to which the leaders and their propaganda replied with the vague but all the more effective promise of a general improvement, a better, proud national future.'[51] Indeed, fascist rallies often had the atmosphere of a revivalist assembly, and the masses shouted: 'The Leader is always right!'

Several historians have stated that—in contrast with all other parties and political movements—the Leader of a fascist party needed charisma, but very little effort has been made to define this charisma, or the social and psychological conditions under which it became effective. Thus Professor Seton-Watson has written: 'An obviously important feature of fascism which often gets left out...is the charismatic leader. Mussolini, Degrelle, and José Antonio Primo de Rivera were clearly men of outstanding abilities. Szálasi and Codreanu were complex personalities combining ruthlessness with strange flashes of nobility of character. Hitler still defies analysis.'[52] Yet it was Hitler before whom battle-hardened generals trembled, who was able to arouse the masses to a fever pitch, whose decisions were unquestioningly accepted by his enthusiastic followers. In a more general form Professor Vierhaus maintains: 'The Leader taking his stand on the basis of the plebiscite can only legitimize himself by his charisma, i.e. the fact that he stands above the ordinary and commonplace, by his personal authority. This has to rely on proving itself every day by deed and success; hence the ever-repeated public appearances of the Leader with a ceremonial which is cunningly adapted to different situations.'[53]

It has often been said that without Hitler there would have been no National Socialism, or that at least National Socialism would have been very different without him. This again seems a field where the historian or the political scientist might have to rely on the help of the social psychologist. A well-known psychologist has recently defined Hitler 'as the quintessential embodiment of Germany's and Austria's many defeat-shattered, uprooted "little men," craving for the security of belonging, for the restoration of power and glory, and for vengeance.' He gave expression 'to a state of mind existing in millions of people, not only in Germany.'[54] This is true, but it does not get us much further.

If the psychological factors which conditioned fascism are difficult to define and have to a large extent defied a more precise analysis, the same need not apply to the social preconditions of its growth. More than fifty years ago, in 1923, Luigi Salvatorelli, who understood fascism as a movement of the lower middle classes, thought that fascism developed in Italy because Italy was economically backward and thus had a particularly numerous petty bourgeoisie.[55] Ten years later the sociologist Franz Borkenau, who understood fascism in the same sense, added that its victory in Italy was due to 'the absence of a politically and economically adequate industrial bourgeoisie.' As fascism destroyed those sections of the working-class movements which were willing to reach a compromise with the bourgeoisie, 'the bourgeoisie of the most developed capitalist countries cannot afford such a policy. In countries where up to 75 per cent of the population belong to the proletariat in the proper sense of the term, democracy, reformism and free trade unions are virtually indispensable factors for the preservation of the status quo. To do without them is only feasible in countries where the proletariat is still weak enough simply to be suppressed. . . . In more developed conditions this is not a question of advantages and disadvantages, but the destruction of the modern working-class movement is a total impossibility.'[56] When these lines were published Hitler had already been appointed chancellor of Germany.

Some years later Otto Bauer attempted another analysis of fascism from a Marxist point of view, which in his opinion rested on a social equilibrium: 'The fascist dictatorship comes into being as the result of a peculiar equilibrium of the social classes. On one side there is the bourgeoisie which con-

trols the means of production and circulation and the power of the state.
. . . On the other side stands the working class which is led by reformist
socialists and the trade unions. Reformism and trade unions have become
stronger than the bourgeoisie is willing to accept. . . . Exactly as the absolutism of the early capitalist epoch. . .developed on the basis of the equilibrium of the forces of the feudal nobility and the bourgeoisie. . .so the new
fascist absolutism is the result of a temporary equilibrium when the bourgeoisie could not force the proletariat to accept its will by the old legal
methods, and the proletariat was unable to liberate itself from the rule of
the bourgeoisie; and thus both classes fell under the dictatorship of the violent mob which the capitalists used against the proletariat until they themselves had to submit to the dictatorship.'[57] Bauer's opinion has more
recently been restated by Dr. Solé-Tura: 'Fascism is the solution found for
the contradictions caused by the development of capitalism at a characteristic point of fundamental class equilibrium.'[58] Yet Bauer's comparison
with the period of absolutism can hardly be maintained: the seventeenth
century was a period when the feudal economy had long disintegrated,
when the power of the nobility was no longer as strong as it had once been,
when a new economic order based on the towns and the urban middle
classes was developing: hence there could be a time of equilibrium when
the princes were able to play off one group against the other. But it would
be vastly overestimating the strength of social democracy and the trade
unions to say that it balanced that of the bourgeoisie; the very ease with
which social democracy was destroyed in Central Europe proves that this
strength was more imaginary than real.

There is, however, another theory which may be more helpful in explaining why certain countries have been more prone to produce fascist
mass movements than others. Professor Nolte has suggested a geographical
classification combined with an approach based on social structure, 'the
path of growing industrialization and a declining share of the agrarian
population, which in Albania and Yugoslavia around 1930 comprised
around 80 per cent of the total but in England counted for hardly more
than 10 per cent. It could obviously be held that in the former group the
social preconditions of fascism did not yet exist, while in the last group they
existed no longer, that only in the centre of Central Europe fascism found
the preconditions for a full development.' Although Nolte then proceeds to
point to the obvious difficulties in accepting this interpretation, he concludes that 'the view which sees the primary cause of fascist movements in a
certain mixture of social forces remains noteworthy and important.'[59]
Indeed, it seems that societies undergoing a rapid social and economic
transformation from a preindustrial to an industrial society proved a
favourite breeding ground of the fascist movements, that members of certain social groups found it particularly difficult to adjust themselves to
social change, to accept a lower social status or the rise of a new social

force, that the period of quick transition was the most difficult one: when the process of industrialization was more or less complete a new equilibrium was established, and with it greater social security, for the individual as well as for the group as a whole. Yet this theory, while it seems worth exploring in greater detail, still does not answer why the fascist movements developed in the 1920s and 1930s, and why they became mass movements in certain countries but not in others. Other factors to be considered here obviously are the stability or instability of political institutions, the strength or weakness of democratic and liberal traditions, the popularity or unpopularity of parliament and the political parties, the marked differences in the political and social structures of the European countries. Perhaps little headway can be made in this field until many more detailed studies have become available.

Another, much more tangible precondition for the *success* of the fascists was their alliance with certain ruling circles and with the political right, and there does not seem to be any disagreement among the historians on this issue, irrespective of their political views. Thus more than ten years ago Nolte stated unequivocally: 'Hardly less than Hitler's oratorical gifts and passion, the German army, the connections of Dietrich Eckart and the protection offered by the director of [the Munich] police Pöhner contributed to make the National Socialist Party into what it was in 1923.... The collaboration of the state and of leading circles in society became at least as important for the development of National Socialism as for that of fascism' in Italy.[60] More recently another German historian has written: 'In reality National Socialism like other fascist movements could only reach power in alliance with the traditional Right, and it received its support because its attacks were to a very large extent directed against the political Left.'[61] From the political left a younger German writer agrees with this thesis: 'The system of rule established by Italian fascism too can be defined as an alliance between the fascist movement and the social upper strata. Yet the balance was different from the German form. Already during the period before the seizure of power Italian fascism had been unable to gain such a strong mass basis as German fascism. The result was that there the fascist movement, even after its "seizure of power," did not obtain the same position of strength in its coalition with the social upper classes as it did in Germany.'[62] Similar is the statement of an American historian: 'The general conclusion one can make from the rise to power of Mussolini and Hitler seems to be this: The radical Right had its best chance in societies where older but still powerful elites see their values and interests eroded by rapid and modernizing social change, change which generates a massive liberal and left threat to "old ways." When this happens conservatives, ultraconservatives and reactionaries of differing ideologies and classes tend to unite and strike back "by any means necessary."[63]

Indeed, one can go further and say: if a fascist party disregards the forging of a firm alliance with the forces of the old order and of the state and tries to seize power relying entirely on its own strength, the attempt is doomed to failure. This is the lesson which Hitler drew from his Munich putsch of 1923 when he aimed at drawing the Bavarian government and army onto his side but ultimately failed to achieve this end; when he came to power in 1933 he was appointed chancellor by the ancient field-marshal, he had the support of the army and of the bureaucracy, and he formed a coalition government with the right-wing German Nationalist party. When Horia Sima, the leader of the powerful Iron Guard, tried to seize power in Bucharest at the beginning of 1941 he failed because the government of Marshal Antonescu and the Rumanian army turned against him. Szálasi, the leader of the Arrow Cross movement, was unable to form a firm alliance with the traditional right in Hungary and the government of the Regent Horthy, hence he was excluded from power until he was raised to the position of a puppet leader by the Germans at the end of the war. Here a striking difference exists between the seizure of power by a fascist party and by a movement of the extreme left.

In spite of these facts, political commentators, historians, and political scientists seem to be agreed in using the term 'fascist revolution,' while they are also aware that the fascist movements contained counter-revolutionary elements. Thus Zibordi wrote as early as 1922: 'It seems to me that fascism is at the same time the following: a counterrevolution of the true middle class against a "red" revolution, . . . a revolution, or rather a convulsion of petty bourgeois, declassed and discontented sections, and a military revolution.'[64] The German former National Socialist Hermann Rauschning in 1938 coined the slogan of 'The Revolution of Nihilism' and declared: 'National Socialism has not only eliminated the positions of power held by the working class, which could justify the verdict that it is a counterrevolutionary movement, but it has equally destroyed the middle class, the political and social positions of the middle class, and of the old, leading social strata. . . . The German revolution therefore is at least both: a social revolution and a counterrevolution.'[65] And from the German left it was stated at about the same time: 'The fascist revolution is thus a genuine revolution insofar as it presents an important scissure in the development of bourgeois society which necessarily is taking place in revolutionary forms and is caused by economic developments. Its typical results are: 1. a new higher form of the organization of the state; 2. a new reactionary form of social organization; 3. a growing check to economic development by reactionary forces which have usurped the power of the state.'[66]

Most modern historians concur that the fascist movements were revolutionary. Thus Professor Mosse speaks of the 'two revolutionary movements' of the twentieth century, of the 'fascist revolution,' which in his opinion in the West 'was primarily a bourgeois revolution.'[67] Professor Sauer has stated in the *American Historical Review:* 'There is virtual agreement among scholars that fascist movements contained, contrary to the Marxist thesis, a true revolutionary potential.'[68] And Professor Bracher has written: 'An interpretation which sees in fascism and National Socialism only the final stage of a reactionary counterrevolution and denies it any revolutionary character amounts to an incorrect simplification of complicated processes. All four basic currents which have contributed to the ideologies of fascism and of National Socialism are simultaneously determined by revolutionary and by reactionary forces.'[69] But there are a few dissentient voices. Thus the American editor of an anthology on fascism maintains: 'Fascism cannot be understood if it is viewed as a revolution. It was a counterrevolution. Its purpose was to prevent the liberalization and radicalization of Italy and Germany. Property and income distribution and the traditional class structure remained roughly the same under fascist rule. What changes there were favoured the old elites or certain segments of the party membership.'[70] A similar view is held by a German left-wing analyst: 'As the beginning of a fascist dictatorship one must see the transfer of power to, or the taking over of power by the most reactionary forces existing which aim at the establishment of a rule of unlimited violence so as to secure the interests of the native, or maybe a foreign, monopoly capitalism. This need not necessarily be fascist parties, but could be the military, or leaders of conservative reactionary parties, or representatives of the higher clergy.'[71]

The issue seems to be confused by the fact that fascist parties—in Germany and in Italy—only came into power through an alliance with conservative and reactionary forces, but an alliance that did not last. Also, in both countries, the opposition of more radical, 'revolutionary' fascist groups had to be overcome before the dictatorship was securely established. Yet it would be silly to deny that there were genuine revolutionary elements in the fascist movements, especially so in central and southeastern Europe, and that important changes in the existing social structure were introduced by the German—but less so by the Italian—dictatorship. As there were only these two fascist regimes, any generalization becomes very difficult. Perhaps the cautious statement by Professor Bracher that revolutionary as well as reactionary elements were present in the fascist ideologies might be extended to the fascist movements as such, and the proportions naturally varied from country to country. Wherever social conditions were particularly antediluvian and radical social reform was urgently necessary, for example in Hungary and Rumania, the revolutionary elements would be stronger, and vice versa.

As the basic elements of fascist ideology, Professor Bracher has identified four currents: national imperialism, étatism, populist socialism, and racialism.[72] To these might be added two more: a kind of national romanticism, glorifying the agrarian and pre-industrial past and military virtues,[73] and corporativism,[74] which had little influence in Germany, but a much stronger one in Italy, Austria, and Spain. Whatever other elements we might add to this list, it seems clear that most of these components were traditional or reactionary, and that only very few could qualify as 'revolutionary.' There were no doubt 'populist' traits in the fascist movements, as several historians have recently emphasized, but the comparison with the *Narodniki* of tsarist Russia seems far-fetched and untenable — precisely because the *Narodniki* were a genuine revolutionary group inspired by a revolutionary creed.[75] In any case, very few historians and political scientists would today accept, without any qualification, Richard Crossman's assertion of 1939: 'In Central Europe, where the economic interpretation of history was the myth of the working-class movement, Racialism became the revolutionary philosophy of a discontented German middle class.'[76] The roots of German racialism went back far into the nineteenth century, and racialist ideas formed part of the traditional armoury of the right.

Discarded too has been the view which so intelligent an historian as Arthur Rosenberg held in 1934 that fascism is 'the counter-revolutionary capitalist, the born foe of the class-conscious working class. Fascism is nothing but a modern, popularly masked form of the bourgeois-capitalist counter-revolution.'[77] This view corresponded to that propounded at the same time by the Communist International that 'fascism is the open and terrorist dictatorship of the most reactionary, chauvinist and imperialist elements of the finance capital.'[78] It has been restated since in exactly the same form in Germany: 'The basic trait of fascism is — in the summarising and still valid definition of Dimitrov — "the open and terroristic dictatorship of the most reactionary, most chauvinist and most imperialist elements of the finance capital." '[79] But the mere repetition of an old cliché does not make it any more correct or fitting a very complex reality. A critic of this view from the New Left was completely justified when he pointed out: 'Not the direct support by big capitalism caused the rise of fascism, but the economic crisis immanent in the capitalist system drove the frightened masses, above all the lower middle classes threatened by proletarianization, into the fascist camp. . . . Only when fascism had become a mass movement support by big capitalists began to a larger extent.'[80] Indeed, large numbers of finance and other big capitalists and many members of the old aristocracies were frightened by the semi-proletarian and pseudo-revolutionary character of the fascist movements — and not without reason.

There can be little doubt that, under the fascist regime, the old ruling circles were partly replaced by 'a new political class,'[81] drawn above all from the leaders of the fascist party whose origins were considerably lower down on the social scale than those of the older groups. This again was the case much more in Germany than in Italy where the old bureaucracy continued to rule almost unchallenged. And even in Germany those party leaders who entered the bureaucracy seem to have taken on its traditional attitudes and to have adopted its standards to a surprising degree.[82] But so far little research has been done in this field, and any more general conclusion must await further investigation. As Professor Schapiro has pointed out, Hitler engaged in bitter and prolonged conflicts with the bureaucracy (from which he often emerged victorious), while 'so far as Mussolini was concerned, he did not succeed in making very serious inroads into the state.'[83] It seems that there is a need here of more comparative studies. It may be the case that National Socialism against its will carried through a modernization of the administrative structure which the Weimar Republic had failed to obtain, while this was not achieved in Italy. It may well turn out, in any case, that the similarities between the two fascist regimes were as pronounced as the differences between them.

What are the conclusions of this brief survey? It seems that no fundamentally new interpretations of fascism have been put forward by the modern historians and political scientists, but that they have taken up and discussed — in one form or the other — the old interpretations of the twenties and thirties. Especially the views and ideas of Italian writers from the early 1920s, formulated from a close observation of the Italian scene, have to a large extent been confirmed by later research. But, in spite of the large volume of modern research and the many dozens of monographs and Ph.D. theses on the subject, a great deal of work remains to be done and in particular there is still a great shortage of good comparative studies. As we have seen, many modern historians are prepared to accept ideas from, and to cooperate with, social psychologists and sociologists, and this may produce more valuable results in the future. If this survey has not produced anything startlingly new, it hopes at least to stimulate further cooperation and research; for fascism remains one of the fundamental issues of the twentieth century and deserves the attention of all concerned about the fundamental traits in the development of our society. Today it is fashionable to call every dictatorship from Greece to Latin America 'fascist': a clear definition of what fascism was and what constituted a fascist movement would eliminate much confused talk and clarify the minds of many students. To equate the terms 'reactionary' and 'fascist,' or to identify military dictatorship with fascism, is to misunderstand the nature of fascism.

## NOTES

1. George L. Mosse, 'The Genesis of Fascism,' *Journal of Contemporary History*, I, 1 (1966), 14.

2. Ernst Nolte, *Der Faschismus in seiner Epoche* (Munich, 1963).

3. Above all, *Die faschistischen Bewegungen* (Munich, 1966), and *Die Krise des liberalen Systems und die faschistischen Bewegungen* (Munich, 1968).

4. *Theorien über den Faschismus* (Cologne and Berlin, 1967).

5. Giovanni Zibordi, *Critica socialista del fascismo* (Bologna, 1922), quoted by Nolte, *Theorien über den Faschismus*, 80, 85.

6. Luigi Salavatorelli, *Nationalfascismo* (Turin, 1923), quoted ibid., 130, 131, 135.

7. P. Togliatti, *A proposito del fascismo* (1928), quoted by Renzo de Felice, *Le interpretazioni del fascismo* (Bari, 1969), 181. The 'arditi' were Italian shock troops of the first world war.

8. A. Rossi (Angelo Tasca), *The Rise of Italian Fascism*, 2d ed. (New York, 1966), 340 (first published in 1938).

9. Erich Fromm, *Die Furcht vor der Freiheit* (Frankfurt, 1966), 206 (written in 1942).

10. Wilhelm Reich, *Die Massenpsychologie des Faschismus* (Cologne, 1971), 68 (written in 1942).

11. Seymour Martin Lipset, *Political Man—The Social Bases of Politics* (New York, 1960), 134, 174.

12. N. Kogan and J. Solé-Tura, in S. J. Woolf (ed.), *The Nature of Fascism* (London, 1968), 13, 43.

13. Ernst Nolte, *Die faschistischen Bewegungen* (Munich, 1966), 65.

14. Manfred Clemenz, *Gesellschaftliche Ursprünge des Faschismus* (Frankfurt, 1972), 147. 228. Compare another more simplified German view which has been put forward recently: 'their [the intellectuals'] arguments would never have brought fascism to power. This was achieved by the support of a whole social class, the lower middle class and the so-called new middle class. The lower middle class, above all the small 'independent' shopkeeper, the enemy of the big concerns, was backward-looking, and was ultimately disappointed with fascism': Otto-Ernst Schüddekopf, *Fascism* (London, 1973), 132.

15. Martin Broszat, 'Soziale und psychologische Grundlagen des Nationalsozialismus,' in E. J. Feuchtwanger, ed., *Deutschland—Wandel und Bestand* (Munich, 1973), 166 (English trans. [London, 1973], 138).

16. See especially Eugen Weber, 'The Men of the Archangel,' *Journal of Contemporary History*, I, 1 (December 1965), 111, 114, 117.

17. See the quotation in n. 5.

18. S. J. Woolf, introduction to *European Fascism* (London, 1968), 4.

19. Wolfgang Sauer, 'National Socialism: Totalitarianism or Fascism?,' *The American Historical Review*, LXXIII (1967), 411.

20. Heinrich August Winkler, 'Extremismus der Mitte?,' *Vierteljahrshefte für Zeitgeschichte*, XX (1972), 187. The article is above all a criticism of the fascism interpretation by Seymour Lipset.

21. Martin Broszat, in *Deutschland—Wandel und Bestand* (Munich, 1973), 170. (I am unable to find this quotation in the English translation, *Upheaval and Continuity—A Century of German History*, ed. E. J. Feuchtwanger [London, 1973], 134 ff.)

22. Clara Zetkin, 'Der Kampf gegen den Faschismus,' protocol of the Enlarged Executive of the Communist International (12-13 June 1923), quoted by Nolte, *Theorien über den Faschismus*, 89, 92.

23. August Thalheimer, 'Über den Faschismus' (1930), in Wolfgang Abendroth, ed., *Otto Bauer, Herbert Marcuse, Arthur Rosenberg u.a.—Faschismus und Kapitalismus* (Frankfurt and Vienna, 1967), 22.

24. Paul Sering, 'Der Faschismus,' *Zeitschrift für Sozialismus*, 24-25 (September-October 1935), 781. This analysis, published in the theoretical journal of the exiled SPD, was the first serious attempt at a Marxist analysis of the problem after Hitler's seizure of power.

25. Wolfgang Sauer, in *The American Historical Review*, LXXIII (1967), 410.

26. G. Germani, 'Fascism and Class,' in S. J. Woolf, ed., *The Nature of Fascism* (London, 1968), 72.

27. Michael Hurst, 'What is Fascism?,' *The Historical Journal*, XI (1968), 179.

28. This has been emphasized by Nolte, *Der Faschismus in seiner Epoche* (Munich, 1963), 397.

29. Giovanni Zibordi, *Critica socialista del fascismo*, quoted by Nolte, *Theorien über den Faschismus*, 80.

30. Otto Bauer, *Zwischen zwei Weltkriegen? Die Krise der Weltwirtschaft, der Demokratie und des Sozialismus* (1936), in Wolfgang Abendroth, ed., *Otto Bauer, Herbert Marcuse, Arthur Rosenberg u.a.—Faschismus und Kapitalismus*, 153-54.

31. Manfred Clemenz, *Gesellschaftliche Ursprünge des Faschismus* (Frankfurt, 1972), 213-14.

32. H. R. Trevor-Roper, 'The Phenomenon of Fascism,' in S. J. Woolf, ed., *European Fascism* (London, 1968), 23-24.

33. R. de Felice, in S. J. Woolf, ed., *The Nature of Fascism* (London, 1968), 250.

34. Reinhard Kühnl, *Formen bürgerlicher Herrschaft—Liberalismus-Faschismus* (Reinbek near Hamburg, 1971), 89-90.

35. Erich Fromm, *Die Furcht vor der Freiheit*, 208-10.

36. G. Germani, 'Fascism and Class,' op. cit., 89.

37. Wilhelm Alff, *Der Begriff Faschismus und andere Aufsätze zur Zeitgeschichte* (Frankfurt, 1971), 124 ff., 141.

38. Fromm, op. cit., 207-08.

39. Wilhelm Reich, *Die Massenpsychologie des Faschismus* (Cologne, 1971), 17.

40. Ibid., 100.

41. Fromm, op. cit., 205-206.

42. George L. Mosse, 'The Genesis of Fascism,' *Journal of Contemporary History*, I, 1 (1966), 21, with special reference to the Iron Guard and the Hungarian Arrow Cross.

43. Z. Barbu, in S. J. Woolf, ed., *The Nature of Fascism* (London, 1968), 111-12.

44. Kühnl, op. cit., p. 89.

45. Adrian Lyttelton, *The Seizure of Power—Fascism in Italy 1919-1929* (London, 1973), 244.

46. These points have above all been made by Adrian Lyttelton, especially during a recent panel discussion at Oxford on 'fascism.' Cp. ibid., 28, 30.

47. Kühnl, op. cit., 94.

48. Filippo Turati, *Fascismo, Socialismo e Democracia* (1928), quoted by Nolte, *Theorien über den Faschismus*, 144.

49. Ibid.

50. Ibid., 149; L. Villari, *The Fascist Experiment*, 41, quoted by Paul Hayes, *Fascism* (London, 1973), 148.

51. Rudolf Vierhaus, 'Faschistisches Führertum,' *Historische Zeitschrift*, 198/3 (June 1964), 629.

52. Hugh Seton-Watson, 'Fascism, Right and Left,' *Journal of Contemporary History*, I, 1 (1966), 194.

53. Vierhaus, in *Historische Zeitschrift*, 198/3, 629.

54. Henry V. Dicks, 'Deadly Fantasies,' *New Statesman*, 16 February 1973, 235.

55. Luigi Salvatorelli, *Nationalfascismo* (1923), quoted by Nolte, *Theorien über den Faschismus*, 135-36.

56. Franz Borkenau, 'Zur Soziologie des Faschismus,' *Archiv für Sozialwissenschaft und Sozialpolitik*, LXVIII (February 1933), 513-47; quoted ibid., 165, 170-71. The argument is further developed ibid., 179-80.

57. Otto Bauer, *Zwischen zwei Weltkriegen? Die Krise der Weltwirtschaft, der Demokratie und des Sozialismus*, 155-56.

58. J. Solé-Tura, 'The Political "Instrumentality" of Fascism,' in S. J. Woolf, ed., *The Nature of Fascism* (London, 1968), 49.

59. Nolte, *Die faschistischen Bewegungen*, 189-90. Cf. the geographical subdivision made by Wolfgang Sauer, in *The American Historical Review*, LXXIII (1967), 421.

60. Nolte, *Der Faschismus in seiner Epoche* (Munich, 1963), 397. See also Lyttelton, *The Seizure of Power*, 40, 118.

61. Heinrich August Winkler, in *Vierteljahrshefte für Zeitgeschichte*, XX (1972), 190; very similarly the same, *Mittelstand, Demokratie und Nationalsozialismus* (Cologne, 1972), 180.

62. Reinhard Kühnl, *Formen bürgerlicher Herrschaft—Liberalismus-Faschismus*, 138.

63. John Weiss, *Nazis and Fascists in Europe* (Chicago, 1969), 15-16.

64. Zibordi, *Critica socialista del fascismo* (1922), quoted by Nolte, *Theorien über den Faschismus*, 83-84.

65. Hermann Rauschning, *Die Revolution des Nihilismus* (Zurich, 1938), quoted ibid., 343.

66. Paul Sering (Richard Löwenthal), 'Der Faschismus,' *Zeitschrift für Sozialismus*, 24-25 (September-October 1935), 787.

67. George L. Mosse, in *Journal of Contemporary History*, I, 1 (1966), 14, 22.

68. Wolfgang Sauer, in *American Historical Review*, LXXIII (December 1967), 412.

69. Karl Dietrich Bracher, *Die deutsche Diktatur* (Cologne-Berlin, 1969), 9.

70. John Weiss, *Nazis and Fascists in Europe*, 21.

71. Kurt Gossweiler, in Kurt Gossweiler, Reinhard Kühnl and Reinhard Opitz, *Entstehung und Verhinderung—Materialien zur Faschismus-Diskussion* (Frankfurt, 1972), 35.

72. Bracher, *Die deutsche Diktatur*, 9.

73. Kühnl, *Formen bürgerlicher Herrschaft—Liberalismus—Faschismus*, 122.

74. J. Solé-Tura, in S. J. Woolf, ed., *The Nature of Fascism*, 57: 'Corporativism, the fascist ideology *par excellence*, was not a modern, but a traditional ideology in Spain.'

75. The opposite has been maintained by Martin Broszat, 'Soziale und psychologische Grundlagen des Nationalsozialismus,' in E. J. Feuchtwanger, ed., *Deutschland—Wandel und Bestand* (Munich, 1973), 166-67.

76. R. H. S. Crossman, *Government and the Governed* (London, 1939), 276.

77. Historikus (Arthur Rosenberg), *Der Faschismus als Massenbewegung* (Karlsbad, 1934), 7.

78. Thus the 13th Plenum of the Executive Committee of the Comintern in December 1933, quoted by Nolte, 'Zur Phänomenologie des Faschismus,' *Vierteljahrshefte für Zeitgeschichte*, X, 20 (1962), 384.

79. Reinhard Opitz, 'Wie bekämpft man den Faschismus?,' in Gossweiler, Kühnl and Opitz, *Entstehung und Verhinderung—Materialien zur Faschismus-Diskussion*, 46.

80. Kühnl, ibid., 41. For financial support of Italian fascism, see Lyttelton, op. cit., 142, 208-11.

81. This is the formulation of S. J. Woolf, in the Introduction to his *European Fascism*, 12. Professor Vierhaus uses the term 'a new "ruling class"': *Historische Zeitschrift*, 198/3 (1964), 627.

82. This emerges very clearly from an important thesis which, however, does not make any comparisons with Italy: A. J. Caplan, 'The Civil Servant in the Third Reich' (Ph.D. diss., Oxford University, 1973).

83. Leonard Schapiro, *Totalitarianism* (London, 1972), 66-67. Cf. N. Kogan, in S. J. Woolf, ed., *The Nature of Fascism*, 16: 'I have serious doubts whether the Fascist Party was ever a ruling party as such. Mussolini ruled as *Capo del Governo*...rather than as *Duce del Fascismo*'; and Lyttelton, op. cit., 158-66, 200-01, 293.

# 12

# Revolution? Counterrevolution? What revolution?

Eugen Weber

Almost any discussion of fascism is bound to involve consideration, explicit or not, of its revolutionary or counterrevolutionary nature. Fascists claimed to engage in a revolution. Their opponents denounced them as counterrevolutionaries. Most students divide unevenly about this: many consider the fascists' counterrevolutionary role self-evident, a few prefer to begin by taking the fascists at their word, some still judge the charges unproven.

At any rate, the debate suggests the high symbolic, hence passional and practical, value of terms like revolution and counterrevolution, increasingly loaded, in intellectual and political intercourse, with an ethical burden that even the mass media perceive. The revolutions of the 18th century stood over the cradle of the modern world; the modern world remembers. It is a long stretch from the fall of the Bastille to the launching of a revolutionary new detergent, but it is worth the trip. As Sellers and Yeatman would have said, revolution is a good thing. One never hears of a counterrevolution in automobile design, though one might be in order. Better accentuate the positive. As a result, the struggle for political advantage involves minor but important skirmishes for semantic advantage. Like the hero in a Western movie, the movement that comes in riding on revolution can, as a rule, expect our sympathy.

I shall suggest that, as of today at least, the issue is wrongly joined. Like 'Left' and 'Right,' Revolution and Counterrevolution have become anachronistic stereotypes, real because installed in vocabulary and minds, but confusing as categories for understanding and scholarly analysis. Misleading, above all, because for a long time now the notion of revolution has been interpreted in one sense only, implying automatically that movements directed to other ends (opposite, or simply different) could not be described as revolutionary, and might well be counterrevolutionary, whether they wanted to be or not.

The very word, revolution, suggests the great modern prototypes: French and Russian. These more than suggest, they impose, a model of what revolution should be because it once was, of expectable actions and stages to which revolutionary developments should conform: the last throes of the dominant classes, the first phase of a bourgeois revolution overtaken

[435]

by more popular challengers, duly put down in a Thermidor easily leading to Brumaire. Moderate change, radical advance, repression, and their dialectic, always open to further challenges. Interpretation provides the recipes of expectation. Sometimes of action too. History is born of history. From Marx's reference to *The Eighteenth Brumaire of Louis Bonaparte*, to Trotsky's description of the Soviet Thermidor when Stalin takes power, through Crane Brinton's *Anatomy of Revolution*, patterns are formulated and roles are prescribed where coming players (or reporters) learn their parts.

A French academic historian, writing about the student revolt of 1968, refers to barricades, red flags, 'the Faculty buildings resembling the Smolny Palace (*sic*) in Petrograd, the lecture halls [resembling] Soviets.'[1] And André Malraux, writing in 1972, resumes the twentieth century in one image: that of a truck bristling with guns. Obviously, the Russian revolution again, and one of the most familiar images of it.

Some responsibility for this lies in organized history and the generalization of historical knowledge, making available that pattern of revolution to which revolutionaries will henceforth conform. Those that fail to conform are not revolutionaries. 'The revolutionary knows his revolution as the wretched knows his want,' writes André Découflé, author of a recent work generally regarded as one of the more sensible treatments of a touchy subject.[2] But the wretched knows his want, precisely because he lives in it, the revolutionary seldom does more than imagine his revolution. And those revolutionaries who, today, in the perspective of history, still claim to know their revolution—in its unfolding beyond means to ends—must be naive indeed.

But history, storehouse of images and recipes that it is, does not exhaust the revolutionary's resources. Gracchus Babeuf could tell his readers, and later his judges, that the Republic was worthless: 'But it is not the real Republic. The real Republic is something we have not yet tried.'[3] The point, frequently made since Babeuf, proceeds from hypothesis to fact, and even against fact. Thus in Découflé: 'The hypothesis of the revolutionary project excludes the destruction of man, since it is [aimed at] his regeneration; and, in fact, it does not destroy him, despite the horrible enterprises of some of its managers. Beyond all the propagandas, the present chronicle of the Soviet Union bears abundant witness to this.'[4]

I like Découflé's reference to the managers of revolution, a handy and expressive term and a revealing one. But it is odd to find, in a book published in 1968, the reaffirmation of an ideal which remains entire though some of its managers betray it, the deliberate denial of historical experience by affirmation of its contrary, and all on the basis of an original hypothesis stronger than any observed fact. The Revolution survives all revolutions.

Far from fearing facts, the hypothesis consumes them, that is it assimilates them to its needs. Boris Porchnev turns the peasant rebellions of the seventeenth century into evidence of class struggles in the early modern period. Découflé hails Eric Hobsbawm's *Primitive Rebels* as a work on *revolutionary* phenomena, despite its French title: *Les primitifs de la revolte*. Even social rebellion of a primitive kind must be mobilized for revolution.[5] Such topical imperialism, perfectly dispensable in Marxist terms, conceals the difference between revolution and rebellion (a difference Hobsbawm himself in no wise ignores!) and deprives the critic of a category he could find useful in refining his terms.

Découflé does distinguish between insurrection, which finds its end in itself, and revolution which is *transhistorical*, 'situated in the realm of duration, temporal site of immanence'; and this permits the keen observer to distinguish between an insurrection, however long-drawn-out, and a revolution, however brief. Thus, the 'revolution' of 1830 was actually an insurrection that lasted 18 years, while the Paris Commune of 1871, though only a few weeks long, can be identified as an authentic revolution, just like...the Crusades![6]

It is Découflé's modest claim that such a conception helps to avoid a lot of shopworn debates and endows 'the category of revolutions with an unusual extension and strictness [of definition].' To the uninitiated, the extensibility of the category and its flexibility appear more striking than its strictness of definition. Events are promoted, excluded, or denied. The Crusades, of course, are there in honour of Alphonse Dupront who (re)invented them. Unless it is to fill the gap left when strict construction eliminated the Agricultural and the Industrial revolutions. But what about the revolution of 1830, demoted to a mere insurrection, yet very much a revolution to its contemporaries: change of regime, of the symbols of state, of the flag, of political personnel — isn't all that enough, until next time?

Clearly, no. Political revolution is not real revolution, not the transhistorical sort. The social aspect is missing when all we get is a change of guard (and of uniforms) among the privileged elites. The wretched continue in their wretchedness. They continue to be exploited: by their exploiters in their time; by intellectuals who have discovered the plus-value of poverty, in ours.

Old-style revolutions ignored the poor.[7] Aristocratic and oligarchic societies made aristocratic and oligarchic revolutions. The poor were enlisted as cannon fodder. Their occasional uses did not entitle them to higher ideological rank. War is waged by soldiers, of course. It is not *about* soldiers, or for them.

Then, from objects of the revolution the poor became its subjects — and its energetic force. The French Revolution said it was about the people. It was not; or only in a special sense. But it did involve mobilizing the masses in a new and, now, doctrinally necessary sense that could not exist before 'the people' had become the subject of politics. And Gracchus Babeuf, more memorably than many, identified 'the people' with the poor people, and the poor people with the majority of the people,[8] a view that contemporary circumstances largely warranted. This new doctrine, due like others to survive the conditions it reflected when it was formulated, would soon coincide with economic and social changes that suggested yet further appeals and further mobilizations.

So, revolution, which had been about political power for people who were far from poor, came to be said to be about the poor, about the poor ceasing to be poor and, even though its efficacy as a means to this end remained dubious, the myth took shape. The poor as energizing agents of real revolution turned into the poor as dynamizing ideal of prospective revolution. They had been other ranks in the armies of the revolution; now they became its flag.

Not everything, of course, went as one might wish. Thus, the revolution that had been supposed to precipitate the participation of excluded social groups (Third Estate, etc.) in the body politic, actually operated by the violent exclusion of other social groups (aristocrats and to some extent, although unplanned, the clergy). This pattern would be repeated on subsequent occasions. Fraternity henceforth would be affirmed by exclusion (of bourgeois, aliens, Jews); just as Justice became the act of taking from the old haves and giving to your supporters. Not, perhaps, the most desirable way of ensuring upward mobility or the redistribution of wealth, but effective enough up to a point.

In any case, the masses that cheered and hooted, stormed and stared, were a necessary stimulant and fuel of action. Revolution came to them less as a promise of better things, though it was that too, than as a gigantic holiday and adventure. For many, its goings-on were the first spectacle they enjoyed. And one of the greatest luxuries revolution afforded was the opportunity to see their 'betters' humbled. Like the peasants of Languedoc who welcome late-summer rains, good for their corn, bad for their landlords' wheat, with 'il pleut des insolences,' the people welcomed the chance to be insolent in its turn, to see its 'betters' cut down to size, not excluding its revolutionary emancipators whom revolution carted through hooting streets that cheered them days before.

So, after all, the people could be wrong.[9] At the very least, its instincts could not be trusted. Not untaught. For Saint-Just, 'the people is an eternal child'; and Robespierre said as much. Lenin would build or rebuild a doctrine on this conviction. And a party. His *What Is To Be Done?* (1902) shows how the spontaneous development of the workers' movement had simply led to its domination by bourgeois ideology. This had to be remedied, a different ideology had to be provided. In due course, in places, it was.

But was this other ideology—creation of rebellious bourgeois and intellectuals—necessarily more revolutionary? I suppose so. More popular?

Hardly, since it denied the possibility of government of the people by the people, and did this more deliberately, with a clearer view of the matter, than Saint-Just would or could have done. This is an issue we need not stir again, except to point out that the superior revolutionary capacity of a movement has little to do with its popular character or representativeness. Quite the contrary: the Leninist argument since 1902 has been that the more popular the movement, the less revolutionary it is likely to be, hence the less objectively representative of true popular interests. A form of elitism no less elitist for coming from the conventional left.

So the people, the poor people, already dubbed *proletariat* by Rousseauist and revolutionary antiquarianism, could continue to enjoy its heroic role, but (a big but) only the role that had been written for it. This is worth bearing in mind, but the point I wish to stress is different: the role in question, sketched at the end of the eighteenth century, written and rewritten through the nineteenth century, falls far short of changed realities in the twentieth century West. When a neo-Marxist declares in 1973: 'The proletariat, producer and not consumer, is the absolute and inalienable ethical order...'[10] he is not only talking nonsense, but anachronistic nonsense. I doubt whether any human group, now or at any time, has been specifically invested with the mission of political liberation and social salvation for mankind. Many such groups have claimed and still claim the daunting responsibility. But that is no excuse for those trained to critical thinking to abandon the thoughtful examination of such claims. Clearly, political messianism and other cargo cults of the West are no monopoly of what we call the Right.[11]

A moment always comes however when revolutionary revelry must give way to discipline, the joys of insolence, the privileges of disorder, to the order of new privileges. The generous, self-indulgent revolution becomes a stern disciplinarian, sterner than the tyrant it displaced. By January 1794, unexpectedly early, the Committee of Public Safety advises its representative in the Calvados to moderate his zeal: 'Today we are less concerned to revolutionize than to set up the revolutionary government.' The fateful words are out. The revolution is made, or can be suspended. It is time to turn it into a regime: the managers of revolution into managers of the state.

This is where the rot sets in. Joseph de Maistre was right. In the end, all governments are monarchies, no matter what you call them, all governments are aristocracies. The young Chateaubriand had said as much in his reactionary essay on revolutions: 'What do I care if it be the King or the Law that drags me to the guillotine?...the greatest misfortune of men is to have laws and a government.'[12] Chateaubriand, writing in exile, had little sympathy for revolution. But many nineteenth century revolutionaries faced that same quandary and failed to solve it: the state is always counter-revolutionary, yet without the state how can a revolution be carried through? Can anything be built except on the ruins — not of the enemy's camp so much as of one's own? Revolutionaries set out to make or remake history. Their opponents say that history is already made, or in the making, and waiting to advance on existing lines. The revolution succeeds, affirms precisely what its opponents used to say, and sets up a government to make sure it is done. That government, like every modern state, will seek the monopoly of violence, conforming not only to Max Weber's thesis on that score but to the more grandiose rule Joseph de Maistre decreed: 'all greatness, all power, all subordination, rest on the executioner: horror and bond of human association.' Remove the executioner and order disintegrates, powers collapse, society disappears. But society must be rebuilt, so it must be the revolution that disappears. A twist of the wrist, then, and the revolution has been juggled away. A great deal has been done. A great deal has been changed. The power of new rulers and freer trade in one case; the power of new rulers and the expansion of productivity in another. Electrification without soviets.

One other novelty: a reversal in the classic relations between state and revolution.[13] Where once upon a time making a revolution meant overthrowing the state, in the new situation it is the state that makes the revolution, becomes identified with it, so that opposition to the state is opposition to revolution. A revolutionary state is a contradiction in terms. But even a socialist state, or one so called, very soon disappears behind administration, institutions, police machinery, bureaucracy — or, rather, it becomes simply the flag that flies over the towering office building of the state.

At this point, presumably, the revolution institutionalized is ready for the challenge of another revolution that will break the frozen flow and set the great glacier of history on the move again. In this respect, a succession of revolutions is but part of the same vast forward movement (necessarily forward, in whatever direction it may face). This may have been what Proudhon had in mind in his toast to the revolution of 1848: 'properly speaking, there haven't been several revolutions, there has been only one and the same revolution.' The revolutionary wheel turns, but each revolution of the wheel propels it farther, each halt only a pause, each apparent failure a spur to further advance. Ce n'est qu'un début, nous continuerons le combat! As Babeuf affirmed, the revolution, the republic, may be worthless, but the true Revolution is still to come, the Common Weal remains to be achieved. Even a 'revolutionary' state, controlled by revolutionary leaders, can further the interests of this immanent force. The Revolution is a constant of history.

Perhaps. But all this begs a question: what revolution? La révolution, says Proudhon, est en permanence dans l'histoire. Not revolution in general, not any particular revolution, but *the* Revolution, identified, vaguely perhaps but enough for all to know, as Babeuf knew it, as Découflé's revolutionaries know it. Reference to revolution, says Proudhon, is necessarily reference to progress. But where does progress go? What is 'forward'? Towards what does the revolution advance?

Towards the Left, of course. It is no good to say that this has become, more than it ever was, an uncertain point of reference. The wretched are still on the earth. Their emancipation can be the pole star of revolutionary progress. If history tells us anything, it is that 'revolutions and revolutionaries are leftist.'[14] There can be debate as to whether the revolution belongs to gradualists, organized revolutionaries, radical leftists. There can be no revolution from other quarters. Any such suggestion is counterrevolutionary by definition.

The term counterrevolution itself evokes, as Joseph de Maistre noticed, violent action in an *opposite* and hence related sense to that of *the* revolution: 'a revolution [the OED tells us] opposed to a previous revolution or reversing its results.' The counterrevolution is condemned to a reflected identity only. It exists in terms of the revolution it opposes, and seeks to reverse. Revolution is the positive term; without it, no counterrevolution.

De Maistre, who understood how awkward such a definition can be if you are saddled with it, sought to escape it. The monarchy reestablished, he insisted, though it is called counterrevolution, ne sera point une révolution contraire, mais le contraire d'une révolution: not an opposite revolution, but the opposite of a revolution. He seems to have been right. If a revolution is more than the violence that it involves, a project for radical change, an attempt at precipitate movement, then the monarchy restored, which conceived no such course, was not revolutionary even in a counterrevolutionary sense. The Restoration was not a revolution against the previous revolution(s), but an attempt to restore the state of things and the rate of evolution, the speed of movement, that had preceded revolution. It wanted to be the opposite of a revolution. That is what, insofar as it could be, it was.[15]

If the Restoration, while antirevolutionary, was not counterrevolutionary, other regimes and movements in later years did adopt revolutionary methods to counterrevolutionary ends—that is, deliberately directed to opposing or reversing a particular revolution. Louis-Napoleon's government appears a case in point, typically adopting not only revolutionary methods but also some of the measures extolled by the revolutionaries with whom it competed. The Action Française was counterrevolutionary: explicitly so. Hungary after 1918 was revealingly torn between antirevolutionaries (Horthy, Bethlen) eager to maintain a regime the very opposite of revolutionary, and counterrevolutionaries (Gömbös, Imrédy) ready to adopt the revolutionary panoply the better to fight what had become a *revolution introuvable*. Franco's insurrection fits the same bill: beginning on the pattern of classic nineteenth-century Spanish revolutions against the 'revolution' of the Popular Front regime, cannibalizing the would-be revolutionaries of the right, and adopting their most visible symbols (as King Carol II of Romania was to do) as a façade for the longest-lasting of antirevolutionary counterrevolutions in captivity.

Can we ever untangle this skein? Many actions described as counter-revolutionary turn out to be simply repressive, though no less odious for that. Charles Maurras said that revolutions are made before they break out. That was the rationale for their preliminary repression. But such repressions did not, as a rule, involve revolutionary means. The *Cagoule* was scotched in France by fairly straightforward police methods. The Iron Guard in Romania was gutted by police and army terror only slightly beyond the country's past experience. The monopoly of violence was reasserted before it slipped away. In some places (Soviet Russia) even before it could be challenged. Both revolutionary and counterrevolutionary regimes rest foursquare on de Maistre's *bourreau*. But is this preemptive counterrevolution, as it has been called? Hardly. It is self-preservation of a conventional sort and, of course, an occasional excuse for the equally conventional elimination of political opponents. And the constant confusion of simple opposition with revolutionary, antirevolutionary or counter-revolutionary action, a confusion that has its roots in fact, fantasy, theory and reality, allows whoever wills to give a dog a bad name before attempting to eliminate it. As Saint-Just explained to Robespierre in December 1793, measures of public safety are justified by the existence of counter-revolutionaries. No more counterrevolutionaries, no more need for public safety or for the dictatorship that is its instrument, *provided* human weakness does not lead people—the people?—into 'that maze in which the revolution and the counterrevolution march pell-mell.'

An illustration, here, not only of the ease with which the image of counterrevolution can justify preemptive repression, but of the difficulty of disentangling revolutionary from counterrevolutionary strands. Only the initiated can tell them apart. But the voice of revelation that addresses the few must, by others, be accepted on faith. No wonder that almost any action, movement, or regime can be interpreted as one wills and that Girondists and Enragés, proudhonians, Trotskyists and Kronstadt sailors have been made to bear the brand of counterrevolution. In Bolivia, for example, where revolutionary activity is very much the order of the day, Trotskyist leader Guillermo Lora denounces the leftists whose radicalism leads only to counterrevolution, while a top figure of the pro-Soviet communist party dismisses Lora's POR as the best ally of reactionary forces.[16] Nor need we be surprised to read that 'the most accomplished contemporary form of the counterrevolutionary project' is North American-style democracy.[17] One does not have to claim a close approach to integral democracy for North American regimes to recognize the prejudice of such a phrase, that can pass unexamined (and often does) only in minds where the case has been pre-judged.

Even denunciation of neo-capitalism does not preserve one from the counterrevolutionary snare (increasingly reminiscent of those children's stories where one character after another tumbles down a trap). The pastures of objective perdition are broader than those of the Lord. Marcuse and the Freudo-Marxists have in their turn been denounced as counter-revolutionaries whose cultural terrorism finally leads to neo-fascism. [18]

In the last resort, counterrevolution does not even deserve rational interpretation. For Découflé, it 'seems to come less under the jurisdiction of sociology than of psychoanalysis: it borrows the modes of revolution and does its best to create its reflected image, determined as it is to take up the contrary position on every score.' A few lines later, Découflé refers very sensibly to Jung's remark that the most dangerous of revolutionaries is the one we carry in ourselves. But this is a predicament attributed to counter-revolutionaries alone. He insists rightly on the anxiety that drives them to extremes, but never on the anxiety that haunts successful (?) revolutionaries, once set in the seats of power. [19] And nary a word about *ideological* divergencies that may set revolutionaries and counterrevolutionaries apart. For the latter alone, doctrinal persuasions must be the rationalizations of unadmissible drives.

Analyses so one-sided are unsatisfactory even in their own terms. Equally important, placing the interpretation of counterrevolution on the psycho-analytic plane minimizes other factors (social, economic, etc.) and denies existence of ideologies or doctrines deserving rational examination: for themselves, and concerning their evolution or corruption, just as with revolutionary ideologies. One side is human and rational, the other is human only in its travesties: a sickness. Thus, one both begs the question and avoids it.

Let us fall back on a more serious work. In 1971, Arno J. Mayer's *Dynamics of Counterrevolution in Europe* set out to examine the concept and to fit it into an analytic framework. My first and chief criticism of the work is that it accepts unquestioningly the Marxist stereotype of *one* revolution in our time, in terms of which counterrevolution must necessarily be defined. In other words, while Professor Mayer's Marxism is explicit, his definition of revolution is implicit. It thus avoids any suggestion that counterrevolution is not alone in need of definition, but revolution too. Mayer's general thesis, with which I disagree, is thoughtful, honest, and forcefully argued. It is therefore with the most sensible exponent of the dominant stereotypes that I take issue.

Mayer distinguishes between conservatives, reactionaries, and counter-revolutionaries. Reactionaries scorn the present for a lost, regretted, past. Conservatives, like Metternich, believe that stability need not mean immo-bility. Counterrevolutionaries are pretty much what we designate as fascists or radicals of the right: equalitarian, dynamic, adept at mass politics, often similar to 'the hated revolutionary rival,' yet only pseudorevolution-ary at best, intending 'to create the impression that they seek fundamental

changes in government, society and community,'[20] but actually anchored
in established order, values, and aspirations. Counterrevolutionaries pretend to represent an alternative revolution; they are, in effect, only an
alternative to revolution. 'In style, method and appearance, their break
with the politics of compromise and mutual concession is very radical
indeed. But in all other major respects the counterrevolutionary project is
in the nature of a stabilizing and rescue operation disguised as a millenarian crusade of heroic vitalism.'[21] True, conservative or reactionary antirevolutionaries (so often the most visible of counterrevolutionaries in everyday politics and parlance) may turn against Mayer's revolutionary counterrevolutionaries, as King Carol of Romania turned against Codreanu. But
this does not affect the ultimate kinship of all three categories in one objectively counterrevolutionary camp. Thus, having begun by brushing aside
the threadbare confusions of the past, Mayer arrives at a more refined version of the same.[22]

We shall meet some of his arguments shortly. But, first, a crucial statement — crucial not only to Mayer's thesis but because it represents a widespread point of view: 'Counterrevolution is essentially a praxis. Its political
doctrine is in the nature of a rationalization and justification of prior
actions. It is a pseudo-doctrine.'[23] If counterrevolution is only the mirror
image of revolution, this makes perfect sense. It is the violent start of reaction to the revolutionary challenge. Doctrine comes later and, dominated
by this same challenge, it can only become a distorting echo of its original
reactions: anger and fear.

So far, so good. But only for that counterrevolution, for those counterrevolutionaries, whose 'project is in the nature of a stabilizing and rescue
operation' for the established order. And that, unless we fall back on
'objective' interpretations which should then include all those denounced
for diversionist and counterrevolutionary strategies, lets out a number of
fascist movements, not least National Socialism, much of whose history was
but the acting out of some fantastic doctrines.

But these are pseudo-doctrines, 'inconsistent' (what political ideology is
not so in practice?) and instrumental. This last suggestion, of ideology as
an instrument of manipulation, confuses the concern of most modern politicians to find the most effective formula for selling their case and themselves, with the ideological constructs embodying their vision. Hitler was
possessed. Obsessed. His obsessions were not 'calculated and instrumental.'
It turned out that they worked that way. But Hitler's doctrine was the
instrument of his dreams. The doctrine, the movement, then the people he
ruled, became the means of their realization. The threat of communist
revolution was only one aspect of the national deterioration he sought to
stem and to reverse. To deal with this he planned a revolution that was not
opposed to, but other than, the model most current at that time. Since

another revolutionary project already held the field, his was an alternative revolution, not a counter-one. Codreanu also postulated a fundamental change. He encountered no revolution in his way, only the established disorder. As for Mussolini, I incline to think that the revolutionary threat, scotched or at least defeated by Giolitti's fabian tactics, seemed less a foil than a convenient pretext. For none of these was counterrevolution, in the sense of the term, the main concern.

Another example and one less debatable may clarify my case. Professor Mayer appears to place the origins of counterrevolutionary ideology in a reaction to socialist challenges.[24] Wherever this may have been so, it was not so in France. There is no evidence that Boulanger, Barrès, Maurras, were particularly concerned with fighting socialism.[25] Boulanger made the most of the Jacobin tradition that inspired both socialists and radicals of his day, Barrès was a socialist fellow-traveller between 1889 and 1896, Maurras's chief quarries were elsewhere. All addressed themselves first and foremost to what they saw as problems of public morality, vitality, and unity. They may have been deluded. They were not insincere.[26]

It is too easy to dismiss their old-fashioned patriotism, their new-fangled nationalism, as convenient derivatives for pressures they (or cleverer men) discerned but could not meet. What they (and cleverer men) thought they discerned was a flabby, deteriorating society. They worried about it. Divisive 'revolutionary' movements that preached class struggle were one aspect of this social decay, but hardly their dominant concern. And social justice, which socialists called for, was also a concern of theirs, because they thought it necessary to the renovation, revivification, unification that they sought. Much of what they said, now has an irrelevant ring. We have discerned, we think, other more crucial seams and strains in the fabric of society. My only point, right here, is that their doctrines were not 'calculated and instrumental.' Not counterrevolutionary either, in intent, except (but I do not think that was Arno Mayer's meaning) in the case of Maurras who, of course, rejected everything that had happened since 1789.

This illustrates the need to be specific, placing events in their context which alone can show what was revolution, counterrevolution, some other kind of revolution, or no revolution at all. If, as Professor Mayer thinks, the reactionary and conservative coordinates of counterrevolution are central to its identification, then we must discriminate between counterrevolutions that may adopt a revolutionary façade, and alternative revolutions that have been found to adopt a conservative façade. Perhaps a reference to the old-fashioned categories of Movement and Resistance (out of July Revolution by André Siegfried) could help in this. Because it can suggest that Movement may direct itself against (post-)revolutionary regimes, and that the latter may find themselves resisting Movement. Only one thing is sure: there is no *juste milieu*, the very notion of it is eccentric. The

more so as politics operate less in concentric ripples than in disorderly
swings—towards extremes. And the motions of extremism matter more
than its directions.

Fascist revolution in Italy, Nazi revolution in Germany, were carried
out—like their forerunners in France and Russia—against the flabbiness
and the failures of the existing regimes. Horthy and Franco led actions
opposed to 'red revolution' in one case,[27] and to a Popular Front regime in
another. They are thus properly counterrevolutionary. Rex, in Belgium,
was neither revolutionary nor counterrevolutionary: political adventurism
dressed up in currently-modish fancy clothes which happened to be fascist
by historical coincidence.[28] And Salazar established his power, like Antonescu, in traditional terms.[29] It is worth repeating that repressive authoritarian regimes may borrow the rhetoric and methods of the class revolution, as others borrow the rhetoric and techniques of the alternative revolution, in order to cloak their inertia or their uncertainties. In both cases the
revolutionaries will be eliminated, or put out of the way, by Franco,
Antonescu, or Stalin.

The confusion becomes patent when all such action against revolutionaries or revolutionary forces is treated as one single phenomenon. In effect,
most antirevolutionary action, especially of the preemptive sort, is taken by
conservative forces worried by threats against their order or their systematic disorder. Police repression, military action, or coup d'état, may be
carried out against national revolutionaries as against Marxist ones. Nor,
given the tug of war for possession of the revolutionary label, is it always
clear, let alone admitted, which side in the conflict is counterrevolutionary.

Which side is revolutionary and which counterrevolutionary in Berlin
1953, Poznan 1956, Budapest 1956, Prague 1968? Or when Moscow and
Belgrade, Belgrade and Tirana, Moscow and Peking, accuse each other of
counterrevolutionism? History will tell if we cannot. But the 'direction' of
history and, hence, its reading can change. In 1939 or 1940 many could
fear with reason that it would confirm the racist dogma of triumphant
nazism. Genetics and biology rather than sociology would have framed the
mythology of the new age. Who can believe that they would have failed to
do so very competently? Revolution, we are told, is the recognition of historical necessity, dyked up by inertia, confronted by counterrevolution.
But history is what happens and, as such, invested with value only by those
who perceive it as good or bad. Like plague or drought, a revolutionary
movement is history because it is in history. So are its rivals, its opponents,
its victims and its beneficiaries. The Spring of Prague proved abortive; the
armies that crushed it got their way. Who stood for revolution? Who represented history?

Is revolution, then, like beauty, only in the eye of the beholder? Who is
to say which is the real revolution and which the sham? Mayer shows no
doubts, but he does not address the question when he explains that 'revolu-

tion is more productive of human growth, betterment and dignity than counterrevolution,'[30] because this only holds for some revolutions, or some parts of some revolutions. We can attempt a list: 1789-92, but not the Terror; 1848 (but which?) but not 1830; the early days in Cuba, but not the repression that followed them. Every man his own historian. And even if the revolution is one block, as the famous phrase insists, the doctrinaire will make sure just what is cemented in it. Which brings us back to the subjective selectivity that we denounced to start with.

We should abandon the notion of one revolution, identified with only one direction or theme; replace the question: 'what is revolution?' by the question: 'what kind of revolution is it?'

In a war we do not say of one side that it wages counterwar. Yet use of the term counterrevolution[31] suggests an authorized version which, misleading as to the motives and ends of movements that do not conform to an approved pattern, implies (though seldom explicitly) the superiority of, the virtue vested in, one kind of revolution only. We remember it as great, so many believe that it was good. Since revolution = good, counterrevolution = bad. Hence the importance of dubbing what we consider bad counterrevolutionary, a description as illuminating as the label 'fascist' freely applied to conservatives, liberals, and portions of the left. When, in the end, fascism and counterrevolution are treated as one, as if identity was self-evident, confusion is complete. Yet evidence at hand, far from justifying confident affirmations, seems to suggest we should proceed with caution — our strongest weapon, doubt.

What are modern revolutions about? The classic formula tells us: Liberty, Equality, Fraternity, or Death. But, as Saint-Just realized as early as 1791, liberty once conquered is easily corrupted into its opposite. Equality is either equality of opportunity, rightly criticized as basic inequality, or it entails injustice and constraint. Fraternity is the vaguest and also the most delusive of the terms. It may reflect the relieved elation of the original release from the constraints of order, but I doubt it. Is it there to compensate for its too-evident absence, or to replace a missing father-figure with a more accessible brother? Latecomer to the original revolutionary duo, fraternity is an invocation, as if for rain at the height of drought; but also a logical outgrowth of the equalitarian ideal: authority is no longer the father, but the brother — a wiser, more experienced, elder brother, standing shoulder to shoulder with you in the struggle, before he is metamorphosed into Big Brother. The figure of authority, thrown out by the door, climbs back through the window. Finally, Death: sole of the revolution's promises that it is certain to make good, whatever its orientation. Bystanders remembered that when, at the feast of the Supreme Being, on 20 Prairial, year II of the Revolution, the symbolic figures of Atheism, Discord, Ambition, and False Simplicity were consumed on a symbolic pyre, the statue of Wisdom that the flames revealed was black with soot.

We might note in passing that, for Marx and Engels, liberty, equality, and fraternity are fine, but hardly serious, since Marx and Engels rejected moral and ethical values, ideas like morality, truth and justice. Marxism, like its contemporary, phrenology, is a science, not an ethics. The revolution it talks about is part of a historical mechanism: hence, purged of values. We have just seen how seriously to take such claims.

Revolution and counterrevolution today both stem from the democratic doctrines of the eighteenth and nineteenth centuries, and from the breakdown of their political outgrowths. While true counterrevolution is the offspring of revolution, revolution is the creature of the regime against which it rises — even to the pettiest things. 'I went to the Convention,' notes Chateaubriand, 'and saw M. Marat; on his lips there floated the banal smile that the Old Regime has placed on everybody's lips.' Marat's smile, like Marat's ideas, had been acquired before the Revolution. It was the old regime that taught Robespierre his self-possession, Saint-Just his strict demeanour and his romanticism, so many deputies their courtesy and manners, Girondists and Jacobins their composure in the face of death. Superficial? Perhaps. But suggestive of more important carry-overs.

When Mayer sees the mainsprings of communism and fascism as 'drastically different, possibly opposite,'[32] he is wrong. The great revolutionary creeds of the twentieth century were (among other things) all inspired by Social Darwinism. Nationalism, fascism, communism, all reflect belief in the survival of the fittest: in terms of nation (or of race, itself a confused notion of the nineteenth century), or in terms of class. This is why, at least one reason why, the distinction between fascism and communism is relative rather than absolute, dynamic rather than fundamental. Both are originally urban ideologies, devised and carried by middle-class intellectuals seeking to appeal to underprivileged and badly integrated sections of society. Both react against liberalism, its injustices, its inefficiencies, its decay; and both are its offspring.[33] Neither represents a revolt of the masses, though both seek to incite one. As the studies published by Lasswell and Lerner indicate, Nazi and Communist elites show striking similarities in recruitment and in evolution. The revolutions they make are, in both cases, 'operated by frustrated segments of the middle classes who...organized violent action to gain what they had been denied.'[34] The fascists benefit from 'the interested collaboration of the old cadres'?[35] Have Communists not done so? Who officered the Red army, or the French revolutionary armies for that matter? How far do the administrative, technological and intellectual establishments of Popular Democracies, so-called, depend on the old cadres and on their scions? And those who do not stem from them, become a 'new class' much like the one that they displaced.[36] This is not what André Malraux had in mind when he declared that every communism that fails calls up its fascism, every fascism that fails calls up its communism;[37] but it is in these terms that the phrase makes good sense.

Mayer is right when he suggests key differences, structural and other, between communism and fascism. They can all be revolutionary, though different.[38] Both preach monistic solutions, establish orthodoxies, define heresies, march on specific ideologies — in Karl Mannheim's terms: 'systems of representations that pretend to offer complete explanation of social phenomena and permit discovery and advancement of solutions required by problems of social change.' They do not only start from a similar gnostic base. They also end in a would-be total system: legally unrestrained government, mass party, rigid ideology, pseudo-elections, systematic terror, state monopoly of mass communications, and a centrally-directed industrial economy. Isn't this fundamental similarity between totalitarian creeds and systems at least as important as their differences of view?

I do not seek to labour points that have long been made, though familiarity is no excuse for indifference to them; and I am not aware of convincing arguments raised against those who find the fundamental similarities of communism and fascism to be highly significant. My purpose here is not to estimate the moral worth of either, even by implication, but to discern their relation to revolution and counterrevolution, and see if the question itself makes sense.

The fact that both communisms and fascisms are violent and monistic in no way proves that they are the same. Merchants of absolutes can hawk different wares. One can choose between them. The question then comes up: is the direction of choice more relevant than the fact of choosing? The answer depends on the importance attributed to the choice. Is it on the level of a new car to buy, or on that of Salvation? In this case, right choice, viewed as a matter of life or death in the struggle for life and for history, is crucial. Both communism and fascism regard as intolerable and intolerably decadent the society which, having created values, tires of them, detaches from them, examines them, organizes uncertainty and tolerates doubt. Both communism and fascism are there to affirm and structure belief. Even their denials are affirmations in reverse. There is no qualitative difference between affirmation and denial, which means that one can shift quite naturally from one to the other, and explains the counterrevolutionary aspects to be found in the propaganda of both.[39]

Not in the propaganda alone: racism, torture, mass murder of genocidal proportions, ideological contortionism, is there much need to insist on similarities that some continue to deny and others to argue that they are superficial? The interest of such characteristic coincidences is not to mark them, but to see why and how they happen, what in the nature of a movement or a situation leads to this blemish and not to another. It isn't so much the state terrorism of modern revolutions that bears witness against

them, as their inability to invent ends different from those of the regimes
they claim to fight. The similarity of their means may be superficial. Yet it
is precisely at the level of means that we place the difference between revolutionary and non-revolutionary creeds. We cannot escape our methods,
and methods are often imposed by the situation, by the demands of the
project. The revolutionary project, the revolutionary situation, have their
corruption built in. One may well feel the justification of the project, the
exaltation of the action. But it is well to note their implications too. We
have failed to draw the conclusions of our findings for far too long.

And yet they differ, we are told, because they appeal to (and benefit)
different social groups. This is far from proven. I have argued the contrary
case in a number of publications;[40] data concerning leadership of the rival
movements appears to support my interpretation; and I suspect that there
has been even more hypocritical dissembling about the attitude of German
workers towards nazism than there has been about the resistance of the
middle classes. Finally, the argument itself is based on the unproved
assumption that true revolution can only stem from a chosen class—or else
represent it, an even more dubious view. Even if this were true, doctrinally
speaking, just what is the difference between a national socialist revolution
partly based on peasants, and a national communist revolution largely
based on peasants? When Mao and Castro find room in the marxist Hall of
Fame, why exclude Strasser, or Hitler? The answer is obvious? Not in these
terms. In all cases, tactics take precedence not over strategy only, but over
ideology too. Tactics are the locomotive of revolutionary history. What
really matters is making the revolution. The revolutionary knows or thinks
he knows what will come of it. The doctrine is there to tell him. Or he
doesn't care. But what comes of the revolution matters less than the event,
the making of revolution. Belief in revolution for its own sake is one more
thing radical Left and Right seem to have in common.[41]

But: they opposed each other. This cannot be denied. It need not be.
Fascist revolutions were in effect directed against Communists—not exclusively, but also. In this sense, which has been treated as decisive and which
is almost accidental, fascisms were counterrevolutionary: revolutions
against a rival revolution. They did not seek, as the Enragés or Babeuf had
done, to carry one revolution beyond a given stage; but to carry another
revolution in a different direction, to define its aims (often similar to the
other's) in terms of other principles, to define its foes (often similar too) in
terms of different values. The coincidences so many have noted[42] were
denounced by communists and their friends as camouflage; they were to be
stressed by the communists' enemies to smear the communists. No one
thought to remark that it is possible to react to similar problems in different ways—even on the immoderate plane. Revolution had been pre-
empted: like the Frigidaire. Ironic, when one remembers that the Jacobins

were nationalists. Convenient, in terms of the way the rival revolutionary movements oriented their appeal.

By doctrine and deliberate choice, communism focused its appeal with narrow intensity. This was (and it is oddly ignored) the basic doctrinal difference between it and fascism which, convinced that the social reality was a national one, accused Marxists of splitting the nation and, thus, weakening it. The fascist net was cast more widely. This has been cited as proof of reactionary opportunism. I incline to see it as a more appropriate response to modern conditions.[43] The debate remains open. But I note that, having at long last read the statistics of thirty years ago, Communist parties have now extended the working class well into what is still denounced as the bourgeoisie; and that doctrinaire internationalism has taken second place to the hard realities of national (and nationalistic) sentiment.[44] It is the tribute that virtue must pay to vice.

Digressions are hard to avoid. But every digression contributes to my case that fascism, too easily described as counterrevolutionary, is not a counterrevolution but a rival revolution: rival of that which claimed to be the only one entitled to the label, and which is still accepted as such. As Jules Monnerot has written, and he is in a good position to know: 'for the fascists, communism is not subversion attacking the established order, it is *a competitor for the foundation of power.*'[45]

If fascism was a rival revolution, what was revolutionary about it, what was it revolutionary about? As far as I can tell, revolutionary projects differed. I have tried to outline that of Codreanu in Romania.[46] In Italy, the Fascist leadership conducted its own Thermidor, and revolutionary élan seeped off between the seats of power. In Germany, however, National Socialism proposed and embarked upon a *sui generis* revolution, and one that was recognized as such by men as different as Hermann Rauschning, Denis de Rougemont and Jacques Ellul.[47]

It is still objected that National Socialism was not a revolution because it did not destroy capitalist economic structures and change the relations of production. But, on the one hand, it showed that control was as effective as formal nationalisation. On the other hand, communist experience suggests that a total change in the relations of production finally leads to results that differ little as regards the relation between producers and the industrial machine. Decisions are still made in one place and executed in another. It would be a help if available facts could be discussed outside models constructed over a hundred years ago. Finally, the objection illustrates my earlier point: inscription in the category 'revolution' is only possible within limited terms. Certainly destruction of capitalist economic structures is a revolutionary achievement. It does not prove that other lines of action, not entailing this, cannot be revolutionary too.

How would the German situation look, as presented in Nazi perspective?

Here was Europe's 'proletarian nation,' encircled by enemies, ruined, powerless, despoiled of its past glories, rebelling against defeat, against the world that caused it, against the forces to which it attributed its straits. The Nazi revolution would build a causeway through the ambient corruption, the loss of confidence and self-respect, the collapse of public (and private) morality, the decadent culture that wore the Germans down and made them flabby, weary and weak. It would reshape man. Manual and intellectual labour would be linked, personality reforged more through service than through schooling, art would become militant and committed to an ideal rather than to negative incoherence. The virtues would be revived: self-denial must replace self-indulgence, self-sacrifice would displace bourgeois selfishness, public spirit would rise where individualism flourished, school and work would contribute to moral, social and political indoctrination. Inspired by communism, perhaps, like the concentration camps with their pious slogans: *Arbeit macht frei.* But also by the practice of successive French Republics, by nationalist tradition, and containing all the themes of more recent cultural revolutions energized by violence and youth, led by a hero leader, inspired by the certainty that if you could first (re)create man, social and economic changes will necessarily follow.[48]

This is an attitude that has often been described as typical of fascism. It seems to belong in other revolutionary traditions. Malraux has spoken of Saint-Just as one who passionately hoped to change man by constraining him to participate in a transfiguring epic. The basic 'fascist' theme, including epic project, theatrical transfiguration, and constraint, appears in the French Revolution as naturally as in China or Cuba today. So does the theme of death and transfiguration: in the Commune of 1871, in the novels of Malraux, in the proclamations of Che Guevara, or in Régis Debray's likening of Che's passion to that of Christ.[49]

The action for action's sake aspect of fascist movements reappears in leftist movements of the 1960s. The student movements that cluster around the year 1968 appear inspired by the thought that first comes action, then an idea of what to do with it. In Latin America, some revolutionary groups develop a mystique of violence for its own sake, comparable to that of the declining Iron Guard. In Colombia one such organization calls itself *La Violencia.*

Incapable of solving, sometimes even of comprehending, the problems that they face, such covenants have recourse to what Ellul has called (in another context) *le terrorisme simplificateur.* Revolutionary war, says Régis Debray, is a sort of destiny for men who have chosen it in order to endow their lives with meaning. Should we attribute such adventurism to social origins and objective counterrevolutionism (remembering that Lenin dismissed leftists as petty bourgeois overwhelmed by the horrors of capitalism), or attribute it to despair—the kind of pessimism often ascribed to fascism? 'Pessimistic as to the issue of the struggle we undertook,' writes

Debray of Guevara, 'disillusioned by the way the revolutionary cause evolved in Latin America,' his revolt was a *mystical* revolt, a Christ-like self-sacrifice. Reminiscent of Albert Béguin's description of the classic road to fascism: 'the way of the revolutionary who has remained revolutionary, but who, by experience of failure or innate propensity, has come to despair of men.'

To despair of them, perhaps, but also to bring them a kind of hope that seems inaccessible otherwise. And so, around Valle Grande, in Bolivia, where Che Guevara's body was brought after he had been shot to death, thousands of photographs of the Che have joined the other pious images on local peasants' walls, and tales of miracles wrought by him are heard throughout the countryside.[50] Evidently, despair and redemptive action— even without hope—are not the preserve of fascists alone, but of other revolutionaries too.[51] Nor are they necessary characteristics of revolutionism of any sort, which readily admits dissatisfaction with men and things as they are, the more forcefully to assert the possibility of changing them.

True, the Nazi revolution was oriented not only against the order of Weimar, which it denounced as disorder (a self-fulfilling prophecy to which Nazis contributed a great deal) and which went bankrupt through its own devices. It was also against modern society itself, or what it denounced as such: the devaluation of values, the destructuring of structures, the liquefaction of familiar references, 'a state of anomie unknown until that time.'[52] Nazi criticism did not limit itself to liberal society and economy, collapsing all around and which, when it worked, worked to demean mankind. It reached out to their concrete incarnations: industrialism, bureaucracy, the mechanization of life, the bourgeois spirit denounced as incarnation of meanness, mediocrity and moderation. Familiar themes today, more difficult perhaps to denounce as purely reactionary than they were at the time.[53]

At any rate, whether we like it or not, whether we trust it or not, the revolutionary project here is clear enough. The more evident in its revivification of the *fête révolutionnaire*, the exhilaration of the great ceremonies and displays that the first revolution inaugurated, the elation of living a vaguely defined but emphatic adventure: dawns when it is a joy to be alive.[54] Sacrilege? It may seem so to us, scarcely to the participants. If revolution is about the people, this was as close to a revolution as Western Europe has known in the past century. And most Germans seem to have perceived it as such at the time.

What were they being promised? The Nazi revolution held out the ultimate revolutionary promise: *changer la vie*, an absurd project unless associated with *changer l'homme*, Nietzsche's *noch nicht festgestellte Tier*. Professor Mayer warns us[55] that this too is typical of counterrevolutionary leaders who 'place greater stress on profound changes in attitude, spirit and outlook than on economic and social structures.' He may be prepared to apply this judgment to men like Régis Debray and Che Guevara too, for whom the true end of communism is the creation of a new man; and to Découflé who seems to adopt Rimbaud's famous words as his slogan. And if he did, Mayer might be right. He would at least be consistent. At any rate, the project that aims to change life and man implies constraint. It did so for the idealists who sat on the Committee of Public Safety. It has done so since. Theories about the revolution are one thing. The practice of revolution is another. Revolution in practice is still another. These are platitudes we sometimes forget.

The Nazi revolution, like other revolutionary projects, proved self-defeating. We have not dismissed other revolutions for that. Babeuf did not do so. Découflé does not do so. Perhaps all revolutions are false: they lead elsewhere than they pretend to do. Why should one revolution be more false than others? In any case, how far does even the best-reasoned revolutionary project reflect the revolutionary perception of the masses? Especially the best-reasoned! Our understanding of this remains on the most impressionistic level. Which may be why we fall back on sociological or theoretical analyses which, in their different ways, provide something we think we can get our teeth into: the security of apparent fact or logical structure. When all that we do, too often, is treat assumptions as solid points of reference: wax fruit for working models of the real.

I do not think it has been often said (although the evidence is not exactly lacking) that most popular perceptions of revolution tend to be reactionary. We have not given enough attention to the nostalgic side of revolution which, when encountered, tends to be dismissed as an irrelevant primitivism similar to the coccyx. Yet a nostalgia for things past informs most visions of the future, if only because imagination has to build with blocks made of past experience, personal or vicarious. We enter the future backwards. The French Revolution itself was conservative, reactionary, aiming not to abolish but to restore (see Tocqueville), and only inadvertently revolutionary (see Hannah Arendt). It executed Louis XVI because Charles I had been executed. It looked back wistfully to the ancient world, and pushed its antiquarianism so far as to revive the notion of the *proletarian*, which Rousseau had fished out of the depths of Roman history. Much nineteenth century revolutionism was consoled or sparked by nostalgic fantasies and yearnings, which survived in fin-de-siècle socialism as they did in explicitly reactionary movements. About the socialist and syndicalist workers he had known before 1914 (and we should remember just how few they were), an old French working man recalls: '. . . their confused dream carried them less towards the founding of a new world than to a return to forms of life they had known or heard tell about; and, the years and distance blurring the bad aspects, made the past appear a new Icaria.'[56]

In a way, all revolution is reaction. Not only in the original sense of the term: an action reacting against other actions or against a state of things;

but in the sense that it draws so many references from the past. Is it so clear, when we look again, that reactionaries demolish in the name of the past (tradition), while revolutionaries demolish in the name of the future (progress)? Is the reality quite so simple? And, if it were, what matters more in the end: the demolition, or the ideals in whose name it is carried out?

Is not, after all, revolution simply the realization of *revolt*, that is of revolt or reaction against conditions or acts that are revolting, so that the only definition of revolution would be: the violent and successful embodiment of one sort of reaction which, in due course, becomes another sort of reaction. This is a question that becomes most pressing in our own time when, most of the traditional revolutions discredited, the torch of revolution seems to have passed to newer nations.

Professor Mayer has avoided discussing the independence and national liberation movements in the Third World.[57] Not surprisingly, since such discussion would reveal profound deviations and confusions in the marxist doctrine of revolution. Yet, in the past score years, the movements and regimes of national liberation have been the chief representatives of revolution, the chief targets of counterrevolution, and any discussion of the two terms that avoids them begs far more questions than it faces.

Reference to the Third World is essential, because it places our question in perspective. Nowhere does the ambiguousness of the 'revolutionary' definition appear more evident. Nasser, surrounded by petty bourgeois or middle-class aides, many like himself once close to fascist-style ideas, adopts a 'socialist' position in 1961 and is recognized as such by the Russians who declare that backward countries, sparing themselves the dictatorship of the proletariat, can pass directly to socialism under the leadership of progressive national forces which include the anticolonialist bourgeoisie. This novel interpretation meant, in effect, that Marxist doctrinaires could endorse 'national revolutions' being made to set up a national state on the nineteenth century pattern, create a nation, institute all the most conventional characteristics of the society against which revolution is supposed to take place in the West. It meant endorsement of dictatorships and coups d'état that had little to do with Marxist theories, and also of millenarian revolutionary ideologies that had even less. It presented doctrinal quandaries (like that which François Bourricaud has outlined for Peru),[58] when in newly developing countries the industrial working class turned out to be a privileged class.

The notion of the privileged proletarian, launched by Frantz Fanon in *The Wretched of the Earth*, has often been applied in Latin America, whose writers seem to have coined the term 'proletarian aristocracy.' In such circumstances, revolution was forced to seek its partisans among the peasants and the urban sub-proletariat—the very social groups whose support was once supposed to prove the counterrevolutionary nature of fascism, and whose revolutionism tends towards nationalism anyway. All of which has led to the development of intricate and seemingly paradoxical patterns of opposition and of doctrinal heresy.

Inspired by Cuban example and by long native tradition, 'leftist' revolutionaries argue that a numerically weak working class, tending to reformism and 'aristocratized in fact by the relatively high salaries paid in large concerns,' precludes adherence to the Marxist-Leninist model; and that, in any case, proletarian hegemony over predominantly peasant countries would be an aberration. 'The vanguard class in Latin America,' declares Debray, 'is the poor peasantry, united under the conscious direction expressed in student ranks.' More orthodox opponents of such 'petty bourgeois intellectuals,' argue that politics cannot be treated as a simple arithmetical operation which holds majorities decisive; and that, faced with a peasantry that is 'backward and hardened in its ways,' the proletariat remains 'the revolutionary class par excellence.' As for the Indian revolution, on behalf of the most oppressed majority of Latin Americans, this is no more than a racist notion designed to drive a wedge between exploited people whether in country or town.[59] In the end, the advocates of *foquismo* and of a 'people's war' appear more like primitive rebel leaders of guerilla bands, while their doctrinaire critics seem fated to revolutionary inactivity.

Such divisions are less interesting than the achievements and the fate of attempts at 'national revolutions' led by those 'national bourgeoisies' that the Russians have come to approve and the leftists to abhor. In Bolivia, for example, the MNR (National Revolutionary Movement), founded during the second world war, has been denounced both as fascist and as communist. Its checkered career, which runs from revolutionism to collaboration with 'imperialism' and American business interests, shows it as a powerful force for change, unafraid of violence, and responsible for 'irreversible structural changes' in Bolivian economy, society, and politics. In its time, and to the extent possible at the time, admirers of Guevara tell us, the MNR 'carried the Bolivian people through the first stages of a revolution without precedent in Latin America.'[60] Yet, by the later 1950s, the MNR had decayed into corruption and opportunism. A more recent representative of revolutionary nationalism, General Juan José Torrès, supported by nationalists, socialists, and orthodox communists, harassed by Trotskyists, Maoists, and leftists who denounced him for refusing to arm the people, could not survive the tug of war between more and less radical revolutionary groups, all accusing each other of objective counterrevolutionism, and was to be swept out by a right-wing army coup in 1972.

Other examples could be cited. But perhaps the point has been made, *not* that would-be revolutionaries disagree among themselves, something that Lenin knew perfectly well, but that there are many ways of attempting a revolution, and even of making one. In conditions prevailing throughout most of the Third World, just as they did in Romania, for one, between the wars, the 'revolutionary patriotism' of Castrism, the 'revolutionary nationalism' of Bolivia or Peru, the 'struggle of national liberation' with its economic implications, can be very revolutionary indeed—especially where, as a Bolivian writer has put it, the nineteenth century is not yet over. This is why the debate between the National Left which places antiimperialism first, and more orthodox doctrinaires who give priority to class war, is very revealing;[61] because the emphasis laid on anti-imperialist struggle, which is simply an aspect of nationalism, shows a perfectly logical direction to which revolution can turn. Just as the decay of the MNR's revolutionism indicates a very natural tendency, to be imputed not to bourgeois corruption but, as we have seen, to built-in factors that manifest themselves in all revolutions, whether they end in the contradictions of an Institutionalized Revolutionary Party as in Mexico, or those of a new class as in Eastern Europe.

Even when a successful revolutionary leader converts to the authorized version, as Pepin did to Rome and for similar reasons, the original revolution seems to harden into something else. Cuban peasants, in 1959, thought that the liberty the new revolution brought meant freedom from work, as well as from their old masters. They were fast enlightened. Their duty was to work even harder to build socialism. There were no more latifundia and no more sugar barons; but the peasants had to carry workbooks like every other worker: the infamous *livret de travail* that stained nineteenth century capitalism and still survives in the Soviet Union. Absenteeism was punished; strikes were banned, salaries frozen, holidays diminished. The chief enterprise of modern states—propaganda—was massively increased, sometimes as education, a guise that can be traced back to the French Revolution and beyond but hardly confused with freedom. The distinction between the centre of decision and the executants persists. What we see in Cuba is a centralized, bureaucratic, police state, basically similar to other modern states, though more to some than to others. Does this go counter to Castro's revolutionary ideals? It does. Does it make the Cuban experience less revolutionary? It does not.

The same point can be made concerning Colonel Qadhafi, the Libyan leader. Qadhafi, who must be counted as revolutionary in the Libyan context, is clearly a reactionary in his ideology. He has, indeed, been denounced as a 'fascist dictator' by the Popular Front for the Liberation of Palestine (Paris *Herald-Tribune*, 20 August 1973). What are we to make of this?

Once abandoned the Marxist model of revolution stemming out of capitalism and industrialization, once adopted the abridged version of precapitalist societies hustling straight into socialism, revolution becomes not the resolution of a developed society's contradictions, but the accelerator of evolution towards development (and towards the contradictions development must bring). In this perspective, socialism is no longer a revolution creative of socio-economic progress of a special kind, but just a way to do more quickly what capitalism has done elsewhere, or has not done fast or well enough. The exploitation of man by state replaces the exploitation of man by man. The difference blurs between the developmental revolutions (Mexico, Bolivia, Cuba, Egypt, Algeria) cited by Edgar Morin,[62] and the developmental dictatorships of Borkenau and Nolte. Professor Mayer was right. Our findings, it would seem, do dilute his heuristic construct and blunt its cutting edge. But if a heuristic approach serves to apprehend some kind of truth or bring us nearer to it, perhaps that's just as well.

No wonder, then, that fascism is included in the category of developmental revolutions by qualified observers, together with the national revolutions of undeveloped or developing countries. We remain uncertain whether either kind or both should be labelled growing pains, revolution, or counterrevolution, unless it be preemptive revolution—a favourite for coups d'état from all quarters since the Ides of March. Only one conclusion seems clear. One cannot exclude fascists and Nazis from the revolutionary category of our times because of the equivocal nature of their rhetoric and their reformist hedging as they jockey for power, without applying the same standards to most 'national revolutions' of our day. So, either the latter are fascist—in which case the fascist model is shown to be actual and appropriate to present circumstances; or they are revolutionary, despite failure to measure up to Marxist definitions, and then the fascists are revolutionary too.

Who can gainsay that Qadhafi, Nasser, Castro, are (were) revolutionaries, their regimes radically different in essentials from preceding ones? The point is not that they have betrayed some ideal pattern of revolution but that, despite non-conformity to the dogmatic pattern, their particular role, action, effects, are very revolutionary.

There is no revolution to betray, because there is not one version of revolution only; and the contortions of Marxist theory reveal not its capacity to assimilate, or to adjust to, practice, but its anachronism.

It is not so much that the Marxist-inspired model of revolution involves us in time-consuming aberrations, as that it is beside the point.

Revolutions, revolts, rebellions, riots, risings, mutinies, insurrections, tumults, troubles, disturbances, coups d'etat and civil wars figure in present history as in that of the past. The first rebels were angels. The first rebellion the Fall. We shall not be rid of the ilk in the foreseeable future. Perhaps we should not be. In any case, they exist, they demand our attention. Treating them in terms of one doctrine, relevant though it was in its time, suggestive though it remains in ours, lessens our grasp of the problem, limits our capacity for comprehension, increases the possibilities of confusion. Incantations hobble analysis. Even the restrictions imposed by terminological conformism pass into our thinking and hamper it. Political terminology becomes a political fact, intellectual terminology becomes a factor of intellectual activity. When we describe something as revolutionary or counterrevolutionary, half the interpretative process has been performed already, the other half will reflect what went — or, rather, what failed to go — before.

Yes, revolution is a continuing historical fact; but the context and objectives of revolutions change. Nineteenth-century revolutions, modelled on that of 1789, were supposed to be for freedom (constitutional, legal, of press, speech and economic enterprise), for the nation (patriotic and nationalist) and the state (a more efficient one, preferably a republic), against tyranny (and monarchy). Twentieth-century revolutions, on a model suggested by Marx and then revised by Lenin, are supposed to eliminate the bourgeoisie (not monarchy), to further the consciousness, unity and struggle of class (not nation), to take over the means of production (rather than free them for private exploitation). The relations that had to be changed in this, second, case lay in the sphere of economics (production) not of politics (the constitutional reflection of economic realities). There was a world of difference between the two revolutionary projects. And Marx, when he came along to say that the changed context of his time called for a changed revolutionary project, could appear as irrelevant in terms of the ruling ideology and terminology, and as counterrevolutionary to the tradition-directed revolutionaries of his time, as one who today denounces the Marxist project and its derivatives as anachronistic when they are applied in a context very different from that of their formulation.

The socialist revolutionary project spoke of and to an industrial society, dominated by the steam engine, by the conditions of life and labour this generated, and by their expression in liberal, individualistic doctrines and competitive economic organization. All this is gone or disappearing in the West. Which is not to say that want and war, injustice or exploitation, national rivalries and overweening states do not endure. But socialism has shown itself no more capable than other systems of solving such persistent problems. In any case, the point about Marxist analysis is not how correct it is in general terms, but how apt it can prove to provide a dynamizing (revolutionary) interpretation and inspiration in specific historical circumstances. Highly appropriate to the needs of certain industrially developing societies, like those of late nineteenth-century Western Europe, its use in conditions like those that prevail in most Latin American or African countries seems restrictive or confusing, condemning would-be revolutionaries to ideological contortions and to awkwardness in practice. Meanwhile, and especially in developed countries that set the pace throughout the world, social mutations from the secondary to the tertiary sector, economic mutations from ownership to management, ideological mutations as the age-old rule of necessity wanes, have all wrought profound changes. New major problems take shape and call for new solutions: growth, the explosive pace of change, technology, automation, demography, mass media, information and propaganda. Many progressive circles view progress as the modern equivalent of the Fall. If only we could be left to die of our ills, they cry, not of our remedies! What has Marxism to propose about all this? The ideal of the nineteenth-century revolution: travail, famille, patrie, more industry, more productivity, eventually more goods to be enjoyed. On such grounds, less revolutionary systems can match and improve on it.

An anachronistic doctrine of revolution hampers its strategy, restricts its tactics and, finally, hamstrings its theory too. In the context of today, reference to socialist or communist theory increasingly suggests the absence of revolutionary theory. This is clear enough in those neo-Marxist variants, neither new nor Marxist, which substitute the poor for the proletariat, the struggle of poor against rich for the struggle between classes (specifically between industrial proletariat and bourgeoisie), the wars of nations for the wars of classes. If such revisionists ignore Marx's views on this score, it may be because reference to Marx would reveal their views as far from Marxist or, more simply, because they ignore Marx. At any rate, viewed in the light of such doctrinal decay, fascism is just one more recent avatar of revolutionary myth,[63] disputing this with ideological rivals with a prior hold upon it; the very assertion of its revolutionism a tribute to the evocative power of the notion.

A tribute, too, to the enduring power of millennarian dreams and to their actuality. For this is what survives in positive as well as negative stereotypes of fascism and communism. If fascism really was the ultimate spasm of capitalist society on its last legs, the need for it must be past today when capitalism, however uneasily, rules the world. The communist revolution, in its ideal form, has shown itself hardly more relevant or more possible. Both fascism and communism have failed, in their own terms, to achieve the fundamental revolutionary dream: *changer la vie*. Yet, at another level, that is beside the point, and the persistence of the issue proves the persistent relevance of revolution as a cause.

The very notion of changing life or man is an inheritance of 1789 and after, the apprehension, novel for mankind, that things can be different from what they have always been. *Belief* that change is possible, fundamental change, even more than the *fact* of change, is characteristic of the modern age. Revolutionary projects answer that belief, which constitutes the chief objective condition of their being. In this perspective, revolutions propose first to define, then to accelerate, what they say should happen and what, without their intervention, would not happen, or would happen otherwise. They express the general situation less in their content than in their form and, above all, in the crucial affirmation that radical change is possible and should take place. Fascists and communists may find themselves revolutionaries without a revolution (we haven't quite got there yet!), but the Revolution as part of the contemporary situation, of the modern view of life, is ready to adopt almost any guise that can express it.

This raises a different question: Do revolutions really change, or do they transform, modifying institutional or ideological expressions of fundamentally similar structures? We know that revolutions wreak great changes, overthrow a regime, break with a given order or state of things. But does this represent a passage from one state to its contrary, or to another form, shape, avatar, of the same? This is not idle speculation or, even, simply an aid to theory. For it would seem as if most modern revolutions are made not to abolish the existing society and state of things but to seek integration in them.

The French and the Russian revolutions were made against societies and regimes incarnated by tangible groups: aristocrats, bourgeoisie. Whom are the new revolutionaries to eliminate? The bureaucrats? Who is their bourgeoisie? Only the workers know quite whom they should redefine as such from time to time, and they do so only because their avenging arm needs to point out some object for their wrath, some enemy in order to ensure their semblance of subsistence as a class. Sorel had sensed this vanishing trick when he tried to make workers fight to force the bourgeoisie to stay bourgeois, which was essential if the bourgeois were to continue to provide one of the two irreducible terms without which (*in ille tempore*) the dialectical evolution would have broken down. No class war, no clash, no synthetic issue into a new society: and that is just what happened. Over the years, the bourgeoisie, that Protean monster, far from eliminated by its successors-to-be, trained and indoctrinated them to assimilate the dominant culture and its values. Not counterrevolution but integration, appropriation, of the Revolution, of revolutions, of revolutionary ideas, mark the practice of the last hundred years.

In the long run, of course. In the short run, society reacts violently to challenges it cannot absorb. But brutal reactions become rarer as we go along. For revolutions are primitive, and primitive rebels are increasingly isolated, assimilated, or entertained to death. So, those who take the place of the 'bourgeoisie' take up only its succession. The new society is not the opposite of the old, but its prolongation and its heir. Undeveloped countries want to industrialize. Developed countries want more of what they have already for more people: immediate satisfactions, regular work, or less work, continuity, security, predictability, comfort, more efficient facilities, and fewer traffic jams. Pursuing the benefits of productivity, bowing to its demands, the parties of Movement and of Resistance both revolve among restricted options. What kind of revolution is there left to make when all revolutionaries propose in the end to establish similar values?

Some time before the March on Rome, Mussolini found occasion to remark, apparently with some surprise, that one could be both revolutionary and conservative. An incriminating remark? Certainly an actual one. As misery and exploitation grow less intense in the West, more complicated elsewhere, the revolutionary project becomes less concrete. In the wealthy West, revolution turns more towards intellectuals and dissatisfied members of the middle classes than to the underprivileged who are not revolutionary but reformist. But a less radical public demanding more costly public services (housing, education, health, social security) can prove more dangerous to the established order than the more vehement (ideological) radicalism of its predecessors. In Bourricaud's Peru, the dream of avenging revolution is replaced by the dream of development: industrial, educational, above all urban. In Lima or in Moscow ideals grow increasingly close: no more classes, only consumers. All revolutions now are oriented not to change existing standards but to enjoy them.

In the beginning was inequality, injustice, hunger, and want. Humanitarianism and political action remedied this (a bit), but only by relying on greatly increased productivity. Man in his numbers and in his way of life depends on technological efficacy and control, seeks to advance by increasing this dependence. What revolution will change this? We are, as Jacques Ellul insists, the prisoners of our technology, the captives of our means. We may diversely estimate this predicament. It may not be a predicament at all, and I for one am far less moved by it than Ellul seems to be. But it is a fact. Consumer society has consumed the revolution. The advances of modernity — production, consumption — have changed the data a would-be revolutionary must consider. Since it is doubtful that revolution now can do much to alter relations of production, perhaps it will return to the more modest project of altering relations of authority. [64] But, judged according to current stereotypes, this would scarcely qualify as revolution at all.

Perhaps the sort of revolution that goes beyond the immediate event, the merely spectacular, is nowadays unlikely. At any rate, what is currently accepted as revolution is not of that sort. The would-be revolutionaries of today would do well to look away from their anachronistic models, which they have abandoned in practice anyway, and try to invent a revolutionary project appropriate to the contemporary context. That is not my concern. But history suggests that such a project must go beyond the spectacular aspects of life, unlock the gate that leads from the familiar to the unexpected, release history to move ahead to a new and unpredictable stage. [65] Marx understood this; and the revolutionary categories that he proposed corresponded to the society of 1850, as it had not yet learned to see itself. But it is not the structures of 1850 that revolutionaries should attack today. Such an attack could still make sense in the first half of the twentieth century, when nineteenth-century structures lingered on. That was when fascist and communist revolutionaries, rooted in nineteenth-century criticisms and ideals, attacked the surviving structures and their conservative, antirevolutionary, or counterrevolutionary defenders. The offensive of the revolutionaries and the ensuing conflicts were part of the preparation of the changes we have lived. They grow less relevant as the modern mutation gains ground throughout the world.

We know too much nowadays to explain very much. We certainly know too little to explain anything thoroughly. But as long as our notions of historical change continue to turn on terms as imprecise as revolution and counterrevolution, they remain blocked, and focused on problems already left behind.

## NOTES

1. Max Gallo, *Gauchisme, réformisme et révolution* (1968), 133. Despite all this, he explains, May 1968 was not the revolution. (Unless otherwise indicated, all books quoted are published in Paris.)

2. Andre Découflé, *Sociologie des révolutions* (1968). There is no point in taking intellectual issue with the lunatic fringe. Découflé is used for reference because he represents the more respectable French students of the subject.

3. Quoted in John Anthony Scott, *The Defense of Gracchus Babeuf* (Amherst, 1967), 42.

4. Découflé, op. cit., 40.

5. Ibid., 7, also 11-12. One might ask in passing whether popular interest in or sympathy for social bandits and some of the other outlaws described by Professor Hobsbawm, who often prey more on their own kind than on the powerful and the rich, reflects even the most primitive form of social revolt. The solidarity of common folk against lawmen and tax collectors is rooted in human and local experience, not in social awareness, however dim. Take the case of smugglers, whom peasants took for granted, buying the salt or matches they sold, accepting their activities as part of the local economy, aiding them when they could. Though differently motivated, such attitudes no more reflect social revolt than our occasional sympathy for those who cheat the Customs or Internal Revenue.

6. Ibid., 13-14.

7. Thus, Cardinal de Retz, a seventeenth-century expert on the matter, in his *Mémoires*, concerning 'les émotions populaires': Les riches n'y viennent que par force; les mendiants y nuisent plus qu'ils n'y servent, parce que la crainte du pillage les fait appréhender. Ceux qui y peuvent le plus sont les gens qui sont assez pressés dans leurs affaires pour désirer du changement dans les publiques et dont la pauvreté ne passe toutefois pas jusques à la mendicité publique.

8. See Herbert Marcuse in J. A. Scott, op. cit., 103. Saint-Just had already declared: 'The miserable are the power of the earth.' (Speech of 8 Ventôse/March 1794).

9. Just how wrong, can be seen from the remark a working man made to Ramon Fernandez, the literary critic, after the Sixth of February riots of 1934: 'Il nous faudrait des fusils et descendre vers les quartiers riches ! ... Avec, à notre tête, un chef, un homme enfin: tenez, un type dans le genre de Gide !' Reported by Ramon Fernandez, 'Politique et littérature,' *Nouvelle revue française* (1935), 286.

10. Michel Clouscard, *Néo-fascisme et idéologie du désir* (1973), 49.

11. Right and Left simply differ in the subject of their messianic fantasies: nation or race for the one, proletarians or intellectuals for the other. Both can be fascinated by heroes. And both, recently, have turned their attention to youth, last brittle hope of those who have bet on so many other horses and lost. But youth (as ideology) is a product of adult society, as the industrial proletariat is a product of capitalist society, and seems as destined for assimilation as its predecessors. Even more so.

12. Chateaubriand, *Essai sur les révolutions* (1797), II (Bruxelles, 1826), 280-81.

13. See Jacques Ellul, *Métamorphose du bourgeois* (1967), 158. I have greatly benefited

from the reading of this and others of his books. Ellul, with whom I do not always agree, is one of the few really original thinkers in France. The mass of those to whom the term is often applied are more liable to run in schools, like fish.

14. Gallo, op. cit., 107.

15. There was White Terror, of course. But the use of terror does not define a counter-revolutionary regime, any more than a revolutionary one. Both may use it and generally do. Yet violence and terror can be found in other regimes as well, with no particular ideological overtones. And let it be understood, once and for all, that the attempt to treat certain phenomena from a detached point of view, does not imply approval.

16. Lora, *Bolivie: de la naissance du POR à l'Assemblée populaire* (1971), 203; Ruben Vasquez Diaz, *La Bolivie à l'heure du Che* (1968), 99.

17. Découflé op. cit., 18. Note the implication of deliberate policy ('project'), where the most one could assert might be an 'objective' role; and the objection that a counterrevolution must have a rival revolution to counter with a revolution of its own, suggesting (a) that the United States (and Canada?) represent a *sui generis* revolutionary cause, yet (b) that the only revolutions deserving the name are those that North Americans oppose.

18. Clouscard, op. cit., 9-10, 72. Clouscard has excellent precedents. Much bandied about during the Terror, the term was even applied to Robespierre, in the Committee of Public Safety, after the vote of the law of 22 Prairial, year II. One danger of such confusionism was pointed out by Eugene Varga in his study of the economic crisis of the 1930's, *La Crise* (1935), 264-65. Communists, he warned, have made the mistake of calling fascist dictatorship what was only 'the accentuated fascisation of bourgeois regimes.' This weakened the antifascist struggle, because workers said that, if that was fascism, then fascism is not as terrible as all that.

19. Découflé, op. cit., 122-23.

20. Mayer, *Dynamics of Counterrevolution*, 115, 116.

21. Ibid., 78.

22. Compare Branco Lazitch, *Lénine et la 3e Internationale* (Neuchâtel, 1951), 211. In 1923 the KPD conference at Frankfurt would define fascism as 'a preventive counterrevolution in that it uses pseudoradical slogans.'

23. Mayer, op. cit., 62. On p. 63 Mayer remarks that the counterrevolutionary project 'is far more militant in rhetoric, style and conduct,' where it can be likened to its revolutionary competitors, 'than in political, social or economic substance,' when in effect the political, economic and, in some ways, social substance of (say) the Nazi politics of the 1930s was more radical and innovative than that of most contemporary socialists.

24. Mayer, op. cit., 62: 'As of the 1870's it became increasingly clear that to be effective, the struggle against Socialism required a distinct popular ideology.'

25. In any case, how intense was the class struggle in France, when Georges Sorel had to initiate a hopeless though brilliant campaign attempting to revive it?

26. There is no vouching for Boulanger. He was certainly an opportunist, and hardly straightforward in his political dealings. But he was not intelligent enough to conceive a manipulative ideology, and hardly a typical revolutionary *or* counterrevolutionary leader.

27. A case where the encounter between straightforward (conservative) and camouflaged counterrevolutionaries is clear appears in Miklós Szinai and László Szúcs, eds., *The Confidential Papers of Admiral Horthy* (Budapest, 1965), 112-18, reprinting a January 14, 1939 memorandum of Count Istvan Bethlen and the 'Rightist' opposition he represented. Bethlen criticizes the pro-Nazi Imrédy for being too sympathetic to the Germans and stirring up a hornets' nest with his anti-Semitic and land-reform proposals, liable to open the way to Arrow Cross overbidding. As for the revolutionary Arrow Cross itself, Horthy's lines of October 14, 1940, addressed to the then prime minister, Pal Teleki, are revealing (150-51). Horthy says he has always been anti-Semitic, but he wants no precipitate measures that would only ruin the country. 'In addition, I consider for example the Arrow Cross men to be by far more danger-

ous and worthless for my country than I do the Jew. The latter is tied to this country from interest, and is more faithful to his adopted country than the Arrow Cross men, who, like the Iron Guard, with their muddled brains, want to play the country into the hands of the Germans.'

28. See Jean-Michel Etienne, *Le Mouvement rexiste jusqu'en 1940* (1968).

29. One can go further and ask if Pétain's National Revolution of 1940, overturning a Republic that all, including the Left, proclaimed was rotten, was less of a revolution than General de Gaulle's raping her faintly consenting successor in 1958, or Revlon's introducing a revolutionary shade of nail polish in 1973.

30. Mayer, op. cit., 2.

31. As when ibid., 66, Mayer speaks of the 'revolutionary opposites' of counterrevolutionary leaders.

32. Ibid., 20.

33. Jacques Ellul, 'Le Fascisme, fils du libéralisme,' *Esprit*, no. 53 (February 1937), 762-63, defines fascism by its formal will to react against liberalism, and not as a true Reaction. But that applies to communism too, 'also formal negation of Liberalism and perhaps also its offspring.'

34. Daniel Lerner and Harold D. Lasswell, *World Revolutionary Elites* (Cambridge, 1966), 230, 461, 463-64 and passim.

35. Mayer, op. cit., 89.

36. It was, of course, against this trend that Mao's cultural revolution was waged, and lost.

37. André Malraux, 'S.O.S.,' *Marianne*, October 11, 1933.

38. Was it the Fourth Congress of the Communist International (1922) which, while recognizing that fascists sought a mass base 'in the peasant class, in the petty bourgeoisie, and even in certain sections of the proletariat,' insisted that the combat organizations they set up were counterrevolutionary, and thus arrogated to itself the coveted revolutionary label? Or was it fascist opportunism, and its incidental (as well as doctrinal) hostility to socialism and communism that gave the label up?

39. See Mayer's remark, op. cit., 66, that counterrevolutionaries favour the conspiratorial rather than the critical-analytic view of history. Is not this characteristic of many creeds addressed to masses? What about the Left's use of bankers, 'merchants of death' and, nowadays, multinational conglomerates?

40. Notably in 'The Men of the Archangel,' *Journal of Contemporary History*, I, 1 (December 1965). And Maurice Thorez, 'holding out his hand' in 1936 to the militants of fascist leagues, 'sons of the people' like the communists, seems to bear out my point.

41. See Malraux speaking in 1929 about the revolutionary characters of his novel, *Les Conquérants*, who were recognized as typical revolutionaries by experts like Trotsky. The revolutionary leader, says Malraux, '...doesn't have to define Revolution, but to make it,' Quoted in Jean Lacouture, *André Malraux* (1973), 136. Similarly, the Second Havana Declaration, quoted in Régis Debray, *Essais sur l'Amérique latine* (1967), 131: 'The duty of a revolutionary is to make the revolution.'

42. See, for example, Talcott Parsons' famous essay of 1942, 'Some Sociological Aspects of the Fascist Movements,' in *Essays in Sociological Theory* (Glencoe, 1954).

43. Note that the question of private property, central both in Marxist doctrine and in categorizing fascism, was regarded as a secondary issue, incidental to major aims: productivity, employment, order, restructuring the society and the productive process. In this respect too, fascists in theory and National Socialists in practice showed themselves more flexible than their rivals.

44. Likewise, petty bourgeoisie and new middle classes, regarded by communists as the chief source of fascist support, are considered to play a positive role when they participate in the national revolutions of the Third World.

45. Jules Monnerot, *Sociologie de la Révolution* (1969), 553. His italics.

46. See above. n. 40, and Rogger and Weber, eds., *The European Right* (Berkeley and Los Angeles, 1965).

47. Ellul, *Autopsie de la révolution* (1969), 338.

48. Philippe Ardant, 'Le Héros maoïste,' *Revue française de science politique* (1969). The hero is characterized by his abandonment of personal selfishness. He is above all devoted to the collectivity, the fatherland, and Mao. As to how exciting it all seemed to the Germans, we can read about in witnesses like Nora Waln, *Reaching for the Stars* (Boston, 1939) or Emmanuel Mounier, *Esprit*, no. 49 (October 1936), 36: '...la fidélité dans la joie...le sourire du régime.... Si vous voulez étonner un nazi, dites-lui qu'il vit sous une dictature.'

49. *Journal Officiel de la Commune*, quoted in Découflé, op. cit., 37: 'Paris a fait un pacte avec la mort.' Guevara, quoted in *Le Monde*, 27 April 1967, calls for two, three, several Vietnams, 'with their share of death and immense tragedies,' for the sake of the blows they can deal to imperialism. As for death, 'let it be welcome provided that our warcry reaches a receptive ear, that another hand takes up our weapons, and that other men rise to strike up the funeral march and the crackling of machine guns and new cries of war and victory.' See also his *Créer deux, trois... de nombreux Vietnams, voilà le mot d'ordre* (1967), 12, 13. Debray is quoted in Ellul, *De la révolution aux révoltes* (1972), 139.

50. Debray, op. cit.; Béguin, *Esprit* (October 1948), quoted in Lacouture, op. cit., 339; González and Sánchez Salazar, *Che Guevara en Bolivie* (1969), 237. The sympathetic Salazars entitle one of their chapters 'A Twentieth-century Don Quixote.' This is as revealing as the legend that has grown around another hero of the revolutionary left, the Colombian priest who died as a guerillero, Camillo Torres. A self-sacrificing and devoted Christian populist, Torres hardly seems a revolutionary leader of the classic pattern: rather, the idealistic chief of primitive rebel bands. See the book of his friend, Mgr. German Guzman-Campos, *Camillo Torres* (1968).

51. Raymond Aron, *Le Développement de la société industrielle et la stratification sociale* (1957), I, 105, points out that in the nineteenth century optimism was on the liberal side: 'Le pessimisme était socialiste.' You could call a catastrophic pessimism (or optimism) the belief that things would have to get much worse before a vast explosion can open the door to betterment. This could, thanks to some confusion, provide a meeting ground for the socially pessimistic right and the doctrinally 'pessimistic' left.

There are less complicated ways of arguing this, by pointing to the frequent recognition that what one sought in one camp was more readily available in the other. Thus, in his *Chiens de paille*, written in the spring of 1943, reread in April 1944, finally published in 1964, Drieu La Rochelle notes his disillusion with Hitlerism, too much of a *juste milieu*: 'Mon idéal d'autorité et d'aristocratie est au fond enfoui dans ce communisme que j'ai tant combattu' (110). About that same time, Konstantin Roszevski, head of the emigré All Russian Fascist party, handed himself over to Soviet authorities and wrote to Stalin that Stalinism was exactly what he had erroneously called fascism, but purged of the exaggerations, errors and illusions of fascism. Rodzevski was to be condemned to death and executed in Moscow in 1946, but his opinion remains suggestive. See Erwin Oberlander, 'The All-Russian Fascist Party,' *Journal of Contemporary History*, I, 1 (1965).

52. Ellul, op. cit., 202.

53. I happen to disagree with them now, as I did then. But that is by the way.

54. The question has been raised how revolutionary such holidays really were. Not only Nuremberg but 1968 suggest equivocal answers. The recent documentary film, 'Français si vous saviez,' shows newsreels of Pétain and de Gaulle being cheered by hundreds of thousands of enthusiastic Parisians at a few weeks' interval.

55. Mayer, op. cit., 65.

56. René Michaud, *J'avais vingt ans. Un jeune ouvrier au début du siècle* (1967), 14.

57. See his statement (Mayer, op. cit., 6-7). To have done so 'would involve diluting the heuristic construct, leaving it with a blunted cutting edge.'

58. François Bourricaud, *Pouvoir et société dans le Pérou contemporain* (1967); Louis Constant, *Avec Douglas Bravo dans le maquis vénézuélien* (1968), 7; Carlos Romeo, *Sur les classes sociales en Amérique latine* (1968), 27 and passim.

59. Debray, op. cit., 86, 202; Lora, op. cit., 188, 203, 204.

60. Salazar, op. cit., 29. Even Trotskyists agree that 'the MNR is indisputably the greatest popular party Bolivia has known.' Lora, op. cit., 210.

61. Compare Lora, op. cit., 185 ff.; Pablo Torres, *La Contre-insurrection et la guerre révolutionnaire* (1971), 39 and passim. Writing to Castro in 1965, Guevara equates revolution, 'the most sacred of tasks,' with 'the struggle against imperialism of whatever kind.' Salazar, op. cit., 42, quote the letter in full. In it we also meet, not for the first time, the Castrist slogan 'Revolution or Death': — another traditional revolutionary reference, hardly restricted to fascists.

62. Edgar Morin, *Introduction à une politique de l'homme* (1965), 92-93. Half-failures all, Morin remarks, 'but isn't half-failure also a formula of life? Isn't that what we call success?'

63. I use the term in the Sorelian sense, to describe a combination of unifying images capable of instinctively evoking the feelings and ideas corresponding to a socio-political movement for the purpose of action.

64. Thus returning, *mutatis mutandis*, to Bossuet's description of an earlier situation: 'Les révolutions des empires...servent à humilier les Princes.' *Discours sur l'histoire universelle*, pt. 3, ch. I.

65. I wonder whether the real revolutions of our time are not our wars. Burckhardt, speaking in 1868, noted that 'modern wars are but an element in modern crises; they do not carry in themselves and do not produce the effects of a true crisis; beside them, bourgeois life goes on its way.' Their short duration, Burckhardt explained, fails to mobilize the forces of despair from which alone could come 'the total renewal of life, the expiatory destruction of what was and its replacement by a new living reality.' The revolutionary projects of the time sought to remedy this. Yet Burckhardt's remark could now apply to their descendants, if we replaced the term 'bourgeois life' with 'bourgeois values.' Meanwhile, the great wars of the twentieth century have proved effective midwives to the 'destruction of what was and its replacement by a new living reality,' even without the help of deliberate revolutions. Perhaps Burckhardt's Basel colleague, Nietzsche, was right when he predicted our entry into 'the classic era of war,' an era in which the functions that the nineteenth century attributed to revolution would be carried out by other means. See Jakob Burckhardt, *Considérations sur l'histoire du monde* (1938), ch. IV, especially 159-60.

# Index

# The Complete Works of
# William Shakespeare

WILLIAM SHAKESPEARE.

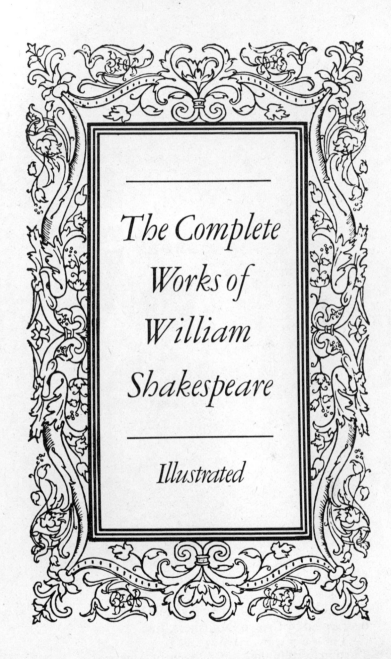

# The Complete Works of William Shakespeare

*Illustrated*

Avenel Books • New York

# CONTENTS

# Contents

# The Complete Works of
# William Shakespeare

TEMPEST.

Act I. Sc. 2.

# THE TEMPEST

## DRAMATIS PERSONÆ

ALONSO, *King of Naples.*
SEBASTIAN, *his brother.*
PROSPERO, *the rightful Duke of Milan.*
ANTONIO, *his brother, the usurping Duke of Milan.*
FERDINAND, *son to the King of Naples.*
GONZALO, *an honest old Counsellor of Naples.*
ADRIAN, } *Lords.*
FRANCISCO, }
CALIBAN, *a savage and deformed Slave.*
TRINCULO, *a Jester.*

STEPHANO, *a drunken Butler.*
*Master of a Ship, Boatswain, and Mariners.*
MIRANDA, *daughter to* PROSPERO.
ARIEL, *an airy Spirit.*
IRIS, }
CERES, }
JUNO, } *Spirits.*
*Nymphs,* }
*Reapers,* }

*Other Spirits attending on* PROSPERO.

SCENE,—*The Sea, with a Ship: afterwards an uninhabited Island.*

## ACT I.

SCENE I.—*On a Ship at Sea.*—*A Storm, with Thunder and Lightning.*

*Enter a* Shipmaster *and a* Boatswain.

*Master.* Boatswain,—
*Boats.* Here, master: what cheer?
*Master.* Good: Speak to the mariners: fall to 't yarely, or we run ourselves aground; bestir, bestir. [*Exit.*

*Enter* Mariners.

*Boats.* Heigh, my hearts; cheerly, cheerly, my hearts; yare, yare: take in the top-sail; 'Tend to the master's whistle.—Blow till thou burst thy wind, if room enough!

*Enter* ALONSO, SEBASTIAN, ANTONIO, FERDINAND, GONZALO, *and others.*

*Alon.* Good Boatswain, have care. Where's the master? Play the men.
*Boats.* I pray now, keep below.
*Ant.* Where is the master, Boatswain?
*Boats.* Do you not hear him? You mar our labour; keep your cabins: you do assist the storm.
*Gon.* Nay, good, be patient.
*Boats.* When the sea is. Hence! What care these roarers for the name of king? To cabin: silence: trouble us not.
*Gon.* Good; yet remember whom thou hast aboard.
*Boats.* None that I more love than myself. You are a counsellor: if you can command these elements to silence, and work the peace of the present, we will not hand a rope more; use your authority. If you cannot, give thanks you have lived so long, and make yourself ready in your cabin for the mischance of the hour, if it so hap.—Cheerly, good hearts.— Out of our way, I say. [*Exit.*

*Gon.* I have great comfort from this fellow: methinks he hath no drowning mark upon him; his complexion is perfect gallows. Stand fast, good fate, to his hanging! make the rope of his destiny our cable, for our own doth little advantage! If he be not born to be hanged, our case is miserable. [*Exeunt.*

*Re-enter* Boatswain.

*Boats.* Down with the top-mast; yare; lower, lower; bring her to try with main-course. *A cry within.*] A plague upon this howling! They are louder than the weather, or our office.—

*Re-enter* SEBASTIAN, ANTONIO, *and* GONZALO.

Yet again? what do you here? Shall we give o'er, and drown? Have you a mind to sink?
*Seb.* A pox o' your throat! you bawling, blasphemous, incharitable dog!
*Boats.* Work you, then.
*Ant.* Hang, cur, hang! you whoreson, insolent noise-maker, we are less afraid to be drowned than thou art.
*Gon.* I'll warrant him from drowning; though the ship were no stronger than a nut-shell, and as leaky as an unstanch'd wench.
*Boats.* Lay her a-hold, a-hold: set her two courses; off to sea again, lay her off.

*Enter* Mariners, *wet.*

*Mar.* All lost! to prayers, to prayers! all lost! [*Exeunt.*
*Boats.* What, must our mouths be cold?
*Gon.* The king and prince at prayers! let us assist them,
For our case is as theirs.
*Seb.* I am out of patience.
*Ant.* We are merely cheated of our lives by drunkards.—
This wide - chapp'd rascal; — Would thou mightst lie drowning,

The washing of ten tides!

*Gon.* He'll be hanged yet;
Though every drop of water swear against it,
And gape at wid'st to glut him.
[*A confused noise within.*]—Mercy on us! We
split, we split!—Farewell, my wife and children!
Farewell, brother!—We split, we split, we
split!—

*Ant.* Let's all sink with the king.    [*Exit.*
*Seb.* Let's take leave of him.    [*Exit.*
*Gon.* Now would I give a thousand furlongs of
sea for an acre of barren ground; long heath,
brown furze, any thing: The wills above be
done! but I would fain die a dry death. [*Exit.*

SCENE II.—*The Island; before the Cell of*
PROSPERO.

*Enter* PROSPERO *and* MIRANDA.

*Mira.* If by your art, my dearest father, you
have
Put the wild waters in this roar, allay them:
The sky, it seems, would pour down stinking
pitch,
But that the sea, mounting to the welkin's
cheek,
Dashes the fire out. O, I have suffer'd
With those that I saw suffer! a brave vessel,
Who had, no doubt, some noble creatures in her,
Dash'd all to pieces. O, the cry did knock
Against my very heart! poor souls! they
perish'd.
Had I been any god of power, I would
Have sunk the sea within the earth, or e'er
It should the good ship so have swallowed, and
The freighting souls within her.
*Pro.*                    Be collected;
No more amazement; tell your piteous heart,
There's no harm done.
*Mira.*              O, woe the day!
*Pro.*                    No harm.
I have done nothing but in care of thee,
(Of thee, my dear one! thee, my daughter!) who
Art ignorant of what thou art, nought knowing
Of whence I am; nor that I am more better
Than Prospero, master of a full poor cell,
And thy no greater father.
*Mira.*              More to know
Did never meddle with my thoughts.
*Pro.*                    'Tis time
I should inform thee further. Lend thy hand,
And pluck my magic garment from me.—So;
              [*Lays down his mantle.*
Lie there my art.—Wipe thou thine eyes; have
comfort.
The direful spectacle of the wreck, which touch'd
The very virtue of compassion in thee,
I have with such provision in mine art
So safely order'd, that there is no soul—
No, not so much perdition as an hair,
Betid to any creature in the vessel
Which thou heard'st cry, which thou saw'st
sink. Sit down;
For thou must now know further.

*Mira.*              You have often
Begun to tell me what I am; but stopp'd,
And left me to a bootless inquisition;
Concluding, *Stay, not yet.*—
*Pro.*              The hour's now come;
The very minute bids thee ope thine ear;
Obey, and be attentive. Canst thou remember
A time before we came unto this cell? [not
I do not think thou canst; for then thou wast
Out three years old.
*Mira.*              Certainly, sir, I can.
*Pro.* By what? by any other house, or person?
Of any thing the image tell me, that
Hath kept with thy remembrance.
*Mira.*              'Tis far off;
And rather like a dream than an assurance
That my remembrance warrants: Had I not
Four or five women once, that tended me?
*Pro.* Thou hadst, and more, Miranda: But how
is it,                    [else
That this lives in thy mind? What seest thou
In the dark backward and abysm of time?
If thou remember'st aught, ere thou cam'st here,
How thou cam'st here, thou mayst.
*Mira.*              But that I do not.
*Pro.* Twelve years since, Miranda, twelve years
since,
Thy father was the Duke of Milan, and
A prince of power.
*Mira.*              Sir, are not you my father?
*Pro.* Thy mother was a piece of virtue, and
She said—thou wast my daughter; and thy
father
Was Duke of Milan; and his only heir
A princess; no worse issued.
*Mira.*              O, the heavens!
What foul play had we that we came from thence;
Or blessed was't, we did?
*Pro.*              Both, both, my girl;
By foul play as thou say'st, were we heaved
thence;
But blessedly holp hither.
*Mira.*              O, my heart bleeds
To think o' the teen that I have turn'd you to,
Which is from my remembrance! Please, you,
further.
*Pro.* My brother, and thy uncle, call'd An-
tonio—
I pray thee, mark me,—that a brother should
Be so perfidious!—he whom, next thyself,
Of all the world I loved, and to him put
The manage of my state; as, at that time,
Through all the signiories it was the first,
And Prospero the prime duke; being so reputed
In dignity, and, for the liberal arts,
Without a parallel: those being all my study,
The government I cast upon my brother,
And to my state grew stranger, being transported
And rapt in secret studies. Thy false uncle—
Dost thou attend me?
*Mira.*              Sir, most heedfully.
*Pro.* Being once perfected how to grant suits,
How to deny them; whom to advance, and
whom

To trash for over-topping; new created
The creatures that were mine; I say, or chang'd
    them,
Or else new form'd them; having both the key
Of officer and office, set all hearts
To what tune pleased his ear; that now he was
The ivy, which had hid my princely trunk,
And suck'd my verdure out on't.—Thou
    attend'st not;
I pray thee, mark me.
*Mira.*                O good sir, I do.
*Pro.* I thus neglecting worldly ends, all dedicate
To closeness, and the bettering of my mind
With that, which, but by being so retired,
O'er-prized all popular rate, in my false brother
Awaked an evil nature: and my trust,
Like a good parent, did beget of him
A falsehood, in its contrary as great
As my trust was; which had, indeed, no limit,
A confidence sans bound. He being thus lorded,
Not only with what my revenue yielded,
But what my power might else exact,—like one,
Who having, unto truth, by telling of it,
Made such a sinner of his memory,
To credit his own lie,—he did believe
He was the duke; out of the substitution,
And executing the outward face of royalty,
With all prerogative:—Hence his ambition
Growing,—Dost hear?
*Mira.* Your tale, sir, would cure deafness.
*Pro.* To have no screen between this part he
    play'd
And him he play'd it for, he needs will be
Absolute Milan: Me, poor man!—my library
Was dukedom large enough; of temporal
    royalties
He thinks me now incapable: confederates
(So dry he was for sway) with the king of Naples,
To give him annual tribute, do him homage;
Subject his coronet to his crown, and bend
The dukedom, yet unbowed, (alas, poor Milan!)
To most ignoble stooping.
*Mira.*                O the heavens!
*Pro.* Mark his condition, and the event; then
If this might be a brother.            [tell me,
*Mira.*                I should sin
To think but nobly of my grandmother:
Good wombs have borne bad sons.
*Pro.*                Now the condition.
This king of Naples being an enemy
To me inveterate, hearkens my brother's suit;
Which was that he in lieu o' the premises,—
Of homage, and I know not how much tribute,—
Should presently extirpate me and mine
Out of the dukedom; and confer fair Milan,
With all the honours, on my brother: Whereon,
A treacherous army levied, one midnight
Fated to the purpose, did Antonio open
The gates of Milan; and i' the dead of darkness,
The ministers for the purpose hurried thence
Me, and thy crying self.
*Mira.*            Alack, for pity!
I, not rememb'ring how I cried out then,
Will cry it o'er again: it is a hint,

That wrings mine eyes to 't.
*Pro.*            Hear a little further,
And then I'll bring thee to the present business
Which now's upon us; without the which, this
Were most impertinent.            [story
*Mira.*            Wherefore did they not,
That hour, destroy us?
*Pro.*            Well demanded, wench;
My tale provokes that question. Dear, they
    durst not;
(So dear the love my people bore me) nor set
A mark so bloody on the business; but
With colours fairer painted their foul ends.
In few, they hurried us aboard a bark;
Bore us some leagues to sea; where they prepar'd
A rotten carcass of a boat, not rigg'd,
Nor tackle, sail, nor mast; the very rats
Instinctively had quit it: there they hoist us,
To cry to the sea that roar'd to us; to sigh
To the winds, whose pity, sighing back again,
Did us but loving wrong.
*Mira.*            Alack! what trouble
Was I then to you!
*Pro.*            O! a cherubim
Thou wast, that did preserve me! Thou didst
    smile,
Infused with a fortitude from heaven,
When I have deck'd the sea with drops full salt;
Under my burden groan'd; which raised in me
An undergoing stomach, to bear up
Against what should ensue.
*Mira.*            How came we ashore?
*Pro.* By Providence divine.
Some food we had, and some fresh water, that
A noble Neapolitan, Gonzalo,
Out of his charity, (who being then appointed
Master of this design,) did give us; with
Rich garments, linens, stuffs, and necessaries,
Which since have steaded much; so, of his
    gentleness,
Knowing I loved my books, he furnish'd me,
From my own library, with volumes that
I prize above my dukedom.
*Mira.*            Would I might
But ever see that man!
*Pro.*            Now I arise:—
Sit still, and hear the last of our sea-sorrow.
Here in this island we arrived; and here
Have I, thy schoolmaster, made thee more profit
Than other princes can, that have more time
For vainer hours, and tutors not so careful.
*Mira.* Heavens thank you for 't! And now, I
    pray you, sir,
(For still 'tis beating in my mind,) your reason
For raising this sea-storm?
*Pro.*            Know thus far forth.—
By accident most strange, bountiful Fortune,
Now my dear lady, hath mine enemies
Brought to this shore: and by my prescience
I find my zenith doth depend upon
A most auspicious star; whose influence
If now I court not, but omit, my fortunes
Will ever after droop.—Here cease more ques-
    tions,

Thou art inclin'd to sleep; 'tis a good dulness,
And give it way;—I know thou canst not choose.
                     [MIRANDA *sleeps.*
Come away, servant, come: I am ready now;
Approach, my Ariel; come.

            *Enter* ARIEL.

*Ari.* All hail, great master! grave sir, hail! I
     come
To answer thy best pleasure; be 't to fly,
To swim, to dive into the fire, to ride
On the curl'd clouds; to thy strong bidding, task
Ariel, and all his quality.
*Pro.*              Hast thou, spirit,
Perform'd to point the tempest that I bade thee?
*Ari.* To every article.
I boarded the king's ship; now on the beak,
Now in the waist, the deck, in every cabin,
I flamed amazement: Sometimes, I'd divide,
And burn in many places; on the top-mast,
The yards, and bowsprit, would I flame dis-
     tinctly,
Then meet and join: Jove's lightnings, the
     precursors
O' the dreadful thunder-claps, more momentary
And sight-out-running were not: The fire, and
     cracks
Of sulphurous roaring, the most mighty Neptune
Seem'd to besiege, and make his bold waves
Yea, his dread trident shake.     [tremble,
*Pro.*              My brave spirit!
Who was so firm, so constant, that this coil
Would not infect his reason?
*Ari.*             Not a soul,
But felt a fever of the mad, and play'd
Some tricks of desperation: All, but mariners,
Plung'd in the foaming brine, and quit the vessel,
Then all afire with me: the king's son, Ferdinand,
With hair up-staring (then like reeds, not hair),
Was the first man that leap'd; cried, *Hell is
And all the devils are here!*     [*empty,*
*Pro.*            Why, that's my spirit!
But was not this nigh shore?
*Ari.*            Close by, my master.
*Pro.* But are they, Ariel, safe?
*Ari.*           Not a hair perish'd;
On their sustaining garments not a blemish,
But fresher than before: and, as thou bad'st me,
In troops I have dispersed them 'bout the isle;
The king's son have I landed by himself;
Whom I left cooling of the air with sighs,
In an odd angle of the isle, and sitting,
His arms in this sad knot.
*Pro.*           Of the king's ship,
The mariners, say, how thou hast disposed,
And all the rest o' the fleet?
*Ari.*           Safely in harbour
Is the king's ship; in the deep nook, where once
Thou call'dst me up at midnight to fetch dew
From the still-vex'd Bermoothes, there she's hid:
The mariners all under hatches stow'd;
Whom, with a charm join'd to their suffer'd
     labour,
I have left asleep: and for the rest o' the fleet,

Which I dispersed, they all have met again;
And are upon the Mediterranean flote,
Bound sadly home for Naples;
Supposing that they saw the king's ship wreck'd,
And his great person perish.
*Pro.*           Ariel, thy charge
Exactly is performed; but there's more work:
What is the time o' the day?
*Ari.*          Past the mid season.
*Pro.* At least two glasses: The time 'twixt six
     and now
Must by us both be spent most preciously.
*Ari.* Is there more toil? Since thou dost give
     me pains.
Let me remember thee what thou hast promis'd,
Which is not yet perform'd me.
*Pro.*          How now? moody?
What is't thou canst demand?
*Ari.*            My liberty.
*Pro.* Before the time be out? No more!
*Ari.*           I pray thee
Remember, I have done thee worthy service;
Told thee no lies, made no mistakings, serv'd
Without or grudge or grumblings: thou didst
     promise
To bate me a full year.
*Pro.*          Dost thou forget
From what a torment I did free thee?
*Ari.*            No.
*Pro.* Thou dost; and think'st
It much to tread the ooze of the salt deep;
To run upon the sharp wind of the north;
To do me business in the veins o' the earth,
When it is bak'd with frost.
*Ari.*          I do not, sir.
*Pro.* Thou liest, malignant thing! Hast thou
     forgot          [envy,
The foul witch, Sycorax, who, with age and
Was grown into a hoop? hast thou forgot her?
*Ari.* No, sir.
*Pro.*        Thou hast: Where was she born?
     speak; tell me.
*Ari.* Sir, in Argier.
*Pro.*        Oh, was she so? I must,
Once in a month, recount what thou has been.
Which thou forget'st. This damn'd witch,
     Sycorax,
For mischiefs manifold, and sorceries terrible
To enter human hearing, from Argier,
Thou know'st, was banished; for one thing she
     did,
They would not take her life: Is not this true?
*Ari.* Ay, sir.
*Pro.* This blear-eyed hag was hither brought
     with child,          [slave,
And here was left by the sailors: Thou, my
As thou report'st thyself, wast then her servant:
And, for thou wast a spirit too delicate
To act her earthy and abhorr'd commands,
Refusing her grand 'hests, she did confine thee,
By help of her more potent ministers,
And in her most unmitigable rage.
Into a cloven pine; within which rift
Imprison'd, thou didst painfully remain

A dozen years; within which space she died,
And left thee there: where thou didst vent thy
    groans,
As fast as mill-wheels strike: Then was this
    island,
(Save for the son that she did litter here,
A freckled whelp, hag-born,) not honour'd with
A human shape.
*Ari.*           Yes: Caliban her son.
*Pro.* Dull thing, I say so; he, that Caliban,
Whom now I keep in service. Thou best know'st
What torment I did find thee in: thy groans
Did make wolves howl, and penetrate the breasts
Of ever-angry bears; it was a torment
To lay upon the damn'd, which Sycorax
Could not again undo; it was mine art,
When I arriv'd, and heard thee that made gape
The pine, and let thee out.
*Ari.*          I thank thee, master.
*Pro.* If thou more murmur'st I will rend an
And peg thee in his knotty entrails, till  [oak,
Thou hast howl'd away twelve winters.
*Ari.*          Pardon, master:
I will be correspondent to command,
And do my spriting gently.
*Pro.*       Do so; and after two days
I will discharge thee.
*Ari.*        That's my noble master!
What shall I do? say what? what shall I do?
*Pro.* Go, make thyself like to a nymph o' the
    sea;
Be subject to no sight but mine; invisible
To every eye-ball else. Go, take this shape
And hither come in 't: hence, with diligence.
               [*Exit* ARIEL.
Awake, dear heart, awake! thou hast slept well;
Awake!
*Mira.* The strangeness of your story put
Heaviness in me.
*Pro.*        Shake it off; Come on;
We'll visit Caliban, my slave, who never
Yields us kind answer.
*Mira.*         'Tis a villain, sir,
I do not love to look on.
*Pro.*         But, as 'tis,
We cannot miss him: he does make our fire,
Fetch in our wood; and serves in offices
That profit us. What ho! slave! Caliban!
Thou earth, thou! speak.
*Cal.* [*Within*] There's wood enough within.
*Pro.* Come forth, I say; there's other business
    for thee:
Come forth, thou tortoise! when?

    *Re-enter* ARIEL, *like a water-nymph.*

Fine apparition! My quaint Ariel,
Hark in thine ear.
*Ari.*     My lord, it shall be done. [*Exit.*
*Pro.* Thou poisonous slave, got by the devil
    himself
Upon thy wicked dam, come forth!

    *Enter* CALIBAN.

*Cal.* As wicked dew as e'er my mother brush'd

With raven's feather from unwholesome fen,
Drop on you both! a south-west blow on ye,
And blister you all o'er.
*Pro.* For this, be sure, to-night thou shalt have
    cramps,
Side-stitches that shall pen thy breath up;
    urchins
Shall, for that vast of night that they may work,
All exercise on thee; thou shalt be pinch'd
As thick as honey-combs, each pinch more
    stinging
Than bees that made them.
*Cal.*       I must eat my dinner.
This island's mine, by Sycorax my mother,
Which thou tak'st from me. When thou camest
    first,
Thou strok'dst me, and mad'st much of me;
    wouldst give me
Water with berries in 't; and teach me how
To name the bigger light, and how the less,
That burn by day and night: and then I lov'd
    thee,
And shew'd thee all the qualities o' the isle,
The fresh springs, brine pits, barren place, and
    fertile;
Cursed be I that did so!—All the charms
Of Sycorax, toads, beetles, bats, light on you!
For I am all the subjects that you have,
Which first was mine own king; and here you
    sty me
In this hard rock, whiles you do keep from me
The rest of the island.
*Pro.*        Thou most lying slave,
Whom stripes may move, not kindness: I have
    used thee,           [thee
Filth as thou art, with human care; and lodged
In mine own cell, till thou didst seek to violate
The honour of my child.
*Cal.* O ho, O ho!—would it had been done!
Thou didst prevent me; I had peopled else
This isle with Calibans.
*Pro.*         Abhorred slave;
Which any print of goodness will not take,
Being capable of all ill! I pitied thee,
Took pains to make thee speak, taught thee
    each hour          [savage,
One thing or other: when thou didst not,
Know thine own meaning, but wouldst gabble
    like
A thing most brutish, I endow'd thy purposes
With words that made them known: But thy
    vile race,        [good natures
Though thou didst learn, had that in't which
Could not abide to be with: therefore wast thou
Deservedly confined into this rock,
Who hadst deserved more than a prison
*Cal* You taught me language; and my profit
    on 't
Is, I know how to curse; the red plague rid you,
For learning me your language!
*Pro.*         Hag-seed, hence!
Fetch us in fuel; and be quick, thou wert best,
To answer other business. Shrug'st thou,
    malice?

If thou neglect'st, or dost unwillingly
What I command, I'll rack thee with old cramps;
Fill all thy bones with aches; make thee roar,
That beasts shall tremble at thy din.
*Cal.*                    No, pray thee!—
I must obey: his art is of such power, [*Aside.*
It would control my dam's god, Setebos,
Ard make a vassal of him.
*Pro.*                    So, slave; hence!
                         [*Exit* CALIBAN.

*Re-enter* ARIEL *invisible, playing and singing;*
FERDINAND *following him.*

### ARIEL'S SONG.

Come unto these yellow sands.
  And then take hands:
Court'sied when you have, and kiss'd.
  (The wild waves whist,)
Foot it featly here and there;
And sweet sprites, the burden bear.
  Hark, hark!
Bur, *Bowgh, wowgh,*          *Dispersedly.*
  The watch-dogs bark:
Bur, *Bowgh, wowgh.*          *Dispersedly.*
Hark, hark! I hear
The strain of strutting chanticlere
Cry, Cock-a-doodle-doo.

*Fer.* Where should this music be? i' the air,
    or the earth?
It sounds no more:—and sure it waits upon
Some god of the island  Sitting on a bank
Weeping again the king my father's wreck,
This music crept by me upon the waters;
Allaying both their fury, and my passion,
With its sweet air: thence I have follow'd it,
Or it hath drawn me rather:—But 'tis gone.
No, it begins again.

*ARIEL sings.*

Full fathom five thy father lies;
  Of his bones are coral made;
Those are pearls that were his eyes:
  Nothing of him that doth fade,
But doth suffer a sea-change
Into something rich and strange.
Sea-nymphs hourly ring his knell:
  Burden, *ding-dong.*
Hark! now I hear them,—ding-dong bell.

*Fer.* The ditty does remember my drown'd
    father:—
This is no mortal business, nor no sound
That the earth owes:—I hear it now above me.
*Pro.* The fringed curtains of thine eye advance,
And say, what thou seest yong'.
*Mira.*                    What is 't? a spirit?
Lord, how it looks about  Believe me, sir,
It carries a brave form:—But 'tis a spirit.
*Pro.* No, wench; it eats and sleeps, and hath
    such senses                    [*seest,*
As we have, such: This gallant, which thou
Was in the wreck: and but he's something
    stain'd                         [*call him*
With grief, that's beauty's canker, thou might'st
A goodly person: he hath lost his fellows,
And strays about to find them.
*Mira.*                    I might call him

A thing divine; for nothing natural
I ever saw so noble.
*Pro.*            It goes on,            [*Aside.*
As my soul prompts it:—Spirit, fine spirit I'll
    free thee
Within two days for this.
*Fer.*            Most sure the goddess
On whom these airs attend!—Vouchsafe, my
    prayer
May know, if you remain upon this island;
And that you will some good instruction give,
How I may bear me here: My prime request,
Which I do last pronounce, is, O you wonder!
If you be maid or no?
*Mira.*            No wonder, sir;
But certainly a maid.
*Fer.*            My language! heavens!—
I am the best of them that speak this speech,
Were I but where 'tis spoken.
*Pro.*            How! the best?
What wert thou, if the king of Naples heard thee?
*Fer.* A single thing, as I am now, that wonders
To hear thee speak of Naples: He does hear me;
And, that he does, I weep: myself am Naples;
Who with mine eyes, ne'er since at ebb, beheld
The king my father wreck'd.
*Mira.*            Alack, for mercy !
*Fer.* Yes, faith, and all his lords: the Duke of
And his brave son, being twain.      [Milan,
*Pro.*            The Duke of Milan,
And his more braver daughter, could control
    thee,                         [*Aside.*
If now 'twere fit to do't:—At the first sight
They have changed eyes:—Delicate Ariel,
I'll set thee free for this!—A word, good sir;
I fear you have done yourself some wrong: a
    word.
*Mira.* Why speaks my father so ungently?
    This
Is the third man that e'er I saw; the first
That e'er I sigh'd for: pity, move my father
To be inclined my way!
*Fer.*            O, if a virgin,
And your affection not gone forth, I'll make you
The queen of Naples.
*Pro.*            Soft, sir; one word more.—
They are both in either's powers; but this swift
    business
I must uneasy make, lest too light winning [*Aside.*
Make the prize light.—One word more; I charge
    thee,
That thou attend me: thou dost here usurp
The name thou ow'st not; and hast put thyself
Upon this island, as a spy, to win it
From me, the lord on 't.
*Fer.*            No, as I am a man.
*Mira.* There's nothing ill can dwell in such a
If the ill spirit have so fair an house, [temple:
Good things will strive to dwell with 't.
*Pro.*                    Follow me.—
                         [*To* FERD.
Speak not you for him; he's a traitor.—Come.
I'll manacle thy neck and feet together:
Sea-water shalt thou drink; thy food shall be

The fresh-brook muscles, wither'd roots, and
    husks
Wherein the acorn cradled: Follow.
*Fer.*                       No;
I will resist such entertainment, till
Mine enemy has more power.     [*He draws.*
*Mira.*              O dear father,
Make not too rash a trial of him, for
He's gentle, and not fearful.
*Pro.*              What, I say,
My foot my tutor! Put thy sword up, traitor;
Who makest a show, but darest not strike, thy
    conscience
Is so possess'd with guilt: come from thy ward;
For I can here disarm thee with this stick,
And make thy weapon drop.
*Mira.*         Beseech you, father!
*Pro.* Hence; hang not on my garments.
*Mira.*           Sir, have pity;
I'll be his surety.
*Pro.*         Silence! one word more
Shall make me chide thee, if not hate thee.
    What!
An advocate for an impostor? hush!
Thou think'st there are no more such shapes
    as he,                [wench!
Having seen but him and Caliban: Foolish
To the most of men this is a Caliban,
And they to him are angels.
*Mira.*         My affections
Are then most humble; I have no ambition
To see a goodlier man.
*Pro.*        Come on; obey: [*To* FERD.
Thy nerves are in their infancy again,
And have no vigour in them.
*Fer.*           So they are:
My spirits, as in a dream, are all bound up.
My father's loss, the weakness which I feel,
The wreck of all my friends, or this man's
    threats,
To whom I am subdued, are but light to me,
Might I but through my prison once a day
Behold this maid: all corners else o' the earth
Let liberty make use of; space enough
Have I, in such a prison.
*Pro.*      It works:—Come on.—
Thou hast done well fine Ariel!—Follow me.—
    [*To* FERD. *and* MIR.
Hark, what thou else shalt do me. [*To* ARIEL.
*Mira.*        Be of comfort;
My father's of a better nature, sir,
Than he appears by speech; this is unwonted,
Which now came from him.
*Pro.*       Thou shalt be as free
As mountain winds: but then exactly do
All points of my command.
*Ari.*          To the syllable.
*Pro.* Come, follow: speak not for him. [*Exeunt.*

## ACT II.

SCENE I.—*Another part of the Island.*

    *Enter* ALONSO, SEBASTIAN, ANTONIO,
  GONZALO, ADRIAN, FRANCISCO, *and others.*

*Gon.* Beseech you, sir, be merry: you have
(So have we all) of joy; for our escape   [cause
Is much beyond our loss: Our hint of woe
Is common: every day, some sailor's wife,
The masters of some merchant, and the mer-
    chant,
Have just our theme of woe: but for the miracle,
I mean our preservation, few in millions
Can speak like us: then wisely, good sir, weigh
Our sorrow with our comfort.
*Alon.*            Pr'ythee, peace.
*Seb.* He receives comfort like cold porridge.
*Ant.* The visitor will not give him o'er so.
*Seb.* Look, he's winding up the watch of his
By and by it will strike.          [wit;
*Gon.* Sir,—
*Seb.* One:—Tell.             [offer'd
*Gon.* When every grief is entertain'd, that's
Comes to the entertainer—
*Seb.* A dollar.
*Gon.* Dolour comes to him, indeed; you have
spoken truer than you purposed.
*Seb.* You have taken it wiselier than I meant
you should.
*Gon.* Therefore, my lord,—
*Ant.* Fye, what a spendthrift is he of his tongue!
*Alon.* I pr'ythee spare.
*Gon.* Well, I have done: But yet—
*Seb.* He will be talking.
*Ant.* Which of them, he, or Adrian, for a good
wager, first begins to crow?
*Seb.* The old cock.
*Ant.* The cockrel.
*Seb.* Done: the wager?
*Ant.* A laughter.
*Seb.* A match.
*Adr.* Though this island seem to be desert,—
*Seb.* Ha, ha, ha!
*Ant.* So, you've paid.
*Adr.* Uninhabitable, and almost inaccessible,—
*Seb.* Yet,—
*Adr.* Yet,—
*Ant.* He could not miss it.
*Adr.* It must needs be of subtle, tender, and
delicate temperance.
*Ant.* Temperance was a delicate wench
*Seb.* Ay, and a subtle; as he most
learnedly delivered.          [sweetly.
*Adr.* The air breathes upon us here most
*Seb.* As if it had lungs, and rotten ones.
*Ant.* Or, as 'twere perfumed by a fen.
*Gon.* Here is everything advantageous to life.
*Ant.* True; save means to live.
*Seb.* Of that there's none, or little.     [green!
*Gon.* How lush and lusty the grass looks! how
*Ant.* The ground, indeed, is tawny.
*Seb.* With an eye of green in 't.
*Ant.* He misses not much.
*Seb.* No; he doth but mistake the truth totally.
*Gon.* But the rarity of it is (which is indeed
almost beyond credit)—
*Seb.* As many vouch'd rarities are.
*Gon.* That our garments, being, as they were,
drenched in the sea, hold, notwithstanding.

their freshness and glosses; being rather new dyed, than stained with salt water.

*Ant.* If but one of his pockets could speak, would it not say, he lies?

*Seb.* Ay, or very falsely pocket up his report.

*Gon.* Methinks, our garments are now as .resh as when we put them on first in Africk, at the marriage of the king's fair daughter Claribel to the king of Tunis.

*Seb.* 'Twas a sweet marriage, and we prosper well in our return.

*Adr.* Tunis was never graced before with such a paragon to their queen.

*Gon.* Not since widow Dido's time.

*Ant.* Widow? a pox o' that! How came that widow in? Widow Dido!

*Seb.* What if he had said, widower Æneas too? good lord, how you take it!

*Adr.* Widow Dido, said you? you make me study of that: She was of Carthage, not of Tunis.

*Gon.* This Tunis, sir, was Carthage.

*Adr.* Carthage?

*Gon.* I assure you, Carthage.

*Ant.* His word is more than the miraculous harp.

*Seb.* He hath raised the wall, and houses too.

*Ant.* What impossible matter will he make easy next?

*Seb.* I think he will carry this island home in his pocket, and give it his son for an apple.

*Ant.* And, sowing the kernels of it in the sea, bring forth more islands.

*Gon.* Ay?

*Ant.* Why, in good time.

*Gon.* Sir, we were talking, that our garments seem now as fresh as when we were at Tunis at the marriage of your daughter, who is now queen.

*Ant.* And the rarest that e'er came there.

*Seb.* 'Bate, I beseech you, widow Dido.

*Ant.* O, widow Dido; ay, widow Dido.

*Gon.* Is not, sir, my doublet as fresh as the first day I wore it? I mean, in a sort.

*Ant.* That sort was well fish'd for.

*Gon.* When I wore it at your daughter's marriage?

*Alon.* You cram these words into mine ears, against
The stomach of my sense: Would I had never
Married my daughter there! for, coming thence,
My son is lost; and, in my rate, she too,
Who is so far from Italy removed,
I ne'er again shall see her. O thou mine heir
Of Naples and of Milan, what strange fish
Hath made his meal on thee!

*Fran.*                    Sir, he may live;
I saw him beat the surges under him,
And ride upon their backs; he trod the water,
Whose enmity he flung aside, and breasted
The surge most swoln that met him; his bold head
'Bove the contentious waves he kept, and oar'd
Himself with his good arms in lusty stroke
To the shore, that o'er his wave-worn basis bow'd,
As stooping to relieve him; I not doubt

He came alive to land.

*Alon.*                    No, no, he's gone.

*Seb.* Sir, you may thank yourself for this great loss;                    [daughter,
That would not bless our Europe with your
But rather lose her to an African;
Where she, at least, is banish'd from your eye,
Who hath cause to wet the grief on 't.

*Alon.*                    Pr'ythee, peace.

*Seb.* You were kneel'd to, and importun'd otherwise.
By all of us; and the fair soul herself
Weigh'd, between lothness and obedience, at
Which end o' the beam she'd bow. We have lost your son,
I fear, for ever: Milan and Naples have
More widows in them of this business' making,
Than we bring men to comfort them: the fault's
Your own.

*Alon.* So is the dearest of the loss.

*Gon.*                    My lord Sebastian,
The truth you speak doth lack some gentleness,
And time to speak it in; you rub the sore,
When you should bring the plaster.

*Seb.*                    Very well.

*Ant.* And most chirurgeonly.

*Gon.* It is foul weather in us all, good sir,
When you are cloudy.

*Seb.*                    Foul weather?

*Ant.*                    Very foul.

*Gon.* Had I a plantation of this isle, my lord,—

*Ant.* He'd sow it with nettle-seed.

*Seb.*                    Or docks, or mallows

*Gon.* And were the king of it, what would I do?

*Seb.* 'Scape being drunk, for want of wine.

*Gon.* I' the commonwealth, I would by con-traries
Execute all things: for no kind of traffic
Would I admit; no name of magistrate;
Letters should not be known; no use of service,
Of riches, or of poverty; no contracts,
Successions; bound of land, tilth, vineyard, none:
No use of metal, corn, or wine, or oil:
No occupation; all men idle, all;
And women too; but innocent and pure:
No sovereignty:—

*Seb.*                    And yet he would be king on 't.

*Ant.* The latter end of his commonwealth for-gets the beginning.                    [duce

*Gon.* All things in common nature should pro-
Without sweat or endeavour: treason, felony,
Sword, pike, knife, gun, or need of any engine,
Would I not have; but nature should bring forth,
Of its own kind, all foison, all abundance,
To feed my innocent people.

*Seb.* No marrying 'mong his subjects?

*Ant.* None, man; all idle; whores and knaves.

*Gon.* I would with such perfection govern, sir,
To excel the golden age.

*Seb.*                    Save his majesty!

*Ant.* Long live Gonzalo!

*Gon.*                    And, do you mark me, sir?—

*Alon.* Pr'ythee, no more: thou dost talk noth-ing to me.

*Gon.* I do well believe your highness; and
did it to minister occasion to these gentlemen,
who are of such sensible and nimble lungs, that
they always use to laugh at nothing.

*Ant.* 'Twas you we laugh'd at.

*Gon.* Who, in this kind of merry fooling, am
nothing to you: so you may continue, and
laugh at nothing still.

*Ant.* What a blow was there given!

*Seb.* An it had not fallen flat-long.

*Gon.* You are gentlemen of brave mettle; you
would lift the moon out of her sphere, if she
would continue in it five weeks without changing.

*Enter* ARIEL *invisible, playing solemn music.*

*Seb.* We would so, and then go a bat-fowling.

*Ant.* Nay, good my lord, be not angry.

*Gon.* No, I warrant you; I will not adventure
my discretion so weakly. Will you laugh me
asleep, for I am very heavy?

*Ant.* Go sleep, and hear us.

[*All sleep but* ALON. SEB. *and* ANT.

*Alon.* What, all so soon asleep! I wish mine
eyes   [I find
Would, with themselves, shut up my thoughts:
They are inclined to do so.

*Seb.*   Please you, sir,
Do not omit the heavy offer of it:
It seldom visits sorrow; when it doth,
It is a comforter.

*Ant.*   We two, my lord,
Will guard your person, while you take your
And watch your safety.   [rest,

*Alon.*   Thank you: wondrous heavy.—

[ALONSO *sleeps. Exit* ARIEL.

*Seb.* What a strange drowsiness possesses
them?

*Ant.* It is the quality o' the climate.

*Seb.*   Why
Doth it not then our eyelids sink! I find not
Myself disposed to sleep.

*Ant.*   Nor I; my spirits are nimble
They fell together all, as by consent;
They dropp'd, as by a thunder-stroke. What
might,   [more:—
Worthy Sebastian?—O, what might?—No
And yet, methinks, I see it in thy face,
What thou shouldst be: the occasion speaks
thee; and
My strong imagination sees a crown
Dropping upon thy head.

*Seb.*   What, art thou waking?

*Ant..* Do you not hear me speak?

*Seb.*   I do; and, surely,
It is a sleepy language; and thou speak'st
Out of thy sleep: What is it thou didst say?
This is a strange repose, to be asleep   [ing,
With eyes wide open, standing, speaking, mov-
And yet so fast asleep.

*Ant.*   Noble Sebastian,   [wink'st
Thou lett'st thy fortune sleep—die rather;
Whiles thou art waking.

*Seb.*   Thou dost snore distinctly;
There's meaning in thy snores.

*Ant.* I am more serious than my custom: you
Must be so too, if heed me; which to do
Trebles thee o'er.

*Seb.*   Well, I am standing water.

*Ant.* I'll teach you how to flow.

*Seb.*   Do so: to ebb,
Hereditary sloth instructs me.

*Ant.*   O,
If you but knew, how you the purpose cherish,
Whiles thus you mock it! how, in stripping it,
You more invest it! Ebbing men, indeed,
Most often do so near the bottom run,
By their own fear, or sloth.

*Seb.*   Pr'ythee, say on:
The setting of thine eye, and cheek, proclaim
A matter from thee; and a birth, indeed,
Which throes thee much to yield.

*Ant.*   Thus, sir:
Although this lord of weak remembrance, this,
Who shall be of as little memory
When he is earth'd, hath here almost persuaded
(For he's a spirit of persuasion only)
The king, his son's alive: 'tis as impossible
That he's undrown'd as he that sleeps here

*Seb.* I have no hope   [swims.
That he's undrown'd.

*Ant.*   O, out of that no hope,
What great hope have you! no hope, that way, is
Another way so high an hope, that even
Ambition cannot pierce a wink beyond,
But doubts discovery there. Will you grant,
with me,
That Ferdinand is drown'd?

*Seb.*   He's gone.

*Ant.*   Then, tell me,
Who's the next heir of Naples?

*Seb.*   Claribel.

*Ant.* She that is queen of Tunis: she that dwells
Ten leagues beyond man's life; she that from
Naples
Can have no note, unless the sun were post
(The man i' the moon's too slow,) till new-born
Be rough and razorable; she, from whom [chins
We were all sea-swallow'd, though some cast
again;
And, by that, destined to perform an act,
Whereof what's past is prologue; what to come,
In yours and my discharge.

*Seb.*   What stuff is this?—How say you?
'Tis true, my brother's daughter's queen of Tunis:
So is she heir of Naples; 'twixt which regions
There is some space.

*Ant.*   A space whose every cubit
Seems to cry out, *How shall that Claribel
Measure us back to Naples?*—Keep in Tunis,
And let Sebastian wake!—Say, this were death
That now hath seized them; why, they were no
worse
Than now they are: There be, that can rule
Naples,
As well as he that sleeps; lords, that can prate
As amply and unnecessarily
As this Gonzalo; I myself could make
A chough of as deep chat. O, that you bore

The mind that I do! what a sleep were this
For your advancement! Do you understand me?
*Seb.* Methinks, I do.
*Ant.*                        And how does your content
Tender your own good fortune?
*Seb.*                              I remember,
You did supplant your brother Prospero.
*Ant.*                                                True:
And, look, how well my garments sit upon me;
Much feater than before: My brother's servants
Were then my fellows, now they are my men.
*Seb.* But, for your conscience—
*Ant.* Ay, sir; where lies that? if it were a kybe,
'Twould put me to my slipper: But I feel not
This deity in my bosom; twenty consciences,
That stand 'twixt me and Milan, candied be
            they,                                            [brother,
And melt, ere they molest! Here lies your
No better than the earth he lies upon,
If he were that which now he's like: whom I,
With this obedient steel, three inches of it,
Can lay to bed for ever: whiles you, doing thus
To the perpetual wink for aye might put
This ancient morsel, this Sir Prudence, who
Should not upbraid our course. For all the rest,
They'll take suggestion, as a cat laps milk;
They'll tell the clock to any business that
We say befits the hour.
*Seb.*                        Thy case, dear friend,
Shall be my precedent; as thou gott'st Milan,
I'll come by Naples. Draw thy sword: one
            stroke                                          [pay'st;
Shall free thee from the tribute which thou
And I the king shall love thee.
*Ant.*                              Draw together:
And when I rear my hand, do you the like,
To fall it on Gonzalo.
*Seb.*                        O, but one word.
                          [*They converse apart.*

*Music. Re-enter* ARIEL, *invisible.*

*Ari.* My master through his art foresees the
            danger                                        [forth,—
That these his friends, are in; and sends me
For else his project dies,—to keep the living.
                          [*Sings in* GONZALO'S *ear.*

While you here do snoring lie,
Open-eyed conspiracy
      His time doth take:
If of life you keep a care,
Shake off slumber, and beware:
      Awake! Awake!

*Ant.* Then let us both be sudden.
*Gon.* Now, good angels, preserve the king!
                          [*They awake.*
*Alon.* Why, how now, ho! awake! Why are
            you drawn?
Wherefore this ghastly looking?
*Gon.*                        What's the matter?
*Seb.* Whiles we stood here securing your repose,
            repose,
Even now, we heard a hollow burst of bellowing

Like bulls, or rather lions; did it not wake you?
It struck mine ear most terribly.
*Alon.*                              I heard nothing.
*Ant.* O, 'twas a din to fright a monster's ear;
To make an earthquake! sure it was the roar
Of a whole herd of lions.
*Alon.*                        Heard you this, Gonzalo?
*Gon.* Upon mine honour, sir, I heard a hum-
            ming.                                          [me;
And that a strange one too, which did awake
I shaked you, sir, and cried; as mine eyes open'd,
I saw their weapons drawn:—there was a noise,
That's verity: 'Best stand upon our guard:
Or that we quit this place: let's draw our
            weapons.                                [further search
*Alon.* Lead off this ground; and let's make
For my poor son.
*Gon.* Heavens keep him from these beasts!
For he is, sure, i' the island.
*Alon.*                              Lead away.
*Ari.* Prospero my lord shall know what I have
            done:                                          [*Aside.*
So, king, go safely on to seek thy son. [*Exeunt.*

SCENE II.—*Another part of the Island.*

*Enter* CALIBAN, *with a burden of wood.*
*A noise of thunder heard.*

*Cal.* All the infections that the sun sucks up
From bogs, fens, flats, on Prosper fall, and
            make him
By inch-meal a disease! His spirits hear me,
And yet I needs must curse. But they'll nor
            pinch,                                        [mire,
Fright me with urchin-shows, pitch me i' the
Nor lead me, like a firebrand, in the dark
Out of my way, unless he bid them; but
For every trifle they are set upon me:
Sometime like apes, that moe and chatter at me,
And after, bite me; then like hedge-hogs, which
Lie tumbling in my bare-foot way, and mount
Their pricks at my foot-fall; sometime am I
All wound with adders, who, with cloven
            tongues,
Do hiss me into madness:—Lo! now! lo!

*Enter* TRINCULO.

Here comes a spirit of his; and to torment me,
For bringing wood in slowly: I'll fall flat;
Perchance he will not mind me.
*Trin.* Here's neither bush nor shrub, to bear
off any weather at all, and another storm brew-
ing; I hear it sing i' the wind; yond same black
cloud, yond huge one, looks like a foul bumbard
that would shed his liquor. If it should thunder,
as it did before, I know not where to hide my
head: yond same cloud cannot choose but fall
by pailfuls.—What have we here? a man or a
fish? dead or alive? A fish: he smells like a fish;
a very ancient and fish-like smell; a kind of,
not of the newest, Poor-John. A strange fish!
Were I in England now (as once I was), and
had but this fish painted, not a holiday fool
there but would give a piece of silver: there

ould this monster make a man; any strange
east there makes a man: when they will not
ve a doit to relieve a lame beggar, they will
y out ten to see a dead Indian. Legg'd like
man! and his fins like arms! Warm, o' my
oth! I do now let loose my opinion, hold it
o longer; this is no fish, but an islander, that
ath lately suffered by a thunder-bolt. [_Thun-
er_] Alas! the storm is come again: my best
ay is to creep under his gaberdine; there is no
ther shelter hereabout: Misery acquaints a
nan with strange bedfellows. I will here
hroud, till the dregs of the storm be past.

_Enter_ STEPHANO _singing, a bottle in his hand._

_te._ I shall no more to sea, to sea,
		Here shall I die ashore;—

This is a very scurvy tune to sing at a man's
uneral: Well, here's my comfort.		[_Drinks._

The master, the swabber, the boatswain, and I,
		The gunner, and his mate,
ov'd Mall, Meg, and Marian, and Margery,
		But none of us car'd for Kate;
		For she had a tongue with a tang,
		Would cry to a sailor, _Go, hang;_
She lov'd not the savour of tar nor of pitch,
Yet a tailor might scratch her where'er she did itch:
		Then to sea, boys, and let her go hang.

This is a scurvy tune too: But here's my comfort.
_Cal._ Do not torment me: Oh!		[_Drinks._
_Ste._ What's the matter? Have we · devils
here? Do you put tricks upon us with savages,
and men of Inde? Ha! I have not 'scaped
drowning, to be afeard now of your four legs;
for it hath been said, As proper a man as ever
went on four legs cannot make him give
ground: and it shall be said so again, while
Stephano breathes at nostrils.
_Cal._ The spirit torments me: Oh!
_Ste._ This is some monster of the isle, with
four legs: who hath got, as I take it, an ague:
Where the devil should he learn our language?
I will give him some relief, if it be but for that:
If I can recover him, and keep him tame, and
get to Naples with him, he's a present for any
emperor that ever trod on neat's leather.
_Cal._ Do not torment me, pr'ythee;
I'll bring my wood home faster.
_Ste._ He's in his fit now; and does not talk
after the wisest. He shall taste of my bottle:
if he have never drunk wine afore, it will go
near to remove his fit. If I can recover him,
and keep him tame, I will not take too much
for him: he shall pay for him that hath him,
and that soundly.		[wilt
_Cal._ Thou dost me yet but little hurt; thou
Anon; I know it by thy trembling;
Now Prosper works upon thee.
_Ste._ Come on your ways; open your mouth:
here is that which will give language to you,
cat; open your mouth: this will shake your shaking, I can tell you, and that soundly: you cannot

tell who's your friend: open your chaps again.
_Trin._ I should know that voice: It should
be—But he is drowned; and these are devils:
Oh! defend me!—
_Ste._ Four legs and two voices; a most delicate
monster! His forward voice now is to speak
well of his friend; his backward voice is to
utter foul speeches, and to detract. If all the
wine in my bottle will recover him, I will help
his ague: Come—Amen! I will pour some in
thy other mouth.
_Trin._ Stephano,—
_Ste._ Doth thy other mouth call me? Mercy,
mercy! This is a devil, and no monster: I will
leave him; I have no long spoon.
_Trin._ Stephano!—if thou beest Stephano,
touch me, and speak to me; for I am Trinculo;
—be not afeard,—thy good friend Trinculo.
_Ste._ If thou beest Trinculo, come forth; I'll
pull thee by the lesser legs: if any be Trinculo's
legs, these are they. Thou art very Trinculo
indeed. How cam'st thou to be the siege of this
moon-calf? Can he vent Trinculos?
_Trin._ I took him to be killed with a thunder-
stroke:—But art thou not drowned, Stephano?
I hope, now, thou art not drowned. Is the
storm over-blown? I hid me under the dead
moon-calf's gaberdine for fear of the storm.
And art thou living, Stephano? O Stephano,
two Neapolitans 'scaped!
_Ste._ Pr'ythee, do not turn me about; my
stomach is not constant.		[sprites,
_Cal._ These are fine things, and if they be not
That's a brave god, and bears celestial liquor:
I will kneel to him
_Ste._ How didst thou 'scape? how cam'st
thou hither? swear by this bottle, how thou
cam'st hither I escaped upon a butt of sack,
which the sailors heaved overboard, by this
bottle! which I made of the bark of a tree,
with mine own hands, since I was cast ashore.
_Cal._ I'll swear, upon that bottle, to be thy
True subject; for the liquor is not earthly.
_Ste._ Here: swear then how thou escap'dst.
_Trin._ Swam ashore, man, like a duck; I can
swim like a duck, I'll be sworn.
_Ste._ Here, kiss the book: Though thou canst
swim like a duck, thou art made like a goose.
_Trin._ O Stephano, hast any more of this?
_Ste._ The whole butt, man; my cellar is in a
rock by the sea-side, where my wine is hid.
How now, moon-calf? how does thine ague?
_Cal._ Hast thou not dropped from heaven?
_Ste._ Out o' the moon, I do assure thee: I
was the man i' the moon, when time was.
_Cal._ I have seen thee in her, and I do adore
		thee;
My mistress showed me thee, and thy dog and
		bush.
_Ste._ Come, swear to that; kiss the book: I
will furnish it anon with new contents: swear.
_Trin._ By this good light, this is a very shal-
low monster:—I afeard of him? a very weak
monster;—The man i' the moon!—a most poor

credulous monster: Well drawn, monster, in good sooth
*Cal.* I'll show thee every fertile inch o' the island;
And kiss thy foot: I pr'ythee, be my god.
*Trin.* By this light, a most perfidious and drunken monster; when his god's asleep, he'll rob his bottle.
*Cal.* I'll kiss thy foot: I'll swear myself thy subject.
*Ste.* Come on, then; down, and swear.
*Trin.* I shall laugh myself to death at this puppy-headed monster: a most scurvy monster! I could find in my heart to beat him,—
*Ste.* Come, kiss.
*Trin.* —but that the poor monster's in drink; An abominable monster!
*Cal.* I'll show thee the best springs; I'll pluck thee berries;
I'll fish for thee, and get thee wood enough.
A plague upon the tyrant that I serve!
I'll bear him no more sticks, but follow thee,
Thou wondrous man.
*Trin.* A most ridiculous monster! to make a wonder of a poor drunkard.
*Cal.* I pr'ythee, let me bring thee where crabs grow;
And I with my long nails will dig thee pig-nuts;
Show thee a jay's nest, and instruct thee how
To snare the nimble marmozet; I'll bring thee
To clust'ring filberts, and sometimes I'll get thee
Young sea-mells from the rock: Wilt thou go with me?
*Ste.* I pr'ythee now lead the way, without any more talking.—Trinculo, the king and all our company else being drowned, we will inherit here.—Here; [*To* CAL.] bear my bottle. Fellow Trinculo, we'll fill him by and by again.
*Cal.* Farewell, master: farewell, farewell.
[*Sings drunkenly.*
*Trin.* A howling monster; a drunken monster.
*Cal.* No more dams I'll make for fish;
  Nor fetch in firing
  At requiring,
  Nor scrape trencher, nor wash dish;
  'Ban 'Ban, Ca—Caliban,
  Has a new master—Get a new man.
Freedom, hey-day hey-day, freedom! freedom, hey-day, freedom!
*Ste.* O brave monster! lead the way. [*Exeunt.*

## ACT III.

SCENE I.—*Before* PROSPERO'S *Cell.*

*Enter* FERDINAND, *bearing a log.*

*Fer.* There be some sports are painful, and their labour
Delight in them sets off: some kinds of baseness
Are nobly undergone; and most poor matters
Point to rich ends. This my mean task would be
As heavy to me, as 'tis odious; but
The mistress which I serve quickens what's dead
And makes my labours pleasures: Oh, she is

Ten times more gentle than her father's crabbed
And he's composed of harshness. I must remov
Some thousands of these logs, and pile them up
Upon a sore injunction: My sweet mistress
Weeps when she sees me work; and says suc]
  baseness
Had never like executor. I forget: [labours
But these sweet thoughts do even refresh my
Most busy, least when I do it.

*Enter* MIRANDA, *and* PROSPERO *at a distance*
*Mira.* Alas, now! pray you
Work not so hard: I would the lightning hac
Burnt up those logs that you are enjoin'd to pile
Pray, set it down, and rest you: when this burns
'Twill weep for having wearied you. My fathe
Is hard at study; pray, now, rest yourself;
He's safe for these three hours.
*Fer.* O most dear mistress
The sun will set before I shall discharge
What I must strive to do.
*Mira.* If you'll sit down,
I'll bear your logs the while: pray, give me that;
I'll carry it to the pile.
*Fer.* No, precious creature:
I had rather crack my sinews, break my back,
Than you should such dishonour undergo,
While I sit lazy by.
*Mira.* It would become me
As well as it does you: and I should do it
With much more ease; for my good will is to it,
And yours against.
*Pro.* [*Aside.*] Poor worm! thou art infected;
This visitation shows it.
*Mira.* You look wearily.
*Fer.* No, noble mistress; 'tis fresh morning with me
When you are by at night. I do beseech you,
Chiefly that I might set it in my prayers,
What is your name?
*Mira.* Miranda:—O my father,
I have broke your 'hest to say so!
*Fer.* Admir'd Miranda!
Indeed the top of admiration! worth
What's dearest to the world! Full many a lady
I have eyed with best regard; and many a time
The harmony of their tongues hath into bondage
Brought my too diligent ear: for several virtues
Have I lik'd several women: never any
With so full soul, but some defect in her
Did quarrel with the noblest grace she owed;
And put it to the foil: but you, O you,
So perfect and so peerless, are created
Of every creature's best.
*Mira.* I do not know
One of my sex! no woman's face remember,
Save, from my glass, mine own; nor have I seen
More that I may call men, than you, good friend,
And my dear father: how features are abroad,
I am skill-less of; but, by my modesty,—
The jewel in my dower,—I would not wish
Any companion in the world but you;
Nor can imagination form a shape,
Besides yourself, to like of. But I **prattle**

Something too wildly, and my father's precepts
Therein forget.

*Fer.*                 I am, in my condition,
A prince, Miranda; I do think, a king,—
I would, not so!—and would no more endure
This wooden slavery than I would suffer
The flesh-fly blow my mouth. Hear my soul
          speak:
The very instant that I saw you, did
My heart fly to your service; there resides,
To make me slave to it; and for your sake
Am I this patient log-man.

*Mira.*                 Do you love me?

*Fer.* O heaven, O earth, bear witness to this
          sound,
And crown what I profess with kind event,
If I speak true! if hollowly, invert
What best is boded me to mischief! I,
Beyond all limit of what else i' the world,
Do love, prize, honour you.

*Mira.*                 I am a fool
To weep at what I am glad of.

*Pro.* [*Aside.*]                 Fair encounter
Of two most rare affections! Heavens rain grace
On that which breeds between them!

*Fer.*                 Wherefore weep you?

*Mira.* At mine unworthiness, that dare not offer
What I desire to give; and much less take
What I shall die to want. But this is trifling;
And all the more it seeks to hide itself,
The bigger bulk it shows. Hence, bashful cun-
          ning;
And prompt me, plain and holy innocence!
I am your wife, if you will marry me;
If not, I'll die your maid: to be your fellow
You may deny me; but I'll be your servant
Whether you will or no.

*Fer.*                 My mistress, dearest,
And I thus humble ever.

*Mir.*                 My husband, then?

*Fer.* Ay, with a heart as willing
As bondage e'er of freedom: here's my hand.

*Mira.* And mine, with my heart in 't: and now
          farewell
Till half an hour hence.

*Fer.*                 A thousand! thousand!
          [*Exeunt* FERD. *and* MIRA.

*Pro.* So glad of this as they I cannot be,
Who are surprised withal; but my rejoicing
At nothing can be more. I'll to my book;
For yet, ere supper time, must I perform
Much business appertaining.                 [*Exit.*

SCENE II.—*Another part of the Island.*

*Enter* STEPHANO *and* TRINCULO; CALIBAN
          *following with a bottle.*

*Ste.* Tell not me;—when the butt is out, we
will drink water; not a drop before: therefore
bear up, and board 'em: Servant-monster,
drink to me.

*Trin.* Servant-monster the folly of this island!
They say there's but five upon this isle: we

are three of them; if the other two be brained
like us, the state totters.

*Ste.* Drink, servant-monster, when I bid thee:
thy eyes are almost set in thy head.

*Trin.* Where should they be set else? he were
a brave monster indeed, if they were set in
his tail.

*Ste.* My man-monster hath drowned his
tongue in sack: for my part, the sea cannot
drown me: I swam, ere I could recover the
shore, five-and-thirty leagues, off and on, by
this light.—Thou shalt be my lieutenant, monster, or my standard.                 [standard.

*Trin.* Your lieutenant, if you list; he's no

*Ste.* We'll not run, monsieur-monster.

*Trin.* Nor go neither: but you'll lie, like dogs;
and yet say nothing neither.

*Ste.* Moon-calf, speak once in thy life, if thou
beest a good moon-calf.

*Cal.* How does thy honour? Let me lick thy
shoe.
I'll not serve him; he is not valiant.

*Trin.* Thou liest, most ignorant monster: I
am in case to justle a constable. Why, thou
deboshed fish thou, was there ever a man a
coward that hath drunk so much sack as I to-
day? Wilt thou tell a monstrous lie, being but
half a fish and half a monster?

*Cal.* Lo, how he mocks me! wilt thou let him,
my lord?

*Trin.* Lord, quoth he!—that a monster should
be such a natural!

*Cal.* Lo, lo again! bite him to death, I pr'ythee.

*Ste.* Trinculo, keep a good tongue in your
head: if you prove a mutineer, the next tree.—
The poor monster's my subject, and he shall
not suffer indignity.

*Cal.* I thank my noble lord. Wilt thou be
pleased to hearken once again to the suit I
made thee?

*Ste.* Marry will I: kneel and repeat it; I will
stand, and so shall Trinculo.

*Enter* ARIEL, *invisible.*

*Cal.* As I told thee before, I am subject to a
tyrant; a sorcerer, that by his cunning hath
cheated me of this island.

*Ari.*                 Thou liest.

*Cal.* Thou liest, thou jesting monkey, thou;
I would my valiant master would destroy thee!
I do not lie.

*Ste.* Trinculo, if you trouble him any more
in his tale, by this hand, I will supplant some
of your teeth.

*Trin.* Why, I said nothing.

*Ste.* Mum, then, and no more.—[*To* CALIBAN.]
Proceed.

*Cal.* I say, by sorcery he got this isle;
From me he got it. If thy greatness will
Revenge it on him—for I know thou dar'st,
But this thing dare not.

*Ste.*                 That's most certain.

*Cal.* Thou shalt be lord of it, and I'll serve thee.

*Ste.* How now shall this be compassed? Canst thou bring me to the party? [asleep,

*Cal.* Yea, yea my lord; I'll yield him thee Where thou mayst knock a nail into his head.

*Ari.* Thou liest; thou canst not.

*Cal.* What a pied ninny's this? Thou scurvy patch!—
I do beseech thy greatness, give him blows, And take his bottle from him: when that's gone He shall drink nought but brine; for I'll not show him
Where the quick freshes are.

*Ste.* Trinculo, run into no further danger; interrupt the monster one word further, and by this hand, I'll turn my mercy out of doors, and make a stock-fish of thee.

*Trin.* Why, what did I? I did nothing. I'll go further off.

*Ste.* Didst thou not say, he lied?

*Ari.* Thou liest.

*Ste.* Do I so? take thou that. [*Strikes him.*] As you like this, give me the lie another time.

*Trin.* I did not give the lie.—Out o' your wits and hearing too?——A pox o' your bottle this can sack and drinking do.—A murrain on your monster, and the devil take your fingers!

*Cal.* Ha, ha, ha!

*Ste.* Now, forward with your tale. Pr'ythee, stand further off.

*Cal.* Beat him enough: after a little time I'll beat him too.

*Ste.* Stand further.—Come, proceed.

*Cal.* Why, as I told thee, 'tis a custom with him I' the afternoon to sleep: there thou mayst brain him,
Having first seized his books; or with a log Batter his skull, or paunch him with a stake, Or cut his wezand with thy knife. Remember, First to possess his books; for without them He's but a sot, as I am, nor hath not One spirit to command: they all do hate him As rootedly as I. Burn but his books.
He has brave utensils,—for so he calls them,— Which, when he has a house, he'll deck withal. And that most deeply to consider is
The beauty of his daughter; he himself Calls her a nonpareil; I never saw woman, But only Sycorax my dam and she;
But she as far surpasseth Sycorax,
As great'st does least.

*Ste.* Is it so brave a lass?

*Cal.* Ay, lord; she will become thy bed, I warrant,
And bring thee forth brave brood.

*Ste.* Monster, I will kill this man: his daughter and I will be king and queen;—save our graces!—and Trinculo and thyself shall be viceroys.—Dost thou like the plot, Trinculo?

*Trin.* Excellent.

*Ste.* Give me thy hand; I am sorry I beat thee: but while thou livest, keep a good tongue in thy head.

*Cal.* Within this half hour will he be asleep; Wilt thou destroy him then?

*Ste.* Ay, on mine honour

*Ari.* This will I tell my master.

*Cal.* Thou mak'st me merry: I am full of pleasure;
Let us be jocund: will you troll the catch You taught me but while-ère?

*Ste.* At thy request, monster, I will do reason, any reason. Come on, Trinculo, let us sing. [*Sings.*

*Flout 'em, and scout 'em; and scout 'em and flout 'em; Thought is free.*

*Cal.* That's not the tune.
[*Ariel plays the tune on a tabor and pipe.*

*Ste.* What is this same?

*Trin.* This is the tune of our catch, played by the picture of Nobody.

*Ste.* If thou beest a man, show thyself in thy likeness: if thou beest a devil, tak't as thou list.

*Trin.* O, forgive me my sins!

*Ste.* He that dies, pays all debts: I defy thee:—Mercy upon us!

*Cal.* Art thou afeard?

*Ste.* No, monster, not I.

*Cal.* Be not afeard; the isle is full of noises, Sounds, and sweet airs, that give delight and hurt not.
Sometimes a thousand twangling instruments Will hum about mine ears; and sometimes voices, That, if I then had waked after long sleep, Will make me sleep again; and then, in dreaming, [riches
The clouds, methought, would open and show Ready to drop upon me: that, when I waked, I cried to dream again.

*Ste.* This will prove a brave kingdom to me, where I shall have my music for nothing.

*Cal.* When Prospero is destroyed.

*Ste.* That shall be by and by: I remember the story.

*Trin.* The sound is going away: let's follow it, and after, do our work.

*Ste.* Lead, monster, we'll follow.—I would I could see this taborer: he lays it on.

*Trin.* Wilt come? I'll follow, Stephano. [*Exeunt.*

SCENE III.—*Another part of the Island.*

*Enter* ALONSO, SEBASTIAN, ANTONIO, GONZALO, ADRIAN, FRANCISCO, *and others.*

*Gon.* By'r lakin, I can go no further, sir; My old bones ache: here's a maze trod, indeed, Through forth-rights and meanders! by your I needs must rest me. [patience.

*Alon.* Old lord, I cannot blame thee, Who am myself attach'd with weariness, To the dulling of my spirits: sit down, and rest. Even here I will put off my hope, and keep it No longer for my flatterer: he is drown'd Whom thus we stray to find: and the sea mocks Our frustrate search on land. Well, let him go.

*Ant.* I am right glad that he's so out of hope. [*Aside to* SEB.

Do not, for one repulse, forego the purpose
That you resolved to effect.
*Seb.*                    The next advantage
Will we take thoroughly.          [*Aside to* Ant.
*Ant.* [*Aside to* Seb.] Let it be to-night;
For, now they are oppress'd with travel, they
Will not, nor cannot, use such vigilance,
As when they are fresh.
*Seb.* [*Aside to* Ant.] I say to-night; no more.

*Solemn and strange music; and* Prospero *above,
invisible. Enter several strange* Shapes, *bringing in a banquet; they dance about it with
gentle actions of salutation, and inviting the
King, &c., to eat, they depart.*

*Alon.* What harmony is this? My good friends
          hark!
*Gon.*          Marvellous sweet music!
*Alon.* Give us kind keepers, heavens! What
          were these?
*Seb.* A living drollery: now I will believe,
That there are unicorns; that, in Arabia
There is one tree, the phœnix' throne; one
At this hour reigning there.          [phœnix
*Ant.*                    I'll believe both;
And what does else want credit, come to me,
And I'll be sworn 'tis true: travellers ne'er did lie,
Though fools at home condemn them.
*Gon.*                    If in Naples
I should report this now, would they believe me?
If I should say, I saw such islanders,—
For, certes, these are people of the island,—
Who, though they are of monstrous shape, yet,
          note,
Their manners are more gentle-kind than of
Our human generation you shall find
Many, nay, almost any.
*Pro.*                    Honest lord,
Thou hast said well; for some of you there
          present
Are worse than devils.                    [*Aside.*
*Alon.*          I cannot too much muse,
Such shapes, such gesture, and such sound,
          expressing,—
Although they want the use of tongue,—a kind
Of excellent dumb discourse.
*Pro.*                    Praise in departing.    [*Aside.*
*Fran.* They vanish'd strangely.
*Seb.*                    No matter, since
They have left their viands behind; for we have
          stomachs,—
Will't please you taste of what is here?
*Alon.*                    Not I.
*Gon.* Faith, sir, you need not fear. When we
          were boys,                         [eers,
Who would believe that there were mountain-
Dew-lapp'd like bulls, whose throats had hang-
          ing at them
Wallets of flesh? or that there were such men,
Whose heads stood in their breasts? which now
          we find,
Each putter-out of one for five, will bring us
Good warrant of.
*Alon.*          I will stand to, and feed,

Although my last: no matter, since I feel,
The best is past:—Brother, my lord the duke,
Stand to, and do as we.

*Thunder and lightning. Enter* Ariel *like a
harpy; claps his wings upon the table, and
with a quaint device the banquet vanishes.*

*Ari.* You are three men of sin, whom destiny,
That hath to instrument this lower world,
And what is in't,—the never-surfeited sea
Hath caused to belch up; and on this island
Where man doth not inhabit; you 'mongst men
Being most unfit to live. I have made you mad;
And even with such like valour, men hang and
Their proper selves.                    [drown
          [Alon., Seb. &c., *draw their swords.*
          You fools! I and my fellows
Are ministers of fate; the elements,
Of whom your swords are temper'd, may as well
Wound the loud winds, or with bemock'd-at stabs
Kill the still-closing waters, as diminish
One dowle that's in my plume; my fellow-
          ministers
Are like invulnerable; if you could hurt,
Your swords are now too massy for your strengths,
And will not be uplifted. But, remember,—
For that's my business to you,—that you three
From Milan did supplant good Prospero;
Expos'd unto the sea, which hath requit it.
Him, and his innocent child: for which foul deed
The powers, delaying, not forgetting have
Incensed the seas and shores, yea, all the
          creatures.
Against your peace: Thee, of thy son, Alonso,
They have bereft; and do pronounce by me,
Ling'ring perdition,—worse than any death
Can be at once,—shall step by step attend
You and your ways; whose wraths to guard
          you from,—
Which here, in this most desolate isle; else falls
Upon your heads,—is nothing but heart's sorrow,
And a clear life ensuing.

*He vanishes in thunder: then, to soft music, enter
the* Shapes *again, and dance with mops and
mows, and carry out the table.*

*Pro.* [*Aside.*] Bravely the figure of this harpy
          hast thou
Perform'd, my Ariel; a grace it had devouring:
Of my instruction hast thou nothing 'bated,
In what thou hadst to say: so, with good life,
And observation strange, my meaner ministers
Their several kinds have done: my high charms
          [work,
And these, mine enemies, are all knit up
In their distractions: they now are in my power;
And in these fits I leave them, whilst I visit
Young Ferdinand,—who they suppose is
And his and my loved darling.          [drown'd,—
          [*Exit* Prospero *from above.*
*Gon.* I' the name of something holy, sir, why
In this strange stare?                    [stand you
*Alon.*          O, it is monstrous! monstrous!
Methought the billows spoke, and told me of it;
The winds did sing it to me; and the thunder,

That deep and dreadful organ-pipe, pronounced
The name of Prosper; it did bass my trespass.
Therefore my son i' the ooze is bedded; and
I'll seek him deeper than e'er plummet sounded
And with him there lie mudded.      [*Exit.*
*Seb.*                  But one fiend at a time,
I'll fight their legions o'er.
*Ant.*                     I'll be thy second.
                        [*Exeunt* SEB. *and* ANT.
*Gon.* All three of them are desperate; their
      great guilt,
Like poison given to work a great time after,
Now 'gins to bite the spirits:—I do beseech you
That are of suppler joints, follow them swiftly,
And hinder them from what this ecstacy
May now provoke them to.
*Adr.*          Follow, I pray you. [*Exeunt.*

## ACT IV.

SCENE I.—*Before* PROSPERO'S *Cell.*

*Enter* PROSPERO, FERDINAND, *and* MIRANDA.

*Pro.* If I have too austerly punished you,
Your compensation makes amends; for I
Have given you here a thread of mine own life,
Or that for which I live; who once again
I tender to thy hand: all thy vexations
Were but my trials of thy love, and thou
Hast strangely stood the test: here, afore Heaven,
I ratify this my rich gift. O Ferdinand,
Do not smile at me, that I boast her off,
For thou shalt find she will outstrip all praise,
And make it halt behind her.
*Fer.*                    I do believe it,
Against an oracle.
*Pro.* Then, as my gift, and thine own acqui-
      sition
Worthily purchas'd, take my daughter: But
If thou dost break her virgin knot before
All sanctimonious ceremonies may
With full and holy rite be minister'd,
No sweet aspersion shall the heavens let fall
To make this contract grow: but barren hate,
Sour-eyed disdain, and discord, shall bestrew
The union of your bed with weeds so loathly,
That you shall hate it both: therefore, take
As Hymen's lamps shall light you.      [heed,
*Fer.*                        As I hope
For quiet days, fair issue, and long life,
With such love as 'tis now; the murkiest den,
The most oppórtune place, the strong'st sugges-
Our worser Genius can, shall never melt   [tion
Mine honour into lust; to take away
The edge of that day's celebration, [founder'd,
When I shall think, or Phœbus' steeds are
Or night kept chain'd below.
*Pro.*                    Fairly spoke:
Sit, then, and talk with her, she is thine own.—
What, Ariel; my industrious servant, Ariel!

*Enter* ARIEL.

*Ari.* What would my potent master? here I
      am.                          [service
*Pro.* Thou and thy meaner fellows your last

Did worthily perform; and I must use you
In such another trick: go, bring the rabble,
O'er whom I give thee power, here, to this place
Incite them to quick motion; for I must
Bestow upon the eyes of this young couple
Some vanity of mine art; it is my promise,
And they expect it from me.
*Ari.*                      Presently?
*Pro.* Ay, with a twink.
*Ari.* Before you can say, *Come* and *go,*
And breathe twice; and cry, *so, so;*
Each one, tripping on his toe,
Will be here with mop and mow:
Do you love me, master? no?            [proach
*Pro.* Dearly, my delicate Ariel. Do not ap-
Till thou dost hear me call.
*Ari.*              Well I conceive.  [*Exit.*
*Pro.* Look thou be true: do not give dalliance
Too much the rein: the strongest oaths are straw
To the fire i' the blood: be more abstemious,
Or else, good night your vow!
*Fer.*              I warrant you, sir.
The white cold virgin snow upon my heart
Abates the ardour of my liver.
*Pro.*                      Well.—
Now come, my Ariel: bring a corollary,
Rather than want a spirit: appear, and pertly.—
No tongue; all eyes; be silent.    [*Soft music.*

*A Masque. Enter* IRIS.

*Iris.* Ceres, most bounteous lady, thy rich leas
Of wheat, rye, barley, vetches, oats, and pease;
Thy turfy mountains, where live nibbling sheep,
And flat meads thatch'd with stover, them to
Thy banks with peonied and lilied brims, [keep,
Which spongy April at thy 'hest betrims,
To make cold nymphs chaste crowns; and thy
      broom groves,
Whose shadow the dismissed bachelor loves,
Being lass-lorn; thy pole-clipt vineyard;
And thy sea-marge, sterile and rocky-hard,
Where thou thyself dost air: The queen o' the sky
Whose watery arch, and messenger, am I,
Bids thee leave these; and with her sovereign
      grace,
Here on this grass-plot, in this very place,
To come and sport: her peacocks fly amain;
Approach, rich Ceres, her to entertain.

*Enter* CERES.

*Cer.* Hail, many-colour'd messenger, that ne'er
Dost disobey the wife of Jupiter;
Who, with thy saffron wings, upon my flowers
Diffusest honey drops, refreshing showers;
And with each end of thy blue bow dost crown
My bosky acres, and my unshrubb'd down,
Rich scarf to my proud earth;—why hath thy
      queen
Summon'd me hither, to this short-grass'd green?
*Iris.* A contract of true love to celebrate;
And some donation freely to estate
On the bless'd lovers.
*Cer.*              Tell me, heavenly bow,
If Venus, or her son, as thou dost know,

Do now attend the queen? since they did plot
The means, that dusky Dis my daughter got,
Her and her blind boy's scandal'd company
I have forsworn.
*Iris.*          Of her society
Be not afraid. I met her deity
Cutting the clouds towards Paphos; and her son
Dove-drawn with her: here thought they to
         have done
Some wanton charm upon this man and maid,
Whose vows are that no bed-rite shall be paid
Till Hymen's torch be lighted; but in vain;
Mars' hot minion is return'd again;
Her waspish-headed son has broke his arrows,
Swears he will shoot no more, but play with
And be a boy right out.      [sparrows,
*Cer.*          Highest queen of state,
Great Juno comes; I know her by her gait.

        *Enter* JUNO.

*Jun.* How does my bounteous sister? Go with
         me,
To bless this twain, that they may prosperous be,
And honour'd in their issue.

         SONG.

*Jun.*—Honour, riches, marriage-blessing,
      Long continuance, and increasing,
      Hourly joys be still upon you!
      Juno sings her blessings on you.
*Cer.*—Earth's increase, and foison plenty,
      Barns and garners never empty;
      Vines, with clust'ring bunches growing;
      Plants, with goodly burden bowing;
      Spring come to you, at the farthest,
      In the very end of harvest!
      Scarcity and want shall shun you
      Ceres' blessing so is on you.

*Fer.* This is a most majestic vision, and
Harmonious charmingly: May I be bold
To think these spirits?
*Pro.*         Spirits, which by mine art
I have from their confines called to enact
My present fancies.
*Fer.*         Let me live here ever;
So rare a wonder'd father, and a wise,
Makes this place Paradise.
      [JUNO *and* CERES *whisper, and*
        *send* IRIS *on employment.*
*Pro.*         Sweet now, silence;
Juno and Ceres whisper seriously;
There's something else to do; hush, and be mute,
Or else our spell is marr'd.
*Iris.* You nymphs, call'd Naiads, of the
      wind'ring brooks,     [looks,
With your sedged crowns, and ever harmless
Leave your crisp channels, and on this green land
Answer your summons: Juno does command.
Come, temperate nymphs, and help to celebrate
A contract of true love; be not too late.

     *Enter certain* Nymphs.

You sun-burn'd sicklemen, of August weary,
Come hither from the furrow, and be merry;

Make holiday: your rye-straw hats put on,
And these fresh nymphs encounter every one
In country footing.

*Enter certain* Reapers, *properly habited; they
join with the* Nymphs *in a graceful dance;
towards the end whereof* PROSPERO *starts suddenly, and speaks; after which, to a strange,
hollow, and confused noise, they heavily vanish.*

*Pro.* [*Aside.*] I had forgot that foul conspiracy
Of the beast Caliban and his confederates
Against my life; the minute of their plot
Is almost come.—[*To the Spirits.*] Well done;
   —avoid;—no more.       passion
*Fer.* This is strange: your father's in some
That works him strongly.
*Mira.*        Never till this day,
Saw I him touch'd with anger so distemper'd.
*Pro.* You do look, my son, in a moved sort,
As if you were dismay'd: be cheerful, sir:
Our revels now are ended: these our actors,
As I foretold you, were all spirits, and
Are melted into air, into thin air:
And, like the baseless fabric of this vision
The cloud-capp'd towers, the gorgeous palaces,
The solemn temples, the great globe itself,
Yea, all which it inherit, shall dissolve,
And, like this insubstantial pageant faded,
Leave not a rack behind: We are such stuff
As dreams are made of, and our little life
Is rounded with a sleep.—Sir, I am vex'd;
Bear with my weakness; my old brain is troubled,
Be not disturb'd with my infirmity;
If you be pleased, retire into my cell,
And there repose; a turn or two I'll walk,
To still my beating mind.
*Fer. Mira.*       We wish your peace.
           [*Exeunt.*
*Pro.* Come, with a thought:—I thank you;
   —Ariel, come.

       *Enter* ARIEL.

*Ari.* Thy thoughts I cleave to: What's thy
         pleasure?
*Pro.*         Spirit,
We must prepare to meet with Caliban.
*Ari.* Ay, my commander; when I presented
         Ceres,
I thought to have told thee of it; but I fear'd
Lest I might anger thee.      [varlets?
*Pro.* Say again, where didst thou leave these
*Ari.* I told you, sir, they were red-hot with
         drinking:
So full of valour that they smote the air
For breathing in their faces; beat the ground
For kissing of their feet; yet always bending
Towards their project: Then I beat my tabor,
At which, like unback'd colts, they prick'd
         their ears,
Advanced their eyelids, lifted up their noses
As they smelt music; so I charm'd their ears,
That, calf-like, they my lowing follow'd through
Tooth'd briers, sharp furzes, pricking goss, and
         thorns.

Which enter'd their frail shins: at last I left them
I' the filthy mantled pool beyond your cell,
There dancing up to the chins, that the foul lake
O'erstunk their feet.
*Pro.* This was well done, my bird;
Thy shape invisible retain thou still:
The trumpery in my house, go, bring it hither,
For stale to catch these thieves.
*Ari.* I go, I go. [*Exit.*
*Pro.* A devil, a born devil, on whose nature
Nurture can never stick; on whom my pains,
Humanely taken, all, all lost, quite lost:
And as, with age, his body uglier grows,
So his mind cankers: I will plague them all,

*Re-enter* ARIEL, *loaden with glistering apparel, &c.*

Even to roaring:—Come, hang them on this line.

PROSPERO *and* ARIEL *remain invisible. Enter* CALIBAN, STEPHANO, *and* TRINCULO, *all wet.*
*Cal.* Pray you, tread softly, that the blind mole may not
Hear a footfall: we now are near his cell.
*Ste.* Monster, your fairy, which you say is a harmless fairy, has done little better than played the Jack with us.
*Trin.* Monster, I do smell all horse-piss; at which my nose is in great indignation.
*Ste.* So is mine. Do you hear, monster? If I should take a displeasure against you; look you,—
*Trin.* Thou wert but a lost monster.
*Cal.* Good, my lord, give me thy favour still:
Be patient, for the prize I'll bring thee to
Shall hood-wink this mischance: therefore speak
All's hush'd as midnight yet. [*softly,*
*Trin.* Ay, but to lose our bottles in the pool—
*Ste.* There is not only disgrace and dishonour in that, monster, but an infinite loss.
*Trin.* That's more to me than my wetting: yet this is your harmless fairy monster.
*Ste.* I will fetch off my bottle, though I be o'er ears for my labour. [*here,*
*Cal.* Pr'ythee, my king, be quiet: Seest thou
This is the mouth o' the cell: no noise, and enter.
Do that good mischief, which may make this island
Thine own for ever, and I, thy Caliban,
For aye thy foot-licker.
*Ste.* Give me thy hand: I do begin to have bloody thoughts.
*Trin.* O king Stephano! O peer! O worthy Stephano! look, what a wardrobe here is for thee.
*Cal.* Let it alone, thou fool; it is but trash.
*Trin.* O, ho, monster; we know what belongs to a frippery.—O king Stephano!
*Ste.* Put off that gown, Trinculo; by this hand, I'll have that gown.
*Trin.* Thy grace shall have it. [*mean,*
*Cal.* The dropsy drown this fool! what do you
To dote thus on such luggage? Let's along,
And do the murder first: if he awake,
From toe to crown he'll fill our skins with pinches;
Make us strange stuff.

*Ste.* Be you quiet, monster.—Mistress line, is not this my jerkin? Now is the jerkin under the line: now, jerkin, you are like to lose your hair, and prove a bald jerkin.
*Trin.* Do, do: We steal by line and level, ain't like your grace.
*Ste.* I thank thee for that jest: here's a garment for 't: wit shall not go unrewarded while I am king of this country: *Steal by line and level*, is an excellent pass of pate; there's another garment for 't.
*Trin.* Monster, come, put some lime upon your fingers, and away with the rest. [*time,*
*Cal.* I will have none on 't: we shall lose our time,
And all be turned to barnacles, or to apes
With foreheads villanous low.
*Ste.* Monster, lay to your fingers; help to bear this away where my hogshead of wine is, or I'll turn you out of my kingdom: go to, carry this.
*Trin.* And this.
*Ste.* Ay, and this.

*A noise of hunters heard. Enter divers* Spirits, *in shape of hounds, and hunt them about.* PROSPERO *and* ARIEL *setting them on.*

*Pro.* Hey, Mountain, hey!
*Ari.* Silver! there it goes, Silver! [*hark!*
*Pro.* Fury, Fury! there, Tyrant, there! hark,
[CAL., STE., *and* TRIN. *are driven out.*
Go, charge my goblins that they grind their joints
With dry convulsions; shorten up their sinews
With aged cramps; and more pinch-spotted make
Than pard or cat o' mountain. [*them,*
*Ari.* Hark, they roar.
*Pro.* Let them be hunted soundly: At this hour
Lie at my mercy all mine enemies:
Shortly shall all my labours end, and thou
Shalt have the air at freedom: for a little
Follow, and do me service. [*Exeunt.*

## ACT V.

SCENE I.—*Before the Cell of* PROSPERO.

*Enter* PROSPERO *in his magic robes; and* ARIEL.

*Pro.* Now does my project gather to a head:
My charms crack not; my spirits obey; and time
Goes upright with his carriage. How's the day?
*Ari.* On the sixth hour; at which time, my lord
You said our work should cease. [*lord,*
*Pro.* I did say so,
When first I raised the tempest. Say, my spirit,
How fares the king and's followers?
*Ari.* Confin'd together
In the same fashion as you gave in charge;
Just as you left them, sir; all prisoners
In the lime-grove which weather-fends your cell;
They cannot budge till your release. The king,
His brother, and yours, abide all three distracted;
And the remainder mourning over them,
Brimful of sorrow and dismay; but chiefly
Him you termed, sir, *The good old lord Gonzalo;*
His tears run down his beard, like winter's drops
From eaves of reeds: your charm so strongly works them,

'hat if you now beheld them, your affections
Vould become tender.
*ro.* Dost thou think so, spirit?
*Ari.* Mine would, sir, were I human.
*Pro.* And mine shall.
Hast thou, which art but air, a touch, a feeling
Of their afflictions? and shall not myself,
One of their kind, that relish all as sharply
Passion as they, be kindlier moved than thou art?
Though with their high wrongs I am struck to
the quick,
Yet, with my nobler reason, 'gainst my fury
Do I take part: the rarer action is
In virtue than in vengeance: they being pentient,
The sole drift of my purpose doth extend
Not a frown further. Go, release them, Ariel;
My charms I'll break, their senses I'll restore,
And they shall be themselves.
*Ari.* I'll fetch them, sir. [*Exit.*
*Pro.* Ye elves of hills, brooks, standing lakes,
and groves;
And ye that on the sands with printless foot
Do chase the ebbing Neptune, and do fly him
When he comes back; you demi-puppets that
By moonshine do the green sour ringlets make,
Whereof the ewe not bites; and you whose pastime
Is to make midnight mushrooms, that rejoice
To hear the solemn curfew; by whose aid,—
Weak masters though ye be,—I have bedimm'd
The noontide sun, call'd forth the mutinous
winds,
And 'twixt the green sea and the azured vault
Set roaring war: to the dread rattling thunder
Have I given fire, and rifted Jove's stout oak
With his own bolt: the strong-based promontory
Have I made shake: and by the spurs pluck'd up
The pine and cedar: graves, at my command,
Have waked their sleepers, oped, and let them
forth
By my so potent art. But this rough magic
I here abjure: and, when I have required
Some heavenly music,—which even now I do,—
To work mine end upon their senses, that
This airy charm is for, I'll break my staff,
Bury it certain fathoms in the earth,
And deeper than did ever plummet sound
I'll drown my book. [*Solemn music.*

*Re-enter* ARIEL: *after him* ALONSO, *with a frantic
gesture, attended by* GONZALO; SEBASTIAN *and*
ANTONIO *in like manner, attended by* ADRIAN
*and* FRANCISCO: *they all enter the circle which*
PROSPERO *had made, and there stand charmed;
which* PROSPERO *observing, speaks.*

A solemn air, and the best comforter
To an unsettled fancy, cure thy brains, [stand,
Now useless, boil'd within thy skull! There
For you are spell-stopp'd.—
Holy Gonzalo, honourable man,
Mine eyes, even sociable to the show of thine,
Fall fellowly drops.—The charm dissolves apace;
And as the morning steals upon the night,
Melting the darkness, so their rising senses
Begin to chase the ignorant fumes that mantle

Their clearer reason.—O good Gonzalo,
My true preserver, and a loyal sir
To him thou follow'st; I will pay thy graces
Home, both in word and deed.—Most cruelly
Didst thou, Alonso, use me and my daughter:
Thy brother was a furtherer in the act;—
Thou'rt pinch'd for't now, Sebastian, flesh and
blood.—
You brother mine, that entertain ambition,
Expell'd remorse and nature; who, with Sebas-
tian,— [strong,—
Whose inward pinches therefore are most
Would here have kill'd your king; I do forgive
thee, [standing
Unnatural though thou art.—Their under-
Begins to swell; and the approaching tide
Will shortly fill the reasonable shore
That now lies foul and muddy. Not one of them
That yet looks on me, or would know me.—Ariel,
Fetch me the hat and rapier in my cell;
[*Exit* ARIEL.
I will discase me, and myself present
As I was sometime Milan: quickly, spirit;
Thou shalt ere long be free.
ARIEL *re-enters, singing, and helps to attire*
PROSPERO.

*Ari.* Where the bee sucks, there suck I;
In the cowslip's bell I lie:
There I couch when owls do cry.
On the bat's back I do fly
After summer merrily:
Merrily, merrily shall I live now,
Under the blossom that hangs on the bough.

*Pro.* Why, that's my dainty Ariel: I shall miss
thee;
But yet thou shalt have freedom: so, so, so.—
To the king's ship, invisible as thou art:
There shalt thou find the mariners asleep
Under the hatches; the master and the boatswain
Being awake, enforce them to this place;
And presently, I pr'ythee.
*Ari.* I drink the air before me, and return
Or e'er your pulse twice beat. [*Exit* ARIEL.
*Gon.* All torment, trouble, wonder, and amaze-
ment
Inhabits here. Some heavenly power guide us
Out of this fearful country!
*Pro.* Behold, sir king,
The wronged Duke of Milan, Prospero:
For more assurance that a living prince
Does now speak to thee, I embrace thy body;
And to thee and thy company I bid
A hearty welcome.
*Alon.* Whether thou beest he or no,
Or some enchanted trifle to abuse me,
As late I have been, I not know: thy pulse
Beats, as of flesh and blood; and, since I saw
thee,
The affliction of my mind amends, with which,
I fear, a madness held me: this must crave,—
An if this be at all,—a most strange story.
Thy dukedom I resign; and do entreat
Thou pardon me my wrongs.—But how should
Prospero

Be living and be here?
*Pro.*                    First, noble friend,
Let me embrace thine age, whose honour cannot
Be measured or confined.
*Gon.*                    Whether this be
Or be not, I'll not swear.
*Pro.*                    You do yet taste
Some subtilties o' the isle, that will not let you
Believe things certain.—Welcome, my friends,
all:—                    [*Aside to* SEB. *and* ANT.
But you, my brace of lords, were I so minded,
I here could pluck his highness' frown upon you,
And justify you traitors; at this time
I'll tell no tales.
*Seb.* The devil speaks in him.          [*Aside.*
*Pro.*                    No:——
For you, most wicked sir, whom to call brother
Would even infect my mouth, I do forgive
Thy rankest fault,—all of them; and require
My dukedom of thee, which, perforce, I know
Thou must restore.
*Alon.*               If thou beest Prospero,
Give us particulars of thy preservation:
How thou hast met us here, who three hours since
Were wreck'd upon this shore; where I have
    lost—
How sharp the point of this remembrance is!—
My dear son Ferdinand.
*Pro.*                    I am woe for 't, sir.
*Alon.* Irreparable is the loss; and patience
Says it is past her cure.
*Pro.*                    I rather think
You have not sought her help; of whose soft grace
For the like loss I have her sovereign aid,
And rest myself content.
*Alon.*                    You the like loss?
*Pro.* As great to me as late; and, supportable
To make the dear loss, have I means much weaker
Than you may call to confort you; for I
Have lost my daughter.
*Alon.*                    A daughter!
O heavens, that they were living both in Naples,
The king and queen there! that they were, I wish
Myself were mudded in that oozy bed
Where my son lies. When did you lose your
          daughter?                    [lords
*Pro.* In this last tempest. I perceive these
At this encounter do so much admire
That they devour their reason, and scarce think
Their eyes do offices of truth, their words
Are natural breath: but, howsoe'er you have
Been justled from your senses, know for certain
That I am Prospero, and that very duke
Which was thrust forth of Milan; who most
          strangely                    [landed,
Upon this shore, where you were wreck'd, was
To be the lord on 't. No more yet of this;
For 'tis a chronicle of day by day,
Not a relation for a breakfast, nor
Befitting this first meeting. Welcome, sir;
This cell's my court: here have I few attendants,
And subjects none abroad: pray you, look in.
My dukedom since you have given me again,
I will requite you with as good a thing:

At least bring forth a wonder, to content y
As much as me my dukedom.

*The entrance of the Cell opens, and discover.*
    FERDINAND *and* MIRANDA *playing at chess.*

*Mira.* Sweet lord, you play me false.
*Fer.*                    No, my dearest love,
I would not for the world.
*Mira.* Yes, for a score of kingdoms you should
          wrangle,
And I would call it fair play.
*Alon.*                    If this prove
A vision of the island, one dear son
Shall I twice lose.
*Seb.*                    A most high miracle!
*Fer.* Though the seas threaten, they are merci-
          ful:
I have cursed them without cause.
                    [FERD. *kneels to* ALON.
*Alon.*                    Now all the blessings
Of a glad father compass thee about!
Arise and say how thou cam'st here.
*Mira.*                    O, wonder!
How many goodly creatures are there here!
How beauteous mankind is! O brave new world
That hath such people in 't!
*Pro.*                    'Tis new to thee.
*Alon.* What is this maid, with whom thou wast
          at play?
Your eld'st acquaintance cannot be three hours:
Is she the goddess that hath sever'd us,
And brought us thus together?
*Fer.*                    Sir, she's mortal;
But by immortal providence she's mine;
I chose her when I could not ask my father
For his advice, nor thought I had one: she
Is daughter to this famous Duke of Milan,
Of whom so often I have heard renown
But never saw before; of whom I have
Received a second life; and second father
This lady makes him to me.
*Alon.*                    I am hers:
But O, how oddly will it sound that I
Must ask my child forgiveness!
*Pro.*                    There, sir, stop;
Let us not burden our remembrances
With a heaviness that's gone.
*Gon.*                    I have inly wept,
Or should have spoke ere this. Look down, you
          gods,
And on this couple drop a blessed crown;
For it is you that have chalk'd forth the way
Which brought us hither!
*Alon.*               I say, Amen, Gonzalo!
*Gon.* Was Milan thrust from Milan, that his
          issue,
Should become kings of Naples? O, rejoice
Beyond a common joy; and set it down
With gold on lasting pillars: in one voyage
Did Claribel her husband find at Tunis;
And Ferdinand, her brother, found a wife
Where he himself was lost; Prospero his duke-
In a poor isle; and all of us ourselves          [dom
When no man was his own.

*Alon.* Give me your hands:
[*To* FERD. *and* MIR.
Let grief and sorrow still embrace his heart
That doth not wish you joy!
*Gon.* Be 't so! Amen!

*Re-enter* ARIEL, *with the* Master *and* Boatswain *amazedly following.*

O look, sir, look, sir; here are more of us!
I prophesied, if a gallows were on land,
This fellow could not drown. Now, blasphemy,
That swear'st grace o'erboard, not an oath on shore?
Hast thou no mouth by land? What is the news?
*Boats.* The best news is, that we have safely found
Our king and company: the next, our ship,—
Which, but three glasses since, we gave out split,
Is tight, and yare, and bravely rigg'd, as when
We first put out to sea.
*Ari.* Sir, all this service }
Have I done since I went. } *Aside.*
*Pro.* My tricksy spirit! }
*Alon.* These are not natural events; they strengthen [hither?
From strange to stranger:—Say, how came you
*Boats.* If I did think, sir, I were well awake,
I'd strive to tell you. We were dead of sleep,
And,—how, we know not,—all clapp'd under hatches, [noises
Where, but even now, with strange and several
Of roaring, shrieking, howling, jingling chains,
And more diversity of sounds, all horrible,
We were awaked; straightway, at liberty:
Where we, in all her trim, freshly beheld
Our royal, good, and gallant ship; our master
Capering to eye her: on a trice, so please you,
Even in a dream, were we divided from them,
And were brought moping hither.
*Ari.* Was 't well done? }
*Pro.* Bravely, my diligence. Thou shalt } *Aside.*
be free. }
*Alon.* This is as strange a maze as e'er men trod:
And there is in this business more than nature
Was ever conduct of: some oracle
Must rectify our knowledge.
*Pro.* Sir, my liege,
Do not infest your mind with beating on
The strangeness of this business: at pick'd leisure,
Which shall be shortly, single I'll resolve you,—
Which to you shall seem probable,—of every
These happen'd accidents: till when, be cheerful,
And think of each thing well.—Come hither, spirit; [*Aside.*
Set Caliban and his companions free.
Untie the spell. [*Exit* ARIEL.] How fares my gracious sir?
There are yet missing of your company
Some few odd lads that you remember not.

*Re-enter* ARIEL, *driving in* CALIBAN, STEPHANO, *and* TRINCULO, *in their stolen apparel.*

*Ste.* Every man shift for all the rest, and let

no man take care for himself; for all is but fortune:—Coragio, bully-monster, coragio!
*Trin.* If these be true spies which I wear in my head, here's a goodly sight.
*Cal.* O Setebos, these be brave spirits indeed!
How fine my master is! I am afraid
He will chastise me.
*Seb.* Ha, ha;—
What things are these, my lord Antonio|
Will money buy them?
*Ant.* Very like; one of them
Is a plain fish, and, no doubt, marketable.
*Pro.* Mark but the badges of these men, my lords, [knave,——
Then say if they be true.—This mis-shapen
His mother was a witch; and one so strong
That could control the moon, make flows and ebbs,
And deal in her command, without her power:
These three have robb'd me: and this demi-devil,—
For he's a bastard one,—had plotted with them
To take my life: two of these fellows you
Must know and own; this thing of darkness I
Acknowledge mine.
*Cal.* I shall be pinch'd to death.
*Alon.* Is not this Stephano, my drunken butler?
*Seb.* He is drunk now: where had he wine?
*Alon.* And Trinculo is reeling ripe: where should they
Find this grand liquor that hath gilded them?—
How cam'st thou in this pickle?
*Trin.* I have been in such a pickle since I saw
you last that, I fear me, will never out of my
bones: I shall not fear fly-blowing.
*Seb.* Why, how now, Stephano?
*Ste.* O, touch me not; I am not Stephano, but
a cramp.
*Pro.* You'd be king of the isle, sirrah!
*Ste.* I should have been a sore one then.
*Alon.* This is as strange a thing as e'er I
look'd on. [*Pointing to* CALIBAN.
*Pro.* He is as disproportioned in his manners
As in his shape.—Go, sirrah, to my cell;
Take with you your companions; as you look
To have my pardon, trim it handsomely.
*Cal.* Ay, that I will; and I'll be wise hereafter,
And seek for grace. What a thrice-double ass
Was I to take this drunkard for a god,
And worship this dull fool!
*Pro.* Go to; away!
*Alon.* Hence, and bestow your luggage where
you found it.
*Seb.* Or stole it, rather.
[*Exeunt* CAL., STE., *and* TRIN.
*Pro.* Sir, I invite your highness and your train
To my poor cell: where you shall take your rest
For this one night; which (part of it) I'll waste
With such discourse as, I not doubt, shall make it
Go quick away,—the story of my life,
And the particular accidents gone by
Since I came to this isle: and in the morn
I'll bring you to your ship, and so to Naples,

Where I have hope to see the nuptial
Of these our dear-belovèd solemniz'd;
And thence retire me to my Milan, where
Every third thought shall be my grave.
*Alon.*             I long
To hear the story of your life, which must
Take the ear strangely.
*Pro.*          I'll deliver all;
And promise you calm seas, auspicious gales,
And sail so expeditious, that shall catch
Your royal fleet afar off.—My Ariel,—chick,—
That is thy charge: then to the elements
Be free, and fare thou well!—[*Aside.*] Please
     you, draw near.         [*Exeunt.*

## EPILOGUE.

SPOKEN BY PROSPERO.

Now my charms are all o'erthrown,

And what strength I have's mine own,—
Which is.most faint: now 'tis true,
I must be here confined by you,
Or sent to Naples. Let me not,
Since I have my dukedom got,
And pardon'd the deceiver, dwell
In this bare island by your spell;
But release me from my bands
With the help of your good hands.
Gentle breath of yours my sails
Must fill, or else my project fails,
Which was to please. Now I want
Spirits to enforce, art to enchant;
And my ending is despair
Unless I be relieved by prayer;
Which pierces so, that it assaults
Mercy itself, and frees all faults.
As you from crimes would pardon'd be,
Let your indulgence set me free.

## THE TWO GENTLEMEN of VERONA.

Page 33.

# TWO GENTLEMEN OF VERONA

## DRAMATIS PERSONÆ

DUKE OF MILAN, *Father to* SILVIA.

VALENTINE,
PROTEUS, } *Gentlemen of Verona.*

ANTONIO, *Father to* PROTEUS.
THURIO, *a foolish Rival to* VALENTINE.
EGLAMOUR, *Agent for* SILVIA *in her escape.*
SPEED, *a clownish Servant to* VALENTINE.
LAUNCE, *Servant to* PROTEUS.
PANTHINO, *Servant to* ANTONIO.

Host, *where* JULIA *lodges in Milan.*
Outlaws.

JULIA, *a lady of Verona, beloved by* PROTEUS.
SILVIA, *the Duke's daughter, beloved by* VALENTINE.
LUCETTA, *Waiting-woman to* JULIA.

*Servants. Musicians.*

SCENE.—*Sometimes in* VERONA; *sometimes in* MILAN; *and on the frontiers of* MANTUA.

## ACT I.

SCENE I.—*An open place in* VERONA.

*Enter* VALENTINE *and* PROTEUS.

*Val.* Cease to persuade, my loving Proteus;
Home-keeping youth have ever homely wits;
Wer't not affection chains thy tender days
To the sweet glances of thy honour'd love,
I rather would entreat thy company
To see the wonders of the world abroad,
Than, living dully sluggardiz'd at home,
Wear out thy youth with shapeless idleness.
But since thou lov'st, love still, and thrive therein,
Even as I would, when I to love begin. [adieu!
*Pro.* Wilt thou be gone? Sweet Valentine,
Think on thy Proteus, when thou haply seest
Some rare noteworthy object in thy travel:
Wish me partaker in thy happiness
When thou dost meet good hap: and in thy danger,
If ever danger do environ thee,
Commend thy grievance to my holy prayers,
For I will be thy beadsman, Valentine.
*Val.* And on a love-book pray for my success.
*Pro.* Upon some book I love I'll pray for thee.
*Val.* That's on some shallow story of deep love,
How young Leander cross'd the Hellespont.
*Pro.* That's a deep story of a deeper love;
For he was more than over shoes in love.
*Val.* 'Tis true; for you are over boots in love,
And yet you never swam the Hellespont.
*Pro.* Over the boots! nay, give me not the boots.
*Val.* No, I will not, for it boots thee not.
*Pro.* What?
*Val.* To be in love, where scorn is bought with groans;
Coy looks with heart-sore sighs; one fading moment's mirth
With twenty watchful, weary, tedious nights:
If haply won, perhaps a hapless gain;
If lost, why then a grievous labour won;
However, but a folly bought with wit,
Or else a wit by folly vanquishèd. [fool.
*Pro.* So, by your circumstance, you call me
*Val.* So, by your circumstance, I fear you'll prove.
*Pro.* 'Tis love you cavil at; I am not Love.
*Val.* Love is your master, for he masters you:
And he that is so yokèd by a fool,
Methinks should not be chronicled for wise.
*Pro.* Yet writers say, As in the sweetest bud
The eating canker dwells, so eating love
Inhabits in the finest wits of all.
*Val.* And writers say, As the most forward bud
Is eaten by the canker ere it blow,
Even so by love the young and tender wit
Is turn'd to folly; blasting in the bud,
Losing his verdure even in the prime,
And all the fair effects of future hopes.
But wherefore waste I time to counsel thee
That art a votary to fond desire?
Once more adieu: my father at the road
Expects my coming, there to see me shipp'd.
*Pro.* And thither will I bring thee, Valentine.
*Val.* Sweet Proteus, no; now let us take our leave.
At Milan let me hear from thee by letters
Of thy success in love, and what news else
Betideth here in absence of thy friend;
And I likewise will visit thee with mine.
*Pro.* All happiness bechance to thee in Milan!
*Val.* As much to you at home! and so farewell.
[*Exit* VALENTINE.
*Pro.* He after honour hunts, I after love:
He leaves his friends to dignify them more;
I leave myself, my friends, and all for love.
Thou, Julia, thou hast metamorphos'd me;
Made me neglect my studies, lose my time,
War with good counsel, set the world at nought:
Made wit with musing weak, heart sick with thought.

*Enter* SPEED.

*Speed.* Sir Proteus, save you. Saw you my master?

*Pro.* But now he parted hence, to embark for
    Milan.
*Speed.* Twenty to one, then, he is shipp'd
    already;
And I have play'd the sheep in losing him.
*Pro.* Indeed a sheep doth very often stray
An if the shepherd be awhile away.
*Speed.* You conclude that my master is a
    shepherd, then, and I a sheep?
*Pro.* I do.
*Speed.* Why, then, my horns are his horns
    whether I wake or sleep.
*Pro.* A silly answer, and fitting well a sheep.
*Speed.* This proves me still a sheep.
*Pro.* True; and thy master a shepherd.
*Speed.* Nay; that I can deny by a circumstance.
*Pro.* It shall go hard but I'll prove it by another.
*Speed.* The shepherd seeks the sheep, and not
the sheep the shepherd; but I seek my master,
and my master seeks not me: therefore, I am
no sheep.
*Pro.* The sheep for fodder follow the shepherd,
the shepherd for food follows not the sheep;
thou for wages followest thy master, thy master for wages follows not thee: therefore, thou
art a sheep.
*Speed.* Such another proof will make me cry
baa.
*Pro.* But dost thou hear? gav'st thou my letter
to Julia?
*Speed.* Ay, sir; I, a lost mutton, gave your
letter to her, a laced mutton; and she, a laced
mutton, gave me, a lost mutton, nothing for
my labour!
*Pro.* Here's too small a pasture for such a store
of muttons.
*Speed.* If the ground be overcharged you were
best stick her?
*Pro.* Nay; in that you are astray: 'twere best
pound you.
*Speed.* Nay, sir; less than a pound shall serve
me for carrying your letter.
*Pro.* You mistake; I mean the pound, a pinfold.
*Speed.* From a pound to a pin? fold it over
    and over.             [your lover.
'Tis threefold too little for carrying a letter to
*Pro.* But what said she? did she nod?
*Speed.* [*Nodding.*] Ay.
*Pro.* Nod—Ay—why, that's noddy.
*Speed.* You mistook, sir; I say she did nod:
and you ask me if she did nod; and I say, Ay.
*Pro.* And that set together is—noddy.
*Speed.* Now you have taken the pains to set it
together, take it for your pains.
*Pro.* No, no; you shall have it for bearing the
letter.
*Speed.* Well, I perceive I must be fain to bear
with you.
*Pro.* Why, sir, how do you bear with me?
*Speed.* Marry, sir, the letter very orderly: hav-
ing nothing but the word noddy for my pains.
*Pro.* Beshrew me, but you have a quick wit.
*Speed.* And yet it cannot overtake your slow
purse.

*Pro.* Come, come; open the matter in brief:
what said she?
*Speed.* Open your purse, that the money and
the matter may be both at once delivered.
*Pro.* Well, sir, here is for your pains: what said
she?
*Speed.* Truly, sir, I think you'll hardly win her.
*Pro.* Why, couldst thou perceive so much from
her?
*Speed.* Sir, I could perceive nothing at all from
her; no, not so much as a ducat for delivering
your letter: and being so hard to me that
brought your mind, I fear she'll prove as hard
to you in telling her mind. Give her no token
but stones; for she's as hard as steel.
*Pro.* What! said she nothing?
*Speed.* No, not so much as—*Take this for thy
pains.* To testify your bounty, I thank you,
you have testern'd me; in requital whereof,
henceforth carry your letters yourself: and, sir,
I'll commend you to my master.     [wreck,
*Pro.* Go, go; begone, to save your ship from
Which cannot perish, having thee aboard,
Being destined to a drier death on shore.
I must go send some better messenger:
I fear my Julia would not deign my lines,
Receiving them from such a worthless post.
                        [*Exeunt.*

SCENE II.—*The same. Garden of* JULIA'S
*House.*

*Enter* JULIA *and* LUCETTA.

*Jul.* But say, Lucetta, now we are alone,
Wouldst thou then counsel me to fall in love?
*Luc.* Ay, madam; so you stumble not unheed-
    fully.
*Jul.* Of all the fair resort of gentlemen
That every day with parle encounter me,
In thy opinion which is worthiest love?
*Luc.* Please you, repeat their names; I'll show
    my mind
According to my shallow simple skill.
*Jul.* What think'st thou of the fair Sir Egla-
    mour?
*Luc.* As of a knight well-spoken, neat, and fine;
But, were I you, he never should be mine.
*Jul.* What think'st thou of the rich Mercatio?
*Luc.* Well of his wealth; but of himself, so so.
*Jul.* What think'st thou of the gentle Proteus?
*Luc.* Lord, Lord! to see what folly reigns in us!
*Jul.* How now! what means this passion at his
    name?
*Luc.* Pardon, dear madam; 'tis a passing shame
That I, unworthy body as I am,
Should censure thus on lovely gentlemen.
*Jul.* Why not on Proteus, as of all the rest?
*Luc.* Then thus: of many good I think him best.
*Jul.* Your reason?
*Luc.* I have no other but a woman's reason;
think him so, because I think him so.
*Jul.* And wouldst thou have me cast my love
    on him?                 [away.
*Luc.* Ay, if you thought your love not cast

*Jul.* Why, he of all the rest hath never moved
 me.      [loves ye.
*Luc.* Yet he of all the rest, I think, best
*Jul.* His little speaking shows his love but
 small.
*Luc.* Fire that is closest kept burns most of all.
*Jul.* They do not love that do not show their
 love.       [love.
*Luc.* O, they love least that let men know their
*Jul.* I would I knew his mind.
*Luc.* Peruse this paper, madam. [*Gives a letter.*
*Jul.* [*reads*] 'To Julia,'—Say, from whom?
*Luc.* That the contents will show.
*Jul.* Say, say; who gave it thee?
*Luc.* Sir Valentine's page; and sent, I think
 'from Proteus:    [the way,
He would have given it you; but I, being in
Did in your name receive it; pardon the fault,
 I pray.
*Jul.* Now, by my modesty, a goodly broker!
Dare you presume to harbour wanton lines?
To whisper and conspire against my youth?
Now, trust me, 'tis an office of great worth,
And you an officer fit for the place.
There, take the paper; see it be return'd;
Or else return no more into my sight.
*Luc.* To plead for love deserves more fee than
*Jul.* Will you be gone?    [hate.
*Luc.*   That you may ruminate. [*Exit.*
*Jul.* And yet, I would I had o'erlook'd the
It were a shame to call her back again, [letter.
And pray her to a fault for which I chid her.
What fool is she, that knows I am a maid,
And would not force the letter to my view?
Since maids, in modesty, say *No* to that
Which they would have the profferer construe *Ay.*
Fie, fie! how wayward is this foolish love,
That, like a testy babe, will scratch the nurse,
And presently, all humbled, kiss the rod!
How churlishly I chid Lucetta hence,
When willingly I would have had her here!
How angrily I taught my brow to frown,
When inward joy enforced my heart to smile!
My penance is to call Lucetta back,
And ask remission for my folly past:—
What, ho! Lucetta?

    *Re-enter* LUCETTA.

*Luc.*    What would your ladyship?
*Jul.* Is it near dinner time?
*Luc.*     I would it were;
That you might kill your stomach on your
And not upon your maid.   [meat,
*Jul.*    What is 't you took up
So gingerly?
*Luc.*  Nothing.
*Jul.*   Why didst thou stoop then?
*Luc.* To take a paper up that I let fall.
*Jul.* And is that paper nothing?
*Luc.*    Nothing concerning me.
*Jul.* Then let it lie for those that it concerns.
*Luc.* Madam, it will not lie where it concerns,
Unless it have a false interpreter.

*Jul.* Some love of yours hath writ to you in
 rhyme.
*Luc.* That I might sing it, madam, to a tune;
Give me a note: your ladyship can set.
*Jul.* As little by such toys as may be possible;
Best sing it to the tune of *Light o' love.*
*Luc.* It is too heavy for so light a tune.
*Jul.* Heavy! belike it hath some burden, then.
*Luc.* Ay; and melodious were it, would you
 sing it.
*Jul.* And why not you?
*Luc.*    I cannot reach so high.
*Jul.* Let's see your song.—How now, minion?
*Luc.* Keep tune there still, so you will sing it out:
And yet methinks I do not like this tune.
*Jul.* You do not?
*Luc.* No, madam; it is too sharp.
*Jul.* You, minion, are too saucy.
*Luc.* Nay, now you are too flat,
And mar the concord with too harsh a descant;
There wanteth but a mean to fill your song.
*Jul.* The mean is drown'd with your unruly
 base.
*Luc.* Indeed, I bid the base for Proteus. [me.
*Jul.* This babble shall not henceforth trouble
Here is a coil with protestation!—
       [*Tears the letter.*
Go, get you gone; and let the papers lie:
You would be fingering them, to anger me.
*Luc.* She makes it strange; but she would be
 best pleased
To be so anger'd with another letter. [*Exit.*
*Jul.* Nay, would I were so anger'd with the
 same!
O hateful hands, to tear such loving words!
Injurious wasps! to feed on such sweet honey,
And kill the bees that yield it, with your stings!
I'll kiss each several paper for amends.
And here is writ—*kind Julia;*—unkind Julia!
As in revenge of thy ingratitude,
I throw thy name against the bruising stones,
Trampling contemptuously on thy disdain.
Look, here is writ—*love-wounded Proteus:*—
Poor wounded name! my bosom, as a bed,
Shall lodge thee till thy wound be thoroughly
 heal'd;
And thus I search it with a sovereign kiss,
But twice or thrice was Proteus written down:
Be calm, good wind, blow not a word away
Till I have found each letter in the letter, [bear
Except mine own name; that some whirlwind
Unto a ragged, fearful, hanging rock,
And throw it thence into the raging sea!
Lo, here in one line is his name twice writ,—
*Poor forlorn Proteus, passionate Proteus,*
*To the sweet Julia;* that I'll tear away;
And yet I will not, sith so prettily
He couples it to his complaining names.
Thus will I fold them one upon another;
Now kiss, embrace, contend, do what you will.

    *Re-enter* LUCETTA.

*Luc.* Madam, dinner's ready, and your father
*Jul.* Well, let us go.    [stays.

*Luc.* What! shall these papers lie like tell-tales
    here?
*Jul.* If you respect them, best to take them up.
*Luc.* Nay, I was taken up for laying them
    down;
Yet here they shall not lie for catching cold.
*Jul.* I see you have a month's mind to them.
*Luc.* Ay, madam, you may say what sights
    you see;
I see things too, although you judge I wink.
*Jul.* Come, come; wilt please you go? [*Exeunt.*

SCENE III.—*The same. A Room in
    ANTONIO'S House.*

*Enter* ANTONIO *and* PANTHINO.

*Ant.* Tell me, Panthino, what sad talk was that
Wherewith my brother held you in the cloister?
*Pan.* 'Twas of his nephew Proteus, your son.
*Ant.* Why, what of him?
*Pan.*           He wonder'd that your lordship
Would suffer him to spend his youth at home,
While other men, of slender reputation,
Put forth their sons to seek preferment out:
Some to the wars, to try their fortune there;
Some to discover islands far away;
Some to the studious universities.
For any, or for all these exercises,
He said that Proteus, your son, was meet;
And did request me to impórtune you
To let him spend his time no more at home,
Which would be great impeachment to his age,
In having known no travel in his youth. [that
*Ant.* Nor need'st thou much impórtune me to
Whereon this month I have been hammering.
I have consider'd well his loss of time,
And how he cannot be a perfect man,
Not being tried and tutor'd in the world:
Experience is by industry achieved,
And perfected by the swift course of time:
Then tell me, whither were I best to send him?
*Pan.* I think your lordship is not ignorant
How his companion, youthful Valentine,
Attends the emperor in his royal court.
*Ant.* I know it well.        [him thither:
*Pan.* 'Twere good, I think, your lordship sent
There shall he practise tilts and tournaments,
Hear sweet discourse, converse with noblemen,
And be in eye of every exercise
Worthy his youth and nobleness of birth.
*Ant.* I like thy counsel; well hast thou advised:
And that thou may'st perceive how well I like
The execution of it shall make known;    [it,
Even with the speediest execution
I will dispatch him to the emperor's court.
*Pan.* To-morrow, may it please you, Don Al-
With other gentlemen of good esteem, [phonso,
Are journeying to salute the emperor,
And to commend their service to his will.
*Ant.* Good company; with them shall Proteus
    go.
And—in good time;—now will we break with
    him.

*Enter* PROTEUS.

*Pro.* Sweet love! sweet lines! sweet life!
Here is her hand, the agent of her heart;
Here is her oath for love, her honour's pawn:
O that our fathers would applaud our loves,
To seal our happiness with their consents!
O heavenly Julia!                [there?
*Ant.* How now? what letter are you reading
*Pro.* May 't please your lordship, 'tis a word or
Of commendation sent from Valentine,    [two
Deliver'd by a friend that came from him.
*Ant.* Lend me the letter; let me see what news.
*Pro.* There is no news, my lord; but that he
    writes.
How happily he lives, how well-beloved
And daily graced by the emperor;
Wishing me with him, partner of his fortune.
*Ant.* And how stand you affected to his wish?
*Pro.* As one relying on your lordship's will,
And not depending on his friendly wish.
*Ant.* My will is something sorted with his wish.
Muse not that I thus suddenly proceed;
For what I will, I will, and there an end.
I am resolved that thou shalt spend some time
With Valentinus in the emperor's court;
What maintenance he from his friends receives,
Like exhibition shalt thou have from me.
To-morrow be in readiness to go:
Excuse it not, for I am peremptory.
*Pro.* My lord, I cannot be so soon provided;
Please you, deliberate a day or two.    [thee:
*Ant.* Look, what thou want'st shall be sent after
No more of stay; to-morrow thou must go.—
Come on, Panthino; you shall be employ'd
To hasten on his expedition.
                [*Exeunt* ANT. *and* PAN.
*Pro.* Thus have I shunn'd the fire, for fear of
burning,                [drown'd;
And drench'd me in the sea, where I am
I fear'd to show my father Julia's letter,
Lest he should take exceptions to my love;
And with the vantage of mine own excuse
Hath he excepted most against my love.
O, how this spring of love resembleth
The uncertain glory of an April day;
Which now shows all the beauty of the sun,
And by and by a cloud takes all away!

*Re-enter* PANTHINO.

*Pan.* Sir Proteus, your father calls for you;
He is in haste; therefore, I pray you, go.
*Pro.* Why, this it is! my heart accords thereto;
And yet a thousand times it answers no.
                        [*Exeunt.*

ACT II.

SCENE I.—MILAN. *An apartment in the
    DUKE'S Palace.*

*Enter* VALENTINE *and* SPEED.

*Speed.* [*Picking up a glove.*] Sir, your glove.
*Val.* Not mine; my gloves are on.
*Speed.* Why, then, this may be yours; for this
    is but one.

*Val.* Ha! let me see: ay, give it me; it's mine:—
Sweet ornament that decks a thing divine!
Ah, Silvia! Silvia!
*Speed.* [*Calling.*] Madam Silvia! Madam Silvia!
*Val.* How now, sirrah?
*Speed.* She is not within hearing, sir.
*Val.* Why, sir, who bade you call her?
*Speed.* Your worship, sir; or else I mistook.
*Val.* Well, you'll still be too forward.
*Speed.* And yet I was last chidden for being too
　　slow.　　　　　　　　　　　　　　[Silvia?
*Val.* Go to, sir; tell me; do you know Madam
*Speed.* She that your worship loves?
*Val.* Why, how know you that I am in love?
*Speed.* Marry, by these special marks: first you
have learned, like Sir Proteus, to wreath your
arms like a mal-content; to relish a love-song,
like a robin redbreast; to walk alone, like one
that had the pestilence; to sigh, like a school-
boy that had lost his A B C; to weep, like a
young wench that had buried her grandam; to
fast, like one that takes diet; to watch, like one
that fears robbing; to speak puling, like a beggar at Hallowmas. You were wont, when you
laughed, to crow like a cock; when you walked,
to walk like one of the lions; when you fasted,
it was presently after dinner; when you looked
sadly, it was for want of money: and now you
are metamorphosed with a mistress, that, when
I look on you, I can hardly think you my master.
*Val.* Are all these things perceived in me?
*Speed.* They are all perceived without you.
*Val.* Without me? they cannot.
*Speed.* Without you? nay, that's certain; for
without you were so simple, none else would:
but you are so without these follies, that these
follies are within you, and shine through you
like the water in a urinal; that not an eye that
sees you but is a physician to comment on your
malady.
*Val.* But tell me, dost thou know my lady
Silvia?
*Speed.* She that you gaze on so, as she sits at
supper?
*Val.* Hast thou observed that? even she I
　　mean.
*Speed.* Why, sir, I know her not.
*Val.* Dost thou know her by my gazing on her,
and yet knowest her not?
*Speed.* Is she not hard favoured, sir?
*Val.* Not so fair, boy, as well favoured.
*Speed.* Sir, I know that well enough.
*Val.* What dost thou know?
*Speed.* That she is not so fair as (of you) well
favoured.
*Val.* I mean that her beauty is exquisite, but
her favour infinite.
*Speed.* That's because the one is painted and
the other out of all count.
*Val.* How painted? and how out of count?
*Speed.* Marry, sir, so painted, to make her fair,
that no man counts of her beauty.
*Val.* How esteemest thou me? I account of
her beauty.

*Speed.* You never saw her since she was de-
formed.
*Val.* How long hath she been deformed?
*Speed.* Ever since you loved her.
*Val.* I have loved her ever since I saw her;
and still I see her beautiful.
*Speed.* If you love her, you cannot see her.
*Val.* Why?
*Speed.* Because love is blind. O that you had
mine eyes; or your own eyes had the lights they
were wont to have when you chid at Sir Pro-
teus for going ungartered!
*Val.* What should I see then?
*Speed.* Your own present folly and her passing
deformity; for he, being in love, could not see
to garter his hose; and you, being in love, can
not see to put on your hose.
*Val.* Belike, boy, then you are in love: for last
morning you could not see to wipe my shoes.
*Speed.* True, sir; I was in love with my bed;
I thank you, you swinged me for my love, which
makes me the bolder to chide you for yours.
*Val.* In conclusion, I stand affected to her.
*Speed.* I would you were set; so your affection
would cease.
*Val.* Last night she enjoined me to write some
lines to one she loves.
*Speed.* And have you?
*Val.* I have.
*Speed.* Are they not lamely writ?
*Val.* No, boy, but as well as I can do them;—
Peace; here she comes.
*Speed.* O excellent motion! O exceeding puppet!
now will he interpret to her.

*Enter* SILVIA.

*Val.* Madam and mistress, a thousand good-
morrows.
*Speed.* O, give you good even!—Here's a mil-
lion of manners.　　　　　　　　　　　[*Aside.*
*Sil.* Sir Valentine and servant, to you two
thousand.
*Speed.* He should give her interest, and she
gives it him.　　　　　　　　　　　　[*Aside.*
*Val.* As you enjoin'd me, I have writ your letter
Unto the secret nameless friend of yours;
Which I was much unwilling to proceed in
But for my duty to your ladyship.
*Sil.* I thank you, gentle servant; 'tis very
clerkly done.
*Val.* Now trust me, madam, it came hardly off;
For, being ignorant to whom it goes
I writ at random, very doubtfully.　　　[pains?
*Sil.* Perchance you think too much of so much
*Val.* No, madam; so it stead you, I will write,
Please you command, a thousand times as much:
And yet,—
*Sil.* A pretty period! Well, I guess the sequel;
And yet I will not name it:—and yet I care not;—
And yet take this again;—and yet I thank you;
Meaning henceforth to trouble you no more.
*Speed.* And yet you will; and yet another yet.
　　　　　　　　　　　　　　　　　　[*Aside.*

*Val.* What means your ladyship? do you not
    like it?
*Sil.* Yes, yes; the lines are very quaintly writ;
But since unwillingly, take them again;
Nay, take them.      *[Gives back the letter.*
*Val.*       Madam, they are for you.
*Sil.* Ay, ay, you writ them, sir, at my request;
But I will none of them; they are for you:
I would have had them writ more movingly.
*Val.* Please you, I'll write your ladyship an-
    other.            *[over;*
*Sil.* And when it's writ, for my sake read it
And if it please you, so; if not, why, so.
*Val.* If it please me, madam! what then?
*Sil.* Why, if it please you, take it for your
    labour.
And so good morrow, servant.    *[Exit* SILVIA.
*Speed.* O jest unseen, inscrutable, invisible,
As a nose on a man's face, or a weather-cock on
    a steeple!
My master sues to her; and she hath taught her
    suitor,
He being her pupil, to become her tutor.
O excellent device! was there ever heard a better,
That my master, being scribe, to himself should
    write the letter?
*Val.* How now, sir? what are you reasoning
with yourself?
*Speed.* Nay, I was rhyming: 'tis you that have
the reason.
*Val.* To do what?
*Speed.* To be a spokesman from Madam Silvia.
*Val.* To whom?
*Speed.* To yourself: why, she woos you by a
figure.
*Val.* What figure?
*Speed.* By a letter, I should say.
*Val.* Why, she hath not writ to me?
*Speed.* What need she when she hath made you
write to yourself? Why, do you not perceive
*Val.* No, believe me.      *[the jest?*
*Speed.* No believing you indeed, sir. But did
you perceive her earnest?
*Val.* She gave me none except an angry word.
*Speed.* Why, she hath given you a letter.
*Val.* That's the letter I writ to her friend.
*Speed.* And that letter hath she deliver'd, and
there an end.
*Val.* I would it were no worse.
*Speed.* I'll warrant you 'tis as well.
*For often you have writ to her; and she, in
    modesty,
Or else for want of idle time, could not again
    reply;
Or fearing else some messenger that might her
    mind discover,
Herself hath taught her love himself to write unto
    her lover.—*
All this I speak in print, for in print I found it.—
Why muse you, sir? 'tis dinner time.
*Val.* I have dined.
*Speed.* Ay, but hearken, sir; though the came-
leon Love can feed on the air, I am one that
am nourished by my victuals, and would fain

have meat; O, be not like your mistress; be
moved, be moved.      *[Exeunt.*

SCENE II.—VERONA. *A Room in* JULIA'S
*House.*

*Enter* PROTEUS *and* JULIA.

*Pro.* Have patience, gentle Julia.
*Jul.* I must, where is no remedy.
*Pro.* When possibly I can I will return.
*Jul.* If you turn not you will return the sooner:
Keep this remembrance for thy Julia's sake.
                *[Giving a ring.*
*Pro.* Why, then, we'll make exchange; here,
    take you this.
*Jul.* And seal the bargain with a holy kiss.
*Pro.* Here is my hand for my true constancy;
And when that hour o'erslips me in the day
Wherein I sigh not, Julia, for thy sake,
The next ensuing hour some foul mischance
Torment me for my love's forgetfulness!
My father stays my coming; answer not:
The tide is now: nay, not thy tide of tears;
That tide will stay me longer than I should:
                *[Exit* JULIA.
Julia, farewell.—What! gone without a word?
Ay; so true love should do: it cannot speak;
For truth hath better deeds than words to
    grace it.

*Enter* PANTHIO.

*Pan.* Sir Proteus, you are stay'd for.
*Pro.* Go; I come, I come:—
Alas! this parting strikes poor lovers dumb.
                *[Exeunt.*

SCENE III.—*The same. A Street.*

*Enter* LAUNCE *leading a dog.*

*Laun.* Nay, 'twill be this hour ere I have done
weeping; all the kind of the Launces have this
very fault: I have received my proportion, like
the prodigious son, and am going with Sir Proteus to the Imperial's court. I think Crab my
dog be the sourest-natured dog that lives: my
mother weeping, my father wailing, my sister
crying, our maid howling, our cat wringing her
hands, and all our house in a great perplexity;
yet did not this cruel-hearted cur shed one tear:
he is a stone, a very pebble stone, and has no
more pity in him than a dog: a Jew would have
wept to have seen our parting; why, my grandam having no eyes, look you, wept herself blind
at my parting. Nay, I'll show you the manner
of it: this shoe is my father,—no, this left shoe
is my father;—no, no, this left shoe is my
mother; nay, that cannot be so neither; yes, it
is so, it is so; it hath the worser sole. This shoe
with the hole in it is my mother, and this my
father. A vengeance on 't! there 'tis. Now, sir,
this staff is my sister; for, look you, she is as
white as a lily and as small as a wand; this hat
is Nan our maid; I am the dog:—no, the dog
is himself, and I am the dog,—O, the dog is
me, and I am myself; ay, so, so. Now come I to

my father; *Father, your blessing;*—now should
not the shoe speak a word for weeping; now
should I kiss my father; well, he weeps on:—
now come I to my mother (O, that she could
speak now!) like a wood woman;—well, I kiss
her:—why there 'tis; here's my mother's breath
up and down; now come I to my sister; mark
the moan she makes: now the dog all this while
sheds not a tear, nor speaks a word; but see
how I lay the dust with my tears.

*Enter* PANTHINO.

*Pan.* Launce, away, away aboard; thy master
is shipped, and thou art to post after with oars.
What's the matter! why weep'st thou, man?
Away, ass; you will lose the tide if you tarry
any longer.
*Laun.* It is no matter if the tied were lost; for
it is the unkindest tied that ever man tied.
*Pan.* What's the unkindest tide?          [dog.
*Laun.* Why, he that's tied here: Crab, my
*Pan.* Tut, man; I mean thou'lt lose the flood:
and, in losing the flood, lose thy voyage; and, in
losing thy voyage, lose thy master; and in los-
ing thy master, lose thy service; and, in losing
thy service,—Why dost thou stop my mouth?
*Laun.* For fear thou shouldst lose thy tongue.
*Pan.* Where should I lose my tongue?
*Laun.* In thy tale.
*Pan.* In thy tail?
*Laun.* Lose the tide, and the voyage, and the
master, and the service? The tide! Why, man,
if the river were dry, I am able to fill it with
my tears; if the wind were down, I could drive
the boat with my sighs.
*Pan.* Come, come away, man; I was sent to
call thee.
*Laun.* Sir, call me what thou darest.
*Pan.* Wilt thou go?
*Laun.* Well, I will go.          [*Exeunt.*

SCENE IV.—MILAN. *An Apartment in the*
DUKE'S *Palace.*

*Enter* VALENTINE, SILVIA, THURIO, *and* SPEED.

*Sil.* Servant—
*Val.* Mistress?
*Speed.* Master, Sir Thurio frowns on you.
*Val.* Ay, boy, it's for love.
*Speed.* Not of you.
*Val.* Of my mistress, then.
*Speed.* 'Twere good you knocked him.
*Sil.* Servant, you are sad.
*Val.* Indeed, madam, I seem so.
*Thu.* Seem you that you are not?
*Val.* Haply I do.
*Thu.* So do counterfeits.
*Val.* So do you.
*Thu.* What seem I that I am not?
*Val.* Wise.
*Thu.* What instance of the contrary?
*Val.* Your folly.
*Thu.* And how quote you my folly?
*Val.* I quote it in your jerkin.

*Thu.* My jerkin is a doublet.
*Val.* Well, then, I'll double your folly.
*Thu.* How?
*Sil.* What, angry, Sir Thurio? do you change
colour?
*Val.* Give him leave, madam: he is a kind of
cameleon.
*Thu.* That hath more mind to feed on your
blood than live in your air.
*Val.* You have said, sir.
*Thu.* Ay, sir, and done too, for this time.
*Val.* I know it well, sir; you always end ere
you begin.          [quickly shot off.
*Sil.* A fine volley of words, gentlemen, and
*Val.* 'Tis indeed, madam; we thank the giver.
*Sil.* Who is that, servant?
*Val.* Yourself, sweet lady; for you gave the fire.
Sir Thurio borrows his wit from your ladyship's
looks, and spends what he borrows kindly in
your company.
*Thu.* Sir, if you spend word for word with me,
I shall make your wit bankrupt.
*Val.* I know it well, sir; you have an exchequer
of words, and, I think, no other treasure to give
your followers; for it appears by their bare
liveries that they live by your bare words.
*Sil.* No more, gentlemen, no more; here comes
my father.

*Enter* DUKE.

*Duke.* Now, daughter Silvia, you are hard beset
Sir Valentine, your father's in good health:
What say you to a letter from your friends
Of much good news?
*Val.*          My lord, I will be thankful
To any happy messenger from thence.
*Duke.* Know you Don Antonio, your country-
man?
*Val.* Ay, my good lord; I know the gentleman
To be of worth, and worthy estimation,
And not without desert so well reputed.
*Duke.* Hath he not a son?
*Val.* Ay, my good lord; a son that well deserves
The honour and regard of such a father.
*Duke.* You know him well?
*Val.* I know him as myself; for from our infancy
We have conversed and spent our hours together:
And though myself have been an idle truant,
Omitting the sweet benefit of time
To clothe mine age with angel-like perfection,
Yet hath Sir Proteus for that's his name—
Made use and fair advantage of his days;
His years but young, but his experience old;
His head unmellow'd, but his judgment ripe;
And, in a word,—for far behind his worth
Come all the praises that I now bestow,—
He is complete in feature and in mind,
With all good grace to grace a gentleman.
*Duke.* Beshrew me, sir, but if he make this
He is as worthy for an empress' love     [good,
As meet to be an emperor's counsellor.
Well, sir; this gentleman is come to me,
With commendation from great potentates;

And here he means to spend his time awhile:
I think 'tis no unwelcome news to you.　　[he.
*Val.* Should I have wished a thing it had been
*Duke.* Welcome him, then, according to his
　　　　worth;
Silvia, I speak to you; and you, Sir Thurio:—
For Valentine, I need not 'cite him to it:
I'll send him hither to you presently.
　　　　　　　　　　[*Exit* DUKE.
*Val.* This is the gentleman I told your ladyship
Had come along with me, but that his mistress
Did hold his eyes lock'd in her crystal looks.
*Sil.* Belike that now she hath enfranchised
Upon some other pawn for fealty.　　[them
*Val.* Nay, sure, I think she holds them pris-
　　oners still.　　　　　　　　[blind,
*Sil.* Nay, then, he should be blind; and, being
How could he see his way to seek out you?
*Val.* Why, lady, love hath twenty pair of eyes.
*Thu.* They say that love hath not an eye at all.
*Val.* To see such lovers, Thurio, as yourself;
Upon a homely object love can wink.

*Enter* PROTEUS.

*Sil.* Have done, have done; here comes the
　　gentleman.　　　　　　　[seech you
*Val.* Welcome, dear Proteus!—Mistress, I be-
Confirm his welcome with some special favour
*Sil.* His worth is warrant for his welcome
　　hither,
If this be he you oft have wish'd to hear from.
*Val.* Mistress, it is: sweet lady, entertain him
To be my fellow-servant to your ladyship.
*Sil.* Too low a mistress for so high a servant.
*Pro.* Not so, sweet lady; but too mean a servant
To have a look of such a worthy mistress.
*Val.* Leave off discourse of disability:—
Sweet lady, entertain him for your servant.
*Pro.* My duty will I boast of, nothing else.
*Sil.* And duty never yet did want his meed.
Servant, you are welcome to a worthless mistress.
*Pro.* I'll die on him that says so but yourself.
*Sil.* That you are welcome?
*Pro.*　　　　　No; that you are worthless.

*Enter* Servant.

*Ser.* Madam, my lord your father would speak
　　with you.
*Sil.* I'll wait upon his pleasure. [*Exit* Servant.
　　　　　　　　Come, Sir Thurio,
Go with me.—Once more, new servant, welcome.
I'll leave you to confer of home affairs;
When you have done we look to hear from you.
*Pro.* We'll both attend upon your ladyship.
　　　　　　　　[*Exeunt* SIL., THU., *and* SPEED.
*Val.* Now, tell me, how do all from whence
　　you came?　　　　[much commended.
*Pro.* Your friends are well, and have them
*Val.* And how do yours?
*Pro.*　　　　I left them all in health.
*Val.* How does your lady? and how thrives
　　your love?
*Pro.* My tales of love were wont to weary you;
I know you joy not in a love-discourse.

*Val.* Ay, Proteus; but that life is alter'd now:
I have done penance for contemning love;
Whose high imperious thoughts have punish'd
With bitter fasts, with penitential groans, [me
With nightly tears, and daily heart-sore sighs;
For, in revenge of my contempt of love,
Love hath chased sleep from my enthralled eyes,
And made them watchers of mine own heart's
　　sorrow.
O, gentle Proteus, love's a mighty lord;
And hath so humbled me, as I confess,
There is no woe to his correction,
Nor, to his service, no such joy on earth!
Now no discourse, except it be of love;
Now can I break my fast, dine, sup, and sleep,
Upon the very naked name of love.
*Pro.* Enough; I read your fortune in your eye:
Was this the idol that you worship so?
*Val.* Even she; and is she not a heavenly saint?
*Pro.* No; but she is an earthly paragon.
*Val.* Call her divine.
*Pro.*　　　　　I will not flatter her.
*Val.* O, flatter me; for love delights in praises.
*Pro.* When I was sick you gave me bitter pills,
And I must minister the like to you.
*Val.* Then speak the truth by her; if not divine,
Yet let her be a principality,
Sovereign to all the creatures on the earth.
*Pro.* Except my mistress.
*Val.*　　　　　Sweet, except not any;
Except thou wilt except against my love.
*Pro.* Have I not reason to prefer mine own?
*Val.* And I will help thee to prefer her too:
She shall be dignified with this high honour—
To bear my lady's train, lest the base earth
Should from her vesture chance to steal a kiss,
And, of so great a favour growing proud,
Disdain to root the summer-swelling flower,
And make rough winter everlastingly.
*Pro.* Why, Valentine, what braggardism is this?
*Val.* Pardon me, Proteus: all I can is nothing
To her whose worth makes other worthies
She is alone.　　　　　　　[nothing;
*Pro.*　　　　Then let her alone.　　[own;
*Val.* Not for the world; why, man, she is mine
And I as rich in having such a jewel
As twenty seas, if all their sand were pearl,
The water nectar, and the rocks pure gold.
Forgive me that I do not dream on thee
Because thou seest me dote upon my love.
My foolish rival, that her father likes
Only for his possessions are so huge,
Is gone with her along; and I must after,
For love, thou know'st is full of jealousy.
*Pro.* But she loves you?
*Val.*　　　　　Ay, we are betroth'd:
Nay, more; our marriage hour,
With all the cunning manner of our flight,
Determined of: how I must climb her window,
The ladder made of cords; and all the means
Plotted and 'greed on for my happiness.
Good Proteus, go with me to my chamber,
In these affairs to aid me with thy counsel.
*Pro.* Go on before; I shall inquire you forth:

I must unto the road to disembark
Some necessaries that I needs must use;
And then I'll presently attend you.
*Val.* Will you make haste?
*Pro.* I will.—                          [*Exit* VAL.
Even as one heat another heat expels,
Or as one nail by strength drives out another,
So the remembrance of my former love
Is by a newer object quite forgotten.
Is it mine eye, or Valentinus' praise,
Her true perfection, or my false transgression,
That makes me, reasonless, to reason thus?
She's fair; and so is Julia that I love,—
That I did love, for now my love is thaw'd;
Which like a waxen image 'gainst a fire
Bears no impression of the thing it was.
Methinks my zeal to Valentine is cold,
And that I love him not as I was wont:
O! but I love his lady too, too much;
And that's the reason I love him so little.
How shall I dote on her with more advice,
That thus without advice begin to love her?
'Tis but her picture I have yet beheld,
And that hath dazzled my reason's light;
But when I look on her perfections,
There is no reason but I shall be blind.
If I can check my erring love, I will:
If not, to compass her I'll use my skill.  [*Exit.*

SCENE V.—*The same.  A Street.*

*Enter* SPEED *and* LAUNCE.

*Speed.* Launce! by mine honesty, welcome to
Milan.
*Laun.* Forswear not thyself, sweet youth; for
I am not welcome. I reckon this always—that
a man is never undone till he be hanged; nor
never welcome to a place till some certain shot
be paid and the hostess say, welcome.
*Speed.* Come on, you madcap; I'll to the ale-
house with you presently; where, for one shot
of fivepence, thou shalt have five thousand
welcomes. But, sirrah, how did thy master
part with Madam Julia?
*Laun.* Marry, after they closed in earnest they
parted very fairly in jest.
*Speed.* But shall she marry him?
*Laun.* No.
*Speed.* How, then? shall he marry her?
*Laun.* No; neither.
*Speed.* What! are they broken?
*Laun.* No; they are both as whole as a fish.
*Speed.* Why, then, how stands the matter with
them?
*Laun.* Marry, thus; when it stands well with
him it stands well with her.
*Speed.* What an ass art thou? I understand
thee not.
*Laun.* What a block art thou, that thou canst
not! My staff understands me.
*Speed.* What thou say'st?
*Laun.* Ay, and what I do, too; look thee, I'll
but lean, and my staff understands me.

*Speed.* It stands under thee, indeed.     [one.
*Laun.* Why, stand under and understand is all
*Speed.* But tell me true, will't be a match?
*Laun.* Ask my dog: if he say ay, it will; if he
say no, it will; if he shake his tail and say
nothing, it will.
*Speed.* The conclusion is, then, that it will.
*Laun.* Thou shalt never get such a secret from
me but by a parable.
*Speed.* 'Tis well that I get it so. But, Launce,
how say'st thou—that my master is become a
notable lover?
*Laun.* I never knew him otherwise.
*Speed.* Than how?
*Laun.* A notable lubber as thou reportest him
to be.
*Speed.* Why, thou whoreson ass, thou mistak-
est me.
*Laun.* Why, fool, I meant not thee, I meant
thy master.
*Speed.* I tell thee, my master is become a hot
lover.
*Laun.* Why, I tell thee I care not though he
burn himself in love. If thou wilt go with me to
the ale-house, so; if not, thou art an Hebrew,
a Jew, and not worth the name of a Christian.
*Speed.* Why?
*Laun.* Because thou hast not so much charity
in thee as to go to the ale with a Christian.
Wilt thou go?
*Speed.* At thy service.              [*Exeunt*

SCENE VI.—*The same.  An Apartment in
the Palace.*

*Enter* PROTEUS.

*Pro.* To leave my Julia, shall I be forsworn;
To love fair Silvia shall I be forsworn;
To wrong my friend, I shall be much forsworn;
And even that power which gave me first my oath
Provokes me to this threefold perjury.
Love bade me swear, and love bids me forswear:
O sweet-suggesting love, if thou hast sinn'd,
Teach me, thy tempted subject, to excuse it.
At first I did adore a twinkling star,
But now I worship a celestial sun.
Unheedful vows may heedfully be broken;
And he wants wit that wants resolved will
To learn his wit to exchange the bad for better.—
Fie, fie, unreverend tongue! to call her bad,
Whose sovereignty so oft thou hast preferr'd
With twenty thousand soul-confirming oaths.
I cannot leave to love, and yet I do;
But there I leave to love where I should love.
Julia I lose, and Valentine I lose:
If I keep them, I needs must lose myself;
If I lose them, thus find I by their loss,
For Valentine, myself; for Julia, Silvia.
I to myself am dearer than a friend,
For love is still more precious in itself: [fair!—
And Silvia—witness heaven, that made her
Shows Julia but a swarthy Ethiope.
I will forget that Julia is alive,
Rememb'ring that my love to her is dead;

And Valentine I'll hold an enemy,
Aiming at Silvia 'as a sweeter friend.
I cannot now prove constant to myself
Without some treachery used to Valentine:—
This night he meaneth with a corded ladder
To climb celestial Silvia's chamber-window—
Myself in counsel, his competitor:
Now presently I'll give her father notice
Of their disguising and pretended flight;
Who, all enraged, will banish Valentine;
For Thurio, he intends, shall wed his daughter:
But, Valentine being gone, I'll quickly cross,
By some sly trick, blunt Thurio's dull proceeding.
Love, lend me wings to make my purpose swift,
As thou has lent me wit to plot this drift! [*Exit*

SCENE VII.—VERONA. *A Room in* JULIA'S
*House.*

*Enter* JULIA *and* LUCETTA.

*Jul.* Counsel, Lucetta! gentle girl, assist me!
And, even in kind love, I do conjure thee,—
Who art the table wherein all my thoughts
Are visibly character'd and engraved,—
To lesson me; and tell me some good mean,
How, with my honour, I may undertake
A journey to my loving Proteus.
*Luc.* Alas! the way is wearisome and long.
*Jul.* A true-devoted pilgrim is not weary
To measure kingdoms with his feeble steps;
Much less shall she that hath love's wings to fly,
And when the flight is made to one so dear,
Of such divine perfection, as Sir Proteus.
*Luc.* Better forbear till Proteus make return.
*Jul.* O, know'st thou not his looks are my
soul's food?
Pity the dearth that I have pined in
By longing for that food so long a time.
Didst thou but know the inly touch of love,
Thou wouldst as soon go kindle fire with snow
As seek to quench the fire of love with words.
*Luc.* I do not seek to quench your love's hot
But qualify the fire's extreme rage,    [fire;
Lest it should burn above the bounds of reason.
*Jul.* The more thou damm'st it up, the more
it burns;
The current that with gentle murmur glides,
Thou know'st, being stopp'd, impatiently doth
rage;
But when his fair course is not hindered,
He makes sweet music with the enamell'd stones,
Giving a gentle kiss to every sedge
He overtaketh in his pilgrimage;
And so by many winding nooks he strays,
With willing sport, to the wild ocean.
Then let me go, and hinder not my course:
I'll be as patient as a gentle stream,
And make a pastime of each weary step,
Till the last step have brought me to my love;
And there I'll rest as, after much turmoil,
A blessed soul doth in Elysium.
*Luc.* But in what habit will you go along?
*Jul.* Not like a woman; for I would prevent
The loose encounters of lascivious men;

Gentle Lucetta, fit me with such weeds
As may beseem some well-reputed page    [hair.
*Luc.* Why, then, your ladyship must cut your
*Jul.* No, girl; I'll knit it up in silken strings,
With twenty odd-conceited true-love knots:
To be fantastic may become a youth
Of greater time than I shall show to be.
*Luc.* What fashion, madam, shall I make your
breeches?    [lord,
*Jul.* That fits as well as—"Tell me, good my
What compass will you wear your farthingale?"
Why. even that fashion thou best lik'st, Lucetta.
*Luc.* You must needs have them with a cod-
piece, madam.
*Jul.* Out, out, Lucetta! that will be ill-favour'd.
*Luc.* A round hose, madam, now's not worth
a. pin,
Unless you have a cod-piece to stick pins on.
*Jul.* Lucetta, as thou lov'st me, let me have
What thou think'st meet, and is most mannerly:
But tell me, wench, how will the world repute
For undertaking so unstaid a journey?    [me
I fear me it will make me scandaliz'd.    [not.
*Luc.* If you think so, then stay at home, and go
*Jul.* Nay, that I will not.
*Luc.* Then never dream on infamy, but go.
If Proteus like your journey when you come,
No matter who's displeas'd when you are gone:
I fear me he will scarce be pleased withal.
*Jul.* That is the least, Lucetta, of my fear:
A thousand oaths, an ocean of his tears,
And instances as infinite of love,
Warrant me welcome to my Proteus.
*Luc.* All these are servants to deceitful men.
*Jul.* Base men, that use them to so base effect!
But truer stars did govern Proteus' birth:
His words are bonds, his oaths are oracles;
His love sincere, his thoughts immaculate;
His tears pure messengers sent from his heart;
His heart as far from fraud as heaven from earth.
*Luc.* Pray heaven he prove so when you come
to him!    [wrong,
*Jul.* Now, as thou lov'st me, do him not that
To bear a hard opinion of his truth;
Only deserve my love by loving him,
And presently go with me to my chamber,
To take a note of what I stand in need of
To furnish me upon my longing journey.
All that is mine I leave at thy dispose,
My goods, my lands, my reputation;
Only, in lieu thereof, dispatch me hence:
Come, answer not, but to it presently:
I am impatient of my tarriance.    [*Exeunt.*

## ACT III.

SCENE I.—MILAN. *An Ante-room in the*
DUKE'S *Palace.*

*Enter* DUKE, THURIO, *and* PROTEUS.

*Duke.* Sir Thurio, give us leave, I pray, awhile;
We have some secrets to confer about.
[*Exit* THURIO.
Now, tell me, Proteus, what's your will with
me?

*Pro.* My gracious lord, that which I would dis-
    cover,
The law of friendship bids me to conceal;·
But, when I call to mind your gracious favours
Done to me, undeserving as I am,
My duty pricks me on to utter that    [me.
Which else no worldly good should draw from
Know, worthy prince, Sir Valentine, my friend,
This night intends to steal away your daughter;
Myself am one made privy to the plot.
I know you have determined to bestow her
On Thurio, whom your gentle daughter hates;
And should she thus be stolen away from you,
It would be much vexation to your age.
Thus, for my duty's sake, I rather chose
To cross my friend in his intended drift,
Than, by concealing it, heap on your head
A pack of sorrows, which would press you down,
Being unprevented, to your timeless grave.
*Duke.* Proteus, I thank thee for thine honest
    care;
Which to requite, command me while I live.
This love of theirs myself have often seen,
Haply when they have judged me fast asleep;
And oftentimes have purposed to forbid
Sir Valentine her company and my court:
But, fearing lest my jealous aim might err,
And so, unworthily, disgrace the man,—
A rashness that I ever yet have shunn'd,—
I gave him gentle looks; thereby to find
That which thyself hast now disclos'd to me.
And, that thou may'st perceive my fear of this,
Knowing that tender youth is soon suggested,
I nightly lodge her in an upper tower,
The key whereof myself have ever kept;
And thence she cannot be conveyed away.
*Pro.* Know, noble lord, they have devised a
    mean
How he her chamber-window will ascend,
And with a corded ladder fetch her down;
For which the youthful lover now is gone,
And this way comes he with it presently;
Where, if it please you, you may intercept him.
But, good my lord, do it so cunningly,
That my discovery be not aimed at;
For love of you, not hate unto my friend,
Hath made me publisher of this pretence.
*Duke.* Upon mine honour, he shall never know
That I had any light from thee of this.
*Pro.* Adieu, my lord; Sir Valentine is coming.
                           [*Exit.*

          *Enter* VALENTINE.

*Duke.* Sir Valentine, whither away so fast?
*Val.* Please it your grace, there is a messenger
That stays to bear my letters to my friends,
And I am going to deliver them.
*Duke.* Be they of much import?
*Val.* The tenor of them doth but signify
My health and happy being at your court.
*Duke.* Nay, then, no matter; stay with me
    awhile;
I am to break with thee of some affairs
That touch me near, wherein thou must be secret.

'Tis not unknown to thee that I have sought
To match my friend, Sir Thurio, to my daughter.
*Val.* I know it well, my lord; and, sure, the
    match          [man
Were rich and honourable; besides, the gentle-
Is full of virtue, bounty, worth, and qualities
Beseeming such a wife as your fair daughter:
Cannot your grace win her to fancy him?
*Duke.* No, trust me; she is peevish, sullen, fro-
    ward,
Proud, disobedient, stubborn, lacking duty;
Neither regarding that she is my child
Nor fearing me as if I were her father:
And, may I say to thee, this pride of hers,
Upon advice, hath drawn my love from her;
And, where I thought the remnant of mine age
Should have been cherished by her child-like
    duty,
I am now full resolved to take a wife,
And turn her out to who will take her in:
Then let her beauty be her wedding-dower;
For me and my possession she esteems not.
*Val.* What would your grace have me to do in
    this?
*Duke.* There is a lady, sir, in Milan, here,
Whom I affect; but she is nice, and coy,
And nought esteems my aged eloquence:
Now, therefore, would I have thee to my tutor,—
For long agone I have forgot to court:
Besides, the fashion of the time is chang'd;—
How and which way I may bestow myself
To be regarded in her sun-bright eye.
*Val.* Win her with gifts, if she respect not words;
Dumb jewels often, in their silent kind,
More than quick words do move a woman's mind.
*Duke.* But she did scorn a present that I sent
    her.              [tents her:
*Val.* A woman sometimes scorns what best con-
Send her another; never give her o'er;
For scorn at first makes after-love the more.
If she do frown, 'tis not in hate of you,
But rather to beget more love in you:
If she do chide, 'tis not to have you gone;
For why, the fools are mad if left alone.
Take no repulse whatever she doth say:
For, *get you gone*, she doth not mean *away:*
Flatter and praise, commend, extol their graces;
Though ne'er so black, say they have angels'
    faces.
That man that hath a tongue, I say, is no man,
If with his tongue he cannot win a woman.
*Duke.* But she I mean is promised by her friends
Unto a youthful gentleman of worth,
And kept severely from resort of men,
That no man hath access by day to her.
*Val.* Why, then, I would resort to her by night.
*Duke.* Ay, but the doors be lock'd, and keys
    kept safe,
That no man hath recourse to her by night.
*Val.* What lets but one may enter at her win-
    dow?             [ground;
*Duke.* Her chamber is aloft, far from the
And built so shelving, that one cannot climb it
Without apparent hazard of his life.

*Val.* Why, then, a ladder, quaintly made of cords,
To cast up with a pair of anchoring hooks
Would serve to scale another Hero's tower,
So bold Leander would adventure it.
*Duke.* Now, as thou art a gentleman of blood,
Advise me where I may have such a ladder.
*Val.* When would you use it? pray, sir, tell me that.
*Duke.* This very night; for love is like a child,
That longs for everything that he can come by.
*Val.* By seven o'clock I'll get you such a ladder.
*Duke.* But, hark thee; I will go to her alone;
How shall I best convey the ladder thither?
*Val.* It will be light, my lord, that you may bear it.
Under a cloak that is of any length.     [turn.
*Duke.* A cloak as long as thine will serve the
*Val.* Ay, my good lord.
*Duke.* Then let me see thy cloak:
I'll get me one of such another length.     [lord.
*Val.* Why, any cloak will serve the turn, my
*Duke.* How shall I fashion me to wear a cloak?—
I pray thee, let me feel thy cloak upon me.—
What letter is this same? What's here?—*To Silvia?*
And here an engine fit for my proceeding!
I'll be so bold to break the seal for once. [*Reads.*
*My thoughts do harbour with my Silvia nightly;*
    *And slaves they are to me, that send them flying.*
*O, could their master come and go as lightly,*
    *Himself would lodge where senseless they are*
       *lying.*
*My herald thoughts in thy pure bosom rest them,*
    *While I, their king, that thither them impor-*
       *tune,*
*Do curse the grace that with such grace hath*
    *bless'd them,*
    *Because myself do want my servants' fortune:*
*I curse myself, for they are sent by me,*
*That they should harbour where their lord should*
       *be.*
What's here?
*Silvia, this night I will enfranchise thee:*
'Tis so; and here's the ladder for the purpose.
Why, Phaeton,—for thou art Merops' son,—
Wilt thou aspire to guide the heavenly car,
And with thy daring folly burn the world?
Wilt thou reach stars because they shine on thee?
Go, base intruder! over-weening slave!
Bestow thy fawning smiles on equal mates;
And think my patience, more than thy desert,
Is privilege for thy departure hence:
Thank me for this, more than for all the favours
Which, all too much, I have bestow'd on thee.
But if thou linger in my territories
Longer than swiftest expedition
Will give thee time to leave our royal court,
By heaven, my wrath shall far exceed the love
I ever bore my daughter or thyself.
Begone, I will not hear thy vain excuse,
But, as thou lov'st thy life, make speed from
       hence.     [*Exit* DUKE.

*Val.* And why not death, rather than living torment?
To die is to be banish'd from myself;
And Silvia is myself: banish'd from her
Is self from self: a deadly banishment!
What light is light if Silvia be not seen?
What joy is joy if Silvia be not by?
Unless it be to think that she is by,
And feed upon the shadow of perfection.
Except I be by Silvia in the night
There is no music in the nightingale;
Unless I look on Silvia in the day
There is no day for me to look upon:
She is my essence; and I leave to be,
If I be not by her fair influence
Foster'd, illumined, cherish'd, kept alive.
I fly not death to fly his deadly doom:
Tarry I here I but attend on death;
But fly I hence I fly away from life.

       *Enter* PROTEUS *and* LAUNCE.

*Pro.* Run, boy, run, run, and seek him out.
*Laun.* So-ho! so-ho!
*Pro.* What seest thou?
*Laun.* Him we go to find: there's not a hair on's head but 'tis a Valentine.
*Pro.* Valentine?
*Val.* No.
*Pro.* Who then? his spirit?
*Val.* Neither.
*Pro.* What then?
*Val.* Nothing.
*Laun.* Can nothing speak? master, shall I strike?
*Pro.* Whom wouldst thou strike?
*Laun.* Nothing.
*Pro.* Villain, forbear.
*Laun.* Why, sir, I'll strike nothing: I pray     [you,—
*Pro.* Sirrah, I say, forbear: Friend Valentine,
       a word.     [good news
*Val.* My ears are stopp'd, and cannot hear
So much of bad already hath possess'd them.
*Pro.* Then in dumb silence will I bury mine,
For they are harsh, untuneable, and bad.
*Val.* Is Silvia dead?
*Pro.* No, Valentine.
*Val.* No Valentine, indeed, for sacred Silvia!—
Hath she forsworn me?
*Pro.* No, Valentine.     [me!—
*Val.* No Valentine, if Silvia have forsworn
What is your news?
*Laun.* Sir, there's a proclamation that you are
       vanish'd.     [news;
*Pro.* That thou art banished; O, that's the
From hence, from Silvia, and from me thy friend.
*Val.* O, I have fed upon this woe already,
And now excess of it will make me surfeit.
Doth Silvia know that I am banished?
*Pro.* Ay, ay; and she hath offer'd to the doom,—
Which unreversed, stands in effectual force,—
A sea of melting pearl, which some call tears:
Those at her father's churlish feet she tender'd,
With them, upon her knees, her humble self;
Wringing her hands, whose whiteness so became them,

As if but now they waxed pale for woe:
But neither bended knees, pure hands held up,
Sad sighs, deep groans, nor silver-shedding tears,
Could penetrate her uncompassionate sire;
But Valentine, if he be ta'en, must die.
Besides, her intercession chafed him so,
When she for thy repeal was suppliant,
That to close prison he commanded her,
With many bitter threats of 'biding there.
*Val.* No more; unless the next word that thou
    speak'st
Have some malignant power upon my life:
If so, I pray thee, breathe it in mine ear,
As ending anthem of my endless dolour. [help,
*Pro.* Cease to lament for that thou canst not
And study help for that which thou lament'st.
Time is the nurse and breeder of all good.
Here if thou stay thou canst not see thy love;
Besides, thy staying will abridge thy life.
Hope is a lover's staff; walk hence with that,
And manage it against despairing thoughts.
Thy letters may be here though thou art hence:
Which, being writ to me, shall be deliver'd
Even in the milk-white bosom of thy love.
The time now serves not to expostulate:
Come, I'll convey thee through the city gate;
And, ere I part with thee, confer at large
Of all that may concern thy love affairs:
As thou lov'st Silvia, though not for thyself,
Regard thy danger, and along with me.
*Val.* I pray thee, Launce, an if thou seest my
    boy,                    [gate.
Bid him make haste and meet me at the north
*Pro.* Go, sirrah, find him out. Come, Valentine.
*Val.* O my dear Silvia, hapless Valentine!
                    [*Exeunt* VAL. *and* PRO.
*Laun.* I am but a fool, look you; and yet I
have the wit to think my master is a kind of
knave: but that's all one if he be but one knave.
He lives not now that knows me to be in love:
yet I am in love; but a team of horse shall not
pluck that from me; nor who 'tis I love, and
yet 'tis a woman: but what woman I will not
tell myself; and yet 'tis a milkmaid; yet 'tis
not a maid, for she hath had gossips: yet 'tis a
maid, for she is her master's maid, and serves
for wages. She hath more qualities than a
water-spaniel,—which is much in a bare Christian. Here is the cat-log [*Pulling out a paper*]
of her conditions. Imprimis, *She can fetch and
carry.* Why, a horse can do no more: nay, a
horse cannot fetch, but only carry; therefore is
she better than a jade. Item, *She can milk;*
look you, a sweet virtue in a maid with clean
hands.

*Enter* SPEED.

*Speed.* How now, Signior Launce? what news
with your mastership?
*Laun.* With my master's ship? why, it is at sea.
*Speed.* Well, your old vice still; mistake the
    word.
What news, then, in your paper?    [heard'st.
*Laun.* The blackest news that ever thou

*Speed.* Why, man, how black?
*Laun.* Why, as black as ink.
*Speed.* Let me read them.                    [read.
*Laun.* Fie on thee, jolthead; thou canst not
*Speed.* Thou liest, I can.
*Laun.* I will try thee: Tell me this: Who begot
    thee?
*Speed.* Marry, the son of my grandfather.
*Laun.* O illiterate loiterer! it was the son of
thy grandmother: this proves that thou canst
not read.
*Speed.* Come, fool, come: try me in thy paper.
*Laun.* There; and St. Nicholas be thy speed!
*Speed.* Imprimis, *She can milk.*
*Laun.* Ay, that she can.
*Speed.* Item, *She brews good ale.*
*Laun.* And thereof comes the proverb,—Bless-
ing of your heart, you brew good ale.
*Speed.* Item, *She can sew.*
*Laun.* That's as much as to say, can she so?
*Speed.* Item, *She can knit.*
*Laun.* What need a man care for a stock with
a wench, when she can knit him a stock.
*Speed.* Item, *She can wash and scour.*
*Laun.* A special virtue; for then she need not
be washed and scoured.
*Speed.* Item, *She can spin.*
*Laun.* Then may I set the world on wheels,
when she can spin for her living.
*Speed.* Item, *She hath many nameless virtues.*
*Laun.* That's as much as to say, bastard vir-
tues; that, indeed, know not their fathers, and
therefore have no names.
*Speed.* Here follow her vices.
*Laun.* Close at the heels of her virtues.
*Speed.* Item, *She is not to be kissed fasting, in
respect of her breath.*
*Laun.* Well, that fault may be mended with a
breakfast. Read on.
*Speed.* Item, *She hath a sweet mouth.*
*Laun.* That makes amends for her sour breath.
*Speed.* Item, *She doth talk in her sleep.*
*Laun.* It's no matter for that, so she sleep not
in her talk.
*Speed.* Item, *She is slow in words.*
*Laun.* O villain, that set this down among her
vices! To be slow in words is a woman's only
virtue: I pray thee, out with't; and place it
for her chief virtue.
*Speed.* Item, *She is proud.*
*Laun.* Out with that too; it was Eve's legacy,
and cannot be ta'en from her.
*Speed.* Item, *She hath no teeth.*
*Laun.* I care not for that neither, because I
love crusts.
*Speed.* Item, *She is curst.*
*Laun.* Well; the best is, she hath no teeth to
bite.
*Speed.* Item, *She will often praise her liquor.*
*Laun.* If her liquor be good, she shall: if she
will not, I will; for good things should be praised.
*Speed.* Item, *She is too liberal.*
*Laun.* Of her tongue she cannot; for that's
writ down she is slow of: of her purse she shall

not; for that I'll keep shut: now of another thing she may; and that I cannot help. Well, proceed.

*Speed.* Item, *She hath more hair than wit, and more faults than hairs, and more wealth than faults.*

*Laun.* Stop there; I'll have her: she was mine, and not mine, twice or thrice in that last article. Rehearse that once more.

*Speed.* Item, *She hath more hair than wit,—*

*Laun.* More hair than wit,—it may be; I'll prove it: The cover of the salt hides the salt, and therefore it is more than the salt; the hair that covers the wit is more than the wit; for the greater hides the less. What's next?

*Speed.—And more faults than hairs,—*

*Laun.* That's monstrous: O, that that were out!

*Speed.—And more wealth than faults.*

*Laun.* Why, that word makes the faults gracious. Well, I'll have her: and if it be a match, as nothing is impossible.

*Speed.* What then?

*Laun.* Why, then will I tell thee,—that thy master stays for thee at the north gate.

*Speed.* For me?

*Laun.* For thee? ay: who art thou? he hath stay'd for a better man than thee.

*Speed.* And must I go to him?

*Laun.* Thou must run to him, for thou hast stay'd so long that going will scarce serve the turn.

*Speed.* Why didst not tell me sooner? 'pox of your love-letters!                    [*Exit.*

*Laun.* Now will he be swinged for reading my letter. An unmannerly slave that will thrust himself into secrets!—I'll after, to rejoice in the boy's correction.                    [*Exit.*

SCENE II.—*The same.  A Room in the Duke's Palace.*

Enter DUKE and THURIO; PROTEUS *behind.*

*Duke.* Sir Thurio, fear not but that she will love you
Now Valentine is banish'd from her sight.

*Thu.* Since his exile she hath despised me most,
Forsworn my company and rail'd at me,
That I am desperate of obtaining her.

*Duke.* This weak impress of love is as a figure
Trenched in ice; which with an hour's heat
Dissolves to water and doth lose his form.
A little time will melt her frozen thoughts,
And worthless Valentine shall be forgot.—
How now, Sir Proteus? Is your countryman,
According to our proclamation, gone?

*Pro.* Gone, my good lord.

*Duke.* My daughter takes his going grievously.

*Pro.* A little time, my lord, will kill that grief.

*Duke.* So I believe; but Thurio thinks not so.—
Proteus, the good conceit I hold of thee,—
For thou hast shown some sign of good desert,—
Makes me the better to confer with thee.

*Pro.* Longer than I prove loyal to your grace,
Let me not live to look upon your grace.

*Duke.* Thou know'st, how willingly I would effect

The match between Sir Thurio and my daughter.

*Pro.* I do, my lord.

*Duke.* And also I think, thou art not ignorant
How she opposes her against my will.

*Pro.* She did, my lord, when Valentine was here.

*Duke.* Ay, and perversely she persévers so.
What might we do to make the girl forget
The love of Valentine and love Sir Thurio?

*Pro.* The best way is to slander Valentine
With falsehood, cowardice, and poor descent;
Three things that women highly hold in hate.

*Duke.* Ay, but she'll think that it is spoke in hate.

*Pro.* Ay, if his enemy deliver it:
Therefore it must, with circumstance, be spoken
by one whom she esteemeth as his friend. [him.

*Duke.* Then you must undertake to slander

*Pro.* And that, my lord, I shall be loth to do:
'Tis an ill office for a gentleman;
Especially against his very friend.    [tage him

*Duke.* Where your good word cannot advan-
Your slander never can endamage him;
Therefore, the office is indifferent,
Being entreated to it by your friend.          [it

*Pro.* You have prevail'd, my lord: if I can do it
By aught that I can speak in his dispraise,
She shall not long continue love to him.
But say this weed her love from Valentine,
It follows not that she will love Sir Thurio.

*Thu.* Therefore, as you unwind her love from him,
Lest it should ravel, and be good to none,
You must provide to bottom it on me:
Which must be done by praising me as much
As you in worth dispraise Sir Valentine.

*Duke.* And, Proteus, we dare trust you in this kind;
Because we know, on Valentine's report,
You are already love's firm votary,
And cannot soon revolt and change your mind.
Upon this warrant shall you have access
Where you with Silvia may confer at large;
For she is lumpish, heavy, melancholy,
And, for your friend's sake, will be glad of you;
Where you may temper her by your persuasion
To hate young Valentine and love my friend.

*Pro.* As much as I can do I will effect:—
But you, Sir Thurio, are not sharp enough;
You must lay lime to tangle her desires
By wailful sonnets, whose composed rhymes
Should be full fraught with serviceable vows.

*Duke.* Ay, much the force of heaven-bred poesy.

*Pro.* Say that upon the altar of her beauty
You sacrifice your tears, your sighs, your heart;
Write till your ink be dry; and with your tears
Moist it again; and frame some feeling line
That may discover such integrity:
For Orpheus' lute was strung with poets' sinews;
Whose golden touch could soften steel and stones,
Make tigers tame and huge leviathans
Forsake unsounded deeps to dance on sands.
After your dire lamenting elegies,

Visit by night your lady's chamber-window
With some sweet concert: to their instruments
Tune a deploring dump; the night's dead silence
Will well become such sweet complaining griev-
    ance.
This, or else nothing, will inherit her.
*Duke.* This discipline shows thou hast been in
    love.                                        [tice:
*Thu.* And thy advice this night I'll put in prac-
Therefore, sweet Proteus, my direction-giver,
Let us into the city presently
To sort some gentlemen well skill'd in music:
I have a sonnet that will serve the turn
To give the onset to thy good advice.
*Duke.* About it, gentlemen.                     [per;
*Pro.* We'll wait upon your grace till after sup-
And afterward determine our proceedings.
*Duke.* Even now about it; I will pardon you.
                                            [*Exeunt.*

### ACT IV.

#### SCENE I.—*A Forest near* MANTUA.

##### *Enter certain* Outlaws.

1 *Out.* Fellows, stand fast; I see a passenger.
2 *Out.* If there be ten, shrink not, but down
    with 'em.

##### *Enter* VALENTINE *and* SPEED.

3 *Out.* Stand, sir, and throw us that you have
    about you;
If not, we'll make you sit, and rifle you.
*Speed.* Sir, we are undone! these are the villains
That all the travellers do fear so much.
*Val.* My friends,—
1 *Out.* That's not so, sir; we are your enemies.
2 *Out.* Peace; we'll hear him.
3 *Out.* Ay, by my beard, will we;
For he's a proper man.                           [lose;
*Val.* Then know that I have little wealth to
A man I am crossed with adversity;
My riches are these poor habiliments,
Of which if you should here disfurnish me,
You take the sum and substance that I have.
2 *Out.* Whither travel you?
*Val.* To Verona.
1 *Out.* Whence came you?
*Val.* From Milan.
3 *Out.* Have you long sojourn'd there?
*Val.* Some sixteen months; and longer might
    have stay'd
If crooked fortune had not thwarted me.
1 *Out.* What! were you banish'd thence?
*Val.* I was.
2 *Out.* For what offence?                       [hearse;
*Val.* For that which now torments me to re-
I kill'd a man, whose death I much repent;
But yet I slew him manfully in fight,
Without false vantage or base treachery.
1 *Out.* Why, ne'er repent it, if it were done so.
But were you banish'd for so small a fault?
*Val.* I was, and held me glad of such a doom.
2 *Out.* Have you the tongues?                   [happy;
*Val.* My youthful travel therein made me

Or else I often had been miserable.             [friar,
3 *Out.* By the bare scalp of Robin Hood's fat
This fellow were a king for our wild faction.
1 *Out.* We'll have him; sirs, a word.
*Speed.*                Master, be one of them;
It is an honourable kind of thievery.
*Val.* Peace, villain!                           [to?
2 *Out.* Tell us this. Have you anything to take
*Val.* Nothing but my fortune.                   [men;
3 *Out.* Know, then, that some of us are gentle-
Such as the fury of ungovern'd youth
Thrust from the company of lawful men:
Myself was from Verona banish'd
For practising to steal away a lady,
An heir, and near allied unto the duke.
2 *Out.* And I from Mantua, for a gentleman,
Whom, in my mood, I stabb'd unto the heart.
1 *Out.* And I for such like petty crimes as these.
But to the purpose,—for we cite our faults
That they may hold excused our lawless lives,—
And, partly, seeing you are beautified
With goodly shape, and by your own report
A linguist, and a man of such perfection
As we do in our quality much want;—
2 *Out.* Indeed, because you are a banish'd man,
Therefore, above the rest, we parley to you.
Are you content to be our general?
To make a virtue of necessity,
And live, as we do, in this wilderness?
3 *Out.* What say'st thou? wilt thou be of our
    consórt?
Say ay, and be the captain of us all:
We'll do thee homage, and be ruled by thee,
Love thee as our commander and our king.
1 *Out.* But if thou scorn our courtesy thou
    diest.                                       [offer'd.
2 *Out.* Thou shalt not live to brag what we have
*Val.* I take your offer, and will live with you,
Provided that you do no outrages
On silly women or poor passengers.
3 *Out.* No; we detest such vile base practices.
Come, go with us, we'll bring thee to our crews,
And show thee all the treasure we have got;
Which, with ourselves, all rest at thy dispose.
                                            [*Exeunt.*

#### SCENE II.—MILAN. *Court of the Palace.*

##### *Enter* PROTEUS.

*Pro.* Already have I been false to Valentine,
And now I must be as unjust to Thurio.
Under the colour of commending him
I have access my own love to prefer;
But Silvia is too fair, too true, too holy,
To be corrupted with my worthless gifts.
When I protest true loyalty to her
She twits me with my falsehood to my friend:
When to her beauty I commend my vows
She bids me think how I have been forsworn
In breaking faith with Julia whom I loved:
And, notwithstanding all her sudden quips,
The least whereof would quell a lover's hope,
Yet, spaniel-like, the more she spurns my love
The more it grows, and fawneth on her still.

But here comes Thurio: now must we to her window,
And give some evening music to her ear.

*Enter* THURIO *and Musicians.*

*Thu.* How now, Sir Proteus? are you crept before us?
*Pro.* Ay, gentle Thurio; for you know that love
Will creep in service where it cannot go. [here.
*Thu.* Ay, but I hope, sir, that you love not
*Pro.* Sir, but I do; or else I would be hence.
*Thu.* Whom? Silvia?
*Pro.* Ay, Silvia—for your sake. [men,
*Thu.* I thank you for your own. Now, gentle-
Let's tune, and to it lustily awhile.

*Enter* HOST, *at a distance; and* JULIA, *in boy's clothes.*

*Host.* Now, my young guest! methinks you're allycholly; I pray you, why is it?
*Jul.* Marry, mine host, because I cannot be merry.
*Host.* Come, we'll have you merry: I'll bring you where you shall hear music, and see the gentleman that you ask'd for.
*Jul.* But shall I hear him speak?
*Host.* Ay, that you shall.
*Jul.* That will be music. [*Music plays.*
*Host.* Hark! Hark!
*Jul.* Is he among these?
*Host.* Ay; but peace, let's hear 'em.

SONG.

Who is Silvia? what is she,
  That all our swains commend her?
Holy, fair, and wise is she,
  The heavens such grace did lend her,
  That she might admired be.

Is she kind as she is fair?
  For beauty lives with kindness:
Love doth to her eyes repair,
  To help him of his blindness;
And, being help'd, inhabits there.

Then to Silvia, let us sing,
  That Silvia is excelling;
She excels each mortal thing
  Upon the dull earth dwelling.
To her let us garlands bring.

*Host.* How now? are you sadder than you were before?
How ao you, man! the music likes you not.
*Jul.* You mistake; the musician likes me not.
*Host.* Why, my pretty youth?
*Jul.* He plays false, father.
*Host.* How! out of tune on the strings?
*Jul.* Not so; but yet so false that he grieves my very heart-strings.
*Host.* You have a quick ear.
*Jul.* Ay, I would I were deaf! it makes me have a slow heart.
*Host.* I perceive you delight not in music.
*Jul.* Not a whit, when it jars so.
*Host.* Hark, what fine change is in the music.

*Jul.* Ay; that change is the spite.
*Host.* You would have them always play but one thing? [thing.
*Jul.* I would always have one play but one
But, host, doth this Sir Proteus, that we talk on, often resort unto this gentlewoman?
*Host.* I'll tell you what, Launce, his man, told me he loved her out of all nick.
*Jul.* Where is Launce?
*Host.* Gone to seek his dog; which, tomorrow, by his master's command, he must carry for a present to his lady.
*Jul.* Peace! stand aside! the company parts.
*Pro.* Sir Thurio, fear not you! I will so plead
That you shall say my cunning drift excels.
*Thu.* Where meet we?
*Pro.* At Saint Gregory's well.
*Thu.* Farewell.

[*Exeunt* THURIO *and Musicians.*

SILVIA *appears above, at her window.*

*Pro.* Madam, good even to your ladyship.
*Sil.* I thank you for your music, gentlemen:
Who is that that spake? [truth,
*Pro.* One, lady, if you knew his pure heart's
You'd quickly learn to know him by his voice.
*Sil.* Sir Proteus, as I take it. [vant.
*Pro.* Sir Proteus, gentle lady, and your ser-
*Sil.* What is your will?
*Pro.* That I may compass yours.
*Sil.* You have your wish; my will is even this,—
That presently you hie you home to bed,
Thou subtle, perjured, false, disloyal man!
Think'st thou I am so shallow, so conceitless,
To be seducèd by thy flattery,
That hast deceived so many with thy vows?
Return, return, and make thy love amends.
For me,—by this pale queen of night I swear
I am so far from granting thy request
That I despise thee for thy wrongful suit,
And by and by intend to chide myself
Even for this time I spend in talking to thee.
*Pro.* I grant, sweet love, that I did love a lady;
But she is dead.
*Jul.* 'Twere false if I should speak it;
For I am sure she is not buried. [*Aside.*
*Sil.* Say that she be; yet Valentine, thy friend,
Survives; to whom, thyself art witness,
I am betrothed. And art thou not ashamed
To wrong him with thy importunacy?
*Pro.* I likewise hear that Valentine is dead.
*Sil.* And so suppose am I; for in his grave
Assure thyself my love is buried.
*Pro.* Sweet lady, let me rake it from the earth.
*Sil.* Go to thy lady's grave, and call hers thence;
Or, at the least, in hers sepulchre thine.
*Jul.* He heard not that. [*Aside.*
*Pro.* Madam, if your heart be so obdúrate,
Vouchsafe me yet your picture for my love;
The picture that is hanging in your chamber;
To that I'll speak, to that I'll sigh and weep:
For, since the substance of your perfect self
Is else devoted, I am but a shadow:
And to your shadow I will make true love.

*Jul.* If 'twere a substance, you would, sure, de-
　　ceive it,
And make it but a shadow, as I am.　　[*Aside.*
*Sil.* I am very loth to be your idol, sir;
But, since your falsehood shall become you well
To worship shadows and adore false shapes,
Send to me in the morning, and I'll send it:
And so, good rest.
*Pro.*　　　　　As wretches have o'er-night,
That wait for execution in the morn.
　　　　　[*Exeunt* PRO.; *and* SIL., *from above.*
*Jul.* Host, will you go?
*Host.* By my hallidom, I was fast asleep.
*Jul.* Pray you, where lies Sir Proteus?
*Host.* Marry, at my house. Trust me, I think
'tis almost day.
*Jul.* Not so; but it hath been the longest night
That e'er I watch'd, and the most heaviest.
　　　　　　　　　　　　[*Exeunt.*

### SCENE III.—*The same.*

#### Enter EGLAMOUR.

*Egl.* This is the hour that Madam Silvia
Entreated me to call and know her mind;
There's some great matter she'd employ me
Madam, madam!　　　　　　　　[*in.*—

#### SILVIA *appears above, at her window.*

*Sil.* Who calls?
*Egl.*　　　　Your servant and your friend;
One that attends your ladyship's command.
*Sil.* Sir Eglamour, a thousand times good mor-
　　row.
*Egl.* As many, worthy lady, to yourself.
According to your ladyship's impose,
I am thus early come to know what service
It is your pleasure to command me in.
*Sil.* O Eglamour, thou art a gentleman,—
Think not I flatter, for I swear I do not,—
Valiant, wise, remorseful, well accomplish'd.
Thou art not ignorant what dear good will
I bear unto the banish'd Valentine;
Nor how my father would enforce me marry
Vain Thurio, whom my very soul abhorr'd.
Thyself hast loved; and I have heard thee say
No grief did ever come so near thy heart
As when thy lady and thy true love died,
Upon whose grave thou vow'dst pure chastity.
Sir Eglamour, I would to Valentine,
To Mantua, where, I hear, he makes abode;
And, for the ways are dangerous to pass,
I do desire thy worthy company,
Upon whose faith and honour I repose.
Urge not my father's anger, Eglamour,
But think upon my grief, a lady's grief;
And on the justice of my flying hence.
To keep me from a most unholy match,
Which heaven and fortune still reward with
I do desire thee, even from a heart　　[plagues.
As full of sorrows as the sea of sands,
To bear me company, and go with me:
If not, to hide what I have said to thee,
That I may venture to depart alone.
*Egl.* Madam, I pity much your grievances;

Which, since I know they virtuously are placed,
I give consent to go along with you;
Recking as little what betideth me
As much I wish all good befortune you.
When will you go?
*Sil.*　　　　　　　This evening coming.
*Egl.* Where shall I meet you?
*Sil.*　　　　　　　At Friar Patrick's cell,
Where I intend holy confession.
*Egl.* I will not fail your ladyship:
Good morrow, gentle lady.
*Sil.* Good morrow, kind Sir Eglamour.
　　　　　　　　　　　　[*Exeunt.*

### SCENE IV.—*The same.*

#### Enter LAUNCE, *with his dog.*

*Laun.* When a man's servant shall play the
cur with him, look you, it goes hard: one that
I brought up of a puppy: one that I saved from
drowning, when three or four of his blind
brothers and sisters went to it! I have taught
him—even as one would say precisely, Thus I
would teach a dog. I was sent to deliver him
as a present to Mistress Silvia from my master;
and I came no sooner into the dining-chamber
but he steps me to her trencher and steals her
capon's leg. O, 'tis a foul thing when a cur
cannot keep himself in all companies! I would
have, as one should say, one that takes upon
him to be a dog indeed, to be, as it were, a dog
at all things. If I had not had more wit than
he, to take a fault upon me that he did, I think
verily he had been hang'd for't; sure as I live
he had suffer'd for't; you shall judge. He
thrusts me himself into the company of three
or four gentleman-like dogs under the duke's
table: he had not been there—bless the mark—
a pissing while, but all the chamber smelt him.
*Out with the dog,* says one; *What cur is that?*
says another; *Whip him out,* says a third;
*Hang him up,* says the duke. I, having been
acquainted with the smell before, knew it was
Crab; and goes me to the fellow that whips
the dogs: *Friend,* quoth I, *you mean to whip
the dog? Ay, marry do I,* quoth he. *You do him
the more wrong,* quoth I; *'twas I did the thing
you wot of.* He makes me no more ado, but
whips me out of the chamber. How many masters would do this for their servant? Nay, I'll
be sworn, I have sat in the stocks for puddings
he hath stolen, otherwise he had been executed: I have stood on the pillory for geese he
hath killed, otherwise he had suffer'd for't:
thou thinkest not of this now!—Nay, I remember the trick you served me when I took my
leave of Madam Silvia; did not I bid thee still
mark me and do as I do? When didst thou see
me heave up my leg and make water against
a gentlewomen's farthingale? didst thou ever
see me do such a trick?

#### Enter PROTEUS *and* JULIA.

*Pro.* Sebastian is thy name? I like thee well,
And will employ thee in some service presently.

*Jul.* In what you please;—I will do what I can.
*Pro.* I hope thou wilt.—How now, you whore-
son peasant?                    [*To* LAUNCE.
Where have you been these two days loitering?
*Laun.* Marry, sir, I carried Mistress Silvia the
dog you bade me.
*Pro.* And what says she to my little jewel?
*Laun.* Marry, she says your dog was a cur;
and tells you currish thanks is good enough for
such a present.
*Pro.* But she received my dog?
*Laun.* No, indeed, she did not; here have I
brought him back again.
*Pro.* What! didst thou offer her this from me?
*Laun.* Ay, sir; the other squirrel was stolen
from me by the hangman's boys in the market-
place: and then I offer'd her mine own; who
is a dog as big as ten of yours, and therefore
the gift the greater.
*Pro.* Go, get thee hence and find my dog again,
Or ne'er return again into my sight.
Away, I say. Stay'st thou to vex me here?
A slave, that still an end turns me to shame.
                              [*Exit* LAUNCE.
Sebastian, I have entertain'd thee,
Partly that I have need of such a youth
That can with some discretion do my business,
For 'tis no trusting to yond foolish lout;
But, chiefly, for thy face and thy behaviour,
Which—if my augury deceive me not—
Witness good bringing up, fortune, and truth:
Therefore, know thou, for this I entertain thee.
Go presently, and take this ring with thee,
Deliver it to Madam Silvia:
She loved me well deliver'd it to me.
*Jul.* It seems you loved not her, to leave her
          token:
She's dead, belike.
*Pro.*              Not so: I think she lives.
*Jul.* Alas!
*Pro.* Why dost thou cry, Alas!
*Jul.* I cannot choose but pity her.
*Pro.* Wherefore shouldst thou pity her?
*Jul.* Because, methinks, that she loved you as
          well
As you do love your lady Silvia:
She dreams on him that has forgot her love;
You dote on her that cares not for your love.
'Tis pity love should be so contrary;
And thinking on it makes me cry, Alas!
*Pro.* Well, give her that ring, and therewithal
This letter;—that's her chamber.—Tell my lady
I claim the promise for her heavenly picture.
Your message done, hie home unto my chamber,
Where thou shalt find me sad and solitary.
                              [*Exit* PROTEUS.
*Jul.* How many women would do such a mes-
          sage?
Alas, poor Proteus! thou hast entertain'd
A fox to be the shepherd of thy lambs;
Alas, poor fool! why do I pity him
That with his very heart despiseth me?
Because he loves her, he despiseth me;
Because I love him, I must pity him.

This ring I gave him, when he parted from me,
To bind him to remember my good will:
And now am I—unhappy messenger—
To plead for that which I would not obtain;
To carry that which I would have refused;
To praise his faith, which I would have dispraised.
I am my master's true confirmèd love,
But cannot be true servant to my master
Unless I prove false traitor to myself.
Yet will I woo for him; but yet so coldly
As, heaven it knows, I would not have him speed.

                  *Enter* SILVIA, *attended*

Gentlewoman, good day! I pray you, be my mean
To bring me where to speak with Madam Silvia.
*Sil.* What would you with her if that I be she?
*Jul.* If you be she I do entreat your patience
To hear me speak the message I am sent on.
*Sil.* From whom?
*Jul.* From my master, Sir Proteus, madam.
*Sil.* Oh!—he sends you for a picture?
*Jul.* Ay, madam.
*Sil.* Ursula, bring my picture there.
                              [*Picture brought.*
Go, give your master this: tell him from me,
One Julia, that his changing thoughts forget,
Would better fit his chamber than this shadow.
*Jul.* Madam, please you peruse this letter.
Pardon me, madam; I have unadvised
Delivered you a paper that I should not.
This is the letter to your ladyship.
*Sil.* I pray thee, let me look on that again.
*Jul.* It may not be; good madam, pardon me.
*Sil.* There, hold.
I will not look upon your master's lines:
I know they are stuff'd with protestations,
And full of new-found oaths; which he will break
As easily as I do tear his paper.
*Jul.* Madam, he sends your ladyship this ring.
*Sil.* The more shame for him that he sends it
          me;
For I have heard him say a thousand times
His Julia gave it him at his departure:
Though his false finger have profaned the ring,
Mine shall not do his Julia so much wrong.
*Jul.* She thanks you.
*Sil.* What say'st thou?
*Jul.* I thank you, madam, that you tender her:
Poor gentlewoman! my master wrongs her much.
*Sil.* Dost thou know her?
*Jul.* Almost as well as I do know myself:
To think upon her woes, I do protest,
That I have wept an hundred several times.
*Sil.* Belike she thinks that Proteus hath for-
          sook her.                    [sorrow.
*Jul.* I think she doth, and that's her cause of
*Sil.* Is she not passing fair?
*Jul.* She hath been fairer, madam, than she is:
When she did think my master loved her well,
She, in my judgment, was as fair as you;
But since she did neglect her looking-glass,
And threw her sun-expelling mask away,
The air hath starv'd the roses in her cheeks,
And pinch'd the lily-tincture of her face,

That now she is become as black as I.
*Sil.* How tall was she?
*Jul.* About my stature: for at Pentecost,
When all our pageants of delight were play'd,
Our youth got me to play the woman's part,
And I was trimm'd in Madam Julia's gown;
Which serv'd me as fit, by all men's judgment,
As if the garment had been made for me:
Therefore, I know she is about my height.
And at that time I made her weep a-good,
For I did play a lamentable part;
Madam, 'twas Ariadne, passioning
For Theseus' perjury and unjust flight;
Which I so lively acted with my tears
That my poor mistress, moved therewithal,
Wept bitterly; and would I might be dead
It I in thought felt not her very sorrow!
*Sil.* She is beholden to thee, gentle youth!—
Alas, poor lady! desolate and left!—
I weep myself, to think upon thy words.
Here, youth, there is my purse: I give thee this
For thy sweet mistress' sake, because thou
          lov'st her.
Farewell.                          [*Exit* SILVIA.
*Jul.* And she shall thank you for 't if e'er you
          know her.
A virtuous gentlewoman, mild and beautiful.
I hope my master's suit will be but cold,
Since she respects my mistress' love so much.
Alas, how love can trifle with itself!
Here is her picture.  Let me see; I think,
If I had such a tire, this face of mine
Were full as lovely as is this of hers:
And yet the painter flatter'd her a little,
Unless I flatter with myself too much.
Her hair is auburn, mine is perfect yellow:
It that be all the difference in his love,
I'll get me such a colour'd periwig.
Her eyes are grey as glass; and so are mine:
Ay, but her forehead's low, and mine's as high.
What should it be that he respects in her
But I can make respective in myself,
If this fond love were not a blinded god?
Come, shadow, come, and take this shadow up,
For 'tis thy rival. O thou senseless form,
Thou shalt be worshipp'd, kiss'd, lov'd, and
          ador'd;
And were there sense in his idolatry
My substance should be statue in thy stead.
I'll use thee kindly for thy mistress' sake,
That used me so; or else, by Jove I vow,
I should have scratch'd out your unseeing eyes,
To make my master out of love with thee.
                                   [*Exit.*

## ACT V.

SCENE I.—*The same.  An Abbey.*

*Enter* EGLAMOUR.

*Egl.* The sun begins to gild the western sky:
And now it is about the very hour
That Silvia at Patrick's cell should meet me.
She will not fail; for lovers break not hours,

Unless it be to come before their time;
So much they spur their expedition.

*Enter* SILVIA.

See where she comes: Lady, a happy evening!
*Sil.* Amen, amen! go on, good Eglamour!
Out at the postern by the abbey wall;
I fear I am attended by some spies.
*Egl.* Fear not: the forest is not three leagues off!
If we recover that, we are sure enough.
                                   [*Exeunt.*

SCENE II.—*The same.  An Apartment in the*
          DUKE'S *Palace.*

*Enter* THURIO, PROTEUS, *and* JULIA.

*Thu.* Sir Proteus, what says Silvia to my suit?
*Pro.* O, sir, I find her milder than she was;
And yet she takes exceptions at your person.
*Thu.* What! that my leg is too long?
*Pro.* No; that it is too little.          [rounder.
*Thu.* I'll wear a boot to make it somewhat
*Pro.* But love will not be spurr'd to what it
          loaths.
*Thu.* What says she to my face?
*Pro.* She says it is a fair one.          [black.
*Thu.* Nay, then, the wanton lies; my face is
*Pro.* But pearls are fair; and the old saying is,
Black men are pearls in beauteous ladies' eyes.
*Jul.* 'Tis true, such pearls as put out ladies'
          eyes;
For I had rather wink than look on them.
                                   [*Aside.*
*Thu.* How likes she my discourse?
*Pro.* Ill when you talk of war.          [peace?
*Thu.* But well when I discourse of love and
*Jul.* But better, indeed, when you hold your
          peace.                          [*Aside.*
*Thu.* What says she to my valour?
*Pro.* O, sir, she makes no doubt of that.
*Jul.* She needs not, when she knows it cow-
          ardice.                          [*Aside.*
*Thu.* What says she to my birth?
*Pro.* That you are well derived.
*Jul.* True; from a gentleman to a fool. [*Aside.*
*Thu.* Considers she my possessions?
*Pro.* O, ay, and pities them.
*Thu.* Wherefore?
*Jul.* That such an ass should owe them. [*Aside.*
*Pro.* That they are out by lease.
*Jul.* Here comes the Duke.

*Enter* DUKE.

*Duke.* How now, Sir Proteus? how now, Thurio?
Which of you saw Sir Eglamour of late?
*Thu.* Not I.
*Pro.*          Nor I.
*Duke.*                    Saw you my daughter?
*Pro.*                                        Neither.
*Duke.* Why, then she's fled unto that peasant
          Valentine;
And Eglamour is in her company.
'Tis true; for Friar Lawrence met them both
As he in penance wander'd through the forest:

Him he knew well, and guess'd that it was she;
But, being mask'd, he was not sure of it:
Besides, she did intend confession
At Patrick's cell this even; and there she was not:
These likelihoods confirm her flight from hence:
Therefore, I pray you, stand not to discourse,
But mount you presently; and meet with me
Upon the rising of the mountain-foot    [fled.
That leads towards Mantua, whither they are
Dispatch, sweet gentlemen, and follow me. [*Exit.*
*Thu.* Why, this it is to be a peevish girl,
That flies her fortune when it follows her:
I'll after; more to be revenged on Eglamour
Than for the love of reckless Silvia.    [*Exit.*
*Pro.* And I will follow, more for Silvia's love
Than hate of Eglamour that goes with her. [*Exit.*
*Jul.* And I will follow, more to cross that love
Than hate for Silvia, that is gone for love. [*Exit.*

### SCENE III.—*Frontiers of* MANTUA. *The Forest.*

*Enter* SILVIA, *and* Outlaws.

1 *Out.* Come, come;
Be patient; we must bring you to our captain.
*Sil.* A thousand more mischances than this one
Have learn'd me how to brook this patiently.
2 *Out.* Come, bring her away.
1 *Out.* Where is the gentleman that was with
    her?
2 *Out.* Being nimble-footed, he hath outrun us,
But Moyses and Valerius follow him.
Go thou with her to the west end of the wood;
There is our captain: we'll follow him that's
The thicket is beset; he cannot 'scape.    [fled.
1 *Out.* Come, I must bring you to our captain's
    cave;
Fear not; he bears an honourable mind,
And will not use a woman lawlessly.
*Sil.* O Valentine, this I endure for thee.
    [*Exeunt.*

### SCENE IV.—*Another part of the Forest.*

*Enter* VALENTINE.

*Val.* How use doth breed a habit in a man!
This shadowy desert, unfrequented woods,
I better brook than flourishing peopled towns:
Here can I sit alone, unseen of any,
And to the nightingale's complaining notes
Tune my distresses and record my woes.
O thou that dost inhabit in my breast,
Leave not the mansion so long tenantless,
Lest, growing ruinous, the building fall,
And leave no memory of what it was!
Repair me with thy presence, Silvia;
Thou gentle nymph, cherish thy forlorn swain!—
What halloing and what stir is this to-day!
These are my mates, that make their wills their
Have some unhappy passenger in chase: [law,
They love me well; yet I have much to do
To keep them from uncivil outrages.
Withdraw thee, Valentine; who's this comes
    here?    [*Steps aside.*

*Enter* PROTEUS, SILVIA, *and* JULIA.

*Pro.* Madam, this service I have done for
    you,—    [doth,—
Though you respect not aught your servant
To hazard life, and rescue you from him [love.
That would have forced your honour and your
Vouchsafe me, for my meed, but one fair look;
A smaller boon than this I cannot beg,
And less than this, I am sure, you cannot give.
*Val.* How like a dream is this I see and hear!
Love, lend me patience to forbear awhile.
    [*Aside.*
*Sil.* O miserable, unhappy that I am!
*Pro.* Unhappy were you, madam, ere I came;
But, by my coming, I have made you happy.
*Sil.* By thy approach thou makest me most
    unhappy.
*Jul.* And me, when he approacheth to your
    presence.    [*Aside.*
*Sil.* Had I been seized by a hungry lion,
I would have been a breakfast to the beast,
Rather than have false Proteus rescue me.
O, heaven be judge how I love Valentine,
Whose life's as tender to me as my soul;
And full as much,—for more there cannot be,—
I do detest false, perjured Proteus:
Therefore begone: solicit me no more.
*Pro.* What dangerous action, stood it next to
    death,
Would I not undergo for one calm look?
O, 'tis the curse in love, and still approved,
When women cannot love where they're be-
    loved.    [loved.
*Sil.* When Proteus cannot love where he's be-
Read over Julia's heart, thy first best love,
For whose dear sake thou didst then rend thy faith
Into a thousand oaths; and all those oaths
Descended into perjury, to love me.    [two,
Thou hast no faith left now, unless thou hadst
And that's far worse than none; better have none
Than plural faith, which is too much by one:
Thou counterfeit to thy true friend!
*Pro.*    In love,
Who respects friends?
*Sil.*    All men but Proteus.
*Pro.* Nay, if the gentle spirit of moving words
Can no way change you to a milder form,
I'll woo you like a soldier, at arms' end; [you.
And love you 'gainst the nature of love—force
*Sil.* O heaven!
*Pro.*    I'll force thee yield to my desire.
*Val.* Ruffian, let go that rude uncivil touch;
Thou friend of an ill fashion!
*Pro.*    Valentine!
*Val.* Thou common friend, that's without faith
    or love,—
For such is a friend now;—treacherous man!
Thou hast beguil'd my hopes; nought but mine
    eye
Could have persuaded me. Now I dare not say
I have one friend alive; thou wouldst disprove
    me.    [hand
Who should be trusted now, when one's right

Is perjured to the bosom? Proteus,
I am sorry I must never trust thee more,
But count the world a stranger for thy sake.
The private wound is deepest :O time, most curst!
'Mongst all foes, that a friend should be the worst.
*Pro.* My shame and guilt confound me.—
Forgive me, Valentine: if hearty sorrow
Be a sufficient ransom for offence,
I tender it here; I do as truly suffer
As e'er I did commit.
*Val.*                     Then I am paid;
And once again I do receive thee honest.—
Who by repentance is not satisfied
Is nor of heaven nor earth; for these are pleased;
By penitence the Eternal's wrath's appeas'd:—
And, that my love may appear plain and free,
All that was mine in Silvia I give thee.
*Jul.* O, me, unhappy!              [*Faints.*
*Pro.* Look to the boy.          [the matter?
*Val.* Why, boy! why, wag! how now? what is
Look up; speak.
*Jul.*          O good sir, my master charged me
To deliver a ring to Madam Silvia;
Which, out of my neglect, was never done.
*Pro.* Where is that ring, boy?
*Jul.*                     Here 'tis: this is it.
                              [*Gives a ring.*
*Pro.* How! let me see:
Why, this is the ring I gave to Julia.
*Jul.* O, cry you mercy, sir I have mistook;
This is the ring you sent to Silvia.
                         [*Shows another ring.*
*Pro.* But how camest thou by this ring? at my
          depart
I gave this unto Julia.
*Jul.* And Julia herself did give it me;
And Julia herself hath brought it hither.
*Pro.* How! Julia!
*Jul.* Behold her that gave aim to all thy oaths,
And entertain'd them deeply in her heart:
How oft hast thou with perjury cleft the root?
O Proteus, let this habit make thee blush!
Be thou asham'd that I have took upon me
Such an immodest raiment; if shame live
In a disguise of love:
It is the lesser blot, modesty finds,     [minds.
Women to change their shapes, than men their
*Pro.* Than men their minds! 'tis true; O heaven!
          were man
But constant, he were perfect: that one error
Fills him with faults; makes him run through
          all th' sins:
Inconstancy falls off ere it begins:
What is in Silvia's face but I may spy
More fresh in Julia's with a constant eye?
*Val.* Come, come, a hand from either:
Let me be blest to make this happy close:
'Twere pity two such friends should be long foes.
*Pro.* Bear witness, Heaven, I have my wish
          for ever.
*Jul.* And I have mine.

*Enter* Outlaws, *with* DUKE *and* THURIO.

*Out.*                     A prize, a prize, a prize!
*Val.* Forbear. I say; it is my lord the duke.
Your grace is welcome to a man disgrac'd,
Banished Valentine.
*Duke.*               Sir Valentine!
*Thu.* Yonder is Silvia; and Silvia's mine.
*Val.* Thurio, give back, or else embrace thy
                         death;
Come not within the measure of my wrath:
Do not name Silvia thine; if once again,
Milan shall not behold thee. Here she stands,
Take but possession of her with a touch;—
I dare thee but to breathe upon my love.—
*Thu.* Sir Valentine, I care not for her, I;
I hold him but a fool that will endanger
His body for a girl that loves him not:
I claim her not, and therefore she is thine.
*Duke.* The more degenerate and base art thou,
To make such means for her as thou hast done,
And leave her on such slight conditions.—
Now, by the honour of my ancestry,
I do applaud thy spirit, Valentine,
And think thee worthy of an empress' love.
Know then, I here forget all former griefs,
Cancel all grudge, repeal thee home again.—
Plead a new state in thy unrivall'd merit,
To which I thus subscribe,—Sir Valentine,
Thou art a gentleman, and well derived;
Take thou thy Silvia. for thou hast deserv'd her.
*Val.* I thank your grace: the gift hath made
          me happy.
I now beseech you, for your daughter's sake,
To grant one boon that I shall ask of you.
*Duke.* I grant it for thine own, whate'er it be.
*Val.* These banish'd men, that I have kept
          withal,
Are men endued with worthy qualities;
Forgive them what they have committed here,
And let them be recall'd from their exile:
They are reform'd, civil, full of good,
And fit for great employment, worthy lord.
*Duke.* Thou hast prevail'd; I pardon them, and
          thee;
Dispose of them as thou know'st their deserts.
Come, let us go; we will include all jars
With triumphs, mirth, and rare solemnity.
*Val.* And, as we walk along, I dare be bold
With our discourse to make your grace to smile:
What think you of this page, my lord?
*Duke.* I think the boy hath grace in him; he
          blushes.                         [boy.
*Val.* I warrant you, my lord; more grace than
*Duke.* What mean you by that saying?
*Val.* Please you, I'll tell you, as we pass along,
That you will wonder what hath fortuned.—
Come, Proteus: 'tis your penance, but to hear
The story of your loves discovered:
That done, our day of marriage shall be yours;
One feast, one house, one mutual happiness.
                                   [*Exeunt.*

MERRY WIVES OF WINDSOR.

Act I. Sc. 1.

# MERRY WIVES OF WINDSOR

## DRAMATIS PERSONÆ

SIR JOHN FALSTAFF.
FENTON.
SHALLOW, a Country Justice.
SLENDER, Cousin to SHALLOW.
MR. FORD, } two Gentlemen dwelling at
MR. PAGE, } Windsor.
WILLIAM PAGE, a boy, Son to MR. PAGE.
SIR HUGH EVANS, a Welsh Parson.
DR. CAIUS, a French Physician.
Host of the Garter Inn.
BARDOLPH, }
PISTOL, } Followers of FALSTAFF.
NYM, }

ROBIN, Page to FALSTAFF.
SIMPLE, Servant to SLENDER.
RUGBY, Servant to DR. CAIUS.

MRS. FORD.
MRS. PAGE.
MRS. ANNE PAGE, her Daughter, in love with
FENTON.
MRS. QUICKLY, Servant to DR. CAIUS.

Servants to PAGE, FORD, &c.

SCENE—WINDSOR; and the parts adjacent.

## ACT I.

SCENE I.—WINDSOR. Before PAGE'S House.

*Enter Justice* SHALLOW, SLENDER, *and Sir* HUGH EVANS.

*Shal.* Sir Hugh, persuade me not; I will make a Star-chamber matter of it; if he were twenty Sir John Falstaffs he shall not abuse Robert Shallow, esquire.

*Slen.* In the county of Gloser, justice of peace, and *coram.*

*Shal.* Ay, cousin Slender, and *Custalorum.*

*Slen.* Ay, and *Ratolorum* too; and a gentleman born, master parson; who writes himself *Armigero;* in any bill, warrant, quittance, or obligation,—*Armigero!*

*Shal.* Ay, that we do; and have done any time these three hundred years.

*Slen.* All his successors, gone before him, have don't; and all his ancestors, that come after him, may: they may give the dozen white luces in their coat.

*Shal.* It is an old coat.

*Eva.* The dozen white louses do become an old coat well; it agrees well, passant: it is a familiar beast to man, and signifies—love.

*Shal.* The luce is the fresh fish; the salt fish is an old coat.

*Slen.* I may quarter, coz?

*Shal.* You may, by marrying.

*Eva.* It is marrying indeed, if he quarter it.

*Shal.* Not a whit.

*Eva.* Yes, py'r lady; if he has a quarter of your coat, there is but three skirts for yourself, in my simple conjectures: but this is all one. If Sir John Falstaff have committed disparagements unto you, I am of the church, and will be glad to do my benevolence to make atonements and compromises between you.

*Shal.* The Council shall hear it; it is a riot.

*Eva.* It is not meet the Council hear a riot; there is no fear of Got in a riot; the Council, look you, shall desire to hear the fear of Got, and not to hear a riot; take your vizaments in that.

*Shal.* Ha! o' my life, if I were young again, the sword should end it.

*Eva.* It is petter that friends is the sword, and end it: and there is also another device in my prain, which, peradventure, prings goot discretions with it. There is Anne Page, which is daughter to Master George Page, which is pretty virginity.

*Slen.* Mistress Anne Page? She has brown hair, and speaks small like a woman.

*Eva.* It is that fery person for all the 'orld, as just as you will desire; and seven hundred pounds of monies, and gold, and silver, is her grandsire, upon his death's bed, (Got deliver to a joyful resurrection!) give, when she is able to overtake seventeen years old: it were a goot motion if we leave our pribbles and prabbles and desire a marriage between Master Abraham and Mistress Anne Page.

*Shal.* Did her grandsire leave her seven hundred pound? [penny.

*Eva.* Ay, and her father is make her a petter

*Shal.* I know the young gentlewoman; she has good gifts.

*Eva.* Seven hundred pounds, and possibilities, is goot gifts.

*Shal.* Well, let us see honest Master Page. Is Falstaff there?

*Eva.* Shall I tell you a lie? I do despise a liar as I do despise one that is false; or, as I despise one that is not true. The knight, Sir John, is there; and, I beseech you, be ruled by your well-willers. I will peat the door [*knocks*] for

[ 45 ]

Master Page. What, hoa! Got pless your house here!

*Enter* PAGE.

*Page.* Who's there?

*Eva.* Here is Got's plessing, and your friend, and Justice Shallow: and here young Master Slender; that, peradventures, shall tell you another tale, if matters grow to your likings.

*Page.* I am glad to see your worships well: I thank you for my venison, Master Shallow.

*Shal.* Master Page, I am glad to see you; much good do it your good heart! I wished your venison better; it was ill killed:—How doth good Mistress Page?—and I love you always with my heart, la; with my heart.

*Page.* Sir, I thank you.

*Shal.* Sir, I thank you; by yea and no, I do.

*Page.* I am glad to see you, good Master Slender.

*Slen.* How does your fallow greyhound, sir? I heard say he was outrun on Cotsale.

*Page.* It could not be judged, sir.

*Slen.* You'll not confess; you'll not confess.

*Shal.* That he will not;—'tis your fault; 'tis your fault:—'Tis a good dog.

*Page.* A cur, sir.

*Shal.* Sir, he's a good dog, and a fair dog. Can there be more said? he is good, and fair. Is Sir John Falstaff here?

*Page.* Sir, he is within; and I would I could do a good office between you.

*Eva.* It is spoke as a Christians ought to speak.

*Shal.* He hath wronged me, Master Page.

*Page.* Sir, he doth in some sort confess it.

*Shal.* If it be confessed, it is not redressed; is not that so, Master Page? He hath wronged me; indeed he hath;—at a word he hath;—believe me; Robert Shallow, esquire, saith he is wronged.

*Page.* Here comes Sir John.

*Enter Sir* JOHN FALSTAFF, BARDOLPH, NYM, *and* PISTOL.

*Fal.* Now, Master Shallow; you'll complain of me to the king?

*Shal.* Knight, you have beaten my men, killed my deer, and broke open my lodge.

*Fal.* But not kissed your keeper's daughter?

*Shal.* Tut, a pin! this shall be answered.

*Fal.* I will answer it straight;—I have done all this:—That is now answered.

*Shal.* The Council shall know this.

*Fal.* 'Twere better for you if it were known in counsel: you'll be laughed at.

*Eva.* Pauca verba, Sir John, goot worts.

*Fal.* Good worts! good cabbage.—Slender, I broke your head; what matter have you against me?

*Slen.* Marry, sir, I have matter in my head against you; and against your coney-catching rascals, Bardolph, Nym, and Pistol. They carried me to the tavern, and made me drunk, and afterwards picked my pocket.

*Bard.* You Banbury cheese!

*Slen.* Ay, it is no matter.

*Pist.* How now, Mephostophilus?

*Slen.* Ay, it is no matter.

*Nym.* Slice, I say! pauca, pauca; slice! that's my humour.                    [cousin?

*Slen.* Where's Simple, my man?—can you tell,

*Eva.* Peace: I pray you! Now let us understand. There is three umpires in this matter as I understand: that is—Master Page, *fidelicit*, Master Page; and there is myself, *fidelicit*, myself; and the three party is, lastly and finally, mine host of the Garter.                    [them.

*Page.* We three to hear it, and end it between

*Eva.* Fery goot. I will make a prief of it in my note-book; and we will afterwards 'ork upon the cause, with as great discreetly as we can.

*Fal.* Pistol,—

*Pist.* He hears with 'ears.

*Eva.* The tevil and his tam! what phrase is this, *He hears with ear?* Why, it is affectations.

*Fal.* Pistol, did you pick Master Slender's purse?

*Slen.* Ay, by these gloves, did he, (or I would I might never come in mine own great chamber again else,) of seven groats in mill-sixpences, and two Edward shovel-boards, that cost me two shilling and two pence a-piece of Yead Miller, by these gloves.

*Fal.* Is this true, Pistol?

*Eva.* No; it is false, if it is a pick-purse.

*Pist.* Ha, thou mountain-foreigner!—Sir John, and master mine,
I combat challenge of this latten bilbo:
Word of denial in thy labras here;
Word of denial: froth and scum, thou liest.

*Slen.* By these gloves, then, 'twas he.

*Nym.* Be advised, sir, and pass good humours: I will say, *marry trap*, with you, if you run the nuthook's humour on me: that is the very note of it.

*Slen.* By this hat, then, he in the red face had it: for though I cannot remember what I did when you made me drunk, yet I am not altogether an ass.

*Fal.* What say you, Scarlet and John?

*Bard.* Why, sir, for my part, I say the gentleman had drunk himself out of his five sentences.

*Eva.* It is his five senses; fie, what the ignorance is!

*Bard.* And being fap, sir, was, as they say, cashiered; and so conclusions passed the careires.

*Slen.* Ay, you spake in Latin then too; but 'tis no matter: I'll ne'er be drunk whilst I live again, but in honest, civil, godly company, for this trick. If I be drunk, I'll be drunk with those that have the fear of God, and not with drunken knaves.

*Eva.* So Got 'udge me, that is a virtuous mind.

*Fal.* You hear all these matters denied, gentlemen; you hear it.

*Enter Mrs.* ANNE PAGE *with wine; Mrs.* FORD *and Mrs.* PAGE *following.*

*Page.* Nay, daughter, carry the wine in; we'll drink within.                    [*Exit* ANNE PAGE.

*Slen.* O heaven! this is Mistress Anne Page.
*Page.* How now, Mistress Ford?
*Fal.* Mistress Ford, by my troth, you are very well met: by your leave, good mistress.
[*Kissing her.*
*Page.* Wife, bid these gentlemen welcome:—Come, we have a hot venison pasty to dinner; come, gentlemen, I hope we shall drink down all unkindness.
[*Exeunt all but* SHAL., SLEN., *and* EVANS.
*Slen.* I had rather than forty shillings I had my Book of Songs and Sonnets here.—

*Enter* SIMPLE.

How now, Simple! Where have you been? I must wait on myself, must I? You have not *The Book of Riddles* about you, have you?
*Sim.* Book of Riddles! why, did you not lend it to Alice Shortcake upon All-hallowmas last, a fortnight afore Michaelmas?
*Shal.* Come, coz; come, coz; we stay for you. A word with you, coz; marry this, coz; there is, as 'twere, a tender, a kind of tender, made afar off by Sir Hugh here.—Do you understand me?
*Slen.* Ay, sir, you shall find me reasonable; if it be so, I shall do that that is reason.
*Shal.* Nay, but understand me.
*Slen.* So I do, sir.
*Eva.* Give ear to his motions, Master Slender: I will description the matter to you, if you be capacity of it.
*Slen.* Nay, I will do as my cousin Shallow says: I pray you, pardon me; he's a justice of peace in his country, simple though I stand here.
*Eva.* But this is not the question; the question is concerning your marriage.
*Shal.* Ay, there's the point, sir.
*Eva.* Marry is it; the very point of it; to Mistress Anne Page.
*Slen.* Why, if it be so, I will marry her upon any reasonable demands.
*Eva.* But can you affection the 'oman? Let us command to know that of your mouth, or of your lips; for divers philosophers hold that the lips is parcel of the mouth.—Therefore, precisely. can you carry your good will to the maid?
*Shal.* Cousin Abraham Slender, can you love her?
*Slen.* I hope, sir,—I will do as it shall become one that would do reason.
*Eva.* Nay, Got's lords and his ladies, you must speak possitable if you can carry her your desires towards her.
*Shal.* That you must. Will you, upon good dowry, marry her?
*Slen.* I will do a greater thing than that upon your request, cousin, in any reason.
*Shal.* Nay, conceive me, conceive me, sweet coz; what I do is to pleasure you, coz. Can you love the maid?
*Slen.* I will marry her, sir, at your request; but if there be no great love in the beginning, yet Heaven may decrease it upon better acquaint-ance, when we are married, and have more occasion to know one another. I hope, upon familiarity will grow more contempt: but if you say, *marry her*, I will marry her, that I am freely dissolved, and dissolutely.
*Eva.* It is a fery discretion answer; save, the faul' is in the 'ort dissolutely: the 'ort is, according to our meaning, resolutely;—his meaning is good.
*Shal.* Ay, I think my cousin meant well.
*Slen.* Ay, or else I would I might be hanged, la.

*Re-enter* ANNE PAGE.

*Shal.* Here comes fair Mistress Anne.—Would I were young for your sake, Mistress Anne!
*Anne.* The dinner is on the table; my father desires your worships' company.
*Shal.* I will wait on him, fair Mistress Anne.
*Eva.* Od's plessed will! I will not be absence at the grace.
[*Exeunt* SHAL. *and Sir* H. EVANS.
*Anne.* Will't please your worship to come in, sir?                      [very well.
*Slen.* No, I thank you, forsooth, heartily; I am
*Anne.* The dinner attends you, sir.
*Slen.* I am not a-hungry, I thank you, forsooth. Go, sirrah, for all you are my man, go wait upon my cousin Shallow [*Exit* SIMPLE.] A justice of peace sometime may be beholden to his friend for a man.—I keep but three men and a boy yet, till my mother be dead: but what though? yet I live like a poor gentleman born.
*Anne.* I may not go in without your worship; they will not sit till you come.
*Slen.* I' faith, I'll eat nothing; I thank you as much as though I did.
*Anne.* I pray you, sir, walk in.
*Slen.* I had rather walk here, I thank you; I bruised my shin the other day with playing at sword and dagger with a master of fence, three veneys for a dish of stewed prunes; and, by my troth, I cannot abide the smell of hot meat since. Why do your dogs bark so? be there bears i' the town?                      [talked of.
*Anne.* I think there are, sir; I heard them
*Slen.* I love the sport well; but I shall as soon quarrel at it as any man in England:—You are afraid, if you see the bear loose, are you not?
*Anne.* Ay, indeed, sir.
*Slen.* That's meat and drink to me now. I have seen Sackerson loose twenty times; and have taken him by the chain: but, I warrant you, the women have so cried and shrieked at it that it passed:—but women, indeed, cannot abide 'em; they are very ill-favoured rough things.

*Re-enter* PAGE.

*Page.* Come, gentle Master Slender, come; we stay for you.
*Slen.* I'll eat nothing, I thank you, sir.
*Page.* By cock and pye, you shall not choose, sir: come, come.
*Slen.* Nay, pray you, lead the way.
*Page.* Come on, sir.

*Slen.* Mistress Anne, yourself shall go first.
*Anne.* Not I, sir; pray you, keep on.
*Slen.* Truly, I will not go first; truly, la: I will not do you that wrong.
*Anne.* I pray you, sir.
*Slen.* I'll rather be unmannerly than troublesome: you do yourself wrong indeed, la.
                                        [*Exeunt.*

SCENE II.—*The same.*

*Enter Sir* HUGH EVANS *and* SIMPLE.

*Eva.* Go your ways, and ask of Doctor Caius' house which is the way: and there dwells one Mistress Quickly, which is in the manner of his nurse, or his dry nurse, or his cook, or his laundry, his washer, and his wringer.
*Simp.* Well, sir.
*Eva.* Nay, it is petter yet:—give her this letter; for it is a 'oman that altogether's acquaintance with Mistress Anne Page: and the letter is, to desire and require her to solicit your master's desires to Mistress Anne Page: I pray you, be-gone; I will make an end of my dinner; there's pippins and cheese to come.        [*Exeunt.*

SCENE III.—*A Room in the* GARTER INN.

*Enter* FALSTAFF, HOST, BARDOLPH, NYM, PISTOL, *and* ROBIN.

*Fal.* Mine host of the Garter,—
*Host.* What says my bully-rook? Speak scholarly and wisely.
*Fal.* Truly, mine host, I must turn away some of my followers.
*Host.* Discard, bully Hercules; cashier: let them wag; trot, trot.
*Fal.* I sit at ten pounds a-week.
*Host.* Thou'rt an emperor, Cæsar, Keisar, and Pheezar. I will entertain Bardolph; he shall draw, he shall tap: said I well, bully Hector?
*Fal.* Do so, good mine host.
*Host.* I have spoke; let him follow. Let me see thee froth and lime: I am at a word: follow.
                                        [*Exit* HOST.
*Fal.* Bardolph, follow him: a tapster is a good trade: an old cloak makes a new jerkin; a with-ered servingman a fresh tapster. Go; adieu.
*Bard.* It is a life that I have desired; I will thrive.                        [*Exit* BARDOLPH.
*Pist.* O base Gongarian wight! wilt thou the spigot wield?
*Nym.* He was gotten in drink: is not the humour conceited? His mind is not heroic, and there's the humour of it.
*Fal.* I am glad I am so acquit of this tinder-box; his thefts were too open; his filching was like an unskilful singer; he kept not time.
*Nym.* The good humour is, to steal at a min-ute's rest.
*Pist.* Convey, the wise it call: Steal! foh; a fico for the phrase!
*Fal.* Well, sirs, I am almost out at heels.
*Pist.* Why, then, let kibes ensue.
*Fal.* There is no remedy; I must coney-catch; I must shift.

*Pist.* Young ravens must have food.
*Fal.* Which of you know Ford of this town?
*Pist.* I ken the wight; he is of substance good.
*Fal.* My honest lads, I will tell you what I am about.
*Pist.* Two yards, and more.
*Fal.* No quips now, Pistol. Indeed I am in the waist two yards about: but I am now about no waste; I am about thrift. Briefly, I do mean to make love to Ford's wife; I spy entertainment in her; she discourses, she carves, she gives the leer of invitation: I can construe the action of her familiar style; and the hardest voice of her behaviour, to be English'd rightly, is, *I am Sir John Falstaff's.*
*Pist.* He hath studied her well, and translated her well; out of honesty into English.    [*pass?*
*Nym.* The anchor is deep: will that humour
*Fal.* Now, the report goes, she has all the rule of her husband's purse; she hath legions of angels.
*Pist.* As many devils entertain; and, *To her,* boy, say I.
*Nym.* The humour rises; it is good: humour me the angels.
*Fal.* I have writ me here a letter to her: and here another to Page's wife; who even now gave me good eyes too, examined my parts with most judicious eyliads: sometimes the beam of her view gilded my foot, sometimes my portly belly.
*Pist.* Then did the sun on dunghill shine.
*Nym.* I thank thee for that humour.
*Fal.* O, she did so course o'er my exteriors with such a greedy intention, that the appetite of her eye did seem to scorch me up like a burn-ing-glass! Here's another letter to her: she bears the purse too; she is a region in Guiana, all gold and bounty. I will be cheater to them both, and they shall be exchequers to me; they shall be my East and West Indies, and I will trade to them both. Go, bear thou this letter to Mistress Page; and thou this to Mistress Ford; we will thrive, lads, we will thrive.
*Pist.* Shall I Sir Pandarus of Troy become, And by my side wear steel? then, Lucifer take all!
*Nym.* I will run no base humour: here, take the humour letter; I will keep the 'haviour of reputation.
*Fal.* Hold, sirrah, [*to* ROB.,] bear you these let-ters tightly;
Sail like my pinnace to these golden shores.—
Rogues, hence, avaunt! vanish like hailstones, go;                                [*pack.*
Trudge, plod, away, o' the hoof; seek shelter, Falstaff will learn the humour of this age,
French thrift, you rogues; myself, and skirted page.                [*Exeunt* FAL. *and* ROB.
*Pist.* Let vultures gripe thy guts! for gourd and fullam holds,
And high and low beguile the rich and poor;
Tester I'll have in pouch when thou shalt lack,
Base Phrygian Turk!
*Nym.* I have operations in my head, which be humours of revenge.
*Pist.* Wilt thou revenge?

*Nym.* By welkin, and her star!
*Pist.* With wit or steel?
*Nym.* With both the humours, I:
I will discuss the humour of this love to Page.
*Pist.* And I to Ford shall eke unfold,
    How Falstaff, varlet vile.
    His dove will prove, his gold will hold,
    And his soft couch defile.
*Nym.* My humour shall not cool: I will incense
Page to deal with poison; I will possess him
with yellowness, for the revolt of mien is dangerous: that is my true humour.
*Pist.* Thou art the Mars of malcontents: I second thee; troop on.    [*Exeunt.*

SCENE IV.—*A Room in Dr.* CAIUS'S *House.*

*Enter Mrs.* QUICKLY, SIMPLE, *and* RUGBY.

*Quick.* What: John Rugby!—I pray thee go to
the casement and see if you can see my master,
Master Doctor Caius, coming: if he do, i' faith,
and find anybody in the house, here will be an
old abusing of God's patience and the king's
English.
*Rug.* I'll go watch.    [*Exit* RUGBY.
*Quick.* Go; and we'll have a posset for't soon
at night, in faith, at the latter end of a sea-coal
fire. An honest, willing, kind fellow, as ever
servant shall come in house withal; and I warrant you, no tell-tale, nor no breed-bate: his
worst fault is that he is given to prayer; he is
something peevish that way; but nobody but
has his fault;—but let that pass. Peter Simple,
you say your name is?
*Sim.* Ay, for fault of a better.
*Quick.* And Master Slender's your master?
*Sim.* Ay, forsooth.
*Quick.* Does he not wear a great round beard,
like a glover's paring-knife?
*Sim.* No, forsooth: he hath but a little wee face,
with a little yellow beard; a Cain-coloured beard.
*Quick.* A softly-sprighted man, is he not?
*Sim.* Ay, forsooth: but he is as tall a man of
his hands as any is between this and his head:
he hath fought with a warrener.
*Quick.* How say you?—O, I should remember
him. Does he not hold up his head, as it were?
and strut in his gait?
*Sim.* Yes, indeed does he.
*Quick.* Well, heaven send Anne Page no worse
fortune! Tell Master Parson Evans, I will do
what I can for your master: Anne is a good
girl, and I wish—

*Re-enter* RUGBY.

*Rug.* Out, alas! here comes my master.
*Quick.* We shall all be shent. Run in here, good
young man; go into his closet. [*Shuts* SIMPLE
*in the closet.*] He will not stay long.—What,
John Rugby! John, what John, I say!—Go,
John, go inquire for my master; I doubt he be
not well that he comes not home:—*and down,
down, adown-a,* &c.    [*Sings.*

*Enter Dr.* CAIUS.

*Caius.* Vat is you sing? I do not like dese toys.
Pray you, go and vetch me in my closet *un
boitier verd;* a box, a green-a box. Do intend
vat I speak? a green-a box.
*Quick.* Ay, forsooth, I'll fetch it you. I am glad
he went not in himself: if he had found the young
man, he would have been horn-mad.   [*Aside.*
*Caius.* Fe, fe, fe, fe! ma foi, il fait fort chaud.
Je m'en vais a la Cour,—la grande affaire.
*Quick.* Is it this, sir?
*Caius.* Ouy; mette le au mon pocket: depeche,
quickly:—Vere is dat knave, Rugby?
*Quick.* What, John Rugby! John?
*Rug.* Here, sir.
*Caius.* You are John Rugby, and you are Jack
Rugby. Come, take-a your rapier, and come
after my heel to de court.
*Rug.* 'Tis ready, sir, here in the porch.
*Caius.* By my trot, I tarry too long:—Od's me!
Qu'ay j' oublié? dere is some simples in my closet
dat I vill not for the varld I shall leave behind.
*Quick.* Ah me! he'll find the young man there,
and be mad!
*Caius.* O diable, diable! vat is in my closet?—
Villany! larron! [*Pulling* SIMPLE *out.*] Rugby,
my rapier.
*Quick.* Good master, be content.
*Caius.* Verefore shall I be content-a!
*Quick.* The young man is an honest man.
*Caius.* Vat shall de honest man do in my closet?
dere is no honest man dat shall come in my closet.
*Quick.* I beseech you, be not so phlegmatic:
hear the truth of it. He came of an errand to
me from Parson Hugh.
*Caius.* Vell?
*Sim.* Ay, forsooth, to desire her to—
*Quick.* Peace, I pray you.    [*tale.*
*Caius.* Peace-a your tongue:—Speak-a your
*Sim.* To desire this honest gentlewoman, your
maid, to speak a good word to Mistress Anne
Page for my master, in the way of marriage.
*Quick.* This is all, indeed, la; but I'll ne'er put
my finger in the fire, and need not.
*Caius.* Sir Hugh send-a you?—Rugby, baille
me some paper. Tarry you a little-a while.
   [*Writes.*
*Quick.* I am glad he is so quiet: if he had been
thoroughly moved, you should have heard him
so loud, and so melancholy;—but not withstanding, man, I'll do your master what good I
can: and the very yea and the no is, the French
doctor, my master,—I may call him my master, look you, for I keep his house: and I wash,
wring, brew, bake, scour, dress meat and drink,
make the beds, and do all myself:—
*Sim.* 'Tis a great charge to come under one
body's hand.
*Quick.* Are you avised o' that? you shall find
it a great charge: and to be up early and down
late;—but notwithstanding,—to tell you in
your ear; I would have no words of it,—my
master himself is in love with Mistress Anne

*Page·* but notwithstanding that,—I know Anne's mind,—that's neither here nor there.

*Caius.* You jack'nape; give-a dis letter to Sir Hugh; by gar, it is a shallenge; I will cut his troat in de park; and I vill teach a scurvy jack-a-nape priest to meddle or make:—you may be gone; it is not good you tarry here:—by gar, I vill cut all his two stones; by gar, he shall not have a stone to trow at his dog.

*[Exit* SIMPLE.

*Quick.* Alas, he speaks but for his friend.

*Caius.* It is no matter-a for dat:—do not you tell-a me dat I shall have Anne Page for my-self?—by gar, I will kill de Jack priest; and I have appointed mine host of *de Jar terre* to measure our weapon:—by gar, I vill myself have Anne Page.

*Quick.* Sir, the maid loves you, and all shall be well: we must give folks leave to prate. What, the good-jer!

*Caius.* Rugby, come to de court vit me.—By gar, if I have not Anne Page, I shall turn your head out of my door:—follow my heels, Rugby.

*[Exeunt* CAIUS *and* RUGBY.

*Quick.* You shall have An fool's-head of your own. No, I know Anne's mind for that: never a woman in Windsor knows more of Anne's mind than I do; nor can do more than I do with her, I thank heaven.

*Fent.* [*Within.*] Who's within there? ho!

*Quick.* Who's there, I trow? Come near the house, I pray you.

*Enter* FENTON.

*Fent.* How now, good woman; how dost thou?

*Quick.* The better that it pleases your good worship to ask.    [*Anne?*

*Fent.* What news? How does pretty Mistress

*Quick.* In truth, sir, and she is pretty, and honest, and gentle; and one that is your friend, I can tell you that by the way; I praise heaven for it.    [*Shall I not lose my suit?*

*Fent.* Shall I do any good, think'st thou?

*Quick.* Troth, sir, all is in his hands above: but notwithstanding, Master Fenton, I'll be sworn on a book she loves you:—Have not your worship a wart above your eye?

*Fent.* Yes, marry, have I; what of that?

*Quick.* Well, thereby hangs a tale; good faith, it is such another Nan;—but, I detest, an honest maid as ever broke bread. We had an hour's talk of that wart:—I shall never laugh but in that maid's company! But, indeed, she is given too much to allicholly and musing: But for you—Well, go to.

*Fent.* Well, I shall see her to-day. Hold, there's money for thee; let me have thy voice in my behalf: if thou seest her before me, commend me—

*Quick.* Will I? i' faith, that we will; and I will tell your worship more of the wart the next time we have confidence; and of other wooers.

*Fent.* Well, farewell; I am in great haste now.

*[Exit.*

*Quick.* Farewell to your worship.—Truly, an honest gentleman; but Anne loves him not; for I know Anne's mind as well as another does:— Out upon't! what have I forgot?    [*Exit.*

# ACT II.

SCENE I.—*Before* PAGE'S *House.*

*Enter Mrs.* PAGE, *with a letter.*

*Mrs. Page.* What! have I 'scaped love-letters in the holiday time of my beauty, and am I now a subject for them? Let me see:    [*Reads.*

Ask me no reason why I love you; for though love use reason for his precisian, he admits him not for his counsellor. You are not young; no more am I: go to then, there's sympathy: you are merry; so am I. Ha! ha! then there's more sympathy; you love sack, and so do I. Would you desire better sympathy? Let it suffice thee, Mistress Page, (at the least, if the love of a soldier can suffice), that I love thee. I will not say, pity me: 'tis not a soldier-like phrase; but I say, love me. By me,

Thine own true knight,
By day or night,
Or any kind of light,
With all his might,
For thee to fight,    JOHN FALSTAFF.

What a Herod of Jewry is this?—O wicked, wicked world!—one that is well-nigh worn to pieces with age to show himself a young gallant! What an unweighed behaviour hath this Flemish drunkard picked (with the devil's name) out of my conversation, that he dares in this manner assay me? Why, he hath not been thrice in my company!—What should I say to him?—I was then frugal of my mirth:—heaven forgive me!—Why, I'll exhibit a bill in the parliament for the putting down of men. How shall I be revenged on him? for revenged I will be, as sure as his guts are made of puddings.

*Enter Mrs.* FORD.

*Mrs. Ford.* Mistress Page! trust me, I was going to your house!

*Mrs. Page.* And, trust me, I was coming to you. You look very ill.

*Mrs. Ford.* Nay, I'll ne'er believe that; I have to show to the contrary.

*Mrs. Page.* 'Faith, but you do, in my mind.

*Mrs. Ford.* Well, I do, then; yet, I say, I could show you to the contrary. O, Mistress Page, give me some counsel!

*Mrs. Page.* What's the matter, woman?

*Mrs. Ford.* O woman, if it were not for one trifling respect, I could come to such honour!

*Mrs. Page.* Hang the trifle, woman; take the honour. What is it?——dispense with trifles;—what is it?

*Mrs. Ford.* If I would but go to hell for an eternal moment, or so, I could be knighted.

*Mrs. Page.* What? thou liest!—Sir Alice Ford! —These knights will hack; and so thou shouldst not alter the article of thy gentry.

*Mrs. Ford.* We burn day-light:—here, read, read;—perceive how I might be knighted.—I shall think the worse of fat men as long as I have an eye to make difference of men's liking. And yet he would not swear; praised women's modesty; and gave such orderly and well-behaved reproof to all uncomeliness, that I would have sworn his disposition would have gone to the truth of his words; but they do no more adhere and keep place together than the hundredth psalm to the tune of *Green sleeves*. What tempest, I trow, threw this whale, with so many tuns of oil in his belly, ashore at Windsor? How shall I be revenged on him? I think the best way were to entertain him with hope till the wicked fire of lust have melted him in his own grease.—Did you ever hear the like?

*Mrs. Page.* Letter for letter; but that the name of Page and Ford differs!—To thy great comfort in this mystery of ill opinions, here's the twin-brother of thy letter: but let thine inherit first; for, I protest, mine never shall. I warrant he hath a thousand of these letters, writ with blank space for different names, (sure more,) and these are of the second edition. He will print them out of doubt; for he cares not what he puts into the press when he would put us two. I had rather be a giantess, and lie under Mount Pelion. Well, I will find you twenty lascivious turtles ere one chaste man.

*Mrs. Ford.* Why, this is the very same; the very hand, the very words. What doth he think of us?

*Mrs. Page.* Nay, I know not; it makes me almost ready to wrangle with mine own honesty. I'll entertain myself like one that I am not acquainted withal; for, sure, unless he know some strain in me that I know not myself, he would never have boarded me in this fury.

*Mrs. Ford.* Boarding, call you it? I'll be sure to keep him above deck.

*Mrs. Page.* So will I; if he come under my hatches, I'll never to sea again. Let's be revenged on him: let's appoint him a meeting; give him a show of comfort in his suit; and lead him on with a fine baited delay, till he hath pawned his horses to mine host of the Garter.

*Mrs. Ford.* Nay, I will consent to act any villany against him that may not sully the chariness of our honesty. O, that my husband saw this letter! it would give eternal food to his jealousy.

*Mrs. Page.* Why, look where he comes; and my good man too; he's as far from jealousy as I am from giving him cause; and that, I hope, is an unmeasurable distance.

*Mrs. Ford.* You are the happier woman.

*Mrs. Page.* Let's consult together against this greasy knight: Come hither.    [*They retire.*

*Enter* FORD, PISTOL, PAGE, *and* NYM.

*Ford.* Well, I hope it be not so.

*Pist.* Hope is a curtail dog in some affairs: Sir John affects thy wife.

*Ford.* Why, sir, my wife is not young.

*Pist.* He woos both high and low, both rich and poor,
Both young and old, one with another, Ford;
He loves thy gally-mawfry; Ford, perpend.

*Ford.* Love my wife?    [thou,

*Pist.* With liver burning hot. Prevent, or go
Like Sir Actæon he, with Ring-wood at thy
O, odious is the name.    [heels:—

*Ford.* What name, sir?

*Pist.* The horn, I say. Farewell.
Take heed; have open eye; for thieves do foot
by night:    [do sing.—
Take heed, ere summer comes, or cuckoo birds
Away, Sir Corporal Nym.—
Believe it, Page; he speaks sense.
[*Exit* PISTOL.

*Ford.* I will be patient; I will find out this.

*Nym.* And this is true [*to* PAGE]. I like not the humour of lying. He hath wronged me in some humours; I should have borne the humoured letter to her; but I have a sword, and it shall bite upon my necessity. He loves your wife; there's the short and the long. My name is Corporal Nym; I speak, and I avouch. 'Tis true:—my name is Nym, and Falstaff loves your wife.—Adieu! I love not the humour of bread and cheese; and there's the humour of it. Adieu.    [*Exit* NYM.

*Page.* The humour of it, quotha! here's a fellow frights humour out of his wits.

*Ford.* I will seek out Falstaff.

*Page.* I never heard such a drawling, affecting rogue.

*Ford.* If I do find it, well.

*Page.* I will not believe such a Cataian though the priest of the town commended him for a true man.

*Ford.* 'Twas a good sensible fellow. Well.

*Page.* How now, Meg?

*Mrs. Page.* Whither go you, George?—Hark you.

*Mrs. Ford.* How now, sweet Frank? why art thou melancholy?

*Ford.* I melancholy! I am not melancholy.—Get you home; go.

*Mrs. Ford.* 'Faith, thou hast some crotchets in thy head now.—Will you go, Mistress Page?

*Mrs. Page.* Have with you.—You'll come to dinner, George? Look, who comes yonder: she shall be our messenger to this paltry knight.
[*Aside to Mrs.* FORD.

*Enter Mrs.* QUICKLY.

*Mrs. Ford.* Trust me, I thought on her: she'll fit it.

*Mrs. Page.* You are come to see my daughter Anne?

*Quick.* Ay, forsooth; and, I pray, how does good Mistress Anne?

*Mrs. Page.* Go in with us and see; we have an hour's talk with you.
[*Exeunt Mrs.* PAGE, *Mrs.* FORD,
*and Mrs.* QUICKLY.

*Page.* How now, Master Ford?

*Ford.* You heard what this knave told me; did you not?

*Page.* Yes; and you heard what the other told me?

*Ford.* Do you think there is truth in them?

*Page.* Hang 'em slaves; I do not think the knight would offer it: but these that accuse him in his intent towards our wives are a yoke of his discarded men: very rogues, now they be out of service.

*Ford.* Were they his men?

*Page.* Marry, were they.

*Ford.* I like it never the better for that.— Does he lie at the Garter?

*Page.* Ay, marry, does he. If he should intend this voyage towards my wife, I would turn her loose to him; and what he gets of her more than sharp words, let it lie on my head.

*Ford.* I do not misdoubt my wife; but I would be loth to turn them together. A man may be too confident: I would have nothing lie on my head: I cannot be thus satisfied.

*Page.* Look where my ranting host of the Garter comes: there is either liquor in his pate or money in his purse when he looks so merrily.— How now, mine host?

*Enter* HOST *and* SHALLOW.

*Host.* How now, bully-rook! thou'rt a gentleman: cavalero-justice, I say.

*Shal.* I follow, mine host, I follow.—Good even, and twenty, good Master Page! Master Page, will you go with us? we have sport in hand.

*Host.* Tell him, cavalero-justice; tell him, bully-rook.

*Shal.* Sir, there is a fray to be fought between Sir Hugh the Welsh priest and Caius the French doctor.

*Ford.* Good mine host o' the Garter, a word with you.

*Host.* What say'st thou, bully-rook?

[*They go aside.*

*Shal.* Will you [*to* PAGE] go with us to behold it? My merry host hath had the measuring of their weapons; and, I think, he hath appointed them contrary places: for, believe me, I hear the parson is no jester. Hark, I will tell you what our sport shall be.

*Host.* Hast thou no suit against my knight, my guest-cavalier?

*Ford.* None, I protest: but I'll give you a pottle of burnt sack to give me recourse to him, and tell him my name is Brook; only for a jest.

*Host.* My hand, bully: thou shalt have egress and regress; said I well? and thy name shall be Brook: it is a merry knight.—Will you go on, hearts?

*Shal.* Have with you, mine host.

*Page.* I have heard the Frenchman hath good skill in his rapier.

*Shal.* Tut, sir, I could have told you more. In these times you stand on distance, your passes, stoccadoes, and I know not what: 'tis the heart,

Master Page; 'tis here, 'tis here. I have seen the time with my long sword I would have made you four tall fellows skip like rats.

*Host.* Here, boys, here, here! shall we wag?

*Page.* Have with you:—I had rather hear them scold than fight. ·

[*Exeunt* HOST, SHAL., *and* PAGE.

*Ford.* Though Page be a secure fool, and stands so firmly on his wife's frailty, yet I cannot put off my opinion so easily. She was in his company at Page's house; and what they made there I know not. Well, I will look further into't: and I have a disguise to sound Falstaff: if I find her honest, I lose not my labour; if she be otherwise, 'tis labour well bestowed. [*Exit.*

SCENE II.—*A Room in the Garter Inn.*

*Enter* FALSTAFF *and* PISTOL.

*Fal.* I will not lend thee a penny.

*Pist.* Why, then the world's mine oyster,
Which I with sword will open.—
I will retort the sum in equipage.—

*Fal.* Not a penny. I have been content, sir, you should lay my countenance to pawn; I have grated upon my good friends for three reprieves for you and your coach fellow, Nym; or else you had looked through the grate, like a geminy of baboons. I am damned in hell for swearing to gentlemen my friends you were good soldiers and tall fellows: and when Mistress Bridget lost the handle of her fan, I took't upon mine honour thou hadst it not.·

*Pist.* Didst thou not share? hadst thou not fifteen pence?

*Fal.* Reason, you rogue, reason. Think'st thou I'll endanger my soul *gratis?* At a word, hang no more about me, I am no gibbet for you;— go.—A short knife and a throng;—to your manor of Pickthatch, go.—You'll not bear a letter for me, you rogue!—you stand upon your honour!—Why, thou unconfinable baseness, it is as much as I can do to keep the terms of my honour precise. I, I, I myself sometimes, leaving the fear of heaven on the left hand, and hiding mine honour in my necessity, am fain to shuffle, to hedge, and to lurch; and yet you, rogue, will ensconce your rags, your cat-a-mountain looks, your red lattice phrases, and your bold-beating oaths, under the shelter of your honour! You will not do it, you?    [man?

*Pist.* I do relent. What wouldst thou more of

*Enter* ROBIN.

*Rob.* Sir, here's a woman would speak with you.

*Fal.* Let her approach.

*Enter Mrs.* QUICKLY.

*Quick.* Give your worship good-morrow.

*Fal.* Good-morrow, good wife.

*Quick.* Not so, an't please your worship.

*Fal.* Good maid, then.

*Quick.* I'll be sworn; as my mother was, the first hour I was born.

*Fal.* I do believe the swearer. What with me?

*Quick.* Shall I vouchsafe your worship a word or two?

*Fal.* Two thousand, fair woman: and I'll vouchsafe thee the hearing.

*Quick.* There is one, Mistress Ford, sir:—I pray, come a little nearer this ways:—I myself dwell with Master Doctor Caius.

*Fal.* Well, on: Mistress Ford, you say,——

*Quick.* Your worship says very true: I pray your worship come a little nearer this ways.

*Fal.* I warrant thee nobody hears;—mine own people, mine own people.

*Quick.* Are they so? Heaven bless them, and make them his servants!

*Fal.* Well: Mistress Ford;—what of her?

*Quick.* Why, sir, she's a good creature. Lord, lord! your worship's a wanton. Well, heaven forgive you, and all of us, I pray!

*Fal.* Mistress Ford;—come, Mistress Ford,—

*Quick.* Marry, this is the short and the long of it; you have brought her into such a canaries as 'tis wonderful. The best courtier of them all, when the court lay at Windsor, could never have brought her to such a canary. Yet there has been knights, and lords, and gentlemen, with their coaches; I warrant you, coach after coach, letter after letter, gift after gift; smelling so sweetly, (all musk) and so rushling, I warrant you, in silk and gold; and in such alligant terms; and in such wine and sugar of the best, and the fairest, that would have won any woman's heart; and, I warrant you, they could never get an eye-wink of her.—I had myself twenty angels given me this morning; but I defy all angels, (in any such sort, as they say,) but in the way of honesty:—and, I warrant you, they could never get her so much as sip on a cup with the proudest of them all: and yet there has been earls, nay, which is more, pensioners; but, I warrant you, all is one with her.

*Fal.* But what says she to me? be brief, my good she Mercury.

*Quick.* Marry, she hath received your letter; for the which she thanks you a thousand times; and she gives you to notify that her husband will be absence from his house between ten and eleven.

*Fal.* Ten and eleven?

*Quick.* Ay, forsooth; and then you may come and see the picture, she says, that you wot of;—Master Ford, her husband, will be from home. Alas! the sweet woman leads an ill life with him: he's a very jealousy man: she leads a very frampold life with him, good heart.

*Fal.* Ten and eleven. Woman, commend me to her; I will not fail her.

*Quick.* Why, you say well: but I have another messenger to your worship. Mistress Page hath her hearty commendations to you too;—and let me tell you in your ear, she's as fartuous a civil, modest wife, and one (I tell you) that will not miss you morning nor evening prayer, as any is in Windsor, whoe'er be the other: and she bade me tell your worship that her husband is seldom from home; but she hopes there will come a time. I never knew a woman so dote upon a man; surely I think you have charms, la; yes, in truth.

*Fal.* Not I, I assure thee; setting the attraction of my good parts aside, I have no other charms.

*Quick.* Blessing on your heart for't!

*Fal.* But, I pray thee, tell me this: has Ford's wife and Page's wife acquainted each other how they love me?

*Quick.* That were a jest indeed!—they have not so little grace, I hope:—that were a trick indeed! But Mistress Page would desire you to send her your little page, of all loves: her husband has a marvellous infection to the little page: and, truly, Master Page is an honest man. Never a wife in Windsor leads a better life than she does; do what she will, say what she will, take all, pay all, go to bed when she list, rise when she list, all is as she will; and truly, she deserves it: for if there be a kind woman in Windsor, she is one. You must send her your page; no remedy.

*Fal.* Why, I will.                    [page; no remedy.

*Quick.* Nay, but do so then: and, look you, he may come and go between you both; and in any case have a nay-word that you may know one another's mind, and the boy never need to understand any thing: for 'tis not good that children should know any wickedness: old folks, you know, have discretion, as they say, and know the world.

*Fal.* Fare thee well: commend me to them both: there's my purse; I am yet thy debtor.—Boy, go along with this woman.——This news distracts me!

[*Exeunt* QUICKLY *and* ROBIN.

*Pist.* This punk is one of Cupid's carriers:—Clap on more sails; pursue; up with your fights; give fire; she is my prize, or ocean whelm them all!                    [*Exit* PISTOL.

*Fal.* Say'st thou so, old Jack? go thy ways; I'll make more of thy old body than I have done. Will they yet look after thee? Wilt thou, after the expense of so much money, be now a gainer? Good body, I thank thee. Let them say 'tis grossly done; so it be fairly done, no matter.

*Enter* BARDOLPH.

*Bard.* Sir John, there's one Master Brook below would fain speak with you, and be acquainted with you; and hath sent your worship a morning's draught of sack.

*Fal.* Brook is his name?

*Bard.* Ay, sir.

*Fal.* Call him in; [*Exit* BARDOLPH.] Such Brooks are welcome to me that o'erflow such liquor. Ah! ha! Mistress Ford and Mistress Page, have I encompassed you? go to; *via!*

*Re-enter* BARDOLPH, *with* FORD *disguised.*

*Ford.* Bless you, sir.

*Fal.* And you, sir. Would you speak with me?

*Ford.* I make bold to press with so little preparation upon you.

*Fal.* You're welcome; what's your will? Give us leave, drawer.        [*Exit* BARDOLPH.

*Ford.* Sir, I am a gentleman that have spent much; my name is Brook.

*Fal.* Good Master Brook, I desire more acquaintance of you.

*Ford.* Good Sir John, I sue for yours: not to charge you; for I must let you understand I think myself in better plight for a lender than you are: the which has something emboldened me to this unseasoned intrusion: for they say if money go before, all ways do lie open.

*Fal.* Money is a good soldier, sir, and will on.

*Ford.* Troth, and I have a bag of money here troubles me; if you will help me to bear it, Sir John, take all or half for easing me of the carriage.

*Fal.* Sir, I know not how I may deserve to be your porter.

*Ford.* I will tell you, sir, if you will give me the hearing.

*Fal.* Speak, good Master Brook; I shall be glad to be your servant.

*Ford.* Sir, I hear you are a scholar,—I will be brief with you,———and you have been a man long known to me, though I had never so good means as desire to make myself acquainted with you. I shall discover a thing to you, wherein I must very much lay open mine own imperfection: but, good Sir John, as you have one eye upon my follies, as you hear them unfolded, turn another into the register of your own; that I may pass with a reproof the easier, sith you yourself know how easy it is to be such an *Fal.* Very well, sir; proceed.        [offender.

*Ford.* There is a gentlewoman in this town, her husband's name is Ford.

*Fal.* Well, sir.

*Ford.* I have long loved her, and I protest to you bestowed much on her; followed her with a doting observance; engrossed opportunities to meet her; fee'd every slight occasion that could but niggardly give me sight of her; not only bought many presents to give her, but have given largely to many to know what she would have given: briefly, I have pursued her as love hath pursued me; which hath been on the wing of all occasions. But whatsoever I have merited, either in my mind or in my means, meed, I am sure, I have received none; unless experience be a jewel; that I have purchased at an infinite rate; and that hath taught me to say this:

*Love like a shadow flies, when substance love*
        *pursues;*
*Pursuing that that flies, and flying what pursues.*

*Fal.* Have you received no promise of satisfaction at her hands?

*Ford.* Never.        [pose?

*Fal.* Have you importuned her to such a pur-

*Ford.* Never.

*Fal.* Of what quality was your love, then?

*Ford.* Like a fair house built upon another man's ground; so that I have lost my edifice by mistaking the place where I erected it.

*Fal.* To what purpose have you unfolded this to me?

*Ford.* When I have told you that, I have told you all. Some say that though she appear honest to me, yet in other places she enlargeth her mirth so far that there is shrewd construction made of her. Now, Sir John, here is the heart of my purpose. You are a gentleman of excellent breeding, admirable discourse, of great admittance, authentic in your place and person, generally allowed for your many war-like, court-like, and learned preparations.

*Fal.* O, sir!

*Ford.* Believe it, for you know it:—There is money; spend it, spend it; spend more; spend all I have; only give me so much of your time in exchange of it as to lay an amiable siege to the honesty of this Ford's wife; use your art of wooing, win her to consent to you; if any man may, you may as soon as any.

*Fal.* Would it apply well to the vehemency of your affection, that I should win what you would enjoy? Methinks you prescribe to yourself very preposterously.

*Ford.* O, understand my drift! She dwells so securely on the excellency of her honour that the folly of my soul dares not present itself; she is too bright to be looked against. Now, could I come to her with any detection in my hand, my desires had instance and argument to commend themselves; I could drive her then from the ward of her purity, her reputation, her marriage vow, and a thousand other her defences, which now are too strongly embattled against me. What say you to't, Sir John?

*Fal.* Master Brook, I will first make bold with your money; next, give me your hand: and last, as I am a gentleman, you shall, if you will, enjoy Ford's wife.

*Ford.* O good sir!

*Fal.* Master Brook, I say you shall.

*Ford.* Want no money, Sir John, you shall want none.

*Fal.* Want no Mistress Ford, Master Brook, you shall want none. I shall be with her (I may tell you) by her own appointment: even as you came in to me her assistant, or go-between, parted from me: I say, I shall be with her between ten and eleven; for at that time the jealous rascally knave, her husband, will be forth. Come you to me at night; you shall know how I speed.

*Ford.* I am blest in your acquaintance. Do you know Ford, sir?

*Fal.* Hang him, poor cuckoldly knave! I know him not:—yet I wrong him to call him poor; they say the jealous wittolly knave hath masses of money; for the which his wife seems to me well-favoured. I will use her as the key of the cuckoldly rogue's coffer; and there's my harvest-home.

*Ford.* I would you knew Ford, sir; that you might avoid him if you saw him.

*Fal.* Hang him, mechanical salt-butter rogue! I will stare him out of his wits; I will awe him with my cudgel: it shall hang like a meteor o'er the cuckold's horns: Master Brook, thou shalt know, I will predominate o'er the peasant, and thou shalt lie with his wife.—Come to me soon at night:—Ford's a knave, and I will aggravate his stile; thou, Master Brook, shalt know him for a knave and cuckold:—come to me soon at night.                                    [*Exit.*

*Ford.* What a damned Epicurean rascal is this! —My heart is ready to crack with impatience.— Who says this is improvident jealousy? My wife hath sent to him, the hour is fixed, the match is made. Would any man have thought this?—See the hell of having a false woman! my bed shall be abused, my coffers ransacked, my reputation gnawn at; and I shall not only receive this villanous wrong, but stand under the adoption of abominable terms, and by him that does me this wrong. Terms! names!—— Amaimon sounds well; Lucifer, well; Barbason, well; yet they are devils' additions, the names of fiends: but cuckold! wittol-cuckold! the devil himself hath not such a name. Page is an ass, a secure ass! he will trust his wife; he will not be jealous! I will rather trust a Fleming with my butter, Parson Hugh the Welshman with my cheese, an Irishman with my aqua-vitæ bottle, or a thief to walk my ambling gelding, than my wife with herself: then she plots, then she ruminates, then she devises: and what they think in their hearts they may effect, they will break their hearts but they will effect. Heaven be praised for my jealousy!—Eleven o'clock the hour:—I will prevent this, detect my wife, be revenged on Falstaff, and laugh at Page. I will about it; better three hours too soon than a minute too late. Fie, fie, fie! cuckold! cuckold! cuckold!                                    [*Exit.*

### Scene III.—*Windsor Park.*

#### Enter CAIUS and RUGBY.

*Caius.* Jack Rugby!

*Rug.* Sir?

*Caius.* Vat is de clock, Jack?

*Rug.* 'Tis past the hour, sir, that Sir Hugh promised to meet.

*Caius.* By gar, he has saved his soul, dat he is no come; he has pray his Pible vell, dat he is no come: by gar, Jack Rugby, he is dead already, if he be come.

*Rug.* He is wise, sir; he knew your worship would kill him if he came.

*Caius.* By gar, de herring is no dead, so as I vill kill him. Take your rapier, Jack; I vill tell you how I vill kill him.

*Rug.* Alas, sir, I cannot fence.

*Caius.* Villany, take your rapier.

*Rug.* Forbear: here's company.

#### Enter HOST, SHALLOW, SLENDER, *and* PAGE.

*Host.* Bless thee, bully doctor.

*Shal.* Save you, Master Doctor Caius.

*Page.* Now, good master doctor!

*Slen.* Give you good morrow, sir.

*Caius.* Vat be all you, one, two, tree, four, come for?

*Host.* To see thee fight, to see thee foin, to see thee traverse, to see thee here, to see thee there; to see thee pass thy punto, thy stock, thy reverse, thy distance, thy montánt. Is he dead, my Ethiopian? is he dead, my Francisco? ha, bully! What says my Æsculapius? my Galen? my heart of elder? ha! is he dead, bully Stale? is he dead?

*Caius.* By gar, he is de coward Jack priest of the vorld; he is not show his face.

*Host.* Thou art a Castilian King Urinal! Hector of Greece, my boy!

*Caius.* I pray you, bear vitness that me have stay six, or seven, two, tree hours for him, and he is no come.

*Shal.* He is the wiser man, master doctor: he is a curer of souls, and you a curer of bodies; if you should fight, you go against the hair of your professions; is it not true, Master Page?

*Page.* Master Shallow, you have yourself been a great fighter, though now a man of peace.

*Shal.* Bodikins, Master Page, though I now be old, and of the peace, if I see a sword out my finger itches to make one: though we are justices, and doctors, and churchmen, Master Page, we have some salt of our youth in us; we are the sons of women, Master Page.

*Page.* 'Tis true, Master Shallow.

*Shal.* It will be found so, Master Page. Master Doctor Caius, I am come to fetch you home. I am sworn of the peace; you have showed yourself a wise physician, and Sir Hugh hath shown himself a wise and patient churchman: you must go with me, master doctor.

*Host.* Pardon, guest justice:—A word, Monsieur Muck-water.

*Caius.* Muck-vater! vat is dat?

*Host.* Muck-water, in our English tongue, is valour, bully.

*Caius.* By gar, then I have as much muck-vater as de Englishman:——Scurvy jack-dog priest! by gar, me vill cut his ears.

*Host.* He will clapper-claw thee tightly, bully.

*Caius.* Clapper-de-claw! vat is dat?

*Host.* That is, he will make thee amends.

*Caius.* By gar, me do look he shall clapper-de-claw me; for, by gar, me vill have it.

*Host.* And I will provoke him to't, or let him wag.

*Caius.* Me tank you for dat.

*Host.* And, moreover, bully,—But first, master guest, and Master Page, and eke Cavalero Slender, go you through the town to Frogmore.                                    [*Aside to them.*

*Page.* Sir Hugh is there, is he?

*Host.* He is there: see what humour he is in;

and I will bring the doctor about by the fields.
Will it do well?

*Shal.* We will do it.

*Page, Shal., and Slen.* Adieu, good master
doctor.     [*Exeunt* PAGE, SHAL., *and* SLEN.

*Caius.* By gar, me vill kill de priest: for he
speak for a jack-an-ape to Anne Page.

*Host.* Let him die; but first sheathe thy impatience; throw cold water on thy choler; go
about the fields with me through Frogmore; I
will bring thee where Mistress Anne Page is,
at a farm-house, a-feasting; and thou shalt woo
her. Cryed game, said I well?

*Caius.* By gar, me tank you for dat: by gar,
I love you; and I shall procure-a you de good
guest, de earl, de knight, de lords, de gentlemen, my patients.

*Host.* For the which I will be thy adversary
towards Anne Page; said I well?

*Caius.* By gar, 'tis good: vell said.

*Host.* Let us wag, then.

*Caius.* Come at my heels, Jack Rugby.
                            [*Exeunt.*

## ACT III.

SCENE I.—*A Field near Frogmore.*

*Enter Sir* HUGH EVANS *and* SIMPLE.

*Eva.* I pray you now, good Master Slender's
serving-man, and friend Simple by your name,
which way have you looked for Master Caius,
that calls himself *Doctor of Physick?*

*Sim.* Marry, sir, the city-ward, the park-wd,ra
every way; old Windsor way, and every way
but the town way.     [also look that way.

*Eva.* I most fehemently desire you, you will

*Sim.* I will, sir.

*Eva.* 'Pless my soul! how full of cholers I am,
and trempling of mind!—I shall be glad if he
have deceived me:—how melancholies I am!—
I will knog his urinals about his knave's costard when I have good opportunities for the
'ork—'pless my soul!     [*Sings.*

To shallow rivers, to whose falls
Melodious birds sing madrigals;
There will we make our peds of roses,
And a thousand fragrant posies.
To shallow——

Mercy on me! I have a great dispositions to cry.

Melodious birds sing madrigals—
When as I sat in Pabylon——
And a thousand vagram posies.
To shallow——

*Sim.* Yonder he is, coming this way, Sir Hugh.

*Eva.* He's welcome:

To shallow rivers, to whose falls——

Heaven prosper the right!—What weapons is
he?

*Sim.* No weapons, sir. There comes my master,
Master Shallow, and another gentleman, from
Frogmore, over the stile, this way.

*Eva.* Pray you, give me my gown; or else keep
it in your arms.

*Enter* PAGE, SHALLOW, *and* SLENDER.

*Shal.* How now, master parson? Good-morrow,
good Sir Hugh. Keep a gamester from the dice,
and a good student from his book, and it is
wonderful.

*Slen.* Ah, sweet Anne Page!

*Page.* Save you, good Sir Hugh!

*Eva.* 'Pless you from his mercy sake, all of you!

*Shall.* What! the sword and the word! Do you
study them both, master parson?

*Page.* And youthful still, in your doublet and
hose, this raw rheumatic day?

*Eva.* There is reasons and causes for it.

*Page.* We are come to you to do a good office,
master parson.

*Eva.* Fery well: what is it?

*Page.* Yonder is a most reverend gentleman,
who, belike having received wrong by some
person, is at most odds with his own gravity
and patience that ever you saw.

*Shal.* I have lived fourscore years and upward;
I never heard a man of his place, gravity, and
learning, so wide of his own respect.

*Eva.* What is he?

*Page.* I think you know him; Master Doctor
Caius, the renowned French physician.

*Eva.* Got's will, and his passion of my heart!
I had as lief you would tell me of a mess of
porridge.

*Page.* Why?

*Eva.* He has no more knowledge in Hibocrates
and Galen,—and he is a knave besides; a cowardly knave, as you would desires to be acquainted withal.

*Page.* I warrant you he's the man shoulc fight
with him.

*Slen.* O, sweet Anne Page!

*Shal.* It appears so, by his weapons.—Keep
them asunder;—here comes Doctor Caius.

*Enter* HOST, CAIUS, *and* RUGBY.

*Page.* Nay, good master parson, keep in your
weapon.

*Shal.* So do you, good master doctor.

*Host.* Disarm them, and let them question; let
them keep their limbs whole and hack our
English.

*Caius.* I pray you, let-a me speak a word vit
your ear. Verefore vill you not meet-a me?

*Eva.* Pray you use your patience: in good time.

*Caius.* By gar, you are de coward, de Jack
dog, John ape.

*Eva.* Pray you, let us not be laughing-stogs to
other men's humours; I desire you in friendship, and I will one way or another make you
amends:—I will knog your urinals about your
knave's cogscomb, for missing your meetings
and appointments.

*Caius.* Diable!—Jack Rugby,—mine *Host de
Jarterre,* have I not stay for him to kill him,
have I not, at de place I did appoint?

*Eva.* As I am a Christians soul, now, look you, this is the place appointed. I'll be judgment by mine host of the Garter.

*Host.* Peace, I say, Gallia and Gaul, French and Welsh; soul-curer and body-curer.

*Caius.* Ay, dat is very good! excellent!

*Host.* Peace, I say; hear mine host of the Garter. Am I politic? am I subtle? am I a Machiavel? Shall I lose my doctor? no; he gives me the potions and the motions. Shall I lose my parson? my priest? my Sir Hugh? no; he gives me the proverbs and the no-verbs. Give me thy hand, terrestrial; so:—Give me thy hand, celestial, so.—Boys of art, I have deceived you both; I have directed you, to wrong places; your hearts are mighty, your skins are whole, and let burnt sack be the issue.—Come, lay their swords to pawn:—Follow me, lad of peace; follow, follow, follow.

*Shal.* Trust me, a mad host:—Follow, gentlemen, follow.

*Slen.* O, sweet Anne Page!

[*Exeunt* SHAL., SLEN., PAGE, *and* HOST.

*Caius.* Ha! do I perceive dat? have you make-a de sot of us? ha, ha!

*Eva.* This is well; he has made us his vlouting-stog,—I desire you that we may be friends; and let us knog our prains together, to be revenge on this same scall, scurvy, cogging companion, the host of the Garter.

*Caius.* By gar, vit all my heart; he promise to bring me vere is Anne Page; by gar, he deceive me too.

*Eva.* Well, I will smite his noddles:—Pray you, follow.  [*Exeunt.*

### SCENE II.—*The Street in Windsor.*

#### Enter Mrs. PAGE *and* ROBIN.

*Mrs. Page.* Nay, keep your way, little gallant; you were wont to be a follower, but now you are a leader. Whether had you rather lead mine eyes or eye your master's heels?

*Rob.* I had rather, forsooth, go before you like a man than follow him like a dwarf.

*Mrs. Page.* O you are a flattering boy; now, I see, you'll be a courtier.

#### Enter FORD.

*Ford.* Well met, Mistress Page. Whither go you?

*Mrs. Page.* Truly, sir, to see your wife. Is she at home?

*Ford.* Ay; and as idle as she may hang together, for want of company; I think, if your husbands were dead, you two would marry.

*Mrs. Page.* Be sure of that,—two other husbands.  [cock?

*Ford.* Where had you this pretty weather-

*Mrs. Page.* I cannot tell what the dickens his name is my husband had him off: What do you call your knight's name, sirrah!

*Rob.* Sir John Falstaff.

*Ford.* Sir John Falstaff!

*Mrs. Page.* He, he; I can never hit on's name. There is such a league between my good man and he!—Is your wife at home indeed?

*Ford.* Indeed she is.

*Mrs. Page.* By your leave, sir;—I am sick till I see her.  [*Exeunt Mrs.* PAGE *and* ROBIN.

*Ford.* Has Page any brains? hath he any eyes? hath he any thinking? Sure, they sleep; he hath no use of them. Why, this boy will carry a letter twenty miles as easy as a cannon will shoot point-blank twelve score. He pieces out his wife's inclination; he gives her folly motion and advantage: and now she's going to my wife, and Falstaff's boy with her. A man may hear this shower sing in the wind!—and Falstaff's boy with her!—Good plots!—they are laid; and our revolted wives share damnation together. Well; I will take him, then torture my wife, pluck the borrowed veil of modesty from the so seeming Mistress Page, divulge Page himself for a secure and wilful Actæon; and to these violent proceedings all my neighbours shall cry aim. [*Clock strikes.*] The clock gives me my cue, and my assurance bids me search; there I shall find Falstaff: I shall be rather praised for this than mocked; for it is as positive as the earth is firm that Falstaff is there. I will go.

#### Enter PAGE, SHALLOW, SLENDER, HOST, Sir HUGH EVANS, CAIUS, *and* RUGBY.

*Shal., Page,* &c. Well met, Master Ford.

*Ford.* Trust me, a good knot: I have good cheer at home; and, I pray you, all go with me.

*Shal.* I must excuse myself, Master Ford.

*Slen.* And so must I, sir; we have appointed to dine with Mistress Anne, and I would not break with her for more money than I'll speak of.

*Shal.* We have lingered about a match between Anne Page and my cousin Slender, and this day we shall have our answer.

*Slen.* I hope I have your good will, father Page.

*Page.* You have, Master Slender; I stand wholly for you:—but my wife, master doctor, is for you altogether.

*Caius.* Ay, by gar; and de maid is love a-me; my nursh-a Quickly tell me so mush.

*Host.* What say you to young Master Fenton? he capers, he dances, he has eyes of youth, he writes verses, he speaks holiday, he smells April and May; he will carry't, he will carry't; 'tis in his buttons; he will carry't.

*Page.* Not by my consent, I promise you. The gentleman is of no having: he kept company with the wild Prince and Poins; he is of too high a region, he knows too much. No; he shall not knit a knot in his fortunes with the finger of my substance: if he take her, let him take her simply; the wealth I have waits on my consent, and my consent goes not that way.

*Ford.* I beseech you, heartily, some of you go home with me to dinner: besides your cheer, you shall have sport; I will show you a monster.—Master doctor, you shall go;—so shall you, Master Page;—and you, Sir Hugh.

*Shal.* Well, fare you well:—we shall have the freer wooing at Master Page's.

[*Exeunt* SHAL. a:d SLEN.

*Caius.* Go home, John Rugby; I come anon.

[*Exit* RUGBY.

*Host.* Farewell, my hearts, I will to my honest knight Falstaff, and drink canary with him.

[*Exit* HOST.

*Ford.* [*Aside.*] I think I shall drink in pipe-wine first with him; I'll make him dance. Will you go, gentles?

*All.* Have with you, to see this monster.

[*Exeunt.*

SCENE III.—*A Room in* FORD'S *House.*

*Enter Mrs.* FORD *and Mrs.* PAGE.

*Mrs. Ford.* What, John! what, Robert!

*Mrs. Page.* Quickly, quickly: Is the buck-basket—

*Mrs. Ford.* I warrant:—What, Robin, I say.

*Enter Servants, with a basket.*

*Mrs. Page.* Come, come, come.

*Mrs. Ford.* Here, set it down.

*Mrs. Page.* Give your men the charge; we must be brief.

*Mrs. Ford.* Marry, as I told you before, John, and Robert, be ready here hard by in the brew-house; and when I suddenly call you, come forth, and, without any pause or staggering, take this basket on your shoulders: that done, trudge with it in all haste, and carry it among the whitsters in Datchet mead, and there emp-ty it in the muddy ditch, close by the Thames

*Mrs. Page.* You will do it?          [side.

*Mrs. Ford.* I have told them over and over; they lack no direction. Begone, and come when you are called.          [*Exeunt* Servants.

*Mrs. Page.* Here comes little Robin.

*Enter* ROBIN.

*Mrs. Ford.* How now, my eyas-musket? what news with you?

*Rob.* My master, Sir John, is come in at your back-door, Mistress Ford, and requests your company.          [been true to us?

*Mrs. Page.* You little Jack-a-lent, have you

*Rob.* Ay, I'll be sworn. My master knows not of your being here; and hath threatened to put me into everlasting liberty. if I tell you of it; for he swears he'll turn me away.

*Mrs. Page.* Thou'rt a good boy; this secrecy of thine shall be a tailor to thee, and shall make thee a new doublet and hose.—I'll go hide me.

*Mrs. Ford.* Do so.—Go tell thy master I am alone. Mrs. Page, remember you your cue.

[*Exit* ROBIN.

*Mrs. Page.* I warrant thee; if I do not act it, hiss me.          [*Exit Mrs.* PAGE.

*Mrs. Ford.* Go to then; we'll use this unwhole-some humidity, this gross watery pumpion;— we'll teach him to know turtles from jays.

*Enter* FALSTAFF.

*Fal.* Have I caught thee, *my heavenly jewel?* Why, now let me die, for I have lived long enough; this is the period of my ambition: O this blessed hour!

*Mrs. Ford.* O sweet Sir John!

*Fal.* Mistress Ford, I cannot cog, I cannot prate, Mrs. Ford. Now shall I sin in my wish. I would thy husband were dead; I'll speak it before the best lord, I would make thee my lady.

*Mrs. Ford.* I your lady, Sir John! alas, I should be a pitiful lady.

*Fal.* Let the court of France show me such another; I see how thine eye would emulate the diamond: thou hast the right arched bent of the brow, that becomes the ship-tire, the tire-val-iant, or any tire of Venetian admittance.

*Mrs. Ford.* A plain kerchief, Sir John: my brows become nothing else; nor that well neither.

*Fal.* Thou art a traitor to say so: thou wouldst make an absolute courtier; and the firm fixture of thy foot would give an excellent motion to thy gait, in a semi-circled farthingale. I see what thou wert, if fortune thy foe were not; na-ture is thy friend. Come, thou canst not hide it.

*Mrs. Ford.* Believe me, there's no such thing in me.

*Fal.* What made me love thee? let that per-suade thee, there's something extraordinary in thee. Come, I cannot cog, and say thou art this and that, like a many of these lisping hawthorn buds that come like women in men's apparel, and smell like Buckler's-bury in simple-time; I cannot: but I love thee; none but thee; and thou deservest it.

*Mrs. Ford.* Do not betray me, sir; I fear you love Mrs. Page.

*Fal.* Thou mightst as well say I love to walk by the counter-gate; which is as hateful to me as the reek of a lime-kiln.

*Mrs. Ford.* Well, heaven knows how I love you; and you shall one day find it.

*Fal.* Keep in that mind; I'll deserve it.

*Mrs. Ford.* Nay, I must tell you, so you do, or else I could not be in that mind.

*Rob.* [*Within.*] Mistress Ford, Mistress Ford! here's Mrs. Page at the door, sweating, and blowing, and looking wildly, and would needs speak with you presently.

*Fal.* She shall not see me; I will ensconce me behind the arras.

*Mrs. Ford.* Pray you, do so: she's a very tat-tling woman.—          [FALSTAFF *hides himself.*

*Enter Mrs.* PAGE *and* ROBIN.

What's the matter? how now?

*Mrs. Page.* O Mistress Ford, what have you done? You're shamed, you are overthrown, you are undone for ever.

*Mrs. Ford.* What's the matter, good Mistress Page?

*Mrs. Page.* O well-a-day, Mistress Ford! hav-ing an honest man to your husband, to give him such cause of suspicion!

*Mrs. Ford.* What cause of suspicion?

*Mrs. Page.* What cause of suspicion!—out upon you! how am I mistook in you?

*Mrs. Ford.* Why, alas! what's the matter?

*Mrs. Page.* Your husband's coming hither, woman, with all the officers in Windsor, to search for a gentleman that, he says, is here now in the house, by your consent, to take an ill advantage of his absence: you are undone.

*Mrs. Ford.* Speak louder.—[*Aside.*]—'Tis not so, I hope.

*Mrs. Page.* Pray heaven it be not so, that you have such a man here; but 'tis more certain your husband's coming with half Windsor at his heels, to search for such a one. I come before to tell you: if you know yourself clear, why, I am glad of it; but if you have a friend here, convey, convey him out. Be not amazed; call all your senses to you; defend your reputation, or bid farewell to your good life for ever.

*Mrs. Ford.* What shall I do?—There is a gentleman, my dear friend; and I fear not mine own shame so much as his peril: I had rather than a thousand pounds he were out of the house.

*Mrs. Page.* For shame, never stand *you had rather*, and *you had rather*; your husband's here at hand, bethink you of some conveyance: in the house you cannot hide him.—O, how have you deceived me!—Look, here is a basket; if he be of any reasonable stature, he may creep in here; and throw foul linen upon him, as if it were going to bucking: or, it is whiting-time, send him by your two men to Datchet mead.

*Mrs. Ford.* He's too big to go in there. What shall I do?

### *Re-enter* FALSTAFF.

*Fal.* Let me see't, let me see't! O let me see't! I'll in, I'll in; follow your friend's counsel:—I'll in.

*Mrs. Page.* What! Sir John Falstaff! Are these your letters, knight?

*Fal.* I love thee, and none but thee; help me away: let me creep in here; I'll never—
[*He goes into the basket; they cover him with foul linen.*

*Mrs. Page.* Help to cover your master, boy. Call your men, Mistress Ford:—You dissembling knight!

*Mrs. Ford.* What, John! Robert! John! [*Exit* ROBIN. *Re-enter* Servants.] Go take up these clothes here, quickly; where's the cowl-staff? look, how you drumble: carry them to the laundress in Datchet mead; quickly, come.

### *Enter* FORD, PAGE, CAIUS, *and Sir* HUGH EVANS.

*Ford.* Pray you, come near: if I suspect without cause, why, then make sport at me, then let me be your jest; I deserve it.—How now? whither bear you this?

*Serv.* To the laundress, forsooth.

*Mrs. Ford.* Why, what have you to do whither they bear it? You were best meddle with buck-washing.

*Ford.* Buck? I would I could wash myself of the buck! Buck, buck, buck? Ay, buck; I warrant you, buck; and of the season too; It shall appear. [*Exeunt* Servants *with the basket.*] Gentlemen, I have dreamed to-night; I'll tell you my dream. Here, here, here be my keys: ascend my chambers, search, seek, find out: I'll warrant we'll unkennel the fox:—Let me stop this way first:—so, now uncape.

*Page.* Good Master Ford, be contented: you wrong yourself too much.

*Ford.* True, Master Page.—Up, gentlemen; you shall see sport anon: follow me, gentlemen.          [*Exit.*

*Eva.* This is fery fantastical humours and jealousies.

*Caius.* By gar, 'tis no de fashion of France: it is not jealous in France.

*Page.* Nay, follow him, gentlemen; see the issue of his search.
[*Exeunt* EVANS, PAGE, *and* CAIUS.

*Mrs. Page.* Is there not a double excellency in this?

*Mrs. Ford.* I know not which pleases me better, that my husband is deceived, or Sir John.

*Mrs. Page.* What a taking was he in when your husband asked who was in the basket!

*Mrs. Ford.* I am half afraid he will have need of washing; so throwing him into the water will do him a benefit.

*Mrs. Page.* Hang him, dishonest rascal! I would all of the same strain were in the same distress.

*Mrs. Ford.* I think my husband hath some special suspicion of Falstaff's being here; for I never saw him so gross in his jealousy till now.

*Mrs. Page.* I will lay a plot to try that: and we will yet have more tricks with Falstaff: his dissolute disease will scarce obey this medicine.

*Mrs. Ford.* Shall we send that foolish carrion, Mrs. Quickly, to him, and excuse his throwing into the water; and give him another hope, to betray him to another punishment?

*Mrs. Page.* We'll do it; let him be sent for to-morrow eight o'clock, to have amends.

### *Re-enter* FORD, PAGE, CAIUS, *and Sir* HUGH EVANS.

*Ford.* I cannot find him: maybe the knave bragged of that he could not compass.

*Mrs. Page.* Heard you that?

*Mrs. Ford.* Ay, ay, peace:—You use me well, Master Ford, do you?

*Ford.* Ay, I do so.          [thoughts!

*Mrs. Ford.* Heaven make you better than your [Master Ford.

*Ford.* Amen.

*Mrs. Page.* You do yourself mighty wrong, Master Ford.

*Ford.* Ay, ay; I must bear it.

*Eva.* If there be any pody in the house, and in the chambers, and in the coffers, and in the presses, heaven forgive my sins at the day of judgment!

*Caius.* By gar, nor I too; dere is no—bodies.

*Page.* Fie, fie, Master Ford! are you not ashamed? What spirit, what devil suggests this imagination? I would not have your distemper in this kind for the wealth of Windsor Castle.

*Ford.* 'Tis my fault, Master Page: I suffer for it.

*Eva.* You suffer for a pad conscience: your wive is as honest a 'omans as I will desires among five thousand, and five hundred too.

*Caius.* By gar, I see 'tis an honest woman.

*Ford.* Well;—I promised you a dinner:—Come, come, walk in the park: I pray you, pardon me; I will hereafter make known to you why I have done this.—Come, wife;—come, Mistress Page; I pray you, pardon me; pray heartily, pardon me.

*Page.* Let's go in, gentlemen; but, trust me, we'll mock him. I do invite you to-morrow morning to my house to breakfast; after, we'll a-birding together; I have a fine hawk for the bush. Shall it be so?

*Ford.* Any thing.                    [company.

*Eva.* If there is one, I shall make two in the

*Caius.* If there be one or two, I shall make-a de turd.

*Eva.* In your teeth: for shame.

*Ford.* Pray you go, Master Page.

*Eva.* I pray you now, remembrance to-morrow on the lousy knave, mine host.

*Caius.* Dat is good; by gar, vit all my heart.

*Eva.* A lousy knave; to have his gibes and his mockeries.                    [*Exeunt.*

SCENE IV.—*A Room in* PAGE'S *House.*

*Enter* FENTON *and Mrs.* ANNE PAGE.

*Fent.* I see, I cannot get thy father's love; Therefore, no more turn me to him, sweet Nan.

*Anne.* Alas! how then?

*Fent.*                    Why, thou must be thyself.
He doth object I am too great of birth;
And that, my state being gall'd with my expense,
I seek to heal it only by his wealth.
Besides these, other bars he lays before me,——
My riots past, my wild societies;
And tells me 'tis a thing impossible.
I should love thee but as a property.

*Anne.* Maybe he tells you true?

*Fent.* No; heaven so speed me in my time to come!
Albeit, I will confess, thy father's wealth
Was the first motive that I woo'd thee, Anne:
Yet, wooing thee, I found thee of more value
Than stamps in gold, or sums in sealed bags;
And 'tis the very riches of thyself
That now I aim at.

*Anne.*                    Gentle Master Fenton,
Yet seek my father's love; still seek it, sir:
If opportunity and humblest suit
Cannot attain it, why then.—Hark you hither.
                    [*They converse apart.*

*Enter* SHALLOW, SLENDER, *and Mrs.* QUICKLY.

*Shal.* Break their talk, Mistress Quickly; my kinsman shall speak for himself.

*Slen.* I'll make a shaft or a bolt on't; 'slid, 'tis but venturing.

*Shal.* Be not dismayed.

*Slen.* No; she shall not dismay me. I care not for that,—but that I am afeard.

*Quick.* Hark ye: Master Slender would speak a word with you.                    [choice.

*Anne.* I come to him.—This is my father's O, what a world of vile ill-favour'd faults. Looks handsome in three hundred pounds a-year!                    [*Aside.*

*Quick.* And how does good Master Fenton? Pray you, a word with you.

*Shal.* She's coming; to her, coz. O boy, thou hadst a father!

*Slen.* I had a father, Mistress Anne—my uncle can tell you good jests of him:—Pray you, uncle, tell Mistress Anne the jest, how my father stole two geese out of a pen, good uncle.

*Shal.* Mistress Anne, my cousin loves you.

*Slen.* Ay, that I do; as well as I love any woman in Gloucestershire.

*Shal.* He will maintain you like a gentlewoman.

*Slen.* Ay, that I will, come cut and long-tail, under the degree of a 'squire.

*Shal.* He will make you a hundred and fifty pounds jointure.                    [himself.

*Anne.* Good Master Shallow, let him woo for

*Shal.* Marry, I thank you for it; I thank you for that good comfort. She calls you, coz; I'll leave you.

*Anne.* Now, Master Slender.

*Slen.* Now, good Mistress Anne.

*Anne.* What is your will?

*Slen.* My will? 'od's heartlings, that's a pretty jest indeed! I ne'er made my will yet, I thank heaven; I am not such a sickly creature, I give heaven praise.                    [with me?

*Anne.* I mean, Master Slender, what would you

*Slen.* Truly, for mine own part I would little or nothing with you. Your father and my uncle have made motions: if it be my luck, so: if not, happy man be his dole! They can tell you how things go better than I can. You may ask your father; here he comes.

*Enter* PAGE *and Mrs.* PAGE.

*Page.* Now, Master Slender:—Love him, daughter Anne.—
Why, how now! what does Master Fenton here? You wrong me, sir, thus still to haunt my house: I told you, sir, my daughter is disposed of.

*Fent.* Nay, Master Page, be not impatient.

*Mrs. Page.* Good Master Fenton, come not to my child.

*Page.* She is no match for you.

*Fent.* Sir, will you hear me?

*Page.*                    No, good Master Fenton.
Come, Master Shallow; come, son Slender, in:—                    [Fenton.
Knowing my mind, you wrong me, Master
                    [*Exeunt* PAGE, SHAL., *and* SLEN.

*Quick.* Speak to Mrs. Page.

*Fent.* Good Mistress Page, for that I love your daughter

In such a righteous fashion as I do,　　　[ners,
Perforce, against all checks, rebukes, and man-
I must advance the colours of my love,
And not retire. Let me have your good will.
*Anne.* Good mother, do not marry me to yond
　　fool.
*Mrs. Page.* I mean it not; I seek you a better
　　husband.
*Quick.* That's my master, master doctor.
*Anne.* Alas! I had rather be set quick i' the
　　earth.
And bowled to death with turnips.
*Mrs. Page.* Come, trouble not yourself, Good
　　Master Fenton.
I will not be your friend, nor enemy:
My daughter will I question how she loves you,
And as I find her, so am I affected;
Till then, farewell, sir:—She must needs go in;
Her father will be angry.
　　　　　　　[*Exeunt Mrs.* PAGE *and* ANNE.
*Fent.* Farewell, gentle mistress; farewell, Nan.
*Quick.* This is my doing, now:—Nay, said I,
will you cast away your child on a fool, and
a physician? Look on Master Fenton:—this is
my doing.
*Fent.* I thank thee; and I pray thee, once to-
　　night
Give my sweet Nan this ring. There's for thy
　　pains.　　　　　　　　　　　　　　[*Exit.*
*Quick.* Now heaven send thee good fortune!
A kind heart he hath: a woman would run
through fire and water for such a kind heart.
But yet I would my master had Mistress Anne:
or I would Master Slender had her: or, in sooth,
I would Master Fenton had her: I will do what
I can for them all three; for so I have promised,
and I'll be as good as my word; but speciously
for Master Fenton. Well, I must of another
errand to Sir John Falstaff from my two mistresses. What a beast am I to slack it! [*Exit.*

SCENE V.—*A Room in the Garter Inn.*

*Enter* FALSTAFF *and* BARDOLPH.

*Fal.* Bardolph, I say,—
*Bard.* Here, sir.
*Fal.* Go fetch me a quart of sack; put a toast
in't. [*Exit* BARD.] Have I lived to be carried
in a basket, like a barrow of butcher's offal;
and to be thrown into the Thames? Well, if I
be served such another trick, I'll have my
brains ta'en out and butter'd, and give them
to a dog for a new year's gift. The rogues
slighted me into the river with as little remorse
as they would have drowned a bitch's blind
puppies, fifteen i' the litter: and you may know
by my size that I have a kind of alacrity in
sinking; if the bottom were as deep as hell I
should down. I had been drowned but that the
shore was shelvy and shallow: a death that I
abhor; for the water swells a man; and what a
thing should I have been when I had been
swelled! I should have been a mountain of
mummy.

*Re-enter* BARDOLPH, *with the wine.*

*Bard.* Here's Mistress Quickly, sir, to speak
with you.
*Fal.* Come, let me pour in some sack to the
Thames water; for my belly's as cold as if I had
swallowed snow-balls for pills to cool the reins.
Call her in.
*Bard.* Come in, woman.

*Enter Mrs.* QUICKLY.

*Quick.* By your leave; I cry you mercy. Give
your worship good-morrow.
*Fal.* Take away these chalices. Go, brew me
a bottle of sack finely.
*Bard.* With eggs, sir?
*Fal.* Simple of itself; I'll no pullet-sperm in
my brewage —[*Exit* BARD.]—How now?
*Quick.* Marry, sir, I come to your worship
from Mistress Ford.
*Fal.* Mistress Ford! I have had ford enough:
I was thrown into the ford: I have my belly
full of ford.
*Quick.* Alas the day! good heart, that was not
her fault: she does so take on with her men;
they mistook their erection.
*Fal.* So did I mine, to build upon a foolish
woman's promise.
*Quick.* Well, she laments, sir, for it, that it
would yearn your heart to see it. Her husband
goes this morning a-birding; she desires you
once more to come to her between eight and
nine; I must carry her word quickly: she'll
make you amends, I warrant you.
*Fal.* Well, I will visit her. Tell her so; and bid
her think what a man is: let her consider his
frailty, and then judge of my merit.
*Quick.* I will tell her.
*Fal.* Do so. Between nine and ten, say'st thou?
*Quick.* Eight and nine, sir.
*Fal.* Well, begone: I will not miss her.
*Quick.* Peace be with you, sir.　　　　[*Exit.*
*Fal.* I marvel I hear not of Master Brook; he
sent me word to stay within: I like his money
well. O, here he comes.

*Enter* FORD.

*Ford.* Bless you, sir!
*Fal.* Now, Master Brook? you come to know
what hath passed between me and Ford's wife.
*Ford.* That, indeed, Sir John, is my business.
*Fal.* Master Brook, I will not lie to you; I
was at her house the hour she appointed me.
*Ford.* And how sped you, sir?
*Fal.* Very ill-favouredly, Master Brook.
*Ford.* How so, sir? Did she change her determination?
*Fal.* No, Master Brook; but the peaking cor-
nuto her husband, Master Brook, dwelling in a
continual 'larum of jealousy, comes me in the
instant of our encounter, after we had embraced,
kissed, protested, and, as it were, spoke the prologue of our comedy; and at his heels a rabble
of his companions, thither provoked and insti-

gated by his distemper, and forsooth, to search his house for his wife's love.

*Ford.* What! while you were there?

*Fal.* While I was there.          [find you?

*Ford.* And did he search for you and could not

*Fal.* You shall hear. As good luck would have it, comes in one Mistress Page; gives intelligence of Ford's approach; and, by her invention and Ford's wife's distraction, they conveyed me into a buck-basket.

*Ford.* A buck-basket!

*Fal.* By the Lord, a buck-basket: rammed me in with foul shirts and smocks, socks, foul stockings, and greasy napkins; that, Master Brook, there was the rankest compound of villanous smell that ever offended nostril.

*Ford.* And how long lay you there?

*Fal.* Nay, you shall hear, Master Brook, what I have suffered to bring this woman to evil for your good. Being thus crammed in the basket, a couple of Ford's knaves, his hinds, were called forth by their mistress to carry me in the name of foul clothes to Datchet-lane: they took me on their shoulders; met the jealous knave their master in the door; who asked them once or twice what they had in their basket: I quaked for fear lest the lunatic knave would have searched it; but fate, ordaining he should be a cuckold, held his hand. Well: on went he for a search, and away went I for foul clothes. But mark the sequel, Master Brook; I suffered the pangs of three several deaths: first, an intolerable fright to be detected with a jealous rotten bell-wether: next, to be compassed, like a good bilbo, in the circumference of a peck, hilt to point, heel to head: and then, to be stopped in, like a strong distillation, with stinking clothes that fretted in their own grease: think of that, —a man of my kidney,—think of that: that am as subject to heat as butter; a man of continual dissolution and thaw; it was a miracle to 'scape suffocation. And in the height of this bath, when I was more than half-stewed in grease, like a Dutch dish, to be thrown into the Thames, and cooled, glowing hot, in that surge, like a horse-shoe; think of that,—hissing hot,— think of that, Master Brook.

*Ford.* In good sadness, sir, I am sorry that for my sake you have suffered all this. My suit, then, is desperate; you'll undertake her no more.

*Fal.* Master Brook, I will be thrown into Etna, as I have been into Thames, ere I will leave her thus. Her husband is this morning gone a-birding: I have received from her another embassy of meeting; 'twixt eight and nine is the hour, Master Brook.

*Ford.* 'Tis past eight already, sir.

*Fal.* Is it? I will then address me to my appointment. Come to me at your convenient leisure, and you shall know how I speed; and the conclusion shall be crowned with your enjoying her. Adieu. You shall have her, Master Brook; Master Brook, you shall cuckold Ford. [*Exit.*

*Ford.* Hum! ha! is this a vision? is this a dream? do I sleep? Master Ford, awake; awake, Master Ford; there's a hole made in your best coat, Master Ford. This 'tis to be married! this 'tis to have linen and buck-baskets!—Well, I will proclaim myself what I am: I will now take the lecher; he is at my house: he cannot 'scape me; 'tis impossible he should; he cannot creep into a halfpenny purse nor into a pepper box; but, lest the devil that guides him should aid him, I will search impossible places. Though what I am I cannot avoid, yet to be what I would not shall not make me tame; if I have horns to make one mad, let the proverb go with me, I'll be horn mad.          [*Exit.*

## ACT IV.

### SCENE I.—*The Street.*

*Enter Mrs.* PAGE, *Mrs.* QUICKLY, *and* WILLIAM.

*Mrs. Page.* Is he at Master Ford's already, think'st thou?

*Quick.* Sure he is by this; or will be presently: but truly he is very courageous mad about his throwing into the water. Mistress Ford desires you to come suddenly.

*Mrs. Page.* I'll be with her by and by; I'll but bring my young man here to school. Look, where his master comes; 'tis a playing day, I see.

*Enter Sir* HUGH EVANS.

How now, Sir Hugh? no school to-day?

*Eva.* No; Master Slender is let the boys leave to play.

*Quick.* Blessing of his heart!

*Mrs. Page.* Sir Hugh, my husband says my son profits nothing in the world at his book; I pray you ask him some questions in his accidence.

*Eva.* Come hither, William; hold up your head; come.

*Mrs. Page.* Come on, sirrah: hold up your head; answer your master; be not afraid.

*Eva.* William, how many numbers is in nouns?

*Will.* Two.

*Quick.* Truly, I thought there had been one number more; because they say od's nouns.

*Eva.* Peace your tattlings. What is *fair*, William?

*Will.* Pulcher.

*Quick.* Polecats! there are fairer things than polecats, sure.

*Eva.* You are a very simplicity, 'oman; I pray you, peace. What is *lapis*, William?

*Will.* A stone.

*Eva.* And what is a stone, William?

*Will.* A pebble.

*Eva.* No, it is *lapis*: I pray you remember in your prain.

*Will.* Lapis.

*Eva.* That is good, William. What is he, William, that does lend articles?

*Will.* Articles are borrowed of the pronoun;

and be thus declined, *Singulariter, nominativo, hic, hæc, hoc.*

*Eva.* Nominativo, hig, hag, hog:—pray you, mark: *genitivo, hujus.* Well, what is your *accusative case?*

*Will.* Accusativo, hinc.

*Eva.* I pray you, have your remembrance, child. *Accusativo, hing, hang, hog.*     [you.

*Quick.* Hang hog is Latin for bacon, I warrant

*Eva.* Leave your prabbles, 'oman. What is the focative case, William?

*Will.* O—vocativo, O.

*Eva.* Remember, William, focative is *caret.*

*Quick.* And that's a good root.

*Eva.* 'Oman, forbear.

*Mrs. Page.* Peace.

*Eva.* What is your *genitive case plural,* William?

*Will.* Genitive case?

*Eva.* Ay.

*Will.* Genitive,—horum, harum, horum.

*Quick.* 'Vengeance of *Jenny's* case! fie on her! —never name her, child, if she be a whore.

*Eva.* For shame, 'oman.

*Quick.* You do ill to teach the child such words: he teaches him to hick and to hack, which they'll do fast enough of themselves, and to call horum: fie upon you!

*Eva.* 'Oman, art thou lunatics? hast thou no understandings for thy cases, and the numbers of the genders? Thou art as foolish Christian creatures as I would desires.

*Mrs. Page.* Pr'ythee, hold thy peace.

*Eva.* Show me now, William, some declensions of your pronouns.

*Will.* Forsooth, I have forgot.

*Eva.* It is *ki, kæ, cod;* if you forget your *kies,* your *kæs,* and your *cods,* you must be preeches. Go your ways and play, go.

*Mrs. Page.* He is a better scholar than I thought he was.

*Eva.* He is a good sprag memory. Farewell, Mistress Page.

*Mrs. Page.* Adieu, good Sir Hugh.     [*Exit Sir Hugh.*] Get you home, boy.—Come, we stay too long.     [*Exeunt.*

### Scene II.—*A Room in* Ford's *House.*

*Enter* Falstaff *and* Mrs. Ford.

*Fal.* Mistress Ford, your sorrow hath eaten up my sufferance: I see you are obsequious in your love, and I profess requital to a hair's breadth; not only, Mistress Ford, in the simple office of love, but in all the accoutrement, complement, and ceremony of it. But are you sure of your husband now?

*Mrs. Ford.* He is a-birding, sweet Sir John.

*Mrs. Page.* [*Within.*] What hoa, gossip Ford, what hoa!

*Mrs. Ford.* Step into the chamber, Sir John.     [*Exit* Falstaff.

*Enter* Mrs. Page.

*Mrs. Page.* How now, sweetheart? who's at home beside yourself?

*Mrs. Ford.* Why, none but mine own people.

*Mrs. Page.* Indeed?

*Mrs. Ford.* No, certainly;—Speak louder.     [*Aside.*

*Mrs. Page.* Truly I am so glad you have nobody here.

*Mrs. Ford.* Why?

*Mrs. Page.* Why, woman, your husband is in his old lunes again: he so takes on yonder with my husband; so rails against all married mankind: so curses all Eve's daughters, of what complexion soever; and so buffets himself on the forehead, crying *Peer-out, peer-out!* that any madness I ever yet beheld seemed but tameness, civility, and patience, to this his distemper he is in now: I am glad the fat knight is not here.

*Mrs. Ford.* Why? does he talk of him?

*Mrs. Page.* Of none but him; and swears he was carried out, the last time he searched for him, in a basket: protests to my husband he is now here; and hath drawn him and the rest of their company from their sport to make another experiment of his suspicion; but I am glad the knight is not here; now he shall see his own foolery.

*Mrs. Ford.* How near is he, Mistress Page?

*Mrs. Page.* Hard by; at street end; he will be here anon.

*Mrs. Ford.* I am undone!—The knight is here.

*Mrs. Page.* Why, then, you are utterly ashamed, and he's but a dead man. What a woman are you!—Away with him, away with him; better shame than murder.

*Mrs. Ford.* Which way should he go? How should I bestow him? Shall I put him into the basket again?

*Re-enter* Falstaff.

*Fal.* No, I'll come no more i' the basket. May I not go out ere he come?

*Mrs. Page.* Alas! three of Master Ford's brothers watch the door with pistols, that none shall issue out: otherwise you might slip away ere he came. But what make you here?

*Fal.* What shall I do?—I'll creep up into the chimney.

*Mrs. Ford.* There they always used to discharge their birding pieces. Creep into the kiln-hole.

*Fal.* Where is it?

*Mrs. Ford.* He will seek there, on my word. Neither press, coffer, chest, trunk, well, vault, but he hath an abstract for the remembrance of such places, and goes to them by his note. There is no hiding you in the house.

*Fal.* I'll go out then.

*Mrs. Page.* If you go out in your own semblance, you die, Sir John. Unless you go out disguised,—

*Mrs. Ford.* How might we disguise him?

*Mrs. Page.* Alas the day, I know not. There is no woman's gown big enough for him; otherwise he might put on a hat, a muffler, and a kerchief, and so escape.

*Fal.* Good hearts, devise something: any extremity rather than a mischief.

*Mrs. Ford.* My maid's aunt, the fat woman of Brentford, has a gown above.

*Mrs. Page.* On my word, it will serve him; she's as big as he is: and there's her thrummed hat, and her muffle too. Run up, Sir John.

*Mrs. Ford.* Go, go, sweet Sir John. Mistress Page and I will look some linen for your head.

*Mrs. Page.* Quick, quick; we'll come dress you straight: put on the gown the while.

[*Exit* FALSTAFF.

*Mrs. Ford.* I would my husband would meet him in this shape: he cannot abide the old woman of Brentford; he swears she's a witch, forbade her my house, and hath threatened to beat her.

*Mrs. Page.* Heaven guide him to thy husband's cudgel; and the devil guide his cudgel afterwards!

*Mrs. Ford.* But is my husband coming?

*Mrs. Page.* Ay, in good sadness is he; and he talks of the basket too, howsoever he hath had intelligence.

*Mrs. Ford.* We'll try that; for I'll appoint my men to carry the basket again to meet him at the door with it as they did last time.

*Mrs. Page.* Nay, but he'll be here presently: let's go dress him like the witch of Brentford.

*Mrs. Ford.* I'll first direct my men what they shall do with the basket. Go up, I'll bring linen for him straight. [*Exit.*

*Mrs. Page.* Hang him, dishonest varlet! we cannot misuse him enough.

We'll leave a proof, by that which we will do,
Wives may be merry and yet honest too:
We do not act that often jest and laugh;
'Tis old but true, *Still swine eat all the draff.*

[*Exit.*

*Re-enter* Mrs. FORD, *with two* Servants.

*Mrs. Ford.* Go, sirs, take the basket again on your shoulders: your master is hard at door; if he bid you set it down, obey him: quickly, despatch. [*Exit.*

*1 Serv.* Come, come, take it up.

*2 Serv.* Pray heaven it be not full of the knight again. [lead.

*1 Serv.* I hope not; I had as lief bear so much

*Enter* FORD, PAGE, SHALLOW, CAIUS, *and* Sir HUGH EVANS.

*Ford.* Ay, but if it prove true, Master Page, have you any way then to unfool me again?—Set down the basket, villain:—Somebody call my wife.—You, youth in a basket, come out here!—O, you panderly rascals! there's a knot, a gin, a pack, a conspiracy against me. Now shall the devil be shamed. What! wife, I say! come, come forth; behold what honest clothes you send forth to bleaching.

*Page.* Why, this passes! Master Ford, you are not to go loose any longer; you must be pinioned.

*Eva.* Why, this is lunatics! this is mad as a mad dog!

*Shal.* Indeed, Master Ford, this is not well: indeed.

*Enter* Mrs. FORD.

*Ford.* So say I too, sir.—Come hither, Mistress Ford; Mistress Ford, the honest woman, the modest wife, the virtuous creature, that hath the jealous fool to her husband!—I suspect without cause, mistress, do I?

*Mrs. Ford.* Heaven be my witness, you do, if you suspect me in any dishonesty.

*Ford.* Well said, brazen-face; hold it out.—Come forth, sirrah.

[*Pulls the clothes out of the basket.*

*Page.* This passes! [clothes alone.

*Mrs. Ford.* Are you not ashamed? Let the

*Ford.* I shall find you anon.

*Eva.* 'Tis unreasonable! Will you take up your wife's clothes? Come away.

*Ford.* Empty the basket, I say.

*Mrs. Ford.* Why, man, why,—

*Ford.* Master Page, as I am a man, there was one conveyed out of my house yesterday in this basket. Why may not he be there again? In my house I am sure he is: my intelligence is true: my jealousy is reasonable. Pluck me out all the linen.

*Mrs. Ford.* If you find a man there he shall die a flea's death.

*Page.* Here's no man.

*Shal.* By my fidelity, this is not well, Master Ford; this wrongs you.

*Eva.* Master Ford, you must pray, and not follow the imaginations of your own heart: this is jealousies.

*Ford.* Well, he's not here I seek for.

*Page.* No, nor no where else but in your brain.

*Ford.* Help to search my house this one time: if I find not what I seek, show no colour for my extremity; let me for ever be your table sport; let them say of me, As jealous as Ford, that searched a hollow walnut for his wife's leman. Satisfy me once more; once more search with me.

*Mrs. Ford.* What, hoa, Mistress Page! come you and the old woman down; my husband will come into the chamber.

*Ford.* Old woman! What old woman's that?

*Mrs. Ford.* Why, it is my maid's aunt of Brentford.

*Ford.* A witch, a quean, an old cozening quean! Have I not forbid her my house? She comes of errands, does she? We are simple men; we do not know what's brought to pass under the profession of fortune telling. She works by charms, by spells, by the figure, and such daubery as this is; beyond our element: we know nothing.——Come down, you witch, you hag you; come down, I say.

*Mrs. Ford.* Nay, good, sweet husband;—good gentlemen, let him not strike the old woman.

*Enter* FALSTAFF *in women's clothes, led by* Mrs. PAGE.

*Mrs. Page.* Come, Mother Prat, come; give me your hand.

'ord. I'll *prat* her:————Out of my door, you
ritch, [*beats him*] you rag, you baggage, you
polecat, you ronyon! out! out! I'll conjure you,
'll fortune-tell you.  [*Exit* FALSTAFF.
*Mrs. Page.* Are you not ashamed? I think you
have killed the poor woman.
*Mrs. Ford.* Nay, he will do it:—'Tis a goodly
credit for you.
*Ford.* Hang her, witch!
*Eva.* By yea and no, I think the 'oman is a
witch indeed: I like not when a 'oman has a
great peard; I spy a great peard under her muffler.
*Ford.* Will you follow, gentlemen? I beseech
you follow; see but the issue of my jealousy:
if I cry out thus upon no trail, never trust me
when I open again.
*Page.* Let's obey his humour a little farther.
Come, gentlemen.
[*Exeunt* PAGE, FORD, SHAL., *and* EVANS.
*Mrs. Page.* Trust me, he beat him most pitifully.
*Mrs. Ford.* Nay, by the mass, that he did not;
he beat him most unpitifully methought.
*Mrs. Page.* I'll have the cudgel hallowed and
hung o'er the altar; it hath done meritorious
service.
*Mrs. Ford.* What think you? May we, with
the warrant of womanhood and the witness of
a good conscience, pursue him with any further
revenge?
*Mrs. Page.* The spirit of wantonness is, sure,
scared out of him; if the devil have him not in
fee-simple, with fine and recovery, he will never,
I think, in the way of waste, attempt us again.
*Mrs. Ford.* Shall we tell our husbands how we
have served him?
*Mrs. Page.* Yes, by all means; if it be but to
scrape the figures out of your husband's brains.
If they can find in their hearts the poor unvir-
tuous fat knight shall be any further afflicted,
we two will still be the ministers.
*Mrs. Ford.* I'll warrant they'll have him publicly shamed: and methinks there would be no
period to the jest should he not be publicly
shamed.
*Mrs. Page.* Come, to the forge with it then,
shape it: I would not have things cool. [*Exeunt.*

SCENE III.—*A Room in the Garter Inn.*

*Enter* HOST *and* BARDOLPH.

*Bard.* Sir, the Germans desire to have three of
your horses: the duke himself will be to-morrow
at court, and they are going to meet him.
*Host.* What duke should that be comes so secretly? I hear not of him in the court. Let me
speak with the gentlemen; they speak English.
*Bard.* Ay, sir; I'll call them to you.
*Host.* They shall have my horses; but I'll make
them pay; I'll sauce them: they have had my
houses a week at command; I have turned
away my other guests: they must come off; I'll
sauce them. Come.  [*Exeunt.*

SCENE IV.—*A Room in* FORD's *House.*

*Enter* PAGE, FORD, *Mrs.* PAGE, *Mrs.* FORD,
*and Sir* HUGH EVANS

*Eva.* 'Tis one of the pest discretions of a 'oman
as ever I did look upon.
*Page.* And did he send you both these letters
at an instant?
*Mrs. Page.* Within a quarter of an hour.
*Ford.* Pardon me, wife. Henceforth, do what
thou wilt;
I rather will suspect the sun with cold
Than thee with wantonness: now doth thy
honour stand,
In him that was of late an heretic,
As firm as faith.
*Page.*     'Tis well, 'tis well; no more.
Be not as extreme in submission
As in offence;
But let our plot go forward: let our wives
Yet once again, to make us public sport,
Appoint a meeting with this old fat fellow,
Where we may take him and disgrace him for it.
*Ford.* There is no better way than that they
spoke of.
*Page.* How! to send him word they'll meet
him in the park at midnight; fie, fie; he'll
never come.
*Eva.* You say he has been thrown into the
rivers; and has been grievously peaten as an old
'oman; methinks there should be terrors in him
that he should not come; methinks his flesh is
punished, he shall have no desires.
*Page.* So think I too.  [he comes,
*Mrs. Ford.* Devise but how you'll use him when
And let us two devise to bring him thither.
*Mrs. Page.* There is an old tale goes, that
Herne the hunter,
Sometime a keeper here in Windsor forest,
Doth all the winter time, at still midnight,
Walk round about an oak, with great ragg'd
horns;
And there he blasts the tree, and takes the cattle,
And makes milch-kine yield blood, and shakes
a chain
In a most hideous and dreadful manner: [know
You have heard of such a spirit; and well you
The supersitious idle-headed eld
Received, and did deliver to our age,
This tale of Herne the hunter for a truth. [fear
*Page.* Why, yet there want not many that do
In deep of night to walk by this Herne's oak:
But what of this?
*Mrs. Ford.*     Marry, this is our device;
That Falstaff at that oak shall meet with us,
Disguised, like Herne, with huge horns on his
head.  [come,
*Page.* Well, let it not be doubted but he'll
And in this shape. When you have brought
him thither,
What shall be done with him? what is your plot?
*Mrs. Page.* That likewise have we thought
upon, and thus:
Nan Page my daughter, and my little son,

And three or four more of their growth, we'll
    dress                  [white,
Like urchins, ouphes, and fairies, green and
With rounds of waxen tapers on their heads,
And rattles in their hands; upon a sudden,
As Falstaff, she, and I, are newly met,
Let them from forth a saw-pit rush at once
With some diffused song; upon their sight
We two in great amazedness will fly:
Then let them all encircle him about,
And fairy-like, to pinch the unclean knight;
And ask him why that hour of fairy revel
In their so sacred paths he dares to tread
In shape profane.
*Mrs. Ford.*       And till he tell the truth,
Let the supposed fairies pinch him sound,
And burn him with their tapers.
*Mrs. Page.*      The truth being known,
We'll all present ourselves, dis-horn the spirit,
And mock him home to Windsor.
*Ford.*          The children must
Be practised well to this or they'll ne'er do't.
*Eva.* I will teach the children their behaviours;
and I will be like a jack-an-apes also, to burn
the knight with my taber.
*Ford.* That will be excellent. I'll go buy them
vizards.                [the fairies,
*Mrs. Page.* My Nan shall be the queen of all
Finely attired in a robe of white.    [time.
*Page.* That silk will I go buy;—and in that
Shall Master Slender steal my Nan away. [*Aside.*
And marry her at Eton.——Go, send to Fal-
    staff straight.
*Ford.* Nay, I'll to him again, in name of Brook;
He'll tell me all his purpose. Sure, he'll come.
*Mrs. Page.* Fear not you that. Go, get us
    properties,
And tricking for our fairies.
*Eva.* Let us about it. It is admirable pleasures,
and fery honest knaveries.
           [*Exeunt* PAGE, FORD, *and* EVANS.
*Mrs. Page.* Go, Mistress Ford,
Send quickly to Sir John to know his mind.
                    [*Exit Mrs.* FORD.
I'll to the doctor; he hath my good-will,
And none but he, to marry with Nan Page.
That Slender, though well landed, is an idiot;
And he my husband best of all affects:
The doctor is well money'd, and his friends
Potent at court; he, none but he, shall have her.
Though twenty thousand worthier come to
    crave her.                [*Exit.*

SCENE V.—*A Room in the Garter Inn.*

*Enter* HOST *and* SIMPLE.

*Host.* What wouldst thou have, boor? what,
thick-skin? speak, breathe, discuss; brief, short,
quick, snap.
*Sim.* Marry, sir, I come to speak with Sir John
Falstaff from Master Slender.
*Host.* There's his chamber, his house, his castle,
his standing-bed and truckle-bed; 'tis painted
about with the story of the Prodigal, fresh and

new. Go, knock and call; he'll speak like an
Anthropophaginian unto thee. Knock, I say.
*Sim.* There's an old woman, a fat woman, gone
up into his chamber; I'll be so bold as stay, sir,
till she come down; I come to speak with her,
indeed.
*Host.* Ha! a fat woman! the knight may be
robbed: I'll call.—Bully knight! Bully Sir
John! speak from thy lungs military. Art thou
there? it is thine host, thine Ephesian, calls.
*Fal.* [*Above.*] How now, mine host?
*Host.* Here's a Bohemian-Tartar tarries the
coming down of thy fat woman. Let her descend, bully, let her descend; my chambers are
honourable. Fie! privacy? fie!

*Enter* FALSTAFF.

*Fal.* There was, mine host, an old fat woman
even now with me; but she's gone.
*Sim.* Pray you, sir, was't not the wise woman
of Brentford?
*Fal.* Ay, marry was it, muscle-shell. What
would you with her?
*Sim.* My master, sir, my Master Slender, sent
to her, seeing her go thorough the streets, to
know, sir, whether one Nym, sir, that beguiled
him of a chain had the chain or no.
*Fal.* I spake with the old woman about it.
*Sim.* And what says she, I pray, sir?
*Fal.* Marry, she says that the very same man
that beguiled Master Slender of his chain coz-
ened him of it.
*Sim.* I would I could have spoken with the
woman herself; I had other things to have
spoken with her too, from him.
*Fal.* What are they? let us know.
*Host.* Ay, come; quick.
*Sim.* I may not conceal them, sir.
*Fal.* Conceal them, or thou diest.
*Sim.* Why, sir, they were nothing but about
Mistress Anne Page; to know if it were my
master's fortune to have her or no.
*Fal.* 'Tis, 'tis his fortune.
*Sim.* What, sir?
*Fal.* To have her,—or no. Go; say the woman
told me so.
*Sim.* May I be so bold to say so, sir?
*Fal.* Ay, Sir Tike; who more bold?
*Sim.* I thank your worship: I shall make my
master glad with these tidings. [*Exit* SIMPLE.
*Host.* Thou art clerkly, thou art clerkly, Sir
John. Was there a wise woman with thee?
*Fal.* Ay, that there was, mine host; one that
hath taught me more wit than ever I learned
before in my life: and I paid nothing for it
neither, but was paid for my learning.

*Enter* BARDOLPH.

*Bard.* Out, alas, sir! cozenage! mere cozenage!
*Host.* Where be my horses? speak well of them,
varletto.
*Bard.* Run away with the cozeners: for so soon
as I came beyond Eton they threw me off from
behind one of them in a slough of mire; and

set spurs and away, like three German devils, three Doctor Faustuses.

*Host.* They are gone but to meet the duke, villain: do not say they be fle̋d; Germans are honest men.

*Enter Sir* HUGH EVANS.

*Eva.* Where is mine host?

*Host.* What is the matter, sir?

*Eva.* Have a care of your entertainments: there is a friend of mine come to town tells me there is three couzin germans that has cozened all the hosts of Readings, of Maidenhead, of Colebrook, of horses and money. I tell you for good-will, look you: you are wise, and full of gibes and vlouting-stogs; and 'tis not convenient you should be cozened: fare you well.          [*Exit.*

*Enter Dr.* CAIUS.

*Caius.* Vere is mine *Host de Jarterre?*

*Host.* Here, master doctor, in perplexity and doubtful dilemma.

*Caius.* I cannot tell vat is dat: but it is tell-a me dat you make grand preparation for a duke de *Jarmany:* by my trot dere is no duke dat de court is know to come; I tell you for good-vill: adieu.          [*Exit.*

*Host.* Hue and cry, villain, go:—assist me, knight; I am undone: fly, run, hue and cry, villain! I am undone!

[*Exeunt* HOST *and* BARD.

*Fal.* I would all the world might be cozened; for I have been cozened and beaten too. If it should come to the ear of the court how I have been transformed, and how my transformation hath been washed and cudgelled, they would melt me out of my fat, drop by drop, and liquor fishermen's boots with me; I warrant they would whip me with their fine wits till I were as crest-fallen as a dried pear. I never prospered since I foreswore myself at *primero.* Well, if my wind were but long enough to say my prayers, I would repent.—

*Enter Mrs.* QUICKLY.

Now! whence come you?

*Quick.* From the two parties, forsooth.

*Fal.* The devil take one party and his dam the other, and so they shall be both bestowed! I have suffered more for their sakes, more than the villanous inconstancy of man's disposition is able to bear.

*Quick.* And have not they suffered? Yes, I warrant; speciously one of them; Mistress Ford, good heart, is beaten black and blue, that you cannot see a white spot about her.

*Fal.* What tell'st thou me of black and blue? I was beaten myself into all the colours of the rainbow; and I was like to be apprehended for the witch of Brentford; but that my admirable dexterity of wit, my counterfeiting the action of an old woman, delivered me, the knave constable had set me i' the stocks, i' the common stocks, for a witch.

*Quick.* Sir, let me speak with you in your chamber: you shall hear how things go; and, I warrant, to your content. Here is a letter will say somewhat. Good hearts, what ado here is to bring you together! Sure, one of you does not serve heaven well, that you are so crossed.

*Fal.* Come up intó my chamber.          [*Exeunt.*

SCENE VI.—*Another Room in the Garter Inn.*

*Enter* FENTON *and* HOST.

*Host.* Master Fenton, talk not to me; my mind is heavy, I will give over all.          [pose,

*Fent.* Yet hear me speak. Assist me in my pur-And, as I am a gentleman, I'll give thee A hundred pound in gold, more than your loss.

*Host.* I will hear you, Master Fenton; and I will, at the least, keep your counsel.

*Fent.* From time to time I have acquainted you With the dear love I bear to fair Anne Page; Who, mutually, hath answer'd my affection,— So far forth as herself might be her chooser,— Even to my wish: I have a letter from her Of such contents as you will wonder at; The mirth whereof so larded with my matter That neither, singly, can be manifested Without the show of both;—wherein fat Falstaff Hath a great scene: the image of the jest
          [*Showing the letter*
I'll show you here at large. Hark, good mine host,          [one,
To-night at Herne's oak, just 'twixt twelve and Must my sweet Nan present the fairy queen: The purpose why is here; in which disguise, While other jests are something rank on foot, Her father hath commanded her to slip Away with Slender, and with him at Eton Immediately to marry: she hath consented: Now, sir, Her mother, ever strong against that match, And firm for Doctor Caius, hath appointed That he shall likewise shuffle her away While other sports are tasking of their minds, And at the deanery, where a priest attends, Straight marry her: to this her mother's plot She, seemingly obedient, likewise hath Made promise to the doctor:—Now thus it rests; Her father means she shall be all in white; And in that habit, when Slender sees his time To take her by the hand and bid her go, She shall go with him: her mother hath intended, The better to denote her to the doctor,— For they must all be mask'd and vizarded,— That, quaint in green, she shall be loose enrobed, With ribands pendant, flaring 'bout her head; And when the doctor spies his vantage ripe, To pinch her by the hand, and, on that token, The maid hath given consent to go with him.

*Host.* Which means she to deceive? father or mother?

*Fent.* Both, my good host, to go along with me: And here it rests,—that you'll procure the vicar To stay for me at church,'twixt twelve and one, And, in the lawful name of marrying,

To give our hearts united ceremony.    [vicar:
*Host.* Well, husband your device; I'll to the Bring you the maid, you shall not lack a priest.
*Fent.* So shall I evermore be bound to thee; Besides, I'll make a present recompense.
     [*Exeunt.*

## ACT V.

### SCENE I.—*A Room in the Garter Inn.*

#### *Enter* FALSTAFF *and Mrs.* QUICKLY.

*Fal.* Pr'ythee, no more prattling:—go.——I'll hold. This is the third time; I hope good luck lies in odd numbers. Away, go; they say there is divinity in odd numbers, either in nativity, chance, or death.—Away.
*Quick.* I'll provide you a chain: and I'll do what I can to get you a pair of horns.
*Fal.* Away, I say; time wears: hold up your head, and mince.     [*Exit Mrs.* QUICKLY.

#### *Enter* FORD.

How now, Master Brook? Master Brook, the matter will be known to-night or never. Be you in the Park about midnight, at Herne's oak, and you shall see wonders.
*Ford.* Went you not to her yesterday, sir, as you told me you had appointed.
*Fal.* I went to her, Master Brook, as you see, like a poor old man; but I came from her, Master Brook, like a poor old woman. That same knave, Ford her husband, hath the finest mad devil of jealousy in him, Master Brook, that ever governed frenzy. I will tell you.— He beat me grievously, in the shape of a woman; for in the shape of man, Master Brook, I fear not Goliath with a weaver's beam: because I know also life is a shuttle. I am in haste; go along with me: I'll tell you all, Master Brook. Since I plucked geese, played truant, and whipped top, I knew not what it was to be beaten till lately. Follow me: I'll tell you strange things of this knave Ford, on whom to-night I will be revenged, and I will deliver his wife into your hand.—Follow. Strange things in hand, Master Brook! follow. [*Exeunt*

### SCENE II.—*Windsor Park.*

#### *Enter* PAGE, SHALLOW, *and* SLENDER.

*Page.* Come, come; we'll couch i' the castle-ditch till we see the light of our fairies.— Remember, son Slender, my daughter.
*Slen.* Ay, forsooth; I have spoke with her, and we have a nay-word how to know one another; I come to her in white and cry *mum;* she cries *budget;* and by that we know one another.
*Shal.* That's good too: but what needs either your *mum* or her *budget?* the white will decipher her well enough.—It hath struck ten o'clock.
*Page.* The night is dark; light and spirits will become it well. Heaven prosper our sport! No man means evil but the devil, and we shall know him by his horns. Let's away; follow me.     [*Exeunt.*

### SCENE III.—*The Street in Windsor.*

#### *Enter Mrs.* PAGE, *Mrs.* FORD, *and Dr.* CAIUS.

*Mrs. Page.* Master doctor, my daughter is in green: when you see your time, take her by the hand, away with her to the deanery, and dispatch it quickly. Go before into the park; we two must go together.
*Caius.* I know vat I have to do; adieu.
*Mrs. Page.* Fare you well, sir.     [*Exit* CAIUS.] My husband will not rejoice so much at the abuse of Falstaff as he will chafe at the doctor's marrying my daughter: but 'tis no matter; better a little chiding than a great deal of heart-break.
*Mrs. Ford.* Where is Nan now, and her troop of fairies? and the Welsh devil, Hugh?
*Mrs. Page.* They are all couched in a pit hard by Herne's oak, with obscured lights; which, at the very instant of Falstaff's and our meeting, they will at once display to the night.
*Mrs. Ford.* That cannot choose but amaze him.
*Mrs. Page.* If he be not amazed he will be mocked; if he be amazed he will every way be mocked.
*Mrs. Ford.* We'll betray him finely.
*Mrs. Page.* Against such lewdsters and their lechery,
Those that betray them do no treachery.
*Mrs. Ford.* The hour draws on. To the oak, to the oak!     [*Exeunt.*

### SCENE IV.—*Windsor Park.*

#### *Enter Sir* HUGH EVANS, *and Fairies.*

*Eva.* Trib, trib, fairies; come; and remember your parts: be pold, I pray you; follow me into the pit; and when I give the watch-'ords, do as I pid you. Come, come; trib, trib.     [*Exeunt.*

### SCENE V.—*Another part of the Park.*

#### *Enter* FALSTAFF *disguised, with a buck's head on.*

*Fal.* The Windsor bell hath struck twelve; the minute draws on. Now the hot-blooded gods assist me:—Remember, Jove, thou wast a bull for thy Europa; love set on thy horns.—O powerful love! that in some respects makes a beast a man; in some other a man a beast.—You were also, Jupiter, a swan, for the love of Leda: —O omnipotent love! how near the god drew to the complexion of a goose?—A fault done first in the form of a beast:—O Jove, a beastly fault! and then another fault in the semblance of a fowl; think on't, Jove; a foul fault.—When gods have hot backs what shall poor men do? For me, I am here a Windsor stag; and the fattest, I think, i' the forest. Send me a cool rut-time, Jove, or who can blame me to piss my tallow? Who comes here? my doe?

#### *Enter Mrs.* FORD *and Mrs.* PAGE.

*Mrs. Ford.* Sir John? art thou there, my deer? my male deer?

*Fal.* My doe with the black scut?—Let the sky rain potatoes; let it thunder to the tune of *Green Sleeves;* hail kissing-comfits, and snow eringoes; let there come a tempest of provocation, I will shelter me here.　[*Embracing her.*

*Mrs. Ford.* Mistress Page is come with me, sweetheart.

*Fal.* Divide me like a bribe-buck, each a haunch: I will keep my sides to myself, my shoulders for the fellow of this walk, and my horns I bequeath your husbands. Am I a woodman? ha! Speak I like Herne the hunter?— Why, now is Cupid a child of conscience; he makes restitution. As I am a true spirit, welcome!　　　　　　　　　[*Noise within.*

*Mrs. Page.* Alas! what noise?

*Mrs. Ford.* Heaven forgive our sins!

*Fal.* What should this be?

*Mrs. Ford.* ⎱
*Mrs. Page.* ⎰　Away, away.　[*They run off.*

*Fal.* I think the devil will not have me damned lest the oil that is in me should set hell on fire; he would never else cross me thus.

*Enter Sir* HUGH EVANS, *like a satyr; Mrs.* QUICKLY *and* PISTOL; ANNE PAGE, *as the Fairy Queen, attended by her brother and others, dressed like fairies, with waxen tapers on their heads.*

*Quick.* Fairies, black, gray, green, and white, You moonshine revellers and shades of night, You orphan-heirs of fixed destiny, Attend your office and your quality. Crier Hobgoblin, make the fairy o-yes.

*Pist.* Elves, list your names; silence, you airy toys.

*Cricket,* to Windsor chimneys shalt thou leap: Where fires thou find'st unrak'd, and hearths unswept, There pinch the maids as blue as bilberry: Our radiant queen hates sluts and sluttery.

*Fal.* They are fairies; he that speaks to them shall die:　　　　　　　　　　[eye. I'll wink and couch: no man their works must [*Lies down upon his face.*

*Eva.* Where's *Pede?*—Go you, and where you find a maid That, ere she sleep, has thrice her prayers said, Raise up the organs of her fantasy, Sleep she as sound as careless infancy; But those as sleep and think not on their sins, Pinch them, arms, legs, backs, shoulders, sides, and shins.

*Quick.* About, about; Search Windsor castle, elves, within and out: Strew good luck, ouphes, on every sacred room; That it may stand till the perpetual doom, In state as wholesome as in state 'tis fit, Worthy the owner and the owner it. The several chairs of order look you scour With juice of balm and every precious flower; Each fair instalment, coat, and several crest, With loyal blazon evermore be blest! And nightly, meadow-fairies, look you sing,

Like to the Garter's compass, in a ring: The expressure that it bears, green let it be, More fertile-fresh than all the field to see; And, *Hony soit qui mal y pense* write, In emerald tufts, flowers purple, blue and white: Like sapphire, pearl, and rich embroidery, Buckled below fair knighthood's bending knee: Fairies use flowers for their charáctery. Away; disperse: but, 'tis one o'clock, Our dance of custom, round about the oak Of Herne the hunter, let us not forget.

*Eva.* Pray you, lock hand in hand; yourselves in order set: And twenty glow-worms shall our lanterns be, To guide our measure round about the tree. But, stay: I smell a man of middle earth.

*Fal.* Heavens defend me from that Welsh fairy! lest he transform me to a piece of cheese!

*Pist.* Vile worm, thou wast o'erlook'd even in thy birth.

*Quick.* With trial-fire touch me his finger end: If he be chaste, the flame will back descend And turn him to no pain; but if he start, It is the flesh of a corrupted heart.

*Pist.* A trial, come.

*Eva.*　　　　Come, will this wood take fire? [*They burn him with their tapers.*

*Fal.* Oh, oh, oh!

*Quick.* Corrupt, corrupt, and tainted in desire! About him, fairies; sing a scornful rhyme; And, as you trip, still pinch him to your time.

*Eva.* It is right; indeed he is full of lecheries and iniquity.

### SONG.

Fye on sinful fantasy!
Fye on lust and luxury!
Lust is but a bloody fire,
Kindled with unchaste desire,
Fed in heart; whose flames aspire,
As thoughts do blow them, higher and higher,
Pinch him, fairies, mutually;
Pinch him for his villany;
Pinch him, and burn him, and turn him about,
Till candles, and star-light, and moonshine be out.

*During this song the fairies pinch* FALSTAFF. *Doctor* CAIUS *comes one way, and steals away a fairy in green;* SLENDER *another way, and takes off a fairy in white; and* FENTON *comes, and steals away Mrs.* ANNE PAGE. *A noise of hunting is made within. All the fairies run away.* FALSTAFF *pulls off his buck's head and rises.*

*Enter* PAGE, FORD, Mrs. PAGE, *and Mrs.* FORD. *They lay hold on him.*

*Page.* Nay, do not fly; I think we have watch'd you now: Will none but Herne the hunter serve your turn?

*Mrs. Page.* I pray you come; hold up the jest no higher:— Now, good Sir John, how like you Windsor wives? See you these, husband? do not these fair yokes Become the forest better than the town?

*Ford.* Now, sir, who's a cuckold now?—Master Brook, Falstaff's a knave, a cuckoldly knave; here are his horns, Master Brook: and,

Master Brook, he hath enjoyed nothing of Ford's but his buck-basket, his cudgel, and twenty pounds of money; which must be paid to Master Brook; his horses are arrested for it, Master Brook.

*Mrs. Ford.* Sir John, we have had ill luck; we could never meet. I will never take you for my love again, but I will always count you my deer.

*Fal.* I do begin to perceive that I am made an ass.

*Ford.* Ay, and an ox too; both the proofs are extant.

*Fal.* And these are not fairies? I was three or four times in the thought they were not fairies: and yet the guiltiness of my mind, the sudden surprise of my powers, drove the grossness of the foppery into a received belief, in despite of the teeth of all rhyme and reason, that they were fairies. See now how wit may be made a Jack-a-lent when 'tis upon ill employment.

*Eva.* Sir John Falstaff, serve Got and leave your desires, and fairies will not pinse you.

*Ford.* Well said, fairy Hugh.

*Eva.* And leave you your jealousies too, I pray you.

*Ford.* I will never mistrust my wife again, till thou art able to woo her in good English.

*Fal.* Have I laid my brain in the sun, and dried it, that it wants matter to prevent so gross o'er-reaching as this? Am I ridden with a Welsh goat too? Shall I have a coxcomb of frize? 'Tis time I were choked with a piece of toasted cheese.

*Eva.* Seese is not good to give putter; your pelly is all putter.

*Fal.* Seese and putter! have I lived to stand at the taunt of one that makes fritters of English? This is enough to be the decay of lust and late-walking through the realm.

*Mrs. Page.* Why, Sir John, do you think, though we would have thrust virtue out of our hearts by the head and shoulders, and have given ourselves without scruple to hell, that ever the devil could have made you our delight?

*Ford.* What! a hodge-pudding? a bag of flax?

*Mrs. Page.* A puffed man?

*Page.* Old, cold, withered, and of intolerable entrails?

*Ford.* And one that is as slanderous as Satan?

*Page.* And as poor as Job?

*Ford.* And as wicked as his wife?

*Eva.* And given to fornications, and to taverns, and sack, and wine, and metheglins, and to drinkings, and swearings, and starings, pribbles, and prabbles?

*Fal.* Well, I am your theme: you have the start of me; I am dejected; I am not able to answer the Welsh flannel: ignorance itself is a plummet o'er me; use me as you will.

*Ford.* Marry, sir, we'll bring you to Windsor, to one Master Brook, that you have cozened of money, to whom you should have been a pander: over and above that you have suffered, I think, to repay that money will be a biting affliction.

*Mrs. Ford.* Nay, husband, let that go to make amends:

Forgive that sum, and so we'll all be friends.

*Ford.* Well, here's my hand; all's forgiven at last.

*Page.* Yet be cheerful, knight: thou shalt eat a posset to-night at my house; where I will desire thee to laugh at my wife, that now laughs at thee. Tell her Master Slender hath married her daughter.

*Mrs. Page.* Doctors doubt that: if Anne Page be my daughter, she is by this Doctor Caius' wife.    [*Aside.*

*Enter* SLENDER.

*Slen.* Who—ho! ho! father Page!

*Page.* Son! how now? how now, son? have you dispatched?

*Slen.* Dispatched!—I'll make the best in Gloucestershire know on't; would I were hanged, la, else.

*Page.* Of what, son?

*Slen.* I came yonder at Eton to marry Mistress Anne Page, and she's a great lubberly boy. If it had not been i' the church I would have swinged him, or he should have swinged me. If I did not think it had been Anne Page, would I might never stir, and 'tis a postmaster's boy.

*Page.* Upon my life then you took the wrong.

*Slen.* What need you tell me that? I think so, when I took a boy for a girl. If I had been married to him, for all he was in woman's apparel, I would not have had him.

*Page.* Why, this is your own folly. Did not I tell you how you should know my daughter by her garments?

*Slen.* I went to her in white and cried *mum*, and she cried *budget*, as Anne and I had appointed; and yet it was not Anne, but a postmaster's boy.

*Eva.* Jeshu! Master Slender, cannot you see but marry boys?

*Page.* Oh, I am vexed at heart: what shall I do?

*Mrs. Page.* Good George, be not angry: I knew of your purpose; turned my daughter into green; and, indeed, she is now with the doctor at the deanery, and there married.

*Enter* CAIUS.

*Caius.* Vere is Mistress Page? By gar, I am cozened! I ha' married *un garçon*, a boy; *un paisan*, by gar, a boy; it is not Anne Page: by gar, I am cozened.

*Mrs. Page.* Why, did you take her in green?

*Caius.* Ay, by gar, and 'tis a boy: by gar, I'll raise all Windsor.    [*Exit* CAIUS.

*Ford.* This is strange. Who hath got the right Anne?

*Page.* My heart misgives me:—here comes Master Fenton.

*Enter* FENTON *and* ANNE PAGE.

How now, Master Fenton?

*Anne.* Pardon, good father! good my mother, pardon!

*Page.* Now, Mistress, how chance you went not with Master Slender?

*Mrs. Page.* Why went you not with master doctor, maid?

*Fent.* You do amaze her: Hear the truth of it.
You would have married her most shamefully,
Where there was no proportion held in love.
The truth is, she and I, long since contracted,
Are now so sure that nothing can dissolve us.
The offence is holy that she hath committed:
And this deceit loses the name of craft,
Of disobedience, or unduteous title;
Since therein she doth evitate and shun
A thousand irreligious cursed hours,
Which forced marriage would have brought upon
her.

*Ford.* Stand not amazed: here is no remedy:—
In love, the heavens themselves do guide the
state;

Money buys lands, and wives are sold by fate.

*Fal.* I am glad, though you have ta'en a special stand to strike at me, that your arrow hath glanced.

*Page.* Well, what remedy? Fenton, heaven give thee joy!
What cannot be eschewed must be embraced.

*Fal.* When night-dogs run all sorts of deer are chased.

*Eva.* I will dance and eat plums at your wedding.

*Mrs. Page.* Well, I will muse no further:—
Master Fenton,
Heaven give you many, many merry days!—
Good husband, let us every one go home,
And laugh this sport o'er by a country fire;
Sir John and all.

*Ford.* Let it be so:—Sir John,
To Master Brook you yet shall hold your word;
For he, to-night, shall lie with Mistress Ford.
                                        [*Exeunt.*

TWELFTH NIGHT.

Act III. Sc. 4.

# TWELFTH NIGHT; OR, WHAT YOU WILL

## DRAMATIS PERSONÆ

ORSINO, *Duke of Illyria.*
SEBASTIAN, *a young Gentleman, brother to* VIOLA.
ANTONIO, *a Sea Captain, friend to* SEBASTIAN.
A SEA CAPTAIN, *friend to* VIOLA.
VALENTINE, } *Gentlemen attending on the*
CURIO, } *Duke.*
SIR TOBY BELCH, *Uncle of* OLIVIA.
SIR ANDREW AGUE-CHEEK.

MALVOLIO, *Steward to* OLIVIA.
FABIAN, } *Servants to* OLIVIA.
CLOWN, }

OLIVIA, *a rich Countess.*
VIOLA, *in love with the Duke.*
MARIA, OLIVIA'S *Woman.*

Lords, Priests, Sailors, Officers, Musicians, *and other* Attendants.

SCENE.—*A City in* ILLYRIA; *and the Sea-coast near it.*

## ACT I.

### SCENE I.—*An Apartment in the* DUKE'S *Palace.*

*Enter* DUKE, CURIO, Lords; Musicians *attending.*

*Duke.* If music be the food of love, play on,
Give me excess of it; that, surfeiting,
The appetite may sicken and so die.—
That strain again;—it had a dying fall;
O, it came o'er my ear like the sweet south,
That breathes upon a bank of violets,
Stealing, and giving odour.—Enough; no more;
'Tis not so sweet now as it was before.
O spirit of love, how quick and fresh art thou!
That, notwithstanding thy capacity
Receiveth as the sea, nought enters there,
Of what validity and pitch soever,
But falls into abatement and low price
Even in a minute! so full of shapes is fancy,
That it alone is high-fantastical.
*Cur.* Will you go hunt, my lord?
*Duke.*                      What, Curio?
*Cur.*                          The hart.
*Duke.* Why, so I do, the noblest that I have:
O, when mine eyes did see Olivia first,
Methought she purg'd the air of pestilence;
That instant was I turn'd into a hart;
And my desires, like fell and cruel hounds,
E'er since pursue me.—How now? what news from her?

*Enter* VALENTINE.

*Val.* So please my lord, I might not be admitted,
But from her handmaid do return this answer:
The element itself, till seven years' heat,
Shall not behold her face at ample view;
But, like a cloistress, she will veiled walk,
And water once a-day her chamber round
With eye-offending brine: all this to season
A brother's dead love, which she would keep fresh
And lasting in her sad remembrance.          [frame,
*Duke.* O, she that hath a heart of that fine
To pay this debt of love but to a brother,
How will she love when the rich golden shaft
Hath kill'd the flock of all affections else
That live in her! when liver, brain, and heart,
These sov'reign thrones, are all supplied and fill'd,
Her sweet perfections,—with one self king!-
Away before me to sweet beds of flowers;
Love-thoughts lie rich when canopied with bowers.          [*Exeunt.*

### SCENE II.—*The Sea-coast.*

*Enter* VIOLA, Captain, *and* Sailors.

*Vio.* What country, friends, is this?
*Cap.*                          Illyria, lady.
*Vio.* And what should I do in Illyria?
My brother he is in Elysium.
Perchance he is not drown'd:—What think you, sailors?          [sav'd.
*Cap.* It is perchance that you yourself were
*Vio.* O my poor brother! and so perchance, may he be.          [chance,
*Cap.* True, madam; and, to comfort you with
Assure yourself, after our ship did split,
When you, and that poor number sav'd with you,
Hung on our driving boat, I saw your brother,
Most provident in peril, bind himself,—
Courage and hope both teaching him the practice,—
To a strong mast that liv'd upon the sea;
Where, like Arion on the dolphin's back,
I saw him hold acquaintance with the waves
So long as I could see.
*Vio.*                For saying so, there's gold:
Mine own escape unfoldeth to my hope,
Whereto thy speech serves for authority,
The like of him. Know'st thou this country?
*Cap.* Ay, madam, well; for I was bred and born
Not three hours' travel from this very place.
*Vio.* Who governs here?

*Cap.*                   A noble duke, in nature
As in his name.

*Vio.*             What is his name?

*Cap.*                         Orsino.

*Vio.* Orsino! I have heard my father name him.
He was a bachelor then.

*Cap.*                   And so is now,
Or was so very late: for but a month
Ago I went from hence; and then 'twas fresh
In murmur,—as you know, what great ones do,
The less will prattle of,—that he did seek
The love of fair Olivia.

*Vio.*               What's she?

*Cap.* A virtuous maid, the daughter of a count
That died some twelvemonth since; then leav-
    ing her
In the protection of his son, her brother,
Who shortly also died: for whose dear love,
They say, she hath abjured the company
And sight of men.

*Vio.*          O that I served that lady!
And might not be delivered to the world,
Till I had made mine own occasion mellow
What my estate is.

*Cap.*            That were hard to compass:
Because she will admit no kind of suit,
No, not the duke's.

*Vio.* There is a fair behaviour in thee, captain;
And though that nature with a beauteous wall
Doth oft close in pollution, yet of thee
I will believe thou hast a mind that suits
With this thy fair and outward character.
I pray thee, and I'll pay thee bounteously,
Conceal me what I am; and be my aid
For such disguise as, haply, shall become
The form of my intent. I'll serve this duke;
Thou shalt present me as an eunuch to him;
It may be worth thy pains; for I can sing,
And speak to him in many sorts of music
That will allow me very worth his service.
What else may hap to time I will commit;
Only shape thou thy silence to my wit.

*Cap.* Be you his eunuch and your mute I'll be;
When my tongue blabs, then let mine eyes not see!

*Vio.* I thank thee. Lead me on.    [*Exeunt.*

SCENE III.—*A Room in* OLIVIA'S *House.*

*Enter Sir* TOBY BELCH *and* MARIA.

*Sir To.* What a plague means my niece, to
take the death of her brother thus? I am sure
care's an enemy to life.

*Mar.* By my troth, Sir Toby, you must come
in earlier o' nights; your cousin, my lady, takes
great exceptions to your ill hours.

*Sir To.* Why, let her except, before excepted.

*Mar.* Ay, but you must confine yourself within
the modest limits of order.

*Sir To.* Confine? I'll confine myself no finer
than I am: these clothes are good enough to drink
in, and so be these boots too; an they be not,
let them hang themselves in their own straps.

*Mar.* That quaffing and drinking will undo
you: I heard my lady talk of it yesterday; and

of a foolish knight that you brought in one
night here to be her wooer.

*Sir To.* Who? Sir Andrew Ague-cheek?

*Mar.* Ay, he.

*Sir To.* He's as tall a man as any's in Illyria.

*Mar.* What's that to the purpose?

*Sir To.* Why, he has three thousand ducats
a-year.

*Mar.* Ay, but he'll have but a year in all these
ducats; he's a very fool, and a prodigal.

*Sir To.* Fye, that you'll say so! he plays o'
the viol-de-gambo, and speaks three or four
languages word for word without book, and
hath all the good gifts of nature.

*Mar.* He hath, indeed,—almost natural: for,
besides that he's a fool, he's a great quarreler;
and, but that he hath the gift of a coward to
allay the gust he hath in quarrelling, 'tis
thought among the prudent he would quickly
have the gift of a grave.

*Sir To.* By this hand, they are scoundrels and
substractors that say so of him. Who are they?

*Mar.* They that add, moreover, he's drunk
nightly in your company.

*Sir To.* With drinking healths to my niece;
I'll drink to her as long as there is a passage in
my throat and drink in Illyria. He's a coward
and a coystril that will not drink to my niece
till his brains turn o' the toe like a parish-top.
What, wench? Castiliano-vulgo! for here comes
Sir Andrew Ague-face.

*Enter Sir* ANDREW AGUE-CHEEK.

*Sir And.* Sir Toby Belch! how now, Sir Toby
Belch?

*Sir To.* Sweet Sir Andrew?

*Sir. And.* Bless you, fair shrew.

*Mar.* And you too, sir.

*Sir To.* Accost, Sir Andrew, accost.

*Sir. And.* What's that?

*Sir To.* My niece's chamber-maid.

*Sir And.* Good Mistress Accost, I desire better
acquaintance.

*Mar.* My name is Mary, sir.

*Sir And.* Good Mistress Mary Accost,—

*Sir To.* You mistake, knight: accost is, front
her, board her, woo her, assail her.

*Sir And.* By my troth, I would not undertake
her in this company. Is that the meaning of
accost?

*Mar.* Fare you well, gentlemen.

*Sir To.* An thou let part so, Sir Andrew, would
thou mightst never draw sword again.

*Sir And.* An you part so, mistress, I would I
might never draw sword again. Fair lady, do
you think you have fools in hand?

*Mar.* Sir, I have not you by the hand.

*Sir And.* Marry, but you shall have; and here's
my hand.

*Mar.* Now, sir, thought is free. I pray you,
bring your hand to the buttery-bar and let it
drink.

*Sir And.* Wherefore, sweetheart? what's your
metaphor?

*Mar.* It's dry, sir.

*Sir And.* Why, I think so; I am not such an ass but I can keep my hand dry. But what's your jest?

*Mar.* A dry jest, sir.

*Sir And.* Are you full of them?

*Mar.* Ay, sir; I have them at my fingers' ends: marry, now I let go your hand I am barren.
[*Exit* MARIA.

*Sir To.* O knight, thou lack'st a cup of canary: When did I see thee so put down?

*Sir And.* Never in your life, I think; unless you see canary put me down. Methinks sometimes I have no more wit than a Christian or an ordinary man has; but I am a great eater of beef, and, I believe, that does harm to my wit.

*Sir To.* No question.

*Sir And.* An I thought that, I'd forswear it. I'll ride home to-morrow, Sir Toby.

*Sir To.* *Pourquoy*, my dear knight?

*Sir And.* What is *pourquoy?* do or not do? I would I had bestowed that time in the tongues that I have in fencing, dancing, and bear-baiting. O, had I but followed the arts!

*Sir To.* Then hadst thou had an excellent head of hair.

*Sir And.* Why, would that have mended my hair?

*Sir To.* Past question; for thou seest it will not curl by nature.

*Sir And.* But it becomes me well enough, does't not?

*Sir To.* Excellent; it hangs like flax on a distaff; and I hope to see a housewife take thee between her legs and spin it off.

*Sir And.* Faith, I'll home to-morrow, Sir Toby; your niece will not be seen; or, if she be, it's four to one she'll none of me; the count himself here hard by woos her.

*Sir To.* She'll none o' the count; she'll not match above her degree, neither in estate, years, nor wit; I have heard her swear it. Tut, there's life in't, man.

*Sir And.* I'll stay a month longer. I am a fellow o' the strangest mind i' the world; I delight in masques and revels sometimes altogether.

*Sir To.* Art thou good at these kick-shaws, knight?

*Sir And.* As any man in Illyria, whatsoever he be, under the degree of my betters; and yet I will not compare with an old man.

*Sir To.* What is thy excellence in a galliard, knight?

*Sir And.* Faith, I can cut a caper.

*Sir To.* And I can cut the mutton to't.

*Sir And.* And, I think, I have the back-trick simply as strong as any man in Illyria.

*Sir To.* Wherefore are these things hid? wherefore have these gifts a curtain before them? are they like to take dust, like Mistress Mall's picture? why dost thou not go to church in a galliard and come home in a coranto? My very walk should be a jig; I would not so much as make water but in a sink-a-pace. What dost thou mean? is it a world to hide virtues in? I did think, by the excellent constitution of thy leg, it was formed under the star of a galliard.

*Sir And.* Ay, 'tis strong, and it does indifferent well in a flame-coloured stock. Shall we set about some revels?

*Sir To.* What shall we do else? were we not born under Taurus?

*Sir And.* Taurus? that's sides and heart.

*Sir To.* No, sir; it is legs and thighs. Let me see thee caper: ha! higher: ha, ha!—excellent!
[*Exeunt.*

SCENE IV.—*A Room in the* DUKE'S *Palace.*

*Enter* VALENTINE, *and* VIOLA *in man's attire.*

*Val.* If the duke continue these favours towards you, Cesario, you are like to be much advanced; he hath known you but three days, and already you are no stranger.

*Vio.* You either fear his humour or my negligence, that you call in question the continuance of his life. Is he inconstant, sir, in his favours?

*Val.* No, believe me.

*Enter* DUKE, CURIO, *and* Attendants.

*Vio.* I thank you. Here comes the count.

*Duke.* Who saw Cesario, ho?

*Vio.* On your attendance, my lord; here.

*Duke.* Stand you awhile aloof.—Cesario, Thou know'st no less but all; I have unclasp'd To thee the book even of my secret soul: Therefore, good youth, address thy gait unto her; Be not denied access, stand at her doors, And tell them there thy fixed foot shall grow Till thou have audience.

*Vio.*                    Sure, my noble lord, If she be so abandon'd to her sorrow As it is spoke, she never will admit me.

*Duke.* Be clamorous, and leap all civil bounds Rather than make unprofited return.

*Vio.* Say I do speak with her, my lord. What then?

*Duke.* O, then unfold the passion of my love, Surprise her with discourse of my dear faith: It shall become thee well to act my woes; She will attend it better in thy youth Than in a nuncio of more grave aspect.

*Vio.* I think not so, my lord.

*Duke.*                    Dear lad, believe it, For they shall yet belie thy happy years That say thou art a man: Diana's lip Is not more smooth and rubious; thy small pipe Is as the maiden's organ, shrill and sound, And all is semblative a woman's part. I know thy constellation is right-apt For this affair:—Some four or five attend him: All, if you will; for I myself am best When least in company:—Prosper well in this And thou shalt live as freely as thy lord, To call his fortunes thine.

*Vio.*                    I'll do my best

To woo your, lady: yet, [*aside*] a barful strife!
Whoe'er I woo, myself would be his wife.

SCENE V.—*A Room in* OLIVIA'S *House.*

*Enter* MARIA *and* CLOWN.

*Mar.* Nay; either tell me where thou hast been,
or I will not open my lips so wide as a bristle
may enter in way of thy excuse: my lady will
hang thee for thy absence.

*Clo.* Let her hang me: he that is well hanged
in this world needs to fear no colours.

*Mar.* Make that good.

*Clo.* He shall see none to fear.

*Mar.* A good lenten answer: I can tell thee
where that saying was born, of, I fear no colours.

*Clo.* Where, good Mistress Mary?

*Mar.* In the wars; and that may you be bold
to say in your foolery.

*Clo.* Well, God give them wisdom that have
it; and those that are fools, let them use their
talents.

*Mar.* Yet you will be hanged for being so long
absent: or, to be turned away; is not that as
good as a hanging to you?

*Clo.* Many a good hanging prevents a bad
marriage; and for turning away, let summer
bear it out.

*Mar.* You are resolute, then?

*Clo.* Not so neither: but I am resolved on two
points.

*Mar.* That, if one break, the other will hold;
or, if both break, your gaskins fall.

*Clo.* Apt, in good faith; very apt! Well, go
thy way; if Sir Toby would leave drinking,
thou wert as witty a piece of Eve's flesh as any
in Illyria.

*Mar.* Peace, you rogue; no more o' that; here
comes my lady: make your excuse wisely; you
were best.                                    [*Exit.*

*Enter* OLIVIA *and* MALVOLIO.

*Clo.* Wit, and 't be thy will, put me into good
fooling! Those wits that think they have thee,
do very oft prove fools; and I, that am sure I
lack thee, may pass for a wise man. For what
says Quinapalus? Better a witty fool than a
foolish wit.——God bless thee, lady!

*Oli.* Take the fool away.                [lady.

*Clo.* Do you not hear, fellows? Take away the

*Oli.* Go to, you're a dry fool; I'll no more of
you: besides, you grow dishonest.

*Clo.* Two faults, madonna, that drink and
good counsel will amend: for give the dry fool
drink, then is the fool not dry; bid the dishonest man mend himself: if he mend, he is no
longer dishonest; if he cannot, let the botcher
mend him. Anything that's mended is but
patched; virtue that transgresses is but patched
with sin; and sin that amends is but patched
with virtue. If that this simple syllogism will
serve, so; if it will not, what remedy? As there
is no true cuckold but calamity, so beauty's

a flower:—the lady bade take away the fool;
therefore, I say again, take her away.

*Oli.* Sir, I bade them take away you.

*Clo.* Misprision in the highest degree!—Lady,
*Cucullus non facit monachum;* that's as much
as to say, I wear not motley in my brain. Good
madonna, give me leave to prove you a fool.

*Oli.* Can you do it?

*Clo.* Dexterously, good madonna.

*Oli.* Make your proof.

*Clo.* I must catechise you for it, madonna.
Good my mouse of virtue, answer me.

*Oli.* Well, sir, for want of other idleness, I'll
'bide your proof.

*Clo.* Good madonna, why mourn'st thou?

*Oli.* Good fool, for my brother's death.

*Clo.* I think his soul is in hell, madonna.

*Oli.* I know his soul is in heaven, fool.

*Clo.* The more fool you, madonna, to mourn
for your brother's soul being in heaven.—Take
away the fool, gentlemen.

*Oli.* What think you of this fool, Malvolio?
doth he not mend?

*Mal.* Yes; and shall do, till the pangs of death
shake him. Infirmity, that decays the wise,
doth ever make the better fool.

*Clo.* God send you, sir, a speedy infirmity, for
the better increasing your folly! Sir Toby will
be sworn that I am no fox; but he will not pass
his word for twopence that you are no fool.

*Oli.* How say you to that, Malvolio?

*Mal.* I marvel your ladyship takes delight in
such a barren rascal; I saw him put down the
other day with an ordinary fool that has no
more brain than a stone. Look you now, he's
out of his guard already; unless you laugh and
minister occasion to him, he is gagged. I protest, I take these wise men, that crow so at
these set kind of fools, no better than the fools'
zanies.

*Oli.* O, you are sick of self-love, Malvolio, and
taste with a distempered appetite. To be generous, guiltless, and of free disposition, is to
take those things for bird-bolts that you deem
cannon-bullets. There is no slander in an allowed fool, though he do nothing but rail; nor
no railing in a known discreet man, though he
do nothing but reprove.

*Clo.* Now Mercury endue thee with leasing, for
thou speakest well of fools!

*Re-enter* MARIA.

*Mar.* Madam, there is at the gate a young
gentleman much desires to speak with you.

*Oli.* From the Count Orsino, is it?

*Mar.* I know not, madam; 'tis a fair young
man, and well attended.

*Oli.* Who of my people hold him in delay?

*Mar.* Sir Toby, madam, your kinsman.

*Oli.* Fetch him off, I pray you; he speaks nothing but madman. Fie on him! [*Exit* MARIA.]
Go you, Malvolio; if it be a suit from the
count, I am sick, or not at home; what you will
to dismiss it. [*Exit* MALVOLIO.] Now you see,

sir, how your fooling grows old, and people dislike it.

*Clo.* Thou hast spoke for us, madonna, as if thy eldest son should be a fool: whose skull Jove cram with brains, for here he comes, one of thy kin, has a most weak *pia mater*.

*Enter Sir* TOBY BELCH.

*Oli.* By mine honour, half drunk.—What is he at the gate, cousin?

*Sir To.* A gentleman.

*Oli.* A gentleman? What gentleman?

*Sir To.* 'Tis a gentleman here—A plague o' these pickle-herrings!—How now, sot?

*Clo.* Good Sir Toby,——

*Oli.* Cousin, cousin, how have you come so early by this lethargy?

*Sir To.* Lechery! I defy lechery. There's one at the gate.

*Oli.* Ay, marry; what is he?

*Sir To.* Let him be the devil an he will, I care not: give me faith, say I. Well, it's all one.                                    [*Exit.*

*Oli.* What's a drunken man like, fool?

*Clo.* Like a drowned man, a fool, and a madman: one draught above heat makes him a fool; the second mads him; and a third drowns him.

*Oli.* Go thou and seek the coroner, and let him sit o' my coz; for he is in the third degree of drink; he's drowned: go, look after him.

*Clo.* He is but mad yet, madonna; and the fool shall look to the madman.    [*Exit* CLOWN.

*Re-enter* MALVOLIO.

*Mal.* Madam, yond young fellow swears he will speak with you. I told him you were sick; he takes on him to understand so much, and therefore comes to speak with you; I told him you were asleep; he seems to have a foreknowledge of that too, and therefore comes to speak with you. What is to be said to him, lady? he's fortified against any denial.

*Oli.* Tell him, he shall not speak with me.

*Mal.* He has been told so; and he says he'll stand at your door like a sheriff's post, and be the supporter of a bench, but he'll speak with you.

*Oli.* What kind of man is he?

*Mal.* Why, of mankind.

*Oli.* What manner of man?

*Mal.* Of very ill manner; he'll speak with you, will you or no.

*Oli.* Of what personage and years is he?

*Mal.* Not yet old enough for a man, nor young enough for a boy; as a squash is before 'tis a peascod, or a codling, when 'tis almost an apple: 'tis with him e'en standing water, between boy and man. He is very well-favoured, and he speaks very shrewishly; one would think his mother's milk were scarce out of him.

*Oli.* Let him approach. Call in my gentlewoman.

*Mal.* Gentlewoman, my lady calls.    [*Exit.*

*Re-enter* MARIA.

*Oli.* Give me my veil: come, throw it o'er my face;
We'll once more hear Orsino's embassy.

*Enter* VIOLA.

*Vio.* The honourable lady of the house, which is she?

*Oli.* Speak to me, I shall answer for her. Your will?

*Vio.* Most radiant, exquisite, and unmatchable beauty,—I pray you, tell me if this be the lady of the house, for I never saw her: I would be loath to cast away my speech; for, besides that it is excellently well penned, I have taken great pains to con it. Good beauties, let me sustain no scorn; I am very comptible, even to the least sinister usage.

*Oli.* Whence came you, sir?

*Vio.* I can say little more than I have studied, and that question's out of my part. Good gentle one, give me modest assurance, if you be the lady of the house, that I may proceed in my speech.

*Oli.* Are you a comedian?

*Vio.* No, my profound heart; and yet, by the very fangs of malice, I swear I am not that I play. Are you the lady of the house?

*Oli.* If I do not usurp myself, I am.

*Vio.* Most certain, if you are she, you do usurp yourself; for what is yours to bestow is not yours to reserve. But this is from my commission: I will on with my speech in your praise, and then show you the heart of my message.

*Oli.* Come to what is important in't: I forgive you the praise.

*Vio.* Alas, I took great pains to study it, and 'tis poetical.

*Oli.* It is the more like to be feigned; I pray you keep it in. I heard you were saucy at my gates; and allowed your approach, rather to wonder at you than to hear you. If you be not mad, be gone; if you have reason, be brief: 'tis not that time of moon with me to make one in so skipping a dialogue.        [way.

*Mar.* Will you hoist sail, sir? here lies your

*Vio.* No, good swabber; I am to hull here a little longer.—Some mollification for your giant, sweet lady.

*Oli.* Tell me your mind.

*Vio.* I am a messenger.

*Oli.* Sure, you have some hideous matter to deliver, when the courtesy of it is so fearful. Speak your office.

*Vio.* It alone concerns your ear. I bring no overture of war, no taxation of homage; I hold the olive in my hand: my words are as full of peace as matter.

*Oli.* Yet you began rudely. What are you? what would you?

*Vio.* The rudeness that hath appeared in me have I learned from my entertainment. What I am and what I would are as sacred as maidenhead: to your ears, divinity; to any other's, profanation.

*Oli.* Give us the place alone: we will hear this divinity. [*Exit* MARIA.] Now, sir, what is your text?

*Vio.* Most sweet lady,——

*Oli.* A comfortable doctrine, and much may be said of it. Where lies your text?

*Vio.* In Orsino's bosom.

*Oli.* In his bosom? In what chapter of his bosom?

*Vio.* To answer by the method, in the first of his heart.

*Oli.* O, I have read it; it is heresy. Have you no more to say?

*Vio.* Good madam, let me see your face.

*Oli.* Have you any commission from your lord to negotiate with my face? you are now out of your text: but we will draw the curtain and show you the picture. Look you, sir, such a one as I was this present. Is't not well done? [*Unveiling.*

*Vio.* Excellently done, if God did all.

*Oli.* 'Tis in grain, sir; 'twill endure wind and weather. [white

*Vio.* 'Tis beauty truly blent, whose red and Nature's own sweet and cunning hand laid on: Lady, you are the cruel'st she alive, If you will lead these graces to the grave, And leave the world no copy.

*Oli.* O, sir, I will not be so hard-hearted; I will give out divers schedules of my beauty. It shall be inventoried; and every particle and utensil labelled to my will: as, item, two lips indifferent red; item, two gray eyes with lids to them; item, one neck, one chin, and so forth. Were you sent hither to praise me? [proud;

*Vio.* I see you what you are: you are too But if you were the devil, you are fair. My lord and master loves you. O, such love Could be but recompens'd though you were crown'd The nonpareil of beauty!

*Oli.*                    How does he love me?

*Vio.* With adorations, with fertile tears, With groans that thunder love, with sighs of fire.

*Oli.* Your lord does know my mind, I cannot love him: Yet I suppose him virtuous, know him noble, Of great estate, of fresh and stainless youth; In voices well divulged, free, learn'd and valiant, And, in dimension and the shape of nature, A gracious person: but yet I cannot love him; He might have took his answer long ago.

*Vio.* If I did love you in my master's flame, With such a suffering, such a deadly life, In your denial I would find no sense, I would not understand it.

*Oli.*                    Why, what would you?

*Vio.* Make me a willow cabin at your gate, And call upon my soul within the house; Write loyal cantons of contemned love, And sing them loud, even in the dead of night; Holla your name to the reverberate hills, And make the babbling gossip of the air Cry out Olivia! O, you should not rest

Between the elements of air and earth, But you should pity me.               [entage?

*Oli.* You might do much. What is your par-

*Vio.* Above my fortunes, yet my state is well: I am a gentleman.

*Oli.*                    Get you to your lord; I cannot love him: let him send no more; Unless, perchance, you come to me again, To tell me how he takes it. Fare you well: I thank you for your pains: spend this for me.

*Vio.* I am no fee'd post, lady; keep your purse; My master, not myself, lacks recompense. Love make his heart of flint that you shall love; And let your fervour, like my master's, be Placed in contempt! Farewell, fair cruelty. [*Exit.*

*Oli.* What is your parentage? *Above my fortunes, yet my state is well: I am a gentleman.*——I'll be sworn thou art; Thy tongue, thy face, thy limbs, actions, and spirit,               [soft! soft! Do give thee fivefold blazon. Not too fast:— Unless the master were the man.—How now? Even so quickly may one catch the plague? Methinks I feel this youth's perfections With an invisible and subtle stealth To creep in at mine eyes. Well, let it be.— What, ho, Malvolio!—

#### Re-enter MALVOLIO.

*Mal.*          Here, madam, at your service.

*Oli.* Run after that same peevish messenger, The county's man: he left this ring behind him, Would I, or not; tell him I'll none of it. Desire him not to flatter with his lord, Nor hold him up with hopes; I am not for him: If that the youth will come this way to-morrow, I'll give him reasons for't. Hie thee, Malvolio.

*Mal.* Madam, I will.               [*Exit.*

*Oli.* I do I know not what: and fear to find Mine eye too great a flatterer for my mind. Fate, show thy force. Ourselves we do not owe; What is decreed must be; and be this so! [*Exit.*

### ACT II.

#### SCENE I.—*The Sea-coast.*

*Enter* ANTONIO *and* SEBASTIAN.

*Ant.* Will you stay no longer? nor will you not that I go with you?

*Seb.* By your patience, no: my stars shine darkly over me; the malignancy of my fate might, perhaps, distemper yours; therefore I shall crave of you your leave that I may bear my evils alone. It were a bad recompense for your love, to lay any of them on you.

*Ant.* Let me yet know of you whither you are bound.

*Seb.* No, 'sooth, sir; my determinate voyage is mere extravagancy. But I perceive in you so excellent a touch of modesty, that you will not extort from me what I am willing to keep in; therefore it charges me in manners the rather to express myself. You must know of me then, Antonio, my name is Sebastian, which I called Rodorigo; my father was that Sebastian of Messaline whom I know you have heard of: he left behind him myself and a sister, both born in an hour. If the heavens had been pleased, would we had so ended! but you, sir, altered that; for some hours before you took me from the breach of the sea was my sister drowned.

*Ant.* Alas the day!

*Seb.* A lady, sir, though it was said she much resembled me, was yet of many accounted beautiful: but though I could not, with such estimable wonder, overfar believe that, yet thus far I will boldly publish her,—she bore a mind that envy could not but call fair. She is drowned already, sir, with salt water, though I seem to drown her remembrance again with more.

*Ant.* Pardon me, sir, your bad entertainment.

*Seb.* O, good Antonio, forgive me your trouble.

*Ant.* If you will not murder me for my love, let me be your servant.

*Seb.* If you will not undo what you have done —that is, kill him whom you have recovered— desire it not. Fare ye well at once; my bosom is full of kindness; and I am yet so near the manners of my mother that, upon the least occasion more, mine eyes will tell tales of me. I am bound to the Count Orsino's court: farewell. [*Exit.*

*Ant.* The gentleness of all the gods go with thee!
I have many enemies in Orsino's court,
Else would I very shortly see thee there:
But come what may, I do adore thee so
That danger shall seem sport, and I will go.
[*Exit.*

SCENE II.—*A Street.*

*Enter* VIOLA; MALVOLIO *following.*

*Mal.* Were not you even now with the Countess Olivia?

*Vio.* Even now, sir; on a moderate pace I have since arrived but hither.

*Mal.* She returns this ring to you, sir; you might have saved me my pains, to have taken it away yourself. She adds moreover, that you should put your lord into a desperate assurance she will none of him: and one thing more; that you be never so hardy to come again in his affairs, unless it be to report your lord's taking of this. Receive it so.

*Vio.* She took the ring of me: I'll none of it.

*Mal.* Come, sir, you peevishly threw it to her; and her will is, it should be so returned. If it be worth stooping for, there it lies in your eye; if not, be it his that finds it. [*Exit.*

*Vio.* I left no ring with her. What means this lady?
Fortune forbid my outside have not charm'd her!
She made good view of me; indeed, so much,
That, sure, methought her eyes had lost her tongue,
For she did speak in starts distractedly

She loves me, sure; the cunning of her passion
Invites me in this churlish messenger.
None of my lord's ring! why, he sent her none.
I am the man;—if it be so,—as 'tis,—
Poor lady, she were better love a dream.
Disguise, I see, thou art a wickedness
Wherein the pregnant enemy does much.
How easy is it for the proper-false
In women's waxen hearts to set their forms!
Alas, our frailty is the cause, not we;
For, such as we are made of, such we be.
How will this fadge? My master loves her dearly;
And I, poor monster, fond as much on him;
And she, mistaken, seems to dote on me.
What will become of this? As I am man,
My state is desperate for my master's love;
As I am woman, now alas the day!
What thriftless sighs shall poor Olivia breathe?
O time, thou must untangle this, not I;
It is too hard a knot for me to untie. [*Exit.*

SCENE III.—*A Room in* OLIVIA'S *House.*

*Enter Sir* TOBY BELCH *and Sir* ANDREW AGUE-CHEEK.

*Sir To.* Approach, Sir Andrew: not to be a-bed after midnight is to be up betimes; and *diluculo surgere,* thou know'st.

*Sir And.* Nay; by my troth, I know not: but I know to be up late is to be up late.

*Sir To.* A false conclusion; I hate it as an unfilled can. To be up after midnight, and to go to bed then is early: so that to go to bed after midnight is to go to bed betimes. Do not our lives consist of the four elements?

*Sir And.* Faith, so they say; but I think it rather consists of eating and drinking.

*Sir To.* Thou art a scholar; let us therefore eat and drink.—Marian, I say!——a stoop of wine.

*Enter* CLOWN.

*Sir And.* Here comes the fool, i' faith.

*Clo.* How now, my hearts? Did you never see the picture of we three?

*Sir To.* Welcome, ass. Now let's have a catch.

*Sir And.* By my troth, the fool has an excellent breast. I had rather than forty shillings I had such a leg; and so sweet a breath to sing as the fool has. In sooth, thou wast in very gracious fooling last night when thou spokest of Pigrogromitus', of the Vapians passing the equinoctial of Queubus; 'twas very good, i' faith. I sent thee sixpence for thy leman. Hads't it?

*Clo.* I did impeticos thy gratillity; for Malvolio's nose is no whipstock. My lady has a white hand, and the Myrmidons are no bottle-ale houses.

*Sir And.* Excellent! Why, this is the best fooling, when all is done. Now, a song.

*Sir To.* Come on; there is sixpence for you: let's have a song.

*Sir And.* There's a testril of me too: if one knight give a——

*Clo.* Would you have a love-song, or a song of good life?
*Sir To.* A love-song, a love-song.
*Sir And.* Ay, ay; I care not for good life.

SONG.

*Clo.* O, mistress mine, where are you roaming?
O stay and hear; your true love's coming,
That can sing both high and low:
Trip no further, pretty sweeting;
Journeys end in lovers' meeting,
Every wise man's son doth know.

*Sir And.* Excellent good, i' faith.
*Sir To.* Good, good.

*Clo.* What is love? 'tis not hereafter;
Present mirth hath present laughter;
What's to come is still unsure:
In delay there lies no plenty;
Then come kiss me, sweet and twenty,
Youth's a stuff will not endure.

*Sir And.* A mellifluous voice, as I am true knight.
*Sir To.* A contagious breath.
*Sir And.* Very sweet and contagious, i' faith.
*Sir To.* To hear by the nose, it is dulcet in contagion. But shall we make the welkin dance indeed? Shall we rouse the night-owl in a catch that will draw three souls out of one weaver? shall we do that?
*Sir And.* An you love me, let's do 't: I am dog at a catch.
*Clo.* By'r lady, sir, and some dogs will catch well.
*Sir And.* Most certain: let our catch be, *Thou knave.*
*Clo.* Hold thy peace, thou knave, knight? I shall be constrained in 't to call thee knave, knight.
*Sir And.* 'Tis not the first time I have constrained one to call me knave. Begin, fool; it begins *Hold thy peace.*
*Clo.* I shall never begin if I hold my peace.
*Sir And.* Good, i' faith! Come begin.
[*They sing a catch.*

*Enter* MARIA.

*Mar.* What a caterwauling do you keep here! If my lady have not called up her steward, Malvolio, and bid him turn you out of doors, never trust me.
*Sir To.* My lady's a Cataian, we are politicians; Malvolio's a Peg-a-Ramsay, and *Three merry men be we.* Am not I consanguineous? am I not of her blood? Tilly-valley, lady! *There dwelt a man in Babylon, lady, lady.* [*Singing.*
*Clo.* Beshrew me, the knight's in admirable fooling.
*Sir And.* Ay, he does well enough if he be disposed, and so do I too; he does it with a better grace, but I do it more natural.
*Sir To.* O, *the twelfth day of December,*— [*Singing.*
*Mar.* For the love o' God, peace.

*Enter* MALVOLIO.

*Mal.* My masters, are you mad? or what are you? Have you no wit, manners, nor honesty, but to gabble like tinkers at this time of night? Do ye make an ale-house of my lady's house, that ye squeak out your coziers' catches without any mitigation or remorse of voice? Is there no respect of place, persons, nor time, in you?
*Sir To.* We did keep time, sir, in our catches. Sneck up!
*Mal.* Sir Toby, I must be round with you. My lady bade me tell you that though she harbours you as her kinsman she's nothing allied to your disorders. If you can separate yourself and your misdemeanours, you are welcome to the house; if not, an it would please you to take leave of her, she is very willing to bid you farewell.
*Sir To.* Farewell, dear heart, since I must needs be gone.
*Mar.* Nay, good Sir Toby.
*Clo.* His eyes do show his days are almost done.
*Mal.* Is 't even so?
*Sir To.* But I will never die.
*Clo.* Sir Toby, there you lie.
*Mal.* This is much credit to you.
*Sir To.* Shall I bid him go?            [*Singing.*
*Clo.* What an if you do?
*Sir To.* Shall I bid him go and spare not?
*Clo.* O no, no, no, no, you dare not.
*Sir To.* Out o' tune? sir, ye lie.—Art any more than a steward? Dost thou think, because thou art virtuous, there shall be no more cakes and ale?
*Clo.* Yes, by Saint Anne; and ginger shall be hot i' the mouth too.
*Sir To.* Thou'rt i' the right.—Go, sir, rub your chain with crumbs:—A stoop of wine, Maria!
*Mal.* Mistress Mary, if you prized my lady's favour at anything more than contempt, you would not give means for this uncivil rule; she shall know of it, by this hand.            [*Exit.*
*Mar.* Go shake your ears.
*Sir And.* 'Twere as good a deed as to drink when a man's a-hungry, to challenge him to the field, and then to break promise with him and make a fool of him.
*Sir To.* Do 't, knight; I'll write thee a challenge; or I'll deliver thy indignation to him by word of mouth.
*Mar.* Sweet Sir Toby, be patient for to-night; since the youth of the count's was to-day with my lady she is much out of quiet. For Monsieur Malvolio, let me alone with him: if I do not gull him into a nayword, and make him a common recreation, do not think I have wit enough to lie straight in my bed. I know I can do it.
*Sir To.* Possess us, possess us; tell us something of him.
*Mar.* Marry, sir, sometimes he is a kind of Puritan.
*Sir And.* O, if I thought that, I'd beat him like a dog.

*Sir To.* What, for being a Puritan? thy exquisite reason, dear knight?

*Sir And.* I have no exquisite reason for 't, but I have reason good enough.

*Mar.* The devil a Puritan that he is, or anything constantly but a time pleaser : an affection'd ass that cons state without book and utters it by great swarths; the best persuaded of himself, so crammed, as he thinks, with excellences, that it is his ground of faith that all that look on him love him; and on that vice in him will my revenge find notable cause to work.

*Sir To.* What wilt thou do?

*Mar.* I will drop in his way some obscure epistles of love; wherein, by the colour of his beard, the shape of his leg, the manner of his gait, the expressure of his eye, forehead, and complexion, he shall find himself most feelingly personated. I can write very like my lady, your niece; on a forgotten matter we can hardly make distinction of our hands.

*Sir To.* Excellent! I smell a device.

*Sir And.* I have 't in my nose too.

*Sir To.* He shall think, by the letters that thou wilt drop, that they come from my niece, and that she is in love with him.       [colour.

*Mar.* My purpose is, indeed, a horse of that

*Sir And.* And your horse now would make him an ass.

*Mar.* Ass, I doubt not.

*Sir And.* O 'twill be admirable.

*Mar.* Sport royal, I warrant you. I know my physic will work with him. I will plant you two, and let the fool make a third, where he shall find the letter; observe his construction of it. For this night, to bed, and dream on the event. Farewell.       [*Exit.*

*Sir To.* Good-night, Penthesilea.

*Sir And.* Before me, she's a good wench.

*Sir To.* She's a beagle, true bred, and one that adores me. What o' that?

*Sir And.* I was adored once too.

*Sir To.* Let's to bed, knight.—Thou hadst need send for more money.

*Sir And.* If I cannot recover your niece I am a foul way out.

*Sir To.* Send for money, knight; if thou hast her not i' the end, call me Cut.

*Sir And.* If I do not, never trust me; take it how you will.

*Sir To.* Come, come; I'll go burn some sack; 'tis too late to go to bed now: come, knight; come, knight.       [*Exeunt.*

SCENE IV.—*A Room in the* DUKE'S *Palace.*

*Enter* DUKE, VIOLA, CURIO, *and others.*

*Duke.* Give me some music:—Now, good morrow, friends:—
Now, good Cesario, but that piece of song,
That old and antique song we heard last night;
Methought it did relieve my passion much;
More than light airs and recollected terms

Of these most brisk and giddy-paced times:——
Come, but one verse.

*Cur.* He is not here, so please your lordship, that should sing it.

*Duke.* Who was it?

*Cur.* Feste, the jester, my lord; a fool that the Lady Olivia's father took much delight in: he is about the house.

*Duke.* Seek him out, and play the tune the
     while.       [*Exit* CURIO.—*Music.*
Come hither, boy. If ever thou shalt love,
In the sweet pangs of it remember me:
For, such as I am, all true lovers are;
Unstaid and skittish in all motions else,
Save in the constant image of the creature
That is belov'd.—How dost thou like this tune?

*Vio.* It gives a very echo to the seat
Where Love is throned.

*Duke.* Thou dost speak masterly:
My life upon 't, young though thou art, thine eye
Hath stayed upon some favour that it loves;
Hath it not, boy?

*Vio.*       A little, by your favour.

*Duke.* What kind of woman is 't?

*Vio.*       Of your complexion.

*Duke.* She is not worth thee, then. What years, i' faith?

*Vio.* About your years, my lord.

*Duke.* Too old, by heaven. Let still the woman take
An elder than herself; so wears she to him,
So sways she level in her husband's heart.
For, boy, however we do praise ourselves,
Our fancies are more giddy and unfirm,
More longing, wavering, sooner lost and worn
Than women's are.

*Vio.*       I think it well, my lord.

*Duke.* Then let thy love be younger than thyself,
Or thy affection cannot hold the bent:
For women are as roses, whose fair flower,
Being once display'd, doth fall that very hour.

*Vio.* And so they are: alas, that they are so;
To die even when they to perfection grow!

*Re-enter* CURIO *and* CLOWN.

*Duke.* O fellow, come, the song we had last night:—
Mark it, Cesario; it is old and plain:
The spinsters and the knitters in the sun,
And the free maids that weave their thread with bones,
Do use to chant it: it is silly sooth,
And dallies with the innocence of love
Like the old age.

*Clo.* Are you ready, sir?

*Duke.* Ay; pr'ythee, sing.       [*Music.*

SONG.

*Clo.*       Come away, come away, death,
          And in sad cypress let me be laid;
          Fly away, fly away, breath;
          I am slain by a fair cruel maid.
          My shroud of white, stuck all with yew,
             O prepare it:

My part of death no one so true
 Did share it.

Not a flower, not a flower sweet,
On my black coffin let there be strown:
 Not a friend, not a friend greet
My poor corpse where my bones shall be
  thrown:
A thousand thousand sighs to save,
 Lay me, O, where
Sad true lover never find my grave,
 To weep there.

*Duke.* There's for thy pains.   [sir.
*Clo.* No pains, sir; I take pleasure in singing,
*Duke.* I'll pay thy pleasure, then.
*Clo.* Truly, sir, and pleasure will be paid one
time or another.
*Duke.* Give me now leave to leave thee.
*Clo.* Now, the melancholy god protect thee;
and the tailor make thy doublet of changeable
taffata, for thy mind is a very opal!—I would
have men of such constancy put to sea, that
their business might be everything, and their
intent everywhere; for that's it that always
makes a good voyage of nothing.—Farewell.
        [*Exit* CLOWN.
*Duke.* Let all the rest give place.——
   [*Exeunt* CURIO *and* Attendants.
     Once more, Cesario,
Get thee to yon same sovereign cruelty:
Tell her my love, more noble than the world,
Prizes not quantity of dirty lands;
The parts that fortune hath bestow'd upon her,
Tell her, I hold as giddily as fortune;
But 'tis that miracle and queen of gems
That Nature pranks her in attracts my soul.
*Vio.* But if she cannot love you, sir?
*Duke.* I cannot be so answer'd.
*Vio.*    'Sooth, but you must.
Say that some lady, as perhaps there is,
Hath for your love as great a pang of heart
As you have for Olivia: you cannot love her;
You tell her so. Must she not then be answer'd?
*Duke.* There is no woman's sides
Can bide the beating of so strong a passion
As love doth give my heart: no woman's heart
So big to hold so much; they lack retention.
Alas, their love may be called appetite,—
No motion of the liver, but the palate,—
That suffer surfeit, cloyment, and revolt;
But mine is all as hungry as the sea,
And can digest as much: make no compare
Between that love a woman can bear me
And that I owe Olivia.
*Vio.*    Ay, but I know,—
*Duke.* What dost thou know?
*Vio.* Too well what love women to men may
  owe.
In faith, they are as true of heart as we.
My father had a daughter loved a man,
As it might be, perhaps, were I a woman,
I should your lordship.
*Duke.*   And what's her history?
*Vio.* A blank, my lord. She never told her love,
But let concealment, like a worm i' the bud,

Feed on her damask cheek: she pined in thought;
And, with a green and yellow melancholy,
She sat like patience on a monument,
Smiling at grief. Was not this love, indeed?
We men may say more, swear more; but, indeed,
Our shows are more than will; for still we prove
Much in our vows, but little in our love.
*Duke.* But died thy sister of her love, my boy?
*Vio.* I am all the daughters of my father's
  house,
And all the brothers too;—and yet I know not.—
Sir, shall I to this lady?
*Duke.*   Ay, that's the theme.
To her in haste: give her this jewel; say
My love can give no place, bide no denay.
         [*Exeunt.*

### SCENE V.—OLIVIA'S *Garden.*

*Enter Sir* TOBY BELCH, *Sir* ANDREW AGUE-
CHEEK, *and* FABIAN.

*Sir To.* Come thy ways, Signior Fabian.
*Fab.* Nay, I'll come; if I lose a scruple of this
sport let me be boiled to death with melancholy.
*Sir To.* Wouldst thou not be glad to have the
niggardly rascally sheep-biter come by some
notable shame?
*Fab.* I would exult, man: you know he brought
me out o' favour with my lady about a bear-
baiting here.
*Sir To.* To anger him we'll have the bear again;
and we will fool him black and blue:—Shall we
not, Sir Andrew?
*Sir And.* An we do not, it is pity of our lives.

*Enter* MARIA.

*Sir To.* Here comes the little villain:—How
now, my nettle of India?
*Mar.* Get ye all three into the box-tree: Malvolio's coming down this walk; he has been
yonder i' the sun, practising behaviour to his
own shadow this half-hour: observe him, for
the love of mockery; for I know this letter will
make a contemplative idiot of him. Close, in
the name of jesting! [*The men hide themselves.*]
Lie thou there; [*throws down a letter*] for here
comes the trout that must be caught with
tickling.       [*Exit* MARIA.

*Enter* MALVOLIO.

*Mal.* 'Tis but fortune; all is fortune. Maria
once told me she did affect me: and I have heard
herself come thus near, that, should she fancy, it
should be one of my complexion. Besides, she
uses me with a more exalted respect than anyone
else that follows her. What should I think on't?
*Sir To.* Here's an overweening rogue!
*Fab.* O, peace! Contemplation makes a rare
turkey-cock of him; how he jets under his advanced plumes!
*Sir And.* 'Slight, I could so beat the rogue:—
*Sir To.* Peace, I say,
*Mal.* To be Count Malvolio;—

*Sir To.* Ah, rogue!

*Sir And.* Pistol him, pistol him.

*Sir To.* Peace, peace.

*Mal.* There is example for 't; the lady of the Strachy married the yeoman of the wardrobe.

*Sir And.* Fie on him, Jezebel!

*Fab.* O, peace! now he's deeply in; look how imagination blows him.

*Mal.* Having been three months married to her, sitting in my state,—

*Sir To.* O for a stone-bow to hit him in the eye!

*Mal.* Calling my officers about me in my branched velvet gown; having come from a day-bed, where I have left Olivia sleeping.

*Sir To.* Fire and brimstone!

*Fab.* O, peace, peace.

*Mal.* And then to have the humour of state: and after a demure travel of regard,—telling them I know my place as I would they should do theirs,—to ask for my kinsman Toby.

*Sir To.* Bolts and shackles!

*Fab.* O, peace, peace, peace! now, now.

*Mal.* Seven of my people, with an obedient start, make out for him: I frown the while; and perchance, wind up my watch, or play with some rich jewel. Toby approaches; court'sies there to me:

*Sir To.* Shall this fellow live?

*Fab.* Though our silence be drawn from us with cars, yet peace.

*Mal.* I extend my hand to him thus, quenching my familiar smile with an austere regard of control:

*Sir To.* And does not Toby take you a blow o' the lips then?

*Mal.* Saying, *Cousin Toby, my fortunes having cast me on your niece, give me this prerogative of speech:—*

*Sir To.* What, what?

*Mal. You must amend your drunkenness.*

*Sir To.* Out, scab!  [our plot.

*Fab.* Nay, patience, or we break the sinews of

*Mal. Besides, you waste the treasure of your time with a foolish knight;*

*Sir And.* That's me, I warrant you.

*Mal. One Sir Andrew:*

*Sir And.* I knew 'twas I; for many do call me fool.

*Mal.* What employment have we here?
                    [*Taking up the letter.*

*Fab.* Now is the woodcock near the gin.

*Sir To.* O, peace! and the spirit of humours intimate reading aloud to him!

*Mal.* By my life, this is my lady's hand: these be her very *C*'s, her *U*'s, and her *T*'s; and thus makes she her great *P*'s. It is in contempt of question, her hand.

*Sir And.* Her *C*'s, her *U*'s, and her *T*'s. Why that?

*Mal.* [*reads.*] *To the unknown beloved, this, and my good wishes:* her very phrases!—By your leave, wax.—Soft!—and the impressure her Lucrece, with which she uses to seal: 'tis my lady. To whom should this be?

*Fab.* This wins him, liver and all.

*Mal.* [*reads.*]

> *Jove knows I love:*
> *But who?*
> *Lips do not move,*
> *No man must know.*

*No man must know.*—What follows? the numbers altered!—*No man must know:*—If this should be thee, Malvolio?

*Sir To.* Marry, hang thee, brock!

*Mal. I may command where I adore:*
> *But silence, like a Lucrece knife,*
> *With bloodiest stroke my heart doth gore;*
> *M, O, A, I, doth sway my life.*

*Fab.* A fustian riddle!

*Sir To.* Excellent wench, say I.

*Mal.* M, O, A, I, *doth sway my life.*—Nay, but first let me see,—let me see,—let me see.

*Fab.* What a dish of poison hath she dressed him!

*Sir To.* And with what wing the stannyel checks at it!

*Mal. I may command where I adore.* Why, she may command me: I serve her, she is my lady. Why, this is evident to any formal capacity. There is no obstruction in this;—And the end, —What should that alphabetical position portend? If I could make that resemble something in me,—Softly!—*M, O, A, I.*—

*Sir To.* O, ay! make up that:—he is now at a cold scent.

*Fab.* Sowter will cry upon 't for all this, though it be as rank as a fox.

*Mal. M,*—Malvolio;—*M,*—why, that begins my name.

*Fab.* Did not I say he would work it out? the cur is excellent at faults.

*Mal. M,*—But then there is no consonancy in the sequel; that suffers under probation: *A* should follow, but *O* does.

*Fab.* And *O* shall end, I hope.  [cry *O*.

*Sir To.* Ay, or I'll cudgel him, and make him

*Mal.* And then *I* comes behind.

*Fab.* Ay, an you had any eye behind you, you might see more detraction at your heels than fortunes before you.

*Mal.* M, O, A, I;—This simulation is not as the former:—and yet, to crush this a little, it would bow to me, for every one of these letters are in my name. Soft; here follows prose.— *If this fall into thy hand, revolve. In my stars I am above thee; but be not afraid of greatness. Some are born great, some achieve greatness, and some have greatness thrust upon them. Thy fates open their hands; let thy blood and spirit embrace them. And, to inure thyself to what thou art like to be, cast thy humble slough and appear fresh. Be opposite with a kinsman, surly with servants: let thy tongue tang arguments of state; put thyself into the trick of singularity: She thus advises thee that sighs for thee. Remember who commended thy yellow stockings, and wished to see thee ever cross-gartered. I say, remember. Go to; thou art made, if thou desirest to be so; if not, let me see thee a steward still, the fellow of servants, and not worthy to touch fortune's fingers. Farewell. She that would alter services with thee,*

*The fortunate unhappy.*

Daylight and champian discovers not more: this is open. I will be proud, I will read politic authors, I will baffle Sir Toby, I will wash off gross acquaintance, I will be point-device, the very man. I do not now fool myself to let imagination jade me; for every reason excites to this, that my lady loves me. She did commend my yellow stockings of late, she did praise my leg being cross-gartered; and in this she manifests herself to my love, and, with a kind of injunction, drives me to these habits of her liking. I thank my stars I am happy. I will be strange, stout, in yellow stockings, and cross-gartered, even with the swiftness of putting on. Jove and my stars be praised!—Here is yet a postscript. *Thou canst not choose but know who I am. If thou entertainest my love, let it appear in thy smiling; thy smiles become thee well: therefore in my presence still smile, dear my sweet, I pr'ythee.* Jove, I thank thee.—I will smile: I will do everything that thou wilt have me.

[*Exit.*

*Fab.* I will not give my part of this sport for a pension of thousands to be paid from the Sophy.
*Sir To.* I could marry this wench for this device:
*Sir And.* So could I too.
*Sir To.* And ask no other dowry with her but such another jest.

*Enter* MARIA.

*Sir And.* Nor I neither.
*Fab.* Here comes my noble gull-catcher.
*Sir To.* Wilt thou set thy foot o' my neck?
*Sir And.* Or o' mine either?
*Sir To.* Shall I play my freedom at tray-trip, and become thy bond-slave?
*Sir And.* I' faith, or I either.
*Sir To.* Why, thou hast put him in such a dream, that, when the image of it leaves him, he must run mad.
*Mar.* Nay, but say true; does it work upon him?
*Sir To.* Like aqua-vitæ with a midwife.
*Mar.* If you will then see the fruits of the sport, mark his first approach before my lady: he will come to her in yellow stockings, and 'tis a colour she abhors; and cross-gartered, a fashion she detests; and he will smile upon her, which will now be so unsuitable to her disposition, being addicted to a melancholy as she is, that it cannot but turn him into a notable contempt: if you will see it, follow me.
*Sir To.* To the gates of Tartar, thou most excellent devil of wit!
*Sir And.* I'll make one too.    [*Exeunt.*

ACT III.

SCENE I.—OLIVIA'S *Garden.*

*Enter* VIOLA, *and* CLOWN *with a tabor.*

*Vio.* Save thee, friend, and thy music. Dost thou live by thy tabor?
*Clo.* No, sir, I live by the church.
*Vio.* Art thou a churchman?
*Clo.* No such matter, sir; I do live by the church; for I do live at my house, and my house doth stand by the church.
*Vio.* So thou mayst say, the king lies by a beggar, if a beggar dwell near him; or the church stands by thy tabor, if thy tabor stand by the church.
*Clo.* You have said, sir.—To see this age!—A sentence is but a cheveril glove to a good wit. How quickly the wrong side may be turned outward!
*Vio.* Nay, that's certain; they that dally nicely with words may quickly make them wanton.
*Clo.* I would, therefore, my sister had had no name, sir.
*Vio.* Why, man?
*Clo.* Why, sir, her name's a word; and to dally with that word might make my sister wanton. But indeed, words are very rascals, since bonds disgraced them.
*Vio.* Thy reason, man?
*Clo.* Troth, sir, I can yield you none without words; and words are grown so false, I am loath to prove reason with them.
*Vio.* I warrant, thou art a merry fellow, and carest for nothing.
*Clo.* Not so, sir, I do care for something: but in my conscience, sir, I do not care for you; if that be to care for nothing, sir, I would it would make you invisible.
*Vio.* Art not thou the Lady Olivia's fool?
*Clo.* No, indeed, sir; the Lady Olivia has no folly: she will keep no fool, sir, till she be married; and fools are as like husbands as pilchards are to herrings, the husband's the bigger; I am, indeed, not her fool, but her corrupter of words.
*Vio.* I saw thee late at the Count Orsino's.
*Clo.* Foolery, sir, does walk about the orb like the sun; it shines everywhere. I would be sorry, sir, but the fool should be as oft with your master as with my mistress: I think I saw your wisdom there.
*Vio.* Nay, an thou pass upon me, I'll no more with thee. Hold, there's expenses for thee.
*Clo.* Now Jove, in his next commodity of hair, send thee a beard!
*Vio.* By my troth, I'll tell thee, I am almost sick for one; though I would not have it grow on my chin. Is thy lady within?
*Clo.* Would not a pair of these have bred, sir?
*Vio.* Yes, being kept together and put to use.
*Clo.* I would play Lord Pandarus of Phrygia, sir, to bring a Cressida to this Troilus.
*Vio.* I understand you, sir; 'tis well begged.
*Clo.* The matter, I hope, is not great, sir, beg-

ging but a beggar: Cressida was a beggar. My
lady is within, sir. I will construe to them
whence you come; who you are and what you
would be out of my welkin: I might say ele-
ment; but the word is overworn.   [*Exit.*
*Vio.* This fellow's wise enough to play the fool;
And, to do that well, craves a kind of wit:
He must observe their mood on whom he jests,
The quality of persons, and the time;
And, like the haggard, check at every feather
That comes before his eye. This is a practice
As full of labour as a wise man's art:
For folly, that he wisely shows, is fit;
But wise men, folly-fallen, quite taint their wit.

*Enter Sir* TOBY BELCH, *and Sir* ANDREW
AGUE-CHEEK.

*Sir To.* Save you, gentleman.
*Vio.* And you, sir.
*Sir And. Dieu vous garde, monsieur.*
*Vio. Et vous aussi: votre serviteur.*
*Sir And.* I hope, sir, you are; and I am yours.
*Sir To.* Will you encounter the house? my
niece is desirous you should enter, if your trade
be to her.
*Vio.* I am bound to your niece, sir: I mean,
she is the list of my voyage.
*Sir To.* Taste your legs, sir; put them to
motion.
*Vio.* My legs do better understand me, sir,
than I understand what you mean by bidding
me taste my legs.
*Sir To.* I mean to go, sir, to enter.
*Vio.* I will answer you with gait and entrance:
but we are prevented.

*Enter* OLIVIA *and* MARIA.

Most excellent accomplished lady, the heavens
rains odours on you.
*Sir And.* That youth's a rare courtier! *Rain
odours!* well.
*Vio.* My matter hath no voice, lady, but to
your own most pregnant and vouchsafed ear.
*Sir And.* Odours, *pregnant*, and *vouchsafed:*—
I'll get 'em all three ready.
*Oli.* Let the garden door be shut, and leave me
to my hearing.
   [*Exeunt Sir* TO., *Sir* AND., *and* MAR.
Give me your hand, sir.   [service.
*Vio.* My duty, madam, and most humble
*Oli.* What is your name?   [princess.
*Vio.* Cesario is your servant's name, fair
*Oli.* My servant, sir! 'Twas never merry world,
Since lowly feigning was call'd compliment:
You are servant to the Count Orsino, youth.
*Vio.* And he is yours, and his must needs be
yours;
Your servant's servant is your servant, madam.
*Oli.* For him, I think not on him: for his
thoughts,   [me!
Would they were blanks rather than fill'd with
*Vio.* Madam, I come to whet your gentle
thoughts
On his behalf:—

*Oli.*          O, by your leave, I pray you;
I bade you never speak again of him:
But, would you undertake another suit,
I had rather hear you to solicit that
Than music from the spheres.
*Vio.*          Dear lady,——
*Oli.* Give me leave, I beseech you: I did send,
After the last enchantment you did here,
A ring in chase of you; so did I abuse
Myself, my servant, and, I fear me, you:
Under your hard construction must I sit;
To force that on you, in a shameful cunning,
Which you knew none of yours. What might
          you think?
Have you not set mine honour at the stake,
And baited it with all the unmuzzl'd thoughts
That tyrannous heart can think? To one of
          your receiving
Enough is shown; a cyprus, not a bosom,
Hides my poor heart: so let me hear you speak.
*Vio.* I pity you.
*Oli.* That's a degree to love.
*Vio.* No, not a grise; for 'tis a vulgar proof
That very oft we pity enemies.   [again:
*Oli.* Why, then, methinks 'tis time to smile
O world, how apt the poor are to be proud!
If one should be a prey, how much the better
To fall before the lion than the wolf!
          [*Clock strikes.*
The clock upbraids me with the waste of time.—
Be not afraid, good youth, I will not have you:
And yet, when wit and youth is come to
          harvest,
Your wife is like to reap a proper man.
There lies your way due-west.
*Vio.*          Then westward-ho:
Grace and good disposition 'tend your ladyship!
You'll nothing, madam, to my lord by me?
*Oli.* Stay:
I pr'ythee tell me what thou think'st of me.
*Vio.* That you do think you are not what you
          are.
*Oli.* If I think so, I think the same of you.
*Vio.* Then think you right; I am not what I am.
*Oli.* I would you were as I would have you be!
*Vio.* Would it be better, madam, that I am,
I wish it might; for now I am your fool.
*Oli.* O what a deal of scorn looks beautiful
In the contempt and anger of his lip!
A murd'rous guilt shows not itself more soon
Than love that would seem hid: love's night is
          noon.
Cesario, by the roses of the spring,
By maidhood, honour, truth, and everything,
I love thee so that, maugre all thy pride,
Nor wit, nor reason, can my passion hide:
Do not extort thy reasons from this clause,
For, that I woo, thou therefore hast no cause:
But, rather, reason thus with reason fetter:
Love sought is good, but given unsought is
          better.
*Vio.* By innocence I swear, and by my youth,
I have one heart, one bosom, and one truth,
And that no woman has; nor never none

Shall mistress be of it, save I alone.
And so adieu, good madam; never more
Will I my master's tears to you deplore.
*Oli.* Yet come again: for thou, perhaps, mayst move
That heart, which now abhors, to like his love.
[*Exeunt.*

SCENE II.—*A Room in* OLIVIA'S *House.*

*Enter Sir* TOBY BELCH, *Sir* ANDREW AGUE-
CHEEK, *and* FABIAN.

*Sir And.* No, faith, I'll not stay a jot longer.
*Sir To.* Thy reason, dear venom: give thy reason.
*Fab.* You must needs yield your reason, Sir Andrew.
*Sir And.* Marry, I saw your niece do more favours to the count's serving man than ever she bestowed upon me; I saw 't i' the orchard.
*Sir To.* Did she see thee the while, old boy? tell me that.
*Sir And.* As plain as I see you now.
*Fab.* This was a great argument of love in her toward you.
*Sir And.* 'Slight! will you make an ass o' me?
*Fab.* I will prove it legitimate, sir, upon the oaths of judgment and reason.
*Sir To.* And they have been grand jurymen since before Noah was a sailor.
*Fab.* She did show favour to the youth in your sight only to exasperate you, to awake your dormouse valour, to put fire in your heart and brimstone in your liver. You should then have accosted her; and with some excellent jests, fire-new from the mint, you should have banged the youth into dumbness. This was looked for at your hand, and this was baulked: the double gilt of this opportunity you let time wash off, and you are now sailed into the north of my lady's opinion; where you will hang like an icicle on a Dutchman's beard, unless you do redeem it by some laudable attempt, either of valour or policy.
*Sir And.* And 't be any way, it must be with valour: for policy I hate; I had as lief be a Brownist as a politician.
*Sir To.* Why, then, build me thy fortunes upon the basis of valour. Challenge me the count's youth to fight with him; hurt him in eleven places; my niece shall take note of it: and assure thyself there is no love-broker in the world can more prevail in man's commendation with woman than report of valour.
*Fab.* There is no way but this, Sir Andrew.
*Sir And.* Will either of you bear me a challenge to him?
*Sir To.* Go, write it in a martial hand; be curst and brief; it is no matter how witty, so it be eloquent and full of invention; taunt him with the licence of ink: if thou *thou's* him some thrice, it shall not be amiss; and as many lies as will lie in thy sheet of paper, although the sheet were big enough for the bed of Ware in England, set 'em down; go about it. Let there be gall enough in thy ink; though thou write with a goose-pen, no matter. About it.
*Sir And.* Where shall I find you?
*Sir To.* We'll call thee at the *cubiculo.* Go.
[*Exit Sir* ANDREW.
*Fab.* This is a dear manikin to you, Sir Toby.
*Sir To.* I have been dear to him, lad; some two thousand strong, or so.
*Fab.* We shall have a rare letter from him: but you'll not deliver it.
*Sir To.* Never trust me then; and by all means stir on the youth to an answer. I think oxen and wainropes cannot hale them together. For Andrew, if he were opened, and you find so much blood in his liver as will clog the foot of a flea, I'll eat the rest of the anatomy.
*Fab.* And his opposite, the youth, bears in his visage no great presage of cruelty.

*Enter* MARIA.

*Sir To.* Look where the youngest wren of nine comes.
*Mar.* If you desire the spleen, and will laugh yourselves into stitches, follow me: yon gull, Malvolio, is turned heathen, a very renegado; for there is no Christian, that means to be saved by believing rightly, can ever believe such impossible passages of grossness. He's in yellow stockings.
*Sir To.* And cross-gartered?
*Mar.* Most villanously; like a pedant that keeps a school i' the church. I have dogged him like his murderer. He does obey every point of the letter that I dropped to betray him. He does smile his face into more lines than are in the new map, with the augmentation of the Indies: you have not seen such a thing as 'tis; I can hardly forbear hurling things at him. I know my lady will strike him; if she do, he'll smile, and tak 't for a great favour.
*Sir To.* Come, bring us, bring us where he is.
[*Exeunt.*

SCENE III.—*A Street.*

*Enter* ANTONIO *and* SEBASTIAN.

*Seb.* I would not by my will have troubled you;
But, since you make your pleasure of your pains,
I will no further chide you.
*Ant.* I could not stay behind you; my desire,
More sharp than filed steel, did spur me forth;
And not all love to see you,—though so much,
As might have drawn one to a longer voyage,—
But jealousy what might befall your travel,
Being skilless in these parts; which to a stranger,
Unguided and unfriended, often prove
Rough and unhospitable. My willing love,
The rather by these arguments of fear,
Set forth in your pursuit.
*Seb.*                My kind Antonio,
I can no other answer make but thanks,
And thanks, and ever thanks. Often good turns
Are shuffled off with such uncurrent pay;

But were my worth, as is my conscience, firm,
You should find better dealing. What's to do?
Shall we go see the reliques of this town?
*Ant.* To-morrow, sir; best, first, go see your
  lodging.
*Seb.* I am not weary, and 'tis long to night;
I pray you, let us satisfy our eyes
With the memorials and the things of fame
That do renown this city.
*Ant.*    Would you'd pardon me:
I do not without danger walk these streets:
Once, in a sea-fight, 'gainst the count, his
  galleys,
I did some service; of such note, indeed,
That were I ta'en here, it would scarce be
  answered.    [people.
*Seb.* Belike you slew great number of his
*Ant.* The offence is not of such a bloody
  nature;
Albeit the quality of the time and quarrel .
Might well have given us bloody argument.
It might have since been answered in repaying
What we took from them; which, for traffic's
  sake,
Most of our city did: only myself stood out:
For which, if I be lapsed in this place,
I shall pay dear.
*Seb.*    Do not then walk too open.
*Ant.* It doth not fit me. Hold, sir, here's my
  purse;
In the south suburbs, at the Elephant,
Is best to lodge: I will bespeak our diet
Whiles you beguile the time and feed your
  knowledge
With viewing of the town; there shall you have
  me.
*Seb.* Why I your purse?
*Ant.* Haply your eye shall light upon some toy
You have desire to purchase; and your store,
I think, is not for idle markets, sir.
*Seb.* I'll be your purse-bearer, and leave you
for an hour.
*Ant.* To the Elephant.—
*Seb.*    I do remember.
          [*Exeunt.*

### Scene IV.—Olivia's *Garden.*

*Enter* Olivia *and* Maria.

*Oli.* I have sent after him. He says he'll come;
How shall I feast him? what bestow on him?
For youth is bought more oft than begged or
  borrowed.
I speak too loud.——
Where is Malvolio?—he is sad and civil,
And suits well for a servant with my fortunes;—
Where is Malvolio?
*Mar.*    He's coming, madam:
But in strange manner. He is sure possessed.
*Oli.* Why, what's the matter? does he rave?
*Mar.*    No, madam,
He does nothing but smile: your ladyship
Were best have guard about you if he come;
For, sure, the man is tainted in his wits.

*Oli.* Go call him hither.—I'm as mad as he,
If sad and merry madness equal be.—

*Enter* Malvolio.

How now, Malvolio?
*Mal.* Sweet lady, ho, ho.
       [*Smiles fantastically.*
*Oli.* Smil'st thou?  .
I sent for thee upon a sad occasion.
*Mal.* Sad, lady? I could be sad: this does make
some obstruction in the blood, this cross-gar-
tering. But what of that; if it please the eye
of one, it is with me as the very true sonnet is:
*Please one and please all.*
*Oli.* Why, how dost thou, man? what is the
matter with thee?
*Mal.* Not black in my mind, though yellow in
my legs. It did come to his hands, and com-
mands shall be executed. I think we do know
the sweet Roman hand.
*Oli.* Wilt thou go to bed, Malvolio?
*Mal.* To bed? ay, sweetheart; and I'll come to
thee.
*Oli.* God comfort thee! Why dost thou smile
on, and kiss thy hand so oft?
*Mar.* How do you, Malvolio?
*Mal.* At your request? Yes; nightingales an-
swer daws.
*Mar.* Why appear you with this ridiculous
boldness before my lady?
*Mal. Be not afraid of greatness:*—'twas well
writ.
*Oli.* What meanest thou by that, Malvolio?
*Mal. Some are born great,*—
*Oli.* Ha?
*Mal. Some achieve greatness,*—
*Oli.* What say'st thou?
*Mal. And some have greatness thrust upon them.*
*Oli.* Heaven restore thee!
*Mal. Remember who commended thy yellow
stockings;*—
*Oli.* Thy yellow stockings?
*Mal. And wished to see thee cross-gartered.*
*Oli.* Cross-gartered?
*Mal. Go to: thou art made, if thou desirest to be
so:*—
*Oli.* Am I made?
*Mal. If not, let me see thee a servant still.*
*Oli.* Why, this is very midsummer madness.

*Enter* Servant.

*Ser.* Madam, the young gentleman of the
Count Orsino's is returned; I could hardly
entreat him back; he attends your ladyship's
pleasure.
*Oli.* I'll come to him. [*Exit* Servant.] Good
Maria, let this fellow be looked to. Where's
my cousin Toby? Let some of my people have
a special care of him; I would not have him
miscarry for the half of my dowry.
      [*Exeunt* Olivia *and* Maria.
*Mal.* Oh, ho! do you come near me now? no
worse man than Sir Toby to look to me? This
concurs directly with the letter: she sends him

on purpose that I may appear stubborn to him; for she incites me to that in the letter. *Cast thy humble slough,* says she;—*be opposite with a kinsman, surly with servants,—let thy tongue tang with arguments of state,—put thyself into the trick of singularity;*——and, consequently, sets down the manner how; as, a sad face, a reverend carriage, a slow tongue, in the habit of some sir of note, and so forth. I have limed her; but it is Jove's doing, and Jove make me thankful! And, when she went away now, *Let this fellow be looked to:* Fellow! not Malvolio, nor after my degree, but fellow. Why, everything adheres together; that no dram of a scruple, no scruple of a scruple, no obstacle, no incredulous or unsafe circumstance,—What can be said? Nothing, that can be, can come between me and the full prospect of my hopes. Well, Jove, not I, is the doer of this, and he is to be thanked.

*Re-enter* MARIA, *with Sir* TOBY BELCH *and* FABIAN.

*Sir To.* Which way is he, in the name of sanctity? If all the devils of hell be drawn in little, and Legion himself possessed him, yet I'll speak to him.

*Fab.* Here he is, here he is:—How is 't with you, sir? how is 't with you, man?

*Mal.* Go off; I discard you; let me enjoy my private; go off.

*Mar.* Lo, how hollow the fiend speaks within him! did not I tell you?—Sir Toby, my lady prays you to have a care of him.

*Mal.* Ah, ah! does she so?

*Sir To.* Go to, go to; peace, peace, we must deal gently with him; let me alone. How do you, Malvolio? how is 't with you? What, man! defy the devil: consider, he's an enemy to mankind.

*Mal.* Do you know what you say?

*Mar.* La you, an you speak ill of the devil, how he takes it at heart! Pray God he be not bewitched.

*Fab.* Carry his water to the wise woman.

*Mar.* Marry, and it shall be done to-morrow morning, if I live. My lady would not lose him for more than I'll say.

*Mal.* How now, mistress?

*Mar.* O lord!

*Sir To.* Pr'ythee, hold thy peace; this is not the way. Do you not see you move him? let me alone with him.

*Fab.* No way but gentleness; gently, gently: the fiend is rough, and will not be roughtly used.

*Sir To.* Why, how now, my bawcock? how dost thou, chuck?

*Mal.* Sir?

*Sir To.* Ay, Biddy, come with me. What, man! 'tis not for gravity to play at cherry-pit with Satan. Hang him, foul collier!

*Mar.* Get him to say his prayers; good Sir Toby, get him to pray.

*Mal.* My prayers, minx?

*Mar.* No, I warrant you, he will not hear of godliness.

*Mal.* Go, hang yourselves all! you are idle shallow things: I am not of your element; you shall know more hereafter.    [*Exit.*

*Sir To.* Is 't possible?

*Fab.* If this were played upon the stage now, I could condemn it as an improbable fiction.

*Sir To.* His very genius hath taken the infection of the device, man.

*Mar.* Nay, pursue him now; lest the device take air and taint.

*Fab.* Why, we shall make him mad indeed.

*Mar.* The house will be the quieter.

*Sir To.* Come, we'll have him in a dark room and bound. My niece is already in the belief that he is mad; we may carry it thus, for our pleasure and his penance, till our very pastime, tired out of breath, prompt us to have mercy on him: at which time we will bring the device to the bar, and crown thee for a finder of madmen. But see, but see.

*Enter Sir* ANDREW AGUE-CHEEK.

*Fab.* More matter for a May morning.

*Sir And.* Here's the challenge, read it; I warrant there's vinegar and pepper in 't.

*Fab.* Is 't so saucy?

*Sir And.* Ay is it, I warrant him; do but read.

*Sir To.* Give me. [*Reads.*] *Youth, whatsoever thou art, thou art but a scurvy fellow.*

*Fab.* Good and valiant.

*Sir To. Wonder not, nor admire not in thy mind, why I do call thee so, for I will show thee no reason for 't.*

*Fab.* A good note: that keeps you from the blow of the law.

*Sir To. Thou comest to the Lady Olivia, and in my sight she uses thee kindly: but thou liest in thy throat; that is not the matter I challenge thee for.*

*Fab.* Very brief, and exceeding good senseless.

*Sir To. I will waylay thee going home; where if it be thy chance to kill me,——*

*Fab.* Good.

*Sir To. Thou killest me like a rogue and a villain.*

*Fab.* Still you keep o' the windy side of the law. Good.

*Sir To. Fare thee well; and God have mercy upon one of our souls! He may have mercy upon mine; but my hope is better, and so look to thyself. Thy friend, as thou usest him, and thy sworn enemy,* ANDREW AGUE-CHEEK.

*Sir To.* If this letter move him not, his legs cannot: I'll give 't him.

*Mar.* You may have very fit occasion for 't; he is now in some commerce with my lady, and will by and by depart.

*Sir To.* Go, Sir Andrew; scout me for him at the corner of the orchard, like a bum-bailiff; so soon as ever thou seest him, draw; and, as thou drawest, swear horrible; for it comes to pass oft that a terrible oath, with a swaggering accent sharply twanged off, gives manhood more approbation than ever proof itself would have earned him. Away.

*Sir And.* Nay, let me alone for swearing. [*Exit.*

*Sir To.* Now will not I deliver his letter; for the behaviour of the young gentleman gives him out to be of good capacity and breeding; his employment between his lord and my niece confirms no less; therefore this letter, being so excellently ignorant, will breed no terror in the youth: he will find it comes from a clodpole. But, sir, I will deliver his challenge by word of mouth, set upon Ague-cheek a notable report of valour, and drive the gentleman,—as I know his youth will aptly receive it,—into a most hideous opinion of his rage, skill, fury, and impetuosity. This will so fright them both that they will kill one another by the look, like cockatrices.

### Enter OLIVIA and VIOLA.

*Fab.* Here he comes with your niece; give them way till he take leave, and presently after him.

*Sir To.* I will meditate the while upon some horrid message for a challenge.

[*Exeunt Sir* To., FAB., *and* MAR.

*Oli.* I have said too much unto a heart of stone, And laid mine honour too unchary on it: There's something in me that reproves my fault; But such a headstrong potent fault it is That it but mocks reproof.                    [*bears*

*Vio.* With the same 'haviour that your passion Go on my master's griefs.                    [*ture;*

*Oli.* Here, wear this jewel for me, 'tis my pic- Refuse it not, it hath no tongue to vex you: And, I beseech you, come again to-morrow. What shall you ask of me that I'll deny, That, honour saved, may upon asking give?

*Vio.* Nothing but this, your true love for my master.                    [*that*

*Oli.* How with mine honour may I give him Which I have given to you?

*Vio.*                    I will acquit you.

*Oli.* Well, come again to-morrow. Fare thee well; A fiend like thee might bear my soul to hell.

[*Exit.*

### Re-enter Sir TOBY BELCH and FABIAN.

*Sir To.* Gentleman, God save thee.

*Vio.* And you, sir.

*Sir To.* That defence thou hast, betake thee to 't. Of what nature the wrongs are thou hast done him, I know not; but thy intercepter, full of despight, bloody as the hunter, attends thee at the orchard end: dismount thy tuck, be yare in thy preparation, for thy assailant is quick, skilful, and deadly.

*Vio.* You mistake, sir; I am sure no man hath any quarrel to me; my remembrance is very free and clear from any image of offence done to any man.

*Sir To.* You'll find it otherwise, I assure you: therefore, if you hold your life at any price, betake you to your guard; for your opposite hath in him what youth, strength, skill, and wrath can furnish man withal.

*Vio.* I pray you, sir, what is he?

*Sir To.* He is a knight, dubbed with unhacked rapier, and on carpet consideration; but he is a devil in private brawl; souls and bodies hath he divorced three; and his incensement at this moment is so implacable that satisfaction can be none but by pangs of death and sepulchre: hob, nob, is his word; give 't or take 't.

*Vio.* I will return again into the house and de- sire some conduct of the lady. I am no fighter. I have heard of some kind of men that put quarrels purposely on others to taste their valour: belike this is a man of that quirk.

*Sir To.* Sir, no; his indignation derives itself out of a very competent injury; therefore, get you on, and give him his desire. Back you shall not to the house, unless you undertake that with me which with as much safety you might answer him: therefore on, or strip your sword stark naked; for meddle you must, that's cer- tain, or forswear to wear iron about you.

*Vio.* This is as uncivil as strange. I beseech you, do me this courteous office as to know of the knight what my offence to him is, it is something of my negligence, nothing of my purpose.

*Sir To.* I will do so. Signior Fabian, stay you by this gentleman till my return.

[*Exit Sir* TOBY.

*Vio.* Pray you, sir, do you know of this matter?

*Fab.* I know the knight is incensed against you, even to a mortal arbitrement; but nothing of the circumstance more.

*Vio.* I beseech you, what manner of man is he?

*Fab.* Nothing of that wonderful promise, to read him by his form, as you are like to find him in the proof of his valour. He is indeed, sir, the most skilful, bloody, and fatal opposite that you could possibly have found in any part of Illyria. Will you walk towards him? I will make your peace with him if I can.

*Vio.* I shall be much bound to you for 't. I am one that would rather go with sir priest than sir knight: I care not who knows so much of my mettle.                    [*Exeunt.*

### Re-enter Sir TOBY with Sir ANDREW.

*Sir To.* Why, man, he's a very devil; I have not seen such a virago. I had a pass with him, rapier, scabbard, and all, and he gives me the stuck-in with such a mortal motion that it is inevitable; and on the answer, he pays you as surely as your feet hit the ground they step on. They say he has been fencer to the Sophy.

*Sir And.* Pox on 't, I'll not meddle with him.

*Sir To.* Ay, but he will not now be pacified: Fabian can scarce hold him yonder.

*Sir And.* Plague on 't; an I thought he had been valiant, and so cunning in fence, I'd have seem him damned ere I'd have challenged him. Let him let the matter slip and I'll give him my horse, gray Capilet.

*Sir To.* I'll make the motion. Stand here, make a good show on 't; this shall end without the perdition of souls. Marry, I'll ride your horse as well as I ride you.          [*Aside.*

#### Re-enter FABIAN and VIOLA.

I have his horse [*to* FAB.] to take up the quarrel; I have persuaded him the youth's a devil.

*Fab.* He is as horribly conceited of him; and pants and looks pale, as if a bear were at his heels.

*Sir To.* There's no remedy, sir; he will fight with you for his oath sake: marry, he hath better bethought him of his quarrel, and he finds that now scarce to be worth talking of: therefore draw, for the supportance of his vow; he protests he will not hurt you.

*Vio.* Pray God defend me! A little thing would make me tell them how much I lack of a man.
          [*Aside.*

*Fab.* Give ground if you see him furious.

*Sir To.* Come, Sir Andrew, there's no remedy; the gentleman will, for his honour's sake, have one bout with you: he cannot by the duello avoid it; but he has promised me, as he is a gentleman and a soldier, he will not hurt you. Come on: to 't.

*Sir And.* Pray God, he kept his oath. [*Draws.*

#### Enter ANTONIO.

*Vio.* I do assure you 'tis against my will.
          [*Draws.*

*Ant.* Put up your sword:—If this young gentleman
Have done offence, I take the fault on me;
If you offend him I for him defy you.
          [*Drawing.*

*Sir To.* You, sir? why, what are you?

*Ant.* One, sir, that for his love dares yet do more
Than you have heard him brag to you he will.

*Sir To.* Nay, if you be an undertaker I am for you.          [*Draws.*

#### Enter two Officers.

*Fab.* O good Sir Toby, hold; here come the officers.

*Sir To.* I'll be with you anon.     [*To* ANTONIO.

*Vio.* Pray, sir, put up your sword, if you please.          [*To Sir* ANDREW.

*Sir And.* Marry, will I, sir; and, for that I promised you, I'll be as good as my word. He will bear you easily and reins well.

1 *Off.* This is the man; do thy office.

2 *Off.* Antonio, I arrest thee at the suit Of Count Orsino.

*Ant.*          You do mistake me, sir.

1 *Off.* No, sir, no jot; I know your favour well, Though now you have no sea-cap on your head.—
Take him away; he knows I know him well.

*Ant.* I must obey.—This comes from seeking you;
But there's no remedy; I shall answer it.

What will you do? Now my necessity     [me
Makes me to ask you for my purse. It grieves
Much more for what I cannot do for you
Than what befalls myself. You stand amazed;
But be of comfort.

2 *Off.* Come, sir, away.

*Ant.* I must entreat of you some of that money.

*Vio.* What money, sir?
For the fair kindness you have showed me here,
And part being prompted by your present trouble,
Out of my lean and low ability
I'll lend you something; my having is not much;
I'll make division of my present with you:.
Hold, there is half my coffer.

*Ant.*          Will you deny me now?
I'st possible that my deserts to you
Can lack persuasion? Do not tempt my misery
Lest that it make me so unsound a man
As to upbraid you with those kindnesses
That I have done for you.

*Vio.*          I know of none,
Nor know I you by voice or any feature:
I hate ingratitude more in a man
Than lying, vainness, babbling, drunkenness,
Or any taint of vice whose strong corruption
Inhabits our frail blood.

*Ant.*          O heavens themselves!

2 *Off.* Come, sir, I pray you go.

*Ant.* Let me speak a little. This youth that you see here
I snatched one half out of the jaws of death,
Relieved him with such sanctity of love,——
And to his image, which methought did promise
Most venerable worth, did I devotion.

1 *Off.* What's that to us? The time goes by; away.

*Ant.* But O how vile an idol proves this god!
Thou hast, Sebastian, done good feature shame.
In nature there's no blemish but the mind;
None can be call'd deform'd but the unkind:
Virtue is beauty; but the beauteous-evil
Are empty trunks o'erflourish'd by the devil.

1 *Off.* The man grows mad; away with him.
Come, come, sir.

*Ant.* Lead me on.
          [*Exeunt* Officers *with* ANTONIO.

*Vio.* Methinks his words do from such passion fly
That he believes himself; so do not I.
Prove true, imagination; O prove true,
That I, dear brother, be now ta'en for you!

*Sir To.* Come hither, knight; come hither, Fabian; we'll whisper o'er a couple or two of most sage saws.

*Vio.* He named Sebastian; I my brother know
Yet living in my glass; even such and so
In favour was my brother; and he went
Still in this fashion, colour, ornament,
For him I imitate. O, if it prove,
Tempests are kind, and salt waves fresh in love!          [*Exit.*

*Sir To.* A very dishonest paltry boy, and more a coward than a hare: his dishonesty appears

in leaving his friend here in necessity, and denying him; and for his cowardice, ask Fabian.
*Fab.* A coward, a most devout coward, religious in it.                          [him.
*Sir And.* 'Slid, I'll after him again and beat
*Sir To.* Do, cuff him soundly, but never draw thy sword.
*Sir And.* An' I do not,—                    [*Exit.*
*Fab.* Come, let's see the event.              •
*Sir To.* I dare lay any money 'twill be nothing yet.                            [*Exeunt.*

## ACT IV.

SCENE I.—*The Street before* OLIVIA'S *House.*

*Enter* SEBASTIAN *and* CLOWN.

*Clo.* Will you make me believe that I am not sent for you?
*Seb.* Go to, go to, thou art a foolish fellow; Let me be clear of thee.
*Clo.* Well held out, i' faith! No, I do not know you; nor I am not sent to you by my lady, to bid you come speak with her; nor your name is not Master Cesario; nor this is not my nose neither.—Nothing that is so is so.
*Seb.* I pr'ythee, vent thy folly somewhere else. Thou knowst not me.
*Clo.* Vent my folly! he has heard that word of some great man, and now applies it to a fool. Vent my folly! I am afraid this great lubber, the world, will prove a cockney.—I pr'ythee now, ungird thy strangeness, and tell me what I shall vent to my lady. Shall I vent to her that thou art coming?
*Seb.* I pr'ythee, foolish Greek, depart from me; There's money for thee; if you tarry longer I shall give worse payment.
*Clo.* By my troth, thou hast an open hand:— These wise men that give fools money get themselves a good report after fourteen years' purchase.

*Enter Sir* ANDREW, *Sir* TOBY, *and* FABIAN.

*Sir And.* Now, sir, have I met you again? there's for you.            [*Striking* SEBASTIAN.
*Seb.* Why, there's for thee, and there, and there.
Are all the people mad?
                       [*Beating Sir* ANDREW.
*Sir To.* Hold, sir, or I'll throw your dagger o'er the house.
*Clo.* This will I tell my lady straight I would not be in some of your coats for twopence.
                               [*Exit* CLOWN.
*Sir To.* Come on, sir; hold.
                       [*Holding* SEBASTIAN.
*Sir And.* Nay, let him alone; I'll go another way to work with him; I'll have an action of battery against him, if there be any law in Illyria: though I struck him first, yet it's no matter for that.
*Seb.* Let go thy hand.
*Sir To.* Come, sir, I will not let you go. Come,

my young soldier, put up your iron: you are well fleshed; come on.
*Seb.* I will be free from thee. What wouldst thou now?
If thou dar'st tempt me further, draw thy sword.                               [*Draws.*
*Sir To.* What, what? Nay, then I must have an ounce or two of this malapert blood from you.                                  [*Draws.*

*Enter* OLIVIA.

*Oli.* Hold, Toby; on thy life, I charge thee, hold.
*Sir To.* Madam?
*Oli.* Will it be ever thus? Ungracious wretch, Fit for the mountains and the barbarous caves, Where manners ne'er were preach'd! Out of my sight!
Be not offended, dear Cesario!——
Rudesby, be gone!—I pr'ythee, gentle friend,
           [*Exeunt Sir* TO., *Sir* AND., *and* FAB.
Let thy fair wisdom, not thy passion, sway
In this uncivil and unjust extent
Against thy peace. Go with me to my house,
And hear thou there how many fruitless pranks
This ruffian hath botch'd up, that thou thereby
Mayst smile at this: thou shalt not choose but go;
Do not deny. Beshrew his soul for me,
He started one poor heart of mine in thee.
*Seb.* What relish is in this? how runs the stream?
Or am I mad? or else this is a dream:—
Let fancy still my sense in Lethe steep;
If it be thus to dream, still let me sleep!
*Oli.* Nay, come, I pr'ythee. Would thou'dst be ruled by me!
*Seb.* Madam, I will.
*Oli.*                  O, say so, and so be!
                              [*Exeunt.*

SCENE II.—*A Room in* OLIVIA'S *House.*

*Enter* MARIA *and* CLOWN.

*Mar.* Nay, I pr'ythee, put on this gown and this beard; make him believe thou art Sir Topas the curate; do it quickly: I'll call Sir Toby the whilst.               [*Exit* MARIA.
*Clo.* Well, I'll put it on, and I will dissemble myself in 't; and I would I were the first that ever dissembled in such a gown. I am not fat enough to become the function well: nor lean enough to be thought a good student: but to be said, an honest man and a good housekeeper, goes as fairly as to say, a careful man and a great scholar. The competitors enter.

*Enter Sir* TOBY BELCH *and* MARIA.

*Sir To.* Jove bless thee, master parson.
*Clo. Bonos dies,* Sir Toby: for as the old hermit of Prague, that never saw pen and ink, very wittily said to a niece of King Gorboduc, *That that is, is:* so I, being master parson, am master parson: for what is that but that? and is but is?
*Sir To* To him, Sir Topas.

*Clo.* What, hoa, I say,—Peace in this prison!

*Sir To.* The knave counterfeits well; a good knave.

*Mal.* [*In an inner chamber.*] Who calls there?

*Clo.* Sir Topas the curate, who comes to visit Malvolio the lunatic.

*Mal.* Sir Topas, Sir Topas, good Sir Topas, go to my lady.

*Clo.* Out, hyperbolical fiend! how vexest thou this man? talkest thou nothing but of ladies?

*Sir To.* Well said, master parson.

*Mal.* Sir Topas, never was man thus wronged: good Sir Topas, do not think I am mad; they have laid me here in hideous darkness.

*Clo.* Fie, thou dishonest Sathan! I call thee by the most modest terms; for I am one of those gentle ones that will use the devil himself with courtesy. Say'st thou that house is dark?

*Mal.* As hell, Sir Topas.

*Clo.* Why, it hath bay-windows, transparent as barricadoes, and the clear storeys towards the south-north are as lustrous as ebony; and yet complainest thou of obstruction?

*Mal.* I am not mad, Sir Topas; I say to you this house is dark.

*Clo.* Madman, thou errest. I say there is no darkness but ignorance; in which thou art more puzzled than the Egyptians in their fog.

*Mal.* I say this house is as dark as ignorance, though ignorance were as dark as hell; and I say there was never man thus abused. I am no more mad than you are; make the trial of it in any constant question.

*Clo.* What is the opinion of Pythagoras concerning wild-fowl?

*Mal.* That the soul of our grandam might haply inhabit a bird.

*Clo.* What thinkest thou of his opinion?

*Mal.* I think nobly of the soul, and no way approve of his opinion.

*Clo.* Fare thee well. Remain thou still in darkness: thou shalt hold the opinion of Pythagoras ere I will allow of thy wits; and fear to kill a woodcock lest thou dispossess the soul of thy grandam. Fare thee well.

*Mal.* Sir Topas, Sir Topas!

*Sir To.* My most exquisite Sir Topas!

*Clo.* Nay, I am for all waters.

*Mar.* Thou mightst have done this without thy beard and gown; he sees thee not.

*Sir To.* To him in thine own voice, and bring me word how thou findest him: I would we were well rid of this knavery. If he may be conveniently delivered, I would he were; for I am now so far in offence with my niece that I cannot pursue with any safety this sport to the upshot. Come by and by to my chamber.

[*Exeunt Sir* To. *and* Mar.

*Clo.*      *Hey, Robin, jolly Robin,*
            *Tell me how thy lady does.*      [*Singing.*

*Mal.* Fool,—

*Clo.* *My lady is unkind, perdy.*

*Mal.* Fool,—

*Clo. Alas, why is she so?*

*Mal.* Fool, I say;—

*Clo. She loves another*—Who calls, ha?

*Mal.* Good fool, as ever thou wilt deserve well at my hand, help me to a candle, and pen, ink, and paper; as I am a gentleman, I will live to be thankful to thee for 't.

*Clo.* Master Malvolio!

*Mal.* Ay, good fool.

*Clo.* Alas, sir, how fell you besides your five wits?

*Mal.* Fool, there was never man so notoriously abused; I am as well in my wits, fool, as thou art.

*Clo.* But as well? then you are mad indeed, if you be no better in your wits than a fool.

*Mal.* They have here propertied me; keep me in darkness, send ministers to me, asses, and do all they can to face me out of my wits.

*Clo.* Advise you what you say; the minister is here.—Malvolio, Malvolio, thy wits the heavens restore! endeavour thyself to sleep, and leave thy vain bibble-babble.

*Mal.* Sir Topas,——

*Clo.* Maintain no words with him, good fellow. Who, I, sir? not I, sir. God b' wi' you, good Sir Topas.—Marry, amen.—I will, sir, I will.

*Mal.* Fool, fool, fool, I say,—

*Clo.* Alas, sir, be patient. What say you, sir? I am shent for speaking to you.

*Mal.* Good fool, help me to some light and some paper; I tell thee I am as well in my wits as any man in Illyria.

*Clo.* Well-a-day,—that you were, sir!

*Mal.* By this hand, I am: Good fool, some ink, paper, and light, and convey what I will set down to my lady; it shall advantage thee more than ever the bearing of letter did.

*Clo.* I will help you to 't. But tell me true, are you not mad indeed? or do you but counterfeit?

*Mal.* Believe me, I am not; I tell thee true.

*Clo.* Nay, I'll ne'er believe a madman till I see his brains. I will fetch you light, and paper, and ink.

*Mal.* Fool, I'll requite it in the highest degree: I pr'ythee, be gone.

*Clo.*          I am gone, sir,
                And anon, sir,
            I'll be with you again,
                In a trice,
                Like to the old vice,
            Your need to sustain;
            Who with dagger of lath,
            In his rage and his wrath,
                Cries ah, ha! to the devil:
            Like a mad lad,
            Pare thy nails, dad,
            Adieu, goodman drivel.      [*Exit.*

### Scene III.—Olivia's *Garden.*

#### Enter Sebastian.

*Seb.* This is the air; that is the glorious sun;
This pearl she gave me, I do feel 't, and see 't:
And though 'tis wonder that enwraps me thus,

Yet 'tis not madness. Where's Antonio, then?
I could not find him at the Elephant;
Yet there he was; and there I found this credit,
That he did range the town to seek me out.
His counsel now might do me golden service:
For though my soul disputes well with my sense,
That this may be some error, but no madness,
Yet doth this accident and flood of fortune
So far exceed all instance, all discourse,
That I am ready to distrust mine eyes
And wrangle with my reason, that persuades me
To any other trust but that I am mad,
Or else the lady's mad; yet if 'twere so,
She could not sway her house, command her
            followers,
Take and give back affairs and their despatch
With such a smooth, discreet, and stable bearing
As I perceive she does: there's something in 't
That is deceivable. But here comes the lady.

*Enter* OLIVIA *and a* Priest.

*Oli.* Blame not this haste of mine. If you mean
            well,
Now go with me and with this holy man
Into the chantry by: there, before him
And underneath that consecrated roof,
Plight me the full assurance of your faith,
That my most jealous and too doubtful soul
May live at peace. He shall conceal it
Whiles you are willing it shall come to note;
What time we will our celebration keep
According to my birth.—What do you say?
*Seb.* I'll follow this good man, and go with you;
And, having sworn truth, ever will be true.
*Oli.* Then lead the way, good father;——And
            heavens so shine
That they may fairly note this act of mine!
                                        [*Exeunt.*

## ACT V.

SCENE I.—*The Street before* OLIVIA'S *House.*

*Enter* CLOWN *and* FABIAN.

*Fab.* Now, as thou lovest me, let me see his
letter.
*Clo.* Good Master Fabian, grant me another
request.
*Fab.* Anything.
*Clo.* Do not desire to see this letter.
*Fab.* That is to give a dog; and in recompense,
desire my dog again.

*Enter* DUKE, VIOLA, *and* Attendants.

*Duke.* Belong you to the Lady Olivia, friends?
*Clo.* Ay, sir; we are some of her trappings.
*Duke.* I know thee well. How dost thou, my
good fellow?
*Clo.* Truly sir, the better for my foes and the
worse for my friends.          [friends.
*Duke.* Just the contrary; the better for thy
*Clo.* No, sir, the worse.
*Duke.* How can that be?
*Clo.* Marry, sir, they praise me, and make an
ass of me; now my foes tell me plainly I am
an ass: so that by my foes, sir, I profit in the
knowledge of myself, and by my friends I am
abused: so that, conclusions to be as kisses, if
your four negatives make your two affirma-
tives, why then, the worse for my friends and
the better for my foes.
*Duke.* Why, this is excellent.
*Clo.* By my troth, sir, no; though it please you
to be one of my friends.
*Duke.* Thou shalt not be the worse for me;
there's gold.
*Clo.* But that it would be double-dealing, sir,
I would you could make it another.
*Duke.* O, you give me ill counsel.
*Clo.* Put your grace in your pocket, sir, for
this once, and let your flesh and blood obey it.
*Duke.* Well, I will be so much a sinner to be a
double-dealer: there's another.
*Clo. Primo, secundo, tertio,* is a good play; and
the old saying is, the third pays for all; the
*triplex,* sir, is a good tripping measure; or the
bells of St. Bennet, sir, may put you in mind;
One, two, three.
*Duke.* You can fool no more money out of me
at this throw: if you will let your lady know I
am here to speak with her, and bring her along
with you, it may awake my bounty further.
*Clo.* Marry, sir, lullaby to your bounty till I
come again. I go, sir; but I would not have
you to think that my desire of having is the sin
of covetousness: but, as you say, sir, let your
bounty take a nap, I will awake it anon.
                                    [*Exit* CLOWN.

*Enter* ANTONIO *and* Officers.

*Vio.* Here comes the man, sir, that did rescue
me.
*Duke.* That face of his I do remember well:
Yet, when I saw it last, it was besmeared
As black as Vulcan in the smoke of war:
A bawbling vessel was he captain of,
For shallow draught and bulk unprizable;
With which such scathful grapple did he make
With the most noble bottom of our fleet,
That very envy and the tongue of loss
Cried fame and honour on him.—What's the
                                    matter?
i *Off.* Orsino, this is that Antonio [Candy:
That took the Phœnix and her fraught from
And this is he that did the Tiger board
When your young nephew Titus lost his leg:
Here in the streets, desperate of shame and state,
In private brabble did we apprehend him.
*Vio.* He did me kindness, sir; drew on my side;
But, in conclusion, put strange speech upon me,
I know not what 'twas, but distraction.
*Duke.* Notable pirate! thou salt-water thief!
What foolish boldness brought thee to their
                                    mercies,
Whom thou, in terms so bloody and so dear,
Hast made thine enemies?
*Ant.*                      Orsino, noble sir,

Be pleased that I shake off these names you
    give me;
Antonio never yet was thief or pirate,
Though, I confess, on base and ground enough,
Orsino's enemy. A witchcraft drew me hither:
That most ingrateful boy there, by your side,
From the rude sea's enraged and foamy mouth
Did I redeem; a wreck past hope he was:
His life I gave him, and did thereto add
My love, without retention or restraint,
All his in dedication: for his sake,
Did I expose myself, pure for his love,
Into the danger of this adverse town;
Drew to defend him when he was beset:
Where being apprehended, his false cunning,—
Not meaning to partake with me in danger,—
Taught him to face me out of his acquaintance,
And grew a twenty-years-removed thing
While one would wink; denied me mine own
    purse,
Which I had recommended to his use
Not half an hour before.
*Vio.*               How can this be?
*Duke.* When came he to this town?
*Ant.* To-dày, my lord; and for three months
    before,—
No interim, not a minute's vacancy,—
Both day and night did we keep company.

    *Enter* OLIVIA *and* Attendants.

*Duke.* Here comes the countess; now heaven
    walks on earth.——
But for thee, fellow, fellow, thy words are
    madness:
Three months this youth hath tended upon me;
But more of that anon.——Take him aside.
*Oli.* What would my lord, but that he may not
    have,
Wherein Olivia may seem serviceable!—
Cesario, you do not keep promise with me.
*Vio.* Madam?
*Duke.* Gracious Olivia,——
*Oli.* What do you say, Cesario?——Good my
    lord,——
*Vio.* My lord would speak, my duth hushes me.
*Oli.* If it be aught to the old tune, my lord,
It is as fat and fulsome to mine ear
As howling after music.
*Duke.*            Still so cruel?
*Oli.* Still so constant, lord.
*Duke.* What! to perverseness? you uncivil lady,
To whose ingrate and unauspicious altars
My soul the faithfull'st offerings hath breathed
    out
That e'er devotion tender'd! What shall I do?
*Oli.* Even what it please my lord, that shall
    become him.             [do it.
*Duke.* Why should I not, had I the heart to
Like to the Egyptian thief, at point of death,
Kill what I love; a savage jealousy    [this:
That sometime savours nobly?—But hear me
Since you to non-regardance cast my faith,
And that I partly know the instrument

That screws me from my true place in your
    favour,
Live you the marble-breasted tyrant still;
But this your minion, whom I know you love,
And whom by heaven I swear, I tender dearly,
Him will I tear out of that cruel eye
Where he sits crownèd in his master's sprite.—
Come, boy, with me; my thoughts are ripe in
    mischief:
I'll sacrifice the lamb that I do love,
To spite a raven's heart within a dove.
                            *[Going.*
*Vio.* And I, most jocund, apt, and willingly,
To do you rest, a thousand deaths would die.
                          *[Following.*
*Oli.* Where goes Cesario?
*Vio.*              After him I love
More than I love these eyes, more than my life,
More, by all mores, than e'er I shall love wife;
If I do feign, you witnesses above
Punish my life for tainting of my love!
*Oli.* Ah me, detested! how am I beguiled?
*Vio.* Who does beguile you? who does do you
    wrong?
*Oli.* Hast thou forgot thyself? Is it so long?
Call forth the holy father.
                 *[Exit an* Attendant.
*Duke.*             Come away. [*To* VIOLA.
*Oli.* Whither, my lord? Cesario, husband, stay.
*Duke.* Husband?
*Oli.*           Ay, husband, can he that deny?
*Duke.* Her husband, sirrah?
*Vio.*             No, my lord, not I
*Oli.* Alas, it is the baseness of thy fear
That makes thee strangle thy propriety:
Fear not, Cesario, take thy fortunes up;
Be that thou know'st thou art, and then thou
    art                     [father!
As great as that thou fear'st—O, welcome,

    *Re-enter* Attendant *and* Priest.

Father, I charge thee, by thy reverence,
Here to unfold—though lately we intended
To keep in darkness what occasion now
Reveals before 'tis ripe,—what thou dost know
Hath newly past between this youth and me.
*Priest.* A contract of eternal bond of love,
Confirmed by mutual joinder of your hands,
Attested by the holy close of lips,
Strengthen'd by interchangement of your rings;
And all the ceremony of this compact
Sealed in my function, by my testimony:
Since when, my watch hath told me, toward
    my grave
I have travelled but two hours.        [be,
*Duke.* O thou dissembling cub! what wilt thou
When time hath sowed a grizzle on thy case?
Or will not else thy craft so quickly grow
That thine own trip shall be thine overthrow?
Farewell, and take her; but direct thy feet
Where thou and I henceforth may never meet.
*Vio.* My lord, I do protest,—
*Oli.*             O, do not swear;
Hold little faith, though thou hast too much fear.

*Enter Sir* ANDREW AGUE-CHEEK, *with his head broke.*

*Sir And.* For the love of God, a surgeon; send one presently to Sir Toby.

*Oli.* What's the matter?

*Sir And.* He has broke my head across, and has given Sir Toby a bloody coxcomb too: for the love of God, your help: I had rather than forty pound I were at home.

*Oli.* Who has done this, Sir Andrew?

*Sir And.* The count's gentleman, one Cesario: we took him for a coward, but he's the very devil incardinate.

*Duke.* My gentleman, Cesario?

*Sir And.* Od's lifelings, here he is:—You broke my head for nothing; and that that I did I was set on to do 't by Sir Toby.            [you:

*Vio.* Why do you speak to me? I never hurt you. You drew your sword upon me without cause; But I bespake you fair and hurt you not.

*Sir And.* If a bloody coxcomb be a hurt, you have hurt me; I think you set nothing by a bloody coxcomb.

*Enter Sir* TOBY BELCH *drunk, led by the* CLOWN.

Here comes Sir Toby halting; you shall hear more: but if he had not been in drink he would have tickled you othergates than he did.

*Duke.* How now, gentleman? how is 't with you?

*Sir To.* That's all one; he has hurt me, and there's the end on 't.—Sot, didst see Dick surgeon, sot?

*Clo.* O he's drunk, Sir Toby, an hour agone; his eyes were set at eight i' the morning.

*Sir To.* Then he's a rogue. After a passymeasure, or a pavin, I hate a drunken rogue.

*Oli.* Away with him. Who hath made this havoc with them?

*Sir And.* I'll help you, Sir Toby, because we'll be dressed together.

*Sir To.* Will you help an ass-head, and a coxcomb, and a knave? a thin-faced knave, a gull?

*Oli.* Get him to bed, and let his hurt be looked to.        [*Exeunt* CLOWN, *Sir* TO., *and Sir* AND.

*Enter* SEBASTIAN.

*Seb.* I am sorry, madam, I have hurt your kinsman;

But, had it been the brother of my blood, I must have done no less, with wit and safety. You throw a strange regard upon me, and By that I do perceive it hath offended you; Pardon me, sweet one, even for the vows We made each other but so late ago.

*Duke.* One face, one voice, one habit, and two persons;

A natural perspective, that is, and is not.

*Seb.* Antonio, O my dear Antonio! How have the hours rack'd and tortur'd me Since I have lost thee.

*Ant.* Sebastian are you?

*Seb.*            Fear'st thou that, Antonio?

*Ant.* How have you made division of yourself?—

An apple, cleft in two, is not more twin Than these two creatures. Which is Sebastian?

*Oli.* Most wonderful!

*Seb.* Do I stand there? I never had a brother: Nor can there be that deity in my nature Of here and everywhere. I had a sister Whom the blind waves and surges have devoured:—

Of charity, what kin are you to me? [*To* VIOLA. Whatcountryman?whatname?whatparentage?

*Vio.* Of Messaline: Sebastian was my father; Such a Sebastian was my brother too; So went he suited to his watery tomb: If spirits can assume both form and suit, You come to fright us.

*Seb.*            A spirit I am indeed: But am in that dimension grossly clad, Which from the womb I did participate. Were you a woman, as the rest goes even, I should my tears let fall upon your cheek, And say—Thrice welcome, drowned Viola!

*Vio.* My father had a mole upon his brow.

*Seb.* And so had mine.

*Vio.* And died that day when Viola from her birth

Had numbered thirteen years.

*Seb.* O, that record is lively in my soul! He finished, indeed, his mortal act That day that made my sister thirteen years.

*Vio.* If nothing lets to make us happy both But this my masculine usurp'd attire, Do not embrace me till each circumstance Of place, time, fortune, do cohere, and jump, That I am Viola: which to confirm, I'll bring you to a captain in this town, [help Where lie my maiden's weeds; by whose gentle I was preserv'd to serve this noble count; All the occurrence of my fortune since Hath been between this lady and this lord.

*Seb.* So comes it, lady, you have been mistook: But nature to her bias drew in that. [*To* OLIVIA. You would have been contracted to a maid; Nor are you therein, by my life, deceived; You are betroth'd both to a maid and man.

*Duke.* Be not amazed; right noble is his blood.— If this be so, as yet the glass seems true, I shall have share in this most happy wreck: Boy, thou hast said to me a thousand times, [*To* VIOLA.

Thou never shouldst love woman like to me.

*Vio.* And all those sayings will I over-swear; And all those swearings keep as true in soul As doth that orbed continent the fire That severs day from night.

*Duke.*            Give me thy hand; And let me see thee in thy woman's weeds.

*Vio.* The captain that did bring me first on shore        [action,

Hath my maid's garments: he, upon some Is now in durance, at Malvolio's suit; A gentleman and follower of my lady's.

*Oli.* He shall enlarge him:—Fetch Malvolio
hither:—
And yet, alas, now I remember me,
They say, poor gentleman, he's much distract.

*Re-enter* CLOWN, *with a letter.*

A most extracting frenzy of mine own
From my remembrance clearly banished his.—
How does he, sirrah?
*Clo.* Truly, madam, he holds Beelzebub at the
stave's end as well as a man in his case may do:
he has here writ a letter to you; I should have
given it you to-day morning; but as a madman's epistles are no gospels, so it skills not
much when they are delivered.
*Oli.* Open it, and read it.
*Clo.* Look then to be well edified when the fool
delivers the madman:—*By the Lord, madam,—*
*Oli.* How now! art thou mad?
*Clo.* No, madam, I do but read madness: an
your ladyship will have it as it ought to be, you
must allow *vox.*
*Oli.* Pr'ythee, read i' thy right wits.
*Clo.* So I do, madonna; but to read his right
wits to read thus: therefore perpend, my princess, and give ear.
*Oli.* Read it you, sirrah.         [*To* FABIAN.
*Fab.* [reads.] *By the Lord, madam, you wrong
me, and the world shall know it: though you have
put me into darkness and given your drunken
cousin rule over me, yet have I the benefit of my
senses as well as your ladyship. I have your own
letter that induced me to the semblance I put on;
with the which I doubt not but to do myself much
right or you much shame. Think of me as you
please. I leave my duty a little unthought of, and
speak out of my injury.*
                *The madly used* MALVOLIO.
*Oli.* Did he write this?
*Clo.* Ay, madam.
*Duke.* This savours not much of distraction.
*Oli.* See him delivered, Fabian: bring him
hither.         [*Exit* FABIAN.
My lord, so please you, these things further
        thought on,
To think me as well a sister as a wife,
One day shall crown the alliance on't, so please
        you,
Here at my house, and at my proper cost.
*Duke.* Madam, I am most apt to embrace your
        offer.—         [*service done him.*
Your master quits you; [*to* VIOLA] and, for your
So much against the metal of your sex,
So far beneath your soft and tender breeding,
And since you called me master for so long,
Here is my hand; you shall from this time be
Your master's mistress.
*Oli.*         A sister?—you are she.

*Re-enter* FABIAN *with* MALVOLIO.

*Duke.* Is this the madman?
*Oli.*         Ay, my lord, this same;
How now, Malvolio?

*Mal.*         Madam, you have done me wrong,
Notorious wrong.
*Oli.*         Have I, Malvolio? no.
*Mal.* Lady, you have. Pray you, peruse that
        letter:
You must not now deny it is your hand,
Write from it, if you can, in hand or phrase;
Or say, 'tis not your seal, nor your invention:
You can say none of this. Well, grant it then,
And tell me, in the modesty of honour,
Why you have given me such clear lights of
        favour;
Bade me come smiling and cross-garter'd to you,
To put on yellow stockings, and to frown
Upon Sir Toby and the lighter people:
And, acting this in an obedient hope,
Why have you suffer'd me to be imprison'd,
Kept in a dark house, visited by the priest,
And made the most notorious geck and gull
That e'er invention play'd on? tell me why.
*Oli.* Alas, Malvolio, this is not my writing,
Though, I confess, much like the character:
But, out of question, 'tis Maria's hand.
And now I do bethink me, it was she
First told me thou wast mad; then cam'st in
        smiling,
And in such forms which here were presuppos'd
Upon thee in the letter. Pr'ythee, be content:
This practice has most shrewdly pass'd upon
        thee:
But, when we know the grounds and authors
        of it,
Thou shalt be both the plaintiff and the judge
Of thine own cause.
*Fab.*         Good madam, hear me speak;
And let no quarrel, nor no brawl to come,
Taint the condition of this present hour,
Which I have wonder'd at. In hope it shall not,
Most freely I confess, myself and Toby
Set this device against Malvolio here,
Upon some stubborn and uncourteous parts
We had conceiv'd against him. Maria writ
The letter, at Sir Toby's great importance;
In recompense whereof he hath married her.
How with a sportful malice it was follow'd
May rather pluck on laughter than revenge,
If that the injuries be justly weigh'd
That have on both sides past.
*Oli.* Alas, poor fool! how have they baffled thee!
*Clo.* Why, *some are born great, some achieve
greatness, and some have greatness thrown upon
them.* I was one, sir, in this interlude; one Sir
Topas, sir; but that's all one:—*By the Lord,
fool, I am not mad;*—But do you remember?
*Madam, why laugh you at such a barren rascal?
an you smile not, he's gagged.* And thus the
whirligig of time brings in his revenges.
*Mal.* I'll be revenged on the whole pack of you.
                [*Exit.*
*Oli.* He hath been most notoriously abus'd.
*Duke.* Pursue him, and entreat him to a peace:—
He hath not told us of the captain yet;
When that is known, and golden time convents,
A solemn combination shall be made

Of our dear souls.—Meantime, sweet sister,
we will not part from hence.—Cesario, come:
For so you shall be while you are a man;
But, when in other habits you are seen,
Orsino's mistress, and his fancy's queen.

[*Exeunt.*

### SONG

*Clo.* When that I was and a little tiny boy,
    With hey, ho, the wind and the rain,
A foolish thing was but a toy,
    For the rain it raineth every day.

But when I came to man's estate,
    With hey, ho, the wind and the rain,
'Gainst knave and thief men shut their gate,
    For the rain it raineth every day.

But when I came, alas! to wive,
    With hey, ho, the wind and the rain,
By swaggering could I never thrive,
    For the rain it raineth every day.

But when I came unto my bed,
    With hey, ho, the wind and the rain,
With toss-pots still had drunken head,
    For the rain it raineth every day.

A great while ago the world began,
    With hey, ho, the wind and the rain,
But that's all one, our play is done,
    And we'll strive to please you every day.

[*Exit.*

MEASURE
FOR
MEASURE.

Act V. Sc. 1.

# MEASURE FOR MEASURE

## DRAMATIS PERSONÆ

VICENTIO, *Duke of Vienna.*
ANGELO, *Lord Deputy in the Duke's absence.*
ESCALUS, *an ancient Lord, joined with AN-GELO in the Deputation.*
CLAUDIO, *a young Gentleman.*
LUCIO, *a Fantastic.*
TWO OTHER LIKE GENTLEMEN.
VARRIUS, *a Gentleman, Servant to the Duke.*
PROVOST.
THOMAS, } *two Friars.*
PETER,
A JUSTICE.
ELBOW, *a simple Constable.*

FROTH, *a foolish Gentleman.*
CLOWN, *Servant to* MRS. OVERDONE.
ABHORSON, *an Executioner.*
BARNARDINE, *a dissolute Prisoner.*

ISABELLA, *Sister to* CLAUDIO.
MARIANA, *betrothed to* ANGELO.
JULIET, *beloved by* CLAUDIO.
FRANCISCA, *a Nun.*
MISTRESS OVERDONE, *a Bawd.*

Lords, Gentlemen, Guards, Officers, and other Attendants.

SCENE,—VIENNA.

## ACT I.

### SCENE I.—*An Apartment in the* DUKE'S *Palace.*

*En er* DUKE, ESCALUS, Lords, *and* Attendants.

*Duke.* Escalus,—
*Escal.* My lord.
*Duke.* Of government the properties to unfold,
Would seem in me to affect speech and discourse;
Since I am put to know that your own science
Exceeds, in that, the lists of all advice
My strength can give you: then no more remains
But that to your sufficiency, as your worth is able,
And let them work. The nature of our people,
Our city's institutions, and the terms
For common justice, you are as pregnant in
As art and practice hath enriched any
That we remember. There is our commission,
From which we would not have you warp.—
        Call hither,
I say, bid come before us Angelo.—
                [*Exit an* Attendant.
What figure of us think you he will bear?
For you must know we have with special soul
Elected him our absence to supply;
Lent him our terror, drest him with our love,
And given his deputation all the organs
Of our own power: what think you of it?
*Escal.* If any in Vienna be of worth
To undergo such ample grace and honour,
It is Lord Angelo.

### *Enter* ANGELO.

*Duke.* Look where he comes.
*Ang.* Always obedient to your grace's will,
I come to know your pleasure.
*Duke.*                Angelo,
There is a kind of character in thy life,
That to the observer doth thy history

Fully unfold. Thyself and thy belongings
Are not thine own so proper as to waste
Thyself upon thy virtues, they on thee.
Heaven doth with us as we with torches do,
Not light them for themselves: for if our virtues
Did not go forth of us, 'twere all alike
As if we had them not. Spirits are not finely
        touch'd
But to fine issues: nor nature never lends
The smallest scruple of her excellence
But, like a thrifty goddess, she determines
Herself the glory of a creditor,
Both thanks and use. But I do bend my speech
To one that can my part in him advertise;
Hold, therefore, Angelo;
In our remove be thou at full ourself:
Mortality and mercy in Vienna
Live in thy tongue and heart! Old Escalus,
Though first in question, is thy secondary:
Take thy commission.
*Ang.*                Now, good my lord,
Let there be some more test made of my metal,
Before so noble and so great a figure
Be stamped upon it.
*Duke.*                No more evasion:
We have with a leaven'd and prepared choice
Proceeded to you; therefore take your honours.
Our haste from hence is of so quick condition
That it prefers itself, and leaves unquestion'd
Matters of needful value. We shall write to you
As time and our concernings shall impórtune
How it goes with us; and do look to know
What doth befall you here. So, fare you well:
To the hopeful execution do I leave you
Of your commissions.
*Ang.*                Yet, give leave, my lord,
That we may bring you something on the way.
*Duke.* My haste may not admit it;
Nor need you, on mine honour, have to do
With any scruple: your scope is as mine own:

So to enforce or qualify the laws
As to your soul seems good. Give me your hand;
I'll privily away: I love the people,
But do not like to stage me to their eyes:
Though it do well, I do not relish well
Their loud applause and *aves* vehement:
Nor do I think the man of safe discretion
That does affect it. Once more, fare you well.
*Ang.* The heavens give safety to your purposes!
*Escal.* Lead forth and bring you back in hap-
         piness.
*Duke.* I thank you. Fare you well.      [*Exit.*
*Escal.* I shall desire you, sir, to give me leave
To have free speech with you; and it concerns me
To look into the bottom of my place:
A power I have, but of what strength and nature
I am not yet instructed.                [gether,
*Ang.* 'Tis so with me.—Let us withdraw to-
And we may soon our satisfaction have
Touching that point.
*Escal.*          I'll wait upon your honour.
                                        [*Exeunt.*

### SCENE II.—*A Street.*

*Enter* LUCIO *and two* GENTLEMEN.

*Lucio.* If the duke, with the other dukes, come
not to composition with the King of Hungary,
why, then, all the dukes fall upon the king.
*1 Gent.* Heaven grant us its peace, but not the
*2 Gent.* Amen.          [king of Hungary's!
*Lucio.* Thou concludest like the sanctimonious
pirate that went to sea with the ten commandments, but scraped one out of the table.
*2 Gent.* Thou shalt not steal?
*Lucio.* Ay, that he razed.
*1 Gent.* Why, 'twas a commandment to command the captain and all the rest from their
functions; they put forth to steal. There's not
a soldier of us all that, in the thanksgiving
before meat, doth relish the petition well that
prays for peace.
*2 Gent.* I never heard any soldier dislike it.
*Lucio.* I believe thee; for I think thou never
wast where grace was said.
*2 Gent.* No? a dozen times at least.
*1 Gent.* What? in metre?
*Lucio.* In any proportion or in any language.
*1 Gent.* I think, or in any religion.
*Lucio.* Ay! why not? Grace is grace, despite of
all controversy. As for example;—thou thyself
art a wicked villain, despite of all grace.
*1 Gent.* Well, there went but a pair of shears
between us.
*Lucio.* I grant; as there may between the lists
and the velvet. Thou art the list.
*1 Gent.* And thou the velvet: thou art good
velvet; thou art a three-piled piece, I warrant
thee: I had as lief be a list of an English kersey
as be piled, as thou art piled, for a French
velvet. Do I speak feelingly now?
*Lucio.* I think thou dost; and, indeed, with
most painful feeling of thy speech. I will, out
of thine own confession, learn to begin thy

health; but, whilst I live, forget to drink after
thee.
*1 Gent.* I think I have done myself wrong; have
I not?
*2 Gent.* Yes, that thou hast; whether thou art
tainted or free.
*Lucio.* Behold, behold, where Madam Mitigation comes! I have purchased as many diseases
under her roof as come to—
*2 Gent.* To what, I pray?
*1 Gent.* Judge.
*2 Gent.* To three thousand dollars a-year.
*1 Gent.* Ay, and more.
*Lucio.* A French crown more.
*1 Gent.* Thou art always figuring diseases in
me, but thou art full of error; I am sound.
*Lucio.* Nay, not as one would say, healthy; but
so sound as things that are hollow: thy bones
are hollow; impiety has made a feast of thee.

### *Enter* BAWD.

*1 Gent.* How now! which of your hips has the
most profound sciatica?
*Bawd.* Well, well; there's one yonder arrested
and carried to prison was worth five thousand
of you all.
*1 Gent.* Who's that, I pray thee?
*Bawd.* Marry, sir, that's Claudio, Signior
Claudio.
*1 Gent.* Claudio to prison! 'tis not so.
*Bawd.* Nay, but I know 'tis so: I saw him arrested; saw him carried away; and, which is
more, within these three days his head's to be
chopped off.
*Lucio.* But, after all his fooling, I would not
have it so. Art thou sure of this?
*Bawd.* I am too sure of it: and it is for getting
Madam Julietta with child.
*Lucio.* Believe me, this may be: he promised to
meet me two hours since; and he was ever precise in promise-keeping.
*2 Gent.* Besides, you know, it draws something
near to the speech we had to such a purpose.
*1 Gent.* But most of all agreeing with the proclamation.
*Lucio.* Away; let's go learn the truth of it.
                [*Exeunt* LUCIO *and* GENTLEMEN.
*Bawd.* Thus, what with the war, what with
the sweat, what with the gallows, and what
with poverty, I am custom-shrunk. How now!
what's the news with you?

### *Enter* CLOWN.

*Clo.* Yonder man is carried to prison.
*Bawd.* Well: what has he done?
*Clo.* A woman.
*Bawd.* But what's his offence?
*Clo.* Groping for trouts in a peculiar river.
*Bawd.* What! is there a maid with child by him?
*Clo.* No; but there's a woman with maid by
him. You have not heard of the proclamation,
have you?
*Bawd.* What proclamation, man?

*Clo.* All houses in the suburbs of Vienna must be plucked down.　　　　　　　　　　[city?

*Bawd.* And what shall become of those in the

*Clo.* They shall stand for seed: they had gone down too, but that a wise burgher put in for them.

*Bawd.* But shall all our houses of resort in the suburbs be pulled down?

*Clo.* To the ground, mistress.

*Bawd.* Why, here's a change indeed in the commonwealth! What shall become of me?

*Clo.* Come; fear not you: good counsellors lack no clients: though you change your place you need not change your trade; I'll be your tapster still. Courage; there will be pity taken on you: you that have worn your eyes almost out in the service, you will be considered.

*Bawd.* What's to do here, Thomas Tapster? Let's withdraw.

*Clo.* Here comes Signior Claudio, led by the provost to prison: and there's Madam Juliet.
　　　　　　　　　　　　　　　　[*Exeunt.*

### SCENE III.—*The same.*

*Enter* PROVOST, CLAUDIO, JULIET, *and* Officers; LUCIO *and two* GENTLEMEN.

*Claud.* Fellow, why dost thou show me thus to the world?
Bear me to prison, where I am committed.

*Prov.* I do it not in evil disposition,
But from Lord Angelo by special charge.

*Claud.* Thus can the demi-god Authority
Make us pay down for our offence by weight.—
The words of heaven;—on whom it will, it will;
On whom it will not, so; yet still 'tis just.

*Lucio.* Why, how now, Claudio? whence comes this restraint?　　　　　　　　　　[erty:

*Claud.* From too much liberty, my Lucio, lib-
As surfeit is the father of much fast,
So every scope by the immoderate use
Turns to restraint. Our natures do pursue,—
Like rats that ravin down their proper bane,—
A thirsty evil; and when we drink we die.

*Lucio.* If I could speak so wisely under an arrest, I would send for certain of my creditors; and yet, to say the truth, I had as lief have the foppery of freedom as the morality of imprisonment.—What's thy offence, Claudio?

*Claud.* What but to speak of would offend again.

*Lucio.* What, is it murder?

*Claud.* No.

*Lucio.* Lechery?

*Claud.* Call it so.

*Prov.* Away, sir; you must go.

*Claud.* One word, good friend:—Lucio, a word with you.　　　　　　　　[*Takes him aside.*

*Lucio.* A hundred, if they'll do you any good. Is lechery so looked after?

*Claud.* Thus it stands with me:—Upon a true contráct
I got possession of Julietta's bed:
You know the lady; she is fast my wife,
Save that we do the denunciation lack

Of outward order: this we came not to
Only for propagation of a dower
Remaining in the coffer of her friends;
From whom we thought it meet to hide our love
Till time had made them for us. But it chances
The stealth of our most mutual entertainment,
With character too gross, is writ on Juliet.

*Lucio.* With child, perhaps?

*Claud.* Unhappily, even so.
And the new deputy now for the duke,—
Whether it be the fault and glimpse of newness,
Or whether that the body public be
A horse whereon the governor doth ride,
Who, newly in the seat, that it may know
He can command, lets it straight feel the spur:
Whether the tyranny be in his place,
Or in his eminence that fills it up,
I stagger in.—But this new governor
Awakes me all the enrolled penalties
Which have, like unscour'd armour, hung by the wall
So long that nineteen zodiacs have gone round
And none of them been worn; and, for a name,
Now puts the drowsy and neglected act
Freshly on me;—'tis surely for a name.

*Lucio.* I warrant it is: and thy head stands so tickle on thy shoulders that a milkmaid, if she be in love, may sigh it off. Send after the duke, and appeal to him.

*Claud.* I have done so, but he's not to be found.
I pr'ythee, Lucio, do me this kind service:
This day my sister should the cloister enter,
And there receive her approbation:
Acquaint her with the danger of my state;
Implore her, in my voice, that she make friends
To the strict deputy; bid herself assay him;
I have great hope in that: for in her youth
There is a prone and speechless dialect
Such as moves men; beside, she hath prosperous art
When she will play with reason and discourse,
And well she can persuade.

*Lucio.* I pray she may; as well for the encouragement of the like, which else would stand under grievous imposition, as for the enjoying of thy life, who I would be sorry should be thus foolishly lost at a game of tick-tack. I'll to her.

*Claud.* I thank you, good friend Lucio.

*Lucio.* Within two hours,——

*Claud.* Come, officer, away.　　　　　[*Exeunt.*

### SCENE IV.—*A Monastery.*

*Enter* DUKE *and Friar* THOMAS.

*Duke.* No; holy father; throw away that thought;
Believe not that the dribbling dart of love
Can pierce a complete bosom: why I desire thee
To give me secret harbour hath a purpose
More grave and wrinkled than the aims and ends
Or burning youth.

*Fri.*　　　　　　May your grace speak of it?

*Duke.* My holy sir, none better knows than you
How I have ever lov'd the life remov'd,
And held in idle price to haunt assemblies

Where youth, and cost, and witless bravery
keeps.
I have deliver'd to Lord Angelo,—
A man of stricture and firm abstinence,—
My absolute power and place here in Vienna
And he supposes me travell'd to Poland;
For so I have strew'd it in the common ear,
And so it is received. Now, pious sir,
You will demand of me why I do this?
*Fri.* Gladly, my lord.
*Duke.* We have strict statutes and most biting
laws,—
The needful bits and curbs for headstrong
steeds,—
Which for these fourteen years we have let sleep,
Even like an o'ergrown lion in a cave,
That goes not out to prey. Now, as fond fathers,
Having bound up the threat'ning twigs of birch,
Only to stick it in their children's sight
For terror, not to use, in time the rod
Becomes more mock'd than fear'd: so our
decrees,
Dead to infliction, to themselves are dead;
And liberty plucks justice by the nose;
The baby beats the nurse, and quite athwart
Goes all decorum.
*Fri.*                It rested in your grace
To unloose this tied-up justice when you
pleas'd:
And it in you more dreadful would have seem'd
Than in Lord Angelo.
*Duke.*              I do fear, too dreadful:
Sith 'twas my fault to give the people scope,
'Twould be my tyranny to strike and gall them
For what I bid them do: for we bid this be done
When evil deeds have their permissive pass
And not the punishment. Therefore, indeed,
my father,
I have on Angelo impos'd the office;
Who may, in the ambush of my name, strike
home,
And yet my nature never in the fight,
To do it slander. And to behold his sway,
I will, as 'twere a brother of your order,
Visit both prince and people: therefore, I
pr'ythee,
Supply me with the habit, and instruct me
How I may formally in person bear me
Like a true friar. More reasons for this action
At our more leisure shall I render you;
Only, this one:—Lord Angelo is precise;
Stands at a guard with envy; scarce confesses
That his blood flows, or that his appetite
Is more to bread than stone: hence shall we see,
If power change purpose, what our seemers
be.
                                    [*Exeunt.*

SCENE V.—*A Nunnery.*

*Enter* ISABELLA *and* FRANCISCA.

*Isab.* And have you nuns no further privileges?
*Fran.* Are not these large enough?
*Isab.* Yes, truly: I speak not as desiring more,

But rather wishing a more strict restraint
Upon the sisterhood, the votaries of St. Clare.
*Lucio.* Ho! Peace be in this place!    [*Within.*
*Isab.*                    Who's that which calls?
*Fran.* It is a man's voice. Gentle Isabella,
Turn you the key, and know his business of him;
You may, I may not; you are yet unsworn:
When you have vow'd, you must not speak
with men
But in the presence of the prioress;    [face.
Then, if you speak, you must not show your
Or, if you show your face, you must not speak.
He calls again; I pray you answer him.
                            [*Exit* FRANCISCA.
*Isab.* Peace and prosperity! Who is 't that calls?

*Enter* LUCIO.

*Lucio.* Hail, virgin, if you be; as those cheek-
roses
Proclaim you are no less! Can you so stead me
As bring me to the sight of Isabella,
A novice of this place, and the fair sister
To her unhappy brother Claudio?
*Isab.* Why her unhappy brother? let me ask;
The rather, for I know must make you know
I am that Isabella, and his sister.
*Lucio.* Gentle and fair, your brother kindly
greets you:
Not to be weary with you, he's in prison.
*Isab.* Woe me! For what?
*Lucio.* For that which, if myself might be his
judge,
He should receive his punishment in thanks:
He hath got his friend with child.
*Isab.* Sir, make me not your story.
*Lucio.*                    It is true.
I would not—though 'tis my familiar sin
With maids to seem the lapwing, and to jest
Tongue far from heart—play with all virgins so:
I hold you as a thing ensky'd and sainted;
By your renouncement an immortal spirit;
And to be talk'd with in sincerity,
As with a saint.                        [me.
*Isab.* You do blaspheme the good in mocking
*Lucio.* Do not believe it. Fewness and truth,
'tis thus:
Your brother and his lover have embraced:
As those that feed grow full: as blossoming time,
That from the seedness the bare fallow brings
To teeming foison; even so her plenteous womb
Expresseth his full tilth and husbandry.
*Isab.* Some one with child by him?—My cousin
Juliet?
*Lucio.* Is she your cousin?
*Isab.* Adoptedly; as schoolmaids change their
names
By vain though apt affection.
*Lucio.*                    She it is.
*Isab.* O, let him marry her!
*Lucio.*                    This is the point.
The duke is very strangely gone from hence;
Bore many gentlemen, myself being one.
In hand, and hope of action: but we do learn
By those that know the very nerves of state,

His givings out were of an infinite distance
From his true-meant design. Upon his place,
And with full line of his authority,
Governs Lord Angelo: a man whose blood
Is very snow-broth; one who never feels
The wanton stings and motions of the sense,
But doth rebate and blunt his natural edge
With profits of the mind, study, and fast.
He,—to give fear to use and liberty,
Which have for long run by the hideous law,
As mice by lions,—hath pick'd out an act,
Under whose heavy sense your brother's life
Falls into forfeit: he arrests him on it;
And follows close the rigour of the statute
To make him an example; all hope is gone,
Unless you have the grace by your fair prayer
To soften Angelo: and that's my pith
Of business 'twixt you and your poor brother.
*Isab.* Doth he so seek his life?
*Lucio.*                    Has censur'd him
Already; and, as I hear, the provost hath
A warrant for his execution.
*Isab.* Alas! what poor ability's in me
To do him good.
*Lucio.*               Assay the power you have.
*Isab.* My power! alas, I doubt,—
*Lucio.*              Our doubts are traitors,
And make us lose the good we oft might win
By fearing to attempt. Go to Lord Angelo,
And let him learn to know, when maidens sue,
Men give like gods; but when they weep and
            kneel,
All their petitions are as freely theirs
As they themselves would owe them.
*Isab.* I'll see what I can do.
*Lucio.*                    But speedily.
*Isab.* I will about it straight;
No longer staying but to give the mother
Notice of my affair. I humbly thank you:
Commend me to my brother: soon at night
I'll send him certain word of my success.
*Lucio.* I take my leave of you.
*Isab.*                    Good sir, adieu.
                              [*Exeunt.*

## ACT II.

### SCENE I—*A Hall in* ANGELO'S *House*

*Enter* ANGELO, ESCALUS, *a* JUSTICE, PROVOST,
Officers, *and other* Attendants.

*Ang.* We must not make a scarecrow of the law,
Setting it up to fear the birds of prey,
And let it keep one shape till custom make it
Their perch, and not their terror.
*Escal.*                    Ay, but yet
Let us be keen, and rather cut a little
Than fall and bruise to death. Alas! this gen-
            tleman,
Whom I would save, had a most noble father.
Let but your honour know,—
Whom I believe to be most strait in virtue,—
That, in the working of your own affections,
Had time coher'd with place, or place with
            wishing,

Or that the resolute acting of your blood
Could have attain'd the effect of your own
            purpose,
Whether you had not sometime in your life
Err'd in this point which now you censure him,
And pull'd the law upon you.
*Ang.* 'Tis one thing to be tempted, Escalus,
Another thing to fall. I not deny,
The jury, passing on the prisoner's life,
May, in the sworn twelve, have a thief or two
Guiltier than him they try. What's open made
            to justice,
That justice seizes. What know the laws
That thieves do pass on thieves? 'Tis very
            pregnant,
The jewel that we find, we stoop and take it,
Because we see it; but what we do not see
We tread upon, and never think of it.
You may not so extenuate his offence
For I have had such faults; but rather tell me,
When I, that censure him, do so offend,
Let mine own judgment pattern out my death,
And nothing come in partial. Sir, he must die.
*Escal.* Be it as your wisdom will.
*Ang.*                    Where is the provost?
*Prov.* Here, if it like your honour.
*Ang.*                    See that Claudio
Be executed by nine to-morrow morning:
Bring him his confessor; let him be prepared;
For that's the utmost of his pilgrimage.
                              [*Exit* PROVOST.
*Escal.* Well, heaven forgive him! and forgive
            us all!
Some rise by sin and some by virtue fall:
Some run from brakes of vice, and answer none;
And some condemnéd for a fault alone.

*Enter* ELBOW, FROTH, CLOWN, Officers, &c.

*Elb.* Come, bring them away: if these be good
people in a commonweal that do nothing but
use their abuses in common houses, I know no
law; bring them away.
*Ang.* How now, sir! What's your name? and
what's the matter?
*Elb.* If it please your honour, I am the poor
duke's constable, and my name is Elbow; I do
lean upon justice, sir, and do bring in here before your good honour two notorious benefactors.
*Ang.* Benefactors! Well; what benefactors are
they? are they not malefactors?
*Elb.* If it please your honour, I know not well
what they are: but precise villains they are,
that I am su re of; and void of all profanation in
the world that good Christians ought to have.
*Escal.* This comes off well; here's a wise officer.
*Ang.* Go to;—what quality are they of? Elbow
is your name? Why dost thou not speak,
Elbow?
*Clo.* He cannot, sir; he's out at elbow.
*Ang.* What are you, sir?
*Elb.* He, sir? a tapster, sir; parcel-bawd; one
that serves a bad woman; whose house, sir,
was, as they say, plucked down in the suburbs;

and now she professes a hot-house, which, I think, is a very ill house too.

*Escal.* How know you that?

*Elb.* My wife, sir, whom I detest before heaven and your honour,—

*Escal.* How! thy wife!

*Elb.* Ay, sir; who, I thank heaven, is an honest woman,—

*Escal.* Dost thou detest her therefore?

*Elb.* I say, sir, I will detest myself also, as well as she, that this house, if it be not a bawd's house, it is pity of her life, for it is a naughty house.

*Escal.* How dost thou know that, constable?

*Elb.* Marry, sir, by my wife; who, if she had been a woman cardinally given, might have been accused in fornication, adultery, and all uncleanliness there.

*Escal.* By the woman's means?

*Elb.* Ay, sir, by Mistress Overdone's means: but as she spit in his face, so she defied him.

*Clo.* Sir, if it please your honour, this is not so.

*Elb.* Prove it before these varlets here, thou honourable man, prove it.

*Escal.* Do you hear how he misplaces?

[*To* ANGELO.

*Clo.* Sir, she came in great with child; and longing—saving your honour's reverence—for stewed prunes, sir; we had but two in the house, which at that very distant time stood as it were, in a fruit-dish, a dish of some three-pence; your honours have seen such dishes; they are not China dishes, but very good dishes.

*Escal.* Go to, go to; no matter for the dish, sir.

*Clo.* No, indeed, sir, not of a pin; you are therein in the right: but to the point. As I say, this Mistress Elbow, being, as I say, with child, and being great-bellied, and longing, as I said, for prunes; and having but two in the dish, as I said, Master Froth here, this very man, having eaten the rest, as I said, and, as I say, paying for them very honestly;—for, as you know, Master Froth, I could not give you threepence again,—

*Froth.* No, indeed.

*Clo.* Very well: you being then, if you be remembered, cracking the stones of the aforesaid prunes,—

*Froth.* Ay, so I did, indeed.

*Clo.* Why, very well: I telling you then, if you be remembered, that such a one and such a one were past cure of the thing you wot of, unless they kept very good diet, as I told you,—

*Froth.* All this is true.

*Clo.* Why, very well then.

*Escal.* Come, you are a tedious fool: to the purpose.—What was done to Elbow's wife that he hath cause to complain of? Come me to what was done to her.

*Clo.* Sir, your honour cannot come to that yet.

*Escal.* No, sir, nor I mean it not.

*Clo.* Sir, but you shall come to it, by your honour's leave. And I beseech you, look into Master Froth here, sir; a man of fourscore

pound a-year; whose father died at Hallowmas:—was't not at Hallowmas, Master Froth?

*Froth.* All-hallond eve.

*Clo.* Why, very well; I hope here be truths: He, sir, sitting, as I say, in a lower chair, sir; —'twas in the *Bunch of Grapes*, where, indeed, you have a delight to sit, have you not?—

*Froth.* I have so; because it is an open room, and good for winter. [truths.

*Clo.* Why, very well then;—I hope here be

*Ang.* This will last out a night in Russia, When nights are longest there: I'll take my leave, And leave you to the hearing of the cause; Hoping you'll find good cause to whip them all.

*Escal.* I think no less. Good morrow to your lordship. [*Exit* ANGELO.

Now, sir, come on: what was done to Elbow's wife, once more? [once.

*Clo.* Once, sir? there was nothing done to her

*Elb.* I beseech you, sir, ask him what this man did to my wife.

*Clo.* I beseech your honour, ask me.

*Escal.* Well, sir: what did this gentleman to her?

*Clo.* I beseech you, sir, look in this gentleman's face.—Good Master Froth, look upon his honour; 'tis for a good purpose.—Doth your honour mark his face?

*Escal.* Ay, sir, very well.

*Clo.* Nay, I beseech you, mark it well.

*Escal.* Well, I do so.

*Clo.* Doth your honour see any harm in his face?

*Escal.* Why, no.

*Clo.* I'll be supposed upon a book, his face is the worst thing about him. Good then; if his face be the worst thing about him, how could Master Froth do the constable's wife any harm? I would know that of your honour.

*Escal.* He's in the right.—Constable, what say you to it?

*Elb.* First, an it like you, the house is a respected house; next, this is a respected fellow; and his mistress is a respected woman.

*Clo.* By this hand, sir, his wife is a more respected person than any of us all.

*Elb.* Varlet, thou liest; thou liest, wicked varlet: the time is yet to come that she was ever respected with man, woman, or child.

*Clo.* Sir, she was respected with him before he married with her.

*Escal.* Which is the wiser here? Justice or Iniquity?—Is this true?

*Elb.* O thou caitiff! O thou varlet! O thou wicked Hannibal! I respected with her before I was married to her? If ever I was respected with her, or she with me, let not your worship think me the poor duke's officer.—Prove this, thou wicked Hannibal, or I'll have mine action of battery on thee.

*Escal.* If he took you a box o' th' ear, you might have your action of slander too.

*Elb.* Marry, I thank your good worship for it. What is't your worship's pleasure I should do with this wicked caitiff?

*Escal.* Truly, officer, because he hath some offences in him that thou wouldst discover if thou couldst, let him continue in his courses till thou knowest what they are.

*Elb.* Marry, I thank your worship for it.—Thou seest, thou wicked varlet, now, what's come upon thee; thou art to continue now, thou varlet; thou art to continue.

*Escal.* Where were you born, friend?

                          [*To* FROTH.

*Froth.* Here in Vienna, sir.

*Escal.* Are you of fourscore pounds a-year?

*Froth.* Yes, an't please you, sir.

*Escal.* So.—What trade are you of, sir?

                        [*To the* CLOWN.

*Clo.* A tapster; a poor widow's tapster.

*Escal.* Your mistress's name?

*Clo.* Mistress Overdone.

*Escal.* Hath she had any more than one husband?

*Clo.* Nine, sir; Overdone by the last.

*Escal.* Nine!—Come hither to me, Master Froth. Master Froth, I would not have you acquainted with tapsters: they will draw you, Master Froth, and you will hang them. Get you gone, and let me hear no more of you.

*Froth.* I thank your worship. For mine own part, I never come into any room in a taphouse but I am drawn in.

*Escal.* Well; no more of it, Master Froth: farewell. [*Exit* FROTH.]—Come you hither to me, master tapster; what's your name, master tapster?

*Clo.* Pompey.

*Escal.* What else?

*Clo.* Bum, sir.

*Escal.* 'Troth, and your bum is the greatest thing about you; so that, in the beastliest sense, you are Pompey the great. Pompey, you are partly a bawd, Pompey, howsoever you colour it in being a tapster. Are you not? come, tell me true; it shall be the better for you.

*Clo.* Truly, sir, I am a poor fellow that would live.

*Escal.* How would you live, Pompey? by being a bawd? What do you think of the trade, Pompey? is it a lawful trade?

*Clo.* If the law would allow it, sir.

*Escal.* But the law will not allow it, Pompey: nor it shall not be allowed in Vienna.

*Clo.* Does your worship mean to geld and splay all the youth in the city?

*Escal.* No, Pompey.

*Clo.* Truly, sir, in my poor opinion, they will to't then. If your worship will take order for the drabs and the knaves, you need not to fear the bawds.

*Escal.* There are pretty orders beginning, I can tell you. It is but heading and hanging.

*Clo.* If you head and hang all that offend that way but for ten year together, you'll be glad to give out a commission for more heads. If this law hold in Vienna ten year, I'll rent the fairest house in it, after threepence a bay. If

you live to see this come to pass, say Pompey told you so.

*Escal.* Thank you, good Pompey: and, in requital of your prophecy, hark you,—I advise you, let me not find you before me again upon any complaint whatsoever, no, not for dwelling where you do; if I do, Pompey, I shall beat you to your tent, and prove a shrewd Cæsar to you; in plain dealing, Pompey, I shall have you whipt: so for this time, Pompey, fare you well.

*Clo.* I thank your worship for your good counsel; but I shall follow it as the flesh and fortune shall better determine.

Whip me? No, no; let carman whip his jade; The valiant heart's not whipt out of his trade.

                             [*Exit.*

*Escal.* Come hither to me, Master Elbow; come hither, Master Constable. How long have you been in this place of constable?

*Elb.* Seven year and a half, sir.

*Escal.* I thought, by your readiness in the office, you had continued in it some time. You say seven years together?

*Elb.* And a half, sir.

*Escal.* Alas! it hath been great pains to you!—They do you wrong to put you so oft upon't. Are there not men in your ward sufficient to serve it?

*Elb.* Faith, sir, few of any wit in such matters: as they are chosen, they are glad to choose me for them; I do it for some piece of money, and go through with all.

*Escal.* Look you, bring me in the names of some six or seven, the most sufficient of your parish.

*Elb.* To your worship's house, sir?

*Escal.* To my house. Fare you well.     [*Exit.* ELBOW.] What's o'clock, think you?

*Just.* Eleven, sir.

*Escal.* I pray you home to dinner with me.

*Just.* I humbly thank you.

*Escal.* It grieves me for the death of Claudio; But there's no remedy.

*Just.* Lord Angelo is severe.

*Escal.*                  It is but needful: Mercy is not itself, that oft looks so; Pardon is still the nurse of second woe: But yet,—Poor Claudio!—There's no remedy. Come, sir.                         [*Exeunt.*

SCENE III.—*Another Room in the same.*

*Enter* PROVOST *and a* Servant.

*Serv.* He's hearing of a cause; he will come straight.
I'll tell him of you.

*Prov.* Pray you do. [*Exit* Servant.] I'll know His pleasure; may be he will relent. Alas, He hath but as offended in a dream! All sects, all ages, smack of this vice; and he To die for it!

*Enter* ANGELO.

*Ang.*            Now, what's the matter, provost?

*Prov.* Is it your will Claudio shall die to-morrow?

*Ang.* Did I not tell thee yea? hadst thou not
　　order?
Why dost thou ask again?
*Prov.*　　　　　Lest I might be too rash:
Under your good correction, I have seen
When, after execution, judgment hath
Repented o'er his doom.
*Ang.*　　　　Go to; let that be mine:
Do you your office, or give up your place,
And you shall well be spared.
*Prov.*　　I crave your honour's pardon:
What shall be done, sir, with the groaning Juliet?
She's very near her hour.
*Ang.*　　　　Dispose of her
To some more fitter place; and that with speed.

　　　　*Re-enter* Servant.

*Serv.* Here is the sister of the man condemned
Desires access to you.
*Ang.*　　　　Hath he a sister?
*Prov.* Ay, my good lord; a very virtuous maid,
And to be shortly of a sisterhood,
If not already.
*Ang.*　　　Well, let her be admitted.
　　　　　　　　　[*Exit* Servant.
See you the fornicatress be remov'd;
Let her have needful but not lavish means;
There shall be order for it.

　　　Enter Lucio *and* Isabella.

*Prov.* Save your honour!　[*Offering to retire.*
*Ang.* Stay a little while.—[*To* Isab.] You are
　　welcome. What's your will?
*Isab.* I am a woeful suitor to your honour,
Please but your honour hear me.
*Ang.*　　　Well; what's your suit?
*Isab.* There is a vice that most I do abhor,
And most desire should meet the blow of justice;
For which I would not plead, but that I must;
For which I must not plead, but that I am
At war 'twixt will and will not.
*Ang.*　　　Well; the matter?
*Isab.* I have a brother is condemn'd to die;
I do beseech you, let it be his fault,
And not my brother.
*Prov.*　　Heaven give thee moving graces.
*Ang.* Condemn the fault and not the actor of it!
Why, every fault's condemn'd ere it be done;
Mine were the very cipher of a function,
To find the fault whose find stands in record,
And let go by the actor.
*Isab.*　　　O just but severe law!
I had a brother, then.—Heaven keep your
　　honour!　　　　　[*Retiring.*
*Lucio.* [*To* Isab.] Giv't not o'er so: to him
　　again, entreat him;
Kneel down before him, hang upon his gown;
You are too cold; if you should need a pin,
You could not with more tame a tongue desire it:
To him, I say.
*Isab.* Must he needs die?
*Ang.*　　　　Maiden, no remedy.
*Isab.* Yes; I do think that you might pardon
　　him,

And neither heaven nor man grieve at the mercy
*Ang.* I will not do 't.
*Isab.*　　　But can you, if you would?
*Ang.* Look, what I will not, that I cannot do
*Isab.* But might you do 't, and do the world
　　no wrong,
If so your heart were touch'd with that remorse
As mine is to him.
*Ang.*　　　He's sentenc'd; 'tis too late.
*Lucio.* You are too cold.　　[*To* Isabella.
*Isab.* Too late? why, no; I, that do speak a
　　word,
May call it back again. Well, believe this,
No ceremony that to great ones 'longs,
Not the king's crown nor the deputed sword,
The marshal's truncheon nor the judge's robe,
Become them with one half so good a grace
As mercy does. If he had been as you,
And you as he, you would have slipp'd like him;
But he, like you, would not have been so stern.
*Ang.* Pray you, be gone.
*Isab.* I would to heaven I had your potency,
And you were Isabel! should it then be thus?
No; I would tell what 'twere to be a judge
And what a prisoner.
*Lucio.* Ay, touch him; there's the vein. [*Aside.*
*Ang.* Your brother is a forfeit of the law,
And you but waste your words.
*Isab.*　　　　Alas! alas!
Why, all the souls that were were forfeit once;
And He that might the vantage best have took
Found out the remedy. How would you be
If He, which is the top of judgment, should
But judge you as you are? O, think on that;
And mercy then will breathe within your lips,
Like man new made.
*Ang.*　　　Be you content, fair maid;
It is the law, not I, condemns your brother:
Were he my kinsman, brother, or my son,
It should be thus with him;—he must die to-
　　morrow.　　　　　[spare him!
*Isab.* To-morrow! O that's sudden! Spare him,
He's not prepared for death. Even for our
　　kitchens
We kill the fowl of season: shall we serve heaven
With less respect than we do minister　[you;
To our gross selves? Good, good my lord, bethink
Who is it that hath died for this offence?
There's many have committed it.
*Lucio.*　　　　Ay, well said.
*Ang.* The law hath not been dead, though it
　　hath slept:
Those many had not dared to do that evil
If the first man that did the edict infringe
Had answer'd for his deed: now 'tis awake;
Takes note of what is done; and, like a prophet,
Looks in a glass that shows what future evils,—
Either now, or by remissness new-conceiv'd,
And so in progress to be hatch'd and born,—
Are now to have no successive degrees,
But, where they live, to end.
*Isab.*　　　Yet show some pity.
*Ang.* I show it most of all when I show justice;
For then I pity those I do not know,

Which a dismiss'd offence would after gall,
And do him right that, answering one foul wrong,
Lives not to act another. Be satisfied;
Your brother dies to-morrow: be content.
*Isab.* So you must be the first that gives this
    sentence;
And he that suffers. O, it is excellent
To have a giant's strength; but it is tyrannous
To use it like a giant.
*Lucio.*          That's well said.
*Isab.* Could great men thunder
As Jove himself does, Jove would ne'er be quiet,
For every pelting petty officer
Would use his heaven for thunder: nothing but
    thunder.——
Merciful heaven!
Thou rather, with thy sharp and sulphurous bolt,
Splitt'st the unwedgeable and gnarled oak
Than the soft myrtle;—but man, proud man!
Dress'd in a little brief authority,—
Most ignorant of what he's most assured,
His glassy essence,—like an angry ape,
Plays such fantastic tricks before high heaven
As make the angels weep; who, with our spleens,
Would all themselves laugh mortal.
*Lucio.* O, to him, to him, wench: he will relent;
He's coming; I perceive 't.
*Prov.*        Pray heaven she win him!
*Isab.* We cannot weigh our brother with our-
    self:
Great men may jest with saints: 'tis wit in them;
But, in the less, foul profanation.
*Lucio.* Thou'rt in the right, girl; more o' that.
*Isab.* That in the captain's but a choleric word
Which in the soldier is flat blasphemy.
*Lucio.* Art advised o' that? more on 't.
*Ang.* Why do you put these sayings upon me?
*Isab.* Because authority, though it err like
    others,
Hath yet a kind of medicine in itself
That skins the vice o' the top. Go to your bosom;
Knock there; and ask your heart what it doth
    know
That's like my brother's fault; if it confess
A natural guiltiness such as is his,
Let it not sound a thought upon your tongue
Against my brother's life.
*Ang.*        She speaks, and 'tis
Such sense that my sense breeds with it.——
    Fare you well.
*Isab.* Gentle, my lord, turn back.
*Ang.* I will bethink me:—Come again to-
    morrow.
*Isab.* Hark how I'll bribe you. Good, my lord,
    turn back.
*Ang.* How! bribe me?
*Isab.* Ay, with such gifts that heaven shall
    share with you.
*Lucio.* You had marr'd all else.
*Isab.* Not with fond shekels of the tested gold,
Or stones, whose rates are either rich or poor
As fancy values them: but with true prayers,
That shall be up at heaven, and enter there,
Ere sunrise: prayers from preserved souls,

From fasting maids, whose minds are dedicate
To nothing temporal.
*Ang.*        Well; come to me
To-morrow.
*Lucio.* Go to; it is well; away.
                   [*Aside to* ISABELLA.
*Isab.* Heaven keep your honour safe!
*Ang.*            Amen: for I
Am that way going to temptation,    [*Aside.*
Where prayers cross.
*Isab.*        At what hour to-morrow
Shall I attend your lordship?
*Ang.*          At any time 'fore noon.
*Isab.* Save your honour!
        [*Exeunt* LUCIO, ISAB., *and* PROV.
*Ang.*    From thee; even from thy virtue!—
What's this? what's this? Is this her fault or
    mine?                     [Ha!
The tempter or the tempted, who sins most?
Not she; nor doth she tempt; but it is I
That, lying by the violet, in the sun
Do, as the carrion does, not as the flower,
Corrupt with virtuous season. Can it be
That modesty may more betray our sense
Than woman's lightness? Having waste ground
    enough,
Shall we desire to raze the sanctuary
And pitch our evils there? O, fie, fie, fie!
What dost thou? or what art thou, Angelo?
Dost thou desire her foully for those things
That make her good? O, let her brother live;
Thieves for their robbery have authority
When judges steal themselves. What! do I love
    her,
That I desire to hear her speak again
And feast upon her eyes? What is 't I dream on?
O cunning enemy, that, to catch a saint,
With saints dost bait thy look! Most dangerous
Is that temptation that doth goad us on
To sin in loving virtue: never could the strumpet,
With all her double vigour, art, and nature,
Once stir my temper; but this virtuous maid
Subdues me quite.—Ever till now,
When men were fond, I smil'd and wonder'd
    how.                      [*Exit.*

SCENE III.—*A Room in a Prison.*

*Enter* DUKE, *habited like a Friar, and* PROVOST.

*Duke.* Hail to you, provost! so I think you are.
*Prov.* I am the provost. What's your will, good
    friar?
*Duke.* Bound by my charity and my bless'd
    order,
I come to visit the afflicted spirits
Here in the prison: do me the common right
To let me see them, and to make me know
The nature of their crimes, that I may minister
To them accordingly.           [needful.
*Prov.* I would do more than that, if more were

*Enter* JULIET.

Look, here comes one; a gentlewoman of mine,
Who, falling in the flames of her own youth,

Hath blister'd her report. She is with child;
And he that got it, sentenc'd: a young man;
More fit to do another such offence
Than die for this.

*Duke.*        When must he die?

*Prov.* As I do think, to-morrow,—
I have provided for you; stay awhile
                 [*To* JULIET.
And you shall be conducted.

*Duke.* Repent you, fair one, of the sin you carry?

*Juliet.* I do; and bear the shame most patiently.

*Duke.* I'll teach you how you shall arraign
       your conscience,
And try your penitence, if it be sound
Or hollowly put on.

*Juliet.*          I'll gladly learn.

*Duke.* Love you the man that wrong'd you?

*Juliet.* Yes, as I love the woman that wrong'd
       him.                   [act

*Duke.* So then, it seems, your most offenceful
Was mutually committed?

*Juliet.*           Mutually.     [his.

*Duke.* Then was your sin of heavier kind than

*Juliet.* I do confess it, and repent it, father.

*Duke.* 'Tis meet so, daughter: but lest you do
       repent             [shame,—
As that the sin hath brought you to this
Which sorrow is always toward ourselves, not
       heaven,            [love it,
Showing we would not spare heaven as we
But as we stand in fear,—

*Juliet.* I do repent me as it is an evil,
And take the shame with joy.

*Duke.*           There rest.
Your partner, as I hear, must die to-morrow,
And I am going with instruction to him.—

*Juliet.* Grace go with you!

*Duke. Benedicite!*             [*Exit.*

*Juliet.* Must die to-morrow! O, injurious law,
That respites me a life whose very comfort
Is still a dying horror!

*Prov.*           'Tis pity of him! [*Exeunt.*

SCENE IV.—*A Room in* ANGELO'S *House.*

*Enter* ANGELO.

*Ang.* When I would pray and think, I think
       and pray           [words;
To several subjects. Heaven hath my empty
Whilst my invention, hearing not my tongue,
Anchors on Isabel: Heaven in my mouth,
As if I did but only chew his name;
And in my heart the strong and swelling evil
Of my conception. The state whereon I studied
Is like a good thing, being often read,
Grown sear'd and tedious; yea, my gravity,
Wherein—let no man hear me—I take pride,
Could I with boot change for an idle plume,
Which the air beats for vain. O place! O form!
How often dost thou with thy case, thy habit,
Wrench awe from fools, and tie the wiser souls
To thy false seeming? Blood, thou still art
       blood:
Let's write good angel on the devil's horn,
'Tis not the devil's crest.

*Enter* Servant.

How now, who's there?

*Serv.*           One Isabel, a sister,
Desires access to you.

*Ang.*          Teach her the way. [*Exit* Serv.
O heavens!
Why does my blood thus muster to my heart,
Making both it unable for itself
And dispossessing all the other parts
Of necessary fitness?          [swoons;
So play the foolish throngs with one that
Come all to help him, and so stop the air
By which he should revive: and even so
The general, subject to a well-wished king,
Quit their own part, and in obsequious fondness
Crowd to his presence, where their untaught love
Must needs appear offence.

*Enter* ISABELLA.

How now, fair maid?

*Isab.*       I am come to know your pleasure.

*Ang.* That you might know it, would much
       better please me          [live.
Than to demand what 'tis. Your brother cannot

*Isab.* Even so?—Heaven keep your honour!
                     [*Retiring.*

*Ang.* Yet may he live awhile: and, it may be,
As long as you or I: yet he must die.

*Isab.* Under your sentence?

*Ang.* Yea.           [prieve,

*Isab.* When, I beseech you? that in his re-
Longer or shorter, he may be so fitted
That his soul sicken not.          [good

*Ang.* Ha! Fie, these filthy vices! It were as
To pardon him that hath from nature stolen
A man already made, as to remit       [image
Their saucy sweetness that do coin heaven's
In stamps that are forbid; 'tis all as easy
Falsely to take away a life true made
As to put metal in restrained means
To make a false one.           [earth.

*Isab.* 'Tis set down so in heaven, but not in

*Ang.* Say you so? then I shall poze you quickly.
Which had you rather,—that the most just law
Now took your brother's life; or, to redeem him
Give up your body to such sweet uncleanness
As she that he hath stain'd?

*Isab.*           Sir, believe this,
I had rather give my body than my soul.

*Ang.* I talk not of your soul; our compell'd sins
Stand more for number than accompt.

*Isab.*           How say you?

*Ang.* Nay, I'll not warrant that; for I can speak
Against the thing I say. Answer to this;—
I, now the voice of the recorded law,
Pronounce a sentence on your brother's life:
Might there not be a charity in sin,
To save this brother's life?

*Isab.*           Please you to do 't,
I'll take it as a peril to my soul
It is no sin at all, but charity.

*Ang.* Pleas'd you to do 't at peril of your soul,
Were equal poise of sin and charity.

*Isab.* That I do beg his life, if it be sin,
Heaven let me bear it! you granting of my suit,
If that be sin, I'll make it my morn prayer
To have it added to the faults of mine,
And nothing of your answer.

*Ang.*	Nay, but hear me:
Your sense pursues not mine: either you are
	ignorant
Or seem so, craftily; and that's not good.

*Isab.* Let me be ignorant, and in nothing good
But graciously to know I am no better.

*Ang.* Thus wisdom wishes to appear most
	bright
When it doth tax itself: as these black masks
Proclaim an enshield beauty ten times louder
Than beauty could, displayed.—But mark me;
To be received plain, I'll speak more gross:
Your brother is to die.

*Isab.* So.

*Ang.* And his offence is so, as it appears
Accountant to the law upon that pain.

*Isab.* True.

*Ang.* Admit no other way to save his life,—
As I subscribe not that, nor any other,
But in the loss of question,—that you, his sister,
Finding yourself desir'd of such a person,
Whose credit with the judge, or own great place,
Could fetch your brother from the manacles
Of the all-binding law; and that there were
No earthly mean to save him but that either
You must lay down the treasures of your body
To this suppos'd, or else let him suffer;
What would you do?

*Isab.* As much for my poor brother as myself:
That is, were I under the terms of death,
The impression of keen whips I'd wear as rubies,
And strip myself to death, as to a bed
That longing I have been sick for, ere I'd yield
My body up to shame.

*Ang.*	Then must your brother die.

*Isab.* And 'twere the cheaper way:
Better it were a brother died at once
Than that a sister, by redeeming him,
Should die for ever.	[tence

*Ang.* Were not you, then, as cruel as the sen-
That you have slandered so?

*Isab.* Ignominy in ransom and free pardon
Are of two houses; lawful mercy is
Nothing akin to foul redemption.	[tyrant;

*Ang.* You seem'd of late to make the law a
And rather prov'd the sliding of your brother
A merriment than a vice.

*Isab.* O, pardon me, my lord; it oft falls out,
To have what we would have, we speak not
	what we mean:
I something do excuse the thing I hate,
For his advantage that I dearly love.

*Ang.* We are all frail.

*Isab.*	Else let my brother die,
If not a feodary, but only he,
Owe, and succeed by weakness.

*Ang.*	Nay, women are frail too.

*Isab.* Ay, as the glasses where they view them-
	selves;

Which are as easy broke as they make forms.
Women!—Help heaven! men their creation mar
In profiting by them. Nay, call us ten times
	frail;
For we are soft as our complexions are,
And credulous to false prints.

*Ang.*	I think it well
And from this testimony of your own sex,—
Since, I suppose, we are made to be no stronger
Than faults may shake our frames,—let me be
	bold;—
I do arrest your words. Be that you are,
That is, a woman; if you be more, you're none;
If you be one,—as you are well express'd
By all external warrants,—show it now
By putting on the destin'd livery.

*Isab.* I have no tongue but one: gentle, my lord,
Let me intreat you, speak the former language.

*Ang.* Plainly conceive, I love you.

*Isab.* My brother did love Juliet; and you tell
	me
That he shall die for it.

*Ang.* He shall not, Isabel, if you give me love.

*Isab.* I know your virtue hath a license in't,
Which seems a little fouler than it is,
To pluck on others.

*Ang.*	Believe me, on mine honour,
My words express my purpose.

*Isab.* Ha! little honour to be much believed,
And most pernicious purpose!—Seeming, seem-
	ing!—
I will proclaim thee, Angelo; look for't:
Sign me a a present pardon for my brother
Or, with an outstretch'd throat, I'll tell the world
Aloud what man thou art.

*Ang.*	Who will believe thee, Isabel?
My unsoil'd name, the austereness of my life,
My vouch against you, and my place i' the state
Will so your accusation overweigh
That you shall stifle in your own report,
And smell of calumny. I have begun;
And now I give my sensual race the rein:
Fit thy consent to my sharp appetite;
Lay by all nicety and prolixious blushes
That banish what they sue for: redeem thy
	brother
By yielding up thy body to my will;
Or else he must not only die the death,
But thy unkindness shall his death draw out
To lingering sufferance: answer me to-morrow,
Or, by the affection that now guides me most,
I'll prove a tyrant to him. As for you,
Say what you can, my false o'erweighs your
	true.	[*Exit.*

*Isab.* To whom shall I complain? Did I tell
	this,
Who would believe me? O perilous mouths,
That bear in them one and the self-same tongue
Either of condemnation or approof!
Bidding the law make court'sy to their will;
Hooking both right and wrong to the appetite,
To follow as it draws! I'll to my brother:
Though he hath fallen by prompture of the
	blood,

Yet hath he in him such a mind of honour
That, had he twenty heads to tender down
On twenty bloody blocks, he'd yield them up
Before his sister should her body stoop
To such abhorr'd pollution
Then, Isabel, live chaste, and, brother, die:
More than our brother is our chastity.
I'll tell him yet of Angelo's request,
And fit his mind to death for his soul's rest.
[*Exit.*

## ACT III.

SCENE I.—*A Room in the Prison.*

*Enter* DUKE, CLAUDIO, *and* PROVOST.

*Duke.* So, then you hope of pardon from Lord
    Angelo?
*Claud.* The miserable have no other medicine
But only hope:
I have hope to live, and am prepar'd to die.
*Duke.* Be absolute for death; either death or
    life    [with life,—
Shall thereby be the sweeter. Reason thus
If I do lose thee, I do lose a thing    [art
That none but fools would keep: a breath thou
Servile to all the skiey influences
That dost this habitation, where thou keep'st,
Hourly afflict; merely, thou art death's fool;
For him thou labour'st by thy flight to shun,
And yet runn'st toward him still. Thou art not
    noble;
For all the accommodations that thou bear'st
Are nurs'd by baseness. Thou art by no means
    valiant;
For thou dost fear the soft and tender fork
Of a poor worm. Thy best of rest is sleep,
And that thou oft provok'st; yet grossly fear'st
Thy death, which is no more. Thou art not
    thyself:
For thou exist'st on many a thousand grains
That issue out of dust. Happy thou art not;
For what thou hast not, still thou striv'st to get;
And what thou hast, forgett'st. Thou art not
    certain;
For thy complexion shifts to strange effects,
After the moon. If thou art rich, thou art poor;
For, like an ass whose back with ingots bows,
Thou bear'st thy heavy riches but a journey,
And death unloads thee. Friend hast thou none;
For thine own bowels, which do call thee sire,
The mere effusion of thy proper loins,
Do curse the gout, serpigo, and the rheum,
For ending thee no sooner. Thou hast nor
    youth nor age,
But, as it were, an after-dinner's sleep,
Dreaming on both: for all thy blessed youth
Becomes as aged, and doth beg the alms
Of palsied eld; and when thou art old and rich
Thou hast neither heat, affection, limb, nor
    beauty.    [this
To make thy riches pleasant. What's yet in
That bears the name of life? Yet in this life
Lie hid more thousand deaths: yet death we
    fear,

That makes these odds all even.
*Claud.*    I humbly thank you.
To sue to live, I find I seek to die;
And, seeking death, find life. Let it come on.
*Isab.* [*Within.*] What, ho! Peace here; grace
    and good company!
*Prov.* Who's there? come in: the wish deserves
    a welcome.
*Duke.* Dear sir, ere long I'll visit you again.
*Claud.* Most holy sir, I thank you.

*Enter* ISABELLA.

*Isab.* My business is a word or two with
    Claudio.    [your sister.
*Prov.* And very welcome. Look, signior, here's
*Duke.* Provost, a word with you.
*Prov.*    As many as you please.
*Duke.* Bring me to hear them speak where I
    may be conceal'd.
    [*Exeunt* DUKE *and* PROVOST.
*Claud.*    Now, sister, what's the comfort?
*Isab.* Why, as all comforts are; most good in
    deed:
Lord Angelo, having affairs to heaven,
Intends you for his swift embassador,
Where you shall be an everlasting lieger.
Therefore, your best appointment make with
    speed;
To-morrow you set on.
*Claud.*    Is there no remedy?
*Isab.* None, but such remedy as, to save a head,
To cleave a heart in twain.
*Claud.*    But is there any?
*Isab.* Yes, brother, you may live:
There is a devilish mercy in the judge,
If you'll implore it, that will free your life,
But fetter you till death.
*Claud.*    Perpetual durance?
*Isab.* Ay, just perpetual durance; a restraint,
Though all the world's vastidity you had,
To a determin'd scope.
*Claud.*    But in what nature?
*Isab.* In such a one as, you consenting to't,
Would bark your honour from that trunk you
    bear,
And leave you naked.
*Claud.*    Let me know the point.
*Isab.* O, I do fear thee, Claudio; and I quake,
Lest thou a feverous life shouldst entertain,
And six or seven winters more respect
Than a perpetual honour. Dar'st thou die?
The sense of death is most in apprehension;
And the poor beetle that we tread upon,
In corporal sufferance finds a pang as great
As when a giant dies.
*Claud.*    Why give you me this shame?
Think you I can a resolution fetch
From flowery tenderness? If I must die
I will encounter darkness as a bride,
And hug it in mine arms.    [father's grave
*Isab.* There spake my brother; there my
Did utter forth a voice! Yes, thou must die:
Thou art too noble to conserve a life

In base appliances. This outward-sainted deputy,—
Whose settled visage and deliberate word
Nips youth i' the head, and follies doth emmew
As falcon doth the fowl,—is yet a devil;
His filth within being cast, he would appear
A pond as deep as hell.

*Claud.*                        The princely Angelo?

*Isab.* O, 'tis the cunning livery of hell,
The damned'st body to invest and cover
In princely guards! Dost thou think, Claudio,
If I would yield him my virginity
Thou mightst be freed?

*Claud.*                        O heavens! it cannot be.

*Isab.* Yes, he would give it thee, from this
rank offence
So to offend him still. This night's the time
That I should do what I abhor to name,
Or else thou diest to-morrow.

*Claud.*                        Thou shalt not do 't.

*Isab.* O, were it but my life,
I'd throw it down for your deliverance
As frankly as a pin.

*Claud.*                        Thanks, dear Isabel.

*Isab.* Be ready, Claudio, for your death to-morrow.

*Claud.* Yes.—Has he affections in him
That thus can make him bite the law by the nose
When he would force it? Sure it is no sin;
Or of the deadly seven it is the least.

*Isab.* Which is the least?

*Claud.* If it were damnable, he, being so wise,
Why would he for the momentary trick
Be perdurably fined?—O Isabel!

*Isab.* What says my brother?

*Claud.* Death is a fearful thing.

*Isab.* And shamed life a hateful.

*Claud.* Ay, but to die, and go we know not
where;
To lie in cold obstruction, and to rot;
This sensible warm motion to become
A kneaded clod; and the delighted spirit
To bathe in fiery floods or to reside
In thrilling regions of thick-ribbed ice;
To be imprison'd in the viewless winds,
And blown with restless violence round about
The pendent world; or to be worse than worst
Of those that lawless and incertain thoughts
Imagine howling!—'tis too horrible!
The weariest and most loathed worldly life
That age, ache, penury, and imprisonment
Can lay on nature is a paradise
To what we fear of death.

*Isab.* Alas! alas!

*Claud.*                        Sweet sister, let me live:
What sin you do to save a brother's life
Nature dispenses with the deed so far
That it becomes a virtue.

*Isab.*                        O you beast!
O faithless coward! O dishonest wretch!
Wilt thou be made a man out of my vice?
Is 't not a kind of incest to take life    [think?
From thine own sister's shame. What should I
Heaven shield my mother play'd my father fair!

For such a warped slip of wilderness
Ne'er issued from his blood. Take my defiance:
Die; perish! might but my bending down
Reprieve thee from thy fate, it should proceed:
I'll pray a thousand prayers for thy death,—
No word to save the.

*Claud.* Nay, hear me, Isabel.

*Isab.*                        O fie, fie, fie!
Thy sin's not accidental, but a trade:
Mercy to thee would prove itself a bawd:
'Tis best that thou diest quickly.    [*Going.*

*Claud.*                        O hear me, Isabella.

### *Re-enter* DUKE.

*Duke.* Vouchsafe a word, young sister, but one
word.

*Isab.* What is your will?

*Duke.* Might you dispense with your leisure
I would by and by have some speech with you:
the satisfaction I would require is likewise your
own benefit.

*Isab.* I have no superfluous leisure; my stay
must be stolen out of other affairs; but I will
attend you awhile.

*Duke.* [*To* CLAUDIO *aside.*] Son, I have overheard what hath passed between you and your
sister. Angelo had never the purpose to corrupt
her; only he hath made an essay of her virtue
to practise his judgment with the disposition
of natures; she, having the truth of honour in
her, hath made him that gracious denial which
he is most glad to receive: I am confessor to
Angelo, and I know this to be true; therefore
prepare yourself to death. Do not satisfy your
resolution with hopes that are fallible: to-
morrow you must die; go to your knees and
make ready.

*Claud.* Let me ask my sister pardon. I am so
out of love with life that I will sue to be rid of it.

*Duke.* Hold you there. Farewell.
                                    [*Exit* CLAUDIO.

### *Re-enter* PROVOST.

Provost, a word with you.

*Prov.* What's your will, father?

*Duke.* That, now you are come, you will be
gone. Leave me a while with the maid; my
mind promises with my habit no loss shall
touch her by my company.

*Prov.* In good time.    [*Exit* PROVOST.

*Duke.* The hand that hath made you fair hath
made you good: the goodness that is cheap in
beauty makes beauty brief in goodness: but
grace, being the soul of your complexion, should
keep the body of it ever fair. The assault that
Angelo hath made to you, fortune hath conveyed to my understanding; and, but that
frailty hath examples for his falling, I should
wonder at Angelo. How will you do to content
this substitute, and to save your brother?

*Isab.* I am now going to resolve him; I had
rather my brother die by the law than my son
should be unlawfully born. But O, how much
is the good duke deceived in Angelo! If ever

he return, and I can speak to him, I will open my lips in vain, or discover his government.

*Duke.* That shall not be much amiss: yet, as the matter now stands, he will avoid your accusation; he made trial of you only.—Therefore fasten your ear on my advisings; to the love I have in doing good a remedy presents itself. I do make myself believe that you may most uprighteously do a poor wronged lady a merited benefit; redeem your brother from the angry law; do no stain to your own gracious person; and much please the absent duke if, peradventure, he shall ever return to have hearing of this business.

*Isab.* Let me hear you speak further; I have spirit to do anything that appears not foul in the truth of my spirit.

*Duke.* Virtue is bold, and goodness never fearful. Have you not heard speak of Mariana, the sister of Frederick the great soldier who miscarried at sea?

*Isab.* I have heard of the lady, and good words went with her name.

*Duke.* Her should this Angelo have married; was affianced to her by oath, and the nuptial appointed: between which time of the contract and limit of the solemnity her brother Frederick was wrecked at sea, having in that perished vessel the dowry of his sister. But mark how heavily this befell to the poor gentlewoman: there she lost a noble and renowned brother, in his love toward her ever most kind and natural; with him the portion and sinew of her fortune, her marriage-dowry; with both, her combinate husband, this well-seeming Angelo.

*Isab.* Can this be so? Did Angelo so leave her?

*Duke.* Left her in her tears, and dried not one of them with his comfort; swallowed his vows whole, pretending, in her, discoveries of dishonour; in few, bestowed her on her own lamentation, which she yet wears for his sake; and he, a marble to her tears, is washed with them, but relents not.

*Isab.* What a merit were it in death to take this poor maid from the world! What corruption in this life that it will let this man live!—But how out of this can she avail?

*Duke.* It is a rupture that you may easily heal; and the cure of it not only saves your brother, but keeps you from dishonour in doing it.

*Isab.* Show me how, good father.

*Duke.* This forenamed maid hath yet in her the continuance of her first affection; his unjust unkindness, that in all reason should have quenched her love, hath, like an impediment in the current, made it more violent and unruly. Go you to Angelo; answer his requiring with a plausible obedience; agree with his demands to the point: only refer yourself to this advantage,—first, that your stay with him may not be long; that the time may have all shadow and silence in it; and the place answer to convenience: this being granted in course, now follows all. We shall advise this wronged maid to

stead up your appointment, go in your place; if the encounter acknowledge itself hereafter, it may compel him to her recompense: and here, by this, is your brother saved, your honour untainted, the poor Mariana advantaged, and the corrupt deputy scaled. The maid will I frame and make fit for his attempt. If you think well to carry this as you may, the doubleness of the benefit defends the deceit from reproof. What think you of it?

*Isab.* The image of it gives me content already; and I trust it will grow to a most prosperous perfection.

*Duke.* It lies much in your holding up. Haste you speedily to Angelo: if for this night he entreat you to his bed, give him promise of satisfaction. I will presently to St. Luke's; there, at the moated grange, resides this dejected Mariana. At that place call upon me; and despatch with Angelo, that it may be quickly.

*Isab.* I thank you for this comfort. Fare you well, good father. [*Exeunt severally.*

SCENE II.—*The Street before the Prison.*

*Enter* DUKE, *as a Friar; to him* ELBOW, CLOWN, *and* Officers.

*Elb.* Nay, if there be no remedy for it, but that you will needs buy and sell men and women like beasts, we shall have all the world drink brown and white bastard.

*Duke.* O heavens! what stuff is here?

*Clo.* 'Twas never merry world since, of two usuries, the merriest was put down, and the worser allowed by order of law a furred gown to keep him warm; and furred with fox and lamb-skins, too, to signify that craft, being richer than innocency, stands for the facing.

*Elb.* Come your way, sir.—Bless you, good father friar.

*Duke.* And you, good brother father. What offence hath this man made you, sir?

*Elb.* Marry, sir, he hath offended the law; and sir, we take him to be a thief too, sir; for we have found upon him, sir, a strange picklock, which we have sent to the deputy.

*Duke.* Fie, sirrah; a bawd, a wicked bawd! The evil that thou causest to be done, That is thy means to live. Do thou but think What 'tis to cram a maw or clothe a back From such a filthy vice: say to thyself,— From their abominable and beastly touches I drink, I eat, array myself, and live. Canst thou believe thy living is a life, So stinkingly depending? Go mend, go mend.

*Clo.* Indeed, it does stink in some sort, sir; but yet, sir, I would prove——

*Duke.* Nay, if the devil have given thee proof for sin, Thou wilt prove his. Take him to prison, officer; Correction and instruction must both work Ere this rude beast will profit.

*Elb.* He must before the deputy, sir; he has

given him warning: the deputy cannot abide a whoremaster: if he be a whoremonger, and comes before him, he were as good go a mile on his errand.

*Duke.* That we were all, as some would seem
    to be,
Free from our faults, as faults from seeming
    free!

*Elb.* His neck will come to your waist, a cord, sir.

*Clo.* I spy comfort; I cry bail! Here's a gentleman, and a friend of mine.

*Enter* LUCIO.

*Lucio.* How now, noble Pompey? What, at the heels of Cæsar! Art thou led in triumph? What, is there none of Pygmalion's images, newly made woman, to be had now, for putting the hand in the pocket and extracting it clutched? What reply, ha? What say'st thou to this tune, matter, and method? Is't not drowned i' the last rain, ha? What say'st thou to't? Is the world as it was, man? Which is the way? Is it sad, and few words? or how? The trick of it?

*Duke.* Still thus, and thus! still worse!

*Lucio.* How doth my dear morsel, thy mistress? Procures she still, ha?

*Clo.* Troth, sir, she hath eaten up all her beef, and she is herself in the tub.

*Lucio.* Why, 'tis good: it is the right of it: it must be so: ever your fresh whore and your powdered bawd: an unshunned consequence; it must be so. Art going to prison, Pompey?

*Clo.* Yes, faith, sir.

*Lucio.* Why, 'tis not amiss, Pompey. Farewell; go, say I sent thee thither. For debt, Pompey? or how?

*Elb.* For being a bawd, for being a bawd.

*Lucio.* Well, then, imprison him: if imprisonment be the due of a bawd, why, 'tis his right; bawd is he doubtless, and of antiquity, too: bawd-born. Farewell, good Pompey. Commend me to the prison, Pompey. You will turn good husband now, Pompey; you will keep the house.

*Clo.* I hope, sir, your good worship will be my bail.

*Lucio.* No, indeed, will I not, Pompey; it is not the wear. I will pray, Pompey, to increase your bondage: if you take it not patiently, why, your mettle is the more. Adieu, trusty Pompey.—Bless you, friar.

*Duke.* And you.

*Lucio.* Does Bridget paint still, Pompey, ha?

*Elb.* Come your ways, sir; come.

*Clo.* You will not bail me then, sir?

*Lucio.* Then, Pompey, nor now.—What news abroad, friar? what news?

*Elb.* Come your ways, sir; come.

*Lucio.* Go,—to kennel, Pompey, go:
    [*Exeunt* ELBOW, CLOWN, *and* Officers.
What news, friar, of the duke?

*Duke.* I know none. Can you tell me of any?

*Lucio.* Some say he is with the Emperor of Russia; other some, he is in Rome: but where is he, think you?

*Duke.* I know not where; but wheresoever, I wish him well.

*Lucio.* It was a mad fantastical trick of him to steal from the state and usurp the beggary he was never born to. Lord Angelo dukes it well in his absence; he puts transgression to't.

*Duke.* He does well in't.

*Lucio.* A little more lenity to lechery would do no harm in him: something too crabbed that way, friar.

*Duke.* It is too general a vice, and severity must cure it.

*Lucio.* Yes, in good sooth, the vice is of a great kindred; it is well allied: but it is impossible to extirp it quite, friar, till eating and drinking be put down. They say this Angelo was not made by man and woman after the downright way of creation: is it true, think you?

*Duke.* How should he be made, then?

*Lucio.* Some report a sea-maid spawned him; some, that he was begot between two stock-fishes.—But it is certain that, when he makes water, his urine is congealed ice; that I know to be true: and he is a motion ungenerative; that's infallible.

*Duke.* You are pleasant, sir, and speak apace.

*Lucio.* Why, what a ruthless thing is this in him, for the rebellion of a cod-piece to take away the life of a man? Would the duke that is absent have done this? Ere he would have hanged a man for the getting a hundred bastards, he would have paid for the nursing a thousand. He had some feeling of the sport; he knew the service, and that instructed him to mercy.

*Duke.* I never heard the absent duke much detected for women; he was not inclined that way.

*Lucio.* O, sir, you are deceived.

*Duke.* 'Tis not possible.

*Lucio.* Who, not the duke? yes, your beggar of fifty;—and his use was to put a ducat in her clack-dish: the duke had crotchets in him. He would be drunk too: that let me inform you.

*Duke.* You do him wrong, surely.

*Lucio.* Sir, I was an inward of his. A shy fellow was the duke: and I believe I know the cause of his withdrawing.

*Duke.* What, I pr'ythee, might be the cause?

*Lucio.* No,—pardon;—'tis a secret must be locked within the teeth and the lips: but this I can let you understand,—the greater file of the subject held the duke to be wise.

*Duke.* Wise? why, no question but he was.

*Lucio.* A very superficial, ignorant, unweighing fellow.

*Duke.* Either this is envy in you, folly, or mistaking; the very stream of his life, and the business he hath helmed, must, upon a warranted need, give him a better proclamation. Let him be but testimonied in his own brings forth, and he shall appear to the envious a scholar, a statesman, and a soldier. Therefore you speak unskilfully; or, if your knowledge be more, it is much darkened in your malice.

*Lucio.* Sir, I know him, and I love him.

*Duke.* Love talks with better knowledge, and knowledge with dearer love.

*Lucio.* Come, sir, I know what I know.

*Duke.* I can hardly believe that, since you know not what you speak. But, if ever the duke return,—as our prayers are he may,—let me desire you to make your answer before him. If it be honest you have spoke, you have courage to maintain it: I am bound to call upon you; and, I pray you, your name?

*Lucio.* Sir, my name is Lucio; well known to the duke.

*Duke.* He shall know you better, sir, if I may live to report you.

*Lucio.* I fear you not.

*Duke.* O, you hope the duke will return no more; or you imagine me too unhurtful an opposite. But, indeed, I can do you little harm: you'll forswear this again.

*Lucio.* I'll be hanged first! thou art deceived in me, friar. But no more of this. Canst thou tell if Claudio die to-morrow or no?

*Duke.* Why should he die, sir?

*Lucio.* Why, for filling a bottle with a tundish. I would the duke we talk of were returned again: this ungenitured agent will unpeople the province with continency; sparrows must not build in his house-eaves because they are lecherous. The duke yet would have dark deeds darkly answered; he would never bring them to light: would he were returned! Marry, this Claudio is condemned for untrussing. Farewell, good friar: I pry'thee, pray for me. The duke, I say to thee again, would eat mutton on Fridays. He's now past it; yet, and I say to thee, he would mouth with a beggar though she smelt brown bread and garlic: say that I said so.—Farewell.     [*Exit.*

*Duke.* No might nor greatness in morality Can censure 'scape; back-wounding calumny The whitest virtue strikes. What king so strong Can tie the gall up in the slanderous tongue? But who comes here?

*Enter* ESCALUS, PROVOST, BAWD, *and* Officers.

*Escal.* Go, away with her to prison.

*Bawd.* Good my lord, be good to me; your honour is accounted a merciful man; good my lord.

*Escal.* Double and treble admonition, and still forfeit in the same kind? This would make mercy swear and play the tyrant.

*Prov.* A bawd of eleven years' continuance, may it please your honour.

*Bawd.* My lord, this is one Lucio's information against me: Mistress Kate Keepdown was with child by him in the duke's time; he promised her marriage; his child is a year and a quarter old come Philip and Jacob: I have kept it myself; and see how he goes about to abuse me.

*Escal.* That fellow is a fellow of much licence:—let him be called before us.—Away with her to prison. Go to; no more words. [*Exeunt* BAWD *and* Officers.] Provost, my brother Angelo will not be altered, Claudio must die to-morrow: let him be furnished with divines, and have all charitable preparation: if my brother wrought by my pity it should not be so with him.

*Prov.* So please you, this friar hath been with him, and advised him for the entertainment of death.

*Escal.* Good even, good father.

*Duke.* Bliss and goodness on you!

*Escal.* Of whence are you?

*Duke.* Not of this country, though my chance is [*now* To use it for my time: I am a brother Of gracious order, late come from the see In special business from his holiness.

*Escal.* What news abroad i' the world?

*Duke.* None, but that there is so great a fever on goodness, that the dissolution of it must cure it: novelty is only in request; and it is as dangerous to be aged in any kind of course as it is virtuous to be constant in any undertaking. There is scarce truth enough alive to make societies secure; but security enough to make fellowships accursed: much upon this riddle runs the wisdom of the world. This news is old enough, yet it is every day's news. I pray you, sir, of what disposition was the duke?

*Escal.* One that, above all other strifes, contended especially to know himself.

*Duke.* What pleasure was he give to?

*Escal.* Rather rejoicing to see another merry, than merry at anything which professed to make him rejoice: a gentleman of all temperance. But leave we him to his events, with a prayer they may prove prosperous; and let me desire to know how you find Claudio prepared. I am made to understand that you have lent him visitation.

*Duke.* He professes to have received no sinister measure from his judge, but most willingly humbles himself to the determination of justice: yet had he framed to himself, by the instruction of his frailty, many deceiving promises of life; which I, by my good leisure, have discredited to him, and how is he resolved to die.

*Escal.* You have paid the heavens your function and the prisoner the very debt of your calling. I have laboured for the poor gentleman to the extremest shore of my modesty; but my brother justice have I found so severe that he hath forced me to tell him he is indeed—justice.

*Duke.* If his own life answer the straitness of his proceeding, it shall become him well; wherein if he chance to fail, he hath sentenced himself.

*Escal.* I am going to visit the prisoner. Fare you well.

*Duke.* Peace be with you!

         [*Exeunt* ESCAL. *and* PROV.

He who the sword of heaven will bear Should be as holy as severe;

Pattern in himself to know,
Grace to stand, and virtue go;
More nor less to others paying
Than by self-offences weighing.
Shame to him whose cruel striking
Kills for faults of his own liking!
Twice treble shame on Angelo,
To weed my vice and let his grow!
O, what man man within him hide,
Though angel on the outward side!
How may likeness, made in crimes,
Making practice on the times,
Draw with idle spiders' strings
Most pond'rous and substantial things!
Craft against vice I must apply;
With Angelo to-night shall lie
His old betrothed but despis'd;
So disguise shall, by the disguis'd,
Pay with falsehood false exacting,
And perform an old contracting.          [*Exit.*

### ACT IV.

Scene I.—*A Room in* Mariana's *House.*

Mariana *discovered sitting; a* Boy *singing.*

SONG.

Take, O take those lips away,
    That so sweetly were forsworn;
And those eyes, the break of day,
    Lights that do mislead the morn:
But my kisses bring again,
        Bring again;
Seals of love, but seal'd in vain,
        Sealed in vain.

*Mari.* Break off thy song, and haste thee quick
    away;
Here comes a man of comfort, whose advice
Hath often still'd my brawling discontent.—
          [*Exit Boy.*

*Enter* Duke.

I cry you mercy, sir; and well could wish
You had not found me here so musical:
Let me excuse me, and believe me so,    [woe.
My mirth it much displeas'd, but pleas'd my
*Duke.* 'Tis good: though music oft hath such
    a charm
To make bad good and good provoke to harm.
I pray you, tell me, hath anybody inquired for
me here to-day? much upon this time have I
promised here to meet.
*Mari.* You have not been inquired after: I
have sat here all day.

*Enter* Isabella.

*Duke.* I do constantly believe you.—The time
is come even now. I shall crave your forbear-
ance a little: may be I will call upon you anon,
for some advantage to yourself.
*Mari.* I am always bound to you.    [*Exit.*
*Duke.* Very well met, and welcome.
What is the news from this good deputy?
*Isab.* He hath a garden circummur'd with brick,

Whose western side is with a vineyard back'd;
And to that vineyard is a planched gate
That makes his opening with this bigger key:
This other doth command a little door
Which from the vineyard to the garden leads;
There have I made my promise to call on him
Upon the heavy middle of the night.
*Duke.* But shall you on your knowledge find
    this way?
*Isab.* I have ta'en a due and wary note upon't;
With whispering and most guilty diligence,
In action all of precept, he did show me
The way twice o'er.
*Duke.*          Are there no other tokens
Between you 'greed concerning her observance?
*Isab.* No, none, but only a repair i' the dark;
And that I have possess'd him my most stay
Can be but brief: for I have made him know
I have a servant comes with me along,
That stays upon me; whose persuasion is
I come about my brother.
*Duke.*                    'Tis well borne up.
I have not yet made known to Mariana.
A word of this.—What, ho! within! come forth.

*Re-enter* Mariana.

I pray you be acquainted with this maid;
She comes to do you good.
*Isab.*                I do desire the like.
*Duke.* Do you persuade yourself that I respect
    you?
*Mari.* Good friar, I know you do, and I have
    found it.                              [hand,
*Duke.* Take, then, this your companion by the
Who hath a story ready for your ear:
I shall attend your leisure; but make haste;
The vaporous night approaches.
*Mari.*              Will't please you walk aside?
          [*Exeunt* Mari. *and* Isab.
*Duke.* O place and greatness, millions of false
    eyes
Are stuck upon thee! volumes of report
Run with these false and most contrarious quests
Upon thy doings! thousand 'scapes of wit
Make thee the father of their idle dream,
And rack thee in their fancies!—Welcome!
    How agreed?

*Re-enter* Mariana *and* Isabella.

*Isab.* She'll take the enterprise upon her, father,
If you advise it.
*Duke.*          It is not my consent,
But my entreaty too.
*Isab.*              Little have you to say,
When you depart from him, but, soft and low,
*Remember now my brother.*
*Mari.*                  Fear me not.
*Duke.* Nor, gentle daughter, fear you not at all:
He is your husband on a pre-contract:
To bring you thus together 'tis no sin,
Sith that the justice of your title to him
Doth flourish the deceit. Come, let us go;
Our corn's to reap, for yet our tilth's to sow.
         [*Exeunt.*

SCENE II.—*A Room in the Prison.*

*Enter* PROVOST *and* CLOWN.

*Prov.* Come hither, sirrah. Can you cut off a man's head?

*Clo.* If the man be a bachelor, sir, I can: but if he be a married man, he is his wife's head, and I can never cut off a woman's head.

*Prov.* Come, sir, leave me your snatches and yield me a direct answer. To-morrow morning are to die Claudio and Barnardine. Here is in our prison a common executioner who in his office lacks a helper; if you will take it on you to assist him, it shall redeem you from your gyves; if not, you shall have your full time of imprisonment, and your deliverance with an unpitied whipping; for you have been a notorious bawd.

*Clo.* Sir, I have been an unlawful bawd time out of mind; but yet I will be content to be a lawful hangman. I would be glad to receive some instruction from my fellow-partner.

*Prov.* What ho, Abhorson! Where's Abhorson, there?

*Enter* ABHORSON.

*Abhor.* Do you call, sir?

*Prov.* Sirrah, here's a fellow will help you to-morrow in your execution. If you think it meet, compound with him by the year, and let him abide here with you; if not, use him for the present, and dismiss him. He cannot plead his estimation with you; he hath been a bawd.

*Abhor.* A bawd, sir? Fie upon him; he will discredit our mystery.

*Prov.* Go to, sir; you weigh equally; a feather will turn the scale.                [*Exit.*

*Clo.* Pray, sir, by your good favour,—for, surely, sir, a good favour you have, but that you have a hanging look,—do you call, sir, your occupation a mystery?

*Abhor.* Ay, sir; a mystery.

*Clo.* Painting, sir, I have heard say, is a mystery; and your whores, sir, being members of my occupation, using painting, do prove my occupation a mystery: but what mystery there should be in hanging, if I should be hanged, I cannot imagine.

*Abhor.* Sir, it is a mystery.

*Clo.* Proof.

*Abhor.* Every true man's apparel fits your thief: if it be too little for your thief, your true man thinks it big enough; if it be too big for your thief, your thief thinks it little enough: so every true man's apparel fits your thief.

*Re-enter* PROVOST.

*Prov.* Are you agreed?

*Clo.* Sir, I will serve him; for I do find your hangman is a more penitent trade than your bawd; he doth oftener ask forgiveness.

*Prov.* You, sirrah, provide your block and your axe to-morrow four o'clock.

*Abhor.* Come on, bawd; I will instruct thee in my trade; follow.

*Clo.* I do desire to learn, sir; and I hope, if you have occasion to use me for your own turn, you shall find me yare: for, truly sir, for your kindness I owe you a good turn.

*Prov.* Call hither Barnardine and Claudio.
                [*Exeunt* CLO. *and* ABHOR.
One has my pity; not a jot the other,
Being a murderer, though he were my brother.

*Enter* CLAUDIO.

Look, here's the warrant, Claudio, for thy death:
'Tis now dead midnight, and by eight to-morrow
Thou must be made immortal. Where's Barnardine?                [labour

*Claud.* As fast lock'd up in sleep as guiltless
When it lies starkly in the traveller's bones:
He will not wake.

*Prov.*                Who can do good on him?
Well, go, prepare yourself. But, hark! what noise?                [*Knocking within.*
Heaven give your spirits comfort!
                [*Exit* CLAUDIO.
                By and by!—
I hope it is some pardon or reprieve
For the most gentle Claudio.—Welcome, father.

*Enter* DUKE.

*Duke.* The best and wholesomest spirits of the night                [of late?
Envelop you, good provost! Who call'd here

*Prov.* None, since the curfew rung.

*Duke.*                Not Isabel?

*Prov.* No.

*Duke.* They will, then, ere't be long.

*Prov.* What comfort is for Claudio?

*Duke.*                There's some in hope.

*Prov.* It is a bitter deputy.

*Duke.* Not so, not so; his life is parallel'd
Even with the stroke and line of his great justice;
He doth with holy abstinence subdue
That in himself which he spurs on his power
To qualify in others: were he meal'd
With that which he corrects, then were he tyrannous;
But this being so, he's just.—Now are they come.
                [*Knocking within.*—PROVOST *goes out.*
This is a gentle provost: seldom when
The steeled gaoler is the friend of men.—
How now? what noise? That spirit's possess'd with haste                [strokes.
That wounds the unsisting postern with these

PROVOST *returns, speaking to one at the door.*

*Prov.* There he must stay until the officer
Arise to let him in; he is call'd up.                [yet,

*Duke.* Have you no countermand for Claudio
But he must die to-morrow?

*Prov.*                None, sir, none.

*Duke.* As near the dawning, Provost, as it is,
You shall hear more ere morning.

*Prov.*                Happily
You something know; yet I believe there comes

No countermand; no such example have we:
Besides, upon the very siege of justice,
Lord Angelo hath to the public ear
Profess'd the contrary.

*Enter a* Messenger.

*Duke.* This is his lordship's man.
*Prov.* And here comes Claudio's pardon.
*Mess.* My lord hath sent you this note; and
by me this further charge, that you swerve not
from the smallest article of it, neither in time,
matter, or other circumstance. Good-morrow;
for as I take it, it is almost day.
*Prov.* I shall obey him.    [*Exit* Messenger.
*Duke.* This is his pardon purchas'd by such
sin,                                [*Aside.*
For which the pardoner himself is in:
Hence hath offence his quick celerity
When it is borne in high authority:
When vice makes mercy, mercy's so extended
That for the fault's love is the offender friended.—
Now, sir, what news?
*Prov.* I told you: Lord Angelo, belike thinking
me remiss in mine office, awakens me with this
unwonted putting on; methinks strangely, for
he hath not used it before.
*Duke.* Pray you, let's hear.
*Prov.* [Reads.] *Whatsoever you may hear to the
contrary, let Claudio be executed by four of the
clock; and, in the afternoon, Barnardine: for my
better satisfaction, let me have Claudio's head sent
me by five. Let this be duly performed; with a
thought that more depends on it than we must yet
deliver. Thus fail not to do your office, as you
will answer it at your peril.*
What say you to this, sir?
*Duke.* What is that Barnardine who is to be
executed in the afternoon?
*Prov.* A Bohemian born; but here nursed up
and bred: one that is a prisoner nine years old.
*Duke.* How came it that the absent duke had
not either delivered him to his liberty or executed him? I have heard it was ever his manner to do so.
*Prov.* His friends still wrought reprieves for
him: and, indeed, his fact, till now in the government of Lord Angelo, came not to an un-
doubtful proof.
*Duke.* Is it now apparent?
*Prov.* Most manifest, and not denied by himself.
*Duke.* Hath he borne himself penitently in
prison? How seems he to be touched?
*Prov.* A man that apprehends death no more
dreadfully but as a drunken sleep; careless,
reckless, and fearless of what's past, present,
or to come; insensible of mortality and desperately mortal.
*Duke.* He wants advice.
*Prov.* He will hear none; he hath evermore had
the liberty of the prison; give him leave to
escape hence, he would not: drunk many times
a-day, if not many days entirely drunk. We

have very often awaked him, as if to carry him
to execution, and showed him a seeming warrant for it: it hath not moved him at all.
*Duke.* More of him anon. There is written in
your brow, Provost, honesty and constancy:
if I read it not truly, my ancient skill beguiles
me; but in the boldness of my cunning I will
lay myself in hazard. Claudio, whom here you
have a warrant to execute, is no greater forfeit
to the law than Angelo who hath sentenced
him. To make you understand this in a manifested effect, I crave but four days' respite; for
the which you are to do me both a present and
a dangerous courtesy.
*Prov.* Pray, sir, in what?
*Duke.* In the delaying death.
*Prov.* Alack! how may I do it? having the
hour limited; and an express command, under
penalty, to deliver his head in the view of
Angelo? I may make my case as Claudio's, to
cross this in the smallest.
*Duke.* By the vow of mine order, I warrant
you, if my instructions may be your guide.
Let this Barnardine be this morning executed,
and his head borne to Angelo.
*Prov.* Angelo hath seen them both, and will
discover the favour.
*Duke.* O, death's a great disguiser: and you
may add to it. Shave the head and tie the
beard; and say it was the desire of the penitent
to be so bared before his death. You know the
course is common. If anything fall to you upon
this, more than thanks and good fortune, by
the saint whom I profess, I will plead against
it with my life.
*Prov.* Pardon me, good father; it is against
my oath.
*Duke.* Were you sworn to the duke, or to the
deputy?
*Prov.* To him and to his substitutes.
*Duke.* You will think you have made no offence
if the duke avouch the justice of your dealing?
*Prov.* But what likelihood is in that?
*Duke.* Not a resemblance, but a certainty. Yet
since I see you fearful that neither my coat,
integrity, nor my persuasion can with ease attempt you, I will go further than I meant, to
pluck all fears out of you. Look you, sir, here
is the hand and seal of the duke. You know
the character, I doubt not; and the signet is
not strange to you.
*Prov.* I know them both.
*Duke.* The contents of this is the return of
the duke; you shall anon over-read it at your
pleasure; where you shall find, within these
two days he will be here. This is a thing that
Angelo knows not: for he this very day receives
letters of strange tenor: perchance of the duke's
death; perchance entering into some monastery; but, by chance, nothing of what is writ.
Look, the unfolding star calls up the shepherd.
Put not yourself into amazement how these
things should be: all difficulties are but easy
when they are known. Call your executioner,

and off with Barnardine's head: I will give him
a present shift, and advise him for a better
place. Yet you are amazed: but this shall absolutely resolve you. Come away; it is almost
clear dawn. [*Exeunt.*

SCENE III.—*Another Room in the same.*

*Enter* CLOWN.

*Clo.* I am as well acquainted here as I was in
our house of profession: one would think it were
Mistress Overdone's own house, for here be
many of her old customers. First, here's young
Master Rash; he's in for a commodity of brown
paper and old ginger, ninescore and seventeen
pounds; of which he made five marks, ready
money: marry, then, ginger was not much in
request, for the old women were all dead. Then
is there here one Master Caper, at the suit of
Master Threepile the mercer, for some four
suits of peach-coloured satin, which now peaches
him a beggar. Then have we here young Dizy,
and young Master Deepvow, and Master Cop-
perspur, and Master Starvelackey the rapier
and dagger-man, and young Dropheir that
killed lusty Pudding, and Master Forthright
the tilter, and brave Master Shootie the great
traveller, and wild Halfcan that stabbed Pots,
and, I think, forty more; all great doers in our
trade, and are now "for the Lord's sake."

*Enter* ABHORSON.

*Abhor.* Sirrah, bring Barnardine hither.
*Clo.* Master Barnardine! you must rise and be
hanged, Master Barnardine!
*Abhor.* What, ho, Barnardine!
*Barnar.* [*Within.*] A pox o' your throats! Who
makes that noise there? What are you?
*Clo.* Your friend, sir; the hangman. You must
be so good, sir, to rise and be put to death.
*Barnar.* [*Within.*] Away, you rogue, away; I
am sleepy.
*Abhor.* Tell him he must awake, and that
quickly too.
*Clo.* Pray, Master Barnardine, awake till you
are executed, and sleep afterwards.
*Abhor.* Go in to him, and fetch him out.
*Clo.* He is coming, sir, he is coming; I hear his
straw rustle.

*Enter* BARNARDINE.

*Abhor.* Is the axe upon the block, sirrah?
*Clo.* Very ready, sir.
*Barnar.* How now, Abhorson? what's the news
with you?
*Abhor.* Truly, sir, I would desire you to clap
into your prayers; for, look you, the warrant's
come.
*Barnar.* You rogue, I have been drinking all
night; I am not fitted for't.
*Clo.* O, the better, sir; for he that drinks all
night and is hanged betimes in the morning
may sleep the sounder all the next day.

*Enter* DUKE.

*Abhor.* Look you, sir, here comes your ghostly
father. Do we jest now, think you?
*Duke.* Sir, induced by my charity, and hearing
how hastily you are to depart, I am come to
advise you, comfort you, and pray with you.
*Barnar.* Friar, not I; I have been drinking
hard all night, and I will have more time to
prepare me, or they shall beat out my brains
with billets: I will not consent to die this day,
that's certain.
*Duke.* O, sir, you must; and therefore, I beseech you,
Look forward on the journey you shall go.
*Barnar.* I swear I will not die to-day for any
man's persuasion.
*Duke.* But hear you,——
*Barnar.* Not a word; if you have anything to
say to me, come to my ward; for thence will
not I to-day. [*Exit.*
*Duke.* Unfit to live or die. O gravel heart!—
After him, fellows; bring him to the block.
[*Exeunt* ABHOR. *and* CLOWN.

*Enter* PROVOST.

*Prov.* Now, sir, how do you find the prisoner?
*Duke.* A creature unprepar'd, unmeet for death;
And to transport him in the mind he is
Were damnable.
*Prov.*    Here in the prison, father,
There died this morning of a cruel fever
One Ragozine, a most notorious pirate,
A man of Claudio's years; his beard and head
Just of his colour. What if we do omit
This reprobate till he were well inclined;
And satisfy the deputy with the visage
Of Ragozine, more like to Claudio?
*Duke.* O, 'tis an accident that Heaven provides!
Despatch it presently; the hour draws on
Prefix'd by Angelo: see this be done,
And sent according to command; whiles I
Persuade this rude wretch willingly to die.
*Prov.* This shall be done, good father, presently.
But Barnardine must die this afternoon:
And how shall we continue Claudio,
To save me from the danger that might come
If he were known alive?
*Duke.*    Let this be done;—
Put them in secret holds; both Barnardine and
   Claudio.    [ing
Ere twice the sun hath made his journal greet-
To the under generation, you shall find
Your safety manifested.
*Prov.* I am your free dependent.
*Duke.*     Quick, despatch,
And send the head to Angelo.
      [*Exit* PROVOST.
Now will I write letters to Angelo,— [tents
The provost, he shall bear them,—whose con-
Shall witness to him I am near at home,
And that, by great injunctions, I am bound
To enter publicly: him I'll desire
To meet me at the consecrated fount,

A league below the city; and from thence,
By cold gradation and weal-balanced form,
We shall proceed with Angelo.

*Re-enter* PROVOST.

*Prov.* Here is the head; I'll carry it myself.
*Duke.* Convenient is it. Make a swift return;
For I would commune with you of such things
That want no ear but yours.
*Prov.*                     I'll make all speed. [*Exit.*
*Isab.* [*Within.*] Peace, ho, be here!
*Duke.* The tongue of Isabel.—She's come to
        know
If yet her brother's pardon be come hither:
But I will keep her ignorant of her good,
To make her heavenly comforts of despair
When it is least expected.

*Enter* ISABELLA

*Isab.* Ho, by your leave!
*Duke.* Good morning to you, fair and gracious
        daughter.
*Isab.* The better, given me by so holy a man.
Hath yet the deputy sent my brother's pardon?
*Duke.* He hath released him, Isabel, from the
        world:
His head is off and sent to Angelo.
*Isab.* Nay, but it is not so.
*Duke.*                     It is no other:
Show your wisdom, daughter, in your close
        patience.
*Isab.* O, I will to him and pluck out his eyes.
*Duke.* You shall not be admitted to his sight.
*Isab.* Unhappy Claudio! Wretched Isabel! In-
jurious world! Most damned Angelo!
*Duke.* This nor hurts him nor profits you a jot:
Forbear it, therefore; give your cause to Heaven.
Mark what I say; which you shall find
By every syllable a faithful verity:
The duke comes home to-morrow;—nay, dry
        your eyes;
One of our convent, and his confessor,
Gives me this instance. Already he hath carried
Notice to Escalus and Angelo,
Who do prepare to meet him at the gates,
There to give up their power. If you can, pace
        your wisdom
In that good path that I would wish it go,
And you shall have your bosom on this wretch,
Grace of the duke, revenges to your heart,
And general honour.
*Isab.*                     I am directed by you.
*Duke.* This letter, then, to Friar Peter give;
'Tis that he sent me of the duke's return:
Say, by this token, I desire his company
At Mariana's house to-night. Her cause and
        yours
I'll perfect him withal; and he shall bring you
Before the duke; and to the head of Angelo
Accuse him home, and home. For my poor self,
I am combined by a sacred vow,
And shall be absent. Wend you with this letter:
Command these fretting waters from your eyes

With a light heart; trust not my holy order
If I pervert your course.—Who's here?

*Enter* LUCIO.

*Lucio.*                     Good even,
Friar; where is the provost?
*Duke.*                     Not within, sir.
*Lucio.* O, pretty Isabella, I am pale at mine
heart to see thine eyes so red: thou must be
patient: I am fain to dine and sup with water
and bran; I dare not for my head fill my belly;
one fruitful meal would set me to 't. But they
say the duke will be here to-morrow. By my
troth, Isabel, I loved thy brother. If the old
fantastical duke of dark corners had been at
home, he had lived.             [*Exit* ISABELLA.
*Duke.* Sir, the duke is marvellous little beholding to your reports; but the best is, he lives
not in them.
*Lucio.* Friar, thou knowest not the duke so
well as I do: he's a better woodman than thou
takest him for.                         [ye well.
*Duke.* Well, you'll answer this one day. Fare
*Lucio.* Nay, tarry; I'll go along with thee; I
can tell thee pretty tales of the duke.
*Duke.* You have told me too many of him already, sir, if they be true: if not true, none
were enough.
*Lucio.* I was once before him for getting a
wench with child.
*Duke.* Did you such a thing?
*Lucio.* Yes, marry, did I: but was fain to forswear it; they would else have married me to
the rotten medlar.
*Duke.* Sir, your company is fairer than honest.
Rest you well.
*Lucio.* By my trot, I'll go with thee to the
lane's end: If bawdy talk offend you, we'll
have very little of it. Nay, friar, I am a kind
of burr; I shall stick.                 [*Exeunt.*

SCENE IV.—*A Room in* ANGELO'S *House.*

*Enter* ANGELO *and* ESCALUS.

*Escal.* Every letter he hath writ hath dis-
vouched other.
*Ang.* In most uneven and distracted manner.
His actions show much like to madness; pray
heaven his wisdom be not tainted! And why
meet him at the gates, and re-deliver our authorities there?
*Escal.* I guess not.
*Ang.* And why should we proclaim it in an
hour before his entering, that if any crave redress of injustice, they should exhibit their petitions in the streets?
*Escal.* He shows his reason for that: to have a
despatch of complaints; and to deliver us from
devices hereafter, which shall then have no
power to stand against us.
*Ang.* Well, I beseech you, let it be proclaimed:
Betimes i' the morn I'll call you at your house:
Give notice to such men of sort and suit
As are to meet him.
*Escal.*                     I shall, sir: fare you well. [*Exit.*

*Ang.* Good night.—                    [pregnant,
This deed unshapes me quite, makes me un-
And dull to all proceedings. A deflower'd maid!
And by an eminent body that enforced
The law against it!—But that her tender shame
Will not proclaim against her maiden loss,
How might she tongue me? Yet reason dares
    her—no:
For my authority bears a credent bulk,
That no particular scandal once can touch
But it confounds the breather. He should have
    liv'd,                    [sense,
Save that his riotous youth, with dangerous
Might in the times to come have ta'en revenge,
By so receiving a dishonour'd life
With ransom of such shame. Would yet he
    had liv'd!
Alack, when once our grace we have forgot,
Nothing goes right; we would, and we would
    not.                    [*Exit.*

SCENE V.—*Fields without the Town.*

*Enter* DUKE *in his own habit, and Friar* PETER.

*Duke.* These letters at fit time deliver me.
                    [*Giving letters.*
The provost knows our purpose and our plot.
The matter being afoot, keep your instruction
And hold you ever to our special drift;
Though sometimes you do blench from this to
    that                    [house,
As cause doth minister. Go, call at Flavius'
And tell him where I stay: give the like notice
To Valentinus, Rowland, and to Crassus,
And bid them bring the trumpets to the gate;
But send me Flavius first.
*F. Peter.*                    It shall be speeded well.
                    [*Exit* FRIAR.

*Enter* VARRIUS.

*Duke.* I thank thee, Varrius; thou hast made
    good haste:                    [friends
Come, we will walk. There's other of our
Will greet us here anon, my gentle Varrius.
                    [*Exeunt.*

SCENE VI.—*Street near the City Gate.*

*Enter* ISABELLA *and* MARIANA.

*Isab.* To speak so indirectly I am loath;
I would say the truth; but to accuse him so,
That is your part: yet I'm advis'd to do it;
He says, to 'vailfull purpose.
*Mari.*                    Be ruled by him.
*Isab.* Besides, he tells me that, if peradventure
He speak against me on the adverse side,
I should not think it strange; for 'tis a physic
That's bitter to sweet end.
*Mari.* I would friar Peter.—
*Isab.*                    O, peace; the friar is come.

*Enter Friar* PETER.

*F. Peter.* Come, I have found you out a stand
    most fit,
Where you may have such vantage on the duke

He shall not pass you. Twice have the trum-
    pets sounded;
The generous and gravest citizens
Have hent the gates, and very near upon
The duke is entering; therefore, hence, away.
                    [*Exeunt.*

ACT V.

SCENE I.—*A public Place near the City Gate.*

MARIANNA (*veiled*), ISABELLA, *and* PETER, *at
    a distance. Enter at opposite doors* DUKE,
    VARRIUS, Lords; ANGELO, ESCALUS, LUCIO,
    PROVOST, Officers, *and* Citizens.

*Duke.* My very worthy cousin, fairly met;—
Our old and faithful friend, we are glad to see
    you.                    [grace!
*Ang. and Escal.* Happy return be to your royal
*Duke.* Many and hearty thankings to you both.
We have made inquiry of you; and we hear
Such goodness of your justice that our soul
Cannot but yield you forth to public thanks,
Forerunning more requital.
*Ang.*                    You make my bonds still greater.
*Duke.* O, your desert speaks loud; and I should
    wrong it
To lock it in the wards of covert bosom,
When it deserves, with characters of brass,
A forted residence 'gainst the tooth of time
And rasure of oblivion. Give me your hand,
And let the subject see, to make them know
That outward courtesies would fain proclaim
Favours that keep within.—Come, Escalus;
You must walk by us on our other hand:
And good supporters are you.

PETER *and* ISABELLA *come forward.*

*F. Peter.* Now is your time; speak loud, and
    kneel before him.
*Isab.* Justice, O royal duke! Vail your regard
Upon a wrong'd, I'd fain have said, a maid!
O worthy prince, dishonour not your eye
By throwing it on any other object
Till you have heard me in my true complaint,
And give me justice, justice, justice, justice!
*Duke.* Relate your wrongs. In what? By whom?
    Be brief:
Here is Lord Angelo shall give you justice.
Reveal yourself to him.
*Isab.*                    O, worthy duke,
You bid me seek redemption of the devil:
Hear me yourself; for that which I must speak
Must either punish me, not being believ'd,
Or wring redress from you; hear me, O, hear
    me here.
*Ang.* My lord, her wits, I fear me, are not firm:
She hath been a suitor to me for her brother,
Cut off by course of justice.
*Isab.*                    By course of justice!
*Ang.* And she will speak most bitterly and
    strange.                    [I speak:
*Isab.* Most strange, but yet most truly, will
That Angelo's forsworn, is it not strange?
That Angelo's a murderer, is 't not strange?

That Angelo is an adulterous thief,
An hypocrite, a virgin-violator,
Is it not strange and strange?
*Duke.*　　　　　Nay, it is ten times strange.
*Isab.* It is not truer he is Angelo.
Than this is all as true as it is strange:
Nay, it is ten times true; for truth is truth
To the end of reckoning.
*Duke.*　　　　Away with her!—Poor soul,
She speaks this in the infirmity of sense.
*Isab.* O prince, I cónjure thee, as thou believ'st
There is another comfort than this world,
That thou neglect me not with that opinion
That I am touch'd with madness: make not
　　　　impossible　　　　　　　　[sible
That which but seems unlike; 'tis not impos-
But one, the wicked'st caitiff on the ground,
May seem as shy, as grave, as just, as absolute
As Angelo; even so may Angelo,
In all his dressings, characts, titles, forms,
Be an arch-villain; believe it, royal prince,
If he be less, he's nothing; but he's more,
Had I more name for badness.
*Duke.*　　　　　　By mine honesty,
If she be mad, as I believe no other,
Her madness hath the oddest frame of sense,
Such a dependency of thing on thing,
As e'er I heard in madness.
*Isab.*　　　　　　O gracious duke,
Harp not on that: nor do not banish reason
For inequality; but let your reason serve
To make the truth appear where it seems hid
And hide the false seems true.
*Duke.*　　　　　Many that are not mad
Have, sure, more lack of reason.—What would
　　　　you say?
*Isab.* I am the sister of one Claudio,
Condemn'd upon the act of fornication
To lose his head; condemn'd by Angelo:
I, in probation of a sisterhood,
Was sent to by my brother: one Lucio
As then the messenger;—
*Lucio.*　　　　That's I, an't like your grace:
I came to her from Claudio, and desir'd her
To try her gracious fortune with Lord Angelo
For her poor brother's pardon.
*Isab.*　　　　　　That's he, indeed.
*Duke.* You were not bid to speak.
*Lucio.*　　　　　No, my good lord:
Nor wish'd to hold my peace.
*Duke.*　　　　　I wish you now, then;
Pray you, take note of it: and when you have
A business for yourself, pray Heaven you then
Be perfect.
*Lucio.* I warrant your honour,　　　[it.
*Duke.* The warrant's for yourself; take heed to
*Isab.* This gentleman told somewhat of my tale.
*Lucio.* Right.
*Duke.* It may be right; but you are in the wrong
To speak before your time.—Proceed.
*Isab.*　　　　　　I went
To this pernicious caitiff deputy.
*Duke.* That's somewhat madly spoken.
*Isab.*　　　　　　Pardon it;

The phrase is to the matter.
*Duke.* Mended again. The matter;—proceed.
*Isab.* In brief,—to set the needless process by,
How I persuaded, how I pray'd, and kneel'd,
How he refell'd me, and how I replied,—
For this was of much length,—the vile con-
　　　clusion
I now begin with grief and shame to utter:
He would not, but by gift of my chaste body
To his concupiscible intemperate lust,　[ment,
Release my brother; and, after much debate-
My sisterly remorse confutes mine honour,
And I did yield to him. But the next morn
　　　betimes,
His purpose surfeiting, he sends a warrant
For my poor brother's head.
*Duke.*　　　　　This is most likely.
*Isab.* O, that it were as like as it is true!
*Duke.* By heaven, fond wretch, thou know'st
　　　not what thou speak'st,
Or else thou art suborn'd against his honour
In hateful practice. First, his integrity
Stands without blemish:—next, it imports no
　　　reason
That with such vehemency he should pursue
Faults proper to himself: if he had so offended,
He would have weigh'd thy brother by himself,
And not have cut him off. Some one hath set
　　　you on;
Confess the truth, and say by whose advice
Thou cam'st here to complain.
*Isab.*　　　　　　And is this all?
Then, O you blessed ministers above,
Keep me in patience; and, with ripen'd time,
Unfold the evil which is here wrapt up
In countenance!—Heaven shield your grace
　　　from woe,
As I, thus wrong'd, hence unbelieved go!
*Duke.* I know you'd fain be gone.—An officer!
To prison with her!—Shall we thus permit
A blasting and a scandalous breath to fall
On him so near us? This needs must be a
　　　practice.
Who knew of your intent and coming hither?
*Isab.* One that I would were here, friar Lodo-
　　　wick.
*Duke.* A ghostly father, belike. Who knows
　　　that Lodowick?
*Lucio.* My lord, I know him; 'tis a meddling
　　　friar.　　　　　　　　　　[lord,
I do not like the man: had he been lay, my
For certain words he spake against your grace
In your retirement, I had swing'd him soundly.
*Duke.* Words against me? This a good friar,
　　　belike!
And to set on this wretched woman here
Against our substitute!—Let this friar be found.
*Lucio.* But yesternight, my lord, she and that
　　　friar
I saw them at the prison: a saucy friar,
A very scurvy fellow.
*F. Peter.*　　　　Bless'd be your royal grace!
I have stood by, my lord, and I have heard
Your royal ear abus'd. First, hath this woman

Most wrongfully accus'd your substitute;
Who is as free from touch or soil with her
As she from one ungot.
*Duke.*              We did believe no less.
Know you that friar Lodowick that she speaks
of?                                    [holy;
*F. Peter.* I know him for a man divine and
Not scurvy, nor a temporary meddler,
As he's reported by this gentleman;
And, on my trust, a man that never yet
Did, as he vouches, misreport your grace.
*Lucio.* My lord, most villanously; believe it.
*F. Peter.* Well, he in time may come to clear
himself;
But at this instant he is sick, my lord,
Of a strange fever. Upon his mere request,—
Being come to knowledge that there was com-
plaint
Intended 'gainst Lord Angelo,—came I hither
To speak, as from his mouth, what he doth know
Is true and false; and what he, with his oath
And all probation, will make up full clear,
Whensoever he's convented. First, for this
woman—
To justify this worthy nobleman,
So vulgarly and personally accus'd,—
Her shall you hear disproved to her eyes,
Till she herself confess it.
*Duke.*              Good friar, let's hear it.
    [ISABELLA *is carried off, guarded; and*
        MARIANA *comes forward.*
Do you not smile at this, Lord Angelo?—
O heaven! the vanity of wretched fools!
Give us some seats.—Come, cousin Angelo;
In this I'll be impartial; be you judge
Of your own cause.—Is this the witness, friar?
First, let her show her face, and after speak.
*Mari.* Pardon, my lord; I will not show my
face
Until my husband bid me.
*Duke.*              What! are you married?
*Mari.* No, my lord.
*Duke.*              Are you a maid?
*Mari.*              No, my lord.
*Duke.* A widow, then?
*Mari.*              Neither, my lord.
*Duke.*              Why, you
Are nothing then:—neither maid, widow, nor
wife?
*Lucio.* My lord, she may be a punk; for many
of them are neither maid, widow, nor wife.
*Duke.* Silence that fellow: I would he had some
cause
To prattle for himself.
*Lucio.* Well, my lord.              [ried;
*Mari.* My lord, I do confess I ne'er was mar-
And I confess, besides, I am no maid:
I have known my husband; yet my husband
knows not
That ever he knew me.
*Lucio.* He was drunk, then, my lord; it can be
no better.
*Duke.* For the benefit of silence, would thou
wert so too.

*Lucio.* Well, my lord.
*Duke.* This is no witness for Lord Angelo.
*Mari.* Now I come to't, my lord:
She that accuses him of fornication.
In self-same manner doth accuse my husband;
And charges him, my lord, with such a time
When I'll depose I had him in mine arms,
With all the effect of love.
*Ang.*              Charges she more than me?
*Mari.* Not that I know.
*Duke.*              No? you say, your husband.
*Mari.* Why, just, my lord, and that is Angelo,
Who thinks he knows that he ne'er knew my
body,
But knows he thinks that he knows Isabel's.
*Ang.* This is a strange abuse.—Let's see thy
face.                                    [mask.
*Mari.* My husband bids me; now I will un-
                                    [*Unveiling.*
This is that face, thou cruel Angelo,        [on:
Which once thou swor'st was worth the looking
This is the hand which, with a vow'd contráct,
Was fast belock'd in thine: this is the body
That took away the match from Isabel,
And did supply thee at thy garden-house
In her imagin'd person.
*Duke.*              Know you this woman?
*Lucio.* Carnally, she says.
*Duke.*              Sirrah, no more.
*Lucio.* Enough, my lord.
*Ang.* My lord, I must confess I know this
woman;
And five years since there was some speech of
marriage
Betwixt myself and her; which was broke off.
Partly for that her promis'd proportions
Came short of composition; but in chief
For that her reputation was disvalued
In levity: since which time of five years [her,
I never spake with her, saw her, nor heard from
Upon my faith and honour.
*Mari.*              Noble prince,
As there comes light from heaven and words
from breath,
As there is sense in truth and truth in virtue,
I am affianc'd this man's wife as strongly
As words could make up vows: and, my good
lord,                                    [house,
But Tuesday night last gone, in his garden-
He knew me as a wife. As this is true,
Let me in safety raise me from my knees,
Or else for ever be confixed here,
A marble monument!
*Ang.*              I did but smile till now:
Now, good my lord, give me the scope of
justice;
My patience here is touch'd. I do perceive
These poor informal women are no more
But instruments of some more mightier member
That sets them on. Let me have way, my lord,
To find this practice out.
*Duke.*              Ay, with my heart;
And punish them unto your height of pleasure.—
Thou foolish friar, and thou pernicious woman,

Compáct with her that's gone, thinkst thou thy
    oaths,        [saint,
Though they would swear down each particular
Were testimonies against his worth and credit,
That's seal'd in approbation?—You, Lord
    Escalus,
Sit with my cousin; lend him your kind pains
To find out this abuse, whence 'tis deriv'd.—
There is another friar that set them on;
Let him be sent for.        [indeed
*F. Peter.* Would he were here, my lord; for he
Hath set the women on this complaint:
Your provost knows the place where he abides,
And he may fetch him.
*Duke.* Go, do it instantly.—[*Exit* Provost.
And you, my noble and well-warranted cousin,
Whom it concerns to hear this matter forth,
Do with your injuries as seems you best
In any chastisement. I for awhile    [well
Will leave you: but stir not you till you have
Determined upon these slanderers.
*Escal.* My lord, we'll do it thoroughly. [*Exit*
Duke.]—Signior Lucio, did not you say you
knew that friar Lodowick to be a dishonest
person?
*Lucio.* *Cucullus non facit monachum:* honest
in nothing but in his clothes; and one that hath
spoke most villanous speeches of the duke.
*Escal.* We shall entreat you to abide here till
he come, and enforce them against him: we
shall find this friar a notable fellow.
*Lucio.* As any in Vienna, on my word.
*Escal.* Call that same Isabel here once again
[*to an* Attendant]; I would speak with her.
Pray you, my lord, give me leave to question;
you shall see how I handle her.
*Lucio.* Not better than he, by her own report.
*Escal.* Say you?
*Lucio.* Marry, sir, I think if you handled her
privately she would sooner confess: perchance,
publicly, she'll be ashamed.

*Re-enter* Officers, *with* Isabella.

*Escal.* I will go darkly to work with her.
*Lucio.* That's the way; for women are light at
midnight.
*Escal.* Come on, mistress [*to* Isabella]: here's
a gentlewoman denies all that you have said.

*Re-enter the* Duke, *in the Friar's habit,*
*and* Provost.

*Lucio.* My lord, here comes the rascal I spoke
of; here with the provost.
*Escal.* In very good time:—speak not you to
him till we call upon you.
*Lucio.* Mum.
*Escal.* Come, sir: did you set these women on
to slander Lord Angelo? they have confessed
you did.
*Duke.* 'Tis false.
*Escal.* How! know you where you are?
*Duke.* Respect to your great place! and let the
    devil

Be sometime honour'd for his burning throne!—
Where is the duke? 'tis he should hear me speak.
*Escal.* The duke's in us; and we will hear you
    speak:
Look you speak justly.
*Duke.* Boldly, at least. But, O, poor souls,
Come you to seek the lamb here of the fox,
Good night to your redress! Is the duke gone!
Then is your cause gone too. The duke's unjust
Thus to retort your manifest appeal,
And put your trial in the villain's mouth
Which here you come to accuse.
*Lucio.* This is the rascal; this is he I spoke of.
*Escal.* Why, thou unreverend and unhallow'd
    friar!
Is 't not enough thou hast suborn'd these women
To accuse this worthy man, but, in foul mouth,
And in the witness of his proper ear,
To call him villain?
And then to glance from him to the duke him-
    self,
To tax him with injustice? Take him hence;
To the rack with him.—We'll touze you joint
    by joint,
But we will know this purpose.—What! unjust?
*Duke.* Be not so hot; the duke
Dare no more stretch this finger of mine than he
Dare rack his own; his subject am I not,
Nor here provincial. My business in this state
Made me a looker-on here in Vienna,
Where I have seen corruption boil and bubble
Till it o'errun the stew: laws for all faults,
But faults so countenanc'd that the strong
    statutes
Stand like the forfeits in a barber's shop,
As much in mock as mark.
*Escal.* Slander to the state! Away with him to
    prison!
*Ang.* What can you vouch against him, Signior
    Lucio?
Is this the man that you did tell us of?
*Lucio.* 'Tis he, my lord. Come hither, good-
man bald-pate. Do you know me?
*Duke.* I remember you, sir, by the sound of
your voice. I met you at the prison, in the ab-
sence of the duke.
*Lucio.* O did you so? And do you remember
what you said of the duke?
*Duke.* Most notedly, sir.
*Lucio.* Do you so, sir? And was the duke a
fleshmonger, a fool, and a coward, as you then
reported him to be?
*Duke.* You must, sir, change persons with me
ere you make that my report: you, indeed,
spoke so of him; and much more, much worse.
*Lucio.* O thou damnable fellow! Did not I
pluck thee by the nose for thy speeches?
*Duke.* I protest I love the duke as I love myself.
*Ang.* Hark how the villain would gloze now,
after his treasonable abuses!
*Escal.* Such a fellow is not to be talked withal.
Away with him to prison!—Where is the provost?—Away with him to prison! lay bolts
enough upon him: let him speak no more.—

Away with those giglots too, and with the other confederate companion!

[*The* PROVOST *lays hands on the* DUKE.

*Duke.* Stay, sir; stay awhile.

*Ang.* What! resists he?—Help him, Lucio.

*Lucio.* Come, sir; come, sir! come, sir; foh, sir. Why, you bald-pated, lying rascal! you must be hooded, must you? Show your knave's visage, with a pox to you! show your sheep-biting face, and be hanged an hour! Will't not off?

[*Pulls off the Friar's hood, and discovers the* DUKE.

*Duke.* Thou art the first knave that e'er made a duke.——

First, Provost, let me bail these gentle three:——

Sneak not away, sir [*to* LUCIO]; for the friar and you

Must have a word anon:—Lay hold on him.

*Lucio.* This may prove worse than hanging.

*Duke.* What you have spoke I pardon; sit you down.—— [*To* ESCALUS.

We'll borrow place of him.—Sir, by your leave:

[*To* ANGELO.

Hast thou or word, or wit, or impudence

That yet can do thee office? If thou hast,

Rely upon it till my tale be heard,

And hold no longer out.

*Ang.*                O my dread lord,

I should be guiltier than my guiltiness,

To think I can be undiscernible,

When I perceive your grace, like power divine,

Hath look'd upon my passes. Then, good prince,

No longer session hold upon my shame,

But let my trial be mine own confession:

Immediate sentence then, and sequent death

Is all the grace I beg.

*Duke.*                Come hither, Mariana:—

Say, wast thou e'er contracted to this woman?

*Ang.* I was, my lord.

*Duke.* Go, take her hence and marry her instantly.

Do you the office, friar; which consummate,

Return him here again.—Go with him, Provost.

[*Exeunt* ANG., MARI., PET., *and* PROV.

*Escal.* My lord, I am more amazed at his dishonour

Than at the strangeness of it.

*Duke.*                Come hither, Isabel:

Your friar is now your prince. As I was then

Advertising and holy to your business,

Not changing heart with habit, I am still

Attorney'd at your service.

*Isab.*                O give me pardon,

That I, your vassal, have employ'd and pain'd

Your unknown sovereignty.

*Duke.*                You are pardon'd, Isabel.

And now, dear maid, be you as free to us.

Your brother's death, I know, sits at your heart;

And you may marvel why I obscur'd myself,

Labouring to save his life, and would not rather

Make rash remonstrance of my hidden power

Than let him so be lost. O most kind maid,

It was the swift celerity of his death,

Which I did think with slower foot came on,

That brain'd my purpose. But peace be with him!

That life is better life, past fearing death,

Than that which lives to fear: make it your comfort,

So happy is your brother.

*Isab.*                I do, my lord.

*Re-enter* ANGELO, MARIANA, PETER, *and* PROVOST.

*Duke.* For this new-married man approaching here,

Whose salt imagination yet hath wrong'd

Your well-defended honour, you must pardon

For Mariana's sake: but as he adjudg'd your brother,—

Being criminal, in double violation

Of sacred chastity and of promise-breach

Thereon dependent, for your brother's life,—

The very mercy of the law cries out

Most audible, even from his proper tongue,

*An Angelo for Claudio, death for death.*

Haste still pays haste, and leisure answers leisure;

Like doth quit like, and measure still for measure.

Then, Angelo, thy fault thus manifested,—

Which though thou wouldst deny, denies thee vantage,—

We do condemn thee to the very block

Where Claudio stoop'd to death, and with like haste.—

Away with him.

*Mari.*                O my most gracious lord,

I hope you will not mock me with a husband!

*Duke.* It is your husband mock'd you with a husband.

Consenting to the safeguard of your honour,

I thought your marriage fit; else imputation,

For that he knew you, might reproach your life,

And choke your good to come: for his possessions,

Although by confiscation they are ours,

We do instate and widow you withal,

To buy you a better husband.

*Mari.*                O my dear lord,

I crave no other, nor no better man.

*Duke.* Never crave him; we are definitive.

*Mari.* Gentle, my liege,—        [*Kneeling.*

*Duke.*                You do but lose your labour.—

Away with him to death.—Now, sir [*to* LUCIO], to you.        [*part.*

*Mari.* O my good lord!—Sweet Isabel, take my part;

Lend me your knees, and all my life to come

I'll lend you all my life to do you service.

*Duke.* Against all sense you do importune her:

Should she kneel down, in mercy of this fact,

Her brother's ghost his pavèd bed would break,

And take her hence in horror.

*Mari.*                Isabel,

Sweet Isabel, do yet but kneel by me;

Hold up your hands, say nothing,—I'll speak all.

They say, best men are moulded out of faults:

And, for the most, become much more the better
For being a little bad: so may my husband.
O Isabel, will you not lend a knee?
*Duke.* He dies for Claudio's death.
*Isab.*          Most bounteous sir, [*Kneeling.*
Look, if it please you, on this man condemn'd,
As if my brother liv'd: I partly think
A due sincerity govern'd his deeds
Till he did look on me; since it is so,
Let him not die. My brother had but justice,
In that he did the thing for which he died:
For Angelo,
His act did not o'ertake his bad intent,
And must be buried but as an intent    [jects;
That perish'd by the way: thoughts are no sub-
Intents but merely thoughts.
*Mari.*              Merely, my lord.
*Duke.* Your suit's unprofitable; stand up, I
          say.—
I have bethought of another fault.—
Provost, how came it Claudio was beheaded
At an unusual hour?
*Prov.*            It was commanded so.
*Duke.* Had you a special warrant for the deed?
*Prov.* No, my good lord; it was by private
          message.
*Duke.* For which I do discharge you of your
          office:
Give up your keys.
*Prov.*            Pardon me, noble lord:
I thought it was a fault, but knew it not;
Yet did repent me, after more advice:
For testimony whereof, one in the prison,
That should by private order else have died,
I have reserved alive.
*Duke.*              What's he?
*Prov.*              His name is Barnardine.
*Duke.* I would thou hadst done so by Claudio.—
Go fetch him hither; let me look upon him.
                              [*Exit* PROVOST.
*Escal.* I am sorry one so learned and so wise
As you, Lord Angelo, have still appear'd,
Should slip so grossly, both in the heat of blood
And lack of temper'd judgment afterward.
*Ang.* I am sorry that such sorrow I procure:
And so deep sticks it in my penitent heart
That I crave death more willingly than mercy;
'Tis my deserving, and I do entreat it.

          *Re-enter* PROVOST, *with* BARNARDINE,

          CLAUDIO (*muffled*), *and* JULIET.

*Duke.* Which is that Barnardine?
*Prov.*                    This, my lord.
*Duke.* There was a friar told me of this man:—
Sirrah, thou art said to have a stubborn soul,
That apprehends no further than this world,
And squar'st thy life according. Thou 'rt con-
          demn'd;
But, for those earthly faults, I quit them all,
And pray thee take this mercy to provide
For better times to come:——Friar, advise him;
I leave him to your hand.—What muffled fel-
low's that?

*Prov.* This is another prisoner that I sav'd,
Who should have died when Claudio lost his
          head;
As like almost to Claudio as himself.
                    [*Unmuffles* CLAUDIO.
*Duke.* If he be like your brother, [*to* ISABELLA],
          for his sake
Is he pardon'd; and, for your lovely sake,
Give me your hand, and say you will be mine;
He is my brother too: but fitter time for that.
By this Lord Angelo perceives he's safe;
Methinks I see a quick'ning in his eye.—
Well, Angelo, your evil quits you well:
Look that you love your wife; her worth worth
          yours.—
I find an apt remission in myself;
And yet here's one in place I cannot pardon.—
You, sirrah [*to* LUCIO], that knew me for a
          fool, a coward,
One all of luxury, an ass, a madman;
Wherein have I so deserved of you
That you extol me thus?
*Lucio.* 'Faith, my lord, I spoke it but accord-
ing to the trick. If you will hang me for it, you
may; but I had rather it would please you I
might be whipped.
*Duke.* Whipp'd first, sir, and hang'd after.—
Proclaim it, Provost, round about the city,
If any woman's wrong'd by this lewd fellow,—
As I have heard him swear himself there's one
Whom he begot with child,—let her appear,
And he shall marry her: the nuptial finish'd,
Let him be whipp'd and hang'd.
*Lucio.* I beseech your highness, do not marry
me to a whore! Your highness said even now I
made you a duke; good my lord, do not recom-
pense me in making me a cuckold.
*Duke.* Upon mine honour, thou shalt marry her.
Thy slanders I forgive; and therewithal
Remit thy other forfeits.—Take him to prison;
And see our pleasure herein executed.
*Lucio.* Marrying a punk, my lord, is pressing
to death, whipping, and hanging.
*Duke.* Slandering a prince deserves it.—
                    [*Exeunt Officers with* LUCIO.
She, Claudio, that you wrong'd, look you re-
          store.—
Joy to you, Mariana!—Love her, Angelo;
I have confess'd her, and I know her virtue.—
Thanks, good friend Escalus, for thy much
          goodness
There's more behind that is more gratulate.
Thanks, Provost, for thy care and secrecy;
We shall employ thee in a worthier place.—
Forgive him, Angelo, that brought you home
The head of Ragozine for Claudio's:
The offence pardons itself.—Dear Isabel,
I have a motion much imports your good;
Whereto if you'll a willing ear incline,
What's mine is yours, and what is yours is
          mine:—
So, bring us to our palace; where we'll show
What's yet behind that's meet you all should
          know.          [*Exeunt.*

MUCH ADO ABOUT NOTHING

Act IV. Sc. 1.

# MUCH ADO ABOUT NOTHING

## DRAMATIS PERSONÆ

DON PEDRO, *Prince of Arragon.*
DON JOHN, *his bastard Brother.*
CLAUDIO, *a young Lord of Florence, favourite to* DON PEDRO.
BENEDICK, *a young Lord of Padua, favourite likewise of* DON PEDRO.
LEONATO, *Governor of Messina.*
ANTONIO, *his Brother.*
BALTHAZAR, *Servant to* DON PEDRO.
BORACHIO, } *Followers of* DON JOHN.
CONRADE, }

DOGBERRY, } *two foolish Officers.*
VERGES, }
A SEXTON.
A FRIAR.
A BOY.

HERO, *Daughter to* LEONATO.
BEATRICE, *Niece to* LEONATO.
MARGARET, } *Gentlewomen attending on*
URSULA, } HERO.

Messengers,. Watch, *and* Attendants.

SCENE,—MESSINA

## ACT I.

### SCENE I.—*Before* LEONATO'S *House.*

*Enter* LEONATO, HERO, BEATRICE, *and others, with a* Messenger.

*Leon.* I learn in this letter that Don Pedro of Arragon comes this night to Messina.

*Mess.* He is very near by this; he was not three leagues off when I left him.

*Leon.* How many gentlemen have you lost in this action?

*Mess.* But few of any sort, and none of name.

*Leon.* A victory is twice itself when the achiever brings home full numbers. I find here that Don Pedro hath bestowed much honour on a young Florentine called Claudio.

*Mess.* Much deserved on his part, and equally remembered by Don Pedro. He hath borne himself beyond the promise of his age; doing, in the figure of a lamb, the feats of a lion: he hath, indeed, better bettered expectation than you must expect of me to tell you how.

*Leon.* He hath an uncle here in Messina will be very much glad of it.

*Mess.* I have already delivered him letters, and there appears much joy in him; even so much that joy could not show itself modest enough without a badge of bitterness.

*Leon.* Did he break out into tears?

*Mess.* In great measure.

*Leon.* A kind overflow of kindness. There are no faces truer than those that are so washed. How much better is it to weep at joy than to joy at weeping?

*Beat.* I pray you, is Signior Montanto returned from the wars or no?

*Mess.* I know none of that name, lady; there was none such in the army of any sort.

*Leon.* What is he that you ask for, niece?

*Hero.* My cousin means Signior Benedick of Padua.

*Mess.* O, he is returned, and as pleasant as ever he was.

*Beat.* He set up his bills here in Messina, and challenged Cupid at the flight: and my uncle's fool, reading the challenge, subscribed for Cupid, and challenged him at the bird-bolt.— I pray you, how many hath he killed and eaten in these wars? But how many hath he killed? for, indeed, I promised to eat all of his killing.

*Leon.* Faith, niece, you tax Signior Benedick too much; but he'll be meet with you, I doubt it not.

*Mess.* He hath done good service, lady, in these wars.

*Beat.* You had musty victual, and he hath holp to eat it: he is a very valiant trencherman; he hath an excellent stomach.

*Mess.* And a good soldier too, lady.

*Beat.* And a good soldier to a lady: but what is he to a lord?

*Mess.* A lord to a lord, a man to a man; stuffed with all honourable virtues.

*Beat* It is so, indeed: he is no less than a stuffed man: but for the stuffing,—well, we are all mortal.

*Leon.* You must not, sir, mistake my niece: there is a kind of merry war betwixt Signior Benedick and her: they never meet but there is a skirmish of wit between them.

*Beat.* Alas, he gets nothing by that. In our last conflict four of his five wits went halting off, and now is the old man governed with one: so that if he have wit enough to keep himself warm, let him bear it for a difference between himself and his horse; for it is all the wealth that he hath left, to be known a reasonable creature.—Who is his companion now? He hath every month a new sworn brother.

*Mess.* Is it possible?

*Beat.* Very easily possible: he wears his faith but as the fashion of his hat; it ever changes with the next block.

*Mess.* I see, lady, the gentleman is not in your books.

*Beat.* No: an he were I would burn my study. But, I pray you, who is his companion? Is there no young squarer, now, that will make a voyage with him to the devil?

*Mess.* He is most in the company of the right noble Claudio.

*Beat.* O Lord! he will hang upon him like a disease: he is sooner caught than the pestilence, and the taker runs presently mad. God help the noble Claudio! if he have caught the Benedick, it will cost him a thousand pound ere he be cured.

*Mess.* I will hold friends with you, lady.

*Beat.* Do, good friend.

*Leon.* You will never run mad, niece.

*Beat.* No, not till a hot January.

*Mess.* Don Pedro is approached.

*Enter* DON PEDRO, *attended by* BALTHAZAR *and others,* DON JOHN, CLAUDIO, *and* BENEDICK.

*D. Pedro.* Good Signior Leonato, you are come to meet your trouble: the fashion of the world is to avoid cost, and you encounter it.

*Leon.* Never came trouble to my house in the likeness of your grace; for trouble being gone, comfort should remain; but when you depart from me, sorrow abides, and happiness takes his leave.

*D. Pedro.* You embrace your charge too willingly.—I think this is your daughter.

*Leon.* Her mother hath many times told me so.

*Bene.* Were you in doubt, sir, that you asked her?                              [a child.

*Leon.* Signior Benedick, no; for then were you

*D. Pedro.* You have it full, Benedick: we may guess by this what you are, being a man. Truly, the lady fathers herself.—Be happy, lady! for you are like an honourable father.

*Bene.* If Signior Leonato be her father, she would not have his head on her shoulders for all Messina, as like him as she is.

*Beat.* I wonder that you will still be talking, Signior Benedick; nobody marks you.

*Bene.* What, my dear lady Disdain! are you yet living?

*Beat.* Is it possible disdain should die while she hath such meet food to feed it as Signior Benedick? Courtesy itself must convert to disdain if you come in her presence.

*Bene.* Then is courtesy a turn-coat.—But it is certain I am loved of all ladies, only you excepted: and I would I could find in my heart that I had not a hard heart: for, truly, I love none.

*Beat.* A dear happiness to women: they would else have been troubled with a pernicious suitor. I thank God, and my cold blood, I am of your humour for that: I had rather hear my dog bark at a crow than a man swear he loves me.

*Bene.* God keep your ladyship still in that mind! so some gentleman or other shall 'scape a predestinate scratched face.

*Beat.* Scratching could not make it worse an 'twere such a face as yours were.

*Bene.* Well, you are a rare parrot-teacher.

*Beat.* A bird of my tongue is better than a beast of yours.

*Bene.* I would my horse had the speed of your tongue, and so good a continuer. But keep your way o' God's name; I have done.

*Beat.* You always end with a jade's trick; I know you of old.

*D. Pedro.* This is the sum of all: Leonato,—Signior Claudio, and Signior Benedick,—my dear friend Leonato hath invited you all. I tell him we shall stay here at the least a month; and he heartily prays some occasion may detain us longer: I dare swear he is no hypocrite, but prays from his heart.

*Leon.* If you swear, my lord, you shall not be forsworn.—Let me bid you welcome, my lord: being reconciled to the prince your brother, I owe you all duty.

*D. John.* I thank you: I am not of many words, but I thank you.

*Leon.* Please it your grace lead on?

*D. Pedro.* Your hand, Leonato; we will go together.          [*Exeunt all but* BENE., *and* CLAUD.

*Claud.* Benedick, didst thou note the daughter of Signior Leonato?

*Bene.* I noted her not, but I looked on her.

*Claud.* Is she not a modest young lady?

*Bene.* Do you question me, as an honest man should do, for my simple true judgment; or would you have me speak after my custom, as being a professed tyrant to their sex?

*Claud.* No, I pray thee, speak in sober judgment.

*Bene.* Why, i' faith, methinks she is too low for a high praise, too brown for a fair praise, and too little for a great praise: only this commendation I can afford her; that were she other than she is, she were unhandsome; and being no other but as she is, I do not like her.

*Claud.* Thou thinkest I am in sport: I pray thee, tell me truly how thou likest her.

*Bene.* Would you buy her, that you inquire after her?

*Claud.* Can the world buy such a jewel?

*Bene.* Yea, and a case to put it into. But speak you this with a sad brow? or do you play the floating Jack, to tell us Cupid is a good hare-finder, and Vulcan a rare carpenter? Come, in what key shall a man take you to go in the song?

*Claud.* In mine eye, she is the sweetest lady that ever I looked on.

*Bene.* I can see yet without spectacles, and I see no such matter: there's her cousin, an she were not possessed with a fury, exceeds her as much in beauty as the first of May doth the last of December. But I hope you have no intent to turn husband, have you?

*Claud.* I would scarce trust myself, though I had sworn the contrary, if Hero would be my wife.

*Bene.* Is it come to this, i' faith? Hath not the world one man but he will wear his cap with suspicion? Shall I never see a bachelor of three-score again? Go to, i' faith; an thou wilt needs thrust thy neck into a yoke, wear the print of it, and sigh away Sundays. Look, Don Pedro is returned to seek you.

*Re-enter* DON PEDRO.

*D. Pedro.* What secret hath held you here, that you followed not to Leonato's?
*Bene.* I would your grace would constrain me to tell.
*D. Pedro.* I charge thee on thy allegiance.
*Bene.* You hear, Count Claudio: I can be secret as a dumb man,—I would have you think so; but on my allegiance,—mark you this,—on my allegiance:—He is in love. With who?—Now that is your grace's part.—Mark how short his answer is:—With Hero, Leonato's short daughter.
*Claud.* If this were so, so were it uttered.
*Bene.* Like the old tale, my lord: "It is not so, nor 'twas not so; but, indeed, God forbid it should be so."
*Claud.* If my passion change not shortly, God forbid it should be otherwise.
*D. Pedro.* Amen, if you love her; for the lady is very well worthy.
*Claud.* You speak this to fetch me in, my lord?
*D. Pedro.* By my troth, I speak my thought.
*Claud.* And, in faith, my lord, I spoke mine.
*Bene.* And, by my two faiths and troths, my lord, I spoke mine.
*Claud.* That I love her, I feel.
*D. Pedro.* That she is worthy, I know.
*Bene.* That I neither feel how she should be loved, nor know how she should be worthy, is the opinion that fire cannot melt out of me: I will die in it at the stake.
*D. Pedro.* Thou wast ever an obstinate heretic in the despite of beauty.
*Claud.* And never could maintain his part but in the force of his will.
*Bene.* That a woman conceived me, I thank her; that she brought me up, I likewise give her most humble thanks; but that I will have a recheat winded in my forehead, or hang my bugle in an invisible baldrick, all women shall pardon me. Because I will not do them the wrong to mistrust any, I will do myself the right to trust none; and the fine is,—for the which I may go the finer,—I will live a bachelor.
*D. Pedro.* I shall see thee, ere I die, look pale with love.
*Bene.* With anger, with sickness, or with hunger, my lord; not with love: prove that ever I lose more blood with love than I will get again with drinking, pick out mine eyes with a ballad-maker's pen, and hang me up at the door of a brothel-house, for the sign of blind Cupid.
*D. Pedro.* Well, if ever thou dost fall from this faith, thou wilt prove a notable argument.

*Bene.* If I do, hang me in a bottle like a cat, and shoot at me; and he that hits me, let him be clapped on the shoulder and called Adam.
*D. Pedro.* Well, as time shall try:
*In time the savage bull doth bear the yoke.*
*Bene.* The savage bull may; but if ever the sensible Benedick bear it, pluck off the bull's horns and set them in my forehead: and let me be vilely painted; and in such great letters as they write *Here is good horse to hire,* let them signify under my sign,—*Here you may see Benedick the married man.*
*Claud.* If this should ever happen, thou wouldst be horn-mad.
*D. Pedro.* Nay, if Cupid have not spent all his quiver in Venice, thou wilt quake for this shortly.
*Bene.* I look for an earthquake too, then.
*D. Pedro.* Well, you will temporise with the hours. In the meantime, good Signior Benedick, repair to Leonato's; commend me to him, and tell him I will not fail him at supper; for, indeed, he hath made great preparation.
*Bene.* I have almost matter enough in me for such an embassage; and so I commit you—
*Claud.* To the tuition of God: From my house,—if I had it—
*D. Pedro.* The sixth of July. Your loving friend, Benedick.
*Bene.* Nay, mock not, mock not. The body of your discourse is sometime guarded with fragments, and the guards are but slightly basted on neither: ere you flout old ends any further, examine your conscience; and so I leave you.
                                    [*Exit* BENEDICK.
*Claud.* My liege, your highness now may do me good.
*D. Pedro.* My love is thine to teach; teach it but how,
And thou shalt see how apt it is to learn
Any hard lesson that may do thee good.
*Claud.* Hath Leonato any son, my lord?
*D. Pedro.* No child but Hero, she's his only heir:
Dost thou affect her, Claudio?
*Claud.*                    O my lord,
When you went onward on this ended action,
I looked upon her with a soldier's eye,
That liked, but had a rougher task in hand
Than to drive liking to the name of love:
But now I am return'd, and that war-thoughts
Have left their places vacant, in their rooms
Come thronging soft and delicate desires,
All prompting me how fair young Hero is,
Saying, I liked her ere I went to wars.
*D. Pedro.* Thou wilt be like a lover presently,
And tire the hearer with a book of words:
If thou dost love fair Hero, cherish it;
And I will break with her, and with her father,
And thou shalt have her. Was't not to this end
That thou began'st to twist so fine a story?
*Claud.* How sweetly do you minister to love,
That know love's grief by his complexion!
But lest my liking might too sudden seem,
I would have slav'd it with a longer treatise.

*D. Pedro.* What need the bridge much broader
　　　　than the flood!
The fairest grant is the necessity.
Look, what will serve is fit: 'tis once, thou lov'st;
And I will fit thee with the remedy.
I know we shall have revelling to-night;
I will assume thy part in some disguise,
And tell fair Hero I am Claudio;
And in her bosom I'll unclasp my heart,
And take her hearing prisoner with the force
And strong encounter of my amorous tale:
Then, after, to her father will I break;
And the conclusion is, she shall be thine:
In practice let us put it presently.　　[*Exeunt.*

SCENE II.—*A Room in* LEONATO'S *House.*

*Enter, severally,* LEONATO *and* ANTONIO.

*Leon.* How now, brother! Where is my cousin,
your son? Hath he provided this music?
*Ant.* He is very busy about it. But, brother, I
can tell you strange news that you yet dreamed
not of.
*Leon.* Are they good?
*Ant.* As the event stamps them; but they have
a good cover; they show well outward. The
prince and Count Claudio, walking in a thick-
pleached alley in my orchard, were thus much
overheard by a man of mine: the prince discovered to Claudio that he loved my niece your
daughter, and meant to acknowledge it this
night in a dance; and, if he found her accord-
ant, he meant to take the present time by the
top, and instantly break with you of it.
*Leon.* Hath the fellow any wit that told you
this?
*Ant.* A good sharp fellow; I will send for him,
and question him yourself.
*Leon.* No, no; we will hold it as a dream, till
it appear itself:—but I will acquaint my daughter withal, that she may be the better prepared
for an answer, if peradventure this be true.
Go you and tell her of it. [*Several persons cross
the stage.*] Cousins, you know what you have to
do.—O, I cry you mercy, friend: you go with
me, and I will use your skill.—Good cousin,
have a care this busy time.　　　　[*Exeunt.*

SCENE III.—*Another Room in* LEONATO'S
*House.*

*Enter* DON JOHN *and* CONRADE.

*Con.* What the good-year, my lord! why are
you thus out of measure sad?
*D. John.* There is no measure in the occasion
that breeds it; therefore the sadness is without
limit.
*Con.* You should hear reason.
*D. John.* And when I have heard it, what
blessing bringeth it?　　　　　[*sufferance.*
*Con.* If not a present remedy, yet a patient
*D. John.* I wonder that thou, being—as thou
say'st thou art—born under Saturn, goest about
to apply a moral medicine to a mortifying mischief. I cannot hide what I am: I must be sad
when I have cause, and smile at no man's jests;

eat when I have stomach, and wait for no man's
leisure; sleep when I am drowsy, and 'tend to
no man's business; laugh when I am merry, and
claw no man in his humour.
*Con.* Yea, but you must not make the full
show of this till you may do it without controlment. You have of late stood out against your
brother, and he hath ta'en you newly into his
grace; where it is impossible you should take
true root but by the fair weather that you make
yourself: it is needful that you frame the season for your own harvest.
*D. John.* I had rather be a canker in a hedge
than a rose in his grace; and it better fits my
blood to be disdained of all than to fashion a
carriage to rob love from any: in this, though
I cannot be said to be a flattering honest man,
it must not be denied that I am a plain-dealing
villain. I am trusted with a muzzle and enfranchised with a clog: therefore I have decreed not
to sing in my cage. If I had my mouth I would
bite; If I had my liberty I would do my liking:
in the meantime let me be that I am, and seek
not to alter me.
*Con.* Can you make no use of your discontent?
*D. John.* I make all use of it, for I use it only.
Who comes here? What news, Borachio?

*Enter* BORACHIO.

*Bora.* I came yonder from a great supper: the
prince, your brother, is royally entertained by
Leonato; and I can give you intelligence of an
intended marriage.
*D. John.* Will it serve for any model to build
mischief on? What is he for a fool that betroths
himself to unquietness?
*Bora.* Marry, it is your brother's right hand.
*D. John.* Who! the most exquisite Claudio?
*Bora.* Even he.
*D. John.* A proper squire! And who, and who?
which way looks he?
*Bora.* Marry, on Hero, the daughter and heir
of Leonato.
*D. John.* A very forward March-chick! How
came you to this?
*Bora.* Being entertained for a perfumer, as I
was smoking a musty room, comes me the
prince and Claudio hand in hand, in sad conference. I whipt me behind the arras, and there
heard it agreed upon that the prince should
woo Hero for himself, and, having obtained
her, give her to Count Claudio.
*D. John.* Come, come, let us thither; this may
prove food to my displeasure: that young start-
up hath all the glory of my overthrow. If I
can cross him any way, I bless myself every
way. You are both sure, and will assist me?
*Con.* To the death, my lord.
*D. John.* Let us to the great supper: their
cheer is the greater that I am subdued. Would
the cook were of my mind!—Shall we go prove
what's to be done?
*Bora.* We'll wait upon your lordship. [*Exeunt.*

## ACT II.

SCENE I.—*A Hall in* LEONATO'S *House.*

*Enter* LEONATO, ANTONIO, HERO, BEATRICE, *and others.*

*Leon.* Was not Count John here at supper?

*Ant.* I saw him not.

*Beat.* How tartly that gentleman looks! I never can see him but I am heart-burned an hour after.

*Hero.* He is of a very melancholy disposition.

*Beat.* He were an excellent man that were made just in the mid-way between him and Benedick: the one is too like an image, and says nothing; and the other too like my lady's eldest son, evermore tattling.

*Leon.* Then half Signior Benedick's tongue in Count John's mouth, and half Count John's melancholy in Signior Benedick's face,—

*Beat.* With a good leg and a good foot, uncle, and money enough in his purse, such a man would win any woman in the world,—if he could get her good-will.

*Leon.* By my troth, niece, thou wilt never get thee a husband if thou be so shrewd of thy tongue.

*Ant.* In faith, she is too curst.

*Beat.* Too curst is more than curst. I shall lessen God's sending that way: for it is said, *God sends a curst cow short horns;* but to a cow too curst he sends none.

*Leon.* So, by being too curst, Good will send you no horns.

*Beat.* Just if he send me no husband; for the which blessing I am at him upon my knees every morning and evening. Lord! I could not endure a husband with a beard on his face: I had rather lie in the woollen.

*Leon.* You may light upon a husband that hath no beard.

*Beat.* What should I do with him? dress him in my apparel, and make him my waiting gentlewoman? He that hath a beard is more than a youth; and he that hath no beard is less than a man: and he that is more than a youth is not for me; and he that is less than a man I am not for him: therefore I will even take sixpence in earnest of the bear-ward, and lead his apes into hell.

*Leon.* Well then, go you into hell?

*Beat.* No; but to the gate; and there will the devil meet me, like an old cuckold, with horns on his head, and say, *Get you to heaven, Beatrice; get you to heaven: here's no place for you maids:* so deliver I up my apes and away to Saint Peter for the heavens; he shows me where the bachelors sit, and there live we as merry as the day is long.

*Ant.* Well, niece [*to* HERO], I trust you will be ruled by your father.

*Beat.* Yes, faith; it's my cousin's duty to make courtesy, and say, *Father, as it please you:*—but yet for all that, cousin, let him be a handsome fellow, or else make another courtesy, and say, *Bather, as it please me.*

*Leon.* Well, niece, I hope to see you one day fitted with a husband.

*Feat.* Not till God make men of some other metal than earth. Would it not grieve a woman to be over-mastered with a piece of valiant dust! to make an account of her life to a clod of wayward marl? No, uncle, I'll none: Adam's sons are my brethren; and, truly, I hold it a sin to match in my kindred.

*Leon.* Daughter, remember what I told you: if the prince do solicit you in that kind, you know your answer.

*Beat.* The fault will be in the music, cousin, if you be not wooed in good time: if the prince be too important, tell him there is measure in everything, and so dance out the answer. For, hear me, Hero, wooing, wedding, and repenting is as a Scotch jig, a measure, and a cinque-pace: the first suit is hot and hasty, like a Scotch jig, and full as fantastical; the wedding, mannerly modest as a measure, full of state and ancientry; and then comes repentance, and, with his bad legs, falls into the cinque-pace faster and faster, till he sink into his grave.

*Leon.* Cousin, you apprehend passing shrewdly.

*Beat.* I have a good eye, uncle; I can see a church by daylight.

*Leon.* The revellers are entering, brother; make good room.

*Enter* DON PEDRO, CLAUDIO, BENEDICK, BALTHAZAR; DON JOHN, BORACHIO, MARGARET, URSULA, *and others, masked.*

*D. Pedro.* Lady, will you walk about with your friend?

*Hero.* So you walk softly, and look sweetly, and say nothing, I am yours for the walk; and, especially, when I walk away.

*D. Pedro.* With me in your company?

*Hero.* I may say so, when I please.

*D. Pedro.* And when please you to say so?

*Hero.* When I like your favour; for God defend the lute should be like the case!

*D. Pedro.* My visor is Philemon's roof; within the house is Jove.

*Hero.* Why, then, your visor should be thatched.

*D. Pedro.* Speak low, if you speak love.
　　　　　　　　　　　　　[*Takes her aside.*

*Balth.* Well, I would you did like me.

*Marg.* So would not I, for your own sake; for I have many ill qualities.

*Balth.* Which is one?

*Marg.* I say my prayers aloud.

*Balth.* I love you the better; the hearers may cry Amen.

*Marg.* God match me with a good dancer!

*Balth.* Amen.

*Marg.* And God keep him out of my sight when the dance is done!—Answer, clerk.

*Balth.* No more words; the clerk is answered.

*Urs.* I know you well enough; you are Signior Antonio.

*Ant.* At a word, I am not.

*Urs.* I know you by the waggling of your head.

*Ant.* To tell you true, I counterfeit him.

*Urs.* You could never do him so ill-well unless you were the very man. Here's his dry hand up and down: you are he; you are he.

*Ant.* At a word, I am not.

*Urs.* Come, come; do you think I do not know you by your excellent wit? Can virtue hide itself? Go to; mum; you are he: graces will appear, and there's an end.

*Beat.* Will you not tell me who told you so?

*Bene.* No, you shall pardon me.

*Beat.* Nor will you not tell me who you are?

*Bene.* Not now.

*Beat.* That I was disdainful!—and that I had my good wit out of the *Hundred Merry Tales!*—Well, this was Signior Benedick that said so.

*Bene.* What's he?

*Beat.* I am sure you know him well enough.

*Bene.* Not I, believe me.

*Beat.* Did he never make you laugh?

*Bene.* I pray you, what is he?

*Beat.* Why, he is the prince's jester: a very dull fool; only his gift is in devising impossible slanders: none but libertines delight in him; and the commendation is not in his wit but in his villany; for he both pleaseth men and angers them, and then they laugh at him and beat him. I am sure he is in the fleet: I would he had boarded me.

*Bene.* When I know the gentleman I'll tell him what you say.

*Beat.* Do, do: he'll but break a comparison or two on me; which, peradventure, not marked, or not laughed at, strikes him into melancholy; and then there's a partridge wing saved, for the fool will eat no supper that night. [*Music within.*] We must follow the leaders.

*Bene.* In every good thing.

*Beat.* Nay, if they lead to any ill, I will leave them at the next turning.

[*Dance. Then exeunt all but* DON JOHN, BORACHIO, *and* CLAUDIO.

*D. John.* Sure, my brother is amorous on Hero, and hath withdrawn her father to break with him about it. The ladies follow her, and but one visor remains. [*bearing.*

*Bora.* And that is Claudio. I know him by his *D. John.* Are not you Signior Benedick?

*Claud.* You know me well; I am he.

*D. John.* Signior, you are very near my brother in his love: he is enamoured on Hero; I pray you dissuade him from her; she is no equal for his birth: you may do the part of an honest man in it.

*Claud.* How know you he loves her?

*D. John.* I heard him swear his affection.

*Bora.* So did I too; and he swore he would marry her to-night.

*D. John.* Come, let us to the banquet.

[*Exeunt* DON JOHN *and* BORACHIO.

*Claud.* Thus answer I in name of Benedick, But hear these ill news with the ears of Claudio.

'Tis certain so;—the prince woos for himself. Friendship is constant in all other things Save in the office and affairs of love: Therefore, all hearts in love use their own tongues: Let every eye negotiate for itself, And trust no agent: for beauty is a witch, Against whose charms faith melteth into blood. This is an accident of hourly proof, [Hero! Which I mistrusted not: farewell, therefore,

*Re-enter* BENEDICK.

*Bene.* Count Claudio?

*Claud.* Yea, the same.

*Bene.* Come, will you go with me?

*Claud.* Whither?

*Bene.* Even to the next willow, about your own business, count. What fashion will you wear the garland of? About your neck, like an usurer's chain? or under your arm like a lieutenant's scarf? You must wear it one way, for the prince hath got your Hero.

*Claud.* I wish him joy of her.

*Bene.* Why, that's spoken like an honest drover; so they sell bullocks. But did you think the prince would have served you thus?

*Claud.* I pray you, leave me.

*Bene.* Ho! now you strike like the blind man; 'twas the boy that stole your meat, and you'll beat the post.

*Claud.* If it will not be, I'll leave you. [*Exit.*

*Bene.* Alas, poor hurt fowl! Now will he creep into sedges.——But, that my Lady Beatrice should know me, and not know me! The prince's fool!—Ha, it may be I go under that title because I am merry.—Yea, but so I am apt to do myself wrong; I am not so reputed: it is the base, the bitter disposition of Beatrice that puts the world into her person, and so gives me out. Well, I'll be revenged as I may.

*Re-enter* DON PEDRO.

*D. Pedro.* Now, signior, where's the count? Did you see him?

*Bene.* Troth, my lord, I have played the part of Lady Fame. I found him here as melancholy as a lodge in a warren; I told him, and I think I told him true, that your grace had got the good-will of this young lady; and I offered him my company to a willow tree, either to make him a garland, as being forsaken, or to bind him up a rod, as being worthy to be whipped.

*D. Pedro.* To be whipped! What's his fault?

*Bene.* The flat transgression of a school-boy, who, being overjoyed with finding a bird's nest, shows it his companion, and he steals it.

*D. Pedro.* Wilt thou make a trust a transgression? The transgression is in the stealer.

*Bene.* Yet it had not been amiss the rod had been made, and the garland too; for the garland he might have worn himself; and the rod he might have bestowed on you, who, as I take it, have stolen his bird's nest.

*D. Pedro.* I will but teach them to sing, and restore them to the owner.

*Bene.* If their singing answer your saying, by my faith, you say honestly.

*D. Pedro.* The Lady Beatrice hath a quarrel to you; the gentleman that danced with her told her she is much wronged by you.

*Bene.* O, she misused me past the endurance of a block; an oak but with one green leaf on it would have answered her; my very visor began to assume life and scold with her: she told me,—not thinking I had been myself,—that I was the prince's jester; that I was duller than a great thaw; huddling jest upon jest with such impossible conveyance upon me, that I stood like a man at a mark, with a whole army shooting at me. She speaks poniards, and every word stabs: if her breath were as terrible as her terminations, there were no living near her; she would infect to the north star. I would not marry her though she were endowed with all that Adam had left him before he transgressed: she would have made Hercules have turned spit; yea, and have cleft his club to make the fire too. Come, talk not of her: you shall find her the infernal Até in good apparel. I would to God some scholar would conjure her; for certainly, while she is here, a man may live as quiet in hell as in a sanctuary; and people sin upon purpose, because they would go thither; so, indeed, all disquiet, horror, and perturbation follows her.

*D. Pedro.* Look, here she comes.

*Re-enter* CLAUDIO *and* BEATRICE, LEONATO *and* HERO.

*Bene.* Will your grace command me any service to the world's end? I will go on the slightest errand now to the antipodes that you can devise to send me on; I will fetch you a toothpicker now from the farthest inch of Asia; bring you the length of Prester John's foot; fetch you a hair off the great Cham's beard; do you any embassage to the Pigmies;—rather than hold three words' conference with this harpy. You have no employment for me?

*D. Pedro.* None, but to desire your good company.

*Bene.* O God, sir, here's a dish I love not; I cannot endure my Lady Tongue.　　[*Exit.*

*D. Pedro.* Come, lady, come; you have lost the heart of Signior Benedick.

*Beat.* Indeed, my lord, he lent it me awhile; and I gave him use for it,—a double heart for his single one: marry, once before he won it of me with false dice, therefore your grace may well say I have lost it.

*D. Pedro.* You have put him down, lady, you have put him down.

*Beat.* So I would not he should do me, my lord, lest I should prove the mother of fools. I have brought Count Claudio, whom you sent me to seek.　　[are you sad?

*D. Pedro.* Why, how now, count! wherefore

*Claud.* Not sad, my lord.

*D. Pedro.* How then? Sick?

*Claud.* Neither, my lord.

*Beat.* The count is neither sad, nor sick, nor merry, nor well: but civil, count; civil as an orange, and something of that jealous complexion.

*D. Pedro.* I' faith, lady, I think your blazon to be true; though I'll be sworn; if he be so, his conceit is false. Here, Claudio, I have wooed in thy name, and fair Hero is won. I have broke with her father, and his good-will obtained: name the day of marriage, and God give thee joy!

*Leon.* Count, take of me my daughter, and with her my fortunes; his grace hath made the match, and all grace say Amen to it!

*Beat.* Speak, count, 'tis your cue.

*Claud.* Silence is the perfectest herald of joy: I were but little happy if I could say how much.
—Lady, as you are mine, I am yours: I give away myself for you, and dote upon the exchange.

*Beat.* Speak, cousin; or, if you cannot, stop his mouth with a kiss, and let not him speak neither.　　[heart.

*D. Pedro.* In faith, lady, you have a merry

*Beat.* Yea, my lord; I thank it,' poor fool, it keeps on the windy side of care.—My cousin tells him in his ear that he is in her heart.

*Claud.* And so she doth, cousin.

*Beat.* Good lord, for alliance!—Thus goes every one to the world but I, and I am sunburnt; I may sit in a corner and cry heigh-ho! for a husband.

*D. Pedro.* Lady Beatrice, I will get you one.

*Beat.* I would rather have one of your father's getting. Hath your grace ne'er a brother like you? Your father got excellent husbands, if a maid could come by them.

*D. Pedro.* Will you have me, lady?

*Beat.* No, my lord, unless I might have another for working-days; your grace is too costly to wear every day. But, I beseech your grace, pardon me; I was born to speak all mirth and no matter.

*D. Pedro.* Your silence most offends me, and to be merry best becomes you; for, out of question, you were born in a merry hour.

*Beat.* No, sure, my lord, my mother cried; but then there was a star danced, and under that was I born. Cousins, God give you joy!

*Leon.* Niece, will you look to those things I told you of?

*Beat.* I cry you mercy, uncle.—By your grace's pardon.　　[*Exit* BEATRICE.

*D. Pedro.* By my troth, a pleasant-spirited lady.

*Leon.* There's little of the melancholy element in her, my lord: she is never sad but when she sleeps; and not ever sad then; for I have heard my daughter say she hath often dreamed of unhappiness, and waked herself with laughing.

*D. Pedro.* She cannot endure to hear tell of a husband.

*Leon.* O, by no means; she mocks all her wooers out of suit.                                    [*dick.*
*D. Pedro.* She were an excellent wife for Bene-
*Leon.* O Lord, my lord, if they were but a week married, they would talk themselves mad.
*D. Pedro.* Count Claudio, when mean you to go to church?
*Claud.* To-morrow, my lord. Time goes on crutches till love have all his rites.
*Leon.* Not till Monday, my dear son, which is hence a just seven-night; and a time too brief too, to have all things answer my mind.
*D. Pedro.* Come, you shake the head at so long a breathing; but I warrant thee, Claudio, the time shall not go dully by us. I will in the interim undertake one of Hercules' labours; which is, to bring Signior Benedick and the Lady Beatrice into a mountain of affection the one with the other. I would fain have it a match; and I doubt not but to fashion it if you three will but minister such assistance as I shall give you direction.
*Leon.* My lord, I am for you, though it cost me ten nights' watchings.
*Claud.* And I, my lord.
*D. Pedro.* And you too, gentle Hero?
*Hero.* I will do any modest office, my lord, to help my cousin to a good husband.
*D. Pedro.* And Benedick is not the unhope-fullest husband that I know: thus far can I praise him; he is of a noble strain, of approved valour, and confirmed honesty. I will teach you how to humour your cousin that she shall fall in love with Benedick:—and I, with your two helps, will so practise on Benedick, that, in despite of his quick wit and his queasy stomach, he shall fall in love with Beatrice. If we can do this, Cupid is no longer an archer; his glory shall be ours, for we are the only love-gods. Go in with me, and I will tell you my drift.                                    [*Exeunt.*

SCENE II.—*Another Room in* LEONATO'S *House.*

*Enter* DON JOHN *and* BORACHIO.

*D. John.* It is so: the Count Claudio shall marry the daughter of Leonato.
*Bora.* Yea, my lord, but I can cross it.
*D. John.* Any bar, any cross, any impediment will be medicinal to me; I am sick in displeasure to him; and whatsoever comes athwart his affection ranges evenly with mine. How canst thou cross this marriage?
*Bora.* Not honestly, my lord; but so covertly that no dishonesty shall appear in me.
*D. John.* Show me briefly how.
*Bora.* I think I told your lordship a year since how much I am in the favour of Margaret, the waiting-gentlewoman to Hero.
*D. John.* I remember.
*Bora.* I can at any unseasonable instant of the night appoint her to look out at her lady's chamber-window.

*D. John.* What life is in that, to be the death of this marriage?
*Bora.* The poison of that lies in you to temper. Go you to the prince your brother; spare not to tell him that he hath wronged his honour in marrying the renowned Claudio—whose estimation do you mightily hold up—to a contaminated stale, such a one as Hero.
*D. John.* What proof shall I make of that?
*Bora.* Proof enough to misuse the prince, to vex Claudio, to undo Hero, and kill Leonato. Look you for any other issue?
*D. John.* Only to despite them I will endeavour anything.
*Bora.* Go, then; find me a meet hour to draw Don Pedro and the Count Claudio alone: tell them that you know that Hero loves me; intend a kind of zeal both to the prince and Claudio, as,—in love of your brother's honour, who hath made this match, and his friend's reputation, who is thus like to be cozened with the semblance of a maid,—that you have discovered thus. They will scarcely believe this without trial: offer them instances; which shall bear no less likelihood than to see me at her chamber-window; hear me call Margaret Hero; hear Margaret term me Borachio; and bring them to see this the very night before the intended wedding: for, in the meantime I will so fashion the matter that Hero shall be absent; and there shall appear such seeming truth of Hero's disloyalty that jealousy shall be called assurance, and all the preparation overthrown.
*D. John.* Grow this to what adverse issue it can, I will put it in practice. Be cunning in the working this, and thy fee is a thousand ducats.
*Bora.* Be you constant in the accusation, and my cunning shall not shame me.
*D. John.* I will presently go learn their day of marriage.                                    [*Exeunt.*

SCENE III.—LEONATO'S *Garden.*

*Enter* BENEDICK *and a* Boy.

*Bene.* Boy,—
*Boy.* Signior.
*Bene.* In my chamber-window lies a book; bring it hither to me in the orchard.
*Boy.* I am here already, sir.
*Bene.* I know that; but I would have thee hence and here again. [*Exit* Boy.] I do much wonder that one man, seeing how much another man is a fool when he dedicates his behaviours to love, will, after he hath laughed at such shallow follies in others, become the argument of his own scorn by falling in love. And such a man is Claudio. I have known when there was no music with him but the drum and fife; and now had he rather hear the tabor and the pipe: I have known when he would have walked ten mile afoot to see a good armour; and now will he lie ten nights awake carving the fashion of a new doublet. He was wont to speak plain and to the purpose, like an honest

man and a soldier; and now is he turned or-
thographer; his words are a very fantastical
banquet, just so many strange dishes. May I.
be so converted, and see with these eyes? I
cannot tell; I think not: I will not be sworn
but Love may transform me to an oyster; but
I'll take my oath on it, till he have made an
oyster of me he shall never make me such a
fool. One woman is fair; yet I am well: another
is wise; yet I am well: another virtuous; yet I
am well: but till all graces be in one woman,
one woman shall not come in my grace. Rich
she shall be, that's certain; wise, or I'll none;
virtuous, or I'll never cheapen her; fair, or I'll
never look on her; mild, or come not near me;
noble, or not I for an angel; of good discourse,
an excellent musician, and her hair shall be of
what colour it please God. Ha! the prince and
Monsieur Love! I will hide me in the arbour.
[*Withdraws.*

*Enter* DON PEDRO, LEONATO, *and* CLAUDIO.

*D. Pedro.* Come, shall we hear this music?
*Claud.* Yea, my good lord.—How still the eve-
ning is,
As hushed on purpose to grace harmony!
*D. Pedro.* See you where Benedick hath hid
himself?
*Claud.* O, very well, my lord: the music ended,
We'll fit the kid-fox with a pennyworth.

*Enter* BALTHAZAR, *with Music.*

*D. Pedro.* Come, Balthazar, we'll hear that
song again.
*Balth.* O, good my lord, tax not so bad a voice
To slander music any more than once.
*D. Pedro.* It is the witness still of excellency
To put a strange face on his own perfection:—
I pray thee, sing, and let me woo no more.
*Balth.* Because you talk of wooing, I will sing:
Since many a wooer doth commence his suit
To her he thinks not worthy; yet he woos;
Yet will he swear he loves.
*D. Pedro.*           Nay, pray thee, come:
Or, if thou wilt hold longer argument,
Do it in notes.
*Balth.*           Note this before my notes,
There's not a note of mine that's worth the
noting.                                   [he speaks;
*D. Pedro.* Why, these are very crotchets that
Note notes, forsooth, and noting!   [*Music.*
*Bene.* Now, divine air! now is his soul ravished!
Is it not strange that sheeps' guts should hale
souls out of men's bodies?—Well, a horn for
my money, when all's done.

BALTHAZAR *sings.*

I.

Sigh no more, ladies, sigh no more;
Men were deceivers ever;
One foot in sea and one on shore,
To one thing constant never;
Then sigh not so,
But let them go,

And be you blithe and bonny;
Converting all your sounds of woe
Into. Hey nonny, nonny.

II.

Sing no more ditties, sing no mo
Of dumps so dull and heavy;
The fraud of men was ever so
Since summer first was leavy.
Then sigh not so, &c.

*D. Pedro.* By my troth, a good song.
*Balth.* And an ill singer, my lord.
*Claud.* Ha, no; no, faith; thou singest well
enough for a shift.
*Bene.* [*Aside.*] An he had been a dog that
should have howled thus they would have
hanged him: and I pray God his bad voice
bode no mischief! I had as lief have heard the
night-raven, come what plague could have
come after it.
*D. Pedro.* Yea, marry [*to* CLAUDIO].—Dost
thou hear, Balthazar! I pray thee get us some
excellent music; for to-morrow night we would
have it at the lady Hero's chamber-window.
*Balth.* The best I can, my lord.
*D. Pedro.* Do so: farewell. [*Exeunt* BALTHAZAR
*and Music.*] Come hither, Leonato. What was
it you told me of to-day,—that your niece
Beatrice was in love with Signior Benedick?
*Claud.* O ay:—stalk on, stalk on; the fowl sits
[*aside to* PEDRO]. I did never think that lady
would have loved any man.
*Leon.* No, nor I neither; but most wonderful
that she should so dote on Signior Benedick,
whom she hath in all outward behaviours
seemed ever to abhor.
*Bene.* Is't possible? Sits the wind in that
corner?                                   [*Aside.*
*Leon.* By my troth, my lord, I cannot tell
what to think of it; but that she loves him with
an enraged affection,—it is past the infinite of
thought.
*D. Pedro.* May be she doth but counterfeit.
*Claud.* 'Faith, like enough.
*Leon.* O Good! counterfeit! There was never
counterfeit of passion came so near the life of
passion as she discovers it.
*D. Pedro.* Why, what effects of passion shows
she?
*Claud.* Bait the hook well; this fish will bite.
[*Aside.*
*Leon.* What effects, my lord! She will sit you,
—You heard my daughter tell you how.
*Claud.* She did, indeed.
*D. Pedro.* How, how, I pray you? You amaze
me: I would have thought her spirit had been
invincible against all assaults of affection.
*Leon.* I would have sworn it had, my lord; es-
pecially against Benedick.
*Bene.* [*Aside.*] I should think this a gull, but
that the white bearded fellow speaks it: knav-
ery cannot, sure, hide itself in such reverence.
*Claud.* He hath ta'en the infection; hold it up.
[*Aside.*

*D. Pedro.* Hath she made her affection known to Benedick.

*Leon.* No; and swears she never will: that's her torment.

*Claud.* 'Tis true, indeed; so your daughter says: *Shall I,* says she, *that have so oft encountered him with scorn, write to him that I love him?*

*Leon.* This says she now, when she is beginning to write to him: for she'll be up twenty times a night: and there will she sit in her smock till she have writ a sheet of paper:—my daughter tells us all.

*Claud.* Now you talk of a sheet of paper, I remember a pretty jest your daughter told us of.

*Leon.* O!—When she had writ it, and was reading it over, she found Benedick and Beatrice between the sheet?—

*Claud.* That.

*Leon.* O! she tore the letter into a thousand halfpence; railed at herself that she should be so immodest to write to one that she knew would flout her. *I measure him,* says she, *by my own spirit; for I should flout him if he writ to me; yea, though I love him, I should.*

*Claud.* Then down upon her knees she falls, weeps, sobs, beats her heart, tears her hair, prays, curses;—*O sweet Benedick! God give me patience!*

*Leon.* She doth indeed; my daughter says so; and the ecstasy hath so much overborne her that my daughter is sometime afraid she will do a desperate outrage to herself. It is very true.

*D. Pedro.* It were good that Benedick knew of it by some other, if she will not discover it.

*Claud.* To what end? He would but make a sport of it, and torment the poor lady worse.

*D. Pedro.* An he should, it were an alms to hang him. She's an excellent sweet lady; and, out of all suspicion, she is virtuous.

*Claud.* And she is exceeding wise.

*D. Pedro.* In everything but in loving Benedick.

*Leon.* O my lord, wisdom and blood combating in so tender a body, we have ten proofs to one that blood hath the victory. I am sorry for her, as I have just cause, being her uncle and her guardian.

*D. Pedro.* I would she had bestowed this dotage on me: I would have daffed all other respects and made her half myself. I pray you, tell Benedick of it, and hear what he will say.

*Leon.* Were it good, think you?

*Claud.* Hero thinks surely she will die; for she says she will die if he love her not; and she will die ere she makes her love known: and she will die if he woo her, rather than she will 'bate one breath of her accustomed crossness.

*D. Pedro.* She doth well; if she should make tender of her love, 'tis very possible he'll scorn it: for the man, as you know all, hath a contemptible spirit.

*Claud.* He is a very proper man.

*D. Pedro.* He hath, indeed, a good outward happiness.

*Claud.* 'Fore God, and in my mind, very wise.

*D. Pedro.* He doth, indeed, show some sparks that are like wit.

*Leon.* And I take him to be valiant.

*D. Pedro.* As Hector, I assure you: and in the managing of quarrels you may say he is wise; for either he avoids them with great discretion, or undertakes them with a most Christian-like fear.

*Leon.* If he do fear God, he must necessarily keep peace; if he break the peace, he ought to enter into a quarrel with fear and trembling.

*D. Pedro.* And so will he do; for the man doth fear God, howsoever it seems not in him by some large jests he will make. Well, I am sorry for your niece. Shall we go see Benedick, and tell him of her love?

*Claud.* Never tell him, my lord; let her wear it out with good counsel.

*Leon.* Nay, that's impossible; she may wear her heart out first.

*D. Pedro.* Well, we'll hear further of it by your daughter: let it cool the while. I love Benedick well: and I could wish he would modestly examine himself, to see how much he is unworthy to have so good a lady.

*Leon.* My lord, will you walk? dinner is ready.

*Claud.* If he do not dote on her upon this, I will never trust my expectation. [*Aside.*

*D. Pedro.* Let there be the same net spread for her: and that must your daughter and her gentlewoman carry. The sport will be when they hold one an opinion of another's dotage, and no such matter; that's the scene that I would see, which will be merely a dumb show. Let us send her to call him in to dinner. [*Aside.*

[*Exeunt* DON PEDRO, CLAUDIO, *and* LEONATO.

BENEDICK *advances from the arbour.*

*Bene.* This can be no trick. The conference was sadly borne.—They have the truth of this from Hero. They seem to pity the lady; it seems her affections have their full bent. Love me! why, it must be requited. I hear how I am censured: they say I will bear myself proudly if I perceive the love come from her; they say, too, that she will rather die than give any sign of affection.—I did never think to marry—I must not seem proud.—Happy are they that hear their detractions and can put them to mending. They say the lady is fair; 'tis a truth, I can bear them witness: and virtuous—'tis so, I cannot reprove it; and wise, but for loving me.—By my troth, it is no addition to her wit;—nor no great argument of her folly, for I will be horribly in love with her.—I may chance have some odd quirks and remnants of wit broken on me because I have railed so long against marriage; but doth not the appetite alter? A man loves the meat in his youth that he cannot endure in his age. Shall quips, and sentences, and these paper bullets of the brain awe a man from the career of his humour? No: the world must be peopled. When I said I would die a bachelor I did not think I should

live till I were married.—Here comes Beatrice.
By this day, she's a fair lady: I do spy some
marks of love in her.

### Enter BEATRICE.

*Beat.* Against my will I am sent to bid you
come in to dinner.                    [pains.
*Bene.* Fair Beatrice, I thank you for your
*Beat.* I took no more pains for those thanks
than you take pains to thank me; if it had
been painful I would not have come.
*Bene.* You take pleasure, then, in the message?
*Beat.* Yea, just so much as you may take upon
a knife's point, and choke a daw withal.—You
have no stomach, signior; fare you well. [*Exit.*
*Bene.* Ha! *Against my will I am sent to bid you
come to dinner*—there's a double meaning in
that. *I took no more pains for those thanks than
you took pains to thank me*—that's as much as
to say, Any pains that I take for you is as easy
as thanks.—If I do not take pity of her, I am
a villain; if I do not love her, I am a Jew: I
will go get her picture.              [*Exit.*

## ACT III.

### SCENE I.—LEONATO'S *Garden.*

#### Enter HERO, MARGARET, *and* URSULA.

*Hero.* Good Margaret, run thee into the parlour;
There shalt thou find my cousin Beatrice
Proposing with the prince and Claudio:
Whisper her ear, and tell her I and Ursula
Walk in the orchard, and our whole discourse
Is all of her; say that thou overheard'st us;
And bid her steal into the pleached bower,
Where honeysuckles, ripen'd by the sun,
Forbid the sun to enter;—like favourites,
Made proud by princes, that advance their pride
Against that power that bred it:—there will
          she hide her,
To listen our propose. This is thy office,
Bear thee well in it, and leave us alone.
*Marg.* I'll make her come, I warrant you,
presently.                            [*Exit.*
*Hero.* Now, Ursula, when Beatrice doth come
As we do trace this alley up and down,
Our talk must only be of Benedick:
When I do name him, let it be thy part
To praise him more than ever man did merit:
My talk to thee must be how Benedick
Is sick in love with Beatrice. Of this matter
Is little Cupid's crafty arrow made,
That only wounds by hearsay. Now begin;

#### Enter BEATRICE, *behind.*

For look where Beatrice, like a lapwing, runs
Close by the ground, to hear our conference.
*Urs.* The pleasant'st angling is to see the fish
Cut with her golden oars the silver stream,
And greedily devour the treacherous bait:
So angle we for Beatrice; who even now
Is couched in the woodbine coverture:
Fear you not my part of the dialogue.

*Hero.* Then go we near her, that her ear lose
          nothing.
Of the false sweet bait that we lay for it.—
                    [*They advance to the bower.*
No, truly, Ursula, she is too disdainful;
I know her spirits are as coy and wild
As haggards of the rock.
*Urs.*                   But are you sure
That Benedick loves Beatrice so entirely?
*Hero.* So says the prince and my new-trothed
lord.                                 [madam?
*Urs.* And did they bid you tell her of it,
*Hero.* They did entreat me to acquaint her
          of it;
But I persuaded them, if they lov'd Benedick,
To wish him wrestle with affection,
And never to let Beatrice know of it.    [man
*Urs.* Why did you so? Doth not the gentle-
Deserve as full, as fortunate a bed
As ever Beatrice shall couch upon?
*Hero.* O God of love! I know he doth deserve
As much as may be yielded to a man:
But nature never framed a woman's heart
Of prouder stuff than that of Beatrice:
Disdain and scorn ride sparkling in her eyes,
Misprizing what they look on; and her wit
Values itself so highly, that to her
All matter else seems weak: she cannot love,
Nor take no shape nor project of affection,
She is so self-endeared.
*Urs.*                   Sure, I think so;
And therefore, certainly, it were not good
She knew his love, lest she make sport at it.
*Hero.* Why, you speak truth: I never yet saw
          man,                        [tured,
How wise, how noble, young, how rarely fea-
But she would spell him backward: if fair-faced,
She'd swear the gentleman should be her sister;
If black, why, Nature, drawing of an antic,
Made a foul blot; if tall, a lance ill-headed;
If low, an agate very vilely cut:
If speaking, why, a vane blown with all winds;
If silent, why, a block moved with none.
So turns she every man the wrong side out;
And never gives to truth and virtue that
Which simpleness and merit purchaseth.
*Urs.* Sure, sure, such carping is not commend-
able.                                 [ions
*Hero.* No: not to be so odd and from all fash-
As Beatrice is, cannot be commendable:
But who dare tell her so? If I should speak,
She'd mock me into air; O, she would laugh me
Out of myself, press me to death with wit.
Therefore let Benedick, like covered fire,
Consume away in sighs, waste inwardly:
It were a better death than die with mocks;
Which is as bad as die with tickling.
*Urs.* Yet tell her of it; hear what she will say.
*Hero.* No; rather I will go to Benedick
And counsel him to fight against his passion:
And truly, I'll devise some honest slanders
To stain my cousin with. One doth not know
How much an ill word may empoison liking.
*Urs.* O, do not do your cousin such a wrong.

She cannot be so much without true judgment,—
Having so swift and excellent a wit
As she is priz'd to have,—as to refuse
So rare a gentleman as Signior Benedick.
*Hero.* He is the only man of Italy,
Always excepted my dear Claudio.
*Urs.* I pray you be not angry with me, madam,
Speaking my fancy; Signior Benedick,
For shape, for bearing, argument, and valour,
Goes foremost in report through Italy.
*Hero.* Indeed, he hath an excellent good name.
*Urs.* His excellence did earn it ere he had it.—
When are you married, madam?        [go in;
*Hero.* Why, every day;—to-morrow. Come,
I'll show thee some attires, and have thy counsel
Which is the best to furnish me to-morrow.
*Urs.* [*Aside.*] She's lim'd, I warrant you; we
        have caught her, madam.
*Hero.* If it prove so, then loving goes by haps:
Some Cupid kills with arrows, some with traps.
        [*Exeunt* HERO *and* URSULA.

BEATRICE *advances.*

*Beat.* What fire is in mine ears? Can this be
        true?        [much?
   Stand I condemn'd for pride, and scorn so
Contempt, farewell! and maiden pride, adieu!
No glory lives behind the back of such.
And, Benedick, love on; I will requite thee;
   Taming my wild heart to thy loving hand:
If thou dost love, my kindness shall incite thee
   To bind our loves up in a holy band:
For others say thou dost deserve, and I
Believe it better than reportingly.        [*Exit.*

SCENE II.—*A Room in* LEONATO'S *House.*

*Enter* DON PEDRO, CLAUDIO, BENEDICK, *and*
        LEONATO.

*D. Pedro.* I do but stay till your marriage be
consummate, and then I go toward Arragon.
*Claud.* I'll bring you thither, my lord, if you'll
vouchsafe me.
*D. Pedro.* Nay, that would be as great a soil
in the new gloss of your marriage as to show a
child his new coat, and forbid him to wear it.
I will only be bold with Benedick for his company; for, from the crown of his head to the
sole of his foot, he is all mirth; he hath twice
or thrice cut Cupid's bow-string, and the little
hangman dare not shoot at him: he hath a heart
as sound as a bell, and his tongue is the clapper;
for what his heart thinks his tongue speaks.
*Bene.* Gallans, I am not as I have been.
*Leon.* So say I; methinks you are sadder.
*Claud.* I hope he be in love.
*D. Pedro.* Hang him, truant; there's no true
drop of blood in him to be truly touched with
love: if he be sad he wants money.
*Bene.* I have the toothache.
*D. Pedro.* Draw it.
*Bene.* Hang it!
*Claud.* You must hang it first and draw it
afterwards.
*D. Pedro.* What, sigh for the toothache!

*Leon.* Where is but a humour or a worm!
*Bene.* Well, every one can master a grief but
he that has it.
*Claud.* Yet, say I, he is in love.
*D. Pedro.* There is no appearance of fancy in
him, unless it be a fancy that he hath to strange
disguises; as, to be a Dutchman to-day, a
Frenchman to-morrow, or in the shape of two
countries at once, as a German from the waist
downward, all slops, and a Spaniard from the
hip upward, no doublet. Unless he have a fancy
to this foolery, as it appears he hath, he is no
fool for fancy, as you would have it appear he is.
*Claud.* If he be not in love with some woman
there is no believing old signs: he brushes his
hat o'mornings: what should that bode?
*D. Pedro.* Hath any man seen him at the
barber's?
*Claud.* No, but the barber's man hath been
seen with him; and the old ornament of his
cheek hath already stuffed tennis-balls.
*Leon.* Indeed, he looks younger than he did,
by the loss of a beard.
*D. Pedro.* Nay, he rubs himself with civet.
Can you smell him out by that?
*Claud.* That's as much as to say the sweet
youth's in love.
*D. Pedro.* The greatest note of it is his mel-
ancholy.
*Claud.* And when was he wont to wash his face?
*D. Pedro.* Yea, or to paint himself? for the
which I hear what they say of him.
*Claud.* Nay, but his jesting spirit; which is
now crept into a lute-string, and now governed
by stops.
*D. Pedro.* Indeed, that tells a heavy tale for
him: conclude, conclude, he is in love.
*Claud.* Nay, but I know who loves him.
*D. Pedro.* That would I know too; I warrant
one that knows him not.
*Claud.* Yes, and his ill conditions; and, in de-
spite of all, dies for him.
*D. Pedro.* She shall be buried with her face
upwards.
*Bene.* Yet is this no charm for the toothache.
—Old signior, walk aside with me; I have
studied eight or nine wise words to speak to
you, which these hobby-horses must not hear.
        [*Exeunt* BENEDICK *and* LEONATO.
*D. Pedro.* For my life, to break with him about
Beatrice.
*Claud.* 'Tis even so: Hero and Margaret have
by this played their parts with Beatrice; and
then the two bears will not bite one another
when they meet.

*Enter* DON JOHN.

*D. John.* My lord and brother, God save you.
*D. Pedro.* Good den, brother.
*D. John.* If your leisure served, I would speak
with you.
*D. Pedro.* In private?
*D. John.* If it please you;—yet Count Claudio

may hear; for what I would speak of concerns him.

*D. Pedro.* What's the matter?

*D. John.* Means your lordship to be married to-morrow?  [*To* CLAUDIO.

*D. Pedro.* You know he does.

*D. John.* I know not that, when he knows what I know.

*Claud.* If there be any impediment, I pray you discover it.

*D. John.* You may think I love you not; let that appear hereafter, and aim better at me by that I now will manifest. For my brother, I think he holds you well, and in dearness of heart hath holp to effect your ensuing marriage; surely suit ill spent, and labour ill bestowed!

*D. Pedro.* Why, what's the matter?

*D. John.* I came hither to tell you: and, circumstances shortened,—for she hath been too long a-talking of,—the lady is disloyal.

*Claud.* Who? Hero?

*D. John.* Even she; Leonato's Hero, your Hero, every man's Hero.

*Claud.* Disloyal?

*D. John.* The word is too good to paint out her wickedness; I could say she were worse: think you of a worse title and I will fit her to it. Wonder not till further warrant: go but with me to-night, you shall see her chamber-window entered, even the night before her wedding-day: if you love her then, to-morrow wed her; but it would better fit your honour to change your mind.

*Claud.* May this be so?

*D. Pedro.* I will not think it.

*D. John.* If you dare not trust that you see, confess not that you know: if you will follow me I will show you enough; and when you have seen more, and heard more, proceed accordingly.

*Claud.* If I see anything to-night why I should not marry her to-morrow, in the congregation where I should wed, there will I shame her.

*D. Pedro.* And, as I wooed for thee to obtain her, I will join with thee to disgrace her.

*D. John.* I will disparage her no farther till you are my witnesses: bear it coldly but till midnight, and let the issue show itself.

*D. Pedro.* O day untowardly turned!

*Claud.* O mischief strangely thwarting!

*D. John.* O plague right well prevented!

So will you say when you have seen the sequel.

[*Exeunt.*

### SCENE III.—*A Street.*

*Enter* DOGBERRY *and* VERGES, *with the* Watch.

*Dogb.* Are you good men and true?

*Verg.* Yea, or else it were pity but they should suffer salvation, body and soul.

*Dogb.* Nay, that were a punishment too good for them, if they should have any allegiance in them, being chosen for the prince's watch.

*Verg.* Well, give them their charge, neighbour Dogberry.

*Dogb.* First, who think you the most desertless man to be constable?

*1 Watch.* Hugh Oatcake, sir, or George Seacoal; for they can write and read.

*Dogb.* Come hither, neighbour Seacoal: God hath blessed you with a good name: to be a well-favoured man is the gift of fortune: but to write and read comes by nature.

*2 Watch.* Both which, master constable,——

*Dogb.* You have; I knew it would be your answer. Well, for your favour, sir, why, give God thanks, and make no boast of it; and for your writing and reading, let that appear when there is no need of such vanity. You are thought here to be the most senseless and fit man for the constable of the watch; therefore bear you the lantern. This is your charge;—you shall comprehend all vagrom men; you are to bid any man stand, in the prince's name.

*2 Watch.* How if 'a will not stand?

*Dogb.* Why, then, take no note of him, but let him go; and presently call the rest of the watch together, and thank God you are rid of a knave.

*Verg.* If he will not stand when he is bidden, he is none of the prince's subjects.

*Dogb.* True, and they are to meddle with none but the prince's subjects.—You shall also make no noise in the streets; for for the watch to babble and talk is most tolerable and not to be endured.

*2 Watch.* We will rather sleep than talk; we know what belongs to a watch.

*Dogb.* Why, you speak like an ancient and most quiet watchman; for I cannot see how sleeping should offend: only, have a care that your bills be not stolen.—Well, you are to call at all the ale-houses, and bid them that are drunk get them to bed.

*2 Watch.* How if they will not?

*Dogb.* Why, then, let them alone till they are sober; if they make you not then the better answer, you may say they are not the men you took them for.

*2 Watch.* Well, sir.

*Dogb.* If you meet a thief, you may suspect him, by virtue of your office, to be no true man: and, for such kind of men, the less you meddle or make with them, why, the more is for your honesty.

*2 Watch.* If we know him to be a thief, shall we not lay hands on him?

*Dogb.* Truly, by your office you may; but I think they that touch pitch will be defiled: the most peaceable way for you, if you do take a thief, is to let him show himself what he is, and steal out of your company.

*Verg.* You have been always called a merciful man, partner.

*Dogb.* Truly, I would not hang a dog by my will; much more a man who hath any honesty in him.

*Verg.* If you hear a child cry in the night you must call to the nurse and bid her still it.

*2 Watch.* How if the nurse be asleep and will not hear us?

*Dogb.* Why, then, depart in peace, and let the child .wake her with crying: for the ewe that will not hear her lamb when it baas will never answer a calf when he bleats.

*Verg.* 'Tis very true.

*Dogb.* This is the end of the charge. You, constable, are to present the prince's own person; if you meet the prince in the night you may stay him.

*Verg.* Nay, by'r lady, that I think'a cannot.

*Dogb.* Five shillings to one on't, with any man that knows the statues, he may stay him: marry, not without the prince be willing: for, indeed, the watch ought to offend no man; and it is an offence to stay a man against his will.

*Verg.* By'r lady, I think it be so.

*Dogb.* Ha, ha, ha! Well, masters, good night: an there be any matter of weight chances, call up me: keep your fellows' counsels and your own, and good night.—Come, neighbour.

*2 Watch.* Well, masters, we hear our charge: let us go sit here upon the church-bench till two, and then all to bed.

*Dogb.* One word more, honest neighbours: I pray you, watch about Signior Leonato's door; for the wedding being there to-morrow, there is a great coil to-night. Adieu, be vigilant, I beseech you. [*Exeunt* DOGBERRY *and* VERGES.

*Enter* BORACHIO *and* CONRADE.

*Bora.* What, Conrade!—

*Watch.* Peace, stir not.          [*Aside.*

*Bora.* Conrade, I say!

*Con.* Here, man, I am at thy elbow.

*Bora.* Mass, and my elbow itched; I thought there would a scab follow.

*Con.* I will owe thee an answer for that; and now forward with thy tale.

*Bora.* Stand thee close then under this penthouse, for it drizzles rain; and I will, like a true drunkard, utter all to thee.

*Watch.* [*Aside.*] Some treason, masters; yet stand close.

*Bora.* Therefore know, I have earned of Don John a thousand ducats.          [so dear?

*Con.* Is it possible that any villany should be

*Bora.* Thou shouldst rather ask if it were possible any villany should be so rich; for when rich villains have need of poor ones, poor ones may make what price they will.

*Con.* I wonder at it.

*Bora.* That shows thou art unconfirmed. Thou knowest that the fashion of a doublet, or a hat, or a cloak is nothing to a man.

*Con.* Yes, it is apparel.

*Bora.* I mean the fashion.

*Con.* Yes, the fashion is the fashion.

*Bora.* Tush! I may as well say the fool's the fool. But seest thou not what a deformed thief this fashion is?

*Watch.* I know that Deformed; 'a has been a vile thief this seven year; 'a goes up and down like a gentleman: I remember his name.

*Bora.* Didst thou not hear somebody?

*Con.* No; 'twas the vane on the house.

*Bora.* Seest thou not, I say, what a deformed thief this fashion is? how giddily he turns about all the hot bloods between fourteen and five-and-thirty? sometimes fashioning them like Pharaoh's soldiers in the reechy painting; sometimes like god Bel's priests in the old church window; sometimes like the shaven Hercules in the smirched worm-eaten tapestry, where his cod-piece seems as massy as his club?

*Con.* All this I see; and see that the fashion wears out more apparel than the man. But art not thou thyself giddy with the fashion too, that thou hast shifted out of thy tale into telling me of the fashion?

*Bora.* Not so neither; but know that I have to-night wooed Margaret, the Lady Hero's gentlewoman, by the name of Hero; she leans me out at her mistress's chamber-window, bids me a thousand times good night,—I tell this tale vilely:—I should first tell thee, how the prince, Claudio, and my master, planted and placed and possessed by my master Don John, saw afar off in the orchard this amiable encounter.

*Con.* And thought they Margaret was Hero?

*Bora.* Two of them did, the prince and Claudio; but the devil my master knew she was Margaret; and partly by his oaths, which first possessed them, partly by the dark night, which did deceive them, but chiefly by my villany, which did confirm any slander that Don John had made, away went Claudio enraged; swore he would meet her, as he was appointed, next morning at the temple, and there, before the whole congregation, shame her with what he saw over-night, and send her home again without a husband.

*1 Watch.* We charge you in the prince's name, stand.

*2 Watch.* Call up the right master constable: we have here recovered the most dangerous piece of lechery that ever was known in the commonwealth.

*1 Watch.* And one Deformed is one of them; I know him, 'a wears a lock.

*Con.* Masters, masters!

*2 Watch.* You'll be made bring Deformed forth, I warrant you.

*Con.* Masters,—

*1 Watch.* Never speak; we charge you, let us obey you to go with us.

*Bora.* We are like to prove a goodly commodity, being taken up of these men's bills.

*Con.* A commodity in question, I warrant you. Come, we'll obey you.          [*Exeunt.*

SCENE IV.—*A Room in* LEONATO'S *House.*

*Enter* HERO, MARGARET, *and* URSULA.

*Hero.* Good Ursula, wake my cousin Beatrice, and desire her to rise.

*Urs.* I will, lady.
*Hero.* And bid her come hither.
*Urs.* Well.                                [*Exit* URSULA.
*Marg.* Troth, I think your other rabato were better.
*Hero.* No, pray thee, good Meg, I'll wear this.
*Marg.* By my troth, it's not so good; and I warrant your cousin will say so.
*Hero.* My cousin's a fool, and thou art another; I'll wear none but this.
*Marg.* I like the new tire within excellently, if the hair were a thought browner: and your gown's a most rare fashion, i' faith. I saw the Duchess of Milan's gown that they praise so.
*Hero.* O, that exceeds, they say.
*Marg.* By my troth, it's but a night-gown in respect of yours. Cloth of gold, and cuts, and laced with silver; set with pearls, down-sleeves, side-sleeves, and skirts round, underborne with a blueish tinsel: but for a fine, quaint, graceful, and excellent fashion, yours is worth ten on't.
*Hero.* God give me joy to wear it, for my heart is exceeding heavy!
*Marg.* 'Twill be heavier soon, by the weight of a man.
*Hero.* Fie upon thee! art not ashamed?
*Marg.* Of what, lady? of speaking honourably? Is not marriage honourable in a beggar? Is not your lord honourable without marriage? I think, you would have me say, saving your reverence,—*a husband:* an bad thinking do not wrest true speaking I'll offend nobody. Is there any harm in—*the heavier for a husband?* None, I think, an it be the right husband and the right wife; otherwise 'tis light, and not heavy. Ask my Lady Beatrice else,—here she comes.

*Enter* BEATRICE.

*Hero.* Good morrow, coz.
*Beat.* Good morrow, sweet Hero.
*Hero.* Why, how now! do you speak in the sick tune?
*Beat.* I am out of all other tune, methinks.
*Marg.* Clap's into *Light o' love;* that goes without a burden: do you sing it and I'll dance it.
*Beat.* Yea, *Light o' love,* with your heels!— then if your husband have stables enough you'll see he shall lack no barns.
*Marg.* O illegitimate construction! I scorn that with my heels.
*Beat.* 'Tis almost five o'clock, cousin; 'tis time you were ready. By my troth, I am exceeding ill:—hey-ho!
*Marg.* For a hawk, a horse, or a husband?
*Beat.* For the letter that begins them all, H.
*Marg.* Well, an you be not turned Turk, there's no more sailing by the star.
*Beat.* What means the fool, trow?
*Marg.* Nothing I; but God send every one their heart's desire!
*Hero.* These gloves the count sent me; they are an excellent perfume.
*Beat.* I am stuffed, cousin, I cannot smell.

*Marg.* A maid and stuffed; there's goodly catching of cold.
*Beat.* O, God help me! God help me! how long have you professed apprehension?
*Marg.* Ever since you left it:—doth not my wit become me rarely?
*Beat.* It is not seen enough; you should wear it in your cap.—By my troth, I am sick.
*Marg.* Get you some of this distilled Carduus Benedictus and lay it to your heart; it is the only thing for a qualm.
*Hero.* There thou prick'st her with a thistle.
*Beat.* Benedictus! why Benedictus? you have some moral in this Benedictus.
*Marg.* Moral? no, by my troth, I have no moral meaning; I meant plain holy-thistle. You may think, perchance, that I think you are in love: nay, by'r lady, I am not such a fool to think what I list; nor I list not to think what I can; nor, indeed, I cannot think, if I would think my heart out of thinking, that you are in love, or that you will be in love, or that you can be in love: yet Benedick was such another, and now is he become a man: he swore he would never marry; and yet now, in despite of his heart, he eats his meat without grudging: and how you may be converted I know not; but methinks you look with your eyes as other women do.
*Beat.* What pace is this that thy tongue keeps?
*Marg.* Not a false gallop.

*Re-enter* URSULA.

*Urs.* Madam, withdraw; the prince, the count, Signior Benedick, Don John, and all the gallants of the town are come to fetch you to church.
*Hero.* Help to dress me, good coz, good Meg, good Ursula.                        [*Exeunt.*

SCENE V.—*Another Room in* LEONATO'S *House.*

*Enter* LEONATO, *with* DOGBERRY *and* VERGES.

*Leon.* What would you with me, honest neighbour?
*Dogb.* Marry, sir, I would have some confidence with you that decerns you nearly.
*Leon.* Brief, I pray you; for you see 'tis a busy time with me.
*Dogb.* Marry, this it is, sir.
*Verg.* Yes, in truth it is, sir.
*Leon.* What is it, my good friends?
*Dogb.* Goodman Verges, sir, speaks a little off the matter: an old man, sir, and his wits are not so blunt as, God help, I would desire they were; but, in faith, honest as the skin between his brows.
*Verg.* Yes, I thank God I am as honest as any man living that is an old man and no honester than I.
*Dogb.* Comparisons are odorous: *palabras,* neighbour Verges.
*Leon.* Neighbours, you are tedious.
*Dogb.* It pleases your worship to say so, but

we are the poor duke's officers: but, truly, for mine own part, if I were as tedious as a king, I could find in my heart to bestow it all of your worship.

*Leon.* All thy tediousness on me! ha!

*Dogb.* Yea, and 'twere a thousand t imes more than 'tis: for I hear as good exclamation on your worship as of any man in the city; and though I be put a poor man, I am glad to hear it.

*Verg.* And so am I.

*Leon.* I would fain know what you have to say.

*Verg.* Marry, sir, our watch to-night, excepting your worship's presence, have ta'en a couple of as arrant knaves as any in Messina.

*Dogb.* A good old man, sir; he will be talking; as they say, When the age is in the wit is out; God help us! it is a world to see!—Well said, i' faith, neighbour Verges:—well, God's a good man; an two men ride of a horse, one must ride behind.—An honest soul, i' faith, sir; by my troth he is, as ever broke bread: but God is to be worshipped. All men are not alike,—alas, good neighbour! [you.

*Leon.* Indeed, neighbour, he comes too short of

*Dogb.* Gifts that God gives.

*Leon.* I must leave you.

*Dogb.* One word, sir: our watch, sir, have indeed comprehended two auspicious persons, and we would have them this morning examined before your worship.

*Leon.* Take their examination yourself, and bring it me; I am now in great haste, as it may appear unto you.

*Dogb.* It shall be suffigance. [well.

*Leon.* Drink some wine ere you go: fare you

*Enter a* Messenger.

*Mess.* My lord, they stay for you to give your daughter to her husband.

*Leon.* I will wait upon them; I am ready.
　　　　　　　[*Exeunt* LEON. *and* Messenger.

*Dogb.* Go, good partner, go, get you to Francis Seacoal; bid him bring his pen and inkhorn to the gaol: we are now to examination these men.

*Verg.* And we must do it wisely.

*Dogb.* We will spare for no wit, I warrant you; here's that [*touching his forehead*] shall drive some of them to a *non com:* only get the learned writer to set down our excommunication, and meet me at the gaol. [*Exeunt.*

ACT IV.

SCENE I.—*The inside of a Church.*

*Enter* DON PEDRO, DON JOHN, LEONATO, FRIAR, CLAUDIO, BENEDICK, HERO, *and* BEATRICE, *&c.*

*Leon.* Come, Friar Francis, be brief; only to the plain form of marriage, and you shall recount their particular duties afterwards.

*Friar.* You come hither, my lord, to marry this lady?

*Claud.* No. [marry her.

*Leon.* To be married to her, friar; you come to

*Friar.* Lady, you come hither to be married to this count?

*Hero.* I do.

*Friar.* If either of you know any inward impediment why you should not be conjoined I charge you, on your souls, to utter it.

*Claud.* Know you any, Hero?

*Hero.* None, my lord.

*Friar.* Know you any, count?

*Leon.* I dare make his answer, none.

*Claud.* O, what men dare do! what men may do! what men daily do! not knowing what they do!

*Bene.* How now! Interjections? Why, then, some be of laughing, as, ha! ha! he!

*Claud.* Stand thee by, friar:—Father, by your leave;

Will you with free and unconstrained soul Give me this maid, your daughter?

*Leon.* As freely, son, as God did give her me.

*Claud.* And what have I to give you back, whose worth

May counterpoise this rich and precious gift?

*D. Pedro.* Nothing, unless you render her again.

*Claud.* Sweet prince, you learn me noble thankfulness.—

There, Leonato, take her back again;

Give not this rotten orange to your friend;

She's but the sign and semblance of her honour.—

Behold, how like a maid she blushes here!

O, what authority and show of truth

Can cunning sin cover itself withal!

Comes not that blood as modest evidence

To witness simple virtue? Would you not swear,

All you that see her, that she were a maid,

By these exterior shows? But she is none:

She knows the heat of a luxurious bed:

Her blush is guiltiness, not modesty.

*Leon.* What do you mean, my lord?

*Claud.* 　　　　　　　Not to be married,

Not to knit my soul to an approved wanton.

*Leon.* Dear, my lord, if you, in your own proof,

Have vanquish'd the resistance of her youth,

And made defeat of her virginity,——

*Claud.* I know what you would say: if I have known her,

You'll say, she did embrace me as a husband,

And so extenuate the 'forehand sin:

No, Leonato,

I never tempted her with word too large;

But, as a brother to his sister, show'd

Bashful sincerity and comely love.

*Hero.* And seem'd I ever otherwise to you?

*Claud.* Out on thy seeming! I will write against it:

You seem to me as Dian in her orb;

As chaste as is the bud ere it be blown;

But you are more intemperate in your blood

Than Venus, or those pamper'd animals

That rage in savage sensuality. [wide?

*Hero.* Is my lord well, that he doth speak so

*Claud.* Sweet prince, why speak not you?

*D. Pedro.* 　　　　　What should I speak?

I stand dishonour'd, that have gone about
To link my dear friend to a common stale.

*Leon.* Are these things spoken? or do I but
dream?

*D. John.* Sir, they are spoken, and these things
are true.

*Bene.* This looks not like a nuptial.

*Hero.* True!—O God!

*Claud.* Leonato, stand I here?
Is this the prince? Is this the prince's brother?
Is this face Hero's? Are our eyes our own?

*Leon.* All this is so; but what of this, my lord?

*Claud.* Let me but move one question to your
daughter;
And, by that fatherly and kindly power
That you have in her, bid her answer truly.

*Leon.* I charge thee do so, as thou art my child.

*Hero.* O God defend me! how am I beset!—
What kind of catechising call you this?

*Claud.* To make you answer truly to your
name.

*Hero.* Is it not Hero? Who can blot that name
With any just reproach?

*Claud.* Marry, that can Hero;
Hero itself can blot out Hero's virtue.
What man was he talk'd with you yesternight
Out at your window, betwixt twelve and one?
Now, if you are a maid, answer to this.

*Hero.* I talk'd with no man at that hour, my
lord.  [Leonato,

*D. Pedro.* Why, then are you no maiden.—
I am sorry you must hear: upon mine honour,
Myself, my brother, and this grieved count,
Did see her, hear her, at that hour last night,
Talk with a ruffian at her chamber-window;
Who hath, indeed, most like a liberal villain,
Confess'd the vile encounters they have had
A thousand times in secret.

*D. John.* Fie, fie! they are
Not to be named, my lord, not to be spoke of;
There is not chastity enough in language,
Without offence, to utter them. Thus, pretty
lady,
I am sorry for thy much misgovernment.

*Claud.* O Hero! what a Hero hadst thou been
If half thy outward graces had been placed
About thy thoughts and counsels of thy heart!
But fare thee well, most foul, most fair! fare-
well,
Thou pure impiety and impious purity!
For thee I'll lock up all the gates of love,
And on my eyelids shall conjecture hang,
To turn all beauty into thoughts of harm,
And never shall it more be gracious.

*Leon.* Hath no man's dagger here a point for
me?  [HERO *swoons.*

*Beat.* Why, how now, cousin? wherefore sink
you down?

*D. John.* Come, let us go: these things, come
thus to light,
Smother her spirits up.
[*Exeunt D.* PEDRO, *D.* JOHN, *and* CLAUD.

*Bene.* How doth the lady?

*Beat.*  Dead, I think;—help, uncle;—

Hero! why, Hero!—Uncle!—Signior Benedick!
—friar!

*Leon.* O fate, take not away thy heavy hand!
Death is the fairest cover for her shame
That may be wish'd for.

*Beat.*  How now, cousin Hero?

*Friar.* Have comfort, lady.

*Leon.*  Dost thou look up?

*Friar.* Yea; wherefore should she not?

*Leon.* Wherefore! Why, doth not every earthly
thing
Cry shame upon her? Could she here deny
The story that is printed in her blood?—
Do not live, Hero; do not ope thine eyes:
For did I think thou wouldst not quickly die,
Thought I thy spirits were stronger than thy
shames,
Myself would, on the rearward of reproaches,
Strike at thy life. Griev'd I I had but one?
Chid I for that at frugal nature's frame?
O, one too much by thee! Why had I one?
Why ever wast thou lovely in my eyes?
Why had I not, with charitable hand,
Took up a beggar's issue at my gates;
Who, smirched thus and mir'd with infamy,
I might have said, *No part of it is mine;*
*This shame derives itself from unknown loins?*
But mine, and mine I lov'd, and mine I prais'd,
And mine that I was proud on; mine so much
That I myself was to myself not mine,
Valuing of her; why, she—O, she is fallen
Into a pit of ink, that the wide sea
Hath drops too few to wash her clean again,
And salt too little, which may season give
To her foul tainted flesh!

*Bene.*  Sir, sir, be patient:
For my part, I am so attir'd in wonder
I know not what to say.

*Beat.* O, on my soul, my cousin is belied!

*Bene.* Lady, were you her bedfellow last night?

*Beat.* No, truly not: although, until last night
I have this twelvemonth been her bedfellow.

*Leon.* Confirm'd, confirm'd! O, that is stronger
made
Which was before barr'd up with ribs of iron!
Would the two princes lie? and Claudio lie,
Who lov'd her so that, speaking of her foulness,
Wash'd it with tears? Hence from her! let her
die.

*Friar.* Hear me a little;
For I have only been silent so long,
And given way unto this course of fortune,
By nothing of the lady: I have mark'd
A thousand blushing apparitions start
Into her face; a thousand innocent shames
In angel whiteness bear away those blushes;
And in her eye there hath appear'd a fire
To burn the errors that these princes hold
Against her maiden truth. Call me a fool;
Trust not my reading, nor my observation,
Which with experimental seal doth warrant
The tenor of my book; trust not my age,
My reverence, calling, nor divinity,
If this sweet lady lie not guiltless here

Under some biting error.
*Leon.*                    Friar, it cannot be:
Thou seest that all the grace that she hath left
Is that she will not add to her damnation
A sin of perjury; she not denies it:
Why seek'st thou then to cover with excuse
That which appears in proper nakedness?
*Friar.* Lady, what man is he you are accused of?
*Hero.* They know that do accuse me; I know
            none:
If I know more of any man alive
Than that which maiden modesty doth warrant,
Let all my sins lack mercy!—O my father,
Prove you that any man with me convers'd
At hours unmeet, or that I yesternight
Maintained the change of words with any
            creature,
Refuse me, hate me, torture me to death!
*Friar.* There is some strange misprison in the
            princes.                                [our;
*Bene.* Two of them have the very bent of hon-
And if their wisdoms be misled in this,
The practice of it lives in John the bastard,
Whose spirits toil in frame of villanies.
*Leon.* I know not. If they speak but truth of
            her,                                    [honour,
These hands shall tear her; if they wrong her
The proudest of them shall well hear of it.
Time hath not yet so dried this blood of mine,
Nor age so eat up my invention,
Nor fortune made such havoc of my means,
Nor my bad life reft me so much of friends,
But they shall find, awak'd in such a kind,
Both strength of limb and policy of mind,
Ability in means and choice of friends,
To quit me of them throughly.
*Friar.*                    Pause awhile,
And let my counsel sway you in this case.
Your daughter here the princes left for dead;
Let her awhile be secretly kept in,
And publish it that she is dead indeed:
Maintain a mourning ostentation,
And on your family's old monument
Hang mournful epitaphs, and do all rites
That appertain unto a burial.
*Leon.* What shall become of this? What will
            this do?                                [behalf
*Friar.* Marry, this, well carried, shall on her
Change slander to remorse; that is some good;
But not for that dream I on this strange course,
But on this travail look for greater birth.
She dying, as it must be so maintain'd,
Upon the instant that she was accus'd,
Shall be lamented, pitied, and excus'd
Of every hearer: for it so falls out
That what we have we prize not to the worth
Whiles we enjoy it; but being lack'd and lost,
Why, then we rack the value; then we find
The virtue that possession would not show us
Whiles it was ours. So will it fare with Claudio:
When he shall hear she died upon his words,
The idea of her life shall sweetly creep
Into his study of imagination;
And every lovely organ of her life

Shall come apparell'd in more precious habit,
More moving delicate, and full of life,
Into the eye and prospect of his soul,
Than when she liv'd indeed:—then shall he
            mourn,—
If ever love had interest in his liver,—
And wish he had not so accused her;
No, though he thought his accusation true.
Let this be so, and doubt not but success
Will fashion the event in better shape
Than I can lay it down in likelihood.
But if all aim but this be levell'd false,
The supposition of the lady's death
Will quench the wonder of her infamy:
And, if it sort not well, you may conceal her,—
As best befits her wounded reputation,—
In some reclusive and religious life,
Out of all eyes, tongues, minds, and injuries.
*Bene.* Signior Leonato, let the friar advise you;
And though you know my inwardness and love
Is very much unto the prince and Claudio,
Yet, by mine honour, I will deal in this
As secretly and justly as your soul
Should with your body.
*Leon.*                    Being that I flow in grief
The smallest twine may lead me.
*Friar.* 'Tis well consented; presently away;
    For to strange sores strangely they strain the
            cure.—
Come, lady, die to live: this wedding-day
    Perhaps is but prolonged; have patience, and
            endure.
                    [*Exeunt* FRIAR, HERO, *and* LEON.
*Bene.* Lady Beatrice, have you wept all this
            while?
*Beat.* Yea, and I will weep a while longer.
*Bene.* I will not desire that.
*Beat.* You have no reason; I do it freely.
*Bene.* Surely, I do believe your fair cousin is
            wrong'd.
*Beat.* Ah, how much might the man deserve of
me that would right her!
*Bene.* Is there any way to show such friendship?
*Beat.* A very even way, but no such friend.
*Bene.* May a man do it?
*Beat.* It is a man's office, but not yours.
*Bene.* I do love nothing in the world so well as
you. Is not that strange?
*Beat.* As strange as the thing I know not. It
were as possible for me to say I loved nothing
so well as you: but believe me not; and yet I
lie not; I confess nothing, nor I deny nothing —
I am sorry for my cousin.
*Bene.* By my sword, Beatrice, thou lovest me.
*Beat.* Do not swear by it and eat it.
*Bene.* I will swear by it that you love me; and
I will make him eat it that says I love you not.
*Beat.* Will you not eat your word?
*Bene.* With no sauce that can be devised to it:
I protest I love thee.
*Beat.* Why, then, God forgive me!
*Bene.* What offence, sweet Beatrice?
*Beat.* You have stayed me in a happy hour: I
was about to protest I loved you.

*Bene.* And do it with all thy heart?

*Beat.* I love you with so much of my heart that none is left to protest.

*Bene.* Come, bid me do anything for thee.

*Beat.* Kill Claudio.

*Bene.* Ha! not for the wide world.

*Beat.* You kill me to deny it. Farewell.

*Bene.* Tarry, sweet Beatrice.

*Beat.* I am gone though I am here;—there is no love in you:—nay, I pray you, let me go.

*Bene.* Beatrice,—

*Beat.* In faith, I will go

*Bene.* We'll be friends first.

*Beat.* You dare easier be friends with me than fight with mine enemy.

*Bene.* Is Claudio thine enemy?

*Beat.* Is he not approved in the height of a villain that hath slandered, scorned, dishonoured my kinswoman?—O that I were a man!—What! bear her in hand until they come to take hands, and then with public accusation, uncovered slander, unmitigated rancour,—O God, that I were a man! I would eat his heart in the market-place!

*Bene.* Hear me, Beatrice;—

*Beat.* Talk with a man out at a window!—a proper saying!

*Bene.* Nay but, Beatrice;—

*Beat.* Sweet Hero!—she is wronged, she is slandered, she is undone.

*Bene.* Beat—

*Beat.* Princes and counties! Surely, a princely testimony, a goodly count-confect; a sweet gallant, surely! O that I were a man for his sake! or that I had any friend would be a man for my sake! But manhood is melted into courtesies, valour into compliment, and men are only turned into tongue, and trim ones too: he is now as valiant as Hercules that only tells a lie and swears it.—I cannot be a man with wishing, therefore I will die a woman with grieving.　　　　　　　　　　[love thee.

*Bene.* Tarry, good Beatrice. By this hand, I

*Beat.* Use it for my love some other way than swearing by it.

*Bene.* Think you in your soul the Count Claudio hath wronged Hero?　　　　[soul.

*Beat.* Yea, as sure as I have a thought or a

*Bene.* Enough, I am engaged; I will challenge him; I will kiss your hand and so leave you. By this hand, Claudio shall render me a dear account. As you hear of me, so think of me. Go, comfort your cousin; I must say she is dead; and so, farewell.　　　　　　[*Exeunt.*

### SCENE II.—*A Prison.*

*Enter* DOGBERRY, VERGES, *and* SEXTON, *in gowns; and the* Watch, *with* CONRADE *and* BORACHIO.

*Dogb.* Is our whole dissembly appeared?

*Verg.* O, a stool and a cushion for the sexton!

*Sexton.* Which be the malefactors?

*Dogb.* Marry, that am I and my partner.

*Verg.* Nay, that's certain; we have the exhibition to examine.

*Sexton.* But which are the offenders that are to be examined? let them come before master constable.

*Dogb.* Yea, marry, let them come before me.—What is your name, friend?

*Bora.* Borachio.

*Dogb.* Pray write down—Borachio.——Yours, sirrah?　　　　　　　　　　　　[Conrade.

*Con.* I am a gentleman, sir, and my name is

*Dogb.* Write down—master gentleman Conrade.—Masters, do you serve God?

*Con.* ⎱ Yea, sir, we hope.
*Bora.* ⎰

*Dogb.* Write down—that they hope they serve God:—and write God first; for God defend but God should go before such villains!—Masters, it is proved already that you are little better than false knaves; and it will go near to be thought so shortly. How answer you for yourselves?

*Con.* Marry, sir, we say we are none.

*Dogb.* A marvellous witty fellow, I assure you; but I will go about with him.—Come you hither, sirrah: a word in your ear, sir; I say to you, it is thought you are false knaves.

*Bora.* Sir, I say to you, we are none.

*Dogb.* Well, stand aside.—'Fore God, they are both in a tale. Have you writ down—that they are none?

*Sexton.* Master constable, you go not the way to examine; you must call forth the Watch that are their accusers.

*Dogb.* Yea, marry, that's the eftest way.—Let the Watch come forth.—Masters, I charge you in the prince's name, accuse these men.

*1 Watch.* This man said, sir, that Don John, the prince's brother, was a villain.

*Dogb.* Write down—Prince John a villain.—Why, this is flat perjury, to call a prince's brother villain.

*Bora.* Master constable,—

*Dogb.* Pray thee, fellow, peace; I do not like thy look, I promise thee.

*Sexton.* What heard you him say else?

*2 Watch.* Marry, that he had received a thousand ducats off Don John for accusing the Lady Hero wrongfully.

*Dogb.* Flat burglary as ever was committed.

*Verg.* Yea, by the mass, that it is.

*Sexton.* What else, fellow?

*1 Watch.* And that Count Claudio did mean, upon his words, to disgrace Hero before the whole assembly, and not marry her.

*Dogb.* O villain! thou wilt be condemned into everlasting redemption for this.

*Sexton.* What else?

*2 Watch.* This is all.

*Sexton.* And this is more, masters, than you can deny. Prince John is this morning secretly stolen away; Hero was in this manner accused, in this very manner refused, and upon the grief of this suddenly died.—Master constable, let

these men be bound and brought to Leonato's;
I will go before and show him their examina-
tion.                             [*Exit.*
*Dogb.* Come, let them be opinioned.
*Verg.* Let them be in band.
*Con.* Off, coxcomb!
*Dogb.* God's my life! where's the sexton? let
him write down—the prince's officer, coxcomb.
—Come, bind them.——Thou naughty varlet!
*Con.* Away! you are an ass, you are an ass.
*Dogb.* Dost thou not suspect my place? Dost
thou not-suspect my years?—O that he were
here to write me down an ass! but, masters,
remember, that I am an ass; though it be not
written down, yet forget not that I am an ass.
—No, thou villain, thou art full of piety, as
shall be proved upon thee by good witness, I
am a wise fellow; and, which is more, an officer;
and, which is more, a householder; and, which
is more, as pretty a piece of flesh as any is in
Messina: and one that knows the law, go to;
and a rich fellow enough, go to; and a fellow
that hath had losses; and one that hath two
gowns, and everything handsome about him.—
Bring him away. O that I had been writ down
an ass!                          [*Exeunt.*

## ACT V.

### Scene I.—*Before* Leonato's *House.*

#### *Enter* Leonato *and* Antonio.

*Ant.* If you go on thus you will kill yourself;
And 'tis not wisdom thus to second grief
Against yourself.
*Leon.*           I pray thee, cease thy counsel,
Which falls into mine ears as profitless
As water in a sieve: give not me counsel;
Nor let no comforter delight mine ear
But such a one whose wrongs do suit with mine.
Bring me a father that so lov'd his child,
Whose joy of her is overwhelm'd like mine,
And bid him speak of patience;         [mine,
Measure his woe the length and breadth· of
And let it answer every strain for strain;
As thus for thus, and such a grief for such,
In every lineament, branch, shape, and form:
If such a one will smile, and stroke his beard,
Cry—sorrow, wag! and hem when he should
         groan,                   [drunk
Patch grief with proverbs, make misfortune
With candle-wasters,—bring him yet to me,
And I of him will gather patience.
But there is no such man: for, brother, men
Can counsel and speak comfort to that grief
Which they themselves not feel; but, tasting it,
Their counsel turns to passion, which before
Would give preceptial medicine to rage,
Fetter strong madness in a silken thread,
Charm ache with air and agony with words:
No, no; 'tis all men's office to speak patience
To those that wring under the load of sorrow;
But no man's virtue nor sufficiency
To be so moral when he shall endure
The like himself: therefore, give me no counsel:

My griefs cry louder than advertisement.
*Ant.* Therein do men from children nothing
       differ.                         [blood;
*Leon.* I pray thee, peace; I will be flesh and
For there was never yet philosopher
That could endure the toothache patiently,
However they have writ the style of gods,
And make a pish at chance and sufferance.
*Ant.* Yet bend not all the harm upon yourself;
Make those that do offend you suffer too.
*Leon.* There thou speak'st reason: nay, I will
       do so.
My soul doth tell me Hero is belied;
And that shall Claudio know; so shall the
       prince,
And all of them that thus dishonour her.
*Ant.* Here comes the prince and Claudio hastily

#### *Enter* Don Pedro *and* Claudio.

*D. Pedro.* Good den, good den.
*Claud.*           Good day to both of you.
*Leon.* Hear you, my lords,—
*D. Pedro.*       We have some haste, Leonato.
*Leon.* Some haste, my lord!—well, fare you
       well, my lord:—
Are you so hasty now?—well, all is one.
*D. Pedro.* Nay, do not quarrel with us, good
       old man.
*Ant.* If he could right himself with quarrelling,
Some of us would lie low.
*Claud.*            Who wrongs him?
*Leon.* Marry, thou dost wrong me: thou dis-
       sembler, thou:—
Nay, never lay thy hand upon thy sword—
I fear thee not.
*Claud.*          Marry, beshrew my hand
If it should give your age such cause of fear:
In faith, my hand meant nothing to my sword.
*Leon.* Tush, tush, man; never fleer and jest at
       me;
I speak not like a dotard nor a fool;
As, under privilege of age, to brag       [do
What I have done being young, or what would
Were I not old. Know, Claudio, to thy head,
Thou hast so wrong'd mine innocent child and
       me
That I am forc'd to lay my reverence by,
And with gray hairs and bruise of many days,
Do challenge thee to trial of a man.
I say thou hast belied mine innocent child;
Thy slander hath gone through and through
       her heart,
And she lies buried with her ancestors,—
O! in a tomb where never scandal slept,
Save this of hers, fram'd by thy villany.
*Claud.* My villany!
*Leon.*          Thine, Claudio; thine, I say.
*D. Pedro.* You say not right, old man.
*Leon.*           My lord, my lord,
I'll prove it on his body if he dare,
Despite his nice fence and his active practice,
His May of youth and bloom of lustihood.
*Claud.* Away! I will not have to do with you.

*Leon.* Canst thou so daff me? Thou hast kill'd
      my child;
If thou kill'st me, boy, thou shalt kill a man.
*Ant.* He shall kill two of us, and men indeed;
But that's no matter; let him kill one first;—
Win me and wear me,—let him answer me.—
Come, follow me, boy; come, boy, follow me:
Sir boy, I'll whip you from your foining fence;
Nay, as I am a gentleman, I will.
*Leon.* Brother,—                    [niece;
*Ant.* Content yourself. God knows I lov'd my
And she is dead, slander'd to death by villains,
That dare as well answer a man, indeed,
As I dare take a serpent by the tongue:
Boys, apes, braggarts, Jacks, milksops!—
*Leon.*                    Brother Anthony,—
*Ant.* Hold you content. What, man! I know
      them, yea,                    [scruple,—
And what they weigh, even to the utmost
Scambling, out-facing, fashion-mong'ring boys,
That lie, and cog, and flout, deprave and slander,
Go anticly, and show outward hideousness,
And speak off half a dozen dangerous words,
How they might hurt their enemies, if they
      durst;
And this is all.
*Leon.* But, brother Anthony,—
*Ant.*                    Come, 'tis no matter;
Do not you meddle, let me deal in this.
*D. Pedro.* Gentlemen both, we will not wake
      your patience.
My heart is sorry for your daughter's death;
But, on my honour, she was charg'd with nothing
But what was true, and very full of proof.
*Leon.* My lord, my lord,—
*D. Pedro.*                    I will not hear you.
*Leon.*                                        No?
Come, brother, away.—I will be heard;—
*Ant.*                              And shall,
Or some of us will smart for it.
                    [*Exeunt* LEON. *and* ANT.
*D. Pedro.* See, see; here comes the man we
went to seek.

                    *Enter* BENEDICK.

*Claud.* Now, signior! what news?
*Bene.* Good day, my lord.
*D. Pedro.* Welcome, signior: you are almost
come to part almost a fray.
*Claud.* We had like to have had our two noses
snapped off with two old men without teeth.
*D. Pedro.* Leonato and his brother. What
think'st thou? Had we fought, I doubt we
should have been too young for them.
*Bene.* In a false quarrel there is no true valour.
I came to seek you both.
*Claud.* We have been up and down to seek
thee; for we are high proof melancholy, and
would fain have it beaten away. Wilt thou use
thy wit?
*Bene.* It is in my scabbard: shall I draw it?
*D. Pedro.* Dost thou wear thy wit by thy side?
*Claud.* Never any did so, though very many
have been beside their wit.—I will bid thee

draw, as we do the minstrels; draw, to pleas-
us us.
*D. Pedro.* As I am an honest man, he looks
pale.—Art thou sick or angry?
*Claud.* What! courage, man! What though care
killed a cat, thou hast mettle enough in thee
to kill care.
*Bene.* Sir, I shall meet your wit in the career,
an you charge it against me.—I pray you,
choose another subject.
*Claud.* Nay, then, give him another staff; this
last was broke cross.
*D. Pedro.* By this light, he changes more and
more; I think he be angry indeed.
*Claud.* If he be, he knows how to turn his girdle.
*Bene.* Shall I speak a word in your ear?
*Claud.* God bless me from a challenge!
*Bene.* You are a villain;—I jest not:—I will
make it good how you dare, with what you
dare, and when you dare.—Do me right, or I
will protest your cowardice. You have killed a
sweet lady, and her death shall fall heavy on
you. Let me hear from you.
*Claud.* Well, I will meet you, so I may have
good cheer.
*D. Pedro.* What, a feast? a feast?
*Claud.* I' faith, I thank him; he hath bid me to
a calf's head and a capon, the which if I do not
carve most curiously, say my knife's naught.—
Shall I not find a woodcock too?
*Bene.* Sir, your wit ambles well; it goes easily.
*D. Pedro.* I'll tell thee how Beatrice praised
thy wit the other day: I said thou hadst a fine
wit; *True*, says she, *a fine little one. No*, said I,
*a great wit; Right*, says she, *a great gross one.*
*Nay*, said I, *a good wit. Just*, said she, *it hurts
nobody. Nay*, said I, *the gentleman is wise. Certain*, said she, *a wise gentleman. Nay*, said I,
*he hath the tongues. That I believe*, said she,
*for he swore a thing to me on Monday night
which he foreswore on Tuesday morning; there's
a double tongue; there's two tongues.* Thus did
she, an hour together, trans-shape thy particular virtues; yet, at last, she concluded, with
a sigh, thou wast the properest man in Italy.
*Claud.* For the which she wept heartily, and
said she cared not.
*D. Pedro.* Yea, that she did; but yet, for all
that, an if she did not hate him deadly, she
would love him dearly: the old man's daughter
told us all.
*Claud.* All, all; and, moreover, *God saw him
when he was hid in the garden.*
*D. Pedro.* But when shall we set the savage
bull's horns on the sensible Benedick's head?
*Claud.* Yea, and text underneath, *Here dwells
Benedick the married man?*
*Bene.* Fare you well, boy; you know my mind.
I will leave you now to your gossip-like humour: you break jests as braggarts do their
blades, which, God be thanked, hurt not.—
My lord, for your many courtesies I thank
you: I must discontinue your company: your
brother the bastard is fled from Messina: you

have among you killed a sweet and innocent lady. For my Lord Lackbeard there, he and I shall meet; and till then, peace be with him.
[*Exit* BENEDICK.

*D. Pedro.* He is in earnest.

*Claud.* In most profound earnest; and I'll warrant you for the love of Beatrice.

*D. Pedro.* And hath challenged thee?

*Claud.* Most sincerely.

*D. Pedro.* What a pretty thing man is when he goes in his doublet and hose, and leaves off his wit!

*Claud.* He is then a giant to an ape: but then is an ape a doctor to such a man.

*D. Pedro.* But, soft, you, let be; pluck up, my heart, and be sad! Did he not say my brother was fled?

*Enter* DOGBERRY, VERGES, *and the* Watch, *with* CONRADE *and* BORACHIO.

*Dogb.* Come, you, sir; if justice cannot tame you, she shall ne'er weigh more reasons in her balance; nay, an you be a cursing hypocrite once, you must be looked to.

*D. Pedro.* How now! two of my brother's men bound! Borachio one!

*Claud.* Hearken after their offence, my lord.

*D. Pedro.* Officers, what offence hath these men done?

*Dogb.* Marry, sir, they have committed false report; moreover, they have spoken untruths; secondarily, they are slanders; sixth and lastly, they have belied a lady; thirdly, they have verified unjust things: and, to conclude, they are lying knaves.

*D. Pedro.* First, I ask thee what they have done; thirdly, I ask thee what's their offence; sixth and lastly, why they are committed; and, to conclude, what you lay to their charge?

*Claud.* Rightly reasoned, and in his own division; and, by my troth, there's one meaning well suited.

*D. Pedro.* Whom have you offended, masters, that you are thus bound to your answer? this learned constable is too cunning to be understood. What's your offence?

*Bora.* Sweet prince, let me go no further to mine answer; do you hear me, and let this count kill me. I have deceived even your very eyes: what your wisdoms could not discover these shallow fools have brought to light; who, in the night, overheard me confessing to this man how Don John your brother incensed me to slander the Lady Hero; how you were brought into the orchard, and saw me court Margaret in Hero's garments; how you disgraced her, when you should marry her: my villany they have upon record; which I had rather seal with my death than repeat over to my shame. The lady is dead upon mine and my master's false accusation; and, briefly, I desire nothing but the reward of a villain.

*D. Pedro.* Runs not this speech like iron through your blood?

*Claud.* I have drunk poison whiles he uttered it.

*D. Pedro.* But did my brother set thee on to this?

*Bora.* Yea, and paid me richly for the practice of it. [ery:

*D. Pedro.* He is compos'd and fram'd of treachery: And fled he is upon this villany. [pear

*Claud.* Sweet Hero! now thy image doth appear In the rare semblance that I lov'd it first.

*Dogb.* Come, bring away the plaintiffs; by this time our sexton hath reformed Signior Leonato of the matter: and, masters, do not forget to specify, when time and place shall serve, that I am an ass.

*Verg.* Here, here comes master Signior Leonato and the sexton too.

*Re-enter* LEONATO *and* ANTONIO, *with the* SEXTON.

*Leon.* Which is the villain? let me see his eyes, That when I note another man like him I may avoid him: which of these is he?

*Bora.* If you would know your wronger, look on me.

*Leon.* Art thou the slave that with thy breath hast kill'd Mine innocent child?

*Bora.*                    Yea, even I alone.

*Leon.* No, not so, villain; thou bely'st thyself: Here stand a pair of honourable men— A third is fled—that had a hand in it.— I thank you, princes, for my daughter's death; Record it with your high and worthy deeds; 'Twas bravely none, if you bethink you of it.

*Claud.* I know not how to pray your patience, Yet I must speak. Choose your revenge yourself; Impose me to what penance your invention Can lay upon my sin: yet sinned I not But in mistaking.

*D. Pedro.*            By my soul, nor I; And yet, to satisfy this good old man, I would bend under any heavy weight That he'll enjoin me to.

*Leon.* I cannot bid you bid my daughter live— That were impossible; but, I pray you both, Possess the people in Messina here How innocent she died: and, if your love Can labour aught in sad invention, Hang her an epitaph upon her tomb, And sing it to her bones; sing it to-night:— To-morrow morning come you to my house; And since you could not be my son-in-law, Be yet my nephew: my brother hath a daughter, Almost the copy of my child that's dead. And she alone is heir to both of us; Give her the right you should have given her cousin, And so dies my revenge.

*Claud.*            O, noble sir, Your overkindness doth wring tears from me! I do embrace your offer; and dispose For henceforth of poor Claudio.

*Leon.* To-morrow, then, I will expect your coming;
To-night I take my leave.—This naughty man
Shall face to face be brought to Margaret,
Who, I believe, was pack'd in all this wrong,
Hir'd to it by your brother.

*Bora.*      No, by my soul, she was not;
Nor knew not what she did when she spoke to me;
But always hath been just and virtuous
In anything that I do know by her.

*Dogb.* Moreover, sir,—which, indeed, is not under white and black,—this plaintiff here, the offender, did call me ass: I beseech you, let it be remembered in this punishment. And also, the Watch heard them talk of one Deformed: they say he wears a key in his ear and a lock hanging by it, and borrows money in God's name; the which he hath used so long, and never paid, that now men grow hard-hearted, and will lend nothing for God's sake: pray you, examine him upon that point.

*Leon.* I thank thee for thy care and honest pains.

*Dogb.* Your worship speaks like a most thankful and reverend youth, and I praise God for you.

*Leon.* There's for thy pains.

*Dogb.* God save the foundation!

*Leon.* Go; I discharge thee of thy prisoner, and I thank thee.

*Dogb.* I leave an arrant knave with your worship; which I beseech your worship to correct yourself, for the example of others. God keep your worship; I wish your worship well; God restore you to health; I humbly give you leave to depart; and if a merry meeting may be wished, God prohibit it.—Come, neighbour.

[*Exeunt* DOGB., VERG., *and* Watch.

*Leon.* Until to-morrow morning, lords, farewell.

*Ant.* Farewell, my lords; we look for you to-morrow.

*D. Pedro.* We will not fail.

*Claud.* To-night I'll mourn with Hero.

[*Exeunt* DON PEDRO *and* CLAUD.

*Leon.* Bring you these fellows on: we'll talk with Margaret
How her acquaintance grew with this lewd fellow.                     [*Exeunt.*

### SCENE II.—LEONATO'S *Garden.*

*Enter* BENEDICK *and* MARGARET, *meeting.*

*Bene.* Pray thee, sweet Mistress Margaret, deserve well at my hands by helping me to the speech of Beatrice.

*Marg.* Will you then write me a sonnet in praise of my beauty?

*Bene.* In so high a style, Margaret, that no man living shall come over it; for, in most comely truth, thou deservest it.

*Marg.* To have no man come over me? why, shall I always keep below stairs?

*Bene.* Thy wit is as quick as the greyhound's mouth; it catches.

*Marg.* And yours as blunt as the fencer's foils, which hit, but hurt not.

*Bene.* A most manly wit, Margaret; it will not hurt a woman; and so, I pray thee, call Beatrice: I give thee the bucklers.

*Marg.* Give us the swords; we have bucklers of our own.

*Bene.* If you use them, Margaret, you must put in the pikes with a vice; and they are dangerous weapons for maids.

*Marg.* Well, I will call Beatrice to you, who I think, hath legs.                     [*Exit* MARGARET.

*Bene.* And therefore will come.          [*Singing.*

The god of love,
That sits above,
And knows me, and knows me,
How pitiful I deserve,——

I mean in singing; but in loving—Leander the good swimmer, Troilus the first employer of panders, and a whole book full of these quondam carpet-mongers, whose names yet run smoothly in the even road of a blank verse, why, they were never so truly turned over and over as my poor self in love. Marry, I cannot show it in rhyme; I have tried; I can find out no rhyme to *lady* but *baby*—an innocent rhyme; for *scorn, horn*—a hard rhyme; for *school, fool* —a babbling rhyme; very ominous endings. No, I was not born under a rhyming planet nor I cannot woo in festival terms.

*Enter* BEATRICE.

Sweet Beatrice, wouldst thou come when I called thee?

*Beat.* Yea, signior, and depart when you bid me.

*Bene.* O, stay but till then!

*Beat. Then* is spoken; fare you well now:— and yet, ere I go, let me go with that I came for, which is, with knowing what hath passed between you and Claudio.

*Bene.* Only foul words; and thereupon I will kiss thee.

*Beat.* Foul words is but foul wind, and foul wind is but foul breath, and foul breath is noisome; therefore I will depart unkissed.

*Bene.* Thou hast frighted the word out of his right sense, so forcible is thy wit. But, I must tell thee plainly, Claudio undergoes my challenge; and either I must shortly hear from him or I will subscribe him a coward. And, I pray thee now, tell me, for which of my bad parts didst thou first fall in love with me?

*Beat.* For them all together; which maintained so politic a state of evil that they will not admit any good part to intermingle with them. But for which of my good parts did you first suffer love for me?

*Bene. Suffer love;* a good epithet! I do suffer love, indeed, for I love thee against my will.

*Beat.* In spite of your heart, I think; alas! poor heart! If you spite it for my sake, I will spite it for yours; for I will never love that which my friend hates.

*Bene.* Thou and I are too wise to woo peaceably.

*Beat.* It appears not in this confession: there's not one wise man among twenty that will praise himself.

*Bene.* An old, an old instance, Beatrice, that lived in the time of good neighbours: if a man do not erect in this age his own tomb ere he dies, he shall live no longer in monument than the bell rings and the widow weeps.

*Beat.* And how long is that, think you?

*Bene.* Question:—why, an hour in clamour, and a quarter in rheum: therefore it is most expedient for the wise (if Don Worm, his conscience, find no impediment to the contrary) to be the trumpet of his own virtues, as I am to myself. So much for praising myself, who, I myself will bear witness, is praiseworthy, and now tell me, how doth your cousin?

*Beat.* Very ill.

*Bene.* And how do you?

*Beat.* Very ill too.

*Bene.* Serve God, love me, and mend: there will I leave you too, for here comes one in haste.

*Enter* URSULA.

*Urs.* Madam, you must come to your uncle. Yonder's old coil at home: it is proved my Lady Hero hath been falsely accused, the prince and Claudio mightily abused; and Don John is the author of all, who is fled and gone. Will you come presently?

*Beat.* Will you go hear this news, signior?

*Bene.* I will live in thy heart, die in thy lap, and be buried in thy eyes; and, moreover, I will go with thee to thy uncle's.    [*Exeunt.*

SCENE III.—*The inside of a Church.*

*Enter* DON PEDRO, CLAUDIO, *and* Attendants, *with music and tapers.*

*Claud.* Is this the monument of Leonato?

*Atten.* It is, my lord.

*Claud. reads from a scroll.*]

Done to death by slanderous tongues
    Was the Hero that here lies:
Death in guerdon of her wrongs,
    Gives her fame which never dies:
So the life, that died with shame,
Lives in death with glorious fame.
Hang thou there upon the tomb,    [*affixing it.*
Praising her when I am dumb.—

Now, music, sound, and sing your solemn hymn.

SONG.

Pardon, Goddess of the night,
Those that slew thy virgin knight;
For the which, with songs of woe,
Round about her tomb they go.
    Midnight, assist our moan!
    Help us to sigh and groan,
        Heavily, heavily;
Graves, yawn, and yield your dead,
Till death be uttered,
    Heavily, heavily.

*Claud.* Now unto thy bones good night:
    Yearly will I do this rite.

*D. Pedro.* Good morrow, masters; put your torches out:
The wolves have prey'd; and look, the gentle day,
Before the wheels of Phœbus, round about
    Dapples the drowsy east with spots of gray.
Thanks to you all, and leave us: fare you well.

*Claud.* Good morrow, masters; each his several way.    [*weeds;*

*D. Pedro.* Come, let us hence, and put on other
And then to Leonato's we will go.

*Claud.* And Hymen now with luckier issue speeds
Than this, for whom we render'd up this woe!
    [*Exeunt.*

SCENE IV.—*A Room in* LEONATO'S *House.*

*Enter* LEONATO, ANTONIO, BENEDICK, BEATRICE, MARGARET, URSULA, FRIAR, *and* HERO.

*Friar.* Did I not tell you she was innocent?

*Leon.* So are the prince and Claudio, who accus'd her
Upon the error that you heard debated:
But Margaret was in some fault for this,
Although against her will, as it appears
In the true course of all the question.

*Ant.* Well, I am glad that all things sort so well.

*Bene.* And so am I, being else by faith enforc'd
To call young Claudio to a reckoning for it.

*Leon.* Well, daughter, and you gentlewomen all,
Withdraw into a chamber by yourselves;
And when I send for you, come hither mask'd:
The prince and Claudio promis'd by this hour
To visit me.—You know your office, brother;
You must be father to your brother's daughter,
And give her to young Claudio.
    [*Exeunt* Ladies.

*Ant.* Which I will do with confirm'd countenance.

*Bene.* Friar, I must entreat your pains, I think.

*Friar.* To do what, signior?

*Bene.* To bind me, or undo me, one of them.—
Signior Leonato, truth it is, good signior,
Your niece regards me with an eye of favour.

*Leon.* That eye my daughter lent her. 'Tis most true.

*Bene.* And I do with an eye of love requite her.

*Leon.* The sight whereof, I think, you had from me,
From Claudio, and the prince. But what's your will?

*Bene.* Your answer, sir, is enigmatical:
But, for my will, my will is your good-will
May stand with ours, this day to be conjoin'd
In the estate of honourable marriage;—
In which, good friar, I shall desire your help.

*Leon.* My heart is with your liking.

*Friar.*                    And my help.—
Here come the prince and Claudio.

*Enter* DON PEDRO *and* CLAUDIO, *with* Attendants.

*D. Pedro.* Good morrow to this fair assembly.

*Leon.* Good morrow, prince; good morrow,
Claudio;
We here attend you. Are you yet determin'd
To-day to marry with my brother's daughter?
*Claud.* I'll hold my mind where she an Ethiope.
*Leon.* Call her forth, brother; here's the friar
ready.                    [*Exit* ANTONIO.
*D. Pedro.* Good morrow, Benedick. Why,
what's the matter,
That you have such a February face,
So full of frost, of storm, and cloudiness?
*Claud.* I think he thinks upon the savage bull.—
Tush, fear not, man; we'll tip thy horns with
gold,
And all Europa shall rejoice at thee,
As once Europa did at lusty Jove,
When he would play the noble beast in love.
*Bene.* Bull Jove, sir, had an amiable low;
And some such strange bull leap'd your father's
cow,
And got a calf in that same noble feat
Much like to you, for you have just his bleat.

*Re-enter* ANTONIO, *with the* Ladies *masked.*

*Claud.* For this I owe you: here come other
reckonings.
Which is the lady I must seize upon?
*Ant.* This same is she, and I do give you her.
*Claud.* Why, then, she's mine. Sweet, let me
see your face.              [hand
*Leon.* No, that you shall not, till you take her
Before this friar, and swear to marry her.
*Claud.* Give me your hand before this holy
friar;
I am your husband if you like of me.
*Hero.* And when I lived I was your other wife:
                    [*Unmasking.*
And when you lov'd you were my other husband.
*Claud.* Another Hero?
*Hero.*             Nothing certainer:
One Hero died defil'd; but I do live,
And, surely as I live, I am a maid.
*D. Pedro.* The former Hero! Hero that is dead!
*Leon.* She died, my lord, but whiles her slan-
der liv'd.
*Friar.* All this amazement can I qualify;
When, after that the holy rites are ended,
I'll tell you largely of fair Hero's death:
Meantime let wonder seem familiar,
And to the chapel let us presently.
*Bene.* Soft and fair, friar.—Which is Beatrice?
*Beat.* I answer to that name;   [*Unmasking.*
What is your will?
*Bene.* Do not you love me?
*Beat.*             No, no more than reason.
*Bene.* Why, then your uncle, and the prince,
and Claudio
Have been deceived; for they swore you did.
*Beat.* Do not you love me?
*Bene.*             No, no more than reason.
*Beat.* Why, then my cousin, Margaret, and
Ursula,
Are much deceived; for they did swear you did.

*Bene.* They swore that you were almost sick
for me.              [for me.
*Beat.* They swore that you were well-nigh dead
*Bene.* 'Tis no such matter.—Then you do not
love me?
*Beat.* No, truly, but in friendly recompense.
*Leon.* Come, cousin, I am sure you love the,
gentleman.
*Claud.* And I'll be sworn upon 't that he loves
her;
For here's a paper written in his hand—
A halting sonnet of his own pure brain,
Fashion'd to Beatrice.
*Hero.*             And here's another,
Writ in my cousin's hand, stolen from her
pocket,
Containing her affection unto Benedick.
*Bene.* A miracle!—here's our own hands against
our hearts!—Come, I will have thee; but, by
this light, I take thee for pity.
*Beat.* I would not deny you;—but, by this
good day, I yield upon great persuasion; and
partly to save your life, for I was told you were
in a consumption.
*Bene.* Peace; I will stop your mouth.
                    [*Kissing her.*
*D. Pedro.* How dost thou, Benedick the married man?
*Bene.* I'll tell thee what, prince; a college of
wit-crackers cannot flout me out of my humour. Dost thou think I care for a satire, or
an epigram? No: if a man will be beaten with
brains, he shall wear nothing handsome about
him. In brief, since I do purpose to marry, I
will think nothing to any purpose that the
world can say against it; and therefore never
flout at me for what I have said against it; for
man is a giddy thing, and this is my conclusion.—For thy part, Claudio, I did think to
have beaten thee; but in that thou art like to
be my kinsman, live unbruised, and love my
cousin.
*Claud.* I had well hoped thou wouldst have
denied Beatrice, that I might have cudgelled
thee out of thy single life, to make thee a
double dealer; which, out of question thou
wilt be if my cousin do not look exceeding
narrowly to thee.
*Bene.* Come, come, we are friends:—let's have
a dance ere we are married, that we may lighten
our own hearts and our wives' heels.
*Leon.* We'll have dancing afterwards.
*Bene.* First, o' my word; therefore, play, music.
—Prince, thou art sad; get thee a wife, get thee
a wife: there is no staff more reverend than one
tipped with horn.

*Enter a* Messenger.

*Mess.* My lord, your brother John is ta'en in
flight,
And brought with arm'd men back to Messina.
*Bene.* Think not on him till to-morrow: I'll devise thee brave punishments for him.—Strike
up, pipers.              [*Dance. Exeunt*

# A MIDSUMMER NIGHT'S DREAM

# A MIDSUMMER NIGHT'S DREAM

## DRAMATIS PERSONÆ

THESEUS, *Duke of Athens.*
EGEUS, *Father to* HERMIA.
LYSANDER, } *in love with* HERMIA.
DEMETRIUS, }
PHILOSTRATE, *Master of the Revels to* THE-
    SEUS.
QUINCE, *the Carpenter.*
SNUG, *the Joiner.*
BOTTOM, *the Weaver.*
FLUTE, *the Bellows-mender.*
SNOUT, *the Tinker.*
STARVELING, *the Tailor.*

HIPPOLYTA, *Queen of the Amazons, betrothed*
    *to* THESEUS.
HERMIA, *Daughter to* EGEUS, *in love with*
    LYSANDER.
HELENA, *in love with* DEMETRIUS.

OBERON, *King of the Fairies.*
TITANIA, *Queen of the Fairies.*
PUCK, *or* ROBIN GOODFELLOW, *a Fairy.*

PEASBLOSSOM, }
COBWEB, }
MOTH, } *Fairies.*
MUSTARDSEED, }

PYRAMUS, }
THISBE, }
WALL, } *Characters in the Interlude*
MOONSHINE, } *performed by the Clowns.*
LION, }

*Other* Fairies *attending their* King *and* Queen.

Attendants *on* THESEUS *and* HIPPOLYTA.

SCENE,—ATHENS, *and a Wood not far from it.*

## ACT I.

SCENE I.—ATHENS. *A Room in the Palace*
    *of* THESEUS.

*Enter* THESEUS, HIPPOLYTA, PHILOSTRATE,
    *and* Attendants.

*The.* Now, fair Hippolyta, our nuptial hour
Draws on apace; four happy days bring in
Another moon: but, oh, methinks, how slow
This old moon wanes! she lingers my desires,
Like to a step-dame or a dowager,
Long withering out a young man's revenue.
*Hip.* Four days will quickly steep themselves
    in nights;
Four nights will quickly dream away the time;
And then the moon, like to a silver bow
New bent in heaven, shall behold the night
Of our solemnities.
*The.*             Go, Philostrate,
Stir up the Athenian youth to merriments;
Awake the pert and nimble spirit of mirth;
Turn melancholy forth to funerals—
The pale companion is not for our pomp.—
               [*Exit* PHILOSTRATE.
Hippolyta, I woo'd thee with my sword,
And won thy love doing thee injuries;
But I will wed thee in another key,
With pomp, with triumph, and with revelling.

*Enter* EGEUS, HERMIA, LYSANDER, *and*
    DEMETRIUS.

*Ege.* Happy be Theseus, our renowned duke!
*The.* Thanks, good Egeus: what's the news
    with thee?

*Ege.* Full of vexation come I, with complaint
Against my child, my daughter Hermia.—
Stand forth, Demetrius.—My noble lord,
This man hath my consent to marry her.—
Stand forth, Lysander;—and, my gracious duke,
This hath bewitch'd the bosom of my child.
Thou, thou, Lysander, thou hast given her
    rhymes,
And interchang'd love-tokens with my child:
Thou hast by moonlight at her window sung,
With feigning voice, verses of feigning love;
And stol'n the impression of her fantasy
With bracelets of thy hair, rings, gawds, con-
    ceits,     [sengers,
Knacks, trifles, nosegays, sweatmeats,—mes-
Of strong prevailment in unharden'd youth;—
With cunning hast thou filch'd my daughter's
    heart;
Turned her obedience, which is due to me,
To stubborn harshness.—And, my gracious
    duke,
Be it so she will not here before your grace
Consent to marry with Demetrius,
I beg the ancient privilege of Athens,—
As she is mine I may dispose of her:
Which shall be either to this gentleman
Or to her death; according to our law
Immediately provided in that case.
*The.* What say you, Hermia? be advis'd, fair
    maid:
To you your father should be as a god;
One that compos'd your beauties; yea, and one
To whom you are but as a form in wax,
By him imprinted, and within his power
To leave the figure, or disfigure it.

Demetrius is a worthy gentleman.

*Her.* So is Lysander.

*The.* In himself he is:
But, in this kind, wanting your father's voice,
The other must be held the worthier. [eyes.

*Her.* I would my father look'd but with my

*The.* Rather your eyes must with his judgment
look.

*Her.* I do entreat your grace to pardon me.
I know not by what power I am made bold,
Nor how it may concern my modesty
In such a presence here to plead my thoughts:
But I beseech your grace that I may know
The worst that may befall me in this case
If I refuse to wed Demetrius.

*The.* Either to die the death, or to abjure
For ever the society of men.
Therefore, fair Hermia, question your desires,
Know of your youth, examine well your blood,
Whether, if you yield not to your father's choice,
You can endure the livery of a nun;
For aye to be in shady cloister mew'd,
To live a barren sister all your life,
Chanting faint hymns to the cold, fruitless moon.
Thrice blessed they that master so their blood
To undergo such maiden pilgrimage:
But earthlier happy is the rose distill'd,
Than that which, withering on the virgin thorn,
Grows, lives, and dies in single blessedness.

*Her.* So will I grow, so live, so die, my lord,
Ere I will yield my virgin patent up
Unto his lordship, whose unwished yoke
My soul consents not to give sovereignty.

*The.* Take time to pause; and by the next new
moon,—
The sealing-day betwixt my love and me,
For everlasting bond of fellowship,—
Upon that day either prepare to die
For disobedience to your father's will;
Or else to wed Demetrius, as he would;
Or on Diana's altar to protest
For aye austerity and single life.

*Dem.* Relent, sweet Hermia;—and, Lysander,
yield
Thy crazed title to my certain right.

*Lys.* You have her father's love, Demetrius;
Let me have Hermia's: do you marry him.

*Ege.* Scornful Lysander! true, he hath my love;
And what is mine my love shall render him;
And she is mine; and all my right of her
I do estate unto Demetrius.

*Lys.* I am, my lord, as well deriv'd as he,
As well possess'd; my love is more than his;
My fortunes every way as fairly rank'd,
If not with vantage, as Demetrius's;
And, which is more than all these boasts can be,
I am belov'd of beauteous Hermia:
Why should not I then prosecute my right?
Demetrius, I'll avouch it to his head,
Made love to Nedar's daughter, Helena,
And won her soul; and she, sweet lady, dotes,
Devoutly dotes, dotes in idolatry,
Upon this spotted and inconstant man.

*The.* I must confess that I have heard so much,

And with Demetrius thought to have spoke
thereof;
But, being over-full of self-affairs,
My mind did lose it.—But, Demetrius, come;
And come, Egeus; you shall go with me;
I have some private schooling for you both.—
For you, fair Hermia, look you arm yourself
To fit your fancies to your father's will,
Or else the law of Athens yields you up,—
Which by no means we may extenuate,—
To death, or to a vow of single life.—
Come, my Hippolyta: what cheer, my love?
Demetrius, and Egeus, go along:
I must employ you in some business
Against our nuptial, and confer with you
Of something nearly that concerns yourselves.

*Ege.* With duty and desire we follow you.

[*Exeunt* THES., HIP., EGE., DEM., *and* TRAIN.

*Lys.* How now, my love! why is your cheek so
pale?
How chance the roses there do fade so fast?

*Her.* Belike for want of rain, which I could well
Beteem them from the tempest of mine eyes.

*Lys.* Ah me! for aught that ever I could read,
Could ever hear by tale or history,
The course of true love never did run smooth:
But either it was different in blood,——

*Her.* O cross! too high to be enthrall'd to low!

*Lys.* Or else misgraffed in respect of years;——

*Her.* O spite! too old to be engag'd to young!

*Lys.* Or else it stood upon the choice of friends:

*Her.* O hell! to choose love by another's eye!

*Lys.* Or, if there were a sympathy in choice!
War, death, or sickness, did lay siege to it,
Making it momentary as a sound,
Swift as a shadow, short as any dream;
Brief as the lightning in the collied night
That, in a spleen, unfolds both heaven and
earth,
And ere a man hath power to say, Behold!
The jaws of darkness do devour it up:
So quick bright things come to confusion.

*Her.* If, then, true lovers have been ever cross'd,
It stands as an edict in destiny:
Then let us teach our trial patience,
Because it is a customary cross;
As due to love as thoughts, and dreams, and sighs,
Wishes, and tears, poor fancy's followers.

*Lys.* A good persuasion; therefore, hear me,
Hermia.
I have a widow aunt, a dowager
Of great revenue, and she hath no child:
From Athens is her house remote seven leagues;
And she respects me as her only son.
There, gentle Hermia, may I marry thee;
And to that place the sharp Athenian law
Cannot pursue us. If thou lov'st me, then,
Steal forth thy father's house to-morrow night;
And in the wood a league without the town,
Where I did meet thee once with Helena,
To do observance to a morn of May,
There will I stay for thee.

*Her.* My good Lysander!
I swear to thee by Cupid's strongest bow,

By his best arrow with the golden head,
By the simplicity of Venus' doves,
By that which knitteth souls and prospers loves,
And by that fire which burn'd the Carthage
    queen,
When the false Trojan under sail was seen,—
By all the vows that ever men have broke,
In number more than ever woman spoke,—
In that same place thou hast appointed me,
To-morrow truly will I meet with thee.
*Lys.* Keep promise, love. Look, here comes
    Helena.

*Enter* HELENA.

*Her.* God speed fair Helena! Whither away?
*Hel.* Call you me fair? that fair again unsay.
Demetrius loves your fair. O happy fair!
Your eyes are lode-stars; and your tongue's
    sweet air
More tuneable than lark to shepherd's ear,
When wheat is green, when hawthorn buds
    appear.
Sickness is catching: O, were favour so,
Yours would I catch, fair Hermia, ere I go;
My ear should catch your voice, my eye your
    eye,      [melody.
My tongue should catch your tongue's sweet
Were the world mine, Demetrius being bated,
The rest I'll give to be to you translated.
O, teach me how you look; and with what art
You sway the motion of Demetrius' heart.
*Her.* I frown upon him, yet he loves me still.
*Hel.* O that your frowns would teach my smiles
    such skill!
*Her.* I give him curses, yet he gives me love.
*Hel.* O that my prayers could such affection
    move!
*Her.* The more I hate, the more he follows me.
*Hel.* The more I love, the more he hateth me.
*Her.* His folly, Helena, is no fault of mine.
*Hel.* None, but your beauty: would that fault
    were mine!      [face.
*Her.* Take comfort; he no more shall see my
Lysander and myself will fly this place.—
Before the time I did Lysander see,
Seem'd Athens like a paradise to me:
O then, what graces in my love do dwell,
That he hath turn'd a heaven unto hell!
*Lys.* Helen, to you our minds we will unfold:
To-morrow night, when Phœbe doth behold
Her silver visage in the watery glass,
Decking with liquid pearl the bladed grass,—
A time that lovers' flights doth still conceal,—
Through Athens' gates have we devis'd to steal.
*Her.* And in the wood where often you and I
Upon faint primrose beds were wont to lie,
Emptying our bosoms of their counsel sweet,
There my Lysander and myself shall meet:
And thence from Athens turn away our eyes,
To seek new friends and stranger companies.
Farewell, sweet playfellow: pray thou for us,
And good luck grant thee thy Demetrius!—
Keep word, Lysander: we must starve our sight
From lovers' food, till morrow deep midnight.

*Lys.* I will, my Hermia.    [*Exit* HERMIA.
              Helena adieu:
As you on him, Demetrius dote on you!
              [*Exit* LYS.
*Hel.* How happy some o'er other some can be!
Through Athens I am thought as fair as she.
But what of that? Demetrius thinks not so;
He will not know what all but he do know.
And as he errs, doting on Hermia's eyes,
So I, admiring of his qualities.
Things base and vile, holding no quantity,
Love can transpose to form and dignity.
Love looks not with the eyes, but with the mind;
And therefore is wing'd Cupid painted blind.
Nor hath love's mind of any judgment taste;
Wings and no eyes figure unheedy haste:
And therefore is love said to be a child,
Because in choice he is so oft beguil'd.
As waggish boys in game themselves forswear,
So the boy Love is perjur'd everywhere:
For ere Demetrius look'd on Hermia's eyne,
He hail'd down oaths that he was only mine;
And when this hail some heat from Hermia felt,
So he dissolv'd, and showers of oaths did melt.
I will go tell him of fair Hermia's flight;
Then to the wood will he to-morrow night
Pursue her; and for this intelligence
If I have thanks, it is a dear expense:
But herein mean I to enrich my pain,
To have his sight thither and back again. [*Exit.*

SCENE II.—*The same. A Room in a Cottage.*

*Enter* SNUG, BOTTOM, FLUTE, SNOUT,
QUINCE, *and* STARVELING.

*Quin.* Is all our company here?
*Bot.* You were best to call them generally, man
by man, according to the scrip.
*Quin.* Here is the scroll of every man's name,
which is thought fit, through all Athens, to play
in our interlude before the duke and duchess
on his wedding-day at night.
*Bot.* First, good Peter Quince, say what the
play treats on; then read the names of the
actors; and so grow to a point.
*Quin.* Marry, our play is—The most lamentable comedy, and most cruel death of Pyramus
and Thisby.
*Bot.* A very good piece of work, I assure you,
and a merry.—Now, good Peter Quince, call
forth your actors by the scroll.—Masters,
spread yourselves.      [weaver.
*Quin.* Answer, as I call you.—Nick Bottom, the
*Bot.* Ready. Name what part I am for, and
proceed.      [Pyramus.
*Quin.* You, Nick Bottom, are set down for
*Bot.* What is Pyramus? a lover, or a tyrant?
*Quin.* A lover, that kills himself most gallantly
for love.
*Bot.* That will ask some tears in the true per-
forming of it. If I do it, let the audience look
to their eyes; I will move storms; I will condole in some measure. To the rest:—yet my
chief humour is for a tyrant: I could play Ercles

rarely, or a part to tear a cat in, to make all split.

| | |
|---|---|
| The raging rocks, | And Phibbus' car |
| With shivering shocks, | Shall shine from far, |
| Shall break the locks | And make and mar |
| Of prison gates: | The foolish Fates. |

This was lofty!—Now, name the rest of the players.—This is Ercles' vein, a tyrant's vein; —a lover is more condoling.

*Quin.* Francis Flute, the bellows-mender.

*Flu.* Here, Peter Quince.

*Quin.* You must take Thisby on you.

*Flu.* What is Thisby? a wandering knight?

*Quin.* It is the lady that Pyramus must love.

*Flu.* Nay, faith, let me not play a woman; I have a beard coming.

*Quin.* That's all one; you shall play it in a mask, and you may speak as small as you will.

*Bot.* An I may hide my face, let me play Thisby too: I'll speak in a monstrous little voice;—*Thisne, Thisne.—Ah, Pyramus, my lover dear; thy Thisby dear! and lady dear!*

*Quin.* No, no, you must play Pyramus; and, Flute, you Thisby.

*Bot.* Well, proceed.

*Quin.* Robin Starveling, the tailor.

*Star.* Here, Peter Quince.

*Quin.* Robin Starveling, you must play Thisby's mother.—Tom Snout, the tinker.

*Snout.* Here, Peter Quince.

*Quin.* You, Pyramus's father; myself, Thisby's father;—Snug, the joiner, you, the lion's part; —and, I hope, here is a play fitted.

*Snug.* Have you the lion's part written? pray you, if it be, give it me, for I am slow of study.

*Quin.* You may do it extempore, for it is nothing but roaring.

*Bot.* Let me play the lion too: I will roar, that I will do any man's heart good to hear me; I will roar, that I will make the duke say, *Let him roar again, let him roar again.*

*Quin.* An you should do it too terribly you would fright the duchess and the ladies, that they would shriek; and that were enough to hang us all.

*All.* That would hang us every mother's son.

*Bot.* I grant you, friends, if that you whould fright the ladies out of their wits, they would have no more discretion but to hang us: but I will aggravate my voice so that I will roar you as gently as any sucking dove; I will roar you an 'twere any nightingale.

*Quin.* You can play no part but Pyramus, for Pyramus is a sweet-faced man; a proper man, as one shall see on a summer's day; a most lovely, gentleman-like man; therefore you must needs play Pyramus.

*Bot.* Well, I will undertake it. What beard were I best to play it in?

*Quin.* Why, what you will.

*Bot.* I will discharge it in either your straw-coloured beard, your orange-tawny beard, your purple-in-grain beard, or your French-crown-colour beard, your perfect yellow.

*Quin.* Some of your French crowns have no hair at all, and then you will play barefaced.— But, masters, here are your parts: and I am to entreat you, request you, and desire you, to con them by to-morrow night; and meet me in the palace wood, a mile without the town, by moonlight; there will we rehearse: for if we meet in the city, we shall be dogg'd with company, and our devices known. In the meantime I will draw a bill of properties, such as our play wants. I pray you, fail me not.

*Bot.* We will meet; and there we may rehearse more obscenely and courageously. Take pains; be perfect; adieu.

*Quin.* At the duke's oak we meet.

*Bot.* Enough; hold, or cut bow-strings.

[*Exeunt.*

## ACT II.

### Scene I.—*A Wood near Athens.*

*Enter a Fairy at one door, and* PUCK *at another.*

*Puck.* How now, spirit! whither wander you?

*Fai.* Over hill, over dale,
  Thorough bush, thorough brier,
Over park, over pale,
  Thorough flood, thorough fire,
I do wander everywhere,
Swifter than the moon's sphere;
And I serve the fairy queen,
To dew her orbs upon the green.
The cowslips tall her pensioners be:
In their gold coats spots you see;
Those be rubies, fairy favours,
In those freckles live their savours:
I must go seek some dew-drops here,
And hang a pearl in every cowslip's ear.
Farewell, thou lob of spirits; I'll be gone:
Our queen and all our elves come here anon.

*Puck.* The king doth keep his revels here to-
  night;
Take heed the queen come not within his sight.
For Oberon is passing fell and wrath,
Because that she, as her attendant, hath
A lovely boy, stol'n from an Indian king;
She never had so sweet a changeling:
And jealous Oberon would have the child
Knight of his train, to trace the forests wild:
But she perforce withholds the loved boy,
Crowns him with flowers, and makes him all
  her joy:
And now they never meet in grove or green,
By fountain clear or spangled starlight sheen,
But they do square; that all their elves, for fear,
Creep into acorn cups, and hide them there.

*Fai.* Either I mistake your shape and making
  quite,
Or else you are that shrewd and knavish sprite
Call'd Robin Goodfellow: are you not he
That frights the maidens of the villagery;
Skim milk, and sometimes labour in the quern,

And bootless make the breathless housewife
　　churn;
And sometime make the drink to bear no barm;
Mislead night-wanderers, laughing at their
　　harm?
Those that Hobgoblin call you, and sweet Puck,
You do their work, and they shall have good luck:
Are not you he?
*Puck.*　　　　　Thou speak'st aright;
I am that merry wanderer of the night.
I jest to Oberon, and make him smile,
When I a fat and bean-fed horse beguile,
Neighing in likeness of a filly foal:
And sometime lurk I in a gossip's bowl,
In very likeness of a roasted crab;
And, when she drinks, against her lips I bob,
And on her wither'd dew-lap pour the ale.
The wisest aunt, telling the saddest tale,
Sometime for three-foot stool mistaketh me;
Then slip I from her bum, down topples she,
And *tailor* cries, and falls into a cough;
And then the whole quire hold their hips and
　　loffe,
And waxen in their mirth, and neeze, and swear
A merrier hour was never wasted there.—
But room, fairy, here comes Oberon.
*Fai.* And here my mistress.—Would that he
　　were gone!

### Scene II.

*Enter* Oberon *at one door, with his* Train,
*and* Titania, *at another, with hers.*

*Obe.* Ill met by moonlight, proud Titania.
*Tita.* What, jealous Oberon! Fairies, skip hence;
I have forsworn his bed and company.
*Obe.* Tarry, rash wanton: am not I thy lord?
*Tita.* Then I must be thy lady: but I know
When thou hast stol'n away from fairy-land,
And in the shape of Corin sat all day,
Playing on pipes of corn, and versing love
To amorous Phillida. Why art thou here,
Come from the farthest steep of India?
But that, forsooth, the bouncing Amazon,
Your buskin'd mistress and your warrior love,
To Theseus must be wedded; and you come
To give their bed joy and prosperity.
*Obe.* How can'st thou thus, for shame, Titania,
Glance at my credit with Hippolyta,
Knowing I know thy love to Theseus?
Didst thou not lead him through the glimmer-
　　ing night
From Perigenia, whom he ravish'd?
And make him with fair Ægle break his faith,
With Ariadne and Antiopa?
*Tita.* These are the forgeries of jealousy:
And never, since the middle summer's spring,
Met we on hill, in dale, forest, or mead,
By paved fountain, or by rushy brook,
Or on the beached margent of the sea,
To dance our ringlets to the whistling wind,
But with thy brawls thou. hast disturb'd our
　　sport.
Therefore the winds, piping to us in vain,
As in revenge. have suck'd up from the sea

Contagious fogs; which, falling in the land,
Have every pelting river made so proud
That they have overborne their continents:
The ox hath therefore stretch'd his yoke in vain,
The ploughman lost his sweat; and the green
　　corn
Hath rotted ere his youth attain'd a beard:
The fold stands empty in the drowned field,
And crows are fatted with the murrain flock;
The nine men's morris is fill'd up with mud;
And the quaint mazes in the wanton green,
For lack of tread, are undistinguishable:
The human mortals want their winter here;
No night is now with hymn or carol blest:—
Therefore the moon, the governess of floods,
Pale in her anger, washes all the air,
That rheumatic diseases do abound:
And thorough this distemperature we see
The seasons alter: hoary-headed frosts
Fall in the fresh lap of the crimson rose;
And on old Hyem's chin and icy crown
An odorous chaplet of sweet summer buds
Is, as in mockery, set: the spring, the summer,
The childing autumn, angry winter, change
Their wonted liveries; and the maz'd world,
By their increase, now knows not which is
　　which:
And this same progeny of evils comes
From our debate, from our dissension:
We are their parents and original.
*Obe.* Do you amend it, then: it lies in you:
Why should Titania cross her Oberon?
I do but beg a little changeling boy
To be my henchman.
*Tita.*　　　　　Set your heart at rest;
The fairy-land buys not the child of me.
His mother was a vot'ress of my order:
And, in the spiced Indian air, by night,
Full often hath she gossip'd by my side;
And sat with me on Neptune's yellow sands,
Marking the embarked traders on the flood;
When we have laugh'd to see the sails conceive,
And grow big-bellied with the wanton wind:
Which she, with pretty and with swimming gait,
Following,—her womb then rich with my young
　　squire,—
Would imitate; and sail upon the land,
To fetch me trifles, and return again,
As from a voyage, rich with merchandise.
But she, being mortal, of that boy did die;
And for her sake I do rear up her boy:
And for her sake I will not part with him.
*Obe.* How long within this wood intend you
　　stay?　　　　　　　　　　　　[day.
*Tita.* Perchance till after Theseus' wedding-
If you will patiently dance in our round,
And see our moonlight revels, go with us;
If not, shun me, and I will spare your haunts.
*Obe.* Give me that boy and I will go with thee.
*Tita.* Not for thy fairy kingdom. Fairies, away:
We shall chide downright if I longer stay.
　　　　　　　　　[*Exit* Titania *and her* Train.
*Obe.* Well, go thy way: thou shalt not from
　　this grove ..

Till I torment thee for this injury —
My gentle Puck, come hither: thou remember'st
Since once I sat upon a promontory,
And heard a mermaid, on a dolphin's back,
Uttering such dulcet and harmonious breath,
That the rude sea grew civil at her song,
And certain stars shot madly from their spheres
To hear the sea-maid's music.

*Puck.*            I remember.

*Obe.* That very time I saw,—but thou couldst
    not,—
Flying between the cold moon and the earth,
Cupid all arm'd: a certain aim he took
At a fair vestal, throned by the west;
And loos'd his love-shaft smartly from his bow,
As it should pierce a hundred thousand hearts,
But I might see young Cupid's fiery shaft
Quench'd in the chaste beams of the watery
    moon;
And the imperial votaress passèd on,
In maiden meditation, fancy-free.
Yet mark'd I where the bolt of Cupid fell:
It fell upon a little western flower,—
Before milk-white, now purple with love's
    wound,
And maidens call it love-in-idleness.
Fetch me that flower; the herb I show'd thee
    once:
The juice of it on sleeping eyelids laid
Will make or man or woman madly dote
Upon the next live creature that it sees.
Fetch me this herb: and be thou here again
Ere the leviathan can swim a league.

*Puck.* I'll put a girdle round about the earth
In forty minutes.          [*Exit* PUCK.

*Obe.*          Having once this juice,
I'll watch Titania when she is asleep,
And drop the liquor of it in her eyes:
The next thing then she waking looks upon,—
Be it on lion, bear, or wolf, or bull,
On meddling monkey, or on busy ape,—
She shall pursue it with the soul of love.
And ere I take this charm off from her sight,—
As I can take it with another herb,
I'll make her render up her page to me.
But who comes here? I am invisible;
And I will overhear their conference.

*Enter* DEMETRIUS, HELENA *following him.*

*Dem.* I love thee not, therefore pursue me not.
Where is Lysander and fair Hermia?
The one I'll slay, the other slayeth me.
Thou told'st me they were stol'n into this wood,
And here am I, and wood within this wood,
Because I cannot meet with Hermia.
Hence, get thee gone, and follow me no more.

*Hel.* You draw me, you hard-hearted adamant;
But yet you draw not iron, for my heart
Is true as steel. Leave you your power to draw,
And I shall have no power to follow you.

*Dem.* Do I entice you? Do I speak you fair?
Or, rather, do I not in plainest truth
Tell you I do not, nor I cannot love you?

*Hel.* And even for that do I love you the more.

I am your spaniel; and, Demetrius,
The more you beat me, I will fawn on you:
Use me but as your spaniel, spurn me, strike me,
Neglect me, lose me; only give me leave,
Unworthy as I am, to follow you.
What worser place can I beg in your love,
And yet a place of high respect with me,—
Than to be used as you use your dog?

*Dem.* Tempt not too much the hatred of my
    spirit;
For I am sick when I do look on thee.

*Hel.* And I am sick when I look not on you.

*Dem.* You do impeach your modesty too much,
To leave the city, and commit yourself
Into the hands of one that loves you not;
To trust the opportunity of night,
And the ill counsel of a desert place,
With the rich worth of your virginity.

*Hel.* Your virtue is my privilege for that.
It is not night when I do see your face,
Therefore I think I am not in the night:
Nor doth this wood lack worlds of company;
For you, in my respect, are all the world:
Then how can it be said I am alone
When all the world is here to look on me?

*Dem.* I'll run from thee, and hide me in the
    brakes,
And leave thee to the mercy of wild beasts.

*Hel.* The wildest hath not such a heart as you.
Run when you will, the story shall be chang'd;
Apollo flies, and Daphne holds the chase;
The dove pursues the griffin; the mild hind
Makes speed to catch the tiger,—bootless speed,
When cowardice pursues and valour flies.

*Dem.* I will not stay thy question; let me go:
Or, if thou follow me, do not believe
But I shall do thee mischief in the wood.

*Hel.* Ay, in the temple, in the town, the field,
You do me mischief. Fie, Demetrius!
Your wrongs do set a scandal on my sex:
We cannot fight for love as men may do:
We should be woo'd, and were not made to woo.
I'll follow thee, and make a heaven of hell,
To die upon the hand I love so well.

         [*Exeunt* DEM. *and* HEL.

*Obe.* Fare thee well, nymph: ere he do leave
    this grove,
Thou shalt fly him, and he shall seek thy love.—

*Re-enter* PUCK.

Hast thou the flower there? Welcome, wanderer.

*Puck.* Ay, there it is.

*Obe.*          I pray thee, give it me.
I know a bank whereon the wild thyme blows,
Where ox-lips and the nodding violet grows;
Quite over-canopied with lush woodbine,
With sweet musk roses, and with eglantine:
There sleeps Titania sometime of the night,
Lulled in these flowers with dances and delight;
And there the snake throws her enamell'd skin,
Weed wide enough to wrap a fairy in:
And with the juice of this I'll streak her eyes,
And make her full of hateful fantasies.

Take thou some of it, and seek through this
grove:
A sweet Athenian lady is in love
With a disdainful youth: anoint his eyes;
But do it when the next thing he espies
May be the lady: thou shalt know the man
By the Athenian garments he hath on.
Effect it with some care, that he may prove
More fond on her than she upon her love:
And look thou meet me ere the first cock crow.
*Puck.* Fear not, my lord, your servant shall do
so.    [*Exeunt.*

SCENE III.—*Another part of the Wood.*

*Enter* TITANIA, *with her* Train.

*Tita.* Come, now a roundel and a fairy song;
Then, for the third part of a minute, hence;
Some to kill cankers in the musk-rose buds;
Some war with rere-mice for their leathern
wings,
To make my small elves coats; and some keep
back    [wonders
The clamorous owl, that nightly hoots and
At our quaint spirits. Sing me now asleep;
Then to your offices, and let me rest.

SONG.

I.

1 *Fai.* You spotted snakes, with double tongue,
Thorny hedgehogs, be not seen;
Newts and blind-worms do no wrong;
Come not near our fairy queen:

CHORUS.

Philomel, with melody,
Sing in our sweet lullaby:
Lulla, lulla, lullaby; lulla, lulla, lullaby:
Never harm, nor spell, nor charm,
Come our lovely lady nigh;
So, good-night, with lullaby:

II.

2 *Fai.* Weaving spiders, come not here;
Hence, you long-legg'd spinners, hence,
Beetles black, approach not near;
Worm nor snail do no offence.

CHORUS.

Philomel, with melody, &c.

1 *Fai.* Hence, away; now all is well:
One, aloof, stand sentinel.
[*Exeunt* Fairies. TITANIA *sleeps.*

*Enter* OBERON.

*Obe.* What thou seest, when thou dost wake,
[*Squeezes the flower on* TITANIA'S *eyelids.*
Do it for thy true-love take;
Love and languish for his sake;
Be it ounce, or cat, or bear,
Pard, or boar with bristled hair,
In thy eye that shall appear
When thou wak'st, it is thy dear;
Wake when some vile thing is near.    [*Exit.*

*Enter* LYSANDER *and* HERMIA.

*Lys.* Fair love, you faint with wandering in
the wood;
And, to speak troth, I have forgot our way;
We'll rest us Hermia, if you think it good,
And tarry for the comfort of the day.
*Her.* Be it so, Lysander: find you out a bed,
For I upon this bank will rest my head.
*Lys.* One turf shall serve as pillow for us both;
One heart, one bed, two bosoms, and one troth.
*Her.* Nay, good Lysander; for my sake, my
dear,
Lie farther off yet, do not lie so near.
*Lys.* O, take the sense, sweet, of my innocence;
Love takes the meaning in love's conference.
I mean, that my heart unto yours is knit;
So that but one heart we can make of it:
Two bosoms interchained with an oath;
So then two bosoms and a single troth.
Then by your side no bed-room me deny;
For lying so, Hermia, I do not lie.
*Her.* Lysander riddles very prettily:—
Now much beshrew my manners and my pride
If Hermia meant to say Lysander lied.
But, gentle friend, for love and courtesy
Lie farther off; in human modesty,
Such separation as may well be said
Becomes a virtuous bachelor and a maid:
So far be distant; and, good night, sweet friend:
Thy love ne'er alter till thy sweet life end!
*Lys.* Amen, amen, to that fair prayer, say I;
And then end life when I end loyalty!
Here is my bed: Sleep give thee all his rest!
*Her.* With half that wish the wisher's eyes be
pressed!    [*They sleep.*

*Enter* PUCK.

*Puck.* Through the forest have I gone,
But Athenian found I none,
On whose eyes I might approve
This flower's force in stirring love.
Night and silence! who is here?
Weeds of Athens he doth wear:
This is he, my master said,
Despised the Athenian maid;
And here the maiden, sleeping sound,
On the dank and dirty ground.
Pretty soul! she durst not lie
Near this lack-love, this kill-courtesy.
Churl, upon thy eyes I throw
All the power this charm doth owe;
When thou wak'st let love forbid
Sleep his seat on thy eyelid:
So awake when I am gone;
For I must now to Oberon.    [*Exit.*

*Enter* DEMETRIUS *and* HELENA, *running.*
*Hel.* Stay, though thou kill me, sweet Deme-
trius.
*Dem.* I charge thee, hence, and do not haunt
me thus.
*Hel.* O, wilt thou darkling leave me? do not so.
*Dem.* Stay on thy peril; I alone will go.
[*Exit* DEMETRIUS.

*Hel.* O, I am out of breath in this fond chase!
The more my prayer the lesser is my grace.
Happy is Hermia, wheresoe'er she lies,
For she hath blessed and attractive eyes. [*tears:*
How came her eyes so bright? Not with salt
If so, my eyes are oftener wash'd than hers.
No, no, I am as ugly as a bear;
For beasts that meet me run away for fear:
Therefore no marvel though Demetrius
Do, as a monster, fly my presence thus.
What wicked and dissembling glass of mine
Made me compare with Hermia's sphery eyne?—
But who is here?—Lysander! on the ground!
Dead? or asleep? I see no blood, no wound.
Lysander, if you live, good sir, awake.

*Lys.* And run through fire I will for thy sweet
    sake.                              [*Waking.*
Transparent Helena! Nature here shows art,
That through thy bosom makes me see thy heart.
Where is Demetrius? O, how fit a word
Is that vile name to perish on my sword!

*Hel.* Do not say so, Lysander; say not so:
What though he love your Hermia? Lord, what
    though?
Yet Hermia still loves you: then be content.

*Lys.* Content with Hermia? No: I do repent
The tedious minutes I with her have spent.
Not Hermia but Helena I love:
Who will not change a raven for a dove?
The will of man is by his reason sway'd;
And reason says you are the worthier maid.
Things growing are not ripe until their season;
So I, being young, till now ripe not to reason;
And touching now the point of human skill,
Reason becomes the marshal to my will,
And leads me to your eyes, where I o'erlook
Love's stories, written in love's richest book.

*Hel.* Wherefore was I to this keen mockery
    born?
When at your hands did I deserve this scorn?
Is't not enough, is't not enough, young man,
That I did never, no, nor never can
Deserve a sweet look from Demetrius' eye,
But you must flout my insufficiency?
Good troth, you do me wrong,—good sooth,
    you do—
In such disdainful manner me to woo.
But fare you well: perforce I must confess,
I thought you lord of more true gentleness.
O, that a lady of one man refus'd,
Should of another therefore be abus'd! [*Exit.*

*Lys.* She sees not Hermia:—Hermia, sleep thou
    there;
And never mayst thou come Lysander near!
For, as a surfeit of the sweetest things
The deepest loathing to the stomach brings;
Or, as the heresies that men do leave
Are hated most of those they did deceive;
So thou, my surfeit and my heresy,
Of all be hated, but the most of me!
And, all my powers, address your love and might
To honour Helen, and to be her knight! [*Exit.*

*Her.* [*Starting.*] Help me, Lysander, help me!
    do thy best

To pluck this crawling serpent from my breast!
Ah me, for pity!—what a dream was here!
Lysander, look how I do quake with fear!
Methought a serpent eat my heart away,
And you sat smiling at his cruel prey.—
Lysander! what, removed? Lysander! lord!
What, out of hearing? gone? no sound, no word?
Alack, where are you? speak, an if you hear;
Speak, of all loves! I swoon almost with fear.
No?—then I well perceive you are not nigh:
Either death or you I'll find immediately.
                                          [*Exit.*

## ACT III.

SCENE I.—*The Wood. The* Queen *of Fairies*
    *lying asleep.*

*Enter* QUINCE, SNUG, BOTTOM, FLUTE,
    SNOUT, *and* STARVELING.

*Bot.* Are we all met?

*Quin.* Pat, pat; and here is a marvellous convenient place for our rehearsal. This green plot
shall be our stage, this hawthorn brake our
tiring-house; and we will do it in action, as we
will do it before the duke.

*Bot.* Peter Quince,—

*Quin.* What say'st thou, bully Bottom?

*Bot.* There are things in this comedy of *Pyramus and Thisby* that will never please. First,
Pyramus must draw a sword to kill himself;
which the ladies cannot abide. How answer
you that?

*Snout.* By'r lakin, a parlous fear.

*Star.* I believe you must leave the killing out,
when all is done.

*Bot.* Not a whit: I have a device to make all
well. Write me a prologue; and let the prologue
seem to say, we will do no harm with our
swords, and that Pyramus is not killed indeed:
and for the more better assurance, tell them
that I Pyramus am not Pyramus, but Bottom
the weaver: this will put them out of fear.

*Quin.* Well, we will have such a prologue; and
it shall be written in eight and six.

*Bot.* No, make it two more; let it be written
in eight and eight.

*Snout.* Will not the ladies be afeard of the lion?

*Star.* I fear it, I promise you.

*Bot.* Masters, you ought to consider with yourselves: to bring in, God shield us! a lion among
ladies is a most dreadful thing: for there is not
a more fearful wild-fowl than your lion living;
and we ought to look to it.

*Snout.* Therefore another prologue must tell
he is not a lion.

*Bot.* Nay, you must name his name, and half
his face must be seen through the lion's neck;
and he himself must speak through, saying
thus, or to the same defect,—"Ladies," or
"Fair Ladies! I would wish you, or, I would
request you, or, I would entreat you, not to
fear, not to tremble: my life for yours. If you
think I come hither as a lion, it were pity of
my life. No, I am no such thing; I am a man

as other men are:"—and there, indeed, let him name his name, and tell them plainly he is Snug the joiner.

*Quin.* Well, it shall be so. But there is two hard things; that is, to bring the moonlight into a chamber: for, you know, Pyramus and Thisby meet by moonlight.

*Snug.* Doth the moon shine that night we play our play?

*Bot.* A calendar, a calendar! look in the almanack; find out moonshine, find out moonshine.

*Quin.* Yes, it doth shine that night.

*Bot.* Why, then you may leave a casement of the great chamber-window, where we play, open; and the moon may shine in at the casement.

*Quin.* Ay; or else one must come in with a bush of thorns and a lantern, and say he comes to disfigure or to present the person of moonshine. Then there is another thing: we must have a wall in the great chamber; for Pyramus and Thisby, says the story, did talk through the chink of a wall.

*Snug.* You never can bring in a wall.—What say you, Bottom?

*Bot.* Some man or other must present wall: and let him have some plaster, or some loam, or some rough-cast about him, to signify wall; or let him hold his fingers thus, and through that cranny shall Pyramus and Thisby whisper.

*Quin.* If that may be, then all is well. Come, sit down, every mother's son, and rehearse your parts. Pyramus, you begin: when you have spoken your speech, enter into that brake; and so every one according to his cue.

*Enter PUCK behind.*

*Puck.* What hempen homespuns have we swaggering here,
So near the cradle of the fairy queen?
What, a play toward! I'll be an auditor;
An actor too, perhaps, if I see cause.

*Quin.* Speak, Pyramus.—Thisby, stand forth.

*Pyr. Thisby, the flowers of odious savours sweet,*

*Quin.* Odours, odours.

*Pyr.* ——*odours savours sweet:*
*So doth they breath, my dearest Thisby dear.—*
*But hark, a voice! stay thou but here awhile,*
*And by and by I will to thee appear.*   [*Exit.*

*Puck.* A stranger Pyramus than e'er played here!   [*Aside.—Exit.*

*This.* Must I speak now?

*Quin.* Ay, marry, must you: for you must understand he goes but to see a noise that he heard, and is to come again.

*This. Most radiant Pyramus, most lily white of hue,*
*Of colour like the red rose on triumphant brier,*
*Most brisky juvenal, and eke most lovely Jew,*
*As true as truest horse, that yet would never tire,*
*I'll meet thee, Pyramus, at Ninny's tomb.*

*Quin.* Ninus' tomb, man: why, you must not speak that yet: that you answer to Pyramus. You speak all your part at once, cues and all.—

Pyramus enter: your cue is past; it is, *never tire.*
*Re-enter* PUCK, *and* BOTTOM *with an ass's head.*

*This. O,—As true as truest horse, that yet would never tire.*

*Pyr. If I were fair, Thisby, I were only thine:—*

*Quin.* O monstrous! O strange! we are haunted. Pray, masters! fly, masters!—Help!   [*Exeunt* Clowns.

*Puck.* I'll follow you; I'll lead you about a round,   [through brier;
Through bog, through bush, through brake,
Sometime a horse I'll be, sometime a hound,
A hog, a headless bear, sometime a fire;
And neigh, and bark, and grunt, and roar, and burn,
Like horse, hound, hog, bear, fire, at every turn.   [*Exit.*

*Bot.* Why do they run away? this is a knavery of them to make me afeard.

*Re-enter* SNOUT.

*Snout.* O Bottom, thou art changed! what do I see on thee?

*Bot.* What do you see? you see an ass-head of your own, do you?

*Re-enter* QUINCE.

*Quin.* Bless thee, Bottom! bless thee! thou art translated.   [*Exit.*

*Bot.* I see their knavery; this is to make an ass of me; to fright me, if they could. But I will not stir from this place, do what they can: I will walk up and down here, and I will sing, that they shall hear I am not afraid.   [*Sings.*

The ousel-cock, so black of hue,
    With orange-tawny bill,
The throstle with his note so true,
    The wren with little quill.

*Tita.* What angel wakes me from my flowery bed?   [*Waking.*

*Bot.*    The finch, the sparrow, and the lark,
        The plain-song cuckoo gray,
    Whose note full many a man doth mark,
        And dares not answer nay;—

for, indeed, who would set his wit to so foolish a bird? who would give a bird the lie, though he cry *cuckoo* never so?

*Tita.* I pray thee, gentle mortal, sing again:
Mine ear is much enamour'd of thy note.
So is mine eye enthralled to thy shape;   [me,
And thy fair virtue's force perforce doth move
On the first view, to say, to swear, I love thee.

*Bot.* Methinks, mistress, you should have little reason for that: and yet, to say the truth, reason and love keep little company together now-a-days: the more the pity that some honest neighbours will not make them friends. Nay, I can gleek upon occasion.

*Tita.* Thou art as wise as thou are beautiful.

*Bot.* Not so, neither: but if I had wit enough

to get out of this wood, I have enough to serve mine own turn.

*Tita.* Out of this wood do not desire to go;
Thou shalt remain here whether thou wilt or no.
I am a spirit of no common rate,—
The summer still doth tend upon my state;
And I do love thee: therefore, go with me,
I'll give thee fairies to attend on thee;
And they shall fetch thee jewels from the deep,
And sing, while thou on pressed flowers dost sleep:
And I will purge thy mortal grossness so
That thou shalt like an airy spirit go.—
Peasblossom! Cobweb! Moth! and Mustard-seed!

*Enter Four* Fairies.

1 *Fai.* Ready.
2 *Fai.*          And I.
3 *Fai.*                    And I.
4 *Fai.*                              Where shall we go?
*Tita.* Be kind and courteous to this gentleman;
Hop in his walks and gambol in his eyes;
Feed him with apricocks and dewberries,
With purple grapes, green figs, and mulberries;
The honey bags steal from the humble-bees,
And, for night-tapers, crop their waxen thighs,
And light them at the fiery glow-worm's eyes,
To have my love to bed and to arise;
And pluck the wings from painted butterflies,
To fan the moonbeams from his sleeping eyes:
Nod to him, elves, and do him courtesies.
1 *Fai.* Hail, mortal!
2 *Fai.* Hail!
3 *Fai.* Hail!
4 *Fai.* Hail!
*Bot.* I cry your worship's mercy heartily.—I beseech your worship's name.
*Cob.* Cobweb.
*Bot.* I shall desire you of more acquaintance, good Master Cobweb. If I cut my finger I shall make bold with you.—Your name, honest gentleman?
*Peas.* Peasblossom.
*Bot.* I pray you, commend me to Mistress Squash, your mother, and to Master Peascod, your father. Good Master Peasblossom, I shall desire you of more acquaintance too.—Your name, I beseech you, sir?
*Mus.* Mustardseed.
*Bot.* Good Master Mustardseed, I know your patience well: that same cowardly giant-like ox-beef hath devoured many a gentleman of your house: I promise you, your kindred hath made my eyes water ere now. I desire you more acquaintance, good Master Mustardseed.
*Tita.* Come, wait upon him; lead him to my bower.
The moon, methinks, looks with a watery eye;
And when she weeps, weeps every little flower,
Lamenting some enforced chastity.
Tie up my love's tongue, bring him silently.
                                        [*Exeunt.*

SCENE II:—*Another part of the Wood.*
*Enter* OBERON.

*Obe.* I wonder if Titania be awak'd;
Then what it was that next came in her eye,
Which she must dote on in extremity.

*Enter* PUCK.

Here comes my messenger.—How now, mad spirit?
What night-rule now about this haunted grove?
*Puck.* My mistress with a monster is in love.
Near to her close and consecrated bower,
While she was in her dull and sleeping hour,
A crew of patches, rude mechanicals,
That work for bread upon Athenian stalls,
Were met together to rehearse a play
Intended for great Theseus' nuptial day.
The shallowest thickskin of that barren sort
Who Pyramus presented in their sport,
Forsook his scene and enter'd in a brake;
When I did him at his advantage take,
An ass's nowl I fixed on his head;
Anon, his Thisbe must be answered,          [spy,
And forth my mimic comes. When they him
As wild geese that the creeping fowler eye,
Or russet-pated choughs, many in sort,
Rising and cawing at the gun's report,
Sever themselves, and madly sweep the sky,
So at his sight away his fellows fly:
And at our stamp here o'er and o'er one falls;
He murder cries, and help from Athens calls.
Their sense, thus weak, lost with their fears, thus strong,
Made senseless things begin to do them wrong:
For briers and thorns at their apparel snatch;
Some sleeves, some hats: from yielders all things catch.
I led them on in this distracted fear,
And left sweet Pyramus translated there:
When in that moment,—so it came to pass,—
Titania wak'd, and straightway lov'd an ass.
*Obe.* This falls out better than I could devise.
But hast thou yet latch'd the Athenian's eyes
With the love-juice, as I did bid thee do?
*Puck.* I took him sleeping,—that is finish'd too,—
And the Athenian woman by his side;
That, when he wak'd, of force she must be ey'd.

*Enter* DEMETRIUS *and* HERMIA.

*Obe.* Stand close; this is the same Athenian.
*Puck.* This is the woman, but not this the man.
*Dem.* O, why rebuke you him that loves you so?
Lay breath so bitter on your bitter foe.
*Her.* Now I but chide, but I should use thee worse;
For thou, I fear, hast given me cause to curse.
If thou hast slain Lysander in his sleep,
Being o'er shoes in blood, plunge in the deep,
And kill me too.
The sun was not so true unto the day
As he to me: would he have stol'n away

From sleeping Hermia? I'll believe as soon
This whole earth may be bor'd; and that the
    moon
May through the centre creep, and so displease
Her brother's noontide with the antipodes.
It cannot be but thou hast murder'd him;
So should a murderer look; so dead, so grim.
*Dem.* So should the murder'd look; and so
    should I,
Pierc'd through the heart with your stern
    cruelty:
Yet you, the murderer, look as bright, as clear,
As yonder Venus in her glimmering sphere.
*Her.* What's this to my Lysander? where is he?
Ah, good Demetrius, wilt thou give him me?
*Dem.* I had rather give his carcass to my
    hounds.
*Her.* Out, dog! out, cur! thou driv'st me past
    the bounds         [then?
Of maiden's patience. Hast thou slain him,
Henceforth be never number'd among men!
Oh! once tell true, tell true, even for my sake;
Durst thou have look'd upon him, being awake,
And hast thou kill'd him sleeping? O brave
    touch!
Could not a worm, an adder, do so much?
An adder did it; for with doubler tongue
Than thine, thou serpent, never adder stung.
*Dem.* You spend your passion on a mispris'd
    mood:
I am not guilty of Lysander's blood;
Nor is he dead, for aught that I can tell.
*Her.* I pray thee, tell me, then, that he is well.
*Dem.* An if I could, what should I get therefore?
*Her.* A privilege never to see me more.—
And from thy hated presence part I so:
See me no more whether he be dead or no.
                      [*Exit.*
*Dem.* There is no following her in this fierce
    vein:
Here, therefore, for awhile I will remain.
So sorrow's heaviness doth heavier grow
For debt that bankrupt sleep doth sorrow owe;
Which now in some light measure it will pay,
If for his tender here I make some stay.
                    [*Lies down.*
*Obe.* What hast thou done? thou hast mistaken
    quite,         [sight:
And laid the love-juice on some true-love's
Of thy misprision must perforce ensue
Some true-love turn'd, and not a false turn'd
    true.         [ing troth,
*Puck.* Then fate o'er-rules, that, one man hold-
A million fail, confounding oath on oath.
*Obe.* About the wood go, swifter than the wind,
And Helena of Athens look thou find:
All fancy-sick she is, and pale of cheer,
With sighs of love, that cost the fresh blood
    dear.
By some illusion see thou bring her here;
I'll charm his eyes against she do appear.
*Puck.* I go, I go; look how I go,—
Swifter than arrow from the Tartar's bow.
                      [*Exit.*

*Obe.* Flower of this purple dye,
Hit with Cupid's archery,
Sink in apple of his eye!
When his love he doth espy,
Let her shine as gloriously
As the Venus of the sky.—
When thou wak'st, if she be by,
Beg of her for remedy.

         *Re-enter* PUCK.

*Puck.* Captain of our fairy band,
Helena is here at hand,
And the youth mistook by me
Pleading for a lover's fee;
Shall we their fond pageant see?
Lord, what fools these mortals be!
*Obe.* Stand aside: the noise they make
Will cause Demetrius to awake.
*Puck.* Then will two at once woo one,—
That must needs be sport alone;
And those things do best please me
That befall preposterously.

    *Enter* LYSANDER *and* HELENA.

*Lys.* Why should you think that I should woo
    in scorn?
Scorn and derision never come in tears.
Look, when I vow, I weep; and vows so born,
In their nativity all truth appears.
How can these things in me seem scorn to you,
Bearing the badge of faith, to prove them true?
*Hel.* You do advance your cunning more and
    more.
When truth kills truth, O devilish-holy fray!
These vows are Hermia's: will you give her o'er?
Weigh oath with oath and you will nothing
    weigh:
Your vows to her and me, put in two scales,
Will even weigh; and both as light as tales.
*Lys.* I had no judgment when to her I swore.
*Hel.* Nor none, in my mind, now you give her
    o'er.         [you.
*Lys.* Demetrius loves her, and he loves not
*Dem.* [*Awaking.*] O Helen, goddess, nymph,
    perfect, divine!
To what, my love, shall I compare thine eyne?
Crystal is muddy. O, how ripe in show
Thy lips, those kissing cherries, tempting grow!
That pure congealed white, high Taurus' snow,
Fann'd with the eastern wind, turns to a crow
When thou hold'st up thy hand: O let me kiss
This princess of pure white, this seal of bliss!
*Hel.* O spite! O hell! I see you all are bent
To set against me for your merriment.
If you were civil, and knew courtesy,
You would not do me thus much injury.
Can you not hate me, as I know you do,
But you must join in souls to mock me too?
If you were men, as men you are in show,
You would not use a gentle lady so;
To vow, and swear, and superpraise my parts,
When I am sure you hate me with your hearts.
You both are rivals, and love Hermia;
And now both rivals, to mock Helena:

A trim exploit, a manly enterprise,
To conjure tears up in a poor maid's eyes
With your derision! None of noble sort
Would so offend a virgin, and extort
A poor soul's patience, all to make you sport.
*Lys.* You are unkind, Demetrius; be not so;
For you love Hermia: this you know I know:
And here, with all good will, with all my heart,
In Hermia's love I yield you up my part;
And yours of Helena to me bequeath,
Whom I do love, and will do to my death.
*Hel.* Never did mockers waste more idle breath.
*Dem.* Lysander, keep thy Hermia; I will none:
If e'er I lov'd her, all that love is gone.
My heart with her but as guest-wise sojourn'd;
And now to Helen is it home return'd,
There to remain.
*Lys.*          Helen, it is not so.
*Dem.* Disparage not the faith thou dost not
          know,
Lest, to thy peril, thou aby it dear.—
Look where thy love comes; yonder is thy dear.

*Enter* HERMIA.

*Her.* Dark night, that from the eye his func-
          tion takes,
The ear more quick of apprehension makes;
Wherein it doth impair the seeing sense,
It pays the hearing double recompense:—
Thou art not by mine eye, Lysander, found;
Mine ear, I thank it, brought me to thy sound.
But why unkindly didst thou leave me so?
*Lys.* Why should he stay whom love doth press
          to go?
*Her.* What love could press Lysander from my
          side?                                    [bide,—
*Lys.* Lysander's love, that would not let him
Fair Helena,—who more engilds the night
Than all yon fiery oes and eyes of light.
Why seek'st thou me? could not this make
          thee know
The hate I bare thee made me leave thee so?
*Her.* You speak not as you think; it cannot be.
*Hel.* Lo, she is one of this confederacy!
Now I perceive they have conjoin'd all three
To fashion this false sport in spite of me.
Injurious Hermia! most ungrateful maid!
Have you conspir'd, have you with these con-
          triv'd
To bait me with this foul derision?
Is all the counsel that we two have shar'd,
The sisters' vows, the hours that we have spent,
When we have chid the hasty-footed time
For parting us,—O, is all forgot?        [cence?
All school-days' friendship, childhood inno-
We, Hermia, like two artificial gods,
Have with our neelds created both one flower,
Both on one sampler, sitting on one cushion,
Both warbling of one song, both in one key;
As if our hands, our sides, voices, and minds
Had been incorporate. So we grew together,
Like to a double cherry, seeming parted;
But yet a union in partition,
Two lovely berries moulded on one stem:

So, with two seeming bodies, but one heart,
Two of the first, like coats in heraldry,
Due but to one, and crowned with one crest.
And will you rent our ancient love asunder,
To join with men in scorning your poor friend?
It is not friendly, 'tis not maidenly:
Our sex, as well as I, may chide you for it,
Though I alone do feel the injury.
*Her.* I am amazed at your passionate words:
I scorn you not; it seems that you scorn me.
*Hel.* Have you not sent Lysander, as in scorn,
To follow me, and praise my eyes and face?
And made your other love, Demetrius,—
Who even but now did spurn me with his foot,—
To call me goddess, nymph, divine, and rare,
Precious, celestial? Wherefore speaks he this
To her he hates? and wherefore doth Lysander
Deny your love, so rich within his soul,
And tender me, forsooth, affection,
But by your setting on, by your consent?
What though I be not so in grace as you,
So hung upon with love, so fortunate;
But miserable most, to love unlov'd?
This you should pity, rather than despise.
*Her.* I understand not what you mean by this.
*Hel.* Ay, do perséver, counterfeit sad looks,
Make mows upon me when I turn my back;
Wink at each other; hold the sweet jest up:
This sport, well carried, shall be chronicled.
If you have any pity, grace, or manners,
You would not make me such an argument.
But, fare ye well: 'tis partly mine own fault;
Which death, or absence, soon shall remedy.
*Lys.* Stay, gentle Helena; hear my excuse;
My love, my life, my soul, fair Helena!
*Hel.* O excellent!
*Her.*          Sweet, do not scorn her so.
*Dem.* If she cannot entreat, I can compel.
*Lys.* Thou canst compel no more than she en-
          treat;
Thy threats have no more strength than her
          weak prayers.—
Helen, I love thee; by my life I do;
I swear by that which I will lose for thee
To prove him false that says I love thee not.
*Dem.* I say I love thee more than he can do.
*Lys.* If thou say so, withdraw, and prove it too.
*Dem.* Quick, come,—
*Her.*          Lysander, whereto tends all this?
*Lys.* Away, you Ethiope!
*Dem.*          No, no, sir:—he will
Seem to break loose; take on as you would
          follow:
But yet come not. You are a tame man; go!
*Lys.* Hang off, thou cat, thou burr: vile thing,
          let loose,
Or I will shake thee from me like a serpent.
*Her.* Why are you grown so rude? what change
          is this,
Sweet love?
*Lys.*          Thy love? out, tawny Tartar, out!
Out, loath'd medicine! hated potion, hence!
*Her.* Do you not jest?
*Hel.*          Yes, 'sooth; and so do you.

*Lys.* Demetrius, I will keep my word with thee.
*Dem.* I would I had your bond; for I perceive
A weak bond holds you; I'll not trust your
    word.         [her dead?
*Lys.* What! should I hurt her, strike her, kill
Although I hate her I'll not harm her so.
*Her.* What! can you do me greater harm than
    hate?         [love?
Hate me! wherefore? O me! what news, my
Am not I Hermia? Are not you Lysander?
I am as fair now as I was erewhile.   [left me:
Since night you lov'd me; yet since night you
Why, then, you left me,—O, the gods forbid!—
In earnest, shall I say?
*Lys.*         Ay, by my life;
And never did desire to see thee more.
Therefore be out of hope, of question, doubt,
Be certain, nothing truer; 'tis no jest
That I do hate thee and love Helena.
*Her.* O me! you juggler! you canker-blossom!
You thief of love! What! have you come by
    night,
And stol'n my love's heart from him?
*Hel.*         Fine, i' faith!
Have you no modesty, no maiden shame,
No touch of bashfulness? What! will you tear
Impatient answers from my gentle tongue?
Fie, fie! you counterfeit, you puppet, you!
*Her.* Puppet! why so? Ay, that way goes the
    game.
    Now I perceive that she hath made compare
Between our statures; she hath urg'd her height;
And with her personage, her tall personage,
Her height, forsooth, she hath prevail'd with
    him.—
And are you grown so high in his esteem
Because I am so dwarfish and so low?
How low am I, thou painted maypole? speak;
How low am I? I am not yet so low
But that my nails can reach unto thine eyes.
*Hel.* I pray you, though you mock me, gentle-
    men,
Let her not hurt me. I was never curst;
I have no gift at all in shrewishness;
I am a right maid for my cowardice;
Let her not strike me. You perhaps may think
Because she's something lower than myself,
That I can match her.
*Her.*         Lower! hark, again.
*Hel.* Good Hermia, do not be so bitter with me.
I evermore did love you, Hermia;     [you;
Did ever keep your counsels; never wrong'd
Save that, in love unto Demetrius,
I told him of your stealth unto this wood:
He follow'd you; for love I follow'd him;
But he hath chid me hence, and threaten'd me
To strike me, spurn me, nay, to kill me too:
And now, so you will let me quiet go,
To Athens will I bear my folly back,
And follow you no farther. Let me go:
You see how simple and how fond I am.
*Her.* Why, get you gone: who is 't that hinders
    you?
*Hel.* A foolish heart that I leave here behind.

*Her.* What! with Lysander?
*Hel.*         With Demetrius.
*Lys.* Be not afraid: she shall not harm thee,
    Helena.
*Dem.* No sir, she shall not, though you take
    her part.
*Hel.* O, when she's angry, she is keen and
    shrewd:
She was a vixen when she went to school;
And, though she be but little, she is fierce.
*Her.* Little again! nothing but low and little!
Why will you suffer her to flout me thus?
Let me come to her.
*Lys.*         Get you gone, you dwarf;
You minimus, of hind'ring knot-grass made;
You bead, you acorn.
*Dem.*         You are too officious
In her behalf that scorns your services.
Let her alone; speak not of Helena;
Take not her part; for if thou dost intend
Never so little show of love to her,
Thou shalt aby it.
*Lys.*         Now she holds me not;
Now follow, if thou dar'st, to try whose right,
Or thine or mine, is most in Helena.
*Dem.* Follow! nay, I'll go with thee, cheek by
    jole.         [*Exeunt* LYS. *and* DEM.
*Her.* You, mistress, all this coil is 'long of you:
Nay, go not back.
*Hel.*         I will not trust you, I;
Nor longer stay in your curst company.
Your hands than mine are quicker for a fray;
My legs are longer though, to run away.
                    [*Exit.*
*Her.* I am amaz'd, and know not what to say.
               [*Exit, pursuing* HELENA.
*Obe.* This is thy negligence: still thou mistak'st,
Or else commit'st thy knaveries wilfully.
*Puck.* Believe me, king of shadows, I mistook.
Did not you tell me I should know the man
By the Athenian garments he had on?
And so far blameless proves my enterprise,
That I have 'nointed an Athenian's eyes:
And so far am I glad it so did sort,
As this their jangling I esteem a sport.
*Obe.* Thou seest these lovers seek a place to
    fight:
Hie therefore, Robin, overcast the night;
The starry welkin cover thou anon
With drooping fog, as black as Acheron;
And lead these testy rivals so astray,
As one come not within another's way.
Like to Lysander sometime frame thy tongue,
Then stir Demetrius up with bitter wrong;
And sometime rail thou like Demetrius;
And from each other look thou lead them thus,
Till o'er their brows death-counterfeiting sleep
With leaden legs and batty wings doth creep:
Then crush this herb into Lysander's eye;
Whose liquor hath this virtuous property,
To take from thence all error with his might,
And make his eyeballs roll with wonted sight.
When they next wake, all this derision
Shall seem a dream and fruitless vision;

And back to Athens shall the lovers wend,
With league whose date till death shall never end
Whiles I in this affair do thee employ,
I'll to my queen, and beg her Indian boy;
And then I will her charmed eye release
From monster's view, and all things shall be
    peace.
*Puck.* My fairy lord, this must be done with
    haste,
For night's swift dragons cut the clouds full fast;
And yonder shines Aurora's harbinger,
At whose approach ghosts, wandering here and
    there,
Troop home to churchyards: damned spirits all,
That in cross-ways and floods have burial,
Already to their wormy beds are gone;
For fear lest day should look their shames upon
They wilfully exile themselves from light,
And must for aye consort with black-brow'd
    night.
*Obe.* But we are spirits of another sort:
I with the morning's love have oft made sport;
And, like a forester, the groves may tread
Even till the eastern gate, all fiery-red,
Opening on Neptune with fair blessed beams,
Turns into yellow gold his salt-green streams.
But, notwithstanding, haste; make no delay:
We may effect this business yet ere day.
                   *[Exit* OBE.
*Puck.* Up and down, up and down;
I will lead them up and down:
I am fear'd in field and town;
Goblin, lead them up and down.
Here comes one.

        *Enter* LYSANDER.

*Lys.* Where art thou, proud Demetrius? speak
    thou now.            [art thou?
*Puck.* Here, villain; drawn and ready. Where
*Lys.* I will be with thee straight.
*Puck.*          Follow me, then,
To plainer ground.
      *[Exit* LYS. *as following the voice.*

        *Enter* DEMETRIUS.

*Dem.*        Lysander! speak again.
Thou runaway, thou coward, art thou fled?
Speak. In some bush? where dost thou hide,
    thy head?            [stars
*Puck.* Thou coward, art thou bragging to the
Telling the bushes that thou look'st for wars,
And wilt not come? Come, recreant; come,
    thou child;
I'll whip thee with a rod: he is defiled
That draws a sword on thee.
*Dem.*        Yea, art thou there?
*Puck.* Follow my voice; we'll try no manhood
    here.           [*Exeunt.*

     *Re-enter* LYSANDER.

*Lys.* He goes before me, and still dares me on;
When I come where he calls, then he is gone.
The villain is much lighter heeled than I:
I follow'd fast, but faster he did fly;

That fallen am I in dark uneven way,
And here will rest me. Come, thou gentle day!
                   *[Lies down.*
For if but once thou show me thy gray light,
I'll find Demetrius, and revenge this spite.
                   [*Sleeps*

   *Re-enter* PUCK *and* DEMETRIUS.

*Puck.* Ho, ho! ho, ho! Coward, why com'st
    thou not?
*Dem.* Abide me if thou dar'st; for well I wot
Thou runn'st before me, shifting every place;
And dar'st not stand, nor look me in the face.
Where art thou?
*Puck.*        Come hither; I am here.
*Dem.* Nay, then, thou mock'st me. Thou shalt
    buy this dear,
If ever I thy face by daylight see:
Now, go thy way. Faintness constraineth me
To measure out my length on this cold bed.—
By day's approach look to be visited.
                *[Lies down and sleeps.*

        *Enter* HELENA.

*Hel.* O weary night, O long and tedious night,
Abate thy hours! Shine comforts from the east,
That I may back to Athens by daylight,
From these that my poor company detest:—
And sleep, that sometimes shuts up sorrow's eye,
Steal me awhile from mine own company.
                   [*Sleeps.*
*Puck.* Yet but three? Come one more;
    Two of both kinds makes up four.
    Here she comes, curst and sad:—
    Cupid is a knavish lad,
    Thus to make poor females mad.

        *Enter* HERMIA.

*Her.* Never so weary, never so in woe,
    Bedabbled with the dew, and torn with briers;
I can no farther crawl, no farther go;
    My legs can keep no pace with my desires.
Here will I rest me till the break of day.
Heaven shield Lysander, if they mean a fray!
                   *[Lies down.*
*Puck.* On the ground
    Sleep sound:
    I'll apply
    To your eye,
Gentle lover, remedy.
    [*Squeezing the juice on* LYSANDER'S *eye.*
    When thou wak'st,
    Thou tak'st
    True delight
    In the sight
Of thy former lady's eye:
And the country proverb known,
That every man should take his own,
In your waking shall be shown:
    Jack shall have Jill;
    Nought shall go ill;        [be well.
The man shall have his mare again, and all shall
    [*Exit* PUCK.—DEM., HEL., &c, *sleep.*

## ACT IV.

### SCENE I.—*The Wood.*

*Enter* TITANIA *and* BOTTOM, Fairies *attending;* OBERON *behind, unseen.*

*Tita.* Come, sit thee down upon this flowery bed,
  While I thy amiable cheeks do coy,
And stick musk-roses in thy sleek smooth head,
  And kiss thy fair large ears, my gentle joy.
*Bot.* Where's Peasblossom?
*Peas.* Ready.
*Bot.* Scratch my head, Peasblossom.—Where's Monsieur Cobweb?
*Cob.* Ready.
*Bot.* Monsieur Cobweb; good monsieur, get your weapons in your hand and kill me a red-hipped humble-bee on the top of a thistle; and, good monsieur, bring me the honey-bag. Do not fret yourself too much in the action, monsieur; and, good monsieur, have a care the honey-bag break not; I would be loath to have you over-flown with a honey-bag, signior.—Where's Monsieur Mustardseed?
*Must.* Ready.                                         [seed.
*Bot.* Give me your neif, Monsieur Mustard-Pray you, leave your courtesy, good monsieur.
*Must.* What's your will?
*Bot.* Nothing, good monsieur, but to help Cavalero Cobweb to scratch. I must to the barber's, monsieur; for methinks I am marvellous hairy about the face: and I am such a tender ass, if my hair do but tickle me I must scratch.
*Tita.* What, wilt thou hear some music, my sweet love?
*Bot.* I have a reasonable good ear in music; let us have the tongs and the bones.                 [eat.
*Tita.* Or say, sweet love, what thou desir'st to
*Bot.* Truly, a peck of provender; I could munch your good dry oats. Methinks I have a great desire to a bottle of hay: good hay, sweet hay, hath no fellow.
*Tita.* I have a venturous fairy that shall seek The squirrel's hoard, and fetch thee new nuts.
*Bot.* I had rather have a handful or two of dried peas. But, I pray you, let none of your people stir me; I have an exposition of sleep come upon me.                                           [arms.
*Tita.* Sleep thou, and I will wind thee in my Fairies, be gone, and be all ways away.
So doth the woodbine the sweet honeysuckle
Gently entwist,—the female ivy so
Enrings the barky fingers of the elm.
O, how I love thee! how I dote on thee!
                                           [*They sleep.*

OBERON *advances. Enter* PUCK.

*Obe.* Welcome, good Robin. Seest thou this sweet sight?
Her dotage now I do begin to pity.
For, meeting her of late behind the wood,
Seeking sweet savours for this hateful fool,
I did upbraid her, and fall out with her:
For she his hairy temples then had rounded
With coronet of fresh and fragrant flowers;
And that same dew, which sometime on the buds
Was wont to swell like round and orient pearls,
Stood now within the pretty flow'rets' eyes,
Like tears that did their own disgrace bewail.
When I had, at my pleasure, taunted her,
And she, in mild terms, begg'd my patience,
I then did ask of her her changeling child;
Which straight she gave me, and her fairy sent
To bear him to my bower in fairy-land.
And now I have the boy, I will undo
This hateful imperfection of her eyes.
And, gentle Puck, take this transformed scalp
From off the head of this Athenian swain;
That he awaking when the other do,
May all to Athens back again repair,
And think no more of this night's accidents
But as the fierce vexation of a dream.
But first I will release the fairy queen.
    Be as thou wast wont to be;
        [*Touching her eyes with an herb.*
    See as thou wast wont to see:
    Dian's bud o'er Cupid's flower
    Hath such force and blessed power.
Now, my Titania; wake you, my sweet queen.
*Tita.* My Oberon! what visions have I seen!
Methought I was enamour'd of an ass.
*Obe.* There lies your love.
*Tita.*                    How came these things to pass?
O, how mine eyes do loathe his visage now!
*Obe.* Silence awhile.—Robin, take off this head.
Titania, music call; and strike more dead
Than common sleep, of all these five, the sense.
*Tita.* Music, ho! music; such as charmeth sleep.
*Puck.* Now, when thou wak'st, with thine own
        fool's eyes peep.
*Obe.* sound, music. [*Still music.*] Come, my
        queen, take hands with me,
And rock the ground whereon these sleepers be.
Now thou and I are new in amity,
And will to-morrow midnight solemnly
Dance in Duke Theseus' house triumphantly,
And bless it to all fair posterity:
There shall the pairs of faithful lovers be
Wedded, with Theseus, all in jollity.
*Puck.* Fairy king, attend and mark;
I do hear the morning lark.
*Obe.* Then, my queen, in silence sad,
Trip we after the night's shade:
We the globe can compass soon,
Swifter than the wand'ring moon.
*Tita.* Come, my lord; and in our flight,
Tell me how it came this night
That I sleeping here was found,
With these mortals on the ground.
                                           [*Exeunt.*
                                   [*Horns sound within.*

*Enter* THESEUS, HIPPOLYTA, EGEUS, *and* Train.

*The.* Go, one of you, find out the forester;—
For now our observation is perform'd;
And since we have the vaward of the day,
My love shall hear the music of my hounds.

Uncouple in the western valley; go:—
Despatch, I say, and find the forester.—
We will, fair queen, up to the mountain's top,
And mark the musical confusion
Of hounds and echo in conjunction.
*Hip.* I was with Hercules and Cadmus once,
When in a wood of Crete they bay'd the bear
With hounds of Sparta: never did I hear
Such gallant chiding; for, besides the groves,
The skies, the fountains, every region near
Seem'd all one mutual cry: I never heard
So musical a discord, such sweet thunder.
*The.* My hounds are bred out of the Spartan
      kind,
So flew'd, so sanded; and their heads are hung
With ears that sweep away the morning dew;
Crook-kneed and dew-lap'd like Thessalian
      bulls;
Slow in pursuit, but match'd in mouth like bells,
Each under each. A cry more tuneable
Was never holla'd to, nor cheer'd with horn,
In Crete, in Sparta, nor in Thessaly:
Judge when you hear.—But, soft, what nymphs
      are these?
*Ege.* My lord, this is my daughter here asleep;
And this Lysander; this Demetrius is;
This Helena, old Nedar's Helena:
I wonder of their being here together.
*The.* No doubt, they rose up early to observe
The rite of May; and, hearing our intent,
Came here in grace of our solemnity.—
But speak, Egeus; is not this the day
That Hermia should give answer of her choice?
*Ege.* It is, my lord.
*The.* Go, bid the huntsmen wake them with
      their horns.
      [*Horns, and shout within.* DEM., LYS.,
            HER., *and* HEL., *awake and start up.*
*The.* Good-morrow, friends. Saint Valentine is
      past;
Begin these wood-birds but to couple now?
*Lys.* Pardon, my lord.
      [*He and the rest kneel to* THESEUS.
*The.*              I pray you all, stand up.
I know you two are rival enemies;
How comes this gentle concord in the world,
That hatred is so far from jealousy
To sleep by hate, and fear no enmity?
*Lys.* My lord, I shall reply amazedly,
Half 'sleep, half waking: but as yet, I swear,
I cannot truly say how I came here:
But, as I think,—for truly would I speak—
And now I do bethink me, so it is,—
I came with Hermia hither: our intent      [be
Was to be gone from Athens, where we might
Without the peril of the Athenian law.
*Ege.* Enough, enough, my lord; you have
      enough;
I beg the law, the law upon his head.—
They would have stol'n away, they would,
      Demetrius,
Thereby to have defeated you and me:
You of your wife, and me of my consent,—
Of my consent that she should be your wife.

*Dem.* My lord, fair Helen told me of their stealth,
Of this their purpose hither to this wood;
And I in fury hither follow'd them,
Fair Helena in fancy following me.
But, my good lord, I wot not by what power,—
But by some power it is,—my love to Hermia
Melted as doth the snow—seems to me now
As the remembrance of an idle gawd
Which in my childhood I did dote upon:
And all the faith, the virtue of my heart,
The object and the pleasure of mine eye,
Is only Helena. To her, my lord,
Was I betroth'd ere I saw Hermia:
But, like in sickness, did I loathe this food;
But, as in health, come to my natural taste,
Now do I wish it, love it, long for it,
And will for evermore be true to it.
*The.* Fair lovers, you are fortunately met:
Of this discourse we more will hear anon.—
Egeus, I will overbear your will;
For in the temple, by and by with us,
These couples shall eternally be knit.
And, for the morning now is something worn,
Our purpos'd hunting shall be set aside.—
Away with us to Athens three and three,
We'll hold a feast in great solemnity.—
Come, Hippolyta.
      [*Exeunt* THE., HIP., EGE., *and* Train.
*Dem.* These things seem small and undistin-
      guishable,
Like far-off mountains turned into clouds.
*Her.* Methinks I see these things with parted
      eye,
When everything seems double.
*Hel.*                        So methinks:
And I have found Demetrius like a jewel.
Mine own, and not mine own.
*Dem.*                     If seems to me
That we yet sleep, we dream.—Do you not
      think
The duke was here, and bid us follow him?
*Her.* Yea, and my father.
*Hel.*                     And Hippolyta.
*Lys.* And he did bid us follow to the temple.
*Dem.* Why, then, we are awake: let's follow him;
And by the way let us recount our dreams.
      [*Exeunt.*

      *As they go out,* BOTTOM *awakes.*

*Bot.* When my cue comes, call me, and I will
answer:—my next is, *Most fair Pyramus.*——
Heigh-ho!—Peter Quince! Flute, the bellows-
mender! Snout, the tinker! Starveling! God's
my life, stolen hence, and left me asleep! I
have had a most rare vision. I have had a
dream—past the wit of man to say what dream
it was.—Man is but an ass if he go about to expound this dream. Methought I was—there is
no man can tell what. Methought I was, and
methought I had,—But man is but a patched
fool, if he will offer to say what methought I
had. The eye of man hath not heard, the ear of
man hath not seen; man's hand is not able to
taste, his tongue to conceive, nor his heart to

report what my dream was. I will get Peter
Quince to write a ballad of this dream: it shall
be called Bottom's Dream, because it hath no
bottom; and I will sing it in the latter end of a
play, before the duke: peradventure, to make
it the more gracious, I shall sing it at her
death.    [*Exit.*

SCENE II.—ATHENS. *A Room in* QUINCE'S
*House.*

*Enter* QUINCE, FLUTE, SNOUT, *and*
STARVELING.

*Quin.* Have you sent to Bottom's house? is he
come home yet?
*Star.* He cannot be heard of. Out of doubt, he
is transported.
*Flu.* If he come not, then the play is marred;
it goes not forward, doth it?
*Quin.* It is not possible: you have not a man in
all Athens able to discharge Pyramus but he.
*Flu.* No; he hath simply the best wit of any
handicraft man in Athens.
*Quin.* Yea, and the best person too: and he is
a very paramour for a sweet voice.
*Flu.* You must say paragon: a paramour is,
God bless us, a thing of naught.

*Enter* SNUG.

*Snug.* Masters, the duke is coming from the
temple; and there is two or three lords and
ladies more married: if our sport had gone forward we had all been made men.
*Flu.* O sweet bully Bottom! Thus hath he lost
sixpence a-day during his life; he could not
have 'scaped sixpence a-day: an the duke had
not given him sixpence a-day for playing Pyramus, I'll be hanged; he would have deserved
it: sixpence a-day in Pyramus, or nothing.

*Enter* BOTTOM.

*Bot.* Where are these lads? where are these
hearts?
*Quin.* Bottom!—O most courageous day! O
most happy hour!
*Bot.* Masters, I am to discourse wonders: but
ask me not what; for if I tell you, I am no true
Athenian. I will tell you everything, right as it
fell out.
*Quin.* Let us hear, sweet Bottom.
*Bot.* Not a word of me. All that I will tell you
is, that the duke hath dined. Get your apparel
together; good strings to your beards, new rib-
bons to your pumps; meet presently at the
palace; every man look over his part; for, the
short and the long is, our play is preferred. In
any case, let Thisby have clean linen; and let
not him that plays the lion pare his nails, for
they shall hang out for the lion's claws. And,
most dear actors, eat no onions nor garlick; for
we are to utter sweet breath; and I do not
doubt but to hear them say it is a sweet comedy.
No more words: away! go; away!    [*Exeunt.*

## ACT V.

SCENE I.—ATHENS. *An Apartment in the
Palace of* THESEUS.

*Enter* THESEUS, HIPPOLYTA, PHILOSTRATE,
Lords *and* Attendants.

*Hip.* 'Tis strange, my Theseus, that these
    lovers speak of.
*The.* More strange than true. I never may
    believe
These antique fables, nor these fairy toys.
Lovers and madmen have such seething brains,
Such shaping fantasies, that apprehend
More than cool reason ever comprehends.
The lunatic, the lover, and the poet
Are of imagination all compact:
One sees more devils than vast hell can hold;
That is the madman: the lover, all as frantic,
Sees Helen's beauty in a brow of Egypt:
The poet's eye, in a fine frenzy rolling,
Doth glance from heaven to earth, from earth
    to heaven,
And, as imagination bodies forth
The forms of things unknown, the poet's pen
Turns them to shapes, and gives to airy nothing
A local habitation and a name.
Such tricks hath strong imagination,
That, if it would but apprehend some joy,
It comprehends some bringer of that joy;
Or in the night, imagining some fear,
How easy is a bush supposed a bear?
*Hip.* But all the story of the night told over,
And all their minds transfigur'd so together,
More witnesseth than fancy's images,
And grows to something of great constancy;
But, howsoever, strange and admirable.

*Enter* LYSANDER, DEMETRIUS, HERMIA, *and*
HELENA.

*The.* Here come the lovers, full of joy and
    mirth.—
Joy, gentle friends! joy and fresh days of love
Accompany your hearts!
*Lys.*                      More than to us
Wait on your royal walks, your board, your bed!
*The.* Come now; what masques, what dances
    shall we have,
To wear away this long age of three hours
Between our after-supper and bed-time?
Where is our usual manager of mirth?
What revels are in hand? Is there no play,
To ease the anguish of a torturing hour?
Call Philostrate.
*Philost.*              Here, mighty Theseus.
*The.* Say, what abridgment have you for this
    evening?
What masque? what music? How shall we
    beguile
The lazy time, if not with some delight?
*Philost.* There is a brief how many sports are
    ripe;
Make choice of which your highness will see
    first.    [*Giving a paper.*

*The.* [*reads.*] *The battle with the Centaurs, to be
    sung
By an Athenian eunuch to the harp.*
We'll none of that: that I have told my love,
In glory of my kinsman Hercules.
*The riot of the tipsy Bacchanals,
    Tearing the Thracian singer in their rage.*
That is an old device, and it was play'd
When I from Thebes came last a conqueror.
*The thrice-three Muses mourning for the death
Of learning, late deceas'd in beggary.*
That is some satire, keen and critical,
Not sorting with a nuptial ceremony.
*A tedious brief scene of young Pyramus,
    And his love Thisbe; very tragical mirth.*
Merry and tragical! tedious and brief!
That is, hot ice and wondrous strange snow.
How shall we find the concord of this discord?
*Philost.* A play there is, my lord, some ten
    words long,
Which is as brief as I have known a play;
But by ten words, my lord, it is too long,
Which makes it tedious: for in all the play
There is not one word apt, one player fitted:
And tragical, my noble lord, it is;
For Pyramus therein doth kill himself:
Which when I saw rehears'd, I must confess,
Made mine eyes water; but more merry tears
The passion of loud laughter never shed.
*The.* What are they that do play it?
*Philost.* Hard-handed men that work in Athens
    here,
Which never labour'd in their minds till now;
And now have toil'd their unbreath'd memories
With this same play against your nuptial.
*The.* And we will hear it.
*Philost.*                    No, my noble lord,
It is not for you: I have heard it over,
And it is nothing, nothing in the world;
Unless you can find sport in their intents,
Extremely stretch'd, and conn'd with cruel pain,
To do you service.
*The.*                    I will hear that play;
For never anything can be amiss
When simpleness and duty tender it.
Go, bring them in: and take your places, ladies.
                        [*Exit* PHILOSTRATE.
*Hip.* I love not to see wretchedness o'er-
    charged,
And duty in his service perishing.    [thing.
*The.* Why, gentle sweet, you shall see no such
*Hip.* He says they can do nothing in this kind.
*The.* The kinder we, to give them thanks for
    nothing.
Our sport shall be to take what they mistake:
And what poor duty cannot do,
Noble respect takes it in might, not merit.
Where I have come, great clerks have purposed
To greet me with premeditated welcomes;
Where I have seen them shiver and look pale,
Make periods in the midst of sentences,
Throttle their practis'd accent in their fears,
And, in conclusion, dumbly have broke off,
Not paying me a welcome. Trust me, sweet,

Out of this silence yet I pick'd a welcome
And in the modesty of fearful duty
I read as much as from the rattling tongue
Of saucy and audacious eloquence.
Love, therefore, and tongue-tied simplicity
In least speak most to my capacity.

*Enter* PHILOSTRATE.

*Philost.* So please your grace, the prologue is
    address'd.
*The.* Let him approach.
                        [*Flourish of Trumpets.*

*Enter* Prologue.

*Prol. If we offend, it is with our good will.
    That you should think we come not to offend
But with good will. To show our simple skill,
    That is the true beginning of our end.
Consider, then, we come but in despite.
    We do not come as minding to content you.
Our true intent is. All for your delight
    We are not here. That you should here repent
        you.
The actors are at hand: and, by their show,
You shall know all that you are like to know.*

*The.* This fellow doth not stand upon points.
*Lys.* He hath rid his prologue like a rough
colt; he knows not the stop. A good moral,
my lord: it is not enough to speak, but to
speak true.
*Hip.* Indeed he hath played on this prologue
like a child on a recorder; a sound, but not in
government.
*The.* His speech was like a tangled chain;
nothing impaired, but all disordered. Who is
next?

*Enter* PYRAMUS *and* THISBE, WALL, MOON-
    SHINE, *and* LION, *as in dumb show.*

*Prol.* Gentles, perchance you wonder at this
    show;                            [plain.
    But wonder on, till truth make all things
This man is Pyramus, if you would know;
    This beauteous lady Thisby is, certáin.
This man, with lime and rough-cast, doth per-
    sent                            [sunder:
    Wall, that vile Wall which did these lovers
And through Wall's chink, poor souls, they are
    content
    To whisper, at the which let no man wonder.
This man, with lantern, dog, and bush of thorn,
    Presenteth Moonshine: for, if you will know,
By moonshine did these lovers think no scorn
    To meet at Ninus' tomb, there, there to woo.
This grisly beast, which by name Lion hight,
    The trusty Thisby, coming first by night,
Did scare away, or rather did affright:
    And as she fled, her mantle she did fall;
    Which Lion vile with bloody mouth did stain:
Anon comes Pyramus, sweet youth, and tall,
    And finds his trusty Thisby's mantle slain;
Whereat with blade, with bloody blameful blade,
    He bravely broach'd his boiling bloody breast;

And Thisby, tarrying in mulberry shade,
　His dagger drew, and died. For all the rest,
Let Lion, Moonshine, Wall, and lovers twain
At large discourse while here they do remain.
　　　[*Exeunt* Prol., Thisb., Lion, *and* Moon.
*The.* I wonder if the lion be to speak.
*Dem.* No wonder, my lord: one lion may, when
many asses do.
*Wall.* In this same interlude it doth befall
That I, one Snout by name, present a wall:
And such a wall as I would have you think
That had in it a crannied hole or chink,
Through which the lovers, Pyramus and Thisby,
Did whisper often very secretly.　　　[show
This loam, this rough-cast, and this stone doth
That I am that same is; the truth is so:
And this the cranny is, right and sinister,
Through which the fearful lovers are to whisper.
*The.* Would you desire lime and hair to speak
　　　better?
*Dem.* It is the wittiest partition that ever I
heard discourse, my lord.
*The.* Pyramus draws near the wall: silence!

*Enter* Pyramus.

*Pyr.* O grim-look'd night! O night with hue so
　　　black!
O night, which ever art when day is not!
O night, O night, alack, alack, alack,
　I fear my Thisby's promise is forgot!—
And thou, O wall, O sweet, O lovely wall,
　That stand'st between her father's ground
　　　and mine;
Thou wall, O wall, O sweet and lovely wall,
　Show me thy chink, to blink through with
　　　mine eyne.
　　　[Wall *holds up his fingers.*
Thanks, courteous wall: Jove shield thee well
　for this!
But what see I? No Thisby do I see.
O wicked wall, through whom I see no bliss;
　Curst be thy stones for thus deceiving me!
*The.* The wall, methinks, being sensible, should
curse again.
*Pyr.* No, in truth, sir, he should not. *Deceiving*
*me* is Thisby's cue: she is to enter now, and I
am to spy her through the wall. You shall see it
will fall pat as I told you.—Yonder she comes.

*Enter* Thisbe.

*This.* O wall, full often hast thou heard my
　　　moans,
For parting my fair Pyramus and me:
My cherry lips have often kiss'd thy stones;
　Thy stones with lime and hair knit up in thee.
*Pyr.* I see a voice; now will I to the chink,
　To spy an I can hear my Thisby's face.
Thisby!
*This.* My love! thou art my love, I think.
*Pyr.* Think what thou wilt, I am thy lover's
　　　grace:
And like Limander am I trusty still.
*This.* And I like Helen, till the fates me kill.
*Pyr.* Not Shafalus to Procrus was so true.

*This.* As Shafalus to Procrus, I to you.
*Pyr.* O, kiss me through the hole of this vile
　　　wall.
*This.* I kiss the wall's hole, not your lips at all.
*Pyr.* Wilt thou at Ninny's tomb meet me
　　　straightway?
*This.* 'Tide life, 'tide death, I come without
　　　delay.
*Wall.* Thus have I, wall, my part discharged so;
And, being done, thus wall away doth go.
　　　[*Exeunt* Wall, Pyr., *and* This.
*The.* Now is the mural down between the two
neighbours.
*Dem.* No remedy, my lord, when walls are so
wilful to hear without warning.
*Hip.* This is the silliest stuff that ever I heard.
*The.* The best in this kind are but shadows;
and the worst are no worse, if imagination
amend them.　　　　　　　　　[not theirs.
*Hip.* It must be your imagination then, and
*The.* If we imagine no worse of them than
they of themselves, they may pass for excellent
men. Here come two noble beasts in, a moon
and a lion.

*Enter* Lion *and* Moonshine.

*Lion.* You, ladies, you, whose gentle hearts do
　　　fear　　　　　　　　　　　　[on floor,
　The smallest monstrous mouse that creeps
May now, perchance, both quake and tremble
　　　here,
　When lion rough in wildest rage doth roar.
Then know that I, one Snug, the joiner, am
A lion fell, nor else no lion's dam:
For if I should as lion come in strife
Into this place, 'twere pity of my life.
*The.* A very gentle beast, and of a good con-
　science.　　　　　　　　　　　　[e'er I saw.
*Dem.* The very best at a beast, my lord, that
*Lys.* This lion is a very fox for his valour.
*The.* True; and a goose for his discretion.
*Dem.* Not so, my lord; for his valour cannot
carry his discretion; and the fox carries the
goose.
*The.* His discretion, I am sure, cannot carry
his valour; for the goose carries not the fox.
It is well: leave it to his discretion, and let us
listen to the moon.
*Moon.* This lantern doth the horned moon pre-
　sent:　　　　　　　　　　　　　　[head.
*Dem.* He should have worn the horns on his
*The.* He is no crescent, and his horns are in-
visible within the circumference.
*Moon.* This lantern doth the horned moon
　present;
Myself the man i' the moon do seem to be.
*The.* This is the greatest error of all the rest:
the man should be put into the lantern. How
is it else the man i' the moon?
*Dem.* He dares not come there for the candle:
for, you see, it is already in snuff.
*Hip.* I am weary of this moon: would he would
change!
*The.* It appears, by his small light of discre-

tion, that he is in the wane: but yet, in courtesy, in all reason, we must stay the time.
*Lys.* Proceed, moon.
*Moon.* All that I have to say, is to tell you that the lantern is the moon; I, the man in the moon; this thorn-bush, my thorn-bush; and this dog, my dog.
*Dem.* Why, all these should be in the lantern; for all these are in the moon. But, silence; here comes Thisbe.

### Enter THISBE.

*This.* This is old Ninny's tomb. Where is my
    love?
*Lion.* Oh!
      [*The* LION *roars.*—THISBE *runs off.*
*Dem.* Well roared, lion.
*The.* Well run, Thisbe.
*Hip.* Well shone, moon.—Truly, the moon shines with a good grace.
*The.* Well moused, lion
    [*The* LION *tears* THISBE'S *mantle and exit.*
*Dem.* And so comes Pyramus.
*Lys.* And then the lion vanishes.

### Enter PYRAMUS.

*Pyr.* Sweet moon, I thank thee for thy sunny
    beams;        [bright:
  I thank thee, moon, for shining now so
For, by thy gracious, golden, glittering streams,
  I trust to taste of truest Thisby's sight.
    But stay;—O spite!
    But mark,—poor knight,
What dreadful dole is here!
    Eyes, do you see?
    How can it be?
O dainty duck! O dear!
    Thy mantle good,
    What! stained with blood?
Approach, ye furies fell!
    O fates! come, come;
    Cut thread and thrum;
Quail, rush, conclude, and quell!
*The.* This passion, and the death of a dear friend, would go near to make a man look sad.
*Hip.* Beshrew my heart, but I pity the man.
*Pyr.* O wherefore, nature, didst thou lions
    frame?
Since lion vile hath here deflower'd my dear:
Which is—no, no—which was the fairest dame
That liv'd, that lov'd, that lik'd, that look'd
    with cheer.
    Come, tears, confound;
    Out, sword, and wound
The pap of Pyramus:
    Ay, that left pap,
    Where heart doth hop:—
Thus die I, thus, thus, thus.
    Now am I dead,
    Now am I fled;
My soul is in the sky:
    Tongue, lose thy light!
    Moon, take thy flight!

    Now die, die, die, die, die.
        [*Dies.—Exit* MOONSHINE.
*Dem.* No die, but an ace, for him; for he is
but one.               [is nothing.
*Lys.* Less than an ace, man; for he is dead; he
*The.* With the help of a surgeon he might yet recover and prove an ass.
*Hip.* How chance moonshine is gone before Thisbe comes back and finds her lover?
*The.* She will find him by starlight.—Here she comes; and her passion ends the play.

### Enter THISBE.

*Hip.* Methinks she should not use a long one for such a Pyramus: I hope she will be brief.
*Dem.* A mote will turn the balance, which Pyramus, which Thisbe, is the better.
*Lys.* She hath spied him already with those sweet eyes.
*Dem.* And thus she moans, *videlicet,*——
*This.*      Asleep, my love?
      What, dead, my dove?
    O Pyramus, arise,
      Speak, speak. Quite dumb?
      Dead, dead? A tomb
Must cover thy sweet eyes.
    These lily brows,
    This cherry nose,
These yellow cowslip cheeks,
    Are gone, are gone:
    Lovers, make moan!
His eyes were green as leeks
    O Sisters Three,
    Come, come to me,
With hands as pale as milk;
    Lay them in gore,
    Since you have shore
With shears his thread of silk.
    Tongue, not a word:—
    Come, trusty sword;
Come, blade, my breast imbrue:
    And farewell, friends:—
    Thus Thisby ends:
Adieu, adieu, adieu.      [*Dies.*
*The.* Moonshine and lion are left to bury the dead.
*Dem.* Ay, and wall too.
*Bot.* No, I assure you; the wall is down that parted their fathers. Will it please you to see the epilogue, or to hear a Bergomask dance between two of our company.
*The.* No epilogue, I pray you; for your play needs no excuse. Never excuse; for when the players are all dead there need none to be blamed. Marry, if he that writ it had played Pyramus, and hanged himself in Thisbe's garter, it would have been a fine tragedy: and so it is, truly; and very notably discharged. But come, your Bergomask: let your epilogue alone.
          [*Here a dance of* CLOWNS.
The iron tongue of midnight hath told twelve:—
Lovers, to bed; 'tis almost fairy time.
I fear we shall out-sleep the coming morn,
As much as we this night have overwatch'd.

This palpable-gross play hath well beguil'd
The heavy gait of night.—Sweet friends, to
    bed.—
A fortnight hold we this solemnity,
In nightly revels and new jollity.    [*Exeunt.*

### SCENE II.

*Enter* PUCK.

*Puck.* Now the hungry lion roars,
    And the wolf behowls the moon;
Whilst the heavy ploughman snores,
    All with weary task fordone.
Now the wasted brands do glow,
    Whilst the scritch-owl, scritching loud,
Puts the wretch that lies in woe
    In remembrance of a shroud.
Now it is the time of night
    That the graves, all gaping wide
Every one lets forth its sprite,
    In the church-way paths to glide:
And we fairies, that do run
    By the triple Hecate's team,
From the presence of the sun
    Following darkness like a dream,
Now are frolic; not a mouse
    Shall disturb this hallow'd house:
I am sent with broom before,
    To sweep the dust behind the door.

*Enter* OBERON *and* TITANIA, *with their* Train.

*Obe.* Through this house give glimmering light,
    By the dead and drowsy fire:
Every elf and fairy sprite
    Hop as light as bird from brier:
And this ditty, after me,
Sing and dance it trippingly.
*Tita.* First, rehearse your song by rote,
    To each word a warbling note,
Hand in hand, with fairy grace,
Will we sing, and bless this place.

SONG AND DANCE.

*Obe.* Now, until the break of day,
Through this house each fairy stray,
To the best bride-bed will we,
Which by us shall blessed be;
And the issue there create
Ever shall be fortunate.
So shall all the couples three
Ever true in loving be;
And the blots of Nature's hand
Shall not in their issue stand:
Never mole, hare-lip, nor scar,
Nor mark prodigious, such as are
Despised in nativity,
Shall upon their children be.—
With this field-dew consecrate,
Every fairy take his gate;
And each several chamber bless,
Through this palace, with sweet peace;
E'er shall it in safety rest,
And the owner of it blest.
    Trip away:
    Make no stay:
Meet me all by break of day.
    [*Exeunt* OBE., TITA., *and* Train.
*Puck.* If we shadows have offended,
Think but this—and all is mended—
That you have but slumber'd here
While these visions did appear.
And this weak and idle theme,
No more yielding but a dream,
Gentles, do not reprehend;
If you pardon, we will mend.
And, as I'm an honest Puck,
If we have unearned luck
Now to 'scape the serpent's tongue,
We will make amends ere long;
Else the Puck a liar call:
So, good night unto you all.
Give me your hands, if we be friends,
And Robin shall restore amends.    [*Exit.*

# LOVE'S LABOUR'S LOST

## DRAMATIS PERSONÆ

FERDINAND, *King of Navarre.*
BIRON,
LONGAVILLE, } *Lords attending on the* KING.
DUMAIN,
BOYET, } *Lords attending on the* PRIN-
MERCADE, } CESS OF FRANCE.
DON ADRIANO DE ARMADO, *a Fantastical*
    *Spaniard.*
SIR NATHANIEL, *a Curate.*
HOLOFERNES, *a Schoolmaster.*
DULL, *a Constable.*
COSTARD, *a Clown.*

MOTH, *Page to* ARMADO.
A Forester.

PRINCESS OF FRANCE.
ROSALINE, }
MARIA, } *Ladies attending on the*
KATHARINE, } PRINCESS.
JAQUENETTA, *a Country Wench.*

Officers *and* Others, *Attendants on the* KING
    *and* PRINCESS.

### SCENE,—NAVARRE.

## ACT I.

SCENE I.—NAVARRE. *A Park, with a Palace*
*in it.*

*Enter the* KING, BIRON, LONGAVILLE, *and*
DUMAIN.

*King.* Let fame, that all hunt after in their
    lives,
Live register'd upon our brazen tombs,
And then grace us in the disgrace of death;
When, spite of cormorant devouring time,
The endeavour of this present breath may buy
That honour which shall bate his scythe's keen
    edge,
And make us heirs of all eternity.
Therefore, brave conquerors,—for so you are,
That war against your own affections,
And the huge army of the world's desires,—
Our late edict shall strongly stand in force:
Navarre shall be the wonder of the world·
Our court shall be a little Academe,
Still and contemplative in living art.
You three, Birón, Dumain, and Longaville,
Have sworn for three years' term to live with me
My fellow-scholars, and to keep those statutes
That are recorded in this schedule here:
Your oaths are pass'd; and now subscribe your
    names,
That his own hand may strike his honour down
That violates the smallest branch herein:
If you are arm'd to do as sworn to do,
Subscribe to your deep oaths, and keep it too.
*Long.* I am resolv'd; 'tis but a three years' fast:
The mind shall banquet though the body pine
Fat paunches have lean pates; and dainty bits.
Make rich the ribs, but bankrupt quite the wits:
*Dum.* My loving lord, Dumain is mortified:
The grosser manner of these world's delights
He throws upon the gross world's baser slaves:

To love, to wealth, to pomp, I pine and die;
With all these living in philosophy.
*Biron.* I can but say their protestation over;
So much, dear liege, I have already sworn,
That is, to live and study here three years.
But there are other strict observances:
As, not to see a woman in that term;
Which I hope well is not enrolled there:
And one day in a week to touch no food,
And but one meal on every day beside;
The which I hope is not enrolled there:
And then, to sleep but three hours in the night,
And not be seen to wink of all the day,—
When I was wont to think no harm all night,
And make a dark night too of half the day,—
Which I hope well is not enrolled there:
O, these are barren tasks too hard to keep;
Not to see ladies—study—fast—not sleep.
*King.* Your oath is pass'd to pass away from
    these. [please;
*Biron.* Let me say no, my liege, and if you
I only swore to study with your grace,
And stay here in your court for three years' space.
*Long.* You swore to that, Birón, and to the rest.
*Biron.* By yea and nay, sir, then I swore in
    jest.—
What is the end of study? let me know.
*King.* Why, that to know which else we should
    not know.
*Biron.* Things hid and barr'd, you mean, from
    common sense?
*King.* Ay, that is study's god-like recompense.
*Biron.* Come on, then, I will swear to study so,
To know the thing I am forbid to know:
As thus,—to study where I well may dine,
    When I to feast expressly am forbid;
Or study where to meet some mistress fine,
    When mistresses from common sense are hid:
Or, having sworn too-hard-a-keeping oath,
Study to break it, and not break my troth.

175

If study's gain be thus, and this be so,
Study knows that which yet it doth not know:
Swear me to this, and I will ne'er say no.
*King.* These be the stops that hinder study
    quite,
And train our intellects to vain delight.
*Biron.* Why, all delights are vain; but that
    most vain
Which, with pain purchas'd, doth inherit pain:
As painfully to pore upon a book
    To seek the light of truth; while truth the
      while
Doth falsely blind the eyesight of his look:
    Light, seeking light, doth light of light beguile.
So, ere you find where light in darkness lies,
Your light grows dark by losing of your eyes.
Study me how to please the eye indeed,
    By fixing it upon a fairer eye;
Who dazzling so, that eye shall be his heed,
    And give him light that it was blinded by.
Study is like the heaven's glorious sun,
    That will not be deep-search'd with saucy
      looks;
Small have continual plodders ever won,
    Save base authority from others' books,
These earthly godfathers of heaven's lights,
    That give a name to every fixed star,
Have no more profit of their shining nights
    Than those that walk and wot not what they
      are.
Too much to know is to know naught but fame;
And every godfather can give a name.
*King.* How well he's read, to reason against
    reading!
*Dum.* Proceeded well, to stop all good pro-
    ceeding!
*Long.* He weeds the corn, and still lets grow
    the weeding.
*Biron.* The spring is near, when green geese are
    a-breeding.
*Dum.* How follows that?
*Biron.*               Fit in his place and time.
*Dum.* In reason nothing.
*Biron.*            Something then in rhyme.
*Long.* Birón is like an envious sneaping frost,
That bites the first-born infants of the spring.
*Biron.* Well, say I am; why should proud sum-
    mer boast
Before the birds have any cause to sing?
Why should I joy in an abortive birth?
At Christmas I no more desire a rose
Than wish a snow in May's new-fangled shows;
But like of each thing that in season grows.
So you, to study now it is too late,
Climb o'er the house to unlock the little gate.
*King.* Well, sit you out: go home, Birón: adieu.
*Biron.* No, my good lord; I have sworn to stay
    with you:
And though I have for barbarism spoke more
    Than for that angel knowledge you can say,
Yet confident I'll keep what I have swore,
    And bide the penance of each three years' day.
Give me the paper, let me read the same;
And to the strict'st decrees I'll write my name.

*King.* How well this yielding rescues thee from
    shame!
*Biron.* [*reads.*] Item, *That no woman shall come
within a mile of my court.*—
And hath this been proclaim'd?
*Long.*                 Four days ago.
*Biron.* Let's see the penalty.
[*Reads.*]—*On pain of losing her tongue.*
                    Who devis'd this?
*Long.* Marry, that did I.
*Biron.* Sweet lord, and why?     [penalty.
*Long.* To fright them hence with that dread
*Biron.* A dangerous law against gentility.
[*Reads.*] Item, *If any man be seen to talk with
a woman within the term of three years, he shall
endure such public shame as the rest of the court
can possibly devise.*—
This article, my liege, yourself must break;
    For well you know here comes in embassy
The French king's daughter, with yourself to
      speak,—
    A maid of grace and cómplete majesty,—
About surrender-up of Aquitain
    To her decrepit, sick, and bed-rid father:
Therefore this article is made in vain.
    Or vainly comes the admired princess hither.
*King.* What say you, lords? why, this was quite
    forgot.
*Biron.* So study evermore is over-shot;
While it doth study to have what it would,
It doth forget to do the thing it should:
And when it hath the thing it hunteth most,
'Tis won as towns with fire,—so won, so lost.
*King.* We must, of force, dispense with this
    decree;
She must lie here on mere necessity.
*Biron.* Necessity will make us all forsworn
    Three thousand times within this three years'
      space:
For every man with his affects is born;
    Not by might master'd, but by special grace:
If I break faith, this word shall speak for me,
I am forsworn on mere necessity.—
So to the laws at large I write my name:
                [*Subscribes.*
    And he that breaks them in the least degree
Stands in attainder of eternal shame.
Suggestions are to others as to me;
But I believe, although I seem so loath;
I am the last that will last keep his oath.
But is there no quick recreation granted?
*King.* Ah, that there is: our court, you know,
    is haunted
With a refined traveller of Spain;
A man in all the world's new fashion planted,
    That hath a mint of phrases in his brain:
One whom the music of his own vain tongue
    Doth ravish, like enchanting harmony;
A man of complements, whom right and wrong
    Have chose as umpire of their mutiny:
This child of fancy, that Armado hight,
    For interim to our studies, shall relate,
In high-born words, the worth of many a knight
    From tawny Spain, lost in the world's debate.

How you delight, my lords, I know not, I;
But, I protest, I love to hear him lie,
And I will use him for my minstrelsy.
*Biron.* Armado is a most illustrious wight,
A man of fire-new words, fashion's own knight.
*Long.* Costard, the swain, and he shall be our
  sport;
And so to study—three years is but short.

*Enter* DULL *with a letter, and* COSTARD.

*Dull.* Which is the duke's own person?
*Biron.* This, fellow; what wouldst?
*Dull.* I myself reprehend his own person, for I
am his grace's tharborough: but I would see
his own person in flesh and blood.
*Biron.* This is he.
*Dull.* Signior Arme—Arme—commends you.
There's villany abroad: this letter will tell you
more.
*Cost.* Sir, the contempts thereof are as touch-
ing me.
*King.* A letter from the magnificent Armado.
*Biron.* How low soever the matter, I hope in
God for high words.
*Long.* A high hope for a low heaven: God grant
us patience!
*Biron.* To hear? or forbear laughing?
*Long.* To hear meekly, sir, and to laugh mod-
erately; or to forbear both.
*Biron.* Well, sir, be it as the style shall give us
cause to climb in the merriness.
*Cost.* The matter is to me, sir, as concerning
Jaquenetta. The manner of it is, I was taken
with the manner.
*Biron.* In what manner?
*Cost.* In manner and form following, sir, all
those three: I was seen with her in the manor
house, sitting with her upon the form, and taken
following her into the park; which, put together,
is in manner and form following. Now, sir, for
the manner,—it is the manner of a man to speak
to a woman: for the form,—in some form.
*Biron.* For the following, sir?
*Cost.* As it shall follow in my correction: and
God defend the right!
*King.* Will you hear this letter with attention?
*Biron.* As we would hear an oracle.
*Cost.* Such is the simplicity of man to hearken
after the flesh.
*King.* [*reads.*] Great deputy, the welkin's vice-
gerent and sole dominator of Navarre, my
soul's earth's God and body's fostering patron,—
*Cost.* Not a word of Costard yet.
*King.* [*reads.*] So it is,—
*Cost.* It may be so: but if he say it is so, he is
in telling true, but so so.
*King.* Peace!
*Cost.* —be to me, and every man that dares
not fight!
*King.* No words!
*Cost.* —of other men's secrets, I beseech you.
*King.* [*reads.*] So it is, besieged with sable-
coloured melancholy, I did commend the black-
oppressing humour to the most wholesome

physic of thy health-giving air; and, as I am a
gentleman, betook myself to walk. The time
when? About the sixth hour; when beasts most
graze, birds best peck, and men sit down to
that nourishment which is called supper: so
much for the time when. Now for the ground
which; which, I mean, I walked upon: it is
ycleped thy park. Then for the place where;
where, I mean, I did encounter that obscene
and most preposterous event that draweth
from my snow-white pen the ebon-coloured
ink, which here thou viewest, beholdest, sur-
veyest, or seest: but to the place where,—it
standeth north-north-east and by-east from
the west corner of thy curious-knotted garden.
There did I see that low-spirited swain, that
base minnow of thy mirth,—
*Cost.* Me.
*King.* —that unlettered small-knowing soul,—
*Cost.* Me.
*King.* —that shallow vassal,—
*Cost.* Still me.
*King.* —which, as I remember, hight Costard,—
*Cost.* O, me.
*King.* —sorted and consorted, contrary to thy
established proclaimed edict and continent
canon, with—with,—O, with—but with this I
passion to say wherewith,—
*Cost.* With a wench.
*King.* —with a child of our grandmother Eve,
a female; or, for thy more sweet understanding,
a woman. Him,—I as my ever esteemed duty
pricks me on,—have sent to thee, to receive the
meed of punishment, by thy sweet grace's officer, Antony Dull, a man of good repute, carriage, bearing, and estimation.
*Dull.* Me, an't shall please you; I am Antony
Dull.
*King.* [*reads.*] For Jaquenetta,—so is the weaker
vessel called, which I apprehended with the
aforesaid swain,—I keep her as a vessel of thy
law's fury; and shall, at the least of thy sweet
notice, bring her to trial. Thine, in all compliments of devoted and heart-burning heat of
duty,          DON ADRIANO DE ARMADO.
*Biron.* This is not so well as I looked for, but
the best that ever I heard.
*King.* Ay, the best for the worst. But, sirrah,
what say you to this?
*Cost.* Sir, I confess the wench.
*King.* Did you hear the proclamation?
*Cost.* I do confess much of the hearing it, but
little of the marking of it.
*King.* It was proclaimed a year's imprison-
ment, to be taken with a wench.
*Cost.* I was taken with none, sir, I was taken
with a damosel.
*King.* Well, it was proclaimed damosel.
*Cost.* This was no damosel neither, sir; she was
a virgin.                               [virgin.
*King.* It is so varied too; for it was proclaimed
*Cost.* If it were, I deny her virginity; I was
taken with a maid.
*King.* This maid will not serve your turn, sir.

*Cost.* This maid will serve my turn, sir.

*King.* Sir, I will pronounce your sentence: you shall fast a week with bran and water.

*Cost.* I had rather pray a month with mutton and porridge.

*King.* And Don Armado shall be your keeper.—
My Lord Birón, see him delivered over.—
And go we, lords, to put in practice that
Which each to other hath so strongly sworn.—
　　　　　[*Exeunt* KING, LONG. *and* DUM.

*Biron.* I'll lay my head to any good man's hat,
These oaths and laws will prove an idle scorn.—
Sirrah, come on.

*Cost.* I suffer for the truth, sir: for true it is, I was taken with Jaquenetta, and Jaquenetta is a true girl; and therefore, Welcome the sour cup of prosperity! Affliction may one day smile again, and till then, Sit thee down, sorrow!
　　　　　[*Exeunt.*

SCENE II.—*Another part of the Park.*

*Enter* ARMADO *and* MOTH.

*Arm.* Boy, what sign is it when a man of great spirit grows melancholy?

*Moth.* A great sign, sir, that he will look sad.

*Arm.* Why, sadness is one and the self-same thing, dear imp.

*Moth.* No, no; O lord, sir, no.

*Arm.* How canst thou part sadness and melancholy, my tender juvenal?

*Moth.* By a familiar demonstration of the working, my tough senior.

*Arm.* Why tough senior? why tough senior?

*Moth.* Why tender juvenal? why tender juvenal?

*Arm.* I spoke it, tender juvenal, as a congruent epitheton appertaining to thy young days, which we may nominate tender.

*Moth.* And I, tough senior, as an appertinent title to your old time, which we may name tough.

*Arm.* Pretty, and apt.

*Moth.* How mean you, sir; I pretty, and my saying apt? or I apt, and my saying pretty?

*Arm.* Thou pretty, because little.

*Moth.* Little pretty, because little. Wherefore apt?

*Arm.* And therefore apt, because quick.

*Moth.* Speak you this in my praise, master?

*Arm.* In thy condign praise.

*Moth.* I will praise an eel with the same praise.

*Arm.* What, that an eel is ingenious?

*Moth.* That an eel is quick.

*Arm.* I do say thou art quick in answers: thou heatest my blood.

*Moth.* I am answered, sir.

*Arm.* I love not to be crossed.

*Moth.* He speaks the mere contrary; crosses love not him.　　　　　[*Aside.*

*Arm.* I have promised to study three years with the duke.

*Moth.* You may do it in an hour, sir.

*Arm.* Impossible.

*Moth.* How many is one thrice told?

*Arm.* I am ill at reckoning; it fitteth the spirit of a tapster.

*Moth.* You are a gentleman and a gamester, sir.

*Arm.* I confess both,—they are both the varnish of a complete man.

*Moth.* Then, I am sure, you know how much the gross sum of deuce-ace amounts to.

*Arm.* It doth amount to one more than two.

*Moth.* Which the base vulgar do call three.

*Arm.* True.

*Moth.* Why, sir, is this such a piece of study? Now here is three studied ere you'll thrice wink: and how easy it is to put years to the word three, and study three years in two words, the dancing horse will tell you.

*Arm.* A most fine figure!

*Moth.* To prove you a cipher.　　　　　[*Aside.*

*Arm.* I will hereupon confess I am in love: and, as it is base for a soldier to love, so am I in love with a base wench. If drawing my sword against the humour of affection would deliver me from the reprobate thought of it, I would take desire prisoner, and ransom him to any French courtier for a new devised courtesy. I think scorn to sigh; methinks, I should outswear Cupid. Comfort me, boy: what great men have been in love?

*Moth.* Hercules, master.

*Arm.* Most sweet Hercules!—More authority, dear boy, name more; and, sweet my child, let them be men of good repute and carriage.

*Moth.* Samson, master; he was a man of good carriage, great carriage,—for he carried the town-gates on his back like a porter: and he was in love.

*Arm.* O well-knit Samson! strong-jointed Samson! I do excel thee in my rapier as much as thou didst me in carrying gates. I am in love too:—who was Samson's love, my dear Moth?

*Moth.* A woman, master.

*Arm.* Of what complexion?

*Moth.* Of all the four, or the three, or the two; or one of the four.

*Arm.* Tell me precisely of what complexion.

*Moth.* Of the sea-water green, sir.

*Arm.* Is that one of the four complexions?

*Moth.* As I have read, sir: and the best of them too.

*Arm.* Green, indeed, is the colour of lovers; but to have a love of that colour, methinks Samson had small reason for it. He surely affected her for her wit.

*Moth.* It was so, sir; for she had a green wit.

*Arm.* My love is most immaculate white and red.

*Moth.* Most maculate thoughts, master, are masked under such colours.

*Arm.* Define, define, well-educated infant.

*Moth.* My father's wit and my mother's tongue, assist me!

*Arm.* Sweet invocation of a child; most pretty, and pathetical!

*Moth.* If she be made of white and red,
　　Her faults will ne'er be known;
For blushing cheeks by faults are bred,

And fears by pale white shown:
Then if she fear, or be to blame,
　By this you shall not know;
For still her cheeks possess the same
　Which native she doth owe.
A dangerous rhyme, master, against the reason
of white and red.

*Arm.* Is there not a ballad, boy, of the King
and the Beggar.

*Moth.* The world was very guilty of such a
ballad some three ages since: but, I think, now
'tis not to be found; or, if it were, it would
neither serve for the writing nor the tune.

*Arm.* I will have the subject newly writ o'er,
that I may example my digression by some
mighty precedent. Boy, I do love that country
girl that I took in the park with the rational
hind Costard: she deserves well.

*Moth.* To be whipped: and yet a better love
than my master.　　　　　　　　　[*Aside.*

*Arm.* Sing, boy; my spirit grows heavy in love.

*Moth.* And that's great marvel, loving a light
　wench.

*Arm.* I say, sing.

*Moth.* Forbear till this company be past.

*Enter* DULL, COSTARD, *and* JAQUENETTA.

*Dull.* Sir, the duke's pleasure is, that you
keep Costard safe: and you must let him take
no delight nor no penance; but 'a must fast
three days a-week. For this damsel, I must
keep her at the park: she is allowed for the
day-woman. Fare you well.　　　　　[*Maid.*

*Arm.* I do betray myself with blushing.—
*Jaq.* Man.

*Arm.* I will visit thee at the lodge.

*Jaq.* That's here by.

*Arm.* I know where it is situate.

*Jaq.* Lord, how wise you are!

*Arm.* I will tell thee wonders.

*Jaq.* With that face?

*Arm.* I love thee.

*Jaq.* So I heard you say.

*Arm.* And so farewell.

*Jaq.* Fair weather after you!

*Dull.* Come, Jaquenetta, away.

　　　　　[*Exeunt* DULL *and* JAQUENETTA.

*Arm.* Villain, thou shalt fast for thy offences
ere thou be pardoned.

*Cost.* Well, sir, I hope, when I do it I shall do
it on a full stomach.

*Arm.* Thou shalt be heavily punished.

*Cost.* I am more bound to you than your fellows, for they are but lightly rewarded.

*Arm.* Take away this villain; shut him up.

*Moth.* Come, you transgressing slave: away.

*Cost.* Let me not be pent up, sir; I will fast,
being loose.

*Moth.* No, sir; that were fast and loose: thou
shalt to prison.

*Cost.* Well, if ever I do see the merry days of
desolation that I have seen, some shall see—

*Moth.* What shall some see?

*Cost.* Nay, nothing, Master Moth, but what

they look upon. It is not for prisoners to be too
silent in their words; and therefore I will say
nothing: I thank God I have as little patience
as another man; and therefore I can be quiet.

　　　　　　　　[*Exeunt* MOTH *and* COSTARD.

*Arm.* I do affect the very ground, which is
base, where her shoe, which is baser, guided by
her foot, which is basest, doth tread. I shall be
forsworn,—which is a great argument of falsehood,—if I love. And how can that be true love
which is falsely attempted? Love is a familiar;
love is a devil; there is no evil angel but love.
Yet Samson was so tempted,—and he had an
excellent strength: yet was Solomon so seduced,
—and he had a very good wit. Cupid's butt-
shaft is too hard for Hercules's club, and therefore too much odds for a Spaniard's rapier.
The first and second cause will not serve my
turn; the passado he respects not, the duello
he regards not: his disgrace is to be called boy;
but his glory is to subdue men. Adieu, valour!
rust, rapier! be still, drum! for your manager
is in love; yea, he loveth. Assist me, some extemporal god of rhyme, for I am sure I shall
turn sonneteer. Devise, wit; write, pen; for I
am for whole volumes in folio.　　　　[*Exit.*

## ACT II.

SCENE I.—*Another part of the Park. A Pavilion and Tents at a distance.*

*Enter the* PRINCESS OF FRANCE, ROSALINE,
MARIA, KATHARINE, BOYET, Lords, *and
other* Attendants.

*Boyet.* Now, madam, summon up your dearest
　　　　　　spirits;
Consider who the king your father sends;
To whom he sends; and what's his embassy:
Yourself, held precious in the world's esteem,
To parley with the sole inheritor
Of all perfections that a man may owe,
Matchless Navarre; the plea of no less weight
Than Aquitain,—a dowry for a queen.
Be now as prodigal of all dear grace
As nature was in making graces dear
When she did starve the general world beside,
And prodigally gave them all to you.

*Prin.* Good Lord Boyet, my beauty, though
　　　　　　but mean,
Needs not be painted flourish of your praise;
Beauty is bought by judgment of the eye,
Not utter'd by base sale of chapmen's tongues:
I am less proud to hear you tell my worth
Than you much willing to be counted wise
In spending your wit in the praise of mine.
But now to task the tasker:—good Boyet,
You are not ignorant, all-telling fame
Doth noise abroad Navarre hath made a vow,
Till painful study shall out-wear three years
No woman may approach his silent court:
Therefore to us seemeth it a needful course,
Before we enter his forbidden gates,
To know his pleasure; and in that behalf,
Bold of your worthiness, we single you

As our best-moving fair solicitor.
Tell him the daughter of the King of France,
On serious business, craving quick despatch,
Importunes personal conference with his grace.
Haste, signify so much; while we attend,
Like humbly-visag'd suitors, his high will.
*Boyet.* Proud of employment, willingly I go.
*Prin.* All pride is willing pride, and yours is
   so.—             [*Exit* BOYET.
Who are the votaries, my loving lords,
That are vow-fellows with this virtuous duke?
*1 Lord.* Longaville is one.
*Prin.*                Know you the man?
*Mar.* I know him, madam; at a marriage feast,
Between Lord Perigort and the beauteous heir
Of Jaques Falconbridge, solémnized
In Normandy, saw I this Longaville:
A man of sovereign parts he is esteem'd;
Well fitted in the arts, glorious in arms:
Nothing becomes him ill that he would well.
The only soil of his fair virtue's gloss,—
If virtue's gloss will stain with any soil,—
Is a sharp wit matched with too blunt a will;
Whose edge hath power to cut, whose will still
   wills
It should none spare that come within his power.
*Prin.* Some merry mocking lord, belike; is't so?
*Mar.* They say so most that most his humours
   know.
*Prin.* Such short-liv'd wits do wither as they
   grow.
Who are the rest?               [youth
*Kath.* The young Dumain, a well-accomplish'd
Of all that virtue love for virtue lov'd:
Most power to do most harm, least knowing ill;
For he hath wit to make an ill shape good,
And shape to win grace though he had no wit.
I saw him at the Duke Alençon's once;
And much too little of that good I saw
Is my report to his great worthiness.
*Ros.* Another of these students at that time
Was there with him; if I have heard a truth,
Biron they call him; but a merrier man,
Within the limit of becoming mirth,
I never spent an hour's talk withal:
His eye begets occasion for his wit:
For every object that the one doth catch,
The other turns to a mirth-moving jest;
Which his fair tongue—conceit's expositor—
Delivers in such apt and gracious words
That aged ears play truant at his tales,
And younger hearings are quite ravished;
So sweet and voluble is his discourse.
*Prin.* God bless my ladies! are they all in love,
That every one her own hath garnished
With such bedecking ornaments of praise?
*Mar.* Here comes Boyet.

*Re-enter* BOYET.

*Prin.*             Now, what admittance, lord?
*Boyet.* Navarre had notice of your fair ap-
   proach;
And he and his competitors in oath
Were all address'd to meet you, gentle lady,

Before I came. Marry, thus much I have
   learnt,—
He rather means to lodge you in the field,
Like one that comes here to besiege his court,
Than seek a dispensation for his oath,
To let you enter his unpeopled house.
Here comes Navarre.       [*The Ladies mask.*

*Enter* KING, LONGAVILLE, DUMAIN, BIRON,
      *and* Attendants.

*King.* Fair princess, welcome to the court of
   Navarre.
*Prin. Fair,* I give you back again; and *welcome*
I have not yet: the roof of this court is too
high to be yours; and welcome to the wide fields
too base to be mine.               [court.
*King.* You shall be welcome, madam, to my
*Prin.* I will be welcome then; conduct me
   thither.                  [oath.
*King.* Hear me, dear lady,—I have sworn an
*Prin.* Our lady help my lord! he'll be forsworn.
*King.* Not for the world, fair madam, by my
   will.                   [ing else.
*Prin.* Why, will shall break it; will, and noth-
*King.* Your ladyship is ignorant what it is.
*Prin.* Were now my lord so, his ignorance were wise,
Where now his knowledge must prove ignorance.
I hear your grace hath sworn-out housekeeping:
'Tis deadly sin to keep that oath, my lord,
And sin to break it:
But pardon me, I am too sudden bold;
To teach a teacher ill beseemeth me.
Vouchsafe to read the purpose of my coming,
And suddenly resolve me in my suit.
                  [*Gives a paper*
*King.* Madam, I will, if suddenly I may.
*Prin.* You will the sooner that I were away;
For you'll prove perjur'd if you make me stay.
*Biron.* Did not I dance with you in Brabant
   once?
*Ros.* Did not I dance with you in Brabant once?
*Biron.* I know you did.
*Ros.*             How needless was it then
To ask the question!
*Biron.*             You must not be so quick.
*Ros.* 'Tis 'long of you, that spur me with such
   questions.
*Biron.* Your wit's too hot, it speeds too fast,
   'twill tire.
*Ros.* Not till it leave the rider in the mire.
*Biron.* What time o' day?
*Ros.* The hour that fools should ask.
*Biron.* Now fair befall your mask!
*Ros.* Fair fall the face it covers!
*Biron.* And send you many lovers!
*Ros.* Amen, so you be none.
*Biron.* Nay, then will I be gone.
*King.* Madam, your father here doth intimate
The payment of a hundred thousand crowns;
Being but the one-half of an entire sum
Disbursed by my father in his wars.
But say that he or we,—as neither have,—
Receiv'd that sum, yet there remains unpaid

A hundred thousand more; in surety of the
    which,
One part of Aquitain is bound to us,
Although not valued to the money's worth.
If, then, the king your father will restore
But that one-half which is unsatisfied,
We will give up our right in Aquitain,
And hold fair friendship with his majesty.
But that, it seems, he little purposeth,
For here he doth demand to have repaid
An hundred thousand crowns; and not demands,
On payment of a hundred thousand crowns,
To have his title live in Aquitain;
Which we much rather had depart withal,
And have the money by our father lent,
Than Aquitain so gelded as it is.
Dear princess, were not his requests so far
From reason's yielding, your fair self should
    make
A yielding, 'gainst some reason, in my breast,
And go well satisfied to France again.
*Prin.* You do the king my father too much
    wrong,
And wrong the reputation of your name,
In so unseeming to confess receipt
Of that which hath so faithfully been paid.
*King.* I do protest I never heard of it;
And if you prove it, I'll repay it back,
Or yield up Aquitain.
*Prin.*     We arrest your word:—
Boyet, you can produce acquittances
For such a sum from special officers
Of Charles his father.
*King.*     Satisfy me so. [come,
*Boyet.* So please your grace, the packet is not
Where that and other specialties are bound;
To-morrow you shall have a sight of them.
*King.* It shall suffice me; at which interview
All liberal reason I will yield unto.
Meantime receive such welcome at my hand
As honour, without breach of honour, may
Make tender of to thy true worthiness:
You may not come, fair princess, in my gates;
But here without you shall be so receiv'd
As you shall deem yourself lodg'd in my heart,
Though so denied fair harbour in my house.
Your own good thoughts excuse me, and farewell:
To-morrow shall we visit you again.
*Prin.* Sweet health and fair desires consort
    your grace!
*King.* Thy own wish wish I thee in every place!
        [*Exeunt* KING *and his* Train.
*Biron.* Lady, I will commend you to my own
    heart.
*Ros.* Pray you, do my commendations; I would
be glad to see it.
*Biron.* I would you heard it groan.
*Ros.* Is the fool sick?
*Biron.* Sick at heart.
*Ros.* Alack, let it blood.
*Biron.* Would that do it good?
*Ros.* My physic says ay.
*Biron.* Will you prick 't with your eye?
*Ros. No poynt,* with my knife.

*Biron.* Now, God save thy life!
*Ros.* And yours from long living!
*Biron.* I cannot stay thanksgiving. [*Retiring.*
*Dum.* Sir, I pray you, a word! what lady is
    that same?
*Boyet.* The heir of Alençon, Katharine her
    name.
*Dum.* A gallant lady! Monsieur, fare you well.
        [*Exit.*
*Long.* I beseech you a word: what is she in the
    white?     [the light.
*Boyet.* A woman sometimes, an you saw her in
*Long.* Perchance, light in the light. I desire her
    name.
*Boyet.* She hath but one for herself; to desire
    that were a shame.
*Long.* Pray you, sir, whose daughter?
*Boyet.* Her mother's, I have heard.
*Long.* God's blessing on your beard!
*Boyet.* Good sir, be not offended:
She is an heir of Falconbridge.
*Long.* Nay, my choler is ended.
She is a most sweet lady.
*Boyet.* Not unlike, sir: that may be.
        [*Exit* LONG.
*Biron.* What's her name in the cap?
*Boyet.* Rosaline, by good hap.
*Biron.* Is she wedded or no?
*Boyet.* To her will, sir, or so.
*Biron.* You are welcome, sir: adieu!
*Boyet.* Farewell to me, sir, and welcome to you.
        [*Exit* BIRON.—Ladies *unmask.*
*Mar.* That last is Biron, the merry mad-cap
    lord;
Not a word with him but a jest.
*Boyet.*     And every jest but a word.
*Prin.* It was well done of you to take him at
    his word.
*Boyet.* I was as willing to grapple as he was to
    board.
*Mar.* Two hot sheeps, marry!
*Boyet.*     And wherefore not ships?
No sheep, sweet lamb, unless we feed on your
    lips.     [ish the jest?
*Mar.* You sheep and I pasture: shall that fin-
*Boyet.* So you grant pasture for me.
        *Offering to kiss her.*
*Mar.*     Not so, gentle beast;
My lips are no common, though several they be.
*Boyet.* Belonging to whom?
*Mar.*     To my fortunes and me.
*Prin.* Good wits will be jangling: but, gentles,
    agree:
The civil war of wits were much better used
On Navarre and his book-men; for here 'tis
    abus'd.     [lies,—
*Boyet.* If my observation,—which very seldom
By the heart's still rhetoric disclos'd with eyes,
Deceive me not now, Navarre is infected.
*Prin.* With what?     [fected.
*Boyet.* With that which we lovers entitle af-
*Prin.* Your reason?     [retire
*Boyet.* Why, all his behaviours did make their
To the court of his eye, peeping thorough desire:

His heart, like an agate, with your print im-
   press'd,
Proud with his form, in his eye pride express'd:
His tongue, all impatient to speak and not see,
Did stumble with haste in his eye-sight to be;
All senses to that sense did make their repair,
To feel only looking on fairest of fair:
Methought all his senses were lock'd in his eye,
As jewels in crystal for some prince to buy;
Who, tend'ring their own worth from where
   they were glass'd,
Did point you to buy them, along as you pass'd
His face's own margent did quote such amazes
That all eyes saw his eyes enchanted with gazes:
I'll give you Aquitain, and all that is his,
An you give him for my sake but one loving kiss.
*Prin.* Come to our pavilion: Boyet is dispos'd—
*Boyet.* But to speak that in words which his
   eye hath disclos'd:
I only have made a mouth of his eye,
By adding a tongue which I know will not lie.
*Ros.* Thou art an old love-monger, and speak'st
   skilfully.       [news of him.
*Mar.* He is Cupid's grandfather, and learns
*Ros.* Then was Venus like her mother; for her
   father is but grim.
*Boyet.* Do you hear, my mad wenches?
*Mar.*                   No.
*Boyet.*       What, then; do you see?
*Ros.* Ay, our way to be gone.
*Boyet.*       You are too hard for me.
                      *[Exeunt.*

## ACT III.

### SCENE I.—*A part of the Park.*

#### Enter ARMADO *and* MOTH.

*Arm.* Warble, child; make passionate my sense
of hearing.
*Moth. Concolinel*——        *[Singing.*
*Arm.* Sweet air!—Go, tenderness of years!
take this key, give enlargement to the swain,
bring him festinately hither; I must employ
him in a letter to my love.
*Moth.* Master, will you win your love with a
French brawl?
*Arm.* How mean'st thou? brawling in French?
*Moth.* No, my complete master: but to jig off
a tune at the tongue's end, canary to it with
your feet, humour it with turning up your eyelids; sigh a note and sing a note; sometime
through the throat, as if you swallowed love
with singing love; sometime through the nose,
as if you snuffed up love by smelling love; with
your hat penthouse-like, o'er the shop of your
eyes; with your arms crossed on your thin belly-
doublet, like a rabbit on a spit; or your hands
in your pocket, like a man after the old painting; and keep not too long in one tune, but a
snip and away. These are complements, these
are humours; these betray nice wenches—that
would be betrayed without those; and make
them men of note,—do you note me?—that
most are affected to these.

*Arm.* How hast thou purchased this experi-
ence?
*Moth.* By my penny of observation.
*Arm.* But O,—but O—
*Moth.* —the hobby-horse is forgot.
*Arm.* Callest thou my love hobby-horse?
*Moth.* No, master; the hobby-horse is but a
colt, and your love perhaps a hackney. But
have you forgot your love?
*Arm.* Almost I had.
*Moth.* Negligent student! learn her by heart.
*Arm.* By heart and in heart, boy.
*Moth.* And out of heart, master: all those three
I will prove.
*Arm.* What wilt thou prove?
*Moth.* A man, if I live; and this, by, in, and
without, upon the instant: by heart you love
her, because your heart cannot come by her; in
heart you love her, because your heart is in love
with her; and out of heart you love her, being
out of heart that you cannot enjoy her.
*Arm.* I am all these three.
*Moth.* And three times as much more, and yet
nothing at all.
*Arm.* Fetch hither the swain; he must carry
me a letter.
*Moth.* A message well sympathized; a horse to
be ambassador for an ass!
*Arm.* Ha, ha! what sayest thou?
*Moth.* Marry, sir, you must send the ass upon
the horse, for he is very slow-gaited. But I go.
*Arm.* The way is but short: away.
*Moth.* As swift as lead, sir.
*Arm.* Thy meaning, pretty ingenious?
Is not lead a metal heavy, dull, and slow?
*Moth. Minimè,* honest master; or rather, mas-
ter, no.
*Arm.* I say lead is slow.
*Moth.*       You are too swift, sir, to say so:
Is that lead slow which is fired from a gun?
*Arm.* Sweet smoke of rhetoric!    [he:—
He reputes me a cannon; and the bullet, that's
I shoot thee at the swain.
*Moth.*           Thump, then, and I flee.
                      *[Exit.*
*Arm.* A most acute juvenal; voluble and free
   of grace!               [face:
By thy favour, sweet welkin, I must sigh in thy
Most rude melancholy, valour gives thee place.
My herald is return'd.

#### Re-enter MOTH *with* COSTARD.

*Moth.* A wonder, master; here's a Costard
   broken in a shin.
*Arm.* Some enigma, some riddle: come,—thy
*l'envoy;*—begin.
*Cost.* No egma, no riddle, no *l'envoy;*—no salve
in the mail, sir: O, sir, plantain, a plain plantain; no *l'envoy,* no *l'envoy,* no salve, sir, but a
plantain!
*Arm.* By virtue thou enforcest laughter; thy
silly thought, my spleen; the heaving of my
lungs provokes me to ridiculous smiling: O,
pardon me, my stars! Doth the inconsiderate

take salve for *l'envoy*, and the word *l'envoy* for
a salve?  [*l'envoy* a salve?
*Moth*. Do the wise think them other? is not
*Arm*. No, page: it is an epilogue or discourse,
    to make plain  [sain.
Some obscure precedence that hath tofore been
I will example it:
    The fox, the ape, and the humble-bee
        Were still at odds, being but three.
There's the moral. Now the *l'envoy*.  [again.
*Moth*. I will add the *l'envoy*. Say the moral
*Arm*. The fox, the ape, and the humble-bee
        Were still at odds, being but three:
*Moth*. Until the goose came out of door,
    And stay'd the odds by adding four.
Now will I begin your moral, and do you follow
with my *l'envoy*.
    The fox, the ape, and the humble-bee,
        Were still at odds, being but three:
*Arm*. Until the goose came out of door.
    Staying the odds by adding four.
*Moth*. A good *l'envoy*, ending in the goose;
Would you desire more?
*Cost*. The boy hath sold him a bargain, a goose,
    that's flat:—  [fat.—
Sir, your pennyworth is good, and your goose be
To sell a bargain well is as cunning as fast and
    loose:
Let me see a fat *l'envoy*; ay, that's a fat goose.
*Arm*. Come hither, come hither. How did this
    argument begin?
*Moth*. By saying that *a Costard* was broken in
    a shin.
Then call'd you for the *l'envoy*.
*Cost*. True, and I for a plantain: thus came
    your argument in;  [bought;
Then the boy's fat *l'envoy*, the goose that you
And he ended the market.
*Arm*. But tell me; how was there a Costard
broken in a shin?
*Moth*. I will tell you sensibly.
*Cost*. Thou hast no feeling of it, Moth; I will
speak that *l'envoy*.
I, Costard, running out, that was safely within,
Fell over the threshold and broke my shin.
*Arm*. We will talk no more of this matter.
*Cost*. Till there be more matter in the shin.
*Arm*. Sirrah, Costard, I will enfranchise thee.
*Cost*. O, marry me to one Frances;—I smell
some *l'envoy*, some goose in this.
*Arm*. By my sweet soul, I mean setting thee
at liberty, enfreedoming thy person; thou wert
immured, restrained, captivated, bound.
*Cost*. True, true; and now you will be my pur-
gation, and let me loose.
*Arm*. I give thee thy liberty, set thee from
durance; and, in lieu thereof, impose on thee
nothing but this:—bear this significant to the
country maid Jaquenetta: there is remuneration [*giving him money*]; for the best ward of
mine honour is rewarding my dependents.
Moth, follow.  [*Exit*.
*Moth*. Like the sequel, I.—Signior Costard,
adieu.

*Cost*. My sweet ounce of man's flesh! my incony Jew!  [*Exit* MOTH.
Now will I look to his remuneration. Remuneration! O, that's the Latin word for three
farthings: three farthings—remuneration.—
*What's the price of this inkle?—A penny.—
No, I'll give you a remuneration*: why, it carries
it.—Remuneration!—why, it is a fairer name
than French crown. I will never buy and sell
out of this word.

        *Enter* BIRON.

*Biron*. O, my good knave Costard! exceedingly
well met.
*Cost*. Pray you, sir, how much carnation rib-
bon may a man buy for a remuneration?
*Biron*. What is a remuneration?
*Cost*. Marry, sir, halfpenny farthing.  [silk.
*Biron*. O, why then, three-farthings-worth of
*Cost*. I thank your worship: God be with you!
*Biron*. O, stay, slave; I must employ thee:
As thou wilt win my favour good my knave,
Do one thing for me that I shall entreat.
*Cost*. When you would have it done, sir?
*Biron*. O, this afternoon.
*Cost*. Well, I will do it, sir: fare you well.
*Biron*. O, thou knowest not what it is.
*Cost*. I shall know, sir, when I have done it.
*Biron*. Why, villain, thou must know first.
*Cost*. I will come to your worship to-morrow
morning.
*Biron*. It must be done this afternoon.
Hark, slave, it is but this:—
The princess comes to hunt here in the park,
And in her train there is a gentle lady;
When tongues speak sweetly, then they name
    her name,
And Rosaline they call her: ask for her;
And to her white hand see thou do commend
This seal'd-up counsel. There's thy guerdon;
    go.  [*Gives him money.*
*Cost*. Gardon,—O sweet gardon! better than
remuneration; elevenpence farthing better:
most sweet gardon!—I will do it, sir, in print.
—Gardon—remuneration.  [*Exit.*
*Biron*. O!—and I, forsooth, in love! I, that
    have been love's whip;
A very beadle to a humourous sigh;
A critic; nay, a night-watch constable;
A domineering pedant o'er the boy,
Than whom no mortal so magnificent!
This wimpled, whining, purblind, wayward boy;
This senior-junior, giant-dwarf, Dan Cupid:
Regent of love-rhymes, lord of folded arms,
The anointed sovereign of sighs and groans,
Liege of all loiterers and malcontents,
Dread prince of plackets, king of codpieces,
Sole imperator, and great general
Of trotting paritors: O my little heart!—
And I to be a corporal of his field,
And wear his colours like a tumbler's hoop!
What! I! I love! I sue! I seek a wife!
A woman, that is like a German clock,
Still a-repairing: ever out of frame:

And never going aright, being a watch,
But being watch'd that it may still go right!
Nay, to be perjur'd, which is worst of all;
And, among three, to love the worst of all;
A whitely wanton with a velvet brow,
With two pitch balls stuck in her face for eyes;
Ay, and, by heaven, one that will do the deed,
Though Argus were her eunuch and her guard:
And I to sigh for her! to watch for her!
To pray for her! Go to; it is a plague
That Cupid will impose for my neglect
Of his almighty dreadful little might.
Well, I will love, write, sigh, pray, sue, watch,
    groan;
Some men must love my lady, and some Joan.
                                        [Exit.

## ACT IV.

### SCENE I.—*A part of the Park.*

*Enter the* PRINCESS, ROSALINE, MARIA, KATH-
ARINE, BOYET, Lords, Attendants, *and a*
Forester.

*Prin.* Was that the king that spurr'd his horse
    so hard
Against the steep uprising of the hill?
*Boyet.* I know not; but I think it was not he.
*Prin.* Whoe'er he was, he show'd a mounting
    mind.
Well, lords, to-day we shall have our despatch;
On Saturday we will return to France.—
Then, forester, my friend, where is the bush
That we must stand and play the murderer in?
*For.* Here by, upon the edge of yonder coppice;
A stand where you may make the fairest shoot.
*Prin.* I thank my beauty, I am fair that shoot,
And thereupon thou speak'st the fairest shoot.
*For.* Pardon me, madam, for I meant not so.
*Prin.* What, what? first praise me, and again
    say no?
O short-liv'd pride! Not fair? alack for woe!
*For.* Yes, madam, fair.
*Prin.*                    Nay, never paint me now;
Where fair is not, praise cannot mend the brow.
Here, good my glass, take this for telling true;
                            [*Giving him money.*
Fair payment for foul words is more than due.
*For.* Nothing but fair is that which you inherit.
*Prin.* See, see, my beauty will be sav'd by merit.
O heresy in fair, fit for these days! [praise.—
A giving hand, though foul, shall have fair
But come, the bow:—now mercy goes to kill,
And shooting well is then accounted ill.
Thus will I save my credit in the shoot:
Not wounding, pity would not let me do't;
If wounding, then it was to show my skill,
That more for praise than purpose meant to kill.
And, out of question, so it is sometimes,—
Glory grows guilty of detested crimes; [part,
When, for fame's sake, for praise, an outward
We bend to that the working of the heart:
As I, for praise alone, now seek to spill [ill
The poor deer's blood, that my heart means no

*Boyet.* Do not curst wives hold that self-
    sovereignty
Only for praise' sake, when they strive to be
Lords o'er their lords?
*Prin.* Only for praise: and praise we may afford
To any lady that subdues a lord.
Here comes a member of the commonwealth.

### *Enter* COSTARD.

*Cost.* God dig-you-den all! Pray you, which is
the head-lady?            [that have no heads.
*Prin.* Thou shalt know her, fellow, by the rest
*Cost.* Which is the greatest lady, the highest?
*Prin.* The thickest and the tallest.
*Cost.* The thickest and the tallest! it is so;
        truth is truth.                     [wit,
An your waist, mistress, were as slender as my
One of these maids' girdles for your waist should
        be fit.                           [est here.
Are not you the chief woman? you are the thick-
*Prin.* What's your will, sir? what's your will?
*Cost.* I have a letter from Monsieur Biron, to
        one Lady Rosaline.
*Prin.* O, thy letter, thy letter; he's a good
        friend of mine:                   [carve;
Stand aside, good bearer.—Boyet, you can
Break up this capon.
*Boyet.*                I am bound to serve.—
This letter is mistook, it importeth none here;
It is writ to Jaquenetta.
*Prin.*              We will read it, I swear:
Break the neck of the wax and every one give
        ear.
*Boyet.* [*reads.*] By heaven, that thou art fair is
most infallible; true that thou art beauteous;
truth itself that thou art lovely. More fairer
than fair, beautiful than beauteous, truer than
truth itself: have commiseration on thy heroical vassal! The magnanimous and most illustrious king *Cophetua* set eye upon the pernicious
and indubitate beggar *Zenelophon;* and he it
was that might rightly say, *veni, vidi, vici;* which
to anatomize in the vulgar,—O base and obscure vulgar!—*videlicet,* he came, saw, and overcame: he came one; saw two; overcame three.
Who came? the king: why did he come? to see:
why did he see? to overcome: to whom came
he? to the beggar: what saw he? the beggar:
who overcame he? the beggar. The conclusion
is victory; on whose side? the king's: the captive is enriched; on whose side? the beggar's:
the catastrophe is a nuptial; on whose side? the
king's?—no on both in one, or one in both. I
am the king; for so stands the comparison: thou
the beggar; for so witnesseth thy lowliness.
Shall I command thy love? I may: shall I enforce thy love? I could: shall I entreat thy love?
I will. What shalt thou exchange for rags?
robes: for tittles? titles: for thyself? me. Thus,
expecting thy reply, I profane my lips on thy
foot, my eyes on thy picture, and my heart on
thy every part.
        Thine in the dearest design of industry,
                DON ADRIANO DE ARMADO.

Thus dost thou hear the Nemean lion roar
'Gainst thee, thou lamb, that standest as his
 prey;
Submissive fall his princely feet before,
 And he from forage will incline to play:
But if thou strive, poor soul, what art thou
 then?
Food for his rage, repasture for his den.
 *Prin.* What plume of feathers is he that in-
 dited this letter?
What vane? what weather-cock? did you ever
 hear better?
 *Boyet.* I am much deceiv'd but I remember
 the style.
 *Prin.* Else your memory is bad, going o'er it
 erewhile.
 *Boyet.* This Armado is a Spaniard, that keeps
 here in court;     [sport
A phantasm, a Monarcho, and one that makes
To the prince and his book-mates.
 *Prin.*    Thou fellow, a word:
Who gave thee this letter?
 *Cost.*    I told you; my lord.
 *Prin.* To whom shouldst thou give it?
 *Cost.*   From my lord to my lady.
 *Prin.* From which lord to which lady?
 *Cost.* From my Lord Biron, a good master of
 mine,
To a lady of France that he call'd Rosaline.
 *Prin.* Thou hast mistaken this letter. Come,
 lords, away.
Here, sweet, put up this; 'twill be thine another
 day.  [*Exeunt* PRINCESS *and* Train.
 *Boyet.* Who is the shooter? who is the shooter?
 *Ros.* Shall I teach you to know?
 *Boyet.* Ay, my continent of beauty.
 *Ros.*   Why, she that bears the bow.
Finely put off!    [thou marry,
 *Boyet.* My lady goes to kill horns; but, if
Hang me by the neck if horns that year mis-
 carry.
Finely put on!
 *Ros.* Well then, I am the shooter.
 *Boyet.*   And who is your deer?
 *Ros.* If we choose by the horns, yourself:
 come near.
Finely put on indeed!—
 *Mar.* You still wrangle with her, Boyet, and
 she strikes at the brow.  [her now?
 *Boyet.* But she herself is hit lower: have I hit
 *Ros.* Shall I come upon thee with an old say-
ing, that was a man when King Pepin of France
was a little boy, as touching the hit it?
 *Boyet.* So I may answer thee with one as old,
that was a woman when Queen Guinever of
Britain was a little wench, as touching the hit it.
          [*Singing.*
 *Ros.*  *Thou canst not hit it, hit it, hit it,*
   *Thou canst not hit it, my good man.*
 *Boyet.*  *An I cannot, cannot, cannot,*
   *An I cannot, another can.*
      [*Exeunt* ROS. *and* KATH.
 *Cost.* By my troth, most pleasant! how both
did fit it!

 *Mar.* A mark marvellous well shot; for they
 both did hit it.
 *Boyet.* A mark! O, mark but that mark! A
 mark, says my lady!   [may be.
Let the mark have a prick in 't, to mete at, if it
 *Mar.* Wide o' the bow-hand! I' faith your
 hand is out.
 *Cost.* Indeed, 'a must shoot nearer, or he'll
 ne'er hit the clout.
 *Boyet.* And if my hand be out, then belike
 your hand is in.    [ing the pin.
 *Cost.* Then will she get the upshot by cleav-
 *Mar.* Come, come, you talk greasily, your
 lips grow foul.
 *Cost.* She's too hard for you at pricks, sir;
 challenge her to bowl.
 *Boyet.* I fear too much rubbing; good-night,
 my good owl.
     [*Exeunt* BOYET *and* MARIA.
 *Cost.* By my soul, a swain! a most simple
 clown!       [down!
Lord, lord! how the ladies and I have put him
O' my troth, most sweet jests! most incony
 vulgar wit!
When it comes so smoothly off, so obscenely, as
 it were, so fit.
Armador o' the one side,—O, a most dainty
 man!        [fan!
To see him walk before a lady and to bear her
To see him kiss his hand! and how most sweetly
 'a will swear!—
And his page o' t' other side, that handful of
 wit!
Ah, heavens, it is a most pathetical nit!
Sola, sola!    [*Shouting within.*
      [*Exit* COSTARD *running.*

SCENE II.—*Another part of the Park.*

*Enter* HOLOFERNES, *Sir* NATHANIEL, *and* DULL.

 *Nath.* Very reverend sport, truly; and done
in the testimony of a good conscience.
 *Hol.* The deer was, as you know, *sanguis*,—
in blood; ripe as a pomewater, who now hangeth like a jewel in the ear of *cælo*,—the sky, the
welkin, the heaven; and anon falleth like a crab
on the face of *terra*,—the soil, the land, the
earth.
 *Nath.* Truly, Master Holofernes, the epithets
are sweetly varied, like a scholar at the least:
but, sir, I assure ye it was a buck of the first
head.
 *Hol.* Sir Nathaniel, *haud credo.*
 *Dull.* 'Twas not a *haud credo;* 'twas a pricket.
 *Hol.* Most barbarous intimation! yet a kind
of insinuation, as it were, *in via*, in way, of
explication; *facere*, as it were, replication, or,
rather, *ostentare*, to show, as it were, his inclination,—after his undressed, unpolished, unedu-
cated, unpruned, untrained, or, rather, unlettered, or, ratherest, unconfirmed fashion,—to
insert again my *haud credo* for a deer.
 *Dull.* I said the deer was not a *haud credo;*
'twas a pricket.
 *Hol.* Twice sod simplicity, *bis coctus!*—

O thou monster Ignorance, how deformed dost
    thou look!

*Nath.* Sir, he hath never fed of the dainties
    that are bred in a book;

He hath not eat paper, as it were; he hath not
drunk ink; his intellect is not replenished; he
is only an animal only sensible in the duller
    parts;

And such barren plants are set before us that
    we thankful should be,—

Which we of taste and feeling are,—for those
    parts that do fructify in us more than he.

For as it would ill become me to be vain, in-
    discreet, or a fool,

So, were there a patch set on learning, to see
    him in a school:

But, *omne, bene,* say I; being of an old father's
    mind,                     [*wind.*

*Many can brook the weather that love not the*

*Dull.* You two are book-men: can you tell
    by your wit

What was a month old at Cain's birth that's
    not five weeks old as yet?

*Hol.* Dictynna, good man Dull; Dictynna,
good man Dull.

*Dull.* What is Dictynna?

*Nath.* A title to Phœbe, to Luna, to the
    moon.

*Hol.* The moon was a month old when Adam
    was no more,         [five-score.

And raught not to five weeks when he came to

The allusion holds in the exchange.

*Dull.* 'Tis true indeed; the collusion holds in
the exchange.

*Hol.* God comfort thy capacity! I say the
allusion holds in the exchange.

*Dull.* And I say the pollusion holds in the
exchange; for the moon is never but a month
old: and I say beside, that 'twas a pricket that
the princess killed.

*Hol.* Sir Nathaniel, will you hear an extemporal epitaph on the death of the deer? and, to
humour the ignorant, I have called the deer the
princess killed a pricket.

*Nath.* *Perge,* good Master Holofernes, *perge;*
so it shall please you to abrogate scurrility.

*Hol.* I will something affect the letter; for it
argues facility.

The praiseful princess pierc'd and prick'd a
    pretty pleasing pricket;

Some say a sore; but not a sore, till now
    made sore with shooting.

The dogs did yell; put l to sore, then sorel
    jumps from thicket;      [a-hooting.

Or pricket, sore, or else sorel; the people fall

If sore be sore, then l to sore makes fifty sores;
    O sore l!         [one more l.

Of one sore I an hundred make by adding but

*Nath.* A rare talent!

*Dull.* If a talent be a claw, look how he
claws him with a talent.

*Hol.* This is a gift that I have, simple, simple; a foolish extravagant spirit, full of forms,
figures, shapes, objects, ideas, apprehensions,
motions, revolutions: these are begot in the
ventricle of memory, nourished in the womb of
*pia mater,* and delivered upon the mellowing
of occasion. But the gift is good in those in
whom it is acute, and I am thankful for it.

*Nath.* Sir, I praise the Lord for you; and so
may my parishioners; for their sons are well
tutored by you, and their daughters profit very
greatly under you: you are a good member of
the commonwealth.

*Hol.* *Mehercle,* if their sons be ingenious,
they shall want no instruction: if their daughters be capable, I will put it to them: but, *vir
sapit qui pauca loquitur:* a soul feminine saluteth us.

*Enter* JAQUENETTA *and* COSTARD.

*Jaq.* God give you good-morrow, master
person.

*Hol.* Master person,—*quasi* pers-on. And if
one should be pierced, which is the one?

*Cost.* Marry, master schoolmaster, he that is
likest to a hogshead.

*Hol.* Of piercing a hogshead! a good lustre
of conceit in a turf of earth; fire enough for a
flint, pearl enough for a swine; 'tis pretty; it is
well.

*Jaq.* Good master person, be so good as read
me this letter; it was given me by Costard, and
sent me from Don Armado: I beseech you,
read it.

*Hol.* *Fauste, precor gelidâ quando pecus omne
    sub umbrâ*        [tuan!

*Ruminat,*—and so forth. Ah, good old Man-
I may speak of thee as the traveller doth of
Venice:

    ——*Vinegia, Vinegia,*
    *Chi non te vede, ei non te pregia.*

Old Mantuan! old Mantuan! who understand-
eth thee not, loves thee not?—*Ut, re, sol, la, mi,
fa.*—Under pardon, sir, what are the contents?
or rather, as Horace says in his—What, my
soul, verses?

*Nath.* Ay, sir, and very learned.

*Hol.* Let me hear a staff, a stanza, a verse;
*Lege, domine.*

*Nath.* [*reads.*] If love make me forsworn,
    how shall I swear to love?      [vow'd!

    Ah, never faith could hold if not to beauty

Though to myself forsworn, to thee I'll faith-
    ful prove;

    Those thoughts to me were oaks, to thee
    like osiers bow'd.

Study his bias leaves, and makes his book
    thine eyes;

    Where all those pleasures live that art
    would comprehend:

If knowledge be the mark, to know thee shall
    suffice;         [thee commend:

    Well learned is that tongue that well can

All ignorant that soul that sees thee without
    wonder,—

    Which is to me some praise that I thy
    parts admire,—

Thy eye Jove's lightning bears, thy voice his
　　dreadful thunder,
　　Which, not to anger bent, is music and
　　　sweet fire.
Celestial as thou art, O pardon, love, this
　　wrong,
That sings heaven's praise with such an
　　earthly tongue.

*Hol.* You find not the apostrophes, and so
miss the accent: let me supervise the canzonet.
Here are only numbers ratified; but, for the
elegancy, facility, and golden cadence of poesy,
*caret.* Ovidius Naso was the man: and why,
indeed, Naso; but for smelling out the oderi-
ferous flowers of fancy, the jerks of invention?
*Imitari* is nothing: so doth the hound his master, the ape his keeper, the tired horse his rider.
But damosella virgin, was this directed to you?

*Jaq.* Ay, sir, from one Monsieur Biron, one
of the strange queen's lords.

*Hol.* I will overglance the superscript.
*To the snow-white hand of the most beauteous
Lady Rosaline.*
I will look again on the intellect of the letter,
for the nomination of the party writing to the
person written unto:
*Your Ladyship's in all desired employment,*
　　　　　　　　　　　　BIRON.
Sir Nathaniel, this Biron is one of the votaries
with the king; and here he hath framed a letter
to a sequent of the stranger queen's, which accidentally, or by the way of progression, hath
miscarried.—Trip and go, my sweet; deliver
this paper into the royal hand of the king; it
may concern much. Stay not thy compliment;
I forgive thy duty: adieu.

*Jaq.* Good Costard, go with me.—Sir, God
save your life!

*Cost.* Have with thee, my girl.
　　　　　　　　　[*Exeunt* COST. *and* JAQ.

*Nath.* Sir, you have done this in the fear of
God, very religiously; and, as a certain father
saith——

*Hol.* Sir, tell not me of the father; I do fear
colourable colours. But to return to the verses:
did they please you, Sir Nathaniel?

*Nath.* Marvellous well for the pen.

*Hol.* I do dine to-day at the father's of a
certain pupil of mine; where if, before repast,
it shall please you to gratify the table with a
grace, I will, on my privilege I have with the
parents of the foresaid child or pupil, undertake your *ben venuto;* where I will prove those
verses to be very unlearned, neither savouring
of poetry, wit, nor invention: I beseech your
society.

*Nath.* And thank you too: for society, saith
the text, is the happiness of life.

*Hol.* And certes, the text most infallibly
concludes it.—Sir [*to* DULL], I do invite you
too; you shall not say me nay: *pauca verba.*
Away! the gentles are at their game, and we
will to our recreation.
　　　　　　　　　　　　　　　[*Exeunt.*

SCENE III.—*Another part of the Park.*

*Enter* BIRON, *with a paper.*

*Biron.* The king he is hunting the deer; I am
coursing myself: they have pitched a toil; I am
toiling in a pitch,—pitch that defiles: defile! a
foul word. Well, sit thee down, sorrow! for so
they say the fool said, and so say I, and I the
fool. Well proved, wit! By the Lord, this love
is as mad as Ajax: it kills sheep; it kills me, I a
sheep: well proved again on my side! I will not
love: if I do, hang me; i' faith, I will not. O,
but her eye,—by this light, but for her eye I
would not love her; yes, for her two eyes. Well,
I do nothing in the world but lie, and lie in my
throat. By heaven, I do love: and it hath
taught me to rhyme, and to be melancholy;
and here is part of my rhyme, and here my
melancholy. Well, she hath one o' my sonnets
already; the clown bore it, the fool sent it, and
the lady hath it: sweet clown, sweeter fool,
sweetest lady! By the world, I would not care
a pin if the other three were in. Here comes one
with a paper; God give him grace to groan.
　　　　　　　　　　　[*Gets up into a tree.*

*Enter the* KING, *with a paper.*

*King.* Ah me!

*Biron.* [*aside.*] Shot, by heaven!—Proceed,
sweet Cupid; thou hast thumped him with thy
bird-bolt under the left pap;—I' faith, secrets.—

*King.* [*reads.*] So sweet a kiss the golden sun
　　gives not
To those fresh morning drops upon the rose,
As thy eyebeams, when their fresh rays have
　　smote　　　　　　　　　　　　[flows]
The night of dew that on my cheeks down
Nor shines the silver moon one half so bright
　Through the transparent bosom of the deep,
As doth thy face through tears of mine give
　　light:
Thou shin'st in every tear that I do weep;
No drop but as a coach doth carry thee;
　So ridest thou triúmphing in my woe.
Do but behold the tears that swell in me,
　And they thy glory through my grief will
　　show:
But do not love thyself; then thou wilt keep
My tears for glasses, and still make me weep.
O queen of queens, how far dost thou excel!
No thought can think nor tongue of mortal
　　tell.—
How shall she know my griefs? I'll drop the
　　paper;
Sweet leaves, shade folly. Who is he comes
　　here?　　　　　　　　　　[*Steps aside.*

*Enter* LONGAVILLE, *with a paper.*

What, Longaville; and reading! listen, ear.

*Biron.* Now, in thy likeness, one more fool,
　　appear!　　　　　　　　　　　[*Aside.*

*Long.* Ah me! I am forsworn.

*Biron.* Why, he comes in like a perjure,
wearing papers.    [*Aside.*
*King.* In love, I hope: sweet fellowship in
shame!    [*Aside.*
*Biron.* One drunkard loves another of the
name.    [*Aside.*
*Long.* Am I the first that have been perjur'd
so?
*Biron.* [*aside.*] I could put thee in comfort;
not by two that I know:
Thou mak'st the triumviry, the corner cap of
society,
The shape of Love's Tyburn that hangs up
simplicity.
*Long.* I fear these stubborn lines lack power
to move:—
O sweet Maria, empress of my love!
These numbers will I tear and write in prose.
*Biron.* [*aside.*] O, rhymes are guards on
wanton Cupid's hose:
Disfigure not his slop.
*Long.*        This same shall go.—
                [*He reads the sonnet.*
Did not the heavenly rhetoric of thine eye,—
'Gainst whom the world cannot hold argu-
ment,—
Persuade my heart to this false perjury?
Vows for thee broke deserve not punishment.
A woman I forswore:    I will prove,
Thou being a goddess, I forswore not thee;
My vow was earthly, thou a heavenly love;
Thy grace being gain'd cures all disgrace in me.
Vows are but breath, and breath a vapour is:
Then thou, fair sun, which on my earth dost
shine,
Exhal'st this vapour vow; in thee it is:
If broken, then it is no fault of mine:
If by me broke, what fool is not so wise
To lose an oath to win a paradise?
*Biron.* [*aside.*] This is the liver vein, which
makes flesh a deity,
A green goose a goddess: pure, pure idolatry.
God amend us, God amend! we are much out
o' the way.
*Long.* By whom shall I send this?—Com-
pany! stay.                [*Stepping aside.*
*Biron.* [*aside.*] All hid, all hid, an old infant
play.
Like a demi-god here sit I in the sky,
And wretched fools' secrets heedfully o'er-eye.
More sacks to the mill! O heavens, I have my
wish!

*Enter* DUMAIN, *with a paper.*

Dumain transform'd: four woodcocks in a dish!
*Dum.* O most divine Kate!
*Biron.*        O most profane coxcomb!
                [*Aside.*
*Dum.* By heaven, the wonder of a mortal eye!
*Biron.* By earth, she is but corporal: there
you lie.                [*Aside.*
*Dum.* Her amber hairs for foul have amber
quoted.

*Biron.* An amber-colour'd raven was well
noted.                [*Aside.*
*Dum.* As upright as the cedar.
*Biron.*        Stoop, I say;
Her shoulder is with child.    [*Aside.*
*Dum.*        As fair as day.
*Biron.* Ay, as some days; but then no sun
must shine.                [*Aside.*
*Dum.* O that I had my wish!
*Long.*        And I had mine!
                [*Aside.*
*King.* And I mine too, good Lord!
                [*Aside.*
*Biron.* Amen, so I had mine: is not that a
good word?                [*Aside.*
*Dum.* I would forget her; but a fever she
Reigns in my blood, and will remember'd be.
*Biron.* A fever in your blood? why, then
incision
Would let her out in saucers: sweet misprison!
                [*Aside.*
*Dum.* Once more I'll read the ode that I
have writ.
*Biron.* Once more I'll mark how love can
vary wit.                [*Aside.*
*Dum.* [*reads.*] On a day,—alack the day!
Love, whose month is ever May,
Spied a blossom passing fair
Playing in the wanton air:
Through the velvet leaves the wind
All unseen, can passage find;
That the lover, sick to death,
Wish'd himself the heaven's breath.
Air, quoth he, thy cheeks may blow:
Air, would I might triumph so!
But, alack, my hand is sworn
Ne'er to pluck thee from thy thorn:
Vow, alack, for youth unmeet;
Youth so apt to pluck a sweet.
Do not call it sin in me
That I am forsworn for thee:
Thou for whom even Jove would swear
Juno but an Ethiope were;
And deny himself for Jove,
Turning mortal for thy love.—
This will I send; and something else more plain,
That shall express my true love's fasting pain.
O, would the King, Birón, and Longaville,
Were lovers too! Ill, to example ill,
Would from my forehead wipe a perjur'd note
For none offend where all alike do dote.
*Long.* Dumain [*advancing*], thy love is far
from charity,
That in love's grief desir'st society:
You may look pale, but I should blush, I know,
To be o'erheard and taken napping so.
*King.* Come, sir [*advancing*], you blush; as
his your case is such;
You chide at him, offending twice as much:
You do not love Maria; Longaville
Did never sonnet for her sake compile;
Nor never lay his wreathed arms athwart
His loving bosom, to keep down his heart.
I have been closely shrouded in this bush,

And mark'd you both, and for you both did
  blush. [fashion;
I heard your guilty rhymes, observ'd your
Saw sighs reek from you, noted well your pas-
  sion:
Ah me! says one; O Jove! the other cries;
One her hairs were gold, crystal the other's
  eyes;
You would for paradise break faith and troth;
  [To LONG.
And Jove for your love would infringe an oath.
  [To DUMAIN.
What will Birón say when that he shall hear
A faith infring'd which such a zeal did swear?
How will he scorn! how will he spend his wit!
How will he triumph, leap, and laugh at it!
For all the wealth that ever I did see
I would not have him know so much by me.
  Biron. Now step I forth to whip hypocrisy.—
  [Descends from the tree.
Ah, good my liege, I pray thee pardon me.
Good heart, what grace hast thou, thus to re-
  prove
These worms for loving, that art most in love?
Your eyes do make no coaches; in your tears
There is no certain princess that appears:
You'll not be perjur'd 'tis a hateful thing;
Tush, none but minstrels like of sonneting.
But are you not asham'd? nay, are you not,
All three of you, to be thus much o'ershot?
You found his mote; the king your mote did see;
But I a beam do find in each of three.
O, what a scene of foolery I have seen,
Of sighs, of groans, of sorrow, and of teen!
O me, with what strict patience have I sat
To see a king transformed to a gnat!
To see great Hercules whipping a gig,
And profound Solomon tuning a jig,
And Nestor play at push-pin with the boys,
And critic Timon laugh at idle toys!
Where lies thy grief, O, tell me, good Dumain?
And, gentle Longaville, where lies thy pain?
And where my liege's? all about the breast:—
A caudle, ho!
  King. Too bitter is thy jest.
Are we betray'd thus to thy over-view?
  Biron. Not you to me, but I betray'd by you:
I, that am honest; I, that hold it sin
To break the vow I am engaged in;
I am betray'd by keeping company
With moon-like men of strange inconstancy.
When shall you see me write a thing in rhyme?
Or groan for Joan? or spend a minute's time
In pruning me? When shall you hear that I
Will praise a hand, a foot, a face, an eye,
A gait, a state, a brow, a breast, a waist,
A leg, a limb?—
  King. Soft! whither away so fast?
A true man or a thief that gallops so?
  Biron. I post from love; good lover, let me
  go.

  Enter JAQUENETTA and COSTARD.
  Jaq. God bless the king!

  King. What present hast thou there?
  Cost. Some certain treason.
  King. What makes treason here?
  Cost. Nay, it makes nothing, sir.
  King. If it mar nothing neither,
The treason and you go in peace away together.
  Jaq. I beseech your grace, let this letter be
  read;
Our parson misdoubts it; 'twas treason he said.
  King. Birón, read it over.
  [Giving him the letter.
Where hadst thou it?
  Jaq. Of Costard.
  King. Where hadst thou it?
  Cost. Of Dun Adramadio, Dun Adramadio.
  King. How now! what is in you? why dost
  thou tear it?
  Biron. A toy, my liege, a toy: your grace
needs not fear it.
  Long. It did move him to passion, and there-
fore let's hear it.
  Dum. It is Birón's writing, and here is his
  name. [Picks up the pieces.
  Biron. Ah, you whoreson loggerhead [to
COSTARD], you were born to do me
  shame.—
Guilty, my lord, guilty; I confess, I confess.
  King. What?
  Biron. That you three fools lack'd me fool
  to make up the mess;
He, he, and you, my liege, and I,
Are pick-purses in love, and we deserve to die.
O, dismiss this audience, and I shall tell you
  more.
  Dum. Now the number is even.
  Biron. True, true; we are four:—
Will these turtles be gone?
  King. Hence, sirs, away.
  Cost. Walk aside the true folk, and let the
  traitors stay.
  [Exeunt COST. and JAQ.
  Biron. Sweet lords, sweet lovers, O let us
  embrace!
As true we are as flesh and blood can be;
The sea will ebb and flow, heaven show his face;
Young blood will not obey an old decree:
We cannot cross the cause why we were born;
Therefore of all hands must we be forsworn.
  King. What! did these rent lines show some
  love of thine?
  Biron. Did they, quoth you? Who sees the
  heavenly Rosaline
That, like a rude and savage man of Inde
  At the first opening of the gorgeous east,
Bows not his vassal head; and, strucken blind,
  Kisses the base ground with obedient breast?
What peremptory eagle-sighted eye
Dares look upon the heaven of her brow,
That is not blinded by her majesty?
  King. What zeal, what fury hath inspir'd
  thee now?
My love, her mistress, is a gracious moon,
She an attending star, scarce seen a light.
  Biron. My eyes are then no eyes, nor I Birón:

O, but for my love, day would turn to night!
Of all complexions the cull'd sovereignty
Do meet, as at a fair, in her fair cheek;
Where several worthies make one dignity;
Where nothing wants that want itself doth
seek.
Lend me the flourish of all gentle tongues,—
Fie, painted rhetoric! O, she needs it not;
To things of sale a seller's praise belongs;
She passes praise: then praise too short doth
blot.
A wither'd hermit, five-score winters worn,
Might shake off fifty, looking in her eye:
Beauty doth varnish age, as if new-born,
And gives the crutch the cradle's infancy.
O, 'tis the sun, that maketh all things shine!
*King.* By heaven, thy love is black as ebony.
*Biron.* Is ebony like her? O wood divine!
A wife of such wood were felicity.
O, who can give an oath? where is a book?
That I may swear beauty doth beauty lack
If that she learn not of her eye to look:
No face is fair that is not full so black.
*King.* O paradox! Black is the badge of hell,
The hue of dungeons, and the scowl of night;
And beauty's crest becomes the heavens well.
*Biron.* Devils soonest tempt, resembling
spirits of light.
O, if in black my lady's brows be deckt,
It mourns that painting and usurping hair
Should ravish doters with a false aspéct;
And therefore is she born to make black fair.
Her favour turns the fashion of the days;
For native blood is counted painting now;
And therefore red, that would avoid dispraise,
Paints itself black, to imitate her brow.
*Dum.* To look like her are chimney-sweepers
black.                              [bright.
*Long.* And, since her time, are colliers counted
*King.* And Ethiopes of their sweet complex-
ion crack.                          [is light.
*Dum.* Dark needs no candles now, for dark
*Biron.* Your mistresses dare never come in
rain,
For fear their colours should be washed away.
*King.* 'Twere good yours did; for, sir, to tell
you plain,
I'll find a fairer face not wash'd to-day.
*Biron.* I'll prove her fair, or talk till dooms-
day here.
*King.* No devil will fright thee then so much
as she.                             [dear.
*Dum.* I never knew man hold vile stuff so
*Long.* Look, here's thy love: my foot and
her face see.               [*Showing his shoe.*
*Biron.* O, if the streets were paved with
thine eyes
Her feet were much too dainty for such tread!
*Dum.* O vile! then, as she goes, what up-
ward lies
The street should see as she walk'd over head.
*King.* But what of this? are we not all in
love?                               [forsworn.
*Biron.* O, nothing so sure; and thereby all

*King.* Then leave this chat; and, good Birón,
now prove
Our loving lawful, and our faith not torn.
*Dum.* Ay, marry, there;—some flattery for
this evil.
*Long.* O, some authority how to proceed;
Some tricks, some quillets, how to cheat the
devil.
*Dum.* Some salve for perjury.
*Biron.*             O, 'tis more than need!—
Have at you, then, affection's men-at-arms:
Consider what you first did swear unto;—
To fast,—to study,—and to see no woman;—
Flat treason 'gainst the kingly state of youth.
Say, can you fast? your stomachs are too young,
And abstinence engenders maladies.
And where that you have vow'd to study, lords,
In that each of you hath forsworn his book,—
Can you still dream, and pore, and thereon
look?
Why, universal plodding prisons up
The nimble spirits in the arteries,
As motion and long-during action tires
The sinewy vigour of the traveller.
Now, for not looking on a woman's face,
You have in that forsworn the use of eyes,
And study, too, the causer of your vow:
For when would you, my liege, or you, or you,
In leaden contemplation, have found out
Such fiery numbers as the prompting eyes
Of beauteous tutors have enrich'd you with?
Other slow arts entirely keep the brain,
And therefore, finding barren practisers,
Scarce show a harvest of their heavy toil;
But love, first learned in a lady's eyes,
Lives not alone immured in the brain,
But, with the motion of all elements,
Courses as swift as thought in every power,
And gives to every power a double power
Above their functions and their offices.
It adds a precious seeing to the eye:
A lover's eyes will gaze an eagle blind;
A lover's ear will hear the lowest sound,
When the suspicious head of theft is stopp'd,
Love's feeling is more soft and sensible
Than are the tender horns of cockled snails;
Love's tongue proves dainty Bacchus gross in
taste:
For valour, is not love a Hercules,
Still climbing trees in the Hesperides?
Subtle as sphinx; as sweet and musical
As bright Apollo's lute, strung with his hair?
And when love speaks, the voice of all the gods
Makes heaven drowsy with the harmony.
Never durst poet touch a pen to write
Until his ink were temper'd with love's sighs:
O, then his lines would ravish savage ears,
And plant in tyrants mild humility.
From women's eyes this doctrine I derive:
They sparkle still the right Promethean fire;
They are the books, the arts, the academes,
That show, contain, and nourish all the world,
Else none at all in aught proves excellent.
Then fools you were these women to forswear;

Or, keeping what is sworn, you will prove fools.
For wisdom's sake—a word that all men love,
Or for love's sake—a word that loves all men,
Or for men's sake, the authors of these women,
Or women's sake, by whom we men are men,
Let us once lose our oaths to find ourselves,
Or else we lose ourselves to keep our oaths:
It is religion to be thus forsworn;
For charity itself fulfils the law,
And who can sever love from charity?
  *King.* Saint Cupid, then! and, soldiers, to
      the field!           [them, lords;
  *Biron.* Advance your standards, and upon
Pell-mell, down with them! but be first advis'd
In conflict that you get the sun of them.
  *Long.* Now to plain-dealing; lay these glozes
      by;
Shall we resolve to woo these girls of France?
  *King.* And win them too: therefore let us
      devise
Some entertainment for them in their tents.
  *Biron.* First, from the park let us conduct
      them thither;
Then homeward every man attach the hand
Of his fair mistress: in the afternoon
We will with some strange pastime solace them,
Such as the shortness of the time can shape;
For revels, dances, masks, and merry hours,
Forerun fair Love, strewing her way with
      flowers.
  *King.* Away, away! no time shall be omitted,
That will be time, and may by us be fitted.
  *Biron. Allons! Allons!*—Sow'd cockle reap'd
      no corn;
And justice always whirls in equal measure:
Light wenches may prove plagues to men for-
      sworn;
If so, our copper buys no better treasure.
                       *[Exeunt.*

## ACT V.

SCENE I.—*Another part of the Park.*

*Enter* HOLOFERNES, *Sir* NATHANIEL, *and*
DULL.

  *Hol. Satis quod sufficit.*
  *Nath.* I praise God for you, sir: your reasons
at dinner have been sharp and sententious;
pleasant without scurrility, witty without affection, audacious without impudency, learned
without opinion, and strange without heresy.
I did converse this *quondam* day with a companion of the king's, who is intituled, nominated, or called, Don Adriano de Armado.
  *Hol. Novi hominem tanquam te:* his humour
is lofty, his discourse peremptory, his tongue
filed, his eye ambitious, his gait majestical, and
his general behaviour vain, ridiculous, and
thrasonical. He is too picked, too spruce, too
affected, too odd, as it were, too peregrinate,
as I may call it.
  *Nath.* A most singular and choice epithet.
              *[Takes out his table-book.*

  *Hol.* He draweth out the thread of his ver-
bosity finer than the staple of his argument. I
abhor such fanatical fantasms, such insociable
and point-devise companions; such rackers of
orthography, as to speak dout, fine, when he
should say doubt; det, when he should pronounce debt, d, e, b, t, not d, e, t: he clepeth
a calf, cauf; half, hauf; neighbour *vocatur*
nebour; neigh abbreviated ne. This is abho-
minable (which he would call abominable), it
insinuateth me of insanie: *Ne intelligis, domine?*
to make frantic, lunatic.
  *Nath. Laus Deo, bone intelligo.*
  *Hol. Bone!*——bone for *bene: Priscian* a little
scratched; 'twill serve.
  *Nath. Videsne quis venit?*
  *Hol. Video, et gaudeo.*

*Enter* ARMADO, MOTH, *and* COSTARD.

  *Arm.* Chirra!          [*To* MOTH.
  *Hol. Quare* Chirra, not sirrah?
  *Arm.* Men of peace, well encountered.
  *Hol.* Most military sir, salutation.
  *Moth.* They have been at a great feast of
languages and stolen the scraps.
            [*To* COSTARD, *aside.*
  *Cost.* O, they have lived long on the alms-
basket of words! I marvel thy master hath not
eaten thee for a word; for thou art not so long
by the head as *honorificabilitudinitatibus:* thou
art easier swallowed than a flap-dragon.
  *Moth.* Peace; the peal begins.   [tered?
  *Arm.* Monsieur [*to* HOL.], are you not let-
  *Moth.* Yes, yes; he teaches boys the horn-
book;—What is a, b, spelt backward with the
horn on his head.
  *Hol.* Ba, *pueritia,* with a horn added.
  *Moth.* Ba, most silly sheep, with a horn.—
You hear his learning.
  *Hol. Quis, quis,* thou consonant?
  *Moth.* The third of the five vowels, if you
repeat them; or the fifth, if I.
  *Hol.* I will repeat them, a, e, i.—
  *Moth.* The sheep; the other two concludes
it; o, u.
  *Arm.* Now, by the salt wave of the Mediter-
raneum, a sweet touch, a quick venew of wit:
snip, snap, quick and home; it rejoiceth my
intellect: true wit.     [which is wit-old.
  *Moth.* Offered by a child to an old man;
  *Hol.* What is the figure? what is the figure?
  *Moth.* Horns.            [thy gig.
  *Hol.* Thou disputest like an infant: go, whip
  *Moth.* Lend me your horn to make one, and
I will whip about your infamy *circum circà;* a
gig of cuckold's horn!
  *Cost.* An I had but one penny in the world
thou shouldst have it to buy gingerbread: hold,
there is the very remuneration I had of thy
master, thou halfpenny purse of wit, thou
pigeon-egg of discretion. O, an the heavens
were so pleased that thou wert but my bastard,
what a joyful father wouldst thou make me!

Go to; thou hast it *ad dunghill*, at the fingers' ends, as they say.        [*unguem.*

*Hol.* O, I smell false Latin; *dunghill* for

*Arm.* Arts-man, *præambula;* we will be singled from the barbarous. Do you not educate youth at the charge-house on the top of the mountain?

*Hol.* Or *mons*, the hill.          [*tain.*

*Arm.* At your sweet pleasure, for the moun-

*Hol.* I do, *sans* question.

*Arm.* Sir, it is the king's most sweet pleasure and affection to congratulate the princess at her pavilion, in the posteriors of this day; which the rude multitude call the afternoon.

*Hol.* The posterior of the day, most generous sir, is liable, congruent, and measurable for the afternoon: the word is well culled, choice; sweet and apt, I do assure you, sir, I do assure.

*Arm.* Sir, the king is a noble gentleman, and my familiar, I do assure you, very good friend:—For what is inward between us, let it pass:—I do beseech thee, remember thy courtesy:—I beseech thee, apparel thy head;—and among other importunate and most serious designs,—and of great import indeed too;—but let that pass;—for I must tell thee, it will please his grace, by the world, sometime to lean upon my poor shoulder; and with his royal finger, thus, dally with my excrement, with my mustachio: but, sweet heart, let that pass. By the world, I recount no fable; some certain special honours it pleaseth his greatness to impart to Armado, a soldier, a man of travel, that hath seen the world: but let that pass.—The very all of all is,—but, sweetheart, I do implore secrecy,—that the king would have me present the princess, sweet chuck, with some delightful ostentation, or show, or pageant, or antic, or firework. Now, understanding that the curate and your sweet self are good at such eruptions and sudden breaking out of mirth, as it were, I have acquainted you withal, to the end to crave your assistance.

*Hol.* Sir, you shall present before her the nine worthies.—Sir Nathaniel, as concerning some entertainment of time, some show in the posterior of this day, to be rendered by our assistance,—the king's command, and this most gallant, illustrate, and learned gentleman,—before the princess, I say, none so fit as to present the nine worthies.

*Nath.* Where will you find men worthy enough to present them?

*Hol.* Joshua, yourself; myself, or this gallant gentleman, Judas Maccabæus; this swain, because of his great limb or joint, shall pass Pompey the Great; the page, Hercules.

*Arm.* Pardon, sir; error: he is not quantity enough for that worthy's thumb: he is not so big as the end of his club.

*Hol.* Shall I have audience? he shall present Hercules in minority; his *enter* and *exit* shall be strangling a snake; and I will have an apology for that purpose.

*Moth.* An excellent device! so, if any of the audience hiss, you may cry: *Well done, Hercules! now thou crushest the snake!* that is the way to make an offence gracious, though few have the grace to do it.

*Arm.* For the rest of the worthies?-

*Hol.* I will play three myself.

*Moth.* Thrice-worthy gentleman!

*Arm.* Shall I tell you a thing?

*Hol.* We attend.

*Arm.* We will have, if this fadge not, an antic. I beseech you, follow.

*Hol.* *Via*, goodman Dull! thou hast spoken no word all this while.

*Dull.* Nor understood none neither, sir.

*Hol.* *Allons!* we will employ thee.

*Dull.* I'll make one in a dance, or so; or I will play on the tabor to the worthies, and let them dance the hay.

*Hol.* Most dull, honest Dull!—to our sport, away.         [*Exeunt.*

SCENE II.—*Another part of the Park.*
*Before the* PRINCESS'S *Pavilion.*

*Enter the* PRINCESS, KATHARINE, ROSALIND, *and* MARIA.

*Prin.* Sweet hearts, we shall be rich ere we depart,
If fairings come thus plentifully in:
A lady wall'd about with diamonds!
Look you what I have from the loving king.

*Ros.* Madam, came nothing else along with that?         [in rhyme

*Prin.* Nothing but this? yes, as much love
As would be cramm'd up in a sheet of paper,
Writ on both sides the leaf, margent and all;
That he was fain to seal on Cupid's name.

*Ros.* That was the way to make his godhead wax;
For he hath been five thousand years a boy.

*Kath.* Ay, and a shrewd unhappy gallows too.

*Ros.* You'll ne'er be friends with him; he kill'd your sister.       [heavy;

*Kath.* He made her melancholy, sad, and heavy;
And so she died: had she been light, like you,
Of such a merry, nimble, stirring spirit,
She might have been a grandam ere she died:
And so may you; for a light heart lives long.

*Ros.* What's your dark meaning, mouse, of this light word?

*Kath.* A light condition in a beauty dark.

*Ros.* We need more light to find your meaning out.       [snuff;

*Kath.* You'll mar the light by taking it in snuff;
Therefore, I'll darkly end the argument.

*Ros.* Look what you do, you do it still i' the dark.       [wench.

*Kath.* So do not you; for you are a light wench.

*Ros.* Indeed, I weigh not you; and therefore light.

*Kath.* You weigh me not?—O, that's you care not for me.       [care.

*Ros.* Great reason; for, Past cure is still past

*Prin.* Well bandied both; a set of wit well
   play'd.
But, Rosaline, you have a favour too:
Who sent it? and what is it?
*Ros.*             I would you knew!
An if my face were but as fair as yours,
My favour were as great; be witness this.
Nay, I have verses too, I thank Birón:
The numbers true; and, were the numb'ring too,
I were the fairest goddess on the ground:
I am compar'd to twenty thousand fairs.
O, he hath drawn my picture in his letter!
  *Prin.* Anything like?
  *Ros.* Much in the letters; nothing in the
   praise.
  *Prin.* Beauteous as ink; a good conclusion.
  *Kath.* Fair as a text B in a copy-book.
  *Ros.* 'Ware pencils, ho! let me not die your
   debtor.
My rod dominical, my golden letter:
O that your face were not so full of O's!
  *Kath.* A pox of that jest! and be shrew all
   shrows!          [from fair Dumain?
  *Prin.* But, Katharine, what was sent to you
  *Kath.* Madam, this glove.
  *Prin.*        Did he not send you twain?
  *Kath.* Yes, madam; and, moreover,
Some thousand verses of a faithful lover;
A huge translation of hypocrisy,
Vilely compil'd, profound simplicity.
  *Mar.* This, and these pearls, to me sent
   Longaville;
The letter is too long by half a mile.  [heart
  *Prin.* I think no less. Dost thou not wish in
The chain were longer and the letter short?
  *Mar.* Ay, or I would these hands might
   never part.
  *Prin.* We are wise girls to mock our lovers so.
  *Ros.* They are worse fools to purchase mock-
   ing so.
That same Birón I'll torture ere I go.
O that I knew he were but in by the week!
How I would make him fawn, and beg, and
  seek,
And wait the season, and observe the times,
And spend his prodigal wits in bootless rhymes,
And shape his service wholly to my 'hests,
And make him proud to make me proud that
  jests!
So portent-like would I o'ersway his state
That he should be my fool and I his fate.
  *Prin.* None are so surely caught, when they
   are catch'd,
As wit turn'd fool: folly, in wisdom hatch'd,
Hath wisdom's warrant, and the help of school,
And wit's own grace to grace a learned fool.
  *Ros.* The blood of youth burns not with such
   excess
As gravity's revolt to wantonness.
  *Mar.* Folly in fools bears not so strong a note
As foolery in the wise, when wit doth dote,
Since all the power thereof it doth apply
To prove, by wit, worth in simplicity.  [face.
  *Prin.* Here comes Boyet, and mirth is in his

*Enter* BOYET.

  *Boyet.* O, I am stabb'd with laughter
   Where's her grace?
  *Prin.* Thy news, Boyet?
  *Boyet.*        Prepare, madam, prepare!—
Arm, wenches, arm! encounters mounted are
Against your peace: Love doth approach dis-
  guis'd,
  Armed in arguments; you'll be surpris'd:
Muster your wits: stand in your own defence;
Or hide your heads like cowards, and fly hence.
  *Prin.* Saint Dennis to Saint Cupid! What
   are they              [ say.
That charge their breath against us? say, scout,
  *Boyet.* Under the cool shade of a sycamore
I thought to close mine eyes some half an hour;
When, lo! to interrupt my purpos'd rest,
Toward that shade I might behold addrest
The king and his companions: warily
I stole into a neighbour thicket by,
And overheard what you shall overhear,
That, by and by, disguis'd they will be here.
Their herald is a pretty knavish page,
That well by heart hath conn'd his embassage:
Action and accent did they teach him there;
*Thus must thou speak and thus thy body bear:*
And ever and anon they made a doubt
Presence majestical would put him out;
*For,* quoth the king, *an angel shalt thou see,*
*Yet fear not thou, but speak audaciously.*
The boy reply'd, *An angel is not evil;*
*I should have fear'd her had she been a devil.*
With that all laugh'd, and clapp'd him on the
  shoulder,
Making the bold wag, by their praises bolder.
One rubb'd his elbow, thus, and fleer'd, and
  swore
A better speech was never spoke before:
Another with his finger and his thumb
Cried, *Via! we will do't, come what will come:*
The third he caper'd, and cried, *All goes well.*
The fourth turn'd on the toe, and down he fell,
With that they all did tumble on the ground,
With such a zealous laughter, so profound,
That in this spleen ridiculous appears,
To check their folly, passion's solemn tears.
  *Prin.* But what, but what, come they to
   visit us?            [thus,—
  *Boyet.* They do, they do; and are apparel'd
Like Muscovites, or Russians, as I guess;
Their purpose is to parle, to court, and dance;
And every one his love-suit will advance
Unto his several mistress; which they'll know
By favours several which they did bestow.
  *Prin.* And will they so? the gallants shall be
   task'd:—
For, ladies, we will every one be mask'd;
And not a man of them shall have the grace,
Despite of suit, to see a lady's face.—
Hold, Rosaline, this favour thou shalt wear;
And then the king will court thee for his dear;
Hold, take thou this, my sweet, and give me
  thine;

So shall Birón take me for Rosaline.—
And change your favours too; so shall your
   loves
Woo contrary, deceiv'd by these removes.

*Ros.* Come on, then; wear the favours most
   in sight.                  [intent?

*Kath.* But, in this changing, what is your

*Prin.* The effect of my intent is to cross
   theirs:
They do it but in mocking merriment;
And mock for mock is only my intent.
Their several counsels they unbosom shall
To loves mistook; and so be mock'd withal
Upon the next occasion that we meet
With visages display'd to talk and greet.

*Ros.* But shall we dance if they desire us
   to't?

*Prin.* No; to the death we will not move a
   foot:
Nor to their penn'd speech render we no graçe:
But while 'tis spoke, each turn away her face.

*Boyet.* Why, that contempt will kill the
   speaker's heart,
And quite divorce his memory from his part.

*Prin.* Therefore I do it; and I make no doubt
The rest will ne'er come in if he be out.
There's no such sport as sport by sport o'er-
   thrown;                 [own:
To make theirs ours, and ours none but our
So shall we stay, mocking intended game;
And they, well mock'd, depart away with
   shame.        [*Trumpets sound within.*

*Boyet.* The trumpet sounds; be mask'd; the
   maskers come.        [*The Ladies mask.*

*Enter the* KING, BIRON, LONGAVILLE, *and*
DUMAIN, *in Russian habits and masked;*
MOTH, Musicians, *and* Attendants.

*Moth.* All hail the richest beauties on the earth!

*Boyet.* Beauties no richer than rich taffeta.

*Moth.* A holy parcel of the fairest dames!
   [*The* Ladies *turn their backs to him.*
*That ever turn'd their—backs—to mortal views!*

*Biron.* Their eyes, villain, *their eyes.*

*Moth.* That ever turn'd their eyes to mortal
   *views!*

*Out—*

*Boyet.* True; *out* indeed.    [*vouchsafe*

*Moth.* Out of your favours, heavenly spirits

*Not to behold—*

*Biron.* Once to behold, rogue.

*Moth.* Once to behold with your sun-beamed
*eyes,*—with your sun-beamed eyes—

*Boyet.* They will not answer to that epithet;
You were best call it daughter-beamed eyes.

*Moth.* They do not mark me, and that brings
   me out.

*Biron.* Is this your perfectness? be gone, you
   rogue.             [*Exit* MOTH.

*Ros.* What would these strangers? Know
   their minds, Boyet:
If they do speak our language, 'tis our will
That some plain man recount our purposes:
Know what they would.

*Boyet.* What would you with the princess?

*Biron.* Nothing but peace and gentle visitation.

*Ros.* What would they, say they?    [tion.

*Boyet.* Nothing but peace and gentle visita-

*Ros.* Why, that they have; and bid them so
   be gone.               [gone.

*Boyet.* She says you have it, and you may be

*King.* Say to her we have measured many
   miles
To tread a measure with her on this grass.

*Boyet.* They say that they have measured
   many a mile
To tread a measure with you on this grass.

*Ros.* It is not so. Ask them how many inches
Is in one mile: if they have measur'd many,
The measure, then, of one is easily told.

*Boyet.* If to come hither you have measur'd
   miles,
And many miles, the princess bids you tell
How many inches do fill up one mile.    [steps.

*Biron.* Tell her we measure them by weary

*Boyet.* She hears herself.

*Ros.*            How many weary steps,
Of many weary miles you have o'ergone,
Are number'd in the travel of one mile?

*Biron.* We number nothing that we spend
   for you;
Our duty is so rich, so infinite,
That we may do it still without accompt.
Vouchsafe to show the sunshine of your face,
That we, like savages, may worship it.

*Ros.* My face is but a moon, and clouded too.

*King.* Blessed are clouds, to do as such
   clouds do!            [shine,—
Vouchsafe, bright moon, and these thy stars, to
Those clouds removed,—upon our wat'ry eyne.

*Ros.* O vain petitioner! beg a greater matter;
Thou now request'st but moonshine in the
   water.

*King.* Then, in our measure do but vouchsafe one change;
Thou bid'st me beg; this begging is not strange.

*Ros.* Play music, then: nay, you must do it
   soon.              [*Music plays.*
Not yet;—no dance:—thus change I like the
   moon.

*King.* Will you not dance? How come you
   thus estrang'd?

*Ros.* You took the moon at full; but now
   she's chang'd.           [man.

*King.* Yet still she is the moon and I the
The music plays; vouchsafe some motion to it.

*Ros.* Our ears vouchsafe it.

*King.*           But your legs should do it.

*Ros.* Since you are strangers, and come here
   by chance,           [dance.
We'll not be nice; take hands;—we will not

*King.* Why take we hands, then?

*Ros.*           Only to part friends;—
Court'sy, sweet hearts; and so the measure
   ends.            [nice.

*King.* More measure of this measure; be not

*Ros.* We can afford no more at such a price.

*King.* Prize you yourselves: what buys your
　company?
*Ros.*　　　　　　Your absence only.
*King.*　　　　　　　That can never be.
*Ros.* Then cannot we be bought: and so
　adieu;
Twice to your visor and half once to you!
*King.* If you deny to dance, let's hold more
　chat.
*Ros.* In private then.
*King.*　　I am best pleas'd with that.
　　　　　　　　[*They converse apart.*
*Biron.* White-handed mistress, one sweet
　word with thee.　　　　　　[three.
*Prin.* Honey, and milk, and sugar; there is
*Biron.* Nay, then, two treys,—an if you
　grow so nice,—
Metheglin, wort, and malmsey;—well run,
　dice!
There's half a dozen sweets.
*Prin.*　　Seventh sweet, adieu!
Since you can cog, I'll play no more with you.
*Biron.* One word in secret.
*Prin.*　　　　Let it not be sweet.
*Biron.* Thou griev'st my gall.
*Prin.*　　　　　Gall? bitter.
*Biron.*　　　　　Therefore meet.
　　　　　　　　[*They converse apart.*
*Dum.* Will you vouchsafe with me to change
　a word?
*Mar.* Name it.
*Dum.*　　　Fair lady,—
*Mar.*　　　Say you so? Fair lord,—
Take that for your fair lady.
*Dum.*　　　　Please it you,
As much in private, and I'll bid adieu.
　　　　　　　　[*They converse apart.*
*Kath.* What, was your visard made without
　a tongue?
*Long.* I know the reason, lady, why you ask.
*Kath.* O for your reason! quickly, sir; I long.
*Long.* You have a double tongue within
　your mask,　　　・
And would afford my speechless visard half.
*Kath.* Veal, quoth the Dutchman;—is not
　veal a calf?
*Long.* A calf, fair lady!
*Kath.*　　　　No, a fair lord calf.
*Long.* Let's part the word.
*Kath.*　　　　No, I'll not be your half:
Take all, and wean it; it may prove an ox.
*Long.* Look how you butt yourself in these
　sharp mocks!
Will you give horns, chaste lady? do not so.
*Kath.* Then die a calf, before your horns do
　grow.
*Long.* One word in private with you ere I die.
*Kath.* Bleat softly, then; the butcher hears
　you cry.　　　　　[*They converse apart.*
*Boyet.* The tongues of mocking wenches are
　as keen
As is the razor's edge invisible,
Cutting a smaller hair than may be seen;
Above the sense of sense; so sensible

Seemeth their conference; their conceits have
　wings,　　　　　　　[swifter things
Fleeter than arrows, bullets, wind, thought,
*Ros.* Not one word more, my maids; break
　of, break off.　　　　　　[scoff!
*Biron.* By heaven, all dry-beaten with pure
*King.* Farewell, mad wenches; you have
　simple wits.
[*Exeunt* KING, LORDS, *Music, and* Attendants.
*Prin.* Twenty adieus, my frozen Musco-
　vites.—
Are these the breed of wits so wonder'd at?
*Boyet.* Tapers they are, with your sweet
　breaths puffed out.
*Ros.* Well-liking wits they have; gross, gross;
　fat, fat.
*Prin.* O poverty in wit, kingly-poor flout!
Will they not, think you, hang themselves to-
　night?
Or ever, but in visards, show their faces?
This pert Birón was out of countenance quite.
*Ros.* O, they were all in lamentable cases!
The king was weeping-ripe for a good word.
*Prin.* Birón did swear himself out of all suit.
*Mar.* Dumain was at my service, and his
　sword:　　　　　　[mute.
No *point*, quoth I; my servant straight was
*Kath.* Lord Longaville said I came o'er his
　heart;
And trow you what he called me?
*Prin.*　　　　Qualm, perhaps.
*Kath.* Yes, in good faith.
*Prin.*　　　Go, sickness as thou art!
*Ros.* Well, better wits have worn plain
　statue-caps.
But will you hear? the king is my love sworn.
*Prin.* And quick Birón hath plighted faith
　to me.　　　　　　[born.
*Kath.* And Longaville was for my service
*Mar.* Dumain is mine, as sure as bark on
　tree.　　　　　　　[ear:
*Boyet.* Madam, and pretty mistresses, give
Immediately they will again be here
In their own shapes; for it can never be
They will digest this harsh indignity.
*Prin.* Will they return?
*Boyet.*　　They will, they will, God knows,
And leap for joy, though they are lame with
　blows;　　　　　　[repair,
Therefore, change favours; and, when they
Blow like sweet roses in this summer air.
*Prin.* How blow? how blow? speak to be
　understood.　　　　　　[bud:
*Boyet.* Fair ladies mask'd are roses in their
Dismask'd, their damask sweet commixture
　shown,
Are angels vailing clouds, or roses blown.
*Prin.* Avaunt, perplexity! What shall we do
If they return in their own shapes to woo?
*Ros.* Good madam, if by me you'll be advis'd,
Let's mock them still, as well known as dis-
　guis'd:
Let us complain to them what fools were here,
Disguis'd like Muscovites, in shapeless gear;

And wonder what they were, and to what end
Their shallow shows and prologue vilely penn'd,
And their rough carries so ridiculous,
Should be presented at our tent to us.     [hand.

*Boyet.* Ladies, withdraw; the gallants are at
*Prin.* Whip to our tents, as roes run over
land.
     [*Exeunt* PRIN., ROS., KATH., *and* MAR.

*Re-enter the* KING, BIRON, LONGAVILLE, *and*
     DUMAIN, *in their proper habits.*

*King.* Fair sir, God save you! Where is the
princess?     [majesty
*Boyet.* Gone to her tent. Please it your
Command me any service to her thither?
*King.* That she vouchsafe me audience for
one word.
*Boyet.* I will; and so will she, I know, my
lord.     [*Exit.*
*Birob.* This fellow pecks up wit as pigeons
peas,
And utters it again when God doth please:
He is wit's pedlar, and retails his wares
At wakes, and wassels, meetings, markets, fairs;
And we that sell by gross, the Lord doth know,
Have not the grace to grace it with such show.
This gallant pins the wenches on his sleeve,—
Had he been Adam, he had tempted Eve:
He can carve too, and lisp: why this is he
That kiss'd away his hand in courtesy:
This is the ape of form, monsieur the nice,
That, when he plays at tables, chides the dice
In honourable terms; nay, he can sing
A mean most meanly; and in ushering,
Mend him who can: the ladies call him sweet;
The stairs, as he treads on them, kiss his feet:
This is the flower that smiles on every one,
To show his teeth as white as whale's bone:
And consciences that will not die in debt
Pay him the due of honey-tongu'd Boyet.
*King.* A blister on his sweet tongue, with my
heart,
That put Armado's page out of his part!
*Biron.* See where it comes!—Behaviour,
what wert thou     [now?
Till this man show'd thee? and what art thou

*Re-enter the* PRINCESS, *ushered by* BOYET;
ROSALINE, MARIA, KATHARINE, *and* Attendants.

*King.* All hail, sweet madam, and fair time
of day!
*Prin.* Fair, in all hail, is foul, as I conceive.
*King.* Construe my speeches better, if you
may.
*Prin.* Then wish me better, I will give you
leave.
*King.* We came to visit you; and purpose now
To lead you to our court: vouchsafe it then.
*Prin.* This field shall hold me; and so hold
your vow:
Nor God, nor I, delight in perjur'd men.
*King.* Rebuke me not for that which you
provoke;

The virtue of your eye must break my oath.
*Prin.* You nickname virtue: vice you should
have spoke:
For virtue's office never breaks men's troth.
Now, by my maiden honour, yet as pure
As the unsullied lily; I protest.
A world of torments though I should endure,
I would not yield to be your house's guest:
So much I hate a breaking cause to be
Of heavenly oaths, vow'd with integrity.
*King.* O, you have liv'd in desolation here,
Unseen, unvisited, much to our shame.
*Prin.* Not so, my lord; it is not so, I swear;
We have had pastime here, and pleasant
game;
A mess of Russians left us but of late.
*King.* How, madam! Russians!
*Prin.*               Ay, in truth, my lord;
Trim gallants, full of courtship and of state.
*Ros.* Madam, speak true.—It is not so, my
lord;
My lady,—to the manner of the days,—
In courtesy, gives undeserving praise.
We four, indeed, confronted here with four
In Russian habit; here they stay'd an hour
And talk'd apace; and in that hour, my lord,
They did not bless us with one happy word.
I dare not call them fools; but this I think,
When they are thirsty, fools would fain have
drink.     [sweet,
*Biron.* This jest is dry to me.—Fair, gentle
Your wit makes wise things foolish; when we
greet
With eyes best seeing heaven's fiery eye,
By light we lose light: your capacity
Is of that nature, that to your huge store
Wise things seem foolish and rich things but
poor.     [my eye,—
*Ros.* This proves you wise and rich, for in
*Biron.* I am a fool, and full of poverty.
*Ros.* But that you take what doth to you
belong,
It were a fault to snatch words from my tongue.
*Biron.* O, I am yours, and all that I possess.
*Ros.* All the fool mine?
*Biron.*               I cannot give you less.
*Ross.* Which of the visards was it that you
wore?
*Biron.* Where? when? what visard? why de-
mand you this?     [ous case
*Ros.* There, then, that visard; that superflu-
That hid the worse and show'd the better face.
*King.* We are descried: they'll mock us now
downright.
*Dum.* Let us confess, and turn it to a jest.
*Prin.* Amaz'd, my lord? why looks your
highness sad?
*Ros.* Help, hold his brows! he'll swoon! Why
look you pale?—
Sea-sick, I think, coming from Muscovy.
*Biron.* Thus pour the stars down plagues for
perjury.
Can any face of brass hold longer out?—
Here stand I, lady: dart thy skill at me;

Bruise me with scorn, confound me with a
　flout;
Thrust thy sharp wit quite through my ignor-
　ance;
Cut me to pieces with thy keen conceit;
And I will wish thee never more to dance,
　Nor never more in Russian habit wait.
O, never will I trust to speeches penn'd,
Nor to the motion of a school-boy's tongue;
Nor never come in visard to my friend;
Nor woo in rhyme, like a blind harper's song:
Taffeta phrases, silken terms precise,
　Three-pil'd hyperboles, spruce affectation,
Figures pedantical; these summer-flies
Have blown me full of maggot ostentation;
I do forswear them: and I here protest,
　By this white glove,—how white the hand,
　　God knows!—
Henceforth my wooing mind shall be express'd
In russet yeas, and honest kersey noes:
And, to begin, wench,—so God help me, la!—
My love to thee is sound, sans crack or flaw.
　*Ros.* Sans sans, I pray you.
　*Biron.*　　　　　Yet I have a trick
Of the old rage:—bear with me, I am sick;
I'll leave it by degrees. Soft, let us see;—
Write, *Lord have mercy on us*, on those three;
They are infected; in their hearts it lies:
They have the plague, and caught it of your
　eyes:
These lords are visited; you are not free,
For the Lord's tokens on you do I see.
　*Prin.* No, they are free that gave these tok-
　　ens to us.　　　　　　　　　[undo us.
　*Biron.* Our states are forfeit: seek not to
　*Ros.* It is not so; for how can this be true,
That you stand forfeit, being those that sue?
　*Biron.* Peace; for I will not have to do with
　you.
　*Ros.* Nor shall not, if I do as I intend.
　*Biron.* Speak for yourselves; my wit is at an
　　end.　　　　　　　　[transgression
　*King.* Teach us, sweet madam, for our rude
Some fair excuse.
　*Prin.*　　　　The fairest is confession.
Were you not here but even now, disguis'd?
　*King.* Madam, I was.
　*Prin.*　　　　And were you well advis'd?
　*King.* I was, fair madam.
　*Prin.*　　　　When you then were here,
What did you whisper in your lady's ear?
　*King.* That more than all the world I did re-
　　spect her.
　*Prin.* When she shall challenge this you will
　　reject her.
　*King.* Upon mine honour, no.
　*Prin.*　　　　Peace, peace, forbear;
Your oath once broke, you force not to for-
　swear.
　*King.* Despise me when I break this oath of
　mine.
　*Prin.* I will: and therefore keep it:—Rosa-
　line,
What did the Russian whisper in your ear?

　*Ros.* Madam, he swore that he did hold me
　　dear
As precious eyesight; and did value me
Above this world: adding thereto, moreover,
That he would wed me, or else die my lover.
　*Prin.* God give thee joy of him! the noble
　　lord
Most honourably doth uphold his word.
　*King.* What mean you, madam? by my life,
　　my troth,
I never swore this lady such an oath.　[plain;
　*Ros.* By heaven you did; and, to confirm it
You gave me this: but take it, sir, again.
　*King.* My faith and this the princess I did
　　give;
I knew her by this jewel on her sleeve.
　*Prin.* Pardon me, sir; this jewel she did wear;
And Lord Birón, I thank him, is my dear:—
What; will you have me, or your pearl again?
　*Biron.* Neither of either; I remit both
　　twain.—
I see the trick on 't;—here was a consent,
Knowing aforehand of our merriment,
To dash it like a Christmas comedy:　[zany,
Some carry-tale, some please-man, some slight
Some mumble-news, some trencher-knight,
　　some Dick,—　　　　　　　　[trick
That smiles his cheek in years, and knows the
To make my lady laugh when she's dispos'd,—
Told our intents before: which once disclos'd,
The ladies did change favours; and then we,
Following the signs, woo'd but the sign of she.
Now, to our perjury to add more terror,
We are again forsworn,—in will and error.
Much upon this it is:—and might not you
　　　　　　　　　　　　[*To* BOYET.
Forestal our sport, to make us thus untrue?
Do not you know my lady's foot by the squire,
　And laugh upon the apple of her eye?
And stand between her back, sir, and the fire,
　Holding a trencher, jesting merrily?
You put our page out: go, you are allow'd;
Die when you will, a smock shall be your
　shroud.
You leer upon me, do you? there's an eye
Wounds like a leaden sword.
　*Boyet.*　　　　　Full merrily
Hath this brave manage, this career, been run.
　*Biron.* Lo, he is tilting straight! Peace; I
　have done.

　　　　　*Enter* COSTARD.

Welcome, pure wit! thou partest a fair fray.
　*Cost.* O Lord, sir, they would know
Whether the three worthies shall come in or no.
　*Biron.* What, are there but three?
　*Cost.*　　　　No, sir; but it is vara fine,
For every one pursents three.
　*Biron.*　　　And three times thrice is nine.
　*Cost.* Not so, sir; under correction, sir; I
　　hope it is not so:
You cannot beg us, sir, I can assure you, sir:
　we know what we know;
I hope, sir, three times thrice, sir,—

*Biron.*                                        Is not nine.
*Cost.* Under correction, sir, we know where-
until it doth amount.                   [for nine.
*Biron.* By Jove, I always took three threes
*Cost.* O Lord, sir, it were pity you should
get your living by reckoning, sir.
*Biron.* How much is it?
*Cost.* O Lord, sir, the parties themselves,
the actors, sir, will show whereuntil it doth
amount; for my own part I am, as they say,
but to parfect one man in one poor man;
Pompion the Great, sir.
*Biron.* Art thou one of the worthies?
*Cost.* It pleased them to think me worthy of
Pompion the Great: for mine own part, I know
not the degree of the worthy; but I am to stand
for him.
*Biron.* Go, bid them prepare.
*Cost.* We will turn it finely off, sir; we will
    take some care.              [*Exit* COSTARD.
*King.* Birón, they will shame us; let them
    not approach.
*Biron.* We are shame-proof, my lord: and
'tis some policy
To have one show worse than the king's and
his company.
*King.* I say they shall not come.      [now:
*Prin.* Nay, my good lord, let me o'errule you
That sport best pleases that doth least know
how;
Where zeal strives to content, and the contents
Die in the zeal of them which it presents,
Their form confounded makes most form in
mirth,
When great things labouring perish in their
birth.
*Biron.* A right description of our sport, my
lord.

*Enter* ARMADO.

*Arm.* Anointed, I implore so much expense
of thy royal sweet breath as will utter a brace
of words.    [ARMADO *converses with the* KING,
                *and delivers him a paper.*
*Prin.* Doth this man serve God?
*Biron.* Why ask you?                 [making.
*Prin.* He speaks not like a man of God's
*Arm.* That's all one, my fair, sweet, honey
monarch: for, I protest, the schoolmaster is exceeding fantastical; too, too vain; too, too vain:
but we will put it, as they say, to *fortuna della
guerra.* I wish you the peace of mind, most
royal couplement!              [*Exit* ARMADO.
*King.* Here is like to be a good presence of
worthies. He presents Hector of Troy; the
swain, Pompey the Great; the parish curate,
Alexander; Armado's page, Hercules; the
pedant, Judas Maccabæus.
And if these four worthies in their first show
thrive,                              [other five.
These four will change habits and present the
*Biron.* There is five in the first show.
*King.* You are deceived, 'tis not so.

*Biron.* The pedant, the braggart, the hedge-
priest, the fool, and the boy;—        [again
Abate throw at novum; and the whole world
Cannot prick out five such, take each one in his
vein.                              [comes amain.
*King.* The ship is under sail, and here she
    [*Seats brought for the* KING, PRIN., *&c.*

*Pageant of the Nine Worthies.*

*Enter* COSTARD, *armed, for* Pompey.

*Cost.* I Pompey am——
*Boyet.*            You lie, you are not he.
*Cost.* I Pompey am——
*Boyet.*        With libbard's head on knee.
*Biron.* Well said, old mocker; I must needs
be friends with thee.                   [Big,—
*Cost.* I Pompey am, Pompey surnamed the
*Dum.* The Great.
*Cost.* It is *Great,* sir;—*Pompey surnamed the
    Great,*
*That oft in field, with targe and shield, did make
    my foe to sweat;*                  [chance,
*And travelling along this coast, I here am come by
*And lay my arms before the legs of this sweet lass
    of France.*                      [had done.
If your ladyship would say, *Thanks, Pompey,* I
*Prin.* Great thanks, great Pompey.
*Cost.* 'Tis not so much worth; but I hope I
was parfect: I made a little fault in *Great.*
*Biron.* My hat to a halfpenny, Pompey
proves the best worthy.

*Enter Sir* NATHANIEL, *armed, for* Alexander.

*Nath. When in the world I liv'd, I was the
    world's commander;*
*By east, west, north, and south I spread my con-
    quering might:*
*My 'scutcheon plain declares that I am Alisander.*
*Boyet.* Your nose says, no, you are not; for
    it stands too right.
*Biron.* Your nose smells no in this, most
    tender-smelling knight.
*Prin.* The conqueror is dismay'd.—Proceed,
    good Alexander.
*Nath. When in the world I liv'd, I was the
    world's commander:*—              [sander.
*Boyet.* Most true, 'tis right; you were so, Ali-
*Biron.* Pompey the Great,—
*Cost.*        Your servant, and Costard.
*Biron.* Take away the conqueror, take away
    Alisander.
*Cost.* O, sir [*to* NATH.], you have overthrown
Alisander the conqueror! You will be scraped
out of the painted cloth for this: your lion, that
holds his poll-ax sitting on a close stool, will be
given to Ajax: he will be the ninth worthy. A
conqueror and afeard to speak! run away for
shame, Alisander. [*Sir* NATH. *retires.*] There,
an't shall please you; á foolish mild man; an
honest man, look you, and soon dashed! he is a
marvellous good neighbour, insooth; and a very
good bowler: but, for Alisander,—alas, you see,
how 'tis,—a little o'erparted.—But there are

worthies a-coming will speak their mind in some other sort.

*Prin.* Stand aside, good Pompey.

*Enter* HOLOFERNES, *armed, for* Judas; *and* MOTH, *armed, for* Hercules.

*Hol.* *Great Hercules is presented by this imp,*
*Whose club kill'd Cerberus, that three-headed* canus;
*And when he was a babe, a child, a shrimp,*
  *Thus did he strangle serpents in his* manus:
Quoniam *he seemeth in minority,*
Ergo *I come with this apology.—*
Keep some state in thy *exit,* and vanish.
                    [MOTH *retires.*

*Judas I am,—*
  *Dum.* A Judas!
  *Hol.* Not Iscariot, sir,—
*Judas I am, ycleped Maccabæus.*
  *Dum.* Judas Maccabæus clipt is plain Judas.
  *Biron.* A kissing traitor. How art thou proved Judas?
  *Hol.* *Judas I am,—*
  *Dum.* The more shame for you, Judas.
  *Hol.* What mean you, sir?
  *Boyet.* To make Judas hang himself.
  *Hol.* Begin, sir; you are my elder.
  *Biron.* Well followed: Judas was hanged on an elder.
  *Hol.* I will not be put out of countenance.
  *Biron.* Because thou hast no face.
  *Hol.* What is this?
  *Boyet.* A cittern head.
  *Dum.* The head of a bodkin.
  *Biron.* A death's face in a ring.   [seen.
  *Long.* The face of an old Roman coin, scarce
  *Boyet.* The pummel of Cæsar's faulchion.
  *Dum.* The carv'd-bone face on a flask.
  *Biron.* St. George's half-cheek in a brooch.
  *Dum.* Ay, and in a brooch of lead.
  *Biron.* Ay, and worn in the cap of a tooth-drawer;
And now, forward; for we have put thee in countenance.
  *Hol.* You have put me out of countenance.
  *Biron.* False: we have given thee faces.
  *Hol.* But you have outfaced them all.
  *Biron.* An thou wert a lion we would do so.
  *Boyet.* Therefore, as he is an ass, let him go.
And so adieu, sweet Jude! nay, why dost thou stay?
  *Dum.* For the latter end of his name.
  *Biron.* For the ass to the Jude; give it him:—Jud-as, away.
  *Hol.* This is not generous, not gentle, not humble.
  *Boyet.* A light for Monsieur Judas! it grows dark, he may stumble.   [been baited!
  *Prin.* Alas, poor Maccabæus, how hath he

*Enter* ARMADO, *armed, for* Hector.

  *Biron.* Hide thy head, Achilles: here comes Hector in arms.

  *Dum.* Though my mocks come home by me, I will now be merry.   [this.
  *King.* Hector was but a Trojan in respect of
  *Boyet.* But is this Hector?
  *Dum.* I think Hector was not so clean-timbered.
  *Long.* His leg is too big for Hector.
  *Dum.* More calf, certain.
  *Boyet.* No; he is best indued in the small.
  *Biron.* This cannot be Hector.   [faces.
  *Dum.* He's a god or a painter, for he makes
  *Arm.* *The armipotent Mars, of lances the al-mighty,*
*Gave Hector a gift,—*
  *Dum.* A gilt nutmeg.
  *Biron.* A lemon.
  *Long.* Stuck with cloves.
  *Dum.* No, cloven.
  *Arm.* Peace!
*The armipotent Mars, of lances the almighty,*
  *Gave Hector a gift, the heir of Ilion;*   [yea,
*A man so breath'd, that certain he would fight,*
  *From morn till night, out of his pavilion.*
*I am that flower,—*
  *Dum.*          That mint.
  *Long.*              That columbine.
  *Arm.* Sweet Lord Longaville, rein thy tongue.
  *Long.* I must rather give it the rein, for it runs against Hector.
  *Dum.* Ay, and Hector's a greyhound.
  *Arm.* The sweet war-man is dead and rotten; sweet chucks, beat not the bones of the buried: when he breathed, he was a man.—But I will forward with my device. Sweet royalty [*to the* PRINCESS], bestow on me the sense of hearing.
                  [BIRON *whispers* COSTARD.
  *Prin.* Speak, brave Hector: we are much delighted.
  *Arm.* I do adore thy sweet grace's slipper.
  *Boyet.* Loves her by the foot.
  *Dum.* He may not by the yard.   [bal,—
  *Arm.* *This Hector far surmounted Hanni-*
  *Cost.* The party is gone, fellow Hector; she is gone: she is two months on her way.
  *Arm.* What meanest thou?
  *Cost.* Faith, unless you play the honest Trojan, the poor wench is cast away: she's quick; the child brags in her belly already; 'tis yours.
  *Arm.* Dost thou infamonize me among potentates? thou shalt die.
  *Cost.* Then shall Hector be whipped for Jaquenetta that is quick by him, and hanged for Pompey that is dead by him.
  *Dum.* Most rare Pompey!
  *Boyet.* Renowned Pompey!
  *Biron.* Greater than great, great, great, great Pompey! Pompey the Huge!
  *Dum.* Hector trembles.
  *Biron.* Pompey is mov'd.—More Ates, more Ates! stir them on! stir them on!
  *Dum.* Hector will challenge him.
  *Biron.* Ay, if he have no more man's blood in 's belly than will sup a flea.
  *Arm.* By the north pole, I do challenge thee.

*Cost.* I will not fight with a pole, like a northern man: I'll slash; I'll do it by the sword.—I pray you, let me borrow my arms again.

*Dum.* Room for the incensed worthies.

*Cost.* I'll do it in my shirt.

*Dum.* Most resolute Pompey!

*Moth.* Master, let me take you a button-hole lower. Do you not see Pompey is uncasing for the combat? What mean you? you will lose your reputation.

*Arm.* Gentlemen and soldiers, pardon me; I will not combat in my shirt.

*Dum.* You may not deny it: Pompey hath made the challenge.

*Arm.* Sweet bloods, I both may and will.

*Biron.* What reason have you for 't?

*Arm.* The naked truth of it is, I have no shirt; I go woolward for penance.

*Boyet.* True, and it was enjoined him in Rome for want of linen; since when, I'll be sworn, he wore none but a dish-clout of Jaquenetta's; and that'a wears next his heart for a favour.

*Enter* NERCADE.

*Mer.* God save you, madam!

*Prin.* Welcome, Mercade;
But that thou interrupt'st our merriment.

*Mer.* I am sorry, madam; for the news I bring
Is heavy in my tongue. The king your father,—

*Prin.* Dead, for my life!

*Mer.* Even so; my tale is told.            [cloud.

*Biron.* Worthies, away; the scene begins to

*Arm.* For mine own part, I breathe free breath: I have seen the day of wrong through the little hole of discretion, and I will right myself like a soldier.            [*Exeunt* Worthies.

*King.* How fares your Majesty?

*Prin.* Boyet, prepare; I will away to-night.

*King.* Madam, not so; I do beseech you, stay.            [lords,

*Prin.* Prepare, I say.—I thank you, gracious
For all your fair endeavours; and entreat
Out of a new-sad soul, that you vouchsafe,
In your rich wisdom, to excuse or hide
The liberal opposition of our spirits;
If over-boldly we have borne ourselves
In the converse of breath, your gentleness
Was guilty of it.—Farewell, worthy lord;
A heavy heart bears not a nimble tongue:
Excuse me so, coming so short of thanks
For my great suit so easily obtain'd.            [form

*King.* The extreme parts of time extremely
All causes to the purpose of his speed;
And often, at his very loose, decides
That which long process could not arbitrate:
And though the mourning brow of progeny
Forbid the smiling courtesy of love
The holy suit which fain it would convince,
Yet, since love's argument was first on foot,
Let not the cloud of sorrow justle it
From what it purpos'd: since to wail friends lost
Is not by much so wholesome-profitable

As to rejoice at friends but newly found.

*Prin.* I understand you not: my griefs are dull.            [ear of grief;—

*Biron.* Honest plain words best pierce the
And by these badges understand the king.
For your fair sakes have we neglected time,
Play'd foul play with our oaths; your beauty, ladies,
Hath much deform'd us, fashioning our humours
Even to the opposed end of our intents:
And what in us hath seem'd ridiculous,—
As love is full of unbefitting strains,—
All wanton as a child, skipping, and vain;
Form'd by the eye, and therefore, like the eye,
Full of strange shapes, of habits, and of forms,
Varying in subjects as the eye doth roll
To every varied object in his glance:
Which party-coated presence of loose love
Put on by us, if in your heavenly eyes
Have misbecom'd our oaths and gravities,
Those heavenly eyes that look into these faults
Suggested us to make. Therefore, ladies,
Our love being yours, the error that love makes
Is likewise yours: we to ourselves prove false,
By being once false, for ever to be true
To those that make us both—fair ladies, you:
And even that falsehood, in itself a sin,
Thus purifies itself and turns to grace.            [love;

*Prin.* We have receiv'd your letters, full of
Your favours, the ambassadors of love;
And, in our maiden council, rated them
At courtship, pleasant jest, and courtesy,
As bombast, and as lining to the time:
But more devout than this in our respects
Have we not been; and therefore met your loves
In their own fashion, like a merriment.

*Dum.* Our letters, madam, show'd much more than jest.

*Long.* So did our looks.

*Ros.*            We did not quote them so.

*King.* Now, at the latest minute of the hour,
Grant us your loves.

*Prin.*            A time, methinks, too short
To make a world-without-end bargain in.
No, no, my lord, your grace is perjur'd much,
Full of dear guiltiness; and therefore this,—
If for my love—as there is no such cause—
You will do aught, this shall you do for me:
Your oath I will not trust; but go with speed
To some forlorn and naked hermitage,
Remote from all the pleasures of the world;
There stay until the twelve celestial signs
Have brought about their annual reckoning.
If this austere insociable life
Change not your offer, made in heat of blood;
If frosts and fasts, hard lodging and thin weeds,
Nip not the gaudy blossoms of your love,
But that it bear this trial, and last love,
Then, at the expiration of the year,
Come, challenge, challenge me by these deserts,
And, by this virgin palm now kissing thine,
I will be thine; and, till that instant, shut
My woeful self up in a mournful house,
Raining the tears of lamentation

For the remembrance of my father's death.
If this thou do deny, let our hands part,
Neither intitled in the other's heart.
  *King.* If this, or more than this, I would deny,
To flatter up these powers of mine with rest,
The sudden hand of death close up mine eye!
Hence ever, then, my heart is in thy breast.
  *Biron.* And what to me, my love? and what
    to me?                              [rank;
  *Ros.* You must be purged too; your sins are
You are attaint with faults and perjury;
Therefore, if you my favour mean to get,
A twelvemonth shall you spend, and never rest,
But seek the weary beds of people sick.
  *Dum.* But what to me, my love? but what
    to me?
  *Kath.* A wife!—A beard, fair health, and
    honesty;
With threefold love I wish you all these three.
  *Dum.* O, shall I say I thank you, gentle
    wife?
  *Kath.* Not so, my lord;—a twelvemonth and
    a day                               [say:
I'll mark no words that smooth-fac'd wooers
Come when the king doth to my lady come,
Then, if I have much love I'll give you some.
  *Dum:* I'll serve thee true and faithfully till
    then.
  *Kath.* Yet swear not, lest you be forsworn
    again.
  *Long.* What says Maria?
  *Mar.*              At the twelvemonth's end
I'll change my black gown for a faithful friend.
  *Long.* I'll stay with patience; but the time
    is long.
  *Mar.* The liker you; few taller are so young.
  *Biron.* Studies my lady? mistress, look on
    me;
Behold the window of my heart, mine eye,
What humble suit attends thy answer there!
Impose some service on me for thy love.
  *Ros.* Oft have I heard of you, my Lord
    Birón,
Before I saw you: and the world's large tongue
Proclaims you for a man replete with mocks,
Full of comparisons and wounding flouts,
Which you on all estates will execute
That lie within the mercy of your wit.
To weed this wormwood from your fruitful
    brain,
And therewithal to win me, if you please,—
Without the which I am not to be won,—
You shall this twelvemonth term from day to
    day
Visit the speechless sick, and still converse
With groaning wretches; and your task shall be,
With all the fierce endeavour of your wit
To enforce the pained impotent to smile.
  *Biron.* To move wild laughter in the throat
    of death!
It cannot be; it is impossible:
Mirth cannot move a soul in agony.
  *Ros.* Why, that's the way to choke a gibing
    spirit,

Whose influence is begot of that loose grace
Which shallow laughing hearers give to fools:
A jest's prosperity lies in the ear
Of him that hears it, never in the tongue
Of him that makes it: then, if sickly ears,
Deaf'd with the clamours of their own dear
    groans,
Will hear your idle scorns, continue them,
And I will have you and that fault withal;
But if they will not, throw away that spirit,
And I shall find you empty of that fault,
Right joyful of your reformation.
  *Biron.* A twelvemonth! well, befall what
    will befall,
I'll jest a twelvemonth in an hospital.
  *Prin.* Ay, sweet my lord; and so I take my
    leave.                         [*To the* KING.
  *King.* No, madam: we will bring you on
    your way.                          [play;
  *Biron.* Our wooing doth not end like an old
Jack hath not Jill: these ladies' courtesy
Might well have made our sport a comedy.
  *King.* Come, sir, it wants a twelvemonth
    and a day,
And then 'twill end.
  *Biron.*              That's too long for a play.

### Enter ARMADO.

  *Arm.* Sweet majesty, vouchsafe me,—
  *Prin.* Was not that Hector?
  *Dum.* The worthy knight of Troy.
  *Arm.* I will kiss thy royal finger, and take
leave: I am a votary; I have vowed to Jaquenetta to hold the plough for her sweet love three
years. But, most esteemed greatness, will you
hear the dialogue that the two learned men
have compiled in praise of the owl and the
cuckoo? it should have followed in the end of
our show.
  *King.* Call them forth quickly, we will do so.
  *Arm.* Holla! approach.

### Enter HOLOFERNES, NATHANIEL, MOTH, COSTARD, *and others*.

This side is Hiems, Winter—this Ver, the
Spring; the one maintained by the owl, the
other by the cuckoo. Ver, begin.

### SONG.

#### I.

*Spring.* When daisies pied, and violets blue,
    And lady-smocks all silver-white,
  And cuckoo-buds of yellow hue,
    Do paint the meadows with delight,
  The cuckoo then, on every tree,
  Mocks married men, for thus sings he—
            Cuckoo;
  Cuckoo, cuckoo,—O word of fear,
  Unpleasing to a married ear!

#### II.

  When shepherds pipe on oaten straws,
    And merry larks are ploughmen's clocks,
  When turtles tread, and rooks and daws,
    And maidens bleach their summer smocks,

The cuckoo then, on every tree,
Mocks married men, for thus sings he—
        Cuckoo;
Cuckoo, cuckoo,—O word of fear,
Unpleasing to a married ear!

### III.

*Winter.* When icicles hang by the wall,
   And *Dick* the shepherd blows his nail,
And *Tom* bears logs into the hall,
   And milk comes frozen home in pail,
When blood is nipp'd and ways be foul,
Then nightly sings the staring owl—
        To-who;
To-whit, to-who, a merry note,
While greasy *Joan* doth keel the pot.

### IV.

When all aloud the wind doth blow,
   And coughing drowns the parson's saw,
And birds sit brooding in the snow,
   And *Marion's* nose looks red and raw,
When roasted crabs hiss in the bowl,
Then nightly sings the staring owl—
        To-who;
Tu-whit, to-who, a merry note,
While greasy *Joan* doth keel the pot.

*Arm.* The words of Mercury are harsh after the songs of Apollo. You that way; we this way.       [*Exeunt.*

# THE MERCHANT OF VENICE

## DRAMATIS PERSONÆ

DUKE OF VENICE.
PRINCE OF MOROCCO, } Suitors to PORTIA.
PRINCE OF ARRAGON, }
ANTONIO, the Merchant of Venice.
BASSANIO, his Friend.

SOLANIO, } Friends to ANTONIO and
SALARINO, } BASSANIO.
GRATIANO, }
LORENZO, in love with JESSICA.
SHYLOCK, a Jew.
TUBAL, a Jew, his Friend.
LAUNCELOT GOBBO, a Clown, Servant to SHYLOCK.

OLD GOBBO, Father to LAUNCELOT.
SALERIO, a Messenger from Venice.
LEONARDO, Servant to BASSANIO.
BALTHAZAR, } Servants to PORTIA.
STEPHANO, }

PORTIA, a rich Heiress.
NERISSA, her Waiting-maid.
JESSICA, Daughter to SHYLOCK.

Magnificoes of Venice, Officers of the Court of Justice, Gaoler, Servants, and other Attendants.

SCENE,—Partly at VENICE, and partly at BELMONT, the Seat of PORTIA, on the Continent.

## ACT I.

### SCENE I.—VENICE. A Street.

*Enter* ANTONIO, SALARINO, *and* SOLANIO.

*Ant.* In sooth, I know not why I am so sad:
It wearies me; you say it wearies you;
But how I caught it, found it, or came by it,
What stuff 'tis made of, whereof it is born,
I am to learn;
And such a want-wit sadness makes of me
That I have much ado to know myself.
  *Salar.* Your mind is tossing on the ocean;
There, where your argosies, with portly sail,—
Like signiors and rich burghers of the flood,
Or, as it were, the pageants of the sea,—
Do overpeer the petty traffickers
That curt'sy to them, do them reverence,
As they fly by them with their woven wings.
  *Solan.* Believe me, sir, had I such venture forth,
The better part of my affections would
Be with my hopes abroad. I should be still
Plucking the grass, to know where sits the wind;
Peering in maps for ports, and piers, and roads;
And every object that might make me fear
Misfortune to my ventures, out of doubt
Would make me sad.
  *Salar.*          My wind, cooling my broth,
Would blow me to an ague when I thought
What harm a wind too great might do at sea.
I should not see the sandy hour-glass run
But I should think of shallows and of flats,
And see my wealthy Andrew dock'd in sand,
Vailing her high-top lower than her ribs,
To kiss her burial. Should I go to church,
And see the holy edifice of stone,
And not bethink me straight of dangerous rocks,
Which, touching but my gentle vessel's side,

Would scatter all her spices on the stream,
Enrobe the roaring waters with my silks,
And, in a word, but even now worth this,
And now worth nothing? Shall I have the thought
To think on this; and shall I lack the thought
That such a thing bechanc'd would make me sad?
But tell not me; I know Antonio
Is sad to think upon his merchandize.          [it,
  *Ant.* Believe me, no: I thank my fortune for
My ventures are not in one bottom trusted,
Nor to one place; nor is my whole estate
Upon the fortune of this present year:
Therefore my merchandize makes me not sad.
  *Solan.* Why, then you are in love.
  *Ant.*                    Fie, fie!
  *Solan.* Not in love neither? Then let's say you are sad
Because you are not merry: and 'twere as easy
For you to laugh, and leap, and say you are merry,
Because you are not sad. Now, by two-headed     [Janus,
Nature hath framed strange fellows in her time:
Some that will ever more peep through their eyes,
And laugh, like parrots, at a bag-piper:
And other of such vinegar aspéct,
That they'll not show their teeth in way of smile,
Though Nestor swear the jest be laughable.
Here comes Bassanio, your most noble kinsman,
Gratiano and Lorenzo. Fare ye well;
We leave you now with better company.
  *Salar.* I would have stay'd till I had made you merry.
If worthier friends had not prevented me.
  *Ant.* Your worth is very dear in my regard.
I take it your own business calls on you,
And you embrace the occasion to depart.

203

*Enter* BASSANIO, LORENZO, *and* GRATIANO.

*Salar.* Good-morrow, my good lords.

*Bass.* Good signiors both, when shall we
laugh? say, when?
You grow exceeding strange: must it be so?

*Salar.* We'll make our leisures to attend on
yours.          [*Exeunt* SALAR. *and* SOLAN.

*Lor.* My Lord Bassanio, since you have
found Antonio,
We two will leave you; but at dinner-time,
I pray you, have in mind where we must meet.

*Bass.* I will not fail you.

*Gra.* You look not well, Signior Antonio;
You have too much respect upon the world:
They lose it that do buy it with much care.
Believe me, you are marvelously chang'd.

*Ant.* I hold the world but as the world,
Gratiano—
A stage, where every man must play a part,
And mine a sad one.

*Gra.*          Let me play the fool:
With mirth and laughter let old wrinkles come;
And let my liver rather heat with wine
Than my heart cool with mortifying groans,
Why should a man, whose blood is warm within,
Sit like his grandsire cut in alabaster?
Sleep when he wakes? and creep into the
jaundice
By being peevish? I tell thee what, Antonio,—
I love thee, and it is my love that speaks,—
There are a sort of men whose visages
Do cream and mantle like a standing pond,
And do a wilful stillness entertain,
With purpose to be dress'd in an opinion
Of wisdom, gravity, profound conceit;
As who should say, *I am Sir Oracle,*
*And, when I ope my lips, let no dog bark!*
O, my Antonio, I do know of these,
That therefore only are reputed wise
For saying nothing; who, I am very sure,
If they should speak, would almost damn those
ears          [fools.
Which, hearing them, would call their brothers
I'll tell thee more of this another time:
But fish not, with this melancholy bait,
For this fool's gudgeon, this opinion.—
Come, good Lorenzo.—Fare ye well awhile;
I'll end my exhortation after dinner.     [time:

*Lor.* Well, we will leave you then till dinner-
I must be one of these same dumb wise men,
For Gratiano never lets me speak.          [moe,

*Gra.* Well, keep me company but two years
Thou shalt not know the sound of thine own
tongue.

*Ant.* Farewell: I'll grow a talker for this
gear.

*Gra.* Thanks, i' faith; for silence is only
commendable          [dible.
In a neat's tongue dried and a maid not ven-
                    [*Exeunt* GRA. *and* LOR.

*Ant.* Is that anything now?

*Bass.* Gratiano speaks an infinite deal of
nothing, more than any man in all Venice.

His reasons are as two grains of wheat hid in
two bushels of chaff: you shall seek all day ere
you find them; and, when you have them, they
are not worth the search.          [same

*Ant.* Well; tell me now, what lady is this
To whom you swore a secret pilgrimage,
That you to-day promis'd to tell me of?

*Bass.* 'Tis not unknown to you, Antonio,
How much I have disabled mine estate
By something showing a more swelling port
Than my faint means would grant continuance:
Nor do I now make moan to be abridg'd
From such a noble rate; but my chief care
Is to come fairly off from the great debts
Wherein my time, something too prodigal,
Hath left me gag'd. To you, Antonio,
I owe the most, in money and in love;
And from your love I have a warranty
To unburthen all my plots and purposes
How to get clear of all the debts I owe.          [it;

*Ant.* I pray you, good Bassanio, let me know
And if it stand, as you yourself still do,
Within the eye of honour, be assur'd
My purse, my person, my extremest means
Lie all unlock'd to your occasions.          [shaft,

*Bass.* In my school-days, when I had lost one
I shot his fellow of the self-same flight
The self-same way, with more advised watch,
To find the other forth; and by advent'ring
both
I oft found both: I urge this childhood proof,
Because what follows is pure innocence.
I owe you much; and, like a wilful youth,
That which I owe is lost: but if you please
To shoot another arrow that self-way
Which you did shoot the first, I do not doubt,
As I will watch the aim, or to find both
Or bring your latter hazard back again,
And thankfully rest debtor for the first.          [time

*Ant.* You know me well, and herein spent but
To wind about my love with circumstance;
And out of doubt you do me now more wrong,
In making question of my uttermost,
Than if you had made waste of all I have.
Then do but say to me what I should do,
That in your knowledge may by me be done,
And I am press'd unto it: therefore, speak.

*Bass.* In Belmont is a lady richly left,
And she is fair, and fairer than that word,
Of wondrous virtues: sometimes from her eyes
I did receive fair speechless messages:
Her name is Portia; nothing undervalued
To Cato's daughter, Brutus' Portia.
Nor is the wide world ignorant of her worth;
For the four winds blow in from every coast
Renowned suitors: and her sunny locks
Hang on her temples like a golden fleece;
Which makes her seat of Belmont Colchos'
strand,
And many Jasons come in quest of her.
O my Antonio, had I but the means
To hold a rival place with one of them,
I have a mind presages me such thrift
That I should questionless be fortunate.

*Ant.* Thou know'st that all my fortunes are
     at sea;
Neither have I money nor commodity
To raise a present sum: therefore go forth;
Try what my credit can in Venice do:
That shall be rack'd, even to the uttermost,
To furnish thee to Belmont, to fair Portia
Go, presently inquire, and so will I,
Where money is; and I no question make
To have it of my trust or for my sake.  [*Exeunt.*

SCENE II.—BELMONT. *A Room in* PORTIA'S
         *House.*

*Enter* PORTIA *and* NERISSA.

*Por.* By my troth, Nerissa, my little body is
a-weary of this great world.

*Ner.* You would be, sweet madam, if your
miseries were in the same abundance as your
good fortunes are: and yet for aught I see, they
are as sick that surfeit with too much as they
that starve with nothing. It is no mean happiness, therefore, to be seated in the mean: superfluity comes sooner by white hairs, but competency lives longer.

*Por.* Good sentences, and well pronounced.

*Ner.* They would be better if well followed.

*Por.* If to do were as easy as to know what
were good to do, chapels had been churches,
and poor men's cottages princes' palaces. It is
a good divine that follows his own instructions:
I can easier teach twenty what were good to be
done, than be one of the twenty to follow mine
own teaching. The brain may devise laws for
the blood, but a hot temper leaps over a cold
decree; such a hare is madness, the youth to
skip o'er the meshes of good council, the cripple.
But this reasoning is not in the fashion to choose
me a husband.—O me, the word choose! I
may neither choose whom I would nor refuse
whom I dislike; so is the will of a living
daughter curbed by the will of a dead father.—
Is it not hard, Nerissa, that I cannot choose
one, nor refuse none?

*Ner.* Your father was ever virtuous; and
holy men, at their death, have good inspira-
tions; therefore, the lottery that he hath devised in these three chests, of gold, silver, and
lead,—whereof who chooses his meaning chooses
you,—will, no doubt, never be chosen by any
rightly, but one who you shall rightly love.
But what warmth is there in your affection
towards any of these princely suitors that are
already come?

*Por.* I pray thee, over-name them; and as
thou namest them, I will describe, them; and
according to my description, level at my affection.

*Ner.* First, there is the Neapolitan prince.

*Por.* Ay, that's a colt indeed, for he doth
nothing but talk of his horse; and he makes it
a great appropriation to his own good parts
that he can shoe him himself: I am much afraid
my lady his mother played false with a smith.

*Ner.* Then is there the County Palatine.

*Por.* He doth nothing but frown; as who
should say, *An if you will not have me, choose:*
he hears merry tales and smiles not: I fear he
will prove the weeping philosopher when he
grows old, being so full of unmannerly sadness
in his youth. I had rather be married to a
death's head with a bone in his mouth than to
either of these. God defend me from these two!

*Ner.* How say you by the French lord,
Monsieur Le Bon?

*Por.* God made him, and therefore let him
pass for a man. In truth, I know it is a sin to
be a mocker: but, he! why, he hath a horse
better than the Neapolitan's; a better bad
habit of frowning than the Count Palatine: he
is every man and no man: if a throstle sing he
falls straight a-capering; he will fence with his
own shadow: if I should marry him I should
marry twenty husbands. If he would despise
me I would forgive him; for if he love me to
madness I shall never requite him.

*Ner.* What say you then to Falconbridge,
the young baron of England?

*Por.* You know I say nothing to him; for he
understands not me, nor I him; he hath neither
Latin, French, nor Italian; and you will come
into the court and swear that I have a poor
pennyworth in the English. He is a proper
man's picture; but, alas! who can converse
with a dumb show? How oddly he is suited!
I think, he bought his doublet in Italy, his
round hose in France, his bonnet in Germany,
and his behaviour everywhere.

*Ner.* What think you of the Scottish lord,
his neighbour?

*Por.* That he hath a neighbourly charity in
him; for he borrowed a box of the ear of the
Englishman, and swore he would pay him again
when he was able: I think the Frenchman became his surety, and sealed under for another.

*Ner.* How like you the young German, the
Duke of Saxony's nephew?

*Por.* Very vilely in the morning when he is
sober; and most vilely in the afternoon when
he is drunk; when he is best he is a little worse
than a man; and when he is worst, he is little
better than a beast. An the worst fall that ever
fell, I hope I shall make shift to go without him.

*Ner.* If he should offer to choose, and choose
the right casket, you should refuse to perform
your father's will if you should refuse to accept
him.

*Por.* Therefore, for fear of the worst, I pray
thee set a deep glass of Rhenish wine on the
contrary casket: for, if the devil be within and
that temptation without, I know he will choose
it. I will do anything, Nerissa, ere I will be
married to a sponge.

*Ner.* You need not fear, lady, the having any
of these lords; they have acquainted me with
their determinations; which is indeed, to return
to their home, and to trouble you with no more
suit, unless you may be won by some other

sort than your father's imposition, depending on the caskets.

*Por.* If I live to be as old as Sibylla, I will die as chaste as Diana, unless I be obtained by the manner of my father's will. I am glad this parcel of wooers are so reasonable; for there is not one among them but I dote on his very absence, and I pray God grant them a fair departure.

*Ner.* Do you not remember, lady, in your father's time, a Venetian, a scholar and a soldier, that came hither in company of the Marquis of Montferrat?

*Por.* Yes, yes, it was Bassanio; as I think, so was he called.

*Ner.* True, madam; he, of all the men that ever my foolish eyes looked upon, was the best deserving a fair lady.

*Por.* I remember him well; and I remember him worthy of thy praise.—

*Enter a* Servant.

How now! what news?

*Serv.* The four strangers seek for you, madam, to take their leave; and there is a forerunner come from a fifth, the prince of Morocco, who brings word, the prince his master will be here to-night.

*Por.* If I could bid the fifth welcome with so good heart as I can bid the other four farewell, I should be glad of his approach: if he have the condition of a saint and the complexion of a devil, I had rather he should shrive me than wive me.

Come, Nerissa.—Sirrah, go before.—Whiles we shut the gate upon one wooer, another knocks at the door. [*Exeunt.*

SCENE III.—VENICE. *A Public Place.*

*Enter* BASSANIO *and* SHYLOCK.

*Shy.* Three thousand ducats,—well.

*Bass.* Ay, sir, for three months.

*Shy.* For three months,—well.

*Bass.* For the which, as I told you, Antonio shall be bound.

*Shy.* Antonio shall become bound,—well.

*Bass.* May you stead me? Will you pleasure me? Shall I know your answer?

*Shy.* Three thousand ducats for three months, and Antonio bound.

*Bass.* Your answer to that.

*Shy.* Antonio is a good man.

*Bass.* Have you heard any imputation to the contrary?

*Shy.* Ho, no, no; no, no;—my meaning, in saying he is a good man, is to have you understand me that he is sufficient: yet his means are in supposition: he hath an argosy bound to Tripolis, another to the Indies; I understand, moreover, upon the Rialto, he hath a third at Mexico, a fourth for England,——and other ventures he hath, squandered abroad. But ships are but boards, sailors but men: there be land-rats and water-rats, water-thieves and land-thieves; I mean pirates; and then there is the peril of waters, winds, and rocks. The man is, notwithstanding, sufficient;—three thousand ducats:—I think I may take his bond.

*Bass.* Be assured you may.

*Shy.* I will be assured I may; and, that I may be assured, I will bethink me. May I speak with Antonio?

*Bass.* If it please you to dine with us.

*Shy.* Yes, to smell pork; to eat of the habitation which your prophet, the Nazarite, conjured the devil into; I will buy with you, sell with you, talk with you, walk with you, and so following; but I will not eat with you, drink with you, nor pray with you.—What news on the Rialto?—Who is he comes here?

*Enter* ANTONIO.

*Bass.* This is Signior Antonio.

*Shy.* [*Aside.*] How like a fawning publican he looks!
I hate him for he is a Christian;
But more for that, in low simplicity.
He lends out money gratis, and brings down
The rate of usance here with us in Venice.
If I can catch him once upon the hip,
I will feed fat the ancient grudge I bear him.
He hates our sacred nation; and he rails,
Even there where merchants most do congregate,
On me, my bargains, and my well-won thrift,
Which he calls interest. Cursed be my tribe
If I forgive him!

*Bass.*                Shylock, do you hear?

*Shy.* I am debating of my present store:
And, by the near guess of my memory,
I cannot instantly raise up the gross
Of full three thousand ducats. What of that?
Tubal, a wealthy Hebrew of my tribe,
Will furnish me. But soft! how many months
Do you desire?—Rest you fair, good signior:
                              [*To* ANTONIO.
Your worship was the last man in our mouths.

*Ant.* Shylock, albeit I neither lend nor borrow,
By taking nor by giving of excess,
Yet, to supply the ripe wants of my friend,
I'll break a custom.—Is he yet possess'd
How much he would?—

*Shy.*                Ay, ay, three thousand ducats.

*Ant.* And for three months.          [me so.

*Shy.* I had forgot,—three months; you told
Well then, your bond; and, let me see,——But hear you:
Methought you said you neither lend nor borrow
Upon advantage.

*Ant.*          I do never use it.

*Shy.* When Jacob graz'd his uncle Laban's sheep,—
This Jacob from our holy Abraham was—
As his wise mother wrought in his behalf—
The third possessor; ay, he was the third,—

*Ant.* And what of him? did he take interest?

*Shy.* No, not take interest; not, as you would say,
Directly interest: mark what Jacob did.
When Laban and himself were compromis'd
That all the eanlings which were streak'd and
pied                [rank,
Should fall as Jacob's hire; the ewes, being
In end of autumn turned to the rams:
And when the work of generation was
Between these wooly breeders in the act,
The skilful shepherd peel'd me certain wands,
And, in the doing of the deed of kind,
He stuck them up before the fulsome ewes,
Who, then conceiving, did in eaning time
Fall party-colour'd lambs, and those were
Jacob's.
This was a way to thrive, and he was blest;
And thrift is blessing if men steal it not.
*Ant.* This was a venture, sir, that Jacob
serv'd for;
A thing not in his power to bring to pass,
But sway'd and fashion'd by the hand of
heaven.
Was this inserted to make interest good?
Or is your gold and silver ewes and rams?
*Shy.* I cannot tell; I make it breed as fast:—
But note me, signior.
*Ant.*                Mark you this, Bassanio,
The devil can cite scripture for his purpose.
An evil soul producing holy witness
Is like a villain with a smiling cheek—
A goodly apple rotten at the heart:
O, what a goodly outside falsehood hath!
*Shy.* Three thousand ducats,—'tis a good
round sum.                [rate.
Three months from twelve, then let me see the
*Ant.* Well, Shylock, shall we be beholden to
you?
*Shy.* Signior Antonio, many a time and oft,
In the Rialto, you have rated me
About my moneys and my usances:
Still have I borne it with a patient shrug;
For sufferance is the badge of all our tribe:
You call me misbeliever, cut-throat dog,
And spit upon my Jewish gaberdine,
And all for use of that which is mine own.
Well, then, it now appears you need my help:
Go to, then; you come to me, and you say,
*Shylock, we would have moneys:*—you say so;
You, that did void your rheum upon my beard,
And foot me as you spurn a stranger cur
Over your threshold: moneys is your suit.
What should I say to you? Should I not say,
*Hath a dog money? is it possible*
*A cur can lend three thousand ducats?* or
Shall I bend low, and in a bondman's key,
With 'bated breath and whispering humbleness
Say this?—
*Fair sir, you spit on me on Wednesday last.*
*You spurn'd me such a day; another time*
*You call'd me dog; and for these courtesies*
*I'll lend you thus much moneys.*
*Ant.* I am as like to call thee so again,
To spit on thee again, to spurn thee too.

If thou wilt lend this money, lend it not
As to thy friends (for when did friendship take
A breed for barren metal of his friend?)
But lend it rather to thine enemy,
Who if he break, thou mayst with better face
Exact the penalty.
*Shy.*        Why, look you, how you storm!
I would be friends with you, and have your love,
Forget the shames that you have stain'd me
with,
Supply your present wants, and take no doit
Of usance for my moneys, and you'll not hear
me:
This is kind I offer.
*Bass.* This were kindness.
*Shy.*            This kindness will I show.—
Go with me to a notary, seal me there
Your single bond; and, in a merry sport,
If you repay me not on such a day,
In such a place, such sum or sums as are
Express'd in the condition, let the forfeit
Be nominated for an equal pound
Of your fair flesh, to be cut off and taken
In what part of your body pleaseth me.  [bond,
*Ant.* Content, in faith: I'll seal to such a
And say there is much kindness in the Jew.
*Bass.* You shall not seal to such a bond for
me:
I'll rather dwell in my necessity.        [it;
*Ant.* Why fear not, man; I will not forfeit
Within these two months—that's a month be-
fore
This bond expires—I do expect return
Of thrice three times the value of this bond.
*Shy.* O father Abraham, what these Chris-
tians are,
Whose own hard dealings teaches them suspect
The thoughts of others! Pray you, tell me this;
If he should break his day, what should I gain
By the exaction of the forfeiture?
A pound of man's flesh, taken from a man,
Is not so estimable, profitable neither,
As flesh of muttons, beefs, or goats. I say,
To buy his favour I extend this friendship;
If he will take it, so; if not, adieu;
And for my love, I pray you wrong me not.
*Ant.* Yes, Shylock, I will seal unto this bond.
*Shy.* Then meet me forthwith at the no-
tary's;
Give him direction for this merry bond,
And I will go and purse the ducats straight,
See to my house, left in the fearful guard
Of an unthrifty knave, and presently
I will be with you.
*Ant.*            Hie thee, gentle Jew:
            [*Exit* SHYLOCK.
This Hebrew will turn Christian: he grows
kind.
*Bass.* I like not fair terms and a villain's
mind.
*Ant.* Come on; in this there can be no dis-
may;
My ships come home a month before the day.
            [*Exeunt.*

## ACT II.

### SCENE I.—BELMONT. *A Room in* PORTIA'S *House.*

*Flourish of Cornets. Enter the* PRINCE OF MO-
ROCCO *and his* Train; PORTIA, NERISSA *and
other of her* Attendants.

*Mor.* Mislike me not for my complexion,
The shadow'd livery of the burnish'd sun,
To whom I am a neighbour, and near bred.
Bring me the fairest creature northward born,
Where Phœbus' fire scarce thaws the icicles,
And let us make incision for your love,
To prove whose blood is reddest, his or mine.
I tell thee lady, this aspect of mine
Hath fear'd the valiant; by my love, I swear,
The best-regarded virgins of our clime
Have lov'd it too: I would not change this hue
Except to steal your thoughts, my gentle queen.
*Por.* In terms of choice I am not solely led
By nice direction of a maiden's eyes:
Besides, the lottery of my destiny
Bars me the right of voluntary choosing:
But, if my father had not scanted me,
And hedg'd me by his wit, to yield myself
His wife who wins me by that means I told you,
Yourself, renowned prince, then stood as fair
As any comer I have look'd on yet
For my affection.
*Mor.*                    Even for that I thank you;
Therefore, I pray you, lead me to the caskets,
To try my fortune. By this scimitar,—
That slew the Sophy, and a Persian prince
That won three fields of Sultan Solyman,—
I would out-stare the sternest eyes that look,
Out-brave the heart most daring on the
    earth,
Pluck the young sucking cubs from the she-
    bear,
Yea, mock the lion when he roars for prey,
To win thee, lady. But, alas the while!
If Hercules and Lichas play at dice
Which is the better man, the greater throw
May turn by fortune from the weaker hand:
So is Alcides beaten by his page;
And so may I, blind fortune leading me,
Miss that which one unworthier may attain,
And die with grieving.
*Por.*                    You must take your chance;
And either not attempt to choose at all,
Or swear before you choose, if you choose
    wrong,
Never to speak to lady afterward
In way of marriage; therefore be advis'd.
*Mor.* Nor will not; come, bring me unto my
    chance.
*Por.* First, forward to the temple: after
    dinner
Your hazard shall be made.
*Mor.*                    Good fortune then!
To make me blest or cursed'st among men.
                            [*Cornets and exeunt.*

### SCENE II.—VENICE. *A Street.*

#### *Enter* LAUNCELOT GOBBO.

*Laun.* Certainly my conscience will serve me
to run from this Jew, my master. The fiend is
at mine elbow, and tempts me, saying to me,
*Gobbo, Launcelot Gobbo, good Launcelot, or good
Gobbo, or good Launcelot Gobbo, use your legs,
take the start, run away.* My conscience says,—
*No; take heed, honest Launcelot; take heed, honest
Gobbo:* or as aforesaid, *honest Launcelot Gobbo;
do not run, scorn running with thy heels.* Well,
the most courageous fiend bids me pack: *Via!*
says the fiend; *away!* says the fiend, *for the
heavens; rouse up a brave mind,* says the fiend,
*and run.* Well, my conscience, hanging about
the neck of my heart, says very wisely to me,—
*My honest friend, Launcelot, being an honest
man's son,* or rather an honest woman's son;—
for indeed, my father did something smack,
something grow to, he had a kind of taste;—
well, my conscience says, *Launcelot, budge not.*
*Budge,* says the fiend. *Budge not,* says my conscience. Conscience, say I, you counsel well;
fiend, say I, you counsel well: to be ruled by
my conscience, I should stay with the Jew, my
master, who (God bless the mark!) is a kind of
devil; and, to run away from the Jew, I should
be ruled by the fiend, who, saving your reverence, is the devil himself. Certainly the Jew is
the very devil incarnation: and, in my conscience, my conscience is but a kind of hard
conscience, to offer to counsel me to stay with
the Jew. The fiend gives the more friendly
counsel: I will run, fiend; my heels are at your
commandment; I will run.

#### *Enter Old* GOBBO, *with a basket.*

*Gob.* Master young man, you, I pray you,
which is the way to master Jew's?
*Laun.* [*Aside.*] O heavens, this is my true
begotten father! who, being more than sand-
blind, high-gravel blind, knows me not:—I will
try confusions with him.
*Gob.* Master young gentleman, I pray you,
which is the way to Master Jew's?
*Laun.* Turn up on your right hand at the
next turning, but, at the next turning of all, on
your left; marry, at the very next turning, turn
of no hand, but turn down indirectly to the
Jew's house.
*Gob.* By God's sonties, 'twill be a hard way
to hit. Can you tell me whether one Launcelot,
that dwells with him, dwell with him or no?
*Laun.* Talk you of young Master Launcelot?
—[*Aside.*] Mark me now; now will I raise the
waters.—Talk you of young Master Launcelot?
*Gob.* No master, sir, but a poor man's son:
his father, though I say it, is an honest exceeding poor man, and, God be thanked, well to live.
*Laun.* Well, let his father be what 'a will,
we talk of young Master Launcelot.      [sir.
*Gob.* Your worship's friend, and Launcelot,
*Laun.* But I pray you, *ergo,* old man, *ergo,* I

beseech you, talk you of young Master Launce-lot?

*Gob.* Of Launcelot, an 't please your master-ship.

*Laun.* *Ergo*, Master Launcelot. Talk not of Master Launcelot, father; for the young gen-tleman,—according to Fates and Destinies, and such odd sayings, the Sisters Three, and such branches of learning,—is indeed deceased; or, as you would say in plain terms, gone to heaven.

*Gob.* Marry, God forbid! the boy was the very staff of my age, my very prop.

*Laun.* Do I look like a cudgel, or a hovel-post, a staff or a prop?—Do you know me, father?

*Gob.* Alack the day, I know you not, young gentleman: but, I pray you, tell me, is my boy (God rest his soul!) alive or dead?

*Laun.* Do you not know me, father?

*Gob.* Alack, sir, I am sand-blind, I know you not.

*Laun.* Nay, indeed, if you had your eyes you might fail of the knowing me: it is a wise father that knows his own child. Well, old man, I will tell you news of your son. Give me your bless-ing; truth will come to light; murder cannot be hid long: a man's son may; but, in the end, truth will out.

*Gob.* Pray you, sir, stand up; I am sure you are not Launcelot, my boy.

*Laun.* Pray you, let's have no more fooling about it, but give me your blessing; I am Launcelot, your boy that was, your son that is, your child that shall be.

*Gob.* I cannot think you are my son.

*Laun.* I know not what I shall think of that; but I am Launcelot, the Jew's man; and I am sure Margery your wife is my mother.

*Gob.* Her name is Margery, indeed: I'll be sworn, if thou be Launcelot, thou art mine own flesh and blood. Lord worshipped might he be! what a beard hast thou got! thou hast got more hair on thy chin than Dobbin my thill-horse has on his tail.

*Laun.* It should seem, then, that Dobbin's tail grows backward; I am sure he had more hair of his tail than I have of my face when I last saw him.

*Gob.* Lord, how thou art changed! How dost thou and thy master agree? I have brought him a present. How 'gree you now?

*Laun.* Well, well; but, for mine own part, as I have set up my rest to run away, so I will not rest till I have run some ground. My master's a very Jew: give him a present! give him a halter: I am famished in his service; you may tell every finger I have with my ribs. Father, I am glad you are come; give me your present to one Master Bassanio, who indeed gives rare new liveries: if I serve not him, I will run as far as God has any ground.—O rare fortune! here comes the man;—to him, father; for I am a Jew if I serve the Jew any longer.

*Enter* BASSANIO, *with* LEONARDO, *and other* Followers.

*Bass.* You may do so;—but let it be so hasted that supper be ready at the farthest by five of the clock. See these letters delivered; put the liveries to making; and desire Gratiano to come anon to my lodging. [*Exit c Servant.*

*Laun.* To him, father.

*Gob.* God bless your worship! [me?

*Bass.* Gramercy: wouldst thou aught with

*Gob.* Here's my son, sir, a poor boy,—

*Laun.* Not a poor boy, sir, but the rich Jew's man, that would, sir, as my father shall specify,—

*Gob.* He hath a great infection, sir, as one would say, to serve,—

*Laun.* Indeed, the short and the long is, I serve the Jew, and have a desire, as my father shall specify,—

*Gob.* His master and he,—saving your wor-ship's reverence,—are scarce cater-cousins,—

*Laun.* To be brief, the very truth is, that the Jew having done me wrong, doth cause me, as my father, being I hope an old man, shall frutify unto you,—

*Gob.* I have here a dish of doves that I would bestow upon your worship; and my suit is,—

*Laun.* In very brief, the suit is impertinent to myself, as your worship shall know by this honest old man; and, though I say it, though old man, yet, poor man, my father.

*Bass.* One speak for both.—What would you?

*Laun.* Serve you, sir.

*Gob.* That is the very defect of the matter, sir.

*Bass.* I know thee well; thou hast obtain'd thy suit:
Shylock, thy master, spoke with me this day,
And hath preferr'd thee—if it be preferment
To leave a rich Jew's service, to become
The follower of so poor a gentleman.

*Laun.* The old proverb is very well parted between my master, Shylock, and you, sir; you have the grace of God, sir, and he hath enough.

*Bass.* Thou speak'st it well. Go, father, with thy son.—
Take leave of thy old master, and inquire
My lodging out.—Give him a livery
　　　　　　　　　　　　[*To his* Followers.
More guarded than his fellows': see it done.

*Laun.* Father, in.—I cannot get a service, no:—I have ne'er a tongue in my head.—Well; [*looking on his palm*] if any man in Italy have a fairer table which doth offer to swear upon a book, I shall have good fortune!—Go to, here's a simple line of life! here's a small trifle of wives: alas, fifteen wives is nothing, eleven widows and nine maids is a simple com-ing in for one man! and then to 'scape drown-ing thrice, and to be in peril of my life with the edge of a feather-bed;—here are simple 'scapes. Well, if Fortune be a woman, she's a

good wench for this gear.—Father, come: I'll
take my leave of the Jew in the twinkling of
an eye.        [*Exeunt* LAUN. *and* Old GOB.

*Bass.* I pray thee, good Leonardo, think on
this:        [stow'd,
These things being bought and orderly be-
Return in haste, for I do feast to-night
My best esteem'd acquaintance: hie thee, go.

*Leon.* My best endeavours shall be done
herein.

### Enter GRATIANO.

*Gra.* Where is your master?
*Leon.*        Yonder, sir, he walks. [*Exit.*
*Gra.* Signior Bassanio,——
*Bass.* Gratiano!
*Gra.* I have a suit to you.
*Bass.*        You have obtain'd it.
*Gra.* You must not deny me: I must go with
you to Belmont.        [Gratiano;
*Bass.* Why, then you must.—But hear thee,
Thou art too wild, too rude, and bold of voice;—
Parts that become thee happily enough,
And in such eyes as ours appear not faults;
But where thou art not known, why, there
they show
Something too liberal. Pray thee, take pain
To allay with some cold drops of modesty
Thy skipping spirit; lest, through thy wild be-
haviour,
I be misconstrued in the place I go to,
And lose my hopes.
*Gra.*        Signior Bassanio, hear me:
If I do not put on a sober habit,
Talk with respect, and swear but now and then,
Wear prayer-books in my pocket, look de-
murely,
Nay more, while grace is saying, hood mine
eyes
Thus with my hat, and sigh, and say amen,
Use all the observance of civility,
Like one well studied in a sad ostent
To please his grandam, never trust me more.
*Bass.* Well, we shall see your bearing.
*Gra.* Nay, but I bar to-night; you shall not
gage me
By what we do to-night.
*Bass.*        No, that were pity;
I would entreat you rather to put on
Your boldest suit of mirth, for we have friends
That purpose merriment. But fare you well:
I have some business.
*Gra.* And I must to Lorenzo and the rest;
But we will visit you at supper-time.
        [*Exeunt.*

### SCENE III.—*The same. A Room in* SHYLOCK'S *House.*

### Enter JESSICA *and* LAUNCELOT.

*Jes.* I am sorry thou wilt leave my father so:
Our house is hell; and thou, a merry devil,
Didst rob it of some taste of tediousness.
But fare thee well; there is a ducat for thee:
And, Launcelot, soon at supper shalt thou see

Lorenzo, who is thy new master's guest:
Give him this letter; do it secretly;—
And so farewell: I would not have my father
See me in talk with thee.
*Laun.* Adieu!—tears exhibit my tongue.—
Most beautiful pagan, most sweet Jew! if a
Christian did not play the knave, and get thee,
I am much deceived. But adieu! these foolish
drops do somewhat drown my manly spirit;
adieu!        [*Exit.*
*Jes.* Farewell, good Launcelot.
Alack, what heinous sin is it in me
To be asham'd to be my father's child!
But though I am a daughter to his blood,
I am not to his manners. O Lorenzo,
If thou keep promise, I shall end this strife,
Become a Christian, and thy loving wife.
        [*Exit.*

### SCENE IV.—*The same. A Street.*

### Enter GRATIANO, LORENZO, SALARINO, *and* SOLANIO.

*Lor.* Nay, we will slink away in supper-time;
Disguise us at my lodging, and return
All in an hour.
*Gra.* We have not made good preparation.
*Salar.* We have not spoke us yet of torch-
bearers.        [order'd;
*Solan.* 'Tis vile, unless it may be quaintly
And better, in my mind, not undertook.
*Lor.* 'Tis now but four o'clock; we have two
hours
To furnish us;—

### Enter LAUNCELOT, *with a letter.*

        Friend Launcelot, what's the news?
*Laun.* An it shall please you to break up
this, it shall seem to signify.
*Lor.* I know the hand: in faith, 'tis a fair
hand;
And whiter than the paper it writ on
Is the fair hand that writ.
*Gra.*        Love-news, in faith.
*Laun.* By your leave, sir.
*Lor.* Whither goest thou?
*Laun.* Marry, sir, to bid my old master, the
Jew, to sup to-night with my new master, the
Christian.        [Jessica
*Lor.* Hold here, take this:—tell gentle
I will not fail her;—speak it privately; go.—
Gentlemen,        [*Exit* LAUNCELOT.
Will you prepare you for this masque to-night?
I am provided of a torch-bearer.
*Salar.* Ay, marry, I'll be gone about it
straight.
*Solan.* And so will I.
*Lor.*        Meet me and Gratiano
At Gratiano's lodging some hour hence.
*Salar.* 'Tis good we do so.
        [*Exeunt* SALAR. *and* SOLAN.
*Gra.* Was not that letter from fair Jessica?
*Lor.* I must needs tell thee all. She hath
directed
How I shall take her from her father's house;

What gold and jewels she is furnish'd with;
What page's suit she hath in readiness.
If e'er the Jew her father come to heaven,
It will be for his gentle daughter's sake:
And never dare misfortune cross her foot,
Unless she do it under this excuse,—
That she is issue to a faithless Jew.
Come, go with me; peruse this as thou goest:
Fair Jessica shall be my torch-bearer.
                                        [*Exeunt.*

SCENE V.—*The same. Before* SHYLOCK'S
                *House.*

*Enter* SHYLOCK *and* LAUNCELOT.

*Shy.* Well, thou shalt see; thy eyes shall be
  thy judge.
The difference of old Shylock and Bassanio:—
What, Jessica!—thou shalt not gormandize
As thou hast done with me;—What, Jessica!—
And sleep and snore, and rend apparel out;—
Why, Jessica, I say!
  *Laun.*                Why, Jessica!   [*call.*
*Shy.* Who bids thee call? I do not bid thee
*Laun.* Your worship was wont to tell me I
could do nothing without bidding.

*Enter* JESSICA.

*Jes.* Call you? what is your will?
*Shy.* I am bid forth to supper, Jessica:
There are my keys.—But wherefore should I
  go?
I am not bid for love; they flatter me:
But yet I'll go in hate, to feed upon
The prodigal Christian.—Jessica, my girl,
Look to my house.—I am right loath to go;
There is some ill a-brewing towards my rest,
For I did dream of money-bags to-night.
  *Laun.* I beseech you, sir, go; my young
master doth expect your reproach.
  *Shy.* So do I his.
  *Laun.* And they have conspired together,—
I will not say you shall see a masque; but if you
do, then it was not for nothing that my nose
fell a-bleeding on Black-Monday last at six
o'clock i' the morning, falling out that year on
Ash-Wednesday was four year in the afternoon.
  *Shy.* What! are there masques? Hear you
me, Jessica:
Lock up my doors; and when you hear the drum,
And the vile squeaking of the wry-neck'd fife,
Clamber not you up to the casements then,
Nor thrust your head into the public street
To gaze on Christian fools with varnish'd faces:
But stop my house's ears,—I mean my case-
  ments:
Let not the sound of shallow foppery enter
My sober house.—By Jacob's staff, I swear
I have no mind of feasting forth to-night:
But I will go.—Go you before me, sirrah;
Say I will come.
  *Laun.*        I will go before, sir.—
Mistress, look out at window for all this;
  There will come a Christian by
  Will be worth a Jewess' eye.     [*Exit.*

*Shy.* What says that fool of Hagar's off-
  spring, ha?        |nothing else.
*Jes.* His words were, Farewell, mistress;
*Shy.* The patch is kind enough, but a huge
  feeder,
Snail-slow in profit, and he sleeps by day
More than the wild cat: drones hive not with
  me;
Therefore I part with him; and part with him
To one that I would have him help to waste
His borrow'd purse.—Well, Jessica, go in;
Perhaps I will return immediately:
Do as I bid you;
Shut doors after you: fast bind, fast find—
A proverb never stale in thrifty mind.   [*Exit.*
  *Jes.* Farewell; and if my fortune be not
  cross'd,
I have a father, you a daughter, lost.   [*Exit.*

SCENE VI.—*The same.*

*Enter* GRATIANO *and* SALARINO, *masked.*

*Gra.* This is the pent-house under which
  Lorenzo
Desir'd us to make stand.
  *Salar.*            His hour is almost past,
*Gra.* And it is marvel he out-dwells his hour,
For lovers ever run before the clock.
  *Salar.* O, ten times faster Venus' pigeons fly
To seal love's bonds new made, than they are
  wont
To keep obliged faith unforfeited!     [*feast*
  *Gra.* That ever holds; who riseth from a
With that keen appetite that he sits down?
Where is the horse that doth untread again
His tedious measures with the unbated fire
That he did pace them first? All things that are,
Are with more spirit chased than enjoy'd.
How like a younker or a prodigal
The scarfed bark puts from her native bay,
Hugg'd and embraced by the strumpet wind!
How like the prodigal doth she return,
With over-weather'd ribs and ragged sails,
Lean, rent, and beggar'd by the strumpet
  wind!
  *Salar.* Here comes Lorenzo;—more of this
  hereafter.

*Enter* LORENZO.

*Lor.* Sweet friends, your patience for my
  long abode;
Not I, but my affairs, have made you wait:
When you shall please to play the thieves for
  wives
I'll watch as long for you then.—Approach;
Here dwells my father Jew.—Ho! who's within?

*Enter* JESSICA, *above, in boy's clothes.*

*Jes.* Who are you? Tell me, for more cer-
  tainty,
Albeit I'll swear that I do know your tongue.
  *Lor.* Lorenzo, and thy love.
  *Jes.* Lorenzo, certain; and my love indeed;
For who love I so much? and now who knows
But you, Lorenzo, whether I am yours?

*Lor.* Heaven and thy thoughts are witness
that thou art.                    [*pains.*
*Jes.* Here, catch this casket; it is worth the
I am glad 'tis night, you do not look on me,
For I am much asham'd of my exchange:
But love is blind, and lovers cannot see
The pretty follies that themselves commit;
For if they could, Cupid himself would blush
To see me thus transformed to a boy.
*Lor.* Descend, for you must be my torch-
bearer.                        [*shames?*
*Jes.* What! must I hold a candle to my
They in themselves, good sooth, are too, too
light.
Why, 'tis an office of discovery, love;
And I should be obscur'd.
*Lor.*                So are you, sweet,
Even in the lovely garnish of a boy.
But come at once;
For the close night doth play the runaway,
And we are stay'd for at Bassanio's feast.
*Jes.* I will make fast the doors, and gild my-
self
With some more ducats, and be with you
straight.                    [*Exit, above.*
*Gra.* Now, by my hood, a Gentile, and no
Jew.
*Lor.* Beshrew me, but I love her heartily:
For she is wise, if I can judge of her;
And fair she is, if that mine eyes be true;
And true she is, as she hath prov'd herself;
And therefore, like herself, wise, fair, and true.
Shall she be placed in my constant soul.

Enter JESSICA, *below.*

What, art thou come?—On, gentlemen, away;
Our masquing mates by this time for us stay.
                [*Exit, with* JES. *and* SALAR.

Enter ANTONIO.

*Ant.* Who's there?
*Gra.* Signior Antonio!
*Ant.* Fie, fie, Gratiano! where are all the
rest?
'Tis nine o'clock: our friends all stay for you:—
No mask to-night; the wind is come about;
Bassanio presently will go aboard:
I have sent twenty out to seek for you.
*Gra.* I am glad on't; I desire no more delight
Than to be under sail. and gone to-night.
                        [*Exeunt.*

SCENE VII.—BELMONT. *A Room in*
PORTIA'S *House.*

*Flourish of Cornets. Enter* PORTIA, *with the*
PRINCE OF MOROCCO, *and their* Trains.

*Por.* Go draw aside the curtains, and dis-
cover
The several caskets to this noble prince.—
Now make your choice.
*Mor.* The first of gold, who this inscription
bears;—                        [*desire.*
*Who chooseth me shall gain what many men*
The second, silver, which this promise carries;—

*Who chooseth me shall get as much as he deserves.*
This third, dull lead, with warning all as
blunt;—                        [*hath.*
*Who chooseth me must give and hazard all he*
How shall I know if I do choose the right?
*Por.* The one of them contains my picture,
prince;
If you choose that, then I am yours withal.
*Mor.* Some god direct my judgment! Let me
see,
I will survey the inscriptions back again:
What says this leaden casket?—        [*hath.*
*Who chooseth me must give and hazard all he*
Must give—for what? for lead? hazard for
lead?
This casket threatens: men that hazard all
Do it in hope of fair advantages:
A golden mind stoops not to shows of dross:
I'll then nor give nor hazard aught for lead.
What says the silver with her virgin hue?
*Who chooseth me shall get as much as he deserves.*
As much as he deserves!—Pause there, Mo-
rocco,
And weigh thy value with an even hand;
If thou be'st rated by thy estimation,
Thou dost deserve enough; and yet enough
May not extend so far as to the lady;
And yet to be afeard of my deserving
Were but a weak disabling of myself.
As much as I deserve!—Why, that's the lady:
I do in birth deserve her, and in fortunes,
In graces, and in qualities of breeding;
But more than these, in love I do deserve.
What if I stray'd no further, but chose here?—
Let's see once more this saying grav'd in gold:
*Who chooseth me shall gain what many men*
*desire.*
Why, that's the lady: all the world desires her:
From the four corners of the earth they come,
To kiss this shrine, this mortal breathing saint.
The Hyrcanian deserts and the vasty wilds
Of wide Arabia are as throughfares now
For princes to come view fair Portia:
The wat'ry kingdom, whose ambitious head
Spits in the face of heaven, is no bar
To stop the foreign spirits; but they come,
As o'er a brook, to see fair Portia.
One of these three contains her heavenly pic-
ture.                            [*nation*
Is't like that lead contains her? 'Twere dam-
To think so base a thought: it were too gross
To rid her cerecloth in the obscure grave.
Or shall I think in silver she's immur'd,
Being ten times undervalued to tried gold?
O sinful thought! Never so rich a gem        [land
Was set in worse than gold. They have in Eng-
A coin that bears the figure of an angel
Stamped in gold; but that's insculp'd upon;
But here an angel in a golden bed
Lies all within.—Deliver me the key;
Here do I choose, and thrive as I may!
*Por.* There, take it, prince; and if my form
lie there,
Then I am yours. [*He opens the golden casket.*

*Mor.* O hell! what have we here?
A carrion Death, within whose empty eye
There is a written scroll! I'll read the writing.

All that glisters is not gold,—
Often have you heard that told;
Many a man his life hath sold
But my outside to behold;
Gilded tombs do worms infold.
Had you been as wise as bold,
Young in limbs, in judgment old,
Your answer had not been inscroll'd
Fare you well; your suit is cold.

Cold indeed, and labour lost:
Then, farewell heat; and, welcome frost.—
Portia, adieu! I have too griev'd a heart
To take a tedious leave: thus losers part.
[*Exit with his Train.*

*Por.* A gentle riddance.—Draw the curtains, go.
Let all of his complexion choose me so.
[*Exeunt.*

SCENE VIII.—VENICE. *A Street.*

*Enter* SALARINO *and* SOLANIO.

*Salar.* Why, man, I saw Bassanio under sail;
With him is Gratiano gone along;
And in their ship I am sure Lorenzo is not.
*Solan.* The villain Jew with outcries rais'd
the duke,
Who went with him to search Bassanio's ship.
*Salar.* He came too late, the ship was under
sail:
But there the duke was given to understand
That in a gondola were seen together
Lorenzo and his amorous Jessica:
Besides, Antonio certify'd the duke
They were not with Bassanio in his ship.
*Solan.* I never heard a passion so confused,
So strange, outrageous, and so variable
As the dog Jew did utter in the streets:
*My daughter!—O my ducats!—O my daughter!
Fled with a Christian!—O my Christian du-
cats!—
Justice! the law! my ducats and my daughter!
A sealed bag, two sealed bags of ducats,
Of double ducats, stolen from me by my daughter!
And jewels,—two stones, two rich and precious
stones,
Stolen by my daughter!—Justice! find the girl!
She hath the stones upon her and the ducats!*
*Salar.* Why, all the boys in Venice follow
him, [ducats.
Crying,—his stones, his daughter, and his
*Solan.* Let good Antonio look he keep his
day,
Or he shall pay for this.
*Salar.* Marry, well remember'd;
I reason'd with a Frenchman yesterday,
Who told me,—in the narrow seas that part
The French and English, there miscarried
A vessel of our country richly fraught:
I thought upon Antonio when he told me,
And wish'd in silence that it were not his.

*Solan.* You were best to tell Antonio what
you hear;
Yet do not suddenly, for it may grieve him.
*Salar.* A kinder gentleman treads not the
earth.
I saw Bassanio and Antonio part:
Bassanio told him he would make some speed
Of his return; he answered—*Do not so;
Slubber not business for my sake, Bassanio,
But stay the very riping of the time;
And for the Jew's bond which he hath of me,
Let it not enter in your mind of love:
Be merry; and employ your chiefest thoughts
To courtship, and such fair ostents of love
As shall conveniently become you there.*
And even there, his eye being big with tears,
Turning his face, he put his hand behind him,
And with affection wondrous sensible
He wrung Bassanio's hand; and so they parted.
*Solan.* I think he only loves the world for
him.
I pray thee, let us go and find him out,
And quicken his embraced heaviness
With some delight or other.
*Salar.* Do we so. [*Exeunt.*

SCENE IX.—BELMONT. *A Room in* PORTIA'S
*House.*

*Enter* NERISSA, *with a* Servant.

*Ner.* Quick, quick, I pray thee; draw the
curtain straight:
The Prince of Arragon hath ta'en his oath,
And comes to his election presently.

*Flourish of Cornets. Enter the* PRINCE OF
ARRAGON, PORTIA, *and their* Trains.

*Por.* Behold, there stands the caskets, noble
prince.
If you choose that wherein I am contain'd.
Straight shall our nuptial rites be solemniz'd:
But if you fail, without more speech, my lord,
You must be gone from hence immediately.
*Ar.* I am enjoin'd by oath to observe three
things:
First, never to unfold to any one
Which casket 'twas I chose; next, if I fail
Of the right casket, never in my life
To woo a maid in way of marriage; lastly,
If I do fail in fortune of my choice,
Immediately to leave you and be gone.
*Por.* To these injunctions every one doth
swear
That comes to hazard for my worthless self.
*Ar.* And so have I address'd me. Fortune
now [lead.
To my heart's hope!—Gold, silver, and base
*Who chooseth me must give and hazard all he
hath:*
You shall look fairer ere I give or hazard.
What says the golden chest? ha! let me see:—
*Who chooseth me shall gain what many men
desire.* [meant
What many men desire.—That many may be
By the fool multitude, that choose by show,

Not learning more than the fond eye doth
    teach;
Which pries not to the interior, but, like the
    martlet,
Builds in the weather on the outward wall,
Even in the force and road of casualty.
I will not choose what many men desire,
Because I will not jump with common spirits,
And rank me with the barbarous multitudes.
Why, then, to thee, thou silver treasure-house;
Tell me once more what title thou dost bear:
*Who chooseth me shall get as much as he deserves:*
And well said too; for who shall go about
To cozen fortune, and be honourable        [sume pre-
Without the stamp of merit! Let none
To wear an undeserved dignity.
O, that estates, degrees, and offices,
Were not deriv'd corruptly! and that clear
    honour
Were purchas'd by the merit of the wearer!
How many then should cover that stand bare!
How many be commanded that command!
How much low peasantry would then be
    glean'd        [honour
From the true seed of honour! and how much
Pick'd from the chaff and ruin of the times,
To be new varnish'd! Well, but to my choice.
*Who chooseth me shall get as much as he deserves:*
I will assume desert.—Give me a key for this,
And instantly unlock my fortunes here.
        [*He opens the silver casket.*
*Por.* Too long a pause for that which you
    find there.        [idiot
*Ar.* What's here? the portrait of a blinking
Presenting me a schedule! I will read it.
How much unlike art thou to Portia!
How much unlike my hopes and my deservings!
*Who chooseth me shall have as much as he de-*
    *serves.*
Did I deserve no more than a fool's head?
Is that my prize? are my deserts no better?
*Por.* To offend and judge are distinct offices
And of opposed natures.
*Ar.*        What is here?

The fire seven times tried this;
Seven times tried that judgment is
That did never choose amiss:
Some there be that shadows kiss;
Such have but a shadow's bliss:
There be fools alive, I wis,
Silver'd o'er; and so was this.
Take what wife you will to bed,
I will ever be your head:
So be gone: you are sped.

Still more fool I shall appear
By the time I linger here:
With one fool's head I came to woo,
But I go away with two.—
Sweet, adieu! I'll keep my oath,
Patiently to bear my roth.
        [*Exit with his* Train.
*Por.* Thus hath the candle singed the moth.
O these deliberate fools! when they do choose,

They have the wisdom by their wit to lose.
*Ner.* The ancient saying is no heresy,—
Hanging and wiving goes by destiny.
*Por.* Come, draw the curtain, Nerissa.

*Enter a* Servant.

*Serv.* Where is my lady?
*Por.*        Here; what would my lord?
*Serv.* Madam, there is alighted at your gate
A young Venetian, one that comes before
To signify the approaching of his lord:
From whom he bringeth sensible regreets;
To wit, besides commends and courteous
    breath,
Gifts of rich value. Yet I have not seen
So likely an ambassador of love:
A day in April never came so sweet,
To show how costly summer was at hand,
As this forespurrer comes before his lord.
*Por.* No more, I pray thee; I am half afeard
Thou wilt say anon he is some kin to thee,
Thou spend'st such high-day wit in praising
    him.—
Come, come, Nerissa; for I long to see
Quick Cupid's post, that comes so mannerly.
*Ner.* Bassanio, lord Love, if thy will it be!
        [*Exeunt.*

## ACT III.

### SCENE I.—VENICE. *A Street.*

*Enter* SOLANIO *and* SALARINO.

*Solan.* Now, what news on the Rialto?
*Salar.* Why, yet it lives there unchecked,
that Antonio hath a ship of rich lading wrecked
on the narrow seas; the Goodwins I think they
call the place; a very dangerous flat and fatal,
where the carcases of many a tall ship lie buried,
as they say, if my gossip report be an honest
woman of her word.
*Solan.* I would she were as lying a gossip in
that as ever knapped ginger or made her neighbours believe she wept for the death of a third
husband. But it is true,—without any slips of
prolixity of crossing the plain highway of talk,
—that the good Antonio, the honest Antonio,
—O that I had a title good enough to keep his
name company!—
*Salar.* Come, the full stop.
*Solan.* Ha,—what sayest thou?—Why the
end is, he hath lost a ship.
*Salar.* I would it might prove the end of his
losses!
*Solan.* Let me say amen betimes, lest the
devil cross my prayer; for here he comes in the
likeness of a Jew.

*Enter* SHYLOCK.

How now, Shylock? what news among the merchants?
*Shy.* You knew, none so well, none so well as
you, of my daughter's flight.
*Salar.* That's certain: I, for my part, knew
the tailor that made the wings she flew withal.

*Solan.* And Shylock, for his own part, knew the bird was fledg'd; and then it is the complexion of them all to leave the dam.

*Shy.* She is damned for it.

*Salar.* That's certain, if the devil may be her judge.

*Shy.* My own flesh and blood to rebel!

*Solan.* Out upon it, old carrion! rebels it at these years?

*Shy.* I say my daughter is my flesh and blood.

*Salar.* There is more difference between thy flesh and hers than between jet and ivory; more between your bloods than there is between red wine and Rhenish.—But tell us, do you hear whether Antonio have had any loss at sea or no?

*Shy.* There I have another bad match: a bankrupt, a prodigal, who dare scarce show his head on the Rialto;—a beggar, that was used to come so smug upon the mart;—let him look to his bond! he was wont to call me usurer;—let him look to his bond! he was wont to lend money for a Christian courtesy;—let him look to his bond.

*Salar.* Why, I am sure if he forfeit thou wilt not take his flesh. What's that good for?

*Shy.* To bait fish withal: if it will feed nothing else it will feed my revenge. He hath disgraced me and hindered me of half a million; laughed at my losses, mocked at my gains, scorned my nation, thwarted my bargains, cooled my friends, heated mine enemies! and what's his reason? I am a Jew! Hath not a Jew eyes? hath not a Jew hands, organs, dimensions, senses, affections, passions? fed with the same food, hurt with the same weapons, subject to the same diseases, healed by the same means, warmed and cooled by the same winter and summer as a Christian is? If you prick us, do we not bleed? if you tickle us, do we not laugh? if you poison us, do we not die? and if you wrong us, shall we not revenge? If we are like you in the rest, we will resemble you in that.—If a Jew wrong a Christian, what is his humility? revenge. If a Christian wrong a Jew, what should his sufferance be by Christian example? why, revenge. The villany you teach me I will execute; and it shall go hard but I will better the instruction.

*Enter a* Servant.

*Serv.* Gentlemen, my master Antonio is at his house, and desires to speak with you both.

*Salar.* We have been up and down to seek him.

*Solan.* Here comes another of the tribe; a third cannot be matched unless the devil himself turn Jew. [*Exeunt* SOLAN., SALAR., *and* Serv.

*Enter* TUBAL.

*Shy.* How now, Tubal, what news from Genoa? hast thou found my daughter?

*Tub.* I often came where I did hear of her, but cannot find her.

*Shy.* Why there, there, there, there! a diamond gone, cost me two thousand ducats in Frankfort! The curse never fell upon our nation till now; I never felt it till now:—two thousand ducats in that; and other precious, precious jewels.—I would my daughter were dead at my foot, and the jewels in her ear! would she were hearsed at my foot, and the ducats in her coffin! No news of them?—Why, so:—and I know not what's spent in the search. Why, thou loss upon loss! the thief gone with so much, and so much to find the thief; and no satisfaction, no revenge: nor no ill luck stirring but what lights o' my shoulders; no sighs but o' my breathing; no tears but o' my shedding.

*Tub.* Yes, other men have ill luck too; Antonio, as I heard in Genoa,—

*Shy.* What, what, what? ill luck, ill luck?

*Tub.* —hath an argosy cast away coming from Tripolis.

*Shy.* I thank God, I thank God.—Is it true? is it true?

*Tub.* I spoke with some of the sailors that escaped the wreck.

*Shy.* I thank thee, good Tubal.—Good news, good news: ha! ha!—Where? in Genoa?

*Tub.* Your daughter spent in Genoa, as I heard, one night, fourscore ducats.

*Shy.* Thou stick'st a dagger in me:—I shall never see my gold again. Fourscore ducats at a sitting! fourscore ducats!

*Tub.* There came divers of Antonio's creditor's in my company to Venice that swear he cannot choose but break.

*Shy.* I am very glad of it: I'll plague him; I'll torture him: I am glad of it.

*Tub.* One of them showed me a ring that he had of your daughter for a monkey.

*Shy.* Out upon her! Thou torturest me, Tubal. It was my turquoise: I had it of Leah when I was a bachelor: I would not have given it for a wilderness of monkeys.

*Tub.* But Antonio is certainly undone.

*Shy.* Nay, that's true; that's very true. Go, Tubal, fee me an officer; bespeak him a fortnight before. I will have the heart of him if he forfeit; for, were he out of Venice, I can make what merchandize I will. Go, go, Tubal, and meet me at our synagogue: go, good Tubal; at our synagogue, Tubal. [*Exeunt.*

SCENE II.—BELMONT. *A Room in* PORTIA'S *House.*

*Enter* BASSANIO, PORTIA, GRATIANO, NERISSA, *and* Attendants.

*Por.* I pray you, tarry: pause a day or two Before you hazard; for, in choosing wrong, I lose your company; therefore forbear awhile: There's something tells me,—but it is not love,—
I would not lose you: and you know yourself

Hate counsels not in such a quality:
But lest you should not understand me well,—
And yet a maiden hath no tongue but thought,—
I would detain you here some month or two
Before you venture for me. I could teach you
How to choose right, but then I am forsworn;
So will I never be; so may you miss me:
But if you do, you'll make me wish a sin,
That I had been forsworn. Beshrew your eyes,
They have o'erlook'd me and divided me;
One half of me is yours, the other half yours,—
Mine own, I would say; but if mine, then yours,
And so all yours. O! these naughty times
Put bars between the owners and their rights;
And so, though yours, not yours.—Prove it so,
Let fortune go to hell for it,—not I.
I speak too long; but 'tis to peise the time,
To eke it, and to draw it out in length,
To stay you from election.
　　*Bass.*　　　　　Let me choose;
For, as I am, I live upon the rack.
　　*Por.*　Upon the rack, Bassanio? then confess
What treason there is mingled with your love.
　　*Bass.*　None but that ugly treason of mistrust,
Which makes me fear the enjoying of my love:
There may as well be amity and life
'Tween snow and fire, as treason and my love.
　　*Por.*　Ay, but I fear you speak upon the rack,
Where men, enforced, do speak anything.
　　*Bass.*　Promise me life, and I'll confess the truth.
　　*Por.*　Well, then, confess and live.
　　*Bass.*　　　　　Confess and love
Had been the very sum of my confession:
O happy torment, when my torturer
Doth teach me answers for deliverance!
But let me to my fortune and the caskets.
　　[*Curtain drawn from before the caskets.*
　　*Por.*　Away, then. I am lock'd in one of them;
If you do love me you will find me out.—
Nerissa and the rest, stand all aloof.—
Let music sound while he doth make his choice;
Then, if he lose, he makes a swan-like end,
Fading in music: that the comparison
May stand more proper, my eye shall be the stream
And wat'ry death-bed for him. He may win,
And what is music then? then music is
Even as the flourish when true subjects bow
To a new-crowned monarch: such it is
As are those dulcet sounds in break of day
That creep into the dreaming bridegroom's ear
And summon him to marriage. Now he goes,
With no less presence but with more love
Than young Alcides when he did redeem
The virgin tribute paid by howling Troy
To the sea-monster. I stand for sacrifice;
The rest aloof are the Dardanian wives,
With bleared visages, come forth to view
The issue of the exploit. Go, Hercules!
Live thou, I live.—With much, much more dismay
I view the fight than thou that mak'st the fray.

*Music and the following Song whilst* BASSANIO
*comments on the caskets to himself.*

　　Tell me, where is fancy bred,
　　Or in the heart, or in the head?
　　How begot, how nourished?
　　　　Reply, reply.
　　It is engender'd in the eyes,
　　With gazing fed; and fancy dies
　　In the cradle where it lies:
　　　Let us all ring fancy's knell;
　　I'll begin it,——Ding, dong, bell.
*All.*　　Ding, dong, bell.

　　*Bass.*　So may the outward shows be least themselves;
The world is still deceiv'd with ornament.
In law, what plea so tainted and corrupt
But, being season'd with a gracious voice,
Obscures the show of evil? In religion,
What damned error but some sober brow
Will bless it, and approve it with a text,
Hiding the grossness with fair ornament?
There is no vice so simple but assumes
Some mark of virtue on his outward parts.
How many cowards, whose hearts are all as false
As stairs of sand, wear yet upon their chins
The beards of Hercules and frowning Mars;
Who, inward search'd, have livers white as milk!
And these assume but valour's excrement
To render them redoubted. Look on beauty
And you shall see 'tis purchas'd by the weight
Which therein works a miracle in nature,
Making them lightest that wear most of it:
So are those crisped snaky golden locks,
Which make such wanton gambols with the wind,
Upon supposed fairness, often known
To be the dowry of a second head—
The skull that bred them in the sepulchre.
Thus ornament is but the guiled shore
To a most dangerous sea; the beauteous scarf
Veiling an Indian beauty; in a word,
The seeming truth which cunning times put on
To entrap the wisest. Therefore, thou gaudy gold,
Hard food for Midas, I will none of thee:
Nor none of thee, thou pale and common drudge
'Tween man and man: but thou, thou meagre lead,
Which rather threat'nest than dost promise  [aught,
Thy plainness moves me more than eloquence,
And here choose I. Joy be the consequence!
　　*Por.*　How all the other passions fleet to air,
As doubtful thoughts, and rash-embrac'd despair,
And shudd'ring fear, and green-ey'd jealousy!
O love, be moderate, allay thy ecstacy,
In measure rain thy joy, scant this excess;
I feel too much thy blessing; make it less,
For fear I surfeit!
　　*Bass.*　　　　What find I here?
　　　　　　[*Opening the leaden casket.*

Fair Portia's counterfeit? What demi-god
Hath come so near creation? Move these eyes?
Or whether, riding on the balls on mine,
Seem they in motion? Here are sever'd lips,
Parted with sugar breath; so sweet a bar [hairs
Should sunder such sweet friends. Here in her
The painter plays the spider, and hath woven
A golden mesh to entrap the hearts of men,
Faster than gnats in cobwebs. But her eyes!—
How could he see to do them? having made one,
Methinks it should have power to steal both
his,
And leave itself unfurnish'd. Yet look how far
The substance of my praise doth wrong this
shadow
In underprizing it, so far this shadow. [scroll,
Doth limp behind the substance.—Here's the
The continent and summary of my fortune.

> You that choose not by the view,
> Chance as fair and choose as true!
> Since this fortune falls to you,
> Be content and seek no new.
> If you be well pleased with this,
> And hold your fortune for your bliss,
> Turn you where your lady is,
> And claim her with a loving kiss.

A gentle scroll.—Fair lady, by your leave:
                              [*Kissing her.*
I come by note, to give and to receive.
Like one of two contending in a prize,
That thinks he hath done well in people's eyes,
Hearing applause and universal shout,
Giddy in spirit, still gazing, in a doubt
Whether those peals of praise be his or no,
So, thrice fair lady, stand I even so;
As doubtful whether what I see be true,
Until confirm'd, sign'd, ratified by you.
    *Por.* You see me, Lord Bassanio, where I
        stand,
Such as I am: though for myself alone
I would not be ambitious in my wish
To wish myself much better; yet for you
I would be trebled twenty times myself;
A thousand times more fair, ten thousand times
More rich;
That only to stand high in your account
I might in virtues, beauties, livings, friends,
Exceed account: but the full sum of me
Is sum of something, which, to term in gross,
Is an unlesson'd girl, unschool'd, unpractis'd:
Happy in this, she is not yet so old
But she may learn; and happier than this,
She is not bred so dull but she can learn;
Happiest of all is, that her gentle spirit
Commits itself to yours to be directed,
As from her lord, her governor, her king.
Myself, and what is mine, to you and yours
Is now converted: but now I was the lord
Of this fair mansion, master of my servants,
Queen o'er myself; and even now, but now
This house, these servants, and this same my-
self
Are yours, my lord; I give them with this ring,

Which when you part from, lose, or give away,
Let it presage the ruin of your love,
And be my vantage to exclaim on you.
    *Bass.* Madam, you have bereft me of all
        words;
Only my blood speaks to you in my veins:
And there is such confusion in my powers,
As, after some oration fairly spoke
By a beloved prince, there doth appear
Among the buzzing pleased multitude,
Where every something, being blent together,
Turns to a wild of nothing, save of joy. [ring
Express'd, and not express'd. But when this
Parts from this finger, then parts life from
    hence;
O, then, be bold to say Bassanio's dead.
    *Ner.* My lord and lady, it is now our time
That have stood by and seen our wishes pros-
    per
To cry, good joy. Good joy, my lord and lady!
    *Gra.* My Lord Bassanio, and my gentle lady,
I wish you all the joy that you can wish;
For I am sure you can wish none from me:
And, when your honours mean to solemnize
The bargain of your faith, I do beseech you,
Even at that time I may be married too.
    *Bass.* With all my heart, so thou canst get a
        wife.
    *Gra.* I thank your lordship; you have got me
        one.
My eyes, my lord, can look as swift as yours:
You saw the mistress, I beheld the maid;
You lov'd, I lov'd; for intermission
No more pertains to me, my lord, than you,
Your fortune stood upon the caskets there,
And so did mine too, as the matter falls:
For wooing here until I sweat again,
And swearing till my very roof was dry
With oaths of love, at last,—if promise last,—
I got a promise of this fair one here,
To have her love provided that your fortune
Achiev'd her mistress.
    *Por.*                    Is this true, Nerissa?
    *Ner.* Madam, it is, so you stand pleas'd
        withal.
    *Bass.* And do you, Gratiano, mean good
        faith?
    *Gra.* Yes, faith, my lord.
    *Bass.* Our feast shall be much honour'd in
        your marriage.
    *Gra.* We'll play with them, the first boy for a
thousand ducats.
    *Ner.* What, and stake down?
    *Gra.* No; we shall ne'er win at that sport,
        and stake down.—
But who comes here? Lorenzo and his infidel?
What, and my old Venetian friend, Solanio!

    *Enter* LORENZO, JESSICA, *and* SOLANIO.

    *Bass.* Lorenzo and Solanio, welcome hither,
If that the youth of my new interest here
Have power to bid you welcome.—By your
    leave,
I bid my very friends and countrymen,

Sweet Portia, welcome.

*Por.*                    So do I, my lord;
They are entirely welcome.                    [lord,
*Lor.* I thank your honour.—For my part, my
My purpose was not to have seen you here;
But meeting with Solanio by the way,
He did entreat me past all saying nay,
To come with him along.
*Solan.*                    I did, my lord,
And I have reason for it. Signior Antonio
Commends him to you.
                    [*Gives* BASSANIO *a letter.*
*Bass.*                    Ere I ope his letter,
I pray you, tell me how my good friend doth.
*Solan.* Not sick, my lord, unless it be in
         mind;
Nor well, unless in mind: his letter there
Will show you his estate.
                    [BASS. *reads the letter.*
*Gra.* Nerissa, cheer yond stranger; bid her
         welcome.                    [Venice?
Your hand, Solanio: what's the news from
How doth that royal merchant, good Antonio?
I know he will be glad of our success:
We are the Jasons; we have won the fleece.
*Solan.* Would you had won the fleece that he
         hath lost!                    [same paper,
*Por.* There are some shrewd contents in yon
That steal the colour from Bassanio's cheek;
Some dear friend dead; else nothing in the world
Could turn so much the contrition [worse?—
Of any constant man. What, worse and
With leave, Bassanio; I am half yourself,
And I must freely have the half of anything
That this same paper brings you.
*Bass.*                    O sweet Portia,
Here are a few of the unpleasant'st words
That ever blotted paper! Gentle lady,
When I did first impart my love to you
I freely told you all the wealth I had
Ran in my veins—I was a gentleman;
And then I told you true: and yet, dear lady,
Rating myself at nothing, you shall see
How much I was a braggart. When I told you
My state was nothing, I should then have told
         you
That I was worse than nothing; for, indeed,
I have engag'd myself to a dear friend,
Engag'd my friend to his mere enemy,
To feed my means. Here is a letter, lady,
The paper as the body of my friend,
And every word in it a gaping wound,
Issuing life-blood. But is it true, Solanio?
Have all his ventures fail'd? What! not one hit?
From Tripolis, from Mexico, and England;
From Lisbon, Barbary, and India?
And not one vessel 'scape the dreadful touch
Of merchant-marring rocks?
*Solan.*                    Not one, my lord.
Besides, it should appear that if he had
The present money to discharge the Jew
He would not take it. Never did I know
A creature that did bear the shape of man
So keen and greedy to confound a man:

He plies the duke at morning and at night,
And doth impeach the freedom of the state
If they deny him justice: twenty merchants,
The duke himself, and the magnificoes
Of greatest port have all persuaded with him;
But none can drive him from the envious plea
Of forfeiture, of justice, and his bond.
*Jes.* When I was with him I have heard him
         swear
To Tubal and to Chus, his countrymen,
That he would rather have Antonio's flesh
Than twenty times the value of the sum
That he did owe him; and I know, my lord,
If law, authority, and power deny not,
It will go hard with poor Antonio.
*Por.* Is it your dear friend that is thus in
         trouble?
*Bass.* The dearest friend to me, the kindest
         man,
The best condition'd and unwearied spirit
In doing courtesies; and one in whom
The ancient Roman honour more appears
Than any that draws breath in Italy.
*Por.* What sum owes he the Jew?
*Bass.* For me, three thousand ducats.
*Por.*                    What! no more?
Pay him six thousand, and deface the bond;
Double six thousand, and then treble that,
Before a friend of this description
Shall lose a hair through Bassanio's fault.
First, go with me to church, and call me wife,
And then away to Venice to your friend;
For never shall you lie by Portia's side
With an unquiet soul. You shall have gold
To pay the petty debt twenty times over;
When it is paid bring your true friend along:
My maid Nerissa and myself, meantime,
Will live as maids and widows. Come, away;
For you shall hence upon your wedding-day:
Bid your friends welcome, show a merry cheer:
Since you are dear bought, I will love you dear.
But let me hear the letter of your friend.
*Bass.* [*Reads.*] *Sweet Bassanio, my ships have
all miscarried, my creditors grow cruel, my estate
is very low, my bond to the Jew is forfeit; and
since, in paying it, it is impossible I should live,
all debts are cleared between you and I, if I might
but see you at my death: notwithstanding, use
your pleasure; if your love do not persuade you to
come, let not my letter.*
*Por.* O love, despatch all business, and be
         gone.
*Bass.* Since I have your good leave to go
         away,
I will make haste: but, till I come again,
No bed shall e'er be guilty of my stay,
No rest be interposer 'twixt us twain.
                    [*Exeunt.*

SCENE III.—VENICE. *A Street.*

*Enter* SHYLOCK, SALARINO, ANTONIO *and*
         Gaoler.

*Shy.* Gaoler, look to him. Tell not me of
         mercy;—

This is the fool that lent out money gratis.—
Gaoler, look to him.

*Ant.* Hear me yet, good Shylock.

*Shy.* I'll have my bond: speak not against
my bond.
I have sworn an oath that I will have my bond.
Thou call'dst me dog before thou hadst a cause:
But, since I am a dog, beware my fangs:
The duke shall grant me justice.—I do wonder,
Thou naughty gaoler, that thou art so fond
To come abroad with him at his request.

*Ant.* I pray thee, hear me speak.

*Shy.* I'll have my bond; I will not hear thee
speak: [more.
I'll have my bond; and therefore speak no
I'll not be made a soft and dull-ey'd fool,
To shake the head, relent, and sigh, and yield
To Christian intercessors. Follow not;
I'll have no speaking: I will have my bond.
[*Exit.*

*Salar.* It is the most impenetrable cur
That ever kept with men.

*Ant.* Let him alone;
I'll follow him no more with bootless prayers.
He seeks my life; his reason well I know:
I oft deliver'd from his forfeitures
Many that have at times made moan to me;
Therefore he hates me.

*Salar.* I am sure the duke
Will never grant this forfeiture to hold.

*Ant.* The duke cannot deny the course of
law;
For the commodity that strangers have
With us in Venice, if it be denied,
Will much impeach the justice of the state;
Since that the trade and profit of the city
Consisteth of all nations. Therefore, go:
These griefs and losses have so 'bated me
That I shall hardly spare a pound of flesh
To-morrow to my bloody creditor.——
Well, gaoler, on.—Pray God, Bassanio come
To see me pay his debt, and then I care not!
[*Exeunt.*

SCENE IV.—BELMONT. *A Room in* PORTIA'S
*House.*

*Enter* PORTIA, NERISSA, LORENZO, JESSICA,
*and* BALTHAZAR.

*Lor.* Madam, although I speak it in your
presence,
You have a noble and a true conceit
Of god-like amity, which appears most strongly
In bearing thus the absence of your lord.
But if you knew to whom you show this honour,
How true a gentleman you send relief,
How dear a lover of my lord your husband,
I know you would be prouder of the work
Than customary bounty can enforce you.

*Por.* I never did repent for doing good,
Nor shall not now: for in companions
That do converse and waste the time together,
Whose souls do bear an equal yoke of love,
There must be needs a like proportion
Of lineaments, of manners, and of spirit,

Which makes me think that this Antonio,
Being the bosom lover of my lord,
Must needs be like my lord. If it be so,
How little is the cost I have bestow'd
In purchasing the semblance of my soul
From out the state of hellish cruelty!
This comes too near the praising of myself;
Therefore, no more of it: hear other things.—
Lorenzo, I commit into your hands
The husbandry and manage of my house
Until my lord's return: for mine own part,
I have toward heaven breath'd a secret vow
To live in prayer and contemplation,
Only attended by Nerissa here,
Until her husband and my lord's return:
There is a monastery two miles off,
And there we will abide. I do desire you
Not to deny this imposition,
The which my love and some necessity
Now lays upon you.

*Lor.* Madam, with all my heart
I shall obey you in all fair commands.

*Por.* My people do already know my mind,
And will acknowledge you and Jessica
In place of Lord Bassanio and myself.
So fare you well till we shall meet again.

*Lor.* Fair thoughts and happy hours attend
on you!

*Jes.* I wish your ladyship all heart's content.

*Por.* I thank you for your wish, and am well
pleas'd
To wish it back on you: fare you well, Jessica.—
[*Exeunt* JESSICA *and* LORENZO.

Now Balthazar,
As I have ever found thee honest, true,
So let me find thee still. Take this same letter,
And use thou all the endeavour of a man
In speed to Padua; see thou render this
Into my cousin's hand, Doctor Bellario;
And, look, what notes and garments he doth
give thee
Bring them, I pray thee, with imagin'd speed
Unto the tranect, to the common ferry [words,
Which trades to Venice:—waste no time in
But get thee gone; I shall be there before thee.

*Balth.* Madam, I go with all convenient
speed. [*Exit.*

*Por.* Come on, Nerissa; I have work in hand
That you yet know not of: we'll see our hus-
bands
Before they think of us.

*Ner.* Shall they see us?

*Por.* They shall, Nerissa; but in such a habit
That they shall think we are accomplished
With that we lack. I'll hold thee any wager,
When we are both accouter'd like young men,
I'll prove the prettier fellow of the two,
And wear my dagger with the braver grace;
And speak, between the change of man and
boy,
With a reed voice; and turn two mincing steps
Into a manly stride; and speak of frays,
Like a fine bragging youth: and tell quaint lies,
How honourable ladies sought my love,

Which I denying, they fell sick and died;
I could not do withal: then I'll repent,
And wish, for all that, that I had not kill'd
  them:
And twenty of these puny lies I'll tell,
That men shall swear I have discontinued
  school
Above a twelvemonth.—I have within my mind
A thousand raw tricks of these bragging Jacks
Which I will practise.
*Ner.*        Why, shall we turn to men?
*Por.* Fie! what a question's that
If thou wert ne'er a lewd interpreter?
But come, I'll tell thee all my whole device
When I am in my coach, which stays for us
At the park-gate; and, therefore, haste away,
For we must measure twenty miles to-day.
                                    [*Exeunt.*

SCENE V.—*The same. A Garden.*

*Enter* LAUNCELOT *and* JESSICA.

*Laun.* Yes, truly;—for, look you, the sins of
the father are to be laid upon the children;
therefore, I promise you, I fear you. I was
always plain with you, and so now I speak my
agitation of the matter: therefore, be of good
cheer; for, truly, I think you are damned.
There is but one hope in it that can do you any
good; and that is but a kind of bastard hope
neither.

*Jes.* And what hope is that, I pray thee?
*Laun.* Marry, you may partly hope that
your father got you not,—that you are not the
Jew's daughter.

*Jes.* That were a kind of bastard hope, indeed; so the sins of my mother should be visited
upon me.

*Laun.* Truly then I fear you are damned
both by father and mother: thus when I shun
Scylla your father, I fall into Charybdis, your
mother; well, you are gone both ways.

*Jes.* I shall be saved by my husband; he hath
made me a Christian.

*Laun.* Truly, the more to blame he: we were
Christians enow before; e'en as many as could
well live, one by another. This making of
Christians will raise the price of hogs; if we
grow all to be pork eaters we shall not shortly
have a rasher on the coals for money.

*Jes.* I'll tell my husband, Launcelot, what
you say; here he comes.

*Enter* LORENZO

*Lor.* I shall grow jealous of you shortly,
Launcelot, if you thus get my wife into corners.

*Jes.* Nay, you need not fear for us, Lorenzo;
Launcelot and I are out: he tells me flatly there
is no mercy for me in heaven, because I am a
Jew's daughter: and he says you are no good
member of the commonwealth; for, in converting Jews to Christians, you raise the price of
pork.

*Lor.* I shall answer that better to the commonwealth than you can the getting up of the
negro's belly; the Moor is with child by you,
Launcelot.

*Laun.* It is much that the Moor should be
more than reason: but if she be less than an
honest woman, she is indeed more than I took
her for.

*Lor.* How every fool can play upon the word!
I think the best grace of wit will shortly turn
into silence, and discourse grow commendable
in none only but parrots.—Go in, sirrah; bid
them prepare for dinner.

*Laun.* That is done, sir; they have all
stomachs.

*Lor.* Goodly lord, what a wit-snapper are
you! then bid them prepare dinner.

*Laun.* That is done too, sir: only. cover is
the word.

*Lor.* Will you cover, then, sir?

*Laun.* Not so, sir, neither; I know my duty.

*Lor.* Yet more quarrelling with occasion!
Wilt thou show the whole wealth of thy wit in
an instant? I pray thee, understand a plain
man in his plain meaning: go to thy fellows;
bid them cover the table, serve in the meat, and
we will come in to dinner.

*Laun.* For the table, sir, it shall be served
in; for the meat, sir, it shall be covered; for
your coming in to dinner, sir, why, let it be as
humours and conceits shall govern.    [*Exit.*

*Lor.* O dear discretion, how his words are
  suited!
The fool hath planted in his memory
An army of good words; and I do know
A many fools that stand in better place,
Garnish'd like him, that for a tricksy word
Defy the matter. How cheer'st thou, Jessica?
And now, good sweet, say thy opinion,—
How dost thou like the Lord Bassanio's wife?

*Jes.* Past all expressing. It is very meet
The Lord Bassanio live an upright life;
For, having such a blessing in his lady,
He finds the joys of heaven here on earth;
And, if on earth he do not mean it, then
In reason he should never come to heaven.
Why, if two gods should play some heavenly
  match,
And on the wager lay two earthly women,
And Portia one, there must be something else
Pawn'd with the other; for the poor rude world
Hath not her fellow.

*Lor.*            Even such a husband
Hast thou of me as she is for a wife.

*Jes.* Nay, but ask my opinion too of that.

*Lor.* I will anon; first let us go to dinner

*Jes.* Nay, let me praise you while I have a
  stomach.

*Lor.* No, pray thee, let it serve for table-talk;
Then, howsoe'er thou speak'st, 'mong other
  things
I shall digest it.

*Jes.*        Well, I'll set you forth.
                                    [*Exeunt.*

## ACT IV.

### SCENE I.—VENICE. *A Court of Justice.*

*Enter the* DUKE, *the* Magnificoes: ANTONIO, BASSANIO, GRATIANO, SALARINO, SOLANIO, *and others.*

*Duke.* What, is Antonio here?

*Ant.* Ready, so please your grace.

*Duke.* I am sorry for thee; thou art come to answer
A stony adversary, an inhuman wretch
Uncapable of pity, void and empty
From any dram of mercy.

*Ant.*　　　　　I have heard
Your grace hath ta'en great pains to qualify
His rigorous course; but since he stands obdurate,
And that no lawful means can carry me
Out of his envy's reach, I do oppose
My patience to his fury, and am arm'd
To suffer, with a quietness of spirit,
The very tyranny and rage of his.

*Duke.* Go one, and call the Jew into the court.　　　　　[my lord.

*Solan.* He's ready at the door: he comes,

### *Enter* SHYLOCK.

*Duke.* Make room, and let him stand before our face.—
Shylock, the world thinks, and I think so too,
Thou thou but lead'st this fashion of thy malice
To the last hour of act; and then, 'tis thought,
Thou'lt show thy mercy and remorse, more strange
Than is thy strange apparent cruelty;
And where thou now exact'st the penalty,—
Which is a pound of this poor merchant's flesh,—
Thou wilt not only lose the forfeiture,
But, touch'd with human gentleness and love,
Forgive a moiety of the principal,
Glancing an eye of pity on his losses,
That have of late so huddled on his back;
Enough to press a royal merchant down,
And pluck commiseration of his state
From brassy bosoms and rough hearts of flint,
From stubborn Turks and Tartars, never train'd
To offices of tender courtesy.
We all expect a gentle answer, Jew.

*Shy.* I have possess'd your grace of what I purpose;
And by our holy Sabbath have I sworn
To have the due and forfeit of my bond.
If you deny it, let the danger light
Upon your charter and your city's freedom.
You'll ask me why I rather choose·to have
A weight of carrion flesh than to receive
Three thousand ducats: I'll not answer that:
But say, it is my humour. Is it answered?
What if my house be troubled with a rat,
And I be pleas'd to give ten thousand ducats
To have it baned? What, are you answer'd yet?
Some men there are love not a gaping pig;
Some that are mad if they behold a cat;

And others, when the bagpipe sings i' the nose,
Cannot contain their urine; for affection,
Master of passion, sways it to the mood
Of what it likes or loathes. Now, for your answer,
As there is no firm reason to be render'd
Why he cannot abide a gaping pig;
Why he, a harmless necessary cat;
Why he, a swollen bagpipe, but of force
Must yield to such inevitable shame
As to offend, himself being offended:
So can I give no reason, nor I will not,
More than a lodg'd hate and a certain loathing
I bear Antonio, that I follow thus
A losing suit against him. Are you answer'd?

*Bass.* This is no answer, thou unfeeling man,
To excuse the current of thy cruelty.

*Shy.* I am not bound to please thee with my answer.　　　　　[love?

*Bass.* Do all men kill the thing they do not

*Shy.* Hates any man the thing he would not kill?

*Bass.* Every offence is not a hate at first.

*Shy.* What! wouldst thou have a serpent sting thee twice?　　　　　[the Jew:

*Ant.* I pray you, think you question with
You may as well go stand upon the beach
And bid the main-flood bait his usual height;
You may as well use question with the wolf
Why he hath made the ewe bleat for the lamb;
You may as well forbid the mountain pines
To wag their high tops, and to make no noise,
When they are fretted with the gusts of heaven;
You may as well do anything most hard
As seek to soften that,—than which what's harder?—　　　　　[you,
His Jewish heart.—Therefore, I do beseech
Make no more offers, use no further means,
But, with all brief and plain conveniency,
Let me have judgment and the Jew his will.

*Bass.* For thy three thousand ducats here is six.

*Shy.* If every ducat in six thousand ducats
Were in six parts, and every part a ducat,
I would not draw them; I would have my bond.

*Duke.* How shalt thou hope for mercy, rend'ring none?　　　　　[no wrong?

*Shy.* What judgment shall I dread, doing
You have among you many a purchas'd slave,
Which, like your asses, and your dogs, and mules,
You use in abject and in slavish parts,
Because you bought them.—Shall I say to you,
Let them be free, marry them to your heirs?
Why sweat they under burdens? let their beds
Be made as soft as yours, and let their palates
Be season'd with such viands? You will answer,
The slaves are ours:—So do I answer you;
The pound of flesh which I demand of him
Is dearly bought, is mine, and I will have it:
If you deny me, fie upon your law!
There is no force in the decrees of Venice.—
I stand for judgment: answer: shall I have it?

*Duke.* Upon my power I may dismiss this court,

Unless Bellario, a learned doctor,
Whom I have sent for to determine this,.
Come here to-day.
 *Solan.*  My lord, here stays without
A messenger with letters from the doctor,
New come from Padua.    [senger.
 *Duke.* Bring us the letters;—call the mes-
 *Bass.* Good cheer, Antonio! What, man,
  courage yet!    [and all,
The Jew shall have my flesh, blood, bones,
Ere thou shalt lose for me one drop of blood.
 *Ant.* I am a tainted wether of the flock,
Meetest for death: the weakest kind of fruit
Drops earliest to the ground, and so let me:
You cannot better be employ'd, Bassanio,
Than to live still, and write mine epitaph.

*Enter* NERISSA, *dressed like a lawyer's clerk.*

 *Duke.* Came you from Padua, from Bellario?
 *Ner.* From both, my lord: Bellario greets
  your grace.   [*Presents a letter.*
 *Bass.* Why dost thou whet thy knife so
  earnestly?    [rupt there.
 *Shy.* To cut the forfeiture from that bank-
 *Gra.* Not on thy sole, but on thy soul,
  harsh Jew,
Thou mak'st thy knife keen: but no metal can,
No, not the hangman's axe, bear half the keen-
  ness
Of thy sharp envy. Can no prayers pierce thee?
 *Shy.* No; none that thou hast wit enough to
  make.
 *Gra.* O, be thou damn'd, inexorable dog!
And for thy life let justice be accus'd.
Thou almost mak'st me waver in my faith,
To hold opinion with Pythagoras,
That souls of animals infuse themselves
Into the trunks of men: thy currish spirit
Govern'd a wolf, who, hang'd for human
  slaughter,
Even from the gallows did his fell soul fleet,
And, whilst thou lay'st in thy unhallow'd dam,
Infus'd itself in thee; for thy desires
Are wolfish, bloody, starv'd, and ravenous.
 *Shy.* Till thou canst rail the seal from off my
  bond
Thou but offend'st thy lungs to speak so loud:
Repair thy wit, good youth, or it will fall
To cureless ruin.—I stand here for law.
 *Duke.* This letter from Bellario doth com-
  mend
A young and learned doctor to our court:—
Where is he?
 *Ner.*  He attendeth here hard by,
To know your answer, whether you'll admit
  him.
 *Duke.* With all my heart:—some three or
  four of you
Go give him courteous conduct to this place.—
Meantime, the court shall hear Bellario's letter.

[*Clerk reads.*] Your grace shall understand that, at
the receipt of your letter, I am very sick; but in the
instant that your messenger came, in loving visitation was with me a young doctor of Rome; his name
is Balthazar: I acquainted him with the cause in
controversy between the Jew and Antonio the
merchant; we turned o'er many books together: he
is furnish'd with my opinion; which, better'd with
his own learning (the greatness whereof I cannot
enough commend), comes with him, at my importunity to fill up your grace's request in my stead.
I beseech you, let his lack of years be no impediment to let him lack a reverend estimation; for I
never knew so young a body with so old a head.
I leave him to your gracious acceptance, whose trial
shall better publish his commendation.

 *Duke.* You hear the learn'd Bellario, what he
  writes:
And here, I take it, is the doctor come.—

*Enter* PORTIA, *dressed like a doctor of laws.*

Give me your hand: came you from old Bellario?
 *Por.* I did, my lord.    [place.
 *Duke.*   You are welcome: take your
Are you acquainted with the difference
That holds this present question in the court?
 *Por.* I am informed throughly of the cause.
Which is the merchant here, and which the
  Jew?    [forth.
 *Duke.* Antonio and old Shylock, both stand
 *Por.* Is your name Shylock?
 *Shy.*   Shylock is my name.
 *Por.* Of a strange nature is the suit you
  follow:
Yet in such rule, that the Venetian law
Cannot impugn you as you do proceed.—
You stand within his danger, do you not?
        [*To* ANTONIO.
 *Ant.* Ay, so he says.
 *Por.*   Do you confess the bond?
 *Ant.* I do.
 *Por.*  Then must the Jew be merciful.
 *Shy.* On what compulsion must I? tell me
  that.
 *Por.* The quality of mercy is not strain'd;
It droppeth as the gentle rain from heaven
Upon the place beneath: it is twice bless'd;
It blesseth him that gives and him that takes:
'Tis mightiest in the mightiest, it becomes
The throned monarch better than his crown,
His sceptre shows the force of temporal power,
The attribute to awe and majesty,
Wherein doth sit the dread and fear of kings;
But mercy is above this scepter'd sway,—
It is enthroned in the heart of kings,
It is an attribute to God himself;
And earthly power doth then show likest God's
When mercy seasons justice. Therefore, Jew,
Though justice be thy plea consider this—
That in the course of justice none of us
Should see salvation: we do pray for mercy;
And that same prayer doth teach us all to
  render
The deeds of mercy. I have spoke thus much
To mitigate the justice of thy plea;
Which if thou follow, this strict court of Venice
Must needs give sentence 'gainst the merchant
  there.

*Shy.* My deeds upon my head! I crave the law,
The penalty and forfeit of my bond.
*Por.* Is he not able to discharge the money?
*Bass.* Yes; here I tender it for him in the court;
Yea, twice the sum: if that will not suffice
I will be bound to pay it ten times o'er,
On forfeit of my hands, my head, my heart:
If this will not suffice, it must appear      [you
That malice bears down truth. And I beseech
Wrest once the law to your authority:
To do a great right do a little wrong,
And curb this cruel devil of his will.
*Por.* It must not be; there is no power in Venice
Can alter a decree established:
'Twill be recorded for a precedent,
And many an error, by the same example,
Will rush into the state: it cannot be.
*Shy.* A Daniel come to judgment! yea, a Daniel!
O wise young judge! how I do honour thee!
*Por.* I pray you, let me look upon the bond.
*Shy.* Here 'tis, most reverend doctor; here it is.
*Por.* Shylock, there's thrice thy money offered thee.
*Shy.* An oath, an oath; I have an oath in heaven:
Shall I lay perjury upon my soul?
No, not for Venice.
*Por.*               Why, this bond is forfeit;
And lawfully by this the Jew may claim
A pound of flesh, to be by him cut off
Nearest the merchant's heart.—Be merciful!
Take thrice thy money; bid me tear the bond.
*Shy.* When it is paid according to the tenor.—
It doth appear you are a worthy judge;
You know the law; your exposition
Hath been most sound: I charge you by the law,
Whereof you are a well-deserving pillar,
Proceed to judgment: by my soul I swear
There is no power in the tongue of man
To alter me.—I stay here on my bond.
*Ant.* Most heartily I do beseech the court
To give the judgment.
*Por.*               Why then, thus it is.
You must prepare your bosom for his knife:
*Shy.* O noble judge! O excellent young man!
*Por.* For the intent and purpose of the law
Hath full relation to the penalty,
Which here appeareth due upon the bond.
*Shy.* 'Tis very true: O wise and upright judge,
How much more elder art thou than thy looks!
*Por.* Therefore, lay bare your bosom.
*Shy.*               Ay, his breast:
So says the bond;—doth it not, noble judge?—
Nearest his heart: those are the very words.
*Por.* It is so. Are there balance here to weigh
The flesh?
*Shy.* I have them ready.

*Por.* Have by some surgeon, Shylock, on your charge,
To stop his wounds, lest he do bleed to death.
*Shy.* Is it so nominated in the bond?
*Por.* It is not so express'd; but what of that?
'Twere good you do so much for charity.
*Shy.* I cannot find it; 'tis not in the bond.
*Por.* Come, merchant, have you anything to say?
*Ant.* But little; I am arm'd and well prepar'd.—
Give me your hand, Bassanio; fare you well.
Grieve not that I am fallen to this for you;
For herein fortune shows herself more kind
Than is her custom: it is still her use
To let the wretched man out-live his wealth,
To view with hollow eye and wrinkled brow
An age of poverty; from which lingering penance
Of such misery doth she cut me off.
Commend me to your honourable wife:
Tell her the process of Antonio's end;
Say how I lov'd you; speak me fair in death;
And, when the tale is told, bid her be judge
Whether Bassanio had not once a love.
Repent not you that you shall lose your friend,
And he repents not that he pays your debt;
For, if the Jew do cut but deep enough,
I'll pay it instantly with all my heart.
*Bass.* Antonio, I am married to a wife
Which is as dear to me as life itself;
But life itself, my wife, and all the world
Are not with me esteem'd above thy life;
I would lose all, ay, sacrifice them all
Here to this devil, to deliver you.
*Por.* Your wife would give you little thanks for that,
If she were by to hear you make the offer.
*Gra.* I have a wife whom, I protest, I love;
I would she were in heaven, so she could
Entreat some power to change this currish Jew.
*Ner.* 'Tis well you offer it behind her back;
The wish would make else an unquiet house.
*Shy.* These be the Christian husbands: I have a daughter;
Would any of the stock of Barrabas
Had been her husband, rather than a Christian!
                                    [*Aside.*
We trifle time;—I pray thee, pursue sentence.
*Por.* A pound of that same merchant's flesh is thine;
The court awards it and the law doth give it.
*Shy.* Most rightful judge!          [his breast;
*Por.* And you must cut this flesh from off
The law allows it and the court awards it.
*Shy.* Most learned judge!—A sentence; come, prepare.          [else.—
*Por.* Tarry a little;—there is something
This bond doth give thee here no jot of blood;
The words expressly are a pound of flesh:
Take then thy bond, take thou thy pound of flesh;
But, in the cutting, if thou dost shed          [goods
One drop of Christian blood, thy lands and
Are, by the laws of Venice, confiscate

Unto the state of Venice.        [learned judge!
*Gra.* O upright judge!—Mark, Jew;—O
*Shy.* Is that the law?
*Por.*        Thyself shall see the act:
For, as thou urgest justice, be assur'd
Thou shalt have justice, more than thou desir'st.
*Gra.* O learned judge!—Mark, Jew;—a
learned judge!        [thrice,
*Shy.* I take this offer then,—pay the bond
And let the Christian go.
*Bass.*        Here is the money.
*Por.* Soft;        [haste:—
The Jew shall have all justice:—soft;—no
He shall have nothing but the penalty.
*Gra.* O Jew! an upright judge, a learned
judge!
*Por.* Therefore, prepare thee to cut off the
flesh.
Shed thou no blood; nor cut thou less nor more
But just a pound of flesh: if thou tak'st more
Or less than a just pound,—be it but so much
As makes it light or heavy in the substance,
Or the division of the twentieth part
Of one poor scruple: nay, if the scale do turn
But in the estimation of a hair,
Thou diest, and all thy goods are confiscate.
*Gra.* A second Daniel, a Daniel, Jew!
Now, infidel, I have thee on the hip.
*Por.* Why doth the Jew pause? take thy for-
feiture.
*Shy.* Give me my principal, and let me go.
*Bass.* I have it ready for thee; here it is.
*Por.* He hath refus'd it in the open court;
He shall have merely justice, and his bond.
*Gra.* A Daniel, still say I; a second Daniel!—
I thank thee, Jew, for teaching me that word.
*Shy.* Shall I not have barely my principal?
*Por.* Thou shalt have nothing but the for-
feiture
To be so taken at thy peril, Jew.
*Shy.* Why, then the devil give him good of it!
I'll stay no longer question.
*Por.*        Tarry, Jew;
The law hath yet another hold on you.
It is enacted in the laws of Venice,—
If it be prov'd against an alien,
That by direct or indirect attempts
He seek the life of any citizen,
The party 'gainst the which he doth contrive
Shall seize one half his goods; the other half
Comes to the privy coffer of the state;
And the offender's life lies in the mercy
Of the duke only, 'gainst all other voice.
In which predicament, I say, thou stand'st;
For it appears by manifest proceeding,
That indirectly, and directly too,
Thou hast contriv'd against the very life
Of the defendant; and thou hast incurr'd
The danger formerly by me rehears'd.
Down, therefore, and beg mercy of the duke.
*Gra.* Beg that thou mayst have leave to hang
thyself;
And yet, thy wealth being forfeit to the state,
Thou hast not left the value of a cord;

Therefore, thou must be hang'd at the state's
charge.        [spirit,
*Duke.* That thou shalt see the difference of our
I pardon thee thy life before thou ask it:
For half thy wealth, it is Antonio's:
The other half comes to the general state,
Which humbleness may drive unto a fine.
*Por.* Ay, for the state; not for Antonio.
*Shy.* Nay, take my life and all, pardon not
that:
You take my house when you do take the prop
That doth sustain my house; you take my life
When you do take the means whereby I live.
*Por.* What mercy can you render him,
Antonio?        [sake.
*Gra.* A halter gratis; nothing else; for God's
*Ant.* So please my lord the duke, and all the
court,
To quit the fine for one half of his goods;
I am content, so he will let me have
The other half in use, to render it,
Upon his death, unto the gentleman
That lately stole his daughter:
Two things provided more,—that for this
favour,
He presently become a Christian;
The other, that he do record a gift,
Here in the court, of all he dies possess'd
Unto his son Lorenzo and his daughter.
*Duke.* He shall do this; or else I do recant
The pardon that I late pronounced here.
*Por.* Art thou contented, Jew? what dost
thou say?
*Shy.* I am content.
*Por.*        Clerk, draw a deed of gift.
*Shy.* I pray you, give me leave to go from
hence:
I am not well; send the deed after me
And I will sign it.
*Duke.*        Get thee gone, but do it.
*Gra.* In christening, thou shalt have two
godfathers;
Had I been judge, thou shouldst have had ten
more,
To bring thee to the gallows, not the font.
        [*Exit* SHYLOCK.
*Duke.* Sir, I entreat you home with me to
dinner.
*Por.* I humbly do desire your grace of par-
don;
I must away this night toward Padua;
And it is meet I presently set forth.
*Duke.* I am sorry that your leisure serves
you not.
Antonio, gratify this gentleman;
For, in my mind, you are much bound to him.
        [*Exeunt* DUKE, Magnificoes, *and* Train.
*Bass.* Most worthy gentleman, I and my
friend
Have by your wisdom been this day acquitted
Of grievous penalties; in lieu whereof,
Three thousand ducats, due unto the Jew,
We freely cope your courteous pains withal.
*Ant.* And stand indebted, over and above

In love and service to you evermore.

*Por.* He is well paid that is-well satisfied,
And I, delivering you, am satisfied,
And therein do account myself well paid:
My mind was never yet more mercenary.
I pray you, know me when we meet again;
I wish you well, and so I take my leave.

*Bass.* Dear sir, of force I must attempt you
    further;
Take some remembrance of us, as a tribute,
Not as a fee; grant me two things, I pray you,
Not to deny me, and to pardon me.

*Por.* You press me far, and therefore I will
    yield.
Give me your gloves, I'll wear them for your
    sake;
And, for your love, I'll take this ring from
    you:—
Do not draw back your hand; I'll take no
    more;
And you in love shall not deny me this.

*Bass.* This ring, good sir,—alas, it is a trifle;
I will not shame myself to give you this.

*Por.* I will have nothing else but only this;
And now, methinks, I have a mind to it.

*Bass.* There's more depends on this than on
    the value.
The dearest ring in Venice will I give you,
And find it out by proclamation;
Only for this, I pray you, pardon me.

*Por.* I see, sir, you are liberal in offers:
You taught me first to beg, and now, methinks,
You teach me how a beggar should be answer'd.

*Bass.* Good sir, this ring was given me by my
    wife,
And, when she put it on, she made me vow
That I should neither sell, nor give, nor lose
    it.

*Por.* That 'scuse serves many men to save
    their gifts.
An if your wife be not a mad woman,
And know how well I have deserv'd this ring,
She would not hold out enemy for ever,
For giving it to me. Well, peace be with you!
                    [*Exeunt* PORTIA *and* NERISSA.

*Ant.* My Lord Bassanio, let him have the
    ring:
Let his deservings, and my love withal,
Be valued 'gainst your wife's commandment.

*Bass.* Go, Gratiano, run and overtake him,
Give him the ring; and bring him, if thou canst,
Unto Antonio's house:—away, make haste.
                    [*Exit* GRATIANO.
Come, you and I will thither presently;
And in the morning early will we both
Fly toward Belmont. Come, Antonio.
                    [*Exeunt.*

SCENE II.—*The same. A Street.*

*Enter* PORTIA *and* NERISSA.

*Por.* Inquire the Jew's house out, give him
    this deed,
And let him sign it; we'll away to-night,

And be a day before our husbands home.
This deed will be well welcome to Lorenzo.

*Enter* GRATIANO.

*Gra.* Fair sir, you are well overta'en:
My Lord Bassanio, upon more advice,
Hath sent you here this ring; and doth entreat
Your company at dinner.

*Por.*                    That cannot be:
His ring I do accept most thankfully.
And so, I pray you, tell him. Furthermore,
I pray you, show my youth old Shylock's house.

*Gra.* That will I do.

*Ner.* Sir, I would speak with you:—
I'll see if I can get my husband's ring,
                    [*To* PORTIA.
Which I did make him swear to keep for ever.

*Por.* Thou mayst, I warrant. We shall have
    old swearing
That they did give the rings away to men;
But we'll outface them and outswear them too.
Away, make haste; thou know'st where I will
    tarry.

*Ner.* Come, good sir, will you show me to
    this house?                    [*Exeunt.*

## ACT V.

SCENE I.—BELMONT. *Pleasure grounds of*
    PORTIA'S *House.*

*Enter* LORENZO *and* JESSICA.

*Lor.* The moon shines bright!—In such a
    night as this,
When the sweet wind did gently kiss the trees,
And they did make no noise; in such a night,
Troilus, methinks, mounted the Trojan walls,
And sigh'd his soul toward the Grecian tents,
Where Cressid lay that night.

*Jes.*                    In such a night
Did Thisbe fearfully o'ertrip the dew,
And saw the lion's shadow ere himself.
And ran dismay'd away.

*Lor.*                    In such a night
Stood Dido with a willow in her hand
Upon the wild sea-banks, and wav'd her love
To come again to Carthage.

*Jes.*                    In such a night
Medea gather'd the enchanted herbs
That did renew old Æson.

*Lor.*                    In such a night
Did Jessica steal from the wealthy Jew
And, with an unthrift love, did run from Venice
As far as Belmont.

*Jes.*                    In such a night
Did young Lorenzo swear he lov'd her well—
Stealing her soul with many vows of faith,
And ne'er a true one

*Lor*                    In such a night
Did pretty Jessica, like a little shrew,
Slander her love, and he forgave it her.

*Jes.* I would out-night you, did nobody
    come:
But hark, I hear the footing of a man.

*Enter* STEPHANO.

*Lor.* Who comes so fast in silence of the night?

*Steph.* A friend.

*Lor.* A friend! what friend? your name, I pray you, friend?

*Steph.* Stepháno is my name; and I bring word
My mistress will before the break of day
Be here at Belmont; she doth stray about
By holy crosses, where she kneels and prays
For happy wedlock hours.

*Lor.*                     Who comes with her?

*Steph.* None but a holy hermit and her maid.
I pray you, is my master yet return'd?

*Lor.* He is not, nor we have not heard from him.—
But go we in, I pray thee, Jessica,
And ceremoniously let us prepare
Some welcome for the mistress of the house.

*Enter* LAUNCELOT.

*Laun.* Sola, sola, wo ha, ho, sola, sola!

*Lor.* Who calls?

*Laun.* Sola! did you see Master Lorenzo and Mistress Lorenzo? sola, sola!

*Lor.* Leave hollaing, man: here.

*Laun.* Sola! where? where?

*Lor.* Here.

*Laun.* Tell him there's a post come from my master with his horn full of good news; my master will be here ere morning.    [*Exit.*

*Lor.* Sweet soul, let's in, and there expect their coming.
And yet no matter;—why should we go in?
My friend Stepháno, signify, I pray you,
Within the house, your mistress is at hand:
And bring your music forth into the air.—
                           [*Exit* STEPHANO.
How sweet the moonlight sleeps upon this bank!
Here will we sit, and let the sounds of music
Creep in our ears; soft stillness and the night
Become the touches of sweet harmony.
Sit, Jessica. Look how the floor of heaven
Is thick inlaid with patines of bright gold;
There's not the smallest orb which thou behold'st
But in his motion like an angel sings,
Still quiring to the young-ey'd cherubims:
Such harmony is in immortal souls;
But, whilst this muddy vesture of decay
Doth grossly close it in, we cannot hear it.—

*Enter* Musicians.

Come, ho, and wake Diana with a hymn;
With sweetest touches pierce your mistress' ear,
And draw her home with music.    [*Music.*

*Jes.* I am never merry when I hear sweet music.

*Lor.* The reason is, your spirits are attentive:
For do but note a wild and wanton herd,
Or race of youthful and unhandled colts,
Fetching mad bounds, bellowing, and neighing loud,
Which is the hot condition of their blood—
If they but hear perchance a trumpet sound,
Or any air of music touch their ears,
You shall perceive them make a mutual stand,
Their savage eyes turn'd to a modest gaze
By the sweet power of music; therefore the poet
Did feign that Orpheus drew trees, stones, and floods;
Since naught so stockish, hard, and full of rage
But music for the time doth change his nature.
The man that hath no music in himself,
Nor is not mov'd with concord of sweet sounds,
Is fit for treasons, stratagems, and spoils;
The motions of his spirit are dull as night,
And his affections dark as Erebus:
Let no such man be trusted.—Mark the music.

*Enter* PORTIA *and* NERISSA, *at a distance.*

*Por.* That light we see is burning in my hall!
How far that little candle throws his beams!
So shines a good deed in a naughty world.

*Ner.* When the moon shone we did not see the candle.

*Por.* So doth the greater glory dim the less:
A substitute shines brightly as a king
Until a king be by; and then his state
Empties itself, as doth an inland brook
Into the main of waters. Music! hark!

*Ner.* It is your music, madam, of the house.

*Por.* Nothing is good, I see, without respect;
Methinks it sounds much sweeter than by day.

*Ner.* Silence bestows that virtue on it, madam.

*Por.* The crow doth sing as sweetly as the lark
When neither in attended; and, I think,
The nightingale, if she should sing by day,
When every goose is cackling, would be thought
No better a musician than the wren.
How many things by season season'd are
To their right praise and true perfection!—
Peace, ho! the moon sleeps with Endymion,
And would not be awaked!    [*Music ceases.*

*Lor.*                  That is the voice,
Or I am much deceived, of Portia.

*Por.* He knows me, as the blind man knows the cuckoo,
By the bad voice.

*Lor.*            Dear lady, welcome home.

*Por.* We have been praying for our husbands' welfare,
Which speed, we hope, the better for our words.
Are they return'd?

*Lor.*             Madam, they are not yet;
But there is come a messenger before,
To signify their coming.

*Por.*                   Go in, Nerissa,
Give order to my servants that they take
No note at all of our being absent hence;—
Nor you, Lorenzo;—Jessica, nor you.
                           [*A tucket sounds.*

*Lor.* Your husband is at hand, I hear his trumpet:

We are no tell-tales, madam; fear you not.

*Por.* This night methinks is but the daylight sick—
It looks a little paler; 'tis a day
Such as the day is when the sun is hid.

*Enter* BASSANIO, ANTONIO, GRATIANO *and their followers.*

*Bass.* We should hold day with the Antipodes
If you would walk in absence of the sun.

*Por.* Let me give light, but let me not be light;
For a light wife doth make a heavy husband,
And never be Bassanio so for me;         [lord.
But God sort all!—you are welcome home, my

*Bass.* I thank you, madam; give welcome to my friend.—
This is the man; this is Antonio,
To whom I am so infinitely bound.          [to him,

*Por.* You should in all sense be much bound
For, as I hear, he was much bound for you.

*Ant.* No more than I am well acquitted of.

*Por.* Sir, you are very welcome to our house:
It must appear in other ways than words,
Therefore, I scant this breathing courtesy.

[GRA. *and* NER. *seem to talk apart.*

*Gra.* By yonder moon, I swear you do me wrong;
In faith, I gave it to the judge's clerk:
Would he were gelt that had it, for my part,
Since you do take it, love, so much at heart.

*Por.* A quarrel, ho, already? what's the matter?

*Gra.* About a hoop of gold, a paltry ring
That she did give me; whose posy was,
For all the world, like cutler's poetry
Upon a knife, *Love me, and leave me not.*

*Ner.* What, talk you of the posy, or the value?
You swore to me, when I did give it you,
That you would wear it till your hour of death;
And that it should lie with you in your grave:
Though not for me, yet for your vehement oaths
You should have been respective, and have kept it.
Gave it a judge's clerk!—no, God's my judge,
The clerk will ne'er wear hair on's face that had it.

*Gra.* He will, an if he live to be a man.

*Ner.* Ay, if a woman live to be a man.

*Gra.* Now, by this hand, I gave it to a youth,—
A kind of boy; a little scrubbed boy
No higher than thyself, the judge's clerk;
A prating boy that begg'd it as a fee;
I could not for my heart deny it him.

*Por.* You were to blame, I must be plain with you,
To part so slightly with your wife's first gift;
A thing stuck on with oaths upon your finger,
And so riveted with faith unto your flesh.
I gave my love a ring, and made him swear
Never to part with it, and here he stands;
I dare be sworn for him, he would not leave it
Nor pluck it from his finger for the wealth
That the world masters. Now, in faith, Gratiano,
You gave your wife too unkind a cause of grief;
An 'twere to me, I should be mad at it.         [off,

*Bass.* Why, I were best to cut my left hand
And swear I lost the ring defending it. [*Aside.*

*Gra.* My Lord Bassanio gave his ring away
Unto the judge that begg'd it, and, indeed,
Deserv'd it too; and then the boy, his clerk,
That took some pains in writing, he begg'd mine:
And neither man nor master would take aught
But the two rings.

*Por.*           What ring gave you, my lord?
Not that, I hope, which you receiv'd of me.

*Bass.* If I could add a lie unto a fault
I would deny it; but you see my finger
Hath not the ring upon it; it is gone.

*Por.* Even so void is your false heart of truth.
By heaven, I will ne'er come in your bed
Until I see the ring.

*Ner.*           Nor I in yours
Till I again see mine.

*Bass.*           Sweet Portia,
If you did know to whom I gave the ring,
If you did know for whom I gave the ring,
And would conceive for what I gave the ring,
And how unwillingly I left the ring,
When naught would be accepted but the ring,
You would abate the strength of your displeasure.

*Por.* If you had known the virtue of the ring,
Or half her worthiness that gave the ring,
Or your own honour to contain the ring,
You would not then have parted with the ring.
What man is there so much unreasonable,
If you had pleas'd to have defended it
With any terms of zeal, wanted the modesty
To urge the thing held as a ceremony?
Nerissa teaches me what to believe;
I'll die for't, but some woman had the ring.

*Bass.* No, by mine honour, madam, by my soul,
No woman had it, but a civil doctor,
Which did refuse three thousand ducats of me,
And begg'd the ring; the which I did deny him,
And suffer'd him to go displeas'd away;
Even he that had held up the very life
Of my dear friend. What should I say, sweet lady?
I was enforc'd to send it after him;
I was beset with shame and courtesy:
My honour would not let ingratitude
So much besmear it. Pardon me, good lady;
For by these blessed candles of the night,
Had you been there, I think you would have begg'd
The ring of me to give the worthy doctor.

*Por.* Let not that doctor e'er come near my house:
Since he hath got the jewel that I lov'd,
And that which you did swear to keep for me,

I will become as liberal as you;
I'll not deny him anything I have,
No, not my body, nor my husband's bed:
Know him I shall, I am well sure of it:
Lie not a night from home; watch me like
        Argus:
If you do not, if I be left alone,
Now, by mine honour, which is yet mine own,
I'll have that doctor for my bedfellow.

   *Ner.* And I his clerk; therefore be well ad-
        vis'd
How you do leave me to mine own protection.

   *Gra.* Well, do you so: let not me take him
        then;
For, if I do, I'll mar the young clerk's pen.

   *Ant.* I am the unhappy subject of these
        quarrels.                    [notwithstanding.

   *Por.* Sir, grieve not you; you are welcome

   *Bass.* Portia, forgive me this enforced wrong;
And, in the hearing of these many friends,
I swear to thee, even by thine own fair eyes,
Wherein I see myself,——

   *Por.*                    Mark you but that!
In both my eyes he doubly sees himself:
In each eye one:—swear by your double self,
And there's an oath of credit.

   *Bass.*                    Nay, but hear me:
Pardon this fault, and by my soul I swear,
I never more will break an oath with thee.

   *Ant.* I once did lend my body for his wealth;
Which, but for him that had your husband's
        ring,
Had quite miscarried: I dare be bound again,
My soul upon the forfeit, that your lord
Will never more break faith advisedly.

   *Por.* Then you shall be his surety: give him
        this;
And bid him keep it better than the other.

   *Ant.* Here, Lord Bassanio; swear to keep
this ring.

   *Bass.* By heaven, it is the same I gave the
doctor!

   *Por.* I had it of him: pardon me, Bassanio;
For by this ring the doctor lay with me.

   *Ner.* And pardon me, my gentle Gratiano;
For that same scrubbed boy, the doctor's clerk,
In lieu of this, last night did lie with me.

   *Gra.* Why, this is like the mending of high-
ways
In summer, where the ways are fair enough:
What! are we cuckolds ere we have deserved it?

   *Por.* Speak not so grossly.—You are all
        amaz'd:
Here is a letter, read it at your leisure;
It comes from Padua, from Bellario:
There you shall find that Portia was the doctor;
Nerissa there, her clerk: Lorenzo here
Shall witness I set forth as soon as you,
And but even now return'd; I have not yet
Enter'd my house.—Antonio, you are welcome;
And I have better news in store for you
Than you expect; unseal this letter soon;
There you shall find three of your argosies
Are richly come to harbour suddenly:
You shall not know by what strange accident
I chanced on this letter.

   *Ant.*                    I am dumb.

   *Bass.* Were you the doctor; and I knew you
        not?                        [cuckold?

   *Gra.* Were you the clerk that is to make me

   *Ner.* Ay, but the clerk that never means to
        do it,
Unless he live until he be a man.        [fellow;

   *Bass.* Sweet doctor, you shall be my bed-
When I am absent, then lie with my wife.

   *Ant.* Sweet lady, you have given me life and
        living;
For here I read for certain that my ships
Are safely come to road.

   *Por.*                    How now, Lorenzo?
My clerk hath some good comforts too for you.

   *Ner.* Ay, and I'll give them him without a
        fee.—
There do I give to you and Jessica,
From the rich Jew, a special deed of gift,
After his death, of all he dies possess'd of.

   *Lor.* Fair ladies, you drop manna in the way
Of starved people.

   *Por.*                    It is almost morning,
And yet, I am sure, you are not satisfied
Of these events at full. Let us go in;
And charge us there upon inter'gatories,
And we will answer all things faithfully.

   *Gra.* Let it be so:—the first inter'gatory
That my Nerissa shall be sworn on is,
Whether till the next night she had rather stay,
Or go to bed now, being two hours to day:
But were the day come, I should wish it dark,
That I were couching with the doctor's clerk.
Well, while I live, I'll fear no other thing
So sore as keeping safe Nerissa's ring.

                                *[Exeunt.*

# AS YOU LIKE IT

## DRAMATIS PERSONÆ

DUKE, *living in exile.*
FREDERICK, *Brother to the* DUKE, *and Usurper of his Dominions.*
AMIENS, } *Lords attending upon the* DUKE
JAQUES, } *in his Banishment.*
LE BEAU, *a Courtier attending upon* FREDERICK.
CHARLES, *his Wrestler.*
OLIVER,
JAQUES, } *Sons of* SIR ROWLAND DE BOIS.
ORLANDO,
ADAM,
DENNIS, } *Servants to* OLIVER.
TOUCHSTONE, *a Clown.*

SIR OLIVER MARTEXT, *a Vicar.*
CORIN, } *Shepherds.*
SILVIUS, }
WILLIAM, *a Country Fellow, in love with* AUDREY.
*A Person representing* HYMEN.

ROSALIND, *Daughter to the banished* DUKE.
CELIA, *Daughter to* FREDERICK.
PHEBE, *a Shepherdess.*
AUDREY, *a Country Wench.*

Lords *belonging to the two Dukes;* Pages, Foresters, *and other* Attendants.

*The* SCENE *lies first near* OLIVER'S *House; afterwards partly in the Usurper's Court and partly in the Forest of* ARDEN.

## ACT I.

SCENE I.—*An Orchard near* OLIVER'S *House.*

*Enter* ORLANDO *and* ADAM.

*Orl.* As I remember, Adam, it was upon this fashion,—bequeathed me by will but poor a thousand crowns, and as thou say'st, charged my brother, on his blessing, to breed me well: and there begins my sadness. My brother Jaques he keeps at school, and report speaks goldenly of his profit: for my part, he keeps me rustically at home, or, to speak more properly, stays me here at home unkept: for call you that keeping for a gentleman of my birth that differs not from the stalling of an ox? His horses are bred better; for, besides that they are fair with their feeding, they are taught their manage, and to that end riders dearly hired: but I, his brother, gain nothing under him but growth; for the which his animals on his dunghills are as much bound to him as I. Besides this nothing that he so plentifully gives me, the something that nature gave me, his countenance seems to take from me: he lets me feed with his hinds, bars me the place of a brother, and as much as in him lies, mines my gentility with my education. This is it, Adam, that grieves me; and the spirit of my father, which I think is within me, begins to mutiny against this servitude: I will no longer endure it, though yet I know no wise remedy how to avoid it.

*Adam.* Yonder comes my master, your brother.

*Orl.* Go apart, Adam, and thou shalt hear how he will shake me up. [ADAM *retires.*

*Enter* OLIVER.

*Oli.* Now, sir! what make you here?

*Orl.* Nothing: I am not taught to make anything.

*Oli.* What mar you then, sir?

*Orl.* Marry, sir, I am helping you to mar that which God made, a poor unworthy brother of yours, with idleness.

*Oli.* Marry, sir, be better employed, and be naught awhile.

*Orl.* Shall I keep your hogs, and eat husks with them? What prodigal portion have I spent that I should come to such penury?

*Oli.* Know you where you are, sir?

*Orl.* O, sir, very well: here in your orchard.

*Oli.* Know you before whom, sir?

*Orl.* Ay, better than him I am before knows me. I know you are my eldest brother: and in the gentle condition of blood you should so know me. The courtesy of nations allows you my better, in that you are the first-born; but the same tradition takes not away my blood, were there twenty brothers betwixt us: I have as much of my father in me as you; albeit, I confess, your coming before me is nearer to his reverence.

*Oli.* What, boy!

*Orl.* Come, come, elder brother, you are too young in this.

*Oli.* Wilt thou lay hands on me, villain?

*Orl.* I am no villain: I am the youngest son of Sir Rowland de Bois: he was my father; and he is thrice a villain that says such a father begot villains. Wert thou not my brother I would not take this hand from thy throat till this other had pulled out thy tongue for saying so: thou hast railed on thyself.

*Adam.* [*Coming forward.*] Sweet masters, be patient; for your father's remembrance, be at accord.

*Oli.* Let me go, I say.

*Orl.* I will not, till I please: you shall hear me. My father charged you in his will to give me good education: you have trained me like a peasant, obscuring and hiding from me all gentleman-like qualities: the spirit of my father grows strong in me, and I will no longer endure it: therefore, allow me such exercises as may become a gentleman, or give me the poor allotery my father left me by testament: with that I will go buy my fortunes.

*Oli.* And what wilt thou do? beg, when that is spent? Well, sir, get you in: I will not long be troubled with you: you shall have some part of your will: I pray you, leave me.

*Orl.* I will no further offend you than becomes me for my good.

*Oli.* Get you with him, you old dog.

*Adam.* Is old dog my reward? Most true, I have lost my teeth in your service.—God be with my old master! he would not have spoke such a word. [*Exeunt* ORLANDO *and* ADAM.

*Oli.* Is it even so? begin you to grow upon me? I will physic your rankness, and yet give no thousand crowns neither. Holla, Dennis!

*Enter* DENNIS.

*Den.* Calls your worship?

*Oli.* Was not Charles, the duke's wrestler, here to speak with me?

*Den.* So please you, he is here at the door, and importunes access to you.

*Oli.* Call him in. [*Exit* DENNIS.]—'Twill be a good way, and to-morrow the wrestling is.

*Enter* CHARLES.

*Cha.* Good morrow to your worship.

*Oli.* Good Monsieur Charles!—what's the new news at the new court?

*Cha.* There's no news at the court, sir, but the old news, that is, the old duke is banished by his younger brother the new duke; and three or four loving lords have put themselves into voluntary exile with him, whose lands and revenues enrich the new duke; therefore he gives them good leave to wander.

*Oli.* Can you tell if Rosalind, the duke's daughter, be banished with her father?

*Cha.* O no; for the duke's daughter, her cousin, so loves her,—being ever from their cradles bred together,—that she would have followed her exile, or have died to stay behind her. She is at the court, and no less beloved of her uncle than his own daughter; and never two ladies loved as they do.

*Oli.* Where will the old duke live?

*Cha.* They say he is already in the forest of Arden, and a many merry men with him; and there they live like the old Robin Hood of England: they say many young gentlemen flock to him every day, and fleet the time carelessly, as they did in the golden world.

*Oli.* What, you wrestle to-morrow before the new duke?

*Cha.* Marry, do I, sir; and I came to acquaint you with a matter. I am given, sir, secretly to understand that your younger brother, Orlando, hath a disposition to come in disguis'd against me to try a fall. To-morrow, sir, I wrestle for my credit; and he that escapes me without some broken limb shall acquit him well. Your brother is but young and tender; and, for your love, I would be loath to foil him, as I must for my own honour, if he come in: therefore, out of my love to you, I came hither to acquaint you withal; that either you might stay him from his intendment, or brook such disgrace well as he shall run into; in that it is a thing of his own search, and altogether against my will.

*Oli.* Charles, I thank thee for thy love to me, which thou shalt find I will most kindly requite. I had myself notice of my brother's purpose herein, and have by underhand means laboured to dissuade him from it; but he is resolute. I'll tell thee, Charles, it is the stubbornest young fellow of France; full of ambition, an envious emulator of every man's good parts, a secret and villanous contriver against me his natural brother; therefore use thy discretion: I had as lief thou didst break his neck as his finger. And thou wert best look to't; for if thou dost him any slight disgrace, or if he do not mightily grace himself on thee, he will practise against thee by poison, entrap thee by some treacherous device, and never leave thee till he hath ta'en thy life by some indirect means or other: for, I assure thee, and almost with tears I speak it, there is not one so young and so villanous this day living. I speak but brotherly of him; but should I anatomize him to thee as he is, I must blush and weep, and thou must look pale and wonder.

*Cha.* I am heartily glad I came hither to you. If he comes to-morrow I'll give him his payment. If ever he go alone again I'll never wrestle for prize more: and so, God keep your worship!                                     [*Exit.*

*Oli.* Farewell, good Charles.—Now will I stir this gamester: I hope I shall see an end of him; for my soul, yet I know not why, hates nothing more than he. Yet he's gentle; never schooled and yet learned; full of noble device of all sorts enchantingly beloved; and, indeed, so much in the heart of the world, and especially of my own people, who best know him, that I am altogether misprised: but it shall not be so long; this wrestler shall clear all: nothing remains but that I kindle the boy thither, which now I'll go about.                                     [*Exit.*

SCENE II.—*A Lawn before the* DUKE'S *Palace*

*Enter* ROSALIND *and* CELIA.

*Cel.* I pray thee, Rosalind, sweet my coz, be merry.

*Ros.* Dear Celia, I show more mirth than I am mistress of; and would you yet I were merrier? Unless you could teach me to forget a banished father, you must not learn me how to remember any extraordinary pleasure.

*Cel.* Herein I see thou lovest me not with the full weight that I love thee; if my uncle, thy banished father, had banished thy uncle, the duke my father, so thou hadst been still with me, I could have taught my love to take thy father for mine; so wouldst thou, if the truth of thy love to me were so righteously tempered as mine is to thee.

*Ros.* Well, I will forget the condition of my estate, to rejoice in yours.

*Cel.* You know my father hath no child but I, nor none is like to have; and, truly, when he dies thou shalt be his heir: for what he hath taken away from thy father perforce, I will render thee again in affection: by mine honour, I will: and when I break that oath, let me turn monster; therefore, my sweet Rose, my dear Rose, be merry.

*Ros.* From henceforth I will, coz, and devise sports: let me see; what think you of falling in love?

*Cel.* Marry, I pr'ythee, do, to make sport withal: but love no man in good earnest; nor no further in sport neither than with safety of a pure blush thou mayst in honour come off again.

*Ros.* What shall be our sport, then?

*Cel.* Let us sit and mock the good housewife Fortune from her wheel, that her gifts may henceforth be bestowed equally.

*Ros.* I would we could do so; for her benefits are mightily misplaced; and the bountiful blind woman doth most mistake in her gifts to women.

*Cel.* 'Tis true: for those that she makes fair she scarce makes honest; and those that she makes honest she makes very ill-favouredly.

*Ros.* Nay; now thou goest from fortune's office to nature's: fortune reigns in gifts of the world, not in the lineaments of nature.

*Cel.* No; when nature hath made a fair creature may she not by fortune fall into the fire?—Though nature hath given us wit to flout at fortune, hath not fortune sent in this fool to cut off the argument?

*Enter* TOUCHSTONE.

*Ros.* Indeed, there is fortune too hard for nature, when fortune makes nature's natural the cutter off of nature's wit.

*Cel.* Peradventure this is not fortune's work neither, but nature's, who perceiveth our natural wits too dull to reason of such goddesses, and hath sent this natural for our whetstone: for always the dulness of the fool is the whetstone of the wits.—How now, wit? whither wander you?

*Touch.* Mistress, you must come away to your father.

*Cel.* Were you made the messenger?

*Touch.* No, by mine honour; but I was bid to come for you.

*Ros.* Where learned you that oath, fool?

*Touch.* Of a certain knight that swore by his honour they were good pancakes, and swore by his honour the mustard was naught; now, I'll stand to it, the pancakes were naught and the mustard was good: and yet was not the knight forsworn.

*Cel.* How prove you that, in the great heap of your knowledge?

*Ros.* Ay, marry; now unmuzzle your wisdom.

*Touch.* Stand you both forth now: stroke your chins, and swear by your beards that I am a knave.

*Cel.* By our beards, if we had them, thou art.

*Touch.* By my knavery, if I had it, then I were: but if you swear by that is not, you are not forsworn: no more was this knight, swearing by his honour, for he never had any; or if he had, he had sworn it away before ever he saw those pancakes or that mustard.

*Cel.* Pr'ythee, who is't that thou mean'st?

*Touch.* One that old Frederick, your father, loves.

*Cel.* My father's love is enough to honour him enough: speak no more of him: you'll be whipp'd for taxation one of these days.

*Touch.* The more pity that fools may not speak wisely what wise men do foolishly.

*Cel.* By my troth, thou say'st true: for since the little wit that fools have was silenced, the little foolery that wise men have makes a great show. Here comes Monsieur Le Beau.

*Ros.* With his mouth full of news.

*Cel.* Which he will put on us as pigeons feed their young.

*Ros.* Then shall we be news-crammed.

*Cel.* All the better; we shall be the more marketable.

*Enter* LE BEAU.

*Bon jour*, Monsieur Le Beau. What's the news?

*Le Beau.* Fair princess, you have lost much good sport.

*Cel.* Sport! of what colour?

*Le Beau.* What colour, madam? How shall I answer you?

*Ros.* As wit and fortune will.

*Touch.* Or as the destinies decree.

*Cel.* Well said; that was laid on with a trowel.

*Touch.* Nay, if I keep not my rank,—

*Ros.* Thou loosest thy old smell.

*Le Beau.* You amaze me, ladies: I would have told you of good wrestling, which you have lost the sight of.

*Ros.* Yet tell us the manner of the wrestling.

*Le Beau.* I will tell you the beginning, and, if it please your ladyships, you may see the end; for the best is yet to do; and here, where you are, they are coming to perform it.

*Cel.* Well,—the beginning, that is dead and buried.

*Le Beau.* There comes an old man and his three sons,—

*Cel.* I could match this beginning with an old tale.

*Le Beau.* Three proper young men, of excellent growth and presence, with bills on their necks,—

*Ros. Be it known unto all men by these presents,—*

*Le Beau.* The eldest of the three wrestled with Charles, the duke's wrestler; which Charles in a moment threw him, and broke three of his ribs, that there is little hope of life in him: so he served the second, and so the third. Yonder they lie; the poor old man, their father, making such pitiful dole over them that all the beholders take his part with weeping.

*Ros.* Alas!

*Touch.* But what is the sport, monsieur, that the ladies have lost?

*Le Beau.* Why, this that I speak of.

*Touch.* Thus men may grow wiser every day! It is the first time that ever I heard breaking of ribs was sport for ladies.

*Cel.* Or I, I promise thee.

*Ros.* But is there any else longs to see this broken music in his sides? is there yet another dotes upon rib-breaking?—Shall we see this wrestling, cousin?

*Le Beau.* You must, if you stay here: for here is the place appointed for the wrestling, and they are ready to perform it.

*Cel.* Yonder, sure, they are coming: let us now stay and see it.

*Flourish. Enter* DUKE FREDERICK, *Lords,* ORLANDO, CHARLES, *and* Attendants.

*Duke F.* Come on; since the youth will not be entreated, his own peril on his forwardness.

*Ros.* Is yonder the man?

*Le Beau.* Even he, madam.

*Cel.* Alas, he is too young: yet he looks successfully.

*Duke F.* How now, daughter, and cousin? are you crept hither to see the wrestling?

*Ros.* Ay, my liege: so please you give us leave.

*Duke F.* You will take little delight in it, I can tell you, there is such odds in the men. In pity of the challenger's youth I would fain dissuade him, but he will not be entreated. Speak to him, ladies; see if you can move him.

*Cel.* Call him hither, good Monsieur Le Beau.

*Duke F.* Do so; I'll not be by.
                          [DUKE F. *goes apart.*
*Le Beau.* Monsieur the challenger, the princesses call for you.

*Orl.* I attend them with all respect and duty.

*Ros.* Young man, have you challenged Charles the wrestler?

*Orl.* No, fair princess; he is the general challenger: I come but in, as others do, to try with him the strength of my youth.

*Cel.* Young gentleman, your spirits are too bold for your years. You have seen cruel proof

of this man's strength: if you saw yourself with your eyes, or knew yourself with your judgment, the fear of your adventure would counsel you to a more equal enterprise. We pray you, for your own sake, to embrace your own safety, and give over this attempt.

*Ros.* Do, young sir; your reputation shall not therefore be misprised: we will make it our suit to the duke that the wrestling might not go forward.

*Orl.* I beseech you, punish me not with your hard thoughts: wherein I confess me much guilty, to deny so fair and excellent ladies anything. But let your fair eyes and gentle wishes go with me to my trial: wherein if I be foiled, there is but one shamed that was never gracious; if killed, but one dead that is willing to be so: I shall do my friends no wrong, for I have none to lament me: the world no injury, for in it I have nothing; only in the world I fill up a place, which may be better supplied when I have made it empty.

*Ros.* The little strength that I have, I would it were with you.

*Cel.* And mine to eke out hers.

*Ros.* Fare you well. Pray heaven, I be deceived in you!

*Cel.* Your heart's desires be with you.

*Cha.* Come, where is this young gallant that is so desirous to lie with his mother earth?

*Orl.* Ready, sir; but his will hath in it a more modest working.

*Duke F.* You shall try but one fall.

*Cha.* No; I warrant your grace, you shall not entreat him to a second, that have so mightily persuaded him from a first.

*Orl.* You mean to mock me after; you should not have mocked me before: but come your ways.

*Ros.* Now, Hercules be thy speed, young man!

*Cel.* I would I were invisible, to catch the strong fellow by the leg.
                   [CHARLES *and* ORLANDO *wrestle.*
*Ros.* O excellent young man!

*Cel.* If I had a thunderbolt in mine eye, I can tell who should down.
                      [CHARLES *is thrown. Shout.*
*Duke F.* No more, no more.

*Orl.* Yes, I beseech your grace; I am not yet well breathed.

*Duke F.* How dost thou, Charles?

*Le Beau.* He cannot speak, my lord.

*Duke F.* Bear him away.
                      [CHARLES *is borne out.*
What is thy name, young man?

*Orl.* Orlando, my liege; the youngest son of Sir Rowland de Bois.                     [man else.

*Duke F.* I would thou hadst been son to some The world esteem'd thy father honourable, But I did find him still mine enemy:     [deed Thou shouldst have better pleas'd me with this Hadst thou descended from another house. But fare thee well; thou art a gallant youth;

I would thou hadst told me of another father.
    [*Exeunt* DUKE F., *Train, and* LE BEAU.
*Cel.* Were I my father, coz, would I do this?
*Orl.* I am more proud to be Sir Rowland's
    son,
His youngest son;—and would not change that
    calling
To be adopted heir to Frederick.
    *Ros.* My father loved Sir Rowland as his
    soul,
And all the world was of my father's mind:
Had I before known this young man his son,
I should have given him tears unto entreaties,
Ere he should thus have ventur'd.
    *Cel.*               Gentle cousin,
Let us go thank him, and encourage him:
My father's rough and envious disposition
Sticks me at heart.—Sir, you have well de-
    serv'd:
If you do keep your promises in love
But justly, as you have exceeded promise,
Your mistress shall be happy.
    *Ros.*            Gentleman,
    [*Giving him a chain from her neck.*
Wear this for me; one out of suits with fortune,
That could give more, but that her hand lacks
    means.—
Shall we go, coz?
    *Cel.*    Ay.—Fare you well, fair gentleman.
    *Orl.* Can I not say, I thank you? My better
    parts                   [*stands up*
Are all thrown down; and that which here
Is but a quintain, a mere lifeless block.
    *Ros.* He calls us back: my pride fell with my
    fortunes:
I'll ask him what he would.—Did you call,
    sir?—
Sir, you have wrestled well, and overthrown
More than your enemies.
    *Cel.*          Will you go, coz?
    *Ros.* Have with you.—Fare you well.
        [*Exeunt* ROSALIND *and* CELIA.
    *Orl.* What passion hangs these weights upon
    my tongue?
I cannot speak to her, yet she urg'd conference.
O poor Orlando! thou art overthrown:
Or Charles, or something weaker, masters thee.

          *Re-enter* LE BEAU.

    *Le Beau.* Good sir, I do in friendship counsel
    you.
To leave this place. Albeit you have deserv'd
High commendation, true applause, and love,
Yet such is now the duke's condition,
That he miscónstrues all that you have done.
The duke is humorous; what he is, indeed,
More suits you to conceive than I to speak of.
    *Orl.* I thank you, sir: and pray you, tell me
    this;
Which of the two was daughter of the duke
That here was at the wrestling?    [*manners.*
    *Le Beau.* Neither his daughter, if we judge by
But yet, indeed, the smaller is his daughter:

The other is daughter to the banish'd duke,
And here detain'd by her usurping uncle,
To keep his daughter company; whose loves
Are dearer than the natural bond of sisters.
But I can tell you that of late this duke
Hath ta'en displeasure 'gainst his gentle niece,
Grounded upon no other argument
But that the people praise her for her virtues
And pity her for her good father's sake;
And, on my life, his malice 'gainst the lady
Will suddenly break forth.—Sir, fare you well!
Hereafter, in a better world than this,
I shall desire more love and knowledge of you.
    *Orl.* I rest much bounden to you: fare you
    well!                [*Exit* LE BEAU.
Thus must I from the smoke into the smother;
From tyrant duke unto a tyrant brother:—
But heavenly Rosalind!          [*Exit.*

SCENE III.—*A Room in the Palace.*

*Enter* CELIA *and* ROSALIND.

    *Cel.* Why, cousin; why, Rosalind;—Cupid
have mercy!—Not a word?
    *Ros.* Not one to throw at a dog.
    *Cel.* No, thy words are too precious to be
cast away upon curs, throw some of them at
me; come, lame me with reasons.
    *Ros.* Then there were two cousins laid up;
when the one should be lamed with reasons and
the other mad without any.
    *Cel.* But is all this for your father?
    *Ros.* No, some of it is for my father's child.
O, how full of briers is this working-day world!
    *Cel.* They are but burs, cousin, thrown upon
thee in holiday foolery; if we walk not in the
trodden paths our very petticoats will catch
them.
    *Ros.* I could shake them off my coat: these
burs are in my heart.
    *Cel.* Hem them away.        [*have him.*
    *Ros.* I would try, if I could cry hem and
    *Cel.* Come, come, wrestle with thy affections.
    *Ros.* O, they take the part of a better
wrestler than myself.
    *Cel.* O, a good wish upon you! you will try
in time, in despite of a fall.—But, turning these
jests out of service, let us talk in good earnest:
is it possible, on such a sudden, you should fall
into so strong a liking with old Sir Rowland's
youngest son?
    *Ros.* The duke my father loved his father
dearly.
    *Cel.* Doth it therefore ensue that you should
love his son dearly? By this kind of chase I
should hate him, for my father hated his father
dearly; yet I hate not Orlando.
    *Ros.* No, 'faith, hate him not, for my sake.
    *Cel.* Why should I not? doth he not deserve
well?
    *Ros.* Let me love him for that; and do you
love him because I do.—Look, here comes the
duke.
    *Cel.* With his eyes full of anger.

*Enter* DUKE FREDERICK, *with* Lords.

*Duke F.* Mistress, despatch you with your safest haste,
And get you from our court.

*Ros.*          Me, uncle?

*Duke F.*          You, cousin:
Within these ten days if that thou be'st found
So near our public court as twenty miles,
Thou diest for it.

*Ros.*       I do beseech your grace,   [me:
Let me the knowledge of my fault bear with
If with myself I hold intelligence,
Or have acquaintance with mine own desires;
If that I do not dream, or be not frantic,—
As I do trust I am not,—then, dear uncle,
Never so much as in a thought unborn
Did I offend your highness.

*Duke F.*       Thus do all traitors;
If their purgation did consist in words,
They are as innocent as grace itself:—
Let it suffice thee that I trust thee not.

*Ros.* Yet your mistrust cannot make me a traitor:
Tell me whereon the likelihood depends.

*Duke F.* Thou art thy father's daughter;
     there's enough.       [dukedom;

*Ros.* So was I when your highness took his
So was I when your highness banish'd him:
Treason is not inherited, my lord;
Or, if we did derive it from our friends,
What's that to me? my father was no traitor!
Then, good my liege, mistake me not so much
To think my poverty is treacherous.

*Cel.* Dear sovereign, hear me speak.   [sake,

*Duke F.* Ay, Celia: we stay'd her for your
Else had she with her father rang'd along.

*Cel.* I did not then entreat to have her stay;
It was your pleasure, and your own remorse:
I was too young that time to value her;
But now I know her: if she be a traitor,
Why so am I: we still have slept together,
Rose at an instant, learn'd, play'd, eat together;
And wheresoe'er we went, like Juno's swans,
Still we went coupled and inseparable.

*Duke F.* She is too subtle for thee; and her smoothness,
Her very silence, and her patience
Speak to the people, and they pity her.
Thou art a fool: she robs thee of thy name;
And thou wilt show more bright and seem more virtuous
When she is gone: then open not thy lips;
Firm and irrevocable is my doom
Which I have pass'd upon her;—she is banish'd.

*Cel.* Pronounce that sentence, then, on me, my liege:      [yourself:
I cannot live out of her company.

*Duke F.* You are a fool.—You, niece, provide
If you outstay the time, upon mine honour,
And in the greatness of my word, you die.

         [*Exeunt* DUKE F. *and* Lords.

*Cel.* O my poor Rosalind! whither wilt thou go?

Wilt thou change fathers? I will give thee mine.
I charge thee, be not thou more griev'd than I am.

*Ros.* I have more cause.

*Cel.*        Thou hast not, cousin;
Pr'ythee, be cheerful: know'st thou not the duke
Hath banish'd me, his daughter?

*Ros.*        That he hath not.

*Cel.* No! hath not? Rosalind lacks, then, the love
Which teacheth thee that thou and I am one:
Shall we be sunder'd? shall we part, sweet girl?
No; let my father seek another heir.
Therefore devise with me how we may fly,
Whither to go, and what to bear with us:
And do not seek to take your change upon you,
To bear your griefs yourself, and leave me out;
For, by this heaven, now at our sorrows pale,
Say what thou canst, I'll go along with thee.

*Ros.* Why, whither shall we go?

*Cel.* To seek my uncle in the forest of Arden.

*Ros.* Alas! what danger will it be to us,
Maids as we are, to travel forth so far?
Beauty provoketh thieves sooner than gold.

*Cel.* I'll put myself in poor and mean attire,
And with a kind of umber smirch my face;
The like do you; so shall we pass along,
And never stir assailants.

*Ros.*        Were it not better,
Because that I am more than common tall,
That I did suit me all points like a man?
A gallant curtle-axe upon my thigh,
A boar spear in my hand; and,—in my heart
Lie there what hidden woman's fear there will—
We'll have a swashing and a martial outside,
As many other mannish cowards have
That do outface it with their semblances.

*Cel.* What shall I call thee when thou art a man?       [own page,

*Ros.* I'll have no worse a name than Jove's
And, therefore, look you call me Ganymede.
But what will you be call'd?      [state:

*Cel.* Something that hath a reference to my
No longer Celia, but Aliena.

*Ros.* But, cousin, what if we assay'd to steal
The clownish fool out of your father's court?
Would he not be a comfort to our travel?

*Cel.* He'll go along o'er the wide world with me;
Leave me alone to woo him. Let's away,
And get our jewels and our wealth together;
Devise the fittest time and safest way
To hide us from pursuit that will be made
After flight. Now go we in content
To liberty, and not to banishment.   [*Exeunt.*

## ACT II.

SCENE I.—*The Forest of Arden.*

*Enter* DUKE *Senior,* AMIENS, *and other* Lords,
*in the dress of Foresters.*

*Duke S.* Now, my co-mates and brothers in exile,

Hath not old custom made this life more sweet
Than that of painted pomp? Are not these
   woods
More free from peril than the envious court?
Here feel we but the penalty of Adam,—
The seasons' difference: as the icy fang
And churlish chiding of the winter's wind,
Which when it bites and blows upon my body,
Even till I shrink with cold, I smile and say,
This is no flattery: these are counsellors
That feelingly persuade me what I am.
Sweet are the uses of adversity,
Which, like the toad, ugly and venomous,
Wears yet a precious jewel in his head;
And this our life, exempt from public haunt,
Finds tongues in trees, books in the running
   brooks,
Sermons in stones, and good in everything.
I would not change it.

*Ami.*    Happy is your grace,
That can translate the stubbornness of fortune
Into so quiet and so sweet a style.    [son?

*Duke S.* Come, shall we go and kill us veni-
And yet it irks me, the poor dappled fools,
Being native burghers of this desert city,
Should, in their own confines, with forked
   heads
Have their round haunches gor'd.

*1 Lord.*    Indeed, my lord,
The melancholy Jaques grieves at that;
And, in that kind, swears you do more usurp
Than doth your brother that hath banish'd
   you.
To-day my lord of Amiens and myself
Did steal behind him as he lay along
Under an oak, whose antique root peeps out
Upon the brook that brawls along this wood:
To the which place a poor sequester'd stag,
That from the hunters' aim had ta'en a hurt,
Did come to languish; and, indeed, my lord,
The wretched animal heav'd forth such groans,
That their discharge did stretch his leathern
   coat
Almost to bursting; and the big round tears
Cours'd one another down his innocent nose
In piteous chase: and thus the hairy fool,
Much marked of the melancholy Jaques,
Stood on the extremest verge of the swift brook,
Augmenting it with tears.

*Duke S.*    But what said Jaques?
Did he not moralize the spectacle?

*1 Lord.* O, yes, into a thousand similies,
First, for his weeping into the needless stream;
*Poor deer,* quoth he, *thou mak'st a testament
As worldlings do, giving thy sum of more
To that which had too much:* then, being there
   alone,
Left and abandon'd of his velvet friends;
*'Tis right,* quoth he; *thus misery doth part
The flux of company:* anon, a careless herd,
Full of the pasture, jumps along by him,
And never stays to greet him; *Ay,* quoth
   Jaques,
*Sweep on, you fat and greasy citizens;*

*'Tis just the fashion; wherefore do you look
Upon that poor and broken bankrupt there?*
Thus most invectively he pierceth through
The body of the country, city, court,
Yea, and of this our life: swearing that we
Are mere usurpers, tyrants, and what's worse,
To fright the animals, and to kill them up
In their assign'd and native dwelling-place.

*Duke S.* And did you leave him in this contemplation?    [menting

*2 Lord.* We did, my lord, weeping and com-
Upon the sobbing deer.

*Duke S.*    Show me the place:
I love to cope him in these sullen fits,
For then he's full of matter.

*2 Lord.* I'll bring you to him straight.
                             *[Exeunt.*

SCENE II.—*A Room in the Palace.*

*Enter* DUKE FREDERICK, Lords, *and* Attendants.

*Duke F.* Can it be possible that no man saw
   them?
It cannot be: some villains of my court
Are of consent and sufferance in this.

*1 Lord.* I cannot hear of any that did see her.
The ladies, her attendants of her chamber,
Saw her a-bed; and in the morning early
They found the bed untreasur'd of their mis-
   tress.    [so oft

*2 Lord.* My lord, the roynish clown, at whom
Your grace was wont to laugh, is also missing.
Hesperia, the princess' gentlewoman,
Confesses that she secretly o'erheard
Your daughter and her cousin much commend
The parts and graces of the wrestler
That did but lately foil the sinewy Charles;
And she believes, wherever they are gone,
That youth is surely in their company.

*Duke F.* Send to his brother; fetch that gal-
   lant hither:
If he be absent, bring his brother to me,
I'll make him find him: do this suddenly;
And let not search and inquisition quail
To bring again these foolish runaways.
                             *[Exeunt.*

SCENE III.—*Before* OLIVER'S *House.*

*Enter* ORLANDO *and* ADAM, *meeting.*

*Orl.* Who's there?

*Adam.* What! my young master?—O, my
   gentle master!
O, my sweet master! O you memory
Of old Sir Rowland! why, what make you here?
Why are you virtuous? why do people love you?
And wherefore are you gentle, strong, and
   valiant?
Why would you be so fond to overcome
The bony prizer of the humorous duke?
Your praise is come too swiftly home before
   you.
Know you not, master, to some kind of men
Their graces serve them but as enemies?
No more do yours; your virtues, gentle master,

Are sanctified and holy traitors to you.
O, what a world is this, when what is comely
Envenoms him that bears it!

*Orl.* Why, what's the matter?

*Adam.* O unhappy youth,
Come not within these doors; within this roof
The enemy of all your graces lives:
Your brother,—no, no brother; yet the son—
Yet not the son; I will not call him son—
Of him I was about to call his father,—
Hath heard your praises; and this night he
means
To burn the lodging where you used to lie.
And you within it: if he fail of that,
He will have other means to cut you off;
I overheard him and his practices.
This is no place; this house is but a butchery:
Abhor it, fear it, do not enter it.     [me go?

*Orl.* Why, whither, Adam, wouldst thou have

*Adam.* No matter whither, so you come not
here.

*Orl.* What, wouldst thou have me go and beg
my food?
Or with a base and boisterous sword enforce
A thievish living on the common road?
This I must do, or know not what to do:
Yet this I will not do, do how I can:
I rather will subject me to the malice
Of a diverted blood and bloody brother.

*Adam.* But do not so. I have five hundred
crowns,
The thrifty hire I sav'd under your father,
Which I did store to be my foster-nurse
When service should in my old limbs lie lame,
And unregarded age in corners thrown;
Take that: and He that doth the ravens feed,
Yea, providently caters for the sparrow,
Be comfort to my age! Here is the gold;
All this I give you. Let me be your servant;
Though I look old, yet I am strong and lusty:
For in my youth I never did apply
Hot and rebellious liquors in my blood;
Nor did not with unbashful forehead woo
The means of weakness and debility;
Therefore my age is as a lusty winter,
Frosty, but kindly: let me go with you;
I'll do the service of a younger man
In all your business and necessities.     [pears

*Orl.* O good old man; how well in thee ap-
The constant service of the antique world,
When service sweat for duty, not for meed!
Thou art not for the fashion of these times,
Where none will sweat but for promotion;
And having that, do choke their service up
Even with the having: it is not so with thee.
But, poor old man, thou prun'st a rotten tree.
That cannot so much as a blossom yield
In lieu of all thy pains and husbandry:
But come thy ways, we'll go along together;
And ere we have thy youthful wages spent
We'll light upon some settled low content.

*Adam.* Master, go on; and I will follow thee
To the last gasp, with truth and loyalty.—
From seventeen years till now almost fourscore

Here lived I, but now live here no more.
At seventeen years many their fortunes seek;
But at fourscore it is too late a week:
Yet fortune cannot recompense me better
Than to die well, and not my master's debtor.
                              [*Exeunt.*

SCENE IV.—*The Forest of Arden.*

*Enter* ROSALIND *in boy's clothes,* CELIA
*dressed like a shepherdess, and* TOUCHSTONE

*Ros.* O Jupiter! how weary are my spirits!

*Touch.* I care not for my spirits if my legs
were not weary.

*Ros.* I could find in my heart to disgrace my
man's apparel, and to cry like a woman: but I
must comfort the weaker vessel, as doublet and
hose ought to show itself courageous to petticoat: therefore, courage, good Aliena.

*Cel.* I pray you, bear with me; I can go no
farther.

*Touch.* For my part, I had rather bear with
you than bear you: yet I should bear no cross if
I did bear you; for, I think, you have no money
in your purse.

*Ros.* Well, this is the forest of Arden.

*Touch.* Ay, now am I in Arden: the more
fool I; when I was at home I was in a better
place; but travellers must be content.

*Ros.* Ay, be so, good Touchstone.—Look
you, who comes here? a young man and an old
in solemn talk.

*Enter* CORIN *and* SILVIUS.

*Cor.* That is the way to make her scorn you
     still.                              [love her!

*Sil.* O Corin, that thou knew'st how I do

*Cor.* I partly guess; for I have lov'd ere now.

*Sil.* No, Corin, being old, thou canst not
     guess;
Though in thy youth thou wast as true a lover
As ever sigh'd upon a midnight pillow:
But if thy love were ever like to mine,—
As sure I think did never man love so,—
How many actions most ridiculous
Hast thou been drawn to by thy fantasy?

*Cor.* Into a thousand that I have forgotten.

*Sil.* O, thou didst then ne'er love so heartily:
If thou remember'st not the slightest folly
That ever love did make thee run into,
Thou hast not lov'd:
Or if thou hast not sat as I do now,
Wearying thy hearer in thy mistress' praise,
Thou hast not lov'd:
Or if thou hast not broke from company
Abruptly, as my passion now makes me,
Thou hast not lov'd: O Phebe, Phebe, Phebe!
                              [*Exit* SILVIUS.

*Ros.* Alas, poor shepherd! searching of thy
     wound,
I have by hard adventure found mine own,

*Touch.* And I mine. I remember, when I was
in love I broke my sword upon a stone, and bid
him take that for coming a-night to Jane Smile:

and I remember the kissing of her batlet, and the cow's dugs that her pretty chapp'd hands had milk'd: and I remember the wooing of a peascod instead of her; from whom I took two cods, and, giving her them again, said with weeping tears, *Wear these for my sake.* We that are true lovers run into strange capers; but as all is mortal in nature, so is all nature in love mortal in folly.

*Ros.* Thou speak'st wiser than thou art 'ware of.

*Touch.* Nay, I shall ne'er be 'ware of mine own wit till I break my shins against it.

*Ros.* Jove, Jove! this shepherd's passion Is much upon my fashion.

*Touch.* And mine: but it grows something stale with me.

*Cel.* I pray you, one of you question yond man If he for gold will give us any food: I faint almost to death.

*Touch.* Holla, you clown!

*Ros.* Peace, fool; he's not thy kinsman.

*Cor.* Who calls?

*Touch.* Your betters, sir.

*Cor.* Else are they very wretched.

*Ros.* Peace, I say.— Good even to you, friend.

*Cor.* And to you, gentle sir, and to you all.

*Ros.* I pr'ythee, shepherd, if that love or gold Can in this desert place buy entertainment, Bring us where we may rest ourselves and feed: Here's a young maid with travel much oppress'd, And faints for succour.

*Cor.* Fair, sir, I pity her, And wish, for her sake more than for mine own, My fortunes were more able to relieve her: But I am shepherd to another man, And do not shear the fleeces that I graze: My master is of churlish disposition, And little recks to find the way to heaven By doing deeds of hospitality: Besides, his cote, his flocks, and bounds of feed Are now on sale; and at our sheepcote now, By reason of his absence, there is nothing That you will feed on; but what is, come see, And in my voice most welcome shall you be.

*Ros.* What is he that shall buy his flock and pasture?

*Cor.* That young swain that you saw here but erewhile, That little cares for buying anything.

*Ros.* I pray thee, if it stand with honesty, Buy thou the cottage, pasture, and the flock, And thou shalt have to pay for it of us.

*Cel.* And we will mend thy wages. I like this place, And willingly could waste my time in it.

*Cor.* Assuredly the thing is to be sold: Go with me: if you like, upon report, The soil, the profit, and this kind of life, I will your very faithful feeder be, And buy it with your gold right suddenly.

[*Exeunt.*

SCENE V.—*Another part of the Forest.*

*Enter* AMIENS, JAQUES, *and others.*

SONG.

*Ami.*　Under the greenwood tree,
　　Who loves to lie with me,
　　And tune his merry note
　　Unto the sweet bird's throat,
Come hither, come hither, come hither;
　　Here shall he see
　　No enemy.
But winter and rough weather.

*Jaq.* More, more, I pr'ythee, more.

*Ami.* It will make you melancholy, Monsieur Jaques.

*Jaq.* I thank it. More, I pr'ythee, more. I can suck melancholy out of a song, as a weasel sucks eggs. More, I pr'ythee, more.

*Ami.* My voice is ragged; I know I cannot please you.

*Jaq.* I do not desire you to please me, I do desire you to sing. Come, more: another stanza: call you them stanzas?

*Ami.* What you will, Monsieur Jaques.

*Jaq.* Nay, I care not for their names; they owe me nothing. Will you sing?　　[myself.

*Ami.* More at your request than to please

*Jaq.* Well then, if ever I thank any man, I'll thank you: but that they call compliment is like the encounter of two dog-apes; and when a man thanks me heartily, methinks I have given him a penny, and he renders me the beggarly thanks. Come, sing; and you that will not, hold your tongues.

*Ami.* Well, I'll end the song.—Sirs, cover the while: the duke will drink under this tree: —he hath been all this day to look you.

*Jaq.* And I have been all this day to avoid him. He is too disputable for my company: I think of as many matters as he; but I give heaven thanks, and make no boast of them. Come, warble, come.

SONG.

Who doth ambition shun, [*All together*
And loves to live i' the sun,　　*here.*
Seeking the food he eats,
And pleas'd with what he gets,
Come hither, come hither, come hither;
　　Here shall he see
　　No enemy,
But winter and rough weather.

*Jaq.* I'll give you a verse to this note, that I made yesterday in despite of my invention.

*Ami.* And I'll sing it.

*Jaq.* Thus it goes:

If it do come to pass
That any man turn ass,
Leaving his wealth and ease
A stubborn will to please,
Ducdame, ducdame, ducdame;
　　Here shall he see
　　Gross fools as he,
An if he will come to Ami.

*Ami.* What's that *ducdame?*

*Jaq.* 'Tis a Greek invocation, to call fools into a circle. I'll go sleep, if I can; if I cannot, I'll rail against all the first-born of Egypt.

*Ami.* And I'll go seek the duke; his banquet is prepared. [*Exeunt severally.*

SCENE VI.—*Another part of the Forest.*

*Enter* ORLANDO *and* ADAM.

*Adam.* Dear master, I can go no farther: O, I die for food! Here lie I down, and measure out my grave. Farewell, kind master.

*Orl.* Why, how now, Adam! no greater heart in thee? Live a little; comfort a little; cheer thyself a little. If this uncouth forest yield anything savage, I will either be food for it or bring it for food to thee. Thy conceit is nearer death than thy powers. For my sake be comfortable: hold death awhile at the arm's end: I will here be with thee presently; and if I bring thee not something to eat, I'll give thee leave to die: but if thou diest before I come, thou art a mocker of my labour. Well said! thou look'st cheerily. and I'll be with thee quickly.—Yet thou liest in the bleak air: come, I will bear thee to some shelter; and thou shalt not die for lack of a dinner if there live anything in this desert. Cheerily, good Adam! [*Exeunt.*

SCENE VII.—*Another part of the Forest.*
*A Table set.*

*Enter* DUKE *Senior,* AMIENS, *and others.*

*Duke S.* I think he be transform'd into a beast;
For I can nowhere find him like a man.

1 *Lord.* My lord, he is but even now gone hence;
Here was he merry, hearing of a song.

*Duke S.* If he, compact of jars, grow musical,
We shall have shortly discord in the spheres.
Go, seek him; tell him I would speak with him.

1 *Lord.* He saves my labour by his own approach.

*Enter* JAQUES.

*Duke S.* Why, how now, monsieur! what a life is this,
That your poor friends must woo your company?
What! you look merrily.

*Jaq.* A fool, a fool!—I met a fool i' the forest,
A motley fool;—a miserable world!—
As I do live by food, I met a fool,
Who laid him down and bask'd him in the sun,
And rail'd on Lady Fortune in good terms,
In good set terms,—and yet a motley fool.
*Good-morrow, fool,* quoth I: *No, sir,* quoth he,
*Call me not fool till heaven hath sent me fortune.*
And then he drew a dial from his poke,
And, looking on it with lack-lustre eye,
Says very wisely, *It is ten o'clock:*
*Thus may we see,* quoth he, *how the world wags.*
'Tis but an hour ago since it was nine;

*And after one hour more 'twill be eleven;*
*And so, from hour to hour, we ripe and ripe,*
*And then, from hour to hour, we rot and rot;*
*And thereby hangs a tale.* When I did hear
The motley fool thus moral on the time,
My lungs began to crow like chanticleer,
That fools should be so deep contemplative;
And I did laugh, sans intermission,
An hour by his dial.—O noble fool!
A worthy fool!—Motley's the only wear.

*Duke S.* What fool is this? [courtier,

*Jaq.* O worthy fool!—One that hath been a
And says, if ladies be but young and fair,
They have the gift to know it: and in his brain,—
Which is as dry as the remainder biscuit
After a voyage,—he hath strange places cramm'd
With observation, the which he vents
In mangled forms.—O that I were a fool!
I am ambitious for a motley coat.

*Duke S.* Thou shalt have one.

*Jaq.*                It is my only suit,
Provided that you weed your better judgments
Of all opinion that grows rank in them
That I am wise. I must have liberty
Withal, as large a charter as the wind,
To blow on whom I please; for so fools have:
And they that are most galled with my folly,
They most must laugh. And why, sir, must they so?
The *why* is plain as way to parish church:
He that a fool doth very wisely hit
Doth very foolishly, although he smart,
Not to seem senseless of the bob; if not,
The wise man's folly is anatomiz'd
Even by the squandering glances of the fool.
Invest me in my motley; give me leave
To speak my mind, and I will through and through
Cleanse the foul body of the infected world,
If they will patiently receive my medicine.

*Duke S.* Fie on thee! I can tell what thou wouldst do.

*Jaq.* What, for a counter, would I do but good?

*Duke S.* Most mischievous foul sin, in chiding sin:
For thou thyself hast been a libertine,
As sensual as the brutish sting itself;
And all the embossed sores and headed evils
That thou with license of free foot hast caught,
Wouldst thou disgorge into the general world.

*Jaq.* Why, who cries out on pride,
That can therein tax any private party?
Doth it not flow as hugely as the sea,
Till that the weary very means do ebb?
What woman in the city do I name
When that I say, The city-woman bears
The cost of princes on unworthy shoulders?
Who can come in and say that I mean her,
When such a one as she, such is her neighbour?
Or what is he of basest function,
That says his bravery is not on my cost,—
Thinking that I mean him,—but therein suits

His folly to the metal of my speech?
There then; how then? what then? Let me see
　　wherein
My tongue hath wrong'd him: if it do him
　　right,
Then he hath wrong'd himself; if he be free,
Why then, my taxing like a wild goose flies,
Unclaim'd of any man.—But who comes here?

*Enter* ORLANDO, *with his sword drawn.*

*Orl.* Forbear, and eat no more.
*Jaq.*　　　　　　Why, I have eat none yet.
*Orl.* Nor shalt not, till necessity be serv'd.
*Jaq.* Of what kind should this cock come of?
*Duke S.* Art thou thus bolden'd, man, by
　　thy distress:
Or else a rude despiser of good manners,
That in civility thou seem'st so empty? [point
*Orl.* You touch'd my vein at first: the thorny
Of bare distress hath ta'en from me the show
Of smooth civility: yet am I inland bred,
And know some nurture. But forbear, I say;
He dies that touches any of this fruit
Till I and my affairs are answered.
*Jaq.* An you will not be answered with
　　reason,
I must die.
*Duke S.* What would you have? your gentle-
　　ness shall force
More than your force move us to gentleness.
*Orl.* I almost die for food, and let me have it.
*Duke S.* Sit down and feed, and welcome to
　　our table.　　　　　　　　　　　[you:
*Orl.* Speak you so gently? Pardon me, I pray
I thought that all things had been savage here;
And therefore put I on the countenance
Of stern commandment. But whate'er you are
That in this desert inaccessible,
Under the shade of melancholy boughs,
Lose and neglect the creeping hours of time;
If ever you have look'd on better days,
If ever been where bells have knoll'd to church,
If ever sat at any good man's feast,
If ever from your eyelids wip'd a tear,
And know what 'tis to pity and be pitied,
Let gentleness my strong enforcement be:
In the which hope I blush, and hide my sword.
*Duke S.* True is it that we have seen better
　　days,
And have with holy bell been knoll'd to
　　church,
And sat at good men's feasts, and wip'd our
　　eyes
Of drops that sacred pity hath engender'd:
And therefore sit you down in gentleness,
And take upon command what help we have,
That to your wanting may be minister'd.
*Orl.* Then but forbear your food a little while
Whiles, like a doe, I go to find my fawn,
And give it food. There is an old poor man,
Who after me hath many a weary step
Limp'd in pure love: till he be first suffic'd,—
Oppress'd with two weak evils, age and hunger,—
I will not touch a bit.

*Duke S.*　　　　　Go find him out,
And we will nothing waste till you return.
*Orl.* I thank ye; and be bless'd for your good
　　comfort!　　　　　　　　　　　　[*Exit.*
*Duke S.* Thou seest we are not all alone un-
　　happy;
This wide and universal theatre
Presents more woeful pageants than the scene
Wherein we play in.
*Jaq.*　　　　　All the world's a stage,
And all the men and women merely players;
They have their exits and their entrances;
And one man in his time plays many parts,
His acts being seven ages. At first the infant,
Mewling and puking in the nurse's arms;
When the whining school-boy, with his satchel
And shining morning face, creeping like snail
Unwillingly to school. And then the lover,
Sighing like furnace, with a woeful ballad
Made to his mistress' eyebrow. Then a soldier,
Full of strange oaths, and bearded like the
　　pard,
Jealous in honour, sudden and quick in quarrel,
Seeking the bubble reputation
Even in the cannon's mouth. And then the
　　justice,
In fair round belly with good capon lin'd,
With eyes severe and beard of formal cut,
Full of wise saws and modern instances;
And so he plays his part. The sixth age shifts
Into the lean and slipper'd pantaloon,
With spectacles on nose and pouch on side;
His youthful hose, well sav'd, a world too wide
For his shrunk shank; and his big manly voice,
Turning again toward childish treble, pipes
And whistles in his sound. Last scene of all,
That ends this strange eventful history,
Is second childishness and mere oblivion;
Sans teeth, sans eyes, sans taste, sans every-
　　thing.

*Re-enter* ORLANDO *with* ADAM.

*Duke S.* Welcome. Set down your venerable
　　burden,
And let him feed.
*Orl.*　　　　　I thank you most for him.
*Adam.* So had you need:
I scarce can speak to thank you for myself.
*Duke S.* Welcome, fall to: I will not trouble
　　you
As yet, to question you about your fortunes.—
Give us some music; and, good cousin, sing.

AMIENS *sings.*

SONG.

I.

Blow, blow, thou winter wind,
Thou art not so unkind
　　As man's ingratitude;
Thy tooth is not so keen,
Because thou art not seen,
　　Although thy breath be rude.
Heigh-ho! sing, heigh-ho! unto the green holly:

Most friendship is feigning, most loving mere folly:
    Then, heigh-ho, the holly!
        This life is most jolly.

#### II.

Freeze, freeze, thou bitter sky,
That dost not bite so nigh
    As benefits forgot:
Though thou the waters warp,
Thy sting is not so sharp
    As friend remember'd not.
Heigh-ho! sing, heigh-ho! &c.

*Duke S.* If that you were the good Sir Row-
    land's son,—
As you have whisper'd faithfully you were,
And as mine eye doth his effigies witness
Mot truly limn'd and living in your face,—
Be truly welcome hither: I am the duke
That lov'd your father. The residue of your
    fortune,
Go to my cave and tell me.—Good old man,
Thou art right welcome as thy master is;
Support him by the arm.—Give me your hand,
And let me all your fortunes understand.
                                        [*Exeunt.*

## ACT III.

### SCENE I.—*A Room in the Palace.*

*Enter* DUKE FREDERICK, OLIVER, Lords,
    *and* Attendants.

*Duke F.* Not see him since? Sir, sir, that
    cannot be:
But were I not the better part made mercy,
I should not seek an absent argument
Of my revenge, thou present. But look to it:
Find out thy brother wheresoe'er he is:
Seek him with candle; bring him dead or living
Within this twelvemonth, or turn thou no more
To seek a living in our territory.
Thy lands, and all things that thou dost call
    thine
Worth seizure, do we seize into our hands,
Till thou canst quit thee by thy brother's
    mouth
Of what we think against thee.

*Oli.* O that your highness knew my heart in
    this!
I never lov'd my brother in my life.

*Duke F.* More villain thou.—Well, push
    him out of doors,
And let my officers of such a nature
Make an extent upon his house and lands:
Do this expediently, and turn him going.
                                        [*Exeunt.*

### SCENE II.—*The Forest of Arden.*

*Enter* ORLANDO, *with a paper.*

*Orl.* Hang there, my verse, in witness of my
    love,                                [survey
And thou, thrice-crowned queen of night,
With thy chaste eye, from thy pale sphere
    above,                               [sway.
Thy huntress' name, that my full life doth

O Rosalind! these trees shall be my books,
    And in their barks my thoughts I'll character,
That every eye which in this forest looks
    Shall see thy virtue witness'd everywhere.
Run, run, Orlando; carve on every tree,
The fair, the chaste, and unexpressive she.
                                        [*Exit.*

*Enter* CORIN *and* TOUCHSTONE.

*Cor.* And how like you this shepherd's life,
Master Touchstone?

*Touch.* Truly, shepherd, in respect of itself,
it is a good life; but in respect that it is a shepherd's life, it is naught. In respect that it is
solitary, I like it very well; but in respect that
it is private, it is a very vile life. Now in respect it is in the fields, it pleaseth me well;
but in respect it is not in the court, it is tedious.
As it is a spare life, look you, it fits my humour
well; but as there is no more plenty in it, it goes
much against my stomach. Hast any philosophy in thee, shepherd?

*Cor.* No more but that I know the more one
sickens the worse at ease he is; and that he that
wants money, means, and content, is without
three good friends; that the property of rain is
to wet, and fire to burn; that good pasture
makes fat sheep; and that a great cause of the
night is lack of the sun; that he that hath
learned no wit by nature nor art may complain
of good breeding, or comes of a very dull kindred.

*Touch.* Such a one is a natural philosopher.
Wast ever in court, shepherd?

*Cor.* No, truly.

*Touch.* Then thou art damned.

*Cor.* Nay, I hope,—

*Touch.* Truly, thou art·damned; like an ill-
roasted egg, all on one side.

*Cor.* For not being at court? Your reason.

*Touch.* Why, if thou never wast at court
thou never saw'st good manners; if thou never
saw'st good manners, then thy manners must
be wicked; and wickedness is sin, and sin is
damnation. Thou art in a parlous state, shepherd.

*Cor.* Not a whit, Touchstone: those that are
good manners at the court are as ridiculous in
the country as the behaviour of the country is
most mockable at the court. You told me you
salute not at the court, but you kiss your
hands; that courtesy would be uncleanly if
courtiers were shepherds.

*Touch.* Instance, briefly; come, instance.

*Cor.* Why, we are still handling our ewes;
and their fells, you know, are greasy.

*Touch.* Why, do not your courtier's hands
sweat? and is not the grease of a mutton as
wholesome as the sweat of a man? Shallow,
shallow: a better instance, I say; come.

*Cor.* Besides, our hands are hard.

*Touch.* Your lips will feel them the sooner.
Shallow again: a more sounder instance; come.

*Cor.* And they are often tarred over with

the surgery of our sheep, and would you have us kiss tar? The courtier's hands are perfumed with civet.

*Touch.* Most shallow man! thou wormsmeat, in respect of a good piece of flesh, indeed!— Learn of the wise, and perpend: civet is of a baser birth than tar,—the very uncleanly flux of a cat. Mend the instance, shepherd.

*Cor.* You have too courtly a wit for me: I'll rest.

*Touch.* Wilt thou rest damned? God help thee, shallow man! God make incision in thee! thou art raw.

*Cor.* Sir, I am a true labourer: I earn that I eat, get that I wear; owe no man hate, envy no man's happiness; glad of other men's good, content with my harm; and the greatest of my pride is, to see my ewes graze and my lambs suck.

*Touch.* That is another simple sin in you; to bring the ewes and the rams together, and to offer to get your living by the copulation of cattle: to be bawd to a bell-wether; and to betray a she-lamb of a twelvemonth to a crooked-pated, old, cuckoldly ram, out of all reasonable match. If thou be'st not damned for this, the devil himself will have no shepherds; I cannot see else how thou shouldst 'scape.

*Cor.* Here comes young Master Ganymede, my new mistress's brother.

*Enter* ROSALIND, *reading a paper.*

*Ros.*   From the east to western Ind,
        No jewel is like Rosalind.
        Her worth, being mounted on the wind,
        Through all the world bears Rosalind.
        All the pictures fairest lin'd
        Are but black to Rosalind.
        Let no face be kept in mind
        But the fair of Rosalind.

*Touch.* I'll rhyme you so eight years together, dinners, and suppers, and sleeping hours excepted: It is the right butter-woman's rank to market.

*Ros.* Out, fool!

*Touch.* For a taste:—

        If a hart do lack a hind,
        Let him seek out Rosalind.
        If the cat will after kind,
        So, be sure, will Rosalind.
        Winter garments must be lin'd,
        So must slender Rosalind.
        They that reap must sheaf and bind, —
        Then to cart with Rosalind.
        Sweetest nut hath sourest rind,
        Such a nut is Rosalind.
        He that sweetest rose will find
        Must find love's prick, and Rosalind.

This is the very false gallop of verses: why do you infect yourself with them?

*Ros.* Peace, you dull fool! I found them on a tree.

*Touch.* Truly, the tree yields bad fruit.

*Ros.* I'll graff it with you, and then I shall graff it with a medlar: then it will be the earliest fruit in the country: for you'll be rotten ere you be half ripe, and that's the right virtue of the medlar.

*Touch.* You have said; but whether wisely or no, let the forest judge.

*Enter* CELIA, *reading a paper.*

*Ros.* Peace!
Here comes my sister, reading: stand aside!

*Cel.*   Why should this a desert be?
            For it is unpeopled? No;
        Tongues I'll hang on every tree,
            That shall civil sayings show:
        Some, how brief the life of man
            Runs his erring pilgrimage,
        That the stretching of a span
            Buckles in his sum of age.
        Some, of violated vows
            'Twixt the souls of friend and friend;
        But upon the fairest boughs,
            Or at every sentence' end,
        Will I Rosalinda write,
            Teaching all that read to know
        The quintessence of every sprite
            Heaven would in little show.
        Therefore heaven nature charg'd
            That one body should be fill'd
        With all graces wide enlarg'd:
            Nature presently distill'd
        Helen's cheek, but not her heart;
            Cleopatra's majesty;
        Atalanta's better part;
            Sad Lucretia's modesty.
        Thus Rosalind of many parts
            By heavenly synod was devis'd,
        Of many faces, eyes, and hearts,
            To have the touches dearest priz'd.
        Heaven would that she these gifts should have,
        And I to live and die her slave.

*Ros.* O most gentle Jupiter!—what tedious homily of love have you wearied your parishioners withal, and never cried, *Have patience, Good people!*

*Cel.* How now! back, friends;—shepherd, go off a little:—go with him, sirrah.

*Touch.* Come, shepherd, let us make an honourable retreat; though not with bag and baggage, yet with scrip and scrippage.
[*Exeunt* CORIN *and* TOUCH.

*Cel.* Didst thou hear these verses?

*Ros.* O yes, I heard them all, and more too; for some of them had in them more feet than the verses would bear.

*Cel.* That's no matter; the feet might bear the verses.

*Ros.* Ay, but the feet were lame, and could not bear themselves without the verse, and therefore stood lamely in the verse.

*Cel.* But didst thou hear without wondering How thy name should be hanged and carved upon these trees?

*Ros.* I was seven of the nine days out of the wonder before you came; for look here what I found on a palm tree: I was never so berhymed since Pythagoras' time, that I was an Irish rat, which I can hardly remember.

*Cel.* Trow you who hath done this?

*Ros.* Is it a man?

*Cel.* And a chain, that you once wore, about his neck. Change you colour?

*Ros.* I pray thee, who?

*Cel.* O lord, lord! it is a hard matter for friends to meet; but mountains may be removed with earthquakes, and so encounter.

*Ros.* Nay, but who is it?

*Cel.* Is it possible?

*Ros.* Nay, I pr'ythee now, with most petitionary vehemence, tell me who it is.

*Cel.* O wonderful, wonderful, and most wonderful wonderful! and yet again wonderful, and after that, out of all whooping!

*Ros.* Good my complexion! dost thou think, though I am caparisoned like a man, I have a doublet and hose in my disposition? One inch of delay more is a South-sea of discovery. I pr'ythee, tell me, who is it? quickly, and speak apace. I would thou couldst stammer, that mightst pour this concealed man out of thy mouth, as wine comes out of a narrow-mouthed bottle; either too much at once or none at all. I pr'ythee take the cork out of thy mouth, that I may drink thy tidings.

*Cel.* So you may put a man in your belly.

*Ros.* Is he of God's making? What manner of man? Is his head worth a hat or his chin worth a beard?

*Cel.* Nay, he hath but a little beard.

*Ros.* Why, God will send more if the man will be thankful: let me stay the growth of his beard if thou delay me not the knowledge of his chin.

*Cel.* It is young Orlando, that tripped up the wrestler's heels and your heart both in an instant.

*Ros.* Nay, but the devil take mocking: speak sad brow and true maid.

*Cel.* I' faith, coz, 'tis he.

*Ros.* Orlando?

*Cel.* Orlando.

*Ros.* Alas the day! what shall I do with my doublet and hose?—What did he when thou saw'st him? What said he? How look'd he? Wherein went he? What makes he here? Did he ask for me? Where remains he? How parted he with thee? and when shalt thou see him again? Answer me in one word.

*Cel.* You must borrow me Gargantua's mouth first: 'tis a word too great for any mouth of this age's size. To say ay and no to these particulars is more than to answer in a catechism.

*Ros.* But doth he know that I am in this forest, and in man's apparel? Looks he as freshly as he did the day he wrestled?

*Cel.* It is as easy to count atomies as to resolve the propositions of a lover:—but take a taste of my finding him, and relish it with good observance. I found him under a tree, like a dropped acorn.

*Ros.* It may well be called Jove's tree, when it drops forth such fruit.

*Cel.* Give me audience, good madam.

*Ros.* Proceed.

*Cel.* There lay he, stretched along like a wounded knight.

*Ros.* Though it be pity to see such a sight, it well becomes the ground.

*Cel.* Cry, holla! to thy tongue, I pr'ythee; it curvets unseasonably. He was furnished like a hunter.

*Ros.* O, ominous! he comes to kill my heart.

*Cel.* I would sing my song without a burden: thou bring'st me out of tune.

*Ros.* Do you not know I am a woman? when I think, I must speak. Sweet, say on.

*Cel.* You bring me out.—Soft! comes he not here?

*Ros.* 'Tis he: slink by, and note him.

[CELIA *and* ROSALIND *retire.*

*Enter* ORLANDO *and* JAQUES.

*Jaq.* I thank you for your company; but, good faith, I had as lief have been myself alone.

*Orl.* And so had I; but yet, for fashion's sake, I thank you too for your society.    [as we can.

*Jaq.* God be with you: let's meet as little

*Orl.* I do desire we may be better strangers.

*Jaq.* I pray you, mar no more trees with writing love-songs in their barks.

*Orl.* I pray you, mar no more of my verses with reading them ill-favouredly.

*Jaq.* Rosalind is your love's name?

*Orl.* Yes, just.

*Jaq.* I do not like her name.

*Orl.* There was no thought of pleasing you when she was christened.

*Jaq.* What stature is she of?

*Orl.* Just as high as my heart.

*Jaq.* You are full of pretty answers. Have you not been acquainted with goldsmiths' wives, and conned them out of rings?

*Orl.* Not so; but I answer you right painted cloth, from whence you have studied your questions.

*Jaq.* You have a nimble wit: I think it was made of Atalanta's heels. Will you sit down with me? and we two will rail against our mistress the world, and all our misery.

*Orl.* I will chide no breather in the world but myself, against whom I know most faults.

*Jaq.* The worst fault you have is to be in love.

*Orl.* 'Tis a fault I will not change for your best virtue. I am weary of you.

*Jaq.* By my troth, I was seeking for a fool when I found you.

*Orl.* He is drowned in the brook; look but in, and you shall see him.

*Jaq.* There I shall see mine own figure.

*Orl.* Which I take to be either a fool or a cipher.

*Jaq.* I'll tarry no longer with you: farewell, good Signior Love.

*Orl.* I am glad of your departure: adieu, good Monsieur Melancholy.

[*Exit* JAQ.—CEL. *and* ROS. *come forward.*

*Ros.* I will speak to him like a saucy lacquey, and under that habit play the knave with him.—Do you hear, forester?

*Orl.* Very well. what would you?

*Ros.* I pray you, what is't o'clock?

*Orl.* You should ask me what time o' day; there's no clock in the forest.

*Ros.* Then there's no true lover in the forest, else sighing every minute and groaning every hour would detect the lazy foot of time as well as a clock.

*Orl.* And why not the swift foot of time? had not that been as proper?

*Ros.* By no means, sir. Time travels in divers paces with divers persons. I will tell you who time ambles withal, who time trots withal, who time gallops withal, and who he stands still withal.

*Orl.* I pr'ythee, who doth he trot withal?

*Ros.* Marry, he trots hard with a young maid between the contract of her marriage and the day it is solemnized; if the interim be but a se'nnight, time's pace is so hard that it seems the length of seven years.

*Orl.* Who ambles time withal?

*Ros.* With a priest that lacks Latin and a rich man that hath not the gout: for the one sleeps easily, because he cannot study; and the other lives merrily, because he feels no pain; the one lacking the burden of lean and wasteful learning; the other knowing no burden of heavy tedious penury. These time ambles withal.

*Orl.* Who doth he gallop withal?

*Ros.* With a thief to the gallows; for though he go as softly as foot can fall, he thinks himself too soon there.

*Orl.* Who stays it still withal?

*Ros.* With lawyers in the vacation; for they sleep between term and term, and then they perceive not how time moves.

*Orl.* Where dwell you, pretty youth?

*Ros.* With this shepherdess, my sister; here in the skirts of the forest, like fringe upon a petticoat.

*Orl.* Are you native of this place?

*Ros.* As the coney, that you see dwell where she is kindled.

*Orl.* Your accent is something finer than you could purchase in so removed a dwelling.

*Ros.* I have been told so of many: but indeed an old religious uncle of mine taught me to speak, who was in his youth an inland man; one that knew courtship too well, for there he fell in love. I have heard him read many lectures against it; and I thank God I am not a woman, to be touched with so many giddy offences as he hath generally taxed their whole sex withal.

*Orl.* Can you remember any of the principal evils that he laid to the charge of women?

*Ros.* There were none principal; they were all like one another as halfpence are; every one fault seeming monstrous till his fellow fault came to match it.

*Orl.* I pr'ythee, recount some of them.

*Ros.* No; I will not cast away my physic but on those that are sick. There is a man haunts the forest that abuses our young plants with carving Rosalind on their barks; hangs odes upon hawthorns, and elegies on brambles, all, forsooth, deifying the name of Rosalind. if I could meet that fancymonger I would give him some good counsel, for he seems to have the quotidian of love upon him.

*Orl.* I am he that is so love-shaked. I pray you, tell me your remedy.

*Ros.* There is none of my uncle's marks upon you: he taught me how to know a man in love; in which cage of rushes I am sure you are not prisoner.

*Orl.* What were his marks?

*Ros.* A lean cheek; which you have not: a blue eye and sunken; which you have not: an unquestionable spirit; which you have not: a beard neglected; which you have not: but I pardon you for that; for simply your having in beard is a younger brother's revenue:—then your hose should be ungartered, your bonnet unbanded, your sleeve unbuttoned, your shoe untied, and everything about you demonstrating a careless desolation. But you are no such man; you are rather point-device in your accoutrements; as loving yourself than seeming the lover of any other.

*Orl.* Fair youth, I would I could make thee believe I love.

*Ros.* Me believe it! you may as soon make her that you love believe it; which, I warrant, she is apter to do than to confess she does: that is one of the points in the which women still give the lie to their consciences. But, in good sooth, are you he that hangs the verses on the trees, wherein Rosalind is so admired?

*Orl.* I swear to thee, youth, by the white hand of Rosalind, I am that he, that unfortunate he.

*Ros.* But are you so much in love as your rhymes speak?

*Orl.* Neither rhyme nor reason can express how much.

*Ros.* Love is merely a madness; and, I tell you, deserves as well a dark house and a whip as madmen do: and the reason why they are not so punished and cured is, that the lunacy is so ordinary that the whippers are in love too. Yet I profess curing it by counsel.

*Orl.* Did you ever cure any so?

*Ros.* Yes, one; and in this manner. He was to imagine me his love, his mistress; and I set him every day to woo me: at which time would I, being but a moonish youth, grieve, be effeminate, changeable, longing, and liking; proud, fantastical, apish, shallow, inconstant, full of tears, full of smiles; for every passion something, and for no passion truly anything, as boys and women are for the most part cattle of this colour: would now like him, now loath him; then entertain him, then forswear him; now weep for him, then spit at him; that I drave my suitor from his mad humour of love to a loving humour of madness; which was, to forswear the full stream of the world, and to live in a nook nearly monastic. And thus I cured him; and this way will I take upon me to wash your liver as clean as a sound sheep's heart, that there shall not be one spot of love in 't.

*Orl.* I would not be cured, youth.

*Ros.* I would cure you if you would but call me Rosalind, and come every day to my cote and woo me.

*Orl.* Now, by the faith of my love, I will. tell me where it is.

*Ros.* Go with me to it, and I'll show it you: and, by the way, you shall tell me where in the forest you live. Will you go?

*Orl.* With all my heart, good youth.

*Ros.* Nay, you must call me Rosalind.— Come, sister, will you go?　　　　　[*Exeunt.*

SCENE III.—*Another part of the Forest.*

*Enter* TOUCHSTONE *and* AUDREY; JAQUES *at a distance observing them.*

*Touch.* Come apace, good Audrey; I will fetch up your goats, Audrey. And how, Audrey? am I the man yet? Doth my simple feature content you?

*Aud.* Your features! Lord warrant us! what features?

*Touch.* I am here with thee and thy goats, as the most capricious poet, honest Ovid, was among the Goths.

*Jaq.* O knowledge ill-inhabited! worse than Jove in a thatch'd house.　　　　　[*Aside.*

*Touch.* When a man's verses cannot be understood, nor a man's good wit seconded with the forward child understanding, it strikes a man more dead than a great reckoning in a little room.—Truly, I would the gods had made thee poetical.

*Aud.* I do not know what poetical is: is it honest in deed and word? is it a true thing?

*Touch.* No, truly: for the truest poetry is the most feigning; and lovers are given to poetry; and what they swear in poetry may be said, as lovers, they do feign.

*Aud.* Do you wish, then, that the gods had made me poetical?

*Touch.* I do, truly, for thou swear'st to me thou art honest; now, if thou wert a poet I might have some hope thou didst feign.

*Aud.* Would you not have me honest?

*Touch.* No, truly, unless thou wert hard-favoured; for honesty coupled to beauty is to have honey a sauce to sugar.

*Jaq.* A material fool!　　　　　[*Aside.*

*Aud.* Well, I am not fair; and therefore I pray the gods make me honest!

*Touch.* Truly, and to cast away honesty upon a foul slut were to put good meat into an unclean dish.

*Aud.* I am not a slut, though I thank the gods I am foul.

*Touch.* Well, praised be the gods for thy foulness! sluttishness may come hereafter. But be it as it may be, I will marry thee: and to that end I have been with Sir Oliver Martext, the vicar of the next village; who hath promised to meet me in this place of the forest, and to couple us.

*Jaq.* I would fain see this meeting.　[*Aside.*

*Aud.* Well, the gods give us joy!

*Touch.* Amen. A man may, if he were of a fearful heart, stagger in this attempt; for here we have no temple but the wood, no assembly but horn-beasts. But what though? Courage! As horns are odious, they are necessary. It is said,—Many a man knows no end of his goods: right; many a man has good horns and knows no end of them. Well, that is the dowry of his wife; 'tis none of his own getting. Horns? Ever to poor men alone?——No, no; the noblest deer hath them as huge as the rascal. Is the single man therefore blessed? No: as a walled town is more worthier than a village, so is the forehead of a married man more honourable than the bare brow of a bachelor: and by how much defence is better than no skill, by so much is a horn more precious than to want. Here comes Sir Oliver.

*Enter Sir* OLIVER MARTEXT.

Sir Oliver Martext, you are well met. Will you despatch us here under this tree, or shall we go with you to your chapel?　　　　　[woman?

*Sir Oli.* Is there none here to give the

*Touch.* I will not take her on gift of any man.

*Sir Oli.* Truly, she must be given, or the marriage is not lawful.

*Jaq.* [*Discovering himself.*] Proceed proceed; I'll give her.

*Touch.* Good even, good Master *What-ye-call 't:* how do you, sir? You are very well met: God 'ild you for your last company: I am very glad to see you:—even a toy in hand here, sir:—nay; pray be covered.

*Jaq.* Will you be married, motley?

*Touch.* As the ox hath his bow, sir, the horse his curb, and the falcon her bells, so man hath his desires; and as pigeons bill, so wedlock would be nibbling.

*Jaq.* And will you, being a man of your breeding, be married under a bush, like a beggar? Get you to church and have a good priest that can tell you what marriage is: this fellow will but join you together as they join wainscot: then one of you will prove a shrunk panel, and like green timber, warp, warp.

*Touch.* I am not in the mind but I were better to be married of him than of another: for he is not like to marry me well; and not being well married, it will be a good excuse for me hereafter to leave my wife.　　　　　[*Aside.*

*Jaq.* Go thou with me and let me counsel thee.

*Touch.* Come, sweet Audrey;
We must be married or we must live in bawdry.
Farewell, good master Oliver!—Not,—

O sweet Oliver,
O brave Oliver,
Leave me not behind thee;

But,—

Wind away,——
Begone I say,
I will not to wedding with thee.

[*Exeunt* JAQ., TOUCH., *and* AUD.
*Sir Oli.* 'Tis no matter; ne'er a fantastical
knave of them all shall flout me out of my calling. [*Exit.*

SCENE IV.—*Another part of the Forest. Before a
Cottage.*

*Enter* ROSALIND *and* CELIA.

*Ros.* Never talk to me; I will weep.
*Cel.* Do, I pr'ythee; but yet have the grace
to consider that tears do not become a man.
*Ros.* But have I not cause to weep?
*Cel.* As good cause as one would desire;
therefore weep.
*Ros.* His very hair is of the dissembling
colour.
*Cel.* Something browner than Judas's:
marry, his kisses are Judas's own children.
*Ros.* I' faith, his hair is of a good colour.
*Cel.* An excellent colour: your chestnut was
ever the only colour.
*Ros.* And his kissing is as full of sanctity as
the touch of holy bread.
*Cel.* He hath bought a pair of cast lips of
Diana: a nun of winter's sisterhood kisses not
more religiously; the very ice of chastity is in
them.
*Ros.* But why did he swear he would come
this morning, and comes not?
*Cel.* Nay, certainly, there is no truth in him.
*Ros.* Do you think so?
*Cel.* Yes; I think he is not a pickpurse nor a
horse-stealer; but for his verity in love, I do
think him as concave as a covered goblet or a
worm-eaten nut.
*Ros.* Not true in love? [in.
*Cel.* Yes, when he is in; but I think he is not
*Ros.* You have heard him swear downright
he was.
*Cel.* *Was* is not *is:* besides, the oath of a
lover is no stronger than the word of a tapster;
they are both the confirmers of false reckonings. He attends here in the forest on the duke,
your father.
*Ros.* I met the duke yesterday, and had
much question with him. He asked me of what
parentage I was; I told him, of as good as he; so
he laughed and let me go. But what talk we of
fathers when there is such a man as Orlando?
*Cel.* O, that's a brave man! he writes brave
verses, speaks brave words, swears brave oaths
and breaks them bravely, quite traverse,

athwart the heart of his lover; as a puny tilter,
that spurs his horse but on one side, breaks his
staff like a noble goose: but all's brave that
youth mounts and folly guides.—Who comes
here?

*Enter* CORIN.

*Cor.* Mistress and master, you have oft in-
quired
After the shepherd that complain'd of love,
Who you saw sitting by me on the turf,
Praising the proud disdainful shepherdess
That was his mistress.
*Cel.* Well, and what of him?
*Cor.* If you will see a pageant truly play'd,
Between the pale complexion of true love
And the red glow of scorn and proud disdain,
Go hence a little, and I shall conduct you,
If you will mark it.
*Ros.* O, come, let us remove:
The sight of lovers feedeth those in love.
Bring us unto this sight, and you shall say
I'll prove a busy actor in their play. [*Exeunt.*

SCENE V.—*Another part of the Forest.*

*Enter* SILVIUS *and* PHEBE.

*Sil.* Sweet Phebe, do not scorn me do not
Phebe:
Say that you love me not; but say not so
In bitterness. The common executioner,
Whose heart the accustom'd sight of death
makes hard,
Falls not the axe upon the humbled neck
But first begs pardon. Will you sterner be
Than he that dies and lives by bloody drops?

*Enter* ROSALIND, CELIA, *and* CORIN, *at a
distance.*

*Phe.* I would not be thy executioner:
I fly thee, for I would not injure thee.
Thou tell'st me there is murder in mine eye:
'Tis pretty, sure, and very probable,
That eyes,—that are the frail'st and softest
things,
Who shut their coward gates on atomies,—
Should be called tyrants, butchers, murderers!
Now I do frown on thee with all my heart;
And if mine eyes can wound, now let them kill
thee:
Now counterfeit to swoon; why, now fall down;
Or, if thou canst not, O, for shame, for shame,
Lie not, to say mine eyes are murderers.
Now show the wound mine eye hath made in
thee:
Scratch thee but with a pin, and there remains
Some scar of it; lean but upon a rush,
The cicatrice and capable impressure [eyes,
Thy palm some moment keeps, but now mine
Which I have darted at thee, hurt thee not;
Nor, I am sure, there is no force in eyes
That can do hurt.
*Sil.* O dear Phebe,
If ever,—as that ever may be near,—

You meet in some fresh cheek the power of
    fancy,
Then shall you know the wounds invisible
That love's keen arrows make.
    *Phe.*                     But till that time
Come not thou near me; and when that time
    comes
Afflict me with thy mocks, pity me not;
As till that time I shall not pity thee.
    *Ros.* [*Advancing.*] And why, I pray you?
    Who might be your mother,
That you insult, exult, and all at once,
Over the wretched? What though you have no
    beauty,—
As, by my faith, I see no more in you
Than without candle may go dark to bed,—
Must you be therefore proud and pitiless?
Why, what means this? Why do you look on
    me?
I see no more in you than in the ordinary
Of nature's sale-work:—Od's my little life,
I think she means to tangle my eyes too!—
No, faith, proud mistress, hope not after it;
'Tis not your inky brows, your black silk hair,
Your bugle eyeballs, nor your cheek of cream,
That can entame my spirits to your worship.—
You foolish shepherd, wherefore do you follow
    her,
Like foggy south, puffing with wind and rain?
You are a thousand times a properer man
Than she a woman. 'Tis such fools as you
That make the world full of ill-favour'd chil-
    dren:
'Tis not her glass, but you that flatters her;
And out of you she sees herself more proper
Than any of her lineaments can show her;—
But, mistress, know yourself; down on your
    knees,
And thank heaven, fasting, for a good man's
    love:
For I must tell you friendly in your ear,—
Sell when you can; you are not for all markets:
Cry the man mercy; love him; take his offer.
Foul is most foul, being foul to be a scoffer.
So take her to thee, shepherd;—fare you well.
    *Phe.* Sweet youth, I pray you chide a year
        together;
I had rather hear you chide than this man woo.
    *Ros.* He's fallen in love with her foulness,
and she'll fall in love with my anger. If it be so,
as fast as she answers thee with frowning looks,
I'll sauce her with bitter words.—Why look
you so upon me?
    *Phe* For no ill-will I bear you.
    *Ros.* I pray you, do not fall in love with me,
For I am falser than vows made in wine:
Besides, I like you not.—If you will know my
    house,
'Tis at the tuft of olives here hard by.—
Will you go, sister?—Shepherd, ply her hard.—
Come, sister.—Shepherdess, look on him better,
And be not proud; though all the world could
    see,
None could be so abus'd in sight as he.

Come to our flock.
                    [*Exeunt* Ros., Cel., *and* Cor.
    *Phe.* Dead shepherd! now I find thy saw of
        might;
*Who ever lov'd that lov'd not at first sight?*
    *Sil.* Sweet Phebe,—
    *Phe.*           Ha! what say'st thou, Silvius?
    *Sil.* Sweet Phebe, pity me.
    *Phe.* Why, I am sorry for thee, gentle Silvius.
    *Sil.* Wherever sorrow is, relief would be:
If you do sorrow at my grief in love,
By giving love, your sorrow and my grief
Were both extermin'd.                  [bourly?
    *Phe.* Thou hast my love: is not that neigh-
    *Sil.* I would have you.
    *Phe.*             Why, that were covetousness.
Silvius, the time was that I hated thee;
And yet it is not that I bear thee love:
But since that thou canst talk of love so well,
Thy company, which erst was irksome to me,
I will endure; and I'll employ thee too:
But do not look for further recompense
Than thine own gladness that thou art em-
    ploy'd.
    *Sil.* So holy and so perfect is my love,
And I in such a poverty of grace,
That I shall think it a most plenteous crop
To glean the broken ears after the man
That the main harvest reaps: lose now and then
A scatter'd smile, and that I'll live upon.
    *Phe.* Know'st thou the youth that spoke to
        me erewhile?
    *Sil.* Not very well; but I have met him oft;
And he hath bought the cottage and the bounds
That the old carlot once was master of. [him;
    *Phe.* Think not I love him, though I ask for
'Tis but a peevish boy:—yet he talks well;—
But what care I for words? yet words do well
When he that speaks them pleases those that
    hear.
It is a pretty youth:—not very pretty:—
But, sure, he's proud; and yet his pride be-
    comes him:
He'll make a proper man: the best thing in him
Is his complexion; and faster than his tongue
Did make offence, his eye did heal it up.
He is not tall; yet for his years he's tall;
His leg is but so-so; and yet 'tis well:
There was a pretty redness in his lip;
A little riper and more lusty red
Than that mix'd in his cheek; 'twas just the
    difference
Betwixt the constant red and mingled damask.
There be some women, Silvius, had they mark'd
    him
In parcels as I did, would have gone near
To fall in love with him: but, for my part,
I love him not, nor hate him not, and yet
I have more cause to hate him than to love
    him:
For what had he to do to chide at me?
He said mine eyes were black, and my hair
    black;
And, now I am remember'd, scorn'd at me:

I marvel why I answer'd not again
But that's all one; omittance is not quittance
I'll write to him a very taunting letter,
And thou shalt bear it; wilt thou, Silvius?

*Sil.* Phebe, with all my heart.

*Phe.*　　　　　　　I'll write it straight,
The matter's in my head and in my heart:
I will be bitter with him, and passing short:
Go with me, Silvius.　　　　　　　[*Exeunt.*

## ACT IV.

### Scene I.—*Forest of Arden.*

*Enter* Rosalind, Celia, *and* Jaques.

*Jaq.* I pr'ythee, pretty youth, let me be better acquainted with thee.

*Ros.* They say you are a melancholy fellow.

*Jaq.* I am so; I do love it better than laughing.

*Ros.* Those that are in extremity of either are abominable fellows, and betray themselves to every modern censure worse than drunkards.

*Jaq.* Why, 'tis good to be sad and say nothing.

*Ros.* Why, then, 'tis good to be a post.

*Jaq.* I have neither the scholar's melancholy, which is emulation; nor the musician's, which is fantastical; nor the courtier's, which is proud; nor the soldier's, which is ambitious; nor the lawyer's, which is politic; nor the lady's, which is nice; nor the lover's, which is all these: but it is a melancholy of mine own, compounded of many simples, extracted from many objects: and, indeed, the sundry contemplation of my travels, in which my often rumination wraps me in a most humorous sadness.

*Ros.* A traveller! By my faith, you have great reason to be sad: I fear you have sold your own land to see other men's; then, to have seen much, and to have nothing, is to have rich eyes and poor hands.

*Jaq.* Yes, I have gained my experience.

*Ros.* And your experience makes you sad: I had rather have a fool to make me merry than experience to make me sad; and to travel for it too.

*Enter* Orlando.

*Orl.* Good day, and happiness, dear Rosalind!

*Jaq.* Nay, then, God be wi' you, an you talk in blank verse.

*Ros.* Farewell, monsieur traveller: look you lisp and wear strange suits; disable all the benefits of your own country, be out of love with your nativity, and almost chide God for making you that countenance you are; or I will scarce think you have swam in a gondola. [*Exit* Jaques.] Why, how now, Orlando! where have you been all this while? You a lover!—An you serve me such another trick, never come in my sight more.

*Orl.* My fair Rosalind, I come within an hour of my promise.

*Ros.* Break an hour's promise in love! He that will divide a minute into a thousand parts, and break but a part of a thousandth part of a minute in the affairs of love, it may be said of him that Cupid hath clapped him o' the shoulder, but I warrant him heart-whole.

*Orl.* Pardon me, dear Rosalind.

*Ros.* Nay, an you be so tardy, come no more in my sight: I had as lief be woo'd of a snail.

*Orl.* Of a snail!

*Ros.* Ay, of a snail; for though he comes slowly, he carries his house on his head; a better jointure, I think, than you can make a woman: besides, he brings his destiny with him.

*Orl.* What's that?

*Ros.* Why, horns; which such as you are fain to be beholden to your wives for: but he comes armed in his fortune, and prevents the slander of his wife.

*Orl.* Virtue is no horn-maker; and my Rosalind is virtuous.

*Ros.* And I am your Rosalind.

*Cel.* It pleases him to call you so; but he hath a Rosalind of a better leer than you.

*Ros.* Come, woo me, woo me; for now I am in a holiday humour, and like enough to consent.—What would you say to me now, an I were your very very Rosalind?

*Orl.* I would kiss before I spoke.

*Ros.* Nay, you were better speak first; and when you were gravelled for lack of matter, you might take occasion to kiss. Very good orators, when they are out, they will spit; and for lovers lacking,—God warn us!—matter, the cleanliest shift is to kiss.

*Orl.* How if the kiss be denied?

*Ros.* Then she puts you to entreaty, and there begins new matter.

*Orl.* Who could be out, being before his beloved mistress?

*Ros.* Marry, that should you, if I were your mistress; or I should think my honesty ranker than my wit.

*Orl.* What, of my suit?

*Ros.* Not out of your apparel, and yet out of your suit. Am not I your Rosalind?

*Orl.* I take some joy to say you are, because I would be talking of her.　　　　[have you.

*Ros.* Well, in her person, I say, I will not

*Orl.* Then, in mine own person, I die.

*Ros.* No, faith, die by attorney. The poor world is almost six thousand years old, and in all this time there was not any man died in his own person, *videlicet*, in a love-cause. Troilus had his brains dashed out with a Grecian club; yet he did what he could to die before; and he is one of the patterns of love. Leander, he would have lived many a fair year, though Hero had turned nun, if it had not been for a hot midsummer-night; for, good youth, he went but forth to wash him in the Hellespont, and, being taken with the cramp, was drawned; and the foolish chroniclers of that age found it was—Hero of Sestos. But these are all lies; men have died from time to time, and worms have eaten them, but not for love.

*Orl.* I would not have my right Rosalind of this mind, for, I protest, her frown might kill me.

*Ros.* By this hand, it will not kill a fly. But come, now I will be your Rosalind in a more coming-on disposition; and ask me what you will, I will grant it.

*Orl.* Then love me, Rosalind.

*Ros.* Yes, faith will I, Fridays and Saturdays, and all.

*Orl.* And wilt thou have me?

*Ros.* Ay, and twenty such.

*Orl.* What say'st thou?

*Ros.* Are you not good?

*Orl.* I hope so.

*Ros.* Why, then, can one desire too much of a good thing?—Come, sister, you shall be the priest, and marry us.—Give me your hand, Orlando:—What do you say, sister?

*Orl.* Pray thee, marry us.

*Cel.* I cannot say the words.          [*lando,*—

*Ros.* You must begin,——*Will you, Or-*

*Cel.* Go to:——Will you, Orlando, have to wife this Rosalind?

*Orl.* I will.

*Ros.* Ay, but when?

*Orl.* Why, now; as fast as she can marry us.

*Ros.* Then you must say,—*I take thee, Rosalind, for wife.*

*Orl.* I take thee, Rosalind, for wife.

*Ros.* I might ask you for your commission; but,—I do take thee, Orlando, for my husband: —there's a girl goes before the priest; and, certainly, a woman's thoughts run before her actions.

*Orl.* So do all thoughts; they are winged.

*Ros.* Now tell me how long you would have her, after you have possessed her.

*Orl.* For ever and a day.

*Ros.* Say a day, without the ever. No, no, Orlando; men are April when they woo, December when they wed: maids are May when they are maids, but the sky changes when they are wives. I will be more jealous of thee than a Barbary cock-pigeon over his hen; more clamorous than a parrot against rain; more new-fangled than an ape; more giddy in my desires than a monkey: I will weep for nothing, like Diana in the fountain, and I will do that when you are disposed to be merry; I will laugh like a hyen, and that when thou art inclined to sleep.

*Orl.* But will my Rosalind do so?

*Ros.* By my life, she will do as I do.

*Orl.* O, but she is wise.

*Ros.* Or else she could not have the wit to do this: the wiser, the waywarder: make the doors upon a woman's wit, and it will out at the casement; shut that, and it will out at the keyhole; stop that, 'twill fly with the smoke out at the chimney.

*Orl.* A man that had a wife with such a wit, he might say,—*Wit, whither wilt?*

*Ros.* Nay, you might keep that check for it, till you met your wife's wit going to your neighbour's bed.                                        [*that?*

*Orl.* And what wit could wit have to excuse

*Ros.* Marry, to say,—she came to seek you there. You shall never take her without her answer, unless you take her without her tongue. O, that woman that cannot make her fault her husband's occasion, let her never nurse her child herself, for she will breed it like a fool.

*Orl.* For these two hours, Rosalind, I will leave thee.                                        [*hours!*

*Ros.* Alas, dear love, I cannot lack thee two

*Orl.* I must attend the duke at dinner: by two o'clock I will be with thee again.

*Ros.* Ay, go your ways, go your ways; I knew what you would prove; my friends told me as much, and I thought no less:—that flattering tongue of yours won me:—'tis but one cast away, and so,—come, death!—Two o'clock is your hour?

*Orl.* Ay, sweet Rosalind.

*Ros.* By my troth, and in good earnest, and so God mend me, and by all pretty oaths that are not dangerous, if you break one jot of your promise, or come one minute behind your hour, I will think you the most pathetical breakpromise, and the most hollow lover, and the most unworthy of her you call Rosalind, that may be chosen out of the gross band of the unfaithful: therefore beware my censure, and keep your promise.

*Orl.* With no less religion than if thou wert indeed my Rosalind: so, adieu!

*Ros.* Well, time is the old justice that examines all such offenders, and let time try: adieu!                                        [*Exit* ORLANDO.

*Cel.* You have simply misus'd our sex in your love-prate: we must have your doublet and hose plucked over your head, and show the world what the bird hath done to her own nest.

*Ros.* O coz, coz, coz, my pretty little coz, that thou didst know how many fathom deep I am in love! But it cannot be sounded: my affection hath an unknown bottom, like the bay of Portugal.

*Cel.* Or rather, bottomless; that as fast as you pour affection in, it runs out.

*Ros.* No; that same wicked bastard of Venus, that was begot of thought, conceived of spleen, and born of madness; that blind rascally boy, that abuses every one's eyes, because his own are out, let him be judge how deep I am in love: —I'll tell thee, Aliena, I cannot be out of the sight of Orlando: I'll go find a shadow, and sigh till he come.

*Cel.* And I'll sleep.                                        [*Exeunt*

SCENE II.—*Another part of the Forest.*

Enter JAQUES *and* Lords, *in the habit of Foresters.*

*Jaq.* Which is he that killed the deer?

1 *Lord.* Sir, it was I.

*Jaq.* Let's present him to the duke, like a Roman conqueror; and it would do well to set the deer's horns upon his head for a branch of victory.—Have you no song, forester, for this purpose?

*2 Lord.* Yes, sir.

*Jaq.* Sing it; 'tis no matter how it be in tune, so it make noise enough.

### SONG.

1. What shall he have that kill'd the deer
2. His leather skin and horns to wear.
   1. Then sing him home:
      [*The rest shall bear this burden.*
Take thou no scorn to wear the horn;
It was a crest ere thou wast born.
   1. Thy father's father wore it;
   2. And thy father bore it:
*All.* The horn, the horn, the lusty horn,
Is not a thing to laugh to scorn.    [*Exeunt.*

### SCENE III.—*Another part of the Forest.*

#### Enter ROSALIND *and* CELIA.

*Ros.* How say you now? Is it not past two o'clock? And here much Orlando!

*Cel.* I warrant you, with pure love and troubled brain, he hath ta'en his bow and arrows, and is gone forth—to sleep. Look, who comes here.

#### Enter SILVIUS.

*Sil.* My errand is to you, fair youth;— My gentle Phebe bid me give you this:
                           [*Giving a letter.*
I know not the contents; but, as I guess
By the stern brow and waspish action
Which she did use as she was writing of it,
It bears an angry tenor: pardon me,
I am but as a guiltless messenger.    [letter,

*Ros.* Patience herself would startle at this
And play the swaggerer; bear this, bear all:
She says I am not fair; that I lack manners;
She calls me proud, and that she could not love me,
Were man as rare as Phœnix. Od's my will!
Her love is not the hare that I do hunt:
Why writes she so to me?—Well, shepherd, well,
This is a letter of your own device.

*Sil.* No, I protest, I know not the contents:
Phebe did write it.

*Ros.*                 Come, come, you are a fool,
And turn'd into the extremity of love.
I saw her hand: she has a leathern hand,
A freestone-colour'd hand: I verily did think
That her old gloves were on, but 'twas her hands;
She has a huswife's hand: but that's no matter:
I say she never did invent this letter:
This is a man's invention, and his hand.

*Sil.* Sure, it is hers.

*Ros.* Why, 'tis a boisterous and a cruel style;
A style for challengers: why, she defies me,
Like Turk to Christian: woman's gentle brain
Could not drop forth such giant-rude invention,

Such Ethiop words, blacker in their effect
Than in their countenance.—Will you hear the letter?

*Sil.* So please you, for I never heard it yet;
Yet heard too much of Phebe's cruelty.

*Ros.* She Phebes me: mark how the tyrant writes. [*Reads.*]

Art thou god to shepherd turn'd,
That a maiden's heart hath burn'd?

Can a woman rail thus?

*Sil.* Call you this railing?

*Ros.* Why, thy godhead laid apart,
Warr'st thou with a woman's heart?

Did you ever hear such railing?

Whiles the eye of man did woo me,
That could do no vengeance to me.—

Meaning me a beast.—

If the scorn of your bright eyne
Have power to raise such love in mind
Alack, in me what strange effect
Would they work in mild aspect
Whiles you chid me I did love;
How then might your prayers move
He that brings this love to thee
Little knows this love in me:
And by him seal up thy mind;
Whether that thy youth and kind
Will the faithful offer take
Of me, and all that I can make;
Or else by him my love deny,
And then I'll study how to die.

*Sil.* Call you this chiding?

*Cel.* Alas, poor shepherd!

*Ros.* Do you pity him? no, he deserves no pity.—Wilt thou love such a woman?—What, to make thee an instrument, and play false strains upon thee! Not to be endured!—Well, go your way to her,—for I see love hath made thee a tame snake,—and say this to her;—that if she love me, I charge her to love thee: if she will not, I will never have her, unless thou entreat for her.—If you be a true lover, hence, and not a word; for here comes more company.
                           [*Exit* SILVIUS.

#### Enter OLIVER.

*Oli.* Good-morrow, fair ones: pray you, if you know
Where in the purlieus of this forest stands
A sheep-cote fenc'd about with olive trees?

*Cel.* West of this place, down in the neighbour bottom:
The rank of osiers, by the murmuring stream,
Left on your right hand, brings you to the place.
But at this hour the house doth keep itself;
There's none within.

*Oli.* If that an eye may profit by a tongue,
Then should I know you by description;
Such garments, and such years. *The boy is fair,*

*Of female favour, and bestows himself*
*Like a ripe sister: the woman low,*
*And browner than her brother.* Are not you
The owner of the house I did inquire for?

*Cel.* It is no boast, being ask'd, to say we are.

*Oli.* Orlando doth commend him to you
both;
And to that youth he calls his Rosalind
He sends this bloody napkin:—are you he?

*Ros.* I am: what must we understand by
this?    [me

*Oli.* Some of my shame; if you will know of
What man I am, and how, and why, and where
This handkerchief was stain'd.

*Cel.*    I pray you, tell it.

*Oli.* When last the young Orlando parted
from you,
He left a promise to return again
Within an hour; and, pacing through the forest,
Chewing the food of sweet and bitter fancy,
Lo, what befell! he threw his eye aside,
And, mark, what object did present itself!
Under an oak, whose boughs were moss'd with
age,
And high top bald with dry antiquity,
A wretched ragged man, o'ergrown with hair,
Lay sleeping on his back: about his neck
A green and gilded snake had wreath'd itself,
Who, with her head, nimble in threats, ap-
proach'd
The opening of his mouth; but suddenly,
Seeing Orlando, it unlink'd itself,
And with indented glides did slip away
Into a bush: under which bush's shade
A lioness, with udders all drawn dry,
Lay crouching, head on ground, with cat-like
watch,    ['tis
When that the sleeping man should stir; for
The royal disposition of that beast
To prey on nothing that doth seem as dead:
This seen, Orlando did approach the man,
And found it was his brother, his elder brother.

*Cel.* O, I have heard him speak of that same
brother;
And he did render him the most unnatural
That liv'd 'mongst men.

*Oli.*    And well he might so do,
For well I know he was unnatural.    [there,

*Ros.* But, to Orlando:—did he leave him
Food to the suck'd and hungry lioness?

*Oli.* Twice did he turn his back, and pur-
pos'd so;
But kindness, nobler ever than revenge,
And nature, stronger than his just occasion,
Made him give battle to the lioness,
Who quickly fell before him; in which hurtling
From miserable slumber I awak'd.

*Cel.* Are you his brother?

*Ros.*    Was it you he rescued?

*Cel.* Was't you that did so oft contrive to
kill him?

*Oli.* 'Twas I; but 'tis not I: I do not shame
To tell you what I was, since my conversion
So sweetly tastes, being the thing I am.

*Ros.* But, for the bloody napkin?—

*Oli.*    By and by.
When from the first to last, betwixt us two,
Tears our recountments had most kindly bath'd,
As, how I came into that desert place;—
In brief, he led me to the gentle duke,
Who gave me fresh array and entertainment,
Committing me unto my brother's love,
Who led me instantly unto his cave,
There stripp'd himself, and here upon his arm
The lioness had torn some flesh away,
Which all this while had bled; and now he fainted,
And cried, in fainting, upon Rosalind.
Brief, I recover'd him, bound up his wound,
And, after some small space, being strong at
heart,
He sent me hither, stranger as I am,
To tell this story, that you might excuse
His broken promise, and to give this napkin,
Dy'd in his blood, unto the shepherd-youth
That he in sport doth call his Rosalind.

*Cel.* Why, how now, Ganymede! sweet
Ganymede!    [ROSALIND *faints.*

*Oli.* Many will swoon when they do look on
blood.

*Cel.* There is more in it:—Cousin—Ganymede!

*Oli.* Look, he recovers.

*Ros.*    I would I were at home.

*Cel.* We'll lead you thither:—
I pray you, will you take him by the arm?

*Oli.* Be of good cheer, youth:—you a man?—
You lack a man's heart.

*Ros.* I do so, I confess it. Ah, sir, a body
'would think this was well counterfeited. I pray
you, tell your brother how well I counterfeited.
—Heigh-ho!—

*Oli.* This was not counterfeit; there is too
great testimony in your complexion that it was
a passion of earnest.

*Ros.* Counterfeit, I assure you.

*Oli.* Well, then, take a good heart, and
counterfeit to be a man.

*Ros.* So I do: but, i' faith, I should have been
a woman by right.

*Cel.* Come, you look paler and paler: pray
you, draw homewards.—Good sir, go with us.

*Oli.* That will I, for I must bear answer back
How you excuse my brother, Rosalind.

*Ros.* I shall devise something: but, I pray
you, commend my counterfeiting to him.—Will
you go?    [*Exeunt.*

## ACT V.

SCENE I.—*The Forest of Arden.*

*Enter* TOUCHSTONE *and* AUDREY.

*Touch.* We shall find a time, Audrey;
patience, gentle Audrey.

*Aud.* Faith, the priest was good enough, for
all the old gentleman's saying.

*Touch.* A most wicked Sir Oliver, Audrey, a
most vile Martext. But, Audrey, there is a
youth here in the forest lays claim to you.

*Aud.* Ay, I know who 'tis: he hath no interest in me in the world: here comes the man you mean.

### Enter WILLIAM.

*Touch.* It is meat and drink to me to see a clown: By my troth, we that have good wits have much to answer for; we shall be flouting; we cannot hold.

*Will.* Good even, Audrey.

*Aud.* God ye good even, William.

*Will.* And good even to you, sir.

*Touch.* Good even, gentle friend. Cover thy head, cover thy head; nay, pr'ythee, be covered. How old are you, friend?

*Will.* Five-and-twenty, sir.

*Touch.* A ripe age. Is thy name William?

*Will.* William, sir.                          [here?

*Touch.* A fair name. Wast born i' the forest

*Will.* Ay, sir, I thank God.                  [rich?

*Touch.* Thank God;—a good answer. Art

*Will.* Faith, sir, so-so.

*Touch.* So-so is good, very good, very excellent good:—and yet it is not; it is but so-so. Art thou wise?

*Will.* Ay, sir, I have a pretty wit.

*Touch.* Why, thou say'st well. I do now remember a saying; *The fool doth think he is wise, but the wise man knows himself to be a fool.* The heathen philosopher, when he had a desire to eat a grape, would open his lips when he put it into his mouth; meaning thereby that grapes were made to eat and lips to open. You do love this maid?

*Will.* I do, sir.

*Touch.* Give me your hand. Art thou learned?

*Will.* No, sir.

*Touch.* Then learn this of me:—to have is to have; for it is a figure in rhetoric that drink, being poured out of a cup into a glass, by filling the one doth empty the other; for all your writers do consent that *ipse* is he; now, you are not *ipse*, for I am he.

*Will.* Which he, sir?

*Touch.* He, sir, that must marry this woman. Therefore, you clown, abandon,—which is in the vulgar, leave,—the society,—which in the boorish is company,—of this female,—which in the common is woman,—which together is abandon the society of this female; or, clown, thou perishest; or, to thy better understanding, diest; or, to wit, I kill thee, make thee away, translate thy life into death, thy liberty into bondage: I will deal in poison with thee, or in bastinado, or in steel; I will bandy with thee in faction; I will o'er-run thee with policy; I will kill thee a hundred and fifty ways; therefore tremble, and depart.

*Aud.* Do, good William.

*Will.* God rest you merry, sir.            [*Exit*

### Enter CORIN.

*Cor.* Our master and mistress seek you; come away, away!

*Touch.* Trip, Audrey, trip, Audrey;—I attend, I attend.                        [*Exeunt.*

### SCENE II.—*Another part of the Forest.*

#### Enter ORLANDO *and* OLIVER.

*Orl.* Is't possible that, on so little acquaintance, you should like her? that, but seeing, you should love her? and, loving, woo? and, wooing, she should grant? and will you perséver to enjoy her?

*Oli.* Neither call the giddiness of it in question, the poverty of her, the small acquaintance, my sudden wooing, nor her sudden consenting; but say with me, I love Aliena; say, with her, that she loves me; consent with both, that we may enjoy each other: it shall be to your good; for my father's house, and all the revenue that was old Sir Rowland's, will I estate upon you, and here live and die a shepherd.

*Orl.* You have my consent. Let your wedding be to-morrow: thither will I invite the duke and all his contented followers. Go you and prepare Aliena; for, look you, here comes my Rosalind.

#### Enter ROSALIND.

*Ros.* God save you, brother.

*Oli.* And you, fair sister.                  [*Exit.*

*Ros.* O, my dear Orlando, how it grieves me to see thee wear thy heart in a scarf.

*Orl.* It is my arm.

*Ros.* I thought thy heart had been wounded with the claws of a lion.

*Orl.* Wounded it is, but with the eyes of a lady.

*Ros.* Did your brother tell you how I counterfeited to swoon when he show'd me your handkercher?

*Orl.* Ay, and greater wonders than that.

*Ros.* O, I know where you are:—nay, 'tis true: there was never anything so sudden but the fight of two rams and Cæsar's thrasonical brag of—*I came, saw, and overcame:* for your brother and my sister no sooner met, but they looked; no sooner looked, but they loved; no sooner loved, but they sighed; no sooner sighed, but they asked one another the reason; no sooner knew the reason, but they sought the remedy: and in these degrees have they made a pair of stairs 'to marriage, which they will climb incontinent, or else be incontinent before marriage: they are in the very wrath of love, and they will together: clubs cannot part them.

*Orl.* They shall be married to-morrow; and I will bid the duke to the nuptial. But O, how bitter a thing it is to look into happiness through another man's eyes! By so much the more shall I to-morrow be at the height of heart-heaviness, by how much I shall think my brother happy in having what he wishes for.

*Ros.* Why, then, to-morrow I cannot serve your turn for Rosalind?

*Orl.* I can live no longer by thinking.

*Ros.* I will weary you, then, no longer with idle talking. Know of me, then,—for now I speak to some purpose,—that I know you are a gentleman of good conceit: I speak not this that you should bear a good opinion of my knowledge, insomuch I say I know you are; neither do I labour for a greater esteem than may in some little measure draw a belief from you, to do yourself good, and not to grace me. Believe, then, if you please, that I can do strange things: I have, since I was three year old, conversed with a magician, most profound in his art, and yet not damnable. If you do love Rosalind so near the heart as your gesture cries it out, when your brother marries Aliena, shall you marry her:—I know into what straits of fortune she is driven; and it is not impossible to me, if it appear not inconvenient to you, to set her before your eyes to-morrow, human as she is, and without any danger.

*Orl.* Speak'st thou in sober meanings?

*Ros.* By my life, I do; which I tender dearly, though I say I am a magician. Therefore, put you in your best array, bid your friends; for if you will be married to-morrow, you shall; and to Rosalind, if you will. Look, here comes a lover of mine, and a lover of hers.

*Enter* SILVIUS *and* PHEBE.

*Phe.* Youth, you have done me much un-gentleness,
To show the letter that I writ to you.

*Ros.* I care not, if I have: it is my study
To seem despiteful and ungentle to you:
You are there follow'd by a faithful shepherd;
Look upon him, love him; he worships you.

*Phe.* Good shepherd, tell this youth what 'tis to love.

*Sil.* It is to be all made of sighs and tears;—
And so am I for Phebe.

*Phe.* And I for Ganymede.

*Orl.* And I for Rosalind.

*Ros.* And I for no woman.

*Sil.* It is to be all made of faith and ser-vice;—
And so am I for Phebe.

*Phe.* And I for Ganymede.

*Orl.* And I for Rosalind.

*Ros.* And I for no woman.

*Sil.* It is to be all made of fantasy,
All made of passion, and all made of wishes;
All adoration, duty, and obedience,
All humbleness, all patience, and impatience,
All purity, all trial, all observance;—
And so am I for Phebe.

*Phe.* And so am I for Ganymede.

*Orl.* And so am I for Rosalind.

*Ros.* And so am I for no woman.

*Phe.* If this be so, why blame you me to love you?            [*To* ROSALIND.

*Sil.* If this be so, why blame you me to love you?            [*To* PHEBE.

*Orl.* If this be so, why blame you me to love you?

*Ros.* Why do you speak too,—*Why blame you me to love you?*

*Orl.* To her that is not here, nor doth not hear.

*Ros.* Pray you, no more of this; 'tis like the howling of Irish wolves against the moon.—I will help you [*to* SILVIUS] if I can:—I would love you [*to* PHEBE] if I could.—To-morrow meet me all together.—I will marry you [*to* PHEBE] if ever I marry woman, and I'll be married to-morrow:—I will satisfy you [*to* OR-LANDO] if ever I satisfied man, and you shall be married to-morrow:—I will content you [*to* SILVIUS] if what pleases you contents you, and you shall be married to-morrow.—As you [*to* ORLANDO] love Rosalind, meet;—as you [*to* SILVIUS] love Phebe, meet; and as I love no woman, I'll meet.—So, fare you well; I have left you commands.

*Sil.* I'll not fail, if I live.

*Phe.*                              Nor I.

*Orl.*                                        Nor I.
                                        [*Exeunt.*

SCENE III.—*Another part of the Forest.*

*Enter* TOUCHSTONE *and* AUDREY.

*Touch.* To-morrow is the joyful day, Audrey; to-morrow will we be married.

*Aud.* I do desire it with all my heart; and I hope it is no dishonest desire to desire to be a woman of the world. Here come two of the banished duke's pages.

*Enter two Pages.*

1 *Page.* Well met, honest gentleman.

*Touch.* By my troth, well met. Come sit, sit, and a song.

2 *Page.* We are for you: sit i' the middle.

1 *Page.* Shall we clap into 't roundly, with-out hawking, or spitting, or saying we are hoarse, which are the only prologues to a bad voice?

2 *Page.* I' faith, i' faith; and both in a tune, like two gipsies on a horse.

SONG.

I.

It was a lover and his lass,
　With a hey, and a ho, and a hey nonino,
That o'er the green corn-field did pass
　In the spring time, the only pretty ring time,
　When birds do sing, hey ding a ding, ding:
Sweet lovers love the spring.

II.

Between the acres of the rye,
　With a hey, and a ho, and a hey nonino,
These pretty country folks would lie,
　In the spring time, &c.

III.

This carol they began that hour,
　With a hey, and a ho, and a hey nonino,
How that a life was but a flower
　In the spring time, &c

IV.

And therefore take the present time,
　With a hey, and a ho, and a hey.nonino,
For love is crowned with the prime
　In the spring time, &c.

*Touch.* Truly, young gentlemen, though there was no great matter in the ditty, yet the note was very untimeable.

1 *Page.* You are deceived, sir; we kept time, we lost not our time.

*Touch.* By my troth, yes; I count it but time lost to hear such a foolish song. God be with you; and God mend your voices! Come, Audrey.
　　　　　　　　　　　　　　[*Exeunt.*

SCENE IV.—*Another part of the Forest.*

*Enter* DUKE *Senior,* AMIENS, JAQUES, OR-
　LANDO, OLIVER, *and* CELIA.

*Duke S.* Dost thou believe, Orlando, that
　the boy
Can do all this that he hath promised?

*Orl.* I sometimes do believe and sometimes
　do not;　　　　　　　　　　　　　　[fear.
As those that fear they hope, and know they

*Enter* ROSALIND, SILVIUS, *and* PHEBE.

*Ros.* Patience once more, whiles our com-
　pact is urg'd:—
You say, if I bring in your Rosalind,
　　　　　　　　　　　　　　[*To the* DUKE.
You will bestow her on Orlando here?

*Duke S.* That would I, had I kingdoms to
　give with her.

*Ros.* And you say you will have her, when I
　bring her?　　　　　　　　[*To* ORLANDO.

*Orl.* That would I, were I of all kingdoms
　king.

*Ros.* You say you'll marry me if I be willing?
　　　　　　　　　　　　　　[*To* PHEBE.

*Phe.* That will I, should I die the hour after.

*Ros.* But if you do refuse to marry me,
You'll give yourself to this most faithful shep-
　herd?

*Phe.* So is the bargain.

*Ros.* You say that you'll have Phebe, if she
　will?　　　　　　　　　　　[*To* SILVIUS.

*Sil.* Though to have her and death were
　both one thing.

*Ros.* I have promis'd to make all this matter
　even.
Keep you your word, O duke, to give your
　daughter;—
You yours, Orlando, to receive his daughter;—
Keep you your word, Phebe, that you'll marry
　me;
Or else, refusing me, to wed this shepherd:—
Keep your word, Silvius, that you'll marry her
If she refuse me:—and from hence I go,
To make these doubts all even.
　　　　　　[*Exeunt* ROSALIND *and* CELIA.

*Duke S.* I do remember in this shepherd-boy
Some lively touches of my daughter's favour.

*Orl.* My lord, the first time that I ever saw
　him,
Methought he was a brother to your daughter:
But, my good lord, this boy is forest-born,
And hath been tutor'd in the rudiments
Of many desperate studies by his uncle,
Whom he reports to be a great magician,
Obscured in the circle of this forest.

*Jaq.* There is, sure, another flood toward, and these couples are coming to the ark. Here comes a pair of very strange beasts, which in all tongues are called fools.

*Enter* TOUCHSTONE *and* AUDREY.

*Touch.* Salutation and greeting to you all!

*Jaq.* Good my lord, bid him welcome. This is the motley-minded gentleman that I have so often met in the forest: he hath been a courtier, he swears.

*Touch.* If any man doubt that, let him put me to my purgation. I have trod a measure; I have flattered a lady; I have been politic with my friend, smooth with mine enemy; I have undone three tailors; I have had four quarrels, and like to have fought one.

*Jaq.* And how was that ta'en up?

*Touch.* Faith, we met, and found the quarrel was upon the seventh cause.

*Jaq.*. How seventh cause? Good my lord, like this fellow.

*Duke S.* I like him very well.

*Touch.* God 'ild you, sir; I desire you of the like. I press in here, sir, amongst the rest of the country copulatives, to swear and to for-swear; according as marriage binds and blood breaks:—A poor virgin, sir, an ill-favoured thing, sir, but mine own; a poor humour of mine, sir, to take that that no man else will: rich honesty dwells like a miser, sir, in a poor-house; as your pearl in your foul oyster.

*Duke S.* By my faith, he is very swift and sententious.

*Touch.* According to the fool's bolt, sir, and such dulcet diseases.

*Jaq.* But, for the seventh cause; how did you find the quarrel on the seventh cause?

*Touch.* Upon a lie seven times removed;— bear your body more seeming, Audrey:—as thus, sir, I did dislike the cut of a certain courtier's beard;'he sent me word, if I said his beard was not cut well, he was in the mind it was: this is called the *Retort courteous*. If I sent him word again, it was not well cut, he would send me word he cut it to please himself: this is called the *Quip modest*. If again, it was not well cut, he disabled my judgment: this is called the *Reply churlish*. If again, it was not well cut, he would answer, I spake not true: this is called the *Reproof valiant*. If again, it was not well cut, he would say, I lie: this is called the *Countercheck quarrelsome*: and so, to the *Lie circumstantial*, and the *Lie direct*.

*Jaq.* And how oft did you say his beard was not well cut?

*Touch.* I durst go no farther than the *Lie circumstantial,* nor he durst not give me the *Lie direct;* and so we measured swords and parted.

*Jaq.* Can you nominate in order now the degrees of the lie?

*Touch.* O, sir, we quarrel in print by the book, as you have books for good manners: I will name you the degrees. The first, the Retort courteous; the second, the Quip modest; the third, the Reply churlish; the fourth, the Reproof valiant; the fifth, the Countercheck quarrelsome; the sixth, the Lie with circumstance; the seventh, the Lie direct. All these you may avoid but the lie direct; and you may avoid that too with an *If.* I knew when seven justices could not take up a quarrel; but when the parties were met themselves, one of them thought but of an *If,* as *If you said so, then I said so;* and they shook hands, and swore brothers. Your *If* is the only peace-maker:—much virtue in *If.*

*Jaq.* Is not this a rare fellow, my lord? he's as good at anything, and yet a fool.

*Duke S.* He uses his folly like a stalking-horse, and under the presentation of that he shoots his wit.

*Enter* HYMEN, *leading* ROSALIND *in woman's clothes: and* CELIA.

### Still Music.

*Hym.* Then is there mirth in heaven,
When earthly things made even
    Atone together.
Good duke, receive thy daughter:
Hymen from heaven brought her,
    Yea, brought her hither,
That thou mightst join her hand with his,
Whose heart within her bosom is.

*Ros.* To you I give myself, for I am yours.
                        [*To* DUKE S.
To you I give myself, for I am yours.
                        [*To* ORLANDO.

*Duke S.* If there be truth in sight, you are my daughter.

*Orl.* If there be truth in sight, you are my Rosalind.

*Phe.* If sight and shape be true,
Why, then, my love, adieu!

*Ros.* I'll have no father, if you be not he:—
                        [*To* DUKE S.
I'll have no husband, if you be not he:—
                        [*To* ORLANDO.
Nor e'er wed woman, if you be not she.
                        [*To* PHEBE.

*Hym.* Peace Ho! I bar confusion:
    'Tis I must make conclusion
    Of these most strange events:
    Here's eight that must take hands,
    To join in Hymen's bands,
    If truth holds true contents.
You and you no crass shall part:
        [*To* ORLANDO *and* ROSALIND.

You and you are heart in heart:
            [*To* OLIVER *and* CELIA.
You to his love must accord,    [*To* PHEBE.
Or have a woman to your lord:—
You and you are sure together,
        [*To* TOUCHSTONE *and* AUDREY.
As the winter to foul weather.
Whiles a wedlock-hymn we sing,
Feed yourselves with questioning,
That reason wonder may diminish,
How thus we met, and these things finish.

### SONG.

Wedding is great Juno's crown;
  O blessed bond of board and bed!
'Tis Hymen peoples every town;
  High wedlock, then, be honoured;
Honour, high honour and renown,
To Hymen, god of every town!

*Duke S.* O my dear niece, welcome thou art to me!
Even daughter, welcome in no less degree.

*Phe.* I will not eat my word, now thou art mine;
Thy faith my fancy to thee doth combine.
                    [*To* SILVIUS.

*Enter* JAQUES DE BOIS.

*Jaq. de B.* Let me have audience for a word or two;
I am the second son of old Sir Rowland,
That bring these tidings to this fair assembly:—
Duke Frederick, hearing how that every day
Men of great worth resorted to this forest,
Address'd a mighty power; which were on foot,
In his own conduct, purposely to take
His brother here, and put him to the sword:
And to the skirts of this wild wood he came;
Where, meeting with an old religious man,
After some question with him, was converted
Both from his enterprise and from the world;
His crown bequeathing to his banish'd brother,
And all their lands restored to them again
That were with him exil'd. This to be true
I do engage my life.

*Duke S.*       Welcome, young man:
Thou offer'st fairly to thy brother's wedding:
To one, his lands withheld; and to the other,
A land itself at large, a potent dukedom.
First, in this forest, let us do those ends
That here were well begun and well begot:
And after, every of this happy number,
That have endur'd shrewd days and nights with us,
Shall share the good of our returned fortune,
According to the measure of their states.
Meantime, forget this new-fall'n dignity,
And fall into our rustic revelry:—
Play, music!—and you, brides and bridegrooms all,
With measure heap'd in joy, to the measures fall.

*Jaq.* Sir, by your patience. If I heard you rightly,

The duke hath put on a religious life,
And thrown into neglect the pompous court?

*Jaq. de B.* He hath.

*Jaq.* To him will I: out of these convertites
There is much matter to be heard and learn'd.—
You to your former honour I bequeath;
                              [*To* DUKE S.
Your patience and your virtue well deserves
    it:—
You [*to* ORLANDO] to a love that your true faith
    doth merit:—
You [*to* OLIVER] to your land, and love, and
    great allies:—
You [*to* SILVIUS] to a long and well-deserved
    bed:—                         [thy loving voyage
And you [*to* TOUCHSTONE] to wrangling; for
Is but for two months victual'd.—So to your
    pleasures;
I am for other than for dancing measures.

*Duke S.* Stay, Jaques, stay.          [have

*Jaq.* To see no pastime I: what you would
I'll stay to know at your abandon'd cave.
                                   [*Exit.*

*Duke S.* Proceed, proceed: we will begin
    these rites,
As we do trust they'll end, in true delights.
                              [*A dance.*

## EPILOGUE.

*Ros.* It is not the fashion to see the lady the
epilogue; but it is no more unhandsome than to
see the lord the prologue. If it be true that good
wine needs no bush, 'tis true that a good play
needs no epilogue. Yet to good wine they do use
good bushes; and good plays prove the better
by the help of good epilogues. What a case am I
in, then, that am neither a good epilogue nor
cannot insinuate with you in the behalf of a
good play! I am not furnished like a beggar;
therefore to beg will not become me: my way is
to conjure you; and I'll begin with the women.
I charge you, O women, for the love you bear to
men, to like as much of this play as please you:
and I charge you, O men, for the love you bear
to women,—as I perceive by your simpering,
none of you hates them,—that between you
and the women the play may please. If I were a
woman, I would kiss as many of you as had
beards that pleased me, complexions that liked
me, and breaths that I defied not: and, I am
sure, as many as have good beards, or good
faces, or sweet breaths, will, for my kind offer,
when I make curtsy, bid me farewell.
                                   [*Exeunt.*

ALL'S WELL THAT ENDS WELL.

Act IV. Sc. 1.

# ALL'S WELL THAT ENDS WELL

## DRAMATIS PERSONÆ

KING OF FRANCE.
DUKE OF FLORENCE.
BERTRAM, *Count of Rousillon.*
LAFEU, *an old Lord.*
PAROLLES, *a Follower of* BERTRAM.
*Several young* French Lords, *that serve with* BERTRAM *in the Florentine War.*

Steward,
Clown,   } *Servants to the* COUNTESS OF
A Page,   }   ROUSILLON.

COUNTESS OF ROUSILLON, *Mother to* BERTRAM.
HELENA, *a Gentlewoman protected by the* COUNTESS.
*An old* Widow *of Florence.*
DIANA, *Daughter to the* Widow.
VIOLENTA, } *Neighbours and Friends to the*
MARIANA, }   Widow.
Lords *attending on the* KING; Officers, Soldiers, &c., *French and Florentine.*

SCENE,—*Partly in* FRANCE, *and partly in* TUSCANY.

## ACT I.

SCENE I.—ROUSILLON. *A Room in the* COUNTESS'S *Palace.*

*Enter* BERTRAM, *the* COUNTESS OF ROUSILLON, HELENA, *and* LAFEU, *in mourning.*

*Count.* In delivering my son from me, I bury a second husband.

*Ber.* And I, in going, madam, weep o'er my father's death anew: but I must attend his majesty's command, to whom I am now in ward, evermore in subjection.

*Laf.* You shall find of the king a husband, madam;—you, sir, a father: he that so generally is at all times good, must of necessity hold his virtue to you; whose worthiness would stir it up where it wanted, rather than lack it where there is such abundance.

*Count.* What hope is there of his majesty's amendment?

*Laf.* He hath abandoned his physicians, madam; under whose practices he hath persecuted time with hope; and finds no other advantage in the process but only the losing of hope by time.

*Count.* This young gentlewoman had a father—O, that *had!* how sad a passage 'tis!—whose skill was almost as great as his honesty; had it stretched so far, would have made nature immortal, and death should have play for lack of work. Would, for the king's sake, he were living! I think it would be the death of the king's disease.

*Laf.* How called you the man you speak of, madam?

*Count.* He was famous, sir, in his profession, and it was his great right to be so,—Gerard de Narbon.

*Laf.* He was excellent, indeed, madam: the king very lately spoke of him admiringly and mourningly: he was skilful enough to have lived still, if knowledge could be set up against mortality.

*Ber.* What is it, my good lord, the king languishes of?

*Laf.* A fistula, my lord.

*Ber.* I heard not of it before.

*Laf.* I would it were not notorious.—Was this gentlewoman the daughter of Gerard de Narbon?

*Count.* His sole child, my lord; and bequeathed to my overlooking. I have those hopes of her good that her education promises: her dispositions she inherits, which make fair gifts fairer; for where an unclean mind carries virtuous qualities, there commendations go with pity,—they are virtues and traitors too: in her they are the better for their simpleness; she derives her honesty, and achieves her goodness.

*Laf.* Your commendations, madam, get from her tears.

*Count.* 'Tis the best brine a maiden can season her praise in. The remembrance of her father never approaches her heart but the tyranny of her sorrows takes all livelihood from her cheek. No more of this, Helena,—go to, no more; lest it be rather thought you affect a sorrow than to have.

*Hel.* I do affect a sorrow indeed; but I have it too.

*Laf.* Moderate lamentation is the right of the dead; excessive grief the enemy to the living.

*Count.* If the living be enemy to the grief, the excess makes it soon mortal.

*Ber.* Madam, I desire your holy wishes.

*Laf.* How understand we that?

*Count.* Be thou blest, Bertram! and succeed thy father
In manners, as in shape! thy blood and virtue
Contend for empire in thee, and thy goodness
Share with thy birthright! Love all, trust a few,

Do wrong to none: be able for thine enemy
Rather in power than use; and keep thy friend
Under thy own life's key: be check'd for silence,
But never tax'd for speech. What heaven more
    will,
That thee may furnish and my prayers pluck
    down,
Fall on thy head! Farewell.—My lord,
'Tis an unseason'd courtier; good my lord,
Advise him.
  *Laf.*    He cannot want the best
That shall attend his love.
  *Count.*  Heaven bless him!—Farewell, Ber-
    tram.            [*Exit* COUNTESS.
  *Ber.*  The best wishes that can be forged in
your thoughts [*to* HELENA] be servants to you!
Be comfortable to my mother, your mistress,
and make much of her.
  *Laf.*  Farewell, pretty lady: you must hold
the credit of your father.
              [*Exeunt* BER. *and* LAF.
  *Hel.*  O, were that all!—I think not on my
    father;                  [more
And these great tears grace his remembrance
Than those I shed for him. What was he like?
I have forgot him; my imagination
Carries no favour in 't but Bertram's.
I am undone: there is no living, none,
If Bertram be away. It were all one
That I should love a bright particular star,
And think to wed it, he is so above me:
In his bright radiance and collateral light
Must I be comforted, not in his sphere.
The ambition in my love thus plagues itself:
The hind that would be mated by the lion
Must die for love. 'Twas pretty, though a
    plague,
To see him every hour; to sit and draw
His arched brows, his hawking eye, his curls,
In our heart's table,—heart too capable
Of every line and trick of his sweet favour:
But now he's gone, and my idolatrous fancy
Must sanctify his relics. Who comes here?
One that goes with him: I love him for his sake;
And yet I know him a notorious liar,
Think him a great way fool, solely a coward;
Yet these fix'd evils sit so fit in him
That they take place when virtue's steely bones
Look bleak i' the cold wind: withal, full oft we
    see
Cold wisdom waiting on superfluous folly.

       *Enter* PAROLLES.

  *Par.*  Save you, fair queen!
  *Hel.*  And you, monarch!
  *Par.*  No.
  *Hel.*  And no.
  *Par.*  Are you meditating on virginity?
  *Hel.*  Ay. You have some stain of soldier in
you: let me ask you a question. Man is enemy
to virginity; how may we barricado it against
him?
  *Par.*  Keep him out.

  *Hel.*  But he assails; and our virginity, though
valiant in the defence, yet is weak: unfold to us
some warlike resistance.
  *Par.*  There is none: man, sitting down before
you, will undermine you, and blow you up.
  *Hel.*  Bless our poor virginity from under-
miners and blowers-up!—Is there no military
policy how virgins might blow up men?
  *Par.*  Virginity being blown down, man will
quicklier be blown up: marry, in blowing him
down again, with the breach yourselves made,
you lose your city. It is not politic in the commonwealth of nature to preserve virginity. Loss
of virginity is rational increase; and there was
never virgin got till virginity was first lost.
That you were made of is metal to make virgins.
Virginity, by being once lost, may be ten times
found; by being ever kept, it is ever lost: 'tis
too cold a companion, away with it!
  *Hel.*  I will stand for 't a little, though therefore I die a virgin.
  *Par.*  There's little can be said in 't; 'tis
against the rule of nature. To speak on the part
of virginity is to accuse your mothers, which is
most infallible disobedience. He that hangs
himself is a virgin: virginity murders itself; and
should be buried in highways, out of all sanctified limit, as a desperate offendress against nature. Virginity breeds mites, much like a cheese;
consumes itself to the very paring, and so dies
with feeding his own stomach. Besides, virginity is peevish, proud, idle, made of self-love,
which is the most inhibited sin in the canon.
Keep it not, you cannot choose but lose by 't:
out with't! within ten years it will make itself
ten, which is a goodly increase, and the principal itself not much the worse: away with it!
  *Hel.*  How might one do, sir, to lose it to her
own liking?
  *Par.*  Let me see: marry, ill, to like him that
ne'er it likes. 'Tis a commodity will lose the
gloss with lying; the longer kept, the less worth:
off with't while 'tis vendible: answer the time
of request. Virginity, like an old courtier, wears
her cap out of fashion; richly suited, but unsuitable: just like the brooch and the toothpick which wear not now. Your date is better in
your pie and your porridge than in your cheek.
And your virginity, your old virginity, is like
one of our French withered pears; it looks ill, it
eats drily; marry, 'tis a withered pear; it was
formerly better; marry, yet 'tis a withered pear.
Will you anything with it?
  *Hel.*  Not my virginity yet.
There shall your master have a thousand loves,
A mother, and a mistress, and a friend,
A phœnix, captain, and an enemy,
A guide, a goddess, and a sovereign,
A counsellor, a traitress, and a dear:
His humble ambition, proud humility,
His jarring concord, and his discord dulcet,
His faith, his sweet disaster; with a world
Of pretty, fond, adoptious christendoms,
That blinking Cupid gossips. Now shall he—

I know not what he shall:—God send him
well!—
The court's a learning-place;—and he is one,—
*Par.* What one, i' faith?
*Hel.* That I wish well.—'Tis pity—
*Par.* What's pity?
*Hel.* That wishing well had not a body in 't
Which might be felt; that we, the poorer born,
Whose baser stars do shut us up in wishes,
Might with effects of them follow our friends,
And show what we alone must think; which
never
Returns us thanks.

*Enter a* Page.

*Page.* Monsieur Parolles, my lord calls for
you.                                    [*Exit* Page.
*Par.* Little Helen, farewell: if I can remem-
ber thee, I will think of thee at court.
*Hel.* Monsieur Parolles, you were born un-
der a charitable star.
*Par.* Under Mars, I.
*Hel.* I especially think, under Mars.
*Par.* Why under Mars?
*Hel.* The wars have so kept you under that
you must needs be born under Mars.
*Par.* When he was predominant.
*Hel.* When he was retrograde, I think, rather.
*Par.* Why think you so?           [fight.
*Hel.* You go so much backward when you
*Par.* That's for advantage.
*Hel.* So is running away, when fear proposes
the safety: but the composition that your valour and fear makes in you is a virtue of a good
wing, and I like the wear well.
*Par.* I am so full of businesses I cannot answer thee acutely. I will return perfect courtier;
in the which my instruction shall serve to nat-
uralize thee, so thou wilt be capable of a courtier's counsel, and understand what advice shall
thrust upon thee; else thou diest in thine unthankfulness, and thine ignorance makes thee
away: farewell. When thou hast leisure, say thy
prayers; when thou hast none, remember thy
friends: get thee a good husband, and use him
as he uses thee: so, farewell.          [*Exit.*
*Hel.* Our remedies oft in ourselves do lie,
Which we ascribe to heaven: the fated sky
Gives us free scope; only doth backward pull
Our slow designs when we ourselves are dull.
What power is it which mounts my love so
high—
That makes me see, and cannot feed mine eye?
The mightiest space in fortune nature brings
To join like likes, and kiss like native things.
Impossible be strange attempts to those
That weigh their pains in sense, and do suppose
What hath been cannot be: who ever strove
To show her merit that did miss her love?
The king's disease,—my project may deceive
me,
But my intents are fix'd, and will not leave me.
                                        [*Exit.*

SCENE II.—PARIS. *A Room in the* KING'S
*Palace.*

*Flourish of cornets. Enter the* KING OF FRANCE,
*with Letters;* Lords *and others attending.*

*King.* The Florentines and Senoys are by the
ears;
Have fought with equal fortune, and continue
A braving war.
*1 Lord.*            So 'tis reported, sir.
*King.* Nay, 'tis most credible; we here re-
ceive it
A certainty, vouch'd from our cousin Austria,
With caution that the Florentine will move us
For speedy aid; wherein our dearest friend
Prejudicates the business, and would seem
To have us make denial.
*1 Lord.*            His love and wisdom,
Approv'd so to your majesty, may plead
For amplest credence.
*King.*            He hath arm'd our answer,
And Florence is denied before he comes:
Yet, for our gentlemen that mean to see
The Tuscan service, freely have they leave
To stand on either part.
*2 Lord.*            It well may serve
A nursery to our gentry, who are sick
For breathing and exploit.
*King.*            What's he comes here?

*Enter* BERTRAM, LAFEU, *and* PAROLLES.

*1 Lord.* It is the Count Rousillon, my good
lord,
Young Bertram.
*King.* Youth, thou bear'st thy father's face;
Frank nature, rather curious than in haste,
Hath well compos'd thee. Thy father's moral
parts
Mayst thou inherit too! Welcome to Paris.
*Ber.* My thanks and duty are your majesty's.
*King.* I would I had that corporal soundness
now,
As when thy father and myself in friendship
First tried our soldiership! He did look far
Into the service of the time, and was
Discipled of the bravest: he lasted long;
But on us both did haggish age steal on,
And wore us out of act. It much repairs me
To talk of your good father. In his youth
He had the wit which I can well observe
To-day in our young lords; but they may jest
Till their own scorn return to them unnoted,
Ere they can hide their levity in honour
So like a courtier: contempt nor bitterness
Were in his pride or sharpness; if they were,
His equal had awak'd them; and his honour,
Clock to itself, knew the true minute when
Exception bid him speak, and at this time
His tongue obey'd his hand: who were below
him
He us'd as creatures of another place;
And bow'd his eminent top to their low ranks,
Making them proud of his humility,
In their poor praise he humbled. Such a man

Might be a copy to these younger times; [now
Which, follow'd well, would demonstrate them
But goers backward.
  *Ber.* His good remembrance, sir,
Lies richer in your thoughts than on his tomb;
So in approof lives not his epitaph
As in your royal speech.   [always say,—
  *King.* Would I were with him! He would
Methinks I hear him now; his plausive words
He scatter'd not in ears, but grafted them,
To grow there, and to bear,—*Let me not live,*—
Thus his good melancholy oft began,
On the catastrophe and heel of pastime,
When it was out,—*Let me not live,* quoth he,
*After my flame lacks oil, to be the snuff*
*Of younger spirits, whose apprehensive senses*
*All but new things disdain; whose judgments are*
*Mere fathers of their garments; whose constancies*
*Expire before their fashions:*—This he wish'd.
I, after him, do after him wish too,
Since I nor wax nor honey can bring home,
I quickly were dissolv'd from my hive,
To give some labourers room.
  *2 Lord.*   You are lov'd, sir.
They that least lend it you shall lack you first.
  *King.* I fill a place, I know't.—How long
    is 't, count,
Since the physician at your father's died?
He was much fam'd.
  *Ber.*   Some six months since, my lord.
  *King.* If he were living I would try him yet;—
Lend me an arm;—the rest have worn me out
With several applications:—nature and sickness
Debate it at their leisure. Welcome, count;
My son's no dearer.
  *Ber.*   Thank your majesty.
      [*Exeunt. Flourish.*

SCENE III.—ROUSILLON. *A Room in the Palace.*

  *Enter* COUNTESS, Steward, *and* Clown.

  *Count.* I will now hear: what say you of this gentlewoman?
  *Stew.* Madam, the care I have had to even your content, I wish might be found in the calendar of my past endeavours; for then we wound our modesty, and make foul the clearness of our deservings, when of ourselves we publish them.
  *Count.* What does this knave here? Get you gone, sirrah: the complaints I have heard of you I do not at all believe; 'tis my slowness that I do not; for I know you lack not folly to commit them, and have ability enough to make such knaveries yours.
  *Clo.* 'Tis not unknown to you, madam, I am a poor fellow.
  *Count.* Well, sir.
  *Clo.* No, madam, 'tis not so well that I am poor; though many of the rich are damned: but if I may have your ladyship's good will to go to the world, Isbel the woman and I will do as we may.
  *Count.* Wilt thou needs be a beggar?
  *Clo* I do beg your good will in this case.

  *Count.* In what case?
  *Clo.* In Isbel's case and mine own. Service is no heritage: and I think I shall never have the blessing of God till I have issue of my body; for they say bairns are blessings.
  *Count.* Tell me thy reason why thou wilt marry.
  *Clo.* My poor body, madam, requires it: I am driven on by the flesh; and he must needs go that the devil drives.
  *Count.* Is this all your worship's reason?
  *Clo.* Faith, madam, I have other holy reasons, such as they are.
  *Count.* May the world know them?
  *Clo.* I have been, madam, a wicked creature, as you and all flesh and blood are; and, indeed, I do marry that I may repent.
  *Count.* Thy marriage, sooner than thy wickedness.
  *Clo.* I am out of friends, madam; and I hope to have friends for my wife's sake.
  *Count.* Such friends are thine enemies, knave.
  *Clo.* You are shallow, madam, in great friends: for the knaves come to do that for me which I am a-weary of. He that ears my land spares my team, and gives me leave to inn the crop: if I be his cuckold, he's my drudge: he that comforts my wife is the cherisher of my flesh and blood; he that cherishes my flesh and blood loves my flesh and blood; he that loves my flesh and blood is my friend; *ergo*, he that kisses my wife is my friend. If men could be contented to be what they are, there were no fear in marriage; for young Charbon the puritan and old Poysam the papist, how-some'er their hearts are severed in religion, their heads are both one; they may joll horns together like any deer i' the herd.
  *Count.* Wilt thou ever be a foul-mouthed and calumnious knave?
  *Clo.* A prophet I, madam; and I speak the truth the next way:

For I the ballad will repeat,
  Which men full true shall find;
Your marriage comes by destiny,
  Your cuckoo sings by kind.

  *Count.* Get you gone, sir; I'll talk with you more anon.
  *Stew.* May it please you, madam, that he bid Helen come to you; of her I am to speak.
  *Count.* Sirrah, tell my gentlewoman I would speak with her; Helen I mean.

  *Clo.* [*Singing.*] Was this fair face the cause, quoth
      she,
Why the Grecians sacked Troy?
Fond done, done fond,
  Was this King Priam's joy?
With that she sighed as she stood,
With that she sighed as she stood,
  And gave this sentence then:—
Among nine bad if one be good,
Among nine bad if one be good,
  There's yet one good in ten.

*Count.* What, one good in ten? you corrupt
the song, sirrah.

*Clo.* One good woman in ten, madam, which
is a purifying o' the song: would God would
serve the world so all the year! we'd find no
fault with the tithe-woman if I were the parson:
one in ten, quoth a'! an we might have a good
woman born but for every blazing star, or at an
earthquake, 'twould mend the lottery well: a
man may draw his heart out ere he pluck one.

*Count.* You'll be gone, sir knave, and do as
I command you!

*Clo.* That man should be at woman's command, and yet no hurt done!—Though honesty
be no puritan, yet it will do no hurt; it will
wear the surplice of humility over the black
gown of a big heart.—I am going, forsooth: the
business is for Helen to come hither.    [*Exit.*

*Count.* Well, now.

*Stew.* I know, madam, you love your gentlewoman entirely.

*Count.* Faith, I do: her father bequeathed
her to me; and she herself, without other advantage, may lawfully make title to as much
love as she finds: there is more owing her than
is paid; and more shall be paid her than she'll
demand.

*Stew.* Madam, I was very late more near her
than I think she wished me: alone she was, and
did communicate to herself her own words to
her own ears; she thought, I dare vow for her,
they touched not any stranger sense. Her matter was, she loved your son: Fortune, she said,
was no goddess, that had put such difference
betwixt their two estates; Love no god, that
would not extend his might only where qualities were level: Diana no queen of virgins, that
would suffer her poor knight surprise, without
rescue in the first assault, or ransom afterward.
This she delivered in the most bitter touch of
sorrow that e'er I heard virgin exclaim in:
which I held my duty speedily to acquaint you
withal; sithence, in the loss that may happen,
it concerns you something to know it.

*Count.* You have discharged this honestly;
keep it to yourself: many likelihoods informed
me of this before, which hung so tottering in
the balance that I could neither believe nor
misdoubt. Pray you, leave me: stall this in your
bosom; and I thank you for your honest care: I
will speak with you further anon.

[*Exit* Steward.

*Count.* Even so it was with me when I was
    young:
If ever we are nature's, these are ours; this
    thorn
Doth to our rose of youth rightly belong;
  Our blood to us, this to our blood is born:
It is the show and seal of nature's truth,
Where love's strong passion is impress'd in
    youth:
By our remembrances of days foregone,
Such were our faults:—or then we thought them
    none.

*Enter* HELENA.

Her eye is sick on't;—I observe her now.

*Hel.* What is your pleasure, madam?

*Count.*                      You know, Helen,
I am a mother to you.

*Hel.* Mine honourable mistress.

*Count.*                      Nay, a mother:
Why not a mother? When I said a mother,
Methought you saw a serpent: what's in mother,
That you start at it? I say I am your mother;
And put you in the catalogue of those
That were emwombed mine. 'Tis often seen
Adoption strives with nature; and choice breeds
A native slip to us from foreign seeds:
You ne'er oppress'd me with a mother's groan,
Yet I express to you a mother's care:—
God's mercy, maiden! does it curd thy blood
To say I am thy mother? What's the matter,
That this distemper'd messenger of wet,
The many-colour'd iris, rounds thine eye?
Why,—that you are my daughter?

*Hel.*                      That I am not.

*Count.* I say, I am your mother.

*Hel.*                      Pardon, madam;
The Count Rousillon cannot be my brother:
I am from humble, he from honour'd name;
No note upon my parents, his all noble;
My master, my dear lord he is; and I
His servant live, and will his vassal die:
He must not be my brother.

*Count.*                      Nor I your mother?

*Hel.* You are my mother, madam; would
    you were,—
So that my lord your son were not my brother,—
Indeed my mother!—or were you both our
    mothers,
I care no more for than I do for heaven,
So I were not his sister. Can't no other,
But, I your daughter, he must be my brother?

*Count.* Yes, Helen, you might be my daugh-
    ter-in-law:                      [mother
God shield you mean it not! daughter and
So strive upon your pulse. What! pale again?
My fear hath catch'd your fondness: now I see
The mystery of your loneliness, and find
Your salt tears' head. Now to all sense 'tis gross
You love my son; invention is asham'd,
Against the proclamation of thy passion,
To say thou dost not: therefore tell me true;
But tell me then, 'tis so;—for, look, thy cheeks
Confess it, one to the other; and thine eyes
See it so grossly shown in thy behaviours,
That in their kind they speak it; only sin
And hellish obstinacy tie thy tongue,
That truth should be suspected Speak, is 't so?
If it be so, you have wound a goodly clue;
If it be not, forswear't: howe'er, I charge thee,
As heaven shall work in me for thine avail,
To tell me truly.

*Hel.*                      Good madam, pardon me!

*Count.* Do you love my son?

*Hel.*                      Your pardon, noble mistress!

*Count.* Love you my son?

*Hel.*          Do not you love him, madam?
*Count.* Go not about; my love hath in't a
          bond,                          [close
Whereof the world takes note: come, come, dis-
The state of your affection; for your passions
Have to the full appeach'd.
     *Hel.*               Then I confess,
Here on my knee, before high heaven and you,
That before you, and next unto high heaven,
I love your son:—
My friends were poor, but honest; so's my love:
Be not offended; for it hurts not him
That he is lov'd of me: I follow him not
By any token of presumptuous suit;
Nor would I have him till I do deserve him;
Yet never know how that desert should be.
I know I love in vain, strive against hope;
Yet in this captious and intenible sieve
I still pour in the waters of my love,
And lack not to lose still: thus, Indian-like,
Religious in mine error, I adore
The sun, that looks upon his worshipper,
But knows of him no more. My dearest madam,
Let not your hate encounter with my love,
For loving where you do; but, if yourself,
Whose aged honours cites a virtuous youth,
Did ever, in so true a frame of liking,
Wish chastely, and love dearly, that your Dian
Was both herself and love; O, then, give pity
To her whose state is such that cannot choose
But lend and give where she is sure to lose;
That seeks not to find that her search implies,
But, riddle-like, lives sweetly where she dies!
     *Count.* Had you not lately an intent,—speak
          truly,—
To go to Paris?
     *Hel.*          Madam, I had.
     *Count.*          Wherefore? tell true.
     *Hel.* I will tell truth; by grace itself I swear.
You know my father left me some prescriptions
Of rare and prov'd effects, such as his reading
And manifest experience had collected
For general sovereignty; and that he will'd me
In heedfulest reservation to bestow them,
As notes whose faculties inclusive were
More than they were in note: amongst the rest
There is a remedy, approv'd, set down,
To cure the desperate languishings whereof
The king is render'd lost.
     *Count.*          This was your motive
For Paris, was it? speak.                    [this;
     *Hel.* My lord your son made me to think of
Else Paris, and the medicine, and the king,
Had from the conversation of my thoughts
Haply been absent then.
     *Count.*          But think you, Helen,
If you should tender your supposed aid,
He would receive it? He and his physicians
Are of a mind; he, that they cannot help him,
They, that they cannot help: how shall they
          credit
A poor unlearned virgin, when the schools,
Embowell'd of their doctrine, have left off
The danger to itself?

*Hel.*               There's something in 't
More than my father's skill, which was the
          greatest
Of his profession, that his good receipt
Shall, for my legacy, be sanctified
By the luckiest stars in heaven: and, would
          your honour
But give me leave to try success, I'd venture
The well-lost life of mine on his grace's cure
By such a day and hour.
     *Count.*               Dost thou believe 't?
     *Hel.* Ay, madam, knowingly.
     *Count.* Why, Helen, thou shalt have my
          leave, and love,
Means, and attendants, and my loving greetings
To those of mine in court: I'll stay at home,
And pray God's blessings into thy attempt:
Be gone to-morrow; and be sure of this,
What I can help thee to thou shalt not miss.
                              [*Exeunt.*

## ACT II.

SCENE I.—PARIS. *A Room in the* KING'S *Palace.*

*Flourish. Enter* KING, *with young* Lords *taking
     leave for the Florentine war;* BERTRAM, PA-
     ROLLES, *and* Attendants.

*King.* Farewell, young lord; these warlike
          principles                    [farewell:—
Do not throw from you:—and you, my lord,
Share the advice betwixt you; if both gain all,
The gift doth stretch itself as 'tis received,
And is enough for both.
     1 *Lord.*          It is our hope, sir,
After well-enter'd soldiers, to return
And find your grace in health.
     *King.* No, no, it cannot be; and yet my heart
Will not confess he owes the malady    [lords;
That doth my life besiege. Farewell, young
Whether I live or die, be you the sons
Of worthy Frenchmen; let higher Italy,—
Those bated that inherit but the fall
Of the last monarchy,—see that you come
Not to woo honour, but to wed it; when
The bravest questant shrinks, find what you
          seek,
That fame may cry you loud: I say, farewell.
     2 *Lord.* Health, at your bidding, serve your
          majesty!
     *King.* Those girls of Italy, take heed of them:
They say our French lack language to deny,
If they demand: beware of being captives
Before you serve
     *Both.*          Our hearts receive your warnings.
     *King.* Farewell.—Come hither to me.
                    [*The* KING *retires to a couch.*
     1 *Lord.* O my sweet lord, that you will stay
          behind us!
     *Par.* 'Tis not his fault; the spark——
     2 *Lord.*          O, 'tis brave wars!
     *Par.* Most admirable: I have seen those
          wars.                              [with,
     *Ber.* I am commanded here, and kept a coil
*Too young, and the next year, and 'tis too early.*

*Par.* An thy mind stand to it, boy, steal
away bravely.                    [smock,
*Ber.* I shall stay here the forehorse to a
Creaking my shoes on the plain masonry,
Till honour be bought up, and no sword worn
But one to dance with! By heaven, I'll steal
away.
1 *Lord.* There's honour in the theft.
*Par.*                    Commit it, count.
2 *Lord.* I am your accessary, and so farewell.
*Ber.* I grow to you, and our parting is a tortured body.
1 *Lord.* Farewell, captain.
2 *Lord.* Sweet Monsieur Parolles!
*Par.* Noble heroes, my sword and yours are
kin. Good sparks and lustrous, a word, good
metals.—You shall find in the regiment of the
Spinii one Captain Spurio, with his cicatrice, an
emblem of war, here on his sinister cheek, it
was this very sword entrenched it: say to him
I live, and observe his reports for me.
2 *Lord.* We shall, noble captain.
*Par.* Mars dote on you for his novices!
[*Exeunt* LORDS.] What will ye do?
*Ber.* Stay; the king——
*Par.* Use a more spacious ceremony to the
noble lords; you have restrained yourself within the list of too cold an adieu: be more expressive to them; for they wear themselves in the
cap of the time; there do muster true gait, eat,
speak, and move under the influence of the
most received star; and though the devil lead
the measure, such are to be followed: after
them, and take a more dilated farewell.
*Ber.* And I will do so.
*Par.* Worthy fellows; and like to prove most
sinewy sword-men.
            [*Exeunt* BERTRAM *and* PAROLLES

*Enter* LAFEU.

*Laf.* Pardon, my lord [*kneeling*], for me and
for my tidings.
*King.* I'll fee thee to stand up.
*Laf.* Then here's a man stands that has
bought his pardon.                    [mercy;
I would you had kneel'd, my lord, to ask me
And that, at my bidding, you could so stand up.
*King.* I would I had; so I had broke thy
pate,
And ask'd thee mercy for't.
*Laf.*                    Good faith, across;
But, my good lord, 'tis thus: Will you be cured
Of your infirmity?
*King.*          No.
*Laf.*               O, will you eat
No grapes, my royal fox? yes, but you will
My noble grapes, and if my royal fox
Could reach them: I have seen a medicine
That's able to breathe life into a stone,
Quicken a rock, and make you dance canary
With spritely fire and motion; whose simple
touch
Is powerful to araise King Pipin, nay,
To give great Charlemain a pen in his hand

And write to her a love-line.
*King.*                    What *her* is that?
*Laf.* Why, doctor *she:* my lord, there's one
arriv'd,                    [honour,
If you will see her,—now, by my faith and
If seriously I may convey my thoughts
In this my light deliverance, I have spoke
With one that in her sex, her years, profession,
Wisdom, and constancy hath amaz'd me more
Than I dare blame my weakness: will you see
her,—                    [ness?
For that is her demand,—and know her busi-
That done, laugh well at me.
*King.*                    Now, good Lafeu,
Bring in the admiration; that we with thee
May spend our wonder too, or take off thine
By wondering how thou took'st it.
*Laf.*                    Nay, I'll fit you,
And not be all day neither.          [*Exit* LAFEU.
*King.* Thus he his special nothing ever pro-
logues.

*Re-enter* LAFEU *with* HELENA.

*Laf.* Nay, come your ways.
*King.*          This haste hath wings indeed.
*Laf.* Nay, come your ways;
This is his majesty: say your mind to him:
A traitor you do look like; but such traitors
His majesty seldom fears: I am Cressid's uncle,
That dare leave two together: fare you well.
                              [*Exit.*
*King.* Now, fair one, does your business fol-
low us?                    [was
*Hel.* Ay, my good lord. Gerard de Narbon
My father; in what he did profess well found.
*King.* I knew him.
*Hel.* The rather will I spare my praises to-
wards him.
Knowing him is enough. On his bed of death
Many receipts he gave me; chiefly one,
Which, as the dearest issue of his practice,
And of his old experience the only darling,
He bade me store up as a triple eye,
Safer than mine own two, more dear: I have so
And, hearing your high majesty is touch'd
With that malignant cause wherein the honour
Of my dear father's gift stands chief in power,
I come to tender it, and my appliance,
With all bound humbleness.
*King.*          We thank you, maiden;
But may not be so credulous of cure,—
When our most learned doctors leave us, and
The congregated college have concluded
That labouring art can never ransom nature
From her inaidable estate,—I say we must not
So stain our judgment, or corrupt our hope,
To prostitute our past-cure malady
To empirics; or, to dissever so
Our great self and our credit, to esteem
A senseless help, when help past sense we deem.
*Hel.* My duty, then, shall pay me for my
pains:
I will no more enforce mine office on you;
Humbly entreating from your royal thoughts

A modest one to bear me back again.

*King.* I cannot give thee less, to be call'd
grateful. [I give
Thou thought'st to help me; and such thanks
As one near death to those that wish him live:
But what at full I know, thou know'st no part;
I knowing all my peril, thou no art.

*Hel.* What I can do can do no hurt to try,
Since you set up your rest 'gainst remedy.
He that of greatest works is finisher
Oft does them by the weakest minister:
So holy writ in babes hath judgment shown,
When judges have been babes. Great floods
have flown
From simple sources; and great seas have dried
When miracles have by the greatest been denied.
Oft expectation fails, and most oft there
Where most it promises; and oft it hits
Where hope is coldest, and despair most fits.

*King.* I must not hear thee: fare thee well,
kind maid;
Thy pains, not used, must by thyself be paid:
Proffers, not took, reap thanks for their reward.

*Hel.* Inspired merit so by breath is barred:
It is not so with Him that all things knows,
As 'tis with us that square our guess by shows:
But most it is presumption in us when
The help of heaven we count the act of men.
Dear sir, to my endeavours give consent:
Of heaven, not me, make an experiment.
I am not an impostor, that proclaim
Myself against the level of mine aim;
But know I think, and think I know most sure,
My art is not past power nor you past cure.

*King.* Art thou so confident? Within what
space
Hop'st thou my cure?

*Hel.* The greatest grace lending grace,
Ere twice the horses of the sun shall bring
Their fiery torcher his diurnal ring;
Ere twice in murk and occidental damp
Moist Hesperus hath quench'd his sleepy lamp;
Or four-and-twenty times the pilot's glass
Hath told the thievish minutes how they pass;
What is infirm from your sound parts shall fly,
Health shall live free, and sickness freely die.

*King.* Upon thy certainty and confidence,
What dars't thou venture?

*Hel.* Tax of impudence,—
A strumpet's boldness, a divulged shame,—
Traduc'd by odious ballads; my maiden's name
Sear'd otherwise; ne worse of worst extended,
With vilest torture let my life be ended.

*King.* Methinks in thee some blessed spirit
doth speak;
His powerful sound within an organ weak:
And what impossibility would slay.
In common sense, sense saves another way.
Thy life is dear; for all that life can rate
Worth name of life in thee hath estimate:
Youth, beauty, wisdom, courage, all
That happiness in prime can happy call;
Thou this to hazard needs must intimate
Skill infinite, or monstrous desperate.

Sweet practiser, thy physic I will try:
That ministers thine own death if I die.

*Hel.* If I break time, or flinch in property
Of what I spoke, unpitied let me die;
And well deserv'd. Not helping, death's my fee;
But, if I help, what do you promise me?

*King.* Make thy demand.

*Hel.* But will you make it even?

*King.* Ay, by my sceptre and my hopes of
heaven. [ly hand,

*Hel.* Then shalt thou give me, with thy king-
What husband in thy power I will command:
Exempted be from me the arrogance
To choose from forth the royal blood of France,
My low and humble name to propagate
With any branch or image of thy state:
But such a one, thy vassal, whom I know
Is free for me to ask, thee to bestow.

*King.* Here is my hand; the premises ob-
serv'd,
Thy will by my performance shall be serv'd;
So make the choice of thy own tie, for I,
Thy resolv'd patient, on thee still rely.
More should I question thee, and more I must,—
Though more to know could not be more to
trust,—
From whence thou cam'st, how tended on.—
But rest
Unquestion'd welcome and undoubted blest.—
Give me some help here, ho!—If thou proceed
As high as word, my deed shall match thy deed.
[*Flourish. Exeunt.*

SCENE II.—ROUSILLON. *A Room in the*
COUNTESS'S *Palace.*

*Enter* COUNTESS *and* CLOWN.

*Count.* Come on, sir; I shall now put you to
the height of your breeding.

*Clo.* I will show myself highly fed and lowly
taught: I know my business is but to the court.

*Count.* To the court! why, what place make
you special, when you put off that with such
contempt? But to the court!

*Clo.* Truly, madam, if God have lent a man
any manners, he may easily put if off at court:
he that cannot make a leg, put off's cap, kiss his
hand, and say nothing, has neither leg, hands,
lip, nor cap; and, indeed, such a fellow, to say
precisely, were not for the court: but, for me, I
have an answer will serve all men.

*Count.* Marry, that's a bountiful answer that
fits all questions.

*Clo.* It is like a barber's chair, that fits all
buttocks,—the pin-buttock, the quatch-but-
tock, the brawn-buttock, or any buttock.

*Count.* Will your answer serve fit to all questions?

*Clo.* As fit as ten groats is for the hand of a
attorney, as your French crown for your taffeta
punk, as Tib's rush for Tom's forefinger, as a
pancake for Shrove-Tuesday, a morris for May-
day, as the nail to his hole, the cuckold to his
horn, as a scolding quean to a wrangling knave,

as the nun's lip to the friar's mouth; nay, as the pudding to his skin.

*Count.* Have you, I say, an answer of such fitness for all questions?

*Clo.* From below your duke to beneath your constable, it will fit any question.

*Count.* It must be an answer of most monstrous size that must fit all demands.

*Clo.* But a trifle neither, in good faith, if the learned should speak truth of it: here it is, and all that belongs to't. Ask me if I am a courtier: it shall do you no harm to learn.

*Count.* To be young again, if we could: I will be a fool in question, hoping to be the wiser by your answer. I pray you, sir, are you a courtier?

*Clo.* O Lord, sir!—There's a simple putting off;—more, more, a hundred of them.

*Count.* Sir, I am a poor friend of yours, that loves you.                                      [me.

*Clo.* O Lord, sir!—Thick, thick; spare not

*Count.* I think, sir, you can eat none of this homely meat.

*Clo.* O Lord, sir!—Nay, put me to't, I warrant you.

*Count.* You were lately whipped, sir, as I think.

*Clo.* O Lord, sir!—spare not me.

*Count.* Do you cry, *O Lord, sir!* at your whipping, and *spare not me?* Indeed, your *O Lord, sir!* is very sequent to your whipping: you would answer very well to a whipping, if you were but bound to't.

*Clo.* I ne'er had worse luck in my life in my —*O Lord, sir!* I see things may serve long, but not serve ever.

*Count.* I play the noble housewife with the time, to entertain it so merrily with a fool.

*Clo.* O Lord, sir!—Why, there't serves well again.

*Count.* An end, sir, to your business. Give
    Helen this,
And urge her to a present answer back:
Commend me to my kinsmen and my son:
This is not much.

*Clo.* Not much commendation to them.

*Count.* Not much employment for you: you understand me?

*Clo.* Most fruitfully: I am there before my legs.

*Count.* Haste you again.     [*Exeunt severally.*

SCENE III.—PARIS. *A Room in the* KING'S
    *Palace.*

*Enter* BERTRAM, LAFEU, *and* PAROLLES.

*Laf.* They say miracles are past; and we have our philosophical persons to make modern and familiar things supernatural and causeless. Hence is it that we make trifles of terrors, ensconcing ourselves into seeming knowledge when we should submit ourselves to an unknown fear.

*Par.* Why, 'tis the rarest argument of wonder that hath shot out in our latter times.

*Ber.* And so 'tis.

*Laf.* To be relinquished of the artists,—

*Par.* So I say; both of Galen and Paracelsus.

*Laf.* Of all the learned and authentic fellows,—

*Par.* Right; so I say.

*Laf.* That gave him out incurable,—

*Par.* Why, there 'tis; so say I too.

*Laf.* Not to be helped,—

*Par.* Right; as 'twere a man assured of a,—

*Laf.* Uncertain life and sure death.     [said.

*Par.* Just; you say well: so would I have

*Laf.* I may truly say, it is a novelty to the world.

*Par.* It is indeed: if you will have it in showing, you shall read it in,—What do you call there?—

*Laf.* A showing of a heavenly effect in an earthly actor.                                      [same.

*Par.* That's it I would have said; the very

*Laf.* Why, your dolphin is not lustier: 'fore me, I speak in respect,—

*Par.* Nay, 'tis strange, 'tis very strange; that is the brief and the tedious of it; and he is of a most facinorous spirit that will not acknowledge it to be the,—

*Laf.* Very hand of heaven.

*Par.* Ay; so I say.

*Laf.* In a most weak,—

*Par.* And debile minister, great power, great transcendence: which should, indeed, give us a further use to be made than alone the recovery of the king, as to be,—

*Laf.* Generally thankful.

*Par.* I would have said it; you say well. Here comes the king.

*Enter* KING, HELENA, *and* Attendants.

*Laf.* Lustic, as the Dutchman says: I'll like a maid the better, whilst I have a tooth in my head: why, he's able to lead her a coranto.

*Par. Mort du Vinaigre!* is not this Helen?

*Laf.* 'Fore God, I think so.

*King.* Go, call before me all the lords in
    court.—                    [*Exit an* Attendant.
Sit, my preserver, by thy patient's side;
And with this healthful hand, whose banish'd sense
Thou hast repeal'd, a second time receive
The confirmation of my promis'd gift,
Which but attends thy naming.

*Enter several* Lords.

Fair maid, send forth thine eye: this youthful parcel
Of noble bachelors stand at my bestowing,
O'er whom both sovereign power and father's voice
I have to use: thy frank election make;
Thou hast power to choose, and they none to forsake.                                      [mistress

*Hel.* To each of you one fair and virtuous
Fall, when love please!—marry, to each, but one!

*Laf.* I'd give bay Curtal, and his furniture,

My mouth no more were broken than these boys',
And writ as little beard.

*King.* Peruse them well:
Not one of those but had a noble father.

*Hel.* Gentlemen,
Heaven hath, through me, restor'd the king to health. [you.

*All.* We understand it, and thank heaven for

*Hel.* I am a simple maid, and therein wealthiest
That I protest I simply am a maid.—
Please it, your majesty, I have done already:
The blushes in my cheeks thus whisper me—
*We blush that thou shouldst choose; but, be refus'd,*
*Let the white death sit on thy cheek for ever;*
*We'll ne'er come there again.*

*King.* Make choice; and, see,
Who shuns thy love shuns all his love in me.

*Hel.* Now, Dian, from thy altar do I fly,
And to imperial Love, that god most high,
Do my sighs stream.—Sir, will you hear my suit?

1 *Lord.* And grant it.

*Hel.* Thanks, sir; all the rest is mute.

*Laf.* I had rather be in this choice than
throw ames-ace for my life. [eyes,

*Hel.* The honour, sir, that flames in your fair
Before I speak, too threateningly replies:
Love make your fortunes twenty times above
Her that so wishes, and her humble love!

2 *Lord.* No better, if you please.

*Hel.* My wish receive,
Which great Love grant! and so I take my leave.

*Laf.* Do all they deny her? An they were
sons of mine I'd have them whipped; or I would
send them to the Turk to make eunuchs of.

*Hel.* [*To third* Lord.] Be not afraid that I
your hand should take;
I'll never do you wrong for your own sake:
Blessing upon your vows! and in your bed
Find fairer fortune, if you ever wed!

*Laf.* These boys are boys of ice; they'll none
have her: sure, they are bastards to the English; the French ne'er got them. [good

*Hel.* You are too young, too happy, and too
To make yourself a son out of my blood.

4 *Lord.* Fair one, I think not so.

*Laf.* There's one grape yet,—I am sure thy
father drank wine.—But if thou beest not an
ass, I am a youth of fourteen; I have known
thee already.

*Hel.* [*To* BERTRAM.] I dare not say I take
you; but I give
Me and my service, ever whilst I live,
Into your guiding power.—This is the man.

*King.* Why, then, young Bertram, take her;
she's thy wife. [highness,

*Ber.* My wife, my liege! I shall beseech your
In such a business give me leave to use
The help of mine own eyes.

*King.* Know'st thou not, Bertram,
What she has done for me?

*Ber.* Yes, my good lord;
But never hope to know why I should marry
her. [my sickly bed.

*King.* Thou know'st she has rais'd me from

*Ber.* But follows it, my lord, to bring me down
Must answer for your raising? I know her well;
She had her breeding at my father's charge;
A poor physician's daughter my wife!—Disdain
Rather corrupt me ever! [the which

*King.* 'Tis only title thou disdain'st in her,
I can build up. Strange is it that our bloods,
Of colour, weight, and heat, pour'd all together,
Would quite confound distinction, yet stand off
In differences so mighty. If she be
All that is virtuous,—save what thou dislik'st,
A poor physician's daughter,—thou dislik'st
Of virtue for the name: but do not so:
From lowest place when virtuous things proceed,
The place is dignified by the doer's deed:
Where great additions swell 's, and virtue none,
It is a dropsied honour: good alone
Is good without a name, vileness is so:
The property by what it is should go,
Not by the title. She is young, wise, fair;
In these to nature she's immediate heir;
And these breed honour: that is honour's scorn
Which challenges itself as honour's born,
And is not like the sire: honours thrive,
When rather from our acts we them derive
Than our fore-goers: the mere word's a slave,
Debauch'd on every tomb; on every grave
A lying trophy; and as oft is dumb
Where dust and damn'd oblivion is the tomb
Of honour'd bones indeed. What should be said?
If thou canst like this creature as a maid,
I can create the rest: virtue and she
Is her own dower; honour and wealth from me.

*Ber.* I cannot love her, nor will strive to do 't.

*King.* Thou wrong'st thyself, if thou shouldst
strive to choose. [am glad:

*Hel.* That you are well restor'd, my lord, I
Let the rest go. [defeat,

*King.* My honour's at the stake; which to
I must produce my power. Here, take her hand,
Proud scornful boy, unworthy this good gift;
That dost in vile misprision shackle up
My love and her desert; that canst not dream
We, poising us in her defective scale,
Shall weigh thee to the beam; that wilt not know
It is in us to plant thine honour where
We please to have it grow. Check thy contempt:
Obey our will, which travails in thy good:
Believe not thy disdain, but presently
Do thine own fortunes that obedient right
Which both thy duty owes and our power claims
Or I will throw thee from my care for ever,
Into the staggers and the careless lapse
Of youth and ignorance; both my revenge and hate
Loosing upon thee in the name of justice,

Without all terms of pity. Speak!—thine
answer!

*Ber.* Pardon, my gracious lord; for I submit
My fancy to your eyes: when I consider
What great creation, and what dole of honour
Flies where you bid it, I find that she, which
late
Was in my nobler thoughts most base, is now
The praised of the king; who, so ennobled,
Is as 'twere born so.

*King.*              Take her by the hand,
And tell her she is thine: to whom I promise
A counterpoise; if not to thy estate,
A balance more replete.

*Ber.*              I take her hand.

*King.* Good fortune and the favour of the king
Smile upon this contract; whose ceremony
Shall seem expedient on the new-born brief,
And be perform'd to-night: the solemn feast
Shall more attend upon the coming space,
Expecting absent friends. As thou lov'st her,
Thy love's to me religious; else, does err.

[*Exeunt* KING, BER., HEL., Lords,
and Attendants.

*Laf.* Do you hear, monsieur? a word with
you.

*Par.* Your pleasure, sir?

*Laf.* Your lord and master did well to make
his recantation.

*Par.* Recantation!—My lord! my master!

*Laf.* Ay; is it not a language I speak?

*Par.* A most harsh one, and not to be understood without bloody succeeding. My master!

*Laf.* Are you companion to the Count
Rousillon?                              [is man.

*Par.* To any count; to all counts; to what

*Laf.* To what is count's man: count's master
is of another style.

*Par.* You are too old, sir; let it satisfy you,
you are too old.

*Laf.* I must tell thee, sirrah, I write man;
to which title age cannot bring thee.

*Par.* What I dare too well do, I dare not do.

*Laf.* I did think thee, for two ordinaries, to
be a pretty wise fellow; thou didst make tolerable vent of thy travel; it might pass: yet the
scarfs and the bannerets about thee did mani-
foldly dissuade me from believing thee a vessel
of two great a burden. I have now found thee,
when I lose thee again I care not: yet art thou
good for nothing but taking up; and that thou
art scarce worth.

*Par.* Hadst thou not the privilege of antiquity upon thee,—

*Laf.* Do not plunge thyself too far in anger,
lest thou hasten thy trial; which if—Lord have
mercy on thee for a hen! So, my good window
of lattice, fare thee well: thy casement I need
not open, for I look through thee. Give me thy
hand.                              [indignity.

*Par.* My lord, you give me most egregious

*Laf.* Ay, with all my heart; and thou art
worthy of it.

*Par.* I have not, my lord, deserved it.

*Laf.* Yes, good faith, every dram of it: and
I will not bate thee a scruple.

*Par.* Well, I shall be wiser.

*Laf.* E'en as soon as thou canst, for thou hast
to pull at a smack o' the contrary. If ever thou
beest bound in thy scarf and beaten, thou shalt
find what it is to be proud of thy bondage. I
have a desire to hold my acquaintance with
thee, or rather my knowledge, that I may say,
in the default, he is a man I know.

*Par.* My lord, you do me most insupportable
vexation

*Laf.* I would it were hell-pains for thy sake,
and my poor doing eternal: for doing I am past;
as I will by thee, in what motion age will give
me leave.                                   [*Exit.*

*Par.* Well, thou hast a son shall take this
disgrace off me; scurvy, old, filthy, scurvy
lord!—Well, I must be patient; there is no fet-
tering of authority. I'll beat him, by my life, if
I can meet him with any convenience, an he
were double and double a lord. I'll have no
more pity of his age than I would have of—I'll
beat him, an if I could but meet him again.

*Re-enter* LAFEU.

*Laf.* Sirrah, your lord and master's married;
there's news for you; you have a new mistress.

*Par.* I most unfeignedly beseech your lordship to make some reservation of your wrongs:
he is my good lord: whom I serve above is my
master.

*Laf.* Who? God?

*Par.* Ay, sir.

*Laf.* The devil it is that's thy master. Why
dost thou garter up thy arms o' this fashion?
dost make hose of thy sleeves? do other servants so? Thou wert best set thy lower part
where thy nose stands. By mine honour, if I
were but two hours younger I'd beat thee:
methink'st thou art a general offence, and
every man should beat thee. I think thou wast
created for men to breathe themselves upon
thee.

*Par.* This is hard and undeserved measure,
my lord.

*Laf.* Go to, sir; you were beaten in Italy for
picking a kernel out of a pomegranate; you are
a vagabond, and no true traveller: you are more
saucy with lords and honourable personages
than the heraldry of your birth and virtue gives
you commission. You are not worth another
word, else I'd call you knave. I leave you.
                                        [*Exit.*

*Par.* Good, very good; it is so then.—Good,
very good; let it be concealed awhile.

*Enter* BERTRAM.

*Ber.* Undone, and forfeited to cares for ever!

*Par.* What is the matter, sweet heart?

*Ber.* Although before the solemn priest I
have sworn,
I will not bed her.

*Par.* What, what, sweet heart?

*Ber.* O my Parolles, they have married me!—
I'll to the Tuscan wars, and never bed her.
  *Par.* France is a dog-hole, and it no more
    merits
The tread of a man's foot:—to the wars!
  *Ber.* There's letters from my mother: what
    the import is
I know not yet.
  *Par.* Ay, that would be known. To the wars,
    my boy, to the wars!
He wears his honour in a box unseen
That hugs his kieksy-wicksy here at home,
Spending his manly marrow in her arms,
Which should sustain the bound and high curvet
Of Mars's fiery steed. To other regions!
France is a stable; we, that dwell in't, jades;
Therefore, to the war!      [house,
  *Ber.* It shall be so; I'll send her tó my house,
Acquaint my mother with my hate to her,
And wherefore I am fled; write to the king
That which I durst not speak: his present gift
Shall furnish me to those Italian fields
Where noble fellows strike: war is no strife
To the dark house and the detested wife.
  *Par.* Will this caprichio hold in thee, art
    sure?      [me.
  *Ber.* Go with me to my chamber and advise
I'll send her straight away: to-morrow
I'll to the wars, she to her single sorrow.
  *Par.* Why, these balls bound; there's noise
    in it. 'Tis hard;
A young man married is a man that's marr'd:
Therefore away, and leave her bravely; go:
The king has done you wrong: but, hush! 'tis
so.      [*Exeunt*

SCENE IV.—*The same. Another Room in the
same.*

*Enter* HELENA *and* Clown.

  *Hel.* My mother greets me kindly: is she
well?
  *Clo.* She is not well; but yet she has her
health: she's very merry; but yet she is not
well: but thanks be given, she's very well, and
wants nothing i' the world; but yet she is not
well.
  *Hel.* If she be very well, what does she ail,
that she's not very well?
  *Clo.* Truly, she's very well indeed, but for
two things.
  *Hel.* What two things?
  *Clo.* One, that she's not in heaven, whither
God send her quickly! the other, that she's in
earth, from whence God send her quickly!

*Enter* PAROLLES.

  *Par.* Bless you, my fortunate lady!
  *Hel.* I hope, sir, I have your good will to
have mine own good fortunes.
  *Par.* You had my prayers to lead them on;
and to keep them on, have them still. O, my
knave,—how does my old lady?
  *Clo.* So that you had her wrinkles and I her
money, I would she did as you say.

  *Par.* Why, I say nothing.
  *Clo.* Marry, you are the wiser man; for many
a man's tongue shakes out his master's undoing: to say nothing, to do nothing, to know
nothing, and to have nothing, is to be a great
part of your title; which is within a verv little
of nothing.
  *Par.* Away! thou'rt a knave.
  *Clo.* You should have said, sir, before a
knave thou art a knave; that is, before me thou
art a knave: this had been truth, sir.
  *Par.* Go to, thou art a witty fool; I have
found thee.
  *Clo.* Did you find me in yourself, sir? or
were you taught to find me? The search, sir,
was profitable; and much fool may you find in
you, even to the world's pleasure and the in-
crease of laughter.
  *Par.* A good knave, i' faith, and well fed.—
Madam, my lord will go away to-night:
A very serious business calls on him.
The great prerogative and right of love,
Which, as your due, time claims, he does ac-
    knowledge;
But puts it off to a compell'd restraint;
Whose want and whose delay is strew'd with
    sweets;
Which they distil now in the curbed time,
To make the coming hour o'erflow with joy,
And pleasure drown the brim.
  *Hel.*        What's his will else?
  *Par.* That you will take your instant leave o'
    the king,      [ing,
And make this haste as your own good proceed-
Strengthen'd with what apology you think
May make it probable need.
  *Hel.*      What more commands he?
  *Par.* That, having this obtain'd, you pre-
    sently
Attend his further pleasure.
  *Hel.* In everything I wait upon his will.
  *Par.* I shall report it so.
  *Hel.*        I pray you.—Come, sirrah.
      [*Exeunt.*

SCENE V.—*Another Room in the same.*

*Enter* LAFEU *and* BERTRAM.

  *Laf.* But I hope your lordship thinks not
him a soldier.
  *Ber.* Yes, my lord, and of very valiant ap-
    proof.
  *Laf.* You have it from his own deliverance.
  *Ber.* And by other warranted testimony.
  *Laf.* Then my dial goes not true: I took this
lark for a bunting.
  *Ber.* I do assure you, my lord, he is very
great in knowledge, and accordingly valiant.
  *Laf.* I have, then, sinned against his experience and transgressed against his valour; and
my state that way is dangerous, since I cannot
yet find in my heart to repent. Here he comes:
I pray you, make us friends; I will pursue the
amity.

*Enter* PAROLLES.

*Par.* These things shall be done, sir.
                              [*To* BER.
*Laf.* Pray you, sir, who's his tailor?
*Par.* Sir!
*Laf.* O, I know him well, I, sir; he, sir, is a good workman, a very good tailor.
*Ber.* Is she gone to the king? [*Aside to* PAR.
*Par.* She is.
*Ber.* Will she away to-night?
*Par.* As you'll have her.                 [treasure,
*Ber.* I have writ my letters, casketed my
Given order for our horses; and to-night,
When I should take possession of the bride,
End ere I do begin.
*Laf.* A good traveller is something at the latter end of a dinner; but one that lies three-thirds and uses a known truth to pass a thousand nothings with, should be once heard and thrice beaten.—God save you, captain.
*Ber.* Is there any unkindness between my lord and you, monsieur?
*Par.* I know not how I have deserved to run into my lord's displeasure.
*Laf.* You have made shift to run into 't, boots and spurs and all, like him that leaped into the custard; and out of it you'll run again, rather than suffer question for your residence.
*Ber.* It may be you have mistaken him, my lord.
*Laf.* And shall do so ever, though I took him at his prayers. Fare you well, my lord; and believe this of me, there can be no kernel in this light nut; the soul of this man is his clothes: trust him not in matter of heavy consequence; I have kept of them tame, and know their natures.—Farewell, monsieur: I have spoken better of you than you have or will deserve at my hand; but we must do good against evil.
                                        [*Exit.*
*Par.* An idle lord, I swear.
*Ber.* I think so.
*Par.* Why, do you not know him?    [speech
*Ber.* Yes, I do know him well; and common
Gives him a worthy pass. Here comes my clog.

*Enter* HELENA.

*Hel.* I have, sir, as I was commanded from
    you,                                [leave
Spoke with the king, and have procur'd his
For present parting; only, he desires
Some private speech with you.
*Ber.*                  I shall obey his will.
You must not marvel, Helen, at my course,
Which holds not colour with the time, nor does
The ministration and required office
On my particular. Prepared I was not
For such a business; therefore am I found
So much unsettled: this drives me to entreat
    you
That presently you take your way for home,
And rather muse than ask why I entreat you:
For my respects are better than they seem;
And my appointments have in them a need

Greater than shows itself at the first view
To you that know them not. This to my
    mother:                        [*Giving a letter.*
'Twill be two days ere I shall see you; so
I leave you to your wisdom.
*Hel.*           Sir, I can nothing say
But that I am your most obedient servant.
*Ber.* Come, come, no more of that.
*Hel.*                     And ever shall
With true obedience seek to eke out that
Wherein toward me my homely stars have
    fail'd
To equal my great fortune.
*Ber.*              Let that go:
My haste is very great. Farewell; hie home.
*Hel.* Pray, sir, your pardon.
*Ber.* Well, what would you say?
*Hel.* I am not worthy of the wealth I owe;
Nor dare I say 'tis mine, and yet it is;   [steal
But, like a timorous thief, most fain would
What law does vouch mine own.
*Ber.*              What would you have?
*Hel.* Something; and scarce so much:—no-
    thing, indeed.—             [faith, yes;—
I would not tell you what I would, my lord:—
Strangers and foes do sunder and not kiss.
*Ber.* I pray you, stay not, but in haste to
    horse.                           [my lord.
*Hel.* I shall not break your bidding, good
*Ber.* Where are my other men, monsieur?—
    Farewell,                      [*Exit* HELENA.
Go thou toward home, where I will never come
Whilst I can shake my sword or hear the
    drum:—
Away, and for our flight.
*Par.*             Bravely, coragio! [*Exeunt.*

## ACT III.

### SCENE I.—FLORENCE. *A Room in the* DUKE'S *Palace.*

*Flourish. Enter the* DUKE OF FLORENCE, *attended; two* French Lords, *and* Soldiers.

*Duke.* So that, from point to point, now have
    you heard
The fundamental reasons of this war;
Whose great decision hath much blood let
    forth,
And more thirsts after.
1 *Lord.*           Holy seems the quarrel
Upon your grace's part; black and fearful
On the opposer.                       [France
*Duke.* Therefore we marvel much our cousin
Would, in so just a business, shut his bosom
Against our borrowing prayers.
1 *Lord.*                 Good my lord,
The reasons of our state I cannot yield,
But like a common and an outward man
That the great figure of a council frames
By self-unable motion: therefore dare not
Say what I think of it, since I have found
Myself in my uncertain grounds to fail
As often as I guess'd.
*Duke.*            Be it his pleasure.

2 *Lord.* But I am sure the younger of our
    nature,
That surfeit on their ease, will day by day
Come here for physic.
    *Duke.*        Welcome shall they be;
And all the honours that can fly from us
Shall on them settle. You know your places
    well;
When better fall, for your avails they fell:
To-morrow to the field.    [*Flourish. Exeunt.*

    SCENE II.—ROUSILLON. *A Room in the*
        COUNTESS'S *Palace.*

    *Enter* COUNTESS *and* CLOWN.

    *Count.* It hath happened all as I would have
had it, save that he comes not along with her.
    *Clo.* By my troth, I take my young lord to
be a very melancholy man.
    *Count.* By what observance, I pray you?
    *Clo.* Why, he will look upon his boot and
sing; mend the ruff and sing; ask questions and
sing; pick his teeth and sing. I know a man that
had this trick of melancholy sold a goodly
manor for a song.
    *Count.* Let me see what he writes, and when
he means to come.    [*Opening a letter.*
    *Clo.* I have no mind to Isbel, since I was at
court: our old ling and our Isbels o' the country
are nothing like your old ling and your Isbels o'
the court: the brains of my Cupid's knocked
out; and I begin to love, as an old man loves
money, with no stomach.
    *Count.* What have we here?
    *Clo.* E'en that you have there.    [*Exit.*
    *Count.* [*Reads.*] *I have sent you a daughter-in-law: she hath recovered the king and undone me. I
have wedded her, not bedded her; and sworn to
make the not eternal. You shall hear I am run
away: know it before the report come. If there
be breadth enough in the world I will hold a long
distance. My duty to you.*

            *Your unfortunate son,*
                BERTRAM.
This is not well, rash and unbridled boy,
To fly the favours of so good a king;
To pluck his indignation on thy head
By the misprizing of a maid too virtuous
For the contempt of empire.

    *Re-enter* Clown.

    *Clo.* O madam, yonder is heavy news within,
between two soldiers and my young lady.
    *Count.* What is the matter?
    *Clo.* Nay, there is some comfort in the news,
some comfort; your son will not be killed so
soon as I thought he would.
    *Count.* Why should he be killed?
    *Clo.* So say I, madam, if he run away, as I
hear he does: the danger is in standing to't;
that's the loss of men, though it be the getting
of children. Here they come will tell you more:
for my part, I only hear your son was run away.
                    [*Exit.*

    *Enter* HELENA *and two* Gentlemen.

    *1 Gent.* Save you, good madam.
    *Hel.* Madam, my lord is gone, for ever gone.
    *2 Gent.* Do not say so.    [gentlemen,—
    *Count.* Think upon patience.—Pray you,
I have felt so many quirks of joy and grief
That the first face of neither, on the start,
Can woman me unto't.—Where is my son, I
    pray you?    [of Florence:
    *2 Gent.* Madam, he's gone to serve the duke
We met him thitherward; for thence we came,
And, after some despatch in hand at court,
Thither we bend again.    [passport.
    *Hel.* Look on his letter, madam; here's my
[*Reads.*] *When thou canst get the ring upon my
finger, which never shall come off, and show me
a child begotten of thy body that I am father to,
then call me husband; but in such a then I
write a* never.
This is a dreadful sentence.
    *Count.* Brought you this letter, gentlemen?
    *1 Gent.*            Ay, madam;
And, for the contents' sake, are sorry for our
    pains.
    *Count.* I pr'ythee, lady, have a better cheer;
If thou engrossest all the griefs are thine,
Thou robb'st me of a moiety. He was my son:
But I do wash his name out of my blood,
And thou art all my child.—Towards Florence
    is he?
    *2 Gent.* Ay, madam.
    *Count.*           And to be a soldier?
    *2 Gent.* Such is his noble purpose; and, be-
    lieve't,
The duke will lay upon him all the honour
That good convenience claims.
    *Count.*           Return you thither?
    *1 Gent.* Ay, madam, with the swiftest wing
    of speed.
    *Hel.* [*Reads.*] *Till I have no wife, I have no-
thing in France.*
'Tis bitter.
    *Count.* Find you that there?
    *Hel.*              Ay, madam.
    *1 Gent.* 'Tis but the boldness of his hand,
    haply,
Which his heart was not consenting to.
    *Count.* Nothing in France until he have no
    wife!
There's nothing here that is too good for him
But only she; and she deserves a lord
That twenty such rude boys might tend upon,
And call her hourly mistress. Who was with
    him?
    *1 Gent.* A servant only, and a gentleman
Which I have sometime known.
    *Count.*          Parolles, was't not?
    *1 Gent.* Ay, my good lady, he.
    *Count.* A very tainted fellow, and full of
    wickedness.
My son corrupts a well-derived nature
With his inducement.
    *1 Gent.*          Indeed, good lady,
The fellow has a deal of that too much,

Which holds him much to have.
  *Count.* You are welcome, gentlemen,
I will entreat you, when you see my son,
To tell him that his sword can never win
The honour that he loses: more I'll entreat you
Written to bear along.
  *2 Gent.*         We serve you, madam,
In that and all your worthiest affairs. [tesies.
  *Count.* Not so, but as we change our cour-
Will you draw near?
        [*Exeunt* COUNT. *and* Gentlemen.
  *Hel.* Till I have no wife, I have nothing in
    France.
Nothing in France until he has no wife!
Thou shalt have none, Rousillon, none in
    France;
Then hast thou all again. Poor lord! is't I
That chase thee from thy country, and expose
Those tender limbs of thine to the event
Of the none-sparing war? and is it I   [thou
That drive thee from the sportive court, where
Wast shot at with fair eyes, to be the mark
Of smoky muskets? O you leaden messengers,
That ride upon the violent speed of fire,
Fly with false aim: move the still-peering air,
That sings with piercing; do not touch my lord!
Whoever shoots at him, I set him there;
Whoever charges on his forward breast,
I am the caitiff that do hold him to it;
And, though I kill him not, I am the cause
His death was so effected: better 'twere
I met the ravin lion when he roar'd
With sharp constraint of hunger; better 'twere
That all the miseries which nature owes
Were mine at once. No; come thou home,
    Rousillon,
Whence honour but of danger wins a scar,
As oft it loses all. I will be gone:
My being here it is that holds thee hence:
Shall I stay here to do't? no, no, although
The air of paradise did fan the house,
And angels offic'd all: I will be gone,
That pitiful rumour may report my flight,
To consolate thine ear. Come, night; end, day!
For with the dark, poor thief, I'll steal away.
                      [*Exit.*

SCENE III.—FLORENCE. *Before the* DUKE'S
    *Palace.*

*Flourish. Enter the* DUKE OF FLORENCE, BER-
  TRAM, PAROLLES, *Lords, Officers, Soldiers,
  and others.*

  *Duke.* The general of our horse thou art; and
    we,
Great in our hope, lay our best love and cre-
    dence
Upon thy promising fortune.
  *Ber.*           Sir, it is
A charge too heavy for my strength; but yet
We'll strive to bear it, for your worthy sake,
To the extreme edge of hazard.
  *Duke.*         Then go thou forth;

And fortune play upon thy prosperous helm,
As thy auspicious mistress!
  *Ber.*            This very day,
Great Mars, I put myself into thy file;
Make me but like my thoughts, and I shall
    prove
A lover of thy drum, hater of love.   [*Exeunt.*

SCENE IV.—ROUSILLON. *A Room in the*
    COUNTESS'S *Palace.*

*Enter* COUNTESS *and* Steward.

  *Count.* Alas! and would you take the letter
    of her?                   [done,
Might you not know she would do as she has
By sending me a letter? Read it again.
  *Stew.* [*Reads.*] *I am St. Jaques' pilgrim,
    thither gone:
Ambitious love hath so in me offended
That barefoot plod I the cold ground upon,
  With sainted vow my faults to have amended.
Write, write, that from the bloody course of war
  My dearest master, your dear son, may hie:
Bless him at home in peace, whilst I from far
  His name with zealous fervour sanctify:
His taken labours bid him me forgive;
  I, his despiteful Juno, sent him forth
From courtly friends, with camping foes to live,
  Where death and danger dog the heels of worth:
He is too good and fair for death and me;
  Whom I myself embrace, to set him free.*
  *Count.* Ah, what sharp stings are in her mild-
    est words!—
Rinaldo, you did never lack advice so much
As letting her pass so; had I spoke with her,
I could have well diverted her intents,
Which thus she hath prevented.
  *Stew.*          Pardon me, madam:
If I had given you this at over-night,   [writes,
She might have been o'erta'en; and yet she
Pursuit would be but vain.
  *Count.*         What angel shall
Bless this unworthy husband? he cannot thrive,
Unless her prayers, whom heaven delights to
    hear,
And loves to grant, reprieve him from the
    wrath
Of greatest justice.—Write, write, Rinaldo,
To this unworthy husband of his wife:
Let every word weigh heavy of her worth,
That he does weigh too light: my greatest grief,
Though little he do feel it, set down sharply,
Despatch the most convenient messenger:—
When, haply, he shall hear that she is gone
He will return; and hope I may that she,
Hearing so much, will speed her foot again,
Led hither by pure love: which of them both
Is dearest to me I have no skill in sense
To make distinction:—provide this messen-
    ger:—
My heart is heavy, and mine age is weak;
Grief would have tears, and sorrow bids me
    speak.                  [*Exeunt.*

SCENE V.—*Without the Walls of* FLORENCE.

*Enter an old* Widow *of Florence,* DIANA, VIO-
LENTA, MARIANA, *and other* Citizens.

*Wid.* Nay, come; for if they do approach the
city we shall lose all the sight.

*Dia.* They say the French count has done
most honourable service.

*Wid.* It is reported that he has taken their
greatest commander; and that with his own
hand he slew the duke's brother. [*A tucket afar
off.*] We have lost our labour; they are gone a
contrary way: hark! you may know by their
trumpets.

*Mar.* Come, let's return again, and suffice
ourselves with the report·of it. Well, Diana,
take heed of this French earl: the honour of a
maid is her name; and no legacy is so rich as
honesty.

*Wid.* I have told my neighbour how you
have been solicited by a gentleman his companion.

*Mar.* I know that knave; hang him! one
Parolles: a filthy officer he is in those suggestions for the young earl.—Beware of them,
Diana; their promises, enticements, oaths,
tokens, and all these engines of lust, are not the
things they go under: many a maid hath been
seduced by them; and the misery is, example,
that so terrible shows in the wreck of maidenhood, cannot for all that dissuade succession,
but that they are limed with the twigs that
threaten them. I hope I need not to advise you
further; but I hope your own grace will keep
you where you are, though there were no further danger known but the modesty which is so
lost.

*Dia.* You shall not need to fear me.

*Wid.* I hope so.—Look, here comes a pilgrim: I know she will lie at my house: thither
they send one another; I'll question her.—

*Enter* HELENA *in the dress of a pilgrim.*

God save you, pilgrim! Whither are you bound?

*Hel.* To Saint Jaques-le-Grand.
Where do the palmers lodge, I do beseech you?

*Wid.* At the Saint Francis here, beside the
port.

*Hel.* Is this the way?

*Wid.* Ay, marry, is it.—Hark you! They
    come this way.    [*A march afar off.*
If you will tarry, holy pilgrim,
But till the troops come by,
I will conduct you where you shall be lodg'd;
The rather for I think I know your hostess
As ample as myself.

*Hel.*    Is it yourself?

*Wid.* If you shall please so, pilgrim.

*Hel.* I thank you, and will stay upon your
    leisure.

*Wid.* You came, I think, from France?

*Hel.*    I did so.

*Wid.* Here you shall see a countryman of
yours

That has done worthy service.

*Hel.*    His name, I pray you.

*Dia.* The Count Rousillon: know you such a
one?    [of him:

*Hel.* But by the ear, that hears most nobly
His face I know not.

*Dia.*    Whatsoe'er he is,
He's bravely taken here. He stole from France,
As 'tis reported, for the king had married him
Against his liking: think you it is so?

*Hel.* Ay, surely, mere the truth; I know his
    lady.    [count

*Dia.* There is a gentleman that serves the
Reports but coarsely of her.

*Hel.*    What's his name?

*Dia.* Monsieur Parolles.

*Hel.*    O, I believe with him,
In argument of praise, or to the worth
Of the great count himself, she is too mean
To have her name repeated; all her deserving
Is a reserved honesty, and that
I have not heard examin'd.

*Dia.*    Alas, poor lady!
'Tis a hard bondage to become the wife
Of a detesting lord.

*Wid.* Ay, right; good creature, wheresoe'er
    she is
Her heart weighs sadly: this young maid might
    do her
A shrewd turn if she pleas'd.

*Hel.*    How do you mean?
May be, the amorous count solicits her
In the unlawful purpose.

*Wid.*    He does, indeed;
And brokes with all that can in such a suit
Corrupt the tender honour of a maid;
But she is arm'd for him, and keeps her guard
In honestest defence.

*Mar.* The gods forbid else!

*Wid.*    So, now they come:—

*Enter, with a drum and colours, a party of the
Florentine army,* BERTRAM, *and* PAROLLES.

That is Antonio, the duke's eldest son;
That, Escalus.

*Hel.* Which is the Frenchman?

*Dia.*    He;
That with the plume: 'tis a most gallant fellow.
I would he lov'd his wife: if he were honester
He were much goodlier:—is't not a handsome
    gentleman?

*Hel.* I like him well.    [same knave

*Dia.* 'Tis pity he is not honest? yond's that
That leads him to these places; were I his lady
I'd poison that vile rascal.

*Hel.*    Which is he?

*Dia.* The jack-an-apes with scarfs. Why is
he melancholy?

*Hel.* Perchance he's hurt i' the battle.

*Par.* Lose our drum! well.

*Mar.* He's shrewdly vexed at something:
look, he has spied us.

*Wid.* Marry, hang you!

*Mar.* And your courtesy, for a ring-carrier!
[*Exeunt* BER., PAR., Officers, *and* Soldiers.
*Wid.* The troop is past. Come, pilgrim, I
　　will bring you
Where you shall host: of enjoin'd penitents
There's four or five, to great Saint Jacques
　　bound,
Already at my house.
　*Hel.*　　　　　　I humbly thank you:
Please it this matron and this gentle maid
To eat with us to-night; the charge and thank-
　　ing
Shall be for me: and, to requite you further,
I will bestow some precepts on this virgin,
Worthy the note.
　*Both.*　　　We'll take your offer kindly.
　　　　　　　　　　　　　　　[*Exeunt.*

SCENE VI.—*Camp before* FLORENCE.

*Enter* BERTRAM, *and the two* French Lords.

　1 *Lord.* Nay, good my lord, put him to't; let
him have his way.
　2 *Lord.* If your lordship find him not a hilding, hold me no more in your respect.
　1 *Lord.* On my life, my lord, a bubble.
　*Ber.* Do you think I am so far deceived in
him?
　1 *Lord.* Believe it, my lord, in mine own direct knowledge, without any malice, but to
speak of him as my kinsman, he's a most notable coward, an infinite and endless liar, an
hourly promise-breaker, the owner of no one
good quality worthy your lordship's entertainment.
　2 *Lord.* It were fit you knew him; lest, reposing too far in his virtue, which he hath not,
he might, at some great and trusty business, in
a main danger, fail you.
　*Ber.* I would I knew in what particular
action to try him.
　2 *Lord.* None better than to let him fetch off
his drum, which you hear him so confidently
undertake to do.
　1 *Lord.* I, with a troop of Florentines, will
suddenly surprise him; such I will have, whom
I am sure he knows not from the enemy: we will
bind and hoodwink him so that he shall suppose
no other but that he is carried into the leaguer
of the adversaries when we bring him to our
tents. Be but your lordship present at his examination: if he do not, for the promise of his
life, and in the highest compulsion of base fear,
offer to betray you, and deliver all the intelligence in his power against you, and that with
the divine forfeit of his soul upon oath, never
trust my judgment in anything.
　2 *Lord.* O, for the love of laughter, let him
fetch off his drum; he says he has a stratagem
for't: when your lordship sees the bottom of his
success in't, and to what metal this counterfeit
lump of ore will be melted, if you give him not
John Drum's entertainment, your inclining
cannot be removed. Here he comes.
　1 *Lord.* O, for the love of laughter, hinder

not the humour of his design: let him fetch off
his drum in any hand.

*Enter* PAROLLES.

　*Ber.* How now, monsieur? this drum sticks
sorely in your disposition.
　2 *Lord.* A pox on't; let it go; 'tis but a drum.
　*Par.* But a drum! Is't but a drum? A drum
so lost!—There was an excellent command! to
charge in with our horse upon our own wings,
and to rend our own soldiers.
　2 *Lord.* That was not to be blamed in the
command of the service; it was a disaster of war
that Cæsar himself could not have prevented, if
he had been there to command.
　*Ber.* Well, we cannot greatly condemn our
success; some dishonour we had in the loss of
that drum; but it is not to be recovered.
　*Par.* It might have been recovered.
　*Ber.* It might, but it is not now.
　*Par.* It is to be recovered: but that the merit
of service is seldom attributed to the true and
exact performer, I would have that drum or another, or *hic jacet.*
　*Ber.* Why, if you have a stomach to't, monsieur, if you think your mystery in stratagem
can bring this instrument of honour again into
his native quarter, be magnanimous in the enterprise, and go on; I will grace the attempt for
a worthy exploit; if you speed well in it the
duke shall both speak of it, and extend to you
what further becomes his greatness, even to the
utmost syllable of your worthiness.
　*Par.* By the hand of a soldier, I will undertake it.
　*Ber.* But you must not now slumber in it.
　*Par.* I'll be about it this evening: and I will
presently pen down my dilemmas, encourage
myself in my certainty, put myself into my
mortal preparation, and, by midnight, look to
hear further from me.
　*Ber.* May I be bold to acquaint his grace you
are gone about it?
　*Par.* I know not what the success will be,
my lord, but the attempt I vow.
　*Ber.* I know thou art valiant; and, to the
possibility of thy soldiership, will subscribe for
thee. Farewell.
　*Par.* I love not many words.　　　[*Exit.*
　1 *Lord.* No more than a fish loves water.—Is
not this a strange fellow, my lord? that so confidently seems to undertake this business, which
he knows is not to be done; damns himself to
do, and dares better be damned than to do't.
　2 *Lord.* You do not know him, my lord, as
we do: certain it is that he will steal himself into a man's favour, and for a week escape a
great deal of discoveries; but when you find
him out, you have him ever after.
　*Ber.* Why, do you think he will make no
deed at all of this, that so seriously he does
address himself unto?
　1 *Lord.* None in the world; but return with
an invention, and clap upon you two or three

probable lies: but we have almost embossed him,—you shall see his fall to-night: for indeed he is not for your lordship's respect.

*2 Lord.* We'll make you some sport with the fox ere we case him. He was first smoked by the old Lord Lafeu: when his disguise and he is parted, tell me what a sprat you shall find him; which you shall see this very night.

*1 Lord.* I must go look my twigs; he shall be caught.

*Ber.* Your brother, he shall go along with me.

*1 Lord.* As't please your lordship: I'll leave you. [*Exit.*

*Ber.* Now will I lead you to the house, and show you

The lass I spoke of.

*2 Lord.* But you say she's honest.

*Ber.* That's all the fault: I spoke with her but once, [her,

And found her wondrous cold; but I sent to

By this same coxcomb that we have i' the wind,

Tokens and letters which she did re-send;

And this is all I have done. She's a fair creature;

Will you go see her?

*2 Lord.* With all my heart, my lord.

[*Exeunt.*

SCENE VII.—FLORENCE. *A Room in the* Widow's *House.*

*Enter* HELENA *and* Widow.

*Hel.* If you misdoubt me that I am not she, I know not how I shall assure you further, But I shall lose the grounds I work upon.

*Wid.* Though my estate be fallen, I was well born, Nothing acquainted with these businesses; And would not put my reputation now In any staining act.

*Hel.* Nor would I wish you.

First give me trust, the count he is my husband, And what to your sworn counsel I have spoken Is so from word to word; and then you cannot, By the good aid that I of you shall borrow, Err in bestowing it.

*Wid.* I should believe you;

For you have show'd me that which well approves

You're great in fortune.

*Hel.* Take this purse of gold,

And let me buy your friendly help thus far, Which I will over-pay, and pay again, When I have found it. The count he wooes your daughter, Lays down his wanton siege before her beauty, Resolv'd to carry her: let her, in fine, consent, As we'll direct her how 'tis best to bear it, Now his important blood will naught deny That she'll demand: a ring the county wears, That downward hath succeeded in his house From son to son, some four or five descents Since the first father wore it: this ring he holds In most rich choice; yet, in his idle fire, To buy his will, it would not seem too dear, Howe'er repented after.

*Wid.* Now I see

The bottom of your purpose.

*Hel.* You see it lawful then: it is no more But that your daughter, ere she seems as won, Desires this ring; appoints him an encounter; In fine, delivers me to fill the time, Herself most chastely absent; after this, To marry her, I'll add three thousand crowns To what is past already.

*Wid.* I have yielded:

Instruct my daughter how she shall perséver, That time and place, with this deceit so lawful, May prove coherent. Every night he comes With musics of all sorts, and songs compos'd To her unworthiness: it nothing steads us To chide him from our eaves; for he persists, As if his life lay on't.

*Hel.* Why, then, to-night

Let us assay our plot; which, if it speed, Is wicked meaning in a lawful deed, And lawful meaning in a lawful act; Where both not sin, and yet a sinful fact: But let's about it. [*Exeunt.*

## ACT IV.

SCENE I.—*Without the* FLORENTINE *Camp.*

*Enter first* LORD, *with five or six* Soldiers *in ambush.*

*1 Lord.* He can come no other way but by this hedge-corner. When you sally upon him, speak what terrible language you will; though you understand it not yourselves, no matter; for we must not seem to understand him, unless some one among us, whom we must produce for an interpreter.

*1 Sold.* Good captain, let me be the interpreter.

*1 Lord.* Art not acquainted with him? knows he not thy voice?

*1 Sold.* No, sir, I warrant you.

*1 Lord.* But what linsey-woolsey hast thou to speak to us again?

*1 Sold.* Even such as you speak to me.

*1 Lord.* He must think us some band of strangers i' the adversary's entertainment. Now he hath a smack of all neighbouring languages; therefore we must every one be a man of his own fancy, not to know what we speak to one another; so we seem to know, is to know straight our purpose: chough's language, gabble enough, and good enough. As for you, interpreter, you must seem very politic. But couch, ho! here he comes; to beguile two hours in a sleep, and then to return and swear the lies he forges.

*Enter* PAROLLES.

*Par.* Ten o'clock: within these three hours 'twill be time enough to go home. What shall I say I have done? It must be a very plausive invention that carries it: they begin to smoke me: and disgraces have of late knocked too often at my door. I find my tongue is too foolhardy; but my heart hath the fear of Mars before it, and of his creatures, not daring the reports of my tongue.

*1 Lord.* This is the first truth that e'er thine own tongue was guilty of.    [*Aside.*

*Par.* What the devil should move me to undertake the recovery of this drum; being not ignorant of the impossibility, and knowing I had no such purpose? I must give myself some hurts, and say I got them in exploit: yet slight ones will not carry it: they will say, Came you off with so little? and great ones I dare not give. Wherefore, what's the instance? Tongue, I must put you into a butter-woman's mouth, and buy myself another of Bajazet's mule, if you prattle me into these perils.

*1 Lord.* Is it possible he should know what he is, and be that he is?    [*Aside.*

*Par.* I would the cutting of my garments would serve the turn, or the breaking of my Spanish sword.

*1 Lord.* We cannot afford you so.    [*Aside.*

*Par.* Or the baring of my beard; and to say it was in stratagem.

*1 Lord.* 'Twould not do.    [*Aside.*

*Par.* Or to drown my clothes, and say I was stripped.

*1 Lord.* Hardly serve.    [*Aside.*

*Par.* Though I swore I leaped from the window of the citadel,—

*1 Lord.* How deep?    [*Aside.*

*Par.* Thirty fathom.

*1 Lord.* Three great oaths would scarce make that be believed.    [*Aside.*

*Par.* I would I had any drum of the enemy's; I would swear I recovered it.

*1 Lord.* You shall hear one anon.    [*Aside.*

*Par.* A drum now of the enemy's!

   [*Alarum within.*

*1 Lord. Throca movousus, cargo, cargo, cargo.*

*All. Cargo, cargo, cargo, villianda par corbo, cargo.*

*Par.* O! ransom, ransom:—Do not hide mine eyes.    [*They seize and blindfold him.*

*1 Sold. Boskos thromuldo boskos.*

*Par.* I know you are the Musko's regiment, And I shall lose my life for want of language: If there be here German, or Dane, low Dutch, Italian, or French, let him speak to me; I will discover that which shall undo The Florentine.

*2 Sold. Boskos vauvado:——*

I understand thee, and can speak thy tongue:— *Kerelybonto:——*Sir, Betake thee to thy faith, for seventeen poniards Are at thy bosom.

*Par.* Oh!

*1 Sold.* O, pray, pray, pray.——

*Manka revania dulche.*

*1 Lord. Oscorbi dulchos volivorco.*

*1 Sold.* The general is content to spare thee yet;

And, hoodwink'd as thou art, will lead thee on To gather from thee: haply thou mayst inform Something to save thy life.

*Par.*    O, let me live, And all the secrets of our camp I'll show, Their force, their purposes: nay, I'll speak that Which you will wonder at.

*1 Sold.*    But wilt thou faithfully?

*Par.* If I do not, damn me.

*1 Sold.*    *A cordo linta.——* Come on; thou art granted space.

   [*Exit, with* PAROLLES *guarded.*

*1 Lord.* Go, tell the Count Rousillon and my brother We have caught the woodcock, and will keep him muffled Till we do hear from them.

*2 Sold.*    Captain, I will.

*1 Lord.* He will betray us all unto ourselves;— Inform 'em that.

*2 Sold.*    So I will, sir.

*1 Lord.* Till then I'll keep him dark, and safely lock'd.    [*Exeunt.*

## SCENE II.—FLORENCE. *A Room in the Widow's House.*

### *Enter* BERTRAM *and* DIANA.

*Ber.* They told me that your name was Fontibell.

*Dia.* No, my good lord, Diana.

*Ber.*    Titled goddess; And worth it, with addition! But, fair soul, In your fine frame hath love no quality? If the quick fire of youth light not your mind, You are no maiden, but a monument; When you are dead, you should be such a one As you are now, for you are cold and stern; And now you should be as your mother was When your sweet self was got.

*Dia.* She then was honest.

*Ber.*    So should you be.

*Dia.*    No: My mother did but duty; such, my lord, As you owe to your wife.

*Ber.*    No more of that! I pr'ythee, do not strive against my vows: I was compell'd to her; but I love thee By love's own sweet constraint, and will for ever Do thee all rights of service.

*Dia.*    Ay, so you serve us Till we serve you: but when you have our roses You barely leave our thorns to prick ourselves, And mock us with our bareness.

*Ber.*    How have I sworn?

*Dia.* 'Tis not the many oaths that make the truth, But the plain single vow that is vow'd true. What is not holy, that we swear not by, But take the Highest to witness: then, pray you, tell me,

If I should swear by Jove's great attributes
I lov'd you dearly, would you believe my oaths,
When I did love you ill? this has no holding,
To swear by him whom I protest to love,
That I will work against him: therefore your
    oaths
Are words and poor conditions; but unseal'd,—
At least in my opinion.

*Ber.*                    Change it, change it;
Be not so holy-cruel: love is holy;
And my integrity ne'er knew the crafts
That you do charge men with. Stand no more
    off,
But give thyself unto my sick desires,
Who then recover: say thou art mine, and ever
My love as it begins shall so persèver.    [case,

*Dia.* I see that men make hopes, in such a
That we'll forsake ourselves. Give me that ring.

*Ber.* I'll lend it thee, my dear, but have no
    power
To give it from me.

*Dia.*                    Will you not, my lord?

*Ber.* It is an honour 'longing to our house,
Bequeathed down from many ancestors;
Which were the greatest obloquy i' the world
In mè to lose.

*Dia.*                    Mine honour's such a ring:
My chastity's the jewel of our house,
Bequeathed down from many ancestors;
Which were the greatest obloquy i' the world
In me to lose. Thus your own proper wisdom
Brings in the champion honour on my part,
Against your vain assault.

*Ber.*                    Here, take my ring:
My house, mine honour, yea, my life be thine,
And I'll be bid by thee.

*Dia.* When midnight comes knock at my
    chamber-window;
I'll order take my mother shall not hear.
Now will I charge you in the band of truth,
When you have conquer'd my yet maiden-bed,
Remain there but an hour, nor speak to me:
My reasons are most strong; and you shall
    know them
When back again this ring shall be deliver'd;
And on your finger, in the night, I'll put
Another ring; that what in time proceeds
May token to the future our past deeds.
Adieu till then; then fail not. You have won
A wife of me, though there my hope be done.

*Ber.* A heaven on earth I have won by woo-
    ing thee.                    [*Exit.*

*Dia.* For which live long to thank both
    heaven and me!
You may so in the end.——
My mother told me just how he would woo,
As if she sat in his heart; she says all men
Have the like oaths: he hath sworn to marry me
When his wife's dead; therefore I'll lie with him
When I am buried. Since Frenchmen are so
    braid,
Marry that will, I'll live and die a maid:
Only, in this disguise, I think't no sin
To cozen him that would unjustly win.    [*Exit.*

SCENE III.—*The Florentine Camp.*

*Enter the two* French Lords, *and two or three*
    Soldiers.

1 *Lord.* You have not given him his mother's
letter?

2 *Lord.* I have delivered it an hour since:
there is something in't that stings his nature;
for, on the reading it, he changed almost into
another man.

1 *Lord.* He has much worthy blame laid upon
him for shaking off so good a wife and so sweet
a lady.

2 *Lord.* Especially he hath incurred the everlasting displeasure of the king, who had even
tuned his bounty to sing happiness to him. I
will tell you a thing, but you shall let it dwell
darkly with you.

1 *Lord.* When you have spoken it, 'tis dead,
and I am the grave of it.

2 *Lord.* He hath perverted a young gentlewoman here in Florence, of a most chaste renown; and this night he fleshes his will in the
spoil of her honour: he hath given her his
monumental ring, and thinks himself made in
the unchaste composition.

1 *Lord.* Now, God delay our rebellion: as
we are ourselves, what things are we!

2 *Lord.* Merely our own traitors. And as in
the common course of all treasons, we still see
them reveal themselves, till they attain to their
abhorred ends; so he that in this action contrives against his own nobility, in his proper
stream o'erflows himself.

1 *Lord.* Is it not meant damnable in us to be
trumpeters of our unlawful intents? We shall
not then have his company to-night?

2 *Lord.* Not till after midnight; for he is
dieted to his hour.

2 *Lord.* That approaches apace: I would
gladly have him see his company anatomized,
that he might take a measure of his own judgments, wherein so curiously he had set this
counterfeit.

2 *Lord.* We will not meddle with him till he
come; for his presence must be the whip of the
other.                    [these wars?

1 *Lord.* In the meantime, what hear you of

2 *Lord.* I hear there is an overture of peace.

1 *Lord.* Nay, I assure you, a peace concluded.

2 *Lord.* What will Count Rousillon do then?
will he travel higher, or return again into
France?

1 *Lord.* I perceive, by this demand, you are
not altogether of his council.

2 *Lord.* Let it be forbid, sir; so should I be a
great deal of his act.

1 *Lord.* Sir, his wife, some two months since,
fled from his house: her pretence is a pilgrimage to St. Jacques-le-Grand; which holy undertaking, with most austere sanctimony, she accomplished; and, there residing, the tenderness
of her nature became as a prey to her grief; in

fine, made a groan of her last breath; and now she sings in heaven.

*2 Lord.* How is this justified?

*1 Lord.* The stronger part of it by her own letters, which make her story true even to the point of her death: her death itself, which could not be her office to say is come, was faithfully confirmed by the rector of the place.

*2 Lord.* Hath the count all this intelligence?

*1 Lord.* Ay, and the particular confirmations, point from point, to the full arming of the verity.

*2 Lord.* I am heartily sorry that he'll be glad of this.

*1 Lord.* How mightily, sometimes, we make us comforts of our losses!

*2 Lord.* And how mightily, some other times, we drown our gain in tears! The great dignity that his valour hath here acquired for him shall at home be encountered with a shame as ample.

*1 Lord.* The web of our life is of a mingled yarn, good and ill together: our virtues would be proud if our faults whipped them not; and our crimes would despair if they were not cherished by our virtues.—

*Enter a Servant.*

How now? where's your master?

*Serv.* He met the duke in the street, sir; of whom he hath taken a solemn leave: his lordship will next morning for France. The duke hath offered him letters of commendations to the king.

*2 Lord.* They shall be no more than needful there, if they were more than they can command.

*1 Lord.* They cannot be too sweet for the king's tartness. Here's his lordship now.

*Enter* BERTRAM.

How now, my lord, is't not after midnight?

*Ber.* I have to-night despatched sixteen businesses, a month's length a-piece, by an abstract of success: I have conge'd with the duke, done my adieu with my nearest; buried a wife, mourned for her; writ to my lady-mother I am returning; entertained my convoy; and, between these main parcels of despatch, effected many nicer needs: the last was the greatest, but that I have not ended yet.

*2 Lord.* If the business be of any difficulty, and this morning your departure hence, it requires haste of your lordship.

*Ber.* I mean, the business is not ended, as fearing to hear of it hereafter. But shall we have this dialogue between the fool and the soldier?——Come, bring forth this counterfeit model: has deceived me like a double-meaning prophesier.

*2 Lord.* Bring him forth. [*Exeunt* Soldiers.] Has sat in the stocks all night, poor gallant knave.

*Ber.* No matter; his heels have deserved it,

in usurping his spurs so long. How does he carry himself?

*1 Lord.* I have told your lordship already; the stocks carry him. But to answer you as you would be understood; he weeps like a wench that had shed her milk: he hath confessed himself to Morgan, whom he supposes to be a friar, from the time of his remembrance to this very instant disaster of his setting i' the stocks: and what think you he hath confessed?

*Ber.* Nothing of me, has he?

*2 Lord.* His confession is taken, and it shall be read to his face: if your lordship be in't, as I believe you are, you must have the patience to hear it.

*Re-enter* Soldiers, *with* PAROLLES.

*Ber.* A plague upon him! muffled! he can say nothing of me; hush, hush!

*1 Lord.* Hoodman comes! *Porto tartarossa.*

*1 Sold.* He calls for the tortures: what will you say without 'em?

*Par.* I will confess what I know without constraint; if ye pinch me like a pasty I can say no more.

*1 Sold. Bosko chimurco.*

*1 Lord. Boblibindo chicurmurco.*

*1 Sold.* You are a merciful general:—Our general bids you answer to what I shall ask you out of a note.

*Par.* And truly, as I hope to live.

*1 Sold. First demand of him how many horse the duke is strong.* What say you to that?

*Par.* Five or six thousand; but very weak and unserviceable: the troops are all scattered, and the commanders very poor rogues, upon my reputation and credit, and as I hope to live.

*1 Sold.* Shall I set down your answer so?

*Par.* Do; I'll take the sacrament on't, how and which way you will.      [slave is this!

*Ber.* All's one to him. What a past-saving

*1 Lord.* You are deceived, my lord; this is Monsieur Parolles, the gallant militarist (that was his own phrase), that had the whole theoric of war in the knot of his scarf, and the practice in the chape of his dagger.

*2 Lord.* I will never trust a man again for keeping his sword clean; nor believe he can have everything in him by wearing his apparel neatly.

*1 Sold.* Well, that's set down.

*Par.* Five or six thousand horse, I said,—I will say true,—or thereabouts, set down,—for I'll speak truth.

*1 Lord.* He's very near the truth in this.

*Ber.* But I con him no thanks for't in the nature he delivers it.

*Par.* Poor rogues, I pray you say.

*1 Sold.* Well, that's set down.

*Par.* I humbly thank you, sir: a truth's a truth, the rogues are marvellous poor.

*1 Sold. Demand of him of what strength they are a-foot.* What say you to that?

*Par.* By my troth, sir, if I were to live this

present hour I will tell true. Let me see: Spurio a hundred and fifty, Sebastian so. many, Corambus so many, Jacques so many; Guiltian, Cosmo, Lodowick, and Gratii, two hundred fifty each: mine own company, Chitopher, Vaumond, Bentii, two hundred fifty each: so that the muster-file, rotten and sound, upon my life, amounts not to fifteen thousand poll; half of the which dare not shake the snow from off their cassocks lest they shake themselves to pieces.

*Ber.* What shall be done to him?

1 *Lord.* Nothing, but let him have thanks. Demand of him my condition, and what credit I have with the duke.

1 *Sold.* Well, that's set down. *You shall demand of him whether one Captain Dumain be i' the camp, a Frenchman; what his reputation is with the duke, what his valour, honesty, expertness in wars; or whether he thinks it were not possible, with well-weighing sums of gold, to corrupt him to a revolt.* What say you to this? what do you know of it?

*Par.* I beseech you, let me answer to the particular of the inter'gatories: demand them singly.

1 *Sold.* Do you know this Captain Dumain?

*Par.* I know him: he was a botcher's 'prentice in Paris, from whence he was whipped for getting the shrieve's fool with child: a dumb innocent that could not say him nay.

[1 *Lord lifts up his hand in anger.*

*Ber.* Nay, by your leave, hold your hands; though I know his brains are forfeit to the next tile that falls.

1 *Sold.* Well, is this captain in the Duke of Florence's camp?

*Par.* Upon my knowledge, he is, and lousy.

1 *Lord.* Nay, look not so upon me; we shall hear of your lordship anon.

1 *Sold.* What is his reputation with the duke?

*Par.* The duke knows him for no other but a poor officer of mine; and writ to me this other day to turn him out o' the band: I think I have his letter in my pocket.

1 *Sold.* Marry, we'll search.

*Par.* In good sadness, I do not know; either it is there or it is upon a file, with the duke's other letters, in my tent.

1 *Sold.* Here 'tis; here's a paper. Shall I read it to you?

*Par.* I do not know if it be or no.

*Ber.* Our interpreter does it well.

1 *Lord.* Excellently.

1 *Sold.* [*Reads.*] *Dian, the Count's a fool, and full of gold,—*

*Par.* That is not the duke's letter, sir; that is an advertisement to a proper maid in Florence, one Diana, to take heed of the allurement of one Count Rousillon, a foolish, idle boy, but, for all that, very ruttish: I pray you, sir, put it up again.

1 *Sold.* Nay, I'll read it first, by your favour.

*Par.* My meaning in't, I protest, was very honest in the behalf of the maid; for I knew the young count to be a dangerous and lascivious boy, who is a whale to virginity, and devours up all the fry it finds.

*Ber.* Damnable! both sides rogue!

1 *Sold. Reads.* When he swears oaths, bid him drop gold, and take it:
After he scores, he never pays the score;
Half won is match well made; match, and well make it;
He ne'er pays after-debts, take it before;
And say a soldier, *Dian,* told thee this,
Men are to mell with, boys are not to kiss;
For count of this, the count 's a fool, I know it,
Who pays before, but not when he does owe it.
 Thine, as he vow'd to thee in thine ear,
     PAROLLES.

*Ber.* He shall be whipped through the army with this rhyme in his forehead.

2 *Lord.* This is your devoted friend, sir, the manifold linguist, and the armipotent soldier.

*Ber.* I could endure anything before but a cat, and now he's a cat to me.

1 *Sold.* I perceive, sir, by our general's looks we shall be fain to hang you.

*Par.* My life, sir, in any case: not that I am afraid to die, but that, my offences being many, I would repent out the remainder of nature: let me live, sir, in a dungeon, i' the stocks, or anywhere, so I may live.

1 *Sold.* We'll see what may be done, so you confess freely; therefore, once more to this Captain Dumain: you have answered to his reputation with the duke, and to his valour: what is his honesty?

*Par.* He will steal, sir, an egg out of a cloister; for rapes and ravishments he parallels Nessus. He professes not keeping of oaths; in breaking them he is stronger than Hercules. He will lie, sir, with such volubility that you would think truth were a fool: drunkenness is his best virtue, for he will be swine-drunk; and in his sleep he does little harm, save to his bedclothes about him; but they know his conditions and lay him in straw. I have but little more to say, sir, of his honesty: he has everything that an honest man should not have; what an honest man should have he has nothing.

1 *Lord.* I begin to love him for this.

*Ber.* For this description of thine honesty? A pox upon him for me; he is more and more a cat.

1 *Sold.* What say you to his expertness in war?

*Par.* Faith, sir, has led the drum before the English tragedians,—to belie him I will not,—and more of his soldiership I know not, except in that country he had the honour to be the officer at a place there called Mile-end, to instruct for the doubling of files: I would do the man what honour I can, but of this I am not certain.

*1 Lord.* He hath out-villanied villany so far
that the rarity redeems him.

*Ber.* A pox on him! he's a cat still.

*1 Sold.* His qualities being at this poor price,
I need not ask you if gold will corrupt him to
revolt.

*Par.* Sir, for a *quart d'ecu* he will sell the fee-
simple of his salvation, the inheritance of it;
and cut the entail from all remainders, and a
perpetual succession for it perpetually.

*1 Sold.* What's his brother, the other Captain Dumain?

*2 Lord.* Why does he ask him of me?

*1 Sold.* What's he?

*Par.* E'en a crow of the same nest; not altogether so great as the first in goodness, but
greater a great deal in evil. He excels his
brother for a coward, yet his brother is reputed
one of the best that is: in a retreat he outruns
any lackey; marry, in coming on he has the
cramp.

*1 Sold.* If your life be saved, will you undertake to betray the Florentine?

*Par.* Ay, and the captain of his horse, Count
Rousillon.

*1 Sold.* I'll whisper with the general, and
know his pleasure.

*Par.* I'll no more drumming; a plague of all
drums! Only to seem to deserve well, and to
beguile the supposition of that lascivious young
boy, the count, have I run into this danger:
yet who would have suspected an ambush
where I was taken? [*Aside.*

*1 Sold.* There is no remedy, sir, but you must
die: the general says, you that have so traitorously discovered the secrets of your army, and,
made such pestiferous reports of men very
nobly held, can serve the world for no honest
use; therefore you must die. Come, headsman,
off with his head.

*Par.* O Lord! sir, let me live, or let me see my
death.

*1 Sold.* That shall you, and take your leave
of all your friends. [*Unmuffling him.*
So look about you: know you any here?

*Ber.* Good morrow, noble captain.

*2 Lord.* Gold bless you, Captain Parolles.

*1 Lord.* God save you, noble captain.

*2 Lord.* Captain, what greeting will you to
my Lord Lafeu? I am for France.

*1 Lord.* Good captain, will you give me a
copy of the sonnet you writ to Diana in behalf
of the Count Rousillon? an I were not a very
coward I'd compel it of you; but fare you well.
[*Exeunt* BERTRAM, Lords, &c.

*1 Sold.* You are undone, captain: all but
your scarf; that has a knot on't yet.

*Par.* Who cannot be crushed with a plot?

*1 Sold.* If you could find out a country where
but women were that had received so much
shame, you might begin an impudent nation.
Fare you well, sir; I am for France too: we
shall speak of you there. [*Exit.*

*Par.* Yet I am thankful: if my heart were
  great,
'Twould burst at this. Captain I'll be no more;
But I will eat and drink, and sleep as soft
As captain shall: simply the thing I am
Shall make me live. Who knows himself a brag-
  gart,
Let him fear this; for it will come to pass
That every braggart shall be found an ass.
Rust, sword! cool, blushes! and, Parolles, live
Safest in shame! being fool'd, by foolery thrive!
There's place and means for every man alive.
I'll after them. [*Exit.*

SCENE IV.—FLORENCE. *A Room in the*
Widow's *House.*

*Enter* HELENA, Widow, *and* DIANA.

*Hel.* That you may well perceive I have not
  wrong'd you,
One of the greatest in the Christian world
Shall be my surety; 'for whose throne 'tis need-
  ful,
Ere I can perfect mine intents, to kneel:
Time was I did him a desired office,
Dear almost as his life; which gratitude
Through flinty Tartar's bosom would peep
  forth,
And answer, thanks: I duly am informed
His grace is at Marseilles; to which place
We have convenient convoy. You must know
I am supposed dead: the army breaking,
My husband hies him home; where, heaven
  aiding,
And by the leave of my good lord the king,
We'll be before our welcome.

*Wid.*              Gentle madam,
You never had a servant to whose trust
Your business was more welcome.

*Hel.*              Nor you, mistress,
Ever a friend whose thoughts more truly labour
To recompense your love: doubt not but
  heaven
Hath brought me up to be your daughter's
  dower,
As it hath fated her to be my motive
And helper to a husband. But, O strange men!
That can such sweet use make of what they
  hate,
When saucy trusting of the cozen'd thoughts
Defiles the pitchy night! so lust doth play
With what it loathes, for that which is away:
But more of this hereafter.—You, Diana,
Under my poor instructions yet must suffer
Something in my behalf.

*Dia.*              Let death and honesty
Go with your impositions, I am yours
Upon your will to suffer.

*Hel.*              Yet, I pray you:
But with the word the time will bring on sum-
  mer,
When briars shall have leaves as well as thorns,
And be as sweet as sharp. We must away;
Our waggon is prepar'd, and time revives us:

All's well that ends well: still the fine's the
    crown:
Whate'er the course, the end is the renown.

                    *[Exeunt.*

SCENE V.—ROUSILLON.  *A Room in the*
        COUNTESS'S *Palace.*

*Enter* COUNTESS, LAFEU, *and* Clown.

*Laf.* No, no, no, your son was misled with
a snipt-taffeta fellow there, whose villanous
saffron would have made all the unbaked and
doughy youth of a nation in his colour: your
daughter-in-law had been alive at this hour,
and your son here at home, more advanced by
the king than by that red-tailed humble-bee I
speak of.

*Count.* I would I had not known him! it was
the death of the most virtuous gentlewoman
that ever nature had praise for creating: if she
had partaken of my flesh, and cost me the
dearest groans of a mother, I could not have
owed her a more rooted love.

*Laf.* 'Twas a good lady, 'twas a good lady:
we may pick a thousand salads ere we light on
such another herb.

*Clo.* Indeed, sir, she was the sweet marjoram of the salad, or rather, the herb of grace.

*Laf.* They are not salad-herbs, you knave;
they are nose-herbs.

*Clo.* I am no great Nebuchadnezzar, sir; I
have not much skill in grass.

*Laf.* Whether dost thou profess thyself,—a
knave or a fool?

*Clo.* A fool, sir, at a woman's service, and a
knave at a man's.

*Laf.* Your distinction?

*Clo.* I would cozen the man of his wife, and
do his service.               *[deed.*

*Laf.* So you were a knave at his service, in-

*Clo.* And I would give his wife my bauble,
sir, to do her service.

*Laf.* I will subscribe for thee; thou art both
knave and fool.

*Clo.* At your service.

*Laf.* No, no, no.

*Clo.* Why, sir, if I cannot serve you, I can
serve as great a prince as you are.

*Laf.* Who's that? a Frenchman?

*Clo.* Faith, sir, 'a has an English name; but
his phisnomy is more hotter in France than
there.

*Laf.* What prince is that?

*Clo.* The black prince, sir; *alias,* the prince
of darkness; *alias,* the devil.

*Laf.* Hold thee, there's my purse: I give thee
not this to suggest thee from thy master thou
talkest of; serve him still.

*Clo.* I am a woodland fellow, sir, that always
loved a great fire; and the master I speak of
ever keeps a good fire. But, sure, he is the
prince of the world; let his nobility remain in
his court. I am for the house with the narrow
gate, which I take to be too little for pomp to
enter: some that humble themselves may; but
the many will be too chill and tender; and
they'll be for the flow'ry way that leads to the
broad gate and the great fire.

*Laf.* Go thy ways, I begin to be a-weary of
thee; and I tell thee so before, because I would
not fall out with thee. Go thy ways; let my
horses be well looked to, without any tricks.

*Clo.* If I put any tricks upon 'em, sir, they
shall be jades' tricks; which are their own
right by the law of nature.         *[Exit.*

*Laf.* A shrewd knave, and an unhappy.

*Count.* So he is. My lord that's gone made
himself much sport out of him: by his authority
he remains here, which he thinks is a patent for
his sauciness; and, indeed, he has no pace, but
runs where he will.

*Laf.* I like him well; 'tis not amiss. And
I was about to tell you, since I heard of the
good lady's death, and that my lord your son
was upon his return home, I moved the king
my master to speak in the behalf of my daughter; which, in the minority of them both, his
majesty, out of a self-gracious remembrance,
did first propose: his highness hath promised
me to do it: and, to stop up the displeasure he
hath conceived against your son, there is no
fitter matter. How does your ladyship like it?

*Count.* With very much content, my lord;
and I wish it happily effected.

*Laf.* His highness comes post from Marseilles, of as able body as when he numbered
thirty; he will be here to-morrow, or I am deceived by him that in such intelligence hath
seldom failed.

*Count.* It rejoices me that I hope I shall see
him ere I die. I have letters that my son will
be here to-night: I shall beseech your lordship
to remain with me till they meet together.

*Laf.* Madam, I was thinking with what
manners I might safely be admitted.

*Count.* You need but plead your honourable
privilege.

*Laf.* Lady, of that I have made a bold charter; but, I thank my God, it holds yet.

*Re-enter* Clown.

*Clo.* O madam, yonder's my lord your son
with a patch of velvet on's face; whether there
be a scar under it or no, the velvet knows; but
'tis a goodly patch of velvet: his left cheek is a
cheek of two pile and a half, but his right cheek
is worn bare.

*Laf.* A scar nobly got, or a noble scar, is a
good livery of honour; so belike is that.

*Clo.* But it is your carbonadoed face.

*Laf.* Let us go see your son, I pray you; I
long to talk with the young noble soldier.

*Clo.* Faith, there's a dozen of 'em, with
delicate fine hats, and most courteous feathers,
which bow the head and nod at every man.

                    *[Exeunt.*

## ACT V.

### SCENE I.—MARSEILLES. *A Street.*

*Enter* HELENA, Widow, *and* DIANA, *with two* Attendants.

*Hel.* But this exceeding posting day and
    night
Must wear your spirits low: we cannot help it:
But since you have made the days and nights
    as one,
To wear you gentle limbs in my affairs,
Be bold you do so grow in my requital
As nothing can unroot you. In happy time;—

*Enter a* Gentleman.

This man may help me to his majesty's ear,
If he would spend his power.—God save you,
    sir.
*Gent.* And you.
*Hel.* Sir, I have seen you in the court of
    France.
*Gent.* I have been sometimes there.
*Hel.* I do presume, sir, that you are not
    fallen
From the report that goes upon your goodness;
And therefore, goaded with most sharp occa-
    sions,
Which lay nice manners by, I put you to
The use of your own virtues, for the which
I shall continue thankful.
*Gent.*               What's your will?
*Hel.* That it will please you
To give this poor petition to the king;
And aid me with that store of power you have
To come into his presence.
*Gent.* The king's not here.
*Hel.*                Not here, sir?
*Gent.*                 Not indeed:
He hence remov'd last night, and with more
    haste
Than is his use.
*Wid.*       Lord, how we lose our pains!
*Hel.* All's well that ends well yet,
Though time seem so adverse and means
    unfit?—
I do beseech you, whither is he gone?
*Gent.* Marry, as I take it, to Rousillon;
Whither I am going.
*Hel.*      I do beseech you, sir,
Since you are like to see the king before me,
Commend the paper to his gracious hand;
Which I presume shall render you no blame,
But rather make you thank your pains for it:
I will come after you, with what good speed
Our means will make us means.
*Gent.*          This I'll do for you.
*Hel.* And you shall find yourself to be well
    thank'd,
Whate'er falls more.—We must to horse
    again;—
Go, go, provide.             [*Exeunt.*

### SCENE II.—ROUSILLON. *The inner Court of the* COUNTESS'S *Palace.*

*Enter* Clown *and* PAROLLES.

*Par.* Good Monsieur Lavatch, give my Lord
Lafeu this letter: I have ere now, sir, been
better known to you, when I have held familiarity with fresher clothes; but I am now, sir,
muddied in fortune's mood, and smell somewhat strong of her strong displeasure.
*Clo.* Truly, fortune's displeasure is but sluttish if it smell so strongly as thou speakest of:
I will henceforth eat no fish of fortune's butter-
ing. Pr'ythee, allow the wind.
*Par.* Nay, you need not to stop your nose,
sir; I spake but by a metaphor.
*Clo.* Indeed, sir, if your metaphor stink, I
will stop my nose; or against any man's metaphor. Pr'ythee, get thee further.
*Par.* Pray you, sir, deliver me this paper.
*Clo.* Foh, pr'ythee, stand away: a paper
from fortune's close-stool to give to a nobleman! Look, here he comes himself.

*Enter* LAFEU.

Here is a pur of fortune's, sir, or of fortune's
cat (but not a musk-cat), that has fallen into
the unclean fishpond of her displeasure, and, as
he says, is muddied withal: pray you, sir, use
the carp as you may; for he looks like a poor,
decayed, ingenious, foolish, rascally knave. I
do pity his distress in my smiles of comfort, and
leave him to your lordship.         [*Exit.*
*Par.* My lord, I am a man whom fortune
hath cruelly scratched.
*Laf.* And what would you have me to do?
'tis too late to pare her nails now. Wherein
have you played the knave with fortune, that
she should scratch you, who of herself is a good
lady, and would not have knaves thrive long
under her? There's a *quart d'ecu* for you: let the
justices make you and fortune friends; I am for
other business.
*Par.* I beseech your honour to hear me one
single word.
*Laf.* You beg a single penny more: come,
you shall ha't: save your word.
*Par.* My name, my good lord, is Parolles.
*Laf.* You beg more than one word then.—
Cox' my passion! give me your hand:—how
does your drum?
*Par.* O my good lord, you were the first that
found me.
*Laf.* Was I, in sooth? and I was the first that
lost thee.
*Par.* It lies in you, my lord, to bring me in
some grace, for you did bring me out.
*Laf.* Out upon thee, knave! dost thou put
upon me at once both the office of God and the
devil? one brings thee in grace, and the other
brings thee out.         [*Trumpets sound.*]
The king's coming; I know by his trumpets.
—Sirrah, inquire further after me; I had talk of

you last night: though you are a fool and a
knave, you shall eat: go to; follow.

*Par.* I praise God for you.     [*Exeunt.*

SCENE III.—*The same. A Room in the*
COUNTESS'S *Palace.*

*Flourish. Enter* KING, COUNTESS, LAFEU,
    Lords, Gentlemen, Guards, &c.

*King.* We lost a jewel of her; and our esteem
Was made much poorer by it: but your son,
As mad in folly, lack'd the sense to know
Her estimation home.

*Count.*       'Tis past, my liege:
And I beseech your majesty to make it
Natural rebellion, done i' the blaze of youth,
When oil and fire, too strong for reason's force,
O'erbears it, and burns on.

*King.*       My honour'd lady,
I have forgiven and forgotten all;
Though my revenges were high bent upon him,
And watch'd the time to shoot.

*Laf.*       This I must say,—
But first, I beg your pardon,—the young lord
Did to his majesty, his mother, and his lady,
Offence of mighty note; but to himself
The greatest wrong of all: he lost a wife
Whose beauty did astonish the survey
Of richest eyes; whose words all ears took cap-
tive;
Whose dear perfection hearts that scorn'd to
serve
Humbly call'd mistress.

*King.*       Praising what is lost
Makes the remembrance dear.—Well, call him
hither;—
We are reconcil'd, and the first view shall kill
All repetition:—let him not ask our pardon;
The nature of his great offence is dead,
And deeper than oblivion do we bury
The incensing relics of it; let him approach,
A stranger, no offender; and inform him,
So 'tis our will he should.

*Gent.*       I shall, my liege.
      [*Exit* Gentleman.

*King.* What says he to your daughter? have
you spoke?

*Laf.* All that he is hath reference to your
highness.

*King.* Then shall we have a match. I have
letters sent me
That set him high in fame.

*Enter* BERTRAM.

*Laf.*       He looks well on't.

*King.* I am not a day of season,
For thou mayst see a sunshine and a hail
In me at once: but to the brightest beams
Distracted clouds give way; so stand thou
forth,
The time is fair again.

*Ber.*       My high-repented blames,
Dear sovereign, pardon to me.

*King.*       All is whole;
Not one word more of the consumed time.

Let's take the instant by the forward top;
For we are old, and on our quick'st decrees
The inaudible and noiseless foot of time
Steals ere we can effect them. You remember
The daughter of this lord?

*Ber.* Admiringly, my liege: at first
I stuck my choice upon her, ere my heart
Durst make too bold a herald of my tongue:
Where the impression of mine eye infixing,
Contempt his scornful perspective did lend me,
Which warp'd the line of every other favour;
Scorn'd a fair colour, or express'd it stolen;
Extended or contracted all proportions
To a most hideous object: thence it came
That she whom all men prais'd, and whom my
self,
Since I have lost, have lov'd, was in mine eye
The dust that did offend it.

*King.*       Well excus'd:
That thou didst love her, strikes some scores
away
From the great compt: but love that comes too
late,
Like a remorseful pardon slowly carried,
To the great sender turns a sour offence,
Crying, That's good that's gone. Our rash
faults
Make trivial price of serious things we have,
Not knowing them until we know their grave:
Oft our displeasures, to ourselves unjust,
Destroy our friends, and after weep their dust:
Our own love waking cries to see what's done,
While shameful hate sleeps out the afternoon.
Be this sweet Helen's knell, and now forget her.
Send forth your amorous token for fair Maud-
lin:
The main consents are had: and here we'll stay
To see our widower's second marriage-day.

*Count.* Which better than the first, O dear
heaven, bless!
Or, ere they meet, in me, O nature, cesse!

*Laf.* Come on, my son, in whom my house's
name
Must be digested, give a favour from you,
To sparkle in the spirits of my daughter,
That she may quickly come.—
      [BERTRAM *gives a ring to* LAFEU.
      By my old beard,
And every hair that's on't, Helen, that's dead,
Was a sweet creature: such a ring as this,
The last that e'er I took her leave at court,
I saw upon her finger.

*Ber.*       Her's it was not.

*King.* Now, pray you, let me see it; for mine
eye,
While I was speaking, oft was fasten'd to it.—
This ring was mine, and when I gave it Helen
I bade her, if her fortunes ever stood
Necessitated to help, that by this token
I would relieve her. Had you that craft to
'reave her
Of what should stead her most?

*Ber.*       My gracious sovereign,
Howe'er it pleases you to take it so,

The ring was never hers.

*Count.*                         Son, on my life,
I have seen her wear it; and she reckon'd it
At her life's rate.

*Laf.*            I'm sure I saw her wear it.

*Ber.* You are deceiv'd, my lord; she never
  saw it:
In Florence was it from a casement thrown me,
Wrapp'd in a paper, which contain'd the name
Of her that threw it: noble she was, and
  thought
I stood engag'd: but when I had subscrib'd
To mine own fortune, and inform'd her fully
I could not answer in that course of honour
As she had made the overture, she ceas'd,
In heavy satisfaction, and would never
Receive the ring again.

*King.*                    Plutus himself,
That knows the tinct and multiplying medi-
  cine,
Hath not in nature's mystery more science
Than I have in this ring: 'twas mine, 'twas
  Helen's,
Whoever gave it you. Then, if you know
That you are well acquainted with yourself,
Confess 'twas hers, and by what rough en-
  forcement
You got it from her: she call'd the saints to
  surety
That she would never put it from her finger
Unless she gave it to yourself in bed,—
Where you have never come,—or sent it us
Upon her great disaster.

*Ber.*                    She never saw it.

*King.* Thou speak'st it falsely, as I love
  mine honour;
And mak'st conjectural fears to come into me
Which I would fain shut out. If it should prove
That thou art so inhuman,—'twill not prove
  so:—
And yet I know not:—thou didst hate her
  deadly.
And she is dead; which nothing, but to close
Her eyes myself, could win me to believe
More than to see this ring.—Take him away.—
                [Guards *seize* BERTRAM.
My fore-past proofs, howe'er the matter fall,
Shall tax my fears of little vanity,
Having vainly fear'd too little.—Away with
  him;—
We'll sift this matter further.

*Ber.*                    If you shall prove
This ring was ever hers, you shall as easy
Prove that I husbanded her bed in Florence,
Where yet she never was.    [*Exit, guarded.*

*King.* I am wrapp'd in dismal thinkings.

*Enter a* Gentleman.

*Gent.*                    Gracious sovereign,
Whether I have been to blame or no, I know
  not:
Here's a petition from a Florentine,
Who hath, for four or five removes, come short
To tender it herself. I undertook it,
Vanquish'd thereto by the fair grace and speech
Of the poor suppliant, who by this, I know,
Is here attending: her business looks in her
With an importing visage; and she told me,
In a sweet verbal brief, it did concern
Your highness with herself.

*King.* [*Reads.*] *Upon his many protestations
to marry me, when his wife was dead, I blush to
say it, he won me. Now is the Count Rousillon a
widower; his vows are forfeited to me, and my
honour's paid to him. He stole from Florence,
taking no leave, and I follow him to his country
for justice: grant it me, O king; in you it best lies;
otherwise a seducer flourishes, and a poor maid is
undone.*                        DIANA CAPULET.

*Laf.* I will buy me a son-in-law in a fair, and
toll this: I'll none of him.

*King.* The heaven's have thought well on
  thee, Lafeu,
To bring forth this discovery.—Seek these
  suitors:—
Go speedily, and bring again the count.
          [*Exeunt* Gentleman, *and some* Attendants.
I am afeard the life of Helen, lady,
Was foully snatch'd.

*Count.*                    Now, justice on the doers!

*Enter* BERTRAM, *guarded.*

*King.* I wonder, sir, since wives are monsters
  to you,
And that you fly them as you swear them lordship,
Yet you desire to marry.—What woman's
  that?

*Re-enter* Gentleman, *with* Widow *and* DIANA.

*Dia.* I am, my lord, a wretched Florentine,
Derived from the ancient Capulet;
My suit, as I do understand, you know,
And therefore know how far I may be pitied.

*Wid.* I am her mother, sir, whose age and
  honour
Both suffer under this complaint we bring,
And both shall cease, without your remedy.

*King.* Come hither, count; do you know
  these women?

*Ber.* My lord, I neither can nor will deny
But that I know them: do they charge me
  further?

*Dia.* Why do you look so strange upon your
  wife.

*Ber.* She's none of mine, my lord.

*Dia.*                    If you shall marry,
You give away this hand, and that is mine;
You give away heaven's vows, and those are
  mine;
You give away myself, which is known mine;
For I by vow am so embodied yours ·
That she which marries you must marry me,
Either both or none.

*Laf.* [*To* BERTRAM.] Your reputation comes
too short for my daughter; you are no husband
for her.

*Ber.* My lord, this is a fond and desperate
  creature

Whom sometimes I have laugh'd with: let your
   highness
Lay a more noble thought upon mine honour
Than for to think I would sink it here.
   *King.* Sir, for my thoughts, you have them
   ill to friend
Till your deeds gain them: fairer prove your
   honour
Than in my thought it lies!
   *Dia.*          Good, my lord,
Ask him upon his oath, if he does think
He had not my virginity.
   *King.* What say'st thou to her?
   *Ber.*        She's impudent, my lord;
And was a common gamester to the camp.
   *Dia.* He does me wrong, my lord; if I were so
He might have bought me at a common price:
Do not believe him. O, behold this ring,
Whose high respect and rich validity
Did lack a parallel; yet, for all that,
He gave it to a commoner o' the camp,
If I be one.
   *Count.* He blushes, and 'tis it:
Of six preceding ancestors, that gem,
Conferr'd by testament to the sequent issue,
Hath it been ow'd and worn. This is his wife;
That ring's a thousand proofs.
   *King.*       Methought you said
You saw one here in court could witness it.
   *Dia.* I did, my lord, but loath am to produce
So bad an instrument; his name's Parolles.
   *Laf.* I saw the man to-day, if man he be.
   *King.* Find him, and bring him hither.
               [*Exit an* Attendant.
   *Ber.*          What of him?
He's quoted for a most perfidious slave,
With all the spots o' the world tax'd and de-
   bosh'd:
Whose nature sickens but to speak a truth:
Am I or that or this for what he'll utter,
That will speak anything?
   *King.*       She hath that ring of yours.
   *Ber.* I think she has: certain it is I lik'd her,
And boarded her i' the wanton way of youth:
She knew her distance, and did angle for me,
Madding my eagerness with her restraint,
As all impediments in fancy's course
Are motives of more fancy; and, in fine,
Her infinite coming with her modern grace,
Subdued me to her rate: she got the ring;
And I had that which any inferior might
At market-price have bought.
   *Dia.*        I must be patient:
You that have turn'd off a first so noble wife
May justly diet me. I pray you yet,—
Since you lack virtue, I will lose a husband,—
Send for your ring, I will return it home,
And give me mine again.
   *Ber.*        I have it not.
   *King.* What ring was yours, I pray you?
   *Dia.*          Sir, much like
The same upon your finger.
   *King.* Know you this ring? this ring was his
   of late.

   *Dia.* And this was it I gave him, being a-bed.
   *King.* The story, then, goes false you threw
   it him
Out of a casement.
   *Dia.* I have spoke the truth.
   *Ber.* My lord, I do confess the ring was hers.
   *King.* You boggle shrewdly; every feather
   starts you.—

   *Re-enter* Attendant, *with* PAROLLES.

Is this the man you speak of?
   *Dia.*          Ay, my lord.
   *King.* Tell me, sirrah, but tell me true, I
   charge you,
Not fearing the displeasure of your master,—
Which, on your just proceeding, I'll keep off,—
By him and by this woman here what know
   you?
   *Par.* So please your majesty, my master hath
been an honourable gentleman; tricks he hath
had in him, which gentlemen have.
   *King.* Come, come, to the purpose: did he
love this woman?
   *Par.* Faith, sir, he did love her; but how?
   *King.* How, I pray you?
   *Par.* He did love her, sir, as a gentleman
loves a woman.
   *King.* How is that?
   *Par.* He loved her, sir, and loved her not.
   *King.* As thou art a knave and no knave.—
What an equivocal companion is this!
   *Par.* I am a poor man, and at your majesty's
command.
   *Laf.* He's a good drum, my lord, but a
naughty orator.
   *Dia.* Do you know he promised me marriage?
   *Par.* Faith, I know more than I'll speak.
   *King.* But wilt thou not speak all thou
know'st?
   *Par.* Yes, so please your majesty; I did go
between them, as I said; but more than that, he
loved her,—for, indeed, he was mad for her,
and talked of Satan, and of limbo, and of furies,
and I know not what: yet I was in that credit
with them at that time that I knew of their going to bed; and of other motions, as promising
her marriage, and things which would derive
me ill-will to speak of; therefore I will not
speak what I know.
   *King.* Thou hast spoken all already, unless
thou canst say they are married: but thou art
too fine in thy evidence; therefore stand aside.
—This ring, you say, was yours?
   *Dia.*         Ay, my good lord.
   *King.* Where did you buy it? or who gave it
   you?                    [it.
   *Dia.* It was not given me, nor I did not buy
   *King.* Who lent it you?
   *Dia.*        It was not lent me neither.
   *King.* Where did you find it then?
   *Dia.*         I found it not.
   *King.* If it were yours by none of all these
   ways,
How could you give it him?

*Dia.* I never gave it him.

*Laf.* This woman's an easy glove, my lord; She goes off and on at pleasure.

*King.* This ring was mine, I gave it his first wife.

*Dia.* It might be yours or hers, for aught I know.

*King.* Take her away, I do not like her now; To prison with her: and away with him.— Unless thou tell'st me where thou hadst this ring, Thou diest within this hour.

*Dia.* I'll never tell you.

*King.* Take her away.

*Dia.* I'll put in bail, my liege.

*King.* I think thee now some common customer.

*Dia.* By Jove, if ever I knew man, 'twas you.

*King.* Wherefore hast thou accus'd him all this while?

*Dia.* Because he's guilty, and he is not guilty:
He knows I am no maid, and he'll swear to't:
I'll swear I am a maid, and he knows not.
Great king, I am no strumpet, by my life;
I am either maid, or else this old man's wife.
[*Pointing to* LAFEU.

*King.* She does abuse our ears; to prison with her.

*Dia.* Good mother, fetch my bail.—Stay, royal sir; [*Exit* Widow.
The jeweller that owes the ring is sent for,
And he shall surety me. But for this lord,
Who hath abus'd me, as he knows himself,
Though yet he never harm'd me, here I quit him:
He knows himself my bed he hath defil'd;
And at that time he got his wife with child.
Dead though she be, she feels her young one kick;
So there's my riddle—One that's dead is quick;
And now behold the meaning.

*Re-enter* Widow *with* HELENA.

*King.* Is there no exorcist

Beguiles the truer office of mine eyes?
Is't real that I see?

*Hel.* No, my good lord;
'Tis but the shadow of a wife you see—
The name, and not the thing.

*Ber.* Both, both; O, pardon!

*Hel.* O, my good lord, when I was like this maid;
I found you wondrous kind. There is your ring,
And, look you, here's your letter. This it says,
*When from my finger you can get this ring,
And are by me with child,* &c.—This is done:
Will you be mine, now you are doubly won?

*Ber.* If she, my liege, can make me know this clearly,
I'll love her dearly, ever, ever dearly.

*Hel.* If it appear not plain, and prove untrue,
Deadly divorce step between me and you!—
O, my dear mother, do I see you living?

*Laf.* Mine eyes smell onions; I shall weep anon:—Good Tom Drum [*to* PAROLLES], lend me a handkercher: so, I thank thee; wait on me home, I'll make sport with thee: let thy courtesies alone, they are scurvy ones.

*King.* Let us from point to point this story know,
To make the even truth in pleasure flow:—
If thou be'st yet a fresh uncropped flower,
[*To* DIANA.
Choose thou thy husband, and I'll pay thy dower;
For I can guess that, by thy honest aid,
Thou kep'st a wife herself, thyself a maid.—
Of that and all the progress, more and less,
Resolvedly more leisure shall express:
All yet seems well; and if it end so meet,
The bitter past, more welcome is the sweet.
[*Flourish.

The king's a beggar, now the play is done:
All is well-ended if this suit be won,
That you express content; which we will pay
With strife to please you, day exceeding day:
Ours be your patience then, and yours our parts;
Your gentle hands lend us, and take our hearts.
[*Exeunt.

TAMING OF THE SHREW. Act III. Sc. 2.

# THE TAMING OF THE SHREW

## DRAMATIS PERSONÆ

A Lord.
CHRISTOPHER SLY, a drunken Tinker ⎫
Hostess, Page, Players, Huntsmen, and Servants. ⎬ Persons in the Induction.

BAPTISTA, a rich Gentleman of Padua.
VINCENTIO, an old Gentleman of Pisa.
LUCENTIO, Son to VINCENTIO, in love with BIANCA.
PETRUCHIO, a Gentleman of Verona, a Suitor to KATHARINA.
GREMIO, ⎫
HORTENSIO, ⎬ Suitors to BIANCA.

TRANIO, ⎫
BIONDELLO, ⎬ Servants to LUCENTIO.
GRUMIO, ⎫
CURTIS, ⎬ Servants to PETRUCHIO.
Pedant, an old fellow set up to personate VINCENTIO.

KATHARINA, the Shrew, ⎫
BIANCA, ⎬ Daughters to BAPTISTA.
Widow.

Tailor, Haberdasher, and Servants attending on BAPTISTA and PETRUCHIO.

SCENE,—Sometimes in PADUA, and sometimes in PETRUCHIO'S House in the Country.

## INDUCTION.

### SCENE I.—Before an Alehouse on a Heath.

*Enter* Hostess *and* SLY.

*Sly.* I'll pheeze you, in faith.
*Host.* A pair of stocks, you rogue!
*Sly.* Y'are a baggage: the Slys are no rogues; look in the chronicles; we came in with Richard Conqueror. Therefore, *paucas pallabris;* let the world slide: sessa!
*Host.* You will not pay for the glasses you have burst?
*Sly.* No, not a denier. Go by, Saint Jeronimy,—go to thy cold bed and warm thee.
*Host.* I know my remedy; I must go fetch the thirdborough. [*Exit.*
*Sly.* Third, or fourth, or fifth borough, I'll answer him by law: I'll not budge an inch, boy: let him come, and kindly.
[*Lies down on the ground and falls asleep.*

*Horns winded. Enter a* Lord *from hunting, with* Huntsmen *and* Servants.

*Lord.* Huntsman, I charge thee, tender well my hounds:
Brach Merriman,—the poor cur is emboss'd,
And couple Clowder with the deep-mouth'd brach.
Saw'st thou not, boy, how Silver made it good
At the hedge-corner, in the coldest fault?
I would not lose the dog for twenty pound.
  *1 Hun.* Why, Belman is as good as he, my lord;
He cried upon it at the merest loss,
And twice to-day pick'd out the dullest scent:
Trust me, I take him for the better dog.
  *Lord.* Thou art a fool: if Echo were as fleet,
I would esteem him worth a dozen such.
But sup them well, and look unto them all:

To-morrow I intend to hunt again.
  *1 Hun.* I will, my lord.
  *Lord.* What's here? one dead, or drunk?
See, doth he breathe?
  *2 Hun.* He breathes, my lord. Were he not warm'd with ale,
This were a bed but cold to sleep so soundly.
  *Lord.* O monstrous beast! how like a swine he lies! [image!
Grim death, how foul and loathsome is thine
Sirs, I will practise on this drunken man.
What think you, if he were convey'd to bed,
Wrapp'd in sweet clothes, rings put upon his fingers,
A most delicious banquet by his bed,
And brave attendants near him when he wakes,
Would not the beggar then forget himself?
  *1 Hun.* Believe me, lord, I think he cannot choose.
  *2 Hun.* It would seem strange unto him when he wak'd. [less fancy.
  *Lord.* Even as a flattering dream or worth-
Then take him up, and manage well the jest:—
Carry him gently to my fairest chamber.
And hang it round with all my wanton pictures:
Balm his foul head in warm distilled waters,
And burn sweet wood to make the lodging sweet:
Procure me music ready when he wakes,
To make a dulcet and a heavenly sound;
And if he chance to speak, be ready straight,
And, with a low, submissive reverence,
Say,—What is it your honour will command?
Let one attend him with a silver basin
Full of rose-water and bestrew'd with flowers;
Another bear the ewer, the third a diaper,
And say,—Will't please your lordship cool your hands?
Some one be ready with a costly suit,

And ask him what apparel he will wear;
Another tell him of his hounds and horse,
And that his lady mourns at his disease:
Persuade him that he hath been lunatic;
And, when he says he is, say that he dreams,
For he is nothing but a mighty lord.
This do, and do it kindly, gentle sirs:
It will be pastime passing excellent,
If it be husbanded with modesty.        [our part,
    1 *Hun.* My lord, I warrant you, we'll play
As he shall think, by our true diligence,
He is no less than what we say he is.        [him;
    *Lord.* Take him up gently, and to bed with
And each one to his office when he wakes.
                [*Some bear out* SLY. *A trumpet sounds.*
Sirrah, go see what trumpet 'tis that sounds:—
                                [*Exit* Servant.
Belike, some noble gentleman, that means,
Travelling some journey, to repose him here.

            *Re-enter a* Servant.

How now! who is it?
    *Serv.*                An it please your honour,
Players that offer service to your lordship.
    *Lord.* Bid them come near.

            *Enter* Players.

                Now, fellows, you are welcome.
    1 *Play.* We thank your honour.
    *Lord.* Do you intend to stay with me to-
        night?
    2 *Play.* So please your lordship to accept our
        duty.                        [member,
    *Lord.* With all my heart.—This fellow I re-
Since once he play'd a farmer's eldest son:—
'Twas where you woo'd the gentlewoman so
        well:
I have forgot your name; but, sure, that part
Was aptly fitted and naturally perform'd.
    1 *Play.* I think 'twas Soto that your honour
        means.
    *Lord.* 'Tis very true: thou didst it excellent.—
Well, you are come to me in happy time;
The rather for I have some sport in hand,
Wherein your cunning can assist me much.
There is a lord will hear you play to-night:
But I am doubtful of your modesties;
Lest, over-eying of his odd behaviour,—
For yet his honour never heard a play,—
You break into some merry passion,
And so offend him; for I tell you, sirs,
If you should smile, he grows impatient.
    1 *Play.* Fear not, my lord; we can contain
        ourselves,
Were he the veriest antic in the world.
    *Lord.* Go, sirrah, take them to the buttery,
And give them friendly welcome every one:
Let them want nothing that my house affords.
                [*Exeunt* Servant *and* Players.
Sirrah, go you to Barthol'mew my page,
                        [*To a* Servant.
And see him dress'd in all suits like a lady:
That done, conduct him to the drunkard's
        chamber:

And call him madam, do him obeisance.
Tell him from me,—as he will win my love,—
He bear himself with honourable action,
Such as he hath observ'd in noble ladies
Unto their lords, by them accomplished:
Such duty to the drunkard let him do,
With soft low tongue and lowly courtesy;
And say,—What is't your honour will com-
        mand,
Wherein your lady and your humble wife
May show her duty and make known her love?
And then,—with kind embracements, tempting
        kisses,
And with declining head into his bosom,—
Bid him shed tears, as being overjoy'd
To see her noble lord restor'd to health,
Who for this seven years hath esteemed him
No better than a poor and loathsome beggar:
And if the boy have not a woman's gift,
To rain a shower of commanded tears,
An onion will do well for such a shift;
Which in a napkin being close conveyed,
Shall in despite enforce a watery eye.        [canst
See this despatch'd with all the haste thou
Anon I'll give thee more instructions.
                            [*Exit* Servant.
I know the boy will well usurp the grace,
Voice, gait, and action of a gentlewoman:
I long to hear him call the drunkard husband;
And how my men will stay themselves from
        laughter
When they do homage to this simple peasant.
I'll to counsel them: haply my presence
May well abate the over-merry spleen,
Which otherwise would grow into extremes.
                                [*Exeunt.*

SCENE II.—*A Bedchamber in the* Lord's *House.*

SLY *is discovered in a rich nightgown, with*
    Attendants; *some with apparel, others with*
    *basin, ewer, and other appurtenances. Enter*
    Lord, *dressed like a Servant.*

    *Sly.* For God's sake, a pot of small ale.
    1 *Serv.* Will't please your lordship drink a
        cup of sack?                [these conserves?
    2 *Serv.* Will't please your honour taste of
    3 *Serv.* What raiment will your honour wear
        to-day?
    *Sly.* I am Christophero Sly; call not me
honour nor lordship: I ne'er drank sack in my
life; and if you give me any conserves, give me
conserves of beef: ne'er ask me what raiment
I'll wear; for I have no more doublets than
backs, no more stockings than legs, nor no more
shoes than feet,—nay, sometime more feet than
shoes, or such shoes as my toes look through
the overleather.                        [honour!
    *Lord.* Heaven cease this idle humour in your
O, that a mighty man, of such descent,
Of such possessions, and so high esteem,
Should be infused with so foul a spirit!
    *Sly.* What, would you make me mad? Am
not I Christopher Sly, old Sly's son of Burton-
heath; by birth a pedler, by education a card-

maker, by transmutation a bear-herd, and now
by present profession a tinker? Ask Marian
Hacket, the fat ale-wife of Wincot, if she know
me not: if she say I am not fourteen-pence on
the score for sheer ale, score me up for the
lyingest knave in Christendom. What! I am
not bestraught: here's—                    [mourn!
  1 Serv.  O, this it is that makes your lady
  2 Serv.  O, this it is that makes your servants
      droop!
  Lord.  Hence comes it that your kindred
      shuns your house,
As beaten hence by your strange lunacy.
O noble lord, bethink thee of thy birth!
Call home thy ancient thoughts from banish-
      ment,
And banish hence these abject lowly dreams.
Look how thy servants do attend on thee,
Each in his office ready at thy beck.
Wilt thou have music? hark! Apollo plays,
                                    [Music.
And twenty caged nightingales do sing:
Or wilt thou sleep? we'll have thee to a couch
Softer and sweeter than the lustful bed
On purpose trimm'd up for Semiramis.
Say thou wilt walk; we will bestrew the ground:
Or wilt thou ride? thy horses shall be trapp'd,
Their harness studded all with gold and pearl.
Dost thou love hawking? thou hast hawks will
      soar
Above the morning lark: or wilt thou hunt?
Thy hounds shall make the welkin answer
      them,
And fetch shrill echoes from the hollow earth.
  1 Serv.  Say thou wilt course; thy greyhounds
      are as swift
As breathed stags; ay, fleeter than the roe.
  2 Serv.  Dost thou love pictures: we will
      fetch thee straight
Adonis painted by a running brook,
And Cytherea all in sedges hid,         [breath,
Which seem to move and wanton with her
Even as the waving sedges play with wind.
  Lord.  We'll show thee Io as she was a maid,
And how she was beguiled and surpris'd,
As lively painted as the deed was done.
  3 Serv.  Or Daphne roaming through a
      thorny wood,                        [bleeds;
Scratching her legs, that one shall swear she
And at that sight shall sad Apollo weep,
So workmanly the blood and tears are drawn.
  Lord.  Thou art a lord, and nothing but a
      lord:
Thou hast a lady far more beautiful
Than any woman in this waning age. [for thee,
  1 Serv.  And, till the tears that she hath shed
Like envious floods, o'er-run her lovely face,
She was the fairest creature in the world;
And yet she is inferior to none.
  Sly.  Am I a lord? and have I such a lady?
Or do I dream? or have I dream'd till now?
I do not sleep: I see, I hear, I speak;
I smell sweet savours, and I feel soft things:—
Upon my life, I am a lord indeed;

And not a tinker, nor Christophero Sly.—
Well, bring our lady hither to our sight;
And once again, a pot o' the smallest ale.
  2 Serv.  Will't please your mightiness to wash
      your hands?
[Servants present a ewer, basin, and napkin.
O, how we joy to see your wit restor'd!
O, that once more you knew but what you are!
These fifteen years you have been in a dream;
Or, when you wak'd, so wak'd as if you slept.
  Sly.  These fifteen years! by my fay, a goodly
      nap.
But did I never speak of all that time?
  1 Serv.  O yes, my lord; but very idle words:
For though you lay here in this goodly chamber,
Yet would you say, ye were beaten out of door;
And rail upon the hostess of the house;
And say, you would present her at the leet,
Because she brought stone jugs and no seal'd
      quarts:
Sometimes you would call out for Cicely
      Hacket.
  Sly.  Ay, the woman's maid of the house.
  3 Serv.  Why, sir, you know no house, nor no
      such maid;
Nor no such men as you have reckon'd up,—
As Stephen Sly, and old John Naps of Greece,
And Peter Turf, and Henry Pimpernell;
And twenty more such names and men as these,
Which never were nor no man ever saw.
  Sly.  Now, Lord be thanked for my good
      amends.
  All.  Amen.
  Sly.  I thank thee: thou shalt not lose by it.

Enter the Page as a lady, with Attendants.

  Page.  How fares my noble lord?   [enough.
  Sly.  Marry, I fare well; for here is cheer
Where is my wife?
  Page.  Here, noble lord: what is thy will with
      her?
  Sly.  Are you my wife, and will not call me
      husband?                            [man.
My men should call me lord: I am your good-
  Page.  My husband and my lord, my lord
      and husband;
I am your wife in all obedience.
  Sly.  I know it well.—What must I call her?
  Lord.  Madam.
  Sly.  Al'ce madam, or Joan madam?
  Lord.  Madam, and nothing else: so lords
      call ladies.                        [dream'd,
  Sly.  Madam wife, they say that I have
And slept above some fifteen year or more.
  Page.  Ay, and the time seems thirty unto
      me,
Being all this time abandoned from your bed.
  Sly.  'Tis much.—Servants, leave me and
      her alone.—
Madam, undress you, and come now to bed.
  Page.  Thrice noble lord, let me entreat of
      you
To pardon me yet for a night or two;
Or, if not so, until the sun be set:

For your physicians have expressly charg'd,
In peril to incur your former malady,
That I should yet absent me from your bed:
I hope this reason stands for my excuse.

*Sly.* Ay, it stands so, that I may hardly
tarry so long. But I would be loath to fall into
my dreams again: I will therefore tarry, in
despite of the flesh and the blood.

*Enter a* Servant.

*Serv.* Your honour's players, hearing your
amendment,
Are come to play a pleasant comedy;
For so your doctors hold it very meet,
Seeing too much sadness hath congeal'd your
blood,
And melancholy is the nurse of frenzy:
Therefore they thought it good you hear a play,
And frame your mind to mirth and merriment,
Which bars a thousand harms and lengthens
life.

*Sly.* Marry, I will; let them play it. Is not a
commonty a Christmas gambol or a tumbling-
trick?                                          [stuff.

*Page.* No, my good lord; it is more pleasing

*Sly.* What, household stuff?

*Page.* It is a kind of history.

*Sly.* Well, we'll see't. Come, madam wife, sit
by my side, and let the world slip: we shall ne'er
be younger.                        [*They sit down.*

## ACT I.

### SCENE I.—PADUA. *A public Place.*

*Enter* LUCENTIO *and* TRANIO.

*Luc.* Tranio, since for the great desire I had
To see fair Padua, nursery of arts,
I am arriv'd for fruitful Lombardy,
The pleasant garden of great Italy;
And, by my father's love and leave, am arm'd
With his good-will and thy good company,
My trusty servant, well approv'd in all;
Here let us breathe, and haply institute
A course of learning and ingenious studies.
Pisa, renowned for grave citizens,
Gave me my being, and my father first,
A merchant of great traffic through the world,
Vincentio, come of the Bentivolii.
Vincentio's son, brought up in Florence,
It shall become, to serve all hopes conceiv'd,
To deck his fortune with his virtuous deeds:
And therefore, Tranio, for the time I study,
Virtue, and that part of philosophy
Will I apply that treats of happiness
By virtue specially to be achiev'd.
Tell me thy mind; for I have Pisa left,
And am to Padua come, as he that leaves
A shallow plash to plunge him in the deep,
And with satiety seeks to quench his thirst.

*Tra. Mi perdonate,* gentle master mine,
I am in all affected as yourself;
Glad that you thus continue your resolve
To suck the sweets of sweet philosophy.
Only, good master, while we do admire

This virtue and this moral discipline,
Let's be no stoics nor no stocks, I pray;
Or so devote to Aristotle's ethics
As Ovid be an outcast quite abjur'd:
Balk logic with acquaintance that you have,
And practise rhetoric in your common talk;
Music and poesy use to quicken you;
The mathematics and the metaphysics,
Fall to them as you find your stomach serves
you;
No profit grows where is no pleasure ta'en:
In brief, sir, study what you most affect.

*Luc.* Gramercies, Tranio, well dost thou ad-
vise.
If Biondello now were come ashore
We could at once put us in readiness,
And take a lodging fit to entertain
Such friends as time in Padua shall beget.
But stay awhile: what company is this?

*Tra.* Master, some show, to welcome us to
town.

*Enter* BAPTISTA, KATHARINA, BIANCA, GREMIO,
*and* HORTENSIO. LUCENTIO *and* TRANIO
*stand aside.*

*Bap.* Gentlemen, impórtune me no further,
For how I firmly am resolv'd you know;
That is, not to bestow my youngest daughter
Before I have a husband for the elder·
If either of you both love Katharina,
Because I know you well, and love you well,
Leave shall you have to court her at your
pleasure.

*Gre.* To cart her rather: she's too rough for
me.—
There, there, Hortensio, will you any wife?

*Kath.* [*To* BAP.] I pray you, sir, is it your will
To make a stale of me amongst these mates?

*Hor.* Mates, maid! how mean you that? no
mates for you,
Unless you were of gentler, milder mould.

*Kath.* I' faith, sir, you shall never need to
fear;
I wis it is not half-way to her heart;
But if it were, doubt not her care should be
To comb your noddle with a three-legg'd stool,
And paint your face, and use you like a fool.

*Hor.* From all such devils, good Lord deliver
us!

*Gre.* And me too, good Lord!

*Tra.* Hush master! here is some good pastime toward;
That wench is stark mad  or wonderful fro-·
ward.

*Luc.* But in the other's silence do I see
Maid's mild behaviour and sobriety.
Peace, Tranio!                        [your fill.

*Tra.* Well said, master; mum! and gaze

*Bap.* Gentlemen, that I may soon make good
What I have said,—Bianca, get you in:
And let it not displease thee, good Bianca;
For I will love thee ne'er the less, my girl.

*Kath.* A pretty peat! it is best
Put finger in the eye,—an she knew why.

*Bian.* Sister, content you in my discontent.—
Sir, to your pleasure humbly I subscribe:
My books and instruments shall be my company,
On them to look, and practise by myself.

*Luc.* Hark, Tranio! thou mayst hear Minerva speak.                    [*Aside.*

*Hor.* Signior Baptista, will you be so strange?
Sorry am I that our good-will effects
Bianca's grief.

*Gre.*        Why will you mew her up,
Signior Baptista, for this fiend of hell,
And make her bear the penance of her tongue?

*Bap.* Gentlemen, content ye; I am resolv'd:—
Go in, Bianca:—                    [*Exit* BIANCA.
And for I know she taketh most delight
In music, instruments, and poetry,
Schoolmasters will I keep within my house,
Fit to instruct her youth.—If you, Hortensio,
Or, Signior Gremio, you,—know any such,
Prefer them hither; for to cunning men
I will be very kind, and liberal
To mine own children in good bringing-up:
And so, farewell. Katharina, you may stay;
For I have more to commune with Bianca.
                              [*Exit.*

*Kath.* Why, and I trust I may go too, may I not?                    [belike,
What! shall I be appointed hours; as though,
I knew not what to take and what to leave? Ha!
                              [*Exit.*

*Gre.* You may go to the devil's dam; your
gifts are so good here is none will hold you.
Their love is not so great, Hortensio, but we
may blow our nails together, and fast it fairly
out; our cake's dough on both sides. Farewell;
—yet, for the love I bear my sweet Bianca, if I
can by any means light on a fit man to teach
her that wherein she delights, I will wish him to
her father.

*Hor.* So will I, Signior Gremio; but a word, I
pray. Though the nature of our quarrel yet
never brooked parle, know now, upon advice,
it toucheth us both—that we may yet again
have access to our fair mistress, and be happy
rivals in Bianca's love—to labour and effect one
thing specially.

*Gre.* What's that, I pray?                    [sister.

*Hor.* Marry, sir, to get a husband for her

*Gre.* A husband! a devil.

*Hor.* I say, a husband.

*Gre.* I say, a devil. Thinkest thou, Hortensio, though her father be very rich, any man
is so very a fool to be married to hell?

*Hor.* Tush, Gremio, though it pass your
patience and mine to endure her loud alarums,
why, man, there be good fellows in the world,
an a man could light on them, would take her
with all faults and money enough.

*Gre.* I cannot tell; but I had as lief take her
dowry with this condition,—to be whipped at
the high-cross every morning.

*Hor.* Faith, as you say, there's small choice

in rotten apples. But, come; since this bar in
law makes us friends, it shall be so far forth
friendly maintained, till, by helping Baptista's
eldest daughter to a husband, we set his
youngest free for a husband, and then have to't
afresh.—Sweet Bianca!—Happy man be his
dole! He that runs fastest gets the ring.
How say you, Signior Gremio?

*Gre.* I am agreed: and would I had given
him the best horse in Padua to begin his wooing, that would thoroughly woo her, wed her,
and bed her, and rid the house of her.   Come
on.                    [*Exeunt* GRE. *and* HOR.

*Tra.* [*Advancing.*] I pray, sir, tell me,—
is it possible
That love should of a sudden take such hold?

*Luc.* O Tranio, till I found it to be true,
I never thought it possible or likely;
But see! while idly I stood looking on
I found the effect of love in idleness:
And now in plainness do confess to thee,—
That art to me as secret and as dear
As Anna to the Queen of Carthage was,—
Tranio, I burn, I pine, I perish, Tranio,
If I achieve not this young modest girl:
Counsel me, Tranio, for I know thou canst;
Assist me, Tranio, for I know thou wilt.

*Tra.* Master, it is no time to chide you now;
Affection is not rated from the heart; [so,—
If love have touch'd you, nought remains but
*Redime te captum quam queas minimo.*

*Luc.* Gramercies, lad; go forward; this contents:
The rest will comfort, for thy counsel's sound.

*Tra.* Master, you look'd so longly on the
maid,
Perhaps you mark'd not what's the pith of all.

*Luc.* O yes, I saw sweet beauty in her face,
Such as the daughter of Agenor had,   [hand,
That made great Jove to humble him to her
When with his knees he kiss'd the Cretan
strand.

*Tra.* Saw you no more? mark'd you not how
her sister
Began to scold, and raise up such a storm,
That mortal ears might hardly endure the din?

*Luc.* Tranio, I saw her coral lips to move,
And with her breath she did perfume the air;
Sacred and sweet was all I saw in her.

*Tra.* Nay, then, 'tis time to stir him from
his trance.
I pray, awake, sir. If you love the maid,
Bend thoughts and wits to achieve her. Thus
it stands:—
Her eldest sister is so curst and shrewd
That, till the father rid his hands of her,
Master, your love must live a maid at home;
And therefore has he closely mew'd her up,
Because she will not be annoy'd with suitors.

*Luc.* Ah, Tranio, what a cruel father's he!
But art thou not advis'd he took some care
To get her cunning schoolmasters to instruct
her?                    [plotted.

*Tra.* Ay, marry, am I, sir: and now 'tis

*Luc.* I have it, Tranio

*Tra.*                    Master, for my hand,
Both our inventions meet and jump in one.

*Luc.* Tell me thine first.

*Tra.*                    You will be schoolmaster,
And undertake the teaching of the maid:
That's your device.

*Luc.*            It is: may it be done?

*Tra.* Not possible; for who shall bear your
      part,
And be in Padua here Vincentio's son;
Keep house, and ply his book; welcome his
      friends;
Visit his countrymen and banquet them?

*Luc.* Basta; content thee; for I have it full.
We have not yet been seen in any house;
Nor can we be distinguished by our faces
For man or master: then it follows thus:—
Thou shalt be master, Tranio, in my stead,
Keep house, and port, and servants, as I should:
I will some other be; some Florentine,
Some Neapolitan, or meaner man of Pisa.
'T is hatch'd, and shall be so:—Tranio, at once
Uncase thee; take my colour'd hat and cloak:
When Biondello comes he waits on thee;
But I will charm him first to keep his tongue.

*Tra.* So you had need.

                    [*They exchange habits.*
In brief, then, sir, sith it your pleasure is,
And I am tied to be obedient,—
For so your father charg'd me at our parting;
*Be serviceable to my son,* quoth he,
Although, I think, 'twas in another sense,—
I am content to be Lucentio,
Because so well I love Lucentio.

*Luc.* Tranio, be so, because Lucentio loves:
And let me be a slave, to achieve that maid
Whose sudden sight hath thrall'd my wounded
      eye.
Here comes the rogue.

### Enter BIONDELLO.

Sirrah, where have you been?

*Bion.* Where have I been? Nay, how now!
      where are you?
Master, has my fellow Tranio stolen your
      clothes?
Or you stolen his? or both? pray, what's the
      news?

*Luc.* Sirrah, come hither; 'tis no time to jest,
And therefore frame your manners to the time.
Your fellow Tranio here, to save my life,
Puts my apparel and my countenance on,
And I for my escape have put on his;
For in a quarrel, since I came ashore,
I kill'd a man, and fear I was descried.
Wait you on him, I charge you, as becomes,
While I make way from hence to save my life:
You understand me?

*Bion.*            I, sir! ne'er a whit.

*Luc.* And not a jot of Tranio in your mouth;
Tranio is chang'd into Lucentio.

*Bion.* The better for him; would I were so
      too!

*Tra.* So could I, faith, boy, to have the next
      wish after,—              [daughter.
That Lucentio indeed had Baptista's youngest
But, sirrah,—not for my sake, but your mas-
      ter's, I advise              [companies:
You use your manners discreetly in all kind of
When I am alone, why, then I am Tranio;
But in all places else, your master Lucentio.

*Luc.* Tranio, let's go:—
One thing more rests, that thyself execute,—
To make one among these wooers. If thou ask
      my why,—
Sufficeth, my reasons are both good and
      weighty.              [*Exeunt.*

[*1 Serv.* My lord, you nod; you do not mind
      the play.

*Sly.* Yes, by Saint Anne do I. A good matter,
surely; comes there any more of it?

*Page.* My lord, 'tis but begun.

*Sly.* 'Tis a very excellent piece of work,
madam lady; would 'twere done!]

SCENE II.—*The same. Before* HORTENSIO'S
      *House.*

### Enter PETRUCHIO *and* GRUMIO.

*Pet.* Verona, for awhile I take my leave,
To see my friends in Padua; but, of all,
My best beloved and approved friend,
Hortensio; and, I trow, this is his house:—
Here, sirrah Grumio; knock, I say.

*Gru.* Knock, sir! whom should I knock? is
there any man has rebused your worship?

*Pet.* Villain, I say, knock me here soundly.

*Gru.* Knock you here, sir? why, sir, what am
I, sir, that I should knock you here, sir?

*Pet.* Villain, I say, knock me at this gate,
And rap me well, of I'll knock your knave's
      pate.

*Gru.* My master is grown quarrelsome: I
      should knock you first,
And then I know after who comes by the worst.

*Pet.* Will it not be?
Faith, sirrah, an you'll not knock I'll wring it:
I'll try how you can *sol, fa,* and sing it.

                    [*He wrings* GRUMIO *by the ears.*

*Gru.* Help, masters, help! my master is mad.

*Pet.* Now, knock when I bid you; sirrah
      villain!

### Enter HORTENSIO.

*Hor.* How now! what's the matter?—My
old friend Grumio! and my good friend Petruchio!—How do you all at Verona?

*Pet.* Signior Hortensio, come you to part the
fray? *Con tutto il core bene trovato,* may I say.

*Hor. Alla nostra casa bene venuto, molto
honorato Signor mio Petruchio.*
Rise, Grumio, rise; we will compound this
      quarrel.

*Gru.* Nay, 'tis no matter, sir, what he 'leges
in Latin.—If this be not a lawful cause for me
to leave his service,—look you, sir,—he bid me
knock him, and rap him soundly, sir: well, was
it fit for a servant to use his master so; being,

perhaps,—for ought I see,—two and thirty,—a
pip out?
Whom would to God I had well knock'd at first,
Then had not Grumio come by the worst.

*Pet.* A senseless villain!—Good Hortensio,
I bade the rascal knock upon your gate,
And could not get him for my heart to do it.

*Gru.* Knock at the gate!—O heavens!
Spake you not these words plain,—*Sirrah,
  knock me here,
Rap me here, knock me well, and knock me
  soundly?*
And come you now with—knocking at the
gate?

*Pet.* Sirrah, be gone, or talk not, I advise
you.                                [pledge:

*Hor.* Petruchio, patience; I am Grumio's
Why, this' a heavy chance 'twixt him and you,
Your ancient, trusty, pleasant servant Grumio.
And tell me now, sweet friend, what happy gale
Blows you to Padua here from old Verona?

*Pet.* Such wind as scatters young men
      through the world,
To seek their fortunes further than at home,
Where small experience grows. But, in a few,
Signior Hortensio, thus it stands with me:—
Antonio, my father, is deceas'd;
And I have thrust myself into this maze,
Haply to wive and thrive as best I may:
Crowns in my purse I have, and goods at home,
And so am come abroad to see the world.

*Hor.* Petruchio, shall I then come roundly to
      thee,
And wish thee to a shrewd ill-favour'd wife?
Thou'dst thank me but a little for my counsel
And yet I'll promise thee she shall be rich,
And very rich:—but thou'rt too much my
      friend,
And I'll not wish thee to her.        [we

*Pet.* Signior Hortensio, 'twixt such friends as
Few words suffice; and, therefore, if thou know
One rich enough to be Petruchio's wife,—
As wealth is burden of my wooing dance,—
Be she as foul as was Florentius' love,
As old as Sibyl, and as curst and shrewd
As Socrates' Xantippe, or a worse,
She moves me not, or not removes, at least,
Affection's edge in me—were she as rough
As are the swelling Adriatic seas:
I come to wive it wealthily in Padua;
If wealthily, then happily in Padua.

*Gru.* Nay, look you, sir, he tells you flatly
what his mind is: why, give him gold enough
and marry him to a puppet or an aglet-baby;
or an old trot with ne'er a tooth in her head,
though she have as many diseases as two and
fifty horses: why, nothing comes amiss, so
money comes withal.               [far in,

*Hor.* Petruchio, since we have stepp'd thus
I will continue that I broach'd in jest.
I can, Petruchio, help thee to a·wife
With wealth enough, and young and beauteous;
Brought up as best becomes a gentlewoman;
Her only fault,—and that is faults enough,—

Is—that she is intolerably curst,
And shrewd, and forward; so beyond all
      measure,
That, were my state far worser than it is,
I would not wed her for a mine of gold.

*Pet.* Hortensio, peace! thou know'st not gold's
      effect:—
Tell me her father's name, and 'tis enough;
For I will board her though she chide as loud
As thunder, when the clouds in autumn crack.

*Hor.* Her father is Baptista Minola,
An affable and courteous gentleman:
Her name is Katharina Minola,
Renown'd in Padua for her scolding tongue.

*Pet.* I know her father though I know not
      her;
And he knew my deceased father well:
I will not sleep Hortensio, till I see her;
And therefore let me be thus bold with you,
To give you over at this first encounter,
Unless you will accompany me thither.

*Gru.* I pray you, sir, let him go while the
humour lasts. O' my word, an she knew him
as well as I do, she would think scolding would
do little good upon him. She may, perhaps,
call him half a score knaves, or so: why, that's
nothing; an he begin once, he'll rail in his rope-
tricks. I'll tell you what sir,—an she stand
him but a little, he will throw a figure in her
face, and so disfigure her with it that she shall
have no more eyes to see withal than a cat.
You know him not, sir.

*Hor.* Tarry, Petruchio, I must go with thee;
For in Baptista's keep my treasure is:
He hath the jewel of my life in hold,
His youngest daughter, beautiful Bianca;
And her withholds from me, and other more,
Suitors to her and rivals in my love:
Supposing it a thing impossible,—
For those defects I have before rehears'd,—
That ever Katharina will be woo'd,
Therefore this order hath Baptista ta'en;
That none shall have access unto Bianca
Till Katharine the curst have got a husband.

*Gru.* Katharine the curst!
A title for a maid, of all titles the worst.

*Hor.* Now shall my friend Petruchio do me
      grace;
And offer me disguis'd in sober robes
To old Baptista as a schoolmaster
Well seen in music, to instruct Bianca;
That so I may, by this device, at least
Have leave and leisure to make love to her,
And, unsuspected, court her by herself.

*Gro.* [*Aside.*] Here's no knavery! See, to beguile the old folks, how the young folks lay
their heads together!

*Enter* GREMIO; *with him* LUCENTIO *dis-*
*guised, with books under his arm.*

Master, master, look about you: who goes
there, ha?

*Hor.* Peace, Grumio! 'tis the rival of my love.
Petruchio, stand by awhile.

*Gru.* A proper stripling, and an amorous!
[*They retire.*

*Gre.* O, very well; I have perused the note.
Hark you, sir; I'll have them very fairly bound:
All books of love, see that at any hand;
And see you read no other lectures to her:
You understand me:—over and beside
Signior Baptista's liberality,          [too,
I'll mend it with a largess:—take your papers
And let me have them very well perfum'd;
For she is sweeter than perfume itself,     [her?
To whom they go to. What will you read to

*Luc.* Whate'er I read to her I'll plead for you
As for my patron,—stand you so assur'd,—
As firmly as yourself were still in place:
Yea, and perhaps with more successful words
Than you, unless you were a scholar, sir.

*Gre.* O this learning! what a thing it is!

*Gru.* O this woodcock! what an ass it is!

*Pet.* Peace, sirrah!

*Hor.* Grumio, mum!—[*Coming forward*].
God save you, Signior Gremio!

*Gre.* And you're well met, Signior Hortensio.
Trow you whither I am going?—To Baptista
Minola.
I promis'd to inquire carefully
About a schoolmaster for the fair Bianca:
And, by good fortune, I have lighted well
On this young man, for learning and behaviour
Fit for her turn; well read in poetry
And other books,—good ones, I warrant you.

*Hor.* 'Tis well; and I have met a gentleman
Hath promis'd me to help me to another,
A fine musician to instruct our mistress;
So shall I no whit be behind in duty
To fair Bianca, so belov'd of me.     [prove.

*Gra.* Belov'd of me,—and that my deeds shall

*Gru.* And that his bags shall prove. [*Aside.*

*Hor.* Gremio, 'tis now no time to vent our
love:
Listen to me, and if you speak me fair
I'll tell you news indifferent good for either.
Here is a gentleman, whom by chance I met,
Upon agreement from us to his liking,
Will undertake to woo curst Katharine;
Yea, and to marry her, if her dowry please.

*Gre.* So said, so done, is well:—
Hortensio, have you told him all her faults?

*Pet.* I know she is an irksome brawling
scold;
If that be all, masters, I hear no harm.

*Gre.* No, say'st me so, friend? What countryman?

*Pet.* Born in Verona, old Antonio's son:
My father dead, my fortune lives for me;
And I do hope good days and long to see.

*Gre.* O, sir, such a life, with such a wife, were
strange:
But if you have a stomach, to't o' God's name;
You shall have me assisting you in all.
But will you woo this wild-cat?

*Pet.*                    Will I live?

*Gru.* Will he woo her? ay, or I'll hang her.

*Pet.* Why came I hither but to that intent?

Think you a little din can daunt mine ears?
Have I not in my time heard lions roar?
Have I not heard the sea, puff'd up with winds,
Rage like an angry boar chafed with sweat?
Have I not heard great ordnance in the field,
And heaven's artillery thunder in the skies?
Have I not in a pitched battle heard     [clang?
Loud 'larums, neighing steeds, and trumpets
And do you tell me of a woman's tongue;
That gives not half so great a blow to hear,
As will a chestnut in a farmer's fire?
Tush! tush! fear boys with bugs.

*Gru.*                 For he fears none.

*Gre.* Hortensio, hark:
This gentleman is happily arriv'd,
My mind presumes, for his own good and ours.

*Hor.* I promis'd we would be contributors,
And bear his charge of wooing, whatsoe'er.

*Gre.* And so we will—provided that he win
her.

*Gru.* I would I were as sure of a good dinner.

*Enter* TRANIO, *bravely apparelled, and*
BIONDELLO.

*Tra.* Gentlemen, God save you! If I may be
bold,                    [way
Tell me, I beseech you, which is the readiest
To the house of Signior Baptista Minola?

*Bion.* He that has the two fair daughters:—
is't [*aside to* TRANIO] he you mean?

*Tra.* Even he, Biondello!

*Gre.* Hark you, sir; you mean not her to,—

*Tra.* Perhaps, him and her, sir; what have
you to do?                    [pray.

*Pet.* Not her that chides, sir, at any hand, I

*Tra.* I love no chiders, sir; Biondello, let's
away.

*Luc.* Well begun, Tranio.          [*Aside.*

*Hor.* Sir, a word ere you go;—     [or no?
Are you a suitor to the maid you talk of, yea

*Tra.* An if I be, sir, is it any offence?

*Gre.* No; if without more words you will get
you hence.                    [free

*Tra.* Why, sir, I pray, are not the streets as
For me as for you?

*Gre.*              But so is not she.

*Tra.* For what reason, I beseech you?

*Gre.* For this reason, if you'll know,—
That she's the choice love of Signior Gremio.

*Hor.* That she's the chosen of Signior Hortensio.

*Tra.* Softly, my masters! if you be gentlemen
Do me this right,—hear me with patience.
Baptista is a noble gentleman,
To whom my father is not all unknown,
And, were his daughter fairer than she is,
She may more suitors have, and me for one.
Fair Leda's daughter had a thousand wooers;
Then well one more may fair Bianca have:
And so she shall; Lucentio shall make one,
Though Paris came in hope to speed alone.

*Gre.* What! this gentleman will out-talk us
all.                    [a jade.

*Luc.* Sir, give him head; I know he'll prove

*Pet.* Hortensio, to what end are all these
  words?
*Hor.* Sir, let me be so bold as ask you,
Did you yet ever see Baptista's daughter?
*Tra.* No, sir; but hear I do that he hath two;
The one as famous for a scolding tongue
As is the other for beauteous modesty.
*Pet.* Sir, sir, the first's for me; let her go by.
*Gre.* Yea, leave that labour to great Her-
  'cules;
And let it be more than Alcides' twelve.
*Pet.* Sir, understand you this of me, in sooth:
The youngest daughter, whom you hearken for,
Her father keeps from all access of suitors,
And will not promise her to any man
Until the elder sister first be wed?
The younger then is free, and not before.
*Tra.* If it be so, sir, that you are the man
Must stead us all, and me amongst the rest;
And if you break the ice, and do this feat,—
Achieve the elder, set the younger free
For our access,—whose hap shall be to have her
Will not so graceless be to be ingrate.
*Hor.* Sir, you say well, and well you do con-
  ceive;
And since you do profess to be a suitor,
You must, as we do, gratify this gentleman,
To whom we all rest generally beholding.
*Tra.* Sir, I shall not be slack: in sign whereof
Please ye we may contrive this afternoon,
And quaff carouses to our mistress' health;
And do as adversaries do in law,—
Strive mightily, but eat and drink as friends.
*Gru. Bion.* O excellent motion! Fellows, let's
  be gone.          [so;—
*Hor.* The motion's good indeed, and be it
Petruchio, I shall be your *ben venuto.*
                    [*Exeunt.*

### ACT II.

SCENE I.—*The same. A Room in* BAP-
  TISTA'S *House.*

*Enter* KATHARINA *and* BIANCA.

*Bian.* Good sister, wrong me not, nor wrong
  yourself,
To make a bondmaid and a slave of me;
That I disdain: but for these other gawds,
Unbind my hands, I'll pull them off myself,
Yea, all my raiment, to my petticoat;
Or what you will command me will I do,
So well I know my duty to my elders.
*Kath.* Of all thy suitors, here I charge thee,
  tell
Whom thou lov'st best: see thou dissemble not.
*Bian.* Believe me, sister, of all the men alive,
I never yet beheld that special face
Which I could fancy more than any other.
*Kath.* Minion, thou liest; is't not Hortensio?
*Bian.* If you affect him, sister, here I swear
I'll plead for you myself, but you shall have
  him.
*Kath.* O then, belike, you fancy riches more;
You will have Gremio to keep you fair.

*Bian.* Is it for him you do envy me so?
Nay, then you jest; and now I well perceive
You have but jested with me all this while:
I pr'ythee, sister Kate, untie my hands.
*Kath.* If that be jest, then all the rest was so.
                    [*Strikes her.*

*Enter* BAPTISTA.

*Bap.* Why, how now, dame! whence grows
  this insolence?—
Bianca, stand aside;—poor girl! she weeps:—
Go ply thy needle; meddle not with her.—
For shame, thou hilding of a devilish spirit,
Why dost thou wrong her that did ne'er wrong
  thee?
When did she cross thee with a bitter word?
*Kath.* Her silence flouts me, and I'll be re-
  veng'd.          [*Flies after* BIANCA.
*Bap.* What, in my sight?—Bianca, get thee
  in.          [*Exit* BIANCA.
*Kath.* What, will you not suffer me? Nay,
  now I see
She is your treasure, she must have a husband;
I must dance bare-foot on her wedding-day,
And for your love to her lead apes in hell.
Talk not to me; I will go sit and weep,
Till I can find occasion of revenge.
                    [*Exit* KATHARINA.
*Bap.* Was ever gentleman thus griev'd as I?
But who comes here?

*Enter* GREMIO, *with* LUCENTIO *in the habit of a
  mean man;* PETRUCHIO, *with* HORTENSIO *as a
  musician; and* TRANIO, *with* BIONDELLO *bearing a lute and books.*

*Gre.* Good-morrow, neighbour Baptista.
*Bap.* Good-morrow, neighbour Gremio: God
save you, gentlemen!          [a daughter
*Pet.* And you, good sir! Pray, have you not
Call'd Katharina, fair and virtuous?
*Bap.* I have a daughter, sir, call'd Katharina.
*Gre.* You are too blunt: go to it orderly.
*Pet.* You wrong me, Signior Gremio: give me
  leave.—
I am a gentleman of Verona, sir,
That,—hearing of her beauty and her wit,
Her affability and bashful modesty,
Her wondrous qualities and mild behaviour,—
Am bold to show myself a forward guest
Within your house, to make mine eye the wit-
  ness
Of that report which I so oft have heard.
And, for an entrance to my entertainment,
I do present you with a man of mine,
                [*Presenting* HORTENSIO.
Cunning in music and the mathematics,
To instruct her fully in those sciences,
Whereof I know she is not ignorant:
Accept of him, or else you do me wrong:
His name is Licio, born in Mantua.
*Bap.* You're welcome, sir; and he for your
  good sake;
But for my daughter Katharine,—this I know,
She is not for your turn, the more my grief.

*Pet.* I see you do not mean to part with her;
Or else you like not of my company.

*Bap.* Mistake me not, I speak but as I find.
Whence are you, sir? what may I call your
  name?

*Pet.* Petruchio is my name; Antonio's son,
A man well known throughout all Italy.

*Bap.* I know him well: you are welcome for
  his sake.

*Gre.* Saving your tale, Petruchio, I pray,
Let us, that are poor petitioners, speak too:
Baccare! you are marvellous forward.

*Pet.* O, pardon me, Signior Gremio: I would
  fain be doing.

*Gre.* I doubt it not, sir; but you will curse
  your wooing.—
Neighbour, this is a gift very grateful, I am
sure of it. To express the like kindness myself,
that have been more kindly beholding to you
than any, I freely give unto you this young
scholar [*presenting* LUCENTIO], that hath been
long studying at Rheims; as cunning in Greek,
Latin, and other languages, as the other in
music and mathematics: his name is Cambio;
pray, accept his service.

*Bap.* A thousand thanks, Signior Gremio:
welcome, good Cambio.—But, gentle sir [*to*
TRANIO], methinks you walk like a stranger.
May I be so bold to know the cause of your
coming?                                    [own;

*Tra.* Pardon me, sir, the boldness is mine
That, being a stranger in this city here,
Do make myself a suitor to your daughter,
Unto Bianco, fair and virtuous.
Nor is your firm resolve unknown to me,
In the preferment of the eldest sister.
This liberty is all that I request,—
That, upon knowledge of my parentage,
I may have welcome 'mongst the rest that woo,
And free access and favour as the rest.
And, toward the education of your daughters,
I here bestow a simple instrument,
And this small packet of Greek and Latin
  books;
If you accept them, then their worth is great.

*Bap.* Lucentio is your name? of whence, I
  pray?

*Tra.* Of Pisa, sir; son to Vincentio.

*Bap.* A mighty man of Pisa: by report
I know him well: you are very welcome, sir.—
Take you [*to* HOR.] the lute, and you [*to* LUC.]
  the set of books;
You shall go see your pupils presently.
Holla, within!

*Enter a* Servant.

        Sirrah, lead these gentlemen
To my daughters; and tell them both,
These are their tutors; bid them use them well.
  [*Exit Serv., with* HOR., LUC., *and* BION.
We will go walk a little in the orchard,
And then to dinner. You are passing welcome,
And so I pray you all to think yourselves.

*Pet.* Signior Baptista, my business asketh
  haste,
And every day I cannot come to woo.
You knew my father well; and in him, me,
Left solely heir to all his lands and goods,
Which I have better'd rather than decreas'd:
Then tell me,—if I get your daughter's love,
What dowry shall I have with her to wife?

*Bap.* After my death, the one half of my
  lands
And, in possession, twenty thousand crowns.

*Pet.* And for that dowry, I'll assure her of
Her widowhood,—be it that she survive me,—
In all my lands and leases whatsoever:
Let specialties be therefore drawn between us,
That covenants may be kept on either hand.

*Bap.* Ay, when the special thing is well obtain'd,
That is, her love; for that is all in all.

*Pet.* Why, that is nothing; for I tell you,
  father,
I am as peremptory as she proud-minded;
And where two raging fires meet together,
They do consume the thing that feeds their
  fury:
Though little fire grows great with little wind,
Yet extreme gusts will blow out fire and all:
So I to her, and so she yields to me;
For I am rough, and woo not like a babe.

*Bap.* Well mayst thou woo, and happy be
  thy speed!
But be thou arm'd for some unhappy words.

*Pet.* Ay, to the proof; as mountains are for
  winds,
That shake not though they blow perpetually.

*Re-enter* HORTENSIO, *with his head broken.*

*Bap.* How now, my friend! why dost thou
  look so pale?

*Hor.* For fear, I promise you, if I look pale.

*Bap.* What, will my daughter prove a good
  musician?

*Hor.* I think she'll sooner prove a soldier:
Iron may hold with her, but never lutes.

*Bap.* Why, then thou canst not break her to
  the lute?

*Hor.* Why, no; for she hath broke the lute
  to me.
I did but tell her she mistook her frets,
And bow'd her hand to teach her fingering,
When, with a most impatient devilish spirit,
*Frets, call you these?* quoth she; *I'll fume with
  them:*
And, with that word, she struck me on the
  head,
And through the instrument my pate made
  way;
And there I stood amazed for awhile,
As on a pillory, looking through the lute,
While she did call me rascal fiddler
And twangling Jack, with twenty such vile
  terms,
As she had studied to misuse me so.

*Pet.* Now, by the world, it is a lusty wench;
I love her ten times more than e'er I did:
O, how I long to have some chat with her! .
  *Bap.* Well, go with me, and be not so dis-
    comfited:
Proceed in practice with my younger daughter:
She's apt to learn, and thankful for good
    turns.—
Signior Petruchio, will you go with us,
Or shall I send my daughter Kate to you?
  *Pet.* I pray you do: I will attend her here,
    [*Exeunt,* BAP., GRE., TRA., *and* HOR.
And woo her with some spirit when she comes.
Say that she rail; why, then I'll tell her plain
She sings as sweetly as a nightingale:
Say that she frown; I'll say she looks as clear
As morning roses newly washed with dew:
Say she be mute, and will not speak a word;
Then I'll commend her volubility,
And say she uttereth piercing eloquence:
If she do bid me pack, I'll give her thanks,
As though she bid me stay by her a week:
If she deny to wed, I'll crave the day
When I shall ask the banns, and when be
    married.—
But here she comes; and now, Petruchio, speak.

*Enter* KATHARINA.

Good-morrow, Kate; for that's your name, I
  hear.
  *Kath.* Well have you heard, but something
    hard of hearing:
They call me Katharine that do talk of me.
  *Pet.* You lie, in faith; for you are call'd plain
    Kate,
And bonny Kate, and sometimes Kate the
    curst;
But, Kate, the prettiest Kate in Christendom,
Kate of Kate-Hall, my super-dainty Kate,
For dainties are all cates; and therefore, Kate,
Take this of me, Kate of my consolation;—
Hearing thy mildness prais'd in every town,
Thy virtues spoke of, and thy beauty sounded,—
Yet not so deeply as to thee belongs,—
Myself am mov'd to woo thee for my wife.
  *Kath.* Mov'd! in good time: let him that
    mov'd you hither
Remove you hence: I knew you at the first
You were a movable.
  *Pet.*        Why, what's a movable?
  *Kath.* A joint-stool.
  *Pet.*      Thou hast hit it: come, sit on me.
  *Kath.* Asses are made to bear, and so are you.
  *Pet.* Women are made to bear, and so are you.
  *Kath.* No such jade as bear you, if me you
    mean.
  *Pet.* Alas, good Kate, I will not burden thee!
For, knowing thee to be but young and light,—
  *Kath.* Too light for such a swain as you to
    catch;
And yet as heavy as my weight should be.
  *Pet.* Should be! should buzz.
  *Kath.*      Well ta'en, and like a buzzard.

  *Pet.* O, slow-wing'd turtle! shall a buzzard
    take thee?
  *Kath.* Ay, for a turtle,—as he takes a buz-
    zard.
  *Pet.* Come, come, you wasp; i' faith, you are
    too angry.
  *Kath.* If I be waspish, best beware my sting.
  *Pet.* My remedy is then, to pluck it out.
  *Kath.* Ay, if the fool could find it where it
    lies.           [wear his sting?
  *Pet.* Who knows not where a wasp doth
In his tail.
  *Kath.*  In his tongue.
  *Pet.*           Whose tongue?
  *Kath.* Yours, if you talk of tails; and so
    farewell.         [come again,
  *Pet.* What, with my tongue in your tail? nay,
Good Kate; I am a gentleman.
  *Kath.*            That I'll try.
            [*Striking him.*
  *Pet.* I swear I'll cuff you, if you strike again.
  *Kath.* So may you lose your arms:
If you strike me, you are no gentleman;
And if no gentleman, why then no arms.
  *Pet.* A herald, Kate? O, put me in thy books!
  *Kath.* What is your crest? a coxcomb?
  *Pet.* A combless cock, so Kate will be my hen.
  *Kath.* No cock of mine; you crow too like a
    craven.           [look so sour.
  *Pet.* Nay, come, Kate, come; you must not
  *Kath.* It is my fashion, when I see a crab.
  *Pet.* Why, here's no crab; and therefore look
    not sour.
  *Kath.* There is, there is.
  *Pet.* Then show it me.
  *Kath.*          Had I a glass I would.
  *Pet.* What, you mean my face?
  *Kath.*      Well aim'd of such a young one.
  *Pet.* Now, by Saint George, I am too young
    for you.
  *Kath.* Yet you are wither'd.
  *Pet.*            'Tis with cares.
  *Kath.*            I care not.
  *Pet.* Nay, hear you, Kate: in sooth, you
    'scape not so.
  *Kath.* I chafe you, if I tarry; let me go.
  *Pet.* No, not a whit: I find you passing
    gentle.
'Twas told me you were rough, and coy, and
    sullen,
And now I find report a very liar;    [teous;
For thou art pleasant, gamesome, passing cour-
But slow in speech, yet sweet as spring-time
    flowers:
Thou canst not frown, thou canst not look as-
    kance,
Nor bite the lip, as angry wenches will;
Nor hast thou pleasure to be cross in talk;
But thou with mildness entertain'st thy wooers
With gentle conference, soft and affable.
Why does the world report that Kate doth
    limp?
O slanderous world! Kate, like the hazel-twig,
Is straight and slender; and as brown in hue

As hazel-nuts, and sweeter than the kernels.
O, let me see thee walk: thou dost not halt.

*Kath.* Go, fool, and whom thou keep'st command.

*Pet.* Did ever Dian so become a grove
As Kate this chamber with her princely gait?
O, be thou Dian, and let her be Kate;
And then let Kate be chaste, and Dian sportful! [speech?

*Kath.* Where did you study all this goodly

*Pet.* It is extempore, from my mother-wit.

*Kath.* A witty mother! witless else her son.

*Pet.* Am I not wise?

*Kath.*                Yes, keep you warm.

*Pet.* Marry, so I mean, sweet Katharine, in
thy bed:
And therefore, setting all this chat aside,
Thus in plain terms:—Your father hath consented [on;
That you shall be my wife; your dowry 'greed
And, will you, nill you, I will marry you.
Now, Kate, I am a husband for your turn;
For, by this light, whereby I see thy beauty,—
Thy beauty that doth make me like thee well—
Thou must be married to no man but me;
For I am he am born to tame you, Kate;
And bring you from a wild Kate to a Kate
Conformable, as other household Kates.
Here comes your father; never make denial;
I must and will have Katharine to my wife.

*Re-enter* BAPTISTA, GREMIO, *and* TRANIO.

*Bap.* Now, Signior Petruchio, how speed you
with my daughter?

*Pet.* How but well, sir? how but well?
It were impossible I should speed amiss.

*Bap.* Why, how now, daughter Katharine!
in your dumps? [you

*Kath.* Call you me daughter? now, I promise
You have show'd a tender fatherly regard
To wish me wed to one half lunatic;
A mad-cap ruffian and a swearing Jack,
That thinks with oaths to face the matter out.

*Pet.* Father, 'tis thus:—yourself and all the
world,
That talked of her, hath talk'd amiss of her;
If she be curst, it is for policy;
For she's not froward, but modest as the dove,
She is not hot, but temperate as the morn;
For patience she will prove a second Grissel,
And Roman Lucrece for her chastity:
And to conclude, we have 'greed so well together,
That upon Sunday is the wedding-day.

*Kath.* I'll see thee hang'd on Sunday first.

*Gre.* Hark, Petruchio; she says she'll see thee
hang'd first.

*Tra.* Is this your speeding? nay, then, goodnight our part! [for myself;

*Pet.* Be patient, gentlemen; I choose her
If she and I be pleas'd, what's that to you?
'Tis bargain'd 'twixt us twain, being alone,
That she shall still be curst in company.
I tell you, 'tis incredible to believe

How much she loves me: O, the kindest Kate!—
She hung about my neck, and kiss on kiss
She vied so fast, protesting oath on oath,
That in a twink she won me to her love.
O, you are novices! 'tis a world to see,
How tame when men and women are alone,
A meacock wretch can make the curstest
shrew.—
Give me thy hand, Kate: I will unto Venice,
To buy apparel 'gainst the wedding-day.—
Provide the feast, father, and bid the guests;
I will be sure my Katharine shall be fine.

*Bap.* I know not what to say: but give me
your hands;
God send you joy, Petruchio! 'tis a match.

*Gre. Tra.* Amen, say we; we will be witnesses.

*Pet.* Father, and wife, and gentlemen, adieu;
I will to Venice; Sunday comes apace:—
We will have rings, and things, and fine array;
And, kiss me, Kate, we will be married o'
Sunday.
                    [*Exeunt* PET. *and* KATH., *severally.*

*Gre.* Was ever match clapp'd up so suddenly?

*Bap.* Faith, gentlemen, now I play a merchant's part,
And venture madly on a desperate mart.

*Tra.* 'Twas a commodity lay fretting by you;
'Twill bring you gain, or perish on the seas.

*Bap.* The gain I seek is quiet in the match.

*Gre.* No doubt but he hath got a quiet catch.
But now, Baptista, to your younger daughter;—
Now is the day we long have looked for;
I am your neighbour, and was suitor first.

*Tra.* And I am one that love Bianca more
Than words can witness or your thoughts can
guess. [as I.

*Gre.* Youngling! thou canst not love so dear

*Tra.* Graybeard! thy love doth freeze.

*Gre.*                But thine doth fry.
Skipper, stand back; 'tis age that nourisheth.

*Tra.* But youth in ladies' eyes that flourisheth. [this strife:

*Bap.* Content you, gentlemen; I'll compound
'Tis deeds must win the prize; and he, of both,
That can assure my daughter greatest dower
Shall have Bianca's love.—
Say, Signior Gremio, what can you assure her?

*Gre.* First, as you know, my house within
the city
Is richly furnished with plate and gold;
Basins and ewers, to lave her dainty hands;
My hangings all of Tyrian tapestry:
In ivory coffers I have stuff'd my crowns;
In cypress chests my arras counterpoints,
Costly apparel, tents, and canopies,
Fine linen, Turkey cushions boss'd with pearl,
Valance of Venice gold in needle-work,
Pewter and brass, and all things that belong
To house or housekeeping: then, at my farm,
I have a hundred milch-kine to the pail,
Six score fat oxen standing in my stalls,
And all things answerable to this portion.
Myself am struck in years, I must confess;

And, if I die to-morrow this is hers:
If, whilst I live, she will be only mine.  [me:
  *Tra.* That *only* came well in.—Sir, list to
I am my father's heir and only son:
If I may have your daughter to my wife,
I'll leave her houses three or four as good,
Within rich Pisa's walls, as any one
Old Signior Gremio has in Padua;
Besides two thousand ducats by the year
Of fruitful land, all which shall be her join-
    ture.—
What, have I pinch'd you Signior Gremio?
  *Gre.* Two thousand ducats by the year of
    land!
My land amounts not to so much in all:
That she shall have; besides an argosy,
That now is lying in Marseilles' road:—
What, have I chok'd you with an argosy?
  *Tra.* Gremio, 'tis known my father hath no
    less
Than three great argosies; besides two gal-
    liases,
And twelve tight galleys: these I will assure
    her,
And twice as much, whate'er thou offer'st next.
  *Gre.* Nay, I have offer'd all,—I have no
    more;
And she can have no more than all I have:—
If you like me, she shall have me and mine.
  *Tra.* Why, then the maid is mine from all
    the world,
By your firm promise: Gremio is out-vied.
  *Bap.* I must confess your offer is the best;
And, let your father make her the assurance,
She is your own; else, you must pardon me:
If you should die before him, where's her
    dower?
  *Tra.* That's but a cavil; he is old, I young.
  *Gre.* And may not young men die as well as
    old?
  *Bap.* Well, gentlemen,
I am thus resolv'd:—On Sunday next you know
My daughter Katharine is to be married:
Now, on the Sunday following shall Bianca
Be bride to you, if you make this assurance;
If not, to Signior Gremio:
And so I take my leave, and thank you both.
  *Gre.* Adieu, good neighbour.—
                [*Exit* BAPTISTA.
        Now I fear thee not:
Sirrah young gamester, your father were a fool
To give thee all, and in his waning age
Set foot under thy table. Tut! a toy!
An old Italian fox is not so kind, my boy.
                      [*Exit.*
  *Tra.* A vengeance on your crafty wither'd
    hide!
Yet I have faced it with a card of ten.
'Tis in my head to do my master good:—
I see no reason but suppos'd Lucentio
Must get a father, call'd—suppos'd Vincentio;
And that's a wonder: fathers commonly
Do get their children; but in this case of woo-
    ing,

A child shall get a sire, if I fail not of my
    cunning.  [*Exit.*

## ACT III.

SCENE I.—PADUA. *A Room in* BAPTISTA'S
    *House.*

*Enter* LUCENTIO, HORTENSIO, *and* BIANCA.

  *Luc.* Fiddler, forbear; you grow too forward,
    sir:
Have you so soon forgot the entertainment
Her sister Katharine welcom'd you withal?
  *Hor.* But, wrangling pedant, this is
The patroness of heavenly harmony:
Then give me leave to have prerogative;
And when in music we have spent an hour,
Your lecture shall have leisure for as much.
  *Luc.* Preposterous ass! that never read so far
To know the cause why music was ordain'd!
Was it not to refresh the mind of man
After his studies or his usual pain?
Then give me leave to read philosophy,
And while I pause serve in your harmony.
  *Hor.* Sirrah, I will not bear these braves of
    thine.
  *Bian.* Why, gentlemen, you do me double
    wrong,
To strive for that which resteth in my choice.
I am no breeching scholar in the schools:
I'll not be tied to hours nor 'pointed times,
But learn my lessons as I please myself.
And, to cut off all strife, here sit we down:—
Take you your instrument, play you the whiles;
His lecture will be done ere you have tun'd.
  *Hor.* You'll leave his lecture when I am in
    tune?
        [*To* BIANCA. HORTENSIO *retires.*
  *Luc.* That will be never:—tune your instru-
    ment.
  *Bian.* Where left we last?
  *Luc.* Here, madam:—
    *Hac ibat Simois; hic est Sigeia tellus;
    Hic steterat Priami regia celsa senis.*
  *Bian.* Construe them.
  *Luc. Hac ibat,* as I told you before,—*Simois,*
I am Lucentio,—*His est,* son unto Vincentio of
Pisa,—*Sigeia tellus,* disguised thus to get your
love;—*Hic steterat,* and that Lucentio that
comes a-wooing,—*Priami,* is my man Tranio,
—*regia,* bearing my port,—*celsa senis,* that we
might beguile the old pantaloon.
  *Hor.* [*Coming forward.*] Madam, my instru-
    ment's in tune.
  *Bian.* Let's hear.—  [HORTENSIO *plays.*
O fie! the treble jars.
  *Luc.* Spit in the hole, man, and tune again.
  *Bian.* Now let me see if I can construe it:
—*Hac ibat Simois,* I know you not,—*hic est
Sigeia tellus,* I trust you not;—*Hic steterat
Priami,* take heed he hear us not,—*regia,* pre-
sume not,—*celsa senis,* despair not.
  *Hor.* Madam, 'tis now in tune.
  *Luc.*                All but the base.
  *Hor.* The base is right; 'tis the base knave
    that jars.

How fiery and forward our pedant is!
Now, for my life, the knave doth court my love:
*Pedascule*, I'll watch you better yet. [*Aside.*
*Bian.* In time I may believe, yet I mistrust.
*Luc.* Mistrust it not; for, sure, Æacides
Was Ajax,—call'd so from his grandfather.
*Bian.* I must believe my master; else, I promise you,
I should be arguing still upon that doubt:
But let it rest.—Now, Licio, to you:—
Good masters, take it not unkindly, pray,
That I have been thus pleasant with you both.
*Hor.* You may go walk [*to* LUCENTIO], and give me leave awhile;
My lessons make no music in three parts.
*Luc.* Are you so formal, sir? well, I must wait,
And watch withal; for, but I be deceiv'd,
Our fine musician groweth amorous. [*Aside.*
*Hor.* Madam, before you touch the instrument,
To learn the order of my fingering,
I must begin with rudiments of art;
To teach you gamut in a briefer sort,
More pleasant, pithy, and effectual,
Than hath been taught by any of my trade:
And there it is in writing, fairly drawn.
*Bian.* Why, I am past my gamut long ago.
*Hor.* Yet read the gamut of Hortensio.
*Bian.* [*Reads.*] Gamut *I am, the ground of all accord,*
A re, *to plead Hortensio's passion;*
B mi, *Bianca, take him for thy lord,*
C fa ut, *that loves with all affection:*
D sol re, *one cliff, two notes have I;*
E la mi, *show pity, or I die.*
Call you this gamut? tut, I like it not:
Old fashions please me best; I am not so nice,
To change true rules for odd inventions.

*Enter a* Servant.

*Serv.* Mistress, your father prays you leave your books,
And help to dress your sister's chamber up:
You know to-morrow is the wedding-day.
*Bian.* Farewell, sweet masters, both; I must be gone!
[*Exeunt* BIANCA *and* Servant.
*Luc.* Faith, mistress, then I have no cause to stay. [*Exit.*
*Hor.* But I have cause to pry into this pedant;
Methinks he looks as though he were in love:—
Yet if thy thoughts, Bianca, be so humble,
To cast thy wand'ring eyes on every stale,
Seize thee that list: if once I find thee ranging,
Hortensio will be quit with thee by changing. [*Exit.*

SCENE II.—*The same. Before* BAPTISTA'S *House.*

*Enter* BAPTISTA, GREMIO, TRANIO, KATHARINA, BIANCA, LUCENTIO, *and* Attendants.

*Bap.* Signior Lucentio [*to* TRANIO], this is the 'pointed day

That Katharine and Petruchio should be married,
And yet we hear not of our son-in-law:
What will be said? what mockery will it be,
To want the bridegroom when the priest attends
To speak the ceremonial rites of marriage?
What says Lucentio to this shame of ours?
*Kath.* No shame but mine: I must, forsooth, be forc'd
To give my hand, oppos'd against my heart,
Unto a mad-brain rudesby, full of spleen;
Who woo'd in haste, and means to wed at leisure.
I told you, I, he was a frantic fool,
Hiding his bitter jests in blunt behaviour:
And, to be noted for a merry man,
He'll woo a thousand, 'point the day of marriage,
Make friends, invite them, and proclaim the banns;
Yet never means to wed where he hath woo'd.
Now must the world point at poor Katharine,
And say, *Lo, there is mad Petruchio's wife,*
*If it would please him come and marry her!*
*Tra.* Patience, good Katharine, and Baptista too.
Upon my life, Petruchio means but well!
Whatever fortune stays him from his word:
Though he be blunt, I know him passing wise;
Though he be merry, yet withal he's honest.
*Kath.* Would Katharine had never seen him though!
[*Exit, weeping, followed by* BIANCA *and others.*
*Bap.* Go, girl; I cannot blame thee now to weep;
For such an injury would vex a very saint,
Much more a shrew of thy impatient humour.

*Enter* BIONDELLO.

*Bion.* Master, master! old news, and such news as you never heard of! [be?
*Bap.* Is it new and old too? how may that
*Bion.* Why, is it not news to hear of Petruchio's coming?
*Bap.* Is he come?
*Bion.* Why, no, sir.
*Bap.* What then?
*Bion.* He is coming.
*Bap.* When will he be here? [you there.
*Bion.* When he stands where I am, and sees
*Tra.* But, say, what to thine old news?
*Bion.* Why, Petruchio is coming, in a new hat and an old jerkin; a pair of old breeches thrice turn'd; a pair of boots that have been candle-cases, one buckled, another laced; an old rusty sword ta'en out of the town armoury, with a broken hilt, and chapeless; with two broken points: his horse hipped with an old mothy saddle, and stirrups of no kindred; besides, possessed with the glanders, and like to mose in the chine; troubled with the lampass, infected with the fashions, fell of windgalls, sped with spavins, rayed with the yellows, past cure of the fives, stark spoiled with the

staggers, begnawn with the bots, swayed in the back, and shoulder-shotten; ne'er legged before and with a half-checked bit; and a head-stall of sheep's leather, which, being restrained to keep him from stumbling, hath been often burst, and now repaired with knots; one girth six times pieced, and a woman's crupper of velure, which hath two letters for her name, fairly set down in studs, and here and there pieced with packthread.

*Bap.*  Who comes with him?

*Bion.*  O, sir, his lackey, for all the world caparisoned like the horse; with a linen stock on one leg and a kersey boot-hose on the other, gartered with a red and blue list; an old hat, and *The humour of forty fancies* pricked in 't for a feather: a monster, a very monster in apparel; and not like a Christian footboy or a gentleman's lackey.

*Tra.*  'Tis some odd humour pricks him to this fashion;
Yet oftentimes he goes but mean apparell'd.

*Bap.*  I am glad he is come, howsoe'er he comes.

*Bion.*  Why, sir, he comes not.

*Bap.*  Didst thou not say he comes?

*Bion.*  Who? that Petruchio came?

*Bap.*  Ay, that Petruchio came.

*Bion.*  No, sir; I say his horse comes with him on his back.

*Bap.*  Why, that's all one.

*Bion.*  Nay, by saint Jamy,
I hold you a penny,
A horse and a man
Is more than one,
And yet not many.

*Enter* PETRUCHIO *and* GRUMIO.

*Pet.*  Come, where be these gallants? who's at home?

*Bap.*  You are welcome, sir.

*Pet.*                    And yet I come not well.

*Bap.*  And yet you halt not.

*Tra.*                    Not so well apparell'd
As I wish you were.

*Pet.*  Were it better, I should rush in thus.
But where is Kate? where is my lovely bride?
How does my father?—Gentles, methinks you frown:
And wherefore gaze this goodly company,
As if they saw some wondrous monument,
Some comet or unusual prodigy?

*Bap.*  Why, sir, you know this is your wedding-day:
First were we sad, fearing you would not come;
Now sadder, that you come so unprovided.
Fie, doff this habit, shame to your estate,
An eye-sore to our solemn festival!

*Tra.*  And tell us, what occasion of import
Hath all so long detain'd you from your wife,
And sent you hither so unlike yourself?

*Pet.*  Tedious it were to tell, and harsh to hear:
Sufficeth, I am come to keep my word,

Though in some part enforced to digress;
Which, at more leisure, I will so excuse
As you shall well be satisfied withal.
But where is Kate? I stay too long from her:
The morning wears, 'tis time we were at church.

*Tra.*  See not your bride in these unreverent robes:
Go to my chamber, put on clothes of mine.

*Pet.*  Not I, believe me: thus I'll visit her.

*Bap.*  But thus, I trust, you will not marry her.

*Pet.*  Good sooth, even thus; therefore ha' done with words;
To me she's married, not unto my clothes
Could I repair what she will wear in me,
As I can change these poor accoutrements,
'Twere well for Kate, and better for myself.
But what a fool am I to chat with you,
When I should bid good-morrow to my bride,
And seal the title with a lovely kiss!
            [*Exeunt* PETRUCHIO *and* GRUMIO.

*Tra.*  He hath some meaning in his mad attire.
We will persuade him, be it possible,
To put on better ere he go to church.

*Bap.*  I'll after him, and see the event of this.
            [*Exeunt* BAP., GREM., *and* BION.

*Tra.*  But, sir, to her love concerneth us to add
Her father's liking: which to bring to pass,
As I before imparted to your worship,
I am to get a man,—whate'er he be,
It skills not much; we'll fit him to our turn,—
And he shall be Vincentio of Pisa;
And make assurance, here in Padua,
Of greater sums than I have promised.
So shall you quietly enjoy your hope,
And marry sweet Bianca with consent.

*Luc.*  Were it not that my fellow-schoolmaster
Doth watch Bianca's steps so narrowly,
'Twere good, methinks, to steal our marriage;
Which once perform'd, let all the world say no,
I'll keep mine own, despite of all the world.

*Tra.*  That by degrees we mean to look into,
And watch our vantage in this business:
We'll over-reach the graybeard, Gremio,
The narrow-prying father, Minola,
The quaint musician, amorous Licio;
All for my master's sake, Lucentio.

*Re-enter* GREMIO.

Signior Gremio,—came you from the church?

*Gre.*  As willingly as e'er I came from school.

*Tra.*  And is the bride and bridegroom coming home?

*Gre.*  A bridegroom, say you? 'tis a groom indeed,
A grumbling groom, and that the girl shall find.

*Tra.*  Curster than she? why, 'tis impossible.

*Gre.*  Why, he's a devil, a devil, a very fiend,

*Tra.*  Why, she's a devil, a devil, the devil's dam.

*Gre.* Tut, she's a lamb, a dove, a fool to him!
I'll tell you, Sir Lucentio: when the priest
Should ask, if Katharine should be his wife,
*Ay, by gogs-wouns,* quoth he; and swore so loud
That, all amaz'd, the priest let fall the book;
And, as he stoop'd again to take it up,
The mad-brain'd bridegroom took him such a
    cuff
That down fell priest and book, and book and
    priest:
*Now take them up,* quoth he, *if any list.*
    *Tra.* What said the wench, when he arose
        again?
    *Gre.* Trembled and shook; for why, he
        stamp'd and swore,
As if the vicar meant to cozen him.
But after many ceremonies done,
He calls for wine: *A health!* quoth he; as if
He had been aboard, carousing to his mates
After a storm: quaff'd off the muscadel,
And threw the sops all in the sexton's face;
Having no other reason
But that his beard grew thin and hungerly,
And seem'd to ask him sops as he was drinking.
This done, he took the bride about the neck,
And kiss'd her lips with such a clamorous
    smack
That, at the parting, all the church did echo.
I, seeing this, came thence for very shame;
And after me, I know, the rout is coming.
Such a mad marriage never was before:
Hark, Hark! I hear the minstrels play.    [*Music.*

*Enter* PETRUCHIO, KATHARINA, BIANCA, BAP-
TISTA, HORTENSIO, GRUMIO, *and* Train.

    *Pet.* Gentlemen and friends, I thank you for
        your pains:
I know you think to dine with me to-day,
And have prepar'd great store of wedding
    cheer;
But so it is, my haste doth call me hence,
And therefore here I mean to take my leave.
    *Bap.* Is't possible you will away to-night?
    *Pet.* I must away to-day, before night come:
Make it no wonder; if you knew my business,
You would entreat me rather go than stay.
And, honest company, I thank you all
That have beheld me give away myself
To this most patient, sweet, and virtuous wife:
Dine with my father, drink a health to me;
For I must hence; and farewell to you all.
    *Tra.* Let us entreat you stay till after dinner.
    *Pet.* It may not be.
    *Gre.*              Let me entreat you.
    *Pet.* It cannot be.
    *Kath.*              Let me entreat you.
    *Pet.* I am content.
    *Kath.*          Are you content to stay?
    *Pet.* I am content you shall entreat me stay;
But yet not stay, entreat me how you can.
    *Kath.* Now, if you love me, stay.
    *Pet.*              Grumio, my horse.

    *Gru.* Ay, sir, they be ready: the oats have
eaten the horses.
    *Kath.* Nay, then,
Do what thou canst, I will not go to-day;
No, nor to-morrow, nor till I please myself.
The door is open, sir; there lies your way;
You may be jogging whiles your boots are
    green;
For me, I'll not be gone till I please myself:
'Tis like you'll prove a jolly surly groom,
That take it on you at the first so roundly.
    *Pet.* O Kate, content thee; pr'ythee, be not
        angry.
    *Kath.* I will be angry; what hast thou to
        do?
Father, be quiet: he shall stay my leisure.
    *Gre.* Ay, marry, sir, now it begins to work.
    *Kath.* Gentlemen, forward to the bridal
        dinner.
I see a woman may be made a fool
If she had not a spirit to resist.
    *Pet.* They shall go forward, Kate, at thy
        command.—
Obey the bride, you that attend on her;
Go to the feast, revel and domineer,
Carouse full measure to her maidenhead;
Be mad and merry,—or go hang yourselves:
But for my bonny Kate, she must with me.
Nay, look not big, nor stamp, nor stare, nor
    fret!
I will be master of what is mine own:
She is my goods, my chattels; she is my house,
My household stuff, my field, my barn,
My horse, my ox, my ass, my anything;
And here she stands, touch her whoever dare;
I'll bring mine action on the proudest he
That stops my way in Padua.—Grumio,
Draw forth thy weapon, we are beset with
    thieves;
Rescue thy mistress, if thou be a man.—
Fear not, sweet wench, they shall not touch
    thee, Kate;
I'll buckler thee against a million.
            [*Exeunt* PET., KATH., *and* GRU.
    *Bap.* Nay, let them go, a couple of quiet
        ones.
    *Gre.* Went they not quickly, I should die
        with laughing.
    *Tra.* Of all mad matches, never was the like!
    *Luc.* Mistress, what's your opinion of your
        sister?                        [*mated.*
    *Bian.* That, being mad herself, she's madly
    *Gre.* I warrant him, Petruchio is Kated.
    *Bap.* Neighbours and friends, though bride
        and bridegroom wants,
For to supply the places at the table,
You know there wants no junkets at the feast.—
Lucentio, you shall supply the bridegroom's
    place;
And let Bianca take her sister's room.
    *Tra.* Shall sweet Bianca practise how to
        bride it?
    *Bap.* She shall, Lucentio.—Come, gentle-
men, let's go.                        [*Exeunt.*

# ACT IV.

SCENE I.—*A Hall in* PETRUCHIO'S *Country House.*

*Enter* GRUMIO.

*Gru.* Fie, fie on all tired jades, on all mad masters, and all foul ways! Was ever man so beaten? was ever man so rayed? was ever man so weary? I am sent before to make a fire, and they are coming after to warm them. Now, were not I a little pot, and soon hot, my very lips might freeze to my teeth, my tongue to the roof of my mouth, my heart in my belly, ere I should come by a fire to thaw me:—but I, with blowing the fire, shall warm myself; for, considering the weather, a taller man than I will take cold.—Holla, ho! Curtis!

*Enter* CURTIS.

*Curt.* Who is that calls so coldly?

*Gru.* A piece of ice: if thou doubt it, thou mayst slide from my shoulder to my heel with no greater a run but my head and my neck. A fire, good Curtis.

*Curt.* Is my master and his wife coming, Grumio?

*Gru.* O, ay, Curtis, ay: and therefore fire, fire; cast on no water.

*Curt.* Is she so hot a shrew as she's reported?

*Gru.* She was, good Curtis, before this frost; but, thou knowest, winter tames man, woman, and beast; for it hath tamed my old master, and my new mistress, and myself, fellow Curtis.

*Curt.* Away, you three-inch fool! I am no beast.

*Gru.* Am I but three inches? why, thy horn is a foot; and so long am I, at the least. But wilt thou make a fire, or shall I complain on thee to our mistress, whose hand,—she being now at hand,—thou shalt soon feel, to thy cold comfort, for being slow in thy hot office?

*Curt.* I pr'ythee, good Grumio, tell me, how goes the world?

*Gru.* A cold world, Curtis, in every office but thine; and, therefore, fire: do thy duty, and have thy duty; for my master and mistress are almost frozen to death.

*Curt.* There's fire ready; and, therefore, good Grumio, the news?

*Gru.* Why, *Jack boy! ho, boy!* and as much news as thou wilt.        [ing!—

*Curt.* Come, you are so full of coney-catch-

*Gru.* Why, therefore, fire; for I have caught extreme cold. Where's the cook? is supper ready, the house trimmed, rushes strewed, cobwebs swept; the serving-men in their new fustian, their white stockings, and every officer his wedding-garment on? Be the jacks fair within, the jills fair without, the carpets laid, and everything in order?        [news?

*Curt.* All ready; and, therefore, I pray thee,

*Gru.* First, know, my horse is tired; my master and mistress fallen out.

*Curt.* How?

*Gru.* Out of their saddles into the dirt; and thereby hangs a tale.

*Curt.* Let's ha't, good Grumio.

*Gru.* Lend thine ear.

*Curt.* Here.

*Gru.* There.        [*Striking him.*

*Curt.* This is to feel a tale, not to hear a tale.

*Gru.* And therefore 'tis called a sensible tale: and this cuff was but to knock at your ear, and beseech listening. Now I begin: *Imprimis*, we came down a foul hill, my master riding behind my mistress:—

*Curt.* Both of one horse?

*Gru.* What's that to thee?

*Curt.* Why, a horse.

*Gru.* Tell thou the tale:—but hadst thou not crossed me, thou shouldst have heard how her horse fell, and she under her horse; thou shouldst have heard, in how miry a place; how she was bemoiled; how he left her with the horse upon her; how he beat me because her horse stumbled; how she waded through the dirt to pluck him off me; how he swore; how she prayed—that never pray'd before; how I cried; how the horses ran away; how her bridle was burst; how I lost my crupper; with many things of worthy memory; which now shall die in oblivion, and thou return unexperienced to thy grave.

*Curt.* By this reckoning, he is more shrew than she.

*Gru.* Ay; and that thou and the proudest of you all shall find when he comes home. But what talk I of this?—Call forth Nathaniel, Joseph, Nicholas, Philip, Walter, Sugarsop, and the rest: let their heads be sleekly combed, their blue coats brushed, and their garters of an indifferent knit: let them curtsy with their left legs; and not presume to touch a hair of my master's horse-tail till they kiss their hands. Are they all ready?

*Curt.* They are.

*Gru.* Call them forth.

*Curt.* Do you hear, ho? you must meet my master, to countenance my mistress.

*Gru.* Why, she hath a face of her own.

*Curt.* Who knows not that?

*Gru.* Thou, it seems, that callest for company to countenance her.

*Curt.* I call them forth to credit her.

*Gru.* Why, she comes to borrow nothing of them.

*Enter several* Servants.

*Nath.* Welcome home, Grumio!

*Phil.* How now, Grumio!

*Jos.* What, Grumio!

*Nich.* Fellow Grumio!

*Nath.* How now, old lad?

*Gru.* Welcome, you;—how now, you; what, you;—fellow, you;—and thus much for greeting. Now, my spruce companions, is all ready, and all things neat?

*Nath.* All things is ready. How near is our master?

*Gru.* E'en at hand, alighted by this;—and therefore be not,—Cock's passion, silence!—I hear my master.

*Enter* PETRUCHIO *and* KATHARINA.

*Pet.* Where be these knaves? What, no man at door
To hold my stirrup nor to take my horse!
Where is Nathaniel, Gregory, Philip?—

*All Serv.* Here, here, sir; here, sir.

*Pet.* Here, sir! here, sir! here, sir! here, sir!—
You logger-headed and unpolish'd grooms!
What, no attendance? no regard? no duty?—
Where is the foolish knave I sent before?

*Gru.* Here, sir; as foolish as I was before.

*Pet.* You peasant swain! you whoreson malt-
horse drudge!
Did I not bid thee meet me in the park,
And bring along these rascal knaves with thee?

*Gru.* Nathaniel's coat, sir, was not fully
made,                                        [heel;
And Gabriel's pumps were all unpink'd i' the
There was no link to colour Peter's hat,
And Walter's dagger was not come from
sheathing:                               [Gregory
There were none fine but Adam, Ralph, and
The rest were ragged, old, and beggarly;
Yet, as they are, here are they come to meet
you.                                           [in.—

*Pet.* Go, rascals, go, and fetch my supper
[*Exeunt some of the* Servants.
Where is the life that late I led—     [*Sings.*
Where are those——Sit down, Kate, and wel-
come.
Soud, soud, soud, soud!

*Re-enter* Servants *with supper.*

Why, when, I say?—Nay, good sweet Kate, be
merry.                                        [when?
Off with my boots, you rogues! you villains,

It was the friar of orders gray;
As he forth walked on his way:—     [*Sings.*

Out, you rogue! you pluck my foot awry;
Take that, and mend the plucking off the
other.—                                   [*Strikes him.*
Be merry, Kate.—Some water, here; what,
ho!—                                         [hence,
Where's my spaniel Troilus?—Sirrah, get you
And bid my cousin Ferdinand come hither:—
[*Exit* Servant.
One, Kate, that you must kiss, and be ac-
quainted with.—                       [water?
Where are my slippers?—Shall I have some
[*A bason is presented to him.*
Come, Kate, and wash, and welcome heartily.—
[Servant *lets the ewer fall.*
You whoreson villain! will you let it fall?
[*Strikes him.*

*Kath.* Patience, I pray you; 'twas a fault
unwilling.                                    [knave!

*Pet.* A whoreson, beetle-headed, flap-ear'd

Come, Kate, sit down; I know you have a
stomach.                                     [shall I?—
Will you give thanks, sweet Kate; or else
What's this? mutton?

*1 Serv.*                Ay.

*Pet.*                Who brought it?

*1 Serv.*                I.

*Pet.* 'Tis burnt; and so is all the meat.
What dogs are these?—Where is the rascal
cook?                                        [dresser,
How durst you, villains, bring it from the
And serve it thus to me that love it not?
There, take it to you, trenchers, cups, and all:
[*Throws the meat, &c., about the stage.*
You heedless joltheads and unmanner'd slaves!
What, do you grumble? I'll be with you straight.

*Kath.* I pray you, husband, be not so disquiet;
The meat was well, if you were so contented.

*Pet.* I tell thee, Kate, 'twas burnt and dried
away;
And I expressly am forbid to touch it,
For it engenders choler, planteth anger;
And better 'twere that both of us did fast,—
Since, of ourselves, ourselves are choleric,—
Then feed it with such over-roasted flesh.
Be patient; to-morrow 't shall be mended,
And, for this night, we'll fast for company:—
Come, I will bring thee to thy bridal chamber.
[*Exeunt* PET., KATH., *and* CURT.

*Nath.* Peter, didst ever see the like?

*Peter.* He kills her in her own humour.

*Re-enter* CURTIS.

*Gru.* Where is he?

*Curt.* In her chamber,
Making a sermon of continency to her,  [soul,
And rails, and swears, and rates, that she, poor
Knows not which way to stand, to look, to
speak,
And sits as one new-risen from a dream.
Away, away! for he is coming hither.
[*Exeunt.*

*Re-enter* PETRUCHIO.

*Pet.* Thus have I politicly begun my reign,
And 'tis my hope to end successfully.
My falcon now is sharp, and passing empty;
And, till she stoop, she must not be full-gorg'd,
For then she never looks upon her lure.
Another way I have to man my haggard,
To make her come, and know her keeper's call,
That is, to watch her, as we watch these kites
That bate, and beat, and will not be obedient.
She eat no meat to-day, nor none shall eat;
Last night she slept not, nor to-night she shall
not;
As with the meat, some undeserved fault
I'll find about the making of the bed;
And here I'll fling the pillow, there the bolster,
This way the coverlet, another way the sheets:—
Ay, and amid this hurly, I intend
That all is done in reverend care of her;
And, in conclusion, she shall watch all night:

And, if she chance to nod, I'll rail and brawl,
And with the clamour keep her still awake.
This is a way to kill a wife with kindness:
And thus I'll curb her mad and headstrong
   humour.
He that knows better how to tame a shrew,
Now let him speak; 'tis charity to show.     [*Exit.*

SCENE II.—PADUA. *Before* BAPTISTA'S
*House.*

*Enter* TRANIO *and* HORTENSIO.

*Tra.* Is't possible, friend Licio, that Bianca
Doth fancy any other but Lucentio?
I tell you, sir, she bears me fair in hand.
  *Hor.* Sir, to satisfy you in what I have said,
Stand by, and mark the manner of his teaching.
                [*They stand aside.*

*Enter* BIANCA *and* LUCENTIO.

*Luc.* Now, mistress, profit you in what you
   read?
  *Bian.* What, master, read you? first resolve
   me that.
  *Luc.* I read that I profess, the Art to Love.
  *Bian.* And may you prove, sir, master of
   your art!
  *Luc.* While you, sweet dear, prove mistress
   of my heart.         [*They retire.*
  *Hor.* Quick proceeders, marry! Now, tell me,
   I pray,
You that durst swear that your Mistress Bianca
Lov'd none in the world so well as Lucentio.
  *Tra.* O despiteful love! unconstant woman-
   kind!—
I tell thee, Licio, this is wonderful.
  *Hor.* Mistake no more: I am not Licio,
Nor a musician, as I seem to be;
But one that scorn to live in this disguise,
For such a one as leaves a gentleman,
And makes a god of such a cullion:
Know, sir, that I am call'd Hortensio.
  *Tra.* Signior Hortensio, I have often heard
Of your entire affection to Bianca;
And since mine eyes are witness of her light-
   ness,
I will with you,—if you be so contented,—
Forswear Bianca and her love for ever.
  *Hor.* See, how they kiss and court!—Signior
   Lucentio,
Here is my hand, and here I firmly vow
Never to woo her more; but do forswear her,
As one unworthy all the former favours
That I have fondly flatter'd her withal.
  *Tra.* And here I take the like unfeigned oath,
Never to marry with her though she would en-
   treat:                [him!
Fie on her! see, how beastly she doth court
  *Hor.* Would all the world but he had quite
   forsworn!
For me, that I may surely keep mine oath,
I will be married to a wealthy widow,

Ere three days pass, which hath as long lov'd
   me
As I have lov'd this proud disdainful haggard:
And so farewell, Signior Lucentio.—
Kindness in women, not their beauteous looks,
Shall win my love: and so I take my leave,
In resolution as I swore before.
    [*Exit* HOR.—LUC. *and* BIAN. *advance.*
  *Tra.* Mistress Bianca, bless you with such
   grace
As 'longeth to a lover's blessed case!
Nay, I have ta'en you napping, gentle love;
And have forsworn you with Hortensio.
  *Bian.* Tranio, you jest; but have you both
   forsworn me?
  *Tra.* Mistress, we have.
  *Luc.*         Then we are rid of Licio.
  *Tra.* I' faith, he'll have a lusty widow now,
That shall be woo'd and wedded in a day.
  *Bian.* God give him joy!
  *Tra.* Ay, and he'll tame her.
  *Bian.*          He says so, Tranio.
  *Tra.* Faith, he is gone unto the taming-
   school.
  *Bian.* The taming-school! what, is there such
   a place?
  *Tra.* Ay, mistress, and Petruchio is the
   master;
That teacheth tricks eleven and twenty long,
To tame a shrew and charm her chattering
   tongue.

*Enter* BIONDELLO.

  *Bion.* O master, master, I have watch'd so
   long
That I'm dog-weary; but at last I spied
An ancient angel coming down the hill,
Will serve the turn.
  *Tra.*         What is he, Biondello?
  *Bion.* Master, a mercatanté, or a pedant,
I know not what; but formal in apparel,
In gait and countenance surely like a father.
  *Luc.* And what of him, Tranio?
  *Tra.* If he be credulous, and trust my tale,
I'll make him glad to seem Vincentio,
And give assurance to Baptista Minola,
As if he were the right Vincentio.
Take in your love, and then let me alone.
      [*Exeunt* LUCENTIO *and* BIANCA.

*Enter a* Pedant.

  *Ped.* God save you, sir!
  *Tra.*       And you, sir! you are welcome.
Travel you far on, or are you at the furthest?
  *Ped.* Sir, at the furthest for a week or two:
But then up further, and as far as Rome;
And so to Tripoli, if God lend me life.
  *Tra.* What countryman, I pray?
  *Ped.*               Of Mantua.
  *Tra.* Of Mantua, sir?—marry, God forbid!
And come to Padua, careless of your life? [hard.
  *Ped.* My life, sir! how, I pray? for that goes
  *Tra.* 'Tis death for any one in Mantua
To come to Padua. Know you not the cause?

Your ships are stayed at Venice; and the duke,—
For private quarrel 'twixt your duke and him,
Have publish'd and proclaim'd it openly:
'Tis marvel, but that you are but newly come,
You might have heard it else proclaim'd about.

*Ped.* Alas, sir, it is worse for me than so!
For I have bills for money by exchange
From Florence, and must here deliver them.

*Tra.* Well, sir, to do you courtesy,
This will I do, and this I will advise you:
First, tell me, have you ever been at Pisa?

*Ped.* Ay, sir, in Pisa have I often been:
Pisa, renowned for grave citizens.

*Tra.* Among them know you one Vincentio?

*Ped.* I know him not, but I have heard of him;
A merchant of incomparable wealth.

*Tra.* He is my father, sir; and, sooth to say,
In countenance somewhat doth resemble you.

*Bion.* As much as an apple doth an oyster,
and all one.        [*Aside.*

*Tra.* To save your life in this extremity,
This favour will I do you for his sake;
And think it not the worst of all your fortunes
That you are like to Sir Vincentio.
His name and credit shall you undertake,
And in my house you shall be friendly lodg'd:—
Look that you take upon you as you should;
You understand me, sir:—so shall you stay
Till you have done your business in the city:
If this be courtesy, sir, accept of it.

*Ped.* O, sir, I do; and will repute you ever
The patron of my life and liberty.        [good.

*Tra.* Then go with me, to make the matter
This, by the way, I let you understand;—
My father is here look'd for every day,
To pass assurance of a dower in marriage
'Twixt me and one Baptista's daughter here:
In all these circumstances I'll instruct you:
Go with me, sir, to clothe you as becomes you.
        [*Exeunt.*

Scene III.—*A Room in* Petruchio's *House.*

*Enter* Katharina *and* Grumio.

*Gru.* No, no, forsooth; I dare not, for my life.

*Kath.* The more my wrong, the more his
        spite appears:
What, did he marry me to famish me?
Beggars, that come unto my father's door,
Upon entreaty have a present alms;
If not, elsewhere they meet with charity:
But I,—who never knew how to entreat,—
Nor never needed that I should entreat,—
Am starved for meat, giddy for lack of sleep;
With oaths kept waking, and with brawling
        fed:
And that which spites me more than all these
        wants,
He does it under the name of perfect love;
As who would say, if I should sleep or eat,
'Twere deadly sickness or else present death.—
I pr'ythee go, and get me some repast;
I care not what, so it be wholesome food.

*Gru.* What say you to a neat's foot?

*Kath.* 'Tis passing good; I pr'ythee let me
        have it.

*Gru.* I fear it is too choleric a meat:
How say you to a fat tripe, finely broil'd?

*Kath.* I like it well: good Grumio, fetch it me.

*Gru.* I cannot tell; I fear 'tis choleric.
What say you to a piece of beef and mustard?

*Kath.* A dish that I do love to feed upon.

*Gru.* Ay, but the mustard is too hot a little.

*Kath.* Why, then the beef, and let the mus-
        tard rest.        [the mustard,

*Gru.* Nay, then I will not; you shall have the
Or else you get no beef of Grumio.

*Kath.* Then both, or one, or anything thou
        wilt.

*Gru.* Why, then the mustard without the
        beef.

*Kath.* Go, get thee gone, thou false deluding
        slave,        [*Beats him.*
That feed'st me with the very name of meat:
Sorrow on thee, and all the pack of you,
That triumph thus upon my misery!
Go, get thee gone, I say.

*Enter* Petruchio *with a dish of meat; and*
        Hortensio.

*Pet.* How fares my Kate? What, sweeting,
        all amort?

*Hor.* Mistress, what cheer?

*Kath.*        Faith, as cold as can be.

*Pet.* Pluck up thy spirits, look cheerfully
        upon me.
Here, love; thou see'st how diligent I am
To dress thy meat myself, and bring it thee:
        [*Sets the dish upon a table.*
I am sure, sweet Kate, this kindness merits
        thanks.        [not;
What! not a word? Nay, then thou lov'st it
And all my pains is sorted to no proof.—
Here, take away this dish.

*Kath.*        I pray you, let it stand.

*Pet.* The poorest service is repaid with
        thanks;
And so shall mine, before you touch the meat.

*Kath.* I thank you, sir.

*Hor.* Signior Petruchio, fie! you are to blame!
Come, Mistress Kate, I'll bear you company.

*Pet.* Eat it up all, Hortensio, if thou lov'st
        me.—        [*Aside.*
Much good do it unto thy gentle heart!
Kate, eat apace:—and now, my honey-love,
Will we return unto thy father's house,
And revel it as bravely as the best,
With silken coats, and caps, and golden rings,
With ruffs and cuffs, and farthingales, and
        things;
With scarfs, and fans, and double change of
        bravery,
With amber bracelets, beads, and all this
        knavery.
What, hast thou din'd? The tailor stays thy
        leisure,
To deck thy body with his ruffling treasure.

*Enter* Tailor.

Come, tailor, let us see these ornaments;
Lay forth the gown.

*Enter* Haberdasher.

What news with you, sir?
*Hab.* Here is the cap your worship did be-
speak.
*Pet.* Why, this was moulded on a porringer;
A velvet dish;—fie, fie! 'tis lewd and filthy;
Why, 'tis a cockle or a walnut-shell,
A knack, a toy, a trick, a baby's cap:
Away with it! come, let me have a bigger.
*Kath.* I'll have no bigger; this doth fit the
time,
And gentlewomen wear such caps as these.
*Pet.* When you are gentle, you shall have one
too,
And not till then.
*Hor.* That will not be in haste. [*Aside.*
*Kath.* Why, sir, I trust I may have leave to
speak;
And speak I will. I am no child, no babe:
Your betters have endur'd me say my mind;
And if you cannot, best you stop your ears.
My tongue will tell the anger of my heart;
Or else my heart concealing it, will break:
And rather than it shall, I will be free
Even to the uttermost, as I please, in words.
*Pet.* Why, thou say'st true; it is a paltry cap,
A custard-coffin, a bauble, a silken pie:
I love thee well, in that thou lik'st it not.
*Kath.* Love me or love me not, I like the cap;
And it I will have, or I will have none.
*Pet.* Thy gown? why, ay;—Come, tailor, let
us see't.
O mercy, God! what masquing stuff is here?
What's this? a sleeve? 'tis like a demi-cannon:
What, up and down, carv'd like an apple-tart?
Here's snip, and nip, and cut, and slish, and
slash,
Like to a censer in a barber's shop:— [this?
Why, what, o' devil's name, tailor, call'st thou
*Hor.* I see she's like to have neither cap nor
gown. [*Aside.*
*Tai.* You bid me make it orderly and well,
According to the fashion and the time. [ber'd,
*Pet.* Marry, and did; but if you be remem-
I did not bid you mar it to the time.
Go, hop me over every kennel home,
For you shall hop without my custom, sir:
I'll none of it: hence! make your best of it.
*Kath.* I never saw a better-fashion'd gown,
More quaint, more pleasing, nor more com-
mendable:
Belike you mean to make a puppet of me.
*Pet.* Why, true; he means to make a puppet
of thee. [a puppet of her.
*Tai.* She says your worship means to make
*Pet.* O monstrous arrogance! Thou liest,
thou thread,
Thou thimble, [nail,
Thou yard, three-quarters, half-yard, quarter,
Thou flea, thou nit, thou-winter-cricket thou!—

Brav'd in mine own house with a skein of
thread?
Away, thou rag, thou quantity, thou remnant;
Or I shall so be-mete thee with thy yard,
As thou shalt think on prating whilst thou
liv'st!
I tell thee, I, that thou hast marr'd her gown.
*Tai.* Your worship is deceiv'd; the gown is
made
Just as my master had direction:
Grumio gave order how it should be done.
*Gru.* I gave him no order; I gave him the
stuff. [made?
*Tai.* But how did you desire it should be
*Gru.* Marry, sir, with needle and thread.
*Tai.* But did you not request to have it cut?
*Gru.* Thou hast faced many things.
*Tai.* I have.
*Gru.* Face not me: thou hast braved many
men; brave not me; I will neither be faced nor
braved. I say unto thee, I bid thy master cut
out the gown; but I did not bid him cut it to
pieces: *ergo*, thou liest. [testify.
*Tai.* Why, here is the note of the fashion to
*Pet.* Read it. [said so.
*Gru.* The note lies in his throat, if he say I
*Tai. Imprimis, a loose-bodied gown:*
*Gru.* Master, if ever I said loose-bodied
gown, sew me in the skirts of it, and beat me to
death with a bottom of brown thread: I said a
gown.
*Pet.* Proceed.
*Tai. With a small compassed cape:*
*Gru.* I confess the cape.
*Tai. With a trunk sleeve:*
*Gru.* I confess two sleeves.
*Tai. The sleeves curiously cut.*
*Pet.* Ay, there's the villany.
*Gru.* Error i' the bill sir; error i' the bill. I
commanded the sleeves should be cut out, and
sewed up again; and that I'll prove upon thee,
though thy little finger be armed in a thimble.
*Tai.* This is true that I say: an I had thee in
place where, thou shouldst know it.
*Gru.* I am for thee straight: take thou the
bill, give me thy mete-yard, and spare not me.
*Hor.* God-a-mercy, Grumio! then he shall
have no odds.
*Pet.* Well, sir, in brief, the gown is not for me.
*Gru.* You are i' the right, sir; 'tis for my
mistress.
*Pet.* Go, take it up unto thy master's use.
*Gru.* Villain, not for thy life! Take up my
mistress' gown for thy master's use!
*Pet.* Why, sir, what's your conceit in that?
*Gru.* O, sir, the conceit is deeper than you
think for:
Take up my mistress' gown to his master's use!
O fie, fie, fie!
*Pet.* Hortensio, say thou wilt see the tailor
paid.— [*Aside.*
Go take it hence; be gone, and say no more.
*Hor.* Tailor, I'll pay thee for thy gown to-
morrow.

Take no unkindness of his hasty words:
Away, I say! commend me to thy master.
                    [*Exeunt* Tailor *and* Haberdasher.
*Pet.* Well, come, my Kate; we will unto your
                    father's
Even in these honest mean habiliments:
Our purses shall be proud, our garments poor;
For 'tis the mind that makes the body rich;
And as the sun breaks through the darkest
        clouds,
So honour peereth in the meanest habit.
What, is the jay more precious than the lark,
Because his feathers are more beautiful?
Or is the adder better than the eel,
Because his painted skin contents the eye?
O no, good Kate; neither art thou the worse
For this poor furniture and mean array.
If thou account'st it shame, lay it on me;
And therefore frolic: we will hence forthwith,
To feast and sport us at thy father's house.—
Go, call my men, and let us straight to him;
And bring our horses unto Long-lane end;
There will we mount, and thither walk on
        foot.—
Let's see; I think 'tis now some seven o'clock,
And well we may come there by dinner-time.
*Kath.* I dare assure you, sir, 'tis almost two;
And 'twill be supper-time ere you come there.
*Pet.* It shall be seven ere I go to horse:
Look, what I speak, or do, or think to do,
You are still crossing it.—Sirs, let't alone:
I will not go to-day; and ere I do,
It shall be what o'clock I say it is.
*Hor.* Why, so, this gallant will command the
sun.                                    [*Exeunt.*

SCENE IV.—PADUA. *Before* BAPTISTA'S *House.*

*Enter* TRANIO, *and the* Pedant *dressed like*
VINCENTIO.

*Tra.* Sir, this is the house: please it you that
        I call?
*Ped.* Ay, what else? and, but I be deceived,
Signior Baptista may remember me,
Near twenty years ago, in Genoa, where
We were lodgers at the Pegasus.          [case,
*Tra.* 'Tis well; and hold your own, in any
With such austerity as 'longeth to a father.
*Ped.* I warrant you. But, sir, here comes
        your boy;
'Twere good he were school'd.

*Enter* BIONDELLO.

*Tra.* Fear you not him.—Sirrah Biondello,
Now do your duty throughly, I advise you:
Imagine 'twere the right Vincentio.
*Bion.* Tut! fear not me.              [tista?
*Tra.* But hast thou done thy errand to Bap-
*Bion.* I told him that your father was at
Venice;
And that you look'd for him this day in Padua.
*Tra.* Thou'rt a tall fellow: hold thee that to
        drink.                            [sir.—
Here comes Baptista:—set your countenance,

*Enter* BAPTISTA *and* LUCENTIO.

Signior Baptista, you are happily met.—
Sir [*to the* Pedant], this is the gentleman I told
        you of:
I pray you, stand good father to me now,
Give me Bianca for my patrimony.
*Ped.* Soft, son!—
Sir, by your leave, having come to Padua
To gather in some debts, my son Lucentio
Made me acquainted with a weighty cause
Of love between your daughter and himself:
And,—for the good report I hear of you;
And for the love he beareth to your daughter,
And she to him,—to stay him not too long,
I am content, in a good father's care,
To have him match'd; and,—if you please to
        like
No worse than I,—upon some agreement,
Me shall you find ready and willing
With one consent to have her so bestow'd;
For curious I cannot be with you,
Signior Baptista, of whom I hear so well.
*Bap.* Sir, pardon me in what I have to say:
Your plainness and your shortness please me
        well.
Right true it is, your son Lucentio here
Doth love my daughter, and she loveth him,
Or both dissemble deeply their affections:
And therefore, if you say no more than this,
That like a father you will deal with him,
And pass my daughter a sufficient dower,
The match is made, and all is done:
Your son shall have my daughter with consent.
*Tra.* I thank you, sir. Where, then, do you
        know best
We be affied, and such assurance ta'en
As shall with either part's agreement stand?
*Bap.* Not in my house, Lucentio; for, you
        know,
Pitchers have ears, and I have many servants:
Besides, old Gremio is heark'ning still;
And, haply, we might be interrupted.
*Tra.* Then at my lodging, an it like you:
There doth my father lie; and there, this night,
We'll pass the business privately and well:
Send for your daughter by your servant here;
My boy shall fetch the scrivener presently.
The worst is this,—that, at so slender warning,
You are like to have a thin and slender pittance.
*Bap.* It likes me well.—Cambio, hie you
        home,
And bid Bianca make her ready straight;
And, if you will, tell what hath happened,—
Lucentio's father is arriv'd in Padua,
And now she's like to be Lucentio's wife.
*Luc.* I pray the gods she may, with all my
        heart.                            [gone.
*Tra.* Dally not with the gods, but get thee
Signior Baptista, shall I lead the way?
Welcome! one mess is like to be your cheer:
Come, sir; we'll better it in Pisa.
*Bap.* I follow you.
                    [*Exeunt* TRA., Ped., *and* BAP.

*Bion.* Cambio.

*Luc.*    What sayest thou, Biondello?

*Bion.* You saw my master wink and laugh upon you?

*Luc.* Biondello, what of that?

*Bion.* Faith, nothing; but has left me here behind, to expound the meaning or moral of his signs and tokens.

*Luc.* I pray thee, moralize them.

*Bion.* Then thus. Baptista is safe, talking with the deceiving father of a deceitful son.

*Luc.* And what of him?

*Bion.* His daughter is to be brought by you to the supper.

*Luc.* And then?—

*Bion.* The old priest at Saint Luke's church is at your command at all hours.

*Luc.* And what of all this?

*Bion.* I cannot tell; expect they are busied about a counterfeit assurance. Take you assurance of her, *cum privilegio ad imprimendum solum:* to the church;—take the priest, clerk, and some sufficient honest witnesses:
If this be not that you look for, I have no more
    to say,
But bid Bianca farewell for ever and a day.
                                                [*Going.*

*Luc.* Hear'st thou, Biondello?

*Bion.* I cannot tarry: I knew a wench married in an afternoon as she went to the garden for parsley to stuff a rabbit; and so may you, sir; and so adieu, sir. My master hath appointed me to go to Saint Luke's, to bid the priest be ready to come against you come with your appendix.                              [*Exit.*

*Luc.* I may, and will, if she be so contented: She will be pleas'd; then wherefore should I doubt?
Hap what hap may, I'll roundly go about her;
It shall go hard if Cambio go without her.
                                                [*Exit.*

SCENE V.—*A Public Road.*

*Enter* PETRUCHIO, KATHARINA, *and* HORTENSIO.

*Pet.* Come on, o' God's name; once more toward our father's.
Good Lord, how bright and goodly shines the
    moon!                            [light now.

*Kath.* The moon! the sun: it is not moon-

*Pet.* I say it is the moon that shines so bright.

*Kath.* I know it is the sun that shines so bright.

*Pet.* Now, by my mother's son, and that's myself,
It shall be moon, or star, or what I list,
Or ere I journey to your father's house.—
Go one, and fetch our horses back again.—
Evermore cross'd and cross'd; nothing but
    cross'd!

*Hor.* Say as he says, or we shall never go.

*Kath.* Forward, I pray, since we have come so far,

And be it moon, or sun, or what you please:
And if you please to call it a rush-candle,
Henceforth I vow it shall be so for me.

*Pet.* I say it is the moon.

*Kath.*                I know it is the moon.

*Pet.* Nay, then you lie: it is the blessed sun.

*Kath.* Then, God be blessed, it is the blessed sun:
But sun it is not, when you say it is not;
And the moon changes even as your mind.
What you will have it nam'd, even that it is;
And so, it shall be so for Katherine.

*Hor.* Petruchio, go thy ways; the field is won.

*Pet.* Well, forward, forward! thus the bowl should run,
And not unluckily against the bias.—
But, soft! company is coming here.

*Enter* VINCENTIO, *in a travelling dress.*

Good-morrow, gentle mistress: where away?—
                                    [*To* VINCENTIO.
Tell me, sweet Kate, and tell me truly too,
Hast thou beheld a fresher gentlewoman?
Such war of white and red within her cheeks!
What stars do spangle heaven with such beauty,
As those two eyes become that heavenly face?—
Fair lovely maid, once more good-day to thee:—
Sweet Kate, embrace her for her beauty's sake.

*Hor.* 'A will make the man mad, to make a woman of him.

*Kath.* Young budding virgin, fair and fresh and sweet,
Whither away; or where is thy abode?
Happy the parents of so fair a child;
Happier the man whom favourable stars
Allot thee for his lovely bed-fellow!

*Pet.* Why, how now, Kate! I hope thou art not mad:
This is a man, old, wrinkled, faded, wither'd;
And not a maiden, as thou sayst he is.

*Kath.* Pardon, old father, my mistaking eyes,
That have been so bedazzled with the sun,
That everything I look on seemeth green:
Now I perceive thou art a reverend father;
Pardon, I pray thee, for my mad mistaking.

*Pet.* Do, good old grandsire; and withal make known
Which way thou travell'st: if along with us,
We shall be joyful of thy company.

*Vin.* Fair sir, and you my merry mistress,
That with your strange encounter much amaz'd me,
My name is call'd Vincentio; my dwelling Pisa;
And bound I am to Padua; there to visit
A son of mine, which long I have not seen.

*Pet.* What is his name?

*Vin.*                Lucentio, gentle sir.

*Pet.* Happily met; the happier for thy son.
And now by law, as well as reverend age,
I may entitle thee my loving father:
The sister to my wife, this gentlewoman,
Thy son by this hath married. Wonder not,
Nor be not griev'd: she is of good esteem

Her dowry wealthy, and of worthy birth;
Beside, so qualified as may beseem
The spouse of any noble gentleman.
Let me embrace with old Vincentio:
And wander we to see thy honest son,
Who will of thy arrival be full joyous.    [sure,
    *Vin.* But is this true? or is it else your plea-
Like pleasant travellers, to break a jest
Upon the company you overtake?
    *Hor.* I do assure thee, father, so it is.
    *Pet.* Come, go along, and see the truth here-
of:
For our first merriment hath made thee jealous.
        [*Exeunt* PET., KATH., *and* VIN.
    *Hor.* Well, Petruchio, this hath put me in
    heart.
Have to my widow; and if she be forward,
Then hast thou taught Hortensio to be un-
    toward.            [*Exit.*

## ACT V.

SCENE I.—PADUA. *Before* LUCENTIO'S *House.*

*Enter on one side* BIONDELLO, LUCENTIO, *and*
BIANCA; GREMIO *walking on the other side.*

    *Bion.* Softly and swiftly, sir; for the priest is
ready.
    *Luc.* I fly, Biondello: but they may chance
to need thee at home, therefore leave us.
    *Bion.* Nay, faith, I'll see the church o' your
back; and then come back to my master as
soon as I can.
        [*Exeunt* LUC., BIAN., *and* BION.
    *Gre.* I marvel Cambio comes not all this
while.

*Enter* PETRUCHIO, KATHARINA, VINCENTIO,
    GRUMIO, *and* Attendants.

    *Pet.* Sir, here's the door; this is Lucentio's
house:                        [place;
My father's bears more toward the market-
Thither must I, and here I leave you, sir.
    *Vin.* You shall not choose but drink before
    you go:
I think I shall command your welcome here,
And, by all likelihood, some cheer is toward.
                        [*Knocks.*
    *Gre.* They're busy within; you were best
knock louder.

*Enter* Pedant *above, at a window.*

    *Ped.* What's he that knocks as he would
beat down the gate?
    *Vin.* Is Signior Lucentio within, sir?
    *Ped.* He's within, sir, but not to be spoken
withal.
    *Vin.* What if a man bring him a hundred
pound or two, to make merry withal?
    *Ped.* Keep your hundred pounds to yourself:
he shall need none so long as I live.
    *Pet.* Nay, I told you your son was well be-
loved in Padua.—Do you hear, sir?—to leave
frivolous circumstances,—I pray you, tell Sig-

nior Lucentio that his father is come from Pisa,
and is here at the door to speak with him.
    *Ped.* Thou liest: his father is come from Pisa,
and here looking out at the window.
    *Vin.* Art thou his father?
    *Ped.* Ay, sir; so his mother says, if I may
believe her.
    *Pet.* Why, how now, gentleman! [*to* VINCEN.]
why, this is flat knavery, to take upon you
another man's name.
    *Ped.* Lay hands on the villain: I believe 'a
means to cozen somebody in this city under my
countenance.

*Re-enter* BIONDELLO.

    *Bion.* I have seen them in the church to-
gether: God send 'em good shipping!—But who
is here? mine old master, Vincentio! now we
are undone, and brought to nothing.
    *Vin.* Come hither, crack-hemp.
                    [*Seeing* BIONDELLO.
    *Bion.* I hope I may choose, sir.
    *Vin.* Come hither, you rogue. What! have
you forgot me?
    *Bion.* Forgot you! no, sir: I could not forget
you, for I never saw you before in all my life.
    *Vin.* What, you notorious villain, didst thou
never see thy master's father, Vincentio?
    *Bion.* What, my old worshipful old master?
yes, marry, sir: see where he looks out of the
window.
    *Vin.* Is't so, indeed?    [*Beats* BIONDELLO.
    *Bion.* Help, help, help! here's a madman will
murder me.                    [*Exit.*
    *Ped.* Help, son! help, Signior Baptista!
                [*Exit from the window.*
    *Pet.* Pr'ythee, Kate, let's stand aside, and
see the end of this controversy.    [*They retire.*

*Re-enter* Pedant *below; and* BAPTISTA,
    TRANIO, *and* Servants.

    *Tra.* Sir, what are you, that offer to beat my
servant?
    *Vin.* What am I, sir! nay, what are you, sir?
—O immortal gods! O fine villain! A silken
doublet! a velvet hose! a scarlet cloak! and a
copatain hat!—O, I am undone! I am undone!
while I play the good husband at home, my son
and my servant spend all at the university.
    *Tra.* How now! what's the matter?
    *Bap.* What, is the man lunatic?
    *Tra.* Sir, you seem a sober ancient gentleman
by your habit, but your words show you a madman. Why, sir, what concerns it you if I wear
pearl and gold? I thank my good father, I am
able to maintain it.
    *Vin.* Thy father! O villain! he is a sailmaker
in Bergamo.
    *Bap.* You mistake, sir; you mistake, sir.
Pray, what do you think is his name?
    *Vin.* His name! as if I knew not his name!
I have brought him up ever since he was three
years old, and his name is Tranio.
    *Ped.* Away, away, mad ass! his name is

Lucentio; and he is mine only son, and heir to the lands of me, Signior Vincentio.

*Vin.* Lucentio! O, he hath murdered his master!—Lay hold on him, I charge you, in the duke's name.—O, my son, my son!—tell me, thou villain, where is my son, Lucentio?

*Tra.* Call forth an officer.

*Enter one with an* Officer.

Carry this mad knave to the gaol.—Father Baptista, I charge you see that he be forthcoming.

*Vin.* Carry me to the gaol!

*Gre.* Stay, officer; he shall not go to prison.

*Bap.* Talk not, Signior Gremio; I say he shall go to prison.

*Gre.* Take heed, Signior Baptista, lest you be coney-catched in this business; I dare swear this is the right Vincentio.

*Ped.* Swear, if thou darest.

*Gre.* Nay, I dare not swear it.  [Lucentio.

*Tra.* Then thou wert best say that I am not

*Gre.* Yes, I know thee to be Signior Lucentio.

*Bap.* Away with the dotard! to the gaol with him!

*Vin.* Thus strangers may be haled and abus'd.—O monstrous villain!

*Re-enter* BIONDELLO, *with* LUCENTIO *and* BIANCA.

*Bion.* O, we are spoiled! and yonder he is: deny him, forswear him, or else we are all undone.

*Luc.* Pardon, sweet father.  [*Kneeling.*

*Vin.*　　　　　Lives my sweet son?
　　　　　　　　[BION., TRA., *and* Ped. *run out.*

*Bian.* Pardon, dear father.  [*Kneeling.*

*Bap.*　　　　How hast thou offended?—Where is Lucentio?

*Luc.*　　　　Here's Lucentio, Right son to the right Vincentio; That hath by marriage made thy daughter mine, While counterfeit supposes blear'd thine eyne.

*Gre.* Here's packing, with a witness, to deceive us all!

*Vin.* Where is that damned villain, Tranio, That fac'd and brav'd me in this matter so?

*Bap.* Why, tell me, is not this my Cambio?

*Bian.* Cambio is chang'd into Lucentio.

*Luc.* Love wrought these miracles. Bianca's love Made me exchange my state with Tranio, While he did bear my countenance in the town; And happily I have arrived at the last Unto the wished-far haven of my bliss. What Tranio did, myself enforc'd him to; Then pardon him, sweet father, for my sake.

*Vin.* I'll slit the villain's nose, that would have sent me to the gaol.

*Bap.* But do you hear, sir? [*to* LUCENTIO] Have you married my daughter without asking my good-will?　　　　　　　　　　[go to:

*Vin.* Fear not, Baptista; we will content you,

But I will in, to be revenged for this villany!
　　　　　　　　　　　　　　　　　[*Exit.*

*Bap.* And I, to sound the depth of this knavery.　　　　　　　　　　　　　　　[*Exit.*

*Luc.* Look not pale, Bianca; thy father will not frown.　　[*Exeunt* LUC. *and* BIAN.

*Gre.* My cake is dough: but I'll in among the rest; Out of hope of all but my share of the feast.
　　　　　　　　　　　　　　　　　[*Exit.*

PETRUCHIO *and* KATHARINA *advance.*

*Kath.* Husband, let's follow, to see the end of this ado.

*Pet.* First kiss me, Kate, and we will.

*Kath.* What, in the midst of the street?

*Pet.* What, art thou ashamed of me?  [kiss.

*Kath.* No, sir; God forbid; but ashamed to

*Pet.* Why, then, let's home again.—Come, sirrah let's away.

*Kath.* Nay, I will give thee a kiss, now, pray thee, love, stay.

*Pet.* Is not this well?—Come, my sweet Kate; Better once than never, for never too late.
　　　　　　　　　　　　　　　　　[*Exeunt.*

SCENE II.—*A Room in* LUCENTIO'S *House.*

*A Banquet set out. Enter* BAPTISTA, VINCENTIO, GREMIO, *the* Pedant, LUCENTIO, BIANCA, PETRUCHIO, KATHARINA, HORTENSIO, *and* Widow. TRANIO, BIONDELLO, GRUMIO, *and others, attending.*

*Luc.* At last, though long, our jarring notes agree: And time it is, when raging war is done, To smile at 'scapes and perils overblown.— My fair Bianca, bid my father welcome, While I with self-same kindness welcome thine.— Brother Petruchio,—sister Katharina,— And thou, Hortensio, with thy loving widow,— Feast with the best, and welcome to my house: My banquet is to close our stomachs up, After our great good cheer. Pray you, sit down; For now we sit to chat, as well as eat.
　　　　　　　　　　　　[*They sit at table.*

*Pet.* Nothing but sit and sit, and eat and eat!

*Bap.* Padua affords this kindness, son Petruchio.

*Pet.* Padua affords nothing but what is kind.

*Hor.* For both our sakes I would that word were true.

*Pet.* Now, for my life, Hortensio fears his widow.

*Wid.* Then never trust me if I be afeard.

*Pet.* You are very sensible, and yet you miss my sense: I mean Hortensio is afeard of you.  [round.

*Wid.* He that is giddy thinks the world turns

*Pet.* Roundly replied.

*Kath.*　　　　Mistress, how mean you that?

*Wid.* Thus I conceive by him.  [that?

*Pet.* Conceives by me!—How likes Hortensio

*Hor.* My widow says thus she conceives her
tale.

*Pet.* Very well mended.—Kiss him for that,
good widow.

*Kath.* He that is giddy thinks the world
turns round:—

I pray you, tell me what you meant by that.

*Wid.* Your husband, being troubled with a
shrew,

Measures my husband's sorrow by his woe:

And now you know my meaning.

*Kath.* A very mean meaning.

*Wid.*                     Right, I mean you.

*Kath.* And I am mean, indeed, respecting
you.

*Pet.* To her, Kate!

*Hor.* To her, widow!                [down.

*Pet.* A hundred marks, my Kate does put her

*Hor.* That's my office.

*Pet.* Spoke like an officer:—ha' to thee, lad.

                    [*Drinks to* HORTENSIO.

*Bap.* How likes Gremio these quick-witted
folks?

*Gre.* Believe me, sir, they butt together well.

*Bian.* Head and butt! an hasty-witted body

Would say your head and butt were head and
horn.                                   [you?

*Vin.* Ay, mistress bride, hath that awaken'd

*Bian.* Ay, but not frighted me; therefore I'll
sleep again.

*Pet.* Nay, that you shall not: since you have
begun,

Have at you for a bitter jest or two.   [bush,

*Bian.* Am I your bird? I mean to shift my

And then pursue me as you draw your bow.—

You are welcome all.

        [*Exeunt* BIAN., KATH., *and* Wid.

*Pet.* She hath prevented me.—Here, Signior
Tranio,

This bird you aim'd at, though you hit her not;

Therefore a health to all that shot and miss'd.

*Tra.* O, sir, Lucentio slipp'd me like his
greyhound,

Which runs himself, and catches for his master.

*Pet.* A good swift simile, but something
currish.                                [self;

*Tra.* 'Tis well, sir, that you hunted for your-

'Tis thought your deer does hold you at a bay.

*Bap.* O ho, Petruchio, Tranio hits you now.

*Luc.* I thank thee for that gird, good Tranio.

*Hor.* Confess, confess, hath he not hit you
here?

*Pet.* 'A has a little gall'd me, I confess;

And, as the jest did glance away from me,

'Tis ten to one it maim'd you two outright.

*Bap.* Now, in good sadness, son Petruchio,

I think thou hast the veriest shrew of all.

*Pet.* Well, I say no: and therefore, for assurance,

Let's each one send unto his wife;

And he whose wife is most obedient

To come at first when he doth send for her,

Shall win the wager which we will propose.

*Hor.* Content. What is the wager?

*Luc.*                     Twenty crowns.

*Pet.* Twenty crowns!

I'll venture so much on my hawk or hound,

But twenty times so much upon my wife.

*Luc.* A hundred then.

*Hor.*                     Content.

*Pet.*                     A match! 'tis done.

*Hor.* Who shall begin?

*Luc.* That will I.—

Go, Biondello, bid your mistress come to me.

*Bion.* I go.                          [*Exit.*

*Bap.* Son, I will be your half, Bianca comes.

*Luc.* I'll have no halves; I'll bear it all myself.

### *Re-enter* BIONDELLO.

How now! what news?

*Bion.*          Sir, my mistress sends you word

That she is busy, and she cannot come.

*Pet.* How! she is busy, and she cannot come!

Is that an answer?

*Gre.*              Ay, and a kind one too:

Pray God, sir, your wife send you not a worse.

*Pet.* I hope better.

*Hor.* Sirrah Biondello, go and entreat my
wife

To come to me forthwith.  [*Exit* BIONDELLO.

*Pet.*                Oh, ho! entreat her!

Nay, then she must needs come.

*Hor.*                     I am afraid, sir,

Do what you can, yours will not be entreated.

### *Re-enter* BIONDELLO.

Now, where's my wife?

*Bion.* She says you have some goodly jest in
hand:

She will not come; she bids you come to her.

*Pet.* Worse and worse; she will not come! O
vile,

Intolerable, not to be endur'd!—

Sirrah Grumio, go to your mistress;

Say I command her come to me.

                              [*Exit* GRUMIO.

*Hor.* I know her answer.

*Pet.*                     What?

*Hor.*                She will not come.

*Pet.* The fouler fortune mine, and there an
end.

*Bap.* Now, by my holidame, here comes
Katharina!

### *Enter* KATHARINA.

*Kath.* What is your will, sir, that you send
for me?                                [wife?

*Pet.* Where is your sister, and Hortensio's

*Kath.* They sit conferring by the parlour fire.

*Pet.* Go, fetch them hither: if they deny to
come,

Swinge me them soundly forth unto their husbands:

Away, I say, and bring them hither straight.

                        [*Exit* KATHARINA.

*Luc.* Here is a wonder, if you talk of a
wonder.

*Hor.* And so it is: I wonder what it bodes.

*Pet.* Marry, peace it bodes, and love, and quiet life,
An awful rule, and right supremacy;    [happy.
And, to be short, what not, that's sweet and

*Bap.* Now fair befall thee, good Petruchio!
The wager thou hast won; and I will add
Unto their losses twenty thousand crowns;
Another dowry to another daughter,
For she is chang'd, as she had never been.

*Pet.* Nay, I will win my wager better yet;
And show more sign of her obedience,
Her new-built virtue and obedience.
See where she comes, and brings your froward wives
As prisoners to her womanly persuasion.—

*Re-enter* KATHARINA, *with* BIANCA *and* Widow.

Katharine, that cap of yours becomes you not:
Off with that bauble, throw it underfoot.
    [KATH. *pulls off her cap and throws it down.*

*Wid.* Lord, let me never have a cause to sigh,
Will I be brought to such a silly pass!

*Bian.* Fie! what a foolish duty call you this?

*Luc.* I would your duty were as foolish too:
The wisdom of your duty, fair Bianca,    [time.
Hath cost me an hundred crowns since supper-

*Bian.* The more fool you, for laying on my duty.

*Pet.* Katharine, I charge thee, tell these headstrong women
What duty they do owe their lords and husbands.

*Wid.* Come, come, you're mocking: we will have no telling.

*Pet.* Come on, I say; and first begin with her.

*Wid.* She shall not.

*Pet.* I say she shall;—and first begin with her.

*Kath.* Fie, fie! unknit that threat'ning unkind brow;
And dart not scornful glances from those eyes,
To wound thy lord, thy king, thy governor:
It blots thy beauty, as frosts do bite the meads;
Confounds thy fame, as whirlwinds shake fair buds;
And in no sense is meet or amiable.
A woman mov'd is like a fountain troubled—
Muddy, ill-seeming, thick, bereft of beauty;
And while it is so, none so dry or thirsty
Will deign to sip or touch one drop of it.

Thy husband is thy lord, thy life, thy keeper,
Thy head, thy sovereign; one that cares for thee
And for thy maintenance; commits his body
To painful labour both by sea and land,
To watch the night in storms, the day in cold,
Whilst thou liest warm at home, secure and safe;
And craves no other tribute at thy hands
But love, fair looks, and true obedience,—
Too little payment for so great a debt!
Such duty as the subject owes the prince,
Even such a woman oweth to her husband;
And when she is froward, peevish, sullen, sour,
And not obedient to his honest will,
What is she but a foul contending rebel,
And graceless traitor to her loving lord?—
I am asham'd that women are so simple
To offer war where they should kneel for peace,
Or seek for rule, supremacy, and sway,
When they are bound to serve, love, and obey.
Why are our bodies soft and weak, and smooth,
Unapt to toil and trouble in the world,
But that our soft conditions and our hearts
Should well agree with our external parts?
Come, come, you froward and unable worms!
My mind hath been as big as one of yours,
My heart as great; my reason, haply, more,
To bandy word for word and frown for frown:
But now I see our lances are but straws;
Our strength as weak, our weakness past com-
    pare,—    [are.
That seeming to be most, which we indeed least
Then vail your stomachs, for it is no boot,
And place your hands below your husband's foot:
In token of which duty, if he please,
My hand is ready, may it do him ease.

*Pet.* Why, there's a wench!—Come on, and kiss me, Kate.    [shalt ha't.

*Luc.* Well, go thy ways, old lad; for thou

*Vin.* 'Tis a good hearing when children are toward.    [froward.

*Luc.* But a harsh hearing when women are

*Pet.* Come, Kate, we'll to bed.—
We three are married, but you two are sped.
'Twas I won the wager, though you hit the white;    [*To* LUCENTIO.
And, being a winner, God give you good-night!
    [*Exeunt* PET. *and* KATH.

*Hor.* Now go thy ways; thou hast tam'd a curst shrew.

*Luc.* 'Tis a wonder, by your leave, she will be tam'd so.    [*Exeunt.*

# WINTER'S TALE.

Act III Sc. 3

# THE WINTER'S TALE

## DRAMATIS PERSONÆ

LEONTES, *King of Sicilia.*
MAMILLIUS, *his Son.*
CAMILLO, ⎫
ANTIGONUS, ⎬ *Sicilian Lords.*
CLEOMENES, ⎪
DION, ⎭
*Other* Sicilian Lords.
Sicilian Gentlemen.
Officers *of a Court of Judicature.*
POLIXENES, *King of Bohemia.*
FLORIZEL, *his Son.*
ARCHIDAMUS, *a Bohemian Lord.*
A Mariner.
Gaoler.
An Old Shepherd, *reputed father of* PERDITA.
Clown, *his Son.*

Servant *to the Old Shepherd.*
AUTOLYCUS, *a Rogue.*
Time, *as Chorus.*

HERMIONE, *Queen to* LEONTES.
PERDITA, *Daughter to* LEONTES *and* HER-
MIONE.
PAULINA, *Wife to* ANTIGONUS.
EMILIA, *a Lady,* ⎫ *attending the* QUEEN.
*Other* Ladies, ⎭
MOPSA, ⎫ *Shepherdesses.*
DORCAS, ⎭

Lords, Ladies, and Attendants; Satyrs *for a
Dance;* Shepherds, Shepherdesses,
Guards, &c.

SCENE,—*Sometimes in* SICILIA; *sometimes in* BOHEMIA.

## ACT I.

### SCENE I.—SICILIA. *An Antechamber in* LEONTES' *Palace.*

*Enter* CAMILLO *and* ARCHIDAMUS.

*Arch.* If you shall chance, Camillo, to visit
Bohemia, on the like occasion whereon my
services are now on foot, you shall see, as I
have said, great difference betwixt our Bohemia
and your Sicilia.

*Cam.* I think this coming summer the King
of Sicilia means to pay Bohemia the visitation
which he justly owes him.

*Arch.* Wherein our entertainment shall
shame us we will be justified in our loves; for,
indeed,—

*Cam.* Beseech you,—

*Arch.* Verily, I speak it in the freedom of my
knowledge: we cannot with such magnificence
—in so rare—I know not what to say.—We will
give you sleepy drinks, that your senses, unin-
telligent of our insufficience, may, though they
cannot praise us, as little accuse us.

*Cam.* You pay a great deal too dear for
what's given freely.

*Arch.* Believe me, I speak as my understanding instructs me, and as mine honesty
puts it to utterance.

*Cam.* Sicilia cannot show himself overkind
to Bohemia. They were trained together in
their childhoods; and there rooted betwixt
them then such an affection which cannot
choose but branch now. Since their more
mature dignities and royal necessities made
separation of their society, their encounters,
though not personal, have been royally attor-
neyed, with interchange of gifts, letters, loving
embassies; that they have seemed to be together, though absent; shook hands, as over a
vast; and embraced, as it were, from the ends
of opposed winds. The heavens continue their
loves!

*Arch.* I think there is not in the world either
malice or matter to alter it. You have an unspeakable comfort of your young Prince
Mamillius: it is a gentleman of the greatest
promise that ever came into my note.

*Cam.* I very well agree with you in the hopes
of him. It is a gallant child; one that, indeed,
physics the subject, makes old hearts fresh:
they that went on crutches ere he was born
desire yet their life to see him a man.

*Arch.* Would they else be content to die?

*Cam.* Yes; if there were no other excuse why
they should desire to live.

*Arch.* If the king had no son they would
desire to live on crutches till he had one.

[*Exeunt.*

### SCENE II.—*The same. A Room of State in the Palace.*

*Enter* LEONTES, POLIXENES, HERMIONE,
MAMILLIUS, CAMILLO, *and* Attendants.

*Pol.* Nine changes of the watery star have
been                                                    [throne
The shepherd's note since we have left our
Without a burden: time as long again
Would be fill'd up, my brother, with our thanks
And yet we should, for perpetuity,
Go hence in debt: and therefore, like a cipher,
Yet standing in rich place, I multiply

With one we-thank-you many thousands more
That go before it.
*Leon.*            Stay your thanks awhile,
And pay them when you part.
*Pol.*                  Sir, that's to-morrow.
I am question'd by my fears, of what may
      chance
Or breed upon our absence; that may blow
No sneaping winds at home, to make us say,
*This is put forth too truly.* Besides, I have stay'd
To tire your royalty.
*Leon.*            We are tougher, brother,
Than you can put us to't.
*Pol.*                  No longer stay.
*Leon.* One seven-night longer.
*Pol.*                  Very sooth, to-morrow.
*Leon.* We'll part the time between's then:
      and in that
I'll no gainsaying.
*Pol.*            Press me not, beseech you, so.
There is no·tongue that moves, none, none i'
      the world            [now,
So soon as yours, could win me: so it should
Were there necessity in your request, although
'Twere needful I denied it. My affairs
Do even drag me homeward: which to hinder,
Were, in your love, a whip to me; my stay,
To you a charge and trouble: to save both,
Farewell, our brother.
*Leon.* Tongue-tied, our queen? Speak you.
*Her.* I had thought, sir, to have held my
      peace until
You had drawn oaths from him not to stay.
You, sir,
Charge him too coldly. Tell him, you are sure
All in Bohemia's well: this satisfaction
The by-gone day proclaim'd: say this to him,
He's beat from his best ward.
*Leon.*            Well said, Hermione.
*Her.* To tell he longs to see his son, were
      strong:
But let him say so then, and let him go;
But let him swear so, and he shall not stay,
We'll thwack him hence with distaffs.—
Yet of your royal presence [*to* POLIXENES] I'll
      adventure
The borrow of a week. When at Bohemia
You take my lord, I'll give him my commission
To let him there a month behind the gest
Prefix'd for his parting:—yet, good deed,
      Leontes,
I love thee not a jar of the clock behind
What lady she her lord.—You'll stay?
*Pol.*            No, madam.
*Her.* Nay, but you will?
*Pol.*            I may not, verily.
*Her.* Verily!
You put me off with limber vows; but I,
Though you would seek to unsphere the stars
      with oaths,
Should yet say, *Sir, no going.* Verily,
You shall not go; a lady's verily is
As potent as a lord's. Will you go yet?
Force me to keep you as a prisoner,

Not like a guest: so you shall pay your fees
When you depart, and save your thanks. How
      say you?
My prisoner or my guest? by your dread verily,
One of them you shall be.
*Pol.*            Your guest, then, madam:
To be your prisoner should import offending;
Which is for me less easy to commit
Than you to punish.
*Her.*            Not your gaoler, then,
But your kind hostess. Come, I'll question you
Of my lord's tricks and yours when you were
      boys:
You were pretty lordlings then.
*Pol.*            We were, fair queen,
Two lads that thought there were no more
      behind
But such a day to-morrow as to-day,
And to be boy eternal.            [two?
*Her.* Was not my lord the verier wag o' the
*Pol.* We were as twinn'd lambs that did
      frisk i' the sun
And bleat the one at the other. What we
      chang'd
Was innocence for innocence; we knew not
The doctrine of ill-doing, nor dream'd
That any did. Had we pursu'd that life,
And our weak spirits ne'er been higher rear'd
With stronger blood, we should have answer'd
      heaven
Boldly, *Not guilty;* the imposition clear'd
Hereditary ours.
*Her.*            By this we gather
You have tripp'd since.
*Pol.*            O my most sacred lady,
Temptations have since then been born to's!
      for
In those unfledg'd days was my wife a girl;
Your precious self had then not cross'd the eyes
Of my young play-fellow.
*Her.*            Grace to boot!
Of this make no conclusion, lest you say
Your queen and I are devils: yet, go on;
The offences we have made you do we'll an-
      swer;
If you first sinn'd with us, and that with us
You did continue fault, and that you slipp'd
      not
With any but with us.
*Leon.*            Is he won yet?
*Her.* He'll stay, my lord.
*Leon.*            At my request he would not.
Hermione, my dearest, thou never spok'st
To better purpose.
*Her.*            Never?
*Leon.*            Never but once.
*Her.* What! have I twice said well? when
      was't before?            [make's
I pr'ythee, tell me: cram's with praise, and
As fat as tame things: one good deed dying
      tongueless
Slaughters a thousand waiting upon that.
Our praises are our wages: you may ride's
With one soft kiss a thousand furlongs ere

With spur we heat an acre. But to the goal:—
My last good deed was to entreat his stay;
What was my first? it has an elder sister,
Or I mistake you: O, would her name were
    Grace!
But once before I spoke to the purpose: when?
Nay, let me have't; I long.
  *Leon.*          Why, that was when
Three crabbed months had sour'd themselves
    to death,
Ere I could make thee open thy white hand,
And clap thyself my love; then didst thou
    utter
*I am yours for ever.*
  *Her.*      It is Grace indeed.—
Why, lo you now, I have spoke to the purpose
    twice;
The one for ever earn'd a royal husband;
The other for some while a friend.
            [*Giving her hand to* POLIXENES.
  *Leon.*      Too hot, too hot! [*Aside.*
To mingle friendship far is mingling bloods.
I have *tremor cordis* on me,—my heart dances;
But not for joy,—not joy.—This entertainment
May a free face put on; derive a liberty
From heartiness, from bounty, fertile bosom,
And well become the agent: 't may, I grant:
But to be paddling palms and pinching fingers,
As now they are; and making practis'd smiles,
As in a looking-glass; and then to sigh, as
    'twere
The mort o' the deer; O, that is entertainment
My bosom likes not, nor my brows,—Mamillius,
Art thou my boy?
  *Mam.*      Ay, my good lord.
  *Leon.*      I' fecks!
Why, that's my bawcock. What! hast smutch'd
    thy nose?—
They say it's a copy out of mine. Come, cap-
    tain,
We must be neat;—not neat, but cleanly, cap-
    tain:
And yet the steer, the heifer, and the calf,
Are all call'd neat.—Still virginalling
            [*Observing* POL. *and* HER.
Upon his palm?—How now, you wanton calf!
Art thou my calf?
  *Mam.*      Yes, if you will, my lord.
  *Leon.*  Thou want'st a rough pash, and the
    shoots that I have,
To be full like me:—yet they say we are
Almost as like as eggs; women say so,
That will say anything: but were they false
As o'erdyed blacks, as wind, as waters,—false
As dice are to be wish'd by one that fixes
No bourn 'twixt his and mine; yet were it true
To say this boy were like me.—Come, sir page,
Look on me with your welkin-eye: sweet vil-
    lain!               [may't be?
Most dear'st! my collop!—Can thy dam?—
Affection! thy intention stabs the centre:
Thou dost make possible things not so held,
Communicat'st with dreams;—how can this
    be?—

With what's unreal thou co-active art,
And fellow'st nothing: then 'tis very credent
Thou mayst co-join with something; and thou
    dost,—
And that beyond commission; and I find it,—
And that to the infection of my brains
And hardening of my brows.
  *Pol.*         What means Sicilia?
  *Her.* He something seems unsettled.
  *Pol.*         How! my lord!
What cheer! how is't with you, best brother?
  *Her.*         You look
As if you held a brow of much distraction:
Are you mov'd, my lord?
  *Leon.*      No, in good earnest.—
How sometimes nature will betray its folly,
Its tenderness, and make itself a pastime
To harder bosoms! Looking on the lines
Of my boy's face, methoughts I did recoil
Twenty-three years; and saw myself unbreech'd,
In my green velvet coat; my dagger muzzled,
Lest it should bite its master, and so prove,
As ornaments oft do, too dangerous.
How like, methought, I then was to this kernel,
This quash, this gentleman.—Mine honest
    friend,
Will you take eggs for money?
  *Mam.* No, my lord, I'll fight.
  *Leon.* You will? Why, happy man be's dole!
    —My brother,
Are you so fond of your young prince as we
Do seem to be of ours?
  *Pol.*        If at home, sir,
He's all my exercise, my mirth, my matter:
Now my sworn friend, and then mine enemy;
My parasite, my soldier, statesman, all:
He makes a July's day short as December;
And with his varying childness cures in me
Thoughts that would thick my blood.
  *Leon.*      So stands this squire
Offic'd with me. We two will walk, my lord,
And leave you to your graver steps.—Her-
    mione,
How thou lov'st us show in our brother's wel-
    come;
Let what is dear in Sicily be cheap:
Next to thyself and my young rover, he's
Apparent to my heart.
  *Her.*        If you would seek us,
We are your's i' the garden: shall's attend you
    there?                [be found,
  *Leon.* To your own bents dispose you: you'll
Be you beneath the sky. [*Aside.*] I am angling
    now.
Though you perceive me not how I give line.
Go to, go to!     [*Observing* POL. *and* HER.
How she holds up the neb, the bill to him!
And arms her with the boldness of a wife
To her allowing husband! Gone already!
        [*Exeunt* POL., HER., *and* Attendants.
Inch-thick, knee-deep, o'er head and ears a
    fork'd one!—
Go, play, boy, play:—thy mother plays, and I
Play too; but so disgrac'd a part, whose issue

Will hiss me to my grave: contempt and
          clamour          [have been,
Will be my knell.—Go, play, boy, play.—There
Or I am much deceiv'd, cuckolds ere now;
And many a man there is, even at this present,
Now while I speak this, holds his wife by the
          arm,          [absence,
That little thinks she has been sluic'd in his
And his pond fish'd by his next neighbour, by
Sir Smile, his neighbour: nay, there's comfort
          in't,          [open'd,
Whiles other men have gates, and those gates
As mine, against their will: should all despair
That have revolted wives, the tenth of mankind.
Would hang themselves. Physic for't there is
          none;
It is a bawdy planet, that will strike
Where 'tis predominant; and 'tis powerful,
          think it,
From east, west, north, and south: be it con-
          cluded,
No barricado for a belly; know't;
It will let in and out the enemy
With bag and baggage: many a thousand of us
Have the disease, and feel't not.—How now,
          boy!
  *Mam.* I am like you, they say.
  *Leon.*          Why, that's some comfort.—
What! Camillo there?
  *Cam.* Ay, my good lord.
  *Leon.* Go play, Mamillius; thou'rt an honest
          man.—          [*Exit* MAMILLIUS.
Camillo, this great sir will yet stay longer.
  *Cam.* You had much ado to make his anchor
          hold:
When you cast out, it still came home.
  *Leon.*          Didst note it?
  *Cam.* He would not stay at your petitions;
          made
His business more material.
  *Leon.*          Didst perceive it?—
They're here with me already; whispering,
          rounding,
*Sicilia is a so-forth:* 'tis far gone
When I shall gust it last.—How cam't, Camillo,
That he did stay?
  *Cam.*          At the good queen's entreaty.
  *Leon.* At the queen's be't: good should be
          pertinent;
But so it is, it is not. Was this taken
By any understanding pate but thine?
For thy conceit is soaking, will draw in
More than the common blocks:—not noted, is't,
But of the finer natures? by some severals
Of head-piece extraordinary? lower messes,
Perchance are to this business purblind? say.
  *Cam.* Business, my lord! I think most under-
          stand
Bohemia stays here longer.
  *Leon.*          Ha!
  *Cam.*          Stays here longer.
  *Leon.* Ay, but why?          [treaties
  *Cam.* To satisfy your highness, and the en-
Of our most gracious mistress.

  *Leon.*          Satisfy
The entreaties of your mistress!—satisfy!—
Let that suffice. I have trusted thee, Camillo,
With all the nearest things to my heart, as well
My chamber-councils, wherein, priest-like,
          thou
Hast cleans'd my bosom; I from thee departed
Thy penitent reform'd: but we have been
Deceiv'd in thy integrity, deceiv'd
In that which seems so.
  *Cam.*          Be it forbid, my lord!
  *Leon.* To bide upon't,—thou art not honest;
          or,
If thou inclin'st that way, thou art a coward,
Which hoxes honesty behind, restraining
From course requir'd; or else thou must be
          counted
A servant grafted in my serious trust,
And therein negligent; or else a fool,
That seest a game play'd home, the rich stake
          drawn,
And tak'st it all for jest.
  *Cam.*          My gracious lord,
I may be negligent, foolish, and fearful;
In every one of these no man is free,
But that his negligence, his folly, fear,
Amongst the infinite doings of the world,
Sometime puts forth: in your affairs, my lord,
If ever I were wilful-negligent,
It was my folly; if industriously
I play'd the fool, it was my negligence,
Not weighing well the end; if ever fearful
To do a thing, where I the issue doubted,
Whereof the execution did cry out
Against the non-performance, 'twas a fear
Which oft affects the wisest: these, my lord,
Are such allow'd infirmities that honesty
Is never free of. But, beseech your grace,
Be plainer with me; let me know my trespass
By its own visage: if I then deny it,
'Tis none of mine.
  *Leon.*          Have you not seen, Camillo,—
But that's past doubt: you have, or your eye-
          glass
Is thicker than a cuckold's horn,—or heard,—
For, to a vision so apparent, rumour
Cannot be mute,—or thought,—for cogitation
Resides not in that man that does not think
          it,—
My wife is slippery? If thou wilt confess,—
Or else be impudently negative,
To have nor eyes nor ears nor thought,—then
          say
My wife's a hobbyhorse; deserves a name
As rank as any flax-wench that puts to
Before her troth-plight: say't and justify't.
  *Cam.* I would not be a stander-by to hear
My sovereign mistress clouded so, without
My present vengeance taken: 'shrew my heart,
You never spoke what did become you less
Than this; which to reiterate were sin
As deep as that, though true.
  *Leon.*          Is whispering nothing?
Is leaning cheek to cheek? is meeting noses?

Kissing with inside lip? stopping the career
Of laughter with a sigh?—a note infallible
Of breaking honesty;—horsing foot on foot?
Skulking in corners? wishing clocks more swift?
Hours, minutes? noon, midnight? and all eyes
Blind with the pin and web, but theirs, theirs
 only,
That would unseen be wicked?—is this nothing?
Why, then the world and all that's in't is no-
 thing;
The covering sky is nothing; Bohemia nothing;
My wife is nothing; nor nothing have these no-
 things,
If this be nothing.
 *Cam.*   Good my lord, be cur'd
Of this diseas'd opinion, and betimes;
For 'tis most dangerous.
 *Leon.*   Say it be, 'tis true.
 *Cam.* No, no, my lord!
 *Leon.*   It is; you lie, you lie:
I say thou liest, Camillo, and I hate thee;
Pronounce thee a gross lout, a mindless slave;
Or else a hovering temporizer, that
Canst with thine eyes at once see good and evil,
Inclining to them both.—Were my wife's liver
Infected as her life, she would not live
The running of one glass.
 *Cam.*   Who does infect her?
 *Leon.* Why, he that wears her like her medal,
 hanging
About his neck, Bohemia: who—if I
Had servants true about me, that bare eyes
To see alike mine honour as their profits,
Their own particular thrifts,—they would do
 that
Which should undo more doing: ay, and thou,
His cupbearer,—whom I from meaner form
Have bench'd and rear'd to worship; who
 mayst see      [heaven,
Plainly, as heaven sees earth, and earth sees
How I am galled,—mightst bespice a cup,
To give mine enemy a lasting wink;
Which draught to me were cordial.
 *Cam.*   Sir, my lord,
I could do this; and that with no rash potion,
But with a ling'ring dram, that should not work
Maliciously like poison: but I cannot
Believe this crack to be in my dread mistress,
So sovereignly being honourable.
I have lov'd thee,—
 *Leon.* Make that thy question, and go rot!
Dost think I am so muddy, so unsettled,
To appoint myself in this vexation; sully
The purity and whiteness of my sheets,—
Which to preserve is sleep; which being spotted
Is goads, thorns, nettles, tails of wasps,—
Give scandal to the blood o' the prince my son,—
Who I do think is mine, and love as mine,—
Without ripe moving to't?—Would I do this?
Could man so blench?
 *Cam.*   I must believe you, sir:
I do; and will fetch off Bohemia for't; [ness
Provided that, when he's remov'd, your high-
Will take again your queen as yours at first,

Even for your son's sake; and thereby for seal-
 ing
The injury of tongues in courts and kingdoms
Known and allied to yours.
 *Leon.*   Thou dost advise me
Even so as I mine own course have set down:
I'll give no blemish to her honour, none.
 *Cam.* My lord,
Go then; and with a countenance as clear
As friendship wears at feasts, keep with Bohemia
And with your queen: I am his cupbearer.
If from me he have wholesome beverage
Account me not your servant.
 *Leon.*   This is all:
Do't and thou hast the one-half of my heart;
Do't not, thou splitt'st thine own.
 *Cam.*   I'll do't, my lord.
 *Leon.* I will seem friendly, as thou hast
 advis'd me.       [*Exit.*
 *Cam.* O miserable lady!—But, for me,
What case stand I in? I must be the poisoner
Of good Polixenes: and my ground to do't
Is the obedience to a master; one
Who, in rebellion with himself, will have
All that are his so too.—To do this deed,
Promotion follows: if I could find example
Of thousands that had struck anointed kings,
And flourish'd after, I'd not do't; but since
Nor brass, nor stone, nor parchment, bears not
 one,
Let villany itself forswear't. I must
Forsake the court: to do't, or no, is certain
To me a break-neck. Happy star, reign now!
Here comes Bohemia.

    *Enter* POLIXENES.

 *Pol.*   This is strange! methinks
My favour here begins to warp. Not speak?—
Good-day, Camillo.
 *Cam.*   Hail, most royal sir!
 *Pol.* What is the news i' the court?
 *Cam.*   None rare, my lord.
 *Pol.* The king hath on him such a counten-
 ance
As he had lost some province, and a region
Lov'd as he loves himself: even now I met him
With customary compliment; when he,
Wafting his eyes to the contrary, and falling
A lip of much contempt, speeds from me; and
So leaves me, to consider what is breeding
That changes thus his manners.
 *Cam.* I dare not know, my lord.
 *Pol.* How! dare not! do not. Do you know,
 and dare not
Be intelligent to me? 'Tis thereabouts;
For, to yourself, what you do know, you must,
And cannot say, you dare not. Good Camillo,
Your chang'd complexions are to me a mirror,
Which shows me mine chang'd too; for I must
 be
A party in this alteration, finding
Myself thus alter'd with it.
 *Cam.*   There is a sickness
Which puts some of us in distemper; but

I cannot name the disease; and it is caught
Of you that yet are well.

*Pol.*　　　　　　　How! caught of me!
Make me not sighted like the basilisk:
I have look'd on thousands, who have sped the
　　better
By my regard, but kill'd none so. Camillo,—
As you are certainly a gentleman; thereto
Clerk-like, experienc'd, which no less adorns
Our gentry than our parents' noble names,
In whose success we are gentle,—I beseech you,
If you know aught which does behove my
　　knowledge
Thereof to be inform'd, imprison't not
In ignorant concealment.

*Cam.*　　　　　　　I may not answer.

*Pol.* A sickness caught of me, and yet I well!
I must be answer'd.—Dost thou hear, Camillo,
I cónjure thee, by all the parts of man,
Which honour does acknowledge,—whereof the
　　least
Is not this suit of mine,—that thou declare
What incidency thou dost guess of harm
Is creeping toward me; how far off, how near;
Which way to be prevented, if to be;
If not, how best to bear it.

*Cam.*　　　　　　Sir, I will tell you;
Since I am charg'd in honour, and by him
That I think honourable: therefore mark my
　　counsel,
Which must be even as swiftly follow'd as
I mean to utter it, or both yourself and me
Cry lost, and so good-night!

*Pol.*　　　　　　　On, good Camillo.

*Cam.* I am appointed him to murder you.

*Pol.* By whom, Camillo?

*Cam.*　　　　　　　By the king.

*Pol.*　　　　　　　For what?

*Cam.* He thinks, nay, with all confidence he
　　swears,
As he had seen't or been an instrument
To vice you to't, that you have touch'd his queen
Forbiddingly.

*Pol.*　　　　O, then my best blood turn
To an infected jelly, and my name
Be yok'd with his that did betray the best!
Turn then my freshest reputation to
A savour that may strike the dullest nostril
Where I arrive, and my approach be shunn'd,
Nay, hated too, worse than the great'st infection
That e'er was heard or read!

*Cam.*　　　　　　Swear his thought over
By each particular star in heaven and
By all their influences, you may as well
Forbid the sea for to obey the moon,
As, or by oath remove, or counsel shake
The fabric of his folly, whose foundation
Is pil'd upon his faith, and will continue
The standing of his body.

*Pol.*　　　　　How should this grow?

*Cam.* I know not: but I am sure 'tis safer to
Avoid what's grown than question how 'tis
　　born.
If, therefore, you dare trust my honesty,—

That lies enclosed in this trunk, which you
Shall bear along impawn'd,—away to-night.
Your followers I will whisper to the business;
And will, by twos and threes, at several pos-
　　terns,
Clear them o' the city: for myself, I'll put
My fortunes to your service, which are here
By this discovery lost. Be not uncertain;
For, by the honour of my parents, I
Have utter'd truth: which if you seek to prove,
I dare not stand by; nor shall you be safer
Than one condemn'd by the king's own mouth,
　　thereon
His execution sworn.

*Pol.*　　　　　　I do believe thee;
I saw his heart in his face. Give me thy hand;
Be pilot to me, and thy places shall
Still neighbour mine. My ships are ready, and
My people did expect my hence departure
Two days ago.—This jealousy
Is for a precious creature: as she's rare,
Must it be great; and, as his person's mighty,
Must it be violent; and as he does conceive
He is dishonour'd by a man which ever
Profess'd to him, why, his revenges must
In that be made more bitter. Fear o'ershades
　　me:
Good expedition be my friend, and comfort
The gracious queen, part of his theme, but no-
　　thing
Of his ill ta'en suspicion! Come, Camillo;
I will respect thee as a father, if
Thou bear'st my life off hence: let us avoid.

*Cam.* It is in mine authority to command
The keys of all the posterns: please your high-
　　ness
To take the urgent hour: come, sir, away.
　　　　　　　　　　　　　　　　*[Exeunt.*

## ACT II.

### SCENE I.—SICILIA. *A Room in the Palace.*

*Enter* HERMIONE, MAMILLIUS, *and* Ladies.

*Her.* Take the boy to you: he so troubles me,
'Tis past enduring.

*1 Lady.*　　　Come, my gracious lord,
Shall I be your playfellow?

*Mam.*　　　　　　No, I'll none of you.

*1 Lady.* Why, my sweet lord?

*Mam.* You'll kiss me hard, and speak to me
　　as if
I were a baby still.—I love you better.

*2 Lady.* And why so, my lord?

*Mam.*　　　　　　Not for because
Your brows are blacker; yet black brows, they
　　say,
Become some women best; so that there be not
Too much hair there, but in a semicircle,
Or a half-moon made with a pen.

*2 Lady.*　　　　　Who taught you this?

*Mam.* I learn'd it out of women's faces.—
　　Pray now,
What colour are your eyebrows?

*1 Lady.*　　　　　Blue, my lord.

*Mam.* Nay, that's a mock: I have seen a
    lady's nose
That has been blue, but not her eyebrows.
  1 *Lady.*               Hark ye;
The queen your mother rounds apace: we shall
Present our services to a fine new prince
One of these days; and then you'd wanton
    with us,
If we would have you.
  2 *Lady.*         She is spread of late
Into a goodly bulk: good time encounter her!
  *Her.* What wisdom stirs amongst you?
    Come, sir, now
I am for you again: pray you, sit by us,
And tell's a tale.
  *Mam.*     Merry or sad shall't be?
  *Her.* As merry as you will.
  *Mam.*       A sad tale's best for winter:
I have one of sprites and goblins.
  *Her.* Let's have that, good sir.
Come on, sit down:—come on, and do your best
To fright me with your sprites: you're powerful
    at it.
  *Mam.* There was a man,—
  *Her.*     Nay, come, sit down: then on.
  *Mam.* Dwelt by a churchyard:—I will tell it
    softly;
Yond crickets shall not hear it.
  *Her.*         Come on, then,
And give't me in mine ear.

*Enter* LEONTES, ANTIGONUS, Lords *and* Guards.

  *Leon.* Was he met there? his train? Camillo
    with him?            [*never*
  1 *Lord.* Behind the tuft of pines I met them;
Saw I men scour so on their way: I ey'd them
Even to their ships.
  *Leon.*       How bless'd am I
In my just censure, in my true opinion!—
Alack, for lesser knowledge!—how accurs'd,
In being so blest!—There may be in the cup
A spider steep'd, and one may drink, depart,
And yet partake no venom; for his knowledge
Is not infected: but if one present
The abhorr'd ingredient to his eye, make
    known            [*sides*
How he hath drunk, he cracks his gorge, his
With violent hefts:—I have drunk, and seen
    the spider.
Camillo was his help in this, his pander:—
There is a plot against my life, my crown;
All's true that is mistrusted:—that false villain,
Whom I employ'd, was pre-employ'd by him:
He has discover'd my design, and I
Remain a pinch'd thing; yea, a very trick
For them to play at will.—How came the
    posterns
So easily open?
  1 *Lord.*   By his great authority;
Which often hath no less prevail'd than so,
On your command.
  *Leon.*     I know't too well.—
Give me the boy:—I am glad you did not
    nurse him:

Though he does bear some signs of me, yet you
Have too much blood in him.
  *Her.*         What is this? sport?
  *Leon.* Bear the boy hence; he shall not come
    about her;
Away with him!—and let her sport herself
    [*Exit* MAMILLIUS, *with some of the* Guards.
With that she's big with;—for 'tis Polixenes
Hath made thee swell thus.
  *Her.*       But I'd say he had not,
And I'll be sworn you would believe my saying,
Howe'er you learn the nayward.
  *Leon.*          You, my lords,
Look on her, mark her well; be but about
To say, *she is a goodly lady,* and
The justice of your hearts will thereto add,
*'Tis pity she's not honest, honourable:*
Praise her but for this her without-door form,—
Which, on my faith, deserves high speech,—
    and straight
The shrug, the hum, or ha,—these petty brands,
That calumny doth use:—O, I am out,
That mercy does; for calumny will sear
Virtue itself:—these shrugs, these hums, and
    ha's,
When you have said *she's goodly,* come between,
Ere you can say *she's honest:* but be it known,
From him that has most cause to grieve it
    should be,
She's an adultress!
  *Her.*       Should a villain say so,
The most replenish'd villain in the world,
He were as much more villain: you, my lord,
Do but mistake.
  *Leon.*     You have mistook, my lady,
Polixenes for Leontes: O thou thing,
Which I'll not call a creature of thy place,
Lest barbarism, making me the precedent,
Should a like language use to all degrees,
And mannerly distinguishment leave out
Betwixt the prince and beggar!—I have said,
She's an adultress; I have said with whom:
More, she's a traitor; and Camillo is
A federary with her; and one that knows
What she should shame to know herself
But with her most vile principal, that she's
A bed-swerver, even as bad as those
That vulgars give boldest titles; ay, and privy
To this their late escape.
  *Her.*      No, by my life,
Privy to none of this. How will this grieve you,
When you shall come to clearer knowledge, that
You thus have publish'd me! Gentle, my lord
You scarce can right me throughly then, to say
You did mistake.
  *Leon.*     No; if I mistake
In those foundations which I build upon,
The centre is not big enough to bear
A school-boy's top.—Away with her to
    prison!
He who shall speak for her is afar off guilty
But that he speaks.
  *Her.*      There's some ill planet reigns:
I must be patient till the heavens look

With an aspect more favourable.—Good my
 lords,
I am not prone to weeping, as our sex
Commonly are; the want of which vain dew
Perchance shall dry your pities; but I have
That honourable grief lodg'd here, which burns
Worse than tears drown: beseech you all, my
 lords,
With thoughts so qualified as your charities
Shall best instruct you, measure me;—and so
The king's will be perform'd!

 *Leon.*        Shall I be heard?
          [*To the* Guards.

 *Her.* Who is't that goes with me?—Beseech
 your highness,
My women may be with me; for you see,
My plight requires it.—Do not weep, good fools;
There is no cause: when you shall know your
 mistress
Has deserv'd prison, then abound in tears
As I come out: this action I now go on
Is for my better grace.—Adieu, my lord:
I never wish'd to see you sorry; now  [leave.
I trust I shall.—My women, come; you have

 *Leon.* Go, do our bidding; hence!
   [*Exeunt* QUEEN *and* Ladies, *with* Guards.

 1 *Lord.* Beseech your highness, call the
 queen again.

 *Ant.* Be certain what you do, sir, lest your
 justice         [suffer,
Prove violence: in the which three great ones
Yourself, your queen, your son.

 1 *Lord.*       For her, my lord,—
I dare my life lay down, and will do't, sir,
Please you to accept it, that the queen is spot-
 less
I' the eyes of heaven and to you; I mean
In this which you accuse her.

 *Ant.*        If it prove
She's otherwise, I'll keep my stables where
I lodge my wife; I'll go in couples with her;
Than when I feel and see her no further trust
 her;
For every inch of woman in the world,
Ay, every dram of woman's flesh, is false,
If she be.

 *Leon.* Hold your peaces.

 1 *Lord.*       Good my lord,—

 *Ant.* It is for you we speak, not for ourselves:
You are abus'd. and by some putter-on,
That will be damn'd for't: would I knew the
 villain,        [flaw'd,—
I would land-damn him. Be she honour-
I have three daughters; the eldest is eleven;
The second and the third, nine and some five;
If this prove true, they'll pay for't: by mine
 honour,
I'll geld 'em all: fourteen they shall not see,
To bring false generations: they are co-heirs;
And I had rather glib myself than they
Should not produce fair issue.

 *Leon.*      Cease; no more.
You smell this business with a sense as cold
As is a dead man's nose: but I do see't and feel't,

As you feel doing thus; and see withal
The instruments that feel.

 *Ant.*       If it be so,
We need no grave to bury honesty;
There's not a grain of it the face to sweeten
Of the whole dungy earth.

 *Leon.*      What! lack I credit?

 1 *Lord.* I had rather you did lack than I, my
 lord,           [me
Upon this ground: and more it would content
To have her honour true than your suspicion;
Be blam'd for't how you might.

 *Leon.*      Why, what need we
Commune with you of this, but rather follow
Our forceful instigation? Our prerogative
Calls not your counsels, but our natural good-
 ness
Imparts this: which, if you,—or stupefied
Or seeming so in skill,—cannot or will not
Relish a truth, like us, inform yourselves
We need no more of your advice: the matter,
The loss, the gain, the ordering on't, is all
Properly ours.

 *Ant.*    And I wish, my liege,
You had only in your silent judgment tried it,
Without more overture.

 *Leon.*      How could that be?
Either thou art most ignorant by age,
Or thou wert born a fool. Camillo's flight,
Added to their familiarity,—
Which was as gross as ever touch'd conjecture,
That lack'd sight only, naught for approbation,
But only seeing, all other circumstances
Made up to the deed,—doth push on this pro-
 ceeding.
Yet, for a greater confirmation,—
For, in an act of this importance, 'twere
Most piteous to be wild,—I have despatch'd in
 post
To sacred Delphos, to Apollo's temple,
Cleomenes and Dion, whom you know
Of stuff'd sufficiency: now, from the oracle
They will bring all; whose spiritual counsel had,
Shall stop or spur me. Have I done well?

 1 *Lord.* Well done, my lord.

 *Leon.* Though I am satisfied, and need no more
Than what I know, yet shall the oracle
Give rest to the minds of others such as he
Whose ignorant credulity will not  [good
Come up to the truth: so have we thought it
From our free person she should be confin'd;
Lest that the treachery of the two fled hence
Be left her to perform. Come, follow us;
We are to speak in public; for this business
Will raise us all.

 *Ant.* [*Aside.*] To laughter, as I take it,
If the good truth were known.   [*Exeunt.*

SCENE II.—*The same. The outer Room of a
Prison.*

*Enter* PAULINA *and* Attendants.

 *Paul.* The keeper of the prison,—call to him;
Let him have knowledge who I am.
        [*Exit an* Attendant.

Good lady!
No court in Europe is too good for thee;
What dost thou, then, in prison?

*Re-enter* Attendant, *with the* Keeper.

Now, good sir.
You know me, do you not?
   *Keep.*           For a worthy lady,
And one who much I honour.
   *Paul.*           Pray you, then,
Conduct me to the queen.
   *Keep.* I may not, madam: to the contrary
I have express commandment.
   *Paul.*           Here's ado,
To lock up honesty and honour from
The access of gentle visitors!—Is't lawful,
Pray you, to see her women? any of them?
Emilia?
   *Keep.* So please you, madam, to put
Apart these your attendants, I shall bring
Emilia forth.
   *Paul.*    I pray now, call her.—
Withdraw yourselves.          [*Exeunt* Attend.
   *Keep.*         And, madam,
I must be present at your conference.
   *Paul.* Well, be't so, pr'ythee. [*Exit* Keeper.
Here's such ado to make no stain a stain,
As passes colouring.

*Re-enter* Keeper, *with* EMILIA.

Dear gentlewoman, how fares our gracious
    lady?
   *Emil.* As well as one so great and so forlorn
May hold together: on her frights and griefs,—
Which never tender lady hath borne greater,—
She is, something before her time, deliver'd.
   *Paul.* A boy?
   *Emil.*    A daughter; and a goodly babe,
Lusty, and like to live: the queen receives
Much comfort in't; says, *My poor prisoner,
I am innocent as you.*
   *Paul.*        I dare be sworn:—
These dangerous unsafe lunes i' the king, be-
    shrew them!
He must be told on't, and he shall: the office
Becomes a woman best: I'll take't upon me:
If I prove honey-mouth'd, let my tongue glis-
    ter;
And never to my red-look'd anger be
The trumpet any more.—Pray you, Emilia,
Commend my best obedience to the queen;
If she dares trust me with her little babe,
I'll show't the king, and undertake to be
Her advocate to the loud'st. We do not know
How he may soften at the sight o' the child:
The silence often of pure innocence
Persuades, when speaking fails.
   *Emil.*    Most worthy madam,
Your honour and your goodness is so evident,
That your free undertaking cannot miss
A thriving issue: there is no lady living
So meet for this great errand. Please your lady-
    ship
To visit the next room, I'll presently

Acquaint the queen of your most noble offer.
Who but to-day hammer'd of this design,
But durst not tempt a minister of honour,
Lest she should be denied.
   *Paul.*       Tell her, Emilia,
I'll use that tongue I have: if wit flow from it,
As boldness from my bosom, let it not be
    doubted
I shall do good.
   *Emil.*    Now be you bless'd for it!
I'll to the queen: please you come something
    nearer.
   *Keep.* Madam, if't please the queen to send
    the babe,
I know not what I shall incur to pass it?
Having no warrant.
   *Paul.* You need not fear it, sir:
The child was prisoner to the womb, and is,
By law and process of great nature, thence
Freed and enfranchis'd, not a party to
The anger of the king, nor guilty of,
If any be, the trespass of the queen.
   *Keep.* I do believe it.
   *Paul.* Do not you fear: upon mine honour, I
Will stand 'twixt you and danger.   [*Exeunt.*

SCENE III.—*The same. A Room in the Palace.*

*Enter* LEONTES, ANTIGONUS, Lords, *and
other* Attendants.

   *Leon.* Nor night nor day no rest: it is but
    weakness
To bear the matter thus,—mere weakness. If
The cause were not in being,—part o' the cause.
She the adultress; for the harlot king
Is quite beyond mine arm, out of the blank
And level of my brain, plot-proof; but she
I can hook to me:—say that she were gone,
Given to the fire, a moiety of my rest
Might come to me again.—Who's there?
   1 *Atten.* [*Advancing.*]          My lord?
   *Leon.* How does the boy?
   1 *Atten.*    He took good rest to-night;
'Tis hop'd his sickness is discharg'd.
   *Leon.* To see his nobleness!
Conceiving the dishonour of his mother,
He straight declin'd, droop'd, took it deeply,
Fasten'd and fix'd the shame on't in himself,
Threw off his spirit, his appetite, his sleep,
And downright languish'd.—Leave me solely:
    —go,
See how he fares. [*Exit* 1 Attend.]—Fie, fie! no
    thought of him;
The very thought of my revenges that way
Recoil upon me: in himself too mighty,
And in his parties, his alliance,—let him be,
Until a time may serve: for present vengeance,
Take it on her. Camillo and Polixenes
Laugh at me; make their pastime at my sorrow.
They should not laugh if I could reach them;
    nor
Shall she, within my power.

*Enter* PAULINA, *with a child.*

   1 *Lord.*        You must not enter.

*Paul.* Nay, rather, good my lords, be second
　　to me:
Fear you his tyrannous passion more, alas,
Than the queen's life? a gracious innocent soul,
More free than he is jealous.

*Ant.*　　　　　　That's enough.

*2 Attend.* Madam, he hath not slept tonight;
　　commanded
None should come at him.

*Paul.*　　　　Not so hot, good sir;
I come to bring him sleep. 'Tis such as you,—
That creep like shadows by him, and do sigh
At each his needless heavings,—such as you
Nourish the cause of his awaking: I
Do come, with words as med'cinal as true,
Honest as either, to purge him of that humour
That presses him from sleep.

*Leon.*　　　　What noise there, ho?

*Paul.* No noise, my lord; but needful con-
　　ference
About some gossips for your highness.

*Leon.*　　　　　　How!—
Away with that audacious lady!—Antigonus,
I charg'd thee that she should not come about
　　me:
I knew she would.

*Ant.*　　　I told her so, my lord,
On your displeasure's peril, and on mine,
She should not visit you.

*Leon.* What, canst not rule her?

*Paul.* From all dishonesty, he can: in this,—
Unless he take the course that you have done,
Commit me for committing honour,—trust it,
He shall not rule me.

*Ant.*　　　La you now, you hear!
When she will take the rein, I let her run;
But she'll not stumble.

*Paul.*　　　Good my liege, I come,—
And, I beseech you, hear me, who professes
Myself your loyal servant, your physician,
Your most obedient counsellor; yet that dares
Less appear so, in comforting your evils,
Than such as most seem yours:—I say, I
　　come
From your good queen.

*Leon.*　　　　Good queen!

*Paul.* Good queen, my lord, good queen: I
　　say, good queen;
And would by combat make her good, so were I
A man, the worst about you.

*Leon.*　　　　Force her hence!

*Paul.* Let him that makes but trifles of his
　　eyes
First hand me: on mine own accord I'll off;
But first I'll do my errand.—The good queen,
For she is good, hath brought you forth a
　　daughter;
Here 'tis; commends it to your blessing.
　　　　　　　　[*Laying down the child.*

*Leon.*　　　　　　Out!
A mankind-witch! Hence with her, out o' door:
A most intelligencing bawd!

*Paul.*　　　　Not so:
I am as ignorant in that as you

In so entitling me; and no less honest　　[rant
Than you are mad; which is enough, I'll war-
As this world goes, to pass for honest.

*Leon.*　　　　　　Traitors!
Will you not push her out? Give her the
　　bastard:—
Thou dotard [*to* ANTIGONUS], thou art woman-
　　tir'd, unroosted
By thy dame Partlet here:—take up the
　　bastard;
Take't up, I say; give't to thy crone.

*Paul.*　　　　　　For ever
Unvenerable be thy hands, if thou
Tak'st up the princess, by that forced baseness
Which he has put upon't!

*Leon.*　　　He dreads his wife.

*Paul.* So I would you did; then 'twere past
　　all doubt,
You'd call your children yours.

*Leon.*　　　　A nest of traitors!

*Ant.* I am none, by this good light.

*Paul.*　　　　Nor I; nor any,
But one, that's here; and that's himself: for he
The sacred honour of himself, his queen's,
His hopeful son's, his babe's, betrays to slander,
Whose sting is sharper than the sword's; and
　　will not,—
For, as the case now stands, it is a curse
He cannot be compell'd to't,—once remove
The root of his opinion, which is rotten
As ever oak or stone was sound.

*Leon.*　　　　　A callat
Of boundless tongue, who late hath beat her
　　husband,
And now baits me!—This brat is none of mine;
It is the issue of Polixenes:
Hence with it! and, together with the dam,
Commit them to the fire.

*Paul.*　　　　It is yours! [*charge,*
And, might we lay the old proverb to your
So like you, 'tis the worse.—Behold, my lords,
Although the print be little, the whole matter
And copy of the father,—eye, nose, lip,
The trick of his frown, his forehead; nay, the
　　valley,　　　　　　　[*smiles;*
The pretty dimples of his chin and cheek; his
The very mould and frame of hand, nail,
　　finger:—　　　　　　[*made it*
And thou, good goddess Nature, which hast
So like to him that got it, if thou hast
The ordering of the mind too, 'mongst all
　　colours
No yellow in't, lest she suspect, as he does,
Her children not her husband's!

*Leon.*　　　　　A gross hag!
And, losel, thou art not worthy to be hang'd,
That wilt not stay her tongue.

*Ant.*　　　Hang all the husbands
That cannot do that feat, you'll leave yourself
Hardly one subject.

*Leon.*　　　Once more, take her hence.

*Paul.* A most unworthy and unnatural lord
Can do no more.

*Leon.*　　　I'll have thee burn'd.

*Paul.*                    I care not.
It is an heretic that makes the fire,    [tyrant;
Not she which burns in't. I'll not call you
But this most cruel usage of your queen,—
Not able to produce more accusation [savours
Than your own weak-hing'd fancy,—something
Of tyranny, and will ignoble make you,
Yea, scandalous to the world.
    *Leon.*            On your allegiance,
Out of the chamber with her! Were I a tyrant,
Where were her life? she durst not call me so,
If she did know me one. Away with her!
    *Paul.* I pray you, do not push me; I'll be
        gone.—                     [send her
Look to your babe, my lord; 'tis yours: Jove
A better guiding spirit!—What needs these
        hands?
You, that are thus so tender o'er his follies,
Will never do him good, not one of you.
So, so:—farewell; we are gone.    [*Exit.*
    *Leon.* Thou, traitor, hast set on thy wife to
        this.—
My child? away with't!—even thou, that hast
A heart so tender o'er it, take it hence,
And see it instantly consum'd with fire;
Even thou, and none but thou. Take it up
        straight:
Within this hour bring me word 'tis done,—
And by good testimony,—or I'll seize thy life,
With what thou else call'st thine. If thou refuse,
And wilt encounter with my wrath, say so;
The bastard-brains with these my proper hands
Shall I dash out. Go, take it to the fire;
For thou sett'st on thy wife.
    *Ant.*                I did not, sir:
These lords, my noble fellows, if they please,
Can clear me in't.
    1 *Lord.*      We can:—my royal liege,
He is not guilty of her coming hither.
    *Leon.* You are liars all.          [credit:
    1 *Lord.* Beseech your highness, give us better
We have always truly serv'd you; and beseech
So to esteem of us: and on our knees we beg,—
As recompense of our dear services,
Past and to come,—that you do change this
        purpose,
Which, being so horrible, so bloody, must
Lead on to some foul issue: we all kneel.
    *Leon.* I am a feather for each wind that
        blows:—
Shall I live on, to see this bastard kneel
And call me father? better burn it now,
Than curse it then. But, be it; let it live:—
It shall not neither.—You, sir, come you hither:
                              [*To* ANTIGONUS.
You that have been so tenderly officious
With Lady Margery, your midwife, there,
To save this bastard's life,—for 'tis a bastard,
So sure as thy beard's gray,—what will you
        adventure
To save this brat's life?
    *Ant.*           Anything, my lord,
That my ability may undergo,
And nobleness impose: at least, thus much;

I'll pawn the little blood which I have left,
To save the innocent:—anything possible.
    *Leon.* It shall be possible. Swear by this
        sword
Thou wilt perform my bidding.
    *Ant.*            I will, my lord.
    *Leon.* Mark, and perform it,—seest thou? for
        the fail
Of any point in't shall not only be
Death to thyself, but to thy lewd-tongu'd wife,
Whom for this time we pardon. We enjoin thee,
As thou art liegeman to us, that thou carry
This female bastard hence; and that thou bear
        it
To some remote and desert place, quite out
Of our dominions; and that there thou leave it,
Without more mercy, to its own protection
And favour of the climate. As by strange for-
        tune
It came to us, I do in justice charge thee,
On thy soul's peril and thy body's torture,
That thou commend it strangely to some place,
Where chance may nurse or end it. Take it up.
    *Ant.* I swear to do this, though a present
        death
Had been more merciful.—Come on, poor babe:
Some powerful spirit instruct the kites and
        ravens
To be thy nurses! Wolves and bears, they say,
Casting their savageness aside, have done
Like offices of pity.—Sir, be prosperous  [ing,
In more than this deed does require!—and bless-
Against this cruelty, fight on thy side,
Poor thing, condemn'd to loss!
                        [*Exit with the child.*
    *Leon.*            No, I'll not rear
Another's issue.
    2 *Attend.*   Please your highness, posts,
From those you sent to the oracle, are come
An hour since: Cleomenes and Dion,
Being well arriv'd from Delphos, are both landed,
Hasting to the court.
    1 *Lord.*     So please you, sir, their speed
Hath been beyond account.
    *Leon.*             Twenty-three days
They have been absent: 'tis good speed; fore-
        tells
The great Apollo suddenly will have
The truth of this appear. Prepare you, lords;
Summon a session, that we may arraign
Our most disloyal lady; for, as she hath
Been publicly accus'd, so shall she have
A just and open trial. While she lives,
My heart will be a burden to me. Leave me;
And think upon my bidding.       [*Exeunt.*

## ACT III.

SCENE I.—SICILIA. *A street in some Town.*

*Enter* CLEOMENES *and* DION.

    *Cleo.* The climate's delicate; the air most
        sweet;
Fertile the isle; the temple much surpassing
The common praise it bears.

*Dion.*                    I shall report,
For most it caught me, the celestial habits,—
Methinks I so should term them,—and the
     reverence
Of the grave wearers. O, the sacrifice!
How ceremonious, solemn, and unearthly
It was i' the offering!
*Cleo.*              But, of all, the burst
And the ear-deafening voice o' the oracle,
Kin to Jove's thunder, so surprised my sense
That I was nothing.
*Dion.*            If the event o' the journey
Prove as successful to the queen,—O, be't so!—
As it hath been to us rare, pleasant, speedy,
The time is worth the use on't.
*Cleo.*                    Great Apollo
Turn all to the best! These proclamations,
So forcing faults upon Hermione,
I little like.
*Dion.*        The violent carriage of it
Will clear or end the business: when the oracle,—
Thus by Apollo's great divine seal'd up,—
Shall the contents discover, something rare
Even then will rush to knowledge.—Go,—
     fresh horses;—
And gracious be the issue!          [*Exeunt.*

SCENE II.—*The same. A Court of Justice.*

LEONTES, Lords, *and* Officers *appear, properly
     seated.*

*Leon.* This sessions,—to our great grief, we
     pronounce,—
Even pushes 'gainst our heart;—the party tried,
The daughter of a king, our wife; and one
Of us too much belov'd. Let us be clear'd
Of being tyrannous, since we so openly
Proceed in justice; which shall have due course,
Even to the guilt or the purgation.—
Produce the prisoner.
*Offi.* It is his highness' pleasure that the
     queen
Appear in person here in court.—
*Crier.* Silence!

HERMIONE *is brought in guarded;* PAULINA *and*
     Ladies *attending.*

*Leon.* Read the indictment.
*Offi.* [*Reads.*] Hermione, *queen to the worthy*
Leontes, *king of* Sicilia, *thou art here accused and
arraigned of high treason, in committing adultery
with* Polixenes, *king of Bohemia; and conspiring
with* Camilio *to take away the life of our sovereign
lord the king, thy royal husband: the pretence
whereof being by circumstances partly laid open,
thou,* Hermione, *contrary to the faith and allegiance of a true subject, didst counsel and aid
them, for their better safety, to fly away by night.*
*Her.* Since what I am to say must be but that
Which contradicts my accusation, and
The testimony on my part no other          [me
But what comes from myself, it shall scarce boot
To say, *Not guilty:* mine integrity
Being counted falsehood, shall, as I express it,

Be so receiv'd. But thus,—if powers divine
Behold our human actions,—as they do,—
I doubt not, then, but innocence shall make
False accusation blush, and tyranny [know,—
Tremble at patience.—You, my lord, best
Who least will seem to do so,—my past life
Hath been as continent, as chaste, as true,
As I am now unhappy: which is more
Than history can pattern, though devis'd
And play'd to take spectators; for, behold
     me,—
A fellow of the royal bed, which owe
A moiety of the throne, a great king's daughter,
The mother to a hopeful prince,—here standing
To prate and talk for life and honour 'fore [it
Who please to come and hear. For life, I prize
As I weigh grief, which I would spare: for honour,
'Tis a derivative from me to mine,
And only that I stand for. I appeal
To your own conscience, sir, before Polixenes
Came to your court, how I was in your grace,
How merited to be so; since he came,
With what encounter so uncurrent I
Have strain'd, to appear thus: if one jot beyond
The bound of honour, or in act or will
That way inclining, harden'd be the hearts
Of all that hear me, and my near'st of kin
Cry, Fie upon my grave!
*Leon.*                I ne'er heard yet
That any of these bolder vices wanted
Less impudence to gainsay what they did
Than to perform it first.
*Her.*                That's true enough;
Though 'tis a saying, sir, not due to me.
*Leon.* You will not own it.
*Her.*                More than mistress of
Which comes to me in name of fault, I must not
At all acknowledge. For Polixenes,—
With whom I am accus'd,—I do confess
I lov'd him, as in honour he requir'd;
With such a kind of love as might become
A lady like me; with a love even such,
So and no other, as yourself commanded:
Which not to have done, I think had been in me
Both disobedience and ingratitude          [spoke
To you and toward your friend; whose love had
Even since it could speak from an infant, freely,
That it was yours. Now, for conspiracy,
I know not how it tastes; though it be dish'd
For me to try how: all I know of it
Is, that Camillo was an honest man,
And why he left your court, the gods themselves,
Wotting no more than I, are ignorant.
*Leon.* You knew of his departure, as you
     know
What you have underta'en to do in's absence.
*Her.* Sir,
You speak a language that I understand not:
My life stands in the level of your dreams,
Which I'll lay down.
*Leon.*            Your actions are my dreams;
You had a bastard by Polixenes,          [shame,—
And I but dream'd it:—as you were past all
Those of your fact are so,—so past all truth:

Which to deny concerns more than avails; for
    as
Thy brat hath been cast out, like to itself,
No father owning it,—which is, indeed,
More criminal in thee than it,—so thou
Shalt feel our justice; in whose easiest passage
Look for no less than death.

  *Her.*         Sir, spare your threats:
The bug which you would fright me with, I seek
To me can life be no commodity:
The crown and comfort of my life, your favour,
I do give lost; for I do feel it gone,
But know not how it went: my second joy,
And first-fruits of my body, from his presence
I am barr'd, like one infectious: my third com-
    fort,
Starr'd most unluckily, is from my breast,—
The innocent milk in its most innocent mouth,—
Hal'd out to murder: myself on every post
Proclaim'd a strumpet; with immodest hatred,
The child-bed privilege denied, which 'longs
To women of all fashion; lastly, hurried
Here to this place, i' the open air, before
I have got strength of limit. Now, my liege,
Tell me what blessings I have here alive,
That I should fear to die? Therefore, proceed.
But yet hear this; mistake me not;—no life,—
I prize it not a straw,—but for mine honour
(Which I would free), if I shall be condemn'd
Upon surmises—all proofs sleeping else,
But what your jealousies awake—I tell you
'Tis rigour, and not law.—Your honours all,
I do refer me to the oracle:
Apollo be my judge!

  *1 Lord.*      This your request
Is altogether just: therefore, bring forth,
And in Apollo's name, his oracle:
              [*Exeunt certain* Officers.

  *Her.* The Emperor of Russia was my father;
O that he were alive, and here beholding
His daughter's trial! that he did but see
The flatness of my misery; yet with eyes
Of pity, not revenge!

*Re-enter* Officers, *with* CLEOMENES *and* DION.

  *Offi.* You here shall swear upon this sword of
    justice,
That you, Cleomenes and Dion, have
Been both at Delphos, and from thence have
    brought
This seal'd-up oracle, by the hand deliver'd
Of great Apollo's priest; and that, since then,
You have not dar'd to break the holy seal,
Nor read the secrets in't.

  *Cleo. Dion.*     All this we swear.

  *Leon.* Break up the seals and read.

  *Offi.* [*Reads.*] Hermione *is chaste; Polixenes
blameless; Camillo a true subject; Leontes a
jealous tyrant; his innocent babe truly begotten;
and the king shall live without an heir, if that
which is lost be not found.*

  *Lords.* Now blessed be the great Apollo!

  *Her.*            Praised!

  *Leon.* Hast thou read truth?

  *Offi.*         Ay, my lord; even so
As it is here set down.

  *Leon.* There is no truth at all i' the oracle:
The sessions shall proceed: this is mere false-
    hood!

*Enter a* Servant *hastily.*

  *Serv.* My lord the king, the king!

  *Leon.*         What is the business?

  *Serv.* O sir, I shall be hated to report it:
The prince your son, with mere conceit and fear
Of the queen's speed, is gone.

  *Leon.*         How! gone?

  *Serv.*            Is dead.

  *Leon.* Apollo's angry; and the heavens them-
    selves
Do strike at my injustice.  [HERMIONE *faints.*
    How now there!

  *Paul.* This news is mortal to the queen:—
Look down
And see what death is doing.

  *Leon.*         Take her hence:
Her heart is but o'ercharg'd; she will recover.—
I have too much believ'd mine own suspicion:—
Beseech you, tenderly apply to her
Some remedies for life.—Apollo, pardon
    [*Exeunt* PAUL. *and* Ladies, *with* HER.
My great profaneness 'gainst thine oracle!—
I'll reconcile me to Polixenes;
New woo my queen; recall the good Camillo,
Whom I proclaim a man of truth, of mercy;
For, being transported by my jealousies
To bloody thoughts and to revenge, I chose
Camillo for the minister, to poison
My friend Polixenes: which had been done,
But that the good mind of Camillo tardied
My swift command, though I with death and
    with
Reward did threaten and encourage him,
Not doing it and being done: he, most humane,
And fill'd with honour, to my kingly guest
Unclasp'd my practice; quit his fortunes here,
Which you knew great; and to the certain
    hazard
Of all incertainties himself commended,
No richer than his honour:—How he glisters
Thorough my rust! and how his piety
Does my deeds make the blacker!

*Re-enter* PAULINA

  *Paul.*         Woe the while!
O, cut my lace, lest my heart, cracking it,
Break too!

  *1 Lord.* What fit is this, good lady?

  *Paul.* What studied torments, tyrant, hast
    for me?            [boiling
What wheels? racks? fires? what flaying?
In leads or oils? what old or newer torture
Must I receive, whose every word deserves
To taste of thy most worst? Thy tyranny
Together working with thy jealousies,—
Fancies too weak for boys, too green and idle
For girls of nine,—O, think what they have
    done,

And then run mad indeed,—stark mad! for all
Thy by-gone fooleries were but spices of it.
That thou betray'dst Polixenes, 'twas nothing;
That did but show thee, of a fool, inconstant,
And damnable ingrateful; nor was't much
Thou wouldst have poison'd good Camillo's
    honour,
To have him kill a king; poor trespasses,—
More monstrous standing by: whereof I reckon
The casting forth to crows thy baby daughter,
To be or none, or little; though a devil
Would have shed water out of fire ere don't:
Nor is't directly laid to thee, the death
Of the young prince, whose honourable
    thoughts,—    [heart
Thoughts high for one so tender,—cleft the
That could conceive a gross and foolish sire
Blemish'd his gracious dam: this is not—no,
Laid to thy answer: but the last,—O lords,
When I have said, cry, Woe!—the queen, the
    queen
The sweetest, dearest creature's dead; and
    vengeance for't
Nor dropp'd down yet.

    1 *Lord.*        The higher powers forbid!
    *Paul.* I say she's dead: I'll swear't. If word
    nor oath
Prevail not, go and see: if you can bring
Tincture, or lustre, in her lip, her eye,
Heat outwardly or breath within, I'll serve you
As I would do the gods.—But, O thou tyrant!
Do not repent these things; for they are heavier
Than all thy woes can stir; therefore betake
    thee
To nothing but despair. A thousand knees
Ten thousand years together, naked, fasting,
Upon a barren mountain, and still winter
In storm perpetual, could not move the gods
To look that way thou wert.

    *Leon.*        Go on, go on:
Thou canst not speak too much; I have de-
    serv'd
All tongues to talk their bitterest!

    1 *Lord.*        Say no more;
Howe'er the business goes, you have made fault
I' the boldness of your speech.

    *Paul.*        I am sorry for't:
All faults I make, when I shall come to know
    them,
I do repent. Alas, I have show'd too much
The rashness of a woman: he is touch'd
To the noble heart.—What's gone, and what's
    past help,
Should be past grief: do not receive affliction
At my petition; I beseech you, rather
Let me be punish'd, that have minded you
Of what you should forget. Now, good my liege,
Sir, royal sir, forgive a foolish woman:
The love I bore your queen,—lo, fool again!—
I'll speak of her no more, nor of your children;
I'll not remember you of my own lord,
Who is lost too: take your patience to you,
And I'll say nothing.

    *Leon.*        Thou didst speak but well,

When most the truth; which I receive much
    better
Than to be pitied of thee. Pr'ythee, bring me
To the dead bodies of my queen and son:
One grave shall be for both; upon them shall
The causes of their death appear, unto
Our shame perpetual. Once a day I'll visit
The chapel where they lie; and tears shed there
Shall be my recreation: so long as nature
Will bear up with this exercise, so long
I daily vow to use it.—Come, and lead me
To these sorrows.        [*Exeunt.*

SCENE III.—BOHEMIA. *A desert Country near*
*the Sea.*

*Enter* ANTIGONUS *with the Child, and a* Mariner.

    *Ant.* Thou art perfect, then, our ship hath
    touch'd upon
The deserts of Bohemia?

    *Mar.* Ay, my lord; and fear
We have landed in ill time: the skies look
    grimly,    [science,
And threaten present blusters. In my con-
The heavens with that we have in hand are
    angry,
And frown upon's.

    *Ant.* Their sacred will be done!—Go, get
    aboard;
Look to thy bark: I'll not be long before
I call upon thee.

    *Mar.* Make your best haste; and go not
Too far i' the land: 'tis like to be loud weather:
Besides, this place is famous for the creatures
Of prey that keep upon't.

    *Ant.*        Go thou away:
I'll follow instantly.

    *Mar.* I am glad at heart
To be so rid o' the business.        [*Exit.*

    *Ant.*        Come, poor babe:—
I have heard (but not believ'd), the spirits of
    the dead
May walk again: if such thing be, thy mother
Appear'd to me last night; for ne'er was dream
So like a waking. To me comes a creature,
Sometimes her head on one side, some another:
I never saw a vessel of like sorrow,
So fill'd and so becoming: in pure white robes,
Like very sanctity, she did approach
My cabin where I lay: thrice bow'd before me:
And, gasping to begin some speech, her eyes
Became two spouts: the fury spent, anon
Did this break from her: *Good* Antigonus,
*Since fate, against thy better disposition,*
*Hath made thy person for the thrower-out*
*Of my poor babe, according to thine oath,—*
*Places remote enough are in* Bohemia,
*There weep, and leave it crying; and, for the babe*
*Is counted lost for ever,* Perdita,
*I pr'ythee call't. For this ungentle business,*
*Put on thee by my lord, thou ne'er shalt see*
*Thy wife* Paulina *more:*—and so, with shrieks,
She melted into air. Affrighted much,
I did in time collect myself; and thought

This was so, and no slumber. Dreams are toys;
Yet, for this once, yea, superstitiously,
I will be squar'd by this. I do believe
Hermione hath suffer'd death; and that
Apollo would, this being indeed the issue
Of King Polixenes, it should here be laid,
Either for life or death, upon the earth
Of its right father. Blossom, speed thee well!
　　　　　　　　　[*Laying down the child.*
There lie; and there thy character: there these;
　　　　　　　　　[*Laying down a bundle.*
Which may if fortune please, both breed thee,
　　　pretty,
And still rest thine.—The storm begins:—poor
　　　wretch,
That, for thy mother's fault, art thus expos'd
To loss and what may follow!—Weep I cannot,
But my heart bleeds: and most accurs'd am I
To be by oath enjoin'd to this.—Farewell!
The day frowns more and more:—thou'rt like
　　　to have
A lullaby too rough:—I never saw
The heavens so dim by day. A savage clamour!—
Well may I get aboard!—This is the chace:
I am gone for ever!   [*Exit, pursued by a bear.*

### Enter an old Shepherd.

*Shep.* I would there were no age between ten
and three-and-twenty, or that youth would
sleep out the rest; for there is nothing in the between but getting wenches with child, wronging
the ancientry, stealing, fighting.—Hark you
now!—Would any but these boiled brains of
nineteen and two-and-twenty hunt this weather? They have scared away two of my best
sheep, which I fear the wolf will sooner find
than the master: if any where I have them, 'tis
by the sea-side, browsing of ivy.—Good luck,
an't be thy will! what have we here? [*Taking up
the child.*] Mercy on 's, a bairn; a very pretty
bairn! A boy or a child, I wonder? A pretty one;
a very pretty one: sure, some scape: though I
am not bookish, yet I can read waiting-gentlewoman in the scape. This has been some stair-
work, some trunk-work, some behind-door-
work: they were warmer that got this than the
poor thing is here. I'll take it up for pity: yet
I'll tarry till my son comes; he hollaed but even
now.—Whoa, ho hoa!

*Clo.* [*Within.*] Hilloa, loa!

*Shep.* What, art so near? If thou'lt see a
thing to talk on when thou art dead and rotten,
come hither.

### Enter Clown.

What ailest thou man?

*Clo.* I have seen two such sights, by sea and
by land!—but I am not to say it is a sea, for it
is now the sky: betwixt the firmament and it,
you cannot thrust a bodkin's point.

*Shep.* Why, boy, how is it?

*Clo.* I would you did but see how it chafes,
how it rages, how it takes up the shore! but
that's not to the point. O, the most piteous cry
of the poor souls! sometimes to see 'em, and not
to see 'em; now the ship boring the moon with
her mainmast, and anon swallowed with yest
and froth, as you'd thrust a cork in a hogshead.
And then for the land service,—to see how the
bear tore out his shoulder-bone; how he cried to
me for help, and said his name was Antigonus,
a nobleman.—But to make an end of the ship,
—to see how the sea flap-dragoned it:—but,
first, how the poor souls roared, and the sea
mocked them;—and how the poor gentleman
roared, and the bear mocked him;—both roaring louder than the sea or weather.

*Shep.* Name of mercy! when was this, boy?

*Clo.* Now, now; I have not winked since I
saw these sights: the men are not yet cold under
water, nor the bear half dined on the gentleman; he's at it now.

*Shep.* Would I had been by to have helped
the old man!

*Clo.* I would you had been by the ship-side,
to have helped her: there your charity would
have lacked footing.   [*Aside.*

*Shep.* Heavy matters! heavy matters! but
look thee here, boy. Now bless thyself: thou
mettest with things dying, I with things new-
born. Here's a sight for thee; look thee, a bearing-cloth for a squire's child! look thee here!
take up, take up, boy; open't. So, let's see:—it
was told me I should be rich by the fairies: this
is some changeling:—open't. What's within,
boy?

*Clo.* You're a made old man; if the sins of
your youth are forgiven you, you're well to live.
Gold! all gold!

*Shep.* This is fairy-gold, boy, and 'twill
prove so: up with it, keep it close: home, home,
the next way! We are lucky, boy; and to be so
still requires nothing but secrecy—Let my
sheep go:—come, good boy, the next way
home.

*Clo.* Go you the next way with your findings.
I'll go see if the bear be gone from the gentleman, and how much he hath eaten: they are
never curst but when they are hungry: if there
be any of him left, I'll bury it.

*Shep.* That's a good deed. If thou mayest
discern by that which is left of him what he is,
fetch me to the sight of him.

*Clo.* Marry, will I; and you shall help to put
him i' the ground.

*Shep.* 'Tis a lucky day, boy; and we'll do
good deeds on't.   [*Exeunt.*

## ACT IV.

### Enter TIME, as Chorus.

*Time.* I,—that please some, try all; both joy
　　　and terror
Of good and bad; that make and unfold error,—
Now take upon me, in the name of Time,
To use my wings. Impute it not a crime
To me or my swift passage, that I slide

O'er sixteen years, and leave the growth un-
   tried
Of that wide gap, since it is in my power
To o'erthrow law, and in one self-born hour
To plant and o'erwhelm custom. Let me pass
The same I am, ere ancient'st order was,
Or what is now received: I witness to
The times that brought them in; so shall I do
To the freshest things now reigning, and make
   stale
The glistering of this present, as my tale
Now seems to it. Your patience this allowing,
I turn my glass, and give my scene such grow-
   ing
As you had slept between. Leontes leaving
The effects of his fond jealousies, so grieving
That he shuts up himself; imagine me,
Gentle spectators, that I now may be
In fair Bohemia; and remember well,
I mention'd a son o' the king's, which Florizel
I now name to you; and with speed so pace
To speak of Perdita, now grown in grace
Equal with wondering: what of her ensues,
I list not prophesy; but let Time's news
Be known when 'tis brought forth:—a shep-
   herd's daughter,
And what to her adheres, which follows after,
Is the argument of Time. Of this allow,
If ever you have spent time worse ere now;
If never, yet that Time himself doth say
He wishes earnestly you never may.    [*Exit.*

SCENE I.—BOHEMIA. *A Room in the Palace of*
POLIXENES.

*Enter* POLIXENES *and* CAMILLO.

*Pol.* I pray thee, good Camillo, be no more
importunate: 'tis a sickness denying thee anything; a death to grant this.

*Cam.* It is fifteen years since I saw my
country; though I have for the most part been
aired abroad, I desire to lay my bones there.
Besides, the penitent king, my master, hath
sent for me; to whose feeling sorrows I might
be some allay, or I o'erween to think so,—
which is another spur to my departure.

*Pol.* As thou lovest me, Camillo, wipe not
out the rest of thy services by leaving me now:
the need I have of thee, thine own goodness
hath made; better not to have had thee than
thus to want thee; thou, having made me businesses which none without thee can sufficiently
manage, must either stay to execute them thyself, or take away with thee the very services
thou hast done; which if I have not enough
considered,—as too much I cannot,—to be
more thankful to thee shall be my study; and
my profit therein the heaping friendships. Of
that fatal country Sicilia, pr'ythee, speak no
more; whose very naming punishes me with the
remembrance of that penitent, as thou call'st
him, and reconciled king, my brother; whose
loss of his most precious queen and children are
even now to be afresh lamented. Say to me,

when sawest thou the Prince Florizel, my son?
Kings are no less unhappy, their issue not being
gracious, than they are in losing them, when
they have approved their virtues.

*Cam.* Sir, it is three days since I saw the
prince. What his happier affairs may be, are
to me unknown; but I have missingly noted he
is of late much retired from court, and is less
frequent to his princely exercises than formerly
he hath appeared.

*Pol.* I have considered so much, Camillo,
and with some care; so far, that I have eyes
under my service which look upon his removed-
ness; from whom I have this intelligence,—that
he is seldom from the house of a most homely
shepherd; a man, they say, that from very
nothing, and beyond the imagination of his
neighbours, is grown into an unspeakable
estate.

*Cam.* I have heard, sir, of such a man, who
hath a daughter of most rare note: the report
of her is extended more than can be thought to
begin from such a cottage.

*Pol.* That's likewise part of my intelligence:
but I fear the angle that plucks our son thither.
Thou shalt accompany us to the place; where
we will, not appearing what we are, have some
question with the shepherd; from whose simplicity I think it not uneasy to get the cause
of my son's resort thither. Pr'ythee, be my
present partner in this business, and lay aside
the thoughts of Sicilia.

*Cam.* I willingly obey your command.

*Pol.* My best Camillo!—We must disguise
ourselves.    [*Exeunt.*

SCENE II.—*The same. A road near the*
Shepherd's *Cottage.*

*Enter* AUTOLYCUS, *singing.*

When daffodils begin to peer,—
   With, hey! the doxy over the dale,—
Why, then comes in the sweet o' the year;
   For the red blood reigns in the winter's pale.

The white sheet bleaching on the hedge,—
   With, hey! the sweet birds, O, how they sing!—
Doth set my pugging tooth on edge;
   For a quart of ale is a dish for a king.

The lark, that tirra-lirra chants,—
   With, hey! with, hey! the thrush and the jay,—
Are summer songs for me and my aunts,
   While we lie tumbling in the hay.

I have served Prince Florizel, and, in my time,
wore three-pile; but now I am out of service:

But shall I go mourn for that, my dear?
   The pale moon shines by night:
And when I wander here and there,
   I then do most go right.

If tinkers may have leave to live,
   And bear the sow-skin budget,
Then my account I well may give
   And in the stocks avouch it.

My traffic is sheets; when the kite builds, look to lesser linen. My father named me Autolycus; who being, as I am, littered under Mercury, was likewise a snapper-up of unconsidered trifles. With die and drab I purchased this caparison; and my revenue is the silly-cheat: gallows and knock are too powerful on the highway; beating and hanging are terrors to me; for the life to come, I sleep out the thought of it.—A prize! a prize!

*Enter* Clown.

*Clo.* Let me see:—every 'leven wether tods; every tod yields pound and odd shilling; fifteen hundred shorn, what comes the wool to?

*Aut.* If the springe hold, the cock's mine.
[*Aside.*

*Clo.* I cannot do't without counters.—Let me see; what am I to buy for our sheep-shearing feast? *Three pound of sugar; five pound of currants; rice*—what will this sister of mine do with rice? But my father hath made her mistress of the feast, and she lays it on. She hath made me four-and-twenty nosegays for the shearers,—three-man song-men all, and very good ones; but they are most of them means and bases; but one puritan amongst them, and he sings psalms to hornpipes. I must have *saffron*, to colour the warden pies; *mace—dates,* —none; that's out of my note; *nutmegs, seven; a race or two of ginger,*—but that I may beg; *four pound of prunes, and as many of raisins o' the sun.*

*Aut.* O that ever I was born!
[*Grovelling on the ground.*

*Clo.* I' the name of me,—

*Aut.* O, help me, help me! pluck but off these rags; and then, death, death!

*Clo.* Alack, poor soul! thou hast need of more rags to lay on thee, rather than have these off.

*Aut.* O, sir, the loathsomeness of them offends me more than the stripes I have received, which are mighty ones and millions.

*Clo.* Alas, poor man! a million of beating may come to a great matter.

*Aut.* I am robbed, sir, and beaten; my money and apparel ta'en from me, and these detestable things put upon me.

*Clo.* What, by a horseman or a footman?

*Aut.* A footman, sweet sir, a footman.

*Clo.* Indeed, he should be a footman, by the garments he has left with thee: if this be a horseman's coat, it hath seen very hot service. Lend me thy hand, I'll help thee: come, lend me thy hand. [*Helping him up.*

*Aut.* O, good sir, tenderly, O!

*Clo.* Alas, poor soul!

*Aut.* Oh, good sir, softly; good sir: I fear, sir, my shoulder blade is out.

*Clo.* How now! canst stand?

*Aut.* Softly, dear sir! [*picks his pocket*] good sir, softly; you ha' done me a charitable office.

*Clo.* Dost lack any money? I have a little money for thee.

*Aut.* No, good sweet sir; no, I beseech you, sir: I have a kinsman not past three quarters of a mile hence, unto whom I was going; I shall there have money or anything I want: offer me no money, I pray you; that kills my heart.

*Clo.* What manner of fellow was he that robbed you?

*Aut.* A fellow, sir, that I have known to go about with troll-my-dames: I knew him once a servant of the prince: I cannot tell, good sir, for which of his virtues it was, but he was certainly whipped out of the court.

*Clo.* His vices, you would say; there's no virtue whipped out of the court: they cherish it, to make it stay there; and yet it will no more but abide.

*Aut.* Vices, I would say, sir. I know this man well: he hath been since an ape-bearer; then a process-server, a bailiff; then he compassed a motion of the Prodigal Son, and married a tinker's wife within a mile where my land and living lies; and, having flown over many knavish professions, he settled only in rogue: some call him Autolycus.

*Clo.* Out upon him! prig, for my life, prig. he haunts wakes, fairs, and bear-baitings.

*Aut.* Very true, sir; he, sir, he; that's the rogue that put me into this apparel.

*Clo.* Not a more cowardly rogue in all Bohemia; if you had but looked big and spit at him, he'd have run.

*Aut.* I must confess to you, sir, I am no fighter: I am false of heart that way; and that he knew, I warrant him.

*Clo.* How do you know?

*Aut.* Sweet sir, much better than I was; I can stand and walk: I will even take my leave of you, and pace softly towards my kinsman's.

*Clo.* Shall I bring thee on the way?

*Aut.* No, good-faced sir; no, sweet sir.

*Clo.* Then fare thee well: I must go buy spices for our sheep-shearing.

*Aut.* Prosper you, sweet sir! [*Exit* Clown.] Your purse is not hot enough to purchase your spice. I'll be with you at your sheep-shearing too. If I make not this cheat bring out another, and the shearers prove sheep, let me be enrolled, and my name put in the book of virtue!
[*Sings.*

Jog on, jog on, the footpath way,
    And merrily hent the stile-a:
A merry heart goes all the day,
    Your sad tires in a mile-a. [*Exit.*

SCENE III.—*The same. A Shepherd's Cottage.*

*Enter* FLORIZEL *and* PERDITA.

*Flo.* These your unusual weeds to each part of you
Do give a life: no shepherdess, but Flora [ing
Peering in April's front. This your sheep-shear-
Is as a meeting of the petty gods,

And you the queen on't.

*Per.*     Sir, my gracious lord,
To chide at your extremes it not becomes me,—
O, pardon that I name them!—your high self,
The gracious mark o' the land, you have
 obscur'd
With a swain's wearing; and me, poor lowly
 maid,
Most goddess-like prank'd up. But that our
 feasts
In every mess have folly, and the feeders
Digest it with a custom, I should blush
To see you so attir'd; swoon, I think,
To show myself a glass.

*Flo.*    I bless the time
When my good falcon made her flight across
Thy father's ground.

*Per.*    Now Jove afford you cause!
To me the difference forges dread: your great-
 ness
Hath not been us'd to fear. Even now I tremble
To think your father, by some accident,
Should pass this way, as you did. O, the fates!
How would he look to see his work, so noble,
Vilely bound up? What would he say? Or how
Should I, in these my borrow'd flaunts, behold
The sternness of his presence?

*Flo.*    Apprehend
Nothing but jollity. The gods themselves,
Humbling their deities to love, have taken
The shapes of beasts upon them: Jupiter
Became a bull, and bellow'd; the green Nep-
 tune
A ram, and bleated; and the fire-rob'd god,
Golden Apollo, a poor humble swain,
As I seem now:—their transformations
Were never for a piece of beauty rarer,—
Nor in a way so chaste, since my desires
Run not before mine honour, nor my lusts
Burn hotter than my faith.

*Per.*    O, but, sir,
Your resolution cannot hold, when 'tis
Oppos'd, as it must be, by the power of the
 king:
One of these two must be necessities,
Which then will speak, that you must change
 this purpose,
Or I my life.

*Flo.*   Thou dearest Perdita, [not
With these forc'd thoughts, I pr'ythee, darken
The mirth o' the feast: or I'll be thine, my fair,
Or not my father's; for I cannot be
Mine own, nor anything to any, if
I be not thine: to this I am most constant,
Though destiny say no. Be merry, gentle:
Strangle such thoughts as these with anything
That you behold the while. Your guests are
 coming:
Lift up your countenance, as it were the day
Of celebration of that nuptial which
We two have sworn shall come.

*Per.*    O lady Fortune,
Stand you auspicious!

*Flo.*   See, your guests approach:

Address yourself to entertain them sprightly,
And let's be red with mirth.

*Enter* Shepherd, *with* POLIXENES *and* CAM-
ILLO *disguised;* Clown, MOPSA, DORCAS,
*with others.*

*Shep.* Fie, daughter! when my old wife liv'd,
 upon
This day she was both pantler, butler, cook;
Both dame and servant; welcom'd all; serv'd
 all;        [here
Would sing her song and dance her turn; now
At upper end o' the table, now i' the middle;
On his shoulder, and his; her face o' fire [it,
With labour; and the thing she took to quench
She would to each one sip. You are retir'd,
As if you were a feasted one, and not
The hostess of the meeting: pray you, bid
These unknown friends to us welcome; for it is
A way to make us better friends, more known.
Come, quench your blushes, and present your-
 self
That which you are, mistress of the feast: come
 on,
And bid us welcome to your sheep-shearing,
As your good flock shall prosper.

*Per.*    Sir, welcome! [*To* POL.
It is my father's will I should take on me
The hostess-ship o' the day:—You're welcome,
 sir!        [*To* CAMILLO.
Give me those flowers there, Dorcas.—Rev-
 erend sirs,
For you there's rosemary and rue; these keep
Seeming and savour all the winter long:
Grace and remembrance be to you both,
And welcome to our shearing!

*Pol.*    Shepherdess—
A fair one are you!—well you fit our ages
With flowers of winter.

*Per.*   Sir, the year growing ancient,—
Not yet on summer's death, nor on the birth
Of trembling winter,—the fairest flowers o' the
 season
Are our carnations, and streak'd gillyvors,
Which some call nature's bastards: of that kind
Our rustic garden's barren; and I care not
To get slips of them.

*Pol.*    Wherefore, gentle maiden,
Do you neglect them?

*Per.*    For I have heard it said
There is an art which, in their piedness, shares
With great creating nature.

*Pol.*    Say there be;
Yet nature is made better by no mean,
But nature makes that mean; so, o'er that
 art
Which you say adds to nature, is an art
That nature makes. You see, sweet maid, we
 marry
A gentler scion to the wildest stock,
And make conceive a bark of baser kind
By bud of nobler race. This is an art [but
Which does mend nature,—change it rather;
The art itself is nature.

*Per.*          So it is.          [vors,
*Pol.* Then make your garden rich in gilly-
And do not call them bastards.
*Per.*          I'll not put
The dibble in earth to set one slip of them;
No more than, were I painted, I would wish
This youth would say, 'twere well, and only
          therefore
Desire to breed by me.—Here's flowers for you;
Hot lavender, mints, savory, marjoram;
The marigold, that goes to bed with the sun,
And with him rises weeping; these are flowers
Of middle summer, and I think they are given
To men of middle age. You're very welcome!
*Cam.* I should leave grazing, were I of your
          flock,
And only live by gazing.
*Per.*          Out, alas!
You'd be so lean that blasts of January
Would blow you through and through.—Now,
          my fairest friend,          [might
I would I had some flowers o' the spring that
Become your time of day;—and yours, and
          yours,
That wear upon your virgin branches yet
Your maidenheads growing.—O Proserpina,
For the flowers now, that, frighted, thou lett'st
          fall
From Dis's waggon!—daffodils,
That come before the swallow dares, and take
The winds of March with beauty; violets dim,
But sweeter than the lids of Juno's eyes
Or Cytherea's breath; pale primroses,
That die unmarried ere they can behold
Bright Phœbus in his strength,—a malady
Most incident to maids; bold oxlips, and
The crown-imperial; lilies of all kinds,
The flower-de-luce being one!—O, these I lack,
To make you garlands of; and, my sweet friend,
To strew him o'er and o'er!
*Flo.*          What, like a corse?
*Per.* No; like a bank for love to lie and play
          on;
Not like a corse; or if,—not to be buried,
But quick, and in mine arms. Come, take your
          flowers;
Methinks I play as I have seen them do
In Whitsun pastorals: sure, this robe of mine
Does change my disposition.
*Flo.*          What you do
Still betters what is done. When you speak,
          sweet,
I'd have you do it ever; when you sing,
I'd have you buy and sell so; so give alms;
Pray so; and, for the ordering your affairs,
To sing them too: when you dance, I wish you
A wave o' the sea, that might ever do
Nothing but that; move still, still so, and own
No other function: each your doing,
So singular in each particular,
Crowns what you are doing in the present
          deeds,
That all your acts are queens.
*Per.*          O Doricles,

Your praises are too large: but that your youth,
And the true blood which peeps fairly through it,
Do plainly give you out an unstained shepherd,
With wisdom I might fear, my Doricles,
You woo'd me the false way.
*Flo.*          I think you have
As little skill to fear as I have purpose
To put you to't.—But, come; our dance, I
          pray:
Your hand, my Perdita; so turtles pair
That never mean to part.
*Per.*          I'll swear for 'em.
*Pol.* This is the prettiest low-born lass that
          ever          [seems
Ran on the green sward: nothing she does or
But smacks of something greater than herself,
Too noble for this place.
*Cam.* He tells her something          [is
That makes her blood look out: good sooth, she
The queen of curds and cream.
*Clo.*          Come on, strike up.
*Dor.* Mopsa must be your mistress: marry,
          garlic,
To mend her kissing with.
*Mop.*          Now, in good time!
*Clo.* Not a word, a word; we stand upon our
          manners.—
Come, strike up.          [*Music.*

*Here a dance of* Shepherds *and* Shepherdesses.
*Pol.* Pray, good shepherd, what
Fair swain is this which dances with your
          daughter?          [himself
*Shep.* They call him Doricles; and boasts
To have a worthy feeding: but I have it
Upon his own report, and I believe it;
He looks like sooth. He says he loves my
          daughter:
I think so too; for never gaz'd the moon
Upon the water as he'll stand, and read,
As 'twere, my daughter's eyes: and, to be plain,
I think there is not half a kiss to choose
Who loves another best.
*Pol.*          She dances featly. [it,
*Shep.* So she does anything; though I report
That should be silent: if young Doricles
Do light upon her, she shall bring him that
Which he not dreams of.

          *Enter a* Servant.

*Serv.* O, master, if you did but hear the pedlar at the door, you would never dance again
after a tabor and pipe; no, the bagpipe could
not move you: he sings several tunes faster
than you'll tell money: he utters them as he
had eaten ballads, and all men's ears grew to
his tunes.
*Clo.* He could never come better: he shall
come in: I love a ballad but even too well; if
it be doleful matter merrily set down, or a very
pleasant thing indeed and sung lamentably.
*Serv.* He hath songs for man or woman of
all sizes; no milliner can so fit his customers
with gloves: he has the prettiest love-songs for

maids; so without bawdry, which is strange; with such delicate burdens of *dildos* and *fadings, jump her and thump her;* and where some stretch-mouth'd rascal would, as it were, mean mischief, and break a foul gap into the matter, he makes the maid to answer, *Whoop, do me no harm, good man;* puts him off, slights him, with *Whoop, do me no harm, good man.*

*Pol.* This is a brave fellow.

*Clo.* Believe me, thou talkest of an admirable conceited fellow. Has he any unbraided wares?

*Serv.* He hath ribands of all the colours i' the rainbow; points more than all the lawyers in Bohemia can learnedly handle, though they come to him by the gross; inkles, caddisses, cambrics, lawns: why he sings 'em over as they were gods or goddesses; you would think a smock were a she-angel, he so chants to the sleeve-hand, and the work about the square on't.

*Clo.* Pr'ythee, bring him in; and let him approach singing.

*Per.* Forewarn him that he use no scurrilous words in his tunes.     [*Exit* Servant.

*Clo.* You have of these pedlars that have more in 'em than you'd think, sister.

*Per.* Ay, good brother, or go about to think.

*Enter* AUTOLYCUS, *singing.*

Lawn as white as driven snow;
Cyprus black as e'er was crow;
Gloves as sweet as damask-roses;
Masks for faces and for noses;
Bugle-bracelet, necklace amber,
Perfume for a lady's chamber;
Golden quoifs and stomachers,
For my lads to give their dears;
Pins and poking-sticks of steel,
What maids lack from head to heel:
Come, buy of me, come; come buy, come buy;
Buy, lads, or else your lasses cry:
Come, buy.

*Clo.* If I were not in love with Mopsa, thou shouldst take no money of me; but being enthralled as I am, it will also be the bondage of certain ribands and gloves.

*Mop.* I was promised them against the feast; but they come not too late now.

*Dor.* He hath promised you more than that, or there be liars.

*Mop.* He hath paid you all he promised you: may be he has paid you more,—which will shame you to give him again.

*Clo.* Is there no manners left among maids? will they wear their plackets where they should bear their faces? Is there not milking-time, when you are going to bed, or kiln-hole, to whistle off these secrets, but you must be tittle-tattling before all our guests? 'tis well they are whispering. Clamour your tongues, and not a word more.

*Mop.* I have done. Come, you promised me a tawdry lace, and a pair of sweet gloves.

*Clo.* Have I not told thee how I was cozened by the way, and lost all my money?

*Aut.* And, indeed, sir, there are cozeners abroad; therefore it behoves men to be wary.

*Clo.* Fear not thou, man, thou shalt lose nothing here.

*Aut.* I hope so, sir; for I have about me many parcels of charge.

*Clo.* What hast here? ballads?

*Mop.* Pray now, buy some: I love a ballad in print a-life; for then we are sure they are true.

*Aut.* Here's one to a very doleful tune. How a usurer's wife was brought to bed of twenty money-bags at a burden, and how she longed to eat adders' heads and toads carbonadoed.

*Mop.* Is it true, think you?

*Aut.* Very true; and but a month old.

*Dor.* Bless me from marrying a usurer!

*Aut.* Here's the midwife's name to't, one Mistress Taleporter, and five or six honest wives that were present. Why should I carry lies abroad?

*Mop.* Pray you now, buy it.

*Clo.* Come on, lay it by; and let's first see more ballads; we'll buy the other things anon.

*Aut.* Here's another ballad, of a fish that appeared upon the coast on Wednesday the fourscore of April, forty thousand fathom above water, and sung this ballad against the hard hearts of maids: it was thought she was a woman, and was turned into a cold fish for she would not exchange flesh with one that loved her. The ballad is very pitiful, and as true.

*Dor.* Is it true too, think you?

*Aut.* Five justices' hands at it; and witnesses more than my pack will hold.

*Clo.* Lay it by too: another.

*Aut.* This is a merry ballad; but a very pretty one.

*Mop.* Let's have some merry ones.

*Aut.* Why, this is a passing merry one, and goes to the tune of *Two maids wooing a man:* there's scarce a maid westward but she sings it: 'tis in request, I can tell you.

*Mop.* We can both sing it: if thou'lt bear a part thou shalt hear; 'tis in three parts.

*Dor.* We had the tune on't a month ago.

*Aut.* I can bear my part; you must know 'tis my occupation: have at it with you.

SONG.

*A.* Get you hence, for I must go;
    Where, it fits not you to know.
      *D.* Whither? *M.* O, whither? *D.* Whither?
*M.* It becomes thy oath full well,
    Thou to me thy secrets tell:
      *D.* Me too, let me go thither.

*M.* Or thou go'st to the grange or mill:
*D.* If to either, thou dost ill.
    *A.* Neither. *D.* What, neither? *A.* Neither.
*D.* Thou hast sworn my love to be;
*M.* Thou hast sworn it more to me;
    Then, whither go'st —say, whither?

*Clo.* We'll have this song out anon by ourselves; my father and the gentlemen are in sad talk, and we'll not trouble them.—Come, bring away thy pack after me.—Wenches, I'll buy for you both:—Pedlar, let's have the first choice.—Follow me, girls.

*Aut.* And you shall pay well for 'em.

[*Aside.*

Will you buy any tape,
　Or lace for your cape,
My dainty duck, my dear-a?
　Any silk, any thread,
　Any toys, for your head,
Of the new'st and fin'st, fin'st wear-a?
　Come to the pedlar;
　Money's a meddler,
That doth utter all men's ware-a.

[*Exeunt* Clown, Aut., Dor., *and* Mop.

*Re-enter* Servant.

*Serv.* Master, there is three carters, three shepherds, three neat-herds, three swine-herds, that have made themselves all men of hair; they call themselves saltiers: and they have a dance which the wenches say is a gallimaufry of gambols, because they are not in't; but they themselves are o' the mind (if it be not too rough for some, that know little but bowling) it will please plentifully.

*Shep.* Away! we'll none on't: here has been too much homely foolery already.—I know, sir, we weary you.

*Pol.* You weary those that refresh us: pray let's see these four threes of herdsmen.

*Serv.* One three of them, by their own report, sir, hath danced before the king; and; not the worst of the three but jumps twelve foot and a half by the squire.

*Shep.* Leave your prating: since these good men are pleased, let them come in; but quickly now.

*Serv.* Why, they stay at door, sir.　　[*Exit.*

*Enter* Twelve Rustics, *habited like Satyrs.*
*They dance, and then exeunt.*

*Pol.* O father, you'll know more of that hereafter.—
Is it not too far gone?—'Tis time to part them.—
He's simple and tells much. [*Aside.*]—How now, fair shepherd!
Your heart is full of something that does take
Your mind from feasting. Sooth, when I was young,
And handed love as you do, I was wont
To load my she with knacks: I would have ransack'd
The pedlar's silken treasury, and have pour'd it
To her acceptance; you have let him go,
And nothing marted with him. If your lass
Interpretation should abuse, and call this
Your lack of love or bounty, you were straited
For a reply, at least if you make a care
Of happy holding her.

*Flo.*　　　　　　Old sir, I know
She prizes not such trifles as these are:
The gifts she looks from me are pack'd and lock'd
Up in my heart; which I have given already,
But not deliver'd.—O, hear me breathe my life
Before this ancient sir, who, it should seem,
Hath sometime lov'd,—I take thy hand! this hand,
As soft as dove's down, and as white as it,
Or Ethiopian's tooth, or the fann'd snow that's bolted
By the northern blasts twice o'er.

*Pol.*　　　　What follows this?—
How prettily the young swain seems to wash
The hand was fair before!—I have put you out:
But to your protestation; let me hear
What you profess.

*Flo.*　　　　Do, and be witness to't.

*Pol.* And this my neighbour, too?

*Flo.*　　　　　　And he, and more
Than he, and men,—the earth, the heavens, and all:—　　　　　　　　[monarch,
That,—were I crown'd the most imperial
Thereof most worthy; were I the fairest youth
That ever made eye swerve; had force and knowledge　　　　　　　　[them
More than was ever man's,—I would not prize
Without her love: for her employ them all;
Commend them, and condemn them, to her service,
Or to their own perdition.

*Pol.*　　　　　　Fairly offer'd.

*Cam.* This shows a sound affection.

*Shep.*　　　　　　But, my daughter,
Say you the like to him?

*Per.*　　　　　I cannot speak
So well, nothing so well; no, nor mean better:
By the pattern of mine own thoughts I cut out
The purity of his.

*Shep.*　　　　Take hands, a bargain!—
And, friends unknown, you shall bear witness to't:
I give my daughter to him, and will make
Her portion equal his.

*Flo.*　　　　　O, that must be
I' the virtue of your daughter: one being dead,
I shall have more than you can dream of yet;
Enough then for your wonder: but come on,
Contract us 'fore these witnesses.

*Shep.*　　　　　Come, your hand;—
And, daughter, yours.

*Pol.*　　Soft, swain, awhile, beseech you;
Have you a father?

*Flo.*　　　　　I have; but what of him?

*Pol.* Knows he of this?

*Flo.*　　　　He neither does nor shall.

*Pol.* Methinks a father
Is, at the nuptial of his son, a guest　　[more;
That best becomes the table. Pray you, once
Is not your father grown incapable
Of reasonable affairs? is he not stupid
With age and altering rheums? can he speak? hear?

Know man from man? dispute his own estate?
Lies he not bed-rid? and again does nothing
But what he did being childish?
*Flo.*                      No, good sir;
He has his health, and ampler strength indeed
Than most have of his age.
*Pol.*                      By my white beard,
You offer him, if this be so, a wrong
Something unfilial: reason my son
Should choose himself a wife; but as good reason
The father,—all whose joy is nothing else
But fair posterity,—should hold some counsel
In such a business.
*Flo.*               I yield all this;
But, for some other reasons, my grave sir,
Which 'tis not fit you know, I not acquaint
My father of this business.
*Pol.*                      Let him know't.
*Flo.* He shall not.
*Pol.*                 Pr'ythee, let him.
*Flo.*                      No, he must not.
*Shep.* Let him, my son: he shall not need to
    grieve
At knowing of thy choice.
*Flo.*            Come, come, he must not.—
Mark our contráct.
*Pol.*           Mark your divorce, young sir,
                            [*Discovering himself.*
Whom son I dare not call; thou art too base
To be acknowledged: thou a sceptre's heir,
That thus affect'st a sheep-hook!—Thou old
    traitor,
I am sorry that, by hanging thee, I can but
Shorten thy life one week.—And thou, fresh
    piece                              [know
Of excellent witchcraft, who, of force, must
The royal fool thou cop'st with,—
*Shep.*                   O, my heart!
*Pol.* I'll have thy beauty scratch'd with
    briers, and made              [boy,—
More homely than thy state.—For thee, fond
If I may ever know thou dost but sigh
That thou no more shalt see this knack,—as
    never                         [cession;
I mean thou shalt,—we'll bar thee from suc-
Not hold thee of our blood, no, not our kin,
Far than Deucalion off,—mark thou my words:
Follow us to the court.—Thou churl, for this
    time,
Though full of our displeasure, yet we free thee
From the dead blow of it.—And you, enchant-
    ment,—
Worthy enough a herdsman; yea, him too
That makes himself, but for our honour therein,
Unworthy thee,—if ever henceforth thou
These rural latches to his entrance open,
Or hoop his body more with thy embraces,
I will devise a death as cruel for thee
As thou art tender to't.             [*Exit.*
*Per.*              Even here undone!
I was not much afeard: for once or twice
I was about to speak, and tell him plainly
The self-same sun that shines upon his court
Hides not his visage from our cottage, but

Looks on alike.—Will't please you, sir, be
    gone?                       [*To* FLORIZEL.
I told you what would come of this! Beseech
    you,
Of your own state take care: this dream of mine,
Being now awake, I'll queen it no inch further,
But milk my ewes, and weep.
*Cam.*               Why, how now, father!
Speak ere thou diest.
*Shep.*              I cannot speak, nor think,
Nor dare to know that which I know.—O, sir,
                            [*To* FLORIZEL
You have undone a man of fourscore-three,
That thought to fill his grave in quiet; yea,
To die upon the bed my father died,
To lie close by his honest bones! but now
Some hangman must put on my shroud, and
    lay me
Where no priest shovels in dust.—O cursed
    wretch,                     [*To* PERDITA.
That knew'st this was the prince, and wouldst
    adventure
To mingle faith with him!—Undone! undone!
If I might die within this hour, I have liv'd
To die when I desire.                  [*Exit.*
*Flo.*              Why look you so upon me.
I am but sorry, not afeard; delay'd,
But nothing alter'd: what I was, I am:
More straining on for plucking back; not fol-
    lowing
My leash unwillingly.
*Cam.*             Gracious, my lord,
You know your father's temper: at this time
He will allow no speech,—which I do guess
You do not purpose to him;—and as hardly
Will he endure your sight as yet, I fear:
Then, till the fury of his highness settle,
Come not before him.
*Flo.*              I not purpose it.
I think Camillo?
*Cam.*          Even he, my lord.
*Per.* How often have I told you 'twould be
    thus!
How often said my dignity would last
But till 'twere known!
*Flo.*              It cannot fail but by
The violation of my faith; and then
Let nature crush the sides o' the earth together.
And mar the seeds within!—Lift up thy looks.—
From my succession wipe me, father; I
Am heir to my affection.
*Cam.*                Be advis'd.
*Flo.* I am,—and by my fancy: if my reason
Will thereto be obedient, I have reason;
If not, my senses, better pleas'd with madness,
Do bid it welcome.
*Cam.*          This is desperate, sir.
*Flo.* So call it: but it does fulfil my vow;
I needs must think it honesty. Camillo,
Not for Bohemia, nor the pomp that may
Be thereat glean'd; for all the sun sees or
The close earth wombs, or the profound seas
    hide
In unknown fathoms, will I break my oath

To this my fair belov'd: therefore, I pray you,
As you have ever been my father's honour'd
    friend                                    [not
When he shall miss me,—as, in faith, I mean
To see him any more,—cast your good counsels
Upon his passion: let myself and fortune
Tug for the time to come. This you may know,
And so deliver,—I am put to sea
With her, whom here I cannot hold on shore;
And, most oppórtune to our need, I have
A vessel rides fast by, but not prepar'd
For this design. What course I mean to hold
Shall nothing benefit your knowledge, nor
Concern me the reporting.
    *Cam.*                    O, my lord.
I would your spirit were easier for advice,
Or stronger for your need.
    *Flo.*        Hark, Perdita.—[*Takes her aside.*
I'll hear you by and by.            [*To* CAMILLO.
    *Cam.*                He's irremovable,
Resolv'd for flight. Now were I happy if
His going I could frame to serve my turn;
Save him from danger, do him love and honour;
Purchase the sight again of dear Sicilia,
And that unhappy king, my master whom
I so much thirst to see.
    *Flo.*            Now, good Camillo,
I am so fraught with curious business that
I leave out ceremony.                [*Going.*
    *Cam.*            Sir, I think
You have heard of my poor services, i' the love
That I have borne your father?
    *Flo.*                Very nobly
Have you deserv'd: it is my father's music
To speak your deeds; not little of his care
To have them recompens'd as thought on.
    *Cam.*                Well, my lord,
If you may please to think I love the king,
And, through him, which is nearest to him,
    which is
Your gracious self, embrace but my direction,—
If your more ponderous and settled project
May suffer alteration,—on mine honour    [ing
I'll point you where you shall have such receiv-
As shall become your highness; where you may
Enjoy your mistress,—from the whom, I see,
There's no disjunction to be made, but by,
As heavens forfend! your ruin,—marry her;
And,—with my best endeavours in your ab-
    sence,—
Your discontenting father strive to qualify,
And bring him up to liking.
    *Flo.*            How, Camillo,
May this, almost a miracle, be done?
That I may call thee something more than man,
And, after that, trust to thee.
    *Cam.*            Have you thought on
A place whereto you'll go?
    *Flo.* Not any yet:
But as the unthought-on accident is guilty
To what we wildly do; so we profess
Ourselves to be the slaves of chance, and flies
Of every wind that blows.
    *Cam.*            Then list to me:

This follows,—if you will not change your pur-
    pose,
But undergo this flight,—make for Sicilia;
And there present yourself and your fair prin-
    cess,—
For so, I see, she must be,—'fore Leontes:
She shall be habited as it becomes
The partner of your bed. Methinks I see
Leonites opening his free arms, and weeping
His welcomes forth; asks thee, the son, forgive-
    ness,
As 'twere i' the father's person; kisses the hands
Of your fresh princess; o'er and o'er divides him
'Twixt his unkindness and his kindness,—the
    one
He chides to hell, and bids the other grow
Faster than thought or time.
    *Flo.*            Worthy Camillo,
What colour for my visitation shall I
Hold up before him?
    *Cam.*        Sent by the king your father
To greet him and to give him comforts. Sir,
The manner of your bearing towards him, with
What you, as from your father, shall deliver,
Things known betwixt us three, I'll write you
    down;
The which shall point you forth at every sitting,
What you must say; that he shall not perceive
But that you have your father's bosom there,
And speak his very heart.
    *Flo.*            I am bound to you:
There is some sap in this.
    *Cam.*        A course more promising
Than a wild dedication of yourselves    [certain
To unpath'd waters, undream'd shores, most
To miseries enough: no hope to help you;
But, as you shake off one, to take another:
Nothing so certain as your anchors; who
Do their best office if they can but stay you
Where you'll be loath to be: besides, you know
Prosperity's the very bond of love,        [gether
Whose fresh complexion and whose heart to-
Affliction alters.
    *Per.*        One of these is true:
I think affliction may subdue the cheek,
But not take in the mind.
    *Cam.*            Yea, say you so?
There shall not, at your father's house, these
    seven years
Be born another such.
    *Flo.*            My good Camillo,
She is as forward of her breeding as
She is i' the rear our birth.
    *Cam.*            I cannot say 'tis pity
She lacks instruction; for she seems a mistress
To most that teach.
    *Per.*        Your pardon, sir, for this:
I'll blush you thanks.
    *Flo.* My prettiest Perdita!—
But, O, the thorns we stand upon!—Camillo,—
Preserver of my father, now of me;
The medicine of our house!—how shall we do?
We are not furnish'd like Bohemia's son;
Nor shall appear in Sicilia.

*Cam.*                    My lord,
Fear none of this: I think you know my for-
    tunes
Do all lie there: it shall be so my care
To have you royally appointed as if          [sir,
The scene you play were mine. For instance,
That you may know you shall not want,—one
    word.                    [*They talk aside.*

### Re-enter AUTOLYCUS.

*Aut.* Ha, ha! what a fool Honesty is! and
Trust, his sworn brother, a very simple gentleman! I have sold all my trumpery; not a
counterfeit stone, not a riband, glass, poman-
der, brooch, table-book, ballad, knife, tape,
glove, shoe-tie, bracelet, horn-ring, to keep my
pack from fasting;—they throng who should
buy first, as if my trinkets had been hallowed,
and brought a benediction to the buyer: by
which means I saw whose purse was best in
picture; and what I saw, to my good use I remembered. My clown (who wants but something to be a reasonable man) grew so in love
with the wenches' song that he would not stir
his pettitoes till he had both tune and words;
which so drew the rest of the herd to me, that
all their other senses stuck in ears: you might
have pinched a placket,—it was senseless; 'twas
nothing to geld a codpiece of a purse; I would
have filed keys off that hung in chains: no hearing, no feeling, but my sir's song, and admiring
the nothing of it. So that, in this time of
lethargy, I picked and cut most of their festival
purses; and had not the old man come in with
a whoobub against his daughter and the king's
son, and scared my choughs from the chaff, I
had not left a purse alive in the whole army.
    [CAM., FLO., *and* PER. *come forward.*

*Cam.* Nay, but my letters, by this means
    being there
So soon as you arrive, shall clear that doubt.

*Flo.* And those that you'll procure from king
    Leontes,—

*Cam.* Shall satisfy your father.

*Per.*                    Happy be you!
All that you speak shows fair.

*Cam.* Who have we here?—
                    [*Seeing* AUTOLYCUS.
We'll make an instrument of this; omit
Nothing may give us aid.

*Aut.* If they have overheard me now,—why,
hanging.                    [*Aside.*

*Cam.* How now, good fellow! why shakest
thou so? Fear not, man; here's no harm intended to thee.

*Aut.* I am a poor fellow, sir.

*Cam.* Why, be so still; here's nobody will
steal that from thee: yet, for the outside of thy
poverty, we must make an exchange; therefore,
discase thee instantly,—thou must think there's
a necessity in't,—and change garments with
this gentleman: though the pennyworth on his
side be the worst, yet hold thee, there's some
boot.                    [*Giving money.*

*Aut.* I am a poor fellow, sir:—I know ye
well enough.                    [*Aside.*

*Cam.* Nay, pr'ythee, despatch: the gentleman is half-flayed already.

*Aut.* Are you in earnest, sir?—I smell the
trick on't.—                    [*Aside.*

*Flo.* Despatch, I pr'ythee.

*Aut.* Indeed, I have had earnest; but I cannot with conscience take it.

*Cam.* Unbuckle, unbuckle.—
            [FLO. *and* AUTOL. *exchange garments.*
Fortunate mistress,—let my prophecy
Come home to you!—you must retire yourself
Into some covert; take your sweetheart's hat,
And pluck it o'er your brows; muffle your face;
Dismantle you; and, as you can, disliken
The truth of your own seeming; that you
    may,—
For I do fear eyes over,—to shipboard
Get undescried.

*Per.*            I see the play so lies
That I must bear a part.

*Cam.*            No remedy.—
Have you done there?

*Flo.*            Should I now meet my father,
He would not call me son.

*Cam.* Nay, you shall have no hat.—
                    [*Giving it to* PERDITA.
Come, lady, come.—Farewell, my friend.

*Aut.* Adieu, sir.

*Flo.* O Perdita, what have we twain forgot?
Pray you, a word.            [*They converse apart.*

*Cam.* What I do next, shall be to tell the
    king                    [*Aside.*
Of this escape, and whither they are bound;
Wherein, my hope is, I shall so prevail
To force him after: in whose company
I shall review Sicilia; for whose sight
I have a woman's longing.

*Flo.*                    Fortune speed us!—
Thus we set on, Camillo, to the sea-side.

*Cam.* The swifter speed the better.
                    [*Exeunt* FLOR., PER., *and* CAM.

*Aut.* I understand the business,—I hear it:
to have an open ear, a quick eye, and a nimble
hand, is necessary for a cut-purse; a good nose
is requisite also, to smell out work for the other
senses. I see this is the time that the unjust
man doth thrive. What an exchange had this
been without boot? what a boot is here with
this exchange? Sure, the gods do this year con-
nive at us, and we may do anything extempore.
The prince himself is about a piece of iniquity,
—stealing away from his father with his clog
at his heels: if I thought it were a piece of honesty to acquaint the king withal, I would not
do't: I hold it the more knavery to conceal it;
and therein am I constant to my profession.

### Re-enter Clown *and* Shepherd.

Aside, aside;—here is more matter for a hot
brain: every lane's end, every shop, church,
session, hanging, yields a careful man work.

*Clo.* See, see: what a man you are now!

There is no other way but to tell the king she's a changeling, and none of your flesh and blood.

*Shep.* Nay, but hear me.

*Clo.* Nay, but hear me.

*Shep.* Go to, then.

*Clo.* She being none of your flesh and blood, your flesh and blood has not offended the king; and so your flesh and blood is not to be punished by him. Show those things you found about her; those secret things,—all but what she has with her: this being done, let the law go whistle; I warrant you.

*Shep.* I will tell the king all, every word,—yea, and his son's pranks too; who, I may say, is no honest man neither to his father nor to me, to go about to make me the king's brother-in-law.

*Clo.* Indeed, brother-in-law was the furthest off you could have been to him; and then your blood had been the dearer by I know how much an ounce.

*Aut.* Very wisely, puppies!　　[*Aside.*

*Shep.* Well, let us to the king: there is that in this fardel will make him scratch his beard!

*Aut.* I know not what impediment this complaint may be to the flight of my master. [*Aside.*

*Clo.* Pray heartily he be at palace.

*Aut.* Though I am not naturally honest, I am so sometimes by chance. Let me pocket up my pedlar's excrement. [*Aside, and takes off his false beard.*]—How now, rustics! whither are you bound?

*Shep.* To the palace, an it like your worship.

*Aut.* Your affairs there, what, with whom, the condition of that fardel, the place of your dwelling, your names, your ages, of what having, breeding, and anything that is fitting to be known? discover.

*Clo.* We are but plain fellows, sir.

*Aut.* A lie; you are rough and hairy. Let me have no lying; it becomes none but tradesmen, and they often give us soldiers the lie: but we pay them for it with stamped coin, not stabing steel; therefore they do not give us the lie.

*Clo.* Your worship had like to have given us one, if you had not taken yourself with the manner.

*Shep.* Are you a courtier, an't like you, sir?

*Aut.* Whether it like me or no, I am a courtier. Seest thou not the air of the court in these enfoldings? hath not my gait in it the measure of the court? receives not thy nose court-odour from me? reflect I not on thy baseness court-contempt? Thinkest thou, for that I insinuate, or toze from thee thy business, I am therefore no courtier? I am courtier cap-a-pé; and one that will either push on or pluck back thy business there: whereupon I command thee to open thy affair.

*Shep.* My business, sir, is to the king.

*Aut.* What advocate hast thou to him?

*Shep.* I know not, an't like you.

*Clo.* Advocate's the court-word for a pheasant, say you have none.

*Shep.* None, sir; I have no pheasant, cock nor hen.　　[men!

*Aut.* How bless'd are we that are not simple Yet nature might have made me as these are, Therefore I will not disdain.

*Clo.* This cannot be but a great courtier.

*Shep.* His garments are rich, but he wears them not handsomely.

*Clo.* He seems to be the more noble in being fantastical: a great man, I'll warrant; I know by the picking on's teeth.

*Aut.* The fardel there? what's i' the fardel? Wherefore that box?

*Shep.* Sir, there lies such secrets in this fardel and box, which none must know but the king; and which he shall know within this hour, if I may come to the speech of him.

*Aut.* Age, thou hast lost thy labour.

*Shep.* Why, sir?

*Aut.* The king is not at the palace; he is gone aboard a new ship to purge melancholy and air himself: for, if thou beest capable of things serious, thou must know the king is full of grief.

*Shep.* So 'tis said, sir,—about his son, that should have married a shepherd's daughter.

*Aut.* If that shepherd be not in hand-fast, let him fly: the curses he shall have, the tortures he shall feel, will break the back of man, the heart of monster.

*Clo.* Think you so, sir?

*Aut.* Not he alone shall suffer what wit can make heavy and vengeance bitter; but those that are germane to him, though removed fifty times, shall all come under the hangman: which, though it be great pity, yet it is necessary. An old sheep-whistling rogue, a ram-tender, to offer to have his daughter come into grace! Some say he shall be stoned; but that death is too soft for him, say I. Draw our throne into a sheep-cote!—all deaths are too few, the sharpest too easy.

*Clo.* Has the old man e'er a son, sir, do you hear, an't like you, sir?

*Aut.* He has a son,—who shall be flayed alive; then 'nointed over with honey, set on the head of a wasp's nest; then stand till he be three quarters and a dram dead; then recovered again with aquavitæ, or some other hot infusion; then, raw as he is, and in the hottest day prognostication proclaims, shall he be set against a brick-wall, the sun looking with a southward eye upon him,—where he is to behold him with flies blown to death. But what talk we of these traitorly rascals, whose miseries are to be smiled at, their offences being so capital? Tell me,—for you seem to be honest plain men,—what have you to the king: being something gently considered, I'll bring you where he is aboard, tender your persons to his presence, whisper him in your behalfs; and if it be in man besides the king to effect your suits, here is man shall do it.

*Clo.* He seems to be of great authority: close

with him, give him gold; and though authority
be a stubborn bear, yet he is oft led by the nose
with gold: show the inside of your purse to the
outside of his hand, and no more ado. Remember,—stoned and flayed alive.

*Shep.* An't please you, sir, to undertake the
business for us, here is that gold I have: I'll
make it as much more, and leave this young
man in pawn till I bring it you.

*Aut.* After I have done what I promised?

*Shep.* Ay, sir.

*Aut.* Well, give me the moiety.—Are you a
party in this business?

*Clo.* In some sort, sir: but though my case be
a pitiful one, I hope I shall not be flayed out of
it.

*Aut.* O, that's the case of the shepherd's son.
Hang him, he'll be made an example!

*Clo.* Comfort, good comfort! We must to the
king, and show our strange sights: he must
know 'tis none of your daughter nor my sister;
we are gone else. Sir, I will give you as much as
this old man does, when the business is performed; and remain, as he says, your pawn till
it be brought you.

*Aut.* I will trust you. Walk before toward
the sea-side; go on the right-hand: I will but
look upon the hedge, and follow you.

*Clo.* We are blessed in this man, as I may
say, even blessed.

*Shep.* Let's before, as he bids us: he was provided to do us good.

[*Exeunt* Shepherd *and* Clown.

*Aut.* If I had a mind to be honest, I see Fortune would not suffer me: she drops booties in
my mouth. I am courted now with a double
occasion,—gold, and a means to do the prince
my master good; which who knows how that
may turn back to my advancement? I will
bring these two moles, these blind ones, aboard
him; if he think it fit to shore them again, and
that the complaint they have to the king concerns him nothing, let him call me rogue for being so far officious; for I am proof against that
title, and what shame else belongs to 't. To him
will I present them: there may be matter in it.

[*Exit.*

## ACT V.

SCENE I.—SICILIA. *A Room in the Palace of*
LEONTES.

*Enter* LEONTES, CLEOMENES, DION, PAULINA,
*and others.*

*Cleo.* Sir, you have done enough, and have
perform'd
A saint-like sorrow: no fault could you make,
Which you have not redeem'd; indeed, paid
down
More penitence than done trespass: at the last,
Do as the heavens have done, forget your evil;
With them, forgive yourself.

*Leon.*                    Whilst I remember
Her and her virtues, I cannot forget
My blemishes in them; and so still think of

The wrong I did myself: which was so much
That heirless it hath made my kingdom, and
Destroy'd the sweet'st companion that e'er man
Bred his hopes out of.

*Paul.*                True, too true, my lord;
If, one by one, you wedded all the world,
Or from the all that are took something good,
To make a perfect woman, she you kill'd
Would be unparallel'd.

*Leon.*                I think so.—Kill'd!
She I kill'd! I did so: but thou strik'st me
Sorely, to say I did: it is as bitter          [now,
Upon thy tongue as in my thought: now, good
Say so but seldom.

*Cleo.*                Not at all, good lady;
You might have spoken a thousand things that
would
Have done the time more benefit, and grac'd
Your kindness better.

*Paul.*                You are one of those
Would have him wed again.

*Dion.*                If you would not so,
You pity not the state, nor the remembrance
Of his most sovereign name; consider little
What dangers, by his highness' fail of issue,
May drop upon his kingdom, and devour
Incertain lookers-on. What were more holy
Than to rejoice the former queen is well?
What holier than,—for royalty's repair,
For present comfort, and for future good,—
To bless the bed of majesty again
With a sweet fellow to 't?

*Paul.*                There is none worthy,
Respecting her that's gone. Besides, the gods
Will have fulfill'd their secret purposes:
For has not the divine Apollo said,
Is 't not the tenor of his oracle,
That king Leontes shall not have an heir
Till his lost child be found? which that it shall,
Is all as monstrous to our human reason
As my Antigonus to break his grave,
And come again to me; who, on my life,
Did perish with the infant. 'Tis your counsel
My lord should to the heavens be contrary,
Oppose against their wills.—Care not for issue;
[*To* LEONTES.
The crown will find an heir: great Alexander
Left his to the worthiest; so his successor
Was like to be the best.

*Leon.*                Good Paulina,—
Who hast the memory of Hermione,
I know, in honour,—O, that ever I          [now,
Had squar'd me to thy counsel!—then, even
I might have look'd upon my queen's full eyes;
Have taken treasure from her lips,—

*Paul.*                And left them
More rich for what they yielded.

*Leon.*                Thou speak'st truth.
No more such wives; therefore, no wife: one
worse,
And better us'd, would make her sainted spirit
Again possess her corpse; and, on this stage,—
Where we offend her now,—appear, soul-vexed,
And begin, *Why to me?*

*Paul.*                    Had she such power,
She had just cause.
    *Leon.*            She had; and would incense me
To murder her I married.
    *Paul.*          I should so.
Were I the ghost that walk'd, I'd bid you mark
Her eye, and tell me for what dull part in't
You chose her: then I'd shriek, that even your
                ears
Should rift to hear me; and the words that
                follow'd
Should be, *Remember mine!*
    *Leon.*            Stars, stars,
And all eyes else dead coals!—fear thou no wife;
I'll have no wife, Paulina.
    *Paul.*            Will you swear
Never to marry but by my free leave?
    *Leon.* Never, Paulina; so be bless'd my
                spirit!
    *Paul.* Then, good my lords, bear witness to
                his oath.
    *Cleo.* You tempt him over-much.
    *Paul.*                Unless another,
As like Hermione as is her picture,
Affront his eye.
    *Cleo.*        Good Madam,—
    *Paul.*                I have done.
Yet, if my lord will marry,—if you will, sir,
No remedy, but you will,—give me the office
To choose you a queen: she shall not be so young
As was your former; but she shall be such
As, walk'd your first queen's ghost, it should
                take joy
To see her in your arms.
    *Leon.*        My true Paulina,
We shall not marry till thou bidd'st us.
    *Paul.*                    That
Shall be when your first queen's again in breath:
Never till then.

            *Enter a* Gentleman.

    *Gent.* One that gives out himself Prince
                Florizel,
Son of Polixenes, with his princess,—she
The fairest I have yet beheld,—desires access
To your high presence.
    *Leon.*        What with him? he comes not
Like to his father's greatness: his approach,
So out of circumstance and sudden, tells us
'Tis not a visitation fram'd, but forc'd
By need and accident. What train?
    *Gent.*                But few,
And those but mean.
    *Leon.*        His princess, say you, with him?
    *Gent.* Ay; the most peerless piece of earth, I
                think,
That e'er the sun shone bright on.
    *Paul.*                O Hermione,
As every present time doth boast itself
Above a better gone, so must thy grave
Give way to what's seen now. Sir, you yourself
Have said and writ so,—but your writing now
Is colder than that theme,—*She had not been,
Nor was not to be equall'd;*—thus your verse

Flow'd with her beauty once; 'tis shrewdly
                ebb'd,
To say you have seen a better.
    *Gent.*            Pardon, madam:
The one I have almost forgot;—your pardon;—
The other, when she has obtain'd your eye,
Will have your tongue too. This is a creature,
Would she begin a sect, might quench the zeal
Of all professors else; make proselytes
Of who she but bid follow.
    *Paul.*            How! not women?
    *Gent.* Women will love her, that she is a
                woman
More worth than any man; men, that she is
The rarest of all women.
    *Leon.*            Go, Cleomenes;
Yourself, assisted with your honour'd friends,
Bring them to our embracement.—Still, tis
                strange,
            [*Exeunt* Cleo., *Lords, and* Gent.
He thus should steal upon us.
    *Paul.*                Had our prince,—
Jewel of children,—seen this hour, he had
                pair'd
Well with this lord: there was not full a month
                between their births.
    *Leon.* Pr'ythee, no more; cease; thou know'st
He dies to me again when talk'd of: sure,
When I shall see this gentleman, thy speeches
Will bring me to consider that which may
Unfurnish me of reason.—They are come.—

*Re-enter* CLEOMENES, *with* FLORIZEL, PERDITA,
                *and* Attendants.

Your mother was most true to wedlock, prince;
For she did print your royal father off,
Conceiving you: were I but twenty-one,
Your father's image is so hit in you,
His very air, that I should call you brother,
As I did him, and speak of something wildly
By us perform'd before. Most dearly welcome!
And your fair princess,—goddess!—O, alas!
I lost a couple that 'twixt heaven and earth
Might thus have stood, begetting wonder, as
You, gracious couple, do! and then I lost,—
All mine own folly,—the society,
Amity too, of your brave father, whom,
Though bearing misery, I desire my life
Once more to look on him.
    *Flo.*            By his command
Have I here touch'd Sicilia, and from him
Give you all greetings that a king, at friend,
Can send his brother: and, but infirmity,—
Which waits upon worn times,—hath some
                thing seiz'd
His wish'd ability, he had himself
The lands and waters 'twixt your throne and his
Measur'd, to look upon you; whom he loves,—
He bade me say so,—more than all the sceptres,
And those that bear them, living.
    *Leon.*        O my brother,—        [stir
Good gentleman!—the wrongs I have done thee
Afresh within me; and these my offices,
So rarely kind, are as interpreters

Of my behind-hand slackness!—Welcome hither,
As is the spring to the earth. And hath he too
Expos'd this paragon to the fearful usage,—
At least ungentle,—of the dreadful Neptune,
To greet a man not worth her pains, much less
The adventure of her person?
   *Flo.*             Good, my lord,
She came from Libya.
   *Leon.*       Where the warlike Smalus,
That noble honour'd lord, is fear'd and lov'd?
   *Flo.* Most royal sir, from thence; from him,
    whose daughter
His tears proclaim'd his, parting with her: thence—
A prosperous south wind friendly,—we have cross'd,
To execute the charge my father gave me,
For visiting your highness: my best train
I have from my Sicilian shores dismiss'd;
Who for Bohemia bend, to signify
Not only my success in Libya, sir,
But my arrival, and my wife's, in safety
Here, where we are.
   *Leon.*       The blessed gods
Purge all infection from our air whilst you
Do climate here! You have a holy father,
A graceful gentleman; against whose person,
So sacred as it is, I have done sin:
For which the heavens, taking angry note,
Have left me issueless; and your father's bless'd,—
As he from heaven merits it,—with you,
Worthy his goodness. What might I have been,
Might I a son and daughter now have look'd on,
Such goodly things as you!

          *Enter a* Lord.

   *Lord.*          Most noble sir,
That which I shall report will bear no credit,
Were not the proof so nigh. Please you, great sir
Bohemia greets you from himself by me.
Desires you to attach his son, who has,
His dignity and duty both cast off,—
Fled from his father, from his hopes, and with
A shepherd's daughter.
   *Leon.*     Where's Bohemia? speak.
   *Lord.* Here in your city; I now came from him:
I speak amazedly; and it becomes
My marvel and my message. To your court
Whiles he was hast'ning,—in the chase, it seems,
Of this fair couple,—meets he on the way
The father of this seeming lady, and
Her brother, both having their country quitted
With this young prince.
   *Flo.*       Camillo has betray'd me;
Whose honour and whose honesty, till now,
Endur'd all weathers.
   *Lord.*      Lay't so to his charge;
He's with the king your father.
   *Leon.*           Who? Camillo?

   *Lord.* Camillo, sir; I spake with him; who now
Has these poor men in question. Never saw I
Wretches so quake: they kneel, they kiss the earth;
Forswear themselves as often as they speak:
Bohemia stops his ears, and threatens them
With divers deaths in death.
   *Per.*         O my poor father!—
The heaven sets spies upon us, will not have
Our contract celebrated.
   *Leon.*         You are married?
   *Flo.* We are not, sir, nor are we like to be;
The stars, I see, will kiss the valleys first:—
The odds for high and low's alike.
   *Leon.*           My lord,
Is this the daughter of a king?
   *Flo.*            She is,
When once she is my wife.
   *Leon.* That once, I see, by your good father's speed,
Will come on very slowly. I am sorry,
Most sorry, you have broken from his liking,
Where you were tied in duty; and as sorry
Your choice is not so rich in worth as beauty,
That you might well enjoy her.
   *Flo.*         Dear, look up:
Though Fortune, visible an enemy,
Should chase us, with my father, power no jot
Hath she to change our loves.—Beseech you, sir,
Remember since you ow'd no more to time
Than I do now: with thought of such affections,
Step forth mine advocate; at your request
My father will grant precious things as trifles.
   *Leon.* Would he do so, I'd beg your precious mistress,
Which he counts but a trifle.
   *Paul.*         Sir, my liege,
Your eye hath too much youth in't: not a month
'Fore your queen died, she was more worth such gazes
Than what you look on now.
   *Leon.*         I thought of her
Even in these looks I made.—But your petition
                 [*To* FLORIZEL.
Is yet unanswer'd. I will to your father:
Your honour not o'erthrown by your desires,
I am friend to them and you: upon which errand
I now go toward him; therefore, follow me,
And mark what way I make. Come, good my lord.
                 [*Exeunt.*

SCENE II.—*The same. Before the Palace.*

   *Enter* AUTOLYCUS *and a* Gentleman.

   *Aut.* Beseech you, sir, were you present at this relation?
   1 *Gent.* I was by at the opening of the fardel, heard the old shepherd deliver the manner how he found it: whereupon, after a little amazedness, we were all commanded out of the cham-

ber; only this, methought I heard the shepherd say he found the child.   [it.

*Aut.* I would most gladly know the issue of

1 *Gent.* I make a broken delivery of the business; but the changes I perceived in the king and Camillo were very notes of admiration: they seemed almost, with staring on one another, to tear the cases of their eyes; there was speech in their dumbness, language in their very gesture; they looked as they had heard of a world ransomed, or one destroyed: a notable passion of wonder appeared in them; but the wisest beholder, that knew no more but seeing, could not say if the importance were joy or sorrow;—but in the extremity of the one, it must needs be. Here comes a gentleman that happily knows more.

*Enter a Gentleman.*

The news, Rogero?

2 *Gent.* Nothing but bonfires: the oracle is fulfilled; the king's daughter is found: such a deal of wonder is broken out within this hour that ballad-makers cannot be able to express it. Here comes the Lady Paulina's steward: he can deliver you more.

*Enter a third Gentleman.*

How goes it now, sir? this news, which is called true, is so like an old tale that the verity of it is in strong suspicion. Has the king found his heir?

3 *Gent.* Most true, if ever truth were pregnant by circumstance: that which you hear you'll swear you see, there is such unity in the proofs. The mantle of Queen Hermione; her jewel about the neck of it; the letters of Antigonus, found with it, which they know to be his character; the majesty of the creature in resemblance of the mother; the affection of nobleness, which nature shows above her breeding; and many other evidences,—proclaim her with all certainty to be the king's daughter. Did you see the meeting of the two kings?

2 *Gent.* No.

3 *Gent.* Then have you lost a sight which was to be seen, cannot be spoken of. There might you have beheld one joy crown another, so and in such manner that it seemed sorrow wept to take leave of them; for their joy waded in tears. There was casting up of eyes, holding up of hands, with countenance of such distraction that they were to be known by garment, not by favour. Our king, being ready to leap out of himself for joy of his found daughter, as if that joy were now become a loss, cries, *O, thy mother, thy mother!* then asks Bohemia forgiveness; then embraces his son-in-law; then again worries he his daughter with clipping her; now he thanks the old shepherd, which stands by like a weather-bitten conduit of many kings' reigns. I never heard of such another encounter, which lames report to follow it, and undoes description to do it.

2 *Gent.* What, pray you, became of Antigonus, that carried hence the child?

3 *Gent.* Like an old tale still, which will have matter to rehearse, though credit be asleep, and not an ear open. He was torn to pieces with a bear: this avouches the shepherd's son; who has not only his innocence,—which seems much,—to justify him, but a handkerchief and rings of his, that Paulina knows.

1 *Gent.* What became of his bark and his followers?

3 *Gent.* Wrecked the same instant of their master's death, and in the view of the shepherd: so that all the instruments which aided to expose the child were even then lost when it was found. But, O, the noble combat that, 'twixt joy and sorrow, was fought in Paulina! She had one eye declined for the loss of her husband, another elevated that the oracle was fulfilled: she lifted the princess from the earth, and so locks her in embracing, as if she would pin her to her heart, that she might no more be in danger of losing.

1 *Gent.* The dignity of this act was worth the audience of kings and princes; for by such was it acted.

3 *Gent.* One of the prettiest touches of all, and that which angled for mine eyes,—caught the water, though not the fish,—was when, at the relation of the queen's death, with the the relation of the queen's death, with the manner how she came to it,—bravely confessed and lamented by the king,—how attentiveness wounded his daughter; till, from one sign of dolour to another, she did, with an *alas!* I would fain say, bleed tears; for I am sure my heart wept blood. Who was most marble there changed colour; some swooned, all sorrowed: if all the world could have seen it, the woe had been universal.

1 *Gent.* Are they returned to the court?

3 *Gent.* No: the princess hearing of her mother's statue, which is in the keeping of Paulina,—a piece many years in doing, and now newly performed by that rare Italian-master, Julio Romano, who, had he himself eternity, and could put breath into his work, would beguile nature of her custom, so perfectly he is her ape. he so near to Hermione hath done Hermione, that they say one would speak to her, and stand in hope of answer:—thither with all greediness of affection are they gone; and there they intend to sup.

2 *Gent.* I thought she had some great matter there in hand; for she hath privately twice or thrice a day, ever since the death of Hermione, visited that removed house. Shall we thither, and with our company piece the rejoicing?

1 *Gent.* Who would be thence that has the benefit of access? every wink of an eye some new grace will be born: our absence makes us unthrifty to our knowledge. Let's along.

[*Exeunt* Gentlemen.

*Aut.* Now, had I not the dash of my former

life in me, would preferment drop on my head. I brought the old man and his son aboard the prince; told him I heard them talk of a fardel, and I know not what; but he at that time over-fond of the shepherd's daughter,—so he then took her to be,—who began to be much sea-sick and himself little better, extremity of weather continuing, this mystery remained undiscovered. But 'tis all one to me; for had I been the finder-out of this secret, it would not have relished among my other discredits. Here come those I have done good to against my will, and already appearing in the blossoms of their fortune.

*Enter* Shepherd *and* Clown.

*Shep.* Come, boy; I am past more children, but thy sons and daughters will be all gentlemen born.

*Clo.* You are well met, sir: you denied to fight with me this other day, because I was no gentleman born. See you these clothes? say you see them not, and think me still no gentleman born: you were best say these robes are not gentlemen born. Give me the lie, do; and try whether I am not now a gentleman born.

*Aut.* I know you are now, sir, a gentleman born.

*Clo.* Ay, and have been so any time these four hours.

*Shep.* And so have I, boy!

*Clo.* So you have:—but I was a gentleman born before my father; for the king's son took me by the hand and called me brother; and then the two kings called my father brother; and then the prince, my brother, and the princess, my sister, called my father father; and so we wept: and there was the first gentleman-like tears that ever we shed.

*Shep.* We may live, son, to shed many more.

*Clo.* Ay; or else 'twere hard luck, being in so preposterous estate as we are.

*Aut.* I humbly beseech you, sir, to pardon me all the faults I have committed to your worship, and to give me your good report to the prince my master.

*Shep.* Pr'ythee, son, do; for we must be gentle, now we are gentlemen.

*Clo.* Thou wilt amend thy life?

*Aut.* Ay, an it like your good worship.

*Clo.* Give me thy hand: I will swear to the prince thou art as honest a true fellow as any is in Bohemia.

*Shep.* You may say it, but not swear it.

*Clo.* Not swear it, now I am a gentleman? Let boors and franklins say it, I'll swear it.

*Shep.* How if it be false, son?

*Clo.* If it be ne'er so false, a true gentleman may swear it in the behalf of his friend.—And I'll swear to the prince, thou art a tall fellow of thy hands, and that thou wilt not be drunk; but I know thou art no tall fellow of thy hands, and that thou wilt be drunk: but I'll swear it;

and I would thou wouldst be a tall fellow of thy hands.

*Aut.* I will prove so, sir, to my power.

*Clo.* Ay, by any means, prove a tall fellow: if I do not wonder how thou darest venture to be drunk, not being a tall fellow, trust me not. —Hark! the kings and the princes, our kindred, are going to see the queen's picture. Come, follow us: we'll be thy good masters. [*Exeunt.*

SCENE III.—*The same. A Room in* PAULINA'S *House.*

*Enter* LEONTES, POLIXENES, FLORIZEL, PERDITA, CAMILLO, PAULINA, Lords, *and* Attendants.

*Leon.* O grave and good Paulina, the great comfort
That I have had of thee!
*Paul.* What, sovereign sir,
I did not well, I meant well. All my services
You have paid home: but that you have vouchsaf'd, [tracted
With your crown'd brother, and these your con-
Heirs of your kingdoms, my poor house to visit,
It is a surplus of your grace which never
My life may last to answer.
*Leon.* O Paulina,
We honour you with trouble:—but we came
To see the statue of our queen: your gallery
Have we pass'd through, not without much content
In many singularities; but we saw not
That which my daughter came to look upon,
The statue of her mother.
*Paul.* As she liv'd peerless,
So her dead likeness, I do well believe,
Excels whatever yet you look'd upon,
Or hand of man hath done; therefore I keep it
Lonely, apart. But here it is: prepare
To see the life as lively mock'd as ever [well.
Still sleep mock'd death: behold; and say 'tis
[PAULINA *undraws a curtain, and discovers*
HERMIONE *standing as a statue.*
I like your silence,—it the more shows off
Your wonder: but yet speak;—first, you, my liege.
Comes it not something near?
*Leon.* Her natural posture!—
Chide me, dear stone, that I may say indeed,
Thou art Hermione; or rather, thou art she,
In thy not chiding; for she was as tender
As infancy and grace.—But yet, Paulina,
Hermione was not so much wrinkled; nothing
So aged, as this seems.
*Pol.* O, not by much.
*Paul.* So much the more our carver's excellence; [her
Which lets go by some sixteen years, and makes
As she liv'd now.
*Leon.* As now she might have done,
So much to my good comfort, as it is
Now piercing to my soul. O, thus she stood,
Even with such life of majesty,—warm life,

As now it coldly stands,—when first I woo'd her!
I am asham'd: does not the stone rebuke me
For being more stone than it?—O royal piece,
There's magic in thy majesty; which has
My evils conjur'd to remembrance; and
From thy admiring daughter took the spirits,
Standing like stone with thee!

*Per.*                        And give me leave;
And do not say 'tis superstition, that
I kneel, and then implore her blessing.—Lady,
Dear queen, that ended when I but began,
Give me that hand of yours to kiss.

*Paul.*                        O, patience!
The statue is but newly fix'd, the colour's
Not dry.                                    [on,

*Cam.* My lord, your sorrow was too sore laid
Which sixteen winters cannot blow away,
So many summers dry: scarce any joy
Did ever so long live; no sorrow
But kill'd itself much sooner.

*Pol.*                        Dear my brother,
Let him that was the cause of this have power
To take off so much grief from you as he
Will piece up in himself.

*Paul.*                        Indeed, my lord,
If I had thought the sight of my poor image
Would thus have wrought you,—for the stone
    is mine,—
I'd not have show'd it.

*Leon.*                        Do not draw the curtain.

*Paul.* No longer shall you gaze on't; lest
    your fancy
May think anon it moves.

*Leon.*                        Let be, let be.—
Would I were dead, but that, methinks, al-
    ready—
What was he that did make it?—See, my lord,
Would you not deem it breath'd? and that
    those veins
Did verily bear blood?

*Pol.*                        Masterly done:
The very life seems warm upon her lip.

*Leon.* The fixture of her eye has motion in't,
As we are mock'd with art.

*Paul.*                        I'll draw the curtain:
My lord's almost so far transported that
He'll think anon it lives.

*Leon.*                        O sweet Paulina,
Make me to think so twenty years together!
No settled senses of the world can match
The pleasure of that madness. Let't alone.

*Paul.* I am sorry, sir, I have thus far stirr'd
    you: but
I could afflict you further.

*Leon.*                        Do, Paulina;
For this affliction has a taste as sweet
As any cordial comfort.—Still, methinks,
There is an air comes from her: what fine chisel
Could ever yet cut breath? Let no man mock
    me,
For I will kiss her!

*Paul.*                        Good my lord, forbear:
The ruddiness upon her lip is wet;
You'll mar it if you kiss it; stain your own

With oily painting. Shall I draw the curtain?

*Leon.* No, not these twenty years.

*Per.*                        So long could I
Stand by, a looker on.

*Paul.*                        Either forbear,
Quit presently the chapel, or resolve you
For more amazement. If you can behold
I'll make the statue move indeed, descend
And take you by the hand: but then you'll
    think,—
Which I protest against,—I am assisted
By wicked powers.

*Leon.*                        What you can make her do
I am content to look on: what to speak?
I am content to hear; for 'tis as easy
To make her speak as move.

*Paul.*                        It is requir'd
You do awake your faith. Then all stand still;
Or those that think it is unlawful business
I am about, let them depart.

*Leon.*                        Proceed:
No foot shall stir.

*Paul.* Music, awake her: strike!—  [*Music.*
'Tis time; descend; be stone no more; approach;
Strike all that look upon with marvel. Come;
I'll fill your grave up: stir; nay, come away;
Bequeath to death your numbness, for from him
Dear life redeems you.—You perceive she stirs:
[HERMIONE *comes down from the pedestal.*
Start not; her actions shall be holy as
You hear my spell is lawful: do not shun her
Until you see her die again; for then
You kill her double. Nay, present your hand:
When she was young you woo'd her; now in age
Is she become the suitor.

*Leon.*                        O, she's warm! [*Embracing her.*
If this be magic, let it be an art
Lawful as eating.

*Pol.*                        She embraces him.

*Cam.* She hangs about his neck:
If she pertain to life, let her speak too.

*Pol.* Ay, and make't manifest where she has
    liv'd,
Or how stol'n from the dead.

*Paul.*                        That she is living,
Were it but told you, should be hooted at
Like an old tale; but it appears she lives,
Though yet she speak not. Mark a little while.—
Please you to interpose, fair madam: kneel,
And pray your mother's blessing.—Turn, good
    lady;
Our Perdita is found.
[*Presenting* PER., *who kneels to* HER.

*Her.*                        You gods, look down,
And from your sacred vials pour your graces
Upon my daughter's head!—Tell me, mine
    own,
Where hast thou been preserv'd? where liv'd?
    how found                                [I,—
Thy father's court? for thou shalt hear that
Knowing by Paulina that the oracle
Gave hope thou wast in being,—have pre-
    serv'd
Myself to see the issue.

*Paul.* There's time enough for that;
Lest they desire, upon this push, to trouble
Your joys with like relation.—Go together,
You precious winners all; your exultation
Partake to every one. I, an old turtle,
Will wing me to some wither'd bough, and
there
My mate, that's never to be found again,
Lament till I am lost.

*Leon.* O peace, Paulina!
Thou shouldst a husband take by my consent,
As I by thine a wife: this is a match,
And made between's by vows. Thou hast found
mine;
But how, is to be question'd: for I saw her,
As I thought, dead; and have, in vain, said
many
A prayer upon her grave. I'll not seek
far,—

For him, I partly know his mind,—to find thee
An honourable husband.—Come, Camillo,
And take her by the hand, whose worth and
honesty
Is richly noted, and here justified
By us, a pair of kings.—Let's from this place.—
What! look upon my brother:—both your par-
dons,
That e'er I put between your holy looks
My ill suspicion.—This your son-in-law,
And son unto the king, whom heavens direct-
ing,
Is troth-plight to your daughter.—Good Paul-
ina,
Lead us from hence; where we may leisurely
Each one demand, and answer to his part
Perform'd in this wide gap of time, since first
We were dissever'd: hastily lead away!

[*Exeunt.*

# THE COMEDY OF ERRORS

## DRAMATIS PERSONÆ

SOLINUS, *Duke of Ephesus.*
ÆGEON, *a Merchant of Syracuse.*
ANTIPHOLUS OF EPHESUS, ANTIPHOLUS OF SYRACUSE, } *Twin Brothers, and sons to ÆGEON and ÆMILIA, but unknown to each other.*
DROMIO OF EPHESUS, DROMIO OF SYRACUSE, } *Twin Brothers, and Attendants on the two* ANTIPHOLUSES.
BALTHAZAR, *a Merchant.*
ANGELO, *a Goldsmith.*
A Merchant, *Friend to* ANTIPHOLUS OF SYRACUSE,

PINCH, *a Schoolmaster and a Conjurer.*

ÆMILIA, *Wife to* ÆGEON, *an Abbess at Ephesus.*
ADRIANA, *Wife to* ANTIPHOLUS OF EPHESUS.
LUCIANA, *her Sister.*
LUCE, *her Servant.*

A Courtezan.

Gaoler, Officers, *and other* Attendants.

SCENE,—EPHESUS.

## ACT I.

SCENE I.—*A Hall in the* DUKE'S *Palace.*

*Enter* DUKE, ÆGEON, Gaoler, Officers, *and other* Attendants.

*Æge.* Proceed, Solinus, to procure my fall,
And, by the doom of death, end woes and all.
*Duke.* Merchant of Syracusa, plead no more;
I am not partial to infringe our laws:
The enmity and discord which of late
Sprung from the rancorous outrage of your duke
To merchants, our well-dealing countrymen,—
Who, wanting gilders to redeem their lives,
Have sealed his rigorous statutes with their bloods,—
Excludes all pity from our threat'ning looks.
For, since the mortal and intestine jars
'Twixt thy seditious countrymen and us,
It hath in solemn synods been decreed,
Both by the Syracusans and ourselves,
To admit no traffic to our adverse towns:
Nay, more,
If any born at Ephesus be seen
At any Syracusan marts and fairs,—
Again, if any Syracusan born
Come to the bay of Ephesus, he dies,
His goods confiscate to the duke's dispose;
Unless a thousand marks be levied,
To quit the penalty and to ransom him.—
Thy substance, valued at the highest rate,
Cannot amount unto a hundred marks:
Therefore, by law thou art condemn'd to die.
*Æge.* Yet this my comfort,—when your words are done,
My woes end likewise with the evening sun.
*Duke.* Well, Syracusan, say, in brief, the cause
Why thou departedst from thy native home,
And for what cause thou cam'st to Ephesus.
*Æge.* A heavier task could not have been impos'd
Than I to speak my griefs unspeakable!
Yet, that the world may witness that my end
Was wrought by nature, not by vile offence,
I'll utter what my sorrow gives me leave.
In Syracusa was I born; and wed
Unto a woman, happy but for me,
And by me too, had not our hap been bad.
With her I liv'd in joy; our wealth increas'd
By prosperous voyages I often made
To Epidamnum, till my factor's death,
And he,—great care of goods at random left,—
Drew me from kind embracements of my spouse: [old,
From whom my absence was not six months
Before herself,—almost at fainting under
The pleasing punishment that women bear,—
Had made provision for her following me,
And soon and safe arrived where I was.
There she had not been long but she became
A joyful mother of two goodly sons; [other
And, which was strange, the one so like the
As could not be distinguish'd but by names.
That very hour, and in the self-same inn,
A poor mean woman was delivered
Of such a burden, male twins, both alike:
Those,—for their parents were exceeding poor,—
I bought, and brought up to attend my sons.
My wife, not meanly proud of two such boys,
Made daily motions for our home return:
Unwilling I agreed; alas, too soon!
We came aboard:
A league from Epidamnum had we sail'd
Before the always-wind-obeying deep
Gave any tragic instance of our harm;
But longer did we not retain much hope:

For what obscured light the heavens did grant
Did but convey unto our fearful minds
A doubtful warrant of immediate death;
Which, though myself would gladly have em-
　　brac'd,
Yet the incessant weepings of my wife,
Weeping before for what she saw must come,
And piteous plainings of the pretty babes,
That mourn'd for fashion, ignorant what to
　　fear,
Forc'd me to seek delays for them and me.
And this it was,—for other means was none.—
The sailors sought for safety by our boat,
And left the ship, then sinking-ripe, to us:
My wife, more careful for the latter-born,
Had fasten'd him unto a small spare mast,
Such as sea-faring men provide for storms:
To him one of the other twins was bound,
Whilst I had been like heedful of the other.
The children thus dispos'd, my wife and I,
Fixing our eyes on whom our care was fix'd,
Fasten'd ourselves at either end the mast;
And floating straight, obedient to the stream,
Were carried towards Corinth, as we thought.
At length the sun, gazing upon the earth,
Dispers'd those vapours that offended us;
And, by the benefit of his wish'd light,
The seas wax'd calm, and we discover'd
Two ships from far making amain to us,—
Of Corinth that, of Epidaurus this:
But ere they came,—O, let me say no more!—
Gather the sequel by that went before.
　　*Duke.* Nay: forward, old man, do not break
　　　　off so;
For we may pity, though not pardon thee.
　　*Æge.* O, had the gods done so, I had not now
Worthily term'd them merciless to us!
For, ere the ships could meet by twice five
　　leagues,
We were encounter'd by a mighty rock,
Which being violently borne upon,
Our helpful ship was splitted in the midst;
So that, in this unjust divorce of us,
Fortune had left to both of us alike
What to delight in, what to sorrow for.
Her part, poor soul! seeming as burdened
With lesser weight, but not with lesser woe,
Was carried with more speed before the wind;
And in our sight they three were taken up
By fishermen of Corinth, as we thought.
At length another ship had seiz'd on us;
And, knowing whom it was their hap to save,
Gave helpful welcome to their shipwreck'd
　　guests;
And would have reft the fishers of their prey,
Had not their bark been very slow of sail,
And therefore homeward did they bend their
　　course.—
Thus have you heard me sever'd from my bliss;
That by misfortunes was my life prolong'd,
To tell sad stories of my own mishaps.
　　*Duke.* And, for the sake of them thou sor-
　　　　rowest for,
Do me the favour to dilate at full

What hath befall'n of them and thee till now.
　　*Æge.* My youngest boy, and yet my eldest
　　　　care,
At eighteen years became inquisitive
After his brother, and impórtun'd me
That his attendant,—for his case was like,
Reft of his brother, but retain'd his name,—
Might bear him company in the quest of him:
Whom whilst I labour'd of a love to see,
I hazarded the loss of whom I lov'd.
Five summers have I spent in furthest Greece,
Roaming clean through the bounds of Asia,
And, coasting homeward, came to Ephesus;
Hopeless to find, yet loath to leave unsought
Or that or any place that harbours men.
But here must end the story of my life;
And happy were I in my timely death,
Could all my travels warrant me they live.
　　*Duke.* Hapless Ægeon, whom the fates have
　　　　mark'd
To bear the extremity of dire mishap!
Now, trust me, were it not against our laws,
Against my crown, my oath, my dignity,
Which princes, would they, may not disannul,
My soul should sue as advocate for thee.
But though thou art adjudged to the death,
And passed sentence may not be recall'd
But to our honour's great disparagement,
Yet will I favour thee in what I can:
Therefore, merchant, I'll limit thee this day
To seek thy help by beneficial help:
Try all the friends thou hast in Ephesus:
Beg thou, or borrow, to make up the sum,
And live; if not, then thou art doom'd to die.—
Gaoler, take him to thy custody.
　　*Gaol.* I will, my lord.
　　*Æge.* Hopeless and helpless doth Ægeon
　　　　wend.
But to procrastinate his lifeless end. [*Exeunt.*

SCENE II.—*A public Place.*

*Enter* ANTIPHOLUS *and* DROMIO OF
SYRACUSE, *and a* Merchant.

　　*Mer.* Therefore, give out you are of Epi-
　　　　damnum,
Lest that your goods too soon be confiscate.
This very day a Syracusan merchant
Is apprehended for arrival here;
And, not being able to buy out his life,
According to the statute of the town,
Dies ere the weary sun set in the west.—
There is your money that I had to keep.
　　*Ant. S.* Go bear it to the Centaur, where
　　　　we host,
And stay there, Dromio, till I come to thee.
Within this hour it will be dinner-time:
Till that, I'll view the manners of the town,
Peruse the traders, gaze upon the buildings,
And then return and sleep within mine inn;
For with long travel I am stiff and weary.—
Get thee away. 　　　　　　　　　　[word,
　　*Dro. S.* Many a man would take you at your
And go indeed, having so good a mean.
　　　　　　　　　　　　　[*Exit* DROMIO S.

*Ant. S.* A trusty villain, sir, that very oft,
When I am dull with care and melancholy,
Lightens my humour with his merry jests.
What, will you walk with me about the town,
And then go to my inn and dine with me?

*Mer.* I am invited, sir, to certain merchants,
Of whom I hope to make much benefit:
I crave your pardon. Soon, at five o'clock,
Please you, I'll meet with you upon the mart,
And afterwards consort you until bed-time:
My present business calls me from you now.

*Ant. S.* Farewell till then: I will go lose
     myself,
And wander up and down to view the city.

*Mer.* Sir, I commend you to your own con-
     tent.                    [*Exit* Merchant.

*Ant. S.* He that commends me to mine own
     content,
Commends me to the thing I cannot get.
I to the world am like a drop of water
That in the ocean seeks another drop;
Who, failing there to find his fellow forth,
Unseen, inquisitive, confounds himself:
So I, to find a mother and a brother,
In quest of them, unhappy, lose myself.

     *Enter* DROMIO OF EPHESUS.

Here comes the almanac of my true date.—
What now? How chance thou art return'd so
     soon?                    [too late:

*Dro. E.* Return'd so soon! rather approach'd
The capon burns, the pig falls from the spit;
The clock hath strucken twelve upon the bell—
My mistress made it one upon my cheek:
She is so hot because the meat is cold;
The meat is cold because you come not home;
You come not home because you have no
     stomach;
You have no stomach, having broke your fast;
But we, that know what 'tis to fast and pray,
Are penitent for your default to-day.

*Ant. S.* Stop—in your wind, sir; tell me this,
     I pray;
Where have you left the money that I gave you?

*Dro. E.* O,—sixpence that I had o' Wednes-
     day last
To pay the saddler for my mistress' crupper;—
The saddler had it, sir, I kept it not.

*Ant. S.* I am not in a sportive humour now:
Tell me, and dally not, where is the money?
We being strangers here, how dar'st thou trust
So great a charge from thine own custody?

*Dro. E.* I pray you, jest, sir, as you sit at
     dinner:
I from my mistress come to you in post:
If I return, I shall be post indeed;
For she will score your fault upon my pate.
Methinks your maw, like mine, should be your
     clock,
And strike you home without a messenger.

*Ant. S.* Come, Dromio, come, these jests are
     out of season;
Reserve them till a merrier hour than this.
Where is the gold I gave in charge to thee?

*Dro. E.* To me, sir? why, you gave no gold
     to me!                    [foolishness,

*Ant. S.* Come on, sir knave; have done your
And tell me how thou hast dispos'd thy charge.

*Dro. E.* My charge was but to fetch you from
     the mart
Home to your house, the Phœnix, sir, to dinner:
My mistress and her sister stay for you.

*Ant. S.* Now, as I am a Christian, answer me,
In what safe place you have bestow'd my
     money:
Or I shall break that merry sconce of yours,
That stands on tricks when I am undispos'd;
Where is the thousand marks thou hadst of me?

*Dro. E.* I have some marks of yours upon
     my pate,
Some of my mistress' marks upon my shoulders,
But not a thousand marks between you both.—
If I should pay your worship those again,
Perchance you will not bear them patiently.

*Ant. S.* Thy mistress' marks! what mistress,
     slave, hast thou?

*Dro. E.* Your worship's wife, my mistress at
     the Phœnix;
She that doth fast till you come home to dinner,
And prays that you will hie you home to dinner.

*Ant. S.* What, wilt thou flout me thus unto
     my face,
Being forbid? There, take you that, sir knave.

*Dro. E.* What mean you, sir? for God's sake,
     hold your hands:
Nay, an you will not, sir, I'll take my heels.
                    [*Exit* DROMIO E.

*Ant. S.* Upon my life, by some device or
     other,
The villain is o'er-raught of all my money.
They say this town is full of cozenage;
As, nimble jugglers that deceive the eye,
Dark-working sorcerers that change the mind,
Soul-killing witches that deform the body,
Disguised cheaters, prating mountebanks,
And many such-like liberties of sin:
If it prove so, I will be gone the sooner.
I'll to the Centaur, to go seek this slave:
I greatly fear my money is not safe.     [*Exit.*

     ACT II.

     SCENE I.—*A public Place.*

     *Enter* ADRIANA *and* LUCIANA.

*Adr.* Neither my husband nor the slave re-
     turn'd,
That in such haste I sent to seek his master!
Sure, Luciana, it is two o'clock.          [him,

*Luc.* Perhaps some merchant hath invited
And from the mart he's somewhere gone to
     dinner.
Good sister, let us dine, and never fret:
A man is master of his liberty;
Time is their master; and, when they see time,
They'll go or come. If so, be patient, sister.

*Adr.* Why should their liberty than ours be
     more?                    [door.

*Luc.* Because their business still lies out o'

*Adr.* Look, when I serve him so, he takes it ill.

*Luc.* O, know he is the bridle of your will.

*Adr.* There's none but asses will be bridled so.                                        [woe.

*Luc.* Why, headstrong liberty is lash'd with
There's nothing situate under heaven's eye
But hath his bound in earth, in sea, in sky:
The beasts, the fishes, and the winged fowls,
Are their males' subject, and at their controls:
Men, more divine, the masters of all these,
Lords of the wide world and wild wat'ry seas,
Indued with intellectual sense and souls
Of more pre-eminence than fish and fowls,
Are masters to their females, and their lords:
Then let your will attend on their accords.

*Adr.* This servitude makes you to keep unwed.                                        [bed.

*Luc.* Not this, but troubles of the marriage-

*Adr.* But, were you wedded, you would bear
some sway.

*Luc.* Ere I learn love, I'll practise to obey.

*Adr.* How if your husband start some other
where?

*Luc.* Till he come home again I would forbear.

*Adr.* Patience unmov'd, no marvel though
she pause:
They can be meek that have no other cause.
A wretched soul, bruis'd with adversity,
We bid be quiet when we hear it cry;
But were we burden'd with like weight of pain,
As much, or more, we should ourselves com-
plain:                                        [thee,
So thou, that hast no unkind mate to grieve
With urging helpless patience wouldst relieve
me:
But if thou live to see like right bereft,
This fool-begg'd patience in thee will be left.

*Luc.* Well, I will marry one day, but to try:—
Here comes your man, now is your husband
nigh.

*Enter* DROMIO OF EPHESUS.

*Adr.* Say, is your tardy master now at hand?

*Dro. E.* Nay, he is at two hands with me,
and that my two ears can witness.

*Adr.* Say, didst thou speak with him?
know'st thou his mind?

*Dro. E.* Ay, ay, he told his mind upon mine
ear. Beshrew his hand, I scarce could understand it.

*Luc.* Spake he so doubtfully thou couldst
not feel his meaning?

*Dro. E.* Nay, he struck so plainly I could too
well feel his blows; and withal so doubtfully
that I could scarce understand them.

*Adr.* But say, I pr'ythee, is he coming home?
It seems he hath great care to please his wife.

*Dro. E.* Why, mistress, sure my master is
horn-mad.

*Adr.* Horn-mad, thou villain?

*Dro. E.* I mean not cuckold-mad; but, sure,
he's stark-mad.
When I desir'd him to come home to dinner,

He ask'd me for a thousand marks in gold:
*'Tis dinner-time*, quoth I; *My gold*, quoth he:
*Your meat doth burn*, quoth I; *My gold*, quoth he:
*Will you come home?* quoth I; *My gold*, quoth he:
*Where is the thousand marks I gave thee, villain?*
*The pig*, quoth I, *is burn'd; My gold*, quoth he:
*My mistress, sir*, quoth I; *Hang up thy mistress;*
*I know not thy mistress; out on thy mistress!*

*Luc.* Quoth who?

*Dro. E.* Quoth my master:
*I know*, quoth he, *no house, no wife, no mistress:*
So that my errand, due unto my tongue,
I thank him, I bare home upon my shoulders;
For, in conclusion, he did beat me there.

*Adr.* Go back again, thou slave, and fetch
him home.                                        [home?

*Dro. E.* Go back again! and be new beaten
For God's sake, send some other messenger.

*Adr.* Back, slave, or I will break thy pate
across.                                        [other beating?

*Dro. E.* And he will bless that cross with
Between you I shall have a holy head.

*Adr.* Hence, prating peasant; fetch thy
master home.                                        [with me,

*Dro. E.* Am I so round with you, as you
That like a football you do spurn me thus?
You spurn me hence, and he will spurn me
hither:
If I last in this service you must case me in
leather.                                        [*Exit.*

*Luc.* Fie, how impatience low'reth in your
face!                                        [grace,

*Adr.* His company must do his minions
Whilst I at home starve for a merry look.
Hath homely age the alluring beauty took
From my poor cheek? then he hath wasted it:
Are my discourses dull? barren my wit?
If voluble and sharp discourse be marr'd,
Unkindness blunts it more than marble hard:
Do their gay vestments his affections bait?
That's not my fault, he's master of my state:
What ruins are in me that can be found
By him not ruin'd? then is he the ground
Of my defeatures: my decayed fair
A sunny look of his would soon repair;
But, too unruly deer, he breaks the pale
And feeds from home; poor I am but his stale.

*Luc.* Self-harming jealousy!—fie, beat it
hence.                                        [dispense.

*Adr.* Unfeeling fools can with such wrongs
I know his eye doth homage otherwhere;
Or else what lets it but he would be here?
Sister, you know he promis'd me a chain;—
Would that alone, alone he would detain,
So he would keep fair quarter with my bed!
I see the jewel best enamelled                                        [still
Will lose his beauty; and though gold 'bides
That others touch, yet often touching will
Wear gold; and so no man that hath a name
But falsehood and corruption doth it shame.
Since that my beauty cannot please his eye,
I'll weep what's left away, and, weeping, die.

*Luc.* How many fond fools serve mad jealousy!                                        [*Exeunt.*

SCENE II.—*The same.*

*Enter* ANTIPHOLUS OF SYRACUSE.

*Ant. S.* The gold I gave to Dromio is laid up
Safe at the Centaur; and the heedful slave
Is wander'd forth in care to seek me out.
By computation and mine host's report
I could not speak with Dromio since at first
I sent him from the mart. See, here he comes.

*Enter* DROMIO OF SYRACUSE.

How now, sir! is your merry humour alter'd?
As you love strokes, so jest with me again.
You know no Centaur? you receiv'd no gold?
Your mistress sent to have me home to dinner?
My house was at the Phœnix? Wast thou mad,
That thus so madly thou didst answer me?

*Dro. S.* What answer, sir? when spake I such
a word?

*Ant. S.* Even now, even here, not half-an-
hour since.

*Dro. S.* I did not see you since you sent me
hence,
Home to the Centaur with the gold you gave
me.

*Ant. S.* Villain, thou didst deny the gold's
receipt;
And told'st me of a mistress and a dinner;
For which, I hope, thou felt'st I was displeas'd.

*Dro. S.* I am glad to see you in this merry
vein:                                         [me.
What means this jest? I pray you, master, tell

*Ant. S.* Yea, dost thou jeer and flout me in
the teeth?
Think'st thou I jest? Hold, take thou that, and
that.                                  [*Beating him.*

*Dro. S.* Hold, sir, for God's sake: now your
jest is earnest:
Upon what bargain do you give it me?

*Ant. S.* Because that I familiarly sometimes
Do use you for my fool, and chat with you,
Your sauciness will jest upon my love,
And make a common of my serious hours.
When the sun shines let foolish gnats make
sport,
But creep in crannies when he hides his beams.
If you will jest with me, know my aspéct,
And fashion your demeanour to my looks,
Or I will beat this method in your sconce.

*Dro. S.* Sconce, call you it? so you would
leave battering, I had rather have it a head: an
you use these blows long, I must get a sconce
for my head, and ensconce it too; or else I shall
seek my wit in my shoulders.—But, I pray sir,
why am I beaten?

*Ant. S.* Dost thou not know?

*Dro. S.* Nothing, sir; but that I am beaten.

*Ant. S.* Shall I tell you why?

*Dro. S.* Ay, sir, and wherefore; for, they say,
every why hath a wherefore,—

*Ant. S.* Why, first,—for flouting me; and
then, wherefore,
For urging it the second time to me.

*Dro. S.* Was there ever any man thus beaten
out of season,
When in the why and the wherefore is neither
rhyme nor reason?—
Well, sir, I thank you.

*Ant. S.* Thank me, sir! for what?

*Dro. S.* Marry, sir, for this something that
you gave me for nothing.

*Ant. S.* I'll make you amends next, to give
you nothing for something.—But say, sir, is it
dinner-time?

*Dro. S.* No, sir; I think the meat wants
that I have.

*Ant. S.* In good time, sir, what's that?

*Dro. S.* Basting.

*Ant. S.* Well, sir, then 'twill be dry.

*Dro. S.* If it be, sir, I pray you eat none of it.

*Ant. S.* Your reason?

*Dro. S.* Lest it make you choleric, and purchase me another dry basting.

*Ant. S.* Well, sir, learn to jest in good time:
There's a time for all things.

*Dro. S.* I durst have denied that before you
were so choleric.

*Ant. S.* By what rule, sir?

*Dro. S.* Marry, sir, by a rule as plain as the
plain bald pate of Father Time himself.

*Ant. S.* Let's hear it.

*Dro. S.* There's no time for a man to recover
his hair, that grows bald by nature.

*Ant. S.* May he not do it by fine and recovery?

*Dro. S.* Yes, to pay a fine for a peruke, and
recover the lost hair of another man.

*Ant. S.* Why is Time such a niggard of hair,
being, as it is, so plentiful an excrement?

*Dro. S.* Because it is a blessing that he bestows on beasts: and what he hath scanted men
in hair he hath given them in wit.

*Ant. S.* Why, but there's many a man hath
more hair than wit.

*Dro. S.* Not a man of those but he hath the
wit to lose his hair.

*Ant. S.* Why, thou didst conclude hairy men
plain dealers without wit.

*Dro. S.* The plainer dealer the sooner lost:
yet he loseth it in a kind of jollity.

*Ant. S.* For what reason?

*Dro. S.* For two; and sound ones too.

*Ant. S.* Nay, not sound, I pray you.

*Dro. S.* Sure ones, then.

*Ant. S.* Nay, not sure, in a thing falsing.

*Dro. S.* Certain ones, then.

*Ant. S.* Name them.

*Dro. S.* The one, to save the money that he
spends in tiring; the other, that at dinner they
should not drop in his porridge.

*Ant. S.* You would all this time have proved
there is no time for all things.

*Dro. S.* Marry, and did, sir; namely, no time
to recover hair lost by nature.

*Ant. S.* But your reason was not substantial
why there is no time to recover.

*Dro. S.* Thus I mend it: Time himself is

bald, and, therefore, to the world's end will
have bald followers.

*Ant. S.* I knew 'twould be a bald conclusion:
But, soft! who wafts us yonder?

*Enter* ADRIANA *and* LUCIANA.

*Adr.* Ay, ay, Antipholus, look strange and
    frown;
Some other mistress hath thy sweet aspécts:
I am not Adriana, nor thy wife.
The time was, once, when thou unurg'd wouldst
    vow
That never words were music to thine ear,
That never object pleasing in thine eye,
That never touch well welcome to thy hand,
That never meat sweet-savour'd in thy taste,
Unless I spake, look'd, touch'd, or carv'd to
    thee.
How comes it now, my husband, oh, how
    comes it,
That thou art then estranged from thyself?
Thyself I call it, being strange to me,
That undividable, incorporate,
Am better than thy dear self's better part.
Ah, do not tear away thyself from me;
For know, my love, as easy mayst thou fall
A drop of water in the breaking gulf,
And take unmingled thence that drop again,
Without addition or diminishing,
As take from me thyself, and not me too.
How dearly would it touch thee to the quick
Shouldst thou but hear I were licentious,
And that this body, consecrate to thee,
By ruffian lust should be contaminate!
Wouldst thou not spit at me, and spurn at me,
And hurl the name of husband in my face,
And tear the stain'd skin off my harlot brow,
And from my false hand cut the wedding-ring,
And break it with a deep-divorcing vow?
I know thou canst; and, therefore, see thou
    do it.
I am possess'd with an adulterate blot;
My blood is mingled with the crime of lust:
For if we two be one, and thou play false,
I do digest the poison of thy flesh,
Being strumpeted by thy contagion.      [bed;
Keep then fair league and truce with thy true
I live dis-stain'd, thou undishonoured.

*Ant. S.* Plead you to me, fair dame? I know
    you not:
In Ephesus I am but two hours old,
As strange unto your town as to your talk;
Who, every word by all my wit being scann'd,
Want wit in all one word to understand.

*Luc.* Fie, brother! how the world is chang'd
    with you:
When were you wont to use my sister thus?
She sent for you by Dromio home to dinner.

*Ant. S.* By Dromio?

*Dro. S.* By me?

*Adr.* By thee; and this thou didst return
    from him,—
That he did buffet thee, and in his blows
Denied my house for his, me for his wife.

*Ant. S.* Did you converse, sir, with this gen-
    tlewoman?
What is the course and drift of your compáct?

*Dro. S.* I, sir? I never saw her till this time.

*Ant. S.* Villain, thou liest; for even her very
    words
Didst thou deliver to me on the mart.

*Dro. S.* I never spake with her in all my life.

*Ant. S.* How can she thus, then, call us by
    our names,
Unless it be by inspiration?

*Adr.* How ill agrees it with your gravity
To counterfeit thus grossly with your slave,
Abetting him to thwart me in my mood!
Be it my wrong, you are from me exempt,
But wrong not that wrong with a more con-
    tempt.
Come, I will fasten on this sleeve of thine:
Thou art an elm, my husband, I a vine,
Whose weakness, married to thy stronger state,
Makes me with thy strength to communicate:
If aught possess thee from me, it is dross,
Usurping ivy, brier, or idle moss;
Who, all for want of pruning, with intrusion
Infect thy sap, and live on thy confusion.

*Ant. S.* To me she speaks; she moves me
    for her theme:
What, was I married to her in my dream?
Or sleep I now, and think I hear all this?
What error drives our eyes and ears amiss?
Until I know this sure uncertainty
I'll entertain the offer'd fallacy.

*Luc.* Dromio, go bid the servants spread for
    dinner.      [sinner.

*Dro. S.* O for my beads! I cross me for a
This is the fairy land;—O spite of spites!
We talk with goblins, owls, and elvish sprites;
If we obey them not, this will ensue,      [blue.
They'll suck our breath, or pinch us black and

*Luc.* Why prat'st thou to thyself, and an-
    swer'st not?      [sot!
Dromio, thou drone, thou snail, thou slug, thou

*Dro. S.* I am transformed, master, am not I?

*Ant. S.* I think thou art, in mind, and so am I.

*Dro. S.* Nay, master, both in mind and in
    my shape.

*Ant. S.* Thou hast thine own form.

*Dro. S.*                    No, I am an ape.

*Luc.* If thou art chang'd to aught, 'tis to an
    ass.      [for grass.

*Dro. S.* 'Tis true; she rides me, and I long
'Tis so, I am an ass; else it could never be
But I should know her as well as she knows me.

*Adr.* Come, come, no longer will I be a fool,
To put the finger in the eye and weep,
Whilst man and master laugh my woes to
    scorn.—      [gate:
Come, sir, to dinner;—Dromio, keep the
Husband, I'll dine above with you to-day,
And shrive you of a thousand idle pranks:—
Sirrah, if any ask you for your master,
Say he dines forth, and let no creature enter.—
Come, sister:—Dromio, play the porter well.

*Ant. S.* Am I in earth, in heaven, or in hell?

Sleeping or waking? mad, or well advis'd?
Known unto these, and to myself disguis'd?
I'll say as they say, and perséver so,
And in this mist at all adventures go.

　*Dro. S.* Master, shall I be porter at the gate?

　*Adr.* Ay; and let none enter, lest I break
　　your pate.

　*Luc.* Come, come, Antipholus, we dine too
　　late. 　　　　　　　　　　　　[*Exeunt.*

### ACT III.

### SCENE I.—*The same.*

*Enter* ANTIPHOLUS OF EPHESUS, DROMIO OF
EPHESUS, ANGELO, *and* BALTHAZAR.

　*Ant. E.* Good signior Angelo, you must ex-
　　cuse us all.
My wife is shrewish when I keep not hours:
Say that I linger'd with you at your shop
To see the making of her carcanet,
And that to-morrow you will bring it home.
But here's a villain that would face me down.
He met me on the mart; and that I beat him,
And charg'd him with a thousand marks in gold;
And that I did deny wife and house:—
Thou drunkard, thou, what didst thou mean
　　by this?

　*Dro. E.* Say what you will, sir, but I know
　　what I know:
That you beat me at the mart I have your
　　hand to show:
If the skin were parchment, and the blows you
　　gave were ink, 　　　　　　　　　[think.
Your own handwriting would tell you what I

　*Ant. E.* I think thou art an ass.

　*Dro. E.* 　　　　Marry, so it doth appear
By the wrongs I suffer and the blows I bear.
I should kick, being kick'd; and, being at that
　　pass, 　　　　　　　　　　　　[an ass.
You would keep from my heels, and beware of

　*Ant. E.* You are sad, Signior Balthazar;
　　pray God, our cheer 　　　　[come here.
May answer my good-will and your good wel-

　*Bal.* I hold your dainties cheap, sir, and
　　your welcome dear.

　*Ant. E.* O, Signior Balthazar, either at flesh
　　or fish,
A table full of welcome makes scarce one dainty
　　dish.

　*Bal.* Good meat, sir, is common; that every
　　churl affords.

　*Ant. E.* And welcome more common; for
　　that's nothing but words.

　*Bal.* Small cheer and great welcome makes
　　a merry feast. 　　　　　　　[sparing guest.

　*Ant. E.* Ay, to a niggardly host and more
But though my cates be mean, take them in
　　good part; 　　　　　　　　　[heart.
Better cheer may you have, but not with better
But, soft; my door is lock'd: go bid them let
　　us in. 　　　　　　　　　　[lian, Jen!

　*Dro. E.* Maud, Bridget, Marian, Cicely, Gil-

　*Dro. S.* [*Within.*] Mome, malt-horse, capon,
　　coxcomb, idiot, patch!

Either get thee from the door or sit down at
　　the hatch:

Dost thou conjure for wenches, that thou
　　call'st for such store, 　　　　　[the door.
When one is one too many? Go, get thee from

　*Dro. E.* What patch is made our porter?
　　My master stays in the street.

　*Dro. S.* Let him walk from whence he came,
　　lest he catch cold on 's feet.

　*Ant. E.* Who talks within there? ho, open
　　the door.

　*Dro. S.* Right, sir, I'll tell you when an
　　you'll tell me wherefore.

　*Ant. E.* Wherefore! for my dinner: I have
　　not dined to-day.

　*Dro. S.* Nor to-day here you must not; come
　　again when you may.

　*Ant. E.* What art thou that keep'st me out
　　from the house I owe?

　*Dro. S.* The porter for this time, sir, and
　　my name is Dromio.

　*Dro. E.* O villain, thou hast stolen both
　　mine office and my name; 　　　[blame.
The one ne'er got me credit, the other mickle
If thou hadst been Dromio to-day in my place,
Thou wouldst have chang'd thy face for a
　　name, or thy name for an ass.

　*Luce.* [*Within.*] What a coil is there! Dromio,
　　who are those at the gate?

　*Dro. E.* Let my master in, Luce.

　*Luce.* 　　　　　Faith, no; he comes too late;
And so tell your master.

　*Dro. E.* 　　　　　O Lord, I must laugh;—
Have at you with a proverb.—Shall I set in
　　my staff?

　*Luce.* Have at you with another: that's,—
　　When? can you tell?

　*Dro. S.* If thy name be called Luce,—Luce,
　　thou hast answer'd him well.

　*Ant. E.* Do you hear, you minion? you'll
　　let us in, I hope?

　*Luce.* I thought to have ask'd you.

　*Dro. S.* 　　　　　　And you said no.

　*Dro. E.* So, come, help: well struck; there
　　was blow for blow.

　*Ant. E.* Thou baggage, let me in.

　*Luce.* 　　　　Can you tell for whose sake?

　*Dro. E.* Master, knock the door hard.

　*Luce.* 　　　　Let him knock till it ache.

　*Ant. E.* You'll cry for this, minion, if I beat
　　the door down.

　*Luce.* What needs all that, and a pair of
　　stocks in the town?

　*Adr.* [*Within.*] Who is that at the door, that
　　keeps all this noise?

　*Dro. S.* By my troth, your town is troubled
　　with unruly boys.

　*Ant. E.* Are you there, wife? you might
　　have come before. 　　　　　　[the door.

　*Adr.* Your wife, sir knave! go, get you from

　*Dro. E.* If you went in pain, master, this
　　knave would go sore.

　*Ang.* Here is neither cheer, sir, nor welcome:
　　we would fain have either.

*Bal.* In debating which was best, we shall
part with neither.

*Dro. E.* They stand at the door, master; bid
them welcome hither.

*Ant. E.* There is something in the wind, that
we cannot get in.

*Dro. E.* You would say so, master, if your
garments were thin.
Your cake here is warm within; you stand here
in the cold:
It would make a man mad as a buck, to be so
bought and sold.

*Ant. E.* Go, fetch me something, I'll break
ope the gate.

*Dro. S.* Break any breaking here, and I'll
break your knave's pate.

*Dro. E.* A man may break a word with you,
sir; and words are but wind;
Ay, and break it in your face, so he break it
not behind.

*Dro. S.* It seems thou wantest breaking; out
upon thee, hind!

*Dro. E.* Here's too much out upon thee: I
pray thee, let me in.

*Dro. S.* Ay, when fowls have no feathers
and fish have no fin.

*Ant. E.* Well, I'll break in; go borrow me
a crow.

*Dro. E.* A crow without a feather; master,
mean you so?                    [a feather:
For a fish without a fin there's a fowl without
If a crow help us in, sirrah, we'll pluck a crow
together.                       [crow.

*Ant. E.* Go, get thee gone; fetch me an iron

*Bal.* Have patience, sir: O, let it not be so:
Herein you war against your reputation,
And draw within the compass of suspect
The unviolated honour of your wife.
Once this,— your long experience of her wisdom,
Her sober virtue, years, and modesty,
Plead on her part some cause to you unknown;
And doubt not, sir, but she will well excuse
Why at this time the doors are made against you.
Be rul'd by me; depart in patience,
And let us to the Tiger all to dinner:
And, about evening, come yourself alone,
To know the reason of this strange restraint.
If by strong hand you offer to break in,
Now in the stirring passage of the day,
A vulgar comment will be made of it;
And that supposed by the common rout
Against your yet ungalled estimation,
That may with foul intrusion enter in,
And dwell upon your grave when you are dead:
For slander lives upon succession,
For ever hous'd where it once gets possession.

*Ant. E.* You have prevail'd. I will depart
in quiet,
And, in despite of mirth, mean to be merry.
I know a wench of excellent discourse,—
Pretty and witty; wild, and yet, too, gentle;—
There will we dine: this woman that I mean,
My wife,—but, I protest, without desert,—
Hath oftentimes upbraided me withal;

To her will we to dinner.—Get you home
And fetch the chain: by this, I know, 'tis made:
Bring it, I pray you, to the Porcupine;
For there's the house; that chain will I be-
stow,—
Be it for nothing but to spite my wife,—
Upon mine hostess there: good sir, make haste:
Since mine own doors refuse to entertain me,
I'll knock elsewhere, to see if they'll disdain me.

*Ang.* I'll meet you at that place some hour
hence.

*Ant. E.* Do so; this jest shall cost me some
expense.                       [*Exeunt.*

SCENE II.—*The same.*

*Enter* LUCIANA *and* ANTIPHOLUS OF SYRACUSE.

*Luc.* And may it be that you have quite
forgot
A husband's office? Shall, Antipholus, hate,
Even in the spring of love, thy love-springs rot?
Shall love, in building, grow so ruinate?
If you did wed my sister for her wealth,
Then, for her wealth's sake, use her with
more kindness:
Of, if you like elsewhere, do it by stealth;
Muffle your false love with some show of
blindness:
Let not my sister read it in your eye;
Be not thy tongue thy own shame's orator;
Look sweet, speak fair, become disloyalty;
Apparel vice like virtue's harbinger:
Bear a fair presence though your heart be
tainted;
Teach sin the carriage of a holy saint;
Be secret-false: what need she be acquainted?
What simple thief brags of his own attaint?
'Tis double wrong, to truant with your bed
And let her read it in thy look at board:—
Shame hath a bastard-fame, well managed;
Ill deeds are doubled with an evil word.
Alas, poor women! make us but believe,
Being compact of credit, that you love us:
Though others have the arm, show us the
sleeve;
We in your motion turn, and you may move
us.
Then, gentle brother, get you in again;
Comfort my sister, cheer her, call her wife:
'Tis holy sport to be a little vain          [strife.
When the sweet breath of flattery conquers

*Ant. S.* Sweet mistress,—what your name is
else, I know not,
Nor by what wonder do you hit on mine,—
Less, in your knowledge and your grace, you
show not                       [divine.
Than our earth's wonder; more than earth
Teach me, dear creature, how to think and
speak;
Lay open to my earthy gross conceit,
Smother'd in errors, feeble, shallow, weak,
The folded meaning of your words' deceit.
Against my soul's pure truth why labour you
To make it wander in an unknown field?

Are you a god? would you create me new?
  Transform me, then, and to your power I'll
    yield.
But if that I am I, then well I know
  Your weeping sister is no wife of mine,
Nor to her bed no homage do I owe:
  Far more, far more, to you do I decline.
O, train me not, sweet mermaid, with thy note,
  To drown me in thy sister's flood of tears:
Sing, siren, for thyself, and I will dote:
  Spread o'er the silver waves thy golden hairs,
And as a bed I'll take thee, and there lie;
  And, in that glorious supposition, think
He gains by death that hath such means to
    die:—
  Let love, being light, be drowned if she sink!
*Luc.* What, are you mad, that you do rea-
    son so?
*Ant. S.* Not mad, but mated; how, I do not
    know.
*Luc.* It is a fault that springeth from your
    eye.
*Ant. S.* For gazing on your beams, fair sun,
    being by.
*Luc.* Gaze where you should, and that will
    clear your sight.          [on night.
*Ant. S.* As good to wink, sweet love, as look
*Luc.* Why call you me love? call my sister so.
*Ant. S.* Thy sister's sister.
*Luc.*                    That's my sister.
*Ant. S.*                             No;
It is thyself, mine own self's better part;
Mine eye's clear eye, my dear heart's dearer
    heart;
My food, my fortune, and my sweet hope's aim,
My sole earth's heaven, and my heaven's claim.
*Luc.* All this my sister is, or else should be.
*Ant. S.* Call thyself sister, sweet, for I aim
    thee:
Thee will I love, and with thee lead my life:
Thou hast no husband yet, nor I no wife;
Give me thy hand.
*Luc.*              O soft, sir, hold you still;
I'll fetch my sister, to get her good-will.
                                   [*Exit* LUCIANA.

*Enter from the House of* ANTIPHOLUS OF
    EPHESUS, DROMIO OF SYRACUSE.

*Ant. S.* Why, how now, Dromio? where
runn'st thou so fast?
*Dro. S.* Do you know me, sir? am I Dromio?
am I your man? am I myself?
*Ant. S.* Thou art Dromio, thou art my man,
thou art thyself.
*Dro. S.* I am an ass, I am a woman's man,
and beside myself.
*Ant. S.* What woman's man? and how beside
thyself?
*Dro. S.* Marry, sir, beside myself, I am due
to a woman; one that claims me, one that
haunts me, one that will have me.
*Ant. S.* What claim lays she to thee?
*Dro. S.* Marry, sir, such claim as you would
lay to your horse: and she would have me as a
beast; not that, I being a beast, she would have
me; but that she, being a very beastly creature,
lays claim to me.
*Ant. S.* What is she?
*Dro. S.* A very reverent body; ay, such a
one as a man may not speak of without he say
sir-reverence: I have but lean luck in the
match, and yet she is a wondrous fat marriage.
*Ant. S.* How dost thou mean?—a fat marriage?
*Dro. S.* Marry, sir, she's the kitchen-wench,
and all grease; and I know not what use to put
her to, but to make a lamp of her, and run
from her by her own light. I warrant, her rags,
and the tallow in them, will burn a Poland
winter: if she lives till doomsday, she'll burn a
week longer than the whole world.
*Ant. S.* What complexion is she of?
*Dro. S.* Swart, like my shoe; but her face
nothing like so clean kept: for why? she sweats;
a man may go over shoes in the grime of it.
*Ant. S.* That's a fault that water will mend.
*Dro. S.* No, sir, 'tis in grain; Noah's flood
could not do it.
*Ant. S.* What's her name?
*Dro. S.* Nell, sir;—but her name and three-
quarters, that is an ell and three-quarters, will
not measure her from hip to hip.
*Ant. S.* Then she bears some breadth?
*Dro. S.* No longer from head to foot than
from hip to hip: she is spherical, like a globe:
I could find out countries in her.      [land?
*Ant. S.* In what part of her body stands Ire-
*Dro. S.* Marry, sir, in her buttocks: I found
it out by the bogs.
*Ant. S.* Where Scotland?
*Dro. S.* I found it by the barrenness; hard
in the palm of the hand.
*Ant. S.* Where France?
*Dro. S.* In her forehead; armed and reverted,
making war against her hair.
*Ant. S.* Where England?
*Dro. S.* I looked for the chalky cliffs, but I
could find no whiteness in them: but I guess it
stood in her chin, by the salt rheum that ran
between France and it.
*Ant. S.* Where Spain?
*Dro. S.* Faith, I saw it not; but I felt it hot
in her breath.
*Ant. S.* Where America—the Indies?
*Dro. S.* O, sir, upon her nose, all o'er embel-
lished with rubies, carbuncles, sapphires, declining their rich aspect to the hot breath of
Spain; who sent whole armadas of carracks to
be ballast at her nose.
*Ant. S.* Where stood Belgia,—the Netherlands?
*Dro. S.* O, sir, I did not look so low.—To
conclude, this drudge or diviner laid claim to
me; called me Dromio; swore I was assured to
her; told me what privy marks I had about me,
as the mark of my shoulder, the mole in my
neck, the great wart on my left arm, that I,
amazed, ran from her as a witch: and, I think,

If my breast had not been made of faith and
my heart of steel, she had transformed me to a
curtail-dog, and made me turn i' the wheel.

*Ant. S.* Go, hie thee presently post to the
  road;
And if the wind blow any way from shore,
I will not harbour in this town to-night.
If any bark put forth, come to the mart,
Where I will walk till thou return to me.
If every one knows us, and we know none,
'Tis time, I think, to trudge, pack, and be gone.

*Dro. S.* As from a bear a man would run for
  life,
So fly I from her that would be my wife.   [*Exit.*

*Ant. S.* There's none but witches do inhabit
  here;
And therefore 'tis high time that I were hence.
She that doth call me husband, even my soul
Doth for a wife abhor; but her fair sister,
Possess'd with such a gentle sovereign grace,
Of such enchanting presence and discourse,
Hath almost made me traitor to myself:
But, lest myself be guilty to self-wrong,
I'll stop mine ears against the mermaid's song.

    *Enter* ANGELO.

*Ang.* Master Antipholus?

*Ant. S.* Ay, that's my name.   [chain;

*Ang.* I know it well, sir. Lo, here is the
I thought to have ta'en you at the Porcupine:
The chain unfinish'd made me stay thus long.

*Ant. S.* What is your will that I shall do with
  this?

*Ang.* What please yourself, sir; I have made
  it for you.

*Ant. S.* Made it for me, sir! I bespoke it not.

*Ang.* Not once nor twice, but twenty times
  you have:
Go home with it, and please your wife withal;
And soon at supper-time I'll visit you,
And then receive my money for the chain.

*Ant. S.* I pray you, sir, receive the money
  now,
For fear you ne'er see chain nor money more.

*Ang.* You are a merry man, sir; fare you
  well.   [*Exit.*

*Ant. S.* What I should think of this I cannot
  tell:
But this I think, there's no man is so vain
That would refuse so fair an offer'd chain.
I see a man here needs not live by shifts,
When in the street he meets such golden gifts.
I'll to the mart, and there for Dromio stay;
If any ship put out, then straight away. [*Exit.*

    ACT IV.

   SCENE I.—*The same.*

*Enter a* Merchant, ANGELO, *and an* Officer.

*Mer.* You know, since Pentecost the sum is
  due,
And since I have not much importun'd you;
Nor now I had not, but that I am bound

To Persia, and want gilders for my voyage;
Therefore make present satisfaction,
Or I'll attach you by this officer.

*Ang.* Even just the sum that I do owe to you
Is growing to me by Antipholus;
And in the instant that I met with you
He had of me a chain; at five o'clock
I shall receive the money for the same:
Pleaseth you walk with me down to his house,
I will discharge my bond, and thank you too.

  *Enter* ANTIPHOLUS OF EPHESUS, *and*
    DROMIO OF EPHESUS.

*Off.* That labour may you save: see where
  he comes.   [go thou

*Ant. E.* While I go to the goldsmith's house,
And buy a rope's end; that will I bestow
Among my wife and her confederates,
For locking me out of doors by day.—
But, soft; I see the goldsmith: get thee gone;
Buy thou a rope, and bring it home to me.

*Dro. E.* I buy a thousand pound a year! I
  buy a rope!   [*Exit* DROMIO.

*Ant. E.* A man is well holp up that trusts
  to you:
I promised your presence, and the chain;
But neither chain nor goldsmith came to me:
Belike you thought our love would last too long,
If it were chained together; and therefore came
  not.   [note.

*Ang.* Saving your merry humour, here's the
How much your chain weighs to the utmost
  carat;
The fineness of the gold, and chargeful fashion;
Which does amount to three odd ducats more
Than I stand debted to this gentleman:
I pray you, see him presently discharg'd,
For he is bound to sea, and stays but for it.

*Ant. E.* I am not furnished with the present
  money;
Besides I have some business in the town:
Good Signior, take the stranger to my house,
And with you take the chain, and bid my wife
Disburse the sum on the receipt thereof;
Perchance I will be there as soon as you.

*Ang.* Then you will bring the chain to her
  yourself?

*Ant. E.* No; bear it with you, lest I come
  not time enough.   [about you?

*Ang.* Well sir, I will: have you the chain

*Ant. E.* An if I have not, sir, I hope you
  have,
Or else you may return without your money.

*Ang.* Nay, come, I pray you, sir, give me
  the chain;
Both wind and tide stays for this gentleman,
And I, to blame, have held him here too long.

*Ant. E.* Good lord, you use this dalliance to
  excuse
Your breach of promise to the Porcupine:
I should have chid you for not bringing it,
But, like a shrew, you first begin to brawl.

*Mer.* The hour steals on; I pray you, sir,
  despatch.

*Ang.* You hear how he importunes me: the chain,—

*Ant. E.* Why, give it to my wife, and fetch your money.                    [even now:

*Ang.* Come, come, you know I gave it you
Either send the chain or send me by some token.

*Ant. E.* Fie! now you run this humour out of breath:                    [see it.
Come, where's the chain? I pray you, let me

*Mer.* My business cannot brook this dalliance:
Good sir, say whe'r you'll answer me or no;
If not, I'll leave him to the officer.          [you?

*Ant. E.* I answer you! What should I answer

*Ang.* The money that you owe me for the chain.                    [chain.

*Ant. E.* I owe you none till I receive the

*Ang.* You know I gave it you half-an-hour since.

*Ant. E.* You gave me none: you wrong me much to say so.

*Ang.* You wrong me more, sir, in denying it:
Consider how it stands upon my credit.

*Mer.* Well, officer, arrest him at my suit.

*Off.* I do, and charge you in the duke's name to obey me.

*Ang.* This touches me in reputation:
Either consent to pay this sum for me,
Or I attach you by this officer.

*Ant. E.* Consent to pay thee that I never had!
Arrest me, foolish fellow, if thou dar'st.

*Ang.* Here is thy fee; arrest him, officer:—
I would not spare my brother in this case,
If he should scorn me so apparently.

*Off.* I do arrest you, sir: you hear the suit.

*Ant. E.* I do obey thee till I give thee bail:—
But, sirrah, you shall buy this sport as dear
As all the metal in your shop will answer.

*Ang.* Sir, sir, I shall have law in Ephesus,
To your notorious shame, I doubt it not.

*Enter* DROMIO OF SYRACUSE.

*Dro. S.* Master, there is a bark of Epidamnum
That stays but till her owner comes aboard,
And then, sir, bears away: our fraughtage, sir,
I have convey'd aboard; and I have bought
The oil, the balsamum, and aqua-vitæ.
The ship is in her trim; the merry wind
Blows fair from land: they stay for naught at all
But for their owner, master, and yourself.

*Ant. E.* How now! a madman? Why, thou peevish sheep,
What ship of Epidamnum stays for me?

*Dro. S.* A ship you sent me to, to hire waftage.

*Ant. E.* Thou drunken slave, I sent thee for a rope;
And told thee to what purpose and what end.

*Dro. S.* You sent me, sir, for a rope's end as soon:
You sent me to the bay, sir, for a bark.

*Ant. E.* I will debate this matter at more leisure,

And teach your ears to listen with more heed.
To Adriana, villain, hie thee straight:
Give her this key, and tell her, in the desk
That's cover'd o'er with Turkish tapestry
There is a purse of ducats; let her send it:
Tell her I am arrested in the street,
And that shall bail me: hie thee, slave; be gone.
On, officer, to prison till it come.

        [*Exeunt* MER., ANG., OFF., *and* ANT. E.

*Dro. S.* To Adriana! that is where we din'd,
Where Dowsabel did claim me for her husband:
She is too big, I hope, for me to compass.
Thither I must, although against my will,
For servants must their masters' minds fulfil.

                    [*Exit.*

### SCENE II.—*The same.*

*Enter* ADRIANA *and* LUCIANA.

*Adr.* Ah, Luciana, did he tempt thee so?
Might'st thou perceive austerely in his eye
That he did plead in earnest, yea or no?
Look'd he or red or pale, or sad or merrily?
What observation mad'st thou in this case
Of his heart's meteors tilting in his face?

*Luc.* First, he denied you had him in no right.                    [my spite.

*Adr.* He meant he did me none; the more

*Luc.* Then swore he that he was a stranger here.                    [he were.

*Adr.* And true he swore, though yet forsworn

*Luc.* Then pleaded I for you.

*Adr.*                    And what said he?

*Luc.* That love I begg'd for you he begg'd of me.                    [love?

*Adr.* With what persuasion did he tempt thy

*Luc.* With words that in an honest suit might move.
First, he did praise my beauty, then my speech.

*Adr.* Didst speak him fair?

*Luc.*                    Have patience, I beseech.

*Adr.* I cannot, nor I will not hold me still:
My tongue, though not my heart, shall have his will.
He is deformed, crooked, old, and sere,
Ill-fac'd, worse bodied, shapeless everywhere;
Vicious, ungentle, foolish, blunt, unkind;
Stigmatical in making, worse in mind.          [one?

*Luc.* Who would be jealous then of such a
No evil lost is wail'd when it is gone.

*Adr.* Ah! but I think him better than I say,
And yet would herein others' eyes were worse:
Far from her nest the lapwing cries, away:
My heart prays for him, though my tongue do curse.

*Enter* DROMIO OF SYRACUSE.

*Dro. S.* Here, go: the desk, the purse: sweet now, make haste.

*Luc.* How hast thou lost thy breath?

*Dro. S.*                    By running fast.

*Adr.* Where is thy master, Dromio? is he well?                    [hell.

*Dro. S.* No, he's in Tartar limbo, worse than

A devil in an everlasting garment hath him;
One whose hard heart is button'd up with steel;
A fiend, a fairy, pitiless and rough;
A wolf—nay worse, a fellow all in buff;
A back-friend, a shoulder-clapper, one that
    countermands    [lands;
The passages of alleys, creeks, and narrow
A hound that runs counter, and yet draws dry
    foot well;    [souls to hell.
One that, before the judgment, carries poor
  *Adr.* Why, man, what is the matter?
  *Dro. S.* I do not know the matter: he is
    'rested on the case.    [suit.
  *Adr.* What, is he arrested? tell me at whose
  *Dro. S.* I know not at whose suit he is ar-
    rested, well;
But he's in a suit of buff which 'rested him,
    that can I tell:
Will you send him, mistress, redemption, the
    money in the desk?
  *Adr.* Go fetch it, sister.—This I wonder at,
                [*Exit* LUCIANA.
That he, unknown to me, should be in debt.—
Tell me, was he arrested on a band?
  *Dro. S.* Not on a band, but on a stronger
    thing;
A chain, a chain: do you not hear it ring?
  *Adr.* What, the chain?    [gone.
  *Dro. S.* No, no, the bell: 'tis time that I were
It was two ere I left him, and now the clock
  strikes one.
  *Adr.* The hours come back! that did I never
    hear.
  *Dro. S.* O yes. If any hour meet a sergeant,
    'a turns back for very fear.
  *Adr.* As if time were in debt! how fondly
    dost thou reason!
  *Dro. S.* Time is a very bankrupt, and owes
    more than he's worth to season.
Nay, he's a thief too: have you not heard men
    say
That Time comes stealing on by night and day?
If he be in debt and theft, and a sergeant in the
    way,    [day?
Hath he not reason to turn back an hour in a

### *Enter* LUCIANA.

  *Adr.* Go, Dromio; there's the money, bear
    it straight;
And bring thy master home immediately.—
Come, sister: I am press'd down with conceit;
Conceit my comfort and my injury.
                [*Exeunt.*

### SCENE III.—*The same.*

### *Enter* ANTIPHOLUS OF SYRACUSE.

  *Ant. S.* There's not a man I meet but doth
    salute me
As if I were their well-acquainted friend;
And every one doth call me by my name.
Some tender money to me, some invite me;
Some other give me thanks for kindnesses;
Some offer me commodities to buy:
Even now a tailor call'd me in his shop,

And show'd me silks that he had bought for me,
And therewithal took measure of my body.
Sure, these are but imaginary wiles,
And Lapland sorcerers inhabit here.

### *Enter* DROMIO OF SYRACUSE.

  *Dro. S.* Master, here's the gold you sent me
    for.
What, have you got the picture of Old Adam
    new apparelled?
  *Ant. S.* What gold is this? What Adam dost
    thou mean?
  *Dro. S.* Not that Adam that kept the paradise, but that Adam that keeps the prison: he
that goes in the calf's-skin that was killed for
the Prodigal; he that came behind you, sir, like
an evil angel, and bid you forsake your liberty.
  *Ant. S.* I understand thee not.
  *Dro. S.* No? why, 'tis a plain case: he that
went like a base-viol in a case of leather; the
man, sir, that, when gentlemen are tired, gives
them a fob, and 'rests them; he, sir, that takes
pity on decayed men, and gives them suits of
durance; he that sets up his rest to do more
exploits with his mace than a morris-pike.
  *Ant. S.* What! thou mean'st an officer?
  *Dro. S.* Ay, sir,—the sergeant of the band:
he that brings any man to answer it that breaks
his band; one that thinks a man always going
to bed, and says, *God give you good rest!*
  *Ant. S.* Well, sir, there rest in your foolery.
Is there any ship puts forth to-night? may we
be gone?
  *Dro. S.* Why, sir, I brought you word an
hour since, that the bark Expedition put forth
tonight; and then were you hindered by the
sergeant, to tarry for the hoy, Delay: here are
the angels that you sent for to deliver you.
  *Ant. S.* The fellow is distract, and so am I;
And here we wander in illusions:
Some blessed power deliver us from hence!

### *Enter a* Courtezan.

  *Cour.* Well met, well met, Master Antipho-
    lus.
I see, sir, you have found the goldsmith now:
Is that the chain you promis'd me to-day?
  *Ant. S.* Satan, avoid! I charge thee, tempt
    me not!
  *Dro. S.* Master, is this Mistress Satan?
  *Ant. S.* It is the devil.
  *Dro. S.* Nay, she is worse—she is the devil's
dam; and here she comes in the habit of a light
wench; and thereof comes that the wenches
say, *God damn me*—that's as much as to say,
*God make me a light wench.* It is written, they
appear to men like angels of light: light is an
effect of fire, and fire will burn; *ergo,* light
wenches will burn: come not near her.
  *Cour.* Your man and you are marvellous
    merry, sir.    [here.
Will you go with me? We'll mend our dinner
  *Dro. S.* Master, if you do; expect spoon-
meat, or bespeak a long spoon.

*Ant. S.* Why, Dromio?

*Dro. S.* Marry, he must have a long spoon that must eat with the devil.

*Ant. S.* Avoid then, fiend! what tell'st thou me of supping?
Thou art, as you are all, a sorceress:
I conjure thee to leave me and be gone.

*Cour.* Give me the ring of mine you had at dinner,
Or, for my diamond, the chain you promis'd,
And I'll be gone, sir, and not trouble you.

*Dro. S.* Some devils ask but the paring of one's nail,
A rush, a hair, a drop of blood, a pin,
A nut, a cherry-stone; but she, more covetous,
Would have a chain.
Master, be wise; an if you give it her,
The devil will shake her chain, and fright us with it.                  [chain:

*Cour.* I pray you, sir, my ring, or else the
I hope you do not mean to cheat me so.

*Ant. S.* Avaunt, thou witch! Come, Dromio, let us go.

*Dro. S.* Fly pride, says the peacock: Mistress, that you know.
                [*Exeunt* ANT. S. *and* DRO. S.

*Cour.* Now, out of doubt, Antipholus is mad,
Else would he never so demean himself:
A ring he hath of mine worth forty ducats,
And for the same he promis'd me a chain;
Both one and other he denies me now:
The reason that I gather he is mad,—
Besides this present instance of his rage,—
Is a mad tale he told to-day at dinner,
Of his own doors being shut against his entrance.
Belike his wife, acquainted with his fits,
On purpose shut the doors against his way.
My way is now to hie home to his house,
And tell his wife that, being lunatic,
He rush'd into my house, and took perforce
My ring away: this course I fittest choose,
For forty ducats is too much to lose.    [*Exit.*

SCENE IV.—*The same.*

*Enter* ANTIPHOLUS OF EPHESUS *and an* Officer.

*Ant. E.* Fear me not, man; I will not break away:
I'll give thee, ere I leave thee, so much money
To warrant thee, as I am 'rested for.
My wife is in a wayward mood to-day;
And will not lightly trust the messenger
That I should be attach'd in Ephesus:
I tell you, 'twill sound harshly in her ears.

*Enter* DROMIO OF EPHESUS, *with a rope's end.*

Here comes my man: I think he brings the money.
How now, sir! have you that I sent you for?

*Dro. E.* Here's that, I warrant you, will pay them all.

*Ant. E.* But where's the money?          [rope.

*Dro. E.* Why, sir, I gave the money for the

*Ant. E.* Five hundred ducats, villain, for a rope?                    [the rate.

*Dro. E.* I'll serve you, sir, five hundred at

*Ant. E.* To what end did I bid thee hie thee home?

*Dro. E.* To a rope's end, sir; and to that end am I return'd.

*Ant. E.* And to that end, sir, I will welcome you.                     [*Beating him.*

*Off.* Good sir, be patient.

*Dro. E.* Nay, 'tis for me to be patient; I am in adversity.

*Off.* Good now, hold thy tongue.

*Dro. E.* Nay, rather persuade him to hold his hands.

*Ant. E.* Thou whoreson senseless villain!

*Dro. E.* I would I were senseless, sir, that I might not feel your blows.

*Ant. E.* Thou art sensible in nothing but blows, and so is an ass.

*Dro. E.* I am an ass indeed: you may prove it by my long ears. I have served him from the hour of my nativity to this instant, and have nothing at his hands for my service but blows: when I am cold he heats me with beating; when I am warm he cools me with beating. I am waked with it when I sleep; raised with it when I sit; driven out of doors with it when I go from home; welcomed home with it when I return: nay, I bear it on my shoulders as a beggar wont her brat; and I think, when he hath lamed me, I shall beg with it from door to door.

*Ant. E.* Come, go along; my wife is coming yonder.

*Enter* ADRIANA, LUCIANA, *and the* Courtezan, *with* PINCH *and others.*

*Dro. E.* Mistress, *respice finem*, respect your end; or rather the prophecy, like the parrot, *Beware the rope's end.*

*Ant. E.* Wilt thou still talk?       [*Beats him.*

*Cour.* How say you now? is not your husband mad?

*Adr.* His incivility confirms no less.—
Good Doctor Pinch, you are a conjurer;
Establish him in his true sense again,
And I will please you what you will demand.

*Luc.* Alas, how fiery and how sharp he looks!

*Cour.* Mark how he trembles in his ecstasy!

*Pinch.* Give me your hand, and let me feel your pulse.

*Ant. E.* There is my hand, and let it feel your ear.

*Pinch.* I charge thee, Satan, hous'd within this man,
To yield possession to my holy prayers,
And to thy state of darkness hie thee straight:
I conjure thee by all the saints in heaven.

*Ant. E.* Peace, doting wizard, peace; I am not mad.

*Adr.* O that thou wert not, poor distressed soul!

*Ant. E.* You minion, you, are these your customers?

Did this companion with the saffron face
Revel and feast it at my house to-day,
Whilst upon me the guilty doors were shut,
And I denied to enter in my house?    [at home,

*Adr.* O husband, God doth know you din'd
Where would you had remain'd until this time,
Free from these slanders and this open shame!

*Ant. E.* I din'd at home! Thou villain, what
   say'st thou?

*Dro. E.* Sir, sooth to say, you did not dine at
   home.

*Ant. E.* Were not my doors lock'd up and I
   shut out?

*Dro. E.* Perdy, your doors were lock'd and
   you shut out.

*Ant. E.* And did not she herself revile me
   there?    [there.

*Dro. E.* Sans fable, she herself revil'd you

*Ant. E.* Did not her kitchen-maid rail,
   taunt, and scorn me?

*Dro. E.* Certes, she did: the kitchen-vestal
   scorn'd you.

*Ant. E.* And did not I in rage depart from
   thence?    [witness,

*Dro. E.* In verity, you did;—my bones bear
That since have felt the vigour of his rage.

*Adr.* Is't good to soothe him in these contraries?    [vein,

*Pinch.* It is no shame: the fellow finds his
And, yielding to him, humours well his frenzy.

*Ant. E.* Thou hast suborn'd the goldsmith
   to arrest me.

*Adr.* Alas! I sent you money to redeem you,
By Dromio here, who came in haste for it.

*Dro. E.* Money by me! heart and good-will
   you might,
But surely, master, not a rag of money.

*Ant. E.* Went'st not thou to her for a purse
   of ducats?

*Adr.* He came to me, and I deliver'd it.

*Luc.* And I am witness with her that she did.

*Dro. E.* God and the rope-maker, bear me
   witness
That I was sent for nothing but a rope!

*Pinch.* Mistress, both man and master is
   possess'd;
I know it by their pale and deadly looks:
They must be bound, and laid in some dark
   room.

*Ant. E.* Say, wherefore didst thou lock me
   forth to-day?—
And why dost thou deny the bag of gold?

*Adr.* I did not, gentle husband, lock thee
   forth.

*Dro. E.* And, gentle master, I receiv'd no
   gold;
But I confess, sir, that we were lock'd out.

*Adr.* Dissembling villain, thou speak'st false
   in both.    [all;

*Ant. E.* Dissembling harlot, thou art false in
And art confederate with a damned pack,
To make a loathsome abject scorn of me:
But with these nails I'll pluck out these false
   eyes,

That would behold me in this shameful sport.
   [PINCH *and* Assistants *bind* ANT. E. *and*
   DRO. E.

*Adr.* O, bind him, bind him; let him not
   come near me.

*Pinch.* More company;—the fiend is strong
   within him.    [looks!

*Luc.* Ah me, poor man! how pale and wan he

*Ant. E.* What, will you murder me? Thou
   gaoler, thou,
I am thy prisoner: wilt thou suffer them
To make a rescue?

*Off.*    Masters, let him go:
He is my prisoner, and you shall not have him.

*Pinch.* Go, bind this man, for he is frantic
   too.

*Adr.* What wilt thou do, thou peevish officer?
Hast thou delight to see a wretched man
Do outrage and displeasure to himself?

*Off.* He is my prisoner: if I let him go,
The debt he owes will be requir'd of me.

*Adr.* I will discharge thee ere I go from thee:
Bear me forthwith unto his creditor,    [it.
And, knowing how the debt grows, I will pay
Good master doctor, see him safe convey'd
Home to my house.—O most unhappy day!

*Ant. E.* O most unhappy strumpet!

*Dro. E.* Master, I am here enter'd in bond
   for you.

*Ant. E.* Out on thee, villain! wherefore dost
   thou mad me?    [mad,

*Dro. E.* Will you be bound for nothing? be
Good master; cry, the devil.—    [talk!

*Luc.* God help, poor souls, how idly do they

*Adr.* Go bear him hence.—Sister, go you
   with me.—
   [*Exeunt* PINCH *and* Assistants, *with*
      ANT. E. *and* DRO. E.
Say now, whose suit is he arrested at?

*Off.* One Angelo, a goldsmith; do you know
   him?    [owes?

*Adr.* I know the man: what is the sum he

*Off.* Two hundred ducats.

*Adr.*    Say, how grows it due?

*Off.* Due for a chain your husband had of
   him.    [it not.

*Adr.* He did bespeak a chain for me, but had

*Cour.* When as your husband, all in rage,
   to-day
Came to my house, and took away my ring,—
The ring I saw upon his finger now,—
Straight after did I meet him with a chain.

*Adr.* It may be so, but I did never see it:
Come, gaoler, bring me where the goldsmith is?
I long to know the truth hereof at large.

*Enter* ANTIPHOLUS OF SYRACUSE, *with his
   rapier drawn, and* DROMIO OF SYRACUSE.

*Luc.* God, for thy mercy! they are loose
   again.    [more help,

*Adr.* And come with naked swords: let's call
To have them bound again.

*Off.*    Away, they'll kill us.
   [*Exeunt* Off., ADR., *and* LUC.

*Ant. S.* I see these witches are afraid of swords.

*Dro. S.* She that would be your wife now ran from you.

*Ant. S.* Come to the Centaur; fetch our stuff from thence:

I long that we were safe and sound aboard.

*Dro. S.* Faith, stay here this night; they will surely do us no harm: you saw they speak us fair, give us gold: methinks, they are such a gentle nation, that but for the mountain of mad flesh that claims marriage of me, I could find in my heart to stay here still and turn witch.                              [town:

*Ant. S.* I will not stay to-night for all the Therefore away to get our stuff aboard.

[*Exeunt.*

## ACT V.

### Scene I.—*The same.*

*Enter* Merchant *and* Angelo.

*Ang.* I am sorry, sir, that I have hinder'd you;

But I protest he had the chain of me,
Though most dishonestly he doth deny it.

*Mer.* How is the man esteem'd here in the city?

*Ang.* Of very reverend reputation, sir;
Of credit infinite, highly belov'd,
Second to none that lives here in the city:
His word might bear my wealth at any time.

*Mer.* Speak softly: yonder, as I think, he walks.

*Enter* Antipholus *and* Dromio of Syracuse.

*Ang.* 'Tis so; and that self chain about his neck

Which he forswore most monstrously to have.
Good sir, draw near to me, I'll speak to him.—
Signior Antipholus, I wonder much
That you would put me to this shame and trouble;
And not without some scandal to yourself,
With circumstance and oaths so to deny
This chain, which now you wear so openly:
Besides the charge, the shame, imprisonment,
You have done wrong to this my honest friend;
Who, but for staying on our controversy,
Had hoisted sail and put to sea to-day:
This chain you had of me; can you deny it?

*Ant. S.* I think I had: I never did deny it.

*Mer.* Yes, that you did, sir; and forswore it too.                              [swear it?

*Ant. S.* Who heard me to deny it or for-

*Mer.* These ears of mine, thou knowest, did hear thee.

Fie on thee, wretch! 'tis pity that thou liv'st
To walk where any honest men resort.  [thus:

*Ant. S.* Thou art a villain to impeach me
I'll prove mine honour and mine honesty
Against thee presently, if thou dar'st stand.

*Mer.* I dare and do defy thee for a villain.

[*They draw.*

*Enter* Adriana, Luciana, Courtezan, *and others.*

*Adr.* Hold, hurt him not, for God's sake; he is mad:

Some get within him, take his sword away:
Bind Dromio too, and bear them to my house.

*Dro. S.* Run, master, run; for God's sake, take a house.

This is some priory;—in, or we are spoil'd.

[*Exeunt* Ant. S. *and* Dro. S. *to the Priory.*

*Enter the* Abbess.

*Abb.* Be quiet, people. Wherefore throng you hither?                              [hence:

*Adr.* To fetch my poor distracted husband
Let us come in, that we may bind him fast,
And bear him home for his recovery.

*Ang.* I knew he was not in his perfect wits.

*Mer.* I am sorry now that I did draw on him.

*Abb.* How long hath this possession held the man?                              [sad,

*Adr.* This week he hath been heavy, sour,
And much, much different from the man he was:
But till this afternoon his passion
Ne'er brake into extremity of rage.  [at sea?

*Abb.* Hath he not lost much wealth by wreck
Buried some dear friend? Hath not else his eye
Stray'd his affection in unlawful love?
A sin prevailing much in youthful men
Who give their eyes the liberty of gazing.
Which of these sorrows is he subject to?

*Adr.* To none of these, except it be the last;
Namely, some love that drew him oft from home.

*Abb.* You should for that have reprehended him.

*Adr.* Why, so I did.

*Abb.*                              Ay, but not rough enough.

*Adr.* As roughly as my modesty would let me.

*Abb.* Haply in private.

*Adr.*                              And in assemblies too.

*Abb.* Ay, but not enough.

*Adr.* It was the copy of our conference:
In bed, he slept not for my urging it;
At board, he fed not for my urging it;
Alone, it was the subject of my theme;
In company, I often glanced it;
Still did I tell him it was vile and bad.

*Abb.* And thereof came it that the man was mad:

The venom clamours of a jealous woman
Poison more deadly than a mad dog's tooth.
It seems his sleeps were hindered by thy railing:
And therefore comes it that his head is light.
Thou say'st his meat was sauc'd with thy up-braidings:
Unquiet meals make ill digestions,
Thereof the raging fire of fever bred;
And what's a fever but a fit of madness?
Thou say'st his sports were hinder'd by thy brawls:
Sweet recreation barr'd, what doth ensue
But moody and dull melancholy,—

Kinsman to grim and comfortless despair,—
And, at her heels, a huge infectious troop
Of pale distemperatures and foes to life?
In food, in sport, and life-preserving rest
To be disturb'd would mad or man or beast:
The consequence is, then, thy jealous fits
Have scar'd thy husband from the use of's wits.

*Luc.* She never reprehended him but mildly,
When he demean'd himself rough, rude, and
wildly.—
Why bear you these rebukes, and answer not?

*Adr.* She did betray me to my own reproof.—
Good people, enter, and lay hold on him.

*Abb.* No, not a creature enters in my house.

*Adr.* Then let your servants bring my husband forth.

*Abb.* Neither: he took this place for sanctu-
ary,
And it shall privilege him from your hands
Till I have brought him to his wits again,
Or lose my labour in assaying it.

*Adr.* I will attend my husband, be his nurse,
Diet his sickness, for it is my office,
And will have no attorney but myself;
And therefore let me have him home with me.

*Abb.* Be patient; for I will not let him stir
Till I have used the approved means I have,
With wholesome syrups, drugs, and holy
prayers,
To make of him a formal man again:
It is a branch and parcel of mine oath,
A charitable duty of my order;
Therefore depart, and leave him here with me.

*Adr.* I will not hence and leave my husband
here;
And ill it doth beseem your holiness
To separate the husband and the wife.

*Abb.* Be quiet, and depart: thou shalt not
have him. [*Exit* Abbess.

*Luc.* Complain unto the duke of this indignity.

*Adr.* Come, go; I will fall prostrate at his
feet,
And never rise until my tears and prayers
Have won his grace to come in person hither,
And take perforce my husband from the abbess.

*Mer.* By this, I think, the dial points at five:
Anon, I am sure, the duke himself in person
Comes this way to the melancholy vale;
The place of death and sorry execution,
Behind the ditches of the abbey here.

*Ang.* Upon what cause?

*Mer.* To see a reverend Syracusan merchant,
Who put unluckily into this bay,
Against the laws and statutes of this town,
Beheaded publicly for his offence. [his death.

*Ang.* See where they come: we will behold

*Luc.* Kneel to the duke before he pass the
abbey.

*Enter* DUKE, *attended;* ÆGEON, *bare-headed;
with the* Headsman *and other* Officers.

*Duke.* Yet once again proclaim it publicly,
If any friend will pay the sum for him,

He shall not die; so much we tender him.

*Adr.* Justice, most sacred duke, against the
abbess!

*Duke.* She is a virtuous and a reverend lady;
It cannot be that she hath done thee wrong.

*Adr.* May it please your grace, Antipholus,
my husband,—
Whom I made lord of me and all I had,
At your important letters,—this ill day
A most outrageous fit of madness took him;
That desperately he hurried through the
street,—
With him his bondman, all as mad as he,—
Doing displeasure to the citizens
By rushing in their houses, bearing thence
Rings, jewels, anything his rage did like.
Once did I get him bound, and sent him home,
Whilst to take order for the wrongs I went,
That here and there his fury had committed.
Anon, I wot not by what strong escape,
He broke from those that had the guard of him;
And, with his mad attendant and himself,
Each one with ireful passion, with drawn swords,
Met us again and, madly bent on us,
Chased us away; till, raising of more aid,
We came again to bind them: then they fled
Into this abbey, whither we pursued them:
And here the abbess shuts the gates on us,
And will not suffer us to fetch him out,
Nor send him forth, that we may bear him hence.
Therefore, most gracious duke, with thy com-
mand, [help.
Let him be brought forth, and borne hence for

*Duke.* Long since thy husband serv'd me in
my wars;
And I to thee engag'd a prince's word,
When thou didst make him master of thy bed,
To do him all the grace and good I could.—
Go, some of you, knock at the abbey-gate,
And bid the lady abbess come to me:
I will determine this before I stir.

*Enter a* Servant.

*Serv.* O mistress, mistress, shift and save
yourself.
My master and his man are both broke loose,
Beaten the maids a-row, and bound the doctor,
Whose beard they have singed off with brands
of fire;
And ever as it blazed they threw on him
Great pails of puddled mire to quench the hair:
My master preaches patience to him, while
His man with scissors nicks him like a fool;
And, sure, unless you send some present help,
Between them they will kill the conjurer.

*Adr.* Peace, fool, thy master and his man
are here;
And that is false thou dost report to us.

*Serv.* Mistress, upon my life, I tell you true:
I have not breath'd almost since I did see it.
He cries for you, and vows, if he can take you,
To scorch your face, and to disfigure you:
[*Cry within.*
Hark, hark, I hear him; mistress, fly; be gone.

*Duke.* Come, stand by me; fear nothing.
  Guard with halberds:
*Adr.* Ah me, it is my husband! Witness you
That he is borne about invisible.
Even now we hous'd him in the abbey here;
And now he's there, past thought of human
  reason.

*Enter* ANTIPHOLUS *and* DROMIO OF EPHESUS.

*Ant. E.* Justice, most gracious duke; oh,
  grant me justice!
Even for the service that long since I did thee,
When I bestrid thee in the wars, and took
Deep scars to save thy life: even for the blood
That then I lost for thee, now grant me justice.
*Æge.* Unless the fear of death doth make
  me doat,
I see my son Antipholus and Dromio.
*Ant. E.* Justice, sweet prince, against that
  woman there.
She whom thou gav'st to me to be my wife;
That hath abused and dishonour'd me,
Even in the strength and height of injury!
Beyond imagination is the wrong
That she this day hath shameless thrown on me.
*Duke.* Discover how, and thou shalt find me
  just.
*Ant. E.* This day, great duke, she shut the
  doors upon me,
While she with harlots feasted in my house.
*Duke.* A grievous fault. Say, woman, didst
  thou so?           [my sister,
*Adr.* No, my good lord;—myself, he, and
To-day did dine together. So befall my soul
As this is false he burdens me withal!
*Luc.* Ne'er may I look on day nor sleep on
  night,
But she tells to your highness simple truth!
*Ang.* O perjur'd woman! they are both for-
  sworn.
In this the madman justly chargeth them.
*Ant. E.* My liege, I am advised what I say;
Neither disturb'd with the effect of wine,
Nor, heady-rash, provok'd with raging ire,
Albeit my wrongs might make one wiser mad.
This woman lock'd me out this day from dinner:
That goldsmith there, were he not pack'd with
  her,
Could witness it, for he was with me then;
Who parted with me to go fetch a chain.
Promising to bring it to the Porcupine,
Where Balthazar and I did dine together.
Our dinner done, and he not coming thither,
I went to seek him. In the street I met him,
And in his company that gentleman.   [down,
There did this perjur'd goldsmith swear me
That I this day of him receiv'd the chain,
Which, God he knows, I saw not: for the which
He did arrest me with an officer.
I did obey, and sent my peasant home
For certain ducats: he with none return'd.
Then fairly I bespoke the officer
To go in person with me to my house.
By the way we met

My wife, her sister, and a rabble more
Of vile confederates: along with them
They brought one Pinch; a hungry lean-faced
  villain,
A mere anatomy, a mountebank,
A thread-bare juggler, and a fortune-teller;
A needy, hollow-ey'd, sharp-looking wretch;
A living dead man: this pernicious slave,
Forsooth, took on him as a conjurer;
And gazing in mine eyes, feeling my pulse,
And with no face, as 'twere outfacing me,
Cries out, I was possess'd: then altogether
They fell upon me, bound me, bore me thence;
And in a dark and dankish vault at home
There left me and my man both bound together;
Till, gnawing with my teeth my bonds in sunder,
I gain'd my freedom, and immediately
Ran hither to your grace; whom I beseech
To give me ample satisfaction
For these deep shames and great indignities.
*Ang.* My lord, in truth, thus far I witness
  with him,
That he dined not at home, but was lock'd out.
*Duke.* But had he such a chain of thee, or no?
*Ang.* He had, my lord: and when he ran in
  here
These people saw the chain about his neck.
*Mer.* Besides, I will be sworn these ears of
  mine
Heard you confess you had the chain of him,
After you first forswore it on the mart,
And thereupon I drew my sword on you;
And then you fled into this abbey here,
From whence, I think, you are come by miracle.
*Ant. E.* I never came within these abbey
  walls,
Nor ever didst thou draw thy sword on me:
I never saw the chain, so help me heaven!
And this is false you burden me withal.
*Duke.* What an intricate impeach is this!
I think you all have drank of Circe's cup.
If here you hous'd him, here he would have
  been:
If he were mad he would not plead so coldly:—
You say he dined at home; the goldsmith here
Denies that saying:—Sirrah, what say you?
*Dro. E.* Sir, he dined with her there at the
  Porcupine.           [that ring.
*Cour.* He did; and from my finger snatch'd
*Ant. E.* 'Tis true, my liege, this ring I had
  of her.           [here?
*Duke.* Saw'st thou him enter at the abbey
*Cour.* Assure, my liege, as I do see your grace.
*Duke.* Why, this is strange:—Go call the
  abbess hither:
I think you are all mated, or stark mad.
           [*Exit an* Attendant.
*Æge.* Most mighty duke, vouchsafe me speak
  a word;
Haply, I see a friend will save my life,
And pay the sum that may deliver me.   [wilt.
*Duke.* Speak freely, Syracusan, what thou
*Æge.* Is not your name, sir, call'd Antipholus?
And is not that your bondman Dromio?

*Dro. E.* Within this hour I was his bondman,
  sir,
But he, I thank him, gnaw'd in two my cords:
Now am I Dromio and his man, unbound.

*Æge.* I am sure you both of you remember
  me. [you;

*Dro. E.* Ourselves we do remember, sir, by
For lately we were bound as you are now.
You are not Pinch's patient, are you, sir?

*Æge.* Why look you strange on me? you
  know me well.

*Ant. E.* I never saw you in my life, till now.

*Æge.* Oh! grief hath chang'd me since you
  saw me last;
And careful hours, with Time's deformed hand,
Have written strange defeatures in my face:
But tell me yet, dost thou not know my voice?

*Ant. E.* Neither.

*Æge.*             Dromio, nor thou?

*Dro. E.* No, trust me, sir, nor I.

*Æge.*             I am sure thou dost.

*Dro. E.* Ay, sir; but I am sure I do not; and
whatsoever a man denies, you are now bound
to believe him.                         [tremity!

*Æge.* Not know my voice! O, time's ex-
Hast thou so crack'd and splitted my poor
  tongue,
In seven short years, that here my only son
Knows not my feeble key of untun'd cares?
Though now this grained face of mine be hid
In sap-consuming winter's drizzled snow,
And all the conduits of my blood.froze up,
Yet hath my night of life some memory,
My wasting lamps some fading glimmer left,
My dull deaf ears a little use to hear:
All these old witnesses,—I cannot err,—
Tell me, thou art my son Antipholus.

*Ant. E.* I never saw my father in my life.

*Æge.* But seven years since, in Syracusa,
  boy,
Thou know'st we parted; but perhaps, my son,
Thou sham'st to acknowledge me in misery.

*Ant. E.* The duke, and all that know me in
  the city,
Can witness with me that it is not so:
I ne'er saw Syracusa in my life.

*Duke.* I tell thee, Syracusan, twenty years
Have I been patron to Antipholus,
During which time he ne'er saw Syracusa:
I see, thy age and dangers make thee dote.

*Enter the* Abbess, *with* ANTIPHOLUS SYRACUSAN
  *and* DROMIO SYRACUSAN.

*Abb.* Most mighty duke, behold a man much
  wrong'd.                    [*All gather to see him.*

*Adr.* I see two husbands, or mine eyes deceive me.

*Duke.* One of these men is genius to the
  other;
And so of these. Which is the natural man,
And which the spirit? Who deciphers them?

*Dro. S.* I, sir, am Dromio; command him
  away.

*Dro. E.* I, sir, am Dromio; pray let me stay.

*Ant. S.* Ægeon, art thou not? or else his
  ghost?

*Dro. S.* O, my old master, who hath bound
  him here?

*Abb.* Whoever bound him, I will loose his
  bonds.
And gain a husband by his liberty.—
Speak, old Ægeon, if thou be'st the man
That hadst a wife once called Æmilia,
That bore thee at a burden two fair sons:
O, if thou be'st the same Ægeon, speak,
And speak unto the same Æmilia!

*Æge.* If I dream not, thou art Æmilia:
If thou art she, tell me where is that son
That floated with thee on the fatal raft?

*Abb.* By men of Epidamnum, he and I,
And the twin Dromio, all were taken up:
But, by and by, rude fishermen of Corinth
By force took Dromio and my son from them,
And me they left with those of Epidamnum:
What then became of them I cannot tell;
I to this fortune that you see me in.    [right;

*Duke.* Why, here begins his morning story
These two Antipholus's, these two so like,
And these two Dromios, one in semblance,—
Besides her urging of her wreck at sea,—
These are the parents to these children,
Which accidentally are met together.
Antipholus, thou cam'st from Corinth first?

*Ant. S.* No, sir, not I; I came from Syracuse.

*Duke.* Stay, stand apart; I know not which
  is which.                         [cious lord.

*Ant. E.* I came from Corinth, my most gra-

*Dro. E.* And I with him.

*Ant. E.* Brought to this town by that most
  famous warrior,
Duke Menaphon, your most renowned uncle.

*Adr.* Which of you two did dine with me
  to-day?

*Ant. S.* I, gentle mistress.

*Adr.*             And are not you my husband?

*Ant. E.* No; I say nay to that.

*Ant. S.* And so do I, yet she did call me so;
And this fair gentlewoman, her sister here,
Did call me brother.—What I told you then,
I hope I shall have leisure to make good;
If this be not a dream I see and hear.    [me.

*Ang.* That is the chain, sir, which you had of

*Ant. S.* I think it be, sir: I deny it not.

*Ant. E.* And you, sir, for this chain arrested
  me.

*Ang.* I think I did, sir: I deny it not.

*Adr.* I sent you money, sir, to be your bail
By Dromio; but I think he brought it not.

*Dro. E.* No, none by me.                 [you,

*Ant. S.* This purse of ducats I receiv'd from
And Dromio my man did bring them me:
I see we still did meet each other's man,
And I was ta'en for him, and he for me,
And thereupon these errors are arose.    [here.

*Ant. E.* These ducats pawn I for my father

*Duke.* It shall not need; thy father hath his
  life.                               [you.

*Cour.* Sir, I must have that diamond from

*Ant. E.* There, take it; and much thanks for
    my good cheer.
*Abb.* Renowned duke, vouchsafe to take the
    pains
To go with us into the abbey here,
And hear at large discoursed all our fortunes:—
And all that are assembled in this place,
That by this sympathized one day's error
Have suffer'd wrong, go, keep us company,
And we shall make full satisfaction.—
Twenty-five years have I but gone in travail
Of you, my sons; nor till this present hour
My heavy burdens are delivered:—
The duke, my husband, and my children both,
And you the calendars of their nativity,
Go to a gossip's feast, and go with me;
After so long grief, such nativity!    [feast.
*Duke.* With all my heart, I'll gossip at this
    [*Exeunt* DUKE, Abb., ÆGE., Cour.,
        Mer., ANG., *and* Attendants.
*Dro. S.* Master, shall I fetch your stuff from
    shipboard?
*Ant. E.* Dromio, what stuff of mine hast thou
    embark'd?

*Dro. S.* Your goods, that lay at host, sir, in
    the Centaur.
*Ant. S.* He speaks to me; I am your master,
    Dromio:
Come, go with us: we'll look to that anon:
Embrace thy brother there; rejoice with him.
    [*Exeunt* ANT. S. *and* E., ADR., *and* LUC.
*Dro. S.* There is a fat friend at your master's
    house,
That kitchen'd me for you to-day at dinner:
She now shall be my sister, not my wife.
*Dro. E.* Methinks you are my glass, and not
    my brother:
I see by you I am a sweet-faced youth.
Will you walk in to see their gossiping?
*Dro. S.* Not I, sir; you are my elder.
*Dro. E.* That's a question: how shall we
    try it?
*Dro. S.* We will draw cuts for the senior:
till then, lead thou first.
*Dro. E.* Nay, then thus:
We came into the world like brother and brother:
And now let's go hand in hand, not one before
    another.     [*Exeunt.*

KING JOHN.

Act IV. Sc. 1.

# KING JOHN

## DRAMATIS PERSONÆ

KING JOHN.
PRINCE HENRY, *his Son; afterwards* KING HENRY III.
ARTHUR, *Duke of Bretagne, Son to* GEFFREY, *late Duke of Bretagne, the Elder Brother to* KING JOHN.
WILLIAM MARESHALL, *Earl of Pembroke.*
GEFFREY FITZ-PETER, *Earl of Essex, Chief Justiciary of England.*
WILLIAM LONGSWORD, *Earl of Salisbury.*
ROBERT BIGOT, *Earl of Norfolk.*
HUBERT DE BURGH, *Chamberlain to the* KING.
ROBERT FALCONBRIDGE, *Son to* SIR ROBERT FALCONBRIDGE.
PHILIP FALCONBRIDGE, *his Half-brother, Bastard Son to* KING RICHARD I.
JAMES GURNEY, *Servant to* LADY FALCONBRIDGE.

PETER *of Pomfret, a Prophet.*
PHILIP, *King of France.*
LOUIS, *the Dauphin.*
ARCHDUKE OF AUSTRIA.
CARDINAL PANDULPH, *the Pope's Legate.*
MELUN, *a French Lord.*
CHATILLON, *Ambassador from France to* KING JOHN.

ELINOR, *Widow of* KING HENRY II., *and Mother to* KING JOHN.
CONSTANCE, *Mother to* ARTHUR.
BLANCH, *Daughter to* ALPHONSO, *King of Castile, and Niece to* KING JOHN.
LADY FALCONBRIDGE, *Mother to the* BASTARD *and* ROBERT FALCONBRIDGE.

Lords, Citizens *of Angiers, Sheriff, Heralds, Officers, Soldiers, Messengers, and other* Attendants.

SCENE,—*Sometimes in* ENGLAND, *and sometimes in* FRANCE.

## ACT I.

SCENE I.—NORTHAMPTON. *A Room of State in the Palace.*

*Enter* KING JOHN, QUEEN ELINOR, PEMBROKE, ESSEX, SALISBURY, *and others, with* CHATILLON.

*K. John.* Now, say, Chatillon, what would France with us? [of France,

*Chat.* Thus, after greeting, speaks the King In my behaviour, to the majesty, The borrow'd majesty of England here.

*Eli.* A strange beginning;—borrow'd majesty!

*K. John.* Silence, good mother; hear the embassy. [behalf

*Chat.* Philip of France, in right and true Of thy deceased brother Geffrey's son, Arthur Plantagenet, lays most lawful claim To this fair island, and the territories,— To Ireland, Poictiers, Anjou, Touraine, Maine; Desiring thee to lay aside the sword Which sways usurpingly these several titles, And put the same into young Arthur's hand, Thy nephew and right royal sovereign.

*K. John.* What follows, if we disallow of this?

*Chat.* The proud control of fierce and bloody war, To enforce these rights so forcibly withheld.

*K. John.* Here have we war for war, and blood for blood, Controlment for controlment: so answer France.

*Chat.* Then take my king's defiance from my mouth, The furthest limit of my embassy. [peace:

*K. John.* Bear mine to him, and so depart in Be thou as lightning in the eyes of France; For ere thou canst report I will be there, The thunder of my cannon shall be heard: So, hence! Be thou the trumpet of our wrath, And sullen presage of your own decay.— An honourable conduct let him have:— Pembroke, look to 't. Farewell, Chatillon.

[*Exeunt* CHATILLON *and* PEMBROKE.

*Eli.* What now, my son! have I not ever said How that ambitious Constance would not cease Till she had kindled France and all the world Upon the right and party of her son? That might have been prevented and made whole, With very easy arguments of love; Which now the manage of two kingdoms must With fearful bloody issue arbitrate.

*K. John.* Our strong possession and our right for us. [your right,

*Eli.* Your strong possession much more than Or else it must go wrong with you and me: So much my conscience whispers in your ear, Which none but heaven and you and I shall hear.

*Enter the* Sheriff of Northamptonshire, *who whispers* ESSEX.

*Essex.* My liege, here is the strangest controversy,

[367]

Come from the country to be judg'd by you,
That e'er I heard: shall I produce the men?
*K. John.* Let them approach.—
        [*Exit* Sheriff.
Our abbeys and our priories shall pay
This expedition's charge.

*Re-enter* Sheriff, *with* ROBERT FALCONBRIDGE,
 *and* PHILIP, *his bastard Brother.*
      What men are you?
 *Bast.* Your faithful subject I, a gentleman
Born in Northamptonshire, and eldest son,
As I suppose, to Robert Falconbridge,—
A soldier, by the honour-giving hand
Of Cœur-de-lion knighted in the field.
 *K. John.* What art thou?
 *Rob.* The son and heir to that same Falcon-
  bridge.       [heir?
 *K. John.* Is that the elder, and art thou the
You came not of one mother, then, it seems.
 *Bast.* Most certain of one mother, mighty
  king,—
That is well known; and, as I think, one father:
But for the certain knowledge of that truth
I put you o'er to heaven and to my mother:—
Of that I doubt, as all men's children may.
 *Eli.* Out on thee, rude man! thou dost shame
  thy mother,
And wound her honour with this diffidence.
 *Bast.* I, madam? no, I have no reason for
  it,—
That is my brother's plea, and none of mine;
The which if he can prove, 'a pops me out
At least from fair five hundred pound a-year:
Heaven guard my mother's honour and my
  land!      [younger born,
 *K. John.* A good blunt fellow.—Why, being
Doth he lay claim to thine inheritance?
 *Bast.* I know not why, except to get the land.
But once he slander'd me with bastardy:
But whe'r I be as true begot or no,
That still I lay upon my mother's head;
But, that I am as well begot, my liege,—
Fair fall the bones that took the pains for me!—
Compare our faces, and be judge yourself.
If old Sir Robert did beget us both,
And were our father, and this son like him,—
O old Sir Robert, father, on my knee
I give heaven thanks I was not like to thee!
 *K. John.* Why, what a madcap hath heaven
  lent us here!
 *Eli.* He hath a trick of Cœur-de-lion's face;
The accent of his tongue affecteth him:
Do you not read some tokens of my son
In the large composition of this man? [parts,
 *K. John.* Mine eye hath well examined his
And finds them perfect Richard.—Sirrah, speak,
What doth move you to claim your brother's
  land?       [father;
 *Bast.* Because he hath a half-face, like my
With that half-face would he have all my land:
A half-fac'd groat five hundred pound a-year!
 *Rob.* My gracious liege, when that my father
  liv'd,

Your brother did employ my father much,—
 *Bast.* Well, sir, by this you cannot get my
  land:
Your tale must be, how he employ'd my mother.
 *Rob.* And once despatch'd him in an embassy
To Germany, there with the emperor
To treat of high affairs touching that time.
The advantage of his absence took the king,
And in the meantime sojourn'd at my father's;
Where how he did prevail I shame to speak,—
But truth is truth: large lengths of seas and
  shores
Between my father and my mother lay,—
As I have heard my father speak himself,—
When this same lusty gentleman was got.
Upon his death-bed he by will bequeath'd
His lands to me; and took it, on his death,
That this, my mother's son, was none of his;
And if he were, he came into the world
Full fourteen weeks before the course of time.
Then, good my liege, let me have what is mine,
My father's land, as was my father's will.
 *K. John.* Sirrah, your brother is legitimate;
Your father's wife did after wedlock bear him;
And if she did play false, the fault was hers;
Which fault lies on the hazards of all husbands
That marry wives. Tell me, how if my brother,
Who, as you say, took pains to get this son,
Had of your father claim'd this son for his?
In sooth, good friend, your father might have
  kept
This calf, bred from his cow, from all the world;
In sooth, he might: then, if he were my
  brother's,      [father,
My brother might not claim him; nor your
Being none of his, refuse him. This concludes,—
My mother's son did get your father's heir;
Your father's heir must have your father's land.
 *Rob.* Shall, then, my father's will be of no
  force
To dispossess that child which is not his?
 *Bast.* Of no more force to dispossess me, sir,
Than was his will to get me, as I think.
 *Eli.* Whether hadst thou rather be a Falcon-
  bridge,
And like thy brother, to enjoy thy land,
Or the reputed son of Cœur-de-lion,
Lord of thy presence, and no land beside?
 *Bast.* Madam, an if my brother had my
  shape
And I had his, Sir Robert his, like him;
And if my legs were two such riding-rods,
My arms such eel-skins stuff'd, my face so thin
That in mine ear I durst not stick a rose
Lest men should say, *Look, where three-farthings
  goes!*
And, to his shape, were heir to all this land,
Would I might never stir from off this place,
I'd give it every foot to have this face;
I would not be Sir Nob in any case.
 *Eli.* I like thee well: wilt thou forsake thy
  fortune,
Bequeath thy land to him, and follow me?
I am a soldier, and now bound to France.

*Bast.* Brother, take you my land, I'll take
   my chance:
Your face hath got five hundred pound a-year;
Yet sell your face for fivepence, and 'tis dear.—
Madam, I'll follow you unto the death.
   *Eli.* Nay, I would have you go before me
      thither.                          [way.
   *Bast.* Our country manners give our betters
   *K. John.* What is thy name?
   *Bast.* Philip, my liege; so is my name begun;
Philip, good old Sir Robert's wife's eldest son.
   *K. John.* From henceforth bear his name
      whose form thou bear'st:
Kneel thou down Philip, but arise more great,—
Arise Sir Richard and Plantagenet.
   *Bast.* Brother by the mother's side, give me
      your hand:
My father gave me honour, yours gave land.—
Now blessed be the hour, by night or day,
When I was got, Sir Robert was away!
   *Eli.* The very spirit of Plantagenet!—
I am thy grandam, Richard; call me so.
   *Bast.* Madam, by chance, but not by truth:
      what though?
Something about, a little from the right,
In at the window, or else o'er the hatch;
Who dares not stir by day must walk by night;
   And have is have, however men do catch:
Near or far off, well won is still well shot;
And I am I, howe'er I was begot.
   *K. John.* Go, Falconbridge; now hast thou
      thy desire;
A landless knight makes thee a landed squire.—
Come, madam,—and come, Richard; we must
      speed
For France, for France; for it is more than need.
   *Bast.* Brother, adieu: good fortune come to
      thee!
For thou wast got i' the way of honesty.
            [*Exeunt all except the* BASTARD.
A foot of honour better than I was;
But many a many foot of land the worse.
Well, now can I make any Joan a lady:—
*Good den, Sir Richard:—God-a-mercy, fellow:—*
And if his name be George, I'll call him Peter:
For new-made honour doth forget men's names:
'Tis too respective and too sociable
For your conversion. Now your traveller,—
He and his toothpick at my worship's mess;
And when my knightly stomach is suffic'd,
Why then I suck my teeth, and catechize
My picked man of countries:—*My dear sir,*—
Thus, leaning on mine elbow, I begin,—
*I shall beseech you*—that is question now;
And then comes answer like an ABC-book:—
*O sir,* says answer, *at your best command;
At your employment; at your service, sir:*—
*No sir,* says question, *I, sweet sir, at yours:*
And so, ere answer knows what question
      would,—
Saving in dialogue of compliment,
And talking of the Alps and Apennines,
The Pyrenean and the river Po,—
It draws towards supper in conclusion so.

But this is worshipful society,
And fits the mounting spirit like myself:
For he is but a bastard to the time,
That doth not smack of observation,—
And so am I, whether I smack or no;
And not alone in habit and device,
Exterior form, outward accoutrement,
But from the inward motion to deliver
Sweet, sweet, sweet poison for the age's tooth:
Which, though I will not practise to deceive,
Yet, to avoid deceit, I mean to learn;
For it shall strew the footsteps of my rising.—
But who comes in such haste in riding-robes?
What woman-post is this? hath she no husband,
That will take pains to blow a horn before her?

   *Enter* LADY FALCONBRIDGE, *and* JAMES
               GURNEY.

O me! it is my mother.—How now, good lady!
What brings you here to court so hastily?
   *Lady F.* Where is that slave, thy brother?
      where is he
That holds in chase mine honour up and down?
   *Bast.* My brother Robert? old Sir Robert's
      son?
Colbrand the giant, that same mighty man?
Is it Sir Robert's son that you seek so?
   *Lady F.* Sir Robert's son! Ay, thou un-
      reverend boy,                   [Robert?
Sir Robert's son: why scorn'st thou at Sir
He is Sir Robert's son; and so art thou.
   *Bast.* James Gurney, wilt thou give us leave
      awhile?
   *Gur.* Good leave, good Philip.
   *Bast.*            Philip?—sparrow!—James,
There's toys abroad: anon I'll tell thee more.
                           [*Exit* GURNEY.
Madam, I was not old Sir Robert's son;
Sir Robert might have eat his part in me
Upon Good-Friday, and ne'er broke his fast:
Sir Robert could do well: marry, to confess,
Could not get me; Sir Robert could not do it,—
We know his handiwork:—therefore, good
      mother,
To whom am I beholding for these limbs?
Sir Robert never holp to make this leg.
   *Lady F.* Hast thou conspired with thy
      brother too,                    [honour?
That for thine own gain shouldst defend mine
What means this scorn, thou most untoward
      knave?                         [isco-like:
   *Bast.* Knight, knight, good mother,—Basil-
What! I am dubb'd; I have it on my shoulder.
But, mother, I am not Sir Robert's son;
I have disclaim'd Sir Robert and my land;
Legitimation, name, and all is gone:
Then, good my mother, let me know my
      father,—
Some proper man, I hope: who was it, mother?
   *Lady F.* Hast thou denied thyself a Falcon-
      bridge?
   *Bast.* As faithfully as I deny the devil.
   *Lady F.* King Richard Cœur-de-lion was thy
      father:

By long and vehement suit I was seduc'd
To make room for him in my husband's bed:—
Heaven lay not my transgression to my
    charge!—
Thou art the issue of my dear offence,
Which was so strongly urg'd, past my defence.
  *Bast.* Now, by this light, were I to get again,
Madam, I would not wish a better father.
Some sins do bear their privilege on earth,
And so doth yours; your fault was not your
    folly:
Needs must you lay your heart at his dispose,—
Subjected tribute to commanding love,—
Against whose fury and unmatched force
The aweless lion could not wage the fight,
Nor keep his princely heart from Richard's
    hand:
He that perforce robs lions of their hearts
May easily win a woman's. Ay, my mother,
With all my heart I thank thee for my father!
Who lives and dares but say, thou didst not well
When I was got, I'll send his soul to hell.
Come, lady, I will show thee to my kin;
  And they shall say, when Richard me begot,
If thou hadst said him nay, it had been sin:
  Who says it was, he lies; I say 'twas not.
                     [*Exeunt.*

## ACT II.

Scene I.—France. *Before the Walls of Angiers.*

*Enter, on one side, the* Archduke of Austria
*and* Forces; *on the other,* Philip, *King of
France,* Louis, Constance, Arthur, *and*
Forces.

  *Lou.* Before Angiers well met, brave Aus-
    tria.—
Arthur, that great forerunner of thy blood,
Richard, that robb'd the lion of his heart,
And fought the holy wars in Palestine,
By this brave duke came early to his grave:
And, for amends to his posterity,
At our importance hither is he come
To spread his colours, boy, in thy behalf;
And to rebuke the usurpation
Of thy unnatural uncle, English John:
Embrace him, love him, give him welcome
    hither.                                        [death
  *Arth.* God shall forgive you Cœur-de-lion's
The rather that you give his offspring life,
Shadowing their right under your wings of war:
I give you welcome with a powerless hand,
But with a heart full of unstained love,—
Welcome before the gates of Angiers, duke.
  *Lou.* A noble boy! Who would not do thee
    right?
  *Aust.* Upon thy cheek lay I this zealous kiss,
As seal to this indenture of my love,—
That to my home I will no more return,
Till Angiers, and the right thou hast in France,
Together with that pale, that white-fac'd shore,
Whose foot spurns back the ocean's roaring
    tides,
And coops from other lands her islanders,—

Even till that England, hedg'd in with the main,
That water-walled bulwark still secure
And confident from foreign purposes,—
Even till that utmost corner of the west
Salute thee for her king: till then, fair boy,
Will I not think of home, but follow arms.
  *Const.* O, take his mother's thanks, a wid-
    ow's thanks,                              [strength
Till your strong hand shall help to give him
To make a more requital to your love!
  *Aust.* The peace of heaven is theirs that lift
    their swords
In such a just and charitable war.
  *K. Phi.* Well, then, to work: our cannon
    shall be bent
Against the brows of this resisting town.—
Call for our chiefest men of discipline,
To cull the plots of best advantages:
We'll lay before this town our royal bones,
Wade to the market-place in Frenchmen's
    blood,
But we will make it subject to this boy.
  *Const.* Stay for an answer to your embassy,
Lest unadvis'd you stain your swords with
    blood:
My Lord Chatillon may from England bring
That right in peace, which here we urge in war;
And then we shall repent each drop of blood
That hot rash haste so indirectly shed.
  *K. Phi.* A wonder, lady!—lo, upon thy wish,
Our messenger Chatillon is arriv'd!

### *Enter* Chatillon.

What England says, say briefly, gentle lord;
We coldly pause for thee; Chatillon, speak.
  *Chat.* Then turn your forces from this paltry
    siege,
And stir them up against a mightier task.
England, impatient of your just demands,
Hath put himself in arms: the adverse winds,
Whose leisure I have stay'd, have given him
    time
To land his legions all as soon as I;
His marches are expedient to this town,
His forces strong, his soldiers confident.
With him along is come the mother-queen,
An Até, stirring him to blood and strife;
With her her niece, the Lady Blanch of Spain;
With them a bastard of the king deceas'd:
And all the unsettled humours of the land,—
Rash, inconsiderate, fiery voluntaries,
With ladies' faces, and fierce dragons' spleens,—
Have sold their fortunes at their native homes,
Bearing their birthrights proudly on their
    backs,
To make a hazard of new fortunes here.
In brief, a braver choice of dauntless spirits,
Than now the English bottoms have waft o'er,
Did never float upon the swelling tide,
To do offence and scath in Christendom.
                  [*Drums beat within.*
The interruption of their churlish drums
Cuts off more circumstance: they are at hand,
To parley or to fight: therefore prepare.

*K. Phi.* How much unlook'd-for is this expedition!

*Aust.* By how much unexpected, by so much
We must awake endeavour for defence;
For courage mounteth with occasion:
Let them be welcome, then; we are prepar'd.

*Enter* KING JOHN, ELINOR, BLANCH, *the*
BASTARD, Lords, *and* Forces.

*K. John.* Peace be to France, if France in peace permit
Our just and lineal entrance to our own!
If not, bleed France, and peace ascend to heaven!
Whiles we, God's wrathful agent, do correct
Their proud contempt that beat his peace to heaven.                                    [*return*

*K. Phi.* Peace be to England, if that war
From France to England, there to live in peace!
England we love; and for that England's sake
With burden of our armour here we sweat.
This toil of ours should be a work of thine;
But thou from loving England art so far,
That thou hast under-wrought his lawful king,
Cut off the sequence of posterity,
Outfaced infant state, and done a rape
Upon the maiden virtue of the crown.
Look here upon thy brother Geffrey's face;—
These eyes, these brows, were moulded out of his:
This little abstract doth contain that large
Which died in Geffrey; and the hand of time
Shall draw this brief into as huge a volume.
That Geffrey was thy elder brother born,
And this his son; England was Geffrey's right,
And this is Geffrey's: in the name of God,
How comes it then, that thou art call'd a king,
When living blood doth in these temples beat,
Which owe the crown that thou o'ermasterest?

*K. John.* From whom hast thou this great commission, France,
To draw my answer from thy articles?

*K. Phi.* From that supernal judge that stirs good thoughts
In any breast of strong authority,
To look into the blots and stains of right.
That judge hath made me guardian to this boy:
Under whose warrant I impeach thy wrong;
And by whose help I mean to chástise it.

*K. John.* Alack, thou dost usurp authority.

*K. Phi.* Excuse,—it is to beat usurping down.

*Eli.* Who is it thou dost call usurper, France?

*Const.* Let me make answer;—thy usurping son.

*Eli.* Out, insolent! thy bastard shall be king,
That thou mayst be a queen, and check the world!

*Const.* My bed was ever to thy son as true
As thine was to thy husband; and this boy
Liker in feature to his father Geffrey    [*like*
Than thou and John in manners,—being as
As rain to water, or devil to his dam.
My boy a bastard! By my soul, I think

His father never was so true begot:
It cannot be, an if thou wert his mother.

*Eli.* There's a good mother, boy, that blots thy father.

*Const.* There's a good grandam, boy, that would blot thee.

*Aust.* Peace!

*Bast.*          Hear the crier.

*Aust.*                    What the devil art thou?

*Bast.* One that will play the devil, sir, with you
An 'a man catch your hide and you alone.
You are the hare of whom the proverb goes,
Whose valour plucks dead lions by the beard:
I'll smoke your skin-coat an I catch you right;
Sirrah, look to 't; i' faith, I will, i' faith.

*Blanch.* O, well did he become that lion's robe
That did disrobe the lion of that robe!

*Bast.* It lies as sightly on the back of him
As great Alcides' shoes upon an ass:—
But, ass, I'll take that burden from your back,
Or lay on that shall make your shoulders crack.

*Aust.* What cracker is this same that deafs our ears
With this abundance of superfluous breath?

*K. Phi.* Louis, determine what we shall do straight.                      [ference.—

*Lou.* Women and fools, break off your con-
King John, this is the very sum of all,—
England and Ireland, Anjou, Touraine, Maine,
In right of Arthur, do I claim of thee:
Wilt thou resign them, and lay down thy arms?

*K. John.* My life as soon:—I do defy thee, France.
Arthur of Bretagne, yield thee to my hand;
And out of my dear love, I'll give thee more
Than e'er the coward hand of France can win:
Submit thee, boy.

*Eli.*          Come to thy grandam, child.

*Const.* Do, child, go to it' grandam, child;
Give grandam kingdom, and it' grandam will
Give it a plum, a cherry, and a fig:
There's a good grandam.

*Arth.*              Good my mother, peace!
I would that I were low laid in my grave:
I am not worth this coil that's made for me.

*Eli.* His mother shames him so, poor boy, he weeps.                      [does or no!

*Const.* Now, shame upon you, whe'r she shames,                      [poor eyes,
His grandam's wrongs, and not his mother's
Draw those heaven-moving pearls from his
Which heaven shall take in nature of a fee:
Ay, with these crystal beads heaven shall be brib'd
To do him justice, and revenge on you.

*Eli.* Thou monstrous slanderer of heaven and earth!                      [and earth!

*Const.* Thou monstrous injurer of heaven
Call not me slanderer; thou and thine usurp
The dominations, royalties, and rights    [son,
Of this oppressed boy: this is thy eldest son's
Infortunate in nothing but in thee:

Thy sins are visited in this poor child;
The canon of the law is laid on him,
Being but the second generation
Removed from thy sin-conceiving womb.

   *K. John.* Bedlam, have done.

   *Const.*          I have but this to say,—
That he is not only plagued for her sin,
But God hath made her sin and her the plague
On this removed issue, plagu'd for her,
And with her plague, her sin; his injury
Her injury,—the beadle to her sin;
All punish'd in the person of this child,
And all for her: a plague upon her!

   *Eli.* Thou unadvised scold, I can produce
A will that bars the title of thy son.    [will;

   *Const.* Ay, who doubts that? a will! a wicked
A woman's will; a canker'd grandam's will!

   *K. Phi.* Peace, lady! pause, or be more temperate:
It ill beseems this presence to cry aim
To these ill-tuned repetitions.—
Some trumpet summon hither to the walls
These men of Angiers: let us hear them speak
Whose title they admit, Arthur's or John's.

*Trumpet sounds. Enter* Citizens *upon the walls.*

   1 *Cit.* Who is it that hath warn'd us to the walls?

   *K. Phi.* 'Tis France, for England.

   *K. John.*        England, for itself:—
You men of Angiers, and my loving subjects,—

   *K. Phi.* You loving men of Angiers, Arthur's subjects,
Our trumpet call'd you to this gentle parle.

   *K. John.* For our advantage; therefore hear us first.
These flags of France, that are advanced here
Before the eye and prospect of your town,
Have hither march'd to your endamagement:
The cannons have their bowels full of wrath,
And ready mounted are they to spit forth
Their iron indignation 'gainst your walls:
All preparation for a bloody siege
And merciless proceeding by these French
Confronts your city's eyes, your winking gates;
And, but for our approach, those sleeping stones,
That as a waist do girdle you about,
By the compulsion of their ordinance
By this time from their fixed beds of lime
Had been dishabited, and wide havoc made
For bloody power to rush upon your peace.
But, on the sight of us, your lawful king,—
Who painfully, with much expedient march,
Have brought a countercheck before your gates,
To save unscratch'd your city's threaten'd cheeks,—
Behold, the French, amaz'd, vouchsafe a parle;
And now, instead of bullets wrapp'd in fire,
To make a shaking fever in your walls,
They shoot but calm words, folded up in smoke,
To make a faithless error in your ears:
Which trust accordingly, kind citizens,
And let us in, your king; whose labour'd spirits,

Forwearied in this action of swift speed,
Crave harbourage within your city-walls.

   *K. Phi.* When I have said, make answer to us both.
Lo, in this right hand, whose protection
Is most divinely vow'd upon the right
Of him it holds, stands young Plantagenet,
Son to the elder brother of this man,
And king o'er him and all that he enjoys:
For this down-trodden equity we tread
In war-like march these greens before your town,
Being no further enemy to you
Than the constraint of hospitable zeal
In the relief of this oppressed child
Religiously provokes. Be pleased, then,
To pay that duty which you truly owe
To him that owes it, namely, this young prince:
And then our arms, like to a muzzled bear,
Save in aspéct, have all offence seal'd up;
Our cannons' malice vainly shall be spent
Against the invulnerable clouds of heaven;
And with a blessed and unvex'd retire,
With unhack'd swords and helmets all unbruis'd,
We will bear home that lusty blood again
Which here we came to spout against your town,
And leave your children, wives, and you in peace.
But if you fondly pass our proffer'd offer,
'Tis not the rondure of your old-fac'd walls
Can hide you from our messengers of war,
Though all these English, and their discipline,
Were harbour'd in their rude circumference.
Then, tell us, shall your city call us lord
In that behalf which we have challeng'd it?
Or shall we give the signal to our rage,
And stalk in blood to our possession?

   1 *Cit.* In brief, we are the King of England's subjects:
For him, and in his right, we hold this town.

   *K. John.* Acknowledge then the king, and let me in.

   1 *Cit.* That can we not; but he that proves the king,
To him will we prove loyal: till that time
Have we ramm'd up our gates against the world.

   *K. John.* Doth not the crown of England prove the king?
And, if not that, I bring you witnesses,
Twice fifteen thousand hearts of England's breed,—

   *Bast.* Bastards, and else.

   *K. John.* To verify our title with their lives.

   *K. Phi.* As many and as well-born bloods as those,—

   *Bast.* Some bastards too.

   *K. Phi.* Stand in his face, to contradict his claim.

   1 *Cit.* Till you compound whose right is worthiest,
We for the worthiest hold the right from both.

*K. John.* Then God forgive the sin of all
　　those souls
That to their everlasting residence,
Before the dew of evening fall, shall fleet,
In dreadful trial of our kingdom's king!
　*K. Phi.* Amen, Amen!—Mount, chevaliers!
　　to arms!
　*Bast.* St. George, that swinged the dragon,
　　and e'er since
Sits on his horse' back at mine hostess' door,
Teach us some fence!—Sirrah [*to* AUSTRIA],
　　were I at home,
At your den, sirrah, with your lioness,
I would set an ox-head to your lion's hide,
And make a monster of you.
　*Aust.*　　　　　　　　Peace! no more.
　*Bast.* O, tremble, for you hear the lion roar.
　*K. John.* Up higher to the plain; where we'll
　　set forth
In best appointment all our regiments. [field.
　*Bast.* Speed, then, to take advantage of the
　*K. Phi.* It shall be so;—[*to* LOUIS] and at
　　the other hill
Command the rest to stand.—God and our
　　right!　　　　　　　[*Exeunt severally.*

*After Excursions, enter a* French Herald, *with*
　　*trumpets, to the gates.*

　*F. Her.* You men of Angiers, open wide your
　　gates,
And let young Arthur, Duke of Bretagne, in,
Who, by the hand of France, this day hath
　　made
Much work for tears in many an English
　　mother,
Whose sons lie scatter'd on the bleeding
　　ground:
Many a widow's husband grovelling lies,
Coldly embracing the discolour'd earth;
And victory, with little loss, doth play
Upon the dancing banners of the French,
Who are at hand triumphantly display'd.
To enter conquerors, and to proclaim
Arthur of Bretagne England's king and yours.

*Enter an* English Herald, *with trumpets.*

　*E. Her.* Rejoice, you men of Angiers, ring
　　your bells;　　　　　　　　　　[proach,
King John, your king and England's, doth ap-
Commander of this hot malicious day:
Their armours, that march'd hence so silver-
　　bright,
Hither return all gilt with Frenchmen's blood;
There stuck no plume in any English crest
That is removed by a staff of France;
Our colours do return in those same hands
That did display them when we first march'd
　　forth;
And, like a jolly troop of huntsmen, come
Our lusty English, all with purpled hands,
Dy'd in the dying slaughter of their foes:
Open your gates, and give the victors way.
　*I Cit.* Heralds, from off our towers we might
　　behold,

From first to last, the onset and retire
Of both your armies, whose equality
By our best eyes cannot be censured:
Blood hath bought blood, and blows have an-
　　swer'd blows;
Strength match'd with strength, and power
　　confronted power:
Both are alike; and both alike we like.
One must prove greatest: while they weigh so
　　even
We hold our town for neither; yet for both.

*Re-enter, on one side,* KING JOHN, ELINOR,
　　BLANCH, *the* BASTARD, *and* Forces; *at the*
　　*other,* KING PHILIP, LOUIS, AUSTRIA, *and*
　　Forces.

　*K. John.* France, hast thou yet more blood
　　to cast away?
Say, shall the current of our right run on?
Whose passage, vex'd with thy impediment,
Shall leave his native channel, and o'erswell
With course disturb'd even thy confining shores,
Unless thou let his silver water keep
A peaceful progress to the ocean.
　*K. Phi.* England, thou hast not sav'd one
　　drop of blood,
In this hot trial, more than we of France;
Rather, lost more: and by this hand I swear,
That sways the earth this climate overlooks,
Before we will lay down our just-borne arms,
We'll put thee down, 'gainst whom these arms
　　we bear,
Or add a royal number to the dead,
Gracing the scroll that tells of this war's loss
With slaughter coupled to the name of kings
　*Bast.* Ha, majesty! how high thy glory
　　towers
When the rich blood of kings is set on fire!
O, now doth Death line his dead chaps with
　　steel;
The swords of soldiers are his teeth, his fangs;
And now he feasts, mousing the flesh of men,
In undetermin'd differences of kings.—
Why stand these royal fronts amazed thus?
Cry, havoc, kings! back to the stained field,
You equal potentates, fiery-kindled spirits!
Then let confusion of one part confirm
The other's peace; till then, blows, blood, and
　　death!　　　　　　　　　　　[admit?
　*K. John.* Whose party do the townsmen yet
　*K. Phi.* Speak, citizens, for England; who's
　　your king?　　　　　　　　　[the king.
　*I Cit.* The king of England, when we know
　*K. Phi.* Know him in us, that here hold up
　　his right.
　*K. John.* In us, that are our own great
　　deputy,
And bear possession of our person here;
Lord of our presence, Angiers, and of you.
　*I Cit.* A greater power than we denies all
　　this;
And till it be undoubted, we do lock
Our former scruple in our strong-barr'd gates;
King'd of our fear, until our fears, resolv'd,

Be by some certain king purg'd and depos'd.

*Bast.* By heaven, these scroyles of Angiers
     flout you, kings,
And stand securely on their battlements
As in a theatre, whence they gape and point
At your industrious scenes and acts of death.
Your royal presences be rul'd by me:—
Do like the mutines of Jerusalem,
Be friends awhile, and both conjointly bend
Your sharpest deeds of malice on this town:
By east and west let France and England mount
Their battering cannon, charged to the mouths,
Till their soul-fearing clamours have brawl'd
     down
The flinty ribs of this contemptuous city:
I'd play incessantly upon these jades,
Even till unfenced desolation
Leave them as naked as the vulgar air.
That done, dissever your united strengths,
And part your mingled colours once again:
Turn face to face, and bloody point to point;
Then, in a moment, fortune shall cull forth
Out of one side her happy minion,
To whom in favour she shall give the day,
And kiss him with a glorious victory.
How like you this wild counsel, mighty states?
Smacks it not something of the policy?

*K. John.* Now, by the sky that hangs above
     our heads,
I like it well.—France, shall we knit our powers,
And lay this Angiers even with the ground;
Then, after, fight who shall be king of it?

*Bast.* And if thou hast the mettle of a king,—
Being wrong'd, as we are, by this peevish
     town,—
Turn thou the mouth of thy artillery,
As we will ours, against these saucy walls;
And when that we have dash'd them to the
     ground,
Why, then defy each other, and, pell-mell,
Make work upon ourselves, for heaven or hell!

*K. Phi.* Let it be so.—Say, where will you
     assault?      }struction

*K. John.* We from the west will send de-
Into this city's bosom.

*Aust.* I from the north.

*K. Phi.* Our thunder from the south
Shall rain their drift of bullets on this town.

*Bast.* O prudent discipline! From north to
     south,—
Austria and France shoot in each other's
     mouth:      [away!
I'll stir them to it. [*Aside.*]—Come, away!

*1 Cit.* Hear us, great kings: vouchsafe awhile
     to stay,
And I shall show you peace and fair-fac'd
     league;
Win you this city without stroke or wound;
Rescue those breathing lives to die in beds,
That here come sacrifices for the field:
Perséver not, but hear me, mighty kings.

*K. John.* Speak on, with favour; we are bent
     to hear.      [Lady Blanch,

*1 Cit.* That daughter there of Spain, the

Is neice to England:—look upon the years
Of Louis the Dauphin, and that lovely maid:
If lusty love should go in quest of beauty,
Where should he find it fairer than in Blanch?
If zealous love should go in search of virtue,
Where should he find it purer than in Blanch?
If love ambitious sought a match of birth,
Whose veins bound richer blood than Lady
     Blanch?
Such as she is, in beauty, virtue, birth,
Is the young Dauphin every way complete,—
If not complete of, say he is not she;
And she again wants nothing, to name want,
If want it be not, that she is not he:
He is the half part of a blessed man,
Left to be finished by such a she;
And she a fair divided excellence,
Whose fulness of perfection lies in him.
O, two such silver currents, when they join
Do glorify the banks that bound them in;
And two such shores to two such streams made
     one,
Two such controlling bounds shall you be,
     kings,
To these two princes, if you marry them.
This union shall do more than battery can
To our fast-closed gates; for, at this match,
With swifter spleen than powder can enforce,
The mouth of passage shall we fling wide ope,
And give you entrance; but without this match,
The sea enraged is not half so deaf,
Lions more confident, mountains and rocks
More free from motion; no, not Death himself
In mortal fury half so peremptory,
As we to keep this city.

*Bast.*      Here's a stay,
That shakes the rotten carcase of old Death
Out of his rags! Here's a large mouth, indeed,
That spits forth death and mountains, rocks
     and seas;
Talks as familiarly of roaring lions
As maids of thirteen do of puppy-dogs!
What cannoneer begot this lusty blood?
He speaks plain cannon,—fire and smoke and
     bounce;
He gives the bastinado with his tongue;
Our ears are cudgell'd; not a word of his
But buffets better than a fist of France:
Zounds! I was never so bethump'd with words
Since I first called my brother's father dad.

*Eli.* Son, list to this conjunction, make this
     match;
Give with our niece a dowry large enough:
For by this knot thou shalt so surely tie
Thy now unsur'd assurance to the crown,
That yon green boy shall have no sun to ripe
The bloom that promiseth a mighty fruit.
I see a yielding in the looks of France;
Mark how they whisper: urge them while their
     souls
Are capable of this ambition,
Lest zeal, now melted by the windy breath
Of soft petitions, pity, and remorse,
Cool and congeal again to what it was.

1 *Cit.* Why answer not the double majesties
This friendly treaty of our threaten'd town?
*K. Phi.* Speak England first, that hath been
　　forward first ·
To speak unto this city: what say you?
*K. John.* If that the Dauphin there, thy
　　princely son,
Can in this book of beauty read, "I love,"
Her dowry shall weigh equal with a queen:
For Anjou, and fair Touraine, Maine, Poictiers,
And all that we upon this side the sea,—
Except this city now by us besieg'd,—
Find liable to our crown and dignity,
Shall gild her bridal bed; and make her rich
In titles, honours, and promotions,
As she in beauty, education, blood,
Holds hand with any princess of the world.
*K. Phi.* What say'st thou, boy? look in the
　　lady's face.
*Lou.* I do, my lord, and in her eye I find
A wonder, or a wondrous miracle,
The shadow of myself form'd in her eye;
Which, being but the shadow of your son,
Becomes a sun, and makes your son a shadow:
I do protest I never lov'd myself
Till now infixed I beheld myself
Drawn in the flattering table of her eye.
　　　　　　　　[*Whispers with* BLANCH.
*Bast.* [*Aside.*] Drawn in the flattering table
　　of her eye!—
Hang'd in the frowning wrinkle of her
　　brow!—
And quarter'd in her heart!—he doth espy
　　Himself love's traitor! This is pity now,
That, hang'd, and drawn, and quarter'd, there
　　should be
In such a love so vile a lout as he.
*Blanch.* My uncle's will in this respect is
　　mine.
If he see aught in you that makes him like,
That anything he sees, which moves his liking,
I can with ease translate it to my will;
Or if you will, to speak more properly,
I will enforce it easily to my love.
Further, I will not flatter you, my lord,
That all I see in you is worthy love,
Than this,—that nothing do I see in you,
Though churlish thoughts themselves should
　　be your judge,—
That I can find should merit any hate.
*K. John.* What say these young ones?—
　　What say you, my niece?　　　　　　[do
*Blanch.* That she is bound in honour still to
What you in wisdom still vouchsafe to say.
*K. John.* Speak then, Prince Dauphin; can
　　you love this lady?
*Lou.* Nay, ask me if I can refrain from love;
For I do love her most unfeignedly.
*K. John.* Then do I give Volquessen, Tou-
　　raine, Maine,
Poictiers, and Anjou, these five provinces,
With her to thee; and this addition more,
Full thirty thousand marks of English coin.—
Philip of France, if thou be pleas'd withal,

Command thy son and daughter to join hands.
*K. Phi.* It likes us well.—Young princes,
　　close your hands.
*Aust.* And your lips too; for I am well assur'd
That I did so when I was first assur'd.
*K. Phi.* Now, citizens of Angiers, ope your
　　gates,
Let in that amity which you have made;
For at Saint Mary's chapel presently
The rites of marriage shall be solemniz'd.—
Is not the Lady Constance in this troop?
I know she is not; for this match made up
Her presence would have interrupted much:
Where is she and her son? tell me, who knows.
*Lou.* She is sad and passionate at your high-
　　ness' tent.
*K. Phi.* And, by my faith, this league that
　　we have made
Will give her sadness very little cure.—
Brother of England, how may we content
This widow lady? In her right we came;
Which we, God knows, have turn'd another
　　way,
To our own vantage.
*K. John.* 　　　　　We will heal up all;
For we'll create young Arthur Duke of Bretagne
And Earl of Richmond; and this rich fair town
We make him lord of.—Call the Lady Con-
　　stance:
Some speedy messenger bid her repair
To our solemnity:—I trust we shall,
If not fill up the measure of her will?
Yet in some measure satisfy her so
That we shall stop her exclamation.
Go we, as well as haste will suffer us,
To this unlook'd-for, unprepared pomp.
　　　　[*Exeunt all but the* BASTARD. *The* Citizens
　　　　　　　*retire from the Walls.*
*Bast.* Mad world! mad kings! mad composi-
　　tion!
John, to stop Arthur's title in the whole,
Hath willingly departed with a part;
And France,—whose armour conscience buck-
　　led on,
Whom zeal and charity brought to the field
As God's own soldier,—rounded in the ear
With that same purpose-changer, that sly devil;
That broker, that still breaks the pate of faith;
That daily break-vow; he that wins of all,
Of kings, of beggars, old men, young men,
　　maids,—
Who having no external thing to lose
But the word maid, cheats the poor maid of
　　that;
That smooth-fac'd gentleman, tickling com-
　　modity,—
Commodity, the bias of the world;
The world, who of itself is peised well,
Made to run even upon even ground,
Till this advantage, this vile-drawing bias,
This sway of motion, this commodity,
Makes it take head from all indifference,
From all direction, purpose, course, intent:
And this same bias, this commodity,

This bawd, this broker, this all-changing word,
Clapp'd on the outward eye of fickle France,
Hath drawn him from his own determin'd aid,
From a resolv'd and honourable war,
To a most base and vile-concluded peace.—
And why rail I on this commodity?
But for because he hath not woo'd me yet:
Not that I have the power to clutch my hand
When his fair angels would salute my palm;
But for my hand, as unattempted yet,
Like a poor beggar, raileth on the rich.
Well, whiles I am a beggar, I will rail,
And say, There is no sin but to be rich;
And, being rich, my virtue then shall be,
To say, There is no vice but beggary:
Since kings break faith upon commodity,
Gain, be my lord!—for I will worship thee.
                                        [*Exit.*

### ACT III.

SCENE I.—FRANCE. *The* French King's *Tent.*

*Enter* CONSTANCE, ARTHUR, *and* SALISBURY.

  *Const.* Gone to be married! gone to swear a
    peace!
False blood to false blood join'd! gone to be
    friends!
Shall Louis have Blanch? and Blanch those
    provinces?
It is not so; thou hast misspoke, misheard;
Be well advis'd, tell o'er thy tale again:
It cannot be; thou dost but say 'tis so:
I trust I may not trust thee; for thy word
Is but the vain breath of a common man:
Believe me, I do not believe thee, man;
I have a king's oath to the contrary.
Thou shalt be punish'd for thus frighting me,
For I am sick, and capable of fears;
Oppress'd with wrongs, and therefore full of
    fears;
A widow, husbandless, subject to fears;
A woman, naturally born to fears;
And though thou now confess thou didst but
    jest,
With my vex'd spirits I cannot take a truce,
But they will quake and tremble all this day.
What dost thou mean by shaking of thy head?
Why dost thou look so sadly on my son?
What means that hand upon that breast of
    thine?
Why holds thine eye that lamentable rheum,
Like a proud river peering o'er its bounds?
Be these sad signs confirmers of thy words?
Then speak again,—not all thy former tale,
But this one word, whether thy tale be true.
  *Sal.* As true as I believe you think them false
That give you cause to prove my saying true.
  *Const.* O, if thou teach me to believe this
    sorrow,
Teach thou this sorrow how to make me die;
And let belief and life encounter so
As doth the fury of two desperate men,
Which in the very meeting fall and die!—

Louis marry Blanch! O boy, then where art
    thou?                              [me?—
France friend with England! what becomes of
Fellow, be gone: I cannot brook thy sight;
This news hath made thee a most ugly man.
  *Sal.* What other harm have I, good lady,
    done,
But spoke the harm that is by others done?
  *Const.* Which harm within itself so heinous is,
As it makes harmful all that speak of it.
  *Arth.* I do beseech you, madam, be content.
  *Const.* If thou, that bid'st me be content,
    wert grim,
Ugly, and slanderous to thy mother's womb,
Full of unpleasing blots and sightless stains,
Lame, foolish, crooked, swart, prodigious,
Patch'd with foul moles and eye-offending
    marks,
I would not care, I then would be content;
For then I should not love thee; no, nor thou
Become thy great birth, nor deserve a crown.
But thou art fair; and at thy birth, dear boy,
Nature and fortune join'd to make thee great:
Of nature's gifts thou mayst with lilies boast,
And with the half-blown rose: but Fortune, O!
She is corrupted, chang'd, and won from thee;
She adulterates hourly with thine uncle John;
And with her golden hand hath pluck'd on
    France
To tread down fair respect of sovereignty,
And make his majesty the bawd to theirs.
France is a bawd to Fortune, and king John—
That strumpet Fortune, that usurping John!—
Tell me, thou fellow, is not France forsworn?
Envenom him with words; or get thee gone,
And leave those woes alone, which I alone
Am bound to under-bear.
  *Sal.*                    Pardon me, madam,
I may not go without you to the kings.
  *Const.* Thou mayst, thou shalt; I will not go
    with thee:
I will instruct my sorrows to be proud;
For grief is proud, and makes his honour stout.
To me, and to the state of my great grief,
Let kings assemble; for my grief's so great
That no supporter but the huge firm earth
Can hold it up: here I and sorrows sit;
Here is my throne, bid kings come bow to it.
                      [*Seats herself on the ground.*

*Enter* KING JOHN, KING PHILIP, LOUIS,
    BLANCH, ELINOR, BASTARD, AUSTRIA, *and*
    Attendants.

  *K. Phi.* 'Tis true, fair daughter; and this
    blessed day
Ever in France shall be kept festival:
To solemnize this day the glorious sun
Stays in his course, and plays the alchemist,
Turning, with splendour of his precious eye,
The meagre cloddy earth to glittering gold:
The yearly course that brings this day about
Shall never see it bud a holiday.
  *Const.* A wicked day, and not a holy day!
                                        [*Rising.*

What hath this day deserv'd? what hath it
　done,
That it in golden letters should be set
Among the high tides in the calendar?
Nay, rather turn this day out of the week,
This day of shame, oppression, perjury:
Or, if it must stand still, let wives with child
Pray that their burdens may not fall this day,
Lest that their hopes prodigiously be cross'd:
But on this day let seamen fear no wreck;
No bargains break that are not this day made:
This day, all things begun come to ill end,—
Yea, faith itself to hollow falsehood change!
　*K. Phi.* By heaven, lady, you shall have no
　cause
To curse the fair proceedings of this day.
Have I not pawn'd to you my majesty?
　*Const.* You have beguil'd me with a counter-
　　feit　　　　　　　　　　　　　　[tried,
Resembling majesty; which, being touch'd and
Proves valueless: you are forsworn, forsworn:
You came in arms to spill mine enemies' blood,
But now in arms you strengthen it with yours:
The grappling vigour and rough frown of war
Is cold in amity and painted peace,　　　·
And our oppression hath made up this league.—
Arm, arm, you heavens, against these perjur'd
　kings!
A widow cries; be husband to me, heavens!
Let not the hours of this ungodly day
Wear out the day in peace; but, ere sunset,
Set armed discord 'twixt these perjur'd kings!
Hear me, O, hear me!
　*Aust.*　　　　　Lady Constance, peace.
　*Const.* War! war! no peace! peace is to me
　a war.
O Lymoges! O Austria! thou dost shame
That bloody spoil: thou slave, thou wretch,
　thou coward!
Thou little valiant, great in villany!
Thou ever strong upon the stronger side!
Thou Fortune's champion that dost never fight
But when her humorous ladyship is by
To teach thee safety!—thou art perjur'd too,
And sooth'st up greatness. What a fool art
　thou,
A ramping fool, to brag, and stamp, and swear
Upon thy party! Thou cold-blooded slave,
Hast thou not spoke like thunder on my side?
Been sworn my soldier? bidding me depend
Upon thy stars, thy fortune, and thy strength?
And dost thou now fall over to my foes?
Thou wear a lion's hide! doff it for shame,
And hang a calf's-skin on those recreant limbs!
　*Aust.* O, that a man should speak those
　　words to me!　　　　　　　　　[limbs.
　*Bast.* And hang a calf's-skin on those recreant
　*Aust.* Thou dar'st not say so, villain, for thy
　life.
　*Bast.* And hang a calf's-skin on those recre-
　ant limbs.
　*K. John.* We like not this; thou dost forget
　　thyself.　　　　　　　　　　　[pope.
　*K. Phi.* Here comes the holy legate of the

*Enter* PANDULPH.

　*Pand.* Hail, you anointed deputies of
　heaven!—
To thee, King John, my holy errand is.
I Pandulph, of fair Milan cardinal,
And from Pope Innocent the legate here,
Do in his name religiously demand,
Why thou against the church, our holy mother,
So wilfully dost spurn; and, force perforce,
Keep Stephen Langton, chosen archbishop
Of Canterbury, from that holy see?
This, in our foresaid holy father's name,
Pope Innocent, I do demand of thee.
　*K. John.* What earthly name to interroga-
　tories
Can task the free breath of a sacred king?
Thou canst not, cardinal, devise a name
So slight, unworthy, and ridiculous,
To charge me to an answer, as the pope.
Tell him this tale; and from the mouth of
　England
Add thus much more,—That no Italian priest
Shall tithe or toll in our dominions:
But as we under heaven are supreme head,
So, under him, that great supremacy,
Where we do reign, we will alone uphold,
Without the assistance of a mortal hand:
So tell the pope; all reverence set apart
To him and his usurp'd authority.
　*K. Phi.* Brother of England, you blaspheme
　in this.　　　　　　　　　　[Christendom,
　*K. John.* Though you, and all the kings of
Are led so grossly by this meddling priest,
Dreading the curse that money may buy out;
And by the merit of vile gold, dross, dust,
Purchase corrupted pardon of a man,
Who in that sale sells pardon from himself;
Though you and all the rest, so grossly led,
This juggling witchcraft with revenue cherish;
Yet I, alone, alone do me oppose
Against the pope, and count his friends my
　foes.
　*Pand.* Then, by the lawful power that I have,
Thou shalt stand curs'd and excommunicate:
And blessed shall he be that doth revolt
From his allegiance to an heretic;
And meritorious shall that hand be call'd,
Canonized, and worship'd as a saint,
That takes away by any secret course
Thy hateful life.
　*Const.*　　　O, lawful let it be
That I have room with Rome to curse awhile!
Good father cardinal, cry thou amen
To my keen curses: for without my wrong
There is no tongue hath power to curse him
　right.　　　　　　　　　　　　[my curse.
　*Pand.* There's law and warrant, lady, for
　*Const.* And for mine too: when law can do
　no right,
Let it be lawful that law bar no wrong:
Law cannot give my child his kingdom here;
For he that holds his kingdom holds the law:
Therefore, since law itself is perfect wrong,

How can the law forbid my tongue to curse?
　*Pand.*　Philip of France, on peril of a curse,
Let go the hand of that arch-heretic;
And raise the power of France upon his head,
Unless he do submit himself to Rome.
　*Eli.*　Look'st thou pale, France; do not let
go thy hand.　　　　　　　　　　　[repent
　*Const.*　Look to that, devil; lest that France
And, by disjoining hands, hell lose a soul.
　*Aust.*　King Philip, listen to the cardinal.
　*Bast.*　And hang a calf's-skin on his recreant
limbs.　　　　　　　　　　　　　　[wrongs,
　*Aust.*　Well, ruffian, I must pocket up these
Because—
　*Bast.*　Your breeches best may carry them.
　*K. John.*　Philip, what say'st thou to the
cardinal?　　　　　　　　　　　　[cardinal?
　*Const.*　What should he say, but as the
　*Lou.*　Bethink you, father; for the difference
Is, purchase of a heavy curse from Rome,
Or the light loss of England for a friend:
Forego the easier.
　*Blanch.*　　　　　　That's the curse of Rome.
　*Const.*　O Louis, stand fast! the devil tempts
thee here
In likeness of a new uptrimmed bride.
　*Blanch.*　The Lady Constance speaks not
from her faith,
But from her need.
　*Const.*　　　　　　O, if thou grant my need,
Which only lives but by the death of faith,
That need must needs infer this principle,—
That faith would live again by death of need!
O, then, tread down my need, and faith mounts
up;
Keep my need up, and faith is trodden down!
　*K. John.*　The king is mov'd, and answers not
to this.　　　　　　　　　　　　　[well!
　*Const.*　O, be remov'd from him, and answer
　*Aust.*　Do so, King Philip; hang no more in
doubt.　　　　　　　　　　　　[sweet lout.
　*Bast.*　Hang nothing but a calf's-skin, most
　*K. Phi.*　I am perplex'd, and know not what
to say.　　　　　　　　　　　　[thee more,
　*Pand.*　What canst thou say, but will preplex
If thou stand excommunicate and curs'd?
　*K. Phi.*　Good reverend father, make my
person yours,
And tell me how you would bestow yourself.
This royal hand and mine are newly knit,
And the conjunction of our inward souls
Married in league, coupled and link'd together
With all religious strength of sacred vows;
The latest breath that gave the sound of words
Was deep-sworn faith, peace, amity, true love,
Between our kingdoms and our royal selves;
And even before this truce, but new before,—
No longer than we well could wash our hands,
To clap this royal bargain up of peace,—
Heaven knows, they were besmear'd and over-
stain'd
With slaughter's pencil, where revenge did
paint
The fearful difference of incensed kings:

And shall these hands, so lately purg'd of blood,
So newly joined in love, so strong in both,
Unyoke this seizure and this kind regreet?
Play fast and loose with faith? so jest with
heaven,
Make such unconstant children of ourselves,
As now again to snatch our palm from palm;
Unswear faith sworn; and on the marriage-bed
Of smiling peace to march a bloody host,
And make a riot on the gentle brow
Of true sincerity? O, holy sir,
My reverend father, let it not be so!
Out of your grace, devise, ordain, impose
Some gentle order; and then we shall be bless'd
To do your pleasure, and continue friends.
　*Pand.*　All form is formless, order orderless,
Save what is opposite to England's love.
Therefore, to arms! be champion of our church!
Or let the church, our mother, breathe her
curse,—
A mother's curse,—on her revolting son.
France, thou mayst hold a serpent by the
tongue,
A chafed lion by the mortal paw,
A fasting tiger safer by the tooth,　　　[hold.
Than keep in peace that hand which thou dost
　*K. Phi.*　I may disjoin my hand, but not my
faith.　　　　　　　　　　　　　　[faith;
　*Pand.*　So mak'st thou faith an enemy to
And, like a civil war, sett'st oath to oath,
Thy tongue against thy tongue. O, let thy vow
First made to heaven, first be to heaven per-
form'd,—
That is, to be the champion of our church!
What since thou swor'st is sworn against thy-
self,
And may not be performed by thyself:
For that which thou hast sworn to do amiss
Is not amiss when it is truly done;
And being not done, where doing tends to ill,
The truth is then most done not doing it:
The better act of purposes mistook
Is to mistake again; though indirect,
Yet indirection thereby grows direct,
And falsehood falsehood cures; as fire cools fire
Within the scorched veins of one new burn'd.
It is religion that doth make vows kept;
But thou hast sworn against religion,
By what thou swear'st against the thing thou
swear'st;
And mak'st an oath the surety for thy truth
Against an oath: the truth thou art unsure
To swear, swears only not to be forsworn;
Else what a mockery should it be to swear!
But thou dost swear only to be forsworn;
And most forsworn, to keep what thou dost
swear.
Therefore thy latter vows against thy first
Is in thyself rebellion to thyself;
And better conquest never canst thou make
Than arm thy constant and thy nobler parts
Against these giddy loose suggestions:
Upon which better part our prayers come in,
If thou vouchsafe them; but if not, then know

The peril of our curses light on thee,
So heavy as thou shalt not shake them off,
But in despair die under their black weight.
  *Aust.* Rebellion, flat rebellion!
  *Bast.*             Will 't not be?
Will not a calf's-skin stop that mouth of thine?
  *Lou.* Father, to arms!
  *Blanch.*      Upon thy wedding-day?
Against the blood that thou hast married?
What, shall our feast be kept with slaughter'd men?
Shall braying trumpets and loud churlish drums,—
Clamours of hell,—be measures to our pomp?
O husband, hear me!—ay, alack, how new
Is husband in my mouth!—even for that name,
Which till this time my tongue did ne'er pronounce,
Upon my knee I beg, go not to arms
Against mine uncle.
  *Const.*      O, upon my knee,
Made hard with kneeling, I do pray to thee,
Thou virtuous Dauphin, alter not the doom
Forethought by heaven.
  *Blanch.* Now shall I see thy love: what motive may
Be stronger with thee than the name of wife?
  *Const.* That which upholdeth him that thee upholds,
His honour:—O, thine honour, Louis, thine honour!
  *Lou.* I muse your majesty doth seem so cold,
When such profound respects do pull you on.
  *Pand.* I will denounce a curse upon his head.
  *K. Phi.* Thou shalt not need.—England, I will fall from thee.
  *Const.* O fair return of banish'd majesty!
  *Eli.* O foul revolt of French inconstancy!
  *K. John.* France, thou shalt rue this hour within this hour.
  *Bast.* Old Time the clock-setter, that bald sexton Time,
Is it as he will? well, then, France shall rue.
  *Blanch.* The sun's o'ercast with blood: fair day, adieu!
Which is the side that I must go withal?
I am with both: each army hath a hand;
And in their rage, I having hold of both,
They whirl asunder and dismember me.
Husband, I cannot pray that thou mayst win;
Uncle, I needs must pray that thou mayst lose;
Father, I may not wish the fortune thine;
Grandam, I will not wish thy wishes thrive:
Whoever wins, on that side shall I lose;
Assured loss before the match be play'd.
  *Lou.* Lady, with me; with me thy fortune lies.
  *Blanch.* There where my fortune lives, there my life dies.
  *K. John.* Cousin, go draw our puissance together.—          [*Exit* BASTARD.
France, I am burn'd up with inflaming wrath;
A rage whose heat hath this condition,
That nothing can allay, nothing but blood,—

The blood, and dearest-valu'd blood of France.
  *K. Phi.* Thy rage shall burn thee up, and thou shalt turn
To ashes, ere our blood shall quench that fire:
Look to thyself, thou art in jeopardy.
  *K. John.* No more than he that threats.—To arms let's hie!      [*Exeunt severally.*

SCENE II.—*The same. Plains near Angiers.*

*Alarums. Excursions. Enter the* BASTARD, *with* AUSTRIA'S *head.*

  *Bast.* Now, by my life, this day grows wondrous hot;
Some airy devil hovers in the sky, [there,
And pours down mischief.—Austria's head lie
While Philip breathes.

*Enter* KING JOHN, ARTHUR, *and* HUBERT.

  *K. John.* Hubert, keep this boy.—Philip, make up:
My mother is assailed in our tent,
And ta'en, I fear.
  *Bast.*      My lord, I rescu'd her;
Her highness is in safety, fear you not:
But on, my liege; for very little pains
Will bring this labour to an happy end.    [*Exeunt.*

SCENE III.—*The same.*

*Alarums, Excursions, Retreat. Enter* KING JOHN, ELINOR, ARTHUR, *the* BASTARD, HUBERT, *and* Lords.

  *K. John.* So shall it be; your grace shall stay behind,      [*To* ELINOR.
So strongly guarded.—Cousin, look not sad:
              [*To* ARTHUR.
Thy grandam loves thee; and thy uncle will
As dear be to thee as thy father was. [grief!
  *Arth.* O, this will make my mother die with
  *K. John.* Cousin [*to the* BASTARD], away for England; haste before:
And, ere our coming, see thou shake the bags
Of hoarding abbots; imprison'd angels
Set at liberty: the fat ribs of peace
Must by the hungry now be fed upon:
Use our commission in his utmost force.
  *Bast.* Bell, book, and candle shall not drive me back,
When gold and silver becks me to come on.
I leave your highness.—Grandam, I will pray,—
If ever I remember to be holy,—
For your fair safety; so, I kiss your hand.
  *Eli.* Farewell, gentle cousin.
  *K. John.* Coz, farewell.    [*Exit* BASTARD.
  *Eli.* Come hither, little kinsman; hark a word.    [*She takes* ARTHUR *aside.*
  *K. John.* Come hither, Hubert. O my gentle Hubert,
We owe thee much! within this wall of flesh
There is a soul counts thee her creditor,
And with advantage means to pay thy love:
And, my good friend, thy voluntary oath

Lives in this bosom, dearly cherished.
Give me thy hand. I had a thing to say,—
But I will fit it with some better time.
By heaven, Hubert, I am almost asham'd
To say what good respect I have of thee.
 *Hub.* I am much bounden to your majesty.
 *K. John.* Good friend, thou hast no cause to
  say so yet:
But thou shalt have; and creep time ne'er so
  slow,
Yet it shall come for me to do thee good.
I had a thing to say,—but let it go:
The sun is in the heaven, and the proud day,
Attended with the pleasures of the world,
Is all too wanton and too full of gawds
To give me audience:—if the midnight bell
Did, with his iron tongue and brazen mouth,
Sound one unto the drowsy ear of night;
If this same were a churchyard where we stand,
And thou possessed with a thousand wrongs;
Or if that surly spirit, melancholy, [thick,—
Had bak'd thy blood, and made it heavy,
Which else runs tickling up and down the veins,
Making that idiot, laughter, keep men's eyes,
And strain their cheeks to idle merriment—
A passion hateful to my purposes;—
Or if that thou couldst see me without eyes,
Hear me without thine ears, and make reply
Without a tongue, using conceit alone,
Without eyes, ears, and harmful sound of
  words,—
Then, in despite of brooded watchful day,
I would into thy bosom pour my thoughts:
But, ah, I will not!—yet I love thee well;
And, by my troth, I think thou lov'st me well.
 *Hub.* So well that what you bid me under-
  take;
Though that my death were adjunct to my act,
By heaven, I would do it.
 *K. John.* Do not I know thou wouldst?
Good Hubert, Hubert, Hubert, throw thine
  eye
On yon young boy: I'll tell thee what, my
  friend,
He is a very serpent in my way;
And wheresoe'er this foot of mine doth tread,
He lies before me:—dost thou understand me?
Thou art his keeper.
 *Hub.* And I'll keep him so
That he shall not offend your majesty.
 *K. John.* Death.
 *Hub.* My lord?
 *K. John.* A grave.
 *Hub.* He shall not live.
 *K. John.* Enough.—
I could be merry now. Hubert, I love thee:
Well, I'll not say what I intend for thee:
Remember.—Madam, fare you well:
I'll send those powers o'er to your majesty.
 *Eli.* My blessing go with thee!
 *K. John.* For England, cousin, go:
Hubert shall be your man, attend on you
With all true duty.—On toward Calais, ho!
          [*Exeunt.*

SCENE IV.—*The same. The* French King's
*Tent.*

*Enter* KING PHILIP, LOUIS, PANDULPH, *and*
Attendants.

 *K. Phi.* So, by a roaring tempest on the
  flood,
A whole armado of convicted sail
Is scatter'd and disjoin'd from fellowship.
 *Pand.* Courage and comfort! all shall yet go
  well.       [run so ill.
 *K. Phi.* What can go well, when we have
Are we not beaten? Is not Angiers lost?
Arthur ta'en prisoner? divers dear friends slain?
And bloody England into England gone,
O'erbearing interruption, spite of France?
 *Lou.* What he hath won, that hath he forti-
  fied:
So hot a speed with such advice dispos'd,
Such temperate order in so fierce a cause,
Doth want example: who hath read or heard
Of any kindred action like to this?
 *K. Phi.* Well could I bear that England had
  this praise,
So we could find some pattern of our shame.—
Look, who comes here! a grave unto a soul;
Holding the eternal spirit, against her will,
In the vile prison of afflicted breath.

*Enter* CONSTANCE.

I pr'ythee, lady, go away with me. [peace!
 *Const.* Lo, now! now see the issue of your
 *K. Phi.* Patience, good lady! comfort, gentle
  Constance!
 *Const.* No, I defy all counsel, all redress,
But that which ends all counsel, true redress,
Death, death:—O amiable lovely death!
Thou odoriferous stench! sound rottenness!
Arise forth from the couch of lasting night,
Thou hate and terror to prosperity,
And I will kiss thy détestable bones;
And put my eyeballs in thy vaulty brows;
And ring these fingers with thy household
  worms;
And stop this gap of breath with fulsome dust,
And be a carrion monster like thyself:
Come, grin on me; and I will think thou smil'st,
And buss thee as thy wife! Misery's love,
O, come to me!
 *K. Phi.* O fair affliction, peace!
 *Const.* No, no, I will not, having breath to
  cry:—
O, that my tongue were in the thunder's mouth!
Then with a passion would I shake the world;
And rouse from sleep that fell anatomy
Which cannot hear a lady's feeble voice,
Which scorns a modern invocation.
 *Pand.* Lady, you utter madness, and not
  sorrow.
 *Const.* Thou art not holy to belie me so;
I am not mad: this hair I tear is mine;
My name is Constance; I was Geffrey's wife;
Young Arthur is my son, and he is lost:

I am not mad;—I would to heaven I were!
For then, 'tis like I should forget myself:
O, if I could, what grief should I forget!—
Preach some philosophy to make me mad,
And thou shalt be canóniz'd, cardinal;
For, being not mad, but sensible of grief,
My reasonable part produces reason
How I may be deliver'd of these woes,
And teaches me to kill or hang myself:
If I were mad I should forget my son,
Or madly think a babe of clouts were he:
I am not mad; too well, too well I feel
The different plague of each calamity.

*K. Phi.* Bind up those tresses.—O, what
　　love I note
In the fair multitude of those her hairs!
Where but by chance a silver drop hath fallen,
Even to that drop ten thousand wiry friends
Do glue themselves in sociable grief;
Like true, inseparable, faithful loves,
Sticking together in calamity.

*Const.* To England, if you will.

*K. Phi.*　　　　　　　　Bind up your hairs.

*Const.* Yes, that I will; and wherefore will
　　I do it?
I tore them from their bonds, and cried aloud,
*O that these hands could so redeem my son,*
*As they have given these hairs their liberty!*
But now I envy at their liberty,
And will again commit them to their bonds,
Because my poor child is a prisoner.—
And, father cardinal, I have heard you say
That we shall see and know our friends in
　　heaven:
If that be true, I shall see my boy again;
For since the birth of Cain, the first male child,
To him that did but yesterday suspire,
There was not such a gracious creature born.
But now will canker sorrow eat my bud,
And chase the native beauty from his cheek,
And he will look as hollow as a ghost,
As dim and meagre as an ague's fit;
And so he'll die; and, rising so again,
When I shall meet him in the court of heaven
I shall not know him: therefore never, never
Must I behold my pretty Arthur more.

*Pand.* You hold too heinous a respect of
　　grief.

*Const.* He talks to me that never had a son.

*K. Phi.* You are as fond of grief as of your
　　child. 　　　　　　　　　　　　　　 [child,

*Const.* Grief fills the room up of my absent
Lies in his bed, walks up and down with me,
Puts on his pretty looks, repeats his words,
Remembers me of all his gracious parts,
Stuffs out his vacant garments with his form;
Then have I reason to be fond of grief.
Fare you well: had you such a loss as I,
I could give better comfort than you do.—
I will not keep this form upon my head,
　　　　　　　[*Tearing off her head-dress.*
When here is such disorder in my wit.
O Lord! my boy, my Arthur, my fair son!
My life, my joy, my food, my all the world!

My widow-comfort, and my sorrow's cure!
　　　　　　　　　　　　　　　　　[*Exit.*

*K. Phi.* I fear some outrage, and I'll follow
　　her. 　　　　　　　　　　　　　　　[*Exit.*

*Lou.* There's nothing in this world can make
　　me joy:
Life is as tedious as a twice-told tale
Vexing the dull ear of a drowsy man; 　　[taste,
And bitter shame hath spoil'd the sweet world's
That it yields naught but shame and bitterness.

*Pand.* Before the curing of a strong disease,
Even in the instant of repair and health,
The fit is strongest; evils that take leave,
On their departure most of all show evil:
What have you lost by losing of this day?

*Lou.* All days of glory, joy, and happiness.

*Pand.* If you had won it, certainly you had.
No, no; when Fortune means to men most good,
She looks upon them with a threatening eye.
'Tis strange to think how much King John hath
　　lost
In this which he accounts so clearly won:
Are not you griev'd that Arthur is his prisoner?

*Lou.* As heartily as he is glad he hath him.

*Pand.* Your mind is all as youthful as your
　　blood.
Now hear me speak with a prophetic spirit;
For even the breath of what I mean to speak
Shall blow each dust, each straw, each little rub,
Out of the path which shall directly lead
Thy foot to England's throne; and therefore
　　mark.
John hath seiz'd Arthur; and it cannot be
That, whiles warm life plays in that infant's
　　veins,
The misplac'd John should entertain an hour,
One minute, nay, one quiet breath of rest:
A sceptre snatch'd with an unruly hand
Must be as boisterously maintain'd as gain'd;
And he that stands upon a slippery place
Makes nice of no vile hole to stay him up:
That John may stand, then Arthur needs must
　　fall;
So be it, for it cannot be but so. 　　　　[fall?

*Lou.* But what shall I gain by young Arthur's

*Pand.* You, in the right of Lady Blanch
　　your wife,
May then make all the claim that Arthur did.

*Lou.* And lose it, life and all, as Arthur did.

*Pand.* How green you are, and fresh in this
　　old world! 　　　　　　　　　　　　 [you;
John lays you plots; the times conspire with
For he that steeps his safety in true blood
Shall find but bloody safety and untrue.
This act, so evilly borne, shall cool the hearts
Of all his people, and freeze up their zeal,
That none so small advantage shall step forth
To check his reign, but they will cherish it;
No natural exhalation in the sky,
No scape of nature, no distemper'd day,
No common wind, no customed event,
But they will pluck away his natural cause,
And call them meteors, prodigies, and signs,
Abortives, présages, and tongues of heaven,

Plainly denouncing vengeance upon John.
  *Lou.* May be he will not touch young Ar-
    thur's life,
But hold himself safe in his prisonment.
  *Pand.* O, sir, when he shall hear of your ap-
    proach,
If that young Arthur be not gone already,
Even at that news he dies; and then the hearts
Of all his people shall revolt from him,
And kiss the lips of unacquainted change;
And pick strong matter of revolt and wrath
Out of the bloody fingers' ends of John.
Methinks I see this hurly all on foot:
And, O, what better matter breeds for you
Than I have nam'd!—The bastard Falcon-
  bridge
Is now in England, ransacking the church,
Offending charity: if but a dozen French
Were there in arms, they would be as a call
To train ten thousand English to their side;
Or as a little snow, tumbled about
Anon becomes a mountain. O noble Dauphin,
Go with me to the king:—'tis wonderful
What may be wrought out of their discontent,
Now that their souls are topful of offence:
For England go:—I will whet on the king.
  *Lou.* Strong reasons make strong actions: let
  us go:
If you say ay, the king will not say no.
                              *[Exeunt.*

### ACT IV.

SCENE I.—NORTHAMPTON. *A Room in the
Castle.*

*Enter* HUBERT *and two* Attendants.

  *Hub.* Heat me these irons hot; and look thou
  stand
Within the arras: when I strike my foot
Upon the bosom of the ground, rush forth,
And bind the boy which you shall find with me
Fast to the chair: be heedful: hence, and watch.
  1 *Attend.* I hope your warrant will bear out
    the deed.
  *Hub.* Uncleanly scruples! Fear not you: look
  to 't.—            *[Exeunt* Attendants.
Young lad, come forth; I have to say with you.

*Enter* ARTHUR.

  *Arth.* Good-morrow, Hubert.
  *Hub.*              Good-morrow, little prince.
  *Arth.* As little prince, having so great a title
To be more prince, as may be.—You are sad.
  *Hub.* Indeed, I have been merrier.
  *Arth.*                Mercy on me!
Methinks no body should be sad but I:
Yet, I remember, when I was in France,
Young gentlemen would be as sad as night,
Only for wantonness. By my christendom,
So I were out of prison, and kept sheep,
I should be as merry as the day is long;
And so I would be here, but that I doubt
My uncle practices more harm to me:
He is afraid of me, and I of him:

Is it my fault that I was Geffrey's son?
No, indeed, is 't not; and I would to heaven
I were your son, so you would love me, Hubert.
  *Hub.* [*Aside.*] If I talk to him, with his inno-
    cent prate
He will awake my mercy, which lies dead:
Therefore I will be sudden and despatch.
  *Arth.* Are you sick, Hubert? you look pale
    to-day:
In sooth, I would you were a little sick,
That I might sit all night and watch with you:
I warrant I love you more than you do me.
  *Hub.* [*Aside.*] His words do take possession
    of my bosom.—
Read here, young Arthur.    [*Showing a paper.*
      [*Aside.*] How now, foolish rheum!
Turning dispiteous torture out of door!
I must be brief, lest resolution drop
Out at mine eyes in tender womanish tears.—
Can you not read it? is it not fair writ?
  *Arth.* Too fairly, Hubert, for so foul effect.
Must you with hot irons burn out both mine
    eyes?
  *Hub.* Young boy, I must.
  *Arth.*                And will you?
  *Hub.*                And I will.
  *Arth.* Have you the heart? When your head
    did but ache
I knit my handkerchief about your brows,—
The best I had, a princess wrought it me,—
And I did never ask it you again;
And, with my hand at midnight held your head;
And, like the watchful minutes to the hour,
Still and anon cheer'd up the heavy time,
Saying, *What lack you?* and, *Where lies your
    grief?*
Or, *What good love may I perform for you?*
Many a poor man's son would have lien still,
And ne'er have spoke a loving word to you;
But you at your sick service had a prince.
Nay, you may think my love was crafty love,
And call it cunning:—do, an if you will:
If heaven be pleas'd that you must use me ill,
Why, then you must.—Will you put out mine
    eyes?
These eyes that never did nor never shall
So much as frown on you?
  *Hub.*           I have sworn to do it!
And with hot irons must I burn them out.
  *Arth.* Ah, none but in this iron age would
    do it!
The iron of itself, though heat red hot,
Approaching near these eyes, would drink my
    tears,
And quench his fiery indignation,
Even in the matter of mine innocence;
Nay, after that, consume away in rust,
But for containing fire to harm mine eye.
Are you more stubborn-hard than hammer'd
    iron?
An if an angel should have come to me
And told me Hubert should put out mine eyes
I would not have believ'd him,—no tongue but
    Hubert's.

*Hub.* Come forth.                    [*Stamps.*

*Re-enter* Attendants, *with cords, irons, &c.*
          Do as I bid you.
*Arth.* O, save me, Hubert, save me! my eyes
     are out
Even with the fierce looks of these bloody men.
*Hub.* Give me the iron, I say, and bind him
     here.                           [rough?
*Arth.* Alas, what need you be so boist'rous-
I will not struggle, I will stand stone-still.
For heaven's sake, Hubert, let me not be bound!
Nay, hear me, Hubert!—drive these men away,
And I will sit as quiet as a lamb;
I will not stir, nor wince, nor speak a word,
Nor look upon the iron angerly:
Thrust but these men away, and I'll forgive
     you,
Whatever torment you do put me to.   [him.
*Hub.* Go, stand within; let me alone with
 1 *Attend.* I am best pleas'd to be from such
     a deed.               [*Exeunt* Attendants.
*Arth.* Alas, I then have chid away my friend!
He hath a stern look but a gentle heart:—
Let him come back, that his compassion may
Give life to yours.
*Hub.*          Come, boy, prepare yourself.
*Arth.* Is there no remedy?
*Hub.*          None, but to lose your eyes.
*Arth.* O heaven!—that there were but a
     mote in yours,
A grain, a dust, a gnat, a wandering hair,
Any annoyance in that precious sense!
Then, feeling what small things are boisterous
     there,
Your vile intent must needs seem horrible.
*Hub.* Is this your promise? go to, hold your
     tongue.
*Arth.* Hubert, the utterance of a brace of
     tongues
Must needs want pleading for a pair of eyes:
Let me not hold my tongue,—let me not,
     Hubert!
Or, Hubert, if you will, cut out my tongue,
So I may keep mine eyes: O, spare mine eyes,
Though to no use but still to look on you!—
Lo, by my troth, the instrument is cold,
And would not harm me.
*Hub.*          I can heat it, boy.
*Arth.* No, in good sooth; the fire is dead with
     grief,
Being create for comfort, to be us'd
In undeserv'd extremes: see else yourself;
There is no malice in this burning coal;
The breath of heaven hath blown his spirit out,
And strew'd repentant ashes on his head.
*Hub.* But with my breath I can revive it,
     boy.
*Arth.* And if you do, you will but make it
     blush,                         [Hubert:
And glow with shame of your proceedings,
Nay, it, perchance, will sparkle in your eyes;
And, like a dog that is compell'd to fight,
Snatch at his master that doth tarre him on.

All things that you should use to do me wrong,
Deny their office: only you do lack
That mercy which fierce fire and iron extends,
Creatures of note for mercy-lacking uses.
*Hub.* Well, see to live; I will not touch thine
     eyes
For all the treasure that thine uncle owes:
Yet am I sworn, and I did purpose, boy,
With this same very iron to burn them out.
*Arth.* O, now you look like Hubert! all this
     while
You were disguised.
*Hub.*          Peace; no more. Adieu!
Your uncle must not know but you are dead;
I'll fill these dogged spies with false reports:
And, pretty child, sleep doubtless and secure,
That Hubert, for the wealth of all the world,
Will not offend thee.
*Arth.*     O heaven! I thank you, Hubert.
*Hub.* Silence; no more: go closely in with me:
Much danger do I undergo for thee.   [*Exeunt.*

SCENE II.—*The same. A Room of State in the
          Palace.*

*Enter* KING JOHN, *crowned;* PEMBROKE, SALIS-
     BURY, *and other* Lords. *The* KING *takes his
     State.*

*K. John.* Here once again we sit, once again
     crown'd,
And look'd upon, I hope, with cheerful eyes.
*Pem.* This once again, but that your high-
     ness pleas'd,
Was once superfluous: you were crown'd before,
And that high royalty was ne'er pluck'd off;
The faiths of men ne'er stained with revolt;
Fresh expectation troubled not the land
With any long'd-for change or better state.
*Sal.* Therefore, to be possess'd with double
     pomp,
To guard a title that was rich before,
To gild refined gold, to paint the lily,
To throw a perfume on the violet,
To smooth the ice, or add another hue
Unto the rainbow, or with taper-light
To seek the beauteous eye of heaven to garnish,
Is wasteful and ridiculous excess.   [done,
*Pem.* But that your royal pleasure must be
This act is as an ancient tale new told;
And in the last repeating troublesome,
Being urged at a time unseasonable.
*Sal.* In this, the antique and well-noted face
Of plain old form is much disfigured;
And, like a shifted wind unto a sail,
It makes the course of thoughts to fetch about;
Startles and frights consideration;
Makes sound opinion sick, and truth suspected,
For putting on so new a fashion'd robe.
*Pem.* When workmen strive to do better
     than well,
They do confound their skill in convetousness;
And oftentimes excusing of a fault
Doth make the fault the worse by the excuse,—
As patches set upon a little breach

Discredit more in hiding of the fault
Than did the fault before it was so patch'd.
  *Sal.* To this effect, before you were new-
    crown'd,       [highness
We breath'd our counsel: but it pleas'd your
To overbear it; and we are all well pleas'd,
Since all and every part of what we would
Doth make a stand at what your highness will.
  *K. John.* Some reasons of this double coro-
    nation
I have possess'd you with, and think them
    strong;
And more, more strong, when lesser is my fear,
I shall indue you with: meantime but ask
What you would have reform'd that is not well,
And well shall you perceive how willingly
I will both hear and grant you your requests.
  *Pem.* Then I,—as one that am the tongue
    of these,
To sound the purposes of all their hearts,—
Both for myself and them,—but, chief of all,
Your safety, for the which myself and them
Bend their best studies,—heartily request
The enfranchisement of Arthur; whose restraint
Doth move the murmuring lips of discontent
To break into this dangerous argument,—
If what in rest you have in right you hold,
Why, then, your fears,—which, as they say,
    attend
The steps of wrong,—should move you to mew
    up
Your tender kinsman, and to choke his days
With barbarous ignorance, and deny his youth
The rich advantage of good exercise?
That the time's enemies may not have this
To grace occasions, let it be our suit
That you have bid us ask his liberty;
Which for our goods we do no further ask
Than whereupon our weal, on you depending,
Counts it your weal he have his liberty.
  *K. John.* Let it be so: I do commit his youth
To your direction.

      *Enter* HUBERT.

Hubert, what news with you?    [deed;
  *Pem.* This is the man should do the bloody
He show'd his warrant to a friend of mine:
The image of a wicked heinous fault
Lives in his eye; that close aspèct of his
Doth show the mood of a much-troubled breast;
And I do fearfully believe 'tis done
What we so fear'd he had a charge to do.  [go
  *Sal.* The colour of the king doth come and
Between his purpose and his conscience,
Like heralds 'twixt two dreadful battles set:
His passion is so ripe it needs must break.
  *Pem.* And when it breaks, I fear will issue
    thence
The foul corruption of a sweet child's death.
  *K. John.* We cannot hold mortality's strong
    hand:—
Good lords, although my will to give is living,
The suit which you demand is gone and dead:
He tells us Arthur is deceas'd to-night.

  *Sal.* Indeed, we fear'd his sickness was past
    cure:      [he was,
  *Pem.* Indeed, we heard how near his death
Before the child himself felt he was sick:
This must be answer'd either here or hence.
  *K. John.* Why do you bend such solemn
    brows on me?
Think you I bear the shears of destiny?
Have I commandment on the pulse of life?
  *Sal.* It is apparent foul-play; and 'tis shame
That greatness should so grossly offer it:
So thrive it in your game! and so, farewell.
  *Pem.* Stay yet, Lord Salisbury; I'll go with
    thee,
And find the inheritance of this poor child,
His little kingdom of a forced grave.    [isle,
That blood which ow'd the breadth of all this
Three foot of it doth hold:—bad world the
    while!      [out
This must not be thus borne: this will break
To all our sorrows, and ere long, I doubt.
            [*Exeunt* Lords.
  *K. John.* They burn in indignation. I repent:
There is no sure foundation set on blood;
No certain life achiev'd by other's death.—

      *Enter a* Messenger.

A fearful eye thou hast: where is that blood
That I have seen inhabit in those cheeks?
So foul a sky clears not without a storm:
Pour down thy weather:—how goes all in
    France?    [such a power
  *Mess.* From France to England.—Never
For any foreign preparation
Was levied in the body of a land.
The copy of your speed is learn'd by them;
For when you should be told they do prepare,
The tidings come that they are all arriv'd.
  *K. John.* O, where hath our intelligence been
    drunk?    [care,
Where hath it slept? Where is my mother's
That such an army could be drawn in France,
And she not hear of it?
  *Mess.*          My liege, her ear
Is stopp'd with dust; the first of April died
Your noble mother: and, as I hear, my lord,
The Lady Constance in a frenzy died    [tongue
Three days before; but this from rumour's
I idly heard,—if true or false I know not.
  *K. John.* Withhold thy speed, dreadful oc-
    casion!
O, make a league with me, till I have pleas'd
My discontented peers!—What! mother dead
How wildly, then, walks my estate in France!—
Under whose conduct came those powers of
    France
That thou for truth giv'st out are landed here?
  *Mess.* Under the Dauphin.
  *K. John.*          Thou hast made me giddy
With these ill tidings.

    *Enter the* BASTARD *and* PETER *of Pomfret.*
        Now, what says the world
To your proceedings? do not seek to stuff

·My head with more ill news, for it is full.

   *Bast.* But if you be afeared to hear the worst,
Then let the worst, unheard, fall on your
   head.

   *K. John.* Bear with me, cousin; for I was
   amaz'd
Under the tide: but now I breathe again
Aloft the flood; and can give audience
To any tongue, speak it of what it will.

   *Bast.* How I have sped among the clergymen,
The sums I have collected shall express.
But as I travell'd hither through the land,
I find the people strangely fantasied;
Possess'd with rumours, full of idle dreams.
Not knowing what they fear, but full of fear:
And here's a prophet that I brought with me
From forth the streets of Pomfret, whom I
   found
With many hundreds treading on his heels;
To whom he sung, in rude harsh-sounding
   rhymes,
That, ere the next Ascension-day at noon,
Your highness should deliver up your crown.

   *K. John.* Thou idle dreamer, wherefore didst
   thou so?             [out so.

   *Peter.* Foreknowing that the truth will fall

   *K. John.* Hubert, away with him; imprison
   him;
And on that day at noon, whereon he says
I shall yield up my crown, let him be hang'd.
Deliver him to safety; and return,
For I must use thee.
               [*Exit* HUBERT *with* PETER.
               O my gentle cousin,
Hear'st thou the news abroad, who are arriv'd?

   *Bast.* The French, my lord; men's mouths
   are full of it:
Besides, I met Lord Bigot and Lord Salis-
   bury,—
With eyes as red as new-enkindled fire,—
And others more, going to seek the grave
Of Arthur, whom they say is kill'd to-night
On your suggestion.

   *K. John.*       Gentle kinsman, go
And thrust thyself into their companies:
I have a way to win their loves again:
Bring them before me.

   *Bast.*        I will seek them out.

   *K. John.* Nay, but make haste; the better
   foot before.
O, let me have no subject enemies
When adverse foreigners affright my towns
With dreadful pomp of stout invasion!
Be Mercury, set feathers to thy heels,
And fly like thought from them to me again.

   *Bast.* The spirit of the time shall teach me
   speed.

   *K. John.* Spoke like a spriteful noble gentle-
   man.               [*Exit* BASTARD.
Go after him; for he perhaps shall need
Some messenger betwixt me and the peers;
And be thou he.

   *Mess.* With all my heart, my liege.   [*Exit.*

   *K. John.* My mother dead!

   *Hub.* My lord, they say five moons were
   seen to-night;
Four fixed; and the fifth did whirl about
The other four in wondrous motion.

   *K. John.* Five moons!

   *Hub.* Old men and beldams in the streets
Do prophesy upon it dangerously:   [mouths:
Young Arthur's death is common in their
And when they talk of him, they shake their
   heads,
And whisper one another in the ear;
And he that speaks doth gripe the hearer's
   wrist;
Whilst he that hears makes fearful action,
With wrinkled brows, with nods, with rolling
   eyes.
I saw a smith stand with his hammer, thus,
The whilst his iron did on the anvil cool,
With open mouth swallowing a tailor's news;
Who, with his shears and measure in his hand,
Standing on slippers,—which his nimble haste
Had falsely thrust upon contráry feet,—
Told of a many thousand warlike French
That were embattailed and rank'd in Kent?
Another lean unwash'd artificer
Cuts off his tale, and talks of Arthur's death?

   *K. John.* Why seek'st thou to possess me
   with these fears?
Why urgest thou so oft young Arthur's death?
Thy hand hath murder'd him: I had a mighty
   cause                [kill him.
To wish him dead, but thou hadst none to

   *Hub.* No hand, my lord! why, did you not
   provoke me?            [tended

   *K. John.* It is the curse of kings to be at-
By slaves that take their humours for a warrant
To break within the bloody house of life;
And, on the winking of authority,
To understand a law; to know the meaning
Of dangerous majesty, when perchance it frowns
More upon humour than advis'd respect.

   *Hub.* Here is your hand and seal for what I
   did.

   *K. John.* O, when the last account 'twixt
   heaven and earth
Is to be made, then shall this hand and seal
Witness against us to damnation!
How oft the sight of means to do ill deeds
Make ill deeds done! Hadst not thou been by,
A fellow by the hand of nature mark'd,
Quoted, and sign'd, to do a deed of shame,
This murder had not come into my mind:
But, taking note of thy abhorr'd aspèct,
Finding thee fit for bloody villany,
Apt, liable to be employ'd in danger,
I faintly broke with thee of Arthur's death;
And thou, to be endeared to a king,
Made it no conscience to destroy a prince.

   *Hub.* My lord,—

   *K. John.* Hadst thou but shook thy head, or
   made a pause,
When I spake darkly what I purpos'd,

Or turn'd an eye of doubt upon my face,
As bid me tell my tale in express words,
Deep shame had struck me dumb, made me
    break off,
And those thy fears might have wrought fears
    in me:
But thou didst understand me by my signs,
And didst in signs again parley with sin;
Yea, without stop, didst let thy heart consent,
And consequently thy rude hand to act
The deed, which both our tongues held vile to
    name.—
Out of my sight, and never see me more!
My nobles leave me; and my state is brav'd,
Even at my gates, with ranks of foreign powers:
Nay, in the body of this fleshly land,
This kingdom, this confine of blood and breath,
Hostility and civil tumult reigns
Between my conscience and my cousin's death.

*Hub.* Arm you against your other enemies,
I'll make a peace between your soul and you.
Young Arthur is alive: this hand of mine
Is yet a maiden and an innocent hand,
Not painted with the crimson spots of blood.
Within this bosom never enter'd yet
The dreadful motion of a murderous thought;
And you have slander'd nature in my form,—
Which, howsoever rude exteriorly,
Is yet the cover of a fairer mind
Than to be butcher of an innocent child.

*K. John.* Doth Arthur live? O, haste thee
    to the peers,
Throw this report on their incensed rage,
And make them tame to their obedience!
Forgive the comment that my passion made
Upon thy feature; for my rage was blind,
And foul imaginary eyes of blood
Presented thee more hideous than thou art.
O, answer not; but to my closet bring
The angry lords with all expedient haste:
I cónjure thee but slowly; run more fast.
                                [*Exeunt.*

SCENE III.—*The same. Before the Castle.*

*Enter* ARTHUR, *on the Walls.*

*Arth.* The wall is high, and yet will I leap
    down:—
Good ground, be pitiful, and hurt me not!—
There's few or none do know me: if they did,
This ship-boy's semblance hath disguis'd me
    quite.
I am afraid; and yet I'll venture it.
If I get down, and do not break my limbs,
I'll find a thousand shifts to get away:
As good to die and go, as die and stay.
                                [*Leaps down.*
O me! my uncle's spirit is in these stones:—
Heaven take my soul, and England keep my
    bones!                          [*Dies.*

*Enter* PEMBROKE, SALISBURY, *and* BIGOT.

*Sal.* Lords, I will meet him at Saint Ed-
    mund's-Bury:
It is our safety, and we must embrace
This gentle offer of the perilous time.

*Pem.* Who brought that letter from the
    cardinal?                       [France;
*Sal.* The Count Melun, a noble lord of
Whose private with me of the Dauphin's love
Is much more general than these lines import.
*Big.* To-morrow morning let us meet him,
    then.
*Sal.* Or rather than set forward; for 'twill be
Two long days' journey, lords, or e'er we meet.

*Enter the* BASTARD.

*Bast.* Once more to-day well met, distem-
    per'd lords!
The king by me requests your presence straight.
*Sal.* The king hath dispossess'd himself of us:
We will not line his thin bestained cloak
With our pure honours, nor attend the foot
That leaves the print of blood where'er it walks.
Return and tell him so: we know the worst.
*Bast.* Whate'er you think, good words, I
    think, were best.                [now.
*Sal.* Our griefs, and not our manners, reason
*Bast.* But there is little reason in your grief;
Therefore 'twere reason you had manners now.
*Pem.* Sir, sir, impatience hath his privilege.
*Bast.* 'Tis true,—to hurt his master, no man
    else.
*Sal.* This is the prison:—what is he lies here?
                                [*Seeing* ARTHUR.
*Pem.* O death, made proud with pure and
    princely beauty!
The earth had not a hole to hide this deed.
*Sal.* Murder, as hating what himself hath
    done,
Doth lay it open to urge on revenge.    [grave,
*Big.* Or, when he doom'd this beauty to a
Found it too precious-princely for a grave.
*Sal.* Sir Richard, what think you? Have you
    beheld,
Or have you read or heard? or could you think?
Or do you almost think, although you see,
That you do see? could thought, without this
    object,
Form such another? This is the very top,
The height, the crest, or crest unto the crest
Of murder's arms: this is the bloodiest shame,
The wildest savagery, the vilest stroke,
That ever wall-ey'd wrath or staring rage
Presented to the tears of soft remorse.   [this.
*Pem.* All murders past do stand excus'd in
And this, so sole and so unmatchable,
Shall give a holiness, a purity,
To the yet unbegotten sin of times;
And prove a deadly bloodshed but a jest,
Exampled by this heinous spectacle.
*Bast.* It is a damned and a bloody work;
The graceless action of a heavy hand,—
If that it be the work of any hand.
*Sal.* If that it be the work of any hand?—
We had a kind of light what would ensue:
It is the shameful work of Hubert's hand;
The practice and the purpose of the king:—
From whose obedience I forbid my soul,
Kneeling before this ruin of sweet life,

And breathing to his breathless excellence
The incense of a vow, a holy vow,
Never to taste the pleasures of the world,
Never to be infected with delight,
Nor conversant with ease and idleness,
Till I have set a glory to this hand,
By giving it the worship of revenge. [words.
*Pem. Big.* Our souls religiously confirm thy

*Enter* HUBERT.

*Hub.* Lords, I am hot with haste in seeking
you:
Arthur doth live; the king hath sent for you.
*Sal.* O, he is bold, and blushes not at
death:—
Avaunt, thou hateful villain, get thee gone!
*Hub.* I am no villain.
*Sal.* Must I rob the law?
[*Drawing his sword.*
*Bast.* Your sword is bright, sir; put it up
again. [skin.
*Sal.* Not till I sheathe it in a murderer's
*Hub.* Stand back, Lord Salisbury,—stand
back, I say; [yours:
By heaven, I think my sword's as sharp as
I would not have you, lord, forget yourself,
Nor tempt the danger of my true defence;
Lest I, by marking of your rage, forget
Your worth, your greatness, and nobility.
*Big.* Out, dunghill! dar'st thou brave a
nobleman?
*Hub.* Not for my life: but yet I dare defend
My innocent life against an emperor.
*Sal.* Thou art a murderer.
*Hub.* Do not prove me so;
Yet I am none: whose tongue soe'er speaks
false,
Not truly speaks; who speaks not truly, lies.
*Pem.* Cut him to pieces.
*Bast.* Keep the peace, I say.
*Sal.* Stand by, or I shall gall you, Falcon-
bridge. [bury.
*Bast.* Thou wert better gall the devil, Salis-
If thou but frown on me, or stir thy foot,
Or teach thy hasty spleen to do me shame,
I'll strike thee dead. Put up thy sword betime;
Or I'll so maul you and your toasting-iron
That you shall think the devil is come from hell.
*Big.* What wilt thou do, renowned Falcon-
bridge?
Second a villain and a murderer?
*Hub.* Lord Bigot, I am none.
*Big.* Who kill'd this prince?
*Hub.* 'Tis not an hour since I left him well:
I honour'd him, I lov'd him; and will weep
My date of life out for his sweet life's loss.
*Sal.* Trust not those cunning waters of his
eyes,
For villany is not without such rheum;
And he, long traded in it, makes it seem
Like rivers of remorse and innocency.
Away with me, all you whose souls abhor
The uncleanly savours of a slaughter-house;
For I am stifled with this smell of sin.

*Big.* Away toward Bury, to the Dauphin
there! [out.
*Pem.* There, tell the king, he may inquire us
[*Exeunt* Lords.
*Bast.* Here's a good world!—Knew you of
this fair work?
Beyond the infinite and boundless reach
Of mercy, if thou didst this deed of death,
Art thou damn'd, Hubert.
*Hub.* Do but hear me, sir.
*Bast.* Ha! I'll tell thee what; [black;
Thou'rt damn'd as black—nay, nothing is so
Thou art more deep damn'd than Prince
Lucifer:
There is not yet so ugly a fiend of hell
As thou shalt be, if thou didst kill this child.
*Hub.* Upon my soul,—
*Bast.* If thou didst but consent
To this most cruel act, do but despair;
And if thou want'st a cord, the smallest thread
That ever spider twisted from her womb
Will serve to strangle thee; a rush will be
A beam to hang thee on; or wouldst thou
drown thyself,
Put but a little water in a spoon,
And it shall be as all the ocean,
Enough to stifle such a villain up.
I do suspect thee very grievously.
*Hub.* If I in act, consent, or sin of thought
Be guilty of the stealing that sweet breath
Which was embounded in this beauteous clay,
Let hell want pains enough to torture me!
I left him well.
*Bast.* Go, bear him in thine arms.—
I am amaz'd, methinks, and lose my way
Among the thorns and dangers of this world.—
How easy dost thou take all England up!
From forth this morsel of dead royalty,
The life, the right, and truth of all this realm
Is fled to heaven; and England now is left
To tug and scamble, and to part by the teeth
The unow'd interest of proud-swelling state.
Now for the bare-pick'd bone of majesty
Doth dogged war bristle his angry crest,
And snarleth in the gentle eyes of peace:
Now powers from home and discontents at home
Meet in one line; and vast confusion waits,
As doth a raven on a sick-fallen beast,
The imminent decay of wrested pomp.
Now happy he whose cloak and cincture can
Hold out this tempest.—Bear away that child,
And follow me with speed: I'll to the king:
A thousand businesses are brief in hand,
And heaven itself doth frown upon the land.
[*Exeunt.*

## ACT V.

SCENE I.—NORTHAMPTON. *A Room in the
Palace.*

*Enter* KING JOHN, PANDULPH *with the crown,
and* Attendants.

*K. John.* Thus have I yielded up into your
hand
The circle of my glory.

*Pand.*                    Take again
                    [*Giving* KING JOHN *the crown.*
From this my hand, as holding of the pope,
Your sovereign greatness and authority.
  *K. John.*  Now keep your holy word: go
      meet the French;
And from his holiness use all your power
To stop their marches 'fore we are inflam'd.
Our discontented counties do revolt;
Our people quarrel with obedience;
Swearing allegiance and the love of soul
To stranger blood, to foreign royalty.
This inundation of mistemper'd humour
Rests by you only to be qualified.
Then pause not; for the present time's so sick
That present medicine must be minister'd,
Or overthrow incurable ensues.
  *Pand.*  It was my breath that blew this tem-
      pest up,
Upon your stubborn usage of the pope:
But since you are a gentle convertite,
My tongue shall hush again this storm of war,
And make fair weather in your blustering land.
On this Ascension-day, remember well,
Upon your oath of service to the pope,
Go I to make the French lay down their arms.
                                              [*Exit.*
  *K. John.*  Is this Ascension-day? Did not the
      prophet
Say that before Ascension-day at noon
My crown I should give off? Even so I have:
I did suppose it should be on constraint;
But, heaven be thank'd, it is but voluntary.

      *Enter the* BASTARD.

  *Bast.*  All Kent hath yielded; nothing there
      holds out
But Dover Castle: London hath receiv'd,
Like a kind host, the Dauphin and his powers:
Your nobles will not hear you, but are gone
To offer service to your enemy;
And wild amazement hurries up and down
The little number of your doubtful friends.
  *K. John.*  Would not my lords return to me
      again,
After they heard young Arthur was alive?
  *Bast.*  They found him dead, and cast into
      the streets;
An empty casket, where the jewel of life
By some damn'd hand was robb'd and ta'en
      away.
  *K. John.*  That villain Hubert told me he did
      live.
  *Bast.*  So, on my soul, he did, for aught he
      knew.
But wherefore do you droop? why look you sad?
Be great in act, as you have been in thought;
Let not the world see fear and sad distrust
Govern the motion of a kingly eye:
Be stirring as the time; be fire with fire;
Threaten the threatener, and outface the brow
Of bragging horror: so shall inferior eyes,
That borrow their behaviours from the great,
Grow great by your example, and put on

The dauntless spirit of resolution.
Away, and glister like the god of war
When he intendeth to become the field:
Show boldness and aspiring confidence.
What, shall they seek the lion in his den,
And fright him there? and make him tremble
      there?
O, let it not be said!—Forage, and run
To meet displeasure further from the doors,
And grapple with him ere he come so nigh.
  *K. John.*  The legate of the pope hath been
      with me,
And I have made a happy peace with him;
And he hath promis'd to dismiss the powers
Led by the Dauphin.
  *Bast.*                  O inglorious league!
Shall we, upon the footing of our land,
Send fair-play orders, and make compromise,
Insinuation, parley, and base truce,
To arms invasive? shall a beardless boy,
A cocker'd silken wanton, brave our fields,
And flesh his spirit in a warlike soil,
Mocking the air with colours idly spread,
And find no check? Let us, my liege, to arms:
Perchance the cardinal cannot make your
      peace;
Or, if he do, let it at least be said,
They saw we had a purpose of defence.
  *K. John.*  Have thou the ordering of this
      present time.                          [I know,
  *Bast.*  Away, then, with good courage! yet,
Our party may well meet a prouder foe.
                                          [*Exeunt.*

      SCENE II.—*Near* ST. EDMUND'S-BURY.
              *The French Camp.*

  *Enter, in arms,* LOUIS, SALISBURY, MELUN,
      PEMBROKE, BIGOT, *and* Soldiers.

  *Lou.*  My Lord Melun, let this be copied out,
And keep it safe for our remembrance:
Return the precedent to these lords again;
That, having our fair order written down,
Both they and we, perusing o'er these notes,
May know wherefore we took the sacrament,
And keep our faiths firm and inviolable.
  *Sal.*  Upon our sides it never shall be broken.
And, noble Dauphin, albeit we swear
A voluntary zeal and unurg'd faith
To your proceedings; yet, believe me, prince,
I am not glad that such a sore of time
Should seek a plaster by contemn'd revolt,
And heal the inveterate canker of one wound
By making many. O, it grieves my soul
That I must draw this metal from my side
To be a widow-maker! O, and there
Where honourable rescue and defence
Cries out upon the name of Salisbury!
But such is the infection of the time,
That, for the health and physic of our right,
We cannot deal but with the very hand
Of stern injustice and confused wrong.—
And is 't not pity, O my grieved friends!
That we, the sons and children of this isle,
Were born to see so sad an hour as this;

Wherein we step after a stranger-march
Upon her gentle bosom, and fill up
Her enemies' ranks—I must withdraw and weep
Upon the spot of this enforc'd cause—
To grace the gentry of a land remote,
And follow unacquainted colours here?
What, here?—O nation, that thou couldst re-
　　move!
That Neptune's arms, who clippeth thee about,
Would bear thee from the knowledge of thyself,
And grapple thee unto a pagan shore,　[bine
Where these two Christian armies might com-
The blood of malice in a vein of league,
And not to spend it so unneighbourly!

　　*Lou.* A noble temper dost thou show in this;
And great affections wrestling in thy bosom
Do make an earthquake of nobility.
O, what a noble combat hast thou fought
Between compulsion and a brave respect!
Let me wipe off this honourable dew
That silverly doth progress on thy cheeks:
My heart hath melted at a lady's tears,
Being an ordinary inundation;
But this effusion of such manly drops,
This shower, blown up by tempest of the soul,
Startles mine eyes, and makes me more amaz'd
Than had I seen the vaulty top of heaven
Figur'd quite o'er with burning meteors.
Lift up thy brow, renowned Salisbury,
And with a great heart heave away this storm:
Commend these waters to those baby eyes
That never saw the giant world enrag'd,
Nor met with fortune other than at feasts,
Full warm of blood, of mirth, of gossiping.
Come, come; for thou shalt thrust thy hand as
　　deep
Into the purse of rich prosperity
As Louis himself:—so, nobles, shall you all,
That knit your sinews to the strength of mine.—
And even there, methinks, an angel spake:
Look, where the holy legate comes apace,
To give us warrant from the hand of heaven,
And on our actions set the name of right
With holy breath.

*Enter* PANDULPH, *attended.*

　　*Pand.*　　　　Hail, noble prince of France!
The next is this,—King John hath reconcil'd
Himself to Rome; his spirit is come in,
That so stood out against the holy church,
The great metropolis and see of Rome:
Therefore thy threatening colours now wind up,
And tame the savage spirit of wild war,
That, like a lion foster'd up at hand,
It may lie gently at the foot of peace,
And be no further harmful than in show.

　　*Lou.* Your grace shall pardon me, I will not
　　back:
I am too high-born to be propertied,
To be a secondary at control,
Or useful serving-man and instrument
To any sovereign state throughout the world.
Your breath first kindled the dead coal of wars
Between this chastis'd kingdom and myself,

And brought in matter that should feed this
　　fire;
And now 'tis far too huge to be blow out
With that same weak wind which enkindled it.
You taught me how to know the face of right,
Acquainted me with interest to this land,
Yea, thrust this enterprise into my heart;
And come ye now to tell me John hath made
His peace with Rome? What is that peace to
　　me?
I, by the honour of my marriage-bed,
After young Arthur, claim this land for mine;
And, now it is half-conquer'd, must I back
Because that John hath made his peace with
　　Rome?　　　　　　　　　　　　[borne,
Am I Rome's slave? What penny hath Rome
What men provided, what munition sent,
To underprop this action? Is't not I
That undergo this charge? who else but I,
And such as to my claim are liable,
Sweat in this business and maintain this war.
Have I not heard these islanders shout out,
*Vive le roi!* as I have bank'd their towns?
Have I not here the best cards for the game,
To win this easy match play'd for a crown?
And shall I now give o'er the yielded set?
No, no, on my soul, it never shall be said.

　　*Pand.* You look but on the outside of this
　　work.

　　*Lou.* Outside or inside, I will not return
Till my attempt so much be glorified
As to my ample hope was promised
Before I drew this gallant head of war,
And cull'd these fiery spirits from the world,
To outlook conquest, and to win renown
Even in the jaws of danger and of death.—
　　　　　　　　　　　　　　*[Trumpet sounds.*
What lusty trumpet thus doth summon us?

*Enter the* BASTARD, *attended.*

　　*Bast.* According to the fair play of the world,
Let me have audience; I am sent to speak:—
My holy lord of Milan, from the king
I come, to learn how you have dealt for him;
And, as you answer, I do know the scope
And warrant limited unto my tongue.

　　*Pand.* The Dauphin is too wilful-opposite,
And will not temporize with my entreaties;
He flatly says he'll not lay down his arms.

　　*Bast.* By all the blood that ever fury breath'd,
The youth says well.—Now hear our English
　　king;
For thus his royalty doth speak in me.
He is prepar'd; and reason too he should:
This apish and unmannerly approach,
This harness'd masque and unadvised revel,
This unhair'd sauciness and boyish troops,
The king doth smile at; and is well prepar'd
To whip this dwarfish war, these pigmy arms,
From out the circle of his territories.　[door,
That hand which had the strength, even at your
To cudgel you, and make you take the hatch;
To dive, like buckets, in concealed wells;
To crouch in litter of your stable planks;

To lie, like pawns, lock'd up in chests and
    trunks;
To hug with swine; to seek sweet safety out
In vaults and prisons; and to thrill and shake
Even at the crying of your nation's crow,
Thinking his voice an armed Englishman;—
Shall that victorious hand be feebled here,
That in your chambers gave you chastisement?
No: know the gallant monarch is in arms;
And like an eagle o'er his aery towers,
To souse annoyance that comes near his nest.—
And you degenerate, you ingrate revolts,
You bloody Neroes, ripping up the womb
Of your dear mother England, blush for shame;
For your own ladies and pale-visag'd maids,
Like Amazons, come tripping after drums,—
Their thimbles into armed gauntlets chang'd,
Their needles to lances, and their gentle hearts
To fierce and bloody inclination.    [in peace;
  *Lou.* There end thy brave, and turn thy face
We grant thou canst outscold us; fare thee well;
We hold our time too precious to be spent
With such a brabbler.
  *Pand.*          Give me leave to speak.
  *Bast.* No, I will speak.
  *Lou.*      We will attend to neither.—
Strike up the drums; and let the tongue of war
Plead for our interest and our being here.
  *Bast.* Indeed, your drums, being beaten, will
    cry out;
And so shall you, being beaten: do but start
An echo with the clamour of thy drum,
And even at hand a drum is ready brac'd
That shall reverberate all as loud as thine;
Sound but another, and another shall,
As loud as thine, rattle the welkin's ear,
And mock the deep-mouth'd thunder: for at
    hand,—
Not trusting to this halting legate here,
Whom he hath us'd rather for sport than need,—
Is warlike John; and in his forehead sits
A bare-ribb'd death, whose office is this day
To feast upon whole thousands of the French.
  *Lou.* Strike up our drums, to find this danger
    out.
  *Bast.* And thou shalt find it, Dauphin, do
    not doubt.               [*Exeunt.*

SCENE III.—*The same. A Field of Battle.*

*Alarums. Enter* KING JOHN *and* HUBERT.

  *K. John.* How goes the day with us? O,
    tell me, Hubert.
  *Hub.* Badly, I fear. How fares your majesty?
  *K. John.* This fever, that hath troubled me
    so long,
Lies heavy on me;—O, my heart is sick!

*Enter a* Messenger.

  *Mess.* My lord, your valiant kinsman, Fal-
    conbridge,
Desires your majesty to leave the field,
And send him word by me which way you go.
  *K. John.* Tell him, toward Swinstead, to the
    abbey there.

  *Mess.* Be of good comfort; for the great
    supply
That was expected by the Dauphin here
Are wreck'd three nights ago on Goodwin
    Sands.                 [now:
This news was brought to Richard but even
The French fight colding, and retire themselves.
  *K. John.* Ay me! this tyrant fever burns me
    up,
And will not let me welcome this good news.—
Set on toward Swinstead: to my litter straight;
Weakness possesseth me, and I am faint.
                        [*Exeunt.*

SCENE IV.—*The same. Another part of the same.*

*Enter* SALISBURY, PEMBROKE, *and others.*

  *Sal.* I did not think the king so stor'd with
    friends.
  *Pem.* Up once again; put spirit in the French:
If they miscarry we miscarry too.
  *Sal.* That misbegotten devil, Falconbridge,
In spite of spite, alone upholds the day.
  *Pem.* They say King John, sore sick, hath
    left the field.

*Enter* MELUN *wounded, and led by* Soldiers.

  *Mel.* Lead me to the revolts of England here.
  *Sal.* When we were happy we had other
    names.
  *Pem.* It is the Count Melun.
  *Sal.*             Wounded to death.
  *Mel.* Fly, noble English, you are bought and
    sold;
Unthread the rude eye of rebellion,
And welcome home again discarded faith.
Seek out King John, and fall before his feet;
For if the French be lords of this loud day,
He means to recompense the pains you take
By cutting off your heads: thus hath he sworn,
And I with him, and many more with me,
Upon the altar at Saint Edmund's-Bury;
Even on that altar where we swore to you
Dear amity and everlasting love.
  *Sal.* May this be possible? may this be true?
  *Mel.* Have I not hideous death within my
    view,
Retaining but a quantity of life,
Which bleeds away even as a form of wax
Resolveth from his figure 'gainst the fire?
What in the world should make me now deceive,
Since I must lose the use of all deceit?
Why should I then be false, since it is true
That I must die here, and live hence by truth?
I say again, if Louis do win the day,
He is forsworn if e'er those eyes of yours
Behold another day break in the east:
But even this night,—whose black contagious
    breath
Already smokes about the burning crest
Of the old, feeble, and day-wearied sun,—
Even this ill night, your breathing shall expire;
Paying the fine of rated treachery
Even with a treacherous fine of all your lives,
If Louis by your assistance win the day.

Commend me to one Hubert, with your king;
The love of him,—and this respect besides,
For that my grandsire was an Englishman,—
Awakes my conscience to confess all this.
In lieu whereof, I pray you, bear me hence
From forth the noise and rumour of the field,
Where I may think the remnant of my thoughts
In peace, and part this body and my soul
With contemplation and devout desires. [soul

*Sal.* We do believe thee:—and beshrew my
But I do love the favour and the form
Of this most fair occasion, by the which
We will entread the steps of damned flight;
And, like a bated and retired flood,
Leaving our rankness and irregular course,
Stoop low within those bounds we have o'er-
    look'd,
And calmly run on in obedience,
Even to our ocean, to our great King John.—
My arm shall give thee help to bear thee hence;
For I do see the cruel pangs of death    [flight,
Right in thine eye.—Away, my friends! New
And happy newness, that intends old right.
        [*Exeunt, leading off* MELUN.

SCENE V.—*The same. The French Camp.*

*Enter* LOUIS *and his train.*

*Lou.* The sun of heaven methought was loth
    to set,
But stay'd, and made the western welkin blush,
When the English measur'd backward their
    own ground
In faint retire. O, bravely came we off,
When with a volley of our needless shot,
After such bloody toil, we bid good-night;
And wound our tattering colours clearly up,
Last in the field, and almost lords of it!

*Enter a* Messenger.

*Mess.* Where is my prince, the Dauphin?
*Lou.*                    Here:—what news?
*Mess.* The Count Melun is slain; the English
    lords,
By his persuasion are again fallen off;
And your supply, which you have wish'd so long,
Are cast away and sunk on Goodwin Sands.
*Lou.* Ah, foul shrewd news!—beshrew thy
    very heart!—
I did not think to be so sad to-night
As this hath made me.—Who was he that said
King John did fly an hour or two before
The stumbling night did part our weary powers?
*Mess.* Whoever spoke it, it is true, my lord.
*Lou.* Well; keep good quarter and good care
    to-night;
The day shall not be up so soon as I,
To try the fair adventure of to-morrow.
        [*Exeunt.*

SCENE VI.—*An open Place in the neighbour-
    hood of Swinstead Abbey.*

*Enter the* BASTARD *and* HUBERT, *meeting.*

*Hub.* Who's there? speak, ho! speak quickly,
    or I shoot.

*Bast.* A friend.—What art thou?
*Hub.*                Of the part of England.
*Bast.* Whither dost thou go?
*Hub.* What's that to thee? Why may I not
    demand
Of thine affairs, as well as thou of mine?
*Bast.* Hubert, I think.
*Hub.*            Thou hast a perfect thought:
I will, upon all hazards, well believe    [well.
Thou art my friend, that know'st my tongue so
Who art thou?
*Bast.*        Who thou wilt: an if thou please,
Thou mayst befriend me so much as to think
I come one way of the Plantagenets.
*Hub.* Unkind remembrance! thou and eye-
    less night        [me,
Have done me shame:—brave soldier, pardon
That any accent breaking from thy tongue
Should 'scape the true acquaintance of mine ear.
*Bast.* Come, come; sans compliment, what
    news abroad?        [night,
*Hub.* Why, here walk I, in the black brow of
To find you out.
*Bast.* Brief, then; and what's the news?
*Hub.* O, my sweet sir, news fitting to the
    night,
Black, fearful, comfortless, and horrible.
*Bast.* Show me the very wound of this ill
    news;
I am no woman, I'll not swoon at it.
*Hub.* The king, I fear, is poison'd by a monk:
I left him almost speechless and broke out
To acquaint you with this evil, that you might
The better arm you to the sudden time,
Than if you had at leisure known of this.
*Bast.* How did he take it; who did taste to
    him?
*Hub.* A monk, I tell you; a resolved villain,
Whose bowels suddenly burst out: the king
Yet speaks, and peradventure may recover.
*Bast.* Who didst thou leave to tend his
    majesty?        [come back,
*Hub.* Why, know you not? the lords are all
And brought Prince Henry in their company;
At whose request the king hath pardon'd them,
And they are all about his majesty.    [heaven,
*Bast.* Withhold thine indignation, mighty
And tempt us not to bear above our power!—
I'll tell thee, Hubert, half my power this night,
Passing these flats, are taken by the tide,—
These Lincoln washes have devoured them;
Myself, well-mounted, hardly have escap'd.
Away, before! conduct me to the king;
I doubt he will be dead or ere I come. [*Exeunt.*

SCENE VII.—*The Orchard of Swinstead Abbey.*

*Enter* PRINCE HENRY, SALISBURY, *and* BIGOT.

*P. Hen.* It is too late: the life of all his blood
Is touch'd corruptibly; and his pure brain,—
Which some suppose the soul's frail dwelling-
    house,—
Doth, by the idle comments that it makes,
Foretell the ending of mortality.

*Enter* PEMBROKE.

*Pem.* His highness yet doth speak; and holds belief
That, being brought into the open air,
It would allay the burning quality
Of that fell poison which assaileth him.
    *P. Hen.* Let him be brought into the orchard here.—
Doth he still rage?                    [*Exit* BIGOT.
    *Pem.*                He is more patient
Than when you left him; even now he sung.
    *P. Hen.* O vanity of sickness! fierce extremes
In their continuance will not feel themselves.
Death, having prey'd upon the outward parts,
Leaves them invisible; and his siege is now
Against the mind, the which he pricks and wounds
With many legions of strange fantasies,
Which, in their throng and press to that last hold,                [should sing.—
Confound themselves. 'Tis strange that death
I am the cygnet to this pale faint swan,
Who chants a doleful hymn to his own death;
And from the organ-pipe of frailty sings
His soul and body to their lasting rest.   [born
    *Sal.* Be of good comfort, prince; for you are
To set a form upon that indigest
Which he hath left so shapeless and so rude.

*Re-enter* BIGOT *and* Attendants, *who bring in*
KING JOHN *in a chair.*

    *K. John.* Ay, marry, now my soul hath elbow-room;
It would not out at windows nor at doors.
There is so hot a summer in my bosom
That all my bowels crumble up to dust;
I am a scribbled form, drawn with a pen
Upon a parchment; and against this fire
Do I shrink up.
    *P. Hen.*            How fares your majesty?
    *K. John.* Poison'd,—ill fare;—dead, forsook, cast off:
And none of you will bid the winter come,
To thrust his icy fingers in my maw;
Nor let my kingdom's rivers take their course
Through my burn'd bosom; nor entreat the north
To make his bleak winds kiss my parched lips,
And comfort me with cold:—I do not ask you much;
I beg cold comfort; and you are so strait,
And so ingrateful, you deny me that.
    *P. Hen.* O, that there were some virtue in my tears,
That might relieve you!
    *K. John.*            The salt in them is hot.—
Within me is a hell; and there the poison
Is, as a fiend, confin'd to tyrannize
On unreprievable condemned blood.

*Enter the* BASTARD.

    *Bast.* O, I am scalded with my violent motion,
And spleen of speed to see your majesty!
    *K. John.* O cousin, thou art come to set mine eye:
The tackle of my heart is crack'd and burn'd;
And all the shrouds, wherewith my life should sail,
Are turned to one thread, one little hair:
My heart hath one poor string to stay it by,
Which holds but till thy news be uttered;
And then all this thou seest is but a clod,
And model of confounded royalty.
    *Bast.* The Dauphin is preparing hitherward,
Where heaven he knows how we shall answer him;
For in a night the best part of my power,
As I upon advantage did remove,
Were in the washes all unwarily
Devoured by the unexpected flood.
                            [*The* KING *dies.*
    *Sal.* You breathe these dead news in as dead an ear.                [thus.
My liege! my lord!—But now a king,—now
    *P. Hen.* Even so must I run on, and even so stop,
What surety of the world, what hope, what stay,
When this was now a king, and now is clay!
    *Bast.* Art thou gone so? I do but stay behind
To do the office for thee of revenge,
And then my soul shall wait on thee to heaven,
As it on earth hath been thy servant still.—
Now, now, you stars that move in your right spheres,                [faiths;
Where be your powers? Show now your mended
And instantly return with me again,
To push destruction and perpetual shame
Out of the weak door of our fainting land.
Straight let us seek, or straight we shall be sought;
The Dauphin rages at our very heels.
    *Sal.* It seems you know not, then, so much as we:
The Cardinal Pandulph is within at rest,
Who half an hour since came from the Dauphin,
And brings from him such offers of our peace
As we with honour and respect may take,
With purpose presently to leave this war.
    *Bast.* He will the rather do it when he sees
Ourselves well sinewed to our defence.
    *Sal.* Nay, it is in a manner done already;
For many carriages he hath despatch'd
To the sea-side, and put his cause and quarrel
To the disposing of the cardinal:
With whom yourself, myself, and other lords,
If you think meet, this afternoon will post
To cónsummate this business happily.
    *Bast.* Let it be so:—And you, my noble prince,
With other princes that may best be spar'd,
Shall wait upon your father's funeral.
    *P. Hen.* At Worcester must his body be interr'd;
For so he will'd it.
    *Bast.*            Thither shall it, then:

And happily may your sweet self put on
The lineal state and glory of the land!
To whom, with all submission, on my knee,
I do bequeath my faithful services
And true subjection everlastingly.

    *Sal.* And the like tender of our love we make,
To rest without a spot for evermore.

    *P. Hen.* I have a kind soul that would give
      you thanks,
And knows not how to do it but with tears.

    *Bast.* O, let us pay the time but needful woe,
Since it hath been beforehand with our griefs.—
This England never did, nor never shall,
Lie at the proud foot of a conqueror,
But when it first did help to wound itself.
Now these her princes are come home again,
Come the three corners of the world in arms,
And we shall shock them: nought shall make
    us rue,
If England to itself do rest but true. [*Exeunt.*

KING
RICHARD
SECOND.

Act II. Sc. I.

# THE LIFE AND DEATH OF KING RICHARD II.

## DRAMATIS PERSONÆ

KING RICHARD THE SECOND.
EDMUND OF LANGLEY, *Duke of York,* } *Uncles to the King.*
JOHN OF GAUNT, *Duke of Lancaster,*
HENRY, *surnamed* BOLINGBROKE, *Duke of Hereford, Son to* JOHN OF GAUNT, *afterwards* KING HENRY IV.
DUKE OF AUMERLE, *Son to the Duke of York.*
THOMAS MOWBRAY, *Duke of Norfolk.*
DUKE OF SURREY.
EARL OF SALISBURY.
EARL BERKLEY.
BUSHY,
BAGOT, } *Creatures to* KING RICHARD.
GREEN,
EARL OF NORTHUMBERLAND.
HENRY PERCY, *his Son.*

LORD ROSS.
LORD WILLOUGHBY.
LORD FITZWATER.
BISHOP OF CARLISLE.
ABBOT OF WESTMINSTER.
Lord Marshal.
SIR PIERCE OF EXTON.
SIR STEPHEN SCROOP.
Captain *of a Band of Welshmen.*

QUEEN *to* KING RICHARD.
DUCHESS OF GLOSTER.
DUCHESS OF YORK.
Lady *attending on the* QUEEN.

Lords, Heralds, Officers, Soldiers, Two Gardeners, Keeper, Messenger, Groom, *and other* Attendants.

SCENE,—*Dispersedly in* ENGLAND *and* WALES.

## ACT I.

### SCENE I.—LONDON. *A Room in the Palace.*

*Enter* KING RICHARD, *attended;* JOHN OF GAUNT, *and other* Nobles.

*K. Rich.* Old John of Gaunt, time-honour'd Lancaster,
Hast thou, according to thy oath and band,
Brought hither Henry Hereford, thy bold son,
Here to make good the boisterous late appeal,
Which then our leisure would not let us hear,
Against the Duke of Norfolk, Thomas Mowbray?
*Gaunt.* I have, my liege.      [sounded him,
*K. Rich.* Tell me, moreover, hast thou
If he appeal the duke on ancient malice;
Or worthily, as a good subject should,
On some known ground of treachery in him?
*Gaunt.* As near as I could sift him on that argument,—
On some apparent danger seen in him,
Aim'd at your highness,—no inveterate malice.
*K. Rich.* Then call them to our presence: face to face.
And frowning brow to brow, ourselves will hear
The accuser and the accused freely speak:—
[*Exeunt some* Attendants.
High-stomach'd are they both, and full of ire,
In rage deaf as the sea, hasty as fire.

*Re-enter* Attendants, *with* BOLINGBROKE *and* NORFOLK.

*Boling.* Many years of happy days befall
My gracious sovereign, my most loving liege!
*Nor.* Each day still better other's happiness;
Until the heavens, envying earth's good hap,
Add an immortal title to your crown!
*K. Rich.* We thank you both: yet one but flatters us,
As well appeareth by the cause you come;
Namely, to appeal each other of high treason.—
Cousin of Hereford, what dost thou object
Against the Duke of Norfolk, Thomas Mowbray?      [speech!—
*Boling.* First,—heaven be the record to my
In the devotion of a subject's love,
Tendering the precious safety of my prince,
And free from other misbegotten hate,
Come I appellant to this princely presence.—
Now, Thomas Mowbray, do I turn to thee;
And mark my greeting well; for what I speak,
My body shall make good upon this earth
Or my divine soul answer it in heaven.
Thou are a traitor and a miscreant;
Too good to be so, and too bad to live;
Since the more fair and crystal is the sky,
The uglier seem the clouds that in it fly.
Once more, the more to aggravate the note,
With a foul traitor's name stuff I thy throat;
And wish,—so please my sovereign,—ere I move,      [may prove.
What my tongue speaks, my right-drawn sword
*Nor.* Let not my cold words here accuse my zeal:
'Tis not the trial of a woman's war,
The bitter clamour of two eager tongues,

[395]

Can arbitrate this cause betwixt us twain:
The blood is hot that must be cool'd for this:
Yet can I not of such tame patience boast
As to be hush'd, and naught at all to say: [me
First, the fair reverence of your highness curbs
From giving reins and spurs to my free speech;
Which else would post until it had return'd
These terms of treason doubled down his throat.
Setting aside his high blood's royalty,
And let him be no kinsman to my liege
I do defy him, and I spit at him;
Call him a slanderous coward and a villain:
Which to maintain, I would allow him odds;
And meet him, were I tied to run a-foot
Even to the frozen ridges of the Alps,
Or any other ground inhabitable,
Wherever Englishman durst set his foot.
Meantime let this defend my loyalty,—
By all my hopes, most falsely doth he lie.
  *Boling.* Pale trembling coward, there I
    throw my gage,
Disclaiming here the kindred of the king;
And lay aside my high blood's royalty, [cept.
Which fear, not reverence, makes thee to ex-
If guilty dread hath left thee so much strength
As to take up mine honour's pawn, then stoop:
By that and all the rites of knighthood else,
Will I make good against thee, arm to arm,
What I have spoke, or thou canst worst devise.
  *Nor.* I take it up; and by that sword I swear,
Which gently laid my knighthood on my
    shoulder,
I'll answer thee in any fair degree,
Or chivalrous design of knightly trial:
And when I mount, alive may I not light,
If I be traitor or unjustly fight!
  *K. Rich.* What doth our cousin lay to Mow-
    bray's charge?
It must be great, that can inherit us
So much as of a thought of ill in him.
  *Boling.* Look, what I speak my life shall
    prove it true;—       [nobles,
That Mowbray hath receiv'd eight thousand
In name of lendings for your highness' soldiers,
The which he hath detain'd for lewd employ-
    ments,
Like a false traitor and injurious villain.
Besides, I say, and will in battle prove,—
Or here, or elsewhere to the farthest verge
That ever was survey'd by English eye,—
That all the treasons for these eighteen years
Complotted and contrived in this land
Fetch'd from false Mowbray their first head
    and spring.
Further, I say,—and further will maintain
Upon his bad life to make all this good,—
That he did plot the Duke of Gloster's death;
Suggest his soon-believing adversaries,
And consequently, like a traitor coward,
Sluic'd out his innocent soul through streams
    of blood: ·
Which blood, like sacrificing Abel's, cries,
Even from the tongueless caverns of the earth,
To me for justice and rough chastisement;

And, by the glorious worth of my descent,
This arm shall do it, or this life be spent!
  *K. Rich.* How high a pitch his resolution
    soars!—
Thomas of Norfolk, what say'st thou to this?
  *Nor.* O, let my sovereign turn away his face,
And bid his ears a little while be deaf,
Till I have told this slander of his blood,
How God and good men hate so foul a liar.
  *K. Rich.* Mowbray, impartial are our eyes
    and ears:
Were he my brother, nay, my kingdom's heir,—
As he is but my father's brother's son,—
Now, by my sceptre's awe, I make a vow,
Such neighbour-nearness to our sacred blood
Should nothing privilege him, nor partialize
The unstooping firmness of my upright soul:
He is our subject, Mowbray, so art thou;
Free speech and fearless I to thee allow.
  *Nor.* Then, Bolingbroke, as low as to thy
    heart,       [liest!
Through the false passage of thy throat, thou
Three parts of that receipt I had for Calais
Disburs'd I duly to his highness' soldiers;
The other part reserv'd I by consent,
For that my sovereign liege was in my debt
Upon remainder of a dear account,
Since last I went to France to fetch his queen:
Now swallow down that lie!—For Gloster's
    death,
I slew him not; but, to mine own disgrace,
Neglected my sworn duty in that case.—
For you, my noble Lord of Lancaster,
The honourable father to my foe,
Once did I lay an ambush for your life,
A trespass that doth vex my grieved soul:
But, ere I last receiv'd the sacrament,
I did confess it; and exactly begg'd
Your grace's pardon, and I hope I had it.
This is my fault: as for the rest appeal'd,
It issues from the rancour of a villain,
A recreant and most degenerate traitor:
Which in myself I boldly will defend;
And interchangeably hurl down my gage
Upon this overweening traitor's foot,
To prove myself a loyal gentleman
Even in the best blood chamber'd in his bosom.
In haste whereof, most heartily I pray
Your highness to assign our trial day.
  *K. Rich.* Wrath-kindled gentlemen, be rul'd
    by me;
Let's purge this choler without letting blood;
This we prescribe, though no physician;
Deep malice makes too deep incision:
Forget, forgive; conclude, and be agreed;
Our doctors say this is no time to bleed.—
Good uncle, let this end where it begun;
We'll calm the Duke of Norfolk, you your son.
  *Gaunt.* To be a make-peace shall become
    my age:       [gage.
Throw down, my son, the Duke of Norfolk's
  *K. Rich.* And, Norfolk, throw down his.
  *Gaunt.*           When, Harry? when?
Obedience bids I should not bid again.

*K. Rich.* Norfolk, throw down; we bid; there
   is no boot.
*Nor.* Myself I throw, dread sovereign at thy
   foot:
My life thou shalt command, but not my shame:
The one my duty owes; but my fair name,—
Despite of death, that lives upon my grave,—
To dark dishonour's use thou shalt not have.
I am disgrac'd, impeach'd, and baffled here;
Pierc'd to the soul with slander's venom'd
   spear,
The which no balm can cure but his heart-blood
Which breath'd this poison.
   *K. Rich.*       Rage must be withstood:
Give me his gage:—lions make leopards tame.
*Nor.* Yea, but not change his spots: take
   but my shame,
And I resign my gage. My dear dear lord,
The purest treasure mortal times afford
Is spotless reputation; that away,
Men are but gilded loam or painted clay.
A jewel in a ten-times-barr'd-up chest
Is a bold spirit in a loyal breast.
Mine honour is my life; both grow in one;
Take honour from me, and my life is done:
Then, dear my liege, mine honour let me try;
In that I live, and for that will I die.
   *K. Rich.* Cousin, throw down your gage; do
   you begin.              [foul sin!
*Boling.* O, God defend my soul from such
Shall I seem crest-fallen in my father's sight?
Or with pale beggar-fear impeach my height
Before this outdar'd dastard? Ere my tongue
Shall wound mine honour with such feeble
   wrong,
Or sound so base a parle, my teeth shall tear
The slavish motive of recanting fear;
And spit it bleeding in his high disgrace,
Where shame doth harbour, even in Mow-
   bray's face!         [*Exit* GAUNT.
   *K. Rich.* We were not born to sue, but to
   command:—
Which since we cannot do to make you friends,
Be ready, as your lives shall answer it,
At Coventry, upon Saint Lambert's day:
There shall your swords and lances arbitrate
The swelling difference of your settled hate:
Since we can not atone you, we shall see
Justice design the victor's chivalry.—
Lord marshal, command our officers-at-arms
Be ready to direct these home-alarms. [*Exeunt.*

SCENE II.—*The same. A Room in the* DUKE OF
LANCASTER'S *Palace.*

*Enter* GAUNT *and* DUCHESS OF GLOSTER.

   *Gaunt.* Alas, the part I had in Gloster's blood
Doth more solicit me than your exclaims,
To stir against the butchers of his life.
But since correction lieth in those hands
Which made the fault that we cannot correct,
Put we our quarrel to the will of heaven;
Who, when they see the hours ripe on earth,
Will rain hot vengeance on offenders' heads.

   *Duch.* Finds brotherhood in thee no sharper
   spur?
Hath love in thy old blood no living fire?
Edward's seven sons, whereof thyself art one,
Were as seven vials of his sacred blood,
Or seven fair branches springing from one root:
Some of those seven are dried by nature's
   course,
Some of those branches by the Destinies cut;
But Thomas, my dear lord, my life, my Glos-
   ter,—
One vial full of Edward's sacred blood,
One flourishing branch of his most royal root,
Is crack'd, and all the precious liquor spilt;
Is hack'd down, and his summer-leaves all
   faded,
By envy's hand and murder's bloody axe.
Ah, Gaunt, his blood was thine! that bed, that
   womb,
That mettle, that self-mould, that fashion'd
   thee,
Made him a man; and though thou liv'st and
   breath'st,
Yet art thou slain in him: thou dost consent
In some large measure to thy father's death,
In that thou seest thy wretched brother die,
Who was the model of thy father's life.
Call it not patience, Gaunt,—it is despair:
In suffering thus thy brother to be slaughter'd,
Thou show'st the naked pathway to thy life,
Teaching stern murder how to butcher thee:
That which in mean men we entitle patience,
Is pale cold cowardice in noble breasts.
What shall I say? to safeguard thine own life,
The best way is to venge my Gloster's death.
   *Gaunt.* God's is the quarrel; for God's sub-
   stitute,
His deputy anointed in his sight,
Hath caus'd his death: the which, if wrongfully,
Let heaven revenge; for I may never lift
An angry arm against his minister.
   *Duch.* Where, then, alas, may I complain
   myself?
   *Gaunt.* To God, the widow's champion and
   defence.              [Gaunt.
   *Duch.* Why, then, I will. Farewell, old
Thou go'st to Coventry, there to behold
Our cousin Hereford and fell Mowbray fight:
O, sit my husband's wrongs on Hereford's
   spear,
That it may enter butcher Mowbray's breast!
Or, if misfortune miss the first career,
Be Mowbray's sins so heavy in his bosom
That they may break his foaming courser's
   back,
And throw the rider headlong in the lists,
A caitiff recreant to my cousin Hereford!
Farewell, old Gaunt; thy sometimes brother's
   wife,
With her companion grief must end her life.
   *Gaunt.* Sister, farewell: I must to Coventry:
As much good stay with thee as go with me!
   *Duch.* Yet one word more:—grief boundeth
   where it falls,

Not with the empty hollowness, but weight:
I take my leave before I have begun;
For sorrow ends not when it seemeth done.
Commend me to my brother, Edmund York.
Lo, this is all:—nay, yet depart not so;
Though this be all, do not so quickly go;
I shall remember more. Bid him—O, what?—
With all good speed at Plashy visit me.
Alack, and what shall good old York there see,
But empty lodgings and unfurnish'd walls,
Unpeopled offices, untrodden stones?
And what hear there for welcome but my
    groans?
Therefore commend me; let him not come there
To seek out sorrow that dwells everywhere.
Desolate, desolate, will I hence and die:
The least leave of thee takes my weeping eye!
                                        [*Exeunt.*

SCENE III.—*Gosford Green, near Coventry.*

*Lists set out, and a throne.* Heralds, &c., *attending. Enter the* Lord Marshal, *and* AUMERLE.

*Mar.* My Lord Aumerle, is Harry Hereford
    arm'd?                                    [in.
*Aum.* Yea, at all points; and longs to enter
*Mar.* The Duke of Norfolk, sprightfully and
    bold,                                     [pet.
Stays but the summons of the appellant's trum-
*Aum.* Why, then, the champions are pre-
    par'd, and stay
For nothing but his majesty's approach.

*Flourish of trumpets. Enter* KING RICHARD,
*who takes his seat on his throne;* GAUNT *and
several Noblemen, who take their places. A
trumpet is sounded, and answered by another
trumpet within. Then enter* NORFOLK *in armour, preceded by a* Herald.

*K. Rich.* Marshal, demand of yonder cham-
    pion
The cause of his arrival here in arms:
Ask him his name; and orderly proceed
To swear him in the justice of his cause.
*Mar.* In God's name and the king's, say
    who thou art,
And why thou com'st thus knightly clad in
    arms;
Against what man thou com'st, and what thy
    quarrel:
Speak truly, on thy knighthood and thine oath;
And so defend thee heaven and thy valour!
*Nor.* My name is Thomas Mowbray, Duke
    of Norfolk;
Who hither come engaged by my oath,—
Which God defend a knight should violate!—
Both to defend my loyalty and truth
To God, my king, and his succeeding issue,
Against the Duke of Hereford that appeals me;
And, by the grace of God and this mine arm,
To prove him in defending of myself,
A traitor to my God, my king, and me:
And as I truly fight, defend me heaven!

*Trumpet sounds. Enter* BOLINGBROKE *in armour, preceded by a* Herald.

*K. Rich.* Marshal, ask yonder knight in arms,
Both who he is, and why he cometh hither
Thus plated in habiliments of war;
And formally, according to our law,
Depose him in the justice of his cause.
*Mar.* What is thy name? and wherefore
    com'st thou hither,
Before King Richard in his royal lists?
Against whom comest thou? and what's thy
    quarrel?
Speak like a true knight, so defend thee heaven!
*Boling.* Harry of Hereford, Lancaster, and
    Derby,
Am I; who ready here do stand in arms,
To prove, by God's grace and my body's valour,
In lists, on Thomas Mowbray, Duke of Norfolk,
That he's a traitor, foul and dangerous,
To God of Heaven, King Richard, and to me:
And as I truly fight, defend me heaven!
*Mar.* On pain of death, no person be so bold
Or daring-hardy as to touch the lists,
Except the marshal and such officers
Appointed to direct these fair designs.
*Boling.* Lord marshal, let me kiss my sove-
    reign's hand,
And bow my knee before his majesty:
For Mowbray and myself are like two men
That vow a long and weary pilgrimage;
Then let us take a ceremonious leave
And loving farewell of our several friends.
*Mar.* The appellant in all duty greets your
    highness,
And craves to kiss your hand and take his leave.
*K. Rich.* We will descend and fold him in
    our arms.—
Cousin of Hereford, as thy cause is right,
So be thy fortune in this royal fight!
Farewell, my blood; which if to-day thou shed,
Lament we may, but not revenge thee dead.
*Boling.* O, let no noble eye profane a tear
For me, if I be gor'd with Mowbray's spear:
As confident as is the falcon's flight
Against a bird, do I with Mowbray fight.—
My loving lord, I take my leave of you;—
Of you, my noble cousin, Lord Aumerle;
Not sick, although I have to do with death,
But lusty, young, and cheerly drawing breath.—
Lo, as at English feasts, so I regreet
The daintiest last, to make the end more sweet:—
O thou, the earthly author of my blood,—
                                    [*To* GAUNT.
Whose youthful spirit, in me regenerate,
Doth with a twofold vigour lift me up
To reach at victory above my head,—
Add proof unto mine armour with thy prayers;
And with thy blessings steel my lance's point,
That it may enter Mowbray's waxen coat,
And furbish new the name of John o' Gaunt,
Even in the lusty 'haviour of his son.   [perous!
*Gaunt.* God in thy good cause make thee pros-
Be swift like lightning in the execution;

And let thy blows, doubly redoubled,
Fall like amazing thunder on the casque
Of thy advérse pernicious enemy:
Rouse up thy youthful blood, be valiant and live.
  *Boling.* Mine innocency and Saint George to
    thrive!
  *Nor.* However God or fortune cast my lot,
There lives or dies, true to King Richard's throne,
A loyal, just, and upright gentleman:
Never did captive with a freer heart
Cast off his chains of bondage, and embrace
His golden uncontroll'd enfranchisement,
More than my dancing soul doth celebrate
This feast of battle with mine adversary.—
Most mighty liege,—and my companion peers,—
Take from my mouth the wish of happy years:
As gentle and as jocund as to jest
Go I to fight: truth hath a quiet breast.
  *K. Rich.* Farewell, my lord: securely I espy
Virtue with valour couched in thine eye.—
Order the trial, marshal, and begin.    [Derby,
  *Mar.* Harry of Hereford, Lancaster, and
Receive thy lance; and God defend the right!
  *Boling.* Strong as a tower in hope, I cry amen.
  *Mar.* Go bear this lance [*to an* Officer] to
Thomas, Duke of Norfolk.    [Derby,
  1 *Her.* Harry of Hereford, Lancaster, and
Stands here for God, his sovereign, and himself,
On pain to be found false and recreant,
To prove the Duke of Norfolk, Thomas Mow-
    bray,
A traitor to his God, his king, and him;
And dares him to set forward to the fight.
  2 *Her.* Here standeth Thomas Mowbray,
    Duke of Norfolk,
On pain to be found false and recreant,
Both to defend himself, and to approve
Henry of Hereford, Lancaster, and Derby,
To God, his sovereign, and to him disloyal;
Courageously, and with a free desire,
Attending but the signal to begin.
  *Mar.* Sound, trumpets; and set forward,
    combatants.    [*A charge sounded.*
Stay, the king hath thrown his warder down.
  *K. Rich.* Let them lay by their helmets and
    their spears,
And both return back to their chairs again:—
Withdraw with us:—and let the trumpets sound
While we return these dukes what we decree.—
    [*A long flourish.*
Draw near,    [*To the combatants.*
And list what with our council we have done.
For that our kingdom's earth should not be soil'd
With that dear blood which it hath fostered;
And for our eyes do hate the dire aspéct
Of civil wounds plough'd up with neighbours'
    swords;
And for we think the eagle-winged pride
Of sky-aspiring and ambitious thoughts,
With rival-hating envy, set on you
To wake our peace, which in our country's cradle
Draws the sweet infant breath of gentle sleep;
Which so rous'd up with boisterous untun'd
    drums,

With harsh-resounding trumpets' dreadful bray,
And grating shock of wrathful iron arms,
Might from our quiet confines fright fair peace,
And make us wade even in our kindred's blood;—
Therefore, we banish you our territories:—
You, cousin Hereford, upon pain of life,
Till twice five summers have enrich'd our fields
Shall not regreet our fair dominions,
But tread the stranger paths of banishment.
  *Boling.* Your will be done: this must my
    comfort be,—    [me;
That sun that warms you here shall shine on
And those his golden beams to you here lent
Shall point on me and gild my banishment.
  *K. Rich.* Norfolk, for thee remains a heavier
    doom,
Which I with some unwillingness pronounce:
The sly-slow hours shall not determinate
The dateless limit of thy dear exile;—
The hopeless word of—never to return
Breathe I against thee, upon pain of life.
  *Nor.* A heavy sentence, my most gracious
    liege,    [mouth:
And all unlook'd-for from your highness'
A dearer merit, not so deep a maim
As to be cast forth in the common air,
Have I deserved at your highness' hands.
The language I have learn'd these forty years,
My native English, now I must forego:
And now my tongue's use is to me no more
Than an unstring'd viol or a harp;
Or like a cunning instrument cas'd up,
Or, being open, put into his hands
That knows no touch to tune the harmony:
Within my mouth you have engaol'd my tongue,
Doubly portcullis'd with my teeth and lips;
And dull, unfeeling, barren ignorance
Is made my gaoler to attend on me.
I am too old to fawn upon a nurse,
Too far in years to be a pupil now:
What is thy sentence, then, but speechless death,
Which robs my tongue from breathing native
    breath?    [sionate:
  *K. Rich.* It boots thee not to be compas-
After our sentence plaining comes too late.
  *Nor.* Then thus I turn me from my country's
    light,
To dwell in solemn shades of endless night.
    [*Retiring.*
  *K. Rich.* Return again, and take an oath
    with thee.
Lay on our royal sword your banish'd hands;
Swear by the duty that you owe to God,—
Our part therein we banish with yourselves,—
To keep the oath that we administer:—
You never shall—so help you truth and God!—
Embrace each other's love in banishment;
Nor never look upon each other's face;
Nor never write, regreet, nor reconcile
This lowering tempest of your home-bred hate;
Nor never by advised purpose meet
To plot, contrive, or complot any ill
'Gainst us, our state, our subjects, or our land.
  *Boling.* I swear.

*Nor.* And I, to keep all this.

*Boling.* Norfolk, so far as to mine enemy;—
By this time, had the king permitted us,
One of our souls had wander'd in the air,
Banish'd this frail sepulchre of our flesh,
As now our flesh is banish'd from this land:
Confess thy treasons, ere thou fly the realm;
Since thou hast far to go, bear not along
The clogging burden of a guilty soul.

*Nor.* No, Bolingbroke: if ever I were traitor,
My name be blotted from the book of life,
And I from heaven banish'd, as from hence!
But what thou art, God, thou, and I do know;
And all too soon, I fear, the king shall rue.—
Farewell, my liege.—Now no way can I stray:
Save back to England, all the world's my way.
                                        [*Exit.*

*K. Rich.* Uncle, even in the glasses of thine
    eyes
I see thy grieved heart: thy sad aspéct
Hath from the number of his banish'd years
Pluck'd four away.—[*To* BOLING.] Six frozen
    winters spent,
Return with welcome home from banishment.

*Boling.* How long a time lies in one little
    word!
Four lagging winters and four wanton springs
End in a word: such is the breath of kings.

*Gaunt.* I thank my liege that in regard of me
He shortens four years of my son's exile:
But little vantage shall I reap thereby;
For, ere the six years that he hath to spend
Can change their moons and bring their times
    about,
My oil-dried lamp and time bewasted light
Shall be extinct with age and endless night;
My inch of taper will be burnt and done,
And blindfold death not let me see my son.

*K. Rich.* Why, uncle, thou hast many years
    to live.

*Gaunt.* But not a minute, king, that thou
    canst give:
Shorten my days thou canst with sullen sorrow,
And pluck nights from me, but not lend a
    morrow;
Thou canst help time to furrow me with age,
But stop no wrinkle in his pilgrimage;
Thy word is current with him for my death,
But dead, thy kingdom cannot buy my breath.

*K. Rich.* Thy son is banish'd upon good
    advice,
Whereto thy tongue a party-verdict gave:
Why at our justice seem'st thou, then, to lower?

*Gaunt.* Things sweet to taste prove in diges-
    tion sour.
You urg'd me as a judge; but I had rather
You would have bid me argue like a father,
O, had it been a stranger, not my child,
To smooth his fault I should have been more
    mild:
A partial slander sought I to avoid,
And in the sentence my own life destroy'd.
Alas, I look'd when some of you should say,
I was too strict to make mine own away;

But you gave leave to mine unwilling tongue
Against my will to do myself this wrong.

*K. Rich.* Cousin, farewell;—and, uncle, bid
    him so:
Six years we banish him, and he shall go.
        [*Flourish. Exeunt* K. RICH. *and* Train.

*Aum.* Cousin, farewell: what presence must
    not know,
From where you do remain let paper show.

*Mar.* My lord, no leave take I; for I will ride
As far as land will let me by your side.

*Gaunt.* O, to what purpose dost thou hoard
    thy words,
That thou return'st no greeting to thy friends?

*Boling.* I have too few to take my leave of
    you,
When the tongue's office should be prodigal
To breathe the abundant dolour of the heart.

*Gaunt.* Thy grief is but thy absence for a
    time.

*Boling.* Joy absent, grief is present for that
    time.                                [gone.

*Gaunt.* What is six winters? they are quickly

*Boling.* To men in joy; but grief makes one
    hour ten.                          [pleasure.

*Gaunt.* Call it a travel that thou tak'st for

*Boling.* My heart will sigh when I miscall
    it so,
Which finds it an enforced pilgrimage.

*Gaunt.* The sullen passage of thy weary steps
Esteem a foil, wherein thou art to set
The precious jewel of thy home-return.

*Boling.* Nay, rather, every tedious stride I
    make
Will but remember me what a deal of world
I wander from the jewels that I love.
Must I not serve a long apprenticehood
To foreign passages; and in the end,
Having my freedom, boast of nothing else
But that I was a journeyman to grief? [visits

*Gaunt.* All places that the eye of heaven
Are to a wise man ports and happy havens,
Teach thy necessity to reason thus;
There is no virtue like necessity.
Think not the king did banish thee,
But thou the king: woe doth the heavier sit
Where it perceives it is but faintly borne.
Go, say I sent thee forth to purchase honour
And not the king exil'd thee; or suppose
Devouring pestilence hangs in our air,
And thou art flying to a fresher clime:
Look, what thy soul holds dear, imagine it
To lie that way thou go'st, not whence thou
    com'st:
Suppose the singing-birds musicians, [strew'd,
The grass whereon thou tread'st the presence
The flowers fair ladies, and thy steps no more
Than a delightful measure or a dance;
For gnarling sorrow hath less power to bite
The man that mocks at it and sets it light.

*Boling.* O, who can hold a fire in his hand
By thinking on the frosty Caucasus?
Or cloy the hungry edge of appetite
By bare imagination of a feast?

Or wallow naked in December snow
By thinking on fantastic summer's heat?
O, no! the apprehension of the good
Gives but the greater feeling to the worse:
Fell sorrow's tooth doth never rankle more
Than when it bites, but lanceth not the sore.

*Gaunt.* Come, come, my son, I'll bring thee
  on thy way:
Had I thy youth and cause, I would not stay.

*Boling.* Then, England's ground, farewell;
  sweet soil, adieu;
My mother, and my nurse, that bears me yet!
Where'er I wander, boast of this I can,—
Though banish'd, yet a true-born Englishman.
                    [*Exeunt.*

SCENE IV.—*The Court.*

*Enter* KING RICHARD, BAGOT, *and* GREEN;
AUMERLE *following.*

*K. Rich.* We did observe.—Cousin Aumerle,
How far brought you high Hereford on his
  way?                          [him so,
*Aum.* I brought high Hereford, if you call
But to the next highway, and there I left him.

*K. Rich.* And say, what store of parting
  tears were shed?              [east wind,
*Aum.* Faith, none for me; except the north-
Which then blew bitterly against our faces,
Awak'd the sleeping rheum, and so by chance
Did grace our hollow parting with a tear.

*K. Rich.* What said our cousin when you
  parted with him?
*Aum.* "Farewell:"
And, for my heart disdained that my tongue
Should so profane the word, that taught me
  craft
To counterfeit oppression of such grief,
That words seem'd buried in my sorrow's grave.
Marry, would the word "farewell" have
  lengthen'd hours,
And added years to his short banishment,
He should have had a volume of farewells;
But since it would not, he had none of me.

*K. Rich.* He is our cousin, cousin; but 'tis
  doubt,
When time shall call him home from banish-
  ment,
Whether our kinsman come to see his friends.
Ourself, and Bushy, Bagot here, and Green,
Observ'd his courtship to the common people;
How he did seem to dive into their hearts
With humble and familiar courtesy;
What reverence he did throw away on slaves;
Wooing poor craftsmen with the craft of smiles,
And patient underbearing of his fortune,
As 'twere to banish their affects with him.
Off goes his bonnet to an oyster-wench;
A brace of draymen bid God speed him well,
And had the tribute of his supple knee,
With *Thanks, my countrymen, my loving friends;*
As were our England in reversion his,
And he our subjects' next degree in hope.

*Green.* Well, he is gone; and with him go
  these thoughts.

Now for the rebels which stand out in Ire-
  land,—
Expedient manage must be made, my liege,
Ere further leisure yield them further means
For their advantage and your highness' loss.

*K. Rich.* We will ourself in person to this
  war:
And, for our coffers,—with too great a court
And liberal largess,—are grown somewhat light,
We are enforc'd to farm our royal realm;
The revenue whereof shall furnish us
For our affairs in hand. If that come short,
Our substitutes at home shall have blank
  charters;                     [rich,
Whereto, when they shall know what men are
They shall subscribe them for large sums of
  gold,
And send them after to supply our wants;
For we will make for Ireland presently.

*Enter* BUSHY.

Bushy, what news?
*Bushy.* Old John of Gaunt is grievous sick,
  my lord,
Suddenly taken; and hath sent post-haste
To entreat your majesty to visit him.

*K. Rich.* Where lies he?
*Bushy.* At Ely House.         [mind
*K. Rich.* Now put it, God, in his physician's
To help him to his grave immediately!
The lining of his coffers shall make coats
To deck our soldiers for these Irish wars.—
Come, gentlemen, let's all go visit him:
Pray God we may make haste, and come too
  late!                        [*Exeunt.*

ACT II.

SCENE I.—LONDON. *A Room in* ELY HOUSE.

GAUNT *on a couch; the* DUKE OF YORK *and
others standing by him.*

*Gaunt.* Will the king come, that I may
  breathe my last
In wholesome counsel to his unstaid youth?
*York.* Vex not yourself, nor strive not with
  your breath;
For all in vain comes counsel to his ear. [men
*Gaunt.* O, but they say the tongues of dying
Enforce attention like deep harmony;
Where words are scarce, they are seldom spent
  in vain;                     [in pain
For they breathe truth that breathe their words
He that no more must say is listen'd more
  Than they whom youth and ease have taught
    to glose;                  [before;
More are men's ends mark'd than their lives
  The setting sun, and music at the close,
As the last taste of sweets, is sweetest last,
Writ in remembrance more than things long
  past;                        [hear,
Though Richard my life's counsel would not
My death's sad tale may yet undeaf his ear.
*York.* No; it is stopp'd with other flattering
  sounds,

As, praises of his state: then there are found
Lascivious metres, to whose venom-sound
The open ear of youth doth always listen;
Report of fashions in proud Italy,
Whose manners still our tardy apish nation
Limps after, in base imitation.
Where doth the world thrust forth a vanity,—
So it be new, there's no respect how vile,—
That is not quickly buzz'd into his ears?
Then all too late comes counsel to be heard,
Where will doth mutiny with wit's regard.
Direct not him, whose way himself will choose:
'Tis breath thou lack'st, and that breath wilt
　　thou lose.　　　　　　　　　　[inspir'd,
　　*Gaunt.* Methinks I am a prophet new
And thus, expiring, do foretell of him:
His rash fierce blaze of riot cannot last,
For violent fires soon burn out themselves;
Small showers last long, but sudden storms are
　　short;
He tires betimes that spurs too fast betimes;
With eager feeding food doth choke the feeder:
Light vanity, insatiate cormorant,
Consuming means, soon preys upon itself.
This royal throne of kings, this scepter'd isle
This earth of majesty, this seat of Mars,
This other Eden, demi-paradise;
This fortress built by Nature for herself
Against infection and the hand of war;
This happy breed of men, this little world;
This precious stone set in the silver sea,
Which serves it in the office of a wall,
Or as a moat defensive to a house,
Against the envy of less happier lands;
This blessed plot, this earth, this realm, this
　　England,
This nurse, this teeming womb of royal kings,
Fear'd by their breed, and famous by their
　　birth,
Renowned for their deeds as far from home,—
For Christian service and true chivalry,—
As is the sepulchre in stubborn Jewry
Of the world's ransom, blessed Mary's Son;—
This land of such dear souls, this dear dear land,
Dear for her reputation through the world,
Is now leas'd out,—I die pronouncing it,—
Like to a tenement or pelting farm:
England, bound in with the triumphant sea,
Whose rocky shore beats back the envious siege
Of watery Neptune, is now bound in with
　　shame,
With inky blots, and rotten parchment bonds:
That England, that was wont to conquer others,
Hath made a shameful conquest of itself.
Ah, would the scandal vanish with my life,
How happy then were my ensuing death!

*Enter* KING RICHARD *and* QUEEN, AUMERLE,
BUSHY, GREEN, BAGOT, ROSS, *and* WIL-
LOUGHBY.

　　*York.* The king is come: deal mildly with
　　his youth;　　　　　　　　　　[more.
For young hot colts, being rag'd, do rage the
　　*Queen.* How fares our noble uncle, Lancaster?

　　*K. Rich.* What comfort, man? How is 't with
　　aged Gaunt?　　　　　　　　　　[position!
　　*Gaunt.* O, how that name befits my com-
Old Gaunt, indeed; and gaunt in being old:
Within me grief hath kept a tedious fast;
And who abstains from meat that is not gaunt?
For sleeping England long time have I watch'd;
Watching breeds leanness, leanness is all gaunt:
The pleasure that some fathers feeds upon
Is my strict fast,—I mean my children's looks;
And therein fasting, hast thou made me gaunt:
Gaunt am I for the grave, gaunt as a grave,
Whose hollow womb inherits naught but bones.
　　*K. Rich.* Can sick men play so nicely with
　　their names?
　　*Gaunt.* No, misery makes sport to mock
　　itself:
Since thou dost seek to kill my name in me,
I mock my name, great king, to flatter thee.
　　*K. Rich.* Should dying men flatter with those
　　that live?　　　　　　　　　　　[die.
　　*Gaunt.* No, no; men living flatter those that
　　*K. Rich.* Thou, now a-dying, say'st thou
　　flatter'st me.
　　*Gaunt.* O, no! thou diest, though I the sicker
　　be.　　　　　　　　　　　　　[thee ill.
　　*K. Rich.* I am in health, I breathe, and see
　　*Gaunt.* Now, He that made me knows I see
　　thee ill;
Ill in myself to see, and in thee seeing ill.
Thy death-bed is no lesser than the land
Wherein thou liest in reputation sick;
And thou, too careless patient as thou art,
Committ'st thy anointed body to the cure
Of those physicians that first wounded thee:
A thousand flatterers sit within thy crown,
Whose compass is no bigger than thy head;
And yet, encaged in so small a verge,
The waste is no whit lesser than thy land.
O, had thy grandsire, with a prophet's eye,
Seen how his son's son should destroy his sons,
From forth thy reach he would have laid thy
　　shame,
Deposing thee before thou wert possess'd,
Which art possess'd now to depose thyself.
Why, cousin, wert thou regent of the world,
It were a shame to let this land by lease;
But for thy world enjoying but this land,
Is it not more than shame to shame it so?
Landlord of England art thou now, not king:
Thy state of law is bondslave to the law;
And—
　　*K. Rich.* And thou a lunatic lean-witted fool,
Presuming on an ague's privilege,
Dar'st with thy frozen admonition
Make pale our cheek, chasing the royal blood
With fury from his native residence.
Now by my seat's right royal majesty,
Wert thou not brother to great Edward's son,
This tongue that runs so roundly in thy head
Should run thy head from thy unreverend
　　shoulders.　　　　　　　　　　[ward's son,
　　*Gaunt.* O, spare me not, my brother Ed-
For that I was his father Edward's son;—

That blood already, like the pelican,
Hast thou tapp'd out, and drunkenly carous'd:
My brother Gloster, plain well-meaning soul—
Whom fair befall in heaven 'mongst happy
    souls!—
May be a precedent and witness good [blood:
That thou respect'st not spilling Edward's
Join with the present sickness that I have:
And thy unkindness be like crooked age,
To crop at once a too-long wither'd flower.
Live in thy shame, but die not shame with
    thee!—
These words hereafter thy tormentors be!—
Convey me to my bed, then to my grave.
Love they to live that love and honour have.
        [*Exit, borne out by his* Attendants.
  *K. Rich.* And let them die that age and
    sullens have;
For both hast thou, and both become the grave.
  *York.* I do beseech your majesty, impute his
    words
To wayward sickliness and age in him:
He loves you, on my life, and holds you dear
As Harry Duke of Hereford, were he here.
  *K. Rich.* Right, you say true: as Hereford's
    love, so his;
As theirs, so mine; and all be as it is.

      *Enter* NORTHUMBERLAND.

  *North.* My liege, old Gaunt commends him
    to your majesty.
  *K. Rich.* What says he?
  *North.*        Nay, nothing; all is said:
His tongue is now a stringless instrument;
Words, life, and all, old Lancaster hath spent.
  *York.* Be York the next that must be bank-
    rupt so!
Though death be poor, it ends a mortal woe.
  *K. Rich.* The ripest fruit first falls, and so
    doth he;
His time is spent, our pilgrimage must be:
So much for that.—Now for our Irish wars:
We must supplant those rough rug-headed kerns,
Which live like venom, where no venom else,
But only they, hath privilege to live.
And for these great affairs do ask some charge:
Towards our assistance we do seize to us
The plate, coin, revenues, and movables,
Whereof our uncle Gaunt did stand possess'd.
  *York.* How long shall I be patient? ah, how
    long
Shall tender duty make me suffer wrong?
Not Gloster's death, nor Hereford's banish-
    ment,    [wrongs,
Not Gaunt's rebukes, nor England's private
Nor the prevention of poor Bolingbroke
About his marriage, nor my own disgrace,
Have ever made me sour my patient cheek,
Or bend one wrinkle on my sovereign's face.
I am the last of noble Edward's sons,
Of whom thy father, Prince of Wales, was first:
In war was never lion rag'd more fierce,
In peace was never gentle lamb more mild,
Than was that young and princely gentleman.

His face thou hast, for even so look'd he,
Accomplish'd with the number of thy hours;
But when he frown'd, it was against the French,
And not against his friends: his noble hand
Did win what he did spend, and spent not that
Which his triumphant father's hand had won:
His hands were guilty of no kindred's blood,
But bloody with the enemies of his kin.
O Richard! York is too far gone with grief,
Or else he never would compare between.
  *K. Rich.* Why, uncle, what's the matter?
  *York.*           O my liege,
Pardon me, if you please; if not, I, pleas'd
Not to be pardon'd, am content withal.
Seek you to seize, and gripe into your hands,
The royalties and rights of banish'd Hereford?
Is not Gaunt dead? and doth not Hereford live?
Was not Gaunt just? and is not Harry true?
Did not the one deserve to have an heir?
Is not his heir a well-deserving son?  [Time
Take Hereford's rights away, and take from
His charters and his customary rights;
Let not to-morrow, then, ensue to-day;
Be not thyself,—for how art thou a king
But by fair sequence and succession?
Now, afore God—God forbid I say true!—
If you do wrongfully seize Hereford's rights,
Call in the letters-patents that he hath
By his attorneys-general to sue
His livery, and deny his offer'd homage,
You pluck a thousand dangers on your head,
You lose a thousand well-disposed hearts,
And prick my tender patience to those thoughts
Which honour and allegiance cannot think.
  *K. Rich.* Think what you will, we seize into
    our hands
His plate, his goods, his money, and his lands.
  *York.* I'll not be by the while: my liege,
    farewell:
What will ensue hereof, there's none can tell:
But by bad courses may be understood
That their events can never fall out good.
               [*Exit.*
  *K. Rich.* Go, Bushy, to the Earl of Wiltshire
    straight:
Bid him repair to us to Ely House
To see this business. To-morrow next
We will for Ireland; and 'tis time, I trow:
And we create, in absence of ourself,
Our uncle York lord governor of England;
For he is just, and always lov'd us well.—
Come on, our queen: to-morrow must we part;
Be merry, for our time of stay is short.
    [*Flourish. Exeunt* KING, QUEEN, BUSHY,
      AUMERLE, GREEN, *and* BAGOT.
  *North.* Well, lords, the Duke of Lancaster
    is dead.
  *Ross.* And living too; for now his son is duke.
  *Willo.* Barely in title, not in revenue.
  *North.* Richly in both, if justice had her
    right.
  *Ross.* My heart is great; but it must break
    with silence,
Ere 't be disburden'd with a liberal tongue.

*North.* Nay, speak thy mind; and let him
　ne'er speak more
That speaks thy words again to do thee harm!
　*Willo.* Tends that thou wouldst speak to the
　　Duke of Hereford?
If it be so, out with it boldly, man;
Quick is mine ear to hear of good towards him.
　*Ross.* No good at all, that I can do for him;
Unless you call it good to pity him,
Bereft and gelded of his patrimony.
　*North.* Now, afore God, 'tis shame such
　　wrongs are borne
In him, a royal prince, and many more
Of noble blood in this declining land.
The king is not himself, but basely led
By flatterers; and what they will inform,
Merely in hate, 'gainst any of us all,
That will the king severely prosecute
'Gainst us, our lives, our children, and our
　heirs.
　*Ross.* The commons hath be pill'd with
　　grievous taxes,
And quite lost their hearts: the nobles hath he
　fin'd
For ancient quarrels, and quite lost their hearts.
　*Willo.* And daily new exactions are devis'd,—
As blanks, benevolences, and I wot not what:
But what, o' God's name, doth become of this?
　*North.* Wars have not wasted it, for warr'd
　　he hath not,
But basely yielded upon compromise
That which his ancestors achiev'd with blows:
More hath he spent in peace than they in wars.
　*Ross.* The Earl of Wiltshire hath the realm
　　in farm.
　*Willo.* The king's grown bankrupt, like a
　　broken man.　　　　　　　　　　[over him.
　*North.* Reproach and dissolution hangeth
　*Ross.* He hath not money for these Irish
　　wars,
His burdenous taxations notwithstanding,
But by the robbing of the banish'd duke.
　*North.* His noble kinsman:—most degener-
　　ate king!
But, lords, we hear this fearful tempest sing,
Yet seek no shelter to avoid the storm;
We see the wind set sore upon our sails,
And yet we strike not, but securely perish.
　*Ross.* We see the very wreck that we must
　　suffer;
And unavoided is the danger now,
For suffering so the causes of our wreck.
　*North.* Not so; even through the hollow eyes
　　of death
I spy life peering; but I dare not say
How near the tidings of our comfort is.
　*Willo.* Nay, let us share thy thoughts, as
　　thou dost ours.　　　　　　　　　　[land:
　*Ross.* Be confident to speak, Northumber-
We three are but thyself; and, speaking so,
Thy words are but as thoughts; therefore, be
　bold.
　*North.* Then thus:—I have from Port le
　　Blanc, a bay

In Brittany, receiv'd intelligence　　　[Cobham,
That Harry Duke of Hereford, Renald Lord
That late broke from the Duke of Exeter,
His brother, Archbishop late of Canterbury,
Sir Thomas Erpingham, Sir John Ramston,
Sir John Norbery, Sir Robert Waterton, and
　　Francis Quoint,—　　　　　　　　　[tagne,
All these, well furnish'd by the Duke of Bre-
With eight tall ships, three thousand men of
　war,
Are making hither with all due expedience,
And shortly mean to touch our northern shore:
Perhaps they had ere this, but that they stay
The first departing of the king for Ireland.
If, then, we shall shake off our slavish yoke,
Imp out our drooping country's broken wing,
Redeem from broking pawn the blemish'd crown,
Wipe off the dust that hides our sceptre's gilt,
And make high majesty look like itself,
Away with me in post to Ravenspurg;
But if you faint, as fearing to do so,
Stay and be secret, and myself will go.
　*Ross.* To horse, to horse! urge doubts to
　　them that fear.
　*Willo.* Hold out my horse, and I will first
　　be there.　　　　　　　　　　[*Exeunt.*

SCENE II.—*The same. A Room in the Palace.*

*Enter* QUEEN, BUSHY, *and* BAGOT.

　*Bushy.* Madam, your majesty is too much
　　sad:
You promis'd, when you parted with the king,
To lay aside life-harming heaviness,
And entertain a cheerful disposition.　[myself,
　*Queen.* To please the king, I did; to please
I cannot do it; yet I know no cause
Why I should welcome such a guest as grief,
Save bidding farewell to so sweet a guest
As my sweet Richard: yet, again, methinks
Some unborn sorrow, ripe in fortune's womb,
Is coming towards me; and my inward soul
With nothing trembles: at some thing it grieves,
More than with parting from my lord the king.
　*Bushy.* Each substance of a grief hath
　　twenty shadows,
Which show like grief itself, but are not so;
For sorrow's eye, glazed with blinding tears,
Divides one thing entire to many objects;
Like perspectives, which, rightly gaz'd upon,
Show nothing but confusion,—ey'd awry,
Distinguish form: so your sweet majesty,
Looking awry upon your lord's departure,
Finds shapes of grief, more than himself, to
　wail;
Which, look'd on as it is, is naught but shadows
Of what it is not. Then, thrice-gracious queen,
More than your lord's departure weep not,—
　more's not seen;
Or if it be, 'tis with false sorrow's eye,
Which for things true weeps things imaginary.
　*Queen.* It may be so; but yet my inward soul
Persuades me it is otherwise: howe'er it be,
I cannot but be sad; so heavy sad,　　[think,—

As,—though, on thinking, on no thought I
Makes me with heavy nothing faint and shrink.
　*Bushy.* 'Tis nothing but conceit, my gracious
lady.　　　　　　　　　　　　[riv'd
　*Queen.* 'Tis nothing less: conceit is still de-
From some forefather grief; mine is not so,
For nothing hath begot my something grief;
Or something hath the nothing that I grieve:
'Tis in reversion that I do possess;
But what it is, that is not yet known; what
I cannot name; 'tis nameless woe, I wot.

*Enter* GREEN.

　*Green.* God save your majesty!—and well
met, gentlemen:—
I hope the king is not yet shipp'd for Ireland.
　*Queen.* Why hop'st thou so? 'tis better hope
he is;
For his designs crave haste, his haste good
hope:
Then wherefore dost thou hope he is not
shipp'd?
　*Green.* That he, our hope, might have retir'd
his power,
And driven into despair an enemy's hope,
Who strongly hath set footing in this land:
The banish'd Bolingbroke repeals himself,
And with uplifted arms is safe arriv'd
At Ravenspurg.
　*Queen.*　　　Now God in heaven forbid!
　*Green.* O madam, 'tis too true: and that is
worse,　　　　　　　　　　[Henry Percy,
The Lord Northumberland, his son young
The Lords of Ross, Beaumond, and Willoughby,
With all their powerful friends, are fled to him.
　*Bushy.* Why have you not proclaim'd
Northumberland,
And all the rest of the revolted faction,
Traitors?　　　　　　　　　[Worcester
　*Green.* We have: whereupon the Earl of
Hath broke his staff, resign'd his stewardship,
And all the household servants fled with him
To Bolingbroke.　　　　　　　　[my woe,
　*Queen.* So, Green, thou art the midwife to
And Bolingbroke my sorrow's dismal heir:
Now hath my soul brought forth her prodigy;
And I, a gasping new-deliver'd mother,
Have woe to woe, sorrow to sorrow join'd.
　*Bushy.* Despair not, madam.
　*Queen.*　　　　Who shall hinder me?
I will despair, and be at enmity
With cozening hope,—he is a flatterer,
A parasite, a keeper-back of death,
Who gently would dissolve the bands of life,
Which false hope lingers in extremity.
　*Green.* Here comes the Duke of York.
　*Queen.* With signs of war about his aged
neck:
O, full of careful business are his looks!

*Enter* YORK.

Uncle, for God's sake, speak comfortable words.
　*York.* Should I do so, I should belie my
thoughts:

Comfort's in heaven; and we are on the earth,
Where nothing lives but crosses, care, and grief.
Your husband, he is gone to save far off,
Whilst others come to make him lose at home:
Here am I left to underprop his land,
Who, weak with age, cannot support myself:
Now comes the sick hour that his surfeit made;
Now shall he try his friends that flatter'd him.

*Enter a* Servant.

　*Serv.* My lord, your son was gone before I
came.
　*York.* He was?—Why, so!—go all which way
it will!—
The nobles they are fled, the commons they are
cold,
And will, I fear, revolt on Hereford's side.—
Sirrah, get thee to Plashy, to my sister Gloster;
Bid her send me presently a thousand pound:—
Hold, take my ring.　　　　　　[ship,
　*Serv.* My lord, I had forgot to tell your lord-
To-day, as I came by, I called there;—
But I shall grieve you to report the rest.
　*York.* What is't, knave?
　*Serv.* An hour before I came, the duchess died.
　*York.* God for his mercy! what a tide of woes
Comes rushing on this woeful land at once!
I know not what to do:—I would to God,
So my untruth had not provok'd him to it,—
The king had cut off my head with my brother's.
What, are there no posts despatch'd for Ire-
land?—
How shall we do for money for these wars?—
Come, sister,—cousin, I would say,—pray,
pardon me.
Go, fellow [*to the* Servant], get thee home, pro-
vide some carts,
And bring away the armour that is there.—
　　　　　　　　　　　　[*Exit* Servant.
Gentlemen, will you go muster men? If I know
How or which way to order these affairs,
Thus thrust disorderly into my hands,
Never believe me. Both are my kinsmen:—
The one's my sovereign, whom both my oath
And duty bids defend; the other, again,
Is my kinsman, whom the king hath wrong'd,
Whom conscience and my kindred bids to right.
Well, somewhat we must do.—Come, cousin,
I'll　　　　　　　　　　　[your men,
Dispose of you.—Gentlemen, go, muster up
And meet me presently at Berkley Castle.
I should to Plashy too;—
But time will not permit:—all is uneven,
And everything is left at six and seven.
　　　　　　　　[*Exeunt* YORK *and* QUEEN.
　*Bushy.* The wind sits fair for news to go to
Ireland,
But none returns. For us to levy power
Proportionable to the enemy
Is all impossible.　　　　　　[love
　*Green.* Besides, our nearness to the king in
Is near the hate of those love not the king.
　*Bagot.* And that's the wavering commons:
for their love

Lies in their purses; and whoso empties them,
By so much fills their hearts with deadly hate.

*Bushy.* Wherein the king stands generally
condemn'd.

*Bagot.* If judgment lie in them, then so do we,
Because we ever have been near the king.

*Green.* Well, I will for refuge straight to
Bristol Castle:
The Earl of Wiltshire is already there. [office

*Bushy.* Thither will I with you: for little
The hateful commons will perform for us,
Except like curs to tear us all to pieces.—
Will you go along with us?

*Bagot.* No; I will to Ireland to his majesty.
Farewell: if heart's presages be not vain,
We three here part that ne'er shall meet again.

*Bushy.* That's as York thrives to beat back
Bolingbroke. [takes

*Green.* Alas, poor duke! the task he under-
Is numbering sands, and drinking oceans dry:
Where one on his side fights, thousands will fly.
Farewell at once,—for once, for all, and ever.

*Bushy.* Well, we may meet again.

*Bagot.* I fear me, never. [*Exeunt.*

SCENE III.—*The Wilds in Glostershire.*

*Enter* BOLINGBROKE *and* NORTHUMBERLAND,
*with* Forces.

*Boling.* How far is it, my lord, to Berkley
now?

*North.* Believe me, noble lord,
I am a stranger here in Glostershire:
These high wild hills and rough uneven ways
Draw out our miles, and make them wearisome;
And yet your fair discourse hath been as sugar,
Making the hard way sweet and délectable.
But I bethink me what a weary way
From Ravenspurg to Cotswold will be found
In Ross and Willoughby, wanting your company,
Which, I protest, hath very much beguil'd
The tediousness and process of my travel:
But theirs is sweeten'd with the hope to have
The present benefit which I possess;
And hope to joy is little less in joy
Than hope enjoy'd: by this the weary lords
Shall make their way seem short; as mine hath
done
By sight of what I have, your noble company.

*Boling.* Of much less value is my company
Than your good words.—But who comes here?

*North.* It is my son, young Harry Percy,
Sent from my brother Worcester, whencesoever.

*Enter* HARRY PERCY.

Harry, how fares your uncle?

*Percy.* I had thought, my lord, to have
learned his health of you.

*North.* Why, is he not with the queen?

*Percy.* No, my good lord; he hath forsook
the court,
Broken his staff of office, and dispers'd
The household of the king.

*North.* What was his reason?

He was not so resolv'd when last we spake together.

*Percy.* Because your lordship was proclaimed
traitor.
But he, my lord, is gone to Ravenspurg,
To offer service to the Duke of Hereford;
And sent me o'er by Berkley, to discover
What power the Duke of York had levied there
Then with direction to repair to Ravenspurg.

*North.* Have you forgot the Duke of Hereford, boy? [forgot

*Percy.* No, my good lord; for that is not
Which ne'er I did remember: to my knowledge,
I never in my life did look on him.

*North.* Then learn to know him now; this is
the duke. [service,

*Percy.* My gracious lord, I tender you my
Such as it is, being tender, raw, and young;
Which elder days shall ripen, and confirm
To more approved service and desert. [sure

*Boling.* I thank thee, gentle Percy; and be
I count myself in nothing else so happy
As in a soul remembering my good friends;
And, as my fortune ripens with thy love,
It shall be still thy true love's recompence:
My heart this covenant makes, my hand thus
seals it.

*North.* How far is it to Berkley? and what stir
Keeps good old York there with his men of war?

*Percy.* There stands the castle, by yon tuft
of trees, [heard:
Mann'd with three hundred men, as I have
And in it are the Lords of York, Berkley, and
Seymour,—
None else of name and noble estimate.

*North.* Here come the Lords of Ross and
Willoughby,
Bloody with spurring, fiery-red with haste.

*Enter* ROSS *and* WILLOUGHBY.

*Boling.* Welcome, my lords. I wot your love
pursues
A banish'd traitor: all my treasury
Is yet but unfelt thanks, which, more enrich'd,
Shall be your love and labour's recompence.

*Ross.* Your presence makes us rich, most
noble lord. [tain it.

*Willo.* And far surmounts our labour to at-

*Boling.* Evermore thanks, the exchequer of
the poor;
Which, till my infant fortune comes to years,
Stands for my bounty.—But, who comes here?

*North.* It is my Lord of Berkley, as I guess.

*Enter* BERKLEY.

*Berk.* My Lord of Hereford, my message is
to you.

*Boling.* My lord, my answer is—to Lan-
caster;
And I am come to seek that name in England;
And I must find that title in your tongue,
Before I make reply to aught you say.

*Berk.* Mistake me not, my lord; 'tis not my
meaning

To raze one title of your honour out:—
To you, my lord, I come,—what lord you will,—
From the most gracious regent of this land,
The Duke of York, to know what pricks you on
To take advantage of the absent time,
And fright our native peace with self-born arms.
    *Boling.* I shall not need transport my words
        by you;
Here comes his grace in person.

*Enter* YORK, *attended.*

            My noble uncle! [*Kneels.*
    *York.* Show me thy humble heart, and not
        thy knee,
Whose duty is deceivable and false.
    *Boling.* My gracious uncle!—
    *York.*                        Tut, tut!
Grace me no grace, nor uncle me no uncle:
I am no traitor's uncle; and that word—grace,
In an ungracious mouth is but profane.
Why have those banish'd and forbidden legs
Dar'd once to touch a dust of England's ground?
But, then, more why,—why have they dar'd to
        march
So many miles upon her peaceful bosom,
Frighting her pale-fac'd villages with war
And ostentation of despised arms?
Com'st thou because the anointed king is hence?
Why, foolish boy, the king is left behind,
And in my loyal bosom lies his power.
Were I but now the lord of such hot youth
As when brave Gaunt thy father, and myself,
Rescued the Black Prince, that young Mars of
        men,
From forth the ranks of many thousand French,
O, then, how quickly should this arm of mine,
Now prisoner to the palsy, chástise thee,
And minister correction to thy fault! [fault;
    *Boling.* My gracious uncle, let me know my
On what condition stands it and wherein?
    *York.* Even in condition of the worst de-
        gree,—
In gross rebellion and detested treason:
Thou art a banish'd man; and here art come
Before the expiration of thy time,
In braving arms against thy sovereign.
    *Boling.* As I was banish'd, I was banish'd
        Hereford;
But as I come, I come for Lancaster.
And, noble uncle, I beseech your grace
Look on my wrongs with an indifferent eye:
You are my father, for methinks in you
I see old Gaunt alive; O, then, my father,
Will you permit that I shall stand condemn'd
A wandering vagabond; my rights and royalties
Pluck'd from my arms perforce, and given away
To upstart unthrifts? Wherefore was I born?
If that my cousin king be king of England,
It must be granted I am Duke of Lancaster.
You have a son, Aumerle, my noble kinsman;
Had you first died, and he been thus trod down,
He should have found his uncle Gaunt a father,
To rouse his wrongs, and chase them to the bay.
I am denied to sue my livery here,

And yet my letters-patents give me leave:
My father's goods are all distrain'd and sold;
And these and all are all amiss employ'd.
What would you have me do? I am a subject,
And challenge law: attorneys are denied me;
And therefore personally I lay my claim
To my inheritance of free descent.    [abus'd.
    *North.* The noble duke hath been too much
    *Ross.* It stands your grace upon to do him
        right.
    *Willo.* Base men by his endowments are
        made great.
    *York.* My lords of England, let me tell you
        this:—
I have had feeling of my cousin's wrongs,
And labour'd all I could to do him right:
But in this kind to come, in braving arms,
Be his own carver, and cut out his way,
To find out right with wrong,—it may not be;
And you that do abet him in this kind
Cherish rebellion, and are rebels all.
    *North.* The noble duke hath sworn his com-
        ing is
But for his own; and for the right of that
We all have strongly sworn to give him aid;
And let him ne'er see joy that breaks that oath!
    *York.* Well, well, I see the issue of these
        arms;—
I cannot mend it, I must needs confess,
Because my power is weak and all ill left:
But if I could, by him that gave me life,
I would attach you all, and make you stoop
Unto the sovereign mercy of the king;
But since I cannot, be it known to you
I do remain as neuter. So, fare you well;—
Unless you please to enter in the castle,
And there repose you for this night.
    *Boling.* An offer, uncle, that we will accept
But we must win your grace to go with us
To Bristol Castle, which they say is held
By Bushy, Bagot, and their complices,
The caterpillars of the commonwealth,
Which I have sworn to weed and pluck away.
    *York.* It may be I will go with you:—but
        yet I'll pause;
For I am loth to break our country's laws.
Nor friends nor foes, to me welcome you are:
Things past redress are now with me past care.
                                    [*Exeunt.*

SCENE IV.—*A Camp in Wales.*

*Enter* SALISBURY *and a* Captain.

    *Cap.* My Lord of Salisbury, we have stay'd
        ten days,
And hardly kept our countrymen together,
And yet we hear no tidings from the king;
Therefore we will disperse ourselves: farewell.
    *Sal.* Stay yet another day, thou trusty
        Welshman:
The king reposeth all his confidence
In thee.                            [not stay.
    *Cap.* 'Tis thought the king is dead; we will
The bay trees in our country all are wither'd,
And meteors fright the fixed stars of heaven;

The pale-fac'd moon looks bloody on the earth,
And lean-look'd prophets whisper fearful
   change;                              [leap,—
Rich men look sad, and ruffians dance and
The one in fear to lose what they enjoy,
The other to enjoy by rage and war:
These signs forerun the death or fall of kings.—
Farewell: our countrymen are gone and fled,
As well assur'd Richard their king is dead.
                                      [*Exit.*

   *Sal.* Ah, Richard, with the eyes of heavy
      mind,
I see thy glory, like a shooting star,
Fall to the base earth from the firmament!
The sun sets weeping in the lowly west,
Witnessing storms to come, woe, and unrest;
Thy friends are fled, to wait upon thy foes;
And crossly to thy good all fortune goes.
                                      [*Exit.*

## ACT III.

SCENE I.—BOLINGBROKE'S *Camp at Bristol.*

*Enter* BOLINGBROKE, YORK, NORTHUMBER-
LAND, PERCY, WILLOUGHBY, ROSS: Officers
*behind, with* BUSHY *and* GREEN, *prisoners.*

   *Boling.* Bring forth these men.—
Bushy and Green, I will not vex your souls,—
Since presently your souls must part your
      bodies,—
With too much urging your pernicious lives,
For 'twere no charity; yet, to wash your blood
From off my hands, here, in the view of men,
I will unfold some causes of your deaths.
You have misled a prince, a royal king,
A happy gentleman in blood and lineaments,
By you unhappied and disfigur'd clean:
You have in manner with your sinful hours
Made a divorce betwixt his queen and him;
Broke the possession of a royal bed,
And stain'd the beauty of a fair queen's cheeks
With tears drawn from her eyes by your foul
      wrongs.
Myself,—a prince by fortune of my birth,
Near to the king in blood, and near in love
Till you did make him misinterpret me,—
Have stoop'd my neck under your injuries,
And sigh'd my English breath in foreign clouds,
Eating the bitter bread of banishment;
Whilst you have fed upon my signories,
Dispark'd my parks, and fell'd my forest-
      woods,                           [coat,
From my own windows torn my household
Raz'd out my impress, leaving me no sign,
Save men's opinions and my living blood,
To show the world I am a gentleman.
This and much more, much more than twice
   all this,
Condemns you to the death.—See them de-
   liver'd over
To execution and the hand of death.
   *Bushy.* More welcome is the stroke of death
      to me                            [well.
Than Bolingbroke to England.—Lords, fare-

   *Green.* My comfort is, that heaven will take
      our souls,
And plague injustice with the pains of hell.
   *Boling.* My Lord Northumberland, see them
      despatch'd.
      [*Exeunt* NORTH. *and others, with* Prisoners.
Uncle, you say the queen is at your house;
For God's sake, fairly let her be entreated:
Tell her I send to her my kind commends;
Take special care my greetings be deliver'd.
   *York.* A gentleman of mine I have despatch'd
With letters of your love to her at large.
   *Boling.* Thanks, gentle uncle.—Come, lords,
      away,
To fight with Glendower and his complices:
Awhile to work, and after holiday.    [*Exeunt.*

SCENE II.—*The Coast of* WALES. *A Castle in
      view.*

*Flourish; drums and trumpets. Enter* KING
   RICHARD, *the* BISHOP OF CARLISLE, AU-
   MERLE, *and* Soldiers.

   *K. Rich.* Barkloughly Castle call they this
      at hand?
   *Aum.* Yea, my lord. How brooks your grace
      the air,
After your late tossing on the breaking seas?
   *K. Rich.* Needs must I like it well: I weep
      for joy
To stand upon my kingdom once again.—
Dear earth, I do salute thee with my hand,
Though rebels wound thee with their horses'
      hoofs:
As a long-parted mother with her child
Plays fondly with her tears and smiles in
      meeting,
So, weeping-smiling, greet I thee, my earth,
And do thee favour with my royal hands.
Feed not thy sovereign's foe, my gentle earth,
Nor with thy sweets comfort his rav'nous sense;
But let thy spiders, that suck up thy venom,
And heavy-gaited toads, lie in their way,
Doing annoyance to the treacherous feet
Which with usurping steps do trample thee:
Yield stinging nettles to mine enemies;
And when they from thy bosom pluck a flower,
Guard it, I pray thee, with a lurking adder,
Whose double tongue may with a mortal touch
Throw death upon thy sovereign's enemies.
Mock not my senseless conjuration, lords:
This earth shall have a feeling, and these stones
Prove armed soldiers, ere her native king
Shall falter under foul rebellion's arms!
   *Car.* Fear not, my lord; that Power that
      made you king
Hath power to keep you king in spite of all.
The means that heaven yields must be embrac'd
And not neglected; else, if heaven would,
And we will not, heaven's offer we refuse,
The proffer'd means of succour and redress.
   *Aum.* He means, my lord, that we are too
      remiss;
Whilst Bolingbroke, through our security,

Grows strong and great in substance and in
friends. [thou not
*K. Rich.* Discomfortable cousin! know'st
That when the searching eye of heaven is hid
Behind the globe that lights the lower world,
Then thieves and robbers range abroad unseen,
In murders and in outrage, boldly here;
But when, from under this terrestrial ball,
He fires the proud tops of the eastern pines,
And darts his light through every guilty hole,
Then murders, treasons, and detested sins,
The cloak of night being pluck'd from off their
backs,
Stand bare and naked, trembling at themselves?
So when this thief, this traitor, Bolingbroke,—
Who all this while hath revell'd in the night,
Whilst we were wandering with the antipodes,—
Shall see us rising in our throne, the east,
His treasons will sit blushing in his face,
Not able to endure the sight of day,
But self-affrighted tremble at his sin.
Not all the water in the rough rude sea
Can wash the balm from an anointed king;
The breath of worldly men cannot depose
The deputy elected by the Lord;
For every man that Bolingbroke hath press'd
To lift shrewd steel against our golden crown,
God for his Richard hath in heavenly pay
A glorious angel: then, if angels fight, [right.
Weak man must fall; for heaven still guards the

*Enter* SALISBURY.

Welcome, my lord: how far off lies your power?
*Sal.* Nor near nor further off, my gracious
lord, [tongue,
Than this weak arm: discomfort guides my
And bids me speak of nothing but despair.
One day too late, I fear, my noble lord,
Hath clouded all thy happy days on earth:
O, call back yesterday, bid time return,
And thou shalt have twelve thousand fighting
men!
To-day, to-day, unhappy day, too late,
O'erthrows thy joys, friends, fortune, and thy
state;
For all the Welshmen, hearing thou wert dead,
Are gone to Bolingbroke, dispers'd, and fled.
*Aum.* Comfort, my liege: why looks your
grace so pale?
*K. Rich.* But now the blood of twenty thou-
sand men
Did triumph in my face, and they are fled;
And, till so much blood thither come again,
Have I not reason to look pale and dead?
All souls that will be safe fly from my side;
For time hath set a blot upon my pride. [are.
*Aum.* Comfort, my liege; remember who you
*K. Rich.* I had forgot myself: am I not king?
Awake, thou sluggard majesty! thou sleep'st.
Is not the king's name forty thousand names?
Arm, arm, my name! a puny subject strikes
At thy great glory.—Look not to the ground,
Ye favourites of a king: are we not high?
High be our thoughts: I know my uncle York

Hath power enough to serve our turn.—But
who comes here?

*Enter* SCROOP.

*Scroop.* More health and happiness betide
my liege
Than can my care-tun'd tongue deliver him.
*K. Rich.* Mine ear is open and my heart
prepar'd:
The worst is worldly loss thou canst unfold.
Say, is my kingdom lost? why, 'twas my care;
And what loss is it to be rid of care?
Strives Bolingbroke to be as great as we?
Greater he shall not be; if he serve God,
We'll serve him too, and be his fellow so:
Revolt our subjects? that we cannot mend;
They break their faith to God, as well as us:
Cry woe, destruction, ruin, loss, decay;
The worst is death, and death will have his day!
*Scroop.* Glad am I that your highness is so
arm'd
To bear the tidings of calamity.
Like an unseasonable stormy day,
Which makes the silver rivers drown their
shores,
As if the world were all dissolv'd to tears;
So high above his limits swells the rage
Of Bolingbroke, covering your fearful land
With hard bright steel, and hearts harder than
steel.
White-beards have arm'd their thin and hair-
less scalps [voices,
Against thy majesty; and boys, with women's
Strive to speak big, and clap their female joints
In stiff unwieldy arms against thy crown:
Thy very beadsmen learn to bend their bows
Of double-fatal yew against thy state;
Yea, distaff-women manage rusty bills
Against thy seat: both old and young rebel,
And all goes worse than I have power to tell.
*K. Rich.* Too well, too well thou tell'st a
tale so ill.
Where is the Earl of Wiltshire? where is Bagot?
What is become of Bushy, where is Green?
That they have let the dangerous enemy
Measure our confines with such peaceful steps?
If we prevail, their heads shall pay for it:
I warrant they have made peace with Boling-
broke.
*Scroop.* Peace have they made with him,
indeed, my lord. [redemption!
*K. Rich.* O villains, vipers, damn'd without
Dogs, easily won to fawn on any man!
Snakes, in my heart-blood warm'd, that sting
my heart! [Judas!
Three Judases, each one thrice worse than
Would they make peace? terrible hell make war
Upon their spotted souls for this offence!
*Scroop.* Sweet love, I see, changing his prop-
erty,
Turns to the sourest and most deadly hate:—
Again uncurse their souls; their peace is made
With heads, and not with hands: those whom
you curse .

Have felt the worst of death's destroying
   wound,
And lie full low, grav'd in the hollow ground.
  *Aum.* Is Bushy, Green, and the Earl of
   Wiltshire dead?           [heads.
  *Scroop.* Yea, all of them at Bristol lost their
  *Aum.* Where is the duke my father with his
   power?
  *K. Rich.* No matter where;—of comfort, no
   man speak:
Let's talk of graves, of worms, and epitaphs;
Make dust our paper, and with rainy eyes
Write sorrow on the bosom of the earth.
Let's choose executors, and talk of wills:
And yet not so,—for what can we bequeath,
Save our deposed bodies to the ground?
Our lands, our lives, and all are Bolingbroke's,
And nothing can we call our own but death,
And that small model of the barren earth
Which serves as paste and cover to our bones.
For God's sake, let us sit upon the ground,
And tell sad stories of the death of kings:—
How some have been depos'd; some slain in
   war;
Some haunted by the ghosts they have depos'd;
Some poison'd by their wives; some sleeping
   kill'd;
All murder'd:—for within the hollow crown
That rounds the mortal temples of a king
Keeps Death his court; and there the antic sits,
Scoffing his state, and grinning at his pomp;
Allowing him a breath, a little scene,
To monarchize, be fear'd, and kill with looks;
Infusing him with self and vain conceit,—
As if this flesh, which walls about our life,
Were brass impregnable; and humour'd thus,
Comes at the last, and with a little pin
Bores through his castle-wall, and—farewell,
   king!           [blood
Cover your heads, and mock not flesh and
With solemn reverence; throw away respect,
Tradition, form, and ceremonious duty;
For you have but mistook me all this while:
I live with bread like you, feel want, taste grief,
Need friends:—subjected thus,
How can you say to me, I am a king?
  *Car.* My lord, wise men ne'er sit and wail
   their woes,
But presently prevent the ways to wail.
To fear the foe, since fear oppresseth strength,
Gives, in your weakness, strength unto your
   foe,
And so your follies fight against yourself.
Fear, and be slain; no worse can come to fight:
And fight and die is death destroying death;
Where fearing dying pays death servile breath.
  *Aum.* My father hath a power; inquire of
   him;
And learn to make a body of a limb.
  *K. Rich.* Thou chid'st me well:—proud Bo-
   lingbroke, I come         [doom.
To change blows with thee for our day of
This ague-fit of fear is over-blown;
An easy task it is to win our own.—

Say, Scroop, where lies our uncle with his
   power?
Speak sweetly, man, although thy looks be
   sour.           [sky
  *Scroop.* Men judge by the complexion of the
The state and inclination of the day:
So may you by my dull and heavy eye,
  My tongue hath but a heavier tale to say.
I play the torturer, by small and small
To lengthen out the worst that must be
   spoken:—
Your uncle York is join'd with Bolingbroke;
And all your northern castles yielded up,
And all your southern gentlemen in arms
Upon his party.
  *K. Rich.*       Thou hast said enough.—
Beshrew thee, cousin, which didst lead me forth
                  [*To* AUMERLE.
Of that sweet way I was in to despair!
What say you now? what comfort have we
   now?
By heaven, I'll hate him everlastingly
That bids me be of comfort any more.
Go to Flint Castle: there I'll pine away;
A king, woe's slave, shall kingly woe obey.
That power I have, discharge; and let them go
To ear the land that hath some hope to grow,
For I have none:—let no man speak again
To alter this, for counsel is but vain.
  *Aum.* My liege, one word.
  *K. Rich.*       He does me double wrong
That wounds me with the flatteries of his
   tongue.
Discharge my followers: let them hence away,
From Richard's night to Bolingbroke's fair
   day.           [*Exeunt.*

SCENE III.—WALES. *Before Flint Castle.*

*Enter, with drum and colours,* BOLINGBROKE
  *and* Forces; YORK, NORTHUMBERLAND, *and*
  *others.*

  *Boling.* So that by this intelligence we learn
The Welshmen are dispers'd; and Salisbury
Is gone to meet the king, who lately landed
With some few private friends upon this coast.
  *North.* The news is very fair and good, my
   lord:
Richard not far from hence hath hid his head.
  *York.* It would beseem the Lord Northum-
   berland
To say, King Richard:—alack the heavy day
When such a sacred king should hide his head.
  *North.* Your grace mistakes; only to be brief,
Left I his title out.
  *York.*        The time hath been,
Would you have been so brief with him, he
   would
Have been so brief with you, to shorten you,
For taking so the head, your whole head's
   length.          [should.
  *Boling.* Mistake not, uncle, further than you
  *York.* Take not, good cousin, further than
   you should,         [heads.
Lest you mistake: the heavens are o'er our

*Boling.* I know it, uncle; and oppose not
    myself
Against their will.—But who comes here?

*Enter* PERCY.

Well, Harry: what, will not this castle yield?
    *Percy.* The castle royally is mann'd, my lord,
Against thy entrance.
    *Boling.* Royally!
Why, it contains no king?
    *Percy.*          Yes, my good lord,
It doth contain a king; King Richard lies
Within the limits of yond lime and stone:
And with him are the Lord Aumerle, Lord
    Salisbury,
Sir Stephen Scroop; besides a clergyman
Of holy reverence, who I cannot learn.
    *North.* O, belike it is the Bishop of Carlisle.
    *Boling.* Noble lord,
                [*To* NORTHUMBERLAND.
Go to the rude ribs of that ancient castle;
Through brazen trumpet send the breath of
    parle
Into his ruin'd ears, and thus deliver:—
Harry Bolingbroke
On both his knees doth kiss King Richard's
    hand,
And sends allegiance and true faith of heart
To his most royal person; hither come
Even at his feet to lay my arms and power,
Provided that, my banishment repeal'd,
And lands restor'd again, be freely granted:
If not, I'll use the advantage of my power,
And lay the summer's dust with showers of
    blood
Rain'd from the wounds of slaughter'd Eng-
    lishmen:
The which, how far off from the mind of Bol-
    ingbroke
It is, such crimson tempest should bedrench
The fresh green lap of fair King Richard's land,
My stooping duty tenderly shall show.
Go, signify as much, while here we march
Upon the grassy carpet of this plain.—
            [NORTH. *advances to the Castle, with a*
                *trumpet.*
Let's march without the noise of threat'ning
    drum,
That from the castle's tatter'd battlements
Our fair appointments may be well perus'd.
Methinks King Richard and myself should meet
With no less terror than the elements
Of fire and water, when their thund'ring shock
At meeting tears the cloudy cheeks of heaven.
Be he the fire, I'll be the yielding water:
The rage be his, while on the earth I rain
My waters,—on the earth, and not on him.
March on, and mark King Richard how he looks.

*A parle sounded, and answered by another trump-*
    *et within. Flourish. Enter on the walls* KING
    RICHARD, *the* BISHOP OF CARLISLE, AUM-
    ERLE, SCROOP, *and* SALISBURY.

See, see, King Richard doth himself appear,

As doth the blushing discontented sun
From out the fiery portal of the east,
When he perceives the envious clouds are bent
To dim his glory, and to stain the track
Of his bright passage to the occident.
    *York.* Yet looks he like a king: behold, his
        eye,
As bright as is the eagle's, lightens forth
Controlling majesty:—alack, alack, for woe,
That any harm should stain so fair a show!
    *K. Rich.* We are amaz'd; and thus long have
        we stood
To watch the fearful bending of thy knee,
                    [*To* NORTHUMBERLAND.
Because we thought ourself thy lawful king:
And if we be, how dare thy joints forget
To pay their awful duty to our presence?
If we be not, show us the hand of God
That hath dismissed us from our stewardship;
For well we know, no hand of blood and bone
Can gripe the sacred handle of our sceptre,
Unless he do profane, steal, or usurp.
And though you think that all, as you have
        done,
Have torn their souls by turning them from us,
And we are barren and bereft of friends;
Yet know,—my master, God omnipotent,
Is mustering in his clouds, on our behalf,
Armies of pestilence; and they shall strike
Your children yet unborn and unbegot,
That lift your vassal hands against my head,
And threat the glory of my precious crown.
Tell Bolingbroke,—for yond methinks he is,—
That every stride he makes upon my land
Is dangerous treason: he is come to ope
The purple testament of bleeding war;
But ere the crown he looks for live in peace,
Ten thousand bloody crowns of mothers' sons
Shall ill become the flower of England's face,
Change the complexion of her maid-pale peace
To scarlet indignation, and bedew
Her pastures' grass with faithful English blood.
    *North.* The king of heaven forbid our lord
        the king
Should so with civil and uncivil arms
Be rush'd upon! Thy thrice-noble cousin,
Harry Bolingbroke, doth humbly kiss thy hand;
And by the honourable tomb he swears,
That stands upon your royal grandsire's bones,
And by the royalties of both your bloods,—
Currents that spring from one most gracious
        head,—
And by the buried hand of warlike Gaunt,
And by the worth and honour of himself,
Comprising all that may be sworn or said,—
His coming hither hath no further scope
Than for his lineal royalties, and to beg
Enfranchisement immediate on his knees:
Which on thy royal party granted once,
His glittering arms he will commend to rust,
His barbed steeds to stables, and his heart
To faithful service of your majesty.
This swears he, as he is a prince, is just;
And, as I am a gentleman, I credit him.

*K. Rich.* Northumberland, say thus the king
    returns:—
His noble cousin is right welcome hither;
And all the number of his fair demands
Shall be accomplish'd without contradiction:
With all the gracious utterance thou hast
Speak to his gentle hearing kind commends.—
We do debase ourself, cousin, do we not,
                    [*To* AUMERLE.
To look so poorly, and to speak so fair?
Shall we call back Northumberland, and send
Defiance to the traitor, and so die?
  *Aum.* No, good my lord; let's fight with
    gentle words
Till time lend friends, and friends their helpful
    swords.
  *K. Rich.* O God, O God! that e'er this tongue
    of mine,
That laid the sentence of dread banishment
On yond proud man, should take it off again
With words of sooth! O that I were as great
As is my grief, or lesser than my name!
Or that I could forget what I have been!
Or not remember what I must be now!
Swell'st thou, proud heart? I'll give thee scope
    to beat,
Since foes have scope to beat both thee and me.
  *Aum.* Northumberland comes back from
    Bolingbroke.
  *K. Rich.* What must the king do now? must
    he submit?
The king shall do it: must he be depos'd?
The king shall be contented: must he lose
The name of king? o' God's name, let it go:
I'll give my jewels for a set of beads,
My gorgeous palace for a hermitage,
My gay apparel for an alms-man's gown,
My figur'd goblets for a dish of wood,
My sceptre for a palmer's walking staff,
My subjects for a pair of carved saints,
And my large kingdom for a little grave,
A little little grave, an obscure grave;—
Or I'll be buried in the king's highway,
Some way of common trade, where subjects'
    feet
May hourly trample on their sovereign's head;
For on my heart they tread now whilst I live;
And buried once, why not upon my head?—
Aumerle, thou weep'st,—my tender-hearted
    cousin!—
We'll make foul weather with despised tears;
Our sighs and they shall lodge the summer corn,
And make a dearth in this revolting land.
Or shall we play the wantons with our woes,
And make some pretty match with shedding
    tears?
As thus;—to drop them still upon one place,
Till they have fretted us a pair of graves
Within the earth; and, therein laid,—there lies
Two kinsmen digg'd their graves with weeping
    eyes.
Would not this ill do well?—Well, well, I see
I talk but idly, and you mock at me.—
Most mighty prince, my Lord Northumberland,

What says King Bolingbroke? will his majesty
Give Richard leave to live till Richard die?
You make a leg, and Bolingbroke says ay.
  *North.* My lord, in the base court he doth
    attend                [down?
To speak with you;—may it please you to come
  *K. Rich.* Down, down I come; like glister-
    ing Phaeton,
Wanting the manage of unruly jades.
             [NORTH. *retires to* BOLING.
In the base court? Base court, where kings
    grow base,
To come at traitors' calls, and do them grace.
In the base court? Come down? Down, court!
    down, king!
For night-owls shriek where mounting larks
    should sing.     [*Exeunt from above.*
  *Boling.* What says his majesty?
  *North.*            Sorrow and grief of heart
Makes him speak fondly, like a frantic man:
Yet he is come.

    *Enter* KING RICHARD, *and his* Attendants,
                  *below.*

  *Boling.* Stand all apart,
And show fair duty to his majesty.—
My gracious lord,—          [*Kneeling.*
  *K. Rich.* Fair cousin, you debase your
    princely knee
To make the base earth proud with kissing it;
Me rather had my heart might feel your love
Than my unpleas'd eye see your courtesy.
Up, cousin, up;—your heart is up, I know,
Thus high at least [*touching his own head*], al-
    though your knee be low.      [own.
  *Boling.* My gracious lord, I come but for mine
  *K. Rich.* Your own is yours, and I am yours,
    and all.                   [lord,
  *Boling.* So far be mine, my most redoubted
As my true service shall deserve your love.
  *K. Rich.* Well you deserve:—they well de-
    serve to have
That know the strong'st and surest way to get.—
Uncle, give me your hand: nay, dry your eyes;
Tears show their love, but want their remedies.—
Cousin, I am too young to be your father,
Though you are old enough to be my heir.
What you will have, I'll give, and willing too;
For do we must what force will have us do.—
Set on towards London:—cousin, is it so?
  *Boling.* Yea, my good lord.
  *K. Rich.*          Then I must not say no.
                 [*Flourish. Exeunt.*

SCENE IV.—LANGLEY. *The* DUKE OF YORK'S
               *Garden.*

    *Enter the* QUEEN *and two* Ladies.

  *Queen.* What sport shall we devise here in
    this garden,
To drive away the heavy thought of care?
  *1 Lady.* Madam, we'll play at bowls.
  *Queen.*          'Twill make me think
The world is full of rubs, and that my fortune
Runs against the bias.

*1 Lady.* Madam, we'll dance.

*Queen.* My legs can keep no measure in delight,
When my poor heart no measure keeps in grief:
Therefore, no dancing, girl; some other sport.

*1 Lady.* Madam, we'll tell tales.

*Queen.* Of sorrow or of joy?

*1 Lady.* Of either, madam.

*Queen.* Of neither, girl:
For if of joy, being altogether wanting,
It doth remember me the more of sorrow;
Or if of grief, being altogether had,
It adds more sorrow to my want of joy:
For what I have, I need not to repeat;
And what I want, it boots not to complain.

*1 Lady.* Madam, I'll sing.

*Queen.* 'Tis well that thou hast cause;
But thou shouldst please me better wouldst thou weep.                    [you good.

*1 Lady.* I could weep, madam, would it do

*Queen.* And I could weep, would weeping do me good,
And never borrow any tear of thee.—
But stay, here come the gardeners:
Let's step into the shadow of these trees.
My wretchedness unto a row of pins,
They'll talk of state; for every one doth so
Against a change: woe is forerun with woe.

[QUEEN *and* Ladies *retire.*

*Enter a* Gardener *and two* Servants.

*Gard.* Go, bind thou up yond dangling apricocks,
Which, like unruly children, make their sire
Stoop with oppression of their prodigal weight:
Give some supportance to the bending twigs.—
Go thou, and like an executioner
Cut off the heads of too-fast-growing sprays,
That look too lofty in our commonwealth:
All must be even in our government.—
You thus employ'd, I will go root away
The noisome weeds, that without profit suck
The soil's fertility from wholesome flowers.

*1 Serv.* Why should we, in the compass of a pale,
Keep law and form and due proportion,
Showing, as in a model, our firm estate,
When our sea-walled garden, the whole land,
Is full of weeds; her fairest flowers chok'd up,
Her fruit-trees all unprun'd, her hedges ruin'd,
Her knots disorder'd, and her wholesome herbs
Swarming with caterpillars?

*Gard.* Hold thy peace:—
He that hath suffer'd this disorder'd spring
Hath now himself met with the fall of leaf:
The weeds that his broad-spreading leaves did shelter,
That seem'd in eating him to hold him up,
Are pluck'd up root and all by Bolingbroke,—
I mean the Earl of Wiltshire, Bushy, Green.

*1 Serv.* What, are they dead?

*Gard.* They are; and Bolingbroke
Hath seiz'd the wasteful king.—Oh! what pity is it.

That he had not so trimm'd and dress'd his land
As we this garden! We at time of year
Do wound the bark, the skin of our fruit-trees,
Lest, being over-proud in sap and blood,
With too much richness it confound itself:
Had he done so to great and growing men,
They might have liv'd to bear, and he to taste
Their fruits of duty. Superfluous branches
We lop away, that bearing boughs may live:
Had he done so, himself had borne the crown,
Which waste of idle hours hath quite thrown down.

*1 Serv.* What, think you, then, the king shall be depos'd?

*Gard.* Depress'd he is already; and depos'd
'Tis doubt he will be: letters came last night
To a dear friend of the good Duke of York's,
That tell black tidings.

*Queen.* O, I am press'd to death through want of speaking!—

Thou, old Adam's likeness [*coming forward with Ladies*], set to dress this garden,
How dares thy harsh-rude tongue sound these unpleasing news?
What Eve, what serpent, hath suggested thee
To make a second fall of cursed man?
Why dost thou say King Richard is depos'd?
Dar'st thou, thou little better thing than earth,
Divine his downfall? Say, where, when, and how
Cam'st thou by this ill tidings? speak, thou wretch.

*Gard.* Pardon me, madam: little joy have I
To breathe these news; yet what I say is true.
King Richard, he is in the mighty hold
Of Bolingbroke: their fortunes both are weigh'd:
In your lord's scale is nothing but himself,
And some few vanities that make him light;
But in the balance of great Bolingbroke,
Besides himself, are all the English peers,
And with that odds he weighs King Richard down.
Post you to London, and you'll find it so;
I speak no more than every one doth know.

*Queen.* Nimble mischance, that art so light of foot,
Doth not thy embassage belong to me,
And am I last that knows it? O, thou think'st
To serve me last, that I may longest keep
Thy sorrow in my breast.—Come, ladies, go
To meet at London London's king in woe.—
What, was I born to this, that my sad look
Should grace the triumph of great Bolingbroke?
Gardener, for telling me this news of woe,
I would the plants thou graft'st may never grow.                    [*Exeunt* QUEEN *and* Ladies.

*Gard.* Poor queen! so that thy state might be no worse,
I would my skill were subject to thy curse.—
Here did she fall a tear; here, in this place,
I'll set a bank of rue, sour herb of grace:
Rue, even for ruth, here shortly shall be seen,
In the remembrance of a weeping queen.                    [*Exeunt.*

ACT IV.

SCENE I.—LONDON. *Westminster Hall. The Lords spiritual on the right side of the throne; the Lords temporal on the left; the Commons below.*

*Enter* BOLINGBROKE, AUMERLE, SURREY, NORTHUMBERLAND, PERCY, FITZWATER, *another* Lord, *the* BISHOP OF CARLISLE, *the* ABBOT OF WESTMINSTER, *and* Attendants. Officers *behind, with* BAGOT.—

*Boling.* Call forth Bagot.—
Now, Bagot, freely speak thy mind;
What thou dost know of noble Gloster's death;
Who wrought it with the king, and who perform'd
The bloody office of his timeless end.
    *Bagot.* Then set before my face the Lord
        Aumerle.                     [that man.
    *Boling.* Cousin, stand forth, and look upon
Bagot. My Lord Aumerle, I know your daring tongue
Scorns to unsay what once it hath deliver'd.
In that dead time when Gloster's death was plotted
I heard thee say,—*Is not my arm of length,
That reacheth from the restful English Court
As far as Calais, to my uncle's head?*
Amongst much other talk, that very time,
I heard you say that you had rather refuse
The offer of an hundred thousand crowns
Than Bolingbroke's return to England;
Adding withal, how blest this land would be
In this your cousin's death.
    *Aum.*                   Princes, and noble lords,
What answer shall I make to this base man?
Shall I so much dishonour my fair stars,
On equal terms to give him chastisement?
Either I must, or have mine honour soil'd
With the attainder of his slanderous lips.—
There is my gage, the manual seal of death,
That marks thee out for hell: I say, thou liest,
And will maintain what thou hast said is false
In thy heart-blood, though being all too base
To stain the temper of my knightly sword.
    *Boling.* Bagot, forbear; thou shalt not take
        it up.                            [best
    *Aum.* Excepting one, I would he were the
In all this presence that hath moved me so.
    *Fitz.* If that thy valour stand on sympathy,
There is my gage, Aumerle, in gage to thine:
By that fair sun that shows me where thou
        stand'st,                          [it,
I heard thee say, and vauntingly thou spak'st
That thou wert cause of noble Gloster's death.
If thou deny'st it twenty times, thou liest;
And I will turn thy falsehood to thy heart,
Where it was forged, with my rapier's point.
    *Aum.* Thou dar'st not, coward, live to see
        that day.                         [hour.
    *Fitz.* Now, by my soul, I would it were this
    *Aum.* Fitzwater, thou art damn'd to hell for
        this.                              [true
    *Percy.* Aumerle, thou liest; his honour is as

In this appeal as thou art all unjust;
And that thou art so, there I throw my gage,
To prove it on thee to the extremest point
Of mortal breathing: seize it, if thou dar'st.
    *Aum.* And if I do not, may my hands rot off,
And never brandish more revengeful steel
Over the glittering helmet of my foe!
    *Lord.* I task the earth to the like, forsworn
        Aumerle;
And spur thee on with full as many lies
As may be holla'd in thy treacherous ear
From sun to sun: there is my honour's pawn;
Engage it to the trial, if thou dar'st.
    *Aum.* Who sets me else? by heaven, I'll
        throw at all:
I have a thousand spirits in one breast,
To answer twenty thousand such as you. [well
    *Surrey.* My Lord Fitzwater, I do remember
The very time Aumerle and you did talk.
    *Fitz.* 'Tis very true: you were in presence
        then;
And you can witness with me this is true.
    *Surrey.* As false, by heaven, as heaven itself
        is true.
    *Fitz.* Surrey, thou liest.
    *Surrey.*                    Dishonourable boy!
That lie shall lie so heavy on my sword
That it shall render vengeance and revenge
Till thou the lie-giver and that lie do lie
In earth as quiet as thy father's skull:
In proof whereof, there is mine honour's pawn;
Engage it to the trial, if thou dar'st.   [horse!
    *Fitz.* How fondly dost thou spur a forward
If I dare eat, or drink, or breathe, or live
I dare meet Surrey in a wilderness,
And spit upon him, whilst I say he lies,
And lies, and lies: there is my bond of faith,
To tie thee to my strong correction.—
As I intend to thrive in this new world,
Aumerle is guilty of my true appeal:
Besides, I heard the banish'd Norfolk say
That thou, Aumerle, didst send two of thy men
To execute the noble duke at Calais.   [a gage,
    *Aum.* Some honest Christian trust me with
That Norfolk lies: here do I throw down this,
If he may be repeal'd, to try his honour. [gage
    *Boling.* These differences shall all rest under
Till Norfolk be repeal'd: repeal'd he shall be,
And, though mine enemy, restor'd again
To all his lands and signories: when he's return'd,
Against Aumerle we will enforce his trial.
    *Car.* That honourable day shall ne'er be
        seen.—
Many a time hath banish'd Norfolk fought
For Jesu Christ in glorious Christian field,
Streaming the ensign of the Christian cross
Against black pagans, Turks, and Saracens:
And toil'd with works of war, retir'd himself
To Italy; and there, at Venice, gave
His body to that pleasant country's earth,
And his pure soul unto his captain Christ,
Under whose colours he had fought so long.
    *Boling.* Why, bishop, is Norfolk dead?

*Car.* As surely as I live, my lord.

*Boling.* Sweet peace conduct his sweet soul
to the bosom
Of good old Abraham!—Lords appellants,
Your differences shall all rest under gage
Till we assign you to your days of trial.

*Enter* YORK, *attended.*

*York.* Great Duke of Lancaster, I come to
thee 　　　　　　　　　　　　　　[soul
From plume-pluck'd Richard; who with willing
Adopts thee heir, and his high sceptre yields
To the possession of thy royal hand:
Ascend his throne, descending now from him,—
And long live Henry, of that name the fourth!

*Boling.* In God's name, I'll ascend the regal
throne.

*Car.* Marry, God forbid!—
Worst in this royal presence may I speak,
Yet best beseeming me to speak the truth.
Would God that any in this noble presence
Were enough noble to be upright judge
Of noble Richard! then true nobless would
Learn him forbearance from so foul a wrong.
What subject can give sentence on his king?
And who sits here that is not Richard's subject?
Thieves are not judg'd but they are by to hear,
Although apparent guilt be seen in them;
And shall the figure of God's majesty,
His captain, steward, deputy elect,
Anointed, crowned, planted many years,
Be judg'd by subject and inferior breath,
And he himself not present? O, forfend it, God,
That, in a Christian climate, souls refin'd
Should show so heinous, black, obscene a deed!
I speak to subjects, and a subject speaks,
Stirr'd up by God, thus boldly for his king.
My Lord of Hereford here, whom you call king,
Is a foul traitor to proud Hereford's king;
And if you crown him, let me prophesy,—
The blood of English shall manure the ground,
And future ages groan for this foul act;
Peace shall go sleep with Turk and infidels,
And in this seat of peace tumultuous wars
Shall kin with kin and kind with kind confound;
Disorder, horror, fear, and mutiny,
Shall here inhabit, and this land be call'd
The field of Golgotha and dead men's skulls.
Or, if you raise this house against this house,
It will the woefullest division prove
That ever fell upon this cursed earth,
Prevent, resist it, let it not be so,
Lest child, child's children, cry against you woe!

*North.* Well have you argu'd, sir; and, for
your pains,
Of capital treason we arrest you here.—
My Lord of Westminster, be it your charge
To keep him safely till his day of trial.—
May't please you, lords, to grant the commons'
suit?

*Boling.* Fetch hither Richard, that in com-
mon view
He may surrender; so we shall proceed
Without suspicion.

*York.* 　　　　　　I will be his conduct. [*Exit.*

*Boling.* Lords, you that are here under our
arrest,
Procure your sureties for your days of answer.—
Little are we beholden to your love,
　　　　　　　　　　　　　　[*To* CARLISLE.
And little look'd for at your helping hands.

*Re-enter* YORK, *with* KING RICHARD, *and
Officers bearing the crown, &c.*

*K. Rich.* Alack, why am I sent for to a king,
Before I have shook off the regal thoughts
Wherewith I reign'd? I hardly yet have learn'd
To insinuate, flatter, bow, and bend my limbs:
Give sorrow leave awhile to tutor me
To this submission. Yet I well remember
The favours of these men: were they not mine?
Did they not sometime cry, All hail! to me?
So Judas did to Christ: but he, in twelve,
Found truth in all but one; I, in twelve thou-
sand, none.
God save the king!—Will no man say amen?
Am I both priest and clerk? well then, amen.
God save the king! although I be not he;
And yet, amen, if heaven do think him me.—
To do what service am I sent for hither?

*York.* To do that office of thine own good-
will
Which tired majesty did make thee offer,—
The resignation of thy state and crown
To Henry Bolingbroke.

*K. Rich.* Give me the crown.—Here, cousin,
seize the crown;
On this side my hand, and on that side yours.
Now is this golden crown like a deep well
That owes two buckets, filling one another;
The emptier ever dancing in the air,
The other down, unseen, and full of water:
That bucket down and full of tears am I,
Drinking my griefs, whilst you mount up on
high. 　　　　　　　　　　　　　[resign.

*Boling.* I thought you had been willing to

*K. Rich.* My crown I am; but still my griefs
are mine:
You may my glories and my state depose,
But not my griefs; still am I king of those.

*Boling.* Part of your cares you give me with
your crown.

*K. Rich.* Your cares set up do not pluck my
cares down.
My care is, loss of care, by old care done;
Your care is, gain of care, by new care won:
The cares I give, I have, though given away;
They tend the crown, yet still with me they
stay. 　　　　　　　　　　　　　[crown?

*Boling.* Are you contented to resign the

*K. Rich.* Ay, no;—no, ay; for I must noth-
ing be;
Therefore no no, for I resign to thee.
Now mark me, how I will undo myself:—
I give this heavy weight from off my head,
And this unwieldy sceptre from my hand,
The pride of kingly sway from out my heart;
With mine own tears I wash away my balm,

With mine own hands I give away my crown,
With mine own tongue deny my sacred state,
With mine own breath release all duty's rites:
All pomp and majesty I do forswear;
My manors, rents. revenues I forego;
My acts, decrees, and statutes I deny:
God pardon all oaths that are broke to me!
God keep all vows unbroke that swear to thee!
Make me, that nothing have, with nothing
    griev'd,
And thou with all pleas'd, that hast all achiev'd!
Long mayst thou live in Richard's seat to sit,
And soon lie Richard in an earthy pit!
God save King Henry, unking'd Richard says,
And send him many years of sunshine days!—
What more remains?

    *North.*        No more, but that you read
             [*Offering a paper.*
These accusations, and these grievous crimes
Committed by your person and your followers
Against the state and profit of this land;
That, by confessing them, the souls of men
May deem that you are worthily depos'd.

    *K. Rich.* Must I do so? and must I ravel out
My weav'd up follies? Gentle Northumberland,
If thy offences were upon record,
Would it not shame thee in so fair a troop
To read a lecture of them? If thou wouldst,
There shouldst thou find one heinous article,—
Containing the deposing of a king,
And cracking the strong warrant of an oath,—
Mark'd with a blot, damn'd in the book of
    heaven:—
Nay, all of you that stand and look upon,
Whilst that my wretchedness doth bait my-
    self,—
Though some of you, with Pilate, wash your
    hands,
Showing an outward pity; yet you Pilates
Have here deliver'd me to my sour cross,
And water cannot wash away your sin.

    *North.* My lord, despatch; read o'er these
    articles.             [see:
    *K. Rich.* Mine eyes are full of tears, I cannot
And yet salt water blinds them not so much
But they can see a sort of traitors here.
Nay, if I turn mine eyes upon myself,
I find myself a traitor with the rest;
For I have given here my soul's consent
To undeck the pompous body of a king;
Make glory base, and sovereignty a slave,
Proud majesty a subject, state a peasant.

    *North.* My lord,—        [sulting man,
    *K. Rich.* No lord of thine, thou haught in-
Nor no man's lord; I have no name, no title,—
No, not that name was given me at the font,—
But 'tis usurp'd:—alack the heavy day,
That I have worn so many winters out,
And know not now what name to call myself!
O that I were a mockery-king of snow,
Standing before the sun of Bolingbroke,
To melt myself away in water-drops!—
Good king,—great king,—and yet not greatly
    good,—

And if my word be sterling yet in England,
Let it command a mirror hither straight,
That it may show me what a face I have,
Since it is bankrupt of his majesty.

    *Boling.* Go some of you and fetch a looking-
    glass.            [*Exit an* Attendant.
    *North.* Read o'er this paper while the glass
    doth come.          [come to hell!
    *K. Rich.* Fiend, thou torment'st me ere I
    *Boling.* Urge it no more, my Lord Northum-
    berland,                [isfied.
    *North.* The commons will not, then, be sat-
    *K. Rich.* They shall be satisfied: I'll read
    enough,
When I do see the very book indeed
Where all my sins are writ, and that's myself.

*Re-enter* Attendant *with a glass.*

Give me the glass, and therein will I read.—
No deeper wrinkles yet? hath sorrow struck
So many blows upon this face of mine,
And made no deeper wounds?—O flattering
    glass,
Like to my followers in prosperity,
Thou dost beguile me! Was this face the face
That every day under his household roof
Did keep ten thousand men? Was this the face
That, like the sun, did make beholders wink?
Was this the face that fac'd so many follies,
And was at last out-fac'd by Bolingbroke?
A brittle glory shineth in this face:
As brittle as the glory is the face;
    [*Dashes the glass against the ground.*
For there it is, crack'd in a hundred shivers.—
Mark, silent king, the moral of this sport,—
How soon my sorrow hath destroy'd my face.

    *Boling.* The shadow of your sorrow hath
    destroy'd
The shadow of your face.

    *K. Rich.*            Say that again.
The shadow of my sorrow? Ha! let's see:—
'Tis very true, my grief lies all within;
And these external manners of laments
Are merely shadows to the unseen grief
That swells with silence in the tortur'd soul;
There lies the substance: and I thank thee,
    king,
For thy great bounty, that not only giv'st
Me cause to wail, but teachest me the way
How to lament the cause. I'll beg one boon,
And then be gone and trouble you no more.
Shall I obtain it?

    *Boling.*         Name it, fair cousin.
    *K. Rich.* Fair cousin! Why, I am greater
    than a king:
For when I was a king, my flatterers
Were then but subjects; being now a subject,
I have a king here to my flatterer.
Being so great, I have no need to beg.

    *Boling.* Yet ask.
    *K. Rich.* And shall I have?
    *Boling.* You shall.
    *K. Rich.* Then give me leave to go.
    *Boling.* Whither?

*K. Rich.* Whither you will, so I were from
　　your sights.　　　　　　　　　　[*Tower.*
*Boling.* Go, some of you convey him to the
*K. Rich.* O, good! Convey?—conveyers are
　　you all.
That rise thus nimbly by a true king's fall.
　　[*Exeunt* K. RICH., *some* Lords, *and a* Guard.
*Boling.* On Wednesday next we solemnly set
　　down
Our coronation: lords, prepare yourselves.
　　[*Exeunt all but the* ABBOT OF WESTMINSTER,
　　BISHOP OF CARLISLE, *and* AUMERLE.
*Abbot.* A woeful pageant have we here be-
　　held.
*Car.* The woe's to come; the children yet un-
　　born
Shall feel this day as sharp to them as thorn.
*Aum.* You holy clergymen, is there no plot
To rid the realm of this pernicious blot?
*Abbot.* Before I freely speak my mind herein,
You shall not only take the sacrament
To bury mine intents, but also to effect
Whatever I shall happen to devise.
I see your brows are full of discontent,
Your hearts of sorrow, and your eyes of tears:
Come home with me to supper; I will lay
A plot shall show us all a merry day.　[*Exeunt.*

## ACT V.

SCENE I.—LONDON. *A Street leading to the*
*Tower.*

*Enter* QUEEN *and* Ladies.

*Queen.* This way the king will come; this is
　　the way
To Julius Cæsar's ill-erected tower,
To whose flint bosom my condemnèd lord
Is doom'd a prisoner by proud Bolingbroke:
Here let us rest, if this rebellious earth
Have any resting for her true king's queen.—
But soft, but see, or rather do not see,
My fair rose wither: yet look up, behold,
That you in pity may dissolve to dew,
And wash him fresh again with true-love tears.

*Enter* KING RICHARD *and* Guards.

Ah, thou, the model where old Troy did stand;
Thou map of honour; thou King Richard's
　　tomb,
And not King Richard; thou most beauteous
　　inn,
Why should hard-favour'd grief be lodg'd in
　　thee,
When triumph is become an alehouse guest?
*K. Rich.* Join not with grief, fair woman, do
　　not so,
To make my end too sudden: learn, good soul,
To think our former state a happy dream;
From which awak'd, the truth of what we are
Shows us but this: I am sworn brother, sweet,
To grim Necessity; and he and I　　[France,
Will keep a league till death. Hie thee to
And cloister thee in some religious house:
Our holy lives must win a new world's crown,

Which our profane hours here have stricken
　　down.　　　　　　　　　[and mind
*Queen.* What, is my Richard both in shape
Transform'd and weaken'd? Hath Bolingbroke
Depos'd thine intellect? Hath he been in thy
　　heart?
The lion, dying, thrusteth forth his paw,
And wounds the earth, if nothing else, with rage
To be o'erpower'd; and wilt thou, pupil-like,
Take thy correction mildly; kiss the rod,
And fawn on rage with base humility,
Which art a lion and a king of beasts?
*K. Rich.* A king of beasts, indeed; if aught
　　but beasts,
I had been still a happy king of men.
Good sometime queen, prepare thee hence for
　　France:
Think I am dead; and that even here thou
　　tak'st,
As from my death-bed, my last living leave.
In winter's tedious nights sit by the fire
With good old folks, and let them tell thee tales
Of woeful ages long ago betid;
And ere thou bid good-night, to quit their grief
Tell thou the lamentable tale of me,
And send the hearers weeping to their beds:
For why, the senseless brands will sympathize
The heavy accent of thy moving tongue,
And in compassion weep the fire out;
And some will mourn in ashes, some coal-black,
For the deposing of a rightful king.

*Enter* NORTHUMBERLAND *attended.*

*North.* My lord, the mind of Bolingbroke is
　　chang'd;
You must to Pomfret, not unto the Tower.—
And, madam, there is order ta'en for you;
With all swift speed you must away to France.
*K. Rich.* Northumberland, thou ladder
　　wherewithal
The mounting Bolingbroke ascends my throne,
The time shall not be many hours of age
More than it is, ere foul sin, gathering head,
Shall break into corruption: thou shalt think,
Though he divide the realm, and give thee half,
It is too little, helping him to all;　[the way
And he shall think that thou, which know'st
To plant unrightful kings, wilt know again,
Being ne'er so little urg'd, another way
To pluck him headlong from the usurped
　　throne.
The love of wicked friends converts to fear;
That fear to hate; and hate turns one or both
To worthy danger and deserved death.
*North.* My guilt be on my head, and there
　　an end.　　　　　　　　　[with.
Take leave, and part; for you must part forth-
*K. Rich.* Doubly divorc'd!—Bad men, ye
　　violate
A twofold marriage,—'twixt my crown and me,
And then betwixt me and my married wife.—
Let me unkiss the oath 'twixt thee and me;
And yet not so, for with a kiss 'twas made.—
Part us, Northumberland; I towards the north,

Where shivering cold and sickness pines the
      clime;                                [pomp,
My wife to France, from whence, set forth in
She came adorned hither like sweet May,
Sent back like Hallowmas or short'st of day.
      *Queen.* And must we be divided? must we
            part?
      *K. Rich.* Ay, hand from hand, my love, and
            heart from heart.              [with me.
      *Queen.* Banish us both, and send the king
*North.* That were some love, but little policy.
      *Queen.* Then whither he goes thither let me
            go.                                 [woe.
      *K. Rich.* So two, together weeping, make one
Weep thou for me in France, I for thee here;
Better far off than near, be ne'er the near.
Go, count thy way with sighs; I, mine with
      groans.                               [moans.
      *Queen.* So longest way shall have the longest
      *K. Rich.* Twice for one step I'll groan, the
      way being short,
And piece the way out with a heavy heart.
Come, come, in wooing sorrow let's be brief,
Since, wedding it, there is such length in grief.
One kiss shall stop our mouths, and dumbly
      part;
Thus give I mine, and thus take I thy heart.
                                          [*They kiss.*
      *Queen.* Give me mine own again; 'twere no
      good part
To take on me to keep and kill thy heart.
                                          [*They kiss again.*
So, now I have mine own again, be gone,
That I may strive to kill it with a groan.
      *K. Rich.* We make woe wanton with this
      fond delay:
Once more, adieu; the rest let sorrow say.
                                          [*Exeunt.*

SCENE II.—*The same. A Room in the* DUKE OF
      YORK'S *Palace.*

      *Enter* YORK *and his* DUCHESS.

      *Duch.* My lord, you told me you would tell
      the rest,
When weeping made you break the story off
Of our two cousins coming into London.
      *York.* Where did I leave?
      *Duch.*                    At that sad stop, my lord,
Where rude misgovern'd hands from windows'
      tops                                  [head.
Threw dust and rubbish on King Richard's
      *York.* Then, as I said, the duke, great
      Bolingbroke,—
Mounted upon a hot and fiery steed,
Which his aspiring rider seem'd to know,—
With slow but stately pace kept on his course,
While all tongues cried, *God save thee, Boling-
broke!*
You would have thought the very windows
      spake,
So many greedy looks of young and old
Through casements darted their desiring eyes
Upon his visage; and that all the walls
With painted imagery had said at once,

*Jesu preserve thee! welcome, Bolingbroke!*
Whilst he, from one side to the other turning,
Bareheaded, lower than his proud steed's neck,
Bespake them this,—*I thank you, countrymen:*
And thus still doing, thus he pass'd along.
      *Duch.* Alas, poor Richard! where rode he
            the whilst?
      *York.* As in a theatre the eyes of men,
After a well-grac'd actor leaves the stage,
Are idly bent on him that enters next,
Thinking his prattle to be tedious;        [eyes
Even so, or with much more contempt, men's
Did scowl on Richard; no man cried, *God save
      him!*
No joyful tongue gave him his welcome home:
But dust was thrown upon his sacred head;
Which with such gentle sorrow he shook off,—
His face still combating with tears and smiles,
The badges of his grief and patience,—
That had not God, for some strong purpose,
      steel'd
The hearts of men, they must perforce have
      melted,
And barbarism itself have pitied him.
But heaven hath a hand in these events,
To whose high will we bound our calm contents.
To Bolingbroke are we sworn subjects now,
Whose state and honour I for aye allow.
      *Duch.* Here comes my son Aumerle.
      *York.*                             Aumerle that was;
But that is lost for being Richard's friend,
And, madam, you must call him Rutland now:
I am in Parliament pledge for his truth
And lasting fealty to the new-made king.

      *Enter* AUMERLE.

      *Duch.* Welcome, my son: who are the violets
      now
That strew the green lap of the new-come
      spring?
      *Aum.* Madam, I know not, nor I greatly
      care not:
God knows I had as lief be none as one.
      *York.* Well, bear you well in this new spring
      of time,
Lest you be cropp'd before you come to prime.
What news from Oxford? hold those justs and
      triumphs?
      *Aum.* For aught I know, my lord, they do.
      *York.* You will be there, I know.
      *Aum.* If God prevent it not, I purpose so.
      *York.* What seal is that that hangs without
      thy bosom?
Yea, look'st thou pale? let me see the writing.
      *Aum.* My lord, 'tis nothing.
      *York.*            No matter, then, who sees it.
I will be satisfied; let me see the writing.
      *Aum.* I do beseech your grace to pardon me:
It is a matter of small consequence,
Which for some reasons I would not have seen.
      *York.* Which for some reasons, sir, I mean
      to see.
I fear, I fear,—
      *Duch.*            What should you fear?

'Tis nothing but some bond that he is enter'd into
For gay apparel against the triumph-day.
  *York.*  Bound to himself! what doth he with a bond
That he is bound to? Wife, thou art a fool.—
Boy, let me see the writing.
  *Aum.*  I do beseech you, pardon me; I may not show it.
  *York.*  I will be satisfied; let me see it, I say.
                    [*Snatches it, and reads.*
Treason! foul treason!—villain! traitor! slave!
  *Duch.*  What's the matter, my lord?
  *York.*  Ho! who's within there?

                *Enter a Servant.*
                    Saddle my horse.
God for his mercy, what treachery is here!
  *Duch.*  Why, what is 't, my lord?
  *York.*  Give me my boots, I say; saddle my horse.—
Now, by mine honour, by my life, my troth,
I will appeach the villain.      [*Exit* Servant.
  *Duch.*                    What's the matter?
  *York.*  Peace, foolish woman.
  *Duch.*  I will not peace.—What is the matter, son?
  *Aum.*  Good mother, be content; it is no more
Than my poor life must answer.
  *Duch.*                    Thy life answer!
  *York.*  Bring me my boots:—I will unto the king.

            *Re-enter* Servant *with boots.*

  *Duch.*  Strike him, Aumerle.—Poor boy, thou art amaz'd.
Hence, villain! never more come in my sight.
                    [*To the* Servant.
  *York.*  Give me my boots, I say.
  *Duch.*  Why, York, what wilt thou do?
Wilt thou not hide the trespass of thine own?
Have we more sons? or are we like to have?
Is not my teeming date drunk up with time?
And wilt thou pluck my fair son from mine age,
And rob me of a happy mother's name?
Is he not like thee? is he not thine own?
  *York.*  Thou fond mad woman,
Wilt thou conceal this dark conspiracy?
A dozen of them here have ta'en the sacrament
And interchangeably set down their hands
To kill the king at Oxford.
  *Duch.*                    He shall be none;
We'll keep him here: then what is that to him?
  *York.*  Away, fond woman! were he twenty times my son
I would appeach him.
  *Duch.*          Hadst thou groan'd for him
As I have done, thou wouldst be more pitiful.
But now I know thy mind; thou dost suspect
That I have been disloyal to thy bed,
And that he is a bastard, not thy son:
Sweet York, sweet husband, be not of that mind:
He is as like thee as a man may be,

Not like to me, nor any of my kin,
And yet I love him.
  *York.*              Make way, unruly woman!
                    [*Exit.*
  *Duch.*  After, Aumerle! mount thee upon his horse;
Spur post, and get before him to the king,
And beg thy pardon ere he do accuse thee.
I'll not be long behind; though I be old,
I doubt not but to ride as fast as York;
And never will I rise up from the ground
Till Bolingbroke have pardon'd thee. Away, be gone!                    [*Exeunt.*

SCENE III.—WINDSOR. *A Room in the Castle.*

        *Enter* BOLINGBROKE *as King,* PERCY, *and other* Lords.

  *Boling.*  Can no man tell of my unthrifty son?
'Tis full three months since I did see him last:—
If any plague hang over us, 'tis he.
I would to God, my lords, he might be found:
Inquire at London, 'mongst the taverns there,
For there, they say, he daily doth frequent,
With unrestrained loose companions,—
Even such, they say, as stand in narrow lanes,
And beat our watch, and rob our passengers;
While he, young, wanton, and effeminate boy,
Takes on the point of honour to support
So dissolute a crew.
  *Percy.*  My lord, some two days since I saw the prince,
And told him of these triumphs held at Oxford.
  *Boling.*  And what said the gallant?
  *Percy.*  His answer was,—he would unto the stews,
And from the common'st creature pluck a glove,
And wear it as a favour; and with that
He would unhorse the lustiest challenger.
  *Boling.*  As dissolute as desperate: yet through both
I see some sparkles of a better hope,
Which elder days may happily bring forth.—
But who comes here?

            *Enter* AUMERLE *hastily.*

  *Aum.*              Where is the king?
  *Boling.*                    What means
Our cousin, that he stares and looks so wildly?
  *Aum.*  God save your grace! I do beseech your majesty,
To have some conference with your grace alone.
  *Boling.*  Withdraw yourselves, and leave us here alone.
                    [*Exeunt* PERCY *and* Lords.
What is the matter with our cousin now?
  *Aum.*  For ever may my knees grow to the earth,                    [*Kneels.*
My tongue cleave to my roof within my mouth,
Unless a pardon ere I rise or speak.
  *Boling.*  Intended or committed was this fault?
If but the first, how heinous e'er it be,
To win thy after-love I pardon thee.

*Aum.* Then give me leave that I may turn the key,
That no man enter till my tale be done.
*Boling.* Have thy desire.
           [AUMERLE *locks the door.*
*York.* [*Within.*] My liege, beware; look to thyself;
Thou hast a traitor in thy presence there.
*Boling.* Villain, I'll make thee safe. /
           [*Drawing.*
*Aum.* Stay thy revengeful hand;
Thou hast no cause to fear.
*York.* [*Within.*] Open the door, secure, foolhardy king:
Shall I, for love, speak treason to thy face?
Open the door, or I will break it open.
    [BOLING. *opens the door and locks it again.*

#### Enter YORK.

*Boling.* What is the matter, uncle? speak;
Recover breath; tell us how near is danger,
That we may arm us to encounter it.
*York.* Peruse this writing here, and thou shalt know
The treason that my haste forbids me show.
*Aum.* Remember, as thou read'st, thy promise pass'd:
I do repent me; read not my name there;
My heart is not confederate with my hand.
*York.* It was, villain, ere thy hand did set it down.—
I tore it from the traitor's bosom, king;
Fear, and not love, begets his penitence:
Forget to pity him, lest thy pity prove
A serpent that will sting thee to the heart.
*Boling.* O heinous, strong, and bold conspiracy!—
O loyal father of a treacherous son!
Thou sheer, immaculate, and silver fountain,
From whence this stream through muddy passages
Hath held his current and defil'd himself!
Thy overflow of good converts to bad;
And thy abundant goodness shall excuse
This deadly blot in thy digressing son.
*York.* So shall my virtue be his vice's bawd;
And he shall spend mine honour with his shame,
As thriftless sons their scraping fathers' gold.
Mine honour lives when his dishonour dies,
Or my sham'd life in his dishonour lies:
Thou kill'st me in his life; giving him breath,
The traitor lives, the true man's put to death.
*Duch.* [*Within.*] What ho, my liege! for God's sake, let me in.
*Boling.* What shrill-voic'd suppliant makes this eager cry?
*Duch.* A woman, and thine aunt, great king; 'tis I.
Speak with me, pity me, open the door:
A beggar begs that never begg'd before.
*Boling.* Our scene is alter'd from a serious thing,
And now chang'd to *The Beggar and the King.*—

My dangerous cousin, let your mother in:
I know she's come to pray for your foul sin.
           [AUMERLE *unlocks the door.*
*York.* If thou do pardon, whosoever pray,
More sins, for this forgiveness, prosper may.
This fester'd joint cut off, the rest rests sound:
This let alone will all the rest confound.

#### Enter DUCHESS.

*Duch.* O king, believe not this hard-hearted man!
Love, loving not itself, none other can.
*York.* Thou frantic woman, what dost thou make here?
Shall thy old dugs once more a traitor rear?
*Duch.* Sweet York, be patient.—Hear me, gentle liege.     [*Kneels.*
*Boling.* Rise up, good aunt.
*Duch.*          Not yet, I thee beseech:
For ever will I walk upon my knees,
And never see day that the happy sees
Till thou give joy; until thou bid me joy,
By pardoning Rutland, my transgressing boy.
*Aum.* Unto my mother's prayers I bend my knee.     [*Kneels.*
*York.* Against them both, my true joints bended be.     [*Kneels.*
Ill mayst thou thrive, if thou grant any grace!
*Duch.* Pleads he in earnest? look upon his face;
His eyes do drop no tears, his prayers are in jest;
His words come from his mouth, ours from our breast:
He prays but faintly, and would be denied;
We pray with heart and soul, and all beside:
His weary joints would gladly rise, I know;
Our knees shall kneel till to the ground they grow:
His prayers are full of false hypocrisy;
Ours of true zeal and deep integrity.
Our prayers do out-pray his; then let them have
That mercy which true prayers ought to have.
*Boling.* Good aunt, stand up.
*Duch.*          Nay, do not say *stand up;*
But *pardon* first, and afterwards *stand up.*
An if I were thy nurse, thy tongue to teach,
*Pardon* should be the first word of thy speech.
I never long'd to hear a word till now;
Say *pardon*, king; let pity teach thee how:
The word is short, but not so short as sweet;
No word like *pardon*, for kings' mouths so meet.
*York.* Speak it in French, king; say *pardonnez-moi.*
*Duch.* Dost thou teach pardon pardon to destroy?
Ah, my sour husband, my hard-hearted lord,
That sett'st the word itself against the word!—
Speak *pardon* as 'tis current in our land;
The chopping French we do not understand.
Thine eye begins to speak, set thy tongue there:
Or in thy piteous heart plant thou thine ear;
That hearing how our plaints and prayers do pierce,

Pity may move thee *pardon* to rehearse.
*Boling.* Good aunt, stand up.
*Duch.*　　　　　　I do not sue to stand;
Pardon is all the suit I have in hand.
*Boling.* I pardon him, as God shall pardon
me.
*Duch.* O happy vantage of a kneeling knee!
Yet am I sick for fear: speak it again;
Twice saying *pardon* doth not pardon twain,
But makes one pardon strong.
*Boling.*　　　　　　With all my heart
I pardon him.
*Duch.*　　　A god on earth thou art.
*Boling.* But for our trusty brother-in-law,
and the abbot,
With all the rest of that consorted crew,
Destruction straight shall dog them at the
heels.
Good uncle, help to order several powers
To Oxford, or where'er these traitors are:
They shall not live within this world, I swear,
But I will have them, if I once know where.
Uncle, farewell:—and, cousin mine, adieu:
Your mother well hath pray'd, and prove you
true.
*Duch.* Come, my old son:—I pray God make
thee new.　　　　　　　　[*Exeunt.*

SCENE IV.—*Another Room in the Castle.*

*Enter* SIR PIERCE OF EXTON *and a* Servant.

*Exton.* Didst thou not mark the king, what
words he spake?—
*Have I no friend will rid me of this living fear?*
Was it not so?
*Serv.*　　　　Those were his very words.
*Exton.* Have I *no friend?* quoth he: he spake
it twice,
And urg'd it twice together,—did he not?
*Serv.* He did.
*Exton.* And, speaking it, he wistly look'd on
me,
As who should say,—I would thou wert the man
That would divorce this terror from my heart,—
Meaning the king at Pomfret. Come, let's go:
I am the king's friend, and will rid his foe.
　　　　　　　　　　　　[*Exeunt.*

SCENE V.—POMFRET. *The Dungeon of the
Castle.*

*Enter* KING RICHARD.

*K. Rich.* I have been studying how I may
compare
This prison where I live unto the world:
And, for because the world is populous,
And here is not a creature but myself,
I cannot do it;—yet I'll hammer't out.
My brain I'll prove the female to my soul,
My soul the father: and these two beget
A generation of still-breeding thoughts,
And these same thoughts people this little
world,
In humours like the people of this world,
For no thought is contented. The better sort,—
As thoughts of things divine,—are intermix'd

With scruples, and do set the word itself
Against the word:
As thus,—*Come, little ones;* and then again,—
*It is as hard to come as for a camel*
*To thread the postern of a needle's eye.*
Thoughts tending to ambition, they do plot
Unlikely wonders: how these vain weak nails
May tear a passage through the flinty ribs
Of this hard world, my ragged prison walls;
And, for they cannot, die in their own pride.
Thoughts tending to content flatter themselves
That they are not the first of fortune's slaves,
Nor shall not be the last; like silly beggars,
Who, sitting in the stocks, refuge their shame,
That many have, and others must sit there;
And in this thought they find a kind of ease,
Bearing their own misfortune on the back
Of such as have before endur'd the like.
Thus play I, in one person, many people,
And none contented: sometimes am I king;
Then treason makes me wish myself a beggar,
And so I am: then crushing penury
Persuades me I was better when a king;
Then am I king'd again: and by and by
Think that I am unking'd by Bolingbroke,
And straight am nothing:—but whate'er I am,
Nor I, nor any man that but man is,
With nothing shall be pleas'd till he be eas'd
With being nothing.—Music do I hear?
　　　　　　　　　　　　　　[*Music.*
Ha, ha! keep time:—how sour sweet music is
When time is broke and no proportion kept!
So is it in the music of men's lives.
And here have I the daintiness of ear
To check time broke in a disorder'd string;
But, for the concord of my state and time,
Had not an ear to hear my true time broke.
I wasted time, and now doth time waste me;
For now hath time made me his numbering
clock:
My thoughts are minutes; and, with sighs, they
jar
Their watches on unto mine eyes, the outward
watch,
Whereto my finger, like a dial's point,
Is pointing still, in cleansing them from tears.
Now, sir, the sound that tells what hour it is,
Are clamorous groans that strike upon my
heart,
Which is the bell: so sighs, and tears, and
groans,
Show minutes, times, and hours:—but my time
Runs posting on in Bolingbroke's proud joy,
While I stand fooling here, his Jack o' the clock.
This music mads me; let it sound no more;
For though it have holp madmen to their wits,
In me it seems it will make wise men mad.
Yet blessing on his heart that gives it me!
For 'tis a sign of love; and love to Richard
Is a strange brooch in this all-hating world.

*Enter* Groom.

*Groom.* Hail, royal prince!
*K. Rich.*　　　　　　Thanks, noble peer;

The cheapest of us is ten groats too dear.
What art thou? and how com'st thou hither,
Where no man ever comes, but that sad dog
That brings me food to make misfortune live?
  *Groom.* I was a poor groom of thy stable,
    king,
When thou wert king; who, travelling towards
    York,
With much ado at length have gotten leave
To look upon my sometimes royal master's
    face.
O, how it yearn'd my heart, when I beheld,
In London streets, that coronation-day,
When Bolingbroke rode on roan Barbary,—
That horse that thou so often hast bestrid,
That horse that I so carefully have dress'd!
  *K. Rich.* Rode he on Barbary? Tell me,
    gentle friend,
How went he under him?      [ground.
  *Groom.* So proudly as if he disdain'd the
  *K. Rich.* So proud that Bolingbroke was on
    his back!
That jade hath eat bread from my royal hand;
This hand hath made him proud with clapping
    him.
Would he not stumble? would he not fall
    down,—      [neck
Since pride must have a fall,—and break the
Of that proud man that did usurp his back?
Forgiveness, horse! why do I rail on thee,
Since thou, created to be aw'd by man,
Wast born to bear? I was not made a horse;
And yet I bear a burden like an ass,
Spur-gall'd and tir'd by jauncing Bolingbroke.

      *Enter* Keeper *with a dish.*

  *Keep.* Fellow, give place; here is no longer
    stay.      [*To the* Groom.
  *K. Rich.* If thou love me, 'tis time thou wert
    away.
  *Groom.* What my tongue dares not, that my
    heart shall say.      [*Exit.*
  *Keep.* My lord, wilt please you to fall to?
  *K. Rich.* Taste of it first as thou art wont to
    do.
  *Keep.* My lord, I dare not. Sir Pierce of Ex-
    ton,
Who lately came from the king, commands the
    contrary.
  *K. Rich.* The devil take Henry of Lancaster
    and thee!
Patience is stale, and I am weary of it.
      [*Beats the* Keeper.
  *Keep.* Help, help, help!

    *Enter* EXTON *and* Servants, *armed.*

  *K. Rich.* How now! what means death in
    this rude assault?
Villain, thine own hand yields thy death's in-
    strument.
      [*Snatching a weapon, and killing one.*
Go thou, and fill another room in hell.
      [*He kills another, then* EXTON *strikes
      him down.*

That hand shall burn in never-quenching fire
That staggers thus my person.—Exton, thy
    fierce hand
Hath with the king's blood stain'd the king's
    own land.
Mount, mount, my soul! thy seat is up on high;
Whilst my gross flesh sinks downward, here to
    die.      [*Dies.*
  *Exton.* As full of valour as of royal blood:
Both have I split;—O, would the deed were
    good!
For now the devil, that told me I did well,
Says that this deed is chronicled in hell.
This dead king to the living king I'll bear:—
Take hence the rest, and give them burial here.
      [*Exeunt.*

SCENE VI.—WINDSOR. *A Room in the Castle.*

    *Flourish. Enter* BOLINGBROKE *as King,*
      YORK, LORDS, *and* Attendants.

  *Boling.* Kind uncle York, the latest news we
    hear
Is that the rebels have consum'd with fire
Our town of Cicester in Glostershire;
But whether they be ta'en or slain we hear not.

      *Enter* NORTHUMBERLAND.

Welcome, my lord: what is the news?
  *North.* First, to thy sacred state wish I all
    happiness.
The next news is, I have to London sent
The heads of Salisbury, Spencer, Blunt, and
    Kent:
The manner of their taking may appear
At large discoursed in this paper here.
      [*Presenting a paper.*
  *Boling.* We thank thee, gentle Percy, for thy
    pains;
And to thy worth will add right worthy gains.

      *Enter* FITZWATER.

  *Fitz.* My lord, I have from Oxford sent to
    London
The heads of Brocas and Sir Bennet Seely;
Two of the dangerous consorted traitors
That sought at Oxford thy dire overthrow.
  *Boling.* Thy pains, Fitzwater, shall not be
    forgot;
Right noble is thy merit, well I wot.

    *Enter* PERCY, *with the* BISHOP OF CARLISLE.

  *Percy.* The grand conspirator, Abbot of
    Westminster,
With clog of conscience and sour melancholy,
Hath yielded up his body to the grave;
But here is Carlisle living, to abide
Thy kingly doom and sentence of his pride.
  *Boling.* Carlisle, this is your doom:—
Choose out some secret place, some reverend
    room,
More than thou hast, and with it joy thy life;
So, as thou liv'st in peace, die free from strife:
For though mine enemy thou hast ever been,
High sparks of honour in thee have I seen.

*Enter* EXTON, *with* Attendants, *bearing a coffin.*
  *Exton.* Great king, within this coffin I pre-
    sent
Thy buried fear: herein all breathless lies
The mightiest of thy greatest enemies,
Richard of Bordeaux, by me hither brought.
  *Boling.* Exton, I thank thee not; for thou
    hast wrought
A deed of slander, with thy fatal hand,
Upon my head and all this famous land.
  *Exton.* From your own mouth, my lord, did
    I this deed.                                   [need,
  *Boling.* They love not poison that do poison
Nor do I thee: though I did wish him dead,
I hate the murderer, love him murdered.

The guilt of conscience take thou for thy la-
  bour,
But neither my good word nor princely favour:
With Cain go wander through the shade of
  night,
And never show thy head by day nor light.—
Lords, I protest, my soul is full of woe,
That blood should sprinkle -me to make me
  grow:
Come, mourn with me for that I do lament.
And put on sullen black incontinent:
I'll make a voyage to the Holy Land,
To wash this blood off from my guilty hand:—
March sadly after; grace my mournings here,
In weeping after this untimely bier.     [*Exeunt.*

King
HENRY the FOURTH.
Part I.

Act II. Sc. 4.

# KING HENRY IV.

## FIRST PART

### DRAMATIS PERSONÆ

KING HENRY THE FOURTH.
HENRY, *Prince of Wales,* } *Sons to the*
PRINCE JOHN *of Lancaster,* } KING.
EARL OF WESTMORELAND, } *Friends to the*
SIR WALTER BLUNT, } KING.
THOMAS PERCY, *Earl of Worcester.*
HENRY PERCY, *Earl of Northumberland.*
HENRY PERCY, *surnamed* HOTSPUR, *his Son.*
EDMUND MORTIMER, *Earl of March.*
SCROOP, *Archbishop of York.*
SIR MICHAEL, *a Friend to the Archbishop.*
ARCHIBALD, *Earl of Douglas.*
OWEN GLENDOWER.
SIR RICHARD VERNON.
SIR JOHN FALSTAFF.

POINS.
GADSHILL.
PETO.
BARDOLPH.

LADY PERCY, *Wife to* HOTSPUR, *and Sister to* MORTIMER.
LADY MORTIMER, *Daughter to* GLENDOWER, *and Wife to* MORTIMER.
MRS. QUICKLY, *Hostess of a Tavern in East-cheap.*

Lords, Officers, Sheriff, Vintner, Chamberlain, Drawers, Two Carriers, Travellers, *and* Attendants.

SCENE,—ENGLAND.

## ACT I.

SCENE I.—LONDON. *A Room in the Palace.*

*Enter* KING HENRY, WESTMORELAND, SIR WALTER BLUNT, *and others.*

*K. Hen.* So shaken as we are, so wan with care,
Find we a time for frighted peace to pant,
And breathe short-winded accents of new broils
To be commenc'd in strands afar remote.
No more the thirsty entrance of this soil
Shall daub her lips with her own children's blood;
No more shall trenching war channel her fields,
Nor bruise her flowerets with the armed hoofs
Of hostile paces: those opposed eyes
Which, like the meteors of a troubled heaven,
All of one nature, of one substance bred,
Did lately meet in the intestine shock
And furious close of civil butchery,
Shall now, in mutual well-beseeming ranks,
March all one way, and be no more oppos'd
Against acquaintance, kindred, and allies:
The edge of war, like an ill-sheathed knife,
No more shall cut his master. Therefore, friends,
As far as to the sepulchre of Christ,—
Whose soldier now, under whose blessed cross
We are impressed and engag'd to fight,—
Forthwith a power of English shall we levy;
Whose arms were moulded in their mothers' womb
To chase these pagans in those holy fields
Over whose acres walk'd those blessed feet
Which fourteen hundred years ago were nail'd
For our advantage on the bitter cross.

But this our purpose is a twelvemonth old,
And bootless 'tis to tell you we will go:
Therefore we meet not now.—Then let me hear
Of you, my gentle cousin Westmoreland,
What yesternight our council did decree
In forwarding this dear expedience.

*West.* My liege, this haste was hot in question,
And many limits of the charge set down
But yesternight: when, all athwart, there came
A post from Wales loaden with heavy news;
Whose worst was,—that the noble Mortimer
Leading the men of Herefordshire to fight
Against the irregular and wild Glendower,
Was by the rude hands of that Welshman taken,
A thousand of his people butchered;
Upon whose dead corpse there was such misuse,
Such beastly, shameless transformation,
By those Welshwomen done, as may not be
Without much shame re-told or spoken of.

*K. Hen.* It seems, then, that the tidings of this broil
Brake off our business for the Holy Land.

*West.* This, match'd with other, did, my gracious Lord;
For more uneven and unwelcome news
Came from the north, and thus it did import:
On Holy-rood day, the gallant Hotspur there,
Young Harry Percy, and brave Archibald,
That ever valiant and approved Scot,
At Holmedon met,
Where they did spend a sad and bloody hour;
As by discharge of their artillery,
And shape of likelihood, the news was told;
For he that brought them, in the very heat

And pride of their contention did take horse,
Uncertain of the issue any way.        [friend,
        K. Hen.    Here is a dear and true-industrious
Sir Walter Blunt, new lighted from his horse,
Stain'd with the variation of each soil
Betwixt that Holmedon and this seat of ours;
And he hath brought us smooth and welcome
        news.
The Earl of Douglas is discomfited:
Ten thousand bold Scots, two-and-twenty
        knights,
Balk'd in their own blood, did Sir Walter see
On Holmedon's plains: of prisoners, Hotspur
        took
Mordake, Earl of Fife and eldest son
To beaten Douglas; and the Earls of Athol,
Of Murray, Angus, and Menteith.
And is not this an honourable spoil?
A gallant prize? ha, cousin, is it not?
        West.                                In faith,
It is a conquest for a prince to boast of.
        K. Hen.    Yea, there thou mak'st me sad, and
        mak'st me sin,
In envy that my Lord Northumberland
Should be the father to so blest a son,—
A son who is the theme of honour's tongue;
Amongst a grove, the very straightest plant;
Who is sweet fortune's minion and her pride:
Whilst I, by looking on the praise of him,
See riot and dishonour stain the brow
Of my young Harry. O that it could be prov'd
That some night-tripping fairy had exchang'd
In cradle-clothes our children where they lay,
And call'd mine Percy, his Plantagenet!
Then would I have his Harry, and he mine:
But let him from my thoughts.—What think
you, coz,
Of this young Percy's pride? The prisoners,
Which he in this adventure hath surpris'd,
To his own use he keeps; and sends me word,
I shall have none but Mordake Earl of Fife.
        West.    This is his uncle's teaching, this is
        Worcester,
Malevolent to you in all aspects;
Which makes him prune himself, and bristle up
The crest of youth against your dignity.
        K. Hen.    But I have sent for him to answer
        this;
And for this cause awhile we must neglect
Our holy purpose to Jerusalem.
Cousin, on Wednesday next our council we
Will hold at Windsor,—so inform the lords:
But come yourself with speed to us again;
For more is to be said and to be done
Than out of anger can be uttered.
        West.    I will, my liege.            [Exeunt.

SCENE II.—The same. Another Room in the
        Palace.

Enter PRINCE HENRY and FALSTAFF.

        Fal.    Now, Hal, what time of day is it, lad?
        P. Hen.    Thou art so fat-witted, with drink-
ing of old sack, and unbuttoning thee after supper, and sleeping upon benches after noon, that
thou hast forgotten to demand that truly which
thou wouldst truly know. What a devil hast
thou to do with the time of the day? unless
hours were cups of sack, and minutes capons,
and cocks the tongues of bawds, and dials the
signs of leaping houses, and the blessed sun
himself a fair hot wench in flame-coloured taffeta,—I see no reason why thou shouldst be so
superfluous to demand the time of the day.
        Fal.    Indeed, you come near me now, Hal;
for we that take purses go by the moon and the
seven stars, and not by Phœbus,—he, that wandering knight so fair. And, I pr'ythee, sweet
wag, when thou art king,—as, God save thy
grace, (majesty, I should say; for grace thou
wilt have none,)—
        P. Hen.    What, none?
        Fal.    No, by my troth; not so much as will
serve to be prologue to an egg and butter.
        P. Hen.    Well, how then? come, roundly,
roundly.
        Fal.    Marry, then, sweet wag, when thou art
king, let not us that are squires of the night's
body be called thieves of the day's beauty: let
us be Diana's foresters, gentlemen of the shade,
minions of the moon; and let men say we be
men of good government, being governed, as
the sea is, by our noble and chaste mistress the
moon, under whose countenance we steal.
        P. Hen.    Thou sayest well, and it holds well
too; for the fortune of us that are the moon's
men doth ebb and flow like the sea, being governed, as the sea is, by the moon. As, for proof,
now: a purse of gold most resolutely snatched
on Monday night, and most dissolutely spent
on Tuesday morning; got with swearing lay by,
and spent with crying bring in; now in as low
an ebb as the foot of the ladder, and by and by
in as high a flow as the ridge of the gallows.
        Fal.    By the Lord, thou sayest true, lad. And
is not my hostess of the tavern a most sweet
wench?
        P. Hen.    As the honey of Hybla, my old lad
of the castle. And is not a buff jerkin a most
sweet robe of durance?
        Fal.    How now, how now, mad wag! what,
in thy quips and thy quiddities? what a plague
have I to do with a buff jerkin?
        P. Hen.    Why, what a pox have I to do with
my hostess of the tavern?
        Fal.    Well, thou hast called her to a reckon-
ing many a time and oft.
        P. Hen.    Did I ever call for thee to pay thy
part?
        Fal.    No; I'll give thee thy due, thou hast
paid all there.
        P. Hen.    Yea, and elsewhere, so far as my
coin would stretch; and where it would not, I
have used my credit.
        Fal.    Yea, and so used it that, were it not
here apparent that thou art heir-apparent,—
but, I pr'ythee, sweet wag, shall there be gallows standing in England when thou art king?
and resolution thus fobbed as it is with the

rusty curb of old father antic the law? Do not thou, when thou art king, hang a thief.

*P. Hen.* No; thou shalt.

*Fal.* Shall I? O rare! By the Lord, I'll be a brave judge.

*P. Hen.* Thou judgest false already: I mean, thou shalt have the hanging of the thieves, and so become a rare hangman.

*Fal.* Well, Hal, well; and in some sort it jumps with my humour as well as waiting in the court, I can tell you.

*P. Hen.* For obtaining of suits?

*Fal.* Yea, for obtaining of suits, whereof the hangman hath no lean wardrobe. 'Sblood, I am as melancholy as a gib-cat or a lugged bear.

*P. Hen.* Or an old lion, or a lover's lute.

*Fal.* Yea, or the drone of a Lincolnshire bagpipe.

*P. Hen.* What sayest thou to a hare, or the melancholy of Moor-ditch?

*Fal.* Thou hast the most unsavoury similes, and art, indeed, the most comparative, rascallest,—sweet young prince,—but, Hal, I pr'ythee, trouble me no more with vanity. I would to God thou and I knew where a commodity of good names were to be bought. An old lord of the council rated me the other day in the street about you, sir,—but I marked him not; and yet he talked very wisely,—but I regarded him not; and yet he talked wisely, and in the street too.

*P. Hen.* Thou didst well; for wisdom cries out in the streets, and no man regards it.

*Fal.* O, thou hast damnable iteration, and art, indeed, able to corrupt a saint. Thou hast done much harm upon me, Hal,—God forgive thee for it! Before I knew thee, Hal, I knew nothing; and now am I, if a man should speak truly, little better than one of the wicked. I must give over this life, and I will give it over; by the Lord, an I do not, I am a villain: I'll be damned for never a king's son in Christendom.

*P. Hen.* Where shall we take a purse tomorrow, Jack?

*Fal.* Where thou wilt, lad; I'll make one; an I do not, call me villain, and baffle me.

*P. Hen.* I see a good amendment of life in thee,—from praying to purse-taking.

*Enter* POINS *at a distance.*

*Fal.* Why, Hal, 'tis my vocation, Hal; 'tis no sin for a man to labour in his vocation.—Poins!—Now shall we know if Gadshill have set a match.—O, if men were to be saved by merit, what hole in hell were hot enough for him? This is the most omnipotent villain that ever cried *stand* to a true man.

*P. Hen.* Good-morrow, Ned.

*Poins.* Good-morrow, sweet Hal.—What says Monsieur Remorse? What says Sir John Sack-and-sugar? Jack, how agrees the devil and thee about thy soul, that thou soldest him on Good-Friday last for a cup of Madeira and a cold capon's leg?

*P. Hen.* Sir John stands to his word,—the devil shall have his bargain; for he was never yet a breaker of proverbs,—he will give the devil his due.

*Poins.* Then art thou damned for keeping thy word with the devil.

*P. Hen.* Else he had been damned for cozening the devil.

*Poins.* But, my lads, my lads, to-morrow morning, by four o'clock, early at Gadshill! there are pilgrims going to Canterbury with rich offerings, and traders riding to London with fat purses: I have visards for you all; you have horses for yourselves: Gadshill lies tonight in Rochester: I have bespoke supper tomorrow night in Eastcheap: we may do it as secure as sleep. If you will go, I will stuff your purses full of crowns; if you will not, tarry at home and be hanged.

*Fal.* Hear ye, Yedward; if I tarry at home and go not, I'll hang you for going.

*Poins.* You will, chops?

*Fal.* Hal, wilt thou make one?

*P. Hen.* Who, I rob? I a thief? not I, by my faith.

*Fal.* There's neither honesty, manhood, nor good fellowship in thee, nor thou camest not of the blood royal, if thou darest not stand for ten shillings.

*P. Hen.* Well, then, once in my days I'll be a madcap.

*Fal.* Why, that's well said.          [home.

*P. Hen.* Well, come what will, I'll tarry at

*Fal.* By the Lord, I'll be a traitor, then, when thou art king.

*P. Hen.* I care not.

*Poins.* Sir John, I pr'ythee, leave the prince and me alone: I will lay him down such reasons for this adventure that he shall go.

*Fal.* Well, God give thee the spirit of persuasion, and him the ears of profiting, that what thou speakest may move, and what he hears may be believed, that the true prince may, for recreation sake, prove a false thief; for the poor abuses of the time want countenance. Farewell: you shall find me in Eastcheap.

*P. Hen.* Farewell, thou latter spring! Farewell, All-hallown summer!          [*Exit* FALSTAFF.

*Poins.* Now, my good sweet honey-lord, ride with us to-morrow: I have a jest to execute that I cannot manage alone. Falstaff, Bardolph, Peto, and Gadshill, shall rob those men that we have already waylaid; yourself and I will not be there; and when they have the booty, if you and I do not rob them, cut this head from my shoulders.

*P. Hen.* But how shall we part with them in setting forth?

*Poins.* Why, we will set forth before or after them, and appoint them a place of meeting, wherein it is at our pleasure to fail; and then will they adventure upon the exploit themselves; which they shall have no sooner achieved, but we'll set upon them.

*P. Hen.* Ay, but 'tis like that they will know us by our horses, by our habits, and by every other appointment, to be ourselves.

*Poins.* Tut, our horses they shall not see,— I'll tie them in the wood; our visards we will change after we leave them; and, sirrah, I have cases of buckram for the nonce, to immask our noted outward garments.

*P. Hen.* But I doubt they will be too hard for us.

*Poins.* Well, for two of them, I know them to be as true-bred cowards as ever turned back; and for the third, if he fight longer than he sees reason, I'll forswear arms. The virtue of this jest will be the incomprehensible lies that this same fat rogue will tell us when we meet at supper: how thirty, at least, he fought with; what wards, what blows, what extremities he endured; and in the reproof of this lies the jest.

*P. Hen.* Well, I'll go with thee: provide us all things necessary, and meet me to-morrow night in Eastcheap; there I'll sup. Farewell.

*Poins.* Farewell, my lord.        [*Exit* POINS.

*P. Hen.* I know you all, and will awhile uphold
The unyok'd humour of your idleness:
Yet herein will I imitate the sun,
Who doth permit the base contagious clouds
To smother up his beauty from the world,
That, when he please again to be himself,
Being wanted, he may be more wonder'd at
By breaking through the foul and ugly mists
Of vapours that did seem to strangle him.
If all the year were playing holidays,
To sport would be as tedious as to work;
But when they seldom come, they wish'd-for come,
And nothing pleaseth but rare accidents.
So, when this loose behaviour I throw off,
And pay the debt I never promised,
By how much better than my word I am,
By so much shall I falsify men's hopes;
And, like bright metal on a sullen ground,
My reformation, glittering o'er my fault,
Shall show more goodly and attract more eyes
Than that which hath no foil to set it off.
I'll so offend, to make offence a skill;
Redeeming time when men think least I will.
                                        [*Exit.*

SCENE III.—*The same. Another Room in the Palace.*

*Enter* KING HENRY, NORTHUMBERLAND, WORCESTER, HOTSPUR, SIR WALTER BLUNT, *and others.*

*K. Hen.* My blood hath been too cold and temperate,
Unapt to stir at these indignities,
And you have found me; for accordingly
You tread upon my patience: but be sure
I will from henceforth rather be myself,
Mighty and to be fear'd, than my condition;
Which hath been smooth as oil, soft as young down,

And therefore lost that title of respect
Which the proud soul ne'er pays but to the proud.

*Wor.* Our house, my sovereign liege, little deserves
The scourge of greatness to be used on it;
And that same greatness, too which our own hands
Have holp to make so portly.

*North.* My lord,—

*K. Hen.* Worcester, get thee gone; for I see danger
And disobedience in thine eye: O, sir,
Your presence is too bold and peremptory
And majesty might never yet endure
The moody frontier of a servant brow.
You have good leave to leave us: when we need
Your use and counsel we shall send for you.
                        [*Exit* WORCESTER.
You were about to speak.
                        [*To* NORTHUMBERLAND.

*North.*                Yea, my good lord.
Those prisoners in your highness' name demanded,
Which Harry Percy here at Holmedon took,
Were, as he says, not with such strength denied
As is delivered to your majesty:
Either envy, therefore, or misprision
Is guilty of this fault, and not my son.

*Hot.* My liege, I did deny no prisoners.
But I remember when the fight was done,
When I was dry with rage and extreme toil,
Breathless and faint, leaning upon my sword,
Came there a certain lord, neat, trimly dress'd,
Fresh as a bridegroom; and his chin new reap'd
Show'd like a stubble-land at harvest-home;
He was perfum'd like a milliner;
And 'twixt his finger and his thumb he held
A pouncet-box, which ever and anon
He gave his nose, and took't away again;—
Who therewith angry, when it next came there,
Took it in snuff:—and still he smil'd and talk'd;
And as the soldiers bore dead bodies by,
He call'd them untaught knaves, unmannerly,
To bring a slovenly unhandsome corse
Betwixt the wind and his nobility.
With many holiday and lady terms
He question'd me; among the rest, demanded
My prisoners in your majesty's behalf.
I, then all smarting with my wounds being cold,
To be so pester'd with a popinjay,
Out of my grief and my impatience,
Answer'd neglectingly, I know not what,—
He should, or he should not;—for he made me mad
To see him shine so brisk, and smell so sweet,
And talk so like a waiting-gentlewoman
Of guns, and drums, and wounds,—God save the mark!—
And telling me the sovereign'st thing on earth
Was parmaceti for an inward bruise;
And that it was great pity, so it was,
This villanous saltpetre should be digg'd
Out of the bowels of the harmless earth,

Which many a good tall fellow had destroy'd
So cowardly; and but for these vile guns
He would himself have been a soldier.
This bald unjointed chat of his, my lord,
I answer'd indirectly, as I said;
And I beseech you, let not his report
Come current for an accusation
Betwixt my love and your high majesty.
    *Blunt.* The circumstance consider'd, good
      my lord,
Whatever Harry Percy then had said
To such a person, and in such a place,
At such a time, with all the rest re-told,
May reasonably die, and never rise
To do him wrong, or any way impeach
What then he said, so he unsay it now.
    *K. Hen.* Why, yet he doth deny his prisoners,
But with proviso and exception,—
That we at our own charge shall ransom straight
His brother-in-law, the foolish Mortimer;
Who, on my soul, hath wilfully betray'd
The lives of those that he did lead to fight
Against the great magician, damn'd Glendower,
Whose daughter, as we hear, that Earl of March
Hath lately married. Shall our coffers, then,
Be emptied to redeem a traitor home?
Shall we buy treason? and indent with fears,
When they have lost and forfeited themselves?
No, on the barren mountains let him starve;
For I shall never hold that man my friend
Whose tongue shall ask me for one penny cost
To ransom home revolted Mortimer.
    *Hot.* Revolted Mortimer!
He never did fall off, my sovereign liege,
But by the chance of war:—to prove that true,
Needs no more but one tongue for all those
    wounds,         [took,
Those mouthed wounds, which valiantly he
When on the gentle Severn's sedgy bank,
In single opposition, hand to hand,
He did confound the best part of an hour
In changing hardiment with great Glendower:
Three times they breath'd, and three times did
    they drink,
Upon agreement, of swift Severn's flood;
Who then, affrighted with their bloody looks,
Ran fearfully among the trembling reeds,
And hid his crisp head in the hollow bank
Blood-stained with these valiant combatants.
Never did base and rotten policy
Colour her working with such deadly wounds;
Nor could the noble Mortimer
Receive so many, and all willingly:
Then let him not be slander'd with revolt.
    *K. Hen.* Thou dost belie him, Percy, thou
      dost belie him;
He never did encounter with Glendower:
I tell thee,
He durst as well have met the devil alone
As Owen Glendower for any enemy.
Art thou not asham'd? But, sirrah, henceforth
Let me not hear you speak of Mortimer:
Send me your prisoners with the speediest
    means,

Or you shall hear in such a kind from me
As will displease you.—My Lord Northumber-
    land,
We license your departure with your son.—
Send us your prisoners, or you'll hear of it.
        [*Exeunt* K. HENRY, BLUNT, *and* Train.
    *Hot.* And if the devil come and roar for
      them,
I will not send them:—I will after straight,
And tell him so; for I will ease my heart,
Albeit I make a hazard of my head.
    *North.* What, drunk with choler? stay, and
      pause awhile;
Here comes your uncle.

        *Re-enter* WORCESTER.)
    *Hot.*         Speak of Mortimer!
Zounds, I will speak of him; and let my soul
Want mercy, if I do not join with him:
Yea, on his part I'll empty all these veins,
And shed my dear blood drop by drop i' the
    dust,
But I will lift the down-trod Mortimer
As high i' the air as this unthankful king,
As this ingrate and canker'd Bolingbroke.
    *North.* Brother, the king hath made your
      nephew mad.     [*To* WORCESTER.
    *Wor.* Who struck this heat up after I was
      gone?
    *Hot.* He will, forsooth, have all my prisoners;
And when I urg'd the ransom once again
Of my wife's brother, then his cheek look'd pale,
And on my face he turn'd an eye of death,
Trembling even at the name of Mortimer.
    *Wor.* I cannot blame him: was he not pro-
      claim'd
By Richard that dead is the next of blood?
    *North.* He was: I heard the proclamation:
And then it was when the unhappy king—
Whose wrongs in us God pardon!—did set forth
Upon his Irish expedition;
From whence he intercepted did return
To be depos'd, and shortly murdered.
    *Wor.* And for whose death we in the world's
      wide mouth
Live scandaliz'd and foully spoken of.
    *Hot.* But, soft, I pray you; did King Richard
      then
Proclaim my brother Edmund Mortimer
Heir to the crown?
    *North.*       He did; myself did hear it.
    *Hot.* Nay, then I cannot blame his cousin
      king,
That wish'd him on the barren mountains
      starve.
But shall it be that you that set the crown
Upon the head of this forgetful man,
And for his sake wear the detested blot
Of murderous subornation,—shall it be
That you a world of curses undergo,
Being the agents, or base second means,
The cords, the ladder, or the hangman rather?—
O, pardon me, that I descend so low
To show the line and the predicament

Wherein you range under this subtle king;—
Shall it, for shame, be spoken in these days,
Or fill up chronicles in time to come,
That men of your nobility and power
Did 'gage them both in an unjust behalf,—
As both of you, God pardon it! have done,—
To put down Richard, that sweet lovely rose,
And plant this thorn, this canker, Bolingbroke?
And shall it, in more shame, be further spoken
That you are fool'd, discarded, and shook off
By him for whom these shames ye underwent?
No; yet time serves, wherein you may redeem
Your banish'd honours, and restore yourselves
Into the good thoughts of the world again,—
Revenge the jeering and disdain'd contempt
Of this proud king, who studies day and night
To answer all the debt he owes to you
Even with the bloody payment of your deaths:
Therefore, I say,—
  *Wor.*        Peace, cousin; say no more:
And now I will unclasp a secret book,
And to your quick-conceiving discontents
I'll read you matter deep and dangerous;
As full of peril and adventurous spirit
As to o'er-walk a current roaring loud
On the unsteadfast footing of a spear.
  *Hot.* If he fall in, good-night!—or sink or
     swim:—
Send danger from the east unto the west,
So honour cross it from the north to south,
And let them grapple.—O, the blood more stirs
To rouse a lion than to start a hare!
  *North.* Imagination of some great exploit
Drives him beyond the bounds of patience.
  *Hot.* By heaven, methinks it were an easy
     leap
To pluck bright honour from the pale-fac'd
     moon;
Or dive into the bottom of the deep,
Where fathom-line could never touch the
     ground,
And pluck up drowned honour by the locks;
So he that doth redeem her thence might wear
Without corrival all her dignities:
But out upon this half-fac'd fellowship!
  *Wor.* He apprehends a world of figures here,
But not the form of what he should attend.—
Good cousin, give me audience for awhile.
  *Hot.* I cry you mercy.
  *Wor.*        Those same noble Scots
That are your prisoners,—
  *Hot.*        I'll keep them all;
By heaven, he shall not have a Scot of them;
No, if a Scot would save his soul, he shall not:
I'll keep them, by this hand.
  *Wor.*        You start away,
And lend no ear unto my purposes.—
Those prisoners you shall keep.
  *Hot.*        Nay, I will; that's flat:—
He said he would not ransom Mortimer;
Forbad my tongue to speak of Mortimer;
But I will find him when he lies asleep,
And in his ear I'll holla—*Mortimer!*
Nay,

I'll have a starling shall be taught to speak
Nothing but *Mortimer,* and give it him,
To keep his anger still in motion.
  *Wor.* Hear you, cousin; a word.
  *Hot.* All studies here I solemnly defy,
Save how to gall and pinch this Bolingbroke:
And that same sword-and-buckler Prince of
     Wales,—
But that I think his father loves him not,
And would be glad he met with some mischance,
I'd have him poison'd with a pot of ale.
  *Wor.* Farewell, kinsman: I will talk to you
When you are better temper'd to attend.
  *North.* Why, what a wasp-tongue and im-
     patient fool
Art thou to break into this woman's mood,
Tying thine ear to no tongue but thine own!
  *Hot.* Why, look you, I am whipp'd and
     scourg'd with rods,
Nettled, and stung with pismires, when I hear
Of this vile politician, Bolingbroke.
In Richard's time,—what do ye call the place?—
A plague upon't—it is in Glostershire;—
'Twas where the madcap duke his uncle kept,
His uncle York:—where I first bow'd my knee
Unto this king of smiles, this Bolingbroke,
When you and he came back from Ravenspurg.
  *North.* At Berkley Castle.
  *Hot.* You say true:—
Why, what a candy deal of courtesy
This fawning greyhound then did proffer me!
Look, *when his infant fortune came to age,*
And, *gentle Harry Percy,* and, *kind cousin,*—
O, the devil take such cozeners!—God forgive
     me!—
Good uncle, tell your tale; for I have done.
  *Wor.* Nay, if you have not, to't again;
We'll stay your leisure.
  *Hot.*        I have done, i' faith.
  *Wor.* Then once more to your Scottish
     prisoners.
Deliver them up without their ransom straight,
And make the Douglas' son your only mean
For powers in Scotland; which, for divers
     reasons
Which I shall send you written, be assur'd,
Will easily be granted.—You, my lord,
            [*To* NORTHUMBERLAND.
Your son in Scotland being thus employ'd,
Shall secretly into the bosom creep
Of that same noble prelate, well belov'd,
The archbishop.
  *Hot.* Of York, is't not?
  *Wor.* True; who bears hard
His brother's death at Bristol, the Lord Scroop.
I speak not this in estimation,
As what I think might be, but what I know
Is ruminated, plotted, and set down,
And only stays but to behold the face
Of that occasion that shall bring it on.
  *Hot.* I smell it: upon my life, it will do well.
  *North.* Before the game's a-foot, thou still
     lett'st slip.             [plot:—
  *Hot.* Why, it cannot choose but be a noble

And then the power of Scotland and of York.—
To join with Mortimer, ha?
*Wor.* And so they shall.
*Hot.* In faith, it is exceedingly well aim'd.
*Wor.* And 'tis no little reason bids us speed,
To save our heads by raising of a head;
For, bear ourselves as even as we can,
The king will always think him in our debt,
And think we think ourselves unsatisfied,
Till he hath found a time to pay us home:
And see already how he doth begin
To make us strangers to his looks of love.
*Hot.* He does, he does: we'll be reveng'd on
him.
*Wor.* Cousin, farewell:—no further go in this
Than I by letters shall direct your course.
When time is ripe,—which will be suddenly,—
I'll steal to Glendower and Lord Mortimer;
Where you and Douglas, and our powers at
once,—
As I will fashion it,—shall happily meet,
To bear our fortunes in our own strong arms,
Which now we hold at much uncertainty.
*North.* Farewell, good brother: we shall
thrive, I trust.
*Hot.* Uncle, adieu:—O, let the hours be short,
Till fields and blows and groans applaud our
sport. [*Exeunt.*

## ACT II.

SCENE I.—ROCHESTER. *An Inn Yard.*

*Enter a* Carrier *with a lantern in his hand.*

1 *Car.* Heigh-ho! an't be not four by the
day, I'll be hanged: Charles' wain is over the
new chimney, and yet our horse not packed.—
What, ostler!
*Ost.* [*Within.*] Anon, anon.
1 *Car.* I pr'ythee, Tom, beat Cut's saddle,
put a few flocks in the point; the poor jade is
wrong in the withers out of all cess.

*Enter another* Carrier.

. 2 *Car.* Peas and beans are as dank here as a
dog, and that is the next way to give poor jades
the bots: this house is turned upside down since
Robin ostler died.
1 *Car.* Poor fellow! never joyed since the
price of oats rose; it was the death of him.
2 *Car.* I think this be the most villanous
house in all London road for fleas: I am stung
like a tench.
1 *Car.* Like a tench! by the mass, there is
ne'er a king in Christendom could be better bit
than I have been since the first cock.
2 *Car.* Why, they will allow us ne'er a jorden, and then we leak in your chimney; and
your chamber-lie breeds fleas like a loach.
1 *Car.* What, ostler! come away, and be
hanged; come away.
2 *Car.* I have a gammon of bacon and two
races of ginger, to be delivered as far as Char-
ing-cross.
1 *Car.* 'Odsbody! the turkeys in my pannier
are quite starved.—What, ostler!—A plague on

thee! hast thou never an eye in thy head?
canst not hear? An 'twere not as good a deed
as drink, to break the pate of thee, I am a very
villain.—Come, and be hanged:—hast no faith
in thee?

*Enter* GADSHILL.

*Gads.* Good-morrow, carriers. What's
o'clock?
1 *Car.* I think it be two o'clock.
*Gads.* I pr'ythee, lend me thy lantern, to see
my gelding in the stable.
1 *Car.* Nay, soft, I pray ye; I know a trick
worth two of that, i' faith.
*Gads.* I pr'ythee, lend me thine.
2 *Car.* Ay, when? canst tell?—Lend me thy
lantern, quoth a?—marry, I'll see thee hanged
first.
*Gads.* Sirrah carrier, what time do you mean
to come to London?
2 *Car.* Time enough to go to bed with a
candle, I warrant thee.—Come, neighbour
Mugs, we'll call up the gentlemen: they will
along with company, for they have great
charge. [*Exeunt* Carriers.
*Gads.* What, ho! chamberlain!
*Cham.* [*Within.*] At hand, quoth pick-purse.
*Gads.* That's even as fair as—at hand, quoth
the chamberlain; for thou variest no more from
picking of purses than giving direction doth
from labouring; thou layest the plot how.

*Enter* Chamberlain.

*Cham.* Good-morrow, Master Gadshill. It
holds current that I told you yesternight:—
there's a franklin in the wild of Kent hath
brought three hundred marks with him in gold:
I heard him tell it to one of his company last
night at supper; a kind of auditor; one that
hath abundance of charge too, God know what.
They are up already, and call for eggs and
butter: they will away presently.
*Gads.* Sirrah, if they meet not with Saint
Nicholas' clerks, I'll give thee this neck.
*Cham.* No, I'll none of it: I pr'ythee, keep
that for the hangman; for I know thou wor-
shippest Saint Nicholas as truly as a man of
falsehood may.
*Gads.* What talkest thou to me of the hangman? If I hang, I'll make a fat pair of gallows;
for if I hang, old Sir John hangs with me; and
thou knowest he's no starveling. Tut! there
are other Trojans that thou dreamest not of,
the which, for sport-sake, are content to do the
profession some grace; that would, if matters
should be looked into, for their own credit-sake,
make all whole. I am joined with no foot land-
rakers, no long-staff sixpenny strikers, none of
these mad mustachio purple-hued malt-worms;
but with nobility and tranquillity; burgomas-
ters and great oneyers, such as can hold in, such
as will strike sooner than speak, and speak
sooner than drink, and drink sooner than pray:
and yet I lie; for they pray continually to their

saint, the commonwealth; or, rather, not pray to her, but prey on her; for they ride up and down on her, and make her their boots.

*Cham.* What, the commonwealth their boots? will she hold out water in foul way?

*Gads.* She will, she will; justice hath liquored her. We steal as in a castle, cock-sure; we have the receipt of fern-seed,—we walk invisible.

*Cham.* Nay, by my faith, I think you are more beholding to the night than to fern-seed for your walking invisible.

*Gads.* Give me thy hand: thou shalt have a share in our purchase, as I am a true man.

*Cham.* Nay, rather let me have it, as you are a false thief.

*Gads.* Go to; *homo* is a common name to all men. Bid the ostler bring my gelding out of the stable. Farewell, you muddy knave. [*Exeunt.*

SCENE II.—*The Road by Gadshill.*

*Enter* PRINCE HENRY *and* POINS; BARDOLPH *and* PETO *at some distance.*

*Poins.* Come, shelter, shelter: I have removed Falstaff's horse, and he frets like a gummed velvet.

*P. Hen.* Stand close.        [*They retire.*

*Enter* FALSTAFF.

*Fal.* Poins! Poins, and be hanged! Poins!

*P. Hen.* [*Coming forward.*] Peace, ye fat-kidneyed rascal! what a brawling dost thou keep!

*Fal.* Where's Poins, Hal?

*P. Hen.* He is walked up to the top of the hill: I'll go seek him. [*Pretends to seek* POINS.

*Fal.* I am accursed to rob in that thief's company: the rascal hath removed my horse, and tied him I know not where. If I travel but four foot by the squire further a-foot, I shall break my wind. Well, I doubt not but to die a fair death for all this, if I 'scape hanging for killing that rogue. I have forsworn his company hourly any time this two-and-twenty year, and yet I am bewitched with the rogue's company. If the rascal have not given me medicines to make me love him, I'll be hanged; it could not be else; I have drunk medicines.—Poins!—Hal!—a plague upon you both!—Bardolph!—Peto!—I'll starve, ere I'll rob a foot further. An 'twere not as good a deed as drink, to turn true man, and leave these rogues, I am the veriest varlet that ever chewed with a tooth. Eight yards of uneven ground is three-score and ten miles a-foot with me; and the stony-hearted villains know it well enough: a plague upon't, when thieves cannot be true to one another! [*They whistle.*] Whew!—a plague upon you all! Give me my horse, you rogues; give me my horse, and be hanged.

*P. Hen.* [*Coming forward.*] Peace, ye fat-guts! lie down; lay thine ear close to the ground, and list if thou canst hear the tread of travellers.

*Fal.* Have you any levers to lift me up again, being down? 'Sblood, I'll not bear mine own flesh so far a-foot again for all the coin in thy father's exchequer. What a plague mean ye to colt me thus?

*P. Hen.* Thou liest; thou art not colted, thou art uncolted.

*Fal.* I pr'ythee, good Prince Hal, help me to my horse, good king's son.

*P. Hen.* Out, you rogue! shall I be your ostler?

*Fal.* Go, hang thyself in thine own heir-apparent garters! If I be ta'en, I'll peach for this. An I have not ballads made on you all, and sung to filthy tunes, let a cup of sack be my poison:—when a jest is so forward, and a-foot too!—I hate it.

*Enter* GADSHILL.

*Gads.* Stand.

*Fal.* So I do, against my will.

*Poins.* O, 'tis our setter: I know his voice. [*Coming forward with* BARD. *and* PETO.

*Bard.* What news?

*Gads.* Case ye, case ye; on with your visards: there's money of the king's coming down the hill; 'tis going to the king's exchequer.

*Fal.* You lie, you rogue; 'tis going to the king's tavern.

*Gads.* There's enough to make us all.

*Fal.* To be hanged.

*P. Hen.* Sirs, you four shall front them in the narrow lane; Ned Poins and I will walk lower: if they 'scape from your encounter, then they light on us.

*Peto.* How many be there of them?

*Gads.* Some eight or ten.

*Fal.* Zounds, will they not rob us?

*P. Hen.* What, a coward, Sir John Paunch?

*Fal.* Indeed, I am not John of Gaunt, your grandfather; but yet no coward, Hal.

*P. Hen.* Well, we leave that to the proof.

*Poins.* Sirrah Jack, thy horse stands behind the hedge: when thou needest him, there thou shalt find him. Farewell, and stand fast.

*Fal.* Now cannot I strike him, if I should be hanged.

*P. Hen.* [*Aside to* POINS.] Ned, where are our disguises?

*Poins.* Here, hard by: stand close. [*Exeunt* P. HENRY *and* POINS.

*Fal.* Now, my masters, happy man be his dole, say I: every man to his business.

*Enter* Travellers.

1 *Trav.* Come, neighbour: the boy shall lead our horses down the hill; we'll walk a-foot awhile, and ease our legs.

*Fal., Gads., &c.* Stand!

*Trav.* Jesu bless us!

*Fal.* Strike; down with them; cut the villains' throats:—ah, whoreson caterpillars! bacon-fed knaves! they hate us youth:—down with them; fleece them.

*Trav.* O, we are undone, both we and ours for ever!

*Fal.* Hang ye, gorbellied knaves, are ye undone? No, ye fat chuffs; I would your store were here! On, bacons on! What, ye knaves! young men must live. You are grand-jurors, are ye? we'll jure ye, i' faith.

[*Exeunt* FAL., &c., *driving the Travellers out.*

*Re-enter* PRINCE HENRY *and* POINS.

*P. Hen.* The thieves have bound the true men. Now could thou and I rob the thieves, and go merrily to London, it would be argument for a week, laughter for a month, and a good jest for ever.

*Poins.* Stand close; I hear them coming.

*Re-enter* FALSTAFF, GADSHILL, BARDOLPH, *and* PETO.

*Fal.* Come, my masters, let us share, and then to horse before day. An the Prince and Poins be not two arrant cowards, there's no equity stirring: there's no more valour in that Poins than in a wild duck.

*P. Hen.* Your money!

[*Rushing out upon them.*

*Poins.* Villains!

[GADS., BARD., *and* PETO *run away; and* FAL. *also, after a blow or two, leaving the booty.*

*P. Hen.* Got with much ease. Now merrily to horse:
The thieves are scatter'd, and possess'd with fear
So strongly that they dare not meet each other;
Each takes his fellow for an officer.
Away, good Ned. Falstaff sweats to death,
And lards the lean earth as he walks along:
Were't not for laughing, I should pity him.

*Poins.* How the rogue roar'd! [*Exeunt.*

SCENE III.—WARKWORTH. *A Room in the Castle.*

*Enter* HOTSPUR, *reading a letter.*

*Hot.* —*But, for mine own part, my lord, I could be well contented to be there, in respect of the love I bear your house.*—He could be contented,—why is he not, then? In respect of the love he bears our house:—he shows in this, he loves his own barn better than he loves our house. Let me see some more. *The purpose you undertake is dangerous.*—Why, that's certain: 'tis dangerous to take a cold, to sleep, to drink; but I tell you, my lord fool, out of this nettle, danger, we pluck this flower, safety. *The purpose you undertake is dangerous; the friends you have named uncertain; the time itself unsorted; and your whole plot too light for the counterpoise of so great an opposition.*—Say you so, say you so? I say unto you again, you are a shallow, cowardly hind, and you lie. What a lack-brain is this! By the Lord, our plot is a good plot as ever was laid; our friends true and constant: a good plot, good friends, and full of expectation; an excellent plot, very good friends. What a frosty-spirited rogue is this! Why, my Lord of York commends the plot and the general course of the action. Zounds, an I were now by this rascal, I could brain him with his lady's fan. Is there not my father, my uncle, and myself? Lord Edmund Mortimer, my Lord of York, and Owen Glendower? Is there not, besides, the Douglas? Have I not all their letters to meet me in arms by the ninth of the next month? and are they not some of them set forward already? What a pagan rascal is this! an infidel! Ha! you shall see now, in very sincerity of fear and cold heart, will he to the king, and lay open all our proceedings. O, I could divide myself, and go to buffets, for moving such a dish of skimmed milk with so honourable an action! Hang him! Let him tell the king: we are prepared. I will set forward to-night.

*Enter* LADY PERCY.

How now, Kate! I must leave you within these two hours.

*Lady.* O, my good lord, why are you thus alone?
For what offence have I this fortnight been
A banish'd woman from my Harry's bed?
Tell me, sweet lord, what is't that takes from thee
Thy stomach, pleasure, and thy golden sleep?
Why dost thou bend thine eyes upon the earth,
And start so often when thou sitt'st alone?
Why hast thou lost the fresh blood in thy cheeks,
And given my treasures and my rights of thee
To thick-ey'd musing and curs'd melancholy?
In thy faint slumbers I by thee have watch'd,
And heard thee murmur tales of iron wars;
Speak terms of manage to thy bounding steed;
Cry, *Courage!—to the field!*—And thou hast talk'd
Of sallies and retires, of trenches, tents,
Of palisadoes, frontiers, parapets,
Of basilisks, of cannon, culverin,
Of prisoners' ransom, and of soldiers slain,
And all the currents of a heady fight.
Thy spirit within thee hath been so at war,
And thus hath so bestirr'd thee in thy sleep
That beads of sweat have stood upon thy brow,
Like bubbles in a late disturbed stream;
And in thy face strange motions have appear'd,
Such as we see when men restrain their breath
On some great sudden hest. O, what portents are these?
Some heavy business hath my lord in hand,
And I must know it, else he loves me not.

*Hot.* What, ho!

*Enter a* Servant.

Is Gilliams with the packet gone?

*Serv.* He is, my lord, an hour ago.

*Hot.* Hath Butler brought those horses from the sheriff?

*Serv.* One horse, my lord, he brought even now.

*Hot.* What horse? a roan, a crop-ear, is it not?

*Serv.* It is, my lord.

*Hot.*    That roan shall be my throne.
Well, I will back him straight: O *esperance!*—
Bid Butler lead him forth into the park.
            [*Exit* Servant.

*Lady.* But hear you, my lord.

*Hot.*    What say'st thou, my lady?

*Lady.* What is it carries you away?

*Hot.* Why, my horse, my love,—my horse.

*Lady.*    Out, you mad-headed ape!
A weasel hath not such a deal of spleen
As you are toss'd with. In faith,
I'll know your business, Harry,—that I will.
I fear my brother Mortimer doth stir
About his title, and hath sent for you
To line his enterprise: but if you go,—

*Hot.* So far a-foot, I shall be weary, love.

*Lady.* Come, come, you paraquito, answer me
Directly to this question that I ask:
In faith, I'll break thy little finger, Harry,
An if thou wilt not tell me all things true.

*Hot.* Away,
Away, you trifler!—Love?—I love thee not,
I care not for thee, Kate: this is no world
To play with mammets and to tilt with lips:
We must have bloody noses and crack'd crowns,
And pass them current too.—Gods me, my horse!—
What say'st thou, Kate? what wouldst thou
    have with me?

*Lady.* Do you not love me? do you not, in-
    deed?
Well, do not, then; for since you love me not,
I will not love myself. Do you not love me?
Nay, tell me if you speak in jest or no.

*Hot.* Come, wilt thou see me ride?
And when I am o' horseback, I will swear
I love thee infinitely. But hark you, Kate;
I must not have you henceforth question me
Whither I go, nor reason whereabout:
Whither I must, I must; and, to conclude,
This evening must I leave you, gentle Kate.
I know you wise; but yet no further wise
Than Harry Percy's wife: constant you are;
But yet a woman: and for secrecy,
No lady closer; for I well believe
Thou wilt not utter what thou dost not know,—
And so far will I trust thee, gentle Kate.

*Lady.* How! so far?        [Kate:

*Hot.* Not an inch further. But hark you,
Whither I go, thither shall you go too;
To-day will I set forth, to-morrow you.—
Will this content you, Kate?

*Lady.*    It must, of force. [*Exeunt.*

SCENE IV.—EASTCHEAP. *A Room in the
    Boar's Head Tavern.*

*Enter* PRINCE HENRY.

*P. Hen.* Ned, pr'ythee, come out of that fat
room, and lend me thy hand to laugh a little.

*Enter* POINS.

*Poins.* Where hast been, Hal?

*P. Hen.* With three or four loggerheads
amongst three or fourscore hogsheads. I have
sounded the very base string of humility.
Sirrah, I am sworn brother to a leash of
drawers; and can call them all by their Christian names, as—Tom, Dick, and Francis. They
take it already upon their salvation, that
though I be but Prince of Wales, yet I am the
king of courtesy; and tell me flatly I am no
proud Jack, like Falstaff, but a Corinthian, a
lad of mettle, a good boy,—by the Lord, so
they call me,—and when I am king of England
I shall command all the good lads in Eastcheap.
They call drinking deep, dying scarlet; and
when you breathe in your watering, they cry
*hem!* and bid you play it off. To conclude, I am
so good a proficient in one quarter of an hour,
that I can drink with any tinker in his own
language during my life. I tell thee, Ned, thou
hast lost much honour, that thou wert not with
me in this action. But, sweet Ned,—to sweeten
which name of Ned, I give thee this pennyworth of sugar, clapped even now into my hand
by an under-skinker; one that never spake
other English in his life than, *Eight shillings
and six-pence,* and *You are welcome;* with this
shrill addition, *Anon, anon, sir! Score a pint of
bastard in the Half-moon,* or so. But, Ned, to
drive away the time till Falstaff come, I pr'y-
thee, do thou stand in some by-room, while I
question my puny drawer to what end he gave
me the sugar; and do thou never leave calling
*Francis,* that his tale to me may be nothing but
*anon.* Step aside, and I'll show thee a precedent.        [*Exit* POINS.

*Poins.* [*Within.*] Francis!

*P. Hen.* Thou art perfect.

*Poins.* [*Within.*] Francis!

*Enter* FRANCIS.

*Fran.* Anon, anon, sir.—Look down into the
Pomegranate, Ralph.

*P. Hen.* Come hither, Francis.

*Fran.* My lord?

*P. Hen.* How long hast thou to serve,
Francis?

*Fran.* Forsooth, five years, and as much
as to,—

*Poins.* [*Within.*] Francis!

*Fran.* Anon, anon, sir.

*P. Hen.* Five years! by'r lady, a long lease
for the clinking of pewter. But, Francis, darest
thou be so valiant as to play the coward with
thy indenture, and show it a fair pair of heels
and run from it?

*Fran.* O Lord, sir, I'll be sworn upon all the
books in England, I could find in my heart,—

*Poins.* [*Within.*] Francis!

*Fran.* Anon, anon, sir.

*P. Hen.* How old art thou, Francis?

*Fran.* Let me see,—about Michaelmas next I shall be,—

*Poins.* [*Within.*] Francis!

*Fran.* Anon, sir,—Pray you, stay a little, my lord.

*P. Hen.* Nay, but hark you, Francis: for the sugar thou gavest me,—'twas a pennyworth, was't not?

*Fran.* O Lord, sir, I would it had been two!

*P. Hen.* I will give thee for it a thousand pound: ask me when thou wilt, and thou shalt have it.

*Poins.* [*Within.*] Francis!

*Fran.* Anon, anon.

*P. Hen.* Anon, Francis? No, Francis; but to-morrow, Francis; or, Francis, on Thursday; or, indeed, Francis, when thou wilt. But, Francis,—

*Fran.* My lord?

*P. Hen.* Wilt thou rob this leathern-jerkin, crystal-button, nott-pated, agate-ring, puke-stocking, caddis-garter, smooth-tongue, Spanish-pouch,—

*Fran.* O Lord, sir, who do you mean?

*P. Hen.* Why, then, your brown bastard is your only drink; for, look you, Francis, your white canvas doublet will sully: in Barbary, sir, it cannot come to so much.

*Fran.* What, sir?

*Poins.* [*Within.*] Francis!

*P. Hen.* Away, you rogue! dost thou not hear them call?

[*Here they both call him;* FRANCIS *stands amazed, not knowing which way to go.*

*Enter* Vintner.

*Vint.* What, standest thou still, and hearest such a calling? Look to the guests within. [*Exit* FRAN.] My lord, old Sir John, with half-a-dozen more, are at the door: shall I let them in?

*P. Hen.* Let them alone awhile, and then open the door. [*Exit* Vintner.] Poins!

*Re-enter* POINS.

*Poins.* Anon, anon, sir.

*P. Hen.* Sirrah, Falstaff and the rest of the thieves are at the door: shall we be merry?

*Poins.* As merry as crickets, my lad. But hark ye; what cunning match have you made with this jest of the drawer? come, what's the issue?

*P. Hen.* I am now of all humours that have showed themselves humours since the old days of goodman Adam to the pupil-age of this present twelve o'clock at midnight.—What's o'clock, Francis?

*Fran.* [*Within.*] Anon, anon, sir.

*P. Hen.* That ever this fellow should have fewer words than a parrot, and yet the son of a woman! His industry is upstairs and downstairs; his eloquence the parcel of a reckoning. I am not yet of Percy's mind, the Hotspur of the north; he that kills me some six or seven dozen Scots at a breakfast, washes his hands, and says to his wife, *Fie upon this quiet life! I want work.* O my sweet Harry, says she, *how many hast thou killed to-day?* Give my roan horse *a drench,* says he; and answers, *Some fourteen,* an hour after,—*a trifle, a trifle.* I pr'ythee, call in Falstaff: I'll play Percy, and that damned brawn shall play Dame Mortimer his wife. *Rivo* says the drunkard. Call in ribs, call in tallow.

*Enter* FALSTAFF, GADSHILL, BARDOLPH, *and* PETO; *followed by* FRANCIS *with wine.*

*Poins.* Welcome, Jack: where hast thou been?

*Fal.* A plague of all cowards, I say, and a vengeance too! marry, and amen!—Give me a cup of sack, boy.—Ere I lead this life long, I'll sew nether-stocks, and mend them and foot them too. A plague of all cowards!—Give me a cup of sack, rogue.—Is there no virtue extant? [*He drinks.*

*P. Hen.* Didst thou never see Titan kiss a dish of butter? pitiful-hearted Titan, that melted at the sweet tale of the sun! if thou didst, then behold that compound.

*Fal.* You rogue, here's lime in this sack too: there is nothing but roguery to be found in villanous man: yet a coward is worse than a cup of sack with lime in it,—a villanous coward.—Go thy ways, old Jack; die when thou wilt, if manhood, good manhood, be not forgot upon the face of the earth, then am I a shotten herring. There live not three good men unhanged in England; and one of them is fat, and grows old: God help the while! a bad world, I say. I would I were a weaver; I could sing psalms or anything. A plague of all cowards, I say still.

*P. Hen.* How now, woolsack! what mutter you?

*Fal.* A king's son! If I do not beat thee out of thy kingdom with a dagger of lath, and drive all thy subjects afore thee like a flock of wild geese, I'll never wear hair on my face more. You Prince of Wales!

*P. Hen.* Why, you whoreson round man, what's the matter?

*Fal.* Are you not a coward? answer me to that:—and Poins there?

*Poins.* Zounds, ye fat paunch, an ye call me coward, I'll stab thee.

*Fal.* I call thee coward! I'll see thee damned ere I call thee coward: but I would give a thousand pound I could run as fast as thou canst. You are straight enough in the shoulders,—you care not who sees your back: call you that backing of your friends? A plague upon such backing! give me them that will face me.—Give me a cup of sack:—I am a rogue if I drunk to-day.

*P. Hen.* O villain! thy lips are scarce wiped since thou drunkest last.

*Fal.* All's one for that. A plague of all cowards, still say I. [*He drinks.*

*P. Hen.* What's the matter?

*Fal.* What's the matter! there be four of us here have ta'en a thousand pound this day morning.

*P. Hen.* Where is it, Jack? where is it?

*Fal.* Where is it! taken from us it is: a hundred upon poor four of us.

*P. Hen.* What, a hundred, man?

*Fal.* I am a rogue, if I were not at half-sword with a dozen of them two hours together. I have 'scaped by miracle. I am eight times thrust through the doublet, four through the hose; my buckler cut through and through; my sword hacked like a hand-saw,—*ecce signum!* I never dealt better since I was a man: all would not do. A plague of all cowards!—Let them speak: if they speak more or less than truth, they are villains, and the sons of darkness.

*P. Hen.* Speak, sirs; how was it?

*Gads.* We four set upon some dozen,—

*Fal.* Sixteen at least, my lord.

*Gads.* And bound them.

*Peto.* No, no, they were not bound.

*Fal.* You rogue, they were bound, every man of them; or I am a Jew else, an Ebrew Jew.

*Gads.* As we were sharing, some six or seven fresh men set upon us,—

*Fal.* An unbound the rest, and then come in the other.

*P. Hen.* What, fought ye with them all?

*Fal.* All! I know not what ye call all; but if I fought not with fifty of them, I am a bunch of radish: if there were not two or three and fifty upon poor old Jack, then am I no two-legged creature.

*P. Hen.* Pray God, you have not murdered some of them.

*Fal.* Nay, that's past praying for: I have peppered two of them; two I am sure I have paid,—two rogues in buckram suits. I tell thee what, Hal,—if I tell thee a lie, spit in my face, call me horse. Thou knowest my old ward;—here I lay, and thus I bore my point. Four rogues in buckram let drive at me,—

*P. Hen.* What, four? thou saidst but two even now.

*Fal.* Four, Hal; I told thee four.

*Poins.* Ay, ay, he said four.

*Fal.* These four came all a-front, and mainly thrust at me. I made me no more ado but took all their seven points in my target, thus.

*P. Hen.* Seven? why, there were but four even now in buckram.

*Poins.* Ay, four in buckram suits.

*Fal.* Seven, by these hilts, or I am a villain else.

*P. Hen.* Pr'ythee, let him alone; we shall have more anon.

*Fal.* Dost thou hear me, Hal?

*P. Hen.* Ay, and mark thee too, Jack.

*Fal.* Do so, for it is worth the listening to. These nine in buckram that I told thee of,—

*P. Hen.* So, two more already.

*Fal.* Their points being broken,—

*Poins.* Down fell their hose.

*Fal.* Began to give me ground: but I followed me close, came in foot and hand; and with a thought seven of the eleven I paid.

*P. Hen.* O monstrous! eleven buckram men grown out of two!

*Fal.* But, as the devil would have it, three misbegotten knaves in Kendal green came at my back and let drive at me;—for it was so dark, Hal, that thou couldst not see thy hand.

*P. Hen.* These lies are like the father that begets them,—gross as a mountain, open, palpable. Why, thou clay-brained guts, thou nott-pated fool, thou whoreson, obscene, greasy tallow-keech,—

*Fal.* What, art thou mad? art thou mad? is not the truth the truth?

*P. Hen.* Why, how couldst thou know these men in Kendal green, when it was so dark thou couldst not see thy hand? come, tell us your reason: what sayest thou to this?

*Poins.* Come, your reason, Jack,—your reason.

*Fal.* What, upon compulsion? No; were I at the strappado, or all the racks in the world, I would not tell you on compulsion. Give you a reason on compulsion! if reasons were as plenty as blackberries I would give no man a reason upon compulsion, I.

*P. Hen.* I'll be no longer guilty of this sin; this sanguine coward, this bed-presser, this horse back-breaker, this huge hill of flesh,—

*Fal.* Away, you starveling, you elf-skin, you dried neat's tongue, bull's pizzle, you stock-fish,—O for breath to utter what is like thee!—you tailor's yard, you sheath, you bow-case, you vile standing-tuck,—

*P. Hen.* Well, breathe awhile, and then to it again: and when thou hast tired thyself in base comparisons, hear me speak but this.

*Poins.* Mark, Jack.

*P. Hen.* We two saw you four set on four; you bound them, and were masters of their wealth.—Mark now, how a plain tale shall put you down.—Then did we two set on you four; and, with a word, out-faced you from your prize, and have it; yea, and can show it you here in the house:—and, Falstaff, you carried your guts away as nimbly, with as quick dexterity, and roared for mercy, and still ran and roared, as ever I heard bull-calf. What a slave art thou, to hack thy sword as thou hast done, and then say it was in fight! What trick, what device, what starting-hole, canst thou now find out to hide thee from this open and apparent shame?

*Poins.* Come, let's hear, Jack; what trick hast thou now?

*Fal.* By the Lord, I knew ye as well as he that made ye. Why, hear ye, my masters: was it for me to kill the heir-apparent? Should I turn upon the true prince? Why, thou knowest I am as valiant as Hercules: but beware instinct; the lion will not touch the true prince. Instinct is a great matter; I was a coward on instinct. I shall think the better of myself and thee during my life; I for a valiant lion, and thou for a true prince. But, by the Lord, lads, I am glad you have the money.—Hostess, clap to the doors [*to* Hostess *within*]:—watch to-night, pray to-morrow.—Gallants, lads, boys, hearts of gold, all the titles of good fellowship come to you! What, shall we be merry? Shall we have a play extempore?

*P. Hen.* Content;—and the argument shall be thy running away.

*Fal.* Ah, no more of that, Hal, an thou lovest me!

### *Enter* Hostess.

*Host.* O Jesu, my lord the prince,—

*P. Hen.* How now, my lady the hostess!—What sayest thou to me?

*Host.* Marry, my lord, there is a nobleman of the court at door would speak with you: he says he comes from your father.

*P. Hen.* Give him as much as will make him a royal man, and send him back again to my mother.

*Fal.* What manner of man is he?

*Host.* An old man.

*Fal.* What doth gravity out of his bed at midnight?—Shall I give him his answer?

*P. Hen.* Pr'ythee, do, Jack.

*Fal.* Faith, and I'll send him packing. [*Exit.*

*P. Hen.* Now, sirs:—by'r lady, you fought fair;—so did you, Peto;—so did you, Bardolph: you are lions too, you ran away upon instinct, you will not touch the true prince; no,—fie!

*Bard.* Faith, I ran when I saw others run.

*P. Hen.* Tell me now in earnest, how came Falstaff's sword so hacked?

*Peto.* Why, he hacked it with his dagger; and said he would swear truth out of England, but he would make you believe it was done in fight; and persuaded us to do the like.

*Bard.* Yea, and to tickle our noses with speargrass to make them bleed; and then to be-slubber our garments with it, and swear it was the blood of true men. I did that I did not this seven year before,—I blushed to hear his monstrous devices.

*P. Hen.* O villain, thou stolest a cup of sack eighteen years ago, and wert taken with the manner, and ever since thou hast blushed extempore. Thou hadst fire and sword on thy side, and yet thou rannest away: what instinct hadst thou for it?

*Bard.* My lord, do you see these meteors? do you behold these exhalations?

*P. Hen.* I do.

*Bard.* What think you they portend?

*P. Hen.* Hot livers and cold purses.

*Bard.* Choler, my lord, if rightly taken.

*P. Hen.* No, if rightly taken, halter.—Here comes lean Jack, here comes bare-bone.

### *Re-enter* FALSTAFF.

How now, my sweet creature of bombast! How long is't ago, Jack, since thou sawest thine own knee?

*Fal.* My own knee! when I was about thy years, Hal, I was not an eagle's talon in the waist; I could have crept into any alderman's thumb-ring: a plague of sighing and grief! it blows a man up like a bladder—There's vilanous news abroad: here was Sir John Bracy from your father; you must to the court in the morning. That same mad fellow of the north, Percy; and he of Wales, that gave Amaimon the bastinado, and made Lucifer cuckold, and swore the devil his true liegeman upon the cross of a Welsh hook,—what, 'a plague, call you him?—

*Poins.* O, Glendower.

*Fal.* Owen, Owen,—the same; and his son-in-law, Mortimer; and old Northumberland; and that sprightly Scot of Scots, Douglas, that runs o' horseback up a hill perpendicular,—

*P. Hen.* He that rides at high speed, and with his pistol kills a sparrow flying?

*Fal.* You have hit it.

*P. Hen.* So did he never the sparrow.

*Fal.* Well, that rascal hath good mettle in him; he will not run;—

*P. Hen.* Why, what a rascal art thou, then, to praise him so for running.

*Fal.* O' horseback, ye cuckoo; but a-foot he will not budge a foot.

*P. Hen.* Yes, Jack, upon instinct.

*Fal.* I grant ye, upon instinct.—Well, he is there too, and one Mordake, and a thousand blue-caps more: Worcester is stolen away to-night; thy father's beard is turned white with the news: you may buy land now as cheap as stinking mackerel.

*P. Hen.* Why, then, it is like, if there come a hot June, and this civil buffeting hold, we shall buy maidenheads as they buy hob-nails, by the hundreds.

*Fal.* By the mass, lad, thou sayest true; it is like we shall have good trading that way.—But tell me, Hal, art thou not horribly afeard? thou being heir-apparent, could the world pick thee out three such enemies again as that fiend Douglas, that spirit Percy, and that devil Glendower? Art thou not horribly afraid? doth not thy blood thrill at it?

*P. Hen.* Not a whit, i' faith; I lack some of thy instinct.

*Fal.* Well, thou wilt be horribly chid to-morrow when thou comest to thy father: if thou love me, practise an answer.

*P. Hen.* Do thou stand for my father! and examine me upon the particulars of my life.

*Fal.* Shall I? content:—this chair shall be my state, this dagger my sceptre, and this cushion my crown.

*P. Hen.* Thy state is taken for a joint-stool, thy golden sceptre for a leaden dagger, and thy precious rich crown for a pitiful bald crown!

*Fal.* Well, an the fire of grace be not quite out of thee, now shalt thou be moved.—Give me a cup of sack to make mine eyes look red, that it may be thought I have wept; for I must speak in passion, and I will do it in King Cambyses' vein.

*P. Hen.* Well, here is my leg.

*Fal.* And here is my speech.—Stand aside, nobility.

*Host.* O Jesu, this is excellent sport, i' faith!

*Fal.* Weep not, sweet queen; for trickling tears are vain.

*Host.* O, the father, how he holds his countenance!

*Fal.* For God's sake, lords, convey my tristful queen;
For tears do stop the floodgates of her eyes.

*Host.* O Jesu, he doth it as like one of these harlotry players as ever I see!

*Fal.* Peace, good pint-pot; peace, good tickle-brain.—Harry, I do not only marvel where thou spendest thy time, but also how thou art accompanied: for though the camomile, the more it is trodden on, the faster it grows, yet youth, the more it is wasted, the sooner it wears. That thou art my son, I have partly thy mother's word, partly my own opinion; but chiefly a villanous trick of thine eye, and a foolish hanging of thy nether lip, that doth warrant me. If, then, thou be son to me, here lies the point;—why, being son to me, art thou so pointed at? Shall the blessed sun of heaven prove a micher, and eat blackberries? a question not to be asked. Shall the son of England prove a thief, and take purses? a question to be asked. There is a thing, Harry, which thou hast often heard of, and it is known to many in our land by the name of pitch: this pitch, as ancient writers do report, doth defile; so doth the company thou keepest: for, Harry, now I do not speak to thee in drink, but in tears; not in pleasure, but in passion; not in words only, but in woes also:—and yet there is a virtuous man whom I have often noted in thy company, but I know not his name.

*P. Hen.* What manner of man, an it like your majesty?

*Fal.* A goodly portly man, i' faith, and a corpulent; of a cheerful look, a pleasing eye, and a most noble carriage; and, as I think, his age some fifty, or, by'r lady, inclining to threescore; and now I remember me, his name is Falstaff: if that man should be lewdly given, he deceiveth me; for, Harry, I see virtue in his looks. If, then, the tree may be known by the fruit, as the fruit by the tree, then, peremptorily I speak it, there is virtue in that Falstaff: him keep with, the rest banish. And tell me now, thou naughty varlet, tell me, where hast thou been this month?

*P. Hen.* Dost thou speak like a king? Do thou stand for me, and I'll play my father.

*Fal.* Depose me? if thou dost it half so gravely, so majestically, both in word and matter, hang me up by the heels for a rabbit-sucker or a poulter's hare.

*P. Hen.* Well, here I am set.

*Fal.* And here I stand:—judge, my masters.

*P. Hen.* Now, Harry, whence come you?

*Fal.* My noble lord, from Eastcheap.

*P. Hen.* The complaints I hear of thee are grievous.

*Fal.* 'Sblood, my lord, they are false:—nay, I'll tickle ye for a young prince, i' faith.

*P. Hen.* Swearest thou, ungracious boy? henceforth ne'er look on me. Thou art violently carried away from grace: there is a devil haunts thee, in the likeness of a fat old man,—a tun of man is thy companion. Why dost thou converse with that trunk of humours, that bolting-hutch of beastliness, that swollen parcel of dropsies, that huge bombard of sack, that stuffed cloak-bag of guts, that roasted Manningtree ox, with the pudding in his belly, that reverend vice, that gray iniquity, that father ruffian, that vanity in years? Wherein is he good, but to taste sack and drink it? wherein neat and cleanly, but to carve a capon and eat it? wherein cunning, but in craft? wherein crafty, but in villany? wherein villanous, but in all things? wherein worthy, but in nothing?

*Fal.* I would your grace would take me with you: whom means your grace?

*P. Hen.* That villanous abominable misleader of youth, Falstaff, that old white-bearded Satan.

*Fal.* My lord, the man I know.

*P. Hen.* I know thou dost.

*Fal.* But to say I know more harm in him than in myself, were to say more than I know. That he is old,—the more the pity,—his white hairs do witness it; but that he is,—saving your reverence,—a whoremaster, that I utterly deny. If sack and sugar be a fault, God help the wicked! If to be old and merry be a sin, then many an old host that I know is damned; if to be fat be to be hated, then Pharaoh's lean kine are to be loved. No, my good lord; banish Peto, banish Bardolph, banish Poins: but, for sweet Jack Falstaff, kind Jack Falstaff, true Jack Falstaff, valiant Jack Falstaff, and therefore more valiant, being, as he is, old Jack Falstaff, banish not him thy Harry's company, banish not him thy Harry's company:—banish plump Jack, and banish all the world.

*P. Hen.* I do, I will.     [*A knocking heard.*
[*Exeunt* Host., Fran., *and* Bard.

*Re-enter* Bardolph, *running.*

*Bard.* O, my lord, my lord! the sheriff with a most monstrous watch is at the door.

*Fal.* Out, you rogue!—play out the play: I have much to say in the behalf of that Falstaff.

*Re-enter* Hostess, *hastily.*

*Host.* O Jesu, my lord, my lord,—

*P. Hen.* Heigh, heigh! the devil rides upon a fiddle-stick: what's the matter?

*Host.* The sheriff and all the watch are at the door: they are come to search the house. Shall I let them in?

*Fal.* Dost thou hear, Hal? never call a true piece of gold a counterfeit: thou art essentially mad, without seeming so.

*P. Hen.* And thou a natural coward, without instinct.

*Fal.* I deny your *major:* if you will deny the sheriff, so; if not, let him enter: if I become not a cart as well as another man, a plague on my bringing up! I hope I shall as soon be strangled with a halter as another.

*P. Hen.* Go, hide thee behind the arras:—the rest walk up above. Now, my masters, for a true face and good conscience.

*Fal.* Both which I have had; but their date is out, and therefore I'll hide me.

[*Exeunt all but the* PRINCE *and* POINS.

*P. Hen.* Call in the sheriff.

*Enter* Sheriff *and* Carrier.

Now, master sheriff, what is your will with me?

*Sher.* First, pardon me, my lord. A hue and cry
Hath followed certain men unto this house.

*P. Hen.* What men?

*Sher.* One of them is well known, my gracious lord,—
A gross fat man.

*Car.*             As fat as butter.

*P. Hen.* The man, I do assure you, is not here;
For I myself at this time have employ'd him.
And, sheriff, I will engage my word to thee,
That I will, by to-morrow dinner-time,
Send him to answer thee, or any man,
For anything he shall be charg'd withal:
And so, let me entreat you leave the house.

*Sher.* I will, my lord. There are two gentlemen
Have in this robbery lost three hundred marks.

*P. Hen.* It may be so: if he have robb'd these men
He shall be answerable; and so, farewell.

*Sher.* Good-night, my noble lord.

*P. Hen.* I think it is good-morrow, is it not?

*Sher.* Indeed, my lord, I think it be two o'clock.   [*Exeunt* Sheriff *and* Carrier.

*P. Hen.* This oily rascal is known as well as Paul's. Go, call him forth.

*Poins.* Falstaff!—fast asleep behind the arras, and snorting like a horse.

*P. Hen.* Hark, how hard he fetches breath. Search his pockets. [POINS *searches.*] What hast thou found?

*Poins.* Nothing but papers, my lord.

*P. Hen.* Let's see what they be: read them.

*Poins.* [*Reads.*] Item, A capon,      2s. 2d.
Item, Sauce, . . . . . . os. 4d.
Item, Sack, two gallons,  . . . 5s. 8d.
Item, Anchovies and sack after
          supper, . . . . . . 2s. 6d.
Item, Bread, . . . . . . . os. o½d.

*P. Hen.* O monstrous! but one halfpennyworth of bread to this intolerable deal of sack!—What there is else, keep close; we'll read it at more advantage: there let him sleep till day. I'll to the court in the morning. We must all to the wars, and thy place shall be honourable. I'll procure this fat rogue a charge of foot; and I know his death will be a march of twelve-score. The money shall be paid back again with advantage. Be with me betimes in the morning; and so, good-morrow, Poins.

*Poins.* Good-morrow, good my lord.

[*Exeunt.*

## ACT III.

SCENE I.—BANGOR. *A Room in the*
ARCHDEACON'S *House.*

*Enter* HOTSPUR, WORCESTER, MORTIMER,
*and* GLENDOWER.

*Mort.* These promises are fair, the parties sure,
And our induction full of prosperous hope.

*Hot.* Lord Mortimer,—and cousin Glendower,—
Will you sit down?—
And uncle Worcester:—a plague upon it!
I have forgot the map.

*Glend.*             No, here it is.
Sit, cousin Percy; sit, good cousin Hotspur,—
For by that name as oft as Lancaster
Doth speak of you, his cheek looks pale, and with
A rising sigh he wishes you in heaven.

*Hot.* And you in hell, as often as he hears
Owen Glendower spoke of.

*Glend.* I cannot blame him: at my nativity
The front of heaven was full of fiery shapes,
Of burning cressets; and at my birth
The frame and huge foundation of the earth
Shak'd like a coward.

*Hot.*              Why, so it would have done,
At the same season, if your mother's cat
Had but kitten'd, though yourself had ne'er
          been born.

*Glend.* I say the earth did shake when I was born.

*Hot.* And I say the earth was not of my mind,
If you suppose as fearing you it shook.

*Glend.* The heavens were all on fire, the earth did tremble.

*Hot.* O, then the earth shook to see the heavens on fire,
And not in fear of your nativity.
Diseased nature oftentimes breaks forth
In strange eruptions; oft the teeming earth
Is with a kind of colic pinch'd and vex'd
By the imprisoning of unruly wind
Within her womb; which, for enlargement striving,
Shakes the old beldame earth, and topples down
Steeples and moss-grown towers. At your birth,

Our grandam earth, having this distemperature,
In passion shook.

*Glend.*                Cousin, of many men
I do not bear these crossings. Give me leave
To tell you once again that at my birth
The front of heaven was full of fiery shapes;
The goats ran from the mountains, and the
herds
Were strangely clamorous to the frighted fields.
These signs have mark'd me extraordinary;
And all the courses of my life do show
I am not in the roll of common men.
Where is he living,—clipp'd in with the sea
That chides the banks of England, Scotland,
Wales,—
Which calls me pupil, or hath read to me?
And bring him out that is but woman's son
Can trace me in the tedious ways of art,
And hold me pace in deep experiments.

*Hot.* I think there is no man speaks better
Welsh.—
I'll to dinner.

*Mort.* Peace, cousin Percy; you will make
him mad.

*Glend.* I can call spirits from the vasty deep.

*Hot.* Why, so can I, or so can any man;
But will they come when you do call for them?

*Glend.* Why, I can teach thee, cousin, to
command
The devil.

*Hot.* And I can teach thee, coz, to shame
the devil
By telling truth: tell truth, and shame the
devil!
If thou have power to raise him, bring him
hither,
And I'll be sworn I have power to shame him
hence.
O, while you live, tell truth, and shame the
devil!

*Mort.* Come, come,
No more of this unprofitable chat.

*Glend.* Three times hath Henry Bolingbroke
made head
Against my power; thrice from the banks of
Wye
And sandy-bottom'd Severn have I sent him
Bootless home and weather-beaten back.

*Hot.* Home without boots, and in foul
weather too!
How 'scapes he agues, in the devil's name?

*Glend.* Come, here's the map: shall we divide our right
According to our threefold order ta'en?

*Mort.* The archdeacon hath divided it
Into three limits very equally:
England, from Trent and Severn hitherto,
By south and east is to my part assign'd:
All westward, Wales beyond the Severn shore,
And all the fertile land within that bound,
To Owen Glendower:—and, dear coz, to you
The remnant northward, lying off from Trent.
And our indentures tripartite are drawn;

Which being sealed interchangeably,—
A business that this night may execute,—
To-morrow, cousin Percy, you, and I,
And my good Lord Worcester, will set forth
To meet your father and the Scottish power,
As is appointed us, at Shrewsbury.
My father Glendower is not ready yet,
Nor shall we need his help these fourteen
days:—
Within that space [*to* GLEND.] you may have
drawn together
Your tenants, friends, and neighbouring gen-
tlemen.

*Glend.* A shorter time shall send me to you,
lords:
And in my conduct shall your ladies come;
From whom you now must steal, and take no
leave;
For there will be a world of water shed
Upon the parting of your wives and you.

*Hot.* Methinks my moiety, north from Bur-
ton here,
In quantity equals not one of yours:
See how this river comes me cranking in,
And cuts me from the best of all my land
A huge half-moon, a monstrous cantle out.
I'll have the current in this place damm'd up;
And here the smug and silver Trent shall run
In a new channel, fair and evenly:
It shall not wind with such a deep indent,
To rob me of so rich a bottom here.

*Glend.* Not wind! it shall, it must; you see
it doth.

*Mort.* Yea.
But mark how he bears his course and runs
me up
With like advantage on the other side;
Gelding the opposed continent as much
As on the other side it takes from you.

*Wor.* Yea, but a little charge will trench
him here,
And on this north side win this cape of land;
And then he runs straight and even.

*Hot.* I'll have it so: a little charge will do it.

*Glend.* I will not have it alter'd.

*Hot.*                Will not you?

*Glend.* No, nor you shall not.

*Hot.*                Who shall say me nay?

*Glend.* Why, that will I.

*Hot.*        Let me not understand you, then;
Speak it in Welsh.

*Glend.* I can speak English, lord, as well as
you;
For I was train'd up in the English court;
Where, being but young, I framed to the harp
Many an English ditty, lovely well,
And gave the tongue a helpful ornament,—
A virtue that was never seen in you.

*Hot.* Marry, and I am glad of it with all my
heart:
I had rather be a kitten and cry mew,
Than one of these same metre ballad-mongers;
I had rather hear a brazen candlestick turn'd,
Or a dry wheel grate on the axle-tree;

And that would set my teeth nothing on edge,
Nothing so much as mincing poetry:—
'Tis like the forc'd gait of a shuffling nag.

*Glend.* Come, you shall have Trent turn'd.

*Hot.* I do not care; I'll give thrice so much
    land
To any well-deserving friend;
But in the way of bargain, mark ye me,
I'll cavil on the ninth part of a hair.
Are the indentures drawn? shall we be gone?

*Glend.* The moon shines fair; you may away
    by night;
I'll haste the writer, and withal
Break with your wives of your departure hence:
I am afraid my daughter will run mad,
So much she doteth on her Mortimer.  [*Exit.*

*Mort.* Fie, cousin Percy! how you cross my
    father!

*Hot.* I cannot choose: sometimes he angers
    me
With telling me of the moldwarp and the ant,
Of the dreamer Merlin and his prophecies,
And of a dragon and a finless fish,
A clip-wing'd griffin and a moulten raven,
A couching lion and a ramping cat,
And such a deal of skimble-skamble stuff
As puts me from my faith. I tell you what,—
He held me last night at least nine hours
In reckoning up the several devils' names
That were has lackeys: I cried *hum*, and *well,*
    *go to,*
But mark'd him not a word. O, he's as tedious
As is a tired horse, a railing wife;
Worse than a smoky house:—I had rather live
With cheese and garlic in a windmill, far,
Than feed on cates and have him talk to me
In any summer-house in Christendom.

*Mort.* In faith, he is a worthy gentleman;
Exceedingly well read, and profited
In strange concealments; valiant as a lion,
And wondrous affable; and as bountiful
As mines of India. Shall I tell you, cousin?
He holds your temper in a high respect,
And curbs himself even of his natural scope
When you do cross his humour; faith, he does:
I warrant you, that man is not alive
Might so have tempted him as you have done,
Without the taste of danger and reproof:
But do not use it oft, let me entreat you.

*Wor.* In faith, my lord, you are too wilful-
    blame;
And since your coming hither have done enough
To put him quite beside his patience.
You must needs learn, lord, to amend this
    fault:    [blood,—
Though sometimes it shows greatness, courage,
And that's the dearest grace it renders you,—
Yet oftentimes it doth present harsh rage,
Defect of manners, want of government,
Pride, haughtiness, opinion, and disdain:
The least of which, haunting a nobleman,
Loseth men's hearts, and leaves behind a stain
Upon the beauty of all parts besides,
Beguiling them of commendation.

*Hot.* Well, I am school'd: good manners be
    your speed!
Here come our wives, and let us take our leave.

*Re-enter* GLENDOWER, *with* LADY MORTIMER
    *and* LADY PERCY.

*Mort.* This is the deadly spite that angers
    me,—
My wife can speak no English, I no Welsh.

*Glend.* My daughter weeps: she will not part
    with you:
She'll be a soldier too, she'll to the wars.

*Mort.* Good father, tell her that she and my
    aunt Percy
Shall follow in your conduct speedily.
    [GLEND. *speaks to* LADY MORT. *in Welsh,*
    *and she answers him in the same.*

*Glend.* She's desperate here; a peevish, self-
    will'd harlotry,
One that no persuasion can do good upon.
    [LADY MORT. *speaks to* MORT. *in Welsh*

*Mort.* I understand thy looks: that pretty
    Welsh
Which thou pour'st down from these welling
    heavens,
I am too perfect in; and, but for shame,
In such a parley should I answer thee.
    [LADY MORT. *speaks again.*
I understand thy kisses, and thou mine,
And that's a feeling disputation:
But I will never be a truant, love,
Till I have learned thy language; for thy tongue
Makes Welsh as sweet as ditties highly penn'd,
Sung by a fair queen in a summer's bower,
With ravishing division, to her lute.

*Glend.* Nay, if you melt, then will she run
    mad.    [LADY MORT. *speaks again.*

*Mort.* O, I am ignorance itself in this!

*Glend.* She bids you on the wanton rushes
    lay you down,
And rest your gentle head upon her lap,
And she will sing the song that pleaseth you,
And on your eyelids crown the god of sleep,
Charming your blood with pleasing heaviness;
Making such difference betwixt wake and sleep
As is the difference betwixt day and night,
The hour before the heavenly harness'd team
Begins his golden progress in the east.

*Mort.* With all my heart I'll sit and hear her
    sing:
By that time will our book, I think, be drawn.

*Glend.* Do so;
And those musicians that shall play to you
Hang in the air a thousand leagues from hence;
And straight they shall be here: sit, and attend.

*Hot.* Come, Kate, thou art perfect in lying
down: come, quick, quick, that I may lay my
head in thy lap.

*Lady P.* Go, ye giddy goose.
    [*The music plays.*

*Hot.* Now I perceive the devil understands
    Welsh;
And 'tis no marvel he's so humorous.
By'r lady, he's a good musician.

*Lady P.* Then should you be nothing but musical; for you are altogether governed by humours. Lie still, ye thief, and hear the lady sing in Welsh.

*Hot.* I had rather hear *Lady*, my brach, howl in Irish.

*Lady P.* Wouldst thou have thy head broken?

*Hot.* No.

*Lady P.* Then be still.

*Hot.* Neither; 'tis a woman's fault.

*Lady P.* Now God help thee!

*Hot.* To the Welsh lady's bed.

*Lady P.* What's that?

*Hot.* Peace! she sings.

[*A Welsh Song sung by* LADY MORT.

*Hot.* Come, Kate, I'll have your song too.

*Lady P.* Not mine, in good sooth.

*Hot.* Not yours, in good sooth! 'Heart, you swear like a comfit-maker's wife! *Not you, in good sooth;* and, *As true as I live;* and, *As God shall mend me;* and, *As sure as day:*
And giv'st such sarcenet surety for thy oaths,
As if thou never walk'dst further than Finsbury.
Swear me, Kate, like a lady as thou art,
A good mouth-filling oath; and leave *in sooth,*
And such protest of pepper-gingerbread,
To velvet guards and Sunday-citizens.
Come, sing.

*Lady P.* I will not sing.

*Hot.* 'Tis the next way to turn tailor, or be redbreast teacher. An the indentures be drawn, I'll away within these two hours; and so, come in when ye will. [*Exit.*

*Glend.* Come, come, Lord Mortimer; you are as slow
As hot Lord Percy is on fire to go.
By this our book is drawn; we will but seal,
And then to horse immediately.

*Mort.*                    With all my heart.
[*Exeunt.*

SCENE II.—LONDON. *A Room in the Palace.*

*Enter* KING HENRY, PRINCE HENRY, *and* Lords.

*K. Hen.* Lords, give us leave; the Prince of Wales and I
Must have some conference; but be near at hand,
For we shall presently have need of you.
[*Exeunt* Lords.
I know not whether God will have it so,
For some displeasing service I have done,
That, in his secret doom, out of my blood
He'll breed revengement and a scourge for me;
But thou dost, in thy passages of life,
Make me believe that thou art only mark'd
For the hot vengeance and the rod of heaven
To punish my mistreadings. Tell me else,
Could such inordinate and low desires,
Such poor, such bare, such lewd, such mean attempts,
Such barren pleasures, rude society,
As thou art match'd withal and grafted to,
Accompany the greatness of thy blood,
And hold their level with thy princely heart?

*P. Hen.* So please your majesty, I would I could
Quit all offences with as clear excuse,
As well as I am doubtless I can purge
Myself of many I am charg'd withal:
Yet such extenuation let me beg,
As, in reproof of many tales devis'd,—
Which oft the ear of greatness needs must hear,—
By smiling pick-thanks and base newsmongers,
I may, for some things true, wherein my youth
Hath faulty wander'd and irregular,
Find pardon on my true submission.

*K. Hen.* God pardon thee!—yet let me wonder, Harry,
At thy affections, which do hold a wing
Quite from the flight of all thy ancestors.
Thy place in council thou hast rudely lost,
Which by thy younger brother is supplied;
And art almost an alien to the hearts
Of all the court and princes of my blood:
The hope and expectation of thy time
Is ruin'd; and the soul of every man
Prophetically does forethink thy fall.
Had I so lavish of my presence been,
So common-hackney'd in the eyes of men,
So stale and cheap to vulgar company,—
Opinion, that did help me to the crown,
Had still kept loyal to possession,
And left me in reputeless banishment,
A fellow of no mark nor likelihood.
By being seldom seen, I could not stir
But, like a comet, I was wonder'd at;
That men would tell their children, *This is he;*
Others would say,—*Where, which is Bolingbroke?*
And then I stole all courtesy from heaven,
And dress'd myself in such humility
That I did pluck allegiance from men's hearts,
Loud shouts and salutations from their mouths,
Even in the presence of the crowned king.
Thus did I keep my person fresh and new;
My presence, like a robe pontifical,
Ne'er seen but wonder'd at: and so my state,
Seldom but sumptuous, showed like a feast,
And won by rareness such solemnity.
The skipping king, he ambled up and down
With shallow jesters and rash bavin wits,
Soon kindled and soon burn'd: carded his state;
Mingled his royalty with carping fools;
Had his great name profaned with their scorns;
And gave his countenance, against his name,
To laugh at gibing boys, and stand the push
Of every beardless vain comparative;
Grew a companion to the common streets,
Enfeoff'd himself to popularity;
That, being daily swallow'd by men's eyes,
They surfeited with honey, and began
To loathe the taste of sweetness, whereof a little
More than a little is by much too much.
So, when he had occasion to be seen,

He was but as the cuckoo is in June,
Heard, not regarded,—seen, but with such
 eyes,
As, sick and blunted with community,
Afford no extraordinary gaze,
Such as is bent on sun-like majesty
When it shines seldom in admiring eyes:
But rather drowz'd, and hung their eyelids
 down,
Slept in his face, and render'd such aspéct
As cloudy men use to their adversaries,
Being with his presence glutted, gorg'd, and
 full.
And in that very line, Harry, stand'st thou;
For thou hast lost thy princely privilege
With vile participation: not an eye
But is a-weary of thy common sight,
Save mine, which hath desir'd to see thee more;
Which now doth that I would not have it do,—
Make blind itself with foolish tenderness.

 *P. Hen.* I shall hereafter, my thrice-gracious
  lord,
Be more myself.

 *K. Hen.* For all the world,
As thou art to this hour, was Richard then
When I from France set foot at Ravenspurg;
And even as I was then is Percy now.
Now, by my sceptre, and my soul to boot,
He hath more worthy interest to the state
Than thou, the shadow of succession:
For, of no right, nor colour like to right,
He doth fill fields with harness in the realm;
Turns head against the lion's armed jaws;
And, being no more in debt to years than thou,
Leads ancient lords and reverend bishops on
To bloody battles and to bruising arms.
What never-dying honour hath he got
Against renowned Douglas! whose high deeds,
Whose hot incursions, and great name in arms,
Holds from all soldiers chief majority
And military title capital
Through all the kingdoms that acknowledge
 Christ:
Thrice hath this Hotspur Mars in swathing-
 clothes,
This infant warrior, in his enterprises
Discomfited great Douglas; ta'en him once,
Enlarged him, and made a friend of him,
To fill the mouth of deep defiance up,
And shake the peace and safety of our throne.
And what say you to this? Percy, Northumber-
 land,
The Archbishop's grace of York, Douglas,
 Mortimer,
Capitulate against us, and are up.
But wherefore do I tell these news to thee?
Why, Harry, do I tell thee of my foes,
Which art my near'st and dearest enemy?
Thou that art like enough,—through vassal
 fear,
Base inclination, and the start of spleen,—
To fight against me under Percy's pay,
To dog his heels, and court'sy at his frowns,
To show how much thou art degenerate.

 *P. Hen.* Do not think so, you shall not find
  it so:
And God forgive them that have so much
 sway'd
Your majesty's good thoughts away from me!
I will redeem all this on Percy's head,
And, in the closing of some glorious day,
Be bold to tell you that I am your son;
When I will wear a garment all of blood,
And stain my favours in a bloody mask,
Which, wash'd away, shall scour my shame
 with it:
And that shall be the day, whene'er it lights,
That this same child of honour and renown,
This gallant Hotspur, this all-praised knight,
And your unthought-of Harry chance to meet.
For every honour sitting on his helm,
Would they were multitudes, and on my head
My shames redoubled! for the time will come
That I shall make this northern youth ex-
 change
His glorious deeds for my indignities.
Percy is but my factor, good my lord,
To engross up glorious deeds on my behalf;
And I will call him to so strict account,
That he shall render every glory up,
Yea, even the slightest worship of his time,
Or I will tear the reckoning from his heart.
This, in the name of God, I promise here:
The which if he be pleas'd I shall perform,
I do beseech your majesty, may salve
The long-grown wounds of my intemperance:
If not, the end of life cancels all bands:
And I will die a hundred thousand deaths
Ere break the smallest parcel of this vow.

 *K. Hen.* A hundred thousand rebels die in
  this:— [herein.
Thou shalt have charge and sovereign trust

 *Enter* SIR WALTER BLUNT.

How now, good Blunt! thy looks are full of
 speed. [speak of.
 *Blunt.* So hath the business that I come to
Lord Mortimer of Scotland hath sent word
That Douglas and the English rebels met
The eleventh of this month at Shrewsbury:
A mighty and a fearful head they are,
If promises be kept on every hand,
As ever offer'd foul play in a state.

 *K. Hen.* The Earl of Westmoreland set forth
  to-day;
With him my son, Lord John of Lancaster;
For this advertisement is five days old:—
On Wednesday next, Harry, you shall set for-
 ward;
On Thursday we ourselves will march:
Our meeting is Bridgenorth: and, Harry, you
Shall march through Glostershire; by which
 account,
Our business valued, some twelve days hence
Our general forces at Bridgenorth shall meet.
Our hands are full of business: let's away;
Advantage feeds him fat while men delay.
 [*Exeunt.*

SCENE III.—EASTCHEAP. *A Room in the Boar's Head Tavern.*

*Enter* FALSTAFF *and* BARDOLPH.

*Fal.* Bardolph, am I not fallen away vilely since this last action? do I not bate? do I not dwindle? Why, my skin hangs about me like an old lady's loose gown; I am withered like an old apple-john. Well, I'll repent, and that suddenly, while I am in some liking; I shall be out of heart shortly, and then I shall have no strength to repent. An I have not forgotten what the inside of a church is made of, I am a pepper-corn, a brewer's horse: the inside of a church! Company, villanous company, hath been the spoil of me.                [not live long.

*Bard.* Sir John, you are so fretful, you can-

*Fal.* Why, there is it: come, sing me a bawdy song; make me merry. I was as virtuously given as a gentleman need to be; virtuous enough; swore little; diced not above seven times a week; went to a bawdy-house not above once in a quarter—of an hour; paid money that I borrowed—three or four times: lived well, and in good compass: and now I live out of all order, out of all compass.

*Bard.* Why, you are so fat, Sir John, that you must needs be out of all compass,—out of all reasonable compass, Sir John.

*Fal.* Do thou amend thy face, and I'll amend my life: thou art our admiral, thou bearest the lantern in the poop,—but 'tis in the nose of thee; thou art the Knight of the Burning Lamp.

*Bard.* Why, Sir John, my face does you no harm.

*Fal.* No, I'll be sworn; I make as good use of it as many a man doth of a Death's head or a *memento mori:* I never see thy face but I think upon hell-fire, and Dives that lived in purple; for there he is in his robes, burning, burning. If thou wert any way given to virtue, I would swear by thy face; my oath should be, *By this fire, that's God's angel;* but thou art altogether given over; and wert indeed, but for the light in thy face, the son of utter darkness. When thou rannest up Gadshill in the night to catch my horse, if I did not think thou hadst been an *ignis fatuus* or a ball of wildfire, there's no purchase in money. O, thou art a perpetual triumph, an everlasting bonfire light! Thou hast saved me a thousand marks in links and torches, walking with thee in the night betwixt tavern and tavern: but the sack that thou hast drunk me would have bought me lights as good cheap at the dearest chandler's in Europe. I have maintained that salamander of yours with fire any time this two-and-thirty years; God reward me for it!                [belly!

*Bard.* 'Sblood, I would my face were in your

*Fal.* God-a-mercy! so should I be sure to be heart-burn'd.

*Enter* Hostess.

How now, Dame Partlet the hen! have you inquired yet who picked my pocket?

*Host.* Why, Sir John, what do you think, Sir John? do you think I keep thieves in my house? I have searched, I have inquired, so has my husband, man by man, boy by boy, servant by servant: the tithe of a hair was never lost in my house before.

*Fal.* You lie, hostess: Bardolph was shaved, and lost many a hair; and I'll be sworn my pocket was picked. Go to, you are a woman, go.

*Host.* Who, I? no; I defy thee: God's light, I was never called so in mine own house before.

*Fal.* Go to, I know you well enough.

*Host.* No, Sir John; you do not know me, Sir John. I know you, Sir John: you owe me money, Sir John; and now you pick a quarrel to beguile me of it: I bought you a dozen of shirts to your back.

*Fal.* Dowlas, filthy dowlas: I have given them away to bakers' wives, and they have made bolters of them.

*Host.* Now, as I am a true woman, holland of eight shillings an ell. You owe money here besides, Sir John, for your diet and by-drinkings, and money lent you, four-and-twenty pound.

*Fal.* He had his part of it; let him pay.

*Host.* He? alas, he is poor; he hath nothing.

*Fal.* How! poor? look upon his face; what call you rich? let them coin his nose, let them coin his cheeks: I'll not pay a denier. What, will you make a younker of me? shall I not take mine ease in mine inn, but I shall have my pocket picked? I have lost a seal-ring of my grandfather's worth forty mark.

*Host.* O Jesu, I have heard the prince tell him, I know not how oft, that that ring was copper!

*Fal.* How! the prince is a Jack, a sneak-cup: 'sblood, an he were here I would cudgel him like a dog if he would say so.

*Enter* PRINCE HENRY *and* POINS, *marching.* FALSTAFF *meets the* PRINCE, *playing on his truncheon like a fife.*

*Fal.* How now, lad! is the wind in that door, i' faith? must we all march?

*Bard.* Yea, two and two, Newgate-fashion.

*Host.* My lord, I pray you, hear me.

*P. Hen.* What sayest thou, Mistress Quickly? How does thy husband? I love him well; he is an honest man.

*Host.* Good my lord, hear me.

*Fal.* Pr'ythee, let her alone, and list to me.

*P. Hen.* What sayest thou, Jack?

*Fal.* The other night I fell asleep here behind the arras, and had my pocket picked: this house is turned bawdy-house; they pick pockets.

*P. Hen.* What didst thou lose, Jack?

*Fal.* Wilt thou believe me, Hal? three or four bonds of forty pound a-piece, and a seal-ring of my grandfather's.

*P. Hen.* A trifle, some eight-penny matter.

*Host.* So I told him, my lord; and I said I heard your grace say so: and, my lord, he speaks most vilely of you, like a foul-mouthed man as he is, and said he would cudgel you.

*P. Hen.* What! he did not?

*Host.* There's neither faith, truth, nor womanhood in me else.

*Fal.* There's no more faith in thee than in a stewed prune; nor no more truth in thee than in a drawn fox; and for womanhood, Maid Marian may be the deputy's wife of the ward to thee. Go, you thing, go.

*Host.* Say, what thing? what thing?

*Fal.* What thing! why, a thing to thank God on.

*Host.* I am no thing to thank God on, I would thou shouldst know it; I am an honest man's wife; and, setting thy knighthood aside, thou art a knave to call me so.

*Fal.* Setting thy womanhood aside, thou art a beast to say otherwise.

*Host.* Say, what beast, thou knave, thou?

*Fal.* What beast! why, an otter⟩

*P. Hen.* An otter, Sir John! why an otter?

*Fal.* Why, she's neither fish nor flesh; a man knows not where to have her.

*Host.* Thou art an unjust man in saying so: thou or any man knows where to have me, thou knave, thou!

*P. Hen.* Thou sayest true, hostess; and he slanders thee most grossly.

*Host.* So he doth you, my lord; and said this other day you ought him a thousand pound.

*P. Hen.* Sirrah, do I owe you a thousand pound?

*Fal.* A thousand pound, Hal! a million: thy love is worth a million; thou owest me thy love.

*Host.* Nay, my lord, he call'd you Jack, and said he would cudgel you.

*Fal.* Did I, Bardolph?

*Bard.* Indeed, Sir John, you said so.

*Fal.* Yea,—if he said my ring was copper.

*P. Hen.* I say 'tis copper: darest thou be as good as thy word now?

*Fal.* Why, Hal, thou knowest, as thou art but man, I dare: but as thou art prince, I fear thee, as I fear the roaring of the lion's whelp.

*P. Hen.* And why not as the lion?

*Fal.* The king himself is to be feared as the lion: dost thou think I'll fear thee as I fear thy father? nay, an I do, I pray God my girdle break.

*P. Hen.* O, if it should, how would thy guts fall about thy knees! But, sirrah, there's no room for faith, truth, nor honesty, in this bosom of thine,—it is all filled up with guts and midriff. Charge an honest woman with picking thy pocket! Why, thou whoreson, impudent, embossed rascal, if there were anything in thy pocket but tavern-reckonings, memorandums of bawdy-houses, and one poor penny-worth of sugar-candy to make thee long-winded,—if thy pocket were enriched with any other injuries but these, I am a villain: and yet you will stand to it; you will not pocket-up wrong: art thou not ashamed?

*Fal.* Dost thou hear, Hal? thou knowest in the state of innocency Adam fell; and what should poor Jack Falstaff do in the days of villany? Thou seest I have more flesh than another man, and therefore more frailty. You confess, then, you picked my pocket?

*P. Hen.* It appears so by the story.

*Fal.* Hostess, I forgive thee: go, make ready breakfast; love thy husband, look to thy servants, cherish thy guests: thou shalt find me tractable to any honest reason: thou seest I am pacified.—Still?—Nay, pr'ythee, be gone. [*Exit* Hostess.] Now, Hal, to the news at court: for the robbery, lad,—how is that answered?

*P. Hen.* O, my sweet beef, I must still be good angel to thee:—the money is paid back again.

*Fal.* O, I do not like that paying back: 'tis a double labour.

*P. Hen.* I am good friends with my father, and may do anything.

*Fal.* Rob me the exchequer the first thing thou doest, and do it with unwashed hands too.

*Bard.* Do, my lord.  [of foot.

*P. Hen.* I have procured thee, Jack, a charge

*Fal.* I would it had been of horse. Where shall I find one that can steal well? O for a fine thief, of the age of two-and-twenty or thereabouts! I am heinously unprovided. Well, God be thanked for these rebels,—they offend none but the virtuous: I laud them, I praise them.

*P. Hen.* Bardolph,—

*Bard.* My lord.  [Lancaster,

*P. Hen.* Go bear this letter to Lord John of To my brother John; this to my Lord of Westmoreland.  [*Exit* BARDOLPH.

Go, Poins, to horse, to horse; for thou and I Have thirty miles to ride yet ere dinner-time.— 
  [*Exit* POINS.

Jack, meet me to-morrow in the Temple-hall At two o'clock in the afternoon:  [receive There shalt thou know thy charge, and there Money and order for their furniture. The land is burning; Percy stands on high; And either they or we must lower lie.  [*Exit.*

*Fal.* Rare words! brave world!—Hostess, my breakfast; come:—

O, I could wish this tavern were my drum! 
  [*Exit.*

## ACT IV.

SCENE I.—*The Rebel Camp near Shrewsbury.*

*Enter* HOTSPUR, WORCESTER, *and* DOUGLAS.

*Hot.* Well said, my noble Scot: if speaking truth
In this fine age were not thought flattery,
Such attribution should the Douglas have,
As not a soldier of this season's stamp
Should go so general current through the world.
By heaven, I cannot flatter; I defy
The tongues of soothers; but a braver place
In my heart's love hath no man than yourself:

Nay, task me to my word; approve me, lord.
*Doug.* Thou art the king of honour:
No man so potent breathes upon the ground
But I will beard him.
*Hot.*            Do so, and 'tis well.—

*Enter a* Messenger *with letters.*

What letters hast thou there?—I can but thank
you.
*Mess.* These letters come from your father,—
*Hot.* Letters from him! why comes he not
himself?            [ous sick.
*Mess.* He cannot come, my lord; he's griev-
*Hot.* Zounds! how has he the leisure to be
sick
In such a justling time? Who leads his power?
Under whose government come they along?
*Mess.* His letters bear his mind, not I, my
lord.            [bed?
*Wor.* I pr'ythee, tell me, doth he keep his
*Mess.* He did, my lord, four days ere I set
forth;
And at the time of my departure thence
He was much fear'd by his physicians.
*Wor.* I would the state of time had first been
whole
Ere he by sickness had been visited:
His health was never better worth than now.
*Hot.* Sick now! droop now! this sickness doth
infect
The very life-blood of our enterprise;
'Tis catching hither, even to our camp.—
He writes me here that inward sickness,—
And that his friends by deputation could not
So soon be drawn; nor did he think it meet
To lay so dangerous and dear a trust
On any soul remov'd, but on his own.
Yet doth he give us bold advertisement,
That with our small conjunction we should on,
To see how fortune is dispos'd to us;
For, as he writes, there is no quailing now,
Because the king is certainly possess'd
Of all our purposes. What say you to it?
*Wor.* Your father's sickness is a maim to us.
*Hot.* A perilous gash, a very limb lopp'd
off:—
And yet, in faith, 'tis not; his present want
Seems more than we shall find it:—were it good
To set the exact wealth of all our states
All at one cast? to set so rich a main
On the nice hazard of one doubtful hour?
It were not good; for therein should we read
The very bottom and the soul of hope,
The very list, the very utmost bound
Of all our fortunes.
*Doug.*            Faith, and so we should;
Where now remains a sweet reversion:
We may boldly spend upon the hope of what
Is to come in:
A comfort of retirement lives in this.
*Hot.* A rendezvous, a home to fly unto,
If that the devil and mischance look big
Upon the maidenhead of our affairs.    [here.
*Wor.* But yet I would your father had been

The quality and hair of our attempt
Brooks no division: it will be thought
By some, that know not why he is away,
That wisdom, loyalty, and mere dislike
Of our proceedings, kept the earl from hence:
And think how such an apprehension
May turn the tide of fearful faction,
And breed a kind of question in our cause;
For well you know we of the offering side
Must keep aloof from strict arbitrement,
And stop all sight-holes, every loop from whence
The eye of reason may pry in upon us:
This absence of your father's draws a curtain
That shows the ignorant a kind of fear
Before not dreamt of.
*Hot.*            You strain too far.
I, rather, of his absence make this use:—
It lends a lustre and more great opinion,
A larger dare to our great enterprise,
Than if the earl were here: for men must think,
If we, without his help, can make a head
To push against the kingdom, with his help
We shall o'erturn it topsy-turvy down.—
Yet all goes well, yet all our joints are whole.
*Doug.* As heart can think: there is not such
a word
Spoke of in Scotland as this term of fear.

*Enter* SIR RICHARD VERNON.

*Hot.* My cousin Vernon! welcome, by my
soul.            [lord.
*Ver.* Pray God my news be worth a welcome,
The Earl of Westmoreland, seven thousand
strong,
Is marching hitherwards; with him Prince
John.
*Hot.* No harm:—what more?
*Ver.*            And further, I have learn'd
The king himself in person is set forth,
Or hitherwards intended speedily,
With strong and mighty preparation.    [son,
*Hot.* He shall be welcome too. Where is his
The nimble-footed madcap Prince of Wales
And his comrades, that daff'd the world aside,
And bid it pass?
*Ver.*            All furnish'd, all in arms;
All plum'd like estridges, that wing the wind;
Bated like eagles having lately bath'd;
Glittering in golden coats, like images;
As full of spirit as the month of May,
And gorgeous as the sun at midsummer;
Wanton as youthful goats, wild as young bulls.
I saw young Harry,—with his beaver on,
His cuisses on his thighs, gallantly arm'd,—
Rise from the ground like feather'd Mercury,
And vaulted with such ease into his seat,
As if an angel dropp'd down from the clouds,
To turn and wind a fiery Pegasus,
And witch the world with noble horsemanship.
*Hot.* No more, no more; worse than the sun
in March,
This praise doth nourish agues. Let them come.
They come like sacrifices in their trim,
And to the fire-ey'd maid of smoky war,

All hot and bleeding, will we offer them:
The mailed Mars shall on his altar sit,
Up to the ears in blood. I am on fire
To hear this rich reprisal is so nigh.
And yet not ours.—Come, let me taste my
    horse,
Who is to bear me, like a thunderbolt,
Against the bosom of the Prince of Wales:
Harry to Harry shall, hot horse to horse,
Meet, and ne'er part till one drop down a
    corse.—
O that Glendower were come!
  *Ver.*            There is more news:
I learn'd in Worcester, as I rode along,
He cannot draw his power this fourteen days.
  *Doug.* That's the worst tidings that I hear
    of yet.
  *Wor.* Ay, by my faith, that bears a frosty
    sound.
  *Hot.* What may the king's whole battle reach
    unto?
  *Ver.* To thirty thousand.
  *Hot.*            Forty let it be:
My father and Glendower being both away,
The powers of us may serve so great a day.
Come, let us take a muster speedily:
Doomsday is near; die all, die merrily.
  *Doug.* Talk not of dying; I am out of fear
Of death or death's hand for this one half-year.
                        *[Exeunt.*

SCENE II.—*A public Road near Coventry.*

*Enter* FALSTAFF *and* BARDOLPH.

  *Fal.* Bardolph, get thee before to Coventry;
fill me a bottle of sack: our soldiers shall march
through; we'll to Sutton-Cop-hill to-night.
  *Bard.* Will you give me money, captain?
  *Fal.* Lay out, lay out.
  *Bard.* This bottle makes an angel.
  *Fal.* An if it do, take it for thy labour; and
if it make twenty, take them all; I'll answer
the coinage. Bid my lieutenant Peto meet me
at the town's end.
  *Bard.* I will, captain: farewell.     *[Exit.*
  *Fal.* If I be not ashamed of my soldiers, I
am a soused gurnet. I have misused the king's
press damnably. I have got, in exchange of a
hundred and fifty soldiers, three hundred and
odd pounds. I press me none but good house-
holders, yeomen's sons; inquire me out contracted bachelors, such as had been asked twice
on the bans; such a commodity of warm slaves
as had as lief hear the devil as a drum; such as
fear the report of a caliver worse than a struck
fowl or a hurt wild-duck. I pressed me none
but such toasts-and-butter, with hearts in their
bellies no bigger than pins' heads, and they
have bought out their services; and now my
whole charge consists of ancients, corporals,
lieutenants, gentlemen of companies, slaves as
ragged as Lazarus in the painted cloth, where
the glutton's dogs licked his sores; and such
as, indeed, were never soldiers, but discarded

unjust serving-men, younger sons to younger
brothers, revolted tapsters, and ostlers trade-
fallen; the cankers of a calm world and a long
peace; ten times more dishonourable ragged
than an old-faced ancient: and such have I, to
fill up the rooms of them that have bought out
their services, that you would think that I had
a hundred and fifty tattered prodigals lately
come from swine-keeping, from eating draff and
husks. A mad fellow met me on the way, and
told me I had unloaded all the gibbets, and
pressed the dead bodies. No eye hath seen such
scarecrows. I'll not march through Coventry
with them, that's flat:—nay, and the villains
march wide betwixt the legs, as if they had
gyves on; for, indeed, I had the most of them
out of prison. There's but a shirt and a half in
all my company; and the half-shirt is two napkins tacked together and thrown over the
shoulders like a herald's coat without sleeves;
and the shirt, to say the truth, stolen from my
host at Saint Alban's, or the red-nose innkeeper
of Daventry. But that's all one; they'll find
linen enough on every hedge.

*Enter* PRINCE HENRY *and* WESTMORELAND.

  *P. Hen.* How now, blown Jack! how now,
quilt!
  *Fal.* What, Hal! how now, mad wag! what
a devil dost thou in Warwickshire?—My good
Lord of Westmoreland, I cry you mercy: I
thought your honour had already been at
Shrewsbury.
  *West.* Faith, Sir John, 'tis more than time
that I were there, and you too; but my powers
are there already. The king, I can tell you,
looks for us all: we must away all night.
  *Fal.* Tut, never fear me: I am as vigilant as
a cat to steal cream.
  *P. Hen.* I think, to steal cream, indeed; for
thy theft hath already made thee butter. But
tell me, Jack, whose fellows are these that come
after?
  *Fal.* Mine, Hal, mine.
  *P. Hen.* I did never see such pitiful rascals.
  *Fal.* Tut, tut; good enough to toss; food for
powder, food for powder; they'll fill a pit as
well as better: tush, man, mortal men, mortal
men.
  *West.* Ay, but, Sir John, methinks they are
exceeding poor and bare,—too beggarly.
  *Fal.* Faith, for their poverty, I know not
where they had that; and for their bareness, I
am sure they never learned that of me.
  *P. Hen.* No, I'll be sworn; unless you call
three fingers on the ribs bare. But, sirrah, make
haste: Percy is already in the field.
  *Fal.* What, is the king encamped?
  *West.* He is, Sir John: I fear we shall stay
too long.
  *Fal.* Well,
To the latter end of a fray and the beginning of
    a feast
Fits a dull fighter and a keen guest.   *[Exeunt.*

SCENE III.—*The Rebel Camp near Shrewsbury.*

*Enter* HOTSPUR, WORCESTER, DOUGLAS, *and*
VERNON.

*Hot.* We'll fight with him to-night.
*Wor.*                                  It may not be.
*Doug.* You give him, then, advantage.
*Ver.*                                  Not a whit.
*Hot.* Why say you so? looks he not for
supply?
*Ver.* So do we.
*Hot.*            His is certain, ours is doubtful.
*Wor.* Good cousin, be advis'd; stir not to-
night.
*Ver.* Do not, my lord.
*Doug.*            You do not counsel well:
You speak it out of fear and cold heart.
*Ver.* Do me no slander, Douglas: by my
life,—
And I dare well maintain it with my life,—
If well-respected honour bid me on,
I hold as little counsel with weak fear
As you, my lord, or any Scot that lives:—
Let it be seen to-morrow in the battle
Which of us fears.
*Doug.*            Yea, or to-night.
*Ver.*                         Content.
*Hot.* To-night, say I.                 [much,
*Ver.* Come, come, it may not be. I wonder
Being men of such great leading as you are,
That you foresee not what impediments
Drag back our expedition: certain horse
Of my cousin Vernon's are not yet come up:
Your uncle Worcester's horse came but to-day;
And now their pride and mettle is asleep,
Their courage with hard labour tame and dull,
That not a horse is half the half of himself.
*Hot.* So are the horses of the enemy
In general, journey-bated and brought low:
The better part of ours is full of rest.
*Wor.* The number of the king exceedeth ours.
For God's sake, cousin, stay till all come in.
            [*The trumpet sounds a parley.*

*Enter* SIR WALTER BLUNT.

*Blunt.* I come with gracious offers from the
king,
If you vouchsafe me hearing and respect.
*Hot.* Welcome, Sir Walter Blunt; and would
to God
You were of our determination!
Some of us love you well; and even those some
Envy your great deservings and good name,
Because you are not of our quality,
But stand against us like an enemy. [stand so,
*Blunt.* And God defend but still I should
So long as out of limit and true rule
You stand against anointed majesty!
But, to my charge.—The king hath sent to
know
The nature of your griefs; and whereupon
You conjure from the breast of civil peace
Such bold hostility; teaching his duteous land
Audacious cruelty. If that the king

Have any way your good deserts forgot,—
Which he confesseth to be manifold,—
He bids you name your griefs; and with all speed
You shall have your desires with interest,
And pardon absolute for yourself, and these
Herein misled by your suggestion.     [king
*Hot.* The king is kind; and well we know the
Knows at what time to promise, when to pay.
My father and my uncle and myself
Did give him that same royalty he wears;
And when he was not six-and-twenty strong,
Sick in the world's regard, wretched and low,
A poor unminded outlaw sneaking home,
My father gave him welcome to the shore;
And when he heard him swear, and vow to God,
He came but to be Duke of Lancaster,
To sue his livery and beg his peace,
With tears of innocency and terms of zeal,—
My father, in kind heart and pity mov'd,
Swore him assistance, and perform'd it too.
Now, when the lords and barons of the realm
Perceiv'd Northumberland did lean to him,
The more and less came in with cap and knee;
Met him in boroughs, cities, villages;
Attended him on bridges, stood in lanes,
Laid gifts before him, proffer'd him their oaths,
Gave him their heirs as pages, follow'd him
Even at the heels in golden multitudes.
He presently,—as greatness knows itself,—
Steps me a little higher than his vow
Made to my father, while his blood was poor,
Upon the naked shore at Ravenspurg;
And now, forsooth, takes on him to reform
Some certain edicts, and some strait decrees,
That lie too heavy on the commonwealth;
Cries out upon abuses, seems to weep
Over his country's wrongs; and, by this face,
This seeming brow of justice, did he win
The hearts of all that he did angle for:
Proceeded further; cut me off the heads
Of all the favourites that the absent king
In deputation left behind him here,
When he was personal in the Irish war.
*Blunt.* Tut, I came not to hear this.
*Hot.*                         Then to the point.
In short time after, he depos'd the king;
Soon after that, depriv'd him of his life;
And, in the neck of that, task'd the whole state:
To make that worse, suffer'd his kinsman
March,—
Who is, if every owner were well plac'd,
Indeed his king,—to be incag'd in Wales
There without ransom to lie forfeited;
Disgrac'd me in my happy victories;
Sought to entrap me by intelligence;
Rated my uncle from the council-board;
In rage dismiss'd my father from the court;
Broke oath on oath, committed wrong on
wrong;
And, in conclusion, drove us to seek out
This head of safety; and withal to pry
Into his title, the which we find
Too indirect for long continuance.
*Blunt.* Shall I return this answer to the king?

*Hot.* Not so, Sir Walter: we'll withdraw
    awhile.
Go to the king; and let there be impawn'd
Some surety for a safe return again,
And in the morning early shall my uncle
Bring him our purposes: and so, farewell.
    *Blunt.* I would you would accept of grace
        and love.
    *Hot.* And may be so we shall.
    *Blunt.*                    Pray God you do!
                                    [*Exeunt.*

SCENE IV.—YORK. *A Room in the* ARCH-
    BISHOP'S *House.*

*Enter the* ARCHBISHOP OF YORK, *and* SIR
    MICHAEL.

    *Arch.* Hie, good Sir Michael; bear this sealed
        brief
With winged haste to the lord marshal;
This to my cousin Scroop; and all the rest
To whom they are directed. If you knew
How much they do import, you would make
    haste.
    *Sir M.* My good lord,
I guess their tenor.
    *Arch.*              Like enough you do.
To-morrow, good Sir Michael, is a day
Wherein the fortune of ten thousand men
Must bide the touch; for, sir, at Shrewsbury,
As I am truly given to understand;
The king, with mighty and quick-raised power,
Meets with Lord Harry: and I fear, Sir
    Michael,
What with the sickness of Northumberland,—
Whose power was in the first proportion,—
And what with Owen Glendower's absence
    thence,—
Who with them was a rated sinew too,
And comes not in, o'erruled by prophecies,—
I fear the power of Percy is too weak
To wage an instant trial with the king.
    *Sir M.* Why, my good lord, you need not
        fear; there is Douglas,
And Lord Mortimer.
    *Arch.*              No, Mortimer is not there.
    *Sir M.* But there is Mordake, Vernon, Lord
        Harry Percy,
And there is my Lord of Worcester; and a head
Of gallant warriors, noble gentlemen.
    *Arch.* And so there is; but yet the king hath
        drawn
The special head of all the land together:—
The Prince of Wales, Lord John of Lancaster,
The noble Westmoreland, and warlike Blunt;
And many more corrivals and dear men
Of estimation and command in arms.
    *Sir M.* Doubt not, my lord, they shall be
        well oppos'd.
    *Arch.* I hope no less, yet needful 'tis to fear;
And, to prevent the worst, Sir Michael, speed:
For if Lord Percy thrive not, ere the king
Dismiss his power, he means to visit us,—
For he hath heard of our confederacy,—

And 'tis but wisdom to make strong against
    him:
Therefore make haste. I must go write again
To other friends; and so, farewell, Sir Michael.
                            [*Exeunt severally.*

## ACT V.

SCENE I.—*The* KING'S *Camp near Shrewsbury.*

*Enter* KING HENRY, PRINCE HENRY, PRINCE
    JOHN OF LANCASTER, SIR WALTER BLUNT,
    *and* SIR JOHN FALSTAFF.

    *K. Hen.* How bloodily the sun begins to peer
Above yon bosky hill! the day looks pale
At his distemperature.
    *P. Hen.*                The southern wind
Doth play the trumpet to his purposes;
And by his hollow whistling in the leaves
Foretells a tempest and a blustering day.
    *K. Hen.* Then with the losers let it sympa-
        thize,
For nothing can seem foul to those that win.
                            [*Trumpet sounds.*

*Enter* WORCESTER *and* VERNON.

How now, my Lord of Worcester! 'tis not well
That you and I should meet upon such terms
As now we meet. You have deceiv'd our trust;
And made us doff our easy robes of peace,
To crush our old limbs in ungentle steel;
This is not well, my lord, this is not well.
What say you to it? will you again unknit
This churlish knot of all-abhorred war?
And move in that obedient orb again
Where you did give a fair and natural light;
And be no more an exhal'd meteor,
A prodigy of fear, and a portent
Of broached mischief to the unborn times?
    *Wor.* Hear me, my liege:
For mine own part, I could be well content
To entertain the lag-end of my life
With quiet hours; for, I do protest,
I have not sought the day of this dislike.
    *K. Hen.* You have not sought it! how comes
        it, then?
    *Fal.* Rebellion lay in his way, and he found it.
    *P. Hen.* Peace, chewet, peace!      [*looks*
    *Wor.* It pleas'd your majesty to turn your
Of favour from myself and all our house;
And yet I must remember you, my lord,
We were the first and dearest of your friends.
For you my staff of office did I break
In Richard's time; and posted day and night
To meet you on the way, and kiss your hand,
When yet you were in place and in account
Nothing so strong and fortunate as I.
It was myself, my brother, and his son,
That brought you home, and boldly did out-
    dare
The dangers of the time: you swore to us,—
And you did swear that oath at Doncaster,—
That you did nothing purpose 'gainst the state;
Nor claim no further than your new-fall'n right,
The seat of Gaunt, dukedom of Lancaster:

To this we swore our aid. But in short space
It rain'd down fortune showering on your head;
And such a flood of greatness fell on you,—
What with our help, what with the absent king,
What with the injuries of a wanton time,
The seeming sufferances that you had borne,
And the contrarious winds that held the king
So long in his unlucky Irish wars
That all in England did repute him dead,—
And, from this swarm of fair advantages,
You took occasion to be quickly woo'd
To gripe the general sway into your hand;
Forgot your oath to us at Doncaster;
And, being fed by us, you us'd us so
As that ungentle gull, the cuckoo's bird,
Useth the sparrow,—did oppress our nest,
Grew by our feeding to so great a bulk    [sight
That even our love durst not come near your
For fear of swallowing; but with nimble wing
We were enforc'd, for safety-sake, to fly
Out of your sight, and raise this present head:
Whereby we stand opposed by such means
As you yourself have forg'd against yourself;
By unkind usage, dangerous countenance,
And violation of all faith and troth
Sworn to us in your younger enterprise.

*K. Hen.* These things, indeed, you have articulated,
Proclaim'd at market-crosses, read in churches;
To face the garment of rebellion
With some fine colour that may please the eye
Of fickle changelings and poor discontents,
Which gape and rub the elbow at the news
Of hurlyburly innovation:
And never yet did insurrection want
Such water-colours to impaint his cause;
Nor moody beggars, starving for a time
Of pellmell havoc and confusion.    [a soul

*P. Hen.* In both our armies there is many
Shall pay full dearly for this encounter,
If once they join in trial. Tell your nephew,
The Prince of Wales doth join with all the world
In praise of Henry Percy: by my hopes,
This present enterprise set off his head,
I do not think a braver gentleman,
More active-valiant or more valiant-young,
More daring or more bold, is now alive
To grace this latter age with noble deeds.
For my part, I may speak it to my shame,
I have a truant been to chivalry;
And so I hear he doth account me too:
Yet this before my father's majesty,—
I am content that he shall take the odds
Of his great name and estimation,
And will, to save the blood on either side,
Try fortune with him in a single fight.

*K. Hen.* And, Prince of Wales, so dare we venture thee,
Albeit considerations infinite
Do make against it.—No, good Worcester, no,
We love our people well; even those we love
That are misled upon your cousin's part;
And, will they take the offer of our grace,

Both he, and they, and you, yea, every man
Shall be my friend again, and I'll be his:
So tell your cousin, and bring me word
What he will do: but if he will not yield,
Rebuke and dread correction wait on us,
And they shall do their office. So, be gone;
We will not now be troubled with reply:
We offer fair; take it advisedly.
                    [*Exeunt* WOR. *and* VER.

*P. Hen.* It will not be accepted, on my life:
The Douglas and the Hotspur both together
Are confident against the world in arms.

*K. Hen.* Hence, therefore, every leader to his charge;
For, on their answer, will we set on them:
And God befriend us, as our cause is just!
                    [*Exeunt* KING, BLUNT, *and* P. JOHN.

*Fal.* Hal, if thou see me down in the battle,
and bestride me, so; 'tis a point of friendship.

*P. Hen.* Nothing but a colossus can do thee
that friendship. Say thy prayers, and farewell.

*Fal.* I would it were bed-time, Hal, and all
well.

*P. Hen.* Why, thou owest God a death.
                    [*Exit.

*Fal.* 'Tis not due yet; I would be loth to
pay him before his day. What need I be so
forward with him that calls not on me? Well,
'tis no matter; honour pricks me on. Yea, but
how if honour prick me off when I come on?
how then? Can honour set-to a leg? no: or an
arm? no: or take away the grief of a wound?
no. Honour hath no skill in surgery, then? no.
What is honour? a word. What is in that word,
honour? What is that honour? air. A trim reckoning!—Who hath it? he that died o' Wednesday. Doth he feel it? no. Doth he hear it? no.
Is it insensible, then? yea, to the dead. But
will it not live with the living? no. Why? detraction will not suffer it:—therefore I'll none
of it: honour is a mere scutcheon: and so ends
my catechism.                    [*Exit.

SCENE II.—*The Rebel Camp.*

*Enter* WORGESTER *and* VERNON.

*Wor.* O, no, my nephew must not know, Sir Richard,
The liberal kind offer of the king.

*Ver.* 'Twere best he did.

*Wor.*                    Then are we all undone.
It is not possible, it cannot be,
The king should keep his word in loving us;
He will suspect us still, and find a time
To punish this offence in other faults:
Suspicion shall be all stuck full of eyes:
For treason is but trusted like the fox,
Who, ne'er so tame, so cherish'd, and lock'd up,
Will have a wild trick of his ancestors.
Look how we can, or sad or merrily,
Interpretation will misquote our looks;
And we shall feed like oxen at a stall,
The better cherish'd still the nearer death.
My nephew's trespass may be well forgot,—

It hath the excuse of youth and heat of blood,
And an adopted name of privilege,—
A hare-brain'd Hotspur, govern'd by a spleen.
All his offences live upon my head
And on his father's: we did train him on;
And, his corruption being ta'en from us,
We, as the spring of all, shall pay for all.
Therefore, good cousin, let not Harry know,
In any case the offer of the king.
　　*Ver.* Deliver what you will, I'll say 'tis so.
Here comes your cousin.

*Enter* HOTSPUR *and* DOUGLAS; Officers *and*
　　Soldiers *behind.*

　　*Hot.* My uncle is return'd:—deliver up
My Lord of Westmoreland.—Uncle, what
　　news?
　　*Wor.* The king will bid you battle presently.
　　*Doug.* Defy him by the Lord of Westmore-
land.
　　*Hot.* Lord Douglas, go you and tell him so.
　　*Doug.* Marry, and shall, and very willingly.
　　　　　　　　　　　　　　　　　　　　[*Exit.*
　　*Wor.* There is no seeming mercy in the king.
　　*Hot.* Did you beg any? God forbid!
　　*Wor.* I told him gently of our grievances,
Of his oath-breaking; which he mended thus,—
By now forswearing that he is forsworn:
He calls us rebels, traitors; and will scourge
With haughty arms this hateful name in us.

*Re-enter* DOUGLAS.

　　*Doug.* Arm, gentlemen; to arms! for I have
　　thrown
A brave defiance in King Henry's teeth,
And Westmoreland, that was engag'd, did bear
　　it;
Which cannot choose but bring him quickly on.
　　*Wor.* The Prince of Wales stepp'd forth be-
fore the king,
And, nephew, challeng'd you to single fight.
　　*Hot.* O, would the quarrel lay upon our
　　heads;
And that no man might draw short breath to-
　　day
But I and Harry Monmouth! Tell me, tell me,
How show'd his tasking? seem'd it in contempt?
　　*Ver.* No, by my soul: I never in my life
Did hear a challenge urg'd more modestly,
Unless a brother should a brother dare
To gentle exercise and proof of arms.
He gave you all the duties of a man;
Trimm'd up your praises with a princely
　　tongue;
Spoke your deservings like a chronicle;
Making you ever better than his praise,
By still dispraising praise valu'd with you:
And, which became him like a prince indeed,
He made a blushing cital of himself;
And chid his truant youth with such a grace,
As if he master'd there a double spirit,
Of teaching and of learning instantly.
There did he pause: but let me tell the world,—
If he outlive the envy of this day,

England did never owe so sweet a hope,
So much misconstru'd in his wantonness.
　　*Hot.* Cousin, I think thou art enamoured
Upon his follies: never did I hear
Of any prince so wild o' liberty.
But be he as he will, yet once ere night
I will embrace him with a soldier's arm,
That he shall shrink under my courtesy.—
Arm, arm with speed:—and, fellows, soldiers,
　　friends,
Better consider what you have to do
Than I, that have not well the gift of tongue,
Can lift your blood up with persuasion.

*Enter a* Messenger.

　　*Mess.* My lord, here are letters for you.
　　*Hot.* I cannot read them now.—
O gentlemen, the time of life is very short!
To spend that shortness basely were too long,
If life did ride upon a dial's point,
Still ending at the arrival of an hour.
An if we live, we live to tread on kings;
If die, brave death, when princes die with us!
Now, for our consciences,—the arms are fair,
When the intent of bearing them is just.

*Enter another* Messenger.

　　*Mess.* My lord, prepare; the king comes on
　　apace.　　　　　　　　　　　　　　　[tale,
　　*Hot.* I thank him that he cuts me from my
For I profess not talking; only this,—
Let each man do his best: and here draw I
A sword, whose temper I intend to stain
With the best blood that I can meet withal
In the adventure of this perilous day.
Now,—*Esperance!*—Percy!—and set on.—
Sound all the lofty instruments of war,
And by that music let us all embrace:
For, heaven to earth, some of us never shall
A second time do such a courtesy.
　　　　[*The trumpets sound. They embrace, and
　　　　　　　　exeunt.*

SCENE III.—*Plain near Shrewsbury.*

*Excursions, and parties fighting. Alarum to the
　　battle. Then enter* DOUGLAS *and* BLUNT,
　　*meeting.*

　　*Blunt.* What is thy name, that in the battle
　　thus
Thou crossest me? What honour dost thou seek
Upon my head?
　　*Doug.* Know, then, my name is Douglas;
And I do haunt thee in the battle thus
Because some tell me that thou art a king.
　　*Blunt.* They tell thee true.　　　[bought
　　*Doug.* The Lord of Stafford dear to-day hath
Thy likeness; for, instead of thee, King Harry,
The sword hath ended him: so shall it thee,
Unless thou yield thee as my prisoner.
　　*Blunt.* I was not born a yielder, thou proud
　　Scot;
And thou shalt find a king that will revenge
Lord Stafford's death.
　　　　　　　[*They fight, and* BLUNT *is slain.*

*Enter* HOTSPUR.

*Hot.* O Douglas, hadst thou fought at Holmedon thus,
I never had triúmph'd upon a Scot.
*Doug.* All's done, all's won; here breathless lies the king.
*Hot.* Where?
*Doug.* Here.
*Hot.* This, Douglas? no; I know this face full well:
A gallant knight he was, his name was Blunt;
Semblably furnish'd like the king himself.
*Doug.* A fool go with thy soul, whither it goes!
A borrow'd title hast thou bought too dear:
Why didst thou tell me that thou wert a king?
*Hot.* The king hath many masking in his coats.
*Doug.* Now, by my sword, I will kill all his coats;
I'll murder all his wardrobe, piece by piece,
Until I meet the king.
*Hot.* Up, and away!
Our soldiers stand full fairly for the day.
[*Exeunt.*

*Other alarums. Enter* FALSTAFF.

*Fal.* Though I could 'scape shot-free at London, I fear the shot here: here's no scoring but upon the pate.—Soft! who art thou? Sir Walter Blunt:—there's honour for you: here's no vanity!—I am as hot as molten lead, and as heavy too: God keep lead out of me! I need no more weight than mine own bowels:—I have led my raggamuffins where they are peppered: there's not three of my hundred and fifty left alive; and they are for the town's end, to beg during life.—But who comes here?

*Enter* PRINCE HENRY.

*P. Hen.* What, stand'st thou idle here? lend me thy sword:
Many a nobleman lies stark and stiff
Under the hoofs of vaunting enemies,
Whose deaths are unreveng'd: pr'ythee, lend me thy sword.
*Fal.* O Hal, I pr'ythee, give me leave to breathe awhile.—Turk Gregory never did such deeds in arms as I have done this day. I have paid Percy, I have made him sure.
*P. Hen.* He is, indeed; and living to kill thee. Lend me thy sword, I pr'ythee.
*Fal.* Nay, before God, Hal, if Percy be alive thou gettest not my sword; but take my pistol, if thou wilt.
*P. Hen.* Give it me: what, is it in the case?
*Fal.* Ay, Hal; 'tis hot, 'tis hot; there's that will sack a city.
[*The* PRINCE *draws out a bottle of sack.*
*P. Hen.* What, is't a time to jest and dally now? [*Throws it at him, and exit.*
*Fal.* Well, if Percy be alive, I'll pierce him. If he do come in my way, so; if he do not, if

I come in his willingly, let him make a carbonado of me. I like not such grinning honour as Sir Walter hath: give me life: which if I can save, so; if not, honour comes unlooked for, and there's an end. [*Exit.*

SCENE IV.—*Another part of the Field.*

*Alarums. Excursions. Enter* KING HENRY, PRINCE HENRY, PRINCE JOHN, *and* WESTMORELAND.

*K. Hen.* I pr'ythee,
Harry, withdraw thyself; thou bleed'st too much.—
Lord John of Lancaster, go you with him.
*P. John.* Not I, my lord, unless I did bleed too.
*P. Hen.* I do beseech your majesty, make up,
Lest your retirement do amaze your friends.
*K. Hen.* I will do so.— [tent.
My Lord of Westmoreland, lead him to his
*West.* Come, my lord, I will lead you to your tent. [your help:
*P. Hen.* Lead me, my lord? I do not need
And God forbid a shallow scratch should drive
The Prince of Wales from such a field as this,
Where stain'd nobility lies trodden on,
And rebels' arms triúmph in massacres!
*P. John.* We breathe too long:—come, cousin Westmoreland,
Our duty this way lies; for God's sake, come.
[*Exeunt* P. JOHN *and* WEST.
*P. Hen.* By heaven, thou hast deceiv'd me, Lancaster;
I did not think thee lord of such a spirit:
Before, I lov'd thee as a brother, John;
But now I do respect thee as my soul.
*K. Hen.* I saw him hold Lord Percy at the point
With lustier maintenance than I did look for
Of such an ungrown warrior.
*P. Hen.* O, this boy
Lends mettle to us all. [*Exit.*

*Alarums. Enter* DOUGLAS.

*Doug.* Another king! they grow like Hydra's heads:
I am the Douglas, fatal to all those
That wear those colours on them:—What art thou,
That counterfeit'st the person of a king?
*K. Hen.* The king himself, who, Douglas, grieves at heart,
So many of his shadows thou hast met,
And not the very king. I have two boys
Seek Percy and thyself about the field:
But, seeing thou fall'st on me so luckily,
I will assay thee; so, defend thyself!
*Doug.* I fear, thou art another counterfeit;
And yet, in faith, thou bear'st thee like a king:
But mine I am sure thou art, whoe'er thou be,
And thus I win thee.
[*They fight; the* KING *being in danger,
re-enter* P. HENRY.

*P. Hen.* Hold up thy head, vile Scot, or thou art like
Never to hold it up again! the spirits
Of Shirley, Stafford, Blunt, are in my arms:
It is the Prince of Wales that threatens thee;
Who never promiseth but he means to pay.
       [*They fight;* DOUGLAS *flies.*
Cheerly, my lord: how fares your grace?—
Sir Nicholas Gawsey hath for succour sent,
And so hath Clifton: I'll to Clifton straight.

*K. Hen.* Stay, and breathe awhile:—
Thou hast redeem'd thy lost opinion;
And show'd thou mak'st some tender of my life
In this fair rescue thou hast brought to me.

*P. Hen.* O God, they did me too much injury
That ever said I hearken'd for your death!
If it were so, I might have let alone
The insulting hand of Douglas over you,
Which would have been as speedy in your end
As all the poisonous potions in the world,
And sav'd the treacherous labour of your son.

*K. Hen.* Make up to Clifton, I'll to Sir Nicholas Gawsey.     [*Exit.*

*Enter* HOTSPUR.

*Hot.* If I mistake not, thou art Harry Monmouth.

*P. Hen.* Thou speak'st as if I would deny my name.

*Hot.* My name is Harry Percy.

*P. Hen.*      Why, then I see
A very valiant rebel of the name.
I am the Prince of Wales; and think not, Percy,
To share with me in glory any more:
Two stars keep not their motion in one sphere;
Nor can one England brook a double reign,
Of Harry Percy and the Prince of Wales.

*Hot.* Nor shall it, Harry, for the hour is come
To end the one of us; and would to God
Thy name in arms were now as great as mine!

*P. Hen.* I'll make it greater ere I part from thee;
And all the budding honours on thy crest
I'll crop, to make a garland for my head.

*Hot.* I can no longer brook thy vanities.
          [*They fight.*

*Enter* FALSTAFF.

*Fal.* Well said, Hal! to it, Hal!—Nay, you shall find no boy's play here, I can tell you.

*Re-enter* DOUGLAS; *he fights with* FALSTAFF' *who falls down as if he were dead, and exit* DOUGLAS. HOTSPUR *is wounded, and falls.*

*Hot.* O, Harry, thou hast robb'd me of my youth!
I better brook the loss of brittle life
Than those proud titles thou hast won of me;
They wound my thoughts worse than thy sword my flesh:—
But thought's the slave of life, and life time's fool;
And time, that takes survey of all the world,
Must have a stop. O, I could prophesy,

But that the earthy and cold hand of death
Lies on my tongue:—No, Percy, thou art dust,
And food for—        [*Dies.*

*P. Hen.* For worms, brave Percy: fare thee well, great heart!—
Ill-weav'd ambition, how much art thou shrunk!
When that this body did contain a spirit,
A kingdom for it was too small a bound;
But now two paces of the vilest earth
Is room enough:—this earth that bears thee dead
Bears not alive so stout a gentleman.
If thou wert sensible of courtesy,
I should not make so dear a show of zeal:—
But let my favours hide thy mangled face;
And, even in thy behalf, I'll thank myself
For doing these fair rites of tenderness.
Adieu, and take thy praise with thee to heaven!
Thy ignominy sleep with thee in the grave,
But not remember'd in thy epitaph!—
     [*He sees* FAL. *on the ground.*
What, old acquaintance! could not all this flesh
Keep in a little life? Poor Jack, farewell!
I could have better spar'd a better man.
O, I should have a heavy miss of thee,
If I were much in love with vanity.
Death hath not struck so fat a deer to-day,
Though many dearer, in this bloody fray.
Embowell'd will I see thee by and by:
Till then in blood by noble Percy lie.  [*Exit.*

*Fal.* [*Rising slowly.*] Embowelled! if thou embowel me to-day, I'll give you leave to powder me and eat me too to-morrow. 'Sblood, 'twas time to counterfeit, or that hot termagant Scot had paid me scot and lot too. Counterfeit? I lie, I am no counterfeit: to die is to be a counterfeit; for he is but the counterfeit of a man who hath not the life of a man; but to counterfeit dying, when a man thereby liveth, is to be no counterfeit, but the true and perfect image of life indeed. The better part of valour is discretion; in the which better part I have saved my life. Zounds, I am afraid of this gunpowder Percy, though he be dead; how if he should counterfeit too, and rise? I am afraid he would prove the better counterfeit. Therefore I'll make him sure: yea, and I'll swear I killed him. Why may not he rise as well as I? Nothing confutes me but eyes, and nobody sees me. Therefore, sirrah [*stabbing him*], with a new wound in your thigh, come you along with me.    [*Takes* HOTSPUR *on his back.*

*Re-enter* PRINCE HENRY *and* PRINCE JOHN.

*P. Hen.* Come, brother John, full bravely hast thou flesh'd
Thy maiden sword.

*P. John.*    But, soft! whom have we here?
Did you not tell me this fat man was dead?

*P. Hen.* I did; I saw him dead, breathless and bleeding
On the ground.—
Art thou alive? or is it fantasy

That plays upon our eyesight? I pr'ythee, speak;
We will not trust our eyes without our ears:—
Thou art not what thou seem'st.

*Fal.* No, that's certain; I am not a double man: but if I be not Jack Falstaff, then am I a Jack. There is Percy [*throwing the body down*]: if your father will do me any honour, so; if not, let him kill the next Percy himself. I look to be either earl or duke, I can assure you.

*P. Hen.* Why, Percy I killed myself, and saw thee dead.

*Fal.* Didst thou?—Lord, Lord, how this world is given to lying!—I grant you I was down and out of breath, and so was he; but we rose both at an instant, and fought a long hour by Shrewsbury clock. If I may be believed, so; if not, let them that should reward valour bear the sin upon their own heads. I'll take it upon my death, I gave him this wound in the thigh: if the man were alive, and would deny it, zounds, I would make him eat a piece of my sword.

*P. John.* This is the strangest tale that e'er I heard.

*P. Hen.* This is the strangest fellow, brother John.—
Come, bring your luggage nobly on your back:
For my part, if a lie may do thee grace,
I'll gild it with the happiest terms I have.

[*A retreat is sounded.*
The trumpet sounds retreat; the day is ours.
Come, brother, let's to the highest of the field,
To see what friends are living, who are dead.

[*Exeunt* P. HENRY *and* P. JOHN.

*Fal.* I'll follow, as they say, for reward. He that rewards me, God reward him! If I do grow great, I'll grow less; for I'll purge, and leave sack, and live cleanly, as a nobleman should do.          [*Exit, bearing off the body.*

SCENE V.—*Another part of the Field.*

*The Trumpets sound. Enter* KING HENRY, PRINCE HENRY, PRINCE JOHN, WESTMORE-LAND, *and others, with* WORCESTER *and* VERNON *prisoners.*

*K. Hen.* Thus ever did rebellion find rebuke.—
Ill-spirited Worcester! did we not send grace,
Pardon, and terms of love to all of you?
And wouldst thou turn our offers contrary?
Misuse the tenor of thy kinsman's trust?

Three knights upon our party slain to-day,
A noble earl, and many a creature else,
Had been alive this hour,
If, like a Christian, thou hadst truly borne
Betwixt our armies true intelligence.

*Wor.* What I have done my safety urg'd me to,
And I embrace this fortune patiently,
Since not to be avoided it falls on me.

*K. Hen.* Bear Worcester to the death, and Vernon too:
Other offenders we will pause upon.

[*Exeunt* WOR. *and* VER., *guarded.*
How goes the field?

*P. Hen.* The noble Scot, Lord Douglas, when he saw
The fortune of the day quite turn'd from him,
The noble Percy slain, and all his men
Upon the foot of fear,—fled with the rest;
And falling from a hill, he was so bruis'd
That the pursuers took him. At my tent
The Douglas is; and I beseech your grace
I may dispose of him.

*K. Hen.* With all my heart.

*P. Hen.* Then, brother John of Lancaster, to you
This honourable bounty shall belong:
Go to the Douglas, and deliver him
Up to his pleasure, ransomless and free:
His valour, shown upon our crests to-day,
Hath taught us how to cherish such high deeds
Even in the bosom of our adversaries.

*P. John.* I thank your grace for this high courtesy,
Which I shall give away immediately.

*K. Hen.* Then this remains,—that we divide our power.—
You, son John, and my cousin Westmoreland,
Towards York shall bend you with your dearest speed,
To meet Northumberland and the prelate Scroop,
Who, as we hear, are busily in arms:
Myself,—and you, son Harry,—will towards Wales,
To fight with Glendower and the Earl of March.
Rebellion in this land shall lose his sway,
Meeting the check of such another day:
And since this business so fair is done,
Let us not leave till all our own be won.

[*Exeunt.*

# KING HENRY IV
## PART II.

Act IV. Sc. 4.

# KING HENRY IV.

## SECOND PART

### DRAMATIS PERSONÆ

KING HENRY THE FOURTH.
HENRY, *Prince of Wales, afterwards* KING HENRY V.,
THOMAS, *Duke of Clarence,*
PRINCE JOHN OF LANCASTER, *afterwards* (Henry V.) *Duke of Bedford,*
PRINCE HUMPHREY OF GLOSTER, *afterwards* (Henry V.) *Duke of Gloster,* } *his Sons.*

EARL OF WARWICK,
EARL OF WESTMORELAND,
EARL OF SURREY,
GOWER,
HARCOURT, } *of the* KING'S *party.*

Lord Chief-Justice *of the King's Bench.*
A Gentleman *attending on the* Chief-Justice.

EARL OF NORTHUMBERLAND,
SCROOP, *Archbishop of York,*
LORD MOWBRAY,
LORD HASTINGS,
LORD BARDOLPH,
SIR JOHN COLEVILE, } *Enemies to the* KING.

TRAVERS *and* MORTON, *Retainers of* NORTHUMBERLAND.
FALSTAFF, BARDOLPH, PISTOL, *and* PAGE.
POINS *and* PETO, *Attendants on* PRINCE HENRY.
SHALLOW *and* SILENCE, *Country Justices.*
DAVY, *Servant to* SHALLOW.
MOULDY, SHADOW, WART, FEEBLE, *and* BULLCALF, *Recruits.*
FANG *and* SNARE, *Sheriff's Officers.*
RUMOUR.
A Porter.
A Dancer, *Speaker of the Epilogue.*

LADY NORTHUMBERLAND.
LADY PERCY.
MISTRESS QUICKLY, *Hostess of a Tavern in Eastcheap.*
DOLL TEARSHEET.

Lords *and other* Attendants; Officers, Soldiers, Messengers, Drawers, Beadles, Grooms, &c.

SCENE,—ENGLAND.

### INDUCTION.

WARKWORTH. *Before* NORTHUMBERLAND'S *Castle.*

*Enter* Rumour, *painted full of tongues.*

*Rum.* Open your ears; for which of you will stop
The vent of hearing when loud Rumour speaks?
I, from the orient to the drooping west,
Making the wind my post-horse, still unfold
The acts commenced on this ball of earth:
Upon my tongues continual slanders ride,
The which in every language I pronounce,
Stuffing the ears of men with false reports.
I speak of peace, while covert enmity,
Under the smile of safety, wounds the world:
And who but Rumour, who but only I,
Make fearful musters and prepar'd defence;
Whilst the big year, swoln with some other grief,
Is thought with child by the stern tyrant war,
And no such matter? Rumour is a pipe
Blown by surmises, jealousies, conjectures;
And of so easy and so plain a stop
That the blunt monster with uncounted heads,
The still-discordant wavering multitude,
Can play upon it. But what need I thus
My well-known body to anatomize
Among my household? Why is Rumour here?

I run before King Harry's victory;
Who, in a bloody field by Shrewsbury,
Hath beaten down young Hotspur and his troops,
Quenching the flame of bold rebellion
Even with the rebel's blood. But what mean I
To speak so true at first? my office is
To noise abroad that Harry Monmouth fell
Under the wrath of noble Hotspur's sword;
And that the king before the Douglas' rage
Stoop'd his anointed head as low as death.
This have I rumour'd through the peasant towns
Between that royal field of Shrewsbury
And this worm-eaten hold of ragged stone,
Where Hotspur's father, old Northumberland,
Lies crafty-sick: the posts come tiring on,
And not a man of them brings other news
Than they have learn'd of me: from Rumour's tongues
They bring smooth comforts false, worse than true wrongs. [*Exit.*

### ACT I.

SCENE I.—*The same.*

*The* Porter *before the Gate; enter* LORD BARDOLPH.

*L. Bard.* Who keeps the gate here, ho?—
Where is the earl?

[455]

*Port.* What shall I say you are?

*L. Bard.*          Tell thou the earl
That the Lord Bardolph doth attend him here.

*Port.* His lordship is walk'd forth into the
    orchard:
Please it your honour, knock but at the gate,
And he himself will answer.

*L. Bard.*          Here comes the earl.
                       [*Exit* Porter.

#### Enter NORTHUMBERLAND.

*North.* What news, Lord Bardolph? every
    minute now
Should be the father of some stratagem:
The times are wild; contention, like a horse,
Full of high feeding, madly hath broke loose
And bears down all before him.

*L. Bard.*          Noble earl,
I bring you certain news from Shrewsbury.

*North.* Good, an God will!

*L. Bard.*     As good as heart can wish:—
The king is almost wounded to the death;
And, in the fortune of my lord your son,
Prince Harry slain outright; and both the
    Blunts
Kill'd by the hand of Douglas: young Prince
    John,
And Westmoreland, and Stafford, fled the field;
And Harry Monmouth's brawn, the hulk Sir
    John,
Is prisoner to your son: O, such a day,
So fought, so follow'd, and so fairly won,
Came not till now to dignify the times,
Since Cæsar's fortunes!

*North.*          How is this deriv'd?
Saw you the field? came you from Shrewsbury?

*L. Bard.* I spake with one, my lord, that
    came from thence;
A gentleman well bred and of good name,
That freely render'd me these news for true.

*North.* Here comes my servant Travers,
    whom I sent
On Tuesday last to listen after news.

*L. Bard.* My lord, I over-rode him on the
    way;
And he is furnish'd with no certainties
More than he haply may retail from me.

#### Enter TRAVERS.

*North.* Now, Travers, what good tidings
    come with you?

*Tra.* My lord, Sir John Umfrevile turn'd me
    back
With joyful tidings; and, being better hors'd,
Out-rode me. After him came spurring hard
A gentleman, almost forspent with speed,
That stopp'd by me to breathe his bloodied
    horse.
He ask'd the way to Chester; and of him
I did demand what news from Shrewsbury.
He told me that rebellion had bad luck,
And that young Harry Percy's spur was cold.
With that, he gave his able horse the head,
And, bending forward, struck his armed heels

Against the panting sides of his poor jade
Up to the rowel-head; and starting so,
He seem'd in running to devour the way,
Staying no longer question.

*North.*          Ha!—Again:
Said he young Harry Percy's spur was cold?
Of Hotspur, coldspur? that rebellion
Had met ill-luck?

*L. Bard.*     My lord, I'll tell you what;
If my young lord your son have not the day,
Upon mine honour, for a silken point
I'll give my barony: never talk of it.

*North.* Why should the gentleman that rode
    by Travers
Give, then, such instances of loss?

*L. Bard.*          Who, he?
He was some hilding fellow, that had stolen
The horse he rode on; and, upon my life,
Spoke at a venture.—Look, here comes more
    news.

#### Enter MORTON.

*North.* Yea, this man's brow, like to a title-
    leaf,
Foretells the nature of a tragic volume:
So looks the strand, whereon the imperious
    flood
Hath left a witness'd usurpation,—
Say, Morton, didst thou come from Shrews-
    bury?

*Mor.* I ran from Shrewsbury, my noble lord;
Where hateful death put on his ugliest mask
To fright our party.

*North.*     How doth my son and brother?
Thou tremblest; and the whiteness in thy cheek
Is apter than thy tongue to tell thy errand.
Even such a man, so faint, so spiritless,
So dull, so dead in look, so woe-begone,
Drew Priam's curtain in the dead of night,
And would have told him half his Troy was
    burn'd;
But Priam found the fire ere he his tongue,
And I my Percy's death ere thou report'st it.
This thou wouldst say,—Your son did thus and
    •thus;
Your brother thus; so fought the noble Douglas;
Stopping my greedy ear with their bold deeds:
But in the end to stop mine ear indeed,
Thou hast a sigh to blow away this praise,
Ending with—brother, son, and all are dead.

*Mor.* Douglas is living, and your brother,
    yet;
But, for my lord your son,—

*North.*          Why, he is dead.
See what a ready tongue suspicion hath!
He that but fears the thing he would not know
Hath by instinct knowledge from others' eyes
That what he fear'd is chanced. Yet speak,
    Morton;
Tell thou thy earl his divination lies,
And I will take it as a sweet disgrace,
And make thee rich for doing me such wrong.

*Mor.* You are too great to be by me gain-
    said:

Your spirit is too true, your fears too certain.

*North.* Yet, for all this, say not that Percy's
    dead.
I see a strange confession in thine eye:
Thou shak'st thy head, and hold'st it fear or sin
To speak a truth. If he be slain, say so;
The tongue offends not that reports his death:
And he doth sin that doth belie the dead;
Not he which says the dead is not alive.
Yet the first bringer of unwelcome news
Hath but a losing office; and his tongue
Sounds ever after as a sullen bell,
Remember'd knolling a departing friend.

*L. Bard.* I cannot think, my lord, your son
    is dead.

*Mor.* I am sorry I should force you to believe
That which I would to God I had not seen;
But these mine eyes saw him in bloody state,
Rend'ring faint quittance, wearied and out-
    breath'd,             [down
To Harry Monmouth; whose swift wrath beat
The never-daunted Percy to the earth,
From whence with life he never more sprang up.
In few, his death,—whose spirit lent a fire
Even to the dullest peasant in his camp,—
Being bruited once, took fire and heat away
From the best-temper'd courage in his troops;
For from his metal was his party steel'd;
Which once in him abated, all the rest
Turn'd on themselves, like dull and heavy lead:
And as the thing that's heavy in itself,
Upon enforcement, flies with greatest speed,
So did our men, heavy in Hotspur's loss,
Lend to this weight such lightness with their
    fear,
That arrows fled not swifter toward their aim
Than did our soldiers, aiming at their safety,
Fly from the field. Then was that noble
    Worcester
Too soon ta'en prisoner; and that furious Scot,
The bloody Douglas, whose well-labouring
    sword           [king,
Had three times slain the appearance of the
'Gan vail his stomach, and did grace the shame
Of those that turn'd their backs; and in his
    flight,
Stumbling in fear, was took. The sum of all
Is, that the king hath won; and hath sent out
A speedy power to encounter you, my lord,
Under the conduct of young Lancaster
And Westmoreland. This is the news at full.

*North.* For this I shall have time enough to
    mourn.
In poison there is physic; and these news,
Having been well, that would have made me
    sick,
Being sick, have in some measure made me
    well:           [joints,
And as the wretch, whose fever-weaken'd
Like strengthless hinges, buckle under life,
Impatient of his fit, breaks like a fire
Out of his keeper's arms; even so my limbs,
Weaken'd with grief, being now enrag'd with
    grief,

Are thrice themselves. Hence, therefore, thou
    nice crutch!
A scaly gauntlet now, with joints of steel,
Must glove this hand: and hence, thou sickly
    quoif!
Thou art a guard too wanton for the head
Which princes, flesh'd with conquest, aim to
    hit.
Now bind my brows with iron, and approach
The rugged'st hour that time and spite dare
    bring
To frown upon the enrag'd Northumberland!
Let heav'n kiss earth! Now let not Nature's
    hand
Keep the wild flood confin'd! let order die!
And let this world no longer be a stage
To feed contention in a lingering act;
But let one spirit of the first-born Cain
Reign in all bosoms, that, each heart being set
On bloody courses, the rude scene may end,
And darkness be the burier of the dead!

*Tra.* This strained passion doth you wrong,
    my lord.

*L. Bard.* Sweet earl, divorce not wisdom
    from your honour.

*Mor.* The lives of all your loving complices
Lean on your health; the which, if you give o'er
To stormy passion, must perforce decay.
You cast the event of war, my noble lord,
And summ'd the account of chance, before you
    said,
Let us make head. It was your presurmise
That in the dole o' blows your son might drop:
You knew he walk'd o'er perils on an edge,
More likely to fall in than to get o'er;
You were advis'd his flesh was capable
Of wounds and scars; and that his forward
    spirit
Would lift him where most trade of danger
    rang'd:
Yet did you say,—Go forth; and none of this
Though strongly apprehended, could restrain
The stiff-borne action. What hath, then, be-
    fallen,
Or what hath this bold enterprise brought forth,
More than that being which was like to be?

*L. Bard.* We all that are engaged to this loss
Knew that we ventur'd on such dangerous seas,
That if we wrought out life, 'twas ten to one:
And yet we ventur'd, for the gain propos'd
Chok'd the respect of likely peril fear'd;
And since we are o'erset, venture again.
Come, we will all put forth, body and goods.

*Mor.* 'Tis more than time: and, my most
    noble lord,
I hear for certain, and do speak the truth,—
The gentle Archbishop of York is up
With well-appointed powers: he is a man
Who with a double surety binds his followers.
My lord your son had only but the corpse,
But shadows and the shows of men, to fight:
For that same word, rebellion, did divide
The action of their bodies from their souls;
And they did fight with queasiness, constrain'd,

As men drink potions; that their weapons only
Seem'd on our side, but, for their spirits and
      souls,
This word, rebellion, it had froze them up,
As fish are in a pond. But now the archbishop
Turns insurrection to religion:
Suppos'd sincere and holy in his thoughts,
He's follow'd both with body and with mind;
And doth enlarge his rising with the blood
Of fair King Richard, scrap'd from Pomfret
      stones;
Derives from heaven his quarrel and his cause;
Tells them he doth bestride a bleeding land,
Gasping for life under great Bolingbroke;
And more and less do flock to follow him.

*North.* I knew of this before; but, to speak
      truth,
This present grief had wip'd it from my mind.
Go in with me; and counsel every man
The aptest way for safety and revenge?
Get posts and letters, and make friends with
      speed,—
Never so few, and never yet more need.
                                    [*Exeunt.*

SCENE II.—LONDON. *A Street.*

*Enter* SIR JOHN FALSTAFF, *with his* Page
      *bearing his sword and buckler.*

*Fal.* Sirrah, you giant, what says the doctor
to my water?

*Page.* He said, sir, the water itself was a good
healthy water; but, for the party that owed it,
he might have more diseases than he knew of.

*Fal.* Men of all sorts take a pride to gird at
me: the brain of this foolish-compounded clay,
man, is not able to invent anything that tends
to laughter, more than I invent or is invented
on me: I am not only witty in myself, but the
cause that wit is in other men. I do here walk
before thee like a sow that hath overwhelmed
all her litter but one. If the prince put thee
into my service for any other reason than to set
me off, why then I have no judgment. Thou
whoreson mandrake, thou art fitter to be worn
in my cap than to wait at my heels. I was never
manned with an agate till now: but I will set
you neither in gold nor silver, but in vile apparel, and send you back again to your master,
for a jewel,—the juvenal, the prince your master, whose chin is not yet fledged. I will sooner
have a beard grow in the palm of my hand than
he shall get one on his cheek; and yet he will
not stick to say his face is a face-royal: God
may finish it when he will, it is not a hair amiss
yet: he may keep it still as a face-royal, for a
barber shall never earn sixpence out of it; and
yet he will be crowing as if he had writ man
ever since his father was a bachelor. He may
keep his own grace, but he is almost out of
mine, I can assure him.—What said Master
Dumbleton about the satin for my short cloak
and my slops?

*Page.* He said, sir, you should procure him

better assurance than Bardolph: he would not
take his bond and yours; he liked not the
security.

*Fal.* Let him be damned, like the glutton!
may his tongue be hotter!—A whoreson Achi-
tophel! a rascally yea-forsooth knave! to bear
a gentleman in hand, and then stand upon
security!—The whoreson smooth-pates do now
wear nothing but high shoes, and bunches of
keys at their girdles; and if a man is thorough
with them in honest taking up, then they must
stand upon security. I had as lief they would
put ratsbane in my mouth as offer to stop it
with security. I looked he should have sent me
two-and-twenty yards of satin, as I am a true
knight, and he sends me security. Well, he may
sleep in security; for he hath the horn of abundance, and the lightness of his wife shines
through it: and yet cannot he see, thou he have
his own lantern to light him.—Where's Bardolph?

*Page.* He's gone into Smithfield to buy your
worship a horse.

*Fal.* I bought him in Paul's, and he'll buy
me a horse in Smithfield: an I could get me
but a wife, in the stews, I were manned, horsed,
and wived.

*Page.* Sir, here comes the nobleman that
committed the prince for striking him about
Bardolph.

*Fal.* Wait close; I will not see him.

*Enter the* Lord Chief-Justice *and an* Attendant.

*Ch. Just.* What's he that goes there?

*Atten.* Falstaff, an't please your lordship.

*Ch. Just.* He that was in question for the
robbery?

*Atten.* He, my lord: but he hath since done
good service at Shrewsbury; and, as I hear, is
now going with some charge to the Lord John
of Lancaster.

*Ch. Just.* What, to York? Call him back
again.

*Atten.* Sir John Falstaff!

*Fal.* Boy, tell him I am deaf.

*Page.* You must speak louder; my master is
deaf.

*Ch. Just.* I am sure he is, to the hearing of
anything good.—Go, pluck him by the elbow;
I must speak with him.

*Atten.* Sir John,—

*Fal.* What! a young knave, and begging!
Is there not wars? is there not employment?
Doth not the king lack subjects? Do not the
rebels need soldiers? Though it be a shame to
be on any side but one, it is worse shame to beg
than to be on the worst side, were it worse than
the name of rebellion can tell how to make it.

*Atten.* You mistake me, sir.

*Fal.* Why, sir, did I say you were an honest
man? setting my knighthood and my soldiership aside, I had lied in my throat if I had
said so.

*Atten.* I pray you, sir, then set your knight

hood and your soldiership aside; and give me leave to tell you, you lie in your throat, if you say I am any other than an honest man.

*Fal.* I give thee leave to tell me so! I lay aside that which grows to me! If thou gettest any leave of me, hang me; if thou takest leave, thou wert better be hanged. You hunt-counter, hence! avaunt!

*Atten.* Sir, my lord would speak with you.

*Ch. Just.* Sir John Falstaff, a word with you.

*Fal.* My good lord!—God give your lordship good time of day. I am glad to see your lordship abroad: I heard say your lordship was sick: I hope your lordship goes abroad by advice. Your lordship, though not clean past your youth, hath yet some smack of age in you, some relish of the saltness of time; and I most humbly beseech your lordship to have a reverend care of your health.

*Ch. Just.* Sir John, I sent for you before your expedition to Shrewsbury.

*Fal.* An't please your lordship, I hear his majesty is returned with some discomfort from Wales.

*Ch. Just.* I talk not of his majesty:—you would not come when I sent for you.

*Fal.* And I hear, moreover, his highness is fallen into this same whoreson apoplexy.

*Ch. Just.* Well, God mend him! I pray you let me speak with you.

*Fal.* This apoplexy is, as I take it, a kind of lethargy, an't please your lordship; a kind of sleeping in the blood, a whoreson tingling.

*Ch. Just.* What tell you me of it? be it as it is.

*Fal.* It hath its original from much grief, from study, and perturbation of the brain: I have read the cause of his effects in Galen; it is a kind of deafness.

*Ch. Just.* I think you are fallen into the disease; for you hear not what I say to you.

*Fal.* Very well, my lord, very well: rather, an't please you, it is the disease of not listening, the malady of not marking, that I am troubled withal.

*Ch. Just.* To punish you by the heels would amend the attention of your ears; and I care not if I do become your physician.

*Fal.* I am as poor as Job, my lord, but not so patient: your lordship may minister the potion of imprisonment to me in respect of poverty; but how I should be your patient to follow your prescriptions, the wise may make some dram of a scruple, or, indeed, a scruple itself.

*Ch. Just.* I sent for you when there were matters against you for your life, to come speak with me.

*Fal.* As I was then advised by my learned counsel in the laws of this land-service, I did not come.

*Ch. Just.* Well, the truth is, Sir John, you live in great infamy.

*Fal.* He that buckles him in my belt cannot live in less.

*Ch. Just.* Your means are very slender, and your waste is great.

*Fal.* I would it were otherwise; I would my means were greater and my waist slenderer.

*Ch. Just.* You have misled the youthful prince.

*Fal.* The young prince hath misled me: I am the fellow with the great belly, and he my dog.

*Ch. Just.* Well, I am loth to gall a new-healed wound: your day's service at Shrewsbury hath a little gilded over your night's exploit on Gadshill: you may thank the unquiet time for your quiet o'erposting that action.

*Fal.* My lord,—

*Ch. Just.* But since all is well, keep it so: wake not a sleeping wolf.

*Fal.* To wake a wolf is as bad as to smell a fox.

*Ch. Just.* What! you are as a candle, the better part burnt out.

*Fal.* A wassail candle, my lord; all tallow: if I did say of wax, my growth would approve the truth.

*Ch. Just.* There is not a white hair on your face but should have his effect of gravity.

*Fal.* His effect of gravy, gravy, gravy.

*Ch. Just.* You follow the young prince up and down, like his ill angel.

*Fal.* Not so, my lord; your ill angel is light; but I hope he that looks upon me will take me without weighing: and yet, in some respects, I grant, I cannot go:—I cannot tell. Virtue is of so little regard in these costermonger times that true valour is turned bear-herd: pregnancy is made a tapster, and hath his quick wit wasted in giving reckonings: all the other gifts appertinent to man, as the malice of this age shapes them, are not worth a gooseberry. You that are old consider not the capacities of us that are young; you measure the heat of our livers with the bitterness of your galls: and we that are in the vaward of our youth, I must confess, are wags too.

*Ch. Just.* Do you set down your name in the scroll of youth, that are written down old with all the characters of age? Have you not a moist eye? a dry hand? a yellow cheek? a white beard? a decreasing leg? an increasing belly? Is not your voice broken? your wind short? your chin double? your wit single? and every part about you blasted with antiquity? and will you yet call yourself young? Fie, fie, fie, Sir John!

*Fal.* My lord, I was born about three of the clock in the afternoon, with a white head, and something a round belly. For my voice,—I have lost it with hollaing and singing of anthems. To approve my youth further, I will not; the truth is, I am only old in judgment and understanding; and he that will caper with me for a thousand marks, let him lend me the money, and have at him. For the box o' the ear that the prince gave you,—he gave it like a rude prince, and you took it like a sensible lord. I have checked him for it; and the young lion repents; marry, not in ashes and sackcloth, but in new silk and old sack.

*Ch. Just.* Well, God send the prince a better companion!

*Fal.* God send the companion a better prince! I cannot rid my hands of him.

*Ch. Just.* Well, the king hath severed you and Prince Harry: I hear you are going with Lord John of Lancaster against the archbishop and the Earl of Northumberland.

*Fal.* Yea; I thank your pretty sweet wit for it. But look you, pray, all you that kiss my Lady Peace at home, that our armies join not in a hot day; for, by the Lord, I take but two shirts out with me, and I mean not to sweat extraordinarily: if it be a hot day, and I brandish anything but my bottle, I would I might never spit white again. There is not a dangerous action can peep out his head but I am thrust upon it: well, I cannot last ever: but it was alway yet the trick of our English nation, if they have a good thing, to make it too common. If you will needs say I am an old man, you should give me rest. I would to God my name were not so terrible to the enemy as it is: I were better to be eaten to death with rust than to be scoured to nothing with perpetual motion.

*Ch. Just.* Well, be honest, be honest; and God bless your expedition!

*Fal.* Will your lordship lend me a thousand pound to furnish me forth?

*Ch. Just.* Not a penny, not a penny; you are too impatient to bear crosses. Fare you well: commend me to my cousin Westmoreland.

[*Exeunt* Chief-Justice *and* Attendant.

*Fal.* If I do, fillip me with a three-man beetle.—A man can no more separate age and covetousness than he can part young limbs and lechery: but the gout galls the one, and the pox pinches the other; and so both the diseases prevent my curses.—Boy!—

*Page.* Sir?

*Fal.* What money is in my purse?

*Page.* Seven groats and two pence.

*Fal.* I can get no remedy against this consumption of the purse: borrowing only lingers and lingers it out, but the disease is incurable. —Go bear this letter to my Lord of Lancaster; this to the prince; this to the Earl of Westmoreland; and this to old Mistress Ursula, whom I have weekly sworn to marry since I perceive the first white hair on my chin. About it; you know where to find me. [*Exit* Page.] A pox of this gout! or, a gout of this pox! for the one or the other plays the rogue with my great toe. It is no matter if I do halt; I have the wars for my colour, and my pension shall seem the more reasonable. A good wit will make use of anything. I will turn diseases to commodity.

[*Exit.*

SCENE III.—YORK. *A Room in the* ARCH-BISHOP'S *Palace.*

*Enter the* ARCHBISHOP OF YORK, *the* LORDS HASTINGS, MOWBRAY, *and* BARDOLPH.

*Arch.* Thus have you heard our cause and know our means;
And, my most noble friends, I pray you all
Speak plainly your opinions of our hopes:—
And first, lord marshal, what say you to it?

*Mowb.* I well allow the occasion of our arms,
But gladly would be better satisfied
How, in our means, we should advance ourselves
To look with forehead bold and big enough
Upon the power and puissance of the king.

*Hast.* Our present musters grow upon the file
To five-and-twenty thousand men of choice;
And our supplies live largely in the hope
Of great Northumberland, whose bosom burns
With an incensed fire of injuries.

*L. Bard.* The question, then, Lord Hastings, standeth thus;—
Whether our present five-and-twenty thousand
May hold up head without Northumberland?

*Hast.* With him, we may.

*L. Bard.*        Ay, marry, there's the point:
But if without him we be thought too feeble,
My judgment is, we should not step too far
Till we had his assistance by the hand;
For, in a theme so bloody-fac'd as this,
Conjecture, expectation, and surmise
Of aids uncertain, should not be admitted.

*Arch.* 'Tis very true, Lord Bardolph; for, indeed,
It was young Hotspur's case at Shrewsbury.

*L. Bard.* It was, my lord; who lin'd himself with hope,
Eating the air on promise of supply,
Flattering himself with project of a power
Much smaller than the smallest of his thoughts:
And so, with great imagination,
Proper to madmen, led his powers to death,
And, winking, leap'd into destruction.

*Hast.* But, by your leave, it never yet did hurt
To lay down likelihoods and forms of hope.

*L. Bard.* Yes, in this present quality of war;—
Indeed, the instant action,—a cause on foot,—
Lives so in hope, as in an early spring
We see the appearing buds; which, to prove fruit,
Hope gives not so much warrant, as despair
That frosts will bite them. When we mean to build,
We first survey the plot, then draw the model;
And when we see the figure of the house,
Then must we rate the cost of the erection;
Which, if we find outweighs ability,
What do we then but draw anew the model
In fewer offices, or at least desist        [work,—
To build at all? Much more, in this great

Which is almost to pluck a kingdom down
And set another up,—should we survey
The plot of situation and the model,
Consent upon a sure foundation,
Question surveyors, know our own estate,
How able such a work to undergo,
To weigh against his opposite; or else,
We fortify in paper and in figures,
Using the names of men instead of men:
Like one that draws the model of a house
Beyond his power to build it; who, half through,
Gives o'er, and leaves his part-created cost
A naked subject to the weeping clouds,
And waste for churlish winter's tyranny.

*Hast.* Grant that our hopes,—yet likely of
fair birth,—
Should be still-born, and that we now possess'd
The utmost man of expectation;
I think we are a body strong enough,
Even as we are, to equal with the king.

*L. Bard.* What, is the king but five-and-
twenty thousand?

*Hast.* To us no more; nay, not so much, Lord
Bardolph;
For his divisions, as the times do brawl,
Are in three heads: one power against the
French,
And one against Glendower; perforce a third
Must take up us: so is the unfirm king
In three divided; and his coffers sound
With hollow poverty and emptiness.

*Arch.* That he should draw his several
strengths together,
And come against us in full puissance,
Need not be dreaded.

*Hast.*            If he should do so,
He leaves his back unarm'd, the French and
Welsh
Baying him at the heels: never fear that.

*L. Bard.* Who is it like should lead his forces
hither?

*Hast.* The Duke of Lancaster and West-
moreland;            [mouth:
Against the Welsh, himself and Harry Mon-
But who is substituted 'gainst the French,
I have no certain notice.

*Arch.*            Let us on,
And publish the occasion of our arms.
The commonwealth is sick of their own choice;
Their over-greedy love hath surfeited:
An habitation giddy and unsure
Hath he that buildeth on the vulgar heart.
O thou fond many! with what loud applause
Didst thou beat heaven with blessing Boling-
broke,
Before he was what thou wouldst have him be!
And being now trimm'd in thine own desires,
Thou, beastly feeder, art so full of him
That thou provok'st thyself to cast him up.
So, so, thou common dog, didst thou disgorge
Thy glutton bosom of the royal Richard;
And now thou wouldst eat thy dead vomit up,
And howl'st to find it. What trust is in these
times?

They that, when Richard liv'd, would have him
die,
Are now become enamour'd on his grave:
Thou, that threw'st dust upon his goodly head,
When through proud London he came sighing
on
After the admired heels of Bolingbroke,
Cry'st now, *O earth yield us that king again,
And take thou this!* O thoughts of men accurst!
Past, and to come, seems best; things present,
worst.

*Mowb.* Shall we go draw our numbers, and
set on?

*Hast.* We are time's subjects, and time bids
be gone.            [*Exeunt.*

## ACT II.

### SCENE I.—LONDON. *A Street.*

*Enter* Hostess, FANG *and his* Boy *with her,
and* SNARE *following.*

*Host.* Master Fang, have you entered the
action?

*Fang.* It is entered.

*Host.* Where is your yeoman? Is it a lusty
yeoman? will he stand to it?

*Fang.* Sirrah, where's Snare?

*Host.* O Lord, ay! good Master Snare.

*Snare.* Here, here.

*Fang.* Snare, we must arrest Sir John Falstaff.

*Host.* Yea, good Master Snare; I have entered him and all.

*Snare.* It may chance cost some of us our
lives, for he will stab.

*Host.* Alas the day! take heed of him; he
stabbed me in mine own house, and that most
beastly: in good faith, he cares not what mischief he doth, if his weapon be out: he will foin
like any devil; he will spare neither man,
woman, nor child.

*Fang.* If I can close with him, I care not for
his thrust.

*Host.* No, nor I neither: I'll be at your elbow.

*Fang.* An I but fist him once; an he come
but within my vice,—

*Host.* I am undone by his going; I warrant
you, he is an infinitive thing upon my score:—
good Master Fang, hold him sure;—good Master Snare, let him not 'scape. He comes continually to Pie-corner,—saving your manhoods,—to buy a saddle; and he is indited to
dinner to the Lubber's Head in Lumbert Street,
to Master Smooth's the silkman: I pray ye,
since my exion is entered, and my case so
openly known to the world, let him be brought
in to his answer. A hundred mark is a long one
for a poor lone woman to bear: and I have
borne, and borne, and borne; and have been
fubbed off, and fubbed off, and fubbed off,
from this day to that day, that it is a shame to
be thought on. There is no honesty in such
dealing; unless a woman should be made an ass

and a beast, to bear every knave's wrong. Yonder he comes; and that arrant malmsey-nose knave, Bardolph, with him. Do your offices, do your offices, Master Fang and Master Snare; do me, do me, do me your offices.

*Enter* SIR JOHN FALSTAFF, Page, *and* BARDOLPH.

*Fal.* How now! whose mare's dead? what's the matter?

*Fang.* Sir John, I arrest you at the suit of Mistress Quickly.

*Fal.* Away, varlets!—Draw, Bardolph: cut me off the villain's head; throw the quean in the channel.

*Host.* Throw me in the channel! I'll throw thee in the channel. Wilt thou? wilt thou? thou bastardly rogue!—Murder, murder! O thou honeysuckle villain! wilt thou kill God's officers and the king's? O thou honey-seed rogue! thou art a honey-seed; a man-queller and a woman-queller.

*Fal.* Keep them off, Bardolph.

*Fang.* A rescue! a rescue!

*Host.* Good people, bring a rescue or two.— Thou wo't, wo't thou? thou wo't, wo't thou? do, do, thou rogue! do, thou hemp-seed!

*Fal.* Away, you scullion! you rampallian! you fustilarian! I'll tickle your catastrophe.

*Enter the* Lord Chief-Justice, *attended.*

*Ch. Just.* What is the matter? keep the peace here, ho!

*Host.* Good my lord, be good to me! I beseech you, stand to me!

*Ch. Just.* How now, Sir John! what, are you brawling here?
Doth this become your place, your time, and business?
You should have been well on your way to York.—
Stand from him, fellow: wherefore hang'st thou on him?

*Host.* O my most worshipful lord, an't please your grace, I am a poor widow of Eastcheap, and he is arrested at my suit.

*Ch. Just.* For what sum?

*Host.* It is more than for some, my lord; it is for all,—all I have. He hath eaten me out of house and home; he hath put all my substance into that fat belly of his:—but I will have some of it out again, or I will ride thee o' nights like the mare.

*Fal.* I think I am as like to ride the mare, if I have any vantage of ground to get up.

*Ch. Just.* How comes this, Sir John? Fie! What man of good temper would endure this tempest of exclamation? Are you not ashamed to enforce a poor widow to so rough a course to come by her own?

*Fal.* What is the gross sum that I owe thee?

*Host.* Marry, if thou wert an honest man, thyself and the money too. Thou didst swear to me upon a parcel-gilt goblet, sitting in my Dolphin-chamber, at the round table, by a sea-coal fire, upon Wednesday in Whitsun-week, when the prince broke thy head for liking his father to a singing-man of Windsor,—thou didst swear to me then, as I was washing thy wound, to marry me, and make me my lady thy wife. Canst thou deny it? Did not goodwife Keech, the butcher's wife, come in then, and call me gossip Quickly? coming in to borrow a mess of vinegar; telling us she had a good dish of prawns; whereby thou didst desire to eat some; whereby I told thee they were ill for a green wound? And didst thou not, when she was gone down stairs, desire me to be no more so familiarity with such poor people; saying that ere long they should call me madam? And didst thou not kiss me, and bid me fetch thee thirty shillings? I put thee now to thy book-oath: deny it, if thou canst!

*Fal.* My lord, this is a poor mad soul; and she says, up and down the town, that her eldest son is like you: she hath been in good case, and, the truth is, poverty hath distracted her. But for these foolish officers, I beseech you I may have redress against them.

*Ch. Just.* Sir John, Sir John, I am well acquainted with your manner of wrenching the true cause the false way. It is not a confident brow, nor the throng of words that come with such more than impudent sauciness from you, can thrust me from a level consideration: you have, as it appears to me, practised upon the easy yielding spirit of this woman, and made her serve your uses both in purse and in person.

*Host.* Yea, in troth, my lord.

*Ch. Just.* Pr'ythee, peace.—Pay her the debt you owe her, and unpay the villany you have done with her: the one you may do with sterling money, and the other with current repentance.

*Fal.* My lord, I will not undergo this sneap without reply. You call honourable boldness impudent sauciness: if a man will make court'sy, and say nothing, he is virtuous:—no, my lord, my humble duty remembered, I will not be your suitor. I say to you, I do desire deliverance from these officers, being upon hasty employment in the king's affairs.

*Ch. Just.* You speak as having power to do wrong: but answer in the effect of your reputation, and satisfy the poor woman.

*Fal.* Come hither, hostess. [*Takes her aside.*

*Enter* GOWER.

*Ch. Just.* Now, Master Gower,—what news?

*Gow.* The king, my lord, and Harry Prince of Wales
Are near at hand: the rest this paper tells.
[*Gives a letter.*

*Fal.* As I am a gentleman,—

*Host.* Nay, you said so before.

*Fal.* As I am a gentleman:—come, no more words of it.

*Host.* By this heavenly ground I tread on, I

must be fain to pawn both my plate and the tapestry of my dining-chambers.

*Fal.* Glasses, glasses, is the only drinking: and for thy walls,—a pretty slight drollery, or the story of the Prodigal, or the German hunting in water-work, is worth a thousand of these bed-hangings and these fly-bitten tapestries. Let it be ten pound, if thou canst. Come, an it were not for thy humours, there is not a better wench in England. Go, wash thy face, and draw thy action. Come, thou must not be in this humour with me; dost not know me? come, come, I know thou wast set on to this.

*Host.* Pray thee, Sir John, let it be but twenty nobles: i' faith, I am loth to pawn my plate, so God save me, la.

*Fal.* Let it alone; I'll make other shift: you'll be a fool still.

*Host.* Well, you shall have it, though I pawn my gown. I hope you'll come to supper. You'll pay me all together?

*Fal.* Will I live?—Go, with her, with her [*to* BARDOLPH]; hook on, hook on.

*Host.* Will you have Doll Tearsheet meet you at supper?

*Fal.* No more words; let's have her.
[*Exeunt* HOST., BARD., Officers, *and* Page.

*Ch. Just.* I have heard better news.

*Fal.* What's the news, my good lord?

*Ch. Just.* Where lay the king last night?

*Gow.* At Basingstoke, my lord.

*Fal.* I hope, my lord, all's well: what's the news, my lord?

*Ch. Just.* Come all his forces back?  [horse,

*Gow.* No; fifteen hundred foot, five hundred Are march'd up to my Lord of Lancaster, Against Northumberland and the archbishop.

*Fal.* Comes the king back from Wales, my noble lord?                                 [ently:

*Ch. Just.* You shall have letters of me pres-Come, go along with me, good master Gower.

*Fal.* My lord!

*Ch. Just.* What's the matter?

*Fal.* Master Gower, shall I entreat you with me to dinner?

*Gow.* I must wait upon my good lord here, —I thank you, good Sir John.

*Ch. Just.* Sir John, you loiter here too long, being you are to take soldiers up in counties as you go.

*Fal.* Will you sup with me, Master Gower?

*Ch. Just.* What foolish master taught you these manners, Sir John?

*Fal.* Master Gower, if they become me not, he was a fool that taught them me.—This is the right fencing grace, my lord; tap for tap, and so part fair.

*Ch. Just.* Now, the Lord lighten thee! thou art a great fool.                          [*Exeunt.*

SCENE II.—*The same. Another Street.*

*Enter* PRINCE HENRY *and* POINS.

*P. Hen.* Before God, I am exceeding weary.

*Poins.* Is it come to that? I had thought weariness durst not have attached one of so high blood.

*P. Hen.* Faith, it does me; though it discolours the complexion of my greatness to acknowledge it. Doth it not show vilely in me to desire small beer?

*Poins.* Why, a prince should not be so loosely studied as to remember so weak a composition.

*P. Hen.* Belike, then, my appetite was not princely got; for, by my troth, I do now remember the poor creature, small beer. But, indeed, these humble considerations make me out of love with my greatness. What a disgrace is it to me to remember thy name? or to know thy face to-morrow? or to take note how many pair of silk stockings thou hast; viz., these, and those that were thy peach-coloured ones? or to bear the inventory of thy shirts, as, one for superfluity, and one other for use?—but that the tennis court-keeper knows better than I; for it is a low ebb of linen with thee when thou keepest not racket there; as thou hast not done a great while, because the rest of thy low-countries have made a shift to eat up thy holland: and God knows, whether those that bawl out the ruins of thy linen shall inherit his kingdom: but the midwives say the children are not in the fault; whereupon the world increases, and kindreds are mightily strengthened.

*Poins.* How ill it follows, after you have laboured so hard, you should talk so idly! Tell me, how many good young princes would do so, their fathers being so sick as yours at this time is?

*P. Hen.* Shall I tell thee one thing, Poins?

*Poins.* Yes, faith; and let it be an excellent good thing.

*P. Hen.* It shall serve among wits of no higher breeding than thine.

*Poins.* Go to; I stand the push of your one thing that you will tell.

*P. Hen.* Marry, I tell thee,—it is not meet that I should be sad, now my father is sick: albeit I could tell to thee,—as to one it pleases me, for fault of a better, to call my friend,—I could be sad and sad indeed too.

*Poins.* Very hardly upon such a subject.

*P. Hen.* By this hand, thou think'st me as far in the devil's book as thou and Falstaff for obduracy and persistency: let the end try the man. But I tell thee, my heart bleeds inwardly that my father is so sick: and keeping such vile company as thou art hath in reason taken from me all ostentation of sorrow.

*Poins.* The reason?

*P. Hen.* What wouldst thou think of me if I should weep?

*Poins.* I would think thee a most princely hypocrite.

*P. Hen.* It would be every man's thought; and thou art a blessed fellow to think as every man thinks: never a man's thought in the world keeps the road-way better than thine: every man would think me an hypocrite indeed. And

What accites your most worshipful thought to think so?

*Poins.* Why, because you have been so lewd, and so much engraffed to Falstaff.

*P. Hen.* And to thee.

*Poins.* By this light, I am well spoke on; I can hear it with mine own ears: the worst that they can say of me is that I am a second brother, and that I am a proper fellow of my hands; and those two things, I confess, I cannot help.—By the mass, here comes Bardolph.

*P. Hen.* And the boy that I gave Falstaff: he had him from me Christian; and look, if the fat villain have not transformed him ape.

*Enter* BARDOLPH *and* Page.

*Bard.* God save your grace!

*P. Hen.* And yours, most noble Bardolph!

*Bard.* Come, you virtuous ass [*to the* Page], you bashful fool, must you be blushing? wherefore blush you now? What a maidenly man-at-arms are you become? Is it such a matter to get a pottle-pot's maidenhead?

*Page.* He called me even now, my lord, through a red lattice, and I could discern no part of his face from the window: at last I spied his eyes; and methought he had made two holes in the alewife's new red petticoat, and so peeped through.

*P. Hen.* Hath not the boy profited?

*Bard.* Away, you whoreson upright rabbit, away!

*Page.* Away, you rascally Althæa's dream, away!

*P. Hen.* Instruct us, boy; what dream, boy?

*Page.* Marry, my lord, Althæa dreamed she was delivered of a fire-brand; and therefore I call him her dream.

*P. Hen.* A crown's worth of good interpretation:—there it is, boy. [*Gives him money.*

*Poins.* O that this good blossom could be kept from cankers!—Well, there is sixpence to preserve thee.

*Bard.* An you do not make him be hanged among you, the gallows shall have wrong.

*P. Hen.* And how doth thy master, Bardolph?

*Bard.* Well, my lord. He heard of your grace's coming to town; there's a letter for you.

*Poins.* Delivered with good respect.—And how doth the martlemas, your master?

*Bard.* In bodily health, sir.

*Poins.* Marry, the immortal part needs a physician; but that moves not him: though that be sick, it dies not.

*P. Hen.* I do allow this wen to be as familiar with me as my dog: and he holds his place; for look you how he writes.

*Poins.* [*Reads.*] *John Falstaff, knight,*—every man must know that, as oft as he has occasion to name himself: even like those that are kin to the king; for they never prick their finger but they say, *There is some of the king's blood spilt.*—*How comes that?* says he, that

takes upon him not to conceive. The answer is as ready as a borrower's cap, *I am the king's poor cousin, sir.*

*P. Hen.* Nay, they will be kin to us, or they will fetch it from Japhet. But to the letter:—

*Poins.* [*Reads.*] *Sir John Falstaff, knight, to the son of the king, nearest his father, Harry Prince of Wales, greeting.*—Why, this is a certificate.

*P. Hen.* Peace!

*Poins.* [*Reads.*] *I will imitate the honourable Romans in brevity:*—sure he means brevity in breath, short-winded.—*I commend me to thee, I commend thee, and I leave thee. Be not too familiar with Poins; for he misuses thy favours so much that he swears thou art to marry his sister Nell. Repent at idle times as thou mayest, and so, farewell.*

> *Thine, by yea and no, (which is as much as to say, as thou usest him,)* JACK FALSTAFF, *with my familiars;* JOHN, *with my brothers and sisters; and* SIR JOHN *with all Europe.*

My lord, I will steep this letter in sack, and make him eat it.

*P. Hen.* That's to make him eat twenty of his words. But do you use me thus, Ned? must I marry your sister?

*Poins.* God send the wench have no worse fortune! but I never said so.

*P. Hen.* Well, thus we play the fools with the time; and the spirits of the wise sit in the clouds and mock us.—Is your master here in London?

*Bard.* Yes, my lord.

*P. Hen.* Where sups he? doth the old boar feed in the old frank?

*Bard.* At the old place, my lord,—in Eastcheap.

*P. Hen.* What company?

*Page.* Ephesians, my lord,—of the old church.

*P. Hen.* Sup any women with him?

*Page.* None, my lord, but old Mistress Quickly and Mistress Doll Tearsheet.

*P. Hen.* What pagan may that be?

*Page.* A proper gentlewoman, sir, and a kinswoman of my master's.

*P. Hen.* Even such kin as the parish heifers are to the town bull.—Shall we steal upon them, Ned, at supper?

*Poins.* I am your shadow, my lord; I'll follow you.

*P. Hen.* Sirrah, you boy,—and Bardolph,—no word to your master that I am yet come to town: there's for your silence.

*Bard.* I have no tongue, sir.

*Page.* And for mine, sir,—I will govern it.

*P. Hen.* Fare ye well; go. [*Exeunt* BARDOLPH *and* Page.]—This Doll Tearsheet should be some road.

*Poins.* I warrant you, as common as the way between Saint Alban's and London.

*P. Hen.* How might we see Falstaff bestow

himself to-night in his true colours, and not
ourselves be seen?

*Poins.* Put on two leathern jerkins and
aprons, and wait upon him at his table as
drawers.

*P. Hen.* From a god to a bull? a heavy de-
scension! it was Jove's case. From a prince to
a prentice? a low transformation! that shall be
mine; for in everything the purpose must weigh
with the folly.—Follow me, Ned.            [*Exeunt.*

SCENE III.—WARKWORTH. *Before the Castle.*

*Enter* NORTHUMBERLAND, LADY NORTHUMBER-
LAND, *and* LADY PERCY.

*North.* I pray thee, loving wife, and gentle
    daughter,
Give even way unto my rough affairs:
Put not you on the visage of the times,
And be, like them, to Percy troublesome.

*Lady N.* I have given over, I will speak no
    more:
Do what you will; your wisdom be your guide.

*North.* Alas, sweet wife, my honour is at
    pawn;
And, but my going, nothing can redeem it.

*Lady P.* O, yet, for God's sake, go not to
    these wars!
The time was, father, that you broke your
    word,
When you were more endear'd to it than now;
When your own Percy, when my heart-dear
    Harry,
Threw many a northward look to see his father
Bring up his powers; but he did long in vain.
Who then persuaded you to stay at home?
There were two honours lost,—yours and your
    son's.
For yours,—may heavenly glory brighten it!
For his,—it stuck upon him, as the sun
In the grey vault of heaven: and by his light
Did all the chivalry of England move
To do brave acts: he was, indeed, the glass
Wherein the noble youth did dress themselves:
He had no legs that practis'd not his gait;
And speaking thick, which nature made his
    blemish,
Became the accents of the valiant;
For those that could speak low and tardily
Would turn their own perfection to abuse
To seem like him: so that in speech, in gait,
In diet, in affections of delight,
In military rules, humours of blood,
He was the mark and glass, copy and book,
That fashion'd others. And him,—O wondrous
    him!
O miracle of men!—him did you leave,—
Second to none, unseconded by you,—
To look upon the hideous god of war
In disadvantage; to abide a field
Where nothing but the sound of Hotspur's
    name
Did seem defensible:—so you left him.
Never, O never, do his ghost the wrong

To hold your honour more precise and nice
With others than with him! let them alone:
The marshal and the archbishop are strong:
Had my sweet Harry had but half their num-
    bers,
To-day might I, hanging on Hotspur's neck,
Have talk'd of Monmouth's grave.

*North.*          Beshrew your heart,
Fair daughter, you do draw my spirits from me
With new lamenting ancient oversights.
But I must go, and meet with danger there;
Or it will seek me in another place,
And find me worse provided.

*Lady N.*         O, fly to Scotland,
Till that the nobles and the armed commons
Have of their puissance made a little taste.

*Lady P.* If they get ground and vantage of
    the king,
Then join you with them, like a rib of steel,
To make strength stronger; but, for all our
    loves,
First let them try themselves. So did your son;
He was so suffer'd: so came I a widow;
And never shall have length of life enough
To rain upon remembrance with mine eyes,
That it may grow and sprout as high as heaven,
For recordation to my noble husband.

*North.* Come, come, go in with me. 'Tis with
    my mind
As with the tide swell'd up unto its height,
That makes a still-stand, running neither way.
Fain would I go to meet the archbishop,
But many thousand reasons hold me back.
I will resolve for Scotland: there am I,
Till time and vantage crave my company.
                        [*Exeunt.*

SCENE IV.—LONDON. *A Room in the Boar's
Head Tavern in Eastcheap.*

*Enter two* DRAWERS.

1 *Draw.* What the devil hast thou brought
there? apple-johns? thou know'st Sir John cannot endure an apple-john.

2 *Draw.* Mass, thou sayest true. The prince
once set a dish of apple-johns before him, and
told him there were five more Sir Johns; and,
putting off his hat, said, *I will now take my
leave of these six dry, round, old, withered knights.*
It angered him to the heart: but he hath forgot
that.

1 *Draw.* Why, then, cover, and set them
down: and see if thou canst find out Sneak's
noise: Mistress Tearsheet would fain hear some
music. Despatch:—the room where they sup-
ped is too hot; they'll come in straight.

2 *Draw.* Sirrah, here will be the prince and
Master Poins anon; and they will put on two
of our jerkins and aprons; and Sir John must
not know of it: Bardolph hath brought word.

1 *Draw.* By the mass, here will be old utis:
it will be an excellent stratagem.

2 *Draw.* I'll see if I can find out Sneak.
                        [*Exit.*

*Enter* Hostess *and* DOLL TEARSHEET.

*Host.* I' faith, sweetheart, methinks now you are in an excellent good temperality: your pulsidge beats as extraordinarily as heart would desire; and your colour, I warrant you, is as red as any rose: but, i' faith, you have drunk too much canaries; and that's a marvellous searching wine, and it perfumes the blood ere one can say, What's this?—How do you now?

*Doll.* Better than I was:—hem.

*Host.* Why, that's well said; a good heart's worth gold.—Look, here comes Sir John.

*Enter* FALSTAFF *singing.*

*Fal.* *When Arthur first in court*—Empty the jorden. [*Exit* 1 Drawer.]—*And was a worthy king.*—How now, Mistress Doll!

*Host.* Sick of a calm; yea, good sooth.

*Fal.* So is all her sect; an they be once in a calm, they are sick.

*Doll.* You muddy rascal, is that all the comfort you give me?

*Fal.* You make fat rascals, Mistress Doll.

*Doll.* I make them! gluttony and diseases make them; I make them not.

*Fal.* If the cook help to make the gluttony, you help to make the diseases, Doll: we catch of you, Doll, we catch of you; grant that, my poor virtue, grant that.

*Doll.* Yea, joy,—our chains and our jewels.

*Fal.* *Your brooches, pearls, and ouches:*—for to serve bravely is to come halting off, you know: to come off the breach with his pike bent bravely, and to surgery bravely; to venture upon the charged chambers bravely,—

*Doll.* Hang yourself, you muddy conger, hang yourself!

*Host.* By my troth, this is the old fashion; you two never meet but you fall to some discord: you are both, in good troth, as rheumatic as two dry toasts; you cannot one bear with another's confirmities. What the good-year! one must bear, and that must be you [*to* DOLL]: you are the weaker vessel, as they say, the emptier vessel.

*Doll.* Can a weak empty vessel bear such a huge full hogshead? there's a whole merchant's venture of Bourdeaux stuff in him; you have not seen a hulk better stuffed in the hold.— Come, I'll be friends with thee, Jack: thou are going to the wars; and whether I shall ever see thee again or no, there is nobody cares.

*Re-enter* First Drawer.

1 *Draw.* Sir, Ancient Pistol is below, and would speak with you.

*Doll.* Hang him, swaggering rascal! let him not come hither: it is the foul-mouth'dst rogue in England.

*Host.* If he swagger, let him not come here: no, by my faith; I must live amongst my neighbours; I'll no swaggerers: I am in good name and fame with the very best:—shut the

door;—there comes no swaggerers here: I have not lived all this while to have swaggering now: —shut the door, I pray you.

*Fal.* Dost thou hear, hostess?—

*Host.* Pray you, pacify yourself, Sir John: there comes no swaggerers here.

*Fal.* Dost thou hear? it is mine ancient.

*Host.* Tilly-fally, Sir John, never tell me: your ancient swaggerer comes not in my doors. I was before Master Tisick, the deputy, the other day; and, as he said to me,—it was no longer ago than Wednesday last,—*Neighbour Quickly,* says he;—Master Dumb, our minister, was by then;—*Neighbour Quickly,* says he, *receive those that are civil; for,* saith he, *you are in an ill-name;*—now he said so, I can tell whereupon; *for,* says he, *you are an honest woman, and well thought on; therefore take heed what guests you receive: receive,* says he, *no swaggering companions.*—There comes none here;— you would bless you to hear what he said:— no, I'll no swaggerers.

*Fal.* He's no swaggerer, hostess; a tame cheater, i' faith; you may stroke him as gently as a puppy greyhound: he will not swagger with a Barbary hen, if her feathers turn back in any show of resistance.—Call him up, drawer.

[*Exit* 1 Drawer.

*Host.* Cheater, call you him? I will bar no honest man my house, nor no cheater: but I do not love swaggering; by my troth, I am the worse when one says swagger: feel, masters, how I shake; look you, I warrant you.

*Doll.* So you do, hostess.

*Host.* Do I? yea, in very truth, do I, an 'twere an aspen leaf: I cannot abide swaggerers.

*Enter* PISTOL, BARDOLPH, *and* Page.

*Pist.* God save you, Sir John!

*Fal.* Welcome, Ancient Pistol. Here, Pistol, I charge you with a cup of sack: do you discharge upon mine hostess.

*Pist.* I will discharge upon her, Sir John, with two bullets.

*Fal.* She is pistol-proof, sir; you shall hardly offend her.

*Host.* Come, I'll drink no proofs nor no bullets; I'll drink no more than will do me good, for no man's pleasure, I.

*Pist.* Then to you, Mrs. Dorothy; I will charge you.

*Doll.* Charge me! I scorn you, scurvy companion. What! you poor, base, rascally, cheating, lack-linen mate! Away, you mouldy rogue, away! I am meat for your master.

*Pist.* I know you, Mistress Dorothy.

*Doll.* Away, you cut-purse rascal! you filthy bung, away! by this wine, I'll thrust my knife in your mouldy chaps, an you play the saucy cuttle with me. Away, you bottle-ale rascal! you basket-hilt stale juggler, you!—Since when, I pray you, sir?—God's light, with two points on your shoulder? much!

*Pist.* I will murder your ruff for this.

*Fal.* No more, Pistol; I would not have you go off here: discharge yourself of our company, Pistol.

*Host.* No, good Captain Pistol; not here, sweet captain.

*Doll.* Captain! thou abominable damned cheater, art thou not ashamed to be called captain? If captains were of my mind, they would truncheon you out, for taking their names upon you before you have earned them. You a captain! you slave, for what? for tearing a poor whore's ruff in a bawdy-house?—He a captain! hang him, rogue! He lives upon mouldy stewed prunes and dried cakes. A captain! God's light, these villains will make the word as odious as the word occupy; which was an excellent good word before it was ill-sorted: therefore captains had need look to it.

*Bard.* Pray thee, go down, good ancient.

*Fal.* Hark thee hither, Mistress Doll.

*Pist.* Not I: I tell thee what, Corporal Bardolph,—I could tear her:—I'll be revenged on her.

*Page.* Pray thee, go down.

*Pist.* I'll see her damned first;—to Pluto's damned lake, by this hand, to the infernal deep, with Erebus and tortures vile also. Hold hook and line, say I. Down, down, dogs! down, faitors! Have we not Hiren here?

*Host.* Good Captain Peesel, be quiet; it is very late, i' faith: I beseek you now, aggravate your choler.

*Pist.* These be good humours, indeed! Shall packhorses,
And hollow pamper'd jades of Asia,
Which cannot go but thirty miles a-day,
Compare with Cæsars, and with Cannibals,
And Trojan Greeks? nay, rather damn them with
King Cerberus; and let the welkin roar.
Shall we fall foul for toys?

*Host.* By my troth, captain, these are very bitter words.

*Bard.* Be gone, good ancient: this will grow to a brawl anon.

*Pist.* Die men like dogs! give crowns like pins! Have we not Hiren here?

*Host.* O' my word, captain; there's none such here. What the good-year! do you think I would deny her? for Godsake, be quiet.

*Pist.* Then feed and be fat, my fair Calipolis. Come, give me some sack.
*Se fortuna mi tormenta, lo sperare mi contenta.*—
Fear we broadsides? no, let the fiend give fire:
Give me some sack:—and, sweetheart, lie thou there. *[Laying down his sword.*
Come we to full points here; and are *et-ceteras* nothing?

*Fal.* Pistol, I would, be quiet.

*Pist.* Sweet knight, I kiss thy neif: what! we have seen the seven stars.

*Doll.* Thrust him downstairs! I cannot endure such a fustian rascal.

*Pist.* Thrust him down stairs! know we not Galloway nags?

*Fal.* Quoit him down, Bardolph, like a shove-groat shilling: nay, an he do nothing but speak nothing, he shall be nothing here.

*Bard.* Come, get you down stairs.

*Pist.* What! shall we have incision? shall we imbrue?— *[Snatching up his sword.*
Then death rock me asleep, abridge my doleful days!
Why, then, let grievous, ghastly, gaping wounds
Untwine the Sisters Three! Come, Atropos, I say!

*Host.* Here's goodly stuff toward!

*Fal.* Give me my rapier, boy.

*Doll.* I pray thee, Jack, I pray thee, do not draw.

*Fal.* Get you down stairs.
*[Drawing, and driving* PIST. *out.*

*Host.* Here's a goodly tumult! I'll forswear keeping house afore I'll be in these tirrits and frights. So; murder, I warrant now.—Alas, alas! put up your naked weapons, put up your naked weapons. *[Exeunt* PIST. *and* BARD.

*Doll.* I pray thee, Jack, be quiet; the rascal is gone.—Ah, you whoreson little valiant villain, you!

*Host.* Are you not hurt i' the groin? methought he made a shrewd thrust at your belly.

*Re-enter* BARDOLPH.

*Fal.* Have you turned him out of doors?

*Bard.* Yes, sir. The rascal's drunk: you have hurt him, sir, in the shoulder.

*Fal.* A rascal! to brave me!

*Doll.* Ah, you sweet little rogue, you! Alas, poor ape, how thou sweatest! come, let me wipe thy face;—come on, you whoreson chops:—ah, rogue! i' faith, I love thee. Thou art as valorous as Hector of Troy, worth five of Agamemnon, and ten times better than the nine worthies: ah, villain!

*Fal.* A rascally slave! I will toss the rogue in a blanket.

*Doll.* Do, if thou darest for thy heart: if thou dost, I'll canvass thee between a pair of sheets.

*Enter* Musicians.

*Page.* The music is come, sir.

*Fal.* Let them play;—play, sirs.—Sit on my knee, Doll.—A rascal-bragging slave! the rogue fled from me like quicksilver.

*Doll.* I' faith, and thou followedst him like a church. Thou whoreson little tidy Bartholomew boar-pig, when wilt thou leave fighting o' days and foining o' nights, and begin to patch up thine old body for heaven?

*Enter, behind,* PRINCE HENRY *and* POINS
*disguised as Drawers.*

*Fal.* Peace, good Doll! do not speak like a

Death's-head; do not bid me remember mine end.

*Doll.* Sirrah, what humour is the prince of?

*Fal.* A good shallow young fellow: he would have made a good pantler; he would have chipped bread well.

*Doll.* They say Poins has a good wit.

*Fal.* He a good wit? hang him, baboon! his wit is as thick as Tewksbury mustard; there is no more conceit in him than is in a mallet.

*Doll.* Why does the prince love him so, then?

*Fal.* Because their legs are both of a bigness; and he plays at quoits well; and eats conger and fennel; and drinks off candles' ends for flap-dragons; and rides the wild mare with the boys; and jumps upon joint-stools; and swears with a good grace; and wears his boot very smooth, like unto the sign of the leg; and breeds no bate with telling of discreet stories; and such other gambol faculties he has, that show a weak mind and an able body, for the which the prince admits him: for the prince himself is such another; the weight of a hair will turn the scales between their avoirdupois.

*P. Hen.* Would not this nave of a wheel have his ears cut off?

*Poins.* Let us beat him before his whore.

*P. Hen.* Look, whether the withered elder hath not his poll clawed like a parrot.

*Poins.* Is it not strange that desire should so many years outlive performance?

*Fal.* Kiss me, Doll.

*P. Hen.* Saturn and Venus this year in conjunction! what says the almanac to that?

*Poins.* And, look, whether the fiery Trigon, his man, be not lisping to his master's old tables, his note-book, his counsel-keeper.

*Fal.* Thou dost give me flattering busses.

*Doll.* By my troth, I kiss thee with a most constant heart.

*Fal.* I am old, I am old.

*Doll.* I love thee better than I love e'er a scurvy young boy of them all.

*Fal.* What stuff wilt thou have a kirtle of? I shall receive money on Thursday; thou shalt have a cap to-morrow. A merry song, come: it grows late; we will to bed. Thou wilt forget me when I am gone.

*Doll.* By my troth, thou wilt set me a weeping, an thou sayest so: prove that ever I dress myself handsome till thy return:—well, harken the end.

*Fal.* Some sack, Francis.

*P. Hen., Poins.* Anon, anon, sir.

[*Advancing.*

*Fal.* Ha! a bastard son of the king's?—And art not thou Poins, his brother?

*P. Hen.* Why, thou globe of sinful continents, what a life dost thou lead!

*Fal.* A better than thou: I am a gentleman; thou art a drawer.

*P. Hen.* Very true, sir, and I come to draw you out by the ears.

*Host.* O, the Lord preserve thy good grace!

by my troth, welcome to London. Now, the Lord bless that sweet face of thine! O Jesu, are you come from Wales?

*Fal.* Thou whoreson mad compound of majesty,—by this light flesh and corrupt blood, thou art welcome.

[*Leaning his hand upon* DOLL.

*Doll.* How, you fat fool! I scorn you.

*Poins.* My lord, he will drive you out of your revenge, and turn all to a merriment, if you take not the heat.

*P. Hen.* You whoreson candle-mine, you, how vilely did you speak of me even now before this honest, virtuous, civil, gentlewoman!

*Host.* God's blessing on your good heart! and so she is, by my troth.

*Fal.* Didst thou hear me?

*P. Hen.* Yes; and you knew me, as you did when you ran away by Gadshill: you knew I was at your back, and spoke it on purpose to try my patience.

*Fal.* No, no, no; not so; I did not think thou wast within hearing.

*P. Hen.* I shall drive you, then, to confess the wilful abuse, and then I know how to handle you.

*Fal.* No abuse, Hal, on mine honour; no abuse.

*P. Hen.* Not! to dispraise me, and call me pantler, and bread-chipper, and I know not what!

*Fal.* No abuse, Hal.

*Poins.* No abuse!

*Fal.* No abuse, Ned, in the world; honest Ned, none. I dispraised him before the wicked, that the wicked might not fall in love with him;—in which doing, I have done the part of a careful friend and a true subject, and thy father is to give me thanks for it. No abuse, Hal;—none, Ned, none;—no, faith, boys, none.

*P. Hen.* See now, whether pure fear and entire cowardice doth not make thee wrong this virtuous gentlewoman to close with us? is she of the wicked? is thine hostess here of the wicked? or is thy boy of the wicked? or honest Bardolph, whose zeal burns in his nose, of the wicked?

*Poins.* Answer, thou dead elm, answer.

*Fal.* The fiend hath pricked down Bardolph irrecoverable; and his face is Lucifer's privy-kitchen, where he doth nothing but roast malt-worms. For the boy,—there is a good angel about him; but the devil outbids him too.

*P. Hen.* For the women?

*Fal.* For one of them,—she is in hell already, and burns, poor soul! For the other,—I owe her money; and whether she be damned for that, I know not.

*Host.* No, I warrant you.

*Fal.* No, I think thou art not; I think thou art quit for that. Marry, there is another indictment upon thee for suffering flesh to be eaten in thy house, contrary to the law; for the which I think thou wilt howl

*Host.* All victuallers do so: what's a joint of mutton or two in a whole Lent?

*P. Hen.* You, gentlewoman,—

*Doll.* What says your grace?

*Fal.* His grace says that which his flesh rebels against. [*Knocking within.*

*Host.* Who knocks so loud at door? Look to the door there, Francis.

#### Enter PETO.

*P. Hen.* Peto, how now! what news?

*Pet.* The king your father is at Westminster;
And there are twenty weak and wearied posts
Come from the north: and as I came along
I met and overtook a dozen captains,
Bare-headed, sweating, knocking at the taverns,
And asking every one for Sir John Falstaff.

*P. Hen.* By heaven, Poins, I feel me much
    to blame,
So idly to profane the precious time;
When tempest of commotion, like the south,
Borne with black vapour, doth begin to melt,
And drop upon our bare unarmed heads.
Give me my sword and cloak.—Falstaff, good-
    night.
        [*Exeunt P. HEN., POINS, PETO, and BARD.*

*Fal.* Now comes in the sweetest morsel of the night, and we must hence, and leave it unpicked. [*Knocking within.*] More knocking at the door!

#### Re-enter BARDOLPH.

How now! what's the matter?

*Bard.* You must away to court, sir, presently; a dozen captains stay at door for you.

*Fal.* Pay the musicians, sirrah [*to the* Page]. —Farewell, hostess;—farewell, Doll.—You see, my good wenches, how men of merit are sought after: the undeserver may sleep, when the man of action is called on. Farewell, good wenches: if I be not sent away post, I will see you again ere I go.

*Doll.* I cannot speak;—if my heart be not ready to burst,—well, sweet Jack, have a care of thyself.

*Fal.* Farewell, farewell.
        [*Exeunt FALSTAFF and BARDOLPH.*

*Host.* Well, fare thee well: I have known thee these twenty-nine years, come peascod-time; but an honester and truer-hearted man,— well, fare thee well.

*Bard.* [*Within.*] Mistress Tearsheet,—

*Host.* What's the matter?

*Bard.* [*Within.*] Bid Mistress Tearsheet come to my master.

*Host.* O, run, Doll, run; run, good Doll.
        [*Exeunt.*

## ACT III.

### SCENE I.—WESTMINSTER. *A Room in the Palace.*

*Enter* KING HENRY *in his nightgown, with a Page*

*K. Hen.* Go call the Earls of Surrey and of
    Warwick;
But, ere they come, bid them o'er-read these
    letters,
And well consider of them: make good speed.
        [*Exit* Page.
How many thousand of my poorest subjects
Are at this hour asleep!—O sleep, O gentle
    sleep,
Nature's soft nurse, how have I frighted thee.
That thou no more wilt weigh my eyelids down,
And steep my senses in forgetfulness?
Why rather, sleep, liest thou in smoky cribs,
Upon uneasy pallets stretching thee,
And hush'd with buzzing night-flies to thy
    slumber,
Than in the perfum'd chambers of the great,
Under high canopies of costly state,
And lull'd with sounds of sweetest melody?
O thou dull god, why liest thou with the vile
In loathsome beds, and leav'st the kingly couch
A watch-case or a common 'larum bell?
Wilt thou upon the high and giddy mast
Seal up the ship-boy's eyes, and rock his brains
In cradle of the rude imperious surge,
And in the visitation of the winds,
Who take the ruffian billows by the top,
Curling their monstrous heads, and hanging
    them
With deafening clamour in the slippery shrouds,
That, with the hurly, death itself awakes?
Canst thou, O partial sleep, give thy repose
To the wet sea-boy in an hour so rude;
And in the calmest and most stillest night,
With all appliances and means to boot,
Deny it to a king? Then, happy low, lie down!
Uneasy lies the head that wears a crown.

#### Enter WARWICK and SURREY.

*War.* Many good-morrows to your majesty!

*K. Hen.* Is it good-morrow, lords?

*War.* 'Tis one o'clock, and past.

*K. Hen.* Why, then, good-morrow to you
    all, my lords.
Have you read o'er the letters that I sent you?

*War.* We have, my liege.

*K. Hen.* Then you perceive the body of our
    kingdom
How foul it is; what rank diseases grow,
And with what danger, near the heart of it.

*War.* It is but as a body yet distemper'd;
Which to his former strength may be restor'd
With good advice and little medicine:—
My lord Northumberland will soon be cool'd.

*K. Hen.* O God! that one might read the
    book of fate,
And see the revolution of the times
Make mountains level, and the continent,—
Weary of solid firmness,—melt itself
Into the sea! and, other times, to see
The beachy girdle of the ocean
Too wide for Neptune's hips; how chances
    mock,
And changes fill the cup of alteration

With divers liquors! Oh, if this were seen,
The happiest youth,—viewing his progress
    through,
What perils past, what crosses to ensue,—
Would shut the book, and sit him down and die.
'Tis not ten years gone         [friends,
Since Richard and Northumberland, great
Did feast together, and in two years after
Were they at wars. It is but eight years since
This Percy was the man nearest my soul;
Who like a brother toil'd in my affairs,
And laid his love and life under my foot;
Yea, for my sake, even to the eyes of Richard
Gave him defiance. But which of you was by,—
You, cousin Nevil, as I may remember,—
                       [To WARWICK.
When Richard,—with his eye brimful of tears,
Then check'd and rated by Northumberland,—
Did speak these words, now prov'd a prophecy?
*Northumberland, thou ladder by the which*
*My cousin Bolingbroke ascends my throne,*—
Though then, God knows, I had no such intent,
But that necessity so bow'd the state
That I and greatness were compell'd to kiss:—
*The time shall come,* thus did he follow it,
*The time will come, that foul sin, gathering head,*
*Shall break into corruption*—so went on,
Foretelling this same time's condition,
And the division of our amity.
  *War.* There is a history in all men's lives,
Figuring the nature of the times deceas'd;
The which observ'd, a man may prophesy,
With a near aim, of the main chance of things
As yet not come to life, which in their seeds
And weak beginnings lie intreasured.
Such things become the hatch and brood of
    time;
And, by the necessary form of this,
King Richard might create a perfect guess
That great Northumberland, then false to him,
Would of that seed grow to a greater falseness;
Which should not find a ground to root upon,
Unless on you.
  *K. Hen.* Are these things, then, necessities?
Then let us meet them like necessities;—
And that the same word even now cries out
    on us:
They say the bishop and Northumberland
Are fifty thousand strong.
  *War.*           It cannot be, my lord;
Rumor doth double, like the voice and echo,
The numbers of the fear'd. Please it your grace
To go to bed. Upon my life, my lord,
The powers that you already have sent forth
Shall bring this prize in very easily.
To comfort you the more, I have receiv'd
A certain instance that Glendower is dead.
Your majesty hath been this fortnight ill;
And these unseason'd hours perforce must add
Unto your sickness.
  *K. Hen.*       I will take your counsel:
And, were these inward wars once out of hand,
We would, dear lords, unto the Holy Land.
                                  *[Exeunt.*

SCENE II.—*Court before* JUSTICE SHALLOW'S
    *House in* Gloucestershire.

*Enter* SHALLOW *and* SILENCE, *meeting;*
    MOULDY, SHADOW, WART, FEEBLE, BULL-
    CALF, *and* Servants, *behind.*

  *Shal.* Come on, come on, come on, sir; give
me your hand, sir, give me your hand, sir: an
early stirrer, by the rood. And how doth my
good cousin Silence?
  *Sil.* Good-morrow, good cousin Shallow.
  *Shal.* And how doth my cousin, your bedfellow? and your fairest daughter and mine, my
god-daughter Ellen?
  *Sil.* Alas, a black ousel, cousin Shallow!
  *Shal.* By yea and nay, sir, I dare say my
cousin William is become a good scholar: he
is at Oxford still, is he not?
  *Sil.* Indeed, sir, to my cost.
  *Shal.* He must, then, to the inns of court
shortly: I was once of Clement's-inn; where l
think they will talk of mad Shallow yet.
  *Sil.* You were called lusty Shallow then,
cousin.
  *Shal.* By the mass, I was called anything;
and I would have done anything indeed, too,
and roundly too. There was I, and little John
Doit of Staffordshire, and black George Bare,
and Francis Pickbone, and Will Squele a Cotswold man,—you had not four such swinge-
bucklers in all the inns of court again: and, I
may say to you, we knew where the *bona-robas*
were, and had the best of them all at commandment. Then was Jack Falstaff, now Sir John,
a boy, and page to Thomas Mowbray, Duke of
Norfolk.
  *Sil.* This Sir John, cousin, that comes hither
anon about soldiers?
  *Shal.* The same Sir John, the very same. I
saw him break Skogan's head at the court gate,
when he was a crack not thus high: and the
very same day did I fight with one Sampson
Stockfish, a fruiterer, behind Gray's-inn. Jesu,
Jesu, the mad days that I have spent! and to see
how many of mine old acquaintance are dead!
  *Sil.* We shall all follow, cousin.
  *Shal.* Certain, 'tis certain; very sure, very
sure: death, as the Psalmist saith, is certain to
all; all shall die.—How a good yoke of bullocks
at Stamford fair?
  *Sil.* Truly, cousin, I was not there.
  *Shal.* Death is certain.—Is old Double of
your town living yet?
  *Sil.* Dead, sir.
  *Shal.* Jesu, Jesu, dead!—he drew a good
bow; and dead!—he shot a fine shoot:—John
of Gaunt loved him well, and betted much
money on his head. Dead!—he would have
clapp'd in the clout at twelve score, and carried
you a forehand shaft a fourteen and fourteen
and a half, that it would have done a man's
heart good to see.—How a score of ewes now?
  *Sil.* Thereafter as they be: a score of good
ewes may be worth ten pounds.

*Shal.* And is old Double dead?

*Sil.* Here come two of Sir John Falstaff's men, as I think.

*Enter* BARDOLPH *and one with him.*

*Bard.* Good-morrow, honest gentlemen: I beseech you, which is Justice Shallow?

*Shal.* I am Robert Shallow, sir, a poor esquire of this county, and one of the king's justices of the peace: what is your good pleasure with me?

*Bard.* My captain, sir, commends him to you; my captain, Sir John Falstaff,—a tall gentleman, by heaven, and a most gallant leader.

*Shal.* He greets me well, sir; I knew him a good backsword man: how doth the good knight? may I ask how my lady his wife doth?

*Bard.* Sir, pardon; a soldier is better accommodated than with a wife.

*Shal.* It is well said, in faith, sir; and it is well said indeed too. Better accommodated!— it is good; yea, indeed, is it: good phrases are surely, and ever were, very commendable. Accommodated!—it comes from *accommodo*: very good; a good phrase.

*Bard.* Pardon me, sir; I have heard the word. Phrase call you it? By this good day, I know not the phrase; but I will maintain the word with my sword to be a soldier-like word, and a word of exceeding good command. Accommodated; that is, when a man is, as they say, accommodated; or, when a man is, being, whereby he may be thought to be accommodated; which is an excellent thing.

*Shal.* It is very just.—Look, here comes good Sir John.

*Enter* FALSTAFF.

Give me your good hand, give me your worship's good hand: by my troth, you look well and bear your years very well: welcome, good Sir John.

*Fal.* I am glad to see you well, good Master Robert Shallow:—Master Surecard, as I think?

*Shal.* No, Sir John, it is my cousin Silence, in commission with me.

*Fal.* Good Master Silence, it well befits you should be of the peace.

*Sil.* Your good worship is welcome.

*Fal.* Fie! this is hot weather.—Gentlemen, have you provided me here half a dozen sufficient men?

*Shal.* Marry, have we, sir. Will you sit?

*Fal.* Let me see them, I beseech you.

*Shal.* Where's the roll? where's the roll? where's the roll?—let me see, let me see. So, so, so, so:—yea, marry, sir:—Ralph Mouldy!— let them appear as I call; let them do so, let them do so.—Let me see; where is Mouldy?

*Moul.* Here, an't please you.

*Shal.* What think you, Sir John? a good limbed fellow; young, strong, and of good friends.

*Fal.* Is thy name Mouldy?

*Moul.* Yea, an't please you.

*Fal.* 'Tis the more time thou wert used.

*Shal.* Ha, ha, ha! most excellent, i' faith! things that are mouldy lack use: very singular good!—in faith, well said, Sir John; very well said.

*Fal.* Prick him.　　　　[*To* SHALLOW.

*Moul.* I was pricked well enough before, an you could have let me alone: my old dame will be undone now for one to do her husbandry and her drudgery: you need not to have pricked me; there are other men fitter to go out than I.

*Fal.* Go to; peace, Mouldy; you shall go. Mouldy, it is time you were spent.

*Moul.* Spent!

*Shal.* Peace, fellow, peace; stand aside: know you where you are?—For the other, Sir John:—let me see;—Simon Shadow!

*Fal.* Yea, marry, let me have him to sit under: he's like to be a cold soldier.

*Shal.* Where's Shadow?

*Shad.* Here, sir.

*Fal.* Shadow, whose son art thou?

*Shad.* My mother's son, sir.

*Fal.* Thy mother's son! like enough; and thy father's shadow: so the son of the female is the shadow of the male: it is often so, indeed; but not much of the father's substance.

*Shal.* Do you like him, Sir John?

*Fal.* Shadow will serve for summer,—prick him; for we have a number of shadows to fill up the muster-book.

*Shal.* Thomas Wart!

*Fal.* Where's he?

*Wart.* Here, sir.

*Fal.* Is thy name Wart?

*Wart.* Yea, sir.

*Fal.* Thou are a very ragged wart.

*Shal.* Shall I prick him, Sir John?

*Fal.* It were superfluous; for his apparel is built upon his back, and the whole frame stands upon pins: prick him no more.

*Shal.* Ha, ha, ha!—you can do it, sir; you can do it: I commend you well.—Francis Feeble!

*Fee.* Here, sir.

*Fal.* What trade art thou, Feeble?

*Fee.* A woman's tailor, sir.

*Shal.* Shall I prick him, sir?

*Fal.* You may: but if he had been a man's tailor, he would have pricked you.—Wilt thou make as many holes in an enemy's battle as thou hast done in a woman's petticoat?

*Fee.* I will do my good will, sir; you can have no more.

*Fal.* Well said, good woman's tailor! well said, courageous Feeble! Thou wilt be as valiant as the wrathful dove or most magnanimous mouse.—Prick the woman's tailor well, Master Shallow; deep, Master Shallow.

*Fee.* I would Wart might have gone, sir.

*Fal.* I would thou wert a man's tailor, that thou mightst mend him, and make him fit to

go. I cannot put him to a private soldier, that
is the leader of so many thousands: let that
suffice, most forcible Feeble.

*Fee.* It shall suffice, sir.

*Fal.* I am bound to thee, Reverend Feeble.—
Who is next?

*Shal.* Peter Bullcalf of the green!

*Fal.* Yea, marry, let us see Bullcalf.

*Bull.* Here, sir.

*Fal.* 'Fore God, a likely fellow!—Come, prick
me, Bullcalf, till he roar again.

*Bull.* O lord! good my lord captain,—

*Fal.* What, dost thou roar before thou art
pricked?

*Bull.* O lord, sir! I am a diseased man.

*Fal.* What disease hast thou?

*Bull.* A whoreson cold, sir,—a cough, sir,—
which I caught with ringing in the king's affairs upon his coronation day, sir.

*Fal.* Come, thou shalt go to the wars in a
gown; we will have away thy cold; and I will
take such order that thy friends shall ring for
thee.—Is here all?

*Shal.* Here is two more called than your
number; you must have but four here, sir:—
and so, I pray you, go in with me to dinner.

*Fal.* Come, I will go drink with you, but I
cannot tarry dinner. I am glad to see you, by
my troth, Master Shallow.

*Shal.* O, Sir John, do you remember since
we lay all night in the windmill in Saint
George's Fields?

*Fal.* No more of that, good Master Shallow,
no more of that.

*Shal.* Ha, it was a merry night. And is Jane
Nightwork alive?

*Fal.* She lives, Master Shallow.

*Shal.* She never could away with me.

*Fal.* Never, never; she would always say she
could not abide Master Shallow.

*Shal.* By the mass, I could anger her to the
heart. She was then a bona-roba. Doth she
hold her own well?

*Fal.* Old, old, Master Shallow.

*Shal.* Nay, she must be old; she cannot
choose but be old; certain she's old; and had
Robin Nightwork, by old Nightwork, before I
came to Clement's-inn.

*Sil.* That's fifty-five year ago.

*Shal.* Ha, cousin Silence, that thou hadst
seen that that this knight and I have seen!—
Ha, Sir John, said I well?

*Fal.* We have heard the chimes at midnight,
Master Shallow.

*Shal.* That we have, that we have, that we
have; in faith, Sir John, we have: our watchword was, *Hem, boys!*—Come, let's to dinner;
come, let's to dinner:—O, the days that we
have seen!—come, come.

[*Exeunt* FAL., SHAL., *and* SIL.

*Bull.* Good Master Corporate Bardolph,
stand my friend; and here is four Harry ten
shillings in French crowns for you. In very
truth, sir, I had as lief be hanged, sir, as go:

and yet, for mine own part, sir, I do not care;
but rather, because I am unwilling, and, for
mine own part, have a desire to stay with my
friends; else, sir, I did not care for mine own
part, so much.

*Bard.* Go to; stand aside.

*Moul.* And, good master corporal captain,
for my old dame's sake, stand my friend: she
has nobody to do anything about her when I
am gone; and she is old, and cannot help herself: you shall have forty, sir.

*Bard.* Go to; stand aside.

*Fee.* By my troth, I care not; a man can die
but once; we owe God a death: I'll ne'er bear
a base mind: an't be my destiny, so; an't be
not, so: no man's too good to serve his prince;
and, let it go which way it will, he that dies
this year is quit for the next.

*Bard.* Well said; thou'rt a good fellow.

*Fee.* Faith, I'll bear no base mind.

*Re-enter* FALSTAFF *and* Justices.

*Fal.* Come, sir, which men shall I have?

*Shal.* Four of which you please.

*Bard.* Sir, a word with you:—I have three
pound to free Mouldy and Bullcalf.

*Fal.* Go to; well.

*Shal.* Come, Sir John, which four will you
have?

*Fal.* Do you choose for me.

*Shal.* Marry, then,—Mouldy, Bullcalf,
Feeble, and Shadow.

*Fal.* Mouldy and Bullcalf:—for you, Mouldy,
stay at home till you are past service: and for
your part, Bullcalf,—grow till you come unto
it: I will none of you.

*Shal.* Sir John, Sir John, do not yourself
wrong: they are your likeliest men, and I would
have you served with the best.

*Fal.* Will you tell me, Master Shallow, how
to choose a man? Care I for the limb, the
thews, the stature, bulk, and big assemblance
of a man! Give me the spirit, Master Shallow.
—Here's Wart;—you see what a ragged appearance it is: he shall charge you and discharge you, with the motion of a pewterer's
hammer; come off, and on, swifter than he that
gibbets on the brewer's bucket. And this same
half-faced fellow, Shadow,—give me this man:
he presents no mark to the enemy; the foeman
may with as great aim level at the edge of a
penknife. And, for a retreat,—how swiftly will
this Feeble, the woman's tailor, run off! O,
give me the spare men, and spare me the great
one.—Put me a caliver into Wart's hand,
Bardolph.

*Bard.* Hold, Wart, traverse; thus, thus,
thus.

*Fal.* Come, manage me your caliver. So:—
very well:—go to:—very good:—exceeding
good.—O, give me always a little, lean, old,
chapped, bald shot.—Well said, i' faith, Wart;
thou'rt a good scab: hold, there's a tester for
thee.

*Shal.* He is not his craft's-master, he doth not do it right. I remember at Mile-end Green,—when I lay at Clement's-inn,—I was then Sir Dagonet in Arthur's show,—there was a little quiver fellow, and he would manage you his piece thus; and he would about and about, and come you in and come you in: *rah, tah, tah*, would he say; *bounce* would he say; and away again would he go, and again would he come:—I shall never see such a fellow.

*Fal.* These fellows will do well, Master Shallow.—God keep you, Master Silence: I will not use many words with you.—Fare you well, gentlemen both: I thank you: I must a dozen mile to-night.—Bardolph, give the soldiers coats.

*Shal.* Sir John, heaven bless you, and prosper your affairs, and send us peace! as you return, visit my house; let our old acquaintance be renewed: peradventure I will with you to the court.

*Fal.* 'Fore God, I would you would, Master Shallow.

*Shal.* Go to; I have spake at a word. Fare you well. [*Exeunt* SHAL. *and* SIL.

*Fal.* Fare you well, gentle gentlemen. On, Bardolph; lead the men away. [*Exeunt* BARDOLPH, *Recruits, &c.*] As I return, I will fetch off these justices: I do see the bottom of Justice Shallow. Lord, Lord, how subject we old men are to this vice of lying! This same starved Justice hath done nothing but prate to me of the wildness of his youth, and the feats he hath done about Turnbull Street; and every third word a lie, duer paid to the hearer than the Turk's tribute. I do remember him at Clement's-inn, like a man made after supper of a cheese-paring: when he was naked, he was, for all the world, like a forked radish, with a head fantastically carved upon it with a knife: he was so forlorn that his dimensions to any thick sight were invincible: he was the very genius of famine: yet lecherous as a monkey, and the whores called him mandrake: he came ever in the reward of the fashion; and sung those tunes to the overscutched huswifes that he heard the carmen whistle, and sware they were his fancies or his good-nights. And now is this Vice's dagger become a squire, and talks as familiarly of John of Gaunt as if he had been sworn brother to him; and I'll be sworn he never saw him but once in the Tilt-yard; and then he burst his head for crowding among the marshal's men. I saw it, and told John of Gaunt he beat his own name; for you might have thrust him and all his apparel into an ell-skin; the case of a treble hautboy was a mansion for him, a court:—and now has he land and beeves. Well, I will be acquainted with him if I return; and it shall go hard but I will make him a philosopher's two stones to me: if the young dace be a bait for the old pike, I see no reason, in the law of nature, but I may snap at him. Let time shape, and there an end. [*Exti.*

## ACT IV.

SCENE I.—*A Forest in Yorkshire.*

*Enter the* ARCHBISHOP OF YORK, MOWBRAY, HASTINGS, *and others.*

*Arch.* What is this forest call'd?

*Hast.* 'Tis Gaultree Forest, an't shall please your grace.

*Arch.* Here stand, my lords; and send discoverers forth
To know the numbers of our enemies.

*Hast.* We have sent forth already.

*Arch.* 'Tis well done.
My friends and brethren in these great affairs,
I must acquaint you that I have receiv'd
New-dated letters from Northumberland;
Their cold intent, tenour, and substance, thus:—
Here doth he wish his person, with such powers
As might hold sortance with his quality,
The which he could not levy; whereupon
He is retir'd, to ripe his growing fortunes,
To Scotland; and concludes in hearty prayers
That your attempts may over-live the hazard
And fearful meeting of their opposite.

*Mowb.* Thus do the hopes we have in him touch ground,
And dash themselves to pieces.

*Enter a* Messenger.

*Hast.* Now, what news?

*Mess.* West of this forest, scarcely off a mile,
In goodly form comes on the enemy;
And, by the ground they hide, I judge their number
Upon or near the rate of thirty thousand.

*Mowb.* The just proportion that we gave them out.
Let us sway on, and face them in the field.

*Arch.* What well-appointed leader fronts us here?

*Mowb.* I think it is my Lord of Westmoreland.

*Enter* WESTMORELAND.

*West.* Health and fair greeting from our general
The prince, Lord John and Duke of Lancaster.

*Arch.* Say, on, my Lord of Westmoreland, in peace,
What doth concern your coming.

*West.* Then, my lord,
Unto your grace do I in chief address
The substance of my speech. If that rebellion
Came like itself, in base and abject routs,
Led on by bloody youth, guarded with rags,
And countenanc'd by boys and beggary,—
I say, if damn'd commotion so appear'd,
In his true, native, and most proper shape,
You, reverend father, and these noble lords,
Had not been here, to dress the ugly form
Of base and bloody insurrection
With your fair honours. You, lord archbishop,—

Whose see is by a civil peace maintain'd;
Whose beard the silver hand of peace hath
touch'd;
Whose learning and good letters peace hath
tutor'd;
Whose white investments figure innocence,
The dove and very blessed spirit of peace,—
Wherefore do you so ill translate yourself
Out of the speech of peace, that bears such
grace,
Into the harsh and boisterous tongue of war;
Turning your books to greaves, your ink to
blood,
Your pens to lances, and your tongue divine
To a loud trumpet and a point of war?
   *Arch.* Wherefore do I this?—so the question
stands.
Briefly to this end:—we are all diseas'd;
And with our surfeiting and wanton hours
Have brought ourselves into a burning fever,
And we must bleed for it: of which disease
Our late king, Richard, being infected, died.
But, my most noble Lord of Westmoreland,
I take not on me here as a physician;
Nor do I, as an enemy to peace,
Troop in the throngs of military men;
But, rather, show awhile like fearful war,
To diet rank minds sick of happiness,
And purge the obstructions which begin to stop
Our very veins of life. Hear me more plainly.
I have in equal balance justly weigh'd
What wrongs our arms may do, what wrongs
we suffer,
And find our griefs heavier than our offences.
We see which way the stream of time doth run,
And are enforc'd from our most quiet sphere
By the rough torrent of occasion;
And have the summary of all our griefs,
When time shall serve, to show in articles;
Which long ere this we offer'd to the king,
And might by no suit gain our audience:
When we are wrong'd, and would unfold our
griefs,
We are denied access unto his person
Even by those men that most have done us
wrong.
The dangers of the days but newly gone,—
Whose memory is written on the earth
With yet appearing blood,—and the examples
Of every minute's instance,—present now,—
Have put us in these ill-beseeming arms;
Not to break peace, or any branch of it,
But to establish here a peace indeed,
Concurring both in name and quality.
   *West.* When ever yet was your appeal
denied;
Wherein have you been galled by the king;
What peer hath been suborn'd to grate on
you;—
That you should seal this lawless bloody book
Of forg'd rebellion with a seal divine,
And consecrate commotion's bitter edge?
   *Arch.* My brother general, the common-
wealth,

To brother born an household cruelty,
I make my quarrel in particular.
   *West.* There is no need of any such redress;
Or if there were, it not belongs to you.
   *Mowb.* Why not to him in part, and to us all
That feel the bruises of the days before,
And suffer the condition of these times
To lay a heavy and unequal hand
Upon our honours?
   *West.*    O, my good Lord Mowbray,
Construe the times to their necessities,
And you shall say indeed, it is the time,
And not the king, that doth you injuries.
Yet, for your part, it not appears to me,
Either from the king or in the present time,
That you should have an inch of any ground
To build a grief on: were you not restor'd
To all the Duke of Norfolk's signiories,
Your noble and right-well-remember'd father's?
   *Mowb.* What thing, in honour, had my
father lost,
That need to be reviv'd and breath'd in me?
The king, that lov'd him, as the state stood
then,
Was, force perforce, compell'd to banish him,
And then that Henry Bolingbroke and he,—
Being mounted and both roused in their seats,
Their neighing coursers daring of the spur,
Their armed staves in charge, their beavers
down,
Their eyes of fire sparkling through sights of
steel,
And the loud trumpet blowing them together,—
Then, then, when there was nothing could have
stay'd
My father from the breast of Bolingbroke,
O, when the king did throw his warder down,
His own life hung upon the staff he threw;
Then threw he down himself, and all their lives
That by indictment and by dint of sword
Have since miscarried under Bolingbroke.
   *West.* You speak, Lord Mowbray, now you
know not what.
The Earl of Hereford was reputed then
In England the most valiant gentleman:
Who knows on whom fortune would then have
smil'd?
But if your father had been victor there,
He ne'er had borne it out of Coventry,
For all the country, in a general voice,
Cried hate upon him; and all their prayers and
love
Were set on Hereford, whom they doted on,
And bless'd and grac'd indeed, more than the
king.
But this is mere digression from my purpose.—
Here come I from our princely general
To know your griefs; to tell you from his grace
That he will give you audience; and wherein
It shall appear that your demands are just,
You shall enjoy them,—everything set off
That might so much as think you enemies.
   *Mowb.* But he hath forc'd us to compel this
offer;

And it proceeds from policy, not love.

*West.* Mowbray, you overween to take it so;
This offer comes from mercy, not from fear:
For, lo! within a ken, our army lies:
Upon mine honour, all too confident
To give admittance to a thought of fear.
Our battle is more full of names than yours,
Our men more perfect in the use of arms,
Our armour all as strong, our cause the best;
Then reason will our hearts should be as good:
Say you not, then, our offer is compell'd.

*Mowb.* Well, by my will we shall admit no
parley.

*West.* That argues but the shame of your
offence:
A rotten case abides no handling.

*Hast.* Hath the Prince John a full commis-
sion,
In very ample virtue of his father,
To hear and absolutely to determine
Of what conditions we shall stand upon?

*West.* That is intended in the general's
name:
I muse you make so slight a question.

*Arch.* Then take, my Lord of Westmoreland,
this schedule,
For this contains our general grievances:
Each several article herein redress'd,
All members of our cause, both here and hence,
That are insinew'd to this action,
Acquitted by a true substantial form,
And present execution of our wills
To us and to our purposes consign'd,—
We come within our awful banks again,
And knit our powers to the arm of peace.

*West.* This will I show the general. Please
you, lords,
In sight of both our battles we may meet;
And either end in peace,—which God so
frame!—
Or to the place of difference call the swords
Which must decide it.

*Arch.* My lord, we will do so.
[*Exit* WESTMORELAND.

*Mowb.* There is a thing within my bosom
tells me
That no conditions of our peace can stand.

*Hast.* Fear you not that: if we can make our
peace
Upon such large terms and so absolute
As our conditions shall consist upon,
Our peace shall stand as firm as rocky moun-
tains.

*Mowb.* Ay, but our valuation shall be such,
That every slight and false-derived cause,
Yea, every idle, nice, and wanton reason,
Shall to the king taste of this action;
That, were our royal faiths martyrs in love,
We shall be winnow'd with so rough a wind
That even our corn shall seem as light as chaff,
And good from bad find no partition.

*Arch.* No, no, my lord. Note this,—the king
is weary
Of dainty and such picking grievances:

For he hath found, to end one doubt by death
Revives two greater in the heirs of life;
And therefore will he wipe his tables clean,
And keep no tell-tale to his memory,
That may repeat and history his loss
To new remembrance: for full well he knows
He cannot so precisely weed this land
As his misdoubts present occasion:
His foes are so enrooted with his friends
That, plucking to unfix an enemy,
He doth unfasten so and shake a friend.
So that this land, like an offensive wife
That hath enrag'd him on to offer strokes,
As he is striking, holds his infant up,
And hangs resolv'd correction in the arm
That was uprear'd to execution.

*Hast.* Besides, the king hath wasted all his
rods
On late offenders, that he now doth lack
The very instruments of chastisement:
So that his power, like to a fangless lion,
May offer, but not hold.

*Arch.* 'Tis very true:
And therefore be assur'd, my good lord mar-
shal,
If we do now make our atonement well,
Our peace will, like a broken limb united,
Grow stronger for the breaking.

*Mowb.* Be it so,
Here is return'd my Lord of Westmoreland.

*Re-enter* WESTMORELAND.

*West.* The prince is here at hand: pleaseth
your lordship
To meet his grace just distance 'tween our
armies?

*Mowb.* Your grace of York, in God's name,
then, set forward.

*Arch.* Before, and greet his grace:—my lord,
we come. [*Exeunt.*

SCENE II.—*Another part of the Forest.*

*Enter, from one side,* MOWBRAY, *the* ARCH-
BISHOP, HASTINGS, *and others: from the other
side,* PRINCE JOHN OF LANCASTER, WEST-
MORELAND, Officers *and* Attendants.

*P. John.* You are well encounter'd here, my
cousin Mowbray:
Good-day to you, gentle lord archbishop;
And so to you, Lord Hastings,—and to all.—
My Lord of York, it better show'd with you
When that your flock, assembled by the bell,
Encircled you to hear with reverence
Your exposition on the holy text,
Than now to see you here an iron man,
Cheering a rout of rebels with your drum,
Turning the word to sword, and life to death.
That man that sits within a monarch's heart,
And ripens in the sunshine of his favour,
Would he abuse the countenance of the king,
Alack, what mischiefs might he set abroach
In shadow of such greatness! With you, lord
bishop,
It is even so. Who hath not heard it spoken

How deep you were within the books of God?
To us the speaker in his parliament;
To us the imagin'd voice of God himself;
The very opener and intelligencer
Between the grace, the sanctities of heaven,
And our dull workings. O, who shall believe
But you misuse the reverence of your place,
Employ the countenance and grace of heaven,
As a false favourite doth his prince's name,
In deeds dishonourable? You have taken up,
Under the counterfeited seal of God,
The subjects of his substitute, my father,
And both against the peace of heaven and him
Have here up-swarm'd them.

*Arch.*          Good my Lord of Lancaster,
I am not here against your father's peace;
But as I told my lord of Westmoreland,
The time misorder'd doth, in common sense,
Crowd us and crush us to this monstrous form,
To hold our safety up. I sent your grace
The parcels and particulars of our grief,—
The which hath been with scorn shov'd from
          the court,—
Whereon this Hydra son of war is born;
Whose dangerous eyes may well be charm'd
          asleep
With grant of our most just and right desires,
And true obedience, of this madness cur'd,
Stoop tamely to the foot of majesty.

*Mowb.* If not, we ready are to try our for-
          tunes
To the last man.

*Hast.*          And though we here fall down,
We have supplies to second our attempt:
If they miscarry, theirs shall second them;
And so success of mischief shall be born,
And heir from heir shall hold this quarrel up
Whiles England shall have generation.

*P. John.* You are too shallow, Hastings,
          much too shallow,
To sound the bottom of the after-times.

*West.* Pleaseth your grace to answer them
          directly,
How far-forth you do like their articles.

*P. John.* I like them all, and do allow them
          well;
And swear here, by the honour of my blood,
My father's purposes have been mistook;
And some about him have too lavishly
Wrested his meaning and authority.—
My lord; these griefs shall be with speed re-
          dress'd;
Upon my soul, they shall. If this may please
          you,
Discharge your powers unto their several coun-
          ties,
As we will ours: and here, between the armies,
Let's drink together friendly, and embrace,
That all their eyes may bear those tokens home
Of our restored love and amity.

*Arch.* I take your princely word for these
          redresses.

*P. John.* I give it you, and will maintain my
          word:

And thereupon I drink unto your grace.

*Hast.* Go, captain [*to an* Officer], and deliver
          to the army
This news of peace; let them have pay, and
          part:
I know it will well please them. Hie thee,
          captain.                    [*Exit* Officer.

*Arch.* To you, my noble Lord of Westmore-
          land.

*West.* I pledge your grace; and, if you knew
          what pains
I have bestow'd to breed this present peace,
You would drink freely: but my love to you
Shall show itself more openly hereafter.

*Arch.* I do not doubt you.

*West.*                    I am glad of it.—
Health to my lord and gentle cousin, Mowbray.

*Mowb.* You wish me health in very happy
          season;
For I am, on the sudden, something ill.

*Arch.* Against ill chances men are ever
          merry;
But heaviness foreruns the good event.

*West.* Therefore be merry, coz; since sudden
          sorrow
Serves to say thus,—Some good thing comes
          to-morrow.

*Arch.* Believe me, I am passing light in spirit.

*Mowb.* So much the worse, if your own rule
          be true.                    [*Shouts within.*

*P. John.* The word of peace is render'd;
          hark, how they shout!

*Mowb.* This had been cheerful after victory.

*Arch.* A peace is of the nature of a conquest;
For then both parties nobly are subdued,
And neither party loser.

*P. John.*                    Go, my lord,
And let our army be discharged too.
                              [*Exit* WESTMORELAND.
And, good my lord, so please you let your trains
March by us, that we may peruse the men
We should have cop'd withal.

*Arch.*                    Go, good Lord Hastings,
And, ere they be dismissed, let them march by.
                              [*Exit* HASTINGS.

*P. John.* I trust, my lords, we shall lie to-
          night together.

*Re-enter* WESTMORELAND.

Now, cousin, wherefore stands our army still?

*West.* The leaders, having charge from you
          to stand,
Will not go off until they hear you speak.

*P. John.* They know their duties.

*Re-enter* HASTINGS.

*Hast.* My lord, our army is dispers'd already:
Like youthful steers unyok'd, they take their
          courses                    [up,
East, west, north, south; or, like a school broke
Each hurries toward his home and sporting-
          place.

*West.* Good tidings, my Lord Hastings; for
          the which

I do arrest thee, traitor, of high treason:—
And you, lord archbishop,—and you, Lord
    Mowbray.—
Of capital treason I attach you both.
*Mowb.* Is this proceeding just and honour-
    able?
*West.* Is your assembly so?
*Arch.* Will you thus break your faith?
*P. John.*            I pawn'd thee none:
I promis'd you redress of these same grievances
Whereof you did complain; which, by mine
    honour,
I will perform with a most Christian care.
But for you, rebels,—look to taste the due
Meet for rebellion and such acts as yours.
Most shallowly did you these arms commence,
Fondly brought here, and foolishly sent hence.—
Strike up our drums, pursue the scatter'd stray:
God, and not we, hath safely fought to-day.—
Some guard these traitors to the block of death,
Treason's true bed and yielder-up of breath.
                                    [*Exeunt.*

SCENE III.—*Another part of the Forest.*

*Alarums: excursions. Enter* FALSTAFF *and*
    COLEVILE, *meeting.*

*Fal.* What's your name, sir? of what condi-
tion are you, and of what place, I pray?
*Cole.* I am a knight, sir; and my name is
Colevile of the dale.
*Fal.* Well, then, Colevile is your name, a
knight is your degree, and your place the dale:
Colevile shall be still your name, a traitor your
degree, and the dungeon your dale,—a dale
deep enough; so shall you be still Colevile of
the dale.
*Cole.* Are not you Sir John Falstaff?
*Fal.* As good a man as he, sir, whoe'er I am.
Do ye yield, sir? or shall I sweat for you? If
I do sweat, they are the drops of thy lovers, and
they weep for thy death; therefore rouse up
fear and trembling, and do observance to my
mercy.
*Cole.* I think you are Sir John Falstaff; and
in that thought yield me.
*Fal.* I have a whole school of tongues in this
belly of mine; and not a tongue of them all
speaks any other word but my name. An I had
but a belly of any indifferency, I were simply
the most active fellow in Europe: my womb,
my womb, my womb undoes me.—Here comes
our general.

*Enter* PRINCE JOHN OF LANCASTER,
    WESTMORELAND, *and others.*

*P. John.* The heat is past, follow no farther
    now:—
Call in the powers, good cousin Westmoreland.
                    [*Exit* WESTMORELAND.
Now, Falstaff, where have you been all this
    while?
When everything is ended, then you come:
These tardy tricks of yours will, on my life,
One time or other break some gallows' back.

*Fal.* I would be sorry, my lord, but it should
be thus: I never knew yet but rebuke and check
was the reward of valour. Do you think me a
swallow, an arrow, or a bullet? have I, in my
poor and old motion, the expedition of thought?
I have speeded hither with the very extremest
inch of possibility; I have foundered nine-score
and odd posts: and here, travel tainted as I am,
have, in my pure and immaculate valour, taken
Sir John Colevile of the dale, a most furious
knight and valorous enemy. But what of that?
he saw me, and yielded; that I may justly say
with the hook-nosed fellow of Rome,—I came,
saw, and overcame.
*P. John.* It was more of his courtesy than
your deserving.
*Fal.* I know not:—here he is, and here I
yield him: and I beseech your grace, let it be
booked with the rest of this day's deeds; or,
by the Lord, I will have it in a particular ballad
else, with mine own picture on the top of it,
Colevile kissing my foot: to the which course
if I be enforced, if you do not all show like gilt
two-pences to me, and I, in the clear sky of
fame, o'ershine you as much as the full moon
doth the cinders of the element, which show
like pins' heads to her, believe not the word of
the noble: therefore let me have right, and let
desert mount.
*P. John.* Thine's too heavy to mount.
*Fal.* Let it shine, then.
*P. John.* Thine's too thick to shine.
*Fal.* Let it do something, my good lord, that
may do me good, and call it what you will.
*P. John.* Is thy name Colevile?
*Cole.*                      It is, my lord.
*P. John.* A famous rebel art thou, Colevile.
*Fal.* And a famous true subject took him.
*Cole.* I am, my lord, but as my betters are
That led me hither: had they been rul'd by me,
You should have won them dearer than you
    have.
*Fal.* I know not how they sold themselves:
but thou, like a kind fellow, gavest thyself
away gratis; and I thank thee for thee.

*Re-enter* WESTMORELAND.

*P. John.* Now, have you left pursuit?
*West.* Retreat is made, and execution stay'd.
*P. John.* Send Colevile, with his confeder-
    ates,
To York, to present execution:—
Blunt, lead him hence; and see you guard him
    sure.      [*Exeunt some with* COLEVILE.
And now despatch we toward the court, my
    lords.
I hear the king, my father, is sore sick:
Our news shall go before us to his majesty,—
Which, cousin, you shall bear,—to comfort him;
And we with sober speed will follow you.
*Fal.* My lord, I beseech you, give me leave
    to go
Through Glostershire: and, when you come to
    court,

Stand, my good lord, pray, in your good report.

*P. John.* Fare you well, Falstaff: I, in my condition,
Shall better speak of you than you deserve.
[*Exeunt all but* FAL.

*Fal.* I would you had but the wit: 'twere better than your dukedom. Good faith, this same young sober-blooded boy doth not love me; nor a man cannot make him laugh;—but that's no marvel; he drinks no wine. There's never any of these demure boys come to any proof; for thin drink doth so over-cool their blood, and making many fish-meals, that they fall into a kind of male green-sickness; and then, when they marry, they get wenches: they are generally fools and cowards;—which some of us should be too, but for inflammation. A good sherris-sack hath a twofold operation in it. It ascends me into the brain; dries me there all the foolish and dull and crudy vapours which environ it; makes it apprehensive, quick, forgetive, full of nimble, fiery, and delectable shapes; which delivered o'er to the voice,—the tongue,—which is the birth, becomes excellent wit. The second property of your excellent sherris is,—the warming of the blood; which, before cold and settled, left the liver white and pale, which is the badge of pusillanimity and cowardice: but the sherris warms it, and makes it course from the inwards to the parts extreme: it illumineth the face; which, as a beacon, gives warning to all the rest of this little kingdom, man, to arm; and then the vital commoners and inland petty spirits muster me all to their captain, the heart, who, great and puffed up with this retinue, doth any deed of courage: and this valour comes of sherris. So that skill in the weapon is nothing without sack, for that sets it a-work; and learning, a mere hoard of gold kept by a devil till sack commences it and sets it in act and use. Hereof comes it that Prince Harry is valiant; for the cold blood he did naturally inherit of his father, he hath, like lean, sterile, and bare land, manured, husbanded, and tilled, with excellent endeavour of drinking good and good store of fertile sherris, that he is become very hot and valiant. If I had a thousand sons, the first human principle I would teach them should be,—to forswear thin potations, and to addict themselves to sack.

*Enter* BARDOLPH.

How now, Bardolph!

*Bard.* The army is discharged all, and gone.

*Fal.* Let them go. I'll through Glostershire: and there will I visit Master Robert Shallow, Esquire: I have him already tempering between my finger and my thumb, and shortly will I seal with him. Come away. [*Exeunt.*

SCENE IV.—WESTMINSTER. *A Room in the Palace.*

*Enter* KING HENRY, CLARENCE, PRINCE HUMPHREY, WARWICK, *and others.*

*K. Hen.* Now, lords, if God doth give successful end
To this debate that bleedeth at our doors,
We will our youth lead on to higher fields,
And draw no swords but what are sanctified.
Our navy is address'd, our power collected,
Our substitutes in absence well invested,
And everything lies level to our wish:
Only, we want a little personal strength;
And pause us till these rebels, now afoot,
Come underneath the yoke of government.

*War.* Both which we doubt not but your majesty
Shall soon enjoy.

*K. Hen.* Humphrey, my son of Gloster,
Where is the prince your brother?

*P. Humph.* I think he's gone to hunt, my lord, at Windsor.

*K. Hen.* And how accompanied?

*P. Humph.* I do not know, my lord.

*K. Hen.* Is not his brother, Thomas of Clarence, with him?

*P. Humph.* No, my good lord, he is in presence here.

*Cla.* What would my lord and father?

*K. Hen.* Nothing but well to thee, Thomas of Clarence.
How chance thou art not with the prince thy brother?
He loves thee, and thou dost neglect him, Thomas;
Thou hast a better place in his affection
Than all thy brothers: cherish it, my boy;
And noble offices thou mayst effect
Of mediation, after I am dead,
Between his greatness and thy other brethren:
Therefore omit him not; blunt not his love,
Nor lose the good advantage of his grace
By seeming cold or careless of his will;
For he is gracious if he be observ'd:
He hath a tear for pity, and a hand
Open as day for melting charity:
Yet notwithstanding, being incens'd, he's flint;
As humorous as winter, and as sudden
As flaws congealed in the spring of day.
His temper, therefore, must be well observ'd
Chide him for faults, and do it reverently,
When you perceive his blood inclin'd to mirth;
But, being moody, give him line and scope,
Till that his passions, like a whale on ground,
Confound themselves with working. Learn this, Thomas,
And thou shalt prove a shelter to thy friends,
A hoop of gold to bind thy brothers in,
That the united vessel of their blood,
Mingled with venom of suggestion,—
As, force perforce, the age will pour it in,—
Shall never leak, though it do work as strong
As aconitum or rash gunpowder. [love.

*Cla.* I shall observe him with all care and

*K. Hen.* Why art thou not at Windsor with him, Thomas?

*Cla.* He is not there to-day; he dines in London.

*K. Hen.* And how accompanied? canst thou tell that?

*Cla.* With Poins, and other his continual followers.

*K. Hen.* Most subject is the fattest soil to weeds;
And he, the noble image of my youth,
Is overspread with them: therefore my grief
Stretches itself beyond the hour of death:
The blood weeps from my heart when I do shape,
In forms imaginary, the unguided days
And rotten times that you shall look upon
When I am sleeping with my ancestors.
For when his headstrong riot hath no curb,
When rage and hot blood are his counsellors,
When means and lavish manners meet together,
O, with what wings shall his affections fly
Towards fronting peril and oppos'd decay!

*Wor.* My gracious lord, you look beyond him quite:
The prince but studies his companions
Like a strange tongue; wherein, to gain the language,
'Tis needful that the most immodest word
Be look'd upon and learn'd; which once attain'd,
Your highness knows, comes to no further use
But to be known and hated. So, like gross terms,
The prince will, in the perfectness of time,
Cast off his followers; and their memory
Shall as a pattern or a measure live,
By which his grace must mete the lives of others,
Turning past evils to advantages.

*K. Hen.* 'Tis seldom when the bee doth leave her comb
In the dead carrion,—

*Enter* WESTMORELAND.

Who's here? Westmoreland?

*West.* Health to my sovereign, and new happiness
Added to that that I am to deliver!
Prince John, your son, doth kiss your grace's hand:
Mowbray, the Bishop Scroop, Hastings, and all,
Are brought to the correction of your law;
There is not now a rebel's sword unsheathed,
But peace puts forth her olive everywhere:
The manner how this action hath been borne,
Here at more leisure may your highness read,
With every course in his particular.

*K. Hen.* O, Westmoreland, thou art a summer bird,
Which ever in the haunch of winter sings
The lifting-up of day. Look, here's more news.

*Enter* HARCOURT.

*Har.* From enemies heaven keep your majesty;
And, when they stand against you, may they fall
As those that I am come to tell you of!

The Earl Northumberland and the Lord Bardolph,
With a great power of English and of Scots,
Are by the sheriff of Yorkshire overthrown:
The manner and true order of the fight
This packet, please it you, contains at large.

*K. Hen.* And wherefore should these good news make me sick?
Will fortune never come with both hands full,
But write her fair words still in foulest letters?
She either gives a stomach, and no food,—
Such are the poor, in health; or else a feast,
And takes away the stomach,—such are the rich,
That have abundance, and enjoy it not.
I should rejoice now at this happy news;
And now my sight fails, and my brain is giddy:—
O me! come near me, now I am much ill.
[*Swoons.*

*P. Humph.* Comfort, your majesty!

*Cla.* O my royal father!

*West.* My sovereign lord, cheer up yourself, look up.

*War.* Be patient, princes; you do know, these fits
Are with his highness very ordinary.
Stand from him, give him air; he'll straight be well.

*Cla.* No, no: he cannot long hold out these pangs:
The incessant care and labour of his mind
Hath wrought the mure, that should confine it in,
So thin, that life looks through, and will break out.

*P. Humph.* The people fear me; for they do observe
Unfather'd heirs and loathly births of nature:
The seasons change their manners, as the year
Had found some months asleep, and leap'd them over.

*Cla.* The river hath thrice flow'd, no ebb between;
And the old folk, time's doting chronicles,
Say it did so a little time before
That our great grandsire, Edward, sick'd and died.

*War.* Speak lower, princes, for the king recovers.

*P. Humph.* This apoplexy will certain be his end. [me hence

*K. Hen.* I pray you, take me up, and bear
Into some other chamber: softly, pray.
[*They convey the* KING *into an inner part of the room, and place him on a bed.*
Let there be no noise made, my gentle friends;
Unless some dull and favourable hand
Will whisper music to my weary spirit.

*War.* Call for the music in the other room.

*K. Hen.* Set me the crown upon my pillow here.

*Cla.* His eye is hollow, and he changes much.

*War.* Less noise, less noise!

*Enter* PRINCE HENRY.

*P. Hen.* Who saw the Duke of Clarence?

*Cla.* I am here, brother, full of heaviness.

*P. Hen.* How now! rain within doors, and none abroad!
How doth the king?

*P. Humph.* Exceeding ill.

*P. Hen.*          Heard he the good news yet?
Tell it him.

*P. Humph.* He alter'd much upon the hearing it.

*P. Hen.* If he be sick
With joy, he will recover without physic.

*War.* Not so much noise, my lords;—sweet prince, speak low;
The king your father is dispos'd to sleep.

*Cla.* Let us withdraw into the other room.

*War.* Will't please your grace to go along with us?

*P. Hen.* No; I will sit and watch here by the king.          [*Exeunt all but* P. HENRY.
Why doth the crown lie there upon his pillow,
Being so troublesome a bedfellow?
O polish'd perturbation! golden care!
That keep'st the ports of slumber open wide
To many a watchful night!—sleep with it now!
Yet not so sound and half so deeply sweet
As he whose brow with homely biggin bound
Snores out the watch of night. O majesty!
When thou dost pinch thy bearer, thou dost sit
Like a rich armour worn in heat of day,
That scalds with safety. By his gates of breath
There lies a downy feather which stirs not:
Did he suspire, that light and weightless down
Perforce must move.—My gracious lord! my father!—
This sleep is sound indeed; this is a sleep
That from this golden rigol hath divorc'd
So many English kings. Thy due from me
Is tears and heavy sorrows of the blood,
Which nature, love, and filial tenderness
Shall, O dear father, pay thee plenteously:
My due from thee is this imperial crown,
Which, as immediate from thy place and blood,
Derives itself to me. Lo, here it sits,—
          [*Putting it on his head.*
Which God shall guard: and put the world's whole strength
Into one giant arm, it shall not force
This lineal honour from me: this from thee
Will I to mine leave, as 'tis left to me.          [*Exit.*

*K. Hen.* Warwick! Gloster! Clarence!

*Re-enter* WARWICK *and the rest.*

*Cla.*          Doth the king call?

*War.* What would your majesty? how fares your grace?

*K. Hen.* Why did you leave me here alone, my lords?

*Cla.* We left the prince my brother here, my liege,
Who undertook to sit and watch by you.

*K. Hen.* The Prince of Wales! Where is he? let me see him:
He is not here.

*War.* This door is open; he is gone this way.

*P. Humph.* He came not through the chamber where we stay'd.

*K. Hen.* Where is the crown? who took it from my pillow?

*War.* When we withdrew, my liege, we left it here.

*K. Hen.* The prince hath ta'en it hence:— go, seek him out.
Is he so hasty that he doth suppose
My sleep my death?—
Find him, my Lord of Warwick; chide him hither.
          [*Exit* WARWICK.
This part of his conjoins with my disease,
And helps to end me.—See, sons, what things you are!
How quickly nature falls into revolt
When gold becomes her object!
For this the foolish over-careful fathers
Have broke their sleep with thoughts, their brains with care,
Their bones with industry;
For this they have engrossed and pil'd up
The canker'd heaps of strange-achieved gold;
For this they have been thoughtful to invest
Their sons with arts and martial exercises:
When, like the bee, tolling from every flower
The virtuous sweets,
Our thighs with wax, our mouths with honey pack'd,
We bring it to the hive: and, like the bees,
Are murder'd for our pains. This bitter taste
Yield his engrossments to the ending father.

*Re-enter* WARWICK.

Now, where is he that will not stay so long
Till his friend sickness hath determin'd me?

*War.* My lord, I found the prince in the next room,
Washing with kindly tears his gentle cheeks;
With such a deep demeanour in great sorrow,
That tyranny, which never quaff'd but blood,
Would, by beholding him, have wash'd his knife
With gentle eye-drops. He is coming hither.

*K. Hen.* But wherefore did he take away the crown?

*Re-enter* PRINCE HENRY.

Lo, where he comes.—Come hither to me, Harry.—
Depart the chamber, leave us here alone.
          [*Exeunt* CLAR., P. HUMPH., Lords, &c.

*P. Hen.* I never thought to hear you speak again.

*K. Hen.* Thy wish was father, Harry, to that thought:
I stay too long by thee, I weary thee.
Dost thou so hunger for my empty chair
That thou wilt needs invest thee with mine honours

Before thy hour be ripe? O foolish youth!
Thou seek'st the greatness that will overwhelm thee.
Stay but a little; for my cloud of dignity
Is held from falling with so weak a wind
That it will quickly drop: my day is dim.
Thou hast stolen that which, after some few hours,
Were thine without offence; and at my death
Thou hast seal'd up my expectation:
Thy life did manifest thou lov'dst me not,
And thou wilt have me die assur'd of it.
Thou hid'st a thousand daggers in thy thoughts,
Which thou hast whetted on thy stony heart,
To stab at half an hour of my life.
What! canst thou not forbear me half an hour?
Then, get thee gone, and dig my grave thyself;
And bid the merry bells ring to thine ear,
That thou art crowned, not that I am dead.
Let all the tears that should bedew my hearse
Be drops of balm to sanctify thy head:
Only compound me with forgotten dust;
Give that which gave thee life unto the worms.
Pluck down my officers, break my decrees;
For now a time is come to mock at form:—
Harry the fifth is crown'd:—up, vanity!
Down, royal state! all you sage counsellors, hence!
And to the English court assemble now,
From every region, apes of idleness!
Now, neighbour confines, purge you of your scum:
Have you a ruffian that will swear, drink, dance,
Revel the night, rob, murder, and commit
The oldest sins the newest kind of ways?
Be happy, he will trouble you no more;
England shall double-gild his treble guilt,—
England shall give him office, honour, might;
For the fifth Harry from curb'd license plucks
The muzzle of restraint, and the wild dog
Shall flesh his tooth in every innocent.
O my poor kingdom, sick with civil blows!
When that my care could not withold thy riots,
What wilt thou do when riot is thy care?
O, thou wilt be a wilderness again,
Peopled with wolves, thy old inhabitants!
  *P. Hen.* O, pardon me, my liege! but for my
    tears,                    [*Kneeling.*
The moist impediments unto my speech,
I had forestall'd this dear and deep rebuke
Ere you with grief had spoke and I had heard
The course of it so far. There is your crown;
And He that wears the crown immortally
Long guard it yours! If I affect it more
Than as your honour and as your renown,
Let me no more from this obedience rise,—
Which my most inward and true duteous spirit
Teacheth,—this prostrate and exterior bending!
God witness with me, when I here came in,
And found no course of breath within your
    majesty,
How cold it struck my heart! If I do feign,
O, let me in my present wildness die,
And never live to show the incredulous world

The noble change that I have purposed!
Coming to look on you, thinking you dead,—
And dead almost, my liege, to think you were,—
I spake unto the crown as having sense,
And thus upbraided it: *The care on the depend-
    ing
Hath fed upon the body of my father;
Therefore, thou, best of gold, art worst of gold:
Other, less fine in carat, is more precious,
Preserving life in medicine potable;
But thou, most fine, most honour'd, most re-
    nown'd,
Hast eat thy bearer up.* Thus, my most royal
    liege,
Accusing it, I put it on my head,
To try with it, as with an enemy
That had before my face murder'd my father,—
The quarrel of a true inheritor.
But if it did infect my blood with joy,
Or swell my thoughts to any strain of pride;
If any rebel or vain spirit of mine
Did with the least affection of a welcome
Give entertainment to the might of it,
Let God for ever keep it from my head,
And make me as the poorest vassal is,
That doth with awe and terror kneel to it!
  *K. Hen.* O my son,
God put it in thy mind to take it hence,
That thou mightst win the more thy father's
    love,
Pleading so wisely in excuse of it!
Come hither, Harry, sit thou by my bed;
And hear, I think, the very latest counsel
That ever I shall breathe. God knows, my son,
By what by-paths and indirect crook'd ways
I met this crown; and I myself know well
How troublesome it sat upon my head:
To thee it shall descend with better quiet,
Better opinion, better confirmation;
For all the soil of the achievement goes
With me into the earth. It seem'd in me
But as an honour snatch'd with boisterous
    hand;
And I had many living to upbraid
My gain of it by their assistances;
Which daily grew to quarrel and to bloodshed,
Wounding supposed peace: all these bold fears
Thou see'st with peril I have answered;
For all my reign hath been but as a scene
Acting that argument: and now my death
Changes the mode; for what in me was pur-
    chas'd,
Falls upon thee in a more fairer sort;
So thou the garland wear'st successively.
Yet, though thou stand'st more sure than I
    could do,
Thou art not firm enough, since griefs are green;
And all my friends, which thou must make thy
    friends,
Have but their stings and teeth newly ta'en out;
By whose fell working I was first advanc'd,
And by whose power I well might lodge a fear
To be again displac'd: which to avoid,
I cut them off, and had a purpose now

To lead out many to the Holy Land,
Lest rest and lying still might make them look
Too near unto my state. Therefore, my Harry,
Be it thy course to busy giddy minds    [out,
With foreign quarrels; that action, hence borne
May waste the memory of the former days.
More would I, but my lungs are wasted so,
That strength of speech is utterly denied me.
How I came by the crown, O God forgive;
And grant it may with thee in true peace live!

  *P. Hen.* My gracious liege,
You won it, wore it, kept it, gave it me;
Then plain and right must my possession be:
Which I with more than with a common pain
'Gainst all the world will rightfully maintain.

  *K. Hen.* Look, look, here comes my John of
    Lancaster.

*Enter* PRINCE JOHN OF LANCASTER,
  WARWICK, Lords, *and others.*

  *P. John.* Health, peace and happiness to my
    royal father!

  *K. Hen.* Thou bring'st me happiness and
    peace, son John;
But health, alack, with youthful wings is flown
From this bare wither'd trunk: upon thy sight,
My worldly business makes a period.—
Where is my Lord of Warwick?

  *P. Hen.*          My Lord of Warwick!

  *K. Hen.* Doth any name particular belong
Unto the lodging where I first did swoon?

  *War.* 'Tis call'd Jerusalem, my noble lord.

  *K. Hen.* Laud be to God!—even there my
    life must end.
It hath been prophesied to me many years,
I should not die but in Jerusalem;
Which vainly I suppos'd the Holy Land:—
But bear me to that chamber; there I'll lie;
In that Jerusalem shall Harry die.    [*Exeunt.*

## ACT V.

SCENE I.—GLOUCESTERSHIRE. *A Hall in*
SHALLOW'S *House.*

*Enter* SHALLOW, FALSTAFF, BARDOLPH, *and*
Page.

  *Shal.* By cock and pie, sir, you shall not
away to-night.—What, Davy, I say!

  *Fal.* You must excuse me, Master Robert
Shallow.

  *Shal.* I will not excuse you; you shall not be
excused; excuses shall not be admitted; there is
no excuse shall serve; you shall not be excused.
—Why, Davy!

*Enter* DAVY.

  *Davy.* Here, sir.

  *Shal.* Davy, Davy, Davy,—let me see,
Davy; let me see:—yea, marry, William cook,
bid him come hither.—Sir John, you shall not
be excused.

  *Davy.* Marry, sir, thus;—those precepts cannot be served: and, again, sir,—shall we sow
the headland with wheat?

  *Shal.* With red wheat, Davy. But for William cook:—are there no young pigeons?

  *Davy.* Yes, sir.—Here is now the smith's
note for shoeing and plough-irons.

  *Shal.* Let it be cast, and paid.—Sir John,
you shall not be excused.

  *Davy.* Now, sir, a new link to the bucket
must needs be had:—and, sir, do you mean to
stop any of William's wages about the sack he
lost the other day at Hinckley fair?

  *Shal.* He shall answer it.—Some pigeons,
Davy, a couple of short-legged hens, a joint of
mutton, and any pretty little tiny kickshaws,
tell William cook.

  *Davy.* Doth the man of war stay all night,
sir?

  *Shal.* Yea, Davy, I will use him well: a
friend i' the court is better than a penny in
purse. Use his men well, Davy; for they are
arrant knaves, and will backbite.

  *Davy.* No worse than they are back-bitten,
sir; for they have marvellous foul linen.

  *Shal.* Well conceited, Davy:—about thy
business, Davy.

  *Davy.* I beseech you, sir, to countenance
William Visor of Wincot against Clement
Perkes of the hill.

  *Shal.* There are many complaints, Davy,
against that Visor: that Visor is an arrant
knave, on my knowledge.

  *Davy.* I grant your worship that he is a
knave, sir; but yet, God forbid, sir, but a knave
should have some countenance at his friend's
request. An honest man, sir, is able to speak for
himself, when a knave is not. I have served
your worship truly, sir, this eight years; and if
I cannot once or twice in a quarter bear out a
knave against an honest man, I have but a very
little credit with your worship. The knave is
mine honest friend, sir; therefore, I beseech
your worship, let him be countenanced.

  *Shal.* Go to; I say, he shall have no wrong.
Look about, Davy. [*Exit* DAVY.] Where are
you, Sir John? Come, come, come, off with
your boots.—Give me your hand, Master Bardolph.

  *Bard.* I am glad to see your worship.

  *Shal.* I thank thee with all my heart, kind
Master Bardolph:—and welcome, my tall fellow [*to the* Page].—Come, Sir John.

  *Fal.* I'll follow you, good Master Robert
Shallow. [*Exit* SHALLOW.] Bardolph, look to
our horses. [*Exeunt* BARDOLPH *and* Page.] If
I were sawed into quantities, I should make
four dozen of such bearded hermits' staves as
Master Shallow. It is a wonderful thing to see
the semblance coherence of his men's spirits
and his: they, by observing of him, do bear
themselves like foolish justices; he, by conversing with them, is turned into a justice-like servingman: their spirits are so married in conjunction with the participation of society that they
flock together in consent, like so many wild
geese. If I had a suit to Master Shallow, I

would humour his men with the imputation of being near their master: if to his men, I would curry with Master Shallow that no man could better command his servants. It is certain that either wise bearing or ignorant carriage is caught, as men take diseases, one of another: therefore, let men take heed of their company. I will devise matter enough out of this Shallow to keep Prince Harry in continual laughter the wearing out of six fashions,—which is four terms, or two actions,—and he shall laugh without *intervallums*. O, it is much that a lie with a slight oath, and a jest with a sad brow, will do with a fellow that never had the ache in his shoulders! O, you shall see him laugh till his face be like a wet cloak ill laid up!

*Shal.* [*Within.*] Sir John!

*Fal.* I come, Master Shallow; I come, Master Shallow.        [*Exit.*

SCENE II.—WESTMINSTER. *A Room in the Palace.*

*Enter, severally,* WARWICK *and the* Lord Chief-Justice.

*War.* How now, my lord chief-justice! whither away?

*Ch. Just.* How doth the king?

*War.* Exceedingly well; his cares are now all ended.

*Ch. Just.* I hope, not dead.

*War.*        He's walk'd the way of nature; And to our purposes he lives no more.

*Ch. Just.* I would his majesty had call'd me with him: The service that I truly did his life Hath left me open to all injuries.

*War.* Indeed I think the young king loves you not.                [myself

*Ch. Just.* I know he doth not; and do arm To welcome the condition of the time; Which cannot look more hideously upon me Than I have drawn it in my fantasy.

*War.* Here come the heavy issue of dead Harry: O that the living Harry had the temper Of him, the worst of these three gentlemen! How many nobles then should hold their places, That must strike sail to spirits of vile sort!

*Ch. Just.* O God, I fear all will be overturn'd.

*Enter* PRINCE JOHN, PRINCE HUMPHREY, CLARENCE, WESTMORELAND, *and others.*

*P. John.* Good-morrow, cousin Warwick, good-morrow.

*P. Humph., Cla.* Good-morrow, cousin.

*P. John.* We meet like men that had forgot to speak.

*War.* We do remember; but our argument Is all too heavy to admit much talk.

*P. John.* Well, peace be with him that hath made us heavy!

*Ch. Just.* Peace be with us, lest we be heavier!

*P. Humph.* O, good my lord, you have lost a friend indeed;

And I dare swear you borrow not that face Of seeming sorrow,—it is sure your own.

*P. John.* Though no man be assur'd what grace to find, You stand in coldest expectation: I am the sorrier; would 'twere otherwise.

*Cla.* Well, you must now speak Sir John Falstaff fair; Which swims against your stream of quality.

*Ch. Just.* Sweet princes, what I did, I did in honour, Led by the impartial conduct of my soul; And never shall you see that I will beg A ragged and forestall'd remission. If truth and upright innocency fail me, I'll to the king my master that is dead, And tell him who hath sent me after him.

*War.* Here comes the prince.

*Enter* KING HENRY V.

*Ch. Just.* Good-morrow; and God save your majesty!

*King.* This new and gorgeous garment, majesty, Sits not so easy on me as you think.— Brothers, you mix your sadness with some fear: This is the English, not the Turkish court; Not Amurath an Amurath succeeds, But Harry Harry. Yet be sad, good brothers, For, to speak truth, it very well becomes you: Sorrow so royally in you appears That I will deeply put the fashion on, And wear it in my heart: why, then, be sad; But entertain no more of it, good brothers, Than a joint burden laid upon us all. For me, by heaven, I bid you be assur'd, I'll be your father and your brother too; Let me but bear your love, I'll bear your cares: Yet weep that Harry's dead; and so will I; But Harry lives, that shall convert those tears, By number, into hours of happiness.

*P. John, &c.* We hope no other from your majesty.

*King.* You all look strangely on me:—and you most;        [*To the* Chief-Justice. You are, I think, assur'd I love you not.

*Ch. Just.* I am assur'd, if I be measur'd rightly, Your majesty hath no just cause to hate me.

*King.* No! How might a prince of my great hopes forget So great indignities you laid upon me? What! rate, rebuke, and roughly send to prison The immediate heir of England! Was this easy? May this be wash'd in Lethe, and forgotten?

*Ch. Just.* I then did use the person of your father; The image of his power lay then in me: And, in the administration of his law, Whiles I was busy for the commonwealth, Your highness pleased to forget my place, And majesty and power of law and justice, The image of the king whom I presented, And struck me in my very seat of judgment;

Whereon, as an offender to your father,
I gave bold way to my authority,
And did commit you. If the deed were ill,
Be you contented, wearing now the garland,
To have a son set your decrees at naught,
To pluck down justice from your awful bench,
To trip the course of law, and blunt the sword
That guards the peace and safety of your person;
Nay, more, to spurn at your most royal image,
And mock your workings in a second body.
Question your royal thoughts, make the case
  yours;
Be now the father, and propose a son;
Hear your own dignity so much profan'd,
See your most dreadful laws so loosely slighted,
Behold yourself so by a son disdain'd;
And then imagine me taking your part,
And, in your power, soft silencing your son:
After this cold considerance, sentence me;
And, as you are a king, speak in your state
What I have done that misbecame my place,
My person, or my liege's sovereignty.
  *King.* You are right, justice, and you weigh
    this well;
Therefore still bear the balance and the sword:
And I do wish your honours may increase
Till you do live to see a son of mine
Offend you, and obey you, as I did.
So shall I live to speak my father's words
*Happy am I, that have a man so bold,*
*That dares do justice on my proper son;*
*And not less happy, having such a son,*
*That would deliver up his greatness so*
*Into the hands of justice.*—You did commit me:
For which I do commit into your hand
The unstain'd sword that you have us'd to
  bear;
With this remembrance,—that you use the
  same
With the like bold, just, and impartial spirit
As you have done 'gainst me. There is my hand;
You shall be as a father to my youth:
My voice shall sound as you do prompt mine
  ear;
And I will stoop and humble my intents
To your well-practis'd wise directions.—
And, princes all, believe me, I beseech you;—
My father is gone wild into his grave,
For in his tomb lie my affections;
And with his spirit sadly I survive,
To mock the expectation of the world,
To frustrate prophecies, and to raze out
Rotten opinion, who hath writ me down
After my seeming. The tide of blood in me
Hath proudly flow'd in vanity till now:
Now doth it turn, and ebb back to the sea,
Where it shall mingle with the state of floods,
And flow henceforth in formal majesty.
Now call we our high court of parliament:
And let us choose such limbs of noble counsel,
That the great body of our state may go
In equal rank with the best-govern'd nation;
That war or peace, or both at once, may be
As things acquainted and familiar to us;

In which you, father, shall have foremost hand.
                    [*To the* Lord Chief-Justice.
Our coronation done, we will accite,
As I before remember'd, all our state:
And,—God consigning to my good intents,—
No prince nor peer shall have just cause to say,
God shorten Harry's happy life one day.
                                    [*Exeunt.*

SCENE III.—GLOUCESTERSHIRE. *The Garden*
        *of* SHALLOW'S *House.*

    *Enter* FALSTAFF, SHALLOW, SILENCE,
        BARDOLPH, *the* Page, *and* DAVY.

  *Shal.* Nay, you shall see mine orchard, where,
in an arbour, we will eat a last year's pippin of
my own graffing, with a dish of carraways, and
so forth:—come, cousin Silence:—and then to
bed.
  *Fal.* 'Fore God, you have here a goodly
dwelling and a rich.
  *Shal.* Barren, barren, barren; beggars all,
beggars all, Sir John:—marry, good air.—
Spread, Davy; spread, Davy: well said, Davy.
  *Fal.* This Davy serves you for good uses; he
is your serving-man and your husband.
  *Shal.* A good varlet, a good varlet, a very
good varlet, Sir John:—by the mass, I have
drunk too much sack at supper:—a good varlet.
Now sit down, now sit down:—come, cousin.
  *Sil.* Ah, sirrah! quoth-a,—we shall
*Do nothing but eat, and make good cheer,*
                                    [*Singing.*
*And praise heaven for the merry year;*
*When flesh is cheap, and females dear,*
*And lusty lads roam here and there,*
        *So merrily,*
        *And ever among so merrily.*
  *Fal.* There's a merry heart!—Good Master
Silence, I'll give you a health for that anon.
  *Shal.* Give Master Bardolph some wine,
Davy.
  *Davy.* Sweet sir, sit [*seating* BARDOLPH *and
the* Page *at another table*]; I'll be with you anon;
most sweet sir, sit.—Master Page, good Master
Page, sit.—Proface! What you want in meat,
we'll have in drink. But you must bear; the
heart's all.                    [*Exit.*
  *Shal.* Be merry, Master Bardolph;—and,
my little soldier there, be merry.
  *Sil.* Be merry, be merry, my wife has all;
                                    [*Singing.*
*For women are shrews, both short and tall;*
*'Tis merry in hall when beards wag all,*
        *And welcome merry shrove-tide.*
*Be merry, be merry, &c.*
  *Fal.* I did not think Master Silence had been
a man of this mettle.
  *Sil.* Who, I? I have been merry twice and
once ere now.

            *Re-enter* DAVY.

  *Davy.* There is a dish of leather-coats for
you.                [*Setting them before* BARD.
  *Shal.* Davy,—

*Davy.* Your worship?—I'll be with you straight [*to* Bard.]—A cup of wine, sir?

*Sil. A cup of wine that's brisk and fine,* [*Singing.*
  *And drink unto the leman mine;*
  *And a merry heart gives long-a.*

*Fal.* Well, said, Master Silence.

*Sil.* And we shall be merry;—now comes in the sweet of the night.

*Fal.* Health and long life to you, Master Silence.

*Sil. Fill the cup, and let it come;* [*Singing.*
  *I'll pledge you a mile to the bottom.*

*Shal.* Honest Bardolph, welcome: if thou wantest anything, and wilt not call, beshrew thy heart.—Welcome, my little tiny thief [*to the* Page]; and welcome indeed too.—I'll drink to Master Bardolph, and to all the cavaleroes about London.

*Davy.* I hope to see London once ere I die.

*Bard.* An I might see you there, Davy,—

*Shal.* By the mass, you'll crack a quart together,—ha! will you not, Master Bardolph?

*Bard.* Yea, sir, in a pottle-pot.

*Shal.* By God's liggens, I thank thee:—the knave will stick by thee, I can assure thee that: he will not out; he is true bred.

*Bard.* And I'll stick by him, sir.

*Shal.* Why, there spoke a king. Lack nothing: be merry. [*Knocking heard.*] Look who's at door there, ho! who knocks? [*Exit* Davy.

*Fal.* Why, now you have done me right.
  [*To* Sil., *who has drunk a bumper.*

*Sil.*     *Do me right,* [*Singing.*
  *And dub me knight:*
    *Samingo.*

Is't not so?

*Fal.* 'Tis so. [do somewhat.

*Sil.* Is't so? Why, then, say an old man can

*Re-enter* Davy.

*Davy.* An it please your worship, there's one Pistol come from the court with news.

*Fal.* From the court! let him come in.

*Enter* Pistol.

How now, Pistol!

*Pist.* Sir John, God save you!

*Fal.* What wind blew you hither, Pistol?

*Pist.* Not the ill wind which blows no man to good.—Sweet knight, thou art now one of the greatest men in the realm.

*Sil.* By'r lady, I think he be, but goodman Puff of Barson.

*Pist.* Puff?

Puff in thy teeth, most recreant coward base!—Sir John, I am thy Pistol and thy friend, And helter-skelter have I rode to thee; And tidings do I bring, and lucky joys, And golden times, and happy news of price.

*Fal.* I pr'ythee now, deliver them like a man of this world. [base!

*Pist.* A foutra for the world and worldlings I speak of Africa and golden joys.

*Fal.* O base Assyrian knight, what is thy news?

Let King Cophetua know the truth thereof.

*Sil. And Robin Hood, Scarlet, and John.* [*Singing.*

*Pist.* Shall dunghill curs confront the Helicons?

And shall good news be baffled?

Then, Pistol, lay thy head in Furies' lap.

*Shal.* Honest gentleman, I know not your breeding.

*Pist.* Why, then, lament, therefore.

*Shal.* Give me pardon, sir:—if, sir, you come with news from the court, I take it there is but two ways; either to utter them, or to conceal them. I am, sir, under the king, in some authority.

*Pist.* Under which king, bezonian? speak, or die.

*Shal.* Under King Harry.

*Pist.* Harry the fourth? or fifth?

*Shal.* Harry the fourth.

*Pist.*     A foutra for thine office!—Sir John, thy tender lambkin now is king; Harry the fifth's the man. I speak the truth: When Pistol lies, do this; and fig me, like The bragging Spaniard.

*Fal.* What! is the old king dead?

*Pist.* As nail in door: the things I speak are just.

*Fal.* Away, Bardolph! saddle my horse.—Master Robert Shallow, choose what office thou wilt in the land,'tis thine.—Pistol, I will double-charge thee with dignities.

*Bard.* O joyful day!

I would not take a knighthood for my fortune.

*Pist.* What, I do bring good news?

*Fal.* Carry Master Silence to bed.—Master Shallow, my Lord Shallow, be what thou wilt; I am fortune's steward. Get on thy boots: we'll ride all night:—O sweet Pistol!—away, Bardolph! [*Exit* Bardolph.]—Come, Pistol, utter more to me; and, withal, devise something to do thyself good.—Boot, boot, Master Shallow: I know the young king is sick for me. Let us take any man's horses; the laws of England are at my commandment. Happy are they which have been my friends; and woe unto my Lord Chief-Justice!

*Pist.* Let vultures vile seize on his lungs also! *Where is the life that late I led?* say they: Why, here it is;—welcome this pleasant day!
  [*Exeunt.*

SCENE IV.—LONDON. *A Street.*

*Enter* Beadles, *dragging in* Hostess Quickly *and* Doll Tearsheet.

*Host.* No, thou arrant knave; I would I might die, that I might have thee hanged: thou hast drawn my shoulder out of joint.

1 *Bead.* The constables have delivered her over to me; and she shall have whipping-cheer enough, I warrant her: there hath been a man or two lately killed about her.

*Doll.* Nut-hook, nut-hook, you lie. Come on; I'll tell thee what, thou damned tripe-visaged rascal, an the child I now go with do miscarry, thou hadst better thou hadst struck thy mother, thou paper-faced villain.

*Host.* O the Lord, that Sir John were come! he would make this a bloody day to somebody. But I pray God the fruit of her womb miscarry!

*1 Bead.* If it do, you shall have a dozen of cushions again; you have but eleven now. Come, I charge you both go with me; for the man is dead that you and Pistol beat among you.

*Doll.* I'll tell thee what, thou thin man in a censer, I will have you as soundly swinged for this,—you blue-bottle rogue, you filthy famished correctioner, if you be not swinged, I'll forswear half-kirtles.

*1 Bead.* Come, come, you she knight-errant, come.

*Host.* O God, that right should thus overcome might! Well, of sufferance comes ease.

*Doll.* Come, you rogue, come; bring me to a justice.

*Host.* Ay, come, you starved bloodhound.

*Doll.* Goodman death, goodman bones!

*Host.* Thou atomy, thou!

*Doll.* Come, you thin thing; come, you rascal.

*1 Bead.* Very well.                    [*Exeunt.*

SCENE V.—*A public Place near Westminster Abbey.*

*Enter two* Grooms, *strewing rushes.*

*1 Groom.* More rushes, more rushes.

*2 Groom.* The trumpets have sounded twice.

*1 Groom.* It will be two o'clock ere they come from the coronation: despatch, despatch.

[*Exeunt.*

*Enter* FALSTAFF, SHALLOW, PISTOL, BARDOLPH, *and the* Page.

*Fal.* Stand here by me, Master Robert Shallow; I will make the king do you grace: I will leer upon him, as he comes by; and do but mark the countenance that he will give me.

*Pist.* God bless thy lungs, good knight.

*Fal.* Come here, Pistol; stand behind me.— O, if I had had time to have made new liveries, I would have bestowed the thousand pound I borrowed of you [*to* SHALLOW]. But 'tis no matter; this poor show doth better: this doth infer the zeal I had to see him,—

*Shal.* It doth so.

*Fal.* It shows my earnestness of affection,—

*Shal.* It doth so.

*Fal.* My devotion,—

*Shal.* It doth, it doth, it doth.

*Fal.* As it were, to ride day and night; and not to deliberate, not to remember, not to have patience to shift me,—

*Shal.* It is most certain.

*Fal.* But to stand stained with travel, and sweating with desire to see him; thinking of nothing else, putting all affairs else in oblivion, as if there were nothing else to be done but to see him.

*Pist.* 'Tis *semper idem,* for *absque hoc nihil est:* 'tis all in every part.

*Shal.* 'Tis so, indeed.                    [liver,

*Pist.* My knight, I will inflame thy noble And make thee rage.

Thy Doll, and Helen of thy noble thoughts,
Is in base durance and contagious prison;
Haul'd thither
By most mechanical and dirty hand:—
Rouse up revenge from ebon den with fell
   Alecto's snake,
For Doll is in. Pistol speaks naught but truth.

*Fal.* I will deliver her.

[*Shouts within, and the trumpets sound*

*Pist.* There roar'd the sea, and trumpets clangor sounds.

*Enter the* KING *and his* Train, *the* Chief-Justice *among them.*

*Fal.* God save thy grace, King Hal; my royal Hal!

*Pist.* The heavens thee guard and keep, most royal imp of fame!

*Fal.* God save thee, my sweet boy!

*King.* My lord chief-justice, speak to that vain man.

*Ch. Just.* Have you your wits? know you what 'tis you speak?

*Fal.* My king! my Jove! I speak to thee, my heart!

*King.* I know thee not, old man: fall to thy prayers;

How ill white hairs become a fool and jester!
I have long dream'd of such a kind of man,
So surfeit-swell'd, so old, and so profane;
But, being awake, I do despise my dream.
Make less thy body hence, and more thy grace;
Leave gormandizing; know the grave doth gape
For thee thrice wider than for other men.—
Reply not to me with a fool-born jest:
Presume not that I am the thing I was;
For God doth know, so shall the world perceive,
That I have turn'd away my former self;
So will I those that kept me company.
When thou dost hear I am as I have been,
Approach me, and thou shalt be as thou wast,
The tutor and the feeder of my riots:
Till then I banish thee, on pain of death,—
As I have done the rest of my misleaders,—
Not to come near our person by ten mile.
For competence of life I will allow you,
That lack of means enforce you not to evil:
And, as we hear you do reform yourselves,
We will, according to your strength and qualities,
Give you advancement.—Be it your charge, my lord,
To see perform'd the tenor of our word.—
Set on.             [*Exeunt* KING *and his* Train.

*Fal.* Master Shallow, I owe you a thousand pound.

*Shal.* Yèa, marry, Sir John; which I beseech you to let me have home with me.

*Fal.* That can hardly be, Master Shallow. Do not you grieve at this; I shall be sent for in private to him: look you, he must seem thus to the world: fear not your advancement; I will be the man yet that shall make you great.

*Shal.* I cannot perceive how,—unless you give me your doublet, and stuff me out with straw. I beseech you, good Sir John, let me have five hundred of my thousand.

*Fal.* Sir, I will be as good as my word: this that you heard was but a colour.

*Shal.* A colour, I fear, that you will die in, Sir John.

*Fal.* Fear no colours: go with me to dinner. Come, Lieutenant Pistol;—come, Bardolph:—I shall be sent for soon at night.

*Re-enter* PRINCE JOHN, *the* Chief-Justice, Officers, &c.

*Ch. Just.* Go, carry Sir John Falstaff to the Fleet;
Take all his company along with him.

*Fal.* My lord, my lord,—

*Ch. Just.* I cannot now speak: I will hear you soon.—
Take them away.

*Pist.* Se fortuna mi tormenta, lo sperare mi contenta.

[*Exeunt* FAL., SHAL., PIST., BARD., Page, *and* Officers.

*P. John.* I like this fair proceeding of the king's:
He hath intent his wonted followers
Shall all be very well provided for;
But all are banish'd till their conversations
Appear more wise and modest to the world.

*Ch. Just.* And so they are.

*P. John.* The king hath call'd his parliament, my lord.

*Ch. Just.* He hath.

*P. John.* I will lay odds that, ere this year expire,

We bear our civil swords and native fire
As far as France: I heard a bird so sing,
Whose music, to my thinking, pleas'd the king.
Come, will you hence? [*Exeunt.*

EPILOGUE.—*Spoken by a Dancer.*

First my fear; then my court'sy; last my speech. My fear is, your displeasure; my court'sy, my duty; and my speech, to beg your pardons. If you look for a good speech now, you undo me: for what I have to say is of mine own making; and what, indeed, I should say will, I doubt, prove mine own marring. But to the purpose, and so to the venture.—Be it known to you,—as it is very well,—I was lately here in the end of a displeasing play, to pray your patience for it, and to promise you a better. I did mean, indeed, to pay you with this; which, if, like an ill venture, it come unluckily home, I break, and you, my gentle creditors, lose. Here I promised you I would be, and here I commit my body to your mercies: bate me some, and I will pay you some, and, as most debtors do, promise you infinitely.

If my tongue cannot entreat you to acquit me, will you command me to use my legs? and yet that were but light payment,—to dance out of your debt. But a good conscience will make any possible satisfaction, and so will I. All the gentlewomen here have forgiven me: if the gentlemen will not, then the gentlemen do not agree with the gentlewomen, which was never seen before in such an assembly.

One word more, I beseech you. If you be not too much cloyed with fat meat, our humble author will continue the story, with Sir John in it, and make you merry with fair Katherine of France: where, for anything I know, Falstaff shall die of a sweat, unless already he be killed with your hard opinions; for Oldcastle died a martyr, and this is not the man. My tongue is weary; when my legs are too, I will bid you good-night: and so kneel down before you;—but, indeed, to pray for the queen.

KING HENRY V.

Act IV. Sc. 7.

# KING HENRY V.

## DRAMATIS PERSONÆ

King Henry the Fifth.

Duke of Gloster, } Brothers to the King.
Duke of Bedford, }

Duke of Exeter, *Uncle to the* King.

Duke of York, *Cousin to the* King.

Earls of Salisbury, Westmoreland, *and* Warwick.

Archbishop of Canterbury.

Bishop of Ely.

Earl of Cambridge, } Conspirators against
Lord Scroop, } the King.
Sir Thomas Grey, }

Sir Thomas Erpingham, Gower, Fluellen, Macmorris, Jamy, *Officers in* King Henry's *Army*.

Bates, Court, Williams, *Soldiers in the same*.

Nym, Bardolph, Pistol, *formerly Servants to* Falstaff, *now Soldiers in the same*.

Boy, *Servant to them*.

A Herald.

Chorus.

Charles the Sixth, *King of France*.

Louis, *the Dauphin*.

Dukes of Burgundy, Orleans, *and* Bourbon.

*The* Constable of France.

Rambures *and* Grandpree, *French Lords*.

Governor of Harfleur.

Montjoy, *a French Herald*.

Ambassadors to the King of England.

Isabel, *Queen of France*.

Katharine, *Daughter to* Charles *and* Isabel.

Alice, *a Lady attending on the* Princess Katharine.

Quickly, Pistol's *Wife, an Hostess*.

Lords, Ladies, Officers, French and English Soldiers, Messengers, *and* Attendants.

Scene,—*At the beginning of the Play, lies in* England; *but afterwards wholly in* France.

---

*Enter* Chorus.

*Chor.* O for a Muse of fire, that would ascend
The brightest heaven of invention!
A kingdom for a stage, princes to act,
And monarchs to behold the swelling scene!
Then should the warlike Harry, like himself,
Assume the port of Mars; and at his heels,
Leash'd in like hounds, should famine, sword, and fire,
Crouch for employment. But pardon, gentles all,
The flat unraised spirit that hath dar'd
On this unworthy scaffold to bring forth
So great an object: can this cockpit hold
The vasty fields of France? or may we cram
Within this wooden O the very casques
That did affright the air at Agincourt?
O, pardon! since a crooked figure may
Attest in little place a million;
And let us, ciphers to this great acompt,
On your imaginary forces work.
Suppose within the girdle of these walls
Are now confin'd two mighty monarchies,
Whose high upreared and abutting fronts
The perilous narrow ocean parts asunder:
Piece out our imperfections with your thoughts:
Into a thousand parts divide one man,
And make imaginary puissance;
Think, when we talk of horses, that you see them
Printing their proud hoof i' the receiving earth;

For 'tis your thoughts that now must deck our kings,
Carry them here and there; jumping o'er times,
Turning the accomplishment of many years
Into an hour-glass: for the which supply,
Admit me Chorus to this history;
Who, prologue-like, your humble patience pray,
Gently to hear, kindly to judge, our play.

## ACT I.

Scene I.—London. *An Ante-chamber in the* King's *Palace*.

*Enter the* Archbishop of Canterbury *and the* Bishop of Ely.

*Cant.* My lord, I'll tell you,—that self bill is urg'd,
Which in the eleventh year of the last king's reign
Was like, and had indeed against us pass'd,
But that the scambling and unquiet time
Did push it out of further question.   [now?
  *Ely.* But how, my lord, shall we resist it
  *Cant.* It must be thought on. If it pass against us,
We lose the better half of our possession:
For all the temporal lands, which men devout
By testament have given to the church,
Would they strip from us; being valu'd thus,—
As much as would maintain, to the king's honour,

[*489*]

Full fifteen earls and fifteen hundred knights,
Six thousand and two hundred good esquires;
And, to relief of lazars and weak age,
Of indigent faint souls past corporal toil,
A hundred alms-houses right well supplied;
And to the coffers of the king, beside,
A thousand pounds by the year: thus runs the
    bill.
*Ely.* This would drink deep.
*Cant.*          'Twould drink the cup and all.
*Ely.* But what prevention?
*Cant.* The king is full of grace and fair re-
    gard.
*Ely.* And a true lover of the holy church.
*Cant.* The courses of his youth promis'd it
    not.
The breath no sooner left his father's body
But that his wildness, mortified in him,
Seem'd to die too: yea, at that very moment,
Consideration, like an angel, came,
And whipp'd the offending Adam out of him,
Leaving his body as a paradise,
To envelop and contain celestial spirits.
Never was such a sudden scholar made;
Never came reformation in a flood,
With such a heady current, scouring faults;
Nor never Hydra-headed wilfulness
So soon did lose his seat, and all at once,
As in this king.
*Ely.*          We are blessed in the change.
*Cant.* Hear him but reason in divinity,
And, all-admiring, with an inward wish
You would desire the king were made a prelate:
Hear him debate of commonwealth affairs,
You would say, it hath been all-in-all his study:
List his discourse of war, and you shall hear
A fearful battle render'd you in music:
Turn him to any cause of policy,
The Gordian knot of it he will unloose,
Familiar as his garter:—that, when he speaks,
The air, a charter'd libertine, is still,
And the mute wonder lurketh in men's ears,
To steal his sweet and honeyed sentences;
So that the art and practice part of life
Must be the mistress to this theoric:
Which is a wonder how his grace should glean
    it,
Since his addiction was to courses vain;
His companies unletter'd, rude, and shallow;
His hours fill'd up with riots, banquets, sports;
And never noted in him any study,
Any retirement, any sequestration
From open haunts and popularity.
*Ely.* The strawberry grows underneath the
    nettle,
And wholesome berries thrive and ripen best
Neighbour'd by fruit of baser quality:
And so the prince obscur'd his contemplation
Under the veil of wildness; which, no doubt,
Grew like the summer grass, fastest by night,
Unseen, yet crescive in his faculty.
*Cant.* It must be so; for miracles are ceas'd;
And therefore we must needs admit the means
How things are perfected.

*Ely.*                        But, my good lord,
How now for mitigation of this bill
Urg'd by the commons? Doth his majesty
Incline to it, or no?
  *Cant.*          He seems indifferent;
Or, rather, swaying more upon our part
Than cherishing the exhibitors against us:
For I have made an offer to his majesty,—
Upon our spiritual convocation,
And in regard of causes now in hand,
Which I have open'd to his grace at large,
As touching France,—to give a greater sum
Than ever at one time the clergy yet
Did to his predecessors part withal.
  *Ely.* How did this offer seem receiv'd, my
    lord?
  *Cant.* With good acceptance of his majesty;
Save that there was not time enough to hear,—
As, I perceiv'd, his grace would fain have
    done,—
The severals and unhidden passages
Of his true titles to some certain dukedoms,
And, generally, to the crown and seat of France,
Deriv'd from Edward, his great-grandfather.
  *Ely.* What was the impediment that broke
    this off?
  *Cant.* The French ambassador upon that
    instant
Crav'd audience: and the hour, I think, is come
To give him hearing: is it four o'clock?
  *Ely.*                              It is.
  *Cant.* Then go we in, to know his embassy;
Which I could, with a ready guess, declare,
Before the Frenchman speak a word of it.
  *Ely.* I'll wait upon you; and I long to hear it.
                         [*Exeunt.*

SCENE II.—*The same. A Room of State in the
    same.*

*Enter* KING HENRY, GLOSTER, BEDFORD,
EXETER, WARWICK, WESTMORELAND, *and*
Attendants.

  *K. Hen.* Where is my gracious Lord of
    Canterbury?
  *Exe.* Not here in presence.
  *K. Hen.* Send for him, good uncle.
  *West.* Shall we call in the ambassador, my
    liege?
  *K. Hen.* Not yet, my cousin; we would be
    resolv'd,
Before we hear him, of some things of weight,
That task our thoughts, concerning us and
    France.

*Enter the* ARCHBISHOP OF CANTERBURY *and*
BISHOP OF ELY.

  *Cant.* God and his angels guard your sacred
    throne,
And make you long become it!
  *K. Hen.*              Sure, we thank you.
My learned lord, we pray you to proceed,
And justly and religiously unfold
Why the law Salique, that they have in France,
Or should, or should not, bar us in our claim:

And God forbid, my dear and faithful lord,
That you should fashion, wrest, or bow your
    reading,
Or nicely charge your understanding soul
With opening titles miscreate, whose right
Suits not in native colours with the truth;
For God doth know how many, now in health,
Shall drop their blood in approbation
Of what your reverence shall incite us to:
Therefore take heed how you impawn our
    person,
How you awake the sleeping sword of war:
We charge you, in the name of God, take heed;
For never two such kingdoms did contend
Without much fall of blood; whose guiltless
    drops
Are every one a woe, a sore complaint
'Gainst him whose wrongs give edge unto the
    swords
That make such waste in brief mortality.
Under this conjuration, speak, my lord;
For we will hear, note, and believe in heart
That what you speak is in your conscience
    wash'd
As pure as sin with baptism.
    *Cant.*  Then hear me, gracious sovereign,—
    and you peers,
That owe yourselves, your lives, and services
To this imperial throne.—There is no bar
To make against your highness' claim to France
But this, which they produce from Phara-
    mond,—
*In terram Salicam muliers ne succedant,*
*No woman shall succeed in Salique land:*
Which Salique land the French unjustly gloze
To be the realm of France, and Pharamond
The founder of this law and female bar.
Yet their own authors faithfully affirm
That the land Salique is in Germany,
Between the floods of Sala and of Elbe;
Where Charles the Great, having subdu'd the
    Saxons,
There left behind and settled certain French;
Who, holding in disdain the German women
For some dishonest manners of their life,
Establish'd then this law,—to wit, no female
Should be inheritrix in Salique land:
Which Salique, as I said, 'twixt Elbe and Sala,
Is at this day in Germany called Meisen.
Then doth it well appear, the Salique law
Was not devised for the realm of France:
Nor did the French possess the Salique land
Until four hundred one-and-twenty years
After defunction of King Pharamond,
Idly suppos'd the founder of this law;
Who died within the year of our redemption
Four hundred twenty-six; and Charles the
    Great
Subdu'd the Saxons, and did seat the French
Beyond the river Sala, in the year
Eight hundred five. Besides, their writers say,
King Pepin, which deposed Childerick,
Did, as heir general, being descended
Of Blithild, which was daughter to King Clothair,

Make claim and title to the crown of France.
Hugh Capet also,—who usurp'd the crown
Of Charles the Duke of Lorraine, sole heir male
Of the true line and stock of Charles the
    Great,—
To fine his title with some show of truth,—
Though, in pure truth, it was corrupt and
    naught,—
Convey'd himself as heir to the Lady Lingare,
Daughter to Charlemain, who was the son
To Louis the emperor, and Louis the son
Of Charles the Great. Also King Louis the
    Tenth,
Who was sole heir to the usurper Capet,
Could not keep quiet in his conscience,
Wearing the crown of France, till satisfied
That fair Queen Isabel, his grandmother,
Was lineal of the Lady Ermengare,
Daughter to Charles the foresaid Duke of Lor-
    raine:
By the which marriage the line of Charles the
    Great
Was re-united to the Crown of France.
So that, as clear as is the summer's sun,
King Pepin's title, and Hugh Capet's claim,
King Louis his satisfaction, all appear
To hold in right and title of the female:
So do the kings of France unto this day;
Howbeit they would hold up this Salique law
To bar your highness claiming from the female;
And rather choose to hide them in a net
Than amply to imbar their crooked titles
Usurp'd from you and your progenitors.
    *K. Hen.*  May I with right and conscience
    make this claim?
    *Cant.*  The sin upon my head, dread sover-
    eign!
For in the book of Numbers is it writ,—
When the man dies, let the inheritance
Descend unto the daughter. Gracious lord,
Stand for your own; unwind your bloody flag;
Look back unto your mighty ancestors:
Go, my dread lord, to your great-grandsire's
    tomb,
From whom you claim; invoke his warlike
    spirit,
And your great-uncle's, Edward the Black
    Prince,
Who on the French ground play'd a tragedy,
Making defeat on the full power of France,
Whiles his most mighty father on a hill
Stood smiling to behold his lion's whelp
Forage in blood of French nobility.
O noble English, that could entertain
With half their forces the full pride of France,
And let another half stand laughing by,
All out of work and cold for action!
    *Ely.*  Awake remembrance of these valiant
    dead,
And with your puissant arm renew their feats:
You are their heir; you sit upon their throne;
The blood and courage that renowned them
Runs in your veins; and my thrice-puissant
    liege

Is in the very May-morn of his youth,
Ripe for exploits and mighty enterprises.
   *Exe.* Your brother kings and monarchs of
     the earth
Do all expect that you should rouse yourself,
As did the former lions of your blood.
   *West.* They know your grace hath cause and
     means and might:—
So hath your highness; never king of England
Had nobles richer and more loyal subjects,
Whose hearts have left their bodies here in
     England,
And lie pavilion'd in the fields of France.
   *Cant.* O, let their bodies follow, my dear
     liege,
With blood and sword and fire to win your
   right:
In aid whereof we of the spiritualty
Will raise your highness such a mighty sum
As never did the clergy at one time
Bring in to any of your ancestors.
   *K. Hen.* We must not only arm to invade the
     French,
But lay down our proportions to defend
Against the Scot, who will make road upon us
With all advantages.
   *Cant.* They of those marches, gracious sove-
     reign,
Shall be a wall sufficient to defend
Our inland from the pilfering borderers.
   *K. Hen.* We do not mean the coursing
     snatchers only,
But fear the main intendment of the Scot,
Who hath been still a giddy neighbour to us;
For you shall read that my great-grandfather
Never went with his forces into France
But that the Scot on his unfurnish'd kingdom
Came pouring, like the tide into a breach,
With ample and brim fulness of his force;
Galling the gleaned land with hot essays,
Girding with grievous siege castles and towns;
That England, being empty of defence,
Hath shook and trembled at the ill neighbour-
     hood.
   *Cant.* She hath been then more fear'd than
     harm'd, my liege;
For hear her but exampled by herself:—
When all her chivalry hath been in France,
And she a mourning widow of her nobles,
She hath herself not only well defended,
But taken, and impounded as a stray,
The king of Scots; whom she did send to
     France,
To fill King Edward's fame with prisoner kings,
And make her chronicle as rich with praise
As is the ooze and bottom of the sea
With sunken wreck and sumless treasuries.
   *West.* But there's a saying, very old and
     true,—
     *If that you will France win,*
     *Then with Scotland first begin:*
For once the eagle England being in prey,
To her unguarded nest the weasel Scot
Comes sneaking, and so sucks her princely eggs;

Playing the mouse in absence of the cat,
To tear and havoc more than she can eat.
   *Exe.* It follows, then, the cat must stay at
     home:
Yet that is but a curs'd necessity,
Since we have locks to safeguard necessaries,
And pretty traps to catch the petty thieves.
While that the armed hand doth fight abroad,
The advised head defends itself at home;
For government, though high, and low, and
     lower,
Put into parts, doth keep in one concent;
Congruing in a full and natural close,
Like music.
   *Cant.* Therefore doth heaven divide
The state of man in divers functions,
Setting endeavour in continual motion;
To which is fixed, as an aim or butt,
Obedience: for so work the honey bees;
Creatures that, by a rule in nature, teach
The act of order to a peopled kingdom.
They have a king, and officers of sorts:
Where some, like magistrates, correct at home;
Others, like merchants, venture trade abroad;
Others, like soldiers, armed in their stings,
Make boot upon the summer's velvet buds;
Which pillage they with merry march bring
     home
To the tent-royal of their emperor:
Who, busied in his majesty, surveys
The singing masons building roofs of gold;
The civil citizens kneading up the honey;
The poor mechanic porters crowding in
Their heavy burdens at his narrow gate;
The sad-ey'd justice, with his surly hum,
Delivering o'er to executors pale
The lazy yawning drone. I this infer,—
That many things, having full reference
To one concent, may work contrariously:
As many arrows, loosed several ways,
Fly to one mark;
As many several ways meet in one town;
As many fresh streams meet in one salt sea;
As many lines close in the dial's centre:
So may a thousand actions, once afoot,
End in one purpose, and be all well borne
Without defeat. Therefore to France, my liege.
Divide your happy England into four;
Whereof take you one quarter into France,
And you withal shall make all Gallia shake.
If we, with thrice such powers left at home,
Cannot defend our own doors from the dog,
Let us be worried, and our nation lose
The name of hardiness and policy.
   *K. Hen.* Call in the messengers sent from
     the Dauphin.      [*Exit an* Attendant.
Now are we well resolv'd: and, by God's help
And yours, the noble sinews of our power,
France being ours, we'll bend it to our awe,
Or break it all to pieces: or there we'll sit,
Ruling in large and ample empery
O'er France and all her almost kingly duke-
     doms,
Or lay these bones in an unworthy urn,

Tombless, with no remembrance over them:
Either our history shall with full mouth
Speak freely of our acts, or else our grave,
Like Turkish mute, shall have a tongueless
　　mouth,
Not worshipp'd with a waxen epitaph.

*Enter* Ambassadors *of France.*

Now are we well prepar'd to know the pleasure
Of our fair cousin Dauphin; for we hear
Your greeting is from him, not from the king.
　1 *Amb.*　May it please your majesty to give
　　us leave
Freely to render what we have in charge;
Or shall we sparingly show you far off
The Dauphin's meaning and our embassy?
　*K. Hen.*　We are no tyrant, but a Christian
　　king;
Unto whose grace our passion is as subject
As are our wretches fetter'd in our prisons:
Therefore with frank and with uncurbed plain-
　　ness
Tell us the Dauphin's mind.
　1 *Amb.*　　　　　Thus, then, in few.
Your highness, lately sending into France,
Did claim some certain dukedoms, in the right
Of your great predecessor, King Edward the
　　Third.
In answer of which claim, the prince our master
Says, that you savour too much of your youth;
And bids you be advis'd there's naught in
　　France
That can be with a nimble galliard won;—
You cannot revel into dukedoms there.
He therefore sends you, meeter for your spirit,
This tun of treasure; and, in lieu of this,
Desires you let the dukedoms that you claim
Hear no more of you. This the Dauphin speaks.
　*K. Hen.*　What treasure, uncle?
　*Exe.*　　　　　Tennis-balls, my liege.
　*K. Hen.*　We are glad the Dauphin is so
　　pleasant with us;
His present and your pains we thank you for:
When we have match'd our rackets to these
　　balls,
We will, in France, by God's grace, play a set
Shall strike his father's crown into the hazard.
Tell him he hath made a match with such a
　　wrangler
That all the courts of France will be disturb'd
With chases. And we understand him well,
How he comes o'er us with our wilder days,
Not measuring what use we made of them.
We never valu'd this poor seat of England;
And therefore, living hence, did give ourself
To barbarous license; as 'tis ever common
That men are merriest when they are from
　　home.
But tell the Dauphin, I will keep my state;
Be like a king, and show my sail of greatness,
When I do rouse me in my throne of France:
For that I have laid by my majesty,
And plodded like a man for working-days;
But I will rise there with so full a glory

That I will dazzle all the eyes of France,
Yea, strike the Dauphin blind to look on us.
And tell the pleasant prince this mock of his
Hath turn'd his balls to gun-stones; and his soul
Shall stand sore charged for the wasteful ven-
　　geance
That shall fly with them; for many a thousand
　　widows
Shall this his mock mock out of their dear
　　husbands;
Mock mothers from their sons, mock castles
　　down;
And some are yet ungotten and unborn
That shall have cause to curse the Dauphin's
　　scorn.
But this lies all within the will of God,
To whom I do appeal; and in whose name,
Tell you the Dauphin, I am coming on,
To venge me as I may, and to put forth
My rightful hand in a well-hallow'd cause.
So, get you hence in peace; and tell the Dauphin
His jest will savour but of shallow wit,
When thousands weep, more than did laugh
　　at it.—
Convey them with safe conduct.—Fare you
　　well.　　　　　[*Exeunt* Ambassadors.
　*Exe.*　This was a merry message.
　*K. Hen.*　We hope to make the sender blush
　　at it.
Therefore, my lords, omit no happy hour
That may give furtherance to our expedition;
For we have now no thought in us but France,
Save those to God, that run before our business.
Therefore let our proportions for these wars
Be soon collected, and all things thought upon
That may with reasonable swiftness add
More feathers to our wings; for, God before,
We'll chide this Dauphin at his father's door.
Therefore let every man now task his thought,
That this fair action may on foot be brought.
　　　　　　　　　　　　[*Exeunt.*

*Enter* Chorus.

　*Chor.*　Now all the youth of England are on
　　fire,
And silken dalliance in the wardrobe lies:
Now thrive the armourers, and honour's thought
Reigns solely in the breast of every man:
They sell the pasture now to buy the horse;
Following the mirror of all Christian kings,
With winged heels, as English Mercuries,
For now sits Expectation in the air;
And hides a sword from hilts unto the point
With crowns imperial, crowns, and coronets,
Promis'd to Harry and his followers.
The French, advis'd by good intelligence
Of this most dreadful preparation,
Shake in their fear; and with pale policy
Seek to divert the English purposes.
O England!—model to thy inward greatness,
Like little body with a mighty heart,—
What mightst thou do, that honour would
　　thee do,
Were all thy children kind and natural!

But see thy fault! France hath in thee found
　　out
A nest of hollow bosoms, which he fills
With treacherous crowns; and three corrupted
　　men,—
One, Richard Earl of Cambridge; and the
　　second,
Henry Lord Scroop of Masham; and the third,
Sir Thomas Grey, knight, of Northumber-
　　land,—
Have, for the guilt of France,—O guilt in-
　　deed!—
Confirm'd conspiracy with fearful France;
And by their hands this grace of kings must
　　die,—
If hell and treason hold their promises,—
Ere he take ship for France, and in South-
　　ampton.
Linger your patience on; and well digest
The abuse of distance, while we force a play.
The sum is paid; the traitors are agreed;
The king is set from London; and the scene
Is now transported, gentles, to Southampton,—
There is the play-house now, there must you
　　sit:
And thence to France shall we convey you safe,
And bring you back, charming the narrow seas
To give you gentle pass; for, if we may,
We'll not offend one stomach with our play.
But, till the king come forth, and not till then,
Unto Southampton do we shift our scene.
　　　　　　　　　　　　　　　　[Exit.

## ACT II.

Scene I.—London. *Before the Boar's Head
Tavern, Eastcheap.*

*Enter, severally,* Nym *and* Bardolph.

*Bard.* Well met, Corporal Nym.

*Nym.* Good-morrow, Lieutenant Bardolph.

*Bard.* What, are Ancient Pistol and you
friends yet?

*Nym.* For my part, I care not: I say little;
but when time shall serve, there shall be smiles;
—but that shall be as it may. I dare not fight;
but I will wink, and hold out mine iron: it is
a simple one; but what though? it will toast
cheese: and it will endure cold as another man's
sword will, and there's the humour of it.

*Bard.* I will bestow a breakfast to make you
friends; and we'll be all three sworn brothers
to France: let it be so, good Corporal Nym.

*Nym.* Faith, I will live so long as I may,
that's the certain of it; and when I cannot live
any longer, I will do as I may: that is my rest,
that is the rendezvous of it.

*Bard.* It is certain, corporal, that he is married to Nell Quickly: and, certainly, she did you
wrong; for you were troth-plight to her.

*Nym.* I cannot tell:—things must be as they
may: men may sleep, and they may have their
throats about them at that time; and, some
say, knives have edges. It must be as it may:
though patience be a tired mare, yet she will

plod. There must be conclusions. Well, I cannot tell.

*Bard.* Here comes Ancient Pistol and his
wife:—good corporal, be patient here.

*Enter* Pistol *and* Hostess.

How now, mine host Pistol!

*Pist.* Base tike, call'st thou me host?
Now, by this hand, I swear, I scorn the term;
Nor shall my Nell keep lodgers.

*Host.* No, by my troth, not long; for we
cannot lodge and board a dozen or fourteen
gentlewomen that live honestly by the prick of
their needles, but it will be thought we keep a
bawdy-house straight. [Nym *draws his sword.*]
O well-a-day, Lady, if he be not drawn! now
we shall see wilful adultery and murder committed.

*Bard.* Good lieutenant,—good corporal,—
offer nothing here.

*Nym.* Pish!

*Pist.* Pish for thee, Iceland dog! thou prick-
ear'd cur of Iceland!

*Host.* Good Corporal Nym, show thy valour,
and put up your sword.

*Nym.* Will you shog off? I would have you
solus. [*Sheathing his sword.*

*Pist.* *Solus*, egregious dog? O viper vile!
The *solus* in thy most marvellous face;
The *solus* in thy teeth, and in thy throat,
And in thy hateful lungs, yea, in thy maw,
　　perdy;
And, which is worse, within thy nasty mouth!
I do retort the *solus* in thy bowels;
For I can take, and Pistol's cock is up,
And flashing fire will follow.

*Nym.* I am not Barbason; you cannot conjure me. I have an humour to knock you indifferently well. If you grow foul with me, Pistol,
I will scour you with my rapier, as I may, in
fair terms: if you would walk off I would prick
your guts a little, in good terms, as I may: and
that's the humour of it.

*Pist.* O braggart vile and damned furious
　　wight!
The grave doth gape and doting death is near;
Therefore exhale. [Pistol *and* Nym *draw.*

*Bard.* Hear me, hear me what I say:—he
that strikes the first stroke I'll run him up to
the hilts, as I am a soldier. [*Draws.*

*Pist.* An oath of mickle might; and fury
shall abate.
Give me thy fist, thy fore-foot to me give:
Thy spirits are most tall.

*Nym.* I will cut thy throat one time or other,
in fair terms: that is the humour of it.

*Pist.* *Coupe la gorge!* That's the word.—I
thee defy again.
O hound of Crete, think'st thou my spouse to
　　get?
No; to the spital go,
And from the powdering tub of infamy
Fetch forth the lazar kite of Cressid's kind,
Doll Tearsheet she by name, and her espouse.

I have, and I will hold, the *quondam* Quickly
For the only she; and—*Pauca*, there's enough.
Go to.

### Enter the Boy.

*Boy.* Mine host Pistol, you must come to
my master,—and you, hostess:—he is very
sick, and would to bed.—Good Bardolph, put
thy nose between his sheets, and do the office of
a warming-pan. Faith, he's very ill.

*Bard.* Away, you rogue.

*Host.* By my troth, he'll yield the crow a
pudding one of these days: the king has killed
his heart.—Good husband, come home presently.　　　　　　　[*Exeunt* Hostess *and* Boy.

*Bard.* Come, shall I make you two friends?
We must to France together: why the devil
should we keep knives to cut one another's
throats?

*Pist.* Let floods o'erswell and fiends for food
howl on!

*Nym.* You'll pay me the eight shillings I
won of you at betting?

*Pist.* Base is the slave that pays.

*Nym.* That now I will have: that's the
humour of it.

*Pist.* As manhood shall compound: push
home.　　　　　　　[Pistol *and* Nym *draw.*

*Bard.* By this sword, he that makes the first
thrust I'll kill him; by this sword, I will.

*Pist.* Sword is an oath, and oaths must have
their course.

*Bard.* Corporal Nym, an thou wilt be friends,
be friends: an thou wilt not, why, then, be
enemies with me too. Pr'ythee, put up.

*Nym.* I shall have my eight shillings I won
of you at betting?

*Pist.* A noble shalt thou have, and present
pay;
And liquor likewise will I give to thee,
And friendship shall combine, and brotherhood:
I'll live by Nym and Nym shall live by me;—
Is not this just?—for I shall sutler be
Unto the camp, and profits will accrue.
Give me thy hand.

*Nym.* I shall have my noble?

*Pist.* In cash most justly paid.

*Nym.* Well, then, that's the humour of it.

### Re-enter Hostess.

*Host.* As ever you came of women, come in
quickly to Sir John. Ah, poor heart! he is so
shaken of a burning quotidian tertian that it is
most lamentable to behold. Sweet men, come
to him.

*Nym.* The king hath run bad humours on
the knight; that's the even of it.

*Pist.* Nym, thou hast spoke the right;
His heart is fracted and corroborate.

*Nym.* The king is a good king: but it must
be as it may; he passes some humours and
careers.

*Pist.* Let us condole the knight; for, lamb-
kins, we will live.　　　　　　　[*Exeunt.*

### SCENE II.—SOUTHAMPTON. *A Council Chamber.*

#### *Enter* EXETER, BEDFORD, *and* WESTMORELAND.

*Bed.* 'Fore God, his grace is bold, to trust
these traitors.

*Exe.* They shall be apprehended by and by

*West.* How smooth and even they do beat
themselves!
As if allegiance in their bosom sat,
Crowned with faith and constant loyalty.

*Bed.* The king hath note of all that they intend,
By interception which they dream not of.

*Exe.* Nay, but the man that was his bed-
fellow,
Whom he hath dull'd and cloy'd with gracious
favours,—
That he should, for a foreign purse, so sell
His sovereign's life to death and treachery!

*Trumpet sounds. Enter* KING HENRY, SCROOP,
CAMBRIDGE, GREY, Lords, *and* Attendants.

*K. Hen.* Now sits the wind fair, and we will
aboard.
My Lord of Cambridge,—and my kind Lord of
Masham,—
And you, my gentle knight,—give me your
thoughts:
Think you not that the powers we bear with us
Will cut their passage through the force of
France,
Doing the execution and the act
For which we have in head assembled them?

*Scroop.* No doubt, my liege, if each man do
his best.

*K. Hen.* I doubt not that; since we are well
persuaded
We carry not a heart with us from hence
That grows not in a fair consent with ours,
Nor leave not one behind that doth not wish
Success and conquest to attend on us.

*Cam.* Never was monarch better fear'd and
lov'd
Than is your majesty: there's not, I think, a
subject
That sits in heart-grief and uneasiness
Under the sweet shade of your government.

*Grey.* True: those that were your father's
enemies
Have steep'd their galls in honey, and do serve
you
With hearts create of duty and of zeal.

*K. Hen.* We therefore have great cause of
thankfulness;
And shall forget the office of our hand
Sooner than quittance of desert and merit
According to the weight and worthiness.

*Scroop.* So service shall with steel'd sinews
toil,
And labour shall refresh itself with hope,
To do your grace incessant services.

*K. Hen.* We judge no less.—Uncle of Exeter

Enlarge the man committed yesterday,
That rail'd against our person: we consider
It was excess of wine that set him on;
And on his more advice we pardon him.

*Scroop.* That's mercy, but too much security:
Let him be punish'd, sovereign; lest example
Breed, by his sufferance, more of such a kind.

*K. Hen.* O, let us yet be merciful.

*Cam.* So may your highness, and yet punish
too.

*Grey.* Sir, you show great mercy if you give
   him life,
After the taste of much correction.

*K. Hen.* Alas, your too much love and care
   of me
Are heavy orisons 'gainst this poor wretch!
If little faults, proceeding on distemper,
Shall not be wink'd at, how shall we stretch
   our eye
When capital crimes, chew'd, swallow'd, and
   digested,
Appear before us?—We'll yet enlarge that man,
Though Cambridge, Scroop, and Grey, in their
   dear care
And tender preservation of our person,
Would have him punish'd. And now to our
   French causes:
Who are the late commissioners?

*Cam.* I one, my lord:
Your highness bade me ask for it to-day.

*Scroop.* So did you me, my liege.

*Grey.* And me, my royal sovereign.

*K. Hen.* Then, Richard Earl of Cambridge,
   there is yours;—
There yours, Lord Scroop of Masham;—and,
   sir knight,
Grey of Northumberland, this same is yours:—
Read them, and know I know your worthi-
   ness.—
My Lord of Westmoreland,—and uncle Ex-
   eter,—
We will aboard to-night.—Why, how now,
   gentlemen!
What see you in those papers, that you lose
So much complexion?—Look ye, how they
   change!
Their cheeks are paper.—Why, what read you
   there
That hath so cowarded and chas'd your blood
Out of appearance?

*Cam.*          I do confess my fault,
And do submit me to your highness' mercy.

*Grey, Scroop.* To which we all appeal.

*K. Hen.* The mercy that was quick in us but
   late
By your own counsel is suppress'd and kill'd:
You must not dare, for shame, to talk of mercy;
For your own reasons turn into your bosoms,
As dogs upon their masters, worrying you.—
See you, my princes and my noble peers,
These English monsters! My Lord of Cam-
   bridge here,—
You know how apt our love was to accord
To furnish him with all appertinents

Belonging to his honour; and this man
Hath, for a few light crowns, lightly conspir'd,
And sworn unto the practices of France,
To kill us here in Hampton: to the which
This knight, no less for bounty bound to us
Than Cambridge is, hath likewise sworn.—
              But, O,        [cruel,
What shall I say to thee, Lord Scroop? thou
Ingrateful, savage, and inhuman creature!
Thou that didst bear the key of all my counsels,
That knew'st the very bottom of my soul,
That almost mightst have coin'd me into gold,
Wouldst thou have practis'd on me for thy
   use,—
May it be possible that foreign hire
Could out of thee extract one spark of evil
That might annoy my finger? 'tis so strange
That, though the truth of it stands off as gross
As black from white, my eye will scarcely see it.
Treason and murder ever kept together,
As two yoke-devils sworn to either's purpose,
Working so grossly in a natural cause
That admiration did not whoop at them:
But thou, 'gainst all proportion, didst bring in
Wonder to wait on treason and on murder:
And whatsoever cunning fiend it was
That wrought upon thee so preposterously
Hath got the voice in hell for excellence: .
And other devils, that suggest by treasons,
Do botch and bungle up damnation
With patches, colours, and with forms being
   fetch'd
From glistering semblances of piety;
But he that temper'd thee bade thee stand up,
Gave thee no instance why thou shouldst do
   treason,
Unless to dub thee with the name of traitor.
If that same demon that hath gull'd thee thus
Should with his lion gait walk the whole world,
He might return to vasty Tartar back,
And tell the legions, *I can never win
A soul so easy as that Englishman's.*
O, how hast thou with jealousy infected
The sweetness of affiance! Show men dutiful?
Why, so didst thou: seem they grave and
   learned?
Why, so didst thou: come they of noble family?
Why, so didst thou: seem they religious?
Why, so didst thou: or are they spare in diet;
Free from gross passion, or of mirth or anger;
Constant in spirit, not swerving with the blood;
Garnish'd and deck'd in modest complement;
Not working with the eye without the ear,
And but in purged judgment trusting neither?
Such and so finely bolted didst thou seem:
And thus thy fall hath left a kind of blot,
To mark the full-fraught man and best indu'd
With some suspicion. I will weep for thee;
For this revolt of thine, methinks, is like
Another fall of man.—Their faults are open:
Arrest them to the answer of the law;—
And God acquit them of their practices!

*Exe.* I arrest thee of high treason, by the
name of Richard Earl of Cambridge.

I arrest thee of high treason, by the name of
Henry Lord Scroop of Masham.

I arrest thee of high treason, by the name of
Thomas Grey, knight, of Northumberland.

*Scroop.* Our purposes God justly hath dis-
    cover'd;
And I repent my fault more than my death;
Which I beseech your highness to forgive,
Although my body pay the price of it.

*Cam.* For me,—the gold of France did not
    seduce;
Although I did admit it as a motive
The sooner to effect what I intended:
But God be thanked for prevention;
Which I in sufferance heartily will rejoice,
Beseeching God and you to pardon me.

*Grey.* Never did faithful subject more rejoice
At the discovery of most dangerous treason
Than I do at this hour joy o'er myself,
Prevented from a damned enterprise:
My fault, but not my body, pardon, sovereign.

*K. Hen.* God quit you in his mercy! Hear
    your sentence.
You have conspir'd against our royal person,
Join'd with an enemy proclaim'd, and from his
    coffers
Receiv'd the golden earnest of our death;
Wherein you would have sold your king to
    slaughter,
His princes and his peers to servitude,
His subjects to oppression and contempt,
And his whole kingdom into desolation.
Touching our person seek we no revenge;
But we our kingdom's safety must so tender,
Whose ruin you have sought, that to her laws
We do deliver you. Get you, therefore, hence,
Poor miserable wretches, to your death:
The taste whereof God of his mercy give you
Patience to endure, and true repentance
Of all your dear offences!—Bear them hence.
              *[Exeunt Conspirators, guarded.*
Now, lords, for France; the enterprise whereof
Shall be to you, as us, like glorious.
We doubt not of a fair and lucky war:
Since God so graciously hath brought to light
This dangerous treason, lurking in our way
To hinder our beginnings, we doubt not now
But every rub is smoothed on our way.
Then, forth, dear countrymen: let us deliver
Our puissance into the hand of God,
Putting it straight in expedition.
Cheerly to sea; the signs of war advance:
No king of England, if not king of France.
                        *[Exeunt.*

SCENE III.—LONDON. *The* Hostess's *House in
Eastcheap.*

*Enter* PISTOL, Hostess, NYM, BARDOLPH, *and*
Boy.

*Host.* Pr'ythee, honey-sweet husband, let me
bring thee to Staines.

*Pist.* No; for my manly heart doth yearn.—
Bardolph, be blithe;—Nym, rouse thy vaunting veins;—

Boy, bristle thy courage up;—for Falstaff he
    is dead,
And we must yearn therefore.

*Bard.* Would I were with him, wheresome'er
he is, either in heaven or in hell!

*Host.* Nay, sure, he's not in hell: he's in
Arthur's bosom, if ever man went to Arthur's
bosom. 'A made a finer end, and went away,
an it had been any christom child; 'a parted
even just between twelve and one, even at the
turning o' the tide: for after I saw him fumble
with the sheets, and play with flowers, and
smile upon his fingers' ends, I knew there was
but one way; for his nose was as sharp as a pen,
and 'a babbled of green fields. *How now, Sir
John!* quoth I: *what, man! be o' good cheer.* So
'a cried out—*God, God, God!* three or four
times. Now I, to comfort him, bid him 'a
should not think of God; I hoped there was no
need to trouble himself with any such thoughts
yet. So 'a bade me lay more clothes on his feet:
I put my hand into the bed and felt them, and
they were as cold as any stone; then I felt to
his knees, and so upward and upward, and all
was as cold as any stone.

*Nym.* They say he cried out of sack.

*Host.* Ay, that 'a did.

*Bard.* And of women.

*Host.* Nay, that 'a did not.

*Boy.* Yes, that 'a did; and said they were
devils incarnate.

*Host.* 'A could never abide carnation; 'twas
a colour he never liked.

*Boy.* 'A said once, the devil would have him
about women.

*Host.* 'A did in some sort, indeed, handle
women; but then he was rheumatic, and talked
of the whore of Babylon.

*Boy.* Do you not remember, 'a saw a flea
stick upon Bardolph's nose, and 'a said it was
a black soul burning in hell?

*Bard.* Well, the fuel is gone that maintained
that fire: that's all the riches I got in his
service.

*Nym.* Shall we shog? the king will be gone
from Southampton.

*Pist.* Come, let's away.—My love, give me
    thy lips.
Look to my chattels and my moveables:
Let senses rule; the word is, Pitch and pay;
Trust none;
For oaths are straws, men's faiths are wafer-
    cakes,
And holdfast is the only dog, my duck:
Therefore *caveto* be thy counsellor.
Go, clear thy crystals.—Yoke-fellows in arms,
Let us to France; like horse-leeches, my boys,
To suck, to suck, the very blood to suck!

*Boy.* And that is but unwholesome food,
    they say.

*Pist.* Touch her soft mouth and march.

*Bard.* Farewell, hostess.    *[Kissing her.*

*Nym.* I cannot kiss, that is the humour of
it; but, adieu.

*Pist.* Let housewifery appear: keep close, I
thee command.

*Host.* Farewell; adieu.          [*Exeunt.*

SCENE IV.—FRANCE. *A Room in the* FRENCH
KING'S *Palace.*

*Flourish. Enter the* FRENCH KING, *attended; the*
DAUPHIN, *the* DUKE OF BURGUNDY, *the* Constable, *and others.*

*Fr. King.* Thus come the English with full
power upon us;
And more than carefully it us concerns
To answer royally in our defences.
Therefore the Dukes of Berri and of Bretagne,
Of Brabant and of Orleans, shall make forth,—
And you, Prince Dauphin,—with all swift de-
spatch,
To line and new repair our towns of war
With men of courage and with means defend-
ant;
For England his approaches makes as fierce
As waters to the sucking of a gulf.
It fits us, then, to be as provident
As fear may teach us, out of late examples
Left by the fatal and neglected English
Upon our fields.

*Dau.*          My most redoubted father,
It is most meet we arm us 'gainst the foe;
For peace itself should not so dull a kingdom,—
Though war, nor no known quarrel, were in
question,—
But that defences, musters, preparations,
Should be maintain'd, assembled, and collected,
As were a war in expectation.
Therefore, I say, 'tis meet we all go forth
To view the sick and feeble parts of France:
And let us do it with no show of fear;      [land
No, with no more than if we heard that Eng-
Were busied with a Whitsun morris-dance:
For, my good liege, she is so idly king'd,
Her sceptre so fantastically borne
By a vain, giddy, shallow, humorous youth,
That fear attends her not.

*Con.*          O peace, Prince Dauphin!
You are too much mistaken in this king:
Question your grace the late ambassadors,—
With what great state he heard their embassy,
How well supplied with noble counsellors,
How modest in exception, and withal
How terrible in constant resolution,—
And you shall find his vanities forespent.
Were but the outside of the Roman Brutus,
Covering discretion with a coat of folly;
As gardeners do with ordure hide those roots
That shall first spring and be most delicate.

*Dau.* Well, 'tis not so, my lord high-
constable;
But though we think it so, it is no matter:
In cases of defence 'tis best to weigh
The enemy more mighty than he seems:
So the proportions of defence are fill'd;
Which, of a weak and niggardly projection,
Doth like a miser spoil his coat with scanting
A little cloth.

*Fr. King.* Think we King Harry strong;
And, princes, look you strongly arm to meet
him.
The kindred of him hath been flesh'd upon us;
And he is bred out of that bloody strain
That haunted us in our familiar paths:
Witness our too-much memorable shame
When Cressy battle fatally was struck,
And all our princes captiv'd by the hand
Of that black name, Edward Black Prince of
Wales;
Whiles that his mountain sire,—on mountain
standing,
Up in the air, crown'd with the golden sun,—
Saw his heroical seed, and smil'd to see him,
Mangle the work of nature, and deface
The patterns that by God and by French
fathers
Had twenty years been made. This is a stem
Of that victorious stock; and let us fear
The native mightiness and fate of him.

*Enter a* Messenger.

*Mess.* Ambassadors from Harry King of
England
Do crave admittance to your majesty.

*Fr. King.* We'll give them present audience.
Go, and bring them.
          [*Exeunt* Mess. *and certain* Lords.
You see this chase is hotly follow'd, friends.

*Dau.* Turn head and stop pursuit; for cow-
ard dogs
Most spend their mouths when what they seem
to threaten
Runs far before them. Good my sovereign,
Take up the English short; and let them know
Of what a monarchy you are the head:
Self-love, my liege, is not so vile a sin
As self-neglecting.

*Re-enter* Lords, *with* EXETER *and* Train.

*Fr. King.*          From our brother England?

*Exe.* From him; and thus he greets your
majesty.
He wills you, in the name of God Almighty,
That you divest yourself, and lay apart
The borrow'd glories that by gift of heaven,
By law of nature and of nations, 'long
To him and to his heirs; namely, the crown,
And all wide stretched honours that pertain,
By custom and the ordinance of times,
Unto the crown of France. That you may know
'Tis no sinister nor no awkward claim,
Pick'd from the worm-holes of long-vanish'd
days,
Nor from the dust of old oblivion rak'd,
He sends you this most memorable line,
          [*Gives a paper.*
In every branch truly demonstrative;
Willing you overlook this pedigree:
And when you find him evenly deriv'd
From his most fam'd of famous ancestors,
Edward the Third, he bids you then resign
Your crown and kingdom, indirectly held

From him the native and true challenger.

*Fr. King.* Or else what follows?

*Exe.* Bloody constraint; for if you hide the
crown
Even in your hearts, there will he rake for it:
Therefore in fierce tempest is he coming,
In thunder and in earthquake, like a Jove,—
That if requiring fail, he will compel;—
And bids you, in the bowels of the Lord,
Deliver up the crown; and to take mercy
On the poor souls for whom this hungry war
Opens his vasty jaws: and on your head
Turns he the widows' tears, the orphans' cries,
The dead men's blood, the pining maidens'
groans,
For husbands, fathers, and betrothed lovers,
That shall be swallow'd in this controversy.
This is his claim, his threatening, and my mes-
sage;
Unless the Dauphin be in presence here,
To whom expressly I bring greeting too.

*Fr. King.* For us, we will consider of this
further:
To-morrow shall you bear our full intent
Back to our brother England.

*Dau.*  For the Dauphin,
I stand here for him: what to him from England?

*Exe.* Scorn and defiance; slight regard, con-
tempt,
And anything that may not misbecome
The mighty sender, doth he prize you at.
Thus says my king: an if your father's highness
Do not, in grant of all demands at large,
Sweeten the bitter mock you sent his majesty,
He'll call you to so hot an answer for it
That caves and womby vaultages of France
Shall chide your trespass and return your mock
In second accent of his ordinance.

*Dau.* Say, if my father render fair return,
It is against my will; for I desire
Nothing but odds with England: to that end,
As matching to his youth and vanity,
I did present him with the Paris balls.

*Exe.* He'll make your Paris Louvre shake
for it,
Were it the mistress court of mighty Europe:
And, be assur'd, you'll find a difference,—
As we, his subjects, have in wonder found,—
Between the promise of his greener days
And these he masters now: now he weighs time
Even to the utmost grain:—that you shall read
In your own losses if he stay in France.

*Fr. King.* To-morrow shall you know our
mind at full.

*Exe.* Despatch us with all speed, lest that
our king
Come here himself to question our delay;
For he is footed in this land already.

*Fr. King.* You shall be soon despatch'd with
fair conditions:
A night is but small breath and little pause
To answer matters of this consequence.
[*Exeunt.*

*Enter* Chorus.

*Cho.* Thus with imagin'd wing our swift
scene flies,
In motion of no less celerity
Than that of thought. Suppose that you have
seen
The well-appointed king at Hampton pier
Embark his royalty; and his brave fleet
With silken streamers the young Phœbus fan-
ning:
Play with your fancies; and in them behold
Upon the hempen tackle ship-boys climbing,
Hear the shrill whistle which doth order give
To sounds confus'd; behold the threaden sails,
Borne with the invisible and creeping wind,
Draw the huge bottoms through the furrow'd
sea,
Breasting the lofty surge: O, do but think
You stand upon the rivage and behold
A city on the inconstant billows dancing;
For so appears this fleet majestical,
Holding due course to Harfleur. Follow, follow!
Grapple your minds to sternage of this navy;
And leave your England, as dead midnight still,
Guarded with grandsires, babies, and old
women,
Either past or not arrived to pith and puis-
sance;
For who is he, whose chin is but enrich'd
With one appearing hair, that will not follow
These cull'd and choice-drawn cavaliers to
France?
Work, work your thoughts, and therein see a
siege;
Behold the ordnance on their carriages,
With fatal mouths gaping on girded Harfleur.
Suppose the ambassador from the French
comes back;
Tells Harry that the king doth offer him
Katharine his daughter; and with her, to
dowry,
Some petty and unprofitable dukedoms.
The offer likes not: and the nimble gunner
With linstock now the devilish cannon touches,
[*Alarum, and chambers go off, within.*
And down goes all before them. Still be kind,
And eke out our performance with your mind.
[*Exit.*

## ACT III.

### SCENE I.—FRANCE. *Before Harfleur.*

*Alarums. Enter* KING HENRY, EXETER, BED-
FORD, GLOSTER, *and* Soldiers, *with scaling-
ladders.*

*K. Hen.* Once more unto the breach, dear
friends, once more;
Or close the wall up with our English dead!
In peace there's nothing so becomes a man
As modest stillness and humility:
But when the blast of war blows in our ears,
Then imitate the action of the tiger;
Stiffen the sinews, summon up the blood,

Disguise fair nature with hard-favour'd rage;
Then lend the eye a terrible aspèct;
Let it pry through the portage of the head [it
Like the brass cannon; let the brow o'erwhelm
As fearfully as doth a galled rock
O'erhang and jutty his confounded base,
Swill'd with the wild and wasteful ocean.
Now set the teeth and stretch the nostril wide;
Hold hard the breath, and bend up every spirit
To his full height!—On, on, you noble English,
Whose blood is fet from fathers of war-proof!—
Fathers, that, like so many Alexanders,
Have in these parts from morn till even fought,
And sheath'd their swords for lack of argu-
    ment:—
Dishonour not your mothers; now attest
That those whom you call'd fathers did beget
    you!
Be copy now to men of grosser blood,
And teach them how to war!—And you, good
    yeomen,
Whose limbs were made in England, show us
    here
The mettle of your pasture; let us swear
That you are worth your breeding: which I
    doubt not;
For there is none of you so mean and base,
That hath not noble lustre in your eyes.
I see you stand like greyhounds in the slips,
Straining upon the start. The game's afoot:
Follow your spirit; and upon this charge
Cry—God for Harry! England! and Saint
    George!
    [Exeunt. Alarum, and chambers go off, within.

Enter NYM, BARDOLPH, PISTOL, and Boy.

*Bard.* On, on, on, on, on! to the breach, to
the breach!

*Nym.* Pray thee, corporal, stay: the knocks
are too hot; and, for mine own part, I have not
a case of lives: the humour of it is too hot, that
is the very plain-song of it.

*Pist.* The plain-song is most just; for humours do abound:

Knocks go and come; God's vassals drop and die;
　　And sword and shield
　　In bloody field
Doth win immortal fame.

*Boy.* Would I were in an alehouse in London! I would give all my fame for a pot of ale
and safety.

*Pist.* And I:

If wishes would prevail with me,
My purpose should not fail with me,
　　But thither would I hie.

*Boy.* As duly, but not as truly,
　　As bird doth sing on bough.

### Enter FLUELLEN.

*Flu.* Up to the preach, you dogs! avaunt,
you cullions!　　[Driving them forward.

*Pist.* Be merciful, great duke, to men of
mould!

Abate thy rage, abate thy manly rage!
Abate thy rage, great duke!
Good bawcock, bate thy rage! use lenity, sweet
    chuck!

*Nym.* These be good humours!—your honour wins bad humours.

    [Exeunt NYM, PISTOL, and BARDOLPH,
        followed by FLUELLEN.

*Boy.* As young as I am, I have observed
these three swashers. I am boy to them all
three: but all they three, though they would
serve me, could not be man to me; for, indeed,
three such antics do not amount to a man. For
Bardolph,—he is white-livered and red-faced;
by the means whereof 'a faces it out, but fights
not. For Pistol,—he hath a killing tongue and
a quiet sword; by the means whereof 'a breaks
words and keeps whole weapons. For Nym,—
he hath heard that men of few words are the
best men; and therefore he scorns to say his
prayers lest 'a should be thought a coward: but
his few bad words are matched with as few
good deeds; for 'a never broke any man's head
but his own, and that was against a post when
he was drunk. They will steal anything, and
call it purchase. Bardolph stole a lute-case,
bore it twelve leagues, and sold it for three
halfpence. Nym and Bardolph are sworn
brothers in filching; and in Calais they stole a
fire-shovel: I knew by that piece of service the
men would carry coals. They would have me
as familiar with men's pockets as their gloves
or their handkerchers: which makes much
against my manhood, if I should take from
another's pocket to put into mine; for it is plain
pocketing up of wrongs. I must leave them,
and seek some better service: their villany goes
against my weak stomach, and therefore I must
cast it up.　　[Exit.

### Re-enter FLUELLEN, GOWER following.

*Gow.* Captain Fluellen, you must come presently to the mines; the Duke of Gloster would
speak with you.

*Flue.* To the mines! tell you the duke it is
not so goot to come to the mines; for, look you,
the mines is not according to the disciplines of
the war: the concavities of it is not sufficient;
for, look you, th' athversary,—you may discuss unto the duke, look you,—is digt himself
four yard under the countermines; by Cheshu,
I think 'a will plow up all, if there is not better
directions.

*Gow.* The Duke of Gloster, to whom the
order of the siege is given, is altogether directed
by an Irishman,—a very valiant gentleman, i'
faith.

*Flu.* It is Captain Macmorris, is it not?

*Gow.* I think it be.

*Flu.* By Cheshu, he is an ass, as in the 'orld:
I will verify as much in his peard: he has no
more directions in the true disciplines of the
wars, look you, of the Roman disciplines, than
is a puppy-dog.

*Gow.* Here 'a comes; and the Scots captain, Captain Jamy, with him.

*Flu.* Captain Jamy is a marvellous falorous gentleman, that is certain, and of great expedition and knowledge in the ancient wars, upon my particular knowledge of his directions: by Cheshu, he will maintain his argument as well as any military man in the 'orld, in the disciplines of the pristine wars of the Romans.

*Enter* MACMORRIS *and* JAMY, *at a distance.*

*Jamy.* I say gud-day, Captain Fluellen.

*Flu.* God-den to your worship, goot Captain Jamy.

*Gow.* How now, Captain Macmorris! have you quit the mines? have the pioneers given o'er?

*Mac.* By Chrish la, tish ill done: the work ish give over, the trumpet sound the retreat. By my hand, I swear, and by my father's soul, the work ish ill done; it ish give over: I would have blowed up the town, so Chrish save me, la, in an hour: O, tish ill done, tish ill done; by my hand, tish ill done!

*Flu.* Captain Macmorris, I peseech you now, will you voutsafe me, look you, a few disputations with you, as partly touching or concerning the disciplines of the war, the Roman wars, in the way of argument, look you, and friendly communication; partly to satisfy my opinion, and partly for the satisfaction, look you, of my mind, as touching the direction of the military discipline; that is the point.

*Jamy.* It sall be very gud, gud feith, gud captains bath: and I sall quit you with gud leve, as I may pick occasion; that sall I, mary.

*Mac.* It is no time to discourse, so Chrish save me: the day is hot, and the weather, and the wars, and the king, and the dukes: it is no time to discourse. The town is beseeched, and the trumpet call us to the breach; and we talk and, by Chrish, do nothing: 'tis shame for us all: so God sa' me, 'tis shame to stand still; it is shame, by my hand: and there is throats to be cut, and works to be done; and there ish nothing done, so Chrish sa' me, la.

*Jamy.* By the mess, ere theise eyes of mine take themselves to slumber, aile do gud service, or aile lig i' the grund for it; ay, or go to death; and aile pay 't as valorously as I may, that sall I surely do, that is the breff and the long. Mary, I wad full fain heard some question 'tween you tway.

*Flu.* Captain Macmorris, I think, look you, under your correction, there is not many of your nation,—

*Mac.* Of my nation! What ish my nation? what ish my nation? Who talks of my nation ish a villain, and a basterd, and a knave, and a rascal.

*Flu.* Look you, if you take the matter otherwise than is meant, Captain Macmorris, peradventure I shall think you do not use me with that affability as in discretion you ought to use

me, look you; being as goot a man as yourself, both in the disciplines of war and in the derivation of my birth, and in other particularities.

*Mac.* I do not know you so good a man as myself: so Chrish save me, I will cut off your head.

*Gow.* Gentlemen both, you will mistake each other.

*Jamy.* Au! that's a foul fault.

[*A parley sounded.*

*Gow.* The town sounds a parley.

*Flu.* Captain Macmorris, when there is more petter opportunity to be required, look you, I will be so pold as to tell you I know the disciplines of war; and there is an end. [*Exeunt.*

SCENE II.—*The same. Before the Gates of Harfleur.*

*The* Governor *and some* Citizens *on the walls; the* English Forces *below. Enter* KING HENRY *and his* Train.

*K. Hen.* How yet resolves the governor of the town?
This is the latest parley we will admit:
Therefore, to our best mercy give yourselves;
Or like to men proud of destruction,
Defy us to our worst: for as I am a soldier,—
A name that, in my thoughts, becomes me best,—
If I begin the battery once again,
I will not leave the half-achieved Harfleur
Till in her ashes she lie buried.
The gates of mercy shall be all shut up;
And the flesh'd soldier,—rough and hard of heart,—
In liberty of bloody hand shall range
With conscience wide as hell; mowing like grass
Your fresh-fair virgins and your flowering infants.
What is it then to me if impious war,—
Array'd in flames, like to the prince of fiends,—
Do, with his smirch'd complexion, all fell feats
Enlink'd to waste and desolation?
What is 't to me when you yourselves are cause,
If your pure maidens fall into the hand
Of hot and forcing violation?
What rein can hold licentious wickedness
When down the hill he holds his fierce career?
We may as bootless spend our vain command
Upon the enraged soldiers in their spoil,
As send précepts to the Leviathan      [fleur,
To come ashore. Therefore, you men of Har-
Take pity of your town and of your people
Whiles yet my soldiers are in my command;
Whiles yet the cool and temperate wind of grace
O'erblows the filthy and contagious clouds
Of heady murder, spoil, and villany.
If not, why, in a moment look to see
The blind and bloody soldier with foul hand
Defile the locks of your shrill-shrieking daughters;
Your fathers taken by the silver beards,
And their most reverend heads dash'd to the walls;

Your naked infants spitted upon pikes,
Whiles the mad mothers with their howls con-
      fus'd
Do break the clouds, as did the wives of Jewry
At Herod's bloody-hunting slaughtermen.
What say you? will you yield, and this avoid?
Or, guilty in defence, be thus destroy'd?

*Gov.* Our expectation hath this day an end:
The Dauphin, whom of succour we entreated,
Returns us that his powers are not yet ready
To raise so great a siege. Therefore, great king,
We yield our town and lives to thy soft mercy.
Enter our gates; dispose of us and ours;
For we no longer are defensible.

*K. Hen.* Open your gates.—Come, uncle
      Exeter,
Go you and enter Harfleur; there remain,
And fortify it strongly 'gainst the French:
Use mercy to them all. For us, dear uncle,—
The winter coming on, and sickness growing
Upon our soldiers,—we will retire to Calais.
To-night in Harfleur will we be your guest;
To-morrow for the march are we addrest.
      [*Flourish. The* KING, *&c., enter the Town.*

SCENE III.—ROUEN. *A Room in the Palace.*

*Enter* KATHARINE *and* ALICE.

*Kath.* Alice, tu as été en Angleterre, et tu
parles bien le langage.

*Alice.* Un peu, madame.

*Kath.* Je te prie, m'enseignez; il faut que
j'apprenne à parler. Comment appelez-vous la
main en Anglais?

*Alice.* La main? elle est appelée de hand.

*Kath.* De hand. Et les doigts?

*Alice.* Les doigts? ma foi, j'oublie les doigts;
mais je me souviendrai. Les doigts? je pense
qu'ils sont appelés de fingres; oui, de fingres.

*Kath.* La main, de hand; les doigts, de
fingres. Je pense que je suis le bon écolier; j'ai
gagné deux mots d'Anglais vîtement. Comment
appelez-vous les ongles?

*Alice.* Les ongles? les appelons de nails.

*Kath.* De nails. Ecoutez; dites-moi, si je parle
bien: de hand, de fingres, et de nails.

*Alice.* C'est bien dit, madame; il est fort bon
Anglais.

*Kath.* Dites-moi l'Anglais pour le bras.

*Alice.* De arm, madame.

*Kath.* Et le coude?

*Alice.* De elbow.

*Kath.* De elbow. Je m'en fais la répétition
de tous les mots que vous m'avez appris dès à
présent.

*Alice.* Il est trop difficile, madame, comme je
pense.

*Kath.* Excusez-moi, Alice; écoutez: de hand,
de fingres, de nails, de arm, de bilbow.

*Alice.* De elbow, madame.

*Kath.* O Seigneur Dieu, je m'en oublie! de
elbow. Comment appelez-vous le col?

*Alice.* De neck, madame.

*Kath.* De nick. Et le menton?

*Alice.* De chin.

*Kath.* De sin. Le col, de nick; le menton,
de sin.

*Alice.* Oui. Sauf votre honneur, en vérité, vous
pronouncez les mots aussi droit que les natifs
d'Angleterre.

*Kath.* Je ne doute point d'apprendre, par la
grace de Dieu, et en peu de temps.

*Alice.* N'avez-vous pas déjà oublié ce que je
vous ai enseigné?

*Kath.* Non, je reciterai à vous promptement:
de hand, de fingres, de mails,—

*Alice.* De nails, madame.

*Kath.* De nails, de arm, de ilbow.

*Alice.* Sauf votre honneur, de elbow.

*Kath.* Ainsi dis-je; de elbow, de nick, et de
sin. Comment appelez-vous le pied et la robe?

*Alice.* De foot, madame; et de coun.

*Kath.* De foot et de coun! O Seigneur Dieu!
ce sont mots de son mauvais, corruptible, gros, et
impudique, et non pour les dames d'honneur d'
user; je ne voudrais prononcer ces mots devant
les seigneurs de France pour tout le monde. Il
faut de foot et de coun néanmoins. Je reciterai
une autre fois ma leçon ensemble: de hand, de
fingres, de nails, de arm, de elbow, de nick, de
sin, de foot, de coun.

*Alice.* Excellent, madame!

*Kath.* C'est assez pour une fois: allons-nous
à dîner.          [*Exeunt.*

SCENE IV.—*The same. Another Room in*
*the same.*

*Enter the* FRENCH KING, *the* DAUPHIN, DUKE
OF BOURBON, *the* Constable of France, *and*
*others.*

*Fr. King.* 'Tis certain he hath pass'd the
      river Somme.

*Con.* And if he be not fought withal, my lord,
Let us not live in France; let us quit all,
And give our vineyards to a barbarous people.

*Dau.* O Dieu vivant! shall a few sprays of us,
The emptying of our fathers' luxury,
Our scions, put in wild and savage stock,
Spurt up so suddenly into the clouds,
And overlook their grafters?

*Bour.* Normans, but bastard Normans, Nor-
      man bastards!
Mort de ma vie! if they march along
Unfought withal, but I will sell my dukedom
To buy a slobbery and a dirty farm
In that nook-shotten isle of Albion.

*Con.* Dieu de batailles! where have they this
      mettle?
Is not their climate foggy, raw, and dull?
On whom, as in despite, the sun looks pale,
Killing their fruit with frowns? Can sodden
      water,          [broth,
A drench for sur-rein'd jades, their barley-
Decoct their cold blood to such valiant heat?
And shall our quick blood, spirited with wine,
Seem frosty? O, for honour of our land,
Let us not hang like roping icicles
Upon our houses' thatch, whiles a more frosty
      people

Sweat drops of gallant youth in our rich
   fields,—
Poor we may call them in their native lords!
  *Dau.* By faith and honour,
Our madams mock at us, and plainly say
Our mettle is bred out, and they will give
Their bodies to the lust of English youth
To new-store France with bastard warriors.
  *Bour.* They bid us to the English dancing-
   schools,
And teach lavoltas high and swift corantos;
Saying our grace is only in our heels,
And that we are most lofty runaways.
  *Fr. King.* Where is Montjoy, the herald?
   speed him hence:
Let him greet England with our sharp defi-
   ance.—
Up, princes! and, with spirit of honour edg'd
More sharper than your swords, hie to the field:
Charles De-la-bret, high-constable of France;
You Dukes of Orleans, Bourbon, and of Berri,
Alençon, Brabant, Bar, and Burgundy;
Jaques Chatillon, Rambures, Vaudemont,
Beaumont, Grandpree, Roussi, and Fauconberg,
Foix, Lestrale, Bouciqualt, and Charolois;
High dukes, great princes, barons, lords, and
   knights,
For your great seats, now quit you of great
   shames.
Bar Harry England, that sweeps through our
   land
With pennons painted in the blood of Harfleur:
Rush on his host as doth the melted snow
Upon the valleys, whose low vassal seat
The Alps doth spit and void his rheum upon:
Go down upon,—you have power enough,—
And in a captive chariot into Rouen
Bring him our prisoner.
  *Con.*            This becomes the great.
Sorry am I his numbers are so few,
His soldiers sick, and famish'd in their march;
For I am sure, when he shall see our army,
He'll drop his heart into the sink of fear,
And for achievement offer us his ransom.
  *Fr. King.* Therefore, lord constable, haste
   on Montjoy;
And let him say to England that we send
To know what willing ransom he will give.—
Prince Dauphin, you shall stay with us in
   Rouen.
  *Dau.* Not so, I do beseech your majesty.
  *Fr. King.* Be patient; for you shall remain
   with us.—
Now forth, lord constable and princes all,
And quickly bring us word of England's fall.
                        [*Exeunt.*

SCENE V.—*The English Camp in Picardy.*

*Enter, severally,* GOWER *and* FLUELLEN.

  *Gow.* How now, Captain Fluellen! come you
from the bridge?
  *Flu.* I assure you there is very excellent services committed at the pridge.
  *Gow.* Is the Duke of Exeter safe?

  *Flu.* The Duke of Exeter is as magnanimous
as Agamemnon; and a man that I love and
honour with my soul, and my heart, and my
duty, and my life, and my living, and my uttermost power: he is not,—God be praised and
plessed!—any hurt in the 'orld; but keeps the
pridge most valiantly, with excellent discipline.
There is an auncient there at the pridge,—I
think in my very conscience he is as valiant a
man as Mark Antony; and he is a man of no
estimation in the 'orld; but I did see him do
as gallant service.
  *Gow.* What do you call him?
  *Flu.* He is called Auncient Pistol.
  *Gow.* I know him not.
  *Flu.* Here is the man.

*Enter* PISTOL.

  *Pist.* Captain, I thee beseech to do me fa-
   vours:
The Duke of Exeter doth love thee well.
  *Flu.* Ay, I praise Got; and I have merited
some love at his hands.
  *Pist.* Bardolph, a soldier, firm and sound of
   heart,
Of buxom valour, hath by cruel fate
And giddy Fortune's furious fickle wheel,—
That goddess blind,
That stands upon the rolling restless stone,—
  *Flu.* By your patience, Auncient Pistol. Fortune is painted plind, with a muffler afore her
eyes, to signify to you that Fortune is plind;
and she is painted also with a wheel, to signify
to you, which is the moral of it, that she is
turning, and inconstant, and mutability, and
variation: and her foot, look you, is fixed upon
a spherical stone, which rolls, and rolls and
rolls.—In good truth, the poet makes a most
excellent description of it: Fortune is an excellent moral.
  *Pist.* Fortune is Bardolph's foe, and frowns
   on him;                   [be,—
For he hath stol'n a pax, and hanged must 'a
A damned death!
Let gallows gape for dog; let man go free,
And let not hemp his windpipe suffocate:
But Exeter hath given the doom of death
For pax of little price.
Therefore, go speak,—the duke will hear thy
   voice;
And let not Bardolph's vital thread be cut
With edge of penny cord and vile reproach:
Speak, captain, for his life, and I will thee re-
   quite.
  *Flu.* Auncient Pistol, I do partly understand
your meaning.
  *Pist.* Why, then, rejoice therefore.
  *Flu.* Certainly, Auncient, it is not a thing to
rejoice at: for if, look you, he were my prother
I would desire the duke to use his goot pleasure,
and put him to execution; for discipline ought
to be used.                [friendship!
  *Pist.* Die and be damn'd! and fico for thy
  *Flu.* It is well.

*Pist.* The fig of Spain! [*Exit.*

*Flu.* Very goot.

*Gow.* Why, this is an arrant counterfeit rascal; I remember him now; a bawd, a cutpurse.

*Flu.* I'll assure you, 'a uttered as prave 'ords at the pridge as you shall see in a summer's day. But it is very well; what he has spoke to me, that is well, I warrant you, when time is serve.

*Gow.* Why, 'tis a gull, a fool, a rogue, that now and then goes to the wars, to grace himself, at his return into London, under the form of a soldier. And such fellows are perfect in the great commanders' names: and they will learn you by rote where services were done;—at such and such a sconce, at such a breach, at such a convoy; who came off bravely, who was shot, who disgraced, what terms the enemy stood on; and this they con perfectly in the phrase of war, which they trick up with new-tuned oaths: and what a beard of the general's cut, and a horrid suit of the camp, will do among foaming bottles and ale-washed wits, is wonderful to be thought on. But you must learn to know such slanders of the age, or else you may be marvellously mistook.

*Flu.* I tell you what, Captain Gower, I do perceive he is not the man that he would gladly make show to the 'orld he is: if I find a hole in his coat I will tell him my mind. [*Drum within.*] Hark you, the king is coming; and I must speak with him from the pridge.

*Enter* KING HENRY, GLOSTER, *and* Soldiers.

Got bless your majesty!

*K. Hen.* How now, Fluellen! cam'st thou from the bridge?

*Flu.* Ay, so please your majesty. The Duke of Exeter has very gallantly maintained the pridge: the French is gone off, look you; and there is gallant and most prave passages: marry, th' athversary was have possession of the pridge; but he is enforced to retire, and the Duke of Exeter is master of the pridge: I can tell your majesty the duke is a prave man.

*K. Hen.* What men have you lost, Fluellen?

*Flu.* The perdition of th' athversary hath been very great, reasonable great: marry, for my part, I think the duke hath lost never a man, but one that is like to be executed for robbing a church,—one Bardolph, if your majesty know the man: his face is all bubukles, and whelks, and knobs, and flames of fire; and his lips plows at his nose, and it is like a coal of fire, sometimes plue and sometimes red; but his nose is executed and his fire's out.

*K. Hen.* We would have all such offenders so cut off:—and we give express charge that in our marches through the country there be nothing compelled from the villages, nothing taken but paid for, none of the French upbraided or abused in disdainful language; for when lenity and cruelty play for a kingdom the gentler gamester is the soonest winner.

*Tucket sounds. Enter* MONTJOY.

*Mont.* You know me by my habit.

*K. Hen.* Well, then, I know thee: what shall I know of thee?

*Mont.* My master's mind.

*K. Hen.* Unfold it.

*Mont.* Thus says my king:—Say thou to Harry of England: Though we seemed dead we did but sleep; advantage is a better soldier than rashness. Tell him we could have rebuked him at Harfleur, but that we thought not good to bruise an injury till it were full ripe:—now we speak upon our cue, and our voice is imperial: England shall repent his folly, see his weakness, and admire our sufferance. Bid him, therefore, consider of his ransom; which must proportion the losses we have borne, the subjects we have lost, the disgrace we have digested; which, in weight to re-answer, his pettiness would bow under. For our losses his exchequer is too poor; for the effusion of our blood the muster of his kingdom too faint a number; and for our disgrace his own person, kneeling at our feet, but a weak and worthless satisfaction. To this add defiance: and tell him, for conclusion, he hath betrayed his followers, whose condemnation is pronounced. So far my king and master; so much my office.

*K. Hen.* What is thy name? I know thy quality.

*Mont.* Montjoy.

*K. Hen.* Thou dost thy office fairly. Turn thee back,
And tell thy king,—I do not seek him now;
But could be willing to march on to Calais
Without impeachment: for, to say the sooth,—
Though 'tis no wisdom to confess so much
Unto an enemy of craft and vantage,—
My people are with sickness much enfeebled;
My numbers lessen'd; and those few I have
Almost no better than so many French;
Who, when they were in health, I tell thee, herald,
I thought upon one pair of English legs
Did march three Frenchmen.—Yet, forgive me, God,
That I do brag thus!—this your air of France
Hath blown that vice in me; I must repent.
Go, therefore, tell thy master here I am;
My ransom is this frail and worthless trunk;
My army but a weak and sickly guard;
Yet, God before, tell him we will come on,
Though France himself, and such another neighbour,
Stand in our way. There's for thy labour, Montjoy.
Go, bid thy master well advise himself:
If we may pass, we will; if we be hinder'd,
We shall your tawny ground with your red blood
Discolour: and so, Montjoy, fare you well.
The sum of all our answer is but this:
We would not seek a battle as we are;

Nor as we are, we say, we will not shun it:
So tell your master.

*Mont.* I shall deliver so. Thanks to your
highness. [*Exit.*

*Glo.* I hope they will not come upon us now.

*K. Hen.* We are in God's hand, brother, not
in theirs.

March to the bridge; it now draws toward
night:—

Beyond the river we'll encamp ourselves;
And on to-morrow bid them march away.
[*Exeunt.*

SCENE VI.—*The French Camp near Agincourt.*

*Enter the* Constable of France, *the* LORD RAM-
BURES, *the* DUKE OF ORLEANS, *the* DAUPHIN,
*and others.*

*Con.* Tut! I have the best armour of the
world.—Would it were day!

*Orl.* You have an excellent armour; but let
my horse have his due.

*Con.* It is the best horse of Europe.

*Orl.* Will it never be morning?

*Dau.* My Lord of Orleans and my lord high-
constable, you talk of horse and armour,—

*Orl.* You are as well provided of both as any
prince in the world.

*Dau.* What a long night is this!—I will not
change my horse with any that treads but on
four pasterns. *Ca, ha!* he bounds from the
earth as if his entrails were hairs; *le cheval
volant,* the Pegasus, *qui a les narines de feu!*
When I bestride him I soar, I am a hawk: he
trots the air; the earth sings when he touches
it; the basest horn of his hoof is more musical
than the pipe of Hermes.

*Orl.* He's of the colour of the nutmeg.

*Dau.* And of the heat of the ginger. It is a
beast for Perseus: he is pure air and fire; and
the dull elements of earth and water never appear in him, but only in patient stillness while
his rider mounts him: he is indeed a horse; and
all other jades you may call beasts.

*Con.* Indeed, my lord, it is a most absolute
and excellent horse.

*Dau.* It is the prince of palfreys; his neigh
is like the bidding of a monarch, and his countenance enforces homage.

*Orl.* No more, cousin.

*Dau.* Nay, the man hath no wit that cannot,
from the rising of the lark to the lodging of the
lamb, vary deserved praise on my palfrey: it
is a theme as fluent as the sea; turn the sands
into eloquent tongues, and my horse is argument for them all: 'tis a subject for a sovereign
to reason on, and for a sovereign's sovereign to
ride on; and for the world,—familiar to us and
unknown,—to lay apart their particular functions and wonder at him. I once writ a sonnet
in his praise, and began thus: *Wonder of
nature,*—

*Orl.* I have heard a sonnet begin so to one's
mistress.

*Dau.* Then did they imitate that which I

composed to my courser: for my horse is my
mistress.

*Orl.* Your mistress bears well.

*Dau.* Me well; which is the prescript praise
and perfection of a good and particular mistress.

*Con.* Nay, for methought yesterday your
mistress shrewdly shook your back.

*Dau.* So, perhaps, did yours.

*Con.* Mine was not bridled.

*Dau.* O, then, belike she was old and gentle;
and you rode like a kern of Ireland, your
French hose off and in your strait strossers.

*Con.* You have good judgment in horsemanship.

*Dau.* Be warned by me, then: they that ride
so, and ride not warily, fall into foul bogs. I
had rather have my horse to my mistress.

*Con.* I had as lief have my mistress a jade.

*Dau.* I tell thee, constable, my mistress
wears his own hair.

*Con.* I could make as true a boast as that if
I had a sow to my mistress.

*Dau. Le chien est retourné à son propre
vomissement, et la truie lavée au bourbier:* thou
makest use of anything.

*Con.* Yet do I not use my horse for my mistress; or any such proverb so little kin to the
purpose.

*Ram.* My lord constable, the armour that I
saw in your tent to-night, are those stars or
suns upon it?

*Con.* Stars, my lord.

*Dau.* Some of them will fall to-morrow, I
hope.

*Con.* And yet my sky shall not want.

*Dau.* That may be, for you bear a many
superfluously, and 'twere more honour some
were away.

*Con.* Even as your horse bears your praises;
who would trot as well were some of your brags
dismounted.

*Dau.* Would I were able to load him with
his desert!—Will it never be day?—I will trot
to-morrow a mile, and my way shall be paved
with English faces.

*Con.* I will not say so, for fear I should be
faced out of my way: but I would it were
morning; for I would fain be about the ears of
the English.

*Ram.* Who will go to hazard with me for
twenty prisoners?

*Con.* You must first go yourself to hazard
ere you have them.

*Dau.* 'Tis midnight; I'll go arm myself.
[*Exit.*

*Orl.* The Dauphin longs for morning.

*Ram.* He longs to eat the English.

*Con.* I think he will eat all he kills.

*Orl.* By the white hand of my lady, he's a
gallant prince.

*Con.* Swear by her foot, that she may tread
out the oath.

*Orl.* He is, simply, the most active gentleman of France.

*Con.* Doing is activity; and he will still be doing.

*Orl.* He never did harm that I heard of.

*Con.* Nor will do none to-morrow: he will keep that good name still.

*Orl.* I know him to be valiant.

*Con.* I was told that by one that knows him better than you.

*Orl.* What's he?

*Con.* Marry, he told me so himself; and he said he cared not who knew it.

*Orl.* He needs not; it is no hidden virtue in him.

*Con.* By my faith, sir, but it is; never anybody saw it but his lackey: 'tis a hooded valour: and when it appears it will bate.

*Orl.* Ill-will never said well.

*Con.* I will cap that proverb with—There is flattery in friendship.

*Orl.* And I will take up that with—Give the devil his due.

*Con.* Well placed: there stands your friend for the devil: have at the very eye of that proverb with—A pox of the devil.

*Orl.* You are the better at proverbs by how much—A fool's bolt is soon shot.

*Con.* You have shot over.

*Orl.* 'Tis not the first time you were overshot.

*Enter a* Messenger.

*Mess.* My lord high-constable, the English lie within fifteen hundred paces of your tents.

*Con.* Who hath measured the ground?

*Mess.* The Lord Grandpree.

*Con.* A valiant and most expert gentleman. —Would it were day!—Alas, poor Harry of England! he longs not for the dawning as we do.

*Orl.* What a wretched and peevish fellow is this King of England, to mope with his fat-brained followers so far out of his knowledge!

*Con.* If the English had any apprehension they would run away.

*Orl.* That they lack; for if their heads had any intellectual armour they could never wear such heavy head-pieces.

*Ram.* That island of England breeds very valiant creatures; their mastiffs are of unmatchable courage.

*Orl.* Foolish curs, that run winking into the mouth of a Russian bear, and have their heads crush like rotten apples! You may as well say, that's a valiant flea that dare eat his breakfast on the lip of a lion.

*Con.* Just, just; and the men do sympathize with the mastiffs in robustious and rough coming-on, leaving their wits with their wives: and then give them great meals of beef, and iron and steel, they will eat like wolves and fight like devils.

*Orl.* Ay, but these English are shrewdly out of beef.

*Con.* Then shall we find to-morrow they have only stomachs to eat, and none to fight. Now is it time to arm: come, shall we about it?

*Orl.* It is now two o'clock: but, let me see,— by ten
We shall have each a hundred Englishmen.
[*Exeunt.*

*Enter* Chorus.

*Chor.* Now entertain conjecture of a time
When creeping murmur and the poring dark
Fills the wide vessel of the universe.
From camp to camp, through the foul womb of night
The hum of either army stilly sounds,
That the fix'd sentinels almost receive
The secret whispers of each other's watch:
Fire answers fire, and through their paly flames
Each battle sees the other's umber'd face:
Steed threatens steed, in high and boastful neighs
Piercing the night's dull ear; and from the tents
The armourers, accomplishing the knights,
With busy hammers closing rivets up,
Give dreadful note of preparation:
The country cocks do crow, the clocks do toll,
And the third hour of drowsy morning name.
Proud of their numbers and secure in soul,
The confident and over-lusty French
Do the low-rated English play at dice;
And chide the cripple tardy-gaited night,
Who, like a foul and ugly witch, doth limp
So tediously away. The poor condemned English,
Like sacrifices, by their watchful fires
Sit patiently, and inly ruminate
The morning's danger; and their gesture sad
Investing lank-lean cheeks and war-worn coats
Presenteth them unto the gazing moon
So many horrid ghosts. O, now, who will behold
The royal captain of this ruin'd band    [tent,
Walking from watch to watch, from tent to
Let him cry, Praise and glory on his head!
For forth he goes and visits all his host;
Bids them good-morrow with a modest smile,
And calls them brothers, friends, and countrymen.
Upon his royal face there is no note
How dread an army hath enrounded him;
Nor doth he dedicate one jot of colour
Unto the weary and all-watched night;
But freshly looks, and over-bears attaint
With cheerful semblance and sweet majesty;
That every wretch, pining and pale before,
Beholding him, plucks comfort from his looks:
A largess universal, like the sun,
His liberal eye doth give to every one,
Thawing cold fear. Then, mean and gentle all,
Behold, as may unworthiness define,
A little touch of Harry in the night:
And so our scene must to the battle fly;
Where,—O for pity!—we shall much disgrace
With four or five most vile and ragged foils,
Right ill-dispos'd in brawl ridiculous,
The name of Agincourt. Yet sit and see;
Minding true things by what their mockeries be.    [*Exit.*

## ACT IV.

SCENE I.—FRANCE. *The English Camp at Agincourt.*

*Enter* KING HENRY, BEDFORD, *and* GLOSTER.

*K. Hen.* Gloster, 'tis true that we are in great danger;
The greater therefore should our courage be.—
Good-morrow, brother Bedford.—God Almighty!
There is some soul of goodness in things evil,
Would men observingly distil it out;
For our bad neighbour makes us early stirrers,
Which is both healthful and good husbandry:
Besides, they are our outward consciences
And preachers to us all: admonishing
That we should dress us fairly for our end.
Thus may we gather honey from the weed,
And make a moral of the devil himself.

*Enter* ERPINGHAM.

Good-morrow, old Sir Thomas Erpingham:
A good soft pillow for that good white head
Were better than a churlish turf of France.

*Erp.* Not so, my liege: this lodging likes me better,
Since I may say, Now lie I like a king.

*K. Hen.* 'Tis good for men to love their present pains
Upon example; so the spirit is eas'd:
And when the mind is quicken'd, out of doubt
The organs, though defunct and dead before,
Break up their drowsy grave, and newly move
With casted slough and fresh legerity.
Lend me thy cloak, Sir Thomas.—Brothers both,
Commend me to the princes in our camp;
Do my good-morrow to them; and anon
Desire them all to my pavilion.

*Glo.* We shall, my liege.

[*Exeunt* GLOSTER *and* BEDFORD.

*Erp.* Shall I attend your grace?

*K. Hen.*　　　　　No, my good knight;
Go with my brothers to my lords of England:
I and my bosom must debate awhile,
And then I would no other company.

*Erp.* The Lord in heaven bless thee, noble Harry!　　　　　[*Exit.*

*K. Hen.* God-a-mercy, old heart! thou speak'st cheerfully.

*Enter* PISTOL.

*Pist. Qui va là?*

*K. Hen.* A friend.

*Pist.* Discuss unto me; art thou officer?
Or art thou base, common, and popular?

*K. Hen.* I am a gentleman of a company.

*Pist.* Trail'st thou the puissant pike?

*K. Hen.* Even so. What are you?

*Pist.* As good a gentleman as the emperor.

*K. Hen.* Then you are a better than the king.

*Pist.* The king's a bawcock and a heart of gold,
A lad of life, an imp of fame;

Of parents good, of fist most valiant:
I kiss his dirty shoe, and from my heart-strings
I love the lovely bully.—What is thy name?

*K. Hen.* Harry *le Roi.*

*Pist. Le Roy!* a Cornish name: art thou of Cornish crew?

*K. Hen.* No, I am a Welshman.

*Pist.* Know'st thou Fluellen?

*K. Hen.* Yes.

*Pist.* Tell him, I'll knock his leek about his pate
Upon Saint Davy's day.

*K. Hen.* Do not you wear your dagger in your cap that day, lest he knock that about yours.

*Pist.* Art thou his friend?

*K. Hen.* And his kinsman too.

*Pist.* The *fico* for thee, then!

*K. Hen.* I thank you: God be with you!

*Pist.* My name is Pistol called.　　　　　[*Exit.*

*K. Hen.* It sorts well with your fierceness.

*Enter* FLUELLEN *and* GOWER, *severally.*

*Gow.* Captain Fluellen!

*Flu.* So! in the name of Cheshu Christ, speak fewer. It is the greatest admiration in the universal 'orld when the true and auncient prerogatifs and laws of the wars is not kept: if you would take the pains but to examine the wars of Pompey the Great, you shall find, I warrant you, that there is no tiddle-taddle nor pibble-pabble in Pompey's camp; I warrant you, you shall find the ceremonies of the wars, and the cares of it, and the forms of it, and the sobriety of it, and the modesty of it, to be otherwise.

*Gow.* Why, the enemy is loud; you hear him all night.

*Flu.* If the enemy is an ass, and a fool, and a prating coxcomb, is it meet, think you, that we should also, look you, be an ass, and a fool, and a prating coxcomb,—in your own conscience, now?

*Gow.* I will speak lower.

*Flu.* I pray you and peseech you that you will.　　　　　[*Exeunt* GOWER *and* FLUELLEN.

*K. Hen.* Though it appear a little out of fashion,
There is much care and valour in this Welshman.

*Enter* BATES, COURT, *and* WILLIAMS.

*Court.* Brother John Bates, is not that the morning which breaks yonder?

*Bates.* I think it be: but we have no great cause to desire the approach of day.

*Will.* We see yonder the beginning of the day, but I think we shall never see the end of it.—Who goes there?

*K. Hen.* A friend.

*Will.* Under what captain serve you?

*K. Hen.* Under Sir Thomas Erpingham.

*Will.* A good old commander and a most kind gentleman: I pray you, what thinks he of our estate?

*K. Hen.* Even as men wrecked upon a sand, that look to be washed off the next tide.

*Bates.* He hath not told his thought to the king?

*K. Hen.* No; nor it is not meet he should. For though I speak it to you, I think the king is but a man as I am: the violet smells to him as it doth to me; the element shows to him as it doth to me; all his senses have but human conditions: his ceremonies laid by, in his nakedness he appears but a man; and though his affections are higher mounted than ours, yet, when they stoop, they stoop with the like wing. Therefore when he sees reason of fears, as we do, his fears, out of doubt, be of the same relish as ours are: yet, in reason, no man should possess him with any appearance of fear, lest he, by showing it, should dishearten his army.

*Bates.* He may show what outward courage he will; but I believe, as cold a night as 'tis, he could wish himself in the Thames up to the neck;—and so I would he were, and I by him, at all adventures, so we were quit here.

*K. Hen.* By my troth, I will speak my conscience of the king: I think he would not wish himself anywhere but where he is.

*Bates.* Then I would he were here alone; so should he be sure to be ransomed, and a many poor men's lives saved.

*K. Hen.* I dare say you love him not so ill, to wish him here alone, howsoever you speak this, to feel other men's minds: methinks I could not die anywhere so contented as in the king's company,—his cause being just and his quarrel honourable.

*Will.* That's more than we know.

*Bates.* Ay, or more than we should seek after; for we know enough if we know we are the king's subjects: if his cause be wrong, our obedience to the king wipes the crime of it out of us.

*Will.* But if the cause be not good, the king himself hath a heavy reckoning to make when all those legs and arms and heads, chopped off in a battle, shall join together at the latter day and cry all, We died at such a place; some swearing; some crying for a surgeon; some upon their wives left poor behind them; some upon the debts they owe; some upon their children rawly left. I am afeared there are few die well that die in a battle; for how can they charitably dispose of anything when blood is their argument? Now, if these men do not die well, it will be a black matter for the king that led them to it; who to disobey were against all proportion of subjection.

*K. Hen.* So if a son, that is by his father sent about merchandise do sinfully miscarry upon the sea, the imputation of his wickedness, by your rule, should be imposed upon his father that sent him: or if a servant, under his master's command, transporting a sum of money, be assailed by robbers, and die in many irreconciled iniquities, you may call the business of the master the author of the servant's damnation: —but this is not so: the king is not bound to answer the particular endings of his soldiers, the father of his son, nor the master of his servant; for they purpose not their death when they purpose their services. Besides, there is no king, be his cause never so spotless, if it come to the arbitrement of swords, can try it out with all unspotted soldiers: some peradventure have on them the guilt of premeditated and contrived murder; some of beguiling virgins with the broken seals of perjury; some making the wars their bulwark that have before gored the gentle bosom of peace with pillage and robbery. Now, if these men have defeated the law and outrun native punishment, though they can outstrip men they have no wings to fly from God: war is his beadle, war is his vengeance; so that here men are punished for before-breach of the king's laws in now the king's quarrel: where they feared the death they have borne life away; and where they would be safe they perish: then if they die unprovided, no more is the king guilty of their damnation than he was before guilty of those impieties for the which they are now visited. Every subject's duty is the king's; but every subject's soul is his own. Therefore should every soldier in the wars do as every sick man in his bed,—wash every mote out of his conscience: and dying so, death is to him advantage; or not dying, the time was blessedly lost wherein such preparation was gained: and in him that escapes it were not sin to think that, making God so free an offer, he let him outlive that day to see his greatness, and to teach others how they should prepare.

*Will.* 'Tis certain, every man that dies ill, the ill upon his own head,—the king is not to answer for it.

*Bates.* I do not desire he should answer for me; and yet I determine to fight lustily for him.

*K. Hen.* I myself heard the king say he would not be ransomed.

*Will.* Ay, he said so, to make us fight cheerfully: but when our throats are cut he may be ransomed, and we ne'er the wiser.

*K. Hen.* If I live to see it I will never trust his word after.

*Will.* You pay him then! That's a perilous shot out of an elder-gun, that a poor and a private displeasure can do against a monarch! you may as well go about to turn the sun to ice with fanning in his face with a peacock's feather. You'll never trust his word after! come, 'tis a foolish saying.

*K. Hen.* Your reproof is something too round: I should be angry with you if the time were convenient.

*Will.* Let it be a quarrel between us if you live.

*K. Hen.* I embrace it.

*Will.* How shall I know thee again?

*K. Hen.* Give me any gage of thine, and I will wear it in my bonnet: then, if ever thou darest acknowledge it, I will make it my quarrel.

*Will.* Here's my glove: give me another of thine.

*K. Hen.* There.

*Will.* This will I also wear in my cap: if ever thou come to me and say, after to-morrow, *This is my glove,* by this hand I will take thee a box on the ear.

*K. Hen.* If ever I live to see it I will challenge it.

*Will.* Thou darest as well be hanged.

*K. Hen.* Well, I will do it though I take thee in the king's company.

*Will.* Keep thy word: fare thee well.

*Bates.* Be friends, you English fools, be friends: we have French quarrels enow, if you could tell how to reckon.

*K. Hen.* Indeed, the French may lay twenty French crowns to one they will beat us; for they bear them on their shoulders: but it is no English treason to cut French crowns; and to-morrow the king himself will be a clipper.

[*Exeunt* Soldiers.

Upon the king!—let us our lives, our souls,
Our debts, our careful wives, our children, and
Our sins lay on the king! We must bear all.
O hard condition, twin-born with greatness,
Subject to the breath of every fool,
Whose sense no more can feel but his own wringing.
What infinite heart's-ease must kings neglect
That private men enjoy!
And what have kings that privates have not too,
Save ceremony,—save general ceremony?
And what art thou, thou idol ceremony?
What kind of god art thou, that suffer'st more
Of mortal griefs than do thy worshippers?
What are thy rents? what are thy comings-in?
O ceremony, show me but thy worth!
What is thy soul of adoration?
Art thou aught else but place, degree, and form,
Creating awe and fear in other men?
Wherein thou art less happy being fear'd
Than they in fearing.
What drink'st thou oft, instead of homage sweet,
But poison'd flattery? O, be sick, great greatness,
And bid thy ceremony give thee cure!
Think'st thou the fiery fever will go out
With titles blown from adulation?
Will it give place to flexure and low bending?
Canst thou, when thou command'st the beggar's knee,
Command the health of it? No, thou proud dream,
That play'st so subtly with a king's repose:
I am a king that find thee; and I know
'Tis not the balm, the sceptre, and the ball,
The sword, the mace, the crown imperial,
The intertissued robe of gold and pearl,

The farced title running 'fore the king,
The throne he sits on, nor the tide of pomp
That beats upon the high shore of this world,—
No, not all these, thrice gorgeous ceremony,
Not all these, laid in bed majestical,
Can sleep so soundly as the wretched slave
Who, with a body fill'd and vacant mind,
Gets him to rest, cramm'd with distressful bread;
Never sees horrid night, the child of hell;
But, like a lackey, from the rise to set
Sweats in the eye of Phœbus, and all night
Sleeps in Elysium; next day, after dawn,
Doth rise and help Hyperion to his horse;
And follows so the ever-running year,
With profitable labour, to his grave:
And but for ceremony, such a wretch,  [sleep,
Winding up days with toil and nights with
Had the fore-hand and vantage of a king.
The slave, a member of the country's peace,
Enjoys it; but in gross brain little wots
What watch the king keeps to maintain the peace
Whose hours the peasant best advantages.

*Enter* ERPINGHAM.

*Erp.* My lord, your nobles, jealous of your absence,
Seek through your camp to find you.

*K. Hen.*                    Good old knight,
Collect them all together at my tent:
I'll be before thee.

*Erp.*                    I shall do't, my lord. [*Exit.*

*K. Hen.* O God of battles! steel my soldiers' hearts;
Possess them not with fear; take from them now
The sense of reckoning, if the opposed numbers
Pluck their hearts from them!—Not to-day, O Lord,
O, not to-day, think not upon the fault
My father made in compassing the crown!
I Richard's body have interred new,
And on it have bestow'd more contrite tears
Than from it issu'd forced drops of blood:
Five hundred poor I have in yearly pay,
Who twice a day their wither'd hands hold up
Toward heaven, to pardon blood; and I have built
Two chantries, where the sad and solemn priests
Sing still for Richard's soul. More will I do;
Though all that I can do is nothing worth,
Since that my penitence comes after all,
Imploring pardon.

*Enter* GLOSTER.

*Glo.* My liege!

*K. Hen.* My brother Gloster's voice?—Ay;
I know thy errand, I will go with thee:—
The day, my friends, and all things stay for me.

[*Exeunt.*

SCENE II.—*The French Camp.*

*Enter* DAUPHIN, ORLEANS, RAMBURES, *and others.*

*Ori.* The sun doth gild our armour; up, my
    lords!
*Dau.* *Montez à cheval!*—My horse! *varlet,
    laquais!* ha!
*Orl.* O brave spirit!
*Dau.* *Via!—les eaux et la terre,*—
*Orl.* *Rienpuis? l'air et le feu,*—
*Dau.* *Ciel!* cousin Orleans.

### Enter Constable.

Now, my lord constable!
*Con.* Hark, how our steeds for present ser-
    vice neigh!
*Dau.* Mount them, and make incision in
    their hides,
That their hot blood may spin in English eyes,
And dout them with superfluous courage, ha!
*Ram.* What, will you have them weep our
    horses' blood?
How shall we, then, behold their natural tears?

### Enter a Messenger.

*Mess.* The English are embattled, you French
    peers.                         [to horse!
*Con.* To horse, you gallant princes! straight
Do but behold yon poor and starved band,
And your fair show shall suck away their souls,
Leaving them but the shales and husks of men.
There is not work enough for all our hands;
Scarce blood enough in all their sickly veins
To give each naked curtle-axe a stain,
That our French gallants shall to-day draw out,
And sheathe for lack of sport: let us but blow
    on them,
The vapour of our valour will o'erturn them.
'Tis positive 'gainst all exceptions, lords,
That our superfluous lackeys and our peas-
    ants,—
Who in unnecessary action swarm
About our squares of battle,—were enow
To purge this field of such a hilding foe;
Though we upon this mountain's basis by
Took stand for idle speculation,—
But that our honours must not. What's to say?
A very little little let us do,
And all is done. Then let the trumpets sound
The tucket-sonance and the note to mount:
For our approach shall so much dare the field
That England shall couch down in fear and
    yield.

### Enter GRANDPREE.

*Grand.* Why do you stay so long, my lords
    of France?
Yond island carrions, desperate of their bones,
Ill-favouredly become the morning field:
Their ragged curtains poorly are let loose,
And our air shakes them passing scornfully:
Big Mars seems bankrupt in their beggar'd
    host,
And faintly through a rusty beaver peeps:
The horsemen sit like fixed candlesticks,
With torch-staves in their hand; and their poor
    jades

Lob down their heads, dropping the hides and
    hips,
The gum down-roping from their pale-dead
    eyes,
And in their pale dull mouths the gimmel-bit
Lies foul with chew'd grass, still and motionless;
And their exécutors, the knavish crows,
Fly o'er them, all impatient for their hour.
Description cannot suit itself in words
To demonstrate the life of such a battle
In life so lifeless as it shows itself.
*Con.* They have said their prayers and they
    stay for death.
*Dau.* Shall we go send them dinners and
    fresh suits,
And give their fasting horses provender,
And after fight with them?
*Con.* I stay but for my guidon:—to the
    field!—
I will the banner from a trumpet take,
And use it for my haste. Come, come, away!
The sun is high, and we outwear the day.
                                    [*Exeunt.*

### SCENE III.—*The English Camp.*

*Enter the English Host;* GLOSTER, BEDFORD,
    EXETER, SALISBURY, *and* WESTMORELAND.

*Glo.* Where is the king?
*Bed.* The king himself is rode to view their
    battle.
*West.* Of fighting men they have full three-
    score thousand.
*Exe.* There's five to one; besides, they all are
    fresh.
*Sal.* God's arm strike with us! 'tis a fearful
    odds.
God b' wi' you, princes all; I'll to my charge:
If we no more meet till we meet in heaven,
Then joyfully,—my noble Lord of Bedford,—
My dear Lord Gloster,—and my good Lord
    Exeter,—
And my kind kinsman,—warriors all, adieu!
*Bed.* Farewell, good Salisbury; and good
    luck go with thee!
*Exe.* Farewell, kind lord; fight valiantly to-
    day:
And yet I do thee wrong to mind thee of it,
For thou art fram'd of the firm truth of valour.
                            [*Exit* SALISBURY.
*Bed.* He is as full of valour as of kindness;
Princely in both.
*West.*                O that we now had here

### Enter KING HENRY.

But one ten thousand of those men in England
That do no work to-day!
*K. Hen.*            What's he that wishes so?
My cousin Westmoreland?—No, my fair cousin:
If we are mark'd to die, we are enow
To do our country loss; and if to live,
The fewer men the greater share of honour.
God's will! I pray thee, wish not one man more.
By Jove, I am not covetous for gold;
Nor care I who doth feed upon my cost;

It yearns me not if men my garments wear;
Such outward things dwell not in my desires:
But if it be a sin to covet honour,
I am the most offending soul alive.
No, faith, my coz, wish not a man from Eng-
land:
God's peace! I would not lose so great an
honour,
As one man more, methinks, would share from
me,
For the best hope I have. O do not wish one
more!
Rather proclaim it, Westmoreland, through my
host,
That he which hath no stomach to this fight,
Let him depart; his passport shall be made,
And crowns for convoy put into his purse:
We would not die in that man's company
That fears his fellowship to die with us.
This day is call'd the feast of Crispian:
He that outlives this day, and comes safe home,
Will stand a tip-toe when this day is nam'd,
And rouse him at the name of Crispian.
He that shall live this day, and see old age,
Will yearly on the vigil feast his neighbours,
And say, To-morrow is Saint Crispian:
Then will he strip his sleeve and show his scars,
And say, These wounds I had on Crispin's day.
Old men forget; yet all shall be forgot,
But he'll remember with advantages
What feats he did that day: then shall our
names,
Familiar in their mouths as household words,—
Harry the king, Bedford and Exeter,
Warwick and Talbot, Salisbury and Gloster,—
Be in their flowing cups freshly remember'd.
This story shall the good man teach his son;
And Crispin Crispian shall ne'er go by,
From this day to the ending of the world,
But we in it shall be remembered,—
We few, we happy few, we band of brothers;
For he to-day that sheds his blood with me
Shall be my brother; be he ne'er so vile,
This day shall gentle his condition:
And gentlemen in England now a-bed
Shall think themselves accurs'd they were not
here,
And hold their manhoods cheap while any
speaks
That fought with us upon Saint Crispin's day.

*Re-enter* SALISBURY.

*Sal.* My sovereign lord, bestow yourself
with speed:
The French are bravely in their battles set,
And will with all expedience charge on us.
*K. Hen.* All things are ready if our minds
be so.
*West.* Perish the man whose mind is back-
ward now!
*K. Hen.* Thou dost not wish more help from
England, coz?
*West.* God's will! my liege, would you and
I alone,

Without more help, could fight this royal battle!
*K. Hen.* Why, now thou hast unwish'd five
thousand men;
Which likes me better than to wish us one.—
You know your places: God be with you all!

*Tucket. Enter* MONTJOY.

*Mont.* Once more I come to know of thee,
King Harry,
If for thy ransom thou wilt now compound,
Before thy most assured overthrow:
For certainly thou art so near the gulf
Thou needs must be englutted. Besides, in
mercy,
The constable desires thee thou wilt mind
Thy followers of repentance; that their souls
May make a peaceful and a sweet retire
From off these fields, where, wretches, their
poor bodies
Must lie and fester.
*K. Hen.*　　　　Who hath sent thee now?
*Mont.* The constable of France.
*K. Hen.* I pray thee, bear my former answer
back:
Bid them achieve me, and then sell my bones.
Good God! why should they mock poor fellows
thus?
The man that once did sell the lion's skin
While the beast liv'd was kill'd with hunting
him.
A many of our bodies shall no doubt
Find native graves; upon the which, I trust,
Shall witness live in brass of this day's work:
And those that leave their valiant bones in
France,
Dying like men, though buried in your dung-
hills,
They shall be fam'd; for there the sun shall
greet them
And draw their honours reeking up to heaven,
Leaving their earthly parts to choke your clime.
The smell whereof shall breed a plague in
France.
Mark, then, abounding valour in our English,
That, being dead, like to the bullet's grazing,
Break out into a second course of mischief,
Killing in rélapse of mortality.
Let me speak proudly:—tell the constable
We are but warriors for the working-day;
Our gayness and our gilt are all besmirch'd
With rainy marching in the painful field;
There's not a piece of feather in our host,—
Good argument, I hope, we will not fly,—
And time hath worn us into slovenry:
But, by the mass, our hearts are in the trim;
And my poor soldiers tell me yet ere night
They'll be in fresher robes; or they will pluck
The gay new coats o'er the French soldiers'
heads,
And turn them out of service. If they do this,—
As, if God please, they shall,—my ransom then
Will soon be levied. Herald, save thou thy
labour;
Come thou no more for ransom, gentle herald:

They shall have none, I swear, but these my
        joints,—
Which if they have as I will leave 'em them,
Shall yield them little, tell the constable.

*Mont.* I shall, King Harry. And so, fare thee
        well:
Thou never shalt hear herald any more. [*Exit.*

*K. Hen.* I fear thou wilt once more come
        again for ransom.

*Enter the* DUKE OF YORK.

*York.* My Lord, most humbly on my knee
        I beg
The leading of the vaward.

*K. Hen.* Take it, brave York.—Now, sol-
        diers, march away:—
And how thou pleasest, God, dispose the day!
                        [*Exeunt.*

SCENE IV.—*The Field of Battle.*

*Alarums. Excursions. Enter* French Soldier,
        PISTOL, *and* Boy.

*Pist.* Yield, cur!

*Fr. Sol.* Je pense que vous êtes le gentil-homme
de bonne qualité.

*Pist.* Quality! Callino, castore me! art thou
a gentleman? what is thy name? discuss.

*Fr. Sol.* O Seigneur Dieu!

*Pist.* O, Signieur Dew should be a gentle-
man:—
Perpend my words, O Signieur Dew, and
        mark;—
O Signieur Dew, thou diest on point of fox,
Except, O Signieur, thou do give to me
Egregious ransom.          [*moi!*

*Fr. Sol.* O prennez miséricorde! ayez pitié de

*Pist.* Moy shall not serve; I will have forty
        moys;
Or I will fetch thy rim out at thy throat
In drops of crimson blood.

*Fr. Sol.* Est-il impossible d'échapper la force
de ton bras?

*Pist.* Brass, cur!
Thou damned and luxurious mountain-goat,
Offer'st me brass?

*Fr. Sol.* O pardonnez-moi!

*Pist.* Say'st thou me so? is that a ton of
moys?—
Come hither, boy: ask me this slave in French
What is his name.

*Boy.* Ecoutez: comment êtes-vous appelé?.

*Fr. Sol.* Monsieur le Fer.

*Boy.* He says his name is Master Fer.

*Pist.* Master Fer! I'll fer him, and firk him,
and ferret him:—discuss the same in French
unto him.

*Boy.* I do not know the French for fer, and
ferret, and firk.

*Pist.* Bid him prepare; for I will cut his
throat.

*Fr. Sol.* Que dit-il, monsieur?

*Boy.* Il me commande de vous dire que vous
faites vous prêt; car ce soldat ici est disposé tout
à cette heure de couper votre gorge.

*Pist.* Oui, coupe la gorge, par ma foi, pesant,
Unless thou give me crowns, brave crowns;
Or mangled shalt thou be by this my sword.

*Fr. Sol.* O, je vous supplie, pour l'amour de
Dieu, me pardonner! Je suis gentilhomme de
bonne maison: gardez ma vie, et je vous donnerai
deux cents écus.

*Pist.* What are his words?

*Boy.* He prays you to save his life: he is a
gentleman of a good house; and for his ransom
he will give you two hundred crowns.

*Pist.* Tell him·my fury shall abate, and I
The crowns will take.

*Fr. Sol.* Petit monsieur, que dit-il?

*Boy.* Encore qu'il est contre son jurement de
pardonner aucun prisonnier, néanmoins, pour
les écus que vous l'avez promis, il est content de
vous donner la liberté, le franchisement.

*Fr. Sol.* Sur mes genoux je vous donne mille
remercîmens; et je m'estine heureux que je suis
tombé entre les mains d'un chevalier, je pense, le
plus brave, vaillant, et très distingué seigneur
d'Angleterre.

*Pist.* Expound unto me, boy.

*Boy.* He gives you, upon his knees, a thousand thanks; and he esteems himself happy
that he hath fallen into the hands of one,—as
he thinks,—the most brave, valorous, and
thrice-worthy signieur of England.

*Pist.* As I suck blood, I will some mercy
show.—Follow me!          [*Exit.*

*Boy.* Suivez-vous le grand capitaine. [*Exit*
French Soldier.] I did never know so full a
voice issue from so empty a heart: but the saying is true,—the empty vessel makes the greatest sound. Bardolph and Nym had ten times
more valour than this roaring devil i' the old
play, that every one may pare his nails with a
wooden dagger; and they are both hanged; and
so would this be if he durst steal anything ad-
venturously. I must stay with the lackeys, with
the luggage of our camp: the French might
have a good prey of us if he knew of it; for there
is none to guard it but boys.          [*Exit.*

SCENE V.—*Another part of the Field of Battle.*

*Alarums. Enter* DAUPHIN, ORLEANS, BOURBON,
        Constable, RAMBURES, *and others.*

*Con.* O diable!

*Orl.* O seigneur! le jour est perdu, tout est
perdu!

*Dau.* Mort de ma vie! all is confounded, all!
Reproach and everlasting shame
Sits mocking in our plumes.—O méchante for-
        tune!—
Do not run away.          [*A short alarum.*

*Con.*          Why, all our ranks are broke.

*Dau.* O perdurable shame!—let's stab our-
        selves.
Be these the wretches that we play'd at dice for?

*Orl.* Is this the king we sent to for his
        ransom?

*Bour.* Shame, and eternal shame, nothing
        but shame!

Let us die in honour: once more back again;
And he that will not follow Bourbon now,
Let him go hence, and with his cap in hand,
Like a base pander, hold the chamber-door
Whilst by a slave, no gentler than my dog,
His fairest daughter is contaminated.

*Con.* Disorder, that hath spoil'd us, friend
us now!
Let us on heaps go offer up our lives
Unto these English, or else die with fame.

*Orl.* We are enow yet living in the field
To smother up the English in our throngs,
If any order might be thought upon.

*Bour.* The devil take order now! I'll to the
throng:
Let life be short, else shame will be too long.
[*Exeunt.*

SCENE VI.—*Another part of the Field.*

*Alarums. Enter* KING HENRY *and* Forces,
EXETER, *and others.*

*K. Hen.* Well have we done, thrice-valiant
countrymen:
But all's not done; yet keep the French the field.

*Exe.* The Duke of York commends him to
your majesty.

*K. Hen.* Lives he, good uncle? thrice within
this hour
I saw him down; thrice up again, and fighting;
From helmet to the spur all blood he was.

*Exe.* In which array, brave soldier, doth he lie
Larding the plain; and by his bloody side,—
Yoke-fellow to his honour-owing wounds,—
The noble Earl of Suffolk also lies.
Suffolk first died: and York, all haggled over,
Comes to him, where in gore he lay insteep'd,
And takes him by the beard; kisses the gashes
That bloodily did yawn upon his face;
And cries aloud, *Tarry, dear cousin Suffolk!*
*My soul shall thine keep company to heaven;*
*Tarry, sweet soul, for mine, then fly a-breast;*
*As in this glorious and well-foughten field*
*We kept together in our chivalry!*
Upon these words I came and cheer'd him up:
He smil'd me in the face, raught me his hand,
And, with a feeble grip, says, *Dear my lord,*
*Commend my service to my sovereign.*
So did he turn, and over Suffolk's neck
He threw his wounded arm, and kiss'd his lips;
And so, espous'd to death, with blood he seal'd
A testament of noble-ending love.
The pretty and sweet manner of it forc'd
Those waters from me which I would have
stopp'd;
But I had not so much of man in me,
And all my mother came into mine eyes,
And gave me up to tears.

*K. Hen.* I blame you not;
For, hearing this, I must perforce compound
With mistful eyes, or they will issue too.—
[*Alarum.*
But, hark! what new alarum is this same?—
The French have reinforc'd their scatter'd
men:—

Then every soldier kill his prisoners;
Give the word through. [*Exeunt.*

SCENE VII.—*Another part of the Field.*

*Alarums. Enter* FLUELLEN *and* GOWER.

*Flu.* Kill the poys and the luggage! 'tis expressly against the law of arms: 'tis as arrant a
piece of knavery, mark you now, as can be
offered; in your conscience, now, is it not?

*Gow.* 'Tis certain there's not a boy left alive;
and the cowardly rascals that ran from the
battle have done this slaughter: besides, they
have burned and carried away all that was in
the king's tent; wherefore the king, most
worthily, hath caused every soldier to cut his
prisoner's throat. O, 'tis a gallant king!

*Flu.* Ay, he was porn at Monmouth, Captain
Gower. What call you the town's name where
Alexander the pig was porn?

*Gow.* Alexander the Great.

*Flu.* Why, I pray you, is not pig great? the
pig, or the great, or the mighty, or the huge, or
the magnanimous, are all one reckonings, save
the phrase is a little variations.

*Gow.* I think Alexander the Great was born
in Macedon: his father was called Philip of
Macedon, as I take it.

*Flu.* I think it is in Macedon where Alexander is porn. I tell you, captain, if you look
in the maps of the 'orld, I warrant you shall
find, in the comparisons between Macedon and
Monmouth, that the situations, look you, is
both alike. There is a river in Macedon; and
there is also moreover a river at Monmouth: it
is called Wye at Monmouth; but it is out of my
prains what is the name of the other river; but
'tis all one, 'tis alike as my fingers is to my
fingers, and there is salmons in both. If you
mark Alexander's life well, Harry of Monmouth's life is come after it indifferent well; for
there is figures in all things. Alexander,—Got
knows, and you know,—in his rages, and his
furies, and his wraths, and his cholers, and his
moods, and his displeasures, and his indigna-
tions, and also being a little intoxicates in his
prains, did, in his ales and his angers, look you,
kill his pest friend, Clytus.

*Gow.* Our king is not like him in that: he
never killed any of his friends.

*Flu.* It is not well done, mark you now, to
take the tales out of my mouth ere it is made
and finished. I speak but in the figures and
comparisons of it: as Alexander is kill his friend
Clytus, being in his ales and his cups; so also
Harry Monmouth, being in his right wits and
his goot judgments, turned away the fat knight
with the great pelly-doublet: he was full of
jests, and gipes, and knaveries, and mocks; I
have forgot his name.

*Gow.* Sir John Falstaff.

*Flu.* That is he:—I can tell you there is goot
men porn at Monmouth.

*Gow.* Here comes his majesty.

*Alarum. Enter* KING HENRY, *with a part of the* English Forces; WARWICK, GLOSTER, EXETER, *and others.*

*K. Hen.* I was not angry since I came to France
Until this instant.—Take a trumpet, herald;
Ride thou unto the horsemen on yond hill:
If they will fight with us, bid them come down,
Or void the field; they do offend our sight:
If they'll do neither, we will come to them,
And make them skirr away as swift as stones
Enforced from the old Assyrian slings:
Besides, we'll cut the throats of those we have;
And not a man of them that we shall take
Shall taste our mercy:—go and tell them so.
*Exe.* Here comes the herald of the French,
my liege.
*Glo.* His eyes are humbler than they us'd
to be.

### Enter MONTJOY.

*K. Hen.* How now! what means this, herald?
know'st thou not
That I have fin'd these bones of mine for
ransom?
Com'st thou again for ransom?
*Mont.*                                   No, great king:
I come to thee for charitable license,
That we may wander o'er this bloody field
To book our dead, and then to bury them;
To sort our nobles from our common men;
For many of our princes,—woe the while!—
Lie drown'd and soak'd in mercenary blood;—
So do our vulgar drench their peasant limbs
In blood of princes;—and their wounded steeds
Fret fetlock deep in gore, and with wild rage
Yerk out their armed heels at their dead masters,
Killing them twice. O, give us leave, great king,
To view the field in safety, and dispose
Of their dead bodies!
*K. Hen.*                    I tell thee truly, herald,
I know not if the day be ours or no;
For yet a many of your horsemen peer
And gallop o'er the field.
*Mont.*                    The day is yours.
*K. Hen.* Praised be God, and not our
strength, for it!—
What is this castle call'd that stands hard by?
*Mont.* They call it Agincourt.
*K. Hen.* Then call we this the field of Agincourt,
Fought on the day of Crispin Crispianus.
*Flu.* Your grandfather of famous memory,
an't please your majesty, and your great-uncle
Edward the Plack Prince of Wales, as I have
read in the chronicles, fought a most prave
pattle here in France.
*K. Hen.* They did, Fluellen.
*Flu.* Your majesty says very true: if your
majesties is remembered of it, the Welshmen
did goot service in a garden where leeks did
grow, wearing leeks in their Monmouth caps;

which, your majesty knows, to this hour is an
honourable padge of the service; and I do pelieve your majesty takes no scorn to wear the
leek upon Saint Tavy's day.
*K. Hen.* I wear it for a memorable honour;
For I am Welsh, you know, good countryman.
*Flu.* All the water in Wye cannot wash your
majesty's Welsh plood out of your pody, I can
tell you that: Got pless it and preserve it as
long as it pleases his grace and his majesty too!
*K. Hen.* Thanks, good my countryman.
*Flu.* By Chesu, I am your majesty's countryman, I care not who know it; I will confess
it to all the 'orld: I need not be ashamed of your
majesty, praised be Got, so long as your majesty is an honest man.
*K. Hen.* God keep me so!—Our heralds go
with him:
Bring me just notice of the numbers dead
On both our parts.—Call yonder fellow hither.
                [*Points to* WILL. *Exeunt* MONT. *and others.*
*Exe.* Soldier, you must come to the king.
*K. Hen.* Soldier, why wearest thou that
glove in thy cap?
*Will.* An't please your majesty, 'tis the gage
of one that I should fight withal, if he be alive.
*K. Hen.* An Englishman?
*Will.* An't please your majesty, a rascal that
swaggered with me last night; who, if alive and
ever dare to challenge this glove, I have sworn
to take him a box o' the ear: or if I can see my
glove in his cap,—which he swore, as he was a
soldier, he would wear if alive,—I will strike it
out soundly.
*K. Hen.* What think you, Captain Fluellen?
is it fit this soldier keep his oath?
*Flu.* He is craven and a villain else, an't
please your majesty, in my conscience.
*K. Hen.* It may be his enemy is a gentleman
of great sort, quite from the answer of his degree.
*Flu.* Though he be as goot a gentleman as
the tevil is, as Lucifer and Belzebub himself, it
is necessary, look your grace, that he keep his
vow and his oath: if he be perjured, see you
now, his reputation is as arrant a villain and a
Jack sauce as ever his plack shoe trod upon
Got's ground and his earth, in my conscience, la.
*K. Hen.* Then keep thy vow, sirrah, when
thou meetest the fellow.
*Will.* So I will, my liege, as I live.
*K. Hen.* Who servest thou under?
*Will.* Under Captain Gower, my liege.
*Flu.* Gower is a goot captain, and is goot
knowledge and literatured in the wars.
*K. Hen.* Call him hither to me, soldier.
*Will.* I will, my liege.            [*Exit.*
*K. Hen.* Here, Fluellen; wear thou this favour for me, and stick it in thy cap: when
Alençon and myself were down together I
pluck'd this glove from his helm: if any man
challenge this, he is a friend to Alençon and an
enemy to our person; if thou encounter any
such, apprehend him, and thou dost love me.

*Flu.* Your grace does me as great honours as can be desired in the hearts of his subjects: I would fain see the man that has but two legs that shall find himself aggriefed at this glove, that is all; but I would fain see it once, and please Got of his grace that I might see it.

*K. Hen.* Knowest thou Gower?

*Flu.* He is my dear friend, and please you.

*K. Hen.* Pray thee, go seek him, and bring him to my tent.

*Flu.* I will fetch him.                    [*Exit.*

*K. Hen.* My Lord of Warwick and my
　　brother Gloster,
Follow Fluellen closely at the heels:
The glove which I have given him for a favour
May haply purchase him a box o' the ear;
It is the soldier's; I, by bargain, should
Wear it myself. Follow, good cousin Warwick:
If that the soldier strike him,—as I judge
By his blunt bearing he will keep his word,—
Some sudden mischief may arise of it;
For I do know Fluellen valiant,
And, touch'd with choler, hot as gunpowder,
And quickly will return an injury:
Follow, and see there be no harm between
　　them.—
Go you with me, uncle of Exeter.    [*Exeunt.*

SCENE VIII.—*Before* KING HENRY's *Pavillion.*

*Enter* GOWER *and* WILLIAMS.

*Will.* I warrant it is to knight you, captain.

*Enter* FLUELLEN.

*Flu.* Got's will and his pleasure, captain, I peseech you now, come apace to the king: there is more goot toward his peradventure than is in your knowledge to dream of.

*Will.* Sir, know you this glove?

*Flu.* Know the glove! I know the glove is a glove.

*Will.* I know this; and thus I challenge it.
　　　　　　　　　　　　　　　[*Strikes him.*

*Flu.* 'Sblood, an arrant traitor as any's in the universal 'orld, or in France, or in England!

*Gow.* How now, sir! you villain!

*Will.* Do you think I'll be forsworn?

*Flu.* Stand away, Captain Gower; I will give treason his payment into plows, I warrant you.

*Will.* I am no traitor.

*Flu.* That's a lie in thy throat.—I charge you in his majesty's name, apprehend him: he's a friend of the Duke Alençon's.

*Enter* WARWICK *and* GLOSTER.

*War.* How now, how now! what's the matter?

*Flu.* My Lord of Warwick, here is,—praised be Got for it!—a most contagious treason come to light, look you, as you shall desire in a summer's day.—Here is his majesty.

*Enter* KING HENRY *and* EXETER.

*K. Hen.* How now! what's the matter?

*Flu.* My liege, here is a villain and a traitor, that, look your grace, has struck the glove which your majesty is take out of the helmet of Alençon.

*Will.* My liege, this was my glove; here is the fellow of it; and he that I gave it to in change promised to wear it in his cap: I promised to strike him if he did: I met this man with my glove in his cap, and I have been as good as my word.

*Flu.* Your majesty hear now,—saving your majesty's manhood,—what an arrant, rascally, beggarly, lousy knave it is: I hope your majesty is pear me testimony and witness, and will avouchment, this is the glove of Alençon that your majesty is give me, in your conscience, now.

*K. Hen.* Give me thy glove, soldier: look, here is the fellow of it.
'Twas I, indeed, thou promisedst to strike;
And thou hast given me most bitter terms.

*Flu.* An please your majesty, let his neck answer for it if there is any martial law in the 'orld.

*K. Hen.* How canst thou make me satisfaction?

*Will.* All offences, my liege, come from the heart: never came any from mine that might offend your majesty.

*K. Hen.* It was ourself thou didst abuse.

*Will.* Your majesty came not like yourself: you appeared to me but as a common man; witness the night, your garments, your lowliness; and what your highness suffered under that shape I beseech you take it for your own fault, and not mine: for had you been as I took you for, I made no offence; therefore, I beseech your highness, pardon me.

*K. Hen.* Here, uncle Exeter, fill this glove
　　with crowns,
And give it to this fellow.—Keep it, fellow;
And wear it for an honour in thy cap
Till I do challenge it.—Give him the crowns:—
And, captain, you must needs be friends with
　　him.

*Flu.* By this day and this light, the fellow has mettle enough in his pelly:—hold, there is twelve pence for you; and I pray you to serve Got, and keep you out of prawls, and prabbles, and quarrels, and dissensions, and, I warrant you, it is the petter for you.

*Will.* I will none of your money.

*Flu.* It is with a goot will; I can tell you it will serve you to mend your shoes: come, wherefore should you be so pashful? your shoes is not so goot: 'tis a goot silling, I warrant you, or I will change it.

*Enter an* English Herald.

*K. Hen.* Now, herald,—are the dead number'd?

*Her.* Here is the number of the slaughter'd French.                    [*Delivers a paper.*

*K. Hen.* What prisoners of good sort are taken, uncle?

*Exe.* Charles Duke of Orleans, nephew to the king;
John Duke of Bourbon, and Lord Bouciqualt:
Of other lords and barons, knights and squires,
Full fifteen hundred, besides common men.

*K. Hen.* This note doth tell me of ten thousand French
That in the field lie slain: of princes, in this number,
And nobles bearing banners, there lie dead
One hundred twenty-six: added to these,
Of knights, esquires, and gallant gentlemen,
Eight thousand and four hundred; of the which
Five hundred were but yesterday dubb'd knights:
So that, in these ten thousand they have lost,
There are but sixteen hundred mercenaries;
The rest are princes, barons, lords, knights, squires,
And gentlemen of blood and quality.
The names of those their nobles that lie dead,—
Charles De-la-bret, high-constable of France;
Jaques of Chatillon, admiral of France;
The master of the cross-bows, Lord Rambures;
Great-master of France, the brave Sir Guischard Dauphin;
John Duke of Alençon; Antony Duke of Brabant,
The brother to the Duke of Burgundy;
And Edward Duke of Bar: of lusty earls,
Grandpree and Roussi, Fauconberg and Foix,
Beaumont and Marle, Vaudemont and Lestrale.
Here was a royal fellowship of death!—
Where is the number of our English dead?
              [Herald *presents another paper.*
Edward the Duke of York, the Earl of Suffolk,
Sir Richard Ketly, Davy Gam, esquire:
None else of name; and of all other men
But five-and-twenty.—O God, thy arm was here;
And not to us, but to thy arm alone,
Ascribe we all!—When, without stratagem,
But in plain shock and even play of battle,
Was ever known so great and little loss
On one part and on the other?—Take it, God,
For it is none but thine!

*Exe.*          'Tis wonderful!

*K. Hen.* Come, go we in procession to the village:
And be it death proclaimed through our host
To boast of this, or take that praise from God
Which is his only.

*Flu.* Is it not lawful, an please your majesty,
to tell how many is killed?

*K. Hen.* Yes, captain; but with this acknowledgment,
That God fought for us.

*Flu.* Yes, my conscience, he did us great goot.

*K. Hen.* Do we all holy rites:
Let there be sung *Non nobis* and *Te Deum;*
The dead with charity enclos'd in clay:
We'll then to Calais; and to England then;
Where ne'er from France arriv'd more happy men.          [*Exeunt.*

*Enter* Chorus.

*Chor.* Vouchsafe to those that have not read the story,
That I may prompt them: and of such as have,
I humbly pray them to admit the excuse
Of time, of numbers, and due course of things,
Which cannot in their huge and proper life
Be here presented. Now we bear the king
Toward Calais: grant him there; there seen,
Heave him away upon your winged thoughts
Athwart the sea. Behold, the English beach
Pales in the flood with men, with wives, and boys,
Whose shouts and claps out-voice the deep-mouth'd sea,
Which, like a mighty whiffler, 'fore the king
Seems to prepare his way: so let him land;
And solemnly see him set on to London.
So swift a pace hath thought that even now
You may imagine him upon Blackheath;
Where that his lords desire him to have borne
His bruised helmet and his bended sword
Before him through the city: he forbids it,
Being free from vainness and self-glorious pride;
Giving full trophy, signal, and ostent,
Quite from himself to God. But now behold,
In the quick forge and working-house of thought,
How London doth pour out her citizens!
The mayor and all his brethren, in best sort,—
Like to the senators of the antique Rome,
With the plebeians swarming at their heels,—
Go forth, and fetch their conquering Cæsar in:
As, by a lower but by loving likelihood,
Were now the general of our gracious empress,—
As in good time he may,—from Ireland coming,
Bringing rebellion broached on his sword,
How many would the peaceful city quit
To welcome him! much more, and much more cause,
Did they this Harry. Now in London place him;—
As yet the lamentation of the French
Invites the King of England's stay at home;
The emperor's coming in behalf of France,
To order peace between them;—and omit
All the occurrences, whatever chanc'd,
Till Harry's back-return again to France:
There must we bring him; and myself have play'd
The interim, by remembering you 'tis past.
Then brook abridgment; and your eyes advance,
After your thoughts, straight back again to France.          [*Exit.*

## ACT V.

SCENE I.—FRANCE. *An English Court of Guard.*

*Enter* FLUELLEN *and* GOWER.

*Gow.* Nay, that's right; but why wear you your leek to-day? Saint Davy's day is past.

*Flu.* There is occasions and causes why and wherefore in all things: I will tell you, as my friend, Captain Gower:—the rascally, scald, peggarly, lousy, pragging knave, Pistol,—which you and yourself, and all the 'orld, know to be no petter than a fellow, look you now, of no merits,—he is come to me, and prings me pread and salt yesterday, look you, and pid me eat my leek: it was in a place where I could not preed no contention with him; but I will be so pold as to wear it in my cap till I see him once again, and then I will tell him a little piece of my desires.

*Gow.* Why, here he comes, swelling like a turkey-cock.

*Flu.* 'Tis no matter for his swellings nor his turkey-cocks.

### Enter PISTOL.

Got pless you, Auncient Pistol! you scurvy, lousy knave, Got pless you!

*Pist.* Ha! art thou bedlam? dost thou thirst, base Trojan,
To have me fold up Parca's fatal web?
Hence! I am qualmish at the smell of leek.

*Flu.* I peseech you heartily, scurvy, lousy knave, at my desires, and my requests, and my petitions, to eat, look you, this leek: because, look you, you do not love it, nor your affections, and your appetites, and your digestions, does not agree with it, I would desire you to eat it.

*Pist.* Not for Cadwallader and all his goats.

*Flu.* There is one goat for you. [*Strikes him.*] Will you be so goot, scald knave, as eat it?

*Pist.* Base Trojan, thou shalt die.

*Flu.* You say very true, scald knave,—when Got's will is: I will desire you to live in the meantime and eat your victuals: come, there is sauce for it. [*Striking him again.*] You called me yesterday mountain-squire; but I will make you to-day a squire of low degree. I pray you, fall to: if you can mock a leek you can eat a leek.

*Gow.* Enough, captain: you have astonished him.

*Flu.* I say, I will make him eat some part of my leek, or I will peat his pate four days.— Pite, I pray you; it is goot for your green wound and your ploody coxcomb.

*Pist.* Must I bite?

*Flu.* Yes, certainly, and out of doubt, and out of question too, and ambiguities.

*Pist.* By this leek, I will most horribly revenge: I eat, and eke, I swear—

*Flu.* Eat, I pray you: will you have some more sauce to your leek? there is not enough leek to swear by.

*Pist.* Quiet thy cudgel; thou dost see I eat.

*Flu.* Much goot do you, scald knave, heartily. Nay, pray you, throw none away; the skin is goot for your proken coxcomb. When you take occasions to see leeks hereafter, I pray you, mock at 'em; that is all.

*Pist.* Good.

*Flu.* Ay, leeks is goot:—hold you, there is a groat to heal your pate.

*Pist.* Me a groat!

*Flu.* Yes, verily and in truth, you shall take it; or I have another leek in my pocket which you shall eat.

*Pist.* I take thy groat in earnest of revenge.

*Flu.* If I owe you anything I will pay you in cudgels: you shall be a woodmonger, and buy nothing of me but cudgels. God b' wi' you, and keep you, and heal your pate.    [*Exit.*

*Pist.* All hell shall stir for this.

*Gow.* Go, go; you are a counterfeit cowardly knave. Will you mock at an ancient tradition,—begun upon an honourable respect, and worn as a memorable trophy of predeceased valour,—and dare not avouch in your deeds any of your words? I have seen you gleeking and galling at this gentleman twice or thrice. You thought, because he could not speak English in the native garb, he could not therefore handle an English cudgel: you find it otherwise; and henceforth let a Welsh correction teach you a good English condition. Fare ye well.    [*Exit.*

*Pist.* Doth Fortune play the huswife with me now?
News have I that my Nell is dead i' the spital
Of malady of France;
And there my rendezvous is quite cut off.
Old I do wax; and from my weary limbs
Honour is cudgell'd. Well, bawd will I turn,
And something lean to cutpurse of quick hand.
To England will I steal, and there I'll steal:
And patches will I get unto these scars,
And swear I got them in the Gallia wars. [*Exit.*

### SCENE II.—TROYES *in Champagne.*
### *An Apartment in the* FRENCH KING'S *Palace.*

*Enter at one door,* KING HENRY, BEDFORD, GLOSTER, EXETER, WARWICK, WESTMORELAND, *and other* Lords; *at another, the* FRENCH KING, QUEEN ISABEL, *the* PRINCESS KATHARINE, Lords, Ladies, &c., *the* DUKE OF BURGUNDY, *and his* Train.

*K. Hen.* Peace to this meeting, wherefore we are met!
Unto our brother France, and to our sister,
Health and fair time of day;—joy and good wishes
To our most fair and princely cousin Katharine;—
And,—as a branch and member of this royalty,
By whom this great assembly is contriv'd,—
We do salute you, Duke of Burgundy;—
And, princes French, and peers, health to you all!

*Fr. King.* Right joyous are we to behold your face,
Most worthy brother England; fairly met:—
So are you, princes English, every one.

*Q. Isa.* So happy be the issue, brother England,
Of this good day and of this gracious meeting

As we are now glad to behold your eyes;
Your eyes, which hitherto have borne in them
Against the French, that met them in their bent,
The fatal balls of murdering basilisks:
The venom of such looks, we fairly hope,
Have lost their quality; and that this day
Shall change all griefs and quarrels into love.

*K. Hen.* To cry amen to that, thus we appear.

*Q. Isa.* You English princes all, I do salute
  you.

*Bur.* My duty to you both, on equal love.
Great Kings of France and England! That I
  have labour'd                              [ours,
With all my wits, my pains, and strong endeav-
To bring your most imperial majesties
Unto this bar and royal interview,
Your mightiness on both parts best can witness.
Since then my office hath so far prevail'd
That face to face and royal eye to eye
You have congreeted, let it not disgrace me
If I demand, before this royal view,
What rub or what impediment there is
Why that the naked, poor, and mangled Peace,
Dear nurse of arts, plenties, and joyful births,
Should not, in this best garden of the world,
Our fertile France, put up her lovely visage?
Alas, she hath from France too long been chas'd!
And all her husbandry doth lie on heaps,
Corrupting in its own fertility.
Her vine, the merry cheerer of the heart,
Unpruned dies; her hedges even-pleach'd,
Like prisoners wildly overgrown with hair,
Put forth disorder'd twigs; her fallow leas
The darnel, hemlock, and rank fumitory
Doth root upon, while that the coulter rusts,
That should deracinate such savagery;
The even mead, that erst brought sweetly forth
The freckled cowslip, burnet, and green clover,
Wanting the scythe, all uncorrected, rank,
Conceives by idleness, and nothing teems
But hateful docks, rough thistles, kecksies, burs,
Losing both beauty and utility.
And as our vineyards, fallows, meads, and
  hedges,
Defective in their natures, grow to wildness,
Even so our houses and ourselves and children
Have lost, or do not learn for want of time,
The sciences that should become our country;
But grow, like savages,—as soldiers will,
That nothing do but meditate on blood,—
To swearing and stern looks, diffus'd attire,
And everything that seems unnatural.
Which to reduce into our former favour
You are assembl'd: and my speech entreats
That I may know the let why gentle Peace
Should not expel these inconveniences,
And bless us with her former qualities.

*K. Hen.* If, Duke of Burgundy, you would
  the peace
Whose want gives growth to the imperfections
Which you have cited, you must buy that peace
With full accord to all our just demands;
Whose tenors and particular effects
You have, enschedul'd briefly, in your hands.

*Bur.* The king hath heard them; to the
  which as yet
There is no answer made.

*K. Hen.*                    Well, then, the peace
Which you before so urg'd lies in his answer.

*Fr. King.* I have but with a cursory eye
O'erglanc'd the articles: pleaseth your grace
To appoint some of your council presently
To sit with us once more, with better heed
To re-survey them, we will suddenly
Pass our accept and peremptory answer.

*K. Hen.* Brother, we shall.—Go, uncle
  Exeter,—
And brother Clarence,—and you, brother
  Gloster,—
Warwick,—and Huntington,—go with the king;
And take with you free power to ratify,
Augment, or alter, as your wisdoms best
Shall see advantageable for our dignity,
Anything in or out of our demands;
And we'll consign thereto.—Will you, fair sister,
Go with the princes or stay here with us?

*Q. Isa.* Our gracious brother, I will go with
  them;
Haply a woman's voice may do some good
When articles too nicely urg'd be stood on.

*K. Hen.* Yet leave our cousin Katharine
  here with us:
She is our capital demand, compris'd
Within the fore-rank of our articles.

*Q. Isa.* She hath good leave.

    [*Exeunt all but* K. HEN., KATH., *and* ALICE.

*K. Hen.*          Fair Katharine, and most fair
Will you vouchsafe to teach a soldier terms
Such as will enter at a lady's ear,
And plead his love-suit to her gentle heart?

*Kath.* Your majesty shall mock at me; I
cannot speak your England.

*K. Hen.* O fair Katharine, if you will love
me soundly with your French heart, I will be
glad to hear you confess it brokenly with your
English tongue. Do you like me, Kate?

*Kath.* Pardonnez-moi, I cannot tell vat is
like me.

*K. Hen.* An angel is like you, Kate, and
you are like an angel.

*Kath.* Que dit-il? que je suis semblable à les
anges?

*Alice.* Oui, vraiment, sauf votre grace, ainsi
dit-il.

*K. Hen.* I said so, dear Katharine; and I
must not blush to affirm it.

*Kath.* O bon Dieu! les langues des hommes
sont pleines de tromperies.

*K. Hen.* What says she, fair one? that the
tongues of men are full of deceits?

*Alice.* Oui, dat de tongues of de mans is be
full of deceits,—dat is de princess.

*K. Hen.* The princess is the better English-
woman. I' faith, Kate, my wooing is fit for thy
understanding: I am glad thou canst speak no
better English; for if thou couldst, thou wouldst
find me such a plain king that thou wouldst
think I had sold my farm to buy my crown. I

know no ways to mince it in love, but directly to say I love you: then, if you urge me further than to say, Do you in faith? I wear out my suit. Give me your answer; i' faith, do; and so clap hands and a bargain: how say you, lady?

*Kath.* Sauf *votre honneur,* me understand vell.

*K. Hen.* Marry, if you would put me to verses or to dance for your sake, Kate, why you undid me: for the one I have neither words nor measure, and for the other I have no strength in measure, yet a reasonable measure in strength. If I could win a lady at leap-frog, or by vaulting into my saddle with my armour on my back, under the correction of bragging be it spoken, I should quickly leap into a wife. Or if I might buffet for my love, or bound my horse for her favours, I could lay on like a butcher, and sit like a jack-an-apes, never off. But, before God, Kate, I cannot look greenly, nor gasp out my eloquence, nor I have no cunning in protestation; only downright oaths, which I never use till urged, nor never break for urging. If thou canst love a fellow of this temper, Kate, whose face is not worth sunburning, that never looks in his glass for love of anything he sees there, let thine eye be thy cook. I speak to thee plain soldier: if thou canst love me for this, take me; if not, to say to thee that I shall die is true,—but for thy love, by the Lord, no; yet I love thee too. And while thou livest, dear Kate, take a fellow of plain and uncoined constancy; for he perforce must do thee right, because he hath not the gift to woo in other places: for these fellows of infinite tongue, that can rhyme themselves into ladies' favours, they do always reason themselves out again. What! a speaker is but a prater; a rhyme is but a ballad. A good leg will fall; a straight back will stoop; a black beard will turn white; a curled pate will grow bald; a fair face will wither; a full eye will wax hollow: but a good heart, Kate, is the sun and the moon; or, rather, the sun, and not the moon,—for it shines bright and never changes, but keeps his course truly. If thou would have such a one, take me: and take me, take a soldier; take a soldier, take a king: and what sayest thou, then, to my love? speak, my fair, and fairly, I pray thee.

*Kath.* Is it possible dat I should love de enemy of France?

*K. Hen.* No; it is not possible you should love the enemy of France, Kate: but in loving me you should love the friend of France; for I love France so well that I will not part with a village of it; I will have it all mine: and, Kate, when France is mine and I am yours, then yours is France and you are mine.

*Kath.* I cannot tell vat is dat.

*K. Hen.* No, Kate? I will tell thee in French; which I am sure will hang upon my tongue like a new-married wife about her husband's neck, hardly to be shook off. *Quand j'ai la possession de France, et quand vous avez la possession de moi,*—let me see, what then? Saint Denis be my speed!—*donc votre est France et vous êtes mienne.* It is as easy for me, Kate, to conquer the kingdom as to speak so much more French: I shall never move thee in French, unless it be to laugh at me.

*Kath.* Sauf *votre honneur, le Français que vous parlez est meilleur que l'Anglais lequel je parle.*

*K. Hen.* No, faith, is't not, Kate: but thy speaking of my tongue, and I thine, most truly falsely, must needs be granted to be much at one. But, Kate, dost thou understand thus much English,—Canst thou love me?

*Kath.* I cannot tell.

*K. Hen.* Can any of your neighbours tell, Kate? I'll ask them. Come, I know thou lovest me: and at night, when you come into your closet, you'll question this gentlewoman about me; and I know, Kate, you will to her dispraise those parts in me that you love with your heart: but, good Kate, mock me mercifully; the rather, gentle princess, because I love thee cruelly. If ever thou be'st mine, Kate,—as I have a saving faith within me tells me thou shalt,—I get thee with scambling, and thou must therefore needs prove a good soldier-breeder: shall not thou and I, between Saint Denis and Saint George, compound a boy, half French, half English, that shall go to Constantinople and take the Turk by the beard? shall we not? what sayest thou, my fair flower-de-luce?

*Kath.* I do not know dat.

*K. Hen.* No; 'tis hereafter to know, but now to promise; do but now promise, Kate, you will endeavour for your French part of such a boy; and for my English moiety take the word of a king and a bachelor. How answer you, *la plus belle Katharine du monde, mon très chère et divine déesse?*

*Kath.* Your *majesté* ave *fausse* French enough to deceive de most *sage damoiselle* dat is *en France.*

*K. Hen.* Now, fie upon my false French! By mine honour, in true English, I love thee, Kate: by which honour I dare not swear thou lovest me; yet my blood begins to flatter me that thou dost, notwithstanding the poor and untempering effect of my visage. Now, beshrew my father's ambition! he was thinking of civil wars when he got me; therefore was I created with a stubborn outside, with an aspect of iron, that when I come to woo ladies I fright them. But, in faith, Kate, the elder I wax the better I shall appear: my comfort is that old age, that ill layer-up of beauty, can do no more spoil upon my face: thou hast me, if thou hast me, at the worst; and thou shalt wear me, if thou wear me, better and better:—and therefore tell me, most fair Katharine, will you have me? Put off your maiden blushes; avouch the thoughts of your heart with the looks of an empress; take me by the hand and say,—Harry of

England', I am thine: which word thou shalt no sooner bless mine ear withal but I will tell thee aloud, England is thine, Ireland is thine, France is thine, and Henry Plantagenet is thine; who, though I speak it before his face, if he be not fellow with the best king, thou shalt find the best king of good fellows. Come, your answer in broken music,—for thy voice is music and thy English broken; therefore, queen of all, Katharine, break thy mind to me in broken English,—wilt thou have me?

*Kath.* Dat is as it sall please de *roi mon père.*

*K. Hen.* Nay, it will please him well, Kate, —it shall please him, Kate.

*Kath.* Den it sall also content me.

*K. Hen.* Upon that I kiss your hand, and I call you my queen.

*Kath. Laissez, mon seigneur, laissez, laissez: ma foi, je ne veux point que vous abaissez votre grandeur en baisant la main d'une votre indigne serviteur; excusez-moi, je vous supplie, mon très puissant seigneur.*

*K. Hen.* Then I will kiss your lips, Kate.

*Kath. Les dames et demoiselles pour être baisées devant leur noces, il n'est pas le coutume de France.*

*K. Hen.* Madam, my intrepreter, what says she?

*Alice.* Dat it is not be de fashion *pour les* ladies of France,—I cannot tell vat is *baiser en* Anglish.

*K. Hen.* To kiss.

*Alice.* Your majesty *entendre* bettre *que moi.*

*K. Hen.* It is not a fashion for the maids in France to kiss before they are married, would she say?

*Alice. Oui, vraiment.*

*K. Hen.* O Kate, nice customs court'sy to great kings. Dear Kate, you and I cannot be confined within the weak list of a country's fashion: we are the makers of manners, Kate; and the liberty that follows our places stops the mouth of all find-faults,—as I will do yours for upholding the nice fashion of your country in denying me a kiss: therefore, patiently and yielding. [*Kissing her.*] You have witchcraft in your lips, Kate: there is more eloquence in a sugar touch of them than in the tongues of the French council; and they should sooner persuade Harry of England than a general petition of monarchs.—Here comes your father.

*Enter the* FRENCH KING *and* QUEEN, BUR-GUNDY, BEDFORD, GLOSTER, EXETER, WAR-WICK, WESTMORELAND, *and other* French *and* English Lords.

*Bur.* God save your majesty! my royal cousin,
Teach you our princess English?

*K. Hen.* I would have her learn, my fair cousin, how perfectly I love her; and that is good English.

*Bur.* Is she not apt?

*K. Hen.* Our tongue is rough, coz, and my condition is not smooth; so that, having neither the voice nor the heart of flattery about me, I cannot so conjure up the spirit of love in her that he will appear in his true likeness.

*Bur.* Pardon the frankness of my mirth if I answer you for that. If you would conjure in her you must make a circle; if conjure up love in her in his true likeness, he must appear naked and blind. Can you blame her, then, being a maid yet rosed-over with the virgin crimson of modesty, if she deny the appearance of a naked blind boy in her naked seeing self? It were, my lord, a hard condition for a maid to consign to.

*K. Hen.* Yet they do wink and yield; as love is blind and enforces.

*Bur.* They are then excused, my lord, when they see not what they do.

*K. Hen.* Then, good my lord, teach your cousin to consent winking.

*Bur.* I will wink on her to consent, my lord, if you will teach her to know my meaning: for maids well summered and warm kept are like flies at Bartholomew-tide, blind, though they have their eyes; and then they will endure handling, which before would not abide looking on.

*K. Hen.* This moral ties me over to time and a hot summer; and so I shall catch the fly, your cousin, in the latter end, and she must be blind too.

*Bur.* As love is, my lord, before it loves.

*K. Hen.* It is so: and you may, some of you, thank love for my blindness, who cannot see many a fair French city for one fair French maid that stands in my way.

*Fr. King.* Yes, my lord, you see them perspectively, the cities turned into a maid; for they are all girdled with maiden walls that war hath never entered.

*K. Hen.* Shall Kate be my wife?

*Fr. King.* So please you.

*K. Hen.* I am content; so the maiden cities you talk of may wait on her: so the maid that stood in the way of my wish shall show me the way to my will.

*Fr. King.* We have consented to all terms of reason.

*K. Hen.* Is't so, my lords of England?

*West.* The king hath granted every article:—
His daughter first; and, in sequel, all,
According to their firm proposed natures.

*Exe.* Only, he hath not yet subscribed this: —Where your majesty demands that the King of France, having any occasion to write for matter of grant, shall name your highness in this form and with this addition, in French,— *Notre très cher fils Henry, roi d'Angleterre, héritier de France;* and thus in Latin, *Præclarissimus filius noster Henricus, rex Angliæ et hæres Franciæ.*　　　　　　　　　　[denied

*Fr. King.* Nor this I have not, brother, so But your request shall make me let it pass.

*K. Hen.* I pray you, then, in love and dear alliance,

Let that one article rank with the rest;
And thereupon give me your daughter.
   *Fr. King.* Take her, fair son; and from her
    blood raise up
Issue to me; that the contending kingdoms
Of France and England, whose very shores
   look pale
With envy of each other's happiness,
May cease their hatred; and this dear conjunc-
   tion
Plant neighbourhood and Christian-like accord
In their sweet bosoms, that never war advance
His bleeding sword 'twixt England and fair
   France.
   *All.* Amen!
   *K. Hen.* Now, welcome, Kate:—and bear
me witness all,
That here I kiss her as my sovereign queen.
                      *[Flourish.*
   *Q. Isa.* God, the best maker of all marriages,
Combine your hearts in one, your realms in one!
As man and wife, being two, are one in love,
So be there 'twixt your kingdoms such a spousal
That never may ill office or fell jealousy,
Which troubles oft the bed of blessed marriage,
Thrust in between the paction of these king-
   doms,
To make divorce of their incorporate league;
That English may as French, French English-
   men,

Receive each other!—God speak this Amen!
   *All.* Amen!
   *K. Hen.* Prepare we for our marriage:—on
   which day,
My Lord of Burgundy, we'll take your oath,
And all the peers', for surety of our leagues.
Then shall I swear to Kate, and you to me;
And may our oaths well kept and prosperous
   be!                 *[Exeunt.*

        *Enter* Chorus.

   *Chor.* Thus far, with rough and all-unable pen,
   Our bending author hath pursu'd the story;
In little room confining mighty men,   [glory.
   Mangling by starts the full course of their
Small time, but, in that small, most greatly
   liv'd
   This star of England: Fortune made his
   sword;
By which the world's best garden he achiev'd,
   And of it left his son imperial lord.
Henry the Sixth, in infant bands crown'd king
   Of France and England, did this king suc-
   ceed;
Whose state so many had the managing
   That they lost France and made his England
   bleed:                [sake
Which oft our stage hath shown; and, for their
In your fair minds let this acceptance take.
                          *[Exit.*

# KING HENRY VI.
## PART I.

Act II. Sc. 3.

# KING HENRY VI.

## FIRST PART

### DRAMATIS PERSONÆ

KING HENRY THE SIXTH.

DUKE OF GLOSTER, *Uncle to the* KING, *and Protector.*

DUKE OF BEDFORD, *Uncle to the* KING, *and Regent of France.*

THOMAS BEAUFORT, *Duke of Exeter, Great-Uncle to the* KING.

HENRY BEAUFORT, *Great-Uncle to the* KING, *Bishop of Winchester, and afterwards Cardinal.*

JOHN BEAUFORT, *Earl of Somerset, afterwards Duke.*

RICHARD PLANTAGENET, *Eldest son of* RICHARD, *late Earl of Cambridge, afterwards Duke of York.*

EARL OF WARWICK.

EARL OF SALISBURY.

EARL OF SUFFOLK.

LORD TALBOT, *afterwards Earl of Shrewsbury.*

JOHN TALBOT, *his Son.*

EDMUND MORTIMER, *Earl of March.*

MORTIMER'S Keepers.

A Lawyer.

SIR JOHN FASTOLFE.

SIR WILLIAM LUCY.

SIR WILLIAM GLANDSDALE.

SIR THOMAS GARGRAVE.

Mayor of London.

WOODVILLE, *Lieutenant of the Tower.*

VERNON, *of the White-rose or York faction.*

BASSET, *of the Red-rose or Lancaster faction.*

CHARLES, *Dauphin, and afterwards King of France.*

REIGNIER, *Duke of Anjou, and Titular King of Naples.*

DUKE OF BURGUNDY.

DUKE OF ALENCON.

BASTARD OF ORLEANS.

Governor of Paris.

Master-Gunner of Orleans, *and his* Son.

General of the French Forces *in Bordeaux.*

A French Sergeant.

A Porter.

An Old Shepherd, *Father to* JOAN LA PUCELLE.

MARGARET, *Daughter to* REIGNIER, *afterwards married to* KING HENRY.

COUNTESS OF AUVERGNE.

JOAN LA PUCELLE, *commonly called* JOAN OF ARC.

Lords, Warders of the Tower, Heralds, Officers, Soldiers, Messengers, *and several* Attendants *both on the English and French.*

Fiends *appearing to* LA PUCELLE.

SCENE,—*Partly in* ENGLAND, *and partly in* FRANCE.

### ACT I.

#### SCENE I.—*Westminster Abbey.*

*Dead March. Corpse of* KING HENRY THE FIFTH, *in state, is brought in, attended on by the* DUKES OF BEDFORD, GLOSTER, *and* EXETER, *the* EARL OF WARWICK, *the* BISHOP OF WINCHESTER, Heralds, &c.

*Bed.* Hung be the heavens with black, yield day to night!
Comets, importing change of times and states,
Brandish your crystal tresses in the sky,
And with them scourge the bad revolting stars
That have consented unto Henry's death!
Henry the Fifth, too famous to live long!
England ne'er lost a king of so much worth.
  *Glo.* England ne'er had a king until his time.
Virtue he had, deserving to command:
His brandish'd sword did blind men with his beams;
His arms spread wider than a dragon's wings;
His sparkling eyes, replete with wrathful fire,
More dazzled and drove back his enemies
Than mid-day sun fierce bent against their faces.
What should I say? his deeds exceed all speech:
He ne'er lift up his hand but conquered.
  *Exe.* We mourn in black: why mourn we not in blood?
Henry is dead, and never shall revive:
Upon a wooden coffin we attend;
And death's dishonourable victory
We with our stately presence glorify,
Like captives bound to a triumphant car.
What! shall we curse the planets of mishap,
That plotted thus our glory's overthrow?
Or shall we think the subtle-witted French
Conjurers and sorcerers, that, afraid of him,
By magic verses have contriv'd his end?
  *Win.* He was a king bless'd of the King of kings,
Unto the French the dreadful judgment-day
So dreadful will not be as was his sight.
The battles of the Lord of hosts he fought:
The church's prayers made him so prosperous.

*Glo.* The church! where is it? Had not
 church-men pray'd,
His thread of life had not so soon decay'd:
None do you like but an effeminate prince,
Whom, like a school-boy, you may overawe.
 *Win.* Gloster, whate'er we like, thou art
 protector,
And lookest to command the prince and realm.
Thy wife is proud; she holdeth thee in awe
More than God or religious churchmen may.
 *Glo.* Name not religion, for thou lov'st the
 flesh;
And ne'er throughout the year to church thou
 go'st,
Except it be to pray against thy foes.
 *Bed.* Cease, cease these jars and rest your
 minds in peace!
Let's to the altar:—heralds, wait on us:—
Instead of gold, we'll offer up our arms;
Since arms avail not, now that Henry's dead.—
Posterity, await for wretched years,
When at their mother's moisten'd eyes babes
 shall suck;
Our isle be made a marish of salt tears,
And none but women left to wail the dead.—
Henry the Fifth! thy ghost I invocate;
Prosper this realm, keep it from civil broils!
Combat with adverse planets in the heavens!
A far more glorious star thy soul will make
Than Julius Cæsar or bright—

   *Enter a Messenger.*

 *Mess.* My honourable lords, health to you all!
Sad tidings bring I to you out of France,
Of loss, of slaughter, and discomfiture:
Guienne, Champaigne, Rheims, Orleans,
Paris, Guysors, Poictiers, are all quite lost.
 *Bed.* What say'st thou, man, before dead
 Henry's corse?
Speak softly; or the loss of those great towns
Will make him burst his lead and rise from
 death.
 *Glo.* Is Paris lost? is Rouen yielded up?
If Henry were recall'd to life again,
These news would cause him once more yield
 the ghost.
 *Exe.* How were they lost? what treachery
 was us'd?
 *Mess.* No treachery but want of men and
 money.
Among the soldiers this is muttered,—
That here you maintain several factions;
And whilst a field should be despatch'd and
 fought,
You are disputing or your generals:
One would have ling'ring wars, with little cost;
Another would fly swift, but wanteth wings;
A third man thinks, without expense at all,
By guileful fair words peace may be obtain'd.
Awake, awake, English nobility!
Let not sloth dim your honours, new-begot:
Cropp'd are the flower-de-luces in your arms;
Of England's coat one half is cut away.
 *Exe.* Were our tears wanting to this funeral,

These tidings would call forth her flowing tides.
 *Bed.* Me they concern; regent I am of
 France.—
Give me my steeled coat! I'll fight for France.—
Away with these disgraceful wailing robes!
Wounds will I lend the French, instead of eyes,
To weep their intermissive miseries.

   *Enter a second Messenger.*

 *2 Mess.* Lords, view these letters, full of bad
 mischance.
France is revolted from the English quite,
Except some petty towns of no import:
The Dauphin Charles is crowned king in
 Rheims;
The Bastard of Orleans with him is join'd;
Reignier, Duke of Anjou, doth take his part;
The Duke of Alençon flieth to his side.
 *Exe.* The Dauphin crowned king! all fly to
 him!
O, whither shall we fly from this reproach?
 *Glo.* We will not fly, but to our enemies'
 throats:—
Bedford, if thou be slack I'll fight it out.
 *Bed.* Gloster, why doubt'st thou of my for-
 wardness?
An army have I muster'd in my thoughts,
Wherewith already France is overrun.

   *Enter a third Messenger.*

 *3 Mess.* My gracious lords,—to add to your
 laments,   [hearse,—
Wherewith you now bedew King Henry's
I must inform you of a dismal fight
Betwixt the stout Lord Talbot and the French.
 *Win.* What! wherein Talbot overcame? is't
 so?    [o'erthrown:
 *3 Mess.* O, no; wherein Lord Talbot was
The circumstance I'll tell you more at large.
The tenth of August last this dreadful lord,
Retiring from the siege of Orleans,
Having full scarce six thousand in his troop,
By three-and-twenty thousand of the French
Was round encompassed and set upon.
No leisure had he to enrank his men;
He wanted pikes to set before his archers;
Instead whereof, sharp stakes, pluck'd out of
 hedges,
They pitched in the ground confusedly,
To keep the horsemen off from breaking in.
More than three hours the fight continued;
Where valiant Talbot, above human thought,
Enacted wonders with his sword and lance:
Hundreds he sent to hell, and none durst stand
 him;
Here, there, and everywhere, enrag'd he flew:
The French exclaim'd the devil was in arms;
All the whole army stood agaz'd on him:
His soldiers, spying his undaunted spirit,
A Talbot! a Talbot! cried out amain,
And rush'd into the bowels of the battle.
Here had the conquest fully been seal'd up
If Sir John Fastolfe had not play'd the coward:
He, being in the vaward,—plac'd behind,

With purpose to relieve and follow them,—
Cowardly fled, not having struck one stroke.
Hence grew the general wreck and massacre;
Enclosed were they with their enemies:
A base Walloon, to win the Dauphin's grace,
Thrust Talbot with a spear into the back;
Whom all France, with their chief assembled strength,
Durst not presume to look once in the face.

*Bed.* Is Talbot slain? then I will slay myself,
For living idly here in pomp and ease,
Whilst such a worthy leader, wanting aid,
Unto his dastard foemen is betray'd.

*3 Mess.* O no, he lives; but is took prisoner,
And Lord Scales with him, and Lord Hungerford:
Most of the rest slaughter'd or took likewise.

*Bed.* His ransom there is none but I shall pay:
I'll hale the Dauphin headlong from his throne,—
His crown shall be the ransom of my friend;
Four of their lords I'll change for one of ours.—
Farewell, my masters; to my task will I;
Bonfires in France forthwith I am to make,
To keep our great Saint George's feast withal:
Ten thousand soldiers with me I will take,
Whose bloody deeds shall make all Europe quake.

*3 Mess.* So you had need; for Orleans is besieg'd;
The English army is grown weak and faint:
The Earl of Salisbury craveth supply,
And hardly keeps his men from mutiny,
Since they, so few, watch such a multitude.

*Exe.* Remember, lords, your oaths to Henry sworn,
Either to quell the Dauphin utterly,
Or bring him in obedience to your yoke.

*Bed.* I do remember it; and here take my leave,
To go about my preparation.       [*Exit.*

*Glo.* I'll to the Tower, with all the haste I can,
To view the artillery and munition;
And then I will proclaim young Henry king.
                                    [*Exit.*

*Exe.* To Eltham will I, where the young king is,
Being ordain'd his special governor;
And for his safety there I'll best devise. [*Exit.*

*Win.* Each hath his place and function to attend:
I am left out; for me nothing remains.
But long I will not be Jack-out-of-office:
The king from Eltham I intend to steal,
And sit at chiefest stern of public weal.
                    [*Exit. Scene closes.*

SCENE II.—FRANCE, *Before Orleans.*

*Enter* CHARLES, *with his* Forces; ALENCON,
      REIGNIER, *and others.*

*Char.* Mars his true moving, even as in the heavens,

So in the earth, to this day is not known:
Late did he shine upon the English side;
Now we are victors, upon us he smiles.
What towns of any moment but we have?
At pleasure here we lie near Orleans;
Otherwhiles the famish'd English, like pale ghosts,
Faintly besiege us one hour in a month.

*Alen.* They want their porridge and their fat bull-beeves:
Either they must be dieted like mules,
And have their provender tied to their mouths,
Or piteous they will look, like drowned mice.

*Reig.* Let's raise the siege: why live we idly here?
Talbot is taken, whom we wont to fear:
Remaineth none but mad-brain'd Salisbury;
And he may well in fretting spend his gall,—
Nor men nor money hath he to make war.

*Char.* Sound, sound alarum! we will rush on them.
Now for the honour of the forlorn French!—
Him I forgive my death that killeth me,
When he sees me go back one foot or flee.
                                    [*Exeunt.*

*Alarums; excursions; afterwards a retreat. Re-
enter* CHARLES, ALENÇON, REIGNIER, *and
others.*

*Char.* Who ever saw the like? what men have I!—
Dogs! cowards! dastards! I would ne'er have fled
But that they left me midst my enemies.

*Reig.* Salisbury is a desperate homicide;
He fighteth as one weary of his life.
The other lords, like lions wanting food,
Do rush upon us as their hungry prey.

*Alen.* Froissart, a countryman of ours, records,
England all Olivers and Rowlands bred
During the time Edward the Third did reign.
More truly now may this be verified;
For none but Samsons and Goliasses
It sendeth forth to skirmish. One to ten!
Lean raw-bon'd rascals! who would e'er suppose
They had such courage and audacity?

*Char.* Let's leave this town; for they are hair-brain'd slaves,
And hunger will enforce them to be more eager:
Of old I know them; rather with their teeth
The walls they'll tear down than forsake the siege.

*Reig.* I think, by some odd gimmers or device,
Their arms are set, like clocks, still to strike on;
Else ne'er could they hold out so as they do.
By my consent, we'll even let them alone.

*Alen.* Be it so.

*Enter the* BASTARD OF ORLEANS.

*Bast.* Where's the Prince Dauphin? I have news for him.

*Char.* Bastard of Orleans, thrice welcome to us.

*Bast.* Methinks your looks are sad, your cheer appall'd:
Hath the late overthrow wrought this offence?
Be not dismay'd, for succour is at hand:
A holy maid hither with me I bring,
Which, by a vision sent to her from heaven,
Ordained is to raise this tedious siege,
And drive the English forth the bounds of France.
The spirit of deep prophecy she hath,
Exceeding the nine sibyls of old Rome:
What's past and what's to come she can descry.
Speak, shall I call her in? Believe my words,
For they are certain and infallible.

*Char.* Go, call her in. [*Exit* BASTARD.] But first, to try her skill,
Reignier, stand thou as Dauphin in my place:
Question her proudly; let thy looks be stern:
By this means shall we sound what skill she hath.                    [*Retires.*

*Re-enter the* BASTARD OF ORLEANS, *with* LA PUCELLE.

*Reig.* Fair maid, is't thou wilt do these wondrous feats?

*Puc.* Reignier, is't thou that thinkest to beguile me?—                    [hind;
Where is the Dauphin?—Come, come from behind;
I know thee well, though never seen before.
Be not amaz'd, there's nothing hid from me:
In private will I talk with thee apart.—
Stand back, you lords, and give us leave awhile.

*Reig.* She takes upon her bravely at first dash.                    [daughter,

*Puc.* Dauphin, I am by birth a shepherd's daughter,
My wit untrain'd in any kind of art.
Heaven and our Lady gracious hath it pleas'd
To shine on my contemptible estate:
Lo, whilst I waited on my tender lambs,
And to sun's parching heat display'd my cheeks,
God's mother deigned to appear to me,
And in a vision full of majesty
Will'd me to leave my base vocation,
And free my country from calamity:
Her aid she promis'd and assur'd success:
In cómplete glory she reveal'd herself;
And whereas I was black and swart before,
With those clear rays which she infus'd on me,
That beauty am I bless'd with which you see.
Ask me what question thou canst possible,
And I will answer unpremeditated:
My courage try by combat if thou dar'st,
And thou shalt find that I exceed my sex.
Resolve on this,—thou shalt be fortunate
If thou receive me for thy warlike mate.

*Char.* Thou hast astonish'd me with thy high terms:
Only this proof I'll of thy valour make,—
In single combat thou shalt buckle with me;
And if thou vanquishest, thy words are true:
Otherwise I renounce all confidence.

*Puc.* I am prepar'd: here is my keen-edg'd sword,
Deck'd with five flower-de-luces on each side;
The which at Touraine, in Saint Katherine's churchyard,
Out of a great deal of old iron I chose forth.

*Char.* Then come, o' God's name; I fear no woman.

*Puc.* And while I live I'll ne'er fly from a man.                    [*They fight.*

*Char.* Stay, stay thy hands! thou art an Amazon,
And fightest with the sword of Deborah.

*Puc.* Christ's mother helps me, else I were too weak.

*Char.* Whoe'er helps thee, 'tis thou that must help me:
Impatiently I burn with thy desire;
My heart and hands thou hast at once subdu'd.
Excellent Pucelle, if thy name be so,
Let me thy servant and not sovereign be:
'Tis the French Dauphin sueth to thee thus.

*Puc.* I must not yield to any rites of love,
For my profession's sacred from above:
When I have chased all thy foes from hence,
Then will I think upon a recompense.

*Char.* Meantime look gracious on thy prostrate thrall.

*Reig.* My lord, methinks, is very long in talk.

*Alen.* Doubtless he shrives this woman to her smock;
Else ne'er could he so long protract his speech.

*Reig.* Shall we disturb him, since he keeps no mean?

*Alen.* He may mean more than we poor men do know:                    [tongues.
These women are shrewd tempters with their tongues.

*Reig.* My lord, where are you? what devise you on?
Shall we give over Orleans, or no?

*Puc.* Why, no, I say, distrustful recreants!
Fight till the last gasp; I will be your guard.

*Char.* What she says I'll confirm: we'll fight it out.

*Puc.* Assign'd am I to be the English scourge.
This night the siege assuredly I'll raise:
Expect Saint Martin's summer, halcyon days,
Since I have entered into these wars.
Glory is like a circle in the water,
Which never ceaseth to enlarge itself,
Till by broad spreading it disperse to naught.
With Henry's death the English circle ends;
Dispersed are the glories it included.
Now am I like that proud insulting ship
Which Cæsar and his fortune bare at once.

*Char.* Was Mahomet inspired with a dove?
Thou with an eagle art inspired, then.
Helen, the mother of great Constantine,
Nor yet Saint Philip's daughters, were like thee.
Bright star of Venus, fall'n down on the earth,
How may I reverently worship thee enough?

*Alen.* Leave off delays, and let us raise the siege.

*Reig.* Woman, do what thou canst to save
  our honours;
Drive them from Orleans, and be immortaliz'd.
*Char.* Presently we'll try:—come, let's away
  about it:—
No prophet will I trust if she prove false.
                                    [*Exeunt.*

SCENE III.—LONDON. *Before the Gates of
  the Tower.*

*Enter the* DUKE OF GLOSTER, *with his*
  Serving-men *in blue coats.*

*Glo.* I am come to survey the Tower this
  day:                            [ance.—
Since Henry's death, I fear, there is convey-
Where be these warders, that they wait not
  here?
Open the gates: Gloster it is that calls.
                          [*Servants knock.*
  1 *Ward.* [*Within.*] Who's there that knocks
    so imperiously?
  1 *Serv.* It is the noble Duke of Gloster.
  2 *Ward.* [*Within.*] Whoe'er he be, you may
    not be let in.                 [tector?
  1 *Serv.* Villains, answer you so the lord pro-
  1 *Ward.* [*Within.*] The Lord protect him!
    so we answer him:
We do no otherwise than we are will'd.
  *Glo.* Who willed you? or whose will stands
    but mine?
There's none protector of the realm but I.—
Break up the gates, I'll be your warrantize:
Shall I be flouted thus by dunghill grooms?
            [GLOSTER'S Servants *rush at the
                      Tower-gates.*
  *Wood.* [*Within.*] What noise is this? what
    traitors have we here?
  *Glo.* Lieutenant, is it you whose voice I hear?
Open the gates; here's Gloster that would
  enter.
  *Wood.* [*Within.*] Have patience, noble Duke;
    I may not come;
The Cardinal of Winchester forbids:
From him I have express commandment
That thou nor none of thine shall be let in.
  *Glo.* Faint-hearted Woodville, prizest him
    'fore me,—
Arrogant Winchester? that haughty prelate
Whom Henry, our late sovereign, ne'er could
  brook?
Thou art no friend to God or to the king:
Open the gates, or I'll shut thee out shortly.
  1 *Serv.* Open the gates unto the lord pro-
    tector,                       [quickly.
Or we'll burst them open if that you come not
        [GLOSTER'S Servants *rush again at the
                  Tower-gates.*

*Enter* WINCHESTER, *with his* Serving-men *in
  tawny coats.*

  *Win.* How now, ambitious Humphry! what
    means this?
  *Glo.* Peel'd priest, dost thou command me
    to be shut out?

*Win.* I do, thou most usurping proditor,
And not protector of the king or realm.
  *Glo.* Stand back, thou manifest conspirator,
Thou that contriv'dst to murder our dead lord;
Thou that giv'st whores indulgences to sin:
I'll canvass thee in thy broad cardinal's hat,
If thou proceed in this thy insolence.
  *Win.* Nay, stand thou back; I will not budge
    a foot:
This be Damascus, be thou cursed Cain,
To slay thy brother Abel, if thou wilt.
  *Glo.* I will not slay thee, but I'll drive thee
    back:
Thy scarlet robes as a child's bearing-cloth
I'll use to carry thee out of this place. .
  *Win.* Do what thou dar'st; I beard thee to
    thy face.                     [face?—
  *Glo.* What! am I dar'd, and bearded to my
Draw, men, for all this privileged place;
Blue-coats to tawny-coats.—Priest, beware
  your beard;
I mean to tug it, and to cuff you soundly:
Under my feet I'll stamp thy cardinal's hat;
In spite of pope or dignities of church,
Here by the cheeks I'll drag thee up and down.
  *Win.* Gloster, thou wilt answer this before
    the pope.                     [rope!—
  *Glo.* Winchester goose! I cry, a rope! a
Now beat them hence, why do you let them
    stay?—
Thee I'll chase hence, thou wolf in sheep's
    array.—
Out, tawny-coats!—Out, scarlet hypocrite!

GLOSTER *and his* Servants *attack the other Party.*
*In the tumult, enter the* Mayor of London *and*
  Officers.

  *May.* Fie, lords! that you, being supreme
    magistrates,
Thus contumeliously should break the peace!
  *Glo.* Peace, mayor! thou know'st little of my
    wrongs:
Here's Beaufort, that regards nor God nor king,
Hath here distrain'd the Tower to his use.
  *Win.* Here's Gloster, too, a foe to citizens;
One that still motions war, and never peace,
O'ercharging your free purses with large fines;
That seeks to overthrow religion,
Because he is protector of the realm;
And would have armour here out of the Tower,
To crown himself king and suppress the prince.
  *Glo.* I will not answer thee with words, but
    blows.          [*Here they skirmish again.*
  *May.* Naught rests for me, in this tumultu-
    ous strife,
But to make open proclamation:—
Come, officer, as loud as e'er thou canst.
  *Off.* [*Reads.*] *All manner of men assembled
here in arms this day against God's peace and
the king's, we charge and command you, in his
highness' name, to repair to your several dwelling-
places; and not to wear, handle, or use any sword,
weapon, or dagger, henceforward, upon pain of
death.*

*Glo.* Cardinal, I'll be no breaker of the law;
But we shall meet and break our minds at large.

*Win.* Gloster, we'll meet, to thy dear cost,
be sure:
Thy heart-blood I will have for this day's work.

*May.* I'll call for clubs if you will not away:—
This cardinal's more haughty than the devil.

*Glo.* Mayor, farewell: thou dost but what
thou mayst.

*Win.* Abominable Gloster! guard thy head;
For I intend to have it ere long.

[*Exeunt severally*, GLO. *and* WIN.,
*with their* Servants.

*May.* See the coast clear'd, and then we will
depart.—
Good God, these nobles should such stomachs
bear!
I myself fight not once in forty year.  [*Exeunt.*

SCENE IV.—FRANCE. *Before Orleans.*

*Enter, on the walls, the* Master-Gunner *and
his* Son.

*M. Gun.* Sirrah, thou know'st how Orleans
is besieg'd,
And how the English have the suburbs won.

*Son.* Father, I know; and oft have shot at
them,
Howe'er, unfortunate, I missed my aim.

*M. Gun.* But now thou shalt not. Be thou
rul'd by me:
Chief master-gunner am I of this town;
Something I must do to procure me grace.
The prince's espials have informed me
How the English, in the suburbs close in-
trench'd,
Wont, through a secret grate of iron bars
In yonder tower, to overpeer the city,
And thence discover how with most advantage
They may vex us with shot or with assault.
To intercept this inconvenience,
A piece of ordnance 'gainst it I have plac'd;
And even these three days have I watch'd if I
Could see them.
Now do thou watch, for I can stay no longer.
If thou spy'st any, run and bring me word;
And thou shalt find me at the governor's.

[*Exit.*

*Son.* Father, I warrant you; take you no
care;
I'll never trouble you if I may spy them.

*Enter, in an upper Chamber of a Tower, the*
LORDS SALISBURY *and* TALBOT, SIR WILLIAM
GLANSDALE, SIR THOMAS GARGRAVE, *and
others.*

*Sal.* Talbot, my life, my joy, again return'd!
How wert thou handled being prisoner?
Or by what means gott'st thou to be releas'd?
Discourse, I pr'ythee, on this turret's top.

*Tal.* The Duke of Bedford had a prisoner
Call'd the brave Lord Ponton de Santrailles;
For him I was exchang'd and ransomed.
But with a baser man of arms by far
Once, in contempt, they would have barter'd
me:
Which I, disdaining, scorn'd; and craved death
Rather than I would be so vile-esteem'd.
In fine, redeem'd I was as I desir'd.
But, O! the treacherous Fastolfe wounds my
heart!
Whom with my bare fists I would execute
If I now had him brought into my power.

*Sal.* Yet tell'st thou not how thou wert entertain'd.

*Tal.* With scoffs, and scorns, and contumeli-
ous taunts.
In open market-place produc'd they me,
To be a public spectacle to all:
Here, said they, is the terror of the French,
The scarecrow that affrights our children so.
Then broke I from the officers that led me,
And with my nails digg'd stones out of the
ground
To hurl at the beholders of my shame:
My grisly countenance made others fly;
None durst come near for fear of sudden death.
In iron walls they deem'd me not secure;
So great fear of my name 'mongst them was
spread
That they suppos'd I could rend bars of steel,
And spurn in pieces posts of adamant:
Wherefore a guard of chosen shot I had,
That walk'd about me every minute-while;
And if I did but stir out of my bed,
Ready they were to shoot me to the heart.

*Sal.* I grieve to hear what torments you en-
dur'd;
But we will be reveng'd sufficiently.
Now it is supper-time in Orleans:
Here, through this grate, I can count each one,
And view the Frenchmen how they fortify:
Let us look in; the sight will much delight
thee.—
Sir Thomas Gargrave and Sir William Glansdale,
Let me have your express opinions
Where is best place to make our battery next.

*Gar.* I think at the north gate; for there
stand lords.

*Glan.* And I here, at the bulwark of the
bridge.

*Tal.* For aught I see, this city must be
famish'd,
Or with light skirmishes enfeebled.

[*Shot from the town.* SAL. *and* SIR
THOMAS GARGRAVE *fall.*

*Sal.* O Lord, have mercy on us, wretched
sinners!

*Gar.* O Lord, have mercy on me, woeful man!

*Tal.* What chance is this that suddenly hath
cross'd us?—
Speak, Salisbury; at least, if thou canst speak:
How far'st thou, mirror of all martial men?
One of thy eyes and thy cheek's side struck
off!—
Accursed tower! accursed fatal hand
That hath contriv'd this woeful tragedy!
In thirteen battles Salisbury o'ercame;

Henry the Fifth he first train'd to the wars;
Whilst any trump did sound or drum struck up,
His sword did ne'er leave striking in the field.—
Yet liv'st thou, Salisbury? though thy speech
    doth fail,
One eye thou hast, to look to heaven for grace:
The sun with one eye vieweth all the world.—
Heaven, be thou gracious to none alive
If Salisbury wants mercy at thy hands!—
Bear hence his body; I will help to bury it.
Sir Thomas Gargrave, hast thou any life?
Speak unto Talbot; nay, look up to him.—
Salisbury, cheer thy spirit with this comfort;
Thou shalt not die whiles—
He beckons with his hand, and smiles on me,
As who should say, *When I am dead and gone,*
*Remember to avenge me on the French.*—
Plantagenet, I will; and like thee, Nero,
Play on the lute, beholding the towns burn:
Wretched shall France be only in my name.
    [*Thunder heard; afterwards an alarum.*
What stir is this? What tumult's in the
    heavens?
Whence cometh this alarum, and the noise?

    *Enter a* Messenger.

*Mess.* My lord, my lord, the French have
    gather'd head:
The Dauphin, with one Joan la Pucelle join'd,—
A holy prophetess new risen up,—
Is come with a great power to raise the siege.
    [Sal. *lifts himself and groans.*
*Tal.* Hear, hear how dying Salisbury doth
    groan!
It irks his heart he cannot be reveng'd.—
Frenchmen, I'll be a Salisbury to you:—
Pucelle or puzzle, dolphin or dogfish,
Your hearts I'll stamp out with my horse's
    heels,
And make a quagmire of your mingled brains.—
Convey me Salisbury into his tent,
And then we'll try what these dastard French-
    men dare.
    [*Exeunt, bearing out the bodies.*

SCENE V.—*The same. Before one of the Gates.*

*Alarum; skirmishings. Enter* TALBOT, *pursu-*
*ing the* DAUPHIN, *drives him in, and exit:*
*then enter* JOAN LA PUCELLE, *driving English-*
*men before her, and exit after them: then re-*
*enter* TALBOT.

*Tal.* Where is my strength, my valour, and
    my force?
Our English troops retire, I cannot stay them;
A woman clad in armour chaseth them.
Here, here she comes.

    *Enter* LA PUCELLE.

I'll have a bout with thee;
Devil or devil's dam, I'll conjure thee:
Blood will I draw on thee,—thou art a witch,—
And straightway give thy soul to him thou
    serv'st.

*Puc.* Come, come, 'tis only I that must dis-
    grace thee.     [*They fight.*
*Tal.* Heavens, can you suffer hell so to pre-
    vail?
My breast I'll burst with straining of my
    courage,
And from my shoulders crack my arms asunder,
But I will chastise this high-minded strumpet.
    [*They fight again.*
*Puc.* [*Retiring.*] Talbot, farewell: thy hour
    is not yet come:
I must go victual Orleans forthwith.
O'ertake me if thou canst; I scorn thy strength.
Go, go, cheer up thy hunger-starved men;
Help Salisbury to make his testament:
This day is ours, as many more shall be.
    [LA PUC. *enters the town with* Soldiers.
*Tal.* My thoughts are whirled like a potter's
    wheel;
I know not where I am nor what I do:
A witch by fear, not force, like Hannibal
Drives back our troops, and conquers as she
    lists:
So bees with smoke and doves with noisome
    stench
Are from their hives and houses driven away.
They call'd us, for our fierceness, English dogs;
Now like to whelps we crying run away.
    [*A short alarum.*
Hark, countrymen! either renew the fight
Or tear the lions out of England's coat;
Renounce your soil, give sheep in lions' stead:
Sheep run not half so timorous from the wolf,
Or horse or oxen from the leopard,
As you fly from your oft-subdued slaves.
    [*Alarum. Another skirmish.*
It will not be:—retire into your trenches:
You all consented unto Salisbury's death,
For none would strike a stroke in his revenge.—
Pucelle is enter'd into Orleans,
In spite of us or aught that we could do.
O, would I were to die with Salisbury!
The shame hereof will make me hide my head!
    [*Alarum. Retreat. Exeunt* TALBOT
    and Forces, &c.

*Flourish. Enter on the walls,* LA PUCELLE,
    CHARLES, REIGNIER, ALENÇON, *and* Soldiers.

*Puc.* Advance our waving colours on the
    walls;
Rescu'd is Orleans from the English:—
Thus Joan la Pucelle hath perform'd her word.
*Char.* Divinest creature, Astræa's daughter,
How shall I honour thee for this success?
Thy promises are like Adonis' gardens,
That one day bloom'd and fruitful were the
    next.—
France, triumph in thy glorious prophetess!—
Recover'd is the town of Orleans:
More blessed hap did ne'er befall our state.
*Reig.* Why ring not out the bells aloud,
    throughout the town?
Dauphin, command the citizens make bonfires,
And feast and banquet in the open streets,

To celebrate the joy that God hath given us.

*Alen.* All France will be replete with mirth and joy
When they shall hear how we have play'd the men.

*Char.* 'Tis Joan, not we, by whom the day is won;
For which I will divide my crown with her;
And all the priests and friars in my realm
Shall in procession sing her endless praise.
A stateli r pyramis to her I'll rear
Than Rhodope's of Memphis ever was:
In memory of 'her when she is dead,
Her ashes, in an urn more precious
Than the rich jewell'd coffer of Darius,
Transported shall be at high festivals
Before the kings and queens of France.
No longer on Saint Denis will we cry,
But Joan la Pucelle shall be France's saint.
Come in, and let us banquet royally,
After this golden day of victory.

[*Flourish. Exeunt.*

## ACT II.

### SCENE I.—*Before Orleans.*

*Enter to the Gate a* French Sergeant *and two* Sentinels.

*Serg.* Sirs, take your places and be vigilant:
If any noise or soldier you perceive
Near to the walls, by some apparent sign
Let us have knowledge at the court of guard.

1 *Sent.* Sergeant, you shall. [*Exit Sergeant.*]
Thus are poor servitors,
When others sleep upon their quiet beds,
Constrain'd to watch in darkness, rain, and cold.

*Enter* TALBOT, BEDFORD, BURGUNDY, *and* Forces, *with scaling-ladders; their drums beating a dead march.*

*Tal.* Lord regent and redoubted Burgundy,—
By whose approach the regions of Artois,
Walloon, and Picardy are friends to us,—
This happy night the Frenchmen are secure,
Having all day carous'd and banqueted:
Embrace we, then, this opportunity,
As fitting best to quittance their deceit,
Contriv'd by art and baleful sorcery.

*Bed.* Coward of France!—how much he wrongs his fame,
Despairing of his own arm's fortitude,
To join with witches and the help of hell.

*Bur.* Traitors have never other company.—
But what's that Pucelle whom they term so pure?

*Tal.* A maid, they say.

*Bed.* A maid! and be so martial!

*Bur.* Pray God she prove not masculine ere long,
If underneath the standard of the French
She carry armour, as she hath begun.

*Tal.* Well, let them practise and converse with spirits:

God is our fortress, in whose conquering name
Let us resolve to scale their flinty bulwarks.

*Bed.* Ascend, brave Talbot; we will follow thee.

*Tal.* Not all together: better far, I guess,
That we do make our entrance several ways;
That, if it chance the one of us do fail,
The other yet may rise against their force.

*Bed.* Agreed: I'll to yon corner.

*Bur.* And I to this.

*Tal.* And here will Talbot mount or make his grave.—
Now, Salisbury, for thee and for the right
Of English Henry, shall this night appear
How much in duty I am bound to both.

[*The* English *scale the walls, crying* St. George! *a* Talbot! *and all enter the Town.*

*Sent.* Arm! arm! the enemy doth make assault!

*The* French *leap over the walls in their shirts.*

*Enter, several ways,* BASTARD, ALENÇON, REIGNIER, *half ready and half unready.*

*Alen.* How now, my lords? what, all unready so?

*Bast.* Unready! ay, and glad we 'scap'd so well.

*Reig.* 'Twas time, I trow, to wake and leave our beds,
Hearing alarums at our chamber-doors.

*Alen.* Of all exploits since first I follow'd arms,
Ne'er heard I of a warlike enterprise
More venturous or desperate than this.

*Bast.* I think this Talbot be a fiend of hell.

*Reig.* If not of hell, the heavens, sure, favour him.

*Alen.* Here cometh Charles: I marvel how he sped.

*Bast.* Tut! holy Joan was his defensive guard.

*Enter* CHARLES *and* LA PUCELLE.

*Char.* Is this thy cunning, thou deceitful dame?
Didst thou at first, to flatter us withal,
Make us partakers of a little gain,
That now our loss might be ten times so much?

*Puc.* Wherefore is Charles impatient with his friend?
At all times will you have my power alike?
Sleeping or waking, must I still prevail,
Or will you blame and lay the fault on me?
Improvident soldiers! had your watch been good
This sudden mischief never could have fall'n.

*Char.* Duke of Alençon, this was your default,
That, being captain of the watch to-night,
Did look no better to that weighty charge.

*Alen.* Had all your quarters been as safely kept
As that whereof I had the government,
We had not been thus shamefully surpris'd.

*Bast.* Mine was secure.

*Reig.* And so was mine, my lord.

*Char.* And, for myself, most part of all this night,
Within her quarter and mine own precinct
I was employ'd in passing to and fro,
About relieving of the sentinels:
Then how or which way should they first break in?     [*case,*
*Puc.* Question, my lords, no further of the
How or which way; 'tis sure they found some place
But weakly guarded, where the breach was made.
And now there rests no other shift but this,—
To gather our soldiers, scatter'd and dispers'd,
And lay new platforms to endamage them.

*Alarum. Enter an* English Soldier, *crying a* Talbot! *a* Talbot! *They fly, leaving their clothes behind.*

*Sold.* I'll be so bold to take what they have left.
The cry of Talbot serves me for a sword;
For I have loaden me with many spoils,
Using no other weapon but his name.    [*Exit.*

SCENE II.—ORLEANS. *Within the Town.*

*Enter* TALBOT, BEDFORD, BURGUNDY,
a Captain, *and others.*

*Bed.* The day begins to break, and night is fled,
Whose pitchy mantle over-veil'd the earth.
Here sound retreat, and cease our hot pursuit.
                 [*Retreat sounded.*
*Tal.* Bring forth the body of old Salisbury,
And here advance it in the market-place,
The middle centre of this cursed town.
Now have I paid my vow unto his soul;
For every drop of blood was drawn from him,
There hath at least five Frenchmen died to-night.
And that hereafter ages may behold
What ruin happen'd in revenge of him,
Within their chiefest temple I'll erect
A tomb, wherein his corpse shall be interr'd:
Upon the which, that every one may read,
Shall be engrav'd the sack of Orleans,
The treacherous manner of his mournful death,
And what a terror he had been to France.
But, lords, in all our bloody massacre,
I muse we meet not with the Dauphin's grace,
His new-come champion, virtuous Joan of Arc,
Nor any of his false confederates.
*Bed.* 'Tis thought, Lord Talbot, when the fight began,
Rous'd on the sudden from their drowsy beds,
They did, amongst the troops of armed men,
Leap o'er the walls for refuge in the field.
*Bur.* Myself,—as far as I could well discern
For smoke and dusky vapours of the night,—
Am sure I scar'd the Dauphin and his trull,
When arm in arm they both came swiftly running,
Like a pair of loving turtle-doves,
That could not live asunder day or night.

After that things are set in order here,
We'll follow them with all the power we have.

*Enter a* Messenger.

*Mess.* All hail, my lords! Which of this princely train
Call ye the warlike Talbot, for his acts
So much applauded through the realm of France?
*Tal.* Here is the Talbot: who would speak with him?     [*Auvergne,*
*Mess.* The virtuous lady, Countess of
With modesty admiring thy renown,    [*safe*
By me entreats, great lord, thou wouldst vouch-
To visit her poor castle where she lies,
That she may boast she hath beheld the man
Whose glory fills the world with loud report.
*Bar.* Is it even so? Nay, then, I see our wars
Will turn unto a peaceful comic sport,
When ladies crave to be encounter'd with.—
You may not, my lord, despise her gentle suit.
*Tal.* Ne'er trust me then; for when a world of men
Could not prevail with all their oratory,
Yet hath a woman's kindness overrul'd:—
And therefore tell her I return great thanks,
And in submission will attend on her.—
Will not your honours bear me company?
*Bed.* No, truly; it is more than manners will:
And I have heard it said, unbidden guests
Are often welcomest when they are gone.
*Tal.* Well then, alone, since there's no remedy,
I mean to prove this lady's courtesy.—
Come hither, captain. [*Whispers.*] You perceive my mind?
*Capt.* I do, my lord, and mean accordingly.
                 [*Exeunt.*

SCENE III.—AUVERGNE. *Court of the Castle.*

*Enter the* COUNTESS *and her* Porter.

*Count.* Porter, remember what I gave in charge;     [*me.*
And when you have done so, bring the keys to
*Port.* Madam, I will.     [*Exit.*
*Count.* The plot is laid: if all things fall out right,
I shall as famous be by this exploit
As Scythian Tomyris by Cyrus' death.
Great is the rumour of this dreadful knight,
And his achievements of no less account:
Fain would mine eyes be witness with mine ears,
To give their censure of these rare reports.

*Enter* Messenger *and* TALBOT.

*Mess.* Madam,
According as your ladyship desir'd,
By message crav'd, so is Lord Talbot come.
*Count.* And he is welcome. What! is this the man?
*Mess.* Madam, it is.
*Count.*         Is this the scourge of France?
Is this the Talbot, so much fear'd abroad

That with his name the mothers still their babes?
I see report is fabulous and false:
I thought I should have seen some Hercules,
A second Hector, for his grim aspect,
And large proportion of his strong-knit limbs.
Alas, this is a child, a silly dwarf!
It cannot be this weak and writhled shrimp
Should strike such terror to his enemies.

*Tal.* Madam, I have been bold to trouble you;
But since your ladyship is not at leisure,
I'll sort some other time to visit you.    [*Going.*

*Count.* What means he now?—Go ask him whither he goes.

*Mess.* Stay, my Lord Talbot; for my lady craves
To know the cause of your abrupt departure.

*Tal.* Marry, for that she's in a wrong belief,
I go to certify her Talbot's here.

*Re-enter* Porter *with keys.*

*Count.* If thou be he, then art thou prisoner.

*Tal.* Prisoner! to whom?

*Count.*    To me, blood-thirsty lord;
And for that cause I train'd thee to my house.
Long time thy shadow hath been thrall to me,
For in my gallery thy picture hangs:
But now the substance shall endure the like;
And I will chain these legs and arms of thine,
That hast by tyranny these many years
Wasted our country, slain our citizens,
And sent our sons and husbands captivate.

*Tal.* Ha, ha, ha!

*Count.* Laughest thou, wretch? thy mirth shall turn to moan.

*Tal.* I laugh to see your ladyship so fond
To think that you have aught but Talbot's shadow
Whereon to practise your severity.

*Count.* Why, art not thou the man?

*Tal.*    I am indeed.

*Count.* Then have I substance too.

*Tal.* No, no, I am but shadow of myself:
You are deceiv'd, my substance is not here;
For what you see is but the smallest part
And least proportion of humanity:
I tell you, madam, were the whole frame here,
It is of such a spacious lofty pitch,
Your roof were not sufficient to contain 't.

*Count.* This is a riddling merchant for the nonce;
He will be here, and yet he is not here:
How can these contrarieties agree?

*Tal.* That will I show you presently.

[*He winds a Horn. Drums heard; then a Peal of Ordnance. The Gates being forced, enter* Soldiers.

How say you, madam? are you now persuaded
That Talbot is but shadow of himself?
These are his substance, sinews, arms, and strength,
With which he yoketh your rebellious necks,
Razeth your cities, and subverts your towns,
And in a moment makes them desolate.

*Count.* Victorious Talbot! pardon my abuse:
I find thou art no less than fame hath bruited,
And more than may be gather'd by thy shape.
Let my presumption not provoke thy wrath;
For I am sorry that with reverence
I did not entertain thee as thou art.

*Tal.* Be not dismay'd, fair lady; nor mis-construe
The mind of Talbot as you did mistake
The outward composition of his body.
What you have done hath not offended me:
No other satisfaction do I crave
But only—with your patience—that we may
Taste of your wine, and see what cates you have;
For soldiers' stomachs always serve them well.

*Count.* With all my heart, and think me honoured
To feast so great a warrior in my house.

[*Exeunt.*

SCENE IV.—LONDON. *The Temple Garden.*

*Enter the* EARLS OF SOMERSET, SUFFOLK, *and* WARWICK; RICHARD PLANTAGENET, VERNON, *and another* Lawyer.

*Plan.* Great lords and gentlemen, what means this silence?
Dare no man answer in a case of truth?

*Suf.* Within the Temple-hall we were too loud;
The garden here is more convenient.    [truth;

*Plan.* Then say at once if I maintain'd the
Or else was wrangling Somerset in the error?

*Suf.* Faith, I have been a truant in the law,
And never yet could frame my will to it;
And therefore frame the law unto my will.

*Som.* Judge you, my lord of Warwick, then, between us.    [higher pitch;

*War.* Between two hawks, which flies the
Between two dogs, which hath the deeper mouth;    [temper;
Between two blades, which bears the better
Between two horses, which doth bear him best;
Between two girls, which hath the merriest eye;—    [ment;
I have, perhaps, some shallow spirit of judg-
But in these nice sharp quillets of the law,
Good faith, I am no wiser than a daw.    [ance:

*Plan.* Tut, tut, here is a mannerly forbear-
The truth appears so naked on my side
That any purblind eye may find it out.

*Som.* And on my side it is so well apparell'd,
So clear, so shining, and so evident,
That it will glimmer through a blind man's eye.

*Plan.* Since you are tongue-tied and so loth to speak,
In dumb significants proclaim your thoughts:
Let him that is a true-born gentleman,
And stands upon the honour of his birth,
If he suppose that I have pleaded truth,
From off this brier pluck a white rose with me.

*Som.* Let him that is no coward nor no flatterer,

But dare maintain the party of the truth,
Pluck a red rose from off this thorn with me.
  *War.* I love no colours; and, without all
    colour
Of base insinuating flattery,
I pluck this white rose with Plantagenet.  [set;
  *Suf.* I pluck this red rose with young Somer-
And say withal, I'think he held the right.
  *Ver.* Stay, lords and gentlemen, and pluck
    no more
Till you conclude that he upon whose side
The fewest roses are cropp'd from the tree
Shall yield the other in the right opinion.
  *Som.* Good Master Vernon, it is well ob-
    jected:
If I have fewest I subscribe in silence.
  *Plan.* And I.
  *Ver.* Then, for the truth and plainness of the
    case,
I pluck this pale and maiden blossom here,
Giving my verdict on the white rose side.
  *Som.* Prick not your finger as you pluck it off,
Lest, bleeding, you do paint the white rose red,
And fall on my side so, against your will.
  *Ver.* If I, my lord, for my opinion bleed,
Opinion shall be surgeon to my hurt,
And keep me on the side where still I am.
  *Som.* Well, well, come on; who else?
  *Law.* Unless my study and my books be false,
The argument you held was wrong in you;
                          [*To* SOMERSET.
In sign whereof I pluck a white rose too.
  *Plan.* Now, Somerset, where is your argu-
    ment?
  *Som.* Here in my scabbard; meditating that
Shall dye your white rose in a bloody red.
  *Plan.* Meantime your cheeks do counterfeit
    our roses;
For pale they look with fear, as witnessing
The truth on our side.
  *Som.*            No, Plantagenet,
'Tis not for fear, but anger that thy cheeks
Blush for pure shame to counterfeit our roses,
And yet thy tongue will not confess thy error.
  *Plan.* Hath not thy rose a canker, Somerset?
  *Som.* Hath not thy rose a thorn, Plantagenet?
  *Plan.* Ay, sharp and piercing, to maintain
    his truth;
Whiles thy consuming canker eats his falsehood.
  *Som.* Well, I'll find friends to wear my
    bleeding roses,
That shall maintain what I have said is true,
Where false Plantagenet dare not be seen.
  *Plan.* Now, by this maiden blossom in my
    hand,
I scorn thee and thy faction, peevish boy.
  *Suf.* Turn not thy scorns this way, Planta-
    genet.
  *Plan.* Proud Poole, I will; and scorn both
    him and thee.
  *Suf.* I'll turn my part thereof into thy throat.
  *Som.* Away, away, good William De-la-
    Poole!
We grace the yeoman by conversing with him.

  *War.* Now, by God's will, thou wrong'st
    him, Somerset;
His grandfather was Lionel Duke of Clarence,
Third son to the third Edward King of England:
Spring crestless yeomen from so deep a root?
  *Plan.* He bears him on the place's privilege,
Or durst not, for his craven heart, say thus.
  *Som.* By him that made me, I'll maintain
    my words
On any plot of ground in Christendom.
Was not thy father, Richard Earl of Cambridge,
For treason executed in our late king's days?
And by his treason stand'st not thou attainted,
Corrupted, and exempt from ancient gentry?
His trespass yet lives guiltv in thy blood;
And till thou be restor'd thou art a yeoman.
  *Plan.* My father was attach'd, not attainted;
Condemn'd to die for treason, but no traitor;
And that I'll prove on better men than Somer-
    set,
Were growing time once ripen'd to my will.
For your partaker Poole, and you yourself,
I'll note you in my book of memory,
To scourge you for this apprehension:
Look to it well, and say you are well warn'd.
  *Som.* Ay, thou shalt find us ready for thee
    still;
And know us by these colours for thy foes,—
For these my friends, in spite of thee, shall
    wear.
  *Plan.* And, by my soul, this pale and angry
    rose,
As cognizance of my blood-drinking hate,
Will I for ever, and my faction, wear,
Until it wither with me to my grave,
Or flourish to the height of my degree.
  *Suf.* Go forward, and be chok'd with thy
    ambition!
And so, farewell, until I meet thee next. [*Exit.*
  *Som.* Have with thee, Poole.—Farewell,
    ambitious Richard.                [*Exit.*
  *Plan.* How I am brav'd, and must perforce
    endure it!                        [house,
  *War.* This blot, that they object against your
Shall be wip'd out in the next Parliament,
Call'd for the truce of Winchester and Gloster:
And if thou be not then created York,
I will not live to be accounted Warwick.
Meantime, in signal of my love to thee,
Against proud Somerset and William Poole,
Will I upon thy party wear this rose:
And here I prophesy,—This brawl to-day,
Grown to this faction, in the Temple-garden,
Shall send, between the red rose and the white,
A thousand souls to death and deadly night.
  *Plan.* Good Master Vernon, I am bound to
    you,
That you on my behalf would pluck a flower.
  *Ver.* In your behalf still will I wear the same.
  *Law.* And so will I.
  *Plan.* Thanks, gentle sir.
Come, let us four to dinner: I dare say
This quarrel will drink blood another day.
                                      [*Exeunt*

SCENE V.—*The same. A Room in the Tower.*

*Enter* MORTIMER, *brought in in a chair by two* Keepers.

*Mor.* Kind keepers of my weak decaying age,
Let dying Mortimer here rest himself.—
Even like a man new-haled from the rack,
So fare my limbs with long imprisonment;
And these gray locks, the pursuivants of death,
Nestor-like aged, in an age of care,
Argue the end of Edmund Mortimer. [spent,—
These eyes,—like lamps whose wasting oil is
Wax dim, as drawing to their exigent: [grief;
Weak shoulders, overborne with burdening
And pithless arms, like to a wither'd vine
That droops his sapless branches to the ground:
Yet are these feet,—whose strengthless stay is
numb,
Unable to support this lump of clay,—
Swift-winged with desire to get a grave,
As witting I no other comfort have.—
But tell me, keeper, will my nephew come?
    1 *Keep.* Richard Plantagenet, my lord, will
come:
We sent unto the Temple, to his chamber;
And answer was return'd that he will come.
    *Mor.* Enough: my soul shall then be satis-
fied.—
Poor gentleman! his wrong doth equal mine.
Since Henry Monmouth first began to reign,—
Before whose glory I was great in arms,—
This loathsome sequestration have I had;
And even since then hath Richard been ob-
scur'd,
Depriv'd of honour and inheritance.
But now the arbitrator of despairs,
Just death, kind umpire of men's miseries,
With sweet enlargement doth dismiss me hence:
I would his troubles likewise were expir'd
That so he might recover what was lost.

*Enter* RICHARD PLANTAGENET.

    1 *Keep.* My lord, your loving nephew now
is come.                                    [come?
    *Mor.* Richard Plantagenet, my friend, is he
    *Plan.* Ay, noble uncle, thus ignobly us'd,
Your nephew, late-despised Richard, comes.
    *Mor.* Direct mine arms I may embrace his
neck,
And in his bosom spend my latter gasp:
O, tell me when my lips do touch his cheeks,
That I may kindly give one fainting kiss.—
And now declare, sweet stem from York's great
stock,
Why didst thou say of late thou wert despis'd?
    *Plan.* First, lean thine aged back against
mine arm;
And, in that ease, I'll tell thee my disease.
This day, in argument upon a case,
Some words there grew 'twixt Somerset and me;
Among which terms he us'd his lavish tongue,
And did upbraid me with my father's death:
Which obloquy set bars before my tongue,
Else with the like I had requited him.

Therefore, good uncle, for my father's sake,
In honour of a true Plantagenet,
And for alliance sake, declare the cause
My father, Earl of Cambridge, lost his head.
    *Mor.* That cause, fair nephew, that impris-
on'd me,
And hath detain'd me all my flowering youth
Within a loathsome dungeon, there to pine,
Was cursed instrument of his decease.
    *Plan.* Discover more at large what cause
that was;
For I am ignorant, and cannot guess.
    *Mor.* I will, if that my fading breath permit,
And death approach not ere my tale be done.
Henry the Fourth, grandfather to this king,
Depos'd his nephew Richard,—Edward's son,
The first-begotten, and the lawful heir
Of Edward king, the third of that descent:
During whose reign the Percies of the north,
Finding his usurpation most unjust,
Endeavour'd my advancement to the throne:
The reason mov'd these warlike lords to this
Was, for that,—young King Richard thus re-
mov'd,
Leaving no heir begotten of his body,—
I was the next by birth and parentage;
For by my mother I derived am
From Lionel Duke of Clarence, the third son
To King Edward the Third; whereas he
From John of Gaunt doth bring his pedigree,
Being but fourth of that heroic line.
But mark: as in this haughty great attempt
They laboured to plant the rightful heir,
I lost my liberty, and they their lives.
Long after this, when Henry the Fifth,
Succeeding his father Bolingbroke, did reign,
Thy father, Earl of Cambridge, then deriv'd
From famous Edmund Langley, Duke of York,
Marrying my sister, that thy mother was,
Again, in pity of my hard distress,
Levied an army, weening to redeem
And have install'd me in the diadem:
But, as the rest, so fell that noble earl,
And was beheaded. Thus the Mortimers,
In whom the title rested, were suppress'd.
    *Plan.* Of which, my lord, your honour is
the last.
    *Mor.* True; and thou see'st that I no issue
have,
And that my fainting words do warrant death:
Thou art my heir; the rest I wish thee gather:
But yet be wary in thy studious care.
    *Plan.* Thy grave admonishments prevail
with me:
But yet methinks my father's execution
Was nothing less than bloody tyranny.
    *Mor.* With silence, nephew, be thou politic;
Strong-fixed is the house of Lancaster,
And, like a mountain, not to be remov'd.
But now thy uncle is removing hence;
As princes do their courts, when they are cloy'd
With long continuance in a settled place.
    *Plan.* O uncle, would some part of my young
years

Might but redeem the passage of your age!

*Mor.* Thou dost then wrong me,—as the slaughterer doth
Which giveth many wounds when one will kill.
Mourn not, except thou sorrow for my good;
Only, give order for my funeral:
And so, farewell; and fair be all thy hopes,
And prosperous be thy life in peace and war!
[*Dies.*

*Plan.* And peace, no war, befall thy parting soul!
In prison hast thou spent a pilgrimage,
And like a hermit overpass'd thy days.—
Well, I will lock his counsel in my breast;
And what I do imagine, let that rest.—
Keepers, convey him hence; and I myself
Will see his burial better than his life.—
[*Exeunt* Keepers, *bearing out the body of* MOR.
Here dies the dusky torch of Mortimer,
Chok'd with ambition of the meaner sort:—
And for those wrongs, those bitter injuries,
Which Somerset hath offer'd to my house,
I doubt not but with honour to redress;
And therefore haste I to the Parliament,
Either to be restored to my blood,
Or make my ill the advantage of my good.
[*Exit.*

## ACT III.

SCENE I.—LONDON. *The Parliament House.*

*Flourish. Enter* KING HENRY, EXETER, GLO-
STER, WARWICK, SOMERSET, *and* SUFFOLK;
*the* BISHOP OF WINCHESTER, RICHARD
PLANTAGENET, *and others.* GLOSTER *offers to
put up a bill;* WINCHESTER *snatches it, and
tears it.*

*Win.* Com'st thou with deep premeditated lines,
With written pamphlets studiously devis'd,
Humphrey of Gloster? if thou canst accuse,
Or aught intend'st to lay unto my charge,
Do it without invention, suddenly:
As I with sudden and extemporal speech
Purpose to answer what thou canst object.

*Glo.* Presumptuous priest! this place com-
mands my patience,
Or thou shouldst find thou hast dishonour'd me.
Think not, although in writing I preferr'd
The manner of thy vile outrageous crimes,
That therefore I have forg'd, or am not able
*Verbatim* to rehearse the method of my pen:
No, prelate; such is thy audacious wickedness,
Thy lewd, pestiferous, and dissentious pranks,
As very infants prattle of thy pride.
Thou art a most pernicious usurer;
Froward by nature, enemy to peace;
Lascivious, wanton, more than well beseems
A man of thy profession and degree;
And for thy treachery, what's more manifest,—
In that thou laid'st a trap to take my life,
As well at London bridge as at the Tower?
Beside, I fear me, if thy thoughts were sifted,
The king, thy sovereign, is not quite exempt
From envious malice of thy swelling heart.

*Win.* Gloster, I do defy thee.—Lords, vouchsafe
To give me hearing what I shall reply.
If I were covetous, ambitious, or perverse,
As he will have me, how am I so poor?
Or how haps it I seek not to advance
Or raise myself, but keep my wonted calling?
And for dissension, who preferreth peace
More than I do,—except I be provok'd?
No, my good lords, it is not that offends;
It is not that that hath incens'd the duke:
It is because no one should sway but he;
No one but he should be about the king;
And that engenders thunder in his breast,
And makes him roar these accusations forth.
But he shall know I am as good—

*Glo.* As good!
Thou bastard of my grandfather!—

*Win.* Ay, lordly sir; for what are you, I pray,
But one imperious in another's throne?

*Glo.* Am I not protector, saucy priest?

*Win.* And am not I a prelate of the church?

*Glo.* Yes, as an outlaw in a castle keeps,
And useth it to patronage his theft.

*Win.* Unreverent Gloster!

*Glo.* Thou art reverent
Touching thy spiritual function, not thy life.

*Win.* Rome shall remedy this.

*War.* Roam thither then.

*Som.* My lord, it were your duty to forbear.

*War.* Ay, see the bishop be not overborne.

*Som.* Methinks my lord should be religious,
And know the office that belongs to such.

*War.* Methinks his lordship should be humbler;
It fitteth not a prelate so to plead. [*near.*

*Som.* Yes, when his holy state is touch'd so

*War.* State holy or unhallow'd, what of that?
Is not his grace protector to the king?

*Plan.* Plantagenet, I see, must hold his tongue,
Lest it be said, *Speak, sirrah, when you should;
Must your bold verdict enter talk with lords?*
Else would I have a fling at Winchester.
[*Aside.*

*K. Hen.* Uncles of Gloster and of Winchester,
The special watchmen of our English weal,
I would prevail, if prayers might prevail,
To join your hearts in love and amity.
O, what a scandal is it to our crown
That two such noble peers as ye should jar!
Believe me, lords, my tender years can tell
Civil dissension is a viperous worm
That gnaws the bowels of the commonwealth.
[*A noise within,* "Down with the tawny coats."
What tumult's this?

*War.* An uproar, I dare warrant,
Begun through malice of the bishop's men!
[*A noise again,* "Stones! Stones!"

*Enter the* Mayor of London, *attended.*

*May.* O, my good lords,—and virtuous Henry,—

Pity the city of London, pity us!
The bishop and the Duke of Gloster's men,
Forbidden late to carry any weapon,
Have fill'd their pockets full of pebble stones,
And, banding themselves in contrary parts,
Do pelt so fast at one another's pate,    [out:
That many have their giddy brains knock'd
Our windows are broke down in every street,
And we, for fear, compell'd to shut our shops.

*Enter, skirmishing, the* Retainers *of* GLOSTER
*and* WINCHESTER, *with bloody pates.*

*K. Hen.* We charge you, on allegiance to
ourself,    [peace.—
To hold your slaught'ring hands, and keep the
Pray, uncle Gloster, mitigate this strife.
*1 Serv.* Nay, if we be
Forbidden stones, we'll fall to it with our teeth.
*2 Serv.* Do what ye dare, we are as resolute.
    [*Skirmish again.*
*Glo.* You of my household, leave this peevish
broil,
And set this unaccustom'd fight aside.    [man
*3 Serv.* My lord, we know your grace to be a
Just and upright; and for your royal birth
Inferior to none but to his majesty:
And ere that we will suffer such a prince,
So kind a father of the commonweal,
To be disgraced by an inkhorn mate,
We, and our wives and children, all will fight,
And have our bodies slaughter'd by thy foes.
*1 Serv.* Ay, and the very parings of our nails
Shall pitch a field when we are dead.
    [*Skirmish again.*
*Glo.*    Stay, stay, I say!
And if you love me, as you say you do,
Let me persuade you to forbear awhile.
*K. Hen.* O, how this discord doth afflict my
soul!—
Can you, my Lord of Winchester, behold
My sighs and tears, and will not once relent?
Who should be pitiful if you be not?
Or who should study to prefer a peace,
If holy churchmen take delight in broils?
*War.* Yield, my lord protector;—yield,
Winchester;—
Except you mean, with obstinate repulse,
To slay your sovereign and destroy the realm.
You see what mischief, and what murder too,
Hath been enacted through your enmity;
Then be at peace, except ye thirst for blood.
*Win.* He shall submit, or I will never yield.
*Glo.* Compassion on the king commands me
stoop;
Or I would see his heart out, ere the priest
Should ever get that privilege of me.
*War.* Behold, my Lord of Winchester, the
duke
Hath banish'd moody discontented fury,
As by his smoothed brows it doth appear:
Why look you still so stern and tragical?
*Glo.* Here, Winchester, I offer thee my hand.
*K. Hen.* Fie, uncle Beaufort! I have heard
you preach

That malice was a great and grievous sin;
And will not you maintain the thing you teach,
But prove a chief offender in the same?
*War.* Sweet king!—the bishop hath a kindly
gird.—
For shame, my Lord of Winchester, relent!
What, shall a child instruct you what to do?
*Win.* Well, Duke of Gloster, I will yield to
thee;
Love for thy love and hand for hand I give.
*Glo.* Ay, but, I fear me, with a hollow heart.—
See here, my friends and loving countrymen;
This token serveth for a flag of truce
Betwixt ourselves and all our followers:
So help me God, as I dissemble not!
*Win.* So help me God, as I intend it not!
    [*Aside.*
*K. Hen.* O loving uncle, kind Duke of
Gloster,
How joyful am I made by this contract!—
Away, my masters! trouble us no more;
But join in friendship, as your lords have done.
*1 Serv.* Content: I'll to the surgeon's.
*2 Serv.*    And so will I.
*3 Serv.* And I will see what physic the tavern
affords. [*Exeunt* Servants, Mayor, *&c.*
*War.* Accept this scroll, most gracious
sovereign;
Which in the right of Richard Plantagenet
We do exhibit to your majesty.
*Glo.* Well urg'd, my Lord of Warwick;—for,
sweet prince,
And if your grace mark every circumstance,
You have great reason to do Richard right;
Especially for those occasions
At Eltham Place I told your majesty.    [force.—
*K. Hen.* And those occasions, uncle, were of
Therefore, my loving lords, our pleasure is
That Richard be restored to his blood.
*War.* Let Richard be restored to his blood;
So shall his father's wrongs be recompens'd.
*Win.* As will the rest, so willeth Winchester.
*K. Hen.* If Richard will be true, not that
alone,
But all the whole inheritance I give
That doth belong unto the house of York,
From whence you spring by lineal descent.
*Plan.* Thy humble servant vows obedience
And humble service till the point of death.
*K. Hen.* Stoop, then, and set your knee
against my foot;
And in reguerdon of that duty done
I girt thee with the valiant sword of York:
Rise, Richard, like a true Plantagenet,
And rise created princely Duke of York.    [fall!
*Plan.* And so thrive Richard as thy foes may
And as my duty springs, so perish they
That grudge one thought against your majesty!
*All.* Welcome, high prince, the mighty Duke
of York!
*Som.* Perish, base prince, ignoble Duke of
York!    [*Aside.*
*Glo.* Now will it best avail your majesty
To cross the seas, and to be crown'd in France:

The presence of a king engenders love
Amongst his subjects and his loyal friends,
As it disanimates his enemies.

*K. Hen.* When Gloster says the word, King
Henry goes;
For friendly counsel cuts off many foes.

*Glo.* Your ships already are in readiness.

[*Flourish. Exeunt all but* EXETER.

*Exe.* Ay, we may march in England or in
France,
Not seeing what is likely to ensue.
This late dissension grown betwixt the peers
Burns under feigned ashes of forg'd love,
And will at last break out into a flame:
As fester'd members rot but by degree,
Till bones and flesh and sinews fall away,
So will this base and envious discord breed.
And now I fear that fatal prophecy
Which in the time of Henry named the Fifth
Was in the mouth of every sucking babe,—
That Henry born at Monmouth should win all,
And Henry born at Windsor should lose all:
Which is so plain that Exeter doth wish
His days may finish ere that hapless time.

[*Exit.*

SCENE II.—FRANCE. *Before Rouen.*

*Enter* LA PUCELLE *disguised, and* Soldiers
*dressed like Countrymen, with sacks upon
their backs.*

*Puc.* These are the city-gates, the gates of
Rouen,
Through which our policy must make a breach:
Take heed, be wary how you place your words;
Talk like the vulgar sort of market-men
That come to gather money for their corn.
If we have entrance,—as I hope we shall,—
And that we find the slothful watch but weak,
I'll by a sign give notice to our friends,
That Charles the Dauphin may encounter
them. [*the city,*

1 *Sold.* Our sacks shall be a mean to sack
And we be lords and rulers over Rouen;
Therefore we'll knock. [*Knocks.*

*Guard.* [*Within.*] *Qui est là?*

*Puc. Paysans, pauvres gens de France,*—
Poor market-folks that come to sell their corn.

*Guard.* [*Opening the gates.*] Enter, go in; the
market-bell is rung.

*Puc.* Now, Rouen, I'll shake thy bulwarks
to the ground.

[LA PUCELLE, &c., *enter the Town.*

*Enter* CHARLES, BASTARD OF ORLEANS,
ALENÇON, *and* Forces.

*Char.* Saint Denis bless this happy stratagem!
And once again we'll sleep secure in Rouen.

*Bast.* Here enter'd Pucelle and her practisants;
Now she is there, how will she specify
Where is the best and safest passage in?

*Alen.* By thrusting out a torch from yonder
tower; [*ing is,—*
Which, once discern'd, shows that her mean-

No way to that, for weakness, which she enter'd.

*Enter* LA PUCELLE, *on a battlement, holding
out a torch burning.*

*Puc.* Behold, this is the happy wedding-torch
That joineth Rouen unto her countrymen,
But burning fatal to the Talbotites.

*Bast.* See, noble Charles, the beacon of our
friend;
The burning torch in yonder turret stands.

*Char.* Now shine it like a comet of revenge,
A prophet to the fall of all our foes!

*Alen.* Defer no time, delays have dangerous
ends;
Enter, and cry *The Dauphine!* presently,
And then do execution on the watch.

[*They enter. Exit* LA PUCELLE *above.*

*Alarum. Enter, from the Town,* TALBOT *and*
English Soldiers.

*Tal.* France, thou shalt rue this treason with
thy tears,
If Talbot but survive thy treachery.—
Pucelle, that witch, that damned sorceress,
Hath wrought this hellish mischief unawares,
That hardly we escap'd the pride of France.

[*Exeunt into the Town.*

*Alarum: excursions. Enter, from the Town,*
BEDFORD, *brought in sick in a chair, with*
TALBOT, BURGUNDY, *and the* English Forces.
*Then enter on the walls* LA PUCELLE,
CHARLES, BASTARD, ALENÇON, *and others.*

*Puc.* Good-morrow, gallants! want ye corn
for bread?
I think the Duke of Burgundy will fast
Before he'll buy again at such a rate:
'Twas full of darnel;—do you like the taste?

*Bur.* Scoff on, vile fiend and shameless cour-
tezan!
I trust ere long to choke thee with thine own,
And make thee curse the harvest of that corn.

*Char.* Your grace may starve, perhaps, before that time. [*treason!*

*Bed.* O let no words, but deeds, revenge this

*Puc.* What will you do, good gray-beard?
break a lance,
And run a tilt at death within a chair? [*spite,*

*Tal.* Foul fiend of France, and hag of all de-
Encompass'd with thy lustful paramours!
Becomes it thee to taunt his valiant age,
And twit with cowardice a man half dead?
Damsel, I'll have a bout with you again,
Or else let Talbot perish with this shame.

*Puc.* Are you so hot, sir?—Yet, Pucelle,
hold thy peace;
If Talbot do but thunder, rain will follow.

[TALBOT *and the rest consult together.*
God speed the parliament! who shall be the
speaker? [*field?*

*Tal.* Dare ye come forth and meet us in the

*Puc.* Belike your lordship takes us then for
fools,

To try if that our own be ours or no.

*Tal.* I speak not to that railing Hecaté,
But unto thee, Alençon, and the rest;
Will ye, like soldiers, come and fight it out?

*Alen.* Signior, no. [France!

*Tal.* Signior, hang!—base muleteers of
Like peasant foot-boys do they keep the walls,
And dare not take up arms like gentlemen.

*Puc.* Away, captains! let's get us from the walls;
For Talbot means no goodness, by his looks.—
God b' wi' you, my lord! we came but to tell you
That we are here.
[*Exeunt* LA PUC., *&c., from the walls.*

*Tal.* And there will we be too, ere it be long,
Or else reproach be Talbot's greatest fame!—
Vow, Burgundy, by honour of thy house,—
Prick'd on by public wrongs sustain'd in France,—
Either to get the town again or die;
And I,—as sure as English Henry lives,
And as his father here was conqueror;
As sure as in this late-betrayed town
Great Cœur-de-lion's heart was buried,—
So sure I swear to get the town or die. [vows.

*Bur.* My vows are equal partners with thy

*Tal.* But ere we go, regard this dying prince,
The valiant Duke of Bedford.—Come, my lord,
We will bestow you in some better place,
Fitter for sickness and for crazy age.

*Bed.* Lord Talbot, do not so dishonour me:
Here will I sit before the walls of Rouen,
And will be partner of your weal or woe.

*Bur.* Courageous Bedford, let us now persuade you. [read

*Bed.* Not to be gone from hence; for once I
That stout Pendragon, in his litter, sick
Came to the field, and vanquished his foes:
Methinks I should revive the soldiers' hearts,
Because I ever found them as myself.

*Tal.* Undaunted spirit in a dying breast!—
Then be it so:—heavens keep old Bedford safe!
And now no more ado, brave Burgundy,
But gather we our forces out of hand,
And set upon our boasting enemy.
[*Exeunt into the Town,* BUR., TAL., *and
Forces, leaving* BED. *and others.*

*Alarum: excursions. Enter* SIR JOHN
FASTOLFE, *and a* Captain.

*Cap.* Whither away, Sir John Fastolfe, in such haste? [flight:

*Fast.* Whither away! to save myself by
We are like to have the overthrow again. [bot?

*Cap.* What! will you fly, and leave Lord Talbot—

*Fast.* Ay,
All the Talbots in the world, to save my life.
[*Exit.*

*Cap.* Cowardly knight! ill fortune follow thee! [*Exit into the Town.*

*Retreat: excursions. Re-enter, from the town,*
LA PUCELLE, ALENÇON, CHARLES, *&c., and
exeunt flying.*

*Bed.* Now, quiet soul, depart when heaven please,
For I have seen our enemies' overthrow.
What is the trust or strength of foolish man?
They that of late were daring with their scoffs
Are glad and fain by flight to save themselves.
[*Dies, and is carried off in his chair.*

*Alarum. Re-enter* TALBOT, BURGUNDY, *and
others.*

*Tal.* Lost and recover'd in a day again!
This is a double honour, Burgundy:
Yet heavens have glory for this victory!

*Bur.* Warlike and martial Talbot, Burgundy
Enshrines thee in his heart; and there erects
Thy noble deeds, as valour's monuments.

*Tal.* Thanks, gentle duke. But where is Pucelle now?
I think her old familiar is asleep:
Now where's the Bastard's braves, and Charles his gleeks? [grief
What, all a-mort? Rouen hangs her head for
That such a valiant company are fled.
Now will we take some order in the town,
Placing therein some expert officers;
And then depart to Paris to the king,
For there young Harry with his nobles lie.

*Bur.* What wills Lord Talbot pleaseth Burgundy.

*Tal.* But yet, before we go, let's not forget
The noble Duke of Bedford, late deceas'd,
But see his exequies fulfill'd in Rouen:
A braver soldier never couched lance,
A gentler heart did never swa in court;
But kings and mightiest potentates must die,
For that's the end of human misery. [*Exeunt.*

SCENE III.—*The Plains near Rouen.*

*Enter* CHARLES, *the* BASTARD, ALENÇON,
LA PUCELLE, *and* Forces.

*Puc.* Dismay not, princes, at this accident,
Nor grieve that Rouen is so recovered:
Care is no cure, but rather corrosive,
For things that are not to be remedied.
Let frantic Talbot triumph for awhile,
And like a peacock sweep along his tail;
We'll pull his plumes and take away his train,
If Dauphin and the rest will be but rul'd.

*Char.* We have been guided by thee hitherto,
And of thy cunning had no diffidence:
One sudden foil shall never breed distrust.

*Bast.* Search out thy wit for secret policies,
And we will make thee famous through the world.

*Alen.* We'll set thy statue in some holy place,
And have thee reverenc'd like a blessed saint:
Employ thee, then, sweet virgin, for our good.

*Puc.* Then thus it must be; this doth Joan devise:
By fair persuasions, mix'd with sugar'd words,
We will entice the Duke of Burgundy
To leave the Talbot and to follow us.

*Char.* Ay, marry, sweeting, if we could do that,

France were no place for Henry's warriors;
Nor should that nation boast it so with us,
But be extirped from our provinces.

*Alen.* For ever should they be expuls'd from France,
And not have title of an earldom here.

*Puc.* Your honours shall perceive how I will work
To bring this matter to the wished end.
　　　　　　　　　　　　　　　　　　　*[Drums heard.*
Hark! by the sound of drum you may perceive
Their powers are marching unto Paris-ward.

*An English March. Enter, and pass over at a distance,* TALBOT *and his* Forces.

There goes the Talbot, with his colours spread,
And all the troops of English after him.

*A French March. Enter the* DUKE OF BURGUNDY *and his* Forces.

Now in the rearward comes the duke and his:
Fortune in favour makes him lag behind.
Summon a parley; we will talk with him.
　　　　　　　　　　　　　　　　　　　*[A parley sounded.*

*Char.* A parley with the Duke of Burgundy!

*Bur.* Who craves a parley with the Burgundy?

*Puc.* The princely Charles of France, thy countryman.

*Bur.* What say'st thou, Charles? for I am marching hence.

*Char.* Speak, Pucelle, and enchant him with thy words.　　　　　　　　　　　*[France!*

*Puc.* Brave Burgundy, undoubted hope of France,
Stay, let thy humble handmaid speak to thee.

*Bur.* Speak on; but be not over-tedious.

*Puc.* Look on thy country, look on fertile France,
And see the cities and the towns defac'd
By wasting ruin of the cruel foe!
As looks the mother on her lovely babe
When death doth close his tender dying eyes,
See, see the pining malady of France;
Behold the wounds, the most unnatural wounds,
Which thou thyself hast given her woeful breast!
O, turn thy edged sword another way;
Strike those that hurt, and hurt not those that help!　　　　　　　　　　　　　*[bosom*
One drop of blood drawn from thy country's
Should grieve thee more than streams of foreign gore:
Return thee, therefore, with a flood of tears,
And wash away thy country's stained spots.

*Bur.* Either she hath bewitch'd me with her words,
Or nature makes me suddenly relent.

*Puc.* Besides, all French and France exclaims on thee,
Doubting thy birth and lawful progeny.
Who join'st thou with but with a lordly nation
That will not trust thee but for profit's sake?
When Talbot hath set footing once in France,
And fashion'd thee that instrument of ill,
Who then but English Henry will be lord.

And thou be thrust out like a fugitive?
Call we to mind,—and mark but this for proof,—
Was not the Duke of Orleans thy foe?
And was he not in England prisoner?
But when they heard he was thine enemy,
They set him free, without his ransom paid,
In spite of Burgundy and all his friends.
See, then, thou fight'st against thy countrymen,
And join'st with them will be thy slaughter-men.
Come, come, return; return, thou wand'ring lord;
Charles and the rest will take thee in their arms.

*Bur.* I am vanquished; these haughty words of hers
Have batter'd me like roaring cannon-shot,
And made me almost yield upon my knees.—
Forgive me, country, and sweet countrymen!
And, lords, accept this hearty kind embrace:
My forces and my power of men are yours:
So, farewell, Talbot; I'll no longer trust thee.

*Puc.* Done like a Frenchman,—turn, and turn again!

*Char.* Welcome, brave duke! thy friendship makes us fresh.　　　　　　　　　　*[breasts.*

*Bast.* And doth beget new courage in our

*Alen.* Pucelle hath bravely play'd her part in this,
And doth deserve a coronet of gold.

*Char.* Now let us on, my lords, and join our powers;
And seek how we may prejudice the foe.
　　　　　　　　　　　　　　　　　　　*[Exeunt.*

SCENE IV.—PARIS. *A Room in the Palace.*

*Enter* KING HENRY, GLOSTER, *and other* Lords, VERNON, BASSET, &c. *To them* TALBOT *and some of his* Officers.

*Tal.* My gracious prince,—and honourable peers,—
Hearing of your arrival in this realm,
I have awhile given truce unto my wars,
To do my duty to my sovereign:
In sign whereof, this arm,—that hath reclaim'd
To your obedience fifty fortresses,
Twelve cities, and seven walled towns of strength,
Beside five hundred prisoners of esteem,—
Lets fall his sword before your highness' feet,
And with submissive loyalty of heart
Ascribes the glory of his conquest got
First to my God and next unto your grace.

*K. Hen.* Is this the Lord Talbot, uncle Gloster,
That hath so long been resident in France?

*Glo.* Yes, if it please your majesty, my liege.

*K. Hen.* Welcome, brave captain and victorious lord!
When I was young,—as yet I am not old,—
I do remember how my father said
A stouter champion never handled sword.
Long since we were resolved of your truth,
Your faithful service, and your toil in war;

Yet never have you tasted our reward,
Or been reguerdon'd with so much as thanks,
Because till now we never saw your face:
Therefore, stand up; and for these good deserts
We here create you Earl of Shrewsbury;
And in our coronation take your place.

[*Exeunt* K. HEN., GLO., TAL., *and* Nobles.

*Ver.* Now, sir, to you, that were so hot at
    sea,
Disgracing of these colours that I wear
In honour of my noble Lord of York,—
Dar'st thou maintain the former words thou
    spak'st?

*Bas.* Yes, sir; as well as you dare patronage
The envious barking of your saucy tongue
Against my lord the Duke of Somerset.

*Ver.* Sirrah, thy lord I honour as he is.

*Bas.* Why, what is he? as good a man as
    York.

*Ver.* Hark ye; not so: in witness, take ye
    that.               [*Strikes him.*

*Bas.* Villain, thou know'st the law of arms
    is such
That whoso draws a sword 'tis present death,
Or else this blow should broach thy dearest
    blood.
But I'll unto his majesty, and crave
I may have liberty to venge this wrong;
When thou shalt see I'll meet thee to thy cost.

*Ver.* Well, miscreant, I'll be there as soon
    as you;
And, after, meet you sooner than you would.
                      [*Exeunt.*

## ACT IV.

### SCENE I.—PARIS. *A Room of State.*

*Enter* KING HENRY, GLOSTER, EXETER, YORK,
SUFFOLK, SOMERSET, WINCHESTER, WAR-
WICK, TALBOT, *the* Governor of Paris, *and*
*others.*

*Glo.* Lord bishop, set the crown upon his
    head.

*Win.* God save King Henry, of that name
    the sixth!

*Glo.* Now, governor of Paris, take your
    oath,—          [Governor *kneels.*
That you elect no other king but him;
Esteem none friends but such as are his friends,
And none your foes but such as shall pretend
Malicious practices against his state:
This shall ye do, so help you righteous God!
          [*Exeunt* GOV. *and his* Train.

### Enter SIR JOHN FASTOLFE.

*Fast.* My gracious sovereign, as I rode from
    Calais,
To haste unto your coronation,
A letter was deliver'd to my hands,
Writ to your grace from the Duke of Burgundy.

*Tal.* Shame to the Duke of Burgundy and
    thee!                    [next,
I vow'd, base knight, when I did meet thee
To tear the garter from thy craven's leg,—
                  [*Plucking it off.*

Which I have done,—because unworthily
Thou wast installed in that high degree.—
Pardon me, princely Henry, and ·the rest:
This dastard, at the battle of Patay,
When but in all I was six thousand strong,
And that the French were almost ten to one,—
Before we met, or that a stroke was given,
Like to a trusty squire, did run away:
In which assault we lost twelve hundred men
Myself, and divers gentlemen beside,
Were there surpris'd and taken prisoners.
Then judge, great lords, if I have done amiss;
Or whether that such cowards ought to wear
This ornament of knighthood, yea or no.

*Glo.* To say the truth, this fact was infamous,
And ill beseeming any common man,
Much more a knight, a captain, and a leader.

*Tal.* When first this order was ordain'd, my
    lords,
Knights of the garter were of noble birth,
Valiant and virtuous, full of haughty courage,
Such as were grown to credit by the wars;
Not fearing death nor shrinking for distress,
But always resolute in most extremes.
He, then, that is not furnish'd in this sort
Doth but usurp the sacred name of knight,
Profaning this most honourable order,
And should,—if I were worthy to be judge,—
Be quite degraded, like a hedge-born swain
That doth presume to boast of gentle blood.

*K. Hen.* Stain to thy countrymen, thou
    hear'st thy doom!
Be packing, therefore, thou that wast a knight:
Henceforth we banish thee, on pain of death.
                [*Exit* FASTOLFE.
And now, my lord protector, view the letter
Sent from our uncle Duke of Burgundy.

*Glo.* What means his grace, that he hath
    chang'd his style?
          [*Viewing the superscription.*
No more but, plain and bluntly, *To the King!*
Hath he forgot he is his sovereign?
Or doth this churlish superscription
Pretend some alteration in good-will?
What's here?—[*Reads.*]—*I have, upon especial*
    *cause,*—
*Mov'd with compassion of my country's wreck,*
*Together with the pitiful complaints*
*Of such as your oppression feeds upon,*—
*Forsaken your pernicious faction,*
*And join'd with Charles, the rightful King of*
    *France.*
O monstrous treachery! Can this be so,—
That in alliance, amity, and oaths,
There should be found such false dissembling
    guile?               [revolt?

*K. Hen.* What! doth my uncle Burgundy

*Glo.* He doth, my lord; and is become your
    foe.               [contain?

*K. Hen.* Is that the worst this letter doth

*Glo.* It is the worst, and all, my lord, he
    writes.

*K. Hen.* Why, then, Lord Talbot there shall
    talk with him,

And give him chastisement for this abuse:—
How say you, my lord, are you not content?

*Tal.* Content, my liege! yes; but that I am
prevented,                          [ploy'd.
I should have begg'd I might have been em-

*K. Hen.* Then gather strength, and march
unto him straight:
Let him perceive how ill we brook his treason,
And what offence it is to flout his friends.

*Tal.* I go, my lord; in heart desiring still
You may behold confusion of your foes.  [*Exit.*

*Enter* VERNON *and* BASSET.

*Ver.* Grant me the combat, gracious sovereign!                               [too!
*Bas.* And me, my lord, grant me the combat

*York.* This is my servant: hear him, noble
prince!                              [him!
*Som.* And this is mine: sweet Henry, favour

*K. Hen.* Be patient, lords; and give them
leave to speak.—
Say, gentlemen, what makes you thus exclaim?
And wherefore crave you combat? or with
whom?

*Ver.* With him, my lord; for he hath done me
wrong.

*Bas.* And I with him; for he hath done me
wrong.

*K. Hen.* What is that wrong whereof you
both complain?
First let me know, and then I'll answer you.

*Bas.* Crossing the sea from England into
France,
This fellow here, with envious carping tongue,
Upbraided me about the rose I wear;
Saying the sanguine colour of the leaves
Did represent my master's blushing cheeks
When stubbornly he did repugn the truth
About a certain question in the law
Argu'd betwixt the Duke of York and him;
With other vile and ignominious terms:
In confutation of which rude reproach,
And in defence of my lord's worthiness,
I crave the benefit of law of arms.

*Ver.* And that is my petition, noble lord:
For though he seem with forged quaint conceit
To set a gloss upon his bold intent,
Yet know, my lord, I was provok'd by him;
And he first took exceptions at this badge,
Pronouncing that the paleness of this flower
Bewray'd the faintness of my master's heart.

*York.* Will not this malice, Somerset, be left?
*Som.* Your private grudge, my Lord of York,
will out,
Though ne'er so cunningly you smother it.

*K. Hen.* Good Lord, what madness rules in
brainsick men,
When for so slight and frivolous a cause
Such factious emulations shall arise!—
Good cousins both, of York and Somerset,
Quiet yourselves, I pray, and be at peace.

*York.* Let this dissension first be tried by
fight,
And then your highness shall command a peace.

*Som.* The quarrel toucheth none but us
alone;
Betwixt ourselves let us decide it them.  [set.
*York.* There is my pledge; accept it, Somer-
*Ver.* Nay, let it rest where it began at first.
*Bas.* Confirm it so, mine honourable lord.
*Glo.* Confirm it so! Confounded be your
strife!
And perish ye, with your audacious prate!
Presumptuous vassals, are you not asham'd
With this immodest clamorous outráge
To trouble and disturb the king and us?—
And you, my lords,—methinks you do not well
To bear with their perverse objections;
Much less to take occasion from their mouths
To raise a mutiny betwixt yourselves:
Let me persuade you take a better course.

*Exe.* It grieves his highness:—good my lords,
be friends.                          [combatants:
*K. Hen.* Come hither, you that would be
Henceforth I charge you, as you love our favour,
Quite to forget this quarrel and the cause.—
And you, my lords, remember where we are;
In France, amongst a fickle wavering nation:
If they perceive dissension in our looks,
And that within ourselves we disagree,
How will their grudging stomachs be provok'd
To wilful disobedience, and rebel!
Beside, what infamy will there arise,
When foreign princes shall be certified
That for a toy, a thing of no regard,
King Henry's peers and chief nobility  [France!
Destroy'd themselves and lost the realm of
O, think upon the conquest of my father;
My tender years; and let us not forego
That for a trifle that was bought with blood!
Let me be umpire in this doubtful strife.
I see no reason, if I wear this rose,
                        [*Putting on a red rose.*
That any one should therefore be suspicious
I more incline to Somerset than York:
Both are my kinsmen, and I love them both:
As well they may upbraid me with my crown,
Because, forsooth, the King of Scots is crown'd.
But your discretions better can persuade
Than I am able to instruct or teach:
And therefore, as we hither came in peace,
So let us still continue peace and love.—
Cousin of York, we institute your grace
To be our regent in these parts of France:—
And, good my Lord of Somerset, unite
Your troops of horsemen with his bands of
foot;
And like true subjects, sons of your progenitors,
Go cheerfully together, and digest
Your angry choler on your enemies.
Ourself, my lord protector, and the rest,
After some respite, will return to Calais;
From thence to England; where I hope ere long
To be presented, by your victories,
With Charles, Alençon, and that traitorous
rout.
            [*Flourish. Exeunt* K. HEN., GLO.,
                SOM., WIN., SUF., *and* BAS.

*War.* My Lord of York, I promise you, the king
Prettily, methought, did play the orator.
*York.* And so he did; but yet I like it not,
In that he wears the badge of Somerset.
*War.* Tush, that was but his fancy, blame him not;                           [harm.
I dare presume, sweet prince, he thought no
*York.* An if I wist he did,—but let it rest;
Other affairs must now be managed.
                    [*Exeunt* YORK, WAR., *and* VER.
*Exe.* Well didst thou, Richard, to suppress thy voice:
For had the passions of thy heart burst out,
I fear we should have seen decipher'd there
More rancorous spite, more furious raging broils,
Than yet can be imagin'd or suppos'd.
But howsoe'er, no simple man that sees
This jarring discord of nobility,
This shouldering of each other in the court,
This factious bandying of their favourites,
But that it doth presage some ill event.
'Tis much when sceptres are in children's hands;
But more when envy breeds unkind division;
There comes the ruin, there begins confusion.
                    [*Exit.*

SCENE II.—FRANCE. *Before Bourdeaux.*

*Enter* TALBOT, *with his* Forces.

*Tal.* Go to the gates of Bourdeaux, trumpeter!
Summon their general unto the wall.

*Trumpet sounds a parley. Enter, on the walls, the*
General of the French Forces, *and others.*

English John Talbot, captains, calls you forth,
Servant in arms to Harry King of England;
And thus he would,—Open your city gates;
Be humble to us; call my sovereign yours,
And do him homage as obedient subjects;
And I'll withdraw me and my bloody power:
But if you frown upon this proffer'd peace
You tempt the fury of my three attendants,
Lean famine, quartering steel, and climbing fire;
Who, in a moment, even with the earth
Shall lay your stately and air-braving towers,
If you forsake the offer of their love.
*Gen.* Thou ominous and fearful owl of death,
Our nation's terror and their bloody scourge!
The period of thy tyranny approacheth.
On us thou canst not enter but by death;
For, I protest, we are well fortified,
And strong enough to issue out and fight:
If thou retire, the Dauphin, well appointed,
Stands with the snares of war to tangle thee:
On either hand thee there are squadrons pitch'd,
To wall thee from the liberty of flight;
And no way canst thou turn thee for redress
But death doth front thee with apparent spoil,
And pale destruction meets thee in the face.
Ten thousand French have ta'en the sacrament,

To rive their dangerous artillery
Upon no Christian soul but English Talbot.
Lo, there thou stand'st, a breathing valiant man,
Of an invincible unconquer'd spirit!
This is the latest glory of thy praise
That I, thy enemy, due thee withal;
For ere the glass that now begins to run
Finish the process of this sandy hour,
These eyes, that see thee now well coloured,
Shall see thee wither'd, bloody, pale, and dead.
                    [*Drum afar off.*
Hark! hark! the Dauphin's drum, a warning bell,
Sings heavy music to thy timorous soul;
And mine shall ring thy dire departure out.
          [*Exeunt* General, *&c. from the Walls.*
*Tal.* He fables not; I hear the enemy:—
Out, some light horsemen, and peruse their wings.—
O, negligent and heedless discipline!
How are we park'd and bounded in a pale,—
A little herd of England's timorous deer,
Maz'd with a yelping kennel of French curs!
If we be English deer, be, then, in blood;
Not rascal-like to fall down with a pinch,
But rather, moody-mad and desperate stags,
Turn on the bloody hounds with heads of steel,
And make the cowards stand aloof at bay:
Sell every man his life as dear as mine,
And they shall find dear deer of us, my friends.—                           [right,
God and Saint George, Talbot and England's
Prosper our colours in this dangerous fight!
                    [*Exeunt.*

SCENE III.—*Plains in Gascony.*

*Enter* YORK, *with* Forces; *to him a* Messenger.

*York.* Are not the speedy scouts return'd again,
That dogg'd the mighty army of the Dauphin?
*Mess.* They are return'd, my lord; and give it out
That he is march'd to Bourdeaux with his power,
To fight with Talbot: as he march'd along,
By your espials were discovered
Two mightier troops than that the Dauphin led,
Which join'd with him, and made their march for Bourdeaux.
*York.* A plague upon that villain Somerset,
That thus delays my promised supply
Of horsemen, that were levied for this siege!
Renowned Talbot doth expect my aid;
And I am louted by a traitor villain,
And cannot help the noble chevalier:
God comfort him in this necessity!
If he miscarry, farewell wars in France.

*Enter* SIR WILLIAM LUCY.

*Lucy.* Thou princely leader of our English strength,
Never so needful on the earth of France,
Spur to the rescue of the noble Talbot,
Who now is girdled with a waist of iron,

And hemm'd about with grim destruction:
To Bourdeaux, warlike duke! to Bourdeaux,
    York!                        [honour.
Else, farewell Talbot, France, and England's
    *York.* O God, that Somerset,—who in proud
heart
Doth stop my cornets,—were in Talbot's place!
So should we save a valiant gentleman
By forfeiting a traitor and a coward.
Mad ire and wrathful fury makes me weep,
That thus we die, while remiss traitors sleep.
    *Lucy.* O, send some succour to the distress'd
    lord!
    *York.* He dies, we lose; I break my warlike
    word;
We mourn, France smiles; we lose, they daily
    get;
All 'long of this vile traitor Somerset.
    *Lucy.* Then God take mercy on brave Tal-
    bot's soul;                  [since
And on his son, young John, who two hours
I met in travel toward his warlike father!
This seven years did not Talbot see his son;
And now they meet where both their lives are
done.
    *York.* Alas, what joy shall noble Talbot have
To bid his young son welcome to his grave?
Away! vexation almost stops my breath,
That sunder'd friends greet in the hour of
    death.—
Lucy, farewell: no more my fortune can,
But curse the cause I cannot aid the man.—
Maine, Blois, Poictiers, and Tours are won
    away,
'Long all of Somerset and his delay.
                  [*Exit,* with Forces.
    *Lucy.* Thus, while the vulture of sedition
Feeds in the bosom of such great commanders,
Sleeping neglection doth betray to loss
The conquest of our scarce-cold conqueror,
That ever-living man of memory,
Henry the Fifth:—whiles they each other cross,
Lives, honours, lands, and all, hurry to loss.
                        [*Exit.*

### SCENE IV.—*Other Plains of Gascony.*

*Enter* SOMERSET, *with his* Forces; *an* Officer
*of* TALBOT'S *with him.*

    *Som.* It is too late; I cannot send them now:
This expedition was by York and Talbot
Too rashly plotted; all our general force
Might with a sally of the very town
Be buckled with: the over-daring Talbot
Hath sullied all his gloss of former honour
By this unheedful, desperate, wild adventure:
York set him on to fight and die in shame.
That, Talbot dead, great York might bear the
    name.
    *Off.* Here is Sir William Lucy, who with me
Set from our o'er-matched forces forth for aid.

### *Enter* SIR WILLIAM LUCY.

    *Som.* How now, Sir William! whither were
you sent?

    *Lucy.* Whither, my lord! from bought and
    sold Lord Talbot;
Who, ring'd about with bold adversity,
Cries out for noble York and Somerset,
To beat assailing death from his weak legions:
And whiles the honourable captain there
Drops bloody sweat from his war-wearied limbs,
And, in advantage lingering, looks for rescue,
You, his false hopes, the trust of England's
    honour,
Keep off aloof with worthless emulation.
Let not your private discord keep away
The levied succours that should lend him aid,
While he, renowned noble gentleman,
Yields up his life unto a world of odds:
Orleans the Bastard, Charles, Burgundy,
Alençon, Reignier, compass him about,
And Talbot perisheth by your default.
    *Som.* York set him on, York should have
    sent him aid.              [claims:
    *Lucy.* And York as fast upon your grace ex-
Swearing that you withhold his levied horse,
Collected for this expedition,     [the horse:
    *Som.* York lies; he might have sent and had
I owe him little duty and less love;
And take foul scorn to fawn on him by sending.
    *Lucy.* The fraud of England, not the force
    of France,
Hath now entrapp'd the noble-minded Talbot:
Never to England shall he bear his life;
But dies betray'd to fortune by your strife.
    *Som.* Come, go; I will despatch the horse-
    men straight:
Within six hours they will be at his aid.
    *Lucy.* Too late comes rescue; he is ta'en or
    slain:
For fly he could not, if he would have fled;
And fly would Talbot never, though he might.
    *Som.* If he be dead, brave Talbot, then,
    adieu!
    *Lucy.* His fame lives in the world, his shame
    in you.                    [*Exeunt.*

### SCENE V.—*The English Camp near Bourdeaux.*

*Enter* TALBOT *and* JOHN *his Son.*

    *Tal.* O young John Talbot! I did send for
    thee
To tutor thee in stratagems of war,
That Talbot's name might be in thee reviv'd
When sapless age and weak unable limbs
Should bring thy father to his drooping chair.
But,—O malignant and ill-boding stars!—
Now thou art come unto a feast of death,
A terrible and unavoided danger:     [horse;
Therefore, dear boy, mount on my swiftest
And I'll direct thee how thou shalt escape
By sudden flight: come, dally not, begone.
    *John.* Is my name Talbot? and am I your
    son?
And shall I fly? O, if you love my mother,
Dishonour not her honourable name,
To make a bastard and a slave of me!
The world will say, he is not Talbot's blood
That basely fled when noble Talbot stood.

*Tal.* Fly to revenge my death, if I be slain.
*John.* He that flies so will ne'er return again.
*Tal.* If we both stay we both are sure to die.
*John.* Then let me stay; and, father, do you fly:
Your loss is great, so your regard should be;
My worth unknown, no loss is known in me.
Upon my death the French can little boast;
In yours they will, in you all hopes are lost.
Flight cannot stain the honour you have won;
But mine it will, that no exploit have done;
You fled for vantage, every one will swear;
But if I bow, they'll say it was for fear,
There is no hope that ever I will stay,
If the first hour I shrink and run away.
Here, on my knee, I beg mortality,
Rather than life preserv'd with infamy.
*Tal.* Shall all thy mother's hopes lie in one tomb?    [womb.
*John.* Ay, rather than I'll shame my mother's
*Tal.* Upon my blessing I command thee go.
*John.* To fight I will, but not to fly the foe.
*Tal.* Part of thy father may be sav'd in thee.
*John.* No part of him but will be shame in me.    [lose it.
*Tal.* Thou never hadst renown, nor canst not
*John.* Yes, your renowned name: shall flight abuse it?
*Tal.* Thy father's charge shall clear thee from that stain.
*John.* You cannot witness for me, being slain.
If death be so apparent, then both fly.
*Tal.* And leave my followers here to fight and die?
My age was never tainted with such shame.
*John.* And shall my youth be guilty of such blame?
No more can I be sever'd from your side
Than can yourself yourself in twain divide:
Stay, go, do what you will, the like do I;
For live I will not if my father die.    [son,
*Tal.* Then here I take my leave of thee, fair
Born to eclipse thy life this afternoon.
Come, side by side together live and die;
And soul with soul from France to heaven fly.
    [*Exeunt.*

SCENE VI.—*A Field of Battle.*

*Alarum: excursions wherein* TALBOT'S Son *is hemmed about, and* TALBOT *rescues him.*

*Tal.* Saint George and victory! fight, soldiers, fight:
The regent hath with Talbot broke his word,
And left us to the rage of France his sword.
Where is John Talbot?—pause, and take thy breath;
I gave thee life and rescu'd thee from death.
*John.* O, twice my father, twice am I thy son!
The life thou gav'st me first was lost and done,
Till with thy warlike sword, despite of fate,
To my determin'd time thou gav'st new date.
*Tal.* When from the Dauphin's crest thy sword struck fire,

It warm'd thy father's heart with proud desire
Of bold-fac'd victory.   Then leaden age,
Quicken'd with youthful spleen and warlike rage,
Beat down Alençon, Orleans, Burgundy,
And from the pride of Gallia rescu'd thee.
The ireful bastard Orleans,—that drew blood
From thee, my boy, and had the maidenhood
Of thy first fight,—I soon encountered,
And, interchanging blows, I quickly shed
Some of his bastard blood; and, in disgrace,
Bespoke him thus,—*Contaminated, base,
And misbegotten blood I spill of thine,
Mean and right poor, for that pure blood of mine
Which thou didst force from Talbot, my brave boy:*—
Here, purposing the Bastard to destroy,
Came in strong rescue.   Speak, thy father's care,—
Art thou not weary, John? how dost thou fare?
Wilt thou yet leave the battle, boy, and fly,
Now thou art seal'd the son of chivalry?
Fly, to revenge my death when I am dead:
The help of one stands me in little stead.
O, too much folly is it, well I wot,
To hazard all our lives in one small boat!
If I to-day die not with Frenchmen's rage,
To-morrow I shall die with mickle age:
By me they nothing gain an if I stay,—
'Tis but the short'ning of my life one day:
In thee thy mother dies, our household's name,
My death's revenge, thy youth, and England's fame:
All these, and more, we hazard by thy stay;
All these are sav'd if thou wilt fly away.
*John.* The sword of Orleans hath not made me smart;    [heart:
These words of yours draw life-blood from my
On that advantage, bought with such a shame,—
To save a paltry life, and slay bright fame,—
Before young Talbot from old Talbot fly,
The coward horse that bears me fall and die!
And like me to the peasant boys of France;
To be shame's scorn, and subject of mischance!
Surely, by all the glory you have won,
An if I fly, I am not Talbot's son:
Then talk no more of flight, it is no boot;
If son to Talbot, die at Talbot's foot.    [Crete,
*Tal.* Then follow thou thy desperate sire of
Thou Icarus; thy life to me is sweet:
If thou wilt fight, fight by thy father's side;
And, commendable prov'd, let's die in pride.
    [*Exeunt.*

SCENE VII.—*Another part of the same.*

*Alarum: excursions. Enter* TALBOT *wounded, supported by a Servant.*

*Tal.* Where is my other life?—mine own is gone;—    [John?—
O, where's young Talbot? where is valiant
Triumphant death, smear'd with captivity,
Young Talbot's valour makes me smile at thee:—

When he perceiv'd me shrink and on my knee,
His bloody sword he brandish'd over me,
And like a hungry lion did commence
Rough deeds of rage and stern impatience;
But when my angry guardant stood alone,
Tendering my ruin, and assail'd of none,
Dizzy-ey'd fury and great rage of heart
Suddenly made him from my side to start
Into the clustering battle of the French;
And in that sea of blood my boy did drench
His overmounting spirit; and there died
My Icarus, my blossom, in his pride.
  *Serv.* O my dear lord! lo where your son is
    borne!

      *Enter* Soldiers, *bearing the body of*
        JOHN TALBOT.

  *Tal.* Thou antic death, which laugh'st us
    here to scorn,
Anon, from thy insulting tyranny,
Coupled in bonds of perpetuity,
Two Talbots, winged through the lither sky,
In thy despite, shall 'scape mortality.—
O thou whose wounds become hard-favour'd
    death,
Speak to thy father ere thou yield thy breath!
Brave death by speaking, whether he will or no;
Imagine him a Frenchman and thy foe.—
Poor boy! he smiles, methinks, as who should
    say,               [to-day.—
Had death been French, then death had died
Come, come, and lay him in his father's arms:
My spirit can no longer bear these harms.
Soldiers, adieu! I have what I would have,
Now my old arms are young Talbot's grave.
                      [*Dies.*

*Alarums. Exeunt* Soldiers *and* Servant, *leaving
   the two bodies. Enter* CHARLES, ALENÇON,
   BURGUNDY, BASTARD, LA PUCELLE, *and*
   Forces.
  *Char.* Had York and Somerset brought
    rescue in,
We should have found a bloody day of this.
  *Bast.* How the young whelp of Talbot's,
    raging-wood,
Did flesh his puny sword in Frenchmen's blood!
  *Puc.* Once I encounter'd him, and thus I
    said,
*Thou maiden youth, be vanquish'd by a maid:*
But, with a proud majestical high scorn,
He answer'd thus, *Young Talbot was not born
To be the pillage of a giglot wench:*
So, rushing in the bowels of the French,
He left me proudly, as unworthy fight.
  *Bur.* Doubtless he would have made a noble
    knight:—
See where he lies inhersed in the arms
Of the most bloody nurser of his harms!
  *Bast.* Hew them to pieces, hack their bones
    asunder,                [der.
Whose life was England's glory, Gallia's won-
  *Char.* O, no; forbear! for that which we
    have fled

During the life, let us not wrong it dead.

    *Enter* SIR WILLIAM LUCY, *attended; a*
        French Herald *preceding.*

  *Lucy.* Herald,
Conduct me to the Dauphin's tent, to know
Who hath obtain'd the glory of the day.
  *Char.* On what submissive message art thou
    sent?
  *Lucy.* Submission, Dauphin! 'tis a mere
    French word;
We English warriors wot not what it means
I come to know what prisoners thou hast ta'en,
And to survey the bodies of the dead.
  *Char.* For prisoners ask'st thou? hell our
    prison is.
But tell me whom thou seek'st.       [field,
  *Lucy.* But where's the great Alcides of the
Valiant Lord Talbot, Earl of Shrewsbury,—
Created, for his rare success in arms,
Great Earl of Washford, Waterford, and Val-
    ence;
Lord Talbot of Goodrig and Urchinfield,
Lord Strange of Blackmere, Lord Verdun of
    Alton,
Lord Cromwell of Wingfield, Lord Furnival of
    Sheffield,
The thrice victorious Lord of Falconbridge;
Knight of the noble order of Saint George,
Worthy Saint Michael, and the Golden Fleece;
Great Marshal to Henry the Sixth
Of all his wars within the realm of France?
  *Puc.* Here is a silly-stately style indeed!
The Turk, that two-and-fifty kingdoms hath,
Writes not so tedious a style as this.—
Him that thou magnifiest with all these titles,
Stinking and fly-blown, lies here at our feet.
  *Lucy.* Is Talbot slain,—the Frenchmen's
    only scourge,
Your kingdom's terror and black Nemesis?
O were mine eye-balls into bullets turn'd,
That I, in rage, might shoot them at your faces!
O that I could but call these dead to life!
It were enough to fright the realm of France:
Were but his picture left among you here,
It would amaze the proudest of you all.
Give me their bodies, that I may bear them
    hence,
And give them burial as beseems their worth.
  *Puc.* I think this upstart is old Talbot's
    ghost,
He speaks with such a proud commanding
    spirit.                 [here,
For God's sake, let him have 'em; to keep them
They would but stink, and putrefy the air.
  *Char.* Go, take their bodies hence.
  *Lucy.*             I'll bear them hence:
But from their ashes shall be rear'd
A phœnix that shall make all France afeard.
  *Char.* So we be rid of them, do with 'em
    what thou wilt.—
And now to Paris in this conquering vein:
All will be ours, now bloody Talbot's slain.
                      [*Exeunt.*

## ACT V.

SCENE I.—LONDON. *A Room in the Palace.*
*Enter* KING HENRY, GLOSTER, *and* EXETER.

*K. Hen.* Have you perus'd the letters from
the pope,
The emperor, and the Earl of Armagnac?
*Glo.* I have, my lord: and their intent is
this,—
They humbly sue unto your excellence
To have a godly peace concluded of
Between the realms of England and of France.
*K. Hen.* How doth your grace affect their
motion?                                    [means
*Glo.* Well, my good lord; and as the only
To stop effusion of our Christian blood,
And stablish quietness on every side.   [thought
*K. Hen.* Ay, marry, uncle; for I always
It was both impious and unnatural
That such immanity and bloody strife
Should reign among professors of one faith.
*Glo.* Beside, my lord, the sooner to effect
And surer bind this knot of amity,
The Earl of Armagnac,—near knit to Charles,
A man of great authority in France,—
Proffers his only daughter to your grace
In marriage, with a large and sumptuous dowry.
*K. Hen.* Marriage, uncle! alas, my years are
young;
And fitter is my study and my books
Than wanton dalliance with a paramour.
Yet, call the ambassadors; and as you please,
So let them have their answers every one:
I shall be well content with any choice
Tends to God's glory and my country's weal.

*Enter a* Legate *and two* Ambassadors, *with*
WINCHESTER, *now* CARDINAL BEAUFORT, *in*
*a Cardinal's habit.*

*Exe.* What! is my Lord of Winchester in-
stall'd,
And call'd unto a cardinal's degree?
Then I perceive that will be verified
Henry the Fifth did sometime prophesy,—
*If once he come to be a cardinal,*
*He'll make his cap co-equal with the crown.*
*K. Hen.* My lords ambassadors, your sev-
eral suits
Have been consider'd and debated on.
Your purpose is both good and reasonable;
And therefore are we certainly resolv'd
To draw conditions of a friendly peace;
Which by my Lord of Winchester we mean
Shall be transported presently to France.
*Glo.* And for the proffer of my lord your
master,
I have inform'd his highness so at large,
As, liking of the lady's virtuous gifts,
Her beauty, and the value of her dower,
He doth intend she shall be England's queen.
*K. Hen.* In argument and proof of which
contract,
Bear her this jewel [*to the* Amb.], pledge of my
affection.
And so, my lord protector, see them guarded
And safely brought to Dover; where, inshipp'd,
Commit them to the fortune of the sea.
          [*Exeunt* K. HEN., GLO., EXE., *and*
                              Ambassadors.
*Win.* Stay, my lord legate: you shall first
receive
The sum of money which I promised
Should be delivered to his holiness
For clothing me in these grave ornaments.
*Leg.* I will attend upon your lordship's
leisure.                                    [*Exit.*
*Win.* Now Winchester will not submit, I
trow,
Or be inferior to the proudest peer.
Humphrey of Gloster, thou shalt well perceive
That neither in birth or for authority
The bishop will be overborne by thee:
I'll either make thee stoop and bend thy knee,
Or sack this country with a mutiny.    [*Exit.*

SCENE II.—FRANCE. *Plains in Anjou.*

*Enter* CHARLES, BURGUNDY, ALENÇON,
LA PUCELLE, *and* Forces, *marching.*

*Char.* These news, my lords, may cheer our
drooping spirits:
'Tis said the stout Parisians do revolt,
And turn again unto the warlike French.
*Alen.* Then march to Paris, royal Charles of
France,
And keep not back your powers in dalliance.
*Puc.* Peace be amongst them if they turn
to us;
Else ruin combat with their palaces!

*Enter a* Messenger.

*Mess.* Success unto our valiant general,
And happiness to his accomplices!
*Char.* What tidings send our scouts? I pr'y-
thee, speak.
*Mess.* The English army, that divided was
Into two parts, is now conjoin'd in one,
And means to give you battle presently.
*Char.* Somewhat too sudden, sirs, the warn-
ing is;
But we will presently provide for them.
*Bur.* I trust the ghost of Talbot is not there:
Now he is gone, my lord, you need not fear.
*Puc.* Of all base passions fear is most ac-
curs'd:—                                    [thine;
Command the conquest, Charles, it shall be
Let Henry fret and all the world repine.
*Char.* Then on, my lords; and France be
fortunate!                                 [*Exeunt.*

SCENE III.—*The same. Before Angiers.*

*Alarums: excursions. Enter* LA PUCELLE.

*Puc.* The regent conquers and the French-
men fly,—
Now help, ye charming spells and periapts;
And ye choice spirits that admonish me,
And give me signs of future accidents,—

You speedy helpers, that are substitutes
Under the lordly monarch of the north,
Appear, and aid me in this enterprise!
                              [*Thunder.*

*Enter* Fiends.

This speedy and quick appearance argues proof
Of your accustom'd diligence to me.
Now, ye familiar spirits that are cull'd
Out of the powerful legions under earth,
Help me this once, that France may get the
          field.   [*They walk about and speak not.*
O, hold me not with silence over-long!
Where I was wont to feed you with my blood
I'll lop a member off and give it you,
In earnest of a further benefit,
So you do condescend to help me now.
                    [*They hang their heads.*
No hope to have redress?—My body shall
Pay recompense if you will grant my suit.
                    [*They shake their heads.*
Cannot my body nor blood sacrifice
Entreat you to your wonted furtherance?
Then take my soul,—my body, soul, and all,
Before that England give the French the foil.
                              [*They depart.*
See! they forsake me. Now the time is come
That France must vail her lofty-plumed crest,
And let her head fall into England's lap.
My ancient incantations are too weak,
And hell too strong for me to buckle with:
Now, France, thy glory droopeth to the dust.
                              [*Exit.*

*Alarums. Enter* French *and* English, *fighting.*
LA PUCELLE *and* YORK *fight hand to hand:*
LA PUCELLE *is taken. The French fly.*

*York.* Damsel of France, I think I have you
          fast:
Unchain your spirits now with spelling charms,
And try if they can gain your liberty.—
A goodly prize, fit for the devil's grace!
See how the ugly witch doth bend her brows,
As if, with Circe, she would change my shape!
*Puc.* Chang'd to a worser shape thou canst
          not be.                    [*man;*
*York.* O, Charles the Dauphin is a proper
No shape but his can please your dainty eye.
*Puc.* A plaguing mischief light on Charles
          and thee!
And may ye both be suddenly surpris'd
By bloody hands, in sleeping on your beds!
*York.* Fell, banning hag; enchantress, hold
          thy tongue!                [*awhile.*
*Puc.* I pr'ythee, give me leave to curse
*York.* Curse, miscreant, when thou comest
          to the stake.                [*Exeunt.*

*Alarums. Enter* SUFFOLK, *leading in* LADY
                  MARGARET.

*Suf.* Be what thou wilt, thou art my pris-
          oner.                    [*Gazes on her.*
O fairest beauty, do not fear nor fly!
For I will touch thee but with reverent hands,

And lay them gently on thy tender side.
I kiss these fingers for eternal peace.
                              [*Kissing her hand.*
Who art thou? say, that I may honour thee.
  *Mar.* Margaret my name, and daughter to
          a king,
The king of Naples—whosoe'er thou art.
  *Suf.* An earl I am, and Suffolk am I call'd.
Be not offended, nature's miracle,
Thou art allotted to be ta'en by me:
So doth the swan her downy cygnets save,
Keeping them prisoners underneath her wings.
Yet, if this servile usage once offend,
Go, and be free again as Suffolk's friend.
                    [*She turns away as going.*
O, stay!—I have no power to let her pass;
My hand would free her, but my heart says no.
As plays the sun upon the glassy streams,
Twinkling another counterfeited beam,
So seems this gorgeous beauty to mine eyes.
Fain would I woo her, yet I dare not speak:
I'll call for pen and ink, and write my mind:
Fie, De-la-Poole! disable not thyself;
Hast not a tongue? is she not here thy prisoner?
Wilt thou be daunted at a woman's sight?
Ay, beauty's princely majesty is such, [*rough*
Confounds the tongue, and makes the senses
  *Mar.* Say, Earl of Suffolk,—if thy name be
          so,—
What ransom must I pay before I pass?
For I perceive I am thy prisoner.       [*suit*
  *Suf.* How canst thou tell she will deny thy
Before thou make a trial of her love?   [*Aside.*
  *Mar.* Why speak'st thou not? what ransom
          must I pay?                [*woo'd.*
  *Suf.* She's beautiful, and therefore to be
She is a woman, therefore to be won.   [*Aside.*
  *Mar.* Wilt thou accept of ransom—yea or no?
  *Suf.* Fond man, remember that thou hast a
          wife;
Then how can Margaret be thy paramour?
                              [*Aside.*
  *Mar.* I were best leave him, for he will not
          hear.
  *Suf.* There all is marr'd; there lies a cooling
          card.                    [*Aside.*
  *Mar.* He talks at random; sure, the man is
          mad.
  *Suf.* And yet a dispensation may be had.
                              [*Aside.*
  *Mar.* And yet I would that you would an-
          swer me.
  *Suf.* I'll win this Lady Margaret. For whom?
Why, for my king: tush, that's a wooden thing!
                              [*Aside.*
  *Mar.* He talks of wood: it is some carpenter.
  *Suf.* Yet so my fancy may be satisfied,
And peace established between these realms.
But there remains a scruple in that too;
For though her father be the King of Naples,
Duke of Anjou and Maine, yet is he poor,
And our nobility will scorn the match. [*Aside.*
  *Mar.* Hear ye, captain,—are ye not at
          leisure?

*Suf.* It shall be so, disdain they ne'er so much:

Henry is youthful, and will quickly yield.— [*Aside.*

Madam, I have a secret to reveal. [*a knight,*

*Mar.* What though I be enthrall'd? he seems And will not any way dishonour me. [*Aside.*

*Suf.* Lady, vouchsafe to listen what I say.

*Mar.* Perhaps I shall be rescued by the French; And then I need not crave his courtesy. [*Aside.*

*Suf.* Sweet madam, give me hearing in a cause—

*Mar.* Tush! women have been captivate ere now. [*Aside.*

*Suf.* Lady, wherefore talk you so?

*Mar.* I cry you mercy, 'tis but *quid* for *quo.*

*Suf.* Say, gentle princess, would you not suppose Your bondage happy, to be made a queen?

*Mar.* To be a queen in bondage is more vile Than is a slave in base servility; For princes should be free.

*Suf.*            And so shall you, If happy England's royal king be free. [*me?*

*Mar.* Why, what concerns his freedom unto

*Suf.* I'll undertake to make thee Henry's queen; To put a golden sceptre in thy hand, And set a precious crown upon thy head, If thou wilt condescend to be my—

*Mar.*            What?

*Suf.*            His love.

*Mar.* I am unworthy to be Henry's wife.

*Suf.* No, gentle madam; I unworthy am To woo so fair a dame to be his wife, And have no portion in the choice myself. How say you, madam,—are you so content?

*Mar.* An if my father please, I am content.

*Suf.* Then call our captains and our colours forth!— [*Troops come forward.* And, madam, at your father's castle-walls We'll crave a parley, to confer with him.

*A Parley sounded. Enter* REIGNIER *on the Walls.*

*Suf.* See, Reignier, see, thy daughter prisoner!

*Reig.* To whom?

*Suf.*            To me.

*Reig.*            Suffolk, what remedy? I am a soldier, and unapt to weep Or to exclaim on fortune's fickleness.

*Suf.* Yes, there is remedy enough, my lord: Consent,—and for thy honour give consent,— Thy daughter shall be wedded to my king; Whom I with pain have woo'd and won thereto; And this her easy-held imprisonment Hath gain'd thy daughter princely liberty.

*Reig.* Speaks Suffolk as he thinks?

*Suf.*            Fair Margaret knows That Suffolk doth not flatter, face, or feign.

*Reig.* Upon thy princely warrant I descend, To give thee answer of thy just demand.

[*Exit* REIGNIER *from the Walls.*

*Suf.* And here I will expect thy coming.

*Trumpets sound. Enter* REIGNER *below.*

*Reig.* Welcome, brave earl, into our territories; Command in Anjou what your honour pleases.

*Suf.* Thanks, Reignier, happy for so sweet a child, Fit to be made companion with a king: What answer makes your grace unto my suit?

*Reig.* Since thou dost deign to woo her little worth To be the princely bride of such a lord, Upon condition I may quietly Enjoy mine own, the county Maine and Anjou Free from oppression or the stroke of war, My daughter shall be Henry's, if he please.

*Suf.* That is her ransom,—I deliver her; And those two counties I will undertake Your grace shall well and quietly enjoy.

*Reig.* And I again, in Henry's royal name, As deputy unto that gracious king, Give thee her hand, for sign of plighted faith.

*Suf.* Reignier of France, I give thee kingly thanks, Because this is in traffic of a king:— And yet, methinks, I could be well content To be mine own attorney in this case.— [*Aside.* I'll over, then, to England with this news, And make this marriage to be solemniz'd. So, farewell, Reignier: set this diamond safe In golden palaces, as it becomes.

*Reig.* I do embrace thee as I would embrace The Christian prince, King Henry, were he here. [*and prayers*

*Mar.* Farewell, my lord: good wishes, praise. Shall Suffolk ever have of Margaret. [*Going*

*Suf.* Farewell, sweet madam: but hark you Margaret,— No princely commendations to my king? [*maid,*

*Mar.* Such commendations as become a A virgin, and his servant, say to him.

*Suf.* Words sweetly plac'd and modestly directed. But, madam, I must trouble you again,— No loving token to his majesty? [*heart,*

*Mar.* Yes, my good lord,—a pure unspotted Never yet taint with love, I send the king.

*Suf.* And this withal. [*Kisses her.*

*Mar.* That for thyself:—I will not so presume To send such peevish tokens to a king.

[*Exeunt* REIG. *and* MAR.

*Suf.* O, wert thou for myself!—But, Suffolk, stay; Thou mayst not wander in that labyrinth: There Minotaurs and ugly treasons lurk. Solicit Henry with her wondrous praise: Bethink thee on her virtues that surmount, And natural graces that extinguish art; Repeat their semblance often on the seas, That when thou com'st to kneel at Henry's feet Thou mayst bereave him of his wits with wonder. [*Exit.*

SCENE IV.—*Camp of the* DUKE OF YORK
*in Anjou.*

*Enter* YORK, WARWICK, *and others.*

*York.* Bring forth that sorceress, condemn'd
to burn.

*Enter* LA PUCELLE, *guarded, and a* Shepherd.

*Shep.* Ah, Joan, this kills thy father's heart
outright!
Have I sought every country far and near,
And now it is my chance to find thee out
Must I behold thy timeless cruel death?
Ah, Joan, sweet daughter Joan, I'll die with
thee!
*Puc.* Decrepit miser! base ignoble wretch!
I am descended of a gentler blood;
Thou art no father nor no friend of mine.
*Shep.* Out, out!—My lords, an please you,
'tis not so;
I did beget her, all the parish knows:
Her mother liveth yet, can testify
She was the first fruit of my bachelorship.
*War.* Graceless, wilt thou deny thy parent-
age?                                    [been,—
*York.* This argues what her kind of life hath
Wicked and vile; and so her death concludes.
*Shep.* Fie, Joan, that thou wilt be so ob-
stacle!
God knows thou art a collop of my flesh;
And for thy sake have I shed many a tear:
Deny me not, I pr'ythee, gentle Joan.
*Puc.* Peasant, avaunt!—You have suborn'd
this man,
Of purpose to obscure my noble birth.
*Shep.* 'Tis true, I gave a noble to the priest
The morn that I was wedded to her mother.—
Kneel down and take my blessing, good my girl.
Wilt thou not stoop? Now cursed be the time
Of thy nativity! I would the milk       [breast
Thy mother gave thee when thou suck'dst her
Had been a little ratsbane for thy sake!
Or else, when thou didst keep my lambs a-field,
I wish some ravenous wolf had eaten thee!
Dost thou deny thy father, cursed drab?
O, burn her, burn her! hanging is too good.
                                    [*Exit.*
*York.* Take her away; for she hath liv'd too
long,
To fill the world with vicious qualities.
*Puc.* First let me tell you whom you have
condemn'd:
Not me begotten of a shepherd swain,
But issu'd from the progeny of kings;
Virtuous and holy; chosen from above,
By inspiration of celestial grace,
To work exceeding miracles on earth.
I never had to do with wicked spirits:
But you,—that are polluted with your lusts,
Stain'd with the guiltless blood of innocents,
Corrupt and tainted with a thousand vices,—
Because you want the grace that others have,
You judge it straight a thing impossible
To compass wonders but by help of devils.

No, misconceived! Joan of Arc hath been
A virgin from her tender infancy,
Chaste and immaculate in very thought;
Whose maiden blood, thus rigorously effus'd,
Will cry for vengeance at the gates of heaven.
*York.* Ay, ay:—away with her to execution!
*War.* And hark ye, sirs; because she is a
maid,
Spare for no fagots, let there be enow:
Place barrels of pitch upon the fatal stake,
That so her torture may be shortened.
*Puc.* Will nothing turn your unrelenting
hearts?
Then, Joan, discover thine infirmity,
That warranteth by law to be thy privilege.—
I am with child, ye bloody homicides:
Murder not, then, the fruit within my womb,
Although ye hale me to a violent death.
*York.* Now heaven forfend! the holy maid
with child!                        [wrought:
*War.* The greatest miracle that e'er ye
Is all your strict preciseness come to this?
*York.* She and the Dauphin have been
juggling:
I did imagine what would be her refuge.  [live;
*War.* Well, go to; we will have no bastards
Especially since Charles must father it.  [his:
*Puc.* You are deceiv'd; my child is none of
It was Alençon that enjoy'd my love.
*York.* Alençon! that notorious Machiavel!
It dies, an if it had a thousand lives.
*Puc.* O, give me leave, I have deluded you;
'Twas neither Charles nor yet the duke I nam'd,
But Reignier, King of Naples, that prevail'd.
*War.* A married man! that's most intoler-
able.
*York.* Why, here's a girl!—I think she
knows not well—
There were so many—whom she may accuse.
*War.* It's sign she hath been liberal and free.
*York.* And yet, forsooth, she is a virgin
pure.—
Strumpet, thy words condemn thy brat and
thee:
Use no entreaty, for it is in vain.
*Puc.* Then lead me hence;—with whom I
leave my curse:
May never glorious sun reflex his beams
Upon the country where you make abode;
But darkness and the gloomy shade of death
Environ you, till mischief and despair
Drive you to break your necks or hang your-
selves!                        [*Exit, guarded.*
*York.* Break thou in pieces and consume to
ashes,
Thou foul accursed minister of hell!

*Enter* CARDINAL BEAUFORT, *attended.*

*Car.* Lord regent, I do greet your excellence
With letters of commission from the king.
For know, my lords, the states of Christendom,
Mov'd with remorse of these outrageous broils,
Have earnestly implor'd a general peace
Betwixt our nation and the aspiring French;

And here at hand the Dauphin and his train
Approacheth, to confer about some matter.
　*York.* Is all our travail turn'd to this effect?
After the slaughter of so many peers,
So many captains, gentlemen, and soldiers,
That in this quarrel have been overthrown,
And sold their bodies for their country's benefit,
Shall we at last conclude effeminate peace?
Have we not lost most part of all the towns,
By treason, falsehood, and by treachery,
Our great progenitors had conquered?—
O Warwick, Warwick! I foresee with grief
The utter loss of all the realm of France.
　*War.* Be patient, York: if we conclude a
　　peace,　　　　　　　　　　　　　　[nants
It shall be with such strict and severe cove-
As little shall the Frenchmen gain thereby.

*Enter* CHARLES, *attended;* ALENÇON,
BASTARD, REIGNIER, *and others.*

　*Char.* Since, lords of England, it is thus
　　agreed　　　　　　　　　　　　　[France,
That peaceful truce shall be proclaim'd in
We come to be informed by yourselves
What the conditions of that league must be.
　*York.* Speak, Winchester; for boiling choler
　　chokes
The hollow passage of my prison'd voice,
By sight of these our baleful enemies.
　*Car.* Charles, and the rest, it is enacted thus:
That in regard King Henry gives consent,
Of mere compassion and of lenity,
To ease your country of distressful war,
And suffer you to breathe in fruitful peace,—
You shall become true liegemen to his crown:
And, Charles, upon condition thou wilt swear
To pay him tribute and submit thyself,
Thou shalt be plac'd as viceroy under him,
And still enjoy thy regal dignity.　　　[self?
　*Alen.* Must he be, then, as shadow of him-
Adorn his temples with a coronet,
And yet, in substance and authority,
Retain but privilege of a private man?
This proffer is absurd and reasonless.　[sess'd
　*Char.* 'Tis known already that I am pos-
With more than half the Gallian territories,
And therein reverenc'd for their lawful king:
Shall I, for lucre of the rest unvanquish'd,
Detract so much from that prerogative
As to be call'd but viceroy of the whole?
No, lord ambassador; I'll rather keep
That which I have than, coveting for more,
Be cast from possibility of all.
　*York.* Insulting Charles! hast thou by secret
　　means
Us'd intercession to obtain a league,
And now the matter grows to compromise
Stand'st thou aloof upon comparison?
Either accept the title thou usurp'st,
Of benefit proceeding from our king,
And not of any challenge of desert,
Or we will plague thee with incessant wars.
　*Reig.* My lord, you do not well in obstinacy
To cavil in the course of this contráct:

If once it be neglected, ten to one
We shall not find like opportunity.
　*Alen.* To say the truth, it is your policy
To save your subjects from such massacre
And ruthless slaughters as are daily seen
By our proceeding in hostility;
And therefore take this compact of a truce,
Although you break it when your pleasure
　　serves.　　　　　　　　[*Aside to* CHARLES.
　*War.* How say'st thou, Charles? shall our
　　condition stand?
　*Char.* It shall;
Only reserv'd, you claim no interest
In any of our towns of garrison.
　*York.* Then swear allegiance to his majesty,
As thou art knight, never to disobey
Nor be rebellious to the crown of England,—
Thou, nor thy nobles, to the crown of England.
　　　[CHARLES *and the rest give tokens of fealty.*
So, now dismiss your army when ye please;
Hang up your ensigns, let your drums be still,
For here we entertain a solemn peace. [*Exeunt.*

SCENE V.—LONDON. *A Room in the Palace.*

*Enter* KING HENRY, *in conference with* SUF-
FOLK; GLOSTER *and* EXETER *following.*

　*K. Hen.* Your wondrous rare description,
　　noble earl,
Of beauteous Margaret hath astonish'd me:
Her virtues, graced with external gifts,
Do breed love's settled passions in my heart:
And like as rigour of tempestuous gusts
Provokes the mightiest hulk against the tide,
So am I driven, by breath of her renown,
Either to suffer shipwreck or arrive
Where I may have fruition of her love.　[tale
　*Suf.* Tush, my good lord,—this superficial
Is but a preface of her worthy praise:
The chief perfections of that lovely dame,—
Had I sufficient skill to utter them,—
Would make a volume of enticing lines,
Able to ravish any dull conceit:
And, which is more, she is not so divine,
So full-replete with choice of all delights,
But, with as humble lowliness of mind,
She is content to be at your command;
Command, I mean, of virtuous chaste intents,
To love and honour Henry as her lord.
　*K. Hen.* And otherwise will Henry ne'er pre-
　　sume.
Therefore, my lord protector, give consent
That Margaret may be England's royal queen.
　*Glo.* So should I give consent to flatter sin.
You know, my lord, your highness is betroth'd
Unto another lady of esteem:　　　　　[tráct,
How shall we, then, dispense with that con-
And not deface your honour with reproach?
　*Suf.* As doth a ruler with unlawful oaths;
Or one that, at a triumph having vow'd
To try his strength, forsaketh yet the lists
By reason of his adversary's odds:
A poor earl's daughter is unequal odds,
And therefore may be broke without offence.

*Glo.* Why, what, I pray, is Margaret more
than that?
Her father is no better than an earl,
Although in glorious titles he excel.
  *Suf.* Yes, my lord, her father is a king,
The King of Naples and Jerusalem;
And of such great authority in France
As his alliance will confirm our peace,
And keep the Frenchmen in allegiance.
  *Glo.* And so the Earl of Armagnac may do,
Because he is near kinsman unto Charles.
  *Exe.* Beside, his wealth doth warrant a lib-
eral dower;
While Reignier sooner will receive than give.
  *Suf.* A dower, my lords! disgrace not so
your king,
That he should be so abject, base, and poor,
To choose for wealth, and not for perfect love.
Henry is able to enrich his queen,
And not to seek a queen to make him rich:
So worthless peasants bargain for their wives,
As market-men for oxen, sheep, or horse.
Marriage is a matter of more worth
Than to be dealt in by attorneyship;
Not whom we will, but whom his grace affects,
Must be companion of his nuptial bed:
And therefore, lords, since he affects her most,
It most of all these reasons bindeth us
In our opinions she should be preferr'd.
For what is wedlock forced but a hell,
An age of discord and continual strife?
Whereas the contrary bringeth bliss,
And is a pattern of celestial peace.          [king,
Whom should we match with Henry, being a
But Margaret, that is daughter to a king?
Her peerless feature, joined with her birth,
Approves her fit for none but for a king;
Her valiant courage and undaunted spirit,—
More than in women commonly is seen,—
Will answer our hope in issue of a king;
For Henry, son unto a conqueror,

Is likely to beget more conquerors,
If with a lady of so high resolve
As is fair Margaret he be link'd in love.   [me
Then yield, my lords; and here conclude with
That Margaret shall be queen, and none but
she.
  *K. Hen.* Whether it be through force of your
report,
My noble Lord of Suffolk, or for that
My tender youth was never yet attaint
With any passion of inflaming love,
I cannot tell; but this I am assur'd.
I feel such sharp dissension in my breast,
Such fierce alarums both of hope and fear,
As I am sick with working of my thoughts.
Take therefore shipping; post, my lord, to
France;
Agree to any covenants; and procure
That Lady Margaret do vouchsafe to come
To cross the seas to England, and be crown'd
King Henry's faithful and anointed queen:
For your expenses and sufficient charge,
Among the people gather up a tenth.
Be gone, I say; for, till you do return,
I rest perplexed with a thousand cares.—
And you, good uncle, banish all offence:
If you do censure me by what you were,
Not what you are, I know it will excuse
This sudden execution of my will.
And so, conduct me where, from company,
I may resolve and ruminate my grief.   [*Exit.*
  *Glo.* Ay, grief, I fear me, both at first and last.
              [*Exeunt* GLOSTER *and* EXETER.
  *Suf.* Thus Suffolk hath prevail'd; and thus
he goes,
As did the youthful Paris once to Greece,
With hope to find the like event in love,
But prosper better than the Trojan did.
Margaret shall now be queen, and rule the king;
But I will rule both her, the king, and realm.
                                        [*Exit.*

KING HENRY VI. PART SECOND.

Act IV. Sc. 2.

# KING HENRY VI.

## SECOND PART

### DRAMATIS PERSONÆ

KING HENRY THE SIXTH.
HUMPHREY, *Duke of Gloster, his Uncle.*
CARDINAL BEAUFORT, *Bishop of Winchester, Great-Uncle to the* KING.
RICHARD PLANTAGENET, *Duke of York.*
EDWARD *and* RICHARD, *his Sons.*
DUKE OF SOMERSET,
DUKE OF SUFFOLK,
DUKE OF BUCKINGHAM, } *of the* KING'S *party.*
LORD CLIFFORD,
YOUNG CLIFFORD, *his Son,*
EARL OF SALISBURY, } *of the York faction.*
EARL OF WARWICK,
LORD SCALES, *Governor of the Tower.*
LORD SAY.
SIR HUMPHREY STAFFORD.
WILLIAM STAFFORD, *his Brother.*
SIR JOHN STANLEY.
A Sea Captain, Master, *and* Master's Mate, *and* WALTER WHITMORE.
Two Gentlemen, *Prisoners with* SUFFOLK.
VAUX.
A Herald.

HUME *and* SOUTHWELL, *two Priests.*
BOLINGBROKE, *a Conjuror.*
A Spirit *raised by him.*
THOMAS HORNER, *an Armourer.*
PETER, *his Man.*
Clerk of Chatham.
Mayor of Saint Alban's.
SIMPCOX, *an Impostor.*
Two Murderers.
JACK CADE, *a Rebel.*
GEORGE, JOHN, DICK, SMITH *the Weaver,* MICHAEL, &c., *his followers.*
ALEXANDER IDEN, *a Kentish Gentleman.*

MARGARET, *Queen to* KING HENRY.
ELEANOR, *Duchess of Gloster.*
MARGERY JOURDAIN, *a Witch.*
Wife *to* SIMPCOX.

Lords, Ladies, *and* Attendants; Petitioners, Aldermen, *a* Beadle, Sheriff, *and* Officers; Citizens, Prentices, Falconers, Guards, Soldiers, Messengers, &c.

SCENE,—*Dispersedly in various parts of* ENGLAND.

## ACT I.

SCENE I.—LONDON. *A Room of State in the Castle.*

*Flourish of trumpets: then hautboys. Enter, on one side,* KING HENRY, DUKE OF GLOSTER, SALISBURY, WARWICK, *and* CARDINAL BEAUFORT; *on the other,* QUEEN MARGARET, *led in by* SUFFOLK; YORK, SOMERSET, BUCKINGHAM, *and others, following.*

*Suf.* As by your high imperial majesty
I had in charge at my depart for France,
As procurator to your excellence,
To marry Princess Margaret for your grace;
So, in the famous ancient city Tours,—
In presence of the Kings of France and Sicil,
The Dukes of Orleans, Calaber, Bretagne, and Alencon,
Seven earls, twelve barons, and twenty reverend bishops,
I have perform'd my task, and was espous'd:
And humbly now, upon my bended knee,
In sight of England and her lordly peers,
Deliver up my title in the queen [substance
To your most gracious hands, that are the
Of that great shadow I did represent;
The happiest gift that ever marquis gave,

The fairest queen that ever king receiv'd.
*K. Hen.* Suffolk, arise.—Welcome, Queen Margaret:
I can express no kinder sign of love [life,
Than this kind kiss.—O Lord, that lends me
Lend me a heart replete with thankfulness!
For thou hast given me, in this beauteous face,
A world of earthly blessings to my soul,
If sympathy of love unite our thoughts.
*Q. Mar.* Great King of England, and my gracious lord,— [had,
The mutual conference that my mind hath
By day, by night, waking and in my dreams,
In courtly company or at my beads,
With you, mine alder-liefest sovereign,
Makes me the bolder to salute my king
With ruder terms, such as my wit affords
And over-joy of heart doth minister.
*K. Hen.* Her sight did ravish; but her grace in speech,
Her words y-clad with wisdom's majesty,
Makes me from wondering fall to weeping joys;
Such is the fulness of my heart's content.—
Lords, with one cheerful voice welcome my love.

553

*All.* [*Kneeling.*] Long live Queen Margaret, England's happiness!

*Q. Mar.* We thank you all.     .[*Flourish.*

*Suf.* My lord protector, so it please your grace,
Here are the articles of contracted peace
Between our sovereign and the French King Charles,
For eighteen months concluded by consent.

*Glo.* [*Reads.*] *Imprimis, It is agreed between the French King Charles and William De-la-Poole, Marquess of Suffolk, ambassador for Henry King of England, that the said Henry shall espouse the Lady Margaret, daughter unto Reignier King of Naples, Sicilia, and Jerusalem; and crown her Queen of England ere the thirtieth of May next ensuing.—Item,—That the duchy of Anjou and the county of Maine shall be released and delivered to the king her father,—*

*K. Hen.* Uncle, how now!

*Glo.*          Pardon me, gracious lord;
Some sudden qualm hath struck me at the heart,
And dimm'd mine eyes, that I can read no further.

*K. Hen.* Uncle of Winchester, I pray read on.

*Car.* [*Reads.*] *Item,—It is further agreed between them that the duchies of Anjou and Maine shall be released and delivered over to the king her father; and she sent over of the King of England's own proper cost and charges, without having any dowry.*

*K. Hen.* They please us well.—Lord marquess, kneel down:
We here create thee the first Duke of Suffolk,
And girt thee with the sword.—Cousin of York,
We here discharge your grace from being regent
I' the parts of France, till term of eighteen months
Be full expir'd.—Thanks, uncle Winchester,
Gloster, York, Buckingham, Somerset,
Salisbury, and Warwick;
We thank you all for this great favour done,
In entertainment to my princely queen.
Come, let us in; and with all speed provide
To see her coronation be perform'd.

     [*Exeunt* KING, QUEEN, *and* SUFFOLK.

*Glo.* Brave peers of England, pillars of the state,
To you Duke Humphrey must unload his grief,—
Your grief, the common grief of all the land.
What! did my brother Henry spend his youth,
His valour, coin, and people in the wars?
Did he so often lodge in open field,
In winter's cold and summer's parching heat,
To conquer France, his true inheritance?
And did my brother Bedford toil his wits

To keep by policy what Henry got?
Have you yourselves, Somerset, Buckingham,
Brave York, Salisbury, and victorious Warwick,
Receiv'd deep scars in France and Normandy?
Or hath mine uncle Beaufort and myself,
With all the learned council of the realm,
Studied so long, sat in the council-house
Early and late, debating to and fro [in awe?
How France and Frenchmen might be kept
And hath his highness in his infancy
Been crown'd in Paris, in despite of foes?
And shall these labours and these honours die?
Shall Henry's conquest, Bedford's vigilance,
Your deeds of war, and all our counsel die?
O peers of England, shameful is this league!
Fatal this marriage! cancelling your fame,
Blotting your names from books of memory,
Razing the characters of your renown.
Defacing monuments of conquer'd France,
Undoing all, as all had never been!

*Car.* Nephew, what means this passionate discourse,
This peroration with such circumstance?
For France, 'tis ours; and we will keep it still.

*Glo.* Ay, uncle, we will keep it if we can;
But now it is impossible we should:
Suffolk, the new-made duke that rules the roast,
Hath given the duchy of Anjou and Maine
Unto the poor King Reignier, whose large style
Agrees not with the leanness of his purse.

*Sal.* Now, by the death of Him that died for all,
These counties were the keys of Normandy:—
But wherefore weeps Warwick, my valiant son?

*War.* For grief that they are past recovery:
For were there hope to conquer them again
My sword should shed hot blood, mine eyes no tears.
Anjou and Maine! myself did win them both;
Those provinces these arms of mine did conquer:
And are the cities that I got with wounds
Deliver'd up again with peaceful words?
*Mort Dieu!*                [focate

*York.* For Suffolk's duke, may he be suffThat dims the honour of this warlike isle!
France should have torn and rent my very heart
Before I would have yielded to this league.
I never read but England's kings have had
Large sums of gold and dowries with their wives;
And our King Henry gives away his own,
To match with her that brings no vantages.

*Glo.* A proper jest, and never heard before,

That Suffolk should demand a whole fif-
    teenth
For costs and charges in transporting her!
She should have stay'd in France, and starv'd
    in France,
Before—
   *Car.* My Lord of Gloster, now you grow
    too hot:
It was the pleasure of my lord the king.
   *Glo.* My Lord of Winchester, I know your
    mind;
'Tis not my speeches that you do mislike,
But 'tis my presence that doth trouble ye.
Rancour will out: proud prelate, in thy face
I see thy fury: if I longer stay
We shall begin our ancient bickerings.—
Lordings, farewell; and say, when I am gone,
I prophesied France will be lost ere long.
                     [*Exit.*
   *Car.* So, there goes our protector in a rage.
'Tis known to you he is mine enemy;
Nay, more, an enemy unto you all,
And no great friend, I fear me, to the king.
Consider, lords, he is the next of blood,
And heir-apparent to the English crown:
Had Henry got an empire by his marriage,
And all the wealthy kingdoms of the west,
There's reason he should be displeas'd at it.
Look to it, lords; let not his smoothing
    words
Bewitch your hearts; be wise and circum-
    spect.
What though the common people favour him,
Calling him—*Humphrey, the good Duke of*
    *Gloster;*            [voice,
Clapping their hands, and crying with loud
*Jesu maintain your royal excellence!*
With *God preserve the good Duke Hum-*
    *phrey!*
I fear me, lords, for all this flattering gloss,
He will be found a dangerous protector.
   *Buck.* Why should he then protect our
    sovereign,
He being of age to govern of himself?—
Cousin of Somerset, join you with me,
And altogether, with the Duke of Suffolk,
We'll quickly hoise Duke Humphrey from his
    seat.                [delay;
   *Car.* This weighty business will not brook
I'll to the Duke of Suffolk presently. [*Exit.*
   *Som.* Cousin of Buckingham, though
    Humphrey's pride
And greatness of his place be grief to us,
Yet let us watch the haughty cardinal:
His insolence is more intolerable
Than all the princes in the land beside:
If Gloster be displac'd, he'll be protector.
   *Buck.* Or thou or I, Somerset, will be pro-
    tector,
Despite Duke Humphrey or the cardinal.
    [*Exeunt* BUCKINGHAM *and* SOMERSET.
   *Sal.* Pride went before, ambition follows
    him.

Whiles these do labour for their own prefer-
    ment,
Behoves it us to labour for the realm.
I never saw but Humphrey Duke of Gloster
Did bear him like a noble gentleman.
Oft have I seen the haughty cardinal,—
More like a soldier than a man o' the church,
As stout and proud as he were lord of all,—
Swear like a ruffian, and demean himself
Unlike the ruler of a commonweal.—
Warwick, my son, the comfort of my age!
Thy deeds, thy plainness, and thy housekeep-
    ing,
Hath won the greatest favour of the com-
    mons,
Excepting none but good Duke Humphrey:—
And, brother York, thy acts in Ireland,
In bringing them to civil discipline;
Thy late exploits done in the heart of France,
When thou wert regent for our sovereign,
Have made thee fear'd and honour'd of the
    people:—
Join we together for the public good
In what we can, to bridle and suppress
The pride of Suffolk and the cardinal,
With Somerset's and Buckingham's ambi-
    tion;
And, as we may, cherish Duke Humphrey's
    deeds
While they do tend the profit of the land.
   *War.* So God help Warwick, as he loves
    the land
And common profit of his country!
   *York.* And so says York, for he hath great-
    est cause.
   *Sal.* Then let's make haste away and look
    unto the main.          [lost,—
   *War.* Unto the main! O father, Maine is
That Maine which by main force Warwick
    did win,             [last!
And would have kept so long as breath did
Main chance, father, you meant; but I meant
    Maine,
Which I will win from France, or else be
    slain.
       [*Exeunt* WARWICK *and* SALISBURY.
   *York.* Anjou and Maine are given to the
    French;
Paris is lost; the state of Normandy
Stands on a tickle point, now they are gone:
Suffolk concluded on the articles;
The peers agreed; and Henry was well pleas'd
To change two dukedoms for a duke's fair
    daughter.
I cannot blame them all: what is 't to them?
'Tis thine they give away, and not their own.
Pirates may make cheap pennyworths of
    their pillage,
And purchase friends, and give to courtezans,
Still revelling like lords till all be gone;
While as the silly owner of the goods
Weeps over them, and wrings his hapless
    hands,

And shakes his head, and trembling stands
aloof,
While all is shar'd, and all is borne away,
Ready to starve, and dare not touch his own:
So York must sit, and fret, and bite his
tongue,
While his own lands are bargain'd for and
sold.
Methinks the realms of England, France, and
Ireland
Bear that proportion to my flesh and blood
As did the fatal brand Althæa burn'd
Unto the prince's heart of Calydon.
Anjou and Maine both given unto the
French!
Cold news for me; for I had hope of France,
Even as I have of fertile England's soil.
A day will come when York shall claim his
own;
And therefore I will take the Nevils' parts,
And make a show of love to proud Duke
Humphrey,
And, when I spy advantage, claim the crown,
For that's the golden mark I seek to hit:
Nor shall proud Lancaster usurp my right,
Nor hold the sceptre in his childish fist,
Nor wear the diadem upon his head,
Whose church-like humours fit not for a
crown.
Then, York, be still awhile, till time do serve:
Watch thou and wake, when others be asleep,
To pry into the secrets of the state;
Till Henry, surfeiting in joys of love
With his new bride and England's dear-
bought queen,
And Humphrey with the peers be fall'n at
jars:
Then will I raise aloft the milk-white rose,
With whose sweet smell the air shall be per-
fum'd;
And in my standard bear the arms of York,
To grapple with the house of Lancaster;
And, force perforce, I'll make him yield the
crown,
Whose bookish rule hath pull'd fair England
down.

[*Exit.*

SCENE II.—LONDON. *A room in the* DUKE
OF GLOSTER'S *House.*

*Enter* GLOSTER *and the* DUCHESS.

*Duch.* Why droops my lord, like over-
ripen'd corn
Hanging the head at Ceres' plenteous load?
Why doth the great Duke Humphrey knit
his brows,
As frowning at the favours of the world?
Why are thine eyes fix'd to the sullen earth,
Gazing on that which seems to dim thy sight?
What see'st thou there? King Henry's dia-
dem.
Enchas'd with all the honours of the world?

If so, gaze on, and grovel on thy face
Until thy head be circled with the same.
Put forth thy hand, reach at the glorious
gold:—
What, is 't too short? I'll lengthen it with
mine;
And, having both together heav'd it up,
We'll both together lift our heads to heaven;
And never more abase our sight so low
As to vouchsafe one glance unto the ground.
*Glo.* O Nell, sweet Nell, if thou dost love
thy lord,
Banish the canker of ambitious thoughts!
And may that thought, when I imagine ill
Against my king and nephew, virtuous
Henry,
Be my last breathing in this mortal world!
My troublous dream this night doth make
me sad.
*Duch.* What dream'd my lord? tell me,
and I'll requite it
With sweet rehearsal of my morning's dream.
*Glo.* Methought this staff, mine office-
badge in court,
Was broke in twain; by whom I have forgot,
But, as I think, it was by the cardinal;
And on the pieces of the broken wand
Were plac'd the heads of Edmund Duke of
Somerset,
And William De-la-Poole, first Duke of Suf-
folk.
This was my dream; what it doth bode God
knows.
*Duch.* Tut, this was nothing but an argu-
ment
That he that breaks a stick of Gloster's grove
Shall lose his head for his presumption.
But list to me, my Humphrey, my sweet
duke:
Methought I sat in seat of majesty
In the cathedral church of Westminster,
And in that chair where kings and queens
are crown'd;
Where Henry and Dame Margaret kneel'd to
me,
And on my head did set the diadem.
*Glo.* Nay, Eleanor, then must I chide out-
right:
Presumptuous dame, ill-nurtur'd Eleanor!
Art thou not second woman in the realm,
And the protector's wife, belov'd of him?
Hast thou not worldly pleasure at command,
Above the reach or compass of thy thought?
And wilt thou still be hammering treachery,
To tumble down thy husband and thyself
From top of honour to disgrace's feet?
Away from me, and let me hear no more!
*Duch.* What, what, my lord! are you so
choleric
With Eleanor for telling but her dream?
Next time I'll keep my dreams unto myself,
And not be check'd.
*Glo.* Nay, be not angry, I am pleas'd again.

*Enter a* Messenger.

*Mess.* My lord protector, 'tis his highness'
  pleasure
You do prepare to ride unto Saint Albans,
Whereas the king and queen do mean to
  hawk.
  *Glo.* I go.—Come, Nell,—thou wilt ride
    with us?                    [sently.
  *Duch.* Yes, my good lord, I'll follow pre-
        [*Exeunt* GLOSTER *and* Messenger.
Follow I must; I cannot go before
While Gloster bears this base and humble
  mind.
Were I a man, a duke, and next of blood,
I would remove these tedious stumbling-
  blocks,
And smooth my way upon their headless
  necks:
And, being a woman, I will not be slack
To play my part in fortune's pageant.—
Where are you there, Sir John? nay, fear
  not, man,
We are alone; here's none but thee and I.

*Enter* HUME.

  *Hume.* Jesus preserve your royal majesty!
  *Duch.* What say'st thou? majesty! I am
    but grace.           [Hume's advice,
  *Hume.* But, by the grace of God and
Your grace's title shall be multiplied.
  *Duch.* What say'st thou, man? hast thou
    as yet conferr'd
With Margery Jourdain, the cunning witch,
With Roger Bolingbroke, the conjurer?
And will they undertake to do me good?
  *Hume.* This they have promised,—to show
    your highness
A spirit rais'd from depth of under-ground,
That shall make answer to such questions
As by your grace shall be propounded him.
  *Duch.* It is enough; I'll think upon the
    questions:
When from Saint Albans we do make return
We'll see these things effected to the full.
Here, Hume, take this reward; make merry,
  man,
With thy confederates in this weighty cause.
                              [*Exit.*
  *Hume.* Hume must make merry with the
    duchess' gold;
Marry, and shall. But, how now, Sir John
  Hume!
Seal up your lips, and give no words but
  mum:
The business asketh silent secrecy.
Dame Eleanor gives gold to bring the witch:
Gold cannot come amiss were she a devil.
Yet have I gold flies from another coast:—
I dare not say from the rich cardinal,
And from the great and new-made Duke of
  Suffolk;

Yet I do find it so: for, to be plain,
They, knowing Dame Eleanor's aspiring hu-
  mour,
Have hired me to undermine the duchess,
And buzz these conjurations in her brain.
They say,—A crafty knave does need no
  broker;
Yet am I Suffolk and the cardinal's broker.
Hume, if you take not heed, you shall go
  near
To call them both a pair of crafty knaves.
Well, so it stands; and thus, I fear, at last
Hume's knavery will be the duchess' wreck
And her attainture will be Humphrey's fall:
Sort how it will, I shall have gold for all.
                              [*Exit.*

SCENE III.—LONDON. *A Room in the Palace.*

*Enter* PETER *and other* Petitioners.

  1 *Pet.* My masters, let's stand close: my
lord protector will come this way by and by,
and then we may deliver our supplications in
the quill.
  2 *Pet.* Marry, the Lord protect him, for
he's a good man! Jesu bless him!
  1 *Pet.* Here 'a comes, methinks, and the
queen with him. I'll be the first, sure.

*Enter* SUFFOLK *and* QUEEN MARGARET.

  2 *Pet.* Come back, fool; this is the Duke of
Suffolk, and not my lord protector.
  *Suf.* How now, fellow! wouldst anything
with me?
  1 *Pet.* I pray, my lord, pardon me: I took
ye for my lord protector.
  *Q. Mar.* [*Glancing at the superscriptions.*]
*To my Lord Protector!* Are your supplications to his lordship? Let me see them:—
what is thine?
  1 *Pet.* Mine is, an 't please your grace,
against John Goodman, my lord cardinal's
man, for keeping my house, and lands, and
wife and all, from me.
  *Suf.* Thy wife too! that is some wrong indeed.—What's yours?—what's here! [*Reads.*]
*Against the Duke of Suffolk, for enclosing
the commons of Melford.*—How now, sir
knave!
  2 *Pet.* Alas, sir, I am but a poor petitioner
of our whole township.
  *Peter.* [*Presenting his petition.*] Against
my master, Thomas Horner, for saying that
the Duke of York was rightful heir to the
crown.
  *Q. Mar.* What say'st thou? did the Duke
of York say he was rightful heir to the
crown?
  *Peter.* That my master was? no, forsooth:
my master said that he was; and that the
king was an usurper.
  *Suf.* Who is there? [*Enter* Servants.]—
Take this fellow in, and send for his master

with a pursuivant presently:—we'll hear
more of your matter before the king.
                [*Exeunt* Servants *with* PETER.
*Q. Mar.* And as for you, that love to be
        protected
Under the wings of our protector's grace,
Begin your suits anew, and sue to him.
                [*Tears the petitions.*
Away, base cullions!—Suffolk, let them go.
*All.* Come, let's be gone.
                [*Exeunt* Petitioners.
*Q. Mar.* My lord of Suffolk, say, is this
        the guise,
Is this the fashion in the court of England?
Is this the government of Britain's isle,
And this the royalty of Albion's king?
What, shall King Henry be a pupil still,
Under the surly Gloster's governance?
Am I a queen in title and in style,
And must be made a subject to a duke?
I tell thee, Poole, when in the city Tours
Thou rann'st a tilt in honour of my love,
And stol'st away the ladies' hearts of France,
I thought King Henry had resembled thee
In courage, courtship, and proportion:
But all his mind is bent to holiness,
To number *Ave-Maries* on his beads:
His champions are, the prophets and apos-
        tles;
His weapons, holy saws of sacred writ;
His study is his tilt-yard, and his loves
Are brazen images of canoniz'd saints.
I would the college of the cardinals
Would choose him pope, and carry him to
        Rome,
And set the triple crown upon his head:—
That were a state fit for his holiness.
*Suf.* Madam, be patient: as I was cause
Your highness came to England, so will I
In England work your grace's full content.
*Q. Mar.* Beside the haughty protector,
        have we Beaufort        [ingham,
The imperious churchman, Somerset, Buck-
And grumbling York; and not the least of
        these
But can do more in England than the king.
*Suf.* And he of these that can do most of
        all
Cannot do more in England than the Nevils:
Salisbury and Warwick are no simple peers.
*Q. Mar.* Not all these lords do vex me half
        so much
As that proud dame, the lord protector's
        wife.
She sweeps it through the court with troops
        of ladies,        [phrey's wife:
More like an empress than Duke Hum-
Strangers in court do take her for the queen:
She bears a duke's revenues on her back,
And in her heart she scorns our poverty:
Shall I not live to be aveng'd on her?
Contemptuous base-born callet as she is,
She vaunted 'mongst her minions t' other day

The very train of her worst wearing gown
Was better worth than all my father's lands,
Till Suffolk gave two dukedoms for his
        daughter.
*Suf.* Madam, myself have lim'd a bush for
        her,
And plac'd a quire of such enticing birds
That she will light to listen to the lays,
And never mount to trouble you again.
So, let her rest: and, madam, list to me;
For I am bold to counsel you in this.
Although we fancy not the cardinal,
Yet must we join with him and with the
        lords,
Till we have brought Duke Humphrey in dis-
        grace.
As for the Duke of York,—this late com-
        plaint
Will make but little for his benefit.
So, one by one, we'll weed them all at last,
And you yourself shall steer the happy helm.

*Enter* KING HENRY, YORK, *and* SOMERSET;
        DUKE *and* DUCHESS OF GLOSTER, CAR-
        DINAL BEAUFORT, BUCKINGHAM, SALISBURY,
        *and* WARWICK.

*K. Hen.* For my part, noble lords, I care
        not which;
Or Somerset or York, all's one to me.
*York.* If York have ill demean'd himself
        in France,
Then let him be denay'd the regentship.
*Som.* If Somerset be unworthy of the
        place,
Let York be regent; I will yield to him.
*War.* Whether your grace be worthy, yea
        or no,
Dispute not that: York is the worthier.
*Car.* Ambitious Warwick, let thy betters
        speak.
*War.* The cardinal's not my better in the
        field.
*Buck.* All in this presence are thy betters,
        Warwick.
*War.* Warwick may live to be the best of
        all.
*Sal.* Peace, son!—and show some reason,
        Buckingham,
Why Somerset should be preferr'd in this.
*Q. Mar.* Because the king, forsooth, will
        have it so.
*Glo.* Madame, the king is old enough him-
        self
To give his censure: these are no women's
        matters.        [your grace
*Q. Mar.* If he be old enough, what needs
To be protector of his excellence?
*Glo.* Madame, I am protector of the
        realm;
And, at his pleasure, will resign my place.
*Suf.* Resign it then, and leave thine inso-
        lence.

Since thou wert king,—as who is king but thou?—
The commonwealth hath daily run to wreck;
The Dauphin hath prevail'd beyond the seas;
And all the peers and nobles of the realm
Have been as bondmen to thy sovereignty.

*Car.* The commons hast thou rack'd; the clergy's bags
Are lank and lean with thy extortions.

*Som.* Thy sumptuous buildings and thy wife's attire
Have cost a mass of public treasury.

*Buck.* Thy cruelty in execution
Upon offenders hath exceeded law,
And left thee to the mercy of the law.

*Q. Mar.* Thy sale of offices and towns in France,—
If they were known, as the suspect is great,—
Would make thee quickly hop without thy head.

    *[Exit* GLOSTER. *The* QUEEN *drops her fan.*

Give me my fan: what, minion! can you not?

    *[Gives the* DUCHESS *a box on the ear.*

I cry you mercy, madam; was it you?

*Duch.* Was't I? yea, I it was, proud Frenchwoman:
Could I come near your beauty with my nails,
I'd set my ten commandments in your face.

*K. Hen.* Sweet aunt, be quiet; 'twas against her will.

*Duch.* Against her will! good king, look to 't in time;
She'll hamper thee, and dandle thee like a baby:     [breeches,
Though in this place most master wear no
She shall not strike Dame Eleanor unreveng'd.     [*Exit.*

*Buck.* Lord cardinal, I will follow Eleanor,
And listen after Humphrey, how he proceeds:
She's tickled now; her fume needs no spurs,
She'll gallop fast enough to her destruction.
    [*Exit.*

### Re-enter GLOSTER.

*Glo.* Now, lords, my choler being over-blown
With walking once about the quadrangle,
I come to talk of commonwealth affairs.
As for your spiteful false objections,
Prove them, and I lie open to the law:
But God in mercy so deal with my soul
As I in duty love my king and country!
But to the matter that we have in hand:—
I say, my sovereign, York is meetest man
To be your regent in the realm of France.

*Suf.* Before we make election, give me leave
To show some reason, of no little force,
That York is most unmeet of any man.

*York.* I'll tell thee, Suffolk, why I am unmeet:
First, for I cannot flatter thee in pride;
Next, if I be appointed for the place,
My Lord of Somerset will keep me here,
Without discharge, money, or furniture,
Till France be won into the Dauphin's hands:
Last time, I danc'd attendance on his will
Till Paris was besieg'd, famished, and lost

*War.* That can I witness; and a fouler fact
Did never traitor in the land commit.

*Suf.* Peace, headstrong Warwick!

*War.* Image of pride, why should I hold my peace?

*Enter Servants of* SUFFOLK, *bringing in* HORNER *and* PETER.

*Suf.* Because here is a man accus'd of treason:
Pray God the Duke of York excuse himself!

*York.* Doth any one accuse York for a traitor?

*K. Hen.* What mean'st thou, Suffolk? tell me, what are these?

*Suf.* Please it your majesty, this is the man
That doth accuse his master of high treason:
His words were these,—that Richard Duke of York
Was rightful heir unto the English crown,
And that your majesty was an usurper.

*K. Hen.* Say, man, were these thy words?

*Hor.* An't shall please your majesty, I never said nor thought any such matter: God is my witness, I am falsely accused by the villain.

*Pet.* By these ten bones, my lords [*holding up his hands,*] he did speak them to me in the garret one night, as we were scouring my Lord of York's armour.

*York.* Base dunghill villain and mechanical,
I'll have thy head for this thy traitor's speech.—
I do beseech your royal majesty,
Let him have all the rigour of the law.

*Hor.* Alas, my lord, hang me if ever I spake the words. My accuser is my prentice; and when I did correct him for his fault the other day, he did vow upon his knees he would be even with me: I have good witness of this; therefore I beseech your majesty, do not cast away an honest man for a villain's accusation.

*K. Hen.* Uncle, what shall we say to this in law?

*Glo.* This doom, my lord, if I may judge:
Let Somerset be regent o'er the French,
Because in York this breeds suspicion;
And let these have a day appointed them
For single combat in convenient place,
For he hath witness of his servant's malice:
This is the law, and this Duke Humphrey's doom.

*K. Hen.* Then be it so.—My Lord of
Somerset,
We make your grace regent over the French.
*Som.* I humbly thank your royal majesty.
*Hor.* And I accept the combat willingly.
*Pet.* Alas, my lord, I cannot fight; for
God's sake, pity my case! the spite of man
prevaileth against me. O Lord, have mercy
upon me! I shall never be able to fight a
blow: O Lord, my heart!
*Glo.* Sirrah, or you must fight, or else be
hang'd.
*K. Hen.* Away with them to prison; and
the day                      [month.—
Of combat shall be the last of the next
Come, Somerset, we'll see thee sent away.
                    [*Flourish. Exeunt.*

SCENE IV.—*The same. The* DUKE OF
    GLOSTER'S *Garden.*

*Enter* MARGERY JOURDAIN, HUME, SOUTH-
    WELL, *and* BOLINGBROKE.

*Hume.* Come, my masters; the duchess, I
tell you, expects performance of your promises.
*Boling.* Master Hume, we are therefore
provided: will her ladyship behold and hear
our exorcisms?
*Hume.* Ay, what else? fear you not her
courage.
*Boling.* I have heard her reported to be a
woman of an invincible spirit: but it shall be
convenient, Master Hume, that you be by her
aloft, while we be busy below; and so, I
pray you, go in God's name, and leave us.
[*Exit* HUME.] Mother Jourdain, be you
prostrate, and grovel on the earth;—John
Southwell, read you;—and let us to our
work.

*Enter* DUCHESS *above, and presently* HUME.

*Duch.* Well said, my masters; and wel-
come all.
To this gear,—the sooner the better.
*Boling.* Patience, good lady; wizards know
their times:
Deep night, dark night, the silent of the
night,
The time of night when Troy was set on
fire;
The time when screech-owls cry, and ban-
dogs howl,
And spirits walk, and ghosts break up their
graves,—
That time best fits the work we have in
hand.
Madam, sit you, and fear not: whom we
raise
We will make fast within a hallow'd verge.
[*Here they perform the ceremonies apper-
taining, and make the circle;* BOLING-
BROKE *or* SOUTHWELL *reads,* "Conjuro

te," &c. *It thunders and lightens ter-
ribly; then the* Spirit *riseth.*
*Spir.* Adsum.
*M. Jourd.* Asmath,
By the eternal God, whose name and power
Thou tremblest at, answer that I shall ask;
For, till thou speak, thou shalt not pass from
hence.                        [and done!
*Spir.* Ask what thou wilt: that I had said
*Boling. First of the king: what shall of
him become?* [*Reading out of a paper.*
*Spir.* The duke yet lives that Henry shall
depose;
But him outlive, and die a violent death.
    [*As the* Spirit *speaks,* SOUTHWELL
              *writes the answers.*
*Boling. What fates await the Duke of
Suffolk?*
*Spir.* By water shall he die and take his
end.
*Boling. What shall befall the Duke of
Somerset?*
*Spir.* Let him shun castles;
Safer shall he be upon the sandy plains
Than where castles mounted stand.—
Have done, for more I hardly can endure.
*Boling.* Descend to darkness and the burn-
ing lake!
False fiend, avoid!
    [*Thunder and lightning.* Spirit *descends.*

*Enter* YORK *and* BUCKINGHAM *hastily, with
    their* Guards *and others.*

*York.* Lay hands upon these traitors and
their trash.—
Beldam, I think we watch'd you at an
inch.—
What, madam, are you there? the king and
commonweal
Are deeply indebted for this piece of pains:
My lord protector will, I doubt it not,
See you well guerdon'd for these good de-
serts.
*Duch.* Not half so bad as thine to Eng-
land's king,
Injurious duke, that threatest where's no
cause.
*Buck.* True, madam, none at all:—what
call you this?
                [*Showing her the papers.*
Away with them! let them be clapp'd up
close,
And kept asunder.—You, madam, shall with
us.—
Stafford, take her to thee.—
We'll see your trinkets here all forthcom-
ing.—
All, away!
    [*Exeunt, above,* DUCHESS *and* HUME,
        *guarded, below,* SOUTH., BOLING.,
        &c., *guarded.*
*York.* Lord Buckingham, methinks you
watch'd her well:

A pretty plot, well chosen to build upon!
Now, pray, my lord, let's see the devil's writ.
What have we here? [*Reads.*
*The duke yet lives that Henry shall depose;*
*But him outlive, and die a violent death.*
Why, this is just,
*Aio te, Æacida, Romanos vincere posse.*
Well, to the rest:
*Tell me what fate awaits the Duke of Suf-*
*folk?*
*By water shall he die and take his end.—*
*What shall betide the Duke of Somerset?*
*Let him shun castles;*
*Safer shall he be upon the sandy plains*
*Than where castles mounted stand.*
Come, come, my lords;
These oracles are hardly attain'd,
And hardly understood. [Albans,
The king is now in progress toward Saint
With him the husband of this lovely lady:
Thither go these news, as fast as horse can
carry them,—
A sorry breakfast for my lord protector.
    *Buck.* Your grace shall give me leave, my
        Lord of York,
To be the post, in hope of his reward.
    *York.* At your pleasure, my good lord.—
Who's within there, ho!

    *Enter a Servant.*

Invite my Lords of Salisbury and Warwick
To sup with me to-morrow night.—Away!
    [*Exeunt.*

### ACT II.

SCENE I.—*Saint Albans.*

*Enter* KING HENRY, QUEEN MARGARET, GLOS-
TER, CARDINAL, *and* SUFFOLK, *with* Falconers *hollaing.*

    *Q. Mar.* Believe me, lords, for flying at the
        brook,
I saw not better sport these seven years' day:
Yet, by your leave, the wind was very high;
And, ten to one, old Joan had not gone out.
    *K. Hen.* But what a point, my lord, your
        falcon made,
And what a pitch she flew above the rest!—
To see how God in all his creatures works!
Yea, man and birds are fain of climbing high.
    *Suf.* No marvel, an it like your majesty,
My lord protector's hawks do tower so well;
They know their master loves to be aloft,
And bears his thoughts above his falcon's
    pitch.
    *Glo.* My lord, 'tis but a base ignoble mind
That mounts no higher than a bird can soar.
    *Car.* I thought as much; he would be
        above the clouds. [by that?
    *Glo.* Ay, my lord cardinal,—how think you
Were it not good your grace could fly to
    heaven?
    *K. Hen.* The treasury of everlasting joy!

    *Car.* Thy heaven is on earth; thine eyes
        and thoughts
Beat on a crown, the treasure of thy heart;
Pernicious protector, dangerous peer,
That smooth'st it so with king and common-
    weal!
    *Glo.* What, cardinal, is your priesthood
        grown peremptory?
*Tantæne animis cælestibus iræ?* [malice;
Churchmen so hot? good uncle, hide such
With such holiness can you do it? [comes
    *Suf.* No malice, sir; no more than well be-
So good a quarrel and so bad a peer.
    *Glo.* As who, my lord?
    *Suf.* Why, as you, my lord,
An't like your lordly lord-protectorship.
    *Glo.* Why, Suffolk, England knows thine
        insolence.
    *Q. Mar.* And thy ambition, Gloster.
    *K. Hen.* I pr'ythee, peace,
Good queen, and whet not on these furious
    peers;
For blessed are the peacemakers on earth.
    *Car.* Let me be blessed for the peace I
        make,
Against this proud protector, with my sword!
    *Glo.* Faith, holy uncle, would 'twere come
        to that [*Aside to* CAR.
    *Car.* Marry, when thou dar'st.
        [*Aside to* GLO.
    *Glo.* Make up no factious numbers for the
        matter;
In thine own person answer thy abuse.
        [*Aside to* CAR.
    *Car.* Ay, where thou dar'st not peep: an
        if thou dar'st,
This evening on the east side of the grove.
        [*Aside to* GLO.
    *K. Hen.* How now, my lords!
    *Car.* Believe me, cousin Gloster,
Had not your man put up the fowl so sud-
    denly,
We had had more sport.—Come with thy
    two-hand sword. [*Aside to* GLO.
    *Glo.* True, uncle.
    *Car.* Are ye advis'd?—the east side of the
        grove? [*Aside to* GLO.
    *Glo.* Cardinal, I am with you.
        [*Aside to* CAR.
    *K. Hen.* Why, how now, uncle Gloster!
    *Glo.* Talking of hawking; nothing else, my
        lord.—
Now, by God's mother, priest, I'll shave your
    crown for this,
Or all my fence shall fail. [*Aside to* CAR.
    *Car. Medice teipsum;*
Protector, see to 't well, protect yourself.
        [*Aside to* GLO.
    *K. Hen.* The winds grow high; so do your
        stomachs, lords.
How irksome is this music to my heart!
When such strings jar, what hope! of har-
    mony?

I pray, my lords, let me compound this strife.

*Enter a* Townsman *of Saint Albans, crying* "A Miracle!"

*Glo.* What means this noise?
Fellow, what miracle dost thou proclaim?
*Towns.* A miracle! a miracle!
*Suf.* Come to the king, and tell him what miracle.        [bans' shrine,
*Towns.* Forsooth, a blind man at St. Al-
Within this half hour hath receiv'd his sight;
A man that ne'er saw in his life before.
*K. Hen.* Now, God be prais'd that to be-
lieving souls
Gives light in darkness, comfort in despair!

*Enter the* Mayor of St. Albans *and his brethren; and* SIMPCOX, *borne between two persons in a chair, his* WIFE *and a multitude following.*

*Car.* Here comes the townsmen on pro-
cession,
To present your highness with the man.
*K. Hen.* Great is his comfort in this earth-
ly vale,
Although by his sight his sin be multiplied.
*Glo.* Stand by, my masters:—bring him near the king;
His highness' pleasure is to talk with him.
*K. Hen.* Good fellow, tell us here the cir-
cumstance,
That we for thee may glorify the Lord.
What, hast thou been long blind and now re-
stor'd?
*Simp.* Born blind, an't please your grace.
*Wife.* Ay, indeed, was he.
*Suf.* What woman is this?
*Wife.* His wife, an't like your worship.
*Glo.* Hadst thou been his mother, thou couldst have better told.
*K. Hen.* Where wert thou born?
*Simp.* At Berwick in the north, an't like your grace.
*K. Hen.* Poor soul, God's goodness hath been great to thee:
Let never day nor night unhallow'd pass,
But still remember what the Lord hath done.
*Q. Mar.* Tell me, good fellow, cam'st thou here by chance,
Or of devotion, to this holy shrine?
*Simp.* God knows, of pure devotion; be-
ing call'd
A hundred times and oftener, in my sleep,
By good Saint Alban; who said, *Simpcox, come,—*
*Come, offer at my shrine, and I will help thee.*
*Wife.* Most true, forsooth; and many time and oft
Myself have heard a voice to call him so.
*Car.* What, art thou lame?
*Simp.* Ay, God Almighty help me!
*Suf.* How cam'st thou so?
*Simp.* A fall off a tree.

*Wife.* A plum-tree, master.
*Glo.* How long hast thou been blind?
*Simp.* O, born so, master.
*Glo.* What, and wouldst climb a tree?
*Simp.* But that in all my life, when I was a youth.        [very dear.
*Wife.* Too true; and bought his climbing
*Glo.* Mass, thou lov'dst plums well that wouldst venture so.
*Simp.* Alas, good master, my wife desir'd some damsons,
And made me climb, with danger of my life.
*Glo.* A subtle knave! but yet it shall not serve.—        [open them:—
Let me see thine eyes:—wink now;—now
In my opinion yet thou see'st not well.
*Simp.* Yes, master, clear as day, I thank God and Saint Alban.
*Glo.* Say'st thou me so? What color is this cloak of?
*Simp.* Red, master; red as blood.
*Glo.* Why, that's well said. What colour is my gown of?
*Simp.* Black, forsooth; coal-black as jet.
*K. Hen.* Why, then, thou know'st what colour jet is of?
*Suf.* And yet, I think, jet did he never see.
*Glo.* But cloaks and gowns, before this day, a many.
*Wife.* Never, before this day, in all his life.
*Glo.* Tell me, sirrah, what's my name?
*Simp.* Alas, master, I know not.
*Glo.* What's his name?
*Simp.* I know not.
*Glo.* Nor his?
*Simp.* No, indeed, master.
*Glo.* What's thine own name?
*Simp.* Saunder Simpcox, an' if it please you, master.
*Glo.* Then, Saunder, sit there, the lyingest knave in Christendom. If thou hadst been born blind, thou mightst as well have known all our names as thus to name the several colours we do wear. Sight may distinguish of colours; but suddenly to nominate them all, it is impossible.—My lords, Saint Alban here hath done a miracle; and would ye not think his cunning to be great that could restore this cripple to his legs again?
*Simp.* O master, that ye could!
*Glo.* My masters of Saint Albans, have you not beadles in your town, and things called whips?
*May.* Yes, my lord, if it please your grace.
*Glo.* Then send for one presently.
*May.* Sirrah, go fetch the beadle hither straight.        [*Exit an* Attendant.
*Glo.* Now fetch me a stool hither by and by.
Now, sirrah, if you mean to save yourself from whipping, leap me over this stool and run away.

*Simp.* Alas, master, I am not able to stand alone:
You go about to torture me in vain.

*Enter a* BEADLE *with whips.*

*Glo.* Well, sir, we must have you find your legs. Sirrah beadle, whip him till he leap over that same stool.

*Bead.* I will, my lord. Come on, sirrah; off with your doublet quickly.

*Simp.* Alas, master, what shall I do? I am not able to stand.

[*After the* BEADLE *hath hit him once, he leaps over the stool and runs away; and they follow and cry, 'A miracle!'*

*King.* O God, seest Thou this, and bearest so long?

*Queen.* It made me laugh to see the villain run.

*Glo.* Follow the knave; and take his drab away.

*Wife.* Alas, sir, we did it for pure need.

*Glo.* Let them be whipped through every market-town, till they come to Berwick, from whence they came.

[*Exeunt* WIFE, BEADLE, MAYOR, *etc.*

*Car.* Duke Humphrey has done a miracle to-day.

*Suf.* True; made the lame to leap and fly away.

*Glo.* But you have done more miracles than I;
You made in a day, my lord, whole towns to fly.

*Enter* BUCKINGHAM.

*King.* What tidings with our cousin Buckingham?

*Buck.* Such as my heart doth tremble to unfold.
A sort of naughty persons, lewdly bent,
Under the countenance and confederacy
Of Lady Eleanor, the protector's wife,
The ringleader and head of all this rout,
Have practiced dangerously against your state,
Dealing with witches and with conjurers:
Whom we have apprehended in the fact;
Raising up wicked spirits from under ground,
Demanding of King Henry's life and death,
And other of your highness' privy-council,
As more at large your grace shall understand.

*Car.* [*Aside to* GLO.] And so, my lord protector, by this means
Your lady is forthcoming yet at London.
This news, I think, hath turn'd your weapon's edge;
'Tis like, my lord, you will not keep your hour.

*Glo.* Ambitious churchman, leave to afflict my heart:
Sorrow and grief have vanquish'd all my powers;

And, vanquish'd as I am, I yield to thee,
Or to the meanest groom.

*King.* O God, what mischief's work the wicked ones,
Heaping confusion on their own heads thereby!

*Queen.* Gloucester, see here the tainture of thy nest,
And look thyself be faultless, thou wert best.

*Glou.* Madam, for myself, to heaven I do appeal,
How I have loved my king and commonweal:
And, for my wife, I know not how it stands;
Sorry I am to hear what I have heard:
Noble she is, but if she have forgot
Honor and virtue and conversed with such
As, like to pitch, defile nobility,
I banish her my bed and company,
And give her as a prey to law and shame,
That hath dishonor'd Gloucester's honest name.

*King.* Well, for this night we will repose us here:
To-morrow toward London back again,
To look into this business thoroughly,
And call these foul offenders to their answers,
And poise the cause in justice's equal scales,
Whose beam stands sure, whose rightful cause prevails.  [*Flourish. Exeunt.*

SCENE II.—LONDON. *The* DUKE OF YORK'S *Garden.*

*Enter* YORK, SALISBURY, *and* WARWICK.

*York.* Now, my good Lords of Salisbury and Warwick,
Our simple supper ended, give me leave
In this close walk to satisfy myself,
In craving your opinion of my title,
Which is infallible, to England's crown.

*Sal.* My lord, I long to hear it at full.

*War.* Sweet York, begin: and if thy claim be good,
The Nevils are thy subjects to command.

*York.* Then thus:
Edward the Third, my lords, had seven sons:
The first, Edward the Black Prince, Prince of Wales;
The second, William of Hatfield, and the third,
Lionel Duke of Clarence; next to whom
Was John of Gaunt, the Duke of Lancaster;
The fifth was Edmund Langley, Duke of York;
The sixth was Thomas of Woodstock, Duke of Gloucester;
William of Windsor was the seventh and last.
Edward the Black Prince died before his father,
And left behind him Richard, his only son,
Who after Edward the Third's death reign'd as king;

Till Henry Bolingbroke, Duke of Lancaster,
The eldest son and heir of John of Gaunt,
Crown'd by the name of Henry the Fourth,
Seized on the realm, deposed the rightful
    king,
Sent his poor queen to France, from whence
    she came,
And him to Pomfret; where, as all you know,
Harmless Richard was murder'd traitorously.
    *War.* Father, the duke hath told the truth;
Thus got the house of Lancaster the crown.
    *York.* Which now they hold by force and
    not by right;
For Richard, the first son's heir, being dead,
The issue of the next son should have reign'd.
    *Sal.* But William of Hatfield died without
    an heir.
    *York.* The third son, Duke of Clarence,
    from whose line
I claim the crown, had issue, Philippe, a
    daughter,
Who married Edmund Mortimer, Earl of
    March:
Edmund had issue, Roger Earl of March;
Roger had issue, Edmund, Anne and Eleanor.
    *Sal.* This Edmund, in the reign of Boling-
    broke,
As I have read, laid claim unto the crown;
And, but for Owen Glendower, had been
    king,
Who kept him in captivity till he died.
But to the rest.
    *York.*         His eldest sister, Anne,
My mother, being heir unto the crown,
Married Richard Earl of Cambridge; who
    was son
To Edmund Langley, Edward the Third's
    fifth son.
By her I claim the kingdom: she was heir
To Roger Earl of March, who was the son
Of Edmund Mortimer, who married Philippe,
Sole daughter unto Lionel Duke of Clarence:
So, if the issue of the elder son
Succeed before the younger, I am king.
    *War.* What plain proceeding is more plain
    than this?
Henry doth claim the crown from John of
    Gaunt,
The fourth son; York claims it from the
    third.
Till Lionel's issue fails, his should not reign:
It fails not yet, but flourishes in thee
And in thy sons, fair slips of such a stock.
Then, father Salisbury, kneel we together;
And in this private plot be we the first
That shall salute our rightful sovereign
With honor of his birthright to the crown.
    *Both.* Long live our sovereign Richard,
    England's king!
    *York.* We thank you, lords. But I am not
    your king
Till I be crown'd, and that my sword be
    stain'd

With heart-blood of the house of Lancaster;
And that's not suddenly to be perform'd,
But with advice and silent secrecy.
Do you as I do in these dangerous days:
Wink at the Duke of Suffolk's insolence,
At Beaufort's pride, at Somerset's ambition,
At Buckingham and all the crew of them,
Till they have snared the shepherd of the
    flock,
That virtuous prince, the good Duke Hum-
    phrey:
'Tis that they seek, and they in seeking that
Shall find their deaths, if York can prophesy.
    *Sal.* My lord, break we off; we know your
    mind at full.
    *War.* My heart assures me that the Earl of
    Warwick
Shall one day make the Duke of York a king.
    *York.* And, Nevil, this I do assure myself:
Richard shall live to make the Earl of War-
    wick
The greatest man in England but the king.
                      *[Exeunt.*

        Scene III.—*A Hall of Justice.*

*Sound trumpets. Enter the* King, *the* Queen,
    Gloucester, York, Suffolk, *and* Salis-
    bury; *the* Duchess of Gloucester, Mar-
    gery Jourdain, Southwell, Hume, *and*
    Bolingbroke, *under guard.*

    *King.* Stand forth, Dame Eleanor Cobham,
    Gloucester's wife:
In sight of God and us, your guilt is great:
Receive the sentence of the law for sins
Such as by God's book are adjudged to death.
You four, from hence to prison back again;
From thence unto the place of execution:
The witch in Smithfield shall be burn'd to
    ashes,
And you three shall be strangled on the gal-
    lows.
You, madam, for you are more nobly born,
Despoiled of your honor in your life,
Shall, after three days' open penance done,
Live in your country here in banishment,
With Sir John Stanley, in the Isle of Man.
    *Duch.* Welcome is banishment; welcome
    were my death.
    *Glo.* Eleanor, the law, thou see'st, hath
    judged thee:
I cannot justify whom the law condemns.
        *[Exeunt* Duchess *and other* prisoners,
                     *guarded.*
Mine eyes are full of tears, my heart of grief.
Ah, Humphrey, this dishonor in thine age
Will bring thy head with sorrow to the
    ground!
I beseech your majesty, give me leave to go;
Sorrow would solace and mine age would
    ease.
    *King.* Stay, Humphrey Duke of Glouces-
    ter: ere thou go,
Give up thy staff: Henry will to himself

Protector be; and God shall be my hope,
My stay, my guide and lantern to my feet:
And go in peace, Humphrey, no less be-
loved
Than when thou wert protector to thy king.

*Queen.* I see no reason why a king of
years
Should be to be protected like a child.
God and King Henry govern England's
realm.
Give up your staff, sir, and the king his
realm.

*Glo.* My staff? here, noble Henry, is my
staff:
As willingly do I the same resign
As e'er thy father Henry made it mine;
And even as willingly at thy feet I leave it
As others would ambitiously receive it.
Farewell, good king: when I am dead and
gone,
May honorable peace attend thy throne!
[*Exit.*

*Queen.* Why, now is Henry king, and Mar-
garet queen;
And Humphrey Duke of Gloucester scarce
himself,
That bears so shrewd a maim; two pulls at
once;
His lady banish'd, and a limb lopp'd off.
This staff of honor raught, there let it stand
Where it best fits to be, in Henry's hand.

*Suf.* Thus droops this lofty pine and hangs
his sprays;
Thus Eleanor's pride dies in her youngest
days.

*York.* Lords, let him go. Please it your
majesty,
This is the day appointed for the combat;
And ready are the appellant and defendant,
The armorer and his man, to enter the lists,
So please your highness to behold the fight.

*Queen.* Aye, good my lord; for purposely
therefore
Left I the court, to see this quarrel tried.

*King.* O' God's name, see the lists and all
things fit:                        [right!
Here let them end it; and God defend the

*York.* I never saw a fellow worse bested,
Or more afraid to fight, than is the appellant,
The servant of this armorer, my lords.

*Enter at one door,* HORNER, *the Armorer, and
his* Neighbors, *drinking to him so much
that he is drunk; and he enters with a
drum before him and his staff with a sand-
bag fastened to it; and at the other door*
PETER, *his man, with a drum and a sand-
bag, and 'Prentices drinking to him.*

*First Neigh.* Here, neighbor Horner, I
drink to you in a cup of sack: and fear not,
neighbor, you shall do well enough.

*Sec. Neigh.* And here, neighbor, here's a
cup of charneco.

*Third Neigh.* And here's a pot of good
double beer, neighbor: drink, and fear not
your man.

*Hor.* Let it come, i' faith, and I'll pledge
you all; and a fig for Peter!

*First 'Pren.* Here, Peter, I drink to thee:
and be not afraid.

*Sec. 'Pren.* Be merry, Peter, and fear not
thy master: fight for credit of the 'prentices.

*Peter.* I thank you all: drink, and pray
for me, I pray you; for I think I have taken
my last draught in this world. Here, Robin,
an if I die, I give thee my apron: and, Will,
thou shalt have my hammer: and here, Tom,
take all the money that I have. O Lord bless
me! I pray God! for I am never able to deal
with my master, he hath learnt so much fence
already.

*Sal.* Come, leave your drinking, and fall
to blows. Sirrah, what's thy name?

*Peter.* Peter, forsooth.

*Sal.* Peter! what more?

*Peter.* Thump.

*Sal.* Thump! then see thou thump thy
master well.

*Hor.* Masters, I am come hither, as it
were, upon my man's instigation, to prove
him a knave and myself an honest man: and
touching the Duke of York, I will take my
death, I never meant him any ill, nor the king,
nor the queen: and therefore, Peter, have at
thee with a downright blow!

*York.* Dispatch: this knave's tongue begins to double. Sound, trumpets, alarum to
the combatants!

[*Alarum. They fight, and* PETER *strikes him
down.*

*Hor.* Hold, Peter, hold! I confess, I confess treason.                        [*Dies.*

*York.* Take away his weapon. Fellow,
thank God, and the good wine in the master's
way.

*Peter.* O God, have I overcome mine enemy in this presence? O Peter, thou hast
prevailed in right!

*King.* Go, take hence that traitor from our
sight;
For by his death we do perceive his guilt:
And God in justice hath reveal'd to us
The truth and innocence of this poor fellow,
Which he had thought to have murder'd
wrongfully.
Come, fellow, follow us for thy reward.
[*Sound a flourish. Exeunt.*

SCENE IV.—*A Street.*

*Enter* GLOUCESTER *and his* Serving-men, *in
mourning cloaks.*

*Glo.* Thus sometimes hath the brightest
day a cloud:
And after summer evermore succeeds

Barren winter, with his wrathful nipping
  cold:
So cares and joys abound, as seasons fleet.
Sirs, what's o'clock?
    *Serv.*                    Ten, my lord.
    *Glo.* Ten is the hour that was appointed
      me
To watch the coming of my punish'd
  duchess:
Uneath may she endure the flinty streets,
To tread them with her tender-feeling feet.
Sweet Nell, ill can thy noble mind abrook
The abject people gazing on thy face,
With envious looks laughing at thy shame,
That erst did follow thy proud chariot-
  wheels,
When thou didst ride in triumph through the
  streets.
But, soft! I think she comes; and I'll prepare
My tear-stain'd eyes to see her miseries.

*Enter the* DUCHESS OF GLOUCESTER *in a
white sheet, and a taper burning in her
hand; with* SIR JOHN STANLEY, *the* Sheriff,
*and* Officers.

    *Serv.* So please your grace, we'll take her
      from the sheriff.
    *Glo.* No, stir not, for your lives; let her
      pass by.
    *Duch.* Come you, my lord, to see my open
      shame?
Now thou dost penance too. Look how they
  gaze!
See how the giddy multitude do point,
And nod their heads, and throw their eyes on
  thee!
Ah, Gloucester, hide thee from their hateful
  looks,
And, in thy closet pent up, rue my shame,
And ban thine enemies, both mine and
  thine!
    *Glo.* Be patient, gentle Nell; forget this
      grief.
    *Duch.* Ah, Gloucester, teach me to forget
      myself.
For whilst I think I am thy married wife,
And thou a prince, protector of this land,
Methinks I should not thus be led along,
Mail'd up in shame, with papers on my back,
And follow'd with a rabble that rejoice
To see my tears and hear my deep-fet groans.
The ruthless flint doth cut my tender feet,
And when I start, the envious people laugh,
And bid me be advised how I tread.
Ah, Humphrey, can I bear this shameful
  yoke?
Trow'st thou that e'er I'll look upon the
  world,
Or count them happy that enjoy the sun?
No; dark shall be my light and night my
  day;
To think upon my pomp shall be my hell.

Sometime I'll say, I am Duke Humphrey's
  wife,
And he a prince and ruler of the land:
Yet so he ruled, and such a prince he was,
As he stood by whilst I, his forlorn duchess,
Was made a wonder and a pointing-stock
To every idle rascal follower.
But be thou mild and blush not at my shame,
Not stir at nothing till the axe of death
Hang over thee, as, sure, it shortly will;
For Suffolk—he that can do all in all
With her that hateth thee and hates us all—
And York and impious Beaufort, that false
  priest,
Have all limed bushes to betray thy wings,
And, fly thou how thou canst, they'll tangle
  thee:
But fear not thou, until thy foot be snared,
Nor never seek prevention of thy foes.
    *Glo.* Ah Nell, forbear! thou aimest all
      awry;
I must offend before I be attainted;
And had I twenty times so many foes,
And each of them had twenty times their
  power,
All these could not procure me any scathe,
So long as I am loyal, true and crimeless.
Wouldst have me rescue thee from this re-
  proach?
Why, yet thy scandal were not wiped away,
But I in danger for the breach of law.
Thy greatest help is quiet, gentle Nell:
I pray thee, sort thy heart to patience;
These few days' wonder will be quickly worn.

*Enter a* Herald.

    *Her.* I summon your grace to his maj-
      esty's parliament,
Holden at Bury the first of this next month.
    *Glo.* And my consent ne'er ask'd herein
      before!
This is close dealing. Well, I will be there.
                              [*Exit* Herald.
My Nell, I take my leave: and, master sher-
  iff,
Let not her penance exceed the king's com-
  mission,
    *Sher.* An't please your grace, here my com-
      mission stays,
And Sir John Stanley is appointed now
To take her with him to the Isle of Man.
    *Glo.* Must you, Sir John, protect my lady
      here?
    *Stan.* So am I given in charge, may't please
      your grace.
    *Glo.* Entreat her not the worse in that I
      pray
You use her well: the world may laugh
  again;
And I may live to do you kindness if
You do it her: and so, Sir John, farewell!
    *Duch.* What, gone, my lord, and bid me
      not farewell!

*Glo.* Witness my tears, I cannot stay to speak.

[*Exeunt* GLOUCESTER *and* Serving-men.

*Duch.* Art thou gone too? all comfort go with thee!
For none abides with me: my joy is death,—
Death, at whose name I oft have been afear'd,
Because I wish'd this world's eternity.
Stanley, I prithee, go, and take me hence;
I care not whither, for I beg no favor,
Only convey me where thou art commanded.

*Stan.* Why, madam, that is to the Isle of Man;
There to be used according to your state.

*Duch.* That's bad enough, for I am but reproach:
And shall I then be used reproachfully?

*Stan.* Like to a duchess, and Duke Humphrey's lady;
According to that state you shall be used.

*Duch.* Sheriff, farewell, and better than I fare,
Although thou hast been conduct of my shame.

*Sher.* It is my office; and, madam, pardon me.

*Duch.* Aye, aye, farewell; thy office is discharged.
Come, Stanley, shall we go?

*Stan.* Madam, your penance done, throw off this sheet,
And go we to attire you for our journey.

*Duch.* My shame will not be shifted with my sheet:
No, it will hang upon my richest robes,
And show itself, attire me how I can.
Go, lead the way; I long to see my prison.

[*Exeunt.*

## ACT III.

SCENE I.—*The Abbey at Bury St. Edmund's.*

*Sound a Sennet. Enter* KING, QUEEN, CARDINAL BEAUFORT, SUFFOLK, YORK, BUCKINGHAM, SALISBURY *and* WARWICK *to the Parliament.*

*King.* I muse my Lord of Gloucester is not come
'Tis not his wont to be the hindmost man,
Whate'er occasion keeps him from us now.

*Queen.* Can you not see? or will ye not observe
The strangeness of his alter'd countenance?
With what a majesty he bears himself,
How insolent of late he is become,
How proud, how peremptory, and unlike himself?
We know the time since he was mild and affable,
And if we did but glance a far-off look,
Immediately he was upon his knee,
That all the court admired him for submission;
But meet him now, and, be it in the morn,
When every one will give the time of day,
He knits his brow and shows an angry eye,
And passeth by with stiff unbowed knee,
Disdaining duty that to us belongs.
Small curs are not regarded when they grin;
But great men tremble when the lion roars;
And Humphrey is no little man in England.
First note that he is near you in descent,
And should you fall, he is the next will mount.
Me seemeth then it is no policy,
Respecting what a rancorous mind he bears,
And his advantage following your decease,
That he should come about your royal person,
Or be admitted to your highness' council.
By flattery hath he won the commons' hearts,
And when he please to make commotion,
'Tis to be feared they all will follow him.
Now 'tis the spring, and weeds are shallow-rooted;
Suffer them now, and they'll o'ergrow the garden,
And choke the herbs for want of husbandry.
The reverent care I bear unto my lord
Made me collect these dangers in the duke.
If it be fond, call it a woman's fear;
Which fear if better reasons can supplant,
I will subscribe and say I wrong'd the duke.
My Lord of Suffolk, Buckingham, and York,
Reprove my allegation, if you can;
Or else conclude my words effectual.

*Suf.* Well hath your highness seen into this duke;
And, had I first been put to speak my mind,
I think I should have told your grace's tale.
The duchess by his subornation,
Upon my life, began her devilish practices:
Or, if he were not privy to those faults,
Yet, by reputing of his high descent,
As next the king he was successive heir,
As such high vaunts of his nobility,
Did instigate the bedlam brain-sick duchess
By wicked means to frame our sovereign's fall.
Smooth runs the water where the brook is deep;
And in his simple show he harbors treason.
The fox barks not when he would steal the lamb.
No, no, my sovereign; Gloucester is a man
Unsounded yet and full of deep deceit.

*Car.* Did he not, contrary to form of law,
Devise strange deaths for small offences done?

*York.* And did he not, in his protectorship,
Levy great sums of money through the realm
For soldiers' pay in France, and never sent it?

By means whereof the towns each day re-
    volted.
*Buck.* Tut, these are petty faults to faults
    unknown,
Which time will bring to light in smooth
    Duke Humphrey.
*King.* My lords, at once: the care you
    have of us,
To mow down thorns that would annoy our
    foot,
Is worthy praise: but, shall I speak my con-
    science,
Our kinsman Gloucester is as innocent
From meaning treason to our royal person,
As is the sucking lamb or harmless dove:
The duke is virtuous, mild and too well given
To dream on evil or to work my downfall.
*Queen.* Ah, what's more dangerous than
    this fond affiance!
Seems he a dove? his feathers are but bor-
    row'd,
For he's disposed as the hateful raven:
Is he a lamb? his skin is surely lent him,
For he's inclined as is the ravenous wolf.
Who cannot steal a shape that means deceit?
Take heed, my lord; the welfare of us all
Hangs on the cutting short that fraudful
    man.

        *Enter* SOMERSET.

*Som.* All health unto my gracious sover-
    eign!
*King.* Welcome, Lord Somerset. What
    news from France?
*Som.* That all your interest in those terri-
    tories
Is utterly bereft you; all is lost.
*King.* Cold news, Lord Somerset: but
    God's will be done!
*York.* [*Aside*] Cold news for me; for I
    had hope of France
As firmly as I hope for fertile England.
Thus are my blossoms blasted in the bud,
And caterpillars eat my leaves away;
But I will remedy this gear ere long,
Or sell my title for a glorious grave.

        *Enter* GLOUCESTER.

*Glo.* All happiness unto my lord the king!
Pardon, my liege, that I have stay'd so long.
*Suf.* Nay, Gloucester, know that thou art
    come too soon,
Unless thou wert more loyal than thou art:
I do arrest thee of high treason here.
*Glo.* Well, Suffolk, thou shalt not see me
    blush,
Nor change my countenance for this arrest:
A heart unspotted is not easily daunted.
The purest spring is not so free from mud
As I am clear from treason to my sovereign:
Who can accuse me? wherein am I guilty?
*York.* 'Tis thought, my lord, that you took
    bribes of France,

And, being protector, stay'd the soldiers' pay;
By means whereof his highness hath lost
    France.
*Glo.* Is it but thought so? what are they
    that think it?
I never robb'd the soldiers of their pay,
Nor ever had one penny bribe from France
So help me God, as I have watch'd the
    night,
Aye, night by night, in studying good for
    England!
That doit that e'er I wrested from the king,
Or any groat I hoarded to my use,
Be brought against me at my trial-day!
No; many a pound of mine own proper store,
Because I would not tax the needy commons,
Have I dispursed to the garrisons,
And never ask'd for restitution.
*Car.* It serves you well, my lord, to say so
    much.
*Glo.* I say no more than truth, so help me
    God!
*York.* In your protectorship you did de-
    vise
Strange tortures for offenders never heard of,
That England was defamed by tyranny.
*Glo.* Why, 'tis well known that, whiles I
    was protector,
Pity was all the fault that was in me;
For I should melt at an offender's tears,
And lowly words were ransom for their fault.
Unless it were a bloody murderer,
Or foul felonious thief that fleeced poor pas-
    sengers,
I never gave them condign punishment:
Murder, indeed, that bloody sin, I tortured
Above the felon or what trespass else.
*Suf.* My lord, these faults are easy,
    quickly answer'd:
But mightier crimes are laid unto your
    charge,
Whereof you cannot easily purge yourself.
I do arrest you in his highness' name;
And here commit you to my lord cardinal
To keep, until your further time of trial.
*King.* My Lord of Gloucester, 'tis my spe-
    cial hope
That you will clear yourself from all suspect:
My conscience tells me you are innocent.
*Glo.* Ah, gracious lord, these days are
    dangerous:
Virtue is choked with foul ambition,
And charity chased hence by rancor's hand;
Foul subordination is predominant,
And equity exiled your highness' land.
I know their complot is to have my life;
And if my death might make this island
    happy,
And prove the period of their tyranny,
I would expend it with all willingness:
But mine is made the prologue to their play;
For thousands more, that yet suspect no
    peril,

Will not conclude their plotted tragedy.
Beaufort's red sparkling eyes blab his heart's
    malice,
And Suffolk's cloudy brow his stormy hate;
Sharp Buckingham unburthens with his
    tongue
The envious load that lies upon his heart;
And dogged York, that reaches at the moon,
Whose overweening arm I have pluck'd back,
By false accuse doth level at my life:
And you, my sovereign lady, with the rest,
Causeless have laid disgraces on my head,
And with your best endeavor have stirr'd up
My liefest liege to be mine enemy:
Aye, all of you have laid your heads to-
    gether—
Myself had notice of your conventicles—
And all to make away my guiltless life.
I shall not want false witness to condemn
    me,
Nor store of treasons to augment my guilt;
The ancient proverb will be well effected:
'A staff is quickly found to beat a dog.'
    *Car.* My liege, his railing is intolerable:
If those that care to keep your royal person
From treason's secret knife and traitors'
    rage
Be thus upbraided, chid and rated at,
And the offender granted scope of speech,
'Twill make them cool in zeal unto your
    grace.
    *Suf.* Hath he not twit our sovereign lady
    here
With ignominious words, though clerkly
    couch'd,
As if she had suborned some to swear
False allegations to o'erthrow his state?
    *Queen.* But I can give the loser leave to
    chide.
    *Glo.* Far truer spoke than meant: I lose,
    indeed;
Beshrew the winners, for they play'd me
    false!                              [speak.
And well such losers may have leave to
    *Buck.* He'll wrest the sense and hold us
    here all day:
Lord cardinal, he is your prisoner.
    *Car.* Sirs, take away the duke, and guard
    him sure.
    *Glo.* Ah! thus King Henry throws away
    his crutch,
Before his legs be firm to bear his body.
Thus is the shepherd beaten from thy side,
And wolves are gnarling who shall gnaw thee
    first.
Ah, that my fear were false! ah, that it were!
For, good King Henry, thy decay I fear.
                              [*Exit, guarded.*
    *King.* My lords, what to your wisdom
    seemeth best,
Do or undo, as if ourself were here.
    *Queen.* What, will your highness leave the
    Parliament?

    *King.* Aye, Margaret; my heart is drown'd
    with grief,
Whose flood begins to flow within mine eyes,
My body round engirt with misery,
For what's more miserable than discontent?
Ah, uncle Humphrey! in thy face I see
The map of honor, truth and loyalty:
And yet, good Humphrey, is the hour to
    come
That e'er I proved thee false or fear'd thy
    faith.
What louring star now envies thy estate,
That these great lords and Margaret our
    queen
Do seek subversion of thy harmless life?
Thou never didst them wrong nor no man
    wrong;
And as the butcher takes away the calf,
And binds the wretch, and beats it when it
    strays,
Bearing it to the bloody slaughter-house,
Even so remorseless have they borne him
    hence;
And as the dam runs lowing up and down,
Looking the way her harmless young one
    went,
And can do nought but wail her darling's
    loss,
Even so myself bewails good Gloucester's
    case
With sad unhelpful tears, and with dimm'd
    eyes
Look after him and cannot do him good,
So mighty are his vowed enemies.
His fortunes I will weep, and 'twixt each
    groan
Say 'Who's a traitor? Gloucester he is none.'
    [*Exeunt all but* QUEEN, CARDINAL BEAU-
    FORT, SUFFOLK *and* YORK. SOMERSET *re-
    mains apart.*
    *Queen.* Free lords, cold snow melts with
    the sun's hot beams.
Henry my lord is cold in great affairs,
Too full of foolish pity, and Gloucester's
    show
Beguiles him, as the mournful crocodile
With sorrow snares relenting passengers,
Or as the snake roll'd in a flowering bank,
With shining checker'd slough, doth sting a
    child
That for the beauty thinks it excellent.
Believe me, lords, were none more wise than
    I—
And yet herein I judge mine own with
    good—
This Gloucester should be quickly rid the
    world
To rid us from the fear we have of him.
    *Car.* That he should die is worthy policy;
But yet we want a color for his death:
'Tis meet he be condemn'd by course of law.
    *Suf.* But, in my mind, that were no policy:
The commons haply rise, to save his life;

The king will labor still to save his life,
And yet we have but trivial argument,
More than mistrust, that shows him worthy death.

*York.* So that, by this, you would not have him die.

*Suf.* Ah, York, no man alive so fain as I!

*York.* 'Tis York that hath more reason for his death.
But, my lord cardinal, and you, my Lord of Suffolk,
Say as you think, and speak it from your souls:
Were't not all one, an empty eagle were set
To guard the chicken from a hungry kite,
As place Duke Humphrey for the king's protector?    [of death.

*Queen.* So the poor chicken should be sure

*Suf.* Madam, 'tis true; and were't not madness, then,
To make the fox surveyor of the fold:
Who being accused a crafty murderer,
His guilt should be but idly posted over,
Because his purpose is not executed.
No; let him die, in that he is a fox,
By nature proved an enemy to the flock,
Before his chaps he stain'd with crimson blood,
As Humphrey, proved by reasons, to my liege.
And do not stand on quillets how to slay him:
Be it by gins, by snares, by subtlety,
Sleeping or waking, 'tis no matter how,
So he be dead; for that is good deceit
Which mates him first that first intends deceit.

*Queen.* Thrice-noble Suffolk, 'tis resolutely spoke.

*Suf.* Not resolute, except so much were done;
For things are often spoke and seldom meant:
But that my heart accordeth with my tongue,
Seeing the deed is meritorious,
And to preserve my sovereign from his foe,
Say but the word, and I will be his priest.

*Car.* But I would have him dead, my lord of Suffolk,
Ere you can take due orders for a priest:
Say you consent and censure well the deed,
And I'll provide his executioner,
I tender so the safety of my liege.

*Suf.* Here is my hand, the deed is worthy doing.

*Queen.* And so say I.

*York.* And I: and now we three have spoke it.
It skills not greatly who impugns our doom.

*Enter a* Post.

*Post.* Great lords, from Ireland am I come amain,
To signify that rebels there are up,
And put the Englishmen unto the sword:
Send succors, lords, and stop the rage betime,
Before the wound do grow uncurable;
For, being green, there is great hope of help.

*Car.* A breach that craves a quick expedient stop!
What counsel give you in this weighty cause?

*York.* That Somerset be sent as regent thither:
'Tis meet that lucky ruler be employ'd;
Witness the fortune he hath had in France.

*Som.* If York, with all his far-fet policy,
Had been the regent there instead of me,
He never would have stay'd in France so long.

*York.* No, not to lose it all, as thou hast done:
I rather would have lost my life betimes
Than bring a burthen of dishonor home,
By staying there so long till all were lost.
Show me one scar character'd on thy skin:
Men's flesh preserved so whole do seldom win.

*Queen.* Nay, then, this spark will prove a raging fire.
If wind and fuel be brought to feed it with:
No more, good York; sweet Somerset, be still:
Thy fortune, York, hadst thou been regent there,
Might happily have proved far worse than his.

*York.* What, worse than nought? nay, then, a shame take all!

*Som.* And, in the number, thee that wishest shame!

*Car.* My Lord of York, try what your fortune is.
The uncivil kernes of Ireland are in arms,
And temper clay with blood of Englishmen:
To Ireland will you lead a band of men,
Collected choicely, from each county some
And try your hap against the Irishmen?

*York.* I will, my lord, so please his majesty.

*Suf.* Why, our authority is his consent,
And what we do establish he confirms:
Then, noble York, take thou this task in hand.

*York.* I am content: provide me soldiers, lords,
Whiles I take order for mine own affairs.

*Suf.* A charge, Lord York, that I will see perform'd.
But now return we to the false Duke Humphrey.

*Car.* No more of him; for I will deal with him,
That henceforth he shall trouble us no more.
And so break off; the day is almost spent:
Lord Suffolk, you and I must talk of that event.

*York.* My Lord of Suffolk, within four-
teen days
At Bristol I expect my soldiers;
For there I'll ship them all for Ireland.
*Suf.* I'll see it truly done, my Lord of
York.  [*Exeunt all but York.*
*York.* Now, York, or never, steel thy fear-
ful thoughts,
And change misdoubt to resolution:
Be that thou hopest to be, or what thou art
Resign to death; it is not worth the en-
joying:
Let pale-faced fear keep with the mean-born
man,
And find no harbor in a royal heart.
Faster than spring-time showers comes
thought on thought,
And not a thought but thinks on dignity.
My brain more busy than the laboring spider
Weaves tedious snares to trap mine enemies.
Well, nobles, well, 'tis politicly done,
To send me packing with an host of men:
I fear me you but warm the starved snake,
Who, cherish'd in your breasts, will sting
your hearts.
'Twas men I lack'd, and you will give them
me:
I take it kindly; yet be well assured
You put sharp weapons in a madman's hands.
Whiles I in Ireland nourish a mighty band,
I will stir up in England some black storm
Shall blow ten thousand souls to heaven or
hell;
And this fell tempest shall not cease to rage
Until the golden circuit on my head,
Like to the glorious sun's transparent beams,
Do calm the fury of this mad-bred flaw.
And, for a minister of my intent,
I have seduced a headstrong Kentishman,
John Cade of Ashford,
To make commotion, as full well he can,
Under the title of John Mortimer.
In Ireland have I seen this stubborn Cade
Oppose himself against a troop of kernes,
And fought so long, till that his thighs with
darts
Were almost like a sharp-quill'd porpentine;
And, in the end being rescued, I have seen
Him caper upright like a wild Morisco,
Shaking the bloody darts as he his bells.
Full often, like a shag-hair'd crafty kerne,
Hath he conversed with the enemy,
And undiscover'd come to me again,
And given me notice of their villanies.
This devil here shall be my substitute;
For that John Mortimer, which now is dead,
In face, in gait, in speech, he doth resemble:
By this I shall perceive the commons' mind,
How they affect the house and claim of York.
Say he be taken, rack'd and tortured,
I know no pain they can inflict upon him
Will make him say I moved him to those
arms.

Say that he thrive, as 'tis great like he will,
Why, then from Ireland come I with my
strength,
And reap the harvest which that rascal
sow'd;
For Humphrey being dead, as he shall be,
And Henry put apart, the next for me.
[*Exit.*

SCENE II

*Bury St. Edmund's. A room of state. Enter
certain* Murderers, *hastily.*

*First Mur.* Run to my Lord of Suffolk;
let him know
We have dispatch'd the duke, as he commanded.
*Sec. Mur.* O that it were to do! What have
we done?
Didst ever hear a man so penitent?

*Enter* SUFFOLK.

*First Mur.* Hence comes my lord.
*Suf.* Now, sirs, have you dispatch'd this
thing?
*First Mur.* Aye, my good lord, he's dead.
*Suf.* Why, that's well said. Go, get you to
my house;
I will reward you for this venturous deed.
The king and all the peers are here at hand.
Have you laid fair the bed? Is all things
well,
According as I gave directions?
*First Mur.* 'Tis, my good lord.
*Suf.* Away, be gone.  [*Exeunt* Murderers.

*Sound trumpets. Enter the* KING, *the* QUEEN,
CARDINAL BEAUFORD, SOMERSET, *with* Attendants.

*King.* Go, call our uncle to our presence
straight;
Say we intend to try his grace to-day,
If he be guilty, as 'tis published.
*Suf.* I'll call him presently, my noble lord.
[*Exit.*
*King.* Lords, take your places; and, I pray
you all,
Proceed no straiter 'gainst our uncle Glouces-
ter
Than from true evidence of good esteem
He be approved in practice culpable.
*Queen.* God forbid any malice should pre-
vail,
That faultless may condemn a nobleman!
Pray God he may acquit him of suspicion!
*King.* I thank thee, Nell; these words con-
tent me much.

*Re-enter* SUFFOLK.

How now! why look'st thou pale? why tremblest thou?
Where is our uncle? what's the matter, Suffolk?

*Suf.* Dead in his bed, my lord; Gloucester is dead.

*Queen.* Marry, God forfend.

*Car.* God's secret judgment: I did dream to-night
The duke was dumb and could not speak a word.    [*The* KING *swoons.*

*Queen.* How fares my lord? Help, lords! the king is dead.    [nose.

*Som.* Rear up his body; wring him by the

*Queen.* Run, go, help, help! O Henry, ope thine eyes!

*Suf.* He doth revive again: Madam, be patient.

*King.* O heavenly God!

*Queen.* How fares my gracious lord?

*Suf.* Comfort, my sovereign! gracious Henry, comfort!

*King.* What, doth my Lord of Suffolk comfort me?
Came he right now to sing a raven's note,
Whose dismal tune bereft my vital powers;
And thinks he that the chirping of a wren,
By crying comfort from a hollow breast,
Can chase away the first-conceived sound?
Hide not thy poison with such sugar'd words;
Lay not thy hands on me; forbear, I say;
Their touch affrights me as a serpent's sting.
Thou baleful messenger, out of my sight!
Upon thy eye-balls murderous tyranny
Sits in grim majesty, to fright the world.
Look not upon me, for thine eyes are wounding:
Yet do not go away: come, basilisk,
And kill the innocent gazer with thy sight;
For in the shade of death I shall find joy;
In life but double death, now Gloucester's dead.

*Queen.* Why do you rate my Lord of Suffolk thus?
Although the duke was enemy to him,
Yet he most Christian-like laments his death:
And for myself, foe as he was to me,
Might liquid tears, or heart-offending groans,
Or blood-consuming sighs recall his life,
I would be blind with weeping, sick with groans,
Look pale as primrose with blood-drinking sighs,
And all to have the noble duke alive.
What know I how the world may deem of me?
For it is known we were but hollow friends:
It may be judged I made the duke away;
So shall my name with slander's tongue be wounded,
And princes' courts be fill'd with my reproach.
This get I by his death: aye me, unhappy!
To be a queen, and crown'd with infamy!

*King.* Ah, woe is me for Gloucester, wretched man!

*Queen.* Be woe for me, more wretched than he is.
What, dost thou turn away and hide thy face?
I am no loathsome leper; look on me.
What! art thou, like the adder, waxen deaf?
Be poisonous too and kill thy forlorn queen.
Is all thy comfort shut in Gloucester's tomb?
Why, then, dame Eleanor was ne'er thy joy.
Erect his statuë and worship it,
And make my image but an alehouse sign.
Was I for this nigh wreck'd upon the sea,
And twice by awkward wind from England's bank
Drove back again unto my native clime?
What boded this, but well forewarning wind
Did seem to say 'Seek not a scorpion's nest,
Nor set no footing on this unkind shore'?
What did I then, but cursed the gentle gusts,
And he that loosed them forth their brazen caves;
And bid them blow towards England's blessed shore,
Or turn our stern upon a dreadful rock?
Yet Æolus would not be a murderer,
But left that hateful office unto thee:
The pretty-vaulting sea refused to drown me,
Knowing that thou wouldst have me drown'd on shore,
With tears as salt as sea, through thy unkindness:
The splitting rocks cower'd in the sinking sands,
And would not dash me with their ragged sides,
Because thy flinty heart, more hard than they,
Might in thy palace perish Eleanor.
As far as I could ken thy chalky cliffs,
When from thy shore the tempest beat us back,
I stood upon the hatches in the storm,
And when the dusky sky began to rob
My earnest-gaping sight of thy land's view,
I took a costly jewel from my neck—
A heart it was, bound in with diamonds—
And threw it towards thy land: the sea received it,
And so I wish'd thy body might my heart:
And even with this I lost fair England's view,
And bid mine eyes be packing with my heart,
And call'd them blind and dusky spectacles,
For losing ken of Albion's wished coast.
How often have I tempted Suffolk's tongue,
The agent of thy foul inconstancy,
To sit and witch me, as Ascanius did,
When he to madding Dido would unfold
His father's acts commenced in burning Troy!
Am I not witch'd like her? or thou not false like him?

Aye me, I can no more! die, Eleanor!
For Henry weeps that thou dost live so long.

*Noise within. Enter* WARWICK, SALISBURY,
*and many Commons.*

*War.* It is reported, mighty sovereign,
That good Duke Humphrey traitorously is
   murder'd                    [means.
By Suffolk and the Cardinal Beaufort's
The commons, like an angry hive of bees
That want their leader, scatter up and down,
And care not who they sting in his revenge.
Myself have calm'd their spleenful mutiny,
Until they hear the order of his death.
*King.* That he is dead, good Warwick, 'tis
   too true;
But how he died God knows, not Henry:
Enter his chamber, view his breathless corpse,
And comment then upon his sudden death.
*War.* That shall I do, my liege. Stay, Sal-
   isbury,
With the rude multitude till I return. [*Exit.*
*King.* O Thou that judgest all things, stay
   my thoughts,
My thoughts, that labor to persuade my soul
Some violent hands were laid on Hum-
   phrey's life!
If my suspect be false, forgive me, God;
For judgment only doth belong to Thee.
Fain would I go to chafe his paly lips
With twenty thousand kisses, and to drain
Upon his face an ocean of salt tears,
To tell my love unto his dumb deaf trunk,
And with my fingers feel his hand unfeeling:
But all in vain are these mean obsequies;
And to survey his dead and earthy image,
What were it but to make my sorrow great-
   er?

*Re-enter* WARWICK *and others, bearing*
GLOUCESTER'S *body on a bed.*

*War.* Come hither, gracious sovereign,
   view this body.
*King.* That is to see how deep my grave is
   made;
For with his soul fled all my worldly solace,
For seeing him I see my life in death.
*War.* As surely as my soul intends to live
With that dread King, that took our state
   upon him
To free us from his father's wrathful curse,
I do believe that violent hands were laid
Upon the life of this thrice-famed duke.
*Suf.* A dreadful oath, sworn with a solemn
   tongue!
What instance gives Lord Warwick for his
   vow?
*War.* See how the blood is settled in his
   face.
Oft have I seen a timely-parted ghost,
Of ashy semblance, meager, pale and blood-
   less,

Being all descended to the laboring heart;
Who, in the conflict that it holds with death,
Attracts the same for aidance 'gainst the
   enemy;
Which with the heart there cools and ne'er
   returneth
To blush and beautify the cheek again.
But see, his face is black and full of blood,
His eye-balls further out than when he lived,
Staring full ghastly like a strangled man;
His hair uprear'd, his nostrils stretch'd with
   struggling;
His hands abroad display'd, as one that
   grasp'd
And tugg'd for life and was by strength sub-
   dued:
Look, on the sheets his hair, you see, is
   sticking;
His well-proportion'd beard made rough and
   rugged,
Like to the summer's corn by tempest lodged
It cannot be but he was murder'd here;
The least of all these signs were probable.
*Suf.* Why, Warwick, who should do the
   duke to death?
Myself and Beaufort had him in protection;
And we, I hope, sir, are no murderers.
*War.* But both of you were vow'd Duke
   Humphrey's foes,
And you, forsooth, had the good duke to
   keep:
'Tis like you would not feast him like a
   friend;
And 'tis well seen he found an enemy.
*Queen.* Then you, belike, suspect these
   noblemen
As guilty of Duke Humphrey's timeless death.
*War.* Who finds the heifer dead and bleed-
   ing fresh,
And sees fast by a butcher with an axe,
But will suspect 'twas he that made the
   slaughter?
Who finds the partridge in the puttock's nest,
But may imagine how the bird was dead,
Although the kite soar with unbloodied
   beak?
Even so suspicious is this tragedy.
*Queen.* Are you the butcher, Suffolk?
   Where's your knife?
Is Beaufort term'd a kite? Where are his tal-
   ons?
*Suf.* I wear no knife to slaughter sleep-
   ing men;
But here's a vengeful sword, rusted with ease.
That shall be scoured in his rancorous heart
That slanders me with murder's crimson
   badge.
Say, if thou darest, proud Lord of Warwick-
   shire,
That I am faulty in Duke Humphrey's death.
   [*Exeunt* CARDINAL, SOMERSET, and *others.*
*War.* What dares not Warwick, if false
   Suffolk dare him?

*Queen.* He dares not calm his contumelious
spirit,
Nor cease to be an arrogant controller,
Though Suffolk dare him twenty thousand
times.
    *War.* Madam, be still; with reverence may
I say;
For every word you speak in his behalf
Is slander to your royal dignity.
    *Suf.* Blunt-witted lord, ignoble in de-
meanor!
If ever lady wrong'd her lord so much.
Thy mother took into her blameful bed
Some stern untutor'd churl, and noble stock
Was graft with crab-tree slip; whose fruit
thou art
And never of the Nevils' noble race.
    *War.* But that the guilt of murder buckles
thee,
And I should rob the deathsman of his fee,
Quitting thee thereby of ten thousand shames,
And that my sovereign's presence makes me
mild,
I would, false murderous coward, on thy
knee
Make thee beg pardon for thy passed speech,
And say it was thy mother that thou
meant'st,
That thou thyself was born in bastardy;
And after all this fearful homage done,
Give thee thy hire and send thy soul to hell,
Pernicious blood-sucker of sleeping men!
    *Suf.* Thou shalt be waking while I shed
thy blood,
If from this presence thou darest go with me.
    *War.* Away even now, or I will drag thee
hence:
Unworthy though thou art, I'll cope with
thee
And do some service to Duke Humphrey's
ghost.
            [*Exeunt* SUFFOLK *and* WARWICK.
    *King.* What stronger breastplate than a
heart untainted!
Thrice is he arm'd that hath his quarrel just,
And he but naked, though lock'd up in steel,
Whose conscience with injustice is corrupted.
                [*A noise within.*
    *Queen.* What noise is this?

*Re-enter* SUFFOLK *and* WARWICK, *with their
weapons drawn.*

    *King.* Why, how now, lords! your wrath-
ful weapons drawn
Here in our presence! dare you be so bold?
Why, what tumultuous clamor have we here?
    *Suf.* The traitorous Warwick with the
men of Bury
Set all upon me, mighty sovereign.
    *Sal.* [*to the Commons, entering*] Sirs,
stand apart; the king shall know your mind.
Dread lord, the commons send you word by
me,

Unless Lord Suffolk straight be done to
death.
Or banished fair England's territories,
They will by violence tear him from your
palace,
And torture him with grievous lingering
death.
They say, by him the good Duke Humphrey
died;
They say, in him they fear your highness'
death;
And mere instinct of love and loyalty,
Free from a stubborn opposite intent,
As being thought to contradict your liking,
Makes them thus forward in his banishment.
They say, in care of your most royal person,
That if your highness should intend to sleep,
And charge that no man should disturb your
rest
In pain of your dislike or pain of death,
Yet, notwithstanding such a strait edict,
Were there a serpent seen, with forked
tongue,
That slily glided towards your majesty,
It were but necessary you were waked,
Lest, being suffer'd in that harmful slumber,
The mortal worm might make the sleep
eternal;
And therefore do they cry, though you for-
bid,
That they will guard you, whether you will
or no,
From such fell serpents as false Suffolk is,
With whose envenomed and fatal sting,
Your loving uncle, twenty times his worth,
They say, is shamefully bereft of life.
    *Commons* [*within*]. An answer from the
king, my Lord of Salisbury!
    *Suf.* 'Tis like the commons, rude unpol-
ish'd hinds,
Could send such message to their sovereign:
But you, my lord, were glad to be employ'd,
To show how quaint an orator you are:
But all the honor Salisbury hath won
Is, that he was the lord ambassador
Sent from a sort of tinkers to the king.
    *Commons* [*within*]. An answer from the
king, or we will all break in!
    *King.* Go, Salisbury, and tell them all from
me,
I thank them for their tender loving care,
And had I not been cited so by them,
Yet did I purpose as they do entreat;
For, sure, my thoughts do hourly prophesy
Mischance unto my state by Suffolk's means:
And therefore, by His majesty I swear,
Whose far unworthy deputy I am,
He shall not breathe infection in this air
But three days longer, on the pain of death.
                [*Exit Salisbury.*
    *Queen.* O Henry, let me plead for gentle
Suffolk!        [Suffolk!
    *King.* Ungentle queen, to call him gentle

No more, I say: if thou dost plead for him,
Thou wilt but add increase unto my wrath.
Had I but said, I would have kept my word,
But when I swear, it is irrevocable.
If, after three days' space, thou here be'st
found
On any ground that I am ruler of,
The world shall not be ransom for thy life.
Come, Warwick, come, good Warwick, go
with me;
I have great matters to impart to thee.
    [*Exeunt all but Queen and Suffolk.*
  *Queen.* Mischance and sorrow go along
with you!
Heart's discontent and sour affliction
Be playfellows to keep you company!
There's two of you; the devil make a third!
And threefold vengeance tend upon your
steps!
  *Suf.* Cease, gentle queen, these execrations,
And let thy Suffolk take his heavy leave.
  *Queen.* Fie, coward woman and soft-
hearted wretch!
Hast thou not spirit to curse thine enemy?
  *Suf.* A plague upon them! wherefore
should I curse them?
Would curses kill, as doth the mandrake's
groan,
I would invent as bitter-searching terms,
As curst, as harsh and horrible to hear,
Deliver'd strongly through my fixed teeth,
With full as many signs of deadly hate,
As lean-faced Envy in her loathsome cave:
My tongue should stumble in mine earnest
words;
Mine eyes should sparkle like the beaten
flint;
Mine hair be fix'd on end, as one distract;
Aye, every joint should seem to curse and
ban:
And even now my burthen'd heart would
break,
Should I not curse them. Poison be their
drink!
Gall, worse than gall, the daintiest that they
taste!
Their sweetest shade a grove of cypress trees!
Their chiefest prospect murdering basilisks!
Their softest touch as smart as lizards' stings!
Their music frightful as the serpent's hiss,
And boding screech-owls make the concert
full!
All the foul terrors in dark-seated hell—
  *Queen.* Enough, sweet Suffolk; thou tor-
ment'st thyself,
And these dread curses, like the sun 'gainst
glass,
Or like an overcharged gun, recoil,
And turn the force of them upon thyself.
  *Suf.* You bade me ban, and will you bid
me leave?
Now, by the ground that I am banish'd from,
Well could I curse away a winter's night,
Though standing naked on a mountain top,

Where biting cold would never let grass grow,
And think it but a minute spent in sport.
  *Queen.* O, let me entreat thee cease. Give
me thy hand,
That I may dew it with my mournful tears;
Nor let the rain of heaven wet this place,
To wash away my woful monuments.
O, could this kiss by printed in thy hand,
That thou mightst think upon these by the
seal,
Through whom a thousand sighs are breathed
for thee!
So, get thee gone, that I may know my
grief;
'Tis but surmised whiles thou art standing by,
As one that surfeits thinking on a want.
I will repeal thee, or, be well assured,
Adventure to be banished myself:
And banished I am, if but from thee.
Go; speak not to me; even now be gone.
O, go not yet! Even thus two friends con-
demn'd
Embrace and kiss and take ten thousand
leaves,
Loather a hundred times to part than die.
Yet now farewell; and farewell life with
thee!
  *Suf.* Thus is poor Suffolk ten times ban-
ished;
Once by the king, and three times thrice by
thee.
'Tis not the land I care for, wert thou
thence;
A wilderness is populous enough,
So Suffolk had thy heavenly company:
For where thou art, there is the world itself,
With every several pleasure in the world,
And where thou art not, desolation.
I can no more: live thou to joy thy life;
Myself no joy in nought but that thou livest.

*Enter* VAUX.

  *Queen.* Wither goes Vaux so fast? what
news, I prithee?
  *Vaux.* To signify unto his majesty
That Cardinal Beaufort is at point of death;
For suddenly a grievous sickness took him.
That makes him gasp and stare and catch
the air,
Blaspheming God and cursing men on earth.
Sometime he talks as if Duke Humphrey's
ghost
Were by his side; sometime he calls the king,
And whispers to his pillow as to him
The secrets of his overcharged soul:
And I am sent to tell his majesty,
That even now he cries aloud for him.
  *Queen.* Go tell this heavy message to the
king.     [*Exit* VAUX.
Aye me! what is this world! what news are
these!
But wherefore grieve I at an hour's poor loss,
Omitting Suffolk's exile, my soul's treasure?
Why only, Suffolk, mourn I not for thee.

And with the southern clouds contend in tears,
Theirs for the earth's increase, mine for my sorrows?
Now get thee hence: the king, thou know'st, is coming;
If thou be found by me, thou art but dead.

*Suf.* If I depart from thee, I cannot live;
And in thy sight to die, what were it else
But like a pleasant slumber in thy lap?
Here could I breathe my soul into the air,
As mild and gentle as the cradle-babe,
Dying with mother's dug between its lips:
Where, from thy sight, I should be raging mad,
And cry out for thee to close up mine eyes,
To have thee with thy lips to stop my mouth;
So shouldst thou either turn my flying soul,
Or I should breathe it so into thy body,
And then it lived in sweet Elysium.
To die by thee were but to die in jest;
From thee to die were torture more than death:
O, let me stay, befall what may befall!

*Queen.* Away! though parting be a fretful corrosive.
It is applied to a deathful wound.
To France, sweet Suffolk: let me hear from thee;
For wheresoe'er thou art in this world's globe,
I'll have an Iris that shall find thee out.

*Suf.* I go.

*Queen.* And take my heart with thee.

*Suf.* A jewel, lock'd into the wofull'st cask
That ever did contain a thing of worth.
Even as a splitted bark, so sunder we:
This way fall I to death.

*Queen.*        This way for me.
                [EXEUNT *severally.*

### SCENE III.—*A bedchamber.*

*Enter the* KING, SALISBURY, WARWICK, *to the* CARDINAL *in bed.*

*King.* How fares my lord? speak, Beaufort, to thy sovereign.

*Car.* If thou be'st death, I'll give thee England's treasure,
Enough to purchase such another island,
So now wilt let me live, and feel no pain.

*King.* Ah, what a sign it is of evil life,
Where death's approach is seen so terrible!

*War.* Beaufort, it is thy sovereign speaks to thee.

*Car.* Bring me unto my trial when you will.
Died he not in his bed? where should he die?
Can I make men live, whether they will or no?
O, torture me no more! I will confess.
Alive again? then show me where he is:
I'll give a thousand pound to look upon him.
He hath no eyes, the dust hath blinded them.

Comb down his hair; look, look! it stands upright,
Like lime-twigs set to catch my winged soul.
Give me some drink; and bid the apothecary
Bring the strong poison that I bought of him.

*King.* O thou eternal mover of the heavens,
Look with a gentle eye upon this wretch!
O, beat away the busy meddling fiend
That lays strong siege unto this wretch's soul,
And from his bosom purge this black despair!

*War.* See, how the pangs of death do make him grin!

*Sal.* Disturb him not; let him pass peaceably.

*King.* Peace to his soul, if God's good pleasure be!
Lord Cardinal, if thou think'st on heaven's bliss,
Hold up thy hand, make signal of thy hope.
He dies, and makes no sign. O God, forgive him!

*War.* So bad a death argues a monstrous life.

*King.* Forbear to judge, for we are sinners all.
Close up his eyes and draw the curtain close;
And let us all to meditation.     [*Exeunt.*

## ACT IV.

### SCENE I.—*The coast of Kent.*

*Alarum. Fight at sea. Ordnance goes off. Enter a* CAPTAIN, *a* MASTER, *a* MASTER'S-MATE, WALTER WHITMORE, *and others; with them* SUFFOLK, *and others, prisoners.*

*Cap.* The gaudy, blabbing and remorseful day
Is crept into the bosom of the sea;
And now loud-howling wolves arouse the jades
That drag the tragic melancholy night;
Who, with their drowsy, slow and flagging wings,
Clip dead men's graves, and from their misty jaws
Breathe foul contagious darkness in the air.
Therefore bring forth the soldiers of our prize;
For, whilst our pinnace anchors in the Downs,
Here shall they make their ransom on the sand,
Or with their blood stain this discolored shore.
Master, this prisoner freely give I thee;
And thou that art his mate, make boot of this;
The other, Walter Whitmore, is thy share.

*First Gent.* What is my ransom, master? let me know.

*Mast.* A thousand crowns, or else lay down your head.

*Mate.* And so much shall you give, or off goes yours.

*Cap.* What, think you much to pay two thousand crowns,
And bear the name and port of gentlemen?
Cut both the villains' throats; for die you shall:
The lives of those which we have lost in fight
Be counterpoised with such a petty sum!

*First Gent.* I'll give it, sir; and therefore spare my life.

*Sec. Gent.* And so will I, and write home for it straight.

*Whit.* I lost mine eye in laying the prize aboard,
And therefore to revenge it, shalt thou die; [*To* Suf.
And so should these, if I might have my will.

*Cap.* Be not so rash; take ransom, let him live.

*Suf.* Look on my George; I am a gentleman:
Rate me at what thou wilt, thou shalt be paid.

*Whit.* And so am I; my name is Walter Whitmore.
How now! why start'st thou? what, doth death affright?

*Suf.* Thy name affrights me, in whose sound is death.
A cunning man did calculate my birth,
And told me that by water I should die:
Yet let not this make thee be bloody-minded;
Thy name is Gaultier, being rightly sounded.

*Whit.* Gaultier or Walter, which it is, I care not:
Never did base dishonor blur our name,
But with our sword we wiped away the blot;
Therefore, when merchant-like I sell revenge,
Broke be my sword, my arms torn and defaced,
And I proclaim'd a coward through the world!

*Suf.* Stay, Whitmore; for thy prisoner is a prince,
The Duke of Suffolk, William de la Pole.

*Whit.* The Duke of Suffolk, muffled up in rags!

*Suf.* Aye, but these rags are no part of the duke:
Jove sometime went disguised, and why not I?

*Cap.* But Jove was never slain, as thou shalt be.

*Suf.* Obscure and lowly swain, King Henry's blood,
The honorable blood of Lancaster,
Must not be shed by such a jaded groom.
Hast thou not kiss'd thy hand and held my stirrup?
Bare-headed plodded by my foot-cloth mule,
And thought thee happy when I shook my head?

How often hast thou waited at my cup,
Fed from my trencher, kneel'd down at the board,
When I have feasted with Queen Margaret?
Remember it and let it make thee crest-fall'n,
Aye, and allay this thy abortive pride;
How in our voiding lobby hast thou stood
And duly waited for my coming forth?
This hand of mine hath writ in thy behalf,
And therefore shall it charm thy riotous tongue.

*Whit.* Speak, captain, shall I stab the forlorn swain?

*Cap.* First let my words stab him, as he hath me.

*Suf.* Base slave, thy words are blunt, and so art thou.

*Cap.* Convey him hence and on our longboat's side
Strike off his head.

*Suf.* Thou darest not, for thy own.

*Cap.* Yes, Pole.

*Suf.* Pole!

*Cap.* Pool! Sir Pool! lord!
Aye, kennel, puddle, sink; whose filth and dirt
Troubles the silver spring where England drinks.
Now will I dam up this thy yawning mouth,
For swallowing the treasure of the realm:
Thy lips that kiss'd the queen shall sweep the ground;
And thou that smiledst at good Duke Humphrey's death
Against the senseless winds shalt grin in vain,
Who in contempt shall hiss at thee again:
And wedded be thou to the hags of hell,
For daring to affy a mighty lord
Unto the daughter of a worthless king,
Having neither subject, wealth, nor diadem.
By devilish policy art thou grown great,
And, like ambitious Sylla, overgorged
With gobbets of thy mother's bleeding heart.
By thee Anjou and Maine were sold to France,
The false revolting Normans thorough thee
Disdain to call us lord, and Picardy
Hath slain their governors, surprised our forts,
And sent the ragged soldiers wounded home.
The princely Warwick, and the Nevils all,
Whose dreadful swords were never drawn in vain,
As hating thee, are rising up in arms:
And now the house of York, thrust from the crown
By shameful murder of a guiltless king,
And lofty proud encroaching tyranny,
Burns with revenging fire; whose hopeful colors
Advance our half-faced sun, striving to shine,
Under the which is writ 'Invitis nubibus.'
The commons here in Kent are up in arms:
And, to conclude, reproach and beggary

Is crept into the palace of our king,
And all by thee. Away! convey him hence.

*Suf.* O that I were a god, to shoot forth
thunder
Upon these paltry, servile, abject drudges!
Small things make base men proud: this villain here,
Being captain of a pinnace, threatens more
Than Bargulus the strong Illyrian pirate.
Drones suck not eagles' blood but rob beehives:
It is impossible that I should die
By such a lowly vassal as thyself.
Thy words move rage and not remorse in me:
I go of message from the queen to France;
I charge thee waft me safely cross the Channel.

*Cap.* Walter,—

*Whit.* Come, Suffolk, I must waft thee to
thy death.

*Suf.* Gelidus timor occupat artus: it is thee
I fear.

*Whit.* Thou shalt have cause to fear before I leave thee.
What, are ye daunted now? now will ye
stoop?

*First Gent.* My gracious lord, entreat him,
speak him fair.

*Suf.* Suffolk's imperial tongue is stern and
rough,
Used to command, untaught to plead for
favor.
Far be it we should honor such as these
With humble suit: no, rather let my head
Stoop to the block than these knees bow to
any
Save to the God of heaven and to my king;
And sooner dance upon a bloody pole
Than stand uncover'd to the vulgar groom
True nobility is exempt from fear.
More can I bear than you dare execute.

*Cap.* Hale him away, and let him talk no
more.

*Suf.* Come, soldiers, show what cruelty ye
can,
That this my death may never be forgot!
Great men oft die by vile bezonians:
A Roman sworder and banditto slave
Murder'd sweet Tully; Brutus' bastard hand
Stabb'd Julius Cæsar; savage islanders
Pompey the Great; and Suffolk dies by
pirates.

[*Exeunt* WHITMORE *and others with*
SUFFOLK.

*Cap.* And as for these whose ransom we
have set,
It is our pleasure one of them depart:
Therefore come you with us and let him go.

[*Exeunt all but the* FIRST GENTLEMAN.

*Re-enter* WHITMORE *with* SUFFOLK'S *body.*

*Whit.* There let his head and lifeless body
lie,

Until the queen his mistress bury it. [*Exit.*

*First Gent.* O barbarous and bloody spectacle!
His body will I bear unto the king:
If he revenge it not, yet will his friends;
So will the queen, that living held him dear.

[*Exit with the body.*

### SCENE II.—*Blackheath.*

*Enter* GEORGE BEVIS *and* JOHN HOLLAND

*Bevis.* Come, and get thee a sword, though
made of a lath: they have been up these
two days.

*Holl.* They have the more need to sleep
now, then,

*Bevis.* I tell thee, Jack Cade the clothier
means to dress the commonwealth, and turn
it, and set a new nap upon it.

*Holl.* So he had need, for 'tis threadbare.
Well, I say it was never merry world in England since gentlemen came up.

*Bevis.* O miserable age! virtue is not regarded in handicrafts-men.

*Holl.* The nobility think scorn to go in
leather aprons.

*Bevis.* Nay, more, the king's council are
no good workmen.

*Holl.* True; and yet it is said, labor in
thy vocation; which is as much to say as, let
the magistrates be laboring men; and therefore should we be magistrates.

*Bevis.* Thou hast hit it; for there's no
better sign of a brave mind than a hard hand.

*Holl.* I see them! I see them! There's
Best's son, the tanner of Wingham,—

*Bevis.* He shall have the skins of our enemies, to make dog's-leather of.

*Holl.* And Dick the butcher,—

*Bevis.* Then is sin struck down like an ox,
and iniquity's throat cut like a calf.

*Holl.* And Smith the weaver,—

*Bevis.* Argo, their thread of life is spun.

*Holl.* Come, come, let's fall in with them.

*Drum. Enter Cade, Dick Butcher, Smith the
Weaver, and a Sawyer, with infinite numbers.*

*Cade.* We John Cade, so termed of our
supposed father,—

*Dick.* [*Aside*]. Or rather stealing a cade of
herrings.

*Cade.* For our enemies shall fall before us,
inspired with the spirit of putting down kings
and princes,—Command silence.

*Dick.* Silence!

*Cade.* My father was a Mortimer,—

*Dick.* [*Aside*] He was an honest man, and
a good bricklayer.

*Cade.* My mother a Plantagenet,—

*Dick.* [*Aside*] I know her well; she was a
midwife.

*Cade.* My wife descended of the Lacies,—

*Dick.* [*Aside*] She was indeed, a peddler's
daughter, and sold many laces.

*Smith* [*Aside*] But now of late, not able to travel with her furred pack, she washes bucks here at home.

*Cade.* Therefore am I of an honorable house.

*Dick.* [*Aside*] Aye, by my faith, the field is honorable; and there was he born, under a hedge, for his father had never a house but the cage.

*Cade.* Valiant I am.

*Smith* [*Aside*] A' must needs; for beggary is valiant.

*Cade.* I am able to endure much.

*Dick.* [*Aside*] No question of that; for I have seen him whipped three market-days together.

*Cade.* I fear neither sword nor fire.

*Smith.* [*Aside*] He need not fear the sword; for his coat is of proof.

*Dick.* [*Aside*] But methinks he should stand in fear of fire, being burnt i' the hand for stealing of sheep.

*Cade.* Be brave, then; for your captain is brave, and vows reformation. There shall be in England seven halfpenny loaves sold for a penny: the three-hooped pot shall have ten hoops; and I will make it felony to drink small beer: all the realm shall be in common; and in Cheapside shall my palfry go to grass: and when I am king, as king I will be,—

*All.* God save your majesty!

*Cade.* I thank you, good people: there shall be no money; all shall eat and drink on my score; and I will apparel them all in one livery, that they may agree like brothers, and worship me their lord.

*Dick.* The first thing we do, let's kill all the lawyers.

*Cade.* Nay, that I mean to do. Is not this a lamentable thing, that of the skin of an innocent lamb should be made parchment? that parchment, being scribbled o'er, should undo man? Some say the bee stings: but I say, 'tis the bee's wax; for I did but seal once to a thing, and I was never mine own man since. How now! who's there?

*Enter some, bringing forward the Clerk of Chatham.*

*Smith.* The clerk of Chatham: he can write and read and cast accompt.

*Cade.* O monstrous!          [copies.

*Smith.* We took him setting of boys'

*Cade.* Here's a villain!

*Smith.* Has a book in his pocket with red letters in 't.

*Cade.* Nay, then, he is a conjurer.

*Dick.* Nay, he can make obligations, and write court-hand.

*Cade.* I am sorry for 't: the man is a proper man, of mine honor; unless I find him guilty, he shall not die. Come hither, sirrah, I must examine thee: what is thy name?

*Clerk.* Emmanuel.

*Dick.* They use to write it on the top of letters: 'twill go hard with you.

*Cade.* Let me alone. Dost thou use to write thy name? or hast thou a mark to thyself, like an honest plain-dealing man?

*Clerk.* Sir, I thank God, I have been so well brought up that I can write my name.

*All.* He hath confessed: away with him! he's a villain and a traitor.

*Cade.* Away with him, I say! hang him with his pen and ink-horn about his neck.

[*Exit one with the Clerk.*

*Enter Michael.*

*Mich.* Where's our general?

*Cade.* Here I am, thou particular fellow.

*Mich.* Fly, fly, fly! Sir Humphrey Stafford and his brother are hard by, with the king's forces.

*Cade.* Stand, villain, stand, or I'll fell thee down. He shall be encountered with a man as good as himself: he is but a knight, is a'?

*Mich.* No.

*Cade.* To equal him, I will make myself a knight presently. [*Kneels*] Rise up, Sir John Mortimer. [*Rises*] Now have at him!

*Enter Sir Humphrey Stafford and his Brother, with drum and soldiers.*

*Staf.* Rebellious hinds, the filth and scum of Kent,
Mark'd for the gallows, lay your weapons down;
Home to your cottages, forsake this groom:
The king is merciful, if you revolt.

*Bro.* But angry, wrathful, and inclined to blood,
If you go forward; therefore yield, or die.

*Cade.* As for these silken-coated slaves, I pass not:
It is to you, good people, that I speak,
Over whom, in time to come, I hope to reign;
For I am rightful heir unto the crown.

*Staf.* Villain, thy father was a plasterer;
And thou thyself a shearman, art thou not?

*Cade.* And Adam was a gardener.

*Bro.* And what of that?

*Cade.* Marry, this: Edmund Mortimer, Earl of March,
Married the Duke of Clarence' daughter, did he not?

*Staf.* Aye, sir.

*Cade.* By her he had two children at one birth.

*Bro.* That's false.

*Cade.* Aye, there's the question; but I say, 'tis true:
The elder of them, being put to nurse,
Was by a beggar-woman stolen away;
And, ignorant of his birth and parentage,
Became a bricklayer when he came to age:
His son am I; deny it, if you can.

*Dick.* Nay, 'tis too true; therefore he shall be king.

*Smith.* Sir, he made a chimney in my father's house, and the bricks are alive at this day to testify it; therefore deny it not.

*Staf.* And will you credit this base drudge's words,
That speaks he knows not what?

*All.* Aye, marry, will we; therefore get ye gone.

*Bro.* Jack Cade, the Duke of York hath taught you this.

*Cade.* [*Aside*] He lies, for I invented it myself. Go to, sirrah, tell the king from me, that, for his father's sake, Henry the fifth, in whose time boys went to span-counter for French crowns, I am content he shall reign; but I'll be protector over him.

*Dick.* And furthermore, we'll have the Lord Say's head for selling the dukedom of Maine.

*Cade.* And good reason; for thereby is England mained, and fain to go with a staff, but that my puissance holds it up. Fellow kings, I tell you that that Lord Say hath gelded the commonwealth, and made it an eunuch; and more than that, he can speak French; and therefore he is a traitor.

*Staf.* O, gross and miserable ignorance!

*Cade.* Nay, answer, if you can: the Frenchmen are our enemies; go to, then, I ask but this: can he that speaks with the tongue of an enemy be a good counsellor, or no?                                         [head.

*All.* No, no; and therefore we'll have his

*Bro.* Well, seeing gentle words will not prevail,
Assail them with the army of the king.

*Staf.* Herald, away; and throughout every town                                         [Cade;
Proclaim them traitors that are up with
That those which fly before the battle ends
May, even in their wives' and children's sight,
Be hang'd up for example at their doors:
And you that be the king's friends, follow me.
[*Exeunt the two Staffords, and soldiers.*

*Cade.* And you that love the commons, follow me.
Now show yourselves men; 'tis for liberty.
We will not leave one lord, one gentleman:
Spare none but such as go in clouted shoon;
For they are thrifty honest men, and such
As would, but that they dare not, take our parts.                                         [ward us.

*Dick.* They are all in order and march to-

*Cade.* But then are we in order when we are most out of order. Come, march forward.
[*Exeunt.*

SCENE III.—*Another part of Blackheath.*

*Alarums to the fight, wherein both the Staffords are slain. Enter Cade and the rest.*

*Cade.* Where's Dick, the butcher of Ashford?

*Dick.* Here, sir.

*Cade.* They fell before thee like sheep and oxen and thou behavedst thyself as if thou hadst been in thine own slaughter-house: therefore thus will I reward thee, the Lent shall be as long again as it is; and thou shalt have a license to kill for a hundred lacking one.

*Dick.* I desire no more.

*Cade.* And, to speak truth, thou deservest no less. This monument of the victory will I bear [*putting on Sir Humphrey's brigandine*]; and the bodies shall be dragged at my horse heels till I do come to London, where we will have the mayor's sword borne before us.

*Dick.* If we mean to thrive and do good, break open the jails and let out the prisoners.

*Cade.* Fear not that, I warrant thee. Come, let's march toward London.            [*Exeunt.*

SCENE IV.—*London.* The palace.

*Enter the King with a supplication, and the Queen with Suffolk's head, the Duke of Buckingham and the Lord Say.*

*Queen.* Oft have I heard that grief softens the mind,
And makes it fearful and degenerate;
Think therefore on revenge and cease to weep.
But who can cease to weep and look on this?
Here may his head lie on my throbbing breast:
But where's the body that I should embrace?

*Buck.* What answer makes your grace to the rebels' supplication?                      [treat;

*King.* I'll send some holy bishop to en-
For God forbid so many simple souls
Should perish by the sword! And I myself,
Rather than bloody war shall cut them short,
Will parley with Jack Cade their general:
But stay, I'll read it over once again.

*Queen.* Ah, barbarous villains! hath this lovely face
Ruled, like a wandering planet, over me,
And could it not enforce them to relent,
That were unworthy to behold the same?

*King.* Lord Say, Jack Cade hath sworn to have thy head.

*Say.* Aye, but I hope your highness shall have his.

*King.* How now, madam!
Still lamenting and mourning for Suffolk's death?
I fear me, love, if that I had been dead,
Thou wouldest not have mourn'd so much for me.

*Queen.* No, my love, I should not mourn, but die for thee.

*Enter a* MESSENGER

*King.* How now! what news? why com-
st thou in such haste?

*Mess.* The rebels are in Southwark; fly
my lord!
Jack Cade proclaims himself Lord Mor-
timer,
Descended from the Duke of Clarence' house,
And calls your grace usurper openly,
And vows to crown himself in Westminster.
His army is a ragged multitude
Of hinds and peasants, rude and merciless:
Sir Humphrey Stafford and his brother's
death
Hath given them heart and courage to pro-
ceed:
All scholars, lawyers, courtiers, gentlemen,
They call false caterpillars and intend their
death.
*King.* O graceless men! they know not
what they do.
*Buck.* My gracious lord, retire to Killing-
worth,
Until a power be raised to put them down.
*Queen.* Ah, were the Duke of Suffolk now
alive,
These Kentish rebels would be soon ap-
peased!
*King.* Lord Say, the traitors hate thee;
Therefore away with us to Killingworth.
*Say.* So might your grace's person be in
danger.
The sight of me is odious in their eyes;
And therefore in this city will I stay,
And live alone as secret as I may.

*Enter another* MESSENGER.

*Mess.* Jack Cade hath gotten London
Bridge:
The citizens fly and forsake their houses:
The rascal people, thirsting after prey,
Join with the traitor, and they jointly swear
To spoil the city and your royal court.
*Buck.* Then linger not, my lord; away,
take horse.
*King.* Come, Margaret; God, our hope,
will succor us.
*Queen.* My hope is gone, now Suffolk is
deceased.
*King.* Farewell, my lord: trust not the
Kentish rebels.
*Buck.* Trust nobody, for fear you be be-
tray'd.
*Say.* The trust I have is in mine inno-
cence,
And therefore am I bold and resolute.
[*Exeunt.*

SCENE V.—LONDON. *The Tower.*

*Enter* LORD SCALES *upon the Tower, walking.
Then enter two or three* CITIZENS *below.*

*Scales.* How now! is Jack Cade slain?
*First Cit.* No, my lord, nor likely to be
slain; for they have won the bridge, killing
all those that withstand them: the lord
mayor craves aid of your honor from the
Tower to defend the city from the rebels.

*Scales.* Such aid as I can spare you shall
command;
But I am troubled here with them myself;
The rebels have assay'd to win the Tower.
But get you to Smithfield and gather head,
And thither I will send you Matthew Goffe;
Fight for your king, your country, and your
lives;
And so, farewell, for I must hence again.
[*Exeunt.*

SCENE VI.—LONDON. *Cannon Street.*

*Enter* JACK CADE *and the rest, and strikes
his staff on London-stone.*

*Cade.* Now is Mortimer lord of this city.
And here, sitting upon London-stone, I
charge and command that, of the city's cost,
the pissing-conduit run nothing but claret
wine this first year of our reign. And now
henceforward it shall be treason for any that
calls me other than Lord Mortimer.

*Enter a* SOLDIER, *running.*

*Sold.* Jack Cade! Jack Cade!
*Cade.* Knock him down there.
[*They kill him.*
*Smith.* If this fellow be wise, he'll never
call ye Jack Cade more: I think he hath a
very fair warning.
*Dick.* My lord, there's an army gathered
together in Smithfield.
*Cade.* Come, then, let's go fight with
them: but first, go and set London bridge on
fire; and, if you can, burn down the Tower
too. Come, let's away. [*Exeunt.*

SCENE VII.—LONDON. *Smithfield.*

*Alarums.* MATTHEW GOFFE *is slain, and all
the rest. Then enter* JACK CADE, *with his
company.*

*Cade.* So, sirs: now go some and pull
down the Savoy; others to the inns of court;
down with them all.
*Dick.* I have a suit upon your lordship.
*Cade.* Be it a lordship, thou shalt have it
for that word.
*Dick.* Only that the laws of England may
come out of your mouth.
*Holl.* [*Aside*] Mass, 'twill be sore law,
then; for he was thrust in the mouth with a
spear, and 'tis not whole yet.
*Smith.* [*Aside*] Nay, John, it will be stinking law; for his breath stinks with eating
toasted cheese.
*Cade.* I have thought upon it, it shall be
so. Away burn all the records of the realm:
my mouth shall be the parliament of England.
*Holl.* [*Aside*] Then we are like to have
biting statutes, unless his teeth be pulled out.
*Cade.* And henceforward all things shall
be in common.

*Enter a* Messenger

*Mess.* My lord, a prize, a prize! here's the Lord Say, which sold the towns in France; he that made us pay one and twenty fifteens, and one shilling to the pound, the last subsidy.

*Enter* GEORGE BEVIS, *with the* LORD SAY

*Cade.* Well, he shall be beheaded for it ten times. Ah, thou say, thou serge, nay, thou buckram lord! now art thou within point-blank of our jurisdiction regal. What canst thou answer to my majesty for giving up of Normandy unto Monsieur Basimecu, the dauphin of France? Be it known unto thee by these presence, even the presence of Lord Mortimer, that I am the besom that must sweep the court clean of such filth as thou art. Thou hast most traitorously corrupted the youth of the realm in erecting a grammar school: and whereas, before, our forefathers had no other books but the score and the tally, thou hast caused printing to be used, and, contrary to the king, his crown and dignity, thou hast built a paper-mill. It will be proved to thy face that thou hast men about thee that usually talk of a noun and a verb, and such abominable words as no Christian ear can endure to hear. Thou hast appointed justices of peace, to call poor men before them about matters they were not able to answer. Moreover, thou hast put them in prison; and because they could not read, thou hast hanged them; when, indeed, only for that cause they have been most worthy to live. Thou dost ride in a foot-cloth, dost thou not?

*Say.* What of that?

*Cade.* Marry, thou oughtest not to let thy horse wear a cloak, when honester men than thou go in their hose and doublets.

*Dick.* And work in their shirt too; as myself, for example, that am a butcher.

*Say.* You men of Kent,—

*Dick.* What say you of Kent?

*Say.* Nothing but this; 'tis 'bona terra, mala gens.'

*Cade.* Away with him, away with him! he speaks Latin.

*Say.* Hear me but speak, and bear me where you will.
Kent, in the Commentaries Cæsar writ,
Is term'd the civil'st place of all this isle:
Sweet is the country, because full of riches;
The people liberal, valiant, active, wealthy;
Which makes me hope you are not void of pity.
I sold not Maine, I lost not Normandy,
Yet, to recover them, would lose my life.
Justice with favor have I always done;
Prayers and tears have moved me, gifts could never.

When have I ought exacted at your hands,
But to maintain the king, the realm, and you?
Large gifts have I bestow'd on learned clerks,
Because my book preferr'd me to the king,
And seeing ignorance is the curse of God,
Knowledge the wing wherewith we fly to heaven,
Unless you be possess'd with devilish spirits,
You cannot but forbear to murder me:
This tongue hath parley'd unto foreign kings
For your behoof,—

*Cade.* Tut, when struck'st thou one blow in the field?

*Say.* Great men have reaching hands: oft have I struck
Those that I never saw and struck them dead.

*Geo.* O monstrous coward! what, to come behind folks?

*Say.* These cheeks are pale for watching for your good.

*Cade.* Give him a box o' the ear and that will make 'em red again.

*Say.* Long sitting to determine poor men's causes
Hath made me full of sickness and diseases.

*Cade.* Ye shall have a hempen caudle then and the help of hatchet.

*Dick.* Why dost thou quiver, man?

*Say.* The palsy, and not fear, provokes me.

*Cade.* Nay, he nods at us, as who should say, I'll be even with you; I'll see if his head will stand steadier on a pole, or no. Take him away, and behead him.

*Say.* Tell me wherein have I offended most?
Have I affected wealth or honor? speak.
And my chests fill'd up with extorted gold?
Is my apparel sumptuous to behold?
Whom have I injured, that ye seek my death?
These hands are free from guiltless blood-shedding,
This breast from harboring foul deceitful thoughts.
O, let me live!

*Cade.* [*Aside*] I feel remorse in myself with his words; but I'll bridle it: he shall die, an it be but for pleading so well for his life. Away with him! he has a familiar under his tongue; he speaks not o' God's name. Go, take him away, I say, and strike off his head presently; and then break into his son-in-law's house, Sir James Cromer, and strike off his head, and bring them both upon two poles hither.

*All.* It shall be done.

*Say.* Ah, countrymen! if when you make your prayers,
God should be so obdurate as yourselves,
How would it fare with your departed souls?
And therefore yet relent, and save my life.

*Cade.* Away with him! and do as I command ye.

[*Exeunt some with* LORD SAY.

The proudest peer in the realm shall not wear a head on his shoulders, unless he pay me tribute; there shall not a maid be married, but she shall pay to me her maidenhead ere they have it: men shall hold of me in capite; and we charge and command that their wives be as free as heart can wish or tongue can tell.

*Dick.* My lord, when shall we go to Cheapside and take up commodities upon our bills?

*Cade.* Marry, presently.

*All.* O, brave!

### Re-enter one with the heads.

*Cade.* But is not this braver? Let them kiss one another, for they loved well when they were alive. Now part them again, lest they consult about the giving up of some more towns in France. Soldiers, defer the spoil of the city until night: for with these borne before us, instead of maces, will we ride through the streets and at every corner have them kiss. Away! [*Exeunt.*

### SCENE VIII.—SOUTHWARK.

*Alarum and retreat. Enter* CADE *and all his rabblement.*

*Cade.* Up Fish Street! down Saint Magnus Corner! kill and knock down! throw them into Thames! [*Sound a parley.*] What noise is this I hear? Dare any be so bold to sound retreat or parley, when I command them kill?

*Enter* BUCKINGHAM *and* CLIFFORD, *attended.*

*Buck.* Aye, here they be that dare and will disturb thee:
Know, Cade, we come ambassadors from the king
Unto the commons whom thou hast misled;
And here pronounce free pardon to them all,
That will forsake thee and go home in peace.

*Clif.* What say ye, countrymen? will ye relent,
And yield to mercy whilst 'tis offer'd you;
Or let a rebel lead you to your deaths?
Who loves the king and will embrace his pardon,
Fling up his cap, and say 'God save his majesty!'
Who hateth him and honors not his father,
Henry the fifth, that made all France to quake,
Shake he his weapon at us and pass by.

*All.* God save the king! God save the king!

*Cade.* What, Buckingham and Clifford, are ye so brave? And you, base peasants, do ye believe him? will you needs be hanged with your pardons about your necks? Hath my sword therefore broke through London gates, that you should leave me at the White Hart in Southwark? I thought ye would never have given out these arms till you had recovered your ancient freedom; but you are all recreants and dastards, and delight to live in slavery to the nobility. Let them break your backs with burthens, take your houses over your heads, ravish your wives and daughters before your faces: for me, I will make shift for one; and so, God's curse light upon you all!

*All.* We'll follow Cade, we'll follow Cade!

*Clif.* Is Cade the son of Henry the Fifth,
That thus you do exclaim you'll go with him?
Will he conduct you through the heart of France,
And make the meanest of you earls and dukes?
Alas, he hath no home, no place to fly to;
Nor knows he how to live but by the spoil,
Unless by robbing of your friends and us.
Were't not a shame, that whilst you live at jar,
The fearful French, whom you late vanquished,
Should make a start o'er seas and vanquish you?
Methinks already in this civil broil
I see them lording it in London streets,
Crying 'Villiago!' unto all they meet.
Better ten thousand base-born Cades miscarry,
Than you should stoop unto a Frenchman's mercy.
To France, to France, and get what you have lost;
Spare England, for it is your native coast:
Henry hath money, you are strong and manly;
God on our side, doubt not of victory.

*All.* A Clifford! a Clifford! we'll follow the king and Clifford.

*Cade.* Was ever feather so lightly blown to and fro as this multitude? The name of Henry the Fifth hales them to an hundred mischiefs and makes them leave me desolate. I see them lay their heads together to surprise me. My sword make way for me, for here is no staying. In despite of the devils and hell, have through the very middest of you! and heavens and honor be witness that no want of resolution in me, but only my followers' base and ignominious treasons, make me betake me to my heels. [*Exit.*

*Buck.* What, is he fled? Go some, and follow him;
And he that brings his head unto the king
Shall have a thousand crowns for his reward.

[*Exeunt some of them.*

Follow me, soldiers: we'll devise a mean
To reconcile you all unto the king.

[*Exeunt.*

SCENE IX.—KENILWORTH CASTLE.

*Sound trumpets. Enter* KING, QUEEN, *and*
SOMERSET, *on the terrace.*

*King.* Was ever king that joy'd an earthly
    throne,
And could command no more content than
    I?
No sooner was I crept out of my cradle
But I was made a king, at nine months old.
Was never subject long'd to be a king
As I do long and wish to be a subject.

*Enter* BUCKINGHAM *and* CLIFFORD.

*Buck.* Health and glad tidings to your
majesty!
*King.* Why, Buckingham, is the traitor
    Cade surprised?
Or is he but retired to make him strong?

*Enter below, multitudes, with halters about
their necks.*

*Clif.* He is fled, my lord, and all his
    powers do yield;
And humbly thus, with halters on their
    necks,
Expect your highness' doom, of life or death.
*King.* Then, heaven, set ope thy everlast-
    ing gates,
To entertain my vows of thanks and praise!
Soldiers, this day have you redeem'd your
    lives,
And show'd how well you love your prince
    and country:
Continue still in this so good a mind,
And Henry, though he be infortunate,
Assure yourselves, will never be unkind:
And so, with thanks and pardon to you all,
I do dismiss you to your several countries.
*All.* God save the king! God save the
    king!

*Enter* Messenger.

*Mess.* Please it your grace to be advertised
The Duke of York is newly come from Ire-
    land,
And with a puissant and mighty power
Of gallowglasses and stout kernes
Is marching hitherward in proud array,
And still proclaimeth, as he comes along,
His arms are only to remove from thee
The Duke of Somerset, whom he terms a
    traitor.
*King.* Thus stands my state, 'twixt Cade
    and York distress'd;
Like to a ship that, having 'scaped a tempest,
Is straightway calm'd and boarded with a
    pirate:                           [persed;
But now is Cade driven back, his men dis-
And now is York in arms to second him.
I pray thee, Buckingham, go and meet him,
And ask him what's the reason of these arms.
Tell him I'll send Duke Edmond to the
    Tower;

And, Somerset, we will commit thee thither,
Until his army be dismiss'd from him.
*Som.* My lord,
I'll yield myself to prison willingly,
Or unto death, to do my country good.
*King.* In any case, be not too rough in
    terms;
For he is fierce and cannot brook hard lan-
    guage.
*Buck.* I will, my lord; and doubt not so
    to deal
As all things shall redound unto your good.
*King.* Come, wife, let's in, and learn to
    govern better;
For yet may England curse my wretched
    reign.                [*Flourish. Exeunt.*

SCENE X.—KENT. *Idens' garden.*

*Enter* CADE.

*Cade.* Fie on ambition! fie on myself, that
have a sword, and yet am ready to famish!
These five days have I hid me in these woods
and durst not peep out, for all the country is
laid for me; but now am I so hungry that if
I might have a lease of my life for a thousand years I could stay no longer. Wherefore, on a brick wall have I climbed into this
garden, to see if I can eat grass, or pick a
sallet another while, which is not amiss to
cool a man's stomach this hot weather. And
I think this word 'sallet' was born to do me
good: for many a time, but for a sallet, my
brain-pan had been cleft with a brown bill;
and many a time, when I have been dry and
bravely marching, it hath served me instead
of a quart pot to drink in; and now the
word 'sallet' must serve me to feed on.

*Enter* IDEN

*Iden.* Lord, who would live turmoiled in
    the court.
And may enjoy such quiet walks as these?
This small inheritance my father left me
Contenteth me, and worth a monarchy.
I seek not to wax great by others' waning,
Or gather wealth, I care not with what envy:
Sufficeth that I have maintains my state,
And sends the poor well pleased from my
    gate.
*Cade.* Here's the lord of the soil come to
seize me for a stray, for entering his fee-
simple without leave. Ah, villain, thou wilt
betray me, and get a thousand crowns of
the king by carrying my head to him: but
I'll make thee eat iron like an ostrich, and
swallow my sword like a great pin, ere thou
and I part.
*Iden.* Why, rude companion, whatsoe'er
    thou be,
I know thee not; why then should I betray
    thee?
Is't not enough to break into my garden,
And, like a thief, to come to rob my grounds,
Climbing my walls in spite of me the owner,

But thou wilt brave me with these saucy
terms?

*Cade.* Brave thee! aye, by the best blood
that ever was broached, and beard thee too.
Look on me well: I have eat no meat these
five days; yet, come thou and thy five men,
and if I do not leave you all as dead as a
door-nail, I pray God I may never eat grass
more.

*Iden.* Nay, it shall ne'er be said, while
England stands,
That Alexander Iden, an esquire of Kent,
Took odds to combat a poor famish'd man,
Oppose thy steadfast-gazing eyes to mine,
See if thou canst outface me with thy looks:
Set limb to limb, and thou are far the lesser:
Thy hand is but a finger to my fist,
Thy leg a stick compared with this trun-
cheon;
My foot shall fight with all the strength thou
hast;
And if mine arm be heaved in the air,
Thy grave is digg'd already in the earth.
As for words, whose greatness answers words,
Let this my sword report what speech for-
bears.

*Cade.* By my valor, the most complete
champion that ever I heard! Steel, if thou
turn the edge, or cut not out the burly-
boned clown in chines of beef ere thou sleep
in thy sheath, I beseech God on my knees
thou mayst be turned to hobnails.
        [*Here they fight.* CADE *falls.*
O, I am slain! famine and no other hath
slain me: let ten thousand devils come
against me, and give me but the ten meals I
have lost, and I'll defy them all. Wither,
garden; and be henceforth a burying-place to
all that do dwell in this house, because the
unconquered soul of Cade is fled.

*Iden.* Is't Cade that I have slain, that
monstrous traitor?
Sword, I will hallow thee for this thy deed,
And hang thee o'er my tomb when I am
dead:
Ne'er shall this blood be wiped from thy
point;
But thou shalt wear it as a herald's coat,
To emblaze the honor that thy master got.

*Cade.* Iden, farewell, and be proud of thy
victory. Tell Kent from me, she hath lost her
best man, and exhort all the world to be
cowards; for I, that never feared any, am
vanquished by famine, not by valor. [*Dies.*

*Iden.* How much thou wrong'st me,
heaven be my judge.
Die, damned wretch, the curse of her that
bare thee;
And as I thrust thy body in with my sword,
So wish I, I might thrust thy soul to hell.
Hence will I drag thee headlong by the heels
Unto a dunghill which shall be thy grave,
And there cut off thy most ungracious head;
Which I will bear in triumph to the king,
Leaving thy trunk for crows to feed upon.
        [*Exit.*

## ACT V.

SCENE I.—*Fields between Dartford and
Blackheath.*

*Enter* YORK, *and his army of Irish, with
drum and colors.*

*York.* From Ireland thus comes York to
claim his right,
And pluck the crown from feeble Henry's
head:
Ring, bells, aloud; burn, bonfires, clear and
bright,
To entertain great England's lawful king.
Ah! sancta majestas, who would not buy
thee dear?
Let them obey that know not how to rule;
This hand was made to handle nought but
gold.
I cannot give due action to my words,
Except a sword or scepter balance it:
A scepter shall it have, have I a soul,
On which I'll toss the flower-de-luce of
France.

*Enter* BUCKINGHAM.

Whom have we here? Buckingham, to disturb me?
The king hath sent him, sure: I must dissemble.

*Buck.* York, if thou meanest well, I greet
thee well.

*York.* Humphrey of Buckingham, I accept
thy greeting.
Art thou a messenger, or come of pleasure?

*Buck.* A messenger from Henry, our dread
liege,
To know the reason of these arms in peace;
Or why thou, being a subject as I am,
Against thy oath and true allegiance sworn,
Should raise so great a power without his
leave,
Or dare to bring thy force so near the court

*York.* [*Aside*] Scarce can I speak my
choler is so great:
O, I could hew up rocks and fight with flint,
I am so angry at these abject terms;
And now, like Ajax Telamonius,
On sheep or oxen could I spend my fury.
I am far better born than is the king,
More like a king, more kingly in my
thoughts:
But I must make fair weather yet a while,
Till Henry be more weak and I more
strong.—
Buckingham, I prithee, pardon me,
That I have given no answer all this while;
My mind was troubled with deep melan-
choly.                                          [hither
The cause why I have brought this army
Is to remove proud Somerset from the king,
Seditious to his grace and to the state.

*Buck.* That is too much presumption on thy part:
But if thy arms be to no other end,
The king hath yielded unto thy demand:
The Duke of Somerset is in the Tower.
*York.* Upon thine honor, is he prisoner?
*Buck.* Upon mine honor, he is prisoner.
*York.* Then, Buckingham, I do dismiss my powers.
Soldiers, I thank you all; disperse yourselves;
Meet me to-morrow in Saint George's field,
You shall have pay and everything you wish.
And let my sovereign, virtuous Henry,
Command my eldest son, nay, all my sons,
As pledges of my fealty and love;
I'll send them all as willing as I live:
Lands, goods, horse, armor, any thing I have,
Is his to use, so Somerset may die.
*Buck.* York, I commend this kind submission:
We twain will go into his highness' tent.

*Enter* KING *and* Attendants.

*King.* Buckingham, doth York intend no harm to us,
That thus he marcheth with thee arm in arm?
*York.* In all submission and humility
York doth present himself unto your highness.
*King.* Then what intends these forces thou dost bring?
*York.* To heave the traitor Somerset from hence,
And fight against that monstrous rebel Cade,
Who since I heard to be discomfited.

*Enter* IDEN, *with* CADE'S *head.*

*Iden.* If one so rude and of so mean condition
May pass into the presence of a king,
Lo, I present your grace a traitor's head,
The head of Cade, whom I in combat slew.
*King.* The head of Cade! Great God, how just art Thou!
O, let me view this visage, being dead,
That living wrought me such exceeding trouble.
Tell me, my friend, art thou the man that slew him?
*Iden.* I was, an't like your majesty.
*King.* How art thou call'd? and what is thy degree?
*Iden.* Alexander Iden, that's my name;
A poor esquire of Kent, that loves his king.
*Buck.* So please it you, my lord, 'twere not amiss
He were created knight for his good service.
*King.* Iden, kneel down. [*He kneels.*] Rise up a knight.
We give thee for reward a thousand marks,
And will that thou henceforth attend on us.
*Iden.* May Iden live to merit such a bounty,

And never live but true unto his liege!
[*Rises.*

*Enter* QUEEN *and* SOMERSET.

*King.* See, Buckingham, Somerset comes with the queen:
Go, bid her hide him quickly from the duke.
*Queen.* For thousand Yorks he shall not hide his head,
But boldly stand and front him to his face.
*York.* How now! is Somerset at liberty?
Then, York, unloose thy long-imprison'd thoughts,
And let thy tongue be equal with thy heart.
Shall I endure the sight of Somerset?
False king! why hast thou broken faith with me,
Knowing how hardly I can brook abuse?
King did I call thee? no, thou art not king,
Not fit to govern and rule multitudes,
Which darest not, no, nor canst not rule a traitor,
That head of thine doth not become a crown;
Thy hand is made to grasp a palmer's staff,
And not to grace an awful princely scepter.
That gold must round engirt these brows of mine,
Whose smile and frown, like to Achilles' spear,
Is able with the change to kill and cure.
Here is a hand to hold a scepter up,
And with the same to act controlling laws.
Give place: by heaven, thou shalt rule no more
O'er him whom heaven created for thy ruler.
*Som.* O monstrous traitor! I arrest thee, York,
Of capital treason 'gainst the king and crown:
Obey, audacious traitor; kneel for grace.
*York.* Wouldst have me kneel? first let me ask of these,
If they can brook I bow a knee to man.
Sirrah, call in my sons to be my bail:
[*Exit* Attendant.
I know, ere they will have me go to ward,
They'll pawn their swords for my enfranchisement.
*Queen.* Call hither Clifford; bid him come amain,
To say if that the bastard boys of York
Shall be the surety for their traitor father.
[*Exit* BUCKINGHAM.
*York.* O blood-bespotted Neapolitan,
Outcast of Naples, England's bloody scourge!
The sons of York, thy betters in their birth,
Shall be their father's bail; and bane to those
That for my surety will refuse the boys!

*Enter* EDWARD *and* RICHARD.

See where they come: I'll warrant they'll make it good.

*Enter* CLIFFORD *and his son.*

*Queen.* And here comes Clifford to deny their bail.

*Clif.* Health and all happiness to my lord the king!    [*Kneels.*

*York.* I thank thee, Clifford: say, what news with thee?
Nay, do not fright us with an angry look:
We are thy sovereign, Clifford, kneel again;
For thy mistaking so, we pardon thee.

*Clif.* This is my king, York, I do not mistake;
But thou mistakest me much to think I do:
To Bedlam with him! is the man grown mad?

*King.* Aye, Clifford; a bedlam and ambitious humor
Makes him oppose himself against his king.

*Clif.* He is a traitor; let him to the Tower,
And chop away that factious pate of his.

*Queen.* He is arrested, but will not obey;
His sons, he says, shall give their words for him.

*York.* Will you not, sons?

*Edw.* Aye, noble father, if our words will serve.

*Rich.* And if words will not, then our weapons shall.

*Clif.* Why, what a brood of traitors have we here!

*York.* Look in a glass, and call thy image so:
I am thy king, and thou a false-heart traitor.
Call hither to the stake my two brave bears,
That with the very shaking of their chains
They may astonish these fell-lurking curs:
Bid Salisbury and Warwick come to me.

*Enter the* EARLS OF WARWICK *and*
SALISBURY.

*Clif.* Are these thy bears? we'll bait thy bears to death,
And manacle the bear-ward in their chains,
If thou darest bring them to the baiting-place.

*Rich.* Oft have I seen a hot o'erweening cur
Run back and bite, because he was withheld;
Who, being suffer'd with the bear's fell paw,
Hath clapp'd his tail between his legs and cried:
And such a piece of service will you do,
If you oppose yourselves to match Lord Warwick.

*Clif.* Hence, heap of wrath, foul indigested lump,
As crooked in thy manners as thy shape!

*York.* Nay, we shall heat you thoroughly anon.

*Clif.* Take heed, lest by your heat you burn yourselves.

*King.* Why, Warwick, hath thy knee forgot to bow?
Old Salisbury, shame to thy silver hair,
Thou mad misleader of thy brain-sick son!
What, wilt thou on thy death-bed play the ruffian,
And seek for sorrow with thy spectacles?
O, where is faith? O, where is loyalty?
If it be banish'd from the frosty head,
Where shall it find a harbor in the earth?
Wilt thou go dig a grave to find out war,
And shame thine honorable age with blood?
Why art thou old, and want'st experience?
Or wherefore dost abuse it, if thou hast it?
For shame! in duty bend thy knee to me,
That bows unto the grave with mickle age.

*Sal.* My lord, I have consider'd with myself
The title of this most renowned duke;
And in my conscience do repute his grace
The rightful heir to England's royal seat.

*King.* Hast thou not sworn allegiance unto me?

*Sal.* I have.

*King.* Canst thou dispense with heaven for such an oath?

*Sal.* It is great sin to swear unto a sin,
But greater sin to keep a sinful oath.
Who can be bound by any solemn vow
To do a murderous deed, to rob a man,
To force a spotless virgin's chastity,
To reave the orphan of his patrimony,
To wring the widow from her custom'd right,
And have no other reason for this wrong
But that he was bound by a solemn oath?

*Queen.* A subtle traitor needs no sophister.

*King.* Call Buckingham, and bid him arm himself.

*York.* Call Buckingham, and all the friends thou hast,
I am resolved for death or dignity.

*Clif.* The first I warrant thee, if dreams prove true.

*War.* You were best to go to bed and dream again,
To keep thee from the tempest of the field.

*Clif.* I am resolved to bear a greater storm
Than any thou canst conjure up to-day;
And that I'll write upon thy burgonet,
Might I but know thee by thy household badge.

*War.* Now, by my father's badge, old Nevil's crest,
The rampant bear chain'd to the ragged staff,
This day I'll wear aloft my burgonet,
As on a mountain top the cedar shows
That keeps his leaves in spite of any storm,
Even to affright thee with the view thereof.

*Clif.* And from the burgonet I'll rend thy bear,
And tread it under foot with all contempt,
Despite the bear-ward that protects the bear.

*Y. Clif.* And so to arms, victorious father,
To quell the rebels and their complices.

*Rich.* Fie! charity, for shame! speak not in spite.

For thou shall sup with Jesu Christ to-night.

*Y. Clif.* Foul stigmatic, that's more than thou canst tell.

*Rich.* If not in heaven, you'll surely sup in hell.                                          [*Exeunt severally.*

SCENE II.—*Saint Alban's.*

ALARUMS *to the battle. Enter* WARWICK.

*War.* Clifford of Cumberland, 'tis Warwick calls:

And if thou dost not hide thee from the bear,
Now, when the angry trumpet sounds alarum,
And dead men's cries do fill the empty air,
Clifford, I say, come forth and fight with me:
Proud northern lord, Clifford of Cumberland,
Warwick is hoarse with calling thee to arms.

*Enter* YORK.

How now, my noble lord! what, all a-foot?

*York.* The deadly-handed Clifford slew my steed,
But match to match I have encounter'd.him,
And made a prey for carrion kites and crows
Even of the bonny beast he loved so well.

*Enter* CLIFFORD.

*War.* Of one or both of us the time is come.

*York.* Hold, Warwick, seek thee out some other chase,
For I myself must hunt this deer to death.

*War.* Then, nobly, York; 'tis for a crown thou fight'st.
As I intend, Clifford, to thrive to-day,
It grieves my soul to leave thee unassail'd.
                                                          [*Exit.*

*Clif.* What seest thou in me, York? why dost thou pause?

*York.* With thy brave bearing should I be in love,
But that thou are so fast mine enemy.

*Clif.* Nor should thy prowess want praise and esteem
But that 'tis shown ignobly and in treason.

*York.* So let it help me now against thy sword,
As I in justice and true right express it.

*Clif.* My soul and body on the action both!                                          [stantly.

*York.* A dreadful lay! Address thee in-
          [*They fight, and* CLIFFORD *falls.*

*Clif.* La fin couronne les œuvres.  [*Dies.*

*York.* Thus war hath given thee peace, for thou art still.
Peace with his soul, heaven, if it be thy will!
                                                          [*Exit.*

*Enter young* CLIFFORD.

*Y. Clif.* Shame and confusion! all is on the rout;
Fear frames disorder, and disorder wounds
Where it should guard. O war, thou son of hell,

Whom angry heavens do make their minister,
Throw in the frozen bosoms of our part
Hot coals of vengeance! Let no soldier fly.
He that is truly dedicate to war
Hath no self-love, nor he that loves himself
Hath not essentially but by circumstance
The name of valor. [*Seeing his dead father*]
          O, let the vile world end,
And the premised flames of the last day
Knit earth and heaven together!
Now let the general trumpet blow his blast,
Particularities and petty sounds
To cease! Wast thou ordain'd, dear father,
To lose thy youth in peace, and to achieve
The silver livery of advised age,
And, in thy reverence and thy chair-days, thus
To die in ruffian battle? Even at this sight
My heart is turn'd to stone: and while 'tis mine,
It shall be stony. York not our old men spares;
No more will I their babes: tears virginal
Shall be to me even as the dew to fire,
And beauty that the tyrant oft reclaims
Shall to my flaming wrath be oil and flax.
Henceforth I will not have to do with pity:
Meet I an infant of the house of York,
Into as many gobbets will I cut it
As wild Medea young Absyrtus did:
In cruelty will I seek out my fame.
Come, thou new ruin of old Clifford's house:
As did Æneas old Anchises bear,
So bear I thee upon my manly shoulders;
But then Æneas bare a living load,
Nothing so heavy as these woes of mine.
          [*Exit, bearing off his father.*

*Enter* RICHARD *and* SOMERSET *to fight.*
          SOMERSET *is killed.*

*Rich.* So, lie thou there;
For underneath an alehouse' paltry sign,
The Castle in Saint Alban's, Somerset
Hath made the wizard famous in his death.
Sword, hold thy temper; heart, be wrathful still:
Priests pray for enemies, but princes kill.
                                                          [*Exit.*

*Fight. Excursions. Enter* KING, QUEEN, *and others.*

*Queen.* Away, my lord! you are slow; for shame, away!

*King.* Can we outrun the heavens? good Margaret, stay.

*Queen.* What are you made of? you'll nor fight nor fly:
Now is it manhood, wisdom and defense,
To give the enemy way, and to secure us
By what we can, which can no more but fly.
                                          [*Alarum afar off.*
If you be ta'en, we then should see the bottom
Of all our fortunes: but if we haply scape,

As well we may, if not through your neglect,
We shall to London get, where you are loved,
And where this breach now in our fortunes made
May readily be stopp'd.

*Re-enter young* CLIFFORD.

*Y. Clif.* But that my heart's on future mis-chief set,
I would speak blasphemy ere bid you fly:
But fly you must; uncurable discomfit
Reigns in the hearts of all our present parts.
Away, for your relief! and we will live
To see their day and them our fortune give:
Away, my lord, away!                    [*Exeunt.*

SCENE III.—*Fields near St. Alban's.*

*Alarum. Retreat. Enter* YORK, RICHARD,
WARWICK, *and soldiers, with drum and colors.*

*York.* Of Salisbury, who can report of him,
That winter lion, who in rage forgets
Aged contusions and all brush of time,
And, like a gallant in the brow of youth,
Repairs him with occasion? This happy day
Is not itself, nor have we won one foot,
If Salisbury be lost.
*Rich.*                    My noble father,
Three times to-day I holp him to his horse,
Three times bestrid him; thrice I led him off,
Persuaded him from any further act:
But still, where danger was, still there I met
him;

And like rich hangings in a homely house,
So was his will in his old feeble body.
But, noble as he is, look where he comes.

*Enter* SALISBURY.

*Sal.* Now, by my sword, well hast thou fought to-day;
By the mass, so did we all. I thank you, Rich-ard:
God knows how long it is I have to live;
And it hath pleased him that three times to-day
You have defended me from imminent death.
Well, lords, we have not got that which we have:
'Tis not enough our foes are this time fled,
Being opposites of such repairing nature.
*York.* I know our safety is to follow them;
For, as I hear, the king is fled to London,
To call a present court of parliament.
Let us pursue him ere the writs go forth.
What says Lord Warwick? shall we after them?
*War.* After them! nay, before them, if we can.
Now, by my faith, lords, 'twas a glorious day:
Saint Alban's battle won by famous York
Shall be eternized in all age to come.
Sound drums and trumpets, and to London all:
And more such days as these to us befall!
                    [*Exeunt.*

King Henry the Sixth, Part Third

Act V. Sc. 5.

# KING HENRY VI.

## THIRD PART

## DRAMATIS PERSONÆ

KING HENRY THE SIXTH.
EDWARD, *Prince of Wales, his Son.*
LOUIS XI., *King of France.*
DUKE OF SOMERSET,
DUKE OF EXETER,
EARL OF OXFORD,                  *Lords on*
EARL OF NORTHUMBERLAND,  *KING*
EARL OF WESTMORELAND,       *HENRY'S*
LORD CLIFFORD,                     *side.*
RICHARD PLANTAGENET, *Duke of York.*
EDWARD, *Earl of March, afterwards*
  KING EDWARD IV.,
EDMUND, *Earl of Rutland,*        *his*
GEORGE, *afterwards Duke of Clarence,* *Sons.*
RICHARD, *afterwards Duke of Gloster,*
DUKE OF NORFOLK,
MARQUIS OF MONTAGUE,
EARL OF WARWICK,                  *of the DUKE OF*
EARL OF PEMBROKE,               *YORK'S party.*
LORD HASTINGS,
LORD STAFFORD,
SIR JOHN MORTIMER,  *Uncles to the DUKE*
SIR HUGH MORTIMER,  *OF YORK.*

HENRY, *Earl of Richmond, a youth.*
LORD RIVERS, *Brother to* LADY GREY.
SIR WILLIAM STANLEY.
SIR JOHN MONTGOMERY.
SIR JOHN SOMERVILLE.
Tutor to RUTLAND.
Mayor of York.
Lieutenant of the Tower.
A Nobleman.
Two Keepers.
A Huntsman.
A Son *that has killed his Father.*
A Father *that has killed his Son.*

QUEEN MARGARET.
LADY GREY, *afterwards Queen to* EDWARD IV
BONA, *Sister to the French Queen.*

Soldiers, and other Attendants on KING
  HENRY and KING EDWARD, Messengers, Watchmen, &c.

SCENE,—*During part of the Third Act in* FRANCE; *during the rest of the Play in* ENGLAND.

## ACT I.

SCENE I.—LONDON. *The Parliament-house.*

*Alarum. Enter the* DUKE OF YORK, EDWARD,
RICHARD, NORFOLK, MONTAGUE, WARWICK,
*and Soldiers.*

*War.* I wonder how the king escaped our
  hands.
*York.* While we pursued the horsemen of
  the north,
He slily stole away and left his men:
Whereat the great Lord of Northumberland,
Whose warlike ears could never brook retreat,
Cheer'd up the drooping army; and himself,
Lord Clifford and Lord Stafford, all a-breast,
Charged our main battle's front, and break-
  ing in
Were by the swords of common soldiers slain.
*Edw.* Lord Stafford's father, Duke of
  Buckingham,
Is either slain or wounded dangerously;
I cleft his beaver with a downright blow:
That this is true, father, behold his blood
*Mont.* And, brother, here's the Earl of
  Wiltshire's blood,
Whom I encounter'd as the battles join'd.

*Rich.* Speak thou for me and tell them
  what I did. [ *Throwing down the
  Duke of Somerset's head.*
*York.* Richard hath best deserved of all
  my sons.                              [set?
But is your grace dead, my Lord of Somer-
*Norf.* Such hope have all the line of John
  of Gaunt!
*Rich.* Thus do I hope to shake King Hen-
  ry's head.
*War.* And so do I. Victorious Prince of
  York,
Before I see thee seated in that throne
Which now the house of Lancaster usurps,
I vow by heaven these eyes shall never close.
This is the palace of the fearful king,
And this the regal seat: possess it, York;
For this is thine, and not King Henry's heirs'.
*York.* Assist me, then, sweet Warwick, and
  I will;
For hither we have broken in by force.
*Norf.* We'll all assist you; he that flies
  shall die.
*York.* Thanks, gentle Norfolk: stay by me,
  my lords;
And, soldiers, stay and lodge by me this
  night                              [*They go up.*

[591]

*War.* And when the king comes, offer him no violence,
Unless he seek to thrust you out perforce.
*York.* The queen this day here holds her parliament,
But little thinks we shall be of her council:
By words or blows here let us win our right.
*Rich.* Arm'd as we are, let's stay within this house.
*War.* The bloody parliament shall this be call'd,
Unless Plantagenet, Duke of York, be king,
And bashful Henry deposed, whose cowardice
Hath made us by-words to our enemies.
*York.* Then leave me not, my lords; be resolute:
I mean to take possession of my right.
*War.* Neither the king, nor he that loves him best,
The proudest he that holds up Lancaster,
Dare stir a wing, if Warwick shake his bells.
I'll plant Plantagenet, root him up who dares:
Resolve thee, Richard; claim the English crown.

*Flourish. Enter* KING HENRY, CLIFFORD, NORTHUMBERLAND, WESTMORELAND, EXETER, *and the rest.*

*K. Hen.* My lords, look where the sturdy rebel sits,
Even in the chair of state: belike he means,
Back'd by the power of Warwick, that false peer,
To aspire unto the crown and reign as king.
Earl of Northumberland, he slew thy father,
And thine, Lord Clifford; and you both have vow'd revenge
On him, his sons, his favorites and his friends.
*North.* If I be not, heavens be revenged on me!
*Clif.* The hope thereof makes Clifford mourn in steel.
*West.* What, shall we suffer this? let's pluck him down:
My heart for anger burns; I cannot brook it.
*K. Hen.* Be patient, gentle Earl of Westmoreland.
*Clif.* Patience is for poltroons, such as he:
He durst not sit there, had your father lived.
My gracious lord, here in the parliament
Let us assail the family of York.
*North.* Well hast thou spoken, cousin: be it so.
*K. Hen.* Ah, know you not the city favors them,
And they have troops of soldiers at their beck?
*Exe.* But when the duke is slain, they'll quickly fly.
*K. Hen.* Far be the thought of this from Henry's heart,
To make a shambles of the parliament-house!

Cousin of Exeter, frowns, words and threats
Shall be the war that Henry means to use.
Thou factious Duke of York, descend my throne,
And kneel for grace and mercy at my feet;
I am thy sovereign.
*York.* I am thine.
*Exe.* For shame, come down: he made thee Duke of York.
*York.* 'Twas my inheritance, as the earldom was.
*Exe.* Thy father was a traitor to the crown.
*War.* Exeter, thou art a traitor to the crown.
In following this usurping Henry.
*Clif.* Whom should he follow but his natural king?
*War.* True, Clifford; and that's Richard Duke of York.
*K. Hen.* And shall I stand, and thou sit in my throne?
*York.* It must and shall be so: content thyself.
*War.* Be Duke of Lancaster; let him be king.
*West.* He is both king and Duke of Lancaster;
And that the Lord of Westmoreland shall maintain.
*War.* And Warwick shall disprove it. You forget,
That we are those which chased you from the field,
And slew your fathers, and with colors spread
March'd through the city to the palace gates.
*North.* Yes, Warwick, I remember it to my grief;
And, by my soul, thou and thy house shall rue it.
*West.* Plantagenet, of thee and these thy sons,
Thy kinsmen and thy friends, I'll have more lives
Than drops of blood were in my father's veins.
*Clif.* Urge it no more; lest that, instead of words,
I send thee, Warwick, such a messenger
As shall revenge his death before I stir.
*War.* Poor Clifford! how I scorn his worthless threats!
*York.* Will you we show our title to the crown?
If not, our swords shall plead it in the field.
*K. Hen.* What title hast thou, traitor, to the crown?
Thy father was, as thou art, Duke of York;
Thy grandfather, Roger Mortimer, Earl of March:
I am the son of Henry the Fifth,
Who made the Dauphin and the French to stoop,
And seized upon their towns and provinces.

*War.* Talk not of France, sith thou hast lost it all.

*K. Hen.* The lord protector lost it, and not I:
When I was crown'd I was but nine months old.

*Rich.* You are old enough now, and yet, methinks, you lose.
Father, tear the crown from the usurper's head.

*Edw.* Sweet father, do so; set it on your head.

*Mont.* Good brother, as thou lovest and honorest arms,
Let's fight it out and not stand caviling thus.

*Rich.* Sound drums and trumpets, and the king will fly.

*York.* Sons, peace!

*K. Hen.* Peace, thou! and give King Henry leave to speak.

*War.* Plantagenet shall speak first: hear him, lords;
And be you silent and attentive too,
For.he that interrupts him shall not live.

*K. Hen.* Think'st thou that I will leave my kingly throne,
Wherein my grandsire and my father sat?
No: first shall war unpeople this my realm;
Ay, and their colors, often borne in France,
And now in England to our heart's great sorrow,
Shall be my winding-sheet. Why faint you, lords?
My title's good, and better far than his.

*War.* Prove it, Henry, and thou shalt be king.

*K. Hen.* Henry the Fourth by conquest got the crown.

*York.* 'Twas by rebellion against his king.

*K. Hen.* [*Aside*] I know not what to say; my title's weak.
Tell me, may not a king adopt an heir?

*York.* What then?

*K. Hen.* An if he may, then am I lawful king;
For Richard, in the view of many lords,
Resign'd the crown to Henry the Fourth,
Whose heir my father was, and I am his.

*York.* He rose against him, being his sovereign,
And made him to resign his crown perforce.

*War.* Suppose, my lords, he did it unconstrain'd,
Think you 'twere prejudicial to his crown?

*Exe.* No; for he could not so resign his crown
But that the next heir should succeed and reign.

*K. Hen.* Art thou against us, Duke of Exeter?

*Exe.* His is the right, and therefore pardon me.

*York.* Why whisper you, my lords, and answer not?

*Exe.* My conscience tells me he is lawful king.

*K. Hen.* [*Aside*] All will revolt from me, and turn to him.

*North.* Plantagenet, for all the claim thou lay'st,
Think not that Henry shall be so deposed.

*War.* Deposed he shall be, in despite of all

*North.* Thou art deceived; 'tis not thy southern power,
Of Essex, Norfolk, Suffolk, nor of Kent,
Which makes thee thus presumptuous and proud,
Can set the duke up in despite of me.

*Clif.* King Henry, be thy title right or wrong,
Lord Clifford vows to fight in thy defense:
May that ground gape and swallow me alive,
Where I shall kneel to him that slew my father!

*K. Hen.* O Clifford, how thy words revive my heart!

*York.* Henry of Lancaster, resign thy crown.
What mutter you, or what conspire you, lords?

*War.* Do right unto this princely Duke of York,
Or I will fill the house with armed men,
And over the chair of state, where now he sits,
Write up his title with usurping blood.
[*He stamps with his foot, and the Soldiers show themselves.*

*K. Hen.* My Lord of Warwick, hear me but one word:
Let me for this my life-time reign as king.

*York.* Confirm the crown to me and to mine heirs,
And thou shalt reign in quiet while thou livest.

*King.* I am content: Richard Plantagenet,
Enjoy the kingdom after my decease.

*Clif.* What wrong is this unto the prince your son!

*War.* What good is this to England and himself!

*West.* Base, fearful and despairing Henry!

*Clif.* How hast thou injured both thyself and us!

*West.* I cannot stay to hear these articles.

*North.* Nor I.

*Clif.* Come, cousin, let us tell the queen these news.

*West.* Farewell, faint-hearted and degenerate king,
In whose cold blood no spark of honor bides.

*North.* Be thou a prey unto the house of York,
And die in bands, for this unmanly deed!

*Clif.* In dreadful war mayst thou be overcome,
Or live in peace, abandon'd and despis'd!
[*Exeunt* NORTH., CLIF., *and* WEST.

*War.* Turn this way, Henry, and regard them not.

*Exe.* They seek revenge, and therefore will not yield.

*K. Hen.* Ah, Exeter!

*War,* Why should you sigh, my lord?

*K. Hen.* Not for myself, Lord Warwick, but my son,
Whom I unnaturally shall disinherit.
But be it as it may:—I here entail
The crown to thee and to thine heirs for ever;
Conditionally, that here thou take an oath
To cease this civil war, and, whilst I live,
To honour me as thy king and sovereign,
And neither by treason nor hostility
To seek to put me down and reign thyself.

*York.* This oath I willingly take, and will perform.        [*Coming from the throne.*

*War.* Long live King Henry!—Plantagenet, embrace him.

*K. Hen.* And long live thou, and these thy forward sons!

*York.* Now York and Lancaster are reconcil'd.

*Exe.* Accurs'd be he that seeks to make them foes!
        [*Sennet. The* Lords *come forward.*

*York.* Farewell, my gracious lord; I'll to my castle.

*War.* And I'll keep London with my soldiers.

*Norf.* And I to Norfolk with my followers.

*Mont.* And I unto the sea, from whence I came.
        [*Exeunt* York *and his* Sons, War.,
        Norf., Mont., Soldiers, *and* Attendants.

*K. Hen.* And I, with grief and sorrow to the court.

*Exe.* Here comes the queen, whose looks bewray her anger;
I'll steal away.

*K. Hen.* Exeter, so will I.        [*Going.*
        [*Going.*

*Enter* Queen Margaret *and the* Prince of Wales.

*Q. Mar.* Nay, go not from me; I will follow thee.        [*will stay.*

*K. Hen.* Be patient, gentle queen, and I

*Q. Mar.* Who can be patient in such extremes?
Ah, wretched man! would I had died a maid,
And never seen thee, never born thee son,
Seeing thou hast prov'd so unnatural a father!
Hath he deserv'd to lose his birthright thus?
Hadst thou but lov'd him half so well as I,
Or felt that pain which I did for him once,
Or nourish'd him as I did with my blood,—
Thou wouldst have left thy dearest heart-blood there,        [heir,
Rather than made that savage duke thine
And disinherited thine only son.

*Prince.* Father, you cannot disinherit me:
If you be king, why should not I succeed?

*K. Hen.* Pardon me, Margaret;—pardon me, sweet son:—
The Earl of Warwick and the duke enforc'd me.

*Q. Mar.* Enforc'd thee! art thou king, and wilt be forc'd?
I shame to hear thee speak. Ah, timorous wretch!
Thou hast undone thyself, thy son, and me;
And given unto the house of York such head
As thou shalt reign but by their sufferance.
To entail him and his heirs unto the crown,
What is it, but to make thy sepulchre,
And creep into it far before thy time?
Warwick is chancellor and the lord of Calais;
Stern Falconbridge commands the narrow seas;
The duke is made protector of the realm;
And yet shalt thou be safe? such safety finds
The trembling lamb environed with wolves.
Had I been there, which am a silly woman,
The soldiers should have toss'd me on their pikes
Before I would have granted to that act.
But thou preferr'st thy life before thine honour:
And seeing thou dost, I here divorce myself
Both from thy table, Henry, and thy bed,
Until that act of parliament be repeal'd,
Whereby my son is disinherited.        [colours
The northern lords that have forsworn thy
Will follow mine, if once they see them spread;
And spread they shall be,—to thy foul disgrace,
And utter ruin of the house of York.
Thus do I leave thee.—Come, son, let's away;
Our army is ready; come, we'll after them.

*K. Hen.* Stay, gentle Margaret, and hear me speak.

*Q. Mar.* Thou hast spoke too much already: get thee gone        [with me?

*K. Hen.* Gentle son Edward, thou wilt stay

*Q. Mar.* Ay, to be murder'd by his enemies.

*Prince.* When I return with victory from the field
I'll see your grace: till then I'll follow her.

*Q. Mar.* Come, son, away; we may not linger thus.
        [*Exeunt* Queen Margaret
        *and the* Prince.

*K. Hen.* Poor queen! how love to me and to her son
Hath made her break out into terms of rage!
Reveng'd may she be on that hateful duke,
Whose haughty spirit, winged with desire,
Will cost my crown, and like an empty eagle
Tire on the flesh of me and my son!
The loss of those three lords torments my heart:
I'll write unto them, and entreat them fair:—
Come, cousin, you shall be the messenger.

*Exe.* And I, I hope, shall reconcile them all. [*Exeunt.*

SCENE II.—*A Room in Sandal Castle, near Wakefield, in Yorkshire.*

*Enter* EDWARD, RICHARD, *and* MONTAGUE.

*Rich.* Brother, though I be youngest, give me leave.

*Edw.* No, I can better play the orator.

*Mont.* But I have reasons strong and forcible.

*Enter* YORK.

*York.* Why, how now, sons and brother! at a strife?
What is your quarrel? how began it first?

*Edw.* No quarrel, but a slight contention.

*York.* About what?

*Rich.* About that which concerns your grace and us,—
The crown of England, father, which is yours.

*York.* Mine, boy? not till King Henry be dead. [death.

*Rich.* Your right depends not on his life or

*Edw.* Now you are heir, therefore enjoy it now: [breathe,
By giving the house of Lancaster leave to
It will outrun you, father, in the end.

*York.* I took an oath that he should quietly reign.

*Edw.* But, for a kingdom, any oath may be broken: [year.
I would break a thousand oaths to reign one

*Rich.* No; God forbid your grace should be forsworn.

*York.* I shall be, if I claim by open war.

*Rich.* I'll prove the contrary, if you'll hear me speak. [sible.

*York.* Thou canst not, son; it is impos-

*Rich.* An oath is of no moment, being not took
Before a true and lawful magistrate,
That hath authority over him that swears;
Henry had none, but did usurp the place;
Then, seeing 'twas he that made you to depose,
Your oath, my lord, is vain and frivolous.
Therefore, to arms. And, father, do but think
How sweet a thing it is to wear a crown;
Within whose circuit is Elysium,
And all that poets feign of bliss and joy.
Why do we linger thus? I cannot rest
Until the white rose that I wear be dy'd
Even in the lukewarm blood of Henry's heart.

*York.* Richard, enough; I will be king, or die.—
Brother, thou shalt to London presently,
And whet on Warwick to this enterprise.—
Thou, Richard, shalt to the Duke of Norfolk,
And tell him privily of our intent,—
You, Edward, shalt unto my Lord Cobham,
With whom the Kentishmen will willingly rise:

In them I trust; for they are soldiers,
Witty, courteous, liberal, full of spirit.—
While you are thus employ'd, what resteth more,
But that I seek occasion how to rise,
And yet the king not privy to my drift,
Nor any of the house of Lancaster?

*Enter a* MESSENGER.

But, stay: what news? Why com'st thou in such post? [earls and lords

*Mess.* The queen with all the northern
Intend here to besiege you in your castle:
She is hard by with twenty thousand men,
And therefore fortify your hold, my lord.

*York.* Ay, with my sword. What! think'st thou that we fear them?—
Edward and Richard, you shall stay with me;—
My brother Montague shall post to London:
Let noble Warwick, Cobham, and the rest,
Whom we have left protectors of the king,
With powerful policy strengthen themselves,
And trust not simple Henry nor his oaths.

*Mont.* Brother, I go; I'll win them, fear it not:
And thus most humbly I do take my leave. [*Exit.*

*Enter* SIR JOHN *and* SIR HUGH MORTIMER.

*York.* Sir John and Sir Hugh Mortimer, mine uncles!
You are come to Sandal in a happy hour;
The army of the queen mean to besiege us.

*Sir John.* She shall not need, we'll meet her in the field.

*York.* What, with five thousand men?

*Rich.* Ay, with five hundred, father, for a need:
A woman's general; what should we fear? [*A march afar off.*

*Edw.* I hear their drums: let's set our men in order,
And issue forth, and bid them battle straight.

*York.* Five men to twenty!—though the odds be great,
I doubt not, uncle, of our victory.
Many a battle have I won in France,
When as the enemy hath been ten to one:
Why should I not now have the like success? [*Exeunt.*

SCENE III.—*Plains near Sandal Castle.*

*Alarum. Enter* RUTLAND *and his* TUTOR.

*Rut.* Ah, whither shall I fly to 'scape their hands?
Ah, tutor, look where bloody Clifford comes!

*Enter* CLIFFORD *and* SOLDIERS.

*Clif.* Chaplain, away! thy priesthood saves thy life.
As for the brat of this accursed duke,
Whose father slew my father,—he shall die.

*Tut.* And I, my lord, will bear him company.

*Clif.* Soldiers, away with him!

*Tut.* Ah, Clifford, murder not this innocent child,
Lest thou be hated both of God and man.

[*Exit, forced off by* SOLDIERS.

*Clif.* How now! is he dead already? or is it fear
That makes him close his eyes?—I'll open them.

*Rut.* So looks the pent-up lion o'er the wretch
That trembles under his devouring paws;
And so he walks, insulting o'er his prey,
And so he comes, to rend his limbs asunder.—
Ah, gentle Clifford, kill me with thy sword,
And not with such a cruel threat'ning look!
Sweet Clifford, hear me speak before I die!—
I am too mean a subject for thy wrath:
Be thou reveng'd on men, and let me live.

*Clif.* In vain thou speak'st, poor boy; my father's blood
Hath stopp'd the passage where thy words should enter.

*Rut.* Then let my father's blood open it again:
He is a man, and, Clifford, cope with him.

*Clif.* Had I thy brethren here, their lives and thine
Were not revenge sufficient for me;
No, if I digg'd up thy forefathers' graves,
And hung their rotten coffins up in chains,
It could not slake mine ire nor ease my heart.
The sight of any of the house of York
Is as a fury to torment my soul;
And till I root out their accursed line
And leave not one alive, I live in hell.
Therefore,— [*Lifting his hand.*

*Rut.* O let me pray before I take my death!
To thee I pray; sweet Clifford, pity me!

*Clif.* Such pity as my rapier's point affords.

*Rut.* I never did thee harm: why wilt thou slay me?

*Clif.* Thy father hath.

*Rut.* But 'twas ere I was born.
Thou hast one son,—for his sake pity me;
Lest in revenge thereof,—sith God is just,—
He be as miserably slain as I.
Ah, let me live in prison all my days;
And when I give occasion of offence
Then let me die, for now thou hast no cause.

*Clif.* No cause!
Thy father slew my father; therefore, die.

[CLIFFORD *stabs him.*

*Rut. Dii faciant, laudis summa sit ista tuæ!* [*Dies.*

*Clif.* Plantagenet! I come, Plantagenet!
And this thy son's blood cleaving to my blade
Shall rust upon my weapon, till thy blood,
Congeal'd with this, do make me wipe off both. [*Exit.*

SCENE IV.—*Another part of the Plains near Sandal Castle.*

*Alarum. Enter* YORK.

*York.* The army of the queen hath got the field:
My uncles both are slain in rescuing me;
And all my followers to the eager foe
Turn back, and fly, like ships before the wind,
Or lambs pursu'd by hunger-starved wolves.
My sons,—God knows what hath bechanced them: [*selves*
But this I know,—they have demean'd themselves
Like men born to renown by life or death.
Three times did Richard make a lane to me;
And thrice cried, *Courage, father! fight it out!*
And full as oft came Edward to my side,
With purple falchion, painted to the hilt
In blood of those that had encounter'd him:
And when the hardiest warriors did retire,
Richard cried, *Charge! and give no foot of ground!*
And cried, *A crown, or else a glorious tomb!
A sceptre, or an earthly sepulchre!*
With this we charg'd again: but, out, alas!
We bodg'd again; as I have seen a swan
With bootless labour swim against the tide,
And spend her strength with over-matching waves. [*A short alarum within.*
Ah, hark! the fatal followers do pursue;
And I am faint, and cannot fly their fury:
And were I strong, I would not shun their fury:
The sands are number'd that make up my life;
Here must I stay, and here my life must end.

*Enter* QUEEN MARGARET, CLIFFORD, NORTHUMBERLAND, *and Soldiers.*

Come, bloody Clifford,—rough Northumberland,—
I dare your quenchless fury to more rage:
I am your butt, and I abide your shot.

*North.* Yield to our mercy, proud Plantagenet.

*Clif.* Ay, to such mercy as his ruthless arm
With downright payment, show'd unto my father.
Now Phaeton hath tumbled from his car,
And made an evening at the noontide prick.

*York.* My ashes, as the phœnix, may bring forth
A bird that will revenge upon you all:
And in that hope I throw mine eyes to heaven,
Scorning whate'er you can afflict me with.
Why come you not? what! multitudes, and fear?

*Clif.* So cowards fight when they can fly no further;
So doves do peck the falcon's piercing talons;

So desperate thieves, all hopeless of their lives,
Breathe out invectives 'gainst the officers.
  *York.* O Clifford, but bethink thee once again,
And in thy thought o'errun my former time;
And, if thou canst, for blushing, view this face,
And bite thy tongue, that slanders him with cowardice                    [this!
Whose frown hath made thee faint and fly ere
  *Clif.* I will not bandy with thee word for word,
But buckle with thee blows, twice two for one.                        [*Draws.*
  *Q. Mar.* Hold, valiant Clifford! for a thousand causes
I would prolong awhile the traitor's life.—
Wrath makes him deaf:—speak thou, Northumberland.              [so much
  *North.* Hold, Clifford! do not honour him
To prick thy finger, though to wound his heart:
What valour were it, when a cur doth grin,
For one to thrust his hand between his teeth,
When he might spurn him with his foot away?
It is war's prize to take all 'vantages;
And ten to one is no impeach of valour.
  [*They lay hands on* YORK, *who struggles.*
  *Clif.* Ay, ay, so strives the woodcock with the gin.
  *North.* So doth the cony struggle in the net.              [YORK *is taken prisoner.*
  *York.* So triumph thieves upon their conquer'd booty;
So true men yield, with robbers so o'ermatch'd.
  *North.* What would your grace have done unto him now?          [thumberland,
  *Q. Mar.* Brave warriers, Clifford and Nor-
Come, make him stand upon this molehill here,
That raught at mountains with outstretched arms,
Yet parted but the shadow with his hand.—
What, was it you that would be England's king?
Was't you that revell'd in our parliament,
And made a preachment of your high descent?
Where are your mess of sons to back you now?
The wanton Edward and the lusty George?
And where's that valiant crook-back prodigy,
Dicky your boy, that with his grumbling voice
Was wont to cheer his dad in mutinies?
Or, with the rest, where is your darling Rutland?
Look, York: I stain'd this napkin with the blood
That valiant Clifford, with his rapier's point,
Made issue from the bosom of the boy:

And if thine eyes can water for his death,
I give thee this to dry thy cheeks withal.
Alas, poor York! but that I hate thee deadly,
I should lament thy miserable state.
I pr'ythee, grieve, to make me merry, York.
What, hath thy fiery heart so parch'd thine entrails
That not a tear can fall for Rutland's death?
Why art thou patient, man? thou shouldst be mad;
And I, to make thee mad, do mock thee thus.
Stamp, rave, and fret, that I may sing and dance.
Thou wouldst be fee'd, I see, to make me sport;
York cannot speak unless he wear a crown.—
A crown for York!—and, lords, bow low to him;—
Hold you his hands whilst I do set it on.
  [*Putting a paper crown on his head.*
Ay, marry, sir, now looks he like a king!
Ay, this is he that took King Henry's chair;
And this is he was his adopted heir.—
But how is it that great Plantagenet
Is crown'd so soon, and broke his solemn oath?
As I bethink me, you should not be king
Till our King Henry had shook hands with death.
And will you pale your head in Henry's glory,
And rob his temples of the diadem
Now in his life, against your holy oath?
O, 'tis a fault too, too unpardonable!—
Off with the crown; and, with the crown, his head;
And whilst we breathe take time to do him dead.
  *Clif.* That is my office, for my father's sake.
  *Q. Mar.* Nay, stay; let's hear the orisons he makes.
  *York.* She-wolf of France, but worse than wolves of France,          [tooth!
Whose tongue more poisons than the adder's
How ill-seeming is it in thy sex.
To triumph, like an Amazonian trull,
Upon their woes whom fortune captivates!
But that thy face is, visard-like, unchanging,
Made impudent with use of evil deeds,
I would assay, proud queen, to make thee blush:
To tell thee whence thou cam'st, of whom deriv'd,
Were shame enough to shame thee, wert thou not shameless.
Thy father bears the type of King of Naples,
Of both the Sicils, and Jerusalem;
Yet not so wealthy as an English yeoman.
Hath that poor monarch taught thee to insult?
It needs not, nor it boots thee not, proud queen:

Unless the adage must be verified,—
That beggars mounted run their horse to death.
'Tis beauty that doth oft make women proud;
But, God he knows, thy share thereof is small:
'Tis virtue that doth make them most admir'd;
The contrary doth make thee wonder'd at:
'Tis government that makes them seem divine;
The want thereof makes thee abominable:
Thou art as opposite to every good
As the antipodes are unto us,
Or as the south to the septentrion.
O tiger's heart wrapp'd in a woman's hide!
How couldst thou drain the life-blood of the child,
To bid the father wipe his eyes withal.
And yet be seen to bear a woman's face?
Women are soft, mild, pitiful, and flexible;
Thou stern, obdurate, flinty, rough, remorseless.
Bidd'st thou me rage? why, now thou hast thy wish:                [thy will:
Wouldst have me weep? why, now thou hast
For raging wind blows up incessant showers,
And when the rage allays, the rain begins.
These tears are my sweet Rutland's obsequies;
And every drop cries vengeance for his death
'Gainst thee, fell Clifford, and thee, false Frenchwoman.                [me so
*North.* Beshrew me, but his passions move
That hardly can I check my eyes from tears.
*York.* That face of his the hungry cannibals
Would not have touch'd, would not have stain'd with blood:
But you are more inhuman, more inexorable,—
O, ten times more,—than tigers of Hyrcania.
See ruthless, queen, a hapless father's tears:
This cloth thou dipp'dst in blood of my sweet boy,
And I with tears do wash the blood away.
Keep thou the napkin, and go boast of this:
                [*He gives back the handkerchief.*
And if thou tell'st the heavy story right,
Upon my soul, the hearers will shed tears;
Yea, even my foes will shed fast-falling tears,
And say, *Alas, it was a piteous deed!*—
There, take the crown, and, with the crown, my curse;
                [*Giving back the paper crown.*
And in thy need such comfort come to thee
As now I reap at thy too cruel hand!—
Hard-hearted Clifford, take me from the world:
My soul to heaven, my blood upon your heads!                [my kin,
*North.* Had he been slaughter-man to all

I should not for my life but weep with him,
To see how inly sorrow gripes his soul.
*Q. Mar.* What, weeping-ripe, my Lord Northumberland?
Think but upon the wrong he did us all,
And that will quickly dry the melting tears.
*Clif.* Here's for my oath, here's for my father's death.                [*Stabbing him.*
*Q. Mar.* And here's to right our gentlehearted king.                [*Stabbing him.*
*York.* Open thy gate of mercy, gracious God!
My soul flies through these wounds to seek out thee.                [*Dies.*
*Q. Mar.* Off with his head, and set it on York gates;
So York may overlook the town of York.
                [*Flourish. Exeunt.*

## ACT II.

SCENE I.—*A plain near Mortimer's Cross in Herefordshire.*

*Drums. Enter* EDWARD *and* RICHARD, *with their* Forces, *marching.*

  *Edw.* I wonder how our princely father 'scap'd,
Or whether he be 'scap'd away or no
From Clifford's and Northumberland's pursuit:
Had he been ta'en we should have heard the news;                [news;
Had he been slain we should have heard the
Or had he 'scap'd, methinks we should have heard
The happy tidings of his good escape.—
How fares my brother? why is he so sad?
  *Rich.* I cannot joy, until I be resolv'd
Where our right valiant father is become.
I saw him in the battle range about;
And watch'd him how he singled Clifford forth.
Methought he bore him in the thickest troop
As doth a lion in a herd of neat;
Or as a bear, encompass'd round with dogs,—
Who having pinch'd a few, and made them cry,
The rest stand all aloof and bark at him.
So far'd our father with his enemies;
So fled his enemies my warlike father:
Methinks 'tis prize enough to be his son.—
See how the morning ope's her golden gates,
And takes her farewell of the glorious sun!
How well resembles it the prime of youth,
Trimm'd like a younker prancing to his love!
  *Edw.* Dazzle mine eyes, or do I see three suns?
  *Rich.* Three glorious suns, each on a perfect sun;
Not separated with the racking clouds,
But sever'd in a pale clear-shining sky.
See, see! they join, embrace, and seem to kiss,
As if they vow'd some league inviolable:

Now are they but one lamp, one light, one sun.
In this the heaven figures some event.

   *Edw.* 'Tis wondrous strange, the like yet never heard of.
I think it cites us, brother, to the field,—
That we, the sons of brave Plantagenet,
Each one already blazing by our meeds,
Should, notwithstanding, join our lights together,
And overshine the earth, as this the world
Whate'er it bodes, henceforward will I bear
Upon my target three fair shining suns.

   *Rich.* Nay, bear three daughters:—by your leave I speak it,
You love the breeder better than the male.

*Enter a* Messenger.

But what are thou, whose heavy looks foretell
Some dreadful story hanging on thy tongue?

   *Mess.* Ah, one that was a woeful looker-on
When as the noble Duke of York was slain,
Your pricely father and my loving lord!

   *Edw.* O, speak no more! for I have heard too much.

   *Rich.* Say how he died, for I will hear it all.

   *Mess.* Environed he was with many foes;
And stood against them as the hope of Troy
Against the Greeks that would have enter'd Troy.
But Hercules himself must yield to odds;
And many strokes, though with a little axe,
Hew down and fell the hardest-timber'd oak.
By many hands your father was subdu'd;
But only slaughter'd by the ireful arm
Of unrelenting Clifford, and the queen,—
Who crown'd the gracious duke in high despite,—
Laugh'd in his face; and when with grief he wept,
The ruthless queen gave him to dry his cheeks
A napkin steeped in the harmless blood
Of sweet young Rutland, by rough Clifford slain:
And after many scorns, many foul taunts,
They took his head, and on the gates of York
They set the same; and there it doth remain,
The saddest spectacle that e'er I view'd.

   *Edw.* Sweet Duke of York, our prop to lean upon,—
Now thou art gone, we have no staff, no stay!—
O Clifford, boisterous Clifford, thou hast slain
The flower of Europe for his chivalry;
And treacherously hast thou vanquish'd him,
For hand to hand he would have vanquish'd thee!—
Now my soul's palace is become a prison:
Ah, would she break from hence, that this my body

Might in the ground be closed up in rest!
For never henceforth shall I joy again,
Never, O never shall I see more joy.

   *Rich.* I cannot weep; for all my body's moisture
Scarce serves to quench my furnace-burning [heart:
Nor can my tongue unload my heart's great burden;
For self-same wind that I should speak withal
Is kindling coals, that fire all my breast,
And burn me up with flames, that tears would quench.
To weep is to make less the depth of grief:
Tears, then, for babes; blows and revenge for me!—
Richard, I bear thy name; I'll venge thy death,
Or die renowned by attempting it.

   *Edw.* His name that valiant duke hath left with thee;
His dukedom and his chair with me is left.

   *Rich.* Nay, if thou be that princely eagle's bird,
Show thy descent by gazing 'gainst the sun:
For chair and dukedom, throne and kingdom say:
Either that is thine, or else thou wert not his.

*March. Enter* WARWICK *and* MONTAGUE, *with* Forces.

   *War.* How now, fair lords! What fare? what news abroad? [should recount

   *Rich.* Great Lord of Warwick, if we
Our baleful news, and at each word's deliverance
Stab poniards in our flesh till all were told,
The words would add more anguish than the wounds.
O valiant lord, the Duke of York is slain!

   *Edw.* O Warwick, Warwick! that Plantagenet
Which held thee dearly as his soul's redemption
Is by the stern Lord Clifford done to death.

   *War.* Ten days ago I drown'd these news in tears;
And now, to add more measure to your woes,
I come to tell you things since then befall'n.
After the bloody fray at Wakefield fought,
Where your brave father breath'd his latest gasp,
Tidings, as swiftly as the posts could run,
Were brought me of your loss and his depart
I, then in London, keeper of the king,
Muster'd my soldiers, gather'd flocks of friends,
And very well appointed, as I thought,
March'd towards Saint Albans to intercept the queen,
Bearing the king in my behalf along;
For by my scouts I was advertised
That she was coming with a full intent
To dash our late decree in parliament

Touching King Henry's oath and your succession.
Short tale to make,—we at St. Albans met,
Our battles join'd, and both sides fiercely fought.
But whether 'twas the coldness of the king,
Who look'd full gently on his warlike queen,
That robb'd my soldiers of their heated spleen;
Or whether 'twas report of her success;
Or more than common fear of Clifford's rigour,
Who thunders to his captives, Blood and death,
I cannot judge: but, to conclude with truth,
Their weapons like to lightning came and went;
Our soldiers',—like the night-owl's lazy flight,
Or like a lazy thrasher with a flail,—
Fell gently down, as if they struck their friends.
I cheer'd them up with justice of our cause,
With promise of high pay and great rewards:
But all in vain; they had no heart to fight,
And we in them no hope to win the day;
So that we fled; the king unto the queen;
Lord George, your brother, Norfolk, and myself,
In haste, post-haste, are come to join with you;
For in the marches here we heard you were
Making another head to fight again.
*Edw.* Where is the Duke of Norfolk, gentle Warwick?    [England?
And when came George from Burgundy to
*War.* Some six miles off the duke is with the soldiers;
And for your brother, he was lately sent
From your kind aunt, Duchess of Burgundy,
With aid of soldiers to this needful war.
*Rich.* 'Twas odds, belike, when valiant Warwick fled:
Oft have I heard his praises in pursuit,
But ne'er till now his scandal of retire.
*War.* Nor now my scandal, Richard, dost thou hear;    [mine
For thou shalt know this strong right hand of
Can pluck the diadem from faint Henry's head,
And wring the awful sceptre from his fist,
Were he as famous and as bold in war
As he is fam'd for mildness, peace, and prayer.
*Rich.* I know it well, Lord Warwick; blame me not:
'Tis love I bear thy glories makes me speak.
But in this troublous time what's to be done?
Shall we go throw away our coats of steel,
And wrap our bodies in black mourning-gowns,
Numbering our Ave-Maries with our beads?
Or shall we on the helmets of our foes
Tell our devotion with revengeful arms?

If for the last, say Ay, and to it, lords.
*War.* Why, therefore Warwick came to seek you out;
And therefore comes my brother Montague.
Attend me, lords. The proud insulting queen,
With Clifford and the haught Northumberland,
And of their feather many more proud birds,
Have wrought the easy-melting king like wax.
He swore consent to your succession,
His oath enrolled in the parliament;
And now to London all the crew are gone,
To frustrate both his oath and what beside
May make against the house of Lancaster.
Their power, I think, is thirty thousand strong:
Now if the help of Norfolk and myself,
With all the friends that thou, brave Earl of March,
Amongst the loving Welshmen canst procure,
Will but amount to five-and-twenty thousand,
Why, *Via!* to London will we march amain;
And once again bestride our foaming steeds,
And once again cry, Charge upon our foes!
But never once again turn back and fly.
*Rich.* Ay, now methinks I hear great Warwick speak:
Ne'er may he live to see a sunshine day
That cries Retire, if Warwick bid him stay.
*Edw.* Lord Warwick, on thy shoulder will I lean;
And when thou fail'st,—as God forbid the hour!—
Must Edward fall, which peril heaven forefend!    [of York:
*War.* No longer Earl of March, but Duke
The next degree is England's royal throne;
For King of England shalt thou be proclaim'd
In every borough as we pass along;
And he that throws not up his cap for joy,
Shall for the fault make forfeit of his head.
King Edward,—valiant Richard,—Montague,—
Stay we no longer, dreaming of renown,
But sound the trumpets and about our task.
*Rich.* Then, Clifford, were thy heart as hard as steel,—
As thou hast shown it flinty by thy deeds,—
I come to pierce it,—or to give thee mine.
*Edw.* Then strike up drums:—God and Saint George for us!

*Enter a* Messenger.

*War.* How now! what news?
*Mess.* The Duke of Norfolk sends you word by me,
The queen is coming with a puissant host;
And craves your company for speedy counsel.
*War.* Why, then it sorts, brave warriors: let's away.    [*Exeunt.*

SCENE II.—*Before York.*

*Flourish. Enter* KING HENRY, QUEEN MAR-
GARET, *the* PRINCE OF WALES, CLIFFORD,
*and* NORTHUMBERLAND, *with* Forces.

*Q. Mar.* Welcome, my lord, to this brave
  town of York.
Yonder's the head of that arch-enemy
That sought to be encompass'd with your
  crown:
Doth not the object cheer your heart, my
  lord?
  *K. Hen.* Ay, as the rocks cheer them that
  fear their wreck:—
To see this sight, it irks my very soul.—
Withhold revenge, dear God! tis not my
  fault,
Nor wittingly have I infring'd my vow.
  *Clif.* My gracious liege, this too much
  lenity
And harmful pity must be laid aside.
To whom do lions cast their gentle looks?
Not to the beast that would usurp their den.
Whose hand is that the forest bear doth lick?
Not his that spoils her young before her
  face.
Who scapes the lurking serpent's mortal
  sting?
Not he that sets his foot upon her back.
The smallest worm will turn, being trodden
  on,
And doves will peck in safeguard of their
  brood.
Ambitious York did level at thy crown,
Thou smiling while he knit his angry brows:
He, but a duke, would have his son a king,
And raise his issue, like a loving sire;
Thou, being a king, bless'd with a goodly
  son,
Didst yield consent to disinherit him,
Which argu'd thee a most unloving father.
Unreasonable creatures feed their young;
And though man's face be fearful to their
  eyes,
Yet, in protection of their tender ones,
Who hath not seen them,—even with those
  wings
Which sometime they have us'd with fearful
  flight,— [nest,
Make war with him that climb'd unto their
Offering their own lives in their young's de-
  fence?
For shame, my liege, make them your prece-
  dent!
Were it not pity that this goodly boy
Should lose his birthright by his father's
  fault,
And long hereafter say unto his child,
*What my great-grandfather and grandsire
  got*
*My careless father fondly gave away?*
Ah, what a shame were this! Look on the
  boy;
And let his manly face, which promiseth

Successful fortune, steel thy melting heart
To hold thine own, and leave thine own with
  him. [orator,
  *K. Hen.* Full well hath Clifford play'd the
Inferring arguments of mighty force.
But, Clifford, tell me, didst thou never hear
That things ill got had ever bad success?
And happy always was it for that son
Whose father for his hoarding went to hell?
I'll leave my son my virtuous deeds behind;
And would my father had left me no more!
For all the rest is held at such a rate
As brings a thousand-fold more care to keep
Than in possession any jot of pleasure.—
Ah, cousin York! would thy best friends did
  know
How it doth grieve me that thy head is here!
  *Q. Mar.* My lord, cheer up your spirits:
  our foes are nigh,
And this soft courage makes your followers
  faint.
You promis'd knighthood to our forward
  son:
Unsheathe your sword, and dub him pres-
  ently.—
Edward, kneel down.
  *K. Hen.* Edward Plantagenet, arise a
  knight;
And learn this lesson,—draw thy sword in
  right.
  *Prince.* My gracious father, by your
  kingly leave,
I'll draw it as apparent to the crown,
And in that quarrel use it to the death.
  *Clif.* Why, that is spoken like a toward
  prince.

*Enter a* Messenger.

  *Mess.* Royal commanders, be in readiness:
For with a band of thirty thousand men
Comes Warwick, backing of the Duke of
  York;
And in the towns, as they do march along,
Proclaims him king, and many fly to him:
Darraign your battle, for they are at hand.
  *Clif.* I would your highness would depart
  the field: [absent.
The queen hath best success when you are
  *Q. Mar.* Ay, good my lord, and leave us
  to our fortune.
  *K. Hen.* Why, that's my fortune too;
  therefore I'll stay.
  *North.* Be it with resolution, then, to
  fight. [lords,
  *Prince.* My royal father, cheer these noble
And hearten those that fight in your defence:
Unsheathe your sword, good father; cry,
  *Saint George!*

*March. Enter* EDWARD, GEORGE, RICHARD,
WARWICK, NORFOLK, MONTAGUE, *and* Soldiers.

  *Edw.* Now, perjur'd Henry! wilt thou
  kneel for grace,

And set thy diadem upon my head;
Or bide the mortal fortune of the field?

*Q. Mar.* Go, rate thy minions, proud insulting boy!
Becomes it thee to be thus bold in terms
Before thy sovereign and thy lawful king?

*Edw.* I am his king, and he should bow
his knee;
I was adopted heir by his consent:
Since when, his oath is broke; for, as I hear,
You, that are king, though he do wear the crown,
Have caus'd him, by new act of parliament,
To blot out me and put his own son in.

*Clif.* And reason too:
Who should succeed the father but the son?

*Rich.* Are you there, butcher?—O, I cannot speak! [swer thee,

*Clif.* Ay, crook-back, here I stand to an-
Or any he the proudest of thy sort.

*Rich.* 'Twas you that kill'd young Rutland, was it not?

*Clif.* Ay, and old York, and yet not satisfied.

*Rich.* For God's sake, lords, give signal to
the fight. [yield the crown?

*War.* What say'st thou, Henry, wilt thou

*Q. Mar.* Why, how now, long-tongu'd
Warwick! dare you speak?
When you and I met at Saint Albans last,
Your legs did better service than your hands.

*War.* Then 'twas my turn to fly, and now
'tis thine. [fled.

*Clif.* You said so much before, and yet you

*War.* 'Twas not your valour, Clifford,
drove me thence. [make you stay.

*North.* No, nor your manhood that durst

*Rich.* Northumberland, I hold thee reverently.—
Break off the parley; for scarce I can refrain
The execution of my big-swoln heart
Upon that Clifford, that cruel child-killer.

*Clif.* I slew thy father,—call'st thou him
a child? [coward,

*Rich.* Ay, like a dastard and a treacherous
As thou didst kill our tender brother Rutland;
But ere sunset I'll make thee curse the deed.

*K. Hen.* Have done with words, my lords,
and hear me speak. [thy lips.

*Q. Mar.* Defy them, then, or else hold close

*K. Hen.* I pr'ythee give no limits to my
tongue:
I am a king, and privileg'd to speak.

*Clif.* My liege, the wound that bred this
meeting here
Cannot be cur'd by words; therefore be still.

*Rich.* Then, executioner, unsheathe thy
sword:
By him that made us all, I am resolv'd
That Clifford's manhood lies upon his
tongue.

*Edw.* Say, Henry, shall I have my right,
or no?

A thousand men have broke their fasts today
That ne'er shall dine unless thou yield the
crown. [head;

*War.* If thou deny, their blood upon thy
For York in justice puts his armour on.

*Prince.* If that be right which Warwick
says is right,
There is no wrong, but everything is right.

*Rich.* Whoever got thee, there thy mother
stands;
For, well I wot, thou hast thy mother's
tongue.

*Q. Mar.* But thou art neither like thy sire
nor dam;
But like a foul misshapen stigmatic,
Mark'd by the destinies to be avoided,
As venom toads, or lizards' dreadful stings.

*Rich.* Iron of Naples hid with English
gilt,
Whose father bears the title of a king,—
As if a channel should be call'd the sea,—
Sham'st thou not, knowing whence thou art
extraught,
To let thy tongue detect thy base-born
heart?

*Edw.* A wisp of straw were worth a thousand crowns,
To make this shameless callet know herself.—
Helen of Greece was fairer far than thou,
Although thy husband may be Menelaus;
And ne'er was Agamemnon's brother
wrong'd
By that false woman as this king by thee.
His father revell'd in the heart of France,
And tam'd the king, and made the dauphin
stoop;
And had he match'd according to his state,
He might have kept that glory to this day;
But when he took a beggar to his bed,
And grac'd thy poor sire with his bridal-day,
Even then that sunshine brew'd a shower for
him
That wash'd his father's fortunes forth of
France,
And heap'd sedition on his crown at home.
For what hath broach'd this tumult but thy
pride?
Hadst thou been meek, our title still had
slept;
And we, in pity of the gentle king,
Had slipp'd our claim until another age.

*Geo.* But when we saw our sunshine made
thy spring,
And that thy summer bred us no increase,
We set the axe to thy usurping root; [selves,
And though the edge hath something hit our-
Yet, know thou, since we have begun to
strike
We'll never leave till we have hewn thee
down,
Or bath'd thy growing with our heated
bloods.

*Edw.* And in this resolution I defy thee;

Not willing any longer conference,
Since thou deniest the gentle king to speak.—
Sound trumpets!—let our bloody colours wave!—
And either victory or else a grave.

*Q. Mar.* Stay, Edward.

*Edw.* No, wrangling woman, we'll no longer stay:
These words will cost ten thousand lives this day.     [*Exeunt.*

SCENE III.—*A Field of Battle between Towton and Saxton, in Yorkshire.*

*Alarums: excursions. Enter* WARWICK.

*War.* Forspent with toil, as runners with a race,
I lay me down a little while to breathe;
For strokes receiv'd and many blows repaid
Have robb'd my strong-knit sinews of their strength,
And, spite of spite, needs must I rest awhile.

*Enter* EDWARD, *running.*

*Edw.* Smile, gentle heaven! or strike, ungentle death!     [clouded.
For this world frowns, and Edward's sun is

*War.* How now, my lord! what hap? what hope of good?

*Enter* GEORGE.

*Geo.* Our hap is loss, our hope but sad despair;
Our ranks are broke, and ruin follows us:
What counsel give you, whither shall we fly?

*Edw.* Bootless is flight,—they follow us with wings;
And weak we are, and cannot shun pursuit.

*Enter* RICHARD.

*Rich.* Ah, Warwick, why hast thou withdrawn thyself?
Thy brother's blood the thirsty earth hath drunk,
Broach'd with the steely point of Clifford's lance;
And in the very pangs of death he cried,
Like to a dismal clangor heard from far,
*Warwick, revenge! brother, revenge my death!*
So, underneath the belly of their steeds,
That stain'd their fetlocks in his smoking blood,
The noble gentleman gave up the ghost.

*War.* Then let the earth be drunken with our blood:
I'll kill my horse, because I will not fly.
Why stand we like soft-hearted women here,
Wailing our losses, whiles the foe doth rage;
And look upon, as if the tragedy
Were play'd in jest by counterfeiting actors?
Here on my knee I vow to God above
I'll never pause again, never stand still,
Till either death hath clos'd these eyes of mine

Or fortune given me measure of revenge.

*Edw.* O Warwick, I do bend my knee with thine;
And in this vow do chain my soul to thine!—
And ere my knee rise from the earth's cold face
I throw my hands, mine eyes, my heart to thee,
Thou setter-up and plucker-down of kings,—
Beseeching thee, if with thy will it stands
That to my foes this body must be prey,
Yet that thy brazen gates of heaven may ope,
And give sweet passage to my sinful soul!—
Now, lords, take leave until we meet again,
Where'er it be, in heaven or in earth.

*Rich.* Brother, give me thy hand;—and, gentle Warwick,
Let me embrace thee in my weary arms:
I, that did never weep, now melt with woe
That winter should cut off our spring-time so.     [lords, farewell.

*War.* Away, away! Once more, sweet

*Geo.* Yet let us all together to our troops,
And give them leave to fly that will not stay;
And call them pillars that will stand to us;
And if we thrive, promise them such rewards
As victors wear at the Olympian games:
This may plant courage in their quailing breasts;
For yet is hope of life and victory.—
Forslow no longer, make we hence amain.     [*Exeunt.*

SCENE IV.—*Another part of the field.*

*Excursions. Enter* RICHARD *and* CLIFFORD.

*Rich.* Now, Clifford, I have singled thee alone:
Suppose this arm is for the Duke of York,
And this for Rutland; both bound to revenge,
Wert thou environ'd with a grazen wall.

*Clif.* Now, Richard, I am with thee here alone:
This is the hand that stabb'd thy father York;
And this the hand that slew thy brother Rutland;
And here's the heart that triumphs in their death,
And cheers these hands that slew thy sire and brother
To execute the like upon thyself;
And so, have at thee!
    [*They fight.* WAR. *enters;* CLIF. *flies.*

*Rich.* Nay, Warwick, single out some other chase;
For I myself will hunt this wolf to death.
    [*Exeunt.*

SCENE V.—*Another part of the Field.*

*Alarum. Enter* KING HENRY.

*K. Hen.* This battle fares like to the morning's war,

When dying clouds contend with growing
    light,
What time the shepherd, blowing of his
    nails,
Can neither call it perfect day nor night.
Now sways it this way, like a mighty sea
Forc'd by the tide to combat with the wind;
Now sways it that way, like the selfsame sea
Forc'd to retire by fury of the wind:
Sometime the flood prevails, and then the
    wind;
Now one the better, then another best;
Both tugging to be victors, breast to breast,
Yet neither conqueror nor conquered:
So is the equal poise of this fell war.
Here on this molehill will I sit me down.
To whom God will, there be the victory!
For Margaret my queen, and Clifford too,
Have chid me from the battle; swearing
    both
They prosper best of all when I am thence.
Would I were dead! if God's good will were
    so;
For what is in this world but grief and woe?
O God! methinks it were a happy life
To be no better than a homely swain;
To sit upon a hill, as I do now,
To carve out dials quaintly, point by point,
Thereby to see the minutes how they run,—
How many make the hour full complete;
How many hours bring about the day;
How many days will finish up the year;
How many years a mortal man may live.
When this is known, then to divide the
    times,—
So many hours must I tend my flock;
So many hours must I take my rest;
So many hours must I contemplate;
So many hours must I sport myself;
So many days my ewes have been with
    young;
So many weeks ere the poor fools will
    yean;
So many years ere I shall shear the fleece:
So minutes, hours, days, months, and years,
Pass'd over to the end they were created,
Would bring white hairs unto a quiet grave.
Ah, what a life were this! how sweet! how
    lovely!
Gives not the hawthorn bush a sweeter shade
To shepherds, looking on their silly sheep,
Than doth a rich embroider'd canopy
To kings that fear their subjects' treachery?
O, yes, it doth; a thousand-fold it doth.
And to conclude,—the shepherd's homely
    curds,
His cold thin drink out of his leather bottle,
His wonted sleep under a fresh tree's shade,
All which secure and sweetly he enjoys,
Is far beyond a prince's delicates,
His viands sparkling in a golden cup,
His body couched in a curious bed,
When care, mistrust, and treason wait on
    him.

*Alarum. Enter a* Son *that has killed his
Father, bringing in the dead body.*

    *Son.* Ill blows the wind that profits no-
      body.
This man, whom hand to hand I slew in
    fight,
May be possessed with some store of crowns;
And I, that haply take them from him now,
May yet ere night yield both my life and
    them
To some man else, as this dead man doth
    me.—
Who's this?—O God! it is my father's face,
Whom in this conflict I unwares have kill'd.
O heavy times, begetting such events!
From London by the king was I press'd
    forth:
My father, being the Earl of Warwick's man,
Came on the part of York, press'd by his
    master;
And I, who at his hands receiv'd my life,
Have by my hands of life bereaved him.—
Pardon me, God, I knew not what I did!—
And pardon father, for I knew not thee!—
My tears shall wipe away these bloody
    marks;
And no more words till they have flow'd
    their fill.
    *K. Hen.* O piteous spectacle! O bloody
      times!
Whilst lions war, and battle for their dens,
Poor harmless lambs abide their enmity.—
Weep, wretched man, I'll aid thee tear for
    tear;
And let our hearts and eyes, like civil war,
Be blind with tears, and break o'ercharged
    with grief.

*Enter a* Father *that has killed his Son, with
the body in his arms.*

    *Fath.* Thou that so stoutly hast resisted
    me.
Give me thy gold, if thou hast any gold;
For I have bought it with an hundred
    blows.—
But let me see: is this our foeman's face?
Ah, no, no, no, it is mine only son!
Ah, boy, if any life be left in thee,    [arise,
Throw up thine eye! see, see what showers
Blown with the windy tempest of my heart,
Upon thy wounds, that kill mine eye and
    heart!—
O pity, God, this miserable age!—
What stratagems, how fell, how butcherly,
Erroneous, mutinous, and unnatural,
This deadly quarrel daily doth beget!—
O boy, thy father gave thee life too soon,
And hath bereft thee of thy life too late!
    *K. Hen.* Woe above woe! grief more than
      common grief!    [deeds!—
O that my death would stay these ruthful
O pity, pity, gentle heaven, pity!—
The red rose and the white are on his face,

The fatal colours of our striving houses:
The one his purple blood right well re-
	sembles;
The other his pale cheeks, methinks, pre-
	senteth:
Wither one rose, and let the other flourish;
If you contend, a thousand lives must
	wither.
	*Son.* How will my mother for a father's
		death
Take on with me, and ne'er be satisfied! [son
	*Fath.* How will my wife for slaughter of my
Shed seas of tears, and ne'er be satisfied!
	*K. Hen.* How will the country for these
		woeful chances
Misthink the king, and not be satisfied!
	*Son.* Was ever son so rued a father's
		death?
	*Fath.* Was ever father so bemoan'd his
		son?
	*K. Hen.* Was ever king so griev'd for sub-
		jects' woe?
Much is your sorrow; mine ten times so
	much.
	*Son.* I'll bear thee hence, where I may
		weep my fill.   [*Exit with the body.*
	*Fath.* These arms of mine shall be thy
		winding-sheet;
My heart, sweet boy, shall be thy sep-
	ulchre,—
For from my heart thine image ne'er shall
	go;
My sighing breast shall be thy funeral bell;
And so obsequious will thy father be,
E'en for the loss of thee, having no more,
As Priam was for all his valiant sons. [will,
I'll bear thee hence; and let them fight that
For I have murder'd where I should not kill.
		[*Exit with the body.*
	*K. Hen.* Sad-hearted men, much overgone
		with care,
Here sits a king more woeful than you are.

*Alarums: excursions. Enter* QUEEN MAR-
GARET, PRINCE OF WALES, *and* EXETER.

	*Prince.* Fly, father, fly! for all your friends
		are fled,
And Warwick rages like a chafed bull:
Away! for death doth hold us in pursuit
	*Q. Mar.* Mount you, my lord; towards
		Berwick post amain:
Edward and Richard, like a brace of grey-
	hounds
Having the fearful flying hare in sight,
With fiery eyes sparkling for very wrath,
And bloody steel grasp'd in their ireful hands,
Are at our backs; and therefore hence
	amain.
	*Exe.* Away! for vengeance comes along
		with them:
Nay, stay not to expostulate,—make speed;
Or else come after: I'll away before.
	*K. Hen.* Nay, take me with thee, good
		sweet Exeter:

Not that I fear to stay, but love to go
Whither the queen intends. Forward; away!
		[*Exeunt.*

SCENE VI.—*Another part of the Field.*

*A loud Alarum. Enter* CLIFFORD, *wounded.*

	*Clif.* Here burns my candle out,—ay, here
		it dies,
Which, whiles it lasted, gave King Henry
		light.
O Lancaster, I fear thy overthrow
More than my body's parting with my soul!
My love and fear glu'd many friends to thee;
And, now I fall, thy tough commixtures
		melt.
Impairing Henry, strengthening misproud
		York,
The common people swarm like summer
		flies;
And whither fly the gnats but to the sun?
And who shines now but Henry's enemies?
O Phœbus, hadst thou never given consent
That Phaeton should check thy fiery steeds,
Thy burning car never had scorch'd the
		earth!
And, Henry, hadst thou sway'd as kings
		should do,
Or as thy father and his father did,
Giving no ground unto the house of York,
They never then had sprung like summer
		flies;
I and ten thousand in this luckless realm
Had left no mourning widows for our death;
And thou this day hadst kept thy chair in
		peace.
For what doth cherish weeds but gentle air?
And what makes robbers bold but too much
		lenity?
Bootless are plaints, and cureless are my
		wounds;
No way to fly, nor strength to hold out
		flight:
The foe is merciless, and will not pity;
For at their hands I have deserv'd no pity.
The air hath got into my deadly wounds,
And much effuse of blood doth make me
		faint.
Come, York and Richard, Warwick and the
		rest;
I stabb'd your fathers' bosoms,—split my
		breast.
			[*He faints.*

*Alarum and retreat. Enter* EDWARD, GEORGE,
RICHARD, MONTAGUE, WARWICK, *and*
Soldiers.

	*Edw.* Now breathe we, lords: good for-
		tune bids us pause,   [ful looks.—
And smooth the frowns of war with peace-
Some troops pursue the bloody-minded
		queen,
That led calm Henry, though he were a king,
As doth a sail, fill'd with a fretting gust,
Command an argosy to stem the waves.

But think you, lords, that Clifford fled with them?

*War.* No, 'tis impossible he should escape;
For though before his face I speak the words,
Your brother Richard mark'd him for the grave:
And, whereso'er he is, he's surely dead.
                    [CLIFFORD *groans, and dies.*

*Edw.* Whose soul is that which takes her heavy leave?              [*departing.*

*Rich.* A deadly groan, like life and death's—

*Edw.* See who it is; and, now the battle's ended,
If friend or foe, let him be gently us'd.

*Rich.* Revoke that doom of mercy, for 'tis Clifford;
Who not contented that he lopp'd the branch
In hewing Rutland when his leaves put forth,
But set his murdering knife unto the root
From whence that tender spray did sweetly spring,—
I mean our princely father, Duke of York.

*War.* From off the gates of York fetch down the head,
Your father's head, which Clifford placed there;
Instead whereof let this supply the room:
Measure for measure must be answered.

*Edw.* Bring forth that fatal screech-owl to our house,
That nothing sung but death to us and ours:
Now death shall stop his dismal threatening sound,
And his ill-boding tongue no more shall speak.
                    [Soldiers *bring the body forward.*

*War.* I think his understanding is bereft.—
Speak, Clifford, dost thou know who speaks to thee?—
Dark cloudy death o'ershades his beams of life,
And he nor sees nor hears us what we say.

*Rich.* O, would he did! and so, perhaps, he doth:
'Tis but his policy to counterfeit,
Because he would avoid such bitter taunts
Which in the time of death he gave our father.

*Geo.* If so thou think'st, vex him with eager words.

*Rich.* Clifford, ask mercy and obtain no grace.

*Edw.* Clifford, repent in bootless penitence.

*War.* Clifford, devise excuses for thy faults.

*Geo.* While we devise fell tortures for thy faults.              [*to York.*

*Rich.* Thou didst love York, and I am son

*Edw.* Thou pitiedst Rutland, I will pity thee.              [*you now?*

*Geo.* Where's Captain Margaret, to fence

*War.* They mock thee, Clifford: swear as thou wast wont.

*Rich.* What, not an oath? nay, then the world goes hard
When Clifford cannot spare his friends an oath.—
I know by that he's dead; and, by my soul,
If this right hand would buy two hours' life,
That I in all despite might rail at him,
This hand should chop it off, and with the issuing blood
Stifle the villain whose unstaunched thirst
York and young Rutland could not satisfy.

*War.* Ay, but he's dead: off with the traitor's head,
And rear it in the place your father's stands.—
And now to London with triumphant march,
There to be crowned England's royal king.
From whence shall Warwick cut the sea to France,
And ask the Lady Bona for thy queen;
So shalt thou sinew both these lands together;
And, having France thy friend, thou shalt not dread
The scatter'd foe that hopes to rise again;
For though they cannot greatly sting to hurt,
Yet look to have them buzz to offend thine ears.
First will I see the coronation;
And then to Brittany I'll cross the sea,
To effect this marriage, so it please my lord.

*Edw.* Even as thou wilt, sweet Warwick, let it be;
For in thy shoulder do I build my seat,
And never will I undertake the thing
Wherein thy counsel and consent is wanting.—
Richard, I will create thee Duke of Gloster,—
And George, of Clarence;—Warwick, as ourself,
Shall do and undo as him pleaseth best.

*Rich.* Let me be Duke of Clarence, George of Gloster;
For Gloster's dukedom is too ominous.

*War.* Tut, that's a foolish observation:
Richard, be Duke of Gloster. Now to London,
To see these honours in possession.
                    [*Exeunt.*

## ACT III

SCENE I.—*A Chase in the North of England.*

*Enter two* KEEPERS, *with cross-bows in their hands.*

1 *Keep.* Under this thick-grown brake we'll shroud ourselves;
For through this laund anon the deer will come;
And in this covert will we make our stand
Culling the principal of all the deer.

2 *Keep.* I'll stay above the hill, so both may shoot.

1 *Keep.* That cannot be; the noise of thy cross-bow
Will scare the herd, and so my shot is lost.
Here stand we both, and aim we at the best:
And, for the time shall not seem tedious,
I'll tell thee what befell me on a day
In this self-place where now we mean to stand.

2 *Keep.* Here comes a man, let's stay till he be past.

*Enter* KING HENRY, *disguised, with a prayer-book.*

K. Hen. From Scotland am I stol'n, even of pure love,
To greet mine own land with my wishful sight.
No, Harry, Harry, 'tis no land of thine;
Thy place is fill'd, thy sceptre wrung from thee,
Thy balm wash'd off wherewith thou wast anointed:
No bending knee will call thee Cæsar now,
No humble suitors press to speak for right,
No, not a man comes for redress of thee;
For how can I help them, and not myself?

1 *Keep.* Ay, here's a deer whose skin's a keeper's fee:
This is the *quondam* king; let's seize upon him.

K. Hen. Let me embrace these sour adversities:
For wise men say it is the wisest course.

2 *Keep.* Why linger we? let us lay hands upon him.                               [more.

1 *Keep.* Forbear awhile; we'll hear a little

K. Hen. My queen and son are gone to France for aid;
And, as I hear, the great commanding Warwick
Is thither gone, to crave the French king's sister
To wife for Edward: if this news be true,
Poor queen and son, your labour is but lost;
For Warwick is a subtle orator,
And Louis a prince soon won with moving words.                               [him;
By this account, then, Margaret may win
For she's a woman to be pitied much:
Her sighs will make a battery in his breast;
Her tears will pierce into a marble heart;
The tiger will be mild while she doth mourn;
And Nero will be tainted with remorse,
To hear and see her plaints, her brinish tears.
Ay, but she's come to beg; Warwick, to give:
She, on his left side, craving aid for Henry;
He, on his right, asking a wife for Edward.
She weeps, and says her Henry is depos'd;
He smiles, and says his Edward is install'd;
That she, poor wretch, for grief can speak no more;                               [wrong,
Whiles Warwick tells his title, smooths the

Inferreth arguments of mighty strength,
And in conclusion wins the king from her,
With promise of his sister, and what else,
To strengthen and support King Edward's place.
O Margaret, thus 'twill be; and thou, poor soul,
Art then forsaken, as thou went'st forlorn!

2 *Keep.* Say, what art thou, that talk'st of kings and queens?

K. Hen. More than I seem, and less than I was born to:
A man at least, for less I should not be;
And men may talk of kings, and why not I?

2 *Keep.* Ay, but thou talk'st as if thou wert a king.                               [that's enough.

K. Hen. Why, so I am—in mind; and

2 *Keep.* But, if thou be a king, where is thy crown?                               [my head;

K. Hen. My crown is in my heart, not on
Not deck'd with diamonds and Indian stones,
Nor to be seen: my crown is call'd content,—
A crown it is that seldom kings enjoy.

2 *Keep.* Well, if you be a king crown'd with content,
Your crown content and you must be contented
To go along with us; for, as we think,
You are the king King Edward hath depos'd;
And we his subjects, sworn in all allegiance,
Will apprehend you as his enemy.

K. Hen. But did you never swear, and break an oath?                               [not now.

2 *Keep.* No, never such an oath; nor will

K. Hen. Where did you dwell when I was King of England?

2 *Keep.* Here in this country, where we now remain.

K. Hen. I was anointed king at nine months old;
My father and my grandfather were kings;
And you were sworn true subjects unto me:
And tell me, then, have you not broke your oaths?

1 *Keep.* No;
For we were subjects but while you were king.

K. Hen. Why, am I dead? do I not breathe a man?
Ah, simple men, you know not what you swear!
Look, as I blow this feather from my face,
And as the air blows it to me again,
Obeying with my wind when I do blow,
And yielding to another when it blows,
Commanded always by the greater gust;
Such is the lightness of you common men.
But do not break your oaths; for of that sin
My mild entreaty shall not make you guilty.
Go where you will, the king shall be commanded;
And be you kings; command, and I'll obey.

1 *Keep.* We are true subjects to the king,
King Edward.
*K. Hen.* So would you be again to Henry,
If he were seated as King Edward is.
1 *Keep.* We charge you, in God's name
and in the king's,
To go with us unto the officers.
*K. Hen.* In God's name, lead; your king's
name be obey'd:
And what God will, that let your king per-
form;
And what he will, I humbly yield unto.
[*Exeunt.*

SCENE II.—LONDON. *A Room in the Palace.*

*Enter* KING EDWARD, GLOSTER, CLARENCE,
*and* LADY GREY.

*K. Edw.* Brother of Gloster, at Saint Al-
bans' field
This lady's husband, Sir John Grey, was
slain,
His lands then seiz'd on by the conqueror:
Her suit is now to repossess those lands;
Which we in justice cannot well deny,
Because in quarrel of the house of York
The worthy gentleman did lose his life.
*Glo.* Your highness shall do well to grant
her suit;
It were dishonour to deny it her.
*K. Edw.* It were no less; but yet I'll make
a pause.
*Glo.* Yea, is it so?
I see the lady hath a thing to grant,
Before the king will grant her humble suit.
[*Aside to* CLARENCE.
*Clar.* He knows the game: how true he
keeps the wind! [*Aside to* GLOSTER.
*Glo.* Silence! [*Aside to* CLARENCE.
*K. Edw.* Widow, we will consider of your
suit;
And come some other time to know our
mind.
*L. Grey.* Right gracious lord, I cannot
brook delay:
May it please your highness to resolve me
now;
And what your pleasure is shall satisfy me.
*Glo.* Ay, widow? then I warrant you all
your lands,
An if what pleases him shall pleasure you:
Fight closer, or good faith, you'll catch a
blow. [*Aside.*
*Clar.* I fear her not, unless she chance to
fall. [*Aside to* GLOSTER.
*Glo.* God forbid that! for he'll take van-
tages. [*Aside to* CLARENCE.
*K. Edw.* How many children hast thou,
widow? tell me.
*Clar.* I think he means to beg a child of
her. [*Aside to* GLOSTER.
*Glo.* Nay, whip me, then; he'll rather give
her two. [*Aside to* CLARENCE.
*L. Grey.* Three, my most gracious lord.

*Glo.* You shall have four if you'll be ruled
by him. [*Aside.*
*K. Edw.* 'Twere pity they should lose
their father's lands. [it then.
*L. Grey.* Be pitiful, dread lord, and grant
*K. Edw.* Lords, give us leave: I'll try
this widow's wit. [will have leave,
*Glo.* Ay, good leave have you; for you
Till youth take leave, and leave you to the
crutch.
[*Aside, and retires with* CLARENCE.
*K. Edw.* Now tell me, madam, do you
love your children?
*L. Grey.* Ay, full as dearly as I love my-
self.
*K. Edw.* And would you not do much to
do them good? [some harm.
*L. Grey.* To do them good I would sustain
*K. Edw.* Then get your husband's lands,
to do them good.
*L. Grey.* Therefore I came unto your
majesty.
*K. Edw.* I'll tell you how these lands are
to be got. [highness' service.
*L. Grey.* So shall you bind me to your
*K. Edw.* What service wilt thou do me if
I give them? [me to do.
*L. Grey.* What you command, that rests in
*K. Edw.* But you will take exceptions to
my boon.
*L. Grey.* No, gracious lord, except I can-
not do it.
*K. Edw.* Ay, but thou canst do what I
mean to ask. [grace commands.
*L. Grey.* Why, then, I will do what your
*Glo.* He plies her hard; and much rain
wears the marble.
[*Aside to* CLARENCE.
*Clar.* As red as fire! nay, then her wax
must melt. [*Aside to* GLOSTER.
*L. Grey.* Why stops my lord? shall I not
hear my task?
*K. Edw.* An easy task; 'tis but to love a
king.
*L. Grey.* That's soon perform'd, because I
am a subject.
*K. Edw.* Why, then, thy husband's lands I
freely give thee. [sand thanks.
*L. Grey.* I take my leave with many thou-
*Glo.* The match is made; she seals it with
a curtsy. [*Aside.*
*K. Edw.* But stay thee,—'tis the fruits of
love I mean. [loving liege.
*L. Grey.* The fruits of love I mean, my
*K. Edw.* Ay, but, I fear me, in another
sense.
What love, thinkst thou, I sue so much to
get?
*L. Grey.* My love till death, my humble
thanks, my prayers;
That love which virtue begs and virtue
grants.
*K. Edw.* No, by my troth, I did not mean
such love.

*L. Grey.* Why, then, you mean not as I thought you did.   [ceive my mind.

*K. Edw.* But now you partly may per-

*L. Grey.* My mind will never grant what I perceive

Your highness aims at, if I aim aright.

*K. Edw.* To tell thee plain, I aim to lie with thee.

*L. Grey.* To tell you plain, I had rather lie in prison.

*K. Edw.* Why, then, thou shalt not have thy husband's lands.   [my dower;

*L. Grey.* Why, then, mine honesty shall be

For by that loss I will not purchase them.

*K. Edw.* Therein thou wrong'st thy children mightily.

*L. Grey.* Herein your highness wrongs both them and me.

But, mighty lord, this merry inclination

Accords not with the sadness of my suit:

Please you dismiss me, either with ay or no.

*K. Edw.* Ay, if thou wilt say ay to my request;

No, if thou dost say no to my demand.

*L. Grey.* Then, no, my lord. My suit is at an end.

*Glo.* The widow likes him not, she knits her brows.   [*Aside to* CLARENCE.

*Clar.* He is the bluntest wooer in Christendom.   [*Aside to* GLOSTER.

*K. Edw.* Her looks do argue her replete with modesty;

Her words do show her wit incomparable;

All her perfections challenge sovereignty;

One way or other, she is for a king;

And she shall be my love, or else my queen.—

   [*Aside.*

Say that King Edward take thee for his queen?

*L. Grey.* 'Tis better said than done, my gracious lord:

I am a subject fit to jest withal,

But far unfit to be a sovereign.

*K. Edw.* Sweet widow, by my state I swear to thee

I speak no more than what my soul intends;

And that is to enjoy thee for my love.

*L. Grey.* And that is more than I will yield unto:

I know I am too mean to be your queen,

And yet too good to be your concubine.

*K. Edw.* You cavil, widow: I did mean my queen.

*L. Grey.* 'Twill grieve your grace my sons should call you father.

*K. Edw.* No more than when my daughters call thee mother.

Thou art a widow, and thou hast some children;   [lor,

And, by God's mother, I, being but a bache-

Have other some: why, 'tis a happy thing

To be the father unto many sons.

Answer no more, for thou shalt be my queen.

*Glo.* The ghostly father now hath done his shrift.   [*Aside to* CLARENCE.

*Clar.* When he was made a shriver, 'twas for shift.   [*Aside to* GLOSTER.

*K. Edw.* Brothers, you muse what chat we two have had.   [very sad.

*Glo.* The widow likes it not, for she looks

*K. Edw.* You'd think it strange if I should marry her.

*Clar.* To whom, my lord?

*K. Edw.*   Why, Clarence, to myself.

*Glo.* That would be ten days' wonder at the least.

*Clar.* That's a day longer than a wonder lasts.

*Glo.* By so much is the wonder in extremes.

*K. Edw.* Well, jest on, brothers: I can tell you both

Her suit is granted for her husband's lands.

*Enter a* Nobleman.

*Nob.* My gracious lord, Henry your foe is taken,

And brought your prisoner to your palace gate.

*K. Edw.* See that he be convey'd unto the Tower:—

And go we, brothers, to the man that took him,

To question of his apprehension.—

Widow, go you along:—lords, use her honourable.

   [*Exeunt* KING EDWARD, LADY GREY, CLARENCE, *and* Nobleman.

*Glo.* Ay, Edward will use women honourably.—

Would he were wasted, marrow, bones, and all,

That from his loins no hopeful branch may spring,

To cross me from the golden time I look for!

And yet, between my soul's desire and me,—

The lustful Edward's title buried,—

Is Clarence, Henry, and his son young Edward,

And all the unlook'd-for issue of their bodies,

To take their rooms, ere I can place myself:

A cold premeditation for my purpose!

Why, then, I do but dream on sovereignty;

Like one that stands upon a promontory,

And spies a far-off shore where he would tread;

Wishing his foot were equal with his eye;

And chides the sea that sunders him from thence

Saying he'll lade it dry to have his way:

So do I wish the crown, being so far off;

And so I chide the means that keep me from it;

And so I say I'll cut the causes off,

Flattering me with impossibilities.—

My eye's too quick, my heart o'erweens too much,

Unless my hand and strength could equal
    them.
Well, say there is no kingdom, then, for
    Richard;
What other pleasure can the world afford?
I'll make my heaven in a lady's lap,
And deck my body in gay ornaments,
And witch sweet ladies with my words and
    looks.
O miserable thought! and more unlikely
Than to accomplish twenty golden crowns!
Why, love forswore me in my mother's
    womb:
And, for I should not deal in her soft
    laws,
She did corrupt frail nature with some bribe,
To shrink mine arm up like a wither'd shrub;
To make an envious mountain on my back,
Where sits deformity to mock my body;
To shape my legs of an unequal size;
To disproportion me in every part,
Like to a chaos, or an unlick'd bear-whelp
That carries no impression like the dam.
And am I, then, a man to be belov'd?
O monstrous fault, to· harbour such a
    thought!
Then, since this earth affords no joy to me
But to command, to check, to o'erbear such
As are of better person than myself,
I'll make my heaven to dream upon the
    crown,
And whiles I live to account this world but
    hell,
Until my misshap'd trunk that bears this
    head
Be round empaled with a glorious crown.
And yet I know not how to get the crown,
For many lives stand between me and home:
And I,—like one lost in a thorny wood,
That rents the thorns, and is rent with the
    thorns,
Seeking a way, and straying from the way;
Not knowing how to find the open air,
But toiling desperately to find it out,—
Torment myself to catch the English crown:
And from that torment I will free myself,
Or hew my way out with a bloody axe.
Why, I can smile, and murder whiles I smile;
And cry content to that which grieves my
    heart,
And wet my cheeks with artificial tears,
And frame my face to all occasions.
I'll drown more sailors than the mermaid
    shall;
I'll slay more gazers than the basilisk;
I'll play the orator as well as Nestor;
Deceive more slily than Ulysses could;
And, like a Sinon, take another Troy:
I can add colours to the cameleon;
Change shapes with Proteus for advantages;
And set the murderous Machiavel to school.
Can I do this, and cannot get a crown?
Tut, were it further off, I'll pluck it down!
                              [*Exit.*

SCENE III.—FRANCE. *A Room in the Palace.*

*Flourish. Enter* LOUIS, *the French King,
and* LADY BONA, *attended; the* KING *takes
his state. Then enter* QUEEN MARGARET,
PRINCE EDWARD *her Son, and the* EARL OF
OXFORD.

*K. Lou.* Fair Queen of England, worthy
    Margaret,             [*Rising.*
Sit down with us: it ill befits thy state
And birth, that thou shouldst stand while
    Louis doth sit.          [Margaret
*Q. Mar.* No, mighty King of France: now
Must strike her sail, and learn awhile to
    serve
Where kings command. I was, I must con-
    fess,
Great Albion's queen in former golden days:
But now mischance hath trod my title down,
And with dishonour laid me on the ground;
Where I must take like seat unto my fortune,
And to my humble seat conform myself.
   *K. Lou.* Why, say, fair queen, whence
      springs this deep despair?
*Q. Mar.* From such a cause as fills mine
    eyes with tears,        [in cares.
And stops my tongue, while heart is drown'd
   *K. Lou.* Whate'er it be, be thou still like
      thyself,
And sit thee by our side: yield not thy neck
                 [*Seats her by him.*
To fortune's yoke, but let thy dauntless mind
Still ride in triumph over all mischance.
Be plain, Queen Margaret, and tell thy grief;
It shall be eas'd, if France can yield relief.
   *Q. Mar.* Those gracious words revive my
      drooping thoughts,
And give my tongue-tied sorrows leave to
    speak.
Now, therefore, be it known to noble Louis
That Henry, sole possessor of my love,
Is, of a king, become a banish'd man,
And forc'd to live in Scotland a forlorn;
While proud ambitious Edward Duke of
    York
Usurps the regal title and the seat
Of England's true-anointed lawful king.
This is the cause that I, poor Margaret,—
With this my son, Prince Edward, Henry's
    heir,—
Am come to crave thy just and lawful aid;
And if thou fail us, all our hope is done:
Scotland hath will to help, but cannot help;
Our people and our peers are both misled,
Our treasure seiz'd, our soldiers put to flight,
And, as thou see'st, ourselves in heavy plight.
   *K. Lou.* Renowned queen, with patience
      calm the storm,
While we bethink a means to break it off.
   *Q. Mar.* The more we stay the stronger
    grows our foe.       [succour thee.
   *K. Lou.* The more I stay the more I'll
   *Q. Mar.* O, but impatience waiteth on true
    sorrow:—

And see where comes the breeder of my sorrow!

*Enter* WARWICK, *attended.*

*K. Lou.* What's he approacheth boldly to our presence?

*Q. Mar.* Our Earl of Warwick, Edward's greatest friend.

*K. Lou.* Welcome, brave Warwick! What brings thee to France?

[*Descending from his state.* Q. MAR. *rises.*

*Q. Mar.* Ay, now begins a second storm to rise;

For this is he that moves both wind and tide.

*War.* From worthy Edward, King of Albion,

My lord and sovereign, and thy vowed friend,

I come, in kindness and unfeigned love,—

First, to do greetings to thy royal person;

And then to crave a league of amity;

And lastly, to confirm that amity

With nuptial knot, if thou vouchsafe to grant

That virtuous Lady Bona, thy fair sister,

To England's king in lawful marriage.

*Q. Mar.* If that go forward, Henry's hope is done.

*War.* And, gracious madam [*to* BONA], in our king's behalf,

I am commanded, with your leave and favour,

Humbly to kiss your hand, and with my tongue

To tell the passion of my sovereign's heart;

Where fame, late entering at his heedful ears,

Hath plac'd thy beauty's image and thy virtue.

*Q. Mar.* King Louis,—and Lady Bona,—hear me speak,

Before you answer Warwick. His demand

Springs not from Edward's well-meant honest love,

But from deceit bred by necessity;

For how can tyrants safely govern home

Unless abroad they purchase great alliance?

To prove him tyrant, this reason may suffice,—

That Henry liveth still; but were he dead,

Yet here Prince Edward stands, King Henry's son. [and marriage

Look therefore, Louis, that by this league

Thou draw not on thy danger and dishonour;

For though usurpers sway the rule awhile,

Yet heavens are just, and time suppresseth wrongs.

*War.* Injurious Margaret!

*Prince.*　　　　And why not queen?

*War.* Because thy father Henry did usurp;

And thou no more art prince than she is queen.

*Oxf.* Then Warwick disannuls great John of Gaunt,

Which did subdue the greatest part of Spain;

And, after John of Gaunt, Henry the Fourth,

Whose wisdom was a mirror to the wisest;

And, after that wise prince, Henry the Fifth,

Who by his prowess conquered all France:

From these our Henry lineally descends.

*War.* Oxford, how haps it, in this smooth discourse,

You told not how Henry the Sixth hath lost

All that which Henry the Fifth had gotten?

Methinks these peers of France should smile at that.

But for the rest,—you tell a pedigree

Of threescore and two years; a silly time

To make prescription for a kingdom's worth.

*Oxf.* Why, Warwick, canst thou speak against thy liege,

Whom thou obey'dst thirty and six years,

And not bewray thy treason with a blush?

*War.* Can Oxford, that did ever fence the right,

Now buckler falsehood with a pedigree?

For shame? leave Henry, and call Edward king.

*Oxf.* Call him my king by whose injurious doom

My elder brother, the Lord Aubrey Vere,

Was done to death? and more than so, my father,

Even in the downfall of his mellow'd years,

When nature brought him to the door of death?

No, Warwick, no; while life upholds this arm,

This arm upholds the house of Lancaster.

*War.* And I the house of York.

*K. Lou.* Queen Margaret, Prince Edward, and Oxford,

Vouchsafe, at our request, to stand aside

While I use further conference with Warwick.

*Q. Mar.* Heavens grant that Warwick's words bewitch him not!

[*Retiring with the* PRINCE *and* OXF.

*K. Lou.* Now, Warwick, tell me, even upon thy conscience,

Is Edward your true king? for I were loth

To link with him that were not lawful chosen.

*War.* Thereon I pawn my credit and mine honour.　　　　[eye?

*K. Lou.* But is he gracious in the people's

*War.* The more that Henry was unfortunate.

*K. Lou.* Then further,—all dissembling set aside,—

Tell me for truth the measure of his love

Unto our sister Bona.

*War.*　　　　Such it seems

As may beseem a monarch like himself.

Myself have often heard him say, and swear,

That this love was an eternal plant,

Whereof the root was fix'd in virtue's ground,

The leaves and fruit maintain'd with beauty's sun:

Exempt from envy, but not from disdain,
Unless the Lady Bona quit his pain. [resolve.
*K. Lou.* Now, sister, let us hear your firm
*Bona.* Your grant or your denial shall be
    mine:—
Yet I confess [*to* WAR.] that often ere this
    day,
When I have heard your king's desert re-
    counted,
Mine ear hath tempted judgment to desire.
*K. Lou.* Then, Warwick, thus,—Our sister
    shall be Edward's;
And now forthwith shall articles be drawn
Touching the jointure that your king must
    make,
Which with her dowry shall be counter-
    pois'd.—
Draw near, Queen Margaret, and be a wit-
    ness
That Bona shall be wife to the English king.
*Prince.* To Edward, but not to the English
    king.
*Q. Mar.* Deceitful Warwick! it was thy
    device
By this alliance to make void my suit:
Before thy coming, Louis was Henry's friend.
*K. Lou.* And still is friend to him and
    Margaret:
But if your title to the crown be weak,—
As may appear by Edward's good success,—
Then 'tis but reason that I be released
From giving aid which late I promised.
Yet shall you have all kindness at my hand
That your estate requires and mine can yield.
*War.* Henry now lives in Scotland at his
    ease,
Where having nothing, nothing can he lose.
And as for you yourself, our *quondam* queen,
You have a father able to maintain you;
And better 'twere you troubled him than
    France.
*Q. Mar.* Peace, impudent and shameless
    Warwick,—
Proud setter-up and puller-down of kings!
I will not hence till, with my talk and tears,
Both full of truth, I make King Louis behold
Thy sly conveyance and thy lord's false love;
For both of you are birds of self-same fea-
    ther.    [*A horn is sounded within.*
*K. Lou.* Warwick, this is some post to us
    or thee.

*Enter a* Messenger.

*Mess.* My lord ambassador, these letters
    are for you,
Sent from your brother, Marquis Mon-
    tague:—
These from our king unto your majesty:—
And, madam, these for you; from whom I
    know not.
    [*To* MAR. *They all read their letters.*
*Oxf.* I like it well that our fair queen and
    mistress    [his.
Smiles at her news, while Warwick frowns at

*Prince.* Nay, mark how Louis stamps, as
    he were nettled:
I hope all's for the best.
*K. Lou.* Warwick, what are thy news?—
    and yours, fair queen? [unhop'd joys.
*Q. Mar.* Mine, such as fill my heart with
*War.* Mine, full of sorrow and heart's dis-
    content.    [Lady Grey?
*K. Lou.* What, has your king married the
And now, to soothe your forgery and his,
Sends me a paper to persuade me patience?
Is this the alliance that he seeks with France?
Dare he presume to scorn us in this manner?
*Q. Mar.* I told your majesty as much be-
    fore:
This proveth Edward's love and Warwick's
    honesty.    [of heaven,
*War.* King Louis, I here protest, in sight
And by the hope I have of heavenly bliss,
That I am clear from this misdeed of Ed-
    ward's,—
No more my king, for he dishonours me,
But most himself, if he could see his shame.
Did I forget that by the house of York
My father came untimely to his death?
Did I let pass the abuse done to my niece?
Did I impale him with the regal crown?
Did I put Henry from his native right?
And am I guerdon'd at the last with shame?
Shame on himself! for my desert is honour:
And, to repair my honour lost for him,
I here renounce him, and return to Henry.—
My noble queen, let former grudges pass,
And henceforth I am thy true servitor:
I will revenge his wrong to Lady Bona,
And replant Henry in his former state.
*Q. Mar.* Warwick, these words have turn'd
    my hate to love;
And I forgive and quite forget old faults,
And joy that thou becom'st King Henry's
    friend.
*War.* So much his friend, ay, his unfeigned
    friend,
That if King Louis vouchsafe to furnish us
With some few bands of chosen soldiers,
I'll undertake to land them on our coast,
And force the tyrant from his seat by war.
'Tis not his new-made bride shall succour
    him:
And as for Clarence,—as my letters tell me,—
He's very likely now to fall from him,
For matching more for wanton lust than
    honour,
Or than for strength and safety of our coun-
    try.
*Bona.* Dear brother, how shall Bona be
    reveng'd
But by thy help to this distressed queen?
*Q. Mar.* Renowned prince, how shall poor
    Henry live,
Unless thou rescue him from foul despair?
*Bona.* My quarrel and this English queen's
    are one.    [yours.
*War.* And mine, fair Lady Bona, joins with

*K. Lou.* And mine with hers, and thine,
and Margaret's.
Therefore, at last, I firmly am resolv'd
You shall have aid.
　*Q. Mar.* Let me give humble thanks for all
at once.　　　　　　　　　　[*in post,*
　*K. Lou.* Then, England's messenger, return
And tell false Edward, thy supposed king,
That Louis of France is sending over mas-
quers
To revel it with him and his new bride:
Thou see'st what's past,—go fear thy king
withal.
　*Bona.* Tell him, in hope he'll prove a wid-
ower shortly,
I'll wear the willow-garland for his sake.
　*Q. Mar.* Tell him, my mourning-weeds are
laid aside,
And I am ready to put armour on.
　*War.* Tell him from me, that he hath done
me wrong;
And therefore I'll uncrown him ere't be long.
There's thy reward: be gone.　[*Exit* Mess.
　*K. Lou.*　　　　　　But, Warwick,
Thou and Oxford, with five thousand men,
Shall cross the seas, and bid false Edward
battle;
And, as occasion serves, this noble queen
And prince shall follow with a fresh supply.
Yet, ere thou go, but answer me one doubt,—
What pledge have we of thy firm loyalty?
　*War.* This shall assure my constant loy-
　alty,—
That if our queen and this young prince
agree
I'll join mine eldest daughter, and my joy,
To him forthwith in holy wedlock-bands.
　*Q. Mar.* Yes, I agree, and thank you for
your motion.—
Son Edward, she is fair and virtuous,
Therefore delay not,—give thy hand to War-
wick;
And, with thy hand, thy faith irrevocable,
That only Warwick's daughter shall be thine.
　*Prince.* Yes, I accept her, for she well de-
serves it;
And here to pledge my vow, I give my hand.
　　　　　[*He gives his hand to* WARWICK.
　*K. Lou.* Why stay we now? These sol-
diers shall be levied,
And thou, Lord Bourbon, our high-admiral,
Shalt waft them over with our royal fleet.—
I long till Edward fall by war's mischance,
For mocking marriage with a dame of
France.
　　　　　　[*Exeunt all but* WARWICK.
　*War.* I come from Edward as ambassador,
But I return his sworn and mortal foe:
Matter of marriage was the charge he gave
me,
But dreadful war shall answer his demand.
Had he none else to make a stale but me?
Then none but I shall turn his jest to sorrow.
I was the chief that rais'd him to the crown,

And I'll be chief to bring him down again:
Not that I pity Henry's misery,
But seek revenge on Edward's mockery.
　　　　　　　　　　　　　　[*Exit.*

## ACT IV.

SCENE I.—LONDON. *A Room in the Palace.*

　*Enter* GLOSTER, CLARENCE, SOMERSET,
　　　　MONTAGUE, *and others.*

　*Glo.* Now tell me, brother Clarence, what
think you
Of this new marriage with the Lady Grey?
Hath not our brother made a worthy choice?
　*Clar.* Alas, you know, 'tis far from hence
to France;
How could he stay till Warwick made re-
turn?
　*Som.* My lords, forbear this talk; here
comes the king.
　*Glo.* And his well-chosen bride.
　*Clar.* I mind to tell him plainly what I
think.

*Flourish. Enter* KING EDWARD, *attended;*
LADY GREY, *as Queen;* PEMBROKE, STAF-
FORD, HASTINGS, *and others.*

　*K. Edw.* Now, brother of Clarence, how
like you our choice,
That you stand pensive, as half malcontent?
　*Clar.* As well as Louis of France or the
Earl of Warwick;
Which are so weak of courage and in judg-
ment
That they'll take no offence at our abuse.
　*K. Edw.* Suppose they take offence with-
out a cause,
They are but Louis and Warwick: I am Ed-
ward,
Your king and Warwick's, and must have my
will.　　　　　　　　　　　　　[*king:*
　*Glo.* And shall have your will, because our
Yet hasty marriage seldom proveth well.
　*K. Edw.* Yea, brother Richard, are you
offended too?
　*Glo.* Not I:
No, God forbid that I should wish them
sever'd
Whom God hath join'd together; ay, and
'twere pity
To sunder them that yoke so well together.
　*K. Edw.* Setting your scorns and your
mislike aside,
Tell me some reason why the Lady Grey
Should not become my wife and England's
queen:—
And you too, Somerset and Montague,
Speak freely what you think.　[*King Louis*
　*Clar.* Then this is mine opinion,—that
Becomes your enemy for mocking him
About the marriage of the Lady Bona.
　*Glo.* And Warwick, doing what you gave
in charge,
Is now dishonoured by this new marriage.

*K. Edw.* What if both Louis and Warwick
be appeas'd
By such invention as I can devise?

*Mont.* Yet to have join'd with France in
such alliance       [monwealth
Would more have strengthen'd this our com-
'Gainst foreign storms than any home-bred
marriage.

*Hast.* Why, knows not Montague that of
itself
England is safe, if true within itself?

*Mont.* But the safer when 'tis back'd with
France.

*Hast.* 'Tis better using France than trust-
ing France:
Let us be back'd with God, and with the seas
Which he hath given for fence impregnable,
And with their helps only defend ourselves;
In them and in ourselves our safety lies.

*Clar.* For this one speech Lord Hastings
well deserves
To have the heir of the Lord Hungerford.

*K. Edw.* Ay, what of that? it was my will
and grant;
And for this once my will shall stand for law.

*Glo.* And yet methinks your grace hath
not done well,
To give the heir and daughter of Lord Scales
Unto the brother of your loving bride;
She better would have fitted me or Clarence:
But in your bride you bury brotherhood.

*Clar.* Or else you would not have bestow'd
the heir
Of the Lord Bonville on your new wife's son,
And leave your brothers to go speed elsewhere.

*K. Edw.* Alas, poor Clarence! is it for a
wife
That thou art malcontent? I will provide
thee.

*Clar.* In choosing for yourself you show'd
your judgment,
Which being shallow, you shall give me leave
To play the broker in mine own behalf;
And to that end I shortly mind to leave you.

*K. Edw.* Leave me or tarry, Edward will
be king,
And not be tied unto his brother's will.

*Q. Eliz.* My lords, before it pleas'd his
majesty
To raise my state to title of a queen,
Do me but right, and you must all confess
That I was not ignoble of descent;
And meaner than myself have had like for-
tune.
But as this title honours me and mine,
So your dislikes, to whom I would be pleas-
ing,
Do cloud my joys with danger and with sor-
row.

*K. Edw.* My love, forbear to fawn upon
their frowns:
What danger or what sorrow can befall thee,
So long as Edward is thy constant friend

And their true sovereign, whom they must
obey?       [too,
Nay, whom they shall obey, and love thee
Unless they seek for hatred at my hands;
Which if they do, yet will I keep thee safe,
And they shall feel the vengeance of my
wrath.

*Glo.* I hear, yet say not much, but think
the more.       [*Aside.*

*Enter a* Messenger.

*K. Edw.* Now, messenger, what letters or
what news
From France?       [few words

*Mess.* My sovereign liege, no letters; and
But such as I, without your special pardon,
Dare not relate.

*K. Edw.* Go to, we pardon thee: therefore,
in brief,       [guess them.
Tell me their words as near as thou canst
What answer makes King Louis unto our
letters?

*Mess.* At my depart, these were his very
words:
*Go tell false Edward, thy supposed king,*
*That Louis of France is sending over masq-*
*uers*
*To revel it with him and his new bride.*

*K. Edw.* Is Louis so brave? belike he
thinks me Henry.
But what said Lady Bona to my marriage?

*Mess.* These were her words, utter'd with
mild disdain:
*Tell him, in hope he'll prove a widower*
*shortly,*
*I'll wear the willow-garland for his sake.*

*K. Edw.* I blame not her, she could say
little less;       [queen?
She had the wrong. But what said Henry's
For I have heard that she was there in place.

*Mess. Tell him,* quoth she, *my mourning-*
*weeds are done,*
*And I am ready to put armour on.*       [zon.

*K. Edw.* Belike she minds to play the Ama-
But what said Warwick to these injuries?

*Mess.* He, more incens'd against your majesty
Than all the rest, discharg'd me with these
words:
*Tell him from me, that he hath done me*
*wrong;*
*And therefore I'll uncrown him ere't be long.*

*K. Edw.* Ha! durst the traitor breathe out
so proud words?
Well, I will arm me, being thus forewarn'd:
They shall have wars, and pay for their pre-
sumption.
But say, is Warwick friends with Margaret?

*Mess.* Ay, gracious sovereign; they are so
link'd in friendship
That young Prince Edward marries Warwick's daughter.

*Clar.* Belike the elder; Clarence will have
the younger.

Now, brother king, farewell, and sit you fast,
For I will hence to Warwick's other daughter;
That, though I want a kingdom, yet in marriage
I may not prove inferior to yourself.—
You that love me and Warwick, follow me.
            [*Exit, and* SOMERSET *follows.*
  *Glo.* Not I:
My thoughts aim at a further matter; I
Stay not for the love of Edward, but the
    crown.                         [*Aside.*
  *K. Edw.* Clarence and Somerset both gone
    to Warwick!
Yet am I arm'd against the worst can happen;
And haste is needful in this desperate case.—
Pembroke and Stafford, you in our behalf
Go levy men, and make prepare for war;
They are already, or quickly will be landed:
Myself in person will straight follow you.
            [*Exeunt* PEM. *and* STAF.
But ere I go, Hastings and Montague,
Resolve my doubt. You twain, of all the rest,
Are near to Warwick by blood and by alliance:
Tell me if you love Warwick more than me?
If it be so, then both depart to him;
I rather wish you foes than hollow friends:
But if you mind to hold your true obedience,
Give me assurance with some friendly vow,
That I may never have you in suspect. [true!
  *Mont.* So God help Montague as he proves
  *Hast.* And Hastings as he favours Edward's cause!             [stand by us?
  *K. Edw.* Now, brother Richard, will you
  *Glo.* Ay, in despite of all that shall withstand you.
  *K. Edw.* Why, so! then am I sure of victory.
Now therefore let us hence; and lose no hour
Till we meet Warwick with his foreign power.
                              [*Exeunt.*

SCENE II.—*A Plain in Warwickshire.*

*Enter* WARWICK *and* OXFORD, *with French and other* Forces.

  *War.* Trust me, my lord, all hitherto goes well;
The common people by numbers swarm to us.—
But see where Somerset and Clarence come!

*Enter* CLARENCE *and* SOMERSET.

Speak suddenly, my lords,—are we all friends?
  *Clar.* Fear not that, my lord. [Warwick;—
  *War.* Then, gentle Clarence, welcome unto
And welcome, Somerset.—I hold it cowardice
To rest mistrustful where a noble heart
Hath pawn'd an open hand in sign of love;

Else might I think that Clarence, Edward's brother,
Were but a feigned friend to our proceedings:
But welcome, sweet Clarence; my daughter shall be thine.
And now, what rests but, in night's coverture,
Thy brother being carelessly encamp'd,
His soldiers lurking in the towns about,
And but attended by a simple guard,
We may surprise and take him at our pleasure?
Our scouts have found the adventure very easy:
That as Ulysses and stout Diomede
With sleight and manhood stole to Rhesus' tents
And brought from thence the Thracian fatal steeds,                        [mantle,
So we, well cover'd with the night's black
At unawares may beat down Edward's guard
And seize himself; I say not, slaughter him,
For I intend but only to surprise him.
You that will follow me to this attempt,
Applaud the name of Henry with your leader.      [*They all cry* "Henry!"
Why, then, let's on our way in silent sort:
For Warwick and his friends, God and Saint George!                   [*Exeunt.*

SCENE III.—EDWARD'S *Camp, near Warwick.*

*Enter certain Watchmen, before the* KING'S *tent.*

  1 *Watch.* Come on, my masters, each man take his stand:
The king by this has set him down to sleep.
  2 *Watch.* What, will he not to bed?
  1 *Watch.* Why, no: for he hath made a solemn vow
Never to lie and take his natural rest
Till Warwick or himself be quite suppress'd.
  2 *Watch.* To-morrow then, belike, shall be the day,
If Warwick be so near as men report.
  3 *Watch.* But say, I pray, what nobleman is that
That with the king here resteth in his tent?
  1 *Watch.* 'Tis the Lord Hastings, the king's chiefest friend.          [the king
  3 *Watch.* O, is it so? But why commands
That his chief followers lodge in towns about him,
While he himself keeps in the cold field?
  2 *Watch.* 'Tis the more honour, because more dangerous.            [quietness,
  3 *Watch.* Ay, but give me worship and
I like it better than a dangerous honour.
If Warwick knew in what estate he stands,
'Tis to be doubted he would waken him.
  1 *Watch.* Unless our halberds did shut up his passage.              [royal tent.
  2 *Watch.* Ay, wherefore else guard we his
But to defend his person from night-foes?

*Enter* WARWICK, CLARENCE, OXFORD,
SOMERSET, *and Forces.*

*War.* This is his tent; and see where
    stand his guard.
Courage, my masters! honour now or never!
But follow me, and Edward shall be ours.
1 *Watch.* Who goes there?
2 *Watch.* Stay, or thou diest.
    [WARWICK *and the rest cry all*—"War-
    wick! Warwick!" *and set upon the*
    Guard, *who fly crying* "Arm! Arm!"
    WARWICK *and the rest following them.*

*The drum beating and trumpets sounding,
re-enter* WARWICK *and the rest, bringing
the* KING *out in his gown, sitting in a
chair;* GLOSTER *and* HASTINGS *are seen
flying.*

*Som.*        What are they that fly there?
*War.* Richard and Hastings: let them go;
    here is the duke.
.*K. Edw.* The duke! Why, Warwick, when
    we parted last
Thou call'dst me king?
*War.*       Ay, but the case is alter'd:
When you disgrac'd me in my embassade,
Then I degraded you from being king,
And come now to create you Duke of York.
Alas, how should you govern any kingdom,
That know not how to use ambassadors?
Nor how to be contented with one wife;
Nor how to use your brothers brotherly;
Nor how to study for the people's welfare;
Nor how to shroud yourself from enemies?
*K. Edw.* Yea, brother of Clarence, art
    thou here too?
Nay, then I see that Edward needs must
    down.—
Yet, Warwick, in despite of all mischance,
Of thee thyself and all thy complices,
Edward will always bear himself as king:
Though fortune's malice overthrow my state,
My mind exceeds the compass of her wheel.
*War.* Then, for his mind, be Edward Eng-
    land's king:     [*Takes off his crown.*
But Henry now shall wear the English
    crown
And be true king indeed; thou but the sha-
    dow.—
My Lord of Somerset, at my request,
See that forthwith Duke Edward be con-
    vey'd
Unto my brother, Archbishop of York.
When I have fought with Pembroke and
    his fellows,
I'll follow you, and tell what answer
Louis and the Lady Bona send to him.—
Now, for awhile farewell, good Duke of
    York.
*K. Edw.* What fates impose, that men
    must needs abide;
It boots not to resist both wind and tide.
    [*Exit. led out;* SOM. *with him.*

*Oxf.* What now remains, my lords, for us
    to do,
But march to London with our soldiers?
*War.* Ay, that's the first thing that we
    have to do;
To free King Henry from imprisonment,
And see him seated in the regal throne.
    [*Exeunt.*

SCENE IV.—LONDON. *A Room in the Palace.*

*Enter* QUEEN ELIZABETH *and* RIVERS.

*Riv.* Madam, what makes you in this sud-
    den change?
*Q. Eliz.* Why, brother Rivers, are you yet
    to learn
What late misfortune is befall'n King Ed-
    ward?
*Riv.* What, loss of some pitch'd battle
    against Warwick?
*Q. Eliz.* No, but the loss of his own royal
    person.
*Riv.* Then, is my sovereign slain?
*Q. Eliz.* Ay, almost slain, for he is taken
    prisoner;
Either betray'd by falsehood of his guard,
Or by his foe surpris'd at unawares:
And, as I further have to understand,
Is new committed to the Bishop of York,
Fell Warwick's brother, and by that our foe.
*Riv.* These news, I must confess, are full
    of grief;
Yet, gracious madam, bear it as you may:
Warwick may lose, that now hath won the
    day.
*Q. Eliz.* Till then, fair hope must hinder
    life's decay.
And I the rather wean me from despair,
For love of Edward's offspring in my womb:
This is it that makes me bridle passion,
And bear with mildness my misfortune's
    cross:
Ay, ay, for this I draw in many a tear,
And stop the rising of blood-sucking sighs,
Lest with my sighs or tears I blast or drown
King Edward's fruit, true heir to the Eng-
    lish crown.     [become?
*Riv.* But, madam, where is Warwick, then?
*Q. Eliz.* I am inform'd that he comes to-
    wards London,
To set the crown once more on Henry's
    head:
Guess thou the rest; King Edward's friends
    must down.
But to prevent the tyrant's violence,—
For trust not him that hath once broken
    faith,—
I'll hence forthwith unto the sanctuary,
To save at least the heir of Edward's right:
There shall I rest secure from force and
    fraud.
Come, therefore, let us fly while we may fly:
If Warwick take us, we are sure to die.
    [*Exeunt.*

SCENE V.—*A Park near Middleham Castle in Yorkshire.*

*Enter* GLOSTER, HASTINGS, SIR WILLIAM STANLEY, *and others.*

*Glo.* Now, my Lord Hastings and Sir William Stanley,
Leave off to wonder why I drew you hither
Into this chiefest thicket of the park.
Thus stands the case: you know our king, my brother,
Is prisoner to the bishop here, at whose hands
He hath good usage and great liberty;
And often, but attended with weak guard,
Comes hunting this way, to disport himself.
I have advértis'd him by secret means
That if about this hour he make this way,
Under the colour of his usual game, [men,
He shall here find his friends, with horse and
To set him free from his captivity.

*Enter* KING EDWARD *and a* Huntsman.

*Hunt.* This way, my lord; for this way lies the game. [the huntsmen stand.—
*K. Edw.* Nay, this way, man: see where
Now, brother of Gloster, Lord Hastings, and the rest,
Stand you thus close to steal the bishop's deer?
*Glo.* Brother, the time and case requireth haste:
Your horse stands ready at the park-corner.
*K. Edw.* But whither shall we then?
*Hast.* To Lynn, my lord; and ship from thence to Flanders. [my meaning.
*Glo.* Well guess'd, believe me; for that was
*K. Edw.* Stanley, I will requite thy forwardness. [to talk.
*Glo.* But wherefore stay we? 'tis no time
*K. Edw.* Huntsmen, what say'st thou? wilt thou go along?
*Hunt.* Better do so than tarry and be hang'd.
*Glo.* Come then, away; let's ha' no more ado.
*K. Edw.* Bishop, farewell: shield thee from Warwick's frown;
And pray that I may repossess the crown.
[*Exeunt.*

SCENE VI.—*A Room in the Tower.*

*Enter* KING HENRY, CLARENCE, WARWICK, SOMERSET, YOUNG RICHMOND, OXFORD, MONTAGUE, Lieutenant of the Tower, *and* Attendants.

*K. Hen.* Master lieutenant, now that God and friends
Have shaken Edward from the regal seat,
And turn'd my captive state to liberty,
My fear to hope, my sorrows unto joys,—
At our enlargement what are thy due fees?

*Lieut.* Subjects may challenge nothing of their sovereigns;
But if an humble prayer may prevail,
I then crave pardon of your majesty.
*K. Hen.* For what, lieutenant? for well-using me?
Nay, be thou sure I'll well requite thy kindness, [ure;
For that it made my imprisonment a pleas-
Ay, such a pleasure as incaged birds
Conceive, when, after many moody thoughts,
At last, by notes of household harmony,
They quite forget their loss of liberty.—
But, Warwick, after God, thou sett'st me free,
And chiefly therefore I thank God and thee;
He was the author, thou the instrument.
Therefore, that I may conquer fortune's spite,
By living low, where fortune cannot hurt me,
And that the people of this blessed land
May not be punish'd with my thwarting stars,—
Warwick, although my head still wear the crown,
I here resign my government to thee,
For thou art fortunate in all thy deeds.
*War.* Your grace hath still been fam'd for virtuous;
And now may seem as wise as virtuous
By spying and avoiding fortune's malice,
For few men rightly temper with the stars:
Yet in this one thing let me blame your grace
For choosing me when Clarence is in place.
*Clar.* No, Warwick, thou art worthy of the sway,
To whom the heavens, in thy nativity,
Adjudg'd an olive-branch and laurel-crown,
As likely to be blest in peace and war;
And therefore I yield thee my free consent.
*War.* And I choose Clarence only for protector.
*K. Hen.* Warwick and Clarence, give me both your hands:
Now join your hands, and with your hands your hearts,
That no dissension hinder government:
I make you both protectors of this land;
While I myself will lead a private life,
And in devotion spend my latter days,
To sin's rebuke and my Creator's praise.
*War.* What answers Clarence to his sovereign's will? [consent;
*Clar.* That he consents if Warwick yield
For on thy fortune I repose myself.
*War.* Why, then, though loth, yet must I be content:
We'll yoke together, like a double shadow
To Henry's body, and supply his place;
I mean, in bearing weight of government,
While he enjoys the honour and his ease
And, Clarence, now then it is more than needful

Forthwith that Edward be pronounc'd a traitor,
And all his lands and goods be confiscate.

*Clar.* What else? and that succession be
determin'd.     [his part.

*War.* Ay, therein Clarence shall not want

*K. Hen.* But, with the first of all your chief affairs,
Let me entreat,—for I command no more,—
That Margaret your queen, and my son Edward,
Be sent for, to return from France with speed;
For till I see them here, by doubtful fear
My joy of liberty is half eclips'd.

*Clar.* It shall be done, my sovereign, with all speed.

*K. Hen.* My Lord of Somerset, what youth is that,
Of whom you seem to have so tender care?

*Som.* My liege, it is young Henry, Earl of Richmond.

*K. Hen.* Come hither, England's hope.—If secret powers
    [*Lays his hand on his head.*
Suggest but truth to my divining thoughts,
This pretty lad will prove our country's bliss.
His looks are full of peaceful majesty;
His head by nature fram'd to wear a crown,
His hand to wield a sceptre; and himself
Likely in time to bless a regal throne.
Make much of him, my lords; for this is he
Must help you more than you are hurt by me.

    *Enter a* Messenger.

*War.* What news, my friend?     [brother,

*Mess.* That Edward is escaped from your
And fled, as he hears since, to Burgundy.

*War.* Unsavoury news! but how made he
escape?     [of Gloster

*Mess.* He was convey'd by Richard Duke
And the Lord Hastings, who attended him
In secret ambush on the forest-side,
And from the bishop's huntsmen rescu'd him;
For hunting was his daily exercise.

*War.* My brother was too careless of his charge.—
But let us hence, my sovereign, to provide
A salve for any sore that may betide.
    [*Exeunt* KING HENRY, WAR., CLAR.,
    Lieut., *and* Attendants.

*Som.* My lord, I like not of this flight of Edward's:
For doubtless Burgundy will yield him help,
And we shall have more wars before 't be long.
As Henry's late presaging prophecy
Did glad my heart with hope of this young Richmond,
So doth my heart misgive me, in these conflicts,
What may befall him, to his harm and ours:

Therefore, Lord Oxford, to prevent the worst,
Forthwith we'll send him hence to Brittany,
Till storms be past of civil enmity.

*Oxf.* Ay, for if Edward repossess the crown,
'Tis like that Richmond with the rest shall down.

*Som.* It shall be so; he shall to Brittany.
Come, therefore, let's about it speedily.
    [*Exeunt.*

    SCENE VII.—*Before York.*

*Enter* KING EDWARD, GLOSTER, HASTINGS,
    *and* Forces.

*K. Edw.* Now, brother Richard, Lord Hastings, and the rest,
Yet thus far fortune maketh us amends,
And says that once more I shall interchange
My waned state for Henry's regal crown.
Well have we pass'd, and now repass'd the seas,
And brought desired help from Burgundy:
What, then, remains, we being thus arriv'd
From Ravenspur haven before the gates of York,
But that we enter, as into our dukedom?

*Glo.* The gates made fast!—Brother, I like not this;
For many men that stumble at the threshold
Are well foretold that danger lurks within.

*K. Edw.* Tush, man, abodements must not now affright us:
By fair or foul means we must enter in,
For hither will our friends repair to us.

*Hast.* My liege, I'll knock once more to summon them.

*Enter, on the Walls, the* Mayor of York *and*
    Aldermen.

*May.* My lords, we were forewarned of your coming,
And shut the gates for safety of ourselves;
For now we owe allegiance unto Henry.

*K. Edw.* But, master mayor, if Henry be your king,
Yet Edward at the least is Duke of York.

*May.* True, my good lord; I know you for no less.

*K. Edw.* Why, and I challenge nothing but my dukedom,
As being well content with that alone.

*Glo.* But when the fox hath once got in his nose,
    He'll soon find means to make the body
follow.     [*Aside.*

*Hast.* Why, master mayor, why stand you in a doubt?
Open the gates, we are King Henry's friends.

*May.* Ay, say you so? the gates shall then be open'd.     [*Exeunt from above.*

*Glo.* A wise stout captain, and soon persuaded!     [all were well,

*Hast.* The good old man would fain that

So 'twere not 'long of him; but being en-
ter'd,
I doubt not, I, but we shall soon persuade
Both him and all his brothers unto reason.

*Re-enter the* Mayor *and* Aldermen, *below.*

*K. Edw.* So, master mayor: these gates
must not be shut
But in the night or in the time of war.
What! fear not, man, but yield me up the
keys; 　　　[*Takes his keys.*
For Edward will defend the town and thee.
And all those friends that deign to follow
me.

*Drum. Enter* MONTGOMERY *and Forces,
marching.*

*Glo.* Brother, this is Sir John Montgom-
ery,
Our trusty friend, unless I be deceiv'd.
*K. Edw.* Welcome, Sir John! But why
come you in arms? 　　　[of storm,
*Mont.* To help King Edward in his time
As every loyal subject ought to do.
*K. Edw.* Thanks, good Montgomery; but
we now forget
Our title to the crown, and only claim
Our dukedom till God please to send the rest.
*Mont.* Then fare you well, for I will
hence again:
I came to serve a king, and not a duke.—
Drummer, strike up, and let us march away.
　　　[*A march begun.*
*K. Edw.* Nay, stay, Sir John, awhile; and
we'll debate
By what safe means the crown may be re-
cover'd.
*Mont.* What talk you of debating? in few
words,—
If you'll not here proclaim yourself our king,
I'll leave you to your fortune, and be gone
To keep them back that come to succour
you:
Why should we fight, if you pretend no title?
*Glo.* Why, brother, wherefore stand you
on nice points?
*K. Edw.* When we grow stronger, then
we'll make our claim:
Till then, 'tis wisdom to conceal our mean-
ing.
*Hast.* Away with scrupulous wit! now
arms must rule.
*Glo.* And fearless minds climb soonest
unto crowns.
Brother, we will proclaim you out of hand;
The bruit thereof will bring you many
friends.
*K. Edw.* Then be it as you will; for 'tis
my right,
And Henry but usurps the diadem.
*Mont.* Ay, now my sovereign speaketh
like himself;
And now will I be Edward's champion.

*Hast.* Sound trumpet; Edward shall be
here proclaim'd:—
Come, fellow-soldier, make thou proclama-
tion. 　　[*Gives him a paper. Flourish.*
*Sold.* [*Reads.*] *Edward the Fourth, by the
grace of God, King of England and France,
and Lord of Ireland, &c.*
*Mont.* And whoso'er gainsays King Ed-
ward's right,
By this I challenge him to single fight.
　　　[*Throws down his gauntlet.*
*All.* Long live Edward the Fourth!
*K. Edw.* Thanks, brave Montgomery;—
and thanks unto you all;
If fortune serve me, I'll requite this kindness.
Now, for this night, let's harbour here in
York;
And when the morning sun shall raise his car
Above the border of this horizon,
We'll forward towards Warwick and his
mates;
For well I wot that Henry is no soldier.—
Ah, froward Clarence! how evil it beseems
thee
To flatter Henry and forsake thy brother!
Yet, as we may, we'll meet both thee and
Warwick.—
Come on, brave soldiers: doubt not of the
day;
And, that once gotten, doubt not of large
pay. 　　　[*Exeunt.*

SCENE VIII.—LONDON. *A Room in the
Palace.*

*Flourish. Enter* KING HENRY, WARWICK,
MONTAGUE, CLARENCE, EXETER, *and* OX-
FORD.

*War.* What counsel, lords? Edward from
Belgia,
With hasty Germans and blunt Hollanders,
Hath pass'd in safety through the narrow
seas,
And with his troops doth march amain to
London;
And many giddy people flock to him.
*Oxf.* Let's levy men, and beat him back
again.
*Clar.* A little fire is quickly trodden out;
Which, being suffer'd, rivers cannot quench.
*War.* In Warwickshire I have true-heart-
ed friends,
Not mutinous in peace, yet bold in war;
Those will I muster up:—and thou, son
Clarence,
Shalt stir up, in Suffolk, Norfolk, and in
Kent,
The knights and gentlemen to come with
thee:—
Thou, brother Montague, in Buckingham,
Northampton, and in Leicestershire, shalt
find
Men well inclin'd to hear what thou com-
mand'st:—

And thou, brave Oxford, wondrous well be-
lov'd,
In Oxfordshire shalt muster up thy friends.
My sovereign, with the loving citizens,—
Like to his island girt in with the ocean,
Or modest Dian circled with her nymphs,—
Shall rest in London till we come to him.—
Fair lords, take leave, and stand not to
reply.—
Farewell, my sovereign.
  *K. Hen.* Farewell, my Hector, and my
Troy's true hope.   [ness' hand.
  *Clar.* In sign of truth, I kiss your high-
  *K. Hen.* Well-minded Clarence, be thou
fortunate!   [my leave.
  *Mont.* Comfort, my lord;—and so I take
  *Oxf.* And thus [*kissing* HENRY's *hand*] I
seal my truth, and bid adieu.
  *K. Hen.* Sweet Oxford, and my loving
Montague,
And all at once, once more a happy farewell.
  *War.* Farewell, sweet lords: let's meet at
Coventry.
  [*Exeunt* WAR., CLAR., OXF., *and* MONT.
  *K. Hen.* Here at the palace will I rest
awhile.
Cousin of Exeter, what thinks your lord-
ship?
Methinks the power that Edward hath in
field
Should not be able to encounter mine.
  *Exe.* The doubt is, that he will seduce the
rest.
  *K. Hen.* That's not my fear; my meed
hath got me fame:
I have not stopp'd mine ears to their de-
mands,
Nor posted off their suits with slow delays;
My pity hath been balm to heal their
wounds,
My mildness hath allay'd their swelling
griefs,
My mercy dried their water-flowing tears;
I have not been desirous of their wealth,
Nor much oppress'd them with great sub-
sidies,
Nor forward of revenge, though they much
err'd:   [than me?
Then why should they love Edward more
No, Exeter, these graces challenge grace:
And, when the lion fawns upon the lamb,
The lamb will never cease to follow him.
  [*Shout within,* "A Lancaster! A Lancaster!"
  *Exe.* Hark, hark, my lord! what shouts
are these?

*Enter* KING EDWARD, GLOSTER, *and* Soldiers.
  *Edw.* Seize on the shame-fac'd Henry,
bear him hence:
And once again proclaim us king of Eng-
land.—
You are the fount that makes small brooks
to flow;   [them dry,
Now stops thy spring; my sea shall suck

And swell so much the higher by their ebb.—
Hence with him to the Tower; let him not
speak.
  [*Exeunt some with* KING HENRY.
And, lords, towards Coventry· bend we our
course,
Where peremptory Warwick now remains:
The sun shines hot; and, if we use delay,
Cold biting winter mars our hop'd-for hay.
  *Glo.* Away betimes, before his forces join,
And take the great-grown traitor unawares:
Brave warriors, march amain towards Cov-
entry.
    [*Exeunt.*

## ACT V.

### SCENE I.—*Coventry.*

*Enter upon the Walls,* WARWICK, *the* Mayor
of Coventry, *two* Messengers, *and others.*
  *War.* Where is the post that came from
valiant Oxford?
How far hence is thy lord, mine honest fellow?
  1 *Mess.* By this at Dunsmore, marching
hitherward.
  *War.* How far off is our brother Montague?—
Where is the post that came from Montague?
  2 *Mess.* By this at Daintry, with a puissant troop.

*Enter* SIR JOHN SOMERVILLE.
  *War.* Say, Somerville, what says my lov-
ing son?
And, by thy guess, how nigh is Clarence
now?   [his forces,
  *Som.* At Southam I did leave him with
And do expect him here some two hours
hence.   [*Drum heard.*
  *War.* Then Clarence is at hand; I hear his
drum.   [am lies;
  *Som.* It is not his, my lord; here South-
The drum your honour hears marcheth from
Warwick.   [look'd-for friends.
  *War.* Who should that be? belike un-
  *Som.* They are at hand, and you shall
quickly know.

*March. Flourish. Enter* KING EDWARD,
GLOSTER, *and* Forces.
  *K. Edw.* Go, trumpet, to the walls, and
sound a parle.   [the wall!
  *Glo.* See how the surly Warwick mans
  *War.* O unbid spite! is sportful Edward
come?   [seduc'd,
Where slept our scouts, or how are they
That we could hear no news of his repair?
  *K. Edw.* Now, Warwick, wilt thou ope
the city gates,
Speak gentle words, and humbly bend thy
knee,
Call Edward king, and at his hands beg
mercy?

And he shall pardon thee these outrages.

*War.* Nay, rather, wilt thou draw thy forces hence,
Confess who set thee up and pluck'd thee down,
Call Warwick patron, and be penitent?
And thou shalt still remain the Duke of York,

*Glo.* I thought, at least, he would have said the king;
Or did he make the jest against his will?

*War.* Is not a dukedom, sir, a goodly gift?

*Glo.* Ay, by my faith, for a poor earl to give:
I'll do thee service for so good a gift.

*War.* 'Twas I that gave the kingdom to thy brother.

*K. Edw.* Why, then, 'tis mine, if but by Warwick's gift.

*War.* Thou art no Atlas for so great a weight:
And, weakling, Warwick takes his gift again;
And Henry is my king, Warwick his subject.

*K. Edw.* But Warwick's king is Edward's prisoner:
And, gallant Warwick, do but answer this,—
What is the body when the head is off?

*Glo.* Alas, that Warwick had no more forecast,
But, whiles he thought to steal the single ten,
The king was slily finger'd from the deck!
You left poor Henry at the bishop's palace,
And, ten to one, you'll meet him in the Tower.

*K. Edw.* 'Tis even so; yet you are Warwick still.

*Glo.* Come, Warwick, take the time; kneel down, kneel down:
Nay, when? strike now, or else the iron cools.

*War.* I had rather chop this hand off at a blow,
And with the other fling it at thy face,
Than bear so low a sail, to strike to thee.

*K. Edw.* Sail how thou canst, have wind and tide thy friend;
This hand, fast wound about thy coal-black hair,
Shall, whiles thy head is warm and new cut off,
Write in the dust this sentence with thy blood,—
*Wind-changing Warwick now can change no more.*

Enter OXFORD, *with* Forces, *drum, and colours.*

*War.* O cheerful colours! see where Oxford comes!

*Oxf.* Oxford, Oxford, for Lancaster!
    [*He and his* Forces *enter the city.*

*Glo.* The gates are open, let us enter too.

*K. Edw.* So other foes may set upon our backs.

Stand we in good array; for they no doubt
Will issue out again and bid us battle:
If not, the city being but of small defence,
We'll quickly rouse the traitors in the same.

*War.* O, welcome, Oxford! for we want thy help.

Enter MONTAGUE, *with* Forces, *drum, and colours.*

*Mont.* Montague, Montague, for Lancaster!
    [*He and his* Forces *enter the city.*

*Glo.* Thou and thy brother both shall buy this treason
Even with the dearest blood your bodies bear.

*K. Edw.* The harder match'd, the greater victory:
My mind presageth happy gain and conquest.

Enter SOMERSET, *with* Forces, *drum, and colours.*

*Som.* Somerset, Somerset, for Lancaster!
    [*He and his* Forces *enter the city.*

*Glo.* Two of thy name, both Dukes of Somerset,
Have sold their lives unto the house of York;
And thou shalt be the third, if this sword hold.

Enter CLARENCE, *with* Forces, *drum and colours.*

*War.* And lo, where George of Clarence sweeps along,
Of force enough to bid his brother battle;
With whom an upright zeal to right prevails
More than the nature of a brother's love!—
Come, Clarence, come; thou wilt, if Warwick call.

*Clar.* Father of Warwick, know you what this means?
    [*Taking the red rose out of his hat.*
Look here, I throw my infamy at thee:
I will not ruinate my father's house,
Who gave his blood to lime the stones together,
And set up Lancaster. Why, trowst thou, Warwick,
That Clarence is so harsh, so blunt, unnatural,
To bend the fatal instruments of war
Against his brother and his lawful king?
Perhaps thou wilt object my holy oath:
To keep that oath were more impiety
Than Jephtha's, when he sacrific'd his daughter.
I am so sorry for my trespass made,
That, to deserve well at my brother's hands,
I here proclaim myself thy mortal foe;
With resolution wheresoe'er I meet thee,—
As I will meet thee, if thou stir abroad,—
To plague thee for thy foul misleading me.
And so, proud-hearted Warwick, I defy thee.

And to my brother turn my blushing
    cheeks.—
Pardon me, Edward, I will make amends;
And, Richard, do not frown upon my faults,
For I will henceforth be no more unconstant.
    *K. Edw.* Now welcome more, and ten
        times more belov'd,
Than if thou never hadst deserv'd our hate.
    *Glo.* Welcome, good Clarence; this is
        brother-like.
    *War.* O passing traitor, perjur'd and un-
        just!
    *K. Edw.* What, Warwick, wilt thou leave
        the town and fight?
Or shall we beat the stones about thine ears?
    *War.* Alas, I am not coop'd here for de-
        fence!
I will away towards Barnet presently,
And bid thee battle, Edward, if thou dar'st.
    *K. Edw.* Yes, Warwick, Edward dares,
        and leads the way
Lords, to the field: Saint George and victory.
                    [*March. Exeunt.*

SCENE II.—*A field of Battle near Barnet.*

*Alarums and excursions. Enter* KING ED-
WARD, *bringing in* WARWICK *wounded.*

    *K. Edw.* So, lie thou there: die thou, and
        die our fear;
For Warwick was a bug that fear'd us all.—
Now, Montague, sit fast; I seek for thee,
That Warwick's bones may keep thine com-
    pany.                  [*Exit.*
    *War.* Ah, who is nigh? come to me, friend
        or foe,
And tell me who is victor, York or Warwick?
Why ask I that? my mangled body shows,
My blood, my want of strength, my sick
    heart shows,
That I must yield my body to the earth,
And, by my fall, the conquest to my foe.
Thus yields the cedar to the axe's edge,
Whose arms gave shelter to the princely
    eagle,
Under whose shade the ramping lion slept,
Whose top-branch overpeer'd Jove's spread-
    ing tree,
And kept low shrubs from winter's powerful
    wind.
These eyes, that now are dimm'd with
    death's black vail,
Have been as piercing as the mid-day sun,
To search the secret treasons of the world:
The wrinkles in my brows, now fill'd with
    blood,
Were liken'd oft to kingly sepulchres;
For who liv'd king, but I could dig his grave?
And who durst smile when Warwick bent his
    brow?
Lo, now my glory smear'd in dust and
    blood!
My parks, my walks, my manors that I had,
Even now forsake me; and of all my lands
Is nothing left me but my body's length!

Why, what is pomp, rule, reign, but earth
    and dust!
And, live we how we can, yet die we must.

        *Enter* OXFORD *and* SOMERSET.

    *Som.* Ah, Warwick, Warwick! wert thou
        as we are,
We might recover all our loss again:
The queen from France hath brought a puis-
    sant power;              [thou fly!
Even now we heard the news: ah, couldst
    *War.* Why, then, I would not fly.—Ah,
        Montague,
If thou be there, sweet brother, take my
    hand,
And with thy lips keep in my soul awhile!
Thou lov'st me not; for, brother, if thou
    didst,
Thy tears would wash this cold congealed
    blood
That glues my lips and will not let me speak.
Come quickly, Montague, or I am dead.
    *Som.* Ah, Warwick! Montague hath
        breath'd his last;
And to the latest gasp cried out for War-
    wick,
And said, *Commend me to my valiant
    brother.*
And more he would have said; and more he
    spoke,
Which sounded like a cannon in a vault,
That might not be distinguish'd; but at last,
I well might hear, deliver'd with a groan,
*O, farewell, Warwick!*
    *War.* Sweet rest his soul!—fly, lords, and
        save yourselves;
For Warwick bids you all farewell, to meet
    in heav'n.              [*Dies.*
    *Oxf.* Away, away, to meet the queen's
        great power!
        [*Exeunt, bearing off* WAR.'s *body.*

SCENE III.—*Another part of the Field.*

*Flourish. Enter* KING EDWARD *in triumph;
with* CLARENCE, GLOSTER, *and the rest.*

    *K. Edw.* Thus far our fortune keeps an
        upward course,
And we are grac'd with wreaths of victory.
But in the midst of this bright-shining day
I spy a black, suspicious, threatening cloud,
That will encounter with our glorious sun
Ere he attain his easeful western bed:
I mean, my lords, those powers that the
    queen
Hath rais'd in Gallia have arriv'd our coast,
And, as we hear, march on to fight with us.
    *Clar.* A little gale will soon disperse that
        cloud
And blow it to the source from whence it
    came:
Thy very beams will dry those vapours up;
For every cloud engenders not a storm.
                        [strong,
    *Glo.* The queen is valu'd thirty thousand

And Somerset, with Oxford, fled to her:
If she have time to breathe, be well assur'd,
Her faction will be full as strong as ours.

*K. Edw.* We are advértis'd by our loving
    friends        [Tewksbury;
That they do hold their course toward
We, having now the best at Barnet field,
Will thither straight, for willingness rids
    way;        [mented
And as we march, our strength will be aug-
In every county as we go along.—
Strike up the drum; cry, Courage! and
    away.        [*Exeunt.*

SCENE IV.—*Plains near Tewksbury.*

*March. Enter* QUEEN MARGARET, PRINCE
EDWARD, SOMERSET, OXFORD, *and* Soldiers.

*Q. Mar.* Great Lords, wise men ne'er sit
    and wail their loss,
But cheerly seek how to redress their harms.
What though the mast be now blown over-
    board,
The cable broke, the holding-anchor lost,
And half our sailors swallow'd in the flood;
Yet lives our pilot still: is't meet that he
Should leave the helm, and, like a fearful lad,
With tearful eyes add water to the sea,
And give more strength to that which hath
    too much;
Whiles, in his moan, the ship splits on the
    rock.
Which industry and courage might have
    sav'd?
Ah, what a shame! ah, what a fault were
    this!
Say Warwick was our anchor; what of that?
And Montague our top-mast; what of him?
Our slaughter'd friends the tackles; what of
    these?
Why, is not Oxford here another anchor?
And Somerset another goodly mast? [lings?
The friends of France our shrouds and tack-
And, though unskilful, why not Ned and I
For once allow'd the skilful pilot's charge?
We will not from the helm to sit and weep;
But keep our course, though the rough wind
    say no,        [wreck.
From shelves and rocks that threaten us with
As good to chide the waves as speak them
    fair.
And what is Edward but a ruthless sea?
What Clarence but a quicksand of deceit?
And Richard but a ragged fatal rock?
All these the enemies to our poor bark.
Say you can swim; alas, 'tis but a while!
Tread on the sand; why, there you quickly
    sink:
Bestride the rock; the tide will wash you off,
Or else you famish,—that's a threefold death.
This speak I, lords, to let you understand,
If case some one of you would fly from us,
That there's no hop'd-for mercy with the
    brothers,        [and rocks.
More than with ruthless waves, with sands,

Why, courage, then! what cannot be avoided,
'Twere childish weakness to lament or fear.

*Prince.* Methinks a woman of this valiant
    spirit
Should, if a coward heard her speak these
    words,
Infuse his breath with magnanimity,
And make him naked foil a man-at-arms.
I speak not this as doubting any here;
For did I but suspect a fearful man,
He should have leave to go away betimes;
Lest in our need he might infect another,
And make him of like spirit to himself.
If any such be here,—as God forbid!—
Let him depart before we need his help.

*Oxf.* Women and children of so high a
    courage,
And warriors faint! why, 'twere perpetual
    shame.—
O brave young prince! thy famous grand-
    father
Doth live again in thee: long mayst thou live
To bear his image and renew his glories!

*Som.* And he that will not fight for such a
    hope,
Go home to bed, and, like the owl by day,
If he arise, be mock'd and wonder'd at.

*Q. Mar.* Thanks, gentle Somerset;—sweet
    Oxford, thanks.        [nothing else.

*Prince.* And take his thanks that yet hath

*Enter a* Messenger.

*Mess.* Prepare you, lords, for. Edward is
    at hand,
Ready to fight; therefore be resolute.

*Oxf.* I thought no less: it is his policy
To haste thus fast, to find us unprovided.

*Som.* But he's deceiv'd; we are in readi-
    ness.

*Q. Mar.* This cheers my heart, to see your
    forwardness.        [not budge.

*Oxf.* Here pitch our battle; hence we will

*Flourish and March. Enter, at a distance,*
KING EDWARD, CLARENCE, GLOSTER, *and*
Forces.

*K. Edw.* Brave followers, yonder stands
    the thorny wood,        [strength,
Which, by the heavens' assistance and your
Must by the roots be hewn up yet ere night.
I need not add more fuel to your fire;
For well I wot ye blaze to burn them out:
Give signal to the fight, and to it, lords.

*Q. Mar.* Lords, knights, and gentlemen,
    what I should say
My tears gainsay; for every word I speak,
Ye see, I drink the water of mine eyes.
Therefore, no more but this:—Henry, your
    sovereign,
Is prisoner to the foe; his state usurp'd,
His realm a slaughter-house, his subjects
    slain,
His statutes cancell'd, and his treasure spent;
And yonder is the wolf that makes this spoil.

You fight in justice: then, in God's name, lords,
Be valiant, and give signal to the fight.

[*Exeunt both armies.*

SCENE V.—*Another part of the Plains.*

*Alarums: excursions: and afterwards a retreat. Then enter* KING EDWARD, CLARENCE, GLOSTER, *and* Forces, *with* QUEEN MARGARET, OXFORD, *and* SOMERSET, *prisoners.*

*K. Edw.* Now, here a period of tumultuous broils.
Away with Oxford to Hammes' Castle straight;
For Somerset, off with his guilty head.

[speak.

Go, bear them hence; I will not hear them
*Oxf.* For my part, I'll not trouble thee with words.                [my fortune.
*Som.* Nor I, but stoop with patience to

[*Exeunt* OXF. *and* SOM., *guarded.*

*Q. Mar.* So part we sadly in this troublous world,
To meet with joy in sweet Jerusalem.
*K. Edw.* Is proclamation made that who finds Edward
Shall have a high reward, and he his life?
*Glo.* It is; and lo, where youthful Edward comes.

*Enter* Soldiers, *with* PRINCE EDWARD.

*K. Edw.* Bring forth the gallant, let us hear him speak.
What, can so young a thorn begin to prick?—
Edward, what satisfaction canst thou make
For bearing arms, for stirring up my subjects,
And all the trouble thou hast turn'd me to?
*Prince.* Speak like a subject, proud ambitious York!
Suppose that I am now my father's mouth;
Resign thy chair, and where I stand kneel thou,
Whilst I propose the self-same words to thee,
Which, traitor, thou wouldst have me answer to.
*Q. Mar.* Ah, that thy father had been so resolv'd!
*Glo.* That you might still have worn the petticoat,
And ne'er have stol'n the breech from Lancaster.
*Prince.* Let Æsop fable in a winter's night;
His currish riddles sort not with this place.
*Glo.* By heaven, brat, I'll plague you for that word.                [to men.
*Q. Mar.* Ay, thou wast born to be a plague
*Glo.* For God's sake, take away this captive scold.
*Prince.* Nay, take away this scolding crook-back rather.

*K. Edw.* Peace, wilful boy, or I will charm your tongue.                [pert.
*Clar.* Untutor'd lad, thou art too malapert.
*Prince.* I know my duty; you are all undutiful:                [George,—
Lascivious Edward,—and thou, perjur'd
And thou, misshapen Dick,—I tell ye all
I am your better, traitors as ye are;—
And thou usurp'st my father's right and mine.
*K. Edw.* Take that, the likeness of this railer here.                [*Stabs him.*
*Glo.* Sprawl'st thou? take that, to end thy agony.                [*Stabs him.*
*Clar.* And there's for twitting me with perjury.                [*Stabs him.*
*Q. Mar.* O, kill me too!
*Glo.* Marry, and shall. [*Offers to kill her.*
*K. Edw.* Hold, Richard, hold; for we have done too much.
*Glo.* Why should she live, to fill the world with words?
*K. Edw.* What, doth she swoon? use means for her recovery.
*Glo.* Clarence, excuse me to the king my brother;
I'll hence to London on a serious matter:
Ere ye come there, be sure to hear some news.
*Clar.* What? what?
*Glo.* The Tower! the Tower!                [*Exit.*
*Q. Mar.* O Ned, sweet Ned! speak to thy mother, boy!                [ers!—
Canst thou not speak?—O traitors! murder—
They that stabb'd Cæsar shed no blood at all,
Did not offend, nor were not worthy blame,
If this foul deed were by to equal it:
He was a man;—this, in respect, a child,—
And men ne'er spend their fury on a child.
What's worse than murderer, that I may name it?
No, no, my heart will burst, an if I speak:—
And I will speak, that so my heart may burst.
Butchers and villains! bloody cannibals!
How sweet a plant have you untimely cropp'd!
You have no children, butchers! if you had,
The thought of them would have stirr'd up remorse:
But if you ever chance to have a child,
Look in his youth to have him so cut off
As, deathsmen, you have rid this sweet young prince!
*K. Edw.* Away with her; go, bear her hence perforce.
*Q. Mar.* Nay, never bear me hence, despatch me here;                [death:
Here, sheathe thy sword, I'll pardon thee my
What, wilt thou not?—then, Clarence, do it thou.                [much ease.
*Clar.* By heaven, I will not do thee so
*Q. Mar.* Good Clarence, do; sweet Clarence, do thou do it.

*Clar.* Didst thou not hear me swear I
　would not do it?

*Q. Mar.* Ay, but thou usest to forswear
　thyself;

'Twas sin before, but now 'tis charity.

What! wilt thou not?—Where is that devil's
　butcher, 　　　　　　[art thou?

Hard-favour'd Richard?—Richard, where

Thou art not here: murder is thy alms-deed;

Petitioners for blood thou ne'er putt'st back.

*K. Edw.* Away, I say; I charge ye, bear
　her hence.

*Q. Mar.* So come to you and yours as to
　this prince!　[*Exit, led out forcibly.*

*K. Edw.* Where's Richard gone?

*Clar.* To London, all in post; and, as I
　guess,

To make a bloody supper in the Tower.

*K. Edw.* He's sudden, if a thing comes in
　his head.　　　　　　[mon sort

Now march we hence: discharge the com-

With pay and thanks, and let's away to
　London,

And see our gentle queen how well she
　fares,—

By this, I hope, she hath a son for me.
　　　　　　　　　　[*Exeunt.*

SCENE VI.—LONDON. *A Room in the Tower.*

KING HENRY *is discovered sitting with a
　book in his hand, the* LIEUTENANT *attending.
　Enter* GLOSTER.

*Glo.* Good-day, my lord. What, at your
　book so hard?

*K. Hen.* Ay, my good lord:—my lord, I
　should say rather;

'Tis sin to flatter, good was little better:

Good Gloster and good devil were alike,

And both preposterous: therefore, not good
　lord.

*Glo.* Sirrah, leave us to ourselves: we
　must confer.　　[*Exit* Lieutenant.

*K. Hen.* So flies the reckless shepherd
　from the wolf;

So first the harmless sheep doth yield his
　fleece,

And next his throat unto the butcher's
　knife.—

What scene of death hath Roscius now to
　act?

*Glo.* Suspicion always haunts the guilty
　mind;

The thief doth fear each bush an officer.

*K. Hen.* The bird that hath been limed in
　a bush,

With trembling wings misdoubteth every
　bush;

And I, the hapless male to one sweet bird,

Have now the fatal object in my eye

Where my poor young was lim'd, was caught,
　and kill'd.

*Glo.* Why, what a peevish fool was that
　of Crete,

That taught his son the office of a fowl!

And yet, for all his wings, the fool was
　drown'd.

*K. Hen.* I, Dædalus, my poor boy, Icarus;

Thy father, Minos, that denied our course;

The sun, that sear'd the wings of my sweet
　boy,

Thy brother Edward; and thyself, the sea,

Whose envious gulf did swallow up his life.

Ah, kill me with thy weapon, not with
　words!

My breast can better brook thy dagger's
　point

Than can my ears that tragic history.

But wherefore dost thou come? is't for my
　life?

*Glo.* Think'st thou I am an executioner?

*K. Hen.* A persecutor, I am sure, thou art:

If murdering innocents be executing,

Why, then thou art an executioner.

*Glo.* Thy son I kill'd for his presumption.

*K. Hen.* Hadst thou been kill'd when first
　thou didst presume,

Thou hadst not liv'd to kill a son of mine.

And thus I prophesy,—that many a thou-
　sand,

Which now mistrust no parcel of my fear,

And many an old man's sigh, and many a
　widow's,

And many an orphan's water-standing
　eye,—

Men for their sons, wives for their hus-
　bands,

And orphans for their parents' timeless
　death,—

Shall rue the hour that ever thou wast born

The owl shriek'd at thy birth,—an evil sign;

The night-crow cried, aboding luckless time;

Dogs howl'd, and hideous tempest shook
　down trees;

The raven rook'd her on the chimney's top,

And chattering pies in dismal discords sung

Thy mother felt more than a mother's pain,

And yet brought forth less than a mother's
　hope,

To wit,—

An indigest deformed lump,

Not like the fruit of such a goodly tree.

Teeth hadst thou in thy head when thou
　wast born,

To signify thou cam'st to bite the world:

And if the rest be true which I have heard,

Thou cam'st—

*Glo.* I'll hear no more:—die, prophet, in
　thy speech:　　　[*Stabs him.*

For this, amongst the rest, was I ordain'd.

*K. Hen.* Ay, and for much more slaughter
　after this.

O God forgive my sins and pardon thee!
　　　　　　　　　　[*Dies.*

*Glo.* What, will the aspiring blood of Lan-
　caster

Sink in the ground? I thought it would have
　mounted.　　　　　　[death!

See how my sword weeps for the poor king's

O may such purple tears be alway shed
From those that wish the downfall of our
 house!—
If any spark of life be yet remaining,
Down, down to hell; and say I sent thee
 thither,—                    [Stabs him again.
I, that have neither pity, love, nor fear.—
Indeed, 'tis true that Henry told me of;
For I have often heard my mother say
I came into the world with my legs forward:
Had I not reason, think ye, to make haste,
And seek their ruin that usurp'd our right:
The midwife wonder'd; and the women
 cried,
*O, Jesus bless us, he is born with teeth!*
And so I was, which plainly signified
That I should snarl, and bite, and play the
 dog.
Then, since the heavens have shap'd my
 body so,
Let hell make crook'd my mind to answer it.
I have no brother, I am like no brother;
And this word *love*, which greybeards call
 divine,
Be resident in men like one another,
And not in me: I am myself alone.—
Clarence, beware; thou keep'st me from the
 light:
But I will sort a pitchy day for thee;
For I will buzz abroad such prophecies
That Edward shall be fearful of his life:
And then, to purge his fear, I'll be thy death.
King Henry and the prince his son are gone:
Clarence, thy turn is next, and then the rest;
Counting myself but bad till I be best.—
I'll throw thy body in another room,
And triumph, Henry, in thy day of doom.
                              [Exit with the body.

SCENE VII.—LONDON. *A Room in the Palace.*

*Flourish.* KING EDWARD *is discovered sitting
on his throne;* QUEEN ELIZABETH *with the
infant* PRINCE, CLARENCE, GLOSTER, HAST-
INGS, *and others, near him.*

K. Edw. Once more we sit in England's
 royal throne.
Repurchas'd with the blood of enemies.
What valiant foemen, like to autumn's corn,
Have we mow'd down in tops of all their
 pride!
Three Dukes of Somerset,—threefold re-
 nown'd
For hardy and undoubted champions;
Two Cliffords, as the father and the son;
And two Northumberlands,—two braver
 men
Ne'er spurr'd their coursers at the trumpet's
 sound;

With them the two brave bears, Warwick
 and Montague,
That in their chains fetter'd the kingly lion,
And made the forest tremble when they
 roar'd.
Thus have we swept suspicion from our seat
And made our footstool of security.—
Come hither, Bess, and let me kiss my boy.—
Young Ned, for thee, thine uncles and my-
 self
Have in our armours watch'd the winter's
 night;
Went all afoot in summer's scalding heat,
That thou mightst repossess the crown in
 peace:
And of our labours thou shalt reap the gain.
 *Glo.* I'll blast his harvest if your head
 were laid;
For yet I am not look'd on in the world.
This shoulder was ordain'd so thick to heave;
And heave it shall some weight, or break my
 back:—
Work thou the way, -and that shalt execute.
                                          [*Aside.*
 *K. Edw.* Clarence and Gloster, love my
 lovely queen;
And kiss your princely nephew, brothers
 both.
 *Clar.* The duty that I owe unto your ma-
 jesty
I seal upon the lips of this sweet babe.
 *K. Edw.* Thanks, noble Clarence; worthy
 brother, thanks.
 *Glo.* And, that I love the tree from whence
 thou sprang'st,
Witness the loving kiss I give the fruit.—
To say the truth, so Judas kiss'd his master,
And cried, all hail! when as he meant all
 harm.                                    [*Aside.*
 *K. Edw.* Now am I seated as my soul de-
 lights,
Having my country's peace and brothers'
 loves.
 *Clar.* What will your grace have done with
 Margaret?
Reignier, her father, to the King of France
Hath pawn'd the Sicils and Jerusalem,
And hither have they sent it for her ransom.
 *K. Edw.* Away with her, and waft her
 hence to France.
And now what rests but that we spend the
 time
With stately triumphs, mirthful comic shows,
Such as befit the pleasure of the court?
Sound drums and trumpets! farewell, sour
 annoy!
For here, I hope, begins our lasting joy.
                                          [*Exeunt.*

# RICHARD III.

Act IV. Sc. 2.

# THE LIFE AND DEATH OF KING RICHARD III.

## DRAMATIS PERSONÆ

KING EDWARD THE FOURTH.

EDWARD, *Prince of Wales, afterwards* KING EDWARD V., } *Sons to the* KING.

RICHARD, *Duke of York,*

GEORGE, *Duke of Clarence,*
RICHARD, *Duke of Gloster, afterwards* KING RICHARD III., } *Brothers to the* KING.

A Young Son of Clarence.
HENRY, *Earl of Richmond, afterwards* KING HENRY VII.
CARDINAL BOUCHER, *Archbishop of Canterbury.*
THOMAS ROTHERAM, *Archbishop of York.*
JOHN MORTON, *Bishop of Ely.*
DUKE OF BUCKINGHAM.
DUKE OF NORFOLK.
EARL OF SURREY, *his Son.*
EARL RIVERS, *Brother to* KING EDWARD'S Queen.
MARQUIS OF DORSET *and* LORD GREY, *her Sons.*
EARL OF OXFORD.
LORD HASTINGS.
LORD STANLEY.

LORD LOVEL.
SIR THOMAS VAUGHAN.
SIR RICHARD RATCLIFF.
SIR WILLIAM CATESBY.
SIR JAMES TYRREL.
SIR JAMES BLOUNT.
SIR WALTER HERBERT.
SIR ROBERT BRAKENBURY, *Lieutenant of the Tower.*
CHRISTOPHER URSWICK, *a Priest.*
Another Priest.
Lord Mayor of London.
Sheriff of Wiltshire.

ELIZABETH, *Queen to* KING EDWARD IV.
MARGARET, *Widow to* KING HENRY VI.
DUCHESS OF YORK, *Mother to* KING EDWARD IV., CLARENCE, *and* GLOSTER.
LADY ANNE, *Widow to* EDWARD, *Prince of Wales, Son to* KING HENRY VI.; *afterwards married to the* DUKE OF GLOSTER.
A Young Daughter of Clarence.

Lords, *and other* Attendants; *two* Gentlemen, *a* Pursuivant, Scrivener, Citizens, Murderers, Messengers, Ghosts, Soldiers, *&c.*

SCENE,—ENGLAND

## ACT I.

### SCENE I.—LONDON. *A Street.*

*Enter* GLOSTER.

*Glo.* Now is the winter of our discontent
Made glorious summer by this sun of York;
And all the clouds that lower'd upon our house
In the deep bosom of the ocean buried.
Now are our brows bound with victorious wreaths;
Our bruised arms hung up for monuments;
Our stern alarums chang'd to merry meetings,
Our dreadful marches to delightful measures.
Grim-visaged war hath smooth'd his wrinkled front;
And now,—instead of mounting barbed steeds
To fright the souls of fearful adversaries,—
He capers nimbly in a lady's chamber
To the lascivious pleasing of a lute.
But I,—that am not shap'd for sportive tricks,

Nor made to court an amorous looking-glass;
I, that am rudely stamp'd, and want love's majesty
To strut before a wanton ambling nymph;
I, that am curtail'd of this fair proportion,
Cheated of feature by dissembling nature,
Deform'd, unfinish'd, sent before my time
Into this breathing world scarce half made up,
And that so lamely and unfashionable
That dogs bark at me as I halt by them;—
Why, I, in this weak piping time of peace,
Have no delight to pass away the time,
Unless to spy my shadow in the sun,
And descant on mine own deformity:
And therefore,—since I cannot prove a lover,
To entertain these fair well-spoken days,—
I am determined to prove a villain,
And hate the idle pleasures of these days.
Plots have I laid, inductions dangerous,
By drunken prophecies, libels, and dreams,
To set my brother Clarence and the king
In deadly hate the one against the other:

And, if King Edward be as true and just
As I am subtle, false, and treacherous,
This day should Clarence closely be mew'd
 up,—
About a prophecy, which says that G
Of Edward's heirs the murderer shall be.
Dive, thoughts, down to my soul:—here
 Clarence comes.

*Enter* CLARENCE, *guarded, and* BRAKENBURY.

Brother, good-day: what means this armed
 guard,
That waits upon your grace?
 *Clar.*                His majesty,
Tendering my person's safety, hath appoint-
 ed
This conduct to convey me to the Tower.
 *Glo.* Upon what cause?
 *Clar.*          Because my name is George.
 *Glo.* Alack, my lord, that fault is none of
 yours;
He should, for that, commit your godfath-
 ers:—
O, belike his majesty hath some intent
That you shall be new-christen'd in the
 Tower.
But what's the matter, Clarence? may I
 know?
 *Clar.* Yea, Richard, when I know; for I
 protest
As yet I do not: but, as I can learn,
He hearkens after prophecies and dreams;
And from the cross-row plucks the letter G,
And says a wizard told him that by G
His issue disinherited should be;
And, for my name of George begins with G,
It follows in his thought that I am he.
These, as I learn, and such like toys as these,
Have mov'd his highness to commit me now.
 *Glo.* Why, this it is, when men are rul'd by
 women:—
'Tis not the king that sends you to the
 Tower;
My Lady Grey, his wife, Clarence, 'tis she
That tempers him to this extremity.
Was it not she, and that good man of wor-
 ship,
Antony Woodville, her brother there,
That made him send Lord Hastings to the
 Tower,
From whence this present day he is deliv-
 er'd?
We are not safe, Clarence; we are not safe.
 *Clar.* By heaven, I think there is no man
 secure                        [heralds
But the queen's kindred, and night-walking
That trudge betwixt the king and Mistress
 Shore.
Heard you not what an humble suppliant
Lord Hastings was to her for his delivery?
 *Glo.* Humbly complaining to her deity
Got my lord chamberlain his liberty.
I'll tell you what,—I think it is our way,
If we will keep in favour with the king,

To be her men, and wear her livery:
The jealous o'er-worn widow and herself,
Since that our brother dubb'd them gentle-
 women,
Are mighty gossips in this monarchy.
 *Brak.* I beseech your graces both to par-
 don me;
His majesty hath straitly given in charge
That no man shall have private conference,
Of what degree soever, with his brother.
 *Glo.* Even so; an please your worship,
 Brakenbury,
You may partake of anything we say:
We speak no treason, man;—we say the king
Is wise and virtuous; and his noble queen
Well struck in years, fair, and not jealous;—
We say that Shore's wife hath a pretty foot,
A cherry lip, a bonny eye, a passing pleasing
 tongue;
And the queen's kindred are made gentle-
 folks:
How say you, sir? can you deny all this?
 *Brak.* With this, my lord, myself have
 naught to do.
 *Glo.* Naught to do with Mistress Shore!
 I tell thee, fellow,
He that doth naught with her, excepting one,
Were best to do it secretly, alone.
 *Brak.* What one, my lord?   [betray me?
 *Glo.* Her husband, knave:—Wouldst thou
 *Brak.* I beseech your grace to pardon me;
 and, withal,
Forbear your conference with the noble
 duke.
 *Clar.* We know thy charge, Brakenbury,
 and will obey.                   [obey.—
 *Glo.* We are the queen's abjects, and must
Brother, farewell: I will unto the king;
And whatsoe'er you will employ me in,—
Were it to call King Edward's widow sis-
 ter,—
I will perform it to enfranchise you.
Meantime, this deep disgrace in brotherhood
Touches me deeper than you can imagine.
 *Clar.* I know it pleaseth neither of us well.
 *Glo.* Well, your imprisonment shall not be
 long;
I will deliver you, or else lie for you:
Meantime, have patience.
 *Clar.*      I must perforce: farewell.
      [*Exeunt* CLAR., BRAK., *and* Guard.
 *Glo.* Go, tread the path that thou shalt
 ne'er return,
Simple, plain Clarence!—I do love thee so
That I will shortly send thy soul to heaven,
If heaven will take the present at our
 hands.—
But who comes here? the new-deliver'd
 Hastings?

*Enter* HASTINGS.

 *Hast.* Good time of day unto my gracious
 lord!                          [berlain!
 *Glo.* As much unto my good lord cham-

Well are you welcome to this open air.
How hath your lordship brook'd imprison-
  ment?
  *Hast.* With patience, noble lord, as pris-
    oners must:
But I shall live, my lord, to give them
    thanks
That were the cause of my imprisonment.
  *Glo.* No doubt, no doubt; and so shall
    Clarence too;
For they that were your enemies are his,
And have prevail'd as much on him as you.
  *Hast.* More pity that the eagle should be
    mew'd
While kites and buzzards prey at liberty.
  *Glo.* What news abroad?
  *Hast.* No news so bad abroad as this at
    home,—
The king is sickly, weak, and melancholy,
And his physicians fear him mightily.
  *Glo.* Now, by Saint Paul, this news is bad
    indeed.
O, he hath kept an evil diet long,
And overmuch consum'd his royal person:
'Tis very grievous to be thought upon.
What, is he in his bed?
  *Hast.*              He is.
  *Glo.* Go you before, and I will follow you.
                              [*Exit* HASTINGS.
He cannot live, I hope; and must not die
Till George be pack'd with posthorse up to
    heaven.
I'll in, to urge his hatred more to Clarence,
With lies well steel'd with weighty argu-
    ments;
And, if I fail not in my deep intent,
Clarence hath not another day to live:
Which done, God take King Edward to his
    mercy,
And leave the world for me to bustle in!
For then I'll marry Warwick's youngest
    daughter:              [father?
What though I kill'd her husband and her
The readiest way to make the wench amends
Is to become her husband and her father:
The which will I; not all so much for love
As for another secret close intent,
By marrying her, which I must reach unto.
But yet I run before my horse to market:
Clarence still breathes; Edward still lives and
    reigns:
When they are gone, then must I count my
    gains.
                              [*Exit.*

### SCENE II.—LONDON. *Another Street.*

*Enter the Corpse of* KING HENRY THE SIXTH,
  *borne in an open coffin,* Gentlemen *bearing
  halberds to guard it; and* LADY ANNE *as
  mourner.*

  *Anne.* Set down, set down your honour-
    able load,—
If honour may be shrouded in a hearse,—

Whilst I awhile obsequiously lament
The untimely fall of virtuous Lancaster.—
Poor key-cold figure of a holy king!
Pale ashes of the house of Lancaster!
Thou bloodless remnant of that royal blood!
Be it lawful that I invocate thy ghost,
To hear the lamentations of poor Anne,
Wife to thy Edward, to thy slaughter'd son,
Stabb'd by the self-same hand that made
    these wounds!
Lo, in these windows that let forth thy life,
I pour the helpless balm of my poor eyes:—
O, cursed be the hand that made these holes!
Cursed the heart that had the heart to do it!
Cursed the blood that let this blood from
    hence!
More direful hap betide that hated wretch
That makes us wretched by the death of thee,
Than I can wish to adders, spiders, toads,
Or any creeping venom'd thing that lives!
If ever he have child, abortive be it,
Prodigious, and untimely brought to light,
Whose ugly and unnatural aspèct
May fright the hopeful mother at the view;
And that be heir to his unhappiness!
If ever he have wife, let her be made
More miserable by the death of him
Than I am made by my young lord and
    thee!—
Come, now towards Chertsey with your holy
    load,
Taken from Paul's to be interred there;
And still, as you are weary of the weight,
Rest you, whiles I lament King Henry's corse.
   [*The* Bearers *take up the Corpse and ad-
    vance.*

#### Enter GLOSTER.

  *Glo.* Stay, you that bear the corse, and set
    it down.
  *Anne.* What black magician conjures up
    this fiend,
To stop devoted charitable deeds?
  *Glo.* Villains, set down the corse; or, by
    Saint Paul,
I'll make a corse of him that disobeys!
  1 *Gent.* My lord, stand back, and let the
    coffin pass.              [command:
  *Glo.* Unmanner'd dog! stand thou, when I
Advance thy halberd higher than my breast,
Or, by Saint Paul, I'll strike thee to my foot,
And spurn upon thee, beggar, for thy bold-
    ness.
              [*The* Bearers *set down the coffin.*
  *Anne.* What, do you tremble? are you all
    afraid?
Alas, I blame you not for you are mortal,
And mortal eyes cannot endure the devil.—
Avaunt, thou dreadful minister of hell!
Thou hadst but power over his mortal body,
His soul thou canst not have; therefore be
    gone.
  *Glo.* Sweet saint, for charity, be not so
    curst.

*Anne.* Foul devil, for God's sake, hence,
     and trouble us not;
For thou hast made the happy earth thy hell,
Fill'd it with cursing cries and deep exclaims.
If thou delight to view thy heinous deeds,
Behold this pattern of thy butcheries.—
O, gentlemen, see, see! dead Henry's wounds
Open their congeal'd mouths and bleed
     afresh!
Blush, blush, thou lump of foul deformity;
For 'tis thy presence that exhales this blood
From cold and empty veins, where no blood
     dwells;
Thy deed, inhuman and unnatural,
Provokes this deluge most unnatural.—
O God, which this blood mad'st, revenge his
     death!
O earth, which this blood drink'st, revenge
     his death!      [derer dead;
Either, heaven, with lightning strike the mur-
Or, earth, gape open wide, and eat him quick,
As thou dost swallow up this good king's
     blood,
Which his hell-govern'd arm hath butchered!
     *Glo.* Lady, you know no rules of charity,
Which renders good for bad, blessings for
     curses.      [nor man:
*Anne.* Villain, thou know'st no law of God
No beast so fierce but knows some touch of
     pity.
     *Glo.* But I know none, and therefore am
     no beast.      [truth!
*Anne.* O wonderful, when devils tell the
     *Glo.* More wonderful when angels are so
     angry.—
Vouchsafe, divine perfection of a woman,
Of these supposed evils to give me leave,
By circumstance, but to acquit myself.
     *Anne.* Vouchsafe, diffus'd infection of a
     man,
For these known evils but to give me leave,
By circumstance, to curse thy cursed self.
     *Glo.* Fairer than tongue can name thee, let
     me have
Some patient leisure to excuse myself.
     *Anne.* Fouler than heart can think thee,
     thou canst make
No excuse current, but to hang thyself.
     *Glo.* By such despair I should accuse my-
     self.
*Anne.* And by despairing shalt thou stand
     excus'd;
For doing worthy vengeance on thyself,
That didst unworthy slaughter upon others.
     *Glo.* Say that I slew them not?
     *Anne.* Then say they were not slain:
But dead they are, and, devilish slave, by
     thee.
     *Glo.* I did not kill your husband.
     *Anne.*      Why, then he is alive.
     *Glo.* Nay, he is dead; and slain by Ed-
     ward's hand.
     *Anne.* In thy foul throat thou liest: Queen
     Margaret saw

Thy murderous falchion smoking in his
     blood;
The which thou once didst bend against her
     breast,
But that thy brothers beat aside the point.
     *Glo.* I was provoked by her slanderous
     tongue,
That laid their guilt upon my guiltless shoul-
     ders.
     *Anne.* Thou wast provoked by thy bloody
     mind,
That never dreamt on aught but butcheries:
Didst thou not kill this king?
     *Glo.*      I grant ye.
     *Anne.* Dost grant me, hedgehog? then, God
     grant me too
Thou mayst be damned for that wicked
     deed!
O, he was gentle, mild, and virtuous.
     *Glo.* The fitter for the King of Heaven,
     that hath him.      [never come.
     *Anne.* He is in heaven, where thou shalt
     *Glo.* Let him thank me, that holp to send
     him thither;
For he was fitter for that place than earth.
     *Anne.* And thou unfit for any place but
     hell.
     *Glo.* Yes, one place else, if you will hear
     me name it.
     *Anne.* Some dungeon.
     *Glo.*      Your bed-chamber.
     *Anne.* Ill rest betide the chamber where
     thou liest!
     *Glo.* So will it, madam, till I lie with you.
     *Anne.* I hope so.
     *Glo.* I know so.—But, gentle Lady Anne,—
To leave this keen encounter of our wits,
And fall somewhat into a slower method,—
Is not the causer of the timeless deaths
Of these Plantagenets, Henry and Edward,
As blameful as the executioner?
     *Anne.* Thou wast the cause and most ac-
     curs'd effect.
     *Glo.* Your beauty was the cause of that
     effect;
Your beauty, that did haunt me in my sleep
To undertake the death of all the world,
So I might live one hour in your sweet bos-
     om.
     *Anne.* If I thought that, I tell thee, ho-
     micide,
These nails should rend that beauty from my
     cheeks.      [beauty's wreck.
     *Glo.* These eyes could not endure that
You should not blemish it if I stood by:
As all the world is cheered by the sun,
So I by that; it is my day, my life.
     *Anne.* Black night o'ershade thy day, and
     death thy life!      [art both.
     *Glo.* Curse not thyself, fair creature; thou
     *Anne.* I would I were, to be reveng'd on
     thee.
     *Glo.* It is a quarrel most unnatural.
To be reveng'd on him that loveth thee.

*Anne.* It is a quarrel just and reasonable,
To be reveng'd on him that kill'd my husband.

*Glo.* He that bereft thee, lady, of thy husband,
Did it to help thee to a better husband.

*Anne.* His better doth not breathe upon the earth. [could.

*Glo.* He lives that loves thee better than he

*Anne.* Name him.

*Glo.* Plantagenet.

*Anne.* Why, that was he.

*Glo.* The self-same name, but one of better nature.

*Anne.* Where is he?

*Glo.* Here. [*She spits at him.*] Why dost thou spit at me? [thy sake!

*Anne.* Would it were mortal poison, for

*Glo.* Never came poison from so sweet a place.

*Anne.* Never hung poison on a fouler toad.
Out of my sight! thou dost infect mine eyes.

*Glo.* Thine eyes, sweet lady, have infected mine.

*Anne.* Would they were basilisks, to strike thee dead! [at once;

*Glo.* I would they were, that I might die
For now they kill me with a living death.
Those eyes of thine from mine have drawn salt tears, [drops:
Sham'd their aspects with store of childish
These eyes, which never shed remorseful tear,
No, when my father York and Edward wept,
To hear the piteous moan that Rutland made
When black-fac'd Clifford shook his sword at him;
Nor when thy warlike father, like a child,
Told the sad story of my father's death,
And twenty times made pause, to sob and weep,
That all the standers-by had wet their cheeks,
Like trees bedash'd with rain; in that sad time
My manly eyes did scorn an humble tear;
And what these sorrows could not thence exhale,
Thy beauty hath, and made them blind with weeping.
I never su'd to friend nor enemy; [ing word;
My tongue could never learn sweet smooth-
But, now thy beauty is propos'd my fee,
My proud heart sues, and prompts my tongue to speak.
[*She looks scornfully at him.*
Teach not thy lip such scorn; for it was made
For kissing, lady, not for such contempt.
If thy revengeful heart cannot forgive,
Lo, here I lend thee this sharp-pointed sword;
Which if thou please to hide in this true breast,
And let the soul forth that adoreth thee,

I lay it naked to the deadly stroke,
And humbly beg the death upon my knee.
Nay, do not pause; for I did kill King Henry,—
[*He lays his breast open; she offers at it with his sword.*
But 'twas thy beauty that provoked me.
Nay, now despatch; 'twas I that stabb'd young Edward,—
[*She again offers at his breast.*
But 'twas thy heavenly face that set me on.
[*She lets fall the sword.*
Take up the sword again, or take up me.

*Anne.* Arise, dissembler: though I wish thy death,
I will not be thy executioner.

*Glo.* Then bid me kill myself, and I will do it.

*Anne.* I have already.

*Glo.* That was in thy rage:
Speak it again, and, even with the word,
This hand, which for thy love did kill thy love,
Shall, for thy love, kill a far truer love;
To both their deaths shalt thou be accessary.

*Anne.* I would I knew thy heart.

*Glo* 'Tis figured in my tongue.

*Anne.* I fear me both are false.

*Glo.* Then never man was true.

*Anne.* Well, well, put up your sword.

*Glo.* Say, then, my peace is made.

*Anne.* That shalt thou know hereafter.

*Glo.* But shall I live in hope?

*Anne.* All men, I hope, live so.

*Glo.* Vouchsafe to wear this ring.

*Anne.* To take is not to give.
[*She puts on the ring.*

*Glo.* Look, how this ring encompasseth thy finger,
Even so thy breast encloseth my poor heart;
Wear both of them, for both of them are thine.
And if thy poor devoted servant may
But beg one favour at thy gracious hand,
Thou dost confirm his happiness for ever.

*Anne.* What is it?

*Glo.* That it may please you leave these sad designs
To him that hath more cause to be a mourner,
And presently repair to Crosby Place;
Where,—after I have solemnly interr'd,
At Chertsey monastery, this noble king,
And wet his grave with my repentant tears,—
I will with all expedient duty see you:
For divers unknown reasons, I beseech you,
Grant me this boon. [joys me too

*Anne.* With all my heart; and much it
To see you are become so penitent.—
Tressel and Berkley, go along with me.

*Glo.* Bid me farewell.

*Anne.* 'Tis more than you deserve;
But since you teach me how to flatter you,

Imagine I have said farewell already.
　　*[Exeunt* Lady Anne, Tress., *and* Berk.
*Glo.* Sirs, take up the corse.
*Gent.*　　　Towards Chertsey, noble lord?
*Glo.* No, to White Friars; there attend my
　　coming.
　　　*[Exeunt the rest, with the Corpse.*
Was ever woman in this humour woo'd?
Was ever woman in this humour won?
I'll have her; but I will not keep her long.
What! I, that kill'd her husband and his
　　father,
To take her in her heart's extremest hate;
With curses in her mouth, tears in her eyes,
The bleeding witness of her hatred by;
Having God, her conscience, and these bars
　　against me,
And I no friends to back my suit withal,
But the plain devil and dissembling looks,
And yet to win her,—all the world to noth-
　　ing!
Ha!
Hath she forgot already that brave prince,
Edward, her lord, whom I, some three
　　months since,
Stabb'd in my angry mood at Tewksbury?
A sweeter and a lovelier gentleman,—
Fram'd in the prodigality of nature,
Young, valiant, wise, and, no doubt, right
　　royal,—
The spacious world cannot again afford:
And will she yet abase her eyes on me,
That cropp'd the golden prime of this sweet
　　prince,
And made her widow to a woeful bed?
On me, whose all not equals Edward's
　　moiety?
On me, that halt and am misshapen thus?
My dukedom to a beggarly denier,
I do mistake my person all this while:
Upon my life, she finds, although I cannot,
Myself to be a marvellous proper man.
I'll be at charges for a looking-glass;
And entertain a score or two of tailors,
To study fashions to adorn my body:
Since I am crept in favour with myself,
I will maintain it with some little cost.
But first I'll turn yon fellow in his grave;
And then return lamenting to my love.—
Shine out, fair sun, till I have bought a glass,
That I may see my shadow as I pass. *[Exit.*

Scene III.—London. *A Room in the Palace.*

*Enter* Queen Elizabeth, Lord Rivers,
　　*and* Lord Grey.

*Riv.* Have patience, madam: there's no
　　doubt his majesty
Will soon recover his accustom'd health.
*Grey.* In that you brook it ill, it makes
　　him worse:　　　　　　　　　[comfort,
Therefore, for God's sake, entertain good
And cheer his grace with quick and merry
　　words.

*Q. Eliz.* If he were dead, what would be-
　　tide on me?
*Grey.* No other harm but loss of such a
　　lord.
*Q. Eliz.* The loss of such a lord includes
　　all harms.　　　　　　　[a goodly son,
*Grey.* The heavens have bless'd you with
To be your comforter when he is gone.
*Q. Eliz.* Ah, he is young; and his minority
Is put unto the trust of Richard Gloster,
A man that loves not me, nor none of you.
*Riv.* Is it concluded he shall be protector?
*Q. Eliz.* It is determin'd, not concluded
　　yet:
But so it must be, if the king miscarry.

*Enter* Buckingham *and* Stanley.

*Grey.* Here come the Lords of Bucking-
　　ham and Stanley.　　　　　　[grace!
*Buck.* Good time of day unto your royal
*Stan.* God make your majesty joyful as
　　you have been!
*Q. Eliz.* The Countess Richmond, good
　　my Lord of Stanley,
To your good prayer will scarcely say amen.
Yet, Stanley, notwithstanding she's your
　　wife,
And loves not me, be you, good lord, as-
　　sur'd
I hate not you for her proud arrogance.
*Stan.* I do beseech you, either not believe
The envious slanders of her false accusers;
Or, if she be accus'd on true report,
Bear with her weakness, which I think pro-
　　ceeds
From wayward sickness, and no grounded
　　malice.　　　　　　　　[Lord of Stanley?
*Q. Eliz.* Saw you the king to-day, my
*Stan.* But now the Duke of Buckingham
　　and I
Are come from visiting his majesty.
*Q. Eliz.* What likelihood of his amend-
　　ment, lords?
*Buck.* Madam, good hope; his grace
　　speaks cheerfully.
*Q. Eliz.* God grant him health! Did you
　　confer with him?　　　　　[atonement
*Buck.* Ay, madam: he desires to make
Between the Duke of Gloster and your
　　brothers,
And between them and my lord chamber-
　　lain;
And sent to warn them to his royal presence.
*Q. Eliz.* Would all were well!—but that
　　will never be:
I fear our happiness is at the height.

*Enter* Gloster, Hastings, *and* Dorset.

*Glo.* They do me wrong, and I will not
　　endure it:—
Who are they that complain unto the king
That I, forsooth, am stern, and love them
　　not?
By Holy Paul, they lov; his grace but lightly

That fill his ears with such dissentious ru-
   mours.
Because I cannot flatter and speak fair,
Smile in men's faces, smooth, deceive, and
   cog,
Duck with French nods and apish courtesy,
I must be held a rancourous enemy.
Cannot a plain man live, and think no harm,
But thus his simple truth must be abus'd
By silken, sly insinuating Jacks? [your grace?
   *Grey.* To whom in all this presence speaks
   *Glo.* To thee, that hast nor honesty nor
   grace.
When have I injur'd thee? when done thee
   wrong?—
Or thee?—or thee?—or any of your faction?
A plague upon you all! His royal grace,—
Whom God preserve better than you would
   wish!—
Cannot be quiet scarce a breathing while,
But you must trouble him with lewd com-
   plaints.  [the matter.
   *Q. Eliz.* Brother of Gloster, you mistake
The king, on his own royal disposition,
And not provok'd by any suitor else—
Aiming, belike, at your interior hatred,
That in your outward action shows itself
Against my children, brothers, and myself—
Makes him to send; that thereby he may
   gather
The ground of your ill-will, and so remove
   it.
   *Glo.* I cannot tell: the world is grown so
   bad,
That wrens may prey where eagles dare not
   perch:
Since every Jack became a gentleman,
There's many a gentle person made a Jack.
   *Q. Eliz.* Come, come, we know your mean-
   ing, brother Gloster;
You envy my advancement, and my
   friends';
God grant we never may have need of you!
   *Glo.* Meantime, God grants that we have
   need of you:
Our brother is imprison'd by your means,
Myself disgrac'd, and the nobility
Held in contempt; while great promotions
Are daily given to ennoble those
That scarce, some two days since, were worth
   a noble.  [careful height
   *Q. Eliz.* By Him that raised me to this
From that contented hap which I enjoy'd,
I never did incense his majesty
Against the Duke of Clarence, but have been
An earnest advocate to plead for him.
My lord, you do me shameful injury,
Falsely to draw me in these vile suspects.
   *Glo.* You may deny that you were not the
   mean
Of my Lord Hastings' late imprisonment.
   *Riv.* She may, my lord; for,—
   *Glo.* She may, Lord Rivers?—why, who
   knows not so?

She may do more, sir, than denying that:
She may help you to many fair preferments;
And then deny her aiding hand therein,
And lay those honours on your high desert.
What may she not? She may, ay, marry, may
   she,—
   *Riv.* What, marry, may she?  [king,
   *Glo.* What, marry, may she! marry with a
A bachelor, a handsome stripling too:
I wis your grandam had a worser match.
   *Q. Eliz.* My Lord of Gloster, I have too
   long borne
Your blunt upbraidings and your bitter
   scoffs:
By heaven, I will acquaint his majesty
Of those gross taunts that oft I have en-
   dur'd.
I had rather be a country servant-maid
Than a great queen, with this condition,—
To be so baited, scorn'd, and stormed at.

*Enter* QUEEN MARGARET, *behind.*

Small joy have I in being England's queen.
   *Q. Mar.* And lessen'd be that small, God,
   I beseech Him!
Thy honour, state, and seat is due to me.
   *Glo.* What! threat you me with telling of
   the king?
Tell him, and spare not: look, what I have
   said
I will avouch in presence of the king:
I dare adventure to be sent to the Tower.
'Tis time to speak,—my pains are quite for-
   got.
   *Q. Mar.* Out, devil! I remember them too
   well:
Thou kill'dst my husband Henry in the
   Tower,
And Edward, my poor son, at Tewksbury.
   *Glo.* Ere you were queen, ay, or your hus-
   band king,
I was a pack-horse in his great affairs;
A weeder-out of his proud adversaries,
A liberal rewarder of his friends:
To royalize his blood I spilt mine own.
   *Q. Mar.* Ay, and much better blood than
   his or thine.  [band Grey
   *Glo.* In all which time you and your hus-
Were factious for the house of Lancaster;—
And, Rivers, so were you: was not your hus-
   band
In Margaret's battle at Saint Albans slain?
Let me put in your minds, if you forget,
What you have been ere this, and what you
   are;
Withal, what I have been, and what I am.
   *Q. Mar.* A murderous villain, and so still
   thou art.  [Warwick;
   *Glo.* Poor Clarence did forsake his father,
Ay, and forswore himself,—which Jesu par-
   don!—
   *Q. Mar.* Which God revenge!  [crown;
   *Glo.* To fight on Edward's party, for the
And for his meed, poor lord, he is mew'd up.

I would to God my heart were flint, like
　　Edward's,
Or Edward's soft and pitiful, like mine:
I am too childish-foolish for this world.
　　*Q. Mar.* Hie thee to hell for shame, and
　　leave this world,
Thou cacodemon! there thy kingdom is.
　　*Riv.* My Lord of Gloster, in those busy
　　days
Which here you urge to prove us enemies,
We follow'd then our lord, our sovereign
　　king:
So should we you, if you should be our king.
　　*Glo.* If I should be!—I had rather be a
　　pedler:
Far be it from my heart, the thought there-
　　of!
　　*Q. Eliz.* As little joy, my lord, as you sup-
　　pose
You should enjoy, were you this country's
　　king,—
As little joy you may suppose in me,
That I enjoy, being the queen thereof.
　　*Q. Mar.* As little joy enjoys the queen
　　thereof;
For I am she, and altogether joyless.
I can no longer hold me patient.—
　　　　　　　　　　　　　　[*Advancing.*
Hear me, you wrangling pirates, that fall out
In sharing that which you have pill'd from
　　me!
Which of you trembles not that looks on
　　me?
If not that, I being queen, you bow like
　　subjects,　　　　　　　　[rebels?—
Yet that, by you depos'd, you quake like
Ah, gentle villain, do not turn away!
　　*Glo.* Foul wrinkled witch, what mak'st
　　thou in my sight?　　　　[marr'd,
　　*Q. Mar.* But repetition of what thou hast
That will I make before I let thee go.
　　*Glo.* Wert thou not banished on pain of
　　death?
　　*Q. Mar.* I was; but I do find more pain in
　　banishment
Than death can yield me here by my abode.
A husband and a son thou ow'st to me,—
And thou a kingdom,—all of you allegiance:
This sorrow that I have, by right is yours;
And all the pleasures you usurp are mine.
　　*Glo.* The curse my noble father laid on
　　thee,
When thou didst crown his warlike brows
　　with paper,　　　　　　　[eyes;
And with thy scorns drew'st rivers from his
And then, to dry them, gav'st the duke a
　　clout
Steep'd in the faultless blood of pretty Rut-
　　land;—
His curses, then from bitterness of soul
Denounc'd against thee, are all fallen upon
　　thee;
And God, not we, hath plagu'd thy bloody
　　deed.

　　*Q. Eliz.* So just is God, to right the inno-
　　cent.
　　*Hast.* O, 'twas the foulest deed to slay
　　that babe,
And the most merciless that e'er was heard
　　of.
　　*Riv.* Tyrants themselves wept when it was
　　reported.
　　*Dor.* No man but prophesied revenge for
　　it.
　　*Buck.* Northumberland, then present,
　　wept to see it.　　　　　[fore I came,
　　*Q. Mar.* What, were you snarling all be-
Ready to catch each other by the throat,
And turn you all your hatred now on me?
Did York's dread curse prevail so much with
　　heaven
That Henry's death, my lovely Edward's
　　death,
Their kingdom's loss, my woeful banish-
　　ment,
Could all but answer for that peevish brat?
Can curses pierce the clouds and enter
　　heaven?—
Why, then, give way, dull clouds, to my
　　quick curses!—
Though not by war, by surfeit die your king,
As ours by murder, to make him a king!
Edward thy son, that now is Prince of
　　Wales,
For Edward my son, that was Prince of
　　Wales,
Die in his youth by like untimely violence!
Thyself a queen, for me that was a queen,
Outlive thy glory, like my wretched self!
Long mayst thou live to wail thy children's
　　loss;
And see another, as I see thee now,
Deck'd in thy rights, as thou art stall'd in
　　mine!
Long die thy happy days before thy death;
And, after many lengthen'd hours of grief,
Die neither mother, wife, nor England's
　　queen!—
Rivers and Dorset, you were standers by,—
And so wast thou, Lord Hastings,—when my
　　son　　　　　　　　　　　[pray him,
Was stabb'd with bloody daggers: God, I
That none of you may live your natural age,
But by some unlook'd accident cut off!
　　*Glo.* Have done thy charm, thou hateful
　　wither'd hag.
　　*Q. Mar.* And leave out thee? stay, dog, for
　　thou shalt hear me.
If heaven have any grievous plague in store,
Exceeding those that I can wish upon thee,
O, let them keep it till thy sins be ripe,
And then hurl down their indignation
On thee, the troubler of the poor world's
　　peace!
The worm of conscience still be-gnaw thy
　　soul!
Thy friends suspect for traitors while thou
　　liv'st,

And take deep traitors for thy dearest friends!
No sleep close up that deadly eye of thine,
Unless it be while some tormenting dream
Affrights thee with a hell of ugly devils!
Thou elvish-mark'd, abortive, rooting hog!
Thou that wast seal'd in thy nativity
The slave of nature and the son of hell!
Thou slander of thy heavy mother's womb!
Thou loathed issue of thy father's loins!
Thou rag of honour! thou detested—
*Glo.* Margaret.
*Q. Mar* Richard!
*Glo.* Ha!
*Q. Mar.* I call thee not.
*Glo.* I cry thee mercy, then; for I did think
That thou hadst call'd me all those bitter names.
*Q. Mar.* Why, so I did; but look'd for no reply.
O, let me make the period to my curse!
*Glo.* 'Tis done by me, and ends in—Margaret.
*Q. Eliz.* Thus have you breath'd your curse against yourself.
*Q. Mar.* Poor painted queen, vain flourish of my fortune!
Why strew'st thou sugar on that bottled spider,
Whose deadly web ensnareth thee about?
Fool, fool! thou whett'st a knife to kill thyself.
The day will come that thou shalt wish for me
To help thee curse this poisonous bunch-back'd toad.
*Hast.* False-boding woman, end thy frantic curse,
Lest to thy harm thou move our patience.
*Q. Mar.* Foul shame upon you! you have all mov'd mine.
*Riv.* Were you well serv'd, you would be taught your duty.   [do me duty,
*Q. Mar.* To serve me well, you all should
Teach me to be your queen, and you my subjects:
O, serve me well, and teach yourselves that duty!
*Dor.* Dispute not with her,—she is lunatic.
*Q. Mar.* Peace, master marquis, you are malapert:
Your fire-new stamp of honour is scarce current:
O, that your young nobility could judge
What 'twere to lose it, and be miserable!
They that stand high have many blasts to shake them;
And if they fall they dash themselves to pieces.
*Glo.* Good counsel, marry:—learn it, learn it, marquis.
*Dor.* It touches you, my lord, as much as me.

*Glo.* Ay, and much more: but I was born so high
Our aery buildeth in the cedar's top,
And dallies with the wind, and scorns the sun.
*Q. Mar.* And turns the sun to shade;—alas! alas!—
Witness my son, now in the shade of death;
Whose bright out-shining beams thy cloudy wrath
Hath in eternal darkness folded up.
Your aery buildeth in our aery's nest:—
O God, that see'st it, do not suffer it;
As it was won with blood, lost be it so!
*Buck.* Peace, peace, for shame, if not for charity.   [to me:
*Q. Mar.* Urge neither charity nor shame
Uncharitably with me have you dealt,
And shamefully my hopes by you are butcher'd.
My charity is outrage, life my shame,—
And in my shame still live my sorrow's rage!
*Buck.* Have done, have done.   [thy hand,
*Q. Mar.* O princely Buckingham, I'll kiss
In sign of league and amity with thee:
Now fair befall thee and thy noble house!
Thy garments are not spotted with our blood,
Nor thou within the compass of my curse.
*Buck.* Nor no one here; for curses never pass
The lips of those that breathe them in the air.
*Q. Mar.* I will not think but they ascend the sky,
And there awake God's gentle sleeping peace.
O Buckingham, take heed of yonder dog!
Look, when he fawns he bites; and when he bites,
His venom tooth will rankle to the death:
Have not to do with him, beware of him;
Sin, death, and hell have set their marks on him,
And all their ministers attend on him.
*Glo.* What doth she say, my Lord of Buckingham?   [lord.
*Buck.* Nothing that I respect, my gracious
*Q. Mar.* What, dost thou scorn me for my gentle counsel?
And soothe the devil that I warn thee from?
O, but remember this another day,
When he shall split thy very heart with sorrow,
And say, poor Margaret was a prophetess!—
Live each of you the subjects to his hate,
And he to yours, and all of you to God's!
[*Exit.*
*Hast.* My hair doth stand on end to hear her curses.   [at liberty.
*Riv.* And so doth mine: I muse why she's
*Glo.* I cannot blame her: by God's holy mother,
She hath had too much wrong; and I repent

My part thereof that I have done to her.

*Q. Eliz.* I never did her any, to my knowledge.          [*wrong.*

*Glo.* Yet you have all the vantage of her
I was too hot to do somebody good,
That is too cold in thinking of it now.
Marry, as for Clarence, he is well repaid;
He is frank'd up to fatting for his pains;
God pardon them that are the cause thereof!

*Riv.* A virtuous and a Christian-like conclusion,
To pray for them that have done scathe to
us.

*Glo.* So do I ever, being well advis'd;
For had I curs'd now, I had curs'd myself.
         [*Aside.*

*Enter* CATESBY.

*Cates.* Madam, his majesty doth call for
you,—
And for your grace,—and you, my noble
lords.

*Q. Eliz.* Catesby, I come.—Lords, will you
go with me?

*Riv.* We wait upon your grace.
         [*Exeunt all but* GLOSTER.

*Glo.* I do the wrong, and first begin to
brawl.
The secret mischiefs that I set abroach
I lay unto the grievous charge of others.
Clarence,—whom I, indeed, have cast in
darkness,—
I do beweep to many simple gulls;
Namely, to Stanley, Hastings, Buckingham;
And tell them 'tis the queen and her allies
That stir the king against the duke my
brother.
Now, they believe it; and withal whet me
To be revenged on Rivers, Vaughan, Grey:
But then I sigh; and, with a piece of Scrip-
ture,
Tell them that God bids us do good for evil:
And thus I clothe my naked villany
With odd old ends stol'n forth of holy writ;
And seem a saint when most I play the
devil.—
But, soft! here come my executioners.

*Enter two* Murderers.

How now, my hardy, stout-resolved mates!
Are you now going to despatch this thing?

1 *Murd.* We are, my lord, and come to
have the warrant,
That we may be admitted where he is.

*Glo.* Well thought upon;—I have it here
about me:          [*Gives the warrant.*
When you have done, repair to Crosby Place.
But, sirs, be sudden in the execution,
Withal obdurate, do not hear him plead;
For Clarence is well-spoken, and perhaps
May move your hearts to pity, if you mark
him.

1 *Murd.* Tut, tut, my lord, we will not
stand to prate;

Talkers are no good doers: be assur'd
We go to use our hands, and not our tongues.

*Glo.* Your eyes drop millstones when
fools' eyes fall tears:
I like you, lads;—about your business
straight;
Go, go, despatch.

1 *Murd.*        We will, my noble lord.
         [*Exeunt.*

SCENE IV.—LONDON. *A Room in the Tower.*

*Enter* CLARENCE *and* BRAKENBURY.

*Brak.* Why looks your grace so heavily to-
day?

*Clar.* O, I have pass'd a miserable night,
So full of fearful dreams, of ugly sights,
That, as I am a Christian faithful man,
I would not spend another such a night
Though 'twere to buy a world of happy
days.—
So full of dismal terror was the time!

*Brak.* What was your dream, my lord? I
pray you, tell me.        [the Tower,

*Clar.* Methought that I had broken from
And was embark'd to cross to Burgundy;
And, in my company, my brother Gloster;
Who from my cabin tempted me to walk
Upon the hatches: thence we look'd toward
England,
And cited up a thousand heavy times,
During the wars of York and Lancaster,
That had befall'n us. As we pac'd along
Upon the giddy footing of the hatches,
Methought that Gloster stumbled; and, in
falling,          [board
Struck me, that thought to stay him, over-
Into the tumbling billows of the main.
O Lord! methought what pain it was to
drown!
What dreadful noise of water in mine ears!
What sights of ugly death within mine eyes!
Methought I saw a thousand fearful wrecks;
A thousand men that fishes gnaw'd upon;
Wedges of gold, great anchors, heaps of
pearl,
Inestimable stones, unvalu'd jewels,
All scatter'd in the bottom of the sea: [holes
Some lay in dead men's skulls; and in those
Where eyes did once inhabit there were
crept,—
As 'twere in scorn of eyes,—reflecting gems,
That woo'd the slimy bottom of the deep,
And mock'd the dead bones that lay scat-
ter'd by.

*Brak.* Had you such leisure in the time of
death
To gaze upon the secrets of the deep? [strive

*Clar.* Methought I had; and often did I
To yield the ghost: but still the envious flood
Stopp'd in my soul, and would not let it
forth
To find the empty, vast, and wandering air;
But smother'd it within my panting bulk,
Which almost burst to belch it in the sea.

*Brak.* Awak'd you not with this sore agony?

*Clar.* No, no, my dream was lengthen'd after life;

O, then began the tempest to my soul!

I pass'd, methought, the melancholy flood

With that grim ferryman which poets write of,

Unto the kingdom of perpetual night.

The first that there did greet my stranger soul

Was my great father-in-law, renowned Warwick;

Who cried aloud, *What scourge for perjury*

*Can this dark monarchy afford false Clarence?*

And so he vanish'd: then came wandering by

A shadow like an Angel, with bright hair

Dabbled in blood; and he shriek'd out aloud,

*Clarence is come,—false, fleeting, perjur'd Clarence,—*

*That stabb'd me in the field by Tewksbury;—*

*Seize on him, Furies, take him to your torments!*

With that, methought, a legion of foul fiends

Environ'd me, and howled in mine ears

Such hideous cries that, with the very noise,

I trembling wak'd, and for a season after

Could not believe but that I was in hell,—

Such terrible impression made my dream.

*Brak.* No marvel, lord, though it affrighted you;

I am afraid, methinks, to hear you tell it.

*Clar.* O Brakenbury, I have done those things

That now give evidence against my soul,

For Edward's sake; and see how he requites me!—　　　　　　　[thee,

O God! If my deep prayers cannot appease

But thou wilt be aveng'd on my misdeeds,

Yet execute thy wrath in me alone,—

O, spare my guiltless wife and my poor children!—

Keeper, I pr'ythee, sit by me awhile;

My soul is heavy, and I fain would sleep.

*Brak.* I will, my lord; God give your grace good rest!—

[CLARENCE *reposes himself on a chair.*

Sorrow breaks seasons and reposing hours,

Makes the night morning, and the noontide night.

Princes have but their titles for their glories,

An outward honour for an inward toil;

And, for, unfelt imaginations,

They often feel a world of restless cares:

So that, between their titles and low name,

There's nothing differs but the outward fame.

*Enter the two* Murderers.

1 *Murd.* Ho! who's here?

*Brak.* What wouldst thou, fellow? and how cam'st thou thither?

1 *Murd.* I would speak with Clarence, and I came hither on my legs.

*Brak.* What, so brief?

2 *Murd.* 'Tis better, sir, than to be tedious.—

Let him see our commission: talk no more.

[*A paper is delivered to* BRAK., *who reads it.*

*Brak.* I am, in this, commanded to deliver

The noble Duke of Clarence to your hands:—

I will not reason what is meant hereby,

Because I will be guiltless of the meaning.

There lies the duke asleep,—and there the keys;

I'll to the king, and signify to him

That thus I have resign'd to you my charge.

1 *Murd.* You may, sir; 'tis a point of wisdom: fare you well.

[*Exit* BRAKENBURY.

2 *Murd.* What, shall we stab him as he sleeps?

1 *Murd.* No; he'll say 'twas done cowardly, when he wakes.

2 *Murd.* When he wakes! why, fool, he shall never wake until the great judgment-day.

1 *Murd.* Why, then he'll say we stabb'd him sleeping.

2 *Murd.* The urging of that word judgment hath bred a kind of remorse in me.

1 *Murd.* What, art thou afraid?

2 *Murd.* Not to kill him, having a warrant for it; but to be damned for killing him, from the which no warrant can defend me.

1 *Murd.* I thought thou hadst been resolute.

2 *Murd.* So I am, to let him live.

1 *Murd.* I'll back to the Duke of Gloster, and tell him so.

2 *Murd.* Nay, I pr'ythee, stay a little: I hope my holy humour will change; it was wont to hold me but while one tells twenty.

1 *Murd.* How dost thou feel thyself now?

2 *Murd.* Faith, some certain dregs of conscience are yet within me.

1 *Murd.* Remember our reward, when the deed's done.

2 *Murd.* Zounds, he dies: I had forgot the reward.

1 *Murd.* Where's thy conscience now?

2 *Murd.* In the Duke of Gloster's purse.

1 *Murd.* So, when he opens his purse to give us our reward, thy conscience flies out.

2 *Murd.* 'Tis no matter; let it go; there's few or none will entertain it.

1 *Murd.* What if it come to thee again?

2 *Murd.* I'll not meddle with it,—it makes a man a coward; a man cannot steal, but it accuseth him; a man cannot swear, but it

checks him; a man cannot lie with his neighbour's wife, but it detects him: 'tis a blushing shame-faced spirit that mutinies in a man's bosom, it fills one full of obstacles: it made me once restore a purse of gold that by chance I found; it beggars any man that keeps it: it is turned out of all towns and cities for a dangerous thing; and every man that means to live well endeavours to trust to himself and live without it.

*1 Murd.* Zounds, it is even now at my elbow, persuading me not to kill the duke.

*2 Murd.* Take the devil in thy mind, and believe him not: he would insinuate with thee but to make thee sigh.

*1 Murd.* I am strong-framed, he cannot prevail with me.

*2 Murd.* Spoke like a tall fellow that respects his reputation. Come, shall we fall to work?

*1 Murd.* Take him on the costard with the hilts of thy sword, and then throw him into the malmsey-butt in the next room.

*2 Murd.* O excellent device! and make a sop of him.

*1 Murd.* Soft! he wakes.

*2 Murd.* Strike!

*1 Murd.* No, we'll reason with him.

*Clar.* Where art thou, keeper? give me a cup of wine.

*1 Murd.* You shall have wine enough, my lord, anon.

*Clar.* In God's name, what art thou?

*1 Murd.* A man, as you are.

*Clar.* But not, as I am, royal.

*1 Murd.* Nor you, as we are, loyal.

*Clar.* Thy voice is thunder, but thy looks are humble.

*1 Murd.* My voice is now the king's, my looks mine own.

*Clar.* How darkly and how deadly dost thou speak!

Your eyes do menace me: why look you pale?

Who sent you hither? Wherefore do you come?

*Both Murd.* To, to, to—

*Clar.* To murder me?

*Both Murd.* Ay, ay.

*Clar.* You scarcely have the hearts to tell me so,

And therefore cannot have the hearts to do it.

Wherein, my friends, have I offended you?

*1 Murd.* Offended us you have not, but the king.

*Clar.* I shall be reconcil'd to him again.

*2 Murd.* Never, my lord; therefore prepare to die.

*Clar.* Are you drawn forth among a world of men

To slay the innocent? What is my offence?

What is the evidence that doth accuse me?

Where lawful quest have given their verdict up

Unto the frowning judge? or who pronounc'd

The bitter sentence of poor Clarence's death?

Before I be convict by course of law,

To threaten me with death is most unlawful.

I charge you, as you hope to have redemption

By Christ's dear blood shed for our grievous sins,

That you depart, and lay no hands on me:

The deed you undertake is damnable.

*1 Murd.* What we will do, we do upon command.

*2 Murd.* And he that hath commanded is our king.                                [kings

*Clar.* Erroneous vassals! the great King of Hath in the table of his law commanded

That thou shalt do no murder: will you then Spurn at his edict, and fulfil a man's?

Take heed; for he holds vengeance in his hand,

To hurl upon their heads that break his law.

*2 Murd.* And that same vengeance doth he hurl on thee

For false forswearing, and for murder too:

Thou didst receive the sacrament to fight

In quarrel of the house of Lancaster.

*1 Murd.* And, like a traitor to the name of God,

Didst break that vow; and with thy treacherous blade

Unripp'dst the bowels of thy sovereign's son.

*2 Murd.* Whom thou wast sworn to cherish and defend.

*1 Murd.* How canst thou urge God's dreadful law to us,

When thou hast broke it in such dear degree?

*Clar.* Alas! for whose sake did I that ill deed?

For Edward, for my brother, for his sake:

He sends you not to murder me for this;

For in that sin he is as deep as I.

If God will be avenged for the deed,

O, know you yet, he doth it publicly:

Take not the quarrel from his powerful arm;

He needs no indirect nor lawless course

To cut off those that have offended him.

*1 Murd.* Who made thee, then, a bloody minister

When gallant-springing brave Plantagenet,

That princely novice, was struck dead by thee?

*Clar.* My brother's love, the devil, and my rage.                              [thy faults,

*1 Murd.* Thy brother's love, our duty, and

Provoke us hither now to slaughter thee.

*Clar.* If you do love my brother, hate not me;

I am his brother, and I love him well.

If you are hir'd for meed, go back again,

And I will send you to my brother Gloster,

Who shall reward you better for my life
Than Edward will for tidings of my death.

  2 *Murd.* You are deceiv'd, your brother
    Gloster hates you.    [me dear:
  *Clar.* O, no, he loves me, and he holds
Go you to him from me.
  *Both Murd.*        Ay, so we will.
  *Clar.* Tell him, when that our princely
    father York
Bless'd his three sons with his victorious arm,
And charg'd us from his soul to love each
    other,
He little thought of this divided friendship:
Bid Gloster think on this, and he will weep.
  1 *Murd.* Ay, millstones; as he lesson'd us
    to weep.
  *Clar.* O, do not slander him, for he is kind.
  1 *Murd.* Right as snow in harvest.—Come,
    you deceive yourself:
'Tis he that sends us to destroy you here.
  *Clar.* It cannot be; for he bewept my for-
    tune,
And hugg'd me in his arms, and swore, with
    sobs,
That he would labour my delivery.
  1 *Murd.* Why, so he doth, when he deliv-
    ers you
From this earth's thraldom to the joys of
    heaven.
  2 *Murd.* Make peace with God, for you
    must die, my lord.
  *Clar.* Have you that holy feeling in your
    souls,
To counsel me to make my peace with God,
And are you yet to your own souls so blind
That you will war with God by murdering
    me?—
O, sirs, consider, they that set you on
To do this deed will hate you for the deed.
  2 *Murd.* What shall we do?
  *Clar.*      Relent, and save your souls.
  1 *Murd.* Relent! 'tis cowardly and wom-
    anish.    [ilish.
  *Clar.* Not to relent is beastly, savage, dev-
Which of you, if you were a prince's son,
Being pent from liberty, as I am now,—
If two such murderers as yourself came to
    you,—
Would not entreat for life?—
My friend, I spy some pity in thy looks;
O, if thine eye be not a flatterer,
Come thou on my side, and entreat for me,
As you would beg, were you in my distress:
A begging prince what beggar pities not?
  2 *Murd.* Look behind you, my lord.
  1 *Murd.* Take that, and that: if all this
    will not do,    [*Stabs him.*
I'll drown you in the malmsey-butt within.
    [*Exit with the body.*
  2 *Murd.* A bloody deed, and desperately
    despatch'd!
How fain, like Pilate, would I wash my
    hands
Of this most grievous guilty murder done!

    *Re-enter* First Murderer.

  1 *Murd.* How now, what mean'st thou,
    that thou help'st me not?
By heaven, the duke shall know how slack
    you have been.    [his brother!
  2 *Murd.* I would he knew that I had sav'd
Take thou the fee, and tell him what I say;
For I repent me that the duke is slain. [*Exit.*
  1 *Murd.* So do not I: go, coward as thou
    art.—
Well, I'll go hide the body in some hole,
Till that the duke give order for his burial:
And when I have my meed, I will away;
For this will out, and then I must not stay.
    [*Exit.*

## ACT II.

SCENE I.—LONDON. *A Room in the Palace.*

*Enter* KING EDWARD, *led in sick;* QUEEN
  ELIZABETH, DORSET, RIVERS, HASTINGS,
  BUCKINGHAM, GREY, *and others.*

  *K. Edw.* Why, so;—now have I done a
    good day's work:—
You peers, continue this united league:
I every day expect an embassage
From my Redeemer, to redeem me hence;
And now in peace my soul shall part to
    heaven,
Since I have made my friends at peace on
    earth.
Rivers and Hastings, take each other's hand;
Dissemble not your hatred, swear your love.
  *Riv.* By heaven, my soul is purg'd from
    grudging hate;
And with my hand I seal my true heart's
    love.
  *Hast.* So thrive I, as I truly swear the
    like!
  *K. Edw.* Take heed you dally not before
    your king;
Lest he that is the supreme King of kings
Confound your hidden falsehood, and award
Either of you to be the other's end.
  *Hast.* So prosper I, as I swear perfect
    love!
  *Riv.* And I, as I love Hastings with my
    heart!
  *K. Edw.* Madam, yourself are not exempt
    from this,—
Nor you, son Dorset,—Buckingham, nor
    you;—
You have been factious one against the other.
Wife, love Lord Hastings, let him kiss your
    hand;
And what you do, do it unfeignedly.
  *Q. Eliz.* There, Hastings; I will never more
    remember
Our former hatred, so thrive I and mine!
  *K. Edw.* Dorset, embrace him;—Hastings,
    love lord marquis.    [test,
  *Dor.* This interchange of love I here pro-
Upon my part shall be inviolable.

*Hast.* And so swear I. [*Embraces* DORSET.

*K. Edw.* Now, princely Buckingham, seal thou this league
With thy embracements to my wife's allies,
And make me happy in your unity.

*Buck.* Whenever Buckingham doth turn his hate
Upon your grace [*to the* QUEEN], but with all duteous love
Doth cherish you and yours, God punish me
With hate in those where I expect most love!
When I have most need to employ a friend,
And most assured that he is a friend,
Deep, hollow, treacherous, and full of guile,
Be he unto me!—this do I beg of heaven
When I am cold in love to you or yours.
[*Embracing* RIVERS, &c.

*K. Edw.* A pleasing cordial, princely Buckingham,
Is this thy vow unto my sickly heart.
There wanteth now our brother Gloster here,
To make the blessed period of this peace.

*Buck.* And, in good time, here comes the noble duke.

*Enter* GLOSTER.

*Glo.* Good-morrow to my sovereign king and queen;
And, princely peers, a happy time of day!

*K. Edw.* Happy, indeed, as we have spent the day.
Gloster, we have done deeds of charity;
Made peace of enmity, fair love of hate,
Between these swelling wrong-incensed peers.

*Glo.* A blessed labour, my most sovereign lord.—
Among this princely heap, if any here,
By false intelligence or wrong surmise,
Hold me a foe;
If I unwittingly, or in my rage,
Have aught committed that is hardly borne
By any in this presence, I desire
To reconcile me to his friendly peace:
'Tis death to me to be at enmity;
I hate it, and desire all good men's love.—
First, madam, I entreat true peace of you,
Which I will purchase with my duteous service;—
Of you, my noble cousin Buckingham,
If ever any grudge were lodg'd between us;—
Of you, and you, Lord Rivers, and of Dorset,
That all without desert have frown'd on me;
Of you, Lord Woodville, and, Lord Scales, of you;—
Dukes, earls, lords, gentlemen;—indeed, of all.
I do not know that Englishman alive
With whom my soul is any jot at odds
More than the infant that is born to-night:
I thank my God for my humility. [after:—

*Q. Eliz.* A holiday shall this be kept here-
I would to God all strifes were well compounded.—
My sovereign lord, I do beseech your highness
To take our brother Clarence to your grace.

*Glo.* Why, madam, have I offer'd love for this,
To be so flouted in this royal presence?
Who knows not that the gentle duke is dead?
[*They all start.*
You do him injury to scorn his corse.

*K. Edw.* Who knows not he is dead! who knows he is? [this!

*Q. Eliz.* All-seeing heaven, what a world is

*Buck.* Look I so pale, Lord Dorset, as the rest? [the presence

*Dor.* Ay, my good lord; and no man in
But his red colour hath forsook his cheeks.

*K. Edw.* Is Clarence dead? the order was revers'd. [died,

*Glo.* But he, poor man, by your first order
And that a winged mercury did bear;
Some tardy cripple bore the countermand
That came too lag to see him buried.
God grant that some, less noble and less royal,
Nearer in bloody thoughts, but not in blood,
Deserve not worse than wretched Clarence did,
And yet go current from suspicion!

*Enter* STANLEY.

*Stan.* A boon, my sovereign, for my service done! [of sorrow.

*K. Edw.* I pr'ythee, peace: my soul is full

*Stan.* I will not rise unless your highness hear me.

*K. Edw.* Then say at once what is it thou request'st.

*Stan.* The forfeit, sovereign, of my servant's life;
Who slew to-day a riotous gentleman
Lately attendant on the Duke of Norfolk.

*K. Edw.* Have I a tongue to doom my brother's death,
And shall that tongue give pardon to a slave?
My brother kill'd no man,—his fault was thought,
And yet his punishment was bitter death.
Who su'd to me for him? who, in my wrath,
Kneel'd at my feet, and bid me be advis'd?
Who spoke of brotherhood? who spoke of love?
Who told me how the poor soul did forsake
The mighty Warwick, and did fight for me?
Who told me, in the field at Tewksbury,
When Oxford had me down, he rescu'd me,
And said, *Dear brother, live, and be a king?*
Who told me, when we both lay in the field
Frozen almost to death, how he did lap me
Even in his garments, and did give himself,
All thin and naked, to the numb-cold night?
All this from my remembrance brutish wrath
Sinfully pluck'd, and not a man of you
Had so much grace to put it in my mind.

But when your carters or your waiting-vas-
sals
Have done a drunken slaughter, and defac'd
The precious image of our dear Redeemer,
You straight are on your knees for pardon,
pardon;
And I, unjustly too, must grant it you:—
But for my brother not a man would speak;—
Nor I, ungracious, speak unto myself
For him, poor soul. The proudest of you all
Have been beholden to him in his life;
Yet none of you would once beg for his
life.—
O God, I fear thy justice will take hold
On me, and you, and mine, and yours, for
this!
Come, Hastings, help me to my closet.
Ah, poor Clarence!
          [*Exeunt* KING, QUEEN, HAST., RIV.,
                    DOR., *and* GREY.
  *Glo.* This is the fruit of rashness!—Mark'd
you not
How the guilty kindred of the queen
Look'd pale when they did hear of Clarence'
death?
O, they did urge it still unto the king!
God will revenge it.—Come, lords, will you
go
To comfort Edward with our company?
  *Buck.* We wait upon your grace. [*Exeunt.*

SCENE II.—*Another Room in the Palace.*

*Enter the* DUCHESS OF YORK, *with a* Son *and*
          Daughter *of* CLARENCE.

  *Son.* Good grandam, tell us, is our father
dead?
  *Duch.* No, boy.                [your breast,
  *Daugh.* Why do you weep so oft, and beat
And cry, *O Clarence, my unhappy son!*
  *Son.* Why do you look on us, and shake
your head,
And call us orphans, wretches, castaways,
If that our noble father be alive?      [both;
  *Duch.* My pretty cousins, you mistake me
I do lament the sickness of the king,
As loth to lose him, not your father's death;
It were lost sorrow to wail one that's lost.
  *Son.* Then you conclude, my grandam, he
is dead.
The king mine uncle is to blame for this:
God will revenge it; whom I will importune
With earnest prayers all to that effect.
  *Daugh.* And so will I.
  *Duch.* Peace, children, peace! the king
doth love you well:
Incapable and shallow innocents,    [death.
You cannot guess who caus'd your father's
  *Son.* Grandam, we can; for my good
uncle Gloster
Told me, the king, provok'd to it by the
queen,
Devis'd impeachments to imprison him:
And when my uncle told me so, he wept,
And pitied me, and kindly kiss'd my cheek;

Bade me rely on him as on my father,
And he would love me dearly as his child.
  *Duch.* Ah, that deceit should steal such
gentle shape,
And with a virtuous visard hide deep vice!
He is my son; ay, and therein my shame;
Yet from my dugs he drew not this deceit.
  *Son.* Think you my uncle did dissemble,
grandam?
  *Duch.* Ay, boy.                [is this?
  *Son.* I cannot think it.—Hark! what noise

*Enter* QUEEN ELIZABETH, *distractedly;*
    RIVERS *and* DORSET *following her.*

  *Q. Eliz.* Ah, who shall hinder me to wail
and weep,
To chide my fortune, and torment myself?
I'll join with black despair against my soul,
And to myself become an enemy. [patience?
  *Duch.* What means this scene of rude im-
  *Q. Eliz.* To make an act of tragic violence:
Edward, my lord, thy son, our king, is
dead.—
Why grow the branches when the root is
gone?
Why wither not the leaves that want their
sap?—
If you will live, lament; if die, be brief,
That our swift-winged souls may catch the
king's;
Or, like obedient subjects, follow him
To his new kingdom of perpetual rest.
  *Duch.* Ah, so much interest have I in thy
sorrow
As I had title in thy noble husband!
I have bewept a worthy husband's death,
And liv'd by looking on his images:
But now two mirrors of his princely sem-
blance
Are crack'd in pieces by malignant death,
And I for comfort have but one false glass,
That grieves me when I see my shame in him.
Thou art a widow; yet thou art a mother,
And hast the comfort of thy children left:
But death hath snatch'd my husband from
mine arms,                      [hands,—
And pluck'd two crutches from my feeble
Clarence and Edward. O, what cause have
I,—
Thine being but a moiety of my moan,—
To overgo thy woes and drown thy cries?
  *Son.* Ah, aunt, you wept not for our fath-
er's death!
How can we aid you with our kindred tears?
  *Daugh.* Our fatherless distress was left
unmoan'd,
Your widow-dolour likewise be unwept!
  *Q. Eliz.* Give me no help in lamentation;
I am not barren to bring forth complaints:
All springs reduce their currents to mine
eyes,
That I, being govern'd by the watery moon,
May send forth plenteous tears to drown the
world!

Ah for my husband, for my dear Lord Ed-
　　ward!

　*Chil.* Ah for our father, for our dear Lord
　　Clarence!　　　　　　　[and Clarence!

*Duch.* Alas for both, both mine, Edward

*Q. Eliz.* What stay had I but Edward?
　　and he's gone.　　　　　[and he's gone.

*Chil.* What stay had we but Clarence?

*Duch.* What stays had I but they? and
　　they are gone.　　　　　　　　[loss!

*Q. Eliz.* Was never widow had so dear a

*Chil.* Were never orphans had so dear a
　　loss!

*Duch.* Was never mother had so dear a
　　loss!

Alas, I am the mother of these griefs!
Their woes are parcell'd, mine are general.
She for an Edward weeps, and so do I;
I for a Clarence weep, so doth not she:
These babes for Clarence weep, and so do I;
I for an Edward weep, so do not they:—
Alas, you three, on me, threefold distress'd,
Pour all your tears! I am your sorrow's
　　nurse,
And I will pamper it with lamentation.

　*Dor.* Comfort, dear mother: God is much
　　displeas'd
That you take with unthankfulness his do-
　　ing:
In common worldly things 'tis call'd ungrate-
　　ful,
With dull unwillingness to repay a debt
Which with a bounteous hand was kindly
　　lent;
Much more to be thus opposite with heaven,
For it requires the royal debt it lent you.

　*Riv.* Madam, bethink you, like a careful
　　mother,　　　　　　　　　　[for him;
Of the young prince your son: send straight
Let him be crown'd; in him your comfort
　　lives:
Drown desperate sorrow in dead Edward's
　　grave,
And plant your joys in living Edward's
　　throne.

*Enter* GLOSTER, BUCKINGHAM, STANLEY,
　　HASTINGS, RATCLIFFE, *and others.*

　*Glo.* Sister, have comfort: all of us have
　　cause
To wail the dimming of our shining star;
But none can cure their harms by wailing
　　them.—
Madam, my mother, I do cry your mercy;
I did not see your grace:—humbly on my
　　knee
I crave your blessing.　　　　[in thy breast,

　*Duch.* God bless thee; and put meekness
Love, charity, obedience, and true duty!

　*Glo.* Amen; and make me die a good old
　　man!—
That is the butt end of a mother's blessing;
I marvel that her grace did leave it out.
　　　　　　　　　　　　　　　　[*Aside.*

　*Buck.* You cloudy princes and heart-sor-
　　rowing peers,
That bear this heavy mutual load of moan,
Now cheer each other in each other's love:
Though we have spent our harvest of this
　　king,
We are to reap the harvest of his son.
The broken rancour of your high-swoln
　　hearts,
But lately splinter'd, knit, and join'd to-
　　gether,
Must gently be preserv'd, cherish'd, and
　　kept:
Me seemeth good that, with some little train.
Forthwith from Ludlow the young prince be
　　fet
Hither to London, to be crown'd our king.

　*Riv.* Why with some little train, my Lord
　　of Buckingham?

　*Buck.* Marry, my lord, lest, by a multi-
　　tude,
The new-heal'd wound of malice should
　　break out;
Which would be so much the more danger-
　　ous
By how much the estate is green and yet un-
　　govern'd:
Where every horse bears his commanding
　　rein,
And may direct his course as please himself,
As well the fear of harm as harm apparent,
In my opinion, ought to be prevented.

　*Glo.* I hope the king made peace with all
　　of us;
And the compact is firm and true in me.

　*Riv.* And so in me; and so, I think, in all:
Yet, since it is but green, it should be put
To no apparent likelihood of breach,
Which haply by much company might be
　　urg'd:
Therefore I say with noble Buckingham,
That it is meet so few should fetch the
　　prince.

　*Hast.* And so say I.

　*Glo.* Then be it so; and go we to deter-
　　mine
Who they shall be that straight shall post to
　　Ludlow.
Madam,—and you, my mother,—will you go
To give your censures in this business?
　　　　　　　[*Exeunt all but* BUCK. *and* GLO.

　*Buck.* My lord, whoever journeys to the
　　prince,
For God's sake, let not us two stay at home;
For by the way I'll sort occasion,
As index to the story we late talk'd of,
To part the queen's proud kindred from the
　　prince.

　*Glo.* My other self, my counsel's consis-
　　tory,
My oracle, my prophet!—my dear cousin,
I, as a child, will go by thy direction.
Toward Ludlow then, for we'll not stay be-
　　hind.　　　　　　　　　　　　[*Exeunt.*

SCENE III.—LONDON. *A Street.*

*Enter two* Citizens, *meeting.*

1 *Cit.* Good-morrow, neighbour: whither away so fast?

2 *Cit.* I promise you, I scarcely know myself:
Hear you the news abroad?

1 *Cit.*　　　Yes,—that the king is dead.

2 *Cit.* Ill news, by'r lady: seldom comes the better:
I fear, I fear 'twill prove a giddy world.

*Enter a third* Citizen.

3 *Cit.* Neighbours, God speed!

1 *Cit.*　　　Give you good-morrow, sir.

3 *Cit.* Doth the news hold of good King Edward's death?　　　[while!

2 *Cit.* Ay, sir, it is too true; God help, the

3 *Cit.* Then, masters, look to see a troublous world.

1 *Cit.* No, no, by God's good grace, his son shall reign.　　　[by a child!

3 *Cit.* Woe to that land that's govern'd

2 *Cit.* In him there is a hope of government,
Which, in his nonage, council under him,
And, in his full and ripen'd years, himself,
No doubt, shall then, and till then, govern well.

1 *Cit.* So stood the state when Henry the Sixth
Was crown'd in Paris but at nine months old.

3 *Cit.* Stood the state so? No, no, good friends, God wot;
For then this land was famously enrich'd
With politic grave counsel; then the king
Had virtuous uncles to protect his grace.

1 *Cit.* Why, so hath this, both by his father and mother.

3 *Cit.* Better it were they all came by his father,
Or by his father there were none at all;
For emulation now, who shall be nearest,
Will touch us all too near if God prevent not.
O, full of danger is the Duke of Gloster!
And the queen's sons and brothers haught and proud:
And were they to be rul'd, and not to rule,
This sickly land might solace as before.

1 *Cit.* Come, come, we fear the worst; all will be well.

3 *Cit.* When clouds are seen, wise men put on their cloaks;
When great leaves fall, then winter is at hand;
When the sun sets, who doth not look for night?
Untimely storms make men expect a dearth.
All may be well; but, if God sort it so,
'Tis more than we deserve or I expect.

2 *Cit.* Truly, the hearts of men are full of fear:
You cannot reason almost with a man
That looks not heavily and full of dread.

3 *Cit.* Before the days of change, still is it so:
By a divine instinct men's minds mistrust
Ensuing danger; as, by proof, we see
The water swell before a boisterous storm.
But leave it all to God.—Whither away?

2 *Cit.* Marry, we were sent for to the justices.

3 *Cit.* And so was I: I'll bear you company.　　　[*Exeunt.*

SCENE IV.—LONDON. *A Room in the Palace.*

*Enter the* ARCHBISHOP OF YORK, *the young* DUKE OF YORK, QUEEN ELIZABETH, *and the* DUCHESS OF YORK.

*Arch.* Last night, I hear, they at Northampton lay;
And at Stony-Stratford will they be to-night:
To-morrow or next day they will be here.

*Duch.* I long with all my heart to see the prince:
I hope he is much grown since last I saw him.

*Q. Eliz.* But I hear no; they say my son of York
Has almost overta'en him in his growth.

*York.* Ay, mother; but I would not have it so.

*Duch.* Why, my young cousin? it is good to grow.　　　[at supper,

*York.* Grandam, one night, as we did sit
My Uncle Rivers talk'd how I did grow
More than my brother: *Ay*, quoth my uncle Gloster,　　　[apace:
*Small herbs have grace, great weeds do grow*
And since, methinks, I would not grow so fast,
Because sweet flowers are slow, and weeds make haste.　　　[did not hold

*Duch.* Good faith, good faith, the saying
In him that did object the same to thee:
He was the wretched'st thing when he was young.
So long a growing, and so leisurely,
That, if his rule were true, he should be gracious.

*Arch.* And so no doubt he is, my gracious madam.

*Duch.* I hope he is; but yet let mothers doubt.

*York.* Now, by my troth, if I had been remember'd,
I could have given my uncle's grace a flout,
To touch his growth nearer than he touch'd mine.

*Duch.* How, my young York? I pr'ythee, let me hear it.

*York.* Marry, they say my uncle grew so fast
That he could gnaw a crust at two hours old:
'Twas full two years ere I could get a tooth.

Grandam, this would have been a biting
jest.
*Duch.* I pr'ythee, pretty York, who told
thee this?
*York* Grandam, his nurse.
*Duch.* His nurse! why she was dead ere
thou wast born.
*York.* If 'twere not she, I cannot tell who
told me.                        [too shrewd.
*Q. Eliz.* A parlous boy:—go to, you are
*Arch.* Good madam, be not angry with
the child.
*Q. Eliz.* Pitchers have ears.
*Arch.* Here comes a messenger.

*Enter a* Messenger.

What news?                        [to report.
*Mess.* Such news, my lord, as grieves me
*Q. Eliz.* How doth the prince?
*Mess.*          Well, madam, and in health.
*Duch.* What is thy news?
*Mess.* Lord Rivers and Lord Grey are
sent to Pomfret,
With them Sir Thomas Vaughan, prisoners.
*Duch.* Who hath committed them?
*Mess.*                The mighty dukes
Gloster and Buckingham.
*Q. Eliz.*                For what offence?
*Mess.* The sum of all I can, I have dis-
clos'd;
Why or for what the nobles were committed
Is all unknown to me, my gracious lady.
*Q. Eliz.* Ah me, I see the ruin of my house!
The tiger now hath seiz'd the gentle hind;
Insulting tyranny begins to jet
Upon the innocent and awless throne:—
Welcome, destruction, blood, and massacre!
I see, as in a map, the end of all.     [days!
*Duch.* Accurs'd and unquiet wrangling
How many of you have mine eyes beheld?
My husband lost his life to get the crown;
And often up and down my sons were toss'd,
For me to joy and weep their gain and loss:
And being seated, and domestic broils
Clean over-blown, themselves, the conquer-
ors,
Make war upon themselves; brother to
brother,
Blood to blood, self against self:—O, prepos-
terous
And frantic outrage, end thy damned spleen;
Or let me die, to look on death no more!
*Q. Eliz.* Come, come, my boy; we will to
sanctuary.—
Madam, farewell.
*Duch.*            Stay, I will go with you.
*Q. Eliz.* You have no cause.
*Arch.*                My gracious lady, go.
                        [*To the* QUEEN.
And thither bear your treasure and your
goods.
For my part, I'll resign unto your grace
The seal I keep; and so betide to me

As well I tender you and all of yours!
Come, I'll conduct you to the sanctuary.
                                [*Exeunt.*

ACT III.

SCENE I.—LONDON. *A Street.*

*The trumpets sound.  Enter the* PRINCE OF
WALES, GLOSTER, BUCKINGHAM, CATESBY,
CARDINAL BOUCHIER, *and others.*

*Buck.* Welcome, sweet prince, to London,
to your chamber.
*Glo.* Welcome, dear cousin, my thought's
sovereign:
The weary way hath made you melancholy.
*Prince.* No, uncle; but our crosses on the
way
Have made it tedious, wearisome, and heavy:
I want more uncles here to welcome me.
*Glo.* Sweet prince, the untainted virtue of
your years
Hath not yet div'd into the world's deceit:
No more can you distinguish of a man
Than of his outward show; which, God he
knows,
Seldom or never jumpeth with the heart.
Those uncles which you want were danger-
ous;
Your grace attended to their sugar'd words,
But look'd not on the poison of their hearts:
God keep you from them, and from such
false friends!
*Prince.* God keep me from false friends!
but they were none.     [to greet you.
*Glo.* My lord, the mayor of London comes

*Enter the* Lord Mayor *and his* Train.

*May.* God bless your grace with health
and happy days!
*Prince.* I thank you, good my lord;—and
thank you all.     [*Exeunt* Mayor, &c.
I thought my mother and my brother York
Would long ere this have met us on the way:
Fie, what a slug is Hastings, that he comes
not
To tell us whether they will come or no!
*Buck.* And, in good time, here comes the
sweating lord.

*Enter* HASTINGS.

*Prince.* Welcome, my lord: what, will our
mother come?
*Hast.* On what occasion, God he knows,
not I,
The queen your mother and your brother
York
Have taken sanctuary: the tender prince
Would fain have come with me to meet your
grace,
But by his mother was perforce withheld.
*Buck.* Fie, what an indirect and peevish
course
Is this of hers?—Lord cardinal, will your
grace

Persuade the queen to send the Duke of York
Unto his princely brother presently?
If she deny, Lord Hastings, go with him,
And from her jealous arms pluck him per-
        force.
    *Card.* My Lord of Buckingham, if my
        weak oratory
Can from his mother win the Duke of York,
Anon expect him here; but if she be obdurate
To mild entreaties, God in heaven forbid
We should infringe the holy privilege
Of blessed sanctuary! not for all this land
Would I be guilty of so great a sin.    [lord,
    *Buck.* You are too senseless-obstinate, my
Too ceremonious and traditional:
Weigh it but with the grossness of this age,
You break not sanctuary in seizing him.
The benefit thereof is always granted
To those whose dealings have deserv'd the
        place,
And those who have the wit to claim the
        place:
This prince hath neither claim'd it nor de-
        serv'd it;
And therefore, in mine opinion, cannot have
        it:
Then, taking him from hence that is not
        there,
You break no privilege nor charter there.
Oft have I heard of sanctuary-men;
But sanctuary-children ne'er till now.
    *Card.* My lord, you shall o'errule my mind
        for once.—
Come on, Lord Hastings, will you go with
        me?
    *Hast.* I go, my lord.
    *Prince.* Good lords, make all the speedy
        haste you may.
                    [*Exeunt* CAR. *and* HAST.
Say, uncle Gloster, if our brother come,
Where shall we sojourn till our coronation?
    *Glo.* Where it seems best unto your royal
        self.
If I may counsel you, some day or two
Your highness shall repose you at the
        Tower:
Then where you please, and shall be thought
        most fit
For your best health and recreation.
    *Prince.* I do not like the Tower, of any
        place—
Did Julius Cæsar build that place, my lord?
    *Glo.* He did, my gracious lord, begin that
        place;
Which, since, succeeding ages have re-edi-
        fied.
    *Prince.* Is it upon record, or else reported
Successively from age to age, he built it?
    *Buck.* Upon record, my gracious lord.
    *Prince.* But say, my lord, it were not reg-
        ister'd,                        [age,
Methinks the truth should live from age to
As 'twere retail'd to all posterity,
Even to the general all-ending day.

    *Glo.* So wise so young, they say, do **never**
        live long.                    [*Aside.*
    *Prince.* What say you, uncle?    [long.—
    *Glo.* I say, without characters, fame lives
Thus, like the formal vice, Iniquity,
I moralize two meanings in one word. [*Aside.*
    *Prince.* That Julius Cæsar was a famous
        man;
With what his valour did enrich his wit,
His wit set down to make his valour live:
Death makes no conquest of this conqueror;
For now he lives in fame, though not in
        life.—
I'll tell you what, my cousin Buckingham,—
    *Buck.* What, my gracious lord?
    *Prince.* And if I live until I be a man,
I'll win our ancient right in France again,
Or die a soldier, as I liv'd a king.
    *Glo.* Short summers lightly have a for-
        ward spring.                [*Aside.*
    *Buck.* Now, in good time, here comes the
        Duke of York.

*Enter* YORK, HASTINGS, *and the* CARDINAL.

    *Prince.* Richard of York! how fares our
        loving brother?            [you now.
    *York.* Well, my dread lord; so must I call
    *Prince.* Ay, brother,—to our grief, as it is
        yours:
Too late he died that might have kept that
        title,
Which by his death hath lost much majesty.
    *Glo.* How fares our cousin, noble Lord of
        York?                        [lord,
    *York.* I thank you, gentle uncle. O, my
You said that idle weeds are fast in growth:
The prince my brother hath outgrown me
        far.
    *Glo.* He hath, my lord.
    *York.*                And therefore is he idle?
    *Glo.* O, my fair cousin, I must not say so.
    *York.* Then is he more beholding to you
        than I.
    *Glo.* He may command me as my sover-
        eign;
But you have power in me as in a kinsman.
    *York.* I pray you, uncle, give me this
        dagger.
    *Glo.* My dagger, little cousin? with all my
        heart.
    *Prince.* A beggar, brother?
    *York.* Of my kind uncle, that I know will
        give;
And being but a toy, which is no grief to give.
    *Glo.* A greater gift than that I'll give my
        cousin.                        [to it.
    *York.* A greater gift! O, that's the sword
    *Glo.* Ay, gentle cousin, were it light
        enough.
    *York.* O then, I see, you will part but
        with light gifts;
In weightier things you'll say a beggar nay.
    *Glo.* It is too weighty for your grace to
        wear.

*York.* I weigh it lightly, were it heavier.

*Glo.* What, would you have my weapon,
　little lord?　　　　　[you call me.

*York.* I would, that I might thank you as

*Glo.* How?

*York.* Little.　　　　[cross in talk:—

*Prince.* My Lord of York will still be
Uncle, your grace knows how to bear with
　him.

*York.* You mean, to bear me, not to bear
　with me:—
Uncle, my brother mocks both you and me;
Because that I am little, like an ape,
He thinks that you should bear me on your
　shoulders.　　　　　　[reasons!

*Buck.* With what a sharp-provided wit he
To mitigate the scorn he gives his uncle,
He prettily and aptly taunts himself:
So cunning and so young is wonderful.

*Glo.* My gracious lord, wil't please to pass
　along?
Myself and my good cousin Buckingham
Will to your mother, to entreat of her
To meet you at the Tower, and welcome
　you.

*York.* What, will you go unto the Tower,
　my lord?　　　　　　[it so.

*Prince.* My lord protector needs will have

*York.* I shall not sleep in quiet at the
　Tower.

*Glo.* Why, what should you fear? [ghost:

*York.* Marry, my uncle Clarence' angry
My grandam told me he was murder'd there.

*Prince.* I fear no uncles dead.

*Glo.* Nor none that live, I hope.　[fear.

*Prince.* An if they live, I hope I need not
But come, my lord; and with a heavy heart,
Thinking on them, go I unto the Tower.
　　[*Sennet. Exeunt* PRINCE, YORK, HAST.,
　　　　CAR., *and* Attendants.

*Buck.* Think you, my lord, this little prat-
　ing York
Was not incensed by his subtle mother
To taunt and scorn you thus opprobriously?

*Glo.* No doubt, no doubt: O, 'tis a parlous
　boy;
Bold, quick, ingenious, forward, capable:
He is all the mother's, from the top to toe.

*Buck.* Well, let them rest.—Come hither,
　Catesby.　　　　　　[intend
Thou art sworn as deeply to effect what we
As closely to conceal what we impart:
Thou know'st our reasons urg'd upon the
　way;—
What think'st thou? is it not an easy matter
To make William Lord Hastings of our mind,
For the instalment of this noble duke
In the seat royal of this famous isle? [prince

*Cate.* He for his father's sake so loves the
That he will not be won to aught against
　him.

*Buck.* What think'st thou then of Stan-
　ley? will not he?

*Cate.* He will do all in all as Hastings doth.

*Buck.* Well, then, no more but this: go,
　gentle Catesby,　　　　　[ings
And, as it were far off, sound thou Lord Hast-
How he doth stand affected to our purpose;
And summon him to-morrow to the Tower,
To sit about the coronation.
If thou dost find him tractable to us,
Encourage him, and tell him all our reasons:
If he be leaden, icy, cold, unwilling,
Be thou so too; and so break off the talk,
And give us notice of his inclination:
For we to-morrow hold divided councils,
Wherein thyself shalt highly be employ'd.

*Glo.* Commend me to Lord William: tell
　him, Catesby,
His ancient knot of dangerous adversaries
To-morrow are let blood at Pomfret Castle;
And bid my lord, for joy of this good news,
Give Mistress Shore one gentle kiss the more.

*Buck.* Good Catesby, go, effect this busi-
　ness soundly.　　　　　[heed I can.

*Cate.* My good lords both, with all the

*Glo.* Shall we hear from you, Catesby, ere
　we sleep?

*Cate.* You shall, my lord.

*Glo.* At Crosby Place, there shall you find
　us both.　　　　　[*Exit* CATESBY.

*Buck.* Now, my lord, what shall we do if
　we perceive
Lord Hastings will not yield to our complots?

*Glo.* Chop off his head, man;—somewhat
　we will do:—
And look, when I am king, claim thou of me
The earldom of Hereford, and all the mov-
　ables
Whereof the king my brother was pos-
　sess'd.

*Buck.* I'll claim that promise at your
　grace's hand.　　　　　[kindness.

*Glo.* And look to have it yielded with all
Come, let us sup betimes, that afterwards
We may digest our complots in some form.
　　　　　　　　　[*Exeunt.*

SCENE II.—*Before* LORD HASTINGS' *House.*

*Enter a Messenger.*

*Mess.* My lord, my lord!—　　[*Knocking.*

*Hast.* [*Within.*] Who knocks?

*Mess.* One from the Lord Stanley.

*Hast.* [*Within.*] What is't o'clock?

*Mess.* Upon the stroke of four.

*Enter* HASTINGS.

*Hast.* Cannot my Lord Stanley sleep these
　tedious nights?

*Mess.* So it appears by that I have to say.
First, he commends him to your noble self.

*Hast.* What then?　　　　　[night

*Mess.* Then certifies your lordship that this
He dreamt the boar had razed off his helm:
Besides, he says there are two councils held;
And that may be determin'd at the one

Which may make you and him to rue at the
   other.              [pleasure,—
Therefore he sends to know your lordship's
If you will presently take horse with him,
And with all speed post with him toward the
   north,
To shun the danger that his soul divines.
   *Hast.* Go, fellow, go, return unto thy lord;
Bid him not fear the separated councils:
His honour and myself are at the one,
And at the other is my good friend Catesby;
Where nothing can proceed that toucheth us
Whereof I shall not have intelligence.
Tell him his fears are shallow, without in-
   stance:
And for his dreams, I wonder he's so simple
To trust the mockery of unquiet slumbers:
To fly the boar before the boar pursues,
Were to incense the boar to follow us,
And make pursuit where he did mean no
   chase.
Go, bid thy master rise and come to me;
And we will both together to the Tower,
Where, he shall see, the boar will use us
   kindly.
   *Mess.* I'll go, my lord, and tell him what
   you say.             [*Exit.*

*Enter* CATESBY.

   *Cate.* Many good-morrows to my noble
   lord!
   *Hast.* Good-morrow, Catesby; you are
   early stirring:          [state?
What news, what news, in this our tottering
   *Cate.* It is a reeling world indeed, my lord;
And I believe will never stand upright
Till Richard wear the garland of the realm.
   *Hast.* How! wear the garland! dost thou
   mean the crown?
   *Cate.* Ay, my good lord.
   *Hast.* I'll have this crown of mine cut
   from my shoulders
Before I'll see the crown so foul misplac'd.
But canst thou guess that he doth aim at it?
   *Cate.* Ay, on my life; and hopes to find
   you forward
Upon his party for the gain thereof:
And thereupon he sends you this good
   news,—
That this same very day your enemies,
The kindred of the queen, must die at Pom-
   fret.
   *Hast.* Indeed, I am no mourner for that
   news,
Because they have been still my adversaries:
But that I'll give my voice on Richard's side,
To bar my master's heirs in true descent,
God knows I will not do it to the death.
   *Cate.* God keep your lordship in that gra-
   cious mind!
   *Hast.* But I shall laugh at this a twelve
   month hence,—        [hate,
That they who brought me in my master's
I live to look upon their tragedy.

Well, Catesby, ere a fortnight make me older,
I'll send some packing that yet think not on't.
   *Cate.* 'Tis a vile thing to die, my gracious
   lord,
When men are unprepar'd, and look not for
   it.
   *Hast.* O monstrous, monstrous! and so falls
   it out
With Rivers, Vaughan, Grey: and so 'twill do
With some men else that think themselves as
   safe
As thou and I; who, as thou know'st, are dear
To princely Richard and to Buckingham.
   *Cate.* The princes both make high account
   of you,—
For they account his head upon the bridge.
                  [*Aside.*
   *Hast.* I know they do; and I have well
   deserv'd it.

*Enter* STANLEY.

Come on, come on; where is your boar-spear,
   man?
Fear you the boar, and go so unprovided?
   *Stan.* My lord, good-morrow; and good-
   morrow, Catesby:—
You may jest on, but, by the holy rood,
I do not like these several councils, I.
   *Hast.* My lord, I hold my life as dear as
   you do yours;
And never in my days, I do protest,
Was it more precious to me than 'tis now:
Think you, but that I know our state secure,
I would be so triumphant as I am?
   *Stan.* The lords at Pomfret, when they
   rode from London,     [sure,—
Were jocund, and suppos'd their states were
And they, indeed, had no cause to mistrust;
But yet, you see, how soon the day o'ercast!
This sudden stab of rancour I misdoubt;
Pray God, I say, I prove a needless coward!
What, shall we toward the Tower? the day
   is spent.
   *Hast.* Come, come, have with you.—Wot
   you what, my lord?
To-day the lords you talk of are beheaded.
   *Stan.* They, for their truth, might better
   wear their heads     [hats,—
Than some that have accus'd them wear their
But come, my lord, let's away.

*Enter a* Pursuivant.

   *Hast.* Go on before; I'll talk with this good
   fellow.     [*Exeunt* STAN. *and* CATE.
How now, sirrah! how goes the world with
   thee?             [to ask.
   *Purs.* The better that your lordship please
   *Hast.* I tell thee, man, 'tis better with me
   now            [we meet:
Than when thou mett'st me last where now
Then was I going prisoner to the Tower.
By the suggestion of the queen's allies;
But now, I tell thee,—keep it to thyself,—
This day those enemies are put to death,

And I in better state than e'er I was.
*Purs.* God hold it, to your honour's good
  content! [for me.
*Hast.* Gramercy, fellow: there, drink that
  [*Throwing him his purse.*
*Purs.* I thank your honour. [*Exit.*

*Enter a Priest.*

*Pr.* Well met, my lord; I am glad to see
  your honour.
*Hast.* I thank thee, good Sir John, with all
  my heart.
I am in your debt for your last exercise;
Come the next Sabbath, and I will content
  you.

*Enter* BUCKINGHAM

*Buck.* What, talking with a priest, lord
  chamberlain!
Your friends at Pomfret, they do need the
  priest;
Your honour hath no shriving-work in hand.
*Hast.* Good faith, and when I met this holy
  man,
The men you talk of came into my mind,—
What, go you toward the Tower?
*Buck.* I do, my lord; but long I cannot
  stay there:
I shall return before your lordship thence.
*Hast.* Nay, like enough, for I stay dinner
  there.
*Buck.* And supper too, although thou
  know'st it not. [*Aside.*
Come, will you go?
*Hast.* I'll wait upon your lordship.
  [*Exeunt.*

SCENE III.—POMFRET. *Before the Castle.*

*Enter* RATCLIFF, *with a* Guard, *conducting*
RIVERS, GREY, *and* VAUGHAN *to execution.*

*Riv.* Sir Richard Ratcliff, let me tell thee
  this,—
To-day shalt thou behold a subject die
For truth, for duty, and for loyalty.
*Grey.* God bless the prince from all the
  pack of you!
A knot you are of damned blood-suckers.
*Vaugh.* You live that shall cry woe for this
  hereafter.
*Rat.* Despatch; the limit of your lives is
  out.
*Riv.* O Pomfret, Pomfret! O thou bloody
  prison.
Fatal and ominous to noble peers!
Within the guilty closure of thy walls
Richard the Second here was hack'd to death:
And, for more slander to thy dismal seat,
We give thee up our guiltless blood to drink.
*Grey.* Now Margaret's curse is fallen upon
  our heads,
When she exclaim'd on Hastings, you, and I,
For standing by when Richard stabb'd her
  son.

*Riv.* Then curs'd she Richard, then curs'd
  she Buckingham,
Then curs'd she Hastings:—O, remember,
  God,
To hear her prayer for them, as now for us!
And for my sister and her princely sons,
Be satisfied, dear God, with our true blood,
Which, as thou know'st, unjustly must be
  spilt!
*Rat.* Make haste; the hour of death is ex-
  piate.
*Riv.* Come, Grey,—come, Vaughan,—let
  us here embrace:
Farewell, until we meet again in heaven.
  [*Exeunt.*

SCENE IV.—LONDON. *A Room in the Tower.*

BUCKINGHAM, STANLEY, HASTINGS, *the*
BISHOP OF ELY, RATCLIFF, LOVEL, *and
others, sitting at a table:* Officers of the
Council *attending.*

*Hast.* Now, noble peers, the cause why we
  are met
Is to determine of the coronation.
In God's name, speak,—when is the royal
  day?
*Buck.* Are all things ready for that royal
  time?
*Stan.* They are; and wants but nomination.
*Ely.* To-morrow, then, I judge a happy
  day.
*Buck.* Who knows the lord protector's mind
  herein?
Who is most inward with the noble duke?
*Ely.* Your grace, we think, should soonest
  know his mind.
*Buck.* We know each other's faces: for our
  hearts,
He knows no more of mine than I of yours;
Nor I of his, my lord, than you of mine.—
Lord Hastings, you and he are near in love.
*Hast.* I thank his grace, I know he loves
  me well;
But for his purpose in the coronation
I have not sounded him, nor he deliver'd
His gracious pleasure any way therein:
But you, my noble lords, may name the time;
And in the duke's behalf I'll give my voice,
Which, I presume, he'll take in gentle part.
*Ely.* In happy time, here comes the duke
  himself.

*Enter* GLOSTER.

*Glo.* My noble lords and cousins all, good-
  morrow.
I have been long a sleeper; but I trust
My absence doth neglect no great design
Which by my presence might have been con-
  cluded.
*Buck.* Had you not come upon your cue,
  my lord, [part,—
William Lord Hastings had pronounc'd your
I mean, your voice,—for crowning of the
  king.

*Glo.* Than my Lord Hastings no man
    might be bolder;     [well.—
His lordship knows me well, and loves me
My lord of Ely, when I was at last in Hol-
    born
I saw good strawberries in your garden there:
I do beseech you send for some of them.
    *Ely.* Marry, and will, my lord, with all my
    heart.          [*Exit.*
    *Glo.* Cousin of Buckingham, a word with
    you.      [*Takes him aside.*
Catesby hath sounded Hastings in our busi-
    ness,
And finds the testy gentleman so hot
That he will lose his head ere give consent
His master's child, as worshipfully he terms
    it,
Shall lose the royalty of England's throne.
    *Buck.* Withdraw yourself awhile; I'll go
    with you.    [*Exeunt* GLO. *and* BUCK.
    *Stan.* We have not yet set down this day
    of triumph.
To-morrow, in my judgment, is too sudden;
For I myself am not so well provided
As else I would be, were the day prolong'd.

       *Re-enter* BISHOP OF ELY.

    *Ely.* Where is my lord the Duke of Glos-
    ter?
I have sent for these strawberries.
    *Hast.* His grace looks cheerfully and
    smooth this morning;
There's some conceit or other likes him well
When that he bids good-morrow with such
    spirit.
I think there's ne'er a man in Christendom
Can lesser hide his love or hate than he;
For by his face straight shall you know his
    heart.
    *Stan.* What of his heart perceive you in his
    face
By any livelihood he showed to-day?
    *Hast.* Marry, that with no man here he is
    offended;
For, were he, he had shown it in his looks.

    *Re-enter* GLOSTER *and* BUCKINGHAM.

    *Glo.* I pray you all, tell me what they de-
    serve
That do conspire my death with devilish
    plots
Of damned witchcraft, and that have pre-
    vail'd
Upon my body with their hellish charms?
    *Hast.* The tender love I bear your grace,
    my lord,
Makes me most forward in this princely pres-
    ence
To doom the offenders: whosoe'er they be,
I say, my lord, they have deserved death.
    *Glo.* Then be your eyes the witness of their
    evil:
Look how I am bewitch'd; behold, mine arm
Is, like a blasted sapling, wither'd up:

And this is Edward's wife, that monstrous
    witch,
Consorted with that harlot-strumpet Shore,
That by their witchcraft thus have marked
    me.
    *Hast.* If they have done this deed, my no-
    ble lord,—     [strumpet,
    *Glo.* If! thou protector of this damned
Talk'st thou to me of *ifs?*—Thou art a
    traitor:—
Off with his head!—now, by Saint Paul I
    swear,
I will not dine until I see the same.—
Lovel and Ratcliff:—look that it be done:—
The rest, that love me, rise and follow me.
    [*Exeunt all except* HAST., LOV., *and*
             RATCLIFF.
    *Hast.* Woe, woe, for England! not a whit
    for me;
For I, too fond, might have prevented this.
Stanley did dream the boar did raze his
    helm;
And I did scorn it, and disdain to fly.
Three times to-day my foot-cloth horse did
    stumble,
And started, when he look'd upon the Tower,
As loth to bear me to the slaughter-house.
O, now I need the priest that spake to me:
I now repent I told the pursuivant,
As too triumphing, how mine enemies
To-day at Pomfret bloodily were butcher'd,
And I myself secure in grace and favour.
O Margaret, Margaret, now thy heavy curse
Is lighted on poor Hastings' wretched head.
    *Rat.* Come, come, despatch; the duke
    would be at dinner:
Make a short shrift; he longs to see your
    head.
    *Hast.* O momentary grace of mortal men,
Which we more hunt for than the grace of
    God!
Who builds his hope in air of your good looks,
Lives like a drunken sailor on a mast,
Ready, with every nod, to tumble down
Into the fatal bowels of the deep.
    *Lov.* Come, come, despatch; 'tis bootless
    to exclaim.       [land!
    *Hast.* O bloody Richard!—miserable Eng-
I prophesy the fearfull'st time to thee
That ever wretched age hath look'd upon.—
Come, lead me to the block; bear him my
    head:
They smile at me who shortly shall be dead.
               [*Exeunt.*

SCENE V.—LONDON. The Tower Walls.

*Enter* GLOSTER *and* BUCKINGHAM *in rusty
    armour, marvellous ill-favoured.*

    *Glo.* Come, cousin, canst thou quake and
    change thy colour,
Murder thy breath in middle of a word,
And then again begin, and stop again,
As if thou wert distraught and mad with
    terror?

*Buck.* Tut, I can counterfeit the deep tragedian;
Speak and look back, and pry on every side,
Tremble and start at wagging of a straw,
Intending deep suspicion: ghastly looks
Are at my service, like enforced smiles;
And both are ready in their offices,
At any time, to grace my stratagems.
But what, is Catesby gone?            [along.
    *Glo.* He is; and, see, he brings the mayor

#### Enter the Lord Mayor and CATESBY.

*Buck.* Lord mayor,—
*Glo.* Look to the drawbridge there!
*Buck.* Hark! a drum.
*Glo.* Catesby, o'erlook the walls.
*Buck.* Lord Mayor, the reason we have sent,—
*Glo.* Look back, defend thee,—here are enemies.
*Buck.* God and our innocency defend and guard us!
*Glo.* Be patient, they are friends,—Ratcliff and Lovel.

#### Enter LOVEL and RATCLIFF, with HASTINGS' head.

*Lov.* Here is the head of that ignoble traitor,
The dangerous and unsuspected Hastings.
    *Glo.* So dear I lov'd the man that I must weep.
I took him for the plainest harmless creature
That breath'd upon the earth a Christian;
Made him my book, wherein my soul recorded
The history of all her secret thoughts:
So smooth he daub'd his vice with show of virtue
That, his apparent open guilt omitted,—
I mean, his conversation with Shore's wife,—
He liv'd from all attainder of suspect.
    *Buck.* Well, well, he was the covert'st shelter'd traitor
That ever liv'd.—
Would you imagine, or almost believe,—
Were't not that by great preservation
We live to tell it you,—the subtle traitor
This day had plotted, in the council-house,
To murder me and my good Lord of Gloster!
    *May.* Had he done so?            [fidels?
    *Glo.* What! think you we are Turks or In-
Or that we would, against the form of law,
Proceed thus rashly in the villain's death,
But that the extreme peril of the case,
The peace of England and our persons' safety,
Enforc'd us to this execution?
    *May.* Now, fair befall you! he deserv'd his death;            [ceeded,
And your good graces both have well pro-
To warn false traitors from the like attempts.
I never look'd for better at his hands
After he once fell in with Mistress Shore.

*Buck.* Yet had we not determin'd he should die
Until your lordship came to see his end;
Which now the loving haste of these our friends,
Something against our meaning, hath prevented:
Because, my lord, we would have had you heard
The traitor speak, and timorously confess
The manner and the purpose of his treasons;
That you might well have signified the same
Unto the citizens, who haply may
Misconstrue us in him, and wail his death.
    *May.* But, my good lord, your grace's word shall serve
As well as I had seen, and heard him speak:
And do not doubt, right noble princes both.
But I'll acquaint our duteous citizens
With all your just proceedings in this case.
    *Glo.* And to that end we wish'd your lordship here,
To avoid the censures of the carping world.
    *Buck.* But since you come too late of our intent,
Yet witness what you hear we did intend:
And so, my good lord mayor, we bid farewell.            [*Exit* LORD MAYOR.
    *Glo.* Go, after, after, cousin Buckingham.
The mayor towards Guildhall hies him in all post:—
There, at your meetest vantage of the time,
Infer the bastardy of Edward's children:
Tell them how Edward put to death a citizen,
Only for saying he would make his son
Heir to the crown; meaning, indeed, his house,
Which, by the sign thereof, was termed so.
Moreover, urge his hateful luxury,
And bestial appetite in change of lust;
Which stretch'd unto their servants, daughters, wives,
Even where his raging eye or savage heart,
Without control, listed to make a prey.
Nay, for a need, thus far come near my person:—            [child
Tell them, when that my mother went with
Of that insatiate Edward, noble York,
My princely father, then had wars in France;
And, by true computation of the time,
Found that the issue was not his begot;
Which well appeared in his lineaments,
Being nothing like the noble duke my father:
Yet touch this sparingly, as 'twere far off;
Because, my lord, you know my mother lives.
    *Buck.* Doubt not, my lord, I'll play the orator
As if the golden plea for which I plead
Were for myself: and so, my lord, adieu.
    *Glo.* If you thrive well, bring them to Baynard's Castle;
Where you shall find me well accompanied
With reverend fathers and well learned bishops.

*Buck.* I go; and towards three or four
o'clock
Look for the news that the Guildhall affords.
                                    [*Exit.*
*Glo.* Go, Lovel, with all speed to Doctor
     Shaw.—            [them both
Go thou [*to* CATE.] to Friar Penker;—bid
Meet me within this hour at Baynard's Castle.
                    [*Exeunt* LOV. *and* CATE.
Now will I in, to take some privy order
To draw the brats of Clarence out of sight;
And to give notice that no manner of person
Have any time recourse unto the prices.
                                    [*Exit.*

SCENE VI.—LONDON. *A Street.*

*Enter a* Scrivener.

*Scriv.* Here is the indictment of the good
     Lord Hastings;
Which in a set hand fairly is engross'd,
That it may be to-day read o'er in Paul's.
And mark how well the sequel hangs to-
     gether:—
Eleven hours I have spent to write it over,
For yesternight by Catesby was it sent me;
The precedent was full as long a-doing:
And yet within these five hours Hastings
     liv'd,
Untainted, unexamin'd, free, at liberty.
Here's a good world the while! Who is so
     gross
That cannot see this palpable device!
Yet who so bold but says he sees it not!
Bad is the world; and all will come to naught
When such ill dealing must be seen in thought.
                                    [*Exit.*

SCENE VII.—LONDON. *Court of Baynard's
     Castle.*

*Enter* GLOSTER *and* BUCKINGHAM, *meeting.*

*Glo.* How now, how now! what say the
     citizens?
*Buck.* Now, by the holy mother of our
     Lord,
The citizens are mum, say not a word.
*Glo.* Touch'd you the bastardy of Ed-
     ward's children?            [Lucy,
*Buck.* I did; with his contract with Lady
And his contract by deputy in France;
The insatiate greediness of his desires,
And his enforcement of the city wives;
His tyranny for trifles; his own bastardy,—
As being got, your father then in France,
And his resemblance, being not like the duke:
Withal I did infer your lineaments,—
Being the right idea of your father,
Both in your form and nobleness of mind;
Laid open all your victories in Scotland,
Your discipline in war, wisdom in peace,
Your bounty, virtue, fair humility;
Indeed, left nothing fitting for your purpose
Untouch'd or slightly handled in discourse:
And when my oratory drew toward end
I bid them that did love their country's good

Cry, *God save Richard, England's royal king!*
*Glo.* And did they so?            [a word;
*Buck.* No, so God help me, they spake not
But, like dumb statuas or breathing stones,
Star'd each on other, and look'd deadly pale.
Which when I saw, I reprehended them;
And ask'd the mayor what meant this wilful
     silence:
His answer was,—the people were not us'd
To be spoke to but by the recorder.
Then he was urg'd to tell my tale again,—
*Thus saith the duke, thus hath the duke in-
     ferr'd*
But nothing spoke in warrant from himself.
When he had done, some followers of mine
     own,
At lower end of the hall, hurl'd up their caps,
And some ten voices cried, *God save King
     Richard!*
And thus I took the vantage of those few,—
*Thanks, gentle citizens and friends,* quoth I;
*This general applause and cheerful shout
Argues your wisdom and your love to Rich-
     ard:*
And even here brake off and came away.
*Glo.* What tongueless blocks were they!
     would they not speak?        [come?
Will not the mayor, then, and his brethren,
*Buck.* The mayor is here at hand. Intend
     some fear;
Be not you spoke with but by mighty suit:
And look you get a prayer-book in your
     hand,
And stand between two churchmen, good my
     lord;
For on that ground I'll make a holy descant:
And be not easily won to our requests;
Play the maid's part,—still answer nay, and
     take it.
*Glo.* I go; and if you plead as well for
     them
As I can say nay to thee for myself,
No doubt we bring it to a happy issue.
*Buck.* Go, go, up to the leads; the lord
     mayor knocks.            [*Exit* GLOSTER.

*Enter the* Lord Mayor, Aldermen, *and*
     Citizens.

Welcome, my lord: I dance attendance here;
I think the duke will not be spoke withal.

*Enter, from the Castle,* CATESBY.

Now, Catesby,—what says your lord to my
     request?            [ble lord,
*Cate.* He doth entreat your grace, my no-
To visit him to-morrow or next day:
He is within, with two right reverend fath-
     ers,
Divinely bent to meditation:
And in no worldly suit would he be mov'd,
To draw him from his holy exercise.
*Buck.* Return, good Catesby, to the gra-
     cious duke;
Tell him, myself, the mayor and aldermen.

In deep designs, in matter of great moment,
No less importing than our general good,
Are come to have some conference with his
　　grace.
　　*Cate.* I'll signify so much unto him straight.
　　　　　　　　　　　　　　　　　[*Exit.*
　　*Buck.* Ah, ha, my lord, this prince is not
　　an Edward!
He is not lolling on a lewd day-bed
But on his knees at meditation;
Not dallying with a brace of courtezans,
But meditating with two deep divines;
Not sleeping, to engross his idle body,
But praying, to enrich his watchful soul:
Happy were England would this virtuous
　　prince
Take on himself the sovereignty thereof:
But, sure, I fear, we shall not win him to it.
　　*May.* Marry, God defend his grace should
　　say us nay!　　　　　　　　　　[again.
　　*Buck.* I fear he will. Here Catesby comes

　　　　　*Re-enter* CATESBY.

Now, Catesby, what says his grace?
　　*Cate.* He wonders to what end you have
　　assembled
Such troops of citizens to come to him:
His grace not being warn'd thereof before,
He fears, my lord, you mean no good to him.
　　*Buck.* Sorry I am my noble cousin should
Suspect me, that I mean no good to him:
By heaven, we come to him in perfect love;
And so once more return and tell his grace.
　　　　　　　　　　　　　[*Exit* CATESBY.
When holy and devout religious men
Are at their beads, 'tis much to draw them
　　thence,—
So sweet is zealous contemplation.

*Enter* GLOSTER, *in a Gallery above, between*
*two* BISHOPS. CATESBY *returns.*

　　*May.* See, where his grace stands 'tween
　　two clergymen!　　　　[prince,
　　*Buck.* Two props of virtue for a Christian
To stay him from the fall of vanity:
And, see, a book of prayer in his hand,—
True ornament to know a holy man.—
Famous Plantagenet, most gracious prince,
Lend favourable ear to our requests;
And pardon us the interruption
Of thy devotion and right Christian zeal.
　　*Glo.* My lord, there needs no such apology:
I rather do beseech you pardon me,
Who, earnest in the service of my God,
Deferr'd the visitation of my friends. [sure?
But, leaving this, what is your grace's plea-
　　*Buck.* Even that, I hope, which pleaseth
　　God above,
And all good men of this ungovern'd isle.
　　*Glo.* I do suspect I have done some offence
That seems disgracious in the city's eye;
And that you come to reprehend my ignor-
　　ance.

　　*Buck.* You have, my lord: would it might
　　please your grace,
On our entreaties, to amend your fault!
　　*Glo.* Else wherefore breathe I in a Chris-
　　tian land?　　　　　　　　[resign
　　*Buck.* Know, then, it is your fault that you
The supreme seat, the throne majestical,
The scepter'd office of your ancestors,
Your state of fortune and your due of birth,
The lineal glory of your royal house,
To the corruption of a blemish'd stock:
Whilst, in the mildness of your sleepy
　　thoughts,—
Which here we waken to our country's
　　good,—
This noble isle doth want her proper limbs;
Her face defac'd with scars of infamy,
Her royal stock graft with ignoble plants,
And almost shoulder'd in the swallowing gulf
Of dark forgetfulness and deep oblivion.
Which to recure, we heartily solicit
Your gracious self to take on you the charge
And kingly government of this your land;—
Not as protector, steward, substitute,
Or lowly factor for another's gain;
But as successively, from blood to blood,
Your right of birth, your empery, your own.
For this, consorted with the citizens
Your very worshipful and loving friends,
And, by their vehement instigation,
In this just suit come I to move your grace.
　　*Glo.* I cannot tell if to depart in silence
Or bitterly to speak in your reproof
Best fitteth my degree or your condition:
If not to answer, you might haply think
Tongue-tied ambition, not replying, yielded
To bear the golden yoke of sovereignty,
Which fondly you would here impose on me;
If to reprove you for this suit of yours,
So season'd with your faithful love to me,
Then, on the other side, I check'd my friends.
Therefore,—to speak, and to avoid the first,
And then, in speaking, not to incur the last,—
Definitively thus I answer you.
Your love deserves my thanks; but my desert
Unmeritable shuns your high request.
First, if all obstacles were cut away,
And that my path were even to the crown,
As the ripe revenue and due of birth,
Yet so much is my poverty of spirit,
So mighty and so many my defects, [ness,—
That I would rather hide me from my great-
Being a bark to brook no mighty sea,—
Than in my greatness covet to be hid,
And in the vapour of my glory smother'd.
But, God be thank'd, there is no need of
　　me,—
And much I need to help you, were there
　　need;—
The royal tree hath left us royal fruit,
Which, mellow'd by the stealing hours of
　　time,
Will well become the seat of majesty,
And make, no doubt, us happy by his reign.

On him I lay that you would lay on me,—
The right and fortune of his happy stars;
Which God defend that I should wring from
　　him!　　　　　　　　　　[your grace;
*Buck.* My lord, this argues conscience in
But the respects thereof are nice and trivial,
All circumstances well considered.
You say that Edward is your brother's son:
So say we too, but not by Edward's wife;
For first was he contract to Lady Lucy,—
Your mother lives a witness to his vow,—
And afterward by substitute betroth'd
To Bona, sister to the King of France.
These both put off, a poor petitioner,
A care-craz'd mother to a many sons,
A beauty-waning and distressed widow,
Even in the afternoon of her best days,
Made prize and purchase of his wanton eye,
Seduc'd the pitch and height of his degree
To base declension and loath'd bigamy:
By her, in his unlawful bed, he got
This Edward, whom our manners call the
　　prince.
More bitterly could I expostulate,
Save that, for reverence to some alive,
I give a sparing limit to my tongue.
Then, good my lord, take to your royal self
This proffer'd benefit of dignity;
If not to bless us and the land withal,
Yet to draw forth your noble ancestry
From the corruption of abusing time
Unto a lineal true-derived course,
　　*May.* Do, good my lord; your citizens en-
　　treat you.
　　*Buck.* Refuse not, mighty lord, this prof-
　　fer'd love.　　　　　　　　　[ful suit!
　　*Cate.* O, make them joyful, grant their law-
　　*Glo.* Alas, why would you heap those
　　cares on me?
I am unfit for state and majesty:—
I do beseech you, take it not amiss;
I cannot nor I will not yield to you.
　　*Buck.* If you refuse it,—as, in love and
　　zeal,
Loth to depose the child, your brother's son—
As well we know your tenderness of heart,
And gentle, kind, effeminate remorse,
Which we have noted in you to your kin-
　　dred,
And equally, indeed, to all estates,—
Yet know, whe'r you accept our suit or no,
Your brother's son shall never reign our king;
But we will plant some other in the throne,
To the disgrace and downfall of your house:
And in this resolution here we leave you.—
Come, citizens, we will entreat no more.
　　　[*Exeunt* BUCK., *the* Mayor *and* Citizens
　　　　　　　　*retiring.*
　　*Cate.* Call them again, sweet prince, ac-
　　cept their suit:
If you deny them, all the land will rue it.
　　*Glo.* Will you enforce me to a world of
　　cares?
Call them again.

　　　　[CATE. *goes to the* Mayor, *&c., and then exit.*
　　　　　　　I am not made of stone,
But penetrable to your kind entreaties,
Albeit against my conscience and my soul.

*Re-enter* BUCKINGHAM *and* CATESBY, *the*
　　Mayor, *&c, coming forward.*

Cousin of Buckingham,—and sage, grave
　　men,
Since you will buckle fortune on my back,
To bear her burden, whe'r I will or no,
I must have patience to endure the load:
But if black scandal or foul-fac'd reproach
Attend the sequel of your imposition,
Your mere enforcement shall acquittance me
From all the impure blots and stains thereof;
For God he knows, and you may partly see,
How far I am from the desire of this.
　　*May.* God bless your grace! we see it, and
　　will say it.
　　*Glo.* In saying so, you shall but say the
　　truth.
　　*Buck.* Then I salute you with this royal
　　title,—
Long live King Richard, England's worthy
　　king!
　　*All.* Amen.　　　　　　　　[crown'd?
　　*Buck.* To-morrow may it please you to be
　　*Glo.* Even when you please, for you will
　　have it so.
　　*Buck.* To-morrow, then, we will attend
　　your grace:
And so, most joyfully, we take our leave.
　　*Glo.* Come, let us to our holy work
　　again.—
　　　　　　　　　　　　　[*To the* Bishops.
Farewell, my cousin;—farewell, gentle
　　friends.　　　　　　　　　　[*Exeunt.*

## ACT IV.

### SCENE I.—LONDON. *Before the Tower.*

*Enter, on one side,* QUEEN ELIZABETH, DUCH-
ESS OF YORK, *and* MARQUIS OF DORSET; *on
the other,* ANNE DUCHESS OF GLOSTER,
*leading* LADY MARGARET PLANTAGENET,
CLARENCE'S *young Daughter.*

　　*Duch.* Who meets us here?—my niece
　　Plantagenet
Led in the hand of her kind aunt of Gloster?
Now, for my life, she's wandering to the
　　Tower,
On pure heart's love, to greet the tender
　　princes.—
Daughter, well met.
　　*Anne.*　　　　　God gives your graces both
A happy and a joyful time of day!
　　*Q. Eliz.* As much to you, good sister!
　　Whither away?
　　*Anne.* No further than the Tower; and, as
　　I guess,
Upon the like devotion as yourselves,
To gratulate the gentle princes there.

*Q. Eliz.* Kind sister, thanks: we'll enter all
   together:—
And, in good time, here the lieutenant comes.

*Enter* BRAKENBURY.

Master lieutenant, pray you, by your leave,
How doth the prince, and my young son of
   York?
   *Brak.* Right well, dear madam. By your
   patience,
I may not suffer you to visit them;
The king has strictly charg'd the contrary.
   *Q. Eliz.* The king! who's that?
   *Brak.*        I mean the lord protector.
   *Q. Eliz.* The lord protect him from that
   kingly title!
Hath he set bounds between their love and
   me?
I am their mother; who shall bar me from
   them?
   *Duch.* I am their father's mother, I will
   see them.           [mother:
   *Anne.* Their aunt I am in law, in love their
Then bring me to their sights; I'll bear thy
   blame,
And take thy office from thee, on my peril.
   *Brak.* No, madam, no,—I may not leave
   it so:
I am bound by oath, and therefore pardon
   me.                    [*Exit.*

*Enter* STANLEY.

   *Stan.* Let me but meet you, ladies, one
   hour hence,
And I'll salute your grace of York as mother
And reverend looker-on of two fair queens.—
Come, madam, you must straight to West-
   minster,
         [*To the* DUCHESS OF GLOSTER.
There to be crowned Richard's royal queen.
   *Q. Eliz.* Ah, cut my lace asunder,    [beat,
That my pent heart may have some scope to
Or else I swoon with this dead-killing news!
   *Anne.* Despiteful tidings! O unpleasing
   news!
   *Dor.* Be of good cheer: mother, how fares
   your grace?           [gone!
   *Q. Eliz.* O Dorset, speak not to me, get thee
Death and destruction dog thee at the heels;
Thy mother's name is ominous to children.
If thou wilt outstrip death, go cross the seas,
And live with Richmond, from the reach of
   hell:
Go, hie thee, hie thee from this slaughter-
   house,
Lest thou increase the number of the dead;
And make me die the thrall of Margaret's
   curse,
Nor mother, wife, nor England's counted
   queen.
   *Stan.* Full of wise care is this your coun-
   sel, madam.—
Take all the swift advantage of the hours;
You shall have letters from me to my son

In your behalf, to meet you on the way:
Be not ta'en tardy by unwise delay.
   *Duch.* O ill-dispersing wind of misery!—
O my accursed womb, the bed of death!
A cockatrice hast thou hatch'd to the world,
Whose unavoided eye is murderous.
   *Stan.* Come, madam, come; I in all haste
   was sent.
   *Anne.* And I with all unwillingness will
   go.—
O, would to God that the inclusive verge
Of golden metal that must round my brow
Were red-hot steel, to sear me to the brain!
Anointed let me be with deadly venom,
And die ere men can say God save the Queen!
   *Q. Eliz.* Go, go, poor soul, I envy not thy
   glory;
To feed my humour, wish thyself no harm.
   *Anne.* No, why?—When he that is my
   husband now
Came to me, as I follow'd Henry's corse;
When scarce the blood was well wash'd from
   his hands
Which issu'd from my other angel husband,
And that dead saint which then I weeping
   follow'd;
O, when, I say, I look'd on Richard's face,
This was my wish,—*Be thou,* quoth I, *ac-*
   *curs'd*
*For making me, so young, so old a widow!*
*And when thou wedd'st, let sorrow haunt thy*
   *bed;*
*And be thy wife,—if any be so mad,—*
*More miserable by the life of thee*   [*death!*
*Than thou hast made me by my dear lord's*
Lo, ere I can repeat this curse again,
Within so small a time, my woman's heart
Grossly grew captive to his honey words,
And prov'd the subject of mine own soul's
   curse,—
Which hitherto hath held mine eyes from
   rest;
For never yet one hour in his bed
Did I enjoy the golden dew of sleep,
But with his timorous dreams was still
   awak'd.
Besides, he hates me for my father Warwick;
And will, no doubt, shortly be rid of me.
   *Q. Eliz.* Poor heart, adieu! I pity thy com-
   plaining.
   *Anne.* No more than with my soul I mourn
   for yours.           [glory!
   *Q. Eliz.* Farewell, thou woeful welcomer of
   *Anne.* Adieu, poor soul, that tak'st thy
   leave of it!
   *Duch.* Go thou to Richmond, and good
   fortune guide thee!—    [*To* DORSET.
Go thou to Richard, and good angels tend
   thee!—            [*To* ANNE.
Go thou to sanctuary, and good thoughts
   possess thee!   [*To* QUEEN ELIZABETH.
I to my grave, where peace and rest lie with
   me!
Eighty odd years of sorrow have I seen,

And each hour's joy wreck'd with a week of
teen.

*Q. Eliz.* Stay yet, look back with me unto
the Tower.—

Pity, you ancient stones, those tender babes,
Whom envy hath immur'd within your walls!
Rough cradle for such little pretty ones!
Rude ragged nurse, old sullen playfellow
For tender princes, use my babies well!
So foolish sorrow bids your stones farewell.

[*Exeunt.*

SCENE II.—LONDON. *A Room of State in the
Palace.*

*Flourish of trumpets.* RICHARD, *as King, upon
his throne;* BUCKINGHAM, CATESBY, *a* Page,
*and others.*

*K. Rich.* Stand all apart.—Cousin of Buckingham,—

*Buck.* My gracious sovereign?

*K. Rich.* Give me thy hand. Thus high, by
thy advice

And thy assistance, is King Richard seated:—
But shall we wear these glories for a day?
Or shall they last, and we rejoice in them?

*Buck.* Still live they, and for ever let them
last!

*K. Rich.* Ah, Buckingham, now do I play
the touch,

To try if thou be current gold indeed:—
Young Edward lives;—think now what I
would speak.

*Buck.* Say on, my loving lord.

*K. Rich.* Why, Buckingham, I say, I
would be king.

*Buck.* Why, so you are, my thrice-re-
nowned liege.     [ward lives.

*K. Rich.* Ha! am I king? 'tis so: but Ed-

*Buck.* True, noble prince.

*K. Rich.*             O bitter consequence,
That Edward still should live,—true, noble
prince!—

Cousin, thou wast not wont to be so dull:—
Shall I be plain?—I wish the bastards dead;
And I would have it suddenly perform'd.
What say'st thou now? speak suddenly, be
brief.

*Buck.* Your grace may do your pleasure.

*K. Rich.* Tut, tut, thou art all ice, thy
kindness freezes:

Say, have I thy consent that they shall die?

*Buck.* Give me some little breath, some
pause, dear lord,

Before I positively speak in this:
I will resolve your grace immediately. [*Exit.*

*Cate.* The king is angry: see, he gnaws his
lip.     [*Aside.*

*K. Rich.* I will converse with iron-witted
fools     [*Descends from his throne.*

And unrespective boys; none are for me
That look into me with considerate eyes:
High-reaching Buckingham grows circum-
spect.

Boy!—

*Page.* My lord?

*K. Rich.* Know'st thou not any whom corrupting gold

Would tempt into a close exploit of death?

*Page.* I know a discontented gentleman,
Whose humble means match not his haughty
spirit:

Gold were as good as twenty orators,
And will, no doubt, tempt him to anything.

*K. Rich.* What is his name?

*Page.*             His name, my lord, is Tyrrel.

*K. Rich.* I partly know the man: go, call
him hither, boy.     [*Exit* Page.

The deep-revolving witty Buckingham
No more shall be the neighbour to my counsels:

Hath he so long held out with me untir'd,
And stops he now for breath?—well, be it so.

*Enter* STANLEY.

How now, Lord Stanley! what's the news?

*Stan.* Know, my loving lord,
The Marquis Dorset, as I hear, is fled
To Richmond, in the parts where he abides.

*K. Rich.* Come hither Catesby: rumour it
abroad

That Anne, my wife, is very grievous sick;
I will take order for her keeping close:
Inquire me out some mean poor gentleman
Whom I will marry straight to Clarence'
daughter;—

The boy is foolish, and I fear not him.—
Look, how thou dream'st!—I say again, give
out

That Anne my queen is sick, and like to die:
About it; for it stands me much upon,
To stop all hopes whose growth may dam-
age me.     [*Exit* CATESBY.

I must be married to my brother's daughter,
Or else my kingdom stands on brittle glass:—
Murder her brothers, and then marry her!
Uncertain way of gain! But I am in
So far in blood that sin will pluck on sin:
Tear-falling pity dwells not in this eye.

*Re-enter* Page, *with* TYRREL.

Is thy name Tyrrel?

*Tyr.* James Tyrrel, and your most obedient
subject.

*K. Rich.* Art thou, indeed?

*Tyr.*             Prove me, my gracious lord.

*K. Rich.* Dar'st thou resolve to kill a
friend of mine?     [enemies.

*Tyr.* Please you. But I had rather kill two

*K. Rich.* Why, then, thou hast it: two
deep enemies,

Foes to my rest, and my sweet sleep's disturbers,

Are they that I would have thee deal upon:—
Tyrrel, I mean those bastards in the Tower.

*Tyr.* Let me have open means to come to
them,

And soon I'll rid you from the fear of them.

*K. Rich.* Thou sing'st sweet music. Hark, come hither, Tyrrel:
Go, by this token:—rise, and lend thine ear: [*Whispers.*
There is no more but so:—say it is done,
And I will love thee, and prefer thee for it.
*Tyr.* I will despatch it straight. [*Exit.*

*Re-enter* BUCKINGHAM.

*Buck.* My lord, I have consider'd in my mind
The late demand that you did sound me in.
*K. Rich.* Well, let that rest. Dorset is fled to Richmond.
*Buck.* I hear the news, my lord.
*K. Rich.* Stanley, he is your wife's son:—well, look to it. [by promise,
*Buck.* My lord, I claim the gift, my due
For which your honour and your faith is pawn'd;
The earldom of Hereford, and the movables,
Which you have promised I shall possess.
*K. Rich.* Stanley, look to your wife: if she convey
Letters to Richmond, you shall answer it.
*Buck.* What says your highness to my just request? [Sixth
*K. Rich.* I do remember me,—Henry the
Did prophesy that Richmond should be king,
When Richmond was a little peevish boy.
A king!—perhaps,—
*Buck.* My lord,—
*K. Rich.* How chance the prophet could not at that time [him?
Have told me, I being by, that I should kill
*Buck.* My lord, your promise for the earldom,— [Exeter,
*K. Rich.* Richmond!—When last I was at
The mayor in courtesy show'd me the castle,
And call'd it Rouge-mont: at which name I started,
Because a bard of Ireland told me once
I should not live long after I saw Richmond.
*Buck.* My lord,—
*K. Rich.* Ay, what's o'clock?· [in mind
*Buck.* I am thus bold to put your grace
Of what you promis'd me.
*K. Rich.* Well, but what's o'clock?
*Buck.* Upon the stroke of ten.
*K. Rich.* Well, let it strike.
*Buck.* Why let it strike?
*K. Rich.* Because that, like a Jack, thou keep'st the stroke
Betwixt thy begging and my meditation.
I am not in the giving vein to-day.
*Buck.* Why, then resolve me whether you will or no. [the vein.
*K. Rich.* Thou troublest me; I am not in
[*Exeunt* K. RICH. *and* Train.
*Buck.* And is it thus? repays he my deep service [this?
With such contempt? made I him king for
O, let me think on Hastings, and be gone
To Brecknock while my fearful head is on! [*Exit.*

SCENE III.—LONDON. *Another Room in the Palace.*

*Enter* TYRREL.

*Tyr.* The tyrannous and bloody act is done,—
The most arch deed of piteous massacre
That ever yet this land was guilty of.
Dighton and Forrest, whom I did suborn
To do this piece of ruthless butchery,
Albeit they were flesh'd villains, bloody dogs,
Melting with tenderness and mild compassion, [story.
Wept like two children in the death's sad
*O thus,* quoth Dighton, *lay the gentle babes,—* [other
*Thus, thus,* quoth Forrest, *girdling one another*
*Within their alabaster innocent arms:*
*Their lips were four red roses on a stalk,*
*Which in their summer beauty kiss'd each other.*
*A book of prayers on their pillow lay;*
*Which one,* quoth Forrest, *almost chang'd my mind;*
*But, O, the devil,—*there the villain stopp'd;
When Dighton thus told on,—*we smothered*
*The most replenished sweet work of nature*
*That from the prime creation e'er she fram'd.—* [remorse
Hence both are gone; with conscience and
They could not speak; and so I left them both,
To bear this tidings to the bloody king:—
And here he comes:—

*Enter* KING RICHARD.

All health, my sovereign lord!
*K. Rich.* Kind Tyrrel, am I happy in thy news? [charge
*Tyr.* If to have done the thing you gave in
Beget your happiness, be happy then,
For it is done.
*K. Rich.* But didst thou see them dead?
*Tyr.* I did, my lord.
*K. Rich.* And buried, gentle Tyrrel?
*Tyr.* The chaplain of the Tower hath buried them;
But where, to say the truth, I do not know.
*K. Rich.* Come to me, Tyrrel, soon, at after supper, [death.
When thou shalt tell the process of their
Meantime, but think how I may do thee good,
And be inheritor of thy desire.
Farewell till then.
*Tyr.* I humbly take my leave. [*Exit.*
*K. Rich.* The son of Clarence have I pent up close; [marriage;
His daughter meanly have I matched in
The sons of Edward sleep in Abraham's bosom, [night.
And Anne my wife hath bid the world good-

Now, for I know the Bretagne Richmond
aims
At young Elizabeth, my brother's daughter,
And by that knot looks proudly on the
crown,
To her go I, a jolly thriving wooer.

*Enter* RATCLIFF.

*Rat.* My lord,—
*K. Rich.* Good news or bad, that thou
com'st in so bluntly?  [Richmond;
*Rat.* Bad news, my lord: Morton is fled to
And Buckingham, back'd with the hardy
Welshmen,
Is in the field, and still his power increaseth.
*K. Rich.* Ely with Richmond troubles me
more near  [strength.
Than Buckingham and his rash-levied
Come,—I have learn'd that fearful com-
menting
Is leaden servitor to dull delay;  [gary:
Delay leads impotent and snail-pac'd beg-
Then fiery expedition be my wing,
Jove's Mercury, and herald for a king!
Go, muster men: my counsel is my shield;
We must be brief when traitors brave the
field.  [*Exeunt.*

SCENE IV.—LONDON. *Before the Palace.*

*Enter* QUEEN MARGARET.

*Q. Mar.* So, now prosperity begins to mel-
low,
And drop into the rotten mouth of death,
Here in these confines slily have I lurk'd,
To watch the waning of mine enemies.
A dire induction am I witness to,
And will to France; hoping the consequence
Will prove as bitter, black and tragical.—
Withdraw thee, wretched Margaret: who
comes here?  [*Retires.*

*Enter* QUEEN ELIZABETH *and the* DUCHESS OF
YORK.

*Q. Eliz.* Ah, my poor princes! ah, my ten-
der babes!
My unblown flowers, new-appearing sweets!
If yet your gentle souls fly in the air,
And be not fix'd in doom perpetual,
Hover about me with your airy wings,
And hear your mother's lamentation!
*Q. Mar.* Hover about her; say, that right
for right  [night.
Hath dimm'd your infant morn to aged
*Duch.* So many miseries have craz'd my
voice
That my woe-wearied tongue is still and
mute.—
Edward Plantagenet, why art thou dead?
*Q. Mar.* Plantagenet doth quit Plantage-
net, Edward for Edward pays a dying debt.
*Q. Eliz.* Wilt thou, O God, fly from such
gentle lambs,
And throw them in the entrails of the wolf?

When didst thou sleep when such a deed was
done?  [sweet son.
*Q. Mar.* When holy Harry died, and my
*Duch.* Dead life, blind sight, poor mortal-
living ghost,  [life usurp'd,
Woe's scene, world's shame, grave's due by
Brief abstract and record of tedious days,
Rest thy unrest on England's lawful earth,
[*Sitting down.*
Unlawfully made drunk with innocent
blood!
*Q. Eliz.* Ah, that thou wouldst as soon af-
ford a grave
As thou canst yield a melancholy seat!
Then would I hide my bones, not rest them
here.
Ah, who hath any cause to mourn but we?
[*Sitting down by her.*
*Q. Mar.* If ancient sorrow be most rev-
erent,
Give mine the benefit of seniory,
[*Coming forward.*
And let my griefs frown on the upper hand.
If sorrow can admit society,
[*Sitting down with them.*
Tell o'er your woes again by viewing mine:—
I had an Edward, till a Richard kill'd him;
I had a Henry, till a Richard kill'd him:
Thou hadst an Edward, till a Richard kill'd
him;  [him.
Thou hadst a Richard, till a Richard kill'd
*Duch.* I had a Richard too, and thou didst
kill him;
I had a Rutland too, thou holp'st to kill him.
*Q. Mar.* Thou hadst a Clarence too, and
Richard kill'd him  [crept
From forth the kennel of thy womb hath
A hell-hound that doth hunt us all to death:
That dog, that had his teeth before his eyes,
To worry lambs and lap their gentle blood;
That foul defacer of God's handiwork;
That excellent grand tyrant of the earth,
That reigns in galled eyes of weeping souls,—
Thy womb let loose, to chase us to our
graves.—
O upright, just, and true-disposing God,
How do I thank thee that this carnal cur
Preys on the issue of his mother's body,
And makes her pew-fellow with others'
moan!  [woes!
*Duch.* O Harry's wife, triumph not in my
God witness with me, I have wept for thine.
*Q. Mar.* Bear with me; I am hungry for
revenge,
And now I cloy me with beholding it.
Thy Edward he is dead, that kill'd my Ed-
ward;
Thy other Edward dead to quit my Edward;
Young York is but boot, because both
they
Match not the high perfection of my loss:
Thy Clarence he is dead that stabb'd my Ed-
ward;
And the beholders of this frantic play,

The adulterate Hastings, Rivers, Vaughan, Grey,
Untimely smother'd in their dusky graves.
Richard yet lives, hell's black intelligencer;
Only reserv'd their factor to buy souls,
And send them thither:—but at hand, at hand,
Ensues his piteous and unpitied end: [pray,
Earth gapes, hell burns, fiends roar, saints
To have him suddenly convey'd from hence.—
Cancel his bond of life, dear God, I pray,
That I may live to say, The dog is dead!
  Q. Eliz. O, thou didst prophesy the time would come
That I should wish for thee to help me curse
That bottled spider, that foul bunch-back'd toad!          [cf my fortune;
  Q. Mar. I call'd thee then, vain flourish
I call'd thee then, poor shadow, painted queen;
The presentation of but what I was,
The flattering index of a direful pageant;
One heav'd a-high, to be hurl'd down below;
A mother only mock'd with two fair babes;
A dream of what thou wast; a garish flag,
To be the aim of every dangerous shot;
A sign of dignity, a breath, a bubble;
A queen in jest, only to fill the scene.
Where is thy husband now? where be thy brothers?          [joy?
Where be thy two sons? wherein dost thou
Who sues, and kneels, and says, God save the queen?          [thee?
Where be the bending peers that flatter'd
Where be the thronging troops that follow'd thee?
Decline all this, and see what now thou art:
For happy wife, a most distressed widow;
For joyful mother, one that wails the name;
For one being su'd to, one that humbly sues;
For queen, a very caitiff crown'd with care;
For one that scorn'd at me, now scorn'd of me;
For one being fear'd of all, now fearing one;
For one commanding all, obey'd of none.
Thus hath the course of justice wheel'd about,
And left thee but a very prey to time:
Having no more but thought of what thou wast,          [art.
To torture thee the more, being what thou
Thou didst usurp my place, and dost thou not
Usurp the just proportion of my sorrow?
Now thy proud neck bears half my burden'd yoke;          [head,
From which even here I slip my wearied
And leave the burden of it all on thee.
Farewell, York's wife, and queen of sad mischance:—          [France.
These English woes shall make me smile in
  Q. Eliz. O thou well skill'd in curses, stay awhile.

And teach me how to curse mine enemies!
  Q. Mar. Forbear to sleep the night, and fast the day;
Compare dead happiness with living woe;
Think that thy babes were fairer than they were,
And he that slew them fouler than he is:
Bettering thy loss makes the bad-causer worse;
Revolving this will teach thee how to curse.
  Q. Eliz. My words are dull; O, quicken them with thine!
  Q. Mar. Thy woes will make them sharp, and pierce like mine.          [Exit.
  Duch. Why should calamity be full of words?          [woes,
  Q. Eliz. Windy attorneys to their client
Airy succeeders of intestate joys,
Poor breathing orators of miseries [impart
Let them have scope: though what they do
Help nothing else, yet do they ease the heart.
  Duch. If so, then be not tongue-tied: go with me,          [smother
And in the breath of bitter words let's
My damned son, that thy two sweet sons smother'd.          [Drum within.
I hear his drum:—be copious in exclaims.

  Enter KING RICHARD and his Train, marching.

  K. Rich. Who intercepts me in my expedition?          [thee,
  Duch. O, she that might have intercepted
By strangling thee in her accursed womb,
From all the slaughters, wretch, that thou hast done!
  Q. Eliz. Hidst thou that forehead with a golden crown,          [right,
Where should be branded, if that right were
The slaughter of the prince that ow'd that crown,          [brothers?
And the dire death of my poor sons and
Tell me, thou villain-slave, where are my children?          [brother Clarence?
  Duch. Thou toad, thou toad, where is thy
And little Ned Plantagenet, his son?
  Q. Eliz. Where is the gentle Rivers, Vaughhan, Grey?
  Duch. Where is kind Hastings?
  K. Rich. A flourish, trumpets! strike alarum, drums!          [women
Let not the heavens hear these tell-tale
Rail on the Lord's anointed: strike, I say!
          [Flourish. Alarums.
Either be patient, and entreat me fair,
Or with the clamorous report of war
Thus will I drown your exclamations.
  Duch. Art thou my son?          [yourself.
  K. Rich. Ay, I thank God, my father, and
  Duch. Then patiently hear my impatience.          [condition,
  K. Rich. Madam, I have a touch of your
That cannot brook the accent of reproof.
  Duch. O, let me speak!

*K Rich.*                Do, then; but I'll not hear.
*Duch.* I will be mild and gentle in my
words.                                [in haste.
*K. Rich.* And brief, good mother; for I am
*Duch.* Art thou so hasty? I have stay'd
for thee,
God knows, in torment and in agony.
*K. Rich.* And came I not at last to com-
fort you?                          [it well
*Duch.* No, by the holy rood, thou know'st
Thou cam'st on earth to make the earth my
hell.
A grievous burden was thy birth to me;
Tetchy and wayward was thy infancy;
Thy school-days frightful, desperate, wild,
and furious                     [venturous;
Thy prime of manhood daring, bold, and
Thy age confirm'd, proud, subtle, sly, and
bloody,                            [hatred:
More mild, but yet more harmful, kind in
What comfortable hour canst thou name
That ever grac'd me in thy company?
*K. Rich.* Faith, none but Humphrey Hour,
that call'd your grace
To breakfast once forth of my company.
If I be so disgracious in your eye,
Let me march on and not offend you,
madam.—
Strike up the drum.
*Duch.*                I pr'ythee, hear me speak.
*K. Rich.* You speak too bitterly.
*Duch.*                            Hear me a word;
For I shall never speak to thee again.
*K. Rich.* So.                    [ordinance
*Duch.* Either thou wilt die by God's just
Ere from this war thou turn a conqueror;
Or I with grief and extreme age shall perish,
And never look upon thy face again.
Therefore take with thee my most heavy
curse;
Which in the day of battle tire thee more
Than all the complete armour that thou
wear'st!
My prayers on the adverse party fight;
And there the little souls of Edward's chil-
dren
Whisper the spirits of thine enemies,
And promise them success and victory.
Bloody thou art, bloody will be thy end;
Shame serves thy life and doth thy death
attend.                            [*Exit.*
*Q. Eliz.* Though far more cause, yet much
less spirit to curse
Abides in me; I say amen to her.  [*Going.*
*K. Rich.* Stay, madam, I must talk a word
with you.                          [blood
*Q. Eliz.* I have no more sons of the royal
For thee to slaughter: for my daughters,
Richard,—                          [queens;
They shall be praying nuns, not weeping
And therefore level not to hit their lives.
*K. Rich.* You have a daughter call'd
Elizabeth,
Virtuous and fair, royal and gracious.

*Q. Eliz.* And must she die for this? O let
her live,                          [beauty;
And I'll corrupt her manners, stain her
Slander myself as false to Edward's bed;
Throw over her the veil of infamy:    [ter,
So she may live unscarr'd of bleeding slaugh-
I will confess she was not Edward's daughter.
*K. Rich.* Wrong not her birth; she is of
royal blood.                        [so.
*Q. Eliz.* To save her life I'll say she is not
*K. Rich.* Her life is safest only in her
birth.                            [brothers.
*Q. Eliz.* And only in that safety died her
*K. Rich.* Lo, at their births good stars
were opposite.                    [contrary.
*Q. Eliz.* No, to their lives bad friends were
*K. Rich.* All unavoided is the doom of
destiny.                          [destiny:
*Q. Eliz.* True, when avoided grace makes
My babes were destined to a fairer death
If grace had bless'd thee with a fairer life.
*K. Rich.* You speak as if that I had slain
my cousins.                  [uncle cozen'd
*Q. Eliz.* Cousins, indeed; and by their
Of comfort, kingdom, kindred, freedom, life
Whose hand soever lanc'd their tender hearts,
Thy head, all indirectly, gave direction:
No doubt the murderous knife was dull and
blunt
Till it was whetted on thy stone-hard heart,
To revel in the entrails of my lambs.  [tame,
But that still use of grief makes wild grief
My tongue should to thy ears not name my
boys                              [eyes;
Till that my nails were anchor'd in thine
And I, in such a desperate bay of death,
Like a poor bark, of sails and tackling reft,
Rush all to pieces on thy rocky bosom.
*K. Rich.* Madam, so thrive I in my enter-
prise
And dangerous success of bloody wars,
As I intend more good to you and yours
Than ever you or yours by me were harm'd!
*Q. Eliz.* What good is cover'd with the
face of heaven,
To be discover'd, that can do me good?
*K. Rich.* The advancement of your chil-
dren, gentle lady.            [their heads?
*Q. Eliz.* Up to some scaffold, there to lose
*K. Rich.* No, to the dignity and height of
honour,
The high imperial type of this earth's glory.
*Q. Eliz.* Flatter my sorrows with report of
it;                              [honour,
Tell me what state, what dignity, what
Canst thou demise to any child of mine?
*K. Rich.* Even all I have; ay, and myself
and all
Will I withal endow a child of thine;
So in the Lethe of thy angry soul    [wrongs
Thou drown the sad remembrance of those
Which thou supposest I have done to thee.
*Q. Eliz.* Be brief, lest that the process of
thy kindness

Last longer telling than thy kindness' date.

*K. Rich.* Then know, that from my soul I
love thy daughter.   '[with her soul.

*Q. Eliz.* My daughter's mother thinks it

*K. Rich.* What do you think?

*Q. Eliz.* That thou dost love my daughter
from thy soul:     [brothers;
So from thy soul's love didst thou love her
And from my heart's love I do thank thee
for it.     [meaning:

*K. Rich.* Be not so hasty so confound my
I mean that with my soul I love thy daugh-
ter,     [land.
And do intend to make her Queen of Eng-

*Q. Eliz.* Well, then, who dost thou mean
shall be her king?

*K. Rich.* Even he that makes her queen:
who else should be?

*Q. Eliz.* What, thou?     [madam?

*K. Rich.* I, even I: what think you of it,

*Q. Eliz.* How canst thou woo her?

*K. Rich.*     That I would learn of you,
As one being best acquainted with her humour.

*Q. Eliz.* And wilt thou learn of me?

*K. Rich.*     Madam, with all my heart.

*Q. Eliz.* Send to her, by the man that slew
her brothers,
A pair of bleeding hearts; thereon engrave
Edward and York; then haply will she weep:
Therefore present to her,—as sometime Mar-
garet     [blood,—
Did to thy father, steep'd in Rutland's
A handkerchief; which, say to her, did drain
The purple sap from her sweet brothers'
bodies,
And bid her wipe her weeping eyes withal,
If this inducement move her not to love,
Send her a letter of thy noble deeds;
Tell her thou mad'st away her uncle Clar-
ence,
Her uncle Rivers; ay, and for her ·sake
Mad'st quick conveyance with her good aunt
Anne.     [not the way

*K. Rich.* You mock me, madam; this is
To win your daughter.

*Q. Eliz.*     There is no other way;
Unless thou couldst put on some other shape,
And not be Richard that hath done all this.

*K. Rich.* Say that I did all this for love of
her?     [choose but hate thee,

*Q. Eliz.* Nay, then indeed she cannot
Having bought love with such a bloody spoil.

*K. Rich.* Look, what is done cannot be
now amended:
Men shall deal unadvisedly sometimes,
Which after-hours give leisure to repent.
If I did take the kingdom from your sons,
To make amends I'll give it to your daughter.
If I have kill'd the issue of your womb,
To quicken your increase I will beget
Mine issue of your blood upon your daugh-
ter:

A grandam's name is little less in love
Than is the doating title of a mother;
They are as children but one step below,
Even of your mettle, of your very blood;
Of all one pain,—save for a night of groans
Endur'd of her, for whom you bid like sor-
row.
Your children were vexation to your youth;
But mine shall be a comfort to your age.
The loss you have is but a son being king,
And by that loss your daughter is made
queen.
I cannot make you what amends I would,
Therefore accept such kindness as I can.
Dorset your son, that with a fearful soul
Leads discontented steps in foreign soil,
This fair alliance quickly shall call home
To high promotions and great dignity: [wife,
The king, that calls your beauteous daughter
Familiarly shall call thy Dorset brother;
Again shall you be mother to a king,
And all the ruins of distressful times
Repair'd with double riches of content.
What! we have many goodly days to see:
The liquid drops of tears that you have shed
Shall come again, transform'd to orient pearl,
Advantaging their loan with interest
Of ten-times-double gain of happiness.
Go, then, my mother, to thy daughter go;
Make bold her bashful years with your ex-
perience;
Prepare her ears to hear a wooer's tale:
Put in her tender heart the aspiring flame
Of golden sovereignty; acquaint the princess
With the sweet silent hours of marriage joys:
And when this arm of mine hath chastised
The petty rebel, dull-brain'd Buckingham,
Bound with triumphant garlands will I come,
And lead thy daughter to a conqueror's bed;
To whom I will retail my conquest won,
And she shall be sole victress, Cæsar's Cæsar

*Q. Eliz.* What were I best to say? her
father's brother
Would be her lord? or shall I say her uncle?
Or he that slew her brothers and her uncles?
Under what title shall I woo for thee,
That God, the law, my honour, and her love
Can make seem pleasing to her tender years?

*K. Rich.* Infer fair England's peace by this
alliance.     [still-lasting war.

*Q. Eliz.* Which she shall purchase with

*K. Rich.* Tell her the king, that may command, entreats.     [king's King forbids.

*Q. Eliz.* That at her hands which the

*K. Rich.* Say she shall be a ·high and
mighty queen.     [doth.

*Q. Eliz.* To wail the title, as her mother

*K. Rich.* Say I will love her everlastingly.

*Q. Eliz.* But how long shall that title,
*ever,* last?     [life's end.

*K. Rich.* Sweetly in force unto her fair

*Q. Eliz.* But how long fairly shall her
sweet life last?

*K. Rich.* As long as heaven and nature lengthens it.

*Q. Eliz.* As long as hell and Richard likes of it.  [ject low.

*K. Rich.* Say I, her sovereign, am her sub-

*Q. Eliz.* But she, your subject, loathes such sovereignty.

*K. Rich.* Be eloquent in my behalf to her.

*Q. Eliz.* An honest tale speeds best being plainly told.  [ing tale.

*K. Rich.* Then, plainly to her tell my lov-

*Q. Eliz.* Plain and not honest is too harsh a style.  [too quick.

*K. Rich.* Your reasons are too shallow and

*Q. Eliz.* O, no, my reasons are too deep and dead;—  [graves.

Too deep and dead, poor infants, in their

*K. Rich.* Harp not on that string, madam; that is past.  [strings break.

*Q. Eliz.* Harp on it still shall I till heart-

*K. Rich.* Now, by my George, my garter, and my crown,—  [third usurp'd.

*Q. Eliz.* Profan'd, dishonour'd, and the

*K. Rich.* I swear.—

*Q. Eliz.* By nothing; for this is no oath:

Thy George, profan'd hath lost his holy honour;  [virtue;

Thy garter, blemish'd, pawn'd his knightly

Thy crown, usurp'd, disgrac'd his kingly glory.  [believ'd,

If something thou wouldst swear to be

Swear, then, by something that thou hast not wrong'd.

*K. Rich.* Now, by the world,—

*Q. Eliz.* 'Tis full of thy foul wrongs.

*K. Rich.* My father's death,—

*Q. Eliz.* Thy life hath that dishonour'd.

*K. Rich.* Then, by myself,—

*Q. Eliz.* Thyself is self-misus'd.

*K. Rich.* Why, then, by God,—

*Q. Eliz.* God's wrong is most of all.

If thou hadst fear'd to break an oath by him,

The unity the king thy brother made

Had not been broken, nor my brother slain:

If thou hadst fear'd to break an oath by him,

The imperial metal, circling now thy head,

Had grac'd the tender temples of my child;

And both the princes had been breathing here,

Which now, two tender bedfellows for dust,

Thy broken faith hath made a prey for worms.

What canst thou swear by now?

*K. Rich.*  The time to come.

*Q. Eliz.* That thou hast wrong'd in the time o'erpast;

For I myself have many tears to wash

Hereafter time, for time past wronged by thee  [slaughter'd,

The children live whose parents thou hast

Ungovern'd youth, to wail it in their age;

The parents live whose children thou hast butcher'd,

Old barren plants, to wail it with their age.

Swear not by time to come; for that thou hast

Misus'd ere used, by times ill-us'd o'erpast.

*K. Rich.* As I intend to prosper and repent!

So thrive I in my dangerous attempt

Of hostile arms! myself myself confound!

Heaven and fortune bar me happy hours!

Day, yield me not thy light; nor, night, thy rest!

Be opposite all planets of good luck

To my proceeding!—if, with pure heart's love,

Immaculate devotion, holy thoughts,

I tender not thy beauteous princely daughter!

In her consists my happiness and thine;

Without her, follows to myself and thee;

Herself, the land, and many a Christian soul,

Death, desolation, ruin, and decay:

It cannot be avoided but by this;

It will not be avoided but by this.

Therefore, dear mother,—I must call you so,—

Be the attorney of my love to her:

Plead what I will be, not what I have been;

Not my deserts, but what I will deserve:

Urge the necessity and state of times,

And be not peevish found in great designs.

*Q. Eliz.* Shall I be tempted of the devil thus?  [good.

*K. Rich.* Ay, if the devil tempt you to do good.

*Q. Eliz.* Shall I forget myself to be myself?  [wrong yourself.

*K. Rich.* Ay, if your self's remembrance wrong yourself.

*Q. Eliz.* But thou didst kill my children.

*K. Rich.* But in your daughter's womb I bury them:  [breed

Where, in that nest of spicery, they shall

Selves of themselves, to your recomforture.

*Q. Eliz.* Shall I go win my daughter to thy will?  [deed.

*K. Rich.* And be a happy mother by the deed.

*Q. Eliz.* I go.—Write to me very shortly,

And you shall understand from me her mind.

*K. Rich.* Bear her my true love's kiss; and so, farewell.

[*Kissing her. Exit* Q. ELIZ.

Relenting fool, and shallow changing woman!

*Enter* RATCLIFF; CATESBY *following.*

How now! what news?

*Rat.* Most mighty sovereign, on the western coast

Rideth a puissant navy; to the short

Throng many doubtful hollow-hearted friends,

Unarm'd, and unresolv'd to beat them back:

'Tis thought that Richmond is their admiral;

And there they hull, expecting but the aid

Of Buckingham to welcome them ashore.

*K. Rich.* Some light-foot friend post to
the Duke of Norfolk:—
Ratcliff, thyself,—or Catesby; where is he?
*Cate.* Here, my good lord.
*K. Rich.*            Catesby, fly to the duke.
*Cate.* I will, my lord, with all convenient
haste.            [Salisbury:
*K. Rich.* Ratcliffe, come hither:—post to
When thou com'st thither,—Dull, unmindful
villain,            [*To* CATESBY.
Why stay'st thou here, and go'st not to the
duke?            [highness' pleasure,
*Cate.* First, mighty liege, tell me your
What from your grace I shall deliver to him.
*K. Rich.* O, true, good Catesby:—bid him
levy straight            [make,
The greatest strength and power he can
And meet me suddenly at Salisbury.
*Cate.* I go.            [*Exit.*
*Rat.* What, may it please you, shall I do
at Salisbury?            [before I go?
*K. Rich.* Why, what wouldst thou do there
*Rat.* Your highness told me I should post
before.

*Enter* STANLEY.

*K. Rich.* My mind is chang'd.—Stanley,
what news with you?
*Stan.* None good, my liege, to please you
with the hearing.
Nor none so bad but well may be reported.
*K. Rich.* Hoyday, a riddle! neither good
nor bad!
What need'st thou run so many miles about,
When thou mayst tell thy tale the nearest
way?
Once more, what news?
*Stan.*            Richmond is on the seas.
*K. Rich.* There let him sink, and be the
seas on him!
White-liver'd runagate, what doth he there?
*Stan.* I know not, mighty sovereign, but
by guess.
*K. Rich.* Well, as you guess?
*Stan.* Stirr'd up by Dorset, Buckingham,
and Morton,            [crown.
He makes for England here, to claim the
*K. Rich.* Is the chair empty? is the sword
unsway'd?
Is the king dead? the empire unpossess'd?
What heir of York is there alive but we?
And who is England's king but great York's
heir?
Then, tell me, what makes he upon the seas?
*Stan.* Unless for that, my liege, I cannot
guess.            [your liege,
*K. Rich.* Unless for that he comes to be
You cannot guess wherefore the Welshman
comes.
Thou wilt revolt, and fly to him I fear.
*Stan.* No, mighty liege; therefore mistrust
me not.            [beat him back?
*K. Rich.* Where is thy power, then, to
Where be thy tenants and thy followers?

Are they not now upon the western shore,
Safe-conducting the rebels from their ships?
*Stan.* No, my good lord, my friends are in
the north.            [in the north,
*K. Rich.* Cold friends to me: what do they
When they should serve their sovereign in
the west?            [mighty king:
*Stan.* They have not been commanded,
Pleaseth your majesty to give me leave,
I'll muster up my friends, and meet your
grace            [please.
Where and what time your majesty shall
*K. Rich.* Ay, ay, thou wouldst be gone to
join with Richmond;
But I'll not trust thee.
*Stan.*            Most mighty sovereign,
You have no cause to hold my friendship
doubtful:
I never was nor never will be false.
*K. Rich.* Go, then, and muster men. But
leave behind            [be firm,
Your son, George Stanley: look your heart
Or else his head's assurance is but frail.
*Stan.* So deal with him as I prove true to
you.            [*Exit.*

*Enter a* Messenger.

*Mess.* My gracious sovereign, now in
Devonshire,
As I by friends am well advertised,
Sir Edward Courtney, and the haughty pre-
late,
Bishop of Exeter, his elder brother,
With many more confederates, are in arms.

*Enter a second* Messenger.

2 *Mess.* In Kent, my liege, the Guilfords
are in arms;
And every hour more competitors            [strong.
Flock to the rebels, and their power grows

*Enter a third* Messenger.

3 *Mess.* My lord, the army of great
Buckingham,—
*K. Rich.* Out on ye, owls! nothing but
songs of death?            [*He strikes him.*
There, take thou that till thou bring better
news.            [jesty
3 *Mess.* The news I have to tell your ma-
Is, that by sudden floods and fall of waters,
Buckingham's army is dispers'd and scat-
ter'd:
And he himself wander'd away alone,
No man knows whither.
*K. Rich.*            I cry you mercy:
There is my purse to cure that blow of thine.
Hath any well-advised friend proclaim'd
Reward to him that brings the traitor in?
3 *Mess.* Such proclamation hath been
made, my liege.

*Enter a fourth* Messenger.

4 *Mess.* Sir Thomas Lovell and Lord Marquis Dorset,

'Tis said, my liege, in Yorkshire are in arms.
But this good comfort bring I to your highness,—
The Bretagne navy is dispers'd by tempest:
Richmond, in Dorsetshire, sent out a boat
Unto the shore, to ask those on the banks
If they were his assistants, yea or no;
Who answer'd him they came from Buckingham
Upon his party: he, mistrusting them,
Hois'd sail, and made his course again for
　　Bretagne. 　　　　[up in arms;
　K. Rich. March on, march on, since we are
If not to fight with foreign enemies,
Yet to beat down these rebels here at home.

*Re-enter* CATESBY.

　Cate. My liege, the Duke of Buckingham
　　is taken,— 　　　　[Richmond
That is the best news: that the Earl of
Is with a mighty power landed at Milford
Is colder news, but yet they must be told.
　K. Rich. Away towards Salisbury! while
　　we reason here
A royal battle might be won and lost:—
Some one take order Buckingham be brought
To Salisbury; the rest march on with me.
　　　　　　　[*Flourish. Exeunt.*

SCENE V.—*A Room in* LORD STANLEY'S
*House.*

*Enter* STANLEY *and* SIR CHRISTOPHER
　　URSWICK.

　Stan. Sir Christopher, tell Richmond this
　　from me:—
That in the sty of the most deadly boar
My son George Stanley is frank'd up in hold:
If I revolt, off goes young George's head;
The fear of that holds off my present aid.
So, get thee gone: commend me to thy lord;
Withal say that the queen hath heartily consented
He should espouse Elizabeth her daughter.
But tell me, where is princely Richmond
　　now? 　　　　　[in Wales.
　Chris. At Pembroke, or at Ha'rford-west,
　Stan. What men of name resort to him?
　Chris. Sir Walter Herbert, a renowned
　　soldier;
Sir Gilbert Talbot, Sir William Stanley;
Oxford, redoubted Pembroke, Sir James
　　Blunt,
And Rice ap Thomas, with a valiant crew;
And many other of great name and worth:
And towards London do they bend their
　　power,
If by the way they be not fought withal.
　Stan. Well, hie thee to thy lord; I kiss his
　　hand;
These letters will resolve him of my mind.
Farewell. 　　[*Gives papers to* SIR CHRIS.
　　　　　　　　　[*Exeunt.*

ACT V.

SCENE I.—SALISBURY. *An open place.*

*Enter the* Sheriff *and* Guard, *with* BUCKINGHAM, *led to execution.*

　Buck. Will not King Richard let me speak
　　with him?
　Sher. No, my good lord; therefore be
　　patient. 　　　　[Grey, and Rivers,
　Buck. Hastings, and Edward's children,
Holy King Henry, and thy fair son Edward,
Vaughan, and all that have miscarried
By underhand corrupted foul injustice,—
If that your moody discontented souls [hour,
Do through the clouds behold this present
Even for revenge mock my destruction!—
This is All-Souls' day, fellows, is it not?
　Sher. It is, my lord.
　Buck. Why, then, All-Souls' day is my
　　body's doomsday. 　　　[time
This is the day which in King Edward's
I wish'd might fall on me, when I was found
False to his children or his wife's allies;
This is the day wherein I wish'd to fall
By the false faith of him whom most I
　　trusted;
This, this All-Souls' day to my fearful soul
Is the determin'd respite of my wrongs;
That high All-Seer which I dallied with
Hath turn'd my feigned prayer on my head,
And given in earnest what I begg'd in jest.
Thus doth he force the swords of wicked men
To turn their own points on their masters'
　　bosoms: 　　　　　[neck,—
Thus Margaret's curse falls heavy on my
When he, quoth she, *shall split thy heart with
　　sorrow,*
*Remember Margaret was a prophetess.*—
Come, sirs, convey me to the block of shame;
Wrong hath but wrong, and blame the due
　　of blame. 　　　　　[*Exeunt.*

SCENE II.—*Plain near Tamworth.*

*Enter, with drum and colours,* RICHMOND,
OXFORD, SIR JAMES BLUNT, SIR WALTER
HERBERT, *and others, with* Forces, *marching.*

　Richm. Fellows in arms, and my most
　　loving friends,
Bruis'd underneath the yoke of tyranny,
Thus far into the bowels of the land
Have we march'd on without impediment;
And here receive we from our father Stanley
Lines of fair comfort and encouragement.
The wretched, bloody, and usurping boar,
That spoil'd your summer fields and fruitful
　　vines, 　　　　　his trough
Swills your warm blood like wash, and makes
In your embowell'd bosoms,—this foul swine
Lies now even in the centre of this isle,
Near to the town of Leicester, as we learn:
From Tamworth thither is but one day's
　　march. 　　　　　[friends
In God's name, cheerly on courageous

To reap the harvest of perpetual peace
By this one bloody trial of sharp war.

*Oxf.* Every man's conscience is a thousand swords,
To fight against that bloody homicide.

*Herb.* I doubt not but his friends will turn to us.     [friends for fear,

*Blunt.* He hath no friends but what are
Which in his dearest need will fly from him.

*Richm.* All for our vantage. Then, in God's name, march:   [wings;
True hope is swift, and flies with swallows' Kings it makes gods, and meaner creatures kings.       [*Exeunt.*

### SCENE III.—*Bosworth Field.*

*Enter* KING RICHARD *and* Forces; *the* DUKE OF NORFOLK, EARL OF SURREY, *and others.*

*K. Rich.* Here pitch our tents, even here in Bosworth field.—
My Lord of Surrey, why look you so sad?

*Sur.* My heart is ten times lighter than my looks.

*K. Rich.* My Lord of Norfolk,—

*Nor.*     Here, most gracious liege.

*K. Rich.* Norfolk, we must have knocks; ha! must we not?    [ing lord.

*Nor.* We must both give and take, my lov-

*K. Rich.* Up with my tent! Here will I lie to-night;

[*Soldiers begin to set up the* KING'S *tent.*
But where to-morrow? Well, all's one for that.—       [tors?
Who hath descried the number of the trai-

*Nor.* Six or seven thousand is their utmost power.      [account:

*K. Rich.* Why, our battalia trebles that
Besides, the king's name is a tower of strength,
Which they upon the adverse faction want.—
Up with the tent!—Come, noble gentlemen,
Let us survey the vantage of the ground;—
Call for some men of sound direction:—
Let's lack no discipline, make no delay;
For, lords, to-morrow is a busy day.
        [*Exeunt.*

*Enter, on the other side of the Field,* RICH-MOND, SIR WILLIAM BRANDON, OXFORD, *and other* Lords. *Some of the* Soldiers *pitch* RICHMOND'S *tent.*

*Richm.* The weary sun hath made a golden set,
And by the bright track of his fiery car
Gives token of a goodly day to-morrow.—
Sir William Brandon, you shall bear my standard.—
Give me some ink and paper in my tent:
I'll draw the form and model of our battle,
Limit each leader to his several charge,
And part in just proportion our small power.—
My Lord of Oxford,—you, Sir William Brandon,—

And you, Sir Walter Herbert,—stay with me.—
The Earl of Pembroke keeps his regiment:—
Good Captain Blunt, bear my good-night to him,
And by the second hour in the morning
Desire the earl to see me in my tent:
Yet one thing more, good captain, do for me,—
Where is Lord Stanley quarter'd, do you know?

*Blunt.* Unless I have mista'en his colours much.—
Which well I am assur'd I have not done,—
His regiment lies half a mile at least
South from the mighty power of the king.

*Richm.* If without peril it be possible,
Sweet Blunt, make some good means to speak with him,
And give him from me this most needful note.

*Blunt.* Upon my life, my lord, I'll undertake it;
And so, God give you quiet rest to-night!

*Richm.* Good-night, good Captain Blunt.
 —Come, gentlemen,
Let us consult upon to-morrow's business:
In to my tent; the air is raw and cold.
     [*They withdraw into the tent.*

*Enter, to his tent,* KING RICHARD, NORFOLK, RATCLIFF, *and* CATESBY.

*K. Rich.* What is't o'clock?

*Cate.*     It's supper-time, my lord;
It's six o'clock.

*K. Rich.*     I will not sup to-night.—
Give me some ink and paper.—
What, is my beaver easier than it was?
And all my armour laid into my tent?

*Cate.* It is, my liege; and all things are in readiness.

*K. Rich.* Good Norfolk, hie thee to thy charge;
Use careful watch, choose trusty sentinels.

*Nor.* I go, my lord.

*K. Rich.* Stir with the lark to-morrow, gentle Norfolk.

*Nor.* I warrant you, my Lord.   [*Exit*

*K. Rich.* Ratcliff,—

*Rat.* My lord?

*K. Rich.* Send out a pursuivant-at-arms
To Stanley's regiment; bid him bring his power
Before sunrising, lest his son George fall
Into the blind cave of eternal night.—
Fill me a bowl of wine.—Give me a watch.—
Saddle white Surrey to the field to-morrow.—
Look that my staves be sound, and not too heavy.—
Ratcliff,—

*Rat.* My lord?

*K. Rich.* Saw'st thou the melancholy Lord Northumberland?

*Rat.* Thomas the Earl of Surrey and himself,
Much about cock-shut time, from troop to troop
Went through the army, cheering up the soldiers.
  *K. Rich.* So, I am satisfied.—Give me a bowl of wine:
I have not that alacrity of spirit
Nor cheer of mind that I was wont to have.
Set it down.—Is ink and paper ready?
  *Rat.* It is, my lord.
  *K. Rich.* Bid my guard watch; leave me.
Ratcliff, about the mid of night come to my tent
And help to arm me. Leave me, I say.
  [K. RICH. *retires into his tent. Exeunt*
    RATCLIFF *and* CATESBY.

RICHMOND'S *tent opens, and discovers him*
    *and his Officers, &c.*

*Enter* STANLEY.

  *Stan.* Fortune and victory sit on thy helm!
  *Richm.* All comfort that the dark night can afford
Be to thy person, noble father-in-law!
Tell me, how fares our loving mother?
  *Stan.* I, by attorney, bless thee from thy mother,
Who prays continually for Richmond's good:
So much for that.—The silent hours steal on,
And flaky darkness breaks within the east.
In brief,—for so the season bids us be,—
Prepare thy battle early in the morning,
And put thy fortune to the arbitrement
Of bloody strokes and mortal-staring war.
I, as I may,—that which I would I cannot,—
With best advantage will deceive the time,
And aid thee in this doubtful stroke of arms:
But on thy side I may not be too forward,
Lest, being seen, thy brother, tender George,
Be executed in his father's sight.
Farewell: the leisure and the fearful time
Cuts off the ceremonious vows of love
And ample interchange of sweet discourse,
Which so-long-sunder'd friends should dwell upon:
God give us leisure for these rites of love!
Once more, adieu: be valiant, and speed well!
  *Richm.* Good lords, conduct him to his regiment:
I'll strive, with troubled thoughts, to take a nap,
Lest leaden slumber peise me down to-morrow,
When I should mount with wings of victory:
Once more, good-night, kind lords and gentlemen.
    [*Exeunt* Lords, &c., *with* STAN.
O Thou whose captain I account myself,
Look on my forces with a gracious eye;
Put in their hands thy bruising irons of wrath,

That they may crush down with a heavy fall
The usurping helmets of our adversaries!
Make us thy ministers of chastisement,
That we may praise thee in thy victory!
To thee I do commend my watchful soul
Ere I let fall the windows of mine eyes:
Sleeping and waking, O, defend me still!
    [*Sleeps.*

*The* Ghost *of* PRINCE EDWARD, *son to* HENRY
    THE SIXTH, *rises between the two tents.*

  *Ghost.* Let me sit heavy on thy soul to-morrow!   [*To* KING RICHARD.
Think how thou stabb'dst me in my prime of youth
At Tewksbury: despair, therefore, and die!—
Be cheerful, Richmond; for the wronged souls
Of butcher'd princes fight in thy behalf:
King Henry's issue, Richmond, comforts thee.

*The* Ghost *of* KING HENRY THE SIXTH *rises.*

  *Ghost.* When I was mortal, my anointed body   [*To* KING RICHARD.
By thee was punched full of deadly holes:
Think on the Tower and me: despair, and die,—
Harry the Sixth bids thee despair and die!—
Virtuous and holy, be thou conqueror!
    [*To* RICHMOND.
Harry, that prophesied thou shouldst be king,
Doth comfort thee in sleep: live, and flourish!

*The* Ghost *of* CLARENCE *rises.*

  *Ghost.* Let me sit heavy on thy soul to-morrow!
    [*To* KING RICHARD.
I, that was wash'd to death with fulsome wine,
Poor Clarence, by thy guile betray'd to death!
To-morrow in the battle think on me,
And fall thy edgeless sword: despair, and die!—
Thou offspring of the house of Lancaster,
    [*To* RICHMOND.
The wronged heirs of York do pray for thee:
Good angels guard thy battle! live, and flourish!

*The* Ghosts *of* RIVERS, GREY, *and* VAUGHAN
    *rise.*

  *G. of R.* Let me sit heavy on thy soul to-morrow,   [*To* KING RICHARD.
Rivers, that died at Pomfret! despair, and die!
  *G. of G.* Think upon Grey, and let thy soul despair!   [*To* KING RICHARD.
  *G. of V.* Think upon Vaughan, and, with guilty fear,
Let fall thy lance: despair, and die!—
    [*To* KING RICHARD.

*All Three.* Awake, and think our wrongs in Richard's bosom     [*To* RICHMOND.
Will conquer him!—awake, and win the day!

*The* Ghost *of* HASTINGS *rises.*

*Ghost.* Bloody and guilty, guiltily awake,
                 [*To* KING RICHARD.
And in a bloody battle end thy days!
Think on Lord Hastings: despair, and die!—
Quiet untroubled soul, awake, awake!
                [*To* RICHMOND.
Arm, fight, and conquer, for fair England's sake!

*The* Ghosts *of the two young* Princes *rise.*

*Ghosts.* Dream on thy cousins smother'd in the Tower:
Let us be lead within thy bosom, Richard,
And weigh thee down to ruin, shame, and death!             [die!—
Thy nephews' souls bid thee despair and die!—
Sleep, Richmond, sleep in peace, and wake in joy;
Good angels guard thee from the boar's annoy!
Live, and beget a happy race of kings!
Edward's unhappy sons do bid thee flourish.

*The* Ghost *of* QUEEN ANNE *rises.*

*Ghost.* Richard, thy wife, that wretched Anne thy wife,
That never slept a quiet hour with thee,
Now fills thy sleep with perturbations:
To-morrow in the battle think on me,
And fall thy edgeless sword: despair, and die!—
Thou quiet soul, sleep thou a quiet sleep;
                [*To* RICHMOND.
Dream of success and happy victory:
Thy adversary's wife doth pray for thee.

*The* Ghost *of* BUCKINGHAM *rises.*

*Ghost.* The first was I that help'd thee to the crown;      [*To* KING RICHARD.
The last was I that felt thy tyranny:
O, in the battle think on Buckingham,
And die in terror of thy guiltiness!
Dream on, dream on of bloody deeds and death:
Fainting, despair; despairing, yield thy breath!—
I died for hope ere I could lend thee aid:
                [*To* RICHMOND.
But cheer thy heart, and be thou not dismay'd:
God and good angels fight on Richmond's side;
And Richard falls in height of all his pride.
     [*The* Ghosts *vanish.* K. RICH. *starts out of his dream.*
*K. Rich.* Give me another horse,—bind up my wounds,—
Have mercy, Jesu!—Soft! I did but dream.—

O coward conscience, how dost thou afflict me!—
The lights burn blue.—It is now dead midnight.
Cold fearful drops stand on my trembling flesh.
What, do I fear myself? there's none else by:
Richard loves Richard; that is, I am I.
Is there a murderer here? No;—yes; I am:
Then fly. What, from myself? Great reason why,—
Lest I revenge. What,—myself upon myself!
Alack, I love myself. Wherefore! for any good
That I myself have done unto myself?
O, no! alas, I rather hate myself
For hateful deeds committed by myself!
I am a villain: yet I lie, I am not.
Fool, of thyself speak well:—fool, do not flatter.
My conscience hath a thousand several tongues,
And every tongue brings in a several tale,
And every tale condemns me for a villain.
Perjury, perjury, in the high'st degree;
Murder, stern murder, in the dir'st degree;
All several sins, all us'd in each degree,
Throng to the bar, crying all, Guilty! guilty!
I shall despair. There is no creature loves me;
And if I die no soul shall pity me:
Nay, wherefore should they,—since that I myself
Find in myself no pity to myself?
Methought the souls of all that I had murder'd
Came to my tent; and every one did threat
To-morrow's vengeance on the head of Richard.

*Enter* RATCLIFF.

*Rat.* My lord,—
*K. Rich.* Who's there?     [village-cock
*Rat.* Ratcliff, my lord; 'tis I. The early
Hath twice done salutation to the morn;
Your friends are up, and buckle on their armour.
*K. Rich.* O Ratcliff, I have dream'd a fearful dream!—         [all true?
What thinkest thou,—will our friends prove
*Rat.* No doubt, my lord.
*K. Rich.*         O Ratcliff, I fear, I fear,—
*Rat.* Nay, good my lord, be not afraid of shadows.           [night
*K. Rich.* By the apostle Paul, shadows to-
Have struck more terror to the soul of Richard
Than can the substance of ten thousand soldiers
Armed in proof and led by shallow Richmond.
It is not yet near day. Come, go with me;
Under our tents I'll play the eaves-dropper,
To hear if any mean to shrink from me.
     [*Exeunt* K. RICH. *and* RATCLIFF.

RICHMOND *wakes. Enter* OXFORD *and others.*

*Lords.* Good-morrow, Richmond!
*Richm.* Cry mercy, lords and watchful
    gentlemen,
That you have ta'en a tardy sluggard here.
*Lords.* How have you slept, my lord?
*Richm.* The sweetest sleep and fairest-
    boding dreams
That ever enter'd in a drowsy head
Have I since your departure had, my lords.
Methought their souls whose bodies Rich-
    ard murder'd
Came to my tent, and cried on victory:
I promise you, my heart is very jocund
In the remembrance of so fair a dream.
How far into the morning is it, lords?
*Lords.* Upon the stroke of four.
*Richm.* Why, then, 'tis time to arm and
    give direction.—
             [*He advances to the* Troops.
More than I have said, loving countrymen,
The leisure and enforcement of the time
Forbids to dwell on: yet remember this,—
God and our good cause fight upon our side;
The prayers of holy saints and wronged
    souls,
Like high-rear'd bulwarks, stand before our
    faces;
Richard except, those whom we fight against
Had rather have us win than him they fol-
    low:               [men,
For what is he they follow? truly, gentle-
A bloody tyrant and a homicide;    [lish'd;
One rais'd in blood, and one in blood estab-
One that made means to come by what he
    hath,
And slaughter'd those that were the means
    to help him.;
A base foul stone, made precious by the foil
Of England's chair, where he is falsely set;
One that hath ever been God's enemy:
Then, if you fight against God's enemy,
God will, in justice, ward you as his soldiers;
If you do sweat to put a tyrant down,
You sleep in peace, the tyrant being slain;
If you do fight against your country's foes,
Your country's fat shall pay your pains the
    hire;
If you do fight in safeguard of your wives,
Your wives shall welcome home the con-
    querors;
If you do free your children from the sword,
Your children's children quit it in your age.
Then, in the name of God and all these rights,
Advance your standards, draw your willing
    swords.
For me, the ransom of my bold attempt
Shall be this cold corpse on the earth's cold
    face;
But if I thrive, the gain of my attempt
The least of you shall share his part thereof.
Sound drums and trumpets boldly and
    cheerfully;

God and Saint George! Richmond and vic-
    tory!               [*Exeunt.*

*Re-enter* KING RICHARD, RATCLIFF,
    Attendants, *and* Forces.

*K. Rich.* What said Northumberland as
    touching Richmond?
*Rat.* That he was never trained up in
    arms.
*K. Rich.* He said the truth: and what said
    Surrey then?           [purpose.
*Rat.* He smil'd, and said, the better for our
*K. Rich.* He was in the right; and so, in-
    deed, it is.        [*Clock strikes.*
Tell the clock there.—Give me a calendar.—
Who saw the sun to-day?
*Rat.*              Not I, my lord.
*K. Rich.* Then he disdains to shine; for by
    the book
He should have brav'd the east an hour ago:
A black day will it be to somebody.—
Ratcliff,—
*Rat.* My lord?
*K. Rich.* The sun will not be seen to-day;
The sky doth frown and lower upon our
    army.
I would these dewy tears were from the
    ground.
Not shine to-day! Why, what is that to me
More than to Richmond? for the selfsame
    heaven
That frowns on me looks sadly upon him.

*Enter* NORFOLK.

*Nor.* Arm, arm, my lord; the foe vaunts in
    the field.          [my horse;—
*K. Rich.* Come, bustle, bustle; caparison
Call up Lord Stanley, bid him bring his
    power:
I will lead forth my soldiers to the plain,
And thus my battle shall be ordered:—
My forward shall be drawn out all in length,
Consisting equally of horse and foot;
Our archers shall be placed in the midst:
John Duke of Norfolk, Thomas Earl of Sur-
    rey,
Shall have the leading of this foot and
    horse.
They thus directed, we ourself will follow
In the main battle; whose puissance on ei-
    ther side
Shall be well winged with our chiefest horse.
This, and Saint George to boot!—What
    think'st thou, Norfolk?
*Nor.* A good direction, warlike sover-
    eign.—
This found I on my tent this morning.
               [*Giving a scroll.*
*K. Rich.* [*Reads.*] *Jocky of Norfolk, be
    not too bold,
    For Dickon thy master is bought and
    sold.*
A thing devised by the enemy.—
Go, gentlemen, every man unto his charge:

Let not our babbling dreams affright our
    souls;
Conscience is but a word that cowards use,
Devis'd at first to keep the strong in awe:
Our strong arms be our conscience, swords
    our law.
March on, join bravely, let us to't pell-mell;
If not to heaven, then hand in hand to hell.—
What shall I say more than I have inferr'd?
Remember whom you are to cope withal;—
A sort of vagabonds, rascals, and runaways,
A scum of Bretagnes, and base lackey peas-
    ants,
Whom their o'er-cloyed country vomits forth
To desperate ventures and assur'd destruc-
    tion.
You sleeping safe, they bring you to unrest;
You having lands, and bless'd with beau-
    teous wives,
They would restrain the one, distain the
    other.
And who doth lead them but a paltry fellow,
Long kept in Bretagne at our mother's cost?
A milk sop, one that never in his life
Felt so much cold as over shoes in snow?
Let's whip these stragglers o'er the seas
    again;
Lash hence these over-weening rags of
    France,
These famish'd beggars, weary of their lives;
Who, but for dreaming on this fond exploit,
For want of means, poor rats, had hang'd
    themselves:
If we be conquer'd, let men conquer us,
And not these bastard Bretagnes; whom our
    fathers                              [thump'd,
Have in their own land beaten, bobb'd, and
And, on record, left them the heirs of shame.
Shall these enjoy our lands? lie with our
    wives?
Ravish our daughters?—Hark! I hear their
    drum.                          [Drum afar off.
Fight, gentlemen of England! fight, bold
    yeomen!
Draw, archers, draw your arrows to the
    head!
Spur your proud horses hard, and ride in
    blood;
Amaze the welkin with your broken staves!

*Enter a* Messenger.

What says Lord Stanley? will he bring his
    power?
*Mess.* My lord, he doth deny to come.
*K. Rich.* Off with his son George's head!
*Nor.* My lord, the enemy is pass'd the
    marsh:
After the battle let George Stanley die.
*K. Rich.* A thousand hearts are great
    within my bosom:
Advance our standards, set upon our foes;
Our ancient word of courage, fair Saint
    George,
Inspire us with the spleen of fiery dragons!

Upon them! Victory sits on our helms.
                                    [*Exeunt.*

SCENE IV.—*Another part of the Field.*
*Alarum: excursions. Enter* NORFOLK *and*
    Forces; *to him* CATESBY.

    *Cate.* Rescue, my Lord of Norfolk, rescue,
        rescue!
The king enacts more wonders than a man,
Daring an opposite to every danger:
His horse is slain, and all on foot he fights,
Seeking for Richmond in the throat of death.
Rescue, fair lord, or else the day is lost!

    *Alarum. Enter* KING RICHARD.

    *K. Rich.* A horse! a horse! my kingdom
        for a horse!
    *Cate.* Withdraw, my lord; I'll help you to
        a horse.
    *K. Rich.* Slave, I have set my life upon a
        cast,
And I will stand the hazard of the die:
I think there be six Richmonds in the field;
Five have I slain to-day instead of him.—
A horse! a horse! my kingdom for a horse!
                                    [*Exeunt.*

SCENE V.—*Another part of the Field.*
*Alarums. Enter, from opposite sides,* KING
    RICHARD *and* RICHMOND; *and exeunt
    fighting. Retreat, and flourish. Then re-
    enter* RICHMOND, *with* STANLEY *bearing
    the crown, and divers other* Lords *and*
    Forces.

    *Richm.* God and your arms be prais'd,
        victorious friends;
The day is ours, the bloody dog is dead.
    *Stan.* Courageous Richmond, well hast
        thou acquit thee!
Lo, here, this long-usurped royalty
From the dead temples of this bloody wretch
Have I pluck'd off, to grace thy brows with-
    al:
Wear it, enjoy it, and make much of it.
    *Richm.* Great God of heaven, say Amen
        to all!—
But, tell me, is young George Stanley living?
    *Stan.* He is, my lord, and safe in Leicester
        town,                              [draw us.
Whither, if it please you, we may now with-
    *Richm.* What men of name are slain on
        either side?
    *Stan.* John Duke of Norfolk, Walter Lord
        Ferrers,                          [Brandon.
Sir Robert Brakenbury, and Sir William
    *Richm.* Inter their bodies as becomes their
        births:
Proclaim a pardon to the soldiers fled
That in submission will return to us:
And then, as we have ta'en the sacrament,
We will unite the white rose and the red:—
Smile heaven upon this fair conjunction,
That long hath frown'd upon their enmity!
What traitor hears me, and says not Amen?

England hath long been mad, and scarr'd
    herself;
The brother blindly shed the brother's blood,
The father rashly slaughter'd his own son,
The son, compell'd, been butcher to the sire:
All this divided York and Lancaster,
Divided in their dire division,—
O, now let Richmond and Elizabeth,
The true succeeders of each royal house,
By God's fair ordinance conjoin together!
And let their heirs,—God, if thy will be so,—
Enrich the time to come with smooth'd-
    fac'd peace,
With smiling plenty, and fair prosperous
    days!
Abate the edge of traitors, gracious Lord,
That would reduce these bloody days again,
And make poor England weep in streams of
    blood!
Let them not live to taste this land's increase
That would with treason wound this fair
    land's peace!
Now civil wounds are stopp'd, peace lives
    again:
That she may long live here, God say Amen!
                                    [*Exeunt.*

HENRY the EIGHTH

Act III. Sc. 2.

# KING HENRY VIII.

## DRAMATIS PERSONÆ

KING HENRY THE EIGHTH.
CARDINAL WOLSEY.
CARDINAL CAMPEIUS.
CAPUCIUS, *Ambas. from the Emperor*
CHARLES V.
CRANMER, *Archbishop of Canterbury.*
DUKE OF NORFOLK.
DUKE OF BUCKINGHAM.
DUKE OF SUFFOLK.
EARL OF SURREY.
Lord Chamberlain. Lord Chancellor.
GARDINER, *Bishop of Winchester.*
BISHOP OF LINCOLN.
LORD ABERGAVENNY.
LORD SANDS.
SIR HENRY GUILDFORD.
SIR THOMAS LOVELL.
SIR ANTHONY DENNY.
SIR NICHOLAS VAUX.
Secretaries *to* WOLSEY.
CROMWELL, *Servant to* WOLSEY.

GRIFFITH, *Gent.-Usher to* QUEEN KATHAR-
INE.
Three Gentlemen.
DR. BUTTS, *Physician to the* KING.
Garter King-at-Arms.
Surveyor *to the* DUKE OF BUCKINGHAM.
BRANDON, *and a* Sergeant-at-Arms.
Doorkeeper of the Council Chamber.
Porter, *and his* Man.
Page *to* GARDINER. A Crier.

QUEEN KATHARINE, *Wife to* KING HENRY,
*afterwards divorced.*
ANNE BULLEN, *her Maid of Honour, after-*
*wards Queen.*
An Old Lady, *Friend to* ANNE BULLEN.
PATIENCE, *Woman to* QUEEN KATHARINE.

*Several* Lords *and* Ladies *in the Dumb Shows;*
Women *attending upon the* QUEEN;
Scribes, Officers, Guards, *and other* At-
tendants; Spirits.

SCENE,—*Chiefly in* LONDON *and* WESTMINSTER; *once at* KIMBOLTON.

## PROLOGUE.

I come no more to make you laugh: things
now
That bear a weighty and a serious brow,
Sad, high, and working, full of state and
woe,
Such noble scenes as draw the eye to flow,
We now present. Those that can pity, here
May, if they think it well, let fall a tear;
The subject will deserve it. Such as give
Their money out of hope they may believe,
May here find truth too. Those that come to
see
Only a show or two, and so agree
The play may pass, if they be still and will-
ing,
I'll undertake may see away their shilling
Richly in two short hours. Only they
That come to hear a merry bawdy play,
A noise of targets, or to see a fellow
In a long motley coat guarded with yellow,
Will be deceiv'd; for, gentle hearers, know,
To rank our chosen truth with such a show
As fool and fight is, beside forfeiting
Our own brains, and the opinion that we
bring,
To make that only true we now intend,
Will leave us never an understanding friend.
Therefore, for goodness' sake, and as you
are known

The first and happiest hearers of the town,
Be sad, as we would make ye: think ye see
The very persons of our noble story
As they were living; think you see them
great,
And follow'd with the general throng and
sweat
Of thousand friends; then, in a moment, see
How soon this mightiness meets misery:
And if you can be merry then I'll say
A man may weep upon his wedding-day.

## ACT I.

SCENE I.—LONDON. *An Ante-chamber in the*
*Palace.*

*Enter the* DUKE OF NORFOLK *at one door; at*
*the other, the* DUKE OF BUCKINGHAM *and*
*the* LORD ABERGAVENNY.

*Buck.* Good-morrow, and well met. How
have you done
Since last we saw in France?
*Nor.*                    I thank your grace,
Healthful; and ever since a fresh admirer
Of what I saw there.
*Buck.*                    An untimely ague
Stay'd me a prisoner in my chamber, when
Those suns of glory, those two lights of men,
Met in the vale of Andren.
*Nor.*                    'Twixt Guynes and Arde:

I was then present, saw them salute on
    horseback;         [clung
Beheld them, when they lighted, how they
In their embracement, as they grew together;
Which had they, what four thron'd ones
    could have weigh'd
Such a compounded one?

   *Buck.*             All the whole time
I was my chamber's prisoner.

   *Nor.*              Then you lost
The view of earthly glory: men might say,
Till this time pomp was single, but now mar-
    ried
To one above itself. Each following day
Became the next day's master, till the last
Made former wonders it's: to-day the
    French,
All clinquant, all in gold, like heathen gods,
Shone down the English; and to-morrow
    they
Made Britain India: every man that stood
Show'd like a mine. Their dwarfish pages
    were
As cherubims, all gilt: the madams too,
Not us'd to toil, did almost sweat to bear
The pride upon them, that their very labour
Was to them as a painting: now this masque
Was cried incomparable; and the ensuing
    night
Made it a fool and beggar. The two kings,
Equal in lustre, were now best, now worst,
As presence did present them; him in eye,
Still him in praise: and, being present both,
'Twas said they saw but one; and no dis-
    cerner
Durst wag his tongue in censure. When these
    suns,—       [challeng'd
For so they phrase 'em,—by their heralds
The noble spirits to arms, they did perform
Beyond thought's compass: that former
    fabulous story,
Being now seen possible enough, got credit,
That Bevis was believ'd.

   *Buck.*             O, you go far.
   *Nor.* As I belong to worship, and affect
In honour honesty, the tract of everything
Would by a good discourser lose some life,
Which action's self was tongue to. All was
    royal;
To the disposing of it naught rebell'd,
Order gave each thing view; the office did
Distinctly his full function.

   *Buck.*            Who did guide—
I mean, who set the body and the limbs
Of this great sport together, as you guess?
   *Nor.* One, certes, that promises no element
In such a business.

   *Buck.*       I pray you, who, my lord?
   *Nor.* All this was order'd by the good dis-
    cretion
Of the right reverend Cardinal of York.
   *Buck.* The devil speed him! no man's pie is
    freed

From his ambitious finger. What had he
To do in these fierce vanities? I wonder
That such a keech can with his very bulk
Take up the rays o' the beneficial sun,
And keep it from the earth.

   *Nor.*             Surely, sir,
There's in him stuff that puts him to these
    ends;            [grace
For, being not propp'd by ancestry, whose
Chalks successors their way; nor call'd upon
For high feats done to the crown; neither
    allied
To eminent assistants; but, spider-like,
Out of his self-drawing web, he gives us note
The force of his own merit makes his way;
A gift that heaven gives for him, which buys
A place next to the king.

   *Aber.*           I cannot tell
What heaven hath given him,—let some
    graver eye
Pierce into that; but I can see his pride
Peep through each part of him: whence has
    he that?
If not from hell, the devil is a niggard;
Or has given all before, and he begins
A new hell in himself.

   *Buck.*             Why the devil,
Upon this French going-out, took he upon
    him,
Without the privity o' the king, to appoint
Who should attend on him? He makes up
    the file
Of all the gentry; for the most part such
To whom as great a charge as little honour
He meant to lay upon: and his own letter,
The honourable board of council out,
Must fetch him in the papers.

   *Aber.*            I do know
Kinsmen of mine, three at the least, that
    have
By this so sicken'd their estates that never
They shall abound as formerly.

   *Buck.*           O, many   [on 'em
Have broke their backs with laying manors
For this great journey. What did this vanity
But minister communication of
A most poor issue?

   *Nor.*          Grievingly I think,
The peace between the French and us not
    values
The cost that did conclude it.

   *Buck.*           Every man,
After the hideous storm that follow'd, was
A thing inspir'd; and, not consulting, broke
Into a general prophecy,—That this tempest,
Dashing the garment of this peace, aboded
The sudden breach on 't.

   *Nor.*          Which is budded out;
For France hath flaw'd the league, and hath
    attach'd
Our merchants' goods at Bourdeaux.

   *Aber.*           Is it therefore
The ambassador is silenc'd?

*Nor.*          Marry, is 't.

*Aber.* A proper title of a peace; and purchas'd
At a superfluous rate!

*Buck.*       Why, all this business
Our reverend cardinal carried.

*Nor.*        Like it your grace,
The state takes notice of the private differ-
ence
Betwixt you and the cardinal. I advise you,—
And take it from a heart that wishes to-
wards you
Honour and plenteous safety,—that you read
The cardinal's malice and his potency
Together; to consider further, that
What his high hatred would effect wants not
A minister in his power. You know his na-
ture,
That he's revengeful; and I know his sword
Hath a sharp edge: it's long, and, 't may be
said,
It reaches far; and where 'twill not extend,
Thither he darts it. Bosom up my counsel,
You'll find it wholesome.—Lo, where comes
that rock
That I advise you shunning.

*Enter* CARDINAL WOLSEY, *the purse borne before him, certain of the* Guard, *and two*
Secretaries *with papers. The* CARDINAL *in
his passage fixeth his eye on* BUCKINGHAM,
*and* BUCKINGHAM *on him, both full of disdain.*

*Wol.* The Duke of Buckingham's surveyor? ha?
Where's his examination?

   1 *Secr.*        Here, so please you.

*Wol.* Is he in person ready?

   1 *Secr.*       Ay, please your grace.

*Wol.* Well, we shall then know more; and
Buckingham
Shall lessen this big look.

           [*Exeunt* WOLSEY *and* Train.

*Buck.* This butcher's cur is venom-
mouth'd, and I
Have not the power to muzzle him; therefore best
Not wake him in his slumber. A beggar's
book
Outworths a noble's blood.

*Nor.*       What, are you chaf'd?
Ask God for temperance; that's the ap-
pliance only
Which your disease requires.

*Buck.*       I read in 's looks
Matter against me; and his eye revil'd
Me, as his abject object: at this instant
He bores me with some trick: he's gone to
the king;
I'll follow, and outstare him.

*Nor.*        Stay, my lord,
And let your reason with your choler question

What 'tis you go about: to climb steep hills
Requires slow pace at first: anger is like
A full-hot horse, who being allow'd his way,
Self-mettle tires him. Not a man in Eng-
land
Can advise me like you: be to yourself
As you would to your friend.

*Buck.*        I'll to the king;
And from a mouth of honour quite cry down
This Ipswich fellow's insolence; or proclaim
There's difference in no persons.

*Nor.*         Be advis'd;
Heat not a furnace for your foe so hot
That it do singe yourself: we may outrun,
By violent swiftness, that which we run at,
And lose by over-running. Know you not,
The fire that mounts the liquor till 't run
o'er,
In seeming to augment it wastes · it? Be
advis'd:
I say again, there is no English soul
More stronger to direct you than yourself,
If with the sap of reason you would quench
Or but allay the fire of passion.

*Buck.*          Sir,
I am thankful to you; and I'll go along
By your prescription: but this top-proud
fellow,—
Whom from the flow of gall I name not, but
From sincere motions,—by intelligence,
And proofs as clear as founts in July, when
We see each grain of gravel, I do know
To be corrupt and treasonous.

*Nor.*       Say not treasonous.

*Buck.* To the king I'll say't; and make my
vouch as strong
As shore of rock. Attend. This holy fox,
Or wolf, or both,—for he is equal ravenous
As he is subtle, and as prone to mischief
As able to perform 't; his mind and place
Infecting one another, yea, reciprocally,—
Only to show his pomp as well in France
As here at home, suggests the king our master
To this last costly treaty, the interview,
That swallow'd so much treasure, and like a
glass
Did break i' the rinsing.

*Nor.*       Faith, and so it did.

*Buck.* Pray, give me favour, sir. This cun-
ning cardinal
The articles o' the combination drew
As himself pleas'd; and they were ratified
As he cried, Thus let be: to as much end
As give a crutch to the dead: but our count-
cardinal
Has done this, and 'tis well; for worthy
Wolsey,
Who cannot err, he did it. Now this fol-
lows,—
Which, as I take it, is a kind of puppy
To the old dam treason,—Charles the em-
peror,
Under pretence to see the queen his aunt,—

For 'twas indeed his colour, but he came
To whisper Wolsey,—here makes visitation:
His fears were that the interview betwixt
England and France might, through their amity,
Breed him some prejudice; for from this league
Peep'd harms that menac'd him: he privily
Deals with our cardinal; and, as I trow,—
Which I do well; for I am sure the emperor
Paid ere he promis'd; whereby his suit was granted
Ere it was ask'd;—but when the way was made,
And pav'd with gold, the emperor thus de-sir'd,—
That he would please to alter the king's course,
And break the foresaid peace. Let the king know,—
As soon he shall by me,—that thus the cardinal
Does buy and sell his honour as he pleases,
And for his own advantage.

*Nor.*                              I am sorry
To hear this of him; and could wish he were
Something mistaken in 't.

*Buck.*                No, not a syllable:
I do pronounce him in that very shape
He shall appear in proof.

*Enter* BRANDON, *a* Sergeant-at-Arms *before
him, and two or three of the* Guard.

*Bran.* Your office, sergeant; execute it.

*Serg.*                                    Sir,
My lord the Duke of Buckingham, and Earl
Of Hereford, Stafford, and Northampton, I
Arrest thee of high treason, in the name
Of our most sovereign king.

*Buck.*                  Lo, you, my lord,
The net has fall'n upon me! I shall perish
Under device and practice.

*Bran.*                  I am sorry
To see you ta'en from liberty, to look on
The business present: 'tis his highness' pleas-ure
You shall to the Tower.

*Buck.*        It will help me nothing
To plead mine innocence; for that dye is on me
Which makes my whit's part black. The will of heaven
Be done in this and all things!—I obey.—
O my Lord Aberga'ny, fare you well!—

*Bran.* Nay, he must bear you company.—
    The king        [*To* ABERGAVENNY.
Is pleas'd you shall to the Tower, till you know
How he determines further.

*Aber.*            As the duke said,
The will of heaven be done, and the king's pleasure
By me obey'd!

*Bran.*        Here is a warrant from

The king to attach Lord Montacute; and the bodies
Of the duke's confessor, John de la Car,
One Gilbert Peck, his chancellor,—

*Buck.*            So, so;
These are the limbs o' the plot:—no more, I hope.

*Bran.* A monk o' the Chartreux.

*Buck.*            O, Nicholas Hopkins?

*Bran.*                          He.

*Buck.* My surveyor is false; the o'er-great cardinal
                              [already:
Hath show'd him gold; my life is spann'd
I am the shadow of poor Buckingham,
Whose figure even this instant cloud puts on,
By darkening my clear sun.—My lord, fare-well.
                              [*Exeunt*

SCENE II.—LONDON. *The Council Chamber*

*Cornets. Enter* KING HENRY, CARDINAL
WOLSEY, the Lords of the Council, SIR
THOMAS LOVELL, Officers, *and* Attendants.
*The* KING *enters, leaning on the* CARD-INAL'S *shoulder.*

*K. Hen.* My life itself, and the best heart of it,
                              [level
Thanks you for this great care: I stood i' the
Of a full-charg'd confederacy, and give thanks
To you that choked it.—Let be call'd before us
That gentleman of Buckingham's: in person
I'll hear him his confessions justify;
And point by point the treasons of his master
He shall again relate.

[*The* KING *takes his state. The* Lords *of
the* Council *take their several places. The*
CARDINAL *places himself under the*
KING'S *feet, on his right side.*

*A noise within, crying,* "Room for the
Queen!" *Enter* QUEEN KATHARINE, *ushered
by the* DUKES OF NORFOLK *and* SUFFOLK:
*she kneels. The* KING *riseth from his state,
takes her up, kisses, and placeth her by
him.*

*Q. Kath.* Nay, we must longer kneel: I am a suitor.
                      [half your suit
*K. Hen.* Arise, and take place by us:—
Never name to us; you have half our power:
The other moiety, ere you ask, is given;
Repeat your will, and take it.

*Q. Kath.*              Thank your majesty.
That you would love yourself, and in that love
Not unconsider'd leave your honour, nor
The dignity of your office, is the point
Of my petition.

*K. Hen.* Lady mine, proceed.

*Q. Kath.* I am solicited, not by a few,
And those of true condition, that your sub-jects
Are in great grievance: there have been com-missions

Sent down among 'em which have flaw'd the
    heart
Of all their loyalties:—wherein, although,
My good lord cardinal, they vent reproaches
Most bitterly on you, as putter-on
Of these exactions, yet the king our master,—
Whose honour Heaven shield from soil!—
    even he escapes not
Language unmannerly, yea, such which
    breaks
The sides of loyalty, and almost appears
In loud rebellion.
    *Nor*        Not almost appears,—
It doth appear; for, upon these taxations,
The clothiers all, not able to maintain
The many to them 'longing, have put off
The spinsters, carders, fullers, weavers, who,
Unfit for other life, compell'd by hunger
And lack of other means, in desperate man-
    ner
Daring the event to the teeth, are all in up-
    roar,
And danger serves among them.
    *K. Hen.*        Taxation!
Wherein? and what taxation?—My lord
    cardinal,
You that are blam'd for it alike with us,
Know you of this taxation?
    *Wol.*        Please you, sir,
I know but of a single part, in aught
Pertains to the state; and front but in that
    file
Where others tell steps with me.
    *Q. Kath.*        No, my lord,
You know no more than others; but you
    frame
Things that are known alike; which are not
    wholesome        [yet must
To those which would not know them, and
Perforce be their acquaintance. These ex-
    actions,
Whereof my sovereign would have note, they
    are
Most pestilent to the hearing; and to bear
    'em
The back is sacrifice to the load. They say
They are devis'd by you; or else you suffer
Too hard an exclamation.
    *K. Hen.*        Still exaction!
The nature of it? in what kind, let's know,
Is this exaction?
    *Q. Kath.*    I am much too venturous
In tempting of your patience; but am bold-
    en'd
Under your promis'd pardon. The subjects'
    grief
Comes through commissions, which compel
    from each
The sixth part of his substance, to be levied
Without delay; and the pretence for this
Is nam'd your wars in France: this makes
    bold mouths;
Tongues spit their duties out, and cold hearts
    freeze

Allegiance in them; their curses now
Live where their prayers did: and it's come
    to pass
This tractable obedience is a slave
To each incensed will. I would your highness
Would give it quick consideration, for
There is no primer business.
    *K. Hen.*        By my life,
This is against our pleasure.
    *Wol.*        And for me,
I have no further gone in this than by
A single voice; and that not pass'd me but
By learned approbation of the judges. If I
    am
Traduc'd by ignorant tongues, which neither
    know
My faculties nor person, yet will be
The chronicles of my doing,—let me say
'Tis but the fate of place, and the rough
    brake
That virtue must go through. We must not
    stint
Our necessary actions, in the fear
To cope malicious censurers; which ever,
As ravenous fishes, do a vessel follow
That is new-trimm'd, but benefit no further
Than vainly longing. What we oft do best,
By sick interpreters, once weak ones, is
Not ours, or not allow'd; what worst, as oft
Hitting a grosser quality, is cried up
For our best act. If we shall stand still,
In fear our motion will be mock'd or carp'd
    at,
We should take root here where we sit, or sit
State-statutes only.
    *K. Hen.*        Things done well
And with a care exempt themselves from
    fear;
Things done without example, in their issue
Are to be fear'd. Have you a precedent
Of this commission? I believe, not any.
We must not rend our subjects from our laws,
And stick them in our will. Sixth part of
    each?
A trembling contribution! Why, we take
From every tree lop, bark, and part o' the
    timber;
And, though we leave it with a root, thus
    hack'd,
The air will drink the sap. To every county
Where this is question'd send our letters, with
Free pardon to each man that has denied
The force of this commission: pray, look to't;
I put it to your care.
    *Wol.*        A word with you.
            [*To the* Secretary.
Let there be letters writ to every shire,
Of the king's grace and pardon. The griev'd
    commons
Hardly conceive of me; let it be nois'd
That through our intercession this revoke-
    ment
And pardon comes: I shall anon advise you
Further in the proceeding.   [*Exit* Secretary.

*Enter Surveyor.*

*Q. Kath.* I am sorry that the Duke of Buckingham
Is run in your displeasure.

*K. Hen.* It grieves many:
The gentleman is learn'd, and a most rare speaker;
To nature none more bound; his training such
That he may furnish and instruct great teachers,
And never seek for aid out of himself. Yet see,
When these so noble benefits shall prove
Not well dispos'd, the mind growing once corrupt,
They turn to vicious forms, ten times more ugly
Then ever they were fair. This man so complete,
[we,
Who was enroll'd 'mongst wonders, and when
Almost with ravish'd list'ning, could not find
His hour of speech a minute; he, my lady,
Hath into monstrous habits put the graces
That once were his, and is become as black
As if besmear'd in hell. Sit by us; you shall hear—
This was his gentleman in trust,—of him
Things to strike honour sad.—Bid him recount
The fore-recited practices; whereof
We cannot feel too little, hear too much.

*Wol.* Stand forth, and with bold spirit relate what you,
Most like a careful subject, have collected
Out of the Duke of Buckingham.

*K. Hen.* Speak freely.

*Surv.* First, it was usual with him, every day
It would infect his speech,—that if the king
Should without issue die, he'll carry it so
To make the sceptre his: these very words
I have heard him utter to his son-in-law,
Lord Aberga'ny; to whom by oath he menac'd
Revenge upon the cardinal.

*Wol.* Please your highness, note
This dangerous conception in this point.
Not friended by his wish, to your high person
His will is most malignant; and it stretches
Beyond you to your friends.

*Q. Kath.* My learn'd lord cardinal,
Deliver all with charity.

*K. Hen.* Speak on:
How grounded he his title to the crown
Upon our fail? to this point hast thou heard him
At any time speak aught?

*Surv.* He was brought to this
By a vain prophecy of Nicholas Hopkins.

*K. Hen.* What was that Hopkins?

*Surv.* Sir, a Chartreux friar,
His confessor; who fed him every minute
With words of sovereignty.

*K. Hen.* How know'st thou this?

*Surv.* Not long before your highness sped to France,
The Duke being at the Rose, within the parish
Saint Lawrence Poultney, did of me demand
What was the speech among the Londoners
Concerning the French journey: I replied,
Men fear'd the French would prove perfidious,
To the king's danger. Presently the duke
Said, 'twas the fear, indeed; and that he doubted
'Twould prove the verity of certain words
Spoke by a holy monk; *That oft,* says he,
*Hath sent to me, wishing me to permit*
*John de la Car, my chaplain, a choice hour*
*To hear from him a matter of some moment:*
*Whom after under the confession's seal*
*He solemnly had sworn, that what he spoke*
*My chaplain to no creature living but*
*To me should utter, with demure confidence*
*This pausingly ensu'd,—Neither the king nor's heirs,*
*Tell you the duke, shall prosper: bid him strive*
*To gain the love o' the commonalty: the duke*
*Shall govern England.*

*Q. Kath.* If I know you well,
You were the duke's surveyor, and lost your office
On the complaint o' the tenants: take good heed
You charge not in your spleen a noble person,
And spoil your nobler soul: I say, take heed;
Yes, heartily beseech you.

*K. Hen.* Let him on:—
Go forward.

*Surv.* On my soul, I'll speak but truth.
I told my lord the duke, by the devil's illusions
The monk might be deceiv'd; and that 'twas dangerous for him
To ruminate on this so far, until
It forg'd him some design, which, being believ'd,
It was much like to do: he answer'd, *Tush,*
*It can do me no damage;* adding further,
That, had the king in his last sickness fail'd,
The cardinal's and Sir Thomas Lovell's heads
Should have gone off.

*K. Hen.* Ha! what, so rank? Ah-ha!
There's mischief in this man:—Canst thou say further?

*Surv.* I can, my liege.

*K. Hen.* Proceed.

*Surv.* Being at Greenwich,
After your highness had reprov'd the duke
About Sir William Blomer,—

*K. Hen.* I remember
Of such a time:—being my sworn servant,
The duke retain'd him his.—But on; what hence?

*Surv.* If, quoth he, *I for this had been committed,*

*As, to the Tower, I thought,—I would have
　　play'd
The part my father meant to act upon
The usurper Richard; who, being at Salis-
　　bury,
Made suit to come in's presence; which, if
　　granted,
As he made semblance of his duty, would
Have put his knife into him.*

　*K. Hen.*　　　　　　　　A giant traitor!

　*Wol.* Now, madam, may his highness live
　　in freedom,
And this man out of prison?

　*Q. Kath.*　　　　　　God mend all!

　*K. Hen.* There's something more would out
　　of thee; what say'st?

　*Surv.* After *the duke his father,* with *the
　　knife,*　　　　　　　　　　　　[dagger,
He stretch'd him, and, with one hand on his
Another spread on's breast, mounting his
　　eyes,
He did discharge a horrible oath; whose tenor
Was, were he evil us'd, he would out-go
His father by as much as a performance
Does an irresolute purpose.

　*K. Hen.*　　　　　　There's his period,
To sheath his knife in us. He is attach'd;
Call him to present trial: if he may
Find mercy in the law, 'tis his; if none,
Let him not seek't of us: by day and night,
He is a daring traitor to the height. [*Exeunt.*

SCENE III.—LONDON. *A Room in the Palace.*

*Enter the* Lord Chamberlain *and* LORD SANDS.

　*Cham.* Is't possible the spells of France
　　should juggle
Men into such strange mysteries?

　*Sands.*　　　　　　　　New customs,
Though they be never so ridiculous,
Nay, let them be unmanly, yet are follow'd.

　*Cham.* As far as I see, all the good our Eng-
　　lish
Have got by the late voyage is but merely
A fit or two o' the face; but they are shrewd
　　ones;
For when they hold them, you would swear
　　directly
Their very noses had been counsellors
To Pepin or Clotharius, they keep state so.

　*Sands.* They have all new legs, and lame
　　ones: one would take it,
That never saw 'em pace before, the spavin
Or springhalt reign'd among 'em.

　*Cham.*　　　　　　　Death! my lord,
Their clothes are after such a pagan cut too,
That sure they have worn out Christendom.

*Enter* SIR THOMAS LOVELL.

　　　　　　　　　　　　　How now?
What news, Sir Thomas Lovell?

　*Lov.*　　　　　　　'Faith, my lord,
I hear of none, but the new proclamation
That's clapp'd upon the court-gate.

　*Cham.*　　　　　　　What is't for?

　*Lov.* The reformation of our travell'd gal-
　　lants,
That fill the court with quarrels, talk, and
　　tailors.

　*Cham.* I am glad 'tis there: now I would
　　pray our monsieurs
To think an English courtier may be wise,
And never see the Louvre.

　*Lov.*　　　　　　They must either—
For so run the conditions—leave those rem-
　　nants
Of fool and feather that they got in France,
With all their honourable points of ignor-
　　ance　　　　　　　　　　　　　[works;
Pertaining thereunto,—as fights and fire-
Abusing better men than they can be,
Out of a foreign wisdom,—renouncing clean
The faith they have in tennis, and tall stock-
　　ings,
Short blister'd breeches, and those types of
　　travel,
And understand again, like honest men;
Or pack to their old playfellows: there, I
　　take it,
They may, *cum privilegio,* wear away
The lag end of their lewdness, and be laugh'd
　　at.

　*Sands.* 'Tis time to give 'em physic, their
　　diseases
Are grown so catching.

　*Cham.*　　　　　　What a loss our ladies
Will have of these trim vanities!

　*Lov.*　　　　　　　　　Ay, marry,
There will be woe indeed, lords: the sly
　　whoresons
Have got a speeding trick to lay down ladies;
A French song and a fiddle has no fellow.

　*Sands.* The devil fiddle 'em! I am glad
　　they're going,—
For, sure, there's no converting of 'em:—now
An honest country lord, as I am, beaten
A long time out of play, may bring his plain-
　　song,
And have an hour of hearing; and, by'r Lady,
Held current music too.

　*Cham.*　　　　　　Well said, Lord Sands;
Your colt's tooth is not cast yet.

　*Sands.*　　　　　　　No, my lord;
Nor shall not, while I have a stump.

　*Cham.*　　　　　　　Sir Thomas,
Whither were you a-going?

　*Lov.*　　　　　　To the cardinal's:
Your lordship is a guest too.

　*Cham.*　　　　　　O, 'tis true;
This night he makes a supper, and a great
　　one,
To many lords and ladies; there will be
The beauty of this kingdom, I'll assure you.

　*Lov.* That churchman bears a bounteous
　　mind indeed,
A hand as fruitful as the land that feeds us;
His dews fall everywhere.

　*Cham.*　　　　　　No doubt he's noble;
He had a black mouth that said other of him.

*Sands.* He may, my lord,—has where-
   withal; in him        [trine:
Sparing would show a worse sin than ill doc-
Men of his way should be most liberal;
They are set here for examples.
   *Cham.*         True, they are so;
But few now give so great ones. My barge
   stays;           [Thomas,
Your lordship shall along.—Come, good Sir
We shall be late else; which I would not be,
For I was spoke to, with Sir Henry Guild-
   ford,
This night to be comptrollers.
   *Sands.*        I am your lordship's.
                  [*Exeunt.*

SCENE IV.—LONDON. *The Presence Chamber*
        *in York Place.*

*Hautboys. A small table under a state for the*
   CARDINAL, *a longer table for the guests.*
   *Enter, at one door,* ANNE BULLEN, *and*
   *divers* Lords, Ladies, *and* Gentlewomen, *as*
   *guests; at another door, enter* SIR HENRY
   GUILDFORD.

   *Guild.* Ladies, a general welcome from his
   grace
Salutes ye all; this night he dedicates
To fair content and you: none here, he hopes,
In all this noble bevy, has brought with her
One care abroad; he would have all as merry
As, first, good company, good wine, good wel-
   come           [tardy:
Can make good people.—O, my lord, you are

*Enter* Lord Chamberlain, LORD SANDS, *and*
   SIR THOMAS LOVELL.

The very thought of this fair company
Clapp'd wings to me.
   *Cham.* You are young, Sir Henry Guild-
   ford.
   *Sands.* Sir Thomas Lovell, had the cardinal
But half my lay-thoughts in him, some of
   these
Should find a running banquet ere they
   rested;
I think would better please 'em: by my life,
They are a sweet society of fair ones.
   *Lov.* O, that your lordship were but now
   confessor
To one or two of these!
   *Sands*          I would I were;
They should find easy penance.
   *Lov.*          Faith, how easy?
   *Sands.* As easy as a down-bed would afford
   it.
   *Cham.* Sweet ladies, will it please you sit?
   Sir Harry,          [this:
Place you that side; I'll take the charge of
His grace is ent'ring.—Nay, you must not
   freeze;         [weather:—
Two women plac'd together makes cold
My Lord Sands, you are one will keep 'em
   waking;
Pray, sit between these ladies.

   *Sands.*          By my faith,
And thank your lordship.—By your leave,
   sweet ladies:
     [*Seats himself between* ANNE BULLEN
              *and another Lady.*
If I chance to talk a little wild, forgive
   me;
I had it from my father.
   *Anne.*          Was he mad, sir?
   *Sands.* O, very mad, exceeding mad, in love
   too:
But he would bite none; just as I do now,—
He would kiss you twenty with a breath.
                  [*Kisses her.*
   *Cham.*         Well said, my lord.—
So, now you're fairly seated.—Gentlemen,
The penance lies on you if these fair ladies
Pass away frowning.
   *Sands.*        For my little cure,
Let me alone.

   *Hautboys. Enter* CARDINAL WOLSEY,
     *attended; and takes his state.*

   *Wol.* Ye're welcome, my fair guests: that
   noble lady
Or gentleman that is not freely merry
Is not my friend: this, to confirm my wel-
   come;
And to you all, good health.     [*Drinks.*
   *Sands.*        Your grace is noble:—
Let me have such a bowl may hold my
   thanks,
And save me so much talking.
   *Wol.*          My Lord Sands,
I am beholden to you: cheer your neigh-
   bours.—
Ladies, you are not merry:—gentlemen,
Whose fault is this?
   *Sands.*       The red wine first must rise
In their fair cheeks, my lord; then we shall
   have 'em
Talk us to silence.
   *Anne.*       You are a merry gamester,
My Lord Sands,
   *Sands.*       Yes, if I make my play.
Here's to your ladyship: and pledge it, ma-
   dam,
For 'tis to such a thing,—
   *Anne.*        You cannot show me.
   *Sands.* I told your grace they would talk
   anon.
     [*Drum and trumpets: Chambers*
            *discharged within.*
   *Wol.*          What's that?
   *Cham.* Look out there, some of ye.
               [*Exit a Servant.*
   *Wol.*        What warlike voice,
And to what end, is this?—Nay, ladies, fear
   not;
By all the laws of war ye're privileg'd.

        *Re-enter* Servant.

   *Cham.* How now! what is 't?
   *Serve.*       A noble troop of strangers,—

For so they seem; they have left their barge,
    and landed;
And hither make, as great ambassadors
From foreign princes.
*Wol.*                   Good lord chamberlain,
Go, give 'em welcome, you can speak the
    French tongue;
And, pray receive 'em nobly, and conduct
    'em
Into our presence, where this heaven of
    beauty
Shall shine at full upon them.—Some attend
    him.
    [*Exit* Chamberlain *attended. All arise,
        and tables removed.*
You have now a broken banquet: but we'll
    mend it.
A good digestion to you all: and once more
I shower a welcome on you;—welcome all.

*Hautboys. Enter the* KING, *and others, as
maskers, habited like shepherds, with
Torchbearers, ushered by the* Lord Chamberlain. *They pass directly before the* CAR-
DINAL, *and gracefully salute him.*

A noble company! what are their pleasures?
*Cham.* Because they speak no English, thus
    they pray'd
To tell your grace,—that, having heard by
    fame
Of this so noble and so fair assembly
This night to meet here, they could do no less,
Out of the great respect they bear to beauty,
But leave their flocks; and, under your fair
    conduct,
Crave leave to view these ladies, and entreat
An hour of revels with 'em.
*Wol.*               Say, lord chamberlain,
They have done my poor house grace; for
    which I pray 'em        [pleasures.
A thousand thanks, and pray 'em take their
    [*Ladies chosen for the dance. The* KING
        *chooses* ANNE BULLEN.
*K. Hen.* The fairest hand I ever touch'd!
    O beauty,
Till now I never knew thee! [*Music. Dance.*
*Wol.* My lord,—
*Cham.*            Your grace?
*Wol.* Pray tell them thus much from me:—
There should be one amongst them, by his
    person,
More worthy this place than myself; to
    whom,
If I but knew him, with my love and duty
I would surrender it.
*Cham.*            I will, my lord.
    [*Goes to the Maskers, and returns.*
*Wol.* What say they?
*Cham.*            Such a one, they all confess,
There is indeed; which they would have your
    grace
Find out, and he will take it.
*Wol.*                   Let me see, then.—
    [*Comes from his state.*

By all your good leaves, gentlemen;—here I'll
    make
My royal choice.
*K. Hen.*         Ye have found him, cardinal:
    [*Unmasking.*
You hold a fair assembly; you do well, lord:
You are a churchman, or I'll tell you, car-
    dinal,
I should judge now unhappily.
*Wol.*                   I am glad
Your grace is grown so pleasant.
*K. Hen.*            My lord chamberlain,
Pr'ythee, come hither: what fair lady's that?
*Cham.* An't please your grace, Sir Thomas
    Bullen's daughter,—        [women.
The Viscount Rochford,—one of her highness'
*K. Hen.* By heaven, she is a dainty one.—
    Sweetheart,
I were unmannerly to take you out,
And not to kiss you.—A health, gentlemen!
Let it go round.
*Wol.* Sir Thomas Lovell, is the banquet
    ready
I' the privy chamber?
*Lov.*            Yes, my lord.
*Wol.*                   Your grace,
I fear, with dancing is a little heated.
*K. Hen.* I fear, too much.
*Wol.*            There's fresher air, my lord,
In the next chamber.        [sweet partner,
*K. Hen.* Lead in your ladies, every one:—
I must not yet forsake you:—let's be
    merry:—
Good my lord cardinal, I have half a dozen
    healths
To drink to these fair ladies, and a measure
To lead 'em once again; and then let's dream
Who's best in favour.—Let the music knock
    it.                [*Exeunt, with trumpets.*

## ACT II.

### SCENE I.—LONDON. *A Street.*

*Enter two* Gentlemen, *meeting.*

1 *Gent.* Whither away so fast?
2 *Gent.*            O, God save ye!
E'en to the hall, to hear what shall become
Of the great Duke of Buckingham.
1 *Gent.*            I'll save you
That labour, sir. All's now done, but the
    ceremony
Of bringing back the prisoner.
2 *Gent.*                   Where you there?
1 *Gent.* Yes, indeed, was I.
2 *Gent.*         Pray, speak what has happen'd.
1 *Gent.* You may guess quickly what.
2 *Gent.*            Is he found guilty?
1 *Gent.* Yes, truly is he, and condemn'd
    upon't.
2 *Gent.* I am sorry for't.
1 *Gent.*            So are a number more.
2 *Gent.* But pray, how pass'd it?        [duke
1 *Gent.* I'll tell you in a little. The great
Came to the bar; where to his accusations
He pleaded still not guilty, and alleg'd

Many sharp reasons to defeat the law.
The king's attorney, on the contrary,
Urg'd on the examinations proofs, confessions
Of divers witnesses; which the duke desir'd
To have brought, *vivâ voce*, to his face:
At which appear'd against him his surveyor;
Sir Gilbert Peck, his chancellor; and John
    Car,
Confessor to him; with that devil-monk,
Hopkins, that made this mischief.

    2 *Gent*.              That was he
That fed him with his prophecies?

    1 *Gent*.              The same.
All these accus'd him strongly; which he fain
Would have flung from him, but, indeed, he
    could not:
And so his peers, upon this evidence,
Have found him guilty of high treason. Much
He spoke, and learnedly, for life; but all
Was either pitied in him or forgotten.

    2 *Gent*. After all this, how did he bear
    himself?

    1 *Gent*. When he was brought again to the
    bar to hear            [stirr'd
His knell rung out, his judgment,—he was
With such an agony, he sweat extremely,
And something spoke in choler, ill, and hasty;
But he fell to himself again, and sweetly
In all the rest show'd a most noble patience.

    2 *Gent*. I do not think he fears death.

    1 *Gent*.           Sure, he does not,
He never was so womanish; the cause
He may a little grieve at.

    2 *Gent*.             Certainly
The cardinal is the end of this.

    1 *Gent*.            'Tis likely,
By all conjectures: first, Kildare's attainder,
Then deputy of Ireland; who remov'd,
Earl Surrey was sent thither, and in haste too,
Lest he should help his father.

    2 *Gent*.          That trick of state
Was a deep envious one.

    1 *Gent*.         At his return
No doubt he will requite it. This is noted,
And generally,—whoever the king favours
The cardinal instantly will find employment,
And far enough from court too.

    2 *Gent*.         All the commons
Hate him perniciously, and, o' my conscience,
Wish him ten fathom deep: this duke as much
They love and dote on; call him bounteous
    Buckingham,
The mirror of all courtesy,—

    1 *Gent*.         Stay there, sir,
And see the noble ruin'd man you speak of.

*Enter* BUCKINGHAM *from his arraignment;
Tip-staves before him; the axe with the
edge towards him; halberds on each side:
with him* SIR THOMAS LOVELL, SIR NICH-
OLAS VAUX, SIR WILLIAM SANDS, *and common people.*

    2 *Gent*. Let's stand close, and behold him.

    *Buck*.            All good people,

You that thus far have come to pity me,
Hear what I say, and then go home and lose
    me.
I have this day receiv'd a traitor's judgment,
And by that name must die: yet, heaven bear
    witness,
And if I have a conscience, let it sink me,
Even as the axe falls, if I be not faithful!
The law I bear no malice for my death;
'T has done, upon the premises, but justice:
But those that sought it I could wish more
    Christians:
Be what they will, I heartily forgive 'em:
Yet let 'em look they glory not in mischief,
Nor build their evils on the graves of great
    men;
For then my guiltless blood must cry against
    'em.
For further like in this world I ne'er hope,
Nor will I sue, although the king have mercies
More than I dare make faults. You few that
    lov'd me,
And dare be bold to weep for Buckingham,
His noble friends and fellows, whom to leave
Is only bitter to him, only dying,
Go with me, like good angels, to my end;
And as the long divorce of steel falls on me
Make of your prayers one sweet sacrifice,
And lift my soul to heaven.—Lead on, o'
    God's name.

    *Lov*. I do beseech your grace, for charity,
If ever any malice in your heart
Were hid against me, now to forgive me
    frankly.

    *Buck*. Sir Thomas Lovell, I as free forgive
    you
As I would be forgiven: I forgive all;
There cannot be those numberless offences
'Gainst me that I cannot take peace with: no
    black envy
Shall make my grave.—Commend me to his
    grace;
And if he speak of Buckingham, pray tell him
You met him half in heaven: my vows and
    prayers
Yet are the king's; and, till my soul forsake,
Shall cry for blessings on him: may he live
Longer than I have time to tell his years!
Ever belov'd and loving may his rule be!
And when old time shall lead him to his end,
Goodness and he fill up one monument!

    *Lov*. To the water side I must conduct
    your grace;
Then give my charge up to Sir Nicholas Vaux,
Who undertakes you to your end.

    *Vaux*.           Prepare there,
The duke is coming: see the barge be ready;
And fit it with such furniture as suits
The greatness of his person.

    *Buck*.          Nay, Sir Nicholas,
Let it alone; my state now will but mock me.
When I came hither I was lord high constable
And Duke of Buckingham; now, poor Ed-
    ward Bohun:

Yet I am richer than by base accusers,
That never knew what truth meant: I now
    seal it;
And with that blood will make 'em one day
    groan for't.
My noble father, Henry of Buckingham,
Who first rais'd head against usurping Rich-
    ard,
Flying for succour to his servant Banister,
Being distress'd, was by that wretch betray'd,
And without trial fell; God's peace be with
    him!
Henry the Seventh succeeding, truly pitying
My father's loss, like a most royal prince,
Restor'd me to my honours, and out of ruins
Made my name once more noble. Now his
    son,
Henry the Eighth, life, honour, name, and all
That made me happy, at one stroke has taken
For ever from the world. I had my trial,
And must needs say a noble one; which
    makes me
A little happier than my wretched father:
Yet thus far we are one in fortunes,—both
Fell by our servants, by those men we lov'd
    most;
A most unnatural and faithless service!
Heaven has an end in all: yet, you that hear
    me,
This from a dying man receive as certain:—
Where you are liberal of your loves and
    counsels,
Be sure you be not loose; for those you make
    friends           [ceive
And give your hearts to, when they once per-
The least rub in your fortunes, fall away
Like water from ye, never found again
But where they mean to sink ye. All good
    people,           [hour
Pray for me! I must now forsake ye: the last
Of my long weary life is come upon me.
Farewell:                    [sad,
And when you would say something that is
Speak how I fell.—I have done; and God for-
    give me!
           *Exeunt* BUCKINGHAM *and* Train.

    1 *Gent.* O, this is full of pity!—Sir, it calls,
I fear, too many curses on their heads
That were the authors.
    2 *Gent.*      If the duke be guiltless,
'Tis full of woe: yet I can give you inkling
Of an ensuing evil, if it fall,
Greater than this.
    1 *Gent.*    Good angels, keep it from us!
Where may it be? You do not doubt my
    faith, sir?             [quire
    2 *Gent.* This secret is so weighty, 'twill re-
A strong faith to conceal it.
    1 *Gent.*         Let me have it;
I do not talk much.
    2 *Gent.*        I am confident;
You shall, sir: did you not of late days hear
A buzzing of a separation
Between the king and Katharine?

    1 *Gent.*         Yes, but it held not:
For when the king once heard it, out of anger
He sent command to the lord mayor straight
To stop the rumour, and allay those tongues
That durst disperse it.
    2 *Gent.*       But that slander, sir,
Is found a truth now: for it grows again
Fresher than e'er it was; and held for certain
The king will venture at it. Either the cardi-
    nal,
Or some about him near, have, out of malice
To the good queen, possess'd him with a
    scruple
That will undo her: to confirm this too,
Cardinal Campeius is arriv'd, and lately;
As all think, for this business.
    1 *Gent.*          'Tis the cardinal;
And merely to revenge him on the emperor
For not bestowing on him, at his asking,
The archbishopric of Toledo, this is purpos'd.
    2 *Gent.* I think you have hit the mark: but
        is't not cruel        [cardinal
That she would feel the smart of this? The
Will have his will, and she must fall.
    1 *Gent.*           'Tis woeful.
We are too open here to argue this;
Let's think in private more.      [*Exeunt.*

SCENE II.—LONDON. *An Ante-chamber in the*
              *Palace.*

*Enter the* Lord Chamberlain *reading a letter.*

    *Cham. My lord,—The horses your lord-
ship sent for, with all the care I had, I saw
well chosen, ridden, and furnished. They were
young and handsome, and of the best breed in
the north. When they were ready to set out
for London, a man of my lord cardinal's, by
commission and main power, took 'em from
me; with this reason,—His master would be
served before a subject, if not before the
king; which stopped our mouths, sir.*
I fear he will indeed: well, let him have them:
He will have all, I think.

*Enter the* DUKES OF NORFOLK *and* SUFFOLK.

    *Nor.* Well met, my Lord Chamberlain.
    *Cham.* Good-day to both your graces.
    *Suf.* How is the king employ'd?
    *Cham.*         I left him private,
Full of sad thoughts and troubles.
    *Nor.*          What's the cause?
    *Cham.* It seems the marriage with his
    brother's wife
Has crept too near his conscience.
    *Suf.*        No, his conscience
Has crept too near another lady.
    *Nor.*          'Tis so:
This is the cardinal's doing, the king-cardinal:
That blind priest, like the eldest son of for-
    tune,
Turns what he lists. The king will know
    him one day.
    *Suf.* Pray God he do! he'll never know
    himself else.

*Nor.* How holily he works in all his business!

And with what zeal! for, now he has crack'd the league [great-nephew,

Between us and the emperor, the queen's

He dives into the king's soul, and there scatters

Dangers, doubts, wringing of the conscience,

Fears, and despairs,—and all these for his marriage:

And out of all these to restore the king,

He counsels a divorce; a loss of her

That, like a jewel, has hung twenty years

About his neck, yet never lost her lustre;

Of her that loves him with that excellence

That angels love good men with; even of her

That, when the greatest stroke of fortune falls, [pious?

Will bless the king: and is not this course

*Cham.* Heaven keep me from such counsel!

'Tis most true [speaks 'em,

These news are everywhere; every tongue

And every true heart weeps for't: all that dare

Look into these affairs see this main end,—

The French king's sister. Heaven will one day open

The king's eyes, that so long have slept upon

This bold bad man.

*Suf.*                 And free us from his slavery.

*Nor.* We had need pray,

And heartily, for our deliverance;

Or this imperious man will work us all

From princes into pages: all men's honours

Lie like one lump before him, to be fashion'd

Into what pitch he please.

*Suf.*                 For me, my lords,

I love him not, nor fear him; there's my creed:

As I am made without him, so I'll stand,

If the king please; his curses and his blessings

Touch me alike, they are breath I not believe in

I knew him, and I know him; so I leave him

To him that made him proud, the pope.

*Nor.*                 Let's in;

And with some other business put the king

From these sad thoughts that work too much upon him:—

My lord, you'll bear us company?

*Cham.*                 Excuse me;

The king has sent me other-where: besides,

You'll find a most unfit time to disturb him:

Health to your lordships.

*Nor.* Thanks, my good lord chamberlain.

[*Exit* Lord Chamberlain.

NORFOLK *opens a folding door. The* KING *is discovered sitting, and reading pensively.*

*Suf.* How sad he looks! sure, he is much afflicted.

*K. Hen.* Who is there, ha?

*Nor.*                 Pray God he be not angry.

*K. Hen.* Who's there, I say? How dare you thrust yourselves

Into my private meditations?

Who am I, ha?

*Nor.* A gracious king, that pardons all offences [way

Malice ne'er meant: our breach of duty this

Is business of estate; in which we come

To know your royal pleasure.

*K. Hen.*                 Ye are too bold;

Go to; I'll make you know your times of business:

Is this an hour for temporal affairs, ha?

*Enter* WOLSEY *and* CAMPEIUS.

Who's there? my good lord cardinal?—O my Wolsey,

The quiet of my wounded conscience,

Thou art a cure fit for a king.—You're welcome, [*To* CAMPEIUS.

Most reverend learned sir, into our kingdom:

Use us and it.—My good lord, have great care

I be not found a talker. [*To* WOLSEY.

*Wol.*                 Sir, you cannot.

I would your grace would give us but an hour

Of private conference.

*K. Hen.*                 We are busy; go.

[*To* NORFOLK *and* SUFFOLK.

*Nor.* [*Aside to* SUF.] This priest has no pride in him!

*Suf.* [*Aside to* NOR.]     Not to speak of:

I would not be so sick though for his place:

But this cannot continue.

*Nor.* [*Aside to* SUF.] If it do,

I'll venture one have-at-him.

*Suf.* [*Aside to* NOR.]     I another.

[*Exeunt* NOR. *and* SUF.

*Wol.* Your grace has given a precedent of wisdom

Above all princes, in committing freely

Your scruple to the voice of Christendom.

Who can be angry now? what envy reach you? [her,

The Spaniard, tied by blood and favour to

Must now confess, if they have any goodness,

The trial just and noble. All the clerks,

I mean the learned ones, in Christian kingdoms,

Have their free voices: Rome the nurse of judgment,

Invited by your noble self, hath sent

One general tongue unto us, this good man,

This just and learned priest, Cardinal Campeius,— [ness.

Whom once more I present unto your high-

*K. Hen.* And once more in mine arms I bid him welcome,

And thank the holy conclave for their loves:

They have sent me such a man I would have wish'd for. [strangers' loves,

*Cam.* Your grace must needs deserve all

You are so noble. To your highness' hand

I tender my commission;—by whose vir-
tue,—                              [lord
The court of Rome commanding,—you, my
Cardinal of York, are join'd with me their
servant,
In the unpartial judging of this business.
  *K. Hen.* Two equal men. The queen shall
    be acquainted                 [Gardiner?
Forthwith for what you come.—Where's
  *Wol.* I know your majesty has always
    lov'd her
So dear in heart, not to deny her that
A woman of less place might ask by law,
Scholars allow'd freely to argue for her.
  *K. Hen.* Ay, and the best she shall have;
    and my favour                 [Cardinal,
To him that does best: God forbid else.
Pr'ythee, call Gardiner to me, my new secre-
    tary:
I find him a fit fellow.       [*Exit* WOLSEY.

  *Re-enter* WOLSEY *with* GARDINER.

  *Wol.* [*Aside to* GARD.] Give me your hand:
    much joy and favour to you;
You are the king's now.
  *Gard.* [*Aside to* WOL.] But to be com-
    manded                        [rais'd me.
For ever by your grace, whose hand has
  *K. Hen.* Come hither, Gardiner.
                    [*They converse apart.*
  *Cam.* My Lord of York, was not one Doc-
    tor Pace
In this man's place before him?
  *Wol.*              Yes, he was.
  *Cam.* Was he not held a learned man?
  *Wol.*                   Yes, surely.
  *Cam.* Believe me, there's an ill opinion
    spread, then,
Even of yourself, lord cardinal.
  *Wol.*           How! of me?
  *Cam.* They will not stick to say you envied
    him;                         [ous,
And fearing he would rise, he was so virtu-
Kept him a foreign man still; which so
    griev'd him
That he ran mad and died.
  *Wol.*       Heaven's peace be with him!
That's Christian care enough: for living mur-
    murers
There's places of rebuke. He was a fool;
For he would needs be virtuous: that good
    fellow,
If I command him, follows my appointment:
I will have none so near else. Learn this,
    brother,
We live not to be grip'd by meaner persons.
  *K. Hen.* Deliver this with modesty to the
    queen.                 [*Exit* GARDINER.
The most convenient place that I can think of
For such receipt of learning is Black-Friars;
There ye shall meet about this weighty busi-
    ness:—
My Wolsey, see it furnish'd—O, my lord,

Would it not grieve an able man to leave
So sweet a bedfellow? But, conscience, con-
    science,—
O, 'tis a tender place! and I must leave her.
                                    [*Exeunt.*

SCENE III.—LONDON. *An Ante-chamber in the*
    QUEEN'S *Apartments.*

  *Enter* ANNE BULLEN *and an* Old Lady.

  *Anne.* Not for that neither: here's the pang
    that pinches:—                [and she
His highness having liv'd so long with her,
So good a lady that no tongue could ever
Pronounce dishonour of her,—by my life,
She never knew harm-doing;—O, now, after
So many courses of the sun enthron'd,
Still growing in a majesty and pomp,—the
    which
To leave a thousand-fold more bitter than
'Tis sweet at first to acquire,—after this proc-
    ess,
To give her the avaunt! it is a pity
Would move a monster.
  *Old L.*       Hearts of most hard temper
Melt and lament for her.
  *Anne.*            O, God's will! much better
She ne'er had known pomp: though it be
    temporal,
Yet, if that quarrel, fortune, do divorce
It from the bearer, 'tis a sufferance panging
As soul and body's severing.
  *Old L.*             Alas, poor lady!
She's a stranger now again.
  *Anne.*              So much the more
Must pity drop upon her. Verily,
I swear, 'tis better to be lowly born,
And range with humble livers in content,
Than to be perk'd up in a glistering grief,
And wear a golden sorrow.
  *Old L.*            Our content
Is our best having
  *Anne*       By my troth and maidenhead,
I would not be a queen.
  *Old L.*        Beshrew me, I would,
And venture maidenhead for't; and so would
    you,
For all this spice of your hypocrisy:
You, that have so fair parts of woman on
    you,
Have too a woman's heart; which ever yet
Affected eminence, wealth, sovereignty;
Which, to say sooth, are blessings;—and
    which gifts,—
Saving your mincing,—the capacity
Of your soft cheveril conscience would receive
If you might please to stretch it.
  *Anne.*              Nay, good troth,—
  *Old L.* Yes, troth and troth; you would
    not be a queen?              [heaven.
  *Anne.* No, not for all the riches under
  *Old L.* 'Tis strange: a threepence bowed
    would hire me,
Old as I am, to queen it: but, I pray you,

What think you of a duchess? have you limbs
To bear that load of title?

*Anne.*                    No, in truth.

*Old L.* Then you are weakly made: pluck
    off a little;
I would not be a young count in your way
For more than blushing comes to: if your
    back
Cannot vouchsafe this burden, 'tis too weak
Ever to get a boy.

*Anne.*                How you do talk!
I swear again I would not be a queen
For all the world.

*Old L.*             In faith, for little England
You'd venture an emballing: I myself
Would for Carnarvonshire, although there
    long'd                        [comes here?
No more to the crown but that. Lo, who

*Enter the* Lord Chamberlain.

*Cham.* Good-morrow, ladies. What wer't
    worth to know
The secret of your conference?

*Anne.*                My good lord,
Not your demand; it values not your asking:
Our mistress' sorrows we were pitying.

*Cham.* It was a gentle business,. and be-
    coming
The action of good women: there is hope
All will be well.

*Anne.*        Now, I pray God, amen!

*Cham.* You bear a gentle mind, and heav-
    enly blessings                    [lady,
Follow such creatures. That you may, fair
Perceive I speak sincerely, and high note's
Ta'en of your many virtues, the king's ma-
    jesty                            [and
Commends his good opinion of you to you,
Does purpose honour to you no less flowing
Than Marchioness of Pembroke; to which
    title
A thousand pound a year, annual support,
Out of his grace he adds.

*Anne.*          I do not know
What kind of my obedience I should tender;
More than my all is nothing: nor my prayers
Are not words duly hallow'd, nor my wishes
More worth than empty vanities; yet prayers
    and wishes
Are all I can return. Beseech your lordship,
Vouchsafe to speak my thanks and my obedi-
    ence,                            [ness;
As from a blushing handmaid, to his high-
Whose health and royalty I pray for.

*Cham.*                Lady,
I shall not fail to approve the fair conceit
The king hath of you.—I have perus'd her
    well;                            [*Aside.*
Beauty and honour in her are so mingled
That they have caught the king: and who
    knows yet
But from this lady may proceed a gem
To lighten all this isle?—I'll to the king
And say I spoke with you.

*Anne.*                My honour'd lord.
                        [*Exit* Lord Chamberlain.

*Old L.* Why, this it is; see, see!
I have been begging sixteen years in court,—
Am yet a courtier beggarly,—nor could
Come pat betwixt too early and too late
For any suit of pounds; and you, O fate!
A very fresh-fish here,—fie, fie, fie upon
This compell'd fortune!—have your mouth
    filled up
Before you open it.

*Anne.*            This is strange to me.

*Old L.* How tastes it? is it bitter? forty
    pence, no.
There was a lady once,—'tis an old story,—
That would not be a queen, that would she
    not,                            [it?
For all the mud in Egypt:—have you heard

*Anne.* Come, you are pleasant.

*Old L.*        With your theme I could
O'ermount the lark. The Marchioness of
    Pembroke!
A thousand pounds a year for pure respect!
No other obligation! By my life,     [train
That promises more thousands: honour's
Is longer than his foreskirt. By this time
I know your back will bear a duchess:—say,
Are you not stronger than you were?

*Anne.*                    Good lady,
Make yourself mirth with your particular
    fancy,
And leave me out on't. Would I had no being,
If this salute my blood a jot: it faints me
To think what follows.
The queen is comfortless, and we forgetful
In our long absence: pray, do not deliver
What here you have heard to her.

*Old L.*        What do you think me?
                                [*Exeunt.*

SCENE IV.—LONDON. *A Hall in* BLACK-FRIARS.

*Trumpet, sennet, and cornets. Enter two* Ver-
gers, *with short silver wands; next them,
two* Scribes, *in the habits of doctors; after
them, the* ARCHBISHOP OF CANTERBURY
*alone; after him, the* BISHOPS OF LINCOLN,
ELY, ROCHESTER, *and* SAINT ASAPH; *next
them, with some small distance, follows a
Gentleman bearing the purse, with the great
seal, and a Cardinal's hat; then two* Priests,
*bearing each a silver cross; then a Gentle-
man-usher bareheaded, accompanied with a
Sergeant-at-Arms bearing a silver mace;
then two* Gentlemen *bearing two great silver pillars; after them, side by side, the
two* Cardinals, WOLSEY *and* CAMPEIUS;
*two Noblemen with the sword and mace.
Then enter the* KING *and* QUEEN *and their
Trains. The* KING *takes place under the
cloth of state; the two Cardinals sit under
him as judges. The* QUEEN *takes place at
some distance from the* KING. *The Bishops
place themselves on each side the court, in
manner of a consistory; between them the*

Scribes. *The* Lords *sit next the* Bishops.
*The* Crier *and the rest of the* Attendants
*stand in convenient order about the hall.*

*Wol.* Whilst our Commission from Rome is
  read,
Let silence be commanded.
  *K. Hen.*                   What's the need?
It hath already publicly been read,
And on all sides the authority allow'd;
You may, then, spare that time.
  *Wol.*                Be't so.—Proceed.
  *Scribe.* Say, Henry King of England, come
    into the court.
  *Crier.* Henry King of England, &c.
  *K. Hen.* Here.
  *Scribe.* Say, Katharine Queen of England,
    come into the court.
  *Crier.* Katharine Queen of England, &c.
  [*The* QUEEN *makes no answer, rises out of
  her chair, goes about the court, comes to
  the* KING, *and kneels at his feet; then
  speaks.*
  *Q. Kath.* Sir, I desire you do me right and
    justice;
And to bestow your pity on me: for
I am a most poor woman, and a stranger,
Born out of your dominions; having here
No judge indifferent, nor no more assurance
Of equal friendship and proceeding. Alas, sir,
In what have I offended you? what cause
Hath my behaviour given to your displeasure,
That thus you should proceed to put me off,
And take your good grace from me? Heaven
  witness,
I have been to you a true and humble wife,
At all times to your will conformable:
Even in fear to kindle your dislike,   [sorry
Yea, subject to your countenance,—glad or
As I saw it inclin'd. When was the hour
I ever contradicted your desire,      [friends
Or made it not mine too? Or which of your
Have I not strove to love, although I knew
He were mine enemy? what friend of mine
That had to him deriv'd your anger, did I
Continue in my liking? nay, gave notice
He was from thence discharg'd? Sir, call to
  mind
That I have been your wife, in this obedience,
Upward of twenty years, and have been blest
With many children by you: if, in the course
And process of this time, you can report,
And prove it too, against mine honour aught,
My bond to wedlock or my love and duty,
Against your sacred person, in God's name,
Turn me away; and let the foul'st contempt
Shut door upon me, and so give me up
To the sharp'st kind of justice. Please you, sir,
The king, your father, was reputed for
A prince most prudent, of an excellent   [nand,
And unmatch'd wit and judgment: Ferdi-
My father, King of Spain, was reckon'd one
The wisest prince that there had reign'd by
  many
A year before: it is not to be question'd

That they had gather'd a wise council to them
Of every realm, that did debate this business,
Who deem'd our marriage lawful: wherefore
  I humbly
Beseech you, sir, to spare me, till I may
Be by my friends in Spain advis'd; whose
  counsel
I will implore; if not, i' the name of God,
Your pleasure be fulfill'd!
  *Wol.*          You have here, lady,—
And of your choice,—these reverend fathers;
  men
Of singular integrity and learning,
Yea, the elect o' the land, who are assembled
To plead your cause: it shall be therefore
  bootless
That longer you desire the court; as well
For your own quiet as to rectify
What is unsettled in the king.
  *Cam.*                   His grace
Hath spoken well and justly: therefore,
  madam,
It's fit this royal session do proceed;
And that, without delay, their arguments
Be now produc'd and heard.
  *Q. Kath.*               Lord cardinal,—
To you I speak.
  *Wol.*        Your pleasure, madam?
  *Q. Kath.*                        Sir,
I am about to weep; but, thinking that
We are a queen,—or long have dream'd so,—
  certain
The daughter of a king, my drops of tears
I'll turn to sparks of fire.
  *Wol.*            Be patient yet.
  *Q. Kath.* I will, when you are humble;
    nay, before,
Or God will punish me. I do believe,
Induc'd by potent circumstances, that
You are mine enemy; and make my challenge
You shall not be my judge: for it is you
Have blown this coal betwixt my lord and
  me,—                               [again,
Which God's dew quench! Therefore I say
I utterly abhor, yea, from my soul    [more,
Refuse you for my judge; whom, yet once
I hold my most malicious foe, and think not
At all a friend to truth.
  *Wol.*          I do profess
You speak not like yourself; who ever yet
Have stood to charity, and display'd the
  effects
Of disposition gentle, and of wisdom
O'ertopping woman's power. Madam, you do
  me wrong:
I have no spleen against you, nor injustice
For you or any: how far I have proceeded,
Or how far further shall, is warranted
By a commission from the consistory,
Yea, the whole consistory of Rome. You
  charge me
That I have blown this coal: I do deny it:
The king is present: if it be known to him
That I gainsay my deed, how may he wound,

And worthily, my falsehood! yea, as much
As you have done my truth. If he know
That I am free of your report, he knows
I am not of your wrong. Therefore in him
It lies to cure me: and the cure is, to  [before
Remove these thoughts from you: the which
His highness shall speak in, I do beseech [ing,
You, gracious madam, to unthink your speak-
And to say so no more.

   *Q. Kath.*        My lord, my lord,
I am a simple woman, much too weak
To oppose your cunning. You're meek and
    humble-mouth'd;        [ing,
You sign your place and calling, in full seem-
With meekness and humility; but your heart
Is crammed with arrogancy, spleen, and pride.
You have, by fortune and his highness' fa-
    vours,        [mounted
Gone slightly o'er low steps, and now are
Where powers are your retainers; and your
    words,
Domestics to you, serve your will as't please
Yourself pronounce their office. I must tell
    you,
You tender more your person's honour than
Your high profession spiritual: that again
I do refuse you for my judge; and here,
Before you all, appeal unto the pope,
To bring my whole cause 'fore his holiness,
And to be judg'd by him.

   [*She curtsies to the* KING, *and offers to*
                   *depart.*

   *Cam.*        The queen is obstinate,
Stubborn to justice, apt to accuse it, and
Disdainful to be tried by it: 'tis not well.
She's going away.

   *K. Hen.*        Call her again.

   *Crier.* Katherine Queen of England, come
    into the court.

   *Grif.* Madam, you are call'd back.

   *Q. Kath.* What need you note it? pray
    you, keep your way;       [help,
When you are call'd, return.—Now the Lord
They vex me past my patience! Pray you,
    pass on:
I will not tarry; no, nor ever more
Upon this business my appearance make
In any of their courts.

   [*Exeunt* QUEEN, GRIF., *and her other*
           Attendants.

   *K. Hen.*        Go thy ways, Kate:
That man i' the world who shall report he has
A better wife, let him in naught be trusted
For speaking false in that: thou art, alone,—
If thy rare qualities, sweet gentleness,
Thy meekness saint-like, wife-like govern-
    ment—
Obeying in commanding—and thy parts
Sovereign and pious else, could speak thee
    out,—        [born;
The queen of earthly queens:—she's noble
And like her true nobility she has
Carried herself towards me.

   *Wol.*        Most gracious sir,
In humblest manner I require your highness
That it shall please you to declare, in hearing
Of all these ears,—for where I am robb'd and
    bound,
There must I be unloos'd; although not there
At once and fully satisfied,—whether ever I
Did broach this business to your highness; or
Laid any scruple in your way, which might
Induce you to the question on't? or ever
Have to you,—but with thanks to God for
    such        [might
A royal lady,—spake one the least word that
Be to the prejudice of her present state,
Or touch of her good person?

   *K. Hen.*        My lord cardinal,
I do excuse you; yea, upon mine honour,
I free you from't. You are not to be taught
That you have many enemies, that know not
Why they are so, but, like to village curs,
Bark when their fellows do: by some of these
The queen is put in anger. You are excus'd:
But will you be more justified? you ever
Have wish'd the sleeping of this business;
    never       [der'd, oft,
Desir'd it to be stirr'd; but oft have hin-
The passages made toward it:—on my hon-
    our,
I speak my good lord cardinal to this point,
And thus far clear him. Now, what mov'd me
    to't,       [tion:—
I will be bold with time and your atten-
Then mark the inducement. Thus it came;—
    give heed to't:—
My conscience first receiv'd a tenderness,
Scruple, and prick, on certain speeches ut-
    ter'd       [ambassador;
By the Bishop of Bayonne, then French
Who had been hither sent on the debating
A marriage 'twixt the Duke of Orleans and
Our daughter Mary: I' the progress of this
    business,
Ere a determinate resolution, he,—
I mean the bishop,—did require a respite;
Wherein he might the king his lord advertise
Whether our daughter were legitimate,
Respecting this our marriage with the do-
    wager,       [shook
Sometimes our brother's wife. This respite
The bosom of my conscience, enter'd me,
Yea, with a splitting power, and made to
    tremble       [way
The region of my breast; which forc'd such
That many maz'd considerings did throng,
And press'd in with this caution. First, me-
    thought
I stood not in the smile of heaven; who had
Commanded nature that my lady's womb,
If it conceiv'd a male child by me, should
Do no more offices of life to't than  [issue
The grave does to the dead; for her male
Or died where they were made, or shortly
    after

This world had air'd them: hence I took a
thought
This was a judgment on me; that my king-
dom,
Well worthy the best heir o' the world,
should not
Be gladded in't by me: then follows that
I weigh'd the danger which my realms stood
in
By this my issue's fail; and that gave to me
Many a groaning throe. Thus hulling in
The wild sea of my conscience, I did steer
Toward this remedy, whereupon we are
Now present here together; that's to say,
I meant to rectify my conscience,—which
I then did feel full sick, and yet not well,—
By all the reverend fathers of the land,
And doctors learn'd:—first, I began in private
With you, my Lord of Lincoln; you remem-
ber
How under my oppression I did reek
When I first mov'd you.
*Lin.*　　　　　　　　Very well, my liege.
*K. Hen.* I have spoke long: be pleas'd
yourself to say
How far you satisfied me.
　　*Lin.*　　　　　So please your highness,
The question did at first so stagger me,—
Bearing a state of mighty moment in 't,
And consequence of dread,—that I committed
The daring'st counsel which I had to doubt;
And did entreat your highness to this course
Which you are running here.
　　*K. Hen.*　　　　　I then mov'd you,
My Lord of Canterbury; and got your leave
To make this present summons:—unsolicited
I left no reverend person in this court;
But by particular consent proceeded
Under your hands and seals: therefore, go on;
For no dislike i' the world against the person
Of the good queen, but the sharp thorny
points
Of my alleged reasons, drive this forward:
Prove but our marriage lawful, by my life
And kingly dignity, we are contented
To wear our mortal state to come with her,
Katharine our queen, before the primest
creature
That's paragon'd o' the world.
　　*Cam.*　　　　So pleasure your highness,
The queen being absent, 'tis a needful fitness
That we adjourn this court till furtherday:
Meanwhile must be an earnest motion
Made to the queen to call back her appeal
She intends unto his holiness.
　　　　　　　　　　　[*They rise to depart.*
　　*K. Hen.*　　　　　I may perceive
These cardinals trifle with me: I abhor
This dilatory sloth and tricks of Rome
　　　　　　　　　　　　　　　[*Aside.*
My learn'd and well-belov'd servant, Cran-
mer,
Pr'ythee, return! with thy approach, I know,

My comfort comes along. Break up the court:
I say, set on.
　　　　　[*Exeunt in manner as they entered.*

## ACT III.

SCENE I.—LONDON. *Palace at Bridewell.*
*A Room in the* QUEEN'S *Apartment.*

*The* QUEEN *and some of her* Women *at work.*

*Q. Kath.* Take thy lute, wench: my soul
grows sad with troubles;　　[*working.*
Sing and disperse 'em if thou canst: leave

### SONG.

Orpheus with his lute made trees,
And the mountain-tops that freeze,
　Bow themselves, when he did sing:
To his music plants and flowers
Ever sprung; as sun and showers
　There had made a lasting spring.

Everything that heard him play,
Even the billows of the sea,
　Hung their heads and then lay by.
In sweet music is such art:
Killing care and grief of heart
　Fall asleep, or, hearing, die.

*Enter a* Gentleman.

*Q. Kath.* How now?　　　[great cardinals
*Gent.* An't please your grace, the two
Wait in the presence.
*Q. Kath.*　　　　Would they speak with me?
*Gent.* They will'd me say so, madam.
*Q. Kath.*　　　　　Pray their graces
To come near. [*Exit* Gent.) What can be
their business　　　　　　[vour?
With me, a poor weak woman, fallen from fa-
I do not like their coming, now I think on't.
They should be good men; their affairs as
righteous:
But all hoods make not monks.

*Enter* WOLSEY *and* CAMPEIUS.

*Wol.*　　　　　Peace to your highness!
*Q. Kath.* Your graces find me here part of
a housewife;　　　　　　[pen.
I would be all, against the worst may hap-
What are your pleasures with me, reverend
lords?　　　　　　[withdraw
*Wol.* May it please you, noble madam, to
Into your private chamber, we shall give you
The full cause of our coming.
*Q. Kath.*　　　　　Speak it here;
There's nothing I have done yet, o' my con-
science,
Deserves a corner: would all other women
Could speak this with as free a soul as I do!
My lords, I care not,—so much I am happy
Above a number,—if my actions　　[em,
Were tried by every tongue, every eye saw
Envy and base opinion set against 'em,
I know my life so even. If your business
Seek me out, and that way I am wife in,
Out with it boldly: truth loves open dealing.

*Wol.* *Tanta est erga te mentis integritas,*
*regina serenissima,*—

*Q. Kath.* O, good my lord, no Latin;
I am not such a truant since my coming
As not to know the language I have lived in:
A strange tongue makes my cause more
strange, suspicious; [thank you,
Pray, speak in English: here are some will
If you speak truth, for their poor mistress'
sake,— [cardinal,
Believe me, she has had much wrong: lord
The willing'st sin I ever yet committed
May be absolv'd in English.

*Wol.* Noble lady,
I am sorry my integrity should breed,—
And service to his majesty and you,—
So deep suspicion, where all faith was meant.
We come not by the way of accusation
To taint that honour every good tongue
blesses,
Nor to betray you any way to sorrow,—
You have too much, good lady; but to know
How you stand minded in the weighty dif-
ference
Between the king and you; and to deliver,
Like free and honest men, our just opinions,
And comforts to your cause.

*Cam.* Most honour'd madam,
My Lord of York,—out of his noble nature,
Zeal and obedience he still bore your grace,—
Forgetting, like a good man, your late censure
Both of his truth and him,—which was too
far,—
Offers, as I do, in a sign of peace,
His service and his counsel.

*Q. Kath.* To betray me. [*Aside.*
My lords, I thank you both for your good-
wills; [prove so!
Ye speak like honest men,—pray God ye
But how to make ye suddenly an answer,
In such a point of weight, so near mine
honour,— [wit,
More near my life, I fear,—with my weak
And to such men of gravity and learning,
In truth, I know not. I was set at work
Among my maids; full little, God knows,
looking
Either for such men or such business.
For her sake that I have been,—for I feel
The last fit of my greatness,—good your
graces,
Let me have time and counsel for my cause:
Alas, I am a woman, friendless, hopeless!

*Wol.* Madam, you wrong the king's love
with these fears:
Your hopes and friends are infinite.

*Q. Kath.* In England
But little for my profit: can you think, lords,
That any Englishman dare give me counsel?
Or be a known friend, 'gainst his highness'
pleasure,— [est,—
Though he be grown so desperate to be hon-
And live a subject? Nay, forsooth, my
friends,

They that must weigh out my afflictions,
They that my trust must grow to, live not
here:
They are, as all my other comforts, far hence,
In mine own country, lords.

*Cam.* I would your grace
Would leave your griefs, and take my counsel.

*Q. Kath.* How, sir?

*Cam.* Put your main cause into the king's
protection; [much
He's loving and most gracious: 'twill be
Both for your honour better and your cause;
For if the trial of the law o'ertake ye
You'll part away disgrac'd.

*Wol.* He tells you rightly.

*Q. Kath.* Ye tell me what ye wish for both,
—my ruin:
Is this your Christian counsel? out upon ye!
Heaven is above all yet; there sits a Judge
That no king can corrupt.

*Cam.* Your rage mistakes us.

*Q. Kath.* The more shame for ye: holy
men I thought ye,
Upon my soul, two reverend cardinal vir-
tues
But cardinal sins and hollow hearts I fear ye:
Mend them, for shame, my lords. Is this your
comfort?
The cordial that ye bring a wretched lady,—
A woman lost among ye, laugh'd at, scorn'd?
I will not wish ye half my miseries;
I have more charity: but say I warn'd ye;
Take heed, for heaven's sake, take heed, lest
at once
The burden of my sorrows fall upon ye.

*Wal.* Madam, this is a mere distraction;
You turn the good we offer into envy.

*Q. Kath.* Ye turn me into nothing: woe
upon ye, [me,—
And all such false professors! would you have
If you have any justice, any pity,
If ye be anything but churchmen's habits,—
Put my sick cause into his hands that hates
me?
Alas! has banish'd me his bed already,
His love too long ago! I am old, my lords,
And all the fellowship I hold now with him
Is only my obedience. What can happen
To me above this wretchedness? all your
studies
Make me a curse like this.

*Cam.* Your fears are worse.

*Q. Kath.* Have I liv'd thus long,—let me
speak myself, [one?
Since virtue finds no friends,—a wife, a true
A woman,—I dare say without vain-glory,—
Never yet branded with suspicion?
Have I with all my full affections
Still met the king? lov'd him next heaven?
obey'd him?
Been, out of fondness, superstitious to him?
Almost forgot my prayers to content him?
And am I thus rewarded? 'tis not well, lords.
Bring me a constant woman to her husband,

One that ne'er dream'd a joy beyond his pleasure;
And to that woman, when she has done most,
Yet will I add an honour,—a great patience.

*Wol.* Madam, you wander from the good
we aim at.  [so guilty,

*Q. Kath.* My lord, I dare not make myself
To give up willingly that noble title
Your master wed me to: nothing but death
Shall e'er divorce my dignities.

*Wol.*  Pray, hear me.

*Q. Kath.* Would I had never trod this English earth,
Or felt the flatteries that grow upon it!
Ye have angels' faces, but heaven knows your hearts.
What will become of me now, wretched lady?
I am the most unhappy woman living.—
Alas, poor wenches, where are now your fortunes?  [*To her* Women.
Shipwreck'd upon a kingdom, where no pity,
No friends, no hope; no kindred weep for me;
Almost no grave allow'd me:—like the lily,
That once was mistress of the field and flourish'd,
I'll hang my head and perish.

*Wol.*  If your grace
Could but be brought to know our ends are honest,  [good lady,
You'd feel more comfort: why should we,
Upon what cause, wrong you? alas, our places,
The way of our profession is against it:
We are to cure such sorrows, not to sow 'em,
For goodness' sake, consider what you do;
How you may hurt yourself, ay, utterly
Grow from the king's acquaintance, by this carriage.
The hearts of princes kiss obedience,
So much they love it; but to stubborn spirits
They swell, and grow as terrible as storms.
I know you have a gentle-noble temper,
A soul as even as a calm: pray, think us
Those we profess, peace-makers, friends, and servants.  [your virtues

*Cam.* Madam, you'll find it so. You wrong
With these weak women's fears: a noble spirit,
As yours was put into you, ever casts
Such doubts, as false coin, from it. The king
loves you;
Beware you lose it not: for us, if you please
To trust us in your business, we are ready
To use our utmost studies in your service.

*Q. Kath.* Do what ye will, my lords: and, pray, forgive me
If I have us'd myself unmannerly;
You know I am a woman, lacking wit
To make a seemly answer to such persons.
Pray, do my service to his majesty:
He has my heart yet; and shall have my prayers  [fathers,
While I shall have my life. Come, reverend

Bestow your counsels on me; she now begs
That little thought, when she set footing here,
She should have bought her dignities so dear.
[*Exeunt.*

SCENE II.—LONDON. *Ante-chamber to the*
KING'S *Apartment in the Palace.*

*Enter the* DUKE OF NORFOLK, *the* DUKE OF
SUFFOLK, *the* EARL OF SURREY, *and the*
Lord Chamberlain.

*Nor.* If you will now unite in your complaints,  [dinal
And force them with a constancy, the car-
Cannot stand under them: if you omit
The offer of this time, I cannot promise
But that you shall sustain more new disgraces,
With these you bear already.

*Sur.*  I am joyful
To meet the least occasion that may give me
Remembrance of my father-in-law, the duke,
To be reveng'd on him.

*Suf.*  Which of the peers
Have uncontemn'd gone by him, or at least
Strangely neglected? when did he regard
The stamp of nobleness in any person
Out of himself?

*Cham.* My lords, you speak your pleasures:
What he deserves of you and me I know;
What we can do to him,—though now the time.  [not
Gives way to us,—I much fear. If you can-
Bar his access to the king, never attempt
Anything on him; for he hath a witchcraft
Over the king in's tongue.

*Nor.*  O, fear him not;
His spell in that is out: the king hath found
Matter against him that for ever mars
The honey of his language. No, he's settled,
Not to come off, in his displeasure

*Sur.*  Sir,
I should be glad to hear such news as this
Once every hour.

*Nor.*  Believe it, this is true;
In the divorce his contrary proceedings
Are all unfolded; wherein he appears
As I would wish mine enemy.

*Sur.*  How came
His practices to light?

*Suf.*  Most strangely.

*Sur.*  O, how, how?

*Suf.* The cardinal's letters to the pope miscarried,  [read
And came to the eye o' the king: wherein was
How that the cardinal did entreat his holiness
To stay the judgment o' the divorce; for if
It did take place, *I do,* quoth he, *perceive
My king is tangled in affection to
A creature of the queen's, Lady Anne Bullen.*

*Sur.* Has the king this?

*Suf.*  Believe it.

*Sur.*  Will this work?

*Cham.* The king in this perceives him how he coasts

And hedges his own way. But in this point
All his tricks founder, and he brings his
physic
After his patient's death: the king already
Hath married the fair lady.

*Sur.*                          Would he had!

*Suf.* May you be happy in your wish, my
lord!
For, I profess, you have it.

*Sur.*                          Now, all my joy
Trace the conjunction!

*Suf.*                    My amen to't!

*Nor.*                              All men's!

*Sur.* There's order given for her corona-
tion:
Marry, this is yet but young, and may be left
To some ears unrecounted.—But, my lords,
She is a gallant creature, and complete
In mind and feature: I persuade me, from her
Will fall some blessing to this land, which
shall
In it be memoriz'd.

*Sur.*                  But will the king
Digest this letter of the cardinal's?
The Lord forbid!

*Nor.*              Marry, amen!

*Suf.*                            No, no;
There be more wasps that buzz about his nose
Will make this sting the sooner. Cardinal
Campeius
Is stol'n away to Rome; hath ta'en no leave;
Has left the cause o' the king unhandled; and
Is posted, as the agent of our cardinal,
To second all his plot. I do assure you
The king cried Ha! at this.

*Cham.*                Now, God incense him,
And let him cry Ha! louder!

*Nor.*                      But, my lord,
When returns Cranmer?

*Suf.* He is return'd, in his opinions; which
Have satisfied the king for his divorce,
Together with all famous colleges
Almost in Christendom: shortly, I believe,
His second marriage shall be publish'd, and
Her coronation. Katharine no more
Shall be call'd queen, but princess dowager
And widow to Prince Arthur.

*Nor.*                      This same Cranmer's
A worthy fellow, and hath ta'en much pain
In the king's business.

*Suf.*              He has; and we shall see him
For it an archbishop.

*Nor.*              So I hear.

*Suf.*                        'Tis so.—
The cardinal!

*Enter* WOLSEY *and* CROMWELL.

*Nor.*              Observe, observe, he's moody.

*Wol.* The packet, Cromwell,
Gave't you the king?

*Crom.* To his own hand, in's bedchamber.

*Wol.* Look'd he o' the inside of the paper?

*Crom.*                          Presently
He did unseal them: and the first he view'd,

He did it with a serious mind; a heed
Was in his countenance. You he bade
Attend him here this morning.

*Wol.*              Is he ready
To come abroad?

*Crom.*        I think by this he is.

*Wol.* Leave me awhile. [*Exit* CROMWELL.
It shall be to the Duchess of Alencon,
The French king's sister: he shall marry
her.—                                    [him:
Anne Bullen! No; I'll no Anne Bullens for
There's more in't than fair visage.—Bullen!
No, we'll no Bullens.—Speedily I wish
To hear from Rome.—The Marchioness of
Pembroke!

*Nor.* He's discontented.

*Suf.*              May be he hears the king
Does whet his anger to him.

*Sur.*                    Sharp enough,
Lord, for thy justice!    [knight's daughter,

*Wol.* The late queen's gentlewoman, a
To be her mistress' mistress! the queen's
queen!—                                  [it;
This candle burns not clear: 'tis I must snuff
Then out it goes.—What though I know her
virtuous
And well deserving? yet I know her for
A spleeny Lutheran; and not wholesome to
Our cause, that she should lie i' the bosom of
Our hard-rul'd king. Again, there is sprung
up
An heretic, an arch one, Cranmer; one
Hath crawl'd into the favour of the king,
And is his oracle.

*Nor.*              He is vex'd at something.

*Sur.* I would 'twere something that would
fret the string,
The master-cord on's heart!

*Suf.*                    The king, the king!

*Enter the* KING, *reading a schedule, and*
LOVELL.

*K. Hen.* What piles of wealth hath he ac-
cumulated                                [the hour
To his own portion! and what expense by
Seems to flow from him! How, i' the name
of thrift,
Does he rake this together?—Now, my lords,
Saw you the cardinal?

*Nor.*              My lord, we have
Stood here observing him: some strange com-
motion
Is in his brain: he bites his lip and starts;
Stops on a sudden, looks upon the ground,
Then lays his finger on his temple; straight
Springs out into fast gait; then stops again,
Strikes his breast hard; and anon he casts
His eye against the moon: in most strange
postures
We have seen him set himself.

*K. Hen.*              It may well be;
There is a mutiny in's mind. This morning
Papers of state he sent me to peruse,
As I requir'd: and wot you what I found

There,—on my conscience, put unwittingly?
Forsooth, an inventory, thus importing,—
The several parcels of his plate, his treasure,
Rich stuffs, and ornaments of household;
which
I find at such proud rate that it out-speaks
Possession of a subject.

*Nor.* It's heaven's will:
Some spirit put this paper in the packet
To bless your eye withal.

*K. Hen.* If we did think
His contemplation were above the earth,
And fix'd on spiritual object, he should still
Dwell in his musings: but I am afraid
His thinkings are below the moon, not worth
His serious considering.

[*He takes his seat and whispers* LOVELL, *who goes to* WOLSEY.

*Wol.* Heaven forgive me!
Ever God bless your highness!

*K. Hen.* Good, my lord,
You are full of heavenly stuff, and bear the
inventory
Of your best graces in your mind; the which
You were now running o'er: you have scarce
time
To steal from spiritual leisure a brief span
To keep your earthly audit: sure, in that
I deem you an ill husband, and am glad
To have you therein my companion.

*Wol.* Sir,
For holy offices I have a time; a time
To think upon the part of business which
I bear i' the state; and nature does require
Her times of preservation, which perforce
I, her frail son, amongst my brethren mortal,
Must give my tendance to.

*K. Hen.* You have said well.

*Wol.* And ever may your highness yoke to-
gether,
As I will lend you cause, my doing well
With my well saying!

*K. Hen.* 'Tis well said again;
And 'tis a kind of good deed to say well:
And yet words are no deeds. My father lov'd
you:
He said he did; and with his deed did crown
His word upon you. Since I had my office
I have kept you next my heart; have not
alone            [home,
Employ'd you where high profits might come
But par'd my present havings to bestow
My bounties upon you.

*Wol.* What should this mean?            [*Aside.*

*Sur.* The Lord increase this business!
[*Aside to others.*

*K. Hen.* Have I not made you
The prime man of the state? I pray you, tell
me            [true:
If what I now pronounce you have found
And, if you may confess it, say withal
If you are bound to us or no. What say you?

*Wol.* My sovereign, I confess your royal
graces,

Shower'd on me daily, have been more than
could
My studied purposes requite; which went
Beyond all man's endeavours:—my endeav-
ours
Have ever come too short of my desires,
Yet fill'd with my abilities: mine own ends
Have been mine so that evermore they
pointed
To the good of your most sacred person and
The profit of the state. For your great graces
Heap'd upon me, poor undeserver, I
Can nothing render but allegiant thanks;
My prayers to heaven for you; my loyalty,
Which ever has and ever shall be growing,
Till death, that winter, kill it.

*K. Hen.* Fairly answer'd;
A loyal and obedient subject is
Therein illustrated: the honour of it
Does pay the act of it: as, i' the contrary,
The foulness is the punishment. I presume
That, as my hand has open'd bounty to you,
My heart dropp'd love, my power rain'd
honour, more
On you than any; so your hand and heart,
Your brain, and every function of your
power,            [duty,
Should, notwithstanding that your bond of
As 'twere in love's particular, be more
To me, your friend, than any.

*Wol.* I do profess
That for your highness' good I ever labour'd
More than mine own; that am, have, and
will be,—            [to you,
Though all the world should crack their duty
And throw it from their soul; though perils
did            [and
Abound as thick as thought could make 'em,
Appear in forms more horrid.—yet my duty,
As doth a rock against the chiding flood,
Should the approach of this wild river break,
And stand unshaken yours.

*K. Hen.* 'Tis nobly spoken:
Take notice, lords, he has a loyal breast,
For you have seen him open't.—Read o'er
this;            [*Giving him papers.*
And after, this: and then to breakfast with
What appetite you have.

[*Exit, frowning upon* CARDINAL WOLSEY:
*the* Nobles *throng after him, smiling
and whispering.*

*Wol.* What should this mean?
What sudden anger's this? how have I reap'd
it?
He parted frowning from me, as if ruin
Leap'd from his eyes: so looks the chafed lion
Upon the daring huntsman that has gall'd
him;
Then makes him nothing. I must read this
paper;
I fear, the story of his anger.—'Tis so;
This paper has undone me:—'tis the account
Of all that world of wealth I have drawn to-
gether

For mine own ends; indeed, to gain the pope-
dom,
And fee my friends in Rome. O negligence,
Fit for a fool to fall by! What cross devil
Made me put this main secret in the packet
I sent the king? Is there no way to cure this?
No new device to beat this from his brains?
I know 'twill stir him strongly; yet I know
A way, if it take right, in spite of fortune,
Will bring me off again.—What's this—*To the
Pope?*
The letter, as I live, with all the business
I writ to 's holiness. Nay then, farewell!
I have touch'd the highest point of all my
greatness;
And from that full meridian of my glory
I haste now to my setting: I shall fall
Like a bright exhalation in the evening,
And no man see me more.

*Re-enter the* DUKES OF NORFOLK *and* SUF-
FOLK, *the* EARL OF SURREY, *and the* Lord
Chamberlain.

*Nor.* Hear the king's pleasure, cardinal:
who commands you
To render up the great seal presently
Into our hands; and to confine yourself
To Asher House, my Lord of Winchester's,
Till you hear further from his highness.
*Wol.*                                Stay,—
Where's your commission, lords? words can-
not carry
Authority so weighty.
*Suf.*          Who dare cross 'em,
Bearing the king's will from his mouth ex-
pressly?
*Wol.* Till I find more than will or words to
do it,—
I mean your malice,—know, officious lords,
I dare and must deny it. Now I feel
Of what coarse metal ye are moulded,—envy:
How eagerly ye follow my disgraces,
As if it fed ye! and how sleek and wanton
Ye appear in everything may bring my ruin!
Follow your envious courses, men of malice;
You have Christian warrant for them, and,
no doubt,
In time will find their fit rewards. That seal,
You ask with such a violence, the king,—
Mine and your master,—with his own hand
gave me;—
Bade me enjoy it, with the place and honours,
During my life; and, to confirm his goodness,
Tied it by letters-patents: now, who'll take
it?
*Sur.* The king, that gave it.
*Wol.*                It must be himself then.
*Sur.* Thou art a proud traitor, priest.
*Wol.*          Proud lord, thou liest:
Within these forty hours Surrey durst better
Have burnt that tongue than said so.
*Sur.*                          Thy ambition,
Thou scarlet sin, robb'd this bewailing land
Of noble Buckingham, my father-in-law:

The heads of all thy brother cardinals,—
With thee and all thy best parts bound to-
gether,—
Weigh'd not a hair of his. Plague of your
policy!
You sent me deputy for Ireland;
Far from his succour, from the king, from all
That might have mercy on the fault thou
gav'st him;
Whilst your great goodness, out of holy pity,
Absolv'd him with an axe.
*Wol.*                This, and all else
This talking lord can lay upon my credit,
I answer, is most false. The duke by law
Found his deserts: how innocent I was
From any private malice in his end,
His noble jury and foul cause can witness.
If I lov'd many words, lord, I should tell you
You have as little honesty as honour,
That in the way of loyalty and truth
Toward the king, my ever royal master,
Dare mate a sounder man than Surrey can
be,
And all that love his follies.
*Sur.*                    By my soul,
Your long coat, priest, protects you; thou
shouldst feel
My sword i' the life-blood of thee else.—My
lords,
Can ye endure to hear this arrogance?
And from this fellow? If we live thus tamely,
To be thus jaded by a piece of scarlet,
Farewell, nobility; let his grace go forward,
And dare us with his cap like larks.
*Wol.*                          All goodness
Is poison to thy stomach.
*Sur.*                Yes, that goodness
Of gleaning all the land's wealth into one,
Into your own hands, cardinal, by extortion;
The goodness of your intercepted packets
You writ to the pope against the king: your
goodness,          [ous.—
Since you provoke me, shall be most notori-
My Lord of Norfolk,—as you are truly noble,
As you respect the common good, the state
Of our despis'd nobility, our issues,
Who, if he live, will scarce be gentlemen,—
Produce the grand sum of his sins, the articles
Collected from his life:—I'll startle you
Worse than the sacring bell, when the brown
wench
Lay kissing in your arms, lord cardinal.
*Wol.* How much, methinks, I could despise
this man,
But that I am bound in charity against it!
*Nor.* Those articles, my lord, are in the
king's hand:
But, thus much, they are foul ones.
*Wol.*                        So much fairer
And spotless shall mine innocence arise,
When the king knows my truth.
*Sur.*                    This cannot save you
I thank my memory I yet remember
Some of these articles; and out they shall.

Now, if you can blush and cry guilty, card-
    inal,
You'll show a little honesty.
    *Wol.*                    Speak on, sir,
I dare your worst objections: if I blush,
It is to see a nobleman want manners.
    *Sur.* I'd rather want those than my head.—
        Have at you!
First, that, without the king's assent or know-
    ledge,
You wrought to be a legate; by which power
You maim'd the jurisdiction of all bishops.
    *Nor.* Then, that in all you writ to Rome,
        or else
To foreign princes, *Ego et Rex meus* [king
Was still inscrib'd; in which you brought the
To be your servant.
    *Suf.*    Then, that, without the knowledge,
Either of king or council, when you went
Ambassador to the emperor, you made bold
To carry into Flanders the great seal.
    *Sur.* Item, you sent a large commission
To Gregory de Cassalis, to conclude,
Without the king's will or the state's allow-
    ance,
A league between his highness and Ferrara.
    *Suf.* That, out of mere ambition, you have
        caus'd
Your holy hat to be stamp'd on the king's
    coin.
    *Sur.* Then, that you have sent innumerable
        substance,                    [science,
By what means got I leave to your own con-
To furnish Rome, and to prepare the ways
You have for dignities; to the mere undoing
Of all the kingdom. Many more there are,
Which, since they are of you, and odious,
I will not taint my mouth with.
    *Cham.*                    O my lord,
Press not a falling man too far! 'tis virtue:
His faults lie open to the laws; let them,
Not you, correct him. My heart weeps to see
    him
So little of his great self.
    *Sur.*        I forgive him. [pleasure is,—
    *Suf.* Lord Cardinal, the king's further
Because all those things you have done of late,
By your power legatine within this kingdom,
Fall into the compass of a *præmunire,*—
That therefore such a writ be sued against
    you;
To forfeit all your goods, lands, tenements,
Chattels, and whatsoever, and to be
Out of the king's protection:—this is my
    charge.
    *Nor.* And so we'll leave you to your medi-
        tations
How to live better. For your stubborn an-
    swer
About the giving back the great seal to us,
The king shall know it, and, no doubt, shall
        thank you.
So fare you well, my little good lord cardinal.
                    [*Exeunt all but* WOLSEY.

    *Wol.* So farewell to the little good you
        bear me.
Farewell, a long farewell, to all my greatness!
This is the state of man: to-day he puts forth
The tender leaves of hope; to-morrow blos-
    soms,
And bears his blushing honours thick upon
    him;
The third day comes a frost, a killing frost,
And,—when he thinks, good easy man, full
    surely
His greatness is a-ripening,—nips his root,
And then he falls, as I do. I have ventur'd,
Like little wanton boys that swim on blad-
    ders,
This many summers in a sea of glory;
But far beyond my depth: my high-blown
    pride
At length broke under me; and now has left
    me,
Weary and old with service, to the mercy
Of a rude stream, that must for ever hide me.
Vain pomp and glory of this world, I hate ye:
I feel my heart new opened. O, how wretched
Is that poor man that hangs on prince's fa-
    vours!                    [to,
There is, betwixt that smile we would aspire
That sweet aspect of princes, and their ruin,
More pangs and fears than wars or women
    have:
And when he falls, he falls like Lucifer,
Never to hope again.

        *Enter* CROMWELL, *amazedly.*
                    Why, how now, Cromwell!
    *Crom.* I have no power to speak, sir.
    *Wol.*                    What, amaz'd
At my misfortunes? can thy spirit wonder
A great man should decline? Nay, an you
        weep,
I am fallen indeed.
    *Crom.*            How does your grace?
    *Wol.*                    Why, well;
Never so truly happy, my good Cromwell.
I know myself now; and I feel within me
A peace above all earthly dignities,
A still and quiet conscience. The king has
        cur'd me,
I humbly thank his grace; and from these
        shoulders,
These ruin'd pillars, out of pity, taken
A load would sink a navy,—too much hon-
        our:
O, 'tis a burden, Cromwell, 'tis a burden
Too heavy for a man that hopes for heaven!
    *Crom.* I am glad your grace has made that
        right use of it.                    [thinks,—
    *Wol.* I hope I have: I am able now, me-
Out of a fortitude of soul I feel,—
To endure more miseries and greater far
Than my weak-hearted enemies dare offer.
What news abroad?
    *Crom.*            The heaviest and the worst
Is your displeasure with the king.

*Wol.*　　　　　　　God bless him!

*Crom.* The next is that Sir Thomas More is chosen
Lord Chancellor in your place.

*Wol.*　　　　　That's somewhat sudden:
But he's a learned man. May he continue
Long in his highness' favour, and do justice,
For truth's sake and his conscience; that his bones,
When he has run his course and sleeps in blessings,
May have a tomb of orphans' tears wept on 'em!
What more?

*Crom.* That Cranmer is return'd with welcome,
Install'd Lord Archbishop of Canterbury.

*Wol.* That's news indeed.

*Crom.*　　　　　Last, that the Lady Anne,
Whom the king has in secrecy long married,
This day was view'd in open as his queen,
Going to chapel; and the voice is now
Only about her coronation.

*Wol.* There was the weight that pull'd me down. O Cromwell,
The king has gone beyond me: all my glories
In that one woman I have lost for ever:
No sun shall ever usher forth mine honours,
Or gild again the noble troops that waited
Upon my smiles. Go, get thee from me, Cromwell;
I am a poor fallen man, unworthy now
To be thy lord and master: seek the king;
That sun, I pray, may never set! I have told him
What and how true thou art: he will advance thee;
Some little memory of me will stir him,—
I know his noble nature,—not to let
Thy hopeful service perish too: good Cromwell,
Neglect him not; make use now, and provide
For thine own future safety.

*Crom.*　　　　　O my lord,
Must I then leave you? must I needs forego
So good, so noble, and so true a master?
Bear witness, all that have not hearts of iron,
With what a sorrow Cromwell leaves his lord.
The king shall have my service; but my prayers
For ever and for ever shall be yours.

*Wol.* Cromwell, I did not think to shed a tear
In all my miseries; but thou hast forc'd me,
Out of thy honest truth, to play the woman.
Let's dry our eyes: and thus far hear me, Cromwell;
And,—when I am forgotten, as I shall be,
And sleep in dull cold marble, where no mention
Of me more must be heard of,—say I taught thee;
Say Wolsey,—that once trod the ways of glory,

And sounded all the depths and shoals of honour,—
Found thee a way, out of his wreck, to rise in;
A sure and safe one, though thy master miss'd it.
Mark but my fall, and that that ruin'd me.
Cromwell, I charge thee, fling away ambition:
By that sin fell the angels; how can man, then,
The image of his Maker, hope to win by it?
Love thyself last: cherish those hearts that hate thee;
Corruption wins not more than honesty.
Still in thy right hand carry gentle peace,
To silence envious tongues. Be just, and fear not:
Let all the ends thou aim'st at be thy country's,
Thy God's, and truth's; then, if thou fall'st, O Cromwell,
Thou fall'st a blessed martyr! Serve the king;
And,—pr'ythee, lead me in:
There take an inventory of all I have,
To the last penny; 'tis the king's: my robe,
And my integrity to heaven, is all
I dare now call mine own. O Cromwell Cromwell!
Had I but serv'd my God with half the zeal
I serv'd my king, he would not in mine age
Have left me naked to mine enemies.

*Crom.* Good sir, have patience.

*Wol.*　　　　　So I have. Farewell
The hopes of court! my hopes in heaven do dwell.　　　　　[*Exeunt.*

## ACT IV.

SCENE I.—*A Street in Westminster.*

*Enter two* Gentlemen, *meeting.*

1 *Gent.* You are well met once again.

2 *Gent.*　　　　　So are you.

1 *Gent.* You come to take your stand here, and behold
The Lady Anne pass from her coronation?

2 *Gent.* 'Tis all my business. At our last encounter
The Duke of Buckingham came from his trial.

1 *Gent.* 'Tis very true: but that time offer'd sorrow;
This, general joy.

2 *Gent.*　　　　　'Tis well: the citizens,
I am sure, have shown at full their royal minds;
As, let 'em have their rights, they are ever forward,
In celebration of this day with shows,
Pageants, and sights of honour.

1 *Gent.*　　　　　Never greater,
Nor, I'll assure you, better taken sir.

2 *Gent.* May I be bold to ask what that contains,
That paper in your hand?

*1 Gent.*                              Yes; 'tis the list
Of those that claim their offices this day,
By custom of the coronation.
The Duke of Suffolk is the first, and claims
To be high-steward; next, the Duke of Nor-
folk,
He to be earl marshal: you may read the
rest.
  *2 Gent.* I thank you, sir; had I not known
those customs,
I should have been beholden to your paper.
But, I beseech you, what's become of Kath-
arine,
The princess dowager? how goes her busi-
ness?
  *1 Gent.* That I can tell you too. The Arch-
bishop
Of Canterbury, accompanied with other
Learned and reverend fathers of his order,
Held a late court at Dunstable, six miles off
From Ampthill, where the princess lay; to
which
She was often cited by them, but appear'd
not:
And, to be short, for not appearance and
The king's late scruple, by the main assent
Of all these learned men, she was divorc'd,
And the late marriage made of none effect:
Since which she was remov'd to Kimbolton,
Where she remains now sick.
  *2 Gent.*                          Alas, good lady!—
                                  [*Trumpets.*
The trumpets sound: stand close, the queen is
coming.

### THE ORDER OF THE PROCESSION.

*A lively flourish of trumpets: then enter,*

1. Two Judges.
2. Lord Chancellor, with the purse and mace before
   him.
3. Choristers singing.                [*Music.*
4. Mayor of London, bearing the mace. Then Garter, in his coat of arms, and on his head a gilt
   copper crown.
5. Marquis Dorset, bearing a sceptre of gold, on his
   head a demi-coronal of gold. With him, the
   Earl of Surrey, bearing the rod of silver with
   the dove, crowned with an earl's coronet. Collars of SS.
6. Duke of Suffolk, in his robe of estate, his coronet
   on his head, bearing a long white wand, as
   high-steward. With him, the Duke of Norfolk,
   with the rod of marshalship, a coronet on his
   head. Collars of SS.
7. A canopy borne by four of the Cinque-ports; under it the Queen in her robe; her hair richly
   adorned with pearl, crowned. On each side of
   her, the Bishops of London and Winchester.
8. The old Duchess of Norfolk, in a coronal of gold,
   wrought with flowers, bearing the Queen's
   train.
9. Certain Ladies or Countesses, with plain circlets
   of gold without flowers.

A royal train, believe me.—These I know:—
Who's that that bears the sceptre?
  *1 Gent.*                          Marquis Dorset:

And that the Earl of Surrey, with the rod.
  *2 Gent.* A bold brave gentleman. That
should be
The Duke of Suffolk?
  *1 Gent.*            'Tis the same,—high-steward.
  *2 Gent.* And that my Lord of Norfolk?
  *1 Gent.*                              Yes.
  *2 Gent.*                    Heaven bless thee!
                      [*Looking on the* QUEEN.
Thou hast the sweetest face I ever look'd
on.—
Sir, as I have a soul, she is an angel;
Our king has all the Indies in his arms,
And more and richer, when he strains that
lady:
I cannot blame his conscience.
  *1 Gent.*                        They that bear
The cloth of honour over her are four barons
Of the Clinque-ports.
  *2 Gent.* Those men are happy; and so are
all are near her.
I take it, she that carries up the train
Is that old noble lady, Duchess of Norfolk.
  *1 Gent.* It is; and all the rest are countesses.
  *2 Gent.* Their coronets say so. These are
stars indeed;
And sometimes falling ones.
  *1 Gent.*                      No more of that.
          [*Exit Procession, with a great flourish
                        of trumpets.*

*Enter a third* Gentleman.

God save you, sir! where have you been broil-
ing?                          [where a finger
  *3 Gent.* Among the crowd i' the abbey;
Could not be wedg'd in more: I am stifled
With the mere rankness of their joy.
  *2 Gent.*                              You saw
The ceremony?
  *3 Gent.*        That I did.
  *1 Gent.*                    How was it?
  *3 Gent.* Well worth the seeing.
  *2 Gent.*                  Good sir, speak it to us.
  *3 Gent.* As well as I am able. The rich
stream
Of lords and ladies, having brought the queen
To a prepar'd place in the choir, fell off
A distance from her: while her grace sat down
To rest awhile, some half an hour or so,
In a rich chair of state, opposing freely
The beauty of her person to the people.
Believe me, sir, she is the goodliest woman
That ever lay by man: which when the peo-
ple
Had the full view of, such a noise arose
As the shrouds make at sea in a stiff tempest,
As loud, and to as many tunes: hats, cloaks,—
Doublets, I think,—flew up; and had their
faces
Been loose, this day they had been lost. Such
joy
I never saw before. Great-bellied women,
That had not half a week to go, like rams

In the old time of war, would shake the press,
And make 'em reel before 'em. No man living
Could say, *This is my wife*, there; all were
   woven
So strangely in one piece.

  *2 Gent.*         But what follow'd?

  *3 Gent.* At length her grace rose, and with
    modest paces        [saintlike,
Came to the altar; where she kneel'd, and,
Cast her fair eyes to heaven, and pray'd de-
  voutly.
Then rose again, and bow'd her to the peo-
  ple:
When by the Archbishop of Canterbury
She had all the royal makings of a queen;
As holy oil, Edward Confessor's crown,
The rod, and bird of peace, and all such em-
  blems,
Laid nobly on her: which perform'd, the
  choir,
With all the choicest music of the kingdom,
Together sung *Te Deum*. So she parted,
And with the same full state pac'd back again
To York Place, where the feast is held.

  *1 Gent.*              Sir,
You must no more call it York Place, that's
  past:
For, since the cardinal fell, that title's lost:
'Tis now the king's, and call'd Whitehall.

  *3 Gent.*            I know it;
But 'tis so lately alter'd that the old name
Is fresh about me.

  *2 Gent.*    What two reverend bishops
Were those that went on each side of the
  queen?

  *3 Gent.* Stokesly and Gardiner; the one of
  Winchester,—
Newly preferr'd from the king's secretary,—
The other, London.

  *2 Gent.*        He of Winchester
Is held no great good lover of the arch-
  bishop's,
The virtuous Cranmer.

  *3 Gent.*        All the land knows that:
However, yet there is no great breach; when
  it comes,           [from him.
Cranmer will find a friend will not shrink

  *2 Gent.* Who may that be, I pray you?

  *3 Gent.*         Thomas Cromwell,
A man in much esteem with the king, and
  truly
A worthy friend.—The king
Has made him master o' the jewel-house,
And one, already, of the privy council.'

  *2 Gent.* He will deserve more.

  *3 Gent.*       Yes, without all doubt.—
Come, gentlemen, ye shall go my way, which
Is to the court, and there ye shall be my
  guests:
Something I can command. As I walk thither
I'll tell ye more.

  *Both.*      You may command us, sir.
                        *[Exeunt.*

SCENE II.—*Kimbolton.*

*Enter* KATHARINE, *Dowager, sick; led between* GRIFFITH *and* PATIENCE.

  *Grif.* How does your grace?

  *Kath.*      O Griffith, sick to death!
My legs, like loaden branches, bow to the
  earth,
Willing to leave their burden. Reach a
  chair:—
So,—now, methinks, I feel a little ease.
Didst thou not tell me, Griffith, as thou
  ledd'st me,
That the great child of honour, Cardinal
  Wolsey,
Was dead?

  *Grif.* Yes, madam; but I think your grace,
Out of the pain you suffer'd, gave no ear
  to 't.

  *Kath.* Pr'ythee, good Griffith, tell me how
  he died:
If well, he stepp'd before me, happily,
For my example.

  *Grif.*      Well, the voice goes, madam:
For after the stout Earl Northumberland
Arrested him at York, and brought him for-
  ward,—
As a man sorely tainted,—to his answer,
He fell sick suddenly, and grew so ill
He could not sit his mule.

  *Kath.*        Alas, poor man!

  *Grif.* At last, with easy roads, he came to
  Leicester,             [abbot,
Lodg'd in the abbey; where the reverend
With all his covent, honourably receiv'd him;
To whom he gave these words,—*O, father
  abbot,
An old man, broken with the storms of state,
Is come to lay his weary bones among ye;
Give him a little earth for charity!*
So went to bed; where eagerly his sickness
Pursu'd him still: and three nights after this,
About the hour of eight,—which he himself
Foretold should be his last,—full of repent-
  ance,
Continual meditations, tears, and sorrows,
He gave his honours to the world again,
His blessed part to heaven, and slept in peace.

  *Kath.* So may he rest; his faults lie gently
  on him!              [him,
Yet thus far, Griffith, give me leave to speak
And yet with charity. He was a man
Of an unbounded stomach, ever ranking
Himself with princes; one that, by suggestion,
Tied all the kingdom: simony was fair play;
His own opinion was his law: i' the presence
He would say untruths; and be ever double
Both in his words and meaning: he was
  never,
But where he meant to ruin, pitiful:
His promises were, as he then was, mighty;
But his performance, as he is now, nothing:

Of his own body he was ill, and gave
The clergy ill example.
  *Grif.*                Noble madam,
Men's evil manners live in brass; their virtues
We write in water. May it please your highness
To hear me speak of his good now!
  *Kath.*                Yes, good Griffith;
I were malicious else.
  *Grif.*                This cardinal,
Though from an humble stock, undoubtedly
Was fashion'd to much honour from his cradle.
He was a scholar, and a ripe and good one;
Exceeding wise, fair-spoken, and persuading:
Lofty and sour to them that lov'd him not;
But to those men that sought him sweet as summer.
And though he were unsatisfied in getting,—
Which was a sin,—yet in bestowing, madam,
He was most princely: ever witness for him
Those twins of learning that he rais'd in you,
Ipswich and Oxford! one of which fell with him,
Unwilling to outlive the good that did it;
The other, though unfinish'd, yet so famous,
So excellent in art, and still so rising,
That Christendom shall ever speak his virtue.
His overthrow heap'd happiness upon him;
For then, and not till then, he felt himself,
And found the blessedness of being little:
And, to add greater honours to his age
Than man could give him, he died fearing God.
  *Kath.* After my death I wish no other herald,
No other speaker of my living actions,
To keep mine honour from corruption,
But such an honest chronicler as Griffith.
Whom I most hated living, thou hast made me,
With thy religious truth and modesty,
Now in his ashes honour: peace be with him!—
Patience, be near me still; and set me lower:
I have not long to trouble thee.—Good Griffith,
Cause the musicians play me that sad note
I nam'd my knell, whilst I sit meditating
On that celestial harmony I go to.
                    [*Sad and solemn music.*
  *Grif.* She is asleep; good wench, let's sit down quiet,
For fear we wake her:—softly, gentle Patience.

THE VISION. *Enter, solemnly tripping one after another, six Personages clad in white robes, wearing on their heads garlands of bays, and golden vizards on their faces; branches of bays or palm in their hands. They first congee unto her, then dance; and, at certain changes, the first two hold a spare garland*

*over her head; at which the other four make reverent courtesies; then the two that held the garland deliver the same to the other next two, who observe the same order in their changes, and holding the garland over her head: which done, they deliver the same garland to the last two, who likewise observe the same order: at which,—as it were by inspiration,—she makes in her sleep signs of rejoicing, and holdeth up her hands to heaven: and so in their dancing they vanish, carrying the garland with them. The music continues.*

  *Kath.* Spirits of peace, where are ye? Are ye all gone?
And leave me here in wretchedness behind ye?
  *Grif.* Madam, we are here.
  *Kath.*                It is not you I call for:
Saw ye none enter since I slept?
  *Grif.*                None, madam.
  *Kath.* No? Saw you not, even now, a blessed troop
Invite me to a banquet; whose bright faces
Cast thousand beams upon me, like the sun?
They promis'd me eternal happiness;
And brought me garlands, Griffith, which I feel
I am not worthy yet to wear: I shall,
Assuredly.                    [*dreams
  *Grif.* I am most joyful, madam, such good
Possess your fancy.
  *Kath.*                Bid the music leave,
They are harsh and heavy to me.
                    [*Music ceases.*
  *Pat.*                Do you note
How much her grace is alter'd on the sudden?
How long her face is drawn? how pale she looks,
And of an earthy cold? Mark you her eyes!
  *Grif.* She is going, wench: pray, pray.
  *Pat.*                Heaven comfort her!

*Enter a* Messenger.

  *Mess.* An't like your grace,—
  *Kath.*                You are a saucy fellow:
Deserve we no more reverence?
  *Grif.*                You are to blame,
Knowing she will not lose her wonted greatness,
To use so rude behaviour: go to, kneel.
  *Mess.* I humbly do entreat your highness'
pardon;                    [*staying
My haste made me unmannerly. There is
A gentleman, sent from the king, to see you.
  *Kath.* Admit him entrance, Griffith: but this fellow
Let me ne'er see again.
                    [*Exeunt* GRIFFITH *and* Messenger.

*Re-enter* GRIFFITH, *with* CAPUCIUS.
                    If my sight fail not,
You should be lord ambassador from the emperor,
My royal nephew, and your name Capucius.

*Cap.* Madam, the same,—your servant.
*Kath.*      O, my Lord,
The times and titles now are alter'd strangely
With me since first you knew me. But, I pray you,
What is your pleasure with me?
    *Cap.*      Noble lady,
First, mine own service to your grace; the next,
The king's request that I would visit you;
Who grieves much for your weakness,.and by me
Sends you his princely commendations,
And heartily entreats you take good comfort.
    *Kath.* O, my good lord, that comfort comes too late;
'Tis like a pardon after execution:
That gentle physic, given in time, had cur'd me;
But now I am past all comforts here, but prayers.
How does his highness?
    *Cap.*      Madam, in good health.
    *Kath.* So may he ever do! and ever flourish,
When I shall dwell with worms, and my poor name
Banish'd the kingdom!—Patience, is that letter
I caus'd you write yet sent away?
    *Pat.*      No, madam.
         [*Giving it to* KATHARINE.
    *Kath.* Sir, I most humbly pray you to deliver
This to my lord the king.
    *Cap.*      Most willing, madam.
    *Kath.* In which I have commended to his goodness      [daughter,—
The model of our chaste loves, his young
The dews of heaven fall thick in blessings on her!—
Beseeching him to give her virtuous breeding;
She is young, and of a noble modest nature,—
I hope she will deserve well;—and a little
To love her for her mother's sake, that lov'd him,
Heaven knows how dearly. My next poor petition
Is, that his noble grace would have some pity
Upon my wretched women, that so long
Have follow'd both my fortunes faithfully:
Of which there is not one, I dare avow,—
And now I should not lie,—but will deserve,
For virtue and true beauty of the soul,
For honesty and decent carriage,
A right good husband, let him be a noble;
And, sure, those men are happy that shall have them.
The last is, for my men,—they are the poorest,
But poverty could never draw 'em from me,—
That they may have their wages duly paid 'em,
And something over to remember me by:
If heaven had pleas'd to have given me longer life
And able means, we had not parted thus.
These are the whole contents:—and, good my lord,
By that you love the dearest in this world,
As you wish Christian peace to souls departed,
Stand these poor people's friend, and urge the king
To do me this last right.
    *Cap.*      By heaven, I will,
Or let me lose the fashion of a man!      [me
    *Kath.* I thank you, honest lord. Remember
In all humility unto his highness:
Say his long trouble now is passing.      [him,
Out of this world, tell him, in death I bless'd
For so I will.—Mine eyes grow dim.—Farewell,
My lord.—Griffith, farewell.—Nay, Patience,
You must not leave me yet: I must to bed;
Call in more women.—When I am dead, good wench,
Let me be us'd with honour: strew me over
With maiden flowers, that all the world may know
I was a chaste wife to my grave: embalm me,
Then lay me forth: although unqueen'd, yet like
A queen, and daughter to a king, inter me.
I can no more. [*Exeunt, leading* KATHARINE.

## ACT V.

SCENE I.—LONDON. *A Gallery in the Palace.*

*Enter* GARDINER, *Bishop of Winchester, a* Page *with a torch before him.*

    *Gar.* It's one o'clock, boy, is 't not?
    *Boy.*      It has struck.
    *Gar.* These should be hours for necessities,
Not for delights; times to repair our nature
With comforting repose, and not for us
To waste these times.

    *Enter* SIR THOMAS LOVELL.

     Good hour of night, Sir Thomas!
Whither so late?
    *Lov.* Came you from the king, my Lord?
    *Gar.* I did, Sir Thomas; and left him at primero
With the Duke of Suffolk.
    *Lov.*      I must to him too,
Before he go to bed. I'll take my leave.
    *Gar.* Not yet, Sir Thomas Lovell. What's the matter?
It seems you are in haste: an if there be
No great offence belongs to 't, give your friend

Some touch of your late business: affairs that
  walk,—
As they say spirits do,—at midnight, have
In them a wilder nature than the business
That seeks despatch by day.

*Lov.*            My lord, I love you;
And durst commend a secret to your ear
Much weightier than this work. The queen's
  in labour,
They say in great extremity; and fear'd
She'll with the labour end.

*Gar.*            The fruit she goes with
I pray for heartily, that it may find [Thomas,
Good time, and live: but for the stock, Sir
I wish it grubb'd up now.

*Lov.*            Methinks I could
Cry thee amen; and yet my conscience says
She's a good creature, and, sweet lady, does
Deserve our better wishes.

*Gar.*            But, sir, sir,—
Hear me, Sir Thomas: you are a gentleman
Of mine own way; I know you wise, relig-
  ious;
And, let me tell you, it will ne'er be well,—
'Twill not, Sir Thomas Lovell, take 't of
  me,—
Till Cranmer, Cromwell, her two hands, and
  she,
Sleep in their graves.

*Lov.*         Now, sir, you speak of two
The most remark'd i' the kingdom. As for
  Cromwell,—            [master
Beside that of the jewel-house, he's made
O' the rolls, and the king's secretary; fur-
  ther, sir,
Stands in the gap and trade of more prefer-
  ments,
With which the time will load him. The arch-
  bishop
Is the king's hand and tongue; and who dare
  speak
One syllable against him?

*Gar.*         Yes, yes, Sir Thomas,
There are that dare; and I myself have ven-
  tur'd
To speak my mind of him: and indeed this
  day,
Sir,—I may tell it you,—I think I have
Incens'd the lords o' the council, that he is,—
For so I know he is, they know he is,—
A most arch heretic, a pestilence      [moved,
That does infect the land: with which they
Have broken with the king; who hath so far
Given ear to our complaint,—of his great
  grace
And princely care; foreseeing those fell mis-
  chiefs
Our reasons laid before him,—hath com-
  manded
To-morrow morning to the council-board
He be convented. He's a rank weed, Sir
  Thomas,
And we must root him out. From your
  affairs

I hinder you too long: good night, Sir
  Thomas.

*Lov.* Many good nights, my lord: I rest
  your servant.
            [*Exeunt* GARDINER *and* Page.

*As* LOVELL *is going out, enter the* KING *and
    the* DUKE OF SUFFOLK.

*K. Hen.* Charles, I will play no more to-
  night;
My mind's not on 't; you are too hard for
  me.

*Suf.* Sir, I did never win of you before.

*K. Hen.* But little, Charles;
Nor shall not, when my fancy's on my play.—
Now, Lovell, from the queen what is the
  news?

*Lov.* I could not personally deliver to her
What you commanded me, but by her woman
I sent your message; who return'd her thanks
In the greatest humbleness, and desir'd your
  highness
Most heartily to pray for her.

*K. Hen.*         What say'st thou, ha?
To pray for her? what, is she crying out?

*Lov.* So said her woman: and that her
  sufferance made
Almost each pang a death.

*K. Hen.*            Alas, good lady!

*Suf.* God safely quit her of her burden, and
With gentle travail, to the gladding of
Your highness with an heir!

*K. Hen.*            'Tis midnight, Charles;
Pr'ythee, to bed; and in thy prayers remem-
  ber
The estate of my poor queen. Leave me
  alone;
For I must think of that which company
Will not be friendly to.

*Suf.*            I wish your highness
A quiet night; and my good mistress will
Remember in my prayers.

*K. Hen.*      Charles, good-night.
            [*Exit* SUFFOLK.

    *Enter* SIR ANTHONY DENNY.

Well, sir, what follows?            [bishop,

*Den.* Sir, I have brought my lord the arch-
As you commanded me.

*K. Hen.*            Ha! Canterbury?

*Den.* Ay, my good lord.

*K. Hen.* 'Tis true: where is he, Denny?

*Den.* He attends your highness' pleasure.

*K. Hen.*            Bring him to us.
            [*Exit* DENNY.

*Lov.* This is about that which the bishop
  spake:
I am happily come hither.            [*Aside.*

    *Re-enter* DENNY, *with* CRANMER.

*K. Hen.* Avoid the gallery.
            [LOVELL *seems to stay.*
            Ha! I have said. Be gone.
What!            [*Exeunt* LOVELL *and* DENNY.

*Cran.* I am fearful:—wherefore frowns he
    thus?
'Tis his aspect of terror. All's not well. [*Aside.*
  *K. Hen.* How now, my lord? you do de-
    sire to know
Wherefore I sent for you.
  *Cran.*           It is my duty
To attend your highness' pleasure.
  *K. Hen.*          Pray you, arise,
My good and gracious Lord of Canterbury.
Come, you and I must walk a turn together;
I have news to tell you: come, come, give me
    your hand.
Ah, my good lord, I grieve at what I speak,
And am right sorry to repeat what follows:
I have, and most unwillingly, of late
Heard many grievous, I do say, my lord,
Grievous complaints of you; which, being
    consider'd,
Have mov'd us and our council that you shall
This morning come before us; where, I know,
You cannot with such freedom purge your-
    self
But that, till further trial in those charges
Which will require your answer, you must
    take
Your patience to you, and be well contented
To make your house our Tower: you a bro-
    ther of us,
It fits we thus proceed, or else no witness
Would come against you.
  *Cran.*     I humbly thank your highness;
And am right glad to catch this good occasion
Most thoroughly to be winnow'd, where my
    chaff
And corn shall fly asunder: for I know
There's none stands under more calumnious
    tongues
Than I myself, poor man.
  *K. Hen.*       Stand up, good Canterbury:
Thy truth and thy integrity is rooted
In us, thy friend: give me thy hand, stand
    up:
Pr'ythee, let's walk. Now, by my holy-dame,
What manner of man are you? My lord, I
    look'd
You would have given me your petition that
I should have ta'en some pains to bring to-
    gether
Yourself and your accusers; and to have
    heard you,
Without indurance, further.
  *Cran.*         Most dread liege,
The good I stand on is my truth and honesty:
If they shall fail, I, with mine enemies, [not,
Will triumph o'er my person; which I weigh
Being of those virtues vacant. I fear nothing
What can be said against me.
  *K. Hen.*         Know you not
How your state stands i' the world, with the
    whole world?
Your enemies are many, and not small; their
    practices
Must bear the same proportion; and not ever

The justice and the truth o' the question
    carries
The due o' the verdict with it: at what ease
Might corrupt minds procure knaves as
    corrupt
To swear against you? such things have been
    done.
You are potently oppos'd; and with a malice
Of as great size. Ween you of better luck,
I mean in perjur'd witness, than your Master,
Whose minister you are, whiles here he liv'd
Upon this naughty earth? Go to, go to;
You take a precipice for no leap of danger,
And woo your own destruction.
  *Cran.*         God and your majesty
Protect mine innocence, or I fall into
The trap is laid for me!
  *K. Hen.*         Be of good cheer;
They shall no more prevail than we give way
    to.
Keep comfort to you; and this morning see
You do appear before them: if they shall
    chance,
In charging you with matters, to commit you,
The best persuasions to the contrary
Fail not to use, and with what vehemency
The occasion shall instruct you: if entreaties
Will render you no remedy, this ring
Deliver them, and your appeal to us
There make before them.—Look, the good
    man weeps!
He's honest, on mine honour. God's bless'd
    mother!
I swear he is true-hearted; and a soul
None better in my kingdom.—Get you gone,
And do as I have bid you. [*Exit* CRANMER.]
    —He has strangled
His language in his tears.

     *Enter an* Old Lady.

  *Gent.* [*Within.*] Come back: what mean
    you?
  *Old L.* I'll not come back; the tidings that
    I bring          [angels
Will make my boldness manners.—Now, good
Fly o'er thy royal head, and shade thy
    person
Under their blessed wings!
  *K. Hen.*        Now, by thy looks
I guess thy message. Is the queen deliver'd?
Say ay; and of a boy.
  *Old L.*        Ay, ay, my liege;
And of a lovely boy: the God of Heaven
Both now and ever bless her!—'tis a girl,—
Promises boys hereafter. Sir, your queen
Desires your visitation, and to be
Acquainted with this stranger; 'tis as like you
As cherry is to cherry.
  *K. Hen.*         Lovell,—

     *Re-enter* LOVELL.

  *Lov.*               Sir?
  *K. Hen.* Give her an hundred marks. I'll
    to the queen.          [*Exit.*

*Old L.* An hundred marks! By this light,
     I'll ha' more.
An ordinary groom is for such payment.
I will have more, or scold it out of him.
Said I for this, the girl was like to him?
I will have more, or else unsay 't; and now,
While it is hot, I'll put it to the issue.
                              [*Exeunt.*

SCENE II.—*Lobby before the Council Chamber.*

*Enter* CRANMER; *Servants, Door-keeper, &c.,
     attending.*

*Cran.* I hope I am not too late; and yet
     the gentleman
That was sent to me from the council pray'd
     me
To make great haste. All fast? what means
     this?—Ho!
Who waits there?—Sure, you know me?
  *D. Keep.*                    Yes, my lord;
But yet I cannot help you.
  *Cran.* Why?
  *D. Keep.* Your grace must wait till you be
     call'd for.

*Enter* DOCTOR BUTTS.

  *Cran.*                              So.
  *Butts.* [*Aside.*] This is a piece of malice. I
     am glad
I came this way so happily: the king
Shall understand it presently.      [*Exits.*
  *Cran.* [*Aside.*]           'Tis Butts,
The King's physician: as he pass'd along,
How earnestly he cast his eyes upon me!
Pray, heaven, he sound not my disgrace! For
     certain,
This is of purpose laid by some that hate
     me,—
God turn their hearts! I never sought their
     malice,—                [to make me
To quench mine honour: they would shame
Wait else at door, a fellow-counsellor,
Among boys, grooms, and lackeys. But their
     pleasures
Must be fulfill'd, and I attend with patience.

*The* KING *and* BUTTS *appear at a window
     above.*

  *Butts.* I'll show your grace the strangest
     sight,—
  *K. Hen.*              What's that, Butts?
  *Butts.* I think your highness saw this many
     a day.
  *K. Hen.* Body o' me, where is it?
  *Butts.*                    There my lord:
The high promotion of his grace of Canter-
     bury;
Who holds his state at door, 'mongst pur-
     suivants,
Pages, and footboys.
  *K. Hen.*           Ha! 'tis he indeed:
Is this the honour they do one another?

'Tis well there's one above them yet. I had
     thought
They had parted so much honesty among
     'em,—
At least good manners,—as not thus to
     suffer
A man of his place, and so near our favour,
To dance attendance on their lordships' plea-
     sures,
And at the door too, like a post with packets.
By holy Mary, Butts, there's knavery:
Let 'em alone, and draw the curtain close;
We shall hear more anon.      [*Exeunt.*

*The Council Chamber.*

*Enter the* Lord Chancellor, *the* DUKE OF
SUFFOLK, *the* DUKE OF NORFOLK, EARL
OF SURREY, *Lord Chamberlain,* GARDINER,
*and* CROMWELL. *The Chancellor places
himself at the upper end of the table on
the left hand; a seat being left void above
him, as for the* ARCHBISHOP OF CANTER-
BURY. *The rest seat themselves in order on
each side.* CROMWELL *at the lower end, as
Secretary.*

  *Chan.* Speak to the business, master secre-
     tary.
Why are we met in council?
  *Crom.*               Please your honours,
The chief cause concerns his grace of Canter-
     bury.
  *Gar.* Has he had knowledge of it?
  *Crom.*                          Yes.
  *Nor.*               Who waits there?
  *D. Keep.* Without, my noble lords?
  *Gar.*                          Yes.
  *D. Keep.*             My lord archbishop;
And has done half an hour, to know your
     pleasures.
  *Chan.* Let him come in.
  *D. Keep.*       Your grace may enter now.
       [CRAN. *approaches the Council-table.*
  *Chan.* My good lord archbishop, I am very
     sorry
To sit here at this present, and behold
That chair stand empty: but we all are men
In our own natures frail, and capable
Of our flesh; few are angels: out of which
     frailty                  [teach us,
And want of wisdom, you, that best should
Have misdemean'd yourself, and not a little,
Toward the king first, then his laws, in filling
The whole realm, by your teaching and your
     chaplains,—
For so we are inform'd,—with new opinions,
Divers and dangerous; which are heresies,
And, not reform'd, may prove pernicious.
  *Gar.* Which reformation must be sudden
     too,
My noble lords; for those that tame wild
     horses
Pace 'em not in their hands to make 'em
     gentle,

But stop their mouths with stubborn bits, and
    spur 'em,
Till they obey the manage. If we suffer,—
Out of our easiness, and childish pity
To one man's honour,—this contagious sick-
    ness,
Farewell all physic: and what follows then?
Commotions, uproars, with a general taint
Of the whole state: as, of late days, our
    neighbours,
The upper Germany, can dearly witness,
Yet freshly pitied in our memories.
  *Cran.* My good lords, hitherto in all the
    progress
Both of my life and office, I have labour'd,
And with no little study, that my teaching
And the strong course of my authority
Might go one way, and safely; and the end
Was ever to do well: nor is there living,—
I speak it with a single heart, my lords,—
A man that more detests, more stirs against,
Both in his private conscience and his place,
Defacers of a public peace, than I do.
Pray heaven, the king may never find a heart
With less allegiance in it! Men that make
Envy and crooked malice nourishment
Dare bite the best. I do beseech your lord-
    ships
That, in this case of justice, my accusers,
Be what they will, may stand forth face to
    face,
And freely urge against me.
  *Suf.*            Nay, my lord,
That cannot be: you are a counsellor,
And, by that virtue, no man dare accuse you.
  *Gar.* My lord, because we have business of
    more moment,     [pleasure,
We will be short with you. 'Tis his highness'
And our consent, for better trial of you,
From hence you be committed to the Tower;
Where, being but a private man again,
You shall know many dare accuse you boldly,
More than, I fear, you are provided for.
  *Cran.* Ah, my good Lord of Winchester,
    I thank you;     [pass
You are always my good friend; if your will
I shall both find your lordship judge and
    juror,
You are so merciful: I see your end,—
'Tis my undoing: love and meekness, lord,
Become a churchman better than ambition:
Win straying souls with modesty again,
Cast none away. That I shall clear myself,
Lay all the weight ye can upon my patience,
I make as little doubt as you do conscience
In doing daily wrongs. I could say more,
But reverence to your calling makes me
    modest.
  *Gar.* My lord, my lord, you are a sectary.
That's the plain truth: your painted gloss
    discovers,     [weakness.
To men that understand you, words and
  *Crom.* My Lord of Winchester, you are a
    little,

By your good favour, too sharp; men so
    noble,   ·
However faulty, yet should find respect
For what they have been: 'tis a cruelty
To load a falling man.
  *Gar.*          Good master secretary,
I cry your honour mercy; you may, worst
Of all this table, say so.
  *Crom.*          Why, my lord?
  *Gar.* Do not I know you for a favourer
Of this new sect? ye are not sound.
  *Crom.*           Not sound?
  *Gar.* Not sound, I say.
  *Crom.*   Would you were half so honest!
Men's prayers then would seek you, not their
    fears.
  *Gar.* I shall remember this bold language.
  *Crom.*              Do.
Remember your bold life too.
  *Chan.*        This is too much;
Forbear, for shame, my lords.
  *Gar.*         I have done.
  *Crom.*           And I.
  *Chan.* Then thus for you, my lord: it
    stands agreed,
I take it, by all voices, that forthwith
You be conveyed to the Tower a prisoner;
There to remain till the king's further
    pleasure
Be known unto us:—are you all agreed,
    lords?
  *All.* We are.
  *Cran.*   Is there no other way of mercy,
But I must needs to the Tower, my lords?
  *Gar.*          What other
Would you expect? You are strangely
    troublesome.—
Let some o' the guard be ready there.

        *Enter* Guard.
  *Cran.*            For me?
Must I go like a traitor thither?
  *Gar.*          Receive him,
And see him safe i' the Tower.
  *Cran.*       Stay, good my lords.
I have a little yet to say. Look there, my
    lords;
By virtue of that ring I take my cause
Out of the gripes of cruel men, and give it
To a most noble judge, the king my master.
  *Cham.* This is the king's ring.
  *Sur.*          'Tis no counterfeit.
  *Suf.* 'Tis the right ring, by heaven: I told
    ye all,     [rolling,
When we first put this dangerous stone a-
'Twould fall upon ourselves.
  *Nor.*     ·  Do you think, my lords,
The king will suffer but the little finger
Of this man to be vex'd?
  *Chan.*       'Tis now too certain:
How much more is his life in value with him?
Would I were fairly out on 't!
  *Crom.*        My mind gave me,
In seeking tales and informations

Against this man,—whose honesty the devil
And his disciples only envy at,—
Ye blew the fire that burns ye: now have at
    ye.

*Enter the* KING *frowning on them; he takes
his seat.*

  *Gar.* Dread sovereign, how much are we
    bound to heaven
In daily thanks, that gave us such a prince;
Not only good and wise, but most religious:
One that, in all obedience, makes the church
The chief aim of his honour; and, to
    strengthen
That holy duty, out of dear respect,
His royal self in judgment comes to hear
The cause betwixt her and this great offender.
  *K. Hen.* You were ever good at sudden
    commendations,
Bishop of Winchester. But know, I come not
To hear such flattery now, and in my presence;
They are too thin and bare to hide offences.
To me you cannot reach: you play the
    spaniel,
And think with wagging of your tongue to
    win me;
But whatsoe'er thou tak'st me for, I am sure
Thou hast a cruel nature, and a bloody.—
Good man [*to* CRANMER], sit down. Now let
    me see the proudest,
He that dares most, but wag his finger at
    thee:
By all that's holy, he had better starve
Than but once think this place becomes thee
    not.
  *Sur.* May it please your grace,—
  *K. Hen.*          No, sir, it does not please me.
I had thought I had had men of some under-
    standing
And wisdom of my council; but I find none.
Was it discretion, lords, to let this man,
This good man,—few of you deserve that
    title,—
This honest man, wait like a lousy footboy
At chamber door? and one as great as you
    are?
Why, what a shame was this! Did my com-
    mission
Bid ye so far forget yourselves? I gave ye
Power as he was a counsellor to try him,
Not as a groom: there's some of ye, I see,
More out of malice than integrity,
Would try him to the utmost, had ye mean;
Which ye shall never have while I live.
  *Chan.*                              Thus far,
My most dread sovereign, may it like your
    grace                              [pos'd
To let my tongue excuse all. What was pur-
Concerning his imprisonment was rather,—
If there be faith in men,—meant for his trial,
And fair purgation to the world, than
    malice,—
I'm sure in me.

  *K. Hen.* Well, well, my lords, respect him;
Take him, and use him well, he's worthy of
    it.
I will say thus much for him,—if a prince
May be beholding to a subject, I
Am, for his love and service, so to him.
Make me no more ado, but all embrace him:
Be friends, for shame, my lords!—My Lord
    of Canterbury,
I have a suit which you must not deny me;
That is, a fair young maid that yet wants
    baptism,
You must be godfather, and answer for her.
  *Cran.* The greatest monarch now alive may
    glory
In such an honour: how may I deserve it,
That am a poor and humble subject to you?
  *K. Hen.* Come, come, my lord, you'd spare
    your spoons: you shall have
Two noble partners with you: the old Duch-
    ess of Norfolk
And Lady Marquis Dorset: will these please
    you?
Once more, my Lord of Winchester, I charge
    you,
Embrace and love this man.
  *Gar.*                              With a true heart
And brother-love I do it.
  *Cran.*                              And let heaven
Witness how dear I hold this confirmation.
  *K. Hen.* Good man, those joyful tears show
    thy true heart:
The common voice, I see, is verified
Of thee, which says thus,—*Do my Lord of
    Canterbury
A shrewd turn, and he is your friend for
    ever.*—
Come, lords, we trifle time away; I long
To have this young one made a Christian.
As I have made ye one, lords, one remain;
So I grow stronger, you more honour gain.
                     [*Exeunt.*

SCENE III.—*The Palace Yard.*

*Noise and tumult within. Enter* Porter *and
his* Man.

  *Port.* You'll leave your noise anon, ye
rascals: do you take the court for Paris garden? ye rude slaves, leave your gaping.
  [*Within*] Good master porter, I belong to
the larder.
  *Port.* Belong to the gallows, and be
hanged, you rogue! is this a place to roar in?
—Fetch me a dozen crab-tree staves, and
strong ones: these are but switches to them.
—I'll scratch your heads: you must be see-
ing christenings? do you look for ale and
cakes here, you rude rascals?
  *Man.* Pray, sir, be patient: 'tis as much
    impossible,—
Unless we sweep them from the door with
    cannons,—
To scatter 'em as 'tis to make 'em sleep
On May-day morning; which will never be:

We may as well push against Paul's as stir
'em.

*Port.* How got they in, and be hang'd?

*Man.* Alas, I know not; how gets the tide
in?
As much as one sound cudgel of four foot,—
You see the poor remainder;—could dis-
tribute,
I made no spare, sir.

*Port.*　　　You did nothing, sir.

*Man.* I am not Samson, nor Sir Guy, nor
Colbrand,
To mow 'em down before me: but if I spar'd
any
That had a head to hit, either young or old,
He or she, cuckold or cuckold-maker,
Let me ne'er hope to see a chine again;
And that I would not for a cow, God save
her!

[*Within.*] Do you hear, master porter?

*Port.* I shall be with you presently, good
master puppy.—Keep the door close, sirrah.

*Man.* What would you have me do?

*Port.* What should you do, but knock them
down by the dozens? Is this Moorfields to
muster in? or have we some strange Indian
with the great tool come to court, the women
so besiege us? Bless me, what a fry of fornication is at door! On my Christian conscience,
this one christening will beget a thousand:
here will be father, godfather, and all together.

*Man.* The spoons will be the bigger, sir.
There is a fellow somewhat near the door, he
should be a brazier by his face, for, o' my
conscience, twenty of the dog-days now reign
in 's nose; all that stand about him are under
the line, they need no other penance: that
fire-drake did I hit three times on the head,
and three times was his nose discharged
against me; he stands there, like a mortar-
piece, to blow us. There was a haberdasher's
wife of small wit near him, that railed upon
me till her pink'd porringer fell off her head,
for kindling such a combustion in the state.
I miss'd the meteor once, and hit that woman, who cried out *Clubs!* when I might see
from far some forty truncheoners draw to
her succour, which were the hope of the
Strand, where she was quartered. They fell
on; I made good my place: at length they
came to the broomstaff to me; I defied them
still: when suddenly a file of boys behind
them, loose shot delivered such a shower of
pebbles, that I was fain to draw mine honour
in, and let them win the work: the devil was
amongst them, I think, surely.

*Port.* These are the youths that thunder at
a play-house and fight for bitten apples; that,
no audience, but the Tribulation of Tower-
hill or the limbs of Limehouse, their dear
brothers, are able to endure. I have some of
them in *Limbo Patrum,* and there they are
like to dance these three days; besides the
running banquet of two beadles that is to
come.

*Enter the* Lord Chamberlain.

*Cham.* Mercy o'me, what a multitude are
here!　　　　　　　　　　　　　[coming,
They grow still too; from all parts they are
As if we kept a fair here! Where are these
porters,
These lazy knaves?—Ye have made a fine
hand, fellows.
There's a trim rabble let in: are all these
Your faithful friends o' the suburbs? We shall
have　　　　　　　　　　　　　　[ladies,
Great store of room, no doubt, left for the
When they pass back from the christening.

*Port.*　　　　　　An't please your honour,
We are but men; and what so many may do,
Not being torn a pieces, we have done:
An army cannot rule 'em.

*Chan.*　　　　　　As I live,
If the king blame me for't, I'll lay ye all
By the heels, and suddenly; and on your
heads
Clap round fines for neglect: you're lazy
knaves;
And here ye lie baiting of bombards, when
Ye should do service. Hark! the trumpets
sound;
They are come already from the christening:
Go, break among the press, and find a way
out
To let the troop pass fairly; or I'll find
A Marshalsea shall hold you play these two
months.

*Port.* Make way there for the princess.

*Man.*　　　　　　　You great fellow,
Stand close up, or I'll make your head ache.

*Port.* You i' the camlet, get up o' the rail;
I'll pick you o'er the pales else.　　[*Exeunt.*

SCENE IV.—The Palace.

*Enter trumpets, sounding; then two* Alder-
men, Lord Mayor, Garter, CRANMER,
DUKE OF NORFOLK, *with his marshal's staff,*
DUKE OF SUFFOLK, *two* Noblemen *bearing
great standing-bowls for the christening
gifts; then four* Noblemen *bearing a can-
opy, under which the* DUCHESS OF NOR-
FOLK, *godmother, bearing the child richly
habited in a mantle, &c. Train borne by a*
Lady; *then follows the* MARCHIONESS OF
DORSET, *the other godmother, and* Ladies.
*The troop pass once about the stage, and*
Garter *speaks.*

*Gart.* Heaven, from thy endless goodness,
send prosperous life, long, and ever-happy, to
the high and mighty princess of England,
Elizabeth!

*Flourish. Enter* KING *and* Train.

*Cran.* [*kneeling.*] And to your royal grace
and the good queen,
My noble partners and myself thus pray;—

All comfort, joy, in this most gracious lady,
Heaven ever laid up to make parents happy,
May hourly fall upon ye!
  *K. Hen.* Thank you, good lord archbishop.
What is her name?
  *Cran.*        Elizabeth.
  *K. Hen.*              Stand up, lord.—
              [*The* KING *kisses the child.*
With this kiss take my blessing: God protect
    thee!
Into whose hand I give thy life.
  *Cran.*              Amen.
  *K. Hen.* My noble gossips, ye have been
    too prodigal.
I thank ye heartily; so shall this lady,
When she has so much English.
  *Cran.*          Let me speak, sir,
For heaven now bids me; and the words I
    utter                [truth.
Let none think flattery, for they'll find 'em
This royal infant,—Heaven still move about
    her!—
Though in her cradle, yet now promises
Upon this land a thousand thousand blessings,
Which time shall bring to ripeness: she shall
    be,—               [ness,
But few now living can behold that good-
A pattern to all princes living with her,
And all that shall succeed: Saba was never
More covetous of wisdom and fair virtue
Than this pure soul shall be: all princely
    graces,
That mould up such a mighty piece as this is,
With all the virtues that attend the good,
Shall still be doubled on her: truth shall nurse
    her,
Holy and heavenly thoughts still counsel her:
She shall be lov'd and fear'd: her own shall
    bless her;
Her foes shake like a field of beaten corn,
And hang their heads with sorrow: good
    grows with her:
In her days every man shall eat in safety,
Under his own vine, what he plants; and
    sing
The merry songs of peace to all his neigh-
    bours:
God shall be truly known; and those about
    her
From her shall read the perfect ways of hon-
    our,
And by those claim their greatness, not by
    blood.              [when
Nor shall this peace sleep with her: but as
The bird of wonder dies, the maiden phœnix,
Her ashes new create another heir,
As great in admiration as herself;
So shall she leave her blessedness to one,—
When heaven shall call her from this cloud of
    darkness,—
Who from the sacred ashes of her honour
Shall star-like rise. as great in fame as she was,

And so stand fix'd: peace, plenty, love, truth,
    terror,
That were the servants to this chosen infant,
Shall then be his, and like a vine grow to him:
Wherever the bright sun of heaven shall shine,
His honour and the greatness of his name
Shall be, and make new nations: he shall
    flourish,
And, like a mountain cedar, reach his
    branches
To all the plains about him:—our children's
    children
Shall see this and bless Heaven.
  *K. Hen.*        Thou speak'st wonders.
  *Cran.* She shall be, to the happiness of
    England,
An aged princess; many days shall see her,
And yet no day without a deed to crown it.
Would I had known no more! but she must
    die,
She must, the saints must have her,—yet a
    virgin;
A most unspotted lily shall she pass
To the ground, and all the world shall mourn
    her.
  *K. Hen.* O lord archbishop,
Thou hast made me now a man; never, before
This happy child, did I get anything:
This oracle of comfort has so pleas'd me
That when I am in heaven I shall desire
To see what this child does, and praise my
    Maker.—
I thank ye all.—To you, my good lord mayor,
And you, good brethren, I am much behold-
    ing;
I have received much honour by your pres-
    ence,
And ye shall find me thankful.—Lead the
    way, lords:—           [ye,
Ye must all see the queen, and she must thank
She will be sick else. This day, no man think
Has business at his house; for all shall stay:
This little one shall make it holiday. [*Exeunt.*

## EPILOGUE.

'Tis ten to one this play can never please
All that are here: some come to take their
    ease,
And sleep an act or two; but those, we fear,
We have frightened with our trumpets; so,
    'tis clear,
They'll say 'tis naught: others to hear the city
Abus'd extremely, and to cry,—*That's witty!*
Which we have not done neither: that, I fear,
All the expected good we're like to hear
For this play at this time, is only in
The merciful construction of good women;
For such a one we show'd 'em: if they smile,
And say 'twill do, I know, within awhile
All the best men are ours; for 'tis ill hap
If they hold when their ladies bid 'em clap.

TROILUS & CRESSIDA.

Act IV. Sc. 4.

# TROILUS AND CRESSIDA

## DRAMATIS PERSONÆ

PRIAM, *King of Troy*

HECTOR,
TROILUS,
PARIS, } *his Sons.*
DEIPHOBUS,
HELENUS,

MARGARELON, *a bastard Son of* PRIAM.

ÆNEAS, } *Trojan Commanders.*
ANTENOR,

CALCHAS, *a Trojan Priest, taking part with the Greeks.*

PANDARUS, *Uncle to* CRESSIDA.
AGAMEMNON, *the Grecian General.*
MENELAUS, *his Brother.*

ACHILLES, } *Grecian Commanders.*
AJAX,

ULYSSES,
NESTOR,
DIOMEDES, } *Grecian Commanders.*
PATROCLUS,

THERSITES, *a deformed and scurrilous Grecian.*

ALEXANDER, *Servant to* CRESSIDA.
Servant *to* TROILUS.
Servant *to* PARIS.
Servant *to* DIOMEDES.

HELEN, *Wife to* MENELAUS.
ANDROMACHE, *Wife to* HECTOR.
CASSANDRA, *Daughter to* PRIAM, *a Prophetess.*
CRESSIDA, *Daughter to* CALCHAS.

Trojan *and* Greek Soldiers, *and* Attendants.

SCENE.—TROY, *and the Grecian Camp before it.*

## PROLOGUE.

In Troy, there lies the scene. From isles of
    Greece
The princes orgulous, their high blood chaf'd,
Have to the port of Athens sent their ships,
Fraught with the ministers and instruments
Of cruel war: sixty and nine, that wore
Their crownets regal, from the Athenian bay
Put forth toward Phrygia: and their vow is
    made
To ransack Troy; within those strong immures
The ravish'd Helen, Menelaus' queen,
With wanton Paris sleeps; and that's the
    quarrel.
To Tenedos they come;
And the deep-drawing barks do there disgorge
Their warlike fraughtage: now on Dardan
    plains
The fresh and yet unbruised Greeks do pitch
Their brave pavilions: Priam's six-gated city,
Dardan, and Tymbria, Helias, Chetas, Troien,
And Antenorides, with massy staples
And corresponsive and fulfilling bolts,
Sperr up the sons of Troy.
Now expectation, tickling skittish spirits,
On one and other side, Trojan and Greek,
Sets all on hazard:—and hither am I come
A prologue arm'd,—but not in confidence
Of author's pen or actor's voice; but suited
In like conditions as our argument,—
To tell you, fair beholders, that our play
Leaps o'er the vaunt and firstlings of those
    broils,

Beginning in the middle; starting thence away
To what may be digested in a play.
Like, or find fault; do as your pleasures are;
Now good or bad, 'tis but the chance of war.

## ACT I.

SCENE I.—TROY. *Before* PRIAM'S *Palace.*

*Enter* TROILUS *armed, and* PANDARUS.

*Tro.* Call here my varlet; I'll unarm again:
Why should I war without the walls of Troy,
That find such cruel battle here within?
Each Trojan that is master of his heart,
Let him to field; Troilus, alas! hath none.

*Pan.* Will the gear ne'er be mended?

*Tro.* The Greeks are strong, and skilful to
    their strength,    [valiant;
Fierce to their skill, and to their fierceness
But I am weaker than a woman's tear,
Tamer than sleep, fonder than ignorance,
Less valiant than the virgin in the night,
And skilless as unpractis'd infancy.

*Pan.* Well, I have told you enough of this:
for my part, I'll not meddle nor make no
further. He that will have a cake out of the
wheat must needs tarry the grinding.

*Tro.* Have I not tarried?

*Pan.* Ay, the grinding; but you must tarry
the bolting.

*Tro.* Have I not tarried?

*Pan.* Ay, the bolting; but you must tarry
the leavening.

*Tro.* Still have I tarried.

*Pan.* Ay, to the leavening; but here's yet

[707]

in the word *hereafter,* the kneading, the making of the cake, the heating of the oven, and the baking; nay, you must stay the cooling too, or you may chance to burn your lips.

*Tro.* Patience herself, what goddess e'er she be,
Doth lesser blench at sufferance than I do.
At Priam's royal table do I sit;
And when fair Cressid comes into my thoughts,—
So, traitor!—when she comes!—When is she thence?

*Pan.* Well, she looked yesternight fairer than ever I saw her look, or any woman else.

*Tro.* I was about to tell thee,—when my heart,
As wedged with a sigh, would rive in twain;
Lest Hector or my father should perceive me,
I have,—as when the sun doth light a storm,—
Buried this sigh in wrinkle of a smile:
But sorrow that is couch'd in seeming gladness
Is like that mirth fate turns to sudden sadness.

*Pan.* An her hair were not somewhat darker than Helen's,—well, go to,—there were no more comparison between the women,—but, for my part, she is my kinswoman; I would not, as they term it, praise her,—but I would somebody had heard her talk yesterday, as I did. I will not dispraise your sister Cassandra's wit; but,—

*Tro.* O Pandarus! I tell thee, Pandarus,—
When I do tell thee there my hopes lie drown'd,
Reply not in how many fathoms deep
They lie indrench'd. I tell thee, I am mad
In Cressid's love: thou answer'st, she is fair;
Pour'st in the open ulcer of my heart [voice;
Her eyes, her hair, her cheek, her gait, her
Handlest in thy discourse, O, that her hand,
In whose comparison all whites are ink,
Writing their own reproach; to whose soft seizure
The cygnet's down is harsh, and spirit of sense
Hard as the palm of ploughman!—This thou tell'st me,
As true thou tell'st me, when I say I love her;
But, saying thus, instead of oil and balm, [me
Thou lay'st in every gash that love hath given
The knife that made it.

*Pan.* I speak no more than truth.

*Tro.* Thou dost not speak so much.

*Pan.* Faith, I'll not meddle in 't. Let her be as she is: if she be fair, 'tis the better for her; an she be not, she has the mends in her own hands.

*Tro.* Good Pandarus,—how now, Pandarus!

*Pan.* I have had my labour for my travail; ill-thought on of her, and ill-thought on of you: gone between and between, but small thanks for my labour.

*Tro.* What, art thou angry, Pandarus? what, with me?

*Pan.* Because she is kin to me, therefore she's not so fair as Helen: an she were not kin to me, she would be as fair on Friday as Helen is on Sunday. But what care I? I care not an she were a blackamoor; 'tis all one to me.

*Tro.* Say I, she is not fair?

*Pan.* I do not care whether you do or no. She's a fool to stay behind her father; let her to the Greeks; and so I'll tell her the next time I see her; for my part, I'll meddle nor make no more in the matter.

*Tro.* Pandarus,—

*Pan.* Not I.

*Tro.* Sweet Pandarus,—

*Pan.* Pray you, speak no more to me: I will leave all as I found it, and there an end.
[*Exit. An alarum.*

*Tro.* Peace, you ungracious clamours! peace, rude sounds!
Fools on both sides! Helen must needs be fair,
When with your blood you daily paint her thus.
I cannot fight upon this argument;
It is too starv'd a subject for my sword.
But Pandarus,—O gods, how do you plague me!
I cannot come to Cressid but by Pandar;
And he's as tetchy to be woo'd to woo
As she is stubborn-chaste against all suit.
Tell me, Apollo, for thy Daphne's love,
What Cressid is, what Pandar, and what we?
Her bed is India; there she lies, a pearl:
Between our Ilium and where she resides
Let it be call'd the wild and wandering flood;
Ourself the merchant; and this sailing Pandar
Our doubtful hope, our convoy, and our bark.

*Alarum. Enter ÆNEAS.*

*Æne.* How now, Prince Troilus! wherefore not afield? [swer sorts,

*Tro.* Because not there: this woman's an-
For womanish it is to be from thence.
What news, Æneas, from the field to-day?

*Æne.* That Paris is returned home, and hurt.

*Tro.* By whom, Æneas?

*Æne.* Troilus, by Menelaus.

*Tro.* Let Paris bleed: 'tis but a scar to scorn;
Paris is gor'd with Menelaus' horn. [*Alarum.*

*Æne.* Hark, what good sport is out of town to-day!

*Tro.* Better at home, if *would I might* were may.— [thither?
But to the sport abroad;—are you bound

*Æne.* In all swift haste.

*Tro.* Come, go we, then, together.
[*Exeunt.*

SCENE II.—TROY. *A Street.*

*Enter* CRESSIDA *and* ALEXANDER.

*Cres.* Who were those went by?

*Alex.* Queen Hecuba and Helen.

*Cres.* And whither go they?

*Alex.*                Up to the eastern tower,
Whose height commands as subject all the
     vale,
To see the battle. Hector, whose patience
Is as a virtue fix'd, to-day was mov'd:
He chid Andromache, and struck his ar-
     mourer;
And, like as there were husbandry in war,
Before the sun rose he was harness'd light,
And to the field goes he; where every flower
Did, as a prophet, weep what it foresaw
In Hector's wrath.
*Cres.*          What was his cause of anger?
*Alex.* The noise goes, this: there is among
     the Greeks
A lord of Trojan blood, nephew to Hector;
They call him Ajax.
*Cres.*                Good; and what of him?
*Alex.* They say he is a very man *per se,*
And stands alone.
*Cres.* So do all men,—unless they are
drunk, sick, or have no legs.
*Alex.* This man, lady, hath robbed many
beasts of their particular additions: he is as
valiant as the lion, churlish as the bear, slow
as the elephant: a man into whom nature
hath so crowded humours that his valour is
crushed into folly, his folly sauced with discretion: there is no man hath a virtue that he
hath not a glimpse of; nor any man an attaint, but he carries some stain of it: he is
melancholy without cause, and merry against
the hair: he hath the joints of everything;
but everything so out of joint that he is a
gouty Briareus, many hands and no use; or
purblind Argus, all eyes and no sight.
*Cres.* But how should this man, that makes
me smile, make Hector angry?
*Alex.* They say he yesterday coped Hector
in the battle, and struck him down; the disdain and shame whereof hath ever since kept
Hector fasting and waking.
*Cres.* Who comes here?
*Alex.* Madam, your uncle Pandarus.

*Enter* PANDARUS.

*Cres.* Hector's a gallant man.
*Alex.* As may be in the world, lady.
*Pan.* What's that? what's that?
*Cres.* Good-morrow, uncle Pandarus.
*Pan.* Good-morrow, cousin Cressid: what
do you talk of?—Good-morrow, Alexander.
—How do you, cousin? When were you at
Ilium?
*Cres.* This morning, uncle.
*Pan.* What were you talking of when I
came? Was Hector armed and gone ere ye
came to Ilium? Helen was not up, was she?
*Cres.* Hector was gone: but Helen was not
up.
*Pan.* E'en so: Hector was stirring early.
*Cres.* That were we talking of, and of his
anger.
*Pan.* Was he angry?

*Cres.* So he says here.
*Pan.* True, he was so; I know the cause
too; he'll lay about him to-day, I can tell
them that: and there is Troilus will not come
far behind him; let them take heed of Troilus,
I can tell them that too.
*Cres.* What, is he angry, too?
*Pan.* Who, Troilus? Troilus is the better
man of the two.
*Cres.* O Jupiter! there's no comparison.
*Pan.* What, not between Troilus and Hec-
tor? Do you know a man if you see him?
*Cres.* Ay, if I ever saw him before, and
knew him.
*Pan.* Well, I say Troilus is Troilus.
*Cres.* Then you say as I say; for I am sure
he is not Hector.
*Pan.* No, nor Hector is not Troilus in some
degrees.
*Cres.* 'Tis just to each of them; he is him-
self.
*Pan.* Himself! Alas, poor Troilus! I would
he were,—
*Cres.* So he is.
*Pan.* Condition, I had gone barefoot to
India.
*Cres.* He is not Hector.
*Pan.* Himself! no, he's not himself,—would
'a were himself! Well, the gods are above;
time must friend or end: well, Troilus, well,—
I would my heart were in her body!—No,
Hector is not a better man than Troilus.
*Cres.* Excuse me.
*Pan.* He is elder.
*Cres.* Pardon me, pardon me.
*Pan.* The other's not come to't; you shall
tell me another tale when the other's come
to't. Hector shall not have his wit this year,—
*Cres.* He shall not need it if he have his
own.
*Pan.* Nor his qualities,—
*Cres.* No matter.
*Pan.* Nor his beauty.
*Cres.* 'Twould not become him,—his own's
better.
*Pan.* You have no judgment, niece: Helen
herself swore the other day that Troilus, for a
brown favour,—for so 'tis, I must confess,—
not brown neither,—
*Cres.* No, but brown.
*Pan.* Faith, to say truth, brown and not
brown.
*Cres.* To say the truth, true and not true.
*Pan.* She praised his complexion above
Paris.
*Cres.* Why, Paris hath colour enough.
*Pan.* So he has.
*Cres.* Then Troilus should have too much:
if she praised him above, his complexion is
higher than his; he having colour enough, and
the other higher, is too flaming a praise for a
good complexion. I had as lief Helen's golden
tongue had commended Troilus for a copper
nose.

*Pan.* I swear to you I think Helen loves him better than Paris.

*Cres.* Then she's a merry Greek indeed.

*Pan.* Nay, I am sure she does. She came to him the other day into the compassed window,—and, you know, he has not past three or four hairs on his chin,—

*Cres.* Indeed, a tapster's arithmetic may soon bring his particulars therein to a total.

*Pan.* Why, he is very young: and yet will he, within three pounds, lift as much as his brother Hector.

*Cres.* Is he so young a man and so old a lifter?

*Pan.* But to prove to you that Helen loves him,—she came, and puts me her white hand to his cloven chin,—

*Cres.* Juno have mercy! how came it cloven?

*Pan.* Why, you know, 'tis dimpled: I think his smiling becomes him better than any man in all Phrygia.

*Cres.* O, he smiles valiantly.

*Pan.* Does he not?

*Cres.* O yes, and 'twere a cloud in autumn.

*Pan.* Why, go to, then:—but to prove to you that Helen loves Troilus,—

*Cres.* Troilus will stand to the proof if you'll prove it so.

*Pan.* Troilus! why, he esteems her no more than I esteem an addle egg.

*Cres.* If you love an addle egg as well as you love an idle head, you would eat chickens i' the shell.

*Pan.* I cannot choose but laugh to think how she tickled his chin;—indeed, she has a marvellous white hand, I must needs confess,—

*Cres.* Without the rack.

*Pan.* And she takes upon her to spy a white hair on his chin.

*Cres.* Alas, poor chin! many a wart is richer.

*Pan.* But there was such laughing!—Queen Hecuba laughed, that her eyes ran o'er,—

*Cres.* With millstones.

*Pan.* And Cassandra laughed,—

*Cres.* But there was more temperate fire under the pot of her eyes.—Did her eyes run o'er too?

*Pan.* And Hector laughed.

*Cres.* At what was all this laughing?

*Pan.* Marry, at the white hair that Helen spied on Troilus' chin.

*Cres.* An't had been a green hair I should have laughed too.

*Pan.* They laughed not so much at the hair as at his pretty answer.

*Cres.* What was his answer?

*Pan.* Quoth she, *Here's but one and fifty hairs on your chin, and one of them is white.*

*Cres.* This is her question.

*Pan.* That's true; make no question of that. *One and fifty hairs,* quoth he, *and one*

white: *that white hair is my father, and all the rest are his sons.*—Jupiter! quoth she, *which of these hairs is Paris my husband?*— *The forked one,* quoth he; *pluck it out and give it him.* But there was such laughing! and Helen so blushed, and Paris so chafed; and all the rest so laughed that it passed.

*Cres.* So let it now; for it has been a great while going by.

*Pan.* Well, cousin, I told you a thing yesterday; think on't.

*Cres.* So I do.

*Pan.* I'll be sworn 'tis true; he will weep you, and 'twere a man born in April.

*Cres.* And I'll spring up in his tears, an 'twere a nettle against May.

          [*A retreat sounded.*

*Pan.* Hark! they are coming from the field: shall we stand up here, and see them as they pass toward Ilium? good niece, do; sweet Cressida.

*Cres.* At your pleasure.

*Pan.* Here, here, here's an excellent place; here we may see most bravely: I'll tell you them all by their names as they pass by; but mark Troilus above the rest.

*Cres.* Speak not so loud.

### ÆNEAS *passes.*

*Pan.* That's Æneas: is not that a brave man? he's one of the flowers of Troy, I can tell you. But mark Troilus; you shall see anon.

### ANTENOR *passes.*

*Cres.* Who's that?

*Pan.* That's Antenor: he has a shrewd wit, I can tell you; and he's a man good enough: he's one o' the soundest judgments in Troy, whosoever, and a proper man of person. When comes Troilus?—I'll show you Troilus anon: if he see me, you shall see him nod at me.

*Cres.* Will he give you the nod?

*Pan.* You shall see.

*Cres.* If he do, the rich shall have more.

### HECTOR *passes.*

*Pan.* That's Hector, that, that look you, that; there's a fellow!—Go thy way, Hector! —There's a brave man, niece.—O brave Hector!—Look how he looks!—There's a countenance! Is't not a brave man?

*Cres.* O, a brave man!

*Pan.* Is 'a not? It does a man's heart good. —Look you what hacks are on his helmet! look you yonder, do you see? look you there: there's no jesting; there's laying on; tak't off who will, as they say: there be hacks!

*Cres.* Be those with swords?

*Pan.* Swords! anything, he cares not; an the devil come to him, it's all one; by god's lid, it does one's heart good. Yonder comes Paris, yonder comes Paris:

PARIS *passes*.

look ye yonder, niece; is't not a gallant man too, is't not?—Why, this is brave now.—Who said he came hurt home to-day? he's not hurt: why, this will do Helen's heart good now, ha!—Would I could see Troilus now!—you shall see Troilus anon.

HELENUS *passes*.

*Cres.* Who's that?

*Pan.* That's Helenus:—I marvel where Troilus is:—that's Helenus:—I think he went not forth to-day:—that's Helenus.

*Cres.* Can Helenus fight, uncle?

*Pan.* Helenus! no;—yes, he'll fight indifferent well.—I marvel where Troilus is.—Hark! do you not hear the people cry *Troilus?*—Helenus is a priest.

*Cres.* What sneaking fellow comes yonder?

TROILUS *passes*.

*Pan.* Where? yonder? that's Deiphobus:—'tis Troilus! there's a man, niece!—Hem!—Brave Troilus! the prince of chivalry!

*Cres.* Peace, for shame, peace!

*Pan.* Mark him; note him:—O brave Troilus!—look well upon him, niece; look you how his sword is bloodied, and his helm more hack'd than Hector's; and how he looks, and how he goes!—O admirable youth! he ne'er saw three and twenty.—Go thy way, Troilus, go thy way!—Had I a sister a grace, or a daughter a goddess, he should take his choice. O admirable man! Paris?—Paris is dirt to him; and, I warrant, Helen, to change, would give an eye to boot.

*Cres.* Here come more.

FORCES *pass*.

*Pan.* Asses, fools, dolts! chaff and bran, chaff and bran! porridge after meat!—I could live and die i' the eyes of Troilus.—Ne'er look, ne'er look; the eagles are gone: crows and daws, crows and daws!—I had rather be such a man as Troilus than Agamemnon and all Greece.

*Cres.* There is among the Greeks Achilles, —a better man than Troilus.

*Pan.* Achilles! a drayman, a porter, a very camel.

*Cres.* Well, well.

*Pan.* Well, well!—Why, have you any discretion? have you any eyes? do you know what a man is? Is not birth, beauty, good shape, discourse, manhood, learning, gentleness, virtue, youth, liberality, and such like, the spice and salt that season a man?

*Cres.* Ay, a minced man: and then to be baked with no date in the pie,—for then the man's date's out.

*Pan.* You are such a woman! one knows not at what ward you lie.

*Cres.* Upon my back, to defend my belly;

upon my wit, to defend my wiles; upon my secrecy, to defend mine honesty; my mask, to defend my beauty; and you, to defend all these: and at all these wards I lie, at a thousand watches.

*Pan.* Say one of your watches.

*Cres.* Nay, I'll watch you for that; and that's one of the chiefest of them too: if I cannot ward what I would not have hit, I can watch you for telling how I took the blow; unless it swell past hiding, and then it is past watching.

*Pan.* You are such another!

*Enter* TROILUS' *Boy*.

*Boy.* Sir, my lord would instantly speak with you.

*Pan.* Where?

*Boy.* At your own house; there he unarms him.

*Pan.* Good boy, tell him I come. [*Exit Boy*. I doubt he be hurt.—Fare ye well, good niece.

*Cres.* Adieu, uncle.

*Pan.* I'll be with you, niece, by and by.

*Cres.* To bring, uncle.

*Pan.* Ay, a token from Troilus.

*Cres.* By the same token—you are a bawd. [*Exit* PANDARUS.

Words, vows, gifts, tears, and love's full sacrifice,
He offers in another's enterprise:
But more in Troilus thousand-fold I see
Than in the glass of Pandar's praise may be;
Yet hold I off. Women are angels, wooing:
Things won are done, joy's soul lies in the doing:
That she belov'd knows naught that knows not this,—
Men prize the thing ungain'd more than it is:
That she was never yet that ever knew
Love got so sweet as when desire did sue:
Therefore this maxim out of love I teach,—
Achievement is command; ungain'd beseech:
Then though my heart's content firm love doth bear,
Nothing of that shall from mine eyes appear.
[*Exit*.

SCENE III.—THE GRECIAN CAMP. *Before* AGAMEMNON'S *Tent*.

*Sennet. Enter* AGAMEMNON, NESTOR, ULYSSES, MENELAUS, *and others*.

*Agam.* Princes,      [cheeks?
What grief hath set the jaundice on your
The ample proposition that hope makes
In all designs begun on earth below [disasters
Fails in the promis'd largeness: checks and
Grow in the veins of actions highest rear'd;.
As knots, by the conflux of meeting sap,
Infect sound pine, and divert his grain
Tortive and errant from his course of growth.
Nor, princes, is it matter new to us
That we come short of our suppose so far

That, after seven years' siege, yet Troy walls
　　stand;
Sith every action that hath gone before,
Whereof we have record, trial did draw
Bias and thwart, not answering the aim,
And that unbodied figure of the thought
That gav't surmised shape. Why, then, you
　　princes,
Do you with cheeks abash'd behold our
　　works;
And call them shames, which are, indeed,
　　naught else
But the protractive trials of great Jove
To find persistive constancy in men?
The fineness of which metal is not found
In fortune's love: for then the bold and
　　coward,
The wise and fool, the artist and unread,
The hard and soft, seem all affin'd and kin:
But, in the wind and tempest of her frown,
Distinction, with a broad and powerful fan,
Puffing at all, winnows the light away;
And what hath mass or matter, by itself
Lies rich in virtue and unmingled.　　[seat,
　　*Nest.* With due observance of thy godlike
Great Agamemnon, Nestor shall apply
Thy latest words. In the reproof of chance
Lies the true proof of men: the sea being
　　smooth,
How many shallow bauble boats dare sail
Upon her patient breast, making their way
With those of nobler bulk!
But let the ruffian Boreas once enrage
The gentle Thetis, and, anon, behold
The strong-ribb'd bark through liquid
　　mountains cut,
Bounding between the two moist elements,
Like Perseus' horse: where's then the saucy
　　boat,
Whose weak untimber'd sides but even now
Co-rivall'd greatness? either to harbour fled
Or made a toast for Neptune. Even so
Doth valour's show and valour's worth
　　divide
In storms of fortune: for in her ray and
　　brightness
The herd hath more annoyance by the
　　breeze
Than by the tiger: but when the splitting
　　wind
Makes flexible the knees of knotted oaks,
And flies fled under shade,—why, then the
　　thing of courage,
As rous'd with rage, with rage doth sympa-
　　thize,
And with an accent tun'd in self-same key
Retorts to chiding fortune.
　　*Ulyss.*　　　　　　　Agamemnon,—
Thou great commander, nerve and bone of
　　Greece,
Heart of our numbers, soul and only spirit,
In whom the tempers and the minds of all
Should be shut up.—hear what Ulysses
　　speaks

Besides the applause and approbation
The which,—most mighty for thy place and
　　sway,—　　　　　　[*To* AGAMEMNON.
And thou most reverend for thy stretch'd-out
　　life,—　　　　　　　[*To* NESTOR.
I give to both your speeches,—which were
　　such
As Agamemnon and the hand of Greece
Should hold up high in brass; and such
　　again
As venerable Nestor, hatch'd in silver,
Should with a bond of air,—strong as the
　　axle-tree
On which heaven rides,—knit all the Greekish
　　ears　　　　　　　　　　[both,—
To his experienc'd tongue,—yet let it please
Thou great,—and wise,—to hear Ulysses
　　speak.
　　*Agam.* Speak, Prince of Ithaca; and be't
　　of less expect,
That matter needless, of importless burden,
Divide thy lips, than we are confident,
When rank Thersites opes his mastiff jaws,
We shall hear music, wit, and oracle.
　　*Ulyss.* Troy, yet upon his basis, had been
　　down,　　　　　　　　　[master,
And the great Hector's sword had lack'd a
But for these instances.
The specialty of rule hath been neglected:
And look, how many Grecian tents do stand
Hollow upon this plain, so many hollow fac-
　　tions.
When that the general is not like the hive,
To whom the foragers shall all repair,
What honey is expected? Degree being viz-
　　arded,
The unworthiest shows as fairly in the mask.
The heavens themselves, the planets, and this
　　centre,
Observe degree, priority, and place,
Insisture, course, proportion, season, form,
Office, and custom, in all line of order:
And therefore is the glorious planet Sol
In noble eminence enthron'd and spher'd
Amidst the other; whose medicinable eye
Corrects the ill aspects of planets evil,
And posts, like the commandment of a king,
Sans check, to good and bad: but when the
　　planets,
In evil mixture, to disorder wander,
What plagues and what portents! what mu-
　　tiny!
What raging of the sea! shaking of earth!
Commotion in the winds! frights, changes,
　　horrors,
Divert and crack, rend and deracinate
The unity and married calm of states [shak'd,
Quite from their fixture! O, when degree is
Which is the ladder to all high designs,
The enterprise is sick! How could communi-
　　ties,
Degrees in schools, and brotherhoods in
　　cities,
Peaceful commérce from dividable shores,

The primogenitive and due of birth,
Prerogative of age, crowns, sceptres, laurels,
But by degree, stand in authentic place?
Take but degree away, untune that string,
And, hark, what discord follows! each thing
    meets
In mere oppugnancy: the bounded waters
Should lift their bosoms higher than the
    shores,
And make a sop of all this solid globe:
Strength should be lord of imbecility,
And the rude son should strike his father
    dead:
Force should be right; or, rather, right and
    wrong,—
Between whose endless jar justice resides,—
Should lose their names, and so should justice
    too.
Then everything includes itself in power,
Power into will, will into appetite;
And appetite, an universal wolf,
So doubly seconded with will and power,
Must make perforce an universal prey,
And last eat up himself. Great Agamemnon,
This chaos, when degree is suffocate,
Follows the choking.
And this neglection of degree it is
That by a pace goes backward, with a pur-
    pose
It hath to climb. The general's disdain'd
By him one step below; he by the next;
That next by him beneath: so every step,
Exampled by the first pace that is sick
Of his superior, grows to an envious fever
Of pale and bloodless emulation;
And 'tis this fever that keeps Troy on foot,
Not her own sinews. To end a tale of length,
Troy in our weakness stands, not in her
    strength.
    *Nest.* Most wisely hath Ulysses here dis-
    cover'd
The fever whereof all our power is sick.
    *Agam.* The nature of the sickness found,
    Ulysses,
What is the remedy?     [crowns
    *Ulyss.* The great Achilles,—whom opinion
The sinew and the forehand of our host,—
Having his ear full of his airy fame,
Grows dainty of his worth, and in his tent
Lies mocking our designs: with him Patroclus,
Upon a lazy bed, the livelong day
Breaks scurril jests;
And with ridiculous and awkward action,—
Which, slanderer, he imitation calls,—
He pageants us. Sometime, great Agamem-
    non,
Thy topless deputation he puts on;
And, like a strutting player,—whose conceit
Lies in his hamstring, and doth think it rich
To hear the wooden dialogue and sound
'Twixt his stretch'd footing and the scaffold-
    age,—
Such to-be-pitied and o'erwrested seeming
He acts thy greatness in: and when he speaks

'Tis like a chime a-mending; with terms un-
    squar'd,     [dropp'd,
Which, from the tongue of roaring Typhon
Would seem hyperboles. At this fusty stuff
The large Achilles, on his press'd bed lolling,
From his deep chest laughs out a loud ap-
    plause;
Cries, *Excellent! 'tis Agamemnon just.*
*Now play me Nestor; hem, and stroke thy
    beard,*
*As he being drest to some oration.*
That's done;—as near as the extremest ends
Of parallels; as like as Vulcan and his wife:
Yet god Achilles still cries, *Excellent!*
*'Tis Nestor right. Now play him me, Pat-
    roclus,*
*Arming to answer in a night alarm.*
And then, forsooth, the faint defects of age
Must be the scene of mirth; to cough and
    spit,
And, with a palsy-fumbling on his gorget,
Shake in and out the rivet: and at this sport
Sir Valour dies; cries, *O, enough, Patroclus;*
*Or give me ribs of steel! I shall split all*
*In pleasure of my spleen.* And in this fashion
All our abilities, gifts, natures, shapes,
Severals and generals of grace exact,
Achievements, plots, orders, preventions,
Excitements to the field or speech for truce,
Success or loss, what is or is not, serves
As stuff for these two to make paradoxes.
    *Nest.* And in the imitation of these
    twain,—
Who, as Ulysses says, opinion crowns
With an imperial voice,—many are infect.
Ajax is grown self-willed; and bears his head
In such a rein, in full as proud a place
As broad Achilles; keeps his tent like him;
Makes factious feasts; rails on our state of
    war
Bold as an oracle; and sets Thersites,—
A slave, whose gall coins slanders like a
    mint,—
To match us in comparisons with dirt,
To weaken and discredit our exposure,
How rank soever rounded in with danger.
    *Ulyss.* They tax our policy, and call it
    cowardice;
Count wisdom as no member of the war;
Forestall prescience, and esteem no act
But that of hand: the still and mental
    parts,—
That do contrive how many hands shall
    strike,
When fitness calls them on; and know, by
    measure
Of their observant toil, the enemies' weight,—
Why, this hath not a finger's dignity:
They call this bed-work, mappery, closet-
    war;
So that the ram that batters down the wall,
For the great swing and rudeness of his poise,
They place before his hand that made the en-
    gine,

Or those that with the fineness of their souls
By reason guide his execution.

*Nest.* Let this be granted, and Achilles'
    horse
Makes many Thetis' sons. [*Trumpet sounds.*

*Agam.* What trumpet? look, Menelaus.

*Men.* From Troy.

#### Enter ÆNEAS.

*Agam.* What would you 'fore our tent?

*Æne.* Is this great Agamemnon's tent, I
    pray you?

*Agam.* Even this.

*Æne.* May one, that is a herald and a
    prince,
Do a fair message to his kingly ears?

*Agam.* With surety stronger than Achilles'
    arm             [voice
'Fore all the Greekish heads, which with one
Call Agamemnon head and general.   [may

*Æne.* Fair leave and large security. How
A stranger to those most imperial looks
Know them from eyes of other mortals?

*Agam.*                   How!

*Æne.* Ay;
I ask, that I might waken reverence,
And bid the cheek be ready with a blush
Modest as morning when she coldly eyes
The youthful Phœbus:
Which is that god in office, guiding men?
Which is the high and mighty Agamemnon?

*Agam.* This Trojan scorns us; or the men
    of Troy
Are ceremonious courtiers.

*Æne.* Courtiers as free, as debonair, un-
    arm'd,
As bending angels; that's their fame in peace:
But when they would seem soldiers, they have
    galls,            [Jove's accord,
Good arms, strong joints, true swords; and,
Nothing so full of heart. But peace, Æneas,
Peace, Trojan; lay thy finger on thy lips!
The worthiness of praise distains his worth,
If that the prais'd himself bring the praise
    forth:
But what the repining enemy commends,
That breath fame blows; that praise, sole
    pure, transcends.         [Æneas?

*Agam.* Sir, you of Troy, call you yourself

*Æne.* Ay, Greek, that is my name.

*Agam.* What's your affair, I pray you?

*Æne.* Sir, pardon; 'tis for Agamemnon's
    ears.

*Agam.* He hears not privately that comes
    from Troy.            [him;

*Æne.* Nor I from Troy come not to whisper
I bring a trumpet to awake his ear;
To set his sense on the attentive bent,
And then to speak.

*Agam.*       Speak frankly as the wind;
It is not Agamemnon's sleeping hour:
That thou shalt know, Trojan, he is awake,
He tells thee so himself.

*Æne.*             Trumpet, blow loud,

Send thy brass voice through all these lazy
    tents;
And every Greek of mettle, let him know
What Troy means fairly shall be spoke aloud.
                [*Trumpet sounds.*
We have, great Agamemnon, here in Troy
A prince called Hector,—Priam is his fath-
    er,—
Who in this dull and long-continued truce
Is rusty grown: he bade me take a trumpet
And to this purpose speak. Kings, princes,
    lords!
If there be one among the fair'st of Greece
That holds his honour higher than his ease;
That seeks his praise more than he fears his
    peril;
That knows his valour and knows not his
    fear;
That loves his mistress more than in confes-
    sion,—
With truant vows to her own lips he loves,—
And dare avow her beauty and her worth
In other arms than hers,—to him this chal-
    lenge.
Hector, in view of Trojans and of Greeks,
Shall make it good, or do his best to do it,
He hath a lady wiser, fairer, truer
Than ever Greek did compass in his arms
And will to-morrow with his trumpet call,
Mid-way between your tents and walls of
    Troy,
To rouse a Grecian that is true in love:
If any come, Hector shall honour him;
If none, he'll say in Troy when he retires,
The Grecian dames are sunburnt, and not
    worth
The splinter of a lance. Even so much.

*Agam.* This shall be told our lovers, Lord
    Æneas;
If none of them have soul in such a kind,
We left them all at home: but we are soldiers;
And may that soldier a mere recreant prove
That means not, hath not, or is not in love!
If then one is, or hath, or means to be,
That one meets Hector; if none else, I am he.

*Nest.* Tell him of Nestor, one that was a
    man
When Hector's grandsire suck'd: he is old
    now;
But if there be not in our Grecian host
One noble man that hath one spark of fire
To answer for his love, tell him from me—
I'll hide my silver beard in a gold beaver,
And in my vantbrace put this wither'd
    brawn;
And, meeting him, will tell him that my lady
Was fairer than his grandame, and as chaste
As may be in the world: his youth in flood,
I'll prove this truth with my three drops of
    blood.            [youth!

*Æne.* Now heavens forbid such scarcity of

*Ulyss.* Amen.               [hand;

*Agam.* Fair Lord Æneas, let me touch your
To our pavilion shall I lead you, sir.

Achilles shall have word of this intent;
So shall each lord of Greece, from tent to
    tent:
Yourself shall feast with us before you go,
And find the welcome of a noble foe.
    [*Exeunt all but* ULYSS. *and* NEST.
*Ulyss.* Nestor,—
    *Nest.* What says Ulysses?        [brain;
*Ulyss.* I have a young conception in my
Be you my time to bring it to some shape.
    *Nest.* What is't?
*Ulyss.* This 'tis:—        [pride
Blunt wedges rive hard knots: the seeded
That hath to this maturity blown up
In rank Achilles must or now be cropp'd,
Or, shedding, breed a nursery of like evil,
To overbulk us all.
    *Nest.*        Well, and how?
*Ulyss.* This challenge that the gallant Hec-
    tor sends,
However it is spread in general name,
Relates in purpose only to Achilles.
    *Nest.* The purpose is perspicuous even as
        substance,
Whose grossness little characters sum up:
And, in the publication, make no strain
But that Achilles, were his brain as barren
As banks of Libya,—though, Apollo knows,
'Tis dry enough,—will, with great speed of
        judgment,
Ay, with celerity, find Hector's purpose
Pointing on him.
    *Ulyss.* And wake him to the answer, think
        you?
    *Nest.* Yes, 'tis most meet: whom may you
        else oppose
That can from Hector bring his honour off,
If not Achilles? Though't be a sportful com-
    bat,
Yet in the trial much opinion dwells;
For here the Trojans taste our dear'st repute
With their fin'st palate: and trust to me,
        Ulysses,
Our imputation shall be oddly pois'd
In this wild action; for the success,
Although particular, shall give a scantling
Of good or bad unto the general;
And in such indexes, although small pricks
To their subsequent volumes, there is seen
The baby figure of the giant mass
Of things to come at large. It is suppos'd
He that meets Hector issues from our choice:
And choice being mutual act of all our souls,
Makes merit her election; and doth boil,
As 'twere from forth us all, a man distill'd
Out of our virtues; who miscarrying,
What heart receives from hence the conquer-
    ing part,
To steal a strong opinion to themselves?
Which entertain'd, limbs are his instruments,
In no less working than are swords and bows
Directive by the limbs.
    *Ulyss.* Give pardon to my speech;—
Therefore 'tis meet Achilles meet not Hector.

Let us, like merchants, show our foulest
    wares,
And think perchance they'll sell; if not,
The lustre of the better shall exceed,
By showing the worst first. Do not consent
That ever Hector and Achilles meet;
For both our honour and our shame in this
Are dogg'd with two strange followers.
    *Nest.* I see them not with my old eyes:
        what are they?
    *Ulyss.* What glory our Achilles shares from
        Hector,        [him:
Were he not proud, we all should share with
But he already is too insolent;
And we were better parch in Afric sun
Than in the pride and salt scorn of his eyes,
Should he 'scape Hector fair: if he were foil'd,
Why, then we did our main opinion crush
In taint of our best man. No, make a lottery;
And, by device, let blockish Ajax draw
The sort to fight with Hector: among our-
    selves,
Give him allowance for the better man;
For that will physic the great Myrmidon
Who broils in loud applause, and make him
    fall
His crest that prouder than blue Iris bends.
If the dull brainless Ajax comes safe off,
We'll dress him up in voices: if he fail,
Yet go we under our opinion still
That we have better men. But, hit or miss,
Our project's life this shape of sense as-
    sumes,—
Ajax employ'd plucks down Achilles' plumes.
    *Nest.* Now, Ulysses, I begin to relish thy
        advice;
And I will give a taste of it forthwith
To Agamemnon: go we to him straight.
Two curs shall tame each other: pride alone
Must tarre the mastiffs on, as 'twere their
    bone.        [*Exeunt.*

## ACT II.

SCENE I.—*Another part of the Grecian Camp.*

*Enter* AJAX *and* THERSITES.

*Ajax.* Thersites,—
*Ther.* Agamemnon,—how if he had boils,—
full, all over, generally?—
*Ajax.* Thersites,—
*Ther.* And those boils did run?—Say so,—
did not the general run then? were not that
a botchy core?—
*Ajax.* Dog.—
*Ther.* Then would come some matter from
him; I see none now.
*Ajax.* Thou bitch-wolf's son, canst thou
not hear? Feel, then.        [*Beating him.*
*Ther.* The plague of Greece upon thee,
thou mongrel beef-witted lord!
*Ajax.* Speak, then, thou vinewedst leaven,
speak: I will beat thee into handsomeness.
*Ther.* I shall sooner rail thee into wit and
holiness: but I think thy horse will sooner

con an oration than thou learn a prayer without book. Thou canst strike, canst thou? a red murrain o' thy jade's tricks!

*Ajax.* Toadstool, learn me the proclamation.

*Ther.* Dost thou think I have no sense, thou strikest me thus?

*Ajax.* The proclamation,—

*Ther.* Thou art proclaimed a fool, I think.

*Ajax.* Do not, porcupine, do not; my fingers itch.

*Ther.* I would thou didst itch from head to foot, and I had the scratching of thee; I would make thee the loathsomest scab in Greece. When thou art forth in incursions, thou strikest as slow as another.

*Ajax.* I say, the proclamation,—

*Ther.* Thou grumblest and railest every hour on Achilles; and thou art as full of envy at his greatness as Cerberus is at Proserpina's beauty, ay, that thou barkest at him.

*Ajax.* Mistress Thersites:

*Ther.* Thou shouldst strike him.

*Ajax.* Cobloaf!

*Ther.* He would pun thee into shivers with his fist, as a sailor breaks a biscuit.

*Ajax.* You whoreson cur!   [*Beating him.*

*Ther.* Do, do.

*Ajax.* Thou stool for a witch!

*Ther.* Ay, do, do; thou sodden-witted lord! thou hast no more brain than I have in mine elbows; an assinego may tutor thee: thou scurvy valiant ass! thou are here but to thrash Trojans; and thou art bought and sold among those of any wit, like a barbarian slave. If thou use to beat me, I will begin at thy heel, and tell what thou art by inches, thou thing of no bowels, thou!

*Ajax.* You dog!

*Ther.* You scurvy lord!

*Ajax.* You cur!         [*Beating him.*

*Ther.* Mars his idiot! do, rudeness; do, camel; do, do.

    *Enter* ACHILLES *and* PATROCLUS.

*Achil.* Why, how now, Ajax! wherefore do you thus?—

How now, Thersites! what's the matter, man?

*Ther.* You see him there, do you?

*Achil.* Ay; what's the matter?

*Ther.* Nay, look upon him.

*Achil.* So I do: what's the matter?

*Ther.* Nay, but regard him well.

*Achil.* Well! why, I do so.

*Ther.* But yet you look not well upon him; for whosoever you take him to be, he is Ajax.

*Achil.* I know that, fool.

*Ther.* Ay, but that fool knows not himself.

*Ajax.* Therefore I beat thee.

*Ther.* Lo, lo, lo, lo, what modicums of wit he utters! his evasions have ears thus long. I have bobbed his brain more than he has beat my bones: I will buy nine sparrows for a

penny, and his *pia mater* is not worth the ninth part of a sparrow. This lord, Achilles, Ajax,—who wears his wit in his belly, and his guts in his head,—I'll tell you what I say of him.

*Achil.* What?

*Ther.* I say, this Ajax,—

    [AJAX *offers to beat him,* ACHILLES *interposes.*

*Achil.* Nay, good Ajax.

*Ther.* Has not so much wit,—

*Achil.* Nay, I must hold you.

*Ther.* As will stop the eye of Helen's needle, for whom he comes to fight.

*Achil.* Peace, fool!

*Ther.* I would have peace and quietness, but the fool will not: he there; that he; look you there.

*Ajax.* O thou damned cur! I shall,—

*Achil.* Will you set your wit to a fool's?

*Ther.* No, I warrant you; for a fool's will shame it.

*Patr.* Good words, Thersites.

*Achil.* What's the quarrel?

*Ajax.* I bade the vile owl go learn me the tenor of the proclamation, and he rails upon me.

*Ther.* I serve thee not.

*Ajax.* Well, go to, go to.

*Ther.* I serve here voluntary.

*Achil.* Your last service was sufferance, 'twas not voluntary,—no man is beaten voluntary: Ajax was here the voluntary, and you as under an impress.

*Ther.* E'en so; a great deal of your wit, too, lies in your sinews, or else there be liars. Hector shall have a great catch if he knock out either of your brains: 'a were as good crack a frusty nut with no kernel.

*Achil.* What, with me too, Thersites?

*Ther.* There's Ulysses and old Nestor,— whose wit was mouldy ere your grandsires had nails on their toes,—yoke you like draught oxen, and make you plough up the wars.

*Achil.* What, what?

*Ther.* Yes, good sooth: to, Achilles! to, Ajax! to!

*Ajax.* I shall cut out your tongue.

*Ther.* 'Tis no matter; I shall speak as much as thou afterwards.

*Patr.* No more words, Thersites; peace!

*Ther.* I will hold my peace when Achilles' brach bids me, shall I?

*Achil.* There's for you, Patroclus.

*Ther.* I will see you hanged, like clotpoles, ere I come any more to your tents: I will keep where there is wit stirring, and leave the faction of fools.         [*Exit.*

*Patr.* A good riddance.

*Achil.* Marry, this, sir, is proclaim'd through all our host:—

That Hector, by the fifth hour of the sun, Will, with a trumpet, 'twixt our tents and Troy,

To-morrow morning call some knight to arms
That hath a stomach; and such a one that
dare
Maintain I know not what; 'tis trash. Fare-
well.
*Ajax.* Farewell. Who shall answer him?
*Achil.* I know not, it is put to lottery;
otherwise
He knew his man.
*Ajax.* O, meaning you.—I'll go learn more
of it.                                 [*Exeunt.*

SCENE II.—TROY. *A Room in* PRIAM'S *Palace.*

*Enter* PRIAM, HECTOR, TROILUS, PARIS,
*and* HELENUS.

*Pri.* After so many hours, lives, speeches
spent,
Thus once again says Nestor from the
Greeks:—
*Deliver Helen, and all damage else,—*
*As honour, loss of time, travail, expense,*
*Wounds, friends, and what else dear that is*
*consum'd*
*In hot digestion of this cormorant war,—*
*Shall be struck off:*—Hector, what say you
to't?
*Hect.* Though no man lesser fears the
Greeks than I,
As far as toucheth my particular,
Yet, dread Priam,
There is no lady of more softer bowels,
More spongy to suck in the sense of fear,
More ready to cry out, *Who knows what fol-*
*lows?*
Than Hector is: the wound of peace is surety,
Surety secure; but modest doubt is call'd
The beacon of the wise, the tent that searches
To the bottom of the worst. Let Helen go:
Since the first sword was drawn about this
question,
Every tithe soul, 'mongst many thousand
dismes,
Hath been as dear as Helen,—I mean, of
ours:
If we have lost so many tenths of ours,
To guard a thing not ours, nor worth to us,
Had it our name, the value of one ten,—
What merit's in that reason which denies
The yielding of her up?
*Tro.*                    Fie, fie, my brother!
Weigh you the worth and honour of a king,
So great as our dread father, in a scale
Of common ounces? will you with counters
sum
The past-proportion of his infinite?
And buckle-in a waist most fathomless
With spans and inches so diminutive
As fears and reasons? fie, for godly shame!
*Hel.* No marvel though you bite so sharp
at reasons:                        [our father
You are so empty of them. Should not
Bear the great sway of his affairs with
reasons,                              [him so?
Because your speech hath none that tells

*Tro.* You are for dreams and slumbers,
brother priest;            [your reasons:
You fur your gloves with reason. Here are
You know an enemy intends you harm;
You know a sword employ'd is perilous,
And reason flies the object of all harm:
Who marvels, then, when Helenus beholds
A Grecian and his sword, if he do set
The very wings of reason to his heels,
And fly like chidden Mercury from Jove,
Or like a star disorb'd?—Nay if we talk of
reason                                [honour
Let's shut our gates and sleep: manhood and
Should have hare hearts would they but fat
their thoughts
With this cramm'd reason: reason and respect
Make livers pale and lustihood deject.
*Hect.* Brother, she is not worth what she
doth cost
The holding.
*Tro.* What is aught but as 'tis valued?
*Hect.* But value dwells not in particular
will;
It holds his estimate and dignity
As well wherein 'tis precious of itself
As in the prizer: 'tis mad idolatry
To make the service greater than the god;
And the will dotes, that is attributive
To what infectiously itself affects,
Without some image of the affected merit.
*Tro.* I take to-day a wife, and my election
Is led on in the conduct of my will;
My will enkindled by mine eyes and ears,
Two traded pilots 'twixt the dangerous shores
Of will and judgment: how may I avoid,
Although my will distaste what it elected,
The wife I chose? there can be no evasion
To blench from this, and to stand firm by
honour:
We turn not back the silks upon the merchant
When we have soil'd them; nor the remainder
viands
We do not throw in unrespective sieve,
Because we now are full. It was thought meet
Paris should do some vengeance on the
Greeks:
Your breath of full consent bellied his sails;
The seas and winds,—old wranglers,—took a
truce,
And did him service: he touch'd the ports
desir'd;
And for an old aunt, whom the Greeks held
captive                          [and freshness
He brought a Grecian queen, whose youth
Wrinkles Apollo's, and makes stale the morn-
ing.
Why keep we her? The Grecians keep our
aunt:
Is she worth keeping? why, she is a pearl,
Whose price hath launch'd above a thousand
ships,
And turn'd crown'd kings to merchants.
If you'll avouch 'twas wisdom Paris went,—
As you must needs, for you all cried, *Go, go,—*

If you'll confess he brought home noble
      prize,—
As you must needs, for you all clapp'd your
      hands,
And cried, *Inestimable!*—why do you now
The issue of your proper wisdoms rate,
And do a deed that fortune never did,—
Beggar the estimation which you priz'd
Richer than sea and land? O theft most base,
That we have stol'n what we do fear to keep!
But thieves, unworthy of a thing so stol'n,
That in their country did them that disgrace,
We fear to warrant in our native place!
*Cas.* [*Within.*] Cry, Trojans, cry!
*Pri.*        What noise? what shriek is this?
*Pro.* 'Tis our mad sister, I do know her
      voice.
*Cas.* [*Within.*] Cry, Trojans!
*Hect.* It is Cassandra.

*Enter* CASSANDRA, *raving.*

*Cas.* Cry, Trojans, cry! lend me ten thou-
      sand eyes,
And I will fill them with prophetic tears.
*Hect.* Peace, sister, peace.        [wrinkled old,
*Cas.* Virgins and boys, mid-age and
Soft infancy, that nothing canst but cry,
Add to my clamours! let us pay betimes
A moiety of that mass of moan to come.
Cry, Trojans, cry! practise your eyes with
      tears!
Troy must not be, nor goodly Ilion stand;
Our firebrand brother, Paris, burns us all.
Cry, Trojans, cry! an Helen and a woe:
Cry, cry! Troy burns, or else let Helen go.
      [*Exit.*
*Hect.* Now, youthful Troilus, do not these
      high strains
Of divination in our sister work
Some touches of remorse? or is your blood
So madly hot that no discourse of reason,
Nor fear of bad success in a bad cause,
Can qualify the same?
*Tro.*        Why, brother Hector,
We may not think the justness of each act
Such and no other than event doth form it;
Nor once deject the courage of our minds
Because Cassandra's mad: her brain-sick
      raptures
Cannot distaste the goodness of a quarrel
Which hath our several honours all engag'd
To make it gracious. For my private part,
I am no more touch'd than all Priam's sons:
And Jove forbid there should be done
      amongst us
Such things as might offend the weakest
      spleen
To fight for and maintain!
*Par.* Else might the world convince of
      levity
As well my undertakings as your counsels:
But I attest the gods, your full consent
Gave wings to my propension, and cut off
All fears attending on so dire a project.

For what, alas, can these my single arms?
What propugnation is in one man's valour,
To stand the push and enmity of those
This quarrel would excite? Yet, I protest,
Were I alone to pass the difficulties,
And had as ample power as I have will,
Paris should ne'er retract what he hath done,
Nor faint in the pursuit.
*Pri.*        Paris, you speak
Like one besotted on your sweet delights:
You have the honey still, but these the gall;
So to be valiant is no praise at all.
*Par.* Sir, I propose not merely to myself
The pleasures such a beauty brings with it:
But I would have the soil of her fair rape
Wip'd off in honourable keeping her.
What treason were it to the ransak'd queen,
Disgrace to your great worths, and shame to
      me,
Now to deliver her possession up
On terms of base compulsion! Can it be
That so degenerate a strain as this
Should once set footing in your generous
      bosoms?
There's not the meanest spirit on our party,
Without a heart to dare or sword to draw,
When Helen is defended; nor none so noble,
Whose life were ill bestow'd or death unfam'd,
Where Helen is the subject: then, I say, [well,
Well may we fight for her, whom, we know
The world's large spaces cannot parallel.
*Hect.* Paris and Troilus, you have both
      said well;
And on the cause and question now in hand
Have gloz'd,—but superficially; not much
Unlike young men, whom Aristotle thought
Unfit to hear moral philosophy:
The reasons you allege do more conduce
To the hot passion of distemper'd blood
Than to make up a free determination
'Twixt right and wrong; for pleasure and
      revenge
Have ears more deaf than adders to the voice
Of any true decision. Nature craves
All dues be render'd to their owners: now,
What nearer debt in all humanity
Than wife is to the husband? If this law
Of nature be corrupted through affection;
And that great minds, of partial indulgence
To their benumbed wills, resist the same;
There is a law in each well-order'd nation
To curb those raging appetites that are
Most disobedient and refractory.
If Helen, then, be wife to Sparta's king,—
As it is known she is,—these moral laws
Of nature and of nations speak aloud
To have her back return'd: thus to persist
In doing wrong extenuates not wrong,
But it makes it much more heavy. Hector's
      opinion
Is this, in way of truth: yet, ne'ertheless,
My spritely brethren, I propend to you
In resolution to keep Helen still;
For 'tis a cause that hath no mean dependence

Upon our joint and several dignities.

*Tro.* Why, there you touch'd the life of our design:
Were it not glory that we more affected
Than the performance of our heaving spleens,
I would not wish a drop of Trojan blood
Spent more in her defence. But, worthy Hector,
She is a theme of honour and renown;
A spur to valiant and magnanimous deeds;
Whose present courage may beat down our foes,
And fame in time to come canónize us:
For, I presume, brave Hector would not lose
So rich advantage of a promis'd glory,
As smiles upon the forehead of this action,
For the wide world's revenue.

*Hect.*                    I am yours,
You valiant offspring of great Priamus.—
I have a roisting challenge sent amongst
The dull and factious nobles of the Greeks
Will strike amazement to their drowsy spirits:
I was advertis'd their great general slept,
Whilst emulation in the army crept:
This, I presume, will wake him.    [*Exeunt.*

SCENE III.—THE GRECIAN CAMP. *Before*
ACHILLES' *Tent.*

*Enter* THERSITES.

*Ther.* How now, Thersites! what, lost in the labyrinth of thy fury! Shall the elephant Ajax carry it thus? he beats me, and I rail at him: O worthy satisfaction! would it were otherwise; that I could beat him, whilst he railed at me. 'Sfoot, I'll learn to conjure and raise devils, but I'll see some issue of my spiteful execrations. Then there's Achilles,—a rare engineer. If Troy be not taken till these two undermine it, the walls will stand till they fall of themselves. O thou great thunder-darter of Olympus, forget that thou art Jove, the king of gods; and, Mercury, lose all the serpentine craft of thy caduceus; if ye take not that little little less-than-little wit from them that they have! which short-aimed ignorance itself knows is so abundant scarce, it will not in circumvention deliver a fly from a spider, without drawing their massy irons and cutting the web. After this, the vengeance on the whole camp! or, rather, the bone-ache! for that, methinks, is the curse dependent on those that war for a placket. I have said my prayers; and devil envy say Amen.—What, ho! my Lord Achilles!

*Enter* PATROCLUS.

*Patr.* Who's there? Thersites! Good Thersites, come in and rail.

*Ther.* If I could have remembered a gilt counterfeit, thou wouldst not have slipped out of my contemplation: but it is no matter; thyself upon thyself! The common curse of mankind, folly and ignorance, be thine in great revenue! beaven bless thee from a tutor, and discipline come not near thee! Let thy blood be thy direction till thy death! then if she that lays thee out says thou art a fair corse, I'll be sworn and sworn upon't she never shrouded any but lazars. Amen.—Where's Achilles?

*Patr.* What, art thou devout? wast thou in prayer?

*Ther.* Ay, the heavens hear me!

*Enter* ACHILLES.

*Achil.* Who's there?

*Patr.* Thersites, my lord.

*Achil.* Where, where?—Art thou come? Why, my cheese, my digestion, why hast thou not served thyself in to my table so many meals? Come,—what's Agamemnon?

*Ther.* Thy commander, Achilles:—then tell me, Patroclus, what's Achilles?

*Patr.* Thy lord, Thersites: then tell me, I pray thee, what's thyself?

*Ther.* Thy knower, Patroclus: then tell me, Patroclus, what art thou?

*Patr.* Thou mayest tell that knowest.

*Achil.* O, tell, tell.

*Ther.* I'll decline the whole question. Agamemnon commands Achilles; Achilles is my lord; I am Patroclus' knower; and Patroclus is a fool.

*Patr.* You rascal!

*Ther.* Peace, fool! I have not done.

*Achil.* He is a privileged man.—Proceed, Thersites.

*Ther.* Agamemnon is a fool; Achilles is a fool; Thersites is a fool; and, as aforesaid, Patroclus is a fool.

*Achil.* Derive this; come.

*Ther.* Agamemnon is a fool to offer to command Achilles; Achilles is a fool to be commanded of Agamemnon; Thersites is a fool to serve such a fool; and Patroclus is a fool positive.

*Patr.* Why am I a fool?

*Ther.* Make that demand of the prover. It suffices me thou art.—Look you, who comes here?

*Achil.* Patroclus, I'll speak with nobody.—Come in with me, Thersites.    [*Exit.*

*Ther.* Here is such patchery,,such juggling, and such knavery! all the argument is a cuckold and a whore; a good quarrel to draw emulous factions and bleed to death upon. Now the dry serpigo on the subject! and war and lechery confound all!    [*Exit.*

*Enter* AGAMEMNON, ULYSSES, NESTOR,
DIOMEDES, *and* AJAX.

*Agam.* Where is Achilles?    [lord·

*Patr.* Within his tent; but ill-dispos'd, my

*Agam.* Let it be known to him that we are here.
He shent our messengers; and we lay by
Our appertainments, visiting of him:
Let him be told so; lest, perchance, he think

We dare not move the question of our place,
Or know not what we are.

*Patr.* I shall say so to him. [*Exit.*

*Ulyss.* We saw him at the opening of his
tent:
He is not sick.

*Ajax.* Yes, lion-sick, sick of proud heart:
you may call it melancholy, if you will favour the man; but, by my head, 'tis pride:
but why, why? let him show us the cause.—
A word, my lord. [*Takes* AGAMEMNON *aside.*

*Nest.* What moves Ajax thus to bay at
him? [*from him.*

*Ulyss.* Achilles hath inveigled his fool

*Nest.* Who, Thersites?

*Ulyss.* He.

*Nest.* Then will Ajax lack matter, if he
have lost his argument.

*Ulyss.* No; you see, he is his argument that
has his argument,—Achilles.

*Nest.* All the better; their fraction is more
our wish than their faction. But it was a
strong composure a fool could disunite.

*Ulyss.* The amity that wisdom knits not,
folly may easily untie. Here comes Patroclus.

*Nest.* No Achilles with him.

*Ulyss.* The elephant hath joints, but none
for courtesy: his legs are legs for necessity,
not for flexure.

*Re-enter* PATROCLUS.

*Patr.* Achilles bids me say, he is much sorry
If anything more than your sport and pleas-
ure
Did move your greatness and this noble state
To call upon him; he hopes it is no other
But for your health and your digestion
sake,—
An after-dinner's breath.

*Agam.* Hear you, Patroclus:—
We are too well acquainted with these an-
swers:
But his evasion, wing'd thus swift with scorn,
Cannot outfly our apprehensions.
Much attribute he hath; and much the
reason [tues,—
Why we ascribe it to him: yet all his vir-
Not virtuously on his own part beheld,—
Do in our eyes begin to lose their gloss;
Yea, like fair fruit in an unwholesome dish,
Are like to rot untasted. Go and tell him
We come to speak with him; and you shall
not sin
If you do say we think him over-proud
And under-honest; in self-assumption greater
Than in the note of judgment; and worthier
than himself
Here tend the savage strangeness he puts on,
Disguise the holy strength of their command,
And underwrite in an observing kind
His humorous predominance; yea, watch
His pettish lunes, his ebbs, his flows, as if
The passage and whole carriage of this action
Rode on his tide. Go tell him this; and add,

That if he overhold his price so much,
We'll none of him; but let him, like an engine
Not portable, lie under this report,—
Bring action hither, this cannot go to war:
A stirring dwarf we do allowance give
Before a sleeping giant:—tell him so.

*Patr.* I shall; and bring his answer presently. [*Exit.*

*Agam.* In second voice we'll not be satis-
fied; [you.
We come to speak with him.—Ulyssus, enter
[*Exit* ULYSSES.

*Ajax.* What is he more than another?

*Agam.* No more than what he thinks he is.

*Ajax.* Is he so much? Do you not think he
thinks himself a better man than I am?

*Agam.* No question.

*Ajax.* Will you subscribe his thought, and
say he is?

*Agam.* No, noble Ajax; you are as strong,
as valiant, as wise, no less noble, much more
gentle, and altogether more tractable.

*Ajax.* Why should a man be proud? How
doth pride grow? I know not what pride is.

*Agam.* Your mind is the clearer, Ajax, and
your virtues the fairer. He that is proud eats
up himself: pride is his own glass, his own
trumpet, his own chronicle; and whatever
praises itself but in the deed devours the deed
in the praise.

*Ajax.* I do hate a proud man as I hate the
engendering of toads.

*Nest.* Yet he loves himself: is't not
strange? [*Aside.*

*Re-enter* ULYSSES.

*Ulyss.* Achilles will not to the fields to-
morrow.

*Agam.* What's his excuse?

*Ulyss.* He doth rely on none;
But carries on the stream of his dispose,
Without observance or respect of any,
In will peculiar and in self-admission.

*Agam.* Why will he not, upon our fair
request,
Untent his person, and share the air with us?

*Ulyss.* Things small as nothing, for re-
quest's sake only, [greatness:
He makes important: possess'd he is with
And speaks not to himself but with a pride
That quarrels at self-breath: imagin'd worth
Holds in his blood such swoln and hot dis-
course
That 'twixt his mental and his active parts
Kingdom'd Achilles in commotion rages,
And batters down himself: what should I
say: [of it
He is so plaguy proud that the death tokens
Cry, *No recovery.*

*Agam.* Let Ajax go to him.—
Dear lord, go you and greet him in his tent:
'Tis said he holds you well; and will be led,
At your request, a little from himself.

*Ulyss.* O Agamemnon, let it not be so!

We'll consecrate the steps that Ajax makes
When they go from Achilles. Shall the proud
    lord,
That bastes his arrogance with his own seam,
And never suffers matter of the world
Enter his thoughts,—save such as do revolve
And ruminate himself,—shall he be wor-
    shipp'd
Of that we hold an idol more than he?
No, this trice-worthy and right valiant lord
Must not so stale his palm, nobly acquir'd;
Nor, by my will, assubjugate his merit,
As amply titled as Achilles is,
By going to Achilles:
That were to enlard his fat-already pride,
And add more coals to Cancer when he burns
With entertaining great Hyperion.
This lord go to him! Jupiter forbid;
And say in thunder, *Achilles go to him.*

*Nest.* O, this is well; he rubs the vein of
    him.                 [*Aside.*
*Dio.* And how his silence drinks up this ap-
    plause!                [*Aside.*
*Ajax.* If I go to him, with my armed fist
I'll pash him o'er the face.
*Agam.* O, no, you shall not go.   [his pride:
*Ajax.* An 'a be proud with me I'll pheeze
Let me go to him.           [our quarrel.
*Ulyss.* Not for the worth that hangs upon
*Ajax.* A paltry, insolent fellow!
*Nest.* How he describes himself! [*Aside.*
*Ajax.* 'Can he not be sociable?
*Ulyss.* The raven chides blackness. [*Aside.*
*Ajax.* I'll let his humours blood.
*Agam.* He will be the physician that should
    be the patient.           [*Aside.*
*Ajax.* An all men were o' my mind,—
*Ulyss.* Wit would be out of fashion. [*Aside.*
*Ajax.* 'A should not bear it so, 'a should eat
swords first: shall pride carry it?
*Nest.* An 'twould, you'd carry half. [*Aside.*
*Ulyss.* 'A would have ten shares. [*Aside.*
*Ajax.* I will knead him, I'll make him sup-
    ple.
*Nest.* He's not yet thorough warm: force
him with praises; pour in, pour in: his ambi-
tion is dry.                [*Aside.*
*Ulyss.* My lord, you feed too much on this
    dislike.          [*To* AGAMEMNON.
*Nest.* Our noble general, do not do so.
*Dio.* You must prepare to fight without
    Achilles.            [him harm.
*Ulyss.* Why 'tis this naming of him does
Here is a man—but 'tis before his face;
I will be silent.
*Nest.*        Wherefore should you so?
He is not emulous, as Achilles is.
*Ulyss.* Know the whole world, he is as
    valiant.           [thus with us!
*Ajax.* A whoreson dog, that shall palter
Would he were a Trojan!
*Nest.* What a vice were it in Ajax now,—
*Ulyss.* If he were proud,—
*Dio.* Or covetous of praise,—

*Ulyss.* Ay, or surly borne,—
*Dio.* Or strange, or self-affected!
*Ulyss.* Thank the heavens, lord, thou art
    of sweet composure;        [suck;
Praise him that got thee, she that gave thee
Fam'd be thy tutor, and thy parts of nature
Thrice-fam'd, beyond all erudition:
But he that disciplin'd thy arms to fight,
Let Mars divide eternity in twain,
And give him half: and, for thy vigour,
Bull-bearing Milo his addition yield
To sinewy Ajax. I will not praise thy wisdom,
Which, like a born, a pale, a shore, confines
Thy spacious and dilated parts: here's Nes-
    ter,—
Instructed by the antiquary times,
He must, he is, he cannot but be wise;—
But pardon, father Nestor, were your days
As green as Ajax', and your brain so tem-
    per'd,
You should not have the eminence of him,
But be as Ajax.
*Ajax.*        Shall I call you father?
*Nest.* Ay, my good son.
*Dio.*        Be rul'd by him, Lord Ajax.
*Ulyss.* There is no tarrying here; the hart
    Achilles
Keeps thicket. Please it our great general
To call together all his state of war;
Fresh kings are come to Troy. To-morrow
We must with all our main of power stand
    fast:               [west,
And here's a lord,—come knights from east to
And cull their flower, Ajax shall cope the best.
*Agam.* Go we to council. Let Achilles sleep:
Light boats sail swift, though greater hulks
    draw deep.           [*Exeunt.*

## ACT III.

SCENE I.—TROY. *A Room in* PRIAM'S *Palace.*

*Enter* PANDARUS *and a* Servant.

*Pan.* Friend, you,—pray you, a word: do
not you follow the young Lord Paris?
*Serv.* Ay, sir, when he goes before me.
*Pan.* You depend upon him, I mean?
*Serv.* Sir, I do depend upon the lord.
*Pan.* You depend upon a noble gentleman!
I must needs praise him.
*Serv.* The lord be praised!
*Pan.* You know me, do you not?
*Serv.* Faith, sir, superficially.
*Pan.* Friend, know me better; I am the
Lord Pandarus.
*Serv.* I hope I shall know your honour
better.
*Pan.* I do desire it.
*Serv.* You are in the state of grace.
                    [*Music within.*
*Pan.* Grace! not so, friend; honour and
lordship are my titles.—What music is this?
*Serv.* I do but partly know, sir: it is music
in parts.
*Pan.* Know you the musicians?

*Serv.* Wholly, sir.

*Pan.* Who play they to?

*Serv.* To the hearers, sir.

*Pan.* At whose pleasure, friend?

*Serv.* At mine, sir, and theirs that love music.

*Pan.* Command, I mean, friend.

*Serv.* Who shall I command, sir?

*Pan.* Friend, we understand not one another: I am too courtly, and thou art too cunning. At whose request do these men play?

*Serv.* That's to 't, indeed, sir. Marry, sir, at the request of Paris my lord, who is there in person; with him, the mortal Venus, the heart-blood of beauty, love's invisible soul,—

*Pan.* Who, my cousin Cressida?

*Serv.* No, sir, Helen: could you not find out that by her attributes?

*Pan.* It should seem, fellow, that thou hast not seen the Lady Cressida. I come to speak with Paris from the Prince Troilus: I will make a complimental assault upon him, for my business seethes.

*Serv.* Sodden business! there's a stewed phrase indeed!

*Enter* PARIS *and* HELEN, *attended.*

*Pan.* Fair be to you, my lord, and to all this fair company! fair desires, in all fair measure, fairly guide them!—especially to you, fair queen! fair thoughts be your fair pillow!

*Helen.* Dear lord, you are full of fair words.

*Pan.* You speak your fair pleasure, sweet queen.—Fair prince, here is good broken music.

*Par.* You have broke it, cousin: and by my life, you shall make it whole again; you shall piece it out with a piece of your performance.—Nell, he is full of harmony.

*Pan.* Truly, lady, no.

*Helen.* O, sir,—

*Pan.* Rude, in sooth; in good sooth, very rude.

*Par.* Well said, my lord! well, you say so in fits.

*Pan.* I have business to my lord, dear queen.—My lord, will you vouchsafe me a word?

*Helen.* Nay, this shall not hedge us out: we'll hear you sing, certainly.

*Pan.* Well, sweet queen, you are pleasant with me.—But, marry, thus, my lord,—My dear lord, and most esteemed friend, your brother Troilus,—

*Helen.* My Lord Pandarus; honey-sweet lord,—

*Pan.* Go to, sweet queen, go to:—commends himself most affectionately to you,—

*Helen.* You shall not bob us out of our melody: if you do, our melancholy upon your head!

*Pan.* Sweet queen, sweet queen; that's a sweet queen, i' faith.

*Helen.* And to make a sweet lady sad is a sour offence.

*Pan.* Nay, that shall not serve your turn; that shall it not, in truth, la. Nay, I care not for such words; no, no.—And, my lord, he desires you that, if the king call for him at supper, you will make his excuse.

*Helen.* My Lord Pandarus,—

*Pan.* What says my sweet queen,—my very very sweet queen?

*Par.* What exploit's in hand? where sups he to-night?

*Helen.* Nay, but, my lord,—

*Pan.* What says my sweet queen?—My cousin will fall out with you. You must not know where he sups.

*Par.* I'll lay my life, with my disposer, Cressida.

*Pan.* No, no, no such matter; you are wide: come, your disposer is sick.

*Par.* Well, I'll make excuse.

*Pan.* Ay, good my lord. Why should you say Cressida? no, your poor disposer's sick.

*Par.* I spy.

*Pan.* You spy! what do you spy?—Come, give me an instrument.—Now, sweet queen.

*Helen.* Why, this is kindly done.

*Pan.* My niece is horribly in love with a thing you have, sweet queen.

*Helen.* She shall have it, my lord, if it be not my Lord Paris.

*Pan.* He! no, she'll none of him; they two are twain.

*Helen.* Falling in, after falling out, may make them three.

*Pan.* Come, come, I'll hear no more of this; I'll sing you a song now.

*Helen.* Ay, ay, pr'ythee now. By my troth, sweet lord, thou hast a fine forehead.

*Pan.* Ay, you may, you may.

*Helen.* Let thy song be love: this love will undo us all. O Cupid, Cupid, Cupid!

*Pan.* Love! ay, that it shall, i' faith. [love.

*Par.* Ay, good now, love, love, nothing but

*Pan.* In good troth, it begins so:

Love, love, nothing but love, still more!
  For, oh, love's bow
  Shoots buck and doe:
  The shaft confounds,
  Not that it wounds,
But tickles still the sore.
These lovers cry—Oh! oh! they die!
  Yet that which seems the wound to kill,
Doth turn oh! oh! to ha! ha! he!
  So dying love lives still:
Oh! oh! a while, but ha! ha! ha!
Oh! oh! groans out for ha! ha! ha!

Heigh ho!

*Helen.* In love, i' faith, to the very tip of the nose.

*Par.* He eats nothing but doves, love; and that breeds hot blood, and hot blood begets hot thoughts, and hot thoughts beget hot deeds, and hot deeds is love.

*Pan.* Is this the generation of love? hot blood, hot thoughts, and hot deeds? Why, they are vipers: is love a generation of vipers?—Sweet lord, who's a-field to-day?

*Par.* Hector, Deiphobus, Helenus, Antenor, and all the gallantry of Troy: I would fain have armed to-day, but my Nell would not have it so. How chance my brother Troilus went not?

*Helen.* He hangs the lip at something:—you know all, Lord Pandarus.

*Pan.* Not I, honey-sweet queen.—I long to hear how they sped to-day. You'll remember your brother's excuse?

*Par.* To a hair.

*Pan.* Farewell, sweet queen.

*Helen.* Commend me to your niece.

*Pan.* I will, sweet queen.          [*Exit.*
                                 [*A retreat sounded.*

*Par.* They are come from field: let us to Priam's hall          [woo you
To greet the warriors. Sweet Helen, I must
To help unarm our Hector: his stubborn buckles,          [touch'd,
With these your white enchanting fingers
Shall more obey than to the edge of steel,
Or force of Greekish sinews; you shall do more          [tor.
Than all the island kings,—disarm great Hec-

*Helen.* 'Twill make us proud to be his servant, Paris;
Yea, what he shall receive of us in duty
Gives us more palm in beauty than we have,
Yea, overshines ourself.

*Par.* Sweet, above thought I love thee.
                                     [*Exeunt.*

### SCENE II.—TROY. PANDARUS' *Orchard.*

*Enter* PANDARUS *and* TROILUS' Boy, *meeting.*

*Pan.* How now! where's thy master? at my cousin Cressida's?          [him thither.

*Boy.* No, sir; he stays for you to conduct

*Pan.* O, here he comes.

#### *Enter* TROILUS.

How now, how now!

*Tro.* Sirrah, walk off.          [*Exit* Boy.

*Pan.* Have you seen my cousin?

*Tro.* No, Pandarus: I stalk about her door,
Like a strange soul upon the Stygian banks
Staying for waftage. O, be thou my Charon,
And give me swift transportation to those fields
Where I may wallow in the lily beds
Propos'd for the deserver! O gentle Pandarus,
From Cupid's shoulder pluck his painted wings,
And fly with me to Cressid!

*Pan.* Walk here i' the orchard, I'll bring her straight.          [*Exit.*

*Tro.* I am giddy; expectation whirls me round.

The imaginary relish is so sweet
That it enchants my sense: what will it be,
When that the wat'ry palate tastes indeed
Love's thrice-repured nectar? death, I fear me;
Swooning destruction; or some joy too fine,
Too subtle-potent, tun'd too sharp in sweetness,
For the capacity of my ruder powers;
I fear it much; and I do fear besides
That I shall lose distinction in my joys;
As doth a battle, when they charge on heaps
The enemy flying.

#### *Re-enter* PANDARUS.

*Pan.* She's making her ready, she'll come straight: you must be witty now. She does so blush, and fetches her wind so short, as if she were frayed with a sprite: I'll fetch her. It is the prettiest villain: she fetches her breath as short as a new-ta'en sparrow.          [*Exit.*

*Tro.* Even such a passion doth embrace my bosom;
My heart beats thicker than a feverous pulse;
And all my powers do their bestowing lose,
Like vassalage at unawares encount'ring
The eye of majesty.

#### *Re-enter* PANDARUS *with* CRESSIDA.

*Pan.* Come, come, what need you blush? shame's a baby.—Here she is now: swear the oaths now to her that you have sworn to me. —What, are you gone again? you must be watched ere you be made tame, must you? Come your ways, come your ways; an you draw backward, we'll put you i' the fills.— Why do you not speak to her?—Come, draw this curtain, and let's see your picture. Alas the day, how loth you are to offend daylight! an 'twere dark, you'd close sooner. So, so; rub on, and kiss the mistress. How now, a kiss in fee-farm! build there, carpenter; the air is sweet. Nay, you shall fight your hearts out ere I part you. The falcon as the tercel, for all the ducks i' the river: go to, go to.

*Tro.* You have bereft me of all words, lady.

*Pan.* Words pay no debts, give her deeds: but she'll bereave you o' the deeds. too, if she call your activity in question. What. billing again? Here's—*In witness whereof the parties interchangeably*—Come in, come in: I'll go get a fire.          [*Exit.*

*Cres.* Will you walk in, my lord?

*Tro.* O Cressida, how often have I wished me thus!

*Cres.* Wished, my lord!—The gods grant, —O my lord!

*Tro.* What should they grant? what makes this pretty abruption? What too curious dreg espies my sweet lady in the fountain of our love?

*Cres.* More dregs than water, if my fears have eyes.

*Tro.* Fears make devils of cherubims; they never see truly.

*Cres.* Blind fear, that seeing reason leads, finds safer footing than blind reason stumbling without fear: to fear the worst oft cures the worse.

*Tro.* O, let my lady apprehend no fear: in all Cupid's pageant there is presented no monster.

*Cres.* Nor nothing monstrous neither?

*Tro.* Nothing, but our undertakings; when we vow to weep seas, live in fire, eat rocks, tame tigers; thinking it harder for our mistress to devise imposition enough than for us to undergo any difficulty imposed. This is the monstruosity in love, lady,—that the will is infinite, and the execution confined; that the desire is boundless, and the act a slave to limit.

*Cres.* They say, all lovers swear more performance than they are able, and yet reserve an ability that they never perform; vowing more than the perfection of ten, and discharging less than the tenth part of one. They that have the voice of lions and the act of hares, are they not monsters?

*Tro.* Are there such? such are not we: praise us as we are tasted, allow us as we prove; our head shall go bare till merit crown it; no perfection in reversion shall have a praise in present: we will not name desert before his birth; and, being born, his addition shall be humble. Few words to fair faith: Troilus shall be such to Cressid as what envy can say worst shall be a mock for his truth; and what truth can speak truest not truer than Troilus.

*Cres.* Will you walk in, my lord?

*Re-enter* PANDARUS.

*Pan.* What, blushing still? have you not done talking yet?

*Cres.* Well, uncle, what folly I commit, I dedicate to you.

*Pan.* I thank you for that: if my lord get a boy of you, you'll give him me. Be true to my lord: if he flinch, chide me for it.

*Tro.* You know now your hostages; your uncle's word and my firm faith.

*Pan.* Nay, I'll give my word for her too: our kindred, though they be long ere they are wooed, they are constant being won: they are burs, I can tell you; they'll stick where they are thrown.

*Cres.* Boldness comes to me now, and brings me heart:—     [day
Prince Troilus, I have lov'd you night and For many weary months.

*Tro.* Why was my Cressid, then, so hard to win?

*Cres.* Hard to seem won; but I was won, my lord,
With the first glance that ever—Pardon me,—
If I confess much, you will play the tyrant.

I love you now; but not, till now, so much
But I might master it:—in faith, I lie;
My thoughts were like unbridl'd children, grown     [fools!
Too headstrong for their mother:—see, we
Why have I blabb'd? who shall be true to us,
When we are so unsecret to ourselves?—
But, though I lov'd you well, I woo'd you not;
And yet, good faith, I wish'd myself a man,
Or that we women had men's privilege
Of speaking first. Sweet, bid me hold my tongue;
For, in this rapture, I shall surely speak
The thing I shall repent. See, see, your silence,     [draws
Cunning in dumbness, from my weakness
My very soul of conscience!—Stop my mouth.

*Tro.* And shall, albeit sweet music issues thence.

*Pan.* Pretty, i' faith.

*Cres.* My lord, I do beseech you, pardon me;
'Twas not my purpose thus to beg a kiss:
I am asham'd;—O heavens! what have I done?
For this time will I take my leave, my lord.

*Tro.* Your leave, sweet Cressid!

*Pan.* Leave! an you take leave till to-morrow morning,—

*Cres.* Pray you, content you.

*Tro.*     What offends you, lady?

*Cres.* Sir, mine own company.

*Tro.*     You cannot shun Yourself.

*Cres.* Let me go and try:
I have a kind of self resides with you;
But an unkind self, that itself will leave
To be another's fool. I would be gone:—
Where is my wit? I know not what I speak.

*Tro.* Well know they what they speak that speak so wisely.

*Cres.* Perchance, my lord, I show more craft than love;
And fell so roundly to a large confession,
To angle for your thoughts: but you are wise;     [love
Or else you love not; for to be wise and
Exceeds man's might; that dwells with gods above.     [woman,—

*Tro.* O that I thought it could be in a
As, if it can, I will presume in you,—
To feed for aye her lamp and flames of love;
To keep her constancy in plight and youth,
Outliving beauty's outward, with a mind
That doth renew swifter than blood decays!
Or, that persuasion could but thus convince me,—
That my integrity and truth to you     [weight
Might be affronted with the match and
Of such a winnow'd purity in love;
How were I then uplifted! but, alas!
I am as true as truth's simplicity

And simpler than the infancy of truth.

*Cres.* In that I'll war with you.

*Tro.*  O virtuous fight,
When right with right wars who shall be
  most right!  [come,
True swains in love shall, in the world to
Approve their truths by Troilus: when their
  rhymes,
Full of protest, of oath, and big compare,
Want similes, truth tir'd with iteration,—
As true as steel, as plantage to the moon,
As son to day, as turtle to her mate,
As iron to adamant, as earth to the centre,—
Yet, after all comparisons of truth,
As truth's authentic author to be cited,
As true as Troilus shall crown up the verse,
And sanctify the numbers.

*Cres.*  Prophet may you be!
If I be false, or swerve a hair from truth,
When time is old and hath forgot itself,
When waterdrops have worn the stones of
  Troy,
And blind oblivion swallow'd cities up,
And mighty states charácterless are grated
To dusty nothing; yet let memory
From false to false, among false maids in love,
Upbraid my falsehood! when they have said
  —as false
As air, as water, wind, or sandy earth,
As fox to lamb, as wolf to heifer's calf,
Pard to the hind, or stepdame to her son;
Yea, let them say, to stick the heart of false-
  hood,
As false as Cressid.

*Pan.* Go to, a bargain made: seal it, seal it;
I'll be the witness. Here I hold your hand;
here my cousin's. If ever you prove false one
to another, since I have taken such pains to
bring you together, let all pitiful goers-be-
tween be called to the world's end after my
name, call them all Pandars; let all constant
men be Troiluses, all false women Cressids,
and all brokers between Pandars! say, amen.

*Tro.* Amen.

*Cres.* Amen.

*Pan.* Amen. Whereupon I will show you a
chamber and a bed; which bed, because it
shall not speak of your pretty encounters,
press it to death: away!
And Cupid grant all tongue-tied maids here,
Bed, chamber, Pandar to provide this geer!
                                    [*Exeunt.*

SCENE III.—THE GRECIAN CAMP.

*Enter* AGAMEMNON, ULYSSES, DIOMEDES,
  NESTOR, AJAX, MENELAUS, *and* CALCHAS.

*Cal.* Now, princes, for the service I. have
  done you
The advantage of the time prompts me aloud
To call for recompense. Appear it to your
  mind  [Jove,
That, through the sight I bear in things to
I have abandon'd Troy, left my possession,

Incurr'd a traitor's name; expos'd myself,
From certain and possess'd conveniences,
To doubtful fortunes; sequest'ring from me
  all  [tion
That time, acquaintance, custom, and condi-
Made tame and most familiar to my nature;
And here, to do you service, am become
As new into the world, strange, unacquainted:
I do beseech you, as in way of taste,
To give me now a little benefit,
Out of those many register'd in promise,
Which, you say, live to come in my behalf.

*Agam.* What wouldst thou of us, Trojan?
  make demand.  [Antenor,

*Cal.* You have a Trojan prisoner, call'd
Yesterday took: Troy holds him very dear.
Oft have you,—often have you thanks there-
  fore,—
Desir'd my Cressid in right great exchange,
Whom Troy hath still denied: but this An-
  tenor,
I know, is such a wrest in their affairs
That their negotiations all must slack
Wanting his manage; and they will almost
Give us a prince of blood, a son of Priam,
In change of him: let him be sent, great prin-
  ces,  [ence
And he shall buy my daughter; and her pres-
Shall quite strike off all service I have done
In most accepted pain.

*Agam.*  Let Diomedes bear him,
And bring us Cressid hither: Calchas shall
  have
What he requests of us.—Good Diomed,
Furnish you fairly for this interchange:
Withal, bring word if Hector will to-morrow
Be answer'd in his challenge: Ajax is ready.

*Dio.* This shall I undertake; and 'tis a
  burden
Which I am proud to bear.
            [*Exeunt* DIOMEDES *and* CALCHAS.

*Enter* ACHILLES *and* PATROCLUS, *before
  their tent.*

*Ulyss.* Achilles stands i' the entrance of his
  tent:—
Please it our general to pass strangely by him,
As if he were forgot; and, princes all,
Lay negligent and loose regard upon him:
I will come last. 'Tis like he'll question me
Why such unplausive eyes are bent on him:
If so, I have derision med'cinable,  [pride,
To use between your strangeness and his
Which his own will shall have desire to drink:
It may do good: pride hath no other glass
To show itself but pride; for supple knees
Feed arrogance, and are the proud man's fees.

*Agam.* We'll execute your purpose, and
  put on
A form of strangeness as we pass along;—
So do each lord; and either greet him not,
Or else disdainfully, which shall shake him
  more
Than if not look'd on. I will lead the way.

*Achil.* What, comes the general to speak
with me?    [*Troy.*
You know my mind, I'll fight no more 'gainst
*Agam.* What says Achilles? would he aught
with us?    [*general?*
*Nest.* Would you, my lord, aught with the
*Achil.* No.
*Nest.* Nothing, my lord.
*Agam.* The better.
    [*Exeunt* AGAMEMNON *and* NESTOR.
*Achil.* Good day, good day.
*Men.* How do you? how do you?    [*Exit.*
*Achil.* What, does the cuckold scorn me?
*Ajax.* How now, Patroclus?
*Achil.* Good-morrow, Ajax.
*Ajax.* Ha?
*Achil.* Good-morrow.
*Ajax.* Ay, and good next day too.    [*Exit.*
*Achil.* What mean these fellows? Know
they not Achilles?    [us'd to bend,
*Patr.* They pass by strangely; they were
To send their smiles before them to Achilles;
To come as humbly as they us'd to creep
To holy altars.
*Achil.*        What, am I poor of late?
'Tis certain, greatness, once fallen out with
fortune,    [clin'd is,
Must fall out with men too. What the de-
He shall as soon read in the eyes of others
As feel on his own fall: for men, like butter-
flies    [mer;
Show not their mealy wings but to the sum-
And not a man, for being simply man,    [ours
Hath any honour; but honour for those hon-
That are without him, as place, riches, and
favour,
Prizes of accident as oft as merit:    [standers,
Which when they fall, as being slippery
The love that lean'd on them as slippery too,
Do one pluck down another, and together
Die in the fall. But 'tis not so with me:
Fortune and I are friends; I do enjoy
At ample point all that I did possess [find out
Save these men's looks; who do, methinks,
Something not worth in me such rich be-
holding
As they have often given. Here is Ulysses:
I'll interrupt his reading.—
How now, Ulysses!
*Ulyss.*        Now, great Thetis' son!
*Achil.* What are you reading?
*Ulyss.*        A strange fellow here
Writes me, That man,—how dearly ever
parted,
How much in having, or without or in,—
Cannot make boast to have that which he
hath,    [tion;
Nor feels not what he owes, but by reflec-
As when his virtues shining upon others
Heat them, and they retort that heat again
To the first giver.
*Achil.*        This is not strange, Ulysses.
The beauty that is borne here in the face
The bearer knows not, but commends itself

To others' eyes: nor doth the eye itself,—
That most pure spirit of sense,—behold itself,
Not going from itself; but eye to eye oppos'd:
Salutes each other with each other's form:
For speculation turns not to itself
Till it hath travell'd, and is mirror'd there
Where it may see itself. This is not strange
at all.
*Ulyss.* I do not strain at the position,—
It is familiar,—but at the author's drift;
Who, in his circumstance, expressly proves
That no man is the lord of anything,—
Though in and of him there be much con-
sisting,—
Till he communicate his parts to others;
Nor doth he of himself know them for aught
Till he behold them form'd in the applause
Where they're extended; who, like an arch,
reverberates
The voice again; or, like a gate of steel
Fronting the sun, receives and renders back
His figure and his heat. I was much rapt in
this;
And apprehended here immediately
The unknown Ajax.
Heavens, what a man is there! a very horse;
That has he knows not what. Nature, what
things there are
Most abject in regard and dear in use!
What things again most dear in the esteem
And poor in worth! Now shall we see to-
morrow    [him,
An act that very chance doth throw upon
Ajax renown'd. O heavens, what some men
do,
While some men leave to do!
How some men creep in skittish fortune's hall,
Whiles others play the idiots in her eyes!
How one man eats into another's pride,
While pride is fasting in his wantonness!
To see these Grecian lords!—why, even al-
ready
They clap the lubber Ajax on the shoulder
As if his foot were on brave Hector's breast,
And great Troy shrinking.
*Achil.* I do believe it; for they pass'd by
me
As misers do by beggars,—neither gave to me
Good word nor look. What, are my deeds
forgot?    [back,
*Ulyss.* Time hath, my lord, a wallet at his
Wherein he puts alms for oblivion,
A great-siz'd monster of ingratitudes:
Those scraps are good deeds past; which are
devour'd
As fast as they are made, forgot as soon
As done: perseverance, dear my lord,
Keeps honour bright: to have done is to hang
Quite out of fashion, like a rusty mail    [way;
In monumental mockery. Take the instant
For honour travels in a strait so narrow
Where one but goes abreast: keep, then, the
path;
For emulation hath a thousand sons

That one by one pursue: if you give way.
Or hedge aside from the direct forthright,
Like to an enter'd tide they all rush by.
And leave you hindmost;
Or, like a gallant horse fall'n in first rank,
Lie there for pavement to the abject rear,
O'er-run and trampl'd on: then what they do
　　　　　　　　　　in present, 　　　　[yours;
Though less than yours in past, must o'ertop
For time is like a fashionable host, 　[hand;
That slightly shakes his parting guest by the
And with his arms out-stretch'd, as he would
　　fly,
Grasps in the comer: welcome ever smiles,
And farewell goes out sighing. O, let not
　　virtue seek
Remuneration for the thing it was;
For beauty, wit,
High birth, vigour of bone, desert in service,
Love, friendship, charity, are subjects all
To envious and calumniating time. 　[kin,—
One touch of nature makes the whole world
That all, with one consent, praise new-born
　　gawds, 　　　　　　　　　　　[past;
Though they are made and moulded of things
And give to dust that is a little gilt 　　[eye
More laud than gilt o'er-dusted. The present
Praises the present object:
Then marvel not, thou great and cómplete
　　man,
That all the Greeks begin to worship Ajax;
Since things in motion sooner catch the eye
Than what not stirs. The cry went once on
　　thee,
And still it might; and yet it may again,
If thou wouldst not entomb thyself alive,
And case thy reputation in thy tent;
Whose glorious deeds but in these fields of
　　late
Made emulous missions 'mongst the gods
　　themselves,
And drave great Mars to faction.
　　*Achil.* 　　　　　　Of this my privacy
I have strong reasons.
　　*Ulyss.* 　　　　But 'gainst your privacy
The reasons are more potent and heroical:
'Tis known, Achilles, that you are in love
With one of Priam's daughters.
　　*Achil.* 　　　　　　　Ha! known!
　　*Ulyss.* Is that a wonder?
The providence that's in a watchful state
Knows almost every grain of Pluto's gold;
Finds bottom in the uncomprehensive deeps;
Keeps place with thought, and almost, like
　　the gods,
Does thoughts unveil in their dumb cradles.
There is a mystery—with whom relation
Durst never meddle—in the soul of state;
Which hath an operation more divine
Than breath or pen can give expressure to:
All the commérce that you have had with
　　Troy
As perfectly is ours as yours, my lord;
And better would it fit Achilles much

To throw down Hector than Polyxena:
But it must grieve young Pyrrhus now at
　　home,
When fame shall in our island sound her
　　trump;
And all the Greekish girls shall tripping sing,
*Great Hector's sister did Achilles win;*
*But our brave Ajax bravely beat down him.*
Farewell, my lord: I as your lover speak;
The fool slides o'er the ice that you should
　　break. 　　　　　　　　　　　　[*Exit.*
　　*Patr.* To this effect, Achilles, have I moved
　　　　you:
A woman impudent and mannish grown
Is not more loath'd than an effeminate man
In time of action. I stand condemn'd for this;
They think my little stomach to the war,
And your great love to me, restrains you
　　thus:
Sweet, rouse yourself; and the weak wanton
　　Cupid
Shall from your neck unloose his amorous
　　fold,
And, like a dew-drop from the lion's mane,
Be shook to air.
　　*Achil.* 　　　Shall Ajax fight with Hector?
　　*Patr.* Ay, and perhaps receive much hon-
　　　　our by him.
　　*Achil.* I see my reputation is at stake;
My fame is shrewdly gor'd.
　　*Patr.* 　　　　　　　O, then, beware;
Those wounds heal ill that men do give them-
　　selves;
Omission to do what is necessary
Seals a commission to a blank of danger;
And danger, like an ague, subtly taints
Even then when we sit idly in the sun.
　　*Achil.* Go call Thersites hither, sweet
　　　　Patroclus:
I'll send the fool to Ajax, and desire him
To invite the Trojan lords, after the combat,
To see us here unarm'd: I have a woman's
　　longing,
An appetite that I am sick withal,
To see great Hector in his weeds of peace;
To talk with him, and to behold his visage,
Even to my full of view. A labour sav'd!

　　　　　*Enter* THERSITES.

　　*Ther.* A wonder!
　　*Achil.* What?
　　*Ther.* Ajax goes up and down the field
asking for himself.
　　*Achil.* How so?
　　*Ther.* He must fight singly to-morrow with
Hector; and is so prophetically proud of an
heroical cudgelling that he raves in saying
nothing.
　　*Achil.* How can that be?
　　*Ther.* Why, he stalks up and down like a
peacock,—a stride and a stand: ruminates like
an hostess that hath no arithmetic but her
brain to set down her reckoning: bites his
lip with a politic regard, as who should say,

There were wit in this head, and 'twould out; and so there is; but it lies as coldly in him as fire in a flint, which will not show without knocking. The man's undone for ever; for if Hector break not his neck i' the combat, he'll break it himself in vain-glory. He knows not me: I said *Good-morrow, Ajax;* and he replies, *Thanks, Agamemnon.* What think you of this man, that takes me for the general? He is grown a very land fish, languageless, a monster. A plague of opinion! a man may wear it on both sides, like a leather jerkin.

*Achil.* Thou must be my ambassador to him, Thersites.

*Ther.* Who, I? why, he'll answer nobody; he professes not answering: speaking is for beggars; he wears his tongue in's arms. I will put on his presence: let Patroclus make demands to me, you shall see the pageant of Ajax.

*Achil.* To him, Patroclus: tell him,—I humbly desire the valiant Ajax to invite the most valorous Hector to come unarmed to my tent; and to procure safe conduct for his person of the magnanimous and most illustrious six-or-seven-times-honoured captain-general of the Grecian army, Agamemnon. Do this.

*Patr.* Jove bless great Ajax!

*Ther.* Hum!

*Patr.* I come from the worthy Achilles,—

*Ther.* Ha!

*Patr.* Who most humbly desires you to invite Hector to his tent,—

*Ther.* Hum!

*Patr.* And to procure safe conduct from Agamemnon.

*Ther.* Agamemnon!

*Patr.* Ay, my lord.

*Ther.* Ha!

*Patr.* What say yo to 't?

*Ther.* God be wi' you, with all my heart.

*Patr.* Your answer, sir.

*Ther.* If to-morrow be a fair day, by eleven o'clock it will go one way or other: howsoever, he shall pay for me ere he has me.

*Patr.* Your answer, sir.

*Ther.* Fare you well, with all my heart.

*Achil.* Why, but he is not in this tune, is he?

*Ther.* No, but he's out o' tune thus. What music will be in him when Hector has knocked out his brains I know not: but, I am sure, none; unless the fiddler Apollo get his sinews to make catlings on.

*Achil.* Come, thou shalt bear a letter to him straight.

*Ther.* Let me bear another to his horse; for that's the more capable creature.

*Achil.* My mind is troubl'd, like a fountain stirr'd;
And I myself see not the bottom of it.

[*Exeunt* ACHIL. *and* PATROCLUS.

*Ther.* Would the fountain of your mind were clear again, that I might water an ass at it! I had rather be a tick in a sheep than such a valiant ignorance. [*Exit.*

## ACT IV.

### SCENE I.—TROY. *A Street.*

*Enter, at one side,* ÆNEAS, *and* Servant *with a torch; at the other,* PARIS, DEIPHOBUS, ANTENOR, DIOMEDES, *and others, with torches.*

*Par.* See, ho! who's that there?

*Dei.* 'Tis the Lord Æneas.

*Æne.* Is the prince there in person?—
Had I so good occasion to lie long　[business
As you, Prince Paris, nothing but heavenly
Should rob my bed-mate of my company.

*Dio.* That's my mind too.—Good-morrow,
　　　Lord Æneas. 　　　[hand,—

*Par.* A valiant Greek, Æneas,—take his
Witness the process of your speech, wherein
You told how Diomed, a whole week by days,
Did haunt you in the field.

*Æne.* 　　　Health to you, valiant sir,
During all question of the gentle truce;
But when I meet you arm'd, as black defiance
As heart can think or courage execute.

*Dio.* The one and other Diomed embraces.
Our bloods are now in calm; and, so long,
　　　health;
But when contention and occasion meet,
By jove, I'll play the hunter for thy life
With all my force, pursuit, and policy.

*Æne.* And thou shalt hunt a lion, that will
　　　fly 　　　[ness,
With his face backward.—In humane gentle-
Welcome to Troy! now, by Anchises' life,
Welcome indeed! By Venus' hand I swear
No man alive can love, in such a sort,
The thing he means to kill, more excellently.

*Dio.* We sympathise.—Jove, let Æneas live
If to my sword his fate be not the glory,
A thousand cómplete courses of the sun!
But, in mine emulous honour, let him die,
With every joint a wound, and that to-mor-
　　　row!

*Æne.* We know each other well.

*Dio.* We do; and long to know each other worse.

*Par.* This is the most despiteful gentle greeting,
The noblest hateful love, that e'er I heard of.—
What business, lord, so early?

*Æne.* I was sent for to the king; but why,
　　　I know not. 　　　[this Greek

*Par.* His purpose meets you: 'twas to bring
To Calchas' house; and there to render him,
For the enfreed Antenor, the fair Cressid:
Let's have your company; or, if you please,
Haste there before us: I constantly do
　　　think,—
Or, rather, call my thought a certain knowl-
　　　edge,—

My brother Troilus lodges there to-night:
Rouse him, and give him note of our ap-
　proach,
With the whole quality wherefore: I fear
We shall be much unwelcome.
　*Æne.*　　　　　That I assure you:
Troilus had rather Troy were borne to Greece
Than Cressid borne from Troy.
　*Par.*　　　　　There is no help;
The bitter disposition of the time.
Will have it so. On, lord; we'll follow you.
　*Æne.* Good-morrow, all.
　　　　　　　[*Exit, with* Servant.
　*Par.* And tell me, noble Diomed,—faith,
　　tell me true,
Even in the soul of sound good-fellowship,—
Who, in your thoughts, merits fair Helen best,
Myself or Menelaus?
　*Dio.*　　　　　Both alike:
He merits well to have her, that doth seek
　her,—
Not making any scruple of her soilure,—
With such a hell of pain and world of charge;
And you as well to keep her, that defend
　her,—
Not palating the taste of her dishonour,—
With such a costly loss of wealth and friends:
He, like a puling cuckold, would drink up
The lees and dregs of a flat tamed piece;
You, like a lecher, out of whorish loins
Are pleas'd to breed out your inheritors:
Both merits pois'd, each weighs nor less nor
　more;
But he as he, each heavier for a whore.
　*Par.* You are too bitter to your country-
　　woman,
　*Dio.* She's bitter to her country. Hear me,
　　Paris:—
For every false drop in her bawdy veins
A Grecian's life hath sunk; for every scruple
Of her contaminated carrion weight　[speak,
A Trojan hath been slain: since she could
She hath not given so many good words
　breath
As for her Greeks and Trojans suffer'd death.
　*Par.* Fair Diomed, you do as chapmen do,
Dispraise the thing that you desire to buy:
But we in silence hold this virtue well.—
We'll not commend what we intend to sell.
Here lies our way.　　　　　[*Exeunt.*

SCENE II.—TROY. *Court of* PANDARUS'
*House.*

*Enter* TROILUS *and* CRESSIDA.

　*Tro.* Dear, trouble not yourself: the morn
　　is cold.　　　　　　[uncle down;
　*Cres.* Then, sweet my lord, I'll call mine
He shall unbolt the gates.
　*Tro.*　　　　　Trouble him not;
To bed, to bed: sleep kill those pretty eyes,
And give as soft attachment to thy senses
As infants empty of all thought!
　*Cres.*　　　　Good-morrow, then.
　*Tro.* I pr'ythee now, to bed.

　*Cres.*　　　　Are you aweary of me?
　*Tro.* O Cressida! but that the busy day,
Wak'd by the lark, hath rous'd the ribald
　crows,
And dreaming night will hide our joys no
　longer,
I would not from thee.
　*Cres.*　　　　Night hath been too brief.
　*Tro.* Beshrew the witch! with venomous
　　wights she stays
As tediously as hell; but flies the grasps of
　love
With wings more momentary-swift than
　thought.
You will catch cold, and curse me.
　*Cres.*　　　　　Pr'ythee, tarry;—
You men will never tarry.—
O foolish Cressid!—I might have still held
　off,
And then you would have tarried. Hark!
　there's one up.　　　　　[here?
　*Pan.* [*Within.*] What, 's all the doors open
　*Tro.* It is your uncle.　　　[mocking:
　*Cres.* A pestilence on him! now will he be
I shall have such a life!—

*Enter* PANDARUS.

　*Pan.* How now, how now? how go maid-
　　enheads?
—Here, you maid! where's my cousin Cres-
　sid?
　*Cres.* Go hang yourself, you naughty
　　mocking uncle!
You bring me to do, and then you flout me
　too.
　*Pan.* To do what? to do what?—let her
say what: what have I brought you to do?
　*Cres.* Come, come, beshrew your heart!
　　you'll ne'er be good,
Nor suffer others.
　*Pan.* Ha, ha! Alas, poor wretch! ah, poor
capocchia! hast not slept to-night? would he
not, a naughty man, let it sleep? a bugbear
take him!
　*Cres.* Did not I tell you?—would he were
　　knock'd i' the head!—　　[*Knocking.*
Who's that at door? good uncle, go and see.—
My lord, come you again into my chamber:
You smile, and mock me, as if I meant
　naughtily.
　*Tro.* Ha! ha!
　*Cres.* Come, you are deceiv'd, I think of no
　　such thing.—　　　　　[*Knocking.*
How earnestly they knock!—Pray you, come
in:
I would not for half Troy have you seen here.
　　　　　[*Exeunt* TROILUS *and* CRESSIDA.
　*Pan.* [*Going to the door.*] Who's there?
what's the matter? will you beat down the
door? How now? what's the matter?

*Enter* ÆNEAS.

　*Æne.* Good-morrow, lord, good-morrow.
　*Pan.* Who's there? my lord Æneas? By

my troth, I knew you not: what news with
you so early?

*Æne.* Is not Prince Troilus here?

*Pan.* Here! what should he do here?

*Æne.* Come, he is here, my lord; do not
deny him:
It doth import him much to speak with me.

*Pan.* Is he here, say you? 'tis more than I
know, I'll be sworn.—For my own part, I
came in late. What should he do here?

*Æne.* Who!—nay, then:—come, come,
you'll do him wrong ere you are ware: you'll
be so true to him to be false to him: do not
you know of him, but yet go fetch him
hither; go.

*As* PANDARUS *is going out, re-enter* TROILUS.

*Tro.* How now! what's the matter?

*Æne.* My lord, I scarce have leisure to
salute you,
My matter is so rash. There is at hand
Paris your brother, and Deiphobus,
The Grecian Diomed, and our Antenor
Deliver'd to us; and for him forthwith,
Ere the first sacrifice, within this hour,
We must give up to Diomedes' hand
The Lady Cressida.

*Tro.*                    Is it so concluded?

*Æne.* By Priam, and the general state of
Troy:
They are at hand, and ready to effect it.

*Tro.* How my achievements mock me!
I will go meet them:—and, my lord Æneas,
We met by chance; you did not find me here.

*Æne.* Good, good, my lord; the secrets of
nature
Have not more gift in taciturnity.
                    [*Exeunt* TROILUS *and* ÆNEAS.

*Pan.* Is't possible? no sooner got but lost?
The devil take Antenor! the young prince will
go mad: a plague upon Antenor! I would
they had broke 's neck!

### Re-enter CRESSIDA.

*Cres.* How now! what is the matter? who
was here?

*Pan.* Ah, ah!

*Cres.* Why sigh you so profoundly? where's
my lord?. gone! tell me, sweet uncle, what's
the matter?

*Pan.* Would I were as deep under the earth
as I am above!

*Cres.* O the gods! what's the matter?

*Pan.* Pr'ythee, get thee in. Would thou
hadst ne'er been born? I knew thou wouldst
be his death!—O, poor gentleman!—A plague
upon Antenor!

*Cres.* Good uncle, I beseech you, on my
knees I beseech you, what's the matter?

*Pan.* Thou must be gone, wench, thou
must be gone; thou art changed for Antenor:
thou must to thy father, and be gone from
Troilus: 'twill be his death; 'twill be his bane;
he cannot bear it.

*Cres.* O you immortal gods!—I will not go.

*Pan.* Thou must.

*Cres.* I will not, uncle: I have forgot my
father;
I know no touch of consanguinity;
No kin, no love, no blood, no soul so near me
As the sweet Troilus.—O you gods divine!
Make Cressid's name the very crown of false-
hood                              [death
If ever she leave Troilus! Time, force, and
Do to this body what extremes you can;
But the strong base and building of my love
Is as the very centre of the earth,
Drawing all things to it.—I'll go in and
weep,—

*Pan.* Do, do.

*Cres.* Tear my bright hair, and scratch my
praised cheeks;
Crack my clear voice with sobs, and break my
heart
With sounding Troilus. I will not go from
Troy.                              [*Exeunt.*

SCENE III.—TROY. *Street before* PANDARUS'
*House.*

*Enter* PARIS, TROILUS, ÆNEAS, DEIPHOBUS,
ANTENOR, *and* DIOMEDES.

*Par.* It is great morning; and the hour
prefix'd
Of her delivery to this valiant Greek
Comes fast upon:—good my brother Troilus,
Tell you the lady what she is to do,
And haste her to the purpose.

*Tro.*                    Walk in to her house;
I'll bring her to the Grecian presently:
And to his hand when I deliver her,
Think it an altar; and thy brother Troilus
A priest, there offering to it his own heart.
                              [*Exit.*

*Par.* I know what 'tis to love;
And would, as I shall pity, I could help!—
Please you walk in, my lords.          [*Exeunt.*

SCENE IV.—TROY. *A Room in* PANDARUS'
*House.*

*Enter* PANDARUS *and* CRESSIDA.

*Pan.* Be moderate, be moderate.

*Cres.* Why tell you me of moderation?
The grief is fine, full, perfect, that I taste,
And violenteth in a sense as strong          [it?
As that which causeth it: how can I moderate
If I could temporize with my affection,
Or brew it to a weak and colder palate,
The like allayment could I give my grief:
My love admits no qualifying dross;
No more my grief, in such a precious loss.

*Pan.* Here, here, here he comes.

### Enter TROILUS.

Ah, sweet ducks!

*Cres.* O Troilus! Troilus! [*Embracing him.*

*Pan.* What a pair of spectacles is here! Let

me embrace too. *O heart,* as the goodly saying is,—

> O heart, heavy heart,
> Why sigh'st thou without breaking?

where he answers again,

> Because thou canst not ease thy smart
> By silence nor by speaking.

There was never a truer rhyme. Let us cast away nothing, for we may live to have need of such a verse: we see it, we see it.—How now, lambs!                              [purity

*Tro.* Cressid, I love thee in so strain'd a
That the bless'd gods,—as angry with my fancy,
More bright in zeal than the devotion which
Cold lips blow to their deities,—take thee from me.

*Cres.* Have the gods envy?

*Pan.* Ay, ay, ay, ay; 'tis too plain a case.

*Cres.* And is it true that I must go from Troy?

*Tro.* A hateful truth.

*Cres.*          What, and from Troilus too?

*Tro.* From Troy and Troilus.

*Cres.*                    Is it possible?

*Tro.* And suddenly; where injury of chance
Puts back leave-taking, justles roughly by
All time of pause, rudely beguiles our lips
Of all rejoindure, forcibly prevents
Our lock'd embrasures, strangles our dear vows
Even in the birth of our own lab'ring breath;
We two, that with so many thousand sighs
Did buy each other, must poorly sell ourselves
With the rude brevity and discharge of one.
Injurious time now, with a robber's haste,
Crams his rich thievery up, he knows not how:
As many farewells as be stars in heaven,
With distinct breath and consign'd kisses to them,
He fumbles up into a loose adieu;
And scants us with a single famish'd kiss,
Distasted with the salt of broken tears.

*Æne.* [*Within.*] My lord, is the lady ready?

*Tro.* Hark! you are call'd. Some say the Genius so
Cries, *Come!* to him that instantly must die.—
Bid them have patience; she shall come anon.

*Pan.* Where are my tears? rain, to lay this wind, or my heart will be blown up by the root?                              [*Exit.*

*Cres.* I must, then, to the Grecians?

*Tro.*                    No remedy.

*Cres.* A woeful Cressid 'mongst the merry Greeks!
When shall we see again?

*Tro.* Hear me, my love. Be thou but true of heart,—                              [is this?

*Cres.* I true! how now! what wicked deem

*Tro.* Nay, we must use expostulation kindly,
For it is parting from us:
I speak not *be thou true,* as fearing thee;
For I will throw my glove to death himself
That there's no maculation in thy heart:
But *be thou true,* say I, to fashion in
My sequent protestation; be thou true,
And I will see thee.                              [dangers

*Cres.* O, you shall be expos'd, my lord, to
As infinite as imminent! but I'll be true.

*Tro.* And I'll grow friend with danger.
Wear this sleeve.                              [see you?

*Cres.* And you this glove. When shall I

*Tro.* I will corrupt the Grecian sentinels,
To give thee nightly visitation.
But yet be true.

*Cres.*          O heavens!—be true, again!

*Tro.* Hear why I speak it, love:
The Grecian youths are full of quality;
They're loving, well compos'd, with gifts of nature flowing,
And swelling o'er with arts and exercise:
How novelty·may move, and parts with person,
Alas, a kind of godly jealousy,—
Which, I beseech you, call a virtuous sin,—
Makes me afeared.

*Cres.*          O heavens! you love me not.

*Tro.* Die I a villain, then!
In this I do not call your faith in question
So mainly as my merit; I cannot sing,
Nor heel the high lavolt, nor sweeten talk,
Nor play at subtle games; fair virtues all,
To which the Grecians are most prompt and pregnant:
But I can tell, that in each grace of these
There lurks a still and dumb-discoursive devil
That tempts most cunningly: but be not tempted.

*Cres.* Do you think I will?

*Tro.* No.
But something may be done that we will not:
And sometimes we are devils to ourselves,
When we will tempt the frailty of our powers,
Presuming on their changeful potency.

*Æne.* [*Within.*] Nay, good my lord,—

*Tro.* Come, kiss; and let us part.

*Par.* [*Within.*] Brother Troilus!

*Tro.*          Good brother, come you hither;
And bring Æneas and the Grecian with you.

*Cres.* My lord, will you be true?

*Tro.* Who, I? alas, it is my vice, my fault:
While others fish with craft for great opinion,
I with great truth catch mere simplicity;
Whilst some with cunning gild their copper crowns,
With truth and plainness I do wear mine bare.
Fear not my truth: the moral of my wit
Is—plain and true; there's all the reach of it.

*Enter* ÆNEAS, PARIS, ANTENOR, DEIPHOBUS, *and* DIOMEDES.

Welcome, Sir Diomed! here is the lady

Which for Antenor we deliver you:
At the port, lord, I'll give her to thy hand;
And by the way posses thee what she is.
Entreat her fair; and, by my soul, fair Greek,
If e'er thou stand at mercy of my sword,
Name Cressid, and thy life shall be as safe
As Priam is in Ilion.

*Dio.* Fair Lady Cressid,
So please you, save the thanks this prince
    expects:
The lustre in your eye, heaven in your cheek,
Pleads your fair usage; and to Diomed
You shall be mistress, and command him
    wholly. [eously,

*Tro.* Grecian, thou dost not use me court-
To shame the zeal of my petition to thee
In praising her: I tell thee, lord of Greece,
She is as far high-soaring o'er thy praises
As thou unworthy to be call'd her servant.
I charge thee use her well, even for my
    charge;
For, by the dreadful Pluto, if thou dost not,
Though the great bulk Achilles be thy guard,
I'll cut thy throat.

*Dio.* O, be not mov'd, Prince Troilus:
Let me be privileg'd by my place and mes-
    sage
To be a speaker free; when I am hence
I'll answer to my lust: and know you, lord,
I'll nothing do on charge: to her own worth
She shall be priz'd; but that you say, be 't so,
I'll speak it in my spirit and honour, no.

*Tro.* Come, to the port.—I'll tell thee,
    Diomed, [head.—
This brave shall oft make thee to hide thy
Lady, give me your hand; and, as we walk,
To our own selves bend we our needful talk.
    [*Exeunt* TRO., CRES., *and* DIOMEDES.
        [*Trumpet within.*

*Par.* Hark! Hector's trumpet.

*Æne.* How have we spent this morning?
The prince must think me tardy and remiss,
That swore to ride before him to the field.

*Par.* 'Tis Troilus' fault. Come, come, to
    field with him.

*Dio.* Let us make ready straight.

*Æne.* Yea, with a bridegroom's fresh
    alacrity
Let us address to tend on Hector's heels:
The glory of our Troy doth this day lie
On his fair worth and single chivalry.
        [*Exeunt.*

SCENE V.—THE GRECIAN CAMP. *Lists set out.*

*Enter* AJAX, *armed;* AGAMEMNON, ACHILLES,
PATROCLUS, MENELAUS, ULYSSES, NESTOR,
*and others.*

*Agam.* Here art thou in appointment fresh
    and fair,
Anticipating time. With starting courage
Give with thy trumpet a loud note to Troy,
Thou dreadful Ajax; that the appalled air
May pierce the head of the great combatant,
And hale him hither.

*Ajax.* Thou, trumpet, there's my purse,
Now crack thy lungs and split thy brazen
    pipe:
Blow, villain, till thy sphered bias cheek
Out-swell the colic of puff'd Aquilon:
Come, stretch thy chest, and let thy eyes
    spout blood;
Thou blow'st for Hector. [*Trumpet sounds.*

*Ulyss.* No trumpet answers.

*Achil.* 'Tis but early day.

*Agam.* Is not yon Diomed, with Calchas'
    daughter?

*Ulyss.* 'Tis he, I ken the manner of his gait;
He rises on the toe: that spirit of his
In aspiration lifts him from the earth.

*Enter* DIOMEDES, *with* CRESSIDA.

*Agam.* Is this the lady Cressid?

*Dio.* Even she?

*Agam.* Most dearly welcome to the Greeks,
    sweet lady.

*Nest.* Our general doth salute you with a
    kiss.

*Ulyss.* Yet is the kindness but particular;
'Twere better she were kiss'd in general.

*Nest.* And very courtly counsel: I'll be-
    gin.—
So much for Nestor.

*Achil.* I'll take that winter from your lips,
    fair lady.
Achilles bids you welcome.

*Men.* I had good argument for kissing once.

*Patr.* But that's no argument for kissing
    now;
For thus popp'd Paris in his hardiment,
And parted thus you and your argument.

*Ulyss.* O deadly gall, and theme of all our
    scorns!
For which we lose our heads to gild his horns.

*Patr.* The first was Menelaus' kiss;—this
    mine;
Patroclus kisses you.

*Men.* O, this is trim!

*Patr.* Paris and I kiss evermore for him.

*Men.* I'll have my kiss, sir.—Lady, by your
    leave.

*Cres.* In kissing, do you render or receive?

*Patr.* Both take and give.

*Cres.* I'll make my match to live,
The kiss you take is better than you give;
Therefore no kiss.

*Men.* I'll give you boot, I'll give you three
    for one. [none.

*Cres.* You're an odd man; give even or give

*Men.* An odd man, lady? every man is odd.

*Cres.* No, Paris is not; for, you know, 'tis
    true,
That you are odd, and he is even with you.

*Men.* You fillip me o' the head.

*Cres.* No, I'll be sworn.

*Ulyss.* It were no match, your nail against
    his horn.—
May I, sweet lady, beg a kiss of you?

*Cres.* You may.

*Ulyss.*                          I do desire it.
*Cres.*                        Why, beg then, do.
*Ulyss.* Why then, for Venus' sake, give me
a kiss
When Helen is a maid again, and his.
*Cres.* I am your debtor, claim it when 'tis
due.                                    [you.
*Ulyss.* Never's my day, and then a kiss of
*Dio.* Lady, a word.—I'll bring you to your
father.

     [DIOMEDES *leads out* CRESSIDA.

*Nest.* A woman of quick sense.
*Ulyss.*                        Fie, fie upon her!
There's language in her eye, her cheek, her
   lip,
Nay, her foot speaks: her wanton spirits look
   out
At every joint and motive of her body.
O, these encounterers, so glib of tongue,
That give a coasting welcome ere it comes,
And wide unclasp the tables of their thoughts
To every ticklish reader! set them down
For sluttish spoils of opportunity,
And daughters of the game. [*Trumpet within.*
*All.* The Trojans' trumpet.
*Agam.*                  Yonder comes the troop.

Enter HECTOR, *armed;* ÆNEAS, TROILUS, *and*
*other* Trojans, *with* Attendants.

  *Æne.* Hail, all you state of Greece! what
    shall be done               [purpose
To him that victory commands? Or do you
A victor shall be known? will you the knights
Shall to the edge of all extremity
Pursue each other: or shall be divided
By any voice or order of the field?
Hector bade ask.
  *Agam.* Which way would Hector have it?
*Æne.* He cares not; he'll obey conditions.
*Achil.* 'Tis done like Hector; but securely
   done,
A little proudly, and great deal misprizing
The knight oppos'd.
  *Æne.*             If not Achilles, sir,
What is your name?
  *Achil.*            If not Achilles, nothing.
*Æne.* Therefore Achilles. But, whate'er,
   know this:—
In the extremity of great and little
Valour and pride excel themselves in Hector;
The one almost as infinite as all,
The other blank as nothing. Weigh him well,
And that which looks like pride is courtesy.
This Ajax is half made of Hector's blood:
In love whereof, half Hector stays at home;
Half heart, half hand, half Hector comes to
   seek                          [Greek.
This blended knight, half Trojan and half
  *Achil.* A maiden battle then?—O, I per-
ceive you.

     *Re-enter* DIOMEDES.

  *Agam.* Here is Sir Diomed.—Go, gentle
knight,

Stand by our Ajax; as you and Lord Æneas
Consent upon the order of their fight
So be it; either to the uttermost,
Or else a breath: the combatants being kin
Half stints their strife before their strokes
   begin.

    [AJAX *and* HECTOR *enter the lists.*
*Ulyss.* They are oppos'd already.
*Agam.* What Trojan is that same that
   looks so heavy?               [knight;
*Ulyss.* The youngest son of Priam, a true
Not yet mature, yet matchless: firm of word;
Speaking in deeds, and deedless in his tongue;
Not soon provok'd, nor, being provok'd, soon
   calm'd;
His heart and hand both open and both free;
For what he has he gives, what thinks he
   shows;
Yet gives he not till judgment guide his
   bounty,
Nor dignifies an impure thought with breath:
Manly as Hector, but more dangerous;
For Hector, in his blaze of wrath, subscribes
To tender objects; but he, in heat of action,
Is more vindicative than jealous love:
They call him Troilus; and on him erect
A second hope, as fairly built as Hector.
Thus says Æneas; one that knows the youth
Even to his inches, and, with private soul,
Did in great Ilion thus translate him to me.

    [*Alarum.* HECTOR *and* AJAX *fight.*
*Agam.* They are in action.
*Nest.* Now, Ajax, hold thine own!
*Tro.*                        Hector, thou sleep'st;
Awake thee!                            [Ajax!
  *Agam.* His blows are well dispos'd:—there,
*Dio.* You must no more. [*Trumpets cease.*
*Æne.* Princes, enough, so please you.
*Ajax.* I am not warm yet, let us fight again.
*Dio.* As Hector pleases.
  *Hect.*            Why, then will I no more:—
Thou art, great lord, my father's sister's son,
A cousin-german to great Priam's seed;
The obligation of our blood forbids
A gory emulation 'twixt us twain;
Were thy commixtion Greek and Trojan so,
That thou could'st say *This hand is Grecian*
   *all,*
*And this is Trojan; the sinews of this leg*
*All Greek, and this all Troy; my mother's*
   *blood*
*Runs on the dexter cheek, and this sinister*
*Bounds-in my father's; by Jove multipotent,*
Thou shouldst not bear from me a Greekish
   member
Wherein my sword had not impressure made
Of our rank feud: but the just gods gainsay
That any drop thou borrow'dst from thy
   mother,
My sacred aunt, should by my mortal sword
Be drain'd! Let me embrace thee, Ajax:
By him that thunders, thou hast lusty arms;
Hector would have them fall upon him thus:
Cousin, all honour to thee!

*Ajax.*                    I thank thee, Hector:
Thou art too gentle and too free a man:
I came to kill thee, cousin, and bear hence
A great addition earned in thy death.
*Hect.* Not Neoptolemus so mirable,—
On whose bright crest Fame with her loud'st
    Oyes
Cries, *This is he,*—could promise to himself
A thought of added honour torn from Hector.
*Æne.* There is expectance here from both
    the sides
What further you will do.
*Hect.*                    We'll answer it;
The issue is embracement:—Ajax, farewell.
*Ajax.* If I might in entreaties find suc-
    cess,—
As seld' I have the chance,—I would desire
My famous cousin to our Grecian tents.
*Dio.* 'Tis Agamemnon's wish; and great
    Achilles
Doth long to see unarm'd the valiant Hector.
*Hect.* Æneas, call my brother Troilus to
    me:
And signify this loving interview
To the expecters of our Trojan part;
Desire them home.—Give me thy hand, my
    cousin;
I will go eat with thee, and see your knights.
*Ajax.* Great Agamemnon comes to meet us
    here.                              [by name;
*Hect.* The worthiest of them tell me name
But for Achilles, mine own searching eyes
Shall find him by his large and portly size.
*Agam.* Worthy of arms! as welcome as to
    one
That would be rid of such an enemy;
But that's no welcome: understand more
    clear,
What's past and what's to come is strew'd
    with husks
And formless ruin of oblivion;
But in this extant moment, faith and troth,
Strain'd purely from all hollow bias-drawing,
Bids thee, with most divine integrity,
From heart of very heart, great Hector, wel-
    come.
*Hect.* I thank thee, most imperious Aga-
    memnon.                           [to you.
*Agam.* My well-fam'd lord of Troy, no less
                              [*To* TROILUS.
*Men.* Let me confirm my princely brother's
    greeting;—
You brace of warlike brothers, welcome
    hither.
*Hect.* Who must we answer?
*Æne.*                    The noble Menelaus.
*Hect.* O you, my lord? by Mars his gaunt-
    let, thanks!
Mock not, that I affect the untraded oath;
Your *quondam* wife swears still by Venus'
    glove:
She's well, but bade me not commend her to
    you.                              [theme.
*Men.* Name her not now, sir; she's a deadly

*Hect.* O, pardon; I offend.          [oft,
*Nest.* I have, thou gallant Trojan, seen thee
Labouring for destiny, make cruel way
Through ranks of Greekish youth; and I
    have seen thee,
As hot as Perseus, spur thy Phrygian steed,
Despising many forfeits and subduements,
When thou hast hung thy advanced sword i'
    the air,
Not letting it decline on the declin'd,
That I have said to some my standers-by,
*Lo, Jupiter is yonder, dealing life!*
And I have seen thee pause, and take thy
    breath,
When that a ring of Greeks have hemm'd
    thee in,
Like an Olympian wrestling: this have I
    seen;
But this thy countenance, still lock'd in steel,
I never saw till now. I knew thy grandsire,
And once fought with him: he was a soldier
    good;
But, by great Mars, the captain of us all,
Never like thee. Let an old man embrace
    thee;
And, worthy warrior, welcome to our tents.
*Æne.* 'Tis the old Nestor.
*Hect.* Let me embrace thee, good old
    chronicle,
That hast so long walk'd hand in hand with
    time:—
Most reverend Nestor, I am glad to clasp thee.
*Nest.* I would my arms could match thee in
    contention,
As they contend with thee in courtesy.
*Hect.* I would they could.
*Nest.* Ha!
By this white beard, I'd fight with thee to-
    morrow:—
Well, welcome, welcome! I have seen the
    time.
*Ulyss.* I wonder now how yonder city
    stands,
When we have here her base and pillar by us.
*Hect.* I know your favour, Lord Ulysses,
    well.
Ah, sir, there's many a Greek and Trojan
    dead,
Since first I saw yourself and Diomed
In Ilion, on your Greekish embassy. [ensue:
*Ulyss.* Sir, I foretold you then what would
My prophecy is but half his journey yet;
For yonder walls, that pertly front your
    town,
Yond towers, whose wanton tops do buss the
    clouds,
Must kiss their own feet.
*Hect.*              I must not believe you:
There they stand yet; and modestly I think
The fall of every Phrygian stone will cost
A drop of Grecian blood: the end crowns all;
And that old common arbitrator, time,
Will one day end it.
*Ulyss.*            So to him we leave it

Most gentle and most valiant Hector, wel-
come:
After the general, I beseech you next
To feast with me, and see me at my tent.
  *Achil.* I shall forestall thee, Lord Ulysses,
    thou!—
Now, Hector, I have fed mine eyes on thee;
I have with exact view perus'd thee, Hector,
And quoted joint by joint.
  *Hect.*             Is this Achilles?
  *Achil.* I am Achilles.       [on thee.
  *Hect.* Stand fair, I pray thee: let me look
  *Achil.* Behold thy fill.
  *Hect.*       Nay, I have done already.
  *Achil.* Thou art too brief: I will the second
    time,
As I would buy thee, view thee limb by limb.
  *Hect.* O, like a book of sport thou'lt read
    me o'er;
But there's more in me than thou under-
    stand'st.
Why dost thou so oppress me with thine eye?
  *Achil.* Tell me, you heavens, in which part
    of his body         [or there,
Shall I destroy him? whither there, or there,
That I may give the local wound a name,
And make distinct the very breach whereout
Hector's great spirit flew: answer me, heav-
    ens!             [proud man,
  *Hect.* It would discredit the bless'd gods,
To answer such a question: stand again:
Think'st thou to catch my life so pleasantly,
As to prenominate in nice conjecture
Where thou wilt hit me dead?
  *Achil.*          I tell thee, yea.
  *Hect.* Wert thou an oracle to tell me so,
I'd not believe thee. Henceforth guard thee
    well;
For I'll not kill thee there, nor there, nor
    there;
But, by the forge that stithied Mars his helm,
I'll kill thee everywhere, yea, o'er and o'er.—
You wisest Grecians, pardon me this brag,
His insolence draws folly from my lips;
But I'll endeavour deeds to match these
    words,
Or may I never,—
  *Ajax.*      Do not chafe thee, cousin:—
And you, Achilles, let these threats alone,
Till accident or purpose bring you to't:
You may have every day enough of Hector,
If you have stomach; the general state, I fear,
Can scarce entreat you to be odd with him.
  *Hect.* I pray you, let us see you in the field:
We have had pelting wars since you refus'd
The Grecians' cause.
  *Achil.*      Dost thou entreat me, Hector?
To-morrow do I meet thee, fell as death;
To-night all friends.
  *Hect.*      Thy hand upon that match.
  *Agam.* First, all you peers of Greece, go to
    my tent;
There in the full convive we: afterwards,
As Hector's leisure and your bounties shall

Concur together, severally entreat him.—
Beat loud the tabourines, let the trumpets
    blow,
That this great soldier may his welcome know.
        [*Exeunt all but* TRO. *and* ULYSSES.
  *Tro.* My Lord Ulysses, tell me, I beseech
    you,
In what place of the field doth Calchas keep?
  *Ulyss.* At Menelaus' tent, most princely
    Troilus:
There Diomed doth feast with him to-night;
Who neither looks upon the heaven nor earth,
But gives all gaze and bent of amorous view
On the fair Cressid.
  *Tro.* Shall I, sweet lord, be bound to you
    so much,
After we part from Agamemnon's tent,
To bring me thither?
  *Ulyss.*      You shall command me, sir.
As gentle tell me, of what honour was
This Cressida in Troy? Had she no lover there
That wails her absence?
  *Tro.* O, sir, to such as boasting show their
    scars
A mock is due. Will you walk on, my lord?
She was belov'd, she lov'd; she is, and doth:
But, still, sweet love is food for fortune's
    tooth.              [*Exeunt.*

## ACT V.

SCENE I.—THE GRECIAN CAMP. *Before*
ACHILLES' *Tent.*

*Enter* ACHILLES *and* PATROCLUS.

  *Achil.* I'll heat his blood with Greekish
    wine to-night.
Which with my scimitar I'll cool to-mor-
    row.—
Patroclus, let us feast him to the height.
  *Patr.* Here comes Thersites.

*Enter* THERSITES.

  *Achil.*       How now, thou core of envy!
Thou crusty batch of nature, what's the
    news?
  *Ther.* Why, thou picture of what thou
seemest, and idol of idiot worshippers, here's
a letter for thee.
  *Achil.* From whence, fragment?
  *Ther.* Why, thou full dish of fool, from
    Troy.
  *Patr.* Who keeps the tent now?    [wound.
  *Ther.* The surgeon's box, or the patient's
  *Patr.* Well said Adversity! and what need
these tricks?
  *Ther.* Pr'ythee, be silent, boy; I profit not
by thy talk; thou art thought to be Achilles'
male varlet.
  *Patr.* Male varlet, you rogue! what's that?
  *Ther.* Why, his masculine whore. Now, the
rotten diseases of the south, the guts griping,
ruptures, catarrhs, loads o' gravel i' the back,
lethargies, cold palsies, raw eyes, dirt-rotten
livers, wheezing lungs, bladders full of im-

posthume, sciaticas, limekilns i' the palm,
incurable bone-ache, and the rivelled fee-
simple of the tetter, take and take again such
preposterous discoveries!

*Patr.* Why, thou damnable box of envy,
thou, what meanest thou to curse thus?

*Ther.* Do I curse thee?

*Patr.* Why, no, you ruinous butt; you
whoreson indistinguishable cur, no.

*Ther.* No! why art thou, then exasperate,
thou idle immaterial skein of sleave-silk, thou
greene sarcenet flap for a sore eye, thou tassel
of a prodigal's purse, thou? Ah, how the poor
world is pestered with such water-flies,—
diminutives of nature!

*Patr.* Out, gall!

*Ther.* Finch egg!        [quite

*Achil.* My sweet Patroclus, I am thwarted
From my great purpose in to-morrow's battle.
Here is a letter from Queen Hecuba;
A token from her daughter, my fair love;
Both taxing me and gaging me to keep
An oath that I have sworn. I will not break
it:
Fall, Greeks; fail, fame; honour; or go or
stay;
My major vow lies here, this I'll obey.—
Come, come, Thersites, help to trim my tent;
This night in banqueting must all be spent.—
Away, Patroclus!

        [*Exeunt* ACHIL. *and* PATR.

*Ther.* With too much blood and too little
brain these two may run man; but, if with
too much brain and too little blood they do,
I'll be a curer of madmen. Here's Agamemnon,—an honest fellow enough, and one that
loves quails; but he has not so much brain as
ear-wax: and the goodly transformation of
Jupiter there, his brother, the bull,—the primitive statue, and oblique memorial of cuckolds; a thrifty shoeing-horn in a chain, hanging at his brother's leg,—to what form, but
that he is, should wit larded with malice, and
malice forced with wit, turn him to? To an
ass, were nothing; he is both ass and ox: to
an ox, were nothing; he is both ox and ass.
To be a dog, a mule, a cat, a fitchew, a toad,
a lizard, an owl, a puttock, or a herring without a roe, I would not care; but to be Menelaus,—I would conspire against destiny. Ask
me not what I would be, if I were not Thersites; for I care not to be the louse of a lazar,
so I were not Menelaus.—Hoy-day! spirits
and fires!

*Enter* HECTOR, TROILUS, AJAX, AGAMEMNON,
ULYSSES, NESTOR, MENELAUS, *and* DIOM-
EDES, *with lights.*

*Agam.* We go wrong, we go wrong.

*Ajax.*                No, yonder 'tis;
There, where we see the lights.

*Hect.*                I trouble you.

*Ajax.* No, not a whit.

*Ulyss.* Here comes himself to guide you.

*Re-enter* ACHILLES.

*Achil.* Welcome, brave Hector; welcome,
princes all.        [good night.

*Agam.* So now, fair prince of Troy, I bid
Ajax commands the guard to tend on you.

*Hect.* Thanks, and good night to the
Greeks' general.

*Men.* Good-night, my lord.

*Hect.* Good-night, sweet Lord Menelaus.

*Ther.* Sweet draught: sweet, quoth'a!
sweet sink, sweet sewer.

*Achil.* Good-night        [or tarry.
And welcome, both at once, to those that go

*Agam.* Good-night.

        [*Exeunt* AGAM. *and* MEN.

*Achil.* Old Nestor tarries; and you too,
Diomed,
Keep Hector company an hour or two.

*Dio.* I cannot, lord; I have important
business,        [Hector.
The tide whereof is now.—Good-night, great

*Hect.* Give me your hand.        [tent;

*Ulyss.* Follow his torch; he goes to Calchas'
I'll keep you company.        [*Aside to* TROILUS.

*Tro.*        Sweet sir, you honour me.

*Hect.* And so good-night.

        [*Exit* DIO.; ULYSS. *and* TRO. *following.*

*Achil.* Come, come, enter my tent.

        [*Exeunt* ACHIL., HECT., AJAX, *and* NEST.

*Ther.* That same Diomed's a false-hearted
rogue, a most unjust knave; I will no more
trust him when he leers than I will a serpent
when he hisses: he will spend his mouth and
promise, like Brabbler the hound; but when
he performs astronomers foretell it; it is
prodigious, there will come some change; the
sun borrows of the moon when Diomed keeps
his word. I will rather leave to see Hector
than not to dog him: they say he keeps a
Trojan drab, and uses the traitor Calchas'
tent: I'll after.—Nothing but lechery! all incontinent varlets!        [*Exit.*

SCENE II.—THE GRECIAN CAMP. *Before*
CALCHAS' *Tent.*

*Enter* DIOMEDES.

*Dio.* What, are you up here, ho? speak.

*Cal.* [*Within.*] Who calls?

*Dio.* Diomed—Calchas, I think.—Where's
your daughter?

*Cal.* [*Within.*] She comes to you.

*Enter* TROILUS *and* ULYSSES, *at a distance;*
*after them* THERSITES.

*Ulyss.* Stand where the torch may not discover us.

*Enter* CRESSIDA.

*Tro.* Cressid comes forth to him.

*Dio.*                How now, my charge!

*Cres.* Now, my sweet guardian!—Hark, a
word with you.        [*Whispers.*

*Tro.* Yea, so familiar!

*Ulyss.* She will sing any man at first sight.

*Ther.* And any man may sing her, if he can take her cliff; she's noted.

*Dio.* Will you remember?

*Cres.*                    Remember? yes.

*Dio.*                    Nay, but do, then;
And let your mind be coupled with your words.

*Tro.* What should she remember?

*Ulyss.* List!                    [more to folly.

*Cres.* Sweet honey Greek, tempt me no

*Ther.* Roguery!

*Dio.* Nay, then,—

*Cres.*                    I'll tell you what,—

*Dio.* Pho, pho! come, tell a pin: you are forsworn.                    [have me do?

*Cres.* In faith, I cannot: what would you

*Ther.* A juggling trick, to be secretly open.

*Dio.* What did you swear you would bestow on me?

*Cres.* I pr'ythee, do not hold me to mine oath;
Bid me do anything but that, sweet Greek.

*Dio.* Good-night.

*Tro.*                    Hold, patience!

*Ulyss.*                    How now, Trojan!

*Cres.*                    Diomed,—

*Dio.* No, no, good-night: I'll be your fool no more.

*Tro.* Thy better must.

*Cres.*                    Hark! one word in your ear.

*Tro.* O' plague and madness!    [I pray you,

*Ulyss.* You are mov'd, prince; let us depart,
Lest your displeasure should enlarge itself
To wrathful terms: this place is dangerous;
The time right deadly; I beseech you, go.

*Tro.* Behold, I pray you!

*Ulyss.*                    Nay, good my lord, go off:
You flow to great destruction; come, my lord.

*Tro.* I pray thee, stay.

*Ulyss.*                    You have not patience; come.

*Tro.* I pray you, stay; by hell and all hell's torments,
I will not speak a word.

*Dio.*                    And so, good-night.

*Cres.* Nay, but you part in anger.

*Tro.*                    Doth that grieve thee?
O wither'd truth!

*Ulyss.*          Why, how now, lord?

*Tro.*                    By Jove,
I will be patient.

*Cres.*          Guardian!—why, Greek!

*Dio.* Pho, pho! adieu; you palter.

*Cres.* In faith, I do not: come hither once again.                    [will you go?

*Ulyss.* You shake, my lord, at something:
You will break out.

*Tro.*          She strokes his cheek!

*Ulyss.*                    Come, come.

*Tro.* Nay, stay; by Jove, I will not speak a word:
There is between my will and all offences
A guard of patience:—stay a little while.

*Ther.* How the devil luxury, with his fat rump and potato finger, tickles these together
Fry, lechery, fry!

*Dio.* But will you, then?

*Cres.* In faith, I will, la; never trust me else.

*Dio.* Give me some token for the surety of it.

*Cres.* I'll fetch you one.                    [*Exit.*

*Ulyss.* You have sworn patience.

*Tro.*                    Fear me not, sweet lord;
I will not be myself, nor have cognition
Of what I feel: I am all patience.

### *Re-enter* CRESSIDA.

*Ther.* Now the pledge; now, now, now!

*Cres.* Here, Diomed, keep this sleeve.

*Tro.* O, beauty! where's thy faith?

*Ulyss.*                    My lord,—

*Tro.* I will be patient; outwardly I will.

*Cres.* You look upon that sleeve; behold it well.—
He lov'd me—O false wench!—Give't me again.

*Dio.* Whose was't?

*Cres.* It is no matter, now I have't again.
I will not meet with you to-morrow night:
I pr'ythee, Diomed, visit me no more. [stone.

*Ther.* Now she sharpens:—Well said, Whet-

*Dio.* I shall have it.

*Cres.*                    What, this?

*Dio.*                    Ay, that.

*Cres.* O, all you gods?—O pretty, pretty pledge!
Thy master now lies thinking in his bed
Of thee and me; and sighs, and takes my glove,
And gives memorial dainty kisses to it,
As I kiss thee.—Nay, do not snatch it from me;
He that takes that doth take my heart withal.

*Dio.* I had your heart before, this follows it.

*Tro.* I did swear patience.

*Cres.* You shall not have it, Diomed; faith, you shall not;
I'll give you something else.

*Dio.* I will have this: whose was it?

*Cres.*                    It is no matter.

*Dio.* Come, tell me whose it was.

*Cres.* 'Twas one's that loved me better than you will.
But, now you have it, take it.

*Dio.*                    Whose was it?

*Cres.* By all Diana's waiting women yond,
And by herself, I will not tell you whose.

*Dio.* To-morrow will I wear it on my helm;                    [it.
And grieve his spirit that dares not challenge

*Tro.* Wert thou the devil, and wor'st it on thy horn,
It should be challeng'd.

*Cres.* Well, well, 'tis done, 'tis past;—and yet it is not;
I will not keep my word.

*Dio.*                Why, then, farewell;
Thou never shalt mock Diomed again.

*Cres.* You shall not go:—one cannot speak
a word
But it straight starts you.

*Dio.*                I do not like this fooling.

*Ther.* Nor I, by Pluto: but that that likes
not you pleases me best.

*Dio.* What, shall I come? the hour?

*Cres.* Ay, come:—O Jove!
Do come:—I shall be plagu'd.

*Dio.* Farewell till then.

*Cres.*            Good-night: I pr'ythee, come.
                    [*Exit* DIOMEDES.
Troilus, farewell! one eye yet looks on thee;
But with my heart the other eye doth see.
Ah, poor our sex! this fault in us I find,
The error of our eye directs our mind:
What error leads must err; O, then conclude,
Minds sway'd by eyes are full of turpitude.
                    [*Exit.*

*Ther.* A proof of strength she could not
    publish more,
Unless she said, My mind is now turn'd whore.

*Ulyss.* All's done, my lord.

*Tro.*                It is.

*Ulyss.*                Why stay we, then?

*Tro.* To make a recordation to my soul
Of every syllable that here was spoke.
But if I tell how these two did co-act,
Shall I not lie in publishing a truth?
Sith yet there is a credence in my heart,
An esperance so obstinately strong,
That doth invert the attest of eyes and ears;
As if those organs had deceptious functions
Created only to calumniate.
Was Cressid here?

*Ulyss.*            I cannot conjure, Trojan.

*Tro.* She was not, sure.

*Ulyss.*                Most sure she was.

*Tro.* Why, my negation hath no taste of
    madness.            [but now.

*Ulyss.* Nor mine, my lord: Cressid was here

*Tro.* Let it not be believ'd for womanhood!
Think, we had mothers; do not give advan-
    tage
To stubborn critics,—apt, without a theme,
For depravation,—to square the general sex
By Cressid's rule: rather think this not Cres-
    sid.

*Ulyss.* What hath she done, prince, that
    can soil our mothers?

*Tro.* Nothing at all, unless that this were
    she.

*Ther.* Will he swagger himself out on's own
    eyes?

*Tro.* This she? no; this is Diomed's Cres-
    sida:
If beauty have a soul, this is not she;
If souls guide vows, if vows be sanctimonies,
If sanctimony be the gods' delight,
If there be rule in unity itself,
This is not she. O madness of discourse,
That cause sets up with and against itself!

Bi-fold authority! where reason can revolt
Without perdition, and loss assume all reason
Without revolt: this is, and is not, Cressid!
Within my soul there doth conduce a fight
Of this strange nature, that a thing inseparate
Divides more wider than the sky and earth;
And yet the spacious breadth of this division
Admits no orifex for a point, as subtle
As Ariachne's broken woof, to enter.
Instance, O instance! strong as Pluto's gates;
Cressid is mine, tied with the bonds of heav-
    en:
Instance, O instance! strong as heaven itself;
The bonds of heaven are slipp'd, dissolv'd,
    and loos'd;
And with another note, five-finger-tied,
The fractions of her faith, orts of her love,
The fragments, scraps, the bits, and greasy
    relics
Of her o'er-eaten faith, are bound to Diomed.

*Ulyss.* May worthy Troilus be but half-
    attach'd
With that which here his passion doth ex-
    press?

*Tro.* Ay, Greek; and that shall be divulged
    well
In characters as red as Mars his heart  [fancy
Inflam'd with Venus: never did young man
With so eternal and so fix'd a soul.
Hark, Greek: as much as I do Cressid love,
So much by weight hate I her Diomed:
That sleeve is mine that he'll bear on his
    helm;
Were it a casque compos'd by Vulcan's skill
My sword should bite it: not the dreadful
    spout
Which shipmen do the hurricano call,
Constring'd in mass by the almighty sun,
Shall dizzy with more clamour Neptune's ear
In his descent, than shall my prompted sword
Falling on Diomed.

*Ther.* He'll tickle it for his concupy.

*Tro.* O Cressid! O false Cressid! false,
    false, false!
Let all untruths stand by thy stained name,
And they'll seem glorious.

*Ulyss.*            O, contain yourself;
Your passion draws ears hither.

*Enter* ÆNEAS.

*Æne.* I have been seeking you this hour,
    my lord:
Hector, by this, is arming him in Troy;
Ajax, your guard, stays to conduct you home.

*Tro.* Have with you, prince.—My cour-
    teous lord, adieu.—
Farewell, revolted fair!—and, Diomed,
Stand fast, and wear a castle on thy head!

*Ulyss.* I'll bring you to the gates.

*Tro.* Accept distracted thanks.
            [*Exeunt* TRO., ÆNE., *and* ULYSS.

*Ther.* Would I could meet that rogue
Diomed! I would croak like a raven; I would
bode, I would bode. Patroclus will give me

anything for the intelligence of this whore: the parrot will not do more for an almond than he for a commodious drab. Lechery, lechery; still wars and lechery; nothing else holds fashion: a burning devil take them!

[*Exit.*

SCENE III.—TROY. *Before* PRIAM'S *Palace.*

*Enter* HECTOR *and* ANDROMACHE.

*And.* When was my lord so much ungently temper'd
To stop his ears against admonishment?
Unarm, unarm, and do not fight to-day.

*Hect.* You train me to offend you; get you in:
By all the everlasting gods, I'll go!

*And.* My dreams will, sure, prove ominous to the day.

*Hect.* No more, I say.

*Enter* CASSANDRA.

*Cas.*　　　　Where is my brother Hector?

*And.* Here, sister; arm'd, and bloody in intent.
Consort with me in loud and dear petition,
Pursue we him on knees; for I have dream'd
Of bloody turbulence, and this whole night
Hath nothing been but shapes and forms of slaughter.

*Cas.* O, 'tis true.

*Hect.*　　　　Ho! bid my trumpet sound!

*Cas.* No notes of sally, for the heavens, sweet brother.　　　　[me swear.

*Hect.* Begone, I say: the gods have heard

*Cas.* The gods are deaf to hot and peevish vows:
They are polluted offerings, more abhorr'd
Than spotted livers in the sacrifice.

*And.* O, be persuaded! do not count it holy
To hurt by being just: it is as lawful,
For we would give much, to use violent thefts,
And rob in the behalf of charity.　　[the vow;

*Cas.* It is the purpose that makes strong
But vows to every purpose must not hold:
Unarm, sweet Hector.

*Hect.*　　　　Hold you still, I say;
Mine honour keeps the weather of my fate:
Life every man holds dear; but the dear man
Holds honour far more precious dear than life.—

*Enter* TROILUS.

How now, young man! mean'st thou to fight to-day?

*And.* Cassandra, call my father to persuade.　　　　[*Exit* CASSANDRA.

*Hect.* No, faith, young Troilus; doff thy harness, youth;
I am to-day i' the vein of chivalry:
Let grow thy sinews till their knots be strong,
And tempt not yet the brushes of the war.
Unarm thee, go; and doubt thou not, brave boy,
I'll stand to-day for thee, and me, and Troy.

*Tro.* Brother, you have a vice of mercy in you,
Which better fits a lion than a man.

*Hect.* What vice is that, good Troilus? chide me for it.　　　　[cians fall,

*Tro.* When many times the captive Gre-
Even in the fan and wind of your fair sword,
You bid them rise and live.

*Hect.* O, 'tis fair play.

*Tro.*　　　　Fool's play, by Heaven, Hector.

*Hect.* How now! how now!

*Tro.*　　　　For the love of all the gods,
Let's leave the hermit pity with our mothers;
And when we have our armours buckled on,
The venom'd vengeance ride upon our swords;
Spur them to ruthful work, rein them from ruth.

*Hect.* Fie, savage, fie!

*Tro.*　　　　Hector, then 'tis wars.

*Hect.* Troilus, I would not have you fight to-day.

*Tro.* Who should withhold me?
Not fate, obedience, nor the hand of Mars
Beckoning with fiery truncheon my retire;
Not Priamus and Hecuba on knees,
Their eyes o'ergalled with recourse of tears;
Nor you, my brother, with your true sword drawn,
Oppos'd to hinder me, should stop my way,
But by my ruin.

*Re-enter* CASSANDRA, *with* PRIAM.

*Cas.* Lay hold upon him, Priam, hold him fast:
He is thy crutch; now if thou lose thy stay
Thou on him leaning and all Troy on thee,
Fall all together.

*Pri.*　　　　Come, Hector, come, go back:
Thy wife hath dream'd; thy mother hath had visions;
Cassandra doth foresee; and I myself
Am like a prophet suddenly enrapt,
To tell thee that this day is ominous:
Therefore, come back.

*Hect.*　　　　Æneas is a-field;
And I do stand engag'd to many Greeks,
Even in the faith of valour, to appear
This morning to them.

*Pri.*　　　　Ay, but thou shalt not go.

*Hect.* I must not break my faith.
You know me dutiful; therefore, dear sir,
Let me not shame respect; but give me leave
To take that course by your consent and voice
Which you do here forbid me, royal Priam.

*Cas.* O Priam, yield not to him!

*And.*　　　　Do not, dear father.

*Hect.* Andromache, I am offended with you:
Upon the love you bear me, get you in.

[*Exit* ANDROMACHE.

*Tro.* This foolish, dreaming, superstitious girl
Makes all these bodements

*Cas.* O, farewell, dear Hector!
Look, how thou diest! look, how thy eye
    turns pale!
Look, how thy wounds do bleed at many
    vents!
Hark, how Troy roars! how Hecuba cries out!
How poor Andromache shrills her dolours
    forth!
Behold, destruction, frenzy, and amazement,
Like witless antics, one another meet,
And all cry, Hector! Hector's dead! O Hector!
    *Tro.* Away! away!     [my leave:
    *Cas.* Farewell:—yet, soft!—Hector I take
Thou dost thyself and all our Troy deceive.
                      *[Exit.*
    *Hect.* You are amaz'd, my liege, at her
    exclaim:         [fight;
Go in, and cheer the town: we'll forth, and
Do deeds worth praise, and tell you them at
    night.         [about thee!
    *Pri.* Farewell: the gods with safety stand
    *[Exeunt severally* PRIAM *and* HECTOR.
           *Alarums.*
    *Tro.* They are at it, hark! Proud Diomed,
    believe,
I come to lose my arm, or win my sleeve.

*As* TROILUS *is going out, enter from the other
    side* PANDARUS.

    *Pan.* Do you hear, my lord? do you hear?
    *Tro.* What now?         [girl.
    *Pan.* Here's a letter come from yond poor
    *Tro.* Let me read.
    *Pan.* A whoreson phtisick, a whoreson
rascally phtisick so troubles me, and the foolish fortune of this girl; and what one thing,
what another, that I shall leave you one o'
these days: and I have a rheum in mine eyes
too; and such an ache in my bones, that unless a man were cursed I cannot tell what to
think on't.—What says she there?
    *Tro.* Words, words, mere words, no mat-
ter from the heart;
The effect doth operate another way.—
           *[Tearing the letter.*
Go, wind, to wind, there turn and change together.—
My love with words and errors still she feeds;
But edifies another with her deeds.
           *[Exeunt severally.*

SCENE IV.—*Plains between Troy and the
    Grecian Camp.*

*Alarums: excursions. Enter* THERSITES.

    *Ther.* Now they are clapper-clawing one
another; I'll go look on. That dissembling
abominable varlet, Diomed, has got that same
scurvy doting foolish young knave's sleeve of
Troy there in his helm: I would fain see them
meet; that that same young Trojan ass, that
loves the whore there, might send that Greekish whoremasterly villain, with the sleeve,
back to the dissembling luxurious drab, of a
sleeve-less errand. O' the t'other side, the
policy of those crafty swearing rascals,—that
stale old mouse-eaten dry cheese, Nestor, and
that same dog-fox, Ulysses,—is not proved
worth a blackberry:—they set me up, in policy, that mongrel cur, Ajax, against that dog
of as bad a kind, Achilles: and now is the cur
Ajax prouder than the cur Achilles, and will
not arm to-day; whereupon the Grecians begin to proclaim barbarism, and policy grows
into an ill opinion. Soft! here come sleeve,
and t'other.

*Enter* DIOMEDES, TROILUS *following.*

    *Tro.* Fly not; for shouldst thou take the
    river Styx
I would swim after.
    *Dio.*         Thou dost miscall retire:
I do not fly; but advantageous care
Withdrew me from the odds of multitude:
Have at thee!
    *Ther.* Hold thy whore, Grecian! now for
thy whore, Trojan!—now the sleeve, now the
sleeve!     *[Exeunt* TRO. *and* DIO., *fighting.*

*Enter* HECTOR.

    *Hect.* What are thou, Greek! art thou for
    Hector's match?
Art thou of blood and honour?
    *Ther.* No, no,—I am a rascal; a scurvy
railing knave; a very filthy rogue.
    *Hect.* I do believe thee;—live.     [*Exit.*
    *Ther.* God-a-mercy, that thou wilt believe
me; but a plague break thy neck for frighting
me!—What's become of the wenching rogues?
I think they have swallowed one another: I
would laugh at that miracle. Yet, in a sort,
lechery eats itself. I'll seek them.     [*Exit.*

SCENE V.—*Another part of the Plains.*

*Enter* DIOMEDES *and a* Servant.

    *Dio.* Go, go, my servant, take thou Troilus'
    horse;
Present the fair steed to my lady Cressid:
Fellow, commend my service to her beauty;
Tell her I have chastis'd the amorous Trojan,
And am her knight by proof.
    *Serv.*         I go, my lord.
                    [*Exit.*

*Enter* AGAMEMNON.

    *Agam.* Renew, renew! The fierce Poly-
    damus
Hath beat down Menon: bastard Margarelon
Hath Doreus prisoner,
And stands colossus-wise, waving his beam,
Upon the pashed corses of the kings
Epistrophus and Cedius: Polixenes is slain;
Amphimacus and Thoas deadly hurt;
Patroclus ta'en, or slain; and Palamedes
Sore hurt and bruis'd: the dreadful Sagittary
Appals our numbers:—haste we, Diomed,
To reinforcement, or we perish all.

*Enter* NESTOR.

*Nest.* Go, bear Patroclus' body to Achilles;
And bid the snail-pac'd Ajax arm for shame.—
There is a thousand Hectors in the field:
Now here he fights on Galathe his horse,
And there lacks work; anon he's there afoot,
And there they fly or die, like scaled skulls
Before the belching whale; then is he yonder,
And there the strawy Greeks, ripe for his edge,
Fall down before him like the mower's swath:
Here, there, and everywhere he leaves and
   takes;
Dexterity so obeying appetite
That what he will he does; and does so much
That proof is call'd impossibility.

*Enter* ULYSSES.

*Ulyss.* O, courage, courage, princes! great
   Achilles
Is arming, weeping, cursing, vowing ven-
   geance:
Patroclus' wounds have rous'd his drowsy
   blood,
Together with his mangl'd Myrmidons,
That noiseless, handless, hack'd and chipp'd,
   come to him,
Crying on Hector. Ajax hath lost a friend,
And foams at mouth, and he is arm'd and at
   it,
Roaring for Troilus; who hath done to-day
Mad and fantastic execution;
Engaging and redeeming of himself
With such a careless force and forceless care
As if that luck, in very spite of cunning,
Bade him win all.

*Enter* AJAX.

*Ajax.* Troilus! thou coward Troilus! [*Exit.*
*Dio.*             Ay, there, there.
*Nest.* So, so, we draw together.

*Enter* ACHILLES.

*Achil.*        Where is this Hector?
Come, come, thou boy-queller, show thy face;
Know what it is to meet Achilles angry:—
Hector! where's Hector? I will none but Hec-
   tor.               [*Exeunt.*

SCENE VI.—*Another Part of the Plains.*

*Enter* AJAX.

*Ajax.* Troilus, thou coward Troilus, show
   thy head!

*Enter* DIOMEDES.

*Dio.* Troilus, I say! where's Troilus?
*Ajax.*         What wouldst thou?
*Dio.* I would correct him.
*Ajax.* Were I the general, thou shouldst
   have my office        [Troilus!
Ere that correction.—Troilus, I say! what,

*Enter* TROILUS.

*Tro.* O traitor Diomed!—turn thy false
   face, thou traitor,
And pay thy life thou owest me for my horse!
*Dio.* Ha! art thou there?
*Ajax.* I'll fight with him alone: stand,
   Diomed.
*Dio.* He is my prize. I will not look upon.
*Tro.* Come, both, you cogging Greeks; have
   at you both.       [*Exeunt fighting.*

*Enter* HECTOR.

*Hect.* Yea, Troilus? O, well fought, my
   youngest brother!

*Enter* ACHILLES.

*Achil.* Now do I see thee, ha! have at thee,
   Hector!
*Hect.* Pause, if thou wilt.      [Trojan:
*Achil.* I do disdain thy courtesy, proud
Be happy that my arms are out of use:
My rest and negligence befriend thee now,
But thou anon shalt hear of me again;  [*Exit.*
*Hect.*          Fare thee well:—
Till when, go seek thy fortune.
I would have been much more a fresher man
Had I expected thee.—How now, my broth-
   er!

*Re-enter* TROILUS.

*Tro.* Ajax hath ta'en Æneas: shall it be?
No, by the flame of yonder glorious heaven,
He shall not carry him; I'll be ta'en too,
Or bring him off:—fate, hear me what I say!
I reck not though I end my life to-day. [*Exit.*

*Enter one in sumptuous armour.*

*Hect.* Stand, stand, thou Greek; thou art a
   goodly mark:—
No? wilt thou not?—I like thy armour well;
I'll frush it, and unlock the rivets all. [abide?
But I'll be master of it:—Wilt thou not, beast,
Why then, fly on, I'll hunt thee for thy hide.
                   [*Exeunt.*

SCENE VII.—*Another Part of the Plains.*

*Enter* ACHILLES, *with* MYRMIDONS.

*Achil.* Come here about me, you my Myr-
   midons;
Mark what I say,—Attend me where I wheel:
Strike not a stroke, but keep yourselves in
   breath:
And when I have the bloody Hector found
Empale him with your weapons round about;
In fellest manner execute your aims.
Follow me, sirs, and my proceedings eye:—
It is decreed Hector the great must die.
                   [*Exeunt.*

*Enter* MENELAUS *and* PARIS, *fighting; then*
           THERSITES.

*Ther.* The cuckold and the cuckold-maker
are at it. Now, bull! now, dog! 'loo, Paris,

'loo! now my double henned sparrow! 'loo,
Paris, 'loo! the bull has the game:—'ware
horns, ho!    [*Exeunt* PARIS *and* MENELAUS.

### Enter MARGARELON.

*Mar.* Turn, slave, and fight.
*Ther.* What art thou?
*Mar.* A bastard son of Priam's.
*Ther.* I am a bastard too; I love bastards:
I am a bastard begot, bastard instructed,
bastard in mind, bastard in valour, in every-
thing illegitimate. One bear will not bite an-
other, and wherefore should one bastard?
Take heed, the quarrel's most ominous to us:
if the son of a whore fight for a whore he
tempts judgment: farewell, bastard.    [*Exit.*
*Mar.* The devil take thee, coward!    [*Exit.*

### SCENE VIII.—*Another Part of the Plains.*

### Enter HECTOR.

*Hect.* Most putrified core, so fair without,
Thy goodly armour thus hath cost thy life.
Now is my day's work done: I'll take good
    breath:
Rest, sword; thou hast thy fill of blood and
    death!
    [*Puts off his helmet and hangs his
        shield behind him.*

### Enter ACHILLES *and* Myrmidons.

*Achil.* Look, Hector, how the sun begins to
    set;
How ugly night comes breathing at his heels;
Even with the vail and dark'ning of the sun,
To close the day up, Hector's life is done.
*Hect.* I am unarm'd; forego this vantage,
    Greek.    [man I seek.
*Achil.* Strike, fellows, strike; this is the
    [HECTOR *falls.*
So, Ilion, fall thou next! now, Troy, sink
    down!    [bore.—
Here lies thy heart, thy sinews, and thy
On, Myrmidons; and cry you all amain,
*Achilles hath the mighty Hector slain.*
    [*A retreat sounded.*
Hark! a retire upon our Grecian part.
*Myr.* The Trojan trumpets sound the like,
    my lord.    [the earth,
*Achil.* The dragon wing of night o'erspreads
And, stickler-like, the armies separate.
My half-supp'd sword, that frankly would
    have fed,    [bed.—
Pleas'd with this dainty bait, thus goes to
    [*Sheathes his sword.*
Come, tie his body to my horse's tail;
Along the field I will the Trojan trail.
    [*Exeunt.*

### SCENE IX.—*Another Part of the Plains.*

*Enter* AGAMEMNON, AJAX, MENELAUS, NES-
TOR, DIOMEDES, *and others, marching.
Shouts within.*

*Agam.* Hark! hark! what shout is that?

*Nest.* Peace, drums!    [Achilles!
[*Within.*] Achilles Achilles! Hector's slain,
*Dio.* The bruit is, Hector's slain, and by
    Achilles.
*Ajax.* If it be so, yet bragless let it be;
Great Hector was a man as good as he.    [sent
*Agam.* March patiently along.—Let one be
To pray Achilles see us at our tent,—
If in his death the gods have us befriended;
Great Troy is ours, and our sharp wars are
    ended.    [*Exeunt, marching.*

### SCENE X.—*Another Part of the Plains.*

### Enter ÆNEAS *and* Trojans.

*Æne.* Stand, ho! yet are we masters of the
    field:
Never go home; here starve we out the night.

### Enter TROILUS.

*Tro.* Hector is slain.
*All.*    Hector!—the gods forbid!
*Tro.* He's dead; and at the murderer's
    horse's tail,    [field.—
In beastly sort, dragg'd through the shameful
Frown on, you heavens, effect your rage with
    speed!    [Troy!
Sit, gods, upon your thrones, and smile at
I say, at once let your brief plagues be mercy.
And linger not our sure destructions on!
*Æne.* My lord, you do discomfort all the
    host.
*Tro.* You understand me not that tell me
    so:
I do not speak of flight, of fear, of death;
But dare all imminence that gods and men
Address their dangers in. Hector is gone:
Who shall tell Priam so, or Hecuba?
Let him that will a screech-owl aye be call'd
Go in to Troy, and say there, Hector's dead:
There is a word will Priam turn to stone;
Make wells and Niobes of the maids and
    wives,
Cold statues of the youth; and, in a word,
Scare Troy out of itself. But, march away:
Hector is dead; there is no more to say.
Stay yet.—You vile abominable tents,
Thus proudly pight upon our Phrygian plains,
Let Titan rise as early as he dare,
I'll through and through you!—And, thou
    great-siz'd coward,
No space of earth shall sunder our two hates:
I'll haunt thee like a wicked conscience still,
That mouldeth goblins swift as frenzy's
    thoughts.—
Strike a free march to Troy!—with comfort
    go:
Hope of revenge shall hide our inward woe.
    [*Exeunt* ÆNEAS *and* Trojans.

*As* TROILUS *is going out, enter, from the other
    side,* PANDARUS.

*Pan.* But hear you, hear you!
*Tro.* Hence, broker lackey! ignomy and

shame pursue thy life, and live aye with thy name!    [*Exit*.

*Pan.* A goodly medicine for my aching bones!—O world! world! world! thus is the poor agent despised! O traitors and bàwds, how earnestly are you set at work, and how ill requited! Why should our endeavour be so loved, and the performance so loathed? what verse for it? what instance for it?—Let me see:—

Full merrily the humble-bee doth sing
Till he hath lost his honey and his sting;
And being once subdued in armed tail,
Sweet honey and sweet notes together fail—

Good traders in the flesh, set this in your painted cloths.
As many as be here of pander's hall,
Your eyes, half out, weep out at Pandar's fall;
Or, if you cannot weep, yet give some groans,
Though not for me, yet for your aching bones.
Brethren and sisters of the old-door trade,
Some two months hence my will shall here be made:
It should be now, but that my fear is this,--
Some galled goose of Winchester would hiss
Till then I'll sweat, and seek about for eases;
And, at that time, bequeath you my diseases.
    [*Exit*

TIMON OF ATHENS.

Act IV. Sc. 3

# TIMON OF ATHENS

## DRAMATIS PERSONÆ

TIMON, *a noble Athenian.*

LUCIUS,
LUCULLUS,  } *Lords and Flatterers of* TIMON.
SEMPRONIUS,

VENTIDIUS, *one of* TIMON'S *false Friends.*
ALCIBIADES, *an Athenian General.*
APEMANTUS, *a churlish Philosopher.*
FLAVIUS, *Steward to* TIMON.

FLAMINIUS,
LUCILIUS,  } TIMON'S *Servants.*
SERVILIUS,

CAPHIS,
PHILOTUS,
TITUS,  } *Servants to* TIMON'S *Creditors.*
LUCIUS,
HORTENSIUS,

*Two Servants of* VARRO.

*The Servants of* ISIDORE.
*Two of* TIMON'S *Creditors.*
Cupid *and* Maskers.
Three Strangers.
Poet.
Painter.
Jeweller.
Merchant.
An Old Athenian.

A Page.
A Fool.

PHRYNIA,
TIMANDRA,  } *Mistresses to* ALCIBIADES.

*Other* Lords, Senators, Officers, Soldiers, Thieves, *and* Attendants.

SCENE,—ATHENS, *and the Woods adjoining.*

## ACT I.

SCENE I.—ATHENS. *A Hall in* TIMON'S *House.*

*Enter* Poet, Painter, Jeweller, Merchant, *and others, at several doors.*

*Poet.* Good-day, sir.
*Pain.* I am glad you are well.
*Poet.* I have not seen you long: how goes the world?
*Pain.* It wears, sir, as it grows.
*Poet.* Ay, that's well known:
But what particular rarity? what strange,
Which manifold record not matches? See,
Magic of bounty! all these spirits thy power
Hath conjur'd to attend. I know the merchant.                [jeweller.
*Pain.* I know them both; the other's a
*Mer.* O, 'tis a worthy lord!
*Jew.*              Nay, that's most fix'd.
*Mer.* A most incomparable man; breath'd, as it were,
To an untirable and continuate goodness:
He passes.
*Jew.* I have a jewel here.
*Mer.* O, pray, let's see't: for the Lord Timon, sir?                [that—
*Jew.* If he will touch the estimate: but, for
*Poet.* [*Reciting to himself.*] *When we for recompense have prais'd the vile,*
*It stains the glory in that happy verse*
*Which aptly sings the good.*
*Mer.*                'Tis a good form.
                [*Looking at the jewel.*
*Jew.* And rich: here is a water, look ye.

*Pain.* You are rapt, sir, in some work, some dedication
To the great lord.
*Poet.*          A thing slipp'd idly from me.
Our poesy is as a gum, which oozes
From whence 'tis nourish'd: the fire i' the flint
Shows not till it be struck; our gentle flame
Provokes itself, and, like the current, flies
Each bound it chafes. What have you there?
*Pain.* A picture, sir.—And when comes your book forth?                [sir,—
*Poet.* Upon the heels of my presentment,
Let's see your piece.
*Pain.*              'Tis a good piece.
*Poet.* So 'tis: this comes off well and excellent.
*Pain.* Indifferent.
*Poet.*          Admirable: how this grace
Speaks his own standing! what a mental power
This eye shoots forth! how big imagination
Moves in this lip! to the dumbness of the gesture
One might interpret.
*Pain.* It is a pretty mocking of the life.
Here is a touch; is't good?
*Poet.*              I will say of it
It tutors nature: artificial strife
Lives in these touches, livelier than life.

*Enter certain* Senators, *and pass over.*

*Pain.* How this lord is follow'd!
*Poet.* The senators of Athens:—happy man!

[745]

*Pain.* Look, more!

*Poet.* You see this confluence, this great flood of visitors,
I have, in this rough work, shap'd out a man,
Whom this beneath world doth embrace and hug
With amplest entertainment: my free drift
Halts not particularly, but moves itself
In a wide sea of wax: no levell'd malice
Infects one comma in the course I hold;
But flies an eagle flight, bold, and forth on
Leaving no track behind.

*Pain.* How shall I understand you?

*Poet.*        I will unbolt to you,
You see how all conditions, how all minds,—
As well of glib and slippery creatures as
Of grave and austere quality,—tender down
Their services to Lord Timon: his large fortune,
Upon his good and gracious nature hanging,
Subdues and properties to his love and tendance       [flatterer
All sorts of hearts; yea, from the glass-fac'd
To Apemantus, that few things loves better
Than to abhor himself: even he drops down
The knee before him, and returns in peace
Most rich in Timon's nod.

*Pain.*       I saw them speak together.

*Poet.* Sir, I have upon a high and pleasant hill
Feign'd Fortune to be thron'd: the base o' the mount
Is rank'd with all deserts, all kinds of natures,
That labour on the bosom of this sphere
To propagate their states: amongst them all,
Whose eyes are on this sovereign lady fix'd,
One do I personate of Lord Timon's frame,
Whom Fortune with her ivory hand wafts to her;       [servants
Whose present grace to present slaves and
Translates his rivals.

*Pain.*       'Tis conceiv'd to scope.
This throne, this Fortune, and this hill, methinks,
With one man beckon'd from the rest below,
Bowing his head against the steepy mount
To climb his happiness, would be well express'd
In our condition.

*Poet.*       Nay, sir, but hear me on.
All those which were his fellows but of late,—
Some better than his value,—on the moment
Follow his strides, his lobbies fill with tendance,
Rain sacrificial whisperings in his ear,
Make sacred even his stirrup, and through him
Drink the free air.

*Pain.*       Ay, marry, what of these?

*Poet.* When Fortune, in her shift and change of mood,
Spurns down her late belov'd, all his dependents,       [top,
Which labour'd after him to the mountain's

Even on their knees and hands, let him slip down,
Not one accompanying his declining foot.

*Pain.* 'Tis common:
A thousand moral paintings I can show
That shall demonstrate these quick blows of Fortune's
More pregnantly than words. Yet you do well
To show Lord Timon that mean eyes have seen
The foot above the head.

*Trumpets sound. Enter* TIMON, *attended, the Servant of* VENTIDIUS *talking with him.*

*Tim.*       Imprison'd is he, say you?

*Ven. Serv.* Ay, my good lord: five talents is his debt;
His means most short, his creditors most strait:
Your honourable letter he desires
To those have shut him up; which failing him,
Periods his comfort.

*Tim.*       Noble Ventidius! Well;
I am not of that feather to shake off       [him
My friend when he most needs me. I do know
A gentleman that well deserves a help,—
Which he shall have: I'll pay the debt, and free him.

*Ven. Serv.* Your lordship ever binds him.

*Tim.* Commend me to him: I will send his ransom;
And, being enfranchis'd, bid him come to me:—
'Tis not enough to help the feeble up,
But to support him after.—Fare you well.

*Ven. Serv.* All happiness to your honour!       [*Exit.*

*Enter an* Old Athenian.

*Old. Ath.* Lord Timon, hear me speak.

*Tim.*       Freely, good father.

*Old. Ath.* Thou hast a servant nam'd Lucilius.

*Tim.* I have so: what of him?

*Old Ath.* Most noble Timon, call the man before thee.

*Tim.* Attends he here, or no?—Lucilius!

LUCILIUS *comes forward from among the Attendants.*

*Luc.* Here, at your lordship's service.

*Old Ath.* This fellow here, Lord Timon, this thy creature,
By night frequents my house. I am a man
That from my first have been inclin'd to thrift;
And my estate deserves an heir more rais'd
Than one which holds a trencher.

*Tim.*       Well; what further?

*Old Ath.* One only daughter have I, no kin else,
On whom I may confer what I have got:
The maid is fair, o' the youngest for a bride,
And I have bred her at my dearest cost

In qualities of the best. This man of thine
Attempts her love: I pr'ythee, noble lord,
Join with me to forbid him her resort;
Myself have spoke in vain.
　*Tim.*　　　　　　　The man is honest.
　*Old Ath.* Therefore he will be, Timon:
His honesty rewards him in itself;
It must not bear my daughter.
　*Tim.*　　　　　　Does she love him?
　*Old Ath.* She is young and apt:
Our own precedent passions do instruct us
What levity's in youth.
　*Tim.* [*To* LUCILIUS.] Love you the maid?
　*Luc.* Ay, my good lord, and she accepts of
it.　　　　　　　　　　　[missing,
　*Old Ath.* If in her marriage my consent be
I call the gods to witness, I will choose
Mine heir from forth the beggars of the world,
And dispossess her all.
　*Tim.*　　　　　How shall she be endow'd,
If she be mated with an equal husband?
　*Old Ath.* Three talents on the present; in
future all.　　　　　　　[me long:
　*Tim.* This gentleman of mine hath serv'd
To build his fortune I will strain a little,
For 'tis a bond in men. Give him thy daugh-
ter:
What you bestow, in him I'll counterpoise,
And make him weigh with her.
　*Old Ath.*　　　　　Most noble lord,
Pawn me to this your honour, she is his.
　*Tim.* My hand to thee; mine honour on
my promise　　　　　　　[may
　*Luc.* Humbly I thank your lordship: never
That state or fortune fall into my keeping
Which is not ow'd to you!
　　　　[*Exeunt* LUCILIUS *and* Old Athenian.
　*Poet.* Vouchsafe my labour, and long live
your lordship!　　　　　[anon:
　*Tim.* I thank you; you shall hear from me
Go not away.—What have you there, my
friend?　　　　　　　　　[seech
　*Pain.* A piece of painting, which I do be-
Your lordship to accept.
　*Tim.*　　　　　Painting is welcome.
The painting is almost the natural man;
For since dishonour traffics with man's nature,
He is but outside: these pencill'd figures are
Even such as they give out. I like your work;
And you shall find I like it: wait attendance
Till you hear further from me.
　*Pain.*　　　　　The gods preserve you!
　*Tim.* Well fare you, gentleman: give me
your hand:
We must needs dine together.—Sir, your jewel
Hath suffer'd under praise.
　*Jew.*　　　　What, my lord! dispraise?
　*Tim.* A mere satiety of commendations,
If I should pay you for't as 'tis extoll'd
It would unclew me quite.
　*Jew.*　　　　My lord, 'tis rated
As those which sell would give. But you well
know,
Things of light value, differing in the owners,

Are prized by their masters: believe't, dear
lord,
You mend the jewel by the wearing it.
　*Tim.* Well mock'd.　　[common tongue,
　*Mer.* No, my good lord; he speaks the
Which all men speak with him.　　[chid?
　*Tim.* Look, who comes here: will you be

　　　　　*Enter* APEMANTUS.

　*Jew.* We'll bear, with your lordship.
　*Mer.*　　　　　　He'll spare none.
　*Tim.* Good-morrow to thee, gentle Ape-
mantus!　　　　　　　[good-morrow;
　*Apem.* Till I be gentle, stay thou for thy
When thou art Timon's dog, and these knaves
honest.
　*Tim.* Why dost thou call them knaves?
thou know'st them not.
　*Apem.* Are they not Athenians?
　*Tim.* Yes.
　*Apem.* Then I repent not.
　*Jew.* You know me, Apemantus?
　*Apem.* Thou knowest I do; I call'd thee by
thy name.
　*Tim.* Thou art proud, Apemantus.
　*Apem.* Of nothing so much as that I am not
like Timon.
　*Tim.* Whither art going?　　　[brains.
　*Apem.* To knock out an honest Athenian's
　*Tim.* That's a deed thou'lt die for.
　*Apem.* Right, if doing nothing be death by
the law.
　*Tim.* How likest thou this picture, Ape-
mantus?
　*Apem.* The best, for the innocence.
　*Tim.* Wrought he not well that painted it?
　*Apem.* He wrought better that made the
painter; and yet he's but a filthy piece of
work.
　*Pain.* You are a dog.
　*Apem.* Thy mother's of my generation:
what's she, if I be a dog?
　*Tim.* Wilt dine with me Apemantus?
　*Apem.* No; I eat not lords.
　*Tim.* An thou shouldst, thou'dst anger
ladies.
　*Apem.* O, they eat lords; so they come by
great bellies.
　*Tim.* That's a lascivious apprehension.
　*Apem.* So thou apprehendest it: take it for
thy labour.
　*Tim.* How dost thou like this jewel, Ape-
mantus?
　*Apem.* Not so well as plain-dealing, which
will not cost a man a doit.
　*Tim.* What dost thou think 'tis worth?
　*Apem.* Not worth my thinking.—How
now, poet!
　*Poet.* How now, philosopher!
　*Apem.* Thou liest.
　*Poet.* Art not one?
　*Apem.* Yes.
　*Poet.* Then I lie not.
　*Apem.* Art not a poet?

*Poet.* Yes.

*Apem.* Then thou liest: look in thy last work, where thou hast feign'd him a worthy fellow.

*Poet.* That's not feign'd,—he is so.

*Apem.* Yes, he is worthy of thee, and to pay thee for thy labour: he that loves to be flatter'd is worthy o' the flatterer. Heavens, that I were a lord!

*Tim.* What wouldst do then, Apemantus?

*Apem.* Even as Apemantus does now, hate a lord with my heart.

*Tim.* What, thyself?

*Apem.* Ay.

*Tim.* Wherefore?

*Apem.* That I had no angry wit to be a lord.—Art not thou a merchant?

*Mer.* Ay, Apemantus.

*Apem.* Traffic confound thee, if the gods will not!

*Mer.* If traffic do it, the gods do it.

*Apem.* Traffic's thy god, and thy god confound thee!

*Trumpet sounds. Enter a* Servant.

*Tim.* What trumpet's that?

*Serv.* 'Tis Alcibiades, and some twenty horse,
All of companionship.

*Tim.* Pray, entertain them; give them guide to us.—
           [*Exeunt some* Attendants.
You must needs dine with me:—go not you hence
Till I have thank'd you:—when dinner's done
Show me this piece.—I am joyful of your sights.

*Enter* ALCIBIADES, *with his company.*

Most welcome, sir!         [*They salute.*

*Apem.*         So, so, there!—
Aches contract and starve your supple joints!—
That there should be small love 'mongst these sweet knaves,       [bred out
And all this court'sy! The strain of man's
Into baboon and monkey.

*Alcib.* Sir, you have sav'd my longing, and I feed
Most hungerly on your sight.

*Tim.*         Right welcome, sir!
Ere we depart we'll share a bounteous time
In different pleasures. Pray you, let us in.
           [*Exeunt all but* APEMANTUS.

*Enter Two* Lords.

1 *Lord.* What time o' day is't, Apemantus?

*Apem.* Time to be honest.

1 *Lord.* That time serves still. [omitt'st it.

*Apem.* The more accursed thou, that still

2 *Lord.* Thou art going to Lord Timon's feast.

*Apem.* Ay; to see meat fill knaves, and wine heat fools.

2 *Lord.* Fare thee well, fare thee well.

*Apem.* Thou art a fool to bid me farewell twice.

2 *Lord.* Why, Apemantus?

*Apem.* Shouldst have kept one to thyself, for I mean to give thee none.

1 *Lord.* Hang thyself.

*Apem.* No, I will do nothing at thy bidding: make thy requests to thy friend.

2 *Lord.* Away, unpeaceable dog, or I'll spurn thee hence.

*Apem.* I will fly, like a dog, the heels o' the ass.           [*Exit.*

1 *Lord.* He's opposite to humanity. Come, shall we in
And taste Lord Timon's bounty? he outgoes
The very heart of kindness.       [gold,

2 *Lord.* He pours it out; Plutus, the god of
Is but his steward: no meed but he repays
Sevenfold above itself; no gift to him
But breeds the giver a return exceeding
All use of quittance.

1 *Lord.*       The noblest mind he carries
That ever govern'd man.     [Shall we in?

2 *Lord.* Long may he line in fortunes!

1 *Lord.* I'll keep you company.    [*Exeunt.*

SCENE II.—ATHENS. *A Room of State in*
TIMON'S *House.*

*Hautboys playing loud music. A great banquet served in;* FLAVIUS *and others attending; then enter* TIMON, ALCIBIADES, LUCIUS, LUCULLUS, SEMPRONIUS, *and other Athenian Senators, with* VENTIDIUS, *and Attendants. Then comes, dropping after all,* APEMANTUS, *discontentedly.*

*Ven.* Most honour'd Timon, [father's age,
It hath pleas'd the gods to remember my
And call him to long peace.
He is gone happy, and has left me rich:
Then, as in grateful virtue I am bound
To your free heart, I do return those talents,
Doubled with thanks and service, from whose help
I deriv'd liberty.

*Tim.*       O, by no means,
Honest Ventidius; you mistake my love:
I gave it freely ever; and there's none
Can truly say he gives if he receives: [dare
If our betters play at that game, we must not
To imitate them; faults that are rich are fair.

*Ven.* A noble spirit!
     [*They all stand ceremoniously looking on* TIMON.

*Tim.* Nay, my lords, ceremony was but devis'd at first
To set a gloss of faint deeds, hollow welcomes,
Recanting goodness, sorry ere 'tis shown;
But where there is true friendship there needs none.
Pray, sit; more welcome are ye to my fortunes
Than my fortunes to me.     [*They sit.*

*1 Lord.* My lord, we always have confess'd
it. [you not?

*Apem.* Ho, ho, confess'd it! hang'd it, have

*Tim.* O, Apemantus!—you are welcome.

*Apem.* No;
You shall not make me welcome.
I come to have thee thrust me out of doors.

*Tim.* Fie, thou art a churl; you have got a
humour there
Does not become a man; 'tis much to blame.—
They say, my lords, *ira furor brevis est;*
But yond man is ever angry.
Go, let him have a table by himself;
For he does neither affect company
Nor is he fit for't, indeed.

*Apem.* Let me stay at thine apparel, Timon:
I come to observe; I give thee warning on't.

*Tim.* I take no heed of thee; thou art an
Athenian, therefore welcome: I myself would
have no power; pr'ythee, let my meat make
thee silent.

*Apem.* I scorn thy meat; 'twould choke
me, for I should ne'er flatter thee.—O you
gods, what a number of men eat Timon, and
he sees 'em not! it grieves me to see
So many dip their meat in one man's blood;
And all the madness is, he cheers them up too.
I wonder men dare trust themselves with
men: [knives;
Methinks they should invite them without
Good for their meat and safer for their lives.
There's much example for't; the fellow that
sits next him now, parts bread with him,
pledges the breadth of him in a divided
draught, is the readiest man to kill him: 't has
been prov'd. If I were a huge man I should
fear to drink at meals,
Lest they should spy my windpipe's dangerous notes: [throats.
Great men should drink with harness on their

*Tim.* My lord, in heart; and let the health
go round. [lord.

*2 Lord.* Let it flow this way, my good

*Apem.* Flow this way! A brave fellow! he
keeps his tides well.—Those healths will make
thee and thy state look ill, Timon.
Here's that which is too weak to be a sinner,
Honest water, which ne'er left man i' the
mire:
This and my food are equals; there's no odds:
Feasts are too proud to give thanks to the
gods.

APEMANTUS' GRACE.

Immortal gods, I crave no pelf;
I pray for no man but myself:
Grant I may never prove so fond,
To trust man on his oath or bond;
Or a harlot for her weeping;
Or a dog that seems a-sleeping;
Or a keeper with my freedom;
Or my friends, if I should need 'em.
Amen. So fall to 't:
Rich men sin, and I eat root.
[*Eats and drinks.*

Much good dich thy good heart, Apemantus!

*Tim.* Captain Alcibiades, your heart's in
the field now.

*Alcib.* My heart is ever at your service, my
lord.

*Tim.* You had rather be at a breakfast of
enemies than a dinner of friends.

*Alcib.* So they were bleeding-new, my
lord, there's no meat like them; I could wish
my best friend at such a feast.

*Apem.* Would all those flatterers were
thine enemies, then; that then thou might'st
kill 'em and bid me to 'em.

*1 Lord.* Might we but have that happiness,
my lord, that you would once use our hearts,
whereby we might express some part of our
zeals, we should think ourselves for ever
perfect.

*Tim.* O, no doubt, my good friends, but
the gods themselves have provided that I
shall have much help from you: how had you
been my friends else? why have you that
charitable title from thousands, did not you
chiefly belong to my heart? I have told more
of you to myself than you can with modesty
speak in your own behalf; and thus far I confirm you. O you gods, think I, what need we
have any friends if we should ne'er have
need of 'em? they were the most needless
creatures living, should we ne'er have use for
'em; and would most resemble sweet instruments hung up in cases, that keep their sounds
to themselves. Why, I have often wished myself poorer, that I might come nearer to you.
We are born to do benefits: and what better
or properer can we call our own than the
riches of our friends? O, what a precious
comfort 'tis to have so many, like brothers,
commanding one another's fortunes! O, joy,
e'en made away ere it can be born! Mine
eyes cannot hold out water, methinks: to forget their faults I drink to you.

*Apem.* Thou weepest to make them drink,
Timon. [eyes,

*2 Lord.* Joy had the like conception in our
And at that instant like a babe sprung up.

*Apem.* Ho, ho! I laugh to think that babe
a bastard. [me much.

*3 Lord.* I promise you, my lord, you mov'd

*Apem.* Much! [*Tucket sounded.*

*Tim.* What means that trump?

*Enter a* Servant.

How now!

*Serv.* Please you, my lord, there are certain ladies most desirous of admittance.

*Tim.* Ladies! what are their wills?

*Serv.* There comes with them a forerunner, my lord, which bears that office, to signify their pleasures.

*Tim.* I pray, let them be admitted.

*Enter* CUPID.

*Cup.* Hail to thee, worthy Timon;—and to
all

That of his bounties taste!—The five best
    senses
Acknowledge thee their patron; and come
    freely
To gratulate thy plenteous bosom:
The ear, taste, touch, smell, pleas'd from thy
    table rise;
They only now come but to feast thine eyes.
   *Tim.* They are welcome all; let 'em have
    kind admittance.
Music, make their welcome!   [*Exit* CUPID.
   1 *Lord.* You see, my lord, how ample
    you're belov'd.

*Music.* Re-enter CUPID, *with a mask of*
Ladies *as Amazons, with lutes in their*
*hands, dancing and playing.*

   *Apem.* Hoy-day, what a sweep of vanity
    comes this way!
They dance! they are mad women.
Like madness is the glory of this life,
As this pomp shows to a little oil and root.
We make ourselves fools to disport ourselves,
And spend our flatteries to drink those men
Upon whose age we void it up again,
With poisonous spite and envy.
Who lives that's not depraved, or depraves?
Who dies that bears not one spurn to their
    graves
Of their friends' gift?
I should fear those that dance before me now
Would one day stamp upon me: 't has been
    done;
Men shut their doors against a setting sun.

*The* Lords *rise from table, with much adoring*
*of* TIMON; *and, to show their loves, each*
*singles out an Amazon, and all dance, men*
*with women, a lofty strain or two to the*
*hautboys, and cease.*

   *Tim.* You have done our pleasures much
    grace, fair ladies,
Set a fair fashion on our entertainment,
Which was not half so beautiful and kind;
You have added worth unto't and lustre,
And entertain'd me with mine own device;
I am to thank you for't.     [best.
   1 *Lady.* My lord, you take us even at the
   *Apem.* Faith, for the worst is filthy; and I
would not hold taking, I doubt me.
   *Tim.* Ladies, there is an idle banquet at-
    tends you:
Please you to dispose yourselves.
   *All Ladies.* Most thankfully, my lord.
         [*Exeunt* CUPID *and* Ladies.
   *Tim.* Flavius,—
   *Flav.* My lord?
   *Tim.*      The little casket bring me hither.
   *Flav.* Yes, my lord.—[*Aside.*] More jewels
    yet!
There is no crossing him in his humour,
Else I should tell him,—well, i' faith, I should,
When all's spent, he'd be cross'd then, an he
    could.

'Tis pity bounty had not eyes behind, [mind.
That man might ne'er be wretched for his
       [*Exit, and returns with the casket.*
   1 *Lord.* Where be our men?
   *Serv.* Here, my lord, in readiness.
   2 *Lord.* Our horses!
   *Tim.*          O my friends,
I have one word to say to you. Look you,
    my good lord,
I must entreat you, honour me so much  [it,
As to advance this jewel; accept it, and wear
Kind my lord.
   1 *Lord.* I am so far already in your gifts,—
   *All.* So are we all.

*Enter a* Servant.

   *Serv.* My lord, there are certain nobles of
    the senate
Newly alighted, and come to visit you.
   *Tim.* They are fairly welcome.
   *Flav.*         I beseech your honour,
Vouchsafe me a word; it does concern you
    near.
   *Tim.* Near; why, then, another time I'll
    hear thee:         [entertainment.
I pr'ythee, let's be provided to show 'em
   *Flav.* I scarce know how.     [*Aside.*

*Enter another* Servant.

   2 *Serv.* May it please your honour, Lord
    Lucius,
Out of his free love, hath presented to you
Four milk-white horses, trapp'd in silver.
   *Tim.* I shall accept them fairly: let the
    presents
Be worthily entertained.

*Enter a third* Servant.

             How now! what news?
   3 *Serv.* Please you, my lord, that honour-
able gentleman, Lord Lucullus, entreats your
company to-morrow to hunt with him; and
has sent your honour two brace of grey-
hounds.
   *Tim.* I'll hunt with him; and let them be
    receiv'd,
Not without fair reward.
   *Flav.* [*Aside.*]      What will this come to?
He commands us to provide, and give great
    gifts,
And all out of an empty coffer:
Nor will he know his purse; or yield me this,
To show him what a beggar his heart is,
Being of no power to make his wishes good:
His promises fly so beyond his state
That what he speaks is all in debt, he owes
For every word: he is so kind that he now
Pays interest for't; his land's put to their
    books.
Well, would I were gently put out of office
Before I were forc'd out!
Happier is he that has no friends to feed
Than such that do e'en enemies exceed.
I bleed inwardly for my lord.     [*Exit.*

*Tim.*               You do yourselves
Much wrong, you bate too much of your own
      merits:
Here, my lord, a trifle of our love.
  2 *Lord.* With more than common thanks I
      will receive it.
  3 *Lord.* O, he is the very soul of bounty!
  *Tim.* And now I remember, my lord, you
      gave
Good words the other day of a bay courser
I rode on; it is yours because you lik'd it.
  3 *Lord.* O, I beseech you, pardon me, my
      lord in that.            [know no man
  *Tim.* You may take my word, my lord; I
Can justly praise but what he does affect:
I weigh my friend's affection with mine own;
I'll tell you true. I'll call to you.
  *All Lords.*          O, none so welcome.
  *Tim.* I take all and your several visitations
So kind to heart, 'tis not enough to give;
Methinks I could deal kingdoms to my
      friends
And ne'er be weary.—Alcibiades,
Thou art a soldier, therefore seldom rich;
It comes in charity to thee: for all thy living
Is 'mongst the dead; and all the lands thou
      hast
Lie in a pitch'd field.
  *Alcib.*          Ay, defil'd land, my lord.
  1 *Lord.* We are so virtuously bound,—
  *Tim.*                And so
Am I to you.
  2 *Lord.*  So infinitely endear'd,—
  *Tim.* All to you.—Lights, more lights.
  1 *Lord.*          The best of happiness,
Honour, and fortunes keep with you, Lord
      Timon!
  *Tim.* Ready for his friends.
          [*Exeunt* ALCIBIADES, Lords, *&c.*
  *Apem.*              What a coil's here!
Serving of becks and jutting-out of bums!
I doubt whether their legs be worth the sums
That are given for 'em. Friendship's full of
      dregs:              [sound legs.
Methinks false hearts should never have
Thus honest fools lay out their wealth on
      court'sies.              [sullen
  *Tim.* Now, Apemantus, if thou wert not
I would be good to thee.
  *Apem.* No, I'll nothing: for if I should be
bribed too, there would be none left to rail
upon thee; and then thou wouldst sin the
faster. Thou givest so long, Timon, I fear me
thou wilt give away thyself in paper shortly:
what need these feasts, pomps, and vain
glories?
  *Tim.* Nay, an you begin to rail on society
once, I am sworn not to give regard to you.
Farewell; and come with better music. [*Exit.*
  *Apem.* So;—thou'lt not hear me now,—
thou shalt not then, I'll lock thy heaven from
thee.
O, that men's ears should be
To counsel deaf, but not to flattery!  [*Exit.*

## ACT II.

SCENE I.—ATHENS. *A Room in a* Senator's
      *House.*

*Enter a* Senator, *with papers in his hand.*

  *Sen.* And late, five thousand;—to Varro
      and to Isidore              [sum,
He owes nine thousand; besides my former
Which makes it five-and-twenty.—Still in
      motion
Of raging waste? It cannot hold; it will not.
If I want gold, steal but a beggar's dog
And give it Timon, why, the dog coins gold:
If I would sell my horse and buy twenty more
Better than he, why, give my horse to Timon,
Ask nothing, give it him, it foals me, straight,
And able horses: no porter at his gate;
But rather one that smiles, and still invites
All that pass by. It cannot hold; no reason
Can found his state in safety. Caphis, ho!
Caphis, I say!

          *Enter* CAPHIS.

  *Caph.*  Here, sir; what is your pleasure?
  *Sen.* Get on your cloak and haste you to
      Lord Timon;
Impórtune him for my moneys; be not ceas'd
With slight denial; nor then silenc'd, when—
*Commend me to your master*—and the cap
Plays in the right hand, thus: but tell him
My uses cry to me, I must serve my turn
Out of mine own; his days and times are past,
And my reliances on his fracted dates
Have smit my credit: I love and honour him;
But must not break my back to heal his fin-
      ger:
Immediate are my needs; and my relief
Must not be toss'd and turn'd to me in words,
But find supply immediate. Get you gone:
Put on a most importunate aspéct,
A visage of demand; for, I do fear,
When every feather sticks in his own wing
Lord Timon will be left a naked gull,
Which flashes now a phœnix. Get you gone
  *Caph.* I go, sir.
  *Sen.* Take the bonds along with you,
And have the dates in compt.
  *Caph.*              I will, sir.
  *Sen.*                Go.
                        [*Exeunt.*

SCENE II.—ATHENS. *A Hall in* TIMON'S
      *House.*

*Enter* FLAVIUS, *with many bills in his hand.*

  *Flav.* No care, no stop! so senseless of
      expense
That he will neither know how to maintain it
Nor cease his flow of riot: takes no account
How things go from him; nor resumes no
      care
Of what is to continue: never mind
Was to be so unwise to be so kind.
What shall be done? he will not hear, till feel:

I must be round with him now he comes from
    hunting.
Fie, fie, fie, fie!

*Enter* CAPHIS, *and the* Servants *of* ISIDORE
*and* VARRO.

*Caph.*          Good-even, Varro: what,
You come for money?
  *Var. Serv.*          Is't not your business too?
  *Caph.* It is:—and yours too, Isidore?
  *Isid. Serv.*               It is so.
  *Caph.* Would we were all discharg'd!
  *Var. Serv.*              I fear it.
  *Caph.* Here comes the lord.

*Enter* TIMON, ALCIBIADES, *and* Lords, &c.

  *Tim.* So soon as dinner's done we'll forth
    again,
My Alcibiades.—With me? what is your will?
  *Caph.* My lord, here is a note of certain
    dues.
  *Tim.* Dues! whence are you?
  *Caph.*          Of Athens here, my lord.
  *Tim.* Go to my steward.      [me off
  *Caph.* Please it your lordship, he hath put
To the succession of new days this month:
My master is awak'd by great occasion
To call upon his own; and humbly prays you
That, with your other noble parts, you'll suit
In giving him his right.
  *Tim.*          Mine honest friend,
I pr'ythee but repair to me next morning.
  *Caph.* Nay, good my lord,—
  *Tim.*          Contain thyself, good friend.
  *Var. Serv.* One Varro's servant, my good
    lord,—
  *Isid. Serv.* From Isidore;
He humbly prays your speedy payment,—
  *Caph.* If you did know, my lord, my mas-
    ter's wants,—      [lord, six weeks
  *Var. Serv.* 'Twas due on forfeiture, my
And past,—
  *Isid. Serv.* Your steward puts me off, my
    lord;
And I am sent expressly to your lordship.
  *Tim.* Give me breath.—
I do beseech you, good my lords, keep on;
I'll wait upon you instantly.—
            [*Exeunt* ALCIBIADES *and* Lords.
Come hither: pray you,      [*To* FLAVIUS.
How goes the world, that I am thus encoun-
    ter'd
With clamorous demands of date-broke
    bonds,
And the detention of long-since-due debts,
Against my honour?
  *Flav.*          Please you, gentlemen,
The time is unagreeable to this business:
Your importunacy cease till after dinner;
That I may make his lordship understand
Wherefore you are not paid.
  *Tim.*          Do so, my friends.—
See them well entertained.      [*Exit.*
  *Flav.*          Pray, draw near. [*Exit.*

*Enter* APEMANTUS *and* Fool.

  *Caph.* Stay, stay, here comes the fool with
Apemantus: let's ha' some sport with 'em.
  *Var. Serv.* Hang him, he'll abuse us.
  *Isid. Serv.* A plague upon him, dog!
  *Var. Serv.* How dost, fool?
  *Apem.* Dost dialogue with thy shadow?
  *Var. Serv.* I speak not to thee.
  *Apem.* No, 'tis to thyself.—Come away.
            [*To the* Fool.
  *Isid. Serv.* [*To* Var. Serv.] There's the fool
hangs on your back already.
  *Apem.* No, thou stand'st single, thou art
not on him yet.
  *Caph.* Where's the fool now?
  *Apem.* He last asked the question.—Poor
rogues and usurers' men! bawds between gold
and want!
  *All Serv.* What are we, Apemantus?
  *Apem.* Asses.
  *All Serv.* Why?
  *Apem.* That you ask me what you are,
and do not know yourselves.—Speak to 'em,
fool.
  *Fool.* How do you, gentlemen?
  *All Serv.* Gramercies, good fool: how does
your mistress?
  *Fool.* She's e'en sitting on water to scald
such chickens as you are. Would we could see
you at Corinth.
  *Apem.* Good! gramercy.      [page.
  *Fool.* Look you, here comes my mistress'

*Enter* Page.

  *Page.* [*To the* Fool.] Why, how now, cap-
tain? what do you in this wise company?
How dost thou, Apemantus?
  *Apem.* Would I had a rod in my mouth
that I might answer thee profitably.
  *Page.* Pr'ythee, Apemantus, read me the
superscription of these letters: I know not
which is which.
  *Apem.* Canst not read?
  *Page.* No.
  *Apem.* There will little learning die, then,
that day thou art hanged. This is to Lord
Timon; this to Alcibiades. Go; thou wast
born a bastard, and thou'lt die a bawd.
  *Page.* Thou wast whelped a dog, and thou
shalt famish a dog's death. Answer not, I am
gone.      [*Exit* Page.
  *Apem.* E'en so thou outrun'st grace.
Fool, I will go with you to Lord Timon's.
  *Fool.* Will you leave me there?
  *Apem.* If Timon stay at home.—You three
serve three usurers?
  *All Serv.* Ay; would they served us!
  *Apem.* So would I,—as good a trick as
ever hangman served thief.
  *Fool.* Are you three usurers' men?
  *All Serv.* Ay, fool.
  *Fool.* I think no usurer but has a fool to
his servant; my mistress is one, and I am her

fool. When men come to borrow of your masters they approach sadly and go away merry; but they enter my mistress' house merrily and go away sadly: the reason of this?

*Var. Serv.* I could render one.

*Apem.* Do it, then, that we may account thee a whoremaster and a knave; which, notwithstanding, thou shalt be no less esteemed.

*Var. Serv.* What is a whoremaster, fool?

*Fool.* A fool in good clothes, and something like thee. 'Tis a spirit: sometime it appears like a lord; sometime like a lawyer; sometime like a philosopher, with two stones more than's artificial one. He is very often like a knight; and, generally, in all shapes that man goes up and down in from fourscore to thirteen this spirit walks in.

*Var. Serv.* Thou art not altogether a fool.

*Fool.* Nor thou altogether a wise man: as much foolery as I have, so much wit thou lackest.

*Apem.* That answer might have become Apemantus.                      [*Timon.*

*Var. Serv.* Aside, aside; here comes Lord

*Re-enter* TIMON *and* FLAVIUS.

*Apem.* Come with me, fool, come.

*Fool.* I do not always follow lover, elder brother, and woman; sometime the philosopher.           [*Exeunt* APEMANTUS *and* Fool.

*Flav.* Pray you, walk near; I'll speak with you anon.                    [*Exeunt* Serv.

*Tim.* You make me marvel: wherefore, ere this time,
Had you not fully laid my state before me;
That I might so have rated my expense
As I had leave of means?

*Flav.*                   You would not hear me
At many leisures I propos'd.

*Tim.*                    Go to:
Perchance some single vantages you took
When my indisposition put you back;
And that unaptness made you minister
Thus to excuse yourself.

*Flav.*                O my good lord
At many times I brought in my accounts,
Laid them before you; you would throw them off,
And say you found them in mine honesty.
When, for some trifling present, you have bid me                    [wept;
Return so much, I have shook my head and
Yea, 'gainst the authority of manners, pray'd you
To hold your hand more close: I did endure
Not seldom, nor no slight checks, when I have
Prompted you, in the ebb of your estate,
And your great flow of debts. My loved lord,
Though you hear now,—too late!—yet now's a time,
The greatest of your having lacks a half
To pay your present debts.

*Tim.*                  Let all my land be sold.

*Flav.* 'Tis all engag'd, some forfeited and gone;
And what remains will hardly stop the mouth
Of present dues: the future comes apace:
What shall defend the interim? and at length
How goes our reckoning?

*Tim.* To Lacedæmon did my land extend.

*Flav.* O my good lord, the world is but a word:
Were it all yours to give it in a breath,
How quickly were it gone!

*Tim.*                 You tell me true.

*Flav.* If you suspect my husbandry or falsehood,
Call me before the exactest auditors
And set me on the proof. So the gods bless me,
When all our offices have been oppress'd
With riotous feeders; when our vaults have wept                    [room
With drunken spilth of wine; when every room
Hath blaz'd with lights and bray'd with minstrelsy;
I have retir'd me to a wasteful cock,
And set mine eyes at flow.

*Tim.*                  Pr'ythee no more.

*Flav.* Heavens, have I said, the bounty of this lord!           [peasants
How many prodigal bits have slaves and
This night englutted! Who is not Timon's?
What heart, head, sword, force, means, but is Lord Timon's?
Great Timon, noble, worthy, royal Timon!
Ah! when the means are gone that buy this praise           [made:
The breath is gone whereof this praise is
Feast-won, fast-lost; one cloud of winter showers,
These flies are couch'd.

*Tim.*               Come, sermon me no further:
No villanous bounty yet hath passed my heart;
Unwisely, not ignobly, have I given.
Why dost thou weep? Canst thou the conscience lack           [heart;
To think I shall lack friends? Secure thy
If I would broach the vessels of my love,
And try the argument of hearts by borrowing,
Men and men's fortunes could I frankly use
As I can bid thee speak.

*Flav.*                Assurance bless your thoughts!

*Tim.* And, in some sort, these wants of mine are crown'd
That I account them blessings for by these
Shall I try friends: you shall perceive how you           [friends.
Mistake my fortunes; I am wealthy in my
Within there! Flaminius! Servilius!

*Enter* FLAMINIUS, SERVILIUS, *and other* Servants.

*Serv.* My lord? my lord?—

*Tim.* I will despatch you severally:—you

to Lord Lucius;—to Lord Lucullus you; I
hunted with his honour to-day;—you to
Sempronius: commend me to their loves; and
I am proud, say, that my occasions have
found time to use 'em toward a supply of
money: let the request be fifty talents.

*Flam.* As you have said, my lord.

*Flav.* Lord Lucius and Lucullus? hum!
                             [*Aside.*

*Tim.* Go you, sir, [*to another* Serv.] to the
senators,—                    [have
Of whom, even to the state's best health, I
Deserv'd this hearing, bid 'em send o' the
   instant
A thousand talents to me.

*Flav.*          I have been bold,—
For that I knew it the most general way,——
To them to use your signet and your name;
But they do shake their heads, and I am here
No richer in return.

*Tim.*          Is't true? can't be?

*Flav.* They answer, in a joint and corpor-
   ate voice,                  [not
That now they are at fall, want treasure, can-
Do what they would; are sorry—you are
   honourable,—              [not—
But yet they could have wish'd—they know
Something hath been amiss—a noble nature
May catch a wrench—would all were well—
   'tis pity;—
And so, intending other serious matters,
After distasteful looks, and these hard frac-
   tions,
With certain half-caps and cold-moving nods,
They froze me into silence.

*Tim.*          You gods, reward them?
Pr'ythee, man, look cheerly. These old fellows
Have their ingratitude in them hereditary:
Their blood is cak'd, 'tis cold, it seldom flows;
'Tis lack of kindly warmth they are not kind;
And nature, as it grows again toward earth,
Is fashion'd for the journey dull and heavy.—
Go to Ventidius [*to a* Serv.]; pr'ythee, [*to*
   FLAVIUS] be not sad,          [speak,
Thou art true and honest; ingeniously I
No blame belongs to thee:—[*To* Serv.] Ven-
   tidius lately             [stepp'd
Buried his father; by whose death he's
Into a great estate: when he was poor,
Imprison'd, and in scarcity of friends,
I clear'd him with five talents: greet him
   from me;
Bid him suppose some good necessity
Touches his friend, which craves to be re-
   member'd
With those five talents:—[*To* FLAV.]—That
   had,—give't these fellows
To whom 'tis instant due. Ne'er speak or
   think                   [sink.
That Timon's fortunes 'mong his friends can

*Flav.* I would I could not think it: that
   thought is bounty's foe;
Being free itself it thinks all others so.
                              [*Exeunt.*

## ACT III.

SCENE I.—ATHENS. *A Room in* LUCULLUS'
*House.*

FLAMINIUS *waiting. Enter a* Servant *to
him.*

*Serv.* I have told my lord of you; he is
coming down to you.

*Flam.* I thank you, sir.

*Enter* LUCULLUS.

*Serv.* Here's my lord.

*Lucul.* [*Aside.*] One of Lord Timon's men?
a gift, I warrant. Why, this hits right; I
dreamt of a silver basin and ewer to-night.—
Flaminius, honest Flaminius; you are very
respectively welcome, sir.—Fill me some wine.
[*Exit* Servant.]—And how does that honourable, complete, free-hearted gentleman of
Athens, thy very bountiful good lord and
master?

*Flam.* His health is well, sir.

*Lucul.* I am right glad that his health is
well, sir: and what hast thou there under thy
cloak, pretty Flaminius?

*Flam.* Faith, nothing but an empty box,
sir; which, in my lord's behalf, I come to entreat your honour to supply; who, having
great and instant occasion to use fifty talents,
hath sent to your lordship to furnish him,
nothing doubting your present assistance
therein.

*Lucul.* La, la, la, la,—nothing doubting,
says he? Alas, good lord! a noble gentleman
'tis, if he would not keep so good a house.
Many a time and often I ha'e dined with him
and told him on't; and come again to supper
to him of purpose to have him spend less; and
yet he would embrace no counsel, take no
warning by my coming. Every man has his
fault, and honesty is his: I ha'e told him on't,
but I could ne'er get him from't.

*Re-enter* Servant, *with wine.*

*Serv.* Please your lordship, here is the wine.

*Lucul.* Flaminius, I have noted thee always
wise. Here's to thee.

*Flam.* Your lordship speaks your pleasure.

*Lucul.* I have observed thee always for a
towardly prompt spirit,—give thee thy due,
—and one that knows what belongs to reason; and canst use the time well, if the time
use thee well: good parts in thee.—Get you
gone, sirrah [*to the* Servant, *who goes out.*]
—Draw nearer, honest Flaminius. Thy lord's
a bountiful gentleman: but thou art wise;
and thou knowest well enough, although thou
comest to me, that this is no time to lend
money; especially upon bare friendship, without security. Here's three solidares for thee:
good boy, wink at me, and say thou saw'st
me not. Fare thee well.       [much differ:

*Flam.* Is't possible the world should so

And we alive that liv'd! Fly, damned base-
ness,
To him that worships thee.
                [*Throwing the money back.*
*Lucul.* Ha! now I see thou art a fool, and
fit for thy master.                    [*Exit.*
*Flam.* May these add to the number that
     may scald thee!
Let molten coin be thy damnation,
Thou disease of a friend and not himself!
Has friendship such a faint and milky heart,
It turns in less than two nights? O you gods,
I feel my master's passion! This slave
Unto his honour has my lord's meat in him:
Why should it thrive and turn to nutriment
When he is turn'd to poison?
O, may diseases only work upon't!
And when he's sick to death, let not that part
     of nature
Which my lord paid for, be of any power
To expel sickness, but prolong his hour!
                                    [*Exit.*

SCENE II.—ATHENS. *A public Place.*

*Enter* LUCIUS, *with Three* Strangers.

*Luc.* Who, the Lord Timon? he is my very
good friend, and an honourable gentleman.
     I *Stran.* We know him for no less, though
we are but strangers to him. But I can tell
you one thing, my lord, and which I hear
from common rumours,—now Lord Timon's
happy hours are done and past, and his estate
shrinks from him.
*Luc.* Fie, no, do not believe it; he cannot
     want for money.
     2 *Stran.* But believe you this, my lord, that
not long ago, one of his men was with the
Lord Lucullus to borrow so many talents;
nay, urged extremely for't, and showed what
necessity belonged to't, and yet was denied.
*Luc.* How?
     2 *Stran.* I tell you, denied, my lord.
*Luc.* What a strange case was that! now,
before the gods, I am ashamed on't. Denied
that honourable man! there was very little
honour showed in't. For my own part, I must
needs confess I have received some small
kindnesses from him, as money, plate, jewels,
and such like trifles, nothing comparing to
his; yet, had he mistook him and sent to me, I
should ne'er have denied his occasion so
many talents.

*Enter* SERVILIUS.

*Ser.* See, by good hap, yonder's my lord; I
have sweat to see his honour.—My honoured
lord,—                              [*To* LUCIUS.
*Luc.* Servilius! you are kindly met, sir.
Fare thee well: commend me to thy honour-
able-virtuous lord, my very exquisite friend.
*Ser.* May it please your honour, my lord
hath sent,—
*Luc.* Ha! what has he sent? I am so much
endeared to that lord; he's ever sending: how

shall I thank him, thinkest thou? And what
has he sent now?
*Ser.* Has only sent his present occasion
now, my lord; requesting your lordship to
supply his instant use with so many talents.
*Luc.* I know his lordship is but merry with
     me;
He cannot want fifty-five hundred talents.
*Ser.* But in the meantime he wants less,
     my lord.
If his occasion were not virtuous
I should not urge it half so faithfully.
*Luc.* Dost thou speak seriously, Servilius?
*Ser.* Upon my soul, 'tis true, sir.
*Luc.* What a wicked beast was I to disfurnish myself against such a good time, when
I might ha' shown myself honourable! how
unluckily it happened that I should purchase
the day before for a little part, and undo a
great deal of honour!—Servilius, now, before
the gods, I am not able to do't,—the more
beast, I say. I was sending to use Lord Timon
myself, these gentlemen can witness; but I
would not for the wealth of Athens I had
done't now. Commend me bountifully to his
good lordship; and I hope his honour will
conceive the fairest of me, because I have no
power to be kind; and tell him this from me,
I count it one of my greatest afflictions, say,
that I cannot pleasure such an honourable
gentleman. Good Servilius, will you befriend
me so far as to use mine own words to him?
*Ser.* Yes, sir, I shall.
*Luc.* I'll look you out a good turn, Servilius.                          [*Exit* SERVILIUS.
True, as you said, Timon is shrunk indeed;
And he that's once denied will hardly speed.
                                    [*Exit.*
     I *Stran.* Do you observe this, Hostilius?
     2 *Stran.*                          Ay, too well.
     I *Stran.* Why, this is the world's soul; and
          just of the same piece
Is every flatterer's spirit. Who can call him
His friend that dips in the same dish? for, in
My knowing, Timon has been this lord's
     father,
And kept his credit with his purse;
Supported his estate; nay, Timon's money
Has paid his men their wages: he ne'er drinks
But Timon's silver treads upon his lip;
And yet,—O see the monstrousness of man
When he looks out in an ungrateful shape!—
He does deny him, in respect of his,
What charitable men afford to beggars.
     3 *Stran.* Religion groans at it.
     I *Stran.*                For mine own part
I never tasted Timon in my life,
Nor came any of his bounties over me
To mark me for his friend; yet I protest,
For his right noble mind, illustrious virtue,
And honourable carriage,
Had his necessity made use of me,
I would have put my wealth into donation,
And the best half should have return'd to him,

So much I love his heart: but, I perceive,
Men must learn now with pity to dispense:
For policy sits above conscience.    [*Exeunt*.

SCENE III.—ATHENS. *A Room in*
SEMPRONIUS' *House*.

*Enter* SEMPRONIUS *and a* Servant *of*
TIMON'S.

*Sem.* Must he needs trouble me in't, hum!
   —'bove all others?
He might have tried Lord Lucius or Lucullus;
And now Ventidius is wealthy too,
Whom he redeem'd from prison: all these
Owe their estates unto him.
   *Serv.*           My lord,
They have all been touch'd and found base
   metal; for
They have all denied him.
   *Sem.*       How! have they denied him?
Has Ventidius and Lucullus denied him?
And does he send to me? Three? hum!—
It shows but little love or judgment in him:
Must I be his last refuge! His friends, like
   physicians,
Thrive, give him over: must I take the cure
   upon me?          [him,
Has much disgrac'd me in't; I am angry at
That might have known my place: I see no
   sense for't,
But his occasions might have woo'd me first;
For, in my conscience, I was the first man
That e'er received gift from him:
And does he think so backardly of me now
That I'll requite it last? No:
So it may prove an argument of laughter
To the rest, and 'mongst the lords I be
   thought a fool.
I had rather than the worth of thrice the sum
Had sent to me first, but for my mind's sake;
I had such a courage to do him good. But
   now return,
And with their faint reply this answer join;
Who bates mine honour shall not know my
   coin.          [*Exit*.
   *Serv.* Excellent! Your lordship's a goodly
villian. The devil knew not what he did when
he made man politic,—he cross'd himself by
't: and I cannot think but, in the end, the
villanies of man will set him clear. How fairly
this lord strives to appear foul! takes virtuous copies to be wicked; like those that under
hot ardent zeal would set whole realms on
fire:
Of such a nature is his politic love.
This was my lord's best hope; now all are
   fled,
Save only the gods: now his friends are dead,
Doors, that were ne'er acquainted with their
   wards
Many a bounteous year, must be employ'd
Now to guard sure their master.
And this is all a liberal course allows;
Who cannot keep his wealth must keep his
   house.          [*Exit*.

SCENE IV.—ATHENS. *A Hall in* TIMON'S
*House*.

*Enter Two* Servants *of* VARRO *and the* Servant *of* LUCIUS, *meeting* TITUS, HORTENSIUS,
*and other* Servants *of* TIMON'S *creditors,
waiting his coming out*.

   1 *Var. Serv.* Well met; good-morrow, Titus
   and Hortensius.
   *Tit.* The like to you, kind Varro.
   *Hor.*             Lucius!
What, do we meet together?
   *Luc. Serv.*         Ay, and I think
One business does command us all; for mine
Is money.
   *Tit.* So is theirs and ours.

*Enter* PHILOTUS.

   *Luc. Serv.*       And Sir Philotus too!
   *Phi.* Good-day at once.
   *Luc. Serv.*      Welcome, good brother.
What do you think the hour?
   *Phi.*          Labouring for nine.
   *Luc. Serv.* So much?
   *Phi.*        Is not my lord seen yet?
   *Luc. Serv.*           Not yet.
   *Phi.* I wonder on't; he was wont to shine
   at seven.
   *Luc. Serv.* Ay, but the days are waxed
   shorter with him:
You must consider that a prodigal course
Is like the sun's; but not, like his, recoverable.
I fear
'Tis deepest winter in Lord Timon's purse;
That is, one may reach deep enough and yet
Find little.
   *Phi.* I am of your fear for that. [event.
   *Tit.* I'll show you how to observe a strange
Your lord sends now for money.
   *Hor.*         Most true, he does.
   *Tit.* And he wears jewels now of Timon's
   gift,
For which I wait for money.
   *Hor.* It is against my heart.
   *Luc. Serv.*    Mark how strange it shows,
Timon in this should pay more than he owes:
And e'en as if your lord should wear rich
   jewels
And send for money for 'em. [can witness:
   *Hor.* I am weary of this charge, the gods
I know my lord hath spent of Timon's wealth,
And now ingratitude makes it worse than
   stealth.
   1 *Var. Serv.* Yes, mine's three thousand
   crowns: what's yours?
   *Luc. Serv.* Five thousand mine.
   1 *Var. Serv.* 'Tis much deep: and it should
   seem by the sum
Your master's confidence was above mine;
Else, surely, his had equall'd.

*Enter* FLAMINIUS.

   *Tit.* One of Lord Timon's men.

*Luc. Serv.* Flaminius! sir, a word; pray, is my lord ready to come forth?

*Flam.* No, indeed, he is not.

*Tit.* We attend his lordship; pray, signify so much.

*Flam.* I need not tell him that; he knows you are too diligent.  [*Exit.*

*Enter* FLAVIUS, *in a cloak, muffled.*

*Luc. Serv.* Ha! is not that his steward muffled so?

He goes away in a cloud: call him, call him.

*Tit.* Do you hear, sir?

*Both Var. Serv.* By your leave, sir,—

*Flav.* What do you ask of me, my friends?

*Tit.* We wait for certain money here, sir.

*Flav.*                    Ay,
If money were as certain as your waiting
'Twere sure enough.
Why then preferr'd you not your sums and bills
When your false masters eat of my lord's meat?
Then they could smile, and fawn upon his debts,    [ous maws.
And take down th' interest into their glutton-
You do yourselves but wrong to stir me up;
Let me pass quietly:
Believe 't my lord and I have made an end;
I have no more to reckon, he to spend.

*Luc. Serv.* Ay, but this answer will not serve.

*Flav.* If 'twill not serve 'tis not so base as you;
For you serve knaves.    [*Exit.*

*1 Var. Serv.* How! What does his cashier'd worship mutter?

*2 Var. Serv.* No matter what; he's poor, and that's revenge enough. Who can speak broader than he that has no house to put his head in? such may rail against great buildings.

*Enter* SERVILIUS.

*Tit.* O, here's Servilius; now we shall know some answer.

*Ser.* If I might beseech you, gentlemen, to repair some other hour, I should much derive from 't; for, take 't of my soul, my lord leans wondrously to discontent: his comfortable temper has forsook him; he is much out of health and keeps his chamber.    [are not sick:

*Luc. Serv.* Many do keep their chambers
And, if it be so far beyond his health,
Methinks he should the sooner pay his debts,
And make a clear way to the gods.

*Ser.*                    Good gods!

*Tit.* We cannot take this for answer, sir.

*Flam.* [*Within.*] Servilius. help!—my lord! my lord!

*Enter* TIMON, *in a rage;* FLAMINIUS *following.*

*Tim.* What, are my doors oppos'd against my passage?

Have I been ever free, and must my house
Be my retentive enemy, my gaol?
The place which I have feasted, does it now,
Like all mankind, show me an iron heart?

*Luc. Serv.* Put in now, Titus.

*Tit.* My lord, here is my bill.

*Luc. Serv.* Here's mine.

*Hor. Serv.* And mine, my lord.

*Both Var. Serv.* And ours, my lord.

*Phi.* All our bills.    [to the girdle.

*Tim.* Knock me down with 'em: cleave me

*Luc. Serv.* Alas, my lord,—

*Tim.* Cut my heart in sums.

*Tit.* Mine, fifty talents.

*Tim.* Tell out my blood.

*Luc. Serv.* Five thousand crowns, my lord.

*Tim.* Five thousand drops pays that.—
What yours?—and yours?—

*1 Var. Serv.* My lord,—

*2 Var. Serv.* My lord,—

*Tim.* Tear me, take me, and the gods fall upon you!    [*Exit.*

*Hor.* Faith, I perceive our masters may throw their caps at their money: these debts may well be called desperate ones, for a madman owes 'em.    [*Exeunt.*

*Re-enter* TIMON *and* FLAVIUS.

*Tim.* They have e'en put my breath from me, the slaves.
Creditors!—devils.

*Flav.* My dear lord,—

*Tim.* What if it should be so?

*Flam.* My lord,—

*Tim.* I'll have it so.—My steward!

*Flav.* Here, my lord.

*Tim.* So fitly? Go, bid all my friends again,
Lucius, Lucullus, and Sempronius; all:
I'll once more feast the rascals.

*Flav.*                    O my lord,
You only speak from your distracted soul;
There is not so much left to furnish out
A moderate table.

*Tim.*                    Be 't not in thy care; go,
I charge thee, invite them all: let in the tide
Of knaves once more; my cook and I'll provide.    [*Exeunt.*

SCENE V.—ATHENS. *The Senate House.*
*The* Senate *sitting.*

*1 Sen.* My lords, you have my voice to it; the fault 's
Bloody; 'tis necessary he should die:
Nothing emboldens sin so much as mercy.

*2 Sen.* Most true; the law shall bruise him.

*Enter* ALCIBIADES, *attended.*

*Alcib.* Honour, health, and compassion to the senate!

*1 Sen.* Now, captain?

*Alcib.* I am an humble suitor to your virtues;
For pity is the virtue of the law,
And none but tyrants use it cruelly.

It pleases time and fortune to lie heavy
Upon a friend of mine, who, in hot blood,
Hath stepp'd into the law, which is past depth
To those that without heed do plunge into 't.
He is a man, setting his fate aside,
Of comely virtues:
Nor did he soil the fact with cowardice,—
An honour in him which buys out his fault,—
But with a noble fury and fair spirit,
Seeing his reputation touch'd to death,
He did oppose his foe:
And with such sober and unnoted passion
He did behove his anger ere 'twas spent,
As if he had but prov'd an argument.

   1 *Sen.* You undergo too strict a paradox.
Striving to make an ugly deed look fair:
Your words have took such pains, as if they
     labour'd      [quarrelling
To bring manslaughter into form, and set
Upon the head of valour; which, indeed,
Is valour misbegot, and came into the world
When sects and factions were newly born:
He's truly valiant that can wisely suffer
The worst that man can breathe; and make
   his wrongs      [carelessly;
His outsides,—to wear them like his raiment,
And ne'er prefer his injuries to his heart,
To bring it into danger.
If wrongs be evils, and enforce us kill,
What folly 'tis to hazard life for ill!

   *Alcib.* My lord,—      [clear:
   1 *Sen.* You cannot make gross sins look
To revenge is no valour, but to bear. [don me,
   *Alcib.* My lords, then, under favour, par-
If I speak like a captain:—
Why do fond men expose themselves to bat-
   tle,
And not endure all threats? sleep upon 't,
And let the foes quietly cut their throats,
Without repugnancy? but if there be
Such valour in the bearing, what make we
Abroad? why, then, women are more valiant,
That stay at home, if bearing carry it;
And th' ass more captain than the lion; the
   fellow
Loaden with irons wiser than the judge,
If wisdom be in suffering. O my lords,
As you are great, be pitifully good:
Who cannot condemn rashness in cold blood?
To kill, I grant, is sin's extremest gust;
But, in defence, by mercy, 'tis more just.
To be in anger is impiety;
But who is man that is not angry?
Weigh but the crime with this.

   2 *Sen.* You breathe in vain.
   *Alcib.*      In vain! his service done
At Lacedæmon and Byzantium
Were a sufficient briber for his life.
   1 *Sen.* What's that?
   *Alcib.* Why, I say, my lords, h'as done fair
   service,
And slain in fight many of your enemies:
How full of valour did he bear himself

In the last conflict, and make plenteous
   wounds!
   2 *Sen.* He has made too much plenty with
   'em, he
Is a sworn rioter: he has a sin that often
Drowns him, and takes his valour prisoner:
If there were no foes, that were enough
To overcome him: in that beastly fury
He has been known to commit outrages
And cherish factions: 'tis inferr'd to us
His days are foul and his drink dangerous.
   1 *Sen.* He dies.
   *Alcib.* Hard fate! he might have died in
   war.
My lords, if not for any parts in him,—
Though his right arm might purchase his own
   time,
And be in debt to none,—yet, more to move
   you,
Take my deserts to his, and join them both:
And, for I know your reverend ages love
Security, I'll pawn my victories, all
My honours to you, upon his good returns.
If by this crime he owes the law his life,
Why, let the war receiv 't in valiant gore;
For law is strict, and war is nothing more.
   1 *Sen.* We are for law,—he dies; urge it no
   more,
On height of our displeasure: friend or
   brother,
He forfeits his own blood that spills another.
   *Alcib.* Must it be so? it must not be. My
   lords,
I do beseech you, know me.
   2 *Sen.* How!
   *Alcib.* Call me to your remembrances.
   3 *Sen.*      What!
   *Alcib.* I cannot think but your age has for-
   got me;
It could not else be, I should prove so base
To sue, and be denied such common grace:
My wounds ache at you.
   1 *Sen.*      Do you dare our anger?
'Tis in few words, but spacious in effect;
We banish thee for ever.
   *Alcib.*      Banish me!
Banish your dotage; banish usury,
That makes the senate ugly.
   1 *Sen.* If, after two day's shine, Athens
   contain thee;
Attend our weightier judgment. And, not to
   swell our spirit,
He shall be executed presently.
                  [*Exeunt* Senators.
   *Alcib.* Now the gods keep you old enough;
   that you may live
Only in bone, that none may look on you!
I am worse than mad: I have kept back their
   foes,
While they have told their money, and let out
Their coin upon large interest; I myself
Rich only in large hurts;—all those for this?
Is this the balsam that the usuring senate

Pours into captains' wounds? Ha! banishment?

It comes not ill; I hate not to be banish'd;
It is a cause worthy my spleen and fury,
That I may strike at Athens. I'll cheer up
My discontented troops, and lay for hearts.
'Tis honour with most lands to be at odds;
Soldiers should brook as little wrongs as gods.

[*Exit.*

SCENE VI.—ATHENS. *A magnificent Room
in* TIMON'S *House.*

*Music. Tables set out:* Servants *attending.*

*Enter divers* Lords *at several doors.*

1 *Lord.* The good time of day to you, sir.

2 *Lord.* I also wish it to you. I think this honourable lord did but try us this other day.

1 *Lord.* Upon that were my thoughts tiring when we encountered: I hope it is not so low with him as he made it seem in the trial of his several friends.

2 *Lord.* It should not be by the persuasion of his new feasting.

1 *Lord.* I should think so: he hath sent me an earnest inviting, which many my near occasions did urge me to put off; but he hath conjured me beyond them, and I must needs appear.

2 *Lord.* In like manner was I in debt to my importunate business, but he would not hear my excuse. I am sorry, when he sent to borrow of me, that my provision was out.

1 *Lord.* I am sick of that grief too, as I understand how all things go.

2 *Lord.* Every man here's so. What would he have borrowed of you?

1 *Lord.* A thousand pieces.

2 *Lord.* A thousand pieces!

1 *Lord.* What of you?

3 *Lord.* He sent to me, sir,—Here he comes.

*Enter* TIMON *and* Attendants.

*Tim.* With all my heart, gentlemen both.—And how fare you?

1 *Lord.* Ever at the best, hearing well of your lordship.

2 *Lord.* The swallow follows not summer more willing than we your lordship.

*Tim.* Nor more willingly leaves winter; such summer-birds are men. [*Aside.*]—Gentlemen, our dinner will not recompense this long stay: feast your ears with the music awhile, if they will fare so harshly o' the trumpet's sound; we shall to 't presently.

1 *Lord.* I hope it remains not unkindly with your lordship that I returned you an empty messenger.

*Tim.* O, sir, let it not trouble you.

2 *Lord.* My noble lord,—

*Tim.* Ah, my good friend! what cheer?

2 *Lord.* My most honourable lord, I am e'en sick of shame that, when your lordship this other day sent to me, I was so unfortunate a beggar.

*Tim.* Think not on't, sir.

2 *Lord.* If you had sent but two hours before,—

*Tim.* Let it not cumber your better remembrance.—Come, bring in all together.

[*The banquet brought in.*

2 *Lord.* All covered dishes!

1 *Lord.* Royal cheer, I warrant you.

3 *Lord.* Doubt not that, if money and the season can yield it.

1 *Lord.* How do you? What's the news?

3 *Lord.* Alcibiades is banished: hear you of it?

1 *& 2 Lord.* Alcibiades banished!

3 *Lord.* 'Tis so, be sure of it.

1 *Lord.* How! how!

2 *Lord.* I pray you, upon what?

*Tim.* My worthy friends, will you draw near?

3 *Lord.* I'll tell you more anon. Here's a noble feast toward.

2 *Lord.* This is the old man still.

3 *Lord.* Will 't hold? will 't hold?

2 *Lord.* It does: but time will—and so,—

3 *Lord.* I do conceive.

*Tim.* Each man to his stool with that spur as he would to the lip of his mistress: your diet shall be in all places alike. Make not a city feast of it, to let the meat cool ere we can agree upon the first place: sit, sit. The gods require our thanks.—

You great benefactors, sprinkle our society with thankfulness. For your own gifts make yourselves praised: but reserve still to give, lest your deities be despised. Lend to each man enough, that one need not lend to another; for, were your godheads to borrow of men, men would forsake the gods. Make the meat be beloved more than the man that gives it. Let no assembly of twenty be without a score of villains: if there sit twelve women at the table, let a dozen of them be—as they are. The rest of your fees, O gods,—the senators of Athens, together with the common tag of people,—what is amiss in them, you gods, make suitable for destruction. For these my present friends,—as they are to me nothing, so in nothing bless them, and to nothing are they welcome.

Uncover, dogs, and lap.

[*The dishes, when uncovered, are seen
to be full of warm water.*

*Some speak.* What does his lordship mean?

*Some other.* I know not.

*Tim.* May you a better feast never behold,
You knot of mouth-friends! smoke and lukewarm water
Is your perfection. This is Timon's last;
Who, stuck and spangled with your flatteries,
Washes it off, and sprinkles in your faces

[*Throwing the water in their faces.*

Your reeking villany. Live loath'd and long,
Most smiling, smooth, detested parasites,
Courteous destroyers, affable wolves, meek bears,                                                                        [flies,
You fools of fortune, trencher-friends, time's

Cap and knee slaves, vapours, and minute-
jacks!
Of man and beast the infinite malady
Crust you quite o'er!—What, dost you go?
Soft, take thy physic first,—thou too,—and
thou;—
Stay, I will lend thee money, borrow none.—
[*Throws the dishes at them, and
drives them out.*
What, all in motion? Henceforth be no feast
Whereat a villain's not a welcome guest.
Burn, house! sink, Athens! henceforth hated
be
Of Timon, man, and all humanity!      [*Exit.*

### Re-enter the Lords.

1 *Lord.* How now, my lords!
2 *Lord.* Know you the quality of Lord
Timon's fury?
    3 *Lord.* Pish! did you see my cap?
    4 *Lord.* I have lost my gown.
    1 *Lord.* He's but a mad lord, and naught
but humour sways him. He gave me a jewel
the other day, and now he has beat it out of
my hat:—did you see my jewel?
    3 *Lord.* Did you see my cap?
    2 *Lord.* Here 'tis.
    4 *Lord.* Here lies my gown.
    1 *Lord.* Let's make no stay.
    2 *Lord.* Lord Timon's mad.
    3 *Lord.*           I feel 't upon my bones.
    4 *Lord.* One day he gives us diamonds, next
day stones.                     [*Exeunt.*

## ACT IV.

Scene I.—*Without the Walls of* Athens.

### Enter Timon.

*Tim.* Let me look back upon thee, O thou
wall
That girdlest in those wolves, dive in the
earth
And fence not Athens! Matrons, turn incon-
tinent!
Obedience fail in children! slaves and fools,
Pluck the grave wrinkled senate from the
bench
And minister in their steads! to general filths
Convert, o' the instant, green virginity,—
Do 't in your parent's eyes! bankrupts, hold
fast;
Rather than render back, out with your
knives
And cut your trusters' throats! bound serv-
ants, steal!
Large-handed robbers your grave masters are,
And pill by law! maid, to thy master's bed,—
Thy mistress is o' the brothel! son of sixteen,
Pluck the lin'd crutch from thy old limping
sire,
With it beat out his brains! piety and fear,
Religion to the gods, peace, justice, truth,
Domestic awe, night-rest, and neighbourhood,
Instruction, manners, mysteries, and trades,

Degrees, observances, customs and laws,
Decline to your confounding contraries, [men,
And let confusion live!—Plagues incident to
Your potent and infectious fevers heap
On Athens, ripe for stroke! thou cold sciatica,
Cripple our senators, that their limbs may
halt
As lamely as their manners! lust and liberty
Creep in the minds and marrows of our
youth,
That 'gainst the stream of virtue they may
strive
And drown themselves in rot! itches, blains,
Sow all the Athenian bosoms; and their crop
Be general leprosy! breath infect breath;
That their society, as their friendship, may
Be merely poison! Nothing I'll bear from thee
But nakedness, thou detestable town!
Take thou that too, with multiplying banns!
Timon will to the woods; where he shall find
The unkindest beast more kinder than man-
kind.                                [all,—
The gods confound,—hear me, ye good gods
The Athenians both within and out that wall!
And grant, as Timon grows, his hate may
grow
To the whole race of mankind, high and low!
Amen.                             [*Exit.*

Scene II.—Athens. *A Room in* Timon's
*House.*

*Enter* Flavius, *with* Two *or* Three *Servants.*

    1 *Serv.* Here you, master steward, where's
our master?
Are we undone? cast off? nothing remain-
ing?
    *Flav.* Alack, my fellows, what I should I
say to you?
Let me be recorded by the righteous gods,
I am as poor as you.
    1 *Serv.*            Such a house broke!
So noble a master fall'n! All gone! and not
One friend to take his fortune by the arm
And go along with him!
    2 *Serv.*             As we do turn our backs
To our companion thrown into his grave,
So his familiars from his buried fortunes
Slink all away; leave their false vows with
him,
Like empty purses pick'd; and his poor self,
A dedicated beggar to the air,
With his disease of all-shunn'd poverty,
Walks, like contempt, alone.—More of our
fellows.

### Enter other Servants.

    *Flav.* All broken implements of a ruin'd
house.                             [livery,
    3 *Serv.* Yet do our hearts wear Timon's
That see I by our faces; we are fellows still,
Serving alike in sorrow: leak'd is our bark;
And we, poor mates, stand on the dying deck
Hearing the surges threat: we must all part
Into this sea of air.

*Flav.*　　　　　　　　Good fellows all,
The latest of my wealth I'll share amongst
　　you.
Wherever we shall meet, for Timon's sake,
Let's yet be fellows; let's shake our heads,
　　and say,
As 'twere a knell unto our master's fortune,
*We have seen better days.* Let each take
　　some.　　　　　　　　[*Giving them money.*
Nay, put out all your hands. Not one word
　　more:
Thus part we rich in sorrow, parting poor.
　　[*Servants embrace, and part several ways.*
O, the fierce wretchedness that glory brings
　　us!
Who would not wish to be from wealth
　　exempt
Since riches point to misery and contempt?
Who would be so mock'd with glory? or to
　　live
But in a dream of friendship?
To have his pomp, and all what state com-
　　pounds,
But only painted, like his varnish'd friends?
Poor honest lord, brought low by his own
　　heart,
Undone by goodness! strange, unusual blood,
When man's worst sin is, he does too much
　　good!
Who then dares to be half so kind again?
For bounty, that makes gods, does still mar
　　men.
My dearest lord,—bless'd to be most accurs'd,
Rich only to be wretched,—thy great for-
　　tunes
Are made thy chief afflictions. Alas, kind
　　lord!
He's flung in rage from this ingrateful seat
Of monstrous friends; nor has he with him to
Supply his life, or that which can command
　　it.
I'll follow and enquire him out:
I'll ever serve his mind with my best will;
Whilst I have gold, I'll be his steward still.
　　　　　　　　　　　　　　　　[*Exit.*

SCENE III.—*The Woods. Before* TIMON'S
　　*Cave.*

*Enter* TIMON.

*Tim.* O blessed breeding sun, draw from
　　the earth
Rotten humidity; below thy sister's orb
Infect the air! Twinn'd brothers of one
　　womb,—
Whose procreation, residence, and birth
Scarce is dividant,—touch them with several
　　fortunes;
The greater scorns the lesser: not nature,
To whom all sores lay siege, can bear great
　　fortune
But by contempt of nature.
Raise me this beggar and deny 't that lord;
The senator shall bear contempt hereditary,
The beggar native honour.

It is the pasture lards the other's sides,
The want that makes him lean. Who dares,
　　who dares,
In purity of manhood stand upright,
And say, *This man's a flatterer?* if one be,
So are they all; for every grise of fortune
Is smooth'd by that below: the learned pate
Ducks to the golden fool: all is oblique;
There's nothing level in our cursed natures
But direct villany. Therefore, be abhorr'd
All feasts, societies, and throngs of men!
His semblable, yea, himself Timon disdains:
Destruction fang mankind!—Earth, yield me
　　roots!　　　　　　　　　　[*Digging.*
Who seeks for better of thee, sauce his palate
With thy most operant poison! What is here?
Gold? yellow, glittering, precious gold? No,
　　gods,
I am no idle votarist. Roots, you clear
　　heavens!
Thus much of this will make black, white;
　　foul, fair;　　　　　　　　[ard, valiant.
Wrong, right; base, noble; old, young; cow-
Ha, you gods! why this? what this, you
　　gods? why, this　　　　　　[sides;
Will lug your priests and servants from your
Pluck stout men's pillows from below their
　　heads:
This yellow slave
Will knit and break religions; bless the ac-
　　curs'd;
Make the hoar leprosy ador'd; place thieves,
And give them title, knee, and approbation,
With senators on the bench: this is it
That makes the wappen'd widow wed again;
She whom the spital-house and ulcerous sores
Would cast the gorge at, this embalms and
　　spices
To the April day again. Come, damned earth,
Thou common whore of mankind, that putt'st
　　odds
Among the rout of nations, I will make thee
Do thy right nature.—[*March afar off.*] Ha!
　　a drum?—Thou 'rt quick,
But yet I'll bury thee: thou 'lt go, strong
　　thief,
When gouty keepers of thee cannot stand:—
Nay, stay thou out for earnest.
　　　　　　　　　　　　[*Keeping some gold.*

*Enter* ALCIBIADES *with drum and fife, in warlike manner;* PHRYNIA *and* TIMANDRA.

*Alcib.*　　　　　　What art thou there? speak.
*Tim.* A beast, as thou art. The canker
　　gnaw thy heart
For showing me again the eyes of man!
*Alcib.* What is thy name? Is man so hate-
　　ful to thee,
That art thyself a man?
*Tim.* I am *misanthropos,* and hate man-
　　kind.
For thy part, I do wish thou wert a dog,
That I might love thee something.
*Alcib.*　　　　　　　　I know thee well;

But in thy fortunes am unlearn'd and strange.

*Tim.* I know thee too; and more than that
I know thee
I not desire to know. Follow thy drum;
With man's blood paint the ground, gules,
gules:
Religious canons, civil laws are cruel;
Then what should war be? This fell whore of
thine
Hath in her more destruction than thy sword,
For all her cherubin look.

*Phry.* Thy lips rot off!

*Tim.* I will not kiss thee; then the rot returns
To thine own lips again. [change?

*Alcib.* How came the noble Timon to this

*Tim.* As the moon does, by wanting light
to give:
But then renew I could not, like the moon;
There were no suns to borrow of.

*Alcib.* Noble Timon,
What friendship may I do thee?

*Tim.* None, but to
Maintain my opinion.

*Alcib.* What is it, Timon?

*Tim.* Promise me friendship, but perform
none: if thou wilt not promise, the gods
plague thee, for thou art a man! if thou dost
perform, confound thee, for thou art a man!

*Alcib.* I have heard in some sort of thy
miseries. [perity.

*Tim.* Thou saw'st them when I had pros-

*Alcib.* I see them now; then was a blessed
time. [harlots.

*Tim.* As thine is now, held with a brace of

*Timan.* Is this the Athenian minion whom
the world
Voic'd so regardfully?

*Tim.* Art thou Timandra?

*Timan.* Yes.

*Tim.* Be a whore still! they love thee not
that use thee;
Give them diseases, leaving with thee their
lust.
Make use of thy salt hours: season the slaves
For tubs and baths; bring down rose-cheek'd
youth to
The tub-fast and the diet.

*Timan.* Hang thee, monster!

*Alcib.* Pardon him, sweet Timandra; for
his wits
Are drown'd and lost in his calamities.—
I have but little gold of late, brave Timon,
The want whereof doth daily make revolt
In my penurious band: I have heard and
griev'd,
How cursed Athens, mindless of thy worth,
Forgetting thy great deeds, when neighbour
states,
But for thy sword and fortune, trod upon
them,—

*Tim.* I pr'ythee, beat thy drum, and get
thee gone. [Timon.

*Alcib.* I am thy friend, and pity thee, dear

*Tim.* How dost thou pity him whom thou
dost trouble?
I had rather be alone.

*Alcib.* Why, fare thee well:
Here is some gold for thee.

*Tim.* Keep it, I cannot eat it.

*Alcib.* When I have laid proud Athens on a
heap,—

*Tim.* Warr'st thou 'gainst Athens?

*Alcib.* Ay, Timon, and have cause.

*Tim.* The gods confound them all in thy
conquest;
And thee after, when thou hast conquer'd!

*Alcib.* Why me, Timon?

*Tim.* That by killing of villains,
Thou wast born to conquer my country.
Put up thy gold: go on,—here's gold,—go on;
Be as a planetary plague, when Jove
Will o'er some high-vic'd city hang his poison
In the sick air: let not thy sword skip one:
Pity not honour'd age for his white beard,
He is an usurer: strike me the counterfeit
matron:
It is her habit only that is honest,
Herself's a bawd: let not the virgin's cheek
Make soft thy trenchant sword; for those
milk paps, [eyes,
That through the window-bars bore at men's
Are not within the leaf of pity writ,
But set them down horrible traitors: spare
not the babe, [their mercy;
Whose dimpled smiles from fools exhaust
Think it a bastard, whom the oracle
Hath doubtfully pronounc'd thy throat shall
cut,
And mince it sans remorse: swear against
objects;
Put armour on thine ears and on thine eyes;
Whose proof nor yells of mothers, maids, nor
babes,
Nor sight of priests in holy vestments bleed-
ing,
Shall pierce a jot. There's gold to pay thy
soldiers:
Make large confusion; and, thy fury spent,
Confounded be thyself! Speak not, be gone.

*Alcib.* Hast thou gold yet? I'll take the
gold thou giv'st me.
Not all thy counsel.

*Tim.* Dost thou, or dost thou not, heaven's
curse upon thee!

*Phr. & Timan.* Give us some gold, good
Timon: hast thou more?

*Tim.* Enough to make a whore forswear
her trade,
And to make whores a bawd. Hold up, you
sluts,
Your aprons mountant: you are not oath-
able,—
Although I know you'll swear, terribly swear,
Into strong shudders and to heavenly agues,
The immortal gods that hear you,—spare
your oaths,
I'll trust to your conditions: be whores still;

And he whose pious breath seeks to convert
　　you,
Be strong in whore, allure him, burn him up;
Let your close fire predominate his smoke,
And be no turncoats: yet may your pains six
　　months　　　　　　　　　　　　[roofs
Be quite contrary: and thatch your poor thin
With burdens of the dead;—some that were
　　hang'd,
No matter:—wear them, betray with them:
　　whore still;
Paint till a horse may mire upon your face:
A pox of wrinkles!
　　*Phr. & Timan.* Well, more gold.—What
　　　　then?—
Believe 't, that we'll do anything for gold.
　　*Tim.* Consumptions sow　　　　[shins,
In hollow bones of man; strike their sharp
And mar men's spurring. Crack the lawyer's
　　voice,
That he may never more false title plead,
Nor sound his quillets shrilly: hoar the
　　flamen,
That scolds against the quality of flesh
And not believes himself: down with the nose,
Down with it flat; take the bridge quite
　　away
Of him that, his particular to foresee,
Smells from the general weal: make curl'd-
　　pate ruffians bald;
And let the unscarr'd braggarts of the war
Derive some pain from you: plague all;
That your activity may defeat and quell
The source of all erection.—There's more
　　gold:—
Do you damn others and let this damn you,
And ditches grave you all!
　　*Phr. & Timan.* More counsel with more
　　　money, bounteous Timon.
　　*Tim.* More whore, more mischief first; I
　　　have given you earnest.
　　*Alcib.* Strike up the drum towards Athens!
　　　Farewell, Timon:
If I thrive well I'll visit thee again.
　　*Tim.* If I hope well I'll never see thee more.
　　*Alcib.* I never did thee harm.
　　*Tim.* Yes, thou spok'st well of me.
　　*Alcib.*　　　　　　Call'st thou that harm?
　　*Tim.* Men daily find it. Get thee away, and
　　　take
Thy beagles with thee.
　　*Alcib.*　　　　We but offend him.—Strike.
　　　　　[*Drum beats. Exeunt* ALCIBIADES,
　　　　　PHRYNIA, *and* TIMANDRA.
　　*Tim.* That nature, being sick of man's un-
　　　kindness,
Should yet be hungry!—Common mother,
　　thou,　　　　　　　　　　　[*Digging.*
Whose womb unmeasurable and infinite
　　breast
Teems and feeds all; whose self-same mettle,
Whereof thy proud child, arrogant man, is
　　puff'd,
Engenders the black toad and adder blue,

The gilded newt and eyeless venom'd worm,
With all the abhorred births below crisp
　　heaven
Whereon Hyperion's quickening fire doth
　　shine;
Yield him, who all thy human sons doth hate,
From forth thy plenteous bosom, one poor
　　root!
Ensear thy fertile and conceptious womb,
Let it no more bring out ingrateful man!
Go great with tigers, dragons, wolves, and
　　bears;　　　　　　　　　　　　[face
Teem with new monsters, whom thy upward
Hath to the marbled mansion all above
Never presented!—O, a root,—dear thanks!
Dry up thy marrows, vines, and plough-torn
　　leas;
Whereof ingrateful man, with liquorish
　　draughts
And morsels unctuous, greases his pure mind,
That from it all consideration slips!

　　　　　*Enter* APEMANTUS.
More man? plague, plague!
　　*Apem.* I was directed hither: men report
Thou dost affect my manners, and dost use
　　them.　　　　　　　　　　　　[a dog
　　*Tim.* 'Tis, then, because thou dost not keep
Whom I would imitate: consumption catch
　　thee!
　　*Apem.* This is in thee a nature but affected;
A poor unmanly melancholy sprung
From change of fortune. Why this spade?
　　this place?
This slave-like habit? and these looks of care?
Thy flatterers yet wear silk, drink wine, lie
　　soft;
Hug their diseas'd perfumes, and have forgot
That ever Timon was. Shame not these woods
By putting on the cunning of a carper.
Be thou a flatterer now, and seek to thrive
By that which has undone thee: hinge thy
　　knee,
And let his very breath whom thou 'lt observe
Blow off thy cap; praise his most vicious
　　strain,
And call it excellent: thou wast told thus;
Thou gav'st thine ears, like tapsters that bid
　　welcome,
To knaves and all approachers: 'tis most just
That thou turn rascal; hadst thou wealth
　　again
Rascals should have 't. Do not assume my
　　likeness.
　　*Tim.* Were I like thee, I'd throw away
　　　myself.
　　*Apem.* Thou hast cast away thyself, being
　　　like thyself;
A madman so long, now a fool. What, think'st
That the bleak air, thy boisterous chamber-
　　lain,
Will put thy shirt on warm? Will these
　　moss'd trees,
That have outliv'd the eagle, page thy heels,

And skip when thou point'st out? Will the
     cold brook,
Candied with ice, caudle thy morning taste
To cure thy o'ernight's surfeit? call the crea-
     tures,—
Whose naked natures live in all the spite
Of wreckful heaven; whose bare unhoused
     trunks,
To the conflicting elements expos'd,
Answer mere nature,—bid them flatter thee;
O, thou shalt find,—

*Tim.*          A fool of thee: depart.
*Apem.* I love thee better now than e'er I
     did.
*Tim.* I hate thee worse.
*Apem.*            Why?
*Tim.*          Thou flatter'st misery.
*Apem.* I flatter not; but say thou art a
     caitiff.
*Tim.* Why dost thou seek me out?
*Apem.*           To vex thee.
*Tim.* Always a villain's office or a fool's.
Dost please thyself in 't?
*Apem.*            Ay.
*Tim.*         What! a knave too?
*Apem.* If thou didst put this sour-cold
     habit on
To castigate thy pride, 'twere well: but thou
Does it enforcedly; thou 'dst courtier be again
Wert thou not beggar. Willing misery
Outlives incertain pomp, is crown'd before:
The one is filling still, never complete;
The other, at high wish: best state, content-
     less,
Hath a distracted and most wretched being,
Worse than the worst, content.
Thou should'st desire to die, being miserable.
    *Tim.* Not by his breath that is more
     miserable.
Thou art a slave, whom Fortune's tender arm
With favour never clasp'd; but bred a dog.
Hadst thou, like us from our first swath, pro-
     ceeded
The sweet degrees that this brief world af-
     fords
To such as may the passive drugs of it
Freely command, thou wouldst have plung'd
     thyself
In general riot; melted down thy youth
In different beds of lust; and never learn'd
The icy precepts of respect, but follow'd
The sugar'd game before thee. But myself,
Who had the world as my confectionary;
The mouths, the tongues, the eyes, and hearts
     of men
At duty, more than I could frame employ-
     ment;
That numberless upon me stuck, as leaves
Do on the oak, have with one winter's brush
Fell from their boughs, and left me open, bare
For every storm that blows;—I, to bear this,
That never knew but better, is some burden:
Thy nature did commence in sufferance, time

Hath made thee hard in 't. Why shouldst thou
     hate men?           [given?
They never flatter'd thee: what hast thou
If thou wilt curse, thy father, that poor rag,
Must be thy subject; who, in spite, put stuff
To some she beggar, and compounded thee
Poor rogue hereditary. Hence! be gone!—
If thou hadst not been born the worst of men,
Thou hadst been a knave and flatterer.
*Apem.*          Art thou proud yet?
*Tim.* Ay, that I am not thee.
*Apem.*            I, that I was
No prodigal.
*Tim.*        I, that I am one now:
Were all the wealth I have shut up in thee,
I'd give thee leave to hang it. Get thee gone.—
That the whole life of Athens were in this!
Thus would I eat it.        [*Eating a root.*
*Apem.*      Here; I will mend thy feast.
                [*Offering him something.*
*Tim.* First mend my company, take away
     thyself.
*Apem.* So I shall mend mine own by the
     lack of thine.
*Tim.* 'Tis not well mended so, it is but
     botch'd;
If not, I would it were.
*Apem.* What wouldst thou have to
     Athens?
*Tim.* Thee thither in a whirlwind. If thou
     wilt,
Tell them there I have gold; look, so I have.
*Apem.* Here is no use for gold.
*Tim.*          The best and truest:
For here it sleeps, and does no hired harm.
*Apem.* Where ly'st o' nights, Timon?
*Tim.*          Under that 's above me.
Where feed'st thou o' days, Apemantus?
*Apem.* Where my stomach finds meat; or,
rather, where I eat it.
*Tim.* Would poison were obedient, and
knew my mind!
*Apem.* Where wouldst thou send it?
*Tim.* To sauce thy dishes.
*Apem.* The middle of humanity thou never
knewest, but the extremity of both ends:
when thou wast in thy gilt and thy perfume
they mocked thee for too much curiosity; in
thy rags thou knowest none, but art despised
for the contrary. There's a medlar for thee,
eat it.
*Tim.* On what I hate I feed not.
*Apem.* Dost hate a medlar?
*Tim.* Ay, though it look like thee.
*Apem.* An thou hadst hated medlars sooner, thou shouldst have loved thyself better
now. What man didst thou ever know unthrift that was beloved after his means?
*Tim.* Who without those means thou talkest of didst thou ever know beloved?
*Apem.* Myself.
*Tim.* I understand thee; thou hadst some
means to keep a dog.

*Apem.* What things in the world canst thou nearest compare to thy flatterers?

*Tim.* Women nearest; but men, men are the things themselves. What wouldst thou do with the world, Apemantus, if it lay in thy power?

*Apem.* Give it to the beasts to be rid of the men.

*Tim.* Wouldst thou have thyself fall in the confusion of men, and remain a beast with the beasts?

*Apem.* Ay, Timon.

*Tim.* A beastly ambition, which the gods grant thee t' attain to! If thou wert the lion, the fox would beguile thee: if thou wert the lamb, the fox would eat thee: if thou wert the fox, the lion would suspect thee, when peradventure, thou wert accused by the ass: if thou wert the ass, thy dulness would torment thee; and still thou livedst but as a breakfast to the wolf: if thou wert the wolf, thy greediness would afflict thee, and oft thou shouldst hazard thy life for thy dinner: wert thou the unicorn, pride and wrath would confound thee, and make thine own self the conquest of thy fury: wert thou a bear, thou wouldst be killed by the horse; wert thou a horse, thou wouldst be seized by the leopard; wert thou a leopard, thou wert german to the lion, and the spots of thy kindred were jurors on thy life: all thy safety were remotion; and thy defence absence. What beast couldst thou be, that were not subject to a beast? and what a beast art thou already, that seest not thy loss in transformation!

*Apem.* If thou couldst please me with speaking to me, thou might'st have hit upon it here: the commonwealth of Athens is become a forest of beasts.

*Tim.* How has the ass broke the wall, that thou art out of the city?

*Apem.* Yonder comes a poet and a painter: the plague of company light upon thee! I will fear to catch it, and give way: when I know not what else to do, I'll see thee again.

*Tim.* When there is nothing living but thee, thou shalt be welcome. I had rather be a beggar's dog than Apemantus.

*Apem.* Thou art the cap of all the fools alive.

*Tim.* Would thou wert clean enough to spit upon!

*Apem.* A plague on thee, thou art too bad to curse.

*Tim.* All villains that do stand by thee are pure.                                    [speak'st.

*Apem.* There is no leprosy but what thou

*Tim.* If I name thee.—
I'll beat thee, but I should infect my hands.

*Apem.* I would my tongue could rot them off!

*Tim.* Away, thou issue of a mangy dog!
Choler does kill me that thou art alive;
I swoon to see thee.

*Apem.*                    Would thou wouldst burst!

*Tim.*                                        Away,
Thou tedious rogue! I am sorry I shall lose
A stone by thee.          [*Throws a stone at him.*

*Apem.*          Beast!

*Tim.*                              Slave!

*Apem.*                                        Toad!

*Tim.*                    Rogue, rogue, rogue!
          [APEM. *retreats backward, as going.*
I am sick of this false world; and will love naught
But even the mere necessities upon 't.
Then, Timon, presently prepare thy grave;
Lie where the light foam of the sea may beat
Thy grave-stone daily: make thine epitaph,
That death in me at others' lives may laugh.
O thou sweet king-killer and dear divorce
          [*Looking on the gold.*
'Twixt natural son and sire! thou bright defiler
Of Hymen's purest bed! thou valiant Mars!
Thou ever young, fresh, lov'd and delicate wooer,
Whose blush doth thaw the consecrated snow
That lies on Dian's lap! thou visible god,
That solder'st close impossibilities,
And mak'st them kiss! that speak'st with every tongue
To every purpose! O thou touch of hearts!
Think, thy slave, man, rebels; and by thy virtue
Set them into confounding odds, that beasts
May have the world in empire!

*Apem.*                    Would 'twere so!—
But not till I am dead.—I'll say thou'st gold:
Thou wilt be throng'd to shortly.

*Tim.*                              Throng'd to?

*Apem.*                                        Ay.

*Tim.* Thy back, I pr'ythee.

*Apem.*          Live, and love thy misery!

*Tim.* Long live so, and so die! [*Exit* APE-
MANTUS.] I am quit.
More things like men?—Eat, Timon, and abhor them.

*Enter* Thieves.

1 *Thief.* Where should he have this gold? It is some poor fragment, some slender ort of his remainder: the mere want of gold and the falling-from of his friends drove him into this melancholy.

2 *Thief.* It is noised he hath a mass of treasure.

3 *Thief.* Let us make the assay upon him: if he care not for't, he will supply us easily; if he covetously reserve it, how shall 's get it?

2 *Thief.* True; for he bears it not about him, 'tis hid.

1 *Thief.* Is not this he?

*Thieves.* Where?

2 *Thief.* 'Tis his description.

3 *Thief.* He; I know him.

*Thieves.* Save thee, Timon.

*Tim.* Now, thieves?

*Thieves.* Soldiers, not thieves.

*Tim.* Both too; and women's sons.

*Thieves.* We are not thieves, but men that much do want.

*Tim.* Your greatest want is, you want much of meat.

Why should you want? Behold, the earth hath roots;

Within this mile break forth a hundred springs:

The oaks bear mast, the briars scarlet hips!

The bounteous housewife, nature, on each bush

Lays her full mess before you. Want! why want?

1 *Thief.* We cannot live on grass, on berries, water,

As beasts and birds and fishes.

*Tim.* Nor on the beasts themselves, the birds, and fishes;

You must eat men. Yet thanks I must you con,

That you are thieves profess'd; that you work not

In holier shapes: for there is boundless theft

In limited professions. Rascal thieves,

Here's gold. Go, suck the subtle blood o' the grape

Till the high fever seethe your blood to froth,

And so 'scape hanging: trust not the physician;

His antidotes are poison, and he slays

More than you rob: take wealth and lives together;

Do villany, do, since you protest to do 't,

Like workmen. I'll example you with thievery:

The sun's a thief, and with his great attraction

Robs the vast sea: the moon's an arrant thief,

And her pale fire she snatches from the sun:

The sea's a thief, whose liquid surge resolves

The moon into salt tears: the earth's a thief,

That feeds and breeds by a composture stolen

From general excrement; each thing's a thief:

The laws, your curb and whip, in their rough power        [away,

Have uncheck'd theft. Love not yourselves;

Rob one another;—there's more gold;—cut throats;

All that you meet are thieves. To Athens go,

Break open shops; nothing can you steal

But thieves do lose it: steal not less for this

I give you; and gold confound you howsoe'er!

Amen.        [TIMON *retires to his cave.*

3 *Thief.* Has almost charmed me from my profession by persuading me to it.

1 *Thief.* 'Tis in the malice of mankind that he thus advises us; not to have us thrive in our mystery.

2 *Thief.* I'll believe him as an enemy, and give over my trade.

1 *Thief.* Let us first see peace in Athens:

there is no time so miserable but a man may be true.        [*Exeunt* Thieves.

*Enter* FLAVIUS.

*Flav.* O you gods!

Is yon despis'd and ruinous man my lord?

Full of decay and failing? O monument

And wonder of good deeds evilly bestow'd!

What an alteration of honour

Has desperate want made!

What viler thing upon the earth than friends

Who can bring noblest minds to basest ends!

How rarely does it meet with this time's guise,

When man was wish'd to love his enemies!

Grant I may ever love, and rather woo

Those that would mischief me than those that do!—

Has caught me in his eye: I will present

My honest grief unto him; and, as my lord,

Still serve him with my life.—My dearest master!

TIMON *comes forward from his cave.*

*Tim.* Away! what art thou?

*Flav.*        Have you forgot me, sir?

*Tim.* Why dost ask that? I have forgot all men;

Then, if thou grant'st thou'rt a man, I have forgot thee.

*Flav.* An honest poor servant of yours.

*Tim.* Then I know thee not:

I ne'er had honest man about me, I; all

I kept were knaves, to serve in meat to villains.

*Flav.* The gods are witness,

Ne'er did poor steward wear a truer grief

For his undone lord than mine eyes for you.

*Tim.* What, dost thou weep?—come nearer;—then I love thee

Because thou art a woman, and disclaim'st

Flinty mankind; whose eyes do never give

But thorough lust and laughter. Pity's sleeping:

Strange times, that weep with laughing, not with weeping!

*Flav.* I beg of you to know me, good my lord,        [wealth lasts,

To accept my grief, and, whilst this poor

To entertain me as your steward still.

*Tim.* Had I a steward

So true, so just, and now so comfortable?

It almost turns my dangerous nature mild.

Let me behold thy face. Surely, this man

Was born of woman.—

Forgive my general and exceptless rashness,

You perpetual-sober gods! I do proclaim

One honest man,—mistake me not,—but one;

No more, I pray,—and he's a steward.—

How fain would I have hated all mankind!

And thou redeem'st thyself: but all, save thee,

I fell with curses.

Methinks thou art more honest now than wise;

For by oppressing and betraying me
Thou might'st have sooner got another ser-
　　vice:
For many so arrive at second masters
Upon their first lord's neck. But tell me true,—
For I must ever doubt, though ne'er so sure,—
Is not thy kindness subtle, covetous,
If not a usuring kindness, and, as rich men
　　deal gifts,
Expecting in return twenty for one?
　　*Flav.* No, my most worthy master; in
　　　　whose breast
Doubt and suspect, alas, are plac'd too late:
You should have fear'd false times when you
　　did feast:
Suspect still comes where an estate is least.
That which I show, heaven knows, is merely
　　love,
Duty, and zeal to your unmatched mind,
Care of your food and living; and, believe it,
My most honour'd lord,
For any benefit that points to me,
Either in hope or present, I'd exchange
For this one wish,—that you had power and
　　wealth
To requite me, by making rich yourself.
　　*Tim.* Look thee, 'tis so!—Thou singly
　　　　honest man,
Here, take:—the gods, out of my misery,
Have sent thee treasure. Go, live rich and
　　happy; 　　　　　　　　　　　[men;
But thus condition'd:—thou shalt build from
Hate all, curse all; show charity to none;
But let the famish'd flesh slide from the bone
Ere thou relieve the beggar: give to dogs
What thou deny'st to men; let prisons swal-
　　low 'em, 　　　　　　　　[blasted woods,
Debts wither 'em to nothing: be men like
And may diseases lick up their false bloods!
And so, farewell and thrive.
　　*Flav.* 　　　　　　　O, let me stay,
And comfort you, my master.
　　*Tim.* 　　　　　　If thou hat'st curses,
Stay not; but fly whilst thou'rt bless'd and
　　free:
Ne'er see thou man, and let me ne'er see thee.
　　　　　　　　　　　[*Exeunt severally.*

## ACT V.

### Scene I.—*The Woods. Before* Timon's
*Cave.*

*Enter* Poet *and* Painter; Timon *watching
them from his cave.*

　　*Pain.* As I took note of the place, it cannot
be far where he abides.
　　*Poet.* What's to be thought of him? Does
the rumour hold for true that he's so full of
gold?
　　*Pain.* Certain: Alcibiades reports it: Phrynia and Timandra had gold of him: he likewise enriched poor straggling soldiers with
great quantity: 'tis said he gave unto his
steward a mighty sum.

　　*Poet.* Then this breaking of his has been
but a try for his friends.
　　*Pain.* Nothing else: you shall see him a
palm in Athens again, and flourish with the
highest. Therefore 'tis not amiss we tender
our loves to him, in this supposed distress of
his: it will show honestly in us; and is very
likely to load our purposes with what they
travail for, if it be a just and true report that
goes of his having.
　　*Poet.* What have you now to present unto
him?
　　*Pain.* Nothing at this time but my visitation: only I will promise him an excellent
piece.
　　*Poet.* I must serve him so too,—tell him of
an intent that's coming toward him.
　　*Pain.* Good as the best. Promising is the
very air o' the time: it opens the eyes of
expectation: performance is ever the duller
for his act; and but in the plainer and simpler kind of people the deed of saying is quite
out of use. To promise is most courtly and
fashionable: performance is a kind of will or
testament which argues a great sickness in his
judgment that makes it.
　　*Tim.* Excellent workman! thou canst not
paint a man so bad as is thyself.
　　*Poet.* I am thinking what I shall say I have
provided for him: it must be a personating of
himself　a satire against the softness of prosperity, with a discovery of the infinite flatteries that follow youth and opulency.
　　*Tim.* Must thou needs stand for a villain in
thine own work? wilt thou whip thine own
faults in other men? Do so, I have gold for
thee.
　　*Poet.* Nay, let's seek him:
Then do we sin against our own estate
When we may profit meet and come too late.
　　*Pain.* True; 　　　　　　　　　[night,
When the day serves, before black-corner'd
Find what thou want'st by free and offer'd
　　light.
Come. 　　　　　　　　　　　[god's gold,
　　*Tim.* I'll meet you at the turn. What a
That he is worship'd in a baser temple
Than where swine feed! 　　　[the foam:
'Tis thou that rigg'st the bark, and plough'st
Settlest admired reverence in a slave:
To thee be worship! and thy saints for aye
Be crown'd with plagues, that thee alone
　　obey!
Fit I meet them. 　　[*Advancing from his cave.*
　　*Poet.* Hail, worthy Timon!
　　*Pain.* 　　　　　　Our late noble master!
　　*Tim.* Have I once liv'd to see two honest
　　men?
　　*Poet.* Sir,
Having often of your open bounty tasted,
Hearing you were retir'd, your friends fall'n
　　off,
Whose thankless natures,—O abhorred spir-
　　its!—

Not all the whips of heaven are large enough:
What! to you,                              [ence
Whose star-like nobleness gave life and influ-
To their whole being! I'm wrapt, and cannot
    cover
The monstrous bulk of this ingratitude
With any size in words.               [better:
    *Tim.* Let it go naked, men may see't the
You that are honest, by being what you are,
Make them best seen and known.
    *Pain.*                        He and myself
Have travail'd in the great shower of your
    gifts,
And sweetly felt it.
    *Tim.*             Ay, you are honest men.
    *Pain.* We are hither come to offer you our
    service.                      [requite you?
    *Tim.* Most honest men! Why, how shall I
Can you eat roots, and drink cold water? no.
    *Both.* What we can do, we'll do, to do you
    service.                      [have gold;
    *Tim.* Ye're honest men: ye've heard that I
I am sure you have: speak truth; ye're honest
    men.
    *Pain.* So it is said, my noble lord: but
    therefore
Came not my friend nor I.
    *Tim.* Good honest men!—Thou draw'st a
    counterfeit
Best in all Athens: thou'rt indeed the best;
Thou counterfeit'st most lively.
    *Pain.*                    So, so, my lord.
    *Tim.* E'en so, sir, as I say.—And, for thy
    fiction,                      [*To the* Poet.
Why, thy verse swells with stuff so fine and
    smooth
That thou art even natural in thine art.—
But for all this, my honest-natur'd friends,
I must needs say you have a little fault:
Marry, 'tis not monstrous in you; neither
    wish I
You take much pains to mend.
    *Both.*                  Beseech your honour
To make it known to us.
    *Tim.*                    You'll take it ill.
    *Both.* Most thankfully, my lord.
    *Tim.*                    Will you indeed?
    *Both.* Doubt it not, worthy lord.
    *Tim.* There's never a one of you but trusts
    a knave
That mightily deceives you.
    *Both.*                    Do we, my lord?
    *Tim.* Ay, and you hear him cog, see him
    dissemble,
Know his gross patchery, love him, feed him,
Keep in your bosom: yet remain assur'd
That he's a made-up villain.
    *Pain.* I know not such, my lord.
    *Poet.*                          Nor I.
    *Tim.* Look you, I love you well; I'll give
    you gold,
Rid me these villains from your companies:
Hang them or stab them, down them in a
    draught,

Confound them by some course, and come to
    me,
I'll give you gold enough.
    *Both.* Name them, my lord; let's know
    them.                        [in company:
    *Tim.* You that way, and you this,—but two
Each man apart, all single and alone,
Yet an arch-villain keeps him company.
If where thou art two villains shall not be,
                              [*To the* Painter.
Come not near him.—If thou wouldst not
    reside                        [*To the* Poet.
But where one villain is, then him abandon.—
Hence! pack! there's gold,—ye came for gold,
    ye slaves:                   [hence!
You have done work for me, there's payment:
You are an alchemist, make gold of that:—
Out, rascal dogs!
            [*Exit, beating and driving them out.*

    *Enter* FLAVIUS *and two* Senators.

    *Flav.* It is in vain that you would speak
    with Timon;
For he is set so only to himself
That nothing but himself, which looks like
    man,
Is friendly with him.
    1 *Sen.*             Bring us to his cave:
It is our part and promise to the Athenians
To speak with Timon.
    2 *Sen.*                   At all times alike
Men are not still the same: 'twas time and
    griefs                       [hand,
That fram'd him thus: time, with his fairer
Offering the fortunes of his former days,
The former man may make him. Bring us to
    him,
And chance it as it may
    *Flav.*                  Here is his cave.—
Peace and content be here! Lord Timon!
    Timon!
Look out, and speak to friends; the Athe-
    nians,                       [thee:
By two of their most reverend senate, greet
Speak to them, noble Timon.

    TIMON *comes from his Cave.*

    *Tim.* Thou sun, that comfort'st, burn!—
    Speak and be hang'd:
For each true word a blister! and each false
Be as a cauterizing to the root o' the tongue,
Consuming it with speaking!
    1 *Sen.*                 Worthy Timon,—
    *Tim.* Of none but such as you, and you of
    Timon.                       [Timon.
    1 *Sen.* The senators of Athens greet thee,
    *Tim.* I thank them; and would send them
    back the plague,
Could I but catch it for them.
    1 *Sen.*                     O, forget
What we are sorry for ourselves in thee.
The senators with one consent of love
Entreat thee back to Athens; who have
    thought

On special dignities, which vacant lie
For thy best use and wearing.

*2 Sen.*                    They confess
Toward thee forgetfulness too general, gross:
Which now the public body,—which doth
    seldom
Play the recanter,—feeling in itself
A lack of Timon's aid, hath sense withal
Of its own fail, restraining aid to Timon;
And send forth us to make their sorrow'd
    render,
Together with a recompense more fruitful
Than their offence can weigh down by the
    dram;
Ay, even such heaps and sums of love and
    wealth
As shall to thee blot out what wrongs were
    theirs,
And write in thee the figures of their love,
Ever to read them thine.

*Tim.*                    You witch me in it;
Surprise me to the very brink of tears;
Lend me a fool's heart and a woman's eyes,
And I'll beweep these comforts, worthy sen-
    ators.                         [with us,

*1 Sen.* Therefore so please thee to return
And of our Athens,—thine and ours,—to take
The captainship, thou shalt be met with
    thanks,                       [name
Allow'd with absolute power, and thy good
Live with authority:—so soon we shall drive
    back
Of Alcibiades the approaches wild;
Who, like a boar too savage, doth root up
His country's peace.

*2 Sen.*    And shakes his threat'ning sword
Against the walls of Athens.

*1 Sen.*                    Therefore, Timon,—

*Tim.* Well, sir, I will; therefore, I will,
    sir; thus,—
If Alcibiades kill my countrymen,
Let Alcibiades know this of Timon, [Athens,
That Timon cares not. But if he sack fair
And take our goodly aged men by the beards,
Giving our holy virgins to the stain
Of contumelious, beastly, mad-brain'd war;
Then let him know,—and tell him Timon
    speaks it,
In pity of our aged and our youth,—
I cannot choose but tell him that I care not,
And let him tak't at worst; for their knives
    care not,
While you have throats to answer; for myself,
There's not a whittle in the unruly camp
But I do prize it at my love, before    [you
The reverend'st throat in Athens. So I leave
To the protection of the prosperous gods,
As thieves to keepers.

*Flav.*                    Stay not, all's in vain.

*Tim.* Why, I was writing of my epitaph;
It will be seen to-morrow: my long sickness
Of health and living now begins to mend,
And nothing brings me all things. Go, live
    still;

Be Alcibiades your plague, you his,
And last so long enough!

*1 Sen.*                    We speak in vain.

*Tim.* But yet I love my country; and am
    not
One that rejoices in the common wreck,
As common bruit doth put it.

*1 Sen.*                    That's well spoke.

*Tim.* Commend me to my loving country-
    men,—

*1 Sen.* These words become your lips as
    they pass through them.    [triumphers

*2 Sen.* And enter in our ears like great
In their applauding gates.

*Tim.*                    Commend me to them;
And tell them that, to ease them of their
    griefs,
Their fears of hostile strokes, their aches,
    losses,                       [throes
Their pangs of love, with other incident
That nature's fragile vessel doth sustain
In life's uncertain voyage, I will some kind-
    ness do them,—               [wrath.
I'll teach them to prevent wild Alcibiades'

*1 Sen.* I like this well; he will return again.

*Tim.* I have a tree, which grows here in my
    close,
That mine own use invites me to cut down,
And shortly must I fell it: tell my friends,
Tell Athens, in the sequence of degree,
From high to low throughout, that whoso
    please
To stop affliction, let him take his halter,
Come hither, ere my tree hath felt the axe,
And hang himself.—I pray you, do my greet-
    ing.

*Flav.* Trouble him no further; thus you
    still shall find him.          [Athens,

*Tim.* Come not to me again: but say to
Timon hath made his everlasting mansion
Upon the beached verge of the salt flood;
Who once a day with his embossed froth
The turbulent surge shall cover: thither come,
And let my grave-stone be your oracle.—
Lips, let sour words go by and language end:
What is amiss, plague and infection mend!
Graves only be men's works and death their
    gain!
Sun, hide thy beams! Timon hath done his
    reign.           [*Retires to his cave.*

*1 Sen.* His discontents are unremovably
Coupled to nature.

*2 Sen.* Our hope in him is dead: let us re-
    turn,
And strain what other means is left unto us
In our dear peril.

*1 Sen.*                    It requires swift foot.
                                [*Exeunt.*

SCENE II.—*The Walls of Athens.*

*Enter two* Senators *and a* Messenger.

*1 Sen.* Thou hast painfully discover'd: are
    his files
As full as thy report?

*Mess.*                    I have spoke the least:
Besides, his expedition promises
Present approach.                    [not Timon.
*2 Sen.* We stand much hazard if they bring
*Mess.* I met a courier, one mine ancient
friend;
Whom, though in general part we were op-
pos'd,
Yet our old love had a particular force,
And made us speak like friends:—this man
was riding
From Alcibiades to Timon's cave
With letters of entreaty, which imported
His fellowship i' the cause against your city,
In part for his sake mov'd.
*1 Sen.*                    Here come our brothers.

    *Enter* Senators *from* TIMON.

*3 Sen.* No talk of Timon, nothing of him
expect.—
The enemies' drum is heard, and fearful scouring
Doth choke the air with dust: in, and prepare:
Ours is the fall, I fear; our foes the snare.
                              [*Exeunt.*

SCENE III.—*The Woods.* TIMON'S *Cave,
and a rude Tomb seen.*

    *Enter a* Soldier *seeking* TIMON.

*Sold.* By all description this should be the
place.                    [is this?
Who's here? speak, ho!—No answer?—What
Timon is dead, who hath outstretch'd his
span;
Some beast rear'd this; there does not live a
man.                    [this tomb
Dead, sure; and this his grave,—what's on
I cannot read; the character I'll take with
wax:
Our captain hath in every figure skill,
An ag'd interpreter, though young in days:
Before proud Athens he's set down by this,
Whose fall the mark of his ambition is. [*Exit.*

SCENE IV.—*Before the Walls of Athens.*

*Trumpets sound. Enter* ALCIBIADES *and*
Forces.

*Alcib.* Sound to this coward and lascivious
town
Our terrible approach.          [*A parley sounded.*

    *Enter* Senators *on the Walls.*

Till now you have gone on, and fill'd the time
With all licentious measure, making your wills
The scope of justice; till now, myself, and
such
As slept within the shadow of your power,
Have wander'd with our travers'd arms, and
breath'd
Our sufferance vainly. Now the time is flush,
When crouching marrow, in the bearer strong,
Cries, of itself, *No more.* now breathless
wrong

Shall sit and pant in your great chairs of ease;
And pursy insolence shall break his wind
With fear and horrid flight.
*1 Sen.*                    Noble and young,
When thy first griefs were but a mere conceit,
Ere thou hadst power or we had cause of fear,
We sent to thee, to give thy rages balm,
To wipe out our ingratitude with loves
Above their quantity.
*2 Sen.*                    So did we woo.
Transformed Timon to our city's love,
By humble message and by promis'd means;
We were not all unkind, nor all deserve
The common stroke of war.
*1 Sen.*                    These walls of ours
Were not erected by their hands from whom
You have receiv'd your griefs: nor are they
such
That these great towers, trophies, and schools
should fall
For private faults in them.
*2 Sen.*                    Nor are they living
Who were the motives that you first went out;
Shame, that they wanted cunning, in excess,
Hath broke their hearts. March, noble lord,
Into our city with thy banners spread:
By decimation and a tithed death,—
If thy revenges hunger for that food  [tenth;
Which nature loathes,—take thou the destin'd
And by the hazard of the spotted die
Let die the spotted.
*1 Sen.*                    All have not offended;
For those that were, it is not square to take.
On those that are, revenges: crimes, like lands,
Are not inherited. Then, dear countryman,
Bring in thy ranks, but leave without thy
rage:
Spare thy Athenian cradle, and those kin
Which, in the bluster of thy wrath, must fall
With those that have offended: like a shepherd
Approach the fold and cull the infected forth,
But kill not all together.
*2 Sen.*                    What thou wilt,
Thou rather shalt enforce it with thy smile
Than hew to't with thy sword.
*1 Sen.*                    Set but thy foot
Against our rampir'd gates and they shall
ope;
So thou wilt send thy gentle heart before
To say thou'lt enter friendly.
*2 Sen.*                    Throw thy glove,
Or any token of thine honour else,
That thou wilt use the wars as thy redress,
And not as our confusion, all thy powers
Shall make their harbour in our town till we
Have seal'd thy full desire.
*Alcib.*                    Then there's my glove;
Descend, and open your uncharged ports;
Those enemies of Timon's and mine own,
Whom you yourselves shall set out for re-
proof,
Fall, and no more: and,—to atone your fears
With my more noble meaning,—not a man
Shall pass his quarter or offend the stream

Of regular justice in your city's bounds,
But shall be render'd to your public.laws
At heaviest answer.
 *Both.*    'Tis most nobly spoken.
 *Alcib.* Descend, and keep your words.
 [*The* Senators *descend and open the gates.*

*Enter a* Soldier.

 *Sol.* My noble general, Timon is dead;
Entomb'd upon the very hem o' the sea;
And on his grave-stone this insculpture, which
With wax I brought away, whose soft impression
Interprets for my poor ignorance.
 *Alcib.* [*Reads.*] *Here lies a wretched corse, of wretched soul bereft:*
*Seek not my name: a plague consume you wicked caitiffs left!*

*Here lie I, Timon; who, alive, all living men did hate:*
*Pass by, and curse thy fill; but pass, and stay not here thy gait.*
These well express in thee thy latter spirits:
Though thou abhorr'dst in us our human griefs, [droplets which
Scorn'dst our brain's flow, and those our
From niggard nature fall, yet rich conceit [aye
Taught thee to make vast Neptune weep for
On thy low grave, on faults forgiven. Dead
Is noble Timon: of whose memory
Hereafter more.—Bring me into your city,
And I will use the olive with my sword:
Make war breed peace; make peace stint war;
make each
Prescribe to other, as each other's leech.
Let our drums strike.    [*Exeunt*

CORNUS.

Act V. Sc. 3.

# CORIOLANUS

## DRAMATIS PERSONÆ

CAIUS MARCIUS CORIOLANUS, *a noble Roman.*
TITUS LARTIUS, } *Generals against the Volscians.*
COMINIUS, }
MENENIUS AGRIPPA, *Friend to* CORIOLANUS.
SICINIUS VELUTUS, } *Tribunes of the People.*
JUNIUS BRUTUS, }
YOUNG MARCIUS, *Son to* CORIOLANUS.
A Roman Herald.
TULLUS AUFIDIUS, *General of the Volscians.*
Lieutenant *to* AUFIDIUS.
Conspirators *with* AUFIDIUS.

A Citizen of Antium.
Two Volscian Guards.

VOLUMNIA, *Mother to* CORIOLANUS.
VIRGILIA, *Wife to* CORIOLANUS.
VALERIA, *Friend to* VIRGILIA.
Gentlewoman *attending on* VIRGILIA.

Roman *and* Volscian Senators, Patricians, Ædiles, Lictors, Soldiers, Citizens, Messengers, Servants *to* AUFIDIUS, *and other* Attendants.

SCENE,—*Partly in* ROME, *and partly in the Territories of the Volscians and Antiates.*

## ACT I.

### SCENE I.—ROME. *A Street.*

*Enter a company of mutinous* Citizens, *with staves, clubs, and other weapons.*

1 *Cit.* Before we proceed any further, hear me speak.

*Citizens.* Speak, speak.

1 *Cit.* You are all resolved rather to die than to famish?

*Citizens.* Resolved, resolved.

1 *Cit.* First, you know Caius Marcius is chief enemy to the people.

*Citizens.* We know't, we know't.

1 *Cit.* Let us kill him, and we'll have corn at our own price. Is't a verdict?

*Citizens.* No more talking on't; let it be done: away, away!

2 *Cit.* One word, good citizens.

1 *Cit.* We are accounted poor citizens; the patricians good. What authority surfeits on would relieve us: if they would yield us but the superfluity, while it were wholesome, we might guess they relieved us humanely; but they think we are too dear: the leanness that afflicts us, the object of our misery, is an inventory to particularize their abundance; our sufferance is a gain to them.—Let us revenge this with our pikes ere we become rakes: for the gods know I speak this in hunger for bread, not in thirst for revenge.

2 *Cit.* Would you proceed especially against Caius Marcius?

1 *Cit.* Against him first: he's a very dog to the commonalty.

2 *Cit.* Consider you what services he has done for his country?

1 *Cit.* Very well; and could be content to give him good report for't, but that he pays himself with being proud.

2 *Cit.* Nay, but speak not maliciously.

1 *Cit.* I say unto you, what he hath done famously he did it to that end: though soft-conscienced men can be content to say it was for his country, he did it to please his mother, and to be partly proud; which he is, even to the altitude of his virtue.

2 *Cit.* What he cannot help in his nature you account a vice in him. You must in no way say he is covetous.

1 *Cit.* If I must not, I need not be barren of accusations; he hath faults, with surplus, to tire in repetition. [*Shouts within.*] What shouts are these? The other side o' the city is risen: why stay we prating here? to the Capitol!

*Citizens.* Come, come.

1 *Cit.* Soft! who comes here?

2 *Cit.* Worthy Menenius Agrippa; one that hath always loved the people.

1 *Cit.* He's one honest enough; would all the rest were so!

*Enter* MENENIUS AGRIPPA.

*Men.* What work's, my countrymen, in hand? where go you
With bats and clubs? the matter? speak, I pray you.

1 *Cit.* Our business is not unknown to the senate; they have had inkling this fortnight what we intend to do, which now we'll show 'em in deeds. They say poor suitors have strong breaths; they shall know we have strong arms too.

*Men.* Why, masters, my good friends, mine honest neighbours,
Will you undo yourselves?

1 *Cit.* We cannot, sir, we are undone already. [*care*

*Men.* I tell you, friends, most charitable

[773]

Have the patricians of you. For your wants,
Your suffering in this dearth, you may as well
Strike at the heaven with your staves as lift
    them
Against the Roman state; whose course will
    on
The way it takes, cracking ten thousand curbs
Of more strong link asunder than can ever
Appear in your impediment: for the dearth,
The gods, not the patricians, make it; and
Your knees to them, not arms, must help.
    Alack,
You are transported by calamity
Thither where more attends you; and you
    slander
The helms o' the state, who care for you like
    fathers.
When you curse them as enemies.

  1 *Cit.* Care for us! True, indeed! They
ne'er cared for us yet. Suffer us to famish,
and their storehouses crammed with grain;
make edicts for usury, to support usurers;
repeal daily any wholesome act established
against the rich; and provide more piercing
statutes daily, to chain up and restrain the
poor. If the wars eat us not up, they will; and
there's all the love they bear us.

  *Men.* Either you must
Confess yourselves wondrous malicious,
Or be accus'd of folly. I shall tell you
A pretty tale: it may be you have heard it;
But, since it serves my purpose, I will venture
To stale't a little more.

  1 *Cit.* Well, I'll hear it, sir: yet you must
not think to fob-off our disgrace with a tale:
but, an't please you, deliver.

  *Men.* There was a time when all the body's
    members
Rebell'd against the belly; thus accus'd it:—
That only like a gulf it did remain
I' the midst o' the body, idle and unactive,
Still cupboarding the viand, never bearing
Like labour with the rest; where the other
    instruments
Did see and hear, devise, instruct, walk, feel,
And, mutually participate, did minister
Unto the appetite and affection common
Of the whole body. The belly answered,—

  1 *Cit.* Well, sir, what answer made the
    belly?

  *Men.* Sir, I shall tell you.—With a kind of
    smile,
Which ne'er came from the lungs, but even
    thus,—
For, look you, I may make the belly smile
As well as speak,—it tauntingly replied
To the discontented members, the mutinous
    parts
That envied his receipt; even so most fitly
As you malign our senators for that
They are not such as you.

  1 *Cit.*             Your belly's answer? What!
The kingly-crowned head, the vigilant eye,

The counsellor heart, the arm our soldier,
Our steed the leg, the tongue our trumpeter,
With other muniments and petty helps
In this our fabric, if that they,—

  *Men.*                     What then?—
'Fore me, this fellow speaks!—what then?
    what then?            [restrain'd

  1 *Cit.* Should by the cormorant belly be
Who is the sink o' the body,—

  *Men.*                   Well, what then?

  1 *Cit.* The former agents, if they did com-
    plain,
What could the belly answer?

  *Men.*                 I will tell you;
If you'll bestow a small,—of what you have
    little,—
Patience awhile, you'll hear the belly's answer.

  1 *Cit.* You are long about it.

  *Men.*            Note me this, good friend;
Your most grave belly was deliberate,
Not rash like his accusers, and thus answer'd:
*True is it, my incorporate friends,* quoth he,
*That I receive the general food at first
Which you do live upon; and fit it is,
Because I am the storehouse and the shop
Of the whole body: but, if you do remember,
I send it through the rivers of your blood,
Even to the court, the heart,—to the seat o'
    the brain;
And, through the cranks and offices of man,
The strongest nerves and small inferior veins
From me receive that natural competency
Whereby they live: and though that all at
    once*

*You, my good friends,*—this says the belly,—
    mark me,—

  1 *Cit.* Ay, sir; well, well.

  *Men.*         *Though all at once cannot
See what I do deliver out to each,
Yet I can make my audit up, that all
From me do back receive the flour of all,
And leave me but the bran.* What say you
    to't?

  1 *Cit.* It was an answer: how apply you
    this?

  *Men.* The senators of Rome are this good
    belly,
And you the mutinous members; for, examine
Their counsels and their cares; digest things
    rightly                [find,
Touching the weal o' the common; you shall
No public benefit which you receive
But it proceeds or comes from them to you,
And no way from yourselves.—What do you
    think,
You, the great toe of this assembly?

  1 *Cit.* I the great toe? why the great toe?

  *Men.* For that, being one o' the lowest,
    basest, poorest,
Of this most wise rebellion, thou go'st fore-
    most:
Thou rascal, that art worst in blood to run,
Lead'st first to win some vantage.—

But make you ready your stiff bats and clubs:
Rome and her rats are at the point of battle;
The one side must have bale.—

*Enter* CAIUS MARCIUS.

                          Hail, noble Marcius!
*Mar.* Thanks.—What's the matter, you
    dissentious rogues,
That, rubbing the poor itch of your opinion,
Make yourselves scabs?
    1 *Cit.*          We have ever your good word.
    *Mar.* He that will give good words to ye
    will flatter                        [you curs,
Beneath abhorring.—What would you have,
That like nor peace nor war? The one affrights
    you,                                [to you
The other makes you proud. He that trusts
Where he should find you lions finds you
    hares;
Where foxes, geese: you are no surer, no,
Than is the coal of fire upon the ice,
Or hailstone in the sun. Your virtue is  [him,
To make him worthy whose offence subdues
And curse that justice did it. Who deserves
    greatness
Deserves your hate; and your affections are
A sick man's appetite, who desires most that
Which would increase his evil. He that de-
    pends
Upon your favours swims with fins of lead,
And hews down oaks with rushes. Hang ye!
    Trust ye!
With every minute you do change a mind;
And call him noble that was now your hate,
Him vile that was your garland. What's the
    matter,
That in these several places of the city
You cry against the noble senate, who,
Under the gods, keep you in awe, which else
Would feed on one another?—What's their
    seeking?                         [they say,
    *Men.* For corn at their own rates; whereof,
The city is well stor'd.
    *Mar.*              Hang 'em! They say!
They'll sit by the fire and presume to know
What's done i' the Capitol; who's like to rise,
Who thrives and who declines; side factions,
    and give out
Conjectural marriages; making parties strong,
And feebling such as stand not in their liking
Below their cobbled shoes. They say there's
    grain enough!
Would the nobility lay aside their ruth
And let me use my sword, I'd make a quarry
With thousands of these quarter'd slaves, as
    high,
As I could pick my lance.
    *Men.* Nay, these are almost thoroughly
    persuaded;
For though abundantly they lack discretion,
Yet are they passing cowardly. But, I beseech
    you,
What says the other troop?
    *Mar.*            They are dissolved: hang 'em!

They said they were an-hungry; sigh'd forth
    proverbs,—                         [eat,
That hunger broke stone walls, that dogs must
That meat was made for mouths, that the
    gods sent not
Corn for the rich men only:—with these
    shreds
They vented their complainings; which being
    answer'd,
And a petition granted them,—a strange one,
To break the heart of generosity,
And make bold power look pale,—they threw
    their caps                         [moon,
As they would hang them on the horns o' the
Shouting their emulation.
    *Men.*              What is granted them?
    *Mar.* Five tribunes, to defend their vulgar
    wisdoms,
Of their own choice: one's Junius Brutus,
Sicinius Velutus, and I know not.—'Sdeath!
The rabble should have first unroof'd the city
Ere so prevail'd with me: it will in time
Win upon power, and throw forth greater
    themes
For insurrection's arguing.
    *Men.*              This is strange.
    *Mar.* Go, get you home, you fragments!

*Enter a* Messenger, *hastily.*

    *Mess.* Where's Caius Marcius?
    *Mar.*              Here: what's the matter?
    *Mess.* The news is, sir, the Volsces are in
    arms.                      [means to vent
    *Mar.* I am glad on't: then we shall ha'
Our musty superfluity.—See, our best elders.

*Enter* COMINIUS, TITUS LARTIUS, *and other*
Senators; JUNIUS BRUTUS *and* SICINIUS
VELUTUS.

    1 *Sen.* Marcius, 'tis true that you have
    lately told us,—
The Volsces are in arms.
    *Mar.*              They have a leader,
Tullus Aufidius, that will put you to't.
I sin in envying his nobility;
And were I anything but what I am,
I would wish me only he.
    *Com.*            You have fought together.
    *Mar.* Were half to half the world by the
    ears, and he
Upon my party, I'd revolt, to make
Only my wars with him: he is a lion
That I am proud to hunt.
    1 *Sen.*            Then, worthy Marcius,
Attend upon Cominius to these wars.
    *Com.* It is your former promise.
    *Mar.*                  Sir, it is;
And I am constant.—Titus Lartius, thou
Shalt see me once more strike at Tullus' face.
What, art thou stiff? stand'st out?
    *Tit.*              No, Caius Marcius;
I'll lean upon one crutch and fight with the
    other
Ere stay behind this business.

*Men.*                              O, true bred!
1 *Sen.* Your company to the Capitol; where
   I know.
Our greatest friends attend us.
*Tit.*                              Lead you on:
Follow, Cominius; we must follow you;
Right worthy your priority.
*Com.*                              Noble Marcius!
1 *Sen.* Hence to your homes; be gone!
                [*To the* Citizens.
*Mar.*                  Nay, let them follow:
The Volsces have much corn; take these rats
   thither
To gnaw their garners.—Worshipful mutin-
   eers,
Your valour puts well forth: pray, follow.
     [*Exeunt* Senators, COM., MAR., TIT.,
        *and* MENEN. Citizens *steal away.*
*Sic.* Was ever man so proud as is this
   Marcius?
*Bru.* He has no equal.           [people,—
*Sic.* When we were chosen tribunes for the
*Bru.* Mark'd you his lip and eyes?
*Sic.*                              Nay, but his taunts.
*Bru.* Being mov'd, he will not spare to gird
   the gods.
*Sic.* Be-mock the modest moon.
*Bru.* The present wars devour him: he is
   grown
Too proud to be so valiant.
*Sic.*                              Such a nature,
Tickled with good success, disdains the
   shadow
Which he treads on at noon: but I do wonder
His insolence can brook to be commanded
Under Cominius.
*Bru.* Fame, at the which he aims,—
In whom already he is well grac'd,—cannot
Better be held, nor more attain'd, than by
A place below the first: for what miscarries
Shall be the general's fault, though he perform
To the utmost of a man; and giddy censure
Will then cry out of Marcius, *O, if he
Had borne the business!*
*Sic.*                  Besides, if things go well,
Opinion, that so sticks on Marcius, shall
Of his demerits rob Cominius.
*Bru.*                              Come:
Half all Cominius' honours are to Marcius,
Though Marcius earn'd them not; and all his
   faults
To Marcius shall be honours, though, indeed,
In aught he merit not.
*Sic.*                  Let's hence, and hear
How the despatch is made; and in what fash-
   ion,
More than in singularity, he goes
Upon this present action.
*Bru.*                  Let's along.
                    [*Exeunt.*

SCENE II.—CORIOLI. *The Senate House.*

*Enter* TULLUS AUFIDIUS *and certain Senators.*

1 *Sen.* So, your opinion is, Aufidius,

That they of Rome are enter'd in our
   counsels,
And know how we proceed.
*Auf.*                              Is it not yours?
What ever hath been thought on in this state,
That could be brought to bodily act ere Rome
Had circumvention! 'Tis not four days gone
Since I heard thence; these are the words: I
   think
I have the letter here; yes, here it is: [*Reads.*
*They have press'd a power, but it is not
   known
Whether for east or west: the dearth is great;
The people mutinous: and it is rumour'd,
Cominius, Marcius your old enemy,—
Who is of Rome worse hated than of you,—
And Titus Lartius, a most valiant Roman,
These three lead on this preparation
Whither 'tis bent: most likely 'tis for you:
Consider of it.*
1 *Sen.*                  Our army's in the field:
We never yet made doubt but Rome was
   ready
To answer us.
*Auf.*                  Nor did you think it folly
To keep your great pretences veil'd till when
They needs must show themselves; which in
   the hatching,
It seem'd, appear'd to Rome. By the discovery
We shall be shorten'd in our aim; which was,
To take in many towns ere, almost, Rome
Should know we were afoot.
2 *Sen.*                  Noble Aufidius,
Take your commission; hie you to your
   bands:
Let us alone to guard Corioli:
If they set down before's, for the remove
Bring up your army; but I think you'll find
They've not prepar'd for us.
*Auf.*                  O, doubt not that;
I speak from certainties. Nay, more,
Some parcels of their power are forth already,
And only hitherward. I leave your honours.
If we and Caius Marcius chance to meet,
'Tis sworn between us we shall ever strike
Till one can do no more.
*All.*                  The gods assist you!
*Auf.* And keep your honours safe!
1 *Sen.*                              Farewell.
2 *Sen.*                              Farewell.
*All.* Farewell.                  [*Exeunt.*

SCENE III.—ROME. *An Apartment in
MARCIUS' House.*

*Enter Volumnia and Virgilia: they sit
down on two low stools and sew.*

*Vol.* I pray you, daughter, sing, or express
yourself in a more comfortable sort: if my
son were my husband, I should freelier rejoice in that absence wherein he won honour
than in the embracements of his bed where he
would show most love. When yet he was but
tenderbodied, and the only son of my womb;
when youth with comeliness plucked all gaze

his way; when, for a day of king's entreaties, a mother should not sell him an hour from her beholding; I,—considering how honour would become such a person; that it was no better than picture-like to hang by the wall if renown made it not stir,—was pleased to let him seek danger where he was like to find fame. To a cruel war I sent him; from whence he returned, his brows bound with oak. I tell thee, daughter, I sprang not more in joy at first hearing he was a man-child than now in first seeing he had proved himself a man.

*Vir.* But had he died in the business, madam? how then?

*Vol.* Then his good report should have been my son; I therein would have found issue. Hear me profess sincerely,—had I a dozen sons, each in my love alike, and none less dear than thine and my good Marcius, I had rather had eleven die nobly for their country than one voluptuously surfeit out of action.

*Enter a* Gentlewoman.

*Gent.* Madam, the Lady Valeria is come to visit you.  [myself.

*Vir.* Beseech you, give me leave to retire

*Vol.* Indeed you shall not.

Methinks I hear hither your husband's drum;
See him pluck Aufidius down by the hair;
As children from a bear, the Volsces shunning him:
Methinks I see him stamp thus, and call thus,—

*Come on, you cowards! you were got in fear Though you were born in Rome:* his bloody brow  [goes,

With his mail'd hand then wiping, forth he
Like to a harvest-man that's task'd to mow
Or all, or lose his hire.

*Vir.* His bloody brow! O Jupiter, no blood!

*Vol.* Away, you fool! it more becomes a man

Than gilt his trophy: the breasts of Hecuba,
When she did suckle Hector, look'd not lovelier  [blood

Than Hector's forehead when it spit forth
At Grecian swords contending.—Tell Valeria
We are fit to bid her welcome.  [*Exit Gent.*

*Vir.* Heavens bless my lord from fell Aufidius!  [knee,

*Vol.* He'll beat Aufidius' head below his
And tread upon his neck.

*Re-enter* Gentlewoman, *with* VALERIA *and her* Usher.

*Val.* My ladies both, good-day to you.

*Vol.* Sweet madam.

*Vir.* I am glad to see your ladyship.

*Val.* How do you both? you are manifest housekeepers. What are you sewing here? A fine spot, in good faith.—How does your little son?

*Vir.* I thank your ladyship; well, good madam.

*Vol.* He had rather see the swords and hear a drum than look upon his schoolmaster.

*Val.* O' my word, the father's son: I'll swear 'tis a very pretty boy. O' my troth, I looked upon him o' Wednesday half an hour together: has such a confirmed countenance. I saw him run after a gilded butterfly; and when he caught it he let it go again; and after it again; and over and over he comes, and up again; catched it again; or whether his fall enraged him, or how 'twas, he did so set his teeth and tear it; O, I warrant, how he mammocked it!

*Vol.* One on's father's moods.

*Val.* Indeed, la, 'tis a noble child.

*Vir.* A crack, madam.

*Val.* Come, lay aside your stitchery; I must have you play the idle huswife with me this afternoon.

*Vir.* No, good madam; I will not out of doors.

*Val.* Not out of doors!

*Vol.* She shall, she shall.

*Vir.* Indeed, no, by your patience; I'll not over the threshold till my lord return from the wars.

*Val.* Fie, you confine yourself most unreasonably; come, you must go visit the good lady that lies in.

*Vir.* I will wish her speedy strength, and visit her with my prayers; but I cannot go thither.

*Vol.* Why, I pray you?

*Vir.* 'Tis not to save labour, nor that I want love.

*Val.* You would be another Penelope: yet they say all the yarn she spun in Ulysses' absence did but fill Ithaca full of moths. Come; I would your cambric were sensible as your finger, that you might leave pricking it for pity.—Come, you shall go with us.

*Vir.* No, good madam pardon me; indeed I will not forth.

*Val.* In truth, la, go with me; and I'll tell you excellent news of your husband.

*Vir.* O, good madam, there can be none yet.

*Val.* Verily I do not jest with you; there came news from him last night.

*Vir.* Indeed madam?

*Val.* In earnest, it's true; I heard a senator speak it. Thus it is:—The Volsces have an army forth; against whom Cominius the general is gone, with one part of our Roman power: your lord and Titus Lartius are set down before their city Corioli; they nothing doubt prevailing, and to make it brief wars. This is true, on mine honour; and so, I pray, go with us.

*Vir.* Give me excuse, good madam; I will obey you in everything hereafter.

*Vol.* Let her alone, lady; as she is now, she will but disease our better mirth.

*Val.* In troth, I think she would.—Fare you well, then.—Come, good sweet lady.—

Pr'ythee, Virgilia, turn thy solemness out o'
door, and go along with us.

*Vir.* No, at a word, madam; indeed I must
not. I wish you much mirth.

*Val.* Well, then, farewell.　　　[*Exeunt.*

### SCENE IV.—*Before Corioli.*

*Enter, with drums and colours,* MARCIUS,
TITUS LARTIUS, *Officers, and* Soldiers.

*Mar.* Yonder comes news:—a wager they
have met.

*Lart.* My horse to yours, no.

*Mar.*　　　　　　　　'Tis done.

*Lart.*　　　　　　　　Agreed.

#### Enter a Messenger.

*Mar.* Say, has our general met the enemy?

*Mess.* They lie in view; but have not spoke
as yet.

*Lart.* So, the good horse is mine.

*Mar.*　　　　　　　I'll buy him of you.

*Lart.* No, I'll nor sell nor give him: lend
you him I will
For half a hundred years.—Summon the town.

*Mar.* How far off lie these armies?

*Mess.*　　　　　　Within this mile and half.

*Mar.* Then shall we hear their 'larum, and
they ours.—　　　　　　　[*work,*
Now, Mars, I pry'thee, make us quick in
That we with smoking swords may march
from hence　　　　　　　[*blast.*
To help our fielded friends!—Come, blow thy

*They sound a parley. Enter, on the Walls,*
*some* Senators *and others.*

Tullus Aufidius, is he within your walls?

1 *Sen.* No, nor a man that fears you less
than he,
That's lesser than a little. Hark, our drums
　　　　　　　　　[*Drums afar off.*
Are bringing forth our youth! we'll break our
walls,
Rather than they shall pound us up: our gates,
Which yet seem shut, we have but pinn'd
with rushes;
They'll open of themselves. Hark you far off!
　　　　　　　　　[*Alarum afar off.*
There is Aufidius; list what work he makes
Amongst your cloven army.

*Mar.*　　　　　　　O, they are at it!

*Lart.* Their noise be our instruction.—
Ladders, ho!

*The* Volsces *enter and pass over.*

*Mar.* They fear us not, but issue forth their
city.　　　　　　　　　[*fight*
Now put your shields before your hearts, and
With hearts more proof than shields.—Ad-
vance, brave Titus:　　　[*thoughts,*
They do disdain us much beyond our
Which makes me sweat with wrath.—Come
on, my fellows:
He that retires, I'll take him for a Volsce,
And he shall feel mine edge.

*Alarums, and exeunt* Romans *and* Volsces
*fighting. The* Romans *are beaten back to*
*their trenches. Re-enter* MARCIUS.

*Mar.* All the contagion of the south light
　　　　　　on you,　　　　[*and plagues*
You shames of Rome!—you herd of—Boils
Plaster you o'er, that you may be abhorr'd
Further than seen, and one infect another
Against the wind a mile! You souls of geese,
That bear the shapes of men, how have you
　　　　　　run　　　　　　[*and hell!*
From slaves that apes would beat! Pluto
All hurt behind; backs red, and faces pale
With flight and agued fear! Mend, and charge
　　　　home,
Or, by the fires of heaven, I'll leave the foe
And make my wars on you: look to't: come
　　　　on;　　　　　　　　[*wives,*
If you'll stand fast we'll beat them to their
As they us to our trenches followed.

*Another alarum. The* Volsces *and* Romans
*re-enter, and the fight is renewed. The*
Volsces *retire into Corioli, and* MARCIUS
*follows them to the gates.*

So, now the gates are ope:—now prove good
　　　　seconds;
'Tis for the followers fortune widens them,
Not for the fliers: mark me, and do the like.
　　　　　　　　　[*He enters the gates.*

1 *Sol.* Fool-hardiness: not I.

2 *Sol.*　　　　　　　　Nor I.
　　　　　　　　　[MARCIUS *is shut in.*

1 *Sol.* See, they have shut him in.

*All.*　　　　　　To the pot, I warrant him.
　　　　　　　　　[*Alarum continues.*

#### Re-enter TITUS LARTIUS.

*Lart.* What is become of Marcius?

*All.*　　　　　　　Slain, sir, doubtless.

1 *Sol.* Following the fliers at the very heels,
With them he enters; who, upon the sudden,
Clapp'd-to their gates: he is himself alone,
To answer all the city.

*Lart.*　　　　　　　O noble fellow!
Who, sensible, outdares his senseless sword,
And when it bows stands up! Thou art left,
　　　　Marcius:
A carbuncle entire, as big as thou art,
Were not so rich a jewel. Thou wast a soldier
Even to Cato's wish, not fierce and terrible
Only in strokes; but with thy grim looks and
The thunder-like percussion of thy sounds
Thou mad'st thine enemies shake, as if the
　　　　world
Were feverous and did tremble.

*Re-enter* MARCIUS, *bleeding, assaulted by the*
*enemy.*

1 *Sol.*　　　　　Look, sir.

*Lart.*　　　　　　　O, 'tis Marcius!
Let's fetch him off, or make remain alike.
　　　　　　　　　[*They fight, and all enter the city.*

SCENE V.—*Within* CORIOLI. *A Street.*

*Enter certain* Romans, *with spoils.*

1 *Rom.* This will I carry to Rome.

2 *Rom.* And I this.

3 *Rom.* A murrain on't! I took this for silver. [*Alarum continues still afar off.*

*Enter* MARCIUS *and* TITUS LARTIUS *with a trumpet.*

*Mar.* See here these movers that do prize their hours
At a crack'd drachm! Cushions, leaden spoons,
Irons of a doit, doublets that hangmen would
Bury with those that wore them, these base slaves, 　　　　　[with them!—
Ere yet the fight be done, pack up:—down
And hark, what noise the general makes!—To him!—
There is the man of my soul's hate, Aufidius,
Piercing our Romans: then, valiant Titus, take
Convenient numbers to make good the city;
Whilst I, with those that have the spirit, will haste
To help Cominius.

*Lart.* 　　　　　Worthy sir, thou bleed'st;
Thy exercise hath been too violent for
A second course of fight.

*Mar.* 　　　　　Sir, praise me not;
My work hath yet not warm'd me: fare you well:
The blood I drop is rather physical
That dangerous to me: to Aufidius thus
I will appear, and fight.

*Lart.* 　　　　Now the fair goddess, Fortune,
Fall deep in love with thee; and her great charms 　　　　　[man,
Misguide thy opposers' swords! Bold gentle-
Prosperity be thy page!

*Mar.* 　　　　　Thy friend no less
Than those she placeth highest!—So farewell.

*Lart.* Thou worthiest Marcius!—
　　　　　　　　　[*Exit* MARCIUS.
Go, sound thy trumpet in the market-place;
Call thither all the officers o' the town,
Where they shall know our mind: away!
　　　　　　　　　[*Exeunt.*

SCENE VI.—*Near the Camp of* COMINIUS.

*Enter* COMINIUS *and* Forces, *retreating.*

*Com.* Breathe you, my friends: well fought; we are come off
Like Romans, neither foolish in our stands
Nor cowardly in retire: believe me, sirs,
We shall be charg'd again. Whiles we have struck,
By interims and conveying gusts we have heard
The charges of our friends. Ye Roman gods,
Lead their successes as we wish our own,
That both our powers, with smiling fronts encountering,
May give you thankful sacrifice!—

*Enter a* Messenger.
　　　　　　　　　Thy news?

*Mess.* The citizens of Corioli have issued,
And given to Lartius and to Marcius battle:
I saw our party to their trenches driven,
And then I came away.

*Com.* 　　　Though thou speak'st truth,
Methinks thou speak'st not well. How long is't since?

*Mess.* Above an hour, my lord.

*Com.* 'Tis not a mile; briefly we heard their drums:
How couldst thou in a mile confound an hour,
And bring thy news so late?

*Mess.* 　　　　　Spies of the Volsces
Held me in chase, that I was forc'd to wheel
Three or four miles about; else had I, sir,
Half an hour since brought my report.

*Com.* 　　　　　Who's yonder,
That does appear as he were flay'd? O gods!
He has the stamp of Marcius; and I have
Before-time seen him thus.

*Mar.* [*Within.*] 　　　　Come I too late?

*Com.* The shepherd knows not thunder from a tabor 　　　　　[tongue
More than I know the sound of Marcius'
From every meaner man.

*Enter* MARCIUS.

*Mar.* 　　　　　Come I too late?

*Com.* Ay, if you come not in the blood of others,
But mantled in your own.

*Mar.* 　　　　　O! let me clip you
In arms as sound as when I woo'd; in heart
As merry as when our nuptial day was done,
And tapers burn'd to bedward!

*Com.* 　　　　Flower of warriors,
How is't with Titus Lartius?

*Mar.* As with a man busied about decrees:
Condemning some to death and some to exile;
Ransoming him or pitying, threat'ning the other;
Holding Corioli in the name of Rome,
Even like a fawning grayhound in the leash,
To let him slip at will.

*Com.* 　　　　Where is that slave
Which told me they had beat you to your trenches?
Where's he? call him hither.

*Mar.* 　　　　　Let him alone;
He did inform the truth: but for our gentle-men,
The common file,—a plague!—tribunes for them!— 　　　　　[budge
The mouse ne'er shunn'd the cat as they did
From rascals worse than they.

*Com.* 　　　But how prevail'd you?

*Mar.* Will the time serve to tell? I do not think.
Where is the enemy? are you lords o' the field?
If not, why cease you till you are so?

*Com.* Marcius,
We have at disadvantage fought, and did
Retire, to win our purpose.
    *Mar.* How lies their battle? know you on
        which side
They have placed their men of trust?
    *Com.* As I guess, Marcius,
Their bands in the vaward are the Antiates,
Of their best trust; o'er them Aufidius,
Their very heart of hope.
    *Mar.* I do beseech you,
By all the battles wherein we have fought,
By the blood we have shed together, by the
        vows                    [directly
We have made to endure friends, that you
Set me against Aufidius and his Antiates;
And that you not delay the present, but,
Filling the air with swords advanc'd and
        darts,
We prove this very hour.
    *Com.* Though I could wish
You were conducted to a gentle bath,
And balms applied to you, yet dare I never
Deny your asking: take your choice of those
That best can aid your action.
    *Mar.* Those are they
That most are willing.—If any such be here,—
As it were sin to doubt,—that love this paint-
        ing
Wherein you see me smear'd; if any fear
Lesser his person than an ill report;
If any think brave death outweighs bad life,
And that his country's dearer than himself;
Let him alone, or so many so minded,
Wave thus [*waving his hand*], to express his
        disposition.
And follow Marcius.
    [*They all shout, and wave their swords;
    take him up in their arms, and cast up
    their caps.*
O, me alone! make you a sword of me?
If these shows be not outward, which of you
But is four Volsces? none of you but is
Able to bear against the great Aufidius
A shield as hard as his. A certain number,
Though thanks to all, must I select from all:
        the rest
Shall bear the business in some other fight,
As cause will be obey'd. Please you to march;
And four shall quickly draw out my com-
        mand,
Which men are best inclin'd.
    *Com.* March on, my fellows:
Make good this ostentation, and you shall
Divide in all with us.                [*Exeunt.*

SCENE VII.—*The Gates of Corioli.*

TITUS LARTIUS, *having set a guard upon
Corioli, going with drum and trumpet toward* COMINIUS *and* CAIUS MARCIUS, *enters with a* Lieutenant, *a party of* Soldiers,
*and a* Scout.

    *Lart.* So, let the ports be guarded: keep
        your duties

As I have set them down. If I do send, de-
        spatch
Those centuries to our aid; the rest will serve
For a short holding: if we lose the field
We cannot keep the town.
    *Lieut.* Fear not our care, sir.
    *Lart.* Hence, and shut your gates upon's.—
Our guider, come; to the Roman camp con-
        duct us.                    [*Exeunt.*

SCENE VIII.—*A Field of Battle between the
        Roman and the Volscian Camps.*

*Alarum. Enter, from opposite sides,* MARCIUS
        *and* AUFIDIUS.

    *Mar.* I'll fight with none but thee; for I
        do hate thee
Worse than a promise-breaker.
    *Auf.* We hate alike:
Not Afric owns a serpent I abhor
More than thy fame and envy. Fix thy foot.
    *Mar.* Let the first budger die the other's
        slave,
And the gods doom him after!
    *Auf.* If I fly, Marcius,
Halloo me like a hare.
    *Mar.* Within these three hours, Tullus,
Alone I fought in your Corioli walls, [*blood*
And made what work I pleas'd: 'tis not my
Wherein thou seest me mask'd; for thy re-
        venge
Wrench up thy power to the highest.
    *Auf.* Wert thou the Hector
That was the whip of your bragg'd progeny,
Thou shouldst not scape me here.—
    [*They fight, and certain* Volsces *come to
        the aid of* AUFIDIUS.
Officious, and not valiant,—you have sham'd
        me
In your condemned seconds.
    [*Exeunt fighting, driven in by* MAR.

SCENE IX.—*The Roman Camp.*

*Alarum. A retreat is sounded. Flourish. En-
ter, at one side,* COMINIUS *and* Romans;
*at the other side,* MARCIUS, *with his arm
in a scarf, and other* Romans.

    *Com.* If I should tell thee o'er this thy
        day's work,
Thou'lt not believe thy deeds: but I'll report
        it
Where senators shall mingle tears with
        smiles;
Where great patricians shall attend, and
        shrug
I' the end admire; where ladies shall be
        frighted,                [*dull tribunes,*
And, gladly quak'd, hear more; where the
That, with the fusty plebeians, hate thine
        honours,
Shall say, against their hearts, *We thank the
        gods
Our Rome hath such a soldier!*
Yet cam'st thou to a morsel of this feast,
Having fully dined before.

*Enter* TITUS LARTIUS, *with his power, from the pursuit.*

*Lart.*                            O general,
Here is the steed, we the caparison:
Hadst thou beheld,—
  *Mar.*    Pray now, no more; my mother,
Who has a charter to extol her blood, [done
When she does praise me grieves me. I have
As you have done,—that's what I can; in-
        duc'd
As you have been,—that's for my country:
He that has but effected his good will
Hath overta'en mine act.
  *Com.*                    You shall not be
The grave of your deserving; Rome must
        know
The value of her own: 'twere a concealment
Worse than a theft, no less than a traduce-
        ment,
To hide your doings, and to silence that
Which, to the spire and top of praises
        vouch'd,                    [seech you,—
Would seem but modest: therefore, I be-
In sign of what you are, not to reward
What you have done,—before our army hear
        me.                        [they smart
  *Mar.*  I have some wounds upon me, and
To hear themselves remember'd.
  *Com.*                    Should they not,
Well might they fester 'gainst ingratitude,
And tent themselves with death. Of all the
        horses,—                    [—of all
Whereof we have ta'en good, and good store,
The treasure in this field achiev'd and city,
We render you the tenth; to be ta'en forth
Before the common distribution at
Your only choice.
  *Mar.*            I thank you, general;
But cannot make my heart consent to take
A bribe to pay my sword: I do refuse it;
And stand upon my common part with those
That have beheld the doing.
  [*A long flourish. They all cry,* "Marcius!
  Marcius!" *cast up their caps and lances:*
  COMINIUS *and* LARTIUS *stand bare.*
  *Mar.*  May these same instruments which
        you profane        [pets shall
Never sound more! When drums and trum-
I' the field prove flatterers, let courts and
        cities be
Made all of false-fac'd soothing!
When steel grows soft as the parasite's silk,
Let him be made a coverture for the wars!
No more, I say! for that I have not wash'd
My nose that bled, or foil'd some debile
        wretch,—                    [done,—
Which, without note, here's many else have
You shout me forth in acclamations hyper-
        bolical;
As if I loved my little should be dieted
In praises sauc'd with lies.
  *Com.*                    Too modest are you;
More cruel to your good report than grate-
        ful

To us that give you truly: by your patience,
If 'gainst yourself you be incens'd, we'll put
        you,—                [manacles,
Like one that means his proper harm,—in
Then reason safely with you.—Therefore be
        it known,                [cius
As to us, to all the world, that Caius Mar-
Wears this war's garland: in token of the
        which,                [him,
My noble steed, known to the camp, I give
With all his trim belonging; and from this
        time,
For what he did before Corioli, call him,
With all the applause and clamour of the
        host,
CAIUS MARCIUS CORIOLANUS.—
Bear the addition nobly ever!
  [*Flourish. Trumpets sound, and drums.*
  *All.*  Caius Marcius Coriolanus!
  *Cor.*  I will go wash;
And when my face is fair you shall perceive
Whether I blush or no: howbeit, I thank
        you.—
I mean to stride your steed; and at all times
To undercrest your good addition
To the fairness of my power.
  *Com.*                    So, to our tent;
Where, ere we do repose us, we will write
To Rome of our success.—You, Titus Lar-
        tius,
Must to Corioli back: send us to Rome
The best, with whom we may articulate,
For their own good and ours.
  *Lart.*                    I shall, my lord.
  *Cor.*  The gods begin to mock me. I, that
        now                        [beg
Refus'd most princely gifts, am bound to
Of my lord general.
  *Com.*        Take 't: 'tis yours.—What is't?
  *Cor.*  I sometime lay here in Corioli
At a poor man's house; he us'd me kindly:
He cried to me; I saw him prisoner;
But then Aufidius was within my view,
And wrath o'erwhelm'd my pity: I request
        you
To give my poor host freedom.
  *Com.*                    O, well begg'd!
Were he the butcher of my son he should
Be free as is the wind. Deliver him, Titus.
  *Lart.* Marcius, his name?
  *Cor.*                    By Jupiter, forgot:—
I am weary; yea, my memory is tir'd.—
Have we no wine here?
  *Com.*                    Go we to our tent:
The blood upon your visage dries; 'tis time
It should be look'd to: come.        [*Exeunt.*

SCENE X.—*The Camp of the* Volsces.

*A flourish. Cornets. Enter* TULLUS AUFI-
DIUS, *bloody, with two or three Soldiers.*

  *Auf.*  The town is ta'en!        [condition
  1 *Sol.*  'Twill be deliver'd back on good
  *Auf.*  Condition!
I would I were a Roman; for I cannot,

Being a Volsce, be that I am.—Condition!
What good condition can a treaty find
I' the part that is at mercy?—Five times,
    Marcius,         [beat me;
I have fought with thee; so often hast thou
And wouldst do so, I think, should we en-
    counter
As often as we eat.—By the elements,
If e'er again I meet him beard to beard,
He's mine or I am his: mine emulation
Hath not that honour in't it had; for where
I thought to crush him in an equal force,—
True sword to sword,—I'll potch at him some
    way,
Or wrath or craft may get him.

    *1 Sol.*             He's the devil.

    *Auf.* Bolder, though not so subtle. My
    valour's poisoned
With only suffering stain by him; for him
Shall fly out of itself: nor sleep nor sanctu-
    ary,
Being naked, sick; nor fane nor Capitol,
The prayers of priests nor times of sacrifice,
Embarquements all of fury, shall lift up
Their rotten privilege and custom 'gainst [it
My hate to Marcius: where I find him, were
At home, upon my brother's guard, even
    there,
Against the hospitable canon, would I
Wash my fierce hand in's heart. Go you to
    the city;         [must
Learn how 'tis held; and what they are that
Be hostages for Rome.

    *1 Sol.*         Will not you go?

    *Auf.* I am attended at the cypress grove:
I pray you,—         [thither
'Tis south the city mills,—bring me word
How the world goes, that to the pace of it
I may spur on my journey.

    *1 Sol.*         I shall, sir. [*Exeunt.*

## ACT II.

### SCENE I.—ROME. *A public Place.*

*Enter* MENENIUS, SICINIUS, *and* BRUTUS.

    *Men.* The augurer tells me we shall have
news to night.

    *Bru.* Good or bad?

    *Men.* Not according to the prayer of the
people, for they love not Marcius.

    *Sic.* Nature teaches beasts to know their
friends.

    *Men.* Pray you, who does the wolf love?

    *Sic.* The lamb.

    *Men.* Ay, to devour him; as the hungry
plebeians would the noble Marcius.

    *Bru.* He's a lamb indeed, that baas like a
bear.

    *Men.* He's a bear indeed, that lives like a
lamb. You two are old men: tell me one
thing that I shall ask you.

    *Both Trib.* Well, sir.

    *Men.* In what enormity is Marcius poor
in, that you two have not in abundance?

    *Bru.* He's poor in no one fault, but stored
with all.

    *Sic.* Especially in pride.

    *Bru.* And topping all others in boasting.

    *Men.* This is strange now: do you two
know how you are censured here in the city,
I mean of us o' the right-hand file? Do you?

    *Both Trib.* Why, how are we censured?

    *Men.* Because you talk of pride now,—
will you not be angry?

    *Both Trib.* Well, well, sir, well.

    *Men.* Why, 'tis no great matter; for a
very little thief of occasion will rob you of a
great deal of patience: give your dispositions
the reins, and be angry at your pleasures; at
the least, if you take it as a pleasure to you in
being so. You blame Marcius for being
proud?

    *Bru.* We do it not alone, sir.

    *Men.* I know you can do very little alone;
for your helps are many, or else your actions
would grow wondrous single: your abilities
are too infant-like for doing much alone.
You talk of pride: O that you could turn you
eyes toward the napes of your necks, and
make but an interior survey of your good
selves! O that you could!

    *Bru.* What then, sir?

    *Men.* Why, then you should discover a
brace of unmeriting, proud, violent, testy
magistrates,—alias, fools,—as any in Rome.

    *Sic.* Menenius, you are known well enough
too.

    *Men.* I am known to be a humorous pa-
trician, and one that loves a cup of hot wine
with not a drop of allaying Tiber in't: said
to be something imperfect in favouring the
first complaint, hasty and tinder-like upon
too trivial motion; one that converses more
with the buttock of the night than with the
forehead of the morning. What I think I
utter, and spend my malice in my breath.
Meeting two such wealsmen as you are,—I
cannot call you Lycurguses,—if the drink
you give me touch my palate adversely, I
make a crooked face at it. I cannot say your
worships have delivered the matter well when
I find the ass in compound with the major
part of your syllables; and though I must be
content to bear with those that say you are
reverend grave men, yet they lie deadly that
tell you have good faces. If you see this in
the map of my microcosm, follows it that I
am known well enough too? What harm can
your bisson conspectuities glean out of this
character, if I be known well enough too?

    *Bru.* Come, sir, come, we know you well
enough.

    *Men.* You know neither me, yourselves,
nor anything. You are ambitious for poor
knaves' caps and legs: you wear out a good
wholesome forenoon in hearing a cause between an orange-wife and a fosset-seller; and
then rejourn the controversy of threepence to

a second day of audience.—When you are hearing a matter between party and party, if you chance to be pinched with the colic, you make faces like mummers; set up the bloody flag against all patience; and, in roaring for a chamber-pot, dismiss the controversy bleeding, the more entangled by your hearing: all the peace you make in their cause is calling both the parties knaves. You are a pair of strange ones.

*Bru.* Come, come, you are well understood to be a perfecter giber for the table than a necessary bencher in the Capitol.

*Men.* Our very priests must become mockers if they shall encounter such ridiculous subjects as you are. When you speak best unto the purpose it is not worth the wagging of your beards; and your beards deserve not so honourable a grave as to stuff a botcher's cushion or to be entombed in an ass's pack-saddle. Yet you must be saying, Marcius is proud; who, in a cheap estimation, is worth all your predecessors since Deucalion; though peradventure some of the best of them were hereditary hangmen. God-den to your worships: more of your conversation would infect my brain, being the herdsmen of the beastly plebeians: I will be bold to take my leave of you.

[BRUTUS *and* SICINIUS *retire.*

*Enter* VOLUMNIA, VIRGILIA, VALERIA, *&c.*

How now, my as fair as noble ladies,—and the moon, were she earthly, no nobler,—whither do you follow your eyes so fast?

*Vol.* Honourable Menenius, my boy Marcius approaches; for the love of Juno let's go.

*Men.* Ha! Marcius coming home!

*Vol.* Ay, worthy Menenius; and with most prosperous approbation.

*Men.* Take my cap, Jupiter, and I thank thee.—Hoo! Marcius coming home!

*Vol. Vir.* Nay, 'tis true.

*Vol.* Look, here's a letter from him: the state hath another, his wife another; and I think there's one at home for you.

*Men.* I will make my very house reel to-night.—A letter for me?

*Vir.* Yes, certain, there's a letter for you; I saw it.

*Men.* A letter for me! It gives me an estate of seven years' health; in which time I will make a lip at the physician: the most sovereign prescription in Galen is but empiricutic, and, to this preservative, of no better report than a horse-drench. Is he not wounded? he was wont to come home wounded.

*Vir.* O, no, no, no.

*Vol.* O, he is wounded, I thank the gods for't.

*Men.* So do I too, if it be not too much.—Brings a victory in his pocket?—The wounds become him.

*Vol.* On's brows: Menenius, he comes the third time home with the oaken garland.

*Men.* Has he disciplined Aufidius soundly?

*Vol.* Titus Lartius writes,—they fought together, but Aufidius got off.

*Men.* And 'twas time for him too. I'll warrant him that: an he had stayed by him, I would not have been so fidiused for all the chests in Corioli, and the gold that's in them. Is the senate possessed of this?

*Vol.* Good ladies, let's go.—Yes, yes, yes; the senate has letters from the general, wherein he gives my son the whole name of the war: he hath in this action outdone his former deeds doubly.

*Val.* In troth, there's wondrous things spoke of him.

*Men.* Wondrous! ay, I warrant you, and not without his true purchasing.

*Vir.* The gods grant them true!

*Vol.* True! pow, wow.

*Men.* True! I'll be sworn they are true.—Where is he wounded?—[*To the* Tribunes, *who come forward.*] God save your good worships! Marcius is coming home: he has more cause to be proud.—Where is he wounded?

*Vol.* I' the shoulder and i' the left arm: there will be large cicatrices to show the people when he shall stand for his place. He received in the repulse of Tarquin seven hurts i' the body.

*Men.* One i' the neck and two i' the thigh,—there's nine that I know.

*Vol.* He had, before this last expedition, twenty-five wounds upon him.

*Men.* Now it's twenty-seven: every gash was an enemy's grave. [*A shout and flourish.*] Hark! the trumpets.

*Vol.* These are the ushers of Marcius: before him [*tears*; He carries noise, and behind him he leaves Death, that dark spirit, in's nervy arm doth lie; [*men die.* Which, being advanc'd, declines, and then

*A sennet. Trumpets sound. Enter* COMINIUS *and* TITUS LARTIUS; *between them,* CORIOLANUS, *crowned with an oaken garland; with* Captains, Soldiers, *and a* Herald.

*Her.* Know, Rome, that all alone Marcius did fight Within Corioli gates: where he hath won, With fame, a name to Caius Marcius; these In honour follows Coriolanus:— Welcome to Rome, renowned Coriolanus!

[*Flourish.*

*All.* Welcome to Rome, renowned Coriolanus! [*heart*;

*Cor.* No more of this, it does offend my Pray now, no more.

*Com.* Look, sir, your mother!

*Cor.* O,
You have, I know, petition'd all the gods For my prosperity! [*Kneels.*

*Vol.*    Nay, my good soldier, up;
My gentle Marcius, worthy Caius, and
By deed-achieving honour newly nam'd,—
What is it?—Coriolanus must I call thee?
But, O, thy wife!

*Cor.*    My gracious silence, hail!
Wouldst thou have laugh'd had I come cof-  [dear,
 fin'd home,
That weep'st to see me triumph? Ah, my
Such eyes the widows in Corioli wear,
And mothers that lack sons.

*Men.*    Now the gods crown thee!

*Cor.* And live you yet?—O my sweet lady,
 pardon.    [*To* VALERIA.

*Vol.* I know not where to turn.—O, wel-  [come all.
 come home;—
And welcome, general;—and you are wel-
*Men.* A hundred thousand welcomes.—I
 could weep
And I could laugh; I am light and heavy.—
 Welcome:
A curse begin at very root on's heart
That is not glad to see thee!—You are three
That Rome should dote on: yet, by the faith
 of men,    [that will not
We have some old crab trees here at home
Be grafted to your relish. Yet welcome, war-
 riors:
We call a nettle but a nettle; and
The faults of fools but folly.

*Com.*    Ever right.

*Cor.* Menenius ever, ever.

*Her.* Give way there, and go on!

*Cor.*    Your hand, and yours:
    [*To his wife and mother.*
Ere in our own house I do shade my head,
The good patricians must be visited;
From whom I have receiv'd not only greet-
 ings,
But with them change of honours.

*Vol.*    I have lived
To see inherited my very wishes,
And the buildings of my fancy: only  [but
There's one thing wanting, which I doubt not
Our Rome will cast upon thee.

*Cor.*    Know, good mother,
I had rather be their servant in my way
Than sway with them in theirs.

*Com.*    On, to the Capitol.
 [*Flourish. Cornets. Exeunt in state, as
  before. The* Tribunes *remain.*

*Bru.* All tongues speak of him, and the
 bleared sights    [nurse
Are spectacled to see him: your prattling
Into a rapture lets her baby cry
While she chats him: the kitchen malkin pins
Her richest lockram 'bout her reechy neck,
Clambering the walls to eye him: stalls,
 bulks, windows,    [hors'd
Are smother'd up, leads fill'd, and ridges
With variable complexions; all agreeing
In earnestness to see him: seld-shown flam-
 ens    [puff
Do press among the popular throngs, and

To win a vulgar station: our veil'd dames
Commit the war of white and damask, in
Their nicely gawded cheeks, to the wanton
 spoil
Of Phœbus' burning kisses: such a pother,
As if that whatsoever god who leads him
Were slily crept into his human powers,
And gave him graceful posture.

*Sic.*    On the sudden,
I warrant him consul.

*Bru.*    Then our office may,
During his power, go sleep.    [honours

*Sic.* He cannot temperately transport his
From where he should begin and end; but
 will
Lose those that he hath won.

*Bru.*    In that there's comfort.

*Sic.* Doubt not the commoners, for whom
 we stand,    [get,
But they, upon their ancient malice, will for-
With the least cause, these his new honours;
 which
That he'll give them make as little question
As he is proud to do't.

*Bru.*    I heard him swear,
Were he to stand for consul, never would he
Appear i' the market-place, nor on him put
The napless vesture of humility;
Nor, showing, as the manner is, his wounds
To the people, beg their stinking breaths.

*Sic.*    'Tis right.

*Bru.* It was his word: O, he would miss it
 rather    [to him,
Than carry it but by the suit of the gentry
And the desire of the nobles.

*Sic.*    I wish no better
Than have him hold that purpose, and to put it
In execution.

*Bru.*  'Tis most like he will.

*Sic.* It shall be to him then, as our good
 wills,
A sure destruction.

*Bru.*    So it must fall out
To him or our authorities. For an end,
We must suggest the people in what hatred
He still hath held them; that to's power he
 would    [ers, and
Have made them mules, silenc'd their plead-
Dispropertied their freedoms: holding them,
In human action and capacity,
Of no more soul nor fitness for the world
Than camels in their war; who have their
 provand
Only for bearing burdens, and sore blows
For sinking under them.

*Sic.*    This, as you say, suggested
At some time when his soaring insolence
Shall touch the people,—which time shall not
 want,
If it be put upon't; and that's as easy
As to set dogs on sheep,—will be his fire
To kindle their dry stubble; and their blaze
Shall darken him for ever.

*Enter a* Messenger.

*Bru.*                    What's the matter?
*Mess.* You are sent for to the Capitol.
   'Tis thought
That Marcius shall be consul:          [and
I have seen the dumb men throng to see him,
The blind to hear his speak: matrons flung
   gloves,                            [chers,
Ladies and maids their scarfs and handker-
Upon him as he pass'd: the nobles bended
As to Jove's statue; and the commons made
A shower and thunder with their caps and
   shouts:
I never saw the like.
   *Bru.*              Let's to the Capitol;
And carry with us ears and eyes for the time,
But hearts for the event.
   *Sic.*           Have with you. [*Exeunt.*

### SCENE II.—ROME. *The Capitol.*

*Enter two* Officers, *to lay cushions.*

1 *Off.* Come, come; they are almost here.
How many stand for consulships?

2 *Off.* Three, they say: but 'tis thought of
every one Coriolanus will carry it.

1 *Off.* That's a brave fellow; but he's vengeance proud, and loves not the common
people.

2 *Off.* Faith, there have been many great
men that have flattered the people, who ne'er
loved them; and there be many that they
have loved, they know not wherefore: so
that, if they love they know not why, they
hate upon no better a ground: therefore, for
Coriolanus neither to care whether they love
or hate him manifests the true knowledge
he has in their disposition; and, out of his
noble carelessness, lets them plainly see't.

1 *Off.* If he did not care whether he had
their love or no, he waved indifferently
'twixt doing them neither good nor harm;
but he seeks their hate with greater devotion
than they can render it him; and leaves
nothing undone that may fully discover him
their opposite. Now, to seem to affect the
malice and displeasure of the people is as bad
as that which he dislikes,—to flatter them
for their love.

2 *Off.* He hath deserved worthily of his
country: and his ascent is not by such easy
degrees as those who, having been supple
and courteous to the people, bonnetted, without any further deed to have them at all
into their estimation and report: but he hath
so planted his honours in their eyes, and his
actions in their hearts, that for their tongues
to be silent, and not confess so much, were a
kind of ingrateful injury; to report otherwise
were a malice 'that, giving itself the lie,
would pluck reproof and rebuke from every
ear that heard it.

1 *Off.* No more of him; he is a worthy
man: make way, they are coming.

*A* Sennet. *Enter, with* Lictors *before them,*
COMINIUS *the* Consul, MENENIUS, CORIO-
LANUS, Senators, SICINIUS, *and* BRUTUS.
*The* Senators *take their places; the* Trib-
unes *take theirs also by themselves.*

*Men.* Having determin'd of the Volsces,
   and
To send for Titus Lartius, it remains,
As the main point of this our after-meeting,
To gratify his noble service that
Hath thus stood for his country: therefore
   please you,
Most reverend and grave elders, to desire
The present consul, and last general
In our well-found successes, to report
A little of that worthy work perform'd
By Caius Marcius Coriolanus; whom  [ber
We meet here, both to thank and to remem-
With honours like himself.
   1 *Sen.*            Speak, good Cominius:
Leave nothing out for length, and make us
   think
Rather our state's defective for requital
Than we to stretch it out.—Masters o' the
   people,
We do request your kindest ears; and, after,
Your loving motion toward the common
   body,
To yield what passes here.
   *Sic.*                We are convented
Upon a pleasing treaty; and have hearts
Inclinable to honour and advance
The theme of our assembly.
   *Bru.*                Which the rather
We shall be bless'd to do, if he remember
A kinder value of the people than
He hath hereto priz'd them at.
   *Men.*                   That's off, that's off;
I would you rather had been silent. Please
   you
To hear Cominius speak?
   *Bru.*                Most willingly:
But yet my caution was more pertinent
Than the rebuke you give it.
   *Men.*                 He loves your people;
But tie him not to be their bedfellow.—
Worthy Cominius, speak.
   [CORIOLANUS *rises, and offers to go away.*
                    Nay, keep your place.
   1 *Sen.* Sit, Coriolanus; never shame to
      hear
What you have nobly done.
   *Cor.*              Your honours' pardon:
I had rather have my wounds to heal again
Than hear say how I got them.
   *Bru.*                  Sir, I hope
My words disbench'd you not.
   *Cor.*                No, sir; yet oft,
When blows have made me stay, I fled from
   words.                            [people,
You sooth'd not, therefore hurt not: but your
I love them as they weigh.
   *Men.*                Pray now, sit down.

*Cor.* I had rather have one scratch my
head i' the sun
When the alarum were struck, than idly sit
To hear my nothings monster'd. [*Exit.*
*Men.* Masters o' the people,
Your multiplying spawn how can he flat-
ter,— [now see
That's thousand to one good one,—when you
He had rather venture all his limbs for hon-
our [Cominius.
Than one on's ears to hear it?—Proceed,
*Com.* I shall lack voice: the deeds of Cor-
iolanus
Should not be utter'd feebly.—It is held
That valour is the chiefest virtue, and
Most dignifies the haver: if it be,
The man I speak of cannot in the world
Be singly counterpois'd. At sixteen years,
When Tarquin made a head for Rome, he
fought [tator,
Beyond the mark of others: our then dic-
Whom with all praise I point at, saw him
fight,
When with his Amazonian chin he drove
The bristled lips before him: he bestrid
An o'erpress'd Roman, and i' the consul's
view
Slew three opposers: Tarquin's self he met,
And struck him on his knee: in that day's
feats,
When he might act the woman in the scene,
He prov'd best man i' the field, and for his
meed [age
Was brow-bound with the oak. His pupil
Man-enter'd thus, he waxed like a sea;
And in the brunt of seventeen battles since
He lurch'd all swords of the garland. For
this last,
Before and in Corioli, let me say, [fliers;
I cannot speak him home: he stopp'd the
And by his rare example made the coward
Turn terror into sport: as weeds before
A vessel under sail, so men obey'd, [stamp,—
And fell below his stem: his sword,—death's
Where it did mark, it took; from face to foot
He was a thing of blood, whose every motion
Was timed with dying cries: alone he enter'd
The mortal gate of the city, which he painted
With shunless destiny; aidless came off,
And with a sudden re-enforcement struck
Corioli like a planet. Now all's his:
When, by and by, the din of war 'gan pierce
His ready sense; then straight his doubled
spirit
Re-quicken'd what in flesh was fatigate,
And to the battle came he; where he did
Run reeking o'er the lives of men as if
'Twere a perpetual spoil; and till we call'd
Both field and city ours he never stood
To ease his breast with panting.
*Men.* Worthy man!
1 *Sen.* He cannot but with measure fit the
honours
Which we devise him.

*Com.* Our spoils he kick'd at;
And look'd upon things precious as they
were [less
The common muck of the world: he covets
Than misery itself would give; rewards
His deeds with doing them; and is content
To spend the time to end it.
*Men.* He's right noble:
Let him be call'd for.
1 *Sen.* Call Coriolanus.
*Off.* He doth appear.

*Re-enter* CORIOLANUS.

*Men.* The senate, Coriolanus, are well
pleas'd
To make thee consul.
*Cor.* I do owe them still
My life and services.
*Men.* It then remains
That you do speak to the people.
*Cor.* I do beseech you
Let me o'erleap that custom; for I cannot
Put on the gown, stand naked, and entreat
them, [please you
For my wounds' sake, to give their suffrage:
That I may pass this doing.
*Sic.* Sir, the people
Must have their voices; neither will they
bate
One jot of ceremony.
*Men.* Put them not to't:—
Pray you, go fit you to the custom; and
Take to you, as your predecessors have,
Your honour with your form.
*Cor.* It is a part
That I shall blush in acting, and might well
Be taken from the people.
*Bru.* Mark you that?
*Cor.* To brag unto them,—thus I did, and
thus;— [should hide
Show them the unaching scars which I
As if I had receiv'd them for the hire
Of their breath only!—
*Men.* Do not stand upon't.—
We recommend to you, tribunes of the
people, [sul
Our purpose to them;—and to our noble con-
Wish we all joy and honour. [our!
*Sen.* To Coriolanus come all joy and hon-
[*Flourish. Exeunt all but* SIC.
*and* BRU.
*Bru.* You see how he intends to use the
people. [requite them
*Sic.* May they perceive's intent! He will
As if he did contemn what he requested
Should be in them to give.
*Bru.* Come, we'll inform them
Of our proceedings here: on the market-place
I know they do attend us. [*Exeunt.*

SCENE III.—ROME. *The Forum.*

*Enter several* Citizens.

1 *Cit.* Once, if he do require our voices, we
ought not to deny him.

2 *Cit.* We may, sir, if we will.

3 *Cit.* We have power in ourselves to do it, but it is a power that we have no power to do: for if he show us his wounds and tell us his deeds, we are to put our tongues into those wounds, and speak for them; so, if he tell us his noble deeds, we must also tell him our noble acceptance of them. Ingratitude is monstrous: and for the multitude to be ingrateful, were to make a monster of the multitude; of the which we, being members, should bring ourselves to be monstrous members.

1 *Cit.* And to make us no better thought of, a little help will serve; for once we stood up about the corn, he himself stuck not to call us the many-headed multitude.

3 *Cit.* We have been called so of many; not that our heads are some brown, some black, some auburn, some bald, but that our wits are so diversely coloured; and truly I think, if all our wits were to issue out of one skull, they would fly east, west, north, south; and their consent of one direct way should be at once to all the points o' the compass.

2 *Cit.* Think you so? Which way do you judge my wit would fly?

3 *Cit.* Nay, your wit will not so soon out as another man's will,—'tis strongly wedged up in a block-head; but if it were at liberty, 'twould, sure, southward.

2 *Cit.* Why that way?

3 *Cit.* To lose itself in a fog; where being three parts melted away with rotten dews, the fourth would return, for conscience' sake, to help to get thee a wife.

2 *Cit.* You are never without your tricks: —you may, you may.

3 *Cit.* Are you all resolved to give your voices? But that's no matter, the greater part carries it. I say, if he would incline to the people, there was never a worthier man. Here he comes, and in the gown of humility: mark his behavior. We are not to stay altogether, but to come by him where he stands, by ones, by twos, and by threes. He's to make his requests by particulars; wherein every one of us has a single honour, in giving him our own voices with our own tongues: therefore follow me, and I'll direct you how you shall go by him.

*All.* Content, content.          [*Exeunt.*

*Enter* CORIOLANUS *and* MENENIUS.

*Men.* O sir, you are not right; have you not known
The worthiest men have done't!
    *Cor.*          What must I say?—
*I pray, sir,—Plague upon't! I cannot bring
My tongue to such a pace.—Look, sir;—my
    wounds;—*
*I got them in my country's service, when
Some certain of your brethren roar'd, and ran
From the noise of our own drums.*

*Men.*                O me, the gods!
You must not speak of that: you must desire
    them
To think upon you.
    *Cor.*          Think upon me! hang 'em!
I would they would forget me, like the virtues
Which our divines lose by 'em.
    *Men.*          You'll mar all:
I'll leave you. Pray you, speak to 'em, I
    pray you,
In wholesome manner.
    *Cor.*          Bid them wash their faces
And keep their teeth clean. [*Exit* MENENIUS.
So, here comes a brace:

*Re-enter two* Citizens.

You know the cause, sirs, of my standing
    here.

1 *Cit.* We do, sir; tell us what hath
    brought you to't.

*Cor.* Mine own desert.

2 *Cit.* Your own desert!

*Cor.* Ay, not mine own desire.

1 *Cit.* How! not your own desire!

*Cor.* No, sir, 'twas never my desire yet to trouble the poor with begging.

1 *Cit.* You must think, if we give you anything, we hope to gain by you.

*Cor.* Well then, I pray, your price o' the consulship?

1 *Cit.* The price is to ask it kindly.

*Cor.* Kindly! sir, I pray, let me ha't: I have wounds to show you, which shall be yours in private.—Your good voice, sir; what say you?

2 *Cit.* You shall ha' it, worthy sir.

*Cor.* A match, sir.—There is in all two worthy voices begg'd.—I have your alms: adieu.

1 *Cit.* But this is something odd.

2 *Cit.* An 'twere to give again,—but 'tis no matter.          [*Exeunt two* Citizens.

*Re-enter other two* Citizens.

*Cor.* Pray you now, if it may stand with the tune of your voices that I may be consul, I have here the customary gown.

3 *Cit.* You have deserved nobly of your country, and you have not deserved nobly.

*Cor.* Your enigma?

3 *Cit.* You have been a scourge to her enemies, you have been a rod to her friends; you have not, indeed, loved the common people.

*Cor.* You should account me the more virtuous, that I have not been common in my love. I will, sir, flatter my sworn brother, the people, to earn a dearer estimation of them; 'tis a condition they account gentle: and since the wisdom of their choice is rather to have my hat than my heart, I will practise the insinuating nod, and be off to them most counterfeitly; that is, sir, I will counterfeit the bewitchment of some popular man, and give it bountifully to the desirers. Therefore, beseech you, I may be consul.

*4 Cit.* We hope to find you our friend; and therefore give you our voices heartily.

*3 Cit.* You have received many wounds for your country.

*Cor.* I will not seal your knowledge with showing them. I will make much of your voices, and so trouble you no further.

*Both Cit.* The gods give you joy, sir, heartily!                    [*Exeunt.*

*Cor.* Most sweet voices!—
Better it is to die, better to starve,
Than crave the hire which first we do deserve.
Why in this wolfish toge should I stand here,
To beg of Hob and Dick, that do appear,
Their needless vouches? Custom calls me to't:—                    [do't,
What custom wills, in all things should we
The dust on antique time would lie unswept,
And mountainous error be too highly heap'd
For truth to o'erpeer. Rather than fool it so,
Let the high office and the honour go
To one that would do thus.—I am half through;
The one part suffer'd, the other will I do.
Here come more voices.

*Re-enter other three* Citizens.

Your voices: for your voices I have fought;
Watch'd for your voices; for your voices bear
Of wounds two dozen odd; battles thrice six
I have seen and heard of; for your voices have                    [your voices:
Done many things, some less, some more:
Indeed, I would be consul.

*5 Cit.* He has done nobly, and cannot go without any honest man's voice.

*6 Cit.* Therefore let him be consul: the gods give him joy, and make him good friend to the people!

*All 3 Citizens.* Amen, amen.—God save thee, noble consul!                    [*Exeunt.*

*Cor.* Worthy voices!

*Re-enter* MENENIUS, *with* BRUTUS *and* SICINIUS.

*Men.* You have stood your limitation; and the tribunes
Endue you with the people's voices:—remains
That, in the official marks invested, you
Anon do meet the senate.

*Cor.*                    Is this done?

*Sic.* The custom of request you have discharg'd:                    [mon'd
The people do admit you; and are summon'd
To meet anon, upon your approbation.

*Cor.* Where? at the senate-house?

*Sic.*                    There, Coriolanus.

*Cor.* May I change these garments?

*Sic.*                    You may, sir.

*Cor.* That I'll straight do; and, knowing myself again,
Repair to the senate-house.                    [along?

*Men.* I'll keep you company.—Will you

*Bru.* We stay here for the people.

*Sic.*                    Fare you well.
                    [*Exeunt* COR. *and* MEN.
He has it now; and by his looks methinks
'Tis warm at his heart.                    [ble weeds.

*Bru.* With a proud heart he wore his humble weeds.
Will you dismiss the people?

*Re-enter* Citizens.

*Sic.* How now, my masters! have you chose this man?

*1 Cit.* He has our voices, sir.                    [your loves

*Bru.* We pray the gods he may deserve

*2 Cit.* Amen, sir:—to my poor unworthy notice,
He mocked us when he begg'd our voices.

*3 Cit.*                    Certainly,
He flouted us downright.

*1 Cit.* No, 'tis his kind of speech,—he did not mock us.

*2 Cit.* Not one amongst us, save yourself, but says                    [us
He us'd us scornfully: he should have show'd
His marks of merit, wounds receiv'd for's country.

*Sic.* Why, so he did, I am sure.

*Citizens.*                    No, no; no man saw 'em.

*3 Cit.* He said he had wounds, which he could show in private;
And with his hat, thus waving it in scorn,
*I would be consul*, says he; *aged custom,
But by your voices, will not so permit me;
Your voices therefore:* when we granted that,
Here was, *I thank you for your voices,—thank you,—
Your most sweet voices:—now you have left your voices
I have no further with you:*—was not this mockery?

*Sic.* Why, either were you ignorant to see't?
Or, seeing it, of such childish friendliness
To yield your voices?

*Bru.*                    Could you not have told him,
As you were lesson'd,—when he had no power,
But was a petty servant to the state,
He was your enemy; ever spake against
Your liberties, and the charters that you bear
I' the body of the weal: and now, arriving
A place of potency and sway o' the state,
If he should still malignantly remain
Fast foe to the plebeii, your voices might
Be curses to yourselves? You should have said,
That as his worthy deeds did claim no less
Than what he stood for, so his gracious nature
Would think upon you for your voices, and

Translate his malice towards you into love,
Standing your friendly lord.

*Sic.*                        Thus to have said,
As you were fore-advis'd, had touch'd his
    spirit
And tried his inclination; from him pluck'd
Either his gracious promise, which you
    might,
As cause had call'd you up, have held him to;
Or else it would have gall'd his surly nature,
Which easily endures not article
Tying him to aught; so, putting him to rage,
You should have ta'en the advantage of his
    choler,
And pass'd him unelected.

*Bru.*                        Did you perceive
He did solicit you in free contempt
When he did need your loves; and do you
    think                                    [you
That his contempt shall not be bruising to
When he hath power to crush? Why, had
    your bodies                              [to cry
No heart among you? Or had you tongues
Against the rectorship of judgment?

*Sic.*                        Have you
Ere now denied the asker? and now again,
On him that did not ask but mock, bestow
Your su'd-for tongues?             [him yet.

3 *Cit.* He's not confirm'd; we may deny
2 *Cit.* And will deny him:
I'll have five hundred voices of that sound.
1 *Cit.* I twice five hundred, and their
    friends to piece 'em.       [those friends
*Bru.* Get you hence instantly; and tell
They have chose a consul that will from
    them take
Their liberties; make them of no more voice
Than dogs, that are as often beat for bark-
    ing
As therefore kept to do so.

*Sic.*                        Let them assemble;
And, on a safer judgment, all revoke
Your ignorant election: enforce his pride
And his old hate unto you: besides, forget not
With what contempt he wore the humble
    weed;                                    [loves,
How in his suit he scorn'd you: but your
Thinking upon his services, took from you
The apprehension of his present portance,
Which, most gibingly, ungravely, he did
    fashion
After the inveterate hate he bears you.

*Bru.*                        Lay
A fault on us, your tribunes; that we la-
    bour'd,—
No impediment between,—but that you must
Cast your election on him.

*Sic.*                        Say you chose him
More after our commandment than as guided
By your own true affections; and that your
    minds,
Pre-occupied with what you rather must do
Than what you should, made you against
    the grain

To voice him consul. Lay the fault on us.

*Bru.* Ay, spare us not. Say we read lec-
    tures to you,
How youngly he began to serve his country,
How long continued: and what stock he
    springs of—                   [whence came
The noble house o' the Marcians; from
That Ancus Marcius, Numa's daughter's son,
Who, after great Hostilius, here was king;
Of the same house Publius and Quintus were,
That our best water brought by conduits
    hither;
And Censorinus, darling of the people,
And nobly nam'd so, twice being censor,
Was his great ancestor.

*Sic.*                        One thus descended,
That hath beside well in his person wrought
To be set high in place, we did commend
To your remembrances: but you have found,
Scaling his present bearing with his past,
That he's your fixed enemy, and revoke
Your sudden approbation.

*Bru.*                        Say you ne'er had done't,—
Harp on that still,—but by our putting on:
And presently when you have drawn your
    number,
Repair to the Capitol.

*Citizens.*                 We will so; almost all
Repent in their election.          [*Exeunt.*
*Bru.*                        Let them go on;
This mutiny were better put in hazard
Than stay, past doubt, for greater:
If, as his nature is, he fall in rage
With their refusal, both observe and answer
The vantage of his anger.

*Sic.*                        To the Capitol,
Come: we will be there before the stream o'
    the people;
And this shall seem, as partly 'tis, their own,
Which we have goaded onward.      [*Exeunt.*

## ACT III.

### Scene I.—Rome. *A Street.*

*Cornets. Enter* Coriolanus, Menenius.
Cominius, Titus Lartius, Senators, *and*
Patricians.

*Cor.* Tullus Aufidius, then, had made new
    head?                        [which caus'd
*Lart.* He had, my lord; and that it was
Our swifter composition.

*Cor.* So then the Volsces stand but as at
    first;                         [make road
Ready, when time shall prompt them, to
Upon's again.

*Com.*                        They are worn, lord consul, so
That we shall hardly in our ages see
Their banners wave again.

*Cor.*                        Saw you Aufidius?
*Lart.* On safeguard he came to me; and
    did curse
Against the Volsces, for they had so vilely
Yielded the town: he is retir'd to **Antium**.
*Cor.* Spoke he of me?

*Lart.*             He did, my lord.
*Cor.*             How? what?
*Lart.* How often he had met you, sword
    to sword;
That of all things upon the earth he hated
Your person most; that he would pawn his
    fortunes
To hopeless restitution, so he might
Be call'd your vanquisher.
*Cor.*             At Antium lives he?
*Lart.* At Antium.
*Cor.* I wish I had a cause to seek him
    there,
To oppose his hatred fully.—Welcome home.
                           [*To* LARTIUS.

*Enter* SICINIUS *and* BRUTUS.

Behold! these are the tribunes of the people,
The tongues o' the common mouth. I do
    despise them;
For they do prank them in authority,
Against all noble sufferance.
*Sic.*             Pass no further.
*Cor.* Ha! what is that?
*Bru.* It will be dangerous to go on: no
    further.
*Cor.* What makes this change?
*Men.* The matter?      [the commons?
*Com.* Hath he not pass'd the nobles and
*Bru.* Cominius, no.
*Cor.*        Have I had children's voices?
1 *Sen.* Tribunes, give way; he shall to the
    market-place.
*Bru.* The people are incens'd against him.
*Sic.*                  Stop,
Or all will fall in broil.
*Cor.*        Are these your herd?—
Must these have voices, that can yield them
    now,          [are your offices?
And straight disclaim their tongues?—What
You being their mouths, why rule you not
    their teeth?
Have you not set them on?
*Men.*          Be calm, be calm.
*Cor.* It is a purpos'd thing, and grows by
    plot,
To curb the will of the nobility:
Suffer't, and live with such as cannot rule,
Nor ever will be rul'd.
*Bru.*          Call't not a plot:
The people cry you mock'd them; and of late,
When corn was given them gratis, you re-
    pin'd;
Scandal'd the suppliants for the people,—
    call'd them
Time-pleasers, flatterers, foes to nobleness.
*Cor.* Why, this was known before.
*Bru.*          Not to them all.
*Cor.* Have you inform'd them sithence?
*Bru.*          How! I inform them!
*Cor.* You are like to do such business.
*Bru.*             Not unlike,
Each way, to better yours.

*Cor.* Why, then, should I be consul? By
    yon clouds,
Let me deserve so ill as you, and make me
Your fellow tribune.
*Sic.*         You show too much of that
For which the people stir: if you will pass
To where you are bound, you must inquire
    your way,
Which you are out of, with a gentler spirit;
Or never be so noble as a consul,
Nor yoke with him for tribune.
*Men.*             Let's be calm.
*Com.* The people are abus'd; set on. This
    palt'ring
Becomes not Rome; nor has Coriolanus
Deserv'd this so dishonour'd rub, laid falsely
I' the plain way of his merit.
*Cor.*          Tell me of corn!
This was my speech, and I will speak't
    again,—
*Men.* Not now, not now.
1 *Sen.*        Not in this heat, sir, now.
*Cor.* Now, as I live, I will.—My nobler
    friends,
I crave their pardons:
For the mutable, rank-scented many, let
    them
Regard me as I do not flatter, and
Therein behold themselves: I say again,
In soothing them we nourish 'gainst our
    senate
The cockle of rebellion, insolence, sedition,
Which we ourselves have plough'd for, sow'd,
    and scatter'd,
By mingling them with us, the honour'd
    number;
Who lack not virtue, no, nor powder, but
    that
Which they have given to beggars.
*Men.*          Well, no more.
1 *Sen.* No more words, we beseech you.
*Cor.*          How! no more!
As for my country I have shed my blood,
Not fearing outward force, so shall my lungs
Coin words till their decay against those
    measles
Which we disdain should tetter us, yet sought
The very way to catch them.
*Bru.*         You speak o' the people
As if you were a god to punish, not
A man of their infirmity.
*Sic.*          'Twere well
We let the people know't.
*Men.*        What, what? his choler?
*Cor.* Choler!
Were I as patient as the midnight sleep,
By Jove, 'twould be my mind!
*Sic.*            It is a mind
That shall remain a poison where it is,
Not poison any further.
*Cor.*          Shall remain!—
Hear you this Triton of the minnows? mark
    you
His absolute *shall?*

*Com.*                    'Twas from the canon.
*Cor.*                                    Shall!
O good, but most unwise patricians! why,
You grave, but reckless senators, have you
    thus
Given Hydra leave to choose an officer,
That with his peremptory *shall*, being but
The horn and noise o' the monster, wants not
    spirit
To say he'll turn your current in a ditch,
And make your channel his? If he have
    power,
Then vail your ignorance: if none, awake
Your dangerous lenity. If you are learn'd
Be not as common fools; if you are not,
Let them have cushions by you. You are
    plebeians
If they be senators: and they are no less
When, both your voices blended, the great'st
    taste
Most palates theirs. They choose their magis-
    trate;
And such a one as he, who puts his *shall*,
His popular *shall*, against a graver bench
Than ever frown'd in Greece. By Jove him-
    self,
It makes the consuls base: and my soul aches
To know, when two authorities are up,
Neither supreme, how soon confusion
May enter 'twixt the gap of both, and take
The one by the other.
*Com.*          Well, on to the market-place.
*Cor.* Whoever gave that counsel, to give
    forth
The corn o' the storehouse gratis, as 'twas
    us'd
Sometime in Greece,—
*Men.*          Well, well, no more of that.
*Cor.* Though there the people had more
    absolute power,—
I say, they nourish'd disobedience, fed
The ruin of the state.
*Bru.*          Why, shall the people give
One that speaks thus their voice?
*Cor.*                    I'll give my reasons,
More worthier than their voices. They know
    the corn
Was not our recompense, resting well assur'd
They ne'er did service for 't: being press'd to
    the war,
Even when the navel of the state was touch'd,
They would not thread the gates,—this kind
    of service
Did not deserve corn gratis: being i' the war,
Their mutinies and revolts, wherein thy
    show'd
Most valour, spoke not for them. The accusa-
    tion
Which they have often made against the
    senate,
All cause unborn, could never be the motive
Of our so frank donation. Well, what then?
How shall this bisson multitude digest
The senate's courtesy? Let deeds express

What's like to be their words:—*We did re-
    quest it;*
*We are the greater poll, and in true fear*
*They gave us our demands:*—thus we debase
The nature of our seats, and make the rabble
Call our cares fears: which will in time
Break ope the locks o' the senate, and bring in
The crows to peck the eagles.—
*Men.*                    Come, enough.
*Bru.* Enough, with over-measure.
*Cor.*                    No, take more:
What may be sworn by, both divine and hu-
    man,
Seal what I end withal!—This double wor-
    ship,—
Where one part does disdain with cause, the
    other          [wisdom,
Insult without all reason; where gentry, title,
Cannot conclude but by the yea and no
Of general ignorance,—it must omit
Real necessities, and give way the while
To unstable slightness: purpose so barr'd, it
    follows,          [seech you,—
Nothing is done to purpose. Therefore, be-
You that will be less fearful than discreet;
That love the fundamental part of state
More than you doubt the change on 't; that
    prefer
A noble life before a long, and wish
To vamp a body with a dangerous physic
That's sure of death without it,—at once
    pluck out
The multitudinous tongue; let them not lick
The sweet which is their poison: your dis-
    honour
Mangles true judgment, and bereaves the
    state
Of that integrity which should become 't;
Not having the power to do the good it
    would,
For the ill which doth control 't.
*Bru.*                    Has said enough.
*Sic.* Has spoken like a traitor, and shall
    answer
As traitors do.
*Cor.* Thou wretch despite o'erwhelm
    thee!—
What should the people do with these bald
    tribunes?
On whom depending, their obedience fails
To the greater bench: in a rebellion,
When what's not meet, but what must be,
    was law,
Then were they chosen; in a better hour
Let what is meet be said it must be meet,
And throw their power i' the dust.
*Bru.* Manifest treason.
*Sic.*                    This a consul? no.
*Bru.* The ædiles, ho!—Let him be appre-
    hended.          [in whose name myself
*Sic.* Go, call the people [*Exit* BRUTUS];—
Attach thee as a traitorous innovator,
A foe to the public weal. Obey, I charge thee,
And follow to thine answer.

*Cor.*                    Hence, old goat!
*Sen. and Pat.* We'll surety him.
*Com.*                    Aged sir, hands off.
*Cor.* Hence, rotten thing! or I shall shake
    thy bones
Out of thy garments.
*Sic.*                    Help, ye citizens!

    *Re-enter* BRUTUS, *with the Ædiles and a*
        *rabble of* Citizens.

*Men.* On both sides more respect.
*Sic.* Here's he that would take from you
    all your power.
*Bru.* Seize him, ædiles.
*Citizens.* Down with him! down with him!
*2 Sen.* Weapons, weapons, weapons!
    [*They all bustle about* CORIOLANUS.
Tribunes, patricians, citizens!—what, ho!—
Sicinius, Brutus, Coriolanus, citizens!
*Citizens.* Peace, peace, peace; stay, hold,
peace!
*Men.* What is about to be?—I am out of
    breath;                    [bunes
Confusion's near; I cannot speak.—You tri-
To the people,—Coriolanus, patience:—
Speak, good Sicinius.
*Sic.*                    Hear me, people; peace!
*Citizens.* Let's hear our tribune: peace!—
    Speak, speak, speak.
*Sic.* You are at point to lose your liberties:
Marcius would have all from you; Marcius,
Whom late you have nam'd for consul.
*Men.*                    Fie, fie, fie!
This is the way to kindle, not to quench.
  *1 Sen.* To unbuild the city, and to lay all
    flat.
*Sic.* What is the city but the people?
*Citizens.*                    True,
The people are the city.
*Bru.* By the consent of all, we were estab-
    lish'd
The people's magistrates.
*Cit.*                    You so remain.
*Men.* And so are like to do.
*Cor.* That is the way to lay the city flat;
To bring the roof to the foundation,
And bury all which yet distinctly ranges,
In heaps and piles of ruin.
*Sic.*                    This deserves death.
*Bru.* Or let us stand to our authority,
Or let us lose it.—We do here pronounce,
Upon the part o' the people, in whose power
We were elected theirs, Marcius is worthy
Of present death.
*Sic.*                    Therefore lay hold of him;
Bear him to the rock Tarpeian, and from
    thence
Into destruction cast him.
*Bru.*                    Ædiles, seize him!
*Citizens.* Yield, Marcius, yield!
*Men.*                    Hear me one word;
Beseech you, tribunes, hear me but a word.
*Æd.* Peace, peace!

*Men.* Be that you seem, truly your coun-
    try's friends,
And temperately proceed to what you would
Thus violently redress.
*Bru.*                    Sir, those cold ways,
That seem like prudent helps, are very
    poisonous
Where the disease is violent.—Lay hands
    upon him,
And bear him to the rock.
*Cor.*                    No; I'll die here.
    [*Draws his sword.*
There's some among you have beheld me
    fighting:                    [seen me.
Come, try upon yourselves what you have
*Men.* Down with that sword!—Tribunes,
    withdraw awhile.
*Bru.* Lay hands upon him.
*Men.*                    Help Marcius, help,
You that be noble; help him, young and old!
*Citizens.* Down with him, down with him!
    [*In this mutiny the* Tribunes, *the* Ædiles,
        *and the* People *are beat in.*
*Men.* Go, get you to your house; be gone,
    away!
All will be naught else.
*2 Sen.*                    Get you gone.
*Cor.*                    Stand fast;
We have as many friends as enemies.
*Men.* Shall it be put to that?
*1 Sen.*                    The gods forbid!
I pr'ythee, noble friend, home to thy house;
Leave us to cure this cause.
*Men.*                    For 'tis a sore upon us,
You cannot tent yourself: be gone, beseech
    you.
*Com.* Come, sir, along with us.  [they are,
*Cor.* I would they were barbarians,—as
Though in Rome litter'd,—not Romans,—as
    they are not,
Though calv'd i' the porch o' the Capitol,—
*Men.*                    Be gone;
Put not your worthy rage into your tongue;
One time will owe another.
*Cor.*                    On fair ground
I could beat forty of them.
*Men.*                    I could myself
Take up a brace o' the best of them; yea, the
    two tribunes.
*Com.* But now 'tis odds beyond arith-
    metic;
And manhood is call'd foolery when it stands
Against a falling fabric.—Will you hence,
Before the tag return? whose rage doth rend
Like interrupted waters, and o'erbear
What they are used to bear.
*Men.*                    Pray you, be gone:
I'll try whether my old wit be in request
With those that have but little: this must be
    patch'd
With cloth of any colour.
*Com.*                    Nay, come away.
    [*Exeunt* COR., COM., *and others.*
  *1 Pat.* This man has marr'd his fortune.

*Men.* His nature is too noble for the
world:
He would not flatter Neptune for his trident,
Or Jove for 's power to thunder. His heart's
    his mouth:
What his breast forges, that his tongue must
    vent;
And, being angry, does forget that ever
He heard the name of death. [*A noise within.*
Here's goodly work!
    2 *Pat.*          I would they were a-bed!
*Men.* I would they were in Tiber! What,
    the vengeance,
Could he not speak 'em fair?

*Re-enter* BRUTUS *and* SICINIUS, *with the
    rabble.*

*Sic.*              Where is this viper
That would depopulate the city and
Be every man himself?
*Men*              You worthy tribunes,—
*Sic.* He shall be thrown down the Tarpeian
    rock
With rigorous hands: he hath resisted law,
And therefore law shall scorn him further
    trial
Than the severity of the public power,
Which he so sets at naught.
    1 *Cit.*          He shall well know
The noble tribunes are the people's mouths,
And we their hands.
    *Citizens.* He shall, sure on 't.
*Men.*              Sir, sir,—
*Sic.*              Peace!
*Men.* Do not cry havoc, where you should
    but hunt
With modest warrant.
*Sic.*          Sir, how comes 't that you
Have holp to make this rescue?
*Men.*              Hear me speak:—
As I do know the consul's worthiness,
So can I name his faults,—
*Sic.*          Consul!—what consul?
*Men.* The consul Coriolanus.
*Bru.*              He consul!
*Citizens.* No, no, no, no, no.
*Men.* If, by the tribunes' leave and yours,
    good people
I may be heard, I would crave a word or
    two;
The which shall turn you to no further harm
Than so much loss of time.
*Sic.*          Speak briefly, then;
For we are peremptory to despatch
This viperous traitor: to eject him hence
Were but one danger; and to keep him here
Our certain death: therefore it is decreed
He dies to-night.
*Men.*          Now the good gods forbid
That our renowned Rome, whose gratitude
Towards her deserved children is enroll'd
In Jove's own book, like an unnatural dam
Should now eat up her own!
*Sic.* He's a disease that must be cut away.

*Men.* O, he's a limb that has but a disease;
Mortal, to cut it off; to cure it, easy.
What has he done to Rome that's worthy
    death?
Killing our enemies, the blood he hath lost,—
Which I dare vouch is more than that he hath
By many an ounce,—he dropt it for his
    country;
And what is left, to lose it by his country
Were to us all, that do 't and suffer it,
A brand to the end o' the world.
*Sic.*              This is clean kam.
*Bru.* Merely awry: when he did love his
    country,
It honour'd him.
*Men.*          The service of the foot,
Being once gangren'd, is not then respected
For what before it was.
*Bru.*              We'll hear no more.—
Pursue him to his house, and pluck him
    thence;
Lest his infection, being of catching nature,
Spread further.
*Men.*          One word more, one word.
This tiger-footed rage, when it shall find
The harm of unscann'd swiftness, will, too
    late,
Tie leaden pounds to 's heels. Proceed by
    process;
Lest parties,—as he is belov'd,—break out,
And sack great Rome with Romans.
*Bru.*              If it were so,—
*Sic.* What do you talk?
Have we not had a taste of his obedience?
Our ædiles smote? ourselves resisted?—
    come,—
*Men.*          Consider this:—he has been bred i'
    the wars
Since he could draw a sword, and is ill
    school'd
In bolted language; meal and bran together
He throws without distinction. Give me leave,
I'll go to him, and undertake to bring him
Where he shall answer, by a lawful form,
In peace, to his utmost peril.
    1 *Sen.*          Noble tribunes,
It is the humane way: the other course
Will prove too bloody; and the end of it
Unknown to the beginning.
*Sic.*              Noble Menenius,
Be you then as the people's officer.—
Masters, lay down your weapons.
*Bru.*              Go not home.
*Sic.* Meet on the market-place.—We'll
    attend you there:
Where, if you bring not Marcius, we'll
    proceed
In our first way.
*Men.*          I'll bring him to you.—
[*To the* Senators.] Let me desire your com-
    pany: he must come,
Or what is worst will follow.
    1 *Sen.*          Pray you, let's to him.
                                        [*Exeunt.*

SCENE II.—ROME. *A Room in* CORIOLANUS'S *House.*

*Enter* CORIOLANUS *and* Patricians.

*Cor.* Let them pull all about mine ears;
present me
Death on the wheel, or at wild horses' heels;
Or pile ten hills on the Tarpeian rock,
That the precipitation might down stretch
Below the beam of sight; yet will I still
Be thus to them.
  1 *Pat.*          You do the nobler.
  *Cor.* I muse my mother
Does not approve me further, who was wont
To call them woollen vassals, things created
To buy and sell with groats; to show bare
heads
In congregations, to yawn, be still, and
wonder,
When one but of my ordinance stood up
To speak of peace or war.

*Enter* VOLUMNIA.

              I talk of you: [*To* VOLUMNIA.
Why did you wish me milder? Would you
have me
False to my nature? Rather say, I play
The man I am.
  *Vol.*         O, sir, sir, sir,
I would have had you put your power well
on
Before you had worn it out.
  *Cor.*         Let go. [you are
  *Vol.* You might have been enough the man
With striving less to be so: lesser had been
The thwartings of your dispositions if
You had not show'd them how ye were
dispos'd
Ere they lack'd power to cross you.
  *Cor.*         Let them hang.
  *Vol.* Ay, and burn too.

*Enter* MENENIUS *and* Senators.

  *Men.* Come, come, you have been too
rough, something too rough;
You must return and mend it.
  1 *Sen.*        There's no remedy;
Unless, by not so doing, our good city
Cleave in the midst, and perish.
  *Vol.*        Pray, be counsell'd;
I have a heart as little apt as yours,
But yet a brain that leads my use of anger
To better vantage.
  *Men.*      Well said, noble woman!
Before he should thus stoop to the herd, but
that
The violent fit o' the time craves it as physic
For the whole state, I would put mine armour
on,
Which I can scarcely bear.
  *Cor.* What must I do?
  *Men.* Return to the tribunes.
  *Cor.* Well, what then? what then?
  *Men.* Repent what you have spoke.

  *Cor.* For them?—I cannot do it to the
gods;
Must I then do 't to them?
  *Vol.*        You are too absolute;
Though therein you can never be too noble
But when extremities speak. I have heard
you say,
Honour and policy, like unsever'd friends,
I' the war do grow together: grant that, and
tell me
In peace what each of them by th' other lose
That they combine not there.
  *Cor.*        Tush, tush!
  *Men.*        A good demand.
  *Vol.* If it be honour in your wars to seem
The same you are not,—which for your best
ends
You adopt your policy,—how is it less or
worse
That it shall hold companionship in peace
With honour as in war; since that to both
It stands in like request?
  *Cor.*        Why force you this?
  *Vol.* Because that now it lies you on to
speak
To the people; not by your own instruction,
Nor by the matter which your heart prompts
you,
But with such words that are but rooted in
Your tongue, though but bastards, and
syllables
Of no allowance, to your bosom's truth,
Now, this no more dishonours you at all
Than to take in a town with gentle words,
Which else would put you to your fortune
and
The hazard of much blood.
I would dissemble with my nature where
My fortunes and my friends at stake
requir'd
I should do so in honour: I am in this
Your wife, your son, these senators, the
nobles;
And you will rather show our general louts
How you can frown, than spend a fawn upon
'em
For the inheritance of their loves and safe-
guard
Of what that want might ruin.
  *Men.*        Noble lady!—
Come, go with us; speak fair: you may salve
so,
Not what is dangerous present, but the loss
Of what is past.
  *Vol.*        I pr'ythee now, my son,
Go to them with this bonnet in thy hand;
And thus far having stretch'd it,—here be
with them,—      [business
Thy knee bussing the stones,—for in such
Action is eloquence, and the eyes of the
ignorant
More learned than the ears,—waving thy
head,
Which often, thus, correcting thy stout heart,

Now humble as the ripest mulberry
That will not hold the handling: or say to
   them
Thou art their soldier, and, being bred in
   broils,
Hast not the soft way which, thou dost
   confess,
Were fit for thee to use, as they to claim,
In asking their good loves; but thou wilt
   frame
Thyself, forsooth, hereafter theirs, so far
As thou hast power and person.
   *Men.*             This but done,
Even as she speaks, why, their hearts were
   yours:
For they have pardons, being ask'd, as free
As words to little purpose.
   *Vol.*            Pr'ythee now,
Go, and be rul'd: although I know thou
   had'st rather
Follow thine enemy in a fiery gulf
Than flatter him in a bower. Here is Comin-
   ius.

     *Enter* COMINIUS.

   *Com.* I have been i' the market-place; and,
   sir, 'tis fit
You make strong party, or defend yourself
By calmness or by absence: all 's in anger.
   *Men.* Only fair speech.
   *Com.*        I think 'twill serve, if he
Can thereto frame his spirit.
   *Vol.*          He must, and will.—
Pr'ythee now, say you will, and go about it.
   *Cor.* Must I go show them my unbarb'd
   sconce? must I,
With my base tongue, give to my noble heart
A lie, that it must bear? Well, I will do 't:
Yet, were there but this single plot to lose,
This mould of Marcius, they to dust should
   grind it,       [market-place:—
And throw 't against the wind.—To the
You have put me now to such a part which
   never
I shall discharge to the life.
   *Com.*      Come, come, we'll prompt you.
   *Vol.* I pr'ythee now, sweet son,—as thou
   hast said
My praises made thee first a soldier, so,
To have my praise for this, perform a part
Thou hast not done before.
   *Cor.*        Well, I must do 't:
Away, my disposition, and possess me
Some harlot's spirit! My throat of war be
   turn'd,
Which quired with my drum, into a pipe
Small as an eunuch, or the virgin voice
That babies lulls asleep! the smiles of knaves
Tent in my cheeks; and school-boys' tears
   take up
The glasses of my sight! a beggar's tongue
Make motion through my lips; and my arm'd
   knees,
Who bow'd but in my stirrup, bend like his

That hath receiv'd an alms!—I will not do
   't;
Lest I surcease to honour mine own truth,
And by my body's action teach my mind
A most inherent baseness.
   *Vol.*          At thy choice, then:
To beg of thee, it is my more dishonour
Than thou of them. Come all to ruin: let
Thy mother rather feel thy pride than fear
Thy dangerous stoutness; for I mock at death
With as big a heart as thou. Do as thou list.
Thy valiantness was mine, thou suck'dst it
   from me;
But owe thy pride thyself.
   *Cor.*         Pray, be content:
Mother, I am going to the market-place;
Chide me no more. I'll mountebank their
   loves,        [belov'd
Cog their hearts from them, and come home
Of all the trades in Rome. Look, I am going:
Commend me to my wife. I'll return consul;
Or never trust to what my tongue can do
I' the way of flattery further.
   *Vol.*         Do your will.    [*Exit.*
   *Com.* Away! the tribunes do attend you;
   arm yourself
To answer mildly; for they are prepar'd
With accusations, as I hear, more strong
Than are upon you yet.
   *Cor.* The word is, mildly.—Pray you, let
   us go:
Let them accuse me by invention, I
Will answer in mine honour.
   *Men.*         Ay, but mildly.
   *Cor.* Well, mildly be it then; mildly.
                   [*Exeunt.*

    SCENE III.—ROME. *The Forum.*
    *Enter* SICINIUS *and* BRUTUS.

   *Bru.* In this point charge him home, that
   he affects
Tyrannical power: if he evade us there,
Enforce him with his envy to the people;
And that the spoil got on the Antiates
Was ne'er distributed.

     *Enter an* ÆDILE.

What, will he come?
   *Æd.*         He's coming.
   *Bru.*         How accompanied?
   *Æd.* With old Menenius, and those
   senators
That always favour'd him.
   *Sic.*         Have you a catalogue
Of all the voices that we have procur'd,
Set down by the poll?
   *Æd.*         I have; 'tis ready.
   *Sic.* Have you collected them by tribes?
   *Æd.*         I have.
   *Sic.* Assemble presently the people hither:
And when they hear me say, *It shall be so
I' the right and strength o' the commons,* be
   it, either        [them,
For death, for fine, or banishment, then let

If I say fine, cry *Fine*—if death, cry *Death;*—
Insisting on the old prerogative
And power i' the truth o' the cause.

&AElig;d.     I shall inform them.

*Bru.* And when such time they have begun
  to cry,
Let them not cease, but with a din confus'd
Enforce the present execution
Of what we chance to sentence.

&AElig;d.      Very well.

*Sic.* Make them be strong, and ready for
  this hint,
When we shall hap to give 't them.

*Bru.*     Go about it.—
         [*Exit* &AElig;dile.
Put him to choler straight: he hath been us'd
Ever to conquer, and to have his worth
Of contradiction: being once chaf'd, he can-
  not
Be rein'd again to temperance; then he speaks
What's in his heart; and that is there which
  looks
With us to break his neck.

*Sic.*. Well, here he comes.

Enter CORIOLANUS, MENENIUS, COMINIUS,
  Senators, *and* Patricians.

*Men.* Calmly, I do beseech you.

*Cor.* Ay, as an ostler, that for the poorest
  piece    [honour'd gods
Will bear the knave by the volume.—The
Keep Rome in safety, and the chairs of
  justice
Supplied with worthy men! plant love among
  's!
Throng our large temples with the shows of
  peace,
And not our streets with war!

1 *Sen.*     Amen, amen!
*Men.* A noble wish.

Re-enter &AElig;dile, *with* Citizens.

*Sic.* Draw near, ye people.  [I say!
&AElig;d. List to your tribunes; audience: peace,
*Cor.* First, hear me speak.
*Both Tri.*  Well, say.—Peace, ho!
*Cor.* Shall I be charg'd no further than this
  present?
Must all determine here?

*Sic.*     I do demand,
If you submit you to the people's voices,
Allow their officers, and are content
To suffer lawful censure for such faults
As shall be proved upon you?

*Cor.*     I am content.

*Men.* Lo, citizens, he says he is content:
The warlike service he has done, consider;
  think       [like
Upon the wounds his body bears, which show
Graves i' the holy churchyard.

*Cor.*    Scratches with briers,
Scars to move laughter only.

*Men.*    Consider further,
That when he speaks not like a citizen,

You find him like a soldier: do not take
His rougher accents for malicious sounds,
But, as I say, such as become a soldier,
Rather than envy you.

*Com.*   Well, well, no more.

*Cor.* What is the matter,
That being pass'd for consul with full voice,
I am so dishonour'd that the very hour
You take it off again?

*Sic.*     Answer to us.

*Cor.* Say then: 'tis true, I ought so.

*Sic.* We charge you that you have con-
  triv'd to take
From Rome all season'd office, and to wind
Yourself into a power tyrannical;
For which you are a traitor to the people.

*Cor.* How! traitor!

*Men.*  Nay, temperately; your promise.

*Cor.* The fires i' the lowest hell fold in the
  people!
Call me their traitor!—Thou injurious tri-
  bune!
Within thine eyes sat twenty thousand
  deaths,
In thy hands clutch'd as many millions, in
Thy lying tongue both numbers, I would say,
Thou liest unto thee, with a voice as free
As I do pray the gods.

*Sic.*    Mark you this, people?

*Citizens.* To the rock, to the rock with
  him!

*Sic.* Peace!
We need not put new matter to his charge:
What you have seen him do and heard him
  speak,
Beating your officers, cursing yourselves,
Opposing laws with strokes, and here defy-
  ing
Those whose great power must try him; even
  this,
So criminal, and in such capital kind,
Deserves the extremest death.

*Bru.*    But since he hath
Serv'd well for Rome,—

*Cor.*   What do you prate of service?

*Bru.* I talk of that, that know it.

*Cor.* You?    [your mother?

*Men.* Is this the promise that you made

*Com.* Know, I pray you,—

*Cor.*    I'll know no further:
Let them pronounce the steep Tarpeian
  death,
Vagabond exile, flaying, pent to linger
But with a grain a day, I would not buy
Their mercy at the price of one fair word,
Nor check my courage for what they can
  give,
To have 't with saying Good-morrow.

*Sic.*    For that he has,—
As much as in him lies,—from time to time
Envied against the people, seeking means
To pluck away their power; as now at last
Given hostile strokes, and that not in the
  presence

Of dreaded justice, but on the ministers
That do distribute it;—in the name o' the
   people,
And in the power of us the tribunes, we,
Even from this instant, banish him our city;
In peril of precipitation
From off the rock Tarpeian, never more
To enter our Roman gates: i' the people's
   name,
I say it shall be so.
   *Citizens.* It shall be so, it shall be so; let
      him away:
He's banished, and it shall be so.
   *Com.* Hear me, my masters, and my com-
      mon friends,—
   *Sic.* He's sentenc'd; no more hearing.
   *Com.*                 Let me speak:
I have been consul, and can show for Rome
Her enemies' marks upon me. I do love
My country's good with a respect more
   tender,
More holy and profound, than mine own life,
My dear wife's estimate, her womb's in-
   crease,
And treasure of my loins; then if I would
Speak that,—
   *Sic.*     We know your drift. Speak what?
   *Bru.* There's no more to be said, but he is
      banish'd,
As enemy to the people and his country:
It shall be so.
   *Citizens.* It shall be so, it shall be so.
   *Cor.* You common cry of curs! whose
      breath I hate       [prize
As reek o' the rotten fens, whose loves I
As the dead carcasses of unburied men
That do corrupt my air,—I banish you;
And here remain with your uncertainty!
Let every feeble rumour shake your hearts!
Your enemies, with nodding of their plumes,
Fan you into despair! Have the power still
To banish your defenders; till at length
Your ignorance,—which finds not till it
   feels,—
Making not reservation of yourselves,—
Still your own foes,—deliver you, as most
Abated captives, to some nation
That won you without blows! Despising,
For you, the city, thus I turn my back:
There is a world elsewhere.
   [*Exeunt* COR., COM., MEN., Senators,
      *and* Patricians.
   *Æd.* The people's enemy is gone, is gone!
   *Citizens.* Our enemy is banish'd! he is
      gone! Hoo! hoo!
      [*Shouting, and throwing up their caps.*
   *Sic.* Go, see him out at gates, and follow
      him,
As he hath follow'd you, with all despite;
Give him deserv'd vexation. Let a guard
Attend us through the city.   [gates; come.
   *Citizens.* Come, come, let us see him out at
The gods preserve our noble tribunes!—
   Come.                            [*Exeunt.*

## ACT IV.

SCENE I.—ROME. *Before a Gate of the City.*

*Enter* CORIOLANUS, VOLUMNIA, VIRGILIA,
MENENIUS, COMINIUS, *and several young*
Patricians.

   *Cor.* Come, leave your tears; a brief fare-
      well:—the beast          [mother,
With many heads butts me away.—Nay,
Where is your ancient courage? you were
   us'd
To say extremity was the trier of spirits;
That common chances common men could
   bear;
That when the sea was calm all boats alike
Show'd mastership in floating; fortune's
   blows,
When most struck home, being gentle
   wounded, craves
A noble cunning: you were us'd to load me
With precepts that would make invincible
The heart that conn'd them.
   *Vir.* O heavens! O heavens!
   *Cor.*            Nay, I pr'ythee, woman,—
   *Vol.* Now the red pestilence strike all
      trades in Rome,
And occupations perish!
   *Cor.*            What, what, what!
I shall be lov'd when I am lack'd. Nay,
   mother,
Resume that spirit when you were wont to
   say,
If you had been the wife of Hercules,
Six of his labours you'd have done, and
   sav'd
Your husband so much sweat.—Cominius,
Droop not; adieu.—Farewell, my wife,—my
   mother:
I'll do well yet.—Thou old and true Mene-
   nius,
Thy tears are salter than a younger man's,
And venomous to thine eyes.—My sometime
   general,
I have seen thee stern, and thou hast oft
   beheld
Heart-hard'ning spectacles; tell these sad
   women
'Tis fond to wail inevitable strokes,
As 'tis to laugh at 'em.—My mother, you wot
   well
My hazards still have been your solace: and
Believe 't not lightly,—though I go alone,
Like to a lonely dragon, that his fen
Makes fear'd and talk'd of more than seen,—
   your son
Will or exceed the common or be caught
With cautelous baits and practice.
   *Vol.*                 My first son,
Whither wilt thou go? Take good Cominius
With thee awhile: determine on some course
More than a wild expósture to each chance
That starts i' the way before thee.
   *Cor.*                        O the gods!

*Com.* I'll follow thee a month, devise with thee     [of us,
Where thou shalt rest, that thou mayst hear
And we of thee: so, if the time thrust forth
A cause for thy repeal, we shall not send
O'er the vast world to seek a single man;
And lose advantage, which doth ever cool
I' the absence of the needer.

*Cor.*               Fare ye well:
Thou hast years upon thee; and thou art too full
Of the wars' surfeits to go rove with one
That's yet unbruis'd: bring me but out at gate.—
Come, my sweet wife, my dearest mother, and
My friends of noble touch; when I am forth,
Bid me farewell, and smile. I pray you, come.
While I remain abòve the ground, you shall
Hear from me still; and never of me aught
But what is like me formerly.

*Men.*               That's worthily
As any ear can hear.—Come, let's not weep.—
If I could shake off but one seven years
From these old arms and legs, by the good gods,
I'd with thee every foot.

*Cor.*               Give me thy hand:—
Come.                    [*Exeunt.*

SCENE II.—ROME. *A Street near the Gate.*

*Enter* SICINIUS, BRUTUS, *and an Æ*dile.

*Sic.* Bid them all home; he's gone, and we'll no further.—
The nobility are vex'd, whom we see have sided
In his behalf.

*Bru.*     Now we have shown our power,
Let us seem humbler after it is done
Than when it was a-doing.

*Sic.*               Bid them home:
Say their great enemy is gone, and they
Stand in their ancient strength.

*Bru.*               Dismiss them home.
                         [*Exit Æ*dile.
Here comes his mother.

*Sic.*               Let's not met her.

*Bru.*                    Why?

*Sic.* They say she's mad.     [your way.

*Bru.* They have ta'en note of us: keep on

*Enter* VOLUMNIA, VIRGILIA, *and* MENENIUS.

*Vol.* O, you're well met: the hoarded plague o' the gods
Requite your love!

*Men.*          Peace, peace, be not so loud.

*Vol.* If that I could for weeping, you should hear,—     [gone?
Nay, and you shall hear some.—Will you be
                         [*To* BRUTUS.

*Vir.* You shall stay too [*To* SICINIUS]: I would I had the power
To say so to my husband.

*Sic.*          Are you mankind?

*Vol.* Ay, fool; is that a shame?—Note but this fool.—
Was not a man my father? Hadst thou fox-ship
To banish him that struck more blows for Rome
Than thou hast spoken words?—

*Sic.*               O blessed heavens!

*Vol.* More noble blows than ever thou wise words;          [yet go;—
And for Rome's good.—I'll tell thee what;—
Nay, but thou shalt stay too:—I would my son
Were in Arabia, and thy tribe before him,
His good sword in his hand.

*Sic.*               What then?

*Vir.*               What then!
He'd make an end of thy posterity.

*Vol.* Bastards and all.—          [Rome!
Good man, the wounds that he does bear for

*Men.* Come, come, peace.          [try

*Sic.* I would he had continu'd to his coun-
As he began, and not unknit himself
The noble knot he made.

*Bru.*               I would he had.

*Vol.* I would he had! 'Twas you incens'd the rabble;—
Cats, that can judge as fitly of his worth
As I can of those mysteries which heaven
Will not have earth to know.

*Bru.*               Pray, let us go.

*Vol.* Now, pray, sir, get you gone:
You have done a brave deed. Ere you go, hear this,—
As far as doth the Capitol exceed
The meanest house in Rome, so far my son,—
This lady's husband here; this, do you see?—
Whom you have banish'd, does exceed you all.

*Bru.* Well, well, we'll leave you.

*Sic.*               Why stay we to be baited
With one that wants her wits?

*Vol.*          Take my prayers with you.—
I would the gods had nothing else to do
                         [*Exeunt* Tribunes.
But to confirm my curses! Could I meet 'em
But once a day, it would unclog my heart
Of what lies heavy to 't.

*Men.*          You have told them home,
And, by my troth, you have cause. You'll sup with me?

*Vol.* Anger's my meat; I sup upon my-self,
And so shall starve with feeding.—Come, let's go:
Leave this faint puling, and lament as I do,
In anger, Juno-like. Come, come, come.

*Men.* Fie, fie, fie!          [*Exeunt.*

SCENE III.—*A Highway between Rome and Antium.*

*Enter a* Roman *and a* Volsce, *meeting.*

*Rom.* I know you well, sir; and you know me: your name, I think, is Adrian.

*Vols.* It is so, sir: truly, I have forgot you.

*Rom.* I am a Roman; and my services are, as you are, against 'em: know you me yet?

*Vols.* Nicanor? no.

*Rom.* The same, sir.

*Vols.* You had more beard when I last saw you; but your favour is well approved by your tongue. What's the news in Rome? I have a note from the Volscian state, to find you out there: you have well saved me a day's journey.

*Rom.* There hath been in Rome strange insurrection; the people against the senators, patricians, and nobles.

*Vols.* Hath been! is it ended, then? Our state thinks not so; they are in a most warlike preparation, and hope to come upon them in the heat of their division.

*Rom.* The main blaze of it is past, but a small thing would make it flame again: for the nobles receive so to heart the banishment of that worthy Coriolanus that they are in a ripe aptness to take all power from the people, and to pluck from them their tribunes for ever. This lies glowing, I can tell you, and is almost mature for the violent breaking out.

*Vols.* Coriolanus banished!

*Rom.* Banished, sir.

*Vols.* You will be welcome with this intelligence, Nicanor.

*Rom.* The day serves well for them now. I have heard it said the fittest time to corrupt a man's wife is when she's fallen out with her husband. Your noble Tullus Aufidius will appear well in these wars, his great opposer, Coriolanus, being now in no request of his country.

*Vols.* He cannot choose. I am most fortunate thus accidentally to encounter you: you have ended my business, and I will merrily accompany you home.

*Rom.* I shall, between this and supper, tell you most strange things from Rome; all tending to the good of their adversaries. Have you an army ready, say you?

*Vols.* A most royal one; the centurions and their charges, distinctly billeted, already in the entertainment, and to be on foot at an hour's warning.

*Rom.* I am joyful to hear of their readiness, and am the man, I think, that shall set them in present action. So, sir, heartily well met, and most glad of your company.

*Vols.* You take my part from me, sir; I have the most cause to be glad of yours.

*Rom.* Well, let us go together. [*Exeunt.*

SCENE IV.—ANTIUM. *Before* AUFIDIUS'S *House.*

*Enter* CORIOLANUS, *in mean apparel, disguised and muffled.*

*Cor.* A goodly city is this Antium.—City,

'Tis I that made thy widows: many an heir
Of these fair edifices 'fore my wars
Have I heard groan and drop: then know me
    not,       [stones
Lest that thy wives with spits and boys with
In puny battle slay me.

*Enter a* Citizen.
              Save you, sir.

*Cit.* And you.

*Cor.*        Direct me, if it be your will,
Where great Aufidius lies: is he in Antium?

*Cit.* He is, and feasts the nobles of the state
At his house this night.

*Cor.*     Which is his house, beseech you?

*Cit.* This, here, before you.

*Cor.*       Thank you, sir: farewell.
                [*Exit* Citizen.

O world, thy slippery turns! Friends now
    fast sworn,
Whose double bosoms seem to wear one
    heart,
Whose house, whose bed, whose meal and
    exercise
Are still together, who twin, as 'twere, in
    love
Unseparable, shall within this hour,
On a dissension of a doit, break out
To bitterest enmity; so fellest foes,
Whose passions and whose plots have broke
    their sleep
To take the one the other, by some chance,
Some trick not worth an egg, shall grow dear
    friends,
And interjoin their issues. So with me:—
My birthplace hate I, and my love's upon
This enemy town.—I'll enter: if he slay me,
He does fair justice; if he give me way,
I'll do his country service.     [*Exit.*

SCENE V.—ANTIUM. *A Hall in* AUFIDIUS'S *House.*

*Music within. Enter a* Servant.

1 *Serv.* Wine, wine, wine! What service is here!
I think our fellows are asleep.     [*Exit.*

*Enter a second* Servant.

2 *Serv.* Where's Cotus? my master calls for him.—Cotus!     [*Exit.*

*Enter* CORIOLANUS.

*Cor.* A goodly house: the feast smells well; but I
Appear not like a guest.

*Re-enter the first* Servant.

1 *Serv.* What would you have, friend? whence are you? Here's no place for you: pray, go to the door.

*Cor.* I have deserv'd no better entertainment
In being Coriolanus.

*Re-enter second* Servant.

*2 Serv.* Whence are you, sir? Has the porter his eyes in his head, that he gives entrance to such companions? Pray, get you out.

*Cor.* Away!

*2 Serv.* Away! Get you away.

*Cor.* Now thou art troublesome.

*2 Serv.* Are you so brave? I'll have you talked with anon.

*Enter a third* Servant. *The first meets him.*

*3 Serv.* What fellow's this?

*1 Serv.* A strange one as ever I looked on: I cannot get him out o' the house: pr'ythee, call my master to him.

*3 Serv.* What have you to do here, fellow? Pray you, avoid the house.

*Cor.* Let me but stand; I will not hurt your hearth.

*3 Serv.* What are you?

*Cor.* A gentleman.

*3 Serv.* A marvellous poor one.

*Cor.* True, so I am.

*3 Serv.* Pray you, poor gentleman, take up some other station; here's no place for you; pray you, avoid: come.

*Cor.* Follow your function, go,
And batten on cold bits. [*Pushes him away.*

*3 Serv.* What, you will not?—Pr'ythee, tell my master what a strange guest he has here.

*2 Serv.* And I shall. [*Exit.*

*3 Serv.* Where dwellest thou?

*Cor.* Under the canopy.

*3 Serv.* Under the canopy!

*Cor.* Ay.

*3 Serv.* Where's that?

*Cor.* I' the city of kites and crows.

*3 Serv.* I' the city of kites and crows!— What an ass it is!—Then thou dwellest with daws too?

*Cor.* No, I serve not thy master.

*3 Serv.* How, sir! Do you meddle with my master?

*Cor.* Ay; 'tis an honester service than to meddle with thy mistress:
Thou prat'st and prat'st; serve with thy trencher, hence! [*Beats him in.*

*Enter* AUFIDIUS *and the second* Servant.

*Auf.* Where is this fellow?

*2 Serv.* Here, sir: I'd have beaten him like a dog, but for disturbing the lords within.

*Auf.* Whence comest thou? what wouldst thou? thy name? [name?
Why speak'st not? speak, man: what's thy

*Cor.* If, Tullus, [*Unmuffling.*
Not yet thou know'st me, and, seeing me, dost not
Think me for the man I am, necessity
Commands me name myself.

*Auf.* What is thy name?
[*Servants retire.*

*Cor.* A name unmusical to the Volscians' ears,
And harsh in sound to thine.

*Auf.* Say, what's thy name?
Thou hast a grim appearance, and thy face
Bears a command in't; though thy tackle's torn,
Thou show'st a noble vessel: what's thy name?

*Cor.* Prepare thy brow to frown:—know'st thou me yet?

*Auf.* I know thee not:—thy name?

*Cor.* My name is Caius Marcius, who hath done
To thee particularly, and to all the Volsces,
Great hurt and mischief; thereto witness may
My surname, Coriolanus: the painful service,
The extreme dangers, and the drops of blood
Shed for my thankless country, are requited
But with that surname; a good memory,
And witness of the malice and displeasure
Which thou shouldst bear me: only that name remains;
The cruelty and envy of the people,
Permitted by our dastard nobles, who
Have all forsook me, hath devour'd the rest,
And suffer'd me by the voice of slaves to be
Whoop'd out of Rome. Now, this extremity
Hath brought me to thy hearth: not out of hope,
Mistake me not, to save my life; for if
I had fear'd death, of all the men i' the world
I would have 'voided thee; but in mere spite,
To be full quit of those my banishers,
Stand I before thee here. Then if thou hast
A heart of wreak in thee, that wilt revenge
Thine own particular wrongs, and stop those maims [thee straight,
Of shame seen through thy country, speed
And make my misery serve thy turn: so use it
That my revengeful services may prove
As benefits to thee; for I will fight
Against my canker'd country with the spleen
Of all the under fiends. But if so be
Thou dar'st not this, and that to prove more fortunes
Thou'rt tir'd, then, in a word, I also am
Longer to live most weary, and present
My throat to thee and to thy ancient malice;
Which not to cut would show thee but a fool,
Since I have ever follow'd thee with hate,
Drawn tuns of blood out of thy country's breast,
And cannot live but to thy shame, unless
It be to do thee service.

*Auf.* O Marcius, Marcius!
Each word thou hast spoke hath weeded from my heart
A root of ancient envy. If Jupiter
Should from yond cloud speak divine things,
And say *'Tis true,* I'd not believe them more
Than thee, all noble Marcius.—Let me twine

Mine arms about that body, where against
My grained ash an hundred times hath broke
And scar'd the moon with splinters: here I
    clip
The anvil of my sword, and do contest
As hotly and as nobly with thy love
As ever in ambitious strength I did
Contend against thy valour. Know thou first,
I lov'd the maid I married; never man
Sighed truer breath; but that I see thee here,
Thou noble thing! more dances my rapt heart
Than when I first my wedded mistress saw
Bestride my threshold. Why, thou Mars! I
    tell thee,
We have a power on foot; and I had purpose
Once more to hew thy target from thy brawn,
Or lose mine arm for't: thou hast beat me out
Twelve several times, and I have nightly
    since
Dreamt of encounters 'twixt thyself and me;
We have been down together in my sleep,
Unbuckling helms, fisting each other's throat,
And wak'd half dead with nothing. Worthy
    Marcius,
Had we no other quarrel else to Rome, but
    that
Thou art thence banish'd, we would muster
    all
From twelve to seventy; and, pouring war
Into the bowels of ungrateful Rome,
Like a bold flood o'erbear. O, come, go in,
And take our friendly senators by the hands;
Who now are here, taking their leaves of me,
Who am prepar'd against your territories,
Though not for Rome itself.
    *Cor.*             You bless me, gods!
    *Auf.* Therefore, most absolute sir, if thou
    wilt have
The leading of thine own revenges, take
The one half of my commission; and set
    down,—
As best thou art experience'd, since thou
    know'st
Thy country's strength and weakness,—thine
    own ways;
Whether to knock against the gates of Rome,
Or rudely visit them in parts remote,
To fright them, ere destroy. But come in:
Let me commend thee first to those that shall
Say yea to thy desires. A thousand welcomes!
And more a friend than e'er an enemy;
Yet, Marcius, that was much. Your hand:
    most welcome!
                 [*Exeunt* COR. *and* AUF.
    1 *Serv.* [*Advancing.*] Here's a strange al-
teration!
    2 *Serv.* By my hand, I had thought to
have strucken him with a cudgel; and yet my
mind gave me his clothes made a false report
of him.
    1 *Serv.* What an arm he has! He turned
me about with his finger and his thumb, as
one would set up a top.
    2 *Serv.* Nay, I knew by his face that there

was something in him: he had, sir, a kind of
face, methought,—I cannot tell how to term
it.
    1 *Serv.* He had so; looking as it were,—
would I were hanged, but I thought there was
more in him than I could think.
    2 *Serv.* So did I, I'll be sworn: he is simply
the rarest man i' the world.
    1 *Serv.* I think he is: but a greater soldier
than he you wot on.
    2 *Serv.* Who, my master?
    1 *Serv.* Nay, it's no matter for that.
    2 *Serv.* Worth six on him.
    1 *Serv.* Nay, not so neither: but I take him
to be the greater soldier.
    2 *Serv.* Faith, look you, one cannot tell
how to say that: for the defence of a town
our general is excellent.
    1 *Serv.* Ay, and for an assault too.

            *Re-enter third* Servant.

    3 *Serv.* O slaves, I can tell you news,—
news, you rascals!
    1 *and* 2 *Serv.* What, what, what? let's par-
take.
    3 *Serv.* I would not be a Roman, of all
nations; I had as lieve be a condemned man.
    1 *and* 2 *Serv.* Wherefore? wherefore?
    3 *Serv.* Why, here's he that was wont to
thwack our general,—Caius Marcius.
    1 *Serv.* Why do you say, thwack our gen-
eral?
    3 *Serv.* I do not say, thwack our general;
but he was always good enough for him.
    2 *Serv.* Come, we are fellows and friends:
he was ever too hard for him; I have heard
him say so himself.
    1 *Serv.* He was too hard for him directly,
to say the troth on't: before Corioli he
scotched him and notched him like a carbonado.
    2 *Serv.* And he had been cannibally given,
he might have broiled and eaten him too.
    1 *Serv.* But more of thy news?
    3 *Serv.* Why, he is so made on here within
as if he were son and heir to Mars; set at
upper end o' the table; no question asked him
by any of the senators, but they stand bald
before him: our general himself makes a mistress of him; sanctifies himself with's hand,
and turns up the white o' the eye to his discourse. But the bottom of the news is, our
general is cut i' the middle, and but one half
of what he was yesterday; for the other has
half, by the entreaty and grant of the whole
table. He'll go, he says, and sowl the porter
of Rome gates by the ears: he will mow all
down before him, and leave his passage
polled.
    2 *Serv.* And he's as like to do't as any man
I can imagine.
    3 *Serv.* Do't! he will do't; for, look you,
sir, he has as many friends as enemies; which
friends, sir, as it were durst not, look you, sir,

show themselves, as we term it, his friends, whilst he's in dejectitude.

1 *Serv.* Dejectitude! what's that?

3 *Serv.* But when they shall see sir, his crest up again, and the man in blood, they will out of their burrows, like conies after rain, and revel all with him.

1 *Serv.* But when goes this forward?

3 *Serv.* To-morrow; to-day; presently; you shall have the drum struck up this afternoon: 'tis as it were a parcel of their feast, and to be executed ere they wipe their lips.

2 *Serv.* Why, then we shall have a stirring world again. This peace is good for nothing but to rust iron, increase tailors, and breed ballad-makers.

1 *Serv.* Let me have war, say I; it exceeds peace as far as day does night; it's spritely, waking, audible, and full of vent. Peace is a very apoplexy, lethargy; mulled, deaf, sleepy, insensible; a getter of more bastard children than wars a destroyer of men.

2 *Serv.* 'Tis so: and as wars in some sort, may be said to be a ravisher, so it cannot be denied but peace is a great maker of cuckolds.

1 *Serv.* Ay, and it makes men hate one another.

3 *Serv.* Reason; because they then less need one another. The wars for my money. I hope to see Romans as cheap as Volscians. They are rising, they are rising.

*All.* In, in, in, in!    [*Exeunt.*

SCENE VI.—ROME. *A public Place.*

*Enter* SICINIUS *and* BRUTUS.

*Sic.* We hear not of him, neither need we fear him;
His remedies are tame i' the present peace
And quietness of the people, which before
Were in wild hurry. Here do we make his
    friends    [had,
Blush that the world goes well; who rather
Though they themselves did suffer by't, behold
Dissentious numbers pestering streets than see
Our tradesmen singing in their shops, and going
About their functions friendly.

*Bru.* We stood to't in good time.—Is this
    Menenius?

*Sic.* 'Tis he, 'tis he: O, he is grown most
    kind
Of late.

*Enter* MENENIUS.

*Bru.* Hail, sir!

*Men.*    Hail to you both!

*Sic.* Your Coriolanus is not much miss'd
But with his friends: the commonwealth doth
    stand;
And so would do, were he more angry at it.

*Men.* All's well; and might have been
    much better if
He could have temporiz'd.

*Sic.*    Where is he, hear you?

*Men.* Nay, I hear nothing: his mother and
    his wife
Hear nothing from him.

*Enter three or four* Citizens.

*Citizens.* The gods preserve you both!

*Sic.*    God-den, our neighbours.

*Bru.* God-den to you all, God-den to you
    all.

1 *Cit.* Ourselves, our wives, and children,
    on our knees,
Are bound to pray for you both.

*Sic.*    Live and thrive!

*Bru.* Farewell, kind neighbours: we wish'd
    Coriolanus
Had lov'd you as we did.

*Citizens.*    Now the gods keep you!

*Both Tri.* Farewell, farewell.

    [*Exeunt* Citizens.

*Sic.* This is a happier and more comely
    time
Than when these fellows ran about the streets
Crying confusion.

*Bru.*    Caius Marcius was
A worthy officer i' the war; but insolent,
O'ercome with pride, ambitious past all
    thinking,
Self-loving,—

*Sic.*    And affecting one sole throne,
Without assistance.

*Men.*    I think not so.    [tion,

*Sic.* We should by this, to all our lamenta-
If he had gone forth consul, found it so.

*Bru.* The gods have well prevented it, and
    Rome
Sits safe and still without him.

*Enter an* ÆDILE.

*Æd.*    Worthy tribunes,
There is a slave, whom we have put in prison,
Reports,—the Volsces with two several pow-
    ers
Are enter'd in the Roman territories;
And with the deepest malice of the war
Destroy what lies before 'em.

*Men.*    'Tis Aufidius,
Who, hearing of our Marcius' banishment,
Thrusts forth his horns again into the world;
Which were inshell'd when Marcius stood for
    Rome,
And durst not once peep out.

*Sic.*    Come, what talk you
Of Marcius?

*Bru.* Go see this rumourer whipp'd.—It
    cannot be
The Volsces dare break with us.

*Men.*    Cannot be!
We have record that very well it can;
And three examples of the like have been
Within my age. But reason with the fellow,
Before you punish him, where he heard this;
Lest you shall chance to whip your informa-
    tion,

And beat the messenger who bids beware
Of what is to be dreaded.
*Sic.*                         Tell not me:
I know this cannot be.
*Bru.*                    Not possible.

*Enter a* Messenger.

*Mess.* The nobles in great earnestness are
        going
All to the senate-house: some news is come
That turns their countenances.
*Sic.*                         'Tis this slave,—
Go whip him 'fore the people's eyes:—his
        raising;
Nothing but his report.
*Mess.*                 Yes, worthy sir,
The slave's report is seconded; and more,
More fearful, is deliver'd.
*Sic.*                What more fearful?
*Mess.* It is spoke freely out of many
        mouths,—
How probable I do not know,—that Marcius,
Join'd with Aufidius, leads a power 'gainst
        Rome,
And vows revenge as spacious as between
The young'st and oldest thing.
*Sic.*                  This is most likely!
*Bru.* Rais'd only, that the weaker sort may
        wish
God Marcius home again.
*Sic.*                The very trick on't.
*Men.* This is unlikely:
He and Aufidius can no more atone
Than violentest contrariety.

*Enter a second* Messenger.

*2 Mess.* You are sent for to the senate:
A fearful army, led by Caius Marcius
Associated with Aufidius, rages
Upon our territories; and have already [took
O'erborne their way, consum'd with fire, and
What lay before them.

*Enter* COMINIUS.

*Com.* O, you have made good work!
*Men.*              What news? what news?
*Com.* You have holp to ravish your own
        daughters, and
To melt the city leads upon your pates;
To see your wives dishonour'd to your
        noses,—
*Men.* What's the news? what's the news?
*Com.* Your temples burned in their ce-
        ment; and
Your franchises, whereon you stood, confin'd
Into an auger's bore.
*Men.*            Pray now, your news?—
You have made fair work, I fear me.—Pray,
        your news?
If Marcius should be join'd with Volscians,—
*Com.*                                    If!
He is their god: he leads them like a thing
Made by some other deity than nature,
That shapes man better; and they follow him,

Against us brats, with no less confidence
Than boys pursuing summer butterflies,
Or butchers killing flies.
*Men.*            You have made good work,
You and your apron men; you that stood so
        much
Upon the voice of occupation and
The breath of garlic-eaters!
*Com.*                  He will shake
Your Rome about your ears.
*Men.*                  As Hercules
Did shake down mellow fruit.—You have
        made fair work!
*Bru.* But is this true, sir?
*Com.*              Ay; and you'll look pale
Before you find it other. All the regions
Do smilingly revolt; and who resist
Are only mock'd for valiant ignorance,
And perish constant fools. Who is't can blame
        him?
Your enemies and his find something in him.
*Men.* We are all undone unless
The noble man have mercy.
*Com.*                Who shall ask it?
The tribunes cannot do't for shame; the
        people
Deserve such pity of him as the wolf  [they
Does of the shepherds: for his best friends, if
Should say, *Be good to Rome,* they charg'd
        him even
As those should do that had deserv'd his hate,
And therein show'd like enemies.
*Men.*                    'Tis true:
If he were putting to my house the brand
That should consume it, I have not the face
To say, *Beseech you, cease.*—You have made
        fair hands,
You and your crafts! you have crafted fair!
*Com.*                You have brought
A trembling upon Rome, such as was never
So incapable of help.
*Both Tri.*              Say not, we brought it.
*Men.* How! Was it we? we lov'd him;
        but, like beasts,         [clusters,
And cowardly nobles, gave way unto your
Who did hoot him out o' the city.
*Com.*                        But I fear.
They'll roar him in again. Tullus Aufidius,
The second name of men, obeys his points
As if he were his officer:—desperation
Is all the policy, strength, and defence,
That Rome can make against them.

*Enter a troop of* Citizens.

*Men.*            Here comes the clusters.—
And is Aufidius with him?—You are they
That made the air unwholesome, when you
        cast
Your stinking greasy caps in hooting at
Coriolanus' exile. Now he's coming;
And not a hair upon a soldier's head  [combs
Which will not prove a whip: as many cox-
As you threw caps up will he tumble down,
And pay you for your voices. 'Tis no matter;

If he could burn us all into one coal,
We have deserv'd it.

*Citizens.* Faith, we hear fearful news.

1 *Cit.*           For mine own part,
When I said banish him, I said 'twas pity.

2 *Cit.* And so did I.

3 *Cit.* And so did I; and, to say the truth,
so did very many of us. That we did, we did
for the best; and though we willingly consented to his banishment, yet it was against
our will.

*Com.* You are goodly things, you voices!

*Men.*           You have made
Good work, you and your cry!—Shall's to
the Capitol?

*Com.* O, ay; what else?
[*Exeunt* COM. *and* MEN.

*Sic.* Go, masters, get you home; be not
dismay'd:
These are a side that would be glad to have
This true which they so seem to fear. Go
home,
And show no sign of fear.

1 *Cit.* The gods be good to us!—Come,
masters, let's home. I ever said we were i'
the wrong when we banished him.

2 *Cit.* So did we all. But come, let's home.
[*Exeunt* Citizens.

*Bru.* I do not like this news.

*Sic.* Nor I.           [wealth

*Bru.* Let's to the Capitol:—would half my
Would buy this for a lie!

*Sic.*         Pray, let us go. [*Exeunt.*

SCENE VII.—*A Camp at a small distance
from Rome.*

*Enter* AUFIDIUS *and his* Lieutenant.

*Auf.* Do they still fly to the Roman?

*Lieu.* I do not know what witchcraft's in
him,, but
Your soldiers use him as the grace 'fore meat,
Their talk at table, and their thanks at end;
And you are darken'd in this action, sir,
Even by your own.

*Auf.*        I cannot help it now,
Unless, by using means, I lame the foot
Of our design. He bares himself more proud-
lier,
Even to my person, than I thought he would
When first I did embrace him: yet his nature
In that's no changeling; and I must excuse
What cannot be amended.

*Lieu.*         Yet I wish, sir,—
I mean, for your particular,—you had not
Join'd in commission with him; but either
Had borne the action of yourself, or else
To him had left it solely.       [sure,

*Auf.* I understand thee well; and be thou
When he shall come to his account, he knows
not           [seems,
What I can urge against him. Although it
And so he thinks, and is no less apparent
To the vulgar eye, that he bears all things
fairly,

And shows good husbandry for the Volscian
state,
Fights dragon-like, and does achieve as soon
As draw his sword: yet he hath left undone
That which shall break his neck or hazard
mine
Whene'er we come to our account.

*Lieu.* Sir, I beseech you, think you he'll
carry Rome?

*Auf.* All places yield to him ere he sits
down;
And the nobility of Rome are his:
The senators and patricians love him too:
The tribunes are no soldiers; and their people
Will be as rash in the repeal as hasty
To expel him thence. I think he'll be to Rome
As is the osprey to the fish, who takes it
By sovereignty of nature. First he was
A noble servant to them; but he could not
Carry his honours even: whether 'twas pride,
Which out of daily fortune ever taints
The happy man; whether defect of judgment,
To fail in the disposing of those chances
Which he was lord of; or whether nature,
Not to be other than one thing, not moving
From the casque to the cushion, but com-
manding peace
Even with the same austerity and garb
As he controll'd the war; but one of these,—
As he hath spices of them all, not all,
For I dare so far free him,—made him fear'd,
So hated, and so banish'd: but he has a merit
To choke it in the utterance. So our virtues
Lie in the interpretation of the time:
And power, unto itself most commendable,
Hath not a tomb so evident as a cheer
To extol what it hath done.
One fire drives out one fire; one nail, one
nail;
Rights by rights falter, strengths by strengths
do fail.
Come, let's away. When, Caius, Rome is thine,
Thou art poor'st of all; then shortly art thou
mine.           [*Exeunt.*

## ACT V.

SCENE I.—ROME. *A public Place.*

*Enter* MENENIUS, COMINIUS, SICINIUS,
BRUTUS, *and others.*

*Men.* No, I'll not go: you hear what he
hath said
Which was sometime his general; who lov'd
him
In a most dear particular. He call'd me father:
But what o' that? Go, you that banish'd
him;
A mile before his tent fall down, and knee
The way into his mercy: nay, if he coy'd
To hear Cominius speak, I'll keep at home.

*Com.* He would not seem to know me.

*Men.*          Do you hear?

*Com.* Yet one time he did call me by my
name:

I urg'd our old acquaintance, and the drops
That we have bled together. Coriolanus
He would not answer to: forbad all names;
He was a kind of nothing, titleless,
Till he had forg'd himself a name o' the fire
Of burning Rome.

*Men.* Why, so,—you have made good
work!
A pair of tribunes that have rack'd for Rome,
To make coals cheap,—a noble memory!

*Com.* I minded him how royal 'twas to
pardon
When it was less expected: he replied,
It was a bare petition of a state
To one whom they had punish'd.

*Men.*   Very well:
Could he say less?

*Com.* I offer'd to awaken his regard
For's private friends: his answer to me was,
He could not stay to pick them in a pile
Of noisome musty chaff: he said 'twas folly
For one poor grain or two to leave unburnt,
And still to nose the offence.

*Men.*   For one poor grain
Or two! I am one of those; his mother, wife,
His child, and this brave fellow too, we are
the grains:
You are the musty chaff; and you are smelt
Above the moon: we must be burnt for you.

*Sic.* Nay, pray, be patient: if you refuse
your aid
In this so never-heeded help, yet do not
Upbraid's with our distress. But, sure, if you
Would be your country's pleader, your good
tongue,
More than the instant army we can make,
Might stop our countryman.

*Men.*   No; I'll not meddle.

*Sic.* Pray you, go to him.

*Men.*   What should I do?

*Bru.* Only make trial what your love can
do
For Rome, towards Marcius.

*Men.*   Well, and say that Marcius
Return me, as Cominius is return'd,
Unheard; what then?
But as a discontented friend, grief-shot
With his unkindness? Say't be so?

*Sic.*   Yet your good-will
Must have that thanks from Rome, after the
measure
As you intended well.

*Men.*   I'll undertake't:
I think he'll hear me. Yet to bite his lip
And hum at good Cominius much unhearts
me.
He was not taken well: he had not din'd:
The veins unfill'd, our blood is cold, and then
We pout upon the morning, are unapt
To give or to forgive; but when we have
stuff'd
These pipes and these conveyances of our
blood
With wine and feeding, we have suppler souls

Than in our priest-like fasts: therefore I'll
watch him
Till he be dieted to my request,
And then I'll set upon him.   [kindness,

*Bru.* You know the very road into his
And cannot lose your way.

*Men.*   Good faith, I'll prove him,
Speed how it will. I shall ere long have
knowledge
Of my success.   [*Exit.*

*Com.*   He'll never hear him.

*Sic.*   Not?

*Com.* I tell you, he does sit in gold, his eye
Red as 'twould burn Rome; and his injury
The gaoler to his pity. I kneel'd before him;
'Twas very faintly he said *Rise;* dismiss'd me
Thus, with his speechless hand: what he
would do,   [not,
He sent in writing after me; what he would
Bound with an oath to yield to his condi-
tions:
So that all hope is vain,
Unless in's noble mother and his wife;
Who, as I hear, mean to solicit him   [hence,
For mercy to his country. Therefore, let's
And with our fair entreaties haste them on.
   [*Exeunt.*

SCENE II.—*An advanced Post of the Volscian
Camp before Rome. The* Guard *at their
stations.*

*Enter to them* MENENIUS.

*1 G.* Stay: whence are you?

*2 G.* Stand, and go back.

*Men.* You guard like men; 'tis well: but,
by your leave,
I am an officer of state, and come
To speak with Coriolanus.

*1 G.*   From whence?

*Men.*   From Rome.

*1 G.* You may not pass, you must return:
our general
Will no more hear from thence.

*2 G.* You'll see your Rome embrac'd with
fire before
You'll speak with Coriolanus.

*Men.*   Good my friends,
If you have heard your general talk of Rome,
And of his friends there, it is lots to blanks
My name hath touch'd your ears: it is
Menenius.

*1 G.* Be it so; go back: the virtue of your
name
Is not here passable.

*Men.*   I tell thee, fellow,
Thy general is my lover: I have been   [read
The book of his good acts, whence men have
His fame unparallel'd, haply amplified;
For I have ever verified my friends,—
Of whom he's chief,—with all the size that
verity
Would without lapsing suffer: nay, sometimes,
Like to a bowl upon a subtle ground, [praise
I have tumbled past the throw: and in his

Have almost stamp'd the leasing: therefore, fellow,
I must have leave to pass

  1 *G.* Faith, sir, if you had told as many lies in his behalf as you have utter'd words in your own, you should not pass here: no, though it were as virtuous to lie as to live chastely. Therefore, go back.

  *Men.* Pr'ythee, fellow, remember my name is Menenius, always factionary on the party of your general.

  2 *G.* Howsoever you have been his liar,—as you say you have,—I am one that, telling true under him, must say, you cannot pass. Therefore, go back.

  *Men.* Has he dined, canst thou tell? for I would not speak with him till after dinner.

  1 *G.* You are a Roman, are you?

  *Men.* I am as thy general is.

  1 *G.* Then you should hate Rome, as he does. Can you, when you have pushed out your gates the very defender of them, and, in a violent popular ignorance, given your enemy your shield, think to front his revenges with the easy groans of old women, the virginal palms of your daughters, or with the palsied intercession of such a decayed dotant as you seem to be? Can you think to blow out the intended fire your city is ready to flame in, with such weak breath as this? No, you are deceived; therefore, back to Rome, and prepare for your execution: you are condemned; our general has sworn you out of reprieve and pardon.

  *Men.* Sirrah, if thy captain knew I were here he would use me with estimation.

  2 *G.* Come, my captain knows you not.

  *Men.* I mean thy general.

  1 *G.* My general cares not for you. Back, I say; go, lest I let forth your half pint of blood;—back; that's the utmost of your having:—back.

  *Men.* Nay, but, fellow, fellow,—

*Enter* CORIOLANUS *and* AUFIDIUS.

  *Cor.* What's the matter?

  *Men.* Now, you companion, I'll say an errand for you; you shall know now that I am in estimation; you shall perceive that a jack guardant cannot office me from my son Coriolanus: guess but by my entertainment with him if thou standest not i' the state of hanging, or of some death more long in spectatorship and crueller in suffering; behold now presently, the swoon for what's to come upon thee.—The glorious gods sit in hourly synod about thy particular prosperity, and love thee no worse than thy old father Menenius does! O my son! my son! thou art preparing fire for us; look thee, here's water to quench it. I was hardly moved to come to thee; but being assured none but myself could move thee, I have been blown out of your gates with sighs; and conjure thee to pardon Rome

and thy petitionary countrymen. The good gods assuage thy wrath, and turn the dregs of it upon this varlet here; this, who, like a block, hath denied my access to thee.

  *Cor.* Away!

  *Men.* How! away!        [affairs

  *Cor.* Wife, mother, child, I know not. My Are servanted to others: though I owe My revenge properly, my remission lies In Volscian breasts. That we have been familiar, Ingrate forgetfulness shall poison, rather Than pity note how much.—Therefore, be gone. Mine ears against your suits are stronger than Your gates against my force. Yet, for I lov'd thee, Take this along; I writ it for thy sake,

                    [*Gives a letter.*

And would have sent it. Another word, Menenius, I will not hear thee speak.—This man, Aufidius, Was my beloved in Rome: yet thou behold'st!

  *Auf.* You keep a constant temper.

             [*Exeunt* COR. *and* AUF.

  1 *G.* Now, sir, is your name Menenius?

  2 *G.* 'Tis a spell, you see, of much power: you know the way home again.

  1 *G.* Do you hear how we are shent for keeping your greatness back?

  2 *G.* What cause, do you think, I have to swoon?

  *Men.* I neither care for the world nor your general: for such things as you, I can scarce think there's any, ye're so slight. He that hath a will to die by himself fears it not from another. Let your general do his worst. For you, be that you are, long; and your misery increase with your age! I say to you, as I was said to, away!        [*Exit.*

  1 *G.* A noble fellow, I warrant him.

  2 *G.* The worthy fellow is our general: he is the rock, the oak not to be wind-shaken.

                     [*Exeunt.*

SCENE III.—*The Tent of* CORIOLANUS.

*Enter* CORIOLANUS, AUFIDIUS, *and others.*

  *Cor.* We will before the walls of Rome tomorrow Set down our host.—My partner in this action, You must report to the Volscian lords how plainly I have borne this business.

  *Auf.*         Only their ends You have respected; stopp'd your ears against The general suit of Rome; never admitted A private whisper, no, not with such friends That thought them sure of you.

  *Cor.*        This last old man, Whom with a crack'd heart I have sent to Rome,

Lov'd me above the measure of a father;
Nay, godded me, indeed. Their latest refuge
Was to send him; for whose old love I
   have,—
Though I show'd sourly to him,—once more
   offer'd
The first conditions, which they did refuse,
And cannot now accept, to grace him only,
That thought he could do more, a very little
I have yielded to: fresh embassies and suits,
Nor from the state nor private friends, here-
   after
Will I lend ear to.—Ha! what shout is this?
                              [*Shout within.*
Shall I be tempted to infringe my vow
In the same time 'tis made? I will not.

*Enter, in mourning habits,* VIRGILIA, VOLUM-
NIA, *leading young* MARCIUS, VALERIA, *and*
Attendants.

My wife comes foremost; then the honour'd
   mould
Wherein this trunk was fram'd, and in her
   hand
The grandchild to her blood. But, out, affec-
   tion!
All bond and privilege of nature, break!
Let it be virtuous to be obstinate.—  [eyes,
What is that curt'sy worth? or those doves'
Which can make gods forsworn?—I melt, and
   am not                  [bows,
Of stronger earth than others.—My mother
As if Olympus to a molehill should
In supplication nod: and my young boy
Hath an aspect of intercession which
Great nature cries, *Deny not.*—Let the
   Volsces
Plough Rome and harrow Italy: I'll never
Be such a gosling to obey instinct; but stand,
As if a man were author of himself,
And knew no other kin.
  *Vir.*          My lord and husband!
  *Cor.*    These eyes are not the same I wore
   in Rome.
  *Vir.*  The sorrow that delivers us thus
   chang'd
Makes you think so.
  *Cor.*        Like a dull actor now,
I have forgot my part, and I am out,
Even to a full disgrace. Best of my flesh,
Forgive my tyranny; but do not say,
For that, *Forgive our Romans.*—O, a kiss
Long as my exile, sweet as my revenge;
Now, by the jealous queen of heaven, that
   kiss
I carried from thee, dear; and my true lip
Hath virgin'd it e'er since.—You gods! I
   prate,
And the most noble mother of the world
Leave unsaluted: sink, my knee, i' the earth;
                               [*Kneels.*
Of thy deep duty more impression show
Than that of common sons.
  *Vol.*         O, stand up bless'd!

Whilst, with no softer cushion than the flint,
I kneel before thee; and unproperly
Show duty, as mistaken all this while
Between the child and parent.     [*Kneels.*
  *Cor.*               What is this?
Your knees to me? to your corrected son?
Then let the pebbles on the hungry beach
Fillip the stars; then let the mutinous winds
Strike the proud cedars 'gainst the fiery sun;
Murdering impossibility, to make
What cannot be, slight work.
  *Vol.*         Thou art my warrior;
I holp to frame thee. Do you know this lady?
  *Cor.*  The noble sister of Publicola,
The moon of Rome; chaste as the icicle
That's curded by the frost from purest snow,
And hangs on Dian's temple:—dear Valeria!
  *Vol.*  This is a poor epitome of yours,
Which, by the interpretation of full time,
May show like all yourself.
  *Cor.*          The god of soldiers,
With the consent of supreme Jove, inform
Thy thoughts with nobleness; that thou
   mayst prove
To shame unvulnerable, and stick i' the wars
Like a great sea-mark, standing every flaw,
And saving those that eye thee!
  *Vol.*         Your knee, sirrah.
  *Cor.*  That's my brave boy.    [myself,
  *Vol.*  Even he, your wife, this lady, and
Are suitors to you.
  *Cor.*  I beseech you, peace:
Or, if you'd ask, remember this before,—
The things I have forsworn to grant may
   never
Be held by you denials. Do not bid me
Dismiss my soldiers, or capitulate
Again with Rome's mechanics.—Tell me not
Wherein I seem unnatural: desire not
To allay my rages and revenges with
Your colder reasons.
  *Vol.*       O, no more, no more!
You have said you will not grant us anything;
For we have nothing else to ask but that
Which you deny already: yet we will ask;
That, if you fail in our request, the blame
May hang upon your hardness; therefore
   hear us.                  [we'll
  *Cor.*  Aufidius, and you Volsces, mark:
Hear naught from Rome in private.—Your
   request?            [our raiment
  *Vol.*  Should we be silent and not speak,
And state of bodies would bewray what life
We have led since thy exile. Think with thy
   self,
How more unfortunate than all living women
Are we come hither: since that thy sight,
   which should       [with comforts,
Make our eyes flow with joy, hearts dance
Constrains them weep, and shake with fear
   and sorrow;
Making the mother, wife, and child to see
The son, the husband, and the father tearing
His country's bowels out. And to poor we,

Thine enmity's most capital: thou barr'st us
Our prayers to the gods, which is a comfort
That all but we enjoy; for how can we,
Alas, how can we for our country pray,
Whereto we are bound,—together with thy
　　　victory,
Whereto we are bound? alack, or we must
　　　lose　　　　　　　　　　　　[person,
The country, our dear nurse; or else thy
Our comfort in the country. We must find
An evident calamity, though we had　　[thou
Our wish, which side should win; for either
Must, as a foreign recreant, be led
With manacles through our streets, or else
Triumphantly tread on thy country's ruin,
And bear the palm for having bravely shed
Thy wife and children's blood. For myself,
　　　son,
I purpose not to wait on fortune till　　[thee
These wars determine: if I cannot persuade
Rather to show a noble grace to both parts
Than seek the end of one, thou shalt no sooner
March to assault thy country than to tread,—
Trust to't, thou shalt not,—on thy mother's
　　　womb,
That brought thee to this world.

*Vir.*　　　　　　　　　　　　Ay, and mine,
That brought you forth this boy, to keep
　　　your name
Living to time.

*Boy.*　　　'A shall not tread on me;
I'll run away till I am bigger; but then I'll
　　　fight.

*Cor.*　Not of a woman's tenderness to be,
Requires nor child nor woman's face to see.
I have sat too long.　　　　　　[*Rising.*

*Vol.*　　　　　　　Nay, go not from us thus.
If it were so that our request did tend
To save the Romans, thereby to destroy
The Volsces whom you serve, you might
　　　condemn us,
As poisonous of your honour: no; our suit
Is, that you reconcile them: while the Volsces
May say, *This mercy we have show'd;* the
　　　Romans,
*This we receiv'd;* and each in either side
Give thee all-hail to thee, and cry, *Be bless'd
For making up this peace!* Thou know'st,
　　　great son,
The end of war's uncertain; but this certain,
That, if thou conquer Rome, the benefit
Which thou shalt thereby reap is such a name,
Whose repetition will be dogg'd with curses;
Whose chronicle thus writ,—*The man was
　　　noble,
But with his last attempt he wip'd it out;
Destroy'd his country; and his name remains
To the ensuing age abhorr'd.* Speak to me,
　　　son:
Thou hast affected the fine strains of honour,
To imitate the graces of the gods,
To tear with thunder the wide cheeks o' the
　　　air,
And yet to charge thy sulphur with a bolt

That should but rive an oak. Why dost not
　　　speak?
Think'st thou it honourable for a noble man
Still to remember wrongs?—Daughter, speak
　　　you:　　　　　　　　　　　　[boy:
He cares not for your weeping.—Speak thou,
Perhaps thy childishness will move him more
Than can our reasons.—There is no man in
　　　the world　　　　　　　　[me prate
More bound to his mother; yet here he lets
Like one i' the stocks. Thou hast never in
　　　thy life
Show'd thy dear mother any courtesy;
When she,—poor hen, fond of no second
　　　brood,　　　　　　　　　　[home,
Has cluck'd thee to the wars, and safely
Loaden with honour. Say my request's unjust,
And spurn me back: but if it be not so,
Thou art not honest; and the gods will plague
　　　thee,
That thou restrain'st from me the duty which
To a mother's part belongs.—He turns away:
Down, ladies; let us shame him with our
　　　knees.
To his surname Coriolanus 'longs more pride
Than pity to our prayers. Down: an end;
This is the last.—So we will home to Rome,
And die among our neighbours.—Nay, be-
　　　hold's:
This boy, that cannot tell what he would
　　　have,
But kneels and holds up hands for fellowship,
Does reason our petition with more strength
Than thou hast to deny't.—Come, let us go:
This fellow had a Volscian to his mother;
His wife is in Corioli, and his child
Like him by chance.—Yet give us our des-
　　　patch:
I am hush'd until our city be afire,
And then I'll speak a little.

*Cor.* [*After holding* VOLUMNIA *by the hands
　　　in silence.*] O mother, mother!
What have you done? Behold, the heavens
　　　do ope,
The gods look down, and this unnatural scene
They laugh at. O my mother, mother! O!
You have won a happy victory to Rome;
But for your son,—believe it, O, believe it,
Most dangerously you have with him pre-
　　　vail'd,
If not most mortal to him. But let it come.—
Aufidius, though I cannot make true wars,
I'll frame convenient peace. Now, good Au-
　　　fidius,　　　　　　　　　　　[heard
If you were in my stead, would you have
A mother less? or granted less, Aufidius?

*Auf.* I was mov'd withal.

*Cor.*　　　　　　I dare be sworn you were:
And, sir, it is no little thing to make
Mine eyes to sweat compassion. But, good sir,
What peace you'll make, advise me: for my
　　　part,
I'll not to Rome, I'll back with you; and,
　　　pray you,

Stand to me in this cause.—O mother! wife!

*Auf.* I am glad thou hast set thy mercy and
　　thy honour
At difference in thee: out of that I'll work
Myself a former fortune.　　　　[*Aside.*
　　[*The* Ladies *make signs to* CORIOLANUS.
*Cor.*　　　　　　　　　Ay, by and by;
　　　　　　[*To* VOLUMNIA, VIRGILIA, *&c.*
But we'll drink together; and you shall bear
A better witness back than words, which we,
On like conditions, will have counter-seal'd.
Come, enter with us. Ladies, you deserve
To have a temple built you: all the swords
In Italy, and her confederate arms,
Could not have made this peace.　　[*Exeunt.*

SCENE IV.—ROME. *A public Place.*

*Enter* MENENIUS *and* SICINIUS.

*Men.* See you yond coigne o' the Capitol,—
yond corner-stone?

*Sic.* Why, what of that?

*Men.* If it be possible for you to displace it
with your little finger, there is some hope the
ladies of Rome, specially his mother, may
prevail with him. But I say there is no hope
in't: our throats are sentenced, and stay upon
execution.

*Sic.* Is't possible that so short a time can
alter the condition of a man?

*Men.* There is difference between a grub
and a butterfly; yet your butterfly was a
grub. This Marcius is grown from man to
dragon: he has wings; he's more than a creeping thing.

*Sic.* He loved his mother dearly.

*Men.* So did he me: and he no more remembers his mother now than an eight-year-
old horse. The tartness of his face sours ripe
grapes: when he walks, he moves like an
engine, and the ground shrinks before his
treading: he is able to pierce a corslet with
his eye; talks like a knell, and his hum is a
battery. He sits in his state as a thing made
for Alexander. What he bids be done is finished with his bidding. He wants nothing of
a god but eternity, and a heaven to throne in.

*Sic.* Yes, mercy, if you report him truly.

*Men.* I paint him in the character. Mark
what mercy his mother shall bring from him:
there is no more mercy in him than there is
milk in a male tiger; that shall our poor city
find: and all this is 'long of you.

*Sic.* The gods be good unto us!

*Men.* No, in such a case the gods will not
be good unto us. When we banished him we
respected not them: and, he returning to
break our necks, they respect not us.

*Enter a* Messenger.

*Mess.* Sir, if you'd save your life, fly to
　　your house:
The plebeians have got your fellow-tribune,

And hale him up and down; all swearing, if
The Roman ladies bring not comfort home,
They'll give him death by inches.

*Enter a second* Messenger.

*Sic.*　　　　　　　　　What's the news?

*2 Mess.* Good news, good news;—the
　　ladies have prevail'd,.
The Volscians are dislodg'd and Marcius gone:
A merrier day did never yet greet Rome,
No, not the expulsion of the Tarquins.

*Sic.*　　　　　　　　　　　　Friend,
Art thou certain this is true? is it most cer-
　　tain?

*2 Mess.* As certain as I know the sun is fire:
Where have you lurk'd, that you make doubt
　　of it?　　　　　　　　　　　　[tide
Ne'er through an arch so hurried the blown
As the recomforted through the gates. Why,
　　hark you!
　　[*Trumpets and hautboys sounded, drums
　　　　beaten, and shouting within.*
The trumpets, sackbuts, psalteries, and fifes,
Tabors and cymbals, and the shouting Ro-
　　mans,
Make the sun dance. Hark you!
　　　　　　　　　　　[*Shouting again.*

*Men.*　　　　　　This is good news.
I will go meet the ladies. This Volumnia
Is worth of consuls, senators, patricians,
A city full: of tribunes such as you, [to-day:
A sea and land full. You have pray'd well
This morning, for ten thousand of your
　　throats
I'd not have given a doit. Hark, how they joy!
　　　　　　　　　　[*Shouting and music.*

*Sic.* First, the gods bless you for your
　　tidings; next,
Accept my thankfulness.

*2 Mess.*　　　　　　　Sir, we have all
Great cause to give great thanks.

*Sic.*　　　　　　　They are near the city?

*Mess.* Almost at point to enter.

*Sic.*　　　　　　　We will meet them,
And help the joy.　　　　　　　[*Exeunt.*

SCENE V.—ROME. *A Street near the Gate.*

*Enter* VOLUMNIA, VIRGILIA, VALERIA, *&c.,
accompanied by* Senators, Patricians, *and*
Citizens.

*1 Sen.* Behold our patroness, the life of
　　Rome!
Call all your tribes together, praise the gods,
And make triumphant fires; strew flowers
　　before them:
Unshout the noise that banish'd Marcius,
Repeal him with the welcome of his mother;
Cry, *Welcome, ladies, welcome!*—

*All.*　　　　　　　Welcome, ladies,
Welcome!
　　[*A flourish with drums and trumpets.*
　　　　　　　　　　　　　　[*Exeunt.*

SCENE VI.—ANTIUM. *A public Place.*
*Enter* TULLUS AUFIDIUS, *with* Attendants.

*Auf.* Go tell the lords of the city I am
        here:
Deliver them this paper; having read it,
Bid them repair to the market-place: where I,
Even in theirs and in the commons' ears,
Will vouch the truth of it. Him I accuse
The city ports by this hath enter'd, and
Intends to appear before the people, hoping
To purge himself with words: despatch.
                        [*Exeunt* Attendants.

*Enter three or four* Conspirators *of*
AUFIDIUS'S *faction.*

Most welcome!
  I *Con.* How is it with our general?
  *Auf.*                        Even so
As with a man by his own alms empoison'd,
And with his charity slain.
  2 *Con.*        Most noble, sir,
If you do hold the same intent wherein
You wish'd us parties, we'll deliver you
Of your great danger.
  *Auf.*        Sir, I cannot tell:
We must proceed as we do find the people.
  3 *Con.* The people will remain uncertain
        whilst                        [either
'Twixt you there's difference: but the fall of
Makes the survivor heir of all.
  *Auf.*        I know it;
And my pretext to strike at him admits
A good construction. I rais'd him, and I
        pawn'd                [heighten'd,
Mine honour for his truth: who being so
He water'd his new plants with dews of flat-
        tery,
Seducing so my friends; and to this end
He bow'd his nature, never known before
But to be rough, unswayable, and free.
  3 *Con.* Sir, his stoutness,
When he did stand for consul, which he lost
By lack of stooping,—
  *Auf.*        That I would have spoke of:
Being banish'd for't, he came unto my hearth;
Presented to my knife his throat: I took him;
Made him joint-servant with me; gave him
        way
In all his own desires; nay, let him choose
Out of my files, his projects to accomplish,
My best and freshest men; serv'd his design-
        ments
In mine own person; holp to reap the fame
Which he made all his; and took some pride
To do myself this wrong: till, at the last,
I seem'd his follower, not partner; and
He wag'd me with his countenance as if
I had been mercenary.
  I *Con.*        So he did, my lord:
The army marvell'd at it; and, in the last,
When he had carried Rome, and that we
        look'd
For no less spoil than glory,—

  *Auf.*                        There was it;—
For which my sinews shall be stretch'd upon
        him.
At a few drops of women's rheum, which are
As cheap as lies, he sold the blood and labour
Of our great action: therefore shall he die,
And I'll renew me in his fall. But, hark!
    [*Drums and trumpets sound, with great
      shouts of the people.*
  I *Con.* Your native town you enter'd like
        a post,
And had no welcomes home; but he returns
Splitting the air with noise.
  2 *Con.*                And patient fools,
Whose children he hath slain, their base
        throats tear
With giving him glory.
  3 *Con.* Therefore, at your vantage,
Ere he express himself, or move the people
With what he would say, let him feel your
        sword,
Which we will second. When he lies along,
After your way his tale pronounc'd shall bury
His reasons with his body.
  *Auf.*                Say no more:
Here come the lords.

    *Enter the* Lords *of the City.*

  *Lords.* You are most welcome home.
  *Auf.*                I have not deserv'd it.
But, worthy lords, have you with heed
        perus'd
What I have written to you?
  *Lords.*                We have.
  I *Lord.*                And grieve to hear't.
What faults he made before the last, I think
Might have found easy fines: but there to end
Where he was to begin, and give away
The benefit of our levies, answering us
With our own charge: making a treaty where
There was a yielding.—This admits no excuse.
  *Auf.* He approaches: you shall hear him.

*Enter* CORIOLANUS, *with drums and colours;
    a crowd of* Citizens *with him.*

  *Cor.* Hail, lords! I am return'd your sol-
        dier;
No more infected with my country's love
Than when I parted hence, but still subsisting
Under your great command. You are to know
That prosperously I have attempted, and
With bloody passage led your wars even to
The gates of Rome. Our spoils we have
        brought home
Do more than counterpoise a full third part
The charges of the action. We have made
        peace
With no less honour to the Antiates
Than shame to the Romans: and we here
        deliver,
Subscribed by the consuls and patricians,
Together with the seal o' the senate, what
We have compounded on.
  *Auf.*                Read it not, noble lords;

But tell the traitor, in the highest degree
He hath abus'd your powers.
　*Cor.* Traitor!—How now!
　*Auf.* 　　·　　Ay, traitor, Marcius.
　*Cor.* 　　　　　　　　　　Marcius!
　*Auf.* Ay, Marcius, Caius Marcius. Dost
　　thou think
I'll grace thee with that robbery, thy stol'n
　name
Coriolanus in Corioli?—
You lords and heads o' the state, perfidiously
He has betray'd your business, and given up,
For certain drops of salt, your city Rome,—
I say your city,—to his wife and mother;
Breaking his oath and resolution, like
A twist of rotten silk; never admitting
Counsel o' the war; but at his nurse's tears
He whin'd and roar'd away your victory;
That pages blush'd at him, and men of heart
Look'd wondering each at other.
　*Cor.* 　　　　　　Hear'st thou, Mars?
　*Auf.* Name not the god, thou boy of
　　tears,—
　*Cor.* 　　　　　　　　　　　　Ha!
　*Auf.* No more.
　*Cor.* Measureless liar, thou hast made my
　　heart　　　　　　　　　　[slave!—
Too great for what contains it. Boy! O
Pardon me, lords, 'tis the first time that ever
I was forc'd to scold. Your judgments, my
　grave lords,
Must give ·this cur the lie: and his own no-
　tion,—　　　　　　　　　[that must bear
Who wears my stripes impress'd upon him;
My beating to his grave,—shall join to thrust
The lie unto him.
　*1 Lord.* Peace, both, and hear me speak.
　*Cor.* Cut me to pieces, Volsces; men and
　　lads,
Stain all your edges on me.—Boy! False
　hound!
If you have writ your annals true, 'tis there,
That, like an eagle in a dove-cote, I
Flutter'd your Volscians in Corioli:
Alone I did it.—Boy!
　*Auf.* 　　　　　Why, noble lords,
Will you be put in mind of his blind fortune,
Which was your shame, by this unholy brag-
　gart,
'Fore your own eyes and ears?
　*Conspirators.* 　　　Let him die for't.
　*Citizens.* Tear him to pieces, do it present-

ly:—he killed my son;—my daughter;—he
killed my cousin Marcus;—he killed my
father,—
　*2 Lord.* Peace, ho!—no outrage;—peace!
The man is noble, and his fame folds in
This orb o' the earth. His last offences to us
Shall have judicious hearing.—Stand, Aufid-
　ius,
And trouble not the peace.
　*Cor.* 　　　　　　　O that I had him,
With six Aufidiuses, or more, his tribe,
To use my lawful sword!
　*Auf.* 　　　　　　Insolent villain!
　*Conspirators.* Kill, kill, kill, kill, kill him!
　　[AUF. *and the* Conspirators *draw, and kill*
　　Cor., *who falls:* AUF. *stands on him.*
　*Lords.* 　　　　Hold, hold, hold, hold!
　*Auf.* My noble masters, hear me speak.
　*1 Lord.* 　　　　　　　O Tullus,—
　*2 Lord.* Thou hast done a deed whereat
　　valour will weep. 　　　　[be quiet;
　*3 Lord.* Tread not upon him.—Masters all,
Put up your swords. 　　　[in this rage,
　*Auf.* My lords, when you shall know,—as
Provok'd by him, you cannot,—the great
　danger　　　　　　　　　[rejoice
Which this man's life did owe you, you'll
That he is thus cut off. Please it your hon-
　ours
To call me to your senate, I'll deliver
Myself your loyal servant, or endure
Your heaviest censure.
　*1 Lord.* 　　　Bear from hence his body,
And mourn you for him. Let him be regarded
As the most noble corse that ever herald
Did follow to his urn.
　*2 Lord.* 　　　　　His own impatience
Takes from Aufidius a great part of blame.
Let's make the best of it.
　*Auf.* 　　　　　　My rage is gone;
And I am struck with sorrow.—Take him
　up:—　　　　　　　　　　[one.—
Help, three o' the chiefest soldiers; I'll be
Beat thou the drum, that it speak mourn-
　fully:
Trail your steel pikes. Though in this city he
Hath widow'd and unchilded many a one,
Which to this hour bewail the injury,
Yet he shall have a noble memory.—
Assist.
　[*Exeunt, bearing the body of* CORIOLANUS.
　　*A dead march sounded.*

JULIUS CÆSAR.

Act III. Sc. 1.

# JULIUS CÆSAR

## DRAMATIS PERSONÆ

JULIUS CÆSAR.

OCTAVIUS CÆSAR, ⎫ Triumvirs after the
MARCUS ANTONIUS, ⎬ death of JULIUS
M. ÆMIL. LEPIDUS, ⎭ CÆSAR.

CICERO, ⎫
PUBLIUS, ⎬ Senators.
POPILIUS LENA, ⎭

MARCUS BRUTUS, ⎫
CASSIUS, ⎪
CASCA, ⎪
TREBONIUS, ⎬ Conspirators against
LIGARIUS, ⎪ JULIUS CÆSAR.
DECIUS BRUTUS, ⎪
METELLUS CIMBER, ⎪
CINNA, . ⎭

FLAVIUS and MARULLUS, Tribunes.
ARTEMIDORUS, a Sophist of Cnidos.
A Soothsayer.
CINNA, a Poet.
Another Poet.
LUCILIUS, TITINIUS MESSALA, YOUNG CATO,
and VOLUMNIUS,—Friends to BRUTUS
and CASSIUS.
VARRO, CLITUS, CLAUDIUS, STRATO, LUCIUS,
DARDANIUS,—Servants to BRUTUS.
PINDARUS, Servant to CASSIUS.

CALPHURNIA, Wife to CÆSAR.
PORTIA, Wife to BRUTUS.

Senators, Citizens, Guards, Attendants, &c.

SCENE,—During a great part of the Play at ROME; afterwards at SARDIS, and near PHILLIPI.

## ACT I.

### SCENE I.—ROME. A Street.

Enter FLAVIUS, MARULLUS, and a rabble of
Citizens.

Flav. Hence! home, you idle creatures,
get you home;
Is this a holiday? What! know you not,
Being mechanical, you ought not walk
Upon a labouring day without the sign
Of your profession?—Speak, what trade art
thou?

1 Cit. Why, sir, a carpenter. [rule?

Mar. Where is thy leather apron and thy
What dost thou with thy best apparel on?—
You, sir, what trade are you? [man,

2 Cit. Truly, sir, in respect of a fine work-
I am but, as you would say, a cobbler.

Mar. But what trade art thou? answer me
directly.

2 Cit. A trade, sir, that I hope I may use
with a safe conscience; which is indeed, sir, a
mender of bad soles.

Mar. What trade, thou knave, thou
naughty knave, what trade?

2 Cit. Nay, I beseech you, sir, be not out
with me: yet, if you be out, sir, I can mend
you.

Mar. What meanest thou by that? mend
me, thou saucy fellow!

2 Cit. Why, sir, cobble you.

Flav. Thou art a cobbler, art thou?

2 Cit. Truly, sir, all that I live by is with
the awl: I meddle with no tradesman's matters, nor women's matters, but with awl. I
am, indeed, sir, a surgeon to old shoes; when

they are in great danger, I re-cover them. As
proper men as ever trod upon neats-leather
have gone upon my handiwork.

Flav. But wherefore art not in thy shop
today? [streets?
Why dost thou lead these men about the

2 Cit. Truly, sir, to wear out their shoes, to
get myself into more work. But, indeed, sir,
we make holiday to see Cæsar, and to rejoice in his triumph.

Mar. Wherefore rejoice? What conquest
brings he home?
What tributaries follow him to Rome,
To grace in captive bonds his chariot wheels?
You blocks, you stones, you worse than
senseless things!
O you hard hearts, you cruel men of Rome,
Knew you not Pompey? Many a time and oft
Have you climb'd up to walls and battle-
ments, [tops,
To towers and windows, yea, to chimney-
Your infants in your arms, and there have sat
The live-long day, with patient expectation,
To see great Pompey pass the streets of
Rome:
And when you saw his chariot but appear,
Have you not made an universal shout,
That Tiber trembled underneath her banks,
To hear the replication of your sounds
Made in her concave shores?
And do you now put on your best attire?
And do you now cull out a holiday?
And do you now strew flowers in his way
That comes in triumph over Pompey's blood?
Be gone!
Run to your houses, fall upon your knees,
Pray to the gods to intermit the plague

That needs must light on this ingratitude.

*Flav.* Go, go, good countrymen, and for
this fault
Assemble all the poor men of your sort;
Draw them to Tiber banks, and weep your
tears
Into the channel, till the lowest stream
Do kiss the most exalted shores of all.
[*Exeunt* Citizens.
See, whe'r their basest metal be not mov'd;
They vanish tongue-tied in their guiltiness.
Go you down that way towards the Capitol:
This way will I: disrobe the images
If you do find them deck'd with ceremonies.

*Mar.* May we do so?
You know it is the feast of Lupercal.

*Flav.* It is no matter; let no images
Be hung with Cæsar's trophies. I'll about,
And drive away the vulgar from the streets:
So do you too, where you perceive them
thick. [wing
These growing feathers pluck'd from Cæsar's
Will make him fly an ordinary pitch;
Who else would soar above the view of men,
And keep us all in servile fearfulness.
[*Exeunt.*

SCENE II.—ROME. *A public Place.*

*Enter, in procession, with music,* CÆSAR;
ANTONY, *for the course;* CALPHURNIA,
PORTIA, DECIUS, CICERO, BRUTUS, CAS-
SIUS, *and* CASA; *a great crowd following:
among them a* Soothsayer.

*Cæs.* Calphurnia,—
*Casca.* Peace, ho! Cæsar speaks.
[*Music ceases.*
*Cæs.* Calphurnia,—
*Cal.* Here, my lord.
*Cæs.* Stand you directly in Antonius' way
When he doth run his course.—Antonius.
*Ant.* Cæsar, my lord.
*Cæs.* Forget not, in your speed, Antonius,
To touch Calphurnia; for our elders say,
The barren, touched in this holy chase,
Shake off their sterile curse.
*Ant.* I shall remember:
When Cæsar says, *Do this,* it is perform'd.
*Cæs.* Set on; and leave no ceremony out.
*Sooth.* Cæsar!
*Cæs.* Ha! who calls?
*Casca.* Bid every noise be still.—Peace yet
again. [*Music ceases.*
*Cæs.* Who is it in the press that calls on
me?
I hear a tongue, shriller than all the music,
Cry, *Cæsar.* Speak; Cæsar is turn'd to hear.
*Sooth.* Beware the ides of March.
*Cæs.* What man is that?
*Bru.* A soothsayer bids you beware the
ides of March.
*Cæs.* Set him before me; let me see his
face [upon Cæsar.
*Cas.* Fellow, come from the throng; look

*Cæs.* What say'st thou to me now? speak
once again.
*Sooth.* Beware the ides of March. [Pass.
*Cæs.* He is a dreamer; let us leave him.—
[*Sennet. Exeunt all but* BRU. *and* CAS.
*Cas.* Will you go see the order of the
course?
*Bru.* Not I.
*Cas.* I pray you do. [part
*Bru.* I am not gamesome: I do lack some
Of that quick spirit that is in Antony.
Let me not hinder, Cassius, your desires;
I'll leave you.
*Cas.* Brutus, I do observe you now of
late:
I have not from your eyes that gentleness
And show of love as I was wont to have:
You bear too stubborn and too strange a
hand
Over your friend that loves you.
*Bru.* Cassius,
Be not deceiv'd: if I have vail'd my look,
I turn the trouble of my countenance
Merely upon myself. Vexed I am
Of late with passions of some difference,
Conceptions only proper to myself, [iours;
Which gives some soil, perhaps, to my behav-
But let not therefore my good friends be
griev'd,—
Among which number, Cassius, be you one,—
Nor construe any further my neglect
Than that poor Brutus, with himself at war,
Forgets the shows of love to other men.
*Cas.* Then, Brutus, I have much mistook
your passion; [buried
By means whereof this breast of mine hath
Thoughts of great value, worthy cogitations.
Tell me, good Brutus, can you see your face?
*Bru.* No, Cassius; for the eye sees not it-
self
But by reflection, by some other things.
*Cas.* 'Tis just;
And it is very much lamented, Brutus,
That you have no such mirrors as will turn
Your hidden worthiness into your eye,
That you might see your shadow. I have
heard,
Where many of the best respect in Rome,—
Except immortal Cæsar,—speaking of Brutus,
And groaning underneath this age's yoke,
Have wish'd that noble Brutus had his eyes.
*Bru.* Into what dangers would you lead
me, Cassius,
That you would have me seek into myself
For that which is not in me? [to hear:
*Cas.* Therefore, good Brutus, be prepar'd
And, since you know you cannot see yourself
So well as by reflection, I, your glass,
Will modestly discover to yourself
That of yourself which you yet know not of.
And be not jealous on me, gentle Brutus:
Were I a common laugher, or did use
To stale with ordinary oaths my love
To every new protester; if you know

That I do fawn on men, and hug them hard,
And after scandal them; or if you know
That I profess myself in banqueting
To all the rout, then hold me dangerous.
                    [*Flourish and shout.*
  *Bru.* What means this shouting? I do
    fear the people
Choose Cæsar for their king.
  *Cas.*              Ay, do you fear it?
Then must I think you would not have it so.
  *Bru.* I would not, Cassius; yet I love him
    well.—
But wherefore do you hold me here so long?
What is it that you would impart to me?
If it be aught toward the general good,
Set honour in one eye and death i' the other,
And I will look on both indifferently;
For, let the gods so speed me as I love
The name of honour more than I fear death.
  *Cas.* I know that virtue to be in you,
    Brutus,
As well as I do know your outward favour.
Well, honour is the subject of my story.—
I cannot tell what you and other men
Think of this life; but, for my single self,
I had as lief not be as live to be
In awe of such a thing as I myself.
I was born free as Cæsar; so were you:
We both have fed as well; and we can both
Endure the winter's cold as well as he.
For once, upon a raw and gusty day,
The troubled Tiber chafing with her shores,
Cæsar said to me, *Dar'st thou, Cassius, now*
*Leap in with me into this angry flood,*
*And swim to yonder point?*—Upon the word,
Accoutred as I was, I plunged in,
And bade him follow: so indeed he did.
The torrent roar'd; and we did buffet it
With lusty sinews, throwing it aside
And stemming it with hearts of controversy:
But ere we could arrive the point propos'd,
Cæsar cried, *Help me, Cassius, or I sink!*
I, as Æneas, our great ancestor,
Did from the flames of Troy upon his shoul-
    der                                  [Tiber
The old Anchises bear, so from the waves of
Did I the tired Cæsar: and this man
Is now become a god; and Cassius is
A wretched creature, and must bend his body
If Cæsar carelessly but nod on him.
He had a fever when he was in Spain,
And, when the fit was on him, I did mark
How he did shake: 'tis true, this god did
    shake:
His coward lips did from their colour fly;
And that same eye, whose bend doth awe the
    world,
Did lose his lustre: I did hear him groan:
Ay, and that tongue of his, that bade the
    Romans                             [books,
Mark him, and write his speeches in their
Alas! it cried, *Give me some drink, Titinius,*
As a sick girl. Ye gods, it doth amaze me,
A man of such a feeble temper should

So get the start of the majestic world,
And bear the palm alone.    [*Shout: flourish.*
  *Bru.* Another general shout!
I do believe that these applauses are
For some new honours that are heap'd on
    Cæsar.
  *Cas.* Why, man, he doth bestride the nar-
    row world
Like a Colossus; and we petty men
Walk under his huge legs, and peep about
To find ourselves dishonourable graves.
Men at some time are masters of their fates:
The fault, dear Brutus, is not in our stars,
But in ourselves, that we are underlings.
Brutus and Cæsar: what should be in that
    Cæsar?                            [than yours?
Why should that name be sounded more
Write them together, yours is as fair a name;
Sound them, it doth become the mouth as
    well;
Weigh them, it is as heavy; conjure with 'em,
Brutus will start a spirit as soon as Cæsar.
                                        [*Shout.*
Now, in the names of all the gods at once,
Upon what meat doth this our Cæsar feed,
That he has grown so great? Age, thou art
    sham'd!                            [bloods!
Rome, thou hast lost the breed of noble
When went there by an age, since the great
    flood,                             [man?
But it was fam'd with more than with one
When could they say, till now, that talk'd of
    Rome,                             [man?
That her wide walls encompass'd but one
Now it is Rome indeed, and room enough,
When there is in it but one only man.
O! you and I have heard our fathers say,
There was a Brutus once that would have
    brook'd
The eternal devil to keep his state in Rome
As easily as a king.                   [jealous;
  *Bru.* That you do love me, I am nothing
What you would work me to, I have some
    aim:
How I have thought of this, and of these
    times,
I shall recount hereafter; for this present,
I would not, so with love I might entreat
    you,
Be any further mov'd. What you have said
I will consider; what you have to say
I will with patience hear: and find a time
Both meet to hear and answer such high
    things.
Till then, my noble friend, chew upon this:
Brutus had rather be a villager
Than to repute himself a son of Rome
Under these hard conditions as this time
Is like to lay upon us.
  *Cas.* I am glad that my weak words
Have struck but thus much show of fire from
    Brutus.
  *Bru.* The games are done, and Cæsar is
    returning.

*Cas.* As they pass by, pluck Casca by the sleeve;
And he will, after his sour fashion, tell you
What hath proceeded worthy note to-day.

*Re-enter* Cæsar *and his* Train.

*Bru.* I will do so.—But, look you, Cassius,
The angry spot doth glow on Cæsar's brow,
And all the rest look like a chidden train:
Calphurnia's cheek is pale; and Cicero
Looks with such ferret and such fiery eyes
As we have seen him in the Capitol,
Being cross'd in conference by some senators.
*Cas.* Casca will tell us what the matter is.
*Cæs.* Antonius.
*Ant.* Cæsar?
*Cæs.* Let me have men about me that are fat;                                    [nights:
Sleek-headed men, and such as sleep o'
Yond Cassius has a lean and hungry look;
He thinks too much: such men are dangerous.
*Ant.* Fear him not, Cæsar, he's not dangerous;
He is a noble Roman, and well given.
*Cæs.* Would he were fatter!—But I fear him not:
Yet if my name were liable to fear,
I do not know the man I should avoid
So soon as that spare Cassius. He reads much;
He is a great observer, and he looks
Quite through the deeds of men: he loves no plays,
As thou dost, Antony; he hears no music:
Seldom he smiles; and smiles in such a sort
As if he mock'd himself, and scorn'd his spirit
That could be mov'd to smile at anything.
Such men as he be never at heart's ease
Whiles they behold a greater than themselves;
And therefore are they very dangerous.
I rather tell thee what is to be fear'd
Than what I fear,—for always I am Cæsar.
Come on my right hand, for this ear is deaf,
And tell me truly what thou think'st of him.
[*Exeunt* Cæsar *and his* Train. Casca
                *stays behind.*
*Casca.* You pull'd me by the cloak; would you speak with me?                [to-day,
*Bru.* Ay, Casca; tell us what hath chanc'd
That Cæsar looks so sad?                            [not?
*Casca.* Why, you were with him, were you
*Bru.* I should not then ask Casca what had chanc'd.
*Casca.* Why, there was a crown offered him: and being offered him, he put it by with the back of his hand, thus; and then the people fell a-shouting.
*Bru.* What was the second noise for?
*Casca.* Why, for that too       [last cry for?
*Cas.* They shouted thrice: what was the
*Casca.* Why, for that too.
*Bru.* Was the crown offer'd him thrice?

*Casca.* Ay, marry, was't, and he put it by thrice, every time gentler than other; and at every putting by mine honest neighbours shouted.
*Cas.* Who offered him the crown?
*Casca.* Why, Antony.
*Bru.* Tell us the manner of it, gentle Casca.
*Casca.* I can as well be hanged, as tell the manner of it: it was mere foolery; I did not mark it. I saw Mark Antony offer him a crown;—yet 'twas not a crown neither, 'twas one of these coronets;—and, as I told you, he put it by once: but for all that, to my thinking, he would fain have had it. Then he offered it to him again; then he put it by again; but, to my thinking, he was very loth to lay his fingers off it. And then he offered it the third time; he put it the third time by: and still, as he refused it, the rabblement hooted, and clapped their chapped hands, and threw up their sweaty night-caps, and uttered such a deal of stinking breath because Cæsar refused the crown, that it had almost choked Cæsar; for he swooned, and fell down at it: and for mine own part I durst not laugh, for fear of opening my lips and receiving the bad air.
*Cas.* But, soft, I pray you: what, did Cæsar swoon?
*Casca.* He fell down in the market-place, and foamed at mouth, and was speechless.
*Bru.* 'Tis very like,—he hath the falling sickness.
*Cas.* No, Cæsar hath it not; but you, and I,                                    [ness.
And honest Casca, we have the falling sick-
*Casca.* I know not what you mean by that: but I am sure Cæsar fell down. If the tag-rag people did not clap him and hiss him, according as he pleased and displeased them, as they use to do the players in the theatre, I am no true man.                            [himself?
*Bru.* What said he when he came unto
*Casca.* Marry, before he fell down, when he perceived the common herd was glad he refused the crown, he plucked me ope his doublet, and offered them his throat to cut. —An I had been a man of any occupation, if I would not have taken him at a word, I would I might go to hell among the rogues. And so he fell. When he came to himself again, he said, If he had done or said anything amiss, he desired their worships to think it was his infirmity. Three or four wenches, where I stood, cried, *Alas, good soul!*—and forgave him with all their hearts: but there's no heed to be taken of them; if Cæsar had stabbed their mothers they would have done no less.
*Bru.* And after that he came, thus sad, away?
*Casca.* Ay.
*Cas.* Did Cicero say anything?

*Casca.* Ay, he spoke Greek.

*Cas.* To what effect?

*Casca.* Nay, an I tell you that, I'll ne'er look you i' the face again: but those that understood him smiled at one another, and shook their heads; but, for mine own part, it was Greek to me. I could tell you more news too: Marullus and Flavius, for pulling scarfs off Cæsar's images, are put to silence. Fare you well. There was more foolery yet, if I could remember it.

*Cas.* Will you sup with me to-night, Casca?

*Casca.* No, I am promised forth.

*Cas.* Will you dine with me to-morrow?

*Casca.* Ay, if I be alive, and your mind hold, and your dinner worth the eating.

*Cas.* Good; I will expect you.

*Casca.* Do so; farewell, both. [*Exit.*

*Bru.* What a blunt fellow is this grown to be! He was quick mettle when he went to school.

*Cas.* So is he now, in execution.
Of any bold or noble enterprise,
However he puts on this tardy form.
This rudeness is a sauce to his good wit,
Which gives men stomach to digest his words
With better appetite.　　　　　[leave you:

*Bru.* And so it is. For this time I will
To-morrow, if you please to speak with me,
I will come home to you; or, if you will,
Come home to me, and I will wait for you.

*Cas.* I will do so: till then, think of the world.　　　　　[*Exit* BRUTUS.
Well, Brutus, thou art noble; yet, I see,
Thy honourable metal may be wrought
From that it is dispos'd: therefore it is meet
That noble minds keep ever with their likes;
For who so firm that cannot be seduc'd?
Cæsar doth bear me hard; but he loves Brutus:
If I were Brutus now, and he were Cassius,
He should not humour me. I will this night,
In several hands, in at his windows throw,
As if they came from several citizens,
Writings, all tending to the great opinion
That Rome holds of his name; wherein obscurely
Cæsar's ambition shall be glanced at:
And, after this, let Cæsar seat him sure;
For we will shake him, or worse days endure.
　　　　　[*Exit.*

### SCENE III.—ROME. *A Street.*

*Thunder and Lightning. Enter, from opposite sides,* CASCA, *with his sword drawn, and* CICERO.

*Cic.* Good-even, Casca: brought you Cæsar home?　　　　　[so?
Why are you breathless? and why stare you

*Casca.* Are you not mov'd, when all the sway of earth
Shakes like a thing unfirm? O Cicero,
I have seen tempests, when the scolding winds

Have riv'd the knotty oaks; and I have seen
The ambitious ocean swell, and rage, and foam,
To be exalted with the threat'ning clouds:
But never till to-night, never till now,
Did I go through a tempest dropping fire.
Either there is a civil strife in heaven;
Or else the world, too saucy with the gods,
Incenses them to send destruction.

*Cic.* Why, saw you anything more wonderful?

*Casca.* A common slave,—you know him well by sight,—　　　　　[burn
Held up his left hand, which did flame and
Like twenty torches join'd; and yet his hand,
Not sensible of fire, remain'd unscorch'd.
Besides,—I ha' not since put up my sword,—
Against the Capitol I met a lion,
Who glar'd upon me, and went surly by,
Without annoying me: and there were drawn
Upon a heap a hundred ghastly women,
Transformed with their fear; who swore they saw　　　　　[streets.
Men, all in fire, walk up and down the
And yesterday the bird of night did sit,
Even at noon-day, upon the market-place,
Hooting and shrieking. When these prodigies
Do so conjointly meet, let not men say,
*These are their reasons,—they are natural;*
For I believe they are portentous things
Unto the climate that they point upon.

*Cic.* Indeed, it is a strange-disposed time:
But men may construe things after their fashion,　　　　　[selves.
Clean from the purpose of the things themComes Cæsar to the Capitol to-morrow?

*Casca.* He doth; for he did bid Antonius
Send word to you he would be there to-morrow.

*Cic.* Good-night, then, Casca: this disturbed sky
Is not to walk in.

*Casca.* Farewell, Cicero. [*Exit* CICERO.

### *Enter* CASSIUS.

*Cas.* Who's there?

*Casca.*　　　　　A Roman.

*Cas.*　　　　　Casca, by your voice.

*Casca.* Your ear is good. Cassius, what night is this!

*Cas.* A very pleasing night to honest men.

*Casca.* Who ever knew the heavens menace so?　　　　　[full of faults.

*Cas.* Those that have known the earth so
For my part, I have walk'd about the streets,
Submitting me unto the perilous night;
And, thus unbraced, Casca, as you see,
Have bar'd my bosom to the thunder-stone:
And when the cross-blue lightning seem'd to open
The breast of heaven, I did present myself
Even in the aim and very flash of it.

*Casca.* But wherefore did you so much tempt the heavens?

It is the part of men to fear and tremble
When the most mighty gods, by tokens, send
Such dreadful heralds to astonish us.

*Cas.* You are dull, Casca; and those sparks of life
That should be in a Roman you do want,
Or else you use not. You look pale, and gaze,
And put on fear, and cast yourself in wonder,
To see the strange impatience of the heavens:
But if you would consider the true cause
Why all these fires, why all these gliding ghosts,
Why birds and beasts, from quality and kind;
Why old men fools, and children calculate;
Why all these things change, from their ordinance,
Their natures, and pre-formed faculties,
To monstrous quality;—why, you shall find
That heaven hath infus'd them with these spirits, [ing
To make them instruments of fear and warn-
Unto some monstrous state.
Now could I, Casca, name to thee a man
Most like this dreadful night [roars
That thunders, lightens, opens graves, and
As doth the lion in the Capitol,—
A man no mightier than thyself or me
In personal action; yet prodigious grown,
And fearful, as these strange eruptions are.

*Casca.* 'Tis Cæsar that you mean; is it not Cassius?

*Cas.* Let it be who it is: for Romans now
Have thews and limbs like to their ancestors;
But, woe the while! our fathers' minds are dead, [spirits;
And we are govern'd with our mothers'
Our yoke and sufferance show us womanish.

*Casca.* Indeed they say the senators tomorrow
Mean to establish Cæsar as a king;
And he shall wear his crown by sea and land,
In every place, save here in Italy.

*Cas.* I know where I will wear this dagger then;
Cassius from bondage will deliver Cassius:
Therein, ye gods, you make the weak most strong;
Therein, ye gods, you tyrants do defeat:
Nor stony tower, nor walls of beaten brass,
Nor airless dungeon, nor strong links of iron,
Can be retentive to the strength of spirit;
But life, being weary of these worldly bars,
Never lacks power to dismiss itself.
If I know this, know all the world besides,
That part of tyranny that I do bear,
I can shake off at pleasure [*Thunder still.*

*Casca.* So can I:
So every bondman in his own hand bears
The power to cancel his captivity. [then?

*Cas.* And why should Cæsar be a tyrant,
Poor man! I know he would not be a wolf,
But that he sees the Romans are but sheep:
He were no lion, were not Romans hinds.
Those that with haste will make a mighty fire

Begin it with weak straws: what trash is Rome,
What rubbish, and what offal, when it serves
For the base matter to illuminate
So vile a thing as Cæsar! But, O grief,
Where hast thou led me? I perhaps speak this
Before a willing bondman; then I know
My answer must be made: but I am arm'd,
And dangers are to me indifferent. [man

*Casca.* You speak to Casca; and to such a
That is no fleering tell-tale. Hold, my hand:
Be factious for redress of all these griefs;
And I will set this foot of mine as far
As who goes farthest.

*Cas.*　　　　　　　　There's a bargain made.
Now know you, Casca, I have mov'd already
Some certain of the noblest-minded Romans
To undergo with me an enterprise
Of honourable-dangerous consequence;
And I do know by this they stay for me
In Pompey's porch: for now, this fearful night,
There is no stir or walking in the streets;
And the complexion of the element
In favour's like the work we have in hand,
Most bloody, fiery, and most terrible.

*Casca.* Stand close awhile, for here comes one in haste. [gait;

*Cas.* 'Tis Cinna,—I do know him by his
He is a friend.

*Enter* CINNA.
　　　　　　Cinna, where haste you so?

*Cin.* To find out you. Who's that? Metellus Cimber?

*Cas.* No, it is Casca; one incorporate
To our attempts. Am I not stay'd for, Cinna?

*Cin.* I am glad on't. What a fearful night is this! [sights.
There's two or three of us have seen strange

*Cas.* Am I not stay'd for? Tell me.

*Cin.*　　　　　　　　Yes, you are.
O Cassius, if you could
But win the noble Brutus to our party,—

*Cas.* Be you content: good Cinna, take this paper,
And look you lay it in the prætor's chair,
Where Brutus may but find it; and throw this
In at his window; set this up with wax
Upon old Brutus' statue: all this done,
Repair to Pompey's porch, where you shall find us.
Is Decius Brutus and Trebonius there?

*Cin.* All but Metellus Cimber; and he's gone
To seek you at your house. Well, I will hie,
And so bestow these papers as you bade me.

*Cas.* That done, repair to Pompey's theatre. [*Exit* CINNA.
Come, Casca, you and I will yet, ere day,
See Brutus at his house: three parts of him
Is ours already; and the man entire,
Upon the next encounter, yields him ours.

*Casca.* O, he sits high in all the people's
　　hearts:
And that which would appear offence in us,
His countenance, like richest alchemy,
Will change to virtue and to worthiness.
　*Cas.* Him, and his worth, and our great
　　need of him,
You have right well conceited. Let us go,
For it is after midnight; and ere day
We will awake him, and be sure of him.
　　　　　　　　　　　　　[*Exeunt.*

### ACT II.

SCENE I.—ROME. BRUTUS'S *Orchard.*

*Enter* BRUTUS.

　*Bru.* What, Lucius, ho!—
I cannot, by the progress of the stars, [say!—
Give guess how near to day.—Lucius, I
I would it were my fault to sleep so sound-
　ly.—　　　　　　　　　　　[Lucius!
When, Lucius, when? awake, I say! what,

*Enter* LUCIUS.

　*Luc.* Call'd you, my lord?
　*Bru.* Get me a taper in my study, Lucius:
When it is lighted, come and call me here.
　*Luc.* I will, my lord.　　　　　[*Exit.*
　*Bru.* It must be by his death: and, for my
　　part,
I know no personal cause to spurn at him,
But for the general. He would be crown'd:
How that might change his nature, there's
　　the question:　　　　　　　　[adder;
It is the bright day that brings forth the
And that craves wary walking. Crown him?
　—that—
And then, I grant, we put a sting in him,
That at his will he may do danger with.
The abuse of greatness is, when it disjoins
Remorse from power: and, to speak truth of
　　Cæsar,
I have not known when his affections sway'd
More than his reason. But 'tis a common
　　proof
That lowliness is young ambition's ladder,
Whereto the climber-upward turns his face;
But when he once attains the utmost round,
He then unto the ladder turns his back,
Looks in the clouds, scorning the base degrees
By which he did ascend. So Cæsar may;
Then, lest he may, prevent. And, since the
　　quarrel
Will bear no colour for the thing he is,
Fashion it thus; that what he is, augmented,
Would run to these and these extremities:
And therefore think him as a serpent's egg,
Which, hatch'd, would as his kind grow
　　mischievous;
And kill him in the shell.

*Re-enter* LUCIUS.

　*Luc.* The taper burneth in your closet, sir.
Searching the window for a flint, I found
　　　　　　　　　[*Giving him a letter.*

This paper, thus seal'd up; and I am sure
It did not lie there when I went to bed.
　*Bru.* Get you to bed again, it is not day.
Is not to-morrow, boy, the ides of March?
　*Luc.* I know not, sir.　　　　[word.
　*Bru.* Look in the calender, and bring me
　*Luc.* I will, sir.　　　　　　　[*Exit.*
　*Bru.* The exhalations, whizzing in the air,
Give so much light that I may read by them.
　　　　　　　[*Opens the letter and reads.*
*Brutus, thou sleep'st: awake, and see thyself.*
*Shall Rome, &c. Speak, strike, redress!*
*Brutus, thou sleep'st: awake.—*
Such instigations have been often dropp'd
Where I have took them up.
*Shall Rome, &c.* Thus must I piece it out,—
Shall Rome stand under one man's awe?
　　What, Rome?
My ancestors did from the streets of Rome
The Tarquin drive, when he was call'd a king.
*Speak, strike, redress!*—Am I entreated then
To speak and strike! O Rome! I make thee
　　promise,
If the redress will follow, thou receivest
Thy full petition at the hand of Brutus!

*Re-enter* LUCIUS.

　*Luc.* Sir, March is wasted fourteen days.
　　　　　　　　　　[*Knocking within.*
　*Bru.* 'Tis good. Go to the gate; somebody
　　knocks.　　　　　　　　[*Exit* LUCIUS.
Since Cassius first did whet me against
　　Cæsar,
I have not slept.
Between the acting of a dreadful thing
And the first motion, all the interim is
Like a phantasma or a hideous dream:
The genius and the mortal instruments
Are then in council; and the state of man,
Like to a little kingdom, suffers then
The nature of an insurrection.

*Re-enter* LUCIUS.

　*Luc.* Sir, 'tis your brother Cassius at the
　　door
Who doth desire to see you.
　*Bru.*　　　　　　　　　Is he alone?
　*Luc.* No, sir, there are more with him.
　*Bru.*　　　　　　　Do you know them?
　*Luc.* No, sir; their hats are pluck'd about
　　their ears,
And half their faces buried in their cloaks,
That by no means I may discover them
By any mark of favour.
　*Bru.*　　　　　　　　Let 'em enter.
　　　　　　　　　　　　[*Exit* LUCIUS.
They are the faction. O conspiracy, [by night,
Sham'st thou to show thy dangerous brow
When evils are most free? O, then, by day
Where wilt thou find a cavern dark enough
To mask thy monstrous visage? Seek none,
　　conspiracy;
Hide it in smiles of affability:
For if thou hath thy native semblance on,

Not Erebus itself were dim enough
To hide thee from prevention.

*Enter* CASSIUS, CASCA, DECIUS, CINNA,
MUTELLUS CIMBER, *and* TREBONIUS.

*Cas.* I think we are too bold upon your
rest:
Good-morrow, Brutus; do we trouble you?
*Bru.* I have been up this hour; awake all
night.                                [you?
Know I these men that come along with
*Cas.* Yes, every man of them; and no man
here
But honours you; and every one doth wish
You had but that opinion of yourself
Which every noble Roman bears of you.
This is Trebonius.
*Bru.*            He is welcome hither.
*Cas.* This, Decius Brutus.
*Bru.*            He is welcome too.
*Cas.* This, Casca; this, Cinna;
And this, Metellus Cimber.
*Bru.*            They are all welcome.
What watchful cares do interpose themselves
Betwixt your eyes and night?
*Cas.* Shall I entreat a word?
            [BRUTUS *and* CASSIUS *whisper.*
*Dec.* Here lies the east; doth not the day
break here?
*Casca.* No.                        [lines
*Cin.* O, pardon, sir, it doth; and yon grey
That fret the clouds are messengers of day.
*Casca.* You shall confess that you are both
deceiv'd.
Here, as I point my sword, the sun arises;
Which is a great way growing on the south,
Weighing the youthful season of the year.
Some two months hence up higher toward
the north
He first presents his fire; and the high east
Stands, as the Capitol, directly here.
*Bru.* Give me your hands all over, one by
one.
*Cas.* And let us swear our resolution.
*Bru.* No, not an oath: if not the face of
men,                                [abuse,—
The sufferance of our souls, the time's
If these be motives weak, break off betimes,
And every man hence to his idle bed;
So let high-sighted tyranny range on,
Till each man drop by lottery. But if these,
As I am sure they do, bear fire enough
To kindle cowards, and to steel with valour
The melting spirits of women; then, coun-
trymen,
What need we any spur, but our own cause,
To prick us to redress? what other bond
Than secret Romans, that have spoke the
word
And will not palter? and what other oath
Than honesty to honesty engag'd
That this shall be, or we will fall for it?
Swear priests, and cowards, and men caute-
lous,

Old feeble carrions, and such suffering souls
That welcome wrongs; unto bad causes swear
Such creatures as men doubt: but do not
stain
The even virtue of our enterprise,
Nor the insuppressive mettle of our spirits,
To think that or our cause or our perform-
ance
Did need an oath; when every drop of blood
That every Roman bears, and nobly bears,
Is guilty of a several bastardy
If he do break the smallest particle
Of any promise that hath pass'd from him.
*Cas.* But what of Cicero? shall we sound
him?
I think he will stand very strong with us.
*Casca.* Let us not leave him out.
*Cin.*                        No, by no means.
*Met.* O, let us have him; for his silver
hairs
Will purchase us a good opinion,
And buy men's voices to commend our deeds:
It shall be said his judgment rul'd our hands;
Our youths and wildness shall no whit ap-
pear,
But all be buried in his gravity.
*Bru.* O, name him not: let us not break
with him;
For he will never follow anything
That other men begin.
*Cas.*            Then leave him out.
*Casa.* Indeed he is not fit.
*Dec.* Shall no man else be touch'd but only
Cæsar?
*Cas.* Decius, well urg'd.—I think it is not
meet
Mark Antony, so well belov'd of Cæsar,
Should outlive Cæsar: we shall find of him
A shrewd contriver; and, you know, his
means,
If he improve them, may well stretch so far
As to annoy us all: which to prevent,
Let Antony and Cæsar fall together.
*Bru.* Our course will seem too bloody,
Caius Cassius,                        [limbs,—
To cut the head off and then hack the
Like wrath in death and envy afterwards;
For Antony is but a limb of Cæsar:
Let's be sacrificers, but not butchers, Caius.
We all stand up against the spirit of Cæsar;
And in the spirit of men there is no blood:
O that we, then, could come by Cæsar's spirit,
And not dismember Cæsar! But, alas,
Cæsar must bleed for it! And, gentle friends,
Let's kill him boldly, but not wrathfully;
Let's carve him as a dish fit for the gods,
Not hew him as a carcase fit for hounds:
And let our hearts, as subtle masters do,
Stir up their servants to an act of rage,
And after seem to chide 'em. This shall make
Our purpose necessary, and not envious:
Which so appearing to the common eyes,
We shall be call'd purgers, not murderers.
And for Mark Antony, think not of him;

For he can do no more than Cæsar's arm
When Cæsar's head is off.
　　*Cas.* 　　　　　Yet I fear him;
For in the engrafted love he bears to Cæsar,—
　　*Bru.* Alas, good Cassius, do not think of
him:
If he love Cæsar, all that he can do [Cæsar:
Is to himself,—take thought and die for
And that were much he should; for he is
given
To sports, to wildness, and much company.
　　*Treb.* There is no fear in him; let him not
die;
For he will live, and laugh at this hereafter.
　　　　　　　　　　　　　　[*Clock strikes.*
　　*Bru.* Peace, count the clock.
　　*Cas.* 　　　The clock hath stricken three.
　　*Treb.* 'Tis time to part.
　　*Cas.* 　　　But it is doubtful yet
Whether Cæsar will come forth to-day or no:
For he is superstitious grown of late;
Quite from the main opinion he held once
Of fantasy, of dreams, and ceremonies:
It may be these apparent prodigies,
The unaccustom'd terror of this night,
And the persuasion of his augurers,
May hold him from the Capitol to-day.
　　*Dec.* Never fear that: if he be so resolv'd
I can o'ersway him; for he loves to hear
That unicorns may be betray'd with trees,
And bears with glasses, elephants with holes.
Lions with toils, and men with flatterers:
But when I tell him he hates flatterers,
He says he does,—being then most flatter'd.
Let me work;
For I can give his humour the true bent,
And I will bring him to the Capitol.
　　*Cas.* Nay, we will all of us be there to
　　　　fetch him. 　　　　　[termost?
　　*Bru.* By the eighth hour: is that the ut-
　　*Cin.* Be that the uttermost, and fail not
then.
　　*Met.* Caius Ligarius doth bear Cæsar hard,
Who rated him for speaking well of Pompey:
I wonder none of you have thought of him.
　　*Bru.* Now, good Metellus, go along by
him:
He loves me well, and I have given him rea-
sons;
Send him but hither, and I'll fashion him.
　　*Cas.* The morning comes upon's: we'll
　　　　leave you, Brutus: 　　　　[member
And, friends, disperse yourselves: but all re-
What you have said, and show yourselves
　　　　true Romans.
　　*Bru.* Good gentlemen, look fresh and mer-
rily;
Let not our looks put on our purposes;
But bear it as our Roman actors do,
With untir'd spirits and formal constancy;
And so, good-morrow to you every one.
　　　　　　　　　　[*Exeunt all but* BRUTUS.
Boy! Lucius!—Fast asleep? it is no matter;
Enjoy the heavy honey-dew of slumber:

Thou hast no figures nor no fantasies
Which busy care draws in the brains of men;
Therefore thou sleep'st so sound.

*Enter* PORTIA.

　　*Por.* 　　　　　Brutus, my lord!
　　*Bru.* Portia, what mean you? wherefore
　　　　rise you now?
It is not for your health thus to commit
Your weak condition to the raw cold morn-
　　　　ing.
　　*Por.* Nor for yours neither. You have un-
　　　　gently, Brutus, 　　　　　[per,
Stole from my bed: and yesternight, at sup-
You suddenly arose, and walk'd about,
Musing and sighing, with your arms across;
And when I ask'd you what the matter was,
You star'd upon me with ungentle looks:
I urg'd you further; then you scratch'd your
　　　　head,
And too impatiently stamp'd with your foot:
Yet I insisted, yet you answer'd not;
But with an angry wafture of your hand
Gave sign for me to leave you: so I did;
Fearing to strengthen that impatience
Which seem'd too much enkindled; and
　　　　withal
Hoping it was but an effect of humour, [man.
Which sometime hath his hour with every
It will not let you eat, nor talk, nor sleep;
And, could it work so much upon your shape
As it hath much prevail'd on your condition,
I should not know you, Brutus. Dear my
　　　　lord, 　　　　　　[grief.
Make me acquainted with your cause of
　　*Bru.* I am not well in health, and that is
　　　　all.
　　*Por.* Brutus is wise, and were he not in
　　　　health,
He would embrace the means to come by it.
　　*Bru.* Why, so I do.—Good Portia, go to
　　　　bed.
　　*Por.* Is Brutus sick? and is it physical
To walk unbraced, and suck up the humours
Of the dank morning? What, is Brutus sick,—
And will he steal out of his wholesome bed,
To dare the vile contagion of the night,
And tempt the rheumy and unpurg'd air
To add unto his sickness? No, my Brutus;
You have some sick offence within your
　　　　mind,
Which by the right and virtue of my place
I ought to know of: and upon my knees
I charm you, by my once-commended
　　　　beauty,
By all your vows of love, and that great vow
Which did incorporate and make us one,
That you unfold to me, yourself, your half,
Why you are heavy; and what men to-night
Have had resort to you,—for here have been
Some six or seven, who did hide their faces
Even from darkness.
　　*Bru.* 　　　　　Kneel not, gentle Portia.

*Por.* I should not need if you were gentle
Brutus.
Within the bond of marriage, tell me, Brutus,
Is it excepted I should know no-secrets
That appertain to you? Am I yourself
But as it were in sort or limitation,—
To keep with you at meals, comfort your
bed, [the suburbs
And talk to you sometimes? Dwell I but in
Of your good pleasure? If it be no more,
Portia is Brutus' harlot, not his wife.
*Bru.* You are my true and honourable
wife;
As dear to me as are the ruddy drops
That visit my sad heart.
*Por.* If this were true, then should I know
this secret.
I grant I am a woman; but withal
A woman that Lord Brutus took to wife:
I grant I am a woman; but withal
A woman well-reputed,—Cato's daughter.
Think you I am no stronger than my sex,
Being so father'd and so husbanded?
Tell me your counsels, I will not disclose 'em:
I have made strong proof of my constancy,
Giving myself a voluntary wound [tience.
Here in the thigh: can I bear that with pa-
And not my husband's secrets?
*Bru.* O ye gods,
Render me worthy of this noble wife!
[*Knocking within.*
Hark, hark! one knocks: Portia, go in
awhile;
And by and by thy bosom shall partake
The secrets of my heart:
All my engagements I will construe to thee,
All the charactery of my sad brows.
Leave me with haste. [*Exit* PORTIA.
Lucius, who's that knocks?

*Enter* LUCIUS *with* LIGARIUS.

*Luc.* Here is a sick man that would speak
with you.
*Bru.* Caius Ligarius, that Metellus spake
of.—
Boy, stand aside.—Caius Ligarius,—how!
*Lig.* Vouchsafe good-morrow from a feeble
tongue.
*Bru.* O, what a time have you chose out,
brave Caius, [sick!
To wear a kerchief! Would you were not
*Lig.* I am not sick if Brutus have in hand
Any exploit worthy the name of honour.
*Bru.* Such an exploit have I in hand,
Ligarius,
Had you a healthful ear to hear of it.
*Lig.* By all the gods that Romans bow
before,
I here discard my sickness! Soul of Rome!
Brave son, deriv'd from honourable loins!
Thou, like an exorcist, hast conjur'd up
My mortified spirit. Now bid me run,
And I will strive with things impossible;
Yea, get the better of them. What's to do?

*Bru.* A piece of work that will make sick
men whole.
*Lig.* But are not some whole that we must
make sick? [Caius,
*Bru.* That must we also. What it is, my
I shall unfold to thee, as we are going
To whom it must be done.
*Lig.* Set on your foot;
And with a heart new fir'd I follow you
To do I know not what: but it sufficeth
That Brutus leads me on.
*Bru.* Follow me, then.
[*Exeunt.*

SCENE II.—ROME. *A Room in* CÆSAR'S
*Palace.*

*Thunder and lightning. Enter* CÆSAR *in his
night-gown.*

*Cæs.* Nor heaven nor earth have been at
peace to-night:
Thrice hath Calphurnia in her sleep cried out,
*Help, ho! They murder Cæsar!*—Who's
within?

*Enter a* Servant.

*Serv.* My lord?
*Cæs.* Go bid the priests do present sacri-
fice,
And bring me their opinions of success.
*Serv.* I will, my lord. [*Exit.*

*Enter* CALPHURNIA.

*Cal.* What mean you, Cæsar? Think you
to walk forth?
You shall not stir out of your house to-day.
*Cæs.* Cæsar shall forth: the things that
threaten'd me [shall see
Ne'er look'd but on my back; when they
The face of Cæsar they are vanished.
*Cal.* Cæsar, I never stood on ceremonies,
Yet now they fright me. There is one within,
Besides the things that we have heard and
seen, [watch.
Recounts most horrid sights seen by the
A lioness hath whelped in the streets;
And graves have yawn'd and yielded up
their dead;
Fierce fiery warriors fight upon the clouds,
In ranks and squadrons and right form of
war,
Which drizzled blood upon the Capitol;
The noise of battle hurtled in the air,
Horses did neigh, and dying men did groan;
And ghosts did shriek and squeal about the
streets.
O Cæsar, these things are beyond all use,
And I do fear them!
*Cæs.* What can be avoided,
Whose end is purpos'd by the mighty gods?
Yet Cæsar shall go forth; for these predic-
tions
Are to the world in general as to Cæsar.

*Cal.* When beggars die there are no com-
ets seen;            [of princes.
The heavens themselves blaze forth the death
*Cæs.* Cowards die many times before their
deaths;
The valiant never taste of death but once.
Of all the wonders that I yet have heard,
It seems to me most strange that men should
fear;
Seeing that death, a necessary end,
Will come when it will come.

*Re-enter* Servant.
                    What say the augurers?
*Serv.* They would not have you to stir
forth to-day.
Plucking the entrails of an offering forth,
They could not find a heart within the beast.
*Cæs.* The gods do this in shame of coward-
ice:
Cæsar should be a beast without a heart
If he should stay at home to-day for fear.
No, Cæsar shall not: danger knows full well
That Cæsar is more dangerous than he:
We are two lions litter'd in one day,
And I the elder and more terrible:—
And Cæsar shall go forth.
*Cal.*                      Alas, my lord,
Your wisdom is consum'd in confidence.
Do not go forth to-day: call it my fear [own.
That keeps you in the house, and not your
We'll send Mark Antony to the senate-house;
And he shall say you are not well to-day:
Let me, upon my knee, prevail in this.
*Cæs.* Mark Antony shall say I am not
well:
And for thy humour I will stay at home.

*Enter* Decius.
Here's Decius Brutus, he shall tell them so.
*Dec.* Cæsar, all hail! Good-morrow,
worthy Cæsar:
I come to fetch you to the senate-house.
*Cæs.* And you are come in very happy
time,
To bear my greeting to the senators,
And tell them that I will not come to-day:
Cannot, is false; and that I dare not, falser:
I will not come to-day,—tell them so, Decius.
*Cal.* Say he is sick.
*Cæs.*                    Shall Cæsar send a lie?
Have I in conquest stretch'd mine arm so far,
To be afeard to tell graybeards the truth?
Decius, go tell them Cæsar will not come.
*Dec.* Most mighty Cæsar, let me know
some cause,
Lest I be laugh'd at when I tell them so.
*Cæs.* The cause is in my will,—I will not
come;
That is enough to satisfy the senate.
But for your private satisfaction,
Because I love you. I will let you know,—
Calphurnia here, my wife, stays me at home:
She dreamt to-night she saw my statua,

Which, like a fountain with a hundred spouts,
Did run pure blood; and many lusty Romans
Came smiling and did bathe their hands in it:
And these does she apply for warnings and
portents,
And evils imminent; and on her knee
Hath begg'd that I will stay at home to-day.
*Dec.* This dream is all amiss interpreted;
It was a vision fair and fortunate:
Your statue spouting blood in many pipes,
In which so many smiling Romans bath'd,
Signifies that from you great Rome shall suck
Reviving blood; and that great men shall
press
For tinctures, stains, relics, and cognizance.
This by Calphurnia's dream is signified.
*Cæs.* And this way have you well ex-
pounded it.
*Dec.* I have, when you have heard what I
can say:               [cluded
And know it now,—the senate have con-
To give this day a crown to mighty Cæsar.
If you shall send them word you will not
come,                    [mock,
Their minds may change. Besides, it were a
Apt to be render'd, for some one to say,
*Break up the senate till another time,*
*When Cæsar's wife shall meet with better*
*dreams.*
If Cæsar hide himself, shall they not whisper,
*Lo, Cæsar is afraid?*
Pardon me, Cæsar; for my dear dear love
To your proceeding bids me tell you this;
And reason to my love is liable.
*Cæs.* How foolish do your fears seem now,
Calphurnia!
I am ashamed I did yield to them.—
Give me my robe for I will go:

*Enter* Publius, Brutus, Ligarius, Metel-
lus, Casca, Trebonis, *and* Cinna.
And look where Publius is come to fetch me.
*Pub.* Good-morrow, Cæsar.
*Cæs.*                        Welcome, Publius.—
What, Brutus, are you stirred so early too?—
Good-morrow, Casca.—Caius Ligarius,
Cæsar was ne'er so much your enemy
As that same ague which hath made you
lean.—
What is't o'clock.
*Bru.*                    Cæsar, 'tis strucken eight.
*Cæs.* I thank you for your pains and
courtesy.

*Enter* Antony.
See! Antony, that revels long o' nights
Is notwithstanding up.—
Good-morrow, Antony.
*Ant.*                        So to most noble Cæsar.
*Cæs.* Bid them prepare within.
I am to blame to be thus waited for.—
Now Cinna;—now Metellus:—what, Tre-
bonius!
I have an hour's talk in store for you;

Remember that you call on me to-day:
Be near me, that I may remember you.

*Treb.* Cæsar, I will:—and so near will I
 be,       [*Aside.*
That your best friends shall wish I had been
 further.

*Cæs.* Good friends, go in and taste some
 wine with me;    [*gether.*
And we, like friends, will straightway go to-

*Bru.* That every like is not the same, O
 Cæsar,
The heart of Brutus yearns to think upon!
        [*Exeunt.*

SCENE III.—ROME. *A Street near the
Capitol.*

*Enter* ARTEMIDORUS *reading a paper.*

*Art.* Cæsar, beware of Brutus; take heed
of Cassius; come nòt near Casca; havè an
eye to Cinna; trust not Trebonius; mark well
Metellus Cimber; Decius Brutus loves thee
not; thou hast wronged Caius Ligarius.
There is but one mind in all these men, and
it is bent against Cæsar. If thou beest not
immortal, look about you: security gives way
to conspiracy. The mighty gods defend thee!
Thy lover, ARTEMIDORUS.
Here will I stand till Cæsar pass along,
And as a suitor will I give him this.
My heart laments that virtue cannot live
Out of the teeth of emulation.
If thou read this, O Cæsar, thou mayst live;
If not, the fates with traitors do contrive.
        [*Exit.*

SCENE IV.—ROME. *Another part of the same
Street, before the House of* BRUTUS.

*Enter* PORTIA *and* LUCIUS.

*Por.* I pr'ythee, boy, run to the senate-
 house;
Stay not to answer me, but get thee gone:
Why dost thou stay?

*Luc.*    To know my errand, madam.

*Por.* I would have had thee there and here
 again      [there.—
Ere I can tell thee what thou shouldst do
O constancy, be strong upon my side!
Set a huge mountain 'tween my heart and
 tongue!
I have a man's mind, but a woman's might.
How hard it is for women to keep counsel!—
Art thou here yet?

*Luc.*    Madam, what should I do?
Run to the Capitol, and nothing else?
And so return to you, and nothing else?

*Por.* Yes, bring me word, boy, if thy lord
 look well,
For he went sickly forth: and take good note
What Cæsar doth, what suitors press to him.
Hark, boy! what noise is that?

*Luc.* I hear none, madam.

*Por.*     Pr'ythee, listen well:
I heard a bustling rumour, like a fray,

And the wind brings it from the Capitol.

*Luc.* Sooth, madam, I hear nothing.

*Enter* ARTEMIDORUS.

*Por.*     Come hither, fellow:
Which way hast thou been?

*Art.*    At mine own house, good lady.

*Por.* What is 't o'clock?

*Art.* About the ninth hour, lady.

*Por.* Is Cæsar yet gone to the Capitol?

*Art.* Madam, not yet: I go to take my
 stand,
To see him pass on to the Capitol.

*Por.* Thou hast some suit to Cæsar, hast
 thou not?

*Art.* That I have, lady: if it will please
 Cæsar
To be so good to Cæsar as to hear me,
I shall beseech him to befriend himself.

*Por.* Why, know'st thou any harm's intended towards him?

*Art.* None that I know will be, much that
 I fear may chance.
Good-morrow to you. Here the street is
 narrow:
The throng that follows Cæsar at the heels
Of senators, of prætors, common suitors,
Will crowd a feeble man almost to death:
I'll get me to a place more void, and there
Speak to great Cæsar as he comes along.
        [*Exit.*

*Por.* I must go in.—Ah me! how weak a
 thing
The heart of woman is! O Brutus,
The heavens speed thee in thine enterprise!—
Sure the boy heard me.—Brutus hath a suit
That Cæsar will not grant.—O, I grow
 faint.—
Run, Lucius, and commend me to my lord;
Say I am merry: come to me again,
And bring me word what he doth say to thee.
      [*Exeunt severally.*

ACT III.

SCENE I.—ROME. *The Capitol; the Senate
sitting.*

*A crowd of* People *in the street leading to the
Capitol; among them* ARTEMIDORUS *and
the* Soothsayer. *Flourish. Enter* CÆSAR,
BRUTUS, CASSIUS, CASCA, DECIUS, ME-
TELLUS, TREBONIUS, CINNA, ANTONY,
LEPIDUS, POPILIUS, *and others.*

*Cæs.* The ides of March are come.

*Sooth.* Ay, Cæsar; but not gone.

*Art.* Hail, Cæsar! Read this schedule.

*Dec.* Trebonius doth desire you to o'er
 read,
At your best leisure, this his humble suit.

*Art.* O Cæsar, read mine first; for mine's
 a suit      [Cæsar.
That touches Cæsar nearer: read it, great

*Cæs.* What touches us ourself shall be last
 serv'd.

*Art.* Delay not, Cæsar; read it instantly.

*Cæs.* What, is the fellow mad?

*Pub.* 　　　　　　Sirrah, give place.

*Cas.* What, urge you your petitions in the street?

Come to the Capitol.

*Cæsar enters the Capitol, the rest following. All the Senators rise.*

*Pop.* I wish your enterprise to-day may thrive.

*Cas.* What enterprise, Popilius?

*Pop.* 　　　　　　　　Fare you well.
　　　　　　　　[*Advances to* Cæsar.

*Bru.* What said Popilius Lena?

*Cas.* He wish'd to-day our enterprise might thrive.

I fear our purpose is discovered.

*Bru.* Look how he makes to Cæsar: mark him. 　　　　　　　[tion.—

*Cas.* Casca, be sudden, for we fear preven-

Brutus, what shall be done? If this be known,

Cassius or Cæsar never shall turn back,

For I will slay myself.

*Bru.* 　　　　　Cassius, be constant:

Popilius Lena speaks not of our purposes;

For, look, he smiles, and Cæsar doth not change.

*Cas.* Trebonius knows his time; for, look you, Brutus,

He draws Mark Antony out of the way.

　　　[*Exeunt* Ant. *and* Treb. Cæsar *and the* Senators *take their seats.*

*Dec.* Where is Metellus Cimber? Let him go,

And presently prefer his suit to Cæsar.

*Bru.* He is address'd: press near and second him.

*Cin.* Casca, you are the first that rears your hand.

*Casca.* Are we all ready?

*Cæs.* What is now amiss

That Cæsar and his senate must redress?

*Met.* Most high, most mighty, and most puissant Cæsar,

Metellus Cimber throws before thy seat

An humble heart,— 　　　　　[*Kneeling.*

*Cæs.* I must prevent thee, Cimber.

These couchings and these lowly courtesies

Might fire the blood of ordinary men,

And turn pre-ordinance and first decree

Into the law of children. Be not fond

To think that Cæsar bears such rebel blood

That will be thaw'd from the true quality

With that which melteth fools; I mean, sweet words,

Low crooked curt'sies, and base spaniel fawning.

Thy brother by decree is banished: 　　[him,

If thou dost bend, and pray, and fawn for

I spurn thee like a cur out of my way.

Know, Cæsar doth not wrong; nor without cause

Will he be satisfied.

*Met.* Is there no voice more worthy than my own,

To sound more sweetly in great Cæsar's ear

For the repealing of my banish'd brother?

*Bru.* I kiss thy hand, but not in flattery, Cæsar,

Desiring thee that Publius Cimber may

Have an immediate freedom of repeal.

*Cæs.* What, Brutus!

*Cas.* 　　　　Pardon, Cæsar; Cæsar, pardon:

As low as to thy foot doth Cassius fall,

To beg enfranchisement for Publius Cimber.

*Cæs.* I could be well mov'd if I were as you;

If I could pray to move, prayers would move me:

But I am constant as the northern star,

Of whose true-fix'd and resting quality

There is no fellow in the firmament.

The skies are painted with unnumber'd sparks,—

They are all fire, and every one doth shine;

But there's but one in all doth hold his place:

So in the world,—'tis furnish'd well with men,

And men are flesh and blood, and apprehensive;

Yet in the number I do know but one

That unassailable holds on his rank,

Unshak'd of motion: and that I am he,

Let me a little show it even in this,—

That I was constant Cimber should be banish'd,

And constant do remain to keep him so.

*Cin.* O Cæsar,—

*Cæs.* 　　Hence! wilt thou lift up Olympus?

*Dec.* Great Cæsar,—

*Cæs.* 　　Doth not Brutus bootless kneel?

*Casca.* Speak, hands, for me!

　　　[Casca *stabs* Cæsar *in the neck.* Cæsar *catches hold of his arm. He is then stabbed by several other Conspirators, and at last by* Marcus Brutus.

*Cæs.* Et tu, Brute?—Then fall, Cæsar!

　　　[*Dies. The* Senators *and* People *retire in confusion.*

*Cin.* Liberty! Freedom! Tyranny is dead!—

Run hence proclaim, cry it about the streets.

*Cas.* Some to the common pulpits, and cry out,

*Liberty, freedom, and enfranchisement!*

*Bru.* People and senators! be not affrighted;

Fly not; stand still: ambition's debt is paid.

*Casca.* Go to the pulpit, Brutus.

*Dec.* 　　　　　And Cassius too.

*Bru.* Where's Publius?

*Cin.* Here, quite confounded with this mutiny.

*Met.* Stand fast together, lest some friend of Cæsar's

Should chance,— 　　　　　　[cheer;

*Bru.* Talk not of standing.—Publius, good

There is no harm intended to your person,
Nor to no Roman else: so tell them, Publius.

*Cas.* And leave us, Publius; lest that the people,
Rushing on us, should do your age some mischief.

*Bru.* Do so: and let no man abide this deed,
But we the doers.

*Re-enter* TREBONIUS.

*Cas.* Where is Antony?

*Tre.*       Fled to his house amaz'd:
Men, wives, and children stare, cry out, and run,
As it were doomsday.

*Bru.* Fates! we will know your pleasures.—
That we shall die, we know; 'tis but the time,
And drawing days out, that men stand upon.

*Cas.* Why, he that cuts off twenty years of life,
Cuts off so many years of fearing death.

*Bru.* Grant that, and then is death a benefit:
So are we Cæsar's friends, that have abridg'd
His time of fearing death.—Stoop, Romans, stoop,
And let us bathe our hands in Cæsar's blood
Up to the elbows, and besmear our swords:
Then walk we forth even to the market-place,
And, waving our red weapons o'er our heads,
Let's all cry, *Peace! freedom! and liberty!*

*Cas.* Stoop then, and wash.—How many ages hence
Shall this our lofty scene be acted over,
In states unborn and accents yet unknown!

*Bru.* How many times shall Cæsar bleed in sport,
That now on Pompey's basis lies along
No worthier than the dust!

*Cas.*       So oft as that shall be,
So often shall the knot of us be call'd
The men that gave their country liberty.

*Dec.* What, shall we forth?

*Cas.*       Ay, every man away:
Brutus shall lead; and we will grace his heels
With the most boldest and best hearts of Rome.

*Bru.* Soft, who comes here?

*Enter a* Servant.

      A friend of Antony's.

*Serv.* Thus, Brutus, did my master bid me kneel;
Thus did Mark Antony bid me fall down;
And, being prostrate, thus he bade me say:—
Brutus is noble, wise, valiant, and honest;
Cæsar was mighty, bold, royal, and loving:
Say I lov'd Brutus, and I honour him; [him.
Say I fear'd Cæsar, honour'd him, and lov'd
If Brutus will vouchsafe that Antony
May safely come to him, and be resolv'd

How Cæsar hath deserv'd to lie in death,
Mark Antony shall not love Cæsar dead
So well as Brutus living; but will follow
The fortunes and affairs of noble Brutus
Through the hazards of this untrod state
With all true faith. So says my master Antony.

*Bru.* Thy master is a wise and valiant Roman:
I never thought him worse.
Tell him, so please him come unto this place,
He shall be satisfied; and, by my honour,
Depart untouch'd.

*Serv.*       I'll fetch him presently. [*Exit.*

*Bru.* I know that we shall have him well to friend.

*Cas.* I wish we may: but yet have I a mind
That fears him much; and my misgiving still
Falls shrewdly to the purpose.

*Bru.* But here comes Antony.

*Re-enter* ANTONY.

      Welcome, Mark Antony.

*Ant.* O mighty Cæsar! dost thou lie so low?
Are all thy conquests, glories, triumphs, spoils, [well.—
Shrunk to this little measure?—Fare thee
I know not, gentlemen, what you intend,
Who else must be let blood, who else is rank:
If I myself, there is no hour so fit
As Cæsar's death's hour; nor no instrument
Of half that worth as those your swords, made rich
With the most noble blood of all this world.
I do beseech ye, if you bear me hard,
Now, whilst your purpled hands do reek and smoke,
Fulfil your pleasure. Live a thousand years,
I shall not find myself so apt to die:
No place will please me so, no mean of death
As here by Cæsar, and by you cut off,
The choice and master spirits of this age.

*Bru.* O Antony! beg not your death of us.
Though now we must appear bloody and cruel,
As by our hands and this our present act
You see we do; yet see you but our hands,
And this the bleeding business they have done:
Our hearts you see not,—they are pitiful;
And pity to the general wrong of Rome,—
As fire drives out fire, so pity pity,—
Hath done this deed on Cæsar. For your part,
To you our swords have leaden points, Mark Antony:
Our arms no strength of malice, and our hearts,
Of brothers' temper, do receive you in
With all kind love, good thoughts, and reverence. [man's

*Cas.* Your voice shall be as strong as any
In the disposing of new dignities.

*Bru.* Only be patient till we have appeas'd
The multitude, beside themselves with fear,
And then we will deliver you the cause
Why I, that did love Cæsar when I struck
him,
Have thus proceeded.
   *Ant.*      I doubt not of your wisdom.
Let each man render me his bloody hand:
First, Marcus Brutus, will I shake with
you;—
Next, Caius Cassius, do I take your hand;—
Now, Decius Brutus, yours;—now yours,
Metellus;—
Yours, Cinna;—and, my valiant Casca,
yours;—
Though last, not least in love, yours, good
Trebonius.
Gentlemen all,—alas, what shall I say?
My credit now stands on such slippery
ground
That one of two bad ways you must conceit
me,
Either a coward or a flatterer.—
That I did love thee, Cæsar, O, 'tis true:
If then, thy spirit look upon us now,
Shall it not grieve thee dearer than thy
death
To see thy Antony making his peace,
Shaking the bloody fingers of thy foes,
Most noble! in the presence of thy corse?
Had I as many eyes as thou hast wounds,
Weeping as fast as they stream forth thy
blood,
It would become me better than to close
In terms of friendship with thine enemies.
Pardon me, Julius!—Here wast thou bay'd,
brave hart;
Here didst thou fall; and here thy hunters
stand,
Sign'd in thy spoil, and crimson'd in thy
Lethe.—
O world, thou wast the forest to this hart;
And this, indeed, O world, the heart of
thee.—
How like a deer strucken by many princes
Dost thou here lie!
   *Cas.* Mark Antony,—
   *Ant.*      Pardon me, Caius Cassius:
The enemies of Cæsar shall say this;
Then in a friend it is cold modesty.
   *Cas.* I blame you not for praising Cæsar
so;
But what compáct mean you to have with
us?
Will you be prick'd in number of our
friends;
Or shall we on, and not depend on you?
   *Ant.* Therefore I took your hands; but
was, indeed,
Sway'd from the point by looking down on
Cæsar.
Friends am I with you all, and love you all;
Upon this hope, that you shall give me
reasons

Why and wherein Cæsar was dangerous.
   *Bru.* Or else were this a savage spectacle:
Our reasons are so full of good regard
That were you, Antony, the son of Cæsar,
You should be satisfied.
   *Ant.*      That's all I seek:
And am moreover suitor that I may
Produce his body to the market-place;
And in the pulpit, as becomes a friend,
Speak in the order of his funeral.
   *Bru.* You shall, Mark Antony.
   *Cas.*      Brutus, a word with you.—
You know not what you do: do not consent
That Antony speak in his funeral:
Know you how much the people may be
mov'd
By that which he will utter?
                [*Aside to* BRUTUS.
   *Bru.*      By your pardon;—
I will myself into the pulpit first,
And show the reason of our Cæsar's death:
What Antony shall speak, I will protest
He speaks by leave and by permission;
And that we are contented Cæsar shall
Have all true rites and lawful ceremonies.
It shall advantage more than do us wrong.
   *Cas.* I know not what may fall; I like it
not.
   *Bru.* Mark Antony, here, take you Cæsar's
body.
You shall not in your funeral speech blame
us,
But speak all good you can devise of Cæsar;
And say you do 't by our permission;
Else shall you not have any hand at all
About his funeral: and you shall speak
In the same pulpit whereto I am going,
After my speech is ended.
   *Ant.*      Be it so;
I do desire no more.
   *Bru.* Prepare the body then, and follow us.
              [*Exeunt all but* ANTONY.
   *Ant.* O, pardon me, thou bleeding piece of
earth,
That I am meek and gentle with these
butchers!
Thou art the ruins of the noblest man
That ever lived in the tide of times.
Woe to the hand that shed this costly blood!
Over thy wounds now do I prophesy,—
Which like dumb mouths do ope their ruby
lips,
To beg the voice and utterance of my
tongue,—
A curse shall light upon the limbs of men;
Domestic fury and fierce civil strife
Shall cumber all the parts of Italy;
Blood and destruction shall be so in use,
And dreadful objects so familiar,
That mothers shall but smile when they be-
hold
Their infants quarter'd with the hands of
war;
All pity chok'd with custom of fell deeds:

And Cæsar's spirit, ranging for revenge,
With Até by his side come hot from hell,
Shall in these confines with a monarch's
   voice
Cry *Havoc*, and let slip the dogs of war;
That this foul deed shall smell above the
   earth
With carrion men, groaning for burial.

        *Enter a* Servant.

You serve Octavius Cæsar, do you not?
   *Serv.* I do, Mark Antony.
   *Ant.* Cæsar did write for him to come to
Rome.                 [ing;
   *Serv.* He did receive his letters, and is com-
And bid me say to you by word of mouth,—
O Cæsar!—         [*Seeing the body.*
   *Ant.* Thy heart is big, get thee apart and
   weep.
Passion, I see, is catching; for mine eyes,
Seeing those beads of sorrow stand in thine,
Began to water. Is thy master coming?
   *Serv.* He lies to-night within· seven leagues
   of Rome.
   *Ant.* Post back with speed, and tell him
   what hath chanc'd:
Here is a mourning Rome, a dangerous Rome,
No Rome of safety for Octavius yet;
Hie hence and tell him so. Yet, stay awhile;
Thou shalt not back till I have borne this
   corse
Into the market-place: there shall I try,
In my oration, how the people take
The cruel issue of these bloody men;
According to the which thou shalt discourse
To young Octavius of the state of things.
Lend me your hand.
        [*Exeunt with* CÆSAR'S *body.*

   SCENE II.—ROME. *The Forum.*

*Enter* BRUTUS *and* CASSIUS, *and a throng of*
        Citizens.

   *Citizens.* We will be satisfied; let us be
satisfied.        [ence, friends.—
   *Bru.* Then follow me, and give me audi-
Cassius, go you into the other street,
And part the numbers.—
Those that will hear me speak, let 'em stay
   here;
Those that will follow Cassius, go with him;
And public reasons shall be rendered
Of Cæsar's death.
   1 *Cit.*        I will hear Brutus speak.
   2· *Cit.* I will hear Cassius; and compare
   their reasons,
When severally we hear them rendered.
   [*Exit* CASSIUS, *with some of the* Citizens.
     BRUTUS *goes into the Rostrum.*
   3 *Cit.* The noble Brutus is ascended:
   silence!
   *Bru.* Be patient till the last.
Romans, countrymen, and lovers! hear me
for my cause; and be silent, that you may

hear: believe me for mine honour; and have
respect to mine honour, that you may believe: censure me in your wisdom; and awake
your senses, that you may the better judge.
If there be any in this assembly, any dear
friend of Cæsar's, to him I say that Brutus'
love to Cæsar was no less than his. If, then,
that friend demand why Brutus rose against
Cæsar, this is my answer,—Not that I loved
Cæsar less, but that I loved Rome more. Had
you rather Cæsar were living, and die all
slaves, than that Cæsar were dead, to live all
free men? As Cæsar loved me, I weep for
him; as he was fortunate, I rejoice at it; as
he was valiant, I honour him: but, as he was
ambitious, I slew him: there is tears for his
love; joy for his fortune; honour for his
valour; and death for his ambition. Who is
here so base that would be a bondman? If
any, speak; for him have I offended. Who is
here so rude that would not be a Roman?
If any, speak; for him have I offended. Who
is here so vile that will not love his country?
If any, speak; for him have I offended. I
pause for a reply.
   *Citizens.* None, Brutus, none.
   *Bru.* Then none have I offended. I have
done no more to Cæsar than you shall do to
Brutus. The question of his death is enrolled
in the Capitol; his glory not extenuated,
wherein he was worthy; nor his offences enforced, for which he suffered death. Here
comes his body, mourn'd by Mark Antony:

*Enter* ANTONY *and others with* CÆSAR'S *body.*
who, though he had no hand in his death,
shall receive the benefit of his dying,—a
place in the commonwealth; as which of you
shall not? With this I depart,—that, as I
slew my best lover for the good of Rome, I
have the same dagger for myself, when it
shall please my country to need my death.
   *Citizens.* Live, Brutus! live, live!
   1 *Cit.* Bring him with triumph home unto
   his house.
   2 *Cit.* Give him a statue with his ancestors.
   3 *Cit.* Let him be Cæsar.
   4 *Cit.*       Cæsar's better parts
Shall be crown'd in Brutus.
   1 *Cit.* We'll bring him to his house with
   shouts and clamours.
   *Bru.* My countrymen,—
   2 *Cit.*    Peace, silence! Brutus speaks.
   1 *Cit.* Peace, ho!
   *Bru.* Good countrymen, let me depart
   alone,
And for my sake stay here with Antony:
Do grace to Cæsar's corse, and grace his
   speech
Tending to Cæsar's glories; which Mark
   Antony,
By our permission, is allow'd to make.
I do entreat you, not a man depart,
Save I alone, till Antony have spoke. [*Exit.*

1 *Cit.* Stay, ho! and let us hear Mark
　Antony.

3 *Cit.* Let him go up into the public chair;
We'll hear him.—Noble Antony, go up.

*Ant.* For Brutus' sake I am behólden to
　you.　　　　　　　　　　　　　[*Goes up.*

4 *Cit.* What does he say of Brutus?

3 *Cit.*　　　　　He says, for Brutus' sake
He finds himself beholden to us all.

4 *Cit.* 'Twere best he speak no harm of
　Brutus here.

1 *Cit.* This Cæsar was a tyrant.

3 *Cit.*　　　　　Nay, that's certain:
We are bless'd that Rome is rid of him.

2 *Cit.* Peace! let us hear what Antony can
　say.

*Ant.* You gentle Romans,—

*Cit.*　　　　　Peace, ho! let us hear him.

*Ant.* Friends, Romans, countrymen, lend
　me your ears;
I come to bury Cæsar, not to praise him.
The evil that men do lives after them;
The good is oft interred with their bones;
So let it be with Cæsar. The noble Brutus
Hath told you Cæsar was ambitious:
If it were so, it was a grievous fault;
And grievously hath Cæsar answer'd it.
Here, under leave of Brutus and the rest,—
For Brutus is an honourable man;
So are they all, all honourable men,—
Come I to speak in Cæsar's funeral.
He was my friend, faithful and just to me:
But Brutus says he was ambitious;
And Brutus is an honourable man.
He hath brought many captives home to
　Rome,　　.
Whose ransoms did the general coffers fill:
Did this in Cæsar seem ambitious?
When that the poor have cried, Cæsar hath
　wept:
Ambition should be made of sterner stuff:
Yet Brutus says he was ambitious;
And Brutus is an honourable man.
You all did see that on the Lupercal
I thrice presented him a kingly crown,
Which he did thrice refuse: was this am-
　bition?
Yet Brutus says he was ambitious;
And, sure, he is an honourable man.
I speak not to disprove what Brutus spoke,
But here I am to speak what I do know.
You all did love him once,—not without
　cause:　　　　　　　　　　　[for him?
What cause withholds you, then, to mourn
O judgment, thou art fled to brutish beasts,
And men have lost their reason!—Bear with
　me;
My heart is in the coffin there with Cæsar,
And I must pause till it come back to me.

1 *Cit.* Methinks there is much reason in
　his sayings.

2 *Cit.* If thou consider rightly of the mat-
　ter,
Cæsar has had great wrong.

3 *Cit.*　　　　　　　　Has he, masters?
I fear there will a worse come in his place.

4 *Cit.* Mark'd ye his words? He would not
　take the crown;
Therefore 'tis certain he was not ambitious.

1 *Cit.* If it be found so, some will dear
　abide it.

2 *Cit.* Poor soul! his eyes are red as fire
　with weeping.

3 *Cit.* There's not a nobler man in Rome
　than Antony.　　　　　　　　　[speak.

4 *Cit.* Now mark him, he begins again to

*Ant.* But yesterday the word of Cæsar
　might
Have stood against the world: now lies he
　there,
And none so poor to do him reverence.
O masters, if I were dispos'd to stir
Your hearts and minds to mutiny and rage,
I should do Brutus wrong, and Cassius
　wrong,
Who, you all know, are honourable men:
I will not do them wrong; I rather choose
To wrong the dead, to wrong myself and
　you,
Than I will wrong such honourable men.
But here's a parchment with the seal of
　Cæsar,—
I found it in his closet,—'tis his will:
Let but the commons hear this testament,—
Which, pardon me, I do not mean to read,—
And they would go and kiss dead Cæsar's
　wounds,
And dip their napkins in his sacred blood;
Yea, beg a hair of him for memory,
And, dying, mention it within their wills,
Bequeathing it as a rich legacy
Unto their issue.

4 *Cit.* We'll hear the will: read it, Mark
　Antony.

*Citizens.* The will, the will! we will hear
　Cæsar's will.

*Ant.* Have patience, gentle friends, I must
　not read it;
It is not meet you know how Cæsar lov'd
　you.
You are not wood, you are not stones, but
　men;
And, being men, hearing the will of Cæsar,
It will inflame you,—it will make you mad:
'Tis good you know not that you are his
　heirs;
For, if you should, O, what would come of it!

4 *Cit.* Read the will; we'll hear it, Antony;
You shall read us the will,—Cæsar's will.

*Ant.* Will you be patient? will you stay
　awhile?
I have o'ershot myself to tell you of it:
I fear I wrong the honourable men
Whose daggers have stabb'd Cæsar; I do fear
　it.

4 *Cit.* They were traitors: honourable
　men!

*Citizens.* The will! the testament!

2 *Cit*. They were villains, murderers: the will! read the will! [will?

*Ant*. You will compel me, then, to read the Then make a ring about the corse of Cæsar, And let me show you him that made the will. Shall I descend? and will you give me leave?

*Citizens*. Come down.

2 *Cit*. Descend. [ANTONY *comes down*.

3 *Cit*. You shall have leave.

4 *Cit*. A ring; stand round. [the body.

1 *Cit*. Stand from the hearse, stand from

2 *Cit*. Room for Antony,—most noble Antony! [off.

*Ant*. Nay, press not so upon me; stand far

*Citizens*. Stand back; room; bear back!

*Ant*. If you have tears, prepare to shed them now.

You all do know this mantle: I remember
The first time ever Cæsar put it on;
'Twas on a summer's evening, in his tent,
That day he overcame the Nervii:—
Look! in this place ran Cassius' dagger through:
See what a rent the envious Casca made:
Through this the well-beloved Brutus stabb'd;
And, as he pluck'd his cursed steel away,
Mark how the blood of Cæsar follow'd it,
As rushing out of doors, to be resolv'd
If Brutus so unkindly knock'd or no;
For Brutus, as you know, was Cæsar's angel:
Judge, O you gods, how dearly Cæsar loved him!
This was the most unkindest cut of all;
For when the noble Cæsar saw him stab,
Ingratitude, more strong than traitors' arms,
Quite vanquish'd him: then burst his mighty heart;
And, in his mantle muffling up his face,
Even at the base of Pompey's statua,
Which all the while ran blood, great Cæsar fell.
O, what a fall was there, my countrymen!
Then I, and you, and all of us fell down,
Whilst bloody treason flourish'd over us.
O, now you weep; and I perceive you feel
The dint of pity: these are gracious drops.
Kind souls, what, weep you when you but behold
Our Cæsar's vesture wounded? Look you here, [ors.
Here is himself, marr'd, as you see, with trait-

1 *Cit*. O piteous spectacle!

2 *Cit*. O noble Cæsar!

3 *Cit*. O woeful day!

4 *Cit*. O traitors, villains!

1 *Cit*. O most bloody sight!

2 *Cit*. We will be revenged: revenge,— about,—seek,— burn,—fire,— kill,—slay,— let not a traitor live!

*Ant*. Stay, countrymen.

1 *Cit*. Peace there! hear the noble Antony.

2 *Cit*. We'll hear him, we'll follow him, we'll die with him.

*Ant*. Good friends, sweet friends, let me not stir you up
To such a sudden flood of mutiny.
They that have done this deed are honourable;—
What private griefs they have, alas, I know not,
That made them do it;—they are wise and honourable,
And will, no doubt, with reasons answer you.
I come not, friends, to steal away your hearts:
I am no orator, as Brutus is;
But, as you know me all, a plain blunt man,
That love my friend; and that they know full well
That gave me public leave to speak of him:
For I have neither wit, nor words, nor worth,
Action, nor utterance, nor the power of speech,
To stir men's blood: I only speak right on;
I tell you that which you yourselves do know;
Show you sweet Cæsar's wounds, poor poor dumb mouths,
And bid them speak for me: but were I Brutus,
And Brutus Antony, there were an Antony
Would ruffle up your spirits, and put a tongue
In every wound of Cæsar, that should move
The stones of Rome to rise and mutiny.

*Citizens*. We'll mutiny.

1 *Cit*. We'll burn the house of Brutus.

3 *Cit*. Away, then! come seek the conspirators.

*Ant*. Yet hear me, countrymen; yet hear me speak.

*Citizens*. Peace, ho! hear Antony, most noble Antony.

*Ant*. Why, friends, you go to do you know not what:
Wherein hath Cæsar thus deserv'd your loves?
Alas, you know not,—I must tell you, then.—
You have forgot the will I told you of.

*Citizens*. Most true;—the will:—let's stay and hear the will.

*Ant*. Here is the will and under Cæsar's seal
To every Roman citizen he gives,
To every several man, seventy-five drachmas.

2 *Cit*. Most noble Cæsar!—we'll revenge his death.

3 *Cit*. O royal Cæsar!

*Ant*. Hear me with patience.

*Citizens*. Peace, ho!

*Ant*. Moreover, he hath left you all his walks, [orchards
His private arbours, and new-planted
On this side Tiber; he hath left them you,
And to your heirs for ever,—common pleasures,

To walk abroad and recreate yourselves.
Here was a Cæsar! when comes such another?
1 *Cit.* Never, never.—Come away, away!
We'll burn his body in the holy place,
And with the brands fire the traitors' houses.
Take up the body.
2 *Cit.* Go, fetch fire.
3 *Cit.* Pluck down benches.
4 *Cit.* Pluck down forms, windows, anything. [*Exeunt* Citizens *with the body.*
*Ant.* Now let it work: mischief, thou art
afoot.
Take thou what course thou wilt!

*Enter a* Servant.

How now, fellow!
*Serv.* Sir, Octavius is already come to
Rome.
*Ant.* Where is he?
*Serv.* He and Lepidus are at Cæsar's house.
*Ant.* And thither will I straight to visit
him:
He comes upon a wish. Fortune is merry,
And in this mood will give us anything.
*Serv.* I heard him say Brutus and Cassius
Are rid like madmen through the gates of
Rome.
*Ant.* Belike they had some notice of the
people,
How I had mov'd them. Bring me to Oc-
tavius. [*Exeunt.*

SCENE III.—ROME. *A Street.*

*Enter* CINNA *the Poet.*

*Cin.* I dreamt to-night that I did feast
with Cæsar,
And things unlucky charge my fantasy:
I have no will to wander forth of doors,
Yet something leads me forth.

*Enter* Citizens.

1 *Cit.* What is your name?
2 *Cit.* Whither are you going?
3 *Cit.* Where do you dwell?
4 *Cit.* Are you a married man or a bachelor?
2 *Cit.* Answer every man directly.
1 *Cit.* Ay, and briefly.
4 *Cit.* Ay, and wisely.
3 *Cit.* Ay, and truly, you were best.
*Cin.* What is my name? Whither am I
going? Where do I dwell? Am I a married
man or a bachelor? Then to answer every
man directly and briefly, wisely and truly.—
Wisely, I say I am a bachelor.
2 *Cit.* That's as much as to say they are
fools that marry: you'll bear me a bang for
that, I fear. Proceed; directly.
*Cin.* Directly, I am going to Cæsar's
funeral.
1 *Cit.* As a friend or an enemy?
*Cin.* As a friend.
2 *Cit.* That matter is answered directly.

4 *Cit.* For your dwelling,—briefly.
*Cin.* Briefly I dwell by the Capitol.
3 *Cit.* Your name, sir, truly.
*Cin.* Truly my name is Cinna.
1 *Cit.* Tear him to pieces; he's a conspirator.
*Cin.* I am Cinna the poet, I am Cinna the
poet.
4 *Cit.* Tear him for his bad verses, tear him
for his bad verses.
*Cin.* I am not Cinna the conspirator.
4 *Cit.* It is no matter, his name's Cinna;
pluck but his name out of his heart, and turn
him going.
3 *Cit.* Tear him, tear him! Come, brands,
ho! fire-brands: to Brutus', to Cassius'; burn
all: some to Decius' house, and some to
Casca's; some to Ligarius': away, go!
[*Exeunt.*

ACT IV.

SCENE I.—ROME. *A room in* ANTONY'S
*House.*

ANTONY, OCTAVIUS, *and* LEPIDUS,
*seated at a table.*

*Ant.* These many, then, shall die; their
names are prick'd.
*Oct.* Your brother too must die; consent
you, Lepidus?
*Lep.* I do consent.
*Oct.* Prick him down, Antony.
*Lep.* Upon condition Publius shall not
live,
Who is your sister's son, Mark Antony.
*Ant.* He shall not live; look, with a spot I
damn him.
But, Lepidus, go you to Cæsar's house;
Fetch the will hither, and we shall determine
How to cut off some charge in legacies.
*Lep.* What, shall I find you here?
*Oct.* Or here or at the Capitol.
[*Exit* LEPIDUS.
*Ant.* This is a slight unmeritable man,
Meet to be sent on errands: is it fit,
The threefold world divided, he should stand
One of the three to share it?
*Oct.* So you thought him;
And took his voice who should be prick'd to
die,
In our black sentence and proscription. [you:
*Ant.* Octavius, I have seen more days than
And though we lay these honours on this
man,
To ease ourselves of divers slanderous loads,
He shall but bear them as the ass bears gold,
To groan and sweat under the business,
Either led or driven as we point the way;
And having brought our treasure where we
will,
Then take we down his load, and turn him
off,
Like to the empty ass, to shake his ears
And graze in commons.

*Oct.*                    You may do your will:
But he's a tried and valiant soldier.
    *Ant.* So is my horse, Octavius; and for
        that
I do appoint him store of provender:
It is a creature that I teach to fight,
To wind, to stop, to run directly on,—
His corporal motion govern'd by my spirit.
And, in some taste, is Lepidus but so;
He must be taught, and train'd, and bid go
        forth;—
A barren-spirited fellow; one that feeds
On abject orts and imitations,
Which, out of use and stal'd by other men,
Begin his fashion: do not talk of him
But as a property. And now, Octavius,
Listen great things.—Brutus and Cassius
Are levying powers: we must straight make
        head:
Therefore let our alliance be combin'd,
Our best friends made, our means stretch'd;
And let us presently go sit in council,
How covert matters may be best disclos'd,
And open perils surest answered.
    *Oct.* Let us do so: for we are at the stake,
And bay'd about with many enemies;    [fear,
And some that smile have in their hearts, I
Millions of mischiefs.                    [*Exeunt.*

SCENE II.—*Before* BRUTUS's *Tent, in the
        Camp near Sardis.*

*Drum. Enter* BRUTUS, LUCILIUS, LUCIUS, *and*
    Soldiers; TITINIUS *and* PINDARUS *meeting
    them.*

    *Bru.* Stand, ho!
    *Lucil.* Give the word, ho! and stand.
    *Bru.* What now, Lucilius! is Cassius near?
    *Lucil.* He is at hand; and Pindarus is
        come
To do you salutation from his master.
            [PIN. *gives a letter to* BRU.
    *Bru.* He greets me well.—Your master,
        Pindarus,
In his own change, or by ill officers,
Hath given me some worthy cause to wish
Things done undone: but if he be at hand
I shall be satisfied.
    *Pin.*            I do not doubt
But that my noble master will appear
Such as he is, full of regard and honour.
    *Bru.* He is not doubted.—A word, Lucil-
        ius;
How he receiv'd you let me be resolv'd.
    *Lucil.* With courtesy and with respect
        enough;
But not with such familiar instances,
Nor with such free and friendly conference
As he hath us'd of old.
    *Bru.*            Thou hast describ'd
A hot friend cooling: ever note, Lucilius,
When love begins to sicken and decay,
It useth an enforced ceremony.
There are no tricks in plain and simple faith:
But hollow men, like horses hot at hand,

Make gallant show and promise of their
        mettle;
But when they should endure the bloody
        spur,
They fall their crests, and, like deceitful
        jades,
Sink in the trial. Comes his army on?
    *Lucil.* They mean this night in Sardis to
        be quarter'd;
The greater part, the horse in general,
Are come with Cassius.        [*March within.*
    *Bru.*            Hark! he is arriv'd:
March gently on to meet him.

        *Enter* CASSIUS *and* Soldiers.

    *Cas.* Stand, ho!
    *Bru.* Stand, ho! speak the word along.
    *Within.* Stand!
    *Within.* Stand!
    *Within.* Stand!                    [me wrong.
    *Cas.* Most noble brother, you have done
    *Bru.* Judge me, you gods! wrong I mine
        enemies?
And, if not so, how should I wrong a bro-
        ther?
    *Cas.* Brutus, this sober form of yours
        hides wrongs;
And when you do them,—
    *Bru.*            Cassius, be content;
Speak your grief softly,—I do know you
        well:—
Before the eyes of both our armies here,
Which should perceive nothing but love from
        us,
Let us not wrangle: bid them move away;
Then in my tent, Cassius, enlarge your griefs,
And I will give you audience.
    *Cas.*            Pindarus,
Bid our commanders lead their charges off
A little from this ground.                [man
    *Bru.* Lucilius, do you the like; and let no
Come to our tent till we have done our con-
    ference.
Let Lucius and Titinius guard our door.
                            [*Exeunt.*

SCENE III.—*Within the Tent of* BRUTUS.

        *Enter* BRUTUS *and* CASSIUS.

    *Cas.* That you have wrong'd me doth
        appear in this,—
You have condemn'd and noted Lucius Pella
For taking bribes here of the Sardians;
Wherein my letters, praying on his side,
Because I knew the man, were slighted off.
    *Bru.* You wrong'd yourself, to write in
        such a case.
    *Cas.* In such a time as this it is not meet
That every nice offence should bear his com-
    ment.
    *Bru.* Let me tell you, Cassius, you your-
        self                            [palm;
Are much condemn'd to have an itching
To sell and mart your offices for gold
To undeservers.

*Cas.* I an itching palm!
You know that you are Brutus that speak
this,
Or, by the gods, this speech were else your
last.
*Bru.* The name of Cassius honours this
corruption,
And chastisement doth therefore hide his
head.
*Cas.* Chastisement!
*Bru.* Remember March, the ides of March
remember!
Did not great Julius bleed for justice' sake?
What villain touch'd his body, that did stab,
And not for justice? What, shall one of us,
That struck the foremost man of all this
world
But for supporting robbers, shall we now
Contaminate our fingers with base bribes,
And sell the mighty space of our large hon-
ours
For so much trash as may be grasped thus?—
I had rather be a dog, and bay the moon,
Than such a Roman.
*Cas.* Brutus, bay not me,—
I'll not endure it: you forget yourself
To hedge me in; I am a soldier, I,
Older in practice, abler than yourself
To make conditions.
*Bru.* Go to; you are not, Cassius.
*Cas.* I am.
*Bru.* I say you are not.
*Cas.* Urge me no more, I shall forget my-
self;
Have mind upon your health, tempt me no
further.
*Bru.* Away, slight man!
*Cas.* Is 't possible?
*Bru.* Hear me, for I will speak.
Must I give way and room to your rash
choler?
Shall I be frighted when a madman stares?
*Cas.* O ye gods, ye gods! must I endure all
this?
*Bru.* All this! ay, more: fret till your
proud heart break;
Go, show your slaves how choleric you are,
And make your bondmen tremble. Must I
budge?
Must I observe you? Must I stand and
crouch
Under your testy humour? By the gods,
You shall digest the venom of your spleen
Though it do split you; for from this day
forth
I'll use you for my mirth, yea, for my laugh-
ter,
When you are waspish.
*Cas.* Is it come to this?
*Bru.* You say you are a better soldier:
Let it appear so; make your vaunting true,
And it shall please me well: for mine own
part,
I shall be glad to learn of noble men.

*Cas.* You wrong me every way; you
wrong me, Brutus;
I said an elder soldier, not a better:
Did I say better?
*Bru.* If you did, I care not.
*Cas.* When Cæsar liv'd, he durst not thus
have mov'd me.
*Bru.* Peace, peace! you durst not so have
tempted him.
*Cas.* I durst not!
*Bru.* No.
*Cas.* What, durst not tempt him!
*Bru.* For your life you durst not.
*Cas.* Do not presume too much upon my
love;
I may do that I shall be sorry for.
*Bru.* You have done that you should be
sorry for.
There is no terror, Cassius, in your threats;
For I am arm'd so strong in honesty
That they pass by me as the idle wind,
Which I respect not. I did send to you
For certain sums of gold, which you denied
me;—
For I can raise no money by vile means:
By heaven, I had rather coin my heart,
And drop my blood for drachmas, than to
wring
From the hard hands of peasants their vile
trash
By any indirection;—I did send
To you for gold to pay my legions, [Cassius?
Which you denied me: was that done like
Should I have answer'd Caius Cassius so?
When Marcus Brutus grows so covetous,
To lock such rascal counters from his friends,
Be ready, gods, with all your thunderbolts,
Dash him to pieces!
*Cas.* I denied you not.
*Bru.* You did.
*Cas.* I did not: he was but a fool that
brought
My answer back.—Brutus hath riv'd my
heart:
A friend should bear his friend's infirmities,
But Brutus makes mine greater than they
are.
*Bru.* I do not, till you practise them on me.
*Cas.* You love me not.
*Bru.* I do not like your faults.
*Cas.* A friendly eye could never see such
faults.
*Bru.* A flatterer's would not, though they
do appear
As huge as high Olympus. [come,
*Cas.* Come, Antony, and young Octavius,
Revenge yourself alone on Cassius,
For Cassius is a weary of the world;
Hated by one he loves; brav'd by his bro-
ther;
Check'd like a bondman; all his faults ob-
serv'd
Set in a notebook, learn'd, and conn'd by
rote,

To cast into my teeth. O, I could weep
My spirit from mine eyes!—There is my dagger,
And here my naked breast; within, a heart
Dearer than Plutus' mine, richer than gold:
If that thou be'st a Roman, take it forth;
I, that denied thee gold, will give my heart:
Strike, as thou didst at Cæsar; for I know,
When thou didst hate him worse, thou lov'dst him better.
Than ever thou lov'dst Cassius.

*Bru.* Sheathe your dagger:
Be angry when you will, it shall have scope;
Do what you will, dishonour shall be humour.
O Cassius, you are yoked with a lamb,
That carries anger as the flint bears fire;
Who, much enforced, shows a hasty spark,
And straight is cold again.

*Cas.* Hath Cassius liv'd
To be but mirth and laughter to his Brutus,
When grief and blood ill-temper'd vexeth him?

*Bru.* When I spoke that I was ill-temper'd too. [your hand.

*Cas.* Do you confess so much? Give me

*Bru.* And my heart too.

*Cas.* O Brutus,—

*Bru.* What's the matter?

*Cas.* Have not you love enough to bear with me, [gave me
When that rash humour which my mother
Makes me forgetful?

*Bru.* Yes, Cassius; and from henceforth,
When you are over-earnest with your Brutus,
He'll think your mother chides, and leave you so. [*Noise within.*

*Poet.* [*Within.*] Let me go in to see the generals;
There is some grudge between 'em; 'tis not meet
They be alone.

*Lucil.* [*Within.*] You shall not come to them. [stay me.

*Poet.* [*Within.*] Nothing but death shall

*Enter* Poet, *followed by* LUCILIUS *and* TITINIUS.

*Cas.* How now! what's the matter?

*Poet.* For shame, you generals! what do you mean? [be;
Love, and be friends, as two such men should
For I have seen more years, I'm sure, than ye.

*Cas.* Ha, ha! how vilely doth this cynic rhyme! [hence!

*Bru.* Get you hence, sirrah; saucy fellow,

*Cas.* Bear with him, Brutus; 'tis his fashion.

*Bru.* I'll know his humour when he knows his time: [fools?
What should the wars do with these jigging
Companion hence!

*Cas.* Away, away, be gone! [*Exit* Poet.

*Bru.* Lucilius and Titinius, bid the commanders
Prepare to lodge their companies to-night.

*Cas.* And come yourselves, and bring Messala with you
Immediately to us.
[*Exeunt* LUCIL. *and* TIT.

*Bru.* Lucius, a bowl of wine!

*Cas.* I did not think you could have been so angry.

*Bru.* O Cassius, I am sick of many griefs.

*Cas.* Of your philosophy you make no use
If you give place to accidental evils.

*Bru.* No man bears sorrow better.—Portia is dead.

*Cas.* Ha! Portia!

*Bru.* She is dead.

*Cas.* How scap'd I killing when I cross'd you so?—
O insupportable and touching loss!—
Upon what sickness?

*Bru.* Impatient of my absence,
And grief that young Octavius with Mark Antony
Have made themselves so strong; for with her death
That tidings came;—with this she fell distract,
And, her attendants absent, swallow'd fire.

*Cas.* And died so?

*Bru.* Even so.

*Cas.* O ye immortal gods.

*Enter* LUCIUS *with wine and tapers.*

*Bru.* Speak no more of her.—Give me a bowl of wine.—
In this I bury all unkindness, Cassius.
[*Drinks.*

*Cas.* My heart is thirsty for that noble pledge.—
Fill, Lucius, till the wine o'erswell the cup;
I cannot drink too much of Brutus' love.
[*Drinks.*

*Bru.* Come in, Titinius!

*Re-enter* TITINIUS, *with* MESSALA.
Welcome, good Messala!—
Now sit we close about this taper here,
And call in question our necessities.

*Cas.* Portia, art thou gone?

*Bru.* No more, I pray you.—
Messala, I have here received letters,
That young Octavius and Mark Antony
Come down upon us with a mighty power,
Bending their expedition toward Philippi.

*Mes.* Myself have letters of the self-same tenor.

*Bru.* With what addition?

*Mes.* That, by proscription and bills of outlawry,
Octavius, Antony, and Lepidus
Have put to death an hundred senators.

*Bru.* Therein our letters do not well agree;
Mine speak of seventy senators that died

By their proscriptions, Cicero being one.
*Cas.* Cicero one!
*Mes.*        Cicero is dead.
And by that order of proscription.—
Had you your letters from your wife, my
    lord?
*Bru.* No, Messala.
*Mes.* Nor nothing in your letters writ of
    her?
*Bru.* Nothing, Messala.
*Mes.*        That, methinks, is strange.
*Bru.* Why ask you? hear you aught of her
    in yours?
*Mes.* No, my lord.
*Bru.* Now, as you are a Roman, tell me
    true.
*Mes.* Then like a Roman bear the truth I
    tell:
For certain she is dead, and by strange man-
    ner.
*Bru.* Why, farewell, Portia.—We must die,
    Messala:
With meditating that she must die once,
I have the patience to endure it now.
*Mes.* Even so great men great losses should
    endure.
*Cas.* I have as much of this in art as you,
But yet my nature could not bear it so.
*Bru.* Well, to our work alive. What do you
    think
Of marching to Philippi presently?
*Cas.* I do nct think it good.
*Bru.*        Your reason?
*Cas.*        This it is:
'Tis better that the enemy seek us:
So shall he waste his means, weary his soldiers,
Doing himself offence; whilst we, lying still,
Are full of rest, defence, and nimbleness.
*Bru.* Good reasons must, of force, give
    place to better.
The people 'twixt Philippi and this ground
Do stand but in a forc'd affection;
For they have grudg'd us contribution:
The enemy, marching along by them,
By them shall make a fuller number up,
Come on refresh'd, new-aided, and encour-
    ag'd;
From which advantage shall we cut him off
If at Philippi we do face him there,
These people at our back.
*Cas.*        Hear me, good brother.
*Bru.* Under your pardon.—You must note
    beside,
That we have tried the utmost of our friends,
Our legions are brimful, our cause is ripe:
The enemy increaseth every day;
We, at the height, are ready to decline.
There is a tide in the affairs of men
Which, taken at the flood, leads on to fortune;
Omitted, all the voyage of their life
Is bound in shallows and in miseries.
On such a full sea are we now afloat;
And we must take the current when it serves,
Or lose our ventures.

*Cas.*        Then, with your will, go on;
We'll along ourselves, and meet them at
    Philippi.        [talk,
*Bru.* The deep of night is crept upon our
And nature must obey necessity;
Which we will niggard with a little rest.
There is no more to say?
*Cas.*        No more. Good-night:
Early to-morrow will we rise, and hence.
*Bru.* Lucius, my gown.        [*Exit* LUCIUS.
    Farewell good Messala:—
Good-night, Titinius;—noble, noble Cassius,
Good-night, and good repose.
*Cas.*        O my dear brother!
This was an ill beginning of the night:
Never come such division 'tween our souls!
Let it not, Brutus.
*Bru.*        Everything is well.
*Cas.* Good-night, my lord.
*Bru.*        Good-night, good brother.
*Tit. and Mes.* Good-night, Lord Brutus.
*Bru.*        Farewell, every one.
    [*Exeunt* CAS., TIT., *and* MES.

*Re-enter* LUCIUS *with the gown.*

Give me the gown. Where is thy instrument?
*Luc.* Here in the tent.
*Bru.*        What, thou speak'st drowsily!
Poor knave, I blame thee not; thou art o'er-
    watch'd.
Call Claudius and some other of my men;
I'll have them sleep on cushions in my tent.
*Luc.* Varro and Claudius!

*Enter* VARRO *and* CLAUDIUS.

*Var.* Calls my lord?        [sleep;
*Bru.* I pray you, sirs, lie in my tent and
It may be I shall raise you by and by
On business to my brother Cassius.
*Var.* So please you we will stand and watch
    your pleasure.        [sirs;
*Bru.* I will not have it so: lie down, good
It may be I shall otherwise bethink me.—
Look, Lucius, here's the book I sought for so;
I put it in the pocket of my gown.
    [VAR. *and* CLAUD. *lie down.*
*Luc.* I was sure your lordship did not give
    it me.        [forgetful.
*Bru.* Bear with me, good boy, I am much
Canst thou hold up thy heavy eyes awhile,
And touch thy instrument a strain or two?
*Luc.* Ay, my lord, an't please you.
*Bru.*        It does, my boy:
I trouble thee too much, but thou art willing.
*Luc.* It is my duty, sir.        [might;
*Bru.* I should not urge thy duty past thy
I know young bloods look for a time of rest.
*Luc.* I have slept, my lord, already.
*Bru.* It was well done; and thou shalt
    sleep again;
I will not hold thee long: if I do live
I will be good to thee.        [*Music and a Song.*
This is a sleepy tune.—O murderous slumber,
Lay'st thou thy leaden mace upon my boy

That plays the music?—Gentle knave, good-
night;
I will not do thee so much wrong to wake
thee:
If thou dost nod, thou break'st thy instru-
ment;
I'll take it from thee; and, good boy, good-
night.—
Let me see, let me see;—is not the leaf turn'd
down
Where I left reading? Here it is, I think.
[Sits down.

*Enter the* Ghost *of* CÆSAR.

How ill this taper burns!—Ha! who comes
here?
I think it is the weakness of mine eyes
That shapes this monstrous apparition.
It comes upon me.—Art thou anything?
Art thou some god, some angel, or some devil,
That mak'st my blood cold and my hair to
stare?
Speak to me what thou art.
*Ghost.* Thy evil spirit, Brutus.
*Bru.*                    Why com'st thou?
*Ghost.* To tell thee thou shalt see me at
Philippi.
*Bru.* Well;
Then I shall see thee again?
*Ghost.*                    Ay, at Philippi.
*Bru.* Why, I will see thee at Philippi,
then.—          [*Exit* Ghost.
Now I have taken heart thou vanishest:
Ill spirit, I would hold more talk with thee,—
Boy Lucius!—Varro! Claudius!—sirs,
awake!—
Claudius!
*Luc.* The strings, my lord, are false.
*Bru.* He thinks he still is at his instru-
ment.—
Lucius, awake!
*Luc.* My lord?
*Bru.* Didst thou dream, Lucius, that thou
so criedst out?
*Luc.* My lord, I do not know that I did cry.
*Bru.* Yes, that thou didst: didst thou see
anything?
*Luc.* Nothing, my lord.          [ius!
*Bru.* Sleep again, Lucius.—Sirrah, Claud-
Fellow, thou, awake!
*Var.* My lord?
*Clau.* My lord?
*Bru.* Why did you cry so out, sirs, in your
sleep?
*Var. and Clau.* Did we, my lord?
*Bru.*                    Ay: saw you anything?
*Var.* No, my lord, I saw nothing.
*Clau.*                    Nor I, my lord.
*Bru.* Go and commend me to my brother
Cassius;
Bid him set on his powers, betimes before,
And we will follow.
*Var. and Clau.* It shall be done, my lord.
[*Exeunt.*

## ACT V.

### SCENE I.—*The Plains of Philippi.*

*Enter* OCTAVIUS, ANTONY, *and their* Army.

*Oct.* Now, Antony, our hopes are an-
swered:
You said the enemy would not come down,
But keep the hills and upper regions;
It proves not so: their battles are at hand
They mean to warn us at Philippi here,
Answering before we do demand of them.
*Ant.* Tut, I am in their bosoms, and I know
Wherefore they do it: they could be content
To visit other places; and come down
With fearful bravery, thinking by this face
To fasten in our thoughts that they have
courage;
But 'tis not so.

*Enter a* Messenger.

*Mess.*                    Prepare you, generals:
The enemy comes on in gallant show;
Their bloody sign of battle is hung out,
And something to be done immediately.
*Ant.* Octavius, lead your battle softly on,
Upon the left hand of the even field.
*Oct.* Upon the right hand I; keep thou
the left.
*Ant.* Why do you cross me in this exigent?
*Oct.* I do not cross you; but I will do so.
[*March.*

*Drum. Enter* BRUTUS, CASSIUS, *and their*
Army; LUCILIUS, TITTINIUS, MESSALA, *and
others.*

*Bru.* They stand, and would have parley.
*Cas.* Stand fast, Titinius: we must out and
talk.          [battle
*Oct.* Mark Antony, shall we give sign of
*Ant.* No, Cæsar, we will answer on their
charge.          [words.
Make forth; the generals would have some
*Oct.* Stir not until the signal.          [men?
*Bru.* Words before blows: is it so, country-
*Oct.* Not that we love words better, as
you do.
*Bru.* Good words are better than bad
strokes, Octavius.
*Ant.* In your bad strokes, Brutus, you give
good words:
Witness the hole you made in Cæsar's heart,
Crying, *Long live! hail, Cæsar!*
*Cas.*                    Antony,
The posture of your blows are yet unknown;
But for your words, they rob the Hybla bees,
And leave them honeyless.
*Ant.*                    Not stingless too.
*Bru.* O yes, and soundless too;
For you have stol'n their buzzing, Antony,
And very wisely threat before you sting.
*Ant.* Villains, you did not so when your
vile daggers
Hack'd one another in the sides of Cæsar:

You show'd your teeth like apes, and fawn'd
    like hounds,           [feet;
And bow'd like bondmen, kissing Cæsar's
Whilst damned Casca, like a cur, behind,
Struck Cæsar on the neck. O you flatterers!
    *Cas.*   Flatterers!—Now, Brutus, thank
    yourself:
This tongue had not offended so to-day
If Cassius might have rul'd.
    *Oct.*   Come, come, the cause: if arguing
    make us sweat,
The proof of it will turn to redder drops.
Look,—
I draw a sword against conspirators;
When think you that the sword goes up
    again?—
Never till Cæsar's three-and-thirty wounds
Be well aveng'd; or till another Cæsar
Have added slaughter to the sword of traitors.
    *Bru.*   Cæsar, thou canst not die by traitors'
    hands,
Unless thou bring'st them with thee.
    *Oct.*              So I hope;
I was not born to die on Brutus' sword.
    *Bru.*   O, if thou wert the noblest of thy
    strain,          [ourable.
Young man, thou couldst not die more hon-
    *Cas.*   A peevish school-boy, worthless of
    such honour,
Join'd with a masker and a reveller!
    *Ant.*   Old Cassius still!
    *Oct.*          Come, Antony; away!—
Defiance, traitors, hurl we in your teeth:
If you dare fight to-day, come to the field;
If not, when you have stomachs.
    [*Exeunt* OCT., ANT., *and their* Army.
    *Cas.*   Why, now, blow wind, swell billow,
    and swim bark!
The storm is up, and all is on the hazard.
    *Bru.*   Ho, Lucilius! hark, a word with you.
    *Lucil.*           My lord.
    [BRU. *and* LUCIL. *converse apart.*
    *Cas.*   Messala,—
    *Mes.*      What says my general?
    *Cas.*              Messala,
This is my birth-day; as this very day
Was Cassius born. Give me thy hand Mes-
    sala:
Be thou my witness that, against my will,
As Pompey was, am I compell'd to set
Upon one battle all our liberties.
You know that I held Epicurus strong,
And his opinion: now I change my mind,
And partly credit things that do presage.
Coming from Sardis, on our former ensign
Two mighty eagles fell; and there they
    perch'd,
Gorging and feeding from our soldiers' hands;
Who to Philippi here consorted us:
This morning are they fled away and gone;
And in their steads do ravens, crows, and kites
Fly o'er our heads, and downward look on us,
As we were sickly prey: their shadows seem
A canopy most fatal, under which

Our army lies, ready to give up the ghost.
    *Mes.*   Believe not so.
    *Cas.*          I but believe it partly,
For I am fresh of spirit; and resolv'd
To meet all perils very constantly.
    *Bru.*   Even so, Lucilius.
    *Cas.*         Now, most noble Brutus,
The gods to-day stand friendly, that we may,
Lovers of peace, lead on our days to age!
But, since the affairs of men rest still incertain,
Let's reason with the worst that may befall.
If we do lose this battle, then is this
The very last time we shall speak together:
What are you, then, determined to do?
    *Bru.*   Even by the rule of that philosophy
By which I did blame Cato for the death
Which he did give himself.—I know not how,
But I do find it cowardly and vile,
For fear of what might fall, so to prevent
The time of life:—arming myself with pa-
    tience
To stay the providence of some high powers
That govern us below.
    *Cas.*        Then, if we lose this battle,
You are contented to be led in triumph
Through the streets of Rome?    [Roman,
    *Bru.*   No, Cassius, no: think not, thou noble
That ever Brutus will go bound to Rome;
He bears too great a mind. But this same day
Must end that work the ides of March began;
And whether we shall meet again I know not.
Therefore our everlasting farewell take:
For ever, and for ever, farewell, Cassius!
If we do meet again, why, we shall smile;
If not, why, then, this parting was well made.
    *Cas.*   For ever and for ever, farewell, Bru-
    tus!
If we do meet again we'll smile indeed;
If not, 'tis true this parting was well made.
    *Bru.*   Why, then, lead on.—O that a man
    might know
The end of this day's business ere it come!
But it sufficeth that the day will end,
And then the end is known.—Come, ho!
    away!          [*Exeunt.*

SCENE II.—THE PLAINS OF PHILIPPI. *The
Field of Battle.*

    *Alarum. Enter* BRUTUS *and* MESSALA.

    *Bru.*   Ride, ride, Messala, ride, and give
    these bills
Unto the legions on the other side:
    [*Loud alarum.*
Let them set on at once; for I perceive
But cold demeanour in Octavius' wing,
And sudden push gives them the overthrow.
Ride, ride, Messala: let them all come down.
    [*Exeunt.*

SCENE III.—THE PLAINS OF PHILIPPI.
*Another part of the Field.*

    *Alarum. Enter* CASSIUS *and* TITINIUS.

    *Cas.*   O look, Titinius, look, the villains fly!
Myself have to mine own turn'd enemy:

This ensign here of mine was turning back;
I slew the coward, and did take it from him.
  *Tit.* O Cassius, Brutus gave the word too
    early;
Who, having some advantage on Octavius,
Took it too eagerly: his soldiers fell to spoil:
Whilst we by Antony are all enclos'd.

### Enter PINDARUS.

  *Pin.* Fly further off, my lord, fly further
    off;
Mark Antony is in your tents, my lord!
Fly, therefore, noble Cassius! fly far off.
  *Cas.* This hill is far enough.—Look, look,
    Titinius;
Are those my tents where I perceive the fire?
  *Tit.* They are, my lord.
  *Cas.*        Titinius, if thou lov'st me,
Mount thou my horse, and hide thy spurs in
    him,
Till he have brought thee up to yonder troops
And here again, that I may rest assur'd
Whether yond troops are friend or enemy.
  *Tit.* I will be here again even with a
    thought.          [*Exit.*
  *Cas.* Go, Pindarus, get higher on that hill;
My sight was ever thick; regard Titinius,
And tell me what thou not'st about the
    field.—        [*Exit* PINDARUS.
This day I breathed first: time is come round,
And where I did begin there shall I end;
My life is run his compass.—Sirrah, what
    news?
  *Pin.* [*Above.*] O my lord!
  *Cas.* What news?
  *Pin.* Titinius is enclosed round about
With horsemen, that make to him on the
    spur;—
Yet he spurs on.—Now they are almost on
    him;—
Now, Titinius!—now some 'light:—O, he
    'lights too:—
He's ta'en;—and, hark! they shout for joy.
              [*Shout.*
  *Cas.*    Come down, behold no more.
O, coward that I am, to live so long,
To see my best friend ta'en before my face!

### Enter PINDARUS.

Come hither, sirrah:
In Parthia did I take thee prisoner;
And then I swore thee, saving of thy life,
That whatsoever I did bid thee do
Thou shouldst attempt it. Come now, keep
    thine oath!
Now be a freeman; and with this good sword,
That ran through Cæsar's bowels, search this
    bosom.
Stand not to answer: here, take thou the hilts;
And when my face is cover'd, as 'tis now,
Guide thou the sword.—Cæsar, thou art re-
    veng'd,
Even with the sword that kill'd thee. [*Dies.*

  *Pin.* So, I am free; yet would not so have
    been,
Durst I have done my will. O Cassius!
Far from this country Pindarus shall run,
Where never Roman shall take note of him.
              [*Exit.*

### Re-enter TITINIUS, *with* MESSALA.

  *Mes.* It is but change, Titinius; for Oc-
    tavius
Is overthrown by noble Brutus' power,
As Cassius' legions are by Antony.
  *Tit.* These tidings will well comfort Cassius.
  *Mes.* Where did you leave him?
  *Tit.*            All disconsolate,
With Pindarus, his bondman, on this hill.
  *Mes.* Is not that he that lies upon the
    ground?
  *Tit.* He lies not like the living. O my heart!
  *Mes.* Is not that he?
  *Tit.*        No, this was he, Messala,
But Cassius is no more.—O setting sun,
As in thy red rays thou dost sink to-night,
So in his red blood Cassius' day is set,—
The sun of Rome is set! Our day is gone;
Clouds, dews, and dangers come; our deeds
    are done!
Mistrust of my success hath done this deed.
  *Mes.* Mistrust of good success hath done
    this deed.
O hateful error, melancholy's child,
Why dost thou show to the apt thoughts of
    men
The things that are not? O error, soon con-
    ceiv'd,
Thou never com'st unto a happy birth,
But kill'st the mother that engender'd thee!
  *Tit.* What, Pindarus! where art thou, Pin-
    darus?
  *Mes.* Seek him, Titinius: whilst I go to
    meet
The noble Brutus, thrusting this report
Into his ears; I may say, thrusting it;
For piercing steel and darts envenomed
Shall be as welcome to the ears of Brutus
As tidings of this sight.
  *Tit.*         Hie you, Messala,
              [*Exit* MESSALA.
And I will seek for Pindarus the while.
Why didst thou send me forth, brave Cassius?
Did I not meet thy friends? and did not they
Put on my brows this wreath of victory,
And bid me giv't thee? Didst thou not hear
    their shouts?
Alas, thou hast misconstru'd everything.
But, hold thee, take this garland on thy
    brow;
Thy Brutus bid me give it thee, and I
Will do his bidding.—Brutus, come apace,
And see how I regarded Caius Cassius.—
By your leave, gods.—This is a Roman's part:
Come, Cassius' sword, and find Titinius'
    heart.              [*Dies.*

*Alarum.* Re-enter Messala, *with* Brutus,
Young Cato, Strato, Volumnius, *and*
Lucilius.

*Bru.* Where, where, Messala, doth his body
lie?
*Mes.* Lo, yonder; and Titinius mourning
it.
*Bru.* Titinius' face is upward.
*Cato.*                          He is slain.
*Bru.* O Julius Cæsar, thou art mighty
yet!
Thy spirit walks abroad, and turns our swords
In our own proper entrails.  [*Low alarums.*
*Cato.*                    Brave Titinius!
Look, whe'r he have not crown'd dead Cas-
sius!
*Bru.* Are yet two Romans living such as
these?—
The last of all the Romans, fare thee well!
It is impossible that ever Rome
Should breed thy fellows.—Friends, I owe
more tears
To this dead man than you shall see me
pay.—
I shall find time, Cassius, I shall find time.—
Come, therefore, and to Thassos send his
body:
His funerals shall not be in our camp,
Lest it discomfort us.—Lucilius, come;—
And come, young Cato; let us to the field.—
Labeo and Flavius, set our battles on:—
'Tis three o'clock; and, Romans, yet ere night
We shall try fortune in a second fight.
[*Exeunt.*

Scene IV.—*Another part of the Field.*

*Alarum. Enter, fighting,* Soldiers *of both
Armies; then* Brutus, Young Cato, Lucilius, *and others.*

*Bru.* Yet, countrymen, O, yet hold up your
heads!                          [with me?
*Cato.* What bastard doth not? Who will go
I will proclaim my name about the field:—
I am the son of Marcus Cato, ho!
A foe to tyrants, and my country's friend;
I am the son of Marcus Cato, ho!
[*Charges the enemy.*
*Bru.* And I am Brutus, Marcus Brutus, I;
Brutus, my country's friend; know me for
Brutus!
[*Exit, charging the enemy.* Young Cato
*is overpowered, and falls.*
*Lucil.* O young and noble Cato, art thou
down?
Why, now thou diest as bravely as Titinius;
And mayst be honour'd, being Cato's son.
1 *Sold.* Yield, or thou diest.
*Lucil.*              Only I yield to die?
There is so much that thou wilt kill me
straight;                    [*Offering money.*
Kill Brutus, and be honour'd in his death.
1 *Sold.* We must not.—A noble prisoner!

2 *Sold.* Room, ho! Tell Antony Brutus is
ta'en.                          [general.—
1 *Sold.* I'll tell the news.—Here comes the

*Enter* Antony.

Brutus is ta'en, Brutus is ta'en, my lord.
*Ant.* Where is he?
*Lucil.* Safe, Antony; Brutus is safe enough:
I dare assure thee that no enemy
Shall ever take alive the noble Brutus:
The gods defend him from so great a shame!
When you do find him, or alive or dead,
He will be found like Brutus, like himself.
*Ant.* This is not Brutus, friend; but, I as-
sure you,
A prize no less in worth: keep this man safe,
Give him all kindness: I had rather have
Such men my friends than enemies. Go on,
And see whe'r Brutus be alive or dead;
And bring us word unto Octavius' tent
How everything is chanc'd.        [*Exeunt.*

Scene V.—*Another part of the Field.*

*Enter* Brutus, Dardanius, Clitus, Strato,
*and* Volumnius.

*Bru.* Come, poor remains of friends, rest
on this rock.
*Cli.* Statilius show'd the torch-light; but,
my lord,
He came not back: he is or ta'en or slain.
*Bru.* Sit thee down, Clitus: slaying is the
word;
It is a deed in fashion. Hark thee, Clitus.
[*Whispering him.*
*Cli.* What, I, my lord? No, not for all the
world.
*Bru.* Peace, then, no words.
*Cli.*                  I'll rather kill myself.
*Bru.* Hark thee, Dardanius!
[*Whispers him.*
*Dar.*          Shall I do such a deed?
*Cli.* O Dardanius!
*Dar.* O Clitus!
*Cli.* What ill request did Brutus make to
thee?
*Dar.* To kill him, Clitus. Look, he medi-
tates.
*Cli.* Now is that noble vessel full of grief,
That it runs over even at his eyes.    [word.
*Bru.* Come hither, good Volumnius; list a
*Vol.* What says my lord?
*Bru.*            Why, this, Volumnius:
The ghost of Cæsar hath appear'd to me
Two several times by night,—at Sardis once,
And this last night here in Philippi fields:
I know my hour is come.
*Vol.*              Not so, my lord.
*Bru.* Nay, I am sure it is, Volumnius.
Thou seest the world, Volumnius, how it
goes;
Our enemies have beat us to the pit:
[*Low alarums.*
It is more worthy to leap in ourselves

Than tarry till they push us. Good Volum-
nius,
Thou know'st that we two went to school to-
gether:
Even for that our love of old, I pray thee,
Hold thou my sword-hilts whilst I run on it.

*Vol.* That's not an office for a friend, my
lord. [*Alarum still.*

*Cli.* Fly, fly, my lord; there is no tarrying
here. [*Volumnius.—*

*Bru.* Farewell to you; and you;—and you,
Strato, thou hast been all this while asleep;
Farewell to thee too, Strato.—Countrymen,
My heart doth joy that yet, in all my life,
I found no man but he was true to me.
I shall have glory by this losing day
More than Octavius and Mark Antony
By this vile conquest shall attain unto.
So, fare you well at once; for Brutus' tongue
Hath almost ended his life's history:
Night hangs upon mine eyes; my bones would
rest,
That have but labour'd to attain this hour.
[*Alarum. Cry within,* "Fly, fly, fly!"

*Cli.* Fly, my lord fly.

*Bru.* Hence! I will follow.
[*Exeunt* CLI., DAR., *and* VOL.
I pr'ythee, Strato, stay thou by thy lord:
Thou art a fellow of a good respect;
Thy life hath had some smatch of honour in
it:
Hold, then, my sword, and turn away thy
face,
While I do run upon it. Wilt thou, Strato?

*Stra.* Give me your hand first: fare you
well, my lord.

*Bru.* Farewell, good Strato.—Cæsar, now
be still:
I kill'd not thee with half so good a will.
[*He runs on his sword, and dies.*

*Alarum. Retreat. Enter* OCTAVIUS, ANTONY,
*and* Army; MESSALA *and* LUCILIUS, *prisoners.*

*Oct.* What man is that?

*Mes.* My master's man.—Strato, where is
thy master? [*Messala:*

*Stra.* Free from the bondage you are in,
The conquerors can but make a fire of him;
For Brutus only overcame himself,
And no man else hath honour by his death.

*Lucil.* So Brutus should be found.—I thank
thee, Brutus,
That thou hast prov'd Lucilius' saying true.

*Oct.* All that serv'd Brutus I will entertain
them.
Fellow, wilt thou bestow thy time with me?

*Stra.* Ay, if Messala will prefer me to you.

*Oct.* Do so, good Messala.

*Mes.* How died my master Strato?

*Stra.* I held the sword, and he did run on it.

*Mes.* Octavius, then take him to follow
thee,
That did the latest service to my master.

*Ant.* This was the noblest Roman of them
all:
All the conspirators, save only he,
Did that they did in envy of great Cæsar;
He only, in a general honest thought,
And common good to all, made one of them.
His life was gentle; and the elements
So mix'd in him that Nature might stand up
And say to all the world, *This was a man!*

*Oct.* According to his virtue, let us use him
With all respect and rites of burial.
Within my tent his bones to-night shall lie,
Most like a soldier, order'd honourably.—
So, call the field to rest: and let's away,
To part the glories of this happy day.
[*Exeunt.*

# ANTONY AND CLEOPATRA

## DRAMATIS PERSONÆ

M. Antony,
Octavius Cæsar, } Triumvirs.
M. Æmil. Lepidus,

Sextus Pompeius.

Domitius Enobarbus,
Ventidius,
Eros,
Scarus, } Friends to
Dercetas, ANTONY.
Demetrius,
Philo,

Mecænas,
Agrippa,
Dolabella, } Friends to Cæsar.
Proculeius,
Thyreus,
Gallus,

Menas,
Menecrates, } Friends to Pompey.
Varrius,
Taurus, Lieutenant-General to Cæsar.
Canidius, Lieutenant-General to Antony.
Silius, an Officer in Ventidius's Army.
Euphronius, an Ambassador from Antony
to Cæsar.
Alexas, Mardian, Seleucus, and Dio-
medes, Attendants on Cleopatra.
A Soothsayer. A Clown.

Cleopatra, Queen of Egypt.
Octavia, Sister to Cæsar and Wife to
Antony.
Charmian and Iras, Attendants on Cleo-
patra.

Officers, Soldiers, Messengers, and other Attendants.

Scene,—Dispersed; in several parts of the Roman Empire.

## ACT I.

Scene I.—Alexandria. A Room in Cleopatra's Palace.

Enter Demetrius and Philo.

*Phi.* Nay, but this dotage of our general's
O'erflows the measure: those his goodly eyes,
That o'er the files and musters of the war
Have glow'd like plated Mars, now bend,
now turn
The office and devotion of their view
Upon a tawny front: his captain's heart,
Which in the scuffles of great fights hath
burst
The buckles of his breast, reneges all temper,
And is become the bellows and the fan
To cool a gipsy's lust. [*Flourish within.*]
Look where they come:
Take but good note, and you shall see in him
The triple pillar of the world transform'd
Into a strumpet's fool: behold and see!

Enter Antony and Cleopatra, with their
Trains; Eunuchs fanning her.

*Cleo.* If it be love, indeed, tell me how
much.
*Ant.* There's beggary in the love that can
be reckon'd.
*Cleo.* I'll set a bourn how far to be belov'd.
*Ant.* Then must thou needs find out new
heaven, new earth.

Enter an Attendant.

*Att.* News, my good lord, from Rome.
*Ant.* Grates me:—the sum.
*Cleo.* Nay, hear them, Antony:
Fulvia perchance is angry; or, who knows
If the scarce-bearded Cæsar have not sent
His powerful mandate to you, *Do this or
this;*
*Take in that kingdom and enfranchise that;
Perform't, or else we damn thee.*
*Ant.* How, my love!
*Cleo.* Perchance! nay, and most like:—
You must not stay here longer,—your dis-
mission
Is come from Cæsar; therefore hear it, An-
tony.—
Where's Fulvia's process?—Cæsar's I would
say?—both?— [queen,
Call in the messengers.—As I am Egypt's
Thou blushest, Antony; and that blood of
thine
Is Cæsar's-homager: else so thy cheek pays
shame [sengers!
When shrill-tongu'd Fulvia scolds.—The mes-
*Ant.* Let Rome in Tiber melt, and the
wide arch
Of the rang'd empire fall! Here is my space.
Kingdoms are clay: our dungy earth alike
Feeds beast as man: the nobleness of life
Is to do thus; when such a mutual pair
[*Embracing.*

[841]

And such a twain can do't, in which I bind,
On pain of punishment, the world to weet
We stand up peerless.

*Cleo.*          Excellent falsehood!
Why did he marry Fulvia, and not love
     her?—
I'll seem the fool I am ·not; Antony
Will be himself.

*Ant.*          But stirr'd by Cleopatra.—
Now, for the love of Love and her soft hours,
Let's not confound the time with conference
     harsh:
There's not a minute of our lives should
     stretch
Without some pleasure now:—what sport to-
     night?

*Cleo.* Hear the ambassadors.

*Ant.*          Fie, wrangling queen!
Whom everything becomes,—to chide, to
     laugh,
To weep; whose every passion fully strives
To make itself in thee fair and admir'd!
No messenger; but thine, and all alone,
To-night we'll wander through the streets and
     note
The qualities of people. Come, my queen;
Last night you did desire it:—speak not to us.
     [*Exeunt* ANT. *and* CLEO., *with their* Train.

*Dem.* Is Cæsar with Antonius priz'd so
     slight?

*Phi.* Sir, sometimes, when he is not An-
     tony,
He comes too short of that great property
Which still should go with Antony.

*Dem.*          I am full sorry
That he approves the common liar, who
Thus speaks of him at Rome: but I will hope
Of better deeds to-morrow. Rest you happy!
     [*Exeunt.*

SCENE II.—ALEXANDRIA. *Another Room in
     Cleopatra's Palace.*

Enter CHARMIAN, IRAS, ALEXAS, *and a*
     Soothsayer.

*Char.* Lord Alexas, sweet Alexas, most
anything Alexas, almost most absolute Alexas,
where's the soothsayer that you praised so to
the queen? O that I knew this husband,
which you say must charge his horns with
garlands!

*Alex.* Soothsayer,—

*Sooth.* Your will?

*Char.* Is this the man?—Is't you, sir, that
know things?

*Sooth.* In nature's infinite book of secrecy
A little I can read.

*Alex.* Show him your hand.

Enter ENOBARBUS.

*Eno.* Bring in the banquet quickly; wine
     enough
Cleopatra's health to drink.

*Char.* Good sir, give me good fortune.

*Sooth.* I make not, but foresee.

*Char.* Pray, then, forsee me one.

*Sooth.* You shall be yet fairer than you are.

*Char.* He means in flesh.

*Iras.* No, you shall paint when you are old.

*Char.* Wrinkles forbid!

*Alex.* Vex not his prescience; be attentive.

*Char.* Hush!

*Sooth.* You shall be more beloving than
beloved.          [drinking.

*Char.* I had rather heat my liver with

*Alex.* Nay, hear him.

*Char.* Good now, some excellent fortune!
Let me be married to three kings in a forenoon, and widow them all: let me have a
child at fifty, to whom Herod of Jewry may
be homage: find me to marry me with Octavius Cæsar, and companion me with my
mistress.

*Sooth.* You shall outlive the lady whom
you serve.

*Char.* O excellent! I love long life better
than figs.

*Sooth.* You have seen and prov'd a fairer
     former fortune
Than that which is to approach.

*Char.* Then belike my children shall have
no names:—pr'ythee, how many boys and
wenches must I have?

*Sooth.* If every of your wishes had a
     womb,
And fertile every wish, a million.

*Char.* Out, fool! I forgive·thee for a witch.

*Alex.* You think none but your sheets are
privy to your wishes.

*Char.* Nay, come, tell Iras hers.

*Alex.* We'll know all our fortunes.

*Eno.* Mine, and most of our fortunes, to-
night, shall be—drunk to bed.

*Iras.* There's a palm presages chastity, if
nothing else.

*Char.* Even as the o'erflowing Nilus presageth famine.

*Iras.* Go, you wild bedfellow, you cannot
soothsay.

*Char.* Nay, if an oily palm be not a fruitful prognostication, I cannot scratch mine ear.
—Pr'ythee, tell her but worky-day fortune.

*Sooth.* Your fortunes are alike.

*Iras.* But how, but how? give me particulars.

*Sooth.* I have said.

*Iras.* Am I not an inch of fortune better
than she?

*Char.* Well, if you were but an inch of
fortune better than I, where would you
choose it?

*Iras.* Not in my husband's nose.

*Char.* Our worser thoughts heavens mend!
—Alexas,—come, his fortune, his fortune!—
O, let him marry a woman that cannot go,
sweet Isis, I beseech thee! And let her die too,
and give him a worse! and let worse follow
worse, till the worst of all follow him laughing to his grave, fiftyfold a cuckold! Good

Isis, hear me this prayer, though thou deny me a matter of more weight; good Isis, I beseech thee!

*Iras.* Amen. Dear goddess, hear that prayer of the people! for, as it is a heart-breaking to see a handsome man loose-wived, so it is a deadly sorrow to behold a foul knave uncuckolded: therefore, dear Isis, keep decorum, and fortune him accordingly!

*Char.* Amen.

*Alex.* Lo, now, if it lay in their hands to make me a cuckold, they would make themselves whores, but they'd do't!

*Eno.* Hush! here comes Antony

*Char.*　　　　　　　Not he; the queen.

*Enter* CLEOPATRA.

*Cleo.* Saw you my lord?

*Eno.*　　　　　　No, lady.

*Cleo.*　　　　　Was he not here?

*Char.* No, madam.　　　　[sudden

*Cleo.* He was dispos'd to mirth; but on the

A Roman thought hath struck him.—Enobarbus,—

*Eno.* Madam?

*Cleo.*　　Seek him, and bring him hither.—Where's Alexas?　　　　[proaches.

*Alex.* Here, at your service.—My lord ap-

*Cleo.* We will not look upon him: go with us.

[*Exeunt* CLEO., ENO., CHAR., IRAS, ALEX. *and* Soothsayer.

*Enter* ANTONY, *with a* Messenger *and* Attendants.

*Mess.* Fulvia thy wife first came into the field.

*Ant.* Against my brother Lucius.

*Mess.* Ay:

But soon that war had end, and the time's state

Made friends of them, jointing their force 'gainst Cæsar;

Whose better issue in the war, from Italy,

Upon the first encounter, drave them.

*Ant.* Well, what worst?　　　[teller.

*Mess.* The nature of bad news infects the

*Ant.* When it concerns the fool or coward.—On:—

Things that are past are done with me.—'Tis thus;

Who tells me true, though in his tale lie death

I hear him as he flatter'd.

*Mess.*　　　　　Labienus,—

This is stiff news,—hath, with his Parthian force,

Extended Asia from Euphrates;

His conquering banner shook from Syria

To Lydia and to Ionia;

Whilst,—

*Ant.* Antony, thou wouldst say,—

*Mess.*　　　　　　O, my lord!

*Ant.* Speak to me home, mince not the general tongue:

Name Cleopatra as she is call'd in Rome;

Rail thou in Fulvia's phrase; and taunt my faults

With such full license as both truth and malice

Have power to utter. O, then we bring forth weeds　　　　　　　[told us

When our quick minds lie still; and our ills

Is as our earing. Fare thee well awhile.

*Mess.* At your noble pleasure.　　[*Exit.*

*Ant.* From Sicyon, ho, the news! Speak there!

*1 Att.* The man from Sicyon,—is there such an one?

*2 Att.* He stays upon your will.

*Ant.*　　　　　Let him appear.—

These strong Egyptian fetters I must break,

Or lose myself in dotage.—

*Enter a second* Messenger.

　　　　　　　What are you?

*2 Mess.* Fulvia thy wife is dead.

*Ant.*　　　　　Where died she?

*2 Mess.* In Sicyon:　　　　　[serious

Her length of sickness, with what else more

Importeth thee to know, this bears.

[*Gives a letter.*

*Ant.*　　　　　Forbear me.

[*Exit second* Messenger.

There's a great spirit gone! Thus did I desire it:

What our contempts do often hurl from us,

We wish it ours again; the present pleasure,

By revolution lowering, does become

The opposite of itself: she's good, being gone;

The hand could pluck her back that shov'd her on.

I must from this enchanting queen break off:

Ten thousand harms, more than the ills I know,

My idleness doth hatch.—Ho, Enobarbus!

*Re-enter* ENOBARBUS.

*Eno.* What's your pleasure, sir?

*Ant.* I must with haste from hence.

*Eno.* Why, then, we kill all our women: we see how mortal an unkindness is to them; if they suffer our departure, death's the word.

*Ant.* I must be gone.

*Eno.* Under a compelling occasion, let women die: it were pity to cast them away for nothing; though, between them and a great cause, they should be esteemed nothing. Cleopatra, catching but the least noise of this, dies instantly; I have seen her die twenty times upon far poorer moment: I do think there is mettle in death, which commits some loving act upon her, she hath such a celerity in dying.

*Ant.* She is cunning past man's thought.

*Eno.* Alack, sir, no; her passions are made of nothing but the finest part of pure love: we cannot call her winds and waters, sighs and tears; they are greater storms and tempests than almanacs can report: this cannot be cunning in her; if it be, she makes a shower of rain as well as Jove.

*Ant.* Would I had never seen her!

*Eno.* O sir, you had then left unseen a wonderful piece of work; which not to have been blessed withal would have discredited your travel.

*Ant.* Fulvia is dead.

*Eno.* Sir?

*Ant.* Fulvia is dead.

*Eno.* Fulvia!

*Ant.* Dead.

*Eno.* Why, sir, give the gods a thankful sacrifice. When it pleaseth their deities to take the wife of a man from him, it shows to man the tailors of the earth; comforting therein that when old robes are worn out there are members of make new. If there were no more women but Fulvia, then had you indeed a cut, and the case to be lamented: this grief is crowned with consolation; your old smock brings forth a new petticoat: —and, indeed, the tears live in an onion that should water this sorrow.            [state

*Ant.* The business she hath broached in the Cannot endure my absence.

*Eno.* And the business you have broached here cannot be without you; especially that of Cleopatra's, which wholly depends on your abode.            [ficers

*Ant.* No more light answers. Let our of-Have notice what we purpose. I shall break The cause of our expedience to the queen, And get her leave to part. For not alone The death of Fulvia, with more urgent touches,
Do strongly speak to us; but the letters too Of many our contriving friends in Rome Petition us at home: Sextus Pompeius Hath given the dare to Cæsar, and commands
The empire of the sea; our slippery people,— Whose love is never link'd to the deserver Till his deserts are past,—begin to throw Pompey the Great, and all his dignities, Upon his son; who, high in name and power, Higher than both in blood and life, stands up For the main soldier: whose quality, going on, The sides o' the world may danger: much is breeding,
Which, like the courser's hair, hath yet but life,
And not a serpent's poison. Say, our pleasure, To such whose place is under us, requires Our quick remove from hence.

*Eno.* I shall do't.            [*Exeunt.*

SCENE III.—ALEXANDRIA. *A Room in* CLEOPATRA'S *Palace.*

*Enter* CLEOPATRA, CHARMIAN, IRAS, *and* ALEXAS.

*Cleo.* Where is he?

*Char.*            I did not see him since.

*Cleo.* See where he is, who's with him, what he does:——
I did not send you:—if you find him sad, Say I am dancing; if in mirth, report That I am sudden sick: quick, and return.
            [*Exit* ALEXAS.

*Char.* Madam, methinks, if you did love him dearly,
You do not hold the method to enforce The like from him.

*Cleo.*            What should I do, I do not?

*Char.* In each thing give him way; cross him in nothing.

*Cleo.* Thou teachest like a fool,—the way to lose him.            [forbear:

*Char.* Tempt him not so too far; I wish, In time we hate that which we often fear. But here comes Antony.

*Cleo.*            I am sick and sullen.

*Enter* ANTONY.

*Ant.* I am sorry to give breathing to my purpose,—

*Cleo.* Help me away, dear Charmian; I shall fall:
It cannot be thus long, the sides of nature Will not sustain it.

*Ant.*            Now, my dearest queen,—

*Cleo.* Pray you, stand further from me.

*Ant.*            What's the matter?

*Cleo.* I know, by that same eye, there's some good news.
What says the married woman?—You may go:
Would she had never given you leave to come! Let her not say 'tis I that keep you here,— I have no power upon you; hers you are.

*Ant.* The gods best know,—

*Cleo.*            O, never was there queen So mightily betray'd! Yet at the first I saw the treasons planted.

*Ant.*            Cleopatra,—

*Cleo.* Why should I think you can be mine and true.
Though you in swearing shake the thronèd gods,  ·
Who have been false to Fulvia? Riotous madness.
To be entangled with those mouth-made vows,
Which break themselves in swearing!

*Ant.*            Most sweet queen,—

*Cleo.* Nay, pray you, seek no colour for your going,
But bid farewell, and go: when you su'd staying,
Then was the time for words: no going then;—
Eternity was in our lips and eyes, Bliss in our brows' bent; none our parts so poor
But was a race of heaven: they are so still, Or thou, the greatèst soldier of the world, Art turn'd the greatest liar.

*Ant.*　　　　　　　　How now, lady!
*Cleo.* I would I had thy inches; thou shouldst know
There were a heart in Egypt.
*Ant.*　　　　　　　Hear me, queen:
The strong necessity of time commands
Our services awhile; but my full heart
Remains in use with you. Our Italy
Shines o'er with civil swords: Sextus Pompeius
Makes his approaches to the port of Rome:
Equality of two domestic powers
Breeds scrupulous faction: the hated, grown
　to strength,
Are newly grown to love: the condemn'd
　Pompey,
Rich in his father's honour, creeps apace
Into the hearts of such as have not thriv'd
Upon the present state, whose numbers
　threaten;
And quietness, grown sick of rest, would
　purge　　　　　　　　　　　[ular,
By any desperate change. My more partic-
And that which most with you should safe
　my going,
Is Fulvia's death.
　*Cleo.* Though age from folly could not give
　me freedom,
It does from childishness:—can Fulvia die?
　*Ant.* She's dead, my queen:
Look here, and, at thy sovereign leisure, read
The garboils she awak'd; at the last, best.
See when and where she died.
　*Cleo.*　　　　　O most false love!
Where be the sacred vials thou shouldst fill
With sorrowful water? Now I see, I see,
In Fulvia's death how mine receiv'd shall be.
　*Ant.* Quarrel no more, but be prepar'd to
　know
The purposes I bear; which are, or cease,
As you shall give the advice. By the fire
That quickens Nilus' slime, I go from hence
Thy soldier, servant; making peace or war
As thou affect'st.
　*Cleo.*　　　Cut my lace, Charmian, come;—
But let it be:—I am quickly ill and well,
So Antony loves.
　*Ant.*　　　My precious queen, forbear;
And give true evidence to his love, which
　stands
An honourable trial.
　*Cleo.*　　　　　So Fulvia told me.
I pr'ythee, turn aside and weep for her;
Then bid adieu to me, and say the tears
Belong to Egypt: good now, play one scene
Of excellent dissembling; and let it look
Like perfect honour.
　*Ant.*　　　You'll heat my blood: no more.
　*Cleo.* You can do better yet; but this is
　meetly.
　*Ant.* Now, by my sword,—
　*Cleo.*　　　And target.—Still he mends;
But this is not the best:—look, pr'ythee,
　Charmian,

How this Herculean Roman does become
The carriage of his chafe.
　*Ant.*　　　　　I'll leave you, lady.
　*Cleo.* Courteous lord, one word.
Sir, you and I must part,—but that's not it:
Sir, you and I have lov'd,—but there's not it;
That you know well: something it is I
　would,—
O, my oblivion is a very Antony,
And I am all forgotten.
　*Ant.*　　　But that your royalty
Holds idleness your subject, I should take you
For idleness itself.
　*Cleo.*　　　　'Tis sweating labour
To bear such idleness so near the heart
As Cleopatra this. But, sir, forgive me;
Since my becomings kill me, when they do not
Eye well to you: your honour calls you
　hence;
Therefore be deaf to my unpitied folly,
And all the gods go with you; upon your
　sword
Sit laurel victory! and smooth success
Be strew'd before your feet!
　*Ant.*　　　　Let us go. Come;
Our separation so abides, and flies,
That thou, residing here, go'st yet with me,
And I, hence fleeting, here remain with thee.
Away!　　　　　　　　　　[*Exeunt.*

SCENE IV.—ROME. *An Apartment in
　　Cæsar's House.*

*Enter* OCTAVIUS CÆSAR, LEPIDUS, *and*
Attendants.

　*Cæs.* You may see, Lepidus, and henceforth
　know,
It is not Cæsar's natural vice to hate
Our great competitor. From Alexandria
This is the news:—he fishes, drinks, and
　wastes　　　　　　　　　　　　[like
The lamps of night in revel: is not more man-
Than Cleopatra; nor the queen of Ptolemy
More womanly than he: hardly gave audi-
　ence, or
Vouchsaf'd to think he had partners: you
　shall find there
A man who is the abstract of all faults
That all men follow.
　*Lep.*　　　I must not think there are
Evils enow to darken all his goodness:
His faults in him seem as the spots of heaven,
More fiery by night's blackness; hereditary
Rather than purchas'd; what he cannot
　change
Than what he chooses.
　*Cæs.* You are too indulgent. Let us grant
　it is not
Amiss to tumble on the bed of Ptolemy;
To give a kingdom for a mirth; to sit
And keep the turn of tippling with a slave;
To reel the streets at noon, and stand the
　buffet
With knaves that smell of sweat: say this
　becomes him,—

As his composure must be rare indeed
Whom these things cannot blemish,—yet must
　　Antony
No way excuse his soils when we do bear
So great weight in his lightness. If he fill'd
His vacancy with his voluptuousness.
Full surfeits and the dryness of his bones
Call on him for't: but to confound such time,
That drums him from his sport, and speaks
　　as loud
As his own state and ours,—'tis to be chid
As we rate boys, who, being mature in
　　knowledge,
Pawn their experience to their present pleas-
　　ure,
And so rebel to judgment.

*Enter a* Messenger.

*Lep.*　　　　　　　Here's more news.
*Mess.* Thy biddings have been done; and
　　every hour,
Most noble Cæsar, shalt thou have report
How 'tis abroad. Pompey is strong at sea;
And it appears he is belov'd of those
That only have fear'd Cæsar: to the ports
The discontents repair, and men's reports
Give him much wrong'd.
*Cæs.*　　　　I should have known no less:
It hath been taught us from the primal state
That he which is was wish'd until he were;
And the ebb'd man, ne'er lov'd till ne'er
　　worth love,　　　　　　　　　　[body,
Comes dear'd by being lack'd. This common
Like to a vagabond flag upon the stream,
Goes to and back, lackeying the varying tide,
To rot itself with motion.
*Mess.*　　　　Cæsar, I bring thee word,
Menecrates and Menas, famous pirates,
Make the sea serve them, which they ear and
　　wound
With keels of every kind: many hot inroads
They make in Italy; the borders maritime
Lack blood to think on't, and flush youth
　　revolt:
No vessel can peep forth but 'tis as soon
Taken as seen; for Pompey's name strikes
　　more
Than could his war resisted.
*Cæs.*　　　　　　　　Antony,
Leave thy lascivious wassails. When thou once
Wast beaten from Modena, where thou slew'st
Hirtius and Pansa, consuls at thy heel
Did famine follow; whom thou fought'st
　　against,　　　　　　　　　　　[more
Though daintily brought up, with patience
Than savages could suffer: thou didst drink
The stale of horses, and the gilded puddle
Which beasts would cough at: thy palate then
　　did deign
The roughest berry on the rudest hedge;
Yea, like the stag, when snow the pastures
　　sheets,
The barks of trees thou browsed'st; on the
　　Alps

It is reported thou didst eat strange flesh,
Which some did die to look on: and all
　　this,—　　　　　　　　　　　　[now,—
It wounds thine honour that I speak it
Was borne so like a soldier that thy cheek
So much as lank'd not.
*Lep.*　　　　　　　'Tis pity of him.
*Cæs.* Let his shames quickly
Drive him to Rome: 'tis time we twain
Did show ourselves i' the field; and to that
　　end
Assemble we immediate council: Pompey
Thrives in our idleness.
*Lep.*　　　　　　　To-morrow, Cæsar,
I shall be furnish'd to inform you rightly
Both what by sea and land I can be able
To front this present time.
*Cæs.*　　　　　　　Till which encounter
It is my business too. Farewell.
*Lep.* Farewell, my lord: what you shall
　　know meantime
Of stirs abroad, I shall beseech you, sir,
To let me be partaker.
*Cæs.*　　　　　　　Doubt not, sir;
I knew it for my bond.　　　　　[*Exeunt.*

SCENE V.—ALEXANDRIA. *A Room in the
Palace.*

*Enter* CLEOPATRA, CHARMIAN, IRAS, *and*
MARDIAN.

*Cleo.* Charmian,—
*Char.* Madam?
*Cleo.* Ha, ha!—
Give me to drink mandragora.
*Char.*　　　　　　　Why, madam?
*Cleo.* That I might sleep out this great gap
　　of time
My Antony is away.
*Char.*　　　You think of him too much.
*Cleo.* O, 'tis treason!
*Char.*　　　　　Madam, I trust, not so.
*Cleo.* Thou, eunuch Mardian!
*Mar.*　　　　What's your highness' pleasure?
*Cleo.* Not now to hear thee sing; I take no
　　pleasure
In aught an eunuch has; 'tis well for thee
That, being unseminar'd, thy freer thoughts
May not fly forth of Egypt. Hast thou affec-
　　tions?
*Mar.* Yes, gracious madam.
*Cleo.* Indeed!　　　　　　　　[nothing
*Mar.* Not in deed, madam; for I can do
But what indeed is honest to be done:
Yet have I fierce affections, and think
What Venus did with Mars.
*Cleo.*　　　　　　　O Charmian,
Where think'st thou he is now? Stands he or
　　sits he?
Or does he walk? or is he on his horse?
O happy horse to bear the weight of Antony!
Do bravely, horse! for wott'st thou whom
　　thou mov'st?
The demi-Atlas of this earth, the arm
And burgonet of men.—He's speaking now,

Or murmuring, *Where's my serpent of old
    Nile?*
For so he calls me.—Now I feed myself
With most delicious poison:—think on me,
That am with Phœbus' amorous pinches
    black,
And wrinkled deep in time? Broad-fronted
    Cæsar,
When thou wast here above the ground I was
A morsel for a monarch: and great Pompey
Would stand and make his eyes grow in my
    brow;
There would he anchor his aspect and die
With looking on his life.

*Enter* ALEXAS.

*Alex.*                Sovereign of Egypt, hail!
*Cleo.* How much unlike art thou Mark
    Antony!                                [hath
Yet, coming from him, that great medicine
With his tinct gilded thee.—
How goes it with my brave Mark Antony?
*Alex.* Last thing he did, dear queen,
He kiss'd,—the last of many doubled kisses,—
This orient pearl:—his speech sticks in my
    heart.
*Cleo.* Mine ear must pluck it thence.
*Alex.*               *Good friend,* quoth he,
*Say, the firm Roman to great Egypt sends
This treasure of an oyster; at whose foot,
To mend the petty present, I will piece
Her opulent throne with kingdoms; all the
    east,*                                  [ded,
*Say thou, shall call her mistress.* So he nod-
And soberly did mount an arm-girt steed,
Who neigh'd so high that what I would have
    spoke
Was beastly dumb'd by him.
*Cleo.*        What, was he sad or merry?
*Alex.* Like to the time o' the year between
    the extremes
Of hot and cold, he was nor sad nor merry.
*Cleo.* O well-divided disposition!—Note
    him,                                [note him:
Note him, good Charmian, 'tis the man; but
He was not sad,—for he would shine on those
That make their looks by his; he was not
    merry,—                                  [lay
Which seem'd to tell them his remembrance
In Egypt with his joy; but between both:
O heavenly mingle!—Be'st thou sad or
    merry,
The violence of either thee becomes,  [posts?
So does it no man else.—Mett'st thou my
*Alex.* Ay, madam, twenty several messen-
    gers:
Why do you send so thick?
*Cleo.*           Who's born that day
When I forget to send to Antony
Shall die a beggar.—Ink and paper, Char-
    mian.—                              [mian.
Welcome, my good Alexas.—Did I, Char-
Ever love Cæsar so?
*Char.*          O that brave Cæsar!

*Cleo.* Be chok'd with such another em-
    phasis!
Say, the brave Antony.
*Char.*                The valiant Cæsar!
*Cleo.* By Isis, I will give thee bloody teeth
If thou with Cæsar paragon again
My man of men.
*Char.*         By your most gracious pardon,
I sing but after you.
*Cleo.*          My salad days,      [blood,
When I was green in judgment:—cold in
To say as I said then!—but, come, away;
Get me ink and paper: he shall have every
    day
A several greeting, or I'll unpeople Egypt.
                                        [*Exeunt.*

ACT II.

SCENE I.—MESSINA. *A Room in* POMPEY'S
*House.*

*Enter* POMPEY, MENECRATES, *and* MENAS.

*Pom.* If the great gods be just, they shall
    assist
The deeds of justest men.
*Mene.*           Know, worthy Pompey,
That what they do delay they not deny.
*Pom.* Whiles we are suitors to their throne,
    decays
The thing we sue for.
*Mene.*         We, ignorant of ourselves,
Beg often our own harms, which the wise
    powers
Deny us for our good; so find we profit
By losing of our prayers.
*Pom.*              I shall do well:
The people love me, and the sea is mine;
My powers are crescent, and my auguring
    hope
Says it will come to the full. Mark Antony
In Egypt sits at dinner, and will make
No wars without doors: Cæsar gets money
    where
He loses hearts: Lepidus flatters both,
Of both is flatter'd; but he neither loves
Nor either cares for him.
*Men.*               Cæsar and Lepidus
Are in the field: a mighty strength they carry.
*Pom.* Where have you this? 'tis false.
*Men.*                       From Silvius, sir.
*Pom.* He dreams: I know they are in
    Rome together,                         [love,
Looking for Antony. But all the charms of
Salt Cleopatra, soften thy wan'd lip! [both!
Let witchcraft join with beauty, lust with
Tie up the libertine in a field of feasts,
Keep his brain fuming; Epicurean cooks
Sharpen with cloyless sauce his appetite;
That sleep and feeding may prorogue his
    honour
Even till a Lethe'd dullness.

*Enter* VARRIUS.

How now, Varrius!

*Var.* This is most certain that I shall deliver:—
Mark Antony is every hour in Rome
Expected: since he went from Egypt 'tis
A space for further travel.

*Pom.* I could have given less matter
A better ear.—Menas, I did not think
This amorous surfeiter would have donn'd his helm
For such a petty war; his soldiership
Is twice the other twain: but let us rear
The higher our opinion, that our stirring
Can from the lap of Egypt's widow pluck
The ne'er lust-wearied Antony.

*Men.* I cannot hope
Cæsar and Antony shall well greet together:
His wife that's dead did trespasses to Cæsar;
His brother warr'd upon him; although, I think,
Not mov'd by Antony.

*Pom.* I know not, Menas.
How lesser enmities may give way to greater.
Were't not that we stand up against them all,
'Twere pregnant they should square between themselves;
For they have entertained cause enough
To· draw their swords: but how the fear of us
May cement their divisions, and bind up
The petty difference, we yet not know.
Be't as our gods will have't! It only stands
Our lives upon to use our strongest hands.
Come, Menas. [*Exeunt.*

SCENE II.—ROME. *A Room in the House of* LEPIDUS.

*Enter* ENOBARBUS *and* LEPIDUS.

*Lep.* Good Enobarbus, 'tis a worthy deed,
And shall become you well, to entreat your captain
To soft and gentle speech.

*Eno.* I shall entreat him
To answer like himself: if Cæsar move him,
Let Antony look over Cæsar's head,
And speak as loud as Mars. By Jupiter,
Were I the wearer of Antonius' beard,
I would not shave't to-day.

*Lep.* 'Tis not a time
For private stomaching.

*Eno.* Every time
Serves for the matter that is then born in't.

*Lep.* But small to greater matters must give way.

*Eno.* Not if the small come first.

*Lep.* Your speech is passion:
But, pray you, stir no embers up. Here comes
The noble Antony.

*Enter* ANTONY *and* VENTIDIUS.

*Eno.* And yonder Cæsar

*Enter* CÆSAR, MECÆNAS, *and* AGRIPPA.

*Ant.* If we compose well here, to Parthia:
Hark, Ventidius.

*Cæs.* I do not know,
Mecænas; ask Agrippa.

*Lep.* Noble friends,
That which combin'd us was most great, and let not
A leaner action rend us. What's amiss,
May it be gently heard: when we debate
Our trivial difference loud, we do commit
Murder in healing wounds: then, noble partners,—
The rather for I earnestly beseech,— [terms,
Touch you the sourest points with sweetest
Nor curstness grow to the matter.

*Ant.* 'Tis spoken well.
Were we before our armies, and to fight,
I should do thus.

*Cæs.* Welcome to Rome.

*Ant.* Thank you.

*Cæs.* Sit.

*Ant.* Sit, sir.

*Cæs.* Nay, then.

*Ant.* I learn, you take things ill which are not so,
Or being, concern you not.

*Cæs.* I must be laugh'd at
If, or for nothing or a little, I
Should say myself offended, and with you
Chiefly i' the world; more laugh'd at that I should [your name
Once name you derogately, when to sound
It not concern'd me.

*Ant.* My being in Egypt, Cæsar,
What was't to you?

*Cæs.* No more than my residing here at Rome
Might be to you in Egypt: yet, if you there
Did practise on my state, your being in Egypt
Might be my question.

*Ant.* How intend you, practis'd?

*Cæs.* You may be pleas'd to catch at mine intent [brother
By what did here befall me. Your wife and
Made wars upon me; and their contestation
Was theme for you, you were the word of war.

*Ant.* You do mistake your business; my brother never
Did urge me in his act: I did inquire it;
And have my learning from some true reports [rather
That drew their swords with you. Did he not
Discredit my authority with yours;
And make the wars alike against my stomach,
Having alike your cause? Of this my letters
Before did satisfy you. If you'll patch a quarrel [with,
As matter whole you have not to make it
It must not be with this.

*Cæs.* You praise yourself
By laying defects of judgment to me; but
You patch'd up your excuses.

*Ant.* Not so, not so;
I know you could not lack, I am certain on't,
Very necessity of this thought, that I,

Your partner in the cause 'gainst which he
 fought,      [wars
Could not with graceful eyes attend those
Which 'fronted mine own peace. As for my
 wife,
I would you had her spirit in such another:
The third o' the world is yours; which with
 a snaffle
You may pace easy, but not such a wife.
 *Eno.* Would we had all such wives, that
 the men
Might go to wars with the women.
 *Ant.* So much uncurable, her garboils,
 Cæsar,      [wanted
Made out of her impatience,—which not
Shrewdness of policy too,—I grieving grant
Did you too much disquiet: for that you
 must
But say I could not help it.
 *Cæs.*     I wrote to you
When rioting in Alexandria; you
Did pocket up my letters, and with taunts
Did gibe my missive out of audience.
 *Ant.*      Sir,
He fell upon me ere admitted: then [want
Three kings I had newly feasted, and did
Of what I was i' the morning: but next day
I told him of myself; which was as much
As to have ask'd him pardon. Let this fellow
Be nothing of our strife; if we contend,
Out of our question wipe him.
 *Cæs.*    You have broken
The article of your oath; which you shall
 never
Have tongue to charge me with.
 *Lep.*     Soft, Cæsar!
 *Ant.* No, Lepidus, let him speak:
The honour is sacred which he talks on now,
Supposing that I lack'd it.—But on, Cæsar;
The article of my oath.
 *Cæs.* To lend me arms and aid when I re-
 quir'd them;
The which you both denied.
 *Ant.*    Neglected, rather;
And then when poison'd hours had bound
 me up      [I may,
From mine own knowledge. As nearly as
I'll play the penitent to you: but mine hon-
 esty      [power
Shall not make poor my greatness, nor my
Work without it. Truth is, that Fulvia,
To have me out of Egypt, made wars here;
For which myself, the ignorant motive, do
So far ask pardon as befits mine honour
To stoop in such a case.
 *Lep.*    'Tis noble spoken.
 *Mec.* If it might please you to enforce no
 further
The griefs between ye: to forget them quite
Were to remember that the present need
Speaks to atone you.
 *Lep.*   Worthily spoken, Mecænas.
 *Eno.* Or, if you borrow one another's love
for the instant, you may, when you hear no

more words of Pompey, return it again: you
shall have time to wrangle in when you have
nothing else to do.
 *Ant.* Thou art a soldier only: speak no
more.
 *Eno.* That truth should be silent I had
almost forgot.
 *Ant.* You wrong this presence; therefore
 speak no more.
 *Eno.* Go to, then; your considerate stone.
 *Cæs.* I do not much dislike the matter,
 but
The manner of his speech; for't cannot be
We shall remain in friendship, our conditions
So differing in their acts. Yet, if I knew
What hoop should hold us staunch, from
 edge to edge
O' the world I would pursue it.
 *Agr.*   Give me leave, Cæsar,—
 *Cæs.* Speak, Agrippa.
 *Agr.* Thou hast a sister by the mother's
 side,
Admir'd Octavia: great Mark Antony
Is now a widower.
 *Cæs.*   Say not so, Agrippa:
If Cleopatra heard you, your reproof
Were well deserv'd of rashness.
 *Ant.* I am not married, Cæsar: let me hear
Agrippa further speak.
 *Agr.* To hold you in perpetual amity,
To make you brothers, and to knit your
 hearts
With an unslipping knot, take Antony
Octavia to his wife; whose beauty claims
No worse a husband than the best of men;
Whose virtue and whose general graces speak
That which none else can utter. By this mar-
 riage,
All little jealousies, which now seem great,
And all great fears, which now import their
 dangers,     [be tales,
Would then be nothing: truths would then
Where now half tales be truths: her love to
 both
Would, each to other and all loves to both,
Draw after her. Pardon what I have spoke;
For 'tis a studied, not a present thought,
By duty ruminated.
 *Ant.*   Will Cæsar speak?
 *Cæs.* Not till he hears how Antony is
 touch'd
With what is spoke already.
 *Ant.*   What power is in Agrippa,
If I would say, *Agrippa, be it so,*
To make this good?
 *Cæs.*   The power of Cæsar, and
His power unto Octavia.
 *Ant.*    May I never
To this good purpose, that so fairly shows,
Dream of impediment!—Let me have thy
 hand:
Further this act of grace; and from this hour
The heart of brothers govern in our loves
And sway our great designs!

*Cæs.*                    There is my hand.
A sister I bequeath you, whom no brother
Did ever love so dearly: let her live [never
To join our kingdoms and our hearts; and
Fly off our loves again!
    *Lep.*                    Happily, amen!
    *Ant.* I did not think to draw my sword
        'gainst Pompey;
For he hath laid strange courtesies and great
Of late upon me: I must thank him only,
Lest my remembrance suffer ill report;
At heel of that, defy him.
    *Lep.*                    Time calls upon's:
Of us must Pompey presently be sought,
Or else he seeks out us.
    *Ant.*                    Where lies he?
    *Cæs.* About the Mount Misenum.
    *Ant.*                    What's his strength
By land?
    *Cæs.* Great and increasing: but by sea
He is an absolute master.
    *Ant.*                    So is the fame.
Would we had spoke together! Haste we for
        it:
Yet, ere we put ourselves in arms, despatch
        we
The business we have talk'd of.
    *Cæs.*                    With most gladness;
And do invite you to my sister's view,
Whither straight I'll lead you.
    *Ant.*                    Let us, Lepidus,
Not lack your company.
    *Lep.*                    Noble Antony,
Not sickness should detain me.
    [*Flourish. Exeunt* Cæs., Ant., *and* Lep.
    *Mec.* Welcome from Egypt, sir.
    *Eno.* Half the heart of Cæsar, worthy
Mecænas!—my honourable friend, Agrippa!—
    *Agr.* Good Enobarbus!
    *Mec.* We have cause to be glad that mat-
ters are so well digested. You stay'd well by
it in Egypt.
    *Eno.* Ay, sir; we did sleep day out of
countenance, and made the night light with
drinking.
    *Mec.* Eight wild boars roasted whole at a
breakfast, and but twelve persons there; is
this true?
    *Eno.* This was but as a fly by an eagle: we
had much more monstrous matter of feasts,
which worthily deserved noting.
    *Mec.* She's a most triumphant lady, if re-
port be square to her.
    *Eno.* When she first met Mark Antony she
pursed up his heart, upon the river of Cydnus.
    *Agr.* There she appeared indeed; or my re-
porter devised well for her.
    *Eno.* I will tell you.
The barge she sat in, like a burnish'd throne,
Burn'd on the water: the poop was beaten
        gold;
Purple the sails, and so perfumed that

The winds were love-sick with them: the
        oars were silver,        [made
Which to the tune of flutes kept stroke, and
The water which they beat to follow faster,
As amorous of their strokes. For her own
        person,
It beggar'd all description: she did lie
In her pavilion,—cloth-of-gold of tissue,—
O'er-picturing that Venus where we see
The fancy out-work nature: on each side her
Stood pretty dimpled boys, like smiling
        Cupids,                    [seem
With divers-colour'd fans, whose wind did,
To glow the delicate cheeks which they did
        cool,
And what they undid did.
    *Agr.*                    O, rare for Antony!
    *Eno.* Her gentlewomen, like the Nereids,
So many mermaids, tended her i' the eyes,
And made their bends adornings: at the helm
A seeming mermaid steers: the silken tackle
Swell with the touches of those flower-soft
        hands
That yarely frame the office. From the barge
A strange invisible perfume hits the sense
Of the adjacent wharfs. The city cast
Her people out upon her; and Antony,
Enthron'd i' the market-place, did sit alone,
Whistling to the air; which, but for vacancy,
Had gone to gaze on Cleopatra too,
And made a gap in nature.
    *Agr.*                    Rare Egyptian!
    *Eno.* Upon her landing, Antony sent to
        her,
Invited her to supper: she replied
It should be better he became her guest;
Which she entreated: our courteous Antony
Whom ne'er the word of *No* woman heard
        speak,                    [feast,
Being barber'd ten times o'er, goes to the
And, for his ordinary, pays his heart
For what his eyes eat only.
    *Agr.*                    Royal wench!
She made great Cæsar lay his sword to bed:
He plough'd her, and she cropp'd.
    *Eno.*                    I saw her once
Hop forty paces through the public street;
And having lost her breath, she spoke and
        panted,
That she did make defect perfection,
And, breathless, power breathe forth.
    *Mec.* Now Antony must leave her utterly.
    *Eno.* Never; he will not:
Age cannot wither her, nor custom stale
Her infinite variety: other women cloy [gry
The appetites they feed; but she makes hun-
Where most she satisfies: for vilest things
Become themselves in her; that the holy
        priests
Bless her when she is riggish.
    *Mec.* If beauty, wisdom, modesty, can
        settle
The heart of Antony, Octavia is
A blessed lottery to him.

*Agr.*                    Let us go.—
Good Enobarbus, make yourself my guest
Whilst you abide here.
      *Eno.* Humbly, sir, I thank you. [*Exeunt.*

SCENE III.—ROME. *A Room in* CÆSAR'S
              *House.*

*Enter* CÆSAR, ANTONY, OCTAVIA *between*
      *them, and* Attendants.

      *Ant.* The world and my great office will
            sometimes
Divide me from your bosom.
      *Octa.*                    All which time
Before the gods my knee shall bow my pray-
            ers
To them for you.
      *Ant.*          Good-night, sir.—My Octavia.
Read not my blemishes in the world's report:
I have not kept my square; but that to come
Shall all be done by the rule. Good-night,
            dear lady.—
      *Octa.* Good-night, sir.
      *Cæs.* Good-night. [*Exeunt* CÆS. *and* OCTA.

      *Enter* Soothsayer.

      *Ant.* Now, sirrah, you do wish yourself in
            Egypt?          [thence, nor you
      *Sooth.* Would I had never come from
Thither!
      *Ant.* If you can, your reason?
      *Sooth.*                    I see it in .
My motion, have it not in my tongue: but
            yet
Hie you to Egypt again.
      *Ant.*                    Say to me, [mine?
Whose fortunes shall rise higher, Cæsar's or
      *Sooth.* Cæsar's.
Therefore, O Antony, stay not by his side:
Thy demon, that's thy spirit which keeps
            thee, is
Noble, courageous, high, unmatchable,
Where Cæsar's is not; but near him thy angel
Becomes afear'd, as being o'erpower'd: there-
            fore
Make space enough between you.
      *Ant.*                    Speak this no more.
      *Sooth.* To none but thee; no more but
            when to thee.
If thou dost play with him at any game,
Thou art sure to lose; and of that natural
            luck          [thickens
He beats thee 'gainst the odds: thy lustre
When he shines by: I say again, thy spirit
Is all afraid to govern thee near him;
But, he away, 'tis noble.
      *Ant.*                    Get thee gone:
Say to Ventidius I would speak with him:—
                    [*Exit* Soothsayer.
He shall to Parthia.—Be it art or hap,
He hath spoken true: the very dice obey
            him;—
And in our sports my better cunning faints
Under his chance: if he draw lots he speeds;
His cocks do win the battle still of mine,

When it is all to naught; and his quails ever
Beat mine, inhoop'd, at odds. I will to Egypt:
And though I make this marriage for my
            peace,
I' the east my pleasure lies.

      *Enter* VENTIDIUS.
                    O, come, Ventidius.
You must to Parthia: your commission's
            ready;
Follow me and receive it.          [*Exeunt.*

SCENE IV.—ROME. *A Street.*

      *Enter* LEPIDUS, MECÆNAS, *and* AGRIPPA.

      *Lep.* Trouble yourselves no further: pray
            you, hasten
Your generals after.
      *Agr.*                    Sir, Mark Antony
Will e'en but kiss Octavia, and we'll follow.
      *Lep.* Till I shall see you in your soldier's
            dress,
Which will become you both, farewell.
      *Mec.*                    We shall,
As I conceive the journey, be at the mount
Before you, Lepidus.
      *Lep.*                    Your way is shorter;
My purposes do draw me much about:
You'll win two days upon me.
      *Mec. and Agr.*          Sir, good success!
      *Lep.* Farewell.          [*Exeunt.*

SCENE V.—ALEXANDRIA. *A Room in the*
              *Palace.*

*Enter* CLEOPATRA, CHARMIAN, IRAS, ALEXAS,
              *and* Attendants.

      *Cleo.* Give me some music,—music, moody
            food
Of us that trade in love.
      *Attend.*                    The music, ho!

      *Enter* MARDIAN.

      *Cleo.* Let it alone; let's to billiards:
Come, Charmian.
      *Char.* My arm is sore; best play with Mar-
            dian.
      *Cleo.* As well a woman with an eunuch
            play'd          [me, sir?
As with a woman.—Come, you'll play with
      *Mar.* As well as I can, madam.
      *Cleo.* And when good-will is show'd,
            though't come too short,
The actor may plead pardon. I'll none now:—
Give me mine angle,—we'll to the river:
            there,
My music playing far off, I will betray
Tawny-finn'd fishes; my bended hook shall
            pierce
Their slimy jaws; and as I draw them up
I'll think them every one an Antony,
And say, *Ah ha! you're caught.*
      *Char.*                    'Twas merry when
You wager'd on your angling; when your
            diver

Did hang a salt fish on his hook, which he
With fervency drew up.
*Cleo*.                That time,—O times!—
I laugh'd him out of patience; and that night
I laugh'd him into patience: and next morn,
Ere the ninth hour, I drunk him to his bed;
Then put my tires and mantles on him, whilst
I wore his sword Philippan.

*Enter a* Messenger.
                    O! from Italy!—
Ram thou thy fruitful tidings in mine ears,
That long time have been barren.
*Mess*.                Madam, madam,—
*Cleo*. Antony's dead!—        [tress:
If thou say so, villain, thou kill'st thy mis-
But well and free,
If thou so yield him, there is gold, and here
My bluest veins to kiss,—a hand that kings
Have lipp'd, and trembled kissing.
*Mess*.            First, madam, he's well.
*Cleo*. Why, there's more gold. But, sirrah,
mark, we use
To say the dead are well: bring it to that,
The gold I give thee will I melt and pour
Down thy ill-uttering throat.
*Mess*. Good madam, hear me.
*Cleo*.            Well, go to, I will;
But there's no goodness in thy face: if An-
tony
Be free and healthful,—why so tart a favour
To trumpet such good tidings! If not well,
Thou shouldst come like a fury crown'd with
snakes,
Not like a formal man.
*Mess*.            Will't please you hear me?
*Cleo*. I have a mind to strike thee ere
thou speak'st:
Yet, if thou say Antony lives, is well,
Or friends with Cæsar, or not captive to him,
I'll set thee in a shower of gold, and hail
Rich pearls upon thee.
*Mess*.            Madam, he's well.
*Cleo*.                Well said.
*Mess*. And friends with Cæsar.
*Cleo*.                Thou'rt an honest man.
*Mess*. Cæsar and he are greater friends
than ever.
*Cleo*. Make thee a fortune from me.
*Mess*.            But yet, madam.—
*Cleo*. I do not like *but yet*, it does ally
The good precedence; fie upon *but yet*!
*But yet* is as a gaoler to bring forth
Some monstrous malefactor. Pr'ythee, friend,
Pour out the pack of matter to mine ear,
The good and bad together: he's friends with
Cæsar;            [say'st, free.
In state of health, thou say'st; and, thou
*Mess*. Free, madam! no; I made no such
report:
He's bound unto Octavia.
*Cleo*.            For what good turn?
*Mess*. For the best turn i' the bed.
*Cleo*.            I am pale, Charmian.

*Mess*. Madam, he's married to Octavia.
*Cleo*. The most infectious pestilence upon
thee!            [*Strikes him down*.
*Mess*. Good madam, patience.
*Cleo*.            What say you?—Hence,
                [*Strikes him again*.
Horrible villain! or I'll spurn thine eyes
Like balls before me; I'll unhair thy head:
            [*She hales him up and down*.
Thou shalt be whipp'd with wire and stew'd
in brine,
Smarting in ling'ring pickle.
*Mess*.            Gracious madam,
I that do bring the news made not the match.
*Cleo*. Say 'tis not so, a province I will give
thee,            [thou hadst
And make thy fortunes proud: the blow
Shall make thy peace for moving me to rage;
And I will boot thee with what gift beside
Thy modesty can beg.
*Mess*.            He's married, madam.
*Cleo*. Rogue, thou hast liv'd too long.
            [*Draws a dagger*.
*Mess*. Nay, then I'll run.
What mean you, madam? I have made no
fault.            [*Exit*.
*Char*. Good madam, keep yourself within
yourself.
The man is innocent.
*Cleo*. Some innocents scape not the thun-
derbolt.—
Melt Egypt into Nile! and kindly creatures
Turn all to serpents!—Call the slave again:—
Though I am mad, I will not bite him:—
call.
*Char*. He is afear'd to come.
*Cleo*.            I will not hurt him.
            [*Exit* CHARMIAN.
These hands do lack nobility, that they strike
A meaner than myself; since I myself
Have given myself the cause.

*Re-enter* CHARMIAN *and* Messenger.
                Come hither, sir.
Though it be honest, it is never good    [sage
To bring bad news: give to a gracious mes-
An host of tongues; but let ill tidings tell
Themselves when they be felt.
*Mess*.            I have done my duty.
*Cleo*. Is he married?
I cannot hate thee worser than I do
If thou again say Yes.
*Mess*.            He is married, madam.
*Cleo*. The gods confound thee! dost thou
hold there still!
*Mess*. Should I lie, madam?
*Cleo*.            O, I would thou didst,
So half my Egypt were submerg'd, and made
A cistern for scal'd snakes! Go, get thee
hence:
Hadst thou Narcissus in thy face, to me
Thou wouldst appear most ugly. He is mar-
ried?
*Mess*. I crave your highness' pardon.

*Cleo.*　　　　　　　　　He is married?

*Mess.* Take no offence that I would not
　　offend you:

To punish me for what you make me do
Seems much unequal: he is married to
　　Octavia.

*Cleo.* O that his fault should make a knave
　　of thee,　　　　　　　　　　　[hence:
Thou art not what thou'rt sure of!—Get thee
The merchandise which thou hast brought
　　from Rome　　　　　　　　　　[hand,
Are all too dear for me: lie they upon thy
And be undone by 'em!　[*Exit* Messenger.

*Char.*　　Good your highness, patience.

*Cleo.* In praising Antony I have dis-
　　prais'd Cæsar.

*Char.* Many times, madam.

*Cleo.*　　　　　　I am paid for't now.
Lead me from hence;
I faint:—O Iras, Charmian!—'tis no mat-
　　ter.—

Go to the fellow, good Alexas; bid him
Report the feature of Octavia, her years,
Her inclination, let him not leave out
The colour of her hair:—bring me word
　　quickly.　　　　　　　　[*Exit* ALEXAS.
Let him for ever go:—let him not—Char-
　　mian,
Though he be painted one way like a Gorgon,
T' other way he's a Mars.—Bid my Alexas
　　　　　　　　　　　　[*To* MARDIAN.
Bring me word how tall she is.—Pity me,
　　Charmian,
But do not speak to me.—Lead me to my
　　chamber.　　　　　　　　　[*Exeunt.*

SCENE VI.—*Near Misenum.*

*Flourish. Enter* POMPEY *and* MENAS *at one
side, with drum and trumpet: at the other,*
CÆSAR, ANTONY, LEPIDUS, ENOBARBUS,
MECÆNAS, *with* Soldiers *marching.*

*Pom.* Your hostages I have, so have you
　　mine;
And we shall talk before we fight.

*Cæs.*　　　　　　　　　　Most meet
That first we come to words; and therefore
　　have we
Our written purposes before us sent;
Which, if thou hast consider'd, let us know
If 'twill tie up thy discontended sword,
And carry back to Sicily much tall youth
That else must perish here.

*Pom.*　　　　　To you all three,
The senators alone of this great world,
Chief factors for the gods,—I do not know
Wherefore my father should revengers want,
Having a son and friends; since Julius Cæsar,
Who at Philippi the good Brutus ghosted,
There saw you labouring for him. What was't
That mov'd pale Cassius to conspire; and
　　what　　　　　　　　　　　　[tus,
Made the all-honour'd, honest Roman, Bru-
With the arm'd rest, courtiers of beauteous
　　freedom

To drench the Capitol, but that they would
Have one man but a man? And that is it
Hath made me rig my navy; at whose burden
The anger'd ocean foams; with which I
　　meant　　　　　　　　　　　　[Rome
To scourge the ingratitude that despiteful
Cast on my noble father.

*Cæs.*　　　　　　Take your time.

*Ant.* Thou canst not fear us, Pompey, with
　　thy sails;　　　　　　　　　[know'st
We'll speak with thee at sea: at land thou
How much we do o'er-count thee.

*Pom.*　　　　　　At land, indeed,
Thou dost o'er-count me of my father's
　　house:
But, since the cuckoo builds not for himself,
Remain in't as thou mayst.

*Lep.*　　　　　Be pleas'd to tell us,—
For this is from the present,—how you take
The offers we have sent you.

*Cæs.*　　　　　　There's the point.

*Ant.* Which do not be entreated to, but
　　weigh
What it is worth embrac'd.

*Cæs.*　　　　　And what may follow,
To try a larger fortune.

*Pom.*　　　　　You have made me offer
Of Sicily, Sardinia; and I must
Rid all the sea of pirates; then to send
Measures of wheat to Rome; this 'greed
　　upon,
To part with unhack'd edges, and bear back
Our targes undinted.

*Cæs., Ant., and Lep.*　　That's our offer.

*Pom.*　　　　　　Know, then,
I came before you here a man prepar'd
To take this offer: but Mark Antony
Put me to some impatience:—though I lose
The praise of it by telling, you must know,
When Cæsar and your brother were at blows,
Your mother came to Sicily, and did find
Her welcome friendly.

*Ant.*　　　　I have heard it, Pompey;
And am well studied for a liberal thanks
Which I do owe you.

*Pom.* Let me have your hand:
I did not think, sir, to have met you here.

*Ant.* The beds i' the east are soft; and,
　　thanks to you,　　　　　　　[hither;
That call'd me, timelier than my purpose,
For I have gain'd by it.

*Cæs.*　　　　　Since I saw you last
There is a change upon you.

*Pom.*　　　　　Well, I know not
What counts harsh fortune casts upon my
　　face;
But in my bosom shall she never come
To make my heart her vassal.

*Lep.*　　　　　　Well met here.

*Pom.* I hope so, Lepidus.—Thus we are
　　agreed:
I crave our composition may be written,
And seal'd between us.

*Cæs.*　　　　　That's the next to do.

*Pom.* We'll feast each other ere we part;
   and let's
Draw lots who shall begin.
   *Ant.*                 That will I, Pompey.
*Pom.* No, Antony, take the lot: but, first
Or last, your fine Egyptian cookery [Cæsar
Shall have the fame. I have heard that Julius
Grew fat with feasting there.
   *Ant.*                 You have heard much.
*Pom.* I have fair meanings, sir.
   *Ant.*                 And fair words to them.
*Pom.* Then so much have I heard:
And I have heard Apollodorus carried,—
   *Eno.* No more of that:—he did so.
*Pom.*                 What, I pray you?
*Eno.* A certain queen to Cæsar in a mat-
   tress.                 [soldier?
*Pom.* I know thee now: how far'st thou,
*Eno.*                 Well;
And well am like to do; for I perceive
Four feasts are toward.
   *Pom.*                 Let me shake thy hand;
I never hated thee: I have seen thee fight,
When I have envied thy behaviour.
   *Eno.*                 Sir,
I never lov'd you much; but I ha' prais'd ye,
When you have well deserv'd ten times as
   much
As I have said you did.
   *Pom.*                 Enjoy thy plainness,
It nothing ill becomes thee.—
Aboard my galley I invite you all:
Will you lead, lords?
   *Cæs., Ant., and Lep.* Show us the way, sir.
*Pom.*                 Come.
         [*Exeunt all but* MEN. *and* ENO.
*Men.* [*Aside.*] Thy father, Pompey, would
ne'er have made this treaty.—You and I
have known, sir.
   *Eno.* At sea, I think.
   *Men.* We have, sir.
   *Eno.* You have done well by water.
   *Men.* And you by land.
   *Eno.* I will praise any man that will
praise me; though it cannot be denied what I
have done by land.
   *Men.* Nor what I have done by water.
   *Eno.* Yes, something you can deny for
your own safety: you have been a great thief
by sea.
   *Men.* And you by land.
   *Eno.* There I deny my land service. But
give me your hand, Menas: if our eyes had
authority, here they might take two thieves
kissing.
   *Men.* All men's faces are true, whatsoe'er
their hands are.
   *Eno.* But there is never a fair woman has
a true face.
   *Men.* No slander; they steal hearts.
   *Eno.* We came hither to fight with you.
   *Men.* For my part, I am sorry it is turned
to a drinking. Pompey doth this day laugh
away his fortune.

*Eno.* If he do, sure, he cannot weep it
back again.
   *Men.* You have said, sir. We looked not
for Mark Antony here: pray you, is he mar-
ried to Cleopatra?
   *Eno.* Cæsar's sister is called Octavia.
   *Men.* True, sir; she was the wife of Caius
Marcellus.
   *Eno.* But she is now the wife of Marcus
Antonius.
   *Men.* Pray you, sir?
   *Eno.* 'Tis true.
   *Men.* Then is Cæsar and he for ever knit
   together.
   *Eno.* If I were bound to divine of this
unity, I would not prophesy so.
   *Men.* I think the policy of that purpose
made more in the marriage than the love of
the parties.
   *Eno.* I think so too. But you shall find the
band that seems to tie their friendship together will be the very strangler of their
amity: Octavia is of a holy, cold, and still
conversation.
   *Men.* Who would not have his wife so?
   *Eno.* Not he that himself is not so; which
is Mark Antony. He will to his Egyptian dish
again: then shall the sighs of Octavia blow
the fire up in Cæsar; and, as I said before,
that which is the strength of their amity
shall prove the immediate author of their
variance. Antony will use his affection where
it is: he married but his occasion here.
   *Men.* And thus it may be. Come, sir, will
you aboard? I have a health for you.
   *Eno.* I shall take it, sir: we have used our
throats in Egypt.
   *Men.* Come, let's away.        [*Exeunt.*

SCENE VII.—*On board* POMPEY's *Galley,
   lying near Misenum.*

*Music. Enter two or three* Servants *with a
   banquet.*

   1 *Serv.* Here they'll be, man. Some o'
their plants are ill-rooted already; the least
wind i' the world will blow them down.
   2 *Serv.* Lepidus is high-coloured.
   1 *Serv.* They have made him drink alms-
drink.
   2 *Serv.* As they pinch one another by the
disposition, he cries out, *no more;* reconciles them to his entreaty and himself to the
drink.
   1 *Serv.* But it raises the greater war between him and his discretion.
   2 *Serv.* Why, this it is to have a name in
great men's fellowship: I had as lief have a
reed that will do me no service as a partizan
I could not heave.
   1 *Serv.* To be called into a huge sphere,
and not to be seen to move in't, are the holes
where eyes should be, which pitifully disaster
the cheeks.

*A sennet sounded. Enter* CÆSAR, ANTONY, LEPIDUS, POMPEY, AGRIPPA, MACÆNAS, ENOBARBUS, MENAS, *with other* Captains.

*Ant.* [*To* CÆSAR:] Thus do they, sir: they take the flow o' the Nile
By certain scales i' the pyramid; they know,
By the height, the lowness, or the mean, if dearth
Or foison follow: the higher Nilus swells
The more it promises: as it ebbs, the seedsman
Upon the slime and ooze scatters his grain,
And shortly comes to harvest.

*Lep.* You've strange serpents there.

*Ant.* Ay, Lepidus.

*Lep.* Your serpent of Egypt is bred now of your mud by the operation of your sun: so is your crocodile.

*Ant.* They are so.　　　[Lepidus!

*Pom.* Sit,—and some wine!—A health to

*Lep.* I am not so well as I should be, but I'll ne'er out.

*Eno.* Not till you have slept; I fear me you'll be in till then.

*Lep.* Nay, certainly, I have heard the Ptolemies' pyramises are very goodly things; without contradiction, I have heard that.

*Men.* [*Aside to* POM.] Pompey, a word.

*Pom.* [*Aside to* MEN.] Say in mine ear: what is't?

*Men.* [*Aside to* POM.] Forsake thy seat, I do beseech thee, captain,
And hear me speak a word.

*Pom.* [*Aside to* MEN.] Forbear me till anon.—
This wine for Lepidus!　　　[dile?

*Lep.* What manner o' thing is your croco-

*Ant.* It is shaped, sir, like itself; and it is as broad as it hath breadth: it is just so high as it is, and moves with its own organs: it lives by that which nourisheth it; and, the elements once out of it, it transmigrates.

*Lep.* What colour is it of?

*Ant.* Of its own colour too.

*Lep.* 'Tis a strange serpent.

*Ant.* 'Tis so. And the tears of it are wet.

*Cæs.* Will this description satisfy him?

*Ant.* With the health that Pompey gives him, else he is a very epicure.

*Pom.* [*Aside to* MEN.] Go, hang, sir, hang! Tell me of that? away!　　　[for?

Do as I bid you.—Where's this cup I call'd

*Men.* [*Aside to* POM.] If for the sake of merit thou wilt hear me,
Rise from thy stool.

*Pom.* [*Aside to* MEN.] I think thou'rt mad. The matter?
　　　　　[*Rises and walks aside.*

*Men.* I have ever held my cap off to thy fortunes.

*Por.* Thou hast serv'd me with much faith. What's else to say?—
Be jolly, lords.

*Ant.*　　　　These quicksands, Lepidus,
Keep off them, for you sink.

*Men.* Wilt thou be lord of all the world?

*Pom.*　　　　What say'st thou?

*Men.* Wilt thou be lord of the whole world? That's twice.

*Pom.* How should that be?

*Men.*　　　　But entertain it, and,
Although thou think me poor, I am the man
Will give thee all the world.

*Pom.*　　　　Hast thou drunk well?

*Men.* No, Pompey, I have kept me from the cup.
Thou art, if thou dar'st be, the earthly Jove:
Whate'er the ocean pales or sky inclips
Is thine, if thou wilt have't.

*Pom.*　　　　Show me which way.

*Men.* These three world-sharers, these competitors,
Are in thy vessel: let me cut the cable;
And, when we are put off, fall to their throats:
All then is thine.

*Pom.*　　　　Ah, this thou shouldst have done,
And not have spoke on't! In me 'tis villany;
In thee't had been good service. Thou must know　　　[our;
'Tis not my profit that does lead mine hon-
Mine honour it. Repent that e'er thy tongue
Hath so betray'd thine act: being done un-known,
I should have found it afterwards well done;
But must condemn it now. Desist, and drink.

*Men.* [*Aside.*] For this
I'll never follow thy pall'd fortunes more.
Who seeks, and will not take when once 'tis offer'd,
Shall never find it more.

*Pom.*　　　　This health to Lepidus!

*Ant.* Bear him ashore. I'll pledge it for him, Pompey.

*Eno.* Here's to thee, Menas!

*Men.*　　　　Enobarbus, welcome!

*Pom.* Fill till the cup be hid.

*Eno.* There's a strong fellow, Menas.
[*Pointing to the* Attendant *who carries off* LEP.

*Men.*　　　　Why?

*Eno.*　　　　'A bears
The third part of the world, man; see'st not?

*Men.* The third part, then, is drunk: would it were all,
That it might go on wheels!

*Eno.* Drink thou; increase the reels.

*Men.* Come.

*Pom.* This is not yet an Alexandrian feast.

*Ant.* It ripens towards it.—Strike the vessels, ho!—
Here is to Cæsar!

*Cæs.*　　　　I could well forbear't.
It's monstrous labour when I wash my brain
And it grows fouler.

*Ant.*　　　　Be a child o' the time.

*Cæs.* Possess it, I'll make answer:

But I had rather fast from all four days
Than drink so much in one.
  *Eno.* Ha, my brave emperor!
                      [*To* ANTONY.
Shall we dance now the Egyptian Bacchanals,
And celebrate our drink?
  *Pom.*        Let's ha't, good soldier.
  *Ant.* Come, let's all take hands, [our sense
Till that the conquering wine hath steep'd
In soft and delicate Lethe.
  *Eno.*          All take hands.—
Make battery to our ears with the loud
    music:—                [sing;
The while I'll place you: then the boy shall
The holding every man shall beat as loud
As his strong sides can volley.
[*Music plays.* ENO. *places them hand in hand.*

           SONG.

    Come, thou monarch of the vine,
    Plumpy Bacchus with pink eyne!
    In thy fats our cares be drown'd,
    With thy grapes our hairs be crown'd:
    Cup us, till the world go round,
    Cup us, till the world go round!

  *Cæs.* What would you more?—Pompey,
    good-night. Good brother,
Let me request you off: our graver business
Frowns at this levity.—Gentle lords, let's
    part;
You see we have burnt our cheeks: strong
    Enobarb            [tongue
Is weaker than the wine; and mine own
Splits what it speaks: the wild disguise hath
    almost.           [Good-night.—
Antick'd us all. What needs more words.
Good Antony, your hand.
  *Pom.*      I'll try you on the shore.
  *Ant.* And shall, sir: give's your hand.
  *Pom.*           O Antony,
You have my father's house,—but, what? we
    are friends.
Come, down into the boat.
  *Eno.*        Take heed you fall not.
[*Exeunt* POM., CÆS., ANT., *and* Attendants.
Menas, I'll not on shore.
  *Men.*         No, to my cabin.—
These drums!—these trumpets, flutes!
    what!—
Let Neptune hear we bid a loud farewell
To these great fellows: sound and be hang'd,
    sound out!
    [*A flourish of trumpets, with drums.*
  *Eno.* Hoo! says 'a.—There's my cap.
  *Men.* Hoo!—noble captain, come.
                    [*Exeunt.*

## ACT III.

### SCENE I.—*A Plain in Syria.*

*Enter* VENTIDIUS, *in triumph, with* SILIUS
*and other* Romans, Officers, *and* Soldiers;
*the dead body of* PACORUS *borne in front.*

  *Ven.* Now, darting Parthia, art thou
    struck; and now

Pleas'd fortune does of Marcus Crassus'
    death
Make me revenger.—Bear the king's son's
    body
Before our army.—Thy Pacorus, Orodes,
Pays this for Marcus Crassus.
  *Sil.*           Noble Ventidius,
Whilst yet with Parthian blood thy sword is
    warm              [Media,
The fugitive Parthians follow; spur through
Mesopotamia, and the shelter whither
The routed fly: so thy grand captain Antony
Shall set thee on triumphant chariots, and
Put garlands on thy head.
  *Ven.*        O Silius, Silius,
I have done enough: a lower place, note well,
May make too great an act; for learn this,
    Silius,—
Better to leave undone, than by our deed
Acquire too high a fame when him we serve's
    away.
Cæsar and Antony have ever won
More in their officer, than person: Sossius,
One of my place in Syria, his lieutenant,
For quick accumulation of renown, [favour.
Which he achiev'd by the minute, lost his
Who does i' the wars more than his captain
    can
Becomes his captain's captain: and ambition,
The soldier's virtue, rather makes choice of
    loss
Than gain which darkens him.
I could do more to do Antonius good,
But 'twould offend him; and in his offence
Should my performance perish.
  *Sil.*        Thou hast, Ventidius, that
Without the which a soldier and his sword
Grants scarce distinction. Thou wilt write to
    Antony?
  *Ven.* I'll humbly signify what in his name,
That magical word of war, we have effected;
How, with his banners, and his well-paid
    ranks,
The ne'er-yet-beaten horse of Parthia
We have jaded out o' the field.
  *Sil.*          Where is he now?
  *Ven.* He purposeth to Athens: whither,
    with what haste         [mit,
The weight we must convey with's will per-
We shall appear before him.—On, there; pass
    along!            [*Exeunt.*

### SCENE II.—ROME. *An Ante-Chamber in* CÆSAR'S *House.*

*Enter* AGRIPPA *and* ENOBARBUS, *meeting.*

  *Agr.* What, are the brothers parted?
  *Eno.* They have despatch'd with Pom-
    pey, he is gone;
The other three are sealing. Octavia weeps
To part from Rome: Cæsar is sad; and
    Lepidus,        [troubled
Since Pompey's feast, as Menas says, is
With the green sickness.

*Agr.*　　　　　　'Tis a noble Lepidus.
*Eno.* A very fine one: O, how he loves
　　Cæsar!　　　　　　　　[Antony!
*Agr.* Nay, but how dearly he adores Mark
*Eno.* Cæsar? Why he's the Jupiter of men.
*Agr.* What's Antony? The god of Jupiter.
*Eno.* Speak you of Cæsar? How! the
　　nonpareil!
*Agr.* Of Antony. O thou Arabian bird!
*Eno.* Would you praise Cæsar, say *Cæsar*,
　　—go no further.
*Agr.* Indeed, he plied them both with ex-
　　cellent praises.　　　　　[loves Antony:
*Eno.* But he loves Cæsar best;—yet he
Hoo! hearts, tongues, figures, scribes, bards,
　　poets cannot　　　　　　[hoo!—
Think, speak, cast, write, sing, number,—
His love to Antony. But as for Cæsar,
Kneel down, kneel down, and wonder.
*Agr.*　　　　　　　　Both he loves.
*Eno.* They are his shards, and he their
　　beetle. [*Trumpets within.*] So,—
This is to horse.—Adieu, noble Agrippa.
*Agr.* Good fortune, worthy soldier; and
　　farewell.

　　*Enter* CÆSAR, ANTONY, LEPIDUS, *and*
　　　　　　OCTAVIA.

*Ant.* No further, sir.
*Cæs.* You take from me a great part of
　　myself;
Use me well in't.—Sister, prove such a wife
As my thoughts make thee, and as my fur-
　　thest band　　　　　　　[tony,
Shall pass on thy approof.—Most noble An-
Let not the piece of virtue which is set
Betwixt us as the cement of our love,
To keep it builded, be the ram to batter
The fortress of it; for better might we
Have lov'd without this mean if on both
　　parts
This be not cherish'd.
*Ant.*　　　　　　Make me not offended
In your distrust.
*Cæs.*　　　　　I have said.
*Ant.*　　　　　　You shall not find,
Though you be therein curious, the least
　　cause　　　　　　　　[keep you,
For what you seem to fear: so, the gods
And make the hearts of Romans serve your
　　ends!
We will here part.　　　　　[well:
*Cæs.* Farewell, my dearest sister, fare thee
The elements be kind to thee, and make
Thy spirits all of comfort! Fare thee well.
*Octa.* My noble brother!—
*Ant.* The April's in her eyes: it is love's
　　spring.　　　　　　　　[cheerful.
And these the showers to bring it on.—Be
*Octa.* Sir, look well to my husband's
　　house; and—
*Cæs.*　　　　　What,
Octavia?
*Octa.* I'll tell you in your ear.

*Ant.* Her tongue will not obey her heart,
　　nor can　　　　　　　[down feather,
Her heart inform her tongue,—the swan's
That stands upon the swell at the full of tide,
And neither way inclines.
*Eno.* [*Aside to* AGRIPPA.] Will Cæsar
　　weep?
*Agr.* [*Aside to* ENO.] He has a cloud in's
　　face.
*Eno.* [*Aside to* AGRIPPA.] He were the
　　worse for that, were he a horse;
So is he, being a man.
*Agr.* [*Aside to* ENO.] Why, Enobarbus,
When Antony found Julius Cæsar dead,
He cried almost to roaring; and he wept
When at Philippi he found Brutus slain.
*Eno.* [*Aside to* AGRIPPA.] That year, in-
　　deed, he was troubled with a rheum;
What willingly he did confound he wail'd;
Believe't till I weep too.
*Cæs.*　　　　　　No, sweet Octavia,
You shall hear from me still; the time shall
　　not
Out-go my thinking on you.
*Ant.*　　　　　　Come, sir, come;
I'll wrestle with you in my strength of love:
Look, here I have you; thus I let you go,
And give you to the gods.
*Cæs.*　　　　　　Adieu; be happy!
*Lep.* Let all the number of the stars give
　　light
To thy fair way!
*Cæs.* Farewell, farewell! [*Kisses* OCTAVIA.
*Ant.*　　　　　　Farewell!
　　[*Trumpets sound within. Exeunt.*

SCENE III.—ALEXANDRIA. *A Room in the
　　Palace.*

　　*Enter* CLEOPATRA, CHARMIAN, IRAS, *and*
　　　　　　ALEXAS.

*Cleo.* Where is the fellow?
*Alex.*　　　　　Half afear'd to come.
*Cleo.* Go to, go to.

　　　　*Enter* a Messenger.
　　　　　　Come hither, sir.
*Alex.*　　　　　Good majesty,
Herod of Jewry dare not look upon you
But when you are well pleas'd.
*Cleo.*　　　　　　That Herod's head
I'll have: but how? when Antony is gone,
Through whom I might command it?—Come
　　thou near.
*Mess.* Most gracious majesty,—
*Cleo.*　　　　　　Didst thou behold
Octavia?
*Mess.* Ay, dread queen.
*Cleo.*　　　　　Where?
*Mess.*　　　　　Madam, in Rome
I look'd her in the face, and saw her led
Between her brother and Mark Antony.
*Cleo.* Is she as tall as me?
*Mess.*　　　　　She is not, madam.

*Cleo.* Didst hear her speak? is she shrill
  tongu'd or low?
*Mess.* Madam, I heard her speak; she is
  low voic'd.                        [her long.
*Cleo.* That's not so good:—he cannot like
*Char.* Like her! O Isis! 'tis impossible.
*Cleo.* I think so, Charmian: dull of tongue
  and dwarfish!—
What majesty is in her gait? Remember,
If e'er thou look'dst on majesty.
  *Mess.*                      She creeps,—
Her motion and her station are as one;
She shows a body rather than a life,
A statue than a breather.
  *Cleo.*            Is this certain?
*Mess.* Or I have no observance.
  *Char.*               Three in Egypt
Cannot make better note.
  *Cleo.*           He's very knowing;
I do perceive't:—there's nothing in her yet:—
The fellow has good judgment.
  *Char.*              Excellent.
*Cleo.* Guess at her years; I pr'ythee.
  *Mess.*                     Madam,
She was a widow.
  *Cleo.*        Widow!—Charmian, hark!
*Mess.* And I do think she's thirty.
*Cleo.* Bear'st thou her face in mind? is't
  long or round?
*Mess.* Round even to faultiness.
*Cleo.* For the most part, too, they are
  foolish that are so.—
Her hair, what colour?
*Mess.* Brown, madam: and her forehead
As low as she would wish it.
  *Cleo.*          There's gold for thee.
Thou must not take my former sharpness
  ill:—
I will employ thee back again; I find thee
Most fit for business: go make thee ready;
Our letters are prepar'd.   [*Exit* Messenger.
  *Char.*            A proper man.
*Cleo.* Indeed, he is so: I repent me much
That so I harried him. Why, methinks, by
  him
This creature's no such thing.
  *Char.*               Nothing, madam.
*Cleo.* The man hath seen some majesty,
  and should know.              [fend,
*Char.* Hath he seen majesty? Isis else de-
And serving you so long!
*Cleo.* I have one thing more to ask him
  yet, good Charmian:
But 'tis no matter; thou shalt bring him to
  me
Where I will write. All may be well enough.
  *Char.* I warrant you, madam.    [*Exeunt.*

SCENE IV.—ATHENS. *A Room in*
  ANTONY'S *House.*

*Enter* ANTONY *and* OCTAVIA.

*Ant.* Nay, nay, Octavia, not only that,—
That were excusable, that and thousands
  more

Of semblable import,—but he hath wag'd
New wars 'gainst Pompey; made his will, and
  read it
To public ear:                  [could not
Spoke scantly of me: when perforce he
But pay me terms of honour, cold and sickly
He vented them; most narrow measure lent
  me:                       [took't,
When the best hint was given him, he not
Or did it from his teeth.          –
  *Octa.*          O my good lord,
Believe not all; or, if you must believe,
Stomach not all. A more unhappy lady,
If this division chance, ne'er stood between,
Praying for both parts:
Sure the good gods will mock me presently
When I shall pray, *O, bless my lord and
  husband!*
Undo that prayer, by crying out as loud,
*O, bless my brother!* Husband win, win
  brother,
Prays and destroys the prayer; no midway
'Twixt these extremes at all.
  *Ant.*                Gentle Octavia,
Let your best love draw to that point which
  seeks
Best to preserve it: if I lose mine honour
I lose myself: better I were not yours
Than yours so branchless. But, as you re-
  quested,                    [lady,
Yourself shall go between's: the meantime,
I'll raise the preparation of a war   [haste;
Shall stain your brother: make you soonest
So your desires are yours.
  *Octa.*             Thanks to my lord.
The Jove of power make me, most weak,
  most weak,                 [would be
Your reconciler! Wars 'twixt you twain
As if the world should cleave, and that slain
  men
Should solder up the rift.          [begins,
  *Ant.* When it appears to you where this
Turn your displeasure that way; for our
  faults
Can never be so equal that your love
Can equally move with them. Provide your
  going;                   [what cost
Choose your own company, and command
Your heart has mind to.           [*Exeunt.*

SCENE V.—ATHENS. *Another Room in*
  ANTONY'S *House.*

*Enter* ENOBARBUS *and* EROS, *meeting.*

*Eno.* How now, friend Eros!
*Eros.* There's strange news come, sir.
*Eno.* What, man?            [upon Pompey.
*Eros.* Cæsar and Lepidus have made wars
*Eno.* This is old: what is the success?
*Eros.* Cæsar, having made use of him in
the wars 'gainst Pompey, presently denied
him rivality; would not let him partake in
the glory of the action: and not resting here,
accuses him of letters he had formerly wrote
to Pompey; upon his own appeal seizes him:

so the poor third is up, till death enlarge his confine.

*Eno.* Then world, thou hast a pair of chaps, no more;　　　　　[hast,
And throw between them all the food thou
They'll grind the one the other. Where's Antony?　　　　　[and spurns

*Eros.* He's walking in the garden—thus;
The rush that lies before him; cries, *Fool Lepidus!*
And threats the throat of that his officer
That murder'd Pompey.

*Eno.*　　　　　Our great navy's rigg'd.

*Eros.* For Italy and Cæsar. More Domitius;
My lord desires you presently: my news
I might have told hereafter.

*Eno.*　　　　　'Twill be naught:
But let it be.—Bring me to Antony.

*Eros.* Come, sir.　　　　　[*Exeunt.*

SCENE VI.—ROME. *A Room in* CÆSAR'S *House.*

*Enter* CÆSAR, AGRIPPA, *and* MECÆNAS.

*Cæs.* Contemning Rome, he has done all this, and more,
In Alexandria: here's the manner of't:—
I' the market-place, on a tribunal silver'd
Cleopatra and himself in chairs of gold
Were publicly enthron'd: at the feet sat
Cæsarion, whom they call my father's son,
And all the unlawful issue that their lust
Since then hath made between them. Unto her　　　　　[her
He gave the 'stablishment of Egypt: made
Of Lower Syria, Cyprus, Lydia,
Absolute queen.

*Mec.*　　　　　This in the public eye?

*Cæs.* I' the common show-place, where they exercise.　　　　　[kings:
His sons he there proclaim'd the kings of
Great Media, Parthia, and Armenia
He gave to Alexander; to Ptolemy he assign'd
Syria, Cilicia, and Phœnicia: she
In the habiliments of the goddess Isis　　[ence,
That day appear'd; and oft before gave audi-
As 'tis reported, so.

*Mec.*　　　　　Let Rome be thus
Inform'd.

*Agr.* Who, queasy with his insolence [him.
Already, will their good thoughts call from

*Cæs.* The people know it: and have now receiv'd
His accusations.

*Agr.*　　　　　Who does he accuse?

*Cæs.* Cæsar: and that, having in Sicily
Sextus Pompeius spoil'd, we had not rated him　　　　　[me
His part o' the isle: then does he say he lent
Some shipping, unrestor'd: lastly, he frets
That Lepidus of the triumvirate　　　　[tain
Should be depos'd; and, being, that we de-
All his revenue.

*Agr.*　　　　　Sir, this should be answer'd.

*Cæs.* 'Tis done already, and the messenger gone.
I have told him Lepidus was grown too cruel;
That he his high authority abus'd,
And did deserve his change: for what I have conquer'd.
I grant him part; but then, in his Armenia
And other of his conquer'd kingdoms, I
Demand the like.

*Mec.*　　　　　He'll never yield to that.

*Cæs.* Nor must not, then, be yielded to in this.

*Enter* OCTAVIA, *with her* Train.

*Octa.* Hail, Cæsar, and my lord! hail, most dear Cæsar!

*Cæs.* That ever I should call thee castaway!

*Octa.* You have not call'd me so, nor have you cause.

*Cæs.* Why have you stol'n upon us thus?
You come not
Like Cæsar's sister: the wife of Antony
Should have an army for an usher, and
The neighs of horse to tell of her approach
Long ere she did appear; the trees by the way
Should have borne men; and expectation fainted,
Longing for what it had not; nay, the dust
Should have ascended to the roof of heaven,
Rais'd by your populous troops: but you are come　　　　　[vented
A market-maid to Rome; and have prevented
The ostentation of our love, which left unshown　　　　　[you
Is often left unlov'd: we should have met
By sea and land; supplying every stage
With an augmented greeting.

*Octa.*　　　　　Good my lord,
To come thus was I not constrain'd, but did it
On my free-will. My lord, Mark Antony,
Hearing that you prepar'd for war, acquainted
My grieved ear withal: whereon I begg'd
His pardon for return.

*Cæs.*　　　　　Which soon he granted,
Being an obstruct 'tween his lust and him.

*Octa.* Do not say so, my lord.

*Cæs.*　　　　　I have eyes upon him,
And his affairs come to me on the wind.
Where is he now?

*Octa.*　　　　　My lord, in Athens.

*Cæs.* No, my most wronged sister; Cleopatra
Hath nodded him to her. He hath given his
Up to a whore; who now are levying
The kings o' the earth for war: he hath assembled
Bocchus, the king of Libya; Archelaus
Of Cappadocia; Philadelphos, king
Of Paphlagonia; the Thracian king, Adallas;
King Malchus of Arabia; King of Pont;

Herod of Jewry; Mithridates, king
Of Comagene; Polemon and Amyntas,
The kings of Mede and Lycaonia, with a
More larger list of sceptres.

*Octa.*          Ay me, most wretched,
That have my heart parted betwixt two
     friends
That do afflict each other!

*Cæs.*          Welcome thither:
Your letters did withhold our breaking forth,
Till we perceiv'd both how you were wrong
     led
And we in negligent danger. Cheer your
     heart:
Be you not troubled with the time, which
     drives
O'er your content these strong necessities;
But let determin'd things to destiny
Hold unbewail'd their way. Welcome to
     Rome;
Nothing more dear to me. You are abus'd
Beyond the mark of thought: and the high
     gods,
To do you justice, make their ministers
Of us and those that love you. Best of com-
     fort;
And ever welcome to us.

*Agr.*          Welcome, lady.
*Mec.* Welcome, dear madam.
Each heart in Rome does love and pity you:
Only the adulterous Antony, most large
In his abominations, turns you off;
And gives his potent regiment to a trull
That noises it against us.

*Octa.*          Is it so, sir? [you
*Cæs.* Most certain. Sister, welcome: pray
Be ever known to patience: my dear'st
     sister!          [*Exeunt.*

SCENE VII.—ANTONY'S CAMP *near the
     Promontory of Actium.*

*Enter* CLEOPATRA *and* ENOBARBUS.

*Cleo.* I will be even with thee, doubt it not.
*Eno.* But why, why, why?          [wars,
*Cleo.* Thou hast forspoke my being in these
And say'st it is not fit.
*Eno.*          Well, is it, is it?
*Cleo.* If not denounc'd against us, why
     should not we
Be there in person?
*Eno.* [*Aside.*]    Well, I could reply:—
If we should serve with horse and mares to-
     gether          [bear
The horse were merely lost; the mares would
A soldier and his horse.
*Cleo.* What is 't you say?
*Eno.* Your presence needs must puzzle
     Antony;          [from's time,
Take from his heart, take from his brain,
What should not then be spar'd. He is al-
     ready
Traduc'd for levity: and 'tis said in Rome
That Photinus an eunuch and your maids
**Manage** this war.

*Cleo.*    Sink Rome, and their tongues rot
That speak against us! A charge we bear i'
     the war,
And, as the president of my kingdom, will
Appear there for a man. Speak not against it;
I will not stay behind.
*Eno.*          Nay, I have done.
Here comes the emperor.

*Enter* ANTONY *and* CANIDIUS.

*Ant.*          Is it not strange, Canidius,
That from Tarentum and Brundusium
He could so quickly cut the Ionian sea,
And take in Toryne?—You have heard on 't,
     sweet?
*Cleo.* Celerity is never more admir'd
Than by the negligent.
*Ant.*          A good rebuke,
Which might have well become the best of
     men
To taunt at slackness.—Canidius, we
Will fight with him by sea.
*Cleo.*          By sea! what else?
*Can.* Why will my lord do so?
*Ant.*          For that he dares us to 't.
*Eno.* So hath my lord dar'd him to single
     fight.
*Can.* Ay, and to wage this battle at Phar-
     salia,
Where Cæsar fought with Pompey: but these
     offers,
Which serve not for his vantage, he shakes
     off;
And so should you.
*Eno.*    Your ships are not well mann'd:
Your mariners are muleteers, reapers, people
Ingross'd by swift impress; in Cæsar's fleet
Are those that often have 'gainst Pompey
     fought:
Their ships are yare; yours heavy: no dis-
     grace
Shall fall you for refusing him at sea,
Being prepar'd for land.
*Ant.*          By sea, by sea.
*Eno.* Most worthy sir, you therein throw
     away
The absolute soldiership you have by land;
Distract your army, which doth most con-
     sist
Of war-mark'd footmen; leave unexecuted
Your own renowned knowledge; quite fore-
     go
The way which promises assurance; and
Give up yourself merely to chance and
     hazard
From firm security.
*Ant.*          I'll fight at sea.
*Cleo.* I have sixty sails, Cæsar none better.
*Ant.* Our overplus of shipping will we
     burn;
And, with the rest full-mann'd, from the
     head of Actium
Beat the approaching Cæsar. But if we fail
We then can do 't at land.

*Enter a* Messenger.

Thy business?

*Mess.* The news is true, my lord; he is
descried;
Cæsar has taken Toryne.              [possible;
*Ant.* Can he be there in person? 'tis im-
Strange that his power should be.—Canidius,
Our nineteen legions thou shalt hold by land,
And our twelve thousand horse.—We'll to
our ship:
Away, my Thetis!

*Enter a* Soldier.

How now, worthy soldier?

*Sold.* O noble emperor, do not fight by sea;
Trust not to rotten planks: do you misdoubt
This sword and these my wounds? Let the
Egyptians
And the Phœnicians go a-ducking: we
Have used to conquer standing on the earth
And fighting foot to foot.
*Ant.*              Well, well:—away.
[*Exeunt* ANT., CLEO., *and* ENO.
*Sold.* By Hercules, I think I am i' the
right.
*Can.* Soldier, thou art: but his whole ac-
tion grows
Not in the power on 't: so our leader's led,
And we are women's men.
*Sold.*              You keep by land
The legions and the horse whole, do you not?
*Can.* Marcus Octavius, Marcius Justeius,
Publicola, and Cælius are for sea:
But we keep whole by land. This speed of
Cæsar's
Carries beyond belief.
*Sold.*              While he was yet in Rome
His power went out in such distractions as
Beguil'd all spies.
*Can.*      Who's his lieutenant, hear you?
*Sold.* They say one Taurus.
*Can.*              Well I know the man.

*Enter a* Messenger.

*Mess.* The emperor calls Canidius.
*Can.* With news the time's with labour:
and throes forth
Each minute some.              [*Exeunt.*

SCENE VIII.—*A Plain near Actium.*

*Enter* CÆSAR, TAURUS, Officers, *and others.*

*Cæs.* Taurus,—
*Taur.*              My lord?
*Cæs.* Strike not by land; keep whole; pro-
voke not battle
Till we have done at sea. Do not exceed
The prescript of this scroll: our fortune lies
Upon this jump.              [*Exeunt.*

SCENE IX.—*Another part of the Plain.*

*Enter* ANTONY *and* ENOBARBUS.

*Ant.* Set we our squadrons on yon side o'
the hill,

In eye of Cæsar's battle; from which place
We may the number of the ships behold,
And so proceed accordingly.

SCENE X.—*Another part of the Plain.*

*Enter* CANIDIUS, *marching with his land
Army one way; and* TAURUS, *the Lieutenant of* CÆSAR, *with his Army, the other
way. After their going in, is heard the noise
of a sea-fight.*

*Alarum. Enter* ENOBARBUS.

*Eno.* Naught, naught, all naught! I can
behold no longer:
The Antoniad, the Egyptian admiral,
With all their sixty, fly and turn the rudder:
To see 't mine eyes are blasted.

*Enter* SCARUS.

*Scar.*              Gods and goddesses,
All the whole synod of them!
*Eno.*              What's thy passion?
*Scar.* The greater cantle of the world is
lost
With very ignorance; we have kiss'd away
Kingdoms and provinces.
*Eno.*              How appears the fight?
*Scar.* On our side like the token'd pesti-
lence,
Where death is sure. Yon ribaudred nag of
Egypt,—              [fight,
Whom leprosy o'ertake!—i' the midst o' the
When vantage like a pair of twins appear'd,
Both as the same, or rather ours the elder,—
The breese upon her, like a cow in June,—
Hoists sails and flies.
*Eno.*              That I beheld:      [not
Mine eyes did sicken at the sight, and could
Endure a further view.
*Scar.*              She once being loof'd
The noble ruin of her magic, Antony,      [lard,
Claps on his sea-wing, and, like a doting mal-
Leaving the fight in height, flies after her:
I never saw an action of such shame;
Experience, manhood, honour, ne'er before
Did violate so itself.
*Eno.*              Alack, alack!

*Enter* CANIDIUS.

*Can.* Our fortune on the sea is out of
breath,
And sinks most lamentably. Had our general
Been what he knew himself, it had gone well:
O, he has given example for our flight
Most grossly by his own!
*Eno.* Ay, are you thereabouts?
Why, then, good-night indeed.
*Can.* Towards Peloponnesus are they fled.
*Scar.* 'Tis easy to 't; and there I will at-
tend
What further comes.
*Can.*              To Cæsar will I render
My legions and my horse; six kings already
Show me the way of yielding.

*Eno.*                    I'll yet follow
The wounded chance of Antony, though my
        reason
Sits in the wind against me.          [*Exeunt.*

SCENE XI.—ALEXANDRIA. *A Room in the
        Palace.*

        *Enter* ANTONY *and* Attendants.

*Ant.* Hark! the land bids me tread no
        more upon 't,—
It is asham'd to bear me!—Friends, come
        hither:
I am so lated in the world that I
Have lost my way for ever:—I have a ship
Laden with gold, take that, divide it; fly,
And make your peace with Cæsar.
*All.*                              Fly! not we.
*Ant.* I have fled myself, and have in-
        structed cowards          [be gone;
To run and show their shoulders.—Friends,
I have myself resolv'd upon a course
Which has no need of you; begone:
My treasure's in the harbour, take it.—O,
I follow'd that I blush to look upon:
My very hairs do mutiny; for the white
Reprove the brown for rashness, and they
        them
For fear and doting.—Friends, be gone: you
        shall
Have letters from me to some friends that
        will
Sweep your way for you. Pray you, look not
        sad,
Nor make replies of loathness: take the hint
Which my despair proclaims; let that be left
Which leaves itself: to the sea-side straight-
        way:
I will possess you of that ship and treasure.
Leave me, I pray, a little: pray you now:—
Nay, do so; for, indeed, I have lost com-
        mand,
Therefore I pray you:—I'll see you by and
        by.                    [*Sits down.*

        *Enter* CLEOPATRA, *led by* CHARMIAN *and*
                IRAS, EROS *following.*

*Eros.* Nay, gentle madam, to him,—com-
        fort him.
*Iras.* Do, most dear queen.
*Char.* Do! why, what else?
*Cleo.* Let me sit down. O Juno!
*Ant.* No, no, no, no, no.
*Eros.* See you here, sir?
*Ant.* O fie, fie, fie!
*Char.* Madam,—
*Iras.* Madam, O good empress,—
*Eros.* Sir, sir,—
*Ant.* Yes, my lord, yes;—he at Philippi
        kept
His sword e'en like a dancer; while I struck
The lean and wrinkled Cassius; and 'twas I
That the mad Brutus ended; he alone
Dealt on lieutenantry, and no practice had

In the brave squares of war: yet now—no
        matter.
*Cleo.* Ah, stand by.
*Eros.* The queen, my lord, the queen.
*Iras.* Go to him, madam, speak to him:
He is unqualitied with very shame.
*Cleo.* Well then,—sustain me:—O!
*Eros.* Most noble sir, arise; the queen ap-
        proaches:                    [but
Her head's declin'd, and death will seize her,
Your comfort make the rescue.
*Ant.* I have offended reputation,—
A most unnoble swerving.
*Eros.*              Sir, the queen.          [See
*Ant.* O, whither hast thou led me, Egypt?
How I convey my shame out of thine eyes
By looking back, what I have left behind
'Stroy'd in dishonour.
*Cleo.*              O my lord, my lord,
Forgive my fearful sails! I little thought
You would have follow'd.
*Ant.*              Egypt, thou knew'st too well
My heart was to thy rudder tied by the
        strings,
And thou shouldst tow me after: o'er my
        spirit
Thy full supremacy thou knew'st, and that
Thy beck might from the bidding of the
        gods
Command me.
*Cleo.*              O, my pardon!
*Ant.*                    Now I must
To the young man send humble treaties,
        dodge
And palter in the shifts of lowness; who
With half the bulk o' the world play'd as I
        pleas'd,
Making and marring fortunes. You did know
How much you were my conqueror; and that
My sword, made weak by my affection,
        would
Obey it on all cause.
*Cleo.*              Pardon, pardon!
*Ant.* Fall not a tear, I say; one of them
        rates
All that is won and lost: give me a kiss;
Even this repays me.—We sent our school-
        master;
Is he come back?—Love, I am full of lead.—
Some wine, within there, and our viands!—
        Fortune knows
We scorn her most when most she offers
        blows.                    [*Exeunt.*

SCENE XII.—CÆSAR'S *Camp in Egypt.*

        *Enter* CÆSAR, DOLABELLA, THYREUS,
                *and others.*

*Cæs.* Let him appear that's come from An-
        tony.—
Know you him?
*Dol.*          Cæsar, 'tis his schoolmaster:
An argument that he is pluck'd, when hither
He sends so poor a pinion of his wing,

Which had superfluous kings for messengers
Not many moons gone by.

*Enter* EUPHRONIUS.

*Cæs.*                    Approach, and speak.
*Eup.* Such as I am, I come from Antony:
I was of late as petty to his ends
As is the morn-dew on the myrtle leaf
To his grand sea.
*Cæs.*         Be 't so: declare thine office.
*Eup.* Lord of his fortunes he salutes thee,
and
Requires to live in Egypt: which not granted,
He lessens his requests; and to thee sues
To let him breathe between the heavens and
earth,
A private man in Athens: this for him.
Next, Cleopatra·does confess thy greatness;
Submits her to thy might; and of thee craves
The circle of the Ptolemies for her heirs,
Now hazarded to thy grace.
*Cæs.*                    For Antony,
I have no ears to his request. The queen
Of audience nor desire shall fail; so she
From Egypt drive her all-disgraced friend,
Or take his life there: this if she perform
She shall not sue unheard. So to them both.
*Eup.* Fortune pursue thee!
*Cæs.*         Bring him through the bands.
                         [*Exit* EUPHRONIUS.
To try thy eloquence, now 'tis time: des-
patch;
From Antony win Cleopatra: promise,
                         [*To* THYR.
And in our name, what she requires; add
more,
From thine invention, offers: women are not
In their best fortunes strong; but want will
perjure
The ne'er-touch'd vestal: try thy cunning,
Thyreus;
Make thine own edict for thy pains, which we
Will answer as a law.
*Thyr.*                  Cæsar, I go.
*Cæs.* Observe how Antony becomes his
flaw,
And what thou think'st his very action speaks
In every power that moves.
*Thyr.*           Cæsar, I shall. [*Exeunt.*

SCENE XIII.—ALEXANDRIA. *A Room in
the Palace.*

*Enter* CLEOPATRA, ENOBARBUS, CHARMIAN,
*and* IRAS.

*Cleo.* What shall we do, Enobarbus?
*Eno.*                    Think, and die.
*Cleo.* Is Antony or we in fault for this?
*Eno.* Antony only, that would make his
will
Lord of his reason. What though you fled
From that great face of war, whose several
ranges
Frighted each other? why should he follow?
The itch of his affection should not then

Have nick'd his captainship; at such a point,
When half to half the world oppos'd, he be-
ing
The mered question: 'twas a shame no less
Than was his loss to course your flying flags
And leave his navy gazing.
*Cleo.*                    Pr'ythee, peace.

*Enter* ANTONY, *with* EUPHRONIUS.

*Ant.* Is that his answer?
*Eup.* Ay, my lord.
*Ant.* The queen shall then have courtesy,
so she
Will yield us up.
*Eup.*           He says so.
*Ant.*                    Let her know 't.—
To the boy Cæsar send this grizzled head,
And he will fill thy wishes to the brim
With principalities.
*Cleo.*           That head, my lord?
*Ant.* To him again: tell him he wears the
rose
Of youth upon him; from which the world
should note
Something particular: his coins, ships, le-
gions,
May be a coward's; whose ministers would
prevail
Under the service of a child as soon [therefore
As i' the command of Cæsar: I dare him
To lay his gay comparisons apart,
And answer me declin'd, sword against
sword,
Ourselves alone. I'll write it: follow me.
                         [*Exeunt* ANTONY *and* EUPHRONIUS.
*Eno.* Yes, like enough, high-battled Cæsar
will
Unstate his happiness, and be stag'd to the
show
Against a sworder.—I see men's judgments
are
A parcel of their fortunes; and things out-
ward
Do draw the inward quality after them,
To suffer all alike. That he should dream,
Knowing all measures, the full Cæsar will
Answer his emptiness!—Cæsar, thou hast
subdu'd
His judgment too.

*Enter an* Attendant.

*Att.*           A messenger from Cæsar.
*Cleo.* What, no more ceremony?—See, my
women!—                    [nose
Against the blown rose may they stop their
That kneel'd unto the buds.—Admit him, sir.
                         [*Exit* Attendant.
*Eno.* [*Aside.*] Mine honesty and I begin
to square.
The loyalty well held to fools does make
Our faith mere folly:—yet he that can en-
dure
To follow with allegiance a fallen lord

Does conquer him that did his master conquer,
And earn a place i' the story.

*Enter* THYREUS.

*Cleo.* Cæsar's will?
*Thyr.* Hear it apart.
*Cleo.* None but friends: say boldly.
*Thyr.* So, haply, are they friends to An-
tony.
*Eno.* He needs as many, sir, as Cæsar has;
Or needs not us. If Cæsar please, our master
Will leap to be his friend: for us, you know
Whose he is we are, and that is Cæsar's.
*Thyr.* So.—
Thus then, thou most renown'd: Cæsar en-
treats
Not to consider in what case thou stand'st,
Further than he is Cæsar.
*Cleo.* Go on: right royal.
*Thyr.* He knows that you embrace not An-
tony
As you did love, but as you fear'd him.
*Cleo.* O!
*Thyr.* The scars upon your honour, there-
fore, he
Does pity, as constrained blemishes,
Not as deserv'd.
*Cleo.* He is a god, and knows
What is most right: mine honour was not
yielded,
But conquer'd merely.
*Eno.* [*Aside.*] To be sure of that,
I will ask Antony.—Sir, sir, thou art so leaky
That we must leave thee to thy sinking, for
Thy dearest quit thee. [*Exit.*
*Thyr.* Shall I say to Cæsar
What you require of him? for he partly begs
To be desir'd to give. It much would please
him
That of his fortunes you should make a staff
To lean upon: but it would warm his spirits
To hear from me you had left Antony,
And put yourself under his shroud, who is
The universal landlord.
*Cleo.* What's your name?
*Thyr.* My name is Thyreus.
*Cleo.* Most kind messenger,
Say to great Cæsar this:—in deputation
I kiss his conquering hand: tell him I am
prompt
To lay my crown at 's feet, and there to
kneel:
Tell him, from his all-obeying breath I hear
The doom of Egypt.
*Thyr.* 'Tis your noblest course.
Wisdom and fortune combating together,
If that the former dare but what it can,
No chance may shake it. Give me grace to
lay
My duty on your hand.
*Cleo.* Your Cæsar's father
Oft, when he hath mus'd of taking king-
doms in,

Bestow'd his lips on that unworthy place,
As it rain'd kisses.

*Re-enter* ANTONY *and* ENOBARBUS.

*Ant.* Favours, by Jove that thunders!—
What art thou, fellow?
*Thyr.* One that but performs
The bidding of the fullest man, and worthiest
To have command obey'd.
*Eno.* [*Aside.*] You will be whipp'd.
*Ant.* Approach there!—Ay, you kite!—
Now, gods and devils! [cried, *Ho!*
Authority melts from me: of late, when I
Like boys unto a muss, kings would start
forth
And cry, *Your will?* Have you no ears? I am
Antony yet.

*Enter* Attendants.

Take hence this Jack and whip him.
*Eno.* 'Tis better playing with a lion's
whelp
Than with an old one dying.
*Ant.* Moon and stars!
Whip him.—Were 't twenty of the greatest
tributaries
That do acknowledge Cæsar, should I find
them
So saucy with the hand of she here,—what's
her name
Since she was Cleopatra?—Whip him, fel-
lows,
Till, like a boy, you see him cringe his face,
And whine aloud for mercy: take him hence.
*Thyr.* Mark Antony.
*Ant.* Tug him away: being whipp'd,
Bring him again.—This Jack of Cæsar's shall
Bear us an errand to him.—
[*Exeunt* Attend. *with* THYR.
You were half blasted ere I knew you.—Ha!
Have I my pillow left unpress'd in Rome,
Forborne the getting of a lawful race,
And by a gem of women, to be abus'd
By one that looks on feeders?
*Cleo.* Good, my lord,—
*Ant.* You have been a boggler ever:—
But when we in our viciousness grow hard,—
O misery on 't!—the wise gods seal our eyes;
In our own filth drop our clear judgments;
make us
Adore our errors; laugh at 's, while we strut
To our confusion.
*Cleo.* O, is 't come to this?
*Ant.* I found you as a morsel cold upon
Dead Cæsar's trencher; nay, you were a frag-
ment
Of Cneius Pompey's; besides what hotter
hours,
Unregister'd in vulgar frame, you have
Luxuriously pick'd out:—for I am sure,
Though you can guess what temperance
should be,
You know not what it is.
*Cleo.* Wherefore is this?

*Ant.* To let a fellow that will take re-
wards,
And say, *God quit you!* be familiar with
My playfellow, your hand; this kingly seal
And plighter of high hearts!—O that I were
Upon the hill of Basan, to outroar
The horned herd! for I have savage cause;
And to proclaim it civilly were like
A halter'd neck which does the hangman
thank
For being yare about him.

*Re-enter* Attendants *with* THYREUS.
Is he whipp'd?
1 *Att.* Soundly, my lord.
*Ant.*    Cried he? and begg'd he pardon?
1 *Att.* He did ask favour.
*Ant.* If that thy father live, let him repent
Thou wast not made his daughter; and be
thou sorry
To follow Cæsar in his triumph, since
Thou hast been whipp'd for following him:
henceforth
The white hand of a lady fever thee,
Shake thou to look on 't.—Get thee back to
Cæsar,
Tell him thy entertainment: look thou say
He makes me angry with him; for he seems
Proud and disdainful, harping on what I am,
Not what he knew I was: he makes me
angry;
And at this time most easy 'tis to do 't,
When my good stars, that were my former
guides,
Have empty left their orbs, and shot their
fires
Into the abysm of hell. If he mislike
My speech and what is done, tell him he has
Hipparchus, my enfranchis'd bondman,
whom
He may at pleasure whip, or hang, or tor-
ture,
As he shall like, to quit me: urge it thou:
Hence with thy stripes, be gone.
[*Exit* THYREUS.
*Cleo.* Have you done yet?
*Ant.*    Alack, our terrene moon
Is now eclips'd; and it portends alone
The fall of Antony!
*Cleo.*    I must stay his time.
*Ant.* To flatter Cæsar, would you mingle
eyes
With one that ties his points?
*Cleo.*    Not know me yet?
*Ant.* Cold-hearted toward me?
*Cleo.*    Ah, dear, if I be so,
From my cold heart let heaven engender hail,
And poison it in the source; and the first
stone
Drop in my neck: as it determines, so
Dissolve my life! The next Cæsarion smite!
Till, by degrees, the memory of my womb,
Together with my brave Egyptians all,
By the discandying of this pelleted storm,

Lie graveless,—till the flies and gnats of Nile
Have buried them for prey!
*Ant.*    I am satisfied.
Cæsar sits down in Alexandria; where
I will oppose his fate. Our force by land
Hath nobly held: our sever'd navy too
Have knit again, and fleet, threat'ning most
sea-like.    [hear, lady?
Where hast thou been, my heart?—Dost thou
If from the field I shall return once more
To kiss these lips, I will appear in blood:
I and my sword will earn our chronicle:
There's hope in 't yet.
*Cleo.*    That's my brave lord!
*Ant.* I will be treble-sinew'd, hearted,
breath'd,
And fight maliciously: for when mine hours
Were nice and lucky, men did ransom lives
Of me for jests; but now I'll set my teeth,
And send to darkness all that stop me.—
Come,
Let's have one other gaudy night: call to me
All my sad captains, fill our bowls; once more
Let's mock the midnight bell.
*Cleo.*    It is my birthday.
I had thought to have held it poor; but since
my lord
Is Antony again I will be Cleopatra.
*Ant.* We will yet do well.
*Cleo.* Call all his noble captains to my lord.
*Ant.* Do so; we'll speak to them: and to-
night I'll force
The wine peep through their scars.—Come
on, my queen;
There's sap in 't yet. The next time I do
fight
I'll make death love me; for I will contend
Even with his pestilent scythe.
[*Exeunt all but* ENO.
*Eno.* Now he'll outstare the lightning. To
be furious
Is to be frighted out of fear; and in that
mood
The dove will peck the estridge; and I see
still
A diminution in our captain's brain
Restores his heart: when valour preys on rea-
son
It eats the sword it fights with. I will seek
Some way to leave him.    [*Exit.*

## ACT IV.

SCENE I.—CÆSAR'S *Camp at Alexandria.*

*Enter* CÆSAR *reading a letter;* AGRIPPA,
MECÆNAS, *and others.*

*Cæs.* He calls me boy; and chides as he
had power
To beat me out of Egypt; my messenger
He hath whipp'd with rods; dares me **to**
personal combat,
Cæsar to Antony:—let the old ruffian know
I have many other ways to die; meantime
Laugh at his challenge.

*Mec.*     [Cæsar must think,
When one so great begins to rage, he's hunted
Even to falling. Give him no breath, but now
Make boot of his distraction:—never anger
Made good guard for itself.

*Cæs.*     Let our best heads
Know that to-morrow the last of many battles
We mean to fight.—Within our files there are,
Of those that serv'd Mark Antony but late,
Enough to fetch him in. See it done:
And feast the army; we have store to do 't,
And they have earn'd the waste. Poor Antony!     [*Exeunt.*

SCENE II.—ALEXANDRIA. *A Room in the Palace.*

*Enter* ANTONY, CLEOPATRA, ENOBARBUS, CHARMIAN, IRAS, ALEXAS, *and others.*

*Ant.* He will not fight with me, Domitius.
*Eno.*     No.
*Ant.* Why should he not?     [ter fortune,
*Eno.* He thinks, being twenty times of bet-
He is twenty men to one.
*Ant.*     Tomorrow, soldier,
By sea and land I'll fight: or I will live,
Or bathe my dying honour in the blood
Shall make it live again. Woo 't thou fight well?
*Eno.* I'll strike, and cry, *Take all.*
*Ant.*     Well said; come on.—
Call forth my household servants: let 's tonight
Be bounteous at our meal.—

*Enter* Servants.

    Give me thy hand,
Thou hast been rightly honest;—so hast thou;—
Thou,—and thou,—and thou;—you have serv'd me well,
And kings have been your fellows.
*Cleo.* [*Aside to* ENO.] What means this?
*Eno.* [*Aside to* CLEO.] 'Tis one of those odd tricks which sorrow shoots
Out of the mind.
*Ant.*     And thou art honest too.
I wish I could be made so many men,
And all of you clapp'd up together in
An Antony, that I might do you service
So good as you have done.
*Serv.*     The gods forbid!
*Ant.* Well, my good fellows, wait on me to-night:
Scant not my cups; and make as much of me
As when mine empire was your fellow too,
And suffer'd my command.
*Cleo.* [*Aside to* ENO.] What does he mean?
*Eno.* [*Aside to* CLEO.] To make his followers weep.
*Ant.*     Tend me to-night;
May be it is the period of your duty:
Haply you shall not see me more; or if,

A mangled shadow: perchance to-morrow
You'll serve another master. I look on you
As one that takes his leave. Mine honest friends,
I turn you not away; but, like a master
Married to your good service, stay till death:
Tend me to-night two hours, I ask no more,
And the gods yield you for 't!
*Eno.*     What mean you, sir,
To give them this discomfort? Look, they weep;
And I, an ass, am onion-ey'd: for shame,
Transform us not to women.
*Ant.*     Ho, ho, ho!
Now the witch take me, if I meant it thus!
Grace grow where those drops fall! My hearty friends,
You take me in too dolorous a sense;
For I spake to you for your comfort,—did desire you     [hearts,
To burn this night with torches: know, my
I hope well of to-morrow; and will lead you
Where rather I'll expect victorious life
Than death and honour. Let's to supper; come,
And drown consideration.     [*Exeunt.*

SCENE III.—ALEXANDRIA. *Before the Palace.*

*Enter two* Soldiers *to their guard.*

1 *Sold.* Brother, good-night: to-morrow is the day.     [you well.
2 *Sold.* It will determine one way: fare
Heard you of nothing strange about the streets?
1 *Sold.* Nothing. What news?     [to you.
2 *Sold.* Belike 'tis but a rumor. Good-night
1 *Sold.* Well, sir, good-night.

*Enter two other* Soldiers.

2 *Sold.* Soldiers, have careful watch.
3 *Sold.* And you. Good-night, good-night.
[*The first two place themselves at their posts.*
4 *Sold.* Here we: [*The third and fourth take their posts.*] and if to-morrow
Our navy thrive, I have an absolute hope
Our landmen will stand up.
3 *Sold.*     'Tis a brave army,
And full of purpose.
    [*Music as of hautboys under the stage.*
4 *Sold.*     Peace, what noise?
1 *Sold.*     List, list!
2 *Sold.* Hark!
1 *Sold.* Music i' the air.
3 *Sold.*     Under the earth.
4 *Sold.* It signs well, does it not?
3 *Sold.*     No.
1 *Sold.*     Peace, I say!
What should this mean?     [tony lov'd,
2 *Sold.* 'Tis the god Hercules, whom An-
Now leaves him.
1 *Sold.* Walk; let's see if other watchmen
Do hear what we do.
    [*They advance to another post.*

*2 Sold.*　　How now, masters!
*Soldiers.* [*Speaking together.*] How now!
How now! do you hear this?
*1 Sold.*　　Ay; is 't not strange?
*3 Sold.* Do you hear, masters? do you
　　hear?
*1 Sold.* Follow the noise so far as we have
　　quarter;
Let's see how 't will give off.
*Soldiers.* [*Speaking together.*] Content. 'Tis
　　strange.　　　　　　　　[*Exeunt.*

SCENE IV.—ALEXANDRIA. *A Room in the
Palace.*

*Enter* ANTONY *and* CLEOPATRA; CHARMIAN,
IRAS, *and others attending.*

*Ant.* Eros! mine armour, Eros!
*Cleo.*　　　　　　　Sleep a little.
*Ant.* No, my chuck.—Eros, come; mine
　armour, Eros!

*Enter* EROS *with armour.*

Come, good fellow, put mine iron on.—
If fortune be not ours to-day, it is
Because we brave her.—Come.
*Cleo.*　　　　Nay, I'll help too.
What's this for?
*Ant.*　　Ah, let be, let be! thou art
The armourer of my heart. False, false; this,
　this.
*Cleo.* Sooth, la, I'll help: thus it must be.
*Ant.*　　　　　　Well, well;
We shall thrive now.—Seest thou, my good
　fellow?
Go put on thy defences.
*Eros.*　　　　　Briefly, sir.
*Cleo.* Is not this buckled well?
*Ant.*　　　　　Rarely, rarely:
He that unbuckles this, till we do please
To doff 't for our repose, shall hear a
　storm.—
Thou fumblest, Eros; and my queen's a
　squire
More tight at this than thou: despatch.—O
　love,　　　　　　　　　[knew'st
That thou couldst see my wars to-day, and
The royal occupation! thou shouldst see
A workman in 't.—

*Enter an* Officer, *armed.*

　　　　Good-morrow to thee; welcome:
Thou look'st like him that knows a warlike
　charge:
To business that we love we rise betime,
And go to 't with delight.
*Off.*　　　　A thousand, sir,
Early though it be, have on their riveted trim,
And at the port expect you.
　　[*Shout. Flourish of Trumpets within.*

*Enter other* Officers *and* Soldiers.

*2 Off.* The morn is fair.—Good-morrow,
　general.
*All.* Good-morrow, general.

*Ant.*　　　　　　'Tis well blown, lads:
This morning, like the spirit of a youth
That means to be of note, begins betimes.—
So, so; come, give me that: this way; well
　said.—　　　　　　　　　　[me:
Fare thee well, dame, whate'er becomes of
This is a soldier's kiss: rebukable, [*Kisses her.*
And worthy shameful check it were, to stand
On more mechanic compliment; I'll leave thee
Now, like a man of steel.—You that will
　fight,
Follow me close; I'll bring you to 't.—Adieu.
　　[*Exeunt* ANT., EROS, Officers, *and* Soldiers.
*Char.* Please you, retire to your chamber.
*Cleo.*　　　　　　　Lead me.
He goes forth gallantly. That he and Cæsar
　might
Determine this great war in single fight!
Then, Antony,—but now—Well, on.
　　　　　　　　　　　　[*Exeunt.*

SCENE V.—ANTONY'S *Camp near Alexandria.*

*Trumpets sound within. Enter* ANTONY *and*
EROS; *a* Soldier *meeting them.*

*Sold.* The gods make this a happy day to
　Antony!
*Ant.* Would thou and those thy scars had
　once prevail'd
To make me fight at land!
*Sold.*　　　　Hadst thou done so,
The kings that have revolted, and the soldier
That has this morning left thee, would have
　still
Follow'd thy heels.
*Ant.*　　Who's gone this morning?
*Sold.*　　　　　　　Who.
One ever near thee: call for Enobarbus,
He shall not hear thee; or from Cæsar's
　camp
Say, *I am none of thine.*
*Ant.*　　　　What say'st thou?
*Sold.*　　　　　　　Sir,
He is with Cæsar.
*Eros.*　　Sir, his chests and treasure
He has not with him.
*Ant.*　　　　Is he gone?
*Sold.*　　　　　　Most certain.
*Ant.* Go, Eros, send his treasure after; do
　it;
Detain no jot, I charge thee; write to him,—
I will subscribe,—gentle adieus and greetings;
Say that I wish he never find more cause
To change a master—O, my fortunes have
Corrupted honest men!—Eros, despatch.
　　　　　　　　　　　　[*Exeunt.*

SCENE VI.—CÆSAR'S *Camp before Alexandria.*

*Flourish. Enter* CÆSAR, *with* AGRIPPA,
ENOBARBUS, *and others.*

*Cæs.* Go forth, Agrippa, and begin the
　fight:
Our will is Antony be took alive;
Make it so known.
*Agr.*　　　Cæsar, I shall.　　[*Exit.*

*Cæs.* The time of universal peace is near:
Prove this a prosperous day, the three-nook'd world
Shall bear the olive freely.

*Enter a* Messenger.

*Mess.*             Antony
Is come into the field.
*Cæs.*           Go charge Agrippa
Plant those that have revolted in the van,
That Antony may seem to spend his fury
Upon himself. [*Exeunt* CÆSAR *and his* Train.
*Eno.* Alexas did revolt; and went to Jewry
On affairs of Antony; there did persuade
Great Herod to incline himself to Cæsar,
And leave his master Antony: for this pains
Cæsar hath hang'd him. Canidius, and the rest
That fell away, have entertainment, but
No honourable trust. I have done ill;
Of which I do accuse myself so sorely
That I will joy no more.

*Enter a* Soldier *of* CÆSAR'S.

*Sold.*         Enobarbus, Antony
Hath after thee sent all thy treasure, with
His bounty overplus: the messenger
Came on my guard, and at thy tent is now
Unloading of his mules.
*Eno.* I give it you.
*Sold.*         Mock not, Enobarbus.
I tell you true: best you saf'd the bringer
Out of the host; I must attend mine office,
Or would have done 't myself. Your emperor
Continues still a Jove.         [*Exit.*
*Eno.* I am alone the villain of the earth,
And feel I am so most. O Antony,     [paid
Thou mine of bounty, how wouldst thou have
My better service, when my turpitude
Thou dost so crown with gold! This blows my heart:
If swift thought break it not, a swifter mean
Shall outstrike thought: but thought will do 't, I feel.
I fight against thee!—No: I will go seek
Some ditch wherein to die; the foul'st best fits
My latter part of life.         [*Exit.*

SCENE VII.—*Field of Battle between the Camps.*

*Alarum. Drums and trumpets. Enter*
AGRIPPA *and others.*

*Agr.* Retire, we have engag'd ourselves too far:
Cæsar himself has work, and our oppression
Exceeds what we expected.       [*Exeunt.*

*Alarum. Enter* ANTONY, *and* SCARUS *wounded.*

*Scar.* O my brave emperor, this is fought indeed!

Had we done so at first, we had driven them home
With clouts about their heads.
*Ant.*         Thou bleed'st apace.
*Scar.* I had a wound here that was like a T,
But now 'tis made an H.
*Ant.*         They do retire.
*Scar.* We'll beat 'em into bench-holes: I have yet
Room for six scotches more.

*Enter* EROS.

*Eros.* They are beaten, sir; and our advantage serves
For a fair victory.
*Scar.*       Let us score their backs,
And snatch 'em up, as we take hares, behind:
'Tis sport to maul a runner.
*Ant.*        I will reward thee
Once for thy spritely comfort, and tenfold
For thy good valour. Come thee on.
*Scar.*         I'll halt after.    [*Exeunt.*

SCENE VIII.—*Under the Walls of Alexandria.*

*Alarum. Enter* ANTONY *marching;* SCARUS *and* Forces.

*Ant.* We have beat him to his camp. Run one before,        [morrow,
And let the queen know of our gests.—To-
Before the sun shall see us, we'll spill the blood
That has to-day escap'd. I thank you all;
For doughty-handed are you, and have fought
Not as you serv'd the cause, but as 't had been
Each man's like mine; you have shown all Hectors.
Enter the city, clip your wives, your friends,
Tell them your feats; whilst they with joyful tears        [and kiss
Wash the congealment from your wounds,
The honour'd gashes whole.—Give me thy hand;         [*To* SCARUS.

*Enter* CLEOPATRA, *attended.*

To this great fairy I'll commend thy acts,
Make her thanks bless thee. O thou day o' the world,        [and all,
Chain mine arm'd neck; leap thou, attire
Through proof of harness to my heart, and there
Ride on the pants triumphing.
*Cleo.*        Lord of lords!
O infinite virtue, com'st thou smiling from
The world's great snare uncaught?
*Ant.*         My nightingale,
We have beat them to their beds. What, girl! though grey    [brown; yet ha' we
Do something mingle with our younger
A brain that nourishes our nerves, and can
Get goal for goal of youth. Behold this man;

Commend unto his lips thy favouring
    hand;—
Kiss it, my warrior: he hath fought to-day
As if a god, in hate of mankind, had
Destroy'd in such a shape.
    *Cleo.*           I'll give thee, friend,
An armour all of gold; it was a king's.
    *Ant.* He has deserv'd it, were it carbuncled
Like holy Phœbus' car.—Give me thy hand:
Through Alexandria make a jolly march;
Bear our hack'd targets like the men that owe
    them:
Had our great palace the capacity
To camp this host, we all would sup together,
And drink carouses to the next day's fate,
Which promises royal peril.—Trumpeters,
With brazen din blast you the city's ear;
Make mingle with our rattling tabourines;
That heaven and earth may strike their
    sounds together,
Applauding our approach.       *[Exeunt.*

### Scene IX.—Cæsar's *Camp.*

#### Sentinels *at their Post.*

    1 *Sold.* If we be not reliev'd within this
    hour,                  [*night*
We must return to the court of guard: the
Is shiny; and they say we shall embattle
By the second hour i' the morn.
    2 *Sold.*         This last day was
A shrewd one to 's.

#### Enter ENOBARBUS.

    *Eno.*      O, bear me witness, night.—
    3 *Sold.* What man is this?
    2 *Sold.*      Stand close and list to him.
    *Eno.* Be witness to me, O thou blessed
    moon,
When men revolted shall upon record
Bear hateful memory, poor Enobarbus did
Before thy face repent!—
    1 *Sold.*      Enobarbus!
    3 *Sold.*              Peace!
Hark further.
    *Eno.* O sovereign mistress of true melon-
    choly,                   [*me,*
The poisonous damp of night disponge upon
That life, a very rebel to my will,
May hang no longer on me: throw my heart
Against the flint and hardness of my fault;
Which, being dried with grief, will break to
    powder,
And finish all foul thoughts, O Antony,
Nobler than my revolt is infamous,
Forgive me in thine own particular;
But let the world rank me in register
A master-leaver and a fugitive:
O Antony! O Antony!           [*Dies.*
    2 *Sold.*          Let's speak
To him.
    1 *Sold.* Let's hear him, for the things he
    speaks
May concern Cæsar.

    3 *Sold.*         Let's do so. But he sleeps.
    1 *Sold.* Swoons rather; for so bad a prayer
    as his
Was never yet fore sleep.
    2 *Sold.*         Go we to him.
    3 *Sold.* Awake, sir, awake; speak to us.
    2 *Sold.*          Hear you, sir?
    1 *Sold.* The hand of death hath raught
    him.
        [*Drums afar off.*] Hark! the drums
Do merrily wake the sleepers. Let us bear
    him
To the court of guard; he is of note: our
    hour
Is fully out.
    3 *Sold.* Come on, then;
He may recover yet. [*Exeunt with the body.*

### Scene X.—*Ground between the two Camps.*

#### Enter ANTONY *and* SCARUS, *with* Forces, *marching.*

    *Ant.* Their preparation is to-day by sea;
We please them not by land.
    *Scar.*         For both, my lord.
    *Ant.* I would they'd fight i' the fire or i' the
    air;
We'd fight there, too. But this it is; our foot
Upon the hills adjoining to the city
Shall stay with us:—order for sea is given;
They have put forth the haven:—forward
    now,
Where their appointment we may best dis-
    cover,
And look on their endeavour.      [*Exeunt*

### Scene XI.—*Another part of the Ground.*

#### Enter CÆSAR, *with his* Forces, *marching.*

    *Cæs.* But being charg'd, we will be still by
    land,
Which, as I take 't, we shall; for his best
    force
Is forth to man his galleys. To the vales,
And hold our best advantage.      [*Exeunt.*

### Scene XII.—*Another part of the Ground.*

#### Enter ANTONY *and* SCARUS.

    *Ant.* Yet they're not join'd: where yond
    pine does stand
I shall discover all: I'll bring thee word
Straight how 'tis like to go.      [*Exeunt.*
    *Scar.*         Swallows have built
In Cleopatra's sails their nests: the augurers
Say they know not,—they cannot tell;—look
    grimly,
And dare not speak their knowledge. An-
    tony
Is valiant and dejected; and, by starts,
His fretted fortunes give him hope and fear
Of what he has and has not.
    [*Alarum afar off, as at a sea-fight.*

#### Re-enter ANTONY.

    *Ant.*          All is lost;

This foul Egyptian hath betrayed me:
My fleet hath yielded to the foe; and
    yonder                              [gether
They cast their caps up, and carouse to-
Like friends long lost.—Triple-turn'd whore!
    'tis thou
Hast sold me to this novice; and my heart
Makes only wars on thee.—Bid them all fly;
For when I am reveng'd upon my charm,
I have done all.—Bid them all fly; begone.
                            [*Exit* SCARUS.
O sun, thy uprise shall I see no more:
Fortune and Antony part here; even here
Do we shake hands.—All come to this!—The
    hearts
That spaniel'd me at heels, to whom I gave
Their wishes, do discandy, melt their sweets
On blossoming Cæsar; and this pine is
    bark'd
That overtopp'd them all. Betray'd I am:
O this false soul of Egypt! this grave charm,
Whose eye beck'd forth my wars and call'd
    them home;                    [end,—
Whose bosom was my crownet, my chief
Like a right gipsy, hath, at fast and loose,
Beguil'd me to the very heart of loss.—
What, Eros, Eros!

#### *Enter* CLEOPATRA.

                Ah, thou spell! Avaunt!
*Cleo.* Why is my lord enrag'd against his
    love?
*Ant.* Vanish; or I shall give thee thy de-
    serving,                        [thee,
And blemish Cæsar's triumph. Let him take
And hoist thee up to the shouting plebeians:
Follow his chariot, like the greatest spot
Of all thy sex; most monster-like, be shown
For poor'st diminutives, for doits; and let
Patient Octavia plough thy visage up
With her prepared nails. [*Exit* CLEO.] 'Tis
    well thou 'rt gone,
If it be well to live; but better 'twere
Thou fell'st into my fury, for one death
Might have prevented many.—Eros, ho!—
The shirt of Nessus is upon me: teach me,
Alcides, thou mine ancestor, thy rage: [moon;
Let me lodge Lichas on the horns o' the
And with those hands, that grasp'd the
    heaviest club,                  [die:
Subdue my worthiest self. The witch shall
To the young Roman boy she hath sold me,
    and I fall
Under this plot: she dies for 't.—Eros, ho!
                            [*Exit.*

#### SCENE XIII.—ALEXANDRIA. *A Room in the Palace.*

#### *Enter* CLEOPATRA, CHARMIAN, IRAS, *and* MARDIAN.

*Cleo.* Help me, my women! O, he is more
    mad                        [Thessaly
Than Telamon for his shield; the boar of
Was never so emboss'd.

*Char.*                To the monument!
There lock yourself, and send him word you
    are dead.
The soul and body rive not more in parting
Than greatness going off.
*Cleo.*                To the monument!—
Mardian, go tell him I have slain myself:
Say that the last I spoke was *Antony,*
And word it, pr'ythee, piteously: hence, Mar-
    dian;
And bring me how he takes my death.—
To the monument!                  [*Exeunt.*

#### SCENE XIV.—ALEXANDRIA. *Another Room.*

#### *Enter* ANTONY *and* EROS.

*Ant.* Eros, thou yet behold'st me?
*Eros.*                Ay, noble lord.
*Ant.* Sometime we see a cloud that's
    dragonish;
A vapour sometime like a bear or lion,
A tower'd citadel, a pendant rock,
A forked mountain, or blue promontory
With trees upon't, that nod unto the world,
And mock our eyes with air: thou hast seen
    these signs;
They are black vesper's pageants.
*Eros.*                Ay, my lord.
*Ant.* That which is now a horse, even with
    a thought
The rack dislimns; and makes it indistinct,
As water is in water.
*Eros.*            It does, my lord.    [is
*Ant.* My good knave Eros, now thy captain
Even such a body: here I am Antony;
Yet cannot hold this visible shape, my knave.
I made these wars for Egypt; and the
    queen,—                      [mine;
Whose heart I thought I had, for she had
Which, whilst it was mine, had annex'd unto't
A million more now lost,—she, Eros, has
Pack'd cards with Cæsar, and false-play'd my
    glory
Unto an enemy's triumph.—
Nay, weep not, gentle Eros; there is left us
Ourselves to end ourselves.—

#### *Enter* MARDIAN.

                O, thy vile lady!
She has robb'd me of my sword.
*Mar.*                No, Antony;
My mistress lov'd thee, and her fortunes
    mingled
With thine entirely.
*Ant.*            Hence, saucy eunuch; peace!
She hath betray'd me, and shall die the death.
*Mar.* Death of one person can be paid but
    once,
And that she has discharg'd: what thou
    wouldst do
Is done unto thy hand: the last she spake
Was, *Antony! most noble Antony!*
Then in the midst a tearing groan did break
The name of Antony; it was divided

Between her heart and lips: she render'd life,
Thy name so buried in her.

*Ant.*                    Dead then?
*Mar.*                          Dead.
*Ant.* Unarm, Eros; the long day's task is
    done,                    [hence safe
And we must sleep.—That thou depart'st
Does pay thy labour richly; go.
                    [*Exit* MARDIAN.
Off, pluck off;—
The sevenfold shield of Ajax cannot keep
The battery from my heart. O, cleave, my
    sides!
Heart, once be stronger than thy continent,
Crack thy frail case!—Apace, Eros, apace.—
No more a soldier.—Bruised pieces, go;
You have been nobly borne.—From me a
    while.—                [*Exit* EROS.
I will o'ertake thee, Cleopatra, and
Weep for my pardon. So it must be, for now
All length is torture.—Since the torch is out,
Lie down, and stray no further: now all la-
    bour
Mars what it does; yea, very force entangles
Itself with strength: seal then, and all is
    done.—
Eros!—I come, my queen.—Eros!—stay for
    me:                    [hand,
Where souls do couch on flowers, we'll hand in
And with our sprightly port make the ghosts
    gaze:
Dido and her Æneas shall want troops,
And all the haunt be ours.—Come, Eros,
    Eros!

            *Re-enter* EROS.

*Eros.* What would my lord?
*Ant.*              Since Cleopatra died,
I have liv'd in such dishonour that the gods
Detest my baseness. I, that with my sword
Quarter'd the world, and o'er green Neptune's
    back
With ships made cities, condemn myself to
    lack
The courage of a woman; less noble mind
Than she which by her death our Cæsar tells,
*I am conqueror of myself.* Thou art sworn,
    Eros,
That, when the exigent should come,—which
    now
Is come indeed—when I should see behind me
The inevitable prosecution of
Disgrace and horror, that, on my command,
Thou then wouldst kill me: do't; the time is
    come:
Thou strik'st not me, 'tis Cæsar thou de-
    feat'st.
Put colour in thy cheek.
*Eros.*          The gods withhold me!
Shall I do that which all the Parthian darts,
Though enemy, lost aim, and could not?
*Ant.*                        Eros,
Wouldst thou be window'd in great Rome,
    and see

Thy master thus with pleach'd arms, bending
    down
His corrigible neck, his face subdu'd
To penetrative shame; whilst the wheel'd seat
Of fortunate Cæsar, drawn before him,
    branded
His baseness that ensu'd?
*Eros.*          I would not see't.
*Ant.* Come, then; for with a wound I must
    be cur'd.                    [worn
Draw that thy honest sword, which thou hast
Most useful for thy country.
*Eros.*          O, sir, pardon me!
*Ant.* When I did make thee free, swor'st
    thou not then
To do this when I bade thee? Do it at once;
Or thy precedent services are all
But accidents unpurpos'd. Draw, and come.
*Eros.* Turn from me then that noble coun-
    tenance,
Wherein the worship of the whole world lies.
*Ant.* Lo thee!          [*Turning from him.*
*Eros.* My sword is drawn.
*Ant.*              Then let it do at once
The thing why thou hast drawn it.
*Eros.*              My dear master,
My captain and my emperor, let me say,
Before I strike this bloody stroke, farewell.
*Ant.* 'Tis said, man;—and farewell. [now?
*Eros.* Farewell, great chief. Shall I strike
*Ant.*                  Now, Eros.
*Eros.* Why, there then [*falls on his
    sword*]:—thus do I escape the sorrow
Of Antony's death.              [*Dies.*
*Ant.*          Thrice nobler than myself!
Thou teachest me, O valiant Eros, what
I should, and thou couldst not. My queen and
    Eros
Have, by their brave instruction, got upon me
A nobleness on record: but I will be
A bridegroom in my death, and run into't
As to a lover's bed. Come, then; and, Eros,
Thy master dies thy scholar: to do thus
                [*Falling on his sword.*
I learn'd of thee. How! not dead? not
    dead?—
The guard, ho!—O, despatch me!

            *Enter* DERCETAS *and* Guard.

1 *Guard.*              What's the noise?
*Ant.* I have done my work ill, friends: O,
    made an end
Of what I have begun.
2 *Guard.*          The star is fallen.
1 *Guard.* And time is at his period.
*All.*                  Alas, and woe!
*Ant.* Let him that loves me, strike me dead.
1 *Guard.*                  Not I.
2 *Guard.* Nor I.
3 *Guard.* Nor any one.      [*Exeunt* Guard.
*Der.* Thy death and fortunes bid thy fol-
    lowers fly.                [ings,
This sword but shown to Cæsar, with this tid-
Shall enter me with him.

*Enter* Diomedes.

*Dio.* Where's Antony?
*Der.* There, Diomed, there.
*Dio.* Lives he?
Wilt thou not answer, man?
[*Exit* Dercetas.
*Ant.* Art thou there, Diomed? Draw thy
sword, and give me
Sufficing strokes for death.
*Dio.* Most absolute lord,
My mistress Cleopatra sent me to thee.
*Ant.* When did she send thee?
*Dio.* Now, my lord.
*Ant.* Where is she?
*Dio.* Lock'd in her monument. She had a
prophesying fear
Of what hath come to pass: for when she
saw,—
Which never shall be found,—you did suspect
She had dispos'd with Cæsar, and that your
rage
Would not be purg'd, she sent you word she
was dead;
But, fearing since how it might work, hath
sent
Me to proclaim the truth; and I am come,
I dread, too late.
*Ant.* Too late, good Diomed.—Call my
guard, I pr'ythee.
*Dio.* What, ho! the emperor's guard! The
guard, what, ho!
Come, your lord calls!

*Enter some of the* Guard.

*Ant.* Bear me, good friends, where Cleo-
patra bides;
'Tis the last service that I shall command
you.
1 *Guard.* Woe, woe are we, sir, you may
not live to wear
All your true followers out.
*All.* Most heavy day!
*Ant.* Nay, good my fellows, do not please
sharp fate [come
To grace it with your sorrows: bid that wel-
Which comes to punish us, and we punish it,
Seeming to bear it lightly. Take me up:
I have led you oft: carry me now, good
friends,
And have my thanks for all.
[*Exeunt, bearing* Antony.

Scene XV.—Alexandria. *A Monument.*

*Enter, above,* Cleopatra, Charmian, *and*
Iras.

*Cleo.* O Charmian, I will never go from
hence.
*Char.* Be comforted, dear madam.
*Cleo.* No, I will not:
All strange and terrible events are welcome,
But comforts we despise; our size of sorrow,
Proportion'd to our cause, must be as great
As that which makes it.—

*Enter, below,* Diomedes.

How now! is he dead?
*Dio.* His death's upon him, but not dead.
Look out o' the other side your monument;
His guard have brought him thither.

*Enter, below,* Antony, *borne by the* Guard.

*Cleo.* O sun,
Burn the great sphere thou mov'st in!—dark-
ling stand
The varying shore o' the world.—O Antony,
Antony, Antony!—Help, Charmian; help,
Iras, help,—
Help, friends below;—let's draw him hither.
*Ant.* Peace!
Not Cæsar's valour hath o'erthrown Antony,
But Antony's hath triumph'd on itself.
*Cleo.* So it should be, that none but An-
tony
Should conquer Antony; but woe 'tis so!
*Ant.* I am dying, Egypt, dying; only
I here impórtune death awhile, until
Of many thousand kisses the poor last
I lay upon thy lips.
*Cleo.* I dare not, dear,—
Dear my lord, pardon,—I dare not,
Lest I be taken: not the imperious show
Of the full-fortun'd Cæsar ever shall [have
Be brooch'd with me; if knife, drugs, serpents
Edge, sting, or operation, I am safe;
Your wife Octavia, with her modest eyes
And still conclusion, shall acquire no honour
Demuring upon me.—But come, come, An-
tony,— [up;—
Help me, my women,—we must draw thee
Assist, good friends.
*Ant.* O, quick, or I am gone.
*Cleo.* Here's sport indeed!—How heavy
weighs my lord!
Our strength is all gone into heaviness,
That makes the weight: had I great Juno's
power,
The strong-wing'd Mercury should fetch thee
up,
And set thee by Jove's side. Yet come a
little,—
Wishers were ever fools,—O, come, come,
come; [*They draw* Antony *up.*
And welcome, welcome! die where thou hast
liv'd;
Quicken with kissing: had my lips that power,
Thus would I wear them out.
*All.* A heavy sight!
*Ant.* I am dying, Egypt, dying:
Give me some wine, and let me speak a little.
*Cleo.* No, let me speak; and let me rail so
high [wheel,
That the false housewife Fortune break her
Provok'd by my offence.
*Ant.* One word, sweet queen:
Of Cæsar seek your honour, with your safe-
ty.—O!
*Cleo.* They do not go together.

*Ant.* Gentle, hear me:
None about Cæsar trust but Proculeius.
  *Cleo.* My resolution and my hands I'll
    trust;
None about Cæsar.
  *Ant.* The miserable change now at my end
Lament nor sorrow at: but please your
    thoughts
In feeding them with those my former for-
    tunes
Wherein I liv'd, the greatest prince o' the
    world,
The noblest; and do now not basely die,
Not cowardly put off my helmet to
My countryman, a Roman by a Roman
Valiantly vanquish'd. Now my spirit is going:
I can no more.
  *Cleo.* Noblest of men, woo't die?
Hast thou no care of me? shall I abide
In this dull world, which in thy absence is
No better than a sty?—O, see, my women,
             [ANTONY *dies.*
The crown o' the earth doth melt.—My
    lord!—
O, wither'd is the garland of the war,  [girls
The soldier's pole is fallen: young boys and
Are level now with men: the odds is gone,
And there is nothing left remarkable
Beneath the visiting moon.     [*Faints.*
  *Char.*       O, quietness, lady!
  *Iras.* She is dead too, our sovereign.
  *Char.*           Lady,—
  *Iras.*           Madam,—
  *Char.* O madam, madam, madam,—
  *Iras.*          Royal Egypt,
Empress,—
  *Char.* Peace, peace, Iras!    [manded
  *Cleo.* No more, but e'en a woman, and com-
By such poor passion as the maid that milks
And does the meanest chares.—It were for me
To throw my sceptre at the injurious gods;
To tell them that this world did equal theirs
Till they had stol'n our jewel. All's but
    naught;
Patience is sottish, and impatience does
Become a dog that's mad: then is it sin
To rush into the secret house of death
Ere death dare come to us?—How do you,
    women?
What, what! good cheer! Why, how now,
    Charmian!
My noble girls!—Ah, women, women, look,
Our lamp is spent, it's out!—Good sirs, take
    heart:—        [what's noble,
We'll bury him; and then, what's brave,
Let's do it after the high Roman fashion,
And make death proud to take us. Come,
    away:
This case of that huge spirit now is cold:
Ah, women, women!—Come; we have no
    friend
But resolution, and the briefest end.
   [*Exeunt; those above bearing off* ANTONY'S
      *body.*

## ACT V.

SCENE I.—CÆSAR'S *Camp before Alexandria.*

*Enter* CÆSAR, AGRIPPA, DOLABELLA, ME-
CÆNAS, GALLUS, PROCULEIUS, *and others.*

  *Cæs.* Go to him, Dolabella, bid him yield;
Being so frustrate, tell him that he mocks
The pauses that he makes.
  *Dol.*         Cæsar, I shall. [*Exit.*

*Enter* DERCETAS *with the sword of* ANTONY.

  *Cæs.* Wherefore is that? and what art thou
    that dar'st
Appear thus to us?
  *Der.*         I am call'd Dercetas;
Mark Antony I serv'd, who best was worthy
Best to be serv'd: whilst he stood up and
    spoke,
He was my master; and I wore my life
To spend upon his haters. If thou please
To take me to thee, as I was to him
I'll be to Cæsar; if thou pleasest not,
I yield thee up my life.
  *Cæs.*        What is't thou say'st?
  *Der.* I say, O Cæsar, Antony is dead.
  *Cæs.* The breaking of so great a thing
    should make
A greater crack: the round world
Should have shook lions into civil streets,
And citizens to their dens. The death of An-
    tony
Is not a single doom; in the name lay
A moiety of the world.
  *Der.*       He is dead, Cæsar;
Not by a public minister of justice,
Nor by a hired knife; but that self hand
Which writ his honour in the acts it did
Hath, with the courage which the heart did
    lend it,
Splitted the heart.—This is his sword;
I robb'd his wound of it; behold it stain'd
With his most noble blood.
  *Cæs.*       Look you sad, friends?
The gods rebuke me, but it is tidings
To wash the eyes of kings.
  *Agr.*       And strange it is
That nature must compel us to lament
Our most persisted deeds.
  *Mec.*       His taints and honours
Weigh'd equal with him.
  *Agr.*      A rarer spirit never    [us
Did steer humanity: but you, gods, will give
Some faults to make us men. Cæsar is touch'd.
  *Mec.* When such a spacious mirror's set
    before him,
He needs must see himself.
  *Cæs.*        O Antony!
I have follow'd thee to this.—But we do lance
Diseases in our bodies: I must perforce
Have shown to thee such a declining day
Or look on thine; we could not stall together
In the whole world: but yet let me lament,
With tears as sovereign as the blood of hearts,

That thou, my brother, my competitor
In top of all design, my mate in empire,
Friend and companion in the front of war,
The arm of mine own body, and the heart
Where mine his thoughts did kindle,—that
　　our stars,
Unreconciliable, should divide　　[friends,—
Our equalness to this.—Hear me, good
But I will tell you at some meeter season:

*Enter a* Messenger.

The business of this man looks out of him;
We'll hear him what he says.—Whence are
　you?　　　　　　　　　　　　　[mistress,
　*Mess.* A poor Egyptian yet. The queen my
Confin'd in all she has, her monument,
Of thy intents desires instruction,
That she preparedly may frame herself
To the way she's forc'd to.
　*Cæs.*　　　Bid her have good heart:
She soon shall know of us, by some of ours,
How honourable and how kindly we
Determine for her; for Cæsar cannot learn
To be ungentle.
　*Mess.*　So the gods preserve thee! [*Exit.*
　*Cæs.* Come hither, Proculeius. Go, and say
We purpose her no shame: give her what
　comforts
The quality of her passion shall require
Lest, in her greatness, by some mortal stroke
She do defeat us; for her life in Rome
Would be eternal in our triumph: go, [says,
And with your speediest bring us what she
And how you find of her.
　*Pro.*　　　Cæsar, I shall. [*Exit.*
　*Cæs.* Gallus, go you along.—
　　　　　　　　　　　　[*Exit* GALLUS.]
　　Where's Dolabella,
To second Proculeius?
　*Agr. and Mec.*　　Dolabella!
　*Cæs.* Let him alone, for I remember now
How he's employ'd: he shall in time be ready.
Go with me to my tent; where you shall see
How hardly I was drawn into this war;
How calm and gentle I proceeded still
In all my writings: go with me, and see
What I can show in this.　　[*Exeunt.*

SCENE II.—ALEXANDRIA. *A Room in the
Monument.*

*Enter* CLEOPATRA, CHARMIAN, *and* IRAS.

　*Cleo.* My desolation does begin to make
A better life. 'Tis paltry to be Cæsar;
Not being Fortune, he's but Fortune's knave,
A minister of her will: and it is great
To do that thing that ends all other deeds;
Which shackles accidents and bolts up change;
Which sleeps, and never palates more the dug,
The beggar's nurse and Cæsar's.

*Enter, to the gates of the Monument,* PRO-
CULEIUS, GALLUS, *and* Soldiers.

　*Pro.* Cæsar sends greeting to the Queen of
　Egypt;

And bids thee study on what fair demands
Thou mean'st to have him grant thee.
　*Cleo.*　　　　What's thy name?
　*Pro.* My name is Proculeius.
　*Cleo.*　　　　　　Antony
Did tell me of you, bade me trust you; but
I do not greatly care to be deceiv'd,
That have no use for trusting. If your master
Would have a queen his beggar, you must tell
　him
That majesty, to keep decorum, must
No less beg than a kingdom: if he please
To give me conquer'd Egypt for my son,
He gives me so much of mine own as I
Will kneel to him with thanks.
　*Pro.*　　　Be of good cheer;
You are fallen into a princely hand, fear
　nothing:
Make your full reference freely to my lord,
Who is so full of grace that it flows over
On all that need: let me report to him
Your sweet dependency; and you shall find
A conqueror that will pray in aid for kindness
Where he for grace is kneel'd to.
　*Cleo.*　　　Pray you, tell him
I am his fortune's vassal, and I send him
The greatness he has got. I hourly learn
A doctrine of obedience; and would gladly
Look him i' the face.
　*Pro.*　　　This I'll report, dear lady.
Have comfort, for I know your plight is pitied
Of him that caus'd it.
　*Gal.* You see how easily she may be sur-
　　pris'd:
[*Here* PROCULEIUS *and two of the* Guard
　*ascend the Monument by a ladder placed
　against a window, and, having descend-
　ed, come behind* CLEOPATRA. *Some of the*
　Guard *unbar and open the gates.*
Guard her till Cæsar come.
　　　　　　[*To* PRO. *and the* Guard. *Exit.*
　*Iras.* Royal queen!
　*Char.* O Cleopatra! thou art taken, queen!
　*Cleo.* Quick, quick, good hands.
　　　　　　　　　　　[*Drawing a dagger.*
　*Pro.*　　　Hold, worthy lady, hold:
　　　　　　　　[*Seizes and disarms her.*
Do not yourself such wrong who are in this
Reliev'd, but not betray'd.
　*Cleo.*　　　What, of death too,
That rids our dogs of languish?
　*Pro.*　　　Cleopatra,
Do not abuse my master's bounty by
The undoing of yourself: let the world see
His nobleness well acted, which your death
Will never let come forth.
　*Cleo.*　　　Where art thou, death?
Come hither, come! come, come, and take a
　queen
Worth many babes and beggars!
　*Pro.*　　　O, temperance, lady!
　*Cleo.* Sir, I will eat no meat, I'll not drink,
　sir;
If idle talk will once be accessary,

I'll not sleep neither: this mortal house I'll
　　ruin,
Do Cæsar what he can. Know, sir, that I
Will not wait pinion'd at your master's court;
Nor once be châstis'd with the sober eye
Of dull Octavia. Shall they hoist me up,
And show me to the shouting varletry
Of censuring Rome? Rather a ditch in Egypt
Be gentle grave unto me! rather on Nilus'
　　mud
Lay me stark nak'd, and let the water-flies
Blow me into abhorring! rather make
My country's high pyramids my gibbet,
And hang me up in chains!
　　*Pro.*　　　　　　　　You do extend
These thoughts of horror further than you
　　shall
Find cause in Cæsar.

*Enter* DOLABELLA.

　　*Dol.*　　　　　　　Proculeius,
What thou hast done thy master Cæsar
　　knows,
And he hath sent for thee: as for the queen,
I'll take her to my guard.
　　*Pro.*　　　　　　　So, Dolabella,
It shall content me best: be gentle to her.—
To Cæsar I will speak what you shall please,
　　　　　　　　　　　　[*To* CLEOPATRA.
If you'll employ me to him.
　　*Cleo.*　　　　　　Say I would die.
　　　　[*Exeunt* PROCULEIUS *and* Soldiers.
　　*Dol.* Most noble empress, you have heard
　　of me?
　　*Cleo.* I cannot tell.
　　*Dol.*　　　　　　Assuredly you know me.
　　*Cleo.* No matter, sir, what I have heard or
　　known.
You laugh when boys or women tell their
　　dreams;
Is't not your trick?
　　*Dol.*　　　　　I understand not, madam.
　　*Cleo.* I dream'd there was an emperor
　　Antony:—
O, such another sleep, that I might see
But such another man!
　　*Dol.*　　　　　If it might please you,—
　　*Cleo.* His face was as the heavens; and
　　therein stuck
A sun and moon, which kept their course,
　　and lighted
The little O, the earth.
　　*Dol.*　　　　Most sovereign creature,—
　　*Cleo.* His legs bestrid the ocean: his
　　rear'd arm
Crested the world: his voice was propertied
As all the tuned spheres, and that to friends;
But when he meant to quail and shake the
　　orb,
He was as rattling thunder. For his bounty,
There was no winter in't; an autumn 'twas
That grew the more by reaping: his delights
Were dolphin-like; they show'd his back
　　above

The element they liv'd in: in his livery
Walk'd crowns and crownets; realms and
　　islands were
As plates dropp'd from his pocket.
　　*Dol.*　　　　　　　　Cleopatra,—
　　*Cleo.* Think you there was or might be
　　such a man
As this I dream'd of?
　　*Dol.*　　　　　Gentle madam, no.
　　*Cleo.* You lie, up to the hearing of the
　　gods.
But if there be, or ever were, one such,
It's past the size of dreaming: nature wants
　　stuff
To vie strange forms with fancy: yet to
　　imagine
An Antony were nature's peace 'gainst fancy,
Condemning shadows quite.
　　*Dol.*　　　　　　Hear me, good madam.
Your loss is, as yourself, great; and you bear
　　it
As answering to the weight: would I might
　　never
O'ertake pursu'd success, but I do feel,
By the rebound of yours, a grief that smites
My very heart at root.
　　*Cleo.*　　　　　　I thank you, sir.
Know you what Cæsar means to do with me?
　　*Dol.* I am loth to tell you what I would
　　you knew.
　　*Cleo.* Nay, pray you, sir,—
　　*Dol.*　　　　　Though he be honourable,—
　　*Cleo.* He'll lead me, then, in triumph?
　　*Dol.*　　　　　　　Madam, he will.
I know it.　　　　　　　[*Flourish within.*
*Within.* Make way there,—Cæsar!

　　*Enter* CÆSAR, GALLUS, PROCULEIUS,
　　MECÆNAS, SELEUCUS, *and* Attendants.

　　*Cæs.* Which is the Queen of Egypt?
　　*Dol.* It is the emperor, madam.
　　　　　　　　　　　[CLEOPATRA *kneels.*
　　*Cæs.* Arise, you shall not kneel:—
I pray you rise; rise, Egypt.
　　*Cleo.*　　　　　　Sir, the gods
Will have it thus; my master and my lord
I must obey.
　　*Cæs.*　　　　Take to you no hard thoughts:
The record of what injuries you did us,
Though written in our flesh, we shall remem-
　　ber
As things but done by chance.
　　*Cleo.*　　　　　Sole sir o' the world,
I cannot project mine own cause so well
To make it clear: but do confess I have
Been laden with like frailties which before
Have often sham'd our sex.
　　*Cæs.*　　　　　　Cleopatra, know
We will extenuate rather than enforce:
If you apply yourself to our intents,—
Which towards you are most gentle,—you
　　shall find
A benefit in this change; but if you seek
To lay on me a cruelty, by taking

Antony's course, you shall bereave yourself
Of my good purposes, and put your children
To that destruction which I'll guard them from,
If thereon you rely. I'll take my leave.

*Cleo.* And may, through all the world: 'tis yours; and we,
Your scutcheons and your signs of conquest, shall [good lord.
Hang in what place you please. Here, my

*Cæs.* You shall advise me in all for Cleopatra.

*Cleo.* This is the brief of money, plate, and jewels
I am possess'd of: 'tis exactly valued; [cus?
Not petty things admitted.—Where's Seleu-

*Sel.* Here, madam. [my lord,

*Cleo.* This is my treasurer: let him speak,
Upon his peril that I have reserv'd
To myself nothing. Speak the truth, Seleucus.

*Sel.* Madam,
I had rather seal my lips than to my peril
Speak that which is not.

*Cleo.* What have I kept back?

*Sel.* Enough to purchase what you have made known.

*Cæs.* Nay, blush not, Cleopatra; I approve
Your wisdom in the deed.

*Cleo.* See, Cæsar! O, behold,
How pomp is follow'd! mine will now be yours; [mine.
And, should we shift estates, yours would be
The ingratitude of this Seleucus does
Even make me wild: O slave, of no more trust
Than love that's hir'd!—What, goest thou back? thou shalt
Go back, I warrant thee; but I'll catch thine eyes [dog!
Though they had wings; slave, soulless villain,
O rarely base!

*Cæs.* Good queen, let us entreat you.

*Cleo.* O Cæsar, what a wounding shame is this,—
That thou, vouchsafing here to visit me,
Doing the honour of thy lordliness
To one so meek, that mine own servant should
Parcel the sum of my disgraces by
Addition of his envy! Say, good Cæsar,
That I some lady trifles have reserv'd,
Immoment toys, things of such dignity
As we greet modern friends withal; and say,
Some nobler token I have kept apart
For Livia and Octavia, to induce
Their mediation; must I be unfolded
With one that I have bred? The gods! It smites me
Beneath the fall I have. Pr'ythee, go hence; [To SELEUCUS.
Or I shall show the cinders of my spirits
Through the ashes of my chance.—Wert thou a man,
Thou wouldst have mercy upon me.

*Cæs.* Forbear, Seleucus. [*Exit* SELEUCUS.

*Cleo.* Be it known that we, the greatest, are misthought
For things that others do; and when we fall
We answer others' merits in our name,
And therefore to be pitied.

*Cæs.* Cleopatra,
Not what you have reserv'd, nor what acknowledg'd,
Put we i' the roll of conquest: still be't yours,
Bestow it at your pleasure; and believe
Cæsar's no merchant, to make prize with you
Of things that merchants sold. Therefore be cheer'd;
Make not your thoughts your prisons: no, dear queen;
For we intend so to dispose you as
Yourself shall give us counsel. Feed and sleep:
Our care and pity is so much upon you
That we remain your friend; and so, adieu.

*Cleo.* My master and my lord!

*Cæs.* Not so. Adieu.
[*Flourish. Exeunt* CÆSAR *and his* Train.

*Cleo.* He words me, girls, he words me, that I should not
Be noble to myself: but hark thee, Charmian!
[*Whispers* CHARMIAN.

*Iras.* Finish, good lady; the bright day is done,
And we are for the dark.

*Cleo.* Hie thee again:
I have spoke already, and it is provided;
Go put it to the haste.

*Char.* Madam, I will.

### Re-enter DOLABELLA.

*Dol.* Where is the queen?

*Char.* Behold, sir. [*Exit.*

*Cleo.* Dolabella!

*Dol.* Madam, as thereto sworn by your command,
Which my love makes religion to obey,
I tell you this: Cæsar through Syria
Intends his journey; and within three days
You with your children will he send before:
Make your best use of this: I have perform'd
Your pleasure and my promise.

*Cleo.* Dolabella,
I shall remain your debtor.

*Dol.* I your servant.
Adieu, good queen; I must attend on Cæsar.

*Cleo.* Farewell, and thanks.
[*Exit* DOLABELLA.
Now, Iras, what think'st thou?
Thou, an Egyptian puppet, shalt be shown
In Rome as well as I: mechanic slaves,
With greasy aprons, rules, and hammers, shall
Uplift us to the view; in their thick breaths,
Rank of gross diet, shall we be enclouded,
And forc'd to drink their vapour.

*Iras.* The gods forbid!

*Cleo.* Nay, 'tis most certain, Iras:— saucy lictors [rhymers
Will catch at us like strumpets; and scald
Ballad us out o' tune: the quick comedians

Extemporally will stage us, and present
Our Alexandrian revels; Antony
Shall be brought drunken forth, and I shall see
Some squeaking Cleopatra boy my greatness
I' the posture of a whore.

    *Iras.*               O the good gods!

    *Cleo.* Nay, that's certain.

    *Iras.* I'll never see't; for I am sure my nails
Are stronger than mine eyes.

    *Cleo.*          Why, that's the way
To fool their preparation and to conquer
Their most absurd intents.

            *Enter* CHARMIAN.

                Now, Charmian!—
Show me, my women, like a queen.—Go fetch
My best attires;—I am again for Cydnus,
To meet Mark Antony:—sirrah, Iras, go.—
Now, noble Charmian, we'll despatch indeed:
And when thou hast done this chare, I'll give
       thee leave          [and all
To play till doomsday.—Bring our crown
Wherefore's this noise?

        [*Exit* IRAS. *A noise within.*

    *Enter one of the* Guard.

    *Guard.*        Here is a rural fellow
That will not be denied your highness' pres-
    ence:
He brings you figs.

    *Cleo.* Let him come in.      [*Exit* Guard.
What poor an instrument
May do a noble deed! he brings me liberty.
My resolution's plac'd, and I have nothing
Of woman in me: now from head to foot
I am marble-constant; now the fleeting moon
No planet is of mine.

    *Re-enter* Guard, *with* Clown *bringing a
        basket.*

    *Guard.*         This is the man.

    *Cleo.* Avoid, and leave him. [*Exit* Guard.
Hast thou the pretty worm of Nilus there
That kills and pains not?

    *Clovin.* Truly, I have him: but I would
not be the party that should desire you to
touch him, for his biting is immortal; those
that do die of it do seldom or never recover.

    *Cleo.* Remember'st thou any that have
died on't?

    *Clown.* Very many, men and women too.
I heard of one of them no longer than yesterday: a very honest woman, but something
given to lie; as a woman should not do but in
the way of honesty: how she died of the biting of it, what pain she felt,—truly she makes
a very good report o' the worm; but he that
will believe all that they say shall never be
saved by half that they do: but this is most
fallible, the worm's an odd worm.

    *Cleo.* Get thee hence; farewell.

    *Clown.* I wish you all joy of the worm.

            [*Sets down the basket.*

    *Cleo.* Farewell.

    *Clown.* You must think this, look you, that
the worm will do his kind.

    *Cleo.* Ay, ay; farewell.

    *Clown.* Look you, the worm is not to be
trusted but in the keeping of wise people; for
indeed there is no goodness in the worm.

    *Cleo.* Take thou no care; it shall be heeded.

    *Clown.* Very good. Give it nothing, I pray
you, for it is not worth the feeding.

    *Cleo.* Will it eat me?

    *Clown.* You must not think I am so simple
but I know the devil himself will not eat a
woman: I know that a woman is a dish for
the gods, if the devil dress her not. But, truly,
these same whoreson devils do the gods great
harm in their women, for in every ten that
they make the devils mar five.

    *Cleo.* Well, get thee gone; farewell.

    *Clown.* Yes, forsooth: I wish you joy o'
the worm.                      [*Exit.*

    *Re-enter* IRAS, *with a robe, crown, &c.*

    *Cleo.* Give me my robe, put on my crown;
    I have
Immortal longings in me: now no more
The juice of Egypt's grape shall moist this
    lip:—
Yare, yare, good Iras; quick.—Methinks I
    hear
Antony call; I see him rouse himself
To praise my noble act; I hear him mock
The luck of Cæsar, which the gods give men
To excuse their after wrath. Husband, I come:
Now to that name my courage prove my title!
I am fire and air; my other elements
I give to baser life.—So,—have you done?
Come then, and take the last warmth of my
    lips.
Farewell, kind Charmian;—Iras, long fare-
    well. [*Kisses them.* IRAS *falls and dies.*
Have I the aspic in my lips? Dost fall?
If thou and nature can so gently part,
The stroke of death is as a lover's pinch,
Which hurts and is desir'd. Dost thou lie still?
If thus thou vanishest, thou tell'st the world
It is not worth leave-taking.

    *Char.* Dissolve, thick cloud, and rain; that
    I may say
The gods themselves do weep!

    *Cleo.*           This proves me base:
If she first meet the curled Antony,    [kiss
He'll make demand of her, and spend that
Which is my heaven to have.—Come, thou
    mortal wretch,
   [*To an asp, which she applies to her breast.*
With thy sharp teeth this knot intrinsicate
Of life at once untie: poor venomous fool,
Be angry, and despatch. O couldst thou speak,
That I might hear thee call great Cæsar ass
Unpolicied!

    *Char.* O eastern star!

    *Cleo.*              Peace, peace!
Dost thou not see my baby at my breast
That sucks the nurse asleep?

*Char.* O, break! O, break!
*Cleo.* As sweet as balm, as soft as air, as gentle:—
O Antony!—Nay, I will take thee too:—
*[Applying another asp to her arm.*
What, should I stay,—
*[Falls on a bed and dies.*
*Char.* In this vile world?—So, fare thee well.—
Now boast thee, death, in thy possession lies
A lass unparallel'd.—Downy windows, close;
And golden Phœbus never be beheld
Of eyes again so royal! Your crown's awry;
I'll mend it and then play.

*Enter the* Guard, *rushing in.*

1 *Guard.* Where is the queen?
*Char.* Speak softly, wake her not.
1 *Guard.* Cæsar hath sent,—
*Char.* Too slow a messenger.
*[Applies an asp.*
O, come apace, despatch: I partly feel thee.
1 *Guard.* Approach, ho! all's not well: Cæsar's beguil'd.
2 *Guard.* There's Dolabella sent from Cæsar; call him.
1 *Guard.* What work is here!—Charmian, is this well done?
*Char.* It is well done, and fitting for a princess
Descended of so many royal kings.
Ah, soldier! *[Dies.*

*Re-enter* DOLABELLA.

*Dol.* How goes it here?
2 *Guard.* All dead.
*Dol.* Cæsar, thy thoughts
Touch their effects in this: thyself art coming
To see perform'd the dreaded act which thou
So sought'st to hinder.
*Within.* A way there, a way for Cæsar!

*Re-enter* CÆSAR *and his* Train.

*Dol.* O, sir, you are too sure an auguerer;
That you did fear is done.

*Cæs.* Bravest at the last,
She levell'd at our purposes, and, being royal,
Took her own way.—The manner of their deaths?
I do not see them bleed.
*Dol.* Who was last with them?
1 *Guard.* A simple countryman that brought her figs.
This was his basket.
*Cæs.* Poison'd then.
1 *Guard.* O Cæsar,
This Charmian liv'd but now; she stood and spake:
I found her trimming up the diadem
On her dead mistress; tremblingly she stood,
And on the sudden dropp'd.
*Cæs.* O noble weakness!—
If they had swallow'd poison 'twould appear
By external swelling: but she looks like sleep,—
As she would catch another Antony
In her strong toil of grace.
*Dol.* Here on her breast
There is a vent of blood, and something blown:
The like is on her arm.
1 *Guard.* This is an aspic's trail: and these fig-leaves
Have slime upon them, such as the aspic leaves
Upon the caves of Nile.
*Cæs.* Most probable
That so she died; for her physician tells me
She hath pursu'd conclusions infinite
Of easy ways to die.—Take up her bed,
And bear her women from the monument:—
She shall be buried by her Antony:
No grave upon the earth shall clip in it
A pair so famous. High events as these
Strike those that make them; and their story is
No less in pity than his glory which
Brought them to be lamented. Our army shall
In solemn show attend this funeral;
And then to Rome.—Come, Dolabella, see
High order in this great solemnity. *[Exeunt.*

# CYMBELINE

## DRAMATIS PERSONÆ

CYMBELINE, *King of Britain.*
CLOTEN, *Son to the Queen by a former Husband.*
POSTHUMUS LEONATUS, *a Gentleman, Husband to* IMOGEN.
BELARIUS, *a banished Lord, disguised under the name of* MORGAN.
{ *Sons to* CYMBELINE, *disguised*
GUIDERIUS, } *under the names of* POLY-
ARVIRAGUS, { DORE *and* CADWAL, *supposed Sons to* BELARIUS.
PHILARIO, *Friend to* POSTHUMUS, } *Italians.*
IACHIMO, *Friend to* PHILARIO, }
A French Gentleman, *Friend to* PHILARIO.
CAIUS LUCIUS, *General of the Roman Forces.*
A Roman Captain.
Two British Captains.

PISANIO, *Servant to* POSTHUMUS.
CORNELIUS, *a Physician.*
Two Lords *of* CYMBELINE'S *Court.*
Two Gentlemen *of the same.*
Two Gaolers.

QUEEN, *Wife to* CYMBELINE.
IMOGEN, *Daughter to* CYMBELINE *by a former Queen.*
HELEN, *Woman to* IMOGEN.

Lords, Ladies, Roman Senators, Tribunes, Apparitions, a Soothsayer, a Dutch Gentleman, a Spanish Gentleman, Musicians, Officers, Captains, Soldiers, Messengers, *and other* Attendants.

SCENE,—*Sometimes in* BRITAIN; *sometimes in* ITALY.

## ACT I.

### SCENE I.—BRITAIN. *The Garden behind* CYMBELINE'S *Palace.*

*Enter two* Gentlemen.

1 *Gent.* You do not meet a man but frowns: our bloods
No more obey the heavens then our courtiers
Still seem as does the king.
  2 *Gent.*            But what's the matter?
  1 *Gent.* His daughter, and the heir of's kingdom, whom
He purpos'd to his wife's sole son,—a widow
That late he married,—hath referr'd herself
Unto a poor but worthy gentleman. She's wedded;
Her husband banish'd; she imprison'd: all
Is outward sorrow; though I think the king
Be touch'd at very heart.
  2 *Gent.*            None but the king?
  1 *Gent.* He that hath lost her too: so is the queen,
That most desir'd the match. But not a [courtier,
Although they wear their faces to the bent
Of the king's looks, hath a heart that is not
Glad at the thing they scowl at.
  2 *Gent.*            And why so?
  1 *Gent.* He that hath miss'd the princess is a thing
Too bad for bad report: and he that hath her,—
I mean that married her—alack, good man!—
And therefore banish'd,—is a creature such
As, to seek through the regions of the earth

For one his like, there would be something failing
In him that should compare. I do not think
So fair an outward and such stuff within
Endows a man but he.
  2 *Gent.*            You speak him far.
  1 *Gent.* I do extend him sir, within himself;
Crush him together, rather than unfold
His measure duly.
  2 *Gent.*            What's his name and birth?
  1 *Gent.* I cannot delve him to the root: his father
Was call'd Sicilius, who did join his honour,
Against the Romans, with Cassibelan,
But had his titles by Tenantius, whom
He serv'd with glory and admir'd success,—
So gain'd the sur-addition Leonatus:
And had, besides this gentleman in question,
Two other sons, who, in the wars o' the time,
Died with their swords in hand; for which their father,—
Then old and fond of issue,—took such sorrow
That he quit being; and his gentle lady,
Big of this gentleman, our theme, deceas'd
As he was born. The king he takes the babe
To his protection; calls him Posthumus Leonatus;
Breeds him, and makes him of his bedchamber:
Puts to him all the learnings that his time
Could make him the receiver of; which he took,
As we do air, fast as 'twas minister'd;

And in's spring became a harvest: liv'd in
    court,—
Which rare it is to do,—most prais'd, most
    lov'd;
A sample to the youngest; to the more ma-
    ture
A glass that feated them; and to the graver
A child that guided dotards: to his mistress,
For whom he now is banish'd,—her own price
Proclaims how she esteem'd him and his vir-
    tue;
By her election may be truly read
What kind of man he is.
    2 *Gent.*             I honour him
Even out of your report. But, pray you, tell
    me,
Is she sole child to the king?
    1 *Gent.*           His only child.
He had two sons,—if this be worth your hear-
    ing,
Mark it,—the eldest of them at three years
    old,
I' the swathing clothes the other, from their
    nursery          [knowledge
Were stol'n; and to this hour no guess in
Which way they went.
    2 *Gent.*        How long is this ago?
    1 *Gent.* Some twenty years.
    2 *Gent.* That a king's children should be so
    convey'd!
So slackly guarded! And the search so slow
That could not trace them!
    1 *Gent.*        Howsoe'er 'tis strange,
Or that the negligence may well be laugh'd at,
Yet is it true, sir.
    2 *Gent.* I do well believe you.
    1 *Gent.* We must forbear: here comes the
    gentleman,
The queen, and princess.        [*Exeunt.*

*Enter the* QUEEN, POSTHUMUS, *and* IMOGEN.

    *Queen.* No, be assur'd you shall not find me,
    daughter,
After the slander of most stepmothers,
Evil-ey'd unto you: you're my prisoner, but
Your gaoler shall deliver you the keys
That lock up your restraint.—For you, Pos-
    thumus,
So soon as I can win the offended king,
I will be known your advocate: marry, yet
The fire of rage is in him; and 'twere good
You lean'd unto his sentence with what pa-
    tience
Your wisdom may inform you.
    *Post.*          Please your highness,
I will from hence to-day.
    *Queen.*        You know the peril.—
I'll fetch a turn about the garden, pitying
The pangs of barr'd affections; though the
    king
Hath charg'd you should not speak together.
                   [*Exit.*
    *Imo.*                      O
Dissembling courtesy! How fine this tyrant

Can tickle where she wounds!—My dearest
    husband,           [ing,—
I something fear my father's wrath; but noth-
Always reserv'd my holy duty,—what
His rage can do on me. You must be gone;
And I shall here abide the hourly shot
Of angry eyes; not comforted to live,
But that there is this jewel in the world
That I may see again.
    *Post.* My queen! my mistress!
O lady, weep no more, lest I give cause
To be suspected of more tenderness
Than doth become a man! I will remain
The loyal'st husband that did e'er plight
    troth:
My residence in Rome at one Philario's,
Who to my father was a friend, to me
Known but by letter: thither write, my
    queen,
And with mine eyes I'll drink the words you
    send,
Though ink be made of gall.

*Re-enter* QUEEN.

    *Queen.*        Be brief, I pray you:
If the king come I shall incur I know not
How much of his displeasure.—[*Aside.*] Yet
    I'll move him
To walk this way: I never do him wrong
But he does buy my injuries to be friends,—
Pays dear for my offences.        [*Exit.*
    *Post.*        Should we be taking leave
As long a term as yet we have to live,
The loathness to depart would grow. Adieu!
    *Imo.* Nay, stay a little:
Were you but riding forth to air yourself,
Such parting were too petty. Look here, love;
This diamond was my mother's: take it,
    heart;
But keep it till you woo another wife,
When Imogen is dead.
    *Post.* How, how! another?—
You gentle gods, give me but this I have,
And sear up my embracements from a next
With bonds of death!—Remain, remain thou
    here          [*Putting on the ring.*
While sense can keep it on! And, sweetest,
    fairest,
As I my poor self did exchange for you,
To your so infinite loss, so in our trifles
I still win of you: for my sake wear this;
It is a manacle of love; I'll place it
Upon this fairest prisoner.
           [*Putting a bracelet on her arm.*
    *Imo.*           O the gods!
When shall we see again?
    *Post.*          Alack, the king!

*Enter* CYMBELINE *and* Lords.

    *Cym.* Thou basest thing, avoid! hence from
    my sight!
If after this command thou fraught the court
With thy unworthiness, thou diest: away!
Thou art poison to my blood.

*Post*.                   The gods protect you!
And bless the good remainders of the court!
I am gone.                              [*Exit*.
   *Imo*. There cannot be a pinch in death
More sharp than this is.
   *Cym*.                        O disloyal thing,
That shouldst repair my youth, thou heapest
A year's age on me!
   *Imo*.                  I beseech you, sir,
Harm not yourself with your vexation: I
Am senseless of your wrath; a touch more
                              rare
Subdues all pangs, all fears.
   *Cym*.                 Past grace? obedience?
   *Imo*. Past hope, and in despair; that way
         past grace.          [of my queen!
   *Cym*. That mightst have had the sole son
   *Imo*. O bless'd that I might not! I chose an
         eagle,
And did avoid a puttock.
   *Cym*. Thou took'st a beggar; wouldst have
         made my throne
A seat for baseness.
   *Imo*.               No; I rather added
A lustre to it.
   *Cym*.               O thou vile one!
   *Imo*.                         Sir,
It is your fault that I have lov'd Posthumus:
You bred him as my playfellow; and he is
A man worth any woman; overbuys me
Almost the sum he pays.
   *Cym*.                What, art thou mad?
   *Imo*. Almost, sir: heaven restore me!—
         Would I were
A neat-herd's daughter, and my Leonatus
Our neighbour shepherd's son!
   *Cym*.                Thou foolish thing!—

*Re-enter* QUEEN.

They were again together: you have done
                              [*To the Queen*.
Not after our command. Away with her,
And pen her up.
   *Queen*. Beseech your patience.—Peace,
Dear lady daughter, peace!—Sweet sovereign,
Leave us to ourselves; and make yourself
         some comfort
Out of your best advice.
   *Cym*.                Nay, let her languish
A drop of blood a day; and, being aged,
Die of this folly!      [*Exit, with* Lords.
   *Queen*.       Fie! you must give way.

*Enter* PISANIO.

Here is your servant.—How now, sir! What
         news?
   *Pis*. My lord your son drew on my master.
   *Queen*.                         Ha!
No harm, I trust, is done!
   *Pis*.              There might have been,
But that my master rather play'd than fought,
And had no help of anger: they were parted
By gentlemen at hand.
   *Queen*.           I am very glad on't.

   *Imo*. Your son's my father's friend; he
         takes his part.—
To draw upon an exile!—O brave sir!—
I would they were in Afric both together;
Myself by with a needle, that I might prick
The goer back.—Why came you from your
         master?                      [me
   *Pis*. On his command: he would not suffer
To bring him to the haven: left these notes
Of what commands I should be subject to,
When't pleas'd you to employ me.
   *Queen*.                This hath been
Your faithful servant: I dare lay mine honour
He will remain so.
   *Pis*.       I humbly thank your highness.
   *Queen*. Pray, walk awhile.
   *Imo*.            About some half hour hence,
I pray you, speak with me: you shall at least
Go see my lord aboard: for this time leave
         me.                          [*Exeunt*.

SCENE II.—BRITAIN.—*A Public Place*.

*Enter* CLOTEN *and two* Lords.

   1 *Lord*. Sir, I would advise you to shift a
shirt; the violence of action hath made you
reek as a sacrifice: where air comes out air
comes in: there's none abroad so wholesome
as that you vent.
   *Clo*. If my shirt were bloody, then to shift
it.—Have I hurt him?
   2 *Lord*. [*Aside*.] No, faith; not so much as
his patience.
   1 *Lord*. Hurt him! His body's a passable
carcass if he be not hurt: it is a throughfare
for steel if it be not hurt.
   2 *Lord*. [*Aside*.] His steel was in debt; it
went o' the back side the town.
   *Clo*. The villain would not stand me.
   2 *Lord*. [*Aside*.] No; but he fled forward
still, toward your face.
   1 *Lord*. Stand you! You have land enough
of your own: but he added to your having;
gave you some ground.
   2 *Lord*. [*Aside*.] As many inches as you
have oceans.—Puppies!
   *Clo*. I would they had not come between
         us.
   2 *Lord*. [*Aside*.] So would I, till you had
measured how long a fool you were upon the
ground.
   *Clo*. And that she should love this fellow,
and refuse me!
   2 *Lord*. [*Aside*.] If it be a sin to make a
true election, she is damned.
   1 *Lord*. Sir, as I told you always, her
beauty and her brain go not together: she's a
good sign, but I have seen small reflection of
her wit.
   2 *Lord*. [*Aside*.] She shines not upon fools,
lest the reflection should hurt her.
   *Clo*. Come, I'll to my chamber. Would
there had been some hurt done!
   2 *Lord*. [*Aside*.] I wish not so; unless it

had been the fall of an ass, which is no great hurt.

*Clo.* You'll go with us?

1 *Lord.* I'll attend your lordship.

*Clo.* Nay, come, let's go together.

2 *Lord.* Well, my lord.    [*Exeunt.*

SCENE III.—BRITAIN. *A Room in* CYMBE-LINE's *Palace.*

*Enter* IMOGEN *and* PISANIO.

*Imo.* I would thou grew'st unto the shores
    o' the heaven,    [write,
And questioned'st every sail: if he should
And I not have it, 'twere a paper lost,
As offer'd mercy is. What was the last
That he spake to thee?

*Pis.*    It was, *His queen, his queen!*

*Imo.* Then wav'd his handkerchief?

*Pis.*    And kiss'd it, madam.

*Imo.* Senseless linen! happier therein than
    I!—

And that was all?

*Pis.*    No, madam; for so long
As he could make me with this eye or ear
Distinguish him from others, he did keep
The deck, with glove, or hat, or handkerchief
Still waving, as the fits and stirs of's mind
Could best express how slow his soul sail'd on,
How swift his ship.

*Imo.*    Thou shouldst have made him
As little as a crow, or less, ere left
To after-eye him.

*Pis.*    Madam, so I did.

*Imo.* I would have broke mine eye-strings,
    crack'd them, but
To look upon him, till the diminution
Of space had pointed him sharp as my needle;
Nay, follow'd him till he had melted from
The smallness of a gnat to air; and then
Have turn'd mine eye and wept.—But, good
    Pisanio,
When shall we hear from him?

*Pis.*    Be assur'd, madam,
With his next vantage.    [had

*Imo.* I did not take my leave of him, but
Most pretty things to say: ere I could tell him
How I would think on him, at certain hours,
Such thoughts and such; or I could make him
    swear
The shes of Italy should not betray    [him
Mine interest and his honour; or have charg'd
At the sixth hour of morn, at noon, at mid-
    night,
To encounter me with orisons, for then
I am in heaven for him; or ere I could
Give him that parting kiss which I had set
Betwixt two charming words, comes in my
    father,
And like the tyrannous breathing of the north
Shakes all our buds from growing.

*Enter a* Lady.

*Lady.*    The queen, madam,
Desires your highness' company.

*Imo.* Those things I bid you do, get them
    despatch'd.—
I will attend the queen.

*Pis.*    Madam, I shall. [*Exeunt.*

SCENE IV.—ROME. *An Apartment in*
    PHILARIO's *House.*

*Enter* PHILARIO, IACHIMO, *a Frenchman, a*
    Dutchman, *and a* Spaniard.

*Iach.* Believe it, sir, I have seen him in
Britain: he was then of a crescent note; expected to prove so worthy as since he hath
been allowed the name of: but I could then
have looked on him without the help of admiration; though the catalogue of his endowments had been tabled by his side, and I to
peruse him by items.

*Phi.* You speak of him when he was less
furnished than now he is with that which
makes him both without and within.

*French.* I have seen him in France: we had
very many there could behold the sun with as
firm eyes as he.

*Iach.* This matter of marrying his king's
daughter,—wherein he must be weighed rather by her value than his own,—words him, I
doubt not, a great deal from the matter.

*French.* And then his banishment,—

*Iach.* Ay, and the approbation of those
that weep this lamentable divorce, under her
colours, are wonderfully to extend him; be it
but to fortify her judgment, which else an
easy battery might lay flat, for taking a beggar without less quality. But how comes it he
is to sojourn with you? How creeps acquaintance?

*Phi.* His father and I were soldiers together; to whom I have been often bound for
no less than my life.—Here comes the Briton:
let him be so entertained amongst you as
suits with gentlemen of your knowing to a
stranger of his quality.

*Enter* POSTHUMUS.

I beseech you all, be better known to this
gentleman; whom I commend to you as a
noble friend of mine: how worthy he is I will
leave to appear hereafter, rather than story
him in his own hearing.

*French.* Sir, we have known together in
Orleans.

*Post.* Since when I have been debtor to
you for courtesies, which I will be ever to pay
and yet pay still.

*French.* Sir, you o'errate my poor kindness: I was glad I did atone my countryman
and you; it had been pity you should have
been put together with so mortal a purpose a-
then each bore, upon importance of so slight
and trivial a nature.

*Post.* By your pardon, sir, I was then a
young traveller; rather shunned to go even
with what I heard than in my every action to

be guided by others' experiences: but, upon my mended judgment,—if I offend not to say it is mended,—my quarrel was not altogether slight.

*French.* Faith, yes, to be put to the arbitriment of swords; and by such two that would, by all likelihood, have confounded one the other, or have fallen both.

*Iach.* Can we, with manners, ask what was the difference?

*French.* Safely, I think: 'twas a contention in public, which may, without contradiction, suffer the report. It was much like an argument that fell out last night, where each of us fell in praise of our country mistresses; this gentleman at that time vouching,—and upon warrant of bloody affirmation,—his to be more fair, virtuous, wise, chaste, constant-qualified, and less attemptible than any the rarest of our ladies in France.

*Iach.* That lady is not now living; or this gentleman's opinion, by this, worn out.

*Post.* She holds her virtue still, and I my mind.

*Iach.* You must not so far prefer her fore ours of Italy.

*Post.* Being so far provoked as I was in France, I would abate her nothing; though I profess myself her adorer, not her friend.

*Iach.* As fair and as good,—a kind of hand-in-hand comparison,—had been something too fair and too good for any lady in Brittany. If she went before others I have seen, as that diamond of yours out-lustres many I have beheld, I could not but believe she excelled many: but I have not seen the most precious diamond that is, nor you the lady.

*Post.* I praised her as I rated her: so do I my stone.

*Iach.* What do you esteem it at?

*Post.* More than the world enjoys.

*Iach.* Either your unparagoned mistress is dead, or she's outprized by a trifle.

*Post.* You are mistaken: the one may be sold or given, if there were wealth enough for the purchase or merit for the gift: the other is not a thing for sale, and only the gift of the gods.

*Iach.* Which the gods have given you?

*Post.* Which, by their graces, I will keep.

*Iach.* You may wear her in title yours: but, you know, strange fowl light upon neighbouring ponds. Your ring may be stolen too: so your brace of unprizeable estimations, the one is but frail and the other casual; a cunning thief or a that-way-accomplished courtier would hazard the winning both of first and last.

*Post.* Your Italy contains none so accomplished a courtier to convince the honour of my mistress, if in the holding or loss of that you term her frail. I do nothing doubt you have store of thieves; notwithstanding I fear not my ring.

*Phi.* Let us leave here, gentlemen.

*Post.* Sir, with all my heart. This worthy signior, I thank him, makes no stranger of me; we are familiar at first.

*Iach.* With five times so much conversation I should get ground of your fair mistress; make her go back even to the yielding, had I admittance and opportunity to friend.

*Post.* No, no.

*Iach.* I dare thereupon pawn the moiety of my estate to your ring; which, in my opinion, o'ervalues it something: but I make my wager rather against your confidence than her reputation: and, to bar your offence herein too, I durst attempt it against any lady in the world.

*Post.* You are a great deal abused in too bold a persuasion; and I doubt not you sustain what you're worthy of by your attempt.

*Iach.* What's that?

*Post.* A repulse: though your attempt, as you call it, deserve more,—a punishment too.

*Phi.* Gentlemen, enough of this: it came in too suddenly; let it die as it was born, and, I pray you, be better acquainted.

*Iach.* Would I had put my estate and my neighbour's on the approbation of what I have spoke!

*Post.* What lady would you choose to assail?

*Iach.* Yours; whom in constancy you think stands so safe. I will lay you ten thousand ducats to your ring, that, commend me to the court where your lady is, with no more advantage than the opportunity of a second conference, and I will bring from thence that honour of hers which you imagine so reserved.

*Post.* I will wage against your gold gold to it: my ring I hold dear as my finger; 'tis part of it.

*Iach.* You are afraid, and therein the wiser. If you buy ladies' flesh at a million a dram, you cannot preserve it from tainting: but I see you have some religion in you, that you fear.

*Post.* This is but a custom in your tongue; you bear a graver purpose, I hope.

*Iach.* I am the master of my speeches; and would undergo what's spoken, I swear.

*Post.* Will you?—I shall but lend my diamond till your return:—let there be covenants drawn between us: my mistress exceeds in goodness the hugeness of your unworthy thinking: I dare you to this match: here's my ring.

*Phi.* I will have it no lay.

*Iach.* By the gods, it is one.—If I bring you no sufficient testimony that I have enjoyed the dearest bodily part of your mistress, my ten thousand ducats are yours; so is your diamond too: if I come off, and leave her in such honour as you have trust in, she your jewel, this your jewel, and my gold are yours;—provided I have your commendation for my more free entertainment.

*Post.* I embrace these conditions; let us have articles betwixt us.—Only, thus far you shall answer: if you make your voyage upon her, and give me directly to understand you have prevail'd, I am no further your enemy; she is not worthy our debate: if she remain unseduced,—you not making it appear otherwise,—for your ill opinion and the assault you have made to her chastity you shall answer me with your sword.

*Iach.* Your hand,—a covenant: we will have these things set down by lawful counsel, and straight away for Britain, lest the bargain should catch cold and starve: I will fetch my gold, and have our two wagers recorded.

*Post.* Agreed.      [*Exeunt* POST. *and* IACH.
*French.* Will this hold, think you?
*Phi.* Signior Iachimo will not from it.
Pray, let us follow 'em.      [*Exeunt.*

SCENE V.—BRITAIN. *A Room in* CYMBELINE'S *Palace.*

*Enter* QUEEN, Ladies, *and* CORNELIUS.

*Queen.* Whiles yet the dew's on ground
            gather those flowers;
Make haste: who has the note of them?
  1 *Lady.*                        I, madam.
*Queen.* Despatch.—      [*Exeunt* Ladies.
Now, master doctor, have you brought those
            drugs?
*Cor.* Pleaseth your highness, ay: here they
            are, madam: [*Presenting a small box.*
But I beseech your grace, without offence,—
My conscience bids me ask,—wherefore you
            have
Commanded of me these most poisonous
            compounds,            [death;
Which are the movers of a languishing
But, though slow, deadly?
*Queen.*                        I wonder, doctor,
Thou ask'st me such a question. Have I not
            been                        [how
Thy pupil long? Hast thou not learn'd me
To make perfumes? distil? preserve? yea, so
That our great king himself doth woo me oft
For my confections? Having thus far proceeded,—            [meet
Unless thou think'st me devilish,—is't not
That I did amplify my judgment in
Other conclusions? I will try the forces
Of these thy compounds on such creatures as
We count not worth the hanging,—but none
            human,—
To try the vigour of them, and apply
Allayments to their act; and by them gather
Their several virtues and effects.
*Cor.*                        Your highness
Shall from this practice but make hard your
            heart:
Besides, the seeing these effects will be
Both noisome and infectious.

*Queen.*                        O, content thee.—
Here comes a flattering rascal; upon him
                                    [*Aside.*
Will I first work: he's for his master,
And enemy to my son.—

*Enter* PISANIO.

How now, Pisanio!—
Doctor, your service for this time is ended;
Take your own way.
*Cor.* [*Aside.*]    I do suspect you, madam;
But you shall do no harm.
*Queen.*                        Hark thee, a word.
                                    [*To* PISANIO.
*Cor.* [*Aside.*]    I do not like her. She doth
            think she has                  [spirit
Strange lingering poisons: I do know her
And will not trust one of her malice with
A drug of such damn'd nature. Those she has
Will stupify and dull the sense awhile;
Which first perchance she'll prove on cats
            and dogs,
Then afterward up higher: but there is
No danger in what show of death it makes,
More than the locking up the spirits a time,
To be more fresh, reviving. She is fool'd
With a most false effect; and I the truer
So to be false with her.
*Queen.*                        No further service, doctor,
Until I send for thee.
*Cor.*                        I humbly take my leave.
                                    [*Exit.*
*Queen.* Weeps she still, say'st thou? Dost
            thou think in time                  [enter
She will not quench, and let instructions
Where folly now possesses? Do thou work:
When thou shalt bring me word she loves my
            son,
I'll tell thee on the instant thou art then
As great as is thy master; greater,—for
His fortunes all lie speechless, and his name
Is at last gasp: return he cannot, nor
Continue where he is: to shift his being
Is to exchange one misery with another;
And every day that comes comes to decay
A day's work in him. What shalt thou expect,
To be depender on a thing that leans,—
Who cannot be new built, nor has no friends
            [*The* QUEEN *drops the box:* PISANIO
                        *takes it up.*
So much as but to prop him?—Thou tak'st
            up                        [labour:
Thou know'st not what; but take it for thy
It is a thing I made, which hath the king
Five times redeem'd from death: I do not
            know                        [it;
What is more cordial:—nay, I pr'ythee, take
It is an earnest of a further good
That I mean to thee. Tell thy mistress how
The case stands with her; do't as from thyself                        [think
Think what a chance thou changest on; but
Thou hast thy mistress still,—to boot, my
            son,

Who shall take notice of thee: I'll move the king
To any shape of thy preferment, such
As thou'lt desire; and then myself, I chiefly,
That set thee on to this desert, am bound
To load thy merit richly. Call my women:
Think on my words. 　　　　[*Exit* PISANIO.
　　　　A sly and constant knave;
Not to be shak'd: the agent for his master;
And the remembrancer of her to hold
The hand-fast to her lord.—I have given him that
Which, if he take, shall quite unpeople her
Of liegers for her sweet; and which she after,
Except she bend her humour, shall be as-sur'd
To taste of too.

*Re-enter* PISANIO *and* Ladies.

So, so;—well done, well done:
The violets, cowslips, and the primroses,
Bear to my closet.—Fare thee well, Pisanio;
Think on my words.
　　　　[*Exeunt* QUEEN *and* Ladies.
*Pis.* 　　　　And shall do:
But when to my good lord I prove untrue
I'll choke myself: there's all I'll do for you.
　　　　[*Exit.*

SCENE VI.—BRITAIN. *Another Room in the Palace.*

*Enter* IMOGEN.

*Imo.* A father cruel and a step-dame false;
A foolish suitor to a wedded lady,
That hath her husband banish'd;—O, that husband!
My supreme crown of grief! and those re-peated
Vexations of it! Had I been thief-stolen,
As my two brothers, happy! but most miser-able
Is the desire that's glorious: bless'd be those,
How mean soe'er, that have their honest wills, 　　　　[Fie!
Which seasons comfort.—Who may this be?

*Enter* PISANIO *and* IACHIMO.

*Pis.* Madam, a noble gentleman of Rome
Comes from my lord with letters.
*Iach.* 　　　　Change you, madam?
The worthy Leonatus is in safety,
And greets your highness dearly.
　　　　[*Presents a letter.*
*Imo.* 　　　　Thanks, good sir:
You're kindly welcome. 　　　　[most rich!
*Iach.* [*Aside.*] All of her that is out of door
If she be furnish'd with a mind so rare,
She is alone the Arabian bird; and I
Have lost the wager. Boldness be my friend!
Arm me, audacity, from head to foot!
Or, like the Parthian, I shall flying fight;
Rather directly fly.
*Imo.* [*Reads.*] *He is one of the noblest note, to whose kindnesses I am most infinitely*

*tied. Reflect upon him accordingly, as you value your truest* 　　　　LEONATUS.
So far I read aloud:
But even the very middle of my heart
Is warm'd by the rest, and takes it thank-fully.—
You are as welcome, worthy sir, as I
Have words to bid you; and shall find it so
In all that I can do.
*Iach.* 　　　　Thanks, fairest lady.—
What, are men mad? Hath nature given them eyes
To see this vaulted arch, and the rich cope
Of sea and land, which can distinguish 'twixt
The fiery orbs above and the twinn'd stones
Upon th' unnumber'd beach? and can we not
Partition make with spectacles so precious
'Twixt fair and foul?
*Imo.* 　　　What makes your admiration?
*Iach.* It cannot be i' the eye; for apes and monkeys,
'Twixt two such shes, would chatter this way and 　　　　[judgment;
Contemn with mows the other: nor i' the
For idiots in this case of favour would
Be wisely definite: nor i' the appetite;
Sluttery, to such neat excellence oppos'd,
Should make desire vomit emptiness,
Not so allur'd to feed.
*Imo.* What is the matter, trow?
*Iach.* 　　　　The cloyed will,—
That satiate yet unsatisfied desire, 　　　　[first
That tub both fill'd and running,—ravening
The lamb, longs after for the garbage.
*Imo.* 　　　　What, dear sir,
Thus raps you? Are you well?
*Iach.* Thanks, madam; well.—Beseech you, sir, desire 　　　　[*To* PISANIO
My man's abode where I did leave him: he
Is strange and peevish.
*Pis.* 　　　　I was going, sir,
To give him welcome. 　　　　[*Exit.*
*Imo.* Continues well my lord? His health, beseech you?
*Iach.* Well, madam.
*Imo.* Is he dispos'd to mirth? I hope he is.
*Iach.* Exceeding pleasant; none a stranger there
So merry and so gamesome: he is call'd
The Briton reveller.
*Imo.* 　　　　When he was here
He did incline to sadness; and ofttimes
Not knowing why.
*Iach.* 　　　　I never saw him sad.
There is a Frenchman his companion, one
An eminent monsieur, that, it seems, much loves
A Gallian girl at home: he furnaces 　　　[ton,—
The thick sighs from him; while the jolly Bri-
Your lord, I mean,—laughs from's free lungs, cries, O, 　　　　[knows
*Can my sides hold, to think that man,—who*
*By history, report, or his own proof,*
*What woman is, yea, what she cannot choose*

But must be,—will his free hours languish
for
Assured bondage?
*Imo.* Will my lord say so?
*Iach.* Ay, madam; with his eyes in flood
with laughter.
It is a recreation to be by [heavens know,
And hear him mock the Frenchman. But,
Some men are much to blame.
*Imo.* Not he, I hope.
*Iach.* Not he: but yet heaven's bounty to-
wards him might
Be us'd more thankfully. In himself 'tis
much;
In you,—which I count his beyond all tal-
ents,—
Whilst I am bound to wonder I am bound
To pity too.
*Imo.* What do you pity, sir?
*Iach.* Two creatures heartily.
*Imo.* Am I one, sir?
You look on me: what wreck discern you in
me
Deserves your pity?
*Iach.* Lamentable! What,
To hide me from the radiant sun, and solace
I' the dungeon by a snuff?
*Imo.* I pray you, sir,
Deliver with more openness your answers
To my demands. Why do you pity me?
*Iach.* That others do,
I was about to say, enjoy your——But
It is an office of the gods to venge it,
Not mine to speak on't.
*Imo.* You do seem to know
Something of me, or what concerns me:
pray you,—
Since doubting things go ill often hurts more
Than to be sure they do: for certainties
Either are past remedies, or, timely knowing,
The remedy then born,—discover to me
What both you spur and stop.
*Iach.* Had I this cheek
To bathe my lips upon; this hand, whose
touch, [soul
Whose every touch, would force the feeler's
To the oath of loyalty; this object, which
Takes prisoner the wild motion of mine eye,
Fixing it only here,—should I,—damn'd
then,—
Slaver with lips as common as the stairs
That mount the Capitol; join gripes with
hands [as
Made hard with hourly falsehood,—falsehood
With labour,—then bo-peeping in an eye
Base and unlustrous as the smoky light
That's fed with stinking tallow,—it were fit
That all the plagues of hell should at one
time
Encounter such revolt.
*Imo.* My lord, I fear,
Has forgot Britain.
*Iach.* And himself. Not I,
Inclin'd to this intelligence, pronounce

The beggary of his change; but 'tis your
graces [tongue
That from my mutest conscience to my
Charms this report out.
*Imo.* Let me hear no more.
*Iach.* O dearest soul! your cause doth
strike my heart
With pity that doth make me sick! A lady
So fair, and fasten'd to an empery,
Would make the great'st king double,—to be
partner'd
With tomboys, hir'd with that self-exhibition
Which your own coffers yield! with diseas'd
ventures,
That play with all infirmities for gold [stuff
Which rottenness can lend nature! such boil'd
As well might poison poison! Be reveng'd;
Or she that bore you was no queen, and you
Recoil from your great stock.
*Imo.* Reveng'd!
How should I be reveng'd? If this be true,—
As I have such a heart that both mine ears
Must not in haste abuse,—if it be true,
How should I be reveng'd?
*Iach.* Should he make me
Live like Diana's priest betwixt cold sheets,
Whiles he is vaulting variable ramps, [it,
In your despite, upon your purse? Revenge
I dedicate myself to your sweet pleasure;
More noble than that runagate to your bed;
And will continue fast to your affection,
Still close as sure.
*Imo.* What ho, Pisanio!
*Iach.* Let me my service tender on your
lips.
*Imo.* Away!—I do condemn mine ears
that have [able
So long attended thee.—If thou wert honour-
Thou wouldst have told this tale for virtue,
not [strange.
For such an end thou seek'st,—as base as
Thou wrong'st a gentleman who is as far
From thy report as thou from honour; and
Solicit'st here a lady that disdains
Thee and the devil alike.—What, ho, Pis-
anio!—
The king my father shall be made ac-
quainted
Of thy assault: if he shall think it fit
A saucy stranger in his court to mart
As in a Romish stew, and to expound
His beastly mind to us,—he hath a cou-
He little cares for, and a daughter who
He not respects at all.—What, ho, Pisanio!
*Iach.* O happy Leonatus! I may say:
The credit that thy lady hath of thee
Deserves thy trust; and thy most perfect
goodness
Her assur'd credit!—Blessed live you long!
A lady to the worthiest sir that ever
Country call'd his! and you his mistress, only
For the most worthiest fit! Give me your
pardon.
I have spoke this to know if your affiance

Were deeply rooted; and shall make your
　　lord
That which he is new o'er: and he is one
The truest manner'd; such a holy witch
That he enchants societies unto him;
Half all men's hearts are his.

*Imo.*　　　　　　　You make amends.

*Iach.* He sits 'mongst men like a descended
　　god:
He hath a kind of honour sets him off
More than a mortal seeming. Be not angry,
Most mighty princess, that I have adven-
　　tur'd　　　　　　　　　　　[hath
To try your taking of a false report; which
Honour'd with confirmation your great judg-
　　ment
In the election of a sir so rare,　　[him
Which you know cannot err: the love I bear
Made me to fan you thus; but the gods made
　　you,　　　　　　　　　　　[don.
Unlike all others, chaffless. Pray, your par-

*Imo.* All's well, sir: take my power i' the
　　court for yours.　　　　　　[got

*Iach.* My humble thanks. I had almost for-
To entreat your grace but in a small request,
And yet of moment too, for it concerns
Your lord, myself, and other noble friends,
Are partners in the business.

*Imo.*　　　　　　　Pray, what is't?

*Iach.* Some dozen Romans of us, and your
　　lord,—　　　　　　　　　[sums
The best feather of our wing,—have mingled
To buy a present for the emperor;
Which I, the factor for the rest, have done
In France: 'tis plate of rare device, and jewels
Of rich and exquisite form; their values
　　great;
And I am something curious, being strange
To have them in safe stowage: may it please
　　you
To take them in protection?

*Imo.*　　　　　　　Willingly;
And pawn mine honour for their safety: since
My lord hath interest in them, I will keep
　　them
In my bedchamber.

*Iach.*　　　　　They are in a trunk,
Attended by my men: I will make bold
To send them to you only for this night;
I must aboard to-morrow.

*Imo.*　　　　　　O, no, no.　　[word

*Iach.* Yes, I beseech; or I shall short my
By length'ning my return. From Gallia
I cross'd the seas on purpose and on promise
To see your grace.

*Imo.*　　　　　I thank you for your pains:
But not away to-morrow!

*Iach.*　　　　　O, I must, madam;
Therefore I shall beseech you, if you please
To greet your lord with writing, do't to-
　　night:
I have outstood my time; which is material
To the tender of our present.

*Imo.*　　　　　　　I will write.

Send your trunk to me; it shall safe be kept
And truly yielded you. You're very welcome.
　　　　　　　　　　　　　　[*Exeunt.*

## ACT II.

SCENE I.—BRITAIN. *Court before* CYM-
BELINE'S *Palace.*

*Enter* CLOTEN *and two* Lords.

*Clo.* Was there ever man had such luck!
when I kissed the jack, upon an up-cast to be
hit away! I had a hundred pound on't: and
then a whoreson jackanapes must take me up
for swearing; as if I borrowed mine oaths of
him, and might not spend them at my
pleasure.

*1 Lord.* What got he by that? You have
broke his pate with your bowl.

*2 Lord.* [*Aside.*] If his wit had been like
him that broke it, it would have run all out.

*Clo.* When a gentleman is disposed to
swear, it is not for any standers-by to curtail his oaths, ha?

*2 Lord.* No, my lord; [*aside*] nor crop
the ears of them.

*Clo.* Whoreson dog!—I give him satisfaction? Would he had been one of my rank!

*2 Lord.* [*Aside.*] To have smelt like a fool.

*Clo.* I am not vexed more at anything in
the earth,—a pox on't! I had rather not be so
noble as I am; they dare not fight with me,
because of the queen my mother: every jack-
slave hath his belly full of fighting, and I
must go up and down like a cock that nobody
can match.

*2 Lord.* [*Aside.*] You are cock and capon
too; and you crow, cock, with your comb on.

*Clo.* Sayest thou?

*1 Lord.* It is not fit your lordship should
undertake every companion that you give
offence to.

*Clo.* No, I know that: but it is fit I should
commit offence to my inferiors.

*2 Lord.* Ay, it is fit for your lordship only.

*Clo.* Why, so I say.

*1 Lord.* Did you hear of a stranger that's
come to court to-night?

*Clo.* A stranger, and I not know on't!

*2 Lord.* [*Aside.*] He's a strange fellow himself, and knows it not.

*1 Lord.* There's an Italian come; and, 'tis
thought, one of Leonatus' friends.

*Clo.* Leonatus! a banished rascal; and he's
another, whatsoever he be. Who told you of
this stranger?

*1 Lord.* One of your lordship's pages.

*Clo.* Is it fit I went to look upon him? Is
there no derogation in't.

*1 Lord.* You cannot derogate, my lord.

*Clo.* Not easily, I think.

*2 Lord.* [*Aside.*] You are a fool granted;
therefore your issues, being foolish, do not
derogate.

*Clo.* Come. I'll go see this Italian: what I

have lost to-day at bowls I'll win to-night of him. Come, go.

*2 Lord.* I'll attend your lordship.

[*Exeunt* CLOTEN *and* first *Lord.*

That such a crafty devil as is his mother
Should yield the world this ass! a woman that [son
Bears all down with her brain; and this her
Cannot take two from twenty, for his heart,
And leave eighteen. Alas, poor princess,
Thou divine Imogen, what thou endur'st,—
Betwixt a father by thy stepdame govern'd:
A mother hourly coining plots; a wooer
More hateful than the foul expulsion is
Of thy dear husband, than that horrid act
Of the divorce he'd make! The heavens hold firm
The walls of thy dear honour; keep unshak'd
That temple, thy fair mind; that thou mayst stand [land!
To enjoy thy banish'd lord and this great [*Exit.*

SCENE II.—BRITAIN. IMOGEN's *Bedchamber; in one part of it a Trunk.*

IMOGEN *in bed reading; a Lady attending.*

*Imo.* Who's there? my woman Helen?
*Lady.* Please you, madam.
*Imo.* What hour is it?
*Lady.* Almost midnight, madam.
*Imo.* I have read three hours, then: mine eyes are weak:
Fold down the leaf where I have left: to bed:
Take not away the taper, leave it burning;
And if thou canst awake by four o' the clock,
I pr'ythee, call me. Sleep hath seiz'd me wholly. [*Exit Lady.*
To your protection I commend me, gods!
From fairies and the tempters of the night
Guard me, beseech ye!

[*Sleeps.* IACHIMO *comes from the trunk.*

*Iach.* The crickets sing, and man's o'er-labour'd sense
Repairs itself by rest. Our Tarquin thus
Did softly press the rushes ere he waken'd
The chastity he wounded.—Cytherea,
How bravely thou becom'st thy bed! fresh lily!
And whiter than the sheets! That I might touch!
But kiss; one kiss!—Rubies unparagon'd,
How dearly they do't!—'Tis her breathing that
Perfumes the chamber thus: the flame o' the taper
Bows toward her, and would underpeep her lids,
To see the enclosed lights, now canopied
Under these windows, white and azure, lac'd
With blue of heaven's own tinct.—But my design
To note the chamber:—I will write all down:—

Such and such pictures;—there the window:
—such [ures,
The adornment of her bed;—the arras, fig-
Why, such and such;—and the contents o' the story,—
Ah, but some natural notes about her body
Above ten thousand meaner movables
Would testify, to enrich mine inventory.
O sleep, thou ape of death, lie dull upon her!
And be her sense but as a monument,
Thus in a chapel lying!—Come off, come off;

[*Taking off her bracelet.*

As slippery as the Gordian knot was hard!—
'Tis mine; and this will witness outwardly,
As strongly as the conscience does within,
To the madding of her lord. On her left breast
A mole cinque-spotted, like the crimson drops
I' the bottom of a cowslip. Here's a voucher
Stronger than ever law could make: this secret [and ta'en
Will force him think I have pick'd the lock,
The treasure of her honour. No more. To what end?
Why should I write this down, that's riveted,
Screw'd to my memory?—She hath been reading late [down
The tale of Tereus; here the leaf's turn'd
Where Philomel gave up.—I have enough.
To the trunk again, and shut the spring of it.
Swift, swift, you dragons of the night, that dawning
May bare the raven's eye! I lodge in fear;
Though this a heavenly angel, hell is here.

[*Clock strikes.*

One, two, three,—Time, time!

[*Goes into the trunk. Scene closes.*

SCENE III.—BRITAIN. *An Ante-chamber adjoining* IMOGEN's *Apartment.*

*Enter* CLOTEN *and* Lords.

*1 Lord.* Your lordship is the most patient man in loss, the most coldest that ever turned up ace.
*Clo.* It would make any man cold to lose.
*1 Lord.* But not every man patient after the noble temper of your lordship. You are most hot and furious when you win.
*Clo.* Winning will put any man into cour-age. If I could get this foolish Imogen, I should have gold enough. It's almost morn-ing, is't not?
*1 Lord.* Day, my lord.
*Clo.* I would this music would come: I am advised to give her music o' mornings; they say it will penetrate.

*Enter* Musicians.

Come on; tune: if you can penetrate her with your fingering, so; we'll try with tongue too: if none will do, let her remain; but I'll never give o'er. First, a very excellent good-conceited thing; after a wonderful sweet air, with admirable rich words to it,—and then let her consider.

SONG.

Hark, hark! the lark at heaven's gate sings,
    And Phœbus 'gins arise,
His steeds to water at those springs
    On chalic'd flowers that lies;
And winking Mary-buds begin
    To ope their golden eyes;
With everything that pretty is:
    My lady sweet, arise;
      Arise, arise!

So, get you gone. If this penetrate, I will consider your music the better: if it do not, it is a vice in her ears; which horse-hairs and calves' guts, nor the voice of unpaved eunuch to boot, can never amend. [*Exeunt* Musicians.

*2 Lord.* Here comes the king.

*Clo.* I am glad I was up so late; for that's the reason I was up so early: he cannot choose but take this service I have done fatherly.—

Enter CYMBELINE *and* QUEEN.

Good-morrow to your majesty and to my gracious mother.     [stern daughter?

*Cym.* Attend you here the door of our Will she not forth?

*Clo.* I have assailed her with music, but she vouchsafes no notice.

*Cym.* The exile of her minion is too new; She hath not yet forgot him: some more time Must wear the print of his remembrance out, And then she's yours.

*Queen.*     You are most bound to the king, Who lets go by no vantages that may Prefer you to his daughter. Frame yourself To orderly solicits, and be friended With aptness of the season; make denials Increase your services; so seem as if You were inspir'd to do those duties which You tender to her; that you in all obey her, Save when command to your dismission tends, And therein you are senseless.

*Clo.*     Senseless! not so.

Enter a Messenger.

*Mess.* So like you, sir, ambassadors from Rome; The one is Caius Lucius.

*Cym.*     A worthy fellow. Albeit he comes on angry purpose now; But that's no fault of his: we must receive him According to the honour of his sender; And towards himself, his goodness forespent on us, We must extend our notice.—Our dear son, When you have given good-morning to your mistress, Attend the queen and us; we shall have need To employ you towards this Roman.—Come, our queen.

[*Exeunt* CYM., QUEEN, Lords, *and* Mess.

*Clo.* If she be up, I'll speak with her; if not,     [ho!— Let her lie still and dream.—By your leave,     [*Knocks.* I know her women are about her: what If I do line one of their hands? 'Tis gold Which buys admittance; oft it doth; yea, and makes Diana's rangers false themselves, yield up Their deer to the stand o' the stealer; and 'tis gold     [the thief; Which makes the true man kill'd and saves Nay, sometimes hangs both thief and true man: what Can it not do and undo? I will make One of her women lawyer to me: for I yet not understand the case myself. By your leave.     [*Knocks.*

Enter a Lady.

*Lady.* Who's there that knocks?

*Clo.*     A gentleman.

*Lady.*     No more?

*Clo.* Yes, and a gentlewoman's son.

*Lady.*     That's more Than some, whose tailors are as dear as yours, Can justly boast of. What's your lordship's pleasure?

*Clo.* Your lady's person: is she ready?

*Lady.*     Ay, To keep her chamber.

*Clo.* There is gold for you; sell me your good report.     [of you

*Lady.* How! my good name? or to report What I shall think is good?—The princess!

Enter IMOGEN.

*Clo.* Good-morrow, fairest: sister, your sweet hand.     [much pains

*Imo.* Good-morrow, sir. You lay out too For purchasing but trouble: the thanks I give Is telling you that I am poor of thanks, And scarce can spare them.

*Clo.*     Still, I swear I love you.

*Imo.* If you but said so, 'twere as deep with me: If you swear still, your recompense is still That I regard it not.

*Clo.*     This is no answer.

*Imo.* But that you shall not say I yield, being silent     [faith, I would not speak. I pray you, spare me: I shall unfold equal discourtesy     [knowing To your best kindness: one of your great Should learn, being taught, forbearance.

*Clo.* To leave you in your madness 'twere my sin: I will not.

*Imo.* Fools are not mad folks.

*Clo.*     Do you call me fool?

*Imo.* As I am mad, I do: If you'll be patient I'll no more be mad; That cures us both. I am much sorry, sir, You put me to forget a lady's manners

By being so verbal: and learn now, for all,
That I, which know my heart, do here pro-
nounce,
By the very truth of it, I care not for you;
And am so near the lack of charity,—
To accuse myself,—I hate you; which I had
rather
You felt that make't my boast.

*Clo.*                    You sin against
Obedience, which you owe your father. For
The contract you pretend with that base
wretch,—                              [dishes,
One bred of alms and foster'd with cold
With scraps o' the court,—it is no contract,
none:
And though it be allow'd in meaner parties,—
Yet who than he more mean?—to knit their
souls,—
On whom there is no more dependency
But brats and beggary,—in self-figur'd knot;
Yet you are curb'd from that enlargement by
The consequence o' the crown; and must not
soil
The precious note of it with a base slave,
A hilding for a livery, a squire's cloth,
A pantler,—not so eminent.

*Imo.*                    Profane fellow!
Wert thou the son of Jupiter, and no more
But what thou art besides, thou wert too base
To be his groom: thou wert dignified enough,
Even to the point of envy, if 'twere made
Comparative for your virtues to be styl'd
The under-hangman of his kingdom; and
hated
For being preferr'd so well.

*Clo.*                    The south fog rot him!

*Imo.* He never can meet more mischance
than come                              ment,
To be but nam'd of thee. His meanest gar-
That ever hath but clipp'd his body, is dearer
In my respect than all the hairs above thee,
Were they all made such men.

*Enter* PISANIO.

                              How now, Pisanio!

*Clo.* His garment! Now, the devil,—

*Imo.* To Dorothy my woman hie thee presently,—

*Clo.* His garment!

*Imo.*              I am spirited with a fool;
Frighted, and anger'd worse.—Go, bid my
woman
Search for a jewel that too casually
Hath left mine arm: it was thy master's;
shrew me
If I would lose it for a revenue
Of any king's in Europe. I do think
I saw't this morning: confident I am
Last night 'twas on mine arm; I kiss'd it:
I hope it be not gone to tell my lord
That I kiss aught but he.

*Pis.*                    'Twill not be lost.

*Imo.* I hope so: go and search.
                              [*Exit* PISANIO.

*Clo.*                    You have abus'd me.—
His meanest garment?

*Imo.*                    Ay, I said so, sir:
If you will make't an action, call witness to't.

*Clo.* I will inform your father.

*Imo.*                    Your mother too:
She's my good lady; and will conceive, I
hope,
But the worse of me. So I leave you, sir,
To the worst of discontent.          [*Exit.*

*Clo.*                    I'll be reveng'd:—
His meanest garment!—Well.          [*Exit.*

SCENE IV.—ROME. *An Apartment in*
PHILARIO'S *House.*

*Enter* POSTHUMUS *and* PHILARIO.

*Post.* Fear it not, sir: I would I were so
sure
To win the king as I am bold her honour
Will remain hers.

*Phi.* What means do you make to him?

*Post.* Not any; but abide the change of
time;
Quake in the present winter's state, and wish
That warmer days would come: in these
sear'd hopes
I barely gratify your love; they failing,
I must die much your debtor.

*Phi.* Your very goodness and your com-
pany
O'erpays all I can do. By this your king
Hath heard of great Augustus: Caius Lucius
Will do's commission throughly: and I think
He'll grant the tribute, send the arrearages,
Or look upon our Romans, whose remem-
brance
Is yet fresh in their grief.

*Post.*                    I do believe,—
Statist though I am none, nor like to be,—
That this will prove a war; and you shall
hear
The legions now in Gallia sooner landed
In our not-fearing Britain than have tidings
Of any penny tribute paid. Our countrymen
Are men more ordered than when Julius
Cæsar                              [courage
Smil'd at their lack of skill, but found their
Worthy his frowning at: their discipline,—
Now mingled with their courage,—will make
known
To their approvers they are people such
That mend upon the world.

*Phi.*                    See! Iachimo!

*Enter* IACHIMO.

*Post.* The swiftest harts have posted you
by land;
And winds of all the corners kiss'd your sails,
To make your vessel nimble.

*Phi.*                    Welcome, sir.

*Post.* I hope the briefness of your answer
made
The speediness of your return.

*Iach.*                    Your lady

Is one of the fairest that I have look'd upon.
　*Post.* And therewithal the best; or let her
　　beauty 　　　　　　　　　　　　[hearts,
Look through a casement to allure false
And be false with them.
　*Iach.*　　　　　　Here are letters for you.
　*Post.* Their tenor good, I trust.
　*Iach.*　　　　　　　　　　'Tis very like.
　*Phi.* Was Caius Lucius in the Britain court
When you were there?
　*Iach.*　　　　　　He was expected then,
But not approach'd.
　*Post.*　　　　　All is well yet.—
Sparkles this stone as it was wont? or is't not
Too dull for your good wearing?
　*Iach.*　　　　　　　　If I had lost it
I should have lost the worth of it in gold.
I'll make a journey twice as far, to enjoy
A second night of such sweet shortness which
Was mine in Britain; for the ring is won.
　*Post.* The stone's too hard to come by.
　*Iach.*　　　　　　　　Not a whit,
Your lady being so easy.
　*Post.*　　　　　　Make not, sir,
Your loss your sport: I hope you know that
　　we
Must not continue friends.
　*Iach.*　　　　　　Good sir, we must,
If you keep covenant. Had I not brought
The knowledge of your mistress home, I
　　grant
We were to question further: but I now
Profess myself the winner of her honour,
Together with your ring; and not the
　　wronger
Of her or you, having proceeded but
By both your wills.
　*Post.*　　　　If you can make't apparent
That you have tasted her in bed, my hand
And ring is yours: if not, the foul opinion
You had of her pure honour gains or loses
Your sword or mine, or masterless leaves
　　both
To who shall find them.
　*Iach.*　　　　Sir, my circumstances,
Being so near the truth as I will make them,
Must first induce you to believe: whose
　　strength
I will confirm with oath; which I doubt not
You'll give me leave to spare when you shall
　　find
You need it not.
　*Post.*　　　　Proceed.
　*Iach.*　　　　First, her bedchamber,—
Where, I confess, I slept not; but profess
Had that was well worth watching,—it was
　　hang'd
With tapestry of silk and silver; the story
Proud Cleopatra, when she met her Roman,
And Cydnus swell'd above the banks, or for
The press of boats or pride: a piece of work
So bravely done, so rich, that it did strive
In workmanship and value; which I won-
　　der'd

Could be so rarely and exactly wrought,
Since the true life on't was,—
　*Post.*　　　　This is true;　　　　[me
And this you might have heard of here, by
Or by some other.
　*Iach.*　　　　　　More particulars
Must justify my knowledge.
　*Post.*　　　　　So they must,
Or do your honour injury.
　*Iach.*　　　　　　The chimney
Is south the chamber; and the chimney-piece
Chaste Dian bathing: never saw I figures
So likely to report themselves: the cutter
Was as another nature, dumb; outwent her,
Motion and breath left out.
　*Post.*　　　　　This is a thing
Which you might from relation likewise reap;
Being, as it is, much spoke of.
　*Iach.*　　　　The roof o' the chamber
With golden cherubins is fretted: her and-
　　irons,—　　　　　　　　　　　[pids
I had forgot them,—were two winking Cu-
Of silver, each on one foot standing, nicely
Depending on their brands.
　*Post.*　　　　This is her honour!—
Let it be granted you have seen all this,—and
　　praise 　　　　　　　　　　　[scription
Be given to your remembrance,—the de-
Of what is in her chamber nothing saves
The wager you have laid.
　*Iach.*　　　　　　Then, if you can,
　　　　　　[*Pulling out the bracelet.*
Be pale; I beg but leave to air this jewel;
　　see!—
And now 'tis up again: it must be married
To that your diamond; I'll keep them.
　*Post.*　　　　　　Jove!—
Once more let me behold it: is it that
Which I left with her?
　*Iach.*　　　　Sir,—I thank her,—that:
She stripp'd it from her arm; I see her yet;
Her pretty action did outsell her gift, 　[said
And yet enrich'd it too: she gave it me, and
She priz'd it once.
　*Post.*　　　　Maybe she pluck'd it off
To send it me.
　*Iach.*　　　She writes so to you? doth she?
　*Post.* O, no, no, no! 'tis true. Here, take
　　this too;　　　　　　　　[*Gives the ring.*
It is a basilisk unto mine eye,
Kills me to look on't.—Let there be no hon-
　　our 　　　　　　　　　　　[blance; love
Where there is beauty; truth where sem-
Where there's another man: the vows of
　　women 　　　　　　　　　　　[made
Of no more bondage be to where they are
Than they are to their virtues; which is
　　nothing.—
O, above measure false!
　*Phi.*　　　　Have patience, sir,
And take your ring again; 'tis not yet won:
It may be probable she lost it; or, 　[rupted,
Who knows if one o' her women, being cor-
Hath stolen it from her?

*Post.*                    Very true;
And so I hope he came by't.—Back my ring:
Render to me some corporal sign about her,
More evident than this; for this was stolen.
*Iach.* By Jupiter, I had it from her arm.
*Post.* Hark you, he swears; by Jupiter he
    swears.                        [sure
'Tis true,—nay, keep the ring,—'tis true: I am
She would not lose it: her attendants are
All sworn and honourable:—they induc'd to
    steal it!                        [her:
And by a stranger!—No, he hath enjoyed
The cognizance of her incontinency
Is this,—she hath bought the name of whore
    thus dearly.—                    [hell
There, take thy hire; and all the fiends of
Divide themselves between you!
*Phi.*                    Sir, be patient:
This is not strong enough to be believ'd
Of one persuaded well of,—
*Post.*                    Never talk on't;
She hath been colted by him.
*Iach.*                    If you seek
For further satisfying, under her breast,—
Worthy the pressing,—lies a mole, right
    proud
Of that most delicate lodging: by my life,
I kiss'd it; and it gave me present hunger
To feed again, though full. You do remember
This stain upon her?
*Post.*                    Ay, and it doth confirm
Another stain, as big as hell can hold,
Were there no more but it.
*Iach.*                    Will you hear more?
*Post.* Spare your arithmetic: never count
    the turns;
Once, and a million!
*Iach.*                    I'll be sworn,—
*Post.*                    No swearing.
If you will swear you have not done't, you
    lie;
And I will kill thee if you dost deny
Thou'st made me cuckold.
*Iach.*                    I'll deny nothing.
*Post.* O, that I had her here to tear her
    limbmeal!
I will go there and do't; i' the court; before
Her father: I'll do something,—        [*Exit.*
*Phi.*                    Quite besides
The government of patience!—You have
    won:
Let's follow him, and pervert the present
    wrath
He hath against himself.
*Iach.*                    With all my heart.
                            [*Exeunt.*

SCENE V.—ROME. *Another Room in*
    PHILARIO'S *House.*

*Enter* POSTHUMUS.

*Post.* Is there no way for men to be, but
    women
Must be half-workers? We are all bastards;
And that most venerable man which I

Did call my father was I know not where
When I was stamp'd; some coiner with his
    tools                        [seem'd
Made me a counterfeit: yet my mother
The Dian of that time: so doth my wife
The nonpareil of this.—O, vengeance, ven-
    geance!—
Me of my lawful pleasure she restrain'd,
And pray'd me oft forbearance: did it with
A pudency so rosy, the sweet view on't
Might well have warm'd old Saturn; that I
    thought her                    [devils!—
As chaste as unsunn'd snow.—O, all the
This yellow Iachimo in an hour,—was't not?
Or less,—at first?—Perchance he spoke not,
    but,
Like a full-acorn'd boar, a German one,
Cried O! and mounted; found no opposition
But what he look'd for should oppose, and
    she                        [out
Should from encounter guard. Could I find
The woman's part in me! For there's no
    motion
That tends to vice in man but I affirm
It is the woman's part: be it lying, note it,
The woman's; flattering, hers; deceiving,
    hers;
Lust and rank thoughts, hers, hers; re-
    venges, hers;
Ambitions, covetings, change of prides, dis-
    dain,
Nice longing, slanders, mutability,    [knows,
All faults that have a name, nay, that hell
Why, hers, in part or all; but rather all;
For ev'n to vice
They are not constant, but are changing still
One vice, but of a minute old, for one [them,
Not half so old as that. I'll write against
Detest them, curse them.—Yet 'tis greater
    skill
In a true hate to pray they have their will:
The very devils cannot plague them better.
                            [*Exit.*

## ACT III.

SCENE I.—BRITAIN. *A Room of State in*
    CYMBELINE'S *Palace.*

*Enter, at one side,* CYMBELINE, QUEEN,
CLOTEN, *and* Lords; *at the other* CAIUS
    LUCIUS *and* Attendants.

*Cym.* Now say, what would Augustus
    Cæsar with us?                [brance yet
*Luc.* When Julius Cæsar,—whose remem-
Lives in men's eyes, and will to ears and
    tongues                        [tain,
Be theme and hearing ever,—was in this Bri-
And conquer'd it, Cassibelan, thine uncle,—
Famous in Cæsar's praises no whit less
Than in his feats deserving it,—for him
And his succession granted Rome a tribute
Yearly three thousand pounds; which by thee
    lately
Is left untender'd.

*Queen.*            And, to kill the marvel,
Shall be so ever.
    *Clo.*            There be many Cæsars
Ere such another Julius. Britain is
A world by itself; and we will nothing pay
For wearing our own noses.
    *Queen.*            That opportunity,
Which then they had to take from's, to re-
    sume
We have again.—Remember, sir, my liege,
The kings your ancestors; together with
The natural bravery of your isle, which
    stands
As Neptune's park, ribbed and paled in
With rocks unscaleable and roaring waters;
With sands that will not bear your enemies'
    boats,            [conquest
But suck them up to the top-mast. A kind of
Cæsar made here; but made not here his brag
Of *came*, and *saw*, and *overcame:* with
    shame,—            [ried
The first that ever touch'd him,—he was car-
From off our coast, twice beaten; and his
    shipping,—
Poor ignorant baubles!—on our terrible seas,
Like egg-shells mov'd upon their surges,
    crack'd
As easily 'gainst our rocks: for joy whereof
The fam'd Cassibelan, who was once at
    point,—
O, giglot fortune!—to master Cæsar's sword,
Made Lud's town with rejoicing fires bright
And Britons strut with courage.
    *Clo.* Come; there's no more tribute to be
paid: our kingdom is stronger than it was at
that time; and, as I said, there is no more
such Cæsars: other of them may have crooked noses; but to owe such straight arms,
none.
    *Cym.* Son, let your mother end.
    *Clo.* We have yet many among us can gripe
as hard as Cassibelan: I do not say I am one;
but I have a hand.—Why tribute? why
should we pay tribute? If Cæsar can hide the
sun from us with a blanket, or put the moon
in his pocket, we will pay him tribute for
light; else, sir, no more tribute, pray you now.
    *Cym.* You must know,
Till the injurious Romans did extort
This tribute from us, we were free: Cæsar's
    ambition,—            [stretch
Which swell'd so much that it did almost
The sides o' the world,—against all colour,
    here            [off
Did put the yoke upon's; which to shake
Becomes a warlike people, whom we reckon
Ourselves to be.
    *Clo.*            We do.
    *Cym.*            Say then to Cæsar,
Our ancestor was that Mulmutius which
Ordain'd our laws,—whose use the sword of
    Cæsar            [franchise
Hath too much mangled; whose repair and
Shall, by the power we hold, be our good

deed,            [tius made our laws,
Though Rome be therefore angry:—Mulmu-
Who was the first of Britain which did put
His brows within a golden crown, and call'd
Himself a king.
    *Luc.*            I am sorry, Cymbeline,
That I am to pronounce Augustus Cæsar,—
Cæsar, that hath more kings his servants than
Thyself domestic officers,—thine enemy:
Receive it from me, then:—War and confu-
    sion            [look
In Cæsar's name pronounce I 'gainst thee:
For fury not to be resisted.—Thus defied,
I thank thee for myself.
    *Cym.*            Thou art welcome, Caius.
Thy Cæsar knighted me; my youth I spent
Much under him; of him I gather'd honour;
Which he to seek of me again, perforce,
Behoves me keep at utterance. I am perfect
That the Pannonians and Dalmatians for
Their liberties are now in arms,—a precedent
Which not to read would show the Britons
    cold:
So Cæsar shall not find them.
    *Luc.*            Let proof speak.
    *Clo.* His majesty bids you welcome. Make
pastime with us a day or two, or longer: if
you seek us afterwards in other terms, you
shall find us in our salt-water girdle: if you
beat us out of it, it is yours; if you fall in the
adventure, our crows shall fare the better for
you; and there's an end.
    *Luc.* So, sir.            [he mine:
    *Cym.* I know your master's pleasure, and
All the remain is, welcome.            [*Exeunt.*

SCENE II.—BRITAIN. *Another Room in the
    Palace.*

*Enter* PISANIO *with a letter.*

    *Pis.* How! of adultery? Wherefore write
        you not.
What monster's her accuser?—Leonatus!
O master! what a strange infection
Is fallen into thy ear! What false Italian,—
As poisonous tongu'd as handed,—hath pre-
    vail'd
On thy too ready hearing?—Disloyal! No:
She's punish'd for her truth; and undergoes,
More goddess-like than wife-like, such as-
    saults
As would take in some virtue.—O my master!
Thy mind to her is now as low as were [her?
Thy fortunes.—How! that I should murder
Upon the love, and truth, and vows which I
Have made to thy command?—I, her?—her
    blood?
If it be so to do good service, never
Let me be counted serviceable. How look I,
That I should seem to lack humanity
So much as this fact comes to? [*Reading.*]
    *Do't: the letter*
*That I have sent her, by her own command*
*Shall give thee opportunity:*—O damn'd
    paper!

Black as the ink that's on thee! Senseless
   bauble,
Art thou a fedary for this act, and look'st
So virgin-like without? Lo, here she comes.
I am ignorant in what I am commanded.

*Enter* IMOGEN.

*Imo.* How now, Pisanio!
*Pis.* Madam, here is a letter from my lord.
*Imo.* Who? thy lord? that is my lord,—
   Leonatus?
O, learn'd indeed were that astronomer
That knew the stars as I his characters;
He'd lay the future open.—You good gods,
Let what is here contain'd relish of love,
Of my lord's health, of his content,—yet not
That we two are asunder,—let that grieve
   him;—                                [them,
Some griefs are med'cinable; that is one of
For it doth physic love;—of his content
All but in that!—Good wax, thy leave:—
   bless'd be                            [Lovers
You bees that make these locks of counsel!
And men in dangerous bonds pray not alike;
Though forfeiters you cast in prison, yet
You clasp young Cupid's tables.—Good news,
   gods!                                 [*Reads.*

*Justice, and your father's wrath, should he
take me in his dominion, could not be so cruel
to me, as you, O the dearest of creatures,
would even renew me with your eyes. Take
notice that I am in Cambria, at Milford-
Haven: what your own love will, out of this,
advise you, follow. So he wishes you all happiness that remains loyal to his vow, and
your, increasing in love,*

            LEONATUS POSTHUMUS.
O for a horse with wings!—Hear'st thou,
   Pisanio?
He is at Milford-Haven: read, and tell me
How far 'tis thither. If one of mean affairs
May plod it in a week, why may not I
Glide thither in a day?—Then, true Pis-
   anio,—                                [long'st—
Who long'st, like me, to see thy lord; who
O, let me 'bate—but not like me; yet long'st,
But in a fainter kind: O, not like me;
For mine's beyond beyond,—say, and speak
   thick,                                [hearing
Love's councillor should fill the bores of
To the smothering of the sense,—how far it is
To this same blessed Milford: and, by the
   way,
Tell me how Wales was made so happy as
To inherit such a haven: but, first of all,
How we may steal from hence; and for the
   gap                                   [going
That we shall make in time, from our hence-
And our return, to excuse. But first, how get
   hence:
Why should excuse be born or e'er begot?
We'll talk of that hereafter. Pr'ythee, speak,
How many score of miles may we well ride
'Twixt hour and hour?

*Pis.*                    One score 'twixt sun and sun,
Madam, 's enough for you, and too much too.
*Imo.* Why, one that rode to's execution,
   man,
Could never go so slow: I have heard of rid-
   ing wagers,
Where horses have been nimbler than the
   sands                                 [foolery:
That run i' the clock's behalf;—but this is
Go bid my women feign a sickness: say
She'll home to her father: and provide me
   presently
A riding suit no costlier than would fit
A franklin's housewife.
*Pis.*                    Madam, you're best consider.
*Imo.* I see before me, man, nor here, nor
   here,
Nor what ensues; but have a fog in them
That I cannot look through. Away, I pr'y-
   thee;
Do as I bid thee: there's no more to say;
Accessible is none but Milford way. [*Exeunt.*

SCENE III.—WALES. *A mountainous Country
           with a Cave.*

*Enter* BELARIUS, GUIDERIUS, *and* ARVIRAGUS.

*Bel.* A goodly day not to keep house, with
   such                                  [this gate
Whose roof's as low as ours! Stoop, boys:
Instructs you how to adore the heavens, and
   bows you                              [archs
To a morning's holy office: the gates of mon-
Are arch'd so high that giants may jet
   through,
And keep their impious turbans on, without
Good-morrow to the sun.—Hail, thou fair
   heaven!                               [hardly
We house i' the rock, yet use thee not so
As prouder livers do.
*Gui.*                    Hail, heaven!
*Arv.*                              Hail, heaven!
*Bel.* Now for our mountain sport: up to
   yond hill,                            [Consider,
Your legs are young; I'll tread these flats.
When you above perceive me like a crow,
That it is place which lessens and sets off:
And you may then revolve what tales I have
   told you
Of courts, of princes, of the tricks in war:
This service is not service so being done,
But being so allow'd: to apprehend thus
Draws us a profit from all things we see;
And often, to our comfort, shall we find
The sharded beetle in a safer hold
Than is the full-wing'd eagle. O, this life
Is nobler than attending for a check,
Richer than doing nothing for a bauble,
Prouder than rustling in unpaid-for silk:
Such gain the cap of him that makes 'em fine,
Yet keeps his book uncross'd: no life to ours.
*Gui.* Out of your proof you speak: we,
   poor unfledg'd,                       [know not
Have never wing'd from view o' the nest; nor
What air's from home. Haply this life is best,

If quiet life be best; sweeter to you [ponding
That have a sharper known; well corres-
With your stiff age: but unto us it is
A cell of ignorance; travelling abed;
A prison for a debtor, that not dares
To stride a limit.
　*Arv.*　　　　What should we speak of
When we are old as you? when we shall hear
The rain and wind beat dark December, how,
In this our pinching cave, shall we discourse
The freezing hours away? We have seen
　nothing:
We are beastly; subtle as the fox for prey;
Like warlike as the wolf for what we eat:
Our valour is to chase what flies; our cage
We make a quire, as doth the prison'd bird,
And sing our bondage freely.
　*Bel.*　　　　　　　How you speak!
Did you but know the city's usuries,
And felt them knowingly: the art o' the
　court,
As hard to leave as keep; whose top to climb
Is certain falling, or so slippery that　[war,
The fear's as bad as falling: the toil o' the
A pain that only seems to seek out danger
I' the name of fame and honour; which dies
　i' the search,
And hath as oft a slanderous epitaph
As record of fair act; nay, many times
Doth ill deserve by doing well; what's worse,
Must court'sy at the censure.—O, boys, this
　story　　　　　　　　　　[mark'd
The world may read in me: my body's
With Roman swords; and my report was
　once　　　　　　　　　　　[me;
First with the best of note: Cymbeline lov'd
And when a soldier was the theme, my name
Was not far off: then was I as a tree [night
Whose boughs did bend with fruit: but in one
A storm or robbery, call it what you will,
Shook down my mellow hangings, nay, my
　leaves,
And left me bare to weather.
　*Gui.*　　　　　　Uncertain favour?
　*Bel.* My fault being nothing,—as I have
　told you oft.—　　　　　　[vail'd
But that two villains, whose false oaths pre-
Before my perfect honour, swore to Cym-
　beline
I was confederate with the Romans: so
Follow'd my banishment; and this twenty
　years　　　　　　　　　　[world:
This rock and these demesnes have been my
Where I have liv'd at honest freedom; paid
More pious debts to heaven than in all
The fore-end of my time.—But up to the
　mountains!　　　　　　　　[strikes
This is not hunters' language.—He that
The venison first shall be the lord o' the
　feast;
To him the other two shall minister;
And we will fear no poison, which attends
In place of greater state. I'll meet you in the
　valleys.　　　　　[*Exeunt* GUI. *and* ARV.

How hard it is to hide the sparks of nature!
These boys know little they are sons to the
　king;
Nor Cymbeline dreams that they are alive.
They think they are mine: and though train'd
　up thus meanly.　　　　　　[do hit
I' the cave wherein they bow, their thoughts
The roofs of palaces; and nature prompts
　them,
In simple and low things, to prince it much
Beyond the trick of others. This Polydore,—
The heir of Cymbeline and Britain, who
The king his father call'd Guiderius,—Jove!
When on my three-foot stool I sit, and tell
The warlike feats I have done, his spirits fly
　out
Into my story: say, *Thus mine enemy fell,*
*And thus I set my foot on's neck;* even then
The princely blood flows in his cheek, he
　sweats,
Strains his young nerves, and puts himself in
　posture　　　　　　　　　[Cadwal,—
That acts my words. The younger brother,
Once Arviragus,—in as like a figure
Strikes life into my speech, and shows much
　more　　　　　　　　　　[rous'd!—
His own conceiving. Hark, the game is
O Cymbeline! heaven and my conscience
　knows
Thou didst unjustly banish me: whereon,
At three and two years old, I stole these
　babes;
Thinking to bar thee of succession, as
Thou reft'st me of my lands. Euriphile,
Thou wast their nurse; they took thee for
　their mother,
And every day do honour to her grave:
Myself, Belarius, that am Morgan call'd,
They take for natural father. The game is up.
　　　　　　　　　　　　　　[*Exit.*

SCENE IV.—*Wales, near Milford-Haven.*

*Enter* PISANIO *and* IMOGEN.

　*Imo.* Thou told'st me, when we came from
　horse, the place
Was near at hand.—Ne'er long'd my mother
　so
To see me first as I have now.—Pisanio!
　Man!
Where is Posthumus? What is in thy mind
That makes thee stare thus? Wherefore
　breaks that sigh
From the inward of thee? One but painted
　thus
Would be interpreted a thing perplex'd
Beyond self-explication: put thyself
Into a 'haviour of less fear, ere wildness
Vanquish my steadier senses. What's the
　matter?
Why tender'st thou that paper to me, with
A look untender? If 't be summer news,
Smile to 't before; if winterly, thou need'st
But keep that countenance still.—My hus-
　band's hand!

That drug-damn'd Italy hath out-craftied
    him,
And he's at some hard point.—Speak, man;
    thy tongue
May take off some extremity, which to read
Would be even mortal to me.
    *Pis.*                 Please you, read;
And you shall find me, wretched man, a
    thing
The most disdain'd of fortune.
    *Imo.* [*Reads.*] *Thy mistress, Pisanio, hath*
*played the strumpet in my bed; the testi-*
*monies whereof lie bleeding in me. I speak*
*not out of weak surmises; but from proof as*
*strong as my grief and as certain as I expect*
*my revenge. That part thou, Pisanio, must act*
*for me, if thy faith be not tainted with the*
*breach of hers. Let thine own hands take*
*away her life; I shall give thee opportunity at*
*Milford-Haven: she hath my letter for the*
*purpose: where, if thou fear to strike, and to*
*make me certain it is done, thou art the*
*pander to her dishonour, and equally to me*
*disloyal.*
    *Pis.* What, shall I need to draw my sword?
    the paper
Hath cut her throat already.—No, 'tis
    slander;
Whose edge is sharper than the sword; whose
    tongue
Outvenoms all the worms of Nile; whose
    breath
Rides on the posting winds, and doth belie
All corners of the world: kings, queens, and
    states,
Maids, matrons, nay, the secrets of the grave
This viperous slander enters.—What cheer,
    madam?                 [*false?*
    *Imo.* False to his bed? What is it to be
To lie in watch there, and to think on him?
To weep 'twixt clock and clock? if sleep
    charge nature,
To break it with a fearful dream of him,
And cry myself awake? that's false to his
    bed,
Is it?
    *Pis.* Alas, good lady!         [*Iachimo,*
    *Imo.* I false! Thy conscience witness:—
Thou didst accuse him of incontinency;
Thou then look'dst like a villain; now, me-
    thinks,
Thy favour's good enough.—Some jay of
    Italy,
Whose mother was her painting, hath be-
    tray'd him:
Poor I am stale, a garment out of fashion;
And for I am richer than to hang by the walls
I must be ripp'd: to pieces with me!—O,
Men's vows are women's traitors! All good
    seeming,
By thy revolt, O husband, shall be thought
Put on for villany,—not born where 't grows,
But worn a bait for ladies.
    *Pis.*             Good madam, hear me.

    *Imo.* True honest men being heard, like
    false Æneas,             [*weeping*
Were, in his time, thought false: and Sinon's
Did scandal many a holy tear; took pity
From most true wretchedness: so thou, Post-
    humus,
Wilt lay the leaven on all proper men;
Goodly and gallant shall be false and perjur'd
From thy great fail.—Come, fellow, be thou
    honest:              [*see'st him,*
Do thou thy master's bidding: when thou
A little witness my obedience: look!
I draw the sword myself: take it, and hit
The innocent mansion of my love, my heart:
Fear not; 'tis empty of all things but grief:
Thy master is not there; who was indeed
The riches of it: do his bidding; strike.
Thou mayst be valiant in a better cause;
But now thou seem'st a coward.
    *Pis.*           Hence, vile instrument!
Thou shalt not damn my hand.
    *Imo.*             Why, I must die;
And if I do not by thy hand, thou art
No servant of thy master's; against self-
    slaughter
There is a prohibition so divine     [*my heart:*
That cravens my weak hand. Come, here's
Something's afore 't.—Soft, soft! we'll no
    defence;
Obedient as the scabbard.—What is here?
The scriptures of the loyal Leonatus
All turn'd to heresy? Away, away,
Corrupters of my faith! you shall no more
Be stomachers to my heart. Thus may poor
    fools
Believe false teachers: though those that are
    betray'd
Do feel the treason sharply, yet the traitor
Stands in worse case of woe.
And thou, Posthumus, that didst set up
My disobedience 'gainst the king my father,
And make me put into contempt the suits
Of princely fellows, shalt hereafter find
It is no act of common passage, but
A strain of rareness: and I grieve myself
To think, when thou shalt be disedg'd by her
That now thou tir'st on, how thy memory
Will then be pang'd by me.—Pr'ythee, des-
    patch:
The lamb entreats the butcher: where 's thy
    knife?
Thou art too slow to do thy master's bidding,
When I desire it too.
    *Pis.*            O gracious lady,
Since I receiv'd command to do this business
I have not slept one wink.
    *Imo.*          Do 't, and to bed then.
    *Pis.* I'll wake mine eyeballs blind first.
    *Imo.*              Wherefore then
Didst undertake it? Why hast thou abus'd
So many miles with a pretence? this place?
Mine action and thine own? our horses'
    labour?
The time inviting thee? the perturb'd court,

For my being absent; whereunto I never
Purpose return? Why hast thou gone so far,
To be unbent when thou hast ta'en thy
　　stand,
The elected deer before thee?

*Pis.*　　　　　　But to win time
To lose so bad employment; in the which
I have consider'd of a course. Good lady,
Hear me with patience.

*Imo.*　　　Talk thy tongue weary: speak:
I have heard I am a strumpet; and mine ear,
Therein false struck, can take no greater
　　wound,
Nor tent to bottom that. But speak.

*Pis.*　　　　　　Then, madam,
I thought you would not back again.

*Imo.*　　　　　　Most like,—
Bringing me here to kill me.

*Pis.*　　　　　Not so neither:
But if I were as wise as honest, then
My purpose would prove well. It cannot be
But that my master is abus'd:
Some villain, ay, and singular in his art,
Hath done you both this cursed injury.

*Imo.* Some Roman courtezan.

*Pis.*　　　　　　No, on my life:
I'll give but notice you are dead, and send
　　him
Some bloody sign of it; for 'tis commanded
I should do so: you shall be miss'd at court,
And that will well confirm it.

*Imo.*　　　　　Why, good fellow,
What shall I do the while? where bide? how
　　live?
Or in my life what comfort when I am
Dead to my husband?

*Pis.*　　If you'll back to the court,—

*Imo.* No court, no father; nor no more ado
With that harsh, noble, simple nothing,—
That Cloten, whose love-suit hath been to me
As fearful as a siege.

*Pis.*　　　　　　If not at court,
Then not in Britain must you bide.

*Imo.*　　　　　　Where then?
Hath Britain all the sun that shines? Day,
　　night,
Are they not but in Britain? I' the world's
　　volume
Our Britain seems as of it, but not in 't;
In a great pool a swan's nest: pr'ythee, think
There's livers out of Britain.

*Pis.*　　　　I am most glad
You think of other place. The ambassador,
Lucius the Roman, comes to Milford-Haven
To-morrow: now, if you could wear a mind
Dark as your fortune is, and but disguise
That which to appear itself must not yet be,
But by self-danger, you should tread a course
Privy and full of view; yea, haply, near
The residence of Posthumus, so nigh at least
That though his actions were not visible, yet
Report should render him hourly to your ear,
As truly as he moves.

*Imo.*　　　　　O, for such means,

Though peril to my modesty, not death on't,
I would adventure.

*Pis.*　　　　Well then, here's the point:
You must forget to be a woman; change
Command into obedience; fear and nice-
　　ness,—
The handmaids of all women, or, more truly,
Woman its pretty self,—into a waggish
　　courage;
Ready in gibes, quick-answer'd, saucy, and
As quarrelous as the weasel; nay, you must
Forget that rarest treasure of your cheek,
Exposing it,—but, O, the harder heart!
Alack, no remedy!—to the greedy touch
Of common-kissing Titan; and forget
Your laboursome and dainty trims, wherein
You made great Juno angry.

*Imo.*　　　　　Nay, be brief;
I see into thy end, and am almost
A man already.

*Pis.*　　　First, make yourself but like one.
Fore-thinking this, I have already fit,—
'Tis in my cloak-bag,—doublet, hat, hose, all
That answer to them: would you, in their
　　serving,
And with what imitation you can borrow
From youth of such a season, 'fore noble
　　Lucius
Present yourself, desire his service, tell him
Wherein you are happy,—which you'll make
　　him know
If that his head have ear in music,—doubtless
With joy he will embrace you; for he's hon-
　　ourable　　　　　　　　　　　　[abroad
And, doubling that, most holy. Your means
You have me, rich; and I will never fail
Beginning nor supplyment.

*Imo.*　　　　Thou art all the comfort
The gods will diet me with. Pr'ythee, away:
There's more to be consider'd; but we'll even
All that good time will give us: this attempt
I am soldier to, and will abide it with
A prince's courage. Away, I pr'ythee.

*Pis.* Well, madam, we must take a short
　　farewell,
Lest, being miss'd, I be suspected of　[tress,
Your carriage from the court. My noble mis-
Here is a box; I had it from the queen;
What 's in 't is precious; if you are sick at
　　sea
Or stomach-qualm'd at land, a dram of this
Will drive away distemper.—To some shade,
And fit you to your manhood:—may the
　　gods
Direct you to the best!

*Imo.*　　　　Amen: I thank thee.
　　　　　　　　　　　　　　　[*Exeunt*

SCENE V.—BRITAIN. *A Room in* CYM-
　　　　BELINE'S *Palace.*

*Enter* CYMBELINE, QUEEN, CLOTEN, LUCIUS
　　　　*and* Lords.

*Cym.* Thus far; and so farewell.
*Luc.*　　　　　Thanks, royal sir

My emperor hath wrote; I must from hence;
And am right sorry that I must report ye
My master's enemy.

*Cym.*                    Our subjects, sir,
Will not endure his yoke; and for ourself
To show less sovereignty than they, must
    needs
Appear unkinglike.

*Luc.*        So, sir, I desire of you
A conduct over-land to Milford-Haven.—
Madam, all joy befall his grace and you!

*Cym.* My lords, you are appointed for that
    office;
The due of honour in no point omit.—
So farewell, noble Lucius.

*Luc.*            Your hand, my lord.

*Clo.* Receive it friendly: but from this
    time forth
I wear it as your enemy.

*Luc.*          Sir, the event
Is yet to name the winner: fare you well.

*Cym.* Leave not the worthy Lucius, good
    my lords,
Till he have cross'd the Severn.—Happiness!
                [*Exeunt* LUCIUS *and* Lords.

*Queen.* He goes hence frowning: but it
    honours us
That we have given him cause.

*Clo.*                'Tis all the better;
Your valiant Britons have their wishes in it.

*Cym.* Lucius hath wrote already to the
    emperor
How it goes here. It fits us therefore ripely
Our chariots and our horsemen be in readi-
    ness:
The powers that he already hath in Gallia
Will soon be drawn to head, from whence he
    moves
His war for Britain.

*Queen.*        'Tis not sleepy business;
But must be look'd to speedily and strongly.

*Cym.* Our expectation that it would be
    thus             [queen,
Hath made us forward. But, my gentle
Where is our daughter? She hath not
    appear'd
Before the Roman, nor to us hath tender'd
The duty of the day: she looks us like
A thing more made of malice than of duty:
We have noted it.—Call her before us; for
We have been too slight in sufferance.
                [*Exit an* Attendant.

*Queen.*                Royal sir,
Since the exile of Posthumus, most retir'd
Hath her life been; the cure whereof, my
    lord,
'Tis time must do. Beseech your majesty,
Forbear sharp speeches to her: she's a lady
So tender of rebukes that words are strokes,
And strokes death to her.

*Re-enter* Attendant.

*Cym.*            Where is she, sir? How
Can her contempt be answer'd?

*Atten.*                Please you, sir,
Her chambers are all lock'd; and there's no
    answer                [make.
That will be given to the loud'st of noise we

*Queen.* My lord, when last I went to visit
    her,
She pray'd me to excuse her keeping close;
Whereto constrain'd by her infirmity
She should that duty leave unpaid to you
Which daily she was bound to proffer: this
She wish'd me to make known; but our great
    court
Made me to blame in memory.

*Cym.*            Her door's lock'd?
Not seen of late? Grant, heavens, that which
    I fear
Prove false!                [*Exit.*

*Queen.* Son, I say, follow the king. [vant,

*Clo.* That man of hers, Pisanio, her old ser-
I have not seen these two days.

*Queen.*                Go, look after.—
                [*Exit* CLOTEN.
Pisanio, thou that stand'st so for Posthu-
    mus!—
He hath a drug of mine; I pray his absence
Proceed by swallowing that; for he believes
It is a thing most precious. But for her, [her;
Where is she gone? Haply despair hath seiz'd
Or, winged with fervour of her love, she's
    flown
To her desir'd Posthumus: gone she is
To death or to dishonour; and my end
Can make good use of either: she being
    down,
I have the placing of the British crown.

*Re-enter* CLOTEN.

How now, my son!

*Clo.*        'Tis certain she is fled.
Go in and cheer the king: he rages; none
Dare come about him.

*Queen.*            All the better: may
This night forestall him of the coming day!
                [*Exit.*

*Clo.* I love and hate her: for she's fair and
    royal,                [quisite
And that she hath all courtly parts more ex-
Than lady, ladies, woman; from every one
The best she hath, and she, of all com-
    pounded,
Outsells them all.—I love her therefore: but,
Disdaining me, and throwing favours on
The low Posthumus, slanders so her judg-
    ment
That what's else rare is chok'd; and in that
    point
I will conclude to hate her, nay, indeed,
To be reveng'd upon her. For when fools
    shall—

*Enter* PISANIO.

Who is here? What, are you packing, sirrah?
Come hither: ah, you precious pander
    Villain,

Where is thy lady? In a word; or else
Thou art straightway with the fiends.
   *Pis.*                 O, good my lord!
   *Clo.* Where is thy lady? or, by Jupiter—
I will not ask again. Close villain,
I'll have this secret from thy heart, or rip
Thy heart to find it. Is she with Posthumus?
From whose so many weights of baseness
    cannot
A dram of worth be drawn.
   *Pis.*           Alas, my lord,
How can she be with him? When was she
    miss'd?
He is in Rome.
   *Clo.*      Where is she, sir? Come nearer;
No further halting: satisfy me home
What is become of her.
   *Pis.* O, my all-worthy lord!
   *Clo.*          All-worthy villain!
Discover where thy mistress is at once,
At the next word,—no more of worthy
    lord,—
Speak, or thy silence on the instant is
Thy condemnation and thy death.
   *Pis.*            Then, sir,
This paper is the history of my knowledge
Touching her flight.   [*Presenting a letter.*
   *Clo.* Let's see 't.—I will pursue her
Even to Augustus' throne.
   *Pis.* [*Aside.*]      Or this or perish.
She's far enough; and what he learns by this
May prove his travel, not her danger.
   *Clo.*              Hum!
   *Pis.* [*Aside.*] I'll write to my lord she's
    dead. O Imogen,
Safe mayst thou wander, safe return again!
   *Clo.* Sirrah, is this letter true?
   *Pis.* Sir, as I think.
   *Clo.* It is Posthumus' hand; I know't.—
Sirrah, if thou wouldst not be a villain, but
do me true service, undergo those employ-
ments wherein I should have cause to use thee
with a serious industry,—that is, what villany
soe'er I bid thee do, to perform it directly
and truly,—I would think thee an honest
man: thou shouldst neither want my means
for thy relief nor my voice for thy preferment.
   *Pis.* Well, my good lord.
   *Clo.* Wilt thou serve me?—for since patiently and constantly thou hast stuck to the
bare fortune of that beggar Posthumus, thou
canst not, in the course of gratitude, but be a
diligent follower of mine,—wilt thou serve
me?
   *Pis.* Sir, I will.
   *Clo.* Give me thy hand; here's my purse.
Hast any of thy late master's garments in thy
possession?
   *Pis.* I have, my lord, at my lodging, the
same suit he wore when he took leave of my
lady and mistress.
   *Clo.* The first service thou dost me, fetch
that suit hither: let it be thy first service; go.

   *Pis.* I shall, my lord.         [*Exit.*
   *Clo.* Meet thee at Milford-Haven!—I forgot to ask him one thing; I'll remember't
anon: even there, thou villain Posthumus,
will I kill thee.—I would these garments were
come. She said upon a time,—the bitterness
of it I now belch from my heart,—that she
held the very garment of Posthumus in more
respect than my noble and natural person, together with the adornment of my qualities.
With that suit upon my back will I ravish
her: first kill him, and in her eyes; there
shall she see my valour, which will then be a
torment to her contempt. He on the ground,
my speech of insultment ended on his dead
body,—and when my lust hath dined,—
which, as I say, to vex her, I will execute in
the clothes that she so praised,—to the court
I'll knock her back, foot her home again. She
hath despised me rejoicingly, and I'll be
merry in my revenge.

      *Re-enter* PISANIO, *with the clothes.*
Be those the garments?
   *Pis.* Ay, my noble lord.
   *Clo.* How long is 't since she went to Mil-
ford-Haven?
   *Pis.* She can scarce be there yet.
   *Clo.* Bring this apparel to my chamber;
that is the second thing that I have com-
manded thee: the third is, that thou wilt be
a voluntary mute to my design. Be but dute-
ous, and true preferment shall tender itself to
thee.—My revenge is now at Milford: would
I had wings to follow it!—Come, and be
true.                            [*Exit.*
   *Pis.* Thou bidd'st me to my loss: for true
    to thee
Were to prove false, which I will never be,
To him that is most true. To Milford go,
And find not her whom thou pursu'st.—Flow,
    flow,
You heavenly blessings on her!—This fool's
    speed
Be cross'd with slowness; labour be his meed!
                           [*Exit.*

SCENE VI.—WALES. *Before the Cave of*
               BELARIUS.

    *Enter* IMOGEN, *in boy's clothes.*

   *Imo.* I see a man's life is a tedious one:
I have tir'd myself; and for two nights to-
    gether
Have made the ground my bed. I should be
    sick,
But that my resolution helps me.—Milford,
When from the mountain-top Pisanio show'd
    thee,
Thou wast within a ken: O Jove! I think
Foundations fly the wretched; such, I mean,
Where they should be reliev'd. Two beggars
    told me
I could not miss my way: will poor folks lie,
That have afflictions on them, knowing 'tis

A punishment or trial? Yes; no wonder,
When rich ones scarce tell true: to lapse in
  fulness
Is sorer than to lie for need; and falsehood
Is worse in kings than beggars.—My dear
  lord!
Thou art one o' the false ones: now I think
  on thee
My hunger's gone; but even before, I was
At point to sink for food.—But what is this?
Here is a path to 't: 'tis some savage hold:
I were best not call; I dare not call: yet
  famine,
Ere clean it o'erthrow nature, makes it
  valiant.
Plenty and peace breeds cowards; hardness
  ever
Of hardiness is mother.—Ho! who's here?
If anything that's civil, speak; if savage,
Take or lend.—Ho! No answer? then I'll
  enter.
Best draw my sword; and if mine enemy
But fear the sword like me, he'll scarcely look
  on 't.
Such a foe, good heavens!
  [Goes into the Cave.

*Enter* BELARIUS, GUIDERIUS, *and*
  ARVIRAGUS.

*Bel.* You, Polydore, have prov'd best
  woodman, and
Are master of the feast: Cadwal and I
Will play the cook and servant; 'tis our
  match:
The sweat of industry would dry and die
But for the end it works to. Come; our
  stomachs
Will make what's homely savoury: weari-
  ness
Can snore upon the flint, when restive sloth
Finds the down pillow hard.—Now, peace be
  here,
Poor house, that keep'st thyself!
*Gui.*                I am throughly weary.
*Arv.* I am weak with toil, yet strong in
  appetite.
*Gui.* There is cold meat i' the cave; we'll
  browse on that
Whilst what we have kill'd be cook'd.
*Bel.*                Stay; come not in.
  [*Looking into the Cave.*
But that it eats our victuals, I should think
Here were a fairy.
*Gui.*          What's the matter, sir?
*Bel.* By Jupiter, an angel! or, if not,
An earthly paragon!—Behold divineness
No elder than a boy!

*Re-enter* IMOGEN.

*Imo.* Good masters, harm me not:
Before I enter'd here I call'd; and thought
To have begg'd or bought what I have took:
  good troth,

I have stol'n nought; nor would not, though
  I had found
Gold strew'd o' the floor. Here's money for
  my meat:
I would have left it on the board, so soon
As I had made my meal; and parted
With prayers for the provider.
*Gui.*                Money, youth?
*Arv.* All gold and silver rather turn to
  dirt!
And 'tis no better reckon'd, but of those
Who worship dirty gods.
*Imo.*              I see you are angry:
Know, if you kill me for my fault, I should
Have died had I not made it.
*Bel.*                Whither bound?
*Imo.* To Milford-Haven.
*Bel.*                What's your name?
*Imo.* Fidele, sir. I have a kinsman who
Is bound for Italy; he embark'd at Milford;
To whom being going, almost spent with
  hunger,
I am fallen in this offence.
*Bel.*                Pr'ythee, fair youth,
Think us no churls, nor measure our good
  minds          [er'd!
By this rude place we live in. Well encount-
'Tis almost night: you shall have better cheer
Ere you depart; and thanks to stay and eat
  it.—
Boys, bid him welcome.
*Gui.*                Were you a woman, youth,
I should woo hard but be your groom.—In
  honesty
I'd bid for you as I do buy.
*Arv.*                I'll make 't my comfort
He is a man; I'll love him as my brother:—
And such a welcome as I'd give to him,
After long absence, such as yours:—most
  welcome!
Be sprightly, for you fall 'mongst friends.
*Imo.*                'Mongst friends,
If brothers.—[*Aside.*] Would it had been so
  that they
Had been my father's sons! then had my
  prize
Been less; and so more equal ballasting
To thee, Posthumus.
*Bel.*              He wrings at some distress.
*Gui.* Would I could free 't!
*Arv.*                Or I; whate'er it be,
What pain it cost, what danger! gods!
*Bel.*                Hark, boys. [*Whispering.*
*Imo.* Great men,
That had a court no bigger than this cave,
That did attend themselves, and had the
  virtue
Which their own conscience seal'd them,—
  laying by
That nothing gift of differing multitudes,—
Could not out-peer these twain. Pardon me,
  gods!          [them,
I'd change my sex to be companion with
Since Leonatus' false.

*Bel.* It shall be so.
Boys, we'll go dress our hunt.—Fair youth,
  come in:
Discourse is heavy, fasting; when we have
  supp'd
We'll mannerly demand thee of thy story,
So far as thou wilt speak it.
  *Gui.* Pray, draw near.
  *Arv.* The night to the owl and morn to the
    lark less welcome.
  *Imo.* Thanks, sir.
  *Arv.* I pray, draw near.
  [*Exeunt.*

SCENE VII.—ROME. *A public Place.*

*Enter two* Senators *and* Tribunes.

  1 *Sen.* This is the tenor of the Emperor's
    writ:
That since the common men are now in
  action
'Gainst the Pannonians and Dalmatians,
And that the legions now in Gallia are
Full weak to undertake our wars against
The fallen-off Britons, that we do incite
The gentry to this business. He creates
Lucius pro-consul: and to you, the tribunes,
For this immediate levy, he commends
His absolute commission. Long live Cæsar!
  1 *Tri.* Is Lucius general of the forces?
  2 *Sen.* Ay.
  1 *Tri.* Remaining now in Gallia?
  1 *Sen.* With those legions
Which I have spoke of, whereunto your levy
Must be supplyant: the words of your com-
  mission
Will tie you to the numbers, and the time
Of their despatch.
  1 *Tri.* We will discharge our duty.
  [*Exeunt.*

## ACT IV.

SCENE I.—WALES. *The Forest near the Cave
of* BELARIUS.

*Enter* CLOTEN.

  *Clo.* I am near to the place where they
should meet, if Pisanio have mapped it truly.
How fit his garments serve me! Why should
his mistress, who was made by him that made
the tailor, not be fit too? the rather,—saving
reverence of the word,—for 'tis said a woman's fitness comes by fits. Therein I must play
the workman. I dare speak it to myself,—for
it is not vainglory for a man and his glass
to confer in his own chamber,—I mean, the
lines of my body are as well drawn as his; no
less young, more strong, not beneath him in
fortunes, beyond him in the advantage of the
time, above him in birth, alike conversant in
general services, and more remarkable in
single oppositions: yet this imperceiverant
thing loves him in my despite. What mortality is! Posthumus, thy head, which now is
growing upon thy shoulders, shall within this

hour be off, thy mistress enforced, thy garments cut to pieces before thy face; and all
this done, spurn her home to her father, who
may haply be a little angry for my so
rough usage; but my mother, having power
of his testiness, shall turn all into my commendations. My horse is tied up safe: out,
sword, and to a sore purpose! Fortune, put
them into my hand! This is the very description of their meeting-place: and the fellow
dares not deceive me. [*Exit.*

SCENE II.—WALES. *Before the Cave.*

*Enter, from the Cave,* BELARIUS, GUIDERIUS,
ARVIRAGUS, *and* IMOGEN.

  *Bel.* [*To* IMOGEN.] You are not well: re-
    main here in the cave;
We'll come to you after hunting.
  *Arv.* [*To* IMOGEN.] Brother, stay here:
Are we not brothers?
  *Imo.* So man and man should be;
But clay and clay differs in dignity,
Whose dust is both alike. I am very sick.
  *Gui.* Go you to hunting. I'll abide with
    him.
  *Imo.* So sick I am not,—yet I am not well;
But not so citizen a wanton as [me;
To seem to die ere sick: so please you, leave
Stick to your journal course: the breach of
  custom [me
Is breach of all. I am ill; but your being by
Cannot amend me: society is no comfort
To one not sociable: I am not very sick,
Since I can reason of it. Pray you, trust me
  here:
I'll rob none but myself; and let me die,
Stealing so poorly.
  *Gui.* I love thee; I have spoke it:
How much the quantity, the weight as much,
As I do love my father.
  *Bel.* What? how! how!
  *Arv.* If it be sin to say so, sir, I yoke me
In my good brother's fault: I know not why
I love this youth; and I have heard you say
Love's reason's without reason: the bier at
  door,
And a demand who is 't shall die, I'd say
*My father, not this youth.*
  *Bel.* [*Aside.*] O noble strain!
O worthiness of nature! breed of greatness!
Cowards father cowards, and base things sire
  base:
Nature hath meal and bran, contempt and
  grace.
I'm not their father; yet who this should be
Doth miracle itself, lov'd before me.—
'Tis the ninth hour o' the morn.
  *Arv.* Brother, farewell.
  *Imo.* I wish ye sport.
  *Arv.* You health,—so please you, sir.
  *Imo.* [*Aside.*] These are kind creatures.
  Gods, what lies I have heard!
Our courtiers say all 's savage but at court:

Experience, O, thou disprov'st report! [dish,
The imperious seas breed monsters; for the
Poor tributary rivers as sweet fish.
I am sick still; heart-sick.—Pisanio,
I'll now taste of thy drug. [*Swallows some.*

*Gui.*                    I could not stir him:
He said he was gentle, but unfortunate;
Dishonestly afflicted, but yet honest. [after

*Arv.* Thus did he answer me: yet said here-
I might know more.

*Bel.*                    To the field, to the field!—
We'll leave you for this time: go in and rest.

*Arv.* We'll not be long away.

*Bel.*                    Pray, be not sick,
For you must be our housewife.

*Imo.*                    Well, or ill,
I am bound to you.

*Bel.*                    And shall be ever.
                    [*Exit* IMOGEN *into the Cave.*
This youth, howe'er distress'd, appears he
        hath had
Good ancestors.

*Arv.*                    How angel-like he sings!

*Gui.* But his neat cookery! He cuts our
        roots in characters;
And sauc'd our broths as Juno had been sick,
And he her dieter.

*Arv.*                    Nobly he yokes
A smiling with a sigh,—as if the sigh
Was that it was for not being such a smile;
The smile mocking the sigh that it would fly
From so divine a temple to commix
With winds that sailors rail at.

*Gui.*                    I do note,
That grief and patience, rooted in him both,
Mingle their spurs together.

*Arv.*                    Grow, patience!
And let the stinking elder, grief, untwine
His perishing root with the increasing vine!

*Bel.* It is great morning. Come, away!—
        Who's there?

### Enter CLOTEN.

*Clo.* I cannot find those runagates; that
        villain
Hath mock'd me.—I am faint.

*Bel.*                    Those runagates!
Means he not us? I partly know him; 'tis
Cloten, the son o' the queen. I fear some
        ambush.
I saw him not these many years, and yet
I know 'tis he.—We are held as outlaws:
        hence!

*Gui.* He is but one: you and my brother
        search
What companies are near: pray you, away;
Let me alone with him.
                    [*Exeunt* BELARIUS *and* ARVIRAGUS.

*Clo.*                    Soft!—What are you
That fly me thus? some villain mountaineers?
I have heard of such.—What slave art thou?

*Gui.*                    A thing
More slavish did I ne'er than answering
A slave without a knock.

*Clo.*                    Thou art a robber,
A law-breaker, a villain: yield thee, thief.

*Gui.* To whom? to thee? What art thou?
        have not I
An arm as big as thine? a heart as big?
Thy words, I grant, are bigger; for I wear
        not
My dagger in my mouth. Say what thou art,
Why I should yield to thee?

*Clo.*                    Thou villain base,
Know'st me not by my clothes?

*Gui.*                    No, nor thy tailor, rascal,
Who is thy grandfather: he made those
        clothes,
Which, as it seems, make thee.

*Clo.*                    Thou precious varlet,
My tailor made them not.

*Gui.*                    Hence, then, and thank
The man that gave them thee. Thou art some
        fool;
I am loth to beat thee.

*Clo.*                    Thou injurious thief,
Hear but my name, and tremble.

*Gui.*                    What's thy name?

*Clo.* Cloten, thou villain.

*Gui.* Cloten, thou double villain, be thy
        name,
I cannot tremble at it; were it toad, or adder,
        spider,
'Twould move me sooner.

*Clo.*                    To thy further fear,
Nay, to thy mere confusion, thou shalt know
I'm son to the queen.

*Gui.*                    I'm sorry for 't; not seeming
So worthy as thy birth.

*Clo.*                    Art not afeard?

*Gui.* Those that I reverence, those I fear,—
        the wise:
At fools I laugh, not fear them.

*Clo.*                    Die the death:
When I have slain thee with my proper
        hand,
I'll follow those that even now fled hence,
And on the gates of Lud's town set your
        heads:
Yield, rustic mountaineer. [*Exeunt fighting.*

### Re-enter BELARIUS and ARVIRAGUS.

*Bel.* No company's abroad?

*Arv.* None in the world: you did mistake
        him, sure.

*Bel.* I cannot tell: long is it since I saw
        him,
But time hath nothing blurr'd those lines of
        favour
Which then he wore; the snatches in his
        voice,
And burst of speaking, were as his: I am
        absolute
'Twas very Cloten.

*Arv.*                    In this place we left them:
I wish my brother make good time with
        him,
You say he is so fell.

*Bel.*          Being scarce made up,
I mean to man, he had not apprehension
Of roaring terrors; for defect of judgment
Is oft the cure of fear.—But, see, thy brother.

*Re-enter* GUIDERIUS *with* CLOTEN'S *head.*

*Gui.* This Cloten was a fool, an empty purse,—
There was no money in 't: not Hercules
Could have knock'd out his brains, for he had none:
Yet I not doing this, the fool had borne
My head as I do his.
          *Bel.*          What hast thou done?
          *Gui.* I am perfect what: cut off one Cloten's head,
Son to the queen, after his own report;
Who call'd me traitor, mountaineer; and swore,
With his own single hand he'd take us in,
Displace our heads where,—thank the gods!—they grow,
And set them on Lud's town.
          *Bel.*          We are all undone.
          *Gui.* Why, worthy father, what have we to lose
But that he swore to take, our lives? The law
Protects not us: then why should we be tender,
To let an arrogant piece of flesh threat us;
Play judge and executioner all himself,
For we do fear the law? What company
Discover you abroad?
          *Bel.*          No single soul
Can we set eye on, but in all safe reason
He must have some attendants. Though his humor
Was nothing but mutation,—ay, and that
From one bad thing to worse; not frenzy, not
Absolute madness could so far have rav'd,
To bring him here alone: although perhaps
It may be heard at court that such as we
Cave here, hunt here, are outlaws, and in time
May make some stronger head: the which he hearing,—
As it is like him,—might break out, and swear
He'd fetch us in; yet is 't not probable
To come alone, either he so undertaking
Or they so suffering: then on good ground we fear,
If we do fear this body hath a tail
More perilous than the head.
          *Arv.*          Let ordinance
Come as the gods foresay it: howsoe'er,
My brother hath done well.
          *Bel.*          I had no mind
To hunt this day: the boy Fidele's sickness
Did make my way long forth.
          *Gui.*          With his own sword,

Which he did wave against my throat, I have ta'en
His head from him: I'll throw 't into the creek
Behind our rock; and let it to the sea,
And tell the fishes he's the queen's son, Cloten:
That's all I reck.          [*Exit.*
          *Bel.*          I fear 'twill be reveng'd;
Would, Polydore, thou hadst not done 't! though valour
Becomes thee well enough.
          *Arv.*          Would I had done 't,
So the revenge alone pursu'd me!—Polydore,
I love thee brotherly; but envy much
Thou hast robb'd me of this deed: I would revenges,          [seek us through,
That possible strength might meet, would
And put us to our answer.
          *Bel.*          Well, 'tis done:—
We'll hunt no more to-day, nor seek for danger
Where there's no profit. I pr'ythee, to our rock;
You and Fidele play the cooks: I'll stay
Till hasty Polydore return, and bring him
To dinner presently.
          *Arv.*          Poor sick Fidele!
I'll willingly to him: to gain his colour
I'd let a parish of such Clotens' blood,
And praise myself for charity.          [*Exit.*
          *Bel.*          O thou goddess,
Thou divine nature, how thyself thou blazon'st
In these two princely boys! They are as gentle
As zephyrs blowing below the violet,
Not wagging his sweet head; and yet as rough,
Their royal blood enchaf'd, as the rud'st wind
That by the top doth take the mountain pine,
And make him stoop to the vale. 'Tis wonder
That an invisible instinct should frame them
To royalty unlearn'd; honour untaught;
Civility not seen from other; valour
That wildly grows in them, but yields a crop
As if it had been sow'd. Yet still it's strange
What Cloten's being here to us portends,
Or what his death will bring us.

*Re-enter* GUIDERIUS.

          *Gui.*          Where's my brother?
I have sent Cloten's clotpoll down the stream,
In embassy to his mother: his body's hostage
For his return.          [*Solemn music.*
          *Bel.*          My ingenious instrument!
Hark, Polydore, it sounds! But what occasion
Hath Cadwal now to give it motion? Hark!
          *Gui.* Is he at home?
          *Bel.*          He went hence even now.
          *Gui.* What does he mean? since death of my dear'st mother

It did not speak before. All solemn things
Should answer solemn accidents. The mat-
  ter?
Triumphs for nothing and lamenting toys
Is jollity for apes and grief for boys.
Is Cadwal mad?
  *Bel.*              Look, here he comes,
And brings the dire occasion in his arms
Of what we blame him for!

*Re-enter* ARVIRAGUS, *bearing* IMOGEN *as dead
  in his arms.*

  *Arv.*              The bird is dead
That we have made so much on. I had
  rather
Have skipp'd from sixteen years of age to
  sixty,
To have turn'd my leaping time into a crutch,
Than have seen this.
  *Gui.*              O sweetest, fairest lily!
My brother wears thee not the one half so
  well
As when thou grew'st thyself.
  *Bel.*              O melancholy!
Who ever yet could sound thy bottom? find
The ooze to show what coast thy sluggish
  crare
Might easiliest harbour in?—Thou blessed
  thing!
Jove knows what man thou might'st have
  made; but I,
Thou diedst, a most rare boy, of melancholy!
How found you him?
  *Arv.*              Stark, as you see:
Thus smiling, as some fly had tickled slumber,
Not as death's dart, being laugh'd at: his
  right cheek
Reposing on a cushion.
  *Gui.*              Where?
  *Arv.*              O' the floor;
His arms thus leagu'd: I thought he slept;
  and put              [rudeness
My clouted brogues from off my feet, whose
Answer'd my steps too loud.
  *Gui.*              Why, he but sleeps:
If he be gone he'll make his grave a bed;
With female fairies will his tomb be haunted,
And worms will not come to thee.
  *Arv.*              With fairest flowers,
Whilst summer lasts and I live here, Fidele,
I'll sweeten thy sad grave: thou shalt not lack
The flower that 's like thy face, pale prim-
  rose; nor
The azure hare-bell, like thy veins; no, nor
The leaf of eglantine, whom not to slander,
Out-sweeten'd not thy breath: the ruddock
  would,
With charitable bill,—O bill, sore shaming
Those rich-left heirs that let their fathers lie
Without a monument!—bring thee all this;
Yea, and furr'd moss besides, when flowers
  are none,
To winter-ground thy corse.
  *Gui.*              Pr'ythee, have done;

And do not play in wench-like words with
  that
Which is so serious. Let us bury him.
And not protract with admiration what
Is now due debt.—To the grave!
  *Arv.*              Say, where shall 's lay him?
  *Gui.* By good Euriphile, our mother.
  *Arv.*              Be 't so:
And let us, Polydore, though now our voices
Have got the mannish crack, sing him to the
  ground,
As once our mother; use like note and words,
Save that Euriphile must be Fidele.
  *Gui.* Cadwal,
I cannot sing: I'll weep, and word it with
  thee;
For notes of sorrow out of tune are worse
Than priests and fanes that lie.
  *Arv.*              We'll speak it, then.
  *Bel.* Great griefs, I see, medicine the less:
  for Cloten
Is quite forgot. He was a queen's son, boys:
And though he came our enemy, remember,
He was paid for that: though mean and mighty,
  rotting
Together, have one dust, yet reverence,—
That angel of the world,—doth make dis-
  tinction
Of place 'tween high and low. Our foe was
  princely;
And though you took his life, as being our
  foe,
Yet bury him as a prince.
  *Gui.*              Pray you, fetch him hither.
Thersites' body is as good as Ajax',
When neither are alive.
  *Arv.*              If you'll go fetch him,
We'll say our song the whilst.—Brother, be-
  gin.              [*Exit* BELARIUS.
  *Gui.* Nay, Cadwal, we must lay his head to
  the east;
My father hath a reason for 't.
  *Arv.*              'Tis true.
  *Gui.* Come on, then, and remove him.
  *Arv.*              So.—Begin.

                    SONG.

*Gui.*   Fear no more the heat o' the sun,
         Nor the furious winter's rages;
       Thou thy worldly task hast done,
         Home art gone, and ta'en thy wages:
       Golden lads and girls all must,
       As chimney-sweepers, come to dust.

*Arv.*   Fear no more the frown o' the great;
         Thou art past the tyrant's stroke:
       Care no more to clothe and eat;
         To thee the reed is as the oak:
       The sceptre, learning, physic, must
       All follow this, and come to dust.

*Gui.*   Fear no more the lightning-flash,
*Arv.*     Nor the all-dreaded thunder-stone;
*Gui.*   Fear not slander, censure rash;
*Arv.*     Thou hast finish'd joy and moan:
*Both.*  All lovers young, all lovers must
       Consign to thee, and come to dust.

*Gui.* No exorciser harm thee!
*Arv.* Nor no witchcraft charm thee!
*Gui.* Ghost unlaid forbear thee!
*Arv.* Nothing ill come near thee!
*Both.* Quiet consummation have;
　　　And renowned be thy grave!

*Re-enter* BELARIUS *with the body of* CLOTEN.

*Gui.* We have done our obsequies: come,
　　lay him down.　　　　　　[night, more:
*Bel.* Here's a few flowers; but 'bout mid-
The herbs that have on them cold dew o' the
　　night　　　　　　　　　　[faces.—
Are strewings fitt'st for graves.—Upon their
You were as flowers, now wither'd: even so
These herblets shall, which we upon you
　　strew.—
Come on, away: apart upon our knees.
The ground that gave them first has them
　　again:
Their pleasures here are past, so is their pain.
　　　　　[*Exeunt* BEL., GUI., *and* ARV.

*Imo.* [*Awaking.*] Yes, sir, to Milford-
Haven; which is the way?—
I thank you.—By yon bush?—Pray, how far
　　thither?
'Ods pittikens! can it be six mile yet?—
I have gone all night. Faith, I'll lie down and
　　sleep.
But, soft! no bedfellow:—O gods and god-
　　desses!　　　　　　[*Seeing the body.*
These flowers are like the pleasures of the
　　world;
This bloody man, the care on 't.—I hope ,I
　　dream;
For so I thought I was a cave-keeper,
And cook to honest creatures: but 'tis not so,
'Twas but a bolt of nothing, shot at nothing,
Which the brain makes of fumes: our very
　　eyes
Are sometimes, like our judgments, blind.
　　Good faith,
I tremble still with fear: but if there be
Yet left in heaven as small a drop of pity
As a wren's eye, fear'd gods, a part of it!
The dream 's here still: even when I wake it
　　is
Without me, as within me; not imagin'd, felt.
A headless man!—The garments of Posthu-
　　mus!
I know the shape of 's leg: this is his hand;
His foot Mercurial; his Martial thigh;
The brawns of Hercules: but his Jovial
　　face—
Murder in heaven?—How!—'Tis gone.—
Pisanio,
All curses madded Hecuba gave the Greeks,
And mine to boot; be darted on thee! Thou,
Conspir'd with that irregulous devil, Cloten,
Hast here cut off my lord.—To write and
　　read
Be henceforth treacherous!—Damn'd Pis-
　　anio
Hath with his forged letters,—damn'd Pis-
　　anio,—

From this most bravest vessel of the world
Struck the main-top!—O Posthumus! alas,
Where is thy head? where's that? Ay me!
　　where's that?
Pisanio might have kill'd thee at the heart,
And left thy head on.—How should this be?
　　Pisanio?
'Tis he and Cloten: malice and lucre in them
Have laid this woe here. O 'tis pregnant,
　　pregnant!
The drug he gave me, which he said was
　　precious
And cordial to me, have I not found it
Murderous to the senses? That confirms it
　　home
This is Pisanio's deed, and Cloten's: O!—
Give colour to my pale cheek with thy blood,
That we the horrider may seem to those
Which chance to find us: O, my lord, my
　　lord!

*Enter* LUCIUS, *a* Captain *and other* Officers,
　　　　*and a* Soothsayer.

*Cap.* To them, the legions garrison'd in
　　Gallia,
After your will, have cross'd the sea; attend-
　　ing
You here at Milford-Haven with your ships:
They are in readiness.
*Luc.*　　　　　But what from Rome?
*Cap.* The senate hath stirr'd up the con-
　　finers
And gentlemen of Italy; most willing spirits,
That promise noble service: and they come
Under the conduct of bold Iachimo,
Sienna's brother.
*Luc.*　　　　　When expect you them?
*Cap.* With the next benefit o' the wind.
*Luc.*　　　　　　This forwardness
Makes our hopes fair. Command our present
　　numbers　　　　　　　　[Now, sir,
Be muster'd; bid the captains look to 't—
What have you dream'd of late of this war's
　　purpose?　　　　　　　　[a vision,
*Sooth.* Last night the very gods show'd me
I fast and pray'd for their intelligence,—
　　thus:—
I saw Jove's bird, the Roman eagle, wing'd
From the spongy south to this part of the
　　west,
There vanish'd in the sunbeams; which por-
　　tends,—
Unless my sins abuse my divination,—
Success to the Roman host.
*Luc.*　　　　　　Dream often so,
And never false.—Soft, ho! what trunk is
　　here　　　　　　　　　　[sometime
Without his top?—The ruin speaks that
It was a worthy building.—How! a page!—
Or dead or sleeping on him? But dead,
　　rather;
For nature doth abhor to make his bed
With the defunct, or sleep upon the dead.—
Let's see the boy's face.

*Cap.*　　　　He's alive, my lord.
*Luc.* He'll, then, instruct us of this body.—
　　Young one,
Inform us of thy fortunes; for it seems
They crave to be demanded. Who is this
Thou mak'st thy bloody pillow? or who was
　　he,
That otherwise then noble nature did,
Hath alter'd that good picture? What's thy
　　interest
In this sad wreck? How came it? Who is it?
What art thou?
　　*Imo.*　　　　I am nothing: or if not,
Nothing to be were better. This was my
　　master,
A very valiant Briton and a good,
That here by mountaineers lies slain: alas!
There is no more such masters: I may
　　wander
From east to occident, cry out for service,
Try many, all good, serve truly, never
Find such another master.
　　*Luc.*　　　　'Lack, good youth!
Thou mov'st no less with thy complaining
　　than
Thy master in bleeding: say his name, good
　　friend.
　　*Imo.* Richard du Champ.—[*Aside.*] If I
　　do lie, and do
No harm by it, though the gods hear, I hope
They'll pardon it.—Say you, sir?
　　*Luc.*　　　　Thy name?
　　*Imo.*　　　　Fidele.
　　*Luc.* Thou dost approve thyself the very
　　same:　　　　[name.
Thy name well fits thy faith, thy faith thy
Wilt take thy chance with me? I will not say
Thou shalt be so well master'd; but, be sure,
No less belov'd. The Roman emperor's letters,
Sent by a counsel to me, should not sooner
Than thine own worth prefer thee: go with
　　me.
　　*Imo.* I'll follow, sir. But first, an 't please
　　the gods,
I'll hide my master from the flies, as deep
As these poor pickaxes can dig: and when
With wild wood-leaves and weeds I ha'
　　strew'd his grave,
And on it said a century of prayers,
Such as I can, twice o'er, I'll weep and sigh;
And leaving so his service, follow you,
So please you entertain me.
　　*Luc.*　　　　Ay, good youth;
And rather father thee than master thee.—
My friends,
The boy hath taught us manly duties: let us
Find out the prettiest daisied plot we can,
And make him with our pikes and partisans
A grave: come, arm him.—Boy, he is pre-
　　ferr'd
By thee to us; and he shall be interr'd
As soldiers can. Be cheerful; wipe thine eyes:
Some falls are means the happier to arise.
　　　　　　　　　　　　[*Exeunt.*

SCENE III.—BRITAIN. *A Room in* CYM-
　　BELINE'S *Palace.*

*Enter* CYMBELINE, Lords, PISANIO, *and*
　　Attendants.

　　*Cym.* Again; and bring me word how 'tis
　　with her.
A fever with the absence of her son;
　　　　　　　　　　　　[*Exit an* Attendant.
A madness, of which her life 's in danger,—
　　Heavens,
How deeply you at once do touch me!
　　Imogen,
The great part of my comfort, gone; my
　　queen
Upon a desperate bed, and in a time
When fearful wars point at me; her son gone,
So needful for this present: it strikes me, past
The hope of comfort.—But for thee, fellow,
Who needs must know of her departure, and
Dost seem so ignorant, we'll enforce it from
　　thee
By a sharp torture.
　　*Pis.*　　　　Sir, my life is yours, [tress,
I humbly set it at your will: but, for my mis-
I nothing know where she remains, why gone,
Nor when she purposes return. Beseech your
　　highness,
Hold me your royal servant.
　　1 *Lord.*　　　　Good my liege,
The day that she was missing he was here:
I dare be bound he 's true, and shall perform
All parts of his subjection loyally. 
For Cloten,—
There wants no diligence in seeking him,
And will no doubt be found.
　　*Cym.*　　　　The time is troublesome,—
We'll slip you for a season; but our jealousy
　　　　　　　　　　　　[*To* PISANIO.
Does yet depend.
　　1 *Lord.*　　　　So please your majesty,
The Roman legions, all from Gallia drawn,
Are landed on your coast; with a supply
Of Roman gentlemen by the senate sent.
　　*Cym.* Now for the counsel of my son and
　　queen!—
I am amaz'd with matter.
　　1 *Lord.*　　　　Good my liege,
Your preparation can affront no less
Than what you hear of: come more, for
　　more you're ready:
The want is but to put those powers in mo-
　　tion
That long to move.
　　*Cym.*　　　　I thank you. Let's withdraw,
And meet the time as it seeks us. We fear not
What can from Italy annoy us; but
We grieve at chances here.—Away!
　　　　　　　　　　　[*Exeunt all but* PISANIO.
　　*Pis.* I heard no letter from my master
　　since
I wrote him Imogen was slain: 'tis strange:
Nor hear I from my mistress, who did prom-
　　ise

To yield me often tidings; neither know I
What is betid to Cloten; but remain
Perplex'd in all: the heavens still must work.
Wherein I am false I am honest; not true to
　　be true:
These present wars shall find I love my coun-
　　try,
Even to the note o' the king, or I'll fall in
　　them.
All other doubts, by time let them be clear'd:
Fortune brings in some boats that are not
　　steer'd.　　　　　　　　　　　[*Exit.*

### SCENE IV.—WALES. *Before the Cave.*

*Enter* BELARIUS, GUIDERIUS, *and*
ARVIRAGUS.

*Gui.* The noise is round about us.
*Bel.*　　　　　　　Let us from it.
*Arv.* What pleasure, sir, find we in life, to
　　lock it
From action and adventure?
*Gui.*　　　　　Nay, what hope
Have we in hiding us? this way the Romans
Must or for Britons slay us or receive us
For barbarous and unnatural revolts
During their use, and slay us after.
*Bel.*　　　　　　　　Sons,
We'll higher to the mountains; there secure
　　us.
To the king's party there 's no going: newness
Of Cloten's death,—we being not known, not
　　muster'd
Among the bands,—may drive us to a render
Where we have liv'd; and so extort from 's
That which we 've done, whose answer would
　　be death,
Drawn on with torture.
*Gui.*　　　　　This is, sir, a doubt
In such a time nothing becoming you
Nor satisfying us.
*Arv.*　　　　　It is not likely
That when they hear the Roman horses neigh,
Behold their quarter'd fires, have both their
　　eyes
And ears so cloy'd importantly as now,
That they will waste their time upon our
　　note,
To know from whence we are.
*Bel.*　　　　　O, I am known
Of many in the army: many years,
Though Cloten then but young, you see, not
　　wore him　　　　　　　　　　[king
From my remembrance. And, besides, the
Hath not deserv'd my service nor your loves;
Who find in my exile the want of breeding
The certainty of this hard life; aye hopeless
To have the courtesy your cradle promis'd,
But to be still hot summer's tanlings and
The shrinking slaves of winter.
*Gui.*　　　　　Than be so,
Better to cease to be. Pray, sir, to the army:
I and my brother are not known; yourself
So out of thought, and thereto so o'ergrown,
Cannot be question'd.

*Arv.*　　　　By this sun that shines,
I'll thither: what thing is it that I never
Did see man die! scarce ever look'd on blood,
But that of coward hares, hot goats, and
　　venison!
Never bestrid a horse, save one that had
A rider like myself, who ne'er wore rowel
Nor iron on his heel! I am asham'd
To look upon the holy sun, to have
The benefit of his blessed beams, remaining
So long a poor unknown.
*Gui.*　　　　By heavens, I'll go:
If you will bless me, sir, and give me leave,
I'll take the better care; but if you will not,
The hazard therefore due fall on me by
The hands of Romans!
*Arv.*　　　　　So say I,—Amen.
*Bel.* No reason I, since of your lives you set
So slight a valuation, should reserve
My crack'd one to more care. Have with you,
　　boys!
If in your country wars you chance to die,
That is my bed too, lads, and there I'll lie:
Lead, lead.—[*Aside.*] The time seems long;
　　their blood thinks scorn
Till it fly out, and show them princes born.
　　　　　　　　　　　　　　　[*Exeunt.*

## ACT V.

### SCENE I.—BRITAIN. *A Field between the British and Roman Camps.*

*Enter* POSTHUMUS *with a bloody handkerchief.*

*Post.* Yea, bloody cloth, I'll keep thee; for
　　I wish'd
Thou shouldst be colour'd thus. You married
　　ones,
If each of you should take this course, how
　　many
Must murder wives much better than them-
　　selves
For wrying but a little! O Pisanio!
Every good servant does not all commands:
No bond but to do just ones.—Gods! if you
Should have ta'en vengeance on my faults, I
　　never
Had liv'd to put on this: so had you sav'd
The noble Imogen to repent; and struck
Me, wretch more worth your vengeance. But
　　alack,
You snatch some hence for little faults; that's
　　love,
To have them fall no more: you some
　　permit
To second ills with ills, each elder worse,
And make them dread it, to the doers' thrift.
But Imogen is your own: do your best wills,
And make me bless'd to obey!—I am brought
　　hither
Among the Italian gentry, and to fight
Against my lady's kingdom: 'tis enough
That, Britain, I have kill'd thy mistress;
　　peace!

I'll give no wound to thee. Therefore, good
　　heavens,
Hear patiently my purpose:—I'll disrobe me
Of these Italian weeds, and suit myself
As does a Briton peasant: so I'll fight
Against the part I come with; so I'll die
For thee, O Imogen, even for whom my life
Is every breath a death: and thus unknown,
Pitied nor hated, to the face of peril
Myself I'll dedicate. Let me make men know
More valour in me than my habits show.
Gods, put the strength o' the Leonati in me!
To shame the guise o' the world, I will begin
The fashion,—less without and more within.
　　　　　　　　　　　　　　　　　[*Exit.*

SCENE II.—BRITAIN. *A Field between the
　　Camps.*

*Enter, at one side,* LUCIUS, IACHIMO, IMOGEN,
*And the* Roman Army; *at the other side,
the* British Army; LEONATUS POSTHUMUS
*following it like a poor soldier. They march
over and go out. Alarums. Then enter
again, in skirmish,* IACHIMO *and* POSTHU-
MUS: *he vanquisheth and disarmeth*
IACHIMO, *and then leaves him.*

*Iach.* The heaviness and guilt within my
　　bosom
Takes off my manhood: I have belied a lady,
The princess of this country, and the air
　　on't
Revengingly enfeebles me; or could this carl,
A very drudge of nature's, have subdu'd me
In my profession? Knighthoods and honours
　　borne
As I wear mine are titles but of scorn.
If that thy gentry, Britain, go before
This lout as he exceeds our lords, the odds
Is that we scarce are men, and you are gods.
　　　　　　　　　　　　　　　　　[*Exit.*

*The battle continues; the Britons fly;* CYM-
BELINE *is taken: then enter to his rescue*
BELARIUS, GUIDERIUS, *and* ARVIRAGUS.

*Bel.* Stand, stand! We have the advantage
　　of the ground;
The lane is guarded: nothing routs us but
The villany of our fears.
　　*Gui. and Arv.*　　Stand, stand, and fight!

*Re-enter* POSTHUMUS, *and seconds the Brit-
ons: they rescue* CYMBELINE, *and exeunt.
Then re-enter* LUCIUS, IACHIMO, *and* IMO-
GEN.

*Luc.* Away, boy, from the troops, and save
　　thyself;
For friends kill friends, and the disorder's such
As war were hoodwink'd.
　　*Iach.*　　　　　'Tis their fresh supplies.
*Luc.* It is a day turn'd strangely: or be-
　　times
Let's re-enforce or fly.　　　　　　[*Exeunt.*

SCENE III.—BRITAIN. *Another part of the
　　Field.*

*Enter* POSTHUMUS *and a* British Lord.

*Lord.* Cam'st thou from where they made
　　the stand?
　　*Post.*　　　　　I did:
Though you, it seems, come from the fliers.
　　*Lord.*　　　　　　　　　　I did.
　　*Post.* No blame be to you, sir; for all was
　　lost,
But that the heavens fought: the king him-
　　self
Of his wings destitute, the army broken,
And but the backs of Britons seen, all flying
Through a straight lane; the enemy full-
　　hearted,
Lolling the tongue with slaughtering, having
　　work
More plentiful than tools to do't, struck down
Some mortally, some slightly touch'd, some
　　falling　　　　　　　　　　　　　　[damn'd
Merely through fear; that the strait path was
With dead men hurt behind, and cowards
　　living,
To die with lengthen'd shame.
　　*Lord.*　　　　　　Where was this lane?
　　*Post.* Close by the battle, ditch'd, and
　　wall'd with turf,
Which gave advantage to an ancient sol-
　　dier,—
An honest one, I warrant; who deserv'd
So long a breeding as his white beard came to,
In doing this for's country:—athwart the lane
He, with two striplings,—lads more like to
　　run
The country base than to commit such slaugh-
　　ter;
With faces fit for masks, or rather fairer
Than those for preservation cas'd, or shame,—
Made good the passage; cried to those that
　　fled,
*Our Britain's harts die flying, not our men:
To darkness fleet, souls that fly backwards!
　　Stand;
Or we are Romans, and will give you that
Like beasts which you shun beastly, and may
　　save,
But to look back in frown: stand, stand!—*
　　These three,
Three thousand confident, in act as many,—
For three performers are the file when all
The rest do nothing,—with this word, *Stand,
　　stand!*
Accommodated by the place, more charming
With their own nobleness,—which could have
　　turn'd
A distaff to a lance,—gilded pale looks,
Part shame, part spirit renew'd; that some,
　　turn'd coward
But by example,—O, a sin in war
Damn'd in the first beginners!—'gan to look
The way that they did, and to grin like lions
Upon the pikes o' the hunters. Then began

A stop i' the chaser, a retire; anon
A rout, confusion thick: forthwith they fly,
Chickens, the way which they stoop'd eagles;
　　　slaves,　　　　　　　　　[cowards,—
The strides they victors made: and now our
Like fragments in hard voyages,—became
The life o' the need; having found the back-
　　　door open　　　　　　　　[wound!
Of the unguarded hearts, heavens, how they
Some slain before; some dying; some their
　　　friends
O'erborne i' the former wave: ten chas'd by
　　　one
Are now each one the slaughter-man of twen-
　　ty:
Those that would die or ere resist are grown
The mortal bugs o' the field.
　　Lord.　　　　　This was strange chance,—
A narrow lane, an old man, and two boys!
　　Post. Nay, do not wonder at it: you are
　　　made
Rather to wonder at the things you hear
Than to work any. Will you rhyme upon't,
And vent it for a mockery? Here is one:
*Two boys, an old man twice a boy, a lane,*
*Preserv'd the Britons, was the Romans' bane,*
　　Lord. Nay, be not angry, sir.
　　Post.　　　　　'Lack, to what end?
Who dares not stand his foe I'll be his friend,
For if he'll do as he is made to do
I know he'll quickly fly my friendship too.
You have put me into rhyme.
　　Lord.　　　　　Farewell; you're angry.
　　　　　　　　　　　　　[*Exit.*
　　Post. Still going?—This is a lord! O noble
　　　misery,—
To be i' the field and ask what news of me!
To-day how many would have given their
　　honours
To have sav'd their carcasses! took heel to
　　do't,
And yet died too! I, in mine own woe
　　charm'd,
Could not find death where I did hear him
　　groan,
Nor feel him where he struck: being an ugly
　　monster,
'Tis strange he hides him in fresh cups, soft
　　beds,
Sweet words; or hath more ministers than we
That draw his knives i' the war.—Well, I will
　　find him:
For being now a favourer to the Briton,
No more a Briton, I have resum'd again
The part I came in: fight I will no more.
But yield me to the veriest hind that shall [is
Once touch my shoulder. Great the slaughter
Here made by the Roman; great the answer
　　be
Britons must take: for me, my ransom's
　　death;
On either side I come to spend my breath;
Which neither here I'll keep nor bear again,
But end it by some means for Imogen.

*Enter two* British Captains *and* Soldiers.

　　1 *Cap.* Great Jupiter be prais'd! Lucius is
　　　taken:
'Tis thought the old man and his sons were
　　angels.
　　2 *Cap.* There was a fourth man, in a silly
　　habit,
That gave the affront with them.
　　1 *Cap.*　　　　　So 'tis reported:
But none of 'em can be found.—Stand! who's
　　there?
　　*Post.* A Roman;　　　　　　[seconds
Who had not now been drooping here if
Had answer'd him.
　　2 *Cap.*　　　Lay hands on him; a dog!—
A leg of Rome shall not return to tell
What crows have peck'd them here:—he
　　brags his service,
As if he were of note: bring him to the king.

*Enter* CYMBELINE *attended;* BELARIUS, GUID-
ERIUS, ARVIRAGUS, PISANIO, *and* Roman
Captives. *The* Captains *present* POSTHU-
MUS *to* CYMBELINE, *who delivers him over
to a* Gaoler: *after which all go out.*

　　SCENE IV.—BRITAIN. *A Prison.*

*Enter* POSTHUMUS *and two* Gaolers.

　　1 *Gaol.* You shall not now be stolen, you
　　　have locks upon you;
So, graze as you find pasture.
　　2 *Gaol.* Ay, or a stomach.
　　　　　　　　　　[*Exeunt* Gaolers.
　　*Post.* Most welcome, bondage! for thou
　　　art a way,
I think, to liberty: yet am I better
Than one that's sick o' the gout; since he
　　had rather
Groan so in perpetuity than be cur'd
By the sure physician death, who is the key
To unbar these locks. My conscience, thou art
　　fetter'd　　　　　　　　[gods, give me
More than my shanks and wrists: you good
The penitent instrument to pick that bolt,
Then free for ever! Is't enough I am sorry?
So children temporal fathers do appease;
Gods are more full of mercy. Must I repent?
I cannot do it better than in gyves,
Desir'd more than constrain'd: to satisfy,
If of my freedom 'tis the main part, take
No stricter render of me than my all.
I know you are more clement than vile men,
Who of their broken debtors take a third,
A sixth, a tenth, letting them thrive again
On their abatement: that's not my desire:
For Imogen's dear life take mine; and though
'Tis not so dear, yet 'tis a life; you coin'd it:
'Tween man and man they weigh not every
　　stamp;
Though light, take pieces for the figure's sake:
You rather mine, being yours: and so, great
　　powers,
If you will take this audit, take this life,

And cancel these cold bonds.—O Imogen!
I'll speak to thee in silence.          [*Sleeps.*

*Solemn Music. Enter, as in an apparition,*
SICILIUS LEONATUS, *father to* POSTHUMUS,
*an old man attired like a warrior, leading in
his hand an ancient matron, his wife and
mother to* POSTHUMUS, *with music before
them: then, after other music, follow the
two young* LEONATI, *brothers to* POSTHU-
MUS, *with wounds, as they died in the
wars. They circle* POSTHUMUS *round as he
lies sleeping.*

*Sici.* No more, thou thunder-master, show
   Thy spite on mortal flies:
With Mars fall out, with Juno chide,
   That thy adulteries
     Rates and revenges.
Hath my poor boy done aught but well,
   Whose face I never saw?
I died whilst in the womb he stay'd
   Attending nature's law;—
Whose father then,—as men report
   Thou orphans' father art,—
Thou shouldst have been, and shielded him
   From this earth-vexing smart.

*Moth.* Lucina lent not me her aid,
   But took me in my throes;
That from me was Posthumus ripp'd,
   Came crying 'mongst his foes,
     A thing of pity!

*Sici.* Great nature, like his ancestry,
   Moulded the stuff so fair
That he deserv'd the praise o' the world
   As great Sicilius' heir.

1 *Bro.* When once he was mature for man,
   In Britain where was he
That could stand up his parallel;
   Or fruitful object be
In eye of Imogen, that best
   Could deem his dignity?

*Moth.* With marriage wherefore was he
   mock'd,
   To be exil'd, and thrown
From Leonati' seat, and cast
   From her his dearest one,
     Sweet Imogen?

*Sici.* Why did you suffer Iachimo,
   Slight thing of Italy,
To taint his nobler heart and brain
   With needless jealousy;
And to become the geck and scorn
   O' the other's villany?

2 *Bro.* For this from stiller seats we came,
   Our parents and us twain,
That, striking in our country's cause,
   Fell bravely and were slain;
Our fealty and Tenantius' right
   With honour to maintain.

1 *Bro.* Like hardiment Posthumus hath
   To Cymbeline perform'd:
Then, Jupiter, thou king of gods,

Why hast thou thus adjourn'd
The graces for his merits due,
   Being all to dolours turn'd?

*Sici.* Thy crystal window ope; look out;
   No longer exercise
Upon a valiant race thy harsh
   And potent injuries.

*Moth.* Since, Jupiter, our son is good,
   Take off his miseries.

*Sici.* Peep through thy marble mansion;
   help;
Or we poor ghosts will cry
To the shining synod of the rest
   Against thy deity.

*Both Bro.* Help, Jupiter; or we appeal,
   And from thy justice fly.

JUPITER *descends in thunder and lightning,
sitting upon an eagle: he throws a thunderbolt. The Ghosts fall on their knees.*

*Jup.* No more, you petty spirits of region
   low,
Offend our hearing; hush!—How dare you
   ghosts
Accuse the thunderer, whose bolt, you know,
   Sky-planted, batters all rebelling coasts?
Poor shadows of Elysium, hence; and rest
   Upon your never-withering banks of flow-
   ers:
Be not with mortal accidents oppress'd;
   No care of yours it is; you know 'tis ours.
Whom best I love I cross; to make my gift,
   The more delay'd, delighted. Be content;
Your low-laid son our godhead will uplift:
   His comforts thrive, his trials well are spent.
Our Jovial star reign'd at his birth, and in
   Our temple was he married.—Rise, and
     fade!—
He shall be lord of Lady Imogen,
   And happier much by his affliction made.
This tablet lay upon his breast, wherein
   Our pleasure his full fortune doth confine:
And so away: no further with your din
   Express impatience, lest you stir up mine.—
Mount, eagle, to my palace crystalline.
                [*Ascends.*

*Sici.* He came in thunder; his celestial
   breath
Was sulphurous to smell: the holy eagle
Stoop'd, as to foot us: his ascension is
More sweet than our bless'd fields: his royal
   bird
Prunes the immortal wing, and cloys his beak,
As when his god is pleas'd.

*All.*             Thanks, Jupiter!

*Sici.* The marble pavement closes, he is
   enter'd
His radiant roof.—Away! and, to be blest,
Let us with care perform his great behest.
                [*Ghosts vanish.*

*Post.* [*Waking.*] Sleep, thou hast been a
   grandsire, and begot
A father to me; and thou hast created

A mother and two brothers: but, O scorn!
Gone! they went hence so soon as they were
　　born.
And so I am awake.—Poor wretches that
　　depend
On greatness' favour dream as I have done,
Wake and find nothing.—But, alas, I swerve:
Many dream not to find, neither deserve,
And yet are steep'd in favours; so am I,
That have this golden chance, and know not
　　why.　　　　　　　　　　　[rare one!
What fairies haunt this ground? A book? O,
Be not, as is our fangled world, a garment
Nobler than that it covers: let thy effects
So follow, to be most unlike our courtiers,
As good as promise.
　　[*Reads.*]　*When as a lion's whelp shall, to
himself unknown, without seeking find, and
be embraced by a piece of tender air; and
when from a stately cedar shall be lopped
branches which, being dead many years, shall
after revive, be jointed to the old stock, and
freshly grow; then shall Posthumus end his
miseries, Britain be fortunate, and flourish in
peace and plenty.*
'Tis still a dream; or else such stuff as mad-
　　men
Tongue, and brain not: either both or noth-
　　ing:
Or senseless speaking, or a speaking such
As sense cannot untie. Be what it is,
The action of my life is like it, which
I'll keep, if but for sympathy.

　　　　　*Re-enter* Gaoler.

　*Gaol.* Come, sir, are you ready for death?
　*Post.* Over-roasted rather; ready long ago.
　*Gaol.* Hanging is the word, sir: if you be
ready for that, you are well cooked.
　*Post.* So, if I prove a good repast to the
spectators, the dish pays the shot.
　*Gaol.* A heavy reckon for you, sir. But the
comfort is, you shall be called to no more
payments, fear no more tavern bills, which
are often the sadness of parting, as the pro-
curing of mirth: you come in faint for want
of meat, depart reeling with too much drink;
sorry that you have paid too much, and
sorry that you are paid too much; purse and
brain both empty,—the brain the heavier for
being too light, the purse too light, being
drawn of heaviness: O, of this contradiction
you shall now be quit.—O, the charity of a
penny cord! it sums up thousands in a trice:
you have no true debitor and creditor but it;
of what's past, is, and to come, the discharge:
—your neck, sir, is pen, book, and counters;
so the acquittance follows.
　*Post.* I am merrier to die than thou art to
live.
　*Gaol.* Indeed, sir, he that sleeps feels not
the toothache: but a man that were to sleep
your sleep, and a hangman to help him to
bed, I think he would change places with his
officer; for, look you, sir, you know **not**
which way you shall go.
　*Post.* Yes, indeed do I, fellow.
　*Gaol.* Your death has eyes in's head, **then**;
I have not seen him so pictured: you **must**
either be directed by some that take up**on**
them to know, or take upon yourself **that**
which I am sure you do not know; or jump
the after-inquiry on your own peril: and how
you shall speed in your journey's end I think
you'll never return to tell one.
　*Post.* I tell thee, fellow, there are none
want eyes to direct them the way I am going, but such as wink and will not use them.
　*Gaol.* What an infinite mock is this, that a
man should have the best use of eyes to see
the way of blindness! I am sure hanging's the
way of winking.

　　　　　*Enter a* Messenger.

　*Mess.* Knock off his manacles; bring your
prisoner to the king.
　*Post.* Thou bringest good news,—I am
called to be made free.
　*Gaol.* I'll be hanged, then.
　*Post.* Thou shalt be then freer than a
gaoler; no bolts for the dead.
　　　　　[*Exeunt* POST. *and* Messenger.
　*Gaol.* Unless a man would marry a gallows
and beget young gibbets I never saw one so
prone. Yet, on my conscience, there are verier
knaves desire to live, for all he be a Roman:
and there be some of them too that die against
their wills; so should I if I were one. I would
we were all of one mind, and one mind good;
O, there were desolation of gaolers and gal-
lowses! I speak against my present profit;
but my wish hath a preferment in't.　　[*Exit.*

　　SCENE V.—BRITAIN. CYMBELINE'S *Tent.*

*Enter* CYMBELINE, BELARIUS, GUIDERIUS,
　ARVIRAGUS, PISANIO, Lords, Officers, *and*
　Attendants.

　*Cym.* Stand by my side, you whom the
　　gods have made
Preservers of my throne. Woe is my heart
That the poor soldier that so richly fought,
Whose rags sham'd gilded arms, whose naked
　　breast
Stepp'd before targes of proof, cannot be
　　found:
He shall be happy that can find him, if
Our grace can make him so.
　*Bel.*　　　　　　　I never saw
Such noble fury in so poor a thing;
Such precious deeds in one that promis'd
　　naught
But beggary and poor looks.
　*Cym.*　　　　　No tidings of him?
　*Pis.* He hath been search'd among the dead
　　and living,
But no trace of him.
　*Cym.*　　　　　To my grief, I am
The heir of his reward, which I will add

To you, the liver, heart, and brain of Britain,
                    [*To* BEL., GUI., *and* ARV.
By whom I grant she lives. 'Tis now the time
To ask of whence you are:—report it.
    *Bel.*                              Sir,
In Cambria are we born, and gentlemen:
Further to boast were neither true nor modest,
Unless I add we are honest.
    *Cym.*                        Bow your knees.
Arise my knights o' the battle: I create you
Companions to our person, and will fit you
With dignities becoming your estates.

        *Enter* CORNELIUS *and* Ladies.

There's business in these faces.—Why so sadly
Greet you our victory? you look like Romans,
And not o' the court of Britain.
    *Cor.*                      Hail, great king!
To sour your happiness, I must report
The queen is dead.
    *Cym.*          Who worse than a physician
Would this report become? But I consider
By medicine life may be prolong'd, yet death
Will seize the doctor too.—How ended she?
    *Cor.* With horror, madly dying, like her
        life;
Which, being cruel to the world, concluded
Most cruel to herself. What she confess'd
I will report, so please you: these her women
Can trip me if I err; who with wet cheeks
Were present when she finish'd.
    *Cym.*                        Pr'ythee, say.
    *Cor.* First, she confess'd she never lov'd
        you; only
Affected greatness got by you, not you:
Married your royalty, was wife to your
        place;
Abhorr'd your person.
    *Cym.*              She alone knew this;
And but she spoke it dying, I would not
Believe her lips in opening it. Proceed.
    *Cor.* Your daughter, whom she bore in
        hand to love
With such integrity, she did confess
Was as a scorpion to her sight; whose life,
But that her flight prevented it, she had
Ta'en off by poison.
    *Cym.*          O most delicate fiend!
Who is't can read a woman?—Is there more?
    *Cor.* More, sir, and worse. She did confess
        she had
For you a mortal mineral; which, being took,
Should by the minute feed on life, and linger-
        ing,
By inches waste you: in which time she pur-
        pos'd,
By watching, weeping, tendance, kissing, to
O'ercome you with her show; and in time,
When she had fitted you with her craft, to
        work
Her son into the adoption of the crown:
But, failing of her end by his strange absence,
Grew shameless-desperate; open'd, in despite
Of heaven and men, her purposes; repented

The evils she hatch'd were not effected; so,
Despairing, died.
    *Cym.* Heard you all this, her women?
    1 *Lady.* We did, so please your highness.
    *Cym.*                          Mine eyes
Were not in fault, for she was beautiful;
Mine ears, that heard her flattery; nor my
        heart
That thought her like her seeming; it had
        been vicious
To have mistrusted her: yet, O my daughter!
That it was folly in me thou mayst say,
And prove it in thy feeling. Heaven mend all!

*Enter* LUCIUS, IACHIMO, *the* Soothsayer, *and
    other* Roman Prisoners, *guarded;* POSTHU-
    MUS *behind, and* IMOGEN.

Thou com'st not, Caius, now for tribute; that
The Britons have raz'd out, though with the
        loss                            [made suit
Of many a bold one, whose kinsmen have
That their good souls may be appeas'd with
        slaughter                      [granted:
Of you their captives, which ourself have
So, think of your estate.              [day
    *Luc.* Consider, sir, the chance of war: the
Was yours by accident; had it gone with us
We should not, when the blood was cool,
        have threaten'd
Our prisoners with the sword. But since the
        gods
Will have it thus, that nothing but our lives
May be call'd ransom, let it come: sufficeth
A Roman with a Roman's heart can suffer;
Augustus lives to think on't: and so much
For my peculiar care. This one thing only
I will entreat; my boy, a Briton born,
Let him be ransom'd; never master had
A page so kind, so duteous, diligent,
So tender over his occasions, true,
So feat, so nurse-like: let his virtue join
With my request which I'll make bold your
        highness
Cannot deny; he hath done no Briton harm
Though he have serv'd a Roman: save him,
        sir,
And spare no blood beside.
    *Cym.*        I have surely seen him:
His favour is familiar to me.—
Boy, thou hast look'd thyself into my grace,
And art mine own.—I know not why nor
        wherefore
To say live, boy: ne'er thank thy master;
        live:
And ask of Cymbeline what boom thou wilt,
Fitting my bounty and thy state, I'll give it;
Yea, though thou do demand a prisoner,
The noblest ta'en.
    *Imo.*      I humbly thank your highness.
    *Luc.* I do not bid thee beg my life, good
        lad;
And yet I know thou wilt.
    *Imo.*                No, no: alack,
There's other work in hand: I see a thing

Bitter to me as death: your life, good master,
Must shuffle for itself.
　　*Luc.*　　　　　　The boy disdains me,
He leaves me, scorns me: briefly die their joys
That place them on the truth of girls and
　　boys.—
Why stands he so perplex'd?
　　*Cym.*　　　　　　What wouldst thou, boy?
I love thee more and more: think more and
　　more　　　　　[on? speak,
What's best to ask. Know'st him thou look'st
Wilt have him live? Is he thy kin? thy
　　friend?
　　*Imo.* He is a Roman; no more kin to me
Than I to your highness; who, being born
　　your vassal,
Am something nearer.
　　*Cym.*　　　　　Wherefore ey'st him so?
　　*Imo.* I'll tell you, sir, in private, if you
　　please
To give me hearing.
　　*Cym.*　　　　　Ay, with all my heart,
And lend my best attention. What's thy
　　name?
　　*Imo.* Fidele, sir.
　　*Cym.*　　Thou'rt my good youth, my page;
I'll be thy master: walk with me; speak
　　freely.
　　　　　　[CYM. *and* IMO. *converse apart.*
　　*Bel.* Is not this boy reviv'd from death?
　　*Arv.*　　　　　　One sand another
Not more resembles that sweet rosy lad
Who died, and was Fidele.—What think you?
　　*Gui.* The same dead thing alive.
　　*Bel.* Peace, peace! see further; he eyes us
　　not; forbear;
Creatures may be alike: were't he, I am sure
He would have spoke to us.
　　*Gui.*　　　　　But we saw him dead.
　　*Bel.* Be silent; let's see further.
　　*Pis.* [*Aside.*]　　　　It is my mistress:
Since she is living, let the time run on
To good or bad.
　　　　　　[CYM. *and* IMO. *come forward.*
　　*Cym.*　　Come, stand thou by our side;
Make thy demand aloud.—[*To* IACH.] Sir,
　　step you forth;
Give answer to this boy, and do it freely;
Or, by our greatness and the grace of it,
Which is our honour, bitter torture shall
Winnow the truth from falsehood.—On,
　　speak to him.　　　　　　[render
　　*Imo.* My boon is that this gentleman may
Of whom he had this ring.
　　*Post.* [*Aside.*]　　What's that to him?
　　*Cym.* That diamond upon your finger, say,
How came it yours?　　　　　　[that
　　*Iach.* Thou'lt torture me to leave unspoken
Which to be spoke would torture thee.
　　*Cym.*　　　　　　How! me?
　　*Iach.* I am glad to be constrain'd to utter
　　that which
Torments me to conceal. By villany
I got this ring: 'twas Leonatus' jewel,

Whom thou didst banish; and,—which more
　　may grieve thee,
As it doth me,—a nobler sir ne'er liv'd
'Twixt sky and ground. Wilt thou hear more,
　　my lord?
　　*Cym.* All that belongs to this.
　　*Iach.*　　　That paragon, thy daughter,—
For whom my heart drops blood, and, my
　　false spirits
Quail to remember,—Give me leave; I faint.
　　*Cym.* My daughter! what of her? Renew
　　thy strength:
I had rather thou shouldst live while nature
　　will
Than die ere I hear more: strive, man, and
　　speak.
　　*Iach.* Upon a time,—unhappy was the
　　clock
That struck the hour!—it was in Rome,—ac-
　　curs'd　　　　　　　　　　[would
The mansion where!—'twas at a feast,—O,
Our viands had been poison'd, or at least
Those which I heav'd to head!—the good
　　Posthumus,—
What should I say? he was too good to be
Where ill men were; and was the best of all
Amongst the rar'st of good ones,—sitting
　　sadly,
Hearing us praise our loves of Italy
For beauty that made barren the swell'd boast
Of him that best could speak; for feature
　　laming
The shrine of Venus, or straight-pight Min-
　　erva,
Postures beyond brief nature; for condition,
A shop of all the qualities that man
Loves woman for; besides that hook of
　　wiving,
Fairness which strikes the eye,—
　　*Cym.*　　　　　　I stand on fire:
Come to the matter.
　　*Iach.*　　　　　All too soon I shall,
Unless thou wouldst grieve quickly.—This
　　Posthumus,—
Most like a noble lord in love, and one
That had a royal lover,—took his hint;
And not dispraising whom we prais'd,—there-
　　in
He was as calm as virtue,—he began
His mistress' picture; which by his tongue
　　being made,
And then a mind put in't, either our brags
Were crack'd of kitchen trulls, or his descrip-
　　tion
Prov'd us unspeaking sots.
　　*Cym.*　　　　　Nay, nay, to the purpose.
　　*Iach.* Your daughter's chastity—there it
　　begins.
He spake of her as Dian had hot dreams
And she alone were cold: whereat I, wretch,
Made scruple of his praise; and wager'd with
　　him
Pieces of gold, 'gainst this, which then he
　　wore

Upon his honour'd finger, to attain
In suit the place of's bed, and win this ring
By hers and mine adultery: he, true knight,
No lesser of her honour confident
Than I did truly find her, stakes this ring;
And would so, had it been a carbuncle
Of Phœbus' wheel; and might so safely, had
  it
Been all the worth of's car. Away to Britain
Post I in this design. Well may you, sir,
Remember me at court, where I was taught
Of your chaste daughter the wide difference
'Twixt amorous and villanous. Being thus
  quench'd
Of hope, not longing, mine Italian brain
'Gan in your duller Britain operate
Most vilely,—for my vantage excellent;
And, to be brief, my practice so prevail'd
That I return'd with simular proof enough
To make the noble Leonatus mad,
By wounding his belief in her renown
With tokens thus and thus; averring notes
Of chamber-hanging, pictures, this her brace-
  let,—
O cunning how I got it!—nay, some marks
Of secret on her person, that he could not
But think her bond of chastity quite crack'd,
I having ta'en the forfeit. Whereupon,—
Methinks I see him now,—

*Post.* [*Coming forward.*] Ay, so thou dost,
Italian fiend!—Ah me, most credulous fool,
Egregious murderer, thief, anything
That's due to all the villains past, in being,
To come!—O, give me cord, or knife, or
  poison,
Some upright justicer! Thou, king, send out
For torturers ingenious: it is I    [amend
That all the abhorred things o' the earth
By being worse than they. I am Posthumus,
That kill'd thy daughter:—villain-like, I lie,—
That caus'd a lesser villain than myself,
A sacrilegious thief, to do't:—the temple
Of virtue was she; yea, and she herself.
Spit, and throw stones, cast mire upon me, set
The dogs o' the street to bay me: every villain
Be call'd Posthumus Leonatus; and
Be villany less than 'twas!—O Imogen!
My queen, my life, my wife! O Imogen,
Imogen, Imogen!

*Imo.*            Peace, my lord; hear, hear,—
*Post.* Shall's have a play of this? Thou
  scornful page,
There lie thy part.    [*Striking her: she falls.*
*Pis.*            O, gentlemen, help! [mus!
Mine and your mistress!—O, my lord Posthu-
You ne'er kill'd Imogen till now.—Help,
  help!—
Mine honour'd lady!
*Cym.*            Does the world go round?
*Post.* How come these staggers on me?
*Pis.*            Wake, my mistress!
*Cym.* If this be so, the gods do mean to
  strike me
To death with mortal joy.

*Pis.*            How fares my mistress?
*Imo.* O, get thee from my sight;
Thou gav'st me poison: dangerous fellow,
  hence!
Breathe not where princes are.
*Cym.*            The tune of Imogen.
*Pis.* Lady,
The gods throw stones of sulphur on me if
That box I gave you was not thought by me
A precious thing: I had it from the queen.
*Cym.* New matter still?
*Imo.*            It poison'd me.
*Cor.*            O gods!—
I left out one thing which the queen confess'd,
Which must approve thee honest: *If Pisanio
Have,* said she, *given his mistress that con-
  fection
Which I gave him for cordial, she is serv'd
As I would serve a rat.*
*Cym.*            What's this, Cornelius?
*Cor.* The queen, sir, very oft importun'd
  me
To temper poisons for her; still pretending
The satisfaction of her knowledge only
In killing creatures vile, as cats and dogs,
Of no esteem: I, dreading that her purpose
Was of more danger, did compound for her
A certain stuff, which, being ta'en, would
  cease
The present power of life; but in short time
All offices of nature should again
Do their due functions.—Have you ta'en of it?
*Imo.* Most like I did, for I was dead.
*Bel.*            My boys,
There was our error.
*Gui.*            This is sure Fidele.
*Imo.* Why did you throw your wedded
  lady from you?
Think that you are upon a rock; and now
Throw me again.    [*Embracing him.*
*Post.*            Hang there like fruit, my soul,
Till the tree die!
*Cym.*            How now, my flesh, my child!
What, mak'st thou me a dullard in this act?
Wilt thou not speak to me?
*Imo.*            Your blessing, sir.
            [*Kneeling.*
*Bel.* Though you did love this youth, I
  blame ye not;
You had a motive for it.
      [*To* Guiderius *and* Arviragus.
*Cym.*            My tears that fall
Prove holy water on thee! Imogen,
Thy mother's dead.
*Imo.*            I am sorry for't, my lord.
*Cym.* O, she was naught; and long of her
  it was
That we meet here so strangely: but her
  son
Is gone, we know not how nor where.
*Pis.*            My lord,
Now fear is from me, I'll speak troth. Lord
  Cloten,
Upon my lady's missing, came to me

With his sword drawn; foam'd at the mouth,
    and swore,
If I discover'd not which way she was gone,
It was my instant death. By accident
I had a feigned letter of my master's
Then in my pocket; which directed him
To seek her on the mountains near to Milford;
Where, in a frenzy, in my master's garments,
Which he enforc'd from me, away he posts
With unchaste purpose, and with oath to
    violate
My lady's honour: what became of him
I further know not.
    *Gui.*            Let me end the story:
I slew him there.
    *Cym.*            Marry, the gods forfend!
I would not thy good deeds should from my
    lips
Pluck a hard sentence: pr'ythee, valiant
    youth,
Deny't again.
    *Gui.*        I have spoke it, and I did it.
    *Cym.* He was a prince.              [me
    *Gui.* A most incivil one: the wrongs he did
Were nothing prince-like; for he did provoke
    me                                  [sea,
With language that would make me spurn the
If it could so roar to me: I cut off's head;
And am right glad he is not standing here
To tell this tale of mine.
    *Cym.*            I am sorry for thee:
By thine own tongue thou art condemn'd, and
    must
Endure our law: thou'rt dead.
    *Imo.*            That headless man
I thought had been my lord.
    *Cym.*            Bind the offender,
And take him from our presence.
    *Bel.*            Stay, sir king:
This man is better than the man he slew,
As well descended as thyself; and hath
More of thee merited than a band of Clotens
Had ever scar for.—Let his arms alone;
                        [*To the* Guard.
They were not born for bondage.
    *Cym.*            Why, old soldier,
Wilt thou undo the worth thou art unpaid for
By tasting of our wrath? How of descent
As good as we?
    *Arv.*        In that he spake too far.
    *Cym.* And thou shalt die for't.
    *Bel.*            We will die all three:
But I will prove that two on's are as good
As I have given out him.—My sons, I must,
For mine own part, unfold a dangerous
    speech,
Though, haply well for you.
    *Arv.*            Your danger's
Ours.
    *Gui.* And our good his.
    *Bel.*            Have at it, then!—
By leave,—thou hadst, great king, a subject
    who
Was call'd Belarius.

    *Cym.*            What of him? he is
A banish'd traitor.
    *Bel.*            He it is that hath
Assum'd this age: indeed, a banish'd man;
I know not how a traitor.
    *Cym.*            Take him hence:
The whole world shall not save him.
    *Bel.*            Not too hot:
First pay me for the nursing of thy sons;
And let it be confiscate all so soon,
As I have receiv'd it.
    *Cym.*            Nursing of my sons!
    *Bel.* I am too blunt and saucy: here's my
    knee:
Ere I arise I will prefer my sons;
Then spare not the old father. Mighty sir,
These two young gentlemen, that call me
    father,
And think they are my sons, are none of mine;
They are the issue of your loins, my liege,
And blood of your begetting.
    *Cym.*            How! my issue!
    *Bel.* So sure as you your father's. I, old
    Morgan,
Am that Belarius whom you sometime ban-
    ish'd.
Your pleasure was my mere offence, my pun-
    ishment
Itself, and all my treason; that I suffer'd
Was all the harm I did. These gentle
    princes,—
For such and so they are,—these twenty years
Have I train'd up: those arts they have as I
Could put into them; my breeding was, sir, as
Your highness knows. Their nurse, Euriphile,
Whom for the theft I wedded, stole these
    children
Upon my banishment: I mov'd her to't;
Having receiv'd the punishment before
For that which I did then: beaten for loyalty
Excited me to treason: their dear loss,
The more of you 'twas felt, the more it shap'd
Unto my end of stealing them. But, gracious
    sir,
Here are your sons again; and I must lose
Two of the sweet'st companions in the
    world:—
The benediction of these covering heavens
Fall on their heads like dew! for they are
    worthy
To inlay heaven with stars.
    *Cym.*            Thou weep'st, and speak'st.
The service that you three have done is
    more
Unlike than this thou tell'st. I lost my chil-
    dren:
If these be they, I know not how to wish
A pair of worthier sons.
    *Bel.*            Be pleas'd awhile.—
This gentleman, whom I call Polydore,
Most worthy prince, as yours, is true Gui-
    derius:
This gentleman, my Cadwal, Arviragus,
Your younger princely son; he, sir, was lapp'd

In a most curious mantle, wrought by the
    hand
Of his queen mother, which, for more proba-
    tion,
I can with ease produce.

*Cym.*            Guiderius had
Upon his neck a mole, a sanguine star;
It was a mark of wonder.

*Bel.*            This is he;
Who hath upon him still that natural stamp:
It was wise nature's end in the donation,
To be his evidence now.

*Cym.*            O, what, am I
A mother to the birth of three? Ne'er mother
Rejoic'd deliverance more.—Bless'd may you
    be,
That, after this strange starting from your
    orbs,
You may reign in them now!—O Imogen,
Thou hast lost by this a kingdom.

*Imo.*            No, my lord;
I have got two worlds by't.—O my gentle
    brothers,
Have we thus met? O, never say hereafter
But I am truest speaker: you call'd me
    brother
When I was but your sister; I you brothers
When you were so indeed.

*Cym.*            Did you e'er meet?

*Arv.* Ay, my good lord.

*Gui.*            And at first meeting lov'd;
Continued so until we thought he died.

*Cor.* By the queen's dram she swallow'd.

*Cym.*            O rare instinct!
When shall I hear all through? This fierce
    abridgment
Hath to it circumstantial branches, which
Distinction should be rich in.—Where? how
    liv'd you?
And when came you to serve our Roman
    captive?
How parted with your brothers? how first
    met them?
Why fled you from the court? and whither?
    These,
And your three motives to the battle, with
I know not how much more, should be de-
    manded;
And all the other by-dependencies,   [place
From chance to chance: but nor the time nor
Will serve our long inter'gatories. See,
Posthumus anchors upon Imogen;
And she, like harmless lightning, throws her
    eye
On him, her brothers, me, her master; hitting
Each object with a joy: the counterchange
Is severally in all.—Let's quit this ground,
And smoke the temple with our sacrifices.—
Thou art my brother; so we'll hold thee ever.
                         [*To* BELARIUS.

*Imo.* You are my father too; and did re-
    lieve me,
To see this gracious season.

*Cym.*            All o'erjoy'd.

Save these in bonds: let them be joyful too,
For they shall taste our comfort.

*Imo.*            My good master,
I will yet do you service.

*Luc.*            Happy be you!

*Cym.* The forlorn soldier, that so nobly
    fought,
He would have well becom'd this place, and
    grac'd
The thankings of a king.

*Post.*            I am, sir,
The soldier that did company these three
In poor beseeming; 'twas a fitment for
The purpose I then follow'd.—That I was he,
Speak, Iachimo: I had you down, and might
Have made you finish.

*Iach.*            I am down again: [*Kneeling.*
But now my heavy conscience sinks my knee,
As then your force did. Take that life, be-
    seech you,
Which I so often owe: but your ring first;
And here the bracelet of the truest princess
That ever swore her faith.

*Post.*            Kneel not to me:
The power that I have on you is to spare you;
The malice towards you to forgive you: live,
And deal with others better.

*Cym.*            Nobly doom'd!
We'll learn our freeness of a son-in-law;
Pardon's the word to all.

*Arv.*            You holp us, sir,
As you did mean indeed to be our brother;
Joy'd are we that you are.

*Post.* Your servant, princes.—Good my lord
    of Rome,
Call forth your soothsayer: as I slept, me-
    thought
Great Jupiter, upon his eagle back,
Appear'd to me, with other spritely shows
Of mine own kindred: when I wak'd I found
This label on my bosom; whose containing
Is so from sense in hardness that I can
Make no collection of it: let him show
His skill in the construction.

*Luc.*            Philarmonus,—

*Sooth.* Here, my good lord.

*Luc.*            Read, and declare the meaning.

*Sooth.* [*Reads.*] *When as a lion's whelp
shall to himself unknown, without seeking
find, and be embraced by a piece of tender
air; and when from a stately cedar shall be
lopped branches, which, being dead many
years, shall after revive, be jointed to the old
stock, and freshly grow; then shall Posthumus end his miseries, Britain be fortunate,
and flourish in peace and plenty.*
Thou, Leonatus, art the lion's whelp;
The fit and apt construction of thy name,
Being Leo-natus, doth import so much:
The piece of tender air, thy virtuous daughter,
                         [*To* CYMBELINE.
Which we call *mollis aer;* and *mollis aer*
We term it *mulier:* which *mulier* I divine
Is his most constant wife: who even now,

Answering the letter of the oracle,
Unknown to you, unsought, were clipp'd
　　about
With this most tender air.
　*Cym.*　　　　　　This hath some seeming.
　*Sooth.* The lofty cedar, royal Cymbeline,
Personates thee: and thy lopp'd branches
　　point
Thy two sons forth, who, by Belarius stol'n,
For many years thought dead, are now re-
　　viv'd,
To the majestic cedar join'd; whose issue
Promises Britain peace and plenty.
　*Cym.*　　　　　　　　　　Well,
By peace we will begin:— and, Caius Lucius,
Although the victor, we submit to Cæsar,
And to the Roman empire; promising
To pay our wonted tribute, from the which
We were dissuaded by our wicked queen;
Whom heavens, in justice both on hers and
　　hers,
Have laid most heavy hand.
　*Sooth.* The fingers of the powers above do
　　tune

The harmony of this peace. The vision,
Which I made known to Lucius ere the stroke
Of this yet scarce-cold battle, at this instant,
Is full accomplish'd; for the Roman eagle,
From south to west on wing soaring aloft,
Lessen'd herself, and in the beams o' the sun
So vanish'd: which foreshow'd our princely
　　eagle,
The imperial Cæsar, should again unite
His favour with the radiant Cymbeline,
Which shines here in the west.
　*Cym.*　　　　　　　　Laud we the gods;
And let our crooked smokes climb to their
　　nostrils
From our bless'd altars. Publish we this peace
To all our subjects. Set we forward: let
A Roman and a British ensign wave
Friendly together: so through Lud's town
　　march:
And in the temple of great Jupiter
Our peace we'll ratify; seal it with feasts.—
Set on there!—Never was a war did cease.
Ere bloody hands were wash'd, with such a
　　peace.　　　　　　　　　　　[*Exeunt.*

Act III. Sc. 1.

# TITUS ANDRONICUS

## DRAMATIS PERSONÆ

SATURNINUS, *Son to the late Emperor of Rome, and afterwards declared Emperor.*
BASSIANUS, *Brother to* SATURNINUS, *in love with* LAVINIA.
TITUS ANDRONICUS, *a noble Roman, General against the Goths.*
MARCUS ANDRONICUS, *Tribune of the People, and Brother to* TITUS.
LUCIUS,
QUINTUS,
MARTIUS,
MUTIUS, } *Sons to* TITUS ANDRONICUS.
YOUNG LUCIUS, *a Boy, Son to* LUCIUS.
PUBLIUS, *Son to* MARCUS *the Tribune.*

ÆMILIUS, *a noble Roman.*
ALARBUS,
DEMETRIUS, } *Sons to* TAMORA.
CHIRON,
AARON, *a Moor, beloved by* TAMORA.
A Captain, Tribune, Messenger, *and* Clown,
—*Romans.*
Goths *and* Romans.

TAMORA, *Queen of the Goths.*
LAVINIA, *Daughter to* TITUS ANDRONICUS.
A Nurse, *and a black* Child.

Kinsmen of TITUS, Senators, Tribunes, Officers, Soldiers, *and* Attendants.

SCENE,—ROME, *and the Country near it.*

## ACT I.

### SCENE I.—ROME. *Before the Capitol.*

*The Tomb of the* ANDRONICI *appearing; the* Tribunes *and* Senators *aloft. Enter, below,* SATURNINUS *and his* Followers *on one side, and* BASSIANUS *and his* Followers *on the other, with drums and colours.*

*Sat.* Noble patricians, patrons of my right,
Defend the justice of my cause with arms;
And, countrymen, my loving followers,
Plead my successive title with your swords:
I am his first-born son that was the last
That wore the imperial diadem of Rome:
Then let my father's honours live in me,
Nor wrong mine age with this indignity.
*Bas.* Romans,—friends, followers, favourers of my right,—
If ever Bassianus, Cæsar's son,
Were gracious in the eyes of royal Rome,
Keep, then, this passage to the Capitol;
And suffer not dishonour to approach
The imperial seat, to virtue consecrate,
To justice, continence, and nobility;
But let desert in pure election shine;
And, Romans, fight for freedom in your choice.

*Enter* MARCUS ANDRONICUS *aloft, with the crown.*

*Marc.* Princes,—that strive by factions and by friends
Ambitiously for rule and empery,— [stand
Know that the people of Rome, for whom we
A special party, have by common voice,
In election for the Roman empery,
Chosen Andronicus, surnamed Pius
For many good and great deserts to Rome:

A nobler man, a braver warrior,
Lives not this day within the city walls:
He by the senate is accited home
From weary wars against the barbarious Goths;
That, with his sons, a terror to our foes,
Hath yok'd a nation strong, train'd up in arms.
Ten years are spent since first he undertook
This cause of Rome, and chastised with arms
Our enemies' pride: five times he hath return'd
Bleeding to Rome, bearing his valiant sons
In coffins from the field;
And now at last, laden with honour's spoils,
Returns the good Andronicus to Rome,
Renowned Titus, flourishing in arms.
Let us entreat,—by honour of his name
Whom worthily you would have now succeed,
And in the Capitol and senate's right,
Whom you pretend to honour and adore,—
That you withdraw you, and abate your strength;
Dismiss your followers, and, as suitors should,
Plead your deserts in peace and humbleness.
*Sat.* How fair the tribune speaks to calm my thoughts!
*Bas.* Marcus Andronicus, so I do affy
In thy uprightness and integrity,
And so I love and honour thee and thine,
Thy noble brother Titus and his sons,
And her to whom my thoughts are humbled all,
Gracious Lavinia, Rome's rich ornament,
That I will here dismiss my loving friends;
And to my fortunes and the people's favour
Commit my cause in balance to be weigh'd.
[*Exeunt the* Followers *of* BAS.

*Sat.* Friends, that have been thus forward
  in my right,
I thank you all, and here dismiss you all;
And to the love and favour of my country
Commit myself, my person, and the cause.
  [*Exeunt the* Followers *of* SAT.
Rome, be as just and gracious unto me
As I am confident and kind to thee.—
Open the gates, tribunes, and let me in.
  *Bas.* Tribunes, and me, a poor competitor.
  [*Flourish. Exeunt;* SAT. *and* BAS. *go up
    into the Capitol.*

### Enter a Captain.

  *Cap.* Romans, make way. The good An-
  dronicus,
Patron of virtue, Rome's best champion,
Successful in the battles that he fights,
With honour and with fortune is return'd
From where he circumscribed with his sword,
And brought to yoke, the enemies of Rome.

*Flourish of trumpets, &c. Enter* MARTIUS
*and* MUTIUS; *after them two* Men *bearing
a coffin covered with black; then* LUCIUS
*and* QUINTUS. *After them* TITUS ANDRONI-
CUS; *and then* TAMORA, *with* ALARBUS,
DEMETRIUS, CHIRON, AARON, *and other*
Goths, *prisoners;* Soldiers *and* People *following. The bearers set down the coffin,
and* TITUS *speaks.*

  *Tit.* Hail, Rome, victorious in thy mourn-
  ing weeds!
Lo, as the bark that hath discharg'd her
  fraught
Returns with precious lading to the bay
From whence at first she weigh'd her an-
  chorage,
Cometh Andronicus, bound with laurel
  boughs,
To re-salute his country with his tears,—
Tears of true joy for his return to Rome.—
Thou great defender of this Capitol,
Stand gracious to the rites that we intend!—
Romans, of five-and-twenty valiant sons,
Half of the number that King Priam had,
Behold the poor remains, alive and dead!
These that survive let Rome reward with
  love;
These that I bring unto their latest home,
With burial amongst their ancestors:
Here Goths have given me leave to sheathe my
  sword.
Titus, unkind, and careless of thine own,
Why suffer'st thou thy sons, unburied yet,
To hover on the dreadful shore of Styx?—
Make way to lay them by their brethren.—
  [*The tomb is opened.*
There greet in silence, as the dead are wont,
And sleep in peace, slain in your country's
  wars!
O sacred receptacle of my joys,
Sweet cell of virtue and nobility,
How many sons of mine hast thou in store,

That thou wilt never render to me more!
  *Luc.* Give us the proudest prisoner of the
  Goths,
That we may hew his limbs, and on a pile
*Ad manes fratrum* sacrifice his flesh
Before this earthly prison of their bones;
That so the shadows be not unappeas'd,
Nor we disturb'd with prodigies on earth.
  *Tit.* I give him you,—the noblest that sur-
  vives,
The eldest son of this distressed queen.
  *Tam.* Stay, Roman brethren!—Gracious
  conqueror,
Victorious Titus, rue the tears I shed,
A mother's tears in passion for her son:
And if thy sons were ever dear to thee,
O, think my son to be as dear to me!
Sufficeth not that we are brought to Rome,
To beautify thy triumphs and return,
Captive to thee and to thy Roman yoke;
But must my sons be slaughter'd in the streets
For valiant doings in their country's cause?
O, if to fight for king and common weal
Were piety in thine, it is in these.
Andronicus, stain not thy tomb with blood:
Wilt thou draw near the nature of the gods?
Draw near them, then, in being merciful:
Sweet mercy is nobility's true badge:
Thrice-noble Titus, spare my first-born son.
  *Tit.* Patient yourself, madam, and pardon
  me.                     [beheld
These are their brethren, whom you Goths
Alive and dead; and for their brethren slain
Religiously they ask a sacrifice:
To this your son is mark'd; and die he must,
To appease their groaning shadows that are
  gone.
  *Luc.* Away with him! and make a fire
  straight;
And with our swords, upon a pile of wood
Let's hew his limbs till they be clean con-
  sum'd.
  [*Exeunt* LUC., QUIN., MARC., *and* MUT.,
    *with* ALARBUS.
  *Tam.* O cruel, irreligious piety!
  *Chi.* Was ever Scythia half so barbarous?
  *Dem.* Oppose not Scythia to ambitious
  Rome.
Alarbus goes to rest; and we survive
To tremble under Titus' threatening looks.
Then, madam, stand resolv'd; but hope withal
The self-same gods that arm'd the Queen of
  Troy
With opportunity of sharp revenge
Upon the Thracian tyrant in his tent,
May favour Tamora, the Queen of Goths,—
When Goths were Goths and Tamora was
  queen,—
To quit the bloody wrongs upon her foes.

*Re-enter* LUCIUS, QUINTAS, MARTIUS, *and*
  MUTIUS, *with their swords bloody.*

  *Luc.* See, lord and father, how we have
  perform'd

Our Roman rites: Alarbus' limbs are lopp'd,
And entrails feed the sacrificing fire,
Whose smoke like incense doth perfume the
    sky.
Remaineth naught but to inter our brethren,
And with loud 'larums welcome them to
    Rome.
  *Tit.* Let it be so, and let Andronicus
Make this his latest farewell to their souls.
  [*Trumpets sounded and the coffin laid in
    the tomb.*
In peace and honour rest you here, my sons;
Rome's readiest champions, repose you here
    in rest,
Secure from worldly chances and mishaps!
Here lurks no treason, here no envy swells,
Here grow no damned grudges; here are no
    storms,
No noise, but silence and eternal sleep:

*Enter* LAVINIA.

In peace and honour rest you here, my sons!
  *Lav.* In peace and honour live Lord Titus
    long;
My noble lord and father, live in fame!
Lo, at this tomb my tributary tears
I render for my brethren's obsequies;
And at thy feet I kneel, with tears of joy
Shed on the earth for thy return to Rome:
O, bless me here with thy victorious hand,
Whose fortunes Rome's best citizens applaud!
  *Tit.* Kind Rome, that hast thus lovingly
    reserv'd
The cordial of mine age to glad my heart!—
Lavinia, live; outlive thy father's days,
And fame's eternal date, for virtue's praise!

*Enter; below,* MARCUS ANDRONICUS *and* Tribunes; *re-enter* SATURNINUS, BASSIANUS,
  *and* Attendants.

  *Marc.* Long live Lord Titus, my beloved
    brother,
Gracious triúmpher in the eyes of Rome!
  *Tit.* Thanks, gentle tribune, noble brother
    Marcus.                        [cessful wars,
  *Marc.* And welcome, nephews, from suc-
You that survive and you that sleep in fame!
Fair lords, your fortunes are alike in all,
That in your country's service drew your
    swords:
But safer triumph is this funeral pomp
That hath aspir'd to Solon's happiness,
And triumphs over chance in honour's bed.—
Titus Andronicus, the people of Rome,
Whose friend in justice thou hast ever been,
Send thee by me, their tribune and their
    trust,
This palliament of white and spotless hue;
And name thee in election for the empire
With these our late-deceased emperor's sons:
Be *candidatus,* then, and put it on,
And help to set a head on headless Rome.
  *Tit.* A better head her glorious body fits
Than his that shakes for age and feebleness:

What, should I don this robe and trouble you?
Be chosen with proclamations to-day,
To-morrow yield up rule, resign my life,
And set abroach new business for you all?
Rome, I have been thy soldier forty years,
And led by country's strength successfully,
And buried one-and-twenty valiant sons,
Knighted in field, slain manfully in arms,
In right and service of their noble country:
Give me a staff of honour for mine age,
But not a sceptre to control the world:
Upright he held it, lords, that held it last.
  *Marc.* Titus, thou shalt obtain and ask the
    empery.
  *Sat.* Proud and ambitious tribune, canst
    thou tell?
  *Tit.* Patience, Prince Saturninus.
  *Sat.*                    Romans, do me right;—
Patricians, draw your swords, and sheathe
    them not
Till Saturninus be Rome's emperor.—
Andronicus, would thou wert shipp'd to hell
Rather than rob me of the people's hearts!
  *Luc.* Proud Saturnine, interrupter of the
    good
That noble-minded Titus means to thee!
  *Tit.* Content thee, prince; I will restore to
    thee                        [themselves.
The people's hearts, and wean them from
  *Bas.* Andronicus, I do not flatter thee,
But honour thee, and will do till I die:
My faction if thou strengthen with thy
    friends,
I will most thankful be; and thanks to men
Of noble minds is honourable meed.   [here,
  *Tit.* People of Rome, and people's tribunes
I ask your voices and your suffrages:
Will you bestow them friendly on Androni-
    cus?
  *Trib.* To gratify the good Andronicus,
And gratulate his safe return to Rome,
The people will accept whom he admits.
  *Tit.* Tribunes, I thank you: and this suit I
    make,
That you create your emperor's eldest son,
Lord Saturnine; whose virtues will, I hope,
Reflect on Rome as Titan's rays on earth,
And ripen justice in this commonweal:
Then, if you will elect by my advice,
Crown him, and say, *Long live our emperor!*
  *Marc.* With voices and applause of every
    sort,
Patricians and plebeians, we create
Lord Saturninus Rome's great emperor;
And say, *Long live our emperor Saturnine!*
                          [*A long flourish.*
  *Sat.* Titus Andronicus, for thy favours done
To us in our election this day
I give thee thanks in part of thy deserts,
And will with deeds requite thy gentleness;
And for an onset, Titus, to advance
Thy name and honourable family,
Lavinia will I make my empress,
Rome's royal mistress, mistress of my heart,

And in the sacred Pantheon her espouse:
Tell me, Andronicus, doth this motion please
　　thee?　　　　　　　　　　　　[match

*Tit.* It doth, my worthy lord; and in this
I hold me highly honour'd of your grace:
And here, in sight of Rome, to Saturnine,—
King and commander of our commonweal,
The wide world's emperor,—do I consecrate
My sword, my chariot, and my prisoners;
Presents well worthy Rome's imperial lord:
Receive them, then, the tribute that I owe,
Mine honour's ensigns humbled at thy feet.

*Sat.* Thanks, noble Titus, father of my
　　life!
How proud I am of thee and of thy gifts
Rome shall record; and when I do forget
The least of these unspeakable deserts,
Romans, forget your fealty to me.

*Tit.* [*To* TAMORA.] Now, madam, are you
　　prisoner to an emperor;
To him that for your honour and your state
Will use you nobly and your followers.

*Sat.* A goodly lady, trust me; of the hue
That I would choose were I to choose anew.—
Clear up, fair queen, that cloudy countenance,
Though chance of war hath wrought this
　　change of cheer,
Thou com'st not to be made a scorn in Rome:
Princely shall be thy usage every way.
Rest on my word, and let not discontent
Daunt all your hopes: madam, he comforts
　　you
Can make you greater than the Queen of
　　Goths.—
Lavinia, you are not displeas'd with this?

*Lav.* Not I, my lord; sith true nobility
Warrants these words in princely courtesy.

*Sat.* Thanks, sweet Lavinia.—Romans, let
　　us go:
Ransomless here we set our prisoners free:
Proclaim our honours, lords, with trump and
　　drum.

　　　[*Flourish.* SAT. *courts* TAMORA *in
　　　　dumb show.*

*Bas.* Lord Titus, by your leave, this maid
　　is mine.　　　　　　[*Seizing* LAVINIA.

*Tit.* How, sir! are you in earnest, then,
　　my lord?

*Bas.* Ay, noble Titus; and resolv'd withal
To do myself this reason and this right.

*Marc. Suum cuique* is our Roman justice:
This prince in justice seizeth but his own.

*Luc.* And that he will and shall, if Lucius
　　live.　　　　　　　　　[peror's guard?—

*Tit.* Traitors, avaunt!—Where is the em-
Treason, my lord,—Lavinia is surpris'd!

*Sat.* Surpris'd! by whom?

*Bas.*　　　　　By him that justly may
Bear his betroth'd from all the world away.

　　　[*Exeunt* BAS. *and* MAR. *with* LAV.

*Mut.* Brothers, help to convey her hence
　　away,
And with my sword I'll keep this door safe.

　　　[*Exeunt* LUC., QUIN., *and* MAR.

*Tit.* Follow, my lord, and I'll soon bring
　　her back.

*Mut.* My lord, you pass not here.

*Tit.*　　　　　　　What, villain boy!
Barr'st me my way in Rome?

　　　　　　　　　　[*Stabbing* MUTIUS.

*Mut.*　　　　Help, Lucius, help!
　　　　　　　　　　　　　　　[*Dies.*

　　　　　*Re-enter* LUCIUS.

*Luc.* My lord, you are unjust; and more
　　than so,
In wrongful quarrel you have slain your son.

*Tit.* Nor thou nor he are any sons of mine;
My sons would never so dishonour me:
Traitor, restore Lavinia to the emperor.

*Luc.* Dead, if you will; but not to be his
　　wife,
That is another's lawful promis'd love. [*Exit.*

*Sat.* No, Titus, no; the emperor needs her
　　not,
Nor her, nor thee, nor any of thy stock:
I'll trust by leisure him that mocks me once;
Thee never, nor thy traitorous haughty sons,
Confederates all thus to dishonour me.
Was there none else in Rome to make a stale
But Saturnine? Full well, Andronicus, [thine,
Agree these deeds with that proud brag of
That said'st I begg'd the empire at thy hands.

*Tit.* O monstrous! what reproachful words
　　are these?　　　　　　　　[ing piece

*Sat.* But go thy ways; go, give that chang-
To him that flourish'd for her with his sword:
A valiant son-in-law thou shalt enjoy;
One fit to bandy with thy lawless sons,
To ruffle in the commonwealth of Rome.

*Tit.* These words are razors to my wound-
　　ed heart.　　　　　　　　[of Goths,

*Sat.* And therefore, lovely Tamora, Queen
That, like the stately Phœbe 'mongst her
　　nymphs,　　　　　　　　　[Rome,—
Dost overshine the gallant'st dames of
If thou be pleas'd with this my sudden choice,
Behold, I choose thee, Tamora, for my bride,
And will create thee empress of Rome.
Speak, Queen of Goths, dost thou applaud my
　　choice?
And here I swear by all the Roman gods,—
Sith priest and holy water are so near,
And tapers burn so bright, and everything
In readiness for Hymenæus stand,—
I will not re-salute the streets of Rome,
Or climb my palace, till from forth this place
I lead espous'd my bride along with me.

*Tam.* And here, in sight of heaven, to
　　Rome I swear,
If Saturnine advance the Queen of Goths,
She will a handmaid be to his desires,
A loving nurse, a mother to his youth.

*Sat.* Ascend, fair queen, Pantheon.—Lords,
　　accompany
Your noble emperor and his lovely bride,
Sent by the heavens for Prince Saturnine,
Whose wisdom hath her fortune conquered·

There shall we consummate our spousal rites.

[*Exeunt* SAT. *and his* Followers; TAM.
*and her sons;* AARON *and* Goths.

*Tit.* I am not bid to wait upon this
bride.—

Titus, when wert thou wont to walk alone,
Dishonour'd thus, and challenged of wrongs?

*Re-enter* MARCUS, LUCIUS, QUINTAS, *and*
MARTIUS.

*Marc.* O Titus, see, O see what thou hast
done!

In a bad quarrel slain a virtuous son.

*Tit.* No, foolish tribune, no; no son of
mine,—      [deed

Nor thou, nor these, confederates in the
That hath dishonour'd all our family;
Unworthy brother and unworthy sons!

*Luc.* But let us give him burial, as becomes;

Give Mutius burial with our brethren.

*Tit.* Traitors, away! he rests not in this
tomb:—      [stood,

This monument five hundred years hath
Which I have sumptuously re-edified:
Here none but soldiers and Rome's servitors
Repose in fame; none basely slain in
brawls:—

Bury him where you can, he comes not here.

*Marc.* My lord, this is impiety in you:
My nephew Mutius' deeds do plead for him;
He must be buried with his brethren.

*Quin. and Mart.* And shall, or him we
will accompany.      [that word?

*Tit.* And shall! What villain was it spake

*Quin.* He that would vouch it in any place
but here.      [despite?

*Tit.* What, would you bury him in my

*Marc.* No, noble Titus; but entreat of thee
To pardon Mutius, and to bury him.

*Tit.* Marcus, even thou hast struck upon
my crest,      [wounded:

And with these boys mine honour thou hast
My foes I do repute you every one;
So trouble me no more, but get you gone.

*Marc.* He is not with himself; let us withdraw.

*Quin.* Not I, till Mutius' bones be buried.

[MARCUS *and the Sons of* TITUS *kneel.*

*Marc.* Brother, for in that name doth nature plead,—      [ture speak,—

*Quin.* Father, and in that name doth na-

*Tit.* Speak thou no more, if all the rest will
speed.

*Marc.* Renowned Titus, more than half
my soul,—

*Luc.* Dear father, soul and substance of
us all,—

*Marc.* Suffer thy brother Marcus to inter
His noble nephew here in virtue's nest,
That died in honour and Lavinia's cause:
Thou art a Roman,—be not barbarous.
The Greeks upon advice did bury Ajax,
That slew himself; and wise Laertes' son

Did graciously plead for his funerals:
Let not young Mutius, then, that was thy joy,
Be barr'd his entrance here.

*Tit.*      Rise, Marcus, rise:
The dismall'st day is this that e'er I saw,
To be dishonour'd by my sons in Rome!—
Well, bury him, and bury me the next.

[MUTIUS *is put into the tomb.*

*Luc.* There lie thy bones, sweet Mutius,
with thy friends,

Till we with trophies do adorn thy tomb.

*All.* [*Kneeling.*] No man shed tears for
noble Mutius;

He lives in fame that died in virtue's cause.

*Marc.* My lord,—to step out of these
dreary dumps,—      [Goths

How comes it that the subtle Queen of
Is of a sudden thus advanc'd in Rome?

*Tit.* I know not, Marcus; but I know it
is,—      [tell:

Whether by device or no, the heavens can
Is she not, then, beholden to the man [so far?
That brought her for this high good turn

*Marc.* Yes, and will nobly him remunerate.

*Flourish. Re-enter, at one side,* SATURNINUS
*attended;* TAMORA, DEMETRIUS, CHIRON,
*and* AARON: *at the other,* BASSIANUS, LA-
VINIA, *and others.*

*Sat.* So, Bassianus, you have play'd your
prize:

God give you joy, sir, of your gallant bride!

*Bas.* And you of yours, my lord! I say no
more,

Nor wish no less; and so I take my leave.

*Sat.* Traitor, if Rome have law or we have
power,

Thou and thy faction shall repent this rape.

*Bas.* Rape, call you it, my lord, to seize
my own,

My true-betrothed love, and now my wife?
But let the laws of Rome determine all;
Meanwhile I am possess'd of that is mine.

*Sat.* 'Tis good, sir: you are very short
with us;

But if we live we'll be as sharp with you.

*Bas.* My lord, what I have done, as best I
may,

Answer I must, and shall do with my life.
Only thus much I give your grace to know,—
By all the duties that I owe to Rome,
This noble gentleman, Lord Titus here,
Is in opinion and in honour wrong'd,
That, in the rescue of Lavinia,
With his own hand did slay his youngest son,
In zeal to you, and highly mov'd to wrath
To be controll'd in that he frankly gave:
Receive him, then, to favour, Saturnine,
That hath express'd himself, in all his deeds,
A father and a friend to thee and Rome.

*Tit.* Prince Bassianus, leave to plead my
deeds:      [me.

'Tis thou and those that have dishonour'd
Rome and the righteous heavens be my judge

How I have lov'd and honour'd Saturnine!

*Tam.* My worthy lord, if ever Tamora
Were gracious in those princely eyes of thine,
Then hear me speak indifferently for all;
And at my suit, sweet, pardon what is past.

*Sat.* What, madam! be dishonour'd openly,
And basely put it up without revenge?

*Tam.* Not so, my lord; the gods of Rome forfend
I should be author to dishonour you!
But on mine honour dare I undertake
For good Lord Titus' innocence in all,
Whose fury not dissembled speaks his griefs:
That at my suit look graciously on him;
Lose not so noble a friend on vain suppose,
Nor with sour looks afflict his gentle heart.—
My lord, be rul'd by me, be won at last;
                     [*Aside.*
Dissemble all your griefs and discontents:
You are but newly planted in your throne;
Lest, then, the people and patricians too,
Upon a just survey, take Titus' part,
And so supplant you for ingratitude,—
Which Rome reputes to be a heinous sin,—
Yield at entreats; and then let me alone:
I'll find a day to massacre them all,
And raze their faction and their family,
The cruel father and his traitorous sons,
To whom I sued for my dear son's life;
And make them know what 'tis to let a queen
Kneel in the streets and beg for grace in
    vain.—            [dronicus,—
Come, come, sweet emperor,—come, An-
Take up this good old man, and cheer the heart
That dies in tempest of thy angry frown.

*Sat.* Rise, Titus, rise; my empress hath prevail'd.

*Tit.* I thank your majesty and her, my lord:                     [me.
These words, these looks, infuse new life in

*Tam.* Titus, I am incorporate in Rome,
A Roman now adopted happily,
And must advise the emperor for his good.
This day all quarrels die, Andronicus;—
And let it be mine honour, good my lord,
That I have reconcil'd your friends and you.—
For you, Prince Bassianus, I have pass'd
My word and promise to the emperor
That you will be more mild and tractable.—
And fear not, lords,—and you, Lavinia,—
By my advice, all humbled on your knees,
You shall ask pardon of his majesty.

*Luc.* We do; and vow to heaven and to his highness
That what we did was mildly as we might,
Tendering our sister's honour and our own.

*Marc.* That on mine honour here I do protest.

*Sat.* Away, and talk not; trouble us no more.              [all be friends:

*Tam.* Nay, nay, sweet emperor, we must
**The** tribune and his nephews kneel for grace;

I will not be denied: sweet heart, look back.

*Sat.* Marcus, for thy sake and thy brother's here,
And at my lovely Tamora's entreats,
I do remit these young men's heinous faults:
Stand up.—
Lavinia, though you left me like a churl,
I found a friend; and sure as death I swore
I would not part a bachelor from the priest.
Come, if the emperor's court can feast two brides,
You are my guest, Lavinia, and your friends.
This day shall be a love-day, Tamora.

*Tit.* To-morrow, an it please your majesty
To hunt the panther and the hart with me,
With horn and hound we'll give your grace
    *bonjour.*

*Sat.* Be it so, Titus, and gramercy too.
                    [*Exeunt.*

## ACT II.

### SCENE I.—ROME. *Before the Palace.*

#### *Enter* AARON.

*Aar.* Now climbeth Tamora Olympus' top,
Safe out of fortune's shot; and sits aloft,
Secure of thunder's crack or lightning's flash;
Advanc'd above pale envy's threatening reach.
As when the golden sun salutes the morn,
And, having gilt the ocean with his beams,
Gallops the zodiac in his glistering coach,
And overlooks the highest-peering hill;
So Tamora:
Upon her will doth earthly honour wait,
And virtue stoops and trembles at her frown.
Then, Aaron, arm thy heart and fit thy thoughts
To mount aloft with thy imperial mistress,
And mount her pitch, whom thou in triumph long            [chains,
Hast prisoner held, fetter'd in amorous
And faster bound to Aaron's charming eyes
Than is Prometheus tied to Caucasus.
Away with slavish weeds and servile thoughts!
I will be bright, and shine in pearl and gold,
To wait upon this new-made empress.
To wait, said I? to wanton with this queen,
This goddess, this Semiramis, this nymph,
This syren, that will charm Rome's Saturnine,            [weal's.—
And see his shipwreck and his common-
Holla! what storm is this?

#### *Enter* DEMETRIUS *and* CHIRON *braving.*

*Dem.* Chiron, thy years want wit, thy wit wants edge
And manners, to intrude where I am grac'd;
And may, for aught thou know'st, affected be.

*Chi.* Demetrius, thou dost over-ween in all;
And so in this, to bear me down with braves.

'Tis not the difference of a year or two [ate:
Makes me less gracious or thee more fortun-
I am as able and as fit as thou
To serve and to deserve my mistress' grace;
And that my sword upon thee shall approve,
And plead my passions for Lavinia's love.

*Aar.* [*Aside.*] Clubs, clubs! these lovers
　　will not keep the peace.

*Dem.* Why, boy, although our mother,
　　unadvis'd,
Gave you a dancing-rapier by your side,
Are you so desperate grown to threat your
　　friends?　　　　　　　　　　[sheath
Go to; have your lath glu'd within your
Till you know better how to handle it.

*Chi.* Meanwhile, sir, with the little skill I
　　have,　　　　　　　　　　　[dare.
Full well shalt thou perceive how much I

*Dem.* Ay, boy, grow ye so brave?
　　　　　　　　　　　　　　[*They draw.*

*Aar.* [*Coming forward.*] Why, how now,
　　lords!
So near the emperor's palace dare you draw,
And maintain such a quarrel openly?
Full well I wot the ground of all this grudge:
I would not for a million of gold　　[cerns:
The cause were known to them it most con-
Nor would your noble mother for much more
Be so dishonour'd in the court of Rome.
For shame, put up.

*Dem.*　　　　　Not I, till I have sheath'd
My rapier in his bosom, and withal　[throat
Thrust these reproachful speeches down' his
That he hath breath'd in my dishonour here.

*Chi.* For that I am prepar'd and full re-
　　solv'd,—　　　　　　　　　[tongue,
Foul-spoken coward, that thunder'st with thy
And with thy weapon nothing dar'st perform.

*Aar.* Away, I say!—
Now, by the gods that warlike Goths adore,
This petty brabble will undo us all.—
Why, lords, and think you not how dangerous
It is to jet upon a prince's right?
What, is Lavinia, then, become so loose,
Or Bassianus so degenerate,　　　[broach'd
That for her love such quarrels may be
Without controlment, justice, or revenge?
Young lords, beware! and should the em-
　　press know　　　　　　　　[please.
This discord's ground, the music would not

*Chi.* I care not, I, knew she and all the
　　world:
I love Lavinia more than all the world.

*Dem.* Youngling, learn thou to make some
　　meaner choice:
Lavinia is thine elder brother's hope.

*Aar.* Why, are you mad? or know ye not
　　in Rome
How furious and impatient they be,
And cannot brook competitors in love?
I tell you, lords, you do but plot your deaths
By this device.

*Chi.*　　　　Aaron, a thousand deaths
Would I propose to achieve her whom I love.

*Aar.* To achieve her!—How?

*Dem.*　　　Why mak'st thou it so strange?
She is a woman, therefore may be woo'd;
She is a woman, therefore may be won;
She is Lavinia, therefore must be lov'd.
What, man! more water glideth by the mill
Than wots the miller of; and easy it is
Of a cut loaf to steal a shive, we know:
Though Bassianus be the emperor's brother,
Better than he have worn Vulcan's badge.

*Aar.* [*Aside.*] Ay, and as good as Saturni-
　　nus may

*Dem.* Then why should he despair that
　　knows to court it
With words, fair looks, and liberality?
What, hast not thou full often struck a doe,
And borne her cleanly by the keeper's nose?

*Aar.* Why, then, it seems some certain
　　snatch or so
Would serve your turns.

*Chi.*　　　　Ay, so the turn were serv'd.

*Dem.* Aaron, thou hast hit it.

*Aar.*　　　　Would you had hit it too!
Then should not we be tir'd with this ado.
Why, hark ye, hark ye,—and are you such
　　fools　　　　　　　　　　　[then,
To square for this? Would it offend you,
That both should speed?

*Chi.*　　　　　　Faith, not me.

*Dem.* Nor me, so I were one.

*Aar.* For shame, be friends, and join for
　　that you jar:
'Tis policy and stratagem must do
That you affect; and so must you resolve
That what you cannot as you would achieve,
You must perforce accomplish as you may.
Take this of me,—Lucrece was not more
　　chaste
Than this Lavinia, Bassianus' love.
A speedier course than lingering languishment
Must we pursue, and I have found the path.
My lords, a solemn hunting is in hand;
There will the lovely Roman ladies troop:
The forest-walks are wide and spacious;
And many unfrequented plots there are
Fitted by kind for rape and villany:
Single you thither, then, this dainty doe,
And strike her home by force if not by
　　words:
This way, or not at all, stand you in hope.
Come, come, our empress, with her sacred wit
To villany and vengeance consecrate,
Will we acquaint with all that we intend;
And she shall file our engines with advice
That will not suffer you to square yourselves,
But to your wishes' height advance you both.
The emperor's court is like the house of fame,
The palace full of tongues, of eyes, and ears:
The woods are ruthless, dreadful, deaf, and
　　dull;　　　　　　　　　　[your turns;
There speak and strike. brave boys, and take
There serve your lust, shadow'd from heav-
　　en's eye,
And revel in Lavinia's treasury.

*Chi.* Thy counsel, lad, smells of no coward-ice.

*Dem.* *Sit fas aut nefas*, till I find the stream
To cool this heat, a charm to calm these fits,
*Per Styga, per manes vehor.* [*Exeunt.*

SCENE II.—*A Forest near Rome: a Lodge seen at a distance. Horns and cry of hounds heard.*

*Enter* TITUS ANDRONICUS, *with* Hunters, &c., MARCUS, LUCIUS, QUINTUS, *and* MARTIUS.

*Tit.* The hunt is up, the morn is bright and gay, [green.
The fields are fragrant, and the woods are
Uncouple here, and let us make a bay,
And wake the emperor and his lovely bride,
And rouse the prince, and ring a hunter's peal,
That all the court may echo with the noise.
Sons, let it be your charge, as it is ours,
To attend the emperor's person carefully:
I have been troubled in my sleep this night,
But dawning day new comfort hath inspir'd.

*Horns wind a peal. Enter* SATURNINUS, TAMORA, BASSIANUS, LAVINIA, DEMETRIUS, CHIRON, *and* Attendants.

Many good-morrows to your majesty;—
Madam, to you as many and as good:—
I promised your grace a hunter's peal.

*Sat.* And you have rung it lustily, my lord;
Somewhat too early for new-married ladies.

*Bas.* Lavinia, how say you?

*Lav.* I say no;
I have been broad awake two hours and more.

*Sat.* Come on, then, horse and chariots let us have, [now shall ye see
And to our sport.—[*To* TAMORA.] Madam,
Our Roman hunting.

*Marc.* I have dogs, my lord,
Will rouse the proudest panther in the chase,
And climb the highest promontory top.

*Tit.* And I have horse will follow where the game [plain.
Makes way, and run like swallows o'er the

*Dem.* Chiron, we hunt not, we, with horse nor hound,
But hope to pluck a dainty doe to ground.
[*Exeunt.*

SCENE III.—*A lonely part of the Forest.*

*Enter* AARON *with a bag of gold.*

*Aar.* He that had wit would think that I had none,
To bury so much gold under a tree,
And never after to inherit it.
Let him that thinks of me so abjectly
Know that this gold must coin a stratagem,
Which, cunningly effected, will beget
A very excellent piece of villany:
And so repose, sweet gold, for their unrest
[*Hides the gold.*

That have their alms out of the empress' chest.

*Enter* TAMORA.

*Tam.* My lovely Aaron, wherefore look'st thou sad
When everything doth make a gleeful boast?
The birds chant melody on every bush;
The snake lies rolled in the cheerful sun;
The green leaves quiver with the cooling wind, [ground:
And make a chequer'd shadow on the
Under their sweet shade, Aaron, let us sit,
And, whilst the babbling echo mocks the hounds,
Replying shrilly to the well-tun'd horns,
As if a double hunt were heard at once,
Let us sit down and mark their yelping noise;
And,—after conflict such as was suppos'd
The wandering prince and Dido once enjoy'd,
When with a happy storm they were sur-pris'd,
And curtain'd with a counsel-keeping cave,—
We may, each wreathed in the other's arms,
Our pastimes done, possess a golden slumber;
While hounds and horns and sweet melodious birds
Be unto us as is a nurse's song
Of lullaby to bring her babe asleep.

*Aar.* Madam, though Venus govern your desires,
Saturn is dominator over mine:
What signifies my deadly-standing eye,
My silence and my cloudy melancholy,
My fleece of woolly hair that now uncurls
Even as an adder when she doth unroll
To do some fatal execution?
No, madam, these are no venereal signs,
Vengeance is in my heart, death in my hand,
Blood and revenge are hammering in my head.
Hark, Tamora,—the empress of my soul,
Which never hopes more heaven than rests in thee,—
This is the day of doom for Bassianus:
His Philomel must lose her tongue to-day;
Thy sons make pillage of her chastity,
And wash their hands in Bassianus' blood.
Seest thou this letter? take it up, I pray thee,
And give the king this fatal-plotted scroll.—
Now question me no more,—we are espied;
Here comes a parcel of our hopeful booty,
Which dreads not yet their lives' destruction.

*Tam.* Ah, my sweet Moor, sweeter to me than life! [comes:

*Aar.* No more, great empress, Bassianus
Be cross with him; and I'll go fetch thy sons
To back thy quarrels, whatsoe'er they be.
[*Exit.*

*Enter* BASSIANUS *and* LAVINIA.

*Bas.* Who have we here? Rome's royal empress,
Unfurnish'd of her well-beseeming troop?

Or is it Dian, habited like her,
Who hath abandoned her holy groves
To see the general hunting in this forest?
  *Tam.*  Saucy controller of our private
     steps!
Had I the power that some say Dian had,
Thy temples should be planted presently
With horns, as was Actæon's; and the hounds
Should drive upon thy new-transformed
    limbs,
Unmannerly intruder as thou art!
  *Lav.*  Under your patience, gentle empress,
'Tis thought you have a goodly gift in horn-
    ing;
And to be doubted that your Moor and you
Are singled forth to try experiments: [to-day!
Jove shield your husband from his hounds
'Tis pity they should take him for a stag.
  *Bas.*  Believe me, queen, your swarth Cim-
    merian
Doth make your honour of his body's hue,
Spotted, detested, and abominable.
Why are you sequester'd from all your train,
Dismounted from your snow-white goodly
    steed,
And wander'd hither to an obscure plot,
Accompanied but with a barbarous Moor,
If foul desire had not conducted you?
  *Lav.*  And, being intercepted in your sport,
Great reason that my noble lord be rated
For sauciness.—I pray you, let us hence,
And let her joy her raven-colour'd love;
This valley fits the purpose passing well.
  *Bas.*  The king my brother shall have note
    of this.                              [noted long:
  *Lav.*  Ay, for these slips have made him
Good king, to be so mightily abus'd!  [this?
  *Tam.*  Why have I patience to endure all

### Enter DEMETRIUS and CHIRON.

  *Dem.*  How, now, dear sovereign, and our
    gracious mother!                        [wan?
Why doth your highness look so pale and
  *Tam.*  Have I not reason, think you, to
    look pale?                             [place:—
These two have 'tic'd me hither to this
A barren detested vale you see it is;  [lean,
The trees, though summer, yet forlorn and
O'ercome with moss and baleful mistletoe:
Here never shines the sun; here nothing
    breeds,
Unless the nightly owl or fatal raven:—
And when they show'd me this abhorred pit
They told me, here at dead time of the night
A thousand fiends, a thousand hissing snakes,
Ten thousand swelling toads, as many ur-
    chins,
Would make such fearful and confused cries
As any mortal body hearing it
Should straight fall mad or else die suddenly.
No sooner had they told this hellish tale
But straight they told me they would bind
    me here
Unto the body of a dismal yew,

And leave me to this miserable death:
And then they call'd me foul adulteress,
Lascivious Goth, and all the bitterest terms
That ever ear did hear to such effect:
And had you not by wondrous fortune come,
This vengeance on me had they executed,
Revenge it, as you love your mother's life,
Or be ye not henceforth call'd my children.
  *Dem.*  This is a witness that I am thy son.
                  [*Stabs* BASSIANUS.
  *Chi.*  And this for me, struck home to
    show my strength.
             [*Also stabs* BAS., *who dies.*
  *Lav.*  Ay, come, Semiramis,—nay, barbar-
    ous Tamora,
For no name fits thy nature but thy own!
  *Tam.*  Give me thy poniard;—you shall
    know, my boys,                          [wrong.
Your mother's hand shall right your mother's
  *Dem.*  Stay, madam; here is more belongs
    to her;                                 [straw:
First thrash the corn, then after burn the
This minion stood upon her chastity,
Upon her nuptial vow, her loyalty,
And with that painted hope braves your
    mightiness:
And shall she carry this unto her grave?
  *Chi.*  An it she do, I would I were an eu-
    nuch.
Drag hence her husband to some secret hole,
And make his dead trunk pillow to our lust.
  *Tam.*  But when ye have the honey ye de-
    sire,
Let not this wasp outlive, us both to sting.
  *Chi.*  I warrant you, madam, we will make
    that sure.—
Come, mistress, now perforce we will enjoy
That nice-preserved honesty of yours. [face,—
  *Lav.*  O Tamora! thou bear'st a woman's
  *Tam.*  I will not hear her speak; away with
    her!                                    [a word.
  *Lav.*  Sweet lords, entreat her hear me but
  *Dem.*  Listen, fair madam: let it be your
    glory
To see her tears; but be your heart to them
As unrelenting flint to drops of rain.
  *Lav.*  When did the tiger's young ones
    teach the dam?                          [thee;
O, do not learn her wrath,—she taught it
The milk thou suck'dst from her did turn to
    marble;
Even at thy teat thou hadst thy tyranny.—
Yet every mother breeds not sons alike:
Do thou entreat her show a woman pity.
                       [*To* CHIRON.
  *Chi.*  What, wouldst thou have me prove
    myself a bastard?                       [lark:
  *Lav.*  'Tis true, the raven doth not hatch a
Yet I have heard,—O, could I find it now!—
The lion, mov'd with pity, did endure
To have his princely paws par'd all away:
Some say that ravens foster forlorn children,
The whilst their own birds famish in their
    nests:

O, be to me, though thy hard heart say no,
Nothing so kind, but something pitiful!

*Tam.* I know not what it means:—away
with her!

*Lav.* O, let me teach thee! for my father's
sake, [slain thee,
That gave thee life, when well he might have
Be not obdurate, open thy deaf ears.

*Tam.* Hadst thou in person ne'er offended
me,
Even for his sake am I pitiless.—
Remember, boys, I pour'd forth tears in vain
To save your brother from the sacrifice;
But fierce Andronicus would not relent:
Therefore away with her, and use her as
you will; [her!
The worse to her the better lov'd of me.

*Lav.* O Tamora, be call'd a gentle queen,
And with thine own hands kill me in this
place!
For 'tis not life that I have begg'd so long;
Poor I was slain when Bassianus died.

*Tam.* What begg'st thou, then? fond woman, let me go. [thing more,

*Lav.* 'Tis present death I beg; and one
That womanhood denies my tongue to tell:
O, keep me from their worse than killing lust,
And tumble me into some loathsome pit,
Where never man's eye may behold my body:
Do this, and be a charitable murderer.

*Tam.* So should I rob my sweet sons of
their fee:
No, let them satisfy their lust on thee.

*Dem.* Away! for thou hast stay'd us here
too long.

*Lav.* No grace? no womanhood? Ah,
beastly creature!
The blot and enemy to our general name!
Confusion fall,—

*Chi.* Nay, then I'll stop your mouth:—
bring thou her husband:
This is the hole where Aaron bid us hide him.
[*Dem.* throws Bas.'s *body into the pit; then
exit with* Chi., *dragging off* Lav.

*Tam.* Farewell, my sons: see that you
make her sure:—
Ne'er let my heart know merry cheer indeed
Till all the Andronici be made away.
Now will I hence to seek my lovely Moor,
And let my spleenful sons this trull deflower.
[*Exit.*

*Re-enter* Aaron, *with* Quintus *and*
Martius.

*Aar.* Come on, my lords, the better foot
before: [pit
Straight will I bring you to the loathsome
Where I espied the panther fast asleep.

*Quin.* My sight is very dull, whate'er it
bodes. [for shame,

*Mart.* And mine, I promise you; were't not
Well could I leave our sport to sleep awhile.
[*Falls into the pit.*

*Quin.* What, art thou fallen?—What sub-
tle hole is this, [briers,
Whose mouth is cover'd with rude-growing
Upon whose leaves are drops of new-shed
blood [ers?
As fresh as morning's dew distill'd on flow-
A very fatal place it seems to me.— [fall?
Speak, brother, hast thou hurt thee with the

*Mart.* O brother, with the dismallest object
hurt
That ever eye with sight made heart lament!

*Aar.* [*Aside.*] Now will I fetch the king to
find them here,
That he thereby may give a likely guess
How these were they that made away his
brother. [*Exit.*

*Mart.* Why dost not comfort me, and help
me out [hole?
From this unhallow'd and blood-stained

*Quin.* I am surprised with an uncouth fear;
A chilling sweat o'er-runs my trembling
joints; [see.
My heart suspects more than mine eye can

*Mart.* To prove thou hast a true divining
heart,
Aaron and thou look down into this den,
And see a fearful sight of blood and death.

*Quin.* Aaron is gone; and my compassion-
ate heart
Will not permit mine eyes once to behold
The thing whereat it trembles by surmise:
O, tell me how it is; for ne'er till now
Was I a child to fear I know not what.

*Mart.* Lord Bassianus lies embrewed here,
All on a heap, like to a slaughter'd lamb,
In this detested, dark, blood-drinking pit.

*Quin.* If it be dark, how dost thou know
'tis he?

*Mart.* Upon his bloody finger he doth wear
A precious ring that lightens all the hole,
Which, like a taper in some monument,
Doth shine upon the dead man's earthy
cheeks,
And shows the ragged entrails of the pit:
So pale did shine the moon on Pyramus
When he by night lay bath'd in maiden blood.
O brother, help me with thy fainting hand,—
If fear hath made thee faint, as me it hath,—
Out of this fell devouring receptacle,
As hateful as Cocytus' misty mouth.

*Quin.* Reach me thy hand, that I may help
thee out;
Or, wanting strength to do thee so much
good,
I may be pluck'd into the swallowing womb
Of this deep pit, poor Bassianus' grave.
I have no strength to pluck thee to the brink.

*Mart.* Nor I no strength to climb without
thy help.

*Quin.* Thy hand once more; I will not lose
again,
Till thou art here aloft, or I below:
Thou canst not come to me,—I come to thee.
[*Falls in.*

*Enter* SATURNINUS *with* AARON.

*Sat.* Along with me: I'll see what hole is here,
And what he is that now is leap'd into it.—
Say, who art thou that lately didst descend
Into this gaping hollow of the earth?
   *Mart.* The unhappy son of old Andronicus,
Brought hither in a most unlucky hour,
To find thy brother Bassianus dead.
   *Sat.* My brother dead! I know thou dost but jest:
He and his lady both are at the lodge
Upon the north side of this pleasant chase;
'Tis not an hour since I left him there.
   *Mart.* We know not where you left him all alive;
But, out, alas! here have we found him dead.

*Re-enter* TAMORA, *with* Attendants; TITUS ANDRONICUS *and* LUCIUS.

   *Tam.* Where is my lord the king?
   *Sat.* Here, Tamora; though griev'd with killing grief.
   *Tam.* Where is thy brother Bassianus?
   *Sat.* Now to the bottom dost thou search my wound:
Poor Bassianus here lies murdered.          [writ,
   *Tam.* Then all too late I bring this fatal
                         [*Giving a letter.*
The complot of this timeless tragedy;
And wonder greatly that man's face can fold
In pleasing smiles such murderous tyranny.
   *Sat.* [*Reads.*] *An if we miss to meet him handsomely,—*
*Sweet huntsman, Bassianus 'tis we mean,—*
*Do thou so much as dig the grave for him:*
*Thou know'st our meaning. Look for thy reward*
*Among the nettles at the elder tree*
*Which overshades the mouth of that same pit*
*Where we decreed to bury Bassianus.*
*Do this, and purchase us thy lasting friends.*
O Tamora! was ever heard the like?—
This is the pit and this the elder tree:—
Look, sirs, if you can find the huntsman out
That should have murder'd Bassianus here.
   *Aar.* My gracious lord, here is the bag of gold.          [*Showing it.*
   *Sat.* [*To* TITUS.] Two of thy whelps, fell curs of bloody kind,
Have here bereft my brother of his life.—
Sirs, drag them from the pit unto the prison:
There let them bide until we have devis'd
Some never-heard-of torturing pain for them.
   *Tam.* What, are they in this pit? O wondrous thing!
How easily murder is discovered!
   *Tit.* High emperor, upon my feeble knee
I beg this boon, with tears not lightly shed,
That this fell fault of my accursed sons,—
Accursed if the fault be prov'd in them,—
   *Sat.* If it be prov'd! you see it is apparent.

—Who found this letter? Tamora, was it you?
   *Tam.* Andronicus himself did take it up.
   *Tit.* I did, my lord: yet let me be their bail;
For, by my father's reverend tomb, I vow
They shall be ready at your highness' will
To answer their suspicion with their lives.
   *Sat.* Thou shalt not bail them: see thou follow me.—          [murderers:
Some bring the murder'd body, some the
Let them not speak a word,—the guilt is plain;          [death,
For, by my soul, were there worse end than
That end upon them should be executed.
   *Tam.* Andronicus, I will entreat the king:
Fear not thy sons; they shall do well enough.
   *Tit.* Come, Lucius, come; stay not to talk with them.
          [*Exeunt severally.* Attendants bearing the body.

SCENE IV.—*Another part of the Forest.*

*Enter* DEMETRIUS *and* CHIRON, *with* LAVINIA *ravished; her hands cut off, and her tongue cut out.*

   *Dem.* So, now go tell, and if thy tongue can speak,          [thee.
Who 'twas that cut thy tongue and ravish'd
   *Chi.* Write down thy mind, bewray thy meaning so,
And if thy stumps will let thee play the scribe.
   *Dem.* See, how with signs and tokens she can scrowl.          [thy hands.
   *Chi.* Go home, call for sweet water, wash
   *Dem.* She hath no tongue to call, nor hands to wash;
And so let's leave her to her silent walks.
   *Chi.* An 'twere my case I should go hang myself.          [the cord.
   *Dem.* If thou hadst hands to help thee knit
          [*Exeunt* DEM. *and* CHI.

*Enter* MARCUS.

   *Marc.* Who is this,—my niece,—that flies away so fast?—
Cousin, a word; where is your husband?—
If I do dream, would all my wealth would wake me!
If I do wake, some planet strike me down,
That I may slumber in eternal sleep!—
Speak, gentle niece,—what stern ungentle hands          [bare
Have lopp'd, and hew'd, and made thy body
Of her two branches,—those sweet ornaments
Whose circling shadows kings have sought to sleep in,
And might not gain so great a happiness
As have thy love? Why dost not speak to me?—
Alas, a crimson river of warm blood,
Like to a bubbling fountain stirr'd with wind,
Doth rise and fall between thy rosed lips,
Coming and going with thy honeyed breath.

But sure some Tereus hath deflowered thee,
And lest thou shouldst detect him, cut thy
    tongue.      [shame!
Ah, now thou turn'st away thy face for
And notwithstanding all this loss of blood,—
As from a conduit with three issuing
    spouts,—
Yet do thy cheeks look red as Titan's face
Blushing to be encounter'd with a cloud.
Shall I speak for thee? shall I say 'tis so?
O, that I knew thy heart, and knew the beast,
That I might rail at him, to ease my mind!
Sorrow concealed, like an oven stopp'd,
Doth burn the heart to cinders where it is.
Fair Philomela, she but lost her tongue,
And in a tedious sampler sew'd her mind:
But, lovely niece, that mean is cut from thee;
A craftier Tereus, cousin, hast thou met,
And he hath cut those pretty fingers off
That could have better sew'd than Philomel.
O, had the monster seen those lily hands
Tremble, like aspen leaves, upon a lute,
And make the silken strings delight to kiss
    them,      [his life!
He would not then have touch'd them for
Or had he heard the heavenly harmony
Which that sweet tongue hath made, [asleep
He would have dropp'd his knife, and fell
As Cerberus at the Thracian poet's feet.
Come, let us go, and make thy father blind;
For such a sight will blind a father's eye:
One hour's storm will drown the fragrant
    meads;      [eyes?
What will whole months of tears thy father's
Do not draw back, for we will mourn with
    thee:
O, could our mourning ease thy misery!
                    [Exeunt.

## ACT III.

### Scene I.—Rome. A Street.

Enter Senators, Tribunes, and Officers of Justice, with Martius and Quintus bound,
passing on to the place of execution; Titus
going before, pleading.

Tit. Hear me, grave fathers! noble trib-
    unes, stay!
For pity of mine age, whose youth was spent
In dangerous wars, whilst you securely slept;
For all my blood in Rome's great quarrel
    shed;
For all the frosty nights that I have watch'd;
And for these bitter tears, which now you see
Filling the aged wrinkles in my cheeks;
Be pitiful to my condemned sons,
Whose souls are not corrupted as 'tis thought.
For two-and-twenty sons I never wept,
Because they died in honour's lofty bed.
For these, good tribunes, in the dust I write
    [Throwing himself on the ground.
My heart's deep languor and my soul's sad
    tears:
Let my tears stanch the earth's dry appetite;

My sons' sweet blood will make it shame and
    blush.

[Exeunt Sen., Trib., &c., with the prisoners.

O earth, I will befriend thee more with rain,
That shall distil from these two ancient ruins,
Than youthful April shall with all his show-
    ers:      [still;
In summer's drought I'll drop upon thee
In winter, with warm tears I'll melt the snow,
And keep eternal spring-time on thy face,
So thou refuse to drink my dear sons' blood.

    Enter Lucius with his sword drawn.

O reverend tribunes! O gentle aged men!
Unbind my sons, reverse the doom of death;
And let me say, that never wept before,
My tears are now prevailing orators.
    Luc. O noble father, you lament in vain:
The tribunes hear you not, no man is by;
And you recount your sorrows to a stone.
    Tit. Ah, Lucius, for thy brothers let me
    plead.—
Grave tribunes, once more I entreat of you.
    Luc. My gracious lord, no tribune hears
    you speak.      [hear
    Tit. Why, 'tis no matter, man: if they did
They would not mark me; or if they did
    mark
They would not pity me; yet plead I must,
And bootless unto them.
Therefore I tell my sorrows to the stones;
Why, though they cannot answer my distress,
Yet in some sort they are better than the
    tribunes,
For that they will not intercept my tale:
When I do weep they humbly at my feet
Receive my tears, and seem to weep with me;
And were they but attired in grave weeds
Rome could afford no tribune like to these.
A stone is soft as wax, tribunes more hard
    than stones;
A stone is silent, and offendeth not,—
And tribunes with their tongues doom men
    to death.      [Rises.
But wherefore stand'st thou with thy wea-
    pon drawn?      [their death:
    Luc. To rescue my two brothers from
For which attempt the judges have pro-
    nounc'd
My everlasting doom of banishment.
    Tit. O happy man! they have befriended
    thee.
Why, foolish Lucius, dost thou not perceive
That Rome is but a wilderness of tigers?
Tigers must prey; and Rome affords no prey
But me and mine: how happy art thou, then,
From these devourers to be banished!—
But who comes with our brother Marcus
    here?

    Enter Marcus and Lavinia.

    Marc. Titus, prepare thy aged eyes to
    weep;

Or if not so, thy noble heart to break:
I bring consuming sorrow to thine age. [then.
 *Tit.* Will it consume me? let me see it
 *Marc.* This was thy daughter.
 *Tit.* Why, Marcus, so she is.
 *Luc.* Ay me! this object kills me!
 *Tit.* Faint-hearted boy, arise, and look
  upon her.—
Speak, my Lavinia, what accursed hand
Hath made thee handless in thy father's
 sight?
What fool hath added water to the sea,
Or brought a fagot to bright-burning Troy?
My grief was at the height before thou
 cam'st;
And now, like Nilus, it disdaineth bounds.
Give me a sword, I'll chop off my hands too;
For they have fought for Rome, and all in
 vain;
And they have nurs'd this woe in feeding life;
In bootless prayer have they been held up,
And they have serv'd me to effectless use:
Now all the service I require of them
Is that the one will help to cut the other.—
'Tis well, Lavinia, that thou hast no hands;
For hands, to do Rome service, are but vain.
 *Luc.* Speak, gentle sister, who hath mar-
  tyr'd thee?   [thoughts,
 *Marc.* O, that delightful engine of her
That blabb'd them with such pleasing elo-
 quence,
Is torn from forth that pretty hollow cage,
Where, like a sweet melodious bird, it sung
Sweet varied notes, enchanting every ear!
 *Luc.* O, say thou for her, who hath done
  this deed?   [park,
 *Marc.* O, thus I found her, straying in the
Seeking to hide herself, as doth the deer
That hath receiv'd some unrecuring wound.
 *Tit.* It was my deer; and he that wounded
  her   [dead:
Hath hurt me more than had he kill'd me
For now I stand as one upon a rock,
Environ'd with a wilderness of sea; [wave,
Who marks the waxing tide grow wave by
Expecting ever when some envious surge
Will in his brinish bowels swallow him.
This way to death my wretched sons are
 gone;
Here stands my other son, a banish'd man;
And here my brother, weeping at my woes:
But that which gives my soul the greatest
 spurn
Is dear Lavinia, dearer than my soul.—
Had I but seen thy picture in this plight
It would have madded me: what shall I do
Now I behold thy lively body so?
Thou hast no hands to wipe away thy tears,
Nor tongue to tell me who hath martyr'd
 thee:
Thy husband he is dead; and for his death
Thy brothers are condemn'd, and dead by
 this.—
Look, Marcus!—ah, son Lucius, look on her!

When I did name her brothers, then fresh
 tears
Stood on her cheeks, as doth the honey dew
Upon a gather'd lily almost wither'd.
 *Marc.* Perchance she weeps because they
  kill'd her husband:
Perchance because she knows them innocent.
 *Tit.* If they did kill thy husband, then be
  joyful,   [them.—
Because the law hath ta'en revenge on
No, no, they would not do so foul a deed;
Witness the sorrow that their sister makes.—
Gentle Lavinia, let me kiss thy lips;
Or make some sign how I may do thee ease:
Shall thy good uncle, and thy brother Lucius,
And thou, and I, sit round about some foun-
 tain
Looking all downwards, to behold our cheeks
How they are stain'd, as meadows, yet not
 dry,
With miry slime left on them by a flood?
And in the fountain shall we gaze so long,
Till the fresh taste be taken from that clear-
 ness,
And made a brine-pit with our bitter tears?
Or shall we cut away our hands like thine?
Or shall we bite our tongues, and in dumb
 shows
Pass the remainder of our hateful days?
What shall we do? let us, that have our
 tongues,
Plot some device of further misery,
To make us wonder'd at in time to come.
 *Luc.* Sweet father, cease your tears; for at
  your grief
See how my wretched sister sobs and weeps.
 *Marc.* Patience, dear niece.—Good Titus,
  dry thine eyes.   [wot
 *Tit.* Ah, Marcus, Marcus! brother, well I
Thy napkin cannot drink a tear of mine,
For thou, poor man, hast drown'd it with
 thine own.
 *Luc.* Ah, my Lavinia, I will wipe thy
  cheeks.
 *Tit.* Mark, Marcus, mark! I understand
  her signs:   [say
Had she a tongue to speak, now would she
That to her brother which I said to thee:
His napkin, with his true tears all bewet,
Can do no service on her sorrowful cheeks.
O, what a sympathy of woe is this,—
As far from help as limbo is from bliss!

   *Enter* AARON.

 *Aar.* Titus Andronicus, my lord, the em-
  peror   [sons,
Sends thee this word,—that if thou love thy
Let Marcus, Lucius, or thyself, old Titus,
Or any one of you, chop off your hand
And send it to the king: he for the same
Will send thee hither both thy sons alive;
And that shall be the ransom for their fault.
 *Tit.* O gracious emperor! O gentle Aaron!
Did ever raven sing so like a lark

That gives sweet tidings of the sun's uprise?
With all my heart I'll send the emperor
My hand:
Good Aaron, wilt thou help to chop it off?
   *Luc.* Stay, father! for that noble hand of
     thine,
That hath thrown down so many enemies,
Shall not be sent: my hand will serve the
     turn:             [you;
My youth can better spare my blood than
And therefore mine shall save my brothers'
     lives.
   *Marc.* Which of your hands hath not de-
     fended Rome,
And rear'd aloft the bloody battle-axe,
Writing destruction on the enemy's castle?
O, none of both but are of high desert:
My hand hath been but idle; let it serve
To ransom my two nephews from their
     death;
Then have I kept it to a worthy end.
   *Aar.* Nay, come, agree whose hand shall
     go along,
For fear they die before their pardon come.
   *Marc.* My hand shall go.
   *Luc.*          By heaven, it shall not go!
   *Tit.* Sirs, strive no more: such wither'd
     herbs as these           [mine.
Are meet for plucking up, and therefore
   *Luc.* Sweet father, if I shall be thought
     thy son,
Let me redeem my brothers both from death.
   *Marc.* And for our father's sake and mo-
     ther's care,
Now let me show a brother's love to thee.
   *Tit.* Agree between you; I will spare my
     hand.
   *Luc.* Then I'll go fetch an axe.
   *Marc.*          But I will use the axe.
          *[Exeunt* LUCIUS *and* MARCUS.
   *Tit.* Come hither, Aaron; I'll deceive them
     both:
Lend me thy hand, and I will give thee mine.
   *Aar.* [*Aside.*] If that be call'd deceit, I
     will be honest,
And never whilst I live deceive men so:—
But I'll deceive you in another sort,
And that you'll say ere half an hour pass.
          *[He cuts off* TITUS'S *hand.*

#### Re-enter LUCIUS and MARCUS.

   *Tit.* Now stay your strife: what shall be is
     despatch'd.—
Good Aaron, give his majesty my hand:
Tell him it was a hand that warded him
From thousand dangers; bid him bury it;
More hath it merited,—that let it have.
As for my sons, say I account of them
As jewels purchas'd at an easy price;
And yet dear too, because I bought mine own.
   *Aar.* I go, Andronicus: and for thy hand
Look by and by to have thy sons with
     thee:—

Their heads I mean. O, how this villany
             [*Aside.*
Doth fat me with the very thoughts of it!
Let fools do good, and fair men call for grace,
Aaron will have his soul black like his face.
             [*Exit.*
   *Tit.* O, here I lift this one hand up to
     heaven,
And bow this feeble ruin to the earth:
If any power pities wretched tears,
To that I call!—[*To* LAVINIA.] What, wilt
     thou kneel with me?
Do, then, dear heart; for heaven shall hear
     our prayers;          [dim,
Or with our sighs we'll breathe the welkin
And stain the sun with fog, as sometime
     clouds            [bosoms.
When they do hug him in their melting
   *Marc.* O brother, speak with possibilities,
And do not break into these deep extremes.
   *Tit.* Is not my sorrow deep, having no
     bottom?
Then be my passions bottomless with them.
   *Marc.* But yet let reason govern thy
     lament.           [eries
   *Tit.* If there were reason for these mis-
Then into limits could I bind my woes:
When heaven doth weep, doth not the earth
     o'erflow?
If the winds rage, doth not the sea wax mad,
Threatening the welkin with his big-swoln
     face?
And wilt thou have a reason for this coil?
I am the sea; hark, how her sighs do flow!
She is the weeping welkin, I the earth:
Then must my sea be moved with her sighs;
Then must my earth with her continual tears
Become a deluge, overflow'd and drown'd:
For why my bowels cannot hide her woes,
But like a drunkard must I vomit them.
Then give me leave; for losers will have leave
To ease their stomachs with their bitter
     tongues.

*Enter* a Messenger, *with two heads and a
     hand.*

   *Mess.* Worthy Andronicus, ill art thou
     repaid
For that good hand thou sent'st the emperor.
Here are the heads of thy two noble sons;
And here's thy hand, in scorn to thee sent
     back,—          [mock'd:
Thy griefs their sports, thy resolution
That woe is me to think upon thy woes,
More than remembrance of my father's
     death.          [*Exit.*
   *Marc.* Now let hot Ætna cool in Sicily,
And be my heart an ever-burning hell!
These miseries are more than may be borne.
To weep with them that weep doth ease some
     deal;
But sorrow flouted at is double death.
   *Luc.* Ah, that this sight should make so
     deep a wound.

And yet detested life not shrink thereat!
That ever death should let life bear his name,
Where life hath no more interest but to
breathe! [LAVINIA *kisses him.*
*Marc.* Alas, poor heart, that kiss is com-
fortless
As frozen water to a starved snake. [an end?
*Tit.* When will this fearful slumber have
*Marc.* Now, farewell, flattery: die, An-
dronicus; [heads,
Thou dost not slumber: see thy two sons'
Thy warlike hand, thy mangled daughter
here;
Thy other banish'd son, with this dear sight
Struck pale and bloodless; and thy brother, I,
Even like a stony image, cold and numb.
Ah! now no more will I control thy griefs:
Rent off thy silver hair, thy other hand
Gnawing with thy teeth; and be this dismal
sight
The closing up of our most wretched eyes:
Now is a time to storm; why art thou still?
*Tit.* Ha, ha, ha! [with this hour.
*Marc.* Why dost thou laugh? it fits not
*Tit.* Why, I have not another tear to shed:
Besides, this sorrow is an enemy,
And would usurp upon my watery eyes,
And make them blind with tributary tears:
Then which way shall I find revenge's cave?
For these two heads do seem to speak to me,
And threat me I shall never come to bliss
Till all these mischiefs be return'd again
Even in their throats that have committed
them.
Come, let me see what task I have to do.—
You heavy people circle me about,
That I may turn me to each one of you,
And swear unto my soul to right your
wrongs.— [head;
The vow is made.—Come, brother, take a
And in this hand the other will I bear.
Lavinia, thou shalt be employ'd in these
things; [thy teeth.
Bear thou my hand, sweet wench, between
As for thee, boy, go, get thee from my sight;
Thou art an exile, and thou must not stay:
Hie to the Goths, and raise an army there:
And if you love me, as I think you do,
Let's kiss and part, for we have much to do.
[*Exeunt* TITUS, MARCUS, *and* LAVINIA.
*Luc.* Farewell, Andronicus, my noble
father,—
The woefull'st man that ever liv'd in Rome:
Farewell, proud Rome; till Lucius come
again,
He leaves his pledges dearer than his life:
Farewell, Lavinia, my noble sister;
O, would thou wert as thou 'tofore hast been!
But now nor Lucius nor Lavinia lives
But in oblivion and hateful griefs.
If Lucius live, he will requite your wrongs,
And make proud Saturnine and his empress
Beg at the gates, like Tarquin and his queen.
New will I to the Goths, and raise a power

To be reveng'd on Rome and Saturnine.
[*Exit.*

SCENE II.—ROME. *A Room in* TITUS'S *House.*
*A Banquet set out.*

*Enter* TITUS, MARCUS, LAVINIA, *and* YOUNG
LUCIUS, *a boy.*

*Tit.* So, so; now sit: and look you eat no
more [us
Than will preserve just so much strength in
As will revenge these bitter woes of ours.
Marcus, unknit that sorrow-wreathen knot:
Thy niece and I, poor creatures, want our
hands,
And cannot passionate our tenfold grief
With folded arms. This poor right hand of
mine
Is left to tyrannize upon my breast;
And when my heart, all mad with misery,
Beats in this hollow prison of my flesh,
Then thus I thump it down.— [signs!
Thou map of woe, that thus dost talk in
[*To* LAVINIA.
When thy poor heart beats with outrageous
beating,
Thou canst not strike it thus to make it still.
Wound it with sighing, girl; kill it with
groans;
Or get some little knife between thy teeth,
And just against thy heart make thou a hole,
That all the tears that thy poor eyes let fall
May run into that sink, and, soaking in,
Drown the lamenting fool in sea-salt tears.
*Marc.* Fie, brother, fie! teach her not thus
to lay
Such violent hands upon her tender life.
*Tit.* How now! has sorrow made thee
dote already?
Why, Marcus, no man should be mad but I.
What violent hands can she lay on her life?
Ah, wherefore dost thou urge the name of
hands;—
To bid Æneas tell the tale twice o'er
How Troy was burnt and he made miserable?
O, handle not the theme, to talk of hands,
Lest we remember still that we have none.—
Fie, fie, how frantically I square my talk,—
As if we should forget we had no hands,
If Marcus did not name the word of hands!—
Come, let's fall to; and, gentle girl, eat this.—
Here is no drink! Hark, Marcus, what she
says;—
I can interpret all her martyr'd signs;—
She says she drinks no other drink but tears,
Brew'd with her sorrow, mesh'd upon her
cheeks:— [thought;
Speechless complainer, I will learn thy
In thy dumb action will I be as perfect
As begging hermits in their holy prayers:
Thou shalt not sigh, nor hold thy stumps to
heaven,
Nor wink, nor nod, nor kneel, nor make a
sign,
But I of these will wrest an alphabet.

And by still practice learn to know thy meaning.

*Y. Luc.* Good grandsire, leave these bitter
deep laments:

Make my aunt merry with some pleasing tale.

*Marc.* Alas, the tender boy, in passion
mov'd,

Doth weep to see his grandsire's heaviness.

*Tit.* Peace, tender sapling; thou art made
of tears,

And tears will quickly melt thy life away.—
[Marcus *strikes the dish with a knife.*

What dost thou strike at, Marcus, with thy
knife?　　　　　　　　　　　　[a fly.

*Marc.* At that that I have kill'd, my lord,—

*Tit.* Out on thee, murderer! thou kill'st my
heart;

Mine eyes are cloy'd with view of tyranny:

A deed of death done on the innocent

Becomes not Titus' brother: get thee gone;

I see thou art not for my company.

*Marc.* Alas, my lord, I have but kill'd a
fly.　　　　　　　　　　　　[mother?

*Tit.* But how if that fly had a father and

How would he hang his slender gilded wings,

And buzz lamenting doings in the air!

Poor harmless fly,

That with his pretty buzzing melody

Came here to make us merry! and thou hast
kill'd him.　　　　　　　　[favour'd fly,

*Marc.* Pardon me, sir, 'twas a black ill-

Like to the empress' Moor; therefore I kill'd
him.

*Tit.* O, O, O.

Then pardon me for reprehending thee,

For thou hast done a charitable deed.

Give me thy knife, I will insult on him

Flattering myself as if it were the Moor

Come hither purposely to poison me.—

There's for thyself, and that's for Tamora.—

Ah, sirrah!

Yet I do think we are not brought so low

But that between us we can kill a fly

That comes in likeness of a coal-black Moor.

*Marc.* Alas, poor man! grief has so
wrought on him,

He takes false shadows for true substances.

*Tit.* Come, take away.—Lavinia, go with
me:

I'll to thy closet; and go read with thee

Sad stories chanced in the times of old.—

Come, boy, and go with me: thy sight is
young,

And thou shalt read when mine begins to
dazzle.　　　　　　　　　　[*Exeunt.*

### ACT IV.

SCENE I.—ROME. *Before* TITUS'S *House.*

*Enter* TITUS *and* MARCUS. *Then enter*
YOUNG LUCIUS *running, with books under
his arm, and* LAVINIA *running after him.*

*Y. Luc.* Help, grandsire, help! my aunt
Lavinia

Follows me everywhere, I know not why.—
Good uncle Marcus, see how swift she
comes!

Alas, sweet aunt, I know not what you mean.

*Marc.* Stand by me, Lucius: do not fear
thine aunt.　　　　　　　　　[harm.

*Tit.* She loves thee, boy, too well to do thee

*Y. Luc.* Ay, when my father was in Rome
she did.　　　　　　　　　[these signs?

*Marc.* What means my niece Lavinia by

*Tit.* Fear her not, Lucius: somewhat doth
she mean:—

See, Lucius, see how much she makes of thee:

Somewhither would she have thee go with her.

Ah, boy, Cornelia never with more care

Read to her sons than she hath read to thee

Sweet poetry and Tully's Orator.

*Marc.* Canst thou not guess wherefore she
plies thee thus?　　　　　　　　[guess,

*Y. Luc.* My lord, I know not, I, nor can I

Unless some fit or frenzy do possess her:

For I have heard my grandsire say full oft

Extremity of griefs would make men mad;

And I have read that Hecuba of Troy

Ran mad through sorrow: that made me to
fear;

Although, my lord, I know my noble aunt

Loves me as dear as e'er my mother did,

And would not, but in fury, fright my youth:

Which made me down to throw my books,
and fly,—

Causeless, perhaps: but pardon me, sweet
aunt:

And, madam, if my uncle Marcus go,

I will most willingly attend your ladyship.

*Marc.* Lucius, I will.

[LAVINIA *turns over with her stumps the
books which* LUCIUS *has let fall.*

*Tit.* How now, Lavinia!—Marcus, what
means this?

Some book there is that she desires to see.

Which is it, girl, of these?—Open them,
boy.—

But thou art deeper read and better skill'd:

Come, and take choice of all my library,

And so beguile thy sorrow, till the heavens

Reveal the damn'd contriver of this deed.—

Why lifts she up her arms in sequence thus?

*Marc.* I think she means that there was
more than one

Confederate in the fact;—ay, more there was,

Or else to heaven she heaves them for revenge.　　　　　　　　　　　　　so?

*Tit.* Lucius, what book is that she tosseth

*Y. Luc.* Grandsire, 'tis Ovid's Metamorphosis;

My mother gave it me.

*Marc.*　　　　For love of her that's gone,

Perhaps she cull'd it from among the rest.

*Tit.* Soft! see how busily she turns the
leaves!

Help her:

What would she find?—Lavinia, shall I
read?

This is the tragic tale of Philomel,
And treats of Tereus' treason and his rape;
And rape, I fear, was root of thine annoy.

  *Marc.* See, brother, see; note how she
    quotes the leaves.

  *Tit.* Lavinia, wert thou thus surpris'd,
    sweet girl,
Ravish'd, and wrong'd, as Philomela was,
Forc'd in the ruthless, vast, and gloomy
    woods?—
See, see!—
Ay, such a place there is where we did hunt.—
O, had we never, never hunted there!—
Pattern'd by that the poet here describes,
By nature made for murders and for rapes.

  *Marc.* O, why should nature build so foul
    a den,
Unless the gods delight in tragedies?

  *Tit.* Give signs, sweet girl,—for here are
    none but friends,—
What Roman lord it was durst do the deed:
Or slunk not Saturnine, as Tarquin erst,
That left the camp to sin in Lucrece' bed?

  *Marc.* Sit down, sweet niece:—brother, sit
    down by me.—
Apollo, Pallas, Jove, or Mercury,
Inspire me, that I may this treason find!—
My lord, look here:—look here, Lavinia:
This sandy plot is plain; guide, if thou canst,
This after me, when I have writ my name
Without the help of any hand at all.

    [*He writes his name with his staff, guid-*
    *ing it with his feet and mouth.*
Curs'd be that heart that forc'd us to this
    shift!—    [last
Write thou, good niece; and here display at
What God will have discover'd for revenge:
Heaven guide thy pen to print thy sorrows
    plain,
That we may know the traitors and the
    truth!

    [*She takes the staff in her mouth, guides*
    *it with her stumps, and writes.*

  *Tit.* O, do ye read, my lord, what she hath
    writ?
*Stuprum—Chiron—Demetrius.*    [Tamora

  *Marc.* What, what!—the lustful sons of
Performers of this heinous, bloody deed?

  *Tit. Magni Dominator poli,*
*Tam lentus audis scelera? tam lentus vides?*

  *Marc.* O, calm thee, gentle lord; although
    I know
There is enough written upon this earth
To stir a mutiny in the mildest thoughts,
And arm the minds of infants to exclaims;
My lord, kneel down with me; Lavinia,
    kneel;
And kneel, sweet boy, the Roman Hector's
    hope;
And swear with me,—as, with the woeful
    fere
And father of that chaste dishonour'd dame,
Lord Junius Brutus sware for Lucrece'
    rape,—

That we will prosecute, by good advice,
Mortal revenge upon these traitorous Goths,
And see their blood, or die with this reproach.

  *Tit.* 'Tis sure enough, an you knew how.
But if you hunt these bear-whelps, then be-
    ware:
The dam will wake; and if she wind you
    once,
She's with the lion deeply still in league,
And lulls him whilst she playeth on her back,
And when he sleeps will she do what she list.
You are a young huntsman, Marcus; let it
    alone;
And, come, I will go get a leaf of brass,
And with a gad of steel will write these
    words,
And lay it by: the angry northern wind
Will blow these sands, like Sybil's leaves,
    abroad,    [say you?
And where's your lesson then?—Boy, what

  *Y. Luc.* I say, my lord, that if I were a
    man,
Their mother's bedchamber should not be
    safe
For these bad-bondmen to the yoke of Rome.

  *Marc.* Ay, that 's my boy! thy father hath
    full oft
For his ungrateful country done the like.

  *Y. Luc.* And, uncle, so will I, an if I live.

  *Tit.* Come, go with me into mine armoury;
Lucius, I'll fit thee; and withal, my boy,
Shalt carry from me to the empress' sons
Presents that I intend to send them both:
Come, come; thou 'lt do thy message, wilt
    thou not?    [bosoms, grandsire.

  *Y. Luc.* Ay, with my dagger in their

  *Tit.* No, boy, not so; I'll teach thee an-
    other course.—
Lavinia, come.—Marcus, look to my house:
Lucius and I'll go brave it at the court;
Ay, marry, will we, sir; and we'll be waited
    on.

    [*Exeunt* TIT., LAV., *and* Y. LUC.

  *Marc.* O heavens, can you hear a good man
    groan,
And not relent, or not compassion him?
Marcus, attend him in his ecstasy,
That hath more scars of sorrow in his heart
Than foemen's marks upon his batter'd
    shield;
But yet so just that he will not revenge:—
Revenge, ye heavens, for old Andronicus!

    [*Exit.*

SCENE II.—ROME. *A Room in the Palace.*

*Enter* AARON, DEMETRIUS *and* CHIRON, *at one*
  *door; at another door,* YOUNG LUCIUS *and*
  *an* Attendant, *with a bundle of weapons,*
  *and verses writ upon them.*

  *Chi.* Demetrius, here's the son of Lucius;
He hath some message to deliver us.

  *Aar.* Ay, some mad message from his mad
    grandfather.    [I may,

  *Y. Luc.* My lords, with all the humbleness

I greet your honours from Andronicus,—
And pray the Roman gods confound you
both!        [Aside.
    Dem. Gramercy, lovely Lucius: what's the
news?
    Boy. [Aside.] That you are both de-
cipher'd, that's the news,        [you,
For villains mark'd with rape.—May it please
My grandsire, well-advis'd, hath sent by me
The goodliest weapons of his armoury
To gratify your honourable youth,
The hope of Rome; for so he bade me say;
And so I do, and with his gifts present
Your lordships, that whenever you have
need,
You may be armed and appointed well:
And so I leave you both,—[aside] like bloody
villains.
        [Exeunt Y. Luc. and Attendant.
    Dem. What 's here? A scroll; and written
round about?
Let's see:—
[Reads.] Integer vitæ, scelerisque purus,
        Non eget Mauri jaculis, nec arcu.
    Chi. O, 'tis a verse in Horace; I know it
well:
I read it in the grammar long ago.
    Aar. Ay, just,—a verse in Horace;—right
you have it.—
Now, what a thing it is to be an ass! [Aside.
Here's no sound jest! the old man hath
found their guilt;        [lines,
And sends them weapons wrapp'd about with
That wound, beyond their feeling, to the
quick.
But were our witty empress well a-foot,
She would applaud Andronicus' conceit.
But let her rest in her unrest awhile.—
And now, young lords, was 't not a happy
star        [so,
Led us to Rome, strangers, and more than
Captives, to be advanced to this height?
It did me good before the palace gate
To brave the tribune in his brother's hear-
ing.
    Dem. But me more good to see so great a
lord
Basely insinuate and send us gifts.
    Aar. Had he not reason, Lord Demetrius?
Did you not use his daughter very friendly?
    Dem. I would we had a thousand Roman
dames
At such a bay, by turn to serve our lust.
    Chi. A charitable wish, and full of love.
    Aar. Here lacks but your mother for to say
amen.
    Chi. And that would she for twenty thou-
sand more.
    Dem. Come, let us go; and pray to all the
gods
For our beloved mother in her pains.
    Aar. [Aside.] Pray to the devils; the gods
have given us over.
        [Flourish within.

    Dem. Why do the emperor's trumpets
flourish thus?
    Chi. Belike, for joy the emperor hath a son.
    Dem. Soft! who comes here?

Enter a Nurse, with a blackamoor Child in
her arms.

    Nur.        Good-morrow, lords:
O, tell me, did you see Aaron the Moor?
    Aar. Well, more or less, or ne'er a whit at
all,
Here Aaron is; and what with Aaron now?
    Nur. O gentle Aaron, we are all undone!
Now help, or woe betide thee evermore!
    Aar. Why, what a caterwauling dost thou
keep!
What dost thou wrap and fumble in thine
arms?
    Nur. O, that which I would hide from
heaven's eye,        [grace!—
Our empress' shame and stately Rome's dis-
She is deliver'd, lords,—she is deliver'd.
    Aar. To whom?
    Nur.        I mean, she's brought a-bed.
    Aar. Well, God give her good rest! What
hath he sent her?
    Nur. A devil.
    Aar. Why, then she is the devil's dam; a
joyful issue.        [ful issue:
    Nur. A joyless, dismal, black and sorrow-
Here is the babe, as loathsome as a toad
Amongst the fairest breeders of our clime:
The empress sends it thee, thy stamp, thy
seal,
And bids thee christen it with thy dagger's
point.
    Aar. Zounds, ye whore! is black so base a
hue?—
Sweet blowse, you are a beauteous blossom,
sure.
    Dem. Villain, what hast thou done?
    Aar. That which thou canst not undo.
    Chi. Thou hast undone our mother.
    Aar. Villain, I have done thy mother.
    Dem. And therein, hellish dog, thou hast
undone.        [choice!
Woe to her chance, and damn'd her loathed
Accurs'd the offspring of so foul a fiend!
    Chi. It shall not live.
    Aar. It shall not die.
    Nur. Aaron, it must; the mother wills it
so.
    Aar. What, must it, nurse? then let no
man but I
Do execution on my flesh and blood.
    Dem. I'll broach the tadpole on my rapier's
point:—
Nurse, give it me; my sword shall soon
despatch it.        [bowels up.
    Aar. Sooner this sword shall plough thy
[Takes the Child from the Nurse, and draws.
Stay, murderous villains! will you kill your
brother?
Now, by the burning tapers of the sky, .

That shone so brightly when this boy was
　　got,
He dies upon my scimitar's sharp point
That touches this my first-born son and heir!
I tell you, younglings, not Enceladus,
With all his threatening band of Typhon's
　　brood,
Nor great Alcides, nor the god of war,
Shall seize this prey out of his father's hands.
What, what, ye sanguine, shallow-hearted
　　boys!　　　　　　　　　　　　　[signs!
Ye white-lim'd walls! ye alehouse-painted
Coal-black is better than another hue,
In that it scorns to bear another hue;
For all the water in the ocean
Can never turn a swan's black legs to white,
Although she lave them hourly in the flood.
Tell the empress from me, I am of age
To keep mine own,—excuse it how she can.

*Dem.* Wilt thou betray thy noble mistress
　　thus?　　　　　　　　　　　　　[self,—
*Aar.* My mistress is my mistress; this, my-
The vigour and the picture of my youth:
This before all the world do I prefer;
This maugre all the world will I keep safe,
Or some of you shall smoke for it in Rome.

*Dem.* By this our mother is for ever
　　sham'd,　　　　　　　　　　　[escape.
*Chi.* Rome will despise her for this foul
*Nur.* The emperor, in his rage, will doom
　　her death.
*Chi.* I blush to think upon this ignomy.
*Aar.* Why, there 's the privilege your
　　beauty bears:
Fie, treacherous hue, that will betray with
　　blushing
The close enacts and counsels of the heart!
Here 's a young lad fram'd of another leer:
Look how the black slave smiles upon the
　　father,
As who should say, *Old lad, I am thine own.*
He is your brother, lords; sensibly fed
Of that self-blood that first gave life to you;
And from that womb where you imprison'd
　　were
He is enfranchised and come to light:
Nay, he is your brother by the surer side,
Although my seal be stamped in his face.
*Nur.* Aaron, what shall I say unto the
　　empress?　　　　　　　　　　　[done,
*Dem.* Advise thee, Aaron, what is to be
And we will all subscribe to thy advice:
Save thou the child, so we may all be safe.
*Aar.* Then sit we down, and let us all con-
　　sult.
My son and I will have the wind of you:
Keep there: now talk at pleasure of your
　　safety.　　　　　　　　　　　[*They sit.*
*Dem.* How many women saw this child of
　　his?　　　　　　　　　　　　[in league
*Aar.* Why, so, brave lords! when we join
I am a lamb: but if you brave the Moor,
The chafed boar, the mountain lioness,
The ocean swells not so as Aaron storms.—

But say, again, how many saw the child?
*Nur.* Cornelia the midwife and myself;
And no one else but the deliver'd empress.
*Aar.* The empress, the midwife, and your-
　　self:　　　　　　　　　　　　　　away:
Two may keep counsel when the third's
Go to the empress, tell her this I said:—
　　　　　　　　　[*Stabs her, and she dies.*
Weke, weke!—so cries a pig prepar'd to the
　　spit.
*Dem.* What mean'st thou, Aaron? Where-
　　fore didst thou this?
*Aar.* O Lord, sir, 'tis a deed of policy:
Shall she live to betray this guilt of ours,—
A long-tongu'd babbling gossip? no, lords,
　　no:
And now be it known to you my full intent.
Not far, one Muliteus lives, my countryman;
His wife but yesternight was brought to bed;
His child is like to her, fair as you are:
Go pack with him, and give the mother gold,
And tell them both the circumstance of all;
And how by this their child shall be ad-
　　vanc'd,
And be received for the emperor's heir,
And substituted in the place of mine,
To calm this tempest whirling in the court;
And let the emperor dandle him for his own.
Hark ye, lords; ye see I have given her
　　physic,　　　　　　[*Pointing to the* Nurse.
And you must needs bestow her funeral;
The fields are near, and you are gallant
　　grooms:
This done, see that you take no longer days,
But send the midwife presently to me.
The midwife and the nurse well made away,
Then let the ladies tattle what they please.
*Chi.* Aaron, I see thou wilt not trust the
　　air
With secrets.
*Dem.*　　　　For this care of Tamora,
Herself and hers are highly bound to thee.
　　[*Exeunt* Dem. *and* Chi., *bearing off the
　　　　　　　dead* Nurse.
*Aar.* Now to the Goths, as swift as swal-
　　low flies;
There to dispose this treasure in mine arms,
And secretly to greet the empress' friends.—
Come on, you thick-lipp'd slave, I'll bear you
　　hence;
For it is you that puts us to our shifts:
I'll make you feed on berries and on roots,
And feed on curds and whey, and suck the
　　goat,
And cabin in a cave; and bring you up
To be a warrior and command a camp. [*Exit.*

SCENE III.—ROME. *A public Place.*

*Enter* TITUS, *bearing arrows, with letters at
the ends of them; with him* MARCUS,
YOUNG LUCIUS, *and other* Gentlemen, *with
bows.*

*Tit.* Come, Marcus, come:—kinsmen, this
　　is the way.—

Sir boy, now let me see your archery;
Look ye draw home enough, and 'tis there
　　straight.—
*Terras Astræa reliquit:*
Be you remember'd, Marcus, she's gone, she's
　　fled.　　　　　　　　　　　　　　　[shall
Sirs, take you to your tools. You, cousins,
Go sound the ocean and cast your nets;
Happily you may catch her in the sea;
Yet there's as little justice as at land.—
No; Publius and Sempronius, you must do it;
'Tis you must dig with mattock and with
　　spade,
And pierce the inmost centre of the earth:
Then, when you come to Pluto's region,
I pray you deliver him this petition;
Tell him it is for justice and for aid,
And that it comes from old Andronicus,
Shaken with sorrows in ungrateful Rome.—
Ah, Rome!—Well, well; I made thee miser-
　　able
What time I threw the people's suffrages
On him that thus doth tyrannize o'er me.—
Go, get you gone; and pray be careful all,
And leave you not a man-of-war unsearch'd:
This wicked emperor may have shipp'd her
　　hence;
And, kinsmen, then we may go pipe for
　　justice.
　*Marc.* O Publius, is not this a heavy case,
To see thy noble uncle thus distract? [cerns
　*Pub.* Therefore, my lord, it highly us con-
By day and night to attend him carefully,
And feed his humour kindly as we may,
Till time beget some careful remedy.
　*Marc.* Kinsmen, his sorrows are past
　　remedy.
Join with the Goths; and with revengeful
　　war
Take wreak on Rome for this ingratitude,
And vengeance on the traitor Saturnine.
　*Tit.* Publius, how now! how now, my
　　masters!
What, have you met with her?　[you word,
　*Pub.* No, my good lord; but Pluto sends
If you will have Revenge from hell, you shall:
Marry, for Justice, she is so employ'd,
He thinks, with Jove in heaven, or some-
　　where else,
So that perforce you must needs stay a time.
　*Tit.* He doth me wrong to feed me with
　　delays.
I'll dive into the burning lake below,
And pull her out of Acheron by the heels.—
Marcus, we are but shrubs, no cedars we,
No big-bon'd men, fram'd of the Cyclops'
　　size;
But metal, Marcus, steel to the very back,
Yet wrung with wrongs more than our backs
　　can bear:
And, sith there is no justice in earth nor hell,
We will solicit heaven, and move the gods
To send down Justice for to wreak our
　　wrongs.—

Come, to this gear.—You are a good archer,
　　Marcus.　　[*He gives them the arrows.*
*Ad Jovem,* that's for you:—here, *ad Apolli-
　　nem:*—
*Ad Martem,* that's for myself:—
Here, boy, to Pallas:—here, to Mercury:—
To Saturn, Caius, not to Saturnine;
You were as good to shoot against the
　　wind.—
To it, boy.—Marcus, loose when I bid.—
Of my word, I have written to effect;
There's not a god left unsolicited. [the court:
　*Marc.* Kinsmen, shoot all your shafts into
We will afflict the emperor in his pride.
　*Tit.* Now, masters, draw. [*They shoot.*]
　　O, well said, Lucius!
Good boy, in Virgo's lap; give it Pallas.
　*Marc.* My lord, I aim a mile beyond the
　　moon:
Your letter is with Jupiter by this.
　*Tit.* Ha! ha!
Publius, Publius, what hast thou done?
See, see, thou hast shot off one of Taurus'
　　horns.
　*Marc.* This was the sport, my lord: when
　　Publius shot,
The Bull, being gall'd, gave Aries such a
　　knock
That down fell both the Ram's horns in the
　　court;
And who should find them but the empress'
　　villain?
She laugh'd, and told the Moor he should not
　　choose
But give them to his master for a present.
　*Tit.* Why, there it goes: God give his lord-
　　ship joy!

*Enter a* Clown, *with a basket and two
　　pigeons in it.*

News, news from heaven! Marcus, the post is
　　come.
Sirrah, what tidings? have you any letters?
Shall I have justice? what says Jupiter?
　*Clo.* Ho, the gibbet-maker? he says that
he hath taken them down again, for the man
must not be hanged till the next week.
　*Tit.* But what says Jupiter, I ask thee?
　*Clo.* Alas, sir, I know not Jupiter; I never
drank with him in all my life.
　*Tit.* Why, villain, art not thou the carrier?
　*Clo.* Ay, of my pigeons, sir; nothing else.
　*Tit.* Why, didst thou not come from
heaven?
　*Clo.* From heaven! alas, sir, I never came
there: God forbid I should be so bold to press
to heaven in my young days. Why, I am going with my pigeons to the tribunal plebs, to
take up a matter of brawl betwixt my uncle
and one of the imperial's men.
　*Marc.* Why, sir, that is as fit as can be to
serve for your oration; and let him deliver
the pigeons to the emperor from you.

*Tit.* Tell me, can you deliver an oration to the emperor with a grace?

*Clo.* Nay, truly, sir, I could never say grace in all my life.

*Tit.* Sirrah, come hither: make no more ado,
But give your pigeons to the emperor:
By me thou shalt have justice at his hands.
Hold, hold; meanwhile here 's money for thy charges.—
Give me pen and ink.—　　　　[cation?
Sirrah, can you with a grace deliver a suppli-

*Clo.* Ay, sir.

*Tit.* Then here is a supplication for you.
And when you come to him, at the first approach you must kneel; then kiss his foot;
then deliver up your pigeons; and then look
for your reward. I'll be at hand, sir; see you
do it bravely.

*Clo.* I warrant you, sir, let me alone.

*Tit.* Sirrah, hast thou a knife? Come, let me see it.
Here, Marcus, fold it in the oration; [ant:—
For thou hast made it like an humble suppli-
And when thou hast given it to the emperor,
Knock at my door, and tell me what he says.

*Clo.* God be with you, sir; I will.

*Tit.* Come, Marcus, let us go.—Publius,
follow me.　　　　　　　　　[*Exeunt.*

SCENE IV.—ROME. *Before the Palace.*

*Enter* SÁTURNINUS, TAMORA, DEMETRIUS,
CHIRON, Lords, *and others;* SATURNINUS
*with the arrows in his hand that* TITUS
*shot.*

*Sat.* Why, lords, what wrongs are these! was ever seen
An emperor in Rome thus overborne,
Troubled, confronted thus; and, for the extent
Of legal justice, us'd in such contempt?
My lords, you know, as do the mightful gods,
However these disturbers of our peace
Buzz in the people's ears, there naught hath pass'd,
But even with law, against the wilful sons
Of old Andronicus. And what an if
His sorrows have so overwhelm'd his wits,
Shall we be thus afflicted in his freaks,
His fits, his frenzy, and his bitterness?
And now he writes to heaven for his redress:
See, here's to Jove, and this to Mercury;
This to Apollo; this to the god of war;—
Sweet scrolls to fly about the streets of Rome!
What 's this but libelling against the senate,
And blazoning our injustice everywhere?
A goodly humour, is it not, my lords?
As who would say, in Rome no justice were.
But if I live, his feigned ecstasies
Shall be no shelter to these outrages:
But he and his shall know that justice lives
In Saturninus' health; whom, if she sleep,
He'll so awake as she in fury shall
Cut off the proud'st conspirator that lives.

*Tam.* My gracious lord, my lovely Saturnine,
Lord of my life, commander of my thoughts,
Calm thee, and bear the faults of Titus' age,
The effects of sorrow for his valiant sons,
Whose loss hath pierc'd him deep, and scarr'd his heart;
And rather comfort his distressed plight
Than prosecute the meanest or the best
For these comtempts.—[*Aside.*] Why, thus it shall become
High-witted Tamora to gloze with all:
But, Titus, I have touch'd thee to the quick,
Thy life-blood on 't: if Aaron now be wise,
Then is all safe, the anchor 's in the port.—

*Enter* Clown.

How now, good follow! wouldst thou speak with us?

*Clo.* Yes, forsooth, an your mistership be imperial.

*Tam.* Empress I am, but yonder sits the emperor.

*Clo.* 'Tis he.—God and Saint Stephen give you good-den: I have brought you a letter and a couple of pigeons here.

[SATURNINUS *reads the letter.*

*Sat.* Go, take him away, and hang him presently.

*Clo.* How much money must I have?

*Tam.* Come, sirrah, you must be hang'd.

*Clo.* Hang'd! By 'r lady, then I have brought up a neck to a fair end.

[*Exit guarded.*

*Sat.* Despiteful and intolerable wrongs!
Shall I endure this monstrous villany?
I know from whence this same device proceeds:
May this be borne,—as if his traitorous sons,
That died by law for murder of our brother,
Have by my means been butcher'd wrongfully?—
Go, drag the villain hither by the hair;
Nor age nor honour shall shape privilege.—
For this proud mock I'll be thy slaughterman;
Sly frantic wretch, that holp'st to make me great,　　　　　　　　　　[me.
In hope thyself should govern Rome and

*Enter* ÆMILIUS.

What news with thee, Æmilius?

*Æmil.* Arm, my lord! Rome never had more cause!
The Goths have gather'd head; and with a power,
Of high resolved men, bent to the spoil,
They hither march amain, under conduct
Of Lucius, son to old Andronicus;
Who threats, in course of this revenge, to do
As much as ever Coriolanus did.

*Sat.* Is warlike Lucius general of the Goths?

These tidings nip me; and I hang the head
As flowers with frost, or grass beat down with
  storms:
Ay, now begin our sorrows to approach:
'Tis he the common people love so much;
Myself hath often overheard them say,—
When I have walked like a private man,—
That Lucius' banishment was wrongfully,
And they have wish'd that Lucius were their
  emperor.
  *Tam.* Why should you fear? is not your
  city strong?
  *Sat.* Ay, but the citizens favour Lucius,
And will revolt from me to succour him.
  *Tam.* King, be thy thoughts imperious, like
  thy name.
Is the sun dimm'd, that gnats do fly in it?
The eagle suffers little birds to sing,
And is not careful what they mean thereby,
Knowing that with the shadow of his wing
He can at pleasure stint their melody:
Even so mayst thou the giddy men of Rome.
Then cheer thy spirit: for know, thou em-
  peror,
I will enchant the old Andronicus
With words more sweet, and yet more
  dangerous,
Than baits to fish or honey-stalks to sheep,
Whenas the one is wounded with the bait,
The other rotted with delicious feed.
  *Sat.* But he will not entreat his son for us.
  *Tam.* If Tamora entreat him, then he will:
For I can smooth and fill his aged ear
With golden promises that, were his heart
Almost impregnable, his old ears deaf,
Yet should both ear and heart obey my
  tongue.—   [bassador:
Go thou before [*to* ÆMILIUS]; be our am-
Say that the emperor requests a parley
Of warlike Lucius, and appoint the meeting
Even at his father's house, the old Androni-
  cus.
  *Sat.* Æmilius, do this message honourably:
And if he stand on hostage for his safety,
Bid him demand what pledge will please him
  best.
  *Æmil.* Your bidding shall I do effectually.
    [*Exit.*
  *Tam.* Now will I to that old Andronicus,
And temper him, with all the art I have,
To pluck proud Lucius from the warlike
  Goths.
And now, sweet emperor, be blithe again,
And bury all thy fear in my devices.
  *Sat.* Then go successfully, and plead to him.
    [*Exeunt.*

## ACT V.

### Scene I.—*Plains near Rome.*

*Enter* LUCIUS *and* Goths, *with drum and
  colours.*

  *Luc.* Approved warriors and my faithful
  friends,

I have received letters from great Rome,
Which signify what hate they bear their
  emperor,
And how desirous of our sight they are.
Therefore, great lords, be as your titles wit-
  ness,
Imperious and impatient of your wrongs;
And wherein Rome hath done you any scath
Let him make treble satisfaction.
  1 *Goth.* Brave slip, sprung from the great
  Andronicus,   [comfort;
Whose name was once our terror, now our
Whose high exploits and honourable deeds
Ingrateful Rome requites with foul contempt,
Be bold in us: we'll follow where thou
  lead'st,—
Like stinging bees in hottest summer's day,
Led by their master to the flowered fields,—
And be aveng'd on cursed Tamora.   [him.
  *Goths.* And as he saith, so say we all with
  *Luc.* I humbly thank him, and I thank you
  all.
But who comes here, led by a lusty Goth?

*Enter a* Goth, *leading* AARON *with his* Child
  *in his arms.*

  2 *Goth.* Renowned Lucius, from our troops
  I stray'd
To gaze upon a ruinous monastery;
And as I earnestly did fix mine eye
Upon the wasted building, suddenly
I heard a child cry underneath a wall.
I made unto the noise; when soon I heard
The crying babe controll'd with this dis-
  course:—
*Peace, tawny slave, half me and half thy
  dam!
Did not thy hue bewray whose brat thou art,
Had nature lent thee but thy mother's look,
Villain, thou mightst have been an emperor:
But where the bull and cow are both milk-
  white
They never do beget a coal-black calf.
Peace, villain, peace!*—even thus he rates the
  babe,—
*For I must bear thee to a trusty Goth;
Who, when he knows thou art the empress'
  babe,
Will hold thee dearly for thy mother's sake.*
With this, my weapon drawn, I rush'd upon
  him,
Surpris'd him suddenly, and brought him
  hither,
To use as you think needful of the man.
  *Luc.* O worthy Goth, this is the incarnate
  devil
That robb'd Andronicus of his good hand;
This is the pearl that pleas'd your empress'
  eye;
And here's the base fruit of his burning
  lust.—
Say, wall-ey'd slave, whither wouldst thou
  convey
This growing image of thy fiend-like face?

Why dost not speak? what, deaf? No; not a
　　word?—
A halter, soldiers; hang him on this tree,
And by his side his fruit of bastardy,
　　*Aar.* Touch not the boy,—he is of royal
　　blood.
　　*Luc.* Too like the sire for ever being
　　good.—
First hang the child, that he may see it
　　sprawl,—
A sight to vex the father's soul withal.
Get me a ladder.
　　　　[*A ladder brought, which* AARON *is
　　　　　　obliged to ascend.*
　　*Aar.*　　　　　Lucius, save the child,
And bear it from me to the empress.
If thou do this, I'll show thee wondrous
　　things
That highly may advantage thee to hear:
If thou wilt not, befall what may befall,
I'll speak no more,—but vengeance rot you
　　all!
　　*Luc.* Say on: an if it please me which thou
　　speak'st,
Thy child shall live, and I will see it
　　nourish'd.
　　*Aar.* An if it please thee! why, assure thee,
　　Lucius,
'Twill vex thy soul to hear what I shall
　　speak;
For I must talk of murders, rapes, and
　　massacres,
Acts of black night, abominable deeds,
Complots of mischief, treason, villanies,
Ruthful to hear, yet pitiously perform'd:
And this shall all be buried by my death,
Unless thou swear to me my child shall live.
　　*Luc.* Tell on thy mind; I say thy child
　　shall live.　　　　　　　　　　[begin.
　　*Aar.* Swear that he shall, and then I will
　　*Luc.* Who should I swear by? thou be-
　　liev'st no god:
That granted, how canst thou believe an
　　oath?
　　*Aar.* What if I do not? as, indeed, I do
　　not;
Yet, for I know thou art religious,
And hast a thing within thee called con-
　　science,
With twenty popish tricks and ceremonies
Which I have seen thee careful to observe,
Therefore I urge thy oath;—for that I know
An idiot holds his bauble for a god,
And keeps the oath which by that god he
　　swears;
To that I'll urge him:—therefore thou shalt
　　vow
By that same god,—what god soe'er it be
That thou ador'st and hast in reverence,—
To save my boy, to nourish and bring him
　　up;
Or else I will discover naught to thee.
　　*Luc.* Even by my god I swear to thee I
　　will.

　　*Aar.* First know thou, I begot him on the
　　empress.
　　*Luc.* O most insatiate luxurious woman!
　　*Aar.* Tut, Lucius, this was but a deed of
　　charity
To that which thou shalt hear of me anon.
'Twas her two sons that murder'd Bassianus;
They cut thy sister's tongue, and ravish'd her,
And cut her hands, and trimm'd her as thou
　　saw'st.　　　　　　　　　　[trimming?
　　*Luc.* O détestable villain! call'st thou that
　　*Aar.* Why, she was wash'd, and cut, and·
　　trimm'd; and 'twas
Trim sport for them that had the doing of it.
　　*Luc.* O barbarous, beastly villains, like
　　thyself!　　　　　　　　　　[them:
　　*Aar.* Indeed, I was their tutor to instruct
That codding spirit had they from their
　　mother,
As sure a card as ever won the set;
That bloody mind, I think, they learn'd of
　　me,
As true a dog as ever fought at head.
Well, let my deeds be witness of my worth.
I train'd thy brethren to that guileful hole
Where the dead corpse of Bassianus lay:
I wrote the letter that thy father found,
And hid the gold within the letter mention'd,
Confederate with the queen and her two
　　sons:
And what not done, that thou hast cause to
　　rue,
Wherein I had no stroke of mischief in 't?
I play'd the cheater for thy father's hand;
And when I had it, drew myself apart,
And almost broke my heart with extreme
　　laughter:
I pry'd me through the crevice of a wall
When, for his hand, he had his two sons'
　　heads;
Beheld his tears, and laugh'd so heartily
That both mine eyes were rainy like to his:
And when I told the empress of this sport,
She swooned almost at my pleasing tale,
And for my tidings gave me twenty kisses.
　　*Goth.* What, canst thou say all this, and
　　never blush?
　　*Aar.* Ay, like a black dog, as the saying is.
　　*Luc.* Art thou not sorry for these heinous
　　deeds?　　　　　　　　　　[more.
　　*Aar.* Ay, that I had not done a thousand
Even now I curse the day,—and yet, I think,
Few come within the compass of my curse,—
Wherein I did not some notorious ill:
As, kill a man, or else devise his death;
Ravish a maid, or plot the way to do it;
Accuse some innocent, and forswear myself;
Set deadly enmity between two friends;
Make poor men's cattle stray and break their
　　necks;
Set fire on barns and hay-stacks in the night,
And bid the owners quench them with their
　　tears.　　　　　　　　　　[graves,
Oft have I digg'd up dead men from their

And set them upright at their dear friends'
    doors,
Even when their sorrows almost were forgot ;
And on their skins, as on the bark of trees,
Have with my knife carved in Roman letters,
*Let not your sorrow die, though I am dead.*
Tut, I have done a thousand dreadful things
As willingly as one would kill a fly ;
And nothing grieves me heartily indeed
But that I cannot do ten thousand more. [*die*
  *Luc.* Bring down the devil ; for he must not
So sweet a death as hanging presently.
  *Aar.* If there be devils, would I were a
    devil,
To live and burn in everlasting fire,
So I might have your company in hell,
But to torment you with my bitter tongue !
  *Luc.* Sirs, stop his mouth, and let him
    speak no more.

*Enter a* Goth.

  3 *Goth.* My lord, there is a messenger from
    Rome
Desires to be admitted to your presence.
  *Luc.* Let him come near.

*Enter* ÆMILIUS.

Welcome, Æmilius : what's the news from
    Rome ?             [the Goths,
  *Æmil.* Lord Lucius, and you princes of
The Roman emperor greets you all by me ;
And, for he understands you are in arms,
He craves a parley at your father's house,
Willing you to demand your hostages,
And they shall be immediately deliver'd.
  1 *Goth.* What says our general ?   [pledges
  *Luc.* Æmilius, let the emperor give his
Unto my father and my uncle Marcus,
And we will come.—March away. [*Exeunt.*

SCENE II.—ROME. *Before* TITUS'S *House.*

*Enter* TAMORA, DEMETRIUS, *and* CHIRON,
*disguised.*

  *Tam.* Thus, in this strange and sad habili-
    ment
I will encounter with Andronicus,
And say I am Revenge, sent from below
To join with him and right his heinous
    wrongs.
Knock at his study, where they say he keeps
To ruminate strange plots of dire revenge ;
Tell him Revenge is come to join with him,
And work confusion on his enemies.
                    [*They knock.*

*Enter* TITUS, *above.*

  *Tit.* Who doth molest my contemplation ?
Is it your trick to make me ope the door,
That so my sad decrees may fly away,
And all my study be to no effect ?
You are deceiv'd : for what I mean to do
See here in bloody lines I have set down ;
And what is written shall be executed.

  *Tam.* Titus, I am come to talk with thee.
  *Tit.* No, not a word : how can I grace my
    talk,
Wanting a hand to give it action ?
Thou hast the odds of me ; therefore no more.
  *Tam.* If thou didst know me, thou wouldst
    talk with me.
  *Tit.* I am not mad ; I know thee well
    enough :
Witness this wretched stump, witness these
    crimson lines ;
Witness these trenches made by grief and
    care ;
Witness the tiring day and heavy night ;
Witness all sorrow, that I know thee well
For our proud empress, mighty Tamora :
Is not thy coming for my other hand ?
  *Tam.* Know thou, sad man, I am not
    Tamora ;
She is thy enemy and I thy friend :
I am Revenge ; sent from the infernal king-
    dom
To ease the gnawing vulture of thy mind
By working wreakful vengeance on thy foes.
Come down and welcome me to this world's
    light ;
Confer with me of murder and of death :
There's not a hollow cave or lurking-place,
No vast obscurity or misty vale,
Where bloody murder or detested rape
Can couch for fear but I will find them out ;
And in their ears tell them my dreadful
    name,—
Revenge, which makes the foul offenders
    quake.
  *Tit.* Art thou Revenge ? and art thou sent
    to me
To be a torment to mine enemies ?
  *Tam.* I am ; therefore come down and wel-
    come me.
  *Tit.* Do me some service ere I come to thee.
Lo, by thy side where Rape and Murder
    stands ;
Now give some 'surance that thou art Re-
    venge,—
Stab them, or tear them on thy chariot
    wheels ;
And then I'll come and be thy waggoner,
And whirl along with thee about the globe.
Provide thee two proper palfreys, black as
    jet,
To hale thy vengeful waggon swift away,
And find out murderers in their guilty caves :
And when thy car is loaden with their heads
I will dismount, and by the waggon-wheel
Trot, like a servile footman, all day long,
Even from Hyperion's rising in the east
Until his very downfall in the sea :
And day by day I'll do this heavy task,
So thou destroy Rapine and Murder there.
  *Tam.* These are my ministers, and come
    with me.
  *Tit.* Are these thy ministers ? what are they
    call'd ?

*Tam.* Rapine and Murder; therefore called
so
'Cause they take vengeance of such kind of
men.
*Tit.* Good lord, how like the empress' sons
they are!
And you the empress! But we worldly men
Have miserable, mad, mistaking eyes.
O sweet Revenge, now do I come to thee;
And, if one arm's embracement will content
thee,
I will embrace thee in it by and by.
                              [*Exit from above.*
*Tam.* This closing with him fits his lunacy:
Whate'er I forge to feed his brain-sick fits,
Do you uphold and maintain in your
speeches,
For now he firmly takes me for Revenge;
And, being credulous in this mad thought,
I'll make him send for Lucius his son;
And, whilst I at a banquet hold him sure,
I'll find some cunning practice out of hand
To scatter and disperse the giddy Goths,
Or, at the least, make them his enemies.
See, here he comes, and I must ply my theme.

*Enter* TITUS.

*Tit.* Long have I been forlorn, and all for
thee:
Welcome, dread fury, to my woeful house;—
Rapine and Murder, you are welcome too:—
How like the empress and her sons you are!
Well are you fitted, had you but a Moor:
Could not all hell afford you such a devil?—
For well I wot the empress never wags
But in her company there is a Moor;
And, would you represent our queen aright,
It were convenient you had such a devil:
But welcome as you are. What shall we do?
*Tam.* What wouldst thou have us do, An-
dronicus?
*Dem.* Show me a murderer, I'll deal with  [him.
*Chi.* Show me a villain that hath done a
rape,
And I am sent to be reveng'd on him.
*Tam.* Show me a thousand that have done
thee wrong,
And I will be revenged on them all.  [of Rome,
*Tit.* Look round about the wicked streets
And when thou find'st a man that 's like
thyself,
Good Murder, stab him; he 's a murderer.—
Go with him; and when it is thy hap
To find another that is like to thee,
Good Rapine, stab him; he's a ravisher.—
Go thou with them; and in the emperor's
court
There is a queen, attended by a Moor;
Well mayst thou know her by thy own pro-
portion,
For up and down she doth resemble thee;
I pray thee, do on them some violent death;
They have been violent to me and mine.

*Tam.* Well hast thou lesson'd us; this shall
we do.
But would it please thee, good Andronicus,
To send for Lucius, thy thrice-valiant son,
Who leads towards Rome a band of warlike
Goths,
And bid him come and banquet at thy house;
When he is here, even at thy solemn feast,
I will bring in the empress and her sons,
The emperor himself and all thy foes;
And at thy mercy shall they stoop and kneel,
And on them shalt thou ease thy angry heart.
What says Andronicus to this device? [calls.
*Tit.* Marcus, my brother!—'tis sad Titus

*Enter* MARCUS.

Go, gentle Marcus, to thy nephew Lucius;
Thou shalt inquire him out among the Goths:
Bid him repair to me, and bring with him
Some of the chiefest princes of the Goths;
Bid him encamp his soldiers where they are:
Tell him the emperor and the empress too
Feast at my house, and he shall feast with
them.
This do thou for my love; and so let him
As he regards his aged father's life.
*Marc.* This will I do, and soon return
again.                                    [*Exit.*
*Tam.* Now will I hence about thy business,
And take my ministers along with me.
*Tit.* Nay, nay, let Rape and Murder stay
with me,
Or else I'll call my brother back again,
And cleave to no revenge but Lucius.
*Tam.* [*Aside to them.*] What say you,
boys? will you abide with him,
Whiles I go tell my lord the emperor
How I have govern'd our determin'd jest?
Yield to his humour, smooth and speak him
fair,
And tarry with him till I come again.
*Tit.* [*Aside.*] I know them all, though
they suppose me mad,            [vices,—
And will o'er-reach them in their own de-
A pair of cursed hell-hounds and their dam.
*Dem.* Madam, depart at pleasure; leave us
here.                                   [goes
*Tam.* Farewell, Andronicus: Revenge now
To lay a complot to betray thy foes.
*Tit.* I know thou dost; and, sweet Re-
venge, farewell!       [*Exit* TAMORA.
*Chi.* Tell us, old man, how shall we be
employ'd?                              [do.—
*Tit.* Tut, I have work enough for you to
Publius, come hither, Caius, and Valentine!

*Enter* PUBLIUS *and others.*

*Pub.* What is your will?
*Tit.* Know you these two?
*Pub.* The empress' sons,
I take them, Chiron and Demetrius.
*Tit.* Fie, Publius, fie! thou art too much
deceiv'd,—
The one is Murder, Rape is the other's name;

And therefore bind them, gentle Publius:—
Caius and Valentine, lay hands on them:—
Oft have you heard me wish for such an hour,
And now I find it; therefore bind them sure;
And stop their mouths if they begin to cry.
   [*Exit.* PUBLIUS, *&c., lay hold on* CHIRON
      *and* DEMETRIUS.
   *Chi.* Villains, forbear! we are the empress'
      sons.           [commanded.—
   *Pub.* And therefore do we what we are
Stop close their mouths, let them not speak a
   word.
Is he sure bound? look that you bind them
   fast.

*Re-enter* TITUS ANDRONICUS, *with* LAVINIA;
   *he bearing a knife and she a basin.*

   *Tit.* Come, come, Lavinia; look, thy foes
      are bound.—           [me;
Sirs, stop their mouths, let them not speak to
But let them hear what fearful words I
   utter.—
O villains, Chiron and Demetrius!
Here stands the spring whom you have
   stain'd with mud;
This goodly summer with your winter mix'd.
You kill'd her husband; and for that vile
   fault
Two of her brothers were condemn'd to
   death,
My hand cut off and made a merry jest;
Both her sweet hands, her tongue, and that,
   more dear
Than hands or tongue, her spotless chastity,
Inhuman traitors, you constrain'd and forc'd.
What would you say, if I should let you
   speak?
Villains, for shame you could not beg for
   grace.
Hark, wretches! how I mean to martyr you.
This one hand yet is left to cut your throats,
Whilst that Lavinia 'tween her stumps doth
   hold
The basin that receives your guilty blood.
You know your mother means to feast with
   me,
And calls herself Revenge, and thinks me
   mad:—
Hark, villains! I will grind your bones to
   dust,
And with your blood and it I'll make a
   paste;
And of the paste a coffin I will rear,
And make two pasties of your shameful
   heads;
And bid that strumpet, your unhallow'd dam,
Like to the earth, swallow her own increase.
This is the feast that I have bid her to,
And this the banquet she shall surfeit on;
For worse than Philomel you us'd my
   daughter,
And worse than Progne I will be reveng'd:
And now prepare your throats. Lavinia,
   come.           [*He cuts their throats.*

Receive the blood: and when that they are
   dead,
Let me go grind their bones to powder small,
And with this hateful liquor temper it;
And in that paste let their vile heads be
   bak'd.
Come, come, be every one officious
To make this banquet; which I wish may
   prove           [feast.
More stern and bloody than the Centaurs'
So, now bring them in, for I will play the
   cook,           [comes.
And see them ready 'gainst their mother
           [*Exeunt, bearing the dead bodies.*

SCENE III.—ROME. *A Pavilion in* TITUS'S
   *Gardens, with tables, &c.*

*Enter* LUCIUS, MARCUS, *and* Goths, *with*
      AARON *prisoner.*

   *Luc.* Uncle Marcus, since 'tis my father's
      mind
That I repair to Rome, I am content.
   1 *Goth.* And ours with thine, befall what
      fortune will.           [barous Moor,
   *Luc.* Good uncle, take you in this bar-
This ravenous tiger, this accursed devil;
Let him receive no sustenance, fetter him,
Till he be brought unto the empress' face,
For testimony of her foul proceedings:
And see the ambush of our friends be strong;
I fear the emperor means no good to us.
   *Aar.* Some devil whisper curses in mine
      ear,
And prompt me, that my tongue may utter
      forth
The venomous malice of my swelling heart!
   *Luc.* Away, inhuman dog! unhallow'd
      slave!—
Sirs, help our uncle to convey him in.—
   [*Exeunt* Goths *with* AAR. *Flourish within.*
The trumpets show the emperor is at hand.

*Enter* SATURNINUS *and* TAMORA, *with*
ÆMILIUS, Tribunes, Senators, *and others.*

   *Sat.* What, hath the firmament more suns
      than one?
   *Luc.* What boots it thee to call thyself the
      sun?
   *Marc.* Rome's emperor, and nephew, break
      the parle;
These quarrels must be quietly debated.
The feast is ready, which the careful Titus
Hath ordain'd to an honourable end,
For peace, for love, for league, and good to
      Rome:           [your places.
Please you, therefore, draw nigh, and take
   *Sat.* Marcus, we will.
   [*Hautboys sound. The company sit at table.*

*Enter* TITUS, *dressed like a cook,* LAVINIA,
   *vailed,* YOUNG LUCIUS, *and others.* TITUS
   *places the dishes on the table.*

   *Tit.* Welcome, my gracious lord; welcome,
      dread queen;

Welcome, ye warlike Goths; welcome, Lucius;
And welcome all: although the cheer be poor,
'Twill fill your stomachs; please you eat of it.
  *Sat.* Why art thou thus attir'd, Andronicus?
  *Tit.* Because I would be sure to have all well
To entertain your highness and your empress.
  *Tam.* We are beholden to you, good Andronicus.       [you were.
  *Tit.* And if your highness knew my heart,
My lord the emperor, resolve me this:
Was it well done of rash Virginius
To slay his daughter with his own right hand,
Because she was enforc'd, stain'd, and deflower'd?
  *Sat.* It was, Andronicus.
  *Tit.* Your reason, mighty lord.    [shame,
  *Sat.* Because the girl should not survive her
And by her presence still renew his sorrows.
  *Tit.* A reason mighty, strong, and effectual;
A pattern, precedent, and lively warrant
For me, most wretched, to perform the like:—
Die, die, Lavinia, and thy shame with thee;
                 [*Kills* LAVINIA.
And with thy shame thy father's sorrow die!
  *Sat.* What hast thou done, unnatural and unkind?
  *Tit.* Kill'd her for whom my tears have made me blind.
I am as woeful as Virginius was,
And have a thousand times more cause than he
To do this outrage;—and it is now done.
  *Sat.* What, was she ravish'd? tell who did the deed.
  *Tit.* Will't please you eat? will't please your highness feed?
  *Tam.* Why hast thou slain thine only daughter thus?
  *Tit.* Not I; 'twas Chiron and Demetrius:
They ravish'd her, and cut away her tongue;
And they, 'twas they that did her all this wrong.
  *Sat.* Go, fetch them hither to us presently.
  *Tit.* Why, there they are both, baked in that pie,
Whereof their mother daintily hath fed,
Eating the flesh that she herself hath bred.
'Tis true, 'tis true; witness my knife's sharp point.         [*Kills* TAMORA.
  *Sat.* Die, frantic wretch, for this accursed deed!         [*Kills* TITUS.
  *Luc.* Can the son's eye behold his father bleed?
There's meed for meed, death for a deadly deed.
[*Kills* SATURNINUS. *A great tumult.* LUCIUS,
MARCUS, *and their partisans, ascend the
steps before* TITUS's *house.*
  *Marc.* You sad-fac'd men, people and sons of Rome,
By uproar sever'd, like a flight of fowl

Scatter'd by winds and high tempestuous gusts,
O, let me teach you how to knit again
This scatter'd corn into one mutual sheaf,
These broken limbs again into one body;
Lest Rome herself be bane unto herself,
And she whom mighty kingdoms court'sy to,
Like a forlorn and desperate castaway,
Do shameful execution on herself.
But if my frosty signs and chaps of age,
Grave witnesses of true experience,
Cannot induce you to attend my words,—
Speak, Rome's dear friend [*to* LUCIUS]: as
  erst our ancestor,
When with his solemn tongue he did discourse
To love-sick Dido's sad attending ear
The story of that baleful burning night
When subtle Greeks surpris'd King Priam's
  Troy,—
Tell us what Sinon hath bewitch'd our ears,
Or who hath brought the fatal engine in
That gives our Troy, our Rome, the civil
  wound.
My heart is not compact of flint nor steel;
Nor can I utter all our bitter grief,
But floods of tears will drown my oratory
And break my very utterance, even in the
  time
When it should move you to attend me most,
Lending your kind commiseration.
Here is a captain, let him tell the tale;
Your hearts will throb and weep to hear him
  speak.              [you
  *Luc.* Then, noble auditory, be it known to
That cursed Chiron and Demetrius
Were they that murdered our emperor's
  brother;
And they it were that ravished our sister:
For their fell faults our brothers were beheaded;
Our father's tears despis'd, and basely cozen'd
Of that true hand that fought Rome's quarrel
  out
And sent her enemies unto the grave.
Lastly, myself unkindly banished,
The gates shut on me, and turn'd weeping
  out,
To beg relief among Rome's enemies;
Who drown'd their enmity in my true tears,
And op'd their arms to embrace me as a
  friend:             [you,
And I am the turn'd-forth, be it known to
That have preserv'd her welfare in my blood;
And from her bosom took the enemy's point,
Sheathing the steel in my adventurous body.
Alas! you know I am no vaunter, I;
My scars can witness, dumb although they
  are,
That my report is just and full of truth.
But, soft! methinks I do digress too much,
Citing my worthless praise: O, pardon me;
For when no friends are by, men praise themselves.             [this child.
  *Marc.* Now is my turn to speak. Behold

[*Pointing to the* Child *in an* Attendant's *arms.*
Of this was Tamora delivered;
The issue of an irreligious Moor,
Chief architect and plotter of these woes:
The villain is alive in Titus' house,
Damn'd as he is, to witness this is true.
Now judge what cause had Titus to revenge
These wrongs unspeakable, past patience,
Or more than any living man could bear.
Now you have heard the truth, what say you,
    Romans?
Have we done aught amiss,—show us wherein,
And, from the place where you behold us now,
The poor remainder of Andronici
Will, hand in hand, all headlong cast us down,
And on the ragged stones beat forth our
    brains,
And make a mutual closure of our house.
Speak, Romans, speak; and if you say we
    shall,
Lo, hand in hand, Lucius and I will fall.
    *Æmil.* Come, come, thou reverend man of
    Rome,
And bring our emperor gently in thy hand,
Lucius our emperor; for well I know
The common voice do cry it shall be so.
    *Romans.* [*Several speak.*] Lucius, all hail,
    Rome's royal emperor!
    *Marc.* Go, go into old Titus' sorrowful
    house,
    [*To* Attendants, *who go into the house.*
And hither hale that misbelieving Moor,
To be adjudg'd some direful slaughtering
    death,
As punishment for his most wicked life.
    [LUCIUS, MARCUS, &c., *descend.*
    *Romans.* [*Several speak.*] Lucius, all hail,
    Rome's gracious governor!
    *Luc.* Thanks, gentle Romans: may I gov-
    ern so
To heal Rome's harms and wipe away her
    woe!
But, gentle people, give me aim awhile,—
For nature puts me to a heavy task:—
Stand all aloof;—but, uncle, draw you near,
To shed obsequious tears upon this trunk—
O, take this warm kiss on thy pale cold lips,
    [*Kisses* TITUS.
These sorrowful drops upon thy blood-stain'd
    face,
The last true duties of thy noble son!
    *Marc.* Tear for tear and loving kiss for kiss
Thy brother Marcus tenders on thy lips:
O, were the sum of these that I should pay
Countless and infinite, yet would I pay them!
    *Luc.* Come hither, boy; come, come, and
    learn of us

To melt in showers: thy grandsire lov'd thee
    well:
Many a time he danc'd thee on his knee,
Sung thee asleep, his loving breast thy pillow;
Many a matter hath he told to thee,
Meet and agreeing with thine infancy;
In that respect, then, like a loving child,
Shed yet some small drops from thy tender
    spring,
Because kind nature doth require it so:
Friends should associate friends in grief and
    woe:
Bid him farewell; commit him to the grave;
Do him that kindness, and take leave of him.
    *Y. Luc.* O grandsire, grandsire! even with
    all my heart
Would I were dead, so you did live again!—
O Lord, I cannot speak to him for weeping,
My tears will choke me if I ope my mouth.

    *Re-enter* Attendants *with* AARON.

    *Æmil.* You sad Andronici, have done with
    woes:
Give sentence on this execrable wretch,
That hath been breeder of these dire events.
    *Luc.* Set him breast-deep in earth, and
    famish him;
There let him stand, and rave, and cry for
    food;
If any one relieves or pities him,
For the offence he dies. This is our doom:
Some stay to see him fasten'd in the earth.
    *Aar.* O, why should wrath be mute and
    fury dumb?
I am no baby, I, that with base prayers
I should repent the evils I have done:
Ten thousand worse than ever yet I did
Would I perform, if I might have my will:
If one good deed in all my life I did,
I do repent it from my very soul.
    *Luc.* Some loving friends convey the em-
    peror hence,
And give him burial in his father's grave.
My father and Lavinia shall forthwith
Be closed in our household's monument.
As for the heinous tiger, Tamora,
No funeral rite, nor man in mournful weeds,
No mournful bell shall ring her burial;
But throw her forth to beasts and birds of
    prey:
Her life was beast-like and devoid of pity;
And, being so, shall have like want of pity.
See justice done on Aaron, that damn'd Moor,
By whom our heavy haps had their beginning:
Then, afterwards, to order well the state,
That like events may ne'er it ruinate.
    [*Exeunt.*

# PERICLES, PRINCE OF TYRE

## DRAMATIS PERSONÆ

ANTIOCHUS, *King of Antioch.*
PERICLES, *Prince of Tyre.*
HELICANUS, } *two Lords of Tyre.*
ESCANES,
SIMONIDES, *King of Pentapolis.*
CLEON, *Governor of Tharsus.*
LYSIMACHUS, *Governor of Mitylene.*
CERIMON, *a Lord of Ephesus.*
THALIARD, *a Lord of Antioch.*
PHILEMON, *Servant to* CERIMON.
LEONINE, *Servant to* DIONYZA.
Marshal.

A Pander; *and* BOULT, *his Servant.*
Gower, *as Chorus.*

The Daughter of ANTIOCHUS.
DIONYZA, *Wife to* CLEON.
THAISA, *Daughter to* SIMONIDES.
MARINA, *Daughter to* PERICLES *and* THASIA.
LYCHORIDA, *Nurse to* MARINA.
DIANA.
A Bawd.

Lords, Ladies, Knights, Gentlemen, Sailors,
Pirates, Fishermen, *and* Messengers.

SCENE,—*Dispersedly in various Countries.*

## ACT I.

*Enter* GOWER.

*Before the Palace of Antioch.*

To sing a song that old was sung,
From ashes ancient Gower is come;
Assuming man's infirmities,
To glad your ear and please your eyes.
It hath been sung at festivals,
On ember-eves and holy-ales;
And lords and ladies in their lives
Have read it for restoratives:
The purchase is to make men glorious;
*Et bonum quo antiquius, eo melius.*
If you, born in these latter times,
When wit's more ripe, accept my rhymes,
And that to hear an old man sing
May to your wishes pleasure bring,
I life would wish, and that I might
Waste it for you, like taper-light.—
This Antioch, then, Antiochus the Great
Built up, this city, for his chiefest seat;
The fairest in all Syria,—
I tell you what mine authors say:
This king unto him took a fere,
Who died and left a female heir,
So buxom, blithe, and full of face,
As heaven had lent her all his grace;
With whom the father liking took,
And her to incest did provoke:—
Bad child; worse father! to entice his own
To evil should be done by none:
But custom what they did begin
Was with long use account no sin.
The beauty of this sinful dame
Made many princes thither frame
To seek her as a bed-fellow,
In marriage-pleasures play-fellow:
Which to prevent he made a law,—
To keep her still, and men in awe,—

That whoso ask'd her for his wife,
His riddle told not, lost his life:
So for her many a wight did die,
As yon grim looks to testify,
What now ensues, to the judgment of your eye
I give, my cause who best can justify. [*Exit.*

SCENE I.—ANTIOCH. *A Room in the Palace.*

*Enter* ANTIOCHUS, PERICLES, *and*
Attendants.

*Ant.* Young Prince of Tyre, you have at
large receiv'd
The danger of the task you undertake.
*Per.* I have, Antiochus, and, with a soul
Embolden'd with the glory of her praise,
Think death no hazard in this enterprise.
*Ant.* Bring in our daughter, clothed like a
bride,
For the embracements even of Jove himself;
At whose conception, till Lucina reign'd,
Nature this dowry gave, to glad her presence,
The senate-house of planets all did sit,
To knit in her their best perfections.

*Music. Enter the* Daughter of ANTIOCHUS.

*Per.* See where she comes, apparell'd like
the spring,
Graces her subjects, and her thoughts the king
Of every virtue gives renown to men!
Her face the book of praises, where is read
Nothing but curious pleasures, as from thence
Sorrow were ever raz'd, and testy wrath
Could never be her mild companion.
Ye gods, that made me man, and sway in love,
That have inflam'd desire in my breast
To taste the fruit of yon celestial tree,
Or die in the adventure, be my helps,
As I am son and servant to your will,
To compass such a boundless happiness!

[947]

*Ant.* Prince Pericles,—
*Per.* That would be son to great Antiochus.
*Ant.* Before thee stands this fair Hes-
 perides,
With golden fruit, but dangerous to be
 touch'd;
For death-like dragons here affright thee
 hard:
Her face, like heaven, enticeth thee to view
Her countless glory, which desert must gain;
And which, without desert, because thine eye
Presumes to reach, all thy whole heap must
 die.
Yon sometime famous princes, like thyself,
Drawn by report, adventurous by desire,
Tell thee, with speechless tongues and sem-
 blance pale,
That, without covering, save yon field of
 stars,
Here they stand martyrs, slain in Cupid's
 wars;
And with dead cheeks advise thee to desist
For going on death's net, whom none resist.
 *Per.* Antiochus, I thank thee, who hath
 taught
My frail mortality to know itself,
And by those fearful objects to prepare
This body, like to them, to what I must;
For death remember'd should be like a mirror,
Who tells us life's but breath, to trust it error.
I'll make my will, then; and, as sick men do,
Who know the world, see heaven, but, feeling
 woe,
Gripe not at earthly joys, as erst they did;
So I bequeath a happy peace to you
And all good men, as every prince should do;
My riches to the earth from whence they
 came;—
But my unspotted fire of love to you.
   [*To the* Daughter *of* ANTIOCHUS.
Thus ready for the way of life or death,
I wait the sharpest blow, Antiochus.
 *Ant.* Scorning advice,—read the conclu-
 sion, then:
Which read and not· expounded, 'tis decreed,
As these before thee, thou thyself shalt bleed.
 *Daugh.* In all save that, mayst thou prove
 prosperous!
In all save that, I wish thee happiness!
 *Per.* Like a bold champion I assume the
 lists,
Nor ask advice of any other thought
But faithfulness and courage.
       [*Reads the Riddle.*

  I am no viper, yet I feed
  On mother's flesh which did me breed.
  I sought a husband, in which labour
  I found that kindness in a father.
  He's father, son, and husband mild;
  I mother, wife, and yet his child.
  How they may be, and yet in two,
  As you will live, resolve it you.

Sharp physic is the last; but, O you powers

That give heaven countless eyes to view men's
 acts,
Why cloud they not their sights perpetually,
If this be true, which makes me pale to read
 it?—
Fair glass of light, I lov'd you, and could still,
  [*Takes hold of the hand of the* Princess.
Were not this glorious casket stor'd with ill:
But I must tell you,—now my thoughts re-
 volt;
For he's no man on whom perfections wait
That, knowing sin within, will touch the gate.
You're a fair viol, and your sense the strings;
Who, finger'd to make man his lawful music,
Would draw heaven down, and all the gods to
 hearken;
But, being play'd upon before your time,
Hell only danceth at so harsh a chime.
Good sooth, I care not for you.
 *Ant.* Prince Pericles, touch not, upon thy
 life,
For that's an article within our law
As dangerous as the rest. Your time's expir'd:
Either expound now, or receive your sen-
 tence.
 *Per.* Great king,
Few love to hear the sins they love to act;
'Twould 'braid yourself too near for me to
 tell it.
Who has a book of all that monarchs do,
He's more secure to keep it shut than shown:
For vice repeated is like the wandering wind,
Blows dust in others' eyes, to spread itself;
And yet the end of all is bought thus dear,
The breath is gone, and the sore eyes see clear:
To stop the air would hurt them. The blind
 mole casts      [is throng'd
Copp'd hills towards heaven, to tell the earth
By man's oppression; and the poor worm doth
 die for't.       [their will;
Kings are earth's gods: in vice their law's
And if Jove stray, who dares say Jove doth
 ill?
It is enough you know; and it is fit,
What being more known grows worse, to
 smother it.
All love the womb that their first being bred.
Then give my tongue like leave to love my
 head.
 *Ant.* [*Aside.*] Heaven, that I had thy head!
  he has found the meaning:   [Tyre
But I will gloze with him.—Young Prince of
Though by the tenor of our strict edict,
Your exposition misinterpreting,
We might proceed to cancel of your days;
Yet hope, succeeding from so fair a tree
As your fair self, doth tune us otherwise:
Forty days longer we do respite you;
If by which time our secret be undone,
This mercy shows we'll joy in such a son:
And until then your entertain shall be
As doth befit our honour and your worth.
  [*Exeunt* ANT., *his* Daughter, *and* Attendants.
 *Per.* How courtesy would seem to cover sin,

When what is done is like an hypocrite,
The which is good in nothing but in sight!
If it be true that I interpret false,
Then were it certain you were not so bad
As with foul incest to abuse your soul;
Where now you're both a father and a son,
By your untimely claspings with your child,—
Which pleasure fits an husband, not a father;—
And she an eater of her mother's flesh,
By the defiling of her parent's bed;
And both like serpents are, who, though they feed
On sweetest flowers, yet they poison breed.
Antioch, farewell! for wisdom sees, those men
Blush not in actions blacker than the night
Will shun no course to keep them from the light.
One sin I know another doth provoke;
Murder's as near to lust as flame to smoke:
Poison and treason are the hands of sin,
Ay, and the targets to put off the shame:
Then, lest my life be cropp'd to keep you clear,
By flight I'll shun the danger which I fear.
　　　　　　　　　　　　　　　　[Exit.

*Re-enter* ANTIOCHUS.

*Ant.* He hath found the meaning, for the which we mean
To have his head.
He must not live to trumpet forth my infamy,
Nor tell the world Antiochus doth sin
In such a loathed manner;
And therefore instantly this prince must die;
For by his fall my honour must keep high.
Who attends us there?

*Enter* THALIARD.

*Thal.*　　　　　　Doth your highness call?
*Ant.* Thaliard, you're of our chamber, and our mind
Partakes her private actions to your secrecy:
And for your faithfulness we will advance you.
Thaliard, behold here's poison and here's gold;
We hate the Prince of Tyre, and thou must kill him:
It fits thee not to ask the reason why,
Because we bid it. Say, is it done?
*Thal.*　　　　　　　　　　My lord,
'Tis done.
*Ant.* Enough.

*Enter a* Messenger.

Let your breath cool yourself, telling your haste.
*Mess.* My lord, Prince Pericles is fled.
　　　　　　　　　　　　　　　　[Exit.
*Ant.*　　　　　　　　　　As thou
Wilt live, fly after: and as an arrow shot
From a well-experienc'd archer hits the mark

His eye doth level at, so thou ne'er return
Unless thou say *Prince Pericles is dead.*
*Thal.* My lord,
If I can get him once within my pistol's length
I'll make him sure enough: so, farewell to your highness.
*Ant.* Thaliard, adieu! [*Exit* THAL.] Till Pericles be dead
My heart can lend no succour to my head.
　　　　　　　　　　　　　　　　[Exit.

SCENE II.—TYRE. *A Room in the Palace.*

*Enter* PERICLES.

*Per.* [*To those without.*] Let none disturb us.—Why should this change of thoughts,
The sad companion, dull-ey'd melancholy,
Be my so us'd a guest as not an hour
In the day's glorious walk, or peaceful night,—
The tomb where grief should sleep,—can breed me quiet?　　　[shun them,
Here pleasures court mine eyes, and mine eyes
And danger, which I fear'd, is at Antioch.
Whose aim seems far too short to hit me here:
Yet neither pleasure's art can joy my spirits,
Nor yet the other's distance comfort me.
Then it is thus: the passions of the mind,
That have their first conception by mis-dread,
Have after-nourishment and life by care;
And what was first but fear what might be done,
Grows elder now, and cares it be not done.
And so with me:—the great Antiochus,
'Gainst whom I am too little to contend,
Since he's so great, can make his will his act,—
Will think me speaking, though I swear to silence;
Nor boots it me to say I honour him,
If he suspect I may dishonour him:
And what may make him blush in being known,
He'll stop the course by which it might be known;
With hostile forces he'll o'spread the land,
And with the ostent of war will look so huge,
Amazement shall drive courage from the state;
Our men be vanquish'd ere they do resist,
And subjects punish'd that ne'er thought offence:
Which care of them, not pity of myself,—
Who once no more but as the tops of trees,
Which fence the roots they grow by, and defend them,—　　　[guish,
Makes both my body pine and soul to lan-
And punish that before that he would punish.

*Enter* HELICANUS *and other* Lords.

1 *Lord.* Joy and all comfort in your sacred breast!　　　　　　　　　[to us,
2 *Lord.* And keep your mind till you return
Peaceful and comfortable!

*Hel.* Peace, peace, my lords, and give experience tongue.

**They** do abuse the king that flatter him:
For flattery is the bellows blows up sin;
The thing the which is flatter'd, but a spark,
To which that blast gives heat and stronger
　glowing;
Whereas reproof, obedient, and in order,
Fits kings, as they are men, for they may err.
When Signior Sooth here does proclaim a
　peace
He flatters you, makes war upon your life.
Prince, pardon me, or strike me if you please;
I cannot be much lower than my knees.

　*Per.* All leave us else; but let your cares
　o'erlook
What shipping and what lading's in our haven,
And then return to us. [*Exeunt* Lords.] Helicanus, thou
Hast moved us: what seest thou in our looks?

　*Hel.* An angry brow, dread lord.

　*Per.* If there be such a dart in princes'
　frowns,
How durst thy tongue move anger to our
　face?

　*Hel.* How dare the plants look up to heaven, from whence
They have their nourishment?

　*Per.*　　　　Thou know'st I have power
To take thy life from thee.

　*Hel.* [*Kneeling.*] I have ground the axe
　myself;
Do you but strike the blow.

　*Per.*　　　　　　Rise, pr'ythee, rise.
Sit down, sit down: thou art no flatterer:
I thank thee for it; and heaven forbid
That kings should let their ears hear their
　faults chid!
Fit counsellor and servant for a prince,
Who by thy wisdom mak'st a prince thy
　servant,
What wouldst thou have me do?

　*Hel.*　　　　　To bear with patience
Such griefs as you yourself do lay upon yourself.

　*Per.* Thou speak'st like a physician, Helicanus,
That minister'st a potion unto me
That thou wouldst tremble to receive thyself.
Attend me, then: I went to Antioch,
Where, as thou know'st, against the face of
　death,
I sought the purchase of a glorious beauty,
From whence an issue I might propagate,
Are arms to princes, and bring joys to subjects.
Her face was to mine eye beyond all wonder;
The rest,—hark in thine ear,—as black as
　incest:
Which by my knowledge found, the sinful
　father
Seem'd not to strike, but smooth: but thou
　know'st this.

'Tis time to fear when tyrants seem to kiss.
Which fear so grew in me, I hither fled,
Under the covering of a careful night,
Who seem'd my good protector; and, being
　here,
Bethought me what was past, what might
　succeed.
I knew him tyrannous; and tyrants' fears
Decrease not, but grow faster than their
　years:
And should he doubt it,—as no doubt he
　doth,—
That I should open to the listening air
How many worthy princes' bloods were shed
To keep his bed of blackness unlaid ope,—
To lop that doubt, he'll fill this land with
　arms,
And make pretence of wrong that I have done
　him;
When all, for mine, if I may call offence,
Must feel war's blow, who spares not innocence:
Which love to all,—of which thyself art one,
Who now reprov'st me for it,—

　*Hel.*　　　　　　Alas, sir!

　*Per.* Drew sleep out of mine eyes, blood
　from my cheeks,
Musings into my mind, with thousand doubts
How I might stop this tempest ere it came;
And, finding little comfort to relieve them,
I thought it princely charity to grieve them.

　*Hel.* Well, my lord, since you have given
　me leave to speak,
Freely will I speak. Antiochus you fear,
And justly too, I think, you fear the tyrant,
Who either by public war or private treason
Will take away your life.
Therefore, my lord, go travel for a while,
Till that his rage and anger be forgot,
Or till the Destinies do cut his thread of life,
Your rule direct to any; if to me,
Day serves not light more faithful than I'll be.

　*Per.* I do not doubt thy faith;
But should he wrong my liberties in my absence?

　*Hel.* We'll mingle our bloods together in
　the earth,
From whence we had our being and our birth.

　*Per.* Tyre, I now look from thee, then, and
　to Tharsus
Intend my travel, where I'll hear from thee;
And by whose letters I'll dispose myself.
The care I had and have of subjects' good
On thee I lay, whose wisdom's strength can
　- bear it.
I'll take thy word for faith, not ask thine
　oath:
Who shuns not to break one will sure crack
　both:
But in our orbs we'll live so round and safe,
That time of both this truth shall ne'er convince,
Thou show'dst a subject's shine, I a true
prince.　　　　　　　　　　　　[*Exeunt.*

SCENE III.—TYRE. *An Ante-chamber in the Palace.*

*Enter* THALIARD.

*Thal.* So, this is Tyre, and this the court. Here must I kill King Pericles; and if I do it not, I am sure to be hanged at home: 'tis dangerous.—Well, I perceive he was a wise fellow, and had good discretion, that, being bid to ask what he would of the king, desired he might know none of his secrets. Now do I see he had some reason for't: for if a king bid a man be a villain, he is bound by the indenture of his oath to be one.—Hush! here come the lords of Tyre.

*Enter* HELICANUS, ESCANES, *and other* Lords.

*Hel.* You shall not need, my fellow peers of Tyre,
Further to question me of your king's departure:
His seal'd commission, left in trust with me,
Doth speak sufficiently he's gone to travel.
*Thal.* [*Aside.*] How! the king gone!
*Hel.* If further yet you will be satisfied,
Why, as it were unlicens'd of your loves,
He would depart, I'll give some light unto you.
Being at Antioch,—
*Thal.* [*Aside.*] What from Antioch?
*Hel.* Royal Antiochus,—on what cause I know not,—
Took some displeasure at him; at least he judg'd so:
And doubting lest that he had err'd or sinn'd,
To show his sorrow, he'd correct himself;
So puts himself unto the shipman's toil,
With whom each minute threatens life or death.
*Thal.* [*Aside.*] Well, I perceive
I shall not be hang'd now although I would;
But since he's gone, the king's ears it must please
He 'scap'd the land to perish on the seas.
I'll present myself.—Peace to the lords of Tyre!
*Hel.* Lord Thaliard from Antiochus is welcome.
*Thal.* From him I come
With message unto princely Pericles;
But since my landing I have understood
Your lord has betook himself to unknown travels,                                [came.
My message must return from whence it
*Hel.* We have no reason to desire it,
Commended to our master, not to us:
Yet, ere you shall depart, this we desire,—
As friends to Antioch, we may feast in Tyre.
[*Exeunt.*

SCENE IV.—THARSUS. *A Room in the Governor's House.*

*Enter* CLEON, DIONYZA, *and* Attendants.

*Cle.* My Dionyza, shall we rest us here,

And by relating tales of others' griefs
See if 'twill teach us to forget our own?
*Dio.* That were to blow at fire in hope to quench it;
For who digs hills because they do aspire
Throws down one mountain to cast up a higher.
O my distressed lord, even such our griefs are;
Here they're but felt, and seen with mischief's eyes,
But like to groves, being topp'd, they higher rise.
*Cle.* O Dionyza,
Who wanteth food, and will not say he wants it,
Or can conceal his hunger till he famish?
Our tongues and sorrows do sound deep
Our woes into the air; our eyes do weep,
Till tongues fetch breath that may proclaim them louder;                     [want,
That, if heaven slumber while their creatures
They may awake their helps to comfort them.
I'll then discourse our woes, felt several years,
And, wanting breath to speak, help me with tears.
*Dio.* I'll do my best, sir.
*Cle.* This Tharsus, o'er which I have the government,
A city on whom plenty held full hand,
For riches strew'd herself even in the streets;
Whose towers bore heads so high they kiss'd the clouds,
And strangers ne'er beheld but wonder'd at;
Whose men and dames so jetted and adorn'd,
Like one another's glass to trim them by:
Their tables were stor'd full, to glad the sight,
And not so much to feed on as delight;
All poverty was scorn'd, and pride so great,
The name of help grew odious to repeat.
*Dio.* O 'tis too true.
*Cle.* But see what heaven can do! By this our change,                       [and air
These mouths, whom but of late earth, sea,
Were all too little to content and please,
Although they gave their creatures in abundance,
As houses are defil'd for want of use,
They are now starv'd for want of exercise:
Those palates who, not us'd to savour hunger,
Must have inventions to delight the taste,
Would now be glad of bread, and beg for it:
Those mothers who, to nousle up their babes,
Thought naught too curious, are ready now
To eat those little darlings whom they lov'd.
So sharp are hunger's teeth, that man and wife
Draw lots who first shall die to lengthen life:
Here stands a lord and there a lady weeping;
Here many sink, yet those which see them fall
Have scarce strength left to give them burial.
Is not this true?                                          [it.
*Dio.* Our cheeks and hollow eyes do witness
*Cle.* O, let those cities that of Plenty's cup
And her prosperities so largely taste,

With their superfluous riots, hear these tears!
The misery of Tharsus may be theirs.

*Enter a* Lord.

*Lord.* Where's the lord governor?
*Cle.*. Here.                            [haste,
Speak out thy sorrows which thou bring'st in
For comfort is too far for us to expect.
*Lord.* We have descried, upon our neigh-
          bouring shore,
A portly sail of ships make hitherward.
*Cle.* I thought as much.
One sorrow never comes but brings an heir
That may succeed as his inheritor;
And so in ours: some neighboring nation,
Taking advantage of our misery,       [power,
Hath stuff'd these hollow vessels with their
To beat us down, the which are down al-
          ready;
And make a conquest of unhappy we,
Whereas no glory's got to overcome.
*Lord.* That's the least fear; for by the sem-
          blance                        [peace,
Of their white flags display'd, they bring us
And come to us as favourers, not as foes.
*Cle.* Thou speak'st like him's untutor'd to
          repeat:
Who makes the fairest show means most de-
          ceit.
But bring they what they will, and what they
          can,
What need we fear?                      [there.
The ground's the lowest, and we are half way
Go tell their general we attend him here,
To know for what he comes, and whence he
          comes,
And what he craves.
*Lord.* I go, my lord.                  [*Exit.*
*Cle.* Welcome is peace, if he on peace con-
          sist;
If wars, we are unable to resist.

*Enter* PERICLES, *with* Attendants.

*Per.* Lord governor, for so we hear you are,
Let not our ships and number of our men
Be, like a beacon fir'd, to amaze your eyes.
We have heard your miseries as far as Tyre,
And seen the desolation of your streets:
Nor come we to add sorrow to your tears,
But to relieve them of their heavy load;
And these our ships, you happily may think
Are like the Trojan horse war-stuff'd within
With bloody veins, expecting overthrow,
Are stor'd with corn to make your needy
          bread,                        [dead.
And give them life whom hunger starv'd half
*All.* The gods of Greece protect you!
And we'll pray for you.
*Per.*                    Rise, O pray you, rise:
We do not look for reverence, but for love,
And harbourage for ourself, our ships, and
          men.
*Cle.* The which when any shall not gratify,
Or pay you with unthankfulness in thought,

Be it our wives, our children, or ourselves,
The curse of heaven and men succeed their
          evils!                        [seen,—
Till when,—the which I hope shall ne'er be
Your grace is welcome to our town and us.
*Per.* Which welcome we'll accept; feast
          here a while,
Until our stars that frown lend us a smile.
                                        [*Exeunt.*

## ACT II.

*Enter* GOWER.

*Gow.* Here have you seen a mighty king
His child, I wis, to incest bring;
A better prince, and benign lord,
That will prove awful both in deed and
          word.
Be quiet, then, as men should be,
Till he hath pass'd necessity.
I'll show you those in troubles reign,
Losing a mite, a mountain gain.
The good in conversation,
To whom I give my benison,—
Is still at Tharsus, where each man
Thinks all is writ he spoken can;
And, to remember what he does,
Gild his statue to make him glorious:
But tidings to the contrary
Are brought your eyes: what need speak I?

*Dumb show.*

*Enter, at one side,* PERICLES, *talking with*
CLEON; *their* Trains *with them. Enter,
at the other, a* Gentleman *with a letter to*
PERICLES, *who shows it to* CLEON, *then
gives the* Messenger *a reward, and knights
him. Exeunt* PERICLES *and* CLEON *with
their* Trains, *severally.*

Good Helicane hath stay'd at home,
Not to eat honey like a drone
From others' labours; for though he strive
To killen bad, keep good alive;
And, to fulfil his prince' desire,
Sends word of all that haps in Tyre:
How Thaliard came full bent with sin
And hid intent to murder him;
And that in Tharsus was not best
Longer for him to make his rest.
He, knowing so, put forth to seas,
Where when men been, there's seldom ease;
For now the wind begins to blow;
Thunder above and deeps below
Make such unquiet that the ship
Should house him safe is wreck'd and split;
And he, good prince, having all lost,
By waves from coast to coast is toss'd:
All perishen of man, of pelf,
Ne aught escapen but himself;
Till fortune, tir'd with doing bad,
Threw him ashore, to give him glad:
And here he comes. What shall be next,
Pardon old Gower,—this longs the text.
                                        [*Exit.*

SCENE I.—PENTAPOLIS. *An open Place by the Sea-side.*

*Enter* PERICLES, *wet.*

*Per.* Yet cease your ire, you angry stars of
　　heaven!　　　　　　　　　　　　　　[man
Wind, rain, and thunder, remember, earthly
Is but a substance that must yield to you;
And I, as fits my nature, do obey you:
Alas, the sea hath cast me on the rocks,
Wash'd me from shore to shore, and left me
　　breath
Nothing to think on but ensuing death:
Let it suffice the greatness of your powers
To have bereft a prince of all his fortunes;
And having thrown him from your watery
　　grave,
Here to have death in peace is all he'll crave.

*Enter three* Fishermen.

*1 Fish.* What, ho, Pilch!

*2 Fish.* Ho, come and bring away the nets!

*1 Fish.* What, Patchbreech, I say!

*3 Fish.* What say you, master?

*1 Fish.* Look how thou stirrest now! come
away, or I'll fetch thee with a wanion.

*3 Fish.* Faith, master, I am thinking of the
poor men that were cast away before us even
now.

*1 Fish.* Alas, poor souls, it grieved my
heart to hear what pitiful cries they made to
us to help them, when, well-a-day, we could
scarce help ourselves.

*3 Fish.* Nay, master, said not I as much
when I saw the porpus how he bounced and
tumbled? they say they're half fish half flesh:
a plague on them, they ne'er come but I look
to be washed. Master, I marvel how the fishes
live in the sea.

*1 Fish.* Why, as men do a-land,—the great
ones eat up the little ones: I can compare our
rich misers to nothing so fitly as to a whale;
'a plays and tumbles, driving the poor fry before him, and at last devours them all at a
mouthful: such whales have I heard on the
land, who never leave gaping till they've swallow'd the whole parish, church, steeple, bells,
and all.

*Per.* [*Aside.*] A pretty moral.

*3 Fish.* But, master, if I had been the sexton, I would have been that day in the belfry.

*2 Fish.* Why, man?

*3 Fish.* Because he should have swallowed
me too: and when I had been in his belly I
would have kept such a jangling of the bells
that he should never have left till he cast
bells, steeple, church, and parish up again.
But if the good King Simonides were of my
mind,—

*Per.* [*Aside.*] Simonides!

*3 Fish.* He would purge the land of these
drones that rob the bee of her honey.

*Per.* [*Aside.*] How from the finny subject
　　of the sea

These fishers tell the infirmities of men;
And from their watery empire recollect
All that may men approve or men detect!—
Peace be at your labour, honest fishermen.

*2 Fish.* Honest! good fellow, what's that?
if it be not a day fits you, scratch it out of
the calendar, and nobody will look after it.

*Per.* Nay, see the sea hath cast upon your
　　coast,—

*2 Fish.* What a drunken knave was the sea
to cast thee in our way.　　　　　　　　[wind

*Per.* A man, whom both the waters and the
In that vast tennis-court hath made the ball
For them to play upon, entreats you pity him;
He asks of you that never used to beg.

*1 Fish.* No, friend, cannot you beg? here's
them in our country of Greece gets more with
begging than we can do with working.

*2 Fish.* Canst thou catch any fishes, then?

*Per.* I never practised it.

*2 Fish.* Nay, then thou wilt starve, sure;
for here's nothing to be got now-a-days unless thou canst fish for't.

*Per.* What I have been I have forgot to
　　know;
But what I am want teaches me to think on:
A man throng'd up with cold; my veins are
　　chill,
And have no more life than may suffice
To give my tongue that heat to ask your
　　help;
Which if you shall refuse, when I am dead,
For that I am a man, pray see me buried.

*1 Fish.* Die quoth-a? Now gods forbid! I
have a gown here; come, put it on; keep thee
warm. Now, afore me, a handsome fellow!
Come, thou shalt go home, and we'll have
flesh for holidays, fish for fasting-days, and
moreo'er puddings and flapjacks; and thou
shalt be welcome.

*Per.* I thank you, sir.

*2 Fish.* Hark you, my friend, you said you
could not beg.

*Per.* I did but crave.

*2 Fish.* But crave! Then I'll turn craver
too, and so I shall scape whipping.

*Per.* Why, are all your beggars whipped,
　　then?

*2 Fish.* O, not all, my friend, not all; for if
all your beggars were whipped, I would wish
no better office than to be beadle. But, master,
I'll go draw up the net.

　　　　　　　[*Exeunt with* Third Fisherman.

*Per.* [*Aside.*] How well this honest mirth
　　becomes their labour!　　　　　　[ye are?

*1 Fish.* Hark you, sir, do you know where

*Per.* Not well.

*1 Fish.* Why, I'll tell you: this is called
Pentapolis, and our king the good Simonides.

*Per.* The good King Simonides, do you
call him?

*1 Fish.* Ay, sir; and he deserves so to be
called for his peaceable reign and good government.

*Per.* He is a happy king, since he gains from his subjects the name of good by his government. How far is his court distant from this shore?

1 *Fish.* Marry, sir, half a day's journey: and I'll tell you, he hath a fair daughter, and tomorrow is her birthday; and there are princes and knights come from all parts of the world to joust and tourney for her love.

*Per.* Were but my fortunes equal my desires I could wish to make one there.

1 *Fish.* O, sir, things must be as they may; and what a man cannot get he may lawfully deal for—his wife's soul.

*Re-enter* Second *and* Third Fishermen, *drawing up a net.*

2 *Fish.* Help, master, help! here's a fish hangs in the net like a poor man's right in the law; 'twill hardly come out. Ha! bots on't, 'tis come at last, and 'tis turned to a rusty armour.

*Per.* An armour, friends! I pray you, let me see it.—

Thanks, fortune, yet, that after all my crosses
Thou giv'st me somewhat to repair myself;
And though it was mine own, part of my heritage,
Which my dead father did bequeath to me,
With this strict charge, even as he left his life,
*Keep it, my Pericles; it hath been a shield
'Twixt me and death;*—and pointed to this brace:—
*For that it sav'd me, keep it; in like necessity,—
The which gods protect thee from!—may defend thee.*
It kept where I kept, I so dearly lov'd it:
Till the rough seas, that spare not any man,
Took it in rage, though calm'd have given't again:
I thank thee for't: my shipwreck now's no ill;
Since I have here my father's gift in's will.

1 *Fish.* What mean you, sir?

*Per.* To beg of you, kind friends, this coat of worth,
For it was sometime target to a king;
I know it by this mark. He lov'd me dearly,
And for his sake I wish the having of it;
And that you'd guide me to your sovereign's court,
Where with it I may appear a gentleman;
And if that ever my low fortunes better,
I'll pay your bounties; till then rest your debtor.

1 *Fish.* Why, wilt thou tourney for the lady?

*Per.* I'll show the virtue I have borne in arms.

1 *Fish.* Why, do you take it, and the gods give thee good on't!

2 *Fish.* Ay, but hark you, my friend; 'twas

we that made up this garment through the rough seams of the waters: there are certain condolements, certain vails. I hope, sir, if you thrive, you'll remember from whence you had it.

*Per.* Believe't, I will.
By your furtherance I am cloth'd in steel;
And spite of all the rupture of the sea
This jewel holds his building on my arm:
Unto thy value I will mount myself
Upon a courser, whose delightful steps
Shall make the gazer joy to see him tread.—
Only, my friends, I yet am unprovided
Of a pair of bases.

2 *Fish.* We'll sure provide: thou shalt have my best gown to make thee a pair; and I'll bring thee to the court myself.

*Per.* Then honour be but a goal to my will;
This day I'll rise, or else add ill to ill. [*Exeunt.*

SCENE II.—PENTAPOLIS. *A public Way or Platform leading to the Lists. A Pavilion by the side of it for the reception of the* King, Princess, Lords, &c.

*Enter* SIMONIDES, THAISA, Lords, *and* Attendants.

*Sim.* Are the knights ready to begin the triumph?

1 *Lord.* They are, my liege;
And stay your coming to present themselves.

*Sim.* Return them, we are ready; and our daughter,
In honour of whose birth these triumphs are,
Sits here, like beauty's child, whom nature gat
For men to see, and seeing wonder at.
[*Exit a* Lord.

*Thai.* It pleaseth you, my royal father, to express
My commendations great, whose merit's less.

*Sim.* It's fit it should be so; for princes are
A model which heaven makes like to itself:
As jewels lose their glory if neglected,
So princes their renown if not respected.
'Tis now your labour, daughter, to explain
The honour of each knight in his device.

*Thai.* Which, to preserve mine honour, I'll perform.

*Enter a* Knight; *he passes over, and his* Squire *presents his shield to the* Princess.

*Sim.* Who is the first that doth prefer himself?

*Thai.* A knight of Sparta, my renowned father;
And the device he bears upon his shield
Is a black Æthiop reaching at the sun;
The word, *Lux tua vita mihi.*

*Sim.* He loves you well that holds his life of you. [*The* Second Knight *passes.*
Who is the second that presents himself?

*Thai.* A prince of Macedon, my royal father;
And the device he bears upon his shield

Is an arm'd knight that's conquer'd by a lady;
The motto thus, in Spanish, *Piu por 'dulzura*
  *que por fuerza.*
          [*The* Third Knight *passes.*
*Sim.* And what's the third?
*Thai.*          The third of Antioch;
And his device a wreath of chivalry;
The word, *Me pompæ provexit apex.*
          [*The* Fourth Knight *passes.*
*Sim.* What is the fourth?
*Thai.* A burning torch that's turned upside
  down;
The word, *Quod me alit, me extinguit.*
*Sim.* Which shows that beauty hath his
  power and will,
Which can as well inflame as it can kill.
          [*The* Fifth Knight *passes.*
*Thai.* The fifth, an hand environed with
  clouds,          [tried;
Holding out gold that's by the touchstone
The motto thus, *Sic spectanda fides.*
          [*The* Sixth Knight (PERICLES) *passes.*
*Sim.* And what's the sixth and last, the
  which the knight himself
With such a graceful courtesy deliver'd?
*Thai.* He seems to be a stranger; but his
  present is
A wither'd branch, that's only green at top;
The motto, *In hac spe vivo.*
*Slim.* A pretty moral;
From the dejected state wherein he is,
He hopes by you his fortunes yet may flour-
  ish.
  1 *Lord.* He had need mean better than his
  outward show
Can any way speak in his just commend;
For, by his rusty outside, he appears
To have practis'd more the whipstock than
  the lance.
  2 *Lord.* He well may be a stranger, for he
  comes
To an honour'd triumph strangely furnished.
  3 *Lord.* And on set purpose let his armour
  rust
Until this day, to scour it in the dust.
*Sim.* Opinion's but a fool, that makes us
  scan
The outward habit by the inward man.
But stay, the knights are coming: we will
  withdraw
Into the gallery.          [*Exeunt.*
  [*Great shouts within, all crying* "The
      mean knight!"

SCENE III.—PENTAPOLIS. *A Hall of State:*
      *A Banquet prepared.*

*Enter* SIMONIDES, THAISA, Lords, Knights,
      *and* Attendants.

*Sim.* Knights,
To say you are welcome were superfluous.
To place upon the volume of your deeds,
As in a title-page, your worth in arms  [fit,
Were more than you expect, or more than's
Since every worth in show commends itself.

Prepare for mirth, for mirth becomes a feast:
You are princes and my guests.
*Thai.*          But you my knight and guest;
To whom this wreath of victory I give,
And crown you king of this day's happiness.
*Per.* 'Tis more by fortune, lady, than by
  merit.          [yours;
*Sim.* Call it by what you will, the day is
And here I hope is none that envies it.
In framing an artist, art hath thus decreed,
To make some good, but others to exceed,
And you're her labour'd scholar.—Come,
  queen o' the feast,—          [place:
For, daughter, so you are,—here take your
Marshal the rest, as they deserve their grace.
*Knights.* We are honour'd much by good
  Simonides.          [our we love;
*Sim.* Your presence glads our days: hon-
For who hates honour hates the gods above.
*Marshal.* Sir, yonder is your place.
*Per.*          Some other is more fit.
1 *Knight.* Contend not, sir; for we are
  gentlemen
That neither in our hearts nor outward eyes
Envy the great, nor do the low despise.
*Per.* You are right courteous knights.
*Sim.*          Sit, sir, sit.
*Per.* By Jove, I wonder, that is king of
  thoughts,
These cates resist me, she but thought upon.
*Thai.* By Juno, that is queen
Of marriage, all viands that I eat
Do seem unsavoury, wishing him my meat.
Sure he's a gallant gentleman.
*Sim.* He's but a country gentleman;
Has done no more than other knights have
  done;
Has broken a staff or so; so let it pass.
*Thai.* To me he seems like diamond to
  glass.
*Per.* Yon king's to me like to my father's
  picture,
Which tells me in that glory once he was;
Had princes sit, like stars, about his throne,
And he the sun, for them to reverence;
None that beheld him but, like lesser lights,
Did vail their crowns to his supremacy:
Where now his son's like a glowworm in the
  night,          [light:
The which hath fire in darkness, none in
Whereby I see that Time's the king of men,
For he's their parent, and he is their grave,
And gives them what he will, not what they
  crave.
*Sim.* What, are you merry, knights?
1 *Knight.* Who can be other in this royal
  presence?
*Sim.* Here, with a cup that's stor'd unto
  the brim,—
As you do love, fill to your mistress' lips,—
We drink this health to you.
*Knights.*          We thank your grace.
*Sim.* Yet pause awhile:          [choly,
Yon knight, methinks, doth sit too melan-

As if the entertainment in our court
Had not a show might countervail his worth.
Note it not you, Thaisa?
 *Thai.*      What is it
To me, my father?
 *Sim.*     O, attend, my daughter:
Princes, in this, should live like gods above,
Who freely give to every one that comes
To honour them:
And princes not doing so are like to gnats,
Which make a sound, but kill'd are wonder'd
 at.
Therefore to make his entrance more sweet,
Here, say we drink this standing-bowl of
 wine to him.
 *Thai.* Alas, my father, it befits not me
Unto a stranger knight to be so bold:
He may my proffer take for an offence,
Since men take women's gifts for impudence.
 *Sim.* How!
Do as I bid you, or you'll move me else.
 *Thai.* [*Aside.*] Now, by the gods, he could
 not please me better.
 *Sim.* And furthermore tell him, we desire
 to know of him
Of whence he is, his name and parentage.
 *Thai.* The king my father, sir, has drunk
 to you.
 *Per.* I thank him.
 *Thai.* Wishing it so much blood unto your
 life.      [pledge him freely.
 *Per.* I thank both him and you, and
 *Thai.* And further he desires to know of
 you
Of whence you are, your name and parentage.
 *Per.* A gentleman of Tyre,—my name,
 Pericles;
My education been in arts and arms;—
Who, looking for adventures in the world,
Was by the rough seas reft of ships and men,
And after shipwreck driven upon this shore.
 *Thai.* He thanks your grace; names him-
 self Pericles,
A gentleman of Tyre,
Who only by misfortune of the seas,
Bereft of ships and men, cast on this shore.
 *Sim.* Now, by the gods, I pity his misfor-
 tune,
And will awake him from his melancholy.—
Come, gentlemen, we sit too long on trifles,
And waste the time which looks for other
 revels,
Even in your armours, as you are address'd,
Will very well become a soldier's dance.
I will not have excuse, with saying this
Loud music is too harsh for ladies' heads,
Since they love men in arms as well as beds.
       [*The* Knights *dance.*
So, this was well ask'd, 'twas so well per-
 form'd.—
Come, sir;
Here is a lady that wants breathing too:
And I have often heard you knights of Tyre
Are excellent in making ladies trip:

And that their measures are as excellent.—
 *Per.* In those that practise them they are,
 my lord.        [denied
 *Sim.* O, that's as much as you would be
Of your fair courtesy.   [*The* Knights *and*
 Ladies *dance.*]—Unclasp, unclasp:
Thanks, gentlemen, to all; all have done well,
But you the best. [*To* PERICLES.]—Pages
 and lights, to conduct [Yours, sir,
These knights unto their several lodgings!—
We have given order to be next our own.
 *Per.* I am at your grace's pleasure.
 *Sim.* Princes, it is too late to talk of love,
And that's the mark I know you level at:
Therefore each one betake him to his rest;
To-morrow all for speeding do their best.
          [*Exeunt.*

SCENE IV.—TYRE. *A room in the* Governor's
      *House.*

  *Enter* HELICANUS *and* ESCANES.

 *Hel.* No, Escanes, no; know this of me,—
Antiochus from incest liv'd not free:
For which, the most high gods not minding
 longer        [store,
To withhold the vengeance that they had in
Due to this heinous capital offence,
Even in the height and pride of all his glory,
When he was seated in a chariot [with him,
Of an inestimable value, and his daughter
A fire from heaven came, and shrivell'd up
Their bodies, even to loathing; for they so
 stunk
That all those eyes ador'd them ere their fall
Scorn now their hand should give them
 burial.
 *Esca.* 'Twas very strange.
 *Hel.*     And yet but justice; for though
This king were great, his greatness was no
 guard
To bar heaven's shaft, but sin had his reward.
 *Esca.* 'Tis very true.

    *Enter three* Lords.

 1 *Lord.* See, not a man in private conference
Or council has respect with him but he.
 2 *Lord.* It shall no longer grieve without
 reproof.        [second it.
 3 *Lord.* And curs'd be he that will not
 1 *Lord.* Follow me, then.—Lord Helicane,
 a word.         [my lords.
 *Hel.* With me? and welcome: happy day,
 1 *Lord.* Know that our griefs are risen to
 the top,
And now at length they overflow their banks.
 *Hel.* Your griefs! for what? wrong not
 your prince you love.    [Helicane;
 1 *Lord.* Wrong not yourself, then, noble
But if the prince do live, let us salute him,
Or know what ground's made happy by his
 breath.
If in the world he live, we'll seek him out;
If in his grave he rest, we'll find him there;

And be resolv'd he lives to govern us,
Or dead, gives cause to mourn his funeral,
And leaves us to our free election.
  2 *Lord.* Whose death's indeed the strong-
      est in our censure:      [head,
And knowing this kingdom, if without a
Like goodly buildings left without a roof,
Will soon to ruins fall,—your noble self,
That best know'st how to rule and how to
    reign,
We thus submit unto,—our sovereign.
  *All.* Live, noble Helicane!    [frages:
  *Hel.* For honour's cause, forbear your suf-
If that you love Prince Pericles, forbear.
Take I your wish, I leap into the seas,
Where's hourly trouble for a minute's ease.
A twelvemonth longer, let me entreat you
To forbear the absence of your king;
If in which time expir'd, he not return,
I shall with aged patience bear your yoke.
But if I cannot win you to this love,
Go search like nobles, like noble subjects,
And in your search spend your adventurous
    worth;
Whom if you find, and win unto return,
You shall like diamonds sit about his crown.
  1 *Lord.* To wisdom he's a fool that will not
    yield;
And since Lord Helicane enjoineth us,
We with our travels will endeavour it.
  *Hel.* Then you love us, we you, and we'll
    clasp hands:
When peers thus knit, a kingdom ever stands.
             [*Exeunt.*

SCENE V.—PENTAPOLIS. *A Room in the
Palace.*

*Enter* SIMONIDES, *reading a letter; the
Knights meet him.*

  1 *Knight.* Good-morrow to the good Si-
    monides.      [you know,
  *Sim.* Knights, from my daughter this I let
That for this twelvemonth she'll not under-
  take
A married life.
Her reason to herself is only known,
Which yet from her by no means can I get.
  2 *Knight.* May we not get access to her,
    my lord?    [strictly tied her
  *Sim.* Faith, by no means; she hath so
To her chamber that it is impossible. [livery;
One twelve moons more she'll wear Diana's
This by the eye of Cynthia hath she vow'd,
And on her virgin honour will not break it.
  3 *Knight.* Loth to bid farewell, we take
    our leaves.    [*Exeunt* Knights.
  *Sim.* So,    [ter's letter:
They are well despatch'd; now to my daugh-
She tells me here she'll wed the stranger
    knight,
Or never more to view nor day nor light.
'Tis well, mistress; your choice agrees with
    mine:

I like that well: nay, how absolute she's in't,
Not minding whether I dislike or no!
Well, I do commend her choice;
And will no longer have it be delay'd.—
Soft! here he comes: I must dissemble it.

*Enter* PERICLES.

  *Per.* All fortune to the good Simonides!
  *Sim.* To you as much, sir! I am beholden
    to you
For your sweet music this last night: I do
Protest my ears were never better fed
With such delightful pleasing harmony.
  *Per.* It is your grace's pleasure to com-
    mend;
Not my desert.
  *Sim.*         Sir, you are music's master.
  *Per.* The worst of all her scholars, my
    good lord.
  *Sim.* Let me ask you one thing:
What do you think of my daughter, sir?
  *Per.* A most virtuous princess.
  *Sim.* And she is fair too, is she not?
  *Per.* As a fair day in summer,—wondrous
    fair.         [you;
  *Sim.* Sir, my daughter thinks very well of
Ay, so well that you must be her master
And she will be your scholar: therefore look
  to it.
  *Per.* I am unworthy for her schoolmaster.
  *Sim.* She thinks not so; peruse this writing
    else.
  *Per.* [*Aside.*] What's here?
A letter, that she loves the knight of Tyre!
'Tis the king's subtilty to have my life.—
O, seek not to entrap me, gracious lord,
A stranger and distressed gentleman,    [ter,
That never aim'd so high to love your daugh-
But bent all offices to honour her.
  *Sim.* Thou hast bewitch'd my daughter,
    and thou art
A villain.
  *Per.* By the gods, I have not:
Never did thought of mine levy offence;
Nor never did my actions yet commence
A deed might gain her love or your dis-
    pleasure.
  *Sim.* Traitor, thou liest.
  *Per.*             Traitor!
  *Sim.*               Ay, traitor.
  *Per.* Even in his throat,—unless it be the
    king,—
That calls me traitor, I return the lie.
  *Sim.* [*Aside.*] Now, by the gods, I do ap-
    plaud his courage.
  *Per.* My actions are as noble as my
    thoughts,
That never relish'd of a base descent.
I came unto your court for honour's cause,
And not to be a rebel to her state;
And he that otherwise accounts of me,
This sword shall prove he's honour's enemy.
  *Sim.* No?
Here comes my daughter, she can witness it.

*Enter* THAISA.

*Per.* Then, as you are as virtuous as fair,
Resolve your angry father if my tongue
Did e'er solicit, or my hand subscribe
To any syllable that made love to you.
  *Thai.* Why, sir, say if you had,      [glad?
Who takes offence at that would make me
  *Sim.* Yea, mistress, are you so peremp-
      tory?—
[*Aside.*] I am glad on't with all my heart.—
I'll tame you; I'll bring you in subjection.
Will you, not having my consent,
Bestow your love and your affections
Upon a stranger?—[*aside*] who, for aught I
      know,
May be,—nor can I think the contrary,—
As great in blood as I myself.—
Therefore, hear you, mistress; either frame
Your will to mine, and you, sir, hear you,
Either be rul'd by me, or I will make you—
Man and wife.
Nay, come, your hands and lips must seal it
      too:                [stroy;—
And being join'd, I'll thus your hopes de-
And for further grief,—God give you joy!—
What, are you both pleas'd?
  *Thai.*              Yes, if you love me, sir.
  *Per.* Even as my life, or blood that fos-
      ters it.
  *Sim.* What, are you both agreed?
  *Both.*       Yes, if't please your majesty.
  *Sim.* It pleaseth me so well that I will see
      you wed;              [to bed.
And then, with what haste you can, get you
                [*Exeunt.*

## ACT III.

### *Enter* GOWER.

  *Gow.* Now sleepy slaked hath the rout;
No din but snores the house about,
Made louder by the o'er-fed breast
Of this most pompous marriage feast.
The cat, with eyne of burning coal,
Now couches fore the mouse's hole;
And crickets sing at the oven's mouth,
Aye the blither for their drouth.
Hymen hath brought the bride to bed,
Where, by the loss of maidenhead,
A babe is moulded.—Be attent,
And time that is so briefly spent
With your fine fancies quaintly eche:
What's dumb in show I'll plain with speech.

### *Dumb-Show*

*Enter* PERICLES *and* SIMONIDES *at one side,
with* Attendants; *a* Messenger *meets them,
kneels, and gives* PERICLES *a letter: he
shows it to* SIMONIDES; *the Lords kneel to*
PERICLES. *Then enter* THAISA, *with child,
and* LYCHORIDA. SIMONIDES *shows his
daughter the letter; she rejoices: she and*
PERICLES *take leave of her father, and depart with* LYCHORIDA *and their* Attendants.
*Then exeunt* SIMONIDES, &c.

By many a dern and painful perch
Of Pericles the careful search,
By the four opposing coigns
Which the world together joins,
Is made with all due diligence
That horse and sail and high expense
Can stead the quest. At last from Tyre,—
Fame answering the most strange in-
      quire,—
To the court of King Simonides
Are letters brought, the tenor these:—
Antiochus and his daughter's dead;
The men of Tyrus on the head
Of Helicanus would set on
The crown of Tyre, but he will none:
The mutiny he there hastes t' oppress;
Says to 'em, if King Pericles
Come not home in twice six moons,
He, obedient to their dooms,
Will take the crown. The sum of this,
Brought hither to Pentapolis,
Y-ravished the regions round,
And every one with claps can sound,
*Our heir-apparent is a king!*
*Who dream'd, who thought of such a*
      *thing?*
Brief, he must hence depart to Tyre:
His queen with child makes her desire,—
Which who shall cross?—along to go:—
Omit we all their dole and woe:—
Lychorida, her nurse, she takes,
And so to sea. Their vessel shakes
On Neptune's billow; half the flood
Hath their keel cut: but fortune's mood
Varies again; the grizzly north
Disgorges such a tempest forth
That, as a duck for life that dives,
So up and down the poor ship drives:
The lady shrieks, and, well-a-near,
Does fall in travail with her fear:
And what ensues in this fell storm
Shall for itself itself perform.
I will relate, action may
Conveniently the rest convey;
Which might not what by me is told.
In your imagination hold
This stage the ship, upon whose deck
The sea-toss'd Pericles appears to speak.
                [*Exit.*

SCENE I.—*Enter* PERICLES, *on a ship at sea.*

  *Per.* Thou god of this great vast, rebuke
      these surges,          [that hast
Which wash both heaven and hell; and thou
Upon the winds command, bind them in
      brass,
Having call'd them from the deep! O, still
Thy deafening, dreadful thunders; gently
      quench
Thy nimble, sulphurous flashes!—O, how,
      Lychorida,

How does my queen?—Thou stormest ven-
　　omously;
Wilt thou spit all thyself?—The seaman's
　　whistle
Is as a whisper in the ears of death,
Unheard.—Lychorida!—Lucina, O
Divinest patroness, and midwife gentle
To those that cry by night, convey thy deity
Aboard our dancing boat; make swift the
　　pangs
Of my queen's travail!

*Enter* LYCHORIDA, *with an* Infant.
　　　　　　　Now, Lychorida!
*Lyc.* Here is a thing too young for such a
　　place,
Who, if it had conceit, would die, as I
Am like to do: take in your arms this piece
Of your dead queen.
　　*Per.*　　　　　　How, how, Lychorida!
　　*Lyc.* Patience, good sir; do not assist the
　　storm.
Here's all that is left living of your queen,—
A little daughter: for the sake of it,
Be manly, and take comfort.
　　*Per.*　　　　　　O you gods!
Why do you make us love your goodly gifts,
And snatch them straight away? We here
　　below
Recall not what we give, and therein may
Vie in honour with you.
　　*Lyc.*　　　　　　Patience, good sir,
Even for this charge.
　　*Per.*　　　　　　Now, mild may be thy life!
For a more blusterous birth had never babe:
Quiet and gentle thy conditions! for
Thou art the rudeliest welcom'd to this world
That ever was prince's child. Happy what
　　follows!
Thou hast as chiding a nativity
As fire, air, water, earth, and heaven can
　　make,　　　　　　　　　　　　　　[first
To herald thee from the womb: even at the
Thy loss is more than can thy portage quit,
With all thou canst find here.—Now, the
　　good gods
Throw their best eyes upon't!

*Enter two* Sailors.

1 *Sail.* What courage, sir? God save you!
*Per.* Courage enough: I do not fear the
　　flaw;　　　　　　　　　　　　　　[love
It hath done to me the worst. Yet, for the
Of this poor infant, this fresh-new seafarer,
I would it would be quiet.
　　1 *Sail.* Slack the bolins there!—Thou wilt
not, wilt thou? Blow, and split thyself.
　　2 *Sail.* But sea-room, and the brine and
cloudy billow kiss the moon, I care not.
　　1 *Sail.* Sir, your queen must overboard:
the sea works high, the wind is loud, and
will not lie till the ship be cleared of the dead.
　　*Per.* That's your superstition.
　　1 *Sail.* Pardon us, sir; with us at sea it

hath been still observed; and we are strong
in custom. Therefore briefly yield her; for she
must overboard straight.　　　　　　　[queen!
　　*Per.* As you think meet.—Most wretched
　　*Lyc.* Here she lies, sir.
　　*Per.* A terrible childbed hast thou had, my
　　dear;
No light, no fire: the unfriendly elements
Forgot thee utterly; nor have I time
To give thee hallow'd to thy grave, but
　　straight
Must cast thee, scarcely coffin'd, in the ooze;
Where, for a monument upon thy bones,
And aye-remaining lamps, the belching whale
And humming water must o'erwhelm thy
　　corpse,
Lying with simple shells.—O Lychorida,
Bid Nestor bring me spices, ink and paper,
My casket and my jewels; and bid Nicander
Bring me the satin coffer: lay the babe
Upon the pillow: hie thee, whiles I say
A priestly farewell to her: suddenly, woman.
　　　　　　　　　　　　　[*Exit* LYCHORIDA.
　　2 *Sail.* Sir, we have a chest beneath the
hatches, caulked and bitumed ready.
　　*Per.* I thank thee.—Mariner, say what
　　coast is this?
　　2 *Sail.* We are near Tharsus.
　　*Per.* Thither, gentle mariner,　　[reach it?
Alter thy course for Tyre. When canst thou
　　2 *Sail.* By break of day, if the wind cease.
　　*Per.* O make for Tharsus!—
There will I visit Cleon, for the babe
Cannot hold out to Tyrus: there I'll leave it
At careful nursing.—Go thy ways, good
　　mariner:
I'll bring the body presently.　　　　[*Exeunt.*

SCENE II.—EPHESUS. *A Room in*
　　　　CERIMON'S *House.*

*Enter* CERIMON, *a* Servant, *and some persons
　　who have been shipwrecked.*

　　*Cer.* Philemon, ho!

*Enter* PHILEMON.

　　*Phil.* Doth my lord call?
　　*Cer.* Get fire and meat for these poor men:
It has been a turbulent and stormy night.
　　*Serv.* I have been in many; but such a
　　night as this,
Till now, I ne'er endur'd.　　　　　　[turn.
　　*Cer.* Your master will be dead ere you re-
There's nothing can be minister'd to nature
That can recover him.—Give this to the
　　'pothecary,
And tell me how it works. [*To* PHILEMON.
　　　　　　　　　[*Exeunt all but* CERIMON.

*Enter two* Gentlemen.

　　1 *Gent.*　　　　　　Good-morrow, sir.
　　2 *Gent.* Good-morrow to your lordship.
　　*Cer.*　　　　　　Gentlemen,
Why do you stir so early?
　　1 *Gent.* Sir,

Our lodgings, standing bleak upon the sea,
Shook as the earth did quake;
The very principals did seem to rend,
And all to topple: pure surprise and fear
Made me to quit the house.            [so early;
    2 *Gent.* That is the cause we trouble you
'Tis not our husbandry.
    *Cer.*            O, you say well.
    1 *Gent.* But I much marvel that your
        lordship, having            [hours
Rich tire about you, should at these early
Shake off the golden slumber of repose.
It is most strange
Nature should be so conversant with pain,
Being thereto not compell'd.
    *Cer.*            I held it ever,
Virtue and cunning were endowments greater
Than nobleness and riches: careless heirs
May the two latter darken and expend;
But immortality attends the former,
Making a man a god. 'Tis known I ever
Have studied physic, through which secret
        art,
By turning o'er authorities, I have,—
Together with my practice,—made familiar
To me and to my aid the blest infusions
That dwell in vegetives, in metals, stones;
And I can speak of the disturbances
That nature works, and of her cures; which
        give me
A more content in course of true delight
Than to be thirsty after tottering honour,
Or tie my treasure up in silken bags,
To please the fool and death      [pour'd forth
    2 *Gent.* Your honour has through Ephesus
Your charity and hundreds call themselves
Your creatures, who by you have been re-
        stor'd:            [but even
And not your knowledge, your personal pain,
Your purse, still open, hath built Lord Ceri-
        mon
Such strong renown as time shall never raze.

    *Enter two* Servants *with a chest.*

    1 *Serv.* So; lift there.
    *Cer.*            What is that?
    1 *Serv.*            Sir, even now
Did the sea toss upon our shore this chest:
'Tis of some wreck.
    *Cer.*            Set't down, let's look upon't.
    2 *Gent.* 'Tis like a coffin, sir.
    *Cer.*            Whate'er it be,
'Tis wondrous heavy. Wrench it open
        straight:
If the sea's stomach be o'ercharg'd with gold,
It is a good constraint of fortune that
It belches upon us.
    2 *Gent.*            'Tis so, my lord.
    *Cer.* How close 'tis caulk'd and bitum'd!—
Did the sea cast it up?
    1 *Serv.* I never saw so huge a billow, sir,
As toss'd it upon shore.
    *Cer.*            Wrench it open;
Soft!—it smells most sweetly in my sense.

    2 *Gent.* A delicate odour.
    *Cer.* As ever hit my nostril.—So, up with
        it.—            [corse!
O you most potent gods! what's here? a
    1 *Gent.* Most strange!    [and entreasur'd
    *Cer.* Shrouded in cloth of state; balm'd
With bags of spices full! A passport too!—
Apollo, perfect me in the characters!
                        [*Reads from a scroll.*

        Here I give to understand,—
        If e'er this coffin drive a-land,—
        I, King Pericles, have lost
        This queen, worth all our mundane cost.
        Who finds her, give her burying;
        She was the daughter of a king:
        Besides this treasure for a fee,
        The gods requite his charity!

If thou liv'st, Pericles, thou hast a heart
That even cracks for woe!—This chanc'd to-
        night.
    2 *Gent.* Most likely, sir.
    *Cer.*            Nay, certainly to-night;
For look how fresh she looks!—They were
        too rough            [within:
That threw her in the sea.—Make a fire
Fetch hither all my boxes in my closet.
                        [*Exit a* Servant.
Death may usurp on nature many hours,
And yet the fire of life kindle again      [tian
The o'erpress'd spirits. I heard of an Egyp-
That had nine hours lien dead,
Who was by good appliances recover'd.

*Re-enter a* Servant, *with boxes, napkins,
        and fire.*

Well said; well said; the fire and cloths.—
The rough and woeful music that we have,
Cause it to sound, beseech you.      [block!—
The viol once more:—how thou stirr'st, thou
The music there!—I pray you, give her air.—
Gentlemen,            [warmth
This queen will live: nature awakes; a
Breathes out of her: she hath not been en-
        tranc'd
Above five hours: see how she 'gins to blow
Into life's flower again!
    1 *Gent.*            The heavens,
Through you, increase our wonder, and set up
Your fame for ever.
    *Cer.*            She is alive; behold,
Her eyelids, cases to those heavenly jewels
Which Pericles hath lost,
Begin to part their fringes of bright gold;
The diamonds of a most praised water [Live,
Do appear, to make the world twice rich.—
And make us weep to hear your fate, fair
        creature,
Rare as you seem to be.            [*She moves.*
    *Thai.*            O dear Diana,
Where am I? Where's my lord? What world
        is this?
    2 *Gent.* Is not this strange?
    1 *Gent.*            Most rare.

*Cer.*                Hush, my gentle neighbours!
Lend me your hands; to the next chamber
    bear her.
Get linen: now this matter must be look'd to,
For her relapse is mortal. Come, come;
And Æsculapius guide us!
            [*Exeunt, carrying out* THAISA.

SCENE III.—THARSUS. *A Room in* CLEON'S
                *House.*

*Enter* PERICLES, CLEON, DIONYZA, *and* LY-
CHORIDA *with* MARINA *in her arms.*

*Per.*  Most honour'd Cleon, I must needs
    be gone;                        [stands
My twelve months are expir'd, and Tyrus
In a litigious peace. You and your lady
Take from my heart all thankfulness! The
    gods
Make up the rest upon you!
*Cle.*  Your shafts of fortune, though they
    hurt you mortally,
Yet glance full wanderingly on us.
*Dion.*                O your sweet queen!
That the strict fates had pleas'd you had
    brought her hither,
To have bless'd mine eyes!
*Per.*                We cannot but obey
The powers above us. Could I rage and roar
As doth the sea she lies in, yet the end
Must be as 'tis. My gentle babe Marina,—
    whom,                           [here
For she was born at sea, I have nam'd so,—
I charge your charity withal, leaving her
The infant of your care; beseeching you
To give her princely training, that she may
    be
Manner'd as she is born.
*Cle.*  Fear not, my lord, but think
Your grace, that fed my country with your
    corn,—                   [upon you,—
For which the people's prayers still fall
Must in your child be thought on. If neg-
    lection                        [body,
Should therein make me vile, the common
By you reliev'd, would force me to my duty:
But if to that my nature need a spur,
The gods revenge it upon me and mine
To the end of generation!
*Per.*                I believe you;
Your honour and your goodness teach me to't
Without your vows. Till she be married,
    madam,
By bright Diana, whom we honour, all
Unscissar'd shall this hair of mine remain,
Though I show ill in't. So I take my leave.
Good madam, make me blessed in your care
In bringing up my child.
*Dion.*                I have one myself,
Who shall not be more dear to my respect
Than yours, my lord.
*Per.*        Madam, my thanks and prayers.
*Cle.*  We'll bring your grace e'en to the
    edge o' the shore,

Then give you up to the vast Neptune and
The gentlest winds of heaven.
*Per.*                I will embrace
Your offer. Come, dearest madam.—O, no
    tears,
Lychorida, no tears:
Look to your little mistress, on whose grace
You may depend hereafter.—Come, my lord.
                            [*Exeunt.*

SCENE IV.—EPHESUS. *A Room in* CERI-
            MON'S *House.*

*Enter* CERIMON *and* THAISA.

*Cer.*  Madam, this letter, and some certain
    jewels,
Lay with you in your coffer: which are now
At your command. Know you the character?
*Thai.*  It is my lord's.
That I was shipp'd at sea I well remember,
Even on my eaning time; but whether there
Deliver'd, by the holy gods,
I cannot rightly say. But since King Pericles,
My wedded lord, I ne'er shall see again,
A vestal livery will I take me to,
And never more have joy.            [speak,
*Cer.*  Madam, if this you purpose as you
Diana's temple is not distant far,
Where you may abide till your date expire.
Moreover, if you please, a niece of mine
Shall there attend you.
*Thai.*  My recompense is thanks, that's all;
Yet my good-will is great, though the gift
    small.                         [*Exeunt.*

## ACT IV.

*Enter* GOWER.

*Gow.*  Imagine Pericles arriv'd at Tyre,
Welcom'd and settled to his own desire.
His woeful queen we leave at Ephesus,
Unto Diana there a votaress.
Now to Marina bend your mind,
Whom our fast growing scene must find
At Tharsus, and by Cleon train'd
In music, letters; who hath gain'd
Of education all the grace,
Which makes her both the heart and place
Of general wonder. But, alack,
That monster envy, oft the wrack
Of earned praise, Marina's life
Seeks to take off by treason's knife.
And in this kind hath our Cleon
One daughter, and a wench full grown,
Even ripe for marriage-rite; this maid
Hight Philoten: and it is said
For certain in our story, she
Would ever with Marina be:
Be't when she weav'd the sleided silk
With fingers long, small, white as milk;
Or when she would with sharp needle
    wound
The cambric, which she made more sound
By hurting it; or when to the lute
She sung, and made the night-bird mute,

That still records with moan; or when
She would with rich and constant pen
Vail to her mistress Dian; still
This Philoten contends in skill
With absolute Marina: so
With the dove of Paphos might the crow
Vie feathers white. Marina gets
All praises, which are paid as debts,
And not as given. This so darks
In Philoten all graceful marks
That Cleon's wife, with envy rare,
A present murderer does prepare
For good Marina, that her daughter
Might stand peerless by this slaughter.
The sooner her vile thoughts to stead,
Lychorida, our nurse, is dead:
And cursed Dionyza hath
The pregnant instrument of wrath
Prest for this blow. The unborn event
I do commend to your content:
Only I carry winged time
Post on the lame feet of my rhyme;
Which never could I so convey
Unless your thoughts went on my way.—
Dionyza does appear,
With Leonine, a murderer.    [*Exit.*

SCENE I.—THARSUS. *An open Place near
the Sea-shore.*

*Enter* DIONYZA *and* LEONINE.

*Dion.* Thy oath remember; thou hast
sworn to do't.
'Tis but a blow, which never shall be known.
Thou canst not do a thing i' the world so
soon
To yield thee so much profit. Let not con-
science,    [bosom,
Which is but cold, inflaming love in thy
Inflame too nicely; nor let pity, which
Even women have cast off, melt thee, but be
A soldier to thy purpose.
*Leon.* I will do't; but yet she is a goodly
creature.    [have her.—
*Dion.* The fitter, then, the gods should
Here she comes weeping for her only mistress'
death.
Thou art resolv'd?
*Leon.*    I am resolv'd.

*Enter* MARINA *with a basket of flowers.*

*Mar.* No, I will rob Tellus of her weed,
To strew thy green with flowers: the yellows,
blues,
The purple violets, and marigolds
Shall as a carpet hang upon thy grave [maid,
While summer-days do last. Ay me! poor
Born in a tempest, when my mother died,
This world to me is like a lasting storm,
Whirring me from my friends.
*Dion.* How now, Marina! why do you
keep alone?
How chance my daughter is not with you?
Do not    [have
Consume your blood with sorrowing: you

A nurse of me. Lord, how your favour's
chang'd
With this unprofitable woe! Come,
Give me your flowers ere the sea mar them.
Walk with Leonine; the air is quick there,
And it pierces and sharpens the stomach.—
Come,
Leonine, take her by the arm, walk with her.
*Mar.* No, I pray you;
I'll not bereave you of your servant.
*Dion.*    Come, come;
I love the king your father, and yourself,
With more than foreign heart. We every day
Expect him here: when he shall come, and
find
Our paragon to all reports thus blasted, [age;
He will repent the breadth of this great voy-
Blame both my lord and me that we have
taken
No care to your best courses. Go, I pray you,
Walk, and be cheerful once again; reserve
That excellent complexion, which did steal
The eyes of young and old. Care not for me;
I can go home alone.
*Mar.*    Well, I will go;
But yet I have no desire to it.    [you.—
*Dion.* Come, come, I know 'tis good for
Walk half an hour, Leonine, at the least:
Remember what I have said.
*Leon.*    I warrant you, madam.
*Dion.* I'll leave you, my sweet lady, for
awhile:
Pray, walk softly, do not heat your blood:
What! I must have a care of you.
*Mar.*    My thanks, sweet madam.—
[*Exit* DIONYZA.
Is this wind westerly that blows?
*Leon.*    South-west.
*Mar.* When I was born the wind was north.
*Leon.*    Was't so?
*Mar.* My father, as nurse said, did never
fear,    [ing
But cried, *Good seamen!* to the sailors, gall-
His kingly hands with hauling of the ropes;
And, clasping to the mast, endur'd a sea
That almost burst the deck.
*Leon.* When was this?
*Mar.* When I was born:
Never was waves nor wind more violent;
And from the ladder-tackle washes off
A canvas-climber: *Ha!* says one, *wilt out?*
And with a dropping industry they skip
From stem to stern: the boatswain whistles,
and
The master calls, and trebles their confusion.
*Leon.* Come, say your prayers.
*Mar.*    What mean you?
*Leon.* If you require a little space for
prayer,
I grant it: pray; but be not tedious,
For the gods are quick of ear, and I am sworn
To do my work with haste.
*Mar.*    Why will you kill me?
*Leon.* To satisfy my lady.

*Mar.* Why would she have me kill'd?
Now, as I can remember, by my troth,
I never did her hurt in all my life:
I never spake bad word, nor did ill turn
To any living creature: believe me, la,
I never kill'd a mouse, nor hurt a fly:
I trod upon a worm against my will,
But I wept for it. How have I offended,
Wherein my death might yield her profit,
Or my life imply her danger?
    *Leon.*          My commission
Is not to reason of the deed, but do it. [hope.
    *Mar.* You will not do't for all the world, I
You are well-favour'd, and your looks fore-
    show
You have a gentle heart. I saw you lately
When you caught hurt in parting two that
    fought:          [now:
Good sooth, it show'd well in you: do so
Your lady seeks my life; come you between,
And save poor me, the weaker.
    *Leon.*          I am sworn,
And will despatch.

*Enter* Pirates *whilst* MARINA *is struggling.*

    1 *Pirate.* Hold, villain!
              [LEONINE *runs away.*
    2 *Pirate.* A prize! a prize!
    3 *Pirate.* Half-part, mates, half-part.
Come, let's have her aboard suddenly.
          [*Exeunt* Pirates *with* MARINA.

*Re-enter* LEONINE.

    *Leon.* These roving thieves serve the great
    pirate Valdes,
And they have seiz'd Marina. Let her go:
There's no hope she will return. I'll swear
    she's dead          [ther:
And thrown into the sea.—But I'll see fur-
Perhaps they will but please themselves upon
    her,
Not carry her aboard. If she remain, [slain.
Whom they have ravish'd must by me be
              [*Exit.*

SCENE II.—MITYLENE. *A Room in a Brothel.*

*Enter* Pander, Bawd, *and* BOULT.

    *Pand.* Boult,—
    *Boult.* Sir?
    *Pand.* Search the market narrowly; Mity-
lene is full of gallants. We lost too much
money this mart by being too wenchless.
    *Bawd.* We were never so much out of
creatures. We have but poor three, and they
can do no more than they can do; and they
with continual action are even as good as
rotten.
    *Pand.* Therefore, let's have fresh ones,
whate'er we pay for them. If there be not
a conscience to be used in every trade we
shall never prosper.
    *Bawd.* Thou sayest true; 'tis not our
bringing up of poor bastards,—as, I think, I
have brought up some eleven,—

    *Boult.* Ay, to eleven; and brought them
down again.—But shall I search the market?
    *Bawd.* What else, man? The stuff we have,
a strong wind will blow it to pieces, they are
so pitifully sodden.
    *Pand.* Thou sayest true; they are too un-
wholesome, o' conscience. The poor Transyl-
vanian is dead, that lay with the little baggage.
    *Boult.* Ay, she quickly pooped him; she
made him roast-meat for worms.—But I'll
go search the market.          [*Exit.*
    *Pand.* Three or four thousand chequins
were as pretty a proportion to live quietly,
and so give over.
    *Bawd.* Why, to give over, I pray you? is it
a shame to get when we are old?
    *Pand.* O, our credit comes not in like the
commodity; nor the commodity wages not
with the danger: therefore, if in our youths
we could pick up some pretty estate, 'twere
not amiss to keep our door hatch'd. Besides,
the sore terms we stand upon with the gods
will be strong with us for giving over. [we.
    *Bawd.* Come, other sorts offend as well as
    *Pand.* As well as we! ay, and better too;
we offend worse. Neither is our profession
any trade; it's no calling.—But here comes
Boult.

*Re-enter* Boult, *with* MARINA *and the* Pirates.

    *Boult.* [*To* MARINA.] Come your ways.—
My masters, you say she's a virgin?
    1 *Pirate.* O, sir, we doubt it not.
    *Boult.* Master, I have gone through for
this piece, you see: if you like her, so; if not,
I have lost my earnest.
    *Bawd.* Boult, has she any qualities?
    *Boult.* She has a good face, speaks well,
and has excellent good clothes: there's no
further necessity of qualities can make her
be refused.
    *Bawd.* What's her price, Boult?
    *Boult.* It cannot be bated one doit of a
thousand pieces.
    *Pand.* Well, follow me, my masters; you
shall have your money presently. Wife, take
her in; instruct her what she has to do, that
she may not be raw in her entertainment.
          [*Exeunt* Pander *and* Pirates.
    *Bawd.* Boult, take you the marks of her,—
the colour of her hair, complexion, height,
age, with warrant of her virginity; and cry,
*He that will give most shall have her first.*
Such a maidenhead were no cheap thing, if
men were as they have been. Get this done as
I command you.
    *Boult.* Performance shall follow.    [*Exit.*
    *Mar.* Alack, that Leonine was so slack, so
    slow!—          [these pirates,—
He should have struck, not spoke;—or that
Not enough barbarous,—had not o'erboard
    thrown me
For to seek my mother!

*Bawd.* Why lament you, pretty one?

*Mar.* 'That I am pretty. [part in you.

*Bawd.* Come, the gods have done their

*Mar.* I accuse them not.

*Bawd.* You are lit into my hands, where you are like to live.

*Mar.* The more my fault
To 'scape his hands where I was like to die.

*Bawd.* Ay, and you shall live in pleasure.

*Mar.* No.

*Bawd.* Yes, indeed shall you, and taste gentlemen of all fashions. You shall fare well: you shall have the difference of all complexions. What! do you stop your ears?

*Mar.* Are you a woman?

*Bawd.* What would you have me be, an I be not a woman?

*Mar.* An honest woman, or not a woman.

*Bawd.* Marry, whip thee, gosling: I think I shall have something to do with you. Come, you are a young foolish sapling, and must be bowed as I would have you.

*Mar.* The gods defend me!

*Bawd.* If it please the gods to defend you by men, then men must comfort you, men must feed you, men must stir you up.— Boult's returned.

### Re-enter BOULT.

Now, sir, hast thou cried her through the market?

*Boult.* I have cried her almost to the number of her hairs; I have drawn her picture with my voice.

*Bawd.* And I pr'ythee tell me, how dost thou find the inclination of the people, especially of the younger sort?

*Boult.* Faith, they listened to me as they would have hearkened to their father's testament. There was a Spaniard's mouth so watered that he went to bed to her very description.

*Bawd.* We shall have him here to-morrow with his best ruff on.

*Boult.* To-night, to-night. But, mistress, do you know the French knight that cowers i' the hams?

*Bawd.* Who? Monsieur Veroles?

*Boult.* Ay: he offered to cut a caper at the proclamation; but he made a groan at it, and swore he would see her to-morrow.

*Bawd.* Well, well; as for him, he brought his disease hither: here he does but repair it. I know he will come in our shadow to scatter his crowns in the sun.

*Boult.* Well, if we had of every nation a traveller, we should lodge them with this sign.

*Bawd.* [*To* MAR.] Pray you, come hither awhile. You have fortunes coming upon you. Mark me: you must seem to do that fearfully which you commit willingly; to despise profit where you have most gain. To weep that you live as you do makes pity in your lovers: seldom but that pity begets you a good opinion, and that opinion a mere profit.

*Mar.* I understand you not.

*Boult.* O, take her home, mistress, take her home: these blushes of hers must be quenched with some present practice.

*Bawd.* Thou sayest true, i' faith, so they must; for your bride goes to that with shame which is her way to go with warrant.

*Boult.* Faith, some do, and some do not. But, mistress, if I have bargained for the joint,—

*Bawd.* Thou mayst cut a morsel off the spit.

*Boult.* I may so.

*Bawd.* Who should deny it? Come, young one, I like the manner of your garments well.

*Boult.* Ay, by my faith, they shall not be changed yet.

*Bawd.* Boult, spend thou that in the town: report what a sojourner we have; you'll lose nothing by custom. When nature framed this piece she meant thee a good turn; therefore say what a paragon she is, and thou hast the harvest out of thine own report.

*Boult.* I warrant you, mistress, thunder shall not so awake the beds of eels as my giving out her beauty stir up the lewdly inclined. I'll bring home some to-night.

*Bawd.* Come your ways; follow me.

*Mar.* If fires be hot, knives sharp, or waters deep,
Untied I still my virgin knot will keep.
Diana, aid my purpose!

*Bawd.* What have we to do with Diana? Pray you, will you go with us? [*Exeunt.*

### SCENE III.—THARSUS. *A Room in* CLEON'S *House.*

### *Enter* CLEON *and* DIONYZA.

*Dion.* Why, are you foolish? Can it be undone?

*Cle.* O Dionyza, such a piece of slaughter The sun and moon ne'er look'd upon!

*Dion.* I think
You'll turn a child again. [world,

*Cle.* Were I chief lord of all the spacious I'd give it to undo the deed. O lady,
Much less in blood than virtue, yet a princess To equal any single crown o' the earth
I' the justice of compare!—O villain Leonine! Whom thou hast poison'd too: [kindness
If thou hadst drunk to him, 't had been a Becoming well thy fact: what canst thou say When noble Pericles shall demand his child?

*Dion.* That she is dead. Nurses are not the fates,
To foster it, nor ever to preserve. [it?
She died at night; I'll say so. Who can cross Unless you play the pious innocent,
And for an honest attribute cry out,
*She died by foul play.*

*Cle.*                    O, go to. Well, well.
Of all the faults beneath the heavens the gods
Do like this worst.
    *Dion.*              Be one of those that think
The petty wrens of Tharsus will fly hence,
And open this to Pericles. I do shame
To think of what a noble strain you are,
And of how coward a spirit.
    *Cle.*                    To such proceeding
Who ever but his approbation added,
Though not his pre-consent, he did not flow
From honourable sources.
    *Dion.*                    Be it so, then:
Yet none does know, but you, how she came
    dead,
Nor none can know, Leonine being gone.
She did distain my child, and stood between
Her and her fortunes: none would look on
    her,
But cast their gazes on Marina's face; [kin,
Whilst ours was blurted at, and held a mal-
Not worth the time of day. It pierc'd me
    thorough
And though you call my course unnatural,
You not your child well loving, yet I find
It greets me as an enterprise of kindness
Perform'd to your sole daughter.
    *Cle.*                Heavens forgive it!
    *Dion.* And as for Pericles,          [hearse,
What should he say? We wept after her
And yet we mourn: her monument
Is almost finish'd, and her epitaphs
In glittering golden characters express
A general praise to her, and care in us
At whose expense 'tis done.
    *Cle.*                Thou art like the harpy,
Which, to betray, dost, with thine angel's
    face,
Seize with thine eagle's talons.
    *Dion.* You are like one that superstitiously
Doth swear to the gods that winter kills the
    flies:
But yet I know you'll do as I advise.
                           *[Exeunt.*

*Enter* GOWER, *before the Monument of*
MARINA *at Tharsus.*

    *Gow.* Thus time we waste, and longest
    leagues make short;
Sail seas in cockles, have an wish but for't;
Making,—to take your imagination,—
From bourn to bourn, region to region.
By you being pardon'd, we commit no crime
To use one language in each several clime,
Where our scenes seem to live. I do beseech
    you
To learn of me, who stand i' the gaps to
    teach you
The stages of our story. Pericles
Is now again thwarting the wayward seas,
Attended on by many a lord and knight,
To see his daughter, all his life's delight.
Old Escanes, whom Helicanus late
Advanc'd in time to great and high estate,

Is left to govern. Bear you it in mind,
Old Helicanus goes along behind.   [brought
Well-sailing ships and bounteous winds have
This king to Tharsus,—think his pilot
    thought;                          [on,—
So with his steerage shall your thoughts grow
To fetch his daughter home, who first is gone.
Like motes and shadows see them move
    awhile;
Your ears unto your eyes I'll reconcile.

    *Dumb show.*

*Enter, at one side,* PERICLES *with his* Train;
    CLEON *and* DIONYZA *at the other.* CLEON
    *shows* PERICLES *the Tomb of* MARINA,
    *whereat* PERICLES *makes lamentation, puts*
    *on sackcloth, and in a mighty passion de-*
    *parts. Then exeunt* CLEON *and* DIONYZA.

See how belief may suffer by foul show!
This borrow'd passion stands for true old
    woe;
And Pericles, in sorrow all devour'd,
With sighs shot through and biggest tears
    o'ershower'd,                        [swears
Leaves Tharsus, and again embarks. He
Never to wash his face nor cut his hairs;
He puts on sackcloth, and to sea. He bears
A tempest which his mortal vessel tears,
And yet he rides it out. Now please you wit
The epitaph is for Marina writ
By wicked Dionyza.
        *[Reads the inscription on* MARINA'S
                *Monument.*

The fairest, sweet'st, and best lies here,
Who wither'd in her spring of year.
She was of Tyrus the king's daughter,
On whom foul death hath made this slaughter;
Marina was she call'd; and at her birth,
Thetis, being proud, swallow'd some part o' the
    earth:
Therefore the earth, fearing to be o'erflow'd,
Hath Thetis' birth-child on the heavens bestow'd:
Wherefore she does,—and swears she'll never stint,—
Make raging battery upon shores of flint.

No visard does become black villany
So well as soft and tender flattery.
Let Pericles believe his daughter's dead,
And bear his courses to be ordered
By Lady Fortune; while our scene must play
His daughter's woe and heavy well-a-day
In her unholy service. Patience, then,
And think you now are all in Mitylen.
                              *[Exit.*

SCENE IV.—MITYLENE. *A Street before the*
                  *Brothel.*

*Enter, from the Brothel, two* Gentlemen.

    1 *Gent.* Did you ever hear the like?
    2 *Gent.* No, nor never shall do in such a
place as this, she being once gone.
    1 *Gent.* But to have divinity preached
there! did you ever dream of such a thing?
    2 *Gent.* No, no. Come, I am for no more

bawdy-houses: shall's go hear the vestals sing?

*z Gent.* I'll do anything now that is virtuous; but I am out of the road of rutting for ever. [*Exeunt.*

SCENE V.—MITYLENE. *A Room in the Brothel.*

*Enter* Pander, Bawd, *and* Boult.

*Pand.* Well, I had rather than twice the worth of her she had ne'er come here.

*Bawd.* Fie, fie upon her! she is able to freeze the god Priapus, and undo a whole generation. We must either get her ravished or be rid of her. When she should do for clients her fitment, and do me the kindness of our profession, she has me her quirks, her reasons, her master-reasons, her prayers, her knees; that she would make a puritan of the devil, if he should cheapen a kiss of her.

*Boult.* Faith, I must ravish her, or she'll disfurnish us of all our cavaliers, and make all our swearers priests. [ness for me!

*Pand.* Now, the pox upon her green-sick-

*Bawd.* Faith there's no way to be rid on't but by the way to the pox. Here comes the Lord Lysimachus disguised.

*Boult.* We should have both lord and lown if the peevish baggage would but give way to customers.

*Enter* LYSIMACHUS.

*Lys.* How now! How a dozen of virginities?

*Bawd.* Now, the gods to-bless your honour!

*Boult.* I am glad to see your honour in good health.

*Lys.* You may so; 'tis the better for you that your resorters stand upon sound legs. How now, wholesome iniquity? Have you that a man may deal withal, and defy the surgeon?

*Bawd.* We have here one, sir, if she would —but there never came her like in Mitylene.

*Lys.* If she'd do the deed of darkness, thou wouldst say. [say well enough.

*Bawd.* Your honour knows what 'tis to

*Lys.* Well, call forth, call forth.

*Boult.* For flesh and blood, sir, white and red, you shall see a rose; and she were a rose indeed, if she had but,—

*Lys.* What, pr'ythee?

*Boult.* O, sir, I can be modest.

*Lys.* That dignifies the renown of a bawd no less than it gives a good report to a number to be chaste. [*Exit* BOULT.

*Bawd.* Here comes that which grows to the stalk,—never plucked yet, I can assure you.

*Re-enter* BOULT *with* MARINA.

Is she not a fair creature?

*Lys.* Faith, she would serve after a long

voyage at sea. Well, there's for you:—leave us.

*Bawd.* I beseech your honour, give me leave: a word, and I'll have done presently.

*Lys.* I beseech you, do.

*Bawd.* First, I would have you note this is an honourable man.

[*To* MAR., *whom she takes aside.*

*Mar.* I desire to find him so, that I may worthily note him.

*Bawd.* Next, he's the governor of this country, and a man whom I am bound to.

*Mar.* If he govern the country you are bound to him indeed; but how honourable he is in that I know not.

*Bawd.* Pray you, without any more virginal fencing, will you use him kindly? He will line your apron with gold.

*Mar.* What he will do graciously I will thankfully receive.

*Lys.* Ha' you done?

*Bawd.* My lord, she's not paced yet: you must take some pains to work her to your manage. Come, we will leave his honour and her together.—Go thy ways.—

[*Exeunt* Bawd, Pander, *and* BOULT.

*Lys.* Now, pretty one, how long have you been at this trade?

*Mar.* What trade, sir?

*Lys.* What I cannot name but I shall offend.

*Mar.* I cannot be offended with my trade. Please you to name it. [fession?

*Lys.* How long have you been of this pro-

*Mar.* E'er since I can remember.

*Lys.* Did you go to't so young? Were you a gamester at five or at seven?

*Mar.* Earlier too, sir, if now I be one.

*Lys.* Why, the house you dwell in proclaims you to be a creature of sale.

*Mar.* Do you know this house to be a place of such resort, and will come into't? I hear say you are of honourable parts, and are the governor of this place.

*Lys.* Why, hath your principal made known unto you who I am?

*Mar.* Who is my principal?

*Lys.* Why, your herb-woman; she that sets seeds and roots of shame and iniquity. O, you have heard something of my power, and so stand aloof for more serious wooing. But I protest to thee, pretty one, my authority shall not see thee, or else look friendly upon thee. Come, come, bring me to some private place: come, come. [it now;

*Mar.* If you were born to honour, show If put upon you, make the judgment good That thought you worthy of it.

*Lys.* How's this? how's this?—Some more;—be sage.

*Mar.* For me, [tune That am a maid, though most ungentle for-Hath plac'd me in this sty, Where, since I came,

Diseases have been sold dearer than physic,—
O that the good gods
Would set me free from this unhallow'd place,
Though they did change me to the meanest
　　bird
That flies i' the purer air!
　*Lys.*　　　　　　　　I did not think
Thou couldst have spoke so well; ne'er
　　dream'd thou couldst.
Had I brought hither a corrupted mind,
Thy speech had alter'd it. Hold, here's gold
　　for thee:
Perséver in that clear way thou goest,
And the gods strengthen thee!
　*Mar.*　　　　　The good gods preserve you!
　*Lys.* For me, be you thoughten
That I came with no ill intent; for to me
The very doors and windows savour vilely.
Fare thee well. Thou art a piece of virtue, and
I doubt not but thy training hath been
　　noble.—
Hold, here's more gold for thee.—
A curse upon him, die he like a thief,
That robs thee of thy goodness! If thou dost
　　hear from me
It shall be for thy good.

*Re-enter* BOULT *as* LYSIMACHUS *is putting up
　　his purse.*

　*Boult.* I beseech your honour, one piece
　　for me.　　　　　　　　[*Your house*,
　*Lys.* Avaunt, thou damned doorkeeper!
But for this virgin that doth prop it,
Would sink and overwhelm you. Away!
　　　　　　　　　　　　　　[*Exit.*
　*Boult.* How's this? We must take another course with you. If your peevish chastity, which is not worth a breakfast in the
cheapest country under the cope, shall undo a
whole household, let me be gelded like a
spaniel. Come your ways.
　*Mar.* Whither would you have me?
　*Boult.* I must have your maidenhead taken
off, or the common hangman shall execute it.
Come your ways. We'll have no more gentlemen driven away. Come your ways, I say.

*Re-enter* Bawd.

　*Bawd.* How now! What's the matter?
　*Boult.* Worse and worse, mistress; she has
here spoken holy words to the Lord Lysimachus.
　*Bawd.* O abominable!
　*Boult.* She makes our profession as it
were to stink afore the face of the gods.
　*Bawd.* Marry, hang her up for ever!
　*Boult.* The nobleman would have dealt with
her like a nobleman, and she sent him away
as cold as a snowball; saying his prayers too.
　*Bawd.* Boult, take her away; use her at
thy pleasure: crack the glass of her virginity,
and make the rest malleable.
　*Boult.* An if she were a thornier piece of
ground than she is, she shall be ploughed.

　*Mar.* Hark, hark, you gods!
　*Bawd.* She conjures: away with her!
Would she had never come within my doors!
Marry, hang you!—She's born to undo us.—
Will you not go the way of womenkind?
Marry, come up, my dish of chastity with
rosemary and bays!　　　　　　[*Exit.*
　*Boult.* Come, mistress; come your ways
with me.
　*Mar.* Whither wilt thou have me?
　*Boult.* To take from you the jewel you
hold so dear.
　*Mar.* Pr'ythee, tell me one thing first.
　*Boult.* Come now, your one thing. [*to be?*
　*Mar.* What canst thou wish thine enemy
　*Boult.* Why, I could wish him to be my
master, or, rather, my mistress.
　*Mar.* Neither of these are so bad as thou
　　art,
Since they do better thee in their command.
Thou hold'st a place for which the pained'st
　　fiend
Of hell would not in reputation change:
Thou'rt the damn'd doorkeeper to every
Coistrel that comes inquiring for his tib;
To the choleric fisting of every rogue
Thy ear is liable; thy very food is such
As hath been belch'd on by infected lungs.
　*Boult.* What would you have me do? go
to the wars, would you? where a man may
serve seven years for the loss of a leg, and
have not money enough in the end to buy
him a wooden one?
　*Mar.* Do anything but this thou doest.
　　Empty
Old receptacles, or common sewers, of filth;
Serve by indenture to the common hangman:
Any of these ways are yet better than this;
For what thou professest, a baboon, could he
　　speak,　　　　　　　　　　　　[*gods*
Would own a name too dear.—O that the
Would safely deliver me from this place!—
Here, here's gold for thee.
If that thy master would gain by me,
Proclaim that I can sing, weave, sew, and
　　dance,　　　　　　　　　　　　[*boast;*
With other virtues which I'll keep from
And I will undertake all these to teach.
I doubt not but this populous city will
Yield many scholars.　　　　　[*speak of?*
　*Boult.* But can you teach all this you
　*Mar.* Prove that I cannot, take me home
　　again,
And prostitute me to the basest groom
That doth frequent your house.
　*Boult.* Well, I will see what I can do for
thee: if I can place thee, I will.
　*Mar.* But amongst honest women?
　*Boult.* Faith, my acquaintance lies little
amongst them. But since my master and mis-
tress have bought you, there's no going but
by their consent: therefore I will make them
acquainted with your purpose, and I doubt
not but I shall find them tractable enough.

Come, I'll do for thee what I can; come
your ways.                              [*Exeunt.*

## ACT V.

### *Enter* GOWER.

*Gow.* Marina thus the brothel scapes, and
        chances
Into an honest house, our story says.
She sings like one immortal, and she dances
As goddess-like to her admired lays;
Deep clerks she dumbs; and with her needle
        composes                        [berry,
Nature's own shape, of bud, bird, branch, or
That even her art sisters the natural roses;
Her inkle, silk, twin with the rubied cherry:
That pupils lacks she none of noble race,
Who pour their bounty on her; and her gain
She gives the cursed bawd. Here we her
        place;
And to her father turn our thoughts again,
Where we left him, on the sea. We there
        him lost;                       [riv'd
Whence, driven before the winds, he is ar-
Here where his daughter dwells; and on this
        coast
Suppose him now at anchor. The city striv'd
God Neptune's annual feast to keep: from
        whence
Lysimachus our Tyrian ship espies,   [pense;
His banners sable, trimm'd with rich ex-
And to him in his barge with fervour hies.
In your supposing once more put your sight
Of heavy Pericles; think this his bark:
Where what is done in action, more, if might,
Shall be discover'd; please you, sit, and hark.
                                        [*Exit.*

SCENE I.—*On board* PERICLES' *ship, off Mitylene. A Pavilion on deck with a curtain
before it;* PERICLES *within it, reclining on
a couch. A barge lying beside the Tyrian
vessel.*

*Enter two* Sailors, *one belonging to the
Tyrian vessel, the other to the barge; to
them* HELICANUS.

*Tyr. Sail.* Where is Lord Helicanus? he
can resolve you.
                    [*To the* Sailor *of Mitylene.*
O, here he is.—
Sir, there's a barge put off from Mitylene,
And in it is Lysimachus the governor, [will?
Who craves to come aboard. What is your
*Hel.* That he have his. Call up some
        gentlemen.
*Tyr. Sail.* Ho, gentlemen! my lord calls.

*Enter two or three* Gentlemen.

1 *Gent.* Doth your lordship call?
*Hel.* Gentlemen,                     [I pray,
There is some of worth would come aboard;
Greet them fairly.
        [*The* Gentlemen *and the two* Sailors
        *descend, and go on board the barge.*

*Enter, from thence,* LYSIMACHUS *and* Lords,
*with the* Gentlemen *and the two* Sailors.

*Tyr. Sail.* Sir,
This is the man that can, in aught you would,
Resolve you.
*Lys.* Hail, reverend sir! The gods preserve
        you!
*Hel.* And you, sir, to outlive the age I am,
And die as I would do.
*Lys.*               You wish me well.
Being on shore, honouring of Neptune's
        triumphs,
Seeing this goodly vessel ride before us,
I made to it, to know of whence you are.
*Hel.* First, what is your place?
*Lys.*                     I am the governor
Of this place you lie before.
*Hel.* Sir,
Our vessel is of Tyre, in it the king; [spoken
A man who for this three months hath not
To any one, nor taken sustenance,
But to prorogue his grief.              [ture?
*Lys.* Upon what ground is his distempera-
*Hel.* 'Twould be too tedious to repeat;
But the main grief springs from the loss
Of a beloved daughter and a wife.
*Lys.* May we not see him?
*Hel.* You may;
But bootless is your sight,—he will not speak
To any.
*Lys.* Yet let me obtain my wish.
*Hel.* Behold him     [PERICLES *discovered*].
        This was a goodly person
Till the disaster that one mortal night
Drove him to this.
*Lys.* Sir king, all hail! the gods preserve
        you!
Hail, royal sir!
*Hel.* It is in vain; he will not speak to you.
1 *Lord.* Sir, we have a maid in Mitylene, I
        durst wager,
Would win some words of him.
*Lys.*                     'Tis well bethought.
She, questionless, with her sweet harmony
And other choice attractions, would allure,
And make a battery through his deafen'd
        parts,
Which now are midway stopp'd:
She is all happy as the fairest of all,
And, with her fellow maids, is now upon
The leafy shelter that abuts against
The island's side.
        [*He whispers first* Lord, *who goes off
        in the barge of* LYSIMACHUS.
*Hel.* Sure, all's effectless; yet nothing we
        'll omit                        [kindness
That bears recovery's name. But, since your
We have stretch'd thus far, let us beseech you
That for our gold we may provision have,
Wherein we are not destitute for want,
But weary for the staleness.
*Lys.*                         O, sir, a courtesy
Which if we should deny, the most just gods

For every graff would send a caterpillar,
And so afflict our province.—Yet once more
Let me entreat to know at large the cause
Of your king's sorrow.
    *Hel.*     Sit, sir, I will recount it to you:—
But, see, I am prevented.

*Re-enter, from the barge,* First Lord, *with*
    MARINA *and a young* Lady.

*Lys.*                    O, here is
The lady that I sent for.—Welcome, fair
    one!—
Is 't not a goodly presence?
    *Hel.*                She 's a gallant lady.
    *Lys.* She 's such a one that, were I well
    assur'd
Came of gentle kind and noble stock, [wed.—
I'd wish no better choice, and think me rarely
Fair one, all goodness that consists in bounty
Expect even here, where is a kingly patient:
If that thy prosperous and artificial feat
Can draw him but to answer thee in aught,
Thy sacred physic shall receive such pay
As thy desires can wish.
    *Mar.*          Sir, I will use
My utmost skill in his recovery,
Provided
That none but I and my companion maid
Be suffer'd to come near him.
    *Lys.*          Come, let us leave her;
And the gods make her prosperous!
                    [MARINA *sings.*

*Lys.* Mark'd he your music?
*Mar.*            No, nor look'd on us.
*Lys.* See, she will speak to him.
*Mar.* Hail, sir! my lord, lend ear.
*Per.* Hum, ha!
*Mar.* I am a maid,
My lord, that ne'er before invited eyes,
But have been gaz'd on like a comet: she
    speaks,
My lord, that, may be, hath endur'd a grief
Might equal yours, if both were justly
    weigh'd.
Though wayward fortune did malign my
    state,
My derivation was from ancestors
Who stood equivalent with mighty kings:
But time hath rooted out my parentage,
And to the world and awkward casaulties
Bound me in servitude.—[*Aside.*] I will
    desist;
But there is something glows upon my cheek,
And whispers in mine ear, *Go not till he
    speak.*
    *Per.* My fortunes—parentage—good par-
    entage—            [you?
To equal mine!—was it not thus? what say
    *Mar.* I said, my lord, if you did know my
    parentage
You would not do me violence.
    *Per.*            I do think so.—
I pray you, turn your eyes upon me.

You are like something that—What country-
    woman?
Here of these shores?
    *Mar.*          No, nor of any shores:
Yet I was mortally brought forth, and am
No other than I appear.          [weeping.
    *Per.* I am great with woe, and shall deliver
My dearest wife was like this maid, and such
    a one          [square brows;
My daughter might have been: my queen's
Her stature to an inch; as wand-like straight;
As silver voic'd; her eyes as jewel-like,
And cas'd as richly; in pace another Juno;
Who starves the ears she feeds, and makes
    them hungry          [you live?
The more she gives them speech.—Where do
    *Mar.* Where I am but a stranger: from the
    deck
You may discern the place.
    *Per.*          Where were you bred?
And how achiev'd you these endowments,
    which
You make more rich to owe?          [seem
    *Mar.* If I should tell my history, it would
Like lies, disdain'd in the reporting.
    *Per.*          Pr'ythee, speak:
Falseness cannot come from thee; for thou
    look'st
Modest as Justice, and thou seem'st a palace
For the crown'd Truth to dwell in: I will
    believe thee,
And make my senses credit thy relation
To points that seem impossible; for thou
    look'st
Like one I lov'd indeed. What were thy
    friends?
Didst thou not say, when I did push thee
    back,—
Which was when I perceiv'd thee,—that thou
    cam'st
From good descending?
    *Mar.*          So indeed I did.
    *Per.* Report thy parentage. I think thou
    said'st
Thou hadst been toss'd from wrong to in-
    jury,
And that thou thought'st thy griefs might
    equal mine,
If both were open'd.
    *Mar.*          Some such thing
I said, and said no more but what my
    thoughts
Did warrant me was likely.
    *Per.*          Tell thy story;
If thine consider'd prove the thousandth
    part
Of my endurance, thou art a man, and I
Have suffer'd like a girl: yet thou dost look
Like Patience gazing on kings' graves, and
    smiling
Extremity out of act. What were thy friends?
How lost thou them? Thy name, my most
    kind virgin?
Recount, I do beseech thee: come, sit by me.

*Mar.* My name is Marina.

*Per.*                              O, I am mock'd,
And thou by some incensed god sent hither
To make the world to laugh at me.

*Mar.*                        Patience, good sir,
Or here I'll cease.

*Per.*                  Nay, I'll be patient.
Thou little know'st how thou dost startle me,
To call thyself Marina.

*Mar.*                        The name
Was given me by one that had some power,—
My father, and a king.

*Per.*                  How! a king's daughter?
And call'd Marina?

*Mar.*        You said you would believe me;
But, not to be a troubler of your peace,
I will end here.

*Per.*          But are you flesh and blood?
Have you a working pulse? and are no fairy?
Motion!—Well; speak on. Where were you
    born?
And wherefore call'd Marina?

*Mar.*                    Call'd Marina
For I was born at sea.

*Per.*                At sea! what mother?

*Mar.* My mother was the daughter of a
    king;
Who died the minute I was born,
As my good nurse Lychorida hath oft
Deliver'd weeping.

*Per.*                O, stop there a little!—
[*Aside.*] This is the rarest dream that e'er dull
    sleep
Did mock sad fools withal: this cannot be:
My daughter's buried.—Well:—where were
    you bred?                          [story,
I'll hear you more, to the bottom of your
And never interrupt you.

*Mar.* You'll scarce believe me: 'twere best
    I did give o'er.

*Per.* I will believe you by the syllable
Of what you shall deliver. Yet give me
    leave,—
How came you in these parts? where were
    you bred?                      [leave me;

*Mar.* The king my father did in Tharsus
Till cruel Cleon, with his wicked wife,
Did seek to murder me: and having woo'd
A villain to attempt it, who having drawn to
    do 't,
A crew of pirates came and rescu'd me;
Brought me to Mitylene. But, good sir,
Whither will you have me? Why do you
    weep? It may be
You think me an imposter: no, good faith;
I am the daughter to King Pericles,
If good King Pericles be.

*Per.* Ho, Helicanus!

*Hel.*                        Calls my lord?

*Per.* Thou art a grave and noble counsel-
    lor,
Most wise in general: tell me, if thou canst,
What this maid is, or what is like to be,
That thus hath made me weep?

*Hel.*                        I know not; but
Here is the regent, sir, of Mitylene
Speaks nobly of her.

*Lys.*                        She would never tell
Her parentage; being demanded that,
She would sit still and weep.

*Per.* O Helicanus, strike me, honour'd sir;
Give me a gash, put me to present pain;
Lest this great sea of joys rushing upon me
O'erbear the shores of my mortality, [hither,
And drown me with their sweetness.—O, come
Thou that begett'st him that did thee beget;
Thou that was born at sea, buried at Thar-
    sus,
And found at sea again!—O Helicanus,
Down on thy knees, thank the holy gods as
    loud
As thunder threatens us: this is Marina.—
What was thy mother's name? tell me but
    that,
For truth can never be confirm'd enough,
Though doubts did ever sleep.

*Mar.*                        First, sir, I pray,
What is your title?

*Per.* I am Pericles of Tyre: but tell me now
My drown'd queen's name,—as in the rest
    you said                [heir of kingdoms,
Thou'st been godlike perfect,—thou 'rt the
And another life to Pericles thy father.

*Mar.* Is it no more to be your daughter
    than
To say my mother's name was Thaisa?
Thaisa was my mother, who did end
The minute I began.

*Per.* Now, blessing on thee! rise; thou art
    my child.—
Give me fresh garments.—Mine own Heli-
    canus,—
She is not dead at Tharsus, as she should
    have been
By savage Cleon: she shall tell thee all;
When thou shalt kneel, and justify in know-
    ledge
She is thy very princess.—Who is this?

*Hel.* Sir, 'tis the governor of Mitylene,
Who, hearing of your melancholy state,
Did come to see you.

*Per.*                    I embrace you.—
Give me my robes.—I am wild in my be-
    holding.—                        [music?—
O heavens bless my girl!—But, hark, what
Tell Helicanus, my Marina, tell him
O'er point by point, for yet he seems to
    doubt,
How sure you are my daughter.—But, what
    music?

*Hel.* My lord, I hear none.

*Per.* None!
The music of the spheres!—List, my Marina.

*Lys.* It is not good to cross him; give him
    way.

*Per.* Rarest sounds! Do ye not hear?

*Lys.*                    My lord, I hear.    [*Music.*

*Per.* Most heavenly music!

It nips me into listening, and thick slumber
Hangs upon mine eyes: let me rest.  [*Sleeps.*
 *Lys.* A pillow for his head:—
So, leave him all.—Well, my companion-
  friends,
If this but answer to my just belief,
I'll well remember you.
                    [*Exeunt all but* PERICLES.

DIANA *appears to* PERICLES *as in a vision.*
 *Dia.* My temple stands in Ephesus: hie
  thee thither,
And do upon mine altar sacrifice.  [gether,
There, when my maiden priests are met to-
Before the people all,
Reveal how thou at sea didst lose thy wife:
To mourn thy crosses, with thy daughter's,
  call,
And give them repetition to the life.
Or perform my bidding or thou liv'st in woe;
Do it, and happy; by my silver bow!
Awake and tell thy dream.  [*Disappears.*
 *Per.* Celestial Dian, goddess argentine,
I will obey thee.—Helicanus!

  *Re-enter* HELICANUS, LYSIMACHUS,
          MARINA, *&c.*

 *Hel.*                Sir?      [strike
 *Per.* My purpose was for Tharsus, there to
The inhospitable Cleon; but I am
For other service first: toward Ephesus
Turn our blown sails; eftsoons I'll tell thee
  why.—                    [*To* HELICANUS.
Shall we refresh us, sir, upon your shore,
                          [*To* LYSIMACHUS.
And give you gold for such provision
As our intents will need?
 *Lys.* Sir,
With all my heart; and when you come
  ashore
I have another suit.
 *Per.*              You shall prevail,
Were it to woo my daughter; for it seems
You have been noble towards her.
 *Lys.*                Sir, lend me your arm.
 *Per.* Come, my Marina.      [*Exeunt.*

*Enter* GOWER, *before the Temple of* DIANA *at
        Ephesus.*

 *Gow.* Now our sands are almost run;
More a little, and then done.
This, my last boon, give me,—
For such kindness must relieve me,—
That you aptly will suppose
What pageantry, what feats, what shows,
What minstrelsy, and pretty din,
The regent made in Mitylin,
To greet the king. So he thriv'd,
That he is promis'd to be wiv'd
To fair Marina; but in no wise
Till he had done his sacrifice,
As Dian bade: whereto being bound
The interim, pray you, all confound.
In feather'd briefness sails are fill'd,

And wishes fall out as they 're will'd.
At Ephesus the temple see,
Our king, and all his company.
That he can hither come so soon,
Is by your fancy's thankful boon.      [*Exit.*

SCENE II.—*The Temple of* DIANA *at Ephesus;*
  THAISA *standing near the altar as high
  priestess; a number of* Virgins *on each side;*
  CERIMON *and other* Inhabitants *of Ephesus
  attending.*

*Enter* PERICLES, *with his* Train; LYSIMA-
  CHUS, HELICANUS, MARINA, *and a* Lady.

 *Per.* Hail, Dian! to perform thy just com-
  mand,
I here confess myself the King of Tyre;
Who, frighted from my country, did wed
At Pentapolis the fair Thaisa.
At sea in childbed died she, but brought forth
A maid-child, call'd Marina; who, O goddess,
Wears yet thy silver livery. She at Tharsus
Was nurs'd with Cleon; who at fourteen
  years
He sought to murder: but her better stars
Brought her to Mitylene; 'gainst whose shore
Riding, her fortunes brought the maid aboard
  us,                                      [she
Where, by her own most clear remembrance,
Made known herself my daughter.
 *Thai.*            Voice and favour!—
You are, you are—O royal Pericles!—[*Faints.*
 *Per.* What means the woman? she dies!
  help, gentlemen!
 *Cer.* Noble sir,
If you have told Diana's altar true,
This is your wife.
 *Per.* Reverend appearer, no;
I threw her o'erboard with these very arms.
 *Cer.* Upon this coast, I warrant you.
 *Per.*                  'Tis most certain.
 *Cer.* Look to the lady;—O, she 's but
  o'erjoy'd.—
Early in blustering morn this lady was
Thrown upon this shore. I op'd the coffin,
Found there rich jewels; recover'd her, and
  plac'd her
Here in Diana's temple.
 *Per.*                May we see them?
 *Cer.* Great sir, they shall be brought you
  to my house,
Whither I invite you.—Look, Thaisa is
Recover'd.
 *Thai.* O, let me look!
If he be none of mine, my sanctity
Will to my sense bend no licentious ear,
But curb it, spite of seeing.—O, my lord,
Are you not Pericles? Like him you speak,
Like him you are: did you not name a
  tempest,
A birth and death?
 *Per.*              The voice of dead Thaisa!
 *Thai.* That Thaisa am I, supposed dead
And drown'd.
 *Per.* Immortal Dian!

*Thai.*                Now I know you better.—
When we with tears parted Pentapolis,
The king my father gave you such a ring.
                                    [*Shows a ring.*
*Per.* This, this: no more, you gods! your
        present kindness           [well,
Makes my past miseries sport: you shall do
That on the touching of her lips I may
Melt, and no more be seen. O, come, be buried
A second time within these arms.
*Mar.*                        My heart
Leaps to be gone into my mother's bosom.
                                [*Kneels to* THAISA.
*Per.* Look, who kneels here! Flesh of thy
        flesh, Thaisa;
Thy burden at the sea, and call'd Marina
For she was yielded there.
*Thai.*                Bless'd, and mine own!
*Hel.* Hail, madam, and my queen!
*Thai.*                        I know you not.
*Per.* You have heard me say, when I did
        fly from Tyre,
I left behind an ancient substitute:
Can you remember what I call'd the man?
I have nam'd him oft.
*Thai.*                'Twas Helicanus then.
*Per.* Still confirmation:
Embrace him, dear Thaisa; this is he.
Now do I long to hear how you were found;
How possibly preserv'd; and who to thank,
Besides the gods, for this great miracle.
*Thai.* Lord Cerimon, my lord; this man,
        through whom
The gods have shown their power; 'tis he
That can from first to last resolve you.
*Per.*                        Reverend sir,
The gods can have no mortal officer
More like a god than you. Will you deliver
How this dead queen re-lives?
*Cer.*                I will, my lord.
Beseech you, first go with me to my house,
Where shall be shown you all was found
        with her;
How she came placed here in the temple;
No needful thing omitted.                [I
*Per.* Pure Dian, bless thee for thy vision!
Will offer night-oblations to thee.—Thaisa,

This prince, the fair-betrothed of your
        daughter,
Shall marry her at Pentapolis.—And now,
This ornament
Makes me look dismal will I clip to form;
And what this fourteen years no razor
        touch'd,
To grace thy marriage-day I'll beautify.
*Thai.* Lord Cerimon hath letters of good
        credit, sir,
My father 's dead.
*Per.* Heavens make a star of him! Yet
        there, my queen,
We'll celebrate their nuptials, and ourselves
Will in that kingdom spend our following
        days:
Our son and daughter shall in Tyrus
        reign.—
Lord Cerimon, we do our longing stay
To hear the rest untold: sir, lead 's the way.
                                    [*Exeunt.*

*Enter* GOWER.

*Gow.* In Antiochus and his daughter you
        have heard
Of monstrous lust the due and just reward:
In Pericles, his queen and daughter, seen,—
Although assail'd with fortune fierce and
        keen,—
Virtue preserv'd from fell destruction 's blast,
Led on by heaven, and crown'd with joy at
        last;
In Helicanus may you well descry
A figure of truth, of faith, of loyalty:
In reverend Cerimon there well appears
The worth that learned charity aye wears:
For wicked Cleon and his wife, when fame
Had spread their cursed deed, and honour'd
        name
Of Pericles, to rage the city turn,
That him and his they in his palace burn;
The gods for murder seemed so content
To punish them,—although not done, but
        meant.
So, on your patience evermore attending,
New joy wait on you! Here our play has
        ending.                        [*Exit.*

# KING LEAR

## DRAMATIS PERSONÆ

LEAR, *King of Britain.*
KING OF FRANCE.
DUKE OF BURGUNDY.
DUKE OF CORNWALL.
DUKE OF ALBANY.
EARL OF KENT.
EARL OF GLOSTER.
EDGAR, *Son to* GLOSTER.
EDMUND, *Bastard Son to* GLOSTER.
CURAN, *a Courtier.*
Old Man, *Tenant to* GLOSTER.
Physician.
Fool.

OSWALD, *Steward to* GONERIL.
An Officer *employed by* EDMUND.
Gentleman *attendant on* CORDELIA.
A Herald.
Servants *to* CORNWALL.

GONERIL,
REGAN,     } *Daughters to* LEAR.
CORDELIA,

Knights *attending on the* KING, Officers, Messengers, Soldiers, *and* Attendants.

SCENE,—BRITAIN.

## ACT I.

### SCENE I.—*A Room of State in* KING LEAR'S *Palace.*

*Enter* KENT, GLOSTER, *and* EDMUND.

*Kent.* I thought the king had more affected the Duke of Albany than Cornwall.

*Glo.* It did always seem so to us: but now, in the division of the kingdom, it appears not which of the dukes he values most; for equalities are so weighed that curiosity in neither can make choice of either's moiety.

*Kent.* Is not this your son, my lord?

*Glo.* His breeding, sir, hath been at my charge: I have so often blushed to acknowledge him that now I am brazed to it.

*Kent.* I cannot conceive you.

*Glo.* Sir, this young fellow's mother could: whereupon she grew round-wombed, and had indeed, sir, a son for her cradle ere she had a husband for her bed. Do you smell a fault?

*Kent.* I cannot wish the fault undone, the issue of it being so proper.

*Glo.* But I have a son, sir, by order of law, some year elder than this, who yet is no dearer in my account: though this knave came something saucily into the world before he was sent for, yet was his mother fair; there was good sport at his making, and the whoreson must be acknowledged.—Do you know this noble gentleman, Edmund?

*Edm.* No, my lord.

*Glo.* My Lord of Kent: remember him hereafter as my honourable friend.

*Edm.* My services to your lordship.

*Kent.* I must love you, and sue to know you better.

*E lm.* Sir, I shall study deserving.

*Glo.* He hath been out nine years, and away he shall again.—The king is coming.

[*Sennet within.*

*Enter* LEAR, CORNWALL, ALBANY, GONERIL, REGAN, CORDELIA, *and* Attendants.

*Lear.* Attend the Lords of France and Burgundy,
Gloster.

*Glo.* I shall, my liege.

[*Exeunt* GLO. *and* EDM.

*Lear.* Meantime we shall express our darker purpose.—    [divided
Give me the map there.—Know that we have
In three our kingdom: and 'tis our fast intent
To shake all cares and business from our age;    [we
Conferring them on younger strengths, while
Unburden'd crawl toward death.—Our son of Cornwall,
And you, our no less loving son of Albany,
We have this hour a constant will to publish
Our daughters' several dowers, that future strife
May be prevented now. The princes, France and Burgundy,
Great rivals in our youngest daughter's love,
Long in our court have made their amorous sojourn,    [daughters.—
And here are to be answer'd.—Tell me, my
Since now we will divest us both of rule,
Interest of territory, cares of state,—
Which of you shall we say doth love us most?
That we our largest bounty may extend
Where nature doth with merit challenge.—
Goneril,
Our eldest-born, speak first.

*Gon.* Sir, I love you more than words can wield the matter;

[973]

Dearer than eyesight, space, and liberty;
Beyond what can be valu'd, rich or rare;
No less than life, with grace, health, beauty,
  honour;
As much as child e'er lov'd, or father found;
A love that makes breath poor and speech
  unable;
Beyond all manner of so much I love you.
  *Cor.* [*Aside.*] What shall Cordelia do?
  Love, and be silent.            [line to this,
  *Lear.* Of all these bounds, even from this
With shadowy forests and with champains
  rich'd,
With plenteous rivers and wide-skirted
  meads,
We make thee lady: to thine and Albany's
  issue
Be this perpetual.—What says our second
  daughter,
Our dearest Regan, wife to Cornwall? Speak.
  *Reg.* I am made of that self metal as my
  sister,
And prize me at her worth. In my true heart
I find she names my very deed of love;
Only she comes too short,—that I profess
Myself an enemy to all other joys
Which the most precious square of sense
  possesses;
And find I am alone felicitate
In your dear highness' love.
  *Cor.* [*Aside.*]            Then poor Cordelia!
And yet not so; since, I am sure, my love's
More ponderous than my tongue.
  *Lear.* To thee and thine hereditary ever
Remain this ample third of our fair kingdom;
No less in space, validity, and pleasure
Than that conferr'd on Goneril.—Now, our
  joy,                            [love
Although the last, not least; to whose young
The vines of France and milk of Burgundy
Strive to be interess'd; what can you say to
  draw                          [Speak.
A third more opulent than your sisters?
  *Cor.* Nothing, my lord.
  *Lear.* Nothing!
  *Cor.* Nothing.              [again.
  *Lear.* Nothing will come of nothing: speak
  *Cor.* Unhappy that I am, I cannot heave
My heart into my mouth: I love your
  majesty
According to my bond; nor more nor less.
  *Lear.* How, how, Cordelia! mend your
  speech a little,
Lest you may mar your fortunes.
  *Cor.*                        Good my lord,
You have begot me, bred me, lov'd me: I
Return those duties back as are right fit,
Obey you, love you, and most honour you.
Why have my sisters husbands if they say
They love you all? Haply, when I shall wed,
That lord whose hand must take my plight
  shall carry
Half my love with him, half my care and
  duty:

Sure I shall never marry like my sisters,
To love my father all.
  *Lear.* But goes thy heart with this?
  *Cor.*                        Ay, good my lord.
  *Lear.* So young and so untender?
  *Cor.* So young, my lord, and true.
  *Lear.* Let it be so,—thy truth, then, be
  thy dower:
For by the sacred radiance of the sun,
The mysteries of Hecate, and the night;
By all the operation of the orbs,
From whom we do exist and cease to be;
Here I disclaim all my paternal care,
Propinquity, and property of blood,
And as a stranger to my heart and me
Hold thee, from this for ever. The barbarous
  Scythian,
Or he that makes his generation messes
To gorge his appetite, shall to my bosom
Be as well neighbour'd, pitied, and reliev'd,
As thou my sometime daughter.
  *Kent.*                        Good my liege,—
  *Lear.* Peace, Kent!
Come not between the dragon and his wrath.
I lov'd her most, and thought to set my rest
On her kind nursery.—Hence, and avoid my
  sight!—                      [*To* Cordelia.
So be my grave my peace, as here I give
Her father's heart from her!—Call France;—
  who stirs?
Call Burgundy.—Cornwall and Albany,
With my two daughters' dowers digest the
  third:                        [her.
Let pride, which she calls plainness, marry
I do invest you jointly with my power,
Pre-eminence, and all the large effects
That troop with majesty.—Ourself, by
  monthly course,
With reservation of an hundred knights,
By you to be sustain'd, shall our abode
Make with you by due turns. Only we still
  retain
The name, and all the additions to a king;
The sway,
Revenue, execution of the rest,
Beloved sons, be yours: which to confirm,
This coronet part between you.
                          [*Giving the crown.*
  *Kent.*                        Royal Lear,
Whom I have ever honour'd as my king,
Lov'd as my father, as my master follow'd,
As my great patron thought on in my
  prayers,—
  *Lear.* The bow is bent and drawn, make
  from the shaft.
  *Kent.* Let it fall rather, though the fork
  invade
The region of my heart: be Kent un-
  mannerly
When Lear is mad. What wouldst thou do,
  old man?                      [speak
Think'st thou that duty shall have dread to
When power to flattery bows? To plainness
  honour's bound

When majesty falls to folly. Reserve thy
state;
And in thy best consideration check
This hideous rashness: answer my life my
judgment,
Thy youngest daughter does not love thee
least;
Nor are those empty-hearted whose low
sound
Reverbs no hollowness.

*Lear.* Kent, on thy life, no more.

*Kent.* My life I never held but as a pawn
To wage against thine enemies; nor fear to
lose it,
Thy safety being the motive.

*Lear.* Out of my sight!

*Kent.* See better, Lear; and let me still
remain
The true blank of thine eye.

*Lear.* Now, by Apollo,—

*Kent.* Now, by Apollo, king,
Thou swear'st thy gods in vain.

*Lear.* O, vassal! miscreant!
[*Laying his hand on his sword.*

*Alb. and Corn.* Dear sir, forbear.

*Kent.* Do;
Kill thy physician, and the fee bestow
Upon the foul disease. Revoke thy gift;
Or, whilst I can vent clamour from my
throat,
I'll tell thee thou dost evil.

*Lear.* Hear me, recreant!
On thine allegiance, hear me!—
Since thou hast sought to make us break our
vow,—
Which we durst never yet,—and with strain'd
pride
To come betwixt our sentence and our pow-
er,—
Which nor our nature nor our place can
bear,—
Our potency made good, take thy reward.
Five days we do allot thee for provision
To shield thee from disasters of the world;
And on the sixth to turn thy hated back
Upon our kingdom: if, on the tenth day
following,
Thy banish'd trunk be found in our domin-
ions,
The moment is thy death. Away! by Jupiter,
This shall not be revok'd.

*Kent.* Fare thee well, king: sith thus thou
wilt appear,
Freedom lives hence, and banishment is
here.—
The gods to their dear shelter take thee,
maid,
[*To* CORDELIA.
That justly think'st, and hast most rightly
said!
And your large speeches may your deeds
approve, [*To* REGAN *and* GONERIL.
That good effects may spring from words of
love.—

Thus Kent, O princes, bids you all adieu;
He'll shape his old course in a country new.
[*Exit.*

*Flourish. Re-enter* GLOSTER, *with* FRANCE,
BURGUNDY, *and* Attendants.

*Glo.* Here 's France and Burgundy, my
noble lord.

*Lear.* My lord of Burgundy,
We first address toward you, who with this
king
Hath rivall'd for our daughter: what in the
least
Will you require in present dower with her,
Or cease your quest of love?

*Bur.* Most royal majesty,
I crave no more than hath your highness
offer'd,
Nor will you tender less.

*Lear.* Right noble Burgundy,
When she was dear to us we did hold her so;
But now her price is fall'n. Sir, there she
stands:
If aught within that little seeming substance,
Or all of it, with our displeasure piec'd,
And nothing more, may fitly like your grace,
She 's there, and she is yours.

*Bur.* I know no answer.

*Lear.* Will you, with those infirmities she
owes,
Unfriended, new-adopted to our hate,
Dower'd with our curse, and stranger'd with
our oath,
Take her or leave her?

*Bur.* Pardon me, royal sir;
Election makes not up on such conditions.

*Lear.* Then leave her, sir; for, by the
power that made me,
I tell you all her wealth.—For you, great
king, [*To* FRANCE.
I would not from your love make such a
stray,
To match you where I hate; therefore be-
seech you
To avert your liking a more worthier way
Than on a wretch whom nature is asham'd
Almost to acknowledge hers.

*France.* This is most strange,
That she, who even but now was your best
object,
The argument of your praise, balm of your
age,
Most best, most dearest, should in this trice
of time
Commit a thing so monstrous, to dismantle
So many folds of favour. Sure her offence
Must be of such unnatural degree
That monsters it, or your fore-vouch'd affec-
tion
Fall into taint: which to believe of her
Must be a faith that reason without miracle
Could never plant in me.

*Cor.* I yet beseech your majesty,—
If for I want that glib and oily art

To speak and purpose not; since what I well
· intend,
I'll do 't before I speak,—that you make
known
It is no vicious blot, murder, or foulness,
No unchaste action or dishonour'd step,
That hath depriv'd me of your grace and
favour;　　　　　　　　　[richer,—
But even for want of that for which I am
A still-soliciting eye, and such a tongue
That I am glad I have not, though not to
have it
Hath lost me in your liking.

*Lear.*　　　　　　　Better thou
Hadst not been born than not to have
pleas'd me better.　　　　[nature,

*France.* Is it but this,—a tardiness in
Which often leaves the history unspoke
That it intends to do?—My lord of Bur-
gundy,
What say you to the lady? Love 's not love
When it is mingled with regards that stand
Aloof from the entire point. Will you have
her?
She is herself a dowry.

*Bur.*　　　　　　　Royal king,
Give me but that portion which yourself
propos'd,
And here I take Cordelia by the hand,
Duchess of Burgundy.

*Lear.* Nothing: I have sworn; I am firm.

*Bur.* I am sorry, then, you have so lost a
father
That you must lose a husband.

*Cor.*　　　　　Peace be with Burgundy!
Since that respects of fortune are his love
I shall not be his wife.　　[rich, being poor;

*France.* Fairest Cordelia, that art most
Most choice, forsaken; and most lov'd,
despis'd!
Thee and thy virtues here I seize upon:
Be it lawful, I take up what 's cast away.
Gods, gods! 'tis strange that from their
cold'st neglect
My love should kindle to inflam'd respect.—
Thy dowerless daughter, king, thrown to my
chance,
Is queen of us, of ours, and our fair France:
Not all the dukes of waterish Burgundy
Can buy this unpriz'd precious maid of me.—
Bid them farewell, Cordelia, though unkind:
Thou losest here, a better where to find.

*Lear.* Thou hast her, France: let her be
thine; for we
Have no such daughter, nor shall ever see
That face of hers again.—Therefore be gone
Without our grace, our love, our benison.—
Come, noble Burgundy.

[*Flourish. Exeunt* LEAR, BURGUNDY, CORN-
WALL, ALBANY, GLOSTER, *and* Attendants.

*France.* Bid farewell to your sisters.

*Cor.* Ye jewels of our father, with wash'd
eyes　　　　　　　　　　　[are;
Cordelia leaves you: I know you what you

And, like a sister, am most loth to call
Your faults as they are nam'd. Love well our
father:
To your professed bosoms I commit him:
But yet, alas, stood I within his grace,
I would prefer him to a better place.
So, farewell to you both.

*Reg.* Prescribe not us our duty.

*Gon.*　　　　　　　Let your study
Be to content your lord, who hath receiv'd
you
At fortune's alms. You have obedience
scanted,
And well are worth the want that you have
wanted.　　　　　　　　[ning hides:

*Cor.* Time shall unfold what plighted cun-
Who cover faults, at last shame them de-
rides.
Well may you prosper!

*France.*　　　　Come, my fair Cordelia.
[*Exeunt* FRANCE *and* CORDELIA.

*Gon.* Sister, it is not little I have to say of
what most nearly appertains to us both. I
think our father will hence to-night.

*Reg.* That 's most certain, and with you;
next month with us.

*Gon.* You see how full of changes his age
is; the observation we have made of it hath
not been little: he always loved our sister
most; and with what poor judgment he hath
now cast her off appears too grossly.

*Reg.* 'Tis the infirmity of his age: yet he
hath ever but slenderly known himself.

*Gon.* The best and soundest of his time
hath been but rash; then must we look to receive from his age not alone the imperfections
of long-engraffed condition, but therewithal
the unruly waywardness that infirm and
choleric years bring with them.

*Reg.* Such unconstant starts are we like to
have from him as this of Kent's banishment.

*Gon.* There is further compliment of leave-
taking between France and him. Pray you,
let us hit together: if our father carry authority with such dispositions as he bears, this
last surrender of his will but offend us.

*Reg.* We shall further think of it.

*Gon.* We must do something, and i' the
heat.　　　　　　　　　　　[*Exeunt.*

SCENE II.—*A Hall in the* EARL OF
GLOSTER'S *Castle.*

*Enter* EDMUND *with a letter.*

*Edm.* Thou, nature, art my goddess; to
thy law
My services are bound. Wherefore should I
Stand in the plague of custom, and permit
The curiosity of nations to deprive me,
For that I am some twelve or fourteen moon-
shines　　　　　　　　　　　[base?
Lag of a brother? Why bastard? wherefore
When my dimensions are as well compact,
My mind as generous, and my shape as true
As honest madam's issue? Why brand they us

With base? with baseness? bastardy? base,
base?
Who, in the lusty stealth of nature, take
More composition and fierce quality
Than doth, within a dull, stale, tired bed,
Go to the creating a whole tribe of fops
Got 'tween asleep and wake?—Well, then,
Legitimate Edgar, I must have your land:
Our father's love is to the bastard Edmund.
As to the legitimate: fine word,—legitimate!
Well, my legitimate, if this letter speed,
And my invention thrive, Edmund the base
Shall top the legitimate. I grow; I prosper.—
Now, gods, stand up for bastards!

*Enter* GLOSTER.

*Glo.* Kent banish'd thus! and France in
    choler parted!       [power!
And the king gone to-night! subscrib'd his
Confin'd to exhibition! All this done [news?
Upon the gad!—Edmund, how now! what
    *Edm.* So please your lordship, none.
              *[Putting up the letter.*
  *Glo.* Why so earnestly seek you to put up
that letter?
  *Edm.* I know no news, my lord.
  *Glo.* What paper were you reading?
  *Edm.* Nothing, my lord.
  *Glo.* No? What needed, then, that terrible
despatch of it into your pocket? the quality
of nothing hath not such need to hide itself.
Let's see: come, if it be nothing, I shall not
need spectacles.
  *Edm.* I beseech you, sir, pardon me: it is
a letter from my brother that I have not all
o'er-read; and for so much as I have perused,
I find it not fit for your over-looking.
  *Glo.* Give me the letter, sir.
  *Edm.* I shall offend either to detain or give
it. The contents, as in part I understand
them, are to blame.
  *Glo.* Let's see, let's see.
  *Edm.* I hope, for my brother's justification, he wrote this but as an essay or taste of
my virtue.
  *Glo.* [*Reads.*] *This policy and reverence of*
*age makes the world bitter to the best of our*
*times; keeps our fortunes from us till our*
*oldness cannot relish them. I begin to find an*
*idle and fond bondage in the oppression of*
*aged tyranny, who sways, not as it hath*
*power, but as it is suffered. Come to me, that*
*of this I may speak more. If our father would*
*sleep till I waked him, you should enjoy half*
*his revenue for ever, and live the beloved of*
*your brother,*            EDGAR.
Hum—Conspiracy!—*Sleep till I waked him,*
—*you should enjoy half his revenue,*—My
son Edgar! Had he a hand to write this? a
heart and a brain to breed it in? When came
this to you? who brought it?
  *Edm.* It was not brought me, my lord,
there's the cunning of it; I found it thrown
in at the casement of my closet.

  *Glo.* You know the character to be your
brother's?
  *Edm.* If the matter were good, my lord, I
durst swear it were his; but in respect of
that, I would fain think it were not.
  *Glo.* It is his.
  *Edm.* It is his hand, my lord; but I hope
his heart is not in the contents.
  *Glo.* Hath he never before sounded you in
this business?
  *Edm.* Never, my lord: but I have heard
him oft maintain it to be fit that sons at
perfect age and fathers declined, the father
should be as ward. to the son, and the son
manage his revenue.
  *Glo.* O villain, villain!—His very opinion
in the letter!—Abhorred villain! Unnatural,
detested, brutish villain! worse than brutish!
—Go, sirrah, seek him; I'll apprehend him.—
Abominable villain!—Where is he?
  *Edm.* I do not well know, my lord. If it
shall please you to suspend your indignation
against my brother till you can derive from
him better testimony of his intent, you shall
run a certain course; where, if you violently
proceed against him, mistaking his purpose, it
would make a great gap in your own honour,
and shake in pieces the heart of his obedience.
I dare pawn down my life for him that he
hath writ this to feel my affection to your
honour, and to no other pretence of danger.
  *Glo.* Think you so?
  *Edm.* If your honour judge it meet, I will
place you where you shall hear us confer of
this, and by an auricular assurance have your
satisfaction; and that without any further
delay than this very evening.
  *Glo.* He cannot be such a monster.
  *Edm.* Nor is not, sure.
  *Glo.* To his father, that so tenderly and
entirely loves him.—Heaven and earth!—
Edmund seek him out; wind me into him, I
pray you: frame the business after your own
wisdom. I would unstate myself to be in a
due resolution.
  *Edm.* I will seek him, sir, presently; convey the business as I shall find means, and
acquaint you withal.
  *Glo.* These late eclipses in the sun and
moon portend no good to us: though the
wisdom of nature can reason it thus and
thus, yet nature finds itself scourged by the
sequent effects: love cools, friendship falls
off, brothers divide: in cities, mutinies; in
countries, discord; in palaces, treason; and
the bond cracked 'twixt son and father. This
villain of mine comes under the prediction;
there 's son against father: the king falls from
bias of nature; there 's father against child.
We have seen the best of our time; machinations, hollowness, treachery, and all ruinous
disorders, follow us disquietly to our graves.
—Find out this villain, Edmund; it shall lose
thee nothing; do it carefully.—And the noble

and true-hearted Kent banished! his offence, honesty!—'Tis strange.                    [*Exit*.

*Edm.* This is the excellent foppery of the world, that, when we are sick in fortune,— often the surfeit of our own behaviour,—we make guilty of our disasters the sun, the moon, and the stars: as if we were villains by necessity; fools by heavenly compulsion; knaves, thieves, and treachers by spherical predominance; drunkards, liars, and adulterers by an enforced obedience of planetary influence; and all that we are evil in, by a divine thrusting on: an admirable evasion of whoremaster man, to lay his goatish disposition to the charge of a star! My father compounded with my mother under the dragon's tail, and my nativity was under *ursa major;* so that it follows I am rough and lecherous.—Tut, I should have been that I am, had the maidenliest star in the firmament twinkled on my bastardizing.

*Enter* EDGAR.

Pat!—he comes like the catastrophe of the old comedy: my cue is villanous melancholy, with a sigh like Tom o' Bedlam.—O, these eclipses do portend these divisions! fa, sol, la, mi.

*Edg.* How now, brother Edmund! what serious contemplation are you in?

*Edm.* I am thinking, brother, of a prediction I read this other day, what should follow these eclipses.

*Edg.* Do you busy yourself with that?

*Edm.* I promise you, the effects he writes of succeed unhappily; as of unnaturalness between the child and the parent; death, dearth, dissolutions of ancient amities; divisions in state, menaces and maledictions against king and nobles; needless diffidences, banishment of friends, dissipation of cohorts, nuptial breaches, and I know not what.

*Edg.* How long have you been a sectary astronomical?                    [father last?

*Edm.* Come, come; when saw you my

*Edg.* The night gone by.

*Edm.* Spake you with him?

*Edg.* Ay, two hours together.

*Edm.* Parted you in good terms? Found you no displeasure in him by word nor countenance?

*Edg.* None at all.

*Edm.* Bethink yourself wherein you may have offended him: and at my entreaty forbear his presence till some little time hath qualified the heat of his displeasure; which at this instant so rageth in him that with the mischief of your person it would scarcely allay.

*Edg.* Some villain hath done me wrong.

*Edm.* That's my fear. I pray you, have a continent forbearance till the speed of his rage goes slower; and, as I say, retire with me to my lodging, from whence I will fitly bring

you to hear my lord speak: pray you, go; there 's my key.—If you do stir abroad, go armed.

*Edg.* Armed, brother!

*Edm.* Brother, I advise you to the best; I am no honest man if there be any good meaning toward you: I have told you what I have seen and heard,but faintly; nothing like the image and horror of it: pray you, away.

*Edg.* Shall I hear from you anon?

*Edm.* I do serve you in this business.

                    [*Exit* EDGAR.

A credulous father! and a brother noble, Whose nature is so far from doing harms That he suspects none; on whose foolish honesty My practices ride easy!—I see the business.— Let me, if not by birth, have lands by wit: All with me's meet that I can fashion fit.

                    [*Exit*.

SCENE III.—*A Room in the* DUKE OF ALBANY'S *Palace*.

*Enter* GONERIL *and* OSWALD.

*Gon.* Did my father strike my gentleman for chiding of his fool?

*Osw.* Ay, madam.                    [every hour

*Gon.* By day and night, he wrongs me; He flashes into one gross crime or other, That sets us all at odds: I'll not endure it: His knights grow riotous, and himself upbraids us                    [ing On every trifle.—When he returns from hunt- I will not speak with him; say I am sick.— If you come slack of former services You shall do well; the fault of it I'll answer.

*Osw.* He's coming, madam: I hear him.

                    [*Horns within*.

*Gon.* Put on what weary negligence you please,                    [question: You and your fellows; I'd have it come to If he distaste it, let him to my sister, [one, Whose mind and mine, I know, in that are Not to be overruled. Idle old man, That still would manage those authorities That he hath given away!—Now, by my life, Old fools are babes again; and must be us'd With checks as flatteries,—when they are seen abus'd. Remember what I have said.

*Osw.*                    Well, madam.

*Gon.* And let his knights have colder looks among you;                    [lows so: What grows of it, no matter; advise your fel- I would breed from hence occasions, and I shall,                    [sister That I may speak.—I'll write straight to my To hold my course.—Prepare for dinner.

                    [*Exeunt*.

SCENE IV.—*A Hall in* ALBANY'S *Palace*.

*Enter* KENT, *disguised*.

*Kent.* If but as well I other accents borrow, That can my speech diffuse, my good intent

May carry through itself to that full issue
For which I rais'd my likeness.—Now, ban-
ish'd Kent, [condemn'd,
If thou canst serve where thou dost stand
So may it come, thy master, whom thou
lov'st,
Shall find thee full of labours.

*Horns within. Enter* KING LEAR, Knights,
*and* Attendants.

*Lear.* Let me not stay a jot for dinner; go
get it ready. [*Exit an* Attendant.] How now!
what art thou?

*Kent.* A man, sir.

*Lear.* What dost thou profess? What
wouldst thou with us?

*Kent.* I do profess to be no less than I
seem; to serve him truly that will put me in
trust; to love him that is honest; to converse
with him that is wise and says little; to fear
judgment; to fight when I cannot choose;
and to eat no fish.

*Lear.* What art thou?

*Kent.* A very honest-hearted fellow, and
as poor as the king.

*Lear.* If thou be'st as poor for a subject as
he's for a king, thou art poor enough. What
wouldst thou?

*Kent.* Service.

*Lear.* Who wouldst thou serve?

*Kent.* You.

*Lear.* Dost thou know me, fellow?

*Kent.* No, sir; but you have that in your
countenance which I would fain call master.

*Lear.* What's that?

*Kent.* Authority.

*Lear.* What services canst thou do?

*Kent.* I can keep honest counsel, ride, run,
mar a curious tale in telling it, and deliver a
plain message bluntly: that which ordinary
men are fit for, I am qualified in: and the best
of me is diligence.

*Lear.* How old art thou?

*Kent.* Not so young, sir, to love a woman
for singing; nor so old to dote on her for anything: I have years on my back forty-eight.

*Lear.* Follow me; thou shalt serve me: if I
like thee no worse after dinner, I will not part
from thee yet.—Dinner, ho, dinner!—Where's
my knave? my fool?—Go you and call my
fool hither. [*Exit an* Attend.

*Enter* OSWALD.

You, you, sirrah, where's my daughter?

*Osw.* So please you,— [*Exit.*

*Lear.* What says the fellow there? Call the
clotpoll back. [*Exit a* Knight.]—Where's my
fool, ho?—I think the world's asleep.

*Re-enter* Knight.

How now! where's that mongrel?

*Knight.* He says, my lord, your daughter is
not well.

*Lear.* Why came not the slave back to me
when I called him?

*Knight.* Sir, he answered me in the round-
est manner, he would not.

*Lear.* He would not!

*Knight.* My lord, I know not what the
matter is; but, to my judgment, your highness is not entertained with that ceremonious
affection as you were wont; there's a great
abatement of kindness appears as well in the
general dependants as in the duke himself
also and your daughter.

*Lear.* Ha! sayest thou so?

*Knight.* I beseech you, pardon me, my
lord, if I be mistaken; for my duty cannot be
silent when I think your highness wronged.

*Lear.* Thou but rememberest me of mine
own conception: I have perceived a most faint
neglect of late; which I have rather blamed
as mine own jealous curiosity than as a very
pretence and purpose of unkindness: I will
look further into't.—But where's my fool? I
have not seen him this two days.

*Knight.* Since my young lady's going into
France, sir, the fool hath much pined away.

*Lear.* No more of that; I have noted it
well.—Go you and tell my daughter I would
speak with her. [*Exit an* Attendant.]—Go
you, call hither my fool.
[*Exit another* Attendant.

*Re-enter* OSWALD.

O, you sir, you, come you hither, sir: who am
I, sir?

*Osw.* My lady's father.

*Lear.* My lady's father! my lord's knave:
you whoreson dog! you slave! you cur!

*Osw.* I am none of these, my lord; I beseech your pardon.

*Lear.* Do you bandy looks with me, you
rascal? [*Striking him.*

*Osw.* I'll not be struck, my lord.

*Kent.* Nor tripped neither, you base football player. [*Tripping up his heels.*

*Lear.* I thank thee, fellow; thou servest
me, and I'll love thee.

*Kent.* Come, sir, arise, away! I'll teach
you differences: away, away! If you will
measure your lubber's length again, tarry:
but away! go to; have you wisdom? so.
[*Pushes* OSWALD *out.*

*Lear.* Now, my friendly knave, I thank
thee: there's earnest of thy service.
[*Giving* KENT *money.*

*Enter* FOOL.

*Fool.* Let me hire him too; here's my coxcomb. [*Giving* KENT *his cap.*

*Lear.* How now, my pretty knave! how
dost thou?

*Fool.* Sirrah, you were best take my coxcomb.

*Kent.* Why, fool?

*Fool.* Why, for taking one's part that's out

of favour. Nay, an thou canst not smile as the wind sits, thou'lt catch cold shortly: there, take my coxcomb: why, this fellow has banish'd, two on's daughters, and did the third a blessing against his will; if thou follow him, thou must needs wear my coxcomb.—How now, nuncle! Would I had two coxcombs and two daughters!

*Lear.* Why, my boy?

*Fool.* If I gave them all my living, I'd keep my coxcombs myself. There's mine; beg another of thy daughters.

*Lear.* Take heed, sirrah,—the whip.

*Fool.* Truth's a dog must to kennel; he must be whipped out, when the lady brach may stand by the fire and stink.

*Lear.* A pestilent gall to me!

*Fool.* Sirrah, I'll teach thee a speech.

*Lear.* Do.

*Fool.* Mark it, nuncle:—
Have more than thou showest,
Speak less than thou knowest,
Lend less than thou owest,
Ride more than thou goest,
Learn more than thou trowest,
Set less than thou throwest;
Leave thy drink and thy whore,
And keep in-a-door,
And thou shalt have more
Than two tens to a score.

*Kent.* This is nothing, fool.

*Fool.* Then 'tis like the breath of an unfee'd lawyer,—you gave me nothing for't.—Can you make no use of nothing, nuncle?

*Lear.* Why, no, boy; nothing can be made out of nothing.

*Fool.* Pr'ythee, tell him, so much the rent of his land comes to: he will not believe a fool.    [*To* KENT.

*Lear.* A bitter fool!

*Fool.* Dost thou know the difference, my boy, between a bitter fool and a sweet one?

*Lear.* No, lad; teach me.

*Fool.* That lord that counsell'd thee
To give away thy land,
Come place him here by me,—
Do thou for him stand:
The sweet and bitter fool
Will presently appear;
The one in motley here,
The other found out there.

*Lear.* Dost thou call me fool, boy?

*Fool.* All thy other titles thou hast given away; that thou wast born with.

*Kent.* This is not altogether fool, my lord.

*Fool.* No, faith, lords and great men will not let me; if I had a monopoly out, they would have part on't, and loads too: they will not let me have all fool to myself; they'll be snatching.—Nuncle, give me an egg, and I'll give thee two crowns.

*Lear.* What two crowns shall they be?

*Fool.* Why, after I have cut the egg i' the middle, and eat up the meat, the two crowns of the egg. When thou clovest thy crown i' the middle, and gavest away both parts, thou borest thine ass on thy back o'er the dirt: thou hadst little wit in thy bald crown when thou gavest thy golden one away. If I speak like myself in this, let him be whipped that first finds it so.

Fools had ne'er less grace in a year;    [*Singing.*
For wise men are grown foppish,
And know not how their wits to wear,
Their manners are so apish.

*Lear.* When were you wont to be so full of songs, sirrah?

*Fool.* I have used it, nuncle, e'er since thou madest thy daughters thy mothers: for when thou gavest them the rod, and puttest down thine own breeches,

Then they for sudden joy did weep,    [*Singing.*
And I for sorrow sung,
That such a king should play bo-peep,
And go the fools among.

Pr'ythee, nuncle, keep a schoolmaster that can teach thy fool to lie: I would fain learn to lie.    [whipped.

*Lear.* An you lie, sirrah, we'll have you

*Fool.* I marvel what kin thou and thy daughters are: they'll have me whipped for speaking true, thou'lt have me whipped for lying; and sometimes I am whipped for holding my peace. I had rather be any kind o' thing than a fool: and yet I would not be thee, nuncle; thou hast pared thy wit o' both sides, and left nothing i' the middle:—here comes one o' the parings.

*Enter* GONERIL.

*Lear.* How now, daughter! what makes that frontlet on? Methinks you are too much of late i' the frown.

*Fool.* Thou wast a pretty fellow when thou hadst no need to care for her frowning; now thou art an O without a figure: I am better than thou art; I am a fool, thou art nothing. —Yes, forsooth, I will hold my tongue; so your face [*to* GON.] bids me, though you say nothing. Mum, mum,
He that keeps nor crust nor crumb,
Weary of all, shall want some.—
That's a shealed peascod. [*Pointing to* LEAR.

*Gon.* Not only, sir, this your all-licens'd fool,
But other of your insolent retinue
Do hourly carp and quarrel; breaking forth
In rank and not-to-be-endured riots. Sir,
I had thought, by making this well known
    unto you,    [fearful,
To have found a safe redress; but now grow
By what yourself too late have spoke and done,
That you protect this course, and put it on
By your allowance; which if you should, the fault

Would not scape censure, nor the redresses
    sleep,
Which, in the tender of a wholesome weal,
Might in their working do you that offence,
Which else were shame, that then necessity
Will call discreet proceeding.
    *Fool.* For, you know, nuncle,
      The hedge-sparrow fed the cuckoo so long
      That it had its head bit off by its young.
So, out went the candle, and we were left
    darkling.
    *Lear.* Are you our daughter?
    *Gon.* I would you would make use of your
    good wisdom,
Whereof I know you are fraught; and put
    away     [you
These dispositions, which of late transport
From what you rightly are.
    *Fool.* May not an ass know when the cart
draws the horse?—Whoop, Jug! I love thee.
    *Lear.* Does any here know me?—This is
    not Lear:     [his eyes?
Does Lear walk thus? speak thus? Where are
Either his notion weakens, his discernings
Are lethargied.—Ha! waking? 'tis not so.—
Who is it that can tell me who I am?
    *Fool.* Lear's shadow.     [of sovereignty,
    *Lear.* I would learn that; for, by the marks
Knowledge, and reason,
I should be false persuaded I had daughters.
    *Fool.* Which they will make an obedient
    father.
    *Lear.* Your name, fair gentlewoman?
    *Gon.* This admiration, sir, is much o' the
    favour
Of other your new pranks. I do beseech you
To understand my purposes aright:
As you are old and reverend, should be wise.
Here do you keep a hundred knights and
    squires;
Men so disorder'd, so debosh'd and bold,
That this our court, infected with their man-
    ners,
Shows like a riotous inn: epicurism and lust
Make it more like a tavern or a brothel
Than a grac'd palace. The shame itself doth
    speak
For instant remedy: be, then, desir'd
By her that else will take the thing she begs,
A little to disquantity your train;
And the remainder, that shall still depend,
To be such men as may besort your age,
Which know themselves and you.
    *Lear.*     Darkness and devils!—
Saddle my horses; call my train together.—
Degenerate bastard! I'll not trouble thee:
Yet have I left a daughter.
    *Gon.* You strike my people; and your dis-
    order'd rabble
Make servants of their betters.

*Enter* ALBANY.

    *Lear.* Woe, that too late repents,—[*to*
    ALB.] O, sir, are you come?

Is it your will? Speak, sir.—Prepare my
    horses.—
Ingratitude, thou marble-hearted fiend,
More hideous when thou show'st thee in a
    child
Than the sea-monster!
    *Alb.*     Pray, sir, be patient.
    *Lear.* Detested kite! thou liest:
                 [*To* GONERIL.
My train are men of choice and rarest parts,
That all particulars of duty know;
And in the most exact regard support   [fault,
The worships of their name.—O most small
How ugly did'st thou in Cordelia show!
Which, like an engine, wrench'd my frame of
    nature     [love,
From the fix'd place; drew from my heart all
And added to the gall. O Lear, Lear, Lear!
Beat at this gate, that let thy folly in
                 [*Striking his head.*
And thy dear judgment out!—Go, go, my
    people.     [ignorant
    *Alb.* My lord, I am guiltless, as I am
Of what hath mov'd you
    *Lear.* It may be so, my lord.
Hear, nature, hear; dear goddess, hear!
Suspend thy purpose if thou didst intend
To make this creature fruitful!
Into her womb convey sterility!
Dry up in her the organs of increase;
And from her derogate body never spring
A babe to honour her! If she must teem,
Create her child of spleen, that it may live
And be athwart disnatur'd torment to her!
Let it stamp wrinkles in her brow of youth;
With cadent tears fret channels in her cheeks;
Turn all her mother's pains and benefits
To laughter and contempt; that she may feel
How sharper than a serpent's tooth it is
To have a thankless child!—Away, away!
                    [*Exit.*
    *Alb.* Now, gods that we adore, whereof
    comes this?     [it;
    *Gon.* Never afflict yourself to know more of
But let his disposition have that scope
That dotage gives it.

*Re-enter* LEAR.

    *Lear.* What, fifty of my followers at a clap!
Within a fortnight!
    *Alb.*     What's the matter, sir?
    *Lear.* I'll tell thee,—Life and death!—I am
    asham'd     [*To* GONERIL.
That thou hast power to shake my manhood
    thus;     [perforce,
That these hot tears, which break from me
Should make thee worth them.—Blasts and
    fogs upon thee!
The untented woundings of a father's curse,
Pierce every sense about thee!—Old fond
    eyes,
Beweep this cause again, I'll pluck you out,
And cast you, with the waters that you lose,
To temper clay.—Ha!

Let it be so: I have another daughter,
Who, I am sure, is kind and comfortable:
When she shall hear this of thee, with her nails
She'll flay thy wolfish visage. Thou shalt find
That I'll resume the shape which thou dost
　　think
I have cast off for ever.

　　　[*Exeunt* LEAR, KENT, *and* Attendants.

*Gon.* Do you mark that?
*Alb.* I cannot be so partial, Goneril,
To the great love I bear you,—　　　　[ho!
*Gon.* Pray you, content.—What, Oswald,
You, sir, more knave than fool, after your
　　master.　　　　　　　　　　[*To the* Fool.
*Fool.* Nuncle Lear nuncle Lear, tarry,—
take the fool with thee.—

　　A fox, when one has caught her,
　　And such a daughter,
　　Should sure to the slaughter,
　　If my cap would buy a halter:
　　So the fool follows after.　　　[*Exit.*

*Gon.* This man hath had good counsel.—A
　　hundred knights!
'Tis politic and safe to let him keep　[dream,
At point a hundred knights: yes, that on every
Each buzz, each fancy, each complaint, dis-
　　like,
He may enguard his dotage with their powers,
And hold our lives in mercy.—Oswald, I
　　say!—
*Alb.* Well, you may fear too far.
*Gon.*　　　　Safer than trust too far:
Let me still take away the harms I fear,
Not fear still to be taken: I know his heart.
What he hath utter'd I have writ my sister:
If she sustain him and his hundred knights,
When I have show'd the unfitness,—

### Re-enter OSWALD.

How now, Oswald!
What, have you writ that letter to my sister?
*Osw.* Ay, madam.　　　　　　[to horse:
*Gon.* Take you some company, and away
Inform her full of my particular fear;
And thereto add such reasons of your own
As may compact it more. Get you gone;
And hasten your return.　　[*Exit* OSWALD.
No, no, my lord,
This milk gentleness and course of yours,
Though I condemned it not, yet, under par-
　　don,　　　　　　　　　　　　[wisdom
You are much more attask'd for want of
Than prais'd for harmful mildness.
*Alb.* How far your eyes may pierce I can-
　　not tell:
Striving to better, oft we mar what's well.
*Gon.* Nay, then,—
*Alb.* Well, well; the event.　　[*Exeunt.*

SCENE V.—*Court before the* DUKE OF
ALBANY'S *Palace.*

*Enter* LEAR, KENT, *and* Fool.

*Lear.* Go you before to Gloster with these
letters: acquaint my daughter no further with

anything you know than comes from her demand out of the letter. If your diligence be
not speedy, I shall be there afore you.
*Kent.* I will not sleep, my lord, till I have
delivered your letter.　　　　　　　[*Exit.*
*Fool.* If a man's brains were in's heels,
were't not in danger of kibes?
*Lear.* Ay, boy.
*Fool.* Then, I pr'ythee, be merry; thy wit
shall not go slipshod.
*Lear.* Ha, ha, ha!
*Fool.* Shalt see thy other daughter will use
thee kindly; for though she's as like this as a
crab's like an apple, yet I can tell what I can
tell.
*Lear.* What canst tell, boy?
*Fool.* She will taste as like this as a crab
does to a crab. Thou canst tell why one's nose
stands i' the middle on's face?
*Lear.* No.
*Fool.* Why to keep one's eyes of either
side's nose, that what a man cannot smell
out, he may spy into.
*Lear.* I did her wrong,—　　　　[shell?
*Fool.* Canst tell how an oyster makes his
*Lear.* No.
*Fool.* Nor I neither; but I can tell why a
snail has a house.
*Lear.* Why?
*Fool.* Why, to put his head in; not to give
it away to his daughters, and leave his horns
without a case.
*Lear.* I will forget my nature. So kind a
father!—Be my horses ready?
*Fool.* Thy asses are gone about 'em. The
reason why the seven stars are no more than
seven is a pretty reason.
*Lear.* Because they are not eight?
*Fool.* Yes, indeed: thou wouldst make a
good fool.　　　　　　　　　　[ingratitude.
*Lear.* To take't again perforce!—Monster
*Fool.* If thou wert my fool, nuncle, I'd
have thee beaten for being old before thy
time.
*Lear.* How's that?
*Fool.* Thou shouldst not have been old till
thou hadst been wise.　　　　[sweet heaven!
*Lear.* O, let me not be mad, not mad,
Keep me in temper: I would not be mad!—

### Enter Gentleman.

How now! are the horses ready?
*Gent.* Ready, my lord.
*Lear.* Come, boy.　　　　　　[my departure,
*Fool.* She that's a maid now, and laughs at
Shall not be a maid long, unless things be cut
　　shorter.　　　　　　　　　　　[*Exeunt.*

## ACT II.

SCENE I.—*A Court within the Castle of the*
EARL OF GLOSTER.

*Enter* EDMUND *and* CURAN, *meeting.*

*Edm.* Save thee, Curan.
*Cur.* And you, sir. I have been with your

father, and given him notice that the Duke
of Cornwall and Regan his duchess will be
here with him this night.

*Edm.* How comes that?

*Cur.* Nay, I know not.—You have heard
of the news abroad; I mean, the whispered
ones, for they are yet but ear-kissing arguments?

*Edm.* Not I: pray you, what are they?

*Cur.* Have you heard of no likely wars
toward, 'twixt the Dukes of Cornwall and
Albany?

*Edm.* Not a word.

*Cur.* You may, then, in time. Fare you
well, sir.                                   [*Exit.*

*Edm.* The duke be here to-night? The
better! best!
This weaves itself perforce into my business.
My father hath set guard to take my brother;
And I have one thing, of a queasy question,
Which I must act:—briefness and fortune
work!—
Brother, a word;—descend:—brother, I say!

*Enter* EDGAR.

My father watches:—O sir, fly this place;
Intelligence is given where you are hid;
You have now the good advantage of the
night.—                                [Cornwall?
Have you not spoken 'gainst the Duke of
He's coming hither; now, i' the night, i' the
haste,
And Regan with him: have you nothing said
Upon his party 'gainst the Duke of Albany?
Advise yourself.

*Edg.*        I am sure on't, not a word.

*Edm.* I hear my father coming:—pardon
me;                                       [you:—
In cunning I must draw my sword upon
Draw: seem to defend yourself: now quit you
well.—                                     [here!
Yield:—come before my father.—Light, ho,
Fly, brother.—Torches, torches!—So, fare-
well.                              [*Exit* EDGAR.
Some blood drawn on me would beget opin-
ion                            [*Wounds his arm.*
Of my more fierce endeavour: I have seen
drunkards
Do more than this in sport.—Father, father!
Stop, stop! No help?

*Enter* GLOSTER, *and* Servants *with torches.*

*Glo.* Now, Edmund, where's the villain?

*Edm.* Here stood he in the dark, his sharp
sword out,                                  [moon
Mumbling of wicked charms, conjuring the
To stand auspicious mistress,—

*Glo.*                    But where is he?

*Edm.* Look, sir, I bleed.

*Glo.*       Where is the villain, Edmund?

*Edm.* Fled this way, sir. When by no means
he could,—

*Glo.* Pursue him, ho!—Go after.  [*Exeunt*
Servants.]—By no means what?

*Edm.* Persuade me to the murder of your
lordship;
But that I told him the revenging gods
'Gainst parricides did all their thunders bend;
Spoke with how manifold and strong a bond
The child was bound to the father;—sir, in
fine,
Seeing how loathly opposite I stood
To his unnatural purpose, in fell motion,
With his prepared sword, he charges home
My unprovided body, lanc'd mine arm:
But when he saw my best alarum'd spirits,
Bold in the quarrel's right, rous'd to the en-
counter,
Or whether gasted by the noise I made,
Full suddenly he fled.

*Glo.*             Let him fly far:
Not in this land shall he remain uncaught;
And found, despatch'd.—The noble duke my
master,
My worthy arch and patron, comes to-night:
By his authority I will proclaim it,  [thanks,
That he which finds him shall deserve our
Bringing the murderous coward to the stake;
He that conceals him, death.

*Edm.* When I dissuaded him from his
intent,
And found him pight to do it, with curst
speech
I threaten'd to discover him: he replied,
*Thou unpossessing bastard! dost thou think,*
*If I would stand against thee, would the
reposal*
*Of any trust, virtue or worth, in thee*
*Make thy words faith'd? No: what I should
deny,—*
*As this I would; ay, though thou didst pro-
duce*
*My very character,—I'd turn it all*
*To thy suggestion, plot, and damned practice:*
*And thou must make a dullard of the world,*
*If they not thought the profits of my death*
*Were very pregnant and potential spurs*
*To make thee seek it.*

*Glo.*           O strong and fasten'd villain!
Would he deny his letter?—I never got him.
                              [*Trumpets within.*
Hark, the duke's trumpets! I know not why
he comes.—
All ports I'll bar; the villain shall not scape;
The duke must grant me that: besides, his
picture
I will send far and near, that all the kingdom
May have due note of him; and of my land,
Loyal and natural boy, I'll work the means
To make thee capable.

*Enter* CORNWALL, REGAN, *and* Attendants.

*Corn.* How now, my noble friend! since I
came hither,—
Which I can call but now,—I have heard
strange news.                            [short

*Reg.* If it be true, all vengeance comes too

Which can pursue the offender. How dost,
my lord?

*Glo.* O, madam, my old heart is crack'd,—
it's crack'd!

*Reg.* What, did my father's godson seek
your life?

He whom my father nam'd? your Edgar?

*Glo.* O lady, lady, shame would have it
hid!

*Reg.* Was he not companion with the riotous knights

That tend upon my father?

*Glo.*            I know not, madam:—

It is too bad, too bad.

*Edm.* Yes, madam, he was of that consort.

*Reg.* No marvel, then, though he were ill
affected:

'Tis they have put him on the old man's
death,

To have the expense and waste of his revenues.

I have this present evening from my sister

Been well inform'd of them; and with such
cautions,

That if they come to sojourn at my house,

I'll not be there.

*Corn.*          Nor I, assure thee, Regan.—

Edmund, I hear that you have shown your
father

A child-like office.

*Edm.*          'Twas my duty, sir.

*Glo.* He did bewray his practice; and receiv'd

This hurt you see, striving to apprehend him.

*Corn.* Is he pursu'd?

*Glo.*               Ay, my good lord.

*Corn.* If he be taken he shall never more

Be fear'd of doing harm: make your own
purpose,

How in my strength you please.—For you,
Edmund,

Whose virtue and obedience doth this instant

So much commend itself, you shall be ours:

Natures of such deep trust we shall much
need;

You we first seize on.

*Edm.*        I shall serve you, sir,

Truly, however else.

*Glo.*          For him I thank your grace.

*Corn.* You know not why we came to visit
you,—                      [ey'd night:

*Reg.* Thus out of season, threading dark-

Occasions, noble Gloster, of some poise, .

Wherein we must have use of your advice:—

Our father he hath writ, so hath our sister,

Of differences, which I best thought it fit

To answer from our home; the several messengers                          [friend,

From hence attend despatch. Our good old

Lay comforts to your bosom; and bestow

Your needful counsel to our businesses,

Which crave the instant use.

*Glo.*              I serve you, madam:

Your graces are right welcome.    [*Exeunt.*

SCENE II.—*Before* GLOSTER'S *Castle.*

*Enter* KENT *and* OSWALD *severally.*

*Osw.* Good dawning to thee, friend: art of
this house?

*Kent.* Ay.

*Osw.* Where may we set our horses?

*Kent.* I' the mire.

*Osw.* Pr'ythee, if thou lovest me, tell me.

*Kent.* I love thee not.

*Osw.* Why, then, I care not for thee.

*Kent.* If I had thee in Lipsbury pinfold I
would make thee care for me.       [thee not.

*Osw.* Why dost thou use me thus? I know

*Kent.* Fellow, I know thee.

*Osw.* What dost thou know me for?

*Kent.* A knave, a rascal, an eater of broken
meats; a base, proud, shallow, beggarly, three-
suited, hundred-pound, filthy, worsted-stock-
ing knave; a lily-livered, action-taking whoreson, glass-gazing, superserviceable, finical
rogue; one-trunk-inheriting slave; one that
wouldst be a bawd, in way of good service,
and art nothing but the composition of a
knave, beggar, coward, pander, and the son
and heir of a mongrel bitch: one whom I
will beat into clamorous whining, if thou
denyest the least syllable of thy addition.

*Osw.* Why, what a monstrous fellow art
thou, thus to rail on one that is neither known
of thee nor knows thee!

*Kent.* What a brazen-faced varlet art thou,
to deny thou knowest me! Is it two days since
I tripped up thy heels and beat thee before
the king? Draw, you rogue: for, though it
be night, yet the moon shines; I'll make a
sop o' the moonshine of you: draw, you
whoreson cullionly barber-monger, draw.

[*Drawing his sword.*

*Osw.* Away! I have nothing to do with
thee.

*Kent.* Draw, you rascal: you come with
letters against the king; and take vanity the
puppet's part against the royalty of her father: draw, you rogue, or I'll so carbonado
your shanks:—draw, you rascal; come your
ways.

*Osw.* Help, ho! murder! help!

*Kent.* Strike, you slave; stand, rogue,
stand; you neat slave, strike. [*Beating him.*

*Osw.* Help, ho! murder! murder!

*Enter* EDMUND, CORNWALL, REGAN,
GLOSTER, *and* Servants.

*Edm.* How now! What's the matter?

*Kent.* With you, goodman boy, if you
please: come, I'll flesh you; come on, young.
master.

*Glo.* Weapons! arms! What's the matter
here?

*Corn.* Keep peace, upon your lives;

He dies that strikes again. What is the matter?                            [the king.

*Reg.* The messengers from our sister and

*Corn.* What is your difference? speak.

*Osw.* I am scarce in breath, my lord.

*Kent.* No marvel, you have so bestirr'd your valour. You cowardly rascal, nature disclaims in thee: a tailor made thee.

*Corn.* Thou art a strange fellow: a tailor make a man?

*Kent.* Ay, a tailor, sir: a stone-cutter or a painter could not have made him so ill, though they had been but two hours at the trade.

*Corn.* Speak yet, how grew your quarrel?

*Osw.* This ancient ruffian, sir, whose life I have spared at suit of his gray beard,—

*Kent.* Thou whoreson zed! thou unnecessary letter!—My lord, if you will give me leave, I will tread this unbolted villain into mortar, and daub the wall of a jakes with him.—Spare my gray beard, you wagtail?

*Corn.* Peace, sirrah!
You beastly knave, know you no reverence?

*Kent.* Yes, sir; but anger hath a privilege.

*Corn.* Why art thou angry?

*Kent.* That such a slave as this should wear a sword, [as these,
Who wears no honesty. Such smiling rogues
Like rats, oft bite the holy cords a-twain
Which are too intrinse t' unloose; smooth every passion
That in the natures of their lords rebel;
Bring oil to fire, snow to their colder moods;
Renege, affirm, and turn their halcyon beaks
With every gale and vary of their masters,
Knowing naught, like dogs, but following.—
A plague upon your epileptic visage!
Smile you my speeches, as I were a fool?
Goose, if I had you upon Sarum plain
I'd drive ye cackling home to Camelot.

*Corn.* What, art thou mad, old fellow?

*Glo.* How fell you out? Say that.

*Kent.* No contraries hold more antipathy
Than I and such a knave.

*Corn.* Why dost thou call him knave? What is his fault?

*Kent.* His countenance likes me not.

*Corn.* No more, perchance, does mine, nor his, nor hers.

*Kent.* Sir, 'tis my occupation to be plain:
I have seen better faces in my time
Than stands on any shoulder that I see
Before me at this instant.

*Corn.* This is some fellow
Who, having been prais'd for bluntness, doth affect
A saucy roughness, and constrains the garb
Quite from his nature: he cannot flatter, he,—
An honest mind and plain,—he must speak truth!
An they will take it, so; if not, he's plain.
These kind of knaves I know, which in this plainness
Harbour more craft and more corrupter ends
Than twenty silly ducking óbservants
That stretch their duties nicely.

*Kent.* Sir, in good faith, in sincere verity,
Under the allowance of your aspéct,
Whose influence, like the wreath of radiant fire
On flickering Phœbus' front,—

*Corn.* What mean'st by this?

*Kent.* To go out of my dialect, which you discommend so much. I know, sir, I am no flatterer: he that beguiled you in a plain accent was a plain knave; which, for my part, I will not be, though I should win your displeasure to entreat me to't.

*Corn.* What was the offence you gave him?

*Osw.* I never gave him any:
It pleas'd the king his master very late
To strike at me, upon his misconstruction;
When he, compact, and flattering his displeasure,
Tripp'd me behind; being down, insulted, rail'd,
And put upon him such a deal of man,
That worthied him, got praises of the king
For him attemping who was self-subdu'd;
And, in the fleshment of this dread exploit,
Drew on me here again.

*Kent.* None of these rogues and cowards
But Ajax is their fool.

*Corn.* Fetch forth the stocks!—
You stubborn ancient knave, you reverend braggart,
We'll teach you,—

*Kent.* Sir, I am too old to learn:
Call not your stocks for me: I serve the king;
On whose employment I was sent to you:
You shall do small respect, show too bold malice
Against the grace and person of my master,
Stocking his messenger.

*Corn.* Fetch forth the stocks!—
As I have life and honour, there shall he sit till noon.

*Reg.* Till noon! till night, my lord; and all night too.

*Kent.* Why, madam, if I were your father's dog
You should not use me so.

*Reg.* Sir, being his knave, I will.

*Corn.* This is a fellow of the self-same colour
Our sister speaks of.—Come, bring away the stocks!  [*Stocks brought out.*

*Glo.* Let me beseech your grace not to do so:
His fault is much, and the good king his master  [rection
Will check him for't: your purpos'd low correction
Is such as basest and contemned'st wretches,
For pilferings and most common trespasses,
Are punish'd with: the king must take it ill
That he, so slightly valu'd in his messenger,
Should have him thus restrain'd.

*Corn.* I'll answer that.

*Reg.* My sister may receive it much more worse

To have her gentleman abus'd, assaulted,
For following her affairs.—Put in his legs.—
　　　　　　　　　[KENT *is put in the stocks*.
Come, my lord, away.
　　　　　　[*Exeunt all but* GLOSTER *and* KENT.
　*Glo.* I am sorry for thee, friend; 'tis the
　　　duke's pleasure,
Whose disposition, all the world well knows,
Will not be rubb'd nor stopp'd: I'll entreat
　　　for thee.
　*Kent.* Pray, do not, sir: I have watch'd,
　　　and travell'd hard;
Some time I shall sleep out, the rest I'll
　　　whistle.
A good man's fortune may grow out at heels:
Give you good-morrow!
　*Glo.* The duke's to blame in this; 'twill be
　　　ill taken.　　　　　　　　　　[*Exit*.
　*Kent.* Good king, that must approve the
　　　common saw,—
Thou out of heaven's benediction com'st
To the warm sun!
Approach, thou beacon to this under globe,
That by thy comfortable beams I may
Peruse this letter!—Nothing almost sees
　　　miracles
But misery:—I know 'tis from Cordelia,
Who hath most fortunately been inform'd
Of my obscured course; and shall find time
From this enormous state,—seeking to give
Losses their remedies,—All weary and o'er-
　　　watch'd,
Take vantage, heavy eyes, not to behold
This shameful lodging.
Fortune, good-night: smile once more; turn
　　　thy wheel!　　　　　　　　[*He sleeps*.

SCENE III.—*The open Country*.

*Enter* EDGAR.

　*Edg.* I heard myself proclaim'd;
And by the happy hollow of a tree
Escap'd the hunt. No port is free; no place,
That guard and most unusual vigilance
Does not attend my taking. While I may
　　　scape
I will preserve myself: and am bethought
To take the basest and most poorest shape
That ever penury, in contempt of man,
Brought near to beast: my face I'll grime
　　　with filth;
Blanket my loins; elf all my hair in knots;
And with presented nakedness outface
The winds and persecutions of the sky.
The country gives me proof and precedent
Of Bedlam beggars, who, with roaring voices,
Strike in their numb'd and mortified bare
　　　arms
Pins, wooden pricks, nails, sprigs of rose-
　　　mary;
And with this horrible object, from low farms,
Poor pelting villages, sheep-cotes, and mills,
Sometime with lunatic bans, sometime with
　　　prayers,　　　　　　　　　　[Tom!
Enforce their charity.—Poor Turlygod! poor

That's something yet:—Edgar I nothing am.
　　　　　　　　　　　　　　　　[*Exit*.

SCENE IV.—*Before* GLOSTER'S *Castle*. KENT
　　　*in the Stocks*.

*Enter* LEAR, Fool, *and* Gentleman.

　*Lear.* 'Tis strange that they should so de-
　　　part from home,
And not send back my messenger.
　*Gent.*　　　　　　　　　　As I learn'd,
The night before there was no purpose in them
Of this remove.
　*Kent.*　　　Hail to thee, noble master!
　*Lear.* Ha!
Mak'st thou this shame thy pastime?
　*Kent.*　　　　　　　　　　No, my lord.
　*Fool.* Ha, ha! he wears cruel garters. Horses
are tied by the head; dogs and bears by the
neck, monkeys by the loins, and men by the
legs: when a man is over-lusty at legs, then
he wears wooden nether-stocks.
　*Lear.* What's he that hath so much thy
　　　place mistook
To set thee here?
　*Kent.*　　　It is both he and she,
Your son and daughter.
　*Lear.* No.
　*Kent.* Yes.
　*Lear.* No, I say.
　*Kent.* I say, yea.
　*Lear.* No, no; they would not.
　*Kent.* Yes, they have.
　*Lear.* By Jupiter, I swear, no.
　*Kent.* By Juno, I swear, ay.
　*Lear.*　　　　　　　They durst not do't.
They could not, would not do't; 'tis worse
　　　than murder,
To do upon respect such violent outrage:
Resolve me, with all modest haste, which way
Thou might'st deserve or they impose this
　　　usage,
Coming from us.
　*Kent.*　　　My lord, when at their home
I did commend your highness' letters to them,
Ere I was risen from the place that show'd
My duty kneeling, came there a reeking post,
Stew'd in his haste, half breathless, panting
　　　forth
From Goneril his mistress salutations;
Deliver'd letters, spite of intermission,
Which presently they read: on whose con-
　　　tents　　　　　　　　　　　　[horse;
They summon'd up their meiny, straight took
Commanded me to follow, and attend
The leisure of their answer; gave me cold
　　　looks:
And meeting here the other messenger,
Whose welcome I perceiv'd had poison'd
　　　mine,—
Being the very fellow which of late
Display'd so saucily against your highness,—
Having more man than wit about me, drew:
He rais'd the house with loud and coward
　　　cries.

Your son and daughter found this trespass
　　worth
The shame which here it suffers.
　　*Fool.* Winter's not gone yet, if the wild-
　　　geese fly that way.
　　Fathers that wear rags
　　　Do make their children blind;
　　But fathers that bear bags
　　　Shall see their children kind.
　　Fortune, that arrant whore,
　　Ne'er turns the key to the poor.—
But, for all this, thou shalt have as many
dolours for thy daughters as thou canst tell
in a year.
　　*Lear.* O, how this mother swells up toward
　　　my heart!
*Hysterica passio,*—down, thou climbing sor-
　　row,　　　　　　　　　　　　　　[ter?
Thy element's below!—Where is this daugh-
　　*Kent.* With the earl, sir, here within.
　　*Lear.*　　　　　　　　Follow me not;
Stay here.　　　　　　　　　　　　[*Exit.*
　　*Gent.* Made you no more offence but what
　　　you speak of?
　　*Kent.* None.　　　　　　　　[number?
How chance the king comes with so small a
　　*Fool.* An thou hadst been set i' the stocks
for that question, thou hadst well deserved it.
　　*Kent.* Why, fool?
　　*Fool.* We'll set thee to school to an ant, to
teach thee there's no labouring in the winter.
All that follow their noses are led by their
eyes but blind men; and there's not a nose
among twenty but can smell him that's stink-
ing. Let go thy hold when a great wheel runs
down a hill, lest it break thy neck with fol-
lowing it; but the great one that goes up the
hill, let him draw thee after. When a wise man
gives thee better counsel, give me mine again.
I would have none but knaves follow it, since
a fool gives it.
　　That sir which serves and seeks for gain,
　　　And follows but for form,
　　Will pack when it begins to rain,
　　　And leave thee in the storm.
　　But I will tarry; the fool will stay,
　　　And let the wise man fly:
　　The knave turns fool that runs away;
　　　The fool no knave, perdy.
　　*Kent.* Where learn'd you this, fool?
　　*Fool.* Not i' the stocks, fool.

　　　*Re-enter* LEAR, *with* GLOSTER.

　　*Lear.* Deny to speak with me? They are
　　　sick? they are weary?
They have travell'd all the night? Mere
　　fetches;
The images of revolt and flying off.
Fetch me a better answer.
　　*Glo.*　　　　　　　My dear lord,
You know the fiery quality of the duke;
How unremovable and fix'd he is
In his own course.　　　　　　　[fusion!—
　　*Lear.* Vengeance! plague! death! con-

Fiery? what quality? why, Gloster, Gloster.
I'd speak with the Duke of Cornwall and his
　　wife.
　　*Glo.* Well, my good lord, I have inform'd
　　　them so.
　　*Lear.* Inform'd them! Dost thou under-
　　　stand me, man?
　　*Glo.* Ay, my good lord.
　　*Lear.* The king would speak with Corn-
　　　wall; the dear father
Would with his daughter speak, commands
　　her service:
Are they inform'd of this?—My breath and
　　blood!—　　　　　　　　　　[that—
Fiery? the fiery duke?—Tell the hot duke
No, but not yet:—may be he is not well:
Infirmity doth still neglect all office
Whereto our health is bound; we are not our-
　　selves　　　　　　　　　　　　[mind
When nature, being oppress'd, commands the
To suffer with the body: I'll forbear;
And am fall'n out with my more headier will
To take the indispos'd and sickly fit
For the sound man.—Death on my state!
　　wherefore　　　　　[*Looking on* KENT.
Should he sit here? This act persuades me
That this remotion of the duke and her
Is practice only. Give me my servant forth.
Go tell the duke and's wife I'd speak with
　　them,
Now, presently: bid them come forth and
　　hear me,
Or at their chamber door I'll beat the drum
Till it cry *Sleep to death.*
　　*Glo.* I would have all well betwixt you.
　　　　　　　　　　　　　　　[*Exit.*
　　*Lear.* O me, my heart, my rising heart!—
　　　but, down!
　　*Fool.* Cry to it, nuncle, as the cockney did
to the eels when she put them i' the paste
alive; she knapped 'em o' the coxcombs with
a stick, and cried, *Down, wantons, down!*
'Twas her brother that, in pure kindness to
his horse, buttered his hay.

　　*Enter* CORNWALL, REGAN, GLOSTER, *and*
　　　　　　　　Servants.

　　*Lear.* Good-morrow to you both.
　　*Corn.*　　　　　Hail to your grace!
　　　　　　　[KENT *is set at liberty.*
　　*Reg.* I am glad to see your highness.
　　*Lear.* Regan, I think you are; I know what
　　　reason
I have to think so: if thou shouldst not be
　　glad,
I would divorce me from thy mother's tomb,
Sepúlchring an adultress.—O, are you free?
　　　　　　　　　　　　　　[*To* KENT.
Some other time for that.—Beloved Regan,
Thy sister's naught: O Regan, she hath tied
Sharp-tooth'd unkindness, like a vulture,
　　here,—　　　　　[*Points to his heart.*
I can scarce speak to thee; thou'lt not believe
With how deprav'd a quality—O Regan!

*Reg.* I pray you sir, take patience: I have hope
You less know how to value her desert
Than she to scant her duty.
*Lear.*      Say, how is that?
*Reg.* I cannot think my sister in the least
Would fail her obligation: if, sir, perchance
She have restrain'd the riots of your followers,
'Tis on such ground, and to such wholesome end,
As clears her from all blame.
*Lear.* My curses on her!
*Reg.*      O, sir, you are old;
Nature in you stands on the very verge
Of her confine: you should be rul'd and led
By some discretion, that discerns your state
Better than you yourself. Therefore, I pray you,
That to our sister you do make return;
Say you have wrong'd her, sir.
*Lear.*      Ask her forgiveness?
Do you but mark how this becomes the house:
*Dear daughter, I confess that I am old;*
                              [*Kneeling.*
*Age is unnecessary: on my knees I beg*
*That you'll vouchsafe me raiment, bed, and food.*
*Reg.* Good sir, no more; these are unsightly tricks:
Return you to my sister.
*Lear.* [*Rising.*]      Never, Regan:
She hath abated me of half my train;
Look'd black upon me; struck me with her tongue,
Most serpent-like, upon the very heart:—
All the stor'd vengeances of heaven fall
On her ingrateful top! Strike her young bones,
You taking airs, with lameness!
*Corn.*      Fie, sir, fie!
*Lear.* You nimble lightnings, dart your blinding flames
Into her scornful eyes! Infect her beauty,
You fen-suck'd fogs, drawn by the powerful sun,
To fall and blast her pride!
*Reg.*      O the blest gods!
So will you wish on me when the rash mood is on.      [*my curse:*
*Lear.* No, Regan, thou shalt never have
Thy tender-hefted nature shall not give
Thee o'er to harshness: her eyes are fierce; but thine
Do comfort, and not burn. 'Tis not in thee
To grudge my pleasures, to cut off my train,
To bandy hasty words, to scant my sizes,
And, in conclusion, to oppose the bolt
Against my coming in: thou better know'st
The offices of nature, bond of childhood,
Effects of courtesy, dues of gratitude;
Thy half o' the kingdom hast thou not forgot,
Wherein I thee endow'd.
*Reg.*      Good sir, to the purpose.
*Lear.* Who put my man i' the stocks?
                              [*Tucket within.*

*Corn.*      What trumpet's that?
*Reg.* I know't,—my sister's: this approves her letter,
That she would soon be here.

*Enter* OSWALD.
                              Is your lady come?
*Lear.* This is a slave whose easy-borrow'd pride
Dwells in the fickle grace of her he follows.—
Out, varlet, from my sight!
*Corn.*      What means your grace?
*Lear.* Who stock'd my servant? Regan, I have good hope      [O heavens,
Thou didst not know on't.—Who comes here?

*Enter* GONERIL.
If you do love old men, if your sweet sway
Allow obedience, if yourselves are old,
Make it your cause; send down, and take my part!—
Art not asham'd to look upon this beard?—
                              [*To* GONERIL.
O Regan, wilt thou take her by the hand?
*Gon.* Why not by the hand, sir? How have I offended?
All's not offence that indiscretion finds,
And dotage terms so.
*Lear.*      O sides, you are too tough!
Will you yet hold?—How came my man i' the stocks?      [orders
*Corn.* I set him there, sir: but his own disDeserv'd much less advancement.
*Lear.*      You! did you?
*Reg.* I pray you, father, being weak, seem so.
If, till the expiration of your month,
You will return and sojourn with my sister,
Dismissing half your train, come then to me:
I am now from home, and out of that provision      [ment.
Which shall be needful for your entertain-
*Lear.* Return to her, and fifty men dismiss'd?
No, rather I abjure all roofs, and choose
To wage against the enmity o' the air;
To be a comrade with the wolf and owl,—
Necessity's sharp pinch!—Return with her?
Why, the hot-blooded France, that dowerless took
Our youngest born, I could as well be brought
To knee his throne, and, squire-like, pension beg
To keep base life a-foot.—Return with her?
Persuade me rather to be slave and sumpter
To this detested groom. [*Pointing to* OSWALD.
*Gon.*      At your choice, sir.
*Lear.* I pr'ythee, daughter, do not make me mad:
I will not trouble thee, my child; farewell:
We'll no more meet, no more see one another:—
But yet thou art my flesh, my blood, my daughter;

Or rather a disease that's in my flesh,
Which I must needs call mine: thou art a boil,
A plague-sore, an embossed carbuncle  [thee;
In my corrupted blood. But I'll not chide
Let shame come when it will, I do not call it:
I do not bid the thunder-bearer shoot,
Nor tell tales of thee to high-judging Jove:
Mend when thou canst; be better at thy
    leisure:
I can be patient; I can stay with Regan,
I and my hundred knights.
    *Reg.*                Not altogether so:
I look'd not for you yet, nor am provided
For your fit welcome. Give ear, sir, to my
    sister;                        [sion
For those that mingle reason with your pas-
Must be content to think you old, and so—
But she knows what she does.
    *Lear.*            Is this well spoken?
    *Reg.* I dare avouch it, sir: what, fifty
    followers?                    [more?
Is it not well? What should you need of
Yea, or so many, sith that both charge and
    danger                        [house
Speak 'gainst so great a number? How in one
Should many people under two commands
Hold amity? 'Tis hard; almost impossible.
    *Gon.* Why might not you, my lord, receive
    attendance                    [mine?
From those that she calls servants, or from
    *Reg.* Why not, my lord? If then they
    chanc'd to slack you,          [me,—
We could control them. If you will come to
For now I spy a danger,—I entreat you
To bring but five-and-twenty: to no more
Will I give place or notice.
    *Lear.* I gave you all,—
    *Reg.*          And in good time you gave it.
    *Lear.* Made you my guardians, my deposi-
    taries;
But kept a reservation to be follow'd  [you
With such a number. What, must I come to
With five-and-twenty, Regan? said you so?
    *Reg.* And speak't again, my lord; no more
    with me.                  [well-favour'd
    *Lear.* Those wicked creatures yet do look
When others are more wicked; not being the
    worst                        [thee:
Stands in some rank of praise.—I'll go with
                        [*To* GONERIL.
Thy fifty yet doth double five-and-twenty,
And thou art twice her love.
    *Gon.*            Hear me, my lord:
What need you five-and-twenty, ten, or five,
To follow in a house where twice so many
Have a command to tend you?
    *Reg.*              What need one?
    *Lear.* O, reason not the need: our basest
    beggars
Are in the poorest thing superfluous:
Allow not nature more than nature needs,
Man's life is cheap as beast's: thou art a lady;
If only to go warm were gorgeous,  [wear'st,
Why, nature needs not what thou gorgeous

Which scarcely keeps thee warm.—But, for
    true need,—
You heavens, give me that patience, patience
    I need!
You see me here, you gods, a poor old man,
As full of grief as age; wretched in both!
If it be you that stir these daughters' hearts
Against their father, fool me not so much
To bear it tamely; touch me with noble anger,
And let not women's weapons, water-drops,
Stain my man's cheeks!—No, you unnatural
    hags,
I will have such revenges on you both
That all the world shall,—I will do such
    things,—                      [be
What they are yet I know not; but they shall
The terrors of the earth. You think I'll weep;
No, I'll not weep:—
I have full cause of weeping; but this heart
Shall break into a hundred thousand flaws
Or ere I'll weep.—O fool, I shall go mad!
        [*Exeunt* LEAR, GLOSTER, KENT, *and* Fool.
            *Storm heard at a distance.*
    *Corn.* Let us withdraw; 'twill be a storm.
    *Reg.* This house is little: the old man and
    his people
Cannot be well bestow'd.          [from rest,
    *Gon.* 'Tis his own blame; hath put himself
And must needs taste his folly.    [gladly,
    *Reg.* For his particular, I'll receive him
But not one follower.
    *Gon.*          So am I purpos'd.
Where is my lord of Gloster?      [return'd.
    *Corn.* Follow'd the old man forth:—he is

            *Re-enter* GLOSTER.

    *Glo.* The king is in high rage.
    *Corn.*            Whither is he going?
    *Glo.* He calls to horse; but will I know not
    whither.                      [himself.
    *Corn.* 'Tis best to give him way; he leads
    *Gon.* My lord, entreat him by no means to
    stay.                        [high winds
    *Glo.* Alack, the night comes on, and the
Do sorely ruffle; for many miles about
There's scarce a bush.
    *Reg.*            O, sir, to wilful men
The injuries that they themselves procure
Must be their schoolmasters. Shut up your
    doors:
He is attended with a desperate train;
And what they may incense him to, being apt
To have his ear abus'd, wisdom bids fear.
    *Corn.* Shut up your doors, my lord; 'tis a
    wild night:
My Regan counsels well: come out o' the
    storm.                        [*Exeunt.*

            ACT III.

        SCENE I.—*A Heath.*

*A storm, with thunder and lightning. Enter*
    KENT *and a* Gentleman, *meeting.*

    *Kent.* Who's there, besides foul weather?

*Gent.* One minded like the weather, most unquietly.

*Kent.* I know you. Where's the king?

*Gent.* Contending with the fretful elements;
Bids the wind blow the earth into the sea,
Or swell the curled waters 'bove the main,
That things might change or cease; tears his white hair,
Which the impetuous blasts, with eyeless rage,
Catch in their fury, and make nothing of;
Strives in his little world of man to out-scorn
The to-and-fro conflicting wind and rain.
This night, wherein the cub-drawn bear would couch,
The lion and the belly-pinched wolf
Keep their fur dry, unbonneted he runs,
And bids what will take all.

*Kent.*                    But who is with him?

*Gent.* None but the fool; who labours to out-jest
His heart-struck injuries.

*Kent.*                    Sir, I do know you;
And dare, upon the warrant of my note,
Commend a dear thing to you. There is division,
Although as yet the face of it be cover'd
With mutual cunning, 'twixt Albany and Cornwall;                    [stars
Who have,—as who have not, that their great
Throne and set high?—servants who seem no less,
Which are to France the spies and speculations
Intelligent of our state; what hath been seen,
Either in snuffs and packings of the dukes;
Or the hard rein which both of them have borne
Against the old kind king; or something deeper,
Whereof perchance these are but furnishings;—
But true it is, from France there comes a power
Into this scatter'd kingdom; who already,
Wise in our negligence, have secret feet
In some of our best ports, and are at point
To show their open banner.—Now to you:
If on my credit you dare build so far
To make your speed to Dover, you shall find
Some that will thank you making just report
Of how unnatural and bemadding sorrow
The king hath cause to plain.
I am a gentleman of blood and breeding;
And from some knowledge and assurance offer
This office to you.

*Gent.* I will talk further with you.

*Kent.*                    No, do not.
For confirmation that I am much more
Than my out wall, open this purse, and take
What it contains. If you shall see Cordelia,—
As fear not but you shall,—show her this ring;
And she will tell you who your fellow is

That yet you do not know. Fie on this storm!
I will go seek the king.          [more to say?

*Gent.* Give me your hand: have you no

*Kent.* Few words, but, to effect, more than all yet,—                    [which your pain
That when we have found the king,—in
That way, I'll this,—he that first lights on him
Holla the other.          [*Exeunt severally.*

SCENE II.—*Another part of the Heath.*
*Storm continues.*

*Enter* LEAR *and* Fool.

*Lear.* Blow, winds, and crack your cheeks! rage! blow!
You cataracts and hurricanoes, spout
Till you have drench'd our steeples, drown'd the cocks!
You sulphurous and thought-executing fires,
Vaunt couriers of oak-cleaving thunderbolts,
Singe my white head! And thou, all-shaking thunder,
Strike flat the thick rotundity o' the world!
Crack nature's moulds, all germens spill at once,
That make ingrateful man!

*Fool.* O nuncle, court holy water in a dry house is better than this rain-water out o' door. Good nuncle, in; ask thy daughters' blessing: here's a night pities neither wise men or fools.

*Lear.* Rumble thy bellyful! Spit, fire! spout, rain!
Nor rain, wind, thunder, fire, are my daughters:
I tax not you, you elements, with unkindness;
I never gave you kingdom, call'd you children;
You owe me no subscription: then let fall
Your horrible pleasure; here I stand, your slave,
A poor, infirm, weak, and despis'd old man:—
But yet I call you servile ministers,
That will with two pernicious daughters join
Your high-engender'd battles 'gainst a head
So old and white as this. O! O! 'tis foul!

*Fool.* He that has a house to put's head in has a good head-piece.
       The cod-piece that will house
           Before the head has any,
       The head and he shall louse;
           So beggars marry many.
       The man that makes his toe
           What he his heart should make
       Shall of a corn cry woe,
           And turn his sleep to wake.
—for there was never yet fair woman but she made mouths in a glass.          [tience;

*Lear.* No, I will be the pattern of all pa-
I will say nothing.

*Enter* KENT.

*Kent.* Who's there?

*Fool.* Marry, here's grace and a cod-piece: that's a wise man and a fool.

*Kent.* Alas, sir, are you here? things that
　　love night
Love not such nights as these; the wrathful
　　skies
Gallow the very wanderers of the dark,
And make them keep their caves: since I was
　　man,　　　　　　　　　　　[thunder,
Such sheets of fire, such bursts of horrid
Such groans of roaring wind and rain I never
Remember to have heard: man's nature can-
　　not carry
The affliction nor the fear.
　　*Lear.*　　　　　　Let the great gods,
That keep this dreadful pother o'er our heads,
Find out their enemies now. Tremble, thou
　　wretch,
That hast within thee undivulged crimes,
Unwhipp'd of justice: hide thee, thou bloody
　　hand;
Thou perjur'd, and thou simular of virtue
That art incestuous: caitiff, to pieces shake,
That under covert and convenient seeming
Hast practis'd on man's life: close pent-up
　　guilts,
Rive your concealing continents, and cry
These dreadful summoners grace.—I am a
　　man
More sinn'd against than sinning.
　　*Kent.*　　　　　　Alack, bare-headed!
Gracious my lord, hard by here is a hovel;
Some friendship will it lend you 'gainst the
　　tempest:
Repose you there, while I to this hard
　　house,—　　　　　　　　[rais'd;
More harder than the stones, whereof 'tis
Which even but now, demanding after you,
Denied me to come in,—return, and force
Their scanted courtesy.
　　*Lear.*　　　　My wits begin to turn.—
Come on, my boy: how dost, my boy? art
　　cold?　　　　　　　　　fellow?
I am cold myself.—Where is this straw, my
The art of our necessities is strange,
That can make vile things precious. Come,
　　your hovel.—　　　　　　[heart
Poor fool and knave, I have one part in my
That's sorry yet for thee.

　　*Fool.* He that has and a little tiny wit,—[*Singing.*
　　　　With heigh, ho, the wind and the rain,—
　　　Must make content with his fortunes fit,
　　　　Though the rain it raineth every day.

　　*Lear.* True, boy.—Come, bring us to this
　　hovel.　　　[*Exeunt* LEAR *and* KENT.
　　*Fool.* This is a brave night to cool a courte-
　　zan.—

I'll speak a prophecy ere I go:—　　　[ter;
　　When priests are more in word than mat-
　　When brewers mar their malt with water;
　　When nobles are their tailors' tutors;
　　No heretics burn'd, but wenches' suitors;
　　When every case in law is right;
　　No squire in debt, nor no poor knight;
　　When slanders do not live in tongues;

　　Nor cutpurses come not to throngs;
　　When userers tell their gold i' the field;
　　And bawds and whores do churches
　　　　build;—
　　Then shall the realm of Albion
　　Come to great confusion:
　　Then comes the time, who lives to see't,
　　That going shall be us'd with feet.
This prophecy Merlin shall make; for I live
before his time.　　　　　　　　[*Exit.*

SCENE III.—*A Room in* GLOSTER'S *Castle.*

*Enter* GLOSTER *and* EDMUND

　　*Glo.* Alack, alack, Edmund, I like not this
unnatural dealing. When I desired their leave
that I might pity him, they took from me
the use of mine own house; charged me, on
pain of perpetual displeasure, neither to speak
of him, entreat for him, nor any way sustain him.
　　*Edm.* Most savage and unnatural!
　　*Glo.* Go to; say you nothing. There is
division between the dukes; and a worse
matter than that: I have received a letter this
night;—'tis dangerous to be spoken;—I have
locked the letter in my closet: these injuries
the king now bears will be revenged home;
there is part of a power already footed: we
must incline to the king. I will seek him, and
privily relieve him: go you and maintain talk
with the duke, that my charity be not of him
perceived: if he ask for me, I am ill, and gone
to bed. If I die for it, as no less is threatened me, the king my old master must be
relieved. There is strange things toward, Edmund; pray you, be careful.　　　　[*Exit.*
　　*Edm.* This courtesy, forbid thee, shall the
　　duke
Instantly know; and of that letter too:—
This seems a fair deserving, and must draw
　　me
That which my father loses,—no less than all:
The younger rises when the old doth fall.
　　　　　　　　　　　　　　[*Exit.*

SCENE IV.—*A part of the Heath with a
　　Hovel. Storm continues.*

*Enter* LEAR, KENT, *and* Fool.

　　*Kent.* Here is the place, my lord; good my
　　lord, enter:
The tyranny of the open night's too rough
For nature to endure.
　　*Lear.*　　　　　　Let me alone.
　　*Kent.* Good my lord, enter here.
　　*Lear.*　　　　　Wilt break my heart?
　　*Kent.* I had rather break mine own. Good
　　my lord, enter.　　　[contentious storm
　　*Lear.* Thou think'st 'tis much that this
Invades us to the skin: so 'tis to thee
But where the greater malady is fix'd, [bear;
The lesser is scarce felt. Thou'dst shun a
But if thy flight lay toward the roaring sea,
Thou'dst meet the bear i' the mouth. When
　　the mind's free

The body's delicate: the tempest in my mind
Doth from my senses take all feeling else
Save what beats there.—Filial ingratitude!
Is it not as this mouth should tear this hand
For lifting food to't?—But I will punish
    home:—
No, I will weep no more.—In such a night
To shut me out!—Pour on; I will endure:—
In such a night as this! O Regan, Goneril!—
Your old kind father, whose frank heart gave
    all,—
O, that way madness lies; let me shun that;
No more of that.

*Kent.*        Good my lord, enter here.

*Lear.* Pr'ythee, go in thyself; seek thine
    own ease:                [der
This tempest will not give me leave to pon-
On things would hurt me more.—But I'll go
    in.—                    [less poverty,—
In, boy; go first [*to the* Fool].—You house-
Nay, get thee in. I'll pray, and then I'll
    sleep.—                [*Fool goes in.*
Poor naked wretches, wheresoe'er you are,
That bide the pelting of this pitiless storm,
How shall your houseless heads and unfed
    sides,                    [fend you
Your loop'd and window'd raggedness, de-
From seasons such as these? O, I have ta'en
Too little care of this! Take physic, pomp;
Expose thyself to feel what wretches feel,
That thou mayst shake the superflux to them,
And show the heavens more just.

*Edg.* [*Within.*] Fathom and half, fathom
    and half! Poor Tom!

        [*The Fool runs out from the hovel.*

*Fool.* Come not in here, nuncle, here's a
    spirit.
Help me, help me!

*Kent.* Give me thy hand.—Who's there?

*Fool.* A spirit, a spirit: he says his name's
    poor Tom.            [there i' the straw?

*Kent.* What art thou that dost grumble
Come forth.

*Enter* EDGAR, *disguised as a madman.*

*Edg.* Away! the foul fiend follows me!—
Through the sharp hawthorn blows the cold
    wind.—
Hum! go to thy cold bed and warm thee.

*Lear.* Didst thou give all to thy daughters?
And art thou come to this?

*Edg.* Who gives anything to poor Tom?
whom the foul fiend hath led through fire
and through flame, through ford and whirl-
pool, o'er bog and quagmire; that hath laid
knives under his pillow, and halters in his
pew; set ratsbane by his porridge; made him
proud of heart, to ride on a bay trotting-
horse over four-inched bridges, to course his
own shadow for a traitor.—Bless thy five
wits!—Tom's a-cold.—O, do de, do de, do de.
—Bless thee from whirlwinds, star-blasting,
and taking! Do poor Tom some charity,
whom the foul fiend vexes:—there could I

have him now,—and there,—and there,—
and there again, and there.

        [*Storm continues.*

*Lear.* What, have his daughters brought
    him to this pass?—
Couldst thou save nothing? Didst thou give
    'em all?

*Fool.* Nay, he reserved a blanket, else we
had been all shamed.

*Lear.* Now, all the plagues that in the
    pendulous air            [daughters!
Tang fated o'er men's faults light on thy

*Kent.* He hath no daughters, sir.

*Lear.* Death, traitor! nothing could have
    subdu'd nature            [ters.—
To such a lowness but his unkind daugh-
Is it the fashion that discarded fathers
Should have thus little mercy on their flesh?
Judicious punishment! 'twas this flesh begot
Those pelican daughters.

*Edg.* Pillicock sat on Pillicock-hill:—
Halloo, halloo, loo loo!

*Fool.* This cold night will turn us all to
fools and madmen.

*Edg.* Take heed o' the foul fiend: obey thy
parents; keep thy word justly; swear not;
commit not with man's sworn spouse; set not
thy sweet heart on proud array. Tom's a-
cold.

*Lear.* What hast thou been?

*Edg.* A serving-man, proud in heart and
mind; that curled my hair; wore gloves in my
cap; served the lust of my mistress's heart,
and did the act of darkness with her; swore
as many oaths as I spake words, and broke
them in the sweet face of heaven: one that
slept in the contriving of lust, and waked to
do it: wine loved I deeply, dice dearly; and
in women out-paramoured the Turk: false of
heart, light of ear, bloody of hand; hog in
sloth, fox in stealth, wolf in greediness, dog
in madness, lion in prey. Let not the creaking of shoes nor the rustling of silks betray
thy poor heart to woman: keep thy foot out
of brothels, thy hand out of plackets, thy pen
from lenders' books, and defy the foul fiend.
—Still through the hawthorn blows the cold
wind: says suum, mun, nonny. Dolphin my
boy, boy, sessa! let him trot by.

        [*Storm still continues.*

*Lear.* Why, thou wert better in thy grave
than to answer with thy uncovered body this
extremity of the skies.—Is man no more than
this? Consider him well. Thou owest the
worm no silk, the beast no hide, the sheep no
wool, the cat no perfume.—Ha! here's three
on's are sophisticated! Thou art the thing
itself: unaccommodated man is no more but
such a poor, bare, forked animal as thou art.
—Off, off, you lendings!—Come, unbutton
here.                [*Tearing off his clothes.*

*Fool.* Pr'ythee, nuncle, be contented; 'tis
a naughty night to swim in.—Now a little
fire in a wild field were like an old lecher's

heart,—a small spark, all the rest on's body cold.—Look, here comes a walking fire.

*Edg.* This is the foul fiend Flibbertigibbet: he begins at curfew, and walks till the first cock; he gives the web and the pin, squints the eye, and makes the hare-lip; mildews the white wheat, and hurts the poor creature of earth.

S.withold footed thrice the old;
He met the nightmare and her nine-fold;
    Bid her alight,
    And her troth plight,
And, aroint thee, witch, aroint thee!

*Kent.* How fares your grace?

*Enter* GLOSTER *with a torch.*

*Lear.* What's he?
*Kent.* Who's there? What is't you seek?
*Glo.* What are you there? Your names?
*Edg.* Poor Tom; that eats the swimming frog, the toad, the tadpole, the wall-newt, and the water; that in the fury of his heart, when the foul fiend rages, eats cow-dung for sallets; swallows the old rat and the ditch-dog; drinks the green mantle of the standing pool; who is whipped from tithing to tithing, and stocked, punished, and imprisoned; who hath had three suits to his back, six shirts to his body, horse to ride, and weapon to wear;—
But mice and rats, and such small deer,
Have been Tom's food for seven long year.
Beware my follower.—Peace, Smulkin; peace, thou fiend! [pany?
*Glo.* What, hath your grace no better com-
*Edg.* The prince of darkness is a gentle-man
Modo he's call'd, and Mahu. [grown so vile
*Glo.* Our flesh and blood, my lord, is
That it doth hate what gets it.
*Edg.* Poor Tom's a-cold. [fer
*Glo.* Go in with me: my duty cannot suf-
To obey in all your daughters' hard com-mands:
Though their injunction be to bar my doors,
And let this tyrannous night take hold upon you,
Yet have I ventur'd to come seek you out,
And bring you where both fire and food is ready.
*Lear.* First let me talk with this philoso-pher.—
What is the cause of thunder?
*Kent.* Good my lord, take his offer;
Go into the house.
*Lear.* I'll talk a word with this same learned Theban.—
What is your study? [vermin.
*Edg.* How to prevent the fiend and to kill
*Lear.* Let me ask you one word in private.
*Kent.* Impórtune him once more to go, my lord;
His wits begin to unsettle.
*Glo.*                    Canst thou blame him?

His daughters seek his death:—ah, that good Kent!—
He said it would be thus,—poor, banish'd man!— [thee, friend,
Thou say'st the king grows mad; I'll tell
I am almost mad myself: I had a son, [life
Now outlaw'd from my blood; he sought my
But lately, very late: I lov'd him, friend,—
No father his son dearer: true to tell thee,
    [*Storm continues.*
The grief hath craz'd my wits.—What a night's this!—
I do beseech your grace,—
*Lear.*                O, cry you mercy, sir.—
Noble philosopher, your company.
*Edg.* Tom's a-cold. [thee warm.
*Glo.* In, fellow, there, into the hovel: keep
*Lear.* Come, let's in all.
*Kent.*                This way, my lord.
*Lear.*                With him;
I will keep still with my philosopher.
*Kent.* Good my lord, soothe him; let him take the fellow.
*Glo.* Take him you on.
*Kent.* Sirrah, come on; go along with us.
*Lear.* Come, good Athenian.
*Glo.*                No words, no words:
Hush. [came,
*Edg.* Child Rowland to the dark tower
His word was still,—Fie, foh, and fum,
I smell the blood of a British man. [*Exeunt.*

SCENE V.—*A Room in* GLOSTER'S *Castle.*

*Enter* CORNWALL *and* EDMUND.

*Corn.* I will have my revenge ere I depart his house.
*Edm.* How, my lord, I may be censured, that nature thus gives way to loyalty, some-thing fears me to think of.
*Corn.* I now perceive, it was not alto-gether your brother's evil disposition made him seek his death; but a provoking merit, set a-work by a reprovable badness in him-self.
*Edm.* How malicious is my fortune, that I must repent to be just! This is the letter he spoke of, which approves him an intelligent party to the advantages of France. O heav-ens! that this treason were not, or not I the detector!
*Corn.* Go with me to the duchess.
*Edm.* If the matter of this paper be cer-tain, you have mighty business in hand.
*Corn.* True or false, it hath made thee earl of Gloster. Seek out where thy father is, that he may be ready for our apprehension.
*Edm.* [*Aside.*] If I find him comforting the king, it will stuff his suspicion more fully.—I will persevere in my course of loyalty, though the conflict be sore between that and my blood.
*Corn.* I will lay trust upon thee; and thou shalt find a dearer father in my love.
    [*Exeunt.*

SCENE VI.—*A Chamber in a Farm-house adjoining the Castle.*

*Enter* GLOSTER, LEAR, KENT, Fool, *and* EDGAR.

*Glo.* Here is better than the open air; take it thankfully. I will piece out the comfort with what addition I can: I will not be long from you.

*Kent.* All the power of his wits have given way to his impatience:—the gods reward your kindness!    [*Exit* GLOSTER.

*Edg.* Fraretetto calls me; and tells me Nero is an angler in the lake of darkness.—Pray, innocent, and beware the foul fiend.

*Fool.* Pr'ythee, nuncle, tell me whether a madman be a gentleman or a yeoman?

*Lear.* A king, a king!

*Fool.* No; he's a yeoman that has a gentleman to his son; for he's a mad yeoman that sees his son a gentleman before him.

*Lear.* To have a thousand with red burning spits
Come hissing in upon 'em,—

*Edg.* The foul fiend bites my back.

*Fool.* He's mad that trusts in the tameness of a wolf, a horse's health, a boy's love, or a whore's oath.    [straight.—

*Lear.* It shall be done; I will arraign them
Come, sit thou here, most learned justicer;—
    [*To* EDGAR.
Thou, sapient sir, sit here [*To the* Fool].—
Now, you she-foxes!—

*Edg.* Look, where he stands and glares!—Wantest thou eyes at trial, madam?
Come o'er the bourn, Bessy, to me,—

*Fool.* Her boat hath a leak,
    And she must not speak
Why she dares not come over to thee.

*Edg.* The foul fiend haunts poor Tom in the voice of a nightingale. Hopdance cries in Tom's belly for two white herring. Croak not, black angel; I have no food for thee.

*Kent.* How do you, sir? Stand you not so amaz'd:    [ions?
Will you lie down and rest upon the cush-

*Lear.* I'll see their trial first.—Bring in the evidence.—

Thou, robed man of justice, take thy place;—
    [*To* EDGAR.
And thou, his yoke-fellow of equity,
    [*To the* Fool.
Bench by his side:—you are o' the commission,
Sit you too.    [*To* KENT.

*Edg.* Let us deal justly.
    Sleepest or wakest thou, jolly shepherd?
        Thy sheep be in the corn;
    And for one blast of thy minikin mouth
        Thy sheep shall take no harm.
Pur! the cat is gray.

*Lear.* Arraign her first; 'tis Goneril. I here take my oath before this honourable assembly, she kicked the poor king her father.

*Fool.* Come hither, mistress. Is your name Goneril?

*Lear.* She cannot deny it.

*Fool.* Cry you mercy, I took you for a jointstool.

*Lear.* And here's another, whose warp'd looks proclaim    [there!
What store her heart is made on.—Stop her
Arms, arms, sword, fire!—Corruption in the place!—
False justicer, why hast thou let her 'scape?

*Edg.* Bless thy five wits!    [now

*Kent.* O pity!—Sir, where is the patience
That you so oft have boasted to retain?

*Edg.* [*Aside.*] My tears begin to take his part so much,
They'll mar my counterfeiting.

*Lear.* The little dogs and all, [bark at me.
Tray, Blanch, and Sweetheart, see, they

*Edg.* Tom will throw his head at them.—Avaunt, you curs!
    Be thy mouth or black or white
    Tooth that poisons if it bite;
    Mastiff, greyhound, mongrel grim,
    Hound or spaniel, brach or lym,
    Or bobtail tike or trundle-tail,—
    Tom will make them weep and wail:
    For, with throwing thus my head,
    Dogs leap the hatch, and all are fled.
Do de, de, de. Sessa! Come, march to wakes and fairs and market-towns.—Poor Tom, thy horn is dry.

*Lear.* Then let them anatomize Regan; see what breeds about her heart. Is there any cause in nature that makes these hard hearts?—[*To* EDGAR.] You, sir, I entertain you for one of my hundred; only I do not like the fashion of your garments: you will say they are Persian; but let them be changed.

*Kent.* Now, good my lord, lie here and rest awhile.    [the curtains:

*Lear.* Make no noise, make no noise; draw
So, so. We'll go to supper i' the morning.

*Fool.* And I'll go to bed at noon.

*Re-enter* GLOSTER.

*Glo.* Come hither, friend: where is the king my master?    [wits are gone.

*Kent.* Here, sir; but trouble him not.—his

*Glo.* Good friend, I pr'ythee, take him in thy arms;
I have o'erheard a plot of death upon him:
There is a litter ready; lay him in't,
And drive toward Dover, friend, where thou shalt meet    [master:
Both welcome and protection. Take up thy
If thou shouldst dally half an hour, his life,
With thine, and all that offer to defend him,
Stand in assured loss: take up, take up;
And follow me, that will to some provision
Give thee quick conduct.

*Kent.*    Oppress'd nature sleeps:—
This rest might yet have balm'd thy broken sinews,

Which, if convenience will not allow,
Stand in hard cure.—Come, help to bear thy
   master;
Thou must not stay behind.        [*To the* Fool.
  *Glo.*                        Come, come, away.
     [*Exeunt* KENT, GLOSTER, *and the* Fool,
         *bearing off* LEAR.
  *Edg.* When we our betters see bearing our
   woes,
We scarcely think our miseries our foes.
Who alone suffers suffers most i' the mind,
Leaving free things and happy shows behind:
But then the mind much sufferance doth
   o'erskip
When grief hath mates and bearing fellowship.
How light and portable my pain seems now,
When that which makes me bend makes the
   king bow;
He childed as I father'd!—Tom, away!
Mark the high noises; and thyself bewray,
When false opinion, whose wrong thought de-
   files thee,
In thy just proof repeals and reconciles thee.
What will hap more to-night, safe 'scape the
   king!
Lurk, lurk.                              [*Exit.*

SCENE VII.—*A Room in* GLOSTER'S *Castle.*

    *Enter* CORNWALL, REGAN, GONERIL,
       EDMUND, *and* Servants.

  *Corn.* Post speedily to my lord your husband; show him this letter:—the army of
France is landed.—Seek out the traitor
Gloster.        [*Exeunt some of the* Servants.
  *Reg.* Hang him instantly.
  *Gon.* Pluck out his eyes.
  *Corn.* Leave him to my displeasure.—Edmund, keep you our sister company: the revenges we are bound to take upon your
traitorous father are not fit for your beholding. Advise the duke, where you are going,
to a most festinate preparation: we are bound
to the like. Our posts shall be swift and intelligent betwixt us. Farewell, dear sister:—
farewell, my lord of Gloster.

          *Enter* OSWALD.

How now! where's the king?        [hence:
  *Osw.* My lord of Gloster hath convey'd him
Some five or six and thirty of his knights,
Hot questrists after him, met him at gate;
Who, with some other of the lord's depend-
   ents,
Are gone with him toward Dover; where
   they boast
To have well-armed friends.
  *Corn.*        Get horses for your mistress.
  *Gon.* Farewell, sweet lord and sister.
  *Corn.* Edmund, farewell.
       [*Exeunt* GON., EDM., *and* OSW.
       Go seek the traitor Gloster,
Pinion him like a thief, bring him before us.
         [*Exeunt other* Servants.
Though well we may not pass upon his life

Without the form of justice, yet our power
Shall do a courtesy to our wrath, which men
May blame, but not control.—Who's there?
   the traitor?

   *Re-enter* Servants, *with* GLOSTER.

  *Reg.* Ingrateful fox! 'tis he.
  *Corn.* Bind fast his corky arms.
  *Glo.* What mean your graces?—Good my
   friends, consider
You are my guests: do me no foul play,
   friends.
  *Corn.* Bind him, I say. [Servants *bind him.*
  *Reg.*              Hard, hard.—O filthy traitor!
  *Glo.* Unmerciful lady as you are, I'm none.
  *Corn.* To this chair bind him.—Villain,
   thou shalt find,—
        [REGAN *plucks his beard.*
  *Glo.* By the kind gods, 'tis most ignobly
   done
To pluck me by the beard.
  *Reg.* So white, and such a traitor!
  *Glo.*                        Naughty lady,
These hairs which thou dost ravish from my
   chin
Will quicken, and accuse thee: I am your
   host:
With robbers' hands my hospitable favours
You should not ruffle thus. What will you do?
  *Corn.* Come, sir, what letters had you late
   from France?                        [truth.
  *Reg.* Be simple-answer'd, for we know the
  *Corn.* And what confederacy have you
   with the traitors
Late footed in the kingdom? [lunatic king?
  *Reg.* To whose hands have you sent the
   Speak.
  *Glo.* I have a letter guessingly set down,
Which came from one that's of a neutral
   heart,
And not from one oppos'd.
  *Corn.*                        Cunning.
  *Reg.*                              And false.
  *Corn.* Where hast thou sent the king?
  *Glo.*                              To Dover.
  *Reg.* Wherefore to Dover? Wast thou not
   charg'd at peril,—
  *Corn.* Wherefore to Dover? Let him an-
   swer that.                [stand the course.
  *Glo.* I am tied to the stake, and I must
  *Reg.* Wherefore to Dover?
  *Glo.* Because I would not see thy cruel
   nails
Pluck out his poor old eyes; nor thy fierce
   sister
In his anointed flesh stick boarish fangs.
The sea, with such a storm as his bare head
In hell-black night endur'd, would have
   buoy'd up,
And quench'd the stelled fires: yet, poor old
   heart,
He holp the heavens to rain.
If wolves had at thy gate howl'd that stern
   time

Thou shouldst have said, *Good porter, turn the key,*
All cruels else subscrib'd:—but I shall see
The winged vengeance overtake such children.
   *Corn.* See't shalt thou never.—Fellows, hold the chair.—
Upon these eyes of thine I'll set my foot.
   [GLOSTER *is held down in his chair, while* CORNWALL *plucks out one of his eyes and sets his foot on it.*
   *Glo.* He that will think to live till he be old
Give me some help!—O cruel!—O you gods!
   *Reg.* One side will mock another; the other too.
   *Corn.* If you see vengeance,—
   1 *Serv.* Hold your hand, my lord:
I have serv'd you ever since I was a child;
But better service have I never done you
Than now to bid you hold.
   *Reg.* How now, you dog!
   1 *Serv.* If you did wear a beard upon your chin,
I'd shake it on this quarrel. What do you mean?
   *Corn.* My villain! [*Draws, and runs at him.*
   1 *Serv.* Nay, then, come on, and take the chance of anger.
   [*Draws. They fight.* CORN. *is wounded.*
   *Reg.* Give me thy sword [*to another* Servant].—A peasant stand up thus!
   [*Snatches a sword, comes behind, and stabs him.*
   1 *Serv.* O, I am slain!—My lord, you have one eye left
To see some mischief on them.—O! [*Dies.*
   *Corn.* Lest it see more, prevent it.—Out, vile jelly!
Where is thy lustre now?
   [*Tears out* GLOSTER'S *other eye, and throws it on the ground.*
   *Glo.* All dark and comfortless.—Where's my son Edmund?
Edmund, enkindle all the sparks of nature,
To quit this horrid act.
   *Reg.* Out, treacherous villain!
Thou call'st on him that hates thee: it was he
That made the overture of thy treasons to us;
Who is too good to pity thee.
   *Glo.* O my follies!
Then Edgar was abus'd.—
Kind gods, forgive me that, and prosper him!
   *Reg.* Go thrust him out at gates, and let him smell.
His way to Dover.—How is't, my lord? How look you?
   *Corn.* I have receiv'd a hurt:—follow me, lady.— [*slave*
Turn out that eyeless villain;—throw this
Upon the dunghill.—Regan, I bleed apace:
Untimely comes this hurt: give me your arm.
   [*Exit* CORNWALL, *led by* REGAN; Servants *unbind* GLOSTER *and lead him out.*

   2 *Serv.* I'll never care what wickedness I do
If this man come to good.
   3 *Serv.* If she live long,
And in the end meet the old course of death,
Women will all turn monsters.
   2 *Serv.* Let's follow the old earl, and get the Bedlam [*madness*
To lead him where he would: his roguish
Allows itself to anything.
   3 *Serv.* Go thou: I'll fetch some flax and whites of eggs
To apply to his bleeding face. Now, heaven help him! [*Exeunt severally.*

## ACT IV.

### SCENE I.—*The Heath.*

*Enter* EDGAR.

   *Edg.* Yet better thus, and known to be contemn'd,
Than still contemn'd and flatter'd. To be worst,
The lowest and most dejected thing of fortune,
Stands still in esperance, lives not in fear:
The lamentable change is from the best;
The worst returns to laughter. Welcome, then,
Thou unsubstantial air that I embrace!
The wretch that thou hast blown unto the worst
Owes nothing to thy blasts.—But who comes here?

*Enter* GLOSTER, *led by an* Old Man.

My father, poorly led?—World, world, O world! [*hate thee,*
But that thy strange mutations make us
Life would not yield to age.
   *Old Man.* O, my good lord, I have been your tenant, and your father's tenant, these fourscore years. [*gone:*
   *Glo.* Away, get thee away; good friend, be Thy comforts can do me no good at all;
Thee they may hurt.
   *Old Man.* You cannot see your way. [*eyes;*
   *Glo.* I have no way, and therefore want no
I stumbled when I saw: full oft 'tis seen
Our means secure us, and our mere defects
Prove our commodities.—O dear son Edgar,
The food of thy abused father's wrath!
Might I but live to see thee in my touch,
I'd say I had eyes again!
   *Old Man.* How now! Who's there?
   *Edg.* [*Aside.*] O gods! Who is't can say,
       *I am at the worst?*
I am worse than e'er I was.
   *Old Man.* 'Tis poor mad Tom.
   *Edg.* [*Aside.*] And worse I may be yet:
       the worst is not
So long as we can say, *This is the worst.*
   *Old Man.* Fellow, where goest?
   *Glo.* Is it a beggar-man?
   *Old Man.* Madman and beggar too.

*Glo.* He has some reason, else he could not beg.
I' the last night's storm I such a fellow saw;
Which made me think a man a worm: my son
Came then into my mind; and yet my mind
Was then scarce friends with him: I have heard more since.
As flies to wanton boys are we to the gods,—
They kill us for their sport.
*Edg.* [*Aside.*] How should this be?—
Bad is the trade that must play fool to sorrow,
Angering itself and others.—Bless thee, master!
*Glo.* Is that the naked fellow?
*Old Man.* Ay, my lord.
*Glo.* Then, pr'ythee, get thee gone: if, for my sake,
Thou wilt o'ertake us, hence a mile or twain,
I' the way toward Dover, do it for ancient love;
And bring some covering for this naked soul,
Which I'll entreat to lead me.
*Old Man.* Alack, sir, he is mad.
*Glo.* 'Tis the times' plague when madmen lead the blind.
Do as I bid thee, or rather do thy pleasure;
Above the rest, be gone. [that I have
*Old Man.* I'll bring him the best 'parel
Come on't what will. [*Exit.*
*Glo.* Sirrah, naked fellow,—
*Edg.* Poor Tom's a-cold.— [*Aside.*] I cannot daub it further.
*Glo.* Come hither, fellow.
*Edg.* [*Aside.*] And yet I must.—Bless thy sweet eyes, they bleed.
*Glo.* Know'st thou the way to Dover?
*Edg.* Both stile and gate, horse-way and footpath. Poor Tom hath been scared out of his good wits:—bless thee, good man's son, from the foul fiend!—five fiends have been in poor Tom at once; of lust, as *Obidicut, Hobbididance,* prince of dumbness; *Mahu,* of stealing; *Modo,* of murder; *Flibbertigibbet,* of mopping and mowing,—who since possesses chambermaids and waiting-women. So, bless thee, master!
*Glo.* Here, take this purse, thou whom the heavens' plagues [wretched
Have humbled to all strokes: that I am
Makes thee the happier;—heavens, deal so still!
Let the superfluous and lust-dieted man,
That slaves your ordinance, that will not see
Because he doth not feel, feel your power quickly;
So distribution should undo excess,
And each man have enough.—Dost thou know Dover?
*Edg.* Ay, master. [head
*Glo.* There is a cliff whose high and bending
Looks fearfully in the confined deep:
Bring me but to the very brim of it,

And I'll repair the misery thou dost bear
With something rich about me: from that place
I shall no leading need.
*Edg.* Give me thy arm:
Poor Tom shall lead thee. [*Exeunt.*

SCENE II.—*Before the* DUKE OF ALBANY'S *Palace.*

*Enter* GONERIL *and* EDMUND; OSWALD *meeting them.*

*Gon.* Welcome, my lord: I marvel our mild husband [master?
Not met us on the way.—Now, where's your
*Osw.* Madam, within; but never man so chang'd.
I told him of the army that was landed;
He smil'd at it: I told him you were coming;
His answer was, *The worse:* of Gloster's treachery,
And of the loyal service of his son,
When I inform'd him, then he call'd me sot,
And told me I had turn'd the wrong side out:—
What most he should dislike seems pleasant to him;
What like offensive.
*Gon.* Then shall you go no further.
[*To* EDMUND.
It is the cowish terror of his spirit,
That dares not undertake: he'll not feel wrongs,
Which tie him to an answer. Our wishes on the way [brother;
May prove effects. Back, Edmund, to my
Hasten his musters and conduct his powers:
I must change arms at home, and give the distaff
Into my husband's hands. This trusty servant
Shall pass between us: ere long you are like to hear,
If you dare venture in your own behalf,
A mistress's command. Wear this; spare speech; [*Giving a favour.*
Decline your head: this kiss, if it durst speak,
Would stretch thy spirits up into the air:—
Conceive, and fare thee well.
*Edm.* Yours in the ranks of death.
*Gon.* My most dear Gloster.
[*Exit* EDMUND.
O, the difference of man and man!
To thee a woman's services are due:
My fool usurps my body.
*Osw.* Madam, here comes my lord.
[*Exit.*

*Enter* ALBANY.

*Gon.* I have been worth the whistle.
*Alb.* O Goneril!
You are not worth the dust which the rude wind
Blows in your face. I fear your disposition:
That nature which contemns its origin

Cannot be border'd certain in itself;
She that herself will silver and disbranch
From her material sap, perforce must wither
And come to deadly use.

  *Gon.* No more; the text is foolish.

  *Alb.* Wisdom and goodness to the vile
    seem vile:                                    [done?
Filths savour but themselves. What have you
Tigers, not daughters, what have you per-
    form'd?
A father, and a gracious aged man,
Whose reverence the head-lugg'd bear would
    lick,                                      [madded.
Most barbarous, most degenerate! have you
Could my good brother suffer you to do it?
A man, a prince, by him so benefited!
If that the heavens do not their visible spirits
Send quickly down to tame these vile of-
    fences,
It will come,
Humanity must perforce prey on itself,
Like monsters of the deep.

  *Gon.*                     Milk-liver'd man!
That bear'st a cheek for blows, a head for
    wrongs;
Who hast not in thy brows an eye discerning
Thine honour from thy suffering; that not
    know'st
Fools do those villains pity who are punish'd
Ere they have done their mischief. Where's
    thy drum?
France spreads his banners in our noiseless
    land;
With plumed helm thy slayer begins threats;
Whiles thou, a moral fool, sitt'st still, and
    criest,
*Alack, why does he so?*

  *Alb.*               See thyself, devil!
Proper deformity seems not in the fiend
So horrid as in woman.

  *Gon.*                     O vain fool!

  *Alb.* Thou changed and self-cover'd thing,
    for shame,
Be-monster not thy feature. Were't my fit-
    ness
To let these hands obey my blood,
They are apt enough to dislocate and tear
Thy flesh and bones:—howe'er thou art a
    fiend,
A woman's shape doth shield thee,

  *Gon.* Marry, your manhood now!

*Enter a* Messenger.

  *Alb.* What news?                    [wall's dead;

  *Mess.* O, my good lord, the Duke of Corn-
Slain by his servant, going to put out
The other eye of Gloster.

  *Alb.*                     Gloster's eyes!

  *Mess.* A servant that he bred, thrill'd with
    remorse,
Oppos'd against the act, bending his sword
To his great master; who, thereat enrag'd,
Flew on him, and amongst them fell'd him
    dead;

But not without that harmful stroke which
    since
Hath pluck'd him after.

  *Alb.*               This shows you are above,
You justicers, that these our nether crimes
So speedily can venge!—But, O poor Gloster!
Lost he his other eye?

  *Mess.*               Both, both, my lord.—
This letter, madman, craves a speedy answer;
'Tis from your sister.

  *Gon.* [*Aside.*] One way I like this well;
But being widow, and my Gloster with her,
May all the building in my fancy pluck
Upon my hateful life: another way
The news is not so tart.—I'll read, and
    answer.                              [*Exit.*

  *Alb.* Where was his son when they did take
    his eyes?

  *Mess.* Come with my lady hither.

  *Alb.*                     He is not here.

  *Mess.* No, my good lord; I met him back
    again.

  *Alb.* Knows he the wickedness?

  *Mess.* Ay, my good lord; 'twas he in-
    form'd against him;            [punishment
And quit the house on purpose that their
Might have the freer course.

  *Alb.*                     Gloster, I live
To thank thee for the love thou show'dst the
    king,                              [friend:
And to revenge thine eyes.—Come hither,
Tell me what more thou knowest. [*Exeunt.*

SCENE III.—*The French Camp near Dover.*

*Enter* KENT *and a* Gentleman.

  *Kent.* Why the King of France is so suddenly gone back know you the reason?

  *Gent.* Something he left imperfect in the
state, which since his coming forth is thought
of; which imports to the kingdom so much
fear and danger that his personal return was
most required and necessary.

  *Kent.* Who hath he left behind him general?

  *Gent.* The Mareschal of France, Monsieur
la Far.

  *Kent.* Did your letters pierce the queen to
any demonstration of grief?     [my presence;

  *Gent.* Ay, sir; she took them, read them in
And now and then an ample tear trill'd down
Her delicate cheek: it seem'd she was a queen
Over her passion; who, most rebel-like,
Sought to be king o'er her.

  *Kent.*               O, then it mov'd her.

  *Gent.* Not to a rage: patience and sorrow
    strove                              [seen
Who should express her goodliest. You have
Sunshine and rain at once: her smiles and
    tears
Were like a better day: those happy smilets
That play'd on her ripe lip seem'd not to
    know
What guests were in her eyes; which parted
    thence

As pearls from diamonds dropp'd—In brief, sorrow
Would be a rarity most beloved if all
Could so become it.
　　*Kent*.　　　　Made she no verbal question?
　　*Gent*. Faith, once or twice she heav'd the name of *father*
Pantingly forth, as if it press'd her heart;
Cried, *Sisters! sisters!—Shame of ladies! sisters!*　　　　[*i' the night?*
*Kent! father! sisters! What, i' the storm?*
*Let pity not be believ'd!*—There she shook
The holy water from her heavenly eyes,
And clamour moisten'd: then away she started
To deal with grief alone.
　　*Kent*.　　　　　It is the stars,
The stars above us, govern our conditions;
Else one self mate and mate could not beget
Such different issues. You spoke not with her since?
　　*Gent*. No.
　　*Kent*. Was this before the king return'd?
　　*Gent*.　　　　　　　No, since.
　　*Kent*. Well, sir, the poor distressed Lear's i' the town;
Who sometime, in his better tune, remembers
What we are come about, and by no means
Will yield to see his daughter.
　　*Gent*.　　　　　　Why, good sir?
　　*Kent*. A sovereign shame so elbows him: his own unkindness,　　　　[*her*
That stripp'd her from his benediction, turn'd
To foreign casualties, gave her dear rights
To his dog-hearted daughters,—these things sting
His mind so venomously that burning shame
Detains him from Cordelia.
　　*Gent*.　　　　Alack, poor gentleman!
　　*Kent*. Of Albany's and Cornwall's powers you heard not?
　　*Gent*. 'Tis so they are a-foot.
　　*Kent*. Well, sir, I'll bring you to our master Lear,
And leave you to attend him: some dear cause
Will in concealment wrap me up awhile;
When I am known aright, you shall not grieve
Lending me this acquaintance. I pray you go
Along with me.　　　　　　[*Exeunt.*

SCENE IV.—*The French Camp. A Tent.*

*Enter* CORDELIA, Physician, *and* Soldiers.

　　*Cor*. Alack, 'tis he: why, he was met even now
As mad as the vex'd sea; singing aloud;
Crown'd with rank fumiter and furrow weeds
With harlocks, hemlock, nettles, cuckoo-flowers,
Darnel, and all the idle weeds that grow
In our sustaining corn.—A century send forth;
Search every acre in the high-grown field,
And bring him to our eye. [*Exit an Officer*.]—
　　　　What can man's wisdom
In the restoring his bereaved sense?

He that helps him take all my outward worth.
　　*Phys*. There is means, madam:
Our foster-nurse of nature is repose,
The which he lacks; that to provoke in him
Are many simples operative, whose power
Will close the eye of anguish.
　　*Cor*.　　　　　　All bless'd secrets,
All you unpublish'd virtues of the earth,
Spring with my tears! be aidant and remediate
In the good man's distress!—Seek, seek for him;
Lest his ungovern'd rage dissolve the life
That wants the means to lead it.

*Enter a* Messenger.

　　*Mess*.　　　　　　News, madam;
The British powers are marching hitherward.
　　*Cor*. 'Tis known before; our preparation stands
In expectation of them.—O dear father,
It is thy business that I go about;
Therefore great France
My mourning and important tears hath pitied.
No blown ambition doth our arms incite,
But love, dear love, and our ag'd father's right:
Soon may I hear and see him!　　[*Exeunt.*

SCENE V.—*A Room in* GLOSTER'S *Castle.*

*Enter* REGAN *and* OSWALD.

　　*Reg*. But are my brother's powers set forth?
　　*Osw*.　　　　　　　Ay, madam.
　　*Reg*. Himself in person there?
　　*Osw*.　　　　Madam, with much ado:
Your sister is the better soldier.
　　*Reg*. Lord Edmund spake not with your lord at home?
　　*Osw*. No, madam.　　　　[*to him?*
　　*Reg*. What might import my sister's letter
　　*Osw*. I know not, lady.　　　[*matter.*
　　*Reg*. Faith, he is posted hence on serious
It was great ignorance, Gloster's eyes being out,
To let him live: where he arrives he moves
All hearts against us: Edmund, I think, is gone,
In pity of his misery, to despatch
His nighted life; moreover, to descry
The strength o' the enemy.
　　*Osw*. I must needs after him, madam, with my letter.　　　　[*with us;*
　　*Reg*. Our troops set forth to-morrow: stay
The ways are dangerous.
　　*Osw*.　　　　I may not, madam:
My lady charg'd my duty in this business.
　　*Reg*. Why should she write to Edmund?
　　　　Might not you
Transport her purposes by word? Belike
Something.—I know not what:—I'll love thee much—
Let me unseal the letter.
　　*Osw*.　　　　Madam, I had rather,—

*Reg.* I know your lady does not love her husband;
I am sure of that: and at her late being here
She gave strange eyeliads and most speaking looks　　　　　　　　[bosom.
To noble Edmund. I know you are of her
*Osw.* I, madam?　　　　　　　[know't:
*Reg.* I speak in understanding; you are, I
Therefore I do advise you, take this note:
My lord is dead; Edmund and I have talk'd;
And more convenient is he for my hand
Than for your lady's.—You may gather more.
If you do find him, pray you, give him this;
And when your mistress hears thus much from you,
I pray, desire her call her wisdom to her.
So, fare you well.
If you do chance to hear of that blind traitor,
Prefermen falls on him that cuts him off.
　　*Osw.* Would I could meet him, madam! I should show
What party I do follow.
　　*Reg.*　　　　　Fare thee well.
　　　　　　　　　　　　　[*Exeunt.*

SCENE VI.—*The Country near Dover.*

*Enter* GLOSTER, *and* EDGAR *dressed like a peasant.*

*Glo.* When shall I come to the top of that same hill?　　　[we labour.
*Edg.* You do climb up it now: look, how
*Glo.* Methinks the ground is even.
*Edg.*　　　　　Horrible steep.
Hark, do you hear the sea?
*Glo.*　　　　　No, truly.
*Edg.* Why, then, your other senses grow imperfect
By your eyes' anguish.
*Glo.*　　　　So may it be indeed:
Methinks thy voice is alter'd; and thou speak'st
In better phrase and matter than thou didst.
*Edg.* You are much deceiv'd: in nothing am I chang'd
But in my garments.
*Glo.*　　　Methinks you're better spoken.
*Edg.* Come on, sir; here's the place:—stand still.—How fearful
And dizzy 'tis to cast one's eyes so low!
The crows and choughs that wing the midway air
Show scarce so gross as beetles: half way down
Hangs one that gathers samphire,—dreadful trade!
Methinks he seems no bigger than his head:
The fishermen that walk upon the beach
Appear like mice; and yond tall anchoring bark
Diminish'd to her cock; her cock a buoy
Almost too small for sight: the murmuring surge,
That on the unnumber'd idle pebbles chafes,
Cannot be heard so high.—I'll look no more;

Lest my brain turn, and the deficient sight
Topple down headlong.
*Glo.*　　　　Set me where you stand.
*Edg.* Give me your hand:—you are now within a foot　　　　[moon
Of the extreme verge: for all beneath the
Would I not leap upright.
*Glo.*　　　　Let go my hand.
Here, friend, 's another purse; in it a jewel
Well worth a poor man's taking: fairies and gods
Prosper it with thee! Go thou further off;
Bid me farewell, and let me hear thee going.
*Edg.* Now, fare you well, good sir.
　　　　　　　　　[*Seems to go.*
*Glo.*　　　　With all my heart.
*Edg.* Why I do trifle thus with his despair
Is done to cure it.
*Glo.*　　　　O you mighty gods!
This world I do renounce, and in your sights
Shake patiently my great affliction off:
If I could bear it longer, and not fall
To quarrel with your great opposeless wills,
My snuff and loathed part of nature should
Burn itself out. If Edgar live, O bless him!—
Now, fellow, fare thee well.
　　*Edg.*　　　　Gone, sir:—farewell,—
　　　　　　[GLOSTER *leaps, and falls along.*
And yet I know not how conceit may rob
The treasury of life, when life itself　[thought,
Yields to the theft: had he been where he
By this had thought been past.—Alive or dead?
Ho, you sir! friend!—Hear you, sir!—speak!
Thus might he pass indeed:—yet he revives.—
What are you, sir?
*Glo.*　　　　Away, and let me die.
*Edg.* Hadst thou been aught but gossamer, feathers, air,
So many fathom down precipitating,
Thou'dst shiver'd like an egg: but thou dost breathe;　　　　　[art sound.
Hast heavy substance; bleed'st not; speak'st;
Ten masts at each make not the altitude
Which thou hast perpendicularly fell:
Thy life's a miracle.—Speak yet again.
*Glo.* But have I fall'n, or no?　　　[bourn.
*Edg.* From the dread summit of this chalky
Look up a-height;—the shrill-gorg'd lark so far
Cannot be seen or heard: do but look up.
*Glo.* Alack, I have no eyes.—
Is wretchedness depriv'd that benefit,　[fort,
To end itself by death? 'Twas yet some com-
When misery could beguile the tyrant's rage
And frustrate his proud will.
*Edg.*　　　　Give me your arm:
Up:—so.—How is't? Feel you your legs? You stand.
*Glo.* Too well, too well.
*Edg.*　　　This is above all strangeness.
Upon the crown o' the cliff what thing was that
Which parted from you?

*Glo.* A poor unfortunate beggar.

*Edg.* As I stood here below, methought his eyes
[noses,
Were two full moons; he had a thousand
Horns whelk'd and wav'd like the enridged sea:
It was some fiend; therefore, thou happy father,
Think that the clearest gods, who make them honours
Of men's impossibilities, have preserv'd thee.

*Glo.* I do remember now: henceforth I'll bear
Affliction till it do cry out itself, [speak of,
*Enough, enough,* and die. That thing you
I took it for a man; often 'twould say,
*The fiend, the fiend:* he led me to that place.

*Edg.* Bear free and patient thoughts.—
But who comes here?

*Enter* LEAR, *fantastically dressed up with flowers.*

The safer sense will ne'er accommodate
His master thus.

*Lear.* No, they cannot touch me for coining; I am the king himself.

*Edg.* O thou side-piercing sight!

*Lear.* Nature's above art in that respect.—
There's your press-money. That fellow handles
his bow like a crow-keeper: draw me a
clothier's yard.—Look, look, a mouse! Peace,
peace;—this piece of toasted cheese will do't.
—There's my gauntlet; I'll prove it on a
giant.—Bring up the brown bills.—O, well
flown, bird!—i' the clout, i' the clout: hewgh!
—Give the word.

*Edg.* Sweet marjoram.

*Lear.* Pass.

*Glo.* I know that voice.

*Lear.* Ha! Goneril, with a white beard!—
They flattered me like a dog; and told me I
had white hairs in my beard ere the black ones
were there. To say *ay* and *no* to everything I
said!—*Ay* and *no,* too, was no good divinity.
When the rain came to wet me once, and the
wind to make me chatter; when the thunder
would not peace at my bidding; there I found
'em, there I smelt 'em out. Go to, they are
not men o' their words: they told me I was
everything; 'tis a lie,—I am not ague-proof.

*Glo.* The trick of that voice I do well remember:
Is't not the king?

*Lear.* Ay, every inch a king:
When I do stare, see how the subject quakes.
I pardon that man's life.—What was thy cause?
Adultery?—
Thou shalt not die: die for adultery! No:
The wren goes to't, and the small gilded fly
Does lecher in my sight.
Let copulation thrive; for Gloster's bastard son
Was kinder to his father than my daughters

Got 'tween the lawful sheets. .
To't, luxury, pell-mell, for I lack soldiers.—
Behold yond simpering dame,
Whose face between her forks presages snow;
That minces virtue, and does shake the head
To hear of pleasure's name;—
The fitchew nor the soiled horse goes to't
With a more riotous appetite.
Down from the waist they are centaurs,
Though women all above:
But to the girdle do the gods inherit,
Beneath is all the fiends'; there's hell, there's darkness,
There is the sulphurous pit, burning, scalding,
stench, consumption;—fie, fie, fie! pah, pah!
Give me an ounce of civet, good apothecary,
to sweeten my imagination: there's money for thee.

*Glo.* O, let me kiss that hand! [tality.

*Lear.* Let me wipe it first; it smells of mor-

*Glo.* O ruin'd piece of nature! This great world
[know me?
Shall so wear out to naught.—Dost thou

*Lear.* I remember thine eyes well enough.
Dost thou squiny at me? No, do thy worst,
blind Cupid; I'll not love.—Read thou this
challenge; mark but the penning of it.

*Glo.* Were all the letters suns, I could not see one.

*Edg.* I would not take this from report;—
it is,
And my heart breaks at it.

*Lear.* Read.

*Glo.* What, with the case of eyes?

*Lear.* O, ho, are you there with me? No
eyes in your head nor no money in your
purse? Your eyes are in a heavy case, your
purse in a light: yet you see how this world goes.

*Glo.* I see it feelingly.

*Lear.* What, art mad? A man may see how
this world goes with no eyes. Look with
thine ears: see how yond justice rails upon
yond simple thief. Hark, in thine ear: change
places; and, handy-dandy, which is the justice, which is the thief?—Thou hast seen a
farmer's dog bark at a beggar?

*Glo.* Ay, sir.

*Lear.* And the creature run from the cur?
There thou mightst behold the great image of
authority: a dog's obeyed in office.—
Thou rascal beadle, hold thy bloody hand!
Why dost thou lash that whore? Strip thine own back;
Thou hotly lust'st to use her in that kind
For which thou whipp'st her. The usurer
hangs the cozener.
Through tatter'd clothes small vices do appear;
Robes and furr'd gowns hide all. Plate sin with gold,
And the strong lance of justice hurtless breaks;
Arm it in rags, a pigmy's straw doth pierce it.

None does offend, none,—I say, none; I'll able 'em:
Take that of me, my friend, who have the power
To seal the accuser's lips. Get thee glass eyes;
And, like a scurvy politician, seem [now, now:
To see the things thou dost not.—Now, now,
Pull off my boots:—harder, harder:—so.
 *Edg.* O, matter and impertinency mix'd!
Reason in madness!   [my eyes.
 *Lear.* If thou wilt weep my fortunes, take
I know thee well enough; thy name is Gloster:
Thou must be patient; we came crying hither:
Thou know'st, the first time that we smell the air
We wawl and cry.—I will preach to thee: mark.
 *Glo.* Alack, alack the day!
 *Lear.* When we are born, we cry that we are come   [block:—
To this great stage of fools—This' a good
It were a delicate stratagem to shoe
A troop of horse with felt: I'll put't in proof;
And when I have stol'n upon these sons-in-law,
Then kill, kill, kill, kill, kill, kill!

*Enter a* Gentleman, *with* Attendants.

 *Gent.* O, here he is: lay hand upon him.—Sir,
Your most dear daughter,—   [even
 *Lear.* No rescue? What, a prisoner? I am
The natural fool of fortune.—Use me well;
You shall have ransom. Let me have surgeons;
I am cut to the brains.
 *Gent.*   You shall have anything.
 *Lear.* No seconds? all myself?
Why, this would make a man a man of salt,
To use his eyes for garden water-pots,
Ay, and for laying Autumn's dust.
 *Gent.*   Good sir,—
 *Lear.* I will die bravely, like a smug bridegroom. What!
I will be jovial: come, come; I am a king,
My masters, know you that.
 *Gent.* You are a royal one, and we obey you.
 *Lear.* Then there's life in't. Nay, an you get it, you shall get it by running. Sa, sa, sa, sa.   [*Exit running;* Attendants *follow.*
 *Gent.* A sight most pitiful in the meanest wretch,   [daughter,
Past speaking of in a king!—Thou hast one
Who redeems nature from the general curse
Which twain have brought her to.
 *Edg.* Hail, gentle sir.
 *Gent.* Sir, speed you: what's your will?
 *Edg.* Do you hear aught, sir, of a battle toward?   [hears that
 *Gent.* Most sure and vulgar: every one Which can distinguish sound.
 *Edg.*   But, by your favour,
How near's the other army?

 *Gent.* Near and on speedy foot; the main descry
Stands on the hourly thought.
 *Edg.*   I thank you, sir: that's all.
 *Gent.* Though that the queen on special cause is here,
Her army is mov'd on.
 *Edg.*   I thank you, sir.  [*Exit Gent.*
 *Glo.* You ever-gentle gods, take my breath from me;
Let not my worser spirit tempt me again
To die before you please!
 *Edg.*   Well pray you, father.
 *Glo.* Now, good sir, what are you?
 *Edg.* A most poor man, made tame by fortune's blows;
Who, by the art of known and feeling sorrows,   [hand,
Am pregnant to good pity. Give me your
I'll lead you to some biding.
 *Glo.*   Hearty thanks:
The bounty and the benison of heaven
To boot, and boot!

*Enter* OSWALD

 *Osw.*  A proclaim'd prize! Most happy!
That eyeless head of thine was first fram'd flesh
To raise my fortunes.—Thou old unhappy traitor,
Briefly thyself remember:—the sword is out
That must destroy thee.
 *Glo.*   Now let thy friendly hand
Put strength enough to it. [EDGAR *interposes.*
 *Osw.*   Wherefore, bold peasant,
Dar'st thou support a publish'd traitor? Hence;
Lest that the infection of this fortune take
Like hold on thee. Let go his arm.  ['casion.
 *Edg.* Chill not let go, zir, without vurther
 *Osw.* Let go, slave, or thou diest!
 *Edg.* Good gentleman, go your gait, and let poor volk pass. And chud ha' been zwaggered out of my life, 'twould not ha' been zo long as 'tis by a vortnight. Nay, come not near the old man; keep out, che vor ye, or ise try whether your costard or my bat be the harder: chill be plain with you.
 *Osw.* Out, dunghill!
 *Edg.* Chill pick your teeth, zir: come; no matter vor your foins.
 [*They fight, and* EDGAR *knocks him down.*
 *Osw.* Slave, thou hast slain me:—villain, take my purse:
If ever thou wilt thrive, bury my body; [me
And give the letters which thou find'st about
To Edmund Earl of Gloster; seek him out
Upon the British party:—O, untimely death!
  [*Dies.*
 *Edg.* I know thee well: a serviceable villain;
As duteous to the vices of thy mistress
As badness would desire.
 *Glo.*   What, is he dead?

*Edg.* Sit you down, father; rest you.—
Let's see these pockets: the letters that he
    speaks of              [sorry
May be my friends.—He's dead; I am only
He had no other death's-man.—Let us see:—
Leave, gentle wax; and, manners, blame us
    not:                [hearts;
To know our enemies' minds we'd rip their
Their papers is more lawful.
    [*Reads.*] *Let our reciprocal vows be re-*
*membered. You have many opportunities to*
*cut him off: if your will want not, time*
*and place will be fruitfully offered. There is*
*nothing done if he return the conqueror: then*
*am I the prisoner, and his bed my goal; from*
*the loathed warmth whereof deliver me, and*
*supply the place for your labour.*
    *Your (wife, so I would say) affectionate*
    *servant,*               GONERIL.
O undistinguish'd space of woman's will!
A plot upon her virtuous husband's life;
And the exchange my brother!—Here, in the
    sands,
Thee I'll rake up, the post unsanctified
Of murderous lechers: and in the mature time
With this ungracious paper strike the sight
Of the death-practis'd duke: for him 'tis well
That of thy death and business I can tell.
    [*Exit* EDGAR, *dragging out the body.*
    *Glo.* The king is mad: how stiff is my vile
    sense,
That I stand up, and have ingenious feeling
Of my huge sorrows! Better I were distract:
So should my thoughts be sever'd from my
    griefs,
And woes by wrong imaginations lose
The knowledge of themselves.

          *Re-enter* EDGAR.

    *Edg.*            Give me your hand:
               [*Drum afar off.*
Far off, methinks, I hear the beaten drum:
Come, father, I'll bestow you with a friend.
                    [*Exeunt.*

SCENE VII.—*A Tent in the French Camp.*
LEAR *on a bed asleep, soft music playing;*
Physician, Gentleman, *and others attending.*

    *Enter* CORDELIA *and* KENT.

    *Cor.* O thou good Kent, how shall I live
    and work            [too short,
To match thy goodness? My life will be
And every measure fail me.       [paid.
    *Kent.* To be acknowledg'd, madam, is o'er-
All my reports go with the modest truth;.
Nor more nor clipp'd, but so.
    *Cor.*           Be better suited:
These weeds are memories of those worser
    hours:
I pr'ythee, put them off.
    *Kent.*        Pardon, dear madam;
Yet to be known shortens my made intent:
My boon I make it that you know me not
Till time and I think meet.

    *Cor.* Then be't so, my good lord.—How
    does the king?     [*To the* Physician.
    *Phys.* Madam, sleeps still.
    *Cor.* O you kind gods,
Cure this great breach in his abused nature!
The untun'd and jarring senses, O, wind up
Of this child-changed father!
    *Phys.*        So please your majesty
That we may wake the king: he hath slept
    long.                [proceed
    *Cor.* Be govern'd by your knowledge, and
I' the sway of your own will. Is he array'd?
    *Gent.* Ay, madam; in the heaviness of sleep
We put fresh garments on him. [awake him;
    *Phys.* Be by, good madam, when we do
I doubt not of his temperance.
    *Cor.*               Very well.
    *Phys.* Please you, draw near.—Louder the
    music there!
    *Cor.* O my dear father! Restoration hang
Thy medicine on my lips; and let this kiss
Repair those violent harms that my two
    sisters
Have in thy reverence made!
    *Kent.*        Kind and dear princess!
    *Cor.* Had you not been their father, these
    white flakes
Had challeng'd pity of them. Was this a face
To be oppos'd against the warring winds?
To stand against the deep dread bolted
    thunder?
In the most terrible and nimble stroke
Of quick, cross lightning? to watch,—poor
    perdu!—
With this thin helm? Mine enemy's dog,
Though he had bit me, should have stood that
    night              [father,
Against my fire; and wast thou fain, poor
To hovel thee with swine and rogues forlorn,
In short and musty straw? Alack, alack!
'Tis wonder that thy life and wits at once
Had not concluded all.—He wakes; speak to
    him.
    *Phys.* Madam, do you; 'tis fittest.
    *Cor.* How does my royal lord? How fares
    your majesty?         [the grave:—
    *Lear.* You do me wrong to take me out o'
Thou art a soul in bliss; but I am bound
Upon a wheel of fire, that mine own tears
Do scald like molten lead.
    *Cor.*          Sir, do you know me?
    *Lear.* You are a spirit, I know: when did
    you die?
    *Cor.* Still, still far wide!      [awhile.
    *Phys.* He's scarce awake: let him alone
    *Lear.* Where have I been? Where am I?—
    Fair daylight?—           [pity
I am mightily abus'd.—I should e'en die with
To see another thus.—I know not what to
    say.—
I will not swear these are my hands:—let's
    see;
I feel this pin prick. Would I were assur'd
Of my condition!

*Cor.*                 O, look upon me, sir,
And hold your hands in benediction o'er me.—
No, sir, you must not kneel.
    *Lear.*            Pray, do not mock me:
I am a very foolish fond old man,        [less;
Fourscore and upward, not an hour more nor
And, to deal plainly,
I fear I am not in my perfect mind.    [man;
Methinks I should know you, and know this
Yet I am doubtful: for I am mainly ignorant
What place this is; and all the skill I have
Remembers not these garments; nor I know
not                              [at me;
Where I did lodge last night. Do not laugh
For, as I am a man, I think this lady
To be my child Cordelia.
    *Cor.*              And so I am, I am.
    *Lear.* Be your tears wet? yes, faith. I
        pray, weep not:
If you have poison for me I will drink it.
I know you do not love me; for your sisters
Have, as I do remember, done me wrong:
You have some cause, they have not.
    *Cor.*              No cause, no cause.
    *Lear.* Am I in France?
    *Kent.*            In your own kingdom, sir.
    *Lear.* Do not abuse me.
    *Phys.* Be comforted, good madam: the
        great rage,
You see, is kill'd in him: and yet it is danger
To make him even o'er the time he has lost.
Desire him to go in; trouble him no more
Till further settling.
    *Cor.* Will't please your highness walk?
    *Lear.*            You must bear with me:
Pray you now, forget and forgive: I am old
        and foolish.
    [*Exeunt* LEAR, COR., Phy., *and* Attendants.
    *Gent.* Holds it true, sir, that the Duke of
Cornwall was so slain?
    *Kent.* Most certain, sir.
    *Gent.* Who is conductor of his people?
    *Kent.* As 'tis said, the bastard son of
        Gloster.
    *Gent.* They say Edgar, his banished son, is
with the Earl of Kent in Germany.
    *Kent.* Report is changeable. 'Tis time to
look about; the powers of the kingdom
approach apace.
    *Gent.* The arbitrement is like to be bloody.
Fare you well, sir.                    [*Exit.*
    *Kent.* My point and period will be thor-
        ough wrought,
Or well or ill, as this day's battle's fought.
                                      [*Exit.*

### ACT V.

SCENE I.—*The Camp of the British Forces
        near Dover.*

Enter, with drum and colours, EDMUND,
    REGAN, Officers, Soldiers, *and others.*

    *Edm.* Know of the duke if his last purpose
        hold,

Or whether since he is advis'd by aught
To change the course: he's full of alteration
And self-reproving:—bring his constant
        pleasure.
                [*To an* Officer, *who goes out.*
    *Reg.* Our sister's man is certainly mis-
        carried.
    *Edm.* 'Tis to be doubted, madam.
    *Reg.*                Now, sweet lord,
You know the goodness I intend upon you:
Tell me,—but truly,—but then speak the
        truth,
Do you not love my sister?
    *Edm.*              In honour'd love.
    *Reg.* But have you never found my
        brother's way
To the forefended place?
    *Edm.*            That thought abuses you.
    *Reg.* I am doubtful that you have been
        conjunct
And bosom'd with her, as far as we call hers.
    *Edm.* No, by mine honour, madam.
    *Reg.* I never shall endure her: dear my
        lord,
Be not familiar with her.
    *Edm.*              Fear me not:—
She and the duke her husband!

*Enter, with drum and colours,* ALBANY,
        GONERIL, *and* Soldiers.

    *Gon.* [*Aside.*] I had rather lose the battle
        than that sister
Should loosen him and me.
    *Alb.* Our very loving sister, well be-met.—
Sir, this I heard,—the king is come to his
        daughter,
With others whom the rigour of our state
Forc'd to cry out. Where I could not be
        honest
I never yet was valiant: for this business,
It toucheth us, as France invades our land,
Not bolds the king, with others whom, I
        fear,
Most just and heavy causes make oppose.
    *Edm.* Sir, you speak nobly.
    *Reg.*              Why is this reason'd?
    *Gon.* Combine together 'gainst the enemy;
For these domestic and particular broils
Are not the question here.
    *Alb.*              Let's, then, determine
With the ancient of war on our proceeding.
    *Edm.* I shall attend you presently at your
        tent.
    *Reg.* Sister, you'll go with us?
    *Gon.* No.
    *Reg.* 'Tis most convenient; pray you, go
        with us.                    [I will go.
    *Gon.* [*Aside.*] O, ho, I know the riddle.—

*As they are going out, enter* EDGAR, *disguised.*

    *Edg.* If e'er your grace had speech with
        man so poor,
Hear me one word.

*Alb.* I'll overtake you.—Speak.
[*Exeunt* EDM., REG., GON., Officers,
Soldiers, *and* Attendants.
*Edg.* Before you fight the battle, ope this
letter.
If you have victory, let the trumpet sound
For him that brought it: wretched though I
seem,
I can produce a champion that will prove
What is avouched there. If you miscarry,
Your business of the world hath so an end,
And machination ceases. Fortune love you!
*Alb.* Stay till I have read the letter.
*Edg.* I was forbid it.
When time shall serve, let but the herald cry,
And I'll appear again.
*Alb.* Why, fare thee well: I will o'erlook
thy paper. [*Exit* EDGAR.

*Re-enter* EDMUND.

*Edm.* The enemy's in view; draw up your
powers. [forces
Here is the guess of their true strength and
By diligent discovery;—but your haste
Is now urg'd on you.
*Alb.* We will greet the time. [*Exit.*
*Edm.* To both these sisters have I sworn
my love;
Each jealous of the other, as the stung
Are of the adder. Which of them shall I
take?
Both? one? or neither? Neither can be en-
joy'd
If both remain alive: to take the widow
Exasperates, makes mad her sister Goneril;
And hardly shall I carry out my side,
Her husband being alive. Now, then, we'll
use
His countenance for the battle; which being
done,
Let her who would be rid of him devise
His speedy taking off. As for the mercy
Which he intends to Lear and to Cordelia,—
The battle done, and they within our power,
Shall never see his pardon: for my state
Stands on me to defend, not to debate. [*Exit.*

SCENE II.—*A Field between the two Camps.*

*Alarum within. Enter with drum and col-
ours,* LEAR, CORDELIA, *and their* Forces;
*and exeunt.*

*Enter* EDGAR *and* GLOSTER.

*Edg.* Here, father, take the shadow of this
tree [may thrive:
For your good host; pray that the right
If ever I return to you again
I'll bring you comfort.
*Glo.* Grace go with you, sir!
[*Exit* EDGAR.

*Alarum and Retreat within. Re-enter* EDGAR.
*Edg.* Away, old man,—give me thy
hand,—away!

King Lear hath lost, he and his daughter
ta'en:
Give me thy hand; come on.
*Glo.* No further, sir; a man may rot even
here. [must endure
*Edg.* What, in ill thoughts again? Men
Their going hence, even as their coming
hither.
Ripeness is all:—come on.
*Glo.* And that's true too.
[*Exeunt.*

SCENE III.—*The British Camp near Dover.*

*Enter, in conquest, with drum and colours,*
EDMUND; LEAR *and* CORDELIA *prisoners;*
Officers, Soldiers, &c.

*Edm.* Some officers take them away: good
guard,
Until their greater pleasures first be known
That are to censure them.
*Cor.* We are not the first
Who, with best meaning, have incurr'd the
worst.
For thee, oppressed king, am I cast down;
Myself could else out-frown false fortune's
frown.— [sisters?
Shall we not see these daughters and these
*Lear.* No, no, no, no! Come, let's away to
prison:
We two alone will sing like birds i' the cage:
When thou dost ask me blessing I'll kneel
down
And ask of thee forgiveness: so we'll live,
And pray, and sing, and tell old tales, and
laugh
At gilded butterflies, and hear poor rogues
Talk of court news; and we'll talk with them
too,— [out;—
Who loses and who wins; who's in, who's
And take upon's the mystery of things
As if we were God's spies: and we'll wear out
In a wall'd prison packs and sects of great
ones
That ebb and flow by the moon.
*Edm.* Take them away.
*Lear.* Upon such sacrifices, my Cordelia,
The gods themselves throw incense. Have I
caught thee? [heaven,
He that parts us shall bring a brand from
And fire us hence like foxes. Wipe thine eyes;
The good years shall devour them, flesh and
fell,
Ere they shall make us weep: we'll see 'em
starve first.
Come. [*Exeunt* LEAR *and* COR., *guarded.*
*Edm.* Come hither, captain; hark.
Take thou this note [*giving him a paper*]; go
follow them to prison:
One step I have advanc'd thee; if thou dost
As this instructs thee, thou dost make thy
way
To noble fortunes: know thou this,—that
men
Are as the time is: to be tender-minded

Does not become a sword:—thy great employment
Will not bear question; either say thou'lt do't,
Or thrive by other means.

*Off.*          I'll do't, my lord.

*Edm.* About it; and write happy when thou hast done.
Mark,—I say, instantly; and carry it so
As I have set it down.

*Off.* I cannot draw a cart nor eat dried oats;
If it be man's work I will do't.      [*Exit.*

*Flourish. Enter* ALBANY, GONERIL, REGAN, Officers *and* Attendants.

*Alb.* Sir, you have shown to-day your valiant strain,
And fortune led you well: you have the captives
Who were the opposites of this day's strife:
We do require them of you, so to use them
As we shall find their merits and our safety
May equally determine.

*Edm.*       Sir, I thought it fit
To send the old and miserable king
To some retention and appointed guard;
Whose age has charms in it, whose title more,
To pluck the common bosom on his side,
And turn our impress'd lances in our eyes
Which do command them. With him I sent the queen;
My reason all the same; and they are ready
To-morrow, or at further space, to appear
Where you shall hold your session. At this time         [friend;
We sweat and bleed: the friend hath lost his
And the best quarrels, in the heat, are curs'd
By those that feel their sharpness:—
The question of Cordelia and her father
Requires a fitter place.

*Alb.*       Sir, by your patience
I hold you but a subject of this war,
Not as a brother.

*Reg.*      That's as we list to grace him.
Methinks our pleasure might have been demanded
Ere you had spoke so far. He led our powers;
Bore the commission of my place and person;
The which immediacy may well stand up
And call itself your brother.

*Gon.*       Not so hot:
In his own grace he doth exalt himself,
More than in your addition.

*Reg.*       In my rights,
By me invested, he compeers the best.

*Gon.* That were the most, if he should husband you.

*Reg.* Jesters do oft prove prophets.

*Gon.*        Holla, holla!
That eye that told you so look'd but asquint.

*Reg.* Lady, I am not well; else I should answer
From a full-flowing stomach.—General,
Take thou my soldiers, prisoners, patrimony;
Dispose of them, of me; the walls are thine:
Witness the world that I create thee here
My lord and master.

*Gon.*      Mean you to enjoy him?

*Alb.* The let-alone lies not in your good-will.

*Edm.* Nor in thine, lord.

*Alb.*       Half-blooded fellow, yes.

*Reg.* Let the drum strike, and prove my title thine.      [*To* EDMUND.

*Alb.* Stay yet; hear reason.—Edmund, I arrest thee
On capital treason; and, in thy arrest,
This gilded serpent [*pointing to* GONERIL].—
For your claim, fair sister,
I bar it in the interest of my wife;
'Tis she is sub-contracted to this lord,
And I, her husband, contradict your bans.
If you will marry, make your loves to me,—
My lady is bespoke.

*Gon.*       An interlude!

*Alb.* Thou art arm'd, Gloster:—let the trumpet sound:
If none appear to prove upon thy person
Thy heinous, manifest, and many treasons,
There is my pledge [*throwing down a glove*];
I'll make it on thy heart,
Ere I taste bread, thou art in nothing less
Than I have here proclaim'd thee.

*Reg.*       Sick, O, sick!

*Gon.* [*Aside.*] If not, I'll ne'er trust medicine.

*Edm.* There's my exchange [*throwing down a glove*]: what in the world he is
That names me traitor, villain-like he lies:
Call by thy trumpet: he that dares approach,
On him, on you, who not? I will maintain
My truth and honour firmly.

*Alb.* A herald, ho!

*Edm.*      A herald, ho, a herald!

*Alb.* Trust to thy single virtue; for thy soldiers,
All levied in my name, have in my name
Took their discharge.

*Reg.*      My sickness grows upon me.

*Alb.* She is not well; convey her to my tent.      [*Exit* REGAN *led.*

*Enter a* Herald.

Come hither, herald,—Let the trumpet sound,—
And read out this.

*Off.* Sound, trumpet! [*A trumpet sounds.*

*Herald.* [*Reads.*] *If any man of quality or degree within the lists of the army will maintain upon Edmund, supposed Earl of Gloster, that he is a manifold traitor, let him appear by the third sound of the trumpet: he is bold in his defence.*

*Edm.* Sound!  [1 *Trumpet.*
*Herald.* Again!  [2 *Trumpet.*
*Herald.* Again!  [3 *Trumpet.*
[*Trumpet answers within.*

Enter EDGAR, *armed, and preceded by a trumpet.*

*Alb.* Ask him his purposes, why he appears
Upon this call o' the trumpet.
*Herald.*  What are you?
Your name, your quality? and why you answer
This present summons?
*Edg.*  Know, my name is lost;
By treason's tooth bare-gnawn and canker-bit:
Yet am I noble as the adversary
I come to cope.
*Alb.*  Which is that adversary?
*Edg.* What's he that speaks for Edmund
Earl of Gloster?
*Edm.* Himself:—what say'st thou to him?
*Edg.*  Draw thy sword,
That, if my speech offend a noble heart,
Thy arm may do thee justice: here is mine.
Behold, it is the privilege of mine honours,
My oath, and my profession: I protest,—
Maugre thy strength, youth, place, and eminence,
Despite thy victor sword and fire-new fortune,
Thy valour and thy heart,—thou art a traitor;
False to thy gods, thy brother, and thy father;
Conspirant 'gainst this high illustrious prince;
And, from the extremest upward of thy head
To the descent and dust below thy foot,
A most toad-spotted traitor. Say thou *No,*
This sword, this arm, and my best spirits, are bent
To prove upon thy heart, whereto I speak,
Thou liest.
*Edm.* In wisdom I should ask thy name;
But, since thy outside looks so fair and war-like,
And that thy tongue some say of breeding breathes,
What safe and nicely I might well delay
By rule of knighthood, I disdain and spurn:
Back do I toss these treasons to thy head;
With the hell-hated lie o'erwhelm thy heart;
Which,—for they yet glance by and scarcely bruise,—
This sword of mine shall give them instant way,
Where they shall rest for ever.—Trumpets, speak!
[*Alarums. They fight.* EDMUND *falls.*
*Alb.* Save him, save him!
*Gon.*  This is practice, Gloster:
By the law of arms thou wast not bound to answer

An unknown opposite; thou art not vanquish'd,
But cozen'd and beguil'd.
*Alb.*  Shut your mouth, dame,
Or with this paper shall I stop it:—hold, sir;
Thou worse than any name, read thine own evil:—
No tearing, lady; I perceive you know it.
[*Gives the letter to* EDMUND.
*Gon.* Say, if I do,—the laws are mine, not thine:
Who can arraign me for't?
*Alb.*  Most monstrous!
Know'st thou this paper?
*Gon.*  Ask me not what I know.
[*Exit.*
*Alb.* Go after her: she's desperate; govern her. [*To an* Officer, *who goes out.*
*Edm.* What you have charg'd me with, that have I done;  [out:
And more, much more; the time will bring it
'Tis past, and so am I.—But what art thou
That hast this fortune on me? If thou'rt noble
I do forgive thee.
*Edg.*  Let's exchange charity.
I am no less in blood than thou art, Edmund;
If more, the more thou hast wrong'd me.
My name is Edgar, and thy father's son.
The gods are just, and of our pleasant vices
Make instruments to plague us:
The dark and vicious place where thee he got
Cost him his eyes.
*Edm.*  Thou hast spoken right, 'tis true;
The wheel is come full circle; I am here.
*Alb.* Methought thy very gait did prophesy
A royal nobleness:—I must embrace thee:
Let sorrow split my heart if ever I
Did hate thee or thy father!
*Edg.* Worthy prince, I know't.
*Alb.* Where have you hid yourself?
How have you known the miseries of your father?  [brief tale;
*Edg.* By nursing them, my lord.—List a
And when 'tis told, O, that my heart would burst!—
The bloody proclamation to escape,
That follow'd me so near,—O, our lives' sweetness!
That with the pain of death we'd hourly die
Rather than die at once!—taught me to shift
Into a madman's rags; to assume a semblance
That very dogs disdain'd: and in this habit
Met I my father with his bleeding rings,
Their precious stones new lost; became his guide,
Led him, begg'd for him, sav'd him from despair;
Never,—O fault!—reveal'd myself unto him
Until some half-hour past, when I was arm'd;

Not sure, though hoping, of this good success,
I ask'd his blessing, and from first to last
Told him my pilgrimage: but his flaw'd heart,—
Alack, too weak the conflict to support!—
'Twixt two extremes of passion, joy and grief,
Burst smilingly.
 *Edm.* This speech of yours hath mov'd me,
And shall perchance do good: but speak you on;
You look as you had something more to say.
 *Alb.* If there be more, more woeful, hold it in;
For I am almost ready to dissolve,
Hearing of this.
 *Edg.*   This would have seem'd a period
To such as love not sorrow; but another,
To amplify too much, would make much more,
And top extremity.     [man
Whilst I was big in clamour, came there a
Who, having seen me in my worst estate,
Shunn'd my abhorr'd society; but then, finding
Who 'twas that so endur'd, with his strong arms
He fasten'd on my neck, and bellow'd out
As he'd burst heaven; threw him on my father;
Told the most piteous tale of Lear and him
That ever ear receiv'd: which in recounting
His grief grew puissant, and the strings of life
Began to crack: twice then the trumpet sounded,
And there I left him tranc'd.
 *Alb.*    But who was this?
 *Edg.* Kent, sir, the banish'd Kent, who in disguise
Follow'd his enemy king, and did him service
Improper for a slave.

*Enter a* Gentleman *hastily, with a bloody knife.*

 *Gent.* Help, help, O, help!
 *Edg.*    What kind of help?
 *Alb.*     Speak, man.
 *Edg.* What means that bloody knife?
 *Gent.*    'Tis hot, it smokes;
It came even from the heart of—O, she's dead!
 *Alb.*    Who dead? speak, man.
 *Gent.* Your lady, sir, your lady: and her sister
By her is poison'd; she hath confess'd it.
 *Edm.* I was contracted to them both: all three
Now marry in an instant.
 *Edg.*    Here comes Kent.
 *Alb.* Produce the bodies, be they alive or dead:—     [tremble,
This judgment of the heavens, that makes us
Touches us not with pity. [*Exit* Gentleman.

*Enter* KENT.

O, is this he?
The time will not allow the compliment
Which very manners urges.
 *Kent.*    I am come
To bid my king and master aye good-night:
Is he not here?
 *Alb.*   Great thing of us forgot!—
Speak, Edmund, where's the king? and where's Cordelia?
[*The bodies of* GON. *and* REG. *are brought in.*
See'st thou this object, Kent?
 *Kent.* Alack, why thus?
 *Edm.*   Yet Edmund was belov'd:
The one the other poison'd for my sake,
And after slew herself.
 *Alb.* Even so.—Cover their faces. [to do,
 *Edm.* I pant for life:—some good I mean
Despite of mine own nature. Quickly send,—
Be brief in it,—to the castle; for my writ
Is on the life of Lear and on Cordelia:—
Nay, send in time.-
 *Alb.* Run, run, O, run! [office? send
 *Edg.* To who, my lord?—Who has the
Thy token of reprieve.
 *Edm.* Well thought on: take my sword,
Give it the captain.
 *Alb.*   Haste thee, for thy life.
        [*Exit* EDGAR.
 *Edm.* He hath commission from thy wife and me
To hang Cordelia in the prison, and
To lay the blame upon her own despair,
That she fordid herself.
 *Alb.* The gods defend her!—Bear him
  hence awhile.  [EDMUND *is borne off.*

*Re-enter* LEAR, *with* CORDELIA *dead in his arms;* EDGAR, Officer, *and others following.*

 *Lear.* Howl, howl, howl, howl!—O, you are men of stones:
Had I your tongues and eyes, I'd use them so
That heaven's vault should crack.—She's gone for ever!—
I know when one is dead and when one lives;
She's dead as earth.—Lend me a looking-glass;
If that her breath will mist or stain the stone,
Why, then she lives.
 *Kent.*   Is this the promis'd end?
 *Edg.* Or image of that horror?
 *Alb.*    Fall, and cease!
 *Lear.* This feather stirs; she lives! if it be so,
It is a chance which does redeem all sorrows
That ever I have felt.
 *Kent.*  O my good master! [*Kneeling.*
 *Lear.* Pr'ythee, away.
 *Edg.*   'Tis noble Kent, your friend.
 *Lear.* A plague upon you, murderers, traitors all!      [ever!—
I might have sav'd her; now she's gone for

Cordelia, Cordelia! stay a little. Ha!
What is't thou say'st?—Her voice was ever
    soft,    [woman.—
Gentle, and low,—an excellent thing in
I kill'd the slave that was a-hanging thee.
    *Off.* 'Tis true, my lords, he did.
    *Lear.*    Did I not, fellow?
I have seen the day, with my good biting
    falchion,
I would have made them skip: I am old now,
And these same crosses spoil me.—Who are
    you?
Mine eyes are not o' the best:—I'll tell you
    straight.    [and hated,
    *Kent.* If fortune brag of two she lov'd
One of them we behold.    [Kent?
    *Lear.* This is a dull sight. Are you not
    *Kent.*    The same,
Your servant Kent.—Where is your servant
    Caius?
    *Lear.* He's a good fellow, I can tell you
    that;
He'll strike, and quickly too:—he's dead and
    rotten.    [man,—
    *Kent.* No, my good lord; I am the very
    *Lear.* I'll see that straight.    [and decay
    *Kent.* That from your first of difference
Have follow'd your sad steps.
    *Lear.*    You are welcome hither.
    *Kent.* Nor no man else:—all's cheerless,
    dark, and deadly.—
Your eldest daughters have foredone them-
    selves,
And desperately are dead.
    *Lear.*    Ay, so I think.
    *Alb.* He knows not what he says; and vain
    is it
That we present us to him.
    *Edg.*    Very bootless.

        *Enter an* Officer.

    *Off.* Edmund is dead, my lord.
    *Alb.*    That's but a trifle here.—
You lords and noble friends, know our in-
    tent.
What comfort to this great decay may come
Shall be applied: for us, we will resign,

During the life of this old majesty,
To him our absolute power:—you to your
    rights;    [*To* EDGAR *and* KENT.
With boot, and such addition as your hon-
    ours
Have more than merited.—All friends shall
    taste
The wages of their virtue, and all foes
The cup of their deservings.—O, see, see!
    *Lear.* And my poor fool is hang'd! No, no,
    no, life!
Why should a dog, a horse, a rat have life,
And thou no breath at all? Thou'lt come no
    more,
Never, never, never, never, never!—
Pray you, undo this button:—thank you,
    sir.—
Do you see this? Look on her, look,—her
    lips,—
Look there, look there!—    [*He dies.*
    *Edg.*    He faints!—My lord, my lord!—
    *Kent.* Break, heart; I pr'ythee, break!
    *Edg.*    Look up, my lord.
    *Kent.* Vex not his ghost: O, let him pass!
    he hates him
That would upon the rack of this rough
    world
Stretch him out longer.
    *Edg.*    He is gone indeed.
    *Kent.* The wonder is he hath endur'd so
    long:
He but usurp'd his life.    [ent business
    *Alb.* Bear them from hence.—Our pres-
Is general woe.—Friends of my soul, you
    twain    [*To* KENT *and* EDGAR.
Rule in this realm, and the gor'd state sus-
    tain.
    *Kent.* I have a journey, sir, shortly to go;
My master calls me,—I must not say no.
    *Alb.* The weight of this sad time we must
    obey;
Speak what we feel, not what we ought to
    say.
The oldest hath borne most: we that are
    young
Shall never see so much nor live so long.
        [*Exeunt, with a dead march.*

# ROMEO AND JULIET.

Act III. Sc. 5.

# ROMEO AND JULIET

## DRAMATIS PERSONÆ

ESCALUS, *Prince of Verona.*
PARIS, *a Young Nobleman, Kinsman to the Prince.*
MONTAGUE, } *Heads of two Houses at vari-*
CAPULET, } *ance with each other.*
An Old Man, *Uncle to* CAPULET.
ROMEO, *Son to* MONTAGUE.
MERCUTIO, *Kinsman to the Prince, and Friend to* ROMEO.
BENVOLIO, *Nephew to* MONTAGUE, *and Friend to* ROMEO.
TYBALT, *Nephew to* LADY CAPULET.
FRIAR LAWRENCE, *a Franciscan.*
FRIAR JOHN, *of the same Order.*
BALTHASAR, *Servant to* ROMEO.
SAMPSON, } *Servants to* CAPULET.
GREGORY, }

PETER, *Servant to* JULIET'S Nurse.
ABRAHAM, *Servant to* MONTAGUE.
An Apothecary.
Three Musicians.
Chorus.
Page *to* PARIS; *another* Page.
An Officer.

LADY MONTAGUE, *Wife to* MONTAGUE.
LADY CAPULET, *Wife to* CAPULET.
JULIET, *Daughter to* CAPULET.
Nurse *to* JULIET.

Citizens *of Verona; several* Men *and* Women, *relations to both Houses;* Maskers, Guards, Watchmen, *and* Attendants.

SCENE,—*During the greater part of the Play in* VERONA; *once, in the Fifth Act, at* MANTUA.

## PROLOGUE

Two households, both alike in dignity,
   In fair Verona, where we lay our scene,
From ancient grudge break to new mutiny,
   Where civil blood makes civil hands unclean.
From forth the fatal loins of these two foes
   A pair of star-cross'd lovers take their life;
Whose misadventùr'd piteous overthrows
   Do with their death bury their parents' strife.
The fearful passage of their death-mark'd love,
And the continuance of their parents' rage,
Which but their children's end naught could remove,
Is now the two hours' traffic of our stage;
The which, if you with patient ears attend,
What here shall miss our toil shall strive to mend.

## ACT I.

### SCENE I.—*A public Place.*

*Enter* SAMPSON *and* GREGORY, *armed with swords and bucklers.*

*Sam.* Gregory, o' my word, we'll not carry coals.

*Gre.* No, for then we should be colliers.

*Sam.* I mean, an we be in choler we'll draw.

*Gre.* Ay, while you live, draw your neck out o' the collar.

*Sam.* I strike quickly, being mcved.

*Gre.* But thou art not quickly moved to strike.

*Sam.* A dog of the house of Montague moves me.

*Gre.* To move is to stir; and to be valiant is to stand: therefore, if thou art moved, thou runn'st away.

*Sam.* A dog of that house shall move me to stand: I will take the wall of any man or maid of Montague's.

*Gre.* That shows thee a weak slave; for the weakest goes to the wall.

*Sam.* True; and therefore women, being the weaker vessels, are ever thrust to the wall: therefore I will push Montague's men from the wall and thrust his maids to the wall.

*Gre.* The quarrel is between our masters and us their men.

*Sam.* 'Tis all one, I will show myself a tyrant: when I have fought with the men I will be cruel with the maids, and cut off their heads.

*Gre.* The heads of the maids?

*Sam.* Ay, the heads of the maids, or their maidenheads; take it in what sense thou wilt.

*Gre.* They must take it in sense that feel it.

*Sam.* Me they shall feel while I am able to stand: and 'tis known I am a pretty piece of flesh.

*Gre.* 'Tis well thou art not fish; if thou hadst, thou hadst been poor-John.—Draw thy tool; here comes two of the house of the Montagues.

*Sam.* My naked weapon is out: quarrel, I will back thee.

*Gre.* How! turn thy back and run?

*Sam.* Fear me not.

*Gre.* No, marry; I fear thee!

*Sam.* Let us take the law of our sides; let them begin.

*Gre.* I will frown as I pass by; and let them take it as they list.

*Sam.* Nay, as they dare. I will bite my thumb at them; which is a disgrace to them if they bear it.

*Enter* ABRAHAM *and* BALTHASAR.

*Abr.* Do you bite your thumb at us, sir?

*Sam.* I do bite my thumb, sir.

*Abr.* Do you bite your thumb at us, sir?

*Sam.* Is the law of our side if I say ay?

*Gre.* No.

*Sam.* No, sir, I do not bite my thumb at you, sir; but I bite my thumb, sir.

*Gre.* Do you quarrel, sir?

*Abr.* Quarrel, sir! no, sir.

*Sam.* If you do, sir, I am for you: I serve as good a man as you.

*Abr.* No better.

*Sam.* Well, sir.

*Gre.* Say better: here comes one of my master's kinsmen.

*Sam.* Yes, better, sir.

*Abr.* You lie.

*Sam.* Draw, if you be men.—Gregory, remember thy swashing blow.    [*They fight.*

*Enter* BENVOLIO.

*Ben.* Part, fools! put up your swords; you know not what you do.

[*Beats down their swords.*

*Enter* TYBALT.

*Tyb.* What, art thou drawn among these heartless hinds?

Turn thee, Benvolio, look upon thy death.

*Ben.* I do but keep the peace: put up thy sword,

Or manage it to part these men with me.

*Tyb.* What, drawn, and talk of peace! I hate the word

As I hate hell, all Montagues, and thee:

Have at thee, coward!    [*They fight.*

*Enter several of both Houses, who join the. fray; then enter* Citizens *with clubs.*

1 *Cit.* Clubs, bills, and partisans! strike! beat them down!    [Montagues!

Down with the Capulets! Down with the

*Enter* CAPULET *in his gown, and* LADY CAPULET.

*Cap.* What noise is this?—Give me my long sword, ho!

*Lady C.* A crutch, a crutch!—Why call you for a sword?

*Cap.* My sword, I say!—Old Montague is come,

And flourishes his blade in spite of me.

*Enter* MONTAGUE *and* LADY MONTAGUE.

*Mon.* Thou villain Capulet!—Hold me not, let me go.

*Lady M.* Thou shalt not stir a foot to seek a foe.

*Enter* PRINCE, *with* Attendants.

*Prin.* Rebellious subjects, enemies to peace,

Profaners of this neighbour-stained steel,—

Will they not hear?—What, ho! you men, you beasts,

That quench the fire of your pernicious rage

With purple fountains issuing from your veins,—-

On pain of torture, from those bloody hands

Throw your mistemper'd weapons to the ground,

And hear the sentence of your moved prince.—

Three civil brawls, bred of an airy word,

By thee, old Capulet and Montague,

Have thrice disturb'd the quiet of our streets;

And made Verona's ancient citizens

Cast by their grave beseeming ornaments,

To wield old partisans in hands as old,

Canker'd with peace, to part your canker'd hate:

If ever you disturb our streets again,

Your lives shall pay the forfeit of the peace.

For this time, all the rest depart away:—

You, Capulet, shall go along with me;—

And, Montague, come you this afternoon,

To know our further pleasure in this case,

To old Free-town, our common judgment-place.—

Once more, on pain of death, all men depart.

[*Exeunt* PRIN. *and* Attendants; CAP., LADY C., TYB., Citizens, *and* Servants.

*Mon.* Who set this ancient quarrel new abroach?—

Speak, nephew, were you by when it began?

*Ben.* Here were the servants of your adversary

And yours close fighting ere I did approach:

I drew to part them: in the instant came

The fiery Tybalt, with his sword prepar'd;

Which, as he breath'd defiance to my ears,

He swung about his head, and cut the winds,

Who, nothing hurt withal, hiss'd him in scorn:

While we were interchanging thrusts and blows,

Came more and more, and fought on part and part,

Till the prince came, who parted either part.

*Lady. M.* O, where is Romeo?—saw you him to-day?—

Right glad I am he was not at this fray.

*Ben.* Madam, an hour before the worshipp'd sun

Peer'd forth the golden window of the east,

A troubled mind drave me to walk abroad;

Where,—underneath the grove of sycamore

That westward rooteth from the city's side,—
So early walking did I see your son:
Towards him I made, but he was ware of me,
And stole into the covert of the wood:
I, measuring his affections by my own,—
That most are busied when they're most
　　alone,—
Pursu'd my humour, not pursuing his,
And gladly shunn'd who gladly fled from me.
　　*Mon.* Many a morning hath he there been
　　　seen,
With tears augmenting the fresh morning's
　　dew,
Adding to clouds more clouds with his deep
　　sighs:
But all so soon as the all-cheering sun
Should in the furthest east begin to. draw
The shady curtains from Aurora's bed,
Away from light steals home my heavy son,
And private in his chamber pens himself;
Shuts up his windows, locks fair daylight out,
And makes himself an artificial night:
Black and portentous must this humour
　　prove,
Unless good counsel may the cause remove.
　　*Ben.* My noble uncle, do you know the
　　　cause?
　　*Mon.* I neither know it nor can learn of
　　　him.
　　*Ben.* Have you importun'd him by any
　　　means?
　　*Mon.* Both by myself and many other
　　　friends:
But he, his own affections' counsellor,
Is to himself,—I will not say how true,—
But to himself so secret and so close,
So far from sounding and discovery,
As is the bud bit with an envious worm
Ere he can spread his sweet leaves to the air,
Or dedicate his beauty to the sun.
Could we but learn from whence his sorrows
　　grow,
We would as willingly give cure as know.
　　*Ben.* See where he comes: so please you,
　　　step aside;
I'll know his grievance or be much denied.
　　*Mon.* I would thou wert so happy by thy
　　　stay
To hear true shift.—Come, madam, let's away.
　　　　　　[*Exeunt* MONTAGUE *and* Lady.

*Enter* ROMEO.

　　*Ben.* Good-morrow, cousin.
　　*Rom.*　　　　　Is the day so young?
　　*Ben.* But new struck nine.
　　*Rom.*　　　　　Ay me! sad hours seem long.
Was that my father that went hence so fast?
　　*Ben.* It was.—What sadness lengthens
　　　Romeo's hours?　[makes them short.
　　*Rom.* Not having that which, having,
　　*Ben.* In love?
　　*Rom.* Out,—
　　*Ben.* Of love?
　　*Rom.* Out of her favour where I am in love.

　　*Ben.* Alas, that love, so gentle in his view,
Should be so tyrannous and rough in proof!
　　*Rom.* Alas, that love, whose view is
　　　muffled still,　　　　　　[will!—
Should, without eyes, see pathways to his
Where shall we dine?—O me!—What fray
　　was here?
Yet tell me not, for I have heard it all.
Here's much to do with hate, but more with
　　love:—
Why, then, O brawling love! O loving hate!
O anything, of nothing first create!
O heavy lightness! serious vanity!
Mis-shapen chaos of well-seeming forms!
Feather of lead, bright smoke, cold fire, sick
　　health!
Still-waking sleep, that is not what it is!—
This love feel I, that feel no love in this.
Does thou not laugh?
　　*Ben.*　　　　　No, coz, I rather weep.
　　*Rom.* Good heart, at what?
　　*Ben.*　　　　　At thy good heart's oppression.
　　*Rom.* Why, such is love's transgression.—
Griefs of mine own lie heavy in my breast;
Which thou wilt propagate, to have it prest
With more of thine: this love that thou hast
　　shown　　　　　　　　　　[own.
Doth add more grief to too much of mine
Love is a smoke rais'd with the fume of sighs;
Being purg'd, a fire sparkling in lovers' eyes;
Being vex'd, a sea nourish'd with lovers' tears:
What is it else? a madness most discreet,
A choking gall, and a preserving sweet.—
Farewell, my coz.　　　　　　[*Going.*
　　*Ben.*　　　　　Soft! I will go along:
An if you leave me so, you do me wrong.
　　*Rom.* Tut, I have lost myself; I am not
　　　here;
This is not Romeo, he's some other where.
　　*Ben.* Tell me in sadness who is that you
　　　love.
　　*Rom.* What, shall I groan and tell thee?
　　*Ben.*　　　　　Groan! why, no;
But sadly tell me who.　　　　　[will,—
　　*Rom.* Bid a sick man in sadness make his
Ah, word ill urg'd to one that is so ill!—
In sadness, cousin, I do love a woman.
　　*Ben.* I aim'd so near when I suppos'd you
　　　lov'd.　　　　　　　[fair I love.
　　*Rom.* A right good marksman!—And she's
　　*Ben.* A right fair mark, fair coz, is soonest
　　　hit.
　　*Rom.* Well, in that hit you miss: she'll
　　　not be hit
With Cupid's arrow,—she hath Dian's wit;
And in strong proof of chastity well arm'd,
From love's weak childish bow she lives un-
　　harm'd.
She will not stay the siege of loving terms
Nor bide the encounter of assailing eyes,
Nor ope her lap to saint-seducing gold:
O, she is rich in beauty; only poor,
That, when she dies, with beauty dies her
　　store.

*Ben.* Then she hath sworn that she will still
live chaste?                               [huge waste;
*Rom.* She hath, and in that sparing makes
For beauty, starv'd with her severity,
Cuts beauty off from all posterity.
She is too fair, too wise; wisely too fair,
To merit bliss by making me despair:
She hath forsworn to love; and in that vow
Do I live dead that live to tell it now.
*Ben.* Be rul'd by me, forget to think of her.
*Rom.* O, teach me how I should forget to
think.
*Ben.* By giving liberty unto thine eyes;
Examine other beauties.
*Rom.*                      'Tis the way
To call hers, exquisite, in question more:
These happy masks that kiss fair ladies'
brows,
Being black, put us in mind they hide the fair;
He that is strucken blind cannot forget
The precious treasure of his eyesight lost:
Show me a mistress that is passing fair,
What doth her beauty serve but as a note
Where I may read who pass'd that passing
fair?
Farewell: thou canst not teach me to forget.
*Ben.* I'll pay that doctrine or else die in
debt.                                      [*Exeunt.*

SCENE II.—*A Street.*

*Enter* CAPULET, PARIS, *and* Servant.

*Cap.* But Montague is bound as well as I,
In penalty alike; and 'tis not hard, I think,
For men so old as we to keep the peace.
*Par.* Of honourable reckoning are you
both;
And pity 'tis you liv'd at odds so long.
But now, my lord, what say you to my suit?
*Cap.* But saying o'er what I have said
before:
My child is yet a stranger in the world,
She hath not seen the change of fourteen
years;
Let two more summers wither in their pride
Ere we may think her ripe to be a bride.
*Par.* Younger than she are happy mothers
made.                                    [early made.
*Cap.* And too soon marr'd are those so
Earth hath swallow'd all my hopes but she,—
She is the hopeful lady of my earth:
But woo her, gentle Paris, get her heart,
My will to her consent is but a part;
An she agree, within her scope of choice
Lies my consent and fair according voice.
This night I hold an old accustom'd feast,
Whereto I have invited many a guest,
Such as I love; and you, among the store,
One more, most welcome, makes my number
more.
At my poor house look to behold this night
Earth-treading stars that make dark heaven
light:
Such comfort as do lusty young men feel
When well-apparell'd April on the heel

Of limping winter treads, even such delight
Among fresh female buds shall you this night
Inherit at my house; hear all, all see,
And like her most whose merit most shall be:
Such, amongst view of many, mine being one,
May stand in number, though in reckoning
none.
Come, go with me.—Go, sirrah, trudge about
Through fair Verona; find those persons out
Whose names are written there [*gives a
paper*], and to them say,
My house and welcome on their pleasure stay.
[*Exeunt* CAPULET *and* PARIS.
*Serv.* Find them out whose names are writ-
ten here! It is written that the shoemaker
should meddle with his yard, and the tailor
with his last, the fisher with his pencil, and
the painter with his nets; but I am sent to
find those persons whose names are here writ,
and can never find what names the writing
person hath here writ. I must to the learned:
—in good time.

*Enter* BENVOLIO *and* ROMEO.

*Ben.* Tut, man, one fire burns out another's
burning,
One pain is is lessen'd by another's anguish,
Turn giddy, and be holp by backward
turning;                                  [languish:
One desperate grief cures with another's
Take thou some new infection to thy eye,
And the rank poison of the old will die.
*Rom.* Your plantain-leaf is excellent for
that.
*Ben.* For what, I pray thee?
*Rom.*                    For your broken shin.
*Ben.* Why, Romeo, art thou mad?
*Rom.* Not mad, but bound more than a
madman is;
Shut up in prison, kept without my food,
Whipp'd and tormented, and—God-den, good
fellow.                                     [read?
*Serv.* God gi' god-den.—I pray, sir, can you
*Rom.* Ay, mine own fortune in my misery.
*Serv.* Perhaps you have learned it without
book: but, I pray, can you read anything you
see?                                      [language.
*Rom.* Ay, if I know the letters and the
*Serv.* Ye say honestly: rest you merry!
*Rom.* Stay, fellow; I can read.       [*Reads.*
*Signior Martino and his wife and daugh-
ters; County Anselme and his beauteous sis-
ters; the lady widow of Vitruvio; Signior
Placentio and his lovely nieces; Mercutio
and his brother Valentine; mine uncle Capu-
let, his wife and daughters; my fair niece
Rosaline; Livia; Signior Valentio and his
cousin Tybalt; Lucio and the lively Helena.*
A fair assembly [*gives back the paper*]:
whither should they come?
*Serv.* Up:
*Rom.* Whither?
*Serv.* To supper; to our house.
*Rom.* Whose house?

*Serv.* My master's.                          [*before.*
*Rom.* Indeed, I should have ask'd you that
*Serv.* Now I'll tell you without asking: my
master is the great rich Capulet; and if you
be not of the house of Montagues, I pray,
come and crush a cup of wine. Rest you
merry!                                      [*Exit.*
*Ben.* At this same ancient feast of
    Capulet's
Sups the fair Rosaline whom thou so lov'st;
With all the admired beauties of Verona:
Go thither; and, with unattainted eye,
Compare her face with some that I shall show,
And I will make thee think thy swan a crow.
*Rom.* When the devout religion of mine
    eye
Maintains such falsehood, then turn tears to
    fires;                                    [*die,—*
And these,—who, often drown'd, could never
    Transparent heretics, be burnt for liars!
One fairer than my love! the all-seeing sun
Ne'er saw her match since first the world
    begun.                               [*ing by,*
*Ben.* Tut, you saw her fair, none else be-
Herself pois'd with herself in either eye:
But in that crystal scales let there be weigh'd
Your lady's love against some other maid
That I will show you shining at this feast,
And she shall scant show well that now shows
    best.                                 [*shown,*
*Rom.* I'll go along, no such sight to be
But to rejoice in splendour of mine own.
                                          [*Exeunt.*

SCENE III.—*A Room in* CAPULET'S *House.*

*Enter* LADY CAPULET *and* Nurse.

*Lady* C. Nurse, where's my daughter? call
    her forth to me.
*Nurse.* Now, by my maidenhead,—at
    twelve year old,—                       [*bird!—*
I bade her come.—What, lamb! what, lady-
God forbid! — where's this girl? — what,
    Juliet!

*Enter* JULIET.

*Jul.* How now, who calls?
*Nurse.*                    Your mother.
*Jul.*                      Madam, I am here.
What is your will?
*Lady* C. This is the matter,—Nurse, give
    leave awhile,                          [*again;*
We must talk in secret:—nurse, come back
I have remember'd me, thou's hear our coun-
    sel.
Thou know'st my daughter's of a pretty age.
*Nurse.* Faith, I can tell her age unto an
    hour.
*Lady* C. She's not fourteen.
*Nurse.*       I'll lay fourteen of my teeth,—
And yet, to my teen be it spoken, I have but
    four,—
She is not fourteen. How long is it now
To Lammas-tide?
*Lady* C.            A fortnight and odd days.

*Nurse.* Even or odd, of all days in the year,
Come Lammas-eve at night shall she be
    fourteen.
Susan and she,—God rest all Christian
    souls!—
Were of an age: well, Susan is with God;
She was too good for me:—but, as I said,
On Lammas-eve at night shall she be
    fourteen;
That shall she, marry; I remember it well.
'Tis since the earthquake now eleven years;
And she was wean'd,—I never shall forget
    it,—
Of all the days of the year, upon that day:
For I had then laid wormwood to my dug,
Sitting in the sun under the dove-house wall;
My lord and you were then at Mantua:
Nay, I do bear a brain:—but, as I said,
When it did taste the wormwood on the
    nipple
Of my dug, and felt it bitter, pretty fool,
To see it tetchy, and fall out with the dug!
Shake, quoth the dove-house: 'twas no need,
    I trow,
To bid me trudge.
And since that time it is eleven years;
For then she could stand alone; nay, by the
    rood
She could have run and waddled all about;
For even the day before, she broke her brow:
And then my husband,—God be with his
    soul!
'A was a merry man,—took up the child:
*Yea, quoth he, dost thou fall upon thy face?*
*Thou wilt fall backward when thou hast more*
    *wit;*
*Wilt thou not, Jule?* and, by my holidame,
The pretty wretch left crying, and said *Ay:*
To see, now, how a jest shall come about!
I warrant, an I should live a thousand years,
I never should forget it: *Wilt thou not, Jule?*
    quoth he;
And, pretty fool, it stinted, and said *Ay.*
*Lady* C. Enough of this; I pray thee, hold
    thy peace.                           [*but laugh,*
*Nurse.* Yes, madam;—yet I cannot choose
To think it should leave crying, and say *Ay:*
And yet, I warrant, it had upon its brow
A bump as big as a young cockerel's stone;
A parlous knock; and it cried bitterly.
*Yea,* quoth my husband, *fall'st upon thy face?*
*Thou wilt fall backward when thou com'st to*
    *age;*
*Wilt thou not, Jule?* it stinted, and said *Ay.*
*Jul.* And stint thou too, I pray thee, nurse,
    say I.                              [*to his grace!*
*Nurse.* Peace, I have done. God mark thee
Thou wast the prettiest babe that e'er I
    nurs'd:
An I might live to see thee married once,
I have my wish.                          [*theme*
*Lady* C. Marry, that marry is the very
I came to talk of.—Tell me, daughter Juliet,
How stands your disposition to be married?

*Jul.* It is an honour that I dream not of.

*Nurse.* An honour! were not I thine only nurse,    [thy teat.

I would say thou hadst suck'd wisdom from

*Lady C.* Well, think of marriage now; younger than you,

Here in Verona, ladies of esteem,

Are made already mothers: by my count

I was your mother much upon these years

That you are now a maid. Thus, then, in brief;—

The valiant Paris seeks you for his love.

*Nurse.* A man, young lady! lady, such a man

As all the world—why, he's a man of wax.

*Lady C.* Verona's summer hath not such a flower.

*Nurse.* Nay, he's a flower; in faith, a very flower.    [gentleman?

*Lady C.* What say you? can you love the

This night you shall behold him at our feast;

Read o'er the volume of young Paris' face,

And find delight writ there with beauty's pen;

Examine every married lineament,

And see how one another lends content;

And what obscur'd in this fair volume lies

Find written in the margent of his eyes.

This precious book of love, this unbound lover

To beautify him, only lacks a cover:

The fish lives in the sea; and 'tis much pride

For fair without the fair within to hide:

That book in many's eyes doth share the glory    [story;

That in gold clasps locks in the golden

So shall you share all that he doth possess,

By having him, making yourself no less.

*Nurse.* No less! nay, bigger; women grow by men.    [Paris' love?

*Lady O.* Speak briefly, can you like of

*Jul.* I'll look to like, if looking liking move:

But no more deep will I endart mine eye [fly.

Than your consent gives strength to make it

### Enter a Servant.

*Serv.* Madam, the guests are come, supper served up, you called, my young lady asked for, the nurse cursed in the pantry, and everything in extremity. I must hence to wait; I beseech you, follow straight.

*Lady C.* We follow thee. [*Exit* Servant.]— Juliet, the county stays.

*Nurse.* Go, girl, seek happy nights to happy days.    [*Exeunt.*

### Scene IV.—*A Street.*

*Enter* Romeo, Mercutio, Benvolio, *with five or six* Maskers, Torch-bearers, *and others.*

*Rom.* What, shall this speech be spoke for our excuse?

Or shall we on without apology?

*Ben.* The date is out of such prolixity:

We'll have no Cupid hoodwink'd with a scarf,

Bearing a Tartar's painted bow of lath,

Scaring the ladies like a crow-keeper;

Nor no without-book prologue, faintly spoke

After the prompter, for our entrance:

But, let them measure us by what they will,

We'll measure them a measure, and be gone.

*Rom.* Give me a torch,—I am not for this ambling;

Being but heavy, I will bear the light.

*Mer.* Nay, gentle Romeo, we must have you dance.

*Rom.* Not I, believe me: you have dancing shoes,

With nimble soles: I have a soul of lead

So stakes me to the ground I cannot move.

*Mer.* You are a lover; borrow Cupid's wings,

And soar with them above a common bound.

*Rom.* I am too sore enpierced with his shaft

To soar with his light feathers; and so bound,

I cannot bound a pitch above dull woe:

Under love's heavy burden do I sink. [love;

*Mer.* And to sink in it should you burden

Too great oppression for a tender thing.

*Rom.* Is love a tender thing? it is too rough,

Too rude, too boisterous; and it pricks like thorn.

*Mer.* If love be rough with you, be rough with love;

Prick love for pricking, and you beat love down.—

Give me a case to put my visage in:

[*Putting on a mask.*

A visard for a visard!—what care I

What curious eye doth quote deformities?

Here are the beetle-brows shall blush for me.

*Ben.* Come, knock and enter; and no sooner in

But every man betake him to his legs.

*Rom.* A torch for me: let wantons, light of heart,

Tickle the senseless rushes with their heels;

For I am proverb'd with a grandsire phrase,—

I'll be a candle-holder, and look on,—

The game was ne'er so fair, and I am done.

*Mer.* Tut, dun's the mouse, the constable's own word:    [mire

If thou art dun, we'll draw thee from the

Of this—sir-reverence—love, wherein thou stick'st

Up to the ears.—Come, we burn daylight, ho.

*Rom.* Nay, that's not so.

*Mer.*                    I mean, sir, in delay

We waste our lights in vain, like lamps by day.

Take our good meaning, for our judgment sits

Five times in that ere once in our five wits.

*Rom.* And we mean well in going to this mask;

But 'tis no wit to go.

*Mer.*                    Why, may one ask?

*Rom.* I dreamt a dream to-night.

*Mer.*                          And so did I.
*Rom.* Well, what was yours?
*Mer.*                    That dreamers often lie.
*Rom.* In bed asleep, while they do dream
    things true.                    [with you.
*Mer.* O, then, I see Queen Mab hath been
She is the fairies' midwife; and she comes
In shape no bigger than an agate-stone
On the fore-finger of an alderman,
Drawn with a team of little atomies
Athwart men's noses as they lie asleep:
Her waggon-spokes made of long spinners'
    legs;
The cover, of the wings of grasshoppers;
The traces, of the smallest spider's web;
The collars, of the moonshine's watery beams;
Her whip, of cricket's bone; the lash, of film;
Her waggoner, a small gray-coated gnat,
Not half so big as a round little worm
Prick'd from the lazy finger of a maid:
Her chariot is an empty hazel-nut,
Made by the joiner squirrel or old grub,
Time out o' mind the fairies' coachmakers.
And in this state she gallops night by night
Through lovers' brains, and then they dream
    of love;
O'er courtiers' knees, that dream on court'sies
    straight;
O'er lawyers' fingers, who straight dream on
    fees;                          [dream,—
O'er ladies' lips, who straight on kisses
Which oft the angry Mab with blisters
    plagues,                    [ed are:
Because their breaths with sweetmeats taint-
Sometimes she gallops o'er a courtier's nose,
And then dreams he of smelling out a suit;
And sometimes comes she with a tithe-pig's
    tail,
Tickling a parson's nose as 'a lies asleep,
Then dreams he of another benefice:
Sometimes she driveth o'er a soldier's neck,
And then dreams he of cutting foreign
    throats,
Of breaches, ambuscadoes, Spanish blades,
Of healths five fathom deep; and then anon
Drums in his ear, at which he starts and
    wakes;                          [two,
And, being thus frighted, swears a prayer or
And sleeps again. This is that very Mab
That plats the manes of horses in the night;
And bakes the elf-locks in foul sluttish hairs,
Which, once untangled, much misfortune
    bodes:                          [backs,
This is the hag, when maids lie on their
That presses them, and learns them first to
    bear,
Making them women of good carriage:
This is she,—
    *Rom.*          Peace, peace, Mercutio, peace,
Thou talk'st of nothing.
    *Mer.*                  True, I talk of dreams,
Which are the children of an idle brain,
Begot of nothing but vain fantasy;
Which is as thin of substance as the air,

And more inconstant than the wind, who
    wooes
Even now the frozen bosom of the north,
And, being anger'd, puffs away from thence,
Turning his face to the dew-dropping south.
  *Ben.* This wind you talk of blows us from
    ourselves:
Supper is done, and we shall come too late.
  *Rom.* I fear, too early: for my mind mis-
    gives
Some consequence, yet hanging in the stars,
Shall bitterly begin his fearful date
With this night's revels; and expire the term
Of a despised life, clos'd in my breast,
By some vile forfeit of untimely death:
But He that hath the steerage of my course
Direct my sail!—On, lusty gentlemen.
  *Ben.* Strike, drum.                    [*Exeunt.*

SCENE V.—*A Hall in* CAPULET'S *House.*

    *Musicians waiting. Enter* Servants.

  1 *Serv.* Where's Potpan, that he helps not
to take away? he shift a trencher! he scrape a
trencher!
  2 *Serv.* When good manners shall lie all in
one or two men's hands, and they unwashed
too, 'tis a foul thing.
  1 *Serv.* Away with the joint-stools, remove
the court-cupboard, look to the plate:—good
thou, save me a piece of marchpane; and as
thou lovest me let the porter let in Susan
Grindstone and Nell.—Antony! and Potpan!
  2 *Serv.* Ay, boy, ready.
  1 *Serv.* You are looked for and called for,
asked for and sought for in the great chamber.
  2 *Serv.* We cannot be here and there too.—
Cheerly, boys; be brisk awhile, and the longer
liver take all.                    [*They retire behind.*

*Enter* CAPULET, *&c., with the* Guests *and
    the* Maskers.

  *Cap.* Welcome, gentlemen! ladies that have
    their toes                    [you.—
Unplagu'd with corns will have a bout with
Ah ha, my mistresses! which of you all
Will now deny to dance? she that makes
    dainty, she,                    [now?
I'll swear hath corns; am I come near you
Welcome, gentlemen! I have seen the day
That I have worn a visard; and could tell
A whispering tale in a fair lady's ear,
Such as would please;—'tis gone, 'tis gone,
    'tis gone:                    [cians, play.—
You are welcome, gentlemen!—Come, musi-
A hall,—a hall! give room, and foot it, girls.—
        [*Music plays, and they dance.*
More light, you knaves; and turn the tables
    up,                          [hot.—
And quench the fire, the room is grown too
Ah, sirrah, this unlook'd-for sport comes well.
Nay, sit, nay, sit, good cousin Capulet;
For you and I are past our dancing days:

How long is't now since last yourself and I
Were in a mask?

2 *Cap.* By-r Lady, thirty years.

*Cap.* What, man! 'tis not so much, 'tis not
so much:

'Tis since the nuptial of Lucentio,
Come Pentecost as quickly as it will,
Some five-and-twenty years; and then we
mask'd. [sir;

2 *Cap.* 'Tis more, 'tis more: his son is elder,
His son is thirty.

*Cap.* Will you tell me that?
His son was but a ward two years ago.

*Rom.* What lady is that which doth enrich
the hand
Of yonder knight?

*Serv.* I know not, sir.

*Rom.* O, she doth teach the torches to
burn bright!

It seems she hangs upon the cheek of night
Like a rich jewel in an Ethiop's ear;
Beauty too rich for use, for earth too dear!
So shows a snowy dove trooping with crows
As yonder lady o'er her fellows shows.
The measure done, I'll watch her place of
stand, [hand.
And, touching hers, make blessed my rude
Did my heart love till now? forswear it,
sight!
For I ne'er saw true beauty till this night.

*Tyb.* This, by his voice, should be a Mon-
tague.— [slave
Fetch me my rapier, boy:—what, dares the
Come hither, cover'd with an antic face,
To fleer and scorn at our solemnity?
Now, by the stock and honour of my kin,
To strike him dead I hold it not a sin.

*Cap.* Why, how now, kinsman! wherefore
storm you so?

*Tyb.* Uncle, this is a Montague, our foe;
A villain, that is hither come in spite,
To scorn at our solemnity this night.

*Cap.* Young Romeo, is it?

*Tyb.* 'Tis he, that villain, Romeo.

*Cap.* Content thee, gentle coz, let him
alone,
He bears him like a portly gentleman;
And, to say truth, Verona brags of him
To be a virtuous and well-govern'd youth:
I would not for the wealth of all the town
Here in my house do him disparagement:
Therefore be patient, take no note of him,—
It is my will; the which if thou respect,
Show a fair presence and put off these frowns,
An ill-beseeming semblance for a feast.

*Tyb.* It fits, when such a villain is a guest:
I'll not endure him.

*Cap.* He shall be endur'd: [to;
What, goodman, boy!—I say he shall;—go
Am I the master here or you? go to. [soul,
You'll not endure him!—God shall mend my
You'll make a mutiny among my guests!
You will set cock-a-hoop! you'll be the man!

*Tyb.* Why, uncle, 'tis a shame.

*Cap.* Go to, go to;
You are a saucy boy. Is't so, indeed?—
This trick may chance to scath you,—I know
what:
You must contrary me! marry, 'tis time.—
Well said, my hearts!—You are a princox;
go:
Be quiet, or—More light, more light!—For
shame! [hearts.
I'll make you quiet.—What,—cheerly, my

*Tyb.* Patience perforce with wilful choler
meeting
Makes my flesh tremble in their different
greeting.
I will withdraw: but this intrusion shall,
Now seeming sweet, convert to bitter gall.
[*Exit.*

*Rom.* If I profane with my unworthiest
hand [*To* JULIET.
This holy shrine, the gentle fine is this,—
My lips, two blushing pilgrims, ready stand
To smooth that rough touch with a tender
kiss.

*Jul.* Good pilgrim, you do wrong, your
hand too much,
Which mannerly devotion shows in this;
For saints have hands that pilgrims' hands
do touch,
And palm to palm is holy palmers' kiss.

*Rom.* Have not saints lips, and holy palmers too? [in prayer.

*Jul.* Ay, pilgrim, lips that they must use

*Rom.* O, then, dear saint, let lips do what
hands do; [despair.
They pray, grant thou, lest faith turn to

*Jul.* Saints do not move, though grant for
prayers' sake. [effect I take.

*Rom.* Then move not while my prayer's
Thus from my lips, by yours, my sin is purg'd.
[*Kissing her.*

*Jul.* Then have my lips the sin that they
have took. [urg'd!

*Rom.* Sin from my lips? O trespass sweetly
Give me my sin again.

*Jul.* You kiss by the book.

*Nurse.* Madam, your mother craves a word
with you.

*Rom.* What is her mother?

*Nurse.* Marry, bachelor,
Her mother is the lady of the house,
And a good lady, and a wise and virtuous;
I nurs'd her daughter that you talk'd withal;
I tell you, he that can lay hold of her
Shall have the chinks.

*Rom.* Is she a Capulet?
O dear account! my life is my foe's debt.

*Ben.* Away, be gone; the sport is at the
best.

*Rom.* Ay, so I fear; the more is my unrest.

*Cap.* Nay, gentlemen, prepare not to be
gone;
We have a trifling foolish banquet towards.—
Is it e'en so? why, then I thank you all;
I thank you, honest gentlemen; good-night.—

More torches here!—Come on, then let's to
　　bed.　　　　　　　　　　　　　　[late:
Ah, sirrah [to 2 *Cap.*], by my fay, it waxes
I'll to my rest.
　　　　　[*Exeunt all but* JULIET *and* Nurse.
*Jul.* Come hither, nurse. What is yon
　　gentleman?
*Nurse.* The son and heir of old Tiberio.
*Jul.* What's he that now is going out of
　　door?　　　　　　　　　　　　　[truchio.
*Nurse.* Marry, that I think be young Pe-
*Jul.* What's he 'that follows there, that
　　would not dance?
*Nurse.* I know not.
*Jul.* Go, ask his name: if he be married,
My grave is like to be my wedding-bed.
*Nurse.* His name is Romeo, and a Mon-
　　tague;
The only son of your great enemy.　[hate!
*Jul.* My only love sprung from my only
Too early seen unknown, and known too late!
Prodigious birth of love it is to me,
That I must love a loathed enemy.
*Nurse.* What's this? What's this?
*Jul.*　　　　　　A rhyme I learn'd even now
Of one I danc'd withal.
　　　　　[*One calls within,* "Juliet."
*Nurse.*　　　　　　　　Anon, anon!
Come, let's away; the strangers are all gone.
　　　　　　　　　　　　　　　　[*Exeunt.*

*Enter* Chorus.

Now old desire doth in his death-bed lie,
　　And young affection gapes to be his heir;
That fair for which love groan'd for, and
　　would die,
　　With tender Juliet match'd, is now not fair.
Now Romeo is belov'd, and loves again,
　　Alike bewitched by the charm of looks,
But to his foe suppos'd he must complain,
　　And she steal love's sweet bait from fearful
　　　　hooks:
Being held a foe, he may not have access
　　To breathe such vows as lovers us'd to
　　　　swear;
And she as much in love, her means much less
　　To meet her new-beloved anywhere: [meet,
But passion lends them power, time means to
Tempering extremities with extreme sweet.
　　　　　　　　　　　　　　　　[*Exit.*

## ACT II.

SCENE I.—*An open place adjoining* CAPULET'S
　　　　　　　　　Garden.

*Enter* ROMEO.

*Rom.* Can I go forward when my heart is
　　here?
Turn back, dull earth, and find thy center out.
　　　　　[*He climbs the wall and leaps down
　　　　　　　　　within it.*

*Enter* BENVOLIO *and* MERCUTIO.

*Ben.* Romeo! my cousin Romeo!

*Mer.*　　　　　　　　　　　He is wise;
And, on my life, hath stol'n him home to bed.
　*Ben.* He ran this way, and leap'd this
　　orchard wall:
Call, good Mercutio.
　*Mer.*　　　　　　Nay, I'll conjure too.—
Romeo! humours! madman! passion! lover!
Appear thou in the likeness of a sigh:
Speak but one rhyme and I am satisfied;
Cry but, Ah me! pronounce but Love and
　　dove;
Speak to my gossip Venus one fair word,
One nickname for her purblind son and heir,
Young auburn Cupid, he that shot so trim
When King Cophetua lov'd the beggar-
　　maid!—　　　　　　　　　　　　[not;
He heareth not, he stirreth not. he moveth
The ape is dead, and I must conjure him.—
I conjure thee by Rosaline's bright eyes,
By her high forehead and her scarlet lip,
By her fine foot, straight leg, and quivering
　　thigh,
And the demesnes that there adjacent lie,
That in thy likeness thou appear to us!
　*Ben.* An if he hear thee, thou wilt anger
　　him.　　　　　　　　　　　　[anger him
　*Mer.* This cannot anger him: 'twould
To raise a spirit in his mistress' circle,
Of some strange nature, letting it there stand
Till she had laid it, and conjur'd it down;
That were some spite: my invocation
Is fair and honest, and, in his mistress' name,
I conjure only but to raise up him.
　*Ben.* Come, he hath hid himself among
　　these trees.
To be consorted with the humorous night:
Blind is his love, and best befits the dark.
　*Mer.* If love be blind, love cannot hit the
　　mark.
Now will he sit under a medlar tree,
And wish his mistress were that kind of fruit
As maids call medlars when they laugh
　　alone.—
Romeo, good-night.—I'll to my truckle-bed;
This field-bed is too cold for me to sleep:
Come, shall we go?
　*Ben.*　　　　　Go, then; for 'tis in vain
To seek him here that means not to be found.
　　　　　　　　　　　　　　　　[*Exeunt.*

SCENE II.—CAPULET'S *Garden.*

*Enter* ROMEO.

*Rom.* He jests at scars that never felt a
　　wound.—
　　　　　[JULIET *appears above at a window.*
But, soft! what light through yonder window
　　breaks?
It is the east, and Juliet is the sun!—
Arise, fair sun, and kill the envious moon,
Who is already sick and pale with grief,
That thou her maid art far more fair than
　　she:
Be not her maid, since she is envious;
Her vestal livery is but sick and green,

And none but fools do wear it; cast it off.—
It is my lady; O, it is my love!
O, that she knew she were!—          [that?
She speaks, yet she says nothing: what of
Her eye discourses, I will answer it.—
I am too bold, 'tis not to me she speaks:
Two of the fairest stars in all the heaven,
Having some business, do entreat her eyes
To twinkle in their spheres till they return.
What if her eyes were there, they in her head?
The brightness of her cheek would shame
          those stars,
As daylight doth a lamp; her eyes in heaven
Would through the airy region stream so
          bright          [not night.—
That birds would sing, and think it were
See how she leans her cheek upon her hand!
O, that I were a glove upon that hand,
That I might touch that cheek!

     *Jul.*                         Ah me!
     *Rom.*                         She speaks:—
O, speak again, bright angel! for thou art
As glorious to this night, being o'er my head,
As is a winged messenger of heaven
Unto the white-upturned wondering eyes
Of mortals that fall back to gaze on him
When he bestrides the lazy-pacing clouds
And sails upon the bosom of the air.
     *Jul.* O Romeo, Romeo! wherefore art thou
          Romeo?
Deny thy father and refuse thy name;
Or, if thou wilt not, be but sworn my love,
And I'll no longer be a Capulet.
     *Rom.* [*Aside.*] Shall I hear more, or shall
          I speak at this?
     *Jul.* 'Tis but thy name that is my enemy;—
Thou art thyself though, not a Montague.
What's Montague? It is nor hand, nor foot,
Nor arm, nor face, nor any other part
Belonging to a man. O, be some other name!
What's in a name? that which we call a rose,
By any other name would smell as sweet;
So Romeo would, were he not Romeo call'd,
Retain that dear perfection which he owes
Without that title:—Romeo, doff thy name;
And for that name, which is no part of thee,
Take all myself.
     *Rom.*          I take thee at thy word:
Call me but love, and I'll be new baptiz'd;
Henceforth I never will be Romeo.
     *Jul.* What man art thou, that, thus be-
          screen'd in night,
So stumblest on my counsel?
     *Rom.*               By a name
I know not how to tell thee who I am:
My name, dear saint, is hateful to myself,
Because it is an enemy to thee;
Had I it written, I would tear the word.
     *Jul.* My ears have not yet drunk a hun-
          dred words          [sound;
Of that tongue's utterance, yet I know the
Art thou not Romeo, and a Montague?
     *Rom.* Neither, fair saint, if either thee dis-
          like.

     *Jul.* How cam'st thou hither, tell me,
          and wherefore?
The orchard walls are high and hard to climb;
And the place death, considering who thou
          art,
If any of my kinsmen find thee here.
     *Rom.* With love's light wings did I o'er-
          perch these walls;
For stony limits cannot hold love out:
And what love can do, that dares love at-
          tempt;
Therefore thy kinsmen are no let to me.
     *Jul.* If they do see thee they will murder
          thee.          [eye
     *Rom.* Alack, there lies more peril in thine
Than twenty of their swords: look thou but
          sweet,
And I am proof against their enmity.
     *Jul.* I would not for the world they saw
          thee here.          [their sight;
     *Rom.* I have night's cloak to hide me from
And, but thou love me, let them find me here:
My life were better ended by their hate
Than death prorogued wanting of thy love.
     *Jul.* By whose direction found'st thou out
          this place?          [inquire;
     *Rom.* By love, who first did prompt me to
He lent me counsel, and I lent him eyes.
I am no pilot; yet, wert thou as far
As that vast shore wash'd with the furthest
          sea,
I would adventure for such merchandise.
     *Jul.* Thou know'st the mask of night is on
          my face,          [cheek
Else would a maiden blush bepaint my
For that which thou hast heard me speak to-
          night.
Fain would I dwell on form, fain, fain deny
What I have spoke: but farewell compli-
          ment!          [Ay,
Dost thou love me? I know thou wilt say
And I will take thy word: yet, if thou
          swear'st,
Thou mayst prove false; at lovers' perjuries
They say Jove laughs. O gentle Romeo,
If thou dost love, pronounce it faithfully:
Or, if thou think'st I am too quickly won,
I'll frown, and be perverse, and say thee nay,
So thou wilt woo; but else, not for the world.
In truth, fair Montague, I am too fond;
And therefore thou mayst think my 'haviour
          light:
But trust me, gentleman, I'll prove more true
Than those that have more cunning to be
          strange.
I should have been more strange, I must con-
          fess,
But that thou over-heard'st, ere I was 'ware,
My true love's passion: therefore pardon me;
And not impute this yielding to light love,
Which the dark night hath so discovered.
     *Rom.* Lady, by yonder blessed moon I
          swear,          [tops,—
That tips with silver all these fruit-tree

*Jul.* O, swear not by the moon,. the incon-
stant moon,
That monthly changes in her circled orb,
Lest that thy love prove likewise variable.
  *Rom.* What shall I swear by?
  *Jul.*                Do not swear at all;
Or, if thou wilt, swear by thy gracious self,
Which is the god of my idolatry,
And I'll believe thee.
  *Rom.*              If my heart's dear love,—
  *Jul.* Well, do not swear: although I joy in
thee,
I have no joy of this contráct to-night:
It is too rash, too unadvis'd, too sudden;
Too like the lightning, which doth cease to be
Ere one can say, It lightens. Sweet, good-
night!
This bud of love, by summer's ripening breath,
May prove a beauteous flower when next we
meet.                                    [rest
Good-night, good-night! as sweet repose and
Come to thy heart as that within my breast!
  *Rom.* O, wilt thou leave me so unsatisfied?
  *Jul.* What satisfaction canst thou have to-
night?
  *Rom.* The exchange of thy love's faithful
vow for mine.                   [request it:
  *Jul.* I gave thee mine before you didst
And yet I would it were to give again.
  *Rom.* Wouldst thou withdraw it? for what
purpose, love?                         [again.
  *Jul.* But to be frank, and give it thee
And yet I wish but for the thing I have:
My bounty is as boundless as the sea,
My love as deep; the more I give to thee
The more I have, for both are infinite.
                          [*Nurse calls within.*
I hear some noise within; dear love, adieu!—
Anon, good nurse!—Sweet Montague, be true.
Stay but a little, I will come again.   [*Exit.*
  *Rom.* O blessed, blessed night! I am afeard,
Being in night, all this is but a dream,
Too flattering-sweet to be substantial.

### Re-enter JULIET above.

  *Jul.* Three words, dear Romeo, and good-
night indeed.
If that thy bent of love be honourable, [row,
Thy purpose marriage, send me word to-mor-
By one that I'll procure to come to thee,
Where and what time thou wilt perform the
rite;
And all my fortunes at thy foot I'll lay,
And follow thee, my lord, throughout the
world.
  *Nurse.* [*Within.*] Madam!       [not well,
  *Jul.* I come anon.—But if thou mean'st
I do beseech thee,—
  *Nurse.* [*Within.*] Madam!
  *Jul.*              By and by, I come:—
To cease thy suit, and leave me to my grief:
To-morrow will I send.
  *Rom.*              So thrive my soul,—
  *Jul.* A thousand times good-night!  [*Exit.*

  *Rom.* A thousand times the worse, to want
thy light.—
Love goes toward love as school-boys from
their books;                           [looks.
But love from love, toward school with heavy
                              [*Retiring slowly.*

### Re-enter JULIET above.

  *Jul.* Hist! Romeo, hist!—O for a falcon-
er's voice,
To lure this tassel-gentle back again!
Bondage is hoarse, and may not speak aloud;
Else would I tear the cave where Echo lies,
And make her airy tongue more hoarse than
mine
With repetition of my Romeo's name.
  *Rom.* It is my soul that calls upon my
name:                                  [night,
How silver-sweet sound lovers' tongues by
Like softest music to attending ears!
  *Jul.* Romeo.
  *Rom.*        My dear?
  *Jul.*                At what o'clock to-morrow
Shall I send to thee?
  *Rom.*              At the hour of nine.
  *Jul.* I will not fail: 'tis twenty years till
then.
I have forgot why I did call thee back.  [it.
  *Rom.* Let me stand here till thou remember
  *Jul.* I shall forget, to have thee still stand
there,
Remembering how I love thy company.
  *Rom.* And I'll still stay, to have thee still
forget,
Forgetting any other home but this.
  *Jul.* 'Tis almost morning; I would have
thee gone:
And yet no further than a wanton's bird;
Who lets it hop a little from her hand,
Like a poor prisoner in his twisted gyves,
And with a silk thread plucks it back again,
So loving-jealous of his liberty.
  *Rom.* I would I were thy bird.
  *Jul.*                        Sweet, so would I:
Yet I should kill thee with much cherishing.
Good-night, good-night! parting is such
sweet sorrow
That I shall say good-night till it be morrow.
                                       [*Exit.*
  *Rom.* Sleep dwell upon thine eyes, peace in
thy breast!—                          [rest!
Would I were sleep and peace, so sweet to
Hence will I to my ghostly father's cell,
His help to crave and my dear hap to tell.
                                       [*Exit.*

### SCENE III.—FRIAR LAWRENCE'S *Cell.*

#### Enter FRIAR LAWRENCE *with a basket.*

  *Fri. L.* The gray-ey'd morn smiles on the
frowning night              [of light;
Chequering the eastern clouds with streaks
And flecked darkness like a drunkard reels
From forth day's path and Titan's fiery
wheels:

Now, ere the sun advance his burning eye,
The day to cheer and night's dank dew to
    dry,
I must up-fill this osier cage of ours
With  baleful  weeds  and  precious-juiced
    flowers.                        [tomb;
The earth, that's nature's mother, is her
What is her burying grave, that is her womb:
And from her womb children of divers kind
We sucking on her natural bosom find;
Many for many virtues excellent,
None but for some, and yet all different.
O, mickle is the powerful grace that lies
In herbs, plants, stones, and their true qual-
    ities:
For naught so vile that on the earth doth live
But to the earth some special good doth give;
Nor aught so good but, strain'd from that
    fair use,
Revolts from true birth, stumbling on abuse:
Virtue itself turns vice, being misapplied;
And vice sometimes by action dignified.
Within the infant rind of this small flower
Poison hath residence, and medicine power:
For this, being smelt, with that part cheers
    each part;
Being tasted, slays all senses with the heart.
To such opposed kings encamp them still
In man as well as herbs,—grace and rude will;
And where the worser is predominant,
Full soon the canker death eats up that plant.

*Enter* ROMEO.

*Rom.* Good-morrow, father!
*Fri. L.*                        *Benedicite!*
What early tongue so sweet saluteth me?—
Young son, it argues a distemper'd head
So soon to bid good-morrow to thy bed:
Care keeps his watch in every old man's eye,
And where care lodges sleep will never lie;
But where unbruised youth with unstuff'd
    brain
Doth couch his limbs, there golden sleep doth
    reign:
Therefore thy earliness doth me assure
Thou art uprous'd by some distemperature;
Or if not so, then here I hit it right,—
Our Romeo hath not been in bed to-night.
*Rom.* That last is true; the sweeter rest
    was mine.
*Fri. L.* God pardon sin! wast thou with
    Rosaline?
*Rom.* With Rosaline,my ghostly father? no;
I have forgot that name, and that name's
    woe.
*Fri. L.* That's my good son: but where
    hast thou been, then?
*Rom.* I'll tell thee ere thou ask it me again.
I have been feasting with mine enemy;
Where, on a sudden, one hath wounded me
That's by me wounded; both our remedies
Within thy help and holy physic lies:
I bear no hatred, blessed man; for, lo,
My intercession likewise steads my foe.

*Fri. L.* Be plain, good son, and homely in
    thy drift;
Riddling confession finds but riddling shrift.
*Rom.* Then plainly know my heart's dear
    love is set
On the fair daughter of rich Capulet:
As mine on hers, so hers is set on mine;
And all combin'd, save what thou must com-
    bine                            [how
By holy marriage: when, and where, and
We met, we woo'd, and made exchange of
    vow,
I'll tell thee as we pass; but this I pray,
That thou consent to marry us to-day.
*Fri. L.* Holy St. Francis! what a change
    is here!
Is Rosaline, whom thou didst love so dear,
So soon forsaken? young men's love, then,
    lies
Not truly in their hearts, but in their eyes.
*Jesu Maria,* what a deal of brine
Hath wash'd thy sallow cheeks for Rosaline!
How much salt water thrown away in waste,
To season love, that of it doth not taste!
The sun not yet thy sighs from heaven clears,
Thy old groans ring yet in my ancient ears;
Lo, here upon thy cheek the stain doth sit
Of an old tear that is not wash'd off yet:
If e'er thou wast thyself, and these woes
    thine,
Thou and these woes were all for Rosaline:
And art thou chang'd? pronounce this sen-
    tence then,—                    [in men.
Women may fall, when there's no strength
*Rom.* Thou chidd'st me oft for loving
    Rosaline.                        [mine.
*Fri. L.* For doting, not for loving, pupil
*Rom.* And bad'st me bury love.
*Fri. L.*                        Not in a grave,
To lay one in, another out to have. [love now
*Rom.* I pray thee, chide not: she whom I
Doth grace for grace and love for love allow;
The other did not so.
*Fri. L.*                        O, she knew well
Thy love did read by rote, and could not
    spell.                            [me,
But come, young waverer, come, go with
In one respect I'll thy assistant be;
For this alliance may so happy prove,
To turn your households' rancour to pure
    love.                            [haste.
*Rom.* O, let us hence; I stand on sudden
*Fri. L.* Wisely and slow; they stumble that
    run fast.                        [*Exeunt.*

SCENE IV.—*A Street.*

*Enter* BENVOLIO *and* MERCUTIO.

*Mer.* Where the devil should this Romeo
    be?—
Came he not home to-night?
*Ben.* Not to his fathers; I spoke with his
    man.
*Mer.* Ah, that same pale hard-hearted
    wench, that Rosaline,

Torments him so that he will sure run mad.

*Ben.* Tybalt, the kinsman of old Capulet, Hath sent a letter to his father's house.

*Mer.* A challenge, on my life.

*Ben.* Romeo will answer it.

*Mer.* Any man that can write may answer a letter.

*Ben.* Nay, he will answer the letter's master, how he dares, being dared.

*Mer.* Alas, poor Romeo, he is already dead! stabbed with a white wench's black eye; shot through the ear with a love-song; the very pin of his heart cleft with the blind bow-boy's butt-shaft: and is he a man to encounter Tybalt?

*Ben.* Why, what is Tybalt?

*Mer.* More than prince of cats, I can tell you. O, he is the courageous captain of compliments. He fights as you sing prick-song, keeps time, distance, and proportion; rests me his minim rest, one, two, and the third in your bosom: the very butcher of a silk button, a duellist, a duellist; a gentleman of the very first house,—of the first and second cause: ah, the immortal passado! the punto reverso! the hay!—

*Ben.* The what?

*Mer.* The pox of such antic, lisping, affecting fantasticoes; these new tuners of accents!— *By Jesu, a very good blade!—a very tall man!—a very good whore!*—Why, is not this a lamentable thing, grandsire, that we should be thus, afflicted with these strange flies, these fashion-mongers, these *pardonnez-mois,* who stand so much on the new form that they cannot sit at ease on the old bench? O, their *bons,* their *bons!*

*Ben.* Here comes Romeo, here comes Romeo.

*Mer.* Without his roe, like a dried herring. —O, flesh, flesh, how art thou fishified!— Now is he for the numbers that Petrarch flowed in: Laura, to his lady, was but a kitchen-wench,—marry, she had a better love to be-rhyme her; Dido, a dowdy; Cleopatra, a gipsy; Helen and Hero, hildings and harlots; Thisbe, a gray eye or so, but not to the purpose,—

*Enter* ROMEO.

Signior Romeo, *bon jour!* there's a French salutation to your French slop. You gave us the counterfeit fairly last night.

*Rom.* Good-morrow to you both. What counterfeit did I give you?

*Mer.* The slip, sir, the slip; can you not conceive?

*Rom.* Pardon, good Mercutio, my business was great; and in such a case as mine a man may strain courtesy.

*Mer.* That's as much as to say, such a case as yours constrains a man to bow in the hams.

*Rom.* Meaning, to court'sy.

*Mer.* Thou hast most kindly hit it.

*Rom.* A most courteous exposition.

*Mer.* Nay, I am the very pink of courtesy.

*Rom.* Pink for flower.

*Mer.* Right.

*Rom.* Why, then is my pump well flowered.

*Mer.* Well said: follow me this jest now till thou hast sworn out thy pump: that when the single sole of it is worn, the jest may remain, after the wearing, sole singular.

*Rom.* O single-soled jest, solely singular for the singleness!

*Mer.* Come between us, good Benvolio; my wits faint.

*Rom.* Switch and spurs, switch and spurs; or I'll cry a match.

*Mer.* Nay, if thy wits run the wild-goose chase, I have done; for thou hast more of the wild-goose in one of thy wits than, I am sure, I have in my whole five: was I with you there for the goose?

*Rom.* Thou wast never with me for anything when thou wast not there for the goose.

*Mer.* I will bite thee by the ear for that jest.

*Rom.* Nay, good goose, bite not.

*Mer.* Thy wit is a very bitter sweeting; it is a most sharp sauce.

*Rom.* And is it not well served in to a sweet goose?

*Mer.* O, here's a wit of cheveril, that stretches from an inch narrow to an ell broad!

*Rom.* I stretch it out for that word, broad: which added to the goose, proves thee far and wide a broad goose.

*Mer.* Why, is not this better now than groaning for love? now art thou sociable, now art thou Romeo; not art thou what thou art, by art as well as by nature: for this drivelling love is like a great natural, that runs lolling up and down to hide his bauble in a hole.

*Ben.* Stop there, stop there.

*Mer.* Thou desirest me to stop in my tale against the hair.

*Ben.* Thou wouldst else have made thy tale large.

*Mer.* O, thou art deceived; I would have made it short: for I was come to the whole depth of my tale; and meant, indeed, to occupy the argument no longer.

*Rom.* Here's goodly gear!

*Enter* NURSE *and* PETER.

*Mer.* A sail, a sail, a sail!

*Ben.* Two, two; a shirt and a smock.

*Nurse.* Peter!

*Peter.* Anon?

*Nurse.* My fan, Peter.

*Mer.* Good Peter, to hide her face; for her fan's the fairer face.

*Nurse.* God ye good-morrow, gentlemen.

*Mer.* God ye good-den, fair gentlewoman.

*Nurse.* Is it good-den?

*Mer.* 'Tis no less, I tell you; for the bawdy hand of the dial is now upon the prick of noon.

*Nurse.* Out upon you! what a man are you!

*Rom.* One, gentlewoman, that God hath made himself to mar.

*Nurse.* By my troth, it is well said;—for himself to mar, quoth 'a?—Gentlemen, can any of you tell me where I may find the young Romeo?

*Rom.* I can tell you: but young Romeo will be older when you have found him than he was when you sought him: I am the youngest of that name, for fault of a worse.

*Nurse.* You say well.

*Mer.* Yea, is the worst well? very well took, i' faith; wisely, wisely.

*Nurse.* If you be he, sir, I desire some confidence with you.

*Ben.* She will indite him to some supper.

*Mer.* A bawd, a bawd, a bawd! So ho!

*Rom.* What hast thou found?

*Mer.* No hare, sir; unless a hare, sir, in a lenten pie, that is something stale and hoar ere it be spent.                    [*Sings.*

> An old hare hoar,
> And an old hare hoar,
> Is very good meat in Lent:
> But a hare that is hoar
> Is too much for a score,
> When it hoars ere it be spent.

Romeo, will you come to your father's? we'll to dinner thither.

*Rom.* I will follow you.

*Mer.* Farewell, ancient lady; farewell,— [*singing*] lady, lady, lady.

[*Exeunt* MERCUTIO *and* BENVOLIO.

*Nurse.* Marry, farewell!—I pray you, sir, what saucy merchant was this, that was so full of his ropery?

*Rom.* A gentleman, nurse, that loves to hear himself talk; and will speak more in a minute than he will stand to in a month.

*Nurse.* An 'a speak anything against me, I'll take him down, an 'a were lustier than he is, and twenty such Jacks; and if I cannot, I'll find those that shall. Scurvy knave! I am none of his flirt-gills; I am none of his skainsmates.—And thou must stand by too, and suffer every knave to use me at his pleasure?

*Pet.* I saw no man use you at his pleasure; if I had, my weapon should quickly have been out, I warrant you: I dare draw as soon as another man, if I see occasion in a good quarrel, and the law on my side.

*Nurse.* Now, afore God, I am so vexed that every part about me quivers. Scurvy knave! —Pray you, sir, a word: and as I told you, my young lady bade me inquire you out; what she bade me say I will keep to myself: but first let me tell ye, if ye should lead her into a fool's paradise, as they say, it were a very gross kind of behaviour, as they say: for the gentlewoman is young; and, therefore, if you should deal double with her, truly it were an ill thing to be offered to any gentlewoman, and very weak dealing.

*Rom.* Nurse, commend me to thy lady and mistress. I protest unto thee,—

*Nurse.* Good heart, and, i' faith, I will tell her as much: Lord, Lord, she will be a joyful woman.

*Rom.* What wilt thou tell her, nurse? thou dost not mark me.

*Nurse.* I will tell her, sir,—that you do protest; which, as I take it, is a gentleman-like offer.                              [to shrift

*Rom.* Bid her devise some means to come
This afternoon;
And there she shall at Friar Lawrence' cell
Be shriv'd and married. Here is for thy pains.

*Nurse.* No, truly, sir; not a penny.

*Rom.* Go to; I say you shall.        [be there.

*Nurse.* This afternoon, sir? well, she shall

*Rom.* And stay, good nurse, behind the abbey-wall:
Within this hour my man shall be with thee,
And bring thee cords made like a tackled stair;
Which to the high top-gallant of my joy
Must be my convoy in the secret night.
Farewell; be trusty, and I'll quit thy pains:
Farewell; commend me to thy mistress.

*Nurse.* Now God in heaven bless thee!— Hark you, sir.

*Rom.* What say'st thou, my dear nurse?

*Nurse.* Is your man secret? Did you ne'er hear say
Two may keep counsel, putting one away?

*Rom.* I warrant thee, my man's as true as steel.

*Nurse.* Well, sir; my mistress is the sweetest lady,—Lord, Lord! when 'twas a little prating thing,—O, there's a nobleman in town, one Paris, that would fain lay knife aboard; but she, good soul, had as lief see a toad, a very toad, as see him. I anger her sometimes, and tell her that Paris is the properer man; but, I'll warrant you, when I say so, she looks as pale as any clout in the versal world. Doth not rosemary and Romeo begin both with a letter?                              [an R.

*Rom.* Ay, nurse; what of that? both with

*Nurse.* Ah, mocker! that's the dog's name. R is for the dog: no; I know it begins with some other letter:—and she hath the prettiest sententious of it, of you and rosemary, that it would do you good to hear it.

*Rom.* Commend me to thy lady.

*Nurse.* Ay, a thousand times.

[*Exit* ROMEO.]

—Peter!

*Pet.* Anon?

*Nurse.* Peter, take my fan and go before.

[*Exeunt.*

SCENE V.—CAPULET'S *Garden.*

*Enter* JULIET.

*Jul.* The clock struck nine when I did
send the nurse;
In half an hour she promis'd to return. [so.—
Perchance she cannot meet him:—that's not
O, she is lame! love's heralds should be
thoughts,    [beams,
Which ten times faster glide than the sun's
Driving back shadows over lowering hills:
Therefore do nimble-pinion'd doves draw
love,    [wings.
And therefore hath the wind-swift Cupid
Now is the sun upon the highmost hill
Of this day's journey; and from nine till
twelve
Is three long hours,—yet she is not come.
Had her affections and warm youthful blood,
She'd be as swift in motion as a ball;
My words would bandy her to my sweet love,
And his to me:
But old folks, many feign as they were dead;
Unwieldy, slow, heavy and pale as lead.—
O God, she comes!

*Enter* Nurse *and* PETER.

O honey nurse, what news?
Hast thou met with him? Send thy man
away.
*Nurse.* Peter, stay at the gate.
[*Exit* PETER.
*Jul.* Now, good sweet nurse,—O Lord, why
look'st thou sad?
Though news be sad, yet tell them merrily;
If good, thou sham'st the music of sweet news
By playing it to me with so sour a face.
*Nurse.* I am a-weary, give me leave a-
while;—    [I had!
Fie, how my bones ache! what a jaunt have
*Jul.* I would thou hadst my bones and I
thy news:    [nurse, speak.
Nay, come, I pray thee, speak;—good, good
*Nurse.* Jesu, what haste? can you not stay
awhile?
Do you not see that I am out of breath?
*Jul.* How art thou out of breath, when
thou hast breath
To say to me that thou art out of breath?
The excuse that thou dost make in this delay
Is longer than the tale thou dost excuse.
Is thy news good or bad? answer to that;
Say either, and I'll stay the circumstance:
Let me be satisfied, is't good or bad?
*Nurse.* Well, you have made a simple
choice; you know not how to choose a man:
Romeo! no, not he; though his face be better
than any man's, yet his leg excels all men's;
and for a hand, and a foot, and a body,—
though they be not to be talked on, yet they
are past compare: he is not the flower of
courtesy,—but I'll warrant him as gentle as a
lamb.—Go thy ways, wench; serve God.—
What, have you dined at home?

*Jul.* No, no: but all this did I know before.
What says he of our marriage? what of that?
*Nurse.* Lord, how my head aches! what a
head have I!
It beats as it would fall in twenty pieces.
My back o' t' other side,—O, my back, my
back!—
Beshrew your heart for sending me about
To catch my death with jaunting up and
down!    [well.
*Jul.* I' faith, I am sorry that thou art not
Sweet, sweet, sweet nurse, tell me, what says
my love?    [gentleman,
*Nurse.* Your love says, like an honest
And a courteous, and a kind, and a handsome,
And, I warrant, a virtuous,—Where is your
mother?
*Jul.* Where is my mother!—why, she is
within;
Where should she be? How oddly thou re-
pliest!
*Your love says, like an honest gentleman,—*
*Where is your mother?*
*Nurse.*    O God's lady dear!
Are you so hot? marry, come up, I trow;
Is this the poultice for my aching bones?
Henceforward, do your messages yourself.
*Jul.* Here's such a coil!—come, what says
Romeo?    [to-day?
*Nurse.* Have you got leave to go to shrift
*Jul.* I have.    [rence' cell;
*Nurse.* Then hie you hence to Friar Law-
There stays a husband to make you a wife:
Now comes the wanton blood up in your
cheeks,
They'll be in scarlet straight at any news.
Hie you to church; I must another way,
To fetch a ladder, by the which your love
Must climb a bird's nest soon when it is dark:
I am the drudge, and toil in your delight;
But you shall bear the burden soon at night.
Go; I'll to dinner; hie you to the cell.
*Jul.* Hie to high fortune!—honest nurse,
farewell.    [*Exeunt.*

SCENE VI.—FRIAR LAWRENCE'S *Cell.*

*Enter* FRIAR LAWRENCE *and* ROMEO.

*Fri. L.* So smile the heavens upon this holy
act
That after-hours with sorrow chide us not!
*Rom.* Amen, amen! but come what sorrow
can,
It cannot countervail the exchange of joy
That one short minute gives me in her sight:
Do thou but close our hands with holy words,
Then love-devouring death do what he dare,—
It is enough I may but call her mine. [ends,
*Fri. L.* These violent delights have violent
And in their triumph die; like fire and
powder,    [honey
Which, as they kiss, consume: the sweetest
Is loathsome in his own deliciousness,
And in the taste confounds the appetite:
Therefore love moderately; long love doth so;

Too swift arrives as tardy as too slow.
Here comes the lady:—O, so light a foot
Will ne'er wear out the everlasting flint:
A lover may bestride the gossamer
That idles in the wanton summer air
And yet not fall; so light is vanity.

*Enter* JULIET.

*Jul.* Good-even to my ghostly confessor.
*Fri. L.* Romeo shall thank thee, daughter,
for us both.
*Jul.* As much to him, else in his thanks
too much.
*Rom.* Ah, Juliet, if the measure of thy joy
Be heap'd like mine, and that thy skill be
more
To blazon it, then sweeten with thy breath
This neighbour air, and let rich music's
tongue
Unfold the imagin'd happiness that both
Receive in either by this dear encounter.
*Jul.* Conceit, more rich in matter than in
words,
Brags of his substance, not of ornament:
They are but beggars that can count their
worth;
But my true love is grown to such excess,
I cannot sum up half my sum of wealth.
*Fri. L.* Come, come with me, and we will
make short work;
For, by your leaves, you shall not stay alone
Till holy church incorporate two in one.
[*Exeunt.*

## ACT III.

SCENE I.—*A public Place.*

*Enter* MERCUTIO, BENVOLIO, Page, *and*
Servants.

*Ben.* I pray thee, good Mercutio, let's retire:
The day is hot, the Capulets abroad,
And, if we meet, we shall not scape a brawl;
For now, these hot days, is the mad blood
stirring.
*Mer.* Thou art like one of those fellows
that, when he enters the confines of a tavern, claps me his sword upon the table, and
says, *God send me no need of thee!* and by
the operation of the second cup draws it on
the drawer, when, indeed, there is no need.
*Ben.* Am I like such a fellow?
*Mer.* Come, come, thou art as hot a Jack
in thy mood as any in Italy; and as soon
moved to be moody, and as soon moody to
be moved.
*Ben.* And what to?
*Mer.* Nay, an there were two such, we
should have none shortly, for one would kill
the other. Thou! why, thou wilt quarrel with
a man that hath a hair more or a hair less in
his beard than thou hast. Thou wilt quarrel
with a man for cracking nuts, having no
other reason but because thou hast hazel

eyes;—what eye but such an eye would spy
out such a quarrel? Thy head is as full of
quarrels as an egg is full of meat; and yet
thy head hath been beaten as addle as an egg
for quarrelling. Thou hast quarrelled with a
man for coughing in the street, because he
hath wakened thy dog that hath lain asleep in
the sun. Didst thou not fall out with a tailor
for wearing his new doublet before Easter?
with another for tying his new shoes with
old riband? and yet thou wilt tutor me from
quarrelling!
*Ben.* An I were so apt to quarrel as thou
art, any man should buy the fee-simple of
my life for an hour and a quarter.
*Mer.* The fee-simple! O simple!
*Ben.* By my head, here come the Capulets.
*Mer.* By my heel, I care not.

*Enter* TYBALT *and others.*

*Tyb.* Follow me close, for I will speak to
them.—Gentlemen, good-den: a word with
one of you.
*Mer.* And but one word with one of us?
Couple it with something; make it a word
and a blow.
*Tyb.* You shall find me apt enough to
that, sir, an you will give me occasion.
*Mer.* Could you not take some occasion
without giving?
*Tyb.* Mercutio, thou consort'st with
Romeo,—
*Mer.* Consort! what, dost thou make us
minstrels? An thou make minstrels of us,
look to hear nothing but discords: here's my
fiddlestick; here's that shall make you dance.
Zounds, consort!
*Ben.* We talk here in the public haunt of
men:
Either withdraw unto some private place,
And reason coldly of your grievances,
Or else depart; here all eyes gaze on us.
*Mer.* Men's eyes were made to look, and
let them gaze;
I will not budge for no man's pleasure, I.
*Tyb.* Well, peace with you, sir.—Here
comes my man.

*Enter* ROMEO.

*Mer.* But I'll be hanged, sir, if he wear
your livery:
Marry, go before to field, he'll be your fol-
lower;
Your worship in that sense may call him
man.
*Tyb.* Romeo, the hate I bear thee can af-
ford
No better term than this,—Thou art a vil-
lain.
*Rom.* Tybalt, the reason that I have to
love thee
Doth much excuse the appertaining rage
To such a greeting. Villain am I none;

Therefore, farewell; I see thou know'st me not.

*Tyb.* Boy, this shall not excuse the injuries `
That thou hast done me; therefore turn and draw.

*Rom.* I do protest I never injur'd thee;
But love thee better than thou canst devise
Till thou shalt know the reason of my love:
And so, good Capulet,—which name I tender
As dearly as my own,—be satisfied.

*Mer.* O calm, dishonourable, vile submission!
*A la stoccata* carries it away.  [*Draws.*
Tybalt, you rat-catcher, will you walk?

*Tyb.* What wouldst thou have with me?

*Mer.* Good king of cats, nothing but one of your nine lives; that I mean to make bold withal, and, as you shall use me hereafter, dry-beat the rest of the eight. Will you pluck your sword out of his pilcher by the ears? make haste, lest mine be about your ears ere it be out.

*Tyb.* I am for you.  [*Drawing.*

*Rom.* Gentle Mercutio, put thy rapier up.

*Mer.* Come, sir, your passado. [*They fight.*

*Rom.* Draw, Benvolio; beat down their weapons.—
Gentlemen, for shame, forbear this outrage!—
Tybalt,—Mercutio,—the prince expressly hath
Forbidden bandying in Verona streets.—
Hold, Tybalt!—good Mercutio.—
[*Exeunt* TYBALT *and his* Partizans.

*Mer.* I am hurt;—
A plague o' both your houses!—I am sped.—
Is he gone, and hath nothing?

*Ben.*                What, art thou hurt?

*Mer.* Ay, ay, a scratch, a scratch; marry, 'tis enough.—
Where is my page?—go, villain, fetch a surgeon.
[*Exit* Page.

*Rom.* Courage, man; the hurt cannot be much.

*Mer.* No, 'tis not so deep as a well, nor so wide as a church-door; but 'tis enough, 'twill serve: ask for me to-morrow, and you shall find me a grave man. I am peppered, I warrant, for this world.—A plague o' both your houses!—Zounds, a dog, a rat, a mouse, a cat, to scratch a man to death! a braggart, a rogue, a villain, that fights by the book of arithmetic!—Why the devil came you between us? I was hurt under your arm.

*Rom.* I thought all for the best.

*Mer.* Help me into some house, Benvolio, Or I shall faint.—A plague o' both your houses!
They have made worm's meat of me:
I have it, and soundly too.—Your houses!
[*Exeunt* MERCUTIO *and* BENVOLIO.

*Rom.* This gentleman, the prince's near ally,
My very friend, hath got his mortal hurt
In my behalf; my reputation stain'd
With Tybalt's slander,—Tybalt, that an hour
Hath been my kinsman.—O sweet Juliet,
Thy beauty hath made me effeminate,
And in my temper soften'd valour's steel.

*Re-enter* BENVOLIO.

*Ben.* O Romeo, Romeo, brave Mercutio's dead!
That gallant spirit hath aspir'd the clouds,
Which too untimely here did scorn the earth.

*Rom.* This day's black fate on more days doth depend;
This but begins the woe others must end.

*Ben.* Here comes the furious Tybalt back again.

*Rom.* Alive, in triumph! and Mercutio slain!
Away to heaven, respective lenity,
And fire-ey'd fury be my conduct now!—

*Re-enter* TYBALT.

Now, Tybalt, take the *villain* back again
That late thou gav'st me; for Mercutio's soul
Is but a little way above our heads,
Staying for thine to keep him company:
Either thou or I, or both, must go with him.

*Tyb.* Thou, wretched boy, that didst consort him here,
Shalt with him hence.

*Rom.*                This shall determine that.
[*They fight;* TYBALT *falls.*

*Ben.* Romeo, away, be gone!
The citizens are up, and Tybalt slain.—
Stand not amaz'd. The prince will doom thee death
If thou art taken. Hence, be gone, away!

*Rom.* O, I am fortune's fool!

*Ben.*                Why dost thou stay?
[*Exit* ROMEO.

*Enter* Citizens, *&c.*

1 *Cit.* Which way ran he that kill'd Mercutio?
Tybalt, that murderer, which way ran he?

*Ben.* There lies that Tybalt.

1 *Cit.*                Up, sir, go with me;
I charge thee in the prince's name, obey.

*Enter* PRINCE, *attended;* MONTAGUE, CAPULET, *their* Wives, *and others.*

*Prin.* Where are the vile beginners of this fray?

*Ben.* O noble prince, I can discover all
The unlucky manage of this fatal brawl:
There lies the man, slain by young Romeo,
That slew thy kinsman, brave Mercutio.

*Lady C.* Tybalt, my cousin! O my brother's child!—
O prince!—O husband!—O, the blood is spill'd

Of my dear kinsman!—Prince, as thou art
 true,
For blood of ours shed blood of Montague.—
O cousin, cousin!
 *Prin.* Benvolio, who began this bloody
  fray?
 *Ben.* Tybalt, here slain, whom Romeo's
  hand did slay;
Romeo that spoke him fair, bade him be-
 think
How nice the quarrel was, and urg'd withal
Your high displeasure.—All this,—uttered
With gentle breath, calm look, knees humbly
 bow'd,—
Could not take truce with the unruly spleen
Of Tybalt, deaf to peace, but that he tilts
With piercing steel at bold Mercutio's breast;
Who, all as hot, turns deadly point to point,
And, with a martial scorn, with one hand
 beats
Cold death aside, and with the other sends
It back to Tybalt, whose dexterity
Retorts it: Romeo he cried aloud,
*Hold, friends! friends, part!* and, swifter
 than his tongue,
His agile arm beats down their fatal points,
And 'twixt them rushes; underneath whose
 arm
An envious thrust from Tybalt hit the life
Of stout Mercutio, and then Tybalt fled:
But by and by comes back to Romeo,
Who had but newly entertain'd revenge,
And to't they go like lightning; for ere I
Could draw to part them was stout Tybalt
 slain;
And as he fell did Romeo turn and fly.
This is the truth, or let Benvolio die.
 *Lady C.* He is a kinsman to the Mon-
  tague,
Affection makes him false, he speaks not
 true:
Some twenty of them fought in this black
 strife,
And all those twenty could but kill one life.
I beg for justice, which thou, prince, must
 give;
Romeo slew Tybalt, Romeo must not live.
 *Prin.* Romeo slew him, he slew Mercutio:
Who now the price of his dear blood doth
 owe?
 *Mon.* Not Romeo, prince, he was Mercu-
  tio's friend; [end,
His fault concludes but what the law should
The life of Tybalt.
 *Prin.* And for that offence,
Immediately we do exile him hence:
I have an interest in your hate's proceeding,
My blood for your rude brawls doth lie a-
 bleeding;
But I'll amerce you with so strong a fine
That you shall all repent the loss of mine:
I will be deaf to pleading and excuses;
Nor tears nor prayers shall purchase out
 abuses,

Therefore use none: let Romeo hence in
 haste,
Else when he's found, that hour is his last.
Bear hence this body, and attend our will:
Mercy but murders, pardoning those that
 kill

 [*Exeunt.*

SCENE II.—*A Room in* CAPULET'S *House.*
 *Enter* JULIET.

 *Jul.* Gallop apace, you fiery-footed steeds,
Towards Phœbus' lodging; such a waggoner
As Phæton would whip you to the west,
And bring in cloudy night immediately.—
Spread thy close curtain, love-performing
 night!
That ru:le day's eyes may wink, and Romeo
Leap to these arms, untalk'd of and unseen.—
Lovers can see to do their amorous rites
By their own beauties: or if love be blind,
It best agrees with night.—Come, civil night,
Thou sober-suited matron, all in black,
And learn me how to lose a winning match,
Play'd for a pair of stainless maidenhoods:
Hood my unmann'd blood, bating in my
 cheeks,
With thy black mantle; till strange love,
 grown bold,
Think true love acted simple modesty.
Come, night;—come, Romeo,—come, thou
 day in night;
For thou wilt lie upon the wings of night
Whiter than new snow on a raven's back.—
Come, gentle night,—come, loving black-
 brow'd night,
Give me my Romeo; and, when he shall die,
Take him and cut him out in little stars,
And he will make the face of heaven so fine
That all the world will be in love with night,
And pay no worship to the garish sun.—
O, I have bought the mansion of a love,
But not possess'd it; and, though I am sold,
Not yet enjoy'd: so tedious is this day,
As is the night before some festival
To an impatient child that hath new robes,
And may not wear them. O, here comes my
 nurse, [speaks
And she brings news; and every tongue that
But Romeo's name speaks heavenly elo-
 quence.—

 *Enter* Nurse *with cords.*

Now, nurse, what news? What hast thou
 there? the cords·
That Romeo bade thee fetch?
 *Nurse.* Ay, ay, the cords.
 [*Throws them down.*
 *Jul.* Ah me! what news? why dost thou
  wring thy hands? [dead, he's dead!
 *Nurse.* Ah, well-a-day! he's dead, he's
We are undone, lady, we are undone!—
Alack the day!—he's gone, he's kill'd, he's
 dead!
 *Jul.* Can heaven be so envious?

*Nurse.*                                    Romeo can,
Though heaven cannot.—O Romeo, Ro-
    meo!—
Who ever would have thought it?—Romeo!
    *Jul.* What devil art thou, that dost tor-
    ment me thus?
This torture should be roar'd in dismal hell.
Hath Romeo slain himself? say thou but I,
And that bare vowel I shall poison more
Than the death-darting eye of cockatrice:
I am not I if there be such an I;
Or those eyes shut that make thee answer I.
If he be slain, say I; or if not, no:
Brief sounds determine of my weal or woe.
    *Nurse.* I saw the wound, I saw it with
    mine eyes,—
God save the mark!—here on his manly
    breast.
A piteous corse, a bloody piteous corse;
Pale, pale as ashes, all bedaub'd in blood,
All in gore-blood;—I swooned at the sight.
    *Jul.* O, break, my heart!—poor bankrupt,
    break at once!
To prison, eyes, ne'er look on liberty!
Vile earth, to earth resign; end motion here;
And thou and Romeo press one heavy bier!
    *Nurse.* O Tybalt, Tybalt! the best friend I
    had!
O courteous Tybalt! honest gentleman!
That ever I should live to see thee dead!
    *Jul.* What storm is this that blows so
    contrary?
Is Romeo slaughter'd, and is Tybalt dead?
My dear-lov'd cousin and my dearer lord?—
Then, dreadful trumpet, sound the general
    doom!
For who is living if those two are gone?
    *Nurse.* Tybalt is gone, and Romeo ban-
    ished;
Romeo that kill'd him, he is banished.
    *Jul.* O God!—did Romeo's hand shed Ty-
    balt's blood?
    *Nurse.* It did, it did; alas the day, it did!
    *Jul.* O serpent heart, hid with a flowering
    face!
Did ever dragon keep so fair a cave?
Beautiful tyrant! fiend angelical!
Dove-feather'd  raven!  wolfish-ravening
    lamb!
Despised substance of divinest show!
Just opposite to what thou justly seem'st,
A damned saint, an honourable villain!—
O nature, what hadst thou to do in hell
When thou didst bower the spirit of a fiend
In mortal paradise of such sweet flesh?—
Was ever book containing such vile matter
So fairly bound? O, that deceit should dwell
In such a gorgeous palace!
    *Nurse.*                     There's no trust,
No faith, no honesty in men; all are per-
    jur'd,
All forsworn, all naught, all dissemblers.—
Ah, where's my man? give me some *aqua
    vitæ.*—

These griefs, these woes, these sorrows make
    me old.
Shame come to Romeo!
    *Jul.*                        Blister'd be thy tongue
For such a wish! he was not born to shame:
Upon his brow shame is asham'd to sit;
For 'tis a throne where honour may be
    crown'd
Sole monarch of the universal earth.
O, what a beast was I to chide at him!
    *Nurse.* Will you speak well of him that
    kill'd your cousin?           [husband?
    *Jul.* Shall I speak ill of him that is my
Ah, poor my lord, what tongue shall smooth
    thy name                      [it?—
When I, thy three-hours' wife, have mangled
But, wherefore, villain, didst thou kill my
    cousin?                        [husband:
That villain cousin would have kill'd my
Back, foolish tears, back to your native
    spring;
Your tributary drops belong to woe,
Which you, mistaking, offer up to joy.
My husband lives, that Tybalt would have
    slain;                         [my husband:
And Tybalt's dead, that would have slain
All this is comfort; wherefore weep I, then?
Some word there was, worser than Tybalt's
    death,
That murder'd me: I would forget it fain;
But, O, it presses to my memory
Like damned guilty deeds to sinners' minds:
*Tybalt is dead, and Romeo banished.*
That *banished*, that one word *banished*,
Hath slain ten thousand Tybalts. Tybalt's
    death
Was woe enough, if it had ended there:
Or, if sour woe delights in fellowship,
And needly will be rank'd with other
    griefs,—
Why follow'd not, when she said Tybalt's
    dead,
Thy father or thy mother, nay, or both,
Which modern lamentation might have
    mov'd?
But, with a rear-ward following Tybalt's
    death,
*Romeo is banished,*—to speak that word
Is father, mother, Tybalt, Romeo, Juliet,
All slain, all dead: *Romeo is banished,*—
There is no end, no limit, measure, bound,
In that word's death; no words can that woe
    sound.—
Where is my father and my mother, nurse?
    *Nurse.* Weeping and wailing over Tybalt's
    corse:
Will you go to them? I will bring you
    thither.
    *Jul.* Wash they his wounds with tears:
    mine shall be spent,
When theirs are dry, for Romeo's banish-
    ment.
Take up those cords. Poor ropes, you are
    beguil'd,

Both you and I; for Romeo is exil'd:
He made you for a highway to my bed;
But I, a maid, die maiden-widowed.
Come, cords; come, nurse; I'll to my wed-
    ding-bed;
And death, not Romeo, take my maiden-
    head!
  *Nurse.* Hie to your chamber, I'll find Ro-
    meo
To comfort you: I wot well where he is.
Hark ye, your Romeo will be here at night:
I'll to him; he is hid at Lawrence's cell.
  *Jul.* O, find him! give this ring to my true
    knight,
And bid him come to take his last farewell.
                                    [*Exeunt.*

### SCENE III.—FRIAR LAWRENCE'S *Cell.*

#### *Enter* FRIAR LAWRENCE.

  *Fri. L.* Romeo, come forth; come forth,
    thou fearful man:
Affliction is enamour'd of thy parts,
And thou art wedded to calamity.

#### *Enter* ROMEO.

  *Rom.* Father, what news? what is the
    prince's doom?
What sorrow craves acquaintance at my
    hand,
That I yet know not?
  *Fri. L.*            Too familiar
Is my dear son with such sour company:
I bring thee tidings of the prince's doom.
  *Rom.* What less than doomsday is the
    prince's doom?                   [his lips,—
  *Fri. L.* A gentler judgment vanish'd from
Not body's death, but body's banishment.
  *Rom.* Ha, banishment! be merciful, say
    death;
For exile hath more terror in his look,
Much more than death: do not say banish-
    ment.
  *Fri. L.* Hence from Verona art thou ban-
    ished:
Be patient, for the world is broad and wide.
  *Rom.* There is no world without Verona
    walls,
But purgatory, torture, hell itself.
Hence-banished is banish'd from the world,
And world's exile is death,—then banished
Is death mis-term'd: calling death banish-
    ment,
Thou cutt'st my head off with a golden axe,
And smil'st upon the stroke that murders me.
  *Fri. L.* O deadly sin! O rude unthankful-
    ness!
Thy fault our law calls death; but the kind
    prince,
Taking thy part, hath brush'd aside the law,
And turn'd that black word death to banish-
    ment:
This is dear mercy, and thou see'st it not.
  *Rom.* 'Tis torture, and not mercy: heaven
    is here

Where Juliet lives; and every cat, and dog,
And little mouse, every unworthy thing,
Live here in heaven, and may look on her;
But Romeo may not.—More validity,
More honourable state, more courtship lives
In carrion flies than Romeo: they may seize
On the white wonder of dear Juliet's hand,
And steal immortal blessing from her lips;
Who, even in pure and vestal modesty,
Still blush, as thinking their own kisses sin;
But Romeo may not; he is banished,-
This may flies do, when I from this must fly.
And say'st thou yet that exile is not death!
Hadst thou no poison mix'd, no sharp-ground
    knife,                            [mean,
No sudden mean of death, though ne'er so
But—banished—to kill me; banished?
O friar, the damned use that word in hell;
Howlings attend it: how hast thou the heart,
Being a divine, a ghostly confessor,
A sin-absolver, and my friend profess'd,
To mangle me with that word banishment?
  *Fri. L.* Thou fond mad man, hear me
    speak a little,—
  *Rom.* O, thou wilt speak again of banish-
    ment.
  *Fri. L.* I'll give thee armour to keep off
    that word;
Adversity's sweet milk, philosophy,
To comfort thee, though thou art banished.
  *Rom.* Yet banished?—Hang up philos-
    ophy!
Unless philosophy can make a Juliet,
Displant a town, reverse a prince's doom,
It helps not, it prevails not,—talk no more.
  *Fri. L.* O, then I see that madmen have no
    ears.                   [men have no eyes?
  *Rom.* How should they, when that wise
  *Fri. L.* Let me dispute with thee of thy
    estate.
  *Rom.* Thou canst not speak of what thou
    dost not feel:
Wert thou as young as I, Juliet thy love,
An hour but married, Tybalt murdered,
Doting like me, and like me banished,
Then mightst thou speak, then mightst thou
    tear thy hair,
And fall upon the ground, as I do now,
Taking the measure of an unmade grave.
  *Fri. L.* Arise; one knocks; good Romeo,
    hide thyself.         [*Knocking within.*
  *Rom.* Not I; unless the breath of heart-
    sick groans,
Mist-like, enfold me from the search of eyes.
                                  [*Knocking.*
  *Fri. L.* Hark how they knock!—Who's
    there?—Romeo, arise;
Thou wilt be taken.—Stay awhile;—stand
    up;                            [*Knocking.*
Run to my study.—By and by.—God's will.
What simpleness is this!—I come, I come.
                                  [*Knocking.*
Who knocks so hard? whence come you?
    what's your will?

*Nurse.* [*Within.*] Let me come in and you
    shall know my errand;
I come from Lady Juliet.
*Fri. L.*            Welcome, then.

        *Enter Nurse.*

*Nurse.* O holy friar, O, tell me, holy friar,
Where is my lady's lord, where's Romeo?
*Fri. L.* There on the ground, with his own
    tears made drunk.
*Nurse.* O, he is even in my mistress' case,—
Just in her case!
*Fri. L.*         O woeful sympathy!
Piteous predicament!
*Nurse.*       Even so lies she,   [bering.—
Blubbering and weeping, weeping and blub-
Stand up, stand up; stand, an you be a man:
For Juliet's sake, for her sake, rise and stand;
Why should you fall into so deep an O?
*Rom.* Nurse!
*Nurse.* Ah, sir! ah, sir!—Well, death's the
    end of all.               [her?
*Rom.* Spak'st thou of Juliet? how is it with
Doth she not think me an old murderer,
Now I have stain'd the childhood of our joy
With blood remov'd but little from her own?
Where is she? and how doth she? and what
    says
My conceal'd lady to our cancell'd love?
*Nurse.* O, she says nothing, sir, but weeps
    and weeps;
And now falls on her bed; and then starts up,
And Tybalt calls; and then on Romeo cries,
And then down falls again.
*Rom.*          As if that name,
Shot from the deadly level of a gun,
Did murder her; as that name's cursed hand
Murder'd her kinsman.—O, tell me, friar, tell
    me,
In what vile part of this anatomy
Doth my name lodge? tell me that I may
    sack
The hateful mansion.   [*Drawing his sword.*
*Fri. L.*       Hold thy desperate hand:
Art thou a man? thy form cries out thou
    art:
Thy tears are womanish; thy wild acts de-
    note
The unreasonable fury of a beast:
Unseemly woman in a seeming man!
Or ill-beseeming beast in seeming both!
Thou hast amaz'd me: by my holy order,
I thought thy disposition better temper'd.
Hast thou slain Tybalt? wilt thou slay thy-
    self?
And slay thy lady, too, that lives in thee,
By doing damned hate upon thyself?
Why rail'st thou on thy birth, the heaven,
    and earth?         [do meet
Since birth, and heaven and earth, all three
In thee at once; which thou at once wouldst
    lose.               [wit;
Fie, fie! thou sham'st thy shape, thy love, thy
Which, like a usurer, abound'st in all,

And usest none in that true use indeed. [wit:
Which should bedeck thy shape, thy love, thy
Thy noble shape is but a form of wax,
Digressing from the valour of a man;
Thy dear love sworn, but hollow perjury,
Killing that love which thou hast vow'd to
    cherish;
Thy wit, that ornament to shape and love,
Mis-shapen in the conduct of them both,
Like powder in a skilless soldier's flask,
Is set a-fire by thine own ignorance,
And thou dismember'd with thine own de-
    fence.
What, rouse thee, man! thy Juliet is alive,
For whose dear sake thou wast but lately
    dead;
There art thou happy: Tybalt would kill
    thee,
But thou slew'st Tybalt; there art thou
    happy too:          [friend,
The law, that threaten'd death, becomes thy
And turns it to exile; there art thou happy:
A pack of blessings lights upon thy back;
Happiness courts thee in her best array;
But, like a misbehav'd and sullen wench,
Thou pout'st upon thy fortune and thy
    love:—
Take heed, take heed, for such die miserable.
Go, get thee to thy love, as was decreed,
Ascend her chamber, hence and comfort her:
But, look, thou stay not till the watch be set,
For then thou canst not pass to Mantua;
Where thou shalt live till we can find a time
To blaze your marriage, reconcile your
    friends,
Beg pardon of the prince, and call thee back
With twenty hundred thousand times more
    joy
Than thou went'st forth in lamentation.—
Go before, nurse: commend me to thy lady;
And bid her hasten all the house to bed,
Which heavy sorrow makes them apt unto:
Romeo is coming.         [the night
*Nurse.* O Lord, I could have stay'd here all
To hear good counsel: O, what learning is!—
My lord, I'll tell my lady you will come.
*Rom.* Do so, and bid my sweet prepare to
    chide.           [you, sir:
*Nurse.* Here, sir, a ring she bid me give
Hie you, make haste, for it grows very late.
                    [*Exit.*
*Rom.* How well my comfort is reviv'd by
    this!
*Fri. L.* Go hence; good-night; and here
    stands all your state:
Either be gone before the watch be set,
Or by the break of day disguis'd from hence:
Sojourn in Mantua; I'll find out your man,
And he shall signify from time to time
Every good hap to you that chances here:
Give me thy hand; 'tis late: farewell; good-
    night.
*Rom.* But that a joy past joy calls out on
    me,

It were a grief so brief to part with thee:
Farewell.  [*Exeunt.*

SCENE IV.—*A Room in* CAPULET'S *House.*

*Enter* CAPULET, LADY CAPULET *and* PARIS.

*Cap.* Things have fallen out, sir, so un-
 luckily
That we have had no time to move our
 daughter:
Look you, she lov'd her kinsman Tybalt
 dearly,
And so did I; well, we were born to die.
'Tis very late, she'll not come down tonignt:
I promise you, but for your company,
I would have been a-bed an hour ago.

*Par.* These times of woe afford no time to
 woo.—  [daughter.
Madam, good-night: commend me to your

*Lady C.* I will, and know her mind early
 to-morrow;
To-night she's mew'd up to her heaviness.

*Cap.* Sir Paris, I will make a desperate
 tender
Of my child's love: I think she will be rul'd
In all respects by me; nay, more, I doubt it
 not.—
Wife, go you to her ere you go to bed;
Acquaint her here of my son Paris' love;
And bid her, mark you me, on Wednesday
 next,—
But, soft, what day is this?

*Par.*  Monday, my lord.

*Cap.* Monday! ha, ha! Well, Wednesday
 is too soon,
O' Thursday let it be;—o' Thursday, tell her,
She shall be married to this noble earl.—
Will you be ready? do you like this haste?
We'll keep no great ado,—a friend or two;
For, hark you, Tybalt being slain so late,
It may be thought we held him carelessly,
Being our kinsman, if we revel much:
Therefore we'll have some half a dozen
 friends,
And there an end. But what say you to
 Thursday?  [to-morrow.

*Par.* My lord, I would that Thursday were

*Cap.* Well, get you gone: o' Thursday be
 it then.—
Go you to Juliet ere you go to bed,
Prepare her, wife, against this wedding-
 day.—
Farewell, my lord.—Light to my chamber,
 ho!—
Afore me, it is so very very late
That we may call it early by and by.—
Good-night.  [*Exeunt.*

SCENE V.—*An open Gallery to* JULIET'S
 *Chamber, overlooking the Garden.*

*Enter* ROMEO *and* JULIET.

*Jul.* Wilt thou be gone? it is not yet near
 day:
It was the nightingale, and not the lark,
That pierc'd the fearful hollow of thine ear;

Nightly she sings on yon pomegranate tree:
Believe me, love, it was the nightingale.

*Rom.* It was the lark, the herald of the
 morn,
No nightingale: look, love, what envious
 streaks
Do lace the severing clouds in yonder east:
Night's candles are burnt out, and jocund day
Stands tiptoe on the misty mountain tops.
I must be gone and live, or stay and die.

*Jul.* Yon light is not daylight, I know it, I:
It is some meteor that the sun exhales,
To be to thee this night a torch-bearer,
And light thee on thy way to Mantua:
Therefore stay yet, thou need'st not to be
 gone.

*Rom.* Let me be ta'en, let me be put to
 death;
I am content, so thou wilt have it so.
I'll say yon gray is not the morning's eye,
'Tis but the pale reflex of Cynthia's brow;
Nor that is not the lark whose notes do beat
The vaulty heaven so high above our heads:
I have more care to stay than will to go.—
Come, death, and welcome! Juliet wills it
 so.—
How is't, my soul? let's talk,—it is not day.

*Jul.* It is, it is,—hie hence, be gone, away!
It is the lark that sings so out of tune,
Straining harsh discords and unpleasing
 sharps.
Some say the lark makes sweet division;
This doth not so, for she divideth us:
Some say the lark and loathed toad change
 eyes;
O, now I would they had chang'd voices too!
Since arm from arm that voice doth us af-
 fray,
Hunting thee hence with hunt's-up to the
 day.
O, now be gone; more light and light it
 grows.

*Rom.* More light and light,—more dark
 and dark our woes!

*Enter* NURSE.

*Nurse.* Madam!

*Jul.* Nurse?  [chamber:

*Nurse.* Your lady mother is coming to your
The day is broke; be wary, look about.
 [*Exit.*

*Jul.* Then, window, let day in and let life
 out.

*Rom.* Farewell, farewell! one kiss, and I'll
 descend.  [*Descends.*

*Jul.* Art thou gone so? my lord, my love,
 my friend!
I must hear from thee every day i' the hour,
For in a minute there are many days:
O, by this count I shall be much in years
Ere I again behold my Romeo!

*Rom.*  Farewell!
I will omit no opportunity
That may convey my greetings, love, to thee.

*Jul.* O, think'st thou we shall ever meet
   again?            [shall serve
*Rom.* I doubt it not; and all these woes
For sweet discourses in our time to come.
*Jul.* O God! I have an ill-divining soul!
Methinks I see thee, now thou art below,
As one dead in the bottom of a tomb:
Either my eyesight fails or thou look'st pale.
*Rom.* And trust me, love, in my eye so do
   you:
Dry sorrow drinks our blood. Adieu, adieu!
                  [*Exit below.*
*Jul.* O fortune, fortune! all men call thee
   fickle:
If thou art fickle, what dost thou with him
That is renown'd for faith? Be fickle, for-
   tune;
For then, I hope, thou wilt not keep him
   long,
But send him back.            [up?
*Lady C.* [*Within.*] Ho, daughter! are you
*Jul.* Who is't that calls? is it my lady
   mother?
Is she not down so late, or up so early?
What unaccustom'd cause procures her
   hither?

       *Enter* LADY CAPULET.

*Lady C.* Why, how now, Juliet!
*Jul.*           Madam, I am not well.
*Lady C.* Evermore weeping for your cous-
   in's death?         [with tears?
What, wilt thou wash him from his grave
An if thou couldst, thou couldst not make
   him live;           [of love;
Therefore have done: some grief shows much
But much of grief shows still some want of
   wit.
*Jul.* Yet let me weep for such a feeling
   loss.
*Lady C.* So shall you feel the loss, but not
   the friend
Which you weep for.
*Jul.*          Feeling so the loss,
I cannot choose but ever weep the friend.
*Lady C.* Well, girl, thou weep'st not so
   much for his death
As that the villain lives which slaughter'd
   him.
*Jul.* What villain, madam?
*Lady C.*       That same villain, Romeo.
*Jul.* Villain and he be many miles asunder.
God pardon him! I do, with all my heart;
And yet no man like he doth grieve my heart.
*Lady C.* That is because the traitor mur-
   derer lives.
*Jul.* Ay, madam, from the reach of these
   my hands.
Would none but I might venge my cousin's
   death!
*Lady C.* We will have vengeance for it,
   fear thou not:
Then weep no more. I'll send to one in Man-
   tua,—

Where that same banish'd runagate doth
   live,—
Shall give him such an unaccustom'd dram
That he shall soon keep Tybalt company:
And then I hope thou wilt be satisfied.
*Jul.* Indeed I never shall be satisfied
With Romeo till I behold him—dead—
Is my poor heart so for a kinsman vex'd:
Madam, if you could find out but a man
To bear a poison, I would temper it,
That Romeo should, upon receipt thereof,
Soon sleep in quiet. O, how my heart abhors
To hear him nam'd,—and cannot come to
   him,—
To wreak the love I bore my cousin Tybalt
Upon his body that hath slaughter'd him!
*Lady C.* Find thou the means, and I'll find
   such a man.
But now I'll tell thee joyful tidings, girl.
*Jul.* And joy comes well in such a needy
   time:
What are they, I beseech your ladyship?
*Lady C.* Well, well, thou hast a careful
   father, child;
One who, to put thee from thy heaviness,
Hath sorted out a sudden day of joy
That thou expect'st not, nor I look'd not for.
*Jul.* Madam, in happy time, what day is
   that?
*Lady C.* Marry, my child, early next
   Thursday morn
The gallant, young, and noble gentleman,
The County Paris, at St. Peter's Church,
Shall happily make thee there a joyful bride.
*Jul.* Now, by St. Peter's Church, and
   Peter too,
He shall not make me there a joyful bride.
I wonder at this haste; that I must wed
Ere he that should be husband comes to woo.
I pray you, tell my lord and father, madam,
I will not marry yet; and when I do, I swear
It shall be Romeo, whom you know I hate,
Rather than Paris:—these are news indeed!
*Lady C.* Here comes your father; tell him
   so yourself,
And see how he will take it at your hands.

     *Enter* CAPULET *and* Nurse.

*Cap.* When the sun sets, the air doth driz-
   zle dew;
But for the sunset of my brother's son
It rains downright.—
How now! a conduit, girl? what, still in
   tears?
Evermore showering? In one little body
Thou counterfeit'st a bark, a sea, a wind:
For still thy eyes, which I may call the sea,
Do ebb and flow with tears; the bark thy
   body is,
Sailing in this salt flood; the winds thy sighs;
Who,—raging with thy tears, and they with
   them,—
Without a sudden calm, will overset
Thy tempest-tossed body.—How now, wife!

Have you deliver'd to her our decree?

*Lady C.* Ay, sir; but she will none, she gives you thanks.

I would the fool were married to her grave!

*Cap.* Soft! take me with you, take me with you, wife.                    [thanks?

How! will she none? doth she not give us

Is she not proud? doth she not count her bless'd,

Unworthy as she is, that we have wrought

So worthy a gentleman to be her bride-groom?

*Jul.* Not proud you have; but thankful that you have:

Proud can I never be of what I hate;

But thankful even for hate that is meant love.

*Cap.* How now, how now, chop-logic! What is this?                    [not;—

Proud,—and, I thank you,—and, I thank you

And yet not proud:—mistress minion, you,

Thank me no thankings, nor proud me no prouds,

But fettle your fine joints 'gainst Thursday next,

To go with Paris to St. Peter's Church,

Or I will drag thee on a hurdle thither.

Out, you green-sickness carrion! out, you baggage!

You tallow-face!

*Lady C.*          Fie, fie! what, are you mad?

*Jul.* Good father, I beseech you on my knees,

Hear me with patience but to speak a word.

*Cap.* Hang thee, young baggage! disobe-dient wretch!                    [Thursday,

I tell thee what,—get thee to church o'

Or never after look me in the face:

Speak not, reply not, do not answer me;

My fingers itch.—Wife, we scarce thought us bless'd

That God had lent us but this only child;

But now I see this one is one too much,

And that we have a curse in having her:

Out on her, hilding!

*Nurse.*          God in heaven bless her!—

You are to blame, my lord, to rate her so.

*Cap.* And why, my lady wisdom? hold your tongue,

Good prudence; smatter with your gossips, go.

*Nurse.* I speak no treason.

*Cap.*          O, God ye good-den!

*Nurse.* May not one speak?

*Cap.*          Peace, you mumbling fool!

Utter your gravity o'er a gossip's bowl,

For here we need it not.

*Lady C.*          You are too hot.

*Cap.* God's bread! it makes me mad:

Day, night, hour, tide, time, work, play,

Alone, in company, still my care hath been

To have her match'd and having now pro-vided

A gentleman of noble parentage

Of fair demesnes, youthful, and nobly train'd,

Stuff'd, as they say, with honourable parts,

Proportion'd as one's heart could wish a man,—

And then to have a wretched puling fool,

A whining mammet, in her fortune's tender,

To answer, *I'll not wed,—I cannot love,*

*I am too young,—I pray you pardon me;—*

But, and you will not wed, I'll pardon you:

Graze where you will you shall not house with me:

Look to't, think on't, I do not use to jest.

Thursday is near; lay hand on heart, advise:

An you be mine, I'll give you to my friend;

And you be not, hang, beg, starve, die i' the streets,

For, by my soul, I'll ne'er acknowledge thee,

Nor what is mine shall never do thee good:

Trust to't, bethink you, I'll not be forsworn.
                                        [*Exit.*

*Jul.* Is there no pity sitting in the clouds,

That sees into the bottom of my grief?

O, sweet my mother, cast me not away!

Delay this marriage for a month, a week;

Or, if you do not, make the bridal bed

In that dim monument where Tybalt lies.

*Lady C.* Talk not to me, for I'll not speak a word.

Do as thou wilt, for I have done with thee.
                                        [*Exit.*

*Jul.* O God!—O nurse! how shall this be prevented?

My husband is on earth, my faith in heaven;

How shall that faith return again to earth,

Unless that husband send it me from heaven

By leaving earth?—comfort me, counsel me.—

Alack, alack, that heaven would practise stratagems

Upon so soft a subject as myself!—      [joy?

What say'st thou? hast thou not a word of

Some comfort, nurse.

*Nurse.*          Faith, here 'tis: Romeo

Is banished; and all the world to nothing

That he dares ne'er come back to challenge you;

Or, if he do, it needs must be by stealth.

Then, since the case so stands as now it doth,

I think it best you married with the county.

O, he's a lovely gentleman!                    [dam,

Romeo's a dishclout to him; an eagle, ma-

Hath not so green, so quick, so fair an eye

As Paris hath. Beshrew my very heart,

I think you are happy in this second match,

For it excels your first: or if it did not,

Your first is dead; or 'twere as good he were,

As living here, and you no use of him.

*Jul.* Speakest thou from thy heart?

*Nurse.*          From my soul too,

Or else beshrew them both.

*Jul.*          Amen!

*Nurse.*          What?

*Jul.* Well, thou hast comforted me marvel-ous much.

Go in; and tell my lady I am gone,

Having displeas'd my father, to Lawrence' cell.
To make confession, and to be absolv'd.
  *Nurse.* Marry, I will; and this is wisely
    done.    [*Exit.*
  *Jul.* Ancient damnation! O most wicked
    fiend!
Is it more sin to wish me thus forsworn,
Or to dispraise my lord with that same tongue
Which she hath prais'd him with above com-
  pare
So many thousand times?—Go, counsellor;
Thou and my bosom henceforth shall be
  twain.—
I'll to the friar, to know his remedy;
If all else fail, myself have power to die.
    [*Exit.*

## ACT IV.

### Scene I.—Friar Lawrence's *Cell.*

*Enter* Friar Lawrence *and* Paris.

  *Fri. L.* On Thursday, sir? the time is very
    short.
  *Par.* My father Capulet will have it so;
And I am nothing slow to slack his haste.
  *Fri. L.* You say you do not know the lady's
    mind:
Uneven is the course, I like it not.    [death,
  *Par.* Immoderately she weeps for Tybalt's
And therefore have I little talk'd of love;
For Venus smiles not in a house of tears.
Now, sir, her father counts it dangerous
That she doth give her sorrow so much sway;
And, in his wisdom, hastes our marriage,
To stop the inundation of her tears;
Which, too much minded by herself alone,
May be put from her by society:
Now do you know the reason of this haste.
  *Fri. L.* [*Aside.*] I would I knew not why it
    should be slow'd.—
Look, sir, hence comes the lady towards my
  cell.

*Enter* Juliet.

  *Par.* Happily met, my lady and my wife!
  *Jul.* That may be, sir, when I may be a
    wife.    [day next.
  *Par.* That may be must be, love, on Thurs-
  *Jul.* What must be shall be.
  *Fri. L.*            That's a certain text.
  *Par.* Come you to make confession to this
    father?
  *Jul.* To answer that, I should confess to
    you.    [me.
  *Par.* Do not deny to him that you love
  *Jul.* I will confess to you that I love him.
  *Par.* So will ye, I am sure, that you love
    me.
  *Jul.* If I do so, it will be of more price
Being spoke behind your back than to your
  face.    [with tears.
  *Par.* Poor soul, thy face is much abus'd
  *Jul.* The tears have got small victory by
    that;

For it was bad enough before their spite.
  *Par.* Thou wrong'st it more than tears with
    that report.    [truth;
  *Jul.* That is no slander, sir, which is a
And what I spake I spake it to my face.
  *Par.* Thy face is mine, and thou hast slan-
    der'd it.
  *Jul.* It may be so, for it is not mine own.—
Are you at leisure, holy father, now;
Or shall I come to you at evening mass?
  *Fri. L.* My leisure serves me, pensive
    daughter, now.—
My lord, we must entreat the time alone.
  *Par.* God shield I should disturb devo-
    tion!—
Juliet, on Thursday early will I rouse you:
Till then, adieu; and keep this holy kiss.
    [*Exit.*
  *Jul.* O, shut the door! and when thou hast
    done so,    [past help!
Come weep with me; past hope, past cure,
  *Fri. L.* Ah, Juliet, I already know thy
    grief;
It strains me past the compass of my wits:
I hear thou must, and nothing may prorogue
  it,
On Thursday next be married to this county.
  *Jul.* Tell me not, friar, that thou hear'st of
    this,
Unless thou tell me how I may prevent it:
If, in thy wisdom, thou canst give no help,
Do thou but call my resolution wise,
And with this knife I'll help it presently.
God join'd my heart and Romeo's, thou our
  hands;
And ere this hand, by thee to Romeo seal'd,
Shall be the label to another deed,
Or my true heart with treacherous revolt
Turn to another, this shall slay them both:
Therefore, out of thy long-experienc'd time,
Give me some present counsel; or, behold,
'Twixt my extremes and me this bloody knife
Shall play the umpire; arbitrating that
Which the commission of thy years and art
Could to no issue of true honour bring.
Be not so long to speak; I long to die,
If what thou speak'st speak not of remedy.
  *Fri. L.* Hold, daughter: I do spy a kind of
    hope,
Which craves as desperate an execution
As that is desperate which we would prevent.
If, rather than to marry County Paris,
Thou hast the strength of will to slay thyself,
Then is it likely thou wilt undertake
A thing like death to chide away this shame,
That cop'st with death himself to scape from
  it;
And, if thou dar'st, I'll give thee remedy.
  *Jul.* O, bid me leap, rather than marry
    Paris,
From off the battlements of yonder tower;
Or walk in thievish ways; or bid me lurk
Where serpents are; chain me with roaring
  bears;

Or shut me nightly in a charnel-house,
O'er-cover'd quite with dead men's rattling
  bones,
With reeky shanks, and yellow chapless skulls;
Or bid me go into a new-made grave,
And hide me with a dead man in his shroud;
Things that, to hear them told, have made me
  tremble;
And I will do it without fear or doubt,
To live an unstain'd wife to my sweet love.
  *Fri. L.* Hold, then; go home, be merry,
  give consent
To marry Paris; Wednesday is to-morrow;
To-morrow night look that thou lie alone,
Let not thy nurse lie with thee in thy
  chamber:
Take thou this vial, being then in bed,
And this distilled liquor drink thou off: [run
When, presently, through all thy veins shall
A cold and drowsy humour; for no pulse
Shall keep his native progress, but surcease:
No warmth, no breath, shall testify thou
  liv'st;
The roses in thy lips and cheeks shall fade
To paly ashes; thy eyes' windows fall,
Like death, when he shuts up the day of life;
Each part, depriv'd of supple government,
Shall, stiff and stark and cold, appear like
  death:
And in this borrow'd likeness of shrunk death
Thou shalt continue two-and-forty hours,
And then awake as from a pleasant sleep.
Now, when the bridegroom in the morning
  comes   [dead:
To rouse thee from thy bed, there art thou
Then,—as the manner of our country is,—
In thy best robes, uncover'd, on the bier,
Thou shalt be borne to that same ancient
  vault
Where all the kindred of the Capulets lie.
In the meantime, against thou shalt awake,
Shall Romeo by my letters know our drift;
And hither shall he come: and he and I
Will watch thy waking, and that very night
Shall Romeo bear thee hence to Mantua.
And this shall free thee from this present
  shame,
If no inconstant toy nor womanish fear
Abate thy valour in the acting it.
  *Jul.* Give me, give me! O, tell not me of
  fear!
  *Fri. L.* Hold; get you gone, be strong and
  prosperous
In this resolve: I'll send a friar with speed
To Mantua, with my letters to thy lord.
  *Jul.* Love give me strength; and strength
  shall help afford.
Farewell, dear father!     [*Exeunt.*

  Scene II.—*Hall in* Capulet's *House.*

*Enter* Capulet, Lady Capulet, Nurse, *and*
  Servants.

  *Cap.* So many guests invite as here are
  writ.—     [*Exit first* Servant.

Sirrah, go hire me twenty cunning cooks.
  *2 Serv.* You shall have none ill, sir; for
I'll try if they can lick their fingers.
  *Cap.* How canst thou try them so?
  *2 Serv.* Marry, sir, 'tis an ill cook that
cannot lick his own fingers: therefore he that
cannot lick his fingers goes not with me.
  *Cap.* Go, be gone.— [*Exit second* Servant.
We shall be much unfurnish'd for this time,—
What, is my daughter gone to Friar Law-
  rence?
  *Nurse.* Ay, forsooth.
  *Cap.* Well, he may chance to do some good
  on her:
A peevish self-will'd harlotry it is.
  *Nurse.* See where she comes from shrift
  with merry look.

    *Enter* Juliet.

  *Cap.* How now, my headstrong! where
  have you been gadding?   [sin
  *Jul.* Where I have learn'd me to repent the
Of disobedient opposition
To you and your behests; and am enjoin'd
By holy Lawrence to fall prostrate here,
And beg your pardon:—pardon, I beseech
  you!
Henceforward I am ever rul'd by you. [this:
  *Cap.* Send for the county; go tell him of
I'll have this knot knit up to-morrow morn-
  ing.     [cell:
  *Jul.* I met the youthful lord at Lawrence'
And gave him what becomed love I might,
Not stepping o'er the bounds of modesty.
  *Cap.* Why, I am glad on't; this is well,—
  stand up.
This is as't should be.—Let me see the county;
Ay, marry, go I say, and fetch him hither.—
Now, afore God, this reverend holy friar,
All our whole city is much bound to him.
  *Jul.* Nurse, will you go with me into my
  closet,
To help me sort such needful ornaments
As you think fit to furnish me to-morrow?
  *Lady C.* No, not till Thursday; there is
  time enough.
  *Cap.* Go, nurse, go with her.—We'll to
  church to-morrow.
    [*Exeunt* Juliet *and* Nurse.
  *Lady C.* We shall be short in our provi-
  sion:
'Tis now near night.
  *Cap.*     Tush, I will stir about,
And all things shall be well, I warrant thee,
  wife:
Go thou to Juliet, help to deck up her;
I'll not to bed to-night;—let me alone; [ho!—
I'll play the housewife for this once.—What,
They are all forth: well, I will walk myself
To County Paris, to prepare him up
Against to-morrow: my heart is wondrous
  light
Since this same wayward girl is so reclaim'd. ·
    [*Exeunt.*

SCENE III.—JULIET's *Chamber*.

*Enter* JULIET *and* Nurse.

*Jul.* Ay, those attires are best:—but, gentle nurse,
I pray thee, leave me to myself to-night;
For I have need of many orisons
To move the heavens to smile upon my state,
Which, well thou know'st, is cross and full of sin.

*Enter* LADY CAPULET.

*Lady C.* What, are you busy, ho? need you my help?                    [necessaries
*Jul.* No, madam; we have cull'd such
As are behoveful for our state to-morrow:
So please you, let me now be left alone,
And let the nurse this night sit up with you;
For I am sure you have your hands full all
In this so sudden business.
*Lady C.*                    Good-night;
Get thee to bed, and rest; for thou hast need.
          [*Exeunt* LADY CAPULET *and* Nurse.
*Jul.* Farewell!—God knows when we shall meet again.                    [veins
I have a faint cold fear thrills through my
That almost freezes up the heat of life:
I'll call them back again to comfort me;—
Nurse!—What should she do here?
My dismal scene I needs must act alone.—
Come, vial.—
What if this mixture do not work at all?
Shall I be married, then, to-morrow morning?—                    [there.—
No, no;—this shall forbid it:—lie thou
          [*Laying down her dagger.*
What if it be a poison, which the friar
Subtly hath minister'd to have me dead,
Lest in this marriage he should be dishonour'd,
Because he married me before to Romeo?
I fear it is: and yet methinks it should not,
For he hath still been tried a holy man:—
I will not entertain so bad a thought.—
How if, when I am laid into the tomb,
I wake before the time that Romeo
Come to redeem me? there's a fearful point!
Shall I not then be stifled in the vault,
To whose foul mouth no healthsome air breathes in,
And there die strangled ere my Romeo comes?
Or, if I live, is it not very like
The horrible conceit of death and night,
Together with the terror of the place,—
As in a vault, an ancient receptacle,                    [bones
Where, for these many hundred years, the
Of all my buried ancestors are pack'd;
Where bloody Tybalt, yet but green in earth,
Lies festering in his shroud; where, as they say,
At some hours in the night spirits resort;—
Alack, alack, is it not like that I,
So early waking,—what with loathsome smells,

And shrieks like mandrakes' torn out of the earth,
That living mortals, hearing them, run mad;—
O, if I wake, shall I not be distraught,
Environed with all these hideous fears?
And madly play with my forefathers' joints?
And pluck the mangled Tybalt from his shroud?                    [man's bone,
And, in this rage, with some great kins-
As with a club, dash out my desperate brains?
O, look! methinks I see my cousin's ghost
Seeking out Romeo, that did spit his body
Upon a rapier's point:—stay, Tybalt, stay!—
Romeo, I come! this do I drink to thee.
          [*Throws herself on the bed.*

SCENE IV.—*Hall in* CAPULET's *House*.

*Enter* LADY CAPULET *and* Nurse.

*Lady C.* Hold, take these keys, and fetch more spices, nurse.
*Nurse.* They call for dates and quinces in the pastry.

*Enter* CAPULET.

*Cap.* Come, stir, stir, stir! the second cock hath crow'd,
The curfew bell hath rung, 'tis three o'clock:—
Look to the bak'd meats, good Angelica:
Spare not for cost.
*Nurse.*                    Go, you cot-quean, go,
Get you to bed; faith, you'll be sick to-morrow
For this night's watching.                    [ere now
*Cap.* No, not a whit: what! I have watch'd
All night for lesser cause, and ne'er been sick.
*Lady C.* Ay, you have been a mouse-hunt in your time;
But I will watch you from such watching now.
          [*Exeunt* LADY CAPULET *and* Nurse.
*Cap.* A jealous-hood, a jealous-hood!—
Now, fellow,

*Enter* Servants, *with spits, logs, and baskets*.

What's there?                    [not what.
    1 *Serv.* Things for the cook, sir; but I know
*Cap.* Make haste, make haste.          [*Exit* 1
    *Serv.*]—Sirrah, fetch drier logs:
Call Peter, he will show thee where they are.
    2 *Serv.* I have a head, sir, that will find out logs,
And never trouble Peter for the matter. [*Exit.*
*Cap.* Mass, and well said; a merry whore-son, ha!                    [day.
Thou shalt be logger-head.—Good faith, 'tis
The county will be here with music straight,
For so he said he would:—I hear him near.—
          [*Music within.*
Nurse!—wife!—what, ho!—what, nurse, I say!

*Re-enter* Nurse.

Go waken Juliet, go and trim her up;

I'll go and chat with Paris:—hie, make haste,
Make haste; the bridegroom he is come already:
Make haste, I say.                    [*Exeunt.*

SCENE V.—JULIET'S *Chamber;* JULIET *on the bed.*

*Enter* Nurse.

*Nurse.* Mistress!—what, mistress!—Juliet!
—fast, I warrant her, she:—
Why, lamb!—why, lady!—fie, you slug-a-bed!—                    [why, bride!—
Why, love, I say!—madam! sweetheart!—
What, not a word?—you take your penny-worths now;                    [rant,
Sleep for a week; for the next night, I war-
The County Paris hath set up his rest
That you shall rest but little.—God forgive me,
Marry, and amen, how sound is she asleep!
I must needs wake her.—Madam, madam, madam!—
Ay, let the county take you in your bed;
He'll fright you up, i' faith.—Will it not be?
What, dress'd! and in your clothes! and down again!                    [lady!—
I must needs wake you:—lady! lady!
Alas, alas!—Help, help! my lady's dead!—
O, well-a-day, that ever I was born!—
Some aqua-vitæ, ho!—my lord, my lady!

*Enter* LADY CAPULET.

*Lady C.* What noise is here?
*Nurse.*                    O lamentable day!
*Lady C.* What is the matter?
*Nurse.*                    Look, look! O heavy day!
*Lady C.* O me, O me!—my child, my only life,
Revive, look up, or I will die with thee!—
Help, help!—call help.

*Enter* CAPULET.

*Cap.* For shame bring Juliet forth; her lord is come.                    [alack the day!
*Nurse.* She's dead, deceas'd, she's dead;
*Lady C.* Alack the day, she's dead, she's dead, she's dead!                    [she's cold;
*Cap.* Ha! let me see her:—out, alas!
Her blood is settled, and her joints are stiff;
Life and these lips have long been separated:
Death lies on her like an untimely frost
Upon the sweetest flower of all the field.
Accursed time! unfortunate old man!
*Nurse.* O lamentable day!
*Lady C.*                    O woeful time!
*Cap.* Death, that hath ta'en her hence to make me wail,
Ties up my tongue, and will not let me speak.

*Enter* FRIAR LAWRENCE *and* PARIS, *with Musicians.*

*Fri. L.* Come, is the bride ready to go to church?
*Cap.* Ready to go, but never to return:—

O son, the night before thy wedding-day
Hath death lain with thy bride:—there she lies,
Flower as she was, deflowered by him.
Death is my son-in-law, death is my heir;
My daughter he hath wedded: I will die,
And leave him all; life, living, all is death's.
*Par.* Have I thought long to see this morning's face,
And doth it give me such a sight as this?
*Lady C.* Accurs'd, unhappy, wretched, hateful day!
Most miserable hour that e'er time saw
In lasting labour of his pilgrimage!
But one, poor one, one poor and loving child,
But one thing to rejoice and solace in,
And cruel death hath catch'd it from my sight!                    [day!
*Nurse.* O woe! O woeful, woeful, woeful
Most lamentable day, most woeful day,
That ever, ever, I did yet behold!
O day! O day! O day! O hateful day!
Never was seen so black a day as this:
O woeful day, O woeful day!                    [slain!
*Par.* Beguil'd, divorced, wronged, spited,
Most detestable death, by thee beguil'd,
By cruel cruel thee quite overthrown!—
O love! O life!—not life, but love in death!
*Cap.* Despis'd, distressed, hated, martyr'd, kill'd!—
Uncomfortable time, why cam'st thou now
To murder, murder our solemnity?—
O child! O child!—my soul, and not my child!—                    [dead;
Dead art thou, dead!—alack, my child is
And with my child my joys are buried!
*Fri. L.* Peace, ho, for shame! confusion's cure lives not
In these confusions. Heaven and yourself
Had part in this fair maid; now heaven hath all,
And all the better is it for the maid:
Your part in her you could not keep from death;
But heaven keeps his part in eternal life.
The most you sought was her promotion;
For 'twas your heaven she should be advanc'd;
And weep ye now, seeing she is advanc'd
Above the clouds, as high as heaven itself?
O, in this love, you love your child so ill
That you run mad, seeing that she is well:
She's not well married that lives married long;                    [young.
But she's best married that dies married
Dry up your tears, and stick your rosemary
On this fair corse; and as the custom is,
In all her best array bear her to church:
For though fond nature bids us all lament,
Yet nature's tears are reason's merriment.
*Cap.* All things that we ordained festival
Turn from their office to black funeral:
Our instruments to melancholy bells;
Our wedding cheer to a sad burial feast;

Our solemn hymns to sullen dirges change;
Our bridal flowers serve for a buried corse,
And all things change them to the contrary.
  *Fri. L.* Sir, go you in,—and, madam, go
      with him;—
And go, Sir Paris;—every one prepare
To follow this fair corse unto her grave:
The heavens do lower upon you for some ill;
Move them no more by crossing their high
    will.
[*Exeunt* CAP., LADY CAP., PARIS, *and* FRIAR.
  1 *Mus.* Faith, we may put up our pipes and
be gone.                            [put up;
  *Nurse.* Honest good fellows, ah, put up,
For, well you know, this is a pitiful case.
                                    [*Exit.*
  1 *Mus.* Ay, by my troth, the case may be
amended.

### Enter PETER.

  *Pet.* Musicians, O, musicians, *Heart's ease,
Heart's ease:* O, an you will have me live,
play *Heart's ease.*
  1 *Mus.* Why *Heart's ease?*
  *Pet.* O, musicians, because my heart itself
plays *My heart is full of woe:* O, play me
some merry dump to comfort me. [play now.
  1 *Mus.* Not a dump we; 'tis no time to
  *Pet.* You will not, then?
  1 *Mus.* No.
  *Pet.* I will, then, give it you soundly.
  1 *Mus.* What will you give us?
  *Pet.* No money, on my faith; but the gleek,
—I will give you the minstrel.   [creature.
  1 *Mus.* Then will I give you the serving-
  *Pet.* Then will I lay the serving-creature's
dagger on your pate. I will carry no crotchets:
I'll *re* you, I'll *fa* you; do you note me?  [us.
  1 *Mus.* An you *re* us and *fa* us, you note
  2 *Mus.* Pray you, put up your dagger, and
put out your wit.
  *Pet.* Then have at you with my wit! I
will dry-beat you with an iron wit, and put
up my iron dagger.—Answer me like men:

  When griping grief the heart doth wound,
    And doleful dumps the mind oppress,
  Then music with her silver sound—

why *silver sound?* why *music with her silver
sound?*—What say you, Simon Catling?
  1 *Mus.* Marry, sir, because silver hath a
sweet sound.                        [beck?
  *Pet.* Pretty!—What say you, Hugh Re-
  2 *Mus.* I say *silver sound* because musicians
sound for silver.               [Sound-post?
  *Pet.* Pretty too!—What say you, James
  3 *Mus.* Faith, I know not what to say.
  *Pet.* O, I cry you mercy; you are the
singer: I will say for you. It is *music with her
silver sound* because musicians have no gold
for sounding:—

  Then music with her silver sound
    With speedy help doth lend redress.  [*Exit.*

  1 *Mus.* What a pestilent knave is this same!
  2 *Mus.* Hang him, Jack!—Come, we'll in
here; tarry for the mourners, and stay dinner.
                                  [*Exeunt.*

## ACT V.

### SCENE I.—MANTUA. *A Street.*

### Enter ROMEO.

  *Rom.* If I may trust the flattering eye of
    sleep,
My dreams presage some joyful news at hand:
My bosom's lord sits lightly in his throne;
And all this day an accustom'd spirit
Lifts me above the ground with cheerful
    thoughts.
I dreamt my lady came and found me dead,—
Strange dream, that gives a dead man leave
    to think!
And breath'd such life with kisses in my lips,
That I reviv'd, and was an emperor.
Ah me! how sweet is love itself possess'd,
When but love's shadows are so rich in joy!

### Enter BALTHASAR.

News from Verona!—How now, Balthasar!
Dost thou not bring me letters from the friar?
How doth my lady? Is my father well?
How fares my Juliet? that I ask again;
For nothing can be ill if she be well.    [ill:
  *Bal.* Then she is well, and nothing can be
Her body sleeps in Capels' monument,
And her immortal part with angels lives.
I saw her laid low in her kindred's vault,
And presently took post to tell it you:
O, pardon me for bringing these ill news,
Since you did leave it for my office, sir.
  *Rom.* Is it even so? then I defy you,
    stars!—
Thou know'st my lodging: get me ink and
    paper,
And hire post-horses; I will hence to-night.
  *Bal.* I do beseech you, sir, have patience:
Your looks are pale and wild, and do import
Some misadventure.
  *Rom.*           Tush, thou art deceiv'd:
Leave me, and do the thing I bid thee do.
Hast thou no letters to me from the friar?
  *Bal.* No, my good lord.
  *Rom.*             No matter: get thee gone,
And hire those horses; I'll be with thee
    straight.           [*Exit* BALTHASAR.
Well, Juliet, I will lie with thee to-night.
Let's see for means:—O mischief, thou art
    swift
To enter in the thoughts of desperate men!
I do remember an apothecary,—
And hereabouts he dwells,—which late I
    noted
In tatter'd weeds, with overwhelming brows,
Culling of simples; meagre were his looks,
Sharp misery had worn him to the bones:
And in his needy shop a tortoise hung,
An alligator stuff'd, and other skins

Of ill-shap'd fishes; and about his shelves
A beggarly account of empty boxes,
Green earthen pots, bladders, and musty
    seeds,                   [roses,
Remnants of packthread, and old cakes of
Were thinly scatter'd, to make up a show.
Noting this penury, to myself I said,
An if a man did need a poison now,
Whose sale is present death in Mantua,
Here lives a caitiff wretch would sell it him.
O, this same thought did but forerun my
    need;
And this same needy man must sell it me.
As I remember, this should be the house:
Being holiday, the beggar's shop is shut.—
What, ho! apothecary!

*Enter* Apothecary.

*Ap.*              Who calls so loud?
*Rom.* Come hither, man.—I see that thou
    art poor;
Hold, there is forty ducats: let me have
A dram of poison; such soon-speeding gear
As will disperse itself through all the veins,
That the life-weary taker may fall dead;
And that the trunk may be discharg'd of
    breath
As violently as hasty powder fir'd
Doth hurry from the fatal cannon's womb.
   *Ap.* Such mortal drugs I have; but Man-
tua's law
Is death to any he that utters them.
   *Rom.* Art thou so bare and full of wretch-
edness,
And fear'st to die? famine is in thy cheeks,
Need and oppression starveth in thine eyes,
Contempt and beggary hangs upon thy back,
The world is not thy friend, nor the world's
    law:
The world affords no law to make thee rich;
Then be not poor, but break it, and take this.
   *Ap.* My poverty, but not my will consents.
   *Rom.* I pay thy poverty, and not thy will.
   *Ap.* Put this in any liquid thing you will,
And drink it off; and, if you had the strength
Of twenty men, it would despatch you
    straight.         [men's souls,
   *Rom.* There is thy gold; worse poison to
Doing more murders in this loathsome world
Than these poor compounds that thou mayst
    not sell:
I sell thee poison, thou hast sold me none.
Farewell: buy food, and get thyself in flesh.—
Come, cordial, and not poison, go with me
To Juliet's grave; for there must I use thee.
                      [*Exeunt.*

SCENE II.—FRIAR LAWRENCE'S *Cell.*

*Enter* FRIAR JOHN.

*Fri. J.* Holy Franciscan friar! brother, ho!

*Enter* FRIAR LAWRENCE.

*Fri. L.* This same should be the voice of
    Friar John.

Welcome from Mantua: what says Romeo?
Or, if his mind be writ, give me his letter.
   *Fri. J.* Going to find a barefoot brother
    out,
One of our order, to associate me,
Here in this city visiting the sick,
And finding him, the searchers of the town,
Suspecting that we both were in a house
Where the infectious pestilence did reign,
Seal'd up the doors, and would not let us
    forth;
So that my speed to Mantua there was stay'd.
   *Fri. L.* Who bare my letter, then, to
    Romeo?
   *Fri. J.* I could not send it,—here it is
    again,—
Nor get a messenger to bring it thee,
So fearful were they of infection.    [hood,
   *Fri. L.* Unhappy fortune! by my brother-
The letter was not nice, but full of charge
Of dear import; and the neglecting it
May do much danger. Friar John, go hence;
Get me an iron crow, and bring it straight
Unto my cell.
   *Fri. J.* Brother, I'll go and bring it thee.
                       [*Exit.*
   *Fri. L.* Now must I to the monument
    alone;
Within this three hours will fair Juliet wake:
She will beshrew me much that Romeo
Hath had no notice of these accidents;
But I will write again to Mantua,
And keep her at my cell till Romeo come;—
Poor living corse, clos'd in a dead man's
    tomb!                  [*Exit.*

SCENE III.—*A Churchyard; in it a Monument belonging to the* CAPULETS.

*Enter* PARIS, *and his* Page *bearing flowers and
    a torch.*

   *Par.* Give me thy torch, boy: hence, and
    stand aloof;—
Yet put it out, for I would not be seen.
Under yond yew trees lay thee all along,
Holding thine ear close to the hollow ground;
So shall no foot upon the churchyard tread,—
Being loose, unfirm, with digging up of
    graves,—
But thou shalt hear it: whistle then to me,
As signal that thou hear'st something ap-
    proach.
Give me those flowers. Do as I bid thee, go.
   *Page. [Aside.]* I am almost afraid to stand
    alone
Here in the churchyard; yet I will adventure.
                      [*Retires.*
   *Par.* Sweet flower, with flowers thy bridal
    bed I strew:
O woe, thy canopy is dust and stones!
Which with sweet water nightly I will dew;
   Or, wanting that, with tears distill'd by
    moans:
The obsequies that I for thee will keep,

Nightly shall be to strew thy grave and weep.
[*The* Page *whistles.*
The boy gives warning something doth approach.
What cursed foot wanders this way to-night,
To cross my obsequies and true love's rite?
What, with a torch!—muffle me, night, a
while.                              [*Retires.*

*Enter* ROMEO *and* BALTHASAR, *with a torch,*
*mattock, &c.*

*Rom.* Give me that mattock and the
wrenching iron.
Hold, take this letter; early in the morning
See thou deliver it to my lord and father.
Give me the light: upon thy life I charge
thee,                             [aloof,
Whate'er thou hear'st or seest, stand all
And do not interrupt me in my course.
Why I descend into this bed of death
Is partly to behold my lady's face,
But chiefly to take thence from her dead
finger
A precious ring,—a ring that I must use
In dear employment: therefore hence, be
gone:—
But if thou, jealous, dost return to pry
In what I further shall intend to do,
By heaven, I will tear thee joint by joint,
And strew this hungry churchyard with thy
limbs:
The time and my intents are savage-wild;
More fierce and more inexorable far
Than empty tigers or the roaring sea.
*Bal.* I will be gone, sir, and not trouble
you.
*Rom.* So shalt thou show me friendship.—
Take thou that:                  [fellow.
Live and be prosperous: and farewell, good
*Bal.* For all this same, I'll hide me hereabout:
His looks I fear and his intents I doubt.
[*Retires.*
*Rom.* Thou detestable maw, thou womb of
death,
Gorg'd with the dearest morsel of the earth,
Thus I enforce thy rotten jaws to open,
[*Breaking open the door of the monument.*
And, in despite, I'll cram thee with more
food!
*Par.* This is that banish'd haughty Montague
That murder'd my love's cousin,—with which
grief,
It is supposed, the fair creature died,—
And here is come to do some villanous shame
To the dead bodies: I will apprehend him.—
[*Advances.*
Stop thy unhallow'd toil, vile Montague!
Can vengeance be pursu'd further than death?
Condemned villain, I do apprehend thee:
Obey, and go with me; for thou must die.
*Rom.* I must indeed; and therefore came I
hither.—

Good gentle youth, tempt not a desperate
man;                              [gone;
Fly hence, and leave me:—think upon these
Let them affright thee.—I beseech thee, youth,
Put not another sin upon my head
By urging me to fury: O, be gone!
By heaven, I love thee better than myself;
For I come hither arm'd against myself:
Stay not, be gone;—live, and hereafter say,
A madman's mercy bade thee run away.
*Par.* I do defy thy conjurations,
And apprehend thee for a felon here.
*Rom.* Wilt thou provoke me? then have at
thee, boy!                        [*They fight.*
*Page.* O lord, they fight! I will go call the
watch.                            [*Exit.*
*Par.* O, I am slain! [*Falls.*]—If thou be
merciful,
Open the tomb, lay me with Juliet. [*Dies.*
*Rom.* In faith, I will.—Let me peruse this
face:—
Mercutio's kinsman, noble County Paris!—
What said my man, when my betossed soul
Did not attend him as we rode? I think
He told me Paris should have married Juliet:
Said he not so? or did I dream it so?
Or am I mad, hearing him talk of Juliet,
To think it was so?—O, give me thy hand,
One writ with me in sour misfortune's book!
I'll bury thee in a triumphant grave;—
A grave? O no, a lantern, slaughter'd youth,
For here lies Juliet, and her beauty makes
This vault a feasting presence full of light.
Death, lie thou there, by a dead man interr'd.
[*Laying* PARIS *in the monument.*
How oft when men are at the point of death
Have they been merry! which their keepers
call
A lightning before death: O, how may I
Call this a lightning?—O my love! my wife!
Death, that hath suck'd the honey of thy
breath,
Hath had no power yet upon thy beauty:
Thou art not conquer'd; beauty's ensign yet
Is crimson in thy lips and in thy cheeks,
And death's pale flag is not advanced there.—
Tybalt, liest thou there in thy bloody sheet?
O, what more favour can I do to thee [twain
Than with that hand that cut thy youth in
To sunder his that was thine enemy?
Forgive me, cousin!—Ah, dear Juliet,
Why are thou yet so fair? Shall I believe
That unsubstantial death is amorous;
And that the lean abhorred monster keeps
Thee here in dark to be his paramour?
For fear of that I still will stay with thee,
And never from this palace of dim night
Depart again: here, here will I remain [here
With worms that are thy chambermaids; O,
Will I set up my everlasting rest;
And shake the yoke of inauspicious stars
From this world-wearied flesh.—Eyes, look
your last!                        [you
Arms, take your last embrace! and, lips, O

The doors of breath, seal with a righteous kiss
A dateless bargain to engrossing death!—
Come, bitter conduct, come, unsavoury guide!
Thou desperate pilot, now at once run on
The dashing rocks thy sea-sick weary bark!
Here's to my love! [*Drinks.*]—O true apothe-
  cary!
Thy drugs are quick.—Thus with a kiss I die.
                                        [*Dies.*

*Enter, at the other end of the Churchyard,*
FRIAR LAWRENCE, *with a lantern, crow,*
           *and spade.*

*Fri. L.*  Saint Francis be my speed! how
  oft to-night                    [there?
Have my old feet stumbled at graves!—Who's
Who is it that consorts, so late, the dead?
*Bal.*  Here's one, a friend, and one that
  knows you well.              [my friend,
*Fri. L.*  Bliss be upon you! Tell me, good
What torch is yond that vainly lends his
  light
To grubs and eyeless skulls? as I discern,
It burneth in the Capels' monument. [master,
*Bal.*  It doth so, holy sir; and there's my
One that you love.
*Fri. L.*          Who is it?
*Bal.*                        Romeo.
*Fri. L.*  How long hath he been there?
*Bal.*                        Full half an hour.
*Fri. L.*  Go with me to the vault.
*Bal.*  I dare not, sir:
My master knows not but I am gone hence;
And fearfully did menace me with death
If I did stay to look on his intents.
*Fri. L.*  Stay, then; I'll go alone:—fear
  comes upon me;
O, much I fear some ill unlucky thing.
*Bal.*  As I did sleep under this yew tree
  here,
I dreamt my master and another fought,
And that my master slew him.
*Fri. L.*          Romeo! [*Advances.*
Alack, alack, what blood is this which stains
The stony entrance of this sepulchre?—
What mean these masterless and gory swords
To lie discolour'd by this place of peace?
                        [*Enters the monument.*
Romeo! O, pale!—Who else? what, Paris too?
And steep'd in blood?—Ah, what an unkind
  hour
Is guilty of this lamentable chance!—
The lady stirs.        [JULIET *wakes and stirs.*
*Jul.*  O comfortable friar! where is my
  lord?—
I do remember well where I should be,
And there I am:—where is my Romeo?
                        [*Noise within.*
*Fri. L.*  I hear some noise.—Lady, come
  from that nest
Of death, contagion, and unnatural sleep:
A greater power than we can contradict
Hath thwarted our intents:—come, come
  away:

Thy husband in thy bosom there lies dead;
And Paris too:—come, I'll dispose of thee
Among a sisterhood of holy nuns:
Stay not to question, for the watch is coming;
Come, go, good Juliet [*noise again*],—I dare
  no longer stay.              [*away.*—
*Jul.*  Go, get thee hence, for I will not
                    [*Exit* FRIAR LAWRENCE.
What's here? a cup, clos'd in my true love's
  hand?
Poison, I see, hath been his timeless end:—
O churl! drink all, and leave no friendly drop
To help me after?—I will kiss thy lips;
Haply some poison yet doth hang on them,
To make me die with a restorative.
                        [*Kisses him.*
Thy lips are warm!
*1 Watch.*  [*Within.*]  Lead, boy:—which
  way?
*Jul.*  Yea, noise?—then I'll be brief.—O
  happy dagger!
                *Snatching* ROMEO's *dagger.*
This is thy sheath [*stabs herself*]; there rest,
  and let me die.
                [*Falls on* ROMEO's *body, and dies.*

*Enter* Watch, *with the Page of* PARIS.

*Page.*  This is the place; there, where the
  torch doth burn.
*1 Watch.*  The ground is bloody; search
  about the churchyard:
Go, some of you, whoe'er you find attach.
                [*Exeunt some of the* Watch.
Pitiful sight! here lies the county slain;—
And Juliet bleeding; warm, and newly dead,
Who here hath lain these two days buried.—
Go, tell the prince,—run to the Capulets,—
Raise up the Montagues,—some others
  search:— [*Exeunt others of the* Watch.
We see the ground whereon these woes do
  lie;
But the true ground of all these piteous woes
We cannot without circumstance descry.

*Re-enter some of the* Watch *with* BALTHASAR.

*2 Watch.*  Here's Romeo's man; we found
  him in the churchyard.
*1 Watch.*  Hold him in safety till the prince
  come hither.

*Re-enter others of the* Watch *with* FRIAR
                LAWRENCE.

*3 Watch.*  Here is a friar, that trembles,
  sighs, and weeps:
We took this mattock and this spade from
  him
As he was coming from this churchyard side.
*1 Watch.*  A great suspicion: stay the friar
  too.

*Enter the* PRINCE *and* Attendants.

*Prince.*  What misadventure is so early up,
That calls our person from our morning's
  rest?

*Enter* CAPULET, LADY CAPULET, *and others.*

*Cap.* What should it be, that they so shriek
　　abroad?　　　　　　　　　　　　[Romeo,
*Lady C.* The people in the street cry
Some Juliet, and some Paris; and all run,
With open outcry, toward our monument.
*Prince.* What fear is this which startles in
　　our ears?
1 *Watch.* Sovereign, here lies the County
　　Paris slain;
And Romeo dead; and Juliet, dead before,
Warm and new kill'd.
*Prince.* Search, seek, and know how this
　　foul murder comes. [Romeo's man,
1 *Watch.* Here is a friar, and slaughter'd
With instruments upon them fit to open
These dead men's tombs.　　[daughter bleeds.]
*Cap.* O heaven!—O wife, look how our
This dagger hath mista'en,—for, lo, his house
Is empty on the back of Montague,—
And is mis-sheathed in my daughter's bosom!
*Lady C.* O me! this sight of death is as a
　　bell
That warns my old age to a sepulchre.

*Enter* MONTAGUE *and others.*

*Prince.* Come, Montague; for thou art
　　early up,
To see thy son and heir more early down.
*Mon.* Alas, my liege, my wife is dead to-
　　night;　　　　　　　　　　　　[breath:
Grief of my son's exile hath stopp'd her
What further woe conspires against my age?
*Prince.* Look, and thou shalt see.　[in this,
*Mon.* O thou untaught! what manners is
To press before thy father to a grave?
*Prince.* Seal up the mouth of outrage for
　　awhile,
Till we can clear these ambiguities,
And know their spring, their head, their true
　　descent;
And then will I be general of your woes,
And lead you even to death: meantime for-
　　bear,
And let mischance be slave to patience.—
Bring forth the parties of suspicion.
*Fri. L.* I am the greatest, able to do least,
Yet most suspected, as the time and place
Doth make against me, of this direful murder;
And here I stand, both to impeach and purge
Myself condemned and myself excus'd.
*Prince.* Then say at once what thou dost
　　know in this.　　　　　　　　　[breath
*Fri. L.* I will be brief, for my short date of
Is not so long as is a tedious tale.　[Juliet;
Romeo, there dead, was husband to that
And she, there dead, that Romeo's faithful
　　wife:　　　　　　　　　　　　　[day
I married them; and their stol'n marriage-
Was Tybalt's dooms day, whose untimely
　　death　　　　　　　　　　　[this city;
Banish'd the new-made bridegroom from
For whom, and not for Tybalt, Juliet pin'd.

You, to remove that siege of grief from her,
Betroth'd, and would have married her per-
　　force,
To County Paris:—then comes she to me,
And, with wild looks, bid me devise some
　　means
To rid her from this second marriage,
Or in my cell there would she kill herself.
Then gave I her, so tutor'd by my art,
A sleeping potion; which so took effect
As I intended, for it wrought on her
The form of death: meantime I writ to
　　Romeo
That he should hither come as this dire night,
To help to take her from her borrow'd grave,
Being the time the potion's force should cease.
But he which bore my letter, Friar John,
Was stay'd by accident; and yesternight
Return'd my letter back. Then all alone
At the prefixed hour of her waking
Came I to take her from her kindred's vault;
Meaning to keep her closely at my cell
Till I conveniently could send to Romeo:
But when I came,—some minute ere the
　　time
Of her awaking,—here untimely lay
The noble Paris and true Romeo dead.
She wakes; and I entreated her come forth,
And bear this work of heaven with patience:
But then a noise did scare me from the tomb;
And she, too desperate, would not go with me,
But, as it seems, did violence on herself.
All this I know; and to the marriage
Her nurse is privy: and if ought in this
Miscarried by my fault, let my old life
Be sacrific'd, some hour before his time,
Unto the rigour of severest law. [holy man.—
*Prince.* We still have known thee for a
Where's Romeo's man? what can he say in
　　this?　　　　　　　　　　　　[death;
*Bal.* I brought my master news of Juliet's
And then in post he came from Mantua
To this same place, to this same monument.
This letter he early bid me give his father;
And threaten'd me with death, going in the
　　vault,
If I departed not, and left him there.
*Prince.* Give me the letter,—I will look on
　　it.—　　　　　　　　　　　　[watch?—
Where is the county's page that rais'd the
Sirrah, what made your master in this place?
*Page.* He came with flowers to strew his
　　lady's grave;
And bid me stand aloof, and so I did:
Anon comes one with light to ope the tomb;
And by and by my master drew on him;
And then I ran away to call the watch.
*Prince.* This letter doth make good the
　　friar's words,
Their course of love, the tidings of her death:
And here he writes that he did buy a poison
Of a poor 'pothecary, and therewithal
Came to this vault to die, and lie with
　　Juliet.—

Where be these enemies?—Capulet,—Montague,—
See what a scourge is laid upon your hate,
That heaven finds means to kill your joys
    with love!
And I, for winking at your discords too,
Have lost a brace of kinsmen:—all are
    punish'd.
  *Cap.* O brother Montague, give me thy
    hand:
This is my daughter's jointure, for no more
Can I demand.
  *Mon.*      But I can give thee more:

For I will raise her statue in pure gold;
That while Verona by that name is known,
There shall be no figure at such rate be set
As that of true and faithful Juliet.
  *Cap.* As rich shall Romeo by his lady lie;
Poor sacrifices of our enmity! [with it brings;
  *Prince.* A glooming peace this morning
    The sun for sorrow will not show his head:
Go hence, to have more talk of these sad
    things;
  Some shall be pardon'd and some punished:
For never was a story of more woe
Than this of Juliet and her Romeo. [*Exeunt.*

# MACBETH

## DRAMATIS PERSONÆ

DUNCAN, *King of Scotland.*
MALCOLM, } *his Sons.*
DONALBAIN,
MACBETH, } *Generals of the King's Army.*
BANQUO,
MACDUFF, ⎤
LENNOX, |
ROSS, ⎬ *Noblemen of Scotland.*
MENTEITH, |
ANGUS, |
CAITHNESS, ⎦
FLEANCE, *Son to* BANQUO.
SIWARD, *Earl of Northumberland, General of
    the English Forces.*
YOUNG SIWARD, *his Son.*

SEYTON, *an Officer attending on* MACBETH.
BOY, *Son to* MACDUFF.
An English Doctor. A Scotch Doctor. A
    Soldier. A Porter. An Old Man.

LADY MACBETH.
LADY MACDUFF.
Gentlewoman *attending on* LADY MACBETH.
HECATE, *and three* Witches.

Lords, Gentlemen, Officers, Soldiers, Mur-
    derers, Attendants, *and* Messengers.

The Ghost of BANQUO, *and several other Ap-
    paritions.*

SCENE,—*In the end of the Fourth Act, in* ENGLAND; *through the rest of the Play, in*
SCOTLAND; *and chiefly at* MACBETH'S *Castle.*

## ACT I.

SCENE I.—*An open Place. Thunder and
    Lightning.*

*Enter three* Witches.

1 *Witch.* When shall we three meet again
In thunder, lightning, or in rain?
2 *Witch.* When the hurlyburly's done,
When the battle's lost and won.
3 *Witch.* That will be ere the set of sun.
1 *Witch.* Where the place?
2 *Witch.*                    Upon the heath.
3 *Witch.* There to meet with Macbeth.
1 *Witch.* I come, Graymalkin!
*All.* Paddock calls:—anon.—
Fair is foul, and foul is fair:
Hover through the fog and filthy air.
                    [Witches *vanish.*

SCENE II.—*A Camp near Forres.*

*Alarum within. Enter* KING DUNCAN, MAL-
COLM, DONALBAIN, LENNOX, *with* Attendants, *meeting a bleeding* Soldier.

*Dun.* What bloody man is that? He can
    report,
As seemeth by his plight, of the revolt
The newest state.
*Mal.*              This is the sergeant,
Who, like a good and hardy soldier, fought
'Gainst my captivity.—Hail, brave friend!
Say to the king the knowledge of the broil,
As thou didst leave it.
*Sold.*              Doubtfully it stood;
As two spent swimmers that do cling together

And choke their art. The merciless Macdon-
    wald,—
Worthy to be a rebel—for to that
The multiplying villanies of nature
Do swarm upon him,—from the Western isles
Of kerns and gallowglasses is supplied;
And fortune, on his damned quarrel smiling,
Show'd like a rebel's whore. But all's too
    weak:                    [name,—
For brave Macbeth,—well he deserves that
Disdaining fortune, with his brandish'd steel,
Which smok'd with bloody execution,
Like valour's minion,
Carv'd out his passage till he fac'd the slave;
And ne'er shook hands, nor bade farewell to
    him,                    [chaps,
Till he unseam'd him from the nave to the
And fix'd his head upon our battlements.
*Dun.* O valiant cousin! worthy gentleman!
*Sold.* As whence the sun 'gins his reflection
Shipwrecking storms and direful thunders
    break;                    [to come,
So from that spring, whence comfort seem'd
Discomfort swells. Mark, King of Scotland,
    mark:
No sooner justice had, with valour arm'd,
Compell'd these skipping kerns to trust their
    heels,
But the Norweyan lord, surveying vantage,
With furbish'd arms and new supplies of men,
Began a fresh assault.
*Dun.*              Dismay'd not this
Our captains, Macbeth and Banquo?
*Sold.*                    Yes;
As sparrows eagles, or the hare the lion.

If I say sooth, I must report they were
As cannons overcharg'd with double cracks;
So they
Doubly redoubled strokes upon the foe:
Except they meant to bathe in reeking
   wounds,
Or memorize another Golgotha,
I cannot tell:—
But I am faint; my gashes cry for help.
   *Dun.* So well thy words become thee as thy
     wounds;
They smack of honour both.—Go, get him
   surgeons.        [*Exit* Soldier, *attended.*
Who comes here?
   *Mal.*            The worthy Thane of Ross.
   *Len.* What a haste looks through his eyes!
So should he look
That seems to speak things strange.

*Enter* Ross.

   *Ross.*           God save the king!
   *Dun.* Whence cam'st thou, worthy thane?
   *Ross.*         From Fife, great king;
Where the Norweyan banners flout the sky
And fan our people cold.
Norway himself, with terrible numbers,
Assisted by that most disloyal traitor
The Thane of Cawdor began a dismal con-
   flict;                  [proof,
Till that Bellona's bridegroom, lapp'd in
Confronted him with self-comparisons,
Point against point rebellious, arm 'gainst
   arm,
Curbing his lavish spirit: and, to conclude,
The victory fell on us.
   *Dun.*           Great happiness!
   *Ross.* That now
Sweno, the Norways' king, craves composi-
   tion;
Nor would we deign him burial of his men
Till he disbursed, at Saint Colmes-inch,
Ten thousand dollars to our general use.
   *Dun.* No more that Thane of Cawdor shall
     deceive           [ent death,
Our bosom interest:—go pronounce his pres-
And with his former title greet Macbeth.
   *Ross.* I'll see it done.
   *Dun.* What he hath lost, noble Macbeth
   hath won.             [*Exeunt.*

SCENE III.—*A Heath.*

*Thunder. Enter the three* Witches.

   1 *Witch.* Where hast thou been, sister?
   2 *Witch.* Killing swine.
   3 *Witch.* Sister, where thou?
   1 *Witch.* A sailor's wife had chestnuts in
     her lap,
And mounch'd, and mounch'd, and mounch'd:
   —*Give me,* quoth I:
*Aroint thee, witch!* the rump-fed ronyon cries.
Her husband's to Aleppo gone, master o' the
   Tiger:
But in a sieve I'll thither sail,
And, like a rat without a tail,

I'll do, I'll do, and I'll do.
   2 *Witch.* I'll give thee a wind.
   1 *Witch.* Thou art kind.
   3 *Witch.* And I another.
   1 *Witch.* I myself have all the other;
And the very ports they blow,
All the quarters that they know
I' the shipman's card.
I will drain him dry as hay:
Sleep shall neither night nor day
Hang upon his pent-house lid;
He shall live a man forbid:
Weary seven-nights nine times nine
Shall he dwindle, peak, and pine:
Though his bark cannot be lost,
Yet it shall be tempest-tost.—
Look what I have.
   2 *Witch.* Show me, show me.
   1 *Witch.* Here I have a pilot's thumb,
Wreck'd as homeward he did come.
                    [*Drum within.*
   3 *Witch.* A drum, a drum!
Macbeth doth come.
   *All.* The weird sisters, hand in hand,
Posters of the sea and land,
Thus do go about, about:
Thrice to thine, and thrice to mine,
And thrice again, to make up nine:—
Peace!—the charm's wound up.

*Enter* MACBETH *and* BANQUO.

   *Macb.* So foul and fair a day I have not
   seen.          [What are these,
   *Ban.* How far is't call'd to Forres?—
So wither'd, and so wild in their attire,
That look not like the inhabitants o' the
   earth,           [aught
And yet are on't?—Live you or are you
That man may question? You seem to un-
   derstand me,
By each at once her chappy finger laying
Upon her skinny lips:—you should be
   women,
And yet your beards forbid me to interpret
That you are so.
   *Macb.* Speak, if you can;—what are you?
   1 *Witch.* All hail, Macbeth! hail to thee,
     Thane of Glamis!
   2 *Witch.* All hail, Macbeth! hail to thee,
     Thane of Cawdor!
   3 *Witch.* All hail, Macbeth; that shalt be
     king hereafter!        [seem to fear
   *Ban.* Good sir, why do you start; and
Things that do sound so fair?—I' the name
   of truth,
Are ye fantastical, or that indeed
Which outwardly ye show? My noble partner
You greet with present grace and great pre-
   diction
Of noble having and of royal hope,    [not:
That he seems rapt withal:—to me you speak
If you can look into the seeds of time,
And say which grain will grow, and which
     will not.

Speak then to me, who neither beg nor fear
Your favours nor your hate.

1 *Witch.*  Hail!

2 *Witch.*  Hail!

3 *Witch.*  Hail!

1 *Witch.*  Lesser than Macbeth, and greater,

2 *Witch.*  Not so happy, yet much happier.

3 *Witch.*  Thou shalt get kings, though thou
be none:

So, all hail, Macbeth and Banquo!

1 *Witch.*  Banquo and Macbeth, all hail!

*Macb.*  Stay, you imperfect speakers, tell
me more:                          [Glamis;
By Sinel's death I know I am Thane of
But how of Cawdor? the Thane of Cawdor
lives,
A prosperous gentleman; and to be king
Stands not within the prospect of belief,
No more than to be Cawdor. Say from whence
You owe this strange intelligence? or why
Upon this blasted heath you stop our way
With such prophetic greeting?—Speak, I
charge you.                [Witches *vanish.*

*Ban.*  The earth hath bubbles, as the water
has,                                [vanish'd?
And these are of them:—whither are they

*Macb.*  Into the air; and what seem'd corporal melted
As breath into the wind.—Would they had
stay'd!                      [speak about?

*Ban.*  Were such things here as we do
Or have we eaten on the insane root
That takes the reason prisoner?

*Macb.*  Your children shall be kings.

*Ban.*                    You shall be king.

*Macb.*  And Thane of Cawdor too; went it
not so?                          [Who's here?

*Ban.*  To the self-same tune and words.

*Enter* Ross *and* ANGUS.

*Ross.*  The king hath happily receiv'd, Mac-
beth,
The news of thy success: and when he reads
Thy personal venture in the rebels' fight,
His wonders and his praises do contend
Which should be thine or his: silenc'd with
that,
In viewing o'er the rest o' the self-same day,
He finds thee in the stout Norweyan ranks,
Nothing afeard of what thyself didst make,
Strange images of death. As thick as hail
Came post with post; and every one did bear
Thy praises in his kingdom's great defence,
And pour'd them down before him.

*Ang.*                        We are sent
To give thee, from our royal master, thanks;
Only to herald thee into his sight,
Not pay thee.                        [our,

*Ross.*  And, for an earnest of a greater hon-
He bade me, from him, call thee Thane of
Cawdor:
In which addition, hail, most worthy thane!
For it is thine.

*Ban.*          What, can the devil speak true?

*Macb.*  The Thane of Cawdor lives: why do
you dress me
In borrow'd robes?

*Ang.*          Who was the thane lives yet;
But under heavy judgment bears that life
Which he deserves to lose. Whether he was
combin'd
With those of Norway, or did line the rebel
With hidden help and vantage, or that with
both                              [not;
He labour'd in his country's wreck, I know
But treasons capital, confess'd, and prov'd,
Have overthrown him.

*Macb.*      Glamis, and Thane of Cawdor:
The greatest is behind [*aside*].—Thanks for
your pains.—                      [kings,
Do you not hope your children shall be
When those that gave the Thane of Cawdor
to me
Promis'd no less to them?

*Ban.*                  That, trusted home,
Might yet enkindle you unto the crown,
Besides the Thane of Cawdor. But 'tis strange:
And oftentimes to win us to our harm,
The instruments of darkness tell us truths;
Win us with honest trifles, to betray's
In deepest consequence.—
Cousins, a word, I pray you.

*Macb.*                  Two truths are told,
As happy prologues to the swelling act
Of the imperial theme [*aside*].—I thank you,
gentlemen.—
This supernatural soliciting            [*Aside.*
Cannot be ill; cannot be good:—if ill,
Why hath it given me earnest of success,
Commencing in a truth? I am Thane of
Cawdor:
If good, why do I yield to that suggestion
Whose horrid image doth unfix my hair,
And make my seated heart knock at my ribs,
Against the use of nature? Present fears
Are less than horrible imaginings:  [tastical,
My thought, whose murder yet is but fan-
Shakes so my single state of man, that
function
Is smother'd in surmise; and nothing is
But what is not.

*Ban.*          Look, how our partner's rapt.

*Macb.*  [*Aside.*]  If chance will have me
king, why, chance may crown me,
Without my stir.

*Ban.*              New honours come upon him,
Like our strange garments, cleave not to their
mould
But with the aid of use.

*Macb.*  [*Aside.*]  Come what come may,
Time and the hour runs through the roughest
day.

*Ban.*  Worthy Macbeth, we stay upon
your leisure.

*Macb.*  Give me your favour:—my dull
brain was wrought                  [pains
With things forgotten. Kind gentlemen, your
Are register'd where every day I turn

The leaf to read them.—Let us toward the king.— [time,
Think upon what hath chanc'd; and, at more
The interim having weigh'd it, let us speak
Our free hearts each to other.
*Ban.* Very gladly.
*Macb.* Till then, enough.—Come, friends.
[*Exeunt.*

Scene IV.—Forres. *A Room in the Palace.*

*Flourish. Enter* Duncan, Malcolm, Donalbain, Lennox *and* Attendants.

*Dun.* Is execution done on Cawdor? Are not
Those in commission yet return'd?
*Mal.* My liege,
They are not yet come back. But I have spoke
With one that saw him die: who did report,
That very frankly he confess'd his treasons;
Implor'd your highness' pardon; and set forth
A deep repentance: nothing in his life
Became him like the leaving it; he died
As one that had been studied in his death,
To throw away the dearest thing he ow'd,
As 'twere a careless trifle.
*Dun.* There's no art
To find the mind's construction in the face:
He was a gentleman on whom I built
An absolute trust.—

*Enter* Macbeth, Banquo, Ross, *and* Angus.
O worthiest cousin!
The sin of my ingratitude even now
Was heavy on me: thou art so far before,
That swiftest wing of recompense is slow
To overtake thee. Would thou hadst less deserv'd [payment
That the proportion both of thanks and
Might have been mine! only I have left to say, [pay.
More is thy due than more than all can
*Macb.* The service and the loyalty I owe,
In doing it, pays itself. Your highness' part
Is to receive our duties: and our duties
Are to your throne and state children and servants;
Which do but what they should, by doing everything
Safe toward your love and honour.
*Dun.* Welcome hither:
I have begun to plant thee, and will labour
To make thee full of growing.—Noble Banquo, [known
That hast no less deserv'd, nor must be
No less to have done so, let me infold thee,
And hold thee to my heart.
*Ban.* There if I grow,
The harvest is your own.
*Dun.* My plenteous joys,
Wanton in fulness, seek to hide themselves
In drops of sorrow.—Sons, kinsmen, thanes,
And you whose places are the nearest, know,
We will establish our estate upon

Our eldest, Malcolm; whom we name hereafter
The Prince of Cumberland: which honour must
Not unaccompanied invest him only,
But signs of nobleness, like stars, shall shine
On all deservers.—From hence to Inverness,
And bind us further to you. [us'd for you:
*Macb.* The rest is labour, which is not
I'll be myself the harbinger, and make joyful
The hearing of my wife with your approach;
So, humbly take my leave.
*Dun.* My worthy Cawdor!
*Macb.* [*Aside.*] The Prince of Cumberland!—That is a step,
On which I must fall down, or else o'er-leap,
For in my way it lies. Stars, hide your fires!
Let not light see my black and deep desires:
The eye wink at the hand! yet let that be,
Which the eye fears, when it is done, to see.
[*Exit.*
*Dun.* True, worthy Banquo,—he is full so valiant;
And in his commendations I am fed,—
It is a banquet to me. Let us after him,
Whose care is gone before to bid us welcome:
It is a peerless kinsman. [*Flourish. Exeunt.*

Scene V.—Inverness. *A Room in* Macbeth's *Castle.*

*Enter* Lady Macbeth, *reading a letter.*

*Lady M. They met me in the day of success; and I have learned by the perfectest report, they have more in them than mortal knowledge. When I burned in desire to question them further, they made themselves air, into which they vanished. Whiles I stood rapt in the wonder of it, came missives from the king, who all-hailed me, Thane of Cawdor; by which title, before, these weird sisters saluted me, and referred me to the coming on of time, with* Hail, king that shalt be! *This have I thought good to deliver thee, my dearest partner of greatness; that thou mightst not lose the dues of rejoicing, by being ignorant of what greatness is promised thee. Lay it to thy heart, and farewell.*
Glamis thou art, and Cawdor; and shalt be
What thou art promis'd: yet do I fear thy nature;
It is too full o' the milk of human kindness
To catch the nearest way: thou wouldst be great;
Art not without ambition; but without
The illness should attend it. What thou wouldst highly, [false,
That wouldst thou holily; wouldst not play
And yet wouldst wrongly win: thou'dst have, great Glamis, [have it:
That which cries, *Thus thou must do, if thou*
*And that which rather thou dost fear to do*
*Than wishest should be undone.* Hie thee hither,
That I may pour my spirits in thine ear;

And chastise with the valour of my tongue
All that impedes thee from the golden round,
Which fate and metaphysical aid doth seem
To have thee crown'd withal.

*Enter an* Attendant.

What is your tidings?
 *Atten.* The king comes here to-night.
 *Lady M.*    Thou'rt mad to say it:
Is not thy master with him? who, were't so,
Would have inform'd for preparation.
 *Atten.* So please you, it is true:—our thane
  is coming:
One of my fellows had the speed of him;
Who, almost dead for breath, had scarcely
  more
Than would make up his message.
 *Lady M.*    Give him tending,
He brings great news.  [*Exit* Attendant.
   The raven himself is hoarse
That croaks the fatal entrance of Duncan
Under my battlements. Come, you spirits
That tend on mortal thoughts, unsex me here;
And fill me, from the crown to the toe, top-
  full
Of direst cruelty! make thick my blood,
Stop up the access and passage to remorse,
That no compunctious visitings of nature
Shake my fell purpose, nor keep peace be-
  tween
The effect and it! Come to my woman's
  breasts,   [ministers,
And take my milk for gall, you murdering
Wherever in your sightless substances [night,
You wait on nature's mischief! Come, thick
And pall thee in the dunnest smoke of hell,
That my keen knife see not the wound it
  makes,
Nor heaven peep through the blanket of the
  dark,
To cry, *Hold, hold!*

*Enter* MACBETH.

   Great Glamis! worthy Cawdor!
Greater than both, by the all-hail hereafter!
Thy letters have transported me beyond
This ignorant present, and I feel now
The future in the instant.
 *Macb.*    My dearest love,
Duncan comes here to-night.
 *Lady M.*   And when goes hence?
 *Macb.* To-morrow,—as he purposes.
 *Lady M.*    O, never
Shall sun that morrow see!
Your face, my thane, is as a book where men
May read strange matters:—to beguile the
  time,
Look like the time; bear welcome in your
  eye,
Your hand, your tongue: look like the inno-
  cent flower,
But be the serpent under't. He that's coming
Must be provided for: and you shall put
This night's great business into my despatch;

Which shall to all our nights and days to
  come
Give solely sovereign sway and masterdom.
 *Macb.* We will speak further.
 *Lady M.*   Only look up clear;
To alter favour ever is to fear:
Leave all the rest to me.   [*Exeunt.*

SCENE VI.—*The same. Before the Castle.*

*Hautboys.* Servants *of* MACBETH *attending.*

*Enter* DUNCAN, MALCOLM, DONALBAIN, BAN-
QUO, LENNOX, MACDUFF, ROSS, ANGUS, *and*
Attendants.

 *Dun.* This castle hath a pleasant seat: the
  air
Nimbly and sweetly recommends itself
Unto our gentle senses.
 *Ban.*    This guest of summer,
The temple-haunting martlet, does approve,
By his lov'd mansionry, that the heaven's
  breath
Smells wooingly here: no jutty, frieze, but-
  tress,
Nor coigne of vantage, but this bird hath
  made
His pendant bed and procreant cradle:
Where they most breed and haunt, I have
  observ'd
The air is delicate.

*Enter* LADY MACBETH.

 *Dun.*   See, see, our honour'd hostess!—
The love that follows us sometime is our
  trouble,
Which still we thank as love. Herein I teach
  you
How you shall bid God ild us for your pains,
And thank us for your trouble.
 *Lady M.*    All our service
In every point twice done, and then done
  double,
Were poor and single business to contend
Against those honours deep and broad where-
  with
Your majesty loads our house: for those of
  old,
And the late dignities heap'd up to them,
We rest your hermits.
 *Dun.*   Where's the Thane of Cawdor?
We cours'd him at the heels, and had a pur-
  pose
To be his purveyor: but he rides well;
And his great love, sharp as his spur, hath
  help him
To his home before us. Fair and noble host-
  ess,
We are your guest to-night.
 *Lady M.*   Your servants ever
Have theirs, themselves, and what is theirs, in
  compt,
To make their audit at your highness' pleas-
  ure,
Still to return your own.
 *Dun.*    Give me your hand;

Conduct me to mine host: we love him
 highly,
And shall continue our graces towards him.
By your leave, hostess.    [*Exeunt.*

SCENE VII.—*The same. A Lobby in the
 Castle.*

*Hautboys and torches. Enter, and pass over,
a Sewer, and divers* Servants *with dishes
and service. Then enter* MACBETH.

*Macb.* If it were done when 'tis done, then
 'twere well
It were done quickly. If the assassination
Could trammel up the consequence, and
 catch,
With his surcease, success; that but this blow
Might be the be-all and the end-all here,
But here, upon this bank and shoal of time,—
We'd jump the life to come. But in these cases
We still have judgment here; that we but
 teach
Bloody instructions, which being taught, re-
 turn
To plague the inventor: this even-handed
 justice
Commends the ingredients of our poison'd
 chalice
To our own lips. He's here in double trust:
First, as I am his kinsman and his subject,
Strong both against the deed: then, as his
 host,
Who should against his murderer shut the
 door,
Not bear the knife myself. Besides, this Dun-
 can
Hath borne his faculties so meek, hath been
So clear in his great office, that his virtues
Will plead like angels, trumpet-tongued,
 against
The deep damnation of his taking-off:
And pity, like a naked new-born babe,
Striding the blast, or heaven's cherubin,
 hors'd
Upon the sightless couriers of the air,
Shall blow the horrid deed in every eye,
That tears shall drown the wind.—I have no
 spur
To prick the sides of my intent, but only
Vaulting ambition, which o'erleaps itself,
And falls on the other.

*Enter* LADY MACBETH.

     How now! what news?
*Lady M.* He has almost supp'd: why have
 you left the chamber?
*Macb.* Hath he ask'd for me?
*Lady M.*    Know you not he has?
*Macb.* We will proceed no further in this
 business:
He hath honour'd me of late; and I have
 bought
Golden opinions from all sorts of people,

Which would be worn now in their newest
 gloss,
Not cast aside so soon.
*Lady M.*    Was the hope drunk
Wherein you dress'd yourself? hath it slept
 since?
And wakes it now, to look so green and pale
At what it did so freely? From this time
Such I account thy love. Art thou afeard
To be the same in thine own act and valour
As thou art in desire? Wouldst thou have
 that
Which thou esteem'st the ornament of life,
And live a coward in thine own esteem;
Letting *I dare not* wait upon *I would,*
Like the poor cat i' the adage?
*Macb.*    Pr'ythee, peace:
I dare do all that may become a man;
Who dares do more is none.
*Lady M.*   What beast was't, then,
That made you break this enterprise to me?
When you durst do it, then you were a man;
And, to be more than what you were, you
 would
Be so much more the man. Nor time nor
 place
Did then adhere, and yet you would make
 both:
They have made themselves, and that their
 fitness now
Does unmake you. I have given suck, and
 know
How tender 'tis to love the babe that milks
 me:
I would, while it was smiling in my face,
Have pluck'd my nipple from his boneless
 gums,
And dash'd the brains out, had I so sworn as
 you
Have done to this.
*Macb.*    If we should fail?
*Lady M.*     We fail!
But screw your courage to the sticking place,
And we'll not fail. When Duncan is asleep,—
Whereto the rather shall his day's hard jour-
 ney
Soundly invite him, his two chamberlains
Will I with wine and wassail so convince
That memory, the warder of the brain,
Shall be a fume, and the receipt of reason
A limbec only: when in swinish sleep
Their drenched natures lie as in a death,
What cannot you and I perform upon
The unguarded Duncan? what not put upon
His spongy officers; who shall bear the guilt
Of our great quell?
*Macb.*   Bring forth men-children only;
For thy undaunted mettle should compose
Nothing but males. Will it not be receiv'd,
When we have mark'd with blood those
 sleepy two
Of his own chamber, and us'd their very dag-
 gers,
That they have done 't?

*Lady M.*　　　　Who dares receive it other,
As we shall make our griefs and clamour
　roar
Upon his death?
　*Macb.*　　　　I am settled, and bend up
Each corporal agent to this terrible feat.
Away, and mock the time with fairest show:
False face must hide what the false heart doth
　know.　　　　　　　　　　*[Exeunt.*

## ACT II.

SCENE I.—INVERNESS. *Court within the
Castle.*

*Enter* BANQUO, *preceded by* FLEANCE *with
a torch.*

　*Ban.* How goes the night, boy?
　*Fle.* The moon is down; I have not heard
　the clock.
　*Ban.* And she goes down at twelve.
　*Fle.*　　　　　I take 't, 'tis later, sir.
　*Ban.* Hold, take my sword,—There's hus-
　bandry in heaven;
Their candles are all out:—take thee that
　too.—
A heavy summons lies like lead upon me,
And yet I would not sleep:—merciful powers,
Restrain me in the cursed thoughts that na-
　ture
Gives way to in repose!—Give me my sword.
Who's there?

*Enter* MACBETH, *and a* Servant *with a torch.*

　*Macb.* A friend.
　*Ban.* What, sir, not yet at rest? The
　king's a-bed:
He hath been in unusual pleasure, and
Sent forth great largess to your officers:
This diamond he greets your wife withal,
By the name of most kind hostess; and shut
　up
In measureless content.
　*Macb.*　　　　　Being unprepar'd,
Our will became the servant to defect;
Which else should free have wrought.
　*Ban.*　　　　　　All's well.
I dreamt last night of the three weird sisters:
To you they have show'd some truth.
　*Macb.*　　　　I think not of them:
Yet, when we can entreat an hour to serve,
We would spend it in some words upon that
　business,
If you would grant the time.
　*Ban.*　　　　At your kind'st leisure.
　*Macb.* If you shall cleave to my consent,—
　when 'tis,
It shall make honour for you.
　*Ban.*　　　　　So I lose none
In seeking to augment it, but still keep
My bosom franchis'd, and allegiance clear,
I shall be counsell'd.
　*Macb.*　　　　Good repose the while!
　*Ban.* Thanks, sir; the like to you!
　　　　　　　*[Exeunt* BANQUO *and* FLEANCE.

　*Macb.* Go bid thy mistress, when my drink
　is ready,
She strike upon the bell. Get thee to bed.
　　　　　　　　　　　*[Exit* Servant.
Is this a dagger which I see before me,
The handle toward my hand? Come, let me
　clutch thee:—
I have thee not, and yet I see thee still.
Art thou not, fatal vision, sensible
To feeling as to sight? or art thou but
A dagger of the mind, a false creation,
Proceeding from the heat-oppressed brain?
I see thee yet, in form as palpable
As this which now I draw.
Thou marshall'st me the way that I was go-
　ing;
And such an instrument I was to use.
Mine eyes are made the fools o' the other
　senses,
Or else worth all the rest: I see thee still;
And on thy blade and dudgeon gouts of
　blood,
Which was not so before.—There's no such
　thing:
It is the bloody business which informs
Thus to mine eyes.—Now o'er the one-half
　world
Nature seems dead, and wicked dreams abuse
The curtain'd sleep; now witchcraft cele-
　brates
Pale Hecate's offerings; and wither'd murder,
Alarum'd by his sentinel, the wolf,
Whose howl's his watch, thus with his
　stealthy pace,　　　　　　[design
With Tarquin's ravishing strides, towards his
Moves like a ghost.—Thou sure and firm-set
　earth,　　　　　　　　[fear
Hear not my steps, which way they walk, for
The very stones prate of my whereabout,
And take the present horror from the time,
Which now suits with it.—Whiles I threat, he
　lives;
Words to the heat of deeds too cold breath
　gives.
　　　　　　　　　　　　*[A bell rings.*
I go, and it is done; the bell invites me.
Hear it not, Duncan, for it is a knell
That summons thee to heaven or to hell.
　　　　　　　　　　　　　　*[Exit.*

*Enter* LADY MACBETH.

　*Lady M.* That which hath made them
　drunk hath made me bold:
What hath quench'd them hath given me
　fire.—Hark!—Peace!
It was the owl that shriek'd, the fatal bell-
　man,
Which gives the stern'st good-night. He is
　about it:
The doors are open; and the surfeited grooms
Do mock their charge with snores: I have
　drugg'd their possets,
That death and nature do contend about
　them,

Whether they live or die.

*Macb.* [*Within.*] Who's there?—what, ho!

*Lady M.* Alack! I am afraid they have awak'd,
And 'tis not done:—the attempt, and not the deed, [ready;
Confounds us.—Hark!—I laid their daggers
He could not miss 'em.—Had he not resembled
My father as he slept, I had done't.—My husband!

*Re-enter* MACBETH.

*Macb.* I have done the deed.—Didst thou not hear a noise? [crickets cry.

*Lady M.* I heard the owl scream and the
Did not you speak?

*Macb.* When?

*Lady M.* Now.

*Macb.* As I descended?

*Lady M.* Ay.

*Macb.* Hark!—
Who lies i' the second chamber?

*Lady M.* Donalbain.

*Macb.* This is a sorry sight.
[*Looking on his hands.*

*Lady M.* A foolish thought to say a sorry sight.

*Macb.* There's one did laugh in's sleep, and one cried *Murder!*
That they did wake each other: I stood and heard them: [dress'd them
But they did say their prayers, and addAgain to sleep.

*Lady M.* There are two lodg'd together.

*Macb.* One cried, *God bless us!* and, *Amen,* the other; [hands.
As they had seen me with these hangman's
Listening their fear, I could not say, *Amen,*
When they did say, *God bless us.*

*Lady M.* Consider it not so deeply.

*Macb.* But wherefore could not I pronounce, *Amen?*
I had most need of blessing, and *Amen*
Stuck in my throat.

*Lady M.* These deeds must not be thought
After these ways; so, it will make us mad.

*Macb.* Methought I heard a voice cry,
*Sleep no more!*
*Macbeth does murder sleep,*—the innocent sleep;
Sleep that knits up the ravell'd sleeve of care,
The death of each day's life, sore labour's bath,
Balm of hurt minds, great nature's second course,
Chief nourisher in life's feast.

*Lady M.* What do you mean?

*Macb.* Still it cried, *Sleep no more!* to all the house: [*Cawdor*
*Glamis hath murder'd sleep: and therefore
Shall sleep no more,—Macbeth shall sleep no more!* [Why, worthy thane,

*Lady M.* Who was it that thus cried?

You do unbend your noble strength to think
So brainsickly of things.—Go get some water,
And wash this filthy witness from your hand.—
Why did you bring these daggers from the place?
They must lie there: go carry them; and smear
The sleepy grooms with blood.

*Macb.* I'll go no more:
I am afraid to think what I have done;
Look on't again I dare not.

*Lady M.* Infirm of purpose!
Give me the daggers: the sleeping and the dead
Are but as pictures: 'tis the eye of childhood
That fears a painted devil. If he do bleed,
I'll gild the faces of the grooms withal,
For it must seem their guilt.
[*Exit. Knocking within.*

*Macb.* Whence is that knocking?
How is't with me, when every noise appals me?
What hands are here? Ha! they pluck out mine eyes!
Will all great Neptune's ocean wash this blood
Clean from my hand? No; this my hand will rather
The multitudinous seas incarnadine,
Making the green one red.

*Re-enter* LADY MACBETH.

*Lady M.* My hands are of your colour; but I shame
To wear a heart so white. [*Knocking within.*]
I hear a knocking
At the south entry:—retire we to our chamber.
A little water clears us of this deed:
How easy is it then! Your constancy
Hath left you unattended.—
[*Knocking within.*]
Hark! more knocking:
Get on your nightgown, lest occasion call us,
And show us to be watchers:—be not lost
So poorly in your thoughts.

*Macb.* To know my deed, 'twere best not know myself. [*Knocking within.*
Wake Duncan with thy knocking! I would thou couldst! [*Exeunt.*

*Enter a* Porter. *Knocking within.*

*Porter.* Here's a knocking indeed! If a man were porter of hell-gate, he should have old turning the key. [*Knocking.*] Knock, knock, knock. Who's there, i' the name of Beelzebub? Here's a farmer that hanged himself on the expectation of plenty: come in time; have napkins enow about you; here you'll sweat for't.—[*Knocking.*] Knock, knock! Who's there, i' the other devil's name? Faith, here's an equivocator, that could swear in both the scales against either scale; who committed treason enough for God's sake, yet could not equivocate to heaven: O, come in, equivocator. [*Knocking.*] Knock, knock, knock! Who's there? Faith, here's an English tailor come hither, for stealing out of a French hose: come in, tailor, here you may roast your goose.—[*Knocking.*] Knock, knock: never at quiet! What are you?—But this place is too cold for hell. I'll devil-porter it no further: I had thought to have let in some of all professions, that go the primrose way to the everlasting bonfire. [*Knocking.*] Anon, anon! I pray you, remember the porter.

[*Opens the gate.*

*Enter* MACDUFF *and* LENNOX.

*Macd.* Was it so late, friend, ere you went to bed, that you do lie so late?

*Port.* Faith, sir, we were carousing till the second cock: and drink, sir, is a great provoker of three things.

*Macd.* What three things does drink especially provoke?

*Port.* Marry, sir, nose-painting, sleep, and urine. Lechery, sir, it provokes and it unprovokes; it provokes the desire, but it takes away the performance: therefore, much drink may be said to be an equivocator with lechery: it makes him, and it mars him; it sets him on, and it takes him off; it persuades him, and disheartens him; makes him stand to, and not stand to: in conclusion, equivocates him in a sleep, and, giving him the lie, leaves him.

*Macd.* I believe drink gave thee the lie last night.

*Port.* That it did, sir, i' the very throat o' me: but I requited him for his lie; and, I think, being too strong for him, though he took up my legs sometime, yet I made a shift to cast him.

*Macd.* Is thy master stirring?—
Our knocking has awak'd him; here he comes.

*Enter* MACBETH.

*Len.* Good-morrow, noble sir!

*Macb.*                Good-morrow, both!

*Macd.* Is the king stirring, worthy thane?

*Macb.*                Not yet.

*Macd.* He did command me to call timely on him:
I have almost slipp'd the hour.

*Macb.*                I'll bring you to him.

*Macd.* I know this is a joyful trouble to you;
But yet 'tis one.

*Macb.* The labour we delight in physics pain.
This is the door.

*Macd.*        I'll make so bold to call.
For 'tis my limited service. [*Exit* MACDUFF.

*Len.* Goes the king hence to-day?

*Macb.*                He does: he did appoint so.

*Len.* The night has been unruly: where we lay,                [say,
Our chimneys were blown down: and, as they
Lamentings heard i' the air; strange screams of death;
And prophesying, with accents terrible,
Of dire combustion and confus'd events,
New hatch'd to the woeful time: the obscure bird                [earth
Clamour'd the live-long night: some say the
Was feverous, and did shake.

*Macb.*                'Twas a rough night.

*Len.* My young remembrance cannot parallel
A fellow to it.

*Re-enter* MACDUFF.

*Macd.* O horror, horror, horror! Tongue nor heart
Cannot conceive nor name thee!

*Macb., Len.*                What's the matter?

*Macd.* Confusion now hath made his masterpiece!
Most sacrilegious murder hath broke ope
The Lord's anointed temple, and stole thence
The life o' the building.

*Macb.*        What is't you say? the life?

*Len.* Mean you his majesty?        [your sight

*Macd.* Approach the chamber, and destroy
With a new Gorgon:—do not bid me speak;
See, and then speak yourselves.

[*Exeunt* MACBETH *and* LENNOX.
Awake! awake!—
Ring the alarum-bell:—murder and treason!
Banquo and Donalbain! Malcolm! awake!
Shake off this downy sleep, death's counterfeit,
And look on death itself! up, up, and see
The great doom's image! Malcolm! Banquo!
As from your graves rise up, and walk like sprites,
To countenance this horror!

[*Alarum-bell rings.*

*Re-enter* LADY MACBETH.

*Lady M.*                What's the business,
That such a hideous trumpet calls to parley
The sleepers of the house? speak, speak!

*Macd.*                O gentle lady,
'Tis not for you to hear what I can speak:
The repetition, in a woman's ear,
Would murder as it fell.

*Re-enter* BANQUO.

*                O Banquo, Banquo!
Our royal master's murder'd!

*Lady M.*                Woe, alas!
What, in our house?

*Ban.*                Too cruel any where.—
Dear Duff, I pr'ythee, contradict thyself,
And say it is not so.

*Re-enter* MACBETH *and* LENNOX

*Macb.* Had I but died an hour before this chance.

I had liv'd a blessed time; for, from this in-
  stant,
There's nothing serious in mortality:
All is but toys: renown and grace is dead;
The wine of life is drawn, and the mere lees
Is left this vault to brag of.

*Enter* MALCOLM *and* DONALBAIN.

*Don.* What is amiss?
*Macb.* You are, and do not know't:
The spring, the head, the fountain of your
  blood
Is stopp'd; the very source of it is stopp'd.
*Macd.* Your royal father's murder'd.
*Mal.* O, by whom?
*Len.* Those of his chamber, as it seem'd,
  had done't: [blood;
Their hands and faces were all badg'd with
So were their daggers, which, unwip'd, we
  found
Upon their pillows:
They star'd, and were distracted; no man's
  life
Was to be trusted with them.
*Macb.* O, yet I do repent me of my fury,
That I did kill them.
*Macd.* Wherefore did you so?
*Macb.* Who can be wise, amaz'd, temper-
  ate, and furious,
Loyal and neutral, in a moment? No man:
The expedition of my violent love
Out-ran the pauser reason. Here lay Duncan,
His silver skin lac'd with his golden blood;
And his gash'd stabs look'd like a breach in
  nature [derers,
For ruin's wasteful entrance: there, the mur-
Steep'd in the colours of their trade, their
  daggers [refrain,
Unmannerly breech'd with gore: who could
That had a heart to love, and in that heart
Courage to make's love known?
*Lady M.* Help me hence, ho!
*Macd.* Look to the lady.
*Mal.* Why do we hold our tongues,
That most may claim this argument for ours?
*Don.* What should be spoken here, where
  our fate,
Hid in an auger-hole, may rush, and seize us?
Let's away;
Our tears are not yet brew'd.
*Mal.* Nor our strong sorrow
Upon the foot of motion.
*Ban.* Look to the lady:—
  [LADY MACBETH *is carried out.*
And when we have our naked frailties hid,
That suffer in exposure, let us meet,
And question this most bloody piece of work,
To know it further. Fears and scruples shake
  us:
In the great hand of God I stand; and
  thence,
Against the undivulg'd pretence I fight
Of treasonous malice.
*Macd.* And so do I.

*All.* So all.
*Macb.* Let's briefly put on manly readi-
  ness,
And meet i' the hall together.
*All.* Well contented.
  [*Exeunt all but* MAL. *and* DON.
*Mal.* What will you do? Let's not consort
  with them:
To show an unfelt sorrow is an office
Which the false man does easy. I'll to Eng-
  land.
*Don.* To Ireland I; our separated fortune
Shall keep us both the safer: where we are,
There's daggers in men's smiles: the near in
  blood,
The nearer bloody.
*Mal.* This murderous shaft that's shot
Hath not yet lighted, and our safest way
Is to avoid the aim. Therefore to horse;
And let us not be dainty of leave-taking,
But shift away: there's warrant in that theft
Which steals itself, when there's no mercy
  left. [*Exeunt.*

SCENE II.—*The same. Without the Castle.*

*Enter* ROSS *and an old Man.*

*Old M.* Threescore and ten I can remem-
  ber well:
Within the volume of which time I have seen
Hours dreadful and things strange; but this
  sore night
Hath trifled former knowings.
*Ross.* Ah, good father,
Thou seest, the heavens, as troubled with
  man's act, [day,
Threaten his bloody stage: by the clock, 'tis
And yet dark night strangles the travelling
  lamp;
Is't night's predominance, or the day's shame,
That darkness does the face of earth entomb,
When living light should kiss it?
*Old M.* 'Tis unnatural,
Even like the deed that's done. On Tuesday
  last,
A falcon, towering in her pride of place,
Was by a mousing owl hawk'd at and kill'd.
*Ross.* And Duncan's horses,—a thing most
  strange and certain,—
Beauteous and swift, the minions of their
  race,
Turn'd wild in nature, broke their stalls, flung
  out, [make
Contending 'gainst obedience, as they would
War with mankind.
*Old M.* 'Tis said they eat each other
*Ross.* They did so; to the amazement of
  mine eyes, [Macduff,
That look'd upon't. Here comes the good

*Enter* MACDUFF.

How goes the world, sir, now?
*Macd.* Why, see you not?
*Ross.* Is't known who did this more than
  bloody deed?

*Macd.* Those that Macbeth hath slain.

*Ross.*                Alas, the day!
What good could they pretend?

*Macd.*            They were suborn'd:
Malcolm and Donalbain, the king's two sons,
Are stol'n away and fled; which puts upon
    them
Suspicion of the deed.

*Ross.*            'Gainst nature still:
Thriftless ambition, that wilt ravin up
Thine own life's means!—Then 'tis most like,
The sovereignty will fall upon Macbeth.

*Macd.* He is already nam'd; and gone to
    Scone
To be invested.

*Ross.*        Where is Duncan's body?

*Macd.* Carried to Colme-kill,
The sacred storehouse of his predecessors,
And guardian of their bones.

*Ross.*                Will you to Scone?

*Macd.* No, cousin, I'll to Fife.

*Ross.*                Well, I will thither.

*Macd.* Well, may you see things well done
    there,—adieu!—
Lest our old robes sit easier than our new!

*Ross.* Farewell, father.        [with those

*Old M.* God's benison go with you; and
That would make good of bad, and friends
    of foes!                [*Exeunt.*

## ACT III.

SCENE I.—FORRES. *A Room in the Palace.*

*Enter* BANQUO.

*Ban.* Thou hast it now,—king, Cawdor,
    Glamis, all
As the weird women promis'd; and, I fear,
Thou play'dst most foully for't; yet it was
    said
It should not stand in thy posterity;
But that myself should be the root and father
Of many kings. If there come truth from
    them,—
As upon thee, Macbeth, their speeches
    shine,—
Why, by the verities on thee made good,
May they not be my oracles as well,
And set me up in hope? But, hush; no more.

*Sennet sounded. Enter* MACBETH *as King;*
LADY MACBETH *as Queen;* LENNOX, ROSS,
Lords, Ladies, *and* Attendants.

*Macb.* Here's our chief guest.

*Lady M.*        If he had been forgotten,
It had been as a gap in our great feast,
And all-thing unbecoming.

*Macb.* To-night we hold a solemn supper,
    sir,
And I'll request your presence.

*Ban.*            Let your highness
Command upon me; to the which my duties
Are with a most indissoluble tie
For ever knit.

*Macb.* Ride you this afternoon?

*Ban.*                Ay, my good lord.

*Macb.* We should have else desir'd your
    good advice,—            [perous,—
Which still hath been both grave and pros-
In this day's council; but we'll take to-mor-
    row.
Is't far you ride?

*Ban.* As far, my lord, as will fill up the
    time
'Twixt this and supper: go not my horse the
    better.
I must become a borrower of the night,
For a dark hour or twain.

*Macb.*            Fail not our feast.

*Ban.* My lord, I will not.        [bestow'd

*Macb.* We hear our bloody cousins are
In England and in Ireland; not confessing
Their cruel parricide, filling their hearers
With strange invention: but of that to-mor-
    row;
When therewithal we shall have cause of
    state
Craving us jointly. Hie you to horse: adieu,
Till you return at night. Goes Fleance with
    you?                [upon's.

*Ban.* Ay, my good lord: our time does call

*Macb.* I wish your horses swift and sure
    of foot;
And so I do commend you to their backs.
Farewell.—                [*Exit* BANQUO.
Let every man be master of his time
Till seven at night; to make society
The sweeter welcome, we will keep ourself
Till supper-time alone: while then, God be
    with you!
            [*Exeunt* LADY MACBETH, Lords,
                    Ladies, &c.
Sirrah, a word with you: attend those men
Our pleasure?            [palace gate.

*Attend.* They are, my lord, without the

*Macb.* Bring them before us.
                [*Exit* Attendant.
                To be thus is nothing;
But to be safely thus:—our fears in Banquo
Stick deep; and in his royalty of nature
Reigns that which would be fear'd: 'tis much
    he dares;
And, to that dauntless temper of his mind,
He hath a wisdom that doth guide his valour
To act in safety. There is none but he
Whose being I do fear: and, under him,
My genius is rebuk'd; as, it is said,    [sisters
Mark Antony's was by Cæsar. He chid the
When first they put the name of king upon
    me,
And bade them speak to him; then, prophet-
    like,
They hail'd him father to a line of kings:
Upon my head they plac'd a fruitless crown,
And put a barren sceptre in my gripe,
Thence to be wrench'd with an unlineal
    hand,
No son of mine succeeding. If't be so,

For Banquo's issue have I fil'd my mind;
For them the gracious Duncan have I murder'd;
Put rancours in the vessel of my peace
Only for them; and mine eternal jewel
Given to the common enemy of man,
To make them kings, the seed of Banquo kings!
Rather than so, come, fate, into the list,
And champion me to the utterance!—Who's there?—

*Re-enter* Attendant, *with two* Murderers.

Now go to the door, and stay there till we call.
                              [*Exit* Attendant.
Was it not yesterday we spoke together?
  1 *Mur.* It was, so please your highness.
  *Macb.*                Well, then, now
Have you consider'd of my speeches? Know
That it was he, in the times past, which held you
So under fortune; which you thought had been
Our innocent self: this I made good to you
In our last conference, pass'd in probation
    with you,             [the instruments,
How you were borne in hand, how cross'd,
Who wrought with them, and all things else that might
To half a soul and to a notion craz'd
Say, *Thus did Banquo.*
  1 *Mur.*          You made it known to us.
  *Macb.* I did so; and went further, which is now
Our point of second meeting. Do you find
Your patience so predominant in your nature,
That you can let this go? Are you so gospell'd,
To pray for this good man and for his issue,
Whose heavy hand hath bow'd you to the grave,
And beggar'd yours for ever?
  1 *Mur.*          We are men, my liege.
  *Macb.* Ay, in the catalogue ye go for men;
As hounds, and greyhounds, mongrels, spaniels curs,
Shoughs, water-rugs, and demi-wolves are clept
All by the name of dogs: the valu'd file
Distinguishes the swift, the slow, the subtle,
The house-keeper, the hunter, every one
According to the gift which bounteous nature
Hath in him clos'd; whereby he does receive
Particular addition, from the bill
That writes them all alike: and so of men.
Now, if you have a station in the file,
And not i' the worst rank of manhood, say it;
And I will put that business in your bosoms,
Whose execution takes your enemy off;
Grapples you to the heart and love of us,
Who wear our health but sickly in his life,

Which in his death were perfect.
  2 *Mur.*          I am one, my liege,
Whom the vile blows and buffets of the world
Have so incens'd that I am reckless what
I do to spite the world.
  1 *Mur.*          And I another,
So weary with disasters, tugg'd with fortune,
That I would set my life on any chance,
To mend it, or be rid on't.
  *Macb.*          Both of you
Know Banquo was your enemy.
  *Both Mur.*          True, my lord.
  *Macb.* So he is mine; and in such bloody distance,
That every minute of his being thrusts
Against my near'st of life: and though I could
With bare-fac'd power sweep him from my sight,
And bid my will avouch it, yet I must not,
For certain friends that are both his and mine,
Whose loves I may not drop, but wail his fall
Who I myself struck down: and thence it is
That I to your assistance do make love;
Masking the business from the common eye
For sundry weighty reasons.
  2 *Mur.*          We shall, my lord,
Perform what you command us.
  1 *Mur.*          Though our lives—
  *Macb.* Your spirits shine through you.
    within this hour at most,
I will advise you where to plant yourselves;
Acquaint you with the perfect spy o' the time,
The moment on't; for't must be done to-night,
                              [thought
And something from the palace; always
That I require a clearness: and with him,—
To leave no rubs nor botches in the work,—
Fleance his son, that keeps him company,
Whose absence is no less material to me
Than is his father's, must embrace the fate
Of that dark hour. Resolve yourselves apart:
I'll come to you anon.
  *Both Mur.* We are resolv'd, my lord.
  *Macb.* I'll call upon you straight: abide within.     [*Exeunt* Murderers.
It is concluded:—Banquo, thy soul's flight,
If it find heaven, must find it out to-night.
                              [*Exit.*

SCENE II.—*The same. Another Room in the Palace.*

*Enter* LADY MACBETH *and a* Servant.

*Lady M.* Is Banquo gone from court?
*Serv.* Ay, madam, but returns again to-night.
*Lady M.* Say to the king, I would attend his leisure
For a few words.
*Serv.*          Madam, I will.     [*Exit.*
*Lady M.*          Naught's had, all's spent,
Where our desire is got without content:

'Tis safer to be that which we destroy,
Than, by destruction, dwell in doubtful joy.

*Enter* MACBETH

How now, my lord! why do you keep alone,
Of sorriest fancies your companions making;
Using those thoughts which should indeed
have died
With them they think on? Things without all
remedy
Should be without regard: what's done is
done.
   *Macb.* We have scotch'd the snake, not
kill'd it;                         [malice
She'll close, and be herself; whilst our poor
Remains in danger of her former tooth.
But let the frame of things disjoint,
Both the worlds suffer,
Ere we will eat our meal in fear, and sleep
In the affliction of these terrible dreams
That shake us nightly: better be with the
dead,                              [peace,
Whom we, to gain our place, have sent to
Than on the torture of the mind to lie
In restless ecstacy. Duncan is in his grave;
After life's fitful fever he sleeps well;
Treason has done his worst: nor steel, nor
poison,
Malice domestic, foreign levy, nothing,
Can touch him further.
   *Lady M.*                       Come on;
Gently my lord, sleek o'er your rugged looks;
Be bright and jovial 'mong your guests to-
night.                             [you:
   *Macb.* So shall I, love; and so, I pray, be
Let your remembrance apply to Banquo;
Present him eminence, both with eye and
tongue:
Unsafe the while, that we          [streams;
Must lave our honours in these flattering
And make our faces vizards to our hearts,
Disguising what they are.
   *Lady M.*                You must leave this.
   *Macb.* O, full of scorpions is my mind,
dear wife!                         [lives.
Thou know'st that Banquo, and his Fleance,
   *Lady M.* But in them nature's copy not
eterne.
   *Macb.* There's comfort yet; they are as-
sailable;
Then be thou jocund: ere the bat hath flown
His cloister'd flight; ere, to black Hecate's
summons,
The shard-borne beetle, with his drowsy
hums,                              [be done
Hath rung night's yawning peal, there shall
A deed of dreadful note.
   *Lady M.*            What's to be done?
   *Macb.* Be innocent of the knowledge, dear-
est chuck,                         [night,
Till thou applaud the deed. Come, seeling
Scarf up the tender eye of pitiful day;
And with thy bloody and invisible hand
Cancel and tear to pieces that great bond

Which keeps me pale!—Light thickens; and
the crow
Makes wing to the rooky wood:
Good things of day begin to droop and
drowse;                            [rouse.—
Whiles night's black agents to their prey do
Thou marvell'st at my words: but hold thee
still;                             [by ill:
Things bad begun make strong themselves
So, pr'ythee, go with me.          [*Exeunt.*

SCENE III.—*The same. A Park or Lawn,
with a gate leading to the Palace.*

*Enter three* Murderers.

   1 *Mur.* But who did bid thee join with us?
   3 *Mur.*                         Macbeth.
   2 *Mur.* He needs not our mistrust; since he
delivers
Our offices, and what we have to do,
To the direction just.
   1 *Mur.*              Then stand with us.
The west yet glimmers with some streaks of
day:
Now spurs the lated traveller apace,
To gain the timely inn; and near approaches
The subject of our watch.
   3 *Mur.*            Hark! I hear horses.
   *Ban.* [*Within.*] Give us a light there, ho!
   2 *Mur.*        Then 'tis he: the rest
That are within the note of expectation
Already are i' the court.
   1 *Mur.*            His horses go about,
   3 *Mur.* Almost a mile; but he does usually,
So all men do, from hence to the palace gate
Make it their walk.
   2 *Mur.*                A light, a light!
   3 *Mur.*                        'Tis he.
   1 *Mur.* Stand to't.

*Enter* BANQUO, *and* FLEANCE *with a torch.*

   *Ban.* It will be rain to-night.
   1 *Mur.*            Let it come down.
                      [*Assaults* BANQUO.
   *Ban.* O, treachery! Fly, good Fleance, fly,
fly, fly!
Thou mayst revenge.—O slave!
                      [*Dies.* FLEANCE *escapes.*
   3 *Mur.* Who did strike out the light?
   1 *Mur.*            Was't not the way?
   3 *Mur.* There's but one down: the son is
fled.                              [fair.
   2 *Mur.* We have lose best half of our af-
   1 *Mur.* Well, let's away, and say how much
is done.                           [*Exeunt.*

SCENE IV.—*The same. A Room of State in
the Palace. A banquet prepared.*

*Enter* MACBETH, LADY MACBETH, ROSS,
LENNOX, Lords, and Attendants.

   *Macb.* You know your own degrees, sit
down: at first
And last the hearty welcome.
   *Lords.*          Thanks to your majesty.
   *Macb.* Ourself will mingle with society,

And play the humble host.
Our hostess keeps her state; but, in best
　　time,
We will require her welcome.　[our friends;
　*Lady M.* Pronounce it for me, sir, to all
For my heart speaks they are welcome.
　*Macb.* See, they encounter thee with their
　　hearts' thanks.—
Both sides are even: here I'll sit i' the midst:

*Enter first Murderer to the door.*

Be large in mirth; anon we'll drink a measure
The table round.—There's blood upon thy
　　face.
　*Mur.* 'Tis Banquo's then.　　[within.
　*Macb.* 'Tis better thee without than he
Is he despatch'd?
　*Mur.* My lord, his throat is cut; that I did
for him.
　*Macb.* Thou art the best o' the cut-throats:
　　yet he's good
That did the like for Fleance: if thou didst it,
Thou art the nonpareil.
　*Mur.*　　　　　　Most royal sir,
Fleance is 'scaped.　　　　[been perfect;
　*Macb.* Then comes my fit again: I had else
Whole as the marble, founded as the rock;
As broad and general as the casing air:
But now I am cabin'd, cribb'd, confin'd,
　　bound in　　　　[safe?
To saucy doubts and fears. But Banquo's
　*Mur.* Ay, my good lord: safe in a ditch he
bides,
With twenty trenched gashes on his head;
The least a death to nature.
　*Macb.*　　　　　　Thanks for that:
There the grown serpent lies; the worm that's
　　fled
Hath nature that in time will venom breed,
No teeth for the present.—Get thee gone; to-
　　morrow
We'll hear, ourselves, again. [*Exit* Murderer.
　*Lady M.*　　　　　My royal lord,
You do not give the cheer: the feast is sold
That is not often vouch'd, while 'tis a-making,
'Tis given with welcome: to feed were best at
　　home;
From thence the sauce to meat is ceremony;
Meeting were bare without it.
　*Macb.*　　　　　Sweet remembrancer!—
Now, good digestion wait on appetite,
And health on both!
　*Len.*　　　May't please your highness sit?
　[*The* Ghost *of* Banquo *rises, and sits in*
　　Macbeth's *place.*
　*Macb.* Here had we now our country's
　　honour roof'd,　　　　[ent;
Were the grac'd person of our Banquo pres-
Who may I rather challenge for unkindness
Than pity for mischance!
　*Ross.*　　　　　His absence, sir,
Lays blame upon his promise. Please't your
　　highness
To grace us with your royal company.

　*Macb.* The table's full.
　*Len.* Here's a place reserv'd, sir.
　*Macb.* Where?
　*Len.*　　　　Here, my lord. What is't
　　that moves your highness?
　*Macb.* Which of you have done this?
　*Lords.*　　　　What, my good lord?
　*Macb.* Thou canst not say I did it: never
　　shake
Thy gory locks at me.　　　　[well.
　*Ross.* Gentlemen, rise; his highness is not
　*Lady M.* Sit, worthy friends:—my lord is
　　often thus,
And hath been from his youth: pray you,
　　keep seat;
The fit is momentary; upon a thought [him
He will again be well: if much you note
You shall offend him, and extend his passion:
Feed, and regard him not.—Are you a man?
　*Macb.* Ay, and a bold one, that dare look
　　on that
Which might appal the devil.
　*Lady M.*　　　　　O proper stuff!
This is the very painting of your fear:
This is the air-drawn dagger which, you said,
Led you to Duncan. O, these flaws, and
　　starts,—
Impostors to true fear,—would well become
A woman's story at a winter's fire,
Authoriz'd by her grandam. Shame itself!
Why do you make such faces? When all's
　　done,
You look but on a stool.
　*Macb.* Pr'ythee, see there! behold! look!
　　lo! how say you?—
Why, what care I? If thou canst nod, speak
　　too.—
If charnel-houses and our graves must send
Those that we bury back, our monuments
Shall be the maws of kites. [Ghost *disappears.*
　*Lady M.* What, quite unmann'd in folly?
　*Macb.* If I stand here, I saw him.
　*Lady M.*　　　　　Fie, for shame!
　*Macb.* Blood hath been shed ere now, i'
　　the olden time,
Ere human statute purg'd the gentle weal;
Ay, and since too, murders have been per-
　　form'd
Too terrible for the ear: the times have been,
That, when the brains were out, the man
　　would die,
And there an end; but now they rise again,
With twenty mortal murders on their crowns,
And push us from our stools: this is more
　　strange
Than such a murder is.
　*Lady M.*　　　　　My worthy lord,
Your noble friends do lack you.
　*Macb.*　　　　　I do forget:—
Do not muse at me, my most worthy friends;
I have a strange infirmity, which is nothing
To those that know me. Come, love and
　　health to all;　　　　[full.—
Then I'll sit down.—Give me some wine, fill

I drink to the general joy o' the whole table,
And to our dear friend Banquo, whom we
    miss;               [thirst,
Would he were here! to all, and him, we
And all to all.
    *Lords.*        Our duties, and the pledge.

               *Ghost rises again.*

    *Macb.* Avaunt! and quit my sight! let the
    earth hide thee!
Thy bones are marrowless, thy blood is cold;
Thou hast no speculation in those eyes
Which thou dost glare with!
    *Lady M.*        Think of this, good peers,
But as a thing of custom: 'tis no other;
Only it spoils the pleasure of the time.
    *Macb.* What man dare, I dare:
Approach thou like the rugged Russian bear,
The arm'd rhinoceros, or the Hyrcan tiger;
Take any shape but that, and my firm nerves
Shall never tremble: or be alive again,
And dare me to the desert with thy sword;
If trembling I inhabit then, protest me
The baby of a girl. Hence, horrible shadow!
Unreal mockery, hence!   [*Ghost disappears.*
             Why, so;—being gone,
I am a man again.—Pray you, sit still.
    *Lady M.* You have displac'd the mirth,
    broke the good meeting,
With most admir'd disorder.
    *Macb.*        Can such things be,
And overcome us like a summer's cloud,
Without our special wonder? You make me
    strange
Even to the disposition that I owe, [sights,
When now I think you can behold such
And keep the natural ruby of your cheeks,
When mine are blanch'd with fear.
    *Ross.*        What sights, my lord?
    *Lady M.* I pray you, speak not; he grows
    worse and worse;
Question enrages him: at once, good-night:—
Stand not upon the order of your going,
But go at once.
    *Len.*        Good-night; and better health
Attend his majesty!
    *Lady M.*        A kind good-night to all!
        [*Exeunt* Lords *and* Attendants.
    *Macb.* It will have blood; they say, blood
    will have blood:       [to speak;
Stones have been known to move, and trees
Augurs, and understood relations, have
By magot-pies, and choughs, and rooks,
    brought forth
The secret'st man of blood.—What is the
    night?       [which is which.
    *Lady M.* Almost at odds with morning,
    *Macb.* How say'st thou, that Macduff de-
    nies his person,
At our great bidding?
    *Lady M.*        Did you send to him, sir?
    *Macb.* I hear it by the way; but I will
    send:
There's not a one of them but in his house

I keep a servant fee'd. I will to-morrow
(And betimes I will) to the weird sisters:
More shall they speak; for now I am bent to
    know,       [own good,
By the worst means, the worst. For mine
All causes shall give way: I am in blood
Stept in so far that, should I wade no more,
Returning were as tedious as go o'er: [hand;
Strange things I have in head, that will to
Which must be acted ere they may be scann'd.
    *Lady M.* You lack the season of all na-
    tures, sleep.       [self-abuse
    *Macb.* Come, we'll to sleep. My strange and
Is the initiate fear, that wants hard use:—
We are yet but young in deed.     [*Exeunt.*

### SCENE V.—*The Heath.*

*Thunder. Enter the three* Witches, *meeting*
            HECATE.

    1 *Witch.* Why, how now, Hecate! you look
    angrily.       [are,
    *Hec.* Have I not reason, beldams as you
Saucy and overbold? How did you dare
To trade and traffic with Macbeth
In riddles and affairs of death;
And I, the mistress of your charms,
The close contriver of all harms,
Was never call'd to bear my part,
Or show the glory of our art?
And, which is worse, all you have done
Hath been but for a wayward son,
Spiteful and wrathful; who, as others do,
Loves for his own ends, not for you.
But make amends now: get you gone,
And at the pit of Acheron
Meet me i' the morning: thither he
Will come to know his destiny.
Your vessels and your spells provide,
Your charms, and everything beside.
I am for the air; this night I'll spend
Unto a dismal and a fatal end.
Great business must be wrought ere noon:
Upon the corner of the moon
There hangs a vaporous drop profound;
I'll catch it ere it come to ground:
And that, distill'd by magic sleights,
Shall raise such artificial sprites,
As, by the strength of their illusion,
Shall draw him on to his confusion:
He shall spurn fate, scorn death, and bear
His hopes 'bove wisdom, grace, and fear:
And you all know, security
Is mortal's chiefest enemy.
    [*Music and song within: Come away,*
            *come away &c.*
Hark! I am call'd; my little spirit, see,
Sits in a foggy cloud, and stays for me. [*Exit.*
    1 *Witch.* Come, let's make haste; she'll
    soon be back again.       [*Exeunt.*

### SCENE VI.—FORRES. *A Room in the Palace.*

*Enter* LENNOX *and another* Lord.

    *Len.* My former speeches have but hit your
    thoughts,

Which can interpret further: only, I say,
Things have been strangely borne. The gra-
    cious Duncan        [dead:—
Was pitied of Macbeth:—marry, he was
And the right-valiant Banquo walk'd too
    late;        [Fleance kill'd,
Whom, you may say, if't please you,
For Fleance fled. Men must not walk too late.
Who cannot want the thought, how mon-
    strous
It was for Malcolm and for Donalbain
To kill their gracious father? damned fact!
How it did grieve Macbeth! did he not
    straight,
In pious rage, the two delinquents tear,
That were the slaves of drink and thralls of
    sleep?
Was not that nobly done? Ay, and wisely too;
For 'twould have anger'd any heart alive,
To hear the men deny't. So that, I say,
He has borne all things well: and I do think,
That had he Duncan's sons under his key,—
As, an't please heaven, he shall not,—they
    should find
What 'twere to kill a father; so should
    Fleance.        ['cause he fail'd
But, peace!—for from broad words, and
His presence at the tyrant's feast, I hear,
Macduff lives in disgrace. Sir, can you tell
Where he bestows himself?
    *Lord.*        The son of Duncan,
From whom this tyrant holds the due of birth,
Lives in the English court; and is receiv'd
Of the most pious Edward with such grace
That the malevolence of fortune nothing
Takes from his high respect: thither Macduff
Is gone to pray the holy king, upon his aid
To wake Northumberland, and warlike
    Siward:        [above
That, by the help of these,—with Him
To ratify the word,—we may again
Give to our tables meat, sleep to our nights;
Free from our feasts and banquets bloody
    knives;        [ours,—
Do faithful homage, and receive free hon-
All which we pipe for now: and this report
Hath so exasperate the king that he
Prepares for some attempt of war.
    *Len.*        Sent he to Macduff?
    *Lord.* He did: and with an absolute, *Sir,*
    *not I,*
The cloudy messenger turns me his back,
And hums, as who should say, *You'll rue the*
    *time*
*That clogs me with this answer.*
    *Len.*        And that well might
Advise him to a caution, to hold what dis-
    tance
His wisdom can provide. Some holy angel
Fly to the court of England, and unfold
His message ere he come; that a swift
    blessing
May soon return to this our suffering country
Under a hand accurs'd!

    *Lord.*      I'll send my prayers with him!
                        *[Exeunt.*

### ACT IV.

Scene I.—*A dark Cave. In the middle, a
    Caldron Boiling.*

*Thunder. Enter the three* Witches.

1 *Witch.* Thrice the brinded cat hath
    mew'd.
2 *Witch.* Thrice; and once the hedge-
    pig whin'd.
3 *Witch.* Harpier cries:—'tis time, 'tis time.
1 *Witch.* Round about the caldron go;
    In the poison'd entrails throw.—
    Toad, that under the cold stone,
    Days and nights hast thirty-one
    Swelter'd venom sleeping got,
    Boil thou first i' the charmed pot!
*All.* Double, double toil and trouble;
    Fire, burn; and, caldron, bubble.
2 *Witch.* Fillet of a fenny snake,
    In the caldron boil and bake;
    Eye of newt, and toe of frog,
    Wool of bat, and tongue of dog,
    Adder's fork, and blind-worm's sting,
    Lizard's leg, and howlet's wing,—
    For a charm of powerful trouble,
    Like a hell-broth boil and bubble.
*All.* Double, double toil and trouble,
    Fire, burn; and, caldron, bubble.
3 *Witch.* Scale of dragon, tooth of wolf,
    Witches' mummy, maw and gulf
    Of the ravin'd salt-sea shark,
    Root of hemlock digg'd i' the dark,
    Liver of blaspheming Jew,
    Gall of goat, and slips of yew
    Sliver'd in the moon's eclipse,
    Nose of Turk; and Tartar's lips,
    Finger of birth-strangl'd babe,
    Ditch-delivr'd by a drab,—
    Make the gruel thick and slab:
    Add thereto a tiger's chaudron,
    For the ingredients of our caldron.
*All.* Double, double toil and trouble;
    Fire, burn; and, caldron, bubble.
2 *Witch.* Cool it with a baboon's blood,
    Then the charm is firm and good.

*Enter* HECATE.

*Hec.* O, well done! I commend your pains;
    And every one shall share i' the gains.
    And now about the caldron sing,
    Like elves and fairies in a ring,
    Enchanting all that you put in.

SONG.

Black spirits and white, red spirits and gray;
    Mingle, mingle, mingle, you that mingle may.

                      *[Exit* HECATE.
2 *Witch.* By the pricking of my thumbs,
Something wicked this way comes:—
Open, locks, whoever knocks!

*Enter* MACBETH.

*Macb.* How now, you secret, black, and
   midnight hags!
What is't you do?
*All.*           A deed without a name.
*Macb.* I cónjure you, by that which you
   profess,—
Howe'er you come to know it,—answer me:
Though you untie the winds, and let them
   fight
Against the churches; though the yesty waves
Confound and swallow navigation up;
Though bladed corn be lodg'd, and trees
   blown down;         [heads;
Though castles topple on their warders'
Though palaces and pyramids do slope
Their heads to their foundations; though the
   treasure
Of nature's germins tumble altogether,
Even till destruction sicken,—answer me
To what I ask you.
 1 *Witch.*        Speak.
 2 *Witch.*        Demand.
 3 *Witch.*        We'll answer.
 1 *Witch.* Say, if thou'dst rather hear it
   from our mouths,
Or from our masters?
 *Macb.*       Call 'em, let me see 'em.
 1 *Witch.* Pour in sow's blood, that hath
   eaten
Her nine farrow; grease that's sweaten
From the murderer's gibbet throw
Into the flame.
 *All.*         Come, high or low;
Thyself and office deftly show!

   *Thunder. An* Apparition *of an armed
     Head rises.*

 *Macb.* Tell me, thou unknown power,—
 1 *Witch.*        He knows thy thought:
Hear his speech, but say thou naught.
 *App.* Macbeth! Macbeth! Macbeth! be-
   ware Macduff;       [enough.
Beware the Thane of Fife.—Dismiss me:—
                   [*Descends.*
 *Macb.* Whate'er 'thou art, for thy good
   caution, thanks;     [word more,—
Thou hast harp'd my fear aright:—but one
 1 *Witch.* He will not be commanded: here's
   another,
More potent than the first.

   *Thunder. An* Apparition *of a bloody Child
     rises.*

 *App.*     Macbeth! Macbeth! Macbeth!—
 *Macb.* Had I three ears, I'd hear thee.
 *App.* Be bloody, bold, and resolute; laugh
   to scorn
The power of man, for none of woman born
Shall harm Macbeth.      [*Descends.*
 *Macb.* Then live, Macduff: what need I
   fear of thee?
But yet I'll make assurance double sure,

And take a bond of fate: thou shalt not live;
That I may tell pale-hearted fear it lies,
And sleep in spite of thunder.—What is this,

   *Thunder. An* Apparition *of a Child crowned,
     with a tree in his hand, rises.*

That rises like the issue of a king,
And wears upon his baby brow the round
And top of sovereignty?
 *All.*        Listen, but speak not to 't.
 *App.* Be lion-mettled, proud; and take no
   care                  [are
Who chafes, who frets, or where conspirers
Macbeth shall never vanquish'd be, until
Great Birnam wood to high Dunsinane hill
Shall come against him.     [*Descends.*
 *Macb.*         That will never be:
Who can impress the forest; bid the tree
Unfix his earth-bound root? Sweet bode-
   ments! good!
Rebellion's head, rise never, till the wood
Of Birnam rise, and our high-plac'd Macbeth
Shall live the lease of nature, pay his breath
To time and mortal custom.—Yet my heart
Throbs to know one thing: tell me,—if your
   art                  [ever
Can tell so much,—shall Banquo's issue
Reign in this kingdom?
 *All.*        Seek to know no more.
 *Macb.* I will be satisfied: deny me this,
And an eternal curse fall on you! Let me
   know:—              [this?
Why sinks that caldron? and what noise is
                   [*Hautboys.*
 1 *Witch.* Show!
 2 *Witch.* Show!
 3 *Witch.* Show!
 *All.* Show his eyes, and grieve his heart;
Come like shadows, so depart!
*Eight* Kings *appear, and pass over in order,
   the last with a glass in his hand;* BANQUO
   following.*
 *Macb.* Thou art too like the spirit of Ban-
   quo; down!           [thy hair,
Thy crown does sear mine eye-balls:—and
Thou other gold-bound brow, is like the
   first:—
A third is like the former.—Filthy hags!
Why do you show me this?—A fourth?—
Start, eyes!             [doom?
What! will the line stretch out to the crack of
Another yet?—A seventh?—I'll see no
   more:—             [glass
And yet the eighth appears, who bears a
Which shows me many more; and some I see
That twofold balls and treble sceptres carry:
Horrible sight!—Now, I see, 'tis true;
For the blood-bolter'd Banquo smiles upon
   me,              [so?
And points at them for his.—What! is this
 1 *Witch.* Ay, sir, all this is so:—but why
Stands Macbeth thus amazedly?—
Come, sisters, cheer we up his sprites,
And show the best of our delights:

I'll charm the air to give a sound,
While you perform your antic round;
That this great king may kindly say,
Our duties did his welcome pay.
[*Music. The* Witches *dance, and then vanish.*
   *Macb.* Where are they? Gone?—Let this
     pernicious hour
Stand aye accursed in the calendar!—
Come in, without there.

          *Enter* LENNOX

*Len.*         What's your grace's will?
*Macb.* Saw you the weird sisters?
*Len.*           No, my lord.
*Macb.* Came they not by you?
*Len.*         No, indeed, my lord.
*Macb.* Infected be the air whereon they
    ride;            [I did hear
And damn'd all those that trust them!—
The galloping of horse: who was't came by?
   *Len.* 'Tis two or three, my lord, that bring
    you word
Macduff is fled to England.
   *Macb.*         Fled to England!
   *Len.* Ay, my good lord.
   *Macb.* Time, thou anticipat'st my dread
    exploits:
The flighty purpose never is o'ertook
Unless the deed go with it: from this moment
The very firstlings of my heart shall be
The firstlings of my hand. And even now,
To crown my thoughts with acts, be it
    thought and done:
The castle of Macduff I will surprise;
Seize upon Fife; give the edge o' the sword
His wife, his babes, and all unfortunate souls
That trace him in his line. No boasting like
    a fool;
This deed I'll do before this purpose cool:
But no more sights!—Where are these gentle-
    men?
Come, bring me where they are.    [*Exeunt.*

SCENE II.—FIFE. *A Room in* MACDUFF'S
       *Castle.*

*Enter* LADY MACDUFF, *her* Son, *and* ROSS.

   *Lady Macd.* What had he done, to make
    him fly the land?
   *Ross.* You must have patience, madam.
   *L. Macd.*         He had none:
His flight was madness: when our actions do
    not,
Our fears do make us traitors.
   *Ross.*         You know not
Whether it was his wisdom or his fear.
   *L. Macd.* Wisdom! to leave his wife, to
    leave his babes,
His mansion, and his titles, in a place  [not:
From whence himself does fly? He loves us
He wants the natural touch; for the poor
    wren,
The most diminutive of birds, will fight,
Her young ones in her nest, against the owl.
All is the fear, and nothing is the love;

As little is the wisdom, where the flight
So runs against all reason.
   *Ross.*         My dearest coz,
I pray you, school yourself: but, for your
    husband,
He is noble, wise, judicious, and best knows
The fits o' the season. I dare not speak much
    further:
But cruel are the times, when we are traitors,
And do not know ourselves; when we hold
    rumour            [fear,
From what we fear, yet know not what we
But float upon a wild and violent sea
Each way and move.—I take my leave of
    you:
Shall not be long but I'll be here again:
Things at the worst will cease, or else climb
    upward
To what they were before.—My pretty cousin,
Blessing upon you!        [fatherless.
   *L. Macd.* Father'd he is, and yet he's
   *Ross.* I am so much a fool, should I stay
    longer.
It would be my disgrace and your discomfort:
I take my leave at once.       [*Exit.*
   *L. Macd.* Sirrah, your father's dead;
And what will you do now? How will you
    live?
   *Son.* As birds do, mother.
   *L. Macd.*      What, with worms and flies?
   *Son.* With what I get, I mean; and so do
    they.           [the net nor lime,
   *L. Macd.* Poor bird! thou'dst never fear
The pit-fall nor the gin.
   *Son.* Why should I, mother? Poor birds
    they are not set for.
My father is not dead, for all your saying.
   *L. Macd.* Yes, he is dead: how wilt thou
    do for a father?
   *Son.* Nay, how will you do for a husband?
   *L. Macd.* Why, I can buy me twenty at
    any market.
   *Son.* Then you'll buy 'em to sell again.
   *L. Macd.* Thou speak'st with all thy wit;
    and yet, i' faith,
With wit enough for thee.
   *Son.* Was my father a traitor, mother?
   *L. Macd.* Ay, that he was.
   *Son.* What is a traitor?
   *L. Macd.* Why, one that swears and lies.
   *Son.* And be all traitors that do so?
   *L. Macd.* Every one that does so is a
traitor, and must be hanged. [swear and lie?
   *Son.* And must they all be hanged that
   *L. Macd.* Every one.
   *Son.* Who must hang them?
   *L. Macd.* Why, the honest men.
   *Son.* Then the liars and swearers are fools:
for there are liars and swearers enow to beat
the honest men, and hang up them.
   *L. Macd.* Now, God help thee, poor mon-
key! But how wilt thou do for a father?
   *Son.* If he were dead, you'd weep for him:
if you would not, it were a good sign that I

should quickly have a new father.

*L. Macd.* Poor prattler! how thou talk'st.

*Enter a* Messenger.

*Mess.* Bless you, fair dame! I am not to
    you known,
Though in your state of honour I am perfect.
I doubt some danger does approach you
    nearly:
If you will take a homely man's advice,
Be not found here; hence, with your little
    ones.                 [age;
To fright you thus, methinks, I am too sav-
To do worse to you were fell cruelty,
Which is too nigh your person. Heaven pre-
    serve you!
I dare abide no longer.         [*Exit.*

*L. Macd.*        Whither should I fly?
I have done no harm. But I remember now
I am in this earthly world; where to do harm
Is often laudable; to do good, sometime
Accounted dangerous folly: why then, alas,
Do I put up that womanly defence,
To say I have done no harm?—What are
    these faces?

*Enter* Murderers.

1 *Mur.* Where is your husband?

*L. Macd.* I hope, in no place so unsancti-
    fied
Where such as thou mayst find him.

1 *Mur.*          He's a traitor.

*Son.* Thou liest, thou shag-hair'd villain.

-1 *Mur.* What, you egg?   [*Stabbing him.*
Young fry of treachery!

*Son.*       He has kill'd me, mother:
Run away, I pray you!         [*Dies.*
    [*Exit* LADY MACDUFF, *crying* Murder,
    *and pursued by the* Murderers.

SCENE III.—ENGLAND. *Before the* KING'S
*Palace.*

*Enter* MALCOLM *and* MACDUFF.

*Mal.* Let us seek out some desolate shade,
    and there
Weep our sad bosoms empty.

*Macd.*           Let us rather
Hold fast the mortal sword, and, like good
    men,              [new morn
Bestride our down-fall'n birthdom: each
New widows howl; new orphans cry; new
    sorrows
Strike heaven on the face, that it resounds
As if it felt with Scotland, and yell'd out
Like syllable of dolour.

*Mal.*        What I believe, I'll wail;
What know, believe; and what I can redress,
As I shall find the time to friend, I will.
What you have spoke, it may be so perchance.
This tyrant, whose sole name blisters our
    tongues,            [him well;
Was once thought honest: you have lov'd
He hath not touch'd you yet. I am young;
    but something

You may deserve of him through me; and
    wisdom
To offer up a weak, poor, innocent lamb
To appease an angry god.

*Macd.* I am not treacherous.

*Mal.*             But Macbeth is.
A good and virtuous nature may recoil
In an imperial charge. But I shall crave your
    pardon;
That which you are my thoughts cannot
    transpose;
Angels are bright still, though the brightest
    fell:
Though all things foul would wear the brows
    of grace,
Yet grace must still look so.

*Macd.*         I have lost my hopes.

*Mal.* Perchance even there where I did
    find my doubts.
Why in that rawness left you wife and child—
Those precious motives, those strong knots of
    love,
Without leave-taking?—I pray you,
Let not my jealousies be your dishonours,
But mine own safeties:—you may be rightly
    just,
Whatever I shall think.

*Macd.*         Bleed, bleed, poor country!
Great tyranny, lay thou thy basis sure,
For goodness dare not check thee! wear thou
    thy wrongs,
Thy title is affeer'd.—Fare thee well, lord:
I would not be the villain that thou think'st
For the whole space that's in the tyrant's
    grasp,
And the rich East to boot.

*Mal.*          Be not offended:
I speak not as in absolute fear of you.
I think our country sinks beneath the yoke;
It weeps, it bleeds; and each new day a gash
Is added to her wounds: I think, withal,
There would be hands uplifted in my right;
And here, from gracious England, have I offer
Of goodly thousands: but, for all this,
When I shall tread upon the tyrant's head,
Or wear it on my sword, yet my poor country
Shall have more vices than it had before;
More suffer, and more sundry ways than ever,
By him that shall succeed.

*Macd.*         What should he be?

*Mal.* It is myself I mean: in whom I know
All the particulars of vice so grafted
That, when they shall be open'd, black Mac-
    beth
Will seem as pure as snow; and the poor state
Esteem him as a lamb, being compar'd
With my confineless harms.

*Macd.*         Not in the legions
Of horrid hell can come a devil more damn'd
In evils to top Macbeth.

*Mal.*         I grant him bloody,
Luxurious, avaricious, false, deceitful,
Sudden, malicious, smacking of every sin
That has a name: but there's no bottom, none,

In my voluptuousness: your wives, your
 daughters,     [up
Your matrons, and your maids, could not fill
The cistern of my lust; and my desire
All continent impediments would o'erbear,
That did oppose my will: better Macbeth
Than such a one to reign.

 *Macd.*    Boundless intemperance
In nature is a tyranny; it hath been
The untimely emptying of the happy throne,
And fall of many kings. But fear not yet
To take upon you what is yours: you may
Convey your pleasures in a spacious plenty,
And yet seem cold, the time you may so
 hoodwink.     [not be
We have willing dames enough; there can-
That vulture in you, to devour so many
As will to greatness dedicate themselves,
Finding it so inclin'd.

 *Mal.*    With this there grows,
In my most ill-compos'd affection, such
A stanchless avarice, that, were I king,
I should cut off the nobles for their lands;
Desire his jewels, and this other's house:
And my more-having would be as a sauce
To make me hunger more; that I should forge
Quarrels unjust against the good and loyal,
Destroying them for wealth.

 *Macd.*    This avarice
Sticks deeper; grows with more pernicious
 root
Than summer-seeming lust; and it hath been
The sword of our slain kings: yet do not fear;
Scotland hath foysons to fill up your will,
Of your mere own: all these are portable,
With other graces weigh'd.    [graces,

 *Mal.* But I have none: the king-becoming
As justice, verity, temperance, stableness,
Bounty, perséverance, mercy, lowliness,
Devotion, patience, courage, fortitude,
I have no relish of them; but abound
In the division of each several crime, [should
Acting it many ways. Nay, had I power, I
Pour the sweet milk of concord into hell,
Uproar the universal peace, confound
All unity on earth.

 *Macd.*    O Scotland! Scotland!

 *Mal.* If such a one be fit to govern, speak:
I am as I have spoken.

 *Macd.*    Fit to govern!
No, not to live!—O nation miserable,
With an untitled tyrant bloody-scepter'd,
When shalt thou see thy wholesome days
 again,
Since that the truest issue of thy throne
By his own interdiction stands accurs'd,
And does blaspheme his breed?—Thy royal
 father     [thee,
Was a most sainted king; the queen that bore
Oftener upon her knees than on her feet,
Died every day she lived. Fare-thee-well!
These evils thou repeat'st upon thyself
Have banish'd me from Scotland.—O my
 breast.

Thy hope ends here!

 *Mal.*    Macduff, this noble passion,
Child of integrity, hath from my soul
Wip'd the black scruples, reconcil'd my
 thoughts
To thy good truth and honour. Devilish Mac-
 beth
By many of these trains hath sought to win
 me     [me
Into his power; and modest wisdom plucks
From over-credulous haste: but God above
Deal between thee and me! for even now
I put myself to thy direction, and
Unspeak mine own detraction; here abjure
The taints and blames I laid upon myself,
For strangers to my nature. I am yet
Unknown to woman; never was forsworn;
Scarcely have coveted what was mine own;
At no time broke my faith; would not betray
The devil to his fellow; and delight [speaking
No less in truth than life: my first false
Was this upon myself:—what I am truly,
Is thine, and my poor country's, to command:
Whither, indeed, before thy here-approach,
Old Siward, with ten thousand warlike men,
Already at a point, was setting forth:
Now we'll together; and the chance of good-
 ness
Be like our warranted quarrel! Why are you
 silent?    [things at once

 *Macd.* Such welcome and unwelcome
'Tis hard to reconcile.

*Enter a* Doctor.

 *Mal.* Well; more anon.—Comes the king
 forth, I pray you?

 *Doct.* Ay, sir: there are a crew of wretched
 souls
That stay his cure: their malady convinces
The great assay of art; but, at his touch,
Such sanctity hath heaven given his hand,
They presently amend.

 *Mal.* I thank you, doctor. [*Exit* Doctor.

 *Macd.* What's the disease he means?

 *Mal.*    'Tis called the evil:
A most miraculous work in this good king;
Which often, since my here-remain in Eng-
 land,
I have seen him do. How he solicits heaven,
Himself best knows: but strangely-visited
 people,
All swoln and ulcerous, pitiful to the eye,
The mere despair of surgery, he cures;
Hanging a golden stamp about their necks,
Put on with holy prayers: and 'tis spoken,
To the succeeding royalty he leaves
The healing benediction. With this strange
 virtue,
He hath a heavenly gift of prophecy;
And sundry blessings hang about his throne,
That speak him full of grace.

 *Macd.*   See, who comes here?

 *Mal.* My countryman; but yet I know him
 not.

*Enter* Ross.

*Macd.* My ever-gentle cousin, welcome hither.     [remove

*Mal.* I know him now. Good God, betimes
The means that makes us strangers!

*Ross.*      Sir, amen.

*Macd.* Stands Scotland where it did?

*Ross.*      Alas, poor country,—
Almost afraid to know itself! It cannot
Be call'd our mother, but our grave: where nothing,     [smile,
But who knows nothing, is once seen to
Where sighs, and groans, and shrieks, that rent the air,
Are made, not mark'd; where violent sorrow seems
A modern ecstacy; the dead man's knell
Is there scarce ask'd for who; and good men's lives
Expire before the flowers in their caps,
Dying or ere they sicken.

*Macd.*      O, relation
Too nice, and yet too true!

*Mal.*      What's the newest grief?

*Ross.* That of an hour's age doth hiss the speaker;
Each minute teems a new one.

*Macd.*      How does my wife?

*Ross.* Why, well.

*Macd.*      And all my children?

*Ross.*      Well too.

*Macd.* The tyrant has not batter'd at their peace?     [I did leave 'em.

*Ross.* No; they were well at peace when

*Macd.* Be not a niggard of your speech: how goes't?     [tidings,

*Ross.* When I came hither to transport the
Which I have heavily borne, there ran a rumour
Of many worthy fellows that were out;
Which was to my belief witness'd the rather,
For that I saw the tyrant's power a-foot:
Now is the time of help; your eye in Scotland
Would create soldiers, make our women fight,
To doff their dire distresses.

*Mal.*      Be't their comfort
We are coming thither: gracious England hath
Lent us good Siward and ten thousand men;
An older and a better soldier none
That Christendom gives out.

*Ross.*      Would I could answer
This comfort with the like! But I have words
That would be howl'd out in the desert air,
Where hearing should not latch them.

*Macd.*      What concern they?
The general cause? or is it a fee-grief
Due to some single breast?

*Ross.*      No mind that's honest
But in it shares some woe; though the main part
Pertains to you alone.

*Macd.*      If it be mine,
Keep it not from me; quickly let me have it.

*Ross.* Let not your ears despise my tongue for ever,     [sound
Which shall possess them with the heaviest
That ever yet they heard.

*Macd.*      Hum! I guess at it.

*Ross.* Your castle is surpris'd; your wife and babes
Savagely slaughter'd: to relate the manner,
Were, on the quarry of these murder'd deer,
To add the death of you.

*Mal.*      Merciful heaven!—
What, man! ne'er pull your hat upon your brows;     [speak
Give sorrow words: the grief that does not
Whispers the o'er-fraught heart, and bids it break.

*Macd.* My children too?

*Ross.*      Wife, children, servants, all
That could be found.

*Macd.*      And I must be from thence!
My wife's kill'd too?

*Ross.*      I have said.

*Mal.*      Be comforted:
Let's make us medicines of our great revenge,
To cure this deadly grief.

*Macd.* He has no children.—All my pretty ones?
Did you say all?—O hell-kite!—All?
What, all my pretty chickens and their dam
At one fell swoop?

*Mal.* Dispute it like a man.

*Macd.*      I shall do so;
But I must also feel it as a man:
I cannot but remember such things were,
That were most precious to me.—Did heaven look on,
And would not take their part? Sinful Macduff,     [I am,
They were all struck for thee! naught that
Not for their own demerits, but for mine,
Fell slaughter on their souls: heaven rest them now!     [let grief

*Mal.* Be this the whetstone of your sword:
Convert to anger; blunt not the heart, enrage it.

*Macd.* O, I could play the woman with mine eye,
And braggart with my tongue!—But, gentle heavens,
Cut short all intermission; front to front
Bring thou this fiend of Scotland and myself;
Within my sword's length set him; if he 'scape,
Heaven forgive him too!

*Mal.*      This tune goes manly.
Come, go we to the king; our power is ready;
Our lack is nothing but our leave: Macbeth
Is ripe for shaking, and the powers above
Put on their instruments. Receive what cheer you may;
The night is long that never finds the day.
     [*Exeunt.*

## ACT V.

### SCENE I.—DUNSINANE. *A Room in the Castle.*

*Enter a* Doctor of Physic *and a* Waiting-Gentlewoman.

*Doct.* I have two nights watched with you, but can perceive no truth in your report. When was it she last walked?

*Gent.* Since his majesty went into the field, I have seen her rise from her bed, throw her nightgown upon her, unlock her closet, take forth paper, fold it, write upon it, read it, afterwards seal it, and again return to bed; yet all this while in a most fast sleep.

*Doct.* A great perturbation in nature,—to receive at once the benefit of sleep, and do the effects of watching!—In this slumbery agitation, besides her walking and other actual performances, what, at any time, have you heard her say?

*Gent.* That, sir, which I will not report after her.

*Doct.* You may to me; and 'tis most meet you should.

*Gent.* Neither to you nor any one; having no witness to confirm my speech. Lo you, here she comes!

*Enter* LADY MACBETH, *with a taper.*
This is her very guise; and, upon my life, fast asleep. Observe her; stand close.

*Doct.* How came she by that light?

*Gent.* Why, it stood by her: she has light by her continually; 'tis her command.

*Doct.* You see, her eyes are open.

*Gent.* Ay, but their sense is shut.

*Doct.* What is it she does now? Look, how she rubs her hands.

*Gent.* It is an accustomed action with her, to seem thus washing her hands: I have known her continue in this a quarter of an hour.

*Lady M.* Yet here's a spot.

*Doct.* Hark! she speaks: I will set down what comes from her, to satisfy my remembrance the more strongly.

*Lady M.* Out, damned spot! out, I say!— One; two: why, then 'tis time to do't:—Hell is murky!—Fie, my lord, fie! a soldier, and afeard? What need we fear who knows it, when none can call our power to account?— Yet who would have thought the old man to have had so much blood in him?

*Doct.* Do you mark that?

*Lady M.* The Thane of Fife had a wife; where is she now?—What, will these hands ne'er be clean?—No more o' that, my lord, no more o' that: you mar all with this starting.

*Doct.* Go to, go to; you have known what you should not.

*Gent.* She has spoke what she should not, I am sure of that: heaven knows what she has known.

*Lady M.* Here's the smell of the blood still: all the perfumes of Arabia will not sweeten this little hand. Oh, oh, oh!

*Doct.* What a sigh is there! The heart is sorely charged.

*Gent.* I would not have such a heart in my bosom for the dignity of the whole body.

*Doct.* Well, well, well,—

*Gent.* Pray God it be, sir.

*Doct.* This disease is beyond my practice: yet I have known those which have walked in their sleep who had died holily in their beds.

*Lady M.* Wash your hands, put on your nightgown; look not so pale:—I tell you yet again, Banquo's buried; he cannot come out on's grave.

*Doct.* Even so?

*Lady M.* To bed, to bed; there's knocking at the gate: come, come, come, come, give me your hand: what's done cannot be undone: to bed, to bed, to bed.            [*Exit.*

*Doct.* Will she go now to bed?

*Gent.* Directly.            [natural deeds

*Doct.* Foul whisperings are abroad: un-Do breed unnatural troubles: infected minds
To their deaf pillows will discharge their
            secrets.
More needs she the divine than the physician.
God, God forgive us all!—Look after her;
Remove from her the means of all annoyance,
And still keep eyes upon her:—so, good-
            night:            [sight:
My mind she has mated, and amaz'd my
I think, but dare not speak.

*Gent.*            Good-night, good doctor.
            [*Exeunt.*

### SCENE II.—*The County near Dunsinane.*

*Enter, with drum and colours,* MENTEITH, CAITHNESS, ANGUS, LENNOX, *and* Soldiers.

*Ment.* The English power is near, led on
            by Malcolm,
His uncle Siward, and the good Macduff.
Revenges burn in them; for their dear causes
Would to the bleeding and the grim alarm
Excite the mortified man.

*Ang.*            Near Birnam wood
Shall we well meet them; that way are they
            coming            [brother?

*Caith.* Who knows if Donalbain be with his

*Len.* For certain, sir, he is not: I have a file
Of all the gentry: there is Siward's son,
And many unrough youths, that even now
Protest their first of manhood.

*Ment.*            What does the tyrant?

*Caith.* Great Dunsinane he strongly forti-
            fies:            [him,
Some say he's mad; others, that lesser hate
Do call it valiant fury: but, for certain,
He cannot buckle his distemper'd course
Within the belt of rule.

*Ang.*            Now does he feel
His secret murders sticking on his hands;

Now minutely revolts upbraid his faith-
　　breach;
Those he commands move only in command,
Nothing in love: now does he feel his title
Hang loose about him, like a giant's robe
Upon a dwarfish thief.
　　*Ment.*　　　　Who, then, shall blame
His pester'd senses to recoil and start,
When all that is within him does condemn
Itself for being there?
　　*Caith.*　　　　Well, march we on,
To give obedience where 'tis truly ow'd:
Meet we the medicine of the sickly weal;
And with him pour we, in our country's
　　purge,
Each drop of us.
　　*Len.*　　　Or so much as it needs,
To dew the sovereign flower, and drown the
　　weeds.
Make we our march towards Birnam.
　　　　　　　　[*Exeunt, marching.*

SCENE III.—DUNSINANE. *A Room in the
　　Castle.*

*Enter* MACBETH, Doctor, *and* Attendants.

*Macb.* Bring me no more reports; let them
　　fly all:
Till Birnam wood remove to Dunsinane
I cannot taint with fear. What's the boy
　　Malcolm?　　　　　　　　　　know
Was he not born of woman? The spirits that
All mortal consequences have pronounc'd me
　　thus,—
*Fear not, Macbeth; no man that's born of
　　woman
Shall e'er have power upon thee.*—Then fly,
　　false thanes,
And mingle with the English epicures:
The mind I sway by, and the heart I bear,
Shall never sag with doubt nor shake with
　　fear.
　　　　　　*Enter a* Servant.
The devil damn thee black, thou cream-fac'd
　　loon!
Where gott'st thou that goose look?
　　*Serv.* There is ten thousand—
　　*Macb.*　　　　　　Geese, villain?
　　*Serv.*　　　　　　Soldiers, sir.
　　*Macb.* Go, prick thy face, and over-red thy
　　fear,
Thou lily-liver'd boy. What soldiers, patch?
Death of thy soul! those linen cheeks of thine
Are counsellors to fear. What soldiers, whey-
　　face?
　　*Serv.* The English force, so please you.
　　*Macb.* Take thy face hence. [*Exit* Servant.
Seyton!—I am sick at heart,
When I behold—Seyton, I say!—This push
Will chair me ever, or disseat me now.
I have liv'd long enough: my way of life
Is fall'n into the sear, the yellow leaf;
And that which should accompany old age,
As honour, love, obedience, troops of friends,
I must not look to have; but, in their stead,

Curses not loud but deep, mouth-honour,
　　breath,　　　　　　　　　　[dare not.
Which the poor heart would fain deny, and
Seyton!—

　　　　　　*Enter* SEYTON.

　　*Sey.* What is your gracious pleasure?
　　*Macb.*　　　　　　What news more?
　　*Sey.* All is confirm'd, my lord, which was
　　reported.　　　　　　　　　[be hack'd.
　　*Macb.* I'll fight till from my bones my flesh
Give me my armour.
　　*Sey.*　　　　　　'Tis not needed yet.
　　*Macb.* I'll put it on.
Send out more horses, skirr the country
　　round;　　　　　　　　　　[armour.—
Hang those that talk of fear.—Give me mine
How does your patient, doctor?
　　*Doct.*　　　　　　Not so sick, my lord,
As she is troubled with thick-coming fancies,
That keep her from her rest.
　　*Macb.*　　　　　　Cure her of that:
Canst thou not minister to a mind diseas'd;
Pluck from the memory a rooted sorrow;
Raze out the written troubles of the brain;
And with some sweet oblivious antidote
Cleanse the stuff'd bosom of that perilous
　　stuff
Which weighs upon the heart?
　　*Doct.*　　　　　　Therein the patient
Must minister to himself　　　　[none of it.—
　　*Macb.* Throw physic to the dogs,—I'll
Come, put mine armour on; give me my
　　staff:—
Seyton, send out.—Doctor, the thanes fly
　　from me.—　　　　　　　　[tor, cast
Come, sir, despatch.—If thou couldst, doc-
The water of my land, find her disease,
And purge it to a sound and pristine health,
I would applaud thee to the very echo,
That should applaud again.—Pull 't off, I
　　say.　　　　　　　　　　　[drug,
What rhubarb, senna, or what purgative
Would scour these English hence? Hear'st
　　thou of them?　　　　　　　[aration
　　*Doct.* Ay, my good lord; your royal prep-
Makes us hear something.
　　*Macb.*　　　　　　Bring it after me.—
I will not be afraid of death and bane,
Till Birnam forest come to Dunsinane.
　　　　　　[*Exeunt all except* Doctor.
　　*Doct.* Were I from Dunsinane away and
　　clear,
Profit again should hardly draw me here.
　　　　　　　　　　　　　　[*Exit.*

SCENE IV.—*Country near Dunsinane: a
　　Wood in view.*

*Enter, with drum and colours,* MALCOLM, *old*
SIWARD *and his* Son, MACDUFF, MENTEITH,
CAITHNESS, ANGUS, LENNOX, ROSS, *and*
Soldiers, *marching.*

　　*Mal.* Cousins, I hope the days are near at
　　hand

That chambers will be safe.

*Ment.* We doubt it nothing.

*Siw.* What wood is this before us?

*Ment.* The wood of Birnam.

*Mal.* Let every soldier hew him down a bough, [shadow
And bear't before him; thereby shall we
The numbers of our host, and make discovery
Err in report of us.

*Sold.* It shall be done. [tyrant

*Siw.* We learn no other but the confident
Keeps still in Dunsinane, and will endure
Our setting down before't.

*Mal.* 'Tis his main hope:
For where there is advantage to be given,
Both more and less have given him the revolt;
And none serve with him but constrained things,
Whose hearts are absent too.

*Macd.* Let our just censures
Attend the true event, and put we on
Industrious soldiership.

*Siw.* The time approaches,
That will with due decision make us know
What we shall say we have, and what we owe. [relate;
Thoughts speculative their unsure hopes
But certain issue strokes must arbitrate:
Towards which advance the war.

[*Exeunt, marching.*

SCENE V.—DUNSINANE. *Within the Castle.*

*Enter, with drum and colours,* MACBETH, SEYTON, *and* Soldiers.

*Macb.* Hang out our banners on the outward walls;
The cry is still, *They come:* our castle's strength
Will laugh a siege to scorn: here let them lie
Till famine and the ague eat them up:
Were they not forc'd with those that should be ours, [beard,
We might have met them dareful, beard to
And beat them backward home.

[*A cry of women within.*
What is that noise?

*Sey.* It is the cry of women, my good lord.

[*Exit.*

*Macb.* I have almost forgot the taste of fears: [cool'd
The time has been, my senses would have
To hear a night-shriek; and my fell of hair
Would at a dismal treatise rouse and stir
As life were in't: I have supp'd full with horrors; [thoughts.
Direness, familiar to my slaught'rous
Cannot once start me.

*Re-enter* SEYTON.

Wherefore was that cry?

*Sey.* The queen, my lord, is dead.

*Macb.* She should have died hereafter;
There would have been a time for such a word.—

To-morrow, and to-morrow, and to-morrow,
Creeps in this petty pace from day to day,
To the last syllable of recorded time;
And all our yesterdays have lighted fools
The way to dusty death. Out, out, brief candle!
Life's but a walking shadow; a poor player,
That struts and frets his hour upon the stage,
And then is heard no more: it is a tale
Told by an idiot, full of sound and fury,
Signifying nothing.

*Enter a* Messenger.

Thou com'st to use thy tongue; thy story quickly.

*Mess.* Gracious my lord,
I should report that which I say I saw,
But know not how to do it.

*Macb.* Well, say, sir.

*Mess.* As I did stand my watch upon the hill, [thought,
I look'd toward Birnam, and anon, methought,
The wood began to move.

*Macb.* Liar, and slave!

[*Striking him.*

*Mess.* Let me endure your wrath, if't be not so.
Within this three mile may you see it coming;
I say, a moving grove.

*Macb.* If thou speak'st false,
Upon the next tree shalt thou hang alive,
Till famine cling thee: if thy speech be sooth,
I care not if thou dost for me as much.—
I pull in resolution; and begin
To doubt the equivocation of the fiend
That lies like truth: *Fear not, till Birnam wood
Do come to Dunsinane;*—and now a wood
Comes toward Dunsinane.—Arm, arm, and out!—
If this which he avouches does appear,
There is nor flying hence nor tarrying here.
I 'gin to be a-weary of the sun, [undone.—
And wish the estate o' the world were now
Ring the alarum-bell!—Blow, wind! come, wrack!
At least we'll die with harness on our back.

[*Exeunt.*

SCENE VI.—*The Same. A Plain before the Castle.*

*Enter, with drum and colours,* MALCOLM, *old* SIWARD, MACDUFF, *&c., and their* Army, *with boughs.*

*Mal.* Now near enough; your leafy screens throw down,
And show like those you are.—You, worthy uncle,
Shall, with my cousin, your right-noble son,
Lead our first battle: worthy Macduff and we
Shall take upon 's what else remains to do,
According to our order.

*Siw.*                    Fare you well—
Do we but find the tyrant's power to-night,
Let us be beaten, if we cannot fight.
  *Macd.* Make all our trumpets speak; give
    them all breath,                    [death.
Those clamorous harbingers of blood and
                                        [*Exeunt.*

SCENE VII.—*The same. Another part of the
    Plain.*

*Alarums. Enter* MACBETH.

  *Macb.* They have tied me to a stake; I
    cannot fly,                    [What's he
But, bear-like, I must fight the course.—
That was not born of woman? Such a one
Am I to fear, or none.

*Enter young* SIWARD.

  *Yo. Siw.* What is thy name?
  *Macb.*                    Thou'lt be afraid to hear it.
  *Yo. Siw.* No; though thou call'st thyself a
    hotter name
Than any is in hell.
  *Macb.*                    My name's Macbeth.
  *Yo. Siw.* The devil himself could not pro-
    nounce a title
More hateful to mine ear.
  *Macb.*                    No, nor more fearful.
  *Yo. Siw.* Thou liest, abhorred tyrant; with
    my sword
I'll prove the lie thou speak'st.
    [*They fight, and young* SIWARD *is slain.*
  *Macb.*                    Thou wast born of woman.—
But swords I smile at, weapons laugh to
    scorn,
Brandish'd by man that's of a woman born.
                                        [*Exit.*
*Alarums. Enter* MACDUFF.
  *Macd.* That way the noise is.—Tyrant,
    show thy face!                    [mine,
If thou be'st slain, and with no stroke of
My wife and children's ghosts will haunt me
    still.                    [arms
I cannot strike at wretched kerns, whose
Are hir'd to bear their staves; either thou,
    Macbeth,
Or else my sword, with an unbatter'd edge,
I sheathe again undeeded. There thou shouldst
    be;
By this great clatter, one of greatest note
Seems bruited. Let me find him, fortune!
And more I beg not.                    [*Exit Alarums.*
*Enter* MALCOLM *and old* SIWARD.
  *Siw.* This way, my lord;—the castle's gent-
    ly render'd:
The tyrant's people on both sides do fight;
The noble thanes do bravely in the war;
The day almost itself professes yours,
And little is to do.
  *Mal.*                    We have met with foes
That strike beside us.
  *Siw.*                    Enter, sir, the castle.
                                        [*Exeunt. Alarums.*

SCENE VIII.—*The same. Another part of the
    Plain.*

*Enter* MACBETH.

  *Macb.* Why, should I play the Roman fool,
    and die                    [gashes
On mine own sword? whiles I see lives, the
Do better upon them.

*Enter* MACDUFF.

  *Macd.*                    Turn, hell-hound, turn!
  *Macb.* Of all men else I have avoided thee:
But get thee back; my soul is too much
    charg'd
With blood of thine already.
  *Macd.*                    I have no words,—
My voice is in my sword: thou bloodier vil-
    lain
Than terms can give thee out!    [*They fight.*
  *Macb.*                    Thou losest labour:
As easy mayst thou the intrenchant air
With thy keen sword impress, as make me
    bleed:
Let fall thy blade on vulnerable crests;
I bear a charmed life, which must not yield
To one of woman born.
  *Macd.*                    Despair thy charm;
And let the angel whom thou still hast serv'd
Tell thee, Macduff was from his mother's
    womb.
Untimely ripp'd.                    [me so,
  *Macb.* Accursed be that tongue that tells
For it hath cow'd my better part of man!
And be these juggling fiends no more believ'd,
That palter with us in a double sense;
That keep the word of promise to our ear,
And break it to our hope!—I'll not fight with
    thee.
  *Macd.* Then yield thee, coward,    [time:
And live to be the show and gaze o' the
We'll have thee, as our rarer monsters are,
Painted upon a pole, and underwrit,
*Here may you see the tyrant.*
  *Macb.*                    I will not yield,
To kiss the ground before young Malcolm's
    feet,
And to be baited with the rabble's curse.
Though Birnam wood be come to Dunsinane,
And thou oppos'd, being of no woman born,
Yet I will try the last. Before my body
I throw my warlike shield: lay on, Macduff;
And damn'd be him that first cries, *Hold,
    enough!*                    [*Exeunt, fighting.*

*Retreat. Flourish. Enter, with drum and
    colours.* MALCOLM, *old* SIWARD, ROSS,
    LENNOX, ANGUS, CAITHNESS, MENTEITH,
    *and* Soldiers.

  *Mal.* I would the friends we miss were safe
    arriv'd.                    [I see,
  *Siw.* Some must go off; and yet, by these
So great a day as this is cheaply bought.
  *Mal.* Macduff is missing, and your noble
    son.                    [soldier's debt:
  *Ross.* Your son, my lord, has paid a

He only liv'd but till he was a man;
The which no sooner had his prowess con-
    firm'd
In the unshrinking station where he fought,
But like a man he died.
  *Siw.* Then he is dead?
  *Ross.* Ay, and brought off the field: your
    cause of sorrow
Must not be measur'd by his worth, for then
It hath no end.
  *Siw.* Had he his hurts before?
  *Ross.* Ay, on the front.
  *Siw.*    Why, then, God's soldier be he!
Had I as many sons as I have hairs,
I would not wish them to a fairer death:
And, so his knell is knoll'd.
  *Mal.*    He's worth more sorrow,
And that I'll spend for him.
  *Siw.*    He's worth no more:
They say he parted well, and paid his score:
And so, God be with him!—Here comes new-
    er comfort.

  *Re-enter* MACDUFF, *with* MACBETH'S *head.*

  *Macd.* Hail, king! for so thou art: behold,
    where stands
The usurper's cursed head: the time is free:
I see thee compass'd with thy kingdom's
    pearl

That speak my salutation in their minds;
Whose voices I desire aloud with mine,—
Hail, King of Scotland!
  *All.*    Hail, King of Scotland!
                      [*Flourish.*
  *Mal.* We shall not spend a large expense of
    time
Before we reckon with your several loves,
And make us even with you. My thanes and
    kinsmen,
Henceforth be earls, the first that ever Scot-
    land               [to do,
In such an honour nam'd.  What's more
Which would be planted newly with the
    time,—
As calling home our exil'd friends abroad,
That fled the snares of watchful tyranny;
Producing forth the cruel ministers
Of this dead butcher, and his fiend-like
    queen,—
Who, as 'tis thought, by self and violent
    hands
Took off her life;—this, and what needful
    else
That calls upon us, by the grace of Grace,
We will perform in measure, time, and place:
So, thanks to all at once, and to each one,
Whom we invite to see us crown'd at Scone.
             [*Flourish. Exeunt.*

# HAMLET, PRINCE OF DENMARK

## DRAMATIS PERSONÆ

CLAUDIUS, *King of Denmark.*
HAMLET, *Son to the former and Nephew to the present King.*
POLONIUS, *Lord Chamberlain.*
HORATIO, *Friend to* HAMLET.
LAERTES, *Son to* POLONIUS.
VOLTIMAND,
CORNELIUS,
ROSENCRANTZ,
GUILDENSTERN, } *Courtiers.*
OSRIC,
A Gentleman,
A Priest.
MARCELLUS, } *Officers.*
BERNARDO,

FRANCISCO, *a Soldier.*
REYNALDO, *Servant to* POLONIUS.
Players.
Two Clowns, *Grave-diggers.*
FORTINBRAS, *Prince of Norway.*
A Captain.
English Ambassadors.
Ghost of HAMLET's Father.

GERTRUDE, *Queen of Denmark, and Mother of* HAMLET.
OPHELIA, *Daughter to* POLONIUS.

Lords, Ladies, Officers, Soldiers, Sailors, Messengers, *and other* Attendants.

SCENE,—ELSINORE.

## ACT I.

SCENE I.—ELSINORE. *A Platform before the Castle.*

FRANCISCO *at his post. Enter to him* BERNARDO.

*Ber.* Who's there?
*Fran.* Nay, answer me: stand, and unfold
Yourself.
*Ber.* Long live the king!
*Fran.* Bernardo?
*Ber.* He.
*Fran.* You come most carefully upon your
hour.
*Ber.* 'Tis now struck twelve; get thee to
bed, Francisco.
*Fran.* For this relief much thanks: 'tis bit-
ter cold,
And I am sick at heart.
*Ber.* Have you had a quiet guard?
*Fran.* Not a mouse stirring.
*Ber.* Well, good-night.
If you do meet Horatio and Marcellus,
The rivals of my watch, bid them make haste.
*Fran.* I think I hear them.—Stand, ho!
Who is there?

*Enter* HORATIO *and* MARCELLUS.

*Hor.* Friends to this ground.
*Mar.* And liegemen to the Dane.
*Fran.* Give you good-night.
*Mar.* O, farewell, honest soldier:
Who hath reliev'd you?
*Fran.* Bernardo has my place.
Give you good-night. [*Exit.*

*Mar.* Holla! Bernardo!
*Ber.* Say.
What, is Horatio there?
*Hor.* A piece of him.
*Ber.* Welcome, Horatio:—welcome, good
Marcellus. [to-night?
*Mar.* What, has this thing appear'd again
*Ber.* I have seen nothing.
*Mar.* Horatio says 'tis but our fantasy,
And will not let belief take hold of him
Touching this dreaded sight, twice seen of us:
Therefore I have entreated him along
With us to watch the minutes of this night;
That, if again this apparition come
He may approve our eyes and speak to it.
*Hor.* Tush, tush, 'twill not appear.
*Ber.* Sit down awhile,
And let us once again assail your ears,
That are so fortified against our story,
What we two nights have seen.
*Hor.* Well, sit we down,
And let us hear Bernardo speak of this.
*Ber.* Last night of all,
When yon same star that's westward from
the pole
Had made his course to illume that part of
heaven
Where now it burns, Marcellus and myself,
The bell then beating one,—
*Mar.* Peace, break thee off; look where it
comes again!

*Enter* Ghost, *armed.*

*Ber.* In the same figure, like the king that's
dead. [Horatio.
*Mar.* Thou art a scholar; speak to it,

[*1071*]

*Ber.* Looks it not like the king? mark it, Horatio.      [and wonder.

*Hor.* Most like:—it harrows me with fear

*Ber.* It would be spoke to.

*Mar.*          Question it, Horatio.

*Hor.* What art thou, that usurp'st this time of night,
Together with that fair and warlike form
In which the majesty of buried Denmark
Did sometimes march? by heaven I charge thee, speak!

*Mar.* It is offended.

*Ber.*          See, it stalks away!

*Hor.* Stay! speak, speak! I charge thee, speak!      [*Exit* Ghost.

*Mar.* 'Tis gone, and will not answer.

*Ber.* How now, Horatio! you tremble and look pale:
Is not this something more than fantasy?
What think you on't?

*Hor.* Before my God, I might not this believe
Without the sensible and true avouch
Of mine own eyes.

*Mar.*          Is it not like the king?

*Hor.* As thou art to thyself:
Such was the very armour he had on
When he the ambitious Norway combated;
So frown'd he once when, in an angry parle,
He smote the sledded Polacks on the ice.
'Tis strange.          [dead hour,

*Mar.* Thus twice before, and just at this
With martial stalk hath he gone by our watch.

*Hor.* In what particular thought to work I know not;
But, in the gross and scope of my opinion,
This bodes some strange eruption to our state.

*Mar.* Good now, sit down, and tell me, he that knows,
Why this same strict and most observant watch
So nightly toils the subject of the land;
And why such daily cast of brazen cannon,
And foreign mart for implements of war;
Why such impress of shipwrights, whose sore task
Does not divide the Sunday from the week;
What might be toward, that this sweaty haste
Doth make the night joint-labourer with the day:
Who is't that can inform me?

*Hor.*          That can I;
At least, the whisper goes so. Our last king,
Whose image even but now appear'd to us,
Was, as you know, by Fortinbras of Norway,
Thereto prick'd on by a most emulate pride,
Dar'd to the combat; in which our valiant Hamlet,—      [him,—
For so this side of our known world esteem'd
Did slay this Fortinbras; who, by a seal'd compact,
Well ratified by law and heraldry,

Did forfeit, with his life, all those his lands,
Which he stood seiz'd of, to the conqueror:
Against the which, a moiety competent
Was gaged by our king; which had return'd
To the inheritance of Fortinbras, [cov'nant,
Had he been vanquisher; as by the same
And carriage of the article design'd,      [bras,
His fell to Hamlet. Now, sir, young Fortin-
Of unimproved mettle hot and full,
Hath in the skirts of Norway, here and there,
Shark'd up a list of landless resolutes,
For food and diet, to some enterprise
That hath a stomach in't: which is no other,—
As it doth well appear unto our state,—
But to recover of us by strong hand,
And terms compulsative, those foresaid lands
So by his father lost: and this, I take it,
Is the main motive of our preparations,
The source of this our watch, and the chief head
Of this post-haste and romage in the land.

*Ber.* I think it be no other, but e'en so:
Well may it sort, that this portentous figure
Comes armed through our watch; so like the king
That was and is the question of these wars.

*Hor.* A mote it is to trouble the mind's eye.
In the most high and palmy state of Rome,
A little ere the mightiest Julius fell,      [dead
The graves stood tenantless, and the sheeted
Did squeak and gibber in the Roman streets:
As, stars with trains of fire and dews of blood,
Disasters in the sun; and the moist star,
Upon whose influence Neptune's empire stands,
Was sick almost to doomsday with eclipse:
And even the like precurse of fierce events,—
As harbingers preceding still the fates,
And prologue to the omen coming on,—
Have heaven and earth together demonstrated
Unto our climature and countrymen.—
But, soft, behold! lo, where it comes again!

*Re-enter* Ghost.

I'll cross it, though it blast me.—Stay, illusion!
If thou hast any sound or use of voice,
Speak to me:
If there be any good thing to be done,
That may to thee do ease, and grace to me,
Speak to me:
If thou art privy to thy country's fate,
Which, happily, foreknowing may avoid,
O, speak!
Or if thou hast uphoarded in thy life
Extorted treasure in the womb of earth,
For which, they say, you spirits oft walk in death,      [*cock crows.*
Speak of it:—stay, and speak!—Stop it, Marcellus.

*Mar.* Shall I strike at it with my partisan?

*Hor.* Do, if it will not stand.

*Ber.* 'Tis here!
*Hor.* 'Tis here!
*Mar.* 'Tis gone! [*Exit* Ghost.
We do it wrong, being so majestical,
To offer it the show of violence;
For it is, as the air, invulnerable,
And our vain blows malicious mockery.
　*Ber.* It was about to speak when the cock
crew.
　*Hor.* And then it started like a guilty thing
Upon a fearful summons. I have heard,
The cock, that is the trumpet to the morn,
Doth with his lofty and shrill-sounding
　throat
Awake the god of day; and at his warning,
Whether in sea or fire, in earth or air,
The extravagant and erring spirit hies
To his confine: and of the truth herein
This present object made probation.
　*Mar.* It faded on the crowing of the cock.
Some say that ever 'gainst that season comes
Wherein our Saviour's birth is celebrated,
The bird of dawning singeth all night long:
And then, they say, no spirit can walk abroad;
The nights are wholesome; then no planets
　strike,
No fairy takes, nor witch hath power to
　charm;
So hallow'd and so gracious is the time.
　*Hor.* So have I heard, and do in part be-
lieve it.
But, look, the morn, in russet mantle clad,
Walks o'er the dew of yon high eastern hill:
Break we our watch up: and, by my advice,
Let us impart what we have seen to-night
Unto young Hamlet; for, upon my life,
This spirit, dumb to us, will speak to him:
Do you consent we shall acquaint him with
　it,
As needful in our loves, fitting our duty?
　*Mar.* Let's do't, I pray; and I this morning
　know
Where we shall find him most conveniently.
　　　　　　　　　　　　　　　[*Exeunt.*

SCENE II.—ELSINORE. *A Room of State in the
Castle.*

*Enter the* KING, QUEEN, HAMLET, POLONIUS,
LAERTES, VOLTIMAND, CORNELIUS, *Lords,
and* Attendants.

　*King.* Though yet of Hamlet our dear
　brother's death
The memory be green; and that it us befitted
To bear our hearts in grief, and our whole
　kingdom
To be contracted in one brow of woe;
Yet so far hath discretion fought with nature
That we with wisest sorrow think on him,
Together with remembrance of ourselves.
Therefore our sometime sister, now our
　queen,
The imperial jointress of this warlike state,
Have we, as 'twere with a defeated joy,—
With one auspicious and one dropping eye,

With mirth and funeral, and with dirge in
　marriage,
In equal scale weighing delight and dole,—
Taken to wife: nor have we herein barr'd
Your better wisdoms, which have freely gone
With this affair along:—for all, our thanks.
Now follows that you know, young Fortin-
　bras,
Holding a weak supposal of our worth,
Or thinking by our late dear brother's death
Our state to be disjoint and out of frame,
Colleagued with the dream of his advantage,
He hath not fail'd to pester us with message,
Importing the surrender of those lands
Lost by his father, with all bonds of law,
To our most valiant brother. So much for
　him.—
Now for ourself, and for this time of meet-
　ing:
Thus much the business is:—we have here
　writ
To Norway, uncle of young Fortinbras,—
Who, impotent and bed-rid, scarcely hears
Of this his nephew's purpose,—to suppress
His further gait herein; in that the levies,
The lists, and full proportions, are all made
Out of his subject:—and we here despatch
You, good Cornelius, and you, Voltimand,
For bearers of this greeting to old Norway;
Giving to you no further personal power
To business with the king more than the
　scope
Of these dilated articles allow. [duty.
Farewell; and let your haste commend your
　*Cor. and Vol.* In that and all things will
　we show our duty.
　*King.* We doubt it nothing: heartily fare-
well.
　　　　　　　　　　　[*Exeunt* VOL. *and* COR.
And now, Laertes, what's the news with you?
You told us of some suit; what is't, Laertes?
You cannot speak of reason to the Dane,
And lose your voice: what wouldst thou beg,
　Laertes,
That shall not be my offer, nor thy asking?
The head is not more native to the heart,
The hand more instrumental to the mouth,
Than is the throne of Denmark to thy father.
What wouldst thou have, Laertes?
　*Laer.* Dread my lord,
Your leave and favour to return to France;
From whence though willingly I came to
　Denmark,
To show my duty in your coronation;
Yet now, I must confess, that duty done,
My thoughts and wishes bend again toward
　France, [pardon.
And bow them to your gracious leave and
　*King.* Have you your father's leave? What
　says Polonius? [slow leave
　*Pol.* He hath, my lord, wrung from me my
By laboursome petition; and at last
Upon his will I seal'd my hard consent:
I do beseech you, give him leave to go.

*King.* Take thy fair hour, Laertes; time be thine,
And thy best graces spend it at thy will!—
But now, my cousin Hamlet, and my son,—
*Ham.* [*Aside.*] A little more than kin, and less than kind.
*King.* How is it that the clouds still hang on you?
*Ham.* Not so, my lord; I am too much i' the sun.
*Queen.* Good Hamlet, cast thy nighted colour off,
And let thine eye look like a friend on Denmark.
Do not for ever with thy vailed lids
Seek for thy noble father in the dust:
Thou know'st 'tis common,—all that live must die,
Passing through nature to eternity.
*Ham.* Ay, madam, it is common.
*Queen.* If it be,
Why seems it so particular with thee?
*Ham.* Seems, madam! nay, it is; I know not seems.
'Tis not alone my inky cloak, good mother,
Nor customary suits of solemn black,
Nor windy suspiration of forc'd breath,
No, nor the fruitful river in the eye,
Nor the dejected 'haviour of the visage,
Together with all forms, moods, shows of grief,
That can denote me truly: these, indeed, seem;
For they are actions that a man might play;
But I have that within me which passeth show;
These but the trappings and the suits of woe.
*King.* 'Tis sweet and commendable in your nature, Hamlet,
To give these mourning duties to your father:
But, you must know, your father lost a father;
That father lost, lost his; and the survivor bound,
In filial obligation, for some term
To do obsequious sorrow: but to persevere
In obstinate condolement is a course
Of impious stubbornness; 'tis unmanly grief:
It shows a will most incorrect to heaven;
A heart unfortified, a mind impatient;
An understanding simple and unschool'd:
For what we know must be, and is as common
As any the most vulgar thing to sense,
Why should we, in our peevish opposition,
Take it to heart? Fie! 'tis a fault to heaven,
A fault against the dead, a fault to nature,
To reason most absurd; whose common theme
Is death of fathers, and who still hath cried,
From the first course till he that died to-day,
*This must be so.* We pray you, throw to earth
This unprevailing woe; and think of us
As of a father: for let the world take note
You are the most immediate to our throne;
And with no less nobility of love
Than that which dearest father bears his son
Do I impart toward you. For your intent
In going back to school in Wittenberg,
It is most retrograde to our desire:
And we beseech you bend you to remain
Here, in the cheer and comfort of our eye,
Our chiefest courtier, cousin, and our son.
*Queen.* Let not thy mother lose her prayers, Hamlet:
I pray thee, stay with us; go not to Wittenberg.
*Ham.* I shall in all my best obey you, madam.
*King.* Why, 'tis a loving and a fair reply:
Be as ourself in Denmark.—Madam, come;
This gentle and unforc'd accord of Hamlet
Sits smiling to my heart: in grace whereof,
No jocund health that Denmark drinks to-day
But the great cannon to the clouds shall tell;
And the king's rouse the heavens shall bruit again,
Re-speaking earthly thunder. Come away.
[*Exeunt all but* HAMLET.
*Ham.* O, that this too too solid flesh would melt,
Thaw, and resolve itself into a dew!
Or that the Everlasting had not fix'd [God!
His canon 'gainst self-slaughter! O God! O
How weary, stale, flat, and unprofitable
Seem to me all the uses of this world!
Fie on't! O fie! 'tis an unweeded garden,
That grows to seed; things rank and gross in nature
Possess it merely. That it should come to this!
But two months dead!—nay, not so much, not two:
So excellent a king; that was, to this,
Hyperion to a satyr: so loving to my mother,
That he might not beteem the winds of heaven
Visit her face too roughly. Heaven and earth!
Must I remember? why, she would hang on him
As if increase of appetite had grown
By what it fed on: and yet, within a month,—
Let me not think on't,—Frailty, thy name is woman!—
A little month; or ere those shoes were old
With which she follow'd my poor father's body,
Like Niobe, all tears;—why she, even she,—
O God! a beast, that wants discourse of reason,
Would have mourn'd longer,—married with mine uncle,
My father's brother; but no more like my father,
Than I to Hercules: within a month;
Ere yet the salt of most unrighteous tears
Had left the flushing in her galled eyes,
She married:—O, most wicked speed, to post
With such dexterity to incestuous sheets!
It is not, nor it cannot come to good;

But break, my heart,—for I must hold my
   tongue!

*Enter* HORATIO, MARCELLUS, *and* BERNARDO.

  *Hor.* Hail to your lordship!
  *Ham.*        I am glad to see you well:
Horatio,—or I do forget myself.
  *Hor.* The same, my lord, and your poor
   servant ever.
  *Ham.* Sir, my good friend; I'll change that
   name with you:      [tio?—
And what make you from Wittenberg, Hora-
Marcellus?
  *Mar.* My good lord,—
  *Ham.* I am very glad to see you.—Good
   even, sir.—
But what, in faith, make you from Witten-
   berg?
  *Hor.* A truant disposition, good my lord.
  *Ham.* I would not hear your enemy say so;
Nor shall you do mine ear that violence,
To make it truster of your own report
Against yourself: I know you are no truant.
But what is your affair in Elsinore?
We'll teach you to drink deep ere you depart.
  *Hor.* My lord, I came to see your father's
   funeral.       [student;
  *Ham.* I pray thee, do not mock me, fellow-
I think it was to see my mother's wedding.
  *Hor.* Indeed, my lord, it follow'd hard
   upon.
  *Ham.* Thrift, thrift, Horatio! the funeral-
   bak'd meats
Did coldly furnish forth the marriage tables.
Would I had met my dearest foe in heaven
Ere I had ever seen that day, Horatio!—
My father,—methinks I see my father.—
  *Hor.* Where, my lord?
  *Ham.*       In my mind's eye, Horatio.
  *Hor.* I saw him once; he was a goodly
   king.
  *Ham.* He was a man, take him for all in
   all,
I shall not look upon his like again.
  *Hor.* My lord, I think I saw him yester-
   night.
  *Ham.* Saw who?
  *Hor.* My lord, the king your father.
  *Ham.*       The king my father!
  *Hor.* Season your admiration for awhile
With an attent ear, till I may deliver,
Upon the witness of these gentlemen,
This marvel to you.
  *Ham.*      For God's love, let me hear.
  *Hor.* Two nights together had these gentle-
   men,
Marcellus and Bernardo, on their watch,
In the dead vast and middle of the night,
Been thus encounter'd. A figure like your
   father,
Arm'd at all points exactly, cap-à-pé,
Appears before them, and with solemn march
Goes slow and stately by them: thrice he
   walk'd

By their oppress'd and fear-surprised eyes,
Within his truncheon's length; whilst they,
   distill'd
Almost to jelly with the act of fear,
Stand dumb, and speak not to him. This to
   me
In dreadful secrecy impart they did;
And I with them the third night kept the
   watch:
Where, as they had deliver'd, both in time,
Form of the thing, each word made true and
   good,
The apparition comes: I knew your father;
These hands are not more like.
  *Ham.*       But where was this?
  *Mar.* My lord, upon the platform where
   we watch'd.
  *Ham.* Did you not speak to it?
  *Hor.*       My lord, I did;
But answer made it none: yet once me-
   thought
It lifted up its head, and did address
Itself to motion, like as it would speak:
But even then the morning cock crew loud,
And at the sound it shrunk in haste away,
And vanish'd from our sight.
  *Ham.*       'Tis very strange.
  *Hor.* As I do live, my honour'd lord, 'tis
   true;
And we did think it writ down in our duty
To let you know of it.       [me.
  *Ham.* Indeed, indeed, sirs, but this troubles
Hold you the watch to-night?
  *Mar. and Ber.*     We do, my lord.
  *Ham.* Arm'd, say you?
  *Mar. and Ber.* Arm'd, my lord.
  *Ham.* From top to toe?
  *Mar. and Ber.* My lord, from head to foot.
  *Ham.* Then saw you not his face?
  *Hor.* O yes, my lord; he wore his beaver
   up.
  *Ham.* What, look'd he frowningly?
  *Hor.* A countenance more in sorrow than
   in anger.
  *Ham.* Pale or red?
  *Hor.* Nay, very pale.
  *Ham.*      And fix'd his eyes upon you?
  *Hor.* Most constantly.
  *Ham.*      I would I had been there.
  *Hor.* It would have much amaz'd you.
  *Ham.* Very like, very like. Stay'd it long?
  *Hor.* While one with moderate haste might
   tell a hundred.
  *Mar. and Ber.* Longer, longer.
  *Hor.* Not when I saw't.
  *Ham.*    His beard was grizzled,—no?
  *Hor.* It was, as I have seen it in his life,
A sable silver'd.
  *Ham.*      I will watch to-night;
Perchance 'twill walk again.
  *Hor.*       I warrant it will.
  *Ham.* If it assume my noble father's person
I'll speak to it, though hell itself should gape
And bid me hold my peace. I pray you all,

If you have hitherto conceal'd this sight,
Let it be tenable in your silence still;
And whatsoever else shall hap to-night,
Give it an understanding, but no tongue:
I will requite your loves. So, fare ye well:
Upon the platform, 'twixt eleven and twelve,
I'll visit you.

*All.*        Our duty to your honour.

*Ham.* Your loves, as mine to you: farewell.

        [*Exeunt* Hor., Mar., *and* Ber.

My father's spirit in arms! all is not well;
I doubt some foul play: would the night were
    come!
Till then sit still, my soul: foul deeds will rise,
Though all the earth o'erwhelm them, to
    men's eyes.        [*Exit.*

Scene III.—*A Room in* Polonius's *House.*

*Enter* Laertes *and* Ophelia.

*Laer.* My necessaries are embark'd: fare-
    well:
And, sister, as the winds give benefit,
And convoy is assistant, do not sleep,
But let me hear from you.

*Oph.*        Do you doubt that?

*Laer.* For Hamlet, and the trifling of his
    favour,
Hold it a fashion and a toy in blood:
A violet in the youth of primy nature,
Forward, not permanent, sweet, not lasting,
The perfume and suppliance of a minute;
No more.

*Oph.*        No more but so?

*Laer.*        Think it no more:
For nature, crescent, does not grow alone
In thews and bulk; but as this temple waxes,
The inward service of the mind and soul
Grows wide withal. Perhaps he loves you
    now;
And now no soil nor cautel doth besmirch
The virtue of his will: but you must fear,
His greatness weigh'd, his will is not his own;
For he himself is subject to his birth:
He may not, as unvalu'd persons do,
Carve for himself; for on his choice depends
The safety and the health of the whole state;
And therefore must his choice be circum-
    scrib'd
Unto the voice and yielding of that body
Whereof he is the head. Then if he says he
    loves you,
It fits your wisdom so far to believe it
As he in his particular act and place
May give his saying deed; which is no further
Than the main voice of Denmark goes withal.
Then weigh what loss your honour may sus-
    tain
If with too credent ear you list his songs,
Or lose your heart, or your chaste treasure
    open
To his unmaster'd importunity.
Fear it, Ophelia, fear it, my dear sister;
And keep within the rear of your affection,
Out of the shot and danger of desire.

The chariest maid is prodigal enough
If she unmask her beauty to the moon:
Virtue itself scapes not calumnious strokes:
The canker galls the infants of the spring
Too oft before their buttons be disclos'd;
And in the morn and liquid dew of youth
Contagious blastments are most imminent.
Be wary, then; best safety lies in fear:
Youth to itself rebels, though none else near.

*Oph.* I shall the effect of this good lesson
    keep        [brother,
As watchman to my heart. But, good my
Do not, as some ungracious pastors do,
Show me the steep and thorny way to
    heaven;
Whilst like a puff'd and reckless libertine,
Himself the primrose path of dalliance treads,
And recks not his own read.

*Laer.*        O, fear me not.
I stay too long:—but here my father comes.

*Enter* Polonius.

A double blessing is a double grace;
Occasion smiles upon a second leave. [shame!

*Pol.* Yet here, Laertes! aboard, aboard, for
The wind sits in the shoulder of your sail,
And you are stay'd for. There,—my blessing
    with you!

        [*Laying his hand on* Laertes's *head.*

And these few precepts in thy memory
See thou character. Give thy thoughts no
    tongue,
Nor any unproportion'd thought his act.
Be thou familiar, but by no means vulgar.
The friends thou hast, and their adoption
    tried,
Grapple them to thy soul with hoops of steel;
But do not dull thy palm with entertainment
Of each new-hatch'd, unfledg'd comrade. Be-
    ware
Of entrance to a quarrel; but, being in,
Bear't that the opposed may beware of thee.
Give every man thine ear, but few thy voice:
Take each man's censure, but reserve thy
    judgment.
Costly thy habit as thy purse can buy,
But not express'd in fancy; rich, not gaudy:
For the apparel oft proclaims the man;
And they in France of the best rank and sta-
    tion
Are most select and generous chief in that.
Neither a borrower nor a lender be:
For loan oft loses both itself and friend;
And borrowing dulls the edge of husbandry.
This above all,—to thine ownself be true;
And it must follow, as the night the day,
Thou canst not then be false to any man.
Farewell: my blessing season this in thee!

*Laer.* Most humbly do I take my leave, my
    lord.        [ants tend.

*Pol.* The time invites you; go, your serv-

*Laer.* Farewell, Ophelia; and remember
    well
What I have said to you.

*Oph.*                        'Tis in my memory lock'd,
And you yourself shall keep the key of it.
   *Laer.* Farewell.                        [*Exit.*
   *Pol.* What is't, Ophelia, he hath said to
   you?
   *Oph.* So please you, something touching
the Lord Hamlet.
   *Pol.* Marry, well bethought:
'Tis told me he hath very oft of late
Given private time to you; and you yourself
Have of your audience been most free and
   bounteous:
If it be so,—as so 'tis put on me,
And that in way of caution,—I must tell you,
You do not understand yourself so clearly
As it behoves my daughter and your honour.
What is between you? give me up the truth.
   *Oph.* He hath, my lord, of late made many
   tenders
Of his affection to me.            [green girl,
   *Pol.* Affection! pooh! you speak like a
Unsifted in such perilous circumstance.
Do you believe his tenders, as you call them?
   *Oph.* I do not know, my lord, what I
   should think.                     [a baby;
   *Pol.* Marry, I'll teach you: think yourself
That you have ta'en these tenders for true
   pay,
Which are not sterling. Tender yourself more
   dearly;
Or,—not to crack the wind of the poor
   phrase,
Wronging it thus,—you'll tender me a fool.
   *Oph.* My lord, he hath impórtun'd me with
   love
In honourable fashion.
   *Pol.* Ay, fashion you may call it; go to, go
   to.
   *Oph.* And hath given countenance to his
   speech, my lord,
With almost all the holy vows of heaven.
   *Pol.* Ay, springes to catch woodcocks. I do
   know,
When the blood burns, how prodigal the soul
Lends the tongue vows: these blazes, daugh-
   ter,
Giving more light than heat,—extinct in both,
Even in their promise, as it is a-making,—
You must not take for fire. From this time
Be somewhat scanter of your maiden pres-
   ence;
Set your entreatments at a higher rate
Than a command to parley. For Lord Ham-
   let,
Believe so much in him, that he is young;
And with a larger tether may he walk
Than may be given you: in few, Ophelia,
Do not believe his vows; for they are
   brokers,—
Not of that dye which their investments
   show,
But mere implorators of unholy suits,
Breathing like sanctified and pious bawds,
The better to beguile. This is for all,—

I would not, in plain terms, from this time
   forth,
Have you so slander any moment leisure
As to give words or talk with the Lord Ham-
   let.
Look to't, I charge you; come your ways.
   *Oph.* I shall obey, my lord.        [*Exeunt.*

SCENE IV.—*The Platform.*

*Enter* HAMLET, HORATIO, *and* MARCELLUS.

   *Ham.* The air bites shrewdly; it is very
   cold.
   *Hor.* It is a nipping and an eager air.
   *Ham.* What hour now?
   *Hor.*              I think it lacks of twelve.
   *Mar.* No, it is struck.
   *Hor.* Indeed? I heard it not: then it draws
   near the season
Wherein the spirit held his wont to walk.
   [*A flourish of trumpets, and ordnance
      shot off within.*
What does this mean, my lord?
   *Ham.* The king doth wake to-night, and
   takes his rouse,                  [reels;
Keeps wassail, and the swaggering up-spring
And, as he drains his draughts of Rhenish
   down,
The kettle-drum and trumpet thus bray out
The triumph of his pledge.
   *Hor.*                Is it a custom?
   *Ham.* Ay, marry, is't:
But to my mind,—though I am native here,
And to the manner born,—it is a custom
More honour'd in the breach than the ob-
   servance.
This heavy-headed revel east and west
Makes us traduc'd and tax'd of other nations:
They clepe us drunkards, and with swinish
   phrase
Soil our addition; and, indeed, it takes
From our achievements, though perform'd at
   height,
The pith and marrow of our attribute.
So oft it chances in particular men
That, for some vicious mole of nature in
   them,
As in their birth,—wherein they are not
   guilty,
Since nature cannot choose his origin,—
By the o'ergrowth of some complexion,
Oft breaking down the pales and forts of rea-
   son;
Or by some habit, that too much o'er-leavens
The form of plausive manners;—that these
   men,—
Carrying, I say, the stamp of one defect,
Being nature's livery or fortune's star,—
Their virtues else,—be they as pure as grace,
As infinite as man may undergo,—
Shall in the general censure take corruption
From that particular fault: the dram of eale
Doth all the noble substance of a doubt
To his own scandal.
   *Hor.*            Look, my lord, it comes!

*Enter* Ghost.

*Ham.* Angels and ministers of grace defend
　　us!—
Be thou a spirit of health or goblin damn'd,
Bring with thee airs from heaven or blasts
　　from hell,
Be thy intents wicked or charitable,
Thou com'st in such a questionable shape
That I will speak to thee: I'll call thee Ham-
　　let,
King, father, royal Dane: O, answer me!
Let me not burst in ignorance; but tell
Why thy canoniz'd bones, hearsed in death,
Have burst their cerements; why the
　　sepulchre,
Wherein we saw thee quietly in-urn'd,
Hath op'd his ponderous and marble jaws
To cast thee up again! What may this mean,
That thou, dead corse, again in cómplete
　　steel,
Revisit'st thus the glimpses of the moon,
Making night hideous, and we fools of nature
So horridly to shake our disposition
With thoughts beyond the reaches of our
　　souls?
Say, why is this? wherefore? what should we
　　do?　　　[Ghost *beckons* HAMLET.
*Hor.* It beckons you to go away with it,
As if it some impartment did desire
To you alone.
*Mar.*　　Look, with what courteous action
It waves you to a more removed ground:
But do not go with it.
*Hor.*　　　　No, by no means.
*Ham.* It will not speak; then will I follow
　　it.
*Hor.* Do not, my lord.
*Ham.*　　Why, what should be the fear?
I do not set my life at a pin's fee;
And for my soul, what can it do to that,
Being a thing immortal as itself?
It waves me forth again;—I'll follow it.
*Hor.* What if it tempts you toward the
　　flood, my lord,
Or to the dreadful summit of the cliff
That beetles o'er his base into the sea,
And there assume some other horrible form,
Which might deprive your sovereignty of
　　reason,
And draw you into madness? think of it:
The very place puts toys of desperation,
Without more motive, into every brain
That looks so many fathoms to the sea
And hears it roar beneath.
*Ham.*　　　　　It waves me still.—
Go on; I'll follow thee.
*Mar.* You shall not go, my lord.
*Ham.*　　　　Hold off your hands.
*Hor.* Be rul'd; you shall not go.
*Ham.*　　　　My fate cries out,
And makes each petty artery in this body
As hardy as the Nemean lion's nerve.—
　　　　　　　　　[Ghost *beckons*.

Still am I call'd;—unhand me, gentlemen;—
　　　　　　　　　　[*Breaking from them.*
By heaven, I'll make a ghost of him that lets
　　me.
I say, away!—Go on; I'll follow thee.
　　　　　　　　[*Exeunt* Ghost *and* HAMLET.
*Hor.* He waxes desperate with imagination.
*Mar.* Let's follow; 'tis not fit thus to obey
　　him.　　　　　　　　　　　[come?
*Hor.* Have after.—To what issue will this
*Mar.* Something is rotten in the state of
　　Denmark.
*Hor.* Heaven will direct it.
*Mar.*　　　　Nay, let's follow him.
　　　　　　　　　　　　　[*Exeunt.*

SCENE V.—*A more remote part of the
　　Platform.*

*Enter* Ghost *and* HAMLET.

*Ham.* Where wilt thou lead me? speak;
　　I'll go no farther.
*Ghost.* Mark me.
*Ham.*　　　　I will.
*Ghost.*　　　　My hour is almost come,
When I to sulphurous and tormenting flames
Must render up myself.
*Ham.*　　　　Alas, poor ghost!
*Ghost.* Pity me not, but lend thy serious
　　hearing
To what I shall unfold.
*Ham.*　　　Speak; I am bound to hear.
*Ghost.* So art thou to revenge, when thou
　　shalt hear.
*Ham.* What?
*Ghost.* I am thy father's spirit;
Doom'd for a certain term to walk the night,
And, for the day, confin'd to waste in fires
Till the foul crimes done in my days of
　　nature　　　　　　　　　　[forbid
Art burnt and purg'd away. But that I am
To tell the secrets of my prison-house,
I could a tale unfold whose lightest word
Would harrow up thy soul; freeze thy young
　　blood;　　　　　　　[their spheres;
Make thy two eyes, like stars, start from
Thy knotted and combined locks to part,
And each particular hair to stand on end,
Like quills upon the fretful porcupine:
But this eternal blazon must not be
To ears of flesh and blood.—List, list, O,
　　list!—
If thou didst ever thy dear father love,—
*Ham.* O God!　　　　　　　[murder.
*Ghost.* Revenge his foul and most unnatural
*Ham.* Murder!
*Ghost.* Murder most foul, as in the best it
　　is;
But this most foul, strange, and unnatural.
*Ham.* Haste me to know't that I, with
　　wings as swift
As meditation or the thoughts of love,
May sweep to my revenge.
*Ghost.*　　　　I find thee apt;
And duller shouldst thou be than the fat weed

That rots itself in ease on Lethe wharf, [hear:
Wouldst thou not stir in this. Now, Hamlet,
'Tis given out that, sleeping in mine orchard,
A serpent stung me; so the whole ear of Den-
mark
Is by a forged process of my death
Rankly abus'd: but know, thou noble youth,
The serpent that did sting thy father's life
Now wears his crown.

*Ham.* O my prophetic soul! mine uncle!

*Ghost.* Ay, that incestuous, that adulterate
beast,
With witchcraft of his wit, with traitorous
gifts,—
O wicked wit and gifts that have the power
So to seduce!—won to his shameful lust
The will of my most seeming virtuous queen:
O Hamlet, what a falling-off was there!
From me, whose love was of that dignity
That it went hand in hand even with the vow
I made to her in marriage; and to decline
Upon a wretch whose natural gifts were poor
To those of mine!
But virtue, as it never will be mov'd,
Though lewdness court it in a shape of
heaven;
So lust, though to a radiant angel link'd,
Will sate itself in a celestial bed
And prey on garbage.
But, soft! methinks I scent the morning air;
Brief let me be.—Sleeping within mine
orchard,
My custom always in the afternoon,
Upon my secure hour thy uncle stole,
With juice or cursed hebenon in a vial,
And in the porches of mine ears did pour
The leperous distilment; whose effect
Holds such an enmity with blood of man
That, swift as quicksilver, it courses through
The natural gates and alleys of the body;
And with a sudden vigour is doth posset
And curd, like eager droppings into milk,
The thin and wholesome blood: so did it
mine;
And a most instant tetter bark'd about,
Most lazar-like, with vile and loathsome
crust,
All my smooth body.
Thus was I, sleeping, by a brother's hand,
Of life, of crown, of queen, at once des-
patch'd:
Cut off even in the blossoms of my sin,
Unhousel'd, unanointed, unanel'd;
No reckoning made, but sent to my account
With all my imperfections on my head:
O, horrible! O, horrible! most horrible!
If thou hast nature in thee, bear it not;
Let not the royal bed of Denmark be
A couch for luxury and damned incest.
But, howsoever thou pursu'st this act,
Taint not thy mind, nor let thy soul contrive
Against thy mother aught: leave her to
heaven,
And to those thorns that in her bosom lodge,

To prick and sting her. Fare thee well at
once!
The glowworm shows the matin to be near,
And 'gins to pale his uneffectual fire:
Adieu, adieu! Hamlet, remember me. [*Exit*.

*Ham.* O all you host of heaven! O earth!
what else? [heart;
And shall I couple hell?—O, fie!—Hold, my
And you, my sinews, grow not instant old,
But bear me stiffly up.—Remember thee!
Ay, thou poor ghost, while memory holds a
seat
In this distracted globe. Remember thee!
Yea, from the table of my memory
I'll wipe away all trivial fond records,
All saws of books, all forms, all pressures past,
That youth and observation copied there;
And thy commandment all alone shall live
Within the book and volume of my brain,
Unmix'd with baser matter: yes, by heaven.—
O most pernicious woman!
O villain, villain, smiling, damned villain!
My tables,—meet it is I set it down,
That one may smile, and smile, and be a
villain; [mark:
At least, I am sure, it may be so in Den-
[*Writing*.
So, uncle, there you are. Now to my word;
It is, *Adieu, adieu! remember me:*
I have sworn't.

*Hor.* [*Within*.] My lord, my lord,—

*Mar.* [*Within*.] Lord Hamlet,—

*Hor.* [*Within*.] Heaven secure him!

*Mar.* [*Within*.] So be it!

*Hor.* [*Within*.] Illo, ho, ho, my lord!

*Ham.* Hillo, ho, ho, boy! come, bird, come.

*Enter* HORATIO *and* MARCELLUS.

*Mar.* How is't, my noble lord?

*Hor.* What news, my lord?

*Ham.* O, wonderful!

*Hor.* Good my lord, tell it.

*Ham.* No; you'll reveal it.

*Hor.* Not I, my lord, by heaven.

*Mar.* Nor I, my lord.

*Ham.* How say you, then; would heart of
man once think it?—
But you'll be secret?

*Hor. and Mar.* Ay, by heaven, my lord.

*Ham.* There's ne'er a villain dwelling in all
Denmark
But he's an arrant knave.

*Hor.* There needs no ghost, my lord, come
from the grave
To tell us this.

*Ham.* Why, right; you are i' the right;
And so, without more circumstance at all,
I hold it fit that we shake hands and part:
You, as your business and desires shall point
you,—
For every man has business and desire,
Such as it is;—and for mine own poor part,
Look you, I'll go pray. [words, my lord.

*Hor.* These are but wild and whirling

*Ham.* I'm sorry they offend you, heartily;
Yes, faith, heartily.

*Hor.*           There's no offence, my lord.

*Ham.* Yes, by Saint Patrick, but there is,
    Horatio,           [here;—
And much offence too. Touching this vision
It is an honest ghost, that let me tell you:
For your desire to know what is between us,
O'ermaster't as you may. And now, good
    friends,
As you are friends, scholars, and soldiers,
Give me one poor request.

*Hor.* What is't, my lord? we will.

*Ham.* Never make known what you have
    seen to-night.

*Hor. and Mar.* My lord, we will not.

*Ham.*           Nay, but swear't.

*Hor.*           In faith,
My lord, not I.

*Mar.*        Nor I, my lord, in faith.

*Ham.* Upon my sword.

*Mar.* We have sworn, my lord, already.

*Ham.* Indeed, upon my sword, indeed.

*Ghost.* [*Beneath.*] Swear.

*Ham.* Ha, ha, boy! say'st thou so? art thou
    there, truepenny?—       [larage,—
Come on.—you hear this fellow in the cel-
Consent to swear.

*Hor.*        Propose the oath, my lord.

*Ham.* Never to speak of this that you have
    seen,
Swear by my sword.

*Ghost.* [*Beneath.*] Swear.    [ground.—

*Ham.* *Hic et ubique?* then we'll shift our
Come hither, gentlemen,
And lay your hands again upon my sword:
Never to speak of this that you have heard,
Swear by my sword.

*Ghost.* [*Beneath.*] Swear. [earth so fast?

*Ham.* Well said, old mole! canst work i' the
A worthy pioneer!—Once more remove, good
    friends.        [drous strange!

*Hor.* O day and night, but this is won-

*Ham.* And therefore as a stranger give it
    welcome.        [Horatio,
There are more things in heaven and earth,
Than are dreamt of in your philosophy.
But come;—
Here, as before, never, so help you mercy,
How strange or odd soe'er I bear myself,—
As I, perchance, hereafter shall think meet
To put an antic disposition on,—    [shall,
That you, at such times seeing me, never
With arms encumber'd thus, or this head-
    shake,
Or by pronouncing of some doubtful phrase,
As, *Well, well, we know;—or, We could, an
    if we would;—*       [*they might;—*
Or, *If we list to speak;—or, There be, an if*
Or such ambiguous giving out, to note
That you know aught of me:—this not to do,
So grace and mercy at your most need help
    you,
Swear.

*Ghost.* [*Beneath.*] Swear.

*Ham.* Rest, rest, perturbed spirit!—So,
    gentlemen,
With all my love I do commend me to you:
And what so poor a man as Hamlet is [you,
May do, to express his love and friending to
God willing, shall not lack. Let us go in to-
    gether;
And still your fingers on your lips, I pray.
The time is out of joint:—O cursed spite,
That ever I was born to set it right!—
Nay, come, let's go together.     [*Exeunt.*

## ACT II.

SCENE I.—*A Room in* POLONIUS'S *House.*

*Enter* POLONIUS *and* REYNALDO.

*Pol.* Give him this money and these notes,
    Reynaldo.

*Rey.* I will, my lord.       [Reynaldo

*Pol.* You shall do marvellous wisely, good
Before you visit him, to make inquiry
Of his behaviour.

*Rey.*        My lord, I did intend it.

*Pol.* Marry, well said; very well said.
    Look you, sir,
Inquire me first what Danskers are in Paris;
And how, and who, what means, and where
    they keep,
What company, at what expense; and finding,
By this encompassment and drift of question,
That they do know my son, come you more
    nearer
Than your particular demands will touch it:
Take you, as 'twere, some distant knowledge
    of him;
As thus, *I know his father and his friends,
And in part him;*—do you mark this, Rey-
    naldo?

*Rey.* Ay, very well, my lord.    [*not well:*

*Pol.* *And in part him;—but,* you may say,
*But if't be he I mean, he's very wild;
Addicted so and so;* and there put on him
What forgeries you please; marry, none so
    rank
As may dishonour him; take heed of that;
But, sir, such wanton, wild, and usual slips
As are companions noted and most known
To youth and liberty.

*Rey.*          As gaming, my lord.

*Pol.* Ay, or drinking, fencing, swearing,
    quarrelling,
Drabbing:—you may go so far.

*Rey.* My lord, that would dishonour him.

*Pol.* Faith, no; as you may season it in the
    charge.
You must not put another scandal on him,
That he is open to incontinency;
That's not my meaning: but breathe his faults
    so quaintly
That they may seem the taints of liberty;
The flash and outbreak of a fiery mind;
A savageness in unreclaimed blood,
Of general assault.

*Rey.*              But, my good lord,—
*Pol.* Wherefore should you do this?
*Rey.*                         Ay, my lord,
I would know that.
*Pol.*              Marry, sir, here's my drift;
And I believe it is a fetch of warrant:
You laying these slight sullies on my son,
As 'twere a thing a little soil'd i' the working,
Mark you,                            [sound,
Your party in converse, him you would
Having ever seen in the prenominate crimes
The youth you breathe of guilty, be assur'd
He closes with you in this consequence;
*Good sir,* or so; or *friend,* or *gentleman,*—
According to the phrase or the addition
Of man and country.
*Rey.*              Very good, my lord.
*Pol.* And then, sir, does he this,—he does,—
What was I about to say?—By the mass, I
was
About to say something:—where did I leave?
*Rey.* At *closes in the consequence,*
At *friend or so,* and *gentleman.*      [marry;
*Pol.* At—closes in the consequence,—ay,
He closes with you thus:—*I know the gentle-
man,*
*I saw him yesterday, or t'other day,* [*you say,*
*Or then, or then; with such, or such; and, as
There was he gaming; there o'ertook in's
rouse;
There falling out at tennis:* or perchance,
*I saw him enter such a house of sale,*—
*Videlicet,* a brothel,—or so forth.—
See you now;
Your bait of falsehood takes this carp of
truth:
And thus do we of wisdom and of reach,
With windlaces, and with assays of bias,
By indirections find directions out:
So, by my former lecture and advice,      [not?
Shall you my son. You have me, have you
*Rey.* My lord, I have,
*Pol.*              God b' wi' you; fare you well.
*Rey.* Good my lord!
*Pol.* Observe his inclination in yourself.
*Rey.* I shall, my lord.
*Pol.* And let him ply his music.
*Rey.*                         Well, my lord.
*Pol.* Farewell!              [*Exit* REYNALDO.

                  *Enter* OPHELIA.

    How now, Ophelia! what's the matter?
*Oph.* Alas, my lord, I have been so af-
frighted!
*Pol.* With what, i' the name of God?
*Oph.* My lord, as I was sewing in my
chamber,
Lord Hamlet,—with his doublet all unbrac'd;
No hat upon his head; his stockings foul'd,
Ungarter'd, and down-gyved to his ankle;
Pale as his shirt; his knees knocking each
other;
And with a look so piteous in purport
As if he had been loosed out of hell

To speak of horrors,—he comes before me.
*Pol.* Mad for thy love?
*Oph.*              My lord, I do not know,
But truly I do fear it.
*Pol.*              What said he?
*Oph.* He took me by the wrist, and held
me hard;
Then goes he to the length of all his arm;
And with his other hand thus o'er his brow,
He falls to such perusal of my face
As he would draw it. Long stay'd he so;
At last,—a little shaking of mine arm,
And thrice his head thus waving up and
down,—
He rais'd a sigh so piteous and profound
That it did seem to shatter all his bulk
And end his being: that done, he lets me go:
And, with his head over his shoulder turn'd,
He seem'd to find his way without his eyes;
For out o' doors he went without their help,
And to the last bended their light on me.
*Pol.* Come, go with me: I will go seek the
king.
This is the very ecstacy of love;
Whose violent property fordoes itself,
And leads the will to desperate undertakings,
As oft as any passion under heaven
That does afflict our natures. I am sorry,—
What, have you given him any hard words of
late?                            [command,
*Oph.* No, my good lord; but, as you did
I did repel his letters, and denied
His access to me.
*Pol.*              That hath made him mad.
I am sorry that with better heed and judg-
ment                            [trifle,
I had not quoted him: I fear'd he did but
And meant to wreck thee; but, beshrew my
jealousy!
It seems it is as proper to our age
To cast beyond ourselves in our opinions
As it is common for the younger sort
To lack discretion. Come, go we to the king:
This must be known; which, being kept close,
might move
More grief to hide than hate to utter love.
                              [*Exeunt.*

            SCENE II.—*A Room in the Castle.*

      *Enter* KING, QUEEN, ROSENCRANTZ,
      GUILDENSTERN, *and* Attendants.

*King.* Welcome, dear Rosencrantz and
Guildenstern!
Moreover that we much did long to see you,
The need we have to use you did provoke
Our hasty sending. Something have you heard
Of Hamlet's transformation; so I call it,
Since nor the exterior nor the inward man
Resembles that it was. What it should be,
More than his father's death, that thus hath
put him
So much from the understanding of himself,
I cannot dream of: I entreat you both,

That being of so young days brought up with him,                    [humour,
And since so neighbour'd to his youth and
That you vouchsafe your rest here in our court
Some little time: so by your companies
To draw him on to pleasures, and to gather,
So much as from occasion you may glean,
Whether aught, to us unknown, afflicts him thus,
That, open'd, lies within our remedy.

*Queen.* Good gentlemen, he hath much talk'd of you;
And sure I am two men there are not living
To whom he more adheres. If it will please you
To show us so much gentry and good-will
As to expend your time with us awhile,
For the supply and profit of our hope,
Your visitation shall receive such thanks
As fits a king's remembrance.

*Ros.*                    Both your majesties
Might, by the sovereign power you have of us,
Put your dread pleasures more into command
Than to entreaty.

*Guil.*                    We both obey,
And here give up ourselves, in the full bent,
To lay our service freely at your feet,
To be commanded.

*King.* Thanks, Rosencrantz and gentle Guildenstern.                    [Rosencrantz:
*Queen.* Thanks, Guildenstern and gentle
And I beseech you instantly to visit    [you,
My too-much-changed son.—Go, some of
And bring these gentlemen where Hamlet is.

*Guil.* Heavens make our presence and our practices
Pleasant and helpful to him!

*Queen.*                    Ay, amen!
[*Exeunt* Ros., Guil., *and some* Attendants.

*Enter* POLONIUS.

*Pol.* The ambassadors from Norway, my good lord,
Are joyfully return'd.

*King.* Thou still hast been the father of good news.

*Pol.* Have I, my lord? Assure you, my good liege,
I hold my duty, as I hold my soul,
Both to my God and to my gracious king:
And I do think,—or else this brain of mine
Hunts not the trail of policy so sure
As it hath us'd to do,—that I have found
The very cause of Hamlet's lunacy.

*King.* O, speak of that; that do I long to hear.

*Pol.* Give first admittance to the ambassadors;
My news shall be the fruit to that great feast.

*King.* Thyself do grace to them, and bring them in.                    [*Exit* POLONIUS.

He tells me, my sweet queen, that he hath found                    [temper.
The head and source of all your son's dis-
*Queen.* I doubt it is no other but the main,—                    [riage.
His father's death and our o'erhasty mar-
*King.* Well, we shall sift him.

*Re-enter* POLONIUS, *with* VOLTIMAND *and* CORNELIUS.

                    Welcome, my good friends!
Say, Voltimand, what from our brother Norway?                    [desires.
*Volt.* Most fair return of greetings and
Upon our first, he sent out to suppress
His nephew's levies; which to him appear'd
To be a preparation 'gainst the Polack;
But, better look'd into, he truly found
It was against your highness: whereat griev'd,—
That so his sickness, age, and impotence
Was falsely borne in hand,—sends out arrests
On Fortinbras; which he, in brief, obeys;
Receives rebuke from Norway; and, in fine,
Makes vow before his uncle never more
To give the assay of arms against your majesty.
Whereon old Norway, overcome with joy,
Gives him three thousand crowns in annual fee;
And his commission to employ those soldiers,
So levied as before, against the Polack:
With an entreaty, herein further shown,
                    [*Gives a paper.*
That it might please you to give quiet pass
Through your dominions for this enterprise,
On such regards of safety and allowance
As therein are set down.

*King.*                    It likes us well;
And at our more consider'd time we'll read,
Answer, and think upon this business.
Meantime we thank you for your well-took labour:
Go to your rest; at night we'll feast together:
Most welcome home!
                    [*Exeunt* VOLT. *and* COR.
*Pol.*                    This business is well ended.—
My liege, and madam,—to expostulate
What majesty should be, what duty is,
Why day is day, night night, and time is time,
Were nothing but to waste night, day, and time.
Therefore, since brevity is the soul of wit,
And tediousness the limbs and outward flourishes.
I will be brief:—your noble son is mad:
Mad call I it; for to define true madness,
What is't but to be nothing else but mad?
But let that go.

*Queen.*                    More matter with less art.
*Pol.* Madam, I swear I use no art at all.
That he is mad, 'tis true: 'tis true 'tis pity;
And pity 'tis 'tis true: a foolish figure;
But farewell it, for I will use no art

Mad let us grant him, then: and now remains
That we find out the cause of this effect;
Or rather say, the cause of this defect,
For this effective defective comes by cause:
Thus it remains, and the remainder thus.
Perpend.                           [mine,—
I have a daughter,—have whilst she is
Who, in her duty and obedience, mark,
Hath given me this: now gather, and surmise.
                                    [Reads.
*To the celestial, and my soul's idol, the most
    beautified Ophelia,—*
That's an ill phrase, a vile phrase,—*beautified*
is a vile phrase: but you shall hear. Thus:
                                    [Reads.
*In her excellent white bosom, these, &c.*
*Queen.* Came this from Hamlet to her?
*Pol.* Good madam, stay awhile; I will be
    faithful.                       [Reads.
    *Doubt thou the stars are fire;*
    *Doubt that the sun doth move;*
    *Doubt truth to be a liar;*
    *But never doubt I love.*
*O dear Ophelia, I am ill at these numbers,*
*I have not art to reckon my groans: but that*
*I love thee best, O most best, believe it. Adieu.*
    *Thine evermore, most dear lady, whilst*
    *this machine is to him,*      HAMLET.
This, in obedience, hath my daughter show'd
    me:
And more above, hath his solicitings,
As they fell out by time, by means, and place,
All given to mine ear.
*King.*                  But how hath she
Receiv'd his love?
*Pol.*                What do you think of me?
*King.* As of a man faithful and honourable.
*Pol.* I would fain prove so. But what might
    you think,
When I had seen this hot love on the wing,—
As I perceiv'd it, I must tell you that,
Before my daughter told me,—what might
    you,
Or my dear majesty your queen here, think,
If I had play'd the desk or table-book;
Or given my heart a winking, mute and
    dumb;
Or look'd upon this love with idle sight;—
What might you think? No, I went round to
    work,
And my young mistress thus I did bespeak:
*Lord Hamlet is a prince out of thy sphere;*
*This must not be:* and then I precepts gave
    her,
That she should lock herself from his resort,
Admit no messengers, receive no tokens.
Which done, she took the fruits of my
    advice;
And he, repulsed,—a short tale to make,—
Fell into a sadness; then into a fast;
Thence to a watch; thence into a weakness;
Thence to a lightness; and, by this declension,
Into the madness wherein now he raves
And all we wail for.

*King.*             Do you think 'tis this?
*Queen.* It may be, very likely.
*Pol.* Hath there been such a time,—I'd
    fain know that,—
That I have positively said, *'Tis so,*
When it prov'd otherwise?
*King.*                Not that I know.
*Pol.* Take this from this, if this be other-
    wise:
    [*Pointing to his head and shoulder.*
If circumstances lead me, I will find
Where truth is hid, though it were hid indeed
Within the centre.
*King.*             How may we try it further?
*Pol.* You know, sometimes he walks for
    · hours together
Here in the lobby.
*Queen.*             So he does, indeed.
*Pol.* At such a time I'll loose my daughter
    to him:
Be you and I behind an arras then;
Mark the encounter: if he love her not,
And be not from his reason fall'n thereon,
Let me be no assistant for a state,
But keep a farm and carters.
*King.*                      We will try it.
*Queen.* But look, where sadly the poor
    wretch comes reading.
*Pol.* Away, I do beseech you, both away:
I'll board him presently:—O, give me leave.
    [*Exeunt* KING, QUEEN, *and* Attendants.

        *Enter* HAMLET, *reading.*
How does my good Lord Hamlet?
*Ham.* Well, God-a-mercy.
*Pol.* Do you know me, my lord?
*Ham.* Excellent, excellent well; you're a
fishmonger.
*Pol.* Not I, my lord.              [man.
*Ham.* Then I would you were so honest a
*Pol.* Honest, my lord!
*Ham.* Ay, sir; to be honest, as this world
goes, is to be one man picked out of ten
thousand.
*Pol.* That's very true, my lord.
*Ham.* For if the sun breed maggots in a
dead dog, being a god-kissing carrion,—Have
you a daughter?
*Pol.* I have, my lord.
*Ham.* Let her not walk i' the sun: con-
ception is a blessing; but not as your daugh-
ter may conceive:—friend, look to't.
*Pol.* How say you by that?—[*Aside.*] Still
harping on my daughter:—yet he knew me
not at first; he said I was a fishmonger: he
is far gone, far gone: and truly in my youth
I suffered much extremity for love; very
near this. I'll speak to him again.—What do
you read, my lord?
*Ham.* Words, words, words.
*Pol.* What is the matter, my lord?
*Ham.* Between who?                [lord.
*Pol.* I mean, the matter that you read, my
*Ham.* Slanders, sir: for the satirical slave

says here that old men have gray beards; that their faces are wrinkled; their eyes purging thick amber and plum-tree gum; and that they have a plentiful lack of wit, together with most weak hams: all which, sir, though I most powerfully and potently believe, yet I hold it not honesty to have it thus set down; for you yourself, sir, should be old as I am, if, like a crab, you could go backward.

*Pol.* [*Aside.*] Though this be madness, yet there is method in't.—Will you walk out of the air, my lord?

*Ham.* Into my grave?

*Pol.* Indeed, that is out o' the air.—[*Aside.*] How pregnant sometimes his replies are! a happiness that often madness hits on, which reason and sanity could not so prosperously be delivered of. I will leave him, and suddenly contrive the means of meeting between him and my daughter.—My honourable lord, I will most humbly take my leave of you.

*Ham.* You cannot, sir, take from me anything that I will more willingly part withal,—except my life, except my life, except my life.

*Pol.* Fare you well, my lord.

*Ham.* These tedious old fools!

*Enter* ROSENCRANTZ *and* GUILDENSTERN.

*Pol.* You go to seek the Lord Hamlet; there he is.

*Ros.* [*To* POLONIUS.] God save you, sir!
　　　　　　　　　　　　　[*Exit* POLONIUS.

*Guil.* Mine honoured lord!

*Ros.* My most dear lord!

*Ham.* My excellent good friends! How dost thou, Guildenstern? Ah, Rosencrantz! Good lads, how do ye both?　　　　[earth.

*Ros.* As the indifferent children of the

*Guil.* Happy in that we are not overhappy; On fortune's cap we are not the very button.

*Ham.* Nor the soles of her shoe?

*Ros.* Neither, my lord.

*Ham.* Then you live about her waist, or in the middle of her favours?

*Guil.* Faith, her privates we.

*Ham.* In the secret parts of fortune? O, most true; she is a strumpet. What's the news?

*Ros.* None, my lord, but that the world's grown honest.

*Ham.* Then is doomsday near: but your news is not true. Let me question more in particular: what have you, my good friends, deserved at the hands of fortune, that she sends you to prison hither?

*Guil.* Prison, my lord!

*Ham.* Denmark's a prison.

*Ros.* Then is the world one.

*Ham.* A goodly one; in which there are many confines, wards, and dungeons, Denmark being one o' the worst.

*Ros.* We think not so, my lord.

*Ham.* Why, then, 'tis none to you; for there is nothing either good or bad, but thinking makes it so: to me it is a prison.

*Ros.* Why, then, your ambition makes it one; 'tis too narrow for your mind.

*Ham.* O God, I could be bounded in a nutshell, and count myself a king of infinite space, were it not that I have bad dreams.

*Guil.* Which dreams, indeed, are ambition; for the very substance of the ambitious is merely the shadow of a dream.

*Ham.* A dream itself is but a shadow.

*Ros.* Truly, and I hold ambition of so airy and light a quality that it is but a shadow's shadow.

*Ham.* Then are our beggars bodies, and our monarchs and outstretched heroes the beggars' shadows. Shall we to the court? for, by my fay, I cannot reason.

*Ros. and Guil.* We'll wait upon you.

*Ham.* No such matter: I will not sort you with the rest of my servants; for, to speak to you like an honest man, I am most dreadfully attended. But, in the beaten way of friendship, what make you at Elsinore?

*Ros.* To visit you, my lord; no other occasion.

*Ham.* Beggar that I am, I am even poor in thanks; but I thank you: and sure, dear friends, my thanks are too dear a halfpenny. Were you not sent for? Is it your own inclining? Is it a free visitation? Come, deal justly with me: come, come; nay, speak.

*Guil.* What should we say, my lord?

*Ham.* Why, anything—but to the purpose. You were sent for; and there is a kind of confession in your looks, which your modesties have not craft enough to colour: I know the good king and queen have sent for you.

*Ros.* To what end, my lord?

*Ham.* That you must teach me. But let me conjure you, by the rights of our fellowship, by the consonancy of our youth, by the obligation of our ever-preserved love, and by what more dear a better proposer could charge you withal, be even and direct with me, whether you were sent for or no?

*Ros.* What say you? [*To* GUILDENSTERN.

*Ham.* [*Aside.*] Nay, then, I have an eye of you.—If you love me, hold not off.

*Guil.* My lord, we were sent for.

*Ham.* I will tell you why; so shall my anticipation prevent your discovery, and your secrecy to the king and queen moult no feather. I have of late,—but wherefore I know not,—lost all my mirth, forgone all custom of exercises; and, indeed, it goes so heavily with my disposition that this goodly frame, the earth, seems to me a sterile promontory; this most excellent canopy, the air, look you, this brave o'erhanging firmament, this majestical roof fretted with golden fire,—why, it appears no other thing to me than a foul and pestilent congregation of vapours. What a piece of work is man! How noble in reason! how infinite in faculties! in form and moving, how express and admirable! in action, how like an angel! in apprehension, how like a god! the beauty of the world! the paragon of animals! And yet, to me, what is this quintessence of dust? man delights not me; no, nor woman neither, though by your smiling you seem to say so.

*Ros.* My lord, there was no such stuff in my thoughts.

*Ham.* Why did you laugh, then, when I said, *Man delights not me?*

*Ros.* To think, my lord, if you delight not in man, what lenten entertainment the players shall receive from you: we coted them on the way; and hither are they coming, to offer you service.

*Ham.* He that plays the king shall be welcome,—his majesty shall have tribute of me; the adventurous knight shall use his foil and target; the lover shall not sigh gratis; the humorous man shall end his part in peace; the clown shall make those laugh whose lungs are tickled o' the sere; and the lady shall say her mind freely, or the blank verse shall halt for't.—What players are they?

*Ros.* Even those you were wont to take delight in,—the tragedians of the city.

*Ham.* How chances it they travel? their residence; both in reputation and profit, was better both ways.

*Ros.* I think their inhibition comes by the means of the late innovation.

*Ham.* Do they hold the same estimation they did when I was in the city? Are they so followed?

*Ros.* No, indeed, they are not.

*Ham.* How comes it? do they grow rusty?

*Ros.* Nay, their endeavour keeps in the wonted pace: but there is, sir, an aery of children, little eyases, that cry out on the top of question, and are most tyrannically clapped for't: these are now the fashion; and so berattle the common stages,—so they call them, —that many wearing rapiers are afraid of goosequills, and dare scarce come thither.

*Ham.* What, are they children? who maintains 'em? how are they escoted? Will they pursue the quality no longer than they can sing? will they not say afterwards, if they should grow themselves to common players, —as it is most like, if their means are no better,—their writers do them wrong, to make them exclaim against their own succession?

*Ros.* Faith, there has been much to do on both sides; and the nation holds it no sin to tarre them to controversy: there was for awhile no money bid for argument, unless the poet and the player went to cuffs in the question.

*Ham.* Is't possible?

*Guil.* O, there has been much throwing about of brains.

*Ham.* Do the boys carry it away?

*Ros.* Ay, that they do, my lord; Hercules and his load too.

*Ham.* It is not strange; for mine uncle is king of Denmark, and those that would make mouths at him while my father lived, give twenty, forty, fifty, an hundred ducats a-piece for his picture in little. 'Sblood, there is something in this more than natural, if philosophy could find it out.

[*Flourish of trumpets within.*

*Guil.* There are the players.

*Ham.* Gentlemen, you are welcome to Elsinore. Your hands, come: the appurtenance of welcome is fashion and ceremony: let me comply with you in this garb; lest my extent to the players, which, I tell you, must show fairly outward, should more appear like entertainment than yours. You are welcome: but my uncle-father and aunt-mother are deceived.

*Guil.* In what, my dear lord?

*Ham.* I am but mad north-north-west: when the wind is southerly I know a hawk from a handsaw.

*Enter* POLONIUS.

*Pol.* Well be with you, gentlemen!

*Ham.* Hark you, Guildenstern;—and you too;—at each ear a hearer: that great baby you see there is not yet out of his swathing-clouts.

*Ros.* Happily he's the second time come to them; for they say an old man is twice a child.

*Ham.* I will prophesy he comes to tell me of the players; mark it.—You say right, sir: o' Monday morning; 'twas so indeed.

*Pol.* My lord, I have news to tell you.

*Ham.* My lord, I have news to tell you. When Roscius was an actor in Rome,—

*Pol.* The actors are come hither, my lord.

*Ham.* Buzz, buzz!

*Pol.* Upon mine honour,—

*Ham.* Then came each actor on his ass,—

*Pol.* The best actors in the world, either for tragedy, comedy, history, pastoral, pastoral-comical, historical-pastoral, tragical-historical, tragical-comical-historical-pastoral, scene individable, or poem unlimited: Seneca cannot be too heavy nor Plautus too light. For the law of writ and the liberty, these are the only men.

*Ham.* O Jephthah, judge of Israel, what a treasure hadst thou!

*Pol.* What a treasure had he, my lord?

*Ham.* Why—

One fair daughter, and no more,
The which he loved passing well.

*Pol.* [*Aside.*] Still on my daughter.

*Ham.* Am I not i 'the right, old Jephthah?

*Pol.* If you call me Jephthah, my lord, I have a daughter that I love passing well.

*Ham.* Nay, that follows not.

*Pol.* What follows, then, my lord?

*Ham.* Why—

       As by lot, God wot,

and then, you know,

       It came to pass, as most like it was,—

the first row of the pious chanson will show you more; for look where my abridgment comes.

*Enter four or five* Players.

You are welcome, masters; welcome, all:—I am glad to see thee well:—welcome, good friends.—O, my old friend! Thy face is valanced since I saw thee last; comest thou to beard me in Denmark?—What, my young lady and mistress! By'r lady, your ladyship is nearer heaven than when I saw you last, by the altitude of a chopine. Pray God, your voice, like a piece of uncurrent gold, be not cracked within the ring.—Masters, you are all welcome. We'll e'en to't like French falconers, fly at anything we see: we'll have a speech straight: come, give us a taste of your quality; come, a passionate speech.

*1 Play.* What speech, my lord?

*Ham.* I heard thee speak me a speech once,—but it was never acted; or, if it was, not above once; for the play, I remember, pleased not the million; 'twas caviare to the general: but it was,—as I received it, and others whose judgments in such matters cried in the top of mine,—an excellent play, well digested in the scenes, set down with as much modesty as cunning. I remember, one said there were no sallets in the lines to make the matter savoury, nor no matter in the phrase that might indite the author of affectation; but called it an honest method, as wholesome as sweet, and by very much more handsome than fine. One speech in it I chiefly loved: 'twas Æneas' tale to Dido; and thereabout of it especially where he speaks of Priam's slaughter: if it live in your memory, begin at this line;—let me see, let me see:—

The rugged Pyrrhus, like the Hyrcanian beast,

—it is not so:—it begins with Pyrrhus:—

The rugged Phyrrhus,—he whose sable arms,
Black as his purpose, did the night resemble
When he lay couched in the ominous horse,—
Hath now this dread and black complexion smear'd
With heraldry more dismal; head to foot
Now is he total gules; horribly trick'd [sons,
With blood of fathers, mothers, daughters,
Bak'd and impasted with the parching streets,
That lend a tyrannous and damned light
To their vile murders: roasted in wrath and fire,

And thus o'er-sized with coagulate gore,
With eyes like carbuncles, the hellish Pyrrhus
Old grandsire Priam seeks.—
So proceed you.

*Pol.* 'Fore God, my lord, well spoken, with good accent and good discretion.

*1 Play.* Anon he finds him       [sword,
Striking too short at Greeks; his antique
Rebellious to his arm, lies where it falls,
Repugnant to command: unequal match'd,
Pyrrhus at Priam drives; in rage strikes wide;
But with the whiff and wind of his fell sword
The unnerved father falls. Then senseless Ilium,
Seeming to feel this blow, with flaming top
Stoops to his base; and with a hideous crash
Takes prisoner Pyrrhus' ear: for, lo! his sword,
Which was declining on the milky head
Of reverend Priam, seem'd i' the air to stick:
So, as a painted tyrant, Pyrrhus stood;
And, like a neutral to his will and matter,
Did nothing.
But as we often see, against some storm,
A silence in the heavens, the rack stand still,
The bold winds speechless, and the orb below
As hush as death, anon the dreadful thunder
Doth rend the region; so, after Pyrrhus' pause,
A roused vengeance sets him new a-work;
And never did the Cyclops' hammers fall
On Mars his armour, forg'd for proof eterne,
With less remorse than Pyrrhus' bleeding sword
Now falls on Priam.—       [gods,
Out, out, thou strumpet, Fortune! All you
In general synod, take away her power;
Break all the spokes and fellies from her wheel,       [of heaven,
And bowl the round knave down the hill
As low as to the fiends!

*Pol.* This is too long.

*Ham.* It shall to the barber's, with your beard.—Pr'ythee, say on.—He's for a jig, or a tale of bawdry, or he sleeps:—say on; come to Hecuba.       [mobled queen,—

*1 Play.* But who, O, who had seen the

*Ham. The mobled queen?*

*Pol.* That's good; *mobled queen* is good.

*1 Play.* Run barefoot up and down, threatening the flames
With bisson rheum; a clout upon that head
Where late the diadem stood; and, for a robe,
About her lank and all o'er-teemed loins,
A blanket, in the alarm of fear caught up;—
Who this had seen, with tongue in venom steep'd,       [pronounc'd:
'Gainst Fortune's state would treason have
But if the gods themselves did see her then,
When she saw Pyrrhus make malicious sport

In mincing with his sword her husband's limbs,
The instant burst of clamour that she made, [all,—
Unless things mortal move them not at
Would have made milch the burning eyes of heaven,
And passion in the gods.

*Pol.* Look, whether he has not turn'd his colour, and has tears in's eyes.—Pray you, no more.

*Ham.* 'Tis well; I'll have thee speak out the rest soon.—Good my lord, will you see the players well bestowed? Do you hear, let them be well used; for they are the abstracts and brief chronicles of the time; after your death you were better have a bad epitaph than their ill report while you live.

*Pol.* My lord, I will use them according to their desert.

*Ham.* Odd's bodikin, man, better: use every man after his desert, and who should scape whipping? Use them after your own honour and dignity: the less they deserve the more merit is in your bounty. Take them in.

*Pol.* Come, sirs.

*Ham.* Follow him, friends: we'll hear a play to-morrow. [*Exit* POLONIUS *with all the* Players *but the* First.]—Dost thou hear me, old friend; can you play the Murder of Gonzago?

*I Play.* Ay, my lord.

*Ham.* We'll ha't to-morrow night. You could, for a need, study a speech of some dozen or sixteen lines which I would set down and insert in't? could you not?

*I Play.* Ay, my lord.

*Ham.* Very well.—Follow that lord; and look you mock him not. [*Exit* First Player.] —My good friends [*to* ROS. *and* GUIL.], I'll leave you till night: you are welcome to Elsinore.

*Ros.* Good my lord!
[*Exeunt* ROS. *and* GUIL.

*Ham.* Ay, so God b' wi' ye!—Now I am alone.

O, what a rogue and peasant slave am I!
Is it not monstrous that this player here,
But in a fiction, in a dream of passion,
Could force his soul so to his own conceit
That from her working all his visage wan'd;
Tears in his eyes, distraction in's aspéct,
A broken voice, and his whole function suiting [ing!
With forms to his conceit? And all for noth-
For Hecuba?
What's Hecuba to him or he to Hecuba, [do,
That he should weep for her? What would he
Had he the motive and the cue for passion
That I have? He would drown the state with tears, [speech;
And cleave the general ear with horrid
Make mad the guilty, and appal the free;

Confound the ignorant, and amaze, indeed,
The very faculties of eyes and ears.
Yet I,
A dull and muddy-mettled rascal, peak,
Like John-a-dreams, unpregnant of my cause,
And can say nothing; no, not for a king
Upon whose property and most dear life
A damn'd defeat was made. Am I a coward?
Who calls me villain? breaks my pate across?
Plucks off my beard and blows it in my face?
Tweaks me by the nose? gives me the lie i' the throat, [ha?
As deep as to the lungs? who does me this,
'Swounds, I should take it: for it cannot be
But I am pigeon-liver'd, and lack gall
To make oppression bitter; or ere this
I should have fatted all the region kites [lain!
With this slave's offal:—bloody, bawdy vil-
Remorseless, treacherous, lecherous, kindless villain!
O, vengeance!
Why, what an ass am I! This is most brave,
That I, the son of a dear father murder'd,
Prompted to my revenge by heaven and hell,
Must, like a whore, unpack my heart with words,
And fall a-cursing like a very drab,
A scullion! [heard
Fie upon't! foh!—About, my brain! I have
That guilty creatures, sitting at a play,
Have by the very cunning of the scene
Been struck so to the soul that presently
They have proclaim'd their malefactions;
For murder, though it have no tongue, will speak
With most miraculous organ. I'll have these players
Play something like the murder of my father
Before mine uncle: I'll observe his looks;
I'll tent him to the quick: if he but blench,
I know my course. The spirit that I have seen
May be the devil: and the devil hath power
To assume a pleasing shape; yea, and perhaps
Out of my weakness and my melancholy,—
As he is very potent with such spirits,—
Abuses me to damn me: I'll have grounds
More relative than this:—the play's the thing
Wherein I'll catch the conscience of the king.
[*Exit.*

## ACT III.

### SCENE I.—*A Room in the Castle.*

*Enter* KING, QUEEN, POLONIUS, OPHELIA, ROSENCRANTZ, *and* GUILDENSTERN.

*King.* And can you, by no drift of circumstance,
Get from him why he puts on this confusion,
Grating so harshly all his days of quiet
With turbulent and dangerous lunacy?

*Ros.* He does confess he feels himself distracted; [speak.
But from what cause he will by no means

*Guil.* Nor do we find him forward to be
  sounded;
But, with a crafty madness, keeps aloof
When we would bring him on to some con-
  fession
Of his true state.
    *Queen.*     Did he receive you well?
  *Ros.* Most like a gentleman.    [tion.
  *Guil.* But with much forcing of his disposi-
  *Ros.* Niggard of question but, of our de-
    mands,
Most free in his reply.
    *Queen.*     Did you assay him
To any pastime?
  *Ros.* Madam, it so fell out that certain
    players    [him;
We o'er-raught on the way: of these we told
And there did seem in him a kind of joy
To hear of it: they are about the court;
And, as I think, they have already order
This night to play before him.
  *Pol.*     'Tis most true:
And he beseech'd me to entreat your majes-
  ties
To hear and see the matter.
    *King.*   With all my heart; and it doth
much content me
To hear him so inclin'd.—
Good gentlemen, give him a further edge,
And drive his purpose on to these delights.
  *Ros.* We shall, my lord.
         [*Exeunt* Ros. *and* Guil.
    *King.*   Sweet Gertrude, leave us too;
For we have closely sent for Hamlet hither
That he, as 'twere by accident, may here
Affront Ophelia:
Her father and myself,—lawful espials,—
Will so bestow ourselves that, seeing, unseen,
We may of their encounter frankly judge;
And gather by him, as he is behav'd,
If't be the affliction of his love or no
That thus he suffers for.
    *Queen.*    I shall obey you:—
And for your part, Ophelia, I do wish
That your good beauties be the happy cause
Of Hamlet's wildness: so shall I hope your
  virtues
Will bring him to his wonted way again,
To both your honours.
  *Oph.*     Madam, I wish it may.
         [*Exit* Queen.
  *Pol.* Ophelia, walk you here.—Gracious, so
please you,
We will bestow ourselves.—[*To* Ophelia.]
  Read on this book;
That show of such an exercise may colour
Your loneliness.—We are oft to blame in
  this,—    [visage.
'Tis too much prov'd,—that with devotion's
And pious action we do sugar o'er
The devil himself.
  *King.* [*Aside.*] O, 'tis too true! [conscience!
How smart a lash that speech doth give my

The harlot's cheek, beautied with plastering
  art,
Is not more ugly to the thing that helps it
Than is my deed to my most painted word:
O heavy burden!    [lord.
  *Pol.* I hear him coming: let's withdraw, my
         [*Exeunt* King *and* Polonius.

       *Enter* Hamlet.

  *Ham.* To be, or not to be,—that is the
    question:—
Whether 'tis nobler in the mind to suffer
The slings and arrows of outrageous fortune,
Or to take arms against a sea of troubles,
And by opposing end them?—To die,—to
  sleep,—
No more; and by a sleep to say we end
The heart-ache and the thousand natural
  shocks
That flesh is heir to,—'tis a consummation
Devoutly to be wish'd. To die,—to sleep;—
To sleep! perchance to dream:—ay, there's
  the rub;    [come,
For in that sleep of death what dreams may
When we have shuffled off this mortal coil,
Must give us pause: there's the respect
That makes calamity of so long life;   [time,
For who would bear the whips and scorns of
The oppressor's wrong, the proud man's con-
  tumely,
The pangs of despis'd love, the law's delay,
The insolence of office, and the spurns
That patient merit of the unworthy takes,
When he himself might his quietus make
With a bare bodkin? who would fardels bear,
To grunt and sweat under a weary life,
But that the dread of something after death,—
The undiscover'd country, from whose bourn
No traveller returns,—puzzles the will,
And makes us rather bear those ills we have
Than fly to others that we know not of?
Thus conscience does make cowards of us all;
And thus the native hue of resolution
Is sicklied o'er with the pale cast of thought;
And enterprises of great pith and moment,
With this regard, their currents turn awry,
And lose the name of action.—Soft you now!
The fair Ophelia.—Nymph, in thy orisons
Be all my sins remember'd.
  *Oph.*     Good my lord,
How does your honour for this many a day?
  *Ham.* I humbly thank you; well, well,
    well.    [yours,
  *Oph.* My lord, I have remembrances of
That I have longed long to re-deliver;
I pray you, now receive them.
  *Ham.*     No, not I;
I never gave you aught.    [well you did;
  *Oph.* My honour'd lord, you know right
And, with them, words of so sweet breath
  compos'd    [lost,
As made the things more rich: their perfume
Take these again; for to the noble mind

Rich gifts wax poor when givers prove unkind.
There, my lord.

*Ham.* Ha, ha! are you honest?

*Oph.* My lord?

*Ham.* Are you fair?

*Oph.* What means your lordship?

*Ham.* That if you be honest and fair, your honesty should admit no discourse to your beauty.

*Oph.* Could beauty, my lord, have better commerce than with honesty?

*Ham.* Ay, truly; for the power of beauty will sooner transform honesty from what it is to a bawd than the force of honesty can translate beauty into his likeness: this was sometime a paradox, but now the time gives it proof. I did love you once.

*Oph.* Indeed, my lord, you made me believe so.

*Ham.* You should not have believed me; for virtue cannot so inoculate our old stock but we shall relish of it: I loved you not.

*Oph.* I was the more deceived.

*Ham.* Get thee to a nunnery: why wouldst thou be a breeder of sinners? I am myself indifferent honest; but yet I could accuse me of such things that it were better my mother had not born me: I am very proud, revengeful, ambitious; with more offences at my beck than I have thoughts to put them in, imagination to give them shape, or time to act them in. What should such fellows as I do crawling between heaven and earth? We are arrant knaves, all; believe none of us. Go thy ways to a nunnery. Where's your father?

*Oph.* At home, my lord.

*Ham.* Let the doors be shut upon him, that he may play the fool nowhere but in's own house. Farewell.

*Oph.* O, help him, you sweet heavens!

*Ham.* If thou dost marry, I'll give thee this plague for thy dowry,—be thou as chaste as ice, as pure as snow, thou shalt not escape calumny. Get thee to a nunnery, go: farewell. Or, if thou wilt needs marry, marry a fool; for wise men know well enough what monsters you make of them. To a nunnery, go; and quickly too. Farewell.

*Oph.* O heavenly powers, restore him!

*Ham.* I have heard of your paintings too, well enough; God has given you one face and you make yourselves another: you jig, you amble, and you lisp, and nickname God's creatures, and make your wantonness your ignorance. Go to, I'll no more on't; it hath made me mad. I say, we will have no more marriages: those that are married already, all but one, shall live; the rest shall keep as they are. To a nunnery, go.  [*Exit.*

*Oph.* O, what a noble mind is here o'erthrown!  [*sword:*
The courtier's, soldier's, scholar's eye, tongue,
The expectancy and rose of the fair state,
The glass of fashion and the mould of form,
The observ'd of all observers,—quite, quite down!
And I, of ladies most deject and wretched
That suck'd the honey of his music vows,
Now see that noble and most sovereign reason,  [harsh;
Like sweet bells jangled, out of tune and
That unmatch'd form and feature of blown youth
Blasted with ecstasy: O, woe is me,  [see!
To have seen what I have seen, see what I

*Re-enter* KING *and* POLONIUS.

*King.* Love! his affections do not that way tend;  [little,
Nor what he spake, though it lack'd form a
Was not like madness. There's something in his soul
O'er which his melancholy sits on brood;
And I do doubt the hatch and the disclose
Will be some danger: which for to prevent,
I have in quick determination  [England
Thus set it down:—he shall with speed to
For the demand of our neglected tribute:
Haply, the seas and countries different,
With variable objects, shall expel
This something-settled matter in his heart;
Whereon his brains still beating puts him thus
From fashion of himself. What think you on't?

*Pol.* It shall do well: but yet do I believe
The origin and commencement of his grief
Sprung from neglected love.—How now, Ophelia!
You need not tell us what Lord Hamlet said;
We heard it all.—My lord, do as you please;
But if you hold it fit, after the play,
Let his queen mother all alone entreat him
To show his grief: let her be round with him;
And I'll be plac'd, so please you, in the ear
Of all their conference. If she find him not,
To England send him; or confine him where
Your wisdom best shall think.

*King.*          It shall be so;
Madness in great ones must not unwatch'd go.  [*Exeunt.*

SCENE II.—*A Hall in the Castle.*

*Enter* HAMLET *and certain* Players.

*Ham.* Speak the speech, I pray you, as I pronounced it to you, trippingly on the tongue: but if you mouth it, as many of your players do, I had as lief the town-crier spoke my lines. Nor do not saw the air too much with your hand, thus; but use all gently: for in the very torrent, tempest, and, as I may say, the whirlwind of passion, you must acquire and beget a temperance that may give it smoothness. O, it offends me to the soul, to hear a robustious periwig-pated fellow tear a passion to tatters, to very rags, to split the ears of the groundlings, who, for the most part, are capable of nothing but inexplicable dumb shows and noise: I could have such a fellow whipped for o'erdoing Termagant; it out-herods Herod: pray you, avoid it.

*1 Play.* I warrant your honour.

*Ham.* Be not too tame neither, but let your own discretion be your tutor: suit the action to the word, the word to the action; with this special observance, that you o'erstep not the modesty of nature: for anything so overdone is from the purpose of playing, whose end, both at the first and now, was and is, to hold, as 'twere, the mirror up to nature; to show virtue her own feature, scorn her own image, and the very age and body of the time his form and pressure. Now, this overdone or come tardy off, though it make the unskilful laugh, cannot but make the judicious grieve; the censure of the which one must, in your allowance, o'erweigh a whole theatre of others. O, there be players that I have seen play,—and heard others praise, and that highly,—not to speak it profanely, that, neither having the accent of Christians, nor the gait of Christian, pagan, nor man, have so strutted and bellowed that I have thought some of nature's journeymen had made men, and not made them well, they imitated humanity so abominably.

*1 Play.* I hope we have reformed that indifferently with us, sir.

*Ham.* O, reform it altogether. And let those that play your clowns speak no more than is set down for them: for there be of them that will themselves laugh, to set on some quantity of barren spectators to laugh too; though, in the meantime, some necessary question of the play be then to be considered: that's villanous, and shows a most pitiful ambition in the fool that uses it. Go, make you ready.                    [*Exeunt* Players.

*Enter* POLONIUS, ROSENCRANTZ, *and* GUILDENSTERN.

How now, my lord! will the king hear this piece of work?

*Pol.* And the queen too, and that presently.

*Ham.* Bid the players make haste.

[*Exit* POLONIUS.

Will you two help to hasten them?

*Ros. and Guil.* We will, my lord.

[*Exeunt* Ros. *and* GUIL.

*Ham.* What, ho, Horatio!

*Enter* HORATIO.

*Hor.* Here, sweet lord, at your service.

*Ham.* Horatio, thou art e'en as just a man As e'er my conversation cop'd withal.

*Hor.* O, my dear lord,—

*Ham.*                    Nay, do not think I flatter;

For what advancement may I hope from thee,
That no revenue hast, but thy good spirits,
To feed and clothe thee? Why should the poor be flatter'd?
No, let the candied tongue lick absurd pomp;
And crook the pregnant hinges of the knee
Where thrift may follow fawning. Dost thou hear?
Since my dear soul was mistress of her choice,
And could of men distinguish, her election
Hath seal'd thee for herself: for thou hast been
As one, in suffering all, that suffers nothing;
A man that Fortune buffets and rewards
Hast ta'en with equal thanks: and bless'd are those                    [mingled
Whose blood and judgment are so well com-
That they are not a pipe for Fortune's finger
To sound what stop she please. Give me that man                    [him
That is not passion's slave, and I will wear
In my heart's core, ay, in my heart of heart,
As I do thee.—Something too much of this.—
There is a play to-night before the king;
One scene of it comes near the circumstance
Which I have told thee of my father's death:
I pr'ythee, when thou see'st that act a-foot,
Even with the very comment of thy soul
Observe mine uncle: if his occulted guilt
Do not itself unkennel in one speech,
It is a damned ghost that we have seen;
And my imaginations are as foul
As Vulcan's stithy. Give him heedful note:
For I mine eyes will rivet to his face;
And, after, we will both our judgments join
In censure of his seeming.

*Hor.*                    Well, my lord:
If he steal aught the whilst this play is playing,
And scape detecting, I will pay the theft.

*Ham.* They are coming to the play; I must be idle:
Get you a place.

*Danish march. A flourish. Enter* KING, QUEEN, POLONIUS, OPHELIA, ROSENCRANTZ, GUILDENSTERN, *and others.*

*King.* How fares our cousin Hamlet?

*Ham.* Excellent, i' faith; of the chameleons dish: I eat the air, promise-crammed: you cannot feed capons so.

*King.* I have nothing with this answer, Hamlet; these words are not mine.

*Ham.* No, nor mine now.—My lord, you played once i' the university, you say?
                    [*To* POL.

*Pol.* That did I, my lord, and was accounted a good actor.

*Ham.* And what did you enact?

*Pol.* I did enact Julius Cæsar: I was killed i' the Capitol; Brutus killed me.

*Ham.* It was a brute part of him to kill so

capital a calf there.—Be the players ready?

*Ros.* Ay, my lord; they stay upon your patience.

*Queen.* Come hither, my good Hamlet, sit by me.     [*attractive.*

*Ham.* No good mother, here's metal more

*Pol.* O, ho! do you mark that?
          [*To the* KING.

*Ham.* Lady, shall I lie in your lap?
        [*Lying down at* OPHELIA's *feet.*

*Oph.* No, my lord.

*Ham.* I mean, my head upon your lap?

*Oph.* Ay, my lord.     [*matters?*

*Ham.* Do you think I meant country

*Oph.* I think nothing, my lord.

*Ham.* That's a fair thought to lie between maids' legs.

*Oph.* What is, my lord?

*Ham.* Nothing.

*Oph.* You are merry, my lord.

*Ham.* Who, I?

*Oph.* Ay, my lord.

*Ham.* O, your only jig-maker. What should a man do but be merry? for, look you, how cheerfully my mother looks, and my father died within's two hours.

*Oph.* Nay, 'tis twice two months, my lord.

*Ham.* So long? Nay, then, let the devil wear black, for I'll have a suit of sables. O heavens! die two months ago, and not forgotten yet? Then there's hope a great man's memory may outlive his life half a year: but, by'r lady, he must build churches, then; or else shall he suffer not thinking on, with the hobby-horse, whose epitaph is, *For, O, for, O, the hobby-horse is forgot.*

*Trumpets sound. The dumb show enters. Enter a* King *and a* Queen, *very lovingly; the* Queen *embracing him and he her. She kneels, and makes show of protestation unto him. He takes her up, and declines his head upon her neck: lays him down upon a bank of flowers: she, seeing him asleep, leaves him. Anon comes in a fellow, takes off his crown, kisses it, and pours poison in the* King's *ears, and exit. The* Queen *returns; finds the* King *dead, and makes passionate action. The* Poisoner, *with some two or three* Mutes, *comes in again, seeming to lament with her. The dead body is carried away. The* Poisoner *woos the* Queen *with gifts: she seems loth and unwilling awhile, but in the end accepts his love.*     [*Exeunt.*

*Oph.* What means this, my lord?

*Ham.* Marry, this is miching mallecho; it means mischief.

*Oph.* Belike this show imports the argument of the play.

### Enter Prologue.

*Ham.* We shall know by this fellow: the players cannot keep counsel; they'll tell all.

*Oph.* Will he tell us what this show meant?

*Ham.* Ay, or any show that you'll show him: be not you ashamed to show, he'll not shame to tell you what it means.

*Oph.* You are naught, you are naught: I'll mark the play.

*Pro.* For us, and for our tragedy,
    Here stooping to your clemency,
    We beg your hearing patiently.

*Ham.* Is this a prologue, or the posy of a ring?

*Oph.* 'Tis brief, my lord.

*Ham.* As woman's love.

### Enter a King and a Queen.

*P. King.* Full thirty minutes hath Phœbus'
    cart gone round     [ground,
Neptune's salt wash and Tellus' orbed
And thirty dozen moons with borrow'd sheen
About the world have times twelve thirties
    been,     [hands
Since love our hearts, and Hymen did our
Unite commutual in most sacred bands.

*P. Queen.* So many journeys may the sun
    and moon
Make us again count o'er ere love be done!
But, woe is me, you are so sick of late,
So far from cheer and from your former
    state,
That I distrust you. Yet, though I distrust,
Discomfort you, my lord, it nothing must:
For women's fear and love holds quantity;
In neither aught, or in extremity.
Now, what my love is, proof hath made you
    know;
And as my love is siz'd, my fear is so:
Where love is great, the littlest doubts are
    fear;     [grows there.
Where little fears grow great, great love

*P. King.* Faith, I must leave thee, love,
    and shortly too;     [do:
My operant powers their functions leave to
And thou shalt live in this fair world behind,
Honour'd, belov'd and haply one as kind
For husband shalt thou,—

*P. Queen.*     O, confound the rest!
Such love must needs be treason in my
    breast:
In second husband let me be accurst!
None wed the second but who kill'd the first.

*Ham.* [*Aside.*] Wormwood, wormwood.

*P. Queen.* The instances that second mar-
    riage move
Are base respects of thrift, but none of love:
A second time I kill my husband dead
When second husband kisses me in bed.

*P. King.* I do believe you think what now
    you speak;
But what we do determine oft we break.
Purpose is but the slave to memory;
Of violent birth, but poor validity:     [tree;
Which now, like fruit unripe, sticks on the

But fall unshaken when they mellow be.
Most necessary 'tis that we forget
To pay ourselves what to ourselves is debt:
What to ourselves in passion we propose,
The passion ending, doth the purpose lose.
The violence of either grief or joy
Their own enactures with themselves de-
　　　stroy:　　　　　　　　　　　　　[ment;
Where joy most revels grief doth most la-
Grief joys, joy grieves, on slender accident.
This world is not for aye; nor 'tis not
　　　strange　　　　　　　　　　　　　[change;
That even our loves should with our fortunes
For 'tis a question left us yet to prove
Whether love lead fortune or else fortune
　　　love.　　　　　　　　　　　　　　[flies;
The great man down, you mark his favourite
The poor advanc'd makes friends of enemies.
And hitherto doth love on fortune tend:
For who not needs shall never lack a friend;
And who in want a hollow friend doth try,
Directly seasons him his enemy.
But, orderly to end where I begun,—
Our wills and fates do so contráry run
That our devices still are overthrown; [own:
Our thoughts are ours, their ends none of our
So think thou wilt no second husband wed;
But die thy thoughts when thy first lord is
　　　dead.
　　*P. Queen.* Nor earth to me give food, nor
　　　heaven light!
Sport and repose lock from me day and
　　　night!
To desperation turn my trust and hope!
An anchor's cheer in prison be my scope!
Each opposite, that blanks the face of joy,
Meet what I would have well, and it destroy!
Both here and hence, pursue me lasting strife,
If, once a widow, ever I be wife!
　　*Ham.* If she should break it now!
　　　　　　　　　　　　　　[*To* OPHELIA.
　　*P. King.* 'Tis deeply sworn. Sweet, leave
　　　me here awhile;　　　　　　　　[guile
My spirits grow dull, and fain I would be-
The tedious day with sleep.　　　　　[*Sleeps.*
　　*P. Queen.*　　　　　Sleep rock thy brain,
And never come mischance between us
　　　twain!　　　　　　　　　　　　　[*Exit.*
　　*Ham.* Madam, how like you this play?
　　*Queen.* The lady protests too much, me-
thinks.
　　*Ham.* O, but she'll keep her word.
　　*King.* Have you heard the argument? Is
there no offence in't?
　　*Ham.* No, no, they do but jest, poison in
jest; no offence i' the world.
　　*King.* What do you call the play?
　　*Ham.* The Mouse-trap. Marry, how?
Tropically. This play is the image of a mur-
der done in Vienna: Gonzago is the duke's
name; his wife, Baptista: you shall see anon;
'tis a knavish piece of work: but what o'
that? your majesty, and we that have free

souls, it touches us not: let the galled jade
wince, our withers are unwrung.

### Enter LUCIANUS.

This is one Lucianus, nephew to the king.
　　*Oph.* You are a good chorus, my lord.
　　*Ham.* I could interpret between you and
your love, if I could see the puppets dally-
ing.
　　*Oph.* You are keen, my lord, you are keen.
　　*Ham.* It would cost you a groaning to
take off my edge.
　　*Oph.* Still better, and worse.
　　*Ham.* So you must take your husbands.—
Begin, murderer; pox, leave thy damnable
faces and begin. Come:—*The croaking raven
doth bellow for revenge.*
　　*Luc.* Thoughts black, hands apt, drugs fit,
　　　and time agreeing;
Confederate season, else no creature seeing;
Thou mixture rank, of midnight weeds col-
　　　lected,　　　　　　　　　　　　　[fected,
With Hecate's ban thrice blasted, thrice in-
Thy natural magic and dire property
On wholesome life usurp immediately.
　　　[*Pours the poison into the sleeper's ears.*
　　*Ham.* He poisons him i' the garden for's
estate. His name's Gonzago: the story is
extant, and writ in choice Italian: you shall
see anon how the murderer gets the love of
Gonzago's wife.
　　*Oph.* The king rises.
　　*Ham.* What, frighted with false fire!
　　*Queen.* How fares my lord?
　　*Pol.* Give o'er the play.
　　*King.* Give me some light:—away!
　　*All.* Lights, lights, lights!
　　　　　　[*Exeunt all but* HAM. *and* HOR.
　　*Ham.* Why, let the strucken deer go weep,
　　　The hart ungalled play;
For some must watch, while some must
　　　sleep:
So runs the world away.—
Would not this, sir, and a forest of feathers,
—if the rest of my fortunes turn Turk with
me,—with two Provencial roses on my razed
shoes, get me a fellowship in a cry of players,
sir?
　　*Hor.* Half a share.
　　*Ham.* A whole one, I.
　　　For thou dost know, O Damon dear,
　　　　This realm dismantled was
　　　Of Jove himself and now reigns here
　　　　A very, very—pajock.
　　*Hor.* You might have rhymed.
　　*Ham.* O good Horatio, I'll take the ghost's
word for a thousand pound. Didst perceive?
　　*Hor.* Very well, my lord.
　　*Ham.* Upon the talk of the poisoning,—
　　*Hor.* I did very well note him.
　　*Ham.* Ah, ha!—Come, some music! come,
the recorders!—
　　For if the king like not the comedy,

Why, then, belike,—he likes it not, perdy.
Come, some music!

*Re-enter* ROSENCRANTZ *and* GUILDENSTERN.

*Guil.* Good my lord, vouchsafe me a word
with you.
*Ham.* Sir, a whole history.
*Guil.* The king, sir,—.
*Ham.* Ay, sir, what of him?    [tempered.
*Guil.* Is, in his retirement, marvellous dis-
*Ham.* With drink, sir?
*Guil.* No, my lord, rather with choler.
*Ham.* Your wisdom should show itself
more richer to signify this to his doctor; for,
for me to put him to his purgation would
perhaps plunge him into far more choler.
*Guil.* Good my lord, put your discourse
into some frame, and start not so wildly from
my affair.
*Ham.* I am tame, sir:—pronounce.
*Guil.* The queen, your mother, in most
great affliction of spirit, hath sent me to you.
*Ham.* You are welcome.
*Guil.* Nay, good my lord, this courtesy is
not of the right breed. If it shall please you
to make me a wholesome answer, I will do
your mother's commandment: if not, your
pardon and my return shall be the end of my
business.
*Ham.* Sir, I cannot.
*Guil.* What, my lord?
*Ham.* Make you a wholesome answer; my
wit's diseased: but, sir, such answer as I can
make, you shall command; or, rather, as
you say, my mother: therefore no more, but
to the matter: my mother, you say,—
*Ros.* Then thus she says: your behaviour
hath struck her into amazement and admiration.
*Ham.* O wonderful son, that can so astonish a mother!—But is there no sequel at the
heels of this mother's admiration?
*Ros.* She desires to speak with you in her
closet ere you go to bed.
*Ham.* We shall obey, were she ten times
our mother. Have you any further trade
with us?
*Ros.* My lord, you once did love me.
*Ham.* So I do still, by these pickers and
stealers.
*Ros.* Good my lord, what is your cause of
distemper? you do, surely, bar the door upon
your own liberty if you deny your griefs to
your friend.
*Ham.* Sir, I lack advancement.
*Ros.* How can that be, when you have the
voice of the king himself for your succession
in Denmark?
*Ham.* Ay, but *While the grass grows,*—the
proverb is something musty.

*Re-enter the* Players, *with* Recorders.

O, the recorders:—let me see one.—To with-
draw with you:—why do you go about to
recover the wind of me, as if you would drive
me into a toil?
*Guil.* O, my lord, if my duty be too bold,
my love is too unmannerly.
*Ham.* I do not well understand that. Will
you play upon this pipe?
*Guil.* My lord, I cannot.
*Ham.* I pray you.
*Guil.* Believe me, I cannot.
*Ham.* I do beseech you.
*Guil.* I know no touch of it, my lord.
*Ham.* 'Tis as easy as lying: govern these
ventages with your finger and thumb, give it
breath with your mouth, and it will discourse
most eloquent music. Look you, these are the
stops.
*Guil.* But these cannot I command to any
utterance of harmony; I have not the skill.
*Ham.* Why, look you now, how unworthy
a thing you make of me! You would play
upon me; you would seem to know my
stops; you would pluck out the heart of my
mystery; you would sound me from my lowest note to the top of my compass: and there
is much music, excellent voice, in this little
organ; yet cannot you make it speak.
'Sblood, do you think that I am easier to be
played on than a pipe? Call me what instrument you will, though you can fret me you
cannot play upon me.

*Enter* POLONIUS.

God bless you, sir!
*Pol.* My lord, the queen would speak with
you, and presently.
*Ham.* Do you see yonder cloud that's al-
most in shape of a camel?
*Pol.* By the mass, and 'tis like a camel
indeed.
*Ham.* Methinks it is like a weasel.
*Pol.* It is backed like a weasel.
*Ham.* Or like a whale?
*Pol.* Very like a whale.
*Ham.* Then will I come to my mother by
and by.—They fool me to the top of my
bent.—I will come by and by.
*Pol.* I will say so.
*Ham.* By and by is easily said. [*Exit*
POLONIUS.]—Leave me, friends.
    [*Exeunt* ROS., GUIL., HOR., *and* Players.
'Tis now the very witching time of night,
When churchyards yawn, and hell itself
        breathes out               [hot blood,
Contagion to this world: now could I drink
And do such bitter business as the day
Would quake to look on. Soft! now to my
        mother.—
O heart, lose not thy nature; let not ever
The soul of Nero enter this firm bosom:
Let me be cruel, not unnatural:
I will speak daggers to her, but use none;
My tongue and soul in this be hypocrites,—

How in my words soever she be shent,
To give them seals never, my soul, consent!
                    [*Exit.*

SCENE III.—*A Room in the Castle.*

*Enter* KING, ROSENCRANTZ, *and* GUILDEN-
       STERN.

   *King.* I like him not; nor stands it safe
    with us                  [you;
To let his madness range. Therefore prepare
I your commission will forthwith despatch,
And he to England shall along with you:
The terms of our estate may not endure
Hazard so dangerous as doth hourly grow
Out of his lunacies.
   *Guil.*         We will ourselves provide:
Most holy and religious fear it is
To keep those many many bodies safe
That live and feed upon your majesty.
   *Ros.* The single and peculiar life is bound,
With all the strength and armour of the
    mind,
To keep itself from 'noyance; but much more
That spirit upon whose weal depend and rest
The lives of many. The cease of majesty
Dies not alone but like a gulf doth draw
What's near it with it: it is a massy wheel,
Fix'd on the summit of the highest mount,
To whose huge spokes ten thousand lesser
    things                  [falls,
Are mortis'd and adjoin'd; which, when it
Each small annexment, petty consequence,
Attends the boisterous ruin. Never alone
Did the king sigh, but with a general groan.
   *King.* Arm you, I pray you, to this speedy
    voyage;
For we will fetters put upon this fear,
Which now goes too free-footed.
   *Ros and Guil.*         We will haste us.
         [*Exeunt* ROS. *and* GUIL.

*Enter* POLONIUS.

   *Pol.* My lord, he's going to his mother's
    closet:
Behind the arras I'll convey myself
To hear the process; I'll warrant she'll tax
    him home:
And, as you said, and wisely was it said,
'Tis meet that some more audience than a
    mother,           [o'erhear
Since nature makes them partial, should
The speech, of vantage. Fare you well, my
    liege:
I'll call upon you ere you go to bed,
And tell you what I know.
   *King.*         Thanks, dear my lord.
              [*Exit* POLONIUS.
O, my offence is rank, it smells to heaven;
It hath the primal eldest curse upon't,—
A brother's murder!—Pray can I not,
Though inclination be as sharp as will:
My stronger guilt defeats my strong intent;
And, like a man to double business bound,

I stand in pause where I shall first begin,
And both neglect. What if this cursed hand
Were thicker than itself with brother's
    blood,—
Is there not rain enough in the sweet heavens
To wash it white as snow? Whereto serves
    mercy
But to confront the visage of offence?
And what's in prayer but this twofold
    force,—
To be forestalled ere we come to fall,
Or pardon'd being down? Then I'll look up;
My fault is past. But, O, what form of
    prayer         [murder!—
Can serve my turn? Forgive me my foul
That cannot be; since I am still possess'd
Of those effects for which I did the murder,—
My crown, mine own ambition, and my
    queen.
May one be pardon'd and retain the offence?
In the corrupted currents of this world
Offence's gilded hand may shove by justice;
And oft 'tis seen the wicked prize itself
Buys out the law: but 'tis not so above;
There is no shuffling,—there the action lies
In his true nature; and we ourselves com-
    pell'd,
Even to the teeth and forehead of our faults,
To give in evidence. What then? what rests?
Try what repentance can: what can it not?
Yet what can it when one can not repent?
O wretched state! O bosom black as death!
O limed soul, that, struggling to be free,
Art more engag'd! Help, angels! make assay:
Bow, stubborn knees and, heart, with strings
    of steel,
Be soft as sinews of the new-born babe!
All may be well.       [*Retires and kneels.*

*Enter* HAMLET.

   *Ham.* Now might I do it pat, now he is
    praying          [heaven;
And now I'll do't;—and so he goes to
And so am I reveng'd:—that would be
    scann'd:
A villain kills my father; and for that,
I, his sole son, do this same villain send
To heaven.
O, this is hire and salary, not revenge.
He took my father grossly, full of bread;
With all his crimes broad blown, as flush as
    May;          [heaven?
And how his audit stands who knows save
But in our circumstance and course of
    thought
Tis heavy with him: and am I, then, reveng'd,
To take him in the purging of his soul,
When he is fit and season'd for his passage?
No.
Up, sword; and know thou a more horrid
    hent:
When he is drunk, asleep, or in his rage;
Or in the incestuous pleasure of his bed;

At gaming, swearing; or about some act
That has no relish of salvation in't;—
Then trip him, that his heels may kick at
　heaven;　　　　　　　　　　　[black
And that his soul may be as damn'd and
As hell, whereto it goes. My mother stays:
This physic but prolongs thy sickly days.
　　　　　　　　　　　　　　　[Exit.
　　　　[The KING rises and advances.
King. My words fly up, my thought re-
　main below:
Words without thoughts never to heaven go.
　　　　　　　　　　　　　　　[Exit.

SCENE IV.—Another Room in the Castle.

Enter QUEEN and POLONIUS.

Pol. He will come straight. Look you lay
home to him:　　　　[bear with,
Tell him his pranks have been too broad to
And that your grace hath screen'd and stood
　between
Much heat and him. I'll silence me e'en here.
Pray you, be round with him.
Ham. [Within.] Mother, mother, mother!
Queen. 　　　　　　　I'll warrant you:
Fear me not:—withdraw, I hear him coming.
　　　　　[POLONIUS goes behind the arras.

Enter HAMLET.

Ham. Now, mother, what's the matter?
Queen. Hamlet, thou hast thy father much
　offended. 　　　　　　　[offended.
Ham. Mother, you have my father much
Queen. Come, come, you answer with an
　idle tongue. 　　　　　[tongue.
Ham. Go, go, you question with a wicked
Queen. Why, how now, Hamlet!
Ham. 　　　　　What's the matter now?
Queen. Have you forgot me?
Ham. 　　　　　No, by the rood, not so:
You are the queen, your husband's brother's
　wife; 　　　　　　　　　　[mother.
And,—would it were not so!—you are my
Queen. Nay, then, I'll set those to you
　that can speak.
Ham. Come, come, and sit you down; you
　shall not budge;
You go not till I set you up a glass
Where you may see the inmost part of you.
Queen. What wilt thou do? thou wilt not
　murder me?—
Help, help, ho!
Pol. [Behind.] What, ho! help, help, help!
Ham. 　　　　　How now! a rat? [Draws.
Dead, for a ducat, dead!
　　　　[Makes a pass through the arras.
Pol. [Behind.] O, I am slain!
　　　　　　　　　　[Falls and dies.
Queen. O me, what hast thou done?
Ham. 　　　　　Nay, I know not:
Is it the king? 　　　[Draws forth POLONIUS.
Queen. O, what a rash and bloody deed is
　this!

Ham. A bloody deed!—almost as bad,
　good mother,
As kill a king and marry with his brother.
Queen. As kill a king!
Ham. 　　　　Ay, lady, 'twas my word.—
Thou wretched, rash, intruding fool, fare-
　well! 　　　　　　　[To POLONIUS.
I took thee for thy better: take thy fortune;
Thou find'st to be too busy is some danger.—
Leave wringing of your hands: peace; sit
　you down,
And let me wring your heart: for so I shall,
If it be made of penetrable stuff;
If damned custom have not braz'd it so
That it is proof and bulwark against sense.
Queen. What have I done, that thou dar'st
　wag thy tongue
In noise so rude against me?
Ham. 　　　　　　　Such an act
That blurs the grace and blush of modesty;
Calls virtue hypocrite; takes off the rose
From the fair forehead of an innocent love,
And sets a blister there; makes marriage-
　vows
As false as dicers' oaths: O, such a deed
As from the body of contraction plucks
The very soul, and sweet religion makes
A rhapsody of words: heaven's face doth
　glow;
Yea, this solidity and compound mass,
With tristful visage, as against the doom,
Is thought-sick at the act.
Queen. 　　　　　Ah me, what act,
That roars so loud, and thunders in the
　index?
Ham. Look here upon this picture and on
　this,—
The counterfeit presentment of two brothers.
See what a grace was seated on this brow;
Hyperion's curls; the front of Jove himself;
An eye like Mars, to threaten and command;
A station like the herald Mercury
New-lighted on a heaven-kissing hill;
A combination and a form, indeed,
Where every god did seem to set his seal,
To give the world assurance of a man:
This was your husband.—Look you now
　what follows:
Here is your husband, like a milldew'd ear
Blasting his wholesome brother. Have you
　eyes? 　　　　　　　　　[feed,
Could you on this fair mountain leave to
And batten on this moor? Ha! have you
　eyes?
You cannot call it love; for at your age
The hey-day in the blood is tame, it's humble,
And waits upon the judgment: and what
　judgment 　　　　　　[you have,
Would step from this to this? Sense, sure,
Else could you not have motion: but sure
　that sense
Is apoplex'd: for madness would not err;
Nor sense to ecstasy was ne'er so thrall'd

But it reserv'd some quantity of choice
To serve in such a difference. What devil
    was't        [blind?
That thus hath cozen'd you at hoodman-
Eyes without feeling, feeling without sight,
Ears without hands or eyes, smelling sans all,
Or but a sickly part of one true sense
Could not so mope.
O shame! where is thy blush? Rebellious hell,
If thou canst mutine in a matron's bones,
To flaming youth let virtue be as wax,
And melt in her own fire: proclaim no shame
When the compulsive ardour gives the charge,
Since frost itself as actively doth burn,
And reason panders will.
  *Queen.*        O Hamlet, speak no more:
Thou turns't mine eyes into my very soul;
And there I see such black and grained spots
As will not leave their tinct.
  *Ham.*        Nay, but to live
In the rank sweat of an enseamed bed, [love
Stew'd in corruption, honeying and making
Over the nasty sty,—
  *Queen.*      O, speak to me no more;
These words like daggers enter in mine ears;
No more, sweet Hamlet.
  *Ham.*       A murderer and a villain;
A slave that is not twentieth part the tithe
Of your precedent lord; a vice of kings;
A cutpurse of the empire and the rule,
That from a shelf the precious diadem stole,
And put it in his pocket!
  *Queen.*       No more.
  *Ham.* A king of shreds and patches,—

*Enter* Ghost.

Save me, and hover o'er me with your wings,
You heavenly guards!—What would your
    gracious figure?
  *Queen.* Alas, he's mad!    [chide,
  *Ham.* Do you not come your tardy son to
That, laps'd in time and passion, lets go by
The important acting of your dread com-
    mand?
O, say!
  *Ghost.* Do not forget: this visitation
Is but to whet thy almost blunted purpose.
But, look, amazement on thy mother sits:
O, step between her and her fighting soul,—
Conceit in weakest bodies strongest works,—
Speak to her, Hamlet.
  *Ham.*      How is it with you, lady?
  *Queen.*      Alas, how is't with you,
That you do bend your eye on vacancy,
And with the incorporal air do hold dis-
    course?
Forth at your eyes your spirits wildly peep;
And, as the sleeping soldiers in the alarm,
Your bedded hair, like life in excrements,
Starts up and stands on end. O gentle son,
Upon the heat and flame of thy distemper
Sprinkle cool patience. Whereon do you
    look?

  *Ham.* On him, on him! Look you, how
    pale he glares!
His form and cause conjoin'd, preaching to
    stones,
Would make them capable.—Do not look
    upon me;
Lest with this piteous action you convert
My stern effects: then what I have to do
Will want true colour; tears perchance for
    blood.
  *Queen.* To whom do you speak this?
  *Ham.*      Do you see nothing there?
  *Queen.* Nothing at all; yet all that is I see.
  *Ham.* Nor did you nothing hear?
  *Queen.*      No, nothing but ourselves.
  *Ham.* Why, look you there! look, how it
    steals away!
My father, in his habit as he liv'd!
Look, where he goes, even now, out at the
    portal!      [*Exit* Ghost.
  *Queen.* This is the very coinage of your
    brain:
This bodiless creation ecstasy
Is very cunning in.
  *Ham.*      Ecstasy!
My pulse, as yours, doth temperately keep
    time,
And makes as healthful music: it is not mad-
    ness,
That I have utter'd; bring me to the test,
And I the matter will re-word; which mad-
    ness
Would gambol from. Mother, for love of
    grace,
Lay not that flattering unction to your soul,
That not your trespass, but my madness
    speaks:
It will but skin and film the ulcerous place,
Whilst rank corruption, mining all within,
Infects unseen. Confess yourself to heaven;
Repent what's past; avoid what is to come;
And do not spread the compost on the weeds,
To make them ranker. Forgive me this my
    virtue;
For in the fatness of these pursy times
Virtue itself of vice must pardon beg,
Yea, curb and woo for leave to do him good.
  *Queen.* O Hamlet, thou hast cleft my heart
    in twain.
  *Ham.* O, throw away the worser part of it,
And live the purer with the other half.
Good-night: but go not to mine uncle's bed;
Assume a virtue, if you have it not.
That monster custom, who all sense doth eat,
Of habits devil, is angel yet in this,—
That to the use of actions fair and good
He likewise gives a frock or livery
That aptly is put on. Refrain to-night;
And that shall lend a kind of easiness
To the next abstinence: the next more easy;
For use almost can change the stamp of na-
    ture,
And either curb the devil or throw him out

With wondrous potency. Once more, good-
night:
And when you are desirous to be bless'd,
I'll blessing beg of you.—For this same lord
                [*Pointing to* POLONIUS.
I do repent: but Heaven hath pleas'd it so,
To punish me with this, and this with me,
That I must be their scourge and minister.
I will bestow him, and will answer well
The death I gave him. So, again, good-
night.—
I must be cruel only to be kind:
Thus bad begins and worse remains behind.—
One word more, good lady.
    *Queen.*          What shall I do?
    *Ham.* Not this, by no means, that I bid
you do:
Let the bloat king tempt you again to bed;
Pinch wanton on your cheek; call you his
mouse;
And let him, for a pair of reechy kisses,
Or paddling in your neck with his damn'd
fingers,
Make you to ravel all this matter out,
That I essentially am not in madness,
But mad in craft. 'Twere good you let him
know;
For who that's but a queen, fair, sober, wise,
Would from a paddock, from a bat, a gib,
Such dear concernings hide? who would do
so?
No, in despite of sense and secrecy,
Unpeg the basket on the house's top,
Let the birds fly, and, like the famous ape,
To try conclusions, in the basket creep,
And break your own neck down.
    *Queen.* Be thou assur'd, if words be made
of breath
And breath of life, I have no life to breathe
What thou hast said to me.
    *Ham.* I must to England; you know that?
    *Queen.*               Alack,
I had forgot: 'tis so concluded on.
    *Ham.* There's letters seal'd: and my two
schoolfellows,—
Whom I will trust as I will adders fang'd,—
They bear the mandate; they must sweep my
way
And marshal me to knavery. Let it work;
For 'tis the sport to have the engineer
Hoist with his own petard: and 't shall go
hard
But I will delve one yard below their mines,
And blow them at the moon: O, 'tis most
sweet,
When in one line two crafts directly meet.—
This man shall set me packing:
I'll lug the guts into the neighbour room.—
Mother, good-night.—Indeed, this counsellor
Is now most still, most secret, and most grave,
Who was in life a foolish prating knave.
Come, sir, to draw toward an end with
you·—

Good-night, mother.
    [*Exeunt severally;* HAM. *dragging out* POL.

## ACT IV.

### SCENE I.—*A Room in the Castle.*

*Enter* KING, QUEEN, ROSENCRANTZ, *and*
GUILDENSTERN.

    *King.* There's matter in these sighs, these
    profound heaves:        [them.
You must translate: 'tis fit we understand
Where is your son?
    *Queen.* Bestow this place on us a little
while.
              [*To* Ros. *and* GUIL., *who go out.*
Ah, my good lord, what have I seen to-night!
    *King.* What, Gertrude? How does Ham-
let?
    *Queen.* Mad as the sea and wind, when
both contend
Which is the mightier: in his lawless fit,
Behind the arras hearing something stir,
He whips his rapier out, and cries, *A rat, a
rat!*
And, in this brainish apprehension, kills
The unseen good old man.
    *King.*           O heavy deed!
It had been so with us had we been there:
His liberty is full of threats to all;
To you yourself, to us, to every one.
Alas, how shall this bloody deed be answer'd?
It will be laid to us, whose providence
Should have kept short, restrain'd, and out of
haunt
This mad young man: but so much was our
love,
We would not understand what was most fit;
But, like the owner of a foul disease,
To keep it from divulging, let it feed
Even on the pith of life. Where is he gone?
    *Queen.* To draw apart the body he hath
kill'd:
O'er whom his very madness, like some ore
Among a mineral of metals base,
Shows itself pure; he weeps for what is done.
    *King.* O Gertrude, come away!
The sun no sooner shall the mountains touch
But we will ship him hence: and this vile deed
We must, with all our majesty and skill,
Both countenance and excuse.—Ho, Guilden-
stern!

*Re-enter* ROSENCRANTZ *and* GUILDENSTERN.

Friends both, go join you with some further
aid:
Hamlet in madness hath Polonius slain,
And from his mother's closet hath he dragg'd
him:               [body
Go seek him out; speak fair, and bring the
Into the chapel. I pray you, haste in this.
               [*Exeunt* Ros. *and* GUIL.
Come, Gertrude, we'll call up our wisest
friends;
And let them know both what we mean to do

And what's untimely done: so haply slander,—
Whose whisper o'er the world's diameter,
As level as the cannon to his blank,          [name,
Transports his poison'd shot,—may miss our
And hit the woundless air.—O, come away!
My soul is full of discord and dismay.

          [*Exeunt.*

SCENE II.—*Another Room in the Castle.*

*Enter* HAMLET.

*Ham.* Safely stowed.

*Ros. and Guil.* [*Within.*] Hamlet! Lord Hamlet!

*Ham.* What noise? who calls on Hamlet? O, here they come.

*Enter* ROSENCRANTZ *and* GUILDENSTERN.

*Ros.* What have you done, my lord, with the dead body?

*Ham.* Compounded it with dust, whereto 'tis kin.

*Ros.* Tell us where 'tis, that we may take it thence,
And bear it to the chapel.

*Ham.* Do not believe it.

*Ros.* Believe what?

*Ham.* That I can keep your counsel, and not mine own. Besides, to be demanded of a sponge!—what replication should be made by the son of a king?

*Ros.* Take you me for a sponge, my lord?

*Ham.* Ay, sir; that soaks up the king's countenance, his rewards, his authorities. But such officers do the king best service in the end: he keeps them, like an ape, in the corner of his jaw first mouthed, to be last swallowed: when he needs what you have gleaned, it is but squeezing you, and, sponge, you shall be dry again.

*Ros.* I understand you not, my lord.

*Ham.* I am glad of it: a knavish speech sleeps in a foolish ear.

*Ros.* My lord, you must tell us where the body is, and go with us to the king.

*Ham.* The body is with the king, but the king is not with the body. The king is a thing,—

*Guil.* A thing, my lord!

*Ham.* Of nothing: bring me to him. Hide fox, and all after.          [*Exeunt.*

SCENE III.—*Another Room in the Castle.*

*Enter* KING, *attended.*

*King.* I have sent to seek him, and to find the body.
How dangerous is it that this man goes loose!
Yet must not we put the strong law on him:
He's lov'd of the distracted multitude,
Who like not in their judgment, but their eyes;
And where 'tis so, the offender's scourge is weigh'd,

But never the offence. To bear all smooth and even,
This sudden sending him away must seem
Deliberate pause: diseases desperate grown
By desperate appliance are reliev'd,
Or not at all.

*Enter* ROSENCRANTZ.

How now! what hath befallen?          [lord,

*Ros.* Where the dead body is bestow'd, my
We cannot get from him.

*King.*          But where is he?

*Ros.* Without, my lord; guarded, to know your pleasure.

*King.* Bring him before us.

*Ros.* Ho, Guildenstern! bring in my lord.

*Enter* HAMLET *and* GUILDENSTERN.

*King.* Now, Hamlet, where's Polonius?

*Ham.* At supper.

*King.* At supper! where?

*Ham.* Not where he eats, but where he is eaten: a certain convocation of politic worms are e'en at him. Your worm is your only emperor for diet: we fat all creatures else to fat us, and we fat ourselves for maggots: your fat king and your lean beggar is but variable service,—two dishes, but to one table: that's the end.

*King.* Alas, alas!

*Ham.* A man may fish with the worm that hath eat of a king, and eat of the fish that hath fed of that worm.

*King.* What dost thou mean by this?

*Ham.* Nothing but to show you how a king may go a progress through the guts of a beggar.

*King.* Where is Polonius?

*Ham.* In heaven; send thither to see: if your messenger find him not there, seek him i' the other place yourself. But, indeed, if you find him not within this month, you shall nose him as you go up the stairs into the lobby.

*King.* Go seek him there.

       [*To some* Attendants.

*Ham.* He will stay till ye come.

       [*Exeunt* Attendants.

*King.* Hamlet, this deed, for thine especial safety,—
Which we do tender, as we dearly grieve
For that which thou hast done,—must send thee hence
With fiery quickness: therefore prepare thyself;
The bark is ready, and the wind at help,
The associates tend, and everything is bent
For England.

*Ham.*          For England!

*King.*          Ay, Hamlet.

*Ham.*          Good.

*King.* So is it, if thou knew'st our purposes.

*Ham.* I see a cherub that sees them.—But,

come; for England!—Farewell, dear mother.
*King.* Thy loving father, Hamlet:
*Ham.* My mother: father and mother is
man and wife; man and wife is one flesh;
and so, my mother.—Come, for England!
[*Exit.*
*King.* Follow him at foot; tempt him with
speed aboard;
Delay it not I'll have him hence to-night:
Away! for everything is seal'd and done
That else leans on the affair: pray you, make
haste.  [*Exeunt* Ros. *and* Guil.
And, England, if my love thou hold'st at
aught,—
As my great power thereof may give thee
sense,
Since yet thy cicatrice looks raw and red
After the Danish sword, and thy free awe
Pays homage to us,—thou mayst not coldly
set
Our sovereign process; which imports at full,
By letters conjuring to that effect,
The present death of Hamlet. Do it, England;
For like the hectic in my blood he rages,
And thou must cure me: till I know 'tis done,
Howe'er my haps, my joys will ne'er begin.
[*Exit.*

SCENE IV.—*A Plain in Denmark.*

*Enter* Fortinbras, *and* Forces *marching.*

*For.* Go, captain, from me greet the Dan-
ish king:
Tell him that, by his license, Fortinbras
Craves the conveyance of a promis'd march
Over his kingdom. You know the rendezvous.
If that his majesty would aught with us,
We shall express our duty in his eye,
And let him know so.
*Cap.*  I will do't, my lord.
*For.* Go softly on.
[*Exeunt* For. *and* Forces.

*Enter* Hamlet, Rosencrantz, Guildenstern, &c.

*Ham.*  Good sir, whose powers are these?
*Cap.* They are of Norway, sir.
*Ham.* How purpos'd, sir, I pray you?
*Cap.* Against some part of Poland.
*Ham.* Who commands them, sir?
*Cap.* The nephew to old Norway, Fortin-
bras.  [sir,
*Ham.* Goes it against the main of Poland,
Or for some frontier?
*Cap.* Truly to speak, and with no addition,
We go to gain a little patch of ground
That hath in it no profit but the name.
To pay five ducats, five, I would not farm it;
Nor will it yield to Norway or the Pole
A ranker rate should it be sold in fee.
*Ham.* Why, then the Polack never will
defend it.
*Cap.* Yes, it is already garrison'd.

*Ham.* Two thousand souls and twenty
thousand ducats
Will not debate the question of this straw:
This is the imposthume of much wealth and
peace,  [without
That inward breaks, and shows no cause
Why the man dies.—I humbly thank you, sir.
*Cap.* God b' wi' you, sir.  [*Exit.*
*Ros.*  Will 't please you go, my lord?
*Ham.* I'll be with you straight. Go a lit-
tle before.  [*Exeunt all but* Hamlet.
How all occasions do inform against me.
And spur my dull revenge! What is a man,
If his chief good and market of his time
Be but to sleep and feed? a beast, no more.
Sure he that made us with such large dis-
course,
Looking before and after, gave us not
That capability and godlike reason
To fust in us unus'd. Now, whether it be
Bestial oblivion or some craven scruple
Of thinking too precisely on the event,—
A thought which, quarter'd, hath but one
part wisdom
And ever three parts coward,—I do not know
Why yet I live to say, *This thing 's to do;*
Sith I have cause, and will, and strength, and
means
To do 't. Examples, gross as earth, exhort me:
Witness this army, of such mass and charge,
Led by a delicate and tender prince;
Whose spirit, with divine ambition puff'd,
Makes mouths at the invisible event;
Exposing what is mortal and unsure
To all that fortune, death, and danger dare,
Even for an egg-shell. Rightly to be great
Is not to stir without great argument,
But greatly to find quarrel in a straw [then,
When honour 's at the stake. How stand I,
That have a father kill'd, a mother stain'd,
Excitements of my reason and my blood,
And let all sleep? while, to my shame, I see
The imminent death of twenty thousand men,
That, for a fantasy and trick of fame,
Go to their graves like beds; fight for a plot
Whereon the numbers cannot try the cause,
Which is not tomb enough and continent
To hide the slain?—O, from this time forth,
My thoughts be bloody, or be nothing worth!
[*Exit.*

SCENE V.—Elsinore. *A Room in the Castle.*

*Enter* Queen *and* Horatio.

*Queen.* I will not speak with her.
*Hor.* She is importunate; indeed, distract:
Her mood will needs be pitied.
*Queen.*  What would she have?
*Hor.* She speaks much of her father; says
she hears
There's tricks i' the world; and hems, and
beats her heart;  [in doubt,
Spurns enviously at straws; speaks things

That carry but half sense: her speech is noth-
ing,
Yet the unshaped use of it doth move
The hearers to collection; they aim at it,
And botch the words up fit to their own
thoughts;
Which, as her winks, and nods, and gestures
yield them,                          [thought,
Indeed would make one think there might be
Though nothing sure, yet much unhappily.
'Twere good she were spoken with; for she
may strew
Dangerous conjectures in ill-breeding minds.
*Queen.* Let her come in.    [*Exit* HORATIO.
To my sick soul, as sin's true nature is,
Each toy seems prologue to some great amiss:
So full of artless jealousy is guilt,
It spills itself in feating to be spilt.

### *Re-enter* HORATIO *with* OPHELIA.

*Oph.* Where is the beauteous majesty of
Denmark?
*Queen.* How now, Ophelia!

*Oph.* How should I your true love know [*Sings.*
From another one?
By his cockle hat and staff,
And his sandal shoon.

*Queen.* Alas, sweet lady, what imports this
song?
*Oph.* Say you? nay, pray you, mark.

He is dead and gone, lady,        [*Sings.*
He is dead and gone;
At his head a grass green turf,
At his heels a stone.

*Queen.* Nay, but, Ophelia,—
*Oph.*                    Pray you, mark.
White his shroud as the mountain [*Sings.*
snow,

### *Enter* KING.

*Queen.* Alas, look here, my lord.

*Oph.* Larded with sweet flowers;    [*Sings.*
Which bewept to the grave did go
With true-love showers.

*King.* How do you, pretty lady?
*Oph.* Well, God 'ild you! They say the owl
was a baker's daughter. Lord, we know what
we are, but know not what we may be. God
be at your table!
*King.* Conceit upon her father.
*Oph.* Pray you, let's have no words of this;
but when they ask you what it means, say
you this:

To-morrow is Saint Valentine's day [*Sings.*
All in the morning betime,
And I a maid at your window,
To be your Valentine.

Then up he rose, and donn'd his clothes,
And dupp'd the chamber-door;
Let in the maid, that out a maid
Never departed more.

*King.* Pretty Ophelia!
*Oph.* Indeed, la, without an oath, I'll make
an end on 't:

By Gis and by Saint Charity,    [*Sings.*
Alack, and fie for shame!
Young men will do 't, if they come to 't;
By cock, they are to blame.

Quoth she, before you tumbled me,
You promis'd me to wed.
So would I ha' done, by yonder sun,
An thou hadst not come to my bed.

*King.* How long hath she been thus?
*Oph.* I hope all will be well. We must be
patient: but I cannot choose but weep, to
think they should lay him i' the cold ground.
My brother shall know of it: and so I thank
you for your good counsel.—Come, my
coach!—Good-night, ladies; good-night,
sweet ladies; good-night, good-night. [*Exit.*
*King.* Follow her close; give her good
watch, I pray you.        [*Exit* HORATIO.
O, this is the poison of deep grief; it springs
All from her father's death. O Gertrude,
Gertrude,
When sorrows come, they come not single
spies,
But in battalias! First, her father slain:
Next, your son gone; and he most violent
author
Of his own just remove: the people muddied,
Thick and unwholesome in their thoughts
and whispers
For good Polonius' death; and we have done
but greenly
In hugger-mugger to inter him: poor Ophelia
Divided from herself and her fair judgment,
Without the which we are pictures, or mere
beasts:
Last, and as much containing as all these,
Her brother is in secret come from France;
Feeds on his wonder, keeps himself in clouds,
And wants not buzzers to infect his ear
With pestilent speeches of his father's death;
Wherein necessity, of matter beggar'd,
Will nothing stick our person to arraign
In ear and ear. O my dear Gertrude, this,
Like to a murdering piece; in many places
Gives me superfluous death. [*A noise within.*
*Queen.*            Alack, what noise is this?
*King.* Where are my Switzers? let them
guard the door.

### *Enter a* Gentleman.

What is the matter?
*Gent.*                Save yourself, my lord:
The ocean, overpeering of his list,
Eats not the flats with more impetuous haste
Than young Laertes, in a riotous head,
O'erbears your officers. The rabble call him
lord;
And, as the world were now but to begin,
Antiquity forgot, custom not known,

The ratifiers and props of every word,
They cry, *Choose we; Laertes shall be king!*
Caps, hands, and tongues applaud it to the
    clouds,
*Laertes shall be king, Laertes king!*
    *Queen.* How cheerfully on the false trail
    they cry!
O, this is counter, you false Danish dogs!
    *King.* The doors are broke. [*Noise within.*

*Enter* LAERTES, *armed;* Danes *following.*

    *Laer.* Where is this king?—Sirs, stand you
    all without.
    *Danes.* No, let's come in.
    *Laer.*           I pray you, give me leave.
    *Danes.* We will, we will.
          [*They retire without the door.*
    *Laer.* I thank you:—keep the door.—O
    thou vile king,
Give me my father!
    *Queen.*          Calmly, good Laertes.
    *Laer.* That drop of blood that's calm pro-
    claims me bastard;
Cries cuckold to my father; brands the harlot
Even here, between the chaste unsmirched
    brow
Of my true mother.
    *King.* What is the cause, Laertes,
That thy rebellion looks so giant-like?—
Let him go, Gertrude; do not fear our per-
    son:
There's such divinity doth hedge a king,
That treason can but peep to what it would,
Acts little of his will.—Tell me, Laertes,
Why thou art thus incens'd.—Let him go,
    Gertrude:—
Speak, man.
    *Laer.* Where is my father?
    *King.*          Dead.
    *Queen.*          But not by him
    *King.* Let him demand his fill. [gled with:
    *Laer.* How came he dead? I'll not be jug-
To hell, allegiance! vows, to the blackest
    devil!
Conscience and grace, to the profoundest pit!
I dare damnation:—to this point I stand,—
That both the worlds I give to negligence,
Let come what comes; only I'll be reveng'd
Most throughly for my father.
    *King.*          Who shall stay you?
    *Laer.* My will, not all the world:
And for my means, I'll husband them so well,
They shall go far with little.
    *King.*          Good Laertes,
If you desire to know the certainty
Of your dear father's death, is 't writ in your
    revenge          [and foe,
That, sweepstake, you will draw both friend
Winner and loser?
    *Laer.* None but his enemies.
    *King.*          Will you know them, then?
    *Laer.* To his good friends thus wide I'll
    ope my arms;

And, like the kind life-rendering pelican,
Repast them with my blood.
    *King.*          Why, now you speak
Like a good child and a true gentleman.
That I am guiltless of your father's death,
And am most sensible in grief for it,
It shall as level to your judgment pierce
As day does to your eye.
    *Danes.* [*Within.*]      Let her come in.
    *Laer.* How now! what noise is that?

*Re-enter* OPHELIA, *fantastically dressed*
    *with straws and flowers.*

O heat, dry up my brains! tears seven times
    salt,
Burn out the sense and virtue of mine eye!—
By heaven, thy madness shall be paid by
    weight,
Till our scale turn the beam. O rose of May!
Dear maid, kind sister, sweet Ophelia!—
O heavens! is 't possible a young maid's wits
Should be as mortal as an old man's life?
Nature is fine in love; and where 'tis fine
It sends some precious instance of itself
After the thing it loves.
    *Oph.*

    They bore him barefac'd on the bier; [*Sings.*
    Hey no nonny, nonny, hey nonny;
    And on his grave rain'd many a tear,—

Fare you well, my dove!
    *Laer.* Hadst thou thy wits, and didst per-
    suade revenge,
It could not move thus.
    *Oph.* You must sing, *Down, a-down, an
you call him a-down-a.* O, how the wheel becomes it! It is the false steward, that stole his
master's daughter.
    *Laer.* This nothing's more than matter.
    *Oph.* There's rosemary, that's for remem-
brance; pray, love, remember: and there is
pansies, that's for thoughts.
    *Laer.* A document is madness,—thoughts
and remembrance fitted.
    *Oph.* There's fennel for you, and colum-
bines:—there's rue for you; and here's some
for me:—we may call it herb-grace o' Sundays:—O, you must wear your rue with a
difference.—There's a daisy:—I would give
you some violets, but they withered all when
my father died:—they say, he made a good
end,—

    For bonny sweet Robin is all my joy,— [*Sings.*

    *Laer.* Thought and affliction, passion, hell
    itself,
She turns to favour and to prettiness.
    *Oph.*

    And will he not come again?      [*Sings*
    And will he not come again?
      No, no, he is dead,
      Go to thy death-bed,
    He never will come again.

His beard was as white as snow
All flaxen was his poll:
    He is gone, he is gone,
    And we cast away moan:
God ha' mercy on his soul!

And of all Christian souls, I pray God.—God
b' wi' ye.                   [*Exit.*

  *Laer.* Do you see this, O God?   [*grief,*

  *King.* Laertes, I must commune with your
Or you deny me right. Go but apart,
Make choice of whom your wisest friends
    you will,             [and me:
And they shall hear and judge 'twixt you
If by direct or by collateral hand
They find us touch'd, we will our kingdom
    give,
Our crown, our life, and all that we call ours,
To you in satisfaction; but if not,
Be you content to lend your patience to us,
And we shall jointly labour with your soul
To give it due content.

  *Laer.*             Let this be so;
His means of death, his obscure burial,—
No trophy, sword, nor hatchment o'er his
    bones,
No noble rite nor formal ostentation,—
Cry to be heard, as 'twere from heaven to
    earth,
That I must call 't in question.

  *King.*            So you shall;
And where the offence is, let the great axe
    fall.
I pray you, go with me.       [*Exeunt.*

### SCENE VI.—*Another Room in the Castle.*

#### Enter HORATIO *and a* Servant.

  *Hor.* What are they that would speak with
me?

  *Serv.* Sailors, sir: they say they have letters for you.

  *Hor.* Let them come in.—   [*Exit* Servant.
I do not know from what part of the world
I should be greeted, if not from Lord Hamlet.

#### Enter Sailors.

  1 *Sail.* God bless you, sir.

  *Hor.* Let him bless thee too.

  1 *Sail.* He shall, sir, an 't please him.
There's a letter for you, sir; it comes from
the ambassador that was bound for England;
if your name be Horatio, as I am let to know
it is.

  *Hor.* [*Reads.*] *Horatio, when thou shalt
have overlooked this, give these fellows some
means to the king: they have letters for him.
Ere we were two days old at sea, a pirate of
very warlike appointment gave us chase.
Finding ourselves too slow of sail, we put on
a compelled valour; and in the grapple I
boarded them: on the instant they got clear
of our ship; so I alone became their prisoner.
They have dealt with me like thieves of
mercy: but they knew what they did; I am*

*to do a good turn for them. Let the king
have the letters I have sent; and repair thou
to me with as much haste as thou wouldst
fly death. I have words to speak in thine ear
will make thee dumb; yet are they much too
light for the bore of the matter. These good
fellows will bring thee where I am. Rosencrantz and Guildenstern hold their course for
England: of them I have much to tell thee.
Farewell. He that thou knowest thine,*
                      HAMLET.

Come, I will give you way for these your
    letters;
And do 't the speedier, that you may direct
    me
To him from whom you brought them.
                      [*Exeunt.*

### SCENE VII.—*Another Room in the Castle.*

#### Enter KING *and* LAERTES.

  *King.* Now must your conscience my ac-
    quittance seal,
And you must put me in your heart for
    friend,
Sith you have heard, and with a knowing ear,
That he which hath your noble father slain
Pursu'd my life.

  *Laer.*         It well appears:—but tell me
Why you proceeded not against these feats,
So crimeful and so capital in nature,
As by your safety, wisdom, all things else,
You mainly were stirr'd up.

  *King.*       O, for two special reasons;
Which may to you, perhaps, seem much un-
    sinew'd,
But yet to me they are strong. The queen his
    mother
Lives almost by his looks; and for myself,—
My virtue or my plague, be it either which,—
She's so conjunctive to my life and soul,
That, as the star moves not but in his sphere,
I could not but by her. The other motive,
Why to a public count I might not go,
Is the great love the general gender bear him;
Who, dipping all his faults in their affection,
Would, like the spring that turneth wood to
    stone,
Convert his gyves to graces; so that my
    arrows,
Too slightly timber'd for so loud a wind,
Would have reverted to my bow again,
And not where I had aim'd them.

  *Laer.* And so have I a noble father lost;
A sister driven into desperate terms,—
Whose worth, if praises may go back again,
Stood challenger on mount of all the age
For her perfections:—but my revenge will
    come.

  *King.* Break not your sleeps for that: you
    must not think
That we are made of stuff so flat and dull
That we can let our beard be shook with
    danger,

And think it pastime. You shortly shall hear
more:
I lov'd your father, and we love ourself;
And that, I hope, will teach you to
imagine,—

*Enter a* Messenger.

How now! what news?

*Mess.* Letters, my lord, from Hamlet:
This to your majesty; this to the queen.

*King.* From Hamlet! Who brought them?

*Mess.* Sailors, my lord, they say; I saw
them not:
They were given me by Claudio,—he receiv'd
them
Of him that brought them.

*King.* Laertes, you shall hear them.—
Leave us. [*Exit* Messenger.
[*Reads.*] *High and mighty,—You 'shall
know I am set naked on your kingdom. To-
morrow shall I beg leave to see your kingly
eyes: when I shall, first asking your pardon
thereunto, recount the occasions of my sudden and more strange return.* HAMLET.
What should this mean? Are all the rest come
back?
Or is it some abuse, and no such thing?

*Laer.* Know you the hand?

*King.* 'Tis Hamlet's character:—*Naked,—*
And in a postscript here, he says, *alone.*
Can you advise me?

*Laer.* I am lost in it, my lord. But let him
come;
It warms the very sickness in my heart,
That I shall live, and tell him to his teeth,
*Thus diddest thou.*

*King.* If it be so, Laertes,—
As how should it be so? how otherwise?—
Will you be rul'd by me?

*Laer.* Ay, my lord;
So you will not o'errule me to a peace.

*King.* To thine own peace. If he be now
return'd,—
As checking at his voyage, and that he means
No more to undertake it,—I will work him
To an exploit, now ripe in my device,
Under the which he shall not choose but fall:
And for his death no wind of blame shall
breathe;
But even his mother shall uncharge the prac-
tice,
And call it accident.

*Laer.* My lord, I will be rul'd;
The rather if you could devise it so
That I might be the organ.

*King.* It falls right.
You have been talk'd of since your travel
much,
And that in Hamlet's hearing, for a quality
Wherein they say you shine: your sum of
parts
Did not together pluck such envy from him
As did that one; and that, in my regard,

Of the unworthiest siege.

*Laer.* What part is that, my lord?

*King.* A very riband in the cap of youth,
Yet needful too; for youth no less becomes
The light and careless livery that it wears
Than settled age his sables and his weeds,
Importing health and graveness.—Two
months since,
Here was a gentleman of Normandy,—
I've seen myself, and serv'd against, the
French,
And they can well on horseback: but this
gallant
Had witchcraft in 't; he grew unto his seat;
And to such wondrous doing brought his
horse,
As he had been incorps'd and demi-natur'd
With the brave beast: so far he topp'd my
thought,
That I, in forgery of shapes and tricks,
Come short of what he did.

*Laer.* A Norman was 't?

*King.* A Norman.

*Laer.* Upon my life, Lamond.

*King.* The very same.

*Laer.* I know him well: he is the brooch,
indeed,
And gem of all the nation.

*King.* He made confession of you;
And gave you such a masterly report
For art and exercise in your defence,
And for your rapier most especially,
That he cried out, 'twould be a sight indeed
If one could match you: the scrimers of
their nation,
He swore, had neither motion, guard, nor
eye,
If you oppos'd them. Sir, this report of his
Did Hamlet so envenom with his envy,
That he could nothing do but wish and beg
Your sudden coming o'er, to play with him.
Now, out of this,—

*Laer.* What out of this, my lord?

*King.* Laertes, was your father dear to
you?
Or are you like the painting of a sorrow,
A face without a heart?

*Laer.* Why ask you this?

*King.* Not that I think you did not love
your father;
But that I know love is begun by time;
And that I see, in passages of proof,
Time qualifies the spark and fire of it.
There lives within the very flame of love
A kind of wick or snuff that will abate it;
And nothing is at a like goodness still;
For goodness, growing to a pleurisy,
Dies in his own too much: that we would do
We should do when we would; for this
*would* changes,
And hath abatements and delays as many
As there are tongues, are hands, are acci-
dents;

And then this *should* is like a spendthrift sigh
That hurts by easing. But to the quick o' the
    ulcer:—
Hamlet comes back: what would you under-
    take
To show yourself your father's son in deed
More than in words?
  *Laer.*         To cut his throat i' the church.
  *King.* No place, indeed, should murder
    sanctuarize;
Revenge should have no bounds. But, good
    Laertes,
Will you do this, keep close within your
    chamber.
Hamlet return'd shall know you are come
    home:
We'll put on those shall praise your excel-
    lence,
And set a double varnish on the fame
The Frenchman gave you; bring you, in fine,
    together,
And wager on your heads: he, being remiss,
Most generous, and free from all contriving,
Will not peruse the foils; so that, with ease,
Or with a little shuffling, you may choose
A sword unbated, and, in a pass of practice,
Requite him for your father.
  *Laer.*         I will do 't:
And, for that purpose, I'll anoint my sword.
I bought an unction of a mountebank,
So mortal that but dip a knife in it,
Where it draws blood no cataplasm so rare,
Collected from all simples that have virtue
Under the moon, can save the thing from
    death
That is but scratch'd withal: I'll touch my
    point
With this contagion, that, if I gall him
    slightly,
It may be death.
  *King.*         Let 's further think of this;
Weigh what convenience both of time and
    means
May fit us to our shape: if this should fail,
And that our drift look through our bad
    performance,
'Twere better not assay'd: therefore this
    project
Should have a back or second, that might
    hold
If this should blast in proof. Soft! let me
    see:—
We'll make a solemn wager on your cun-
    nings,—
I ha 't:
When in your motion you are hot and dry,—
As make your bouts more violent to that
    end,—
And that he calls for drink I'll have prepar'd
    him
A chalice for the nonce; whereon but sipping
If he by chance escape your venom'd stuck
Our purpose may hold there.

*Enter* QUEEN.

               How now, sweet queen!
  *Queen.* One woe doth tread upon another's
    heel,                  [Laertes.
So fast they follow:—your sister's drown'd,
  *Laer.* Drown'd! O, where?
  *Queen.* There is a willow grows aslant a
    brook,
That shows his hoar leaves in the glassy
    stream;
There with fantastic garlands did she come
Of crowflowers, nettles, daisies, and long
    purples,
That liberal shepherds give a grosser name,
But our cold maids do dead men's fingers call
    them.
There, on the pendant boughs her coronet
    weeds
Clambering to hang, an envious sliver broke;
When down her weedy trophies and herself
Fell in the weeping brook. Her clothes spread
    wide;
And, mermaid-like, awhile they bore her up:
Which time she chanted snatches of old
    tunes;
As one incapable of her own distress,
Or like a creature native and indu'd
Unto that element: but long it could not be
Till that her garments, heavy with their
    drink,
Pull'd the poor wretch from her melodious
    lay
To muddy death.
  *Laer.*         Alas, then, she is drown'd?
  *Queen.* Drown'd, drown'd.       [Ophelia,
  *Laer.* Too much of water hast thou, poor
And therefore I forbid my tears: but yet
It is our trick; nature her custom holds,
Let shame say what it will: when these are
    gone,
The woman will be out.—Adieu, my lord:
I have a speech of fire, that fain would blaze,
But that this folly douts it.       [*Exit.*
  *King.*         Let's follow, Gertrude;
How much I had to do to calm his rage!
Now fear I this will give it start again;
Therefore let's follow.         [*Exeunt.*

## ACT V.

### SCENE I.—*A Churchyard.*

*Enter two* Clowns *with spades, &c.*

  *1 Clo.* Is she to be buried in Christian
burial that wilfully seeks her own salvation?
  *2 Clo.* I tell thee she is; and therefore
make her grave straight: the crowner hath sat
on her, and finds it Christian burial.
  *1 Clo.* How can that be, unless she
drowned herself in her own defence?
  *2 Clo.* Why, 'tis found so.
  *1 Clo.* It must be *se offendendo;* it cannot
be else. For here lies the point: if I drown

myself wittingly, it argues an act: and an act hath three branches; it is to act, to do, and to perform: argal, she drowned herself wittingly.

*2 Clo.* Nay, but hear you, goodman delver,—

*1 Clo.* Give me leave. Here lies the water; good: here stands the man; good: if the man go to this water and drown himself, it is, will he, nill he, he goes,—mark you that: but if the water come to him and drown him, he drowns not himself: argal, he that is not guilty of his own death shortens not his own life.

*2 Clo.* But is this law?

*1 Clo.* Ay, marry, is 't; crowner's quest law.

*2 Clo.* Will you ha' the truth on 't? If this had not been a gentlewoman she should have been buried out of Christian burial.

*1 Clo.* Why, there thou say'st: and the more pity that great folk should have countenance in this world to drown or hang themselves more than their even Christian.—Come, my spade. There is no ancient gentlemen but gardeners, ditchers, and gravemakers: they hold up Adam's profession.

*2 Clo.* Was he a gentleman?

*1 Clo.* He was the first that ever bore arms.

*2 Clo.* Why, he had none.

*1 Clo.* What, art a heathen? How dost thou understand the Scripture? The Scripture says, Adam digged: could he dig without arms? I'll put another question to thee: if thou answerest me not to the purpose, confess thyself,—

*2 Clo.* Go to.

*1 Clo.* What is he that builds stronger than either the mason, the shipwright, or the carpenter?

*2 Clo.* The gallows-maker; for that frame outlives a thousand tenants.

*1 Clo.* I like thy wit well, in good faith: the gallows does well; but how does it well? it does well to those that do ill: now thou dost ill to say the gallows is built stronger than the church: argal, the gallows may do well to thee. To 't again, come.

*2 Clo.* Who builds stronger than a mason, a shipwright, or a carpenter?

*1 Clo.* Ay, tell me that, and unyoke.

*2 Clo.* Marry, now I can tell.

*1 Clo.* To 't.

*2 Clo.* Mass, I cannot tell.

*Enter* HAMLET *and* HORATIO, *at a distance.*

*1 Clo.* Cudgel thy brains no more about it, for your dull ass will not mend his pace with beating; and when you are asked this question next, say a grave-maker; the houses that he makes last till doomsday. Go, get thee to

Yaughan; fetch me a stoup of liquor.

[*Exit* Second Clown.

In youth, when I did love, did love, [*Ligs and sings.*
  Methought it was very sweet,
To contract, O, the time, for, ah, my behove,
  O, methought there was nothing meet.

*Ham.* Has this fellow no feeling of his business, that he sings at grave-making?

*Hor.* Custom hath made it in him a property of easiness.

*Ham.* 'Tis e'en so: the hand of little employment hath the daintier sense.

*1 Clo.*

  But age, with his stealing steps,  [*Sings.*
    Hath claw'd me in his clutch,
  And hath shipp'd me intil the land,
    As if I had never been such.

[*Throws up a skull.*

*Ham.* That skull had a tongue in it, and could sing once: how the knave jowls it to the ground, as if it were Cain's jawbone, that did the first murder! This might be the pate of a politician, which this ass now o'erreaches; one that would circumvent God, might it not?

*Hor.* It might, my lord.

*Ham.* Or of a courtier; which could say, *Good-morrow, sweet lord! How dost thou, good lord?* This might be my lord such-a-one, that praised my lord such-a-one's horse, when he meant to beg it,—might it not?

*Hor.* Ay, my lord.

*Ham.* Why, e'en so: and now my Lady Worm's; chapless, and knocked about the mazard with a sexton's spade: here's fine revolution, an we had the trick to see't. Did these bones cost no more the breeding but to play at loggats with 'em? mine ache to think on 't.

*1 Clo.*

  A pick-axe and a spade, a spade,  [*Sings*
    For and a shrouding sheet:
  O, a pit of clay for to be made
    For such a guest is meet.

[*Throws up another skull.*

*Ham.* There's another: why may not that be the skull of a lawyer? Where be his quiddits now, his quillets, his cases, his tenures, and his tricks? why does he suffer this rude knave now to knock him about the sconce with a dirty shovel, and will not tell him of his action of battery? Hum! This fellow might be in 's time a great buyer of land, with his statutes, his recognizances, his fines, his double vouchers, his recoveries: is this the fine of his fines, and the recovery of his recoveries, to have his fine pate full of dirt? will his vouchers vouch him no more of his purchases, and double ones too, than the length and breadth of a pair of indentures? The very conveyances of his lands will hardly lie in this box; and must the inheritor himself have no more, ha?

*Hor.* Not a jot more, my lord.

*Ham.* Is not parchment made of sheep-skins?

*Hor.* Ay, my lord, and of calf-skins too.

*Ham.* They are sheep and calves which seek out assurance in that. I will speak to this fellow.—Whose grave's this, sir?

*1 Clo.* Mine, sir.—

　　O, a pit of clay for to be made　[*Sings.*
　　For such a guest is meet.

*Ham.* I think it be thine indeed; for thou liest in 't.

*1 Clo.* You lie out on 't, sir, and therefore it is not yours: for my part, I do not lie in 't, and yet it is mine.

*Ham.* Thou does lie in 't, to be in 't, and say it is thine: 'tis for the dead, not for the quick; therefore thou liest.

*1 Clo.* 'Tis a quick lie, sir; 't will away again from me to you.

*Ham.* What man dost thou dig it for?

*1 Clo.* For no man, sir.

*Ham.* What woman, then?

*1 Clo.* For none, neither.

*Ham.* Who is to be buried in 't?

*1 Clo.* One that was a woman, sir; but, rest her soul, she's dead.

*Ham.* How absolute the knave is! we must speak by the card, or equivocation will undo us. By the Lord, Horatio, these three years I have taken note of it; the age is grown so picked that the toe of the peasant comes so near the heel of the courtier, he galls his kibe.—How long hast thou been a grave-maker?

*1 Clo.* Of all the days i' the year, I came to 't that day that our last King Hamlet o'er-came Fortinbras.

*Ham.* How long is that since?

*1 Clo.* Cannot you tell that? every fool can tell that: it was the very day that young Hamlet was born,—he that is mad, and sent into England.

*Ham.* Ay, marry, why was he sent into England?

*1 Clo.* Why, because he was mad: he shall recover his wits there; or, if he do not, it's no great matter there.

*Ham.* Why?

*1 Clo.* 'Twill not be seen in him there; there the men are as mad as he.

*Ham.* How came he mad?

*1 Clo.* Very strangely, they say.

*Ham.* How strangely?

*1 Clo.* Faith, e'en with losing his wits.

*Ham.* Upon what ground?

*1 Clo.* Why, here in Denmark: I have been sexton here, man and boy, thirty years.

*Ham.* How long will a man lie i' the earth ere he rot?

*1 Clo.* Faith, if he be not rotten before he die,—as we have many pocky corses now-a-days, that will scarce hold the laying,—he will last you some eight year or nine year: a tanner will last you nine year.

*Ham.* Why he more than another?

*1 Clo.* Why, sir, his hide is so tanned with his trade that he will keep out water a great while; and your water is a sore decayer of your whoreson dead body. Here's a skull now; this skull has lain in the earth three-and-twenty years.

*Ham.* Whose was it?

*1 Clo.* A whoreson mad fellow's it was: whose do you think it was?

*Ham.* Nay, I know not.

*1 Clo.* A pestilence on him for a mad rogue! 'a poured a flagon of Rhenish on my head once. This same skull, sir, was Yorick's skull, the king's jester.

*Ham.* This?

*1 Clo.* E'en that.

*Ham.* Let me see. [*Takes the skull.*]—Alas, poor Yorick!—I knew him, Horatio; a fellow of infinite jest, of most excellent fancy: he hath borne me on his back a thousand times and now, how abhorred in my imagination it is! my gorge rises at it. Here hung those lips that I have kissed I know not how oft. Where be your gibes now? your gambols? your songs? your flashes of merriment, that were wont to set the table on a roar? Not one now, to mock your own grinning? quite chap-fallen? Now get you to my lady's chamber, and tell her, let her paint an inch thick, to this favour she must come; make her laugh at that.—Pr'ythee, Horatio, tell me one thing.

*Hor.* What's that, my lord?

*Ham.* Dost thou think Alexander looked o' this fashion i' the earth?

*Hor.* E'en so.

*Ham.* And smelt so? pah!

　　　　　　　　[*Throws down the skull.*

*Hor.* E'en so, my lord.

*Ham.* To what base uses we may return, Horatio! Why not imagination trace the noble dust of Alexander till he find it stopping a bung-hole?

*Hor.* 'Twere to consider too curiously to consider so.

*Ham.* No, faith, not a jot; but to follow him thither with modesty enough, and likelihood to lead it: as thus; Alexander died, Alexander was buried, Alexander returneth into dust; the dust is earth; of earth we make loam; and why of that loam whereto he was converted might they not stop a beer-barrel?

Imperious Cæsar, dead and turn'd to clay,
Might stop a hole to keep the wind away:
O, that that earth which kept the world in awe

Should patch a wall to expel the winter's
flaw!—
But soft! but soft! aside.—Here comes the
king.

*Enter* Priests, *&c., in procession; the Corpse
of* OPHELIA, LAERTES *and Mourners following;* KING, QUEEN, *their* Trains, &c.

The queen, the courtiers: who is that they
follow?
And with such maimed rites? This doth be-
token
The corse they follow did with desperate
hand
Fordo its own life: 'twas of some estate.
Couch we awhile and mark.
      *[Retiring with* HOR.
 *Laer.* What ceremony else?
 *Ham.*      That is Laertes,
A very noble youth: mark.
 *Laer.* What ceremony else?
 1 *Priest.* Her obsequies have been as far
         enlarg'd  [ful;
As we have warrantise: her death was doubt-
And, but that great command o'ersways the
order,
She should in ground unsanctified have lodg'd
Till the last trumpet; for charitable prayers,
Shards, flints, and pebbles, should be thrown
on her,
Yet here she is allowed her virgin rites,
Her maiden strewments, and the bringing
home
Of bell and burial.
 *Laer.* Must there no more be done?
 1 *Priest.*     No more be done:
We should profane the service of the dead
To sing a *requiem,* and such rest to her
As to peace-parted souls.
 *Laer.*    Lay her i' the earth,—
And from her fair and unpolluted flesh
May violets spring!—I tell thee, churlish
priest,
A ministering angel shall my sister be
When thou liest howling.
 *Ham.*    What, the fair Ophelia!
 *Queen.* Sweets to the sweet: farewell!
      *[Scattering flowers.*
I hop'd thou shouldst have been my Hamlet's
wife;      [sweet maid,
I thought thy bride-bed to have deck'd,
And not have strew'd thy grave.
 *Laer.*     O, treble woe
Fall ten times treble on that cursed head
Whose wicked deed thy most ingenious sense
Depriv'd thee of!—Hold off the earth awhile,
Till I have caught her once more in mine
arms:
    *[Leaps into the grave.*
Now pile your dust upon the quick and dead,
Till of this flat a mountain you have made,
To o'er-top old Pelion or the skyish head
Of blue Olympus.

 *Ham.* [*Advancing.*] What is he whose
     grief
Bears such an emphasis? whose phrase of
sorrow     [them stand
Conjures the wandering stars, and makes
Like wonder-wounded hearers? this is I,
Hamlet the Dane.   [*Leaps into the grave.*
 *Laer.*    'The devil take thy soul!
      *[Grappling with him.*
 *Ham.* Thou pray'st not well.
I pr'ythee, take thy fingers from my throat;
For, though I am not splenitive and rash,
Yet have I in me something dangerous,
Which let thy wiseness fear: away thy hand.
 *King.* Pluck them asunder.
 *Queen.*     Hamlet! Hamlet!
 *All.* Gentlemen,—
 *Hor.*    Good my lord, be quiet.
  [*The* Attendants *part them, and they
    come out of the grave.*
 *Ham.* Why, I will fight with him upon
  this theme
Until my eyelids will no longer wag.
 *Queen.* O my son, what theme?
 *Ham.* I lov'd Ophelia; forty thousand
  brothers
Could not, with all their quantity of love,
Make up my sum.—What wilt thou do for
her?
 *King.* O, he is mad, Laertes.
 *Queen.* For love of God, forbear him.
 *Ham.* 'Swounds, show me what thou'lt
  do:    [woul't tear thyself?
Woul't weep? woul't fight? woul't fast?
Woul't drink up eisel? eat a crocodile?
I'll do't.—Dost thou come here to whine?
To outface me with leaping in her grave?
Be buried quick with her, and so will I:
And, if thou prate of mountains, let them
throw
Millions of acres on us, till our ground,
Singeing his pate against the burning zone,
Make Ossa like a wart! Nay, an thou'lt
mouth,
I'll rant as well as thou.
 *Queen.*    This is mere madness:
And thus awhile the fit will work on him;
Anon, as patient as the female dove,
When that her golden couplets are disclos'd,
His silence will sit drooping.
 *Ham.*     Hear you, sir;
What is the reason that you use me thus?
I lov'd you ever: but it is no matter;
Let Hercules himself do what he may,
The cat will mew, and dog will have his day.
         [*Exit.*
 *King.* I pray thee, good Horatio, wait
  upon him.—   [*Exit* HORATIO.
Strengthen your patience in our last night's
speech:     [*To* LAERTES.
We'll put the matter to the present push.—
Good Gertrude, set some watch over your
son.—

This grave shall have a living monument;
An hour of quiet shortly shall we see;
Till then, in patience our proceeding be.

[*Exeunt.*

### SCENE II.—*A Hall in the Castle.*

*Enter* HAMLET *and* HORATIO.

*Ham.* So much for this, sir: now let me
see the other;
You do remember all the circumstance?
  *Hor.* Remember it, my lord!  [of fighting
  *Ham.* Sir, in my heart there was a kind
That would not let me sleep: methought I
  ¹ay
Worse than the mutines in the bilboes.
  Rashly,
And prais'd be rashness for it,—let us know,
Our indiscretion sometimes serves us well,
When our deep plots do fail: and that should
  teach us
There's a divinity that shapes our ends,
Rough-hew them how we will.
  *Hor.*        That is most certain.
  *Ham.* Up from my cabin,
My sea-gown scarf'd about me, in the dark
Grop'd I to find out them: had my desire;
Finger'd their packet; and, in fine, withdrew
To mine own room again: making so bold,
My fears forgetting manners, to unseal
Their grand commission; where I found,
  Horatio,
O royal knavery! an exact command,—
Larded with many several sorts of reasons,
Importing Denmark's health and England's
  too,
With, ho! such bugs and goblins in my life,—
That, on the supervise, no leisure bated,
No, not to stay the grinding of the axe,
My head should be struck off.
  *Hor.*            Is't possible?
  *Ham.* Here's the commission: read it at
  more leisure.
But wilt thou hear me how I did proceed?
  *Hor.* I beseech you.       [villanies.—
  *Ham.* Being thus benetted round with
Ere I could make a prologue to my brains,
They had begun the play,—I sat me down;
Devis'd a new commission; wrote it fair:
I once did hold it, as our statists do,
A baseness to write fair, and labour'd much
How to forget that learning; but, sir, now
It did me yeoman's service. Wilt thou know
The effect of what I wrote?
  *Hor.*        Ay, good my lord.
  *Ham.* An earnest conjuration from the
  king,—
As England was his faithful tributary;
As love between them like the palm might
  flourish;       [wear
As peace should still her wheaten garland
And stand a comma 'tween their amities;
And many such like as's of great charge,—

That, on the view and kr.ow of these con-
  tents,
Without debatement further, more or less,
He should the bearers put to sudden death,
Not shriving-time allow'd.
  *Hor.*        How was this seal'd?
  *Ham.* Why, even in that was heaven or-
  dinant.
I had my father's signet in my purse,
Which was the model of that Danish seal:
Folded the writ up in form of the other;
Subscrib'd it; gave't the impression; plac'd it
  safely,       [day
The changeling never known. Now, the next
Was our sea-fight; and what to this was se-
  quent
Thou know'st already.       [to't.
  *Hor.* So Guildenstern and Rosencrantz go
  *Ham.* Why, man, they did make love to
  this employment;       [feat
They are not near my conscience; their de-
Does by their own insinuation grow:
'Tis dangerous when the baser nature comes
Between the pass and fell incensed points
Of mighty opposites.
  *Hor.*        Why, what a king is this!
  *Ham.* Does it not, think'st thee, stand me
  now upon,—        [mother;
He that hath kill'd my king and whor'd my
Popp'd in between the election and my
  hopes;
Thrown out his angle for my proper life,
And with such cozenage,—is't not perfect
  conscience        [damn'd,
To quit him with this arm? and is't not to be
To let this canker of our nature come
In further evil?        [from England
  *Hor.* It must be shortly known to him
What is the issue of the business there.
  *Ham.* It will be short: the interim is mine;
And a man's life's no more than to say One.
But I am very sorry, good Horatio,
That to Laertes I forgot myself;
For by the image of my cause I see
The portraiture of his: I'll court his favours;
But, sure, the bravery of his grief did put me
Into a towering passion.
  *Hor.*        Peace; who comes here?

*Enter* OSRIC.

  *Osr.* Your lordship is right welcome back
to Denmark.
  *Ham.* I humbly thank you, sir.—Dost
know this water-fly?
  *Hor.* No, my good lord.
  *Ham.* Thy state is the more gracious; for
'tis a vice to know him. He hath much land,
and fertile: let a beast be lord of beasts, and
his crib shall stand at the king's mess: 'tis a
chough; but, as I say, spacious in the possession of dirt.
  *Osr.* Sweet lord, if your lordship were at
  leisure,

I should impart a thing to you from his majesty.

*Ham.* I will receive it with all diligence of spirit.

Put your bonnet to his right use; 'tis for the head.

*Osr.* I thank your lordship, 'tis very hot.

*Ham.* No, believe me, 'tis very cold; the wind is northerly.

*Osr.* It is indifferent cold, my lord, indeed.

*Ham.* Methinks it is very sultry and hot for my complexion.

*Osr.* Exceedingly, my lord; it is very sultry,—as 't were,—I cannot tell how.—But, my lord, his majesty bade me signify to you that he has laid a great wager on your head. Sir, this is the matter,—

*Ham.* I beseech you, remember,—

[HAMLET *moves him to put on his hat.*

*Osr.* Nay, in good faith; for mine ease, in good faith. Sir, here is newly come to court Laertes; believe me, an absolute gentleman, full of most excellent differences, of very soft society and great showing: indeed, to speak feelingly of him, he is the card or calendar of gentry, for you shall find in him the continent of what part a gentleman would see.

*Ham.* Sir, his definement suffers no perdition in you;—though, I know, to divide him inventorially would dizzy the arithmetic of memory, and it but yaw neither, in respect of his quick sail. But, in the verity of extolment, I take him to be a soul of great article; and his infusion of such dearth and rareness as, to make true diction of him, his semblable is his mirror; and who else would trace him, his umbrage, nothing more.  [of him.

*Osr.* Your lordship speaks most infallibly

*Ham.* The concernancy, sir? why do we wrap the gentleman in our more rawer breath?

*Osr.* Sir?

*Hor.* Is't not possible to understand in another tongue? You will do't sir, really.

*Ham.* What imports the nomination of this gentleman?

*Osr.* Of Laertes?

*Hor.* His purse is empty already; all's golden words are spent.

*Ham.* Of him, sir.

*Osr.* I know, you are not ignorant,—

*Ham.* I would you did, sir; yet, in faith, if you did, it would not much approve me.—Well, sir.

*Osr.* You are not ignorant of what excellence Laertes is,—

*Ham.* I dare not confess that, lest I should compare with him in excellence; but to know a man well were to know himself.

*Osr.* I mean, sir, for his weapon; but in the imputation laid on him by them, in his meed he's unfellowed.

*Ham.* What's his weapon?

*Osr.* Rapier and dagger.

*Ham.* That's two of his weapons: but, well.

*Osr.* The king, sir, hath wagered with him six Barbary horses: against the which he has imponed, as I take it, six French rapiers and poniards, with their assigns, as girdle, hangers, and so: three of the carriages, in faith, are very dear to fancy, very responsive to the hilts, most delicate carriages, and of very liberal conceit.

*Ham.* What call you the carriages?

*Hor.* I knew you must be edified by the margent ere you had done.

*Osr.* The carriages, sir, are the hangers.

*Ham.* The phrase would be more german to the matter if we could carry cannon by our sides: I would it might be hangers till then. But, on: six Barbary horses against six French swords, their assigns, and three liberal conceited carriages; that's the French bet against the Danish: why is this imponed, as you call it?

*Osr.* The king, sir, hath laid, that in a dozen passes between you and him he shall not exceed you three hits: he hath laid on twelve for nine; and it would come to immediate trial if your lordship would vouchsafe the answer.

*Ham.* How if I answer no?

*Osr.* I mean, my lord, the opposition of your person in trial.

*Ham.* Sir, I will walk here in the hall: if it please his majesty, it is the breathing time of day with me: let the foils be brought, the gentleman willing, and the king hold his purpose, I will win for him if I can; if not, I will gain nothing but my shame and the odd hits.

*Osr.* Shall I re-deliver you e'en so?

*Ham.* To this effect, sir; after what flourish your nature will.

*Osr.* I commend my duty to your lordship.

*Ham.* Yours, yours. [*Exit* OSRIC.]—He does well to commend it himself; there are no tongues else for's turn.

*Hor.* This lapwing runs away with the shell on his head.

*Ham.* He did comply with his dug before he sucked it. Thus has he,—and many more of the same bevy, that I know the drossy age dotes on,—only got the tune of the time, and outward habit of encounter; a kind of yesty collection, which carries them through and through the most fanned and winnowed opinions; and do but blow them to their trial, the bubbles are out.

*Enter a Lord.*

*Lord.* My lord, his majesty commended him to you by young Osric, who brings back to him that you attend him in the hall: he sends to know if your pleasure hold to play with Laertes, or that you will take longer time.

*Ham.* I am constant to my purposes; they follow the king's pleasure: if his fitness speaks, mine is ready; now or whensoever, provided I be so able as now. [*ing down.*

*Lord.* The king and queen and all are com—

*Ham.* In happy time.

*Lord.* The queen desires you to use some gentle entertainment to Laertes before you fall to play.

*Ham.* She well instructs me. [*Exit Lord.*

*Hor.* You will lose this wager, my lord.

*Ham.* I do not think so; since he went into France I have been in continual practice: I shall win at the odds. But thou wouldst not think how ill all's here about my heart: but it is no matter.

*Hor.* Nay, good my lord,—

*Ham.* It is but foolery; but it is such a kind of gain-giving as would perhaps trouble a woman.

*Hor.* If your mind dislike anything, obey it: I will forestall their repair hither, and say you are not fit.

*Ham.* Not a whit, we defy augury: there's a special providence in the fall of a sparrow. If it be now, 'tis not to come; if it be not to come, it will be now; if it be not now, yet it will come: the readiness is all: since no man has aught of what he leaves, what is't to leave betimes?

*Enter* KING, QUEEN, LAERTES, *Lords,* OSRIC, *and* Attendants *with foils, &c.*

*King.* Come, Hamlet, come, and take this hand from me.

[*The* KING *puts* LAERTES's *hand into* HAMLET's.

*Ham.* Give me your pardon, sir: I have done you wrong;
But pardon't as you are a gentleman.
This presence knows, and you must needs have heard,
How I am punish'd with sore distraction.
What I have done,                          [*tion*
That might your nature, honour, and excep-
Roughly awake, I here proclaim was mad-
ness.                                       [*Hamlet:*
Was't Hamlet wrong'd Laertes? Never
If Hamlet from himself be ta'en away,
And when he's not himself does wrong Laer-
tes,
Then Hamlet does it not, Hamlet denies it.
Who does it, then? His madness: if't be so,
Hamlet is of the fraction that is wrong'd;
His madness is poor Hamlet's enemy.
Sir, in this audience,
Let my disclaiming from a purpos'd evil
Free me so far in your most generous thoughts
That I have shot mine arrow o'er the house
And hurt my brother.

*Laer.*                          I am satisfied in nature,
Whose motive, in this case, should stir me most
To my revenge: but in my terms of honour
I stand aloof; and will no reconcilement
Till by some elder masters of known honour
I have a voice and precedent of peace
To keep my name ungor'd. But till that time
I do receive your offer'd love like love,
And will not wrong it.

*Ham.*                          I embrace it freely;
And will this brother's wager frankly play.—
Give us the foils; come on.

*Laer.*                          Come, one for me.

*Ham.* I'll be your foil, Laertes; in mine ignorance
Your skill shall, like a star in the darkest night,
Stick fiery off indeed.

*Laer.*                          You mock me, sir.

*Ham.* No, by this hand.

*King.* Give them the foils, young Osric. Cousin Hamlet,
You know the wager?

*Ham.*                          Very well, my lord;
Your grace hath laid the odds o' the weaker side.

*King.* I do not fear it; I have seen you both;
But since he's better'd, we have therefore odds.

*Laer.* This is too heavy, let me see another.

*Ham.* This likes me well. These foils have all a length? [*They prepare to play.*

*Osr.* Ay, my good lord.

*King.* Set me the stoups of wine upon that table,—
If Hamlet give the first or second hit,
Or quit in answer of the third exchange,
Let all the battlements their ordnance fire;
The king shall drink to Hamlet's better breath;
And in the cup an union shall he throw,
Richer than that which four successive kings
In Denmark's crown have worn. Give me the cups;
And let the kettle to the trumpet speak,
The trumpet to the cannoneer without,
The cannons to the heavens, the heavens to earth,
*Now the king drinks to Hamlet.*—Come, begin;—
And you, the judges, bear a wary eye.

*Ham.* Come on, sir.

*Laer.*                          Come, my lord.
[*They play.*

*Ham.*                          One.

*Laer.*                          No.

*Ham.*                          Judgment.

*Osr.* A hit, a very palpable hit.

*Laer.*                          Well;—again.

*King.* Stay, give me drink.—Hamlet, this pearl is thine;

Here's to thy health.—

[*Trumpets sound, and cannon shot
off within.*

Give him the cup.  [awhile.—

*Ham.* I'll play this bout first; set it by
Come.—Another hit; what say you?

[*They play.*

*Laer.* A touch, a touch, I do confess.

*King.* Our son shall win.

*Queen.* He's fat, and scant of breath.—
Here, Hamlet, take my napkin, rub thy
brows:

The queen carouses to thy fortune, Hamlet.

*Ham.* Good madam!

*King.*  Gertrude, do not drink.

*Queen.* I will my lord; I pray you, pardon
me.  [too late.

*King.* [*Aside.*] It is the poison'd cup; it is

*Ham.* I dare not drink yet, madam; by
and by.

*Queen.* Come, let me wipe thy face.

*Laer.* My lord, I'll hit him now.

*King.*  I do not think't.

*Laer.* [*Aside.*] And yet 'tis almost 'gainst
my conscience.

*Ham.* Come, for the third, Laertes: you
but dally;

I pray you, pass with your best violence:
I am afeard you make a wanton of me.

*Laer.* Say you so? come on.  [*They play.*

*Osr.* Nothing, neither way.

*Laer.* Have at you now!

[*LAER. wounds HAM.; then, in scuffling, they
change rapiers, and HAM. wounds
LAER.*

*King.* Part them; they are incens'd.

*Ham.* Nay, come, again. [*The QUEEN falls.*

*Osr.* Look to the queen there, ho!

*Hor.* They bleed on both sides.—How is it,
my lord?

*Osr.* How is't, Laertes?

*Laer.* Why, as a woodcock to my own
springe, Osric;

I am justly kill'd with mine own treachery.

*Ham.* How does the queen?

*King.* She swoons to see them bleed.

*Queen.* No, no, the drink, the drink,—O
my dear Hamlet,—

The drink, the drink!—I am poison'd. [*Dies.*

*Ham.* O villany!—Ho! let the door be
lock'd:

Treachery! seek it out.  [*LAERTES falls.*

*Laer.* It is here, Hamlet: Hamlet, thou art
slain;

No medicine in the world can do thee good;
In thee there is not half an hour of life;
The treacherous instrument is in thy hand,
Unbated and envenom'd: the foul practice
Hath turn'd itself on me; lo, here I lie,
Never to rise again: thy mother's poison'd:
I can no more:—the king, the king's to
blame.

*Ham.* The point envenom'd too!—

Then venom to thy work.  [*Stabs the KING.*

*Osr. and Lords.* Treason! treason!

*King.* O, yet defend me, friends; I am but
hurt.

*Ham.* Here, thou incestuous, murderous,
damned Dane,

Drink off this potion.—Is thy union here?
Follow my mother.  [*KING dies.*

*Laer.* He is justly serv'd;
It is a poison temper'd by himself.—
Exchange forgiveness with me, noble Ham-
let:  [thee,
Mine and my father's death come not upon
Nor thine on me!  [*Dies.*

*Ham.* Heaven make thee free of it! I
follow thee.—

I am dead, Horatio.—Wretched queen,
adieu!—  [chance,
You that look pale and tremble at this
That are but mutes or audience to this act,
Had I but time,—as this fell sergeant, death,
Is strict in his arrest,—O, I could tell you,—
But let it be.—Horatio, I am dead;
Thou liv'st; report me and my cause aright
To the unsatisfied.

*Hor.* Never believe it:
I am more an antique Roman than a Dane,—
Here's yet some liquor left.

*Ham.*  As thou'rt a man,
Give me the cup; let go; by heaven, I'll
have't.—

O good Horatio, what a wounded name,
Things standing thus unknown, shall live
behind me!

If thou didst ever hold me in thy heart,
Absent thee from felicity awhile,
And in this harsh world draw thy breath in
pain,

To tell my story.—

[*March afar off, and shot within.*

What warlike noise is this?

*Osr.* Young Fortinbras, with conquest
come from Poland,

To the ambassadors of England gives
This warlike volley.

*Ham.* O, I die, Horatio;
The potent poison quite o'er-crows my spirit:
I cannot live to hear the news from England;
But I do prophesy the election lights
On Fortinbras: he has my dying voice;
So tell him, with the occurrents, more and
less,

Which have solicited.—The rest is silence.

[*Dies.*

*Hor.* Now cracks a noble heart.—Good-
night, sweet prince,

And flights of angels sing thee to thy rest!
Why does the drum come hither?

[*March within.*

*Enter* FORTINBRAS, *the* English Ambassadors,
*and others.*

*Fort.* Where is this sight?

*Hor.*          What is it you would see?
If aught of woe or wonder, cease your search.

*Fort.*   This quarry cries on havoc.—O
     proud death,
What feast is toward in thine eternal cell,
That thou so many princes at a shot
So bloodily hast struck?

*1 Amb.*               The sight is dismal;
And our affairs from England come too late:
The ears are senseless that should give us
     hearing,
To tell him his commandment is fulfill'd,
That Rosencrantz and Guildenstern are dead:
Where should we have our thanks?

*Hor.*               Not from his mouth,
Had it the ability of life to thank you:
He never gave commandment for their death.
But since, so jump upon this bloody question,
You from the Polack wars, and you from
     England,
Are here arriv'd, give order that these bodies
High on a stage be placed to the view;
And let me speak to the yet unknowing world
How these things came about: so shall you
     hear
Of carnal, bloody, and unnatural acts;
Of accidental judgments, casual slaughters;
Of deaths put on by cunning and forc'd
     cause;
And, in this upshot, purposes mistook

Fall'n on the inventors' heads: all this can I
Truly deliver.

*Fort.*          Let us haste to hear it,
And call the noblest to the audience.
For me, with sorrow I embrace my fortune:
I have some rights of memory in this king-
     dom,
Which now to claim my vantage doth invite
     me.

*Hor.* Of that I shall have also cause to
     speak,
And from his mouth whose voice will draw
     on more:
But let this same be presently perform'd,
Even while men's minds are wild: lest more
     mischance
On plots and errors happen.

*Fort.*               Let four captains
Bear Hamlet like a soldier to the stage;
For he was likely, had he been put on,
To have prov'd most royally: and, for his
     passage,
The soldier's music and the rites of war
Speak loudly for him.—
Take up the bodies.—Such a sight as this
Becomes the field, but here shows much
     amiss.
Go, bid the soldiers shoot.   *[A dead march.*
   *[Exeunt, bearing off the dead bodies; after
     which a peal of ordnance is shot off.*

# OTHELLO, THE MOOR OF VENICE

## DRAMATIS PERSONÆ

DUKE OF VENICE.
BRABANTIO, *a Senator.*
Other Senators.
GRATIANO, *Brother to* BRABANTIO.
LODOVICO, *Kinsman to* BRABANTIO.
OTHELLO, *a noble Moor, in the service of Venice.*
CASSIO, *his Lieutenant.*
IAGO, *his Ancient.*
RODERIGO, *a Venetian Gentleman.*
MONTANO, OTHELLO'S *predecessor in the government of Cyprus.*

Clown, *Servant to* OTHELLO.
Herald.

DESDEMONA, *Daughter to* BRABANTIO, *and Wife to* OTHELLO.
EMILIA, *Wife to* IAGO.
BIANCA, *Mistress to* CASSIO.

Officers, Gentlemen, Messenger, Musicians, Herald, Sailor, Attendants, &c.

SCENE,—*The First Act in* VENICE; *during the rest of the Play at a Seaport in* CYPRUS.

## ACT I.

### SCENE I.—VENICE. *A Street.*

*Enter* RODERIGO *and* IAGO.

*Rod.* Never tell me; I take it much unkindly
That thou, Iago, who hast had my purse
As if the strings were thine, shouldst know of this,—
*Iago.* 'Sblood, but you will not hear me:—
If ever I did dream of such a matter,
Abhor me.
*Rod.* Thou told'st me thou didst hold him in thy hate.
*Iago.* Despise me if I do not. Three great ones of the city,
In personal suit to make me his lieutenant,
Off-capp'd to him:—and, by the faith of man,
I know my price, I am worth no worse a place:—
But he, as loving his own pride and purposes,
Evades them, with a bombast circumstance
Horribly stuff'd with epithets of war:
And, in conclusion, nonsuits
My mediators; for, *Certes,* says he,
*I have already chose my officer.*
And what was he?
Forsooth, a great arithmetician,
One Michael Cassio, a Florentine,
A fellow almost damn'd in a fair wife;
That never set a squadron in the field,
Nor the division of a battle knows
More than a spinster; unless the bookish theoric,
Wherein the toged consuls can propose
As masterly as he: mere prattle, without practice,
Is all his soldiership. But he, sir, had the election:
And I,—of whom his eyes had seen the proof
At Rhodes, at Cyprus, and on other grounds,
Christian and heathen,—must be be-lee'd and calm'd
By debitor and creditor, this counter-caster;
He, in good time, must be his lieutenant be,
And I, God bless the mark! his Moorship's ancient.                [his hangman.
*Rod.* By heaven, I rather would have been
*Iago.* Why, there's no remedy; 'tis the curse of service,
Preferment goes by letter and affection,
And not by old gradation, where each second
Stood heir to the first. Now, sir, be judge yourself
Whether I in any just term am affin'd
To love the Moor.
*Rod.*           I would not follow him, then.
*Iago.* O, sir, content you;
I follow him to serve my turn upon him:
We cannot all be masters, nor all masters
Cannot be truly follow'd. You shall mark
Many a duteous and knee-crooking knave
That, doting on his own obsequious bondage,
Wears out his time, much like his master's ass,
For naught but provender; and when he's old, cashier'd:                [are
Whip me such honest knaves. Others there
Who, trimm'd in forms and visages of duty,
Keep yet their hearts attending on themselves;                [lords,
And, throwing but shows of service on their
Do well thrive by them, and when they have lin'd their coats,
Do themselves homage: these fellows have some soul;

And such a one do I profess myself.
For, sir,
It is as sure as you are Roderigo,
Were I the Moor I would not be Iago:
In following him I follow but myself;
Heaven is my judge, not I for love and duty,
But seeming so for my peculiar end:
For when my outward action doth demon-
strate
The native act and figure of my heart
In compliment extern, 'tis not long after
But I will wear my heart upon my sleeve
For daws to peck at: I am not what I am.
   *Rod.* What a full fortune does the thick
lips owe,
If he can carry't thus!
   *Iago.*           Call up her father.
Rouse him:—make after him, poison his de-
light,         [kinsmen,
Proclaim him in the streets; incense her
And, though he in a fertile climate dwell,
Plague him with flies: though that his joy be
joy,
Yet throw such changes of vexation on't.
As it may lose some colour.     [aloud.
   *Rod.* Here is her father's house: I'll call
   *Iago.* Do; with like timorous accent and
dire yell
As when, by night and negligence, the fire
Is spied in populous cities.     [bantio, ho!
   *Rod.* What, ho, Brabantio! Signior Bra-
   *Iago.*   Awake! what, ho, Brabantio!
thieves! thieves! thieves!     [bags!
Look to your house, your daughter, and your
Thieves! thieves!

   BRABANTIO *appears above at a window.*
   *Bra.* What is the reason of this terrible
summons?
What is the matter there?
   *Rod.* Signior, is all your family within?
   *Iago.* Are your doors locked?
   *Bra.*     Why, wherefore ask you this?
   *Iago.* Zounds, sir, you're robb'd; for
shame, put on your gown;     [soul;
Your heart is burst, you have lost half your
Even now, now, very now, an old black ram
Is tupping your white ewe. Arise, arise;
Awake the snorting citizens with the bell,
Or else the devil will make a grandsire of
you:
Arise, I say.
   *Bra.*   What, have you lost your wits?
   *Rod.* Most reverend signior, do you know
my voice?
   *Bra.* Not I; what are you?
   *Rod.* My name is Roderigo.
   *Bra.*     The worser welcome:
I have charg'd thee not to haunt about my
doors;
In honest plainness thou hast heard me say
My daughter is not for thee; and now, in
madness,

Being full of supper and distempering
draughts,
Upon malicious bravery dost thou come
To start my quiet.
   *Rod.* Sir, sir, sir,—
   *Bra.*       But thou must needs be sure,
My spirit and my place have in them power
To make this bitter to thee.
   *Rod.*           Patience, good sir.
   *Bra.* What tell'st thou me of robbing? this
is Venice;
My house is not a grange.
   *Rod.*         Most grave Brabantio,
In simple and pure soul I come to you.
   *Iago.* Zounds, sir, you are one of those
that will not serve God if the devil bid you.
Because we come to do you service, and you
think we are ruffians, you'll have your
daughter covered with a Barbary horse;
you'll have your nephews neigh to you; you'll
have coursers for cousins and gennets for
germans.
   *Bra.* What profane wretch art thou?
   *Iago.* I am one, sir, that comes to tell you
your daughter and the Moor are now making
the beast with two backs.
   *Bra.* Thou art a villain.
   *Iago.*         You are—a senator.
   *Bra.* This thou shalt answer; I know thee,
Roderigo.     [seech you,
   *Rod.* Sir, I will answer anything. But I be-
If't be your pleasure and most wise consent,—
As partly I find it is,—that your fair daugh-
ter,
At this odd-even and dull watch o' the night,
Transported with no worse nor better guard
But with a knave of common hire, a gon-
dolier,
To the gross clasps of a lascivious Moor,—
If this be known to you, and your allowance,
We then have done you bold and saucy
wrongs;     [me
But if you know not this, my manners tell
We have your wrong rebuke. Do not believe
That, from the sense of all civility,
I thus would play and trifle with your rever-
ence:     [leave,—
Your daughter,—if you have not given her
I say again, hath made a gross revolt;
Tying her duty, beauty, wit, and fortunes
In an extravagant and wheeling stranger
Of here and everywhere. Straight satisfy
yourself:
If she be in her chamber or your house
Let loose on me the justice of the state
For thus deluding you.
   *Bra.*       Strike on the tinder, ho!
Give me a taper!—call up all my people!—
This accident is not unlike my dream:
Belief of it oppresses me already.—
Light, I say! light!     [*Exit from above.*
   *Iago.*    Farewell; for I must leave you:
It seems not meet nor wholesome to my place

to be produc'd,—as if I stay I shall,—
Against the Moor: for I do know the state,—
However this may gall him with some
    check,—            [bark'd
Cannot with safety cast him; for he's em-
With such loud reason to the Cyprus wars,—
Which even now stand in act,—that, for their
    souls,
Another of his fathom they have none
To lead their business: in which regard,
Though I do hate him as I do hell pains,
Yet, for necessity of present life,
I must show out a flag and sign of love,
Which is indeed but sign. That you shall
    surely find him,
Lead to the Sagittary the raised search;
And there will I be with him. So, farewell.
                                [*Exit.*

*Enter below,* BRABANTIO, *and* Servants *with
    torches.*

*Bra.* It is too true an evil: gone she is;
And what's to come of my despised time
Is naught but bitterness.—Now, Roderigo,
Where didst thou see her?—O unhappy
    girl!—
With the Moor, say'st thou?—Who would be
    a father!                [ceives me
How didst thou know 'twas she?—O, she de-
Past thought.—What said she to you?—Get
    more tapers;
Raise all my kindred.—Are they married,
    think you?
*Rod.* Truly, I think they are.
*Bra.* O heaven!—How got she out?—O
    treason of the blood!—
Fathers, from hence trust not your daughters'
    minds
By what you see them act.—Are there not
    charms
By which the property of youth and maid-
    hood                    [igo,
May be abused? Have you not read, Roder-
Of some such thing?
*Rod.*              Yes, sir, I have indeed.
*Bra.* Call up my brother.—O, would you
    had her!—
Some one way some another.—Do you know
Where we may apprehend her and the Moor?
*Rod.* I think I can discover him, if you
    please
To get good guard, and go along with me.
*Bra.* Pray you, lead on. At every house
    I'll call;
I may command at most.—Get weapons, ho!
And raise some special officers of night.—
On, good Roderigo:—I'll deserve your pains.
                                [*Exeunt.*

SCENE II.—VENICE. *Another Street.*

*Enter* OTHELLO, IAGO, *and* Attendants *with
    torches.*

*Iago.* Though in the trade of war I have
    slain men,

Yet do I hold it very stuff o' the conscience
To do no cóntriv'd murder: I lack iniquity
Sometimes to do me service: nine or ten
    times
I had thought to have yerk'd him here under
    the ribs.
*Oth.* 'Tis better as it is.
*Iago.*              Nay, but he prated,
And spoke such scurvy and provoking terms
Against your honour,
That, with the little godliness I have,
I did full hard forbear him. But I pray you,
    sir,
Are you fast married? Be assured of this,
That the magnifico is much beloved;
And hath, in his effect, a voice potential
As double as the duke's: he will divorce you;
Or put upon you what restraint and griev-
    ance              [on,—
The law,—with all his might to enforce it
Will give him cable.
*Oth.*              Let him do his spite:
My services which I have done the signiory
Shall out-tongue his complaints. 'Tis yet to
    know,—
Which, when I know that boasting is an
    honour,
I shall promulgate,—I fetch my life and being
From men of royal siege; and my demerits
May speak unbonneted to as proud a fortune
As this that I have reach'd: for know, Iago,
But that I love the gentle Desdemona,
I would not my unhoused free condition
Put into circumscription and confine
For the sea's worth. But, look! what lights
    come yond?
*Iago.* Those are the raised father and his
    friends:
You were best go in.
*Oth.*              Not I; I must be found:
My parts, my title, and my perfect soul.
Shall manifest me rightly. Is it they?
*Iago.* By Janus, I think no.

*Enter* CASSIO *and certain* Officers *with
    torches.*

*Oth.* The servants of the duke and my
    lieutenant.
The goodness of the night upon you, friends!
What is the news?
*Cas.*     The duke does greet you, general;
And he requires your haste-post-haste ap-
    pearance
Even on the instant.
*Oth.*          What is the matter, think you?
*Cas.* Something from Cyprus, as I may
    divine:
It is a business of some heat: the galleys
Have sent a dozen sequent messengers
This very night at one another's heels;
And many of the consuls, rais'd and met,
Are at the duke's already: you have been
    hotly call'd for;

When, being not at your lodging to be found,
The senate hath sent about three several
    quests
To search you out.
   *Oth.*      'Tis well I am found by you.
I will but spend a word here in the house,
And go with you.           [*Exit.*
   *Cas.*     Ancient, what makes he here?
   *Iago.* Faith, he to-night hath boarded a
    land carack.
If it prove lawful prize, he's made for ever.
   *Cas.* I do not understand.
   *Iago.*           He's married.
   *Cas.*            To who?

       *Re-enter* OTHELLO.

   *Iago.* Marry, to—Come, captain, will you
    go?
   *Oth.*    Have with you.
   *Cas.* Here comes another troop to seek for
    you.
   *Iago.* It is Brabantio.—General, be advis'd;
He comes to bad intent.

   *Enter* BRABANTIO, RODERIGO, *and* Officers
      *with torches and weapons.*

   *Oth.*          Holla! stand there!
   *Rod.* Signior, it is the Moor.
   *Bra.*         Down with him, thief!
          [*They draw on both sides.*
   *Iago.* You, Roderigo! come, sir, I am for
    you.
   *Oth.* Keep up your bright swords, for the
    dew will rust them.—       [years
Good signior, you shall more command with
Than with your weapons.
   *Bra.* O thou foul thief, where hast thou
    stow'd my daughter?
Damn'd as thou art, thou hast enchanted her;
For I'll refer me to all things of sense,
If she in chains of magic were not bound,
Whether a maid so tender, fair, and happy,
So opposite to marriage that she shunn'd
The wealthy curled darlings of our nation,
Would ever have, to incur a general mock,
Run from her guardage to the sooty bosom
Of such a thing as thou,—to fear, not to de-
    light.
Judge me the world, if 'tis not gross in sense
That thou hast practis'd on her with foul
    charms;
Abus'd her delicate youth with drugs or
    minerals
That weaken motion:—I'll have't disputed
    on;
'Tis probable, and palpable to thinking.
I therefore apprehend and do attach thee
For an abuser of the world, a practiser
Of arts inhibited and out of warrant.—
Lay hold upon him: if he do resist,
Subdue him at his peril.
   *Oth.*          Hold your hands,
Both you of my inclining, and the rest:

Were it my cue to fight, I should have known
    it           [I go
Without a prompter.—Where will you that
To answer this your charge?
   *Bra.*         To prison, till fit time
Of law and course of direct session
Call thee to answer.
   *Oth.*          What if I do obey?
How may the duke be therewith satisfied,
Whose messengers are here about my side,
Upon some present business of the state,
To bring me to him.
   1 *Off.*       'Tis true, most worthy signior;
The duke's in council, and your noble self,
I am sure, is sent for.
   *Bra.*         How! the duke in council!
In this time of the night!—Bring him away:
Mine's not an idle cause: the duke himself,
Or any of my brothers of the state,
Cannot but feel this wrong as 'twere their
    own;
For if such actions may have passage free,
Bond-slaves and pagans shall our statesmen
    be.           [*Exeunt.*

   SCENE III.—VENICE. *A Council-chamber.*

   *The* DUKE *and* Senators *sitting at a table;*
      Officers *attending.*

   *Duke.* There is no composition in these
    news
That gives them credit.
   1 *Sen.* Indeed, they are disproportion'd;
My letter say a hundred and seven galleys.
   *Duke.* And mine a hundred and forty.
   2 *Sen.*         And mine two hundred:
But though they jump not on a just ac-
    count,—
As in these cases, where the aim reports,
'Tis oft with difference,—yet do they all
    confirm
A Turkish fleet, and bearing up to Cyprus.
   *Duke.* Nay, it is possible enough to judg-
    ment:
I do not so secure me in the error,
But the main article I do approve
In fearful sense.
   *Sailor.* [*Within*] What, ho! what, ho!
    what, ho!
   1 *Off.* A messenger from the galleys.

       *Enter a* Sailor.

   *Duke.*       Now,—what's the business?
   *Sail.* The Turkish preparation makes for
    Rhodes;
So was I bid report here to the state
By Signior Angelo.
   *Duke.* How say you by this change?
   1 *Sen.*         This cannot be,
By no assay of reason: 'tis a pageant
To keep us in false gaze. When we consider
The importancy of Cyprus to the Turk;
And let ourselves again but understand

That, as it more concerns the Turk than
Rhodes,
So may he with more facile question bear it,
For that it stands not in such warlike brace,
But altogether lacks the abilities
That Rhodes is dress'd in: if we make
thought of this,
We must not think the Turk is so unskilful
To leave that latest which concerns him first;
Neglecting an attempt of ease and gain
To wake and wage a danger profitless.

*Duke.* Nay, in all confidence, he's not for
Rhodes.

1 *Off.* Here is more news.

*Enter a* Messenger.

*Mess.* The Ottomites, reverend and gra-
cious, [Rhodes,
Steering with due course toward the isle of
Have there injointed them with an after fleet.

1 *Sen.* Ay, so I thought.—How many, as
you guess? [stem

*Mess.* Of thirty sail: and now do they re-
Their backward course, bearing with frank
appearance [Montano,
Their purposes toward Cyprus,—Signior
Your trusty and most valiant servitor,
With his free duty recommends you thus,
And prays you to believe him.

*Duke.* 'Tis certain, then, for Cyprus.—
Marcus Luccicos, is not he in town?

1 *Sen.* He's now in Florence.

*Duke.* Write from us to him; post-post-
haste despatch. [valiant Moor.

1 *Sen.* Here comes Brabantio and the

*Enter* BRABANTIO, OTHELLO, IAGO,
RODERIGO, *and* Officers.

*Duke.* Valiant Othello, we must straight
employ you
Against the general enemy Ottoman.—
I did not see you; welcome, gentle signior;
[*To* BRABANTIO.
We lack'd your counsel and your help to-
night.

*Bra.* So did I yours. Good your grace,
pardon me;
Neither my place, nor aught I heard of busi-
ness [general care
Hath rais'd me from my bed; nor doth the
Take hold on me for my particular grief
Is of so flood-gate and o'erbearing nature
That it engluts and swallows other sorrows,
And it is still itself.

*Duke.* Why, what's the matter?

*Bra.* My daughter! O, my daughter!

*Duke and Senators.* Dead?

*Bra.* Ay, to me;
She is abus'd, stol'n from me, and corrupted
By spells and medicines bought of mounte-
banks;
For nature so preposterously to err,

Being not deficient, blind, or lame of sense,
Sans witchcraft could not. [ceeding.

*Duke.* Whoe'er he be that, in this foul pro-
Hath thus beguil'd your daughter of herself,
And you of her, the bloody book of law
You shall yourself read in the bitter letter
After your own sense; yea, though our prop-
er son
Stood in your action.

*Bra.* Humbly I thank your grace.
Here is the man, this Moor; whom now, it
seems,
Your special mandate for the state affairs
Hath hither brought. [for't.

*Duke and Senators.* We are very sorry

*Duke.* What, in your own part, can you
say to this? [*To* OTHELLO.

*Bra.* Nothing, but this is so. [signiors,

*Oth.* Most potent, grave, and reverend
My very noble and approv'd good masters,—
That I have ta'en away this old man's daugh-
ter,
It is most true; true, I have married her:
The very head and front of my offending
Hath this extent, no more. Rude am I in my
speech, [peace;
And little bless'd with the soft phrase of
For since these arms of mine had seven years'
pith, [us'd
Till now some nine moons wasted, they have
Their dearest action in the tented field;
And little of this great world can I speak,
More than pertains to feats of broil and
battle;
And therefore little shall I grace my cause
In speaking for myself. Yet, by your gracious
patience,
I will a round unvarnish'd tale deliver
Of my whole course of love; what drugs,
what charms,
What conjuration, and what mighty magic,—
For such proceeding I am charg'd withal,—
I won his daughter.

*Bra.* A maiden never bold:
Of spirit so still and quiet that her motion
Blush'd at herself; and she,—in spite of na-
ture,
Of years, of country, credit, everything,—
To fall in love with what she fear'd to look
on!
It is a judgment maim'd and most imperfect
That will confess perfection so could err
Against all rules of nature; and must be
driven
To find out practices of cunning hell,
Why this should be. I therefore vouch again,
That with some mixtures powerful o'er the
blood,
Or with some dram conjur'd to this effect,
He wrought upon her.

*Duke.* To vouch this is no proof;
Without more wider and more overt test
Than these thin habits and poor likelihoods

Of modern seeming do prefer against him.
　1 *Sen.* But, Othello, speak:
Did you by indirect and forced courses
Subdue and poison this young maid's affec-
　tions?
Or came it by request, and such fair question
As soul to soul affordeth?
　*Oth.*　　　　　　　　　　I do beseech you,
Send for the lady to the Sagittary,
And let her speak of me before her father
If you do find me foul in her report,
The trust, the office I do hold of you,
Not only take away, but let your sentence
Even fall upon my life.
　*Duke.*　　　　　Fetch Desdemona hither.
　*Oth.* Ancient, conduct them; you best
　　know the place.—
　　　　　　　[*Exeunt* IAGO *and* Attendants.
And, till she come, as truly as to heaven
I do confess the vices of my blood,
So justly to your grave ears I'll present
How I did thrive in this fair lady's love,
And she in mine.
　*Duke.* Say it, Othello.
　*Oth.* Her father lov'd me; oft invited me;
Still question'd me the story of my life,
From year to year,—the battles, sieges, for-
　　tunes,
That I have pass'd.
I ran it through, even from my boyish days
To the very moment that he bade me tell it:
Wherein I spake of most disastrous chances,
Of moving accidents by flood and field;
Of hairbreadth scapes i' the imminent deadly
　　breach;
Of being taken by the insolent foe,
And sold to slavery; of my redemption
　　thence,
And portance in my travel's history:
Wherein of antres vast and deserts idle,
Rough quarries, rocks, and hills whose heads
　　touch heaven,
It was my hint to speak,—such was the proc-
　　ess;
And of the Cannibals that each other eat,
The Anthropophagi, and men whose heads
Do grow beneath their shoulders. This to hear
Would Desdemona seriously incline:
But still the house affairs would draw her
　　thence;
Which ever as she could with haste despatch,
She'd come again, and with a greedy ear
Devour up my discourse: which I observing,.
Took once a pliant hour; and found good
　　means
To draw from her a prayer of earnest heart
That I would all my pilgrimage dilate,
Whereof by parcels she had something heard,
But not intentively: I did consent;
And often did beguile her of her tears,
When I did speak of some distressful stroke
That my youth suffer'd. My story being done,
She gave me for my pains a world of sighs:

She swore,—in faith, 'twas strange, 'twas
　　passing strange;
'Twas pitiful, 'twas wondrous pitiful:
She wish'd she had not heard it; yet she
　　wish'd
That heaven had made her such a man: she
　　thank'd me;
And bade me, if I had a friend that lov'd her,
I should but teach him how to tell my story,
And that would woo her. Upon this hint I
　　spake:
She lov'd me for the dangers I had pass'd;
And I lov'd her that she did pity them.
This only is the witchcraft I have us'd:—
Here comes the lady; let her witness it.

　*Enter* DESDEMONA, IAGO, *and* Attendants.
　*Duke.* I think this tale would win my
　　daughter too.—
Good Brabantio,
Take up this mangled matter at the best.
Men do their broken weapons rather use
Than their bare hands.
　*Bra.*　　　　　I pray you, hear her speak:
If she confess that she was half the wooer,
Destruction on my head if my bad blame
Light on the man!—Come hither, gentle mis-
　　tress:
Do you perceive in all this noble company
Where most you owe obedience?
　*Des.*　　　　　　　　My noble father
I do perceive here a divided duty:
To you I am bound for life and education;
My life and education both do learn me
How to respect you; you are the lord of
　　duty,—
I am hitherto your daughter: but here's my
　　husband;
And so much duty as my mother show'd
To you, preferring you before her father,
So much I challenge that I may profess
Due to the Moor, my lord.
　*Bra.*　　　God be with you!—I have done.—
Please it your grace, on to the state affairs:
I had rather to adopt a child than get it.—
Come hither, Moor:
I here do give thee that with all my heart,
Which, but thou hast already, with all my
　　heart
I would keep from thee.—For your sake,
　　jewel,
I am glad at soul I have no other child;
For thy escape would teach me tyranny,
To hang clogs on them.—I have done, my
　　lord.
　*Duke.* Let me speak like yourself; and lay
　　a sentence,
Which, as a grise or step, may help these lov-
　　ers
Into your favour.
When remedies are past, the griefs are ended
By seeing the worst, which late on hopes de-
　　pended.

To mourn a mischief that is past and gone
Is the next way to draw new mischief on.
What cannot be preserv'd when fortune takes,
Patience her injury a mockery makes.
The robb'd that smiles steals something from
   the thief;
He robs himself that spends a bootless grief.
  *Bra.* So let the Turk of Cyprus us beguile;
We lose it not so long as we can smile;
He bears the sentence well that nothing bears
But the free comfort which from thence he
   hears;
But he bears both the sentence and the sor-
   row
That, to pay grief, must of poor patience bor-
   row.
These sentences, to sugar or to gall,
Being strong on both sides, are equivocal:
But words are words; I never yet did hear
That the bruis'd heart was pierced through
   the ear.—
I humbly beseech you, proceed to the affairs
  of state.
  *Duke.* The Turk with a most mighty preparation makes for Cyprus.—Othello, the fortitude of the place is best known to you; and
though we have there a substitute of most
allowed sufficiency, yet opinion, a sovereign
mistress of effects, throws a more safer voice
on you: you must therefore be content
to slubber the gloss of your new fortunes
with this more stubborn and boisterous expe-
dition.
  *Oth.* The tyrant custom, most grave sena-
  tors,
Hath made the flinty and steel couch of war
My thrice-driven bed of down: I do agnize
A natural and prompt alacrity
I find in hardness; and do undertake
These present wars against the Ottomites.
Most humbly, therefore, bending to your
  state,
I crave fit disposition for my wife;
Due reference of place and exhibition;
With such accommodation and besort
As levels with her breeding.
  *Duke.*            If you please,
Be't at her father's.
  *Bra.*         I'll not have it so.
  *Oth.* Nor I.
  *Des.*       Nor I; I would not there reside,
To put my father in impatient thoughts,
By being in his eye. Most gracious duke,
To my unfolding lend a gracious ear;
And let me find a charter in your voice
To assist my simpleness.
  *Duke.* What would you, Desdemona?
  *Des.* That I did love the Moor to live with
  him,
My downright violence and scorn of fortunes
May trumpet to the world: my heart's sub-
  du'd
Even to the very quality of my lord:

I saw Othello's visage in his mind;
And to his honours and his valiant parts
Did I my soul and fortunes consecrate.
So that, dear lords, if I be left behind,
A moth of peace, and he go to the war,
The rites for which I love him are bereft
  me,
And I a heavy interim shall support
By his dear absence. Let me go with him.
  *Oth.* Let her have your voices.
Vouch with me, heaven, I therefore beg it not
To please the palate of my appetite;
Nor to comply with heat,—the young affects
In me defunct,—and proper satisfaction;
But to be free and bounteous to her mind:
And heaven defend your good souls, that you
  think
I will your serious and great business scant
For she is with me: no, when light-wing'd
  toys
Of feather'd Cupid seel with wanton dullness
My speculative and offic'd instruments,
That my disports corrupt and taint my busi-
  ness,
Let housewives make a skillet of my helm,
And all indign and base adversities
Make head against my estimation!
  *Duke.* Be it as you shall privately deter-
  mine,
Either for her stay or going: the affair cries
  haste,
And speed must answer it.
  1 *Sen:* You must away to-night.
  *Oth.*              With all my heart.
  *Duke.* At nine i' the morning here we'll
  meet again.—
Othello, leave some officer behind,
And he shall our commission bring to you;
With such things else of quality and respect
As doth import you.
  *Oth.*     So please your grace, my ancient,—
A man he is of honesty and trust,—
To his conveyance I assign my wife,
With what else needful your good grace shall
  think
To be sent after me.
  *Duke.*          Let it be so.—
Good-night to everyone.—And, noble signior,
                [*To* BRABANTIO.
If virtue no delighted beauty lack,
Your son-in-law is far more fair than black.
  1 *Sen.* Adieu, brave Moor; use Desdemona
  well.
  *Bra.* Look to her, Moor, if thou hast eyes
  to see:
She has deceiv'd her father, and may thee.
      [*Exeunt* DUKE, Senators, Officers, &c.
  *Oth.* My life upon her faith!—Honest Iago,
My Desdemona must I leave to thee:
I pr'ythee, let thy wife attend on her;
And bring them after in the best advantage.—
Come, Desdemona, I have but an hour
Of love, of worldly matters and direction,

To spend with thee: we must obey the time.

[*Exeunt* OTHELLO *and* DESDEMONA.

*Rod.* Iago,—

*Iago.* What say'st thou, noble heart?

*Rod.* What will I do, thinkest thou?

*Iago.* Why, go to bed and sleep.

*Rod.* I will incontinently drown myself.

*Iago.* If thou dost, I shall never love thee after. Why, thou silly gentleman!

*Rod.* It is silliness to live when to live is torment; and then have we a prescription to die when death is our physician.

*Iago.* O villanous! I have looked upon the world for four times seven years; and since I could distinguish betwixt a benefit and an injury, I never found man that knew how to love himself. Ere I would say I would drown myself for the love of a Guinea-hen, I would change my humanity with a baboon.

*Rod.* What should I do? I confess it is my shame to be so fond; but it is not in my virtue to amend it.

*Iago.* Virtue! a fig! 'tis in ourselves that we are thus or thus. Our bodies are gardens, to the which our wills are gardeners; so that if we will plant nettles or sow lettuce, set hyssop and weed up thyme, supply it with one gender of herbs or distract it with many, either to have it sterile with idleness or manured with industry; why, the power and corrigible authority of this lies in our wills. If the balance of our lives had not one scale of reason to poise another of sensuality, the blood and baseness of our natures would conduct us to most preposterous conclusions: but we have reason to cool our raging motions, our carnal stings, our unbitted lusts; whereof I take this, that you call love, to be a sect or scion.

*Rod.* It cannot be.

*Iago.* It is merely a lust of the blood and a permission of the will. Come, be a man: drown thyself! drown cats and blind puppies. I have professed me thy friend, and I confess me knit to thy deserving with cables of perdurable toughness; I could never better stead thee than now. Put money in thy purse; follow thou the wars; defeat thy favour with an usurped beard; I say, put money in thy purse. It cannot be that Desdemona should long continue her love to the Moor,—put money in thy purse,—nor he his to her: it was a violent commencement, and thou shalt see an answerable sequestration;—put but money in thy purse.—These Moors are changeable in their wills;—fill thy purse with money: the food that to him now is as luscious as locusts shall be to him shortly as bitter as coloquintida. She must change for youth: when she is sated with his body she will find the error of her choice: she must have change, she must: therefore put money in thy purse.—If thou wilt needs damn thyself, do it a more delicate way than drowning. Make all the money thou canst: if sanctimony and a frail vow betwixt an erring barbarian and a supersubtle Venetian be not too hard for my wits and all the tribe of hell, thou shalt enjoy her; therefore make money. A pox of drowning thyself! it is clean out of the way: seek thou rather to be hanged in compassing thy joy than to be drowned and go without her.

*Rod.* Wilt thou be fast to my hopes if I depend on the issue?

*Iago.* Thou art sure of me:—go, make money:—I have told thee often, and I re-tell thee again and again, I hate the Moor: my cause is hearted; thine hath no less reason. Let us be conjunctive in our revenge against him: if thou canst cuckold him, thou dost thyself a pleasure, me a sport. There are many events in the womb of time which will be delivered. Traverse; go; provide thy money. We will have more of this to-morrow. Adieu.

*Rod.* Where shall we meet i' the morning?

*Iago.* At my lodging.

*Rod.* I'll be with thee betimes.

*Iago.* Go to; farewell. Do you hear, Roderigo?

*Rod.* What say you?

*Iago.* No more of drowning, do you hear?

*Rod.* I am changed: I'll go sell all my land.

[*Exit.*

*Iago.* Thus do I ever make my fool my purse;

For I mine own gain'd knowledge should profane

If I would time expend with such a snipe

But for my sport and profit. I hate the Moor;

And it is thought abroad that 'twixt my sheets

He has done my office: I know not if't be true;

But I, for mere suspicion in that kind,

Will do as if for surety. He holds me well;

The better shall my purpose work on him.

Cassio's a proper man: let me see now;

To get his place, and to plume up my will

In double knavery,—How, how?—Let's see:—

After some time to abuse Othello's ear

That he is too familiar with his wife:—

He hath a person, and a smooth dispose,

To be suspected; fram'd to make women false.

The Moor is of a free and open nature,

That thinks men honest that but seem to be so;

And will as tenderly be led by the nose

As asses are.

I have't;—it is engender'd:—hell and night

Must bring this monstrous birth to the world's light. [*Exit.*

### ACT II.

SCENE I.—*A Seaport Town in Cyprus. A Platform.*

*Enter* MONTANO *and two* Gentlemen.

*Mon.* What from the cape can you discern at sea?

1 *Gent.* Nothing at all: it is a high-wrought flood;
I cannot, 'twixt the heaven and the main,
Descry a sail.

*Mon.* Methinks the wind hath spoke aloud at land;
A fuller blast ne'er shook our battlements:
If it hath ruffian'd so upon the sea,
What ribs of oak, when mountains melt on them,
Can hold the mortise? What shall we hear of this?

2 *Gent.* A segregation of the Turkish fleet:
For do but stand upon the foaming shore,
The chidden billow seems to pelt the clouds;
The wind-shak'd surge, with high and monstrous main,
Seems to cast water on the burning Bear,
And quench the guards of the ever-fixed pole:
I never did like molestation view
On the enchafed flood.

*Mon.*               If that the Turkish fleet
Be not enshelter'd and embay'd, they are drown'd;
It is impossible to bear it out.

*Enter a third* Gentleman.

3 *Gent.* News, lads! our wars are done.
The desperate tempest hath so bang'd the Turks
That their designment halts: a noble ship of Venice
Hath seen a grievous wreck and sufferance
On most part of their fleet.

*Mon.*               How! is this true?

3 *Gent.* The ship is here put in,
A Veronessa; Michael Cassio,
Lieutenant to the warlike Moor Othello,
Is come on shore: the Moor himself's at sea,
And is in full commission here for Cyprus.

*Mon.* I am glad on't; 'tis a worthy governor.

3 *Gent.* But this same Cassio,—though he speak of comfort
Touching the Turkish loss,—yet he looks sadly,
And prays the Moor be safe; for they were parted
With foul and violent tempest.

*Mon.*               Pray heavens he be;
For I have serv'd him, and the man commands
Like a full soldier. Let's to the sea-side, ho!
As well to see the vessel that's come in
As to throw out our eyes for brave Othello,
Even till we make the main and the aerial blue
An indistinct regard.

3 *Gent.*               Come, let's do so;
For every minute is expectancy
Of more arrivance.

*Enter* CASSIO.

*Cas.* Thanks you, the valiant of this warlike isle,
That so approve the Moor! O, let the heavens
Give him defence against the elements,
For I have lost him on a dangerous sea!

*Mon.* Is he well shipp'd?

*Cas.* His bark is stoutly timber'd, and his pilot
Of very expert and approv'd allowance;
Therefore my hopes, not surfeited to death,
Stand in bold cure.

  [*Within.*]       A sail, a sail, a sail!

*Enter a fourth* Gentleman.

*Cas.* What noise?

4 *Gent.* The town is empty; on the brow o' the sea
Stand ranks of people, and they cry, *A sail!*

*Cas.* My hopes do shape him for the governor.       [*Guns within.*

2 *Gent.* They do discharge their shot of courtesy:
Our friends at least.

*Cas.*               I pray you, sir, go forth,
And give us truth who 'tis that is arriv'd.

2 *Gent.* I shall.       [*Exit.*

*Mon.* But, good lieutenant, is your general wiv'd?

*Cas.* Most fortunately: he hath achiev'd a maid
That paragons description and wild fame;
One that excels the quirks of blazoning pens,
And in the essential vesture of creation
Does tire the ingener.—

*Re-enter second* Gentleman.

How now! who has put in?

2 *Gent.* 'Tis one Iago, ancient to the general.

*Cas.* Has had most favourable and happy speed:       [winds,
Tempests themselves, high seas, and howling
The gutter'd rocks, and congregated sands,—
Traitors ensteep'd to clog the guiltless keel,—
As having sense of beauty, do omit
Their mortal natures, letting go safely by
The divine Desdemona.

*Mon.*               What is she?

*Cas.* She that I spake of, our great captain's captain,
Left in the conduct of the bold Iago;
Whose footing here anticipates our thoughts
A se'nnight's speed.—Great Jove, Othello guard,       [breath,
And swell his sail with thine own powerful

That he may bless this bay with his tall ship,
Make love's quick pants in Desdemona's
arms,
Give renew'd fire to our extincted spirits,
And bring all Cyprus comfort!—O, behold,

*Enter* DESDEMONA, EMILIA, IAGO, RODER-
IGO, *and* Attendants.

The riches of the ship is come on shore!
Ye men of Cyprus, let her have your knees.—
Hail to thee, lady! and the grace of heaven,
Before, behind thee, and on every hand,
Enwheel thee round!
  *Des.*                I thank you, valiant Cassio.
What tidings can you tell me of my lord?
  *Cas.* He is not yet arriv'd: nor know I
    aught
But that he's well, and will be shortly here.
  *Des.* O, but I fear—How lost you com-
    pany?
  *Cas.* The great contention of the sea and
    skies
Parted our fellowship:—but, hark! a sail.
  [*Within.*] A sail, a sail!      [*Guns within.*
  2 *Gent.* They give their greeting to the
    citadel:
This likewise is a friend.
  *Cas.*            See for the news.—
                  [*Exit* Gentlemen.
Good ancient, you are welcome:—welcome,
    mistress:—            [*To* EMILIA.
Let it not gall your patience, good Iago,
That I extend my manners; 'tis my breeding
That gives me this bold show of courtesy.
                  [*Kissing her.*
  *Iago.* Sir, would she give you so much of
    her lips
As of her tongue she oft bestows on me,
You'd have enough.
  *Des.*            Alas, she has no speech.
  *Iago.* In faith, too much;
I find it still when I have list to sleep:
Marry, before your ladyship, I grant,
She puts her tongue a little in her heart,
And chides with thinking.
  *Emil.* You have little cause to say so.
  *Iago.* Come on, come on; you are pictures
    out of doors,            [kitchens,
Bells in your parlours, wild cats in your
Saints in your injuries, devils being offended,
Players in your housewifery, and housewifes
    in your beds.
  *Des.* O, fie upon thee, slanderer!
  *Iago.* Nay, it is true, or else I am a Turk:
You rise to play, and go to bed to work.
  *Emil.* You shall not write my praise.
  *Iago.*                No, let me not.
  *Des.* What wouldst thou write of me if
    thou shouldst praise me?
  *Iago.* O gentle lady, do not put me to't;
For I am nothing if not critical.
  *Des.* Come on, assay—There's one gone to
    the harbour?

  *Iago.* Ay, madam.
  *Des.* I am not merry; but I do beguile
The thing I am, by seeming otherwise.—
Come, how wouldst thou praise me?
  *Iago.* I am about it; but, indeed, my in-
    vention
Comes from my pate as birdlime does from
    frize,—            [labours,
It plucks out brains and all: but my muse
And thus she is deliver'd.
If she be fair and wise,—fairness and wit,
The one's for use, the other useth it.
  *Des.* Well prais'd! How if she be black and
    witty?
  *Iago.* If she be black, and thereto have a
    wit,
She'll find a white that shall her blackness fit.
  *Des.* Worse and worse.
  *Emil.* How if fair and foolish?
  *Iago.* She never yet was foolish that was
    fair;
For even her folly help'd her to an heir.
  *Des.* These are old fond paradoxes to make
fools laugh i' the alehouse. What miserable
praise hast thou for her that's foul and fool-
ish?
  *Iago.* There's none so foul, and foolish
    thereunto,
But does foul pranks which fair and wise ones
    do.
  *Des.* O heavy ignorance!—thou praisest
the worst best. But what praise couldst thou
bestow on a deserving woman indeed,—one
that, in the authority of her merit, did justly
put on the vouch of very malice itself?
  *Iago.* She that was ever fair, and never
    proud;
Had tongue at will, and yet was never loud;
Never lack'd gold, and yet went never gay;
Fled from her wish, and yet said, *Now I may;*
She that, being anger'd, her revenge being
    nigh,
Bade her wrong stay and her displeasure fly;
She that in wisdom never was so frail
To change the cod's head for the salmon's
    tail;
She that could think, and ne'er disclose her
    mind;
See suitors following, and not look behind;
She was a wight, if ever such wight were,—
  *Des.* To do what?
  *Iago.* To suckle fools and chronicle small
    beer.
  *Des.* O most lame and impotent conclu-
sion!—Do not learn of him, Emilia, though
he be thy husband.—How say you, Cassio?
is he not a most profane and liberal counsel-
lor?
  *Cas.* He speaks home, madam: you may
relish him more in the soldier than in the
scholar.
  *Iago.* [*Aside.*] He takes her by the palm:
ay, well said, whisper: with as little a web as

this will I ensnare as great a fly as Cassio. Ay, smile upon her, do; I will gyve thee in thine own courtship. You say true; 'tis so, indeed: if such tricks as these strip you out of your lieutenantry, it had been better you had not kissed your three fingers so oft, which now again you are most apt to play the sir in. Very good; well kissed! an excellent courtesy! 'tis so, indeed. Yet again your fingers to your lips? would they were cylster-pipes for your sake! [*Trumpet within.*]—The Moor! I know his trumpet.

*Cas.* 'Tis truly so.

*Des.* Let's meet him, and receive him.

*Cas.* Lo, here he comes!

*Enter* OTHELLO *and* Attendants.

*Oth.* O my fair warrior!

*Des.*                    My dear Othello!

*Oth.* It gives me wonder great as my content
To see you here before me. O my soul's joy!
If after every tempest come such calms,
May the winds blow till they have waken'd death!
And let the labouring bark climb hills of seas
Olympus-high, and duck again as low
As hell's from heaven! If it were now to die,
'Twere now to be most happy; for, I fear,
My soul hath her content so absolute
That not another comfort like to this
Succeeds in unknown fate.

*Des.*                    The heavens forbid
But that our loves and comforts should increase
Even as our days do grow!

*Oth.*          Amen to that, sweet powers!—
I cannot speak enough of this content;
It stops me here; it is too much of joy:
And this, and this, the greatest discords be
                              [*Kissing her.*
That e'er our hearts shall make!

*Iago.* [*Aside.*] O, you are well tun'd now!
But I'll set down the pegs that make this music,
As honest as I am.

*Oth.*          Come, let us to the castle.—
News, friends; our wars are done, the Turks are drown'd.
How does my old acquaintance of this isle?
Honey, you shall be well desir'd in Cyprus;
I have found great love amongst them. O my sweet,
I prattle out of fashion, and I dote
In mine own comforts.—I pr'ythee, good Iago,
Go to the bay, and disembark my coffers:
Bring thou the master to the citadel;
He is a good one, and his worthiness
Does challenge much respect.—Come, Desdemona,
Once more well met at Cyprus.
                    [*Exeunt* OTH., DES., *and* Attend.

*Iago.* Do thou meet me presently at the harbour. Come hither. If thou be'st valiant,—as, they say, base men being in love have then a nobility in their natures more than is native to them,—list me. The lieutenant to-night watches on the court of guard: first, I must tell thee this—Desdemona is directly in love with him.

*Rod.* With him! why, 'tis not possible.

*Iago.* Lay thy finger thus, and let thy soul be instructed. Mark me with what violence she first loved the Moor, but for bragging, and telling her fantastical lies: and will she love him still for prating? let not thy discreet heart think it. Her eye must be fed; and what delight shall she have to look on the devil? When the blood is made dull with the act of sport, there should be,—again to inflame it, and to give satiety a fresh appetite,—loveliness in favour; sympathy in years, manners, and beauties; all which the Moor is defective in: now, for want of these required conveniences, her delicate tenderness will find itself abused, begin to heave the gorge, disrelish and abhor the Moor; very nature will instruct her in it, and compel her to some second choice. Now, sir, this granted,—as it is a most pregnant and unforced position,—who stands so eminently in the degree of this fortune as Cassio does? a knave very voluble; no further conscionable than in putting on the mere form of civil and human seeming, for the better compassing of his salt and most hidden loose affection? why, none; why, none: a slippery and subtle knave; a finder of occasions; that has an eye can stamp and counterfeit advantages, though true advantage never present itself: a devilish knave! besides, the knave is handsome, young, and hath all those requisites in him that folly and green minds look after: a pestilent complete knave; and the woman hath found him already.

*Rod.* I cannot believe that in her; she is full of most blessed condition.

*Iago.* Blessed fig's end! the wine she drinks is made of grapes: if she had been blessed, she would never have loved the Moor: blessed pudding! Didst thou not see her paddle with the palm of his hand? didst not mark that?

*Rod.* Yes, that I did; but that was but courtesy.

*Iago.* Lechery, by this hand; an index and obscure prologue to the history of lust and foul thoughts. They met so near with their lips that their breaths embraced together. Villanous thoughts, Roderigo! when these mutualities so marshal the way, hard at hand comes the master and main exercise, the incorporate conclusion: pish!—But, sir, be you ruled by me: I have brought you from Venice. Watch you to-night; for the command, I'll lay't upon you: Cassio knows you not:—I'll not be far from you: do you find some occasion to anger Cassio, either by speaking too loud, or tainting his discipline, or from what other course you please, which the time shall more favourably minister.

*Rod.* Well.

*Iago.* Sir, he is rash, and very sudden in choler, and haply with his truncheon may strike at you: provoke him that he may; for even out of that will I cause these of Cyprus to mutiny, whose qualifications shall come into no true taste again but by the displanting of Cassio. So shall you have a shorter journey to your desires by the means I shall then have to prefer them; and the impediment most profitably removed, without the which there were no expectation of our prosperity. [opportunity.

*Rod.* I will do this, if I can bring it to any

*Iago.* I warrant thee. Meet me by and by at the citadel: I must fetch his necessaries ashore. Farewell.

*Rod.* Adieu. [*Exit.*

*Iago.* That Cassio loves her, I do well believe it; [credit:
That she loves him, 'tis apt, and of great
The Moor,—howbeit that I endure him not,—
Is of a constant, loving, noble nature;
And, I dare think, he'll prove to Desdemona
A most dear husband. Now, I do love her too;
Not out of absolute lust,—though, peradventure,
I stand accountant for as great a sin,—
But partly led to diet my revenge,
For that I do suspect the lusty Moor
Hath leap'd into my seat: the thought whereof
Doth, like a poisonous mineral, gnaw my inwards;
And nothing can or shall content my soul
Till I am even'd with him, wife for wife;
Or, failing so, yet that I put the Moor
At least into a jealousy so strong
That judgment cannot cure. Which thing to do,—
If this poor trash of Venice, whom I trash
For his quick hunting, stand the putting on,
I'll have our Michael Cassio on the hip;
Abuse him to the Moor in the rank garb,—
For I fear Cassio with my night-cap too;
Make the Moor thank me, love me, and reward me
For making him egregiously an ass,
And practising upon his peace and quiet
Even to madness. 'Tis here, but yet confus'd:
Knavery's plain face is never seen till us'd.
[*Exit.*

SCENE II.—*A Street.*

*Enter* a Herald *with a proclamation;* People *following.*

*Her.* It is Othello's pleasure, our noble and valiant general, that, upon certain tidings now arrived, importing the mere perdition of the Turkish fleet, every man put himself into triumph; some to dance, some to make bonfires, each man to what sport and revels his addiction leads him: for, besides these beneficial news, it is the celebration of his nuptial:—so much was his pleasure should be proclaimed. All offices are open; and there is full liberty of feasting from this present hour of five till the bell have told eleven. Heaven bless the isle of Cyprus and our noble general Othello! [*Exeunt.*

SCENE III.—*A Hall in the Castle.*

*Enter* OTHELLO, DESDEMONA, CASSIO, *and* Attendants.

*Oth.* Good Michael, look you to the guard to-night:
Let's teach ourselves that honorable stop,
Not to out-sport discretion.

*Cas.* Iago hath direction what to do;
But, notwithstanding, with my personal eye
Will I look to't.

*Oth.* Iago is most honest.
Michael, good-night: to-morrow with your earliest
Let me have speech with you.—Come, my dear love,— [*To* DESDEMONA.
The purchase made, the fruits are to ensue;
That profit's yet to come 'tween me and you.—
Good-night.
[*Exeunt* OTH., DES., *and* Attend.

*Enter* IAGO.

*Cas.* Welcome, Iago; we must to the watch.

*Iago.* Not this hour, lieutenant; 'tis not yet ten o' the clock. Our general cast us thus early for the love of his Desdemona; who let us not therefore blame: he hath not yet made wanton the night with her; and she is sport for Jove.

*Cas.* She's a most exquisite lady.

*Iago.* And, I'll warrant her, full of game.

*Cas.* Indeed, she is a most fresh and delicate creature.

*Iago.* What an eye she has! methinks it sounds a parley to provocation.

*Cas.* An inviting eye; and yet methinks right modest.

*Iago.* And when she speaks, is it not an alarm to love?

*Cas.* She is, indeed, perfection.

*Iago.* Well, happiness to their sheets! Come, lieutenant, I have a stoup of wine; and here without are a brace of Cyprus gallants that would fain have a measure to the health of black Othello.

*Cas.* Not to-night, good Iago: I have very poor and unhappy brains for drinking: I could well wish courtesy would invent some other custom of entertainment.

*Iago.* O, they are our friends; but one cup: I'll drink for you.

*Cas.* I have drunk but one cup to-night, and that was craftily qualified too, and, behold, what innovation it makes here: I am unfortunate in the infirmity, and dare not task my weakness with any more.

*Iago.* What, man! 'tis a night of revels: the gallants desire it.

*Cas.* Where are they?     [them in.

*Iago.* Here at the door; I pray you, call

*Cas.* I'll do't; but it dislikes me.   [*Exit.*

*Iago.* If I can fasten but one cup upon him,
With that which he hath drunk to-night already,
He'll be as full of quarrel and offence
As my young mistress' dog. Now, my sick
   fool Roderigo,      [out,
Whom love hath turn'd almost the wrong side
To Desdemona hath to-night carous'd
Potations pottle deep; and he's to watch:
Three lads of Cyprus,—noble swelling
   spirits,
That hold their honours in a wary distance,
The very elements of this warlike isle,—
Have I to-night fluster'd with flowing cups,
And they watch too. Now, 'mongst this flock
   of drunkards,
Am I to put our Cassio in some action
That may offend the isle:—but here they
   come:
If consequence do but approve my dream,
My boat sails freely, both with wind and
   stream.

*Re-enter* CASSIO, *with him* MONTANO *and* Gentlemen, *followed by* Servant *with wine.*

*Cas.* 'Fore heaven, they have given me a rouse already.

*Mon.* Good faith, a little one; not past a pint, as I am a soldier.

*Iago.* Some wine, ho!

  And let me the canakin clink, clink;   [*Sings.*
  And let me the canakin clink:
    A soldier's a man;
    O, man's life's but a span;
    Why, then, let a soldier drink.

Some wine, boys.

*Cas.* 'Fore heaven, an excellent song.

*Iago.* I learned it in England, where, indeed, they are most potent in potting: your Dane, your German, and your swag-bellied Hollander,—Drink, ho!—are nothing to your English.

*Cas.* Is your Englishman so expert in his drinking?

*Iago.* Why, he drinks you, with facility, your Dane dead drunk; he sweats not to overthrow your Almain; he gives your Hollander a vomit ere the next pottle can be filled.

*Cas.* To the health of our general!

*Mon.* I am for it, lieutenant; and I'll do you justice.

*Iago.* O sweet England!

  King Stephen was and a worthy peer,   [*Sings.*
    His breeches cost him but a crown;
  He held them sixpence all too dear,
    With that he call'd the tailor lown.
  He was a wight of high renown,
    And thou art but of low degree:
  'Tis pride that pulls the country down;
    Then take thine auld cloak about thee.

Some wine, ho!

*Cas.* Why, this is a more exquisite song than the other.

*Iago.* Will you hear it again?

*Cas.* No; for I hold him to be unworthy of his place that does those things.—Well,—heaven's above all; and there be souls must be saved, and there be souls must not be saved.

*Iago.* It's true, good lieutenant.

*Cas.* For mine own part,—no offence to the general, nor any man of quality,—I hope to be saved.

*Iago.* And so do I too, lieutenant.

*Cas.* Ay, but, by your leave, not before me; the lieutenant is to be saved before the ancient. Let's have no more of this; let's to our affairs.—Forgive us our sins!—Gentlemen, let's look to our business. Do not think, gentlemen, I am drunk: this is my ancient,—this is my right hand, and this is my left hand:—I am not drunk now; I can stand well enough, and speak well enough.

*All.* Excellent well.

*Cas.* Why, very well, then: you must not think, then, that I am drunk.    [*Exit.*

*Mon.* To the platform, masters; come, let's set the watch.       [before;—

*Iago.* You see this fellow that is gone
He is a soldier fit to stand by Cæsar
And give direction: and do but see his vice;
'Tis to his virtue a just equinox,
The one as long as the other: 'tis pity of
   him.
I fear the trust Othello puts him in,
On some odd time of his infirmity,
Will shake this island.

*Mon.*         But is he often thus?

*Iago.* 'Tis evermore the prologue to his
   sleep:
He'll watch the horologe a double set
If drink rock not his cradle.

*Mon.*         It were well
The general were put in mind of it.
Perhaps he sees it not; or his good nature
Prizes the virtue that appears in Cassio,
And looks not on his evils: is not this true?

*Enter* RODERIGO.

*Iago.* How, now, Roderigo! [*Aside to him.*

I pray you, after the lieutenant; go.

[*Exit* Rod.

*Mon.* And 'tis great pity that the noble Moor
Should hazard such a place as his own second
With one of an ingraft infirmity:
It were an honest action to say
So to the Moor.

*Iago.* Not I, for this fair island;
I do love Cassio well; and would do much
To cure him of this evil.—But, hark! what
noise? [*Cry within,*—"Help! help!"

*Re-enter* Cassio, *driving in* Roderigo.

*Cas.* You rogue! you rascal!

*Mon.* What's the matter, lieutenant?

*Cas.* A knave teach me my duty!
I'll beat the knave into a twiggen bottle.

*Rod.* Beat me!

*Cas.* Dost thou prate, rogue?

[*Striking* Roderigo.

*Mon.* Nay, good lieutenant;

[*Staying him.*

I pray you, sir, hold your hand.

*Cas.* Let me go, sir,
Or I'll knock you o'er the mazard.

*Mon.* Come, come, you're drunk.

*Cas.* Drunk! [*They fight.*

*Iago.* Away, I say! go out, and cry a mu-
tiny! [*Aside to* Rod., *who goes out.*
Nay, good lieutenant,—alas, gentlemen;—
Help, ho!—Lieutenant,—sir,—Montano,—
sir:—
Help, masters!—Here's a goodly watch in-
deed! [*Bell rings.*
Who's that which rings the bell?—Diablo,
ho!
The town will rise: God's will, lieutenant,
hold;
You will be sham'd for ever.

*Re-enter* Othello *and* Attendants

*Oth.* What is the matter here?

*Mon.* Zounds, I bleed still; I am hurt to
the death.

*Oth.* Hold, for your lives!

*Iago.* Hold, ho! lieutenant,—sir,—Montano,—gentlemen,—
Have you forgot all sense of place and duty?
Hold! the general speaks to you; hold, for
shame! [ariseth this?

*Oth.* Why, how now, ho! from whence
Are we turned Turks, and to ourselves do
that
Which Heaven hath forbid the Ottomites?
For Christian shame, put by this barbarous
brawl:
He that stirs next to carve for his own rage
Holds his soul light; he dies upon his mo-
tion.—
Silence that dreadful bell! it frights the isle
From her propriety.—What is the matter,
masters?—

Honest Iago, that look'st dead with grieving,
Speak, who began this? on thy love, I
charge thee.

*Iago.* I do not know:—friends all but now,
even now,
In quarter, and in terms like bride and groom
Divesting them for bed; and then, but now,—
As if some planet had unwitted men,—
Swords out, and tilting one at other's breast
In opposition bloody. I cannot speak
Any beginning to this peevish odds;
And would in action glorious I had lost
Those legs that brought me to a part of it!

*Oth.* How comes it, Michael, you are thus
forgot?

*Cas.* I pray you, pardon me; I cannot
speak.

*Oth.* Worthy Montano, you were wont to
be civil;
The gravity and stillness of your youth
The world hath noted, and your name is
great
In mouths of wisest censure: what's the mat-
ter,
That you unlace your reputation thus,
And spend your rich opinion for the name
Of a night-brawler? give me answer to it.

*Mon.* Worthy Othello, I am hurt to dan-
ger:
Your officer, Iago, can inform you,—
While I spare speech, which something now
offends me,—
Of all that I do know: nor know I aught
By me that's said or done amiss this night.
Unless self-charity be sometimes a vice,
And to defend ourselves it be a sin
When violence assails us.

*Oth.* Now, by heaven,
My blood begins my safer guides to rule;
And passion, having my best judgment col-
lied,
Assays to lead the way. If I once stir,
Or do but lift this arm, the best of you
Shall sink in my rebuke. Give me to know
How this foul rout began, who set it on;
And he that is approv'd in this offence,
Though he had twinn'd with me, both at a
birth,
Shall lose me.—What! in a town of war
Yet wild, the people's hearts brimful of fear,
To manage private and domestic quarrel,
In night, and on the court and guard of
safety!
'Tis monstrous.—Iago, who began't?

*Mon.* If partially affin'd, or leagu'd in
office,
Thou dost deliver more or less than truth,
Thou art no soldier.

*Iago.* Touch me not so near:
I had rather have this tongue cut from my
mouth
Than it should do offence to Michael Cassio;
Yet, I persuade myself, to speak the truth

Shall nothing wrong him.—Thus it is, general.
Montano and myself being in speech,
There comes a fellow crying out for help;
And Cassio following him with determin'd sword,
To execute upon him. Sir, this gentleman
Steps in to Cassio, and entreats his pause:
Myself the crying fellow did pursue,
Lest by his clamour,—as it so fell out,—
The town might fall in fright: he, swift of foot,
Outran my purpose; and I return'd the rather
For that I heard the clink and fall of swords,
And Cassio high in oath; which till-to-night
I ne'er might say before. When I came back,—
For this was brief,—I found them close together
At blow and thrust; even as again they were
When you yourself did part them.
More of this matter cannot I report;—
But men are men; the best sometimes forget:—
Though Cassio did some little wrong to him,—
As men in rage strike those that wish them best,—
Yet surely Cassio, I believe, receiv'd
From him that fled some strange indignity
Which patience could not pass.
 *Oth.*     I know, Iago,
Thy honesty and love doth mince this matter,
Making it light to Cassio. Cassio, I love thee;
But never more be officer of mine.—

 *Re-enter* DESDEMONA, *attended.*

Look, if my gentle love be not rais'd up!—
I'll make thee an example.
 *Des.*    What's the matter?
 *Oth.* All's well now, sweeting; come away to bed.
Sir, for your hurts, myself will be your surgeon:
Lead him off. [*To* MONTANO, *who is led off.*
Iago, look with care about the town,
And silence those whom this vile brawl distracted.—
Come, Desdemona: 'tis the soldier's life
To have their balmy slumbers wak'd with strife.
   [*Exeunt all but* IAGO *and* CASSIO.
 *Iago.* What, are you hurt, lieutenant?
 *Cas.* Ay, past all surgery.
 *Iago.* Marry, heaven forbid!
 *Cas.* Reputation, reputation, reputation! O, I have lost my reputation! I have lost the immortal part of myself, and what remains is bestial.—My reputation, Iago, my reputation!
 *Iago.* As I am an honest man, I thought you had received some bodily wound; there is more sense in that than in reputation. Reputation is an idle and most false imposition; oft got without merit, and lost without deserving: you have lost no reputation at all, unless you repute yourself such a loser. What, man! there are ways to recover the general again: you are but now cast in his mood, a punishment more in policy than in malice; even so as one would beat his offenceless dog to affright an imperious lion: sue to him again, and he is yours.
 *Cas.* I will rather sue to be despised than to deceive so good a commander with so slight, so drunken, and so indiscreet an officer. Drunk? and speak parrot? and squabble? swagger? swear? and discourse fustian with one's own shadow?—O thou invisible spirit of wine, if thou hast no name to be known by, let us call thee devil!
 *Iago.* What was he that you followed with your sword? What had he done to you?
 *Cas.* I know not.
 *Iago.* Is't possible?
 *Cas.* I remember a mass of things, but nothing distinctly; a quarrel, but nothing wherefore.—O God, that men should put an enemy in their mouths to steal away their brains! that we should, with joy, pleasance, revel, and applause, transform ourselves into beasts!
 *Iago.* Why, but you are now well enough: how come you thus recovered?
 *Cas.* It hath pleased the devil drunkenness to give place to the devil wrath: one unperfectness shows me another, to make me frankly despise myself.
 *Iago.* Come, you are too severe a moraler: as the time, the place, and the condition of this country stands, I could heartily wish this had not fallen; but, since it is as it is, mend it for your own good.
 *Cas.* I will ask him for my place again,— he shall tell me I am a drunkard! Had I as many mouths as Hydra, such an answer would stop them all. To be now a sensible man, by and by a fool, and presently a beast! O strange!—Every inordinate cup is unbless'd, and the ingredient is a devil.
 *Iago.* Come, come, good wine is a good familiar creature if it be well used: exclaim no more against it. And, good lieutenant, I think you think I love you.
 *Cas.* I have well approved it, sir.—I drunk!
 *Iago.* You, or any man living, may be drunk at a time, man. I'll tell you what you shall do. Our general's wife is now the general;—I may say so in this respect, for that he hath devoted and given up himself to the contemplation, mark, and denotement of her parts and graces:—confess yourself freely to her; importune her help to put you in your

place again: she is of so free, so kind, so apt,
so blessed a disposition, she holds it a vice in
her goodness not to do more than she is requested: this broken joint between you and
her husband entreat her to splinter; and, my
fortunes against any lay worth naming, this
crack of your love shall grow stronger than
it was before.

*Cas.* You advise me well.

*Iago.* I protest, in the sincerity of love and
honest kindness.

*Cas.* I think it freely; and betimes in the
morning I will beseech the virtuous Desdemona to undertake for me: I am desperate
of my fortunes if they check me here.

*Iago.* You are in the right. Good-night,
lieutenant; I must to the watch.

*Cas.* Good-night, honest Iago. [*Exit.*

*Iago.* And what's he, then, that says I play
 the villain?
When this advice is free I give and honest,
Probal to thinking, and, indeed, the course
To win the Moor again? For 'tis most easy
The inclining Desdemona to subdue
In any honest suit: she's fram'd as fruitful
As the free elements. And then for her
To win the Moor,—were't to renounce his
 baptism,
All seals and symbols of redeemed sin,—
His soul is so enfetter'd to her love
That she may make, unmake, do what she
 list,
Even as her appetite shall play the god
With his weak function. How am I, then, a
 villain
To counsel Cassio to this parallel course,
Directly to his good? Divinity of hell!
When devils will their blackest sins put on,
They do suggest at first with heavenly
 shows,
As I do now: for whiles this honest fool
Plies Desdemona to repair his fortunes,
And she for him pleads strongly to the
 Moor,
I'll pour this pestilence into his ear,—
That she repeals him for her body's lust;
And by how much she strives to do him good
She shall undo her credit with the Moor.
So will I turn her virtue into pitch;
And out of her own goodness make the net
That shall enmesh them all.

   *Enter* RODERIGO.

     How now, Roderigo!

*Rod.* I do follow here in the chase, not
like a hound that hunts, but one that fills up
the cry. My money is almost spent; I have
been to-night exceedingly well cudgelled; and
I think the issue will be—I shall have so
much experience for my pains: and so, with
no money at all, and a little more wit, return
again to Venice. [*patience!*

*Iago.* How poor are they that have not

What wound did ever heal but by degrees?
Thou know'st we work by wit, and not by
 witchcraft;
And wit depends on dilatory time.
Does't not go well? Cassio hath beaten thee,
And thou, by that small hurt, hast cashier'd
 Cassio;
Though other things grow fair against the
 sun,
Yet fruits that blossom first will first be
 ripe:
Content thyself awhile.—By the mass, 'tis
 morning;
Pleasure and action make the hours seem
 short.—
Retire thee; go where thou art billeted:
Away, I say; thou shalt know more here-
 after:
Nay, get thee gone. [*Exit* ROD.]—Two things
 are to be done,—
My wife must move for Cassio to her mis-
 tress;
I'll set her on;
Myself the while to draw the Moor apart,
And bring him jump when he may Cassio
 find
Soliciting his wife. Ay, that's the way;
Dull not device by coldness and delay. [*Exit.*

## ACT III.

### SCENE I.—CYPRUS. *Before the Castle.*

*Enter* CASSIO *and some* Musicians.

*Cas.* Masters, play here,—I will content
 your pains,
Something that's brief; and bid good-morrow, general.   [*Music.*

    *Enter* Clown.

*Clo.* Why, masters, have your instruments
been in Naples, that they speak i' the nose
thus?

1 *Mus.* How, sir, how!

*Clo.* Are these, I pray you, wind instruments?

1 *Mus.* Ay, marry, are they, sir.

*Clo.* O, thereby hangs a tale.

1 *Mus.* Whereby hangs a tale, sir?

*Clo.* Marry, sir, by many a wind instrument that I know. But, masters, here's money
for you: and the general so likes your music
that he desires you, for love's sake, to make
no more noise with it.

1 *Mus.* Well, sir, we will not.

*Clo.* If you have any music that may not
be heard, to't again: but, as they say, to hear
music the general does not greatly care.

1 *Mus.* We have none such, sir.

*Clo.* Then put up your pipes in your bag,
for I'll away: go, vanish into air; away.

     [*Exeunt* Musicians.

*Cas.* Dost thou hear, mine honest friend?

*Clo.* No, I hear not your honest friend; I hear you.

*Cas.* Pr'ythee, keep up thy quillets. There's a poor piece of gold for thee: if the gentlewoman that attends the general's wife be stirring, tell her there's one Cassio entreats her a little favour of speech: wilt thou do this?

*Clo.* She is stirring, sir; if she will stir hither I shall seem to notify unto her.

*Cas.* Do, good my friend. [*Exit* Clown.

### Enter IAGO.

In happy time, Iago.

*Iago.* You have not been a-bed, then?

*Cas.* Why, no; the day had broke
Before we parted. I have made bold, Iago,
To send in to your wife: my suit to her
Is, that she will to virtuous Desdemona
Procure me some access.

*Iago.* I'll send her to you presently;
And I'll devise a mean to draw the Moor
Out of the way, that your converse and business
May be more free.

*Cas.* I humbly thank you for't.
I never knew [*Exit* IAGO.]
A Florentine more kind and honest.

### Enter EMILIA.

*Emil.* Good-morrow, good lieutenant: I am sorry
For your displeasure; but all will soon be well.
The general and his wife are talking of it;
And she speaks for you stoutly: the Moor replies
That he you hurt is of great fame in Cyprus,
And great affinity, and that, in wholesome wisdom, [he loves you,
He might not but refuse you; but he protests
And needs no other suitor but his likings
To take the saf'st occasion by the front
To bring you in again.

*Cas.* Yet, I beseech you,—
If you think fit, or that it may be done,—
Give me advantage of some brief discourse
With Desdemon alone.

*Emil.* Pray you, come in:
I will bestow you where you shall have time
To speak your bosom freely.

*Cas.* I am much bound to you.
[*Exeunt.*

### SCENE II.—CYPRUS. *A Room in the Castle.*

*Enter* OTHELLO, IAGO, *and* Gentlemen.

*Oth.* These letters give, Iago, to the pilot;
And by him do my duties to the senate:
That done, I will be walking on the works;
Repair there to me.

*Iago.* Well, my good lord, I'll do't.

*Oth.* This fortification, gentlemen,—shall we see't?

*Gent.* We'll wait upon your lordship.
[*Exeunt.*

### SCENE III.—CYPRUS. *The Garden of the Castle.*

*Enter* DESDEMONA, CASSIO, *and* EMILIA.

*Des.* Be thou assur'd, good Cassio, I will do
All my abilities in thy behalf. [my husband

*Emil.* Good madam, do: I warrant it grieves
As if the case were his. [doubt, Cassio,

*Des.* O, that's an honest fellow.—Do not
But I will have my lord and you again
As friendly as you were.

*Cas.* Bounteous madam,
Whatever shall become of Michael Cassio,
He's never anything but your true servant.

*Des.* I know't,—I thank you. You do love my lord: [assur'd
You have known him long; and be you well
He shall in strangeness stand no further off
Than in a politic distance.

*Cas.* Ay, but, lady,
That policy may either last so long,
Or feed upon such nice and waterish diet,
Or breed itself so out of circumstance,
That, I being absent, and my place supplied,
My general will forget my love and service.

*Des.* Do not doubt that; before Emilia here
I give thee warrant of thy place: assure thee,
If I do vow a friendship, I'll perform it
To the last article: my lord shall never rest;
I'll watch him tame, and talk him out of patience;
His bed shall seem a school, his board a shrift;
I'll intermingle everything he does
With Cassio's suit: therefore be merry, Cassio;
For thy solicitor shall rather die
Than give thy cause away.

*Emil.* Madam, here comes
My lord.

*Cas.* Madam, I'll take my leave.

*Des.* Why, stay,
And hear me speak.

*Cas.* Madam, not now: I am very ill at ease,
Unfit for mine own purposes.

*Des.* Well, do your discretion.
[*Exit* CASSIO.

### Enter OTHELLO and IAGO.

*Iago.* Ha! I like not that.

*Oth.* What dost thou say? [what.

*Iago.* Nothing, my lord: or if—I know not

*Oth.* Was not that Cassio parted from my wife? [think it,

*Iago.* Cassio, my lord! No, sure, I cannot
That he would steal away so guilty-like,
Seeing you coming.

*Oth.* I do believe 'twas he.

*Des.* How now, my lord!
I have been talking with a suitor here,
A man that languishes in your displeasure.
   *Oth.* Who is't you mean?    [lord,
   *Des.* Why, your lieutenant, Cassio. Good my
If I have any grace or power to move you,
His present reconciliation take;
For if he be not one that truly loves you,
That errs in ignorance, and not in cunning,
I have no judgment in an honest face:
I pr'ythee, call him back.
   *Oth.*          Went he hence now?
   *Des.* Ay, sooth; so humbled
That he hath left part of his grief with me,
To suffer with him. Good love, call him back.
   *Oth.* Not now, sweet Desdemon; some
    other time.
   *Des.* But shall't be shortly?
   *Oth.*        The sooner, sweet, for you.
   *Des.* Shall't be to-night at supper?
   *Oth.*          No, not to-night.
   *Des.* To-morrow dinner, then?
   *Oth.*        I shall not dine at home;
I meet the captains at the citadel.
   *Des.* Why, then, to-morrow night; or
    Tuesday morn;    [morn:—
On Tuesday noon, or night; on Wednesday
I pr'ythee, name the time; but let it not
Exceed three days: in faith, he's penitent;
And yet his trespass, in our common rea-
    son,—
Save that, they say, the wars must make
    examples
Out of the best,—is not almost a fault
To incur a private check. When shall he
    come?
Tell me, Othello: I wonder in my soul
What you would ask me that I should deny,
Or stand so mammering on. What! Michael
    Cassio,    [a time,
That came a-wooing with you; and so many
When I have spoke of you dispraisingly,
Hath ta'en your part; to have so much to do
To bring him in! Trust me, I could do
    much,—    [when he will;
   *Oth.* Pr'ythee, no more; let him come
I will deny thee nothing.
   *Des.*        Why, this is not a boon;
'Tis as I should entreat you wear your gloves,
Or feed on nourishing dishes, or keep you
    warm,
Or sue to you to do a peculiar profit
To your own person: nay, when I have a suit
Wherein I mean to touch your love indeed,
It shall be full of poise and difficult weight,
And fearful to be granted.
   *Oth.*        I will deny thee nothing:
Whereon, I do beseech thee, grant me this,
To leave me but a little to myself.
   *Des.* Shall I deny you? no: farewell, my
    lord.
   *Oth.* Farewell, my Desdemona: I'll come
to thee straight.

   *Des.* Emilia, come.—Be as your fancies
    teach you;
Whate'er you be, I am obedient.
              [*Exit with* EMILIA.
   *Oth.* Excellent wretch! Perdition catch my
    soul,
But I do love thee! and when I love thee not
Chaos is come again.
   *Iago.* My noble lord,—
   *Oth.*         What dost thou say, Iago?
   *Iago.* Did Michael Cassio, when you
    woo'd my lady,
Know of your love?    [thou ask?
   *Oth.* He did, from first to last; why dost
   *Iago.* But for a satisfaction of my thought;
No further harm.
   *Oth.*        Why of thy thought, Iago?
   *Iago.* I did not think he had been ac-
    quainted with her.
   *Oth.* O, yes; and went between us very
    oft.
   *Iago.* Indeed!
   *Oth.* Indeed! ay, indeed:—discern'st thou
    aught in that?
Is he not honest?
   *Iago.*        Honest, my lord!
   *Oth.*         Honest! ay, honest.
   *Iago.* My lord, for aught I know.
   *Oth.* What dost thou think?
   *Iago.*         Think, my lord!
   *Oth.*         Think, my lord!
By heaven, he echoes me,
As if there were some monster in his thought
Too hideous to be shown.—Thou dost mean
    something:    [not that,
I heard thee say even now,—thou lik'dst
When Cassio left my wife: what didst not
    like?
And when I told thee he was of my counsel
In my whole course of wooing, thou criedst,
    *Indeed!*    [gether,
And didst contract and purse thy brow to-
As if thou then hadst shut up in thy brain
Some horrible conceit: if thou dost love me,
Show me thy thought.
   *Iago.* My lord, you know I love you.
   *Oth.*        I think thou dost;
And,—for I know thou'rt full of love and
    honesty,
And weigh'st thy words before thou giv'st
    them breath,—
Therefore these stops of thine fright me the
    more:
For such things in a false disloyal knave
Are tricks of custom; but in a man that's
    just
They're close delations, working from the
    heart,
That passion cannot rule.
   *Iago.*       For Michael Cassio,
I dare be sworn I think that he is honest.
   *Oth.* I think so too.
   *Iago.*       Men should be what they seem;

Or those that be not, would they might seem
    none!
  *Oth.* Certain, men should be what they
    seem.
  *Iago.*             Why, then,
I think Cassio's an honest man.
  *Oth.* Nay, yet there's more in this:
I pr'ythee, speak to me as to thy thinkings,
As thou dost ruminate; and give thy worst
    of thoughts
The worst of words.
  *Iago.*       Good my lord, pardon me:
Though I am bound to every act of duty,
I am not bound to that all slaves are free to.
Utter my thoughts? Why, say they are vile
    and false,—
As where's that palace whereunto foul things
Sometimes intrude not? who has a breast so
    pure
But some uncleanly apprehensions
Keep leets and law-days, and in session sit
With meditations lawful?     [friend, Iago,
  *Oth.* Thou dost conspire against thy
If thou think'st him wrong'd, and mak'st his
    ear
A stranger to thy thoughts.
  *Iago.*       I do beseech you,—
Though I perchance am vicious in my guess,
As, I confess, it is my nature's plague
To spy into abuses, and of my jealousy [yet,
Shape faults that are not,—that your wisdom
From one that so imperfectly conceits,
Would take no notice; nor build yourself a
    trouble
Out of his scattering and unsure observ-
    ance:—
It were not for your quiet nor your good,
Nor for my manhood, honesty, or wisdom,
To let you know my thoughts.
  *Oth.*         What dost thou mean?
  *Iago.* Good name in man and woman,
    dear my lord,
Is the immediate jewel of their souls:
Who steals my purse steals trash; 'tis some-
    thing, nothing;     [thousands;
'Twas mine, 'tis his, and has been slave to
But he that filches from me my good name
Robs me of that which not enriches him,
And makes me poor indeed.
  *Oth.* By heaven, I'll know thy thoughts.
  *Iago.* You cannot, if my heart were in
    your hand;
Nor shall not, whilst 'tis in my custody.
  *Oth.* Ha!
  *Iago.*     O, beware, my lord, of jealousy;
It is the green-ey'd monster which doth mock
The meat it feeds on: that cuckold lives in
    bliss
Who, certain of his fate, loves not his wrong-
    er;
But, O what damned minutes tells he o'er
Who dotes, yet doubts—suspects, yet strongly
    loves!

  *Oth.* O misery!           [enough;
  *Iago.* Poor and content is rich, and rich
But riches fineless is as poor as winter
To him that ever fears he shall be poor:—
Good heaven, the souls of all my tribe defend
From jealousy!
  *Oth.*      Why, why is this?
Think'st thou I'd make a life of jealousy,
To follow still the changes of the moon
With fresh suspicions? No; to be once in
    doubt
Is once to be resolv'd: exchange me for a goat
When I shall turn the business of my soul
To such exsufflicate and blown surmises,
Matching thy inference. 'Tis not to make me
    jealous,
To say my wife is fair, feeds well, loves com-
    pany,
Is free of speech, sings, plays, and dances
    well;
Where virtue is, these are more virtuous:
Nor from mine own weak merits will I draw
The smallest fear or doubt of her revolt;
For she had eyes, and chose me. No, Iago;
I'll see before I doubt; when I doubt, prove;
And, on the proof, there is no more but
    this,—
Away at once with love or jealousy!
  *Iago.* I am glad of it; for now I shall have
    reason
To show the love and duty that I bear you
With franker spirit: therefore, as I am bound,
Receive it from me:—I speak not yet of
    proof.
Look to your wife; observe her well with
    Cassio;
Wear your eye thus, not jealous nor secure:
I would not have your free and noble nature,
Out of self-bounty, be abus'd; look to't:
I know our country disposition well;
In Venice they do let heaven see the pranks
They dare not show their husbands; their
    best conscience
Is not to leave undone, but keep unknown.
  *Oth.* Dost thou say so?      [you;
  *Iago.* She did deceive her father, marrying
And when she seem'd to shake and fear your
    looks,
She lov'd them most.
  *Oth.*          And so she did.
  *Iago.*         Why, go to, then;
She that, so young, could give out such a
    seeming,
To seal her father's eyes up close as oak,—
He thought 'twas witchcraft,—But I am
    much to blame;
I humbly do beseech you of your pardon
For too much loving you.
  *Oth.*         I am bound to thee for ever.
  *Iago.* I see this hath a little dash'd your
    spirits.
  *Oth.* Not a jot, not a jot.
  *Iago.*         Trust me, I fear it has.

I hope you will consider what is spoke
Comes from my love; but I do see you're
　　mov'd:—
I am to pray you not to strain my speech
To grosser issues nor to larger reach
Than to suspicion.

*Oth.* I will not.

*Iago.*　　　　　Should you do so, my lord,
My speech should fall into such vile success
Which my thoughts aim'd not. Cassio's my
　　worthy friend:—
My lord, I see you're mov'd.

*Oth.*　　　　　No, not much mov'd:
I do not think but Desdemona's honest.

*Iago.* Long live she so! and long live you
　　to think so!　　　　　　　[self,—

*Oth.* And yet, how nature erring from it-

*Iago.* Ay, there's the point:—as,—to be
　　bold with you,—
Not to affect many proposed matches
Of her own clime, complexion, and degree,
Whereto we see in all things nature tends,—
Foh! one may smell in such a will most rank,
Foul disproportion, thoughts unnatural:—
But pardon me: I do not in position
Distinctly speak of her; though I may fear
Her will, recoiling to her better judgment,
May fall to match you with her country
　　forms,
And happily repent.

*Oth.*　　　　　Farewell, farewell:
If more thou dost perceive, let me know
　　more;
Set on thy wife to observe: leave me, Iago.

*Iago.* My lord, I take my leave. 　[*Going.*

*Oth.* Why did I marry?—This honest crea-
　　ture doubtless 　　　　　　[unfolds.
Sees and knows more, much more, than he

*Iago.* [*Returning.*] My lord, I would I
　　might entreat your honour
To scan this thing no further; leave it to
　　time:
Although 'tis fit that Cassio have his place,—
For, sure, he fills it up with great ability,—
Yet, if you please to hold him off awhile,
You shall by that perceive him and his
　　means:
Note if your lady strain his entertainment
With any strong or vehement importunity;
Much will be seen in that. In the meantime
Let me be thought too busy in my fears,—
As worthy cause I have to fear I am,—
And hold her free, I do beseech your honour.

*Oth.* Fear not my government.

*Iago.* I once more take my leave. 　[*Exit.*

*Oth.* This fellow's of exceeding honesty,
And knows all qualities, with a learned spirit,
Of human dealings. If I do prove her haggard,
Though that her jesses were my dear heart-
　　strings,
I'd whistle her off, and let her down the wind
To prey at fortune. Haply, for I am black,
And have not those soft parts of conversation

That chamberers have; or, for I am declin'd
Into the vale of years,—yet that's not
　　much,—
She's gone; I am abus'd; and my relief
Must be to loathe her. O curse of marriage,
That we can call these delicate creatures
　　ours,
And not their appetites! I had rather be a
　　toad,
And live upon the vapour of a dungeon,
Than keep a corner in the thing I love
For others' uses. Yet 'tis the plague of great
　　ones;
Prerogativ'd are they less than the base;
'Tis destiny unshunnable, like death:
Even then this forked plague is fated to us
When we do quicken. Desdemona comes:
If she be false, O, then heaven mocks itself!—
I'll not believe't.

*Re-enter* DESDEMONA *and* EMILIA.

*Des.*　　　　　How now, my dear Othello!
Your dinner, and the generous islanders
By you invited, do attend your presence.

*Oth.* I am to blame.

*Des.*　　　　　Why do you speak so faintly?
Are you not well?

*Oth.* I have a pain upon my forehead here.

*Des.* Faith, that's with watching; 'twill
　　away again:
Let me but bind it hard, within this hour
It will be well.

*Oth.*　　　　　Your napkin is too little;
　　　[*He puts the handkerchief from him,
　　　　　and she drops it.*
Let it alone. Come, I'll go in with you.

*Des.* I am very sorry that you are not well.
　　　　　　[*Exeunt* OTH. *and* DES.

*Emil.* I am glad I have found this napkin:
This was her first remembrance from the
　　Moor:
My wayward husband hath a hundred times
Woo'd me to steal it; but she so loves the
　　token,—
For he conjur'd her she should ever keep it,—
That she reserves it evermore about her
To kiss and talk to. I'll have the work ta'en
　　out,
And give't Iago:
What he'll do with it heaven knows, not I;
I nothing but to please his fantasy.

*Re-enter* IAGO.

*Iago.* How now! what do you here alone?

*Emil.* Do not you chide; I have a thing for
　　you.

*Iago.* A thing for me!—it is a common
　　thing.

*Emil.* Ha!

*Iago.* To have a foolish wife. 　　[now

*Emil.* O, is that all? What will you give me
For that same handkerchief?

*Iago.*　　　　　What handkerchief?

*Emil.* What handkerchief!
Why, that the Moor first gave to Desdemona;
That which so often you did bid me steal.
*Iago.* Hast stol'n it from her?
*Emil.* No, faith; she let it drop by negligence,
And, to the advantage, I, being here, took't up.
Look, here it is.
*Iago.*            A good wench; give it me.
*Emil.* What will you do with't, that you have been so earnest
To have me filch it?
*Iago.*            Why, what's that to you?
                                   [*Snatching it.*
*Emil.* If it be not for some purpose of import,
Give't me again: poor lady, she'll run mad
When she shall lack it.                    [it.
*Iago.* Be not acknown on't; I have use for
Go, leave me.                  [*Exit* EMILIA.
I will in Cassio's lodging lose this napkin,
And let him find it. Trifles light as air
Are to the jealous confirmation strong
As proofs of holy writ: this may do something,
The Moor already changes with my poison:
Dangerous conceits are in their natures poisons,
Which at the first are scarce found to distaste,
But, with a little act upon the blood,
Burn like the mines of sulphur.—I did say so:—              [dragora,
Look, where he comes! Not poppy, nor mandragora,
Nor all the drowsy syrups of the world,
Shall ever medicine thee to that sweet sleep
Which thou ow'dst yesterday.

                *Re-enter* OTHELLO.

*Oth.*              Ha! ha! false to me?
*Iago.* Why, how now, general! no more of that.              [the rack:—
*Oth.* Avaunt! be gone! thou hast set me on
I swear 'tis better to be much abus'd
Than but to know't a little.
*Iago.*              How now, my lord!
*Oth.* What sense had I of her stol'n hours of lust?
I saw it not, thought it not, it harm'd not me:
I slept the next night well, was free and merry;
I found not Cassio's kisses on her lips:
He that is robb'd, not wanting what is stol'n,
Let him not know't, and he's not robb'd at all.
*Iago.* I am sorry to hear this.
*Oth.* I had been happy if the general camp,
Pioneers and all, had tasted her sweet body,
So I had nothing known. O, now, for ever
Farewell the tranquil mind! farewell content!
Farewell the plumed troop and the big wars
That make ambition virtue! O, farewell!

Farewell the neighing steed and the shrill trump,
The spirit-stirring drum, the ear-piercing fife,
The royal banner, and all quality,
Pride, pomp, and circumstance of glorious war!
And, O you mortal engines, whose rude throats
The immortal Jove's dread clamours counterfeit,
Farewell! Othello's occupation's gone!
*Iago.* Is't possible, my lord?—
*Oth.* Villain, be sure thou prove my love a whore,—        [*Taking him by the throat.*
Be sure of it; give me the ocular proof;
Or, by the worth of mine eternal soul,
Thou hadst been better have been born a dog
Than answer my wak'd wrath!
*Iago.*              Is't come to this?
*Oth.* Make me to see't; or, at the least, so prove it
That the probation bear no hinge nor loop
To hang a doubt on; or woe upon thy life!
*Iago.* My noble lord,—
*Oth.* If thou dost slander her and torture me,
Never pray more; abandon all remorse;
On horror's head horrors accumulate;
Do deeds to make heaven weep, all earth amaz'd;
For nothing canst thou to damnation add
Greater than that.
*Iago.*      O grace! O heaven forgive me!
Are you a man? have you a soul or sense?—
God b' wi' you; take mine office.—O wretched fool,
That liv'st to make thine honesty a vice!—
O monstrous world! Take note, take note, O world,
To be direct and honest is not safe.—
I thank you for this profit; and from hence
I'll love no friend, sith love breeds such offence.
*Oth.* Nay, stay:—thou shouldst be honest.
*Iago.* I should be wise; for honesty's a fool,
And loses that it works for.
*Oth.*              By the world,
I think my wife be honest, and think she is not;
I think that thou art just, and think thou art not:
I'll have some proof: her name, that was as fresh
As Dian's visage, is now begrim'd and black
As mine own face.—If there be cords or knives,
Poison, or fire, or suffocating streams,
I'll not endur't.—Would I were satisfied!
*Iago.* I see, sir, you are eaten up with passion:
I do repent me that I put it to you.
You would be satisfied?
*Oth.*              Would! nay, I will.

*Iago.* And may: but how? how satisfied,
my lord?
Would you, the supervisor, grossly gape on,—
Behold her tupp'd?
   *Oth.*         Death and damnation! O!
*Iago.* It were a tedious difficulty, I think,
To bring them to that prospect: damn them,
then,
If ever mortal eyes do see them bolster
More than their own! What then? how then?
What shall I say? Where's satisfaction?
It is impossible you should see this,
Were they as prime as goats, as hot as mon-
keys,
As salt as wolves in pride, and fools as gross
As ignorance made drunk. But yet, I say,
If imputation and strong circumstances,—
Which lead directly to the door of truth,—
Will give you satisfaction, you may have't.
   *Oth.* Give me a living reason she's disloyal.
   *Iago.* I do not like the office:
But, sith I am enter'd in this cause so far,—
Prick'd to it by foolish honesty and love,—
I will go on. I lay with Cassio lately;
And, being troubled with a raging tooth,
I could not sleep.
There are a kind of men so loose of soul
That in their sleeps will mutter their affairs:
One of this kind is Cassio:
In sleep I heard him say, *Sweet Desdemona,*
*Let us be wary, let us hide our loves;*
And then, sir, would he gripe and wring my
hand,
Cry, *O sweet creature!* and then kiss me hard,
As if he pluck'd up kisses by the roots,
That grew upon my lips: then laid his leg
Over my thigh, and sigh'd, and kiss'd; and
then
Cried, *Cursed fate that gave thee to the*
   \*Moor!*
   *Oth.* O monstrous! monstrous!
   *Iago.*        Nay, this was but his dream.
   *Oth.* But this denoted a foregone conclu-
sion:
'Tis a shrewd doubt, though it be but a
dream.
   *Iago.* And this may help to thicken other
   proofs
That do demonstrate thinly.
   *Oth.*       I'll tear her all to pieces.
   *Iago.* Nay, but be wise: yet we see nothing
   done;
She may be honest yet. Tell me but this,—
Have you not sometimes seen a handkerchief
Spotted with strawberries in your wife's
hand?
   *Oth.* I gave her such a one; 'twas my first
   gift.           [chief,—
   *Iago.* I know not that: but such a handker-
I am sure it was your wife's,—did I to-day
See Cassio wipe his beard with.
   *Oth.*          If it be that,—
   *Iago.* If it be that, or any that was hers,

It speaks against her with the other proofs.
   *Oth.* O, that the slave had forty thousand
   lives,—
One is too poor, too weak for my revenge!
Now do I see 'tis true.—Look here, Iago;
All my fond love thus do I blow to heaven:
'Tis gone.—
Arise, black vengeance, from the hollow hell!
Yield up, O love, thy crown and hearted
   throne
To tyrannous hate! swell, bosom, with thy
   fraught,
For 'tis of aspics' tongues!
   *Iago.* Yet be content.
   *Oth.*         O, blood, Iago, blood!
   *Iago.* Patience, I say; your mind perhaps
   may change.
   *Oth.* Never, Iago. Like to the Pontic sea,
Whose icy current and compulsive course
Ne'er feels retiring ebb, but keeps due on
To the Propontic and the Hellespont;
Even so my bloody thoughts, with violent
   pace,
Shall ne'er look back, ne'er ebb to humble
   love,
Till that a capable and wide revenge
Swallow them up.—Now, by yond marble
   heaven,
In the due reverence of a sacred vow [*Kneels.*
I here engage my words.
   *Iago.*       Do not rise yet.—[*Kneels.*
Witness, you ever-burning lights above,
You elements that clip us round about,—
Witness that here Iago doth give up
The execution of his wit, hands, heart,
To wrong'd Othello's service! Let him com-
   mand,
And to obey shall be in me remorse,
What bloody business ever.
   *Oth.*         I greet thy love,
Not with vain thanks, but with acceptance
   bounteous,
And will upon the instant put thee to't:
Within these three days let me hear thee say
That Cassio's not alive.        [request:
   *Iago.* My friend is dead; 'tis done at your
But let her live.
   *Oth.* Damn her, lewd minx! O, damn her!
Come, go with me apart; I will withdraw
To furnish me with some swift means of
   death
For the fair devil. Now art thou my lieu-
   tenant.
   *Iago.* I am your own for ever.    [*Exeunt.*

SCENE IV. CYPRUS. *Before the Castle.*

*Enter* DESDEMONA, EMILIA, *and* Clown.

   *Des.* Do you know, sirrah, where Lieu-
tenant Cassio lies?
   *Clo.* I dare not say he lies anywhere.
   *Des.* Why, man?
   *Clo.* He's a soldier; and for one to say a
soldier lies is stabbing.

*Des.* Go to: where lodges he?

*Clo.* To tell you where he lodges is to tell you where I lie.

*Des.* Can anything be made of this?

*Clo.* I know not where he lodges; and for me to devise a lodging, and say he lies here or he lies there were to lie in mine own throat.

*Des.* Can you inquire him out, and be edified by report?

*Clo.* I will catechize the world for him; that is, make questions, and by them answer.

*Des.* Seek him, bid him come hither: tell him I have moved my lord on his behalf, and hope all will be well.

*Clo.* To do this is within the compass of man's wit; and therefore I will attempt the doing it.  [*Exit*.

*Des.* Where should I lose that handkerchief, Emilia?

*Emil.* I know not, madam.  [*purse*

*Des.* Believe me, I had rather have lost my
Full of crusadoes: and, but my noble Moor
Is true of mind, and made of no such baseness
As jealous creatures are, it were enough
To put him to ill thinking.

*Emil.*  Is he not jealous?

*Des.* Who, he? I think the sun where he
was born
Drew all such humours from him.

*Emil.*  Look, where he comes.

*Des.* I will not leave him now till Cassio
Be call'd to him.

### *Enter* OTHELLO.

How is't with you, my lord?

*Oth.* Well, my good lady.—[*Aside.*] O,
hardness to dissemble!—
How do you, Desdemona?

*Des.* Well, my good lord.

*Oth.* Give me your hand: this hand is
moist, my lady.  [*sorrow.*

*Des.* It yet hath felt no age nor known no

*Oth.* This argues fruitfulness and liberal
heart:—  [*quires*
Hot, hot, and moist: this hand of yours re-
A sequester from liberty, fasting and prayer,
Must castigation, exercise devout;
For here's a young and sweating devil here
That commonly rebels. 'Tis a good hand,
A frank one.

*Des.* You may indeed say so;
For 'twas that hand that gave away my heart.

*Oth.* A liberal hand: the hearts of old gave
hands;
But our new heraldry is hands, not hearts.

*Des.* I cannot speak of this. Come now,
your promise.

*Oth.* What promise, chuck?

*Des.* I have sent to bid Cassio come speak
with you.  [*me;*

*Oth.* I have a salt and sorry rheum offends
Lend me thy handkerchief.

*Des.*  Here, my lord.

*Oth.* That which I gave you.

*Des.*  I have it not about me.

*Oth.* Not?

*Des.*  No, indeed, my lord.

*Oth.*  That is a fault.
That handkerchief
Did an Egyptian to my mother give;
She was a charmer, and could almost read
The thoughts of people: she told her, while
she kept it,  [*father*
'Twould make her amiable, and subdue my
Entirely to her love; but if she lost it,
Or made a gift of it, my father's eye
Should hold her loathed, and his spirits
should hunt
After new fancies: she, dying, gave it me;
And bid me, when my fate would have me
wive,
To give it her. I did so: and take heed on't;
Make it a darling like your precious eye;
To lose't or give't away were such perdition
As nothing else could match.

*Des.*  Is't possible?

*Oth.* 'Tis true: there's magic in the web of
it:
A sibyl, that had number'd in the world
The sun to course two hundred compasses,
In her prophetic fury sew'd the work;
The worms were hallow'd that did breed the
silk;
And it was dy'd in mummy which the skilful
Conserv'd of maidens' hearts.

*Des.*  Indeed! is't true?

*Oth.* Most veritable, therefore look to't
well.

*Des.* Then would to God that I had never
seen't!

*Oth.* Ha! wherefore?

*Des.* Why do you speak so startingly and
rash?  [*the way?*

*Oth.* Is't lost? is't gone? speak, is it out of

*Des.* Heaven bless us!

*Oth.*  Say you?

*Des.* It is not lost; but what an if it were?

*Oth.* How!

*Des.* I say, it is not lost.

*Oth.*  Fetch't, let me see't.

*Des.* Why, so I can, sir, but I will not now.
This is a trick to put me from my suit:
Pray you, let Cassio be receiv'd again.

*Oth.* Fetch me the handkerchief: my mind
misgives.

*Des.* Come, come;
You'll never meet a more sufficient man.

*Oth.* The handkerchief!

*Des.*  I pray, talk me of Cassio.

*Oth.* The handkerchief!

*Des.*  A man that all his time
Hath founded his good fortunes on your love,
Shar'd dangers with you,—

*Oth.*  The handkerchief!

*Des.* In sooth, you are to blame.

*Oth.* Away!  [*Exit.*

*Emil.* Is not this man jealous?
*Des.* I ne'er saw this before.
Sure there's some wonder in this handkerchief:
I am most unhappy in the loss of it.
*Emil.* 'Tis not a year or two shows us a man:
They are all but stomachs, and we all but food:
They eat us hungerly, and when they are full,
They belch us.—Look you, Cassio and my husband.

*Enter* CASSIO *and* IAGO.

*Iago.* There is no other way; 'tis she must do't:
And, lo, the happiness! go and importune her.
*Des.* How now, good Cassio! what's the news with you? [you
*Cas.* Madam, my former suit: I do beseech
That by your virtuous means I may again
Exist, and be a member of his love,
Whom I, with all the office of my heart,
Entirely honour: I would not be delay'd.
If my offence be of such mortal kind
That nor my service past, nor present sorrows,
Nor purpos'd merit in futurity,
Can ransom me into his love again,
But to know so must be my benefit;
So shall I clothe me in a forc'd content,
And shut myself up in some other course,
To fortune's alms.
*Des.* Alas, thrice-gentle Cassio!
My advocation is not now in tune;
My lord is not my lord; nor should I know him,
Were. he in favour as in humour alter'd.
So help me every spirit sanctified,
As I have spoken for you all my best,
And stood within the blank of his displeasure
For my free speech! You must awhile be patient:
What I can do I will; and more I will
Than for myself I dare: let that suffice you.
*Iago.* Is my lord angry?
*Emil.* He went hence but now,
And certainly in strange unquietness.
*Iago.* Can he be angry? I have seen the cannon,
When it hath blown his ranks into the air,
And, like the devil, from his very arm
Puff'd his own brother;—and can he be angry?
Something of moment, then: I will go meet him:
There's matter in't indeed if he be angry.
*Des.* I pr'ythee, do so. [*Exit* IAGO.] Something, sure, of state,—
Either from Venice, or some unhatch'd practice
Made démonstrable here in Cyprus to him,—

Hath puddled his clear spirit, and in such cases
Men's natures wrangle with inferior things,
Though great ones are their object. 'Tis even so;
For let our finger ache, and it endures
Our other healthful members even to that sense
Of pain: nay, we must think men are not gods,
Nor of them look for such observancy
As fits the bridal.—Bestrew me much, Emilia,
I was,—unhandsome warrior as I am,—
Arraigning his unkindness with my soul;
But now I find I had suborn'd the witness,
And he's indicted falsely. [you think,
*Emil.* Pray heaven it be state matters, as
And no conception nor no jealous toy
Concerning you.
*Des.* Alas the day, I never gave him cause!
*Emil.* But jealous souls will not be answer'd so;
They are not ever jealous for the cause,
But jealous for they are jealous: 'tis a monster
Begot upon itself, born on itself.
*Des.* Heaven keep that monster from Othello's mind!
*Emil.* Lady, amen.
*Des.* I will go seek him.—Cassio, walk hereabout:
If I do find him fit, I'll move your suit,
And seek to effect it to my uttermost.
*Cas.* I humbly thank your ladyship.
[*Exeunt* DESDEMONA *and* EMILIA.

*Enter* BIANCA.

*Bian.* Save you, friend Cassio!
*Cas.* What make you from home?
How is it with you, my most fair Bianca?
I' faith, sweet love, I was coming to your house.
*Bian.* And I was going to your lodging, Cassio.
What, keep a week away? seven days and nights?
Eight score eight hours? and lovers' absent hours,
More tedious than the dial eight score times?
O weary reckoning!
*Cas.* .Pardon me, Bianca:
I have this while with leaden thoughts been press'd;
But I shall in a more continuate time
Strike off this score of absence. Sweet Bianca,
[*Giving her* DESDEMONA'S *handkerchief.*
Take me this work out.
*Bian.* O Cassio, whence came this?
This is some token from a newer friend:
To the felt absence now I feel a cause:
Is't come to this? Well, well.
*Cas.* Go to, woman!
Throw your vile guesses in the devil's teeth,

From whence you have them. You are jealous now
That this is from some mistress, some remembrance:
No, in good troth, Bianca.
*Bian.* Why, whose is it?
*Cas.* I know not neither: I found it in my chamber.
I like the work well: ere it be demanded,—
As like enough it will,—I'd have it copied:
Take it, and do't; and leave me for this time.
*Bian.* Leave you! wherefore?
*Cas.* I do attend here on the general;
And think it no addition, nor my wish,
To have him see me woman'd.
*Bian.* Why, I pray you?
*Cas.* Not that I love you not.
*Bian.* But that you do not love me
I pray you, bring me on the way a little;
And say if I shall see you soon at night.
*Cas.* 'Tis but a little way that I can bring you,
For I attend here: but I'll see you soon.
*Bian.* 'Tis very good; I must be circumstanc'd. [*Exeunt.*

### ACT IV.

#### SCENE I.—CYPRUS. *Before the Castle.*

*Enter* OTHELLO *and* IAGO.

*Iago.* Will you think so?
*Oth.* Think so, Iago?.
*Iago.* What,
To kiss in private?
*Oth.* An unauthoriz'd kiss.
*Iago.* Or to be naked with her friend in bed
An hour or more, not meaning any harm?
*Oth.* Naked in bed, Iago, and not mean harm!
It is hypocrisy against the devil:
They that mean virtuously, and yet do so,
The devil their virtue tempts, and they tempt heaven.
*Iago.* So they do nothing, 'tis a venial slip:
But if I give my wife a handkerchief,—
*Oth.* What then? [being hers,
*Iago.* Why, then, 'tis hers, my lord; and,
She may, I think, bestow't on any man.
*Oth.* She is protectress of her honour too:
May she give that? [seen?
*Iago.* Her honour is an essence that's not
They have it very oft that have it not:
But, for the handkerchief,— [forgot it:—
*Oth.* By heaven, I would most gladly have
Thou said'st,—O, it comes o'er my memory
As doth the raven o'er the infected house,
Boding to all,—he had my handkerchief.
*Iago.* Ay, what of that?
*Oth.* That's not so good now.
*Iago.* What,
If I had said I had seen him do you wrong?
Or heard him say,—as knaves be such abroad,
Who having, by their own importunate suit,

Or voluntary dotage of some mistress,
Convinced or supplied them, cannot choose
But they must blab,—
*Oth.* Hath he said anything?
*Iago.* He hath, my lord; but be you well assur'd,
No more than he'll unswear.
*Oth.* What hath he said?
*Iago.* Faith, that he did,—I know not what he did.
*Oth.* What? what?
*Iago.* Lie,—
*Oth.* With her?
*Iago.* With her, on her; what you will.
*Oth.* Lie with her! lie on her!—We say lie
on her when they belie her.—Lie with her!
that's fulsome.—Handkerchief,—confessions,
—handkerchief!—To confess, and be hanged
for his labour;—first, to be hanged, and then
to confess.—I tremble at it. Nature would
not invest herself in such shadowing passion
without some instruction. It is not words that
shake me thus:—pish!—noses, ears, and lips.
—Is't possible?—Confess,—handkerchief!—O
devil!— [*Falls in a trance.*
*Iago.* Work on, [caught;
My medicine, work! Thus credulous fools are
And many worthy and chaste dames even thus,
All guiltless, meet reproach.—What, ho! my lord!
My lord, I say! Othello!

*Enter* CASSIO.

How now, Cassio!
*Cas.* What's the matter?
*Iago.* My lord is fallen into an epilepsy:
This is his second fit; he had one yesterday.
*Cas.* Rub him about the temples.
*Iago.* No, forbear;
The lethargy must have his quiet course:
If not, he foams at mouth, and by and by
Breaks out to savage madness. Look, he stirs:
Do you withdraw yourself a little while,
He will recover straight: when he is gone,
I would on great occasion speak with you.
[*Exit* CASSIO.
How is it, general? have you not hurt your head?
*Oth.* Dost thou mock me?
*Iago.* I mock you! no, by heaven.
Would you would bear your fortune like a man!
*Oth.* A horned man's a monster and a beast.
*Iago.* There's many a beast, then, in a populous city,
And many a civil monster.
*Oth.* Did he confess it?
*Iago.* Good sir, be a man;
Think every bearded fellow that's but yok'd
May draw with you: there's millions now alive
That nightly lie in those unproper beds

Which they dare swear peculiar: your case is
   better.
O, 'tis the spite of hell, the fiend's arch-mock,
To lip a wanton in a secure couch,
And to suppose her chaste! No,.let me know;
And knowing what I am, I know what she
   shall be.
   *Oth.*     O, thou art wise; 'tis certain.
   *Iago.*        Stand you awhile apart;
Confine yourself but in a patient list.
Whilst you were here o'erwhelmed with your
   grief,—
A passion most unsuiting such a man,—
Cassio came hither: I shifted him away,
And laid good 'scuse upon your ecstasy;
Bade him anon return, and here speak with
   me;
The which he promis'd. Do but encave your-
   self,
And mark the fleers, the gibes, and notable
   scorns,
That dwell in every region of his face;
For I will make him tell the tale anew,—
Where, how, how oft, how long ago, and
   when
He hath, and is again to cope your wife:
I say, but mark his gesture. Marry, patience;
Or I shall say you are all in all in spleen,
And nothing of a man.
   *Oth.*        Dost thou hear, Iago?
I will be found most cunning in my patience;
But,—dost thou hear?—most bloody.
   *Iago.*        That's not amiss;
But yet keep time in all. Will you withdraw?
                 [OTHELLO *withdraws.*
Now will I question Cassio of Bianca,
A housewife that, by selling her desires,
Buys herself bread and clothes: it is a crea-
   ture
That dotes on Cassio,—as 'tis the strumpet's
   plague
To beguile many and be beguil'd by one:—
He, when he hears of her, cannot refrain
From the excess of laughter:—here he
   comes:—
As he shall smile Othello shall go mad;
And his unbookish jealousy must construe
Poor Cassio's smiles, gestures, and light be-
   haviour
Quite in the wrong.

           *Re-enter* CASSIO.

           How do you now, lieutènant?
   *Cas.* The worser that you give me the ad-
   dition
Whose want even kills me.        [on't.
   *Iago.* Ply Desdemona well, and you are sure
Now, if this suit lay in Bianca's power,
                 [*Speaking lower.*
How quickly should you speed!
   *Cas.*        Alas, poor caitiff!
   *Oth.* [*Aside.*] Look, how he laughs already!
   *Iago.* I never knew woman love man so.

   *Cas.* Alas, poor rogue! I think, i' faith, she
   loves me.
   *Oth.* [*Aside.*] Now he denies it faintly, and
   laughs it out.
   *Iago.* Do you hear, Cassio?
   *Oth.* [*Aside.*]     Now he importunes him
To tell it o'er:—go to; well said, well said.
   *Iago.* She gives it out that you shall marry
   her:
Do you intend it?
   *Cas.*        Ha, ha, ha!
   *Oth.* [*Aside.*] Do you triumph, Roman? do
   you triumph?
   *Cas.* I marry her!—what, a customer! I
pr'ythee, bear some charity to my wit; do not
think it so unwholesome:—ha, ha, ha!
   *Oth.* [*Aside.*] So, so, so, so: they laugh
   that win.        [marry her.
   *Iago.* Faith, the cry goes that you shall
   *Cas.* Pr'ythee, say true.
   *Iago.* I am a very villain else.
   *Oth.* [*Aside.*] Have you scored me? Well.
   *Cas.* This is the monkey's own giving out:
she is persuaded I will marry her, out of her
own love and flattery, not out of my promise.
   *Oth.* [*Aside.*] Iago beckons me; now he
begins the story.
   *Cas.* She was here even now; she haunts me
in every place. I was the other day talking on
the sea-bank with certain Venetians, and
thither comes the bauble, and falls thus about
my neck,—
   *Oth.* [*Aside.*] Crying, *O dear Cassio!* as it
were: his gesture imports it.
   *Cas.* So hangs, and lolls, and weeps upon
me; so hales, and pulls me:—ha, ha, ha!
   *Oth.* [*Aside.*] Now he tells how she plucked
him to my chamber. O, I see that nose of
yours, but not that dog I shall throw it to.
   *Cas.* Well, I must leave her company.
   *Iago.* Before me! look where she comes.
   *Cas.* 'Tis such another fitchew! marry, a
perfumed one.

           *Enter* BIANCA.

What do you mean by this haunting of me?
   *Bian.* Let the devil and his dam haunt
you! What did you mean by that same handkerchief you gave me even now? I was a fine
fool to take it. I must take out the work?—A
likely piece of work that you should find it in
your chamber, and not know who left it
there! This is some minx's token, and I must
take out the work? There,—give it your
hobby-horse: wheresoever you had it, I'll
on't.
   *Cas.* How now, my sweet Bianca! how
now! how now!
   *Oth.* [*Aside.*] By heaven, that should be
my handkerchief!
   *Bian.* An you'll come to supper to-night,
you may; an you will not, come when you
are next prepared for.        [*Exit.*

*Iago.* After her, after her.

*Cas.* Faith, I must; she'll rail in the street else.

*Iago.* Will you sup there?

*Cas.* Faith, I intend so.

*Iago.* Well, I may chance to see you; for I would very fain speak with you.

*Cas.* Pr'ythee, come; will you?

*Iago.* Go to; say no more. [*Exit* CASSIO.

*Oth.* [*Coming forward.*] How shall I murder him, Iago?

*Iago.* Did you perceive how he laughed at his vice?

*Oth.* O Iago!

*Iago.* And did you see the handkerchief?

*Oth.* Was that mine?

*Iago.* Yours, by this hand: and to see how he prizes the foolish woman your wife! she gave it him, and he hath given it his whore.

*Oth.* I would have him nine years a-killing. —A fine woman! a fair woman! a sweet woman!

*Iago.* Nay, you must forget that.

*Oth.* Ay, let her rot, and perish, and be damned to-night; for she shall not live: no, my heart is turned to stone; I strike it, and it hurts my hand.—O, the world hath not a sweeter creature: she might lie by an emperor's side, and command him tasks.

*Iago.* Nay, that's not your way.

*Oth.* Hang her! I do but say what she is:— so delicate with her needle!—an admirable musician! O, she will sing the savageness out of a bear!—Of so high and plenteous wit and invention!—

*Iago.* She's the worse for all this.

*Oth.* O, a thousand thousand times:—and then of so gentle a condition!

*Iago.* Ay, too gentle.

*Oth.* Nay, that's certain:—but yet the pity of it, Iago! O Iago, the pity of it, Iago!

*Iago.* If you are so fond over her iniquity, give her patent to offend; for, if it touch not you, it comes near nobody. [me!

*Oth.* I will chop her into messes.—Cuckold

*Iago.* O, 'tis foul in her.

*Oth.* With mine officer!

*Iago.* That's fouler.

*Oth.* Get me some poison, Iago; this night. —I'll not expostulate with her, lest her body and beauty unprovide my mind again:—this night, Iago.

*Iago.* Do it not with poison; strangle her in her bed, even the bed she hath contaminated.

*Oth.* Good, good: the justice of it pleases: very good.

*Iago.* And for Cassio,—let me be his undertaker: you shall hear more by midnight.

*Oth.* Excellent good. [*A trumpet within.*] What trumpet is that same?

*Iago.* Something from Venice, sure. 'Tis Lodovico

Come from the duke: and, see, your wife is with him.

*Enter* LODOVICO, DESDEMONA, *and* Attendants.

*Lod.* Save you, worthy general!

*Oth.* With all my heart, sir

*Lod.* The duke and senators of Venice greet you. [*Gives him a packet.*

*Oth.* I kiss the instrument of their pleasures. [*Opens the packet and reads.*

*Des.* And what's the news, good cousin Lodovico?

*Iago.* I am very glad to see you, signior; Welcome to Cyprus. [Cassio?

*Lod.* I thank you. How does Lieutenant

*Iago.* Lives, sir. [and my lord

*Des.* Cousin, there's fall'n between him An unkind breach: but you shall make all well.

*Oth.* Are you sure of that?

*Des.* My lord? [*you will,*—

*Oth.* [*Reads.*] *This fail you not to do as*

*Lod.* He did not call; he's busy in the paper.

Is there division 'twixt my lord and Cassio?

*Des.* A most unhappy one: I would do much

To atone them, for the love I bear to Cassio.

*Oth.* Fire and brimstone!

*Des.* My lord?

*Oth.* Are you wise?

*Des.* What, is he angry?

*Lod.* May be the letter mov'd him;

For, as I think, they do command him home,

Deputing Cassio in his government.

*Des.* Trust me, I am glad on't.

*Oth.* Indeed!

*Des.* My lord?

*Oth.* I am glad to see you mad.

*Des.* Why, sweet Othello,—

*Oth.* Devil! [*Striking her.*

*Des.* I have not deserv'd this.

*Lod.* My lord, this would not be believ'd in Venice,

Though I should swear I saw't: 'tis very much:

Make her amends; she weeps.

*Oth.* O devil, devil!

If that the earth could teem with woman's tears,

Each drop she falls would prove a crocodile.—

Out of my sight!

*Des.* I will not stay to offend you. [*Going.*

*Lod.* Truly, an obedient lady:—

I do beseech your lordship, call her back.

*Oth.* Mistress!

*Des.* My lord?

*Oth.* What would you with her, sir?

*Lod.* Who, I, my lord? [her turn:

*Oth.* Ay; you did wish that I would make

Sir, she can turn, and turn, and yet go on,
And turn again; and she can weep, sir, weep;
And she's obedient, as you say,—obedient,—
Very obedient.—Proceed you in your tears.—
Concerning this, sir,—O well-painted passion!
I am commanded home.—Get you away;
I'll send for you anon.—Sir, I obey the mandate,
And will return to Venice.—Hence, avaunt!
[*Exit* DESDEMONA.
Cassio shall have my place. And, sir, to-night,
I do entreat that we may sup together:
You are welcome, sir, to Cyprus.—Goats and monkeys! [*Exit.*
*Lod.* Is this the noble Moor whom our full senate
Call all-in-all sufficient?—Is this the nature
Whom passion could not shake? whose solid virtue
The shot of accident nor dart of chance
Could neither graze nor pierce?
*Iago.* He is much chang'd.
*Lod.* Are his wits safe? is he not light of brain?
*Iago.* He is that he is: I may not breathe my censure. [not,—
What he might be,—if what he might he is
I would to heaven he were!
*Lod.* What, strike his wife!
*Iago.* Faith, that was not so well; yet would I knew
That stroke would prove the worst!
*Lod.* Is it his use?
Or did the letters work upon his blood,
And new-create this fault?
*Iago.* Alas, alas!
It is not honesty in me to speak
What I have seen and known. You shall observe him;
And his own courses will denote him so
That I may save my speech: do but go after,
And mark how he continues.
*Lod.* I am sorry that I am deceiv'd in him. [*Exeunt.*

SCENE II.—CYPRUS. *A Room in the Castle.*
*Enter* OTHELLO *and* EMILIA.
*Oth.* You have seen nothing, then?
*Emil.* Nor ever heard, nor ever did suspect.
*Oth.* Yes, you have seen Cassio and she together.
*Emil.* But then I saw no harm, and then I heard [them.
Each syllable that breath made up between
*Oth.* What, did they never whisper?
*Emil.* Never, my lord.
*Oth.* Nor send you out o' the way?
*Emil.* Never. [nor nothing?
*Oth.* To fetch her fan, her gloves, her mask,
*Emil.* Never, my lord.

*Oth.* That's strange. [honest,
*Emil.* I durst, my lord, to wager she is
Lay down my soul at stake: if you think other,
Remove your thought,—it doth abuse your bosom.
If any wretch hath put this in your head,
Let heaven requite it with the serpent's curse!
For, if she be not honest, chaste, and true,
There's no man happy; the purest of their wives
Is foul as slander.
*Oth.* Bid her come hither.—Go.
[*Exit* EMILIA.
She says enough;—yet she's a simple bawd
That cannot say as much. This is a subtle whore,
A closet-lock-and-key of villanous secrets:
And yet she'll kneel and pray; I have seen her do't.

*Re-enter* EMILIA *with* DESDEMONA.

*Des.* My lord, what is your will?
*Oth.* Pray, chuck, come hither.
*Des.* What is your pleasure?
*Oth.* Let me see your eyes;
Look in my face.
*Des.* What horrible fancy's this?
*Oth.* Some of your function, mistress;
[*To* EMIL.
Leave procreants alone, and shut the door;
Cough, or cry hem, if any body come:
Your mystery, your mystery;—nay, despatch. [*Exit* EMILIA.
*Des.* Upon my knees, what doth your speech import?
I understand a fury in your words,
But not the words.
*Oth.* Why, what art thou?
*Des.* Your wife, my lord; your true
And loyal wife.
*Oth.* Come, swear it, damn thyself;
Lest, being like one of heaven, the devils themselves [double-damn'd.—
Should fear to seize thee: therefore be
Swear thou art honest.
*Des.* Heaven doth truly know it.
*Oth.* Heaven truly knows that thou art false as hell. [How am I false?
*Des.* To whom, my lord? with whom?
*Oth.* Ah, Desdemona!—away! away!
*Des.* Alas the heavy day!—Why do you weep?
Am I the motive of these tears, my lord?
If haply you my father do suspect
An instrument of this your calling back,
Lay not your blame on me: if you have lost him,
Why, I have lost him too.
*Oth.* Had it pleas'd heaven
To try me with affliction; had they rain'd

All kinds of sores and shames on my bare
head;
Steep'd me in poverty to the very lips;
Given to captivity me and my utmost hopes;
I should have found in some place of my
soul
A drop of patience: but, alas, to make me
The fixed figure of the time, for scorn
To point his slow and moving finger at!—
Yet could I bear that too; well, very well:
But there, where I have garner'd up my
heart;
Where either I must live, or bear no life,—
The fountain from the which my current
runs,
Or else dries up; to be discarded thence!
Or keep it as a cistern for foul toads
To knot and gender in!—turn thy complexion
there,
Patience, thou young and rose-lipp'd cheru-
bin,—
Ay, there, look grim as hell!
 *Des.* I hope my noble lord esteems me
  honest.
 *Oth.* O, ay; as summer flies are in the
  shambles,
That quicken even with blowing. O thou
weed,
Who art so lovely fair, and smell'st so sweet,
That the sense aches at thee,—would thou
hadst ne'er been born!
 *Des.* Alas, what ignorant sin have I com-
  mitted?
 *Oth.* Was this fair paper, this most goodly
  book,
Made to write whore upon? What com-
mitted!
Committed!—O thou public commoner!
I should make very forges of my cheeks,
That would to cinders burn up modesty,
Did I but speak thy deeds.—What com-
mitted!
Heaven stops the nose at it, and the moon
winks;
The bawdy wind, that kisses all it meets,
Is hush'd within the hollow mine of earth,
And will not hear it.—What committed!—
Impudent strumpet!
 *Des.*  By heaven, you do me wrong.
 *Oth.* Are not you a strumpet?
 *Des.*  No, as I am a Christian:
If to preserve this vessel for my lord
From any other foul unlawful touch
Be not to be a strumpet, I am none.
 *Oth.* What, not a whore?
 *Des.*  No, as I shall be sav'd.
 *Oth.* Is't possible?
 *Des.* O, heaven forgive us!
 *Oth.*  I cry you mercy, then:
I took you for that cunning whore of Venice
That married with Othello.—You, mistress,
That have the office opposite to Saint Peter,
And keep the gate of hell!

   *Re-enter* EMILIA.

    You, you, ay you!
We have done our course; there's money for
your pains:
I pray you, turn the key, and keep our
counsel.      [*Exit.*
 *Emil.* Alas, what does this gentleman con-
  ceive?—      [lady?
How do you, madam? how do you, my good
 *Des.* Faith, half asleep.  [with my lord?
 *Emil.* Good madam, what's the matter
 *Des.* With who?
 *Emil.* Why, with my lord, madam.
 *Des.* Who is thy lord?
 *Emil.* He that is yours, sweet lady.
 *Des.* I have none: do not talk to me,
  Emilia;
I cannot weep; ror answer have I none,
But what should go by water. Pr'ythee, to-
night      [member;—
Lay on my bed my wedding sheets,—re-
And call thy husband hither.
 *Emil.* Here's a change indeed!  [*Exit.*
 *Des.* 'Tis meet I should be us'd so, very
  meet.
How have I been behav'd, that he might
stick
The small'st opinion on my least misuse?

  *Re-enter* EMILIA *with* IAGO.

 *Iago.* What is your pleasure, madam? How
  is't with you?    [young babes
 *Des.* I cannot tell. Those that do teach
Do it with gentle means and easy tasks:
He might have chid me so; for, in good
faith,
I am a child to chiding.
 *Iago.*   What's the matter, lady?
 *Emil.* Alas, Iago, my lord hath so bewhor'd
  her,
Thrown such despite and heavy terms upon
her
As true hearts cannot bear.
 *Des.* Am I that name, Iago?
 *Iago.*   What name, fair lady?
 *Des.* Such as she says my lord did say I
  was.
 *Emil.* He call'd her whore: a beggar in his
  drink
Could not have laid such terms upon his cal-
lat.
 *Iago.* Why did he so?    [such.
 *Des.* I do not know; I am sure I am none
 *Iago.* Do not weep, do not weep:—alas,
  the day!     [matches,
 *Emil.* Hath she forsook so many noble
Her father, and her country, and her friends,
To be call'd whore? would it not make one
weep?
 *Des.* It is my wretched fortune.
 *Iago.*   Beshrew him for't!
How comes this trick upon him?

*Des.*                    Nay, heaven doth know.
*Emil.* I will be hang'd if some eternal villain,
Some busy and insinuating rogue,
Some cogging, cozening slave, to get some office,
Have not devis'd this slander; I'll be hang'd else.                          [possible.
*Iago.* Fie, there is no such man; it is im-
*Des.* If any such there be, heaven pardon him!                          [his bones!
*Emil.* A halter pardon him! and hell gnaw
Why should he call her whore? who keeps her company?
What place? what time? what form? what likelihood?
The Moor's abus'd by some most villanous knave,
Some base notorious knave, some scurvy fellow:—
O heaven, that such companions thou'dst unfold,
And put in every honest hand a whip
To lash the rascals naked through the world
Even from the east to the west!
*Iago.*                    Speak within door.
*Emil.* O, fie upon him! some such squire he was
That turn'd your wit the seamy side without,
And made you to suspect me with the Moor.
*Iago.* You are a fool; go to.
*Des.*                    Alas, Iago,
What shall I do to win my lord again?
Good friend, go to him; for, by this light of heaven,
I know not how I lost him. Here I kneel:—
If e'er my will did trespass 'gainst his love,
Either in discourse of thought or actual deed;
Or that mine eyes, mine ears, or any sense,
Delighted them in any other form;
Or that I do not yet, and ever did,
And ever will,—though he do shake me off
To beggarly divorcement,—love him dearly,
Comfort forswear me! Unkindness may do much;
And his unkindness may defeat my life,
But never taint my love. I cannot say whore,—
It does abhor me now I speak the word;
To do the act that might the addition earn,
Not the world's mass of vanity could make me.
*Iago.* I pray you, be content; 'tis but his humour:
The business of the state does him offence,
And he does chide with you.
*Des.*                    If 'twere no other,—
*Iago.* It is but so, I warrant.
                          [*Trumpets within.*
Hark, how these instruments summon to supper!

The messengers of Venice stay the meat:
Go in, and weep not; all things shall be well.
                          [*Exeunt* DESDEMONA *and* EMILIA.

                    *Enter* RODERIGO.
How now, Roderigo!
*Rod.* I do not find that thou dealest justly with me.
*Iago.* What in the contrary?
*Rod.* Every day thou daffest me with some device, Iago; and rather, as it seems to me now, keepest from me all conveniency than suppliest me with the least advantage of hope. I will, indeed, no longer endure it; nor am I yet persuaded to put up in peace what already I have foolishly suffered.
*Iago.* Will you hear me, Roderigo?
*Rod.* Faith, I have heard too much; for your words and performances are no kin together.
*Iago.* You charge me most unjustly.
*Rod.* With naught but truth. I have wasted myself out of my means. The jewels you have had from me to deliver to Desdemona would half have corrupted a votarist: you have told me she hath received them, and returned me expectations and comforts of sudden respect and acquaintance; but I find none.
*Iago.* Well; go to; very well.
*Rod.* Very well! go to! I cannot go to, man; nor 'tis not very well: nay, I think it is scurvy, and begin to find myself fobbed in it.
*Iago.* Very well.
*Rod.* I tell you 'tis not very well. I will make myself known to Desdemona: if she will return me my jewels, I will give over my suit, and repent my unlawful solicitation; if not, assure yourself I will seek satisfaction of you.
*Iago.* You have said now.
*Rod.* Ay, and said nothing but what I protest intendment of doing.
*Iago.* Why, now I see there's mettle in thee; and even from this instant do build on thee a better opinion than ever before. Give me thy hand, Roderigo: thou hast taken against me a most just exception; but yet, I protest, I have dealt most directly in thy affair.
*Rod.* It hath not appeared.
*Iago.* I grant, indeed, it hath not appeared; and your suspicion is not without wit and judgment. But, Roderigo, if thou hast that in thee indeed, which I have greater reason to believe now than ever,—I mean purpose, courage, and valour,—this night show it: if thou the next night following enjoy not Desdemona, take me from this world with treachery, and devise engines for my life.
*Rod.* Well, what is it? is it within reason and compass?

*Iago.* Sir, there is especial commission come from Venice to depute Cassio in Othello's place.

*Rod.* Is that true? why, then Othello and Desdemona return again to Venice.

*Iago.* O, no; he goes into Mauritania, and takes away with him the fair Desdemona, unless his abode be lingered here by some accident: wherein none can be so determinate as the removing of Cassio.

*Rod.* How do you mean removing of him?

*Iago.* Why, by making him uncapable of Othello's place,—knocking out his brains.

*Rod.* And that you would have me to do?

*Iago.* Ay, if you dare do yourself a profit and a right. He sups to-night with a harlotry, and thither will I go to him:—he knows not yet of his honourable fortune. If you will watch his going thence,—which I will fashion to fall out between twelve and one,—you may take him at your pleasure: I will be near to second your attempt, and he shall fall between us. Come, stand not amazed at it, but go along with me; I will show you such a necessity in his death that you shall think yourself bound to put it on him. It is now high supper-time, and the night grows to waste: about it.

*Rod.* I will hear further reason for this.

*Iago.* And you shall be satisfied. [*Exeunt.*

SCENE III.—CYPRUS. *Another Room in the Castle.*

*Enter* OTHELLO, LODOVICO, DESDEMONA, EMILIA, *and* Attendants.

*Lod.* I do beseech you, sir, trouble yourself no further.                [*walk.*

*Oth.* O, pardon me; 'twill do me good to walk.

*Lod.* Madam, good-night; I humbly thank your ladyship.

*Des.* Your honour is most welcome.

*Oth.*                Will you walk, sir?— O,—Desdemona,—

*Des.* My lord?

*Oth.* Get you to bed on the instant; I will be returned forthwith: dismiss your attendant there: look't be done.

*Des.* I will, my lord.

[*Exeunt* OTH., LOD., *and* Attendants.

*Emil.* How goes it now? he looks gentler than he did.

*Des.* He says he will return incontinent: He hath commanded me to go to bed, And bade me to dismiss you.

*Emil.*            Dismiss me!

*Des.* It was his bidding; therefore, good Emilia, Give me my nightly wearing, and adieu: We must not now displease him.

*Emil.* I would you had never seen him!

*Des.* So would not I: my love doth so approve him,                [*frowns,—* That even his stubbornness, his checks, his

Pr'ythee, unpin me,—have grace and favour in them.            [*me on the bed.*

*Emil.* I have laid those sheets you bade

*Des.* All's one.—Good faith, how foolish are our minds!— If I do die before thee, pr'ythee, shroud me In one of those same sheets.

*Emil.*        Come, come, you talk.

*Des.* My mother had a maid call'd Barbara:            [*mad.* She was in love; and he she lov'd prov'd And did forsake her: she had a song of *willow;* An old thing 'twas, but it express'd her fortune, And she died singing it: that song to-night Will not go from my mind; I have much to do, But to go hang my head all at one side, And sing it like poor Barbara.—Pr'ythee, despatch.

*Emil.* Shall I go fetch your night-gown?

*Des.*            No, unpin me here.— This Lodovico is a proper man.

*Emil.* A very handsome man.

*Des.*            He speaks well.

*Emil.* I know a lady in Venice would have walked barefoot to Palestine for a touch of his nether lip.

*Des.* The poor soul sat sighing by a sycamore tree            [*Sings.* Sing all a green willow: Her hand on her bosom, her head on her knee, Sing willow, willow, willow: The fresh streams ran by her, and murmur'd her moans: Sing willow, willow, willow: Her salt tears fell from her and soften'd the stones;—

Lay by these:—

Sing willow, willow, willow;—            [*Sings.*

Pr'ythee, hie thee; he'll come anon:—

Sing all a green willow must be my garland.            [*Sings.* Let nobody blame him; his scorn I approve,—

Nay, that's not next.—Hark! who is't that knocks?

*Emil.* It's the wind.

*Des.* I call'd my love false love; but what said he then?            [*Sings.* Sing willow, willow, willow: If I court mo women, you 'll couch with mo men.—

So, get thee gone; good-night. Mine eyes do itch; Doth that bode weeping?

*Emil.* 'Tis neither here nor there.

*Des.* I have heard it said so.—O, these men, these men!— Dost thou in conscience think,—tell me, Emilia,—

That there be women do abuse their husbands
In such gross kind?

*Emil.* There be some such, no question.

*Des.* Wouldst thou do such a deed for all
the world?

*Emil.* Why, would not you?

*Des.* No, by this heavenly light!

*Emil.* Nor I neither by this heavenly
light;
I might do't as well i' the dark. [the world?

*Des.* Wouldst thou do such a deed for all

*Emil.* The world's a huge thing: it is a
great price
For a small vice.

*Des.* In troth, I think thou wouldst not.

*Emil.* In troth, I think I should; and undo't when I had done. Marry, I would not
do such a thing for a joint-ring, nor for
measures of lawn, nor for gowns, petticoats,
nor caps, nor any petty exhibition; but for
the whole world,—why, who would not
make her husband a cuckold to make him a
monarch? I should venture purgatory for't.

*Des.* Beshrew me, if I would do such a
wrong for the whole world.

*Emil.* Why, the wrong is but a wrong i'
the world; and having the world for your
labour, 'tis a wrong in your own world, and
you might quickly make it right.

*Des.* I do not think there is any such
woman.

*Emil.* Yes, a dozen; and as many to the
vantage as would store the world they play'd
for.
But I do think it is their husbands' faults
If wives do fall: say that they slack their
duties,
And pour our treasures into foreign laps;
Or else break out in peevish jealousies,
Throwing restraint upon us; or say they
strike us,
Or scant our former having in despite;
Why, we have galls; and though we have
some grace,
Yet have we some revenge. Let husbands
know
Their wives have sense like them: they see
and smell,
And have their palates both for sweet and
sour,
As husbands have. What is it that they do
When they change us for others? Is it sport?
I think it is: and doth affection breed it?
I think it doth: is't frailty that thus errs?
It is so too. And have not we affections,
Desires for sport, and frailty, as men have?
Then let them use us well: else let them know
The ills we do their ills instruct us to.

*Des.* Good-night, good-night: heaven me
such usage send,
Not to pick bad from bad, but by bad mend!

[*Exeunt.*

## ACT V.

### SCENE I.—CYPRUS. *A Street.*

*Enter* IAGO *and* RODERIGO.

*Iago.* Here, stand behind this bulk;
straight will he come:
Wear thy good rapier bare, and put it home:
Quick, quick; fear nothing; I'll be at thy
elbow:
It makes us or it mars us; think on that,
And fix most firm thy resolution.

*Rod.* Be near at hand; I may miscarry
in't.

*Iago.* Here, at thy hand: be bold, and
take thy stand.
[*Retires to a little distance.*

*Rod.* I have no great devotion to the
deed;
And yet he hath given me satisfying reasons:—
'Tis but a man gone.—Forth, my sword; he
dies. [*Goes to his stand.*

*Iago.* I have rubb'd this young quat al-
most to the sense, [*Cassio*
And he grows angry. Now, whether he kill
Or Cassio him, or each do kill the other,
Every way makes my gain: live Roderigo,
He calls me to a restitution large
Of gold and jewels that I bobb'd from him
As gifts to Desdemona;
It must not be: if Cassio do remain,
He hath a daily beauty in his life
That makes me ugly; and, besides, the Moor
May unfold me to him; there stand I in much
peril:
No, he must die.—But, so, I hear him com-
ing.

### *Enter* CASSIO.

*Rod.* I know his gait, 'tis he.—Villain,
thou diest!
[*Rushes out, and makes a pass at* CASSIO.

*Cas.* That thrust had been mine enemy
indeed,
But that my coat is better than thou know'st:
I will make proof of thine.
[*Draws, and wounds* RODERIGO.

*Rod.* O, I am slain!
[IAGO *rushes from his post, cuts* CASSIO
*behind in the leg, and exit.*

*Cas.* I am maim'd for ever.—Help, ho!
murder! murder! [*Falls.*

### *Enter* OTHELLO *at a distance.*

*Oth.* The voice of Cassio:—Iago keeps his
word.

*Rod.* O, villain that I am!

*Oth.* It is even so.

*Cas.* O, help, ho! light! a surgeon!

*Oth.* 'Tis he:—O brave Iago, honest and
just,

That hath such noble sense of thy friend's
    wrong!
Thou teachest me,—minion, your dear lies
    dead,
And your unbless'd fate hies.—Strumpet, I
    come!          [are blotted;
Forth of my heart those charms, thine eyes,
Thy bed, lust-stain'd, shall with lust's blood
    be spotted.          [*Exit.*

*Enter* LODOVICO *and* GRATIANO *at a distance.*

*Cas.* What, ho! no watch? no passage?
    murder! murder!        [very direful.
*Gra.* 'Tis some mischance; the voice is
*Cas.* O, help!
*Lod.* Hark!
*Rod.* O wretched villain!        [night:
*Lod.* Two or three groan:—it is a heavy
These may be counterfeits: let's think't un-
    safe
To come in to the cry without more help.
*Rod.* Nobody come? then shall I bleed to
    death.
*Lod.* Hark!
*Gra.* Here's one comes in his shirt, with
    light and weapons.

*Re-enter* IAGO *with a light.*

*Iago.* Who's there? whose noise is this that
    cries on murder?
*Lod.* We do not know.
*Iago.*          Did not you hear a cry?
*Cas.* Here, here! for heaven's sake, help
    me!
*Iago.*          What's the matter?
*Gra.* This is Othello's ancient, as I take it.
*Lod.* The same indeed; a very valiant
    fellow.
*Iago.* What are you here that cry so griev-
    ously?          [villains!
*Cas.* Iago? O, I am spoil'd, undone by
Give me some help.        [done this?
*Iago.* O me, lieutenant! what villains have
*Cas.* I think that one of them is here-
    about,
And cannot make away.
*Iago.*          O treacherous villains!—
What are you there? come in, and give some
    help.        [*To* LODOVICO *and* GRATIANO.
*Rod.* O, help me here!
*Cas.* That's one of them.
*Iago.*          O murderous slave! O villain!
          [*Stabs* RODERIGO.
*Rod.* O damn'd Iago! O inhuman dog!
*Iago.* Kill men i' the dark!—Where be
    these bloody thieves?—
How silent is this town!—Ho! murder! mur-
    der!—
What may you be? are you of good or evil?
*Lod.* As you shall prove us, praise us.
*Iago.* Signior Lodovico?
*Lod.* He, sir.

*Iago.* I cry you mercy. Here's Cassio hurt
    by villains.
*Gra.* Cassio!
*Iago.* How is't, brother?
*Cas.* My leg is cut in two.
*Iago.*          Marry, heaven forbid!—
Light, gentlemen:—I'll bind it with my
    shirt.

*Enter* BIANCA.

*Bian.* What is the matter, ho? who is't
    that cried?
*Iago.* Who is't that cried!
*Bian.* O my dear Cassio! my sweet Cas-
    sio! O Cassio, Cassio, Cassio!
*Iago.* O notable strumpet!—Cassio, may
    you suspect        [you?
Who they should be that have thus mangled
*Cas.* No.
*Gra.* I am sorry to find you thus: I have
    been to seek you.
*Iago.* Lend me a garter:—so.—O, for a
    chair,
To bear him easily hence!        [Cassio!
*Bian.* Alas, he faints!—O Cassio, Cassio,
*Iago.* Gentlemen all, I do suspect this trash
To be a party in this injury.—
Patience awhile, good Cassio.—Come, come;
Lend me a light.—Know we this face or no?
Alas, my friend and my dear countryman
Roderigo? no:—yes, sure; O heaven! Rod-
    erigo.
*Gra.* What, of Venice?
*Iago.* Even he, sir: did you know him?
*Gra.*          Know him! ay.
*Iago.* Signior Gratiano? I cry you gentle
    pardon;
These bloody accidents must excuse my man-
    ners,
That so neglected you.
*Gra.*          I am glad to see you.
*Iago.* How do you, Cassio?—O, a chair, a
    chair!
*Gra.* Roderigo!
*Iago.* He, he, 'tis he.—O, that's well said;
    —the chair:—    [*A chair brought in.*
Some good man bear him carefully from
    hence;
I'll fetch the general's surgeon.—For you,
    mistress,        [*To* BIANCA.
Save you your labour.—He that lies slain
    here, Cassio,        [tween you?
Was my dear friend: what malice was be-
*Cas.* None in the world; nor do I know
    the man.
*Iago.* [*To* BIAN.] What, look you pale?—
    O, bear him out o' the air.—
        [*CAS. and* ROD. *are borne off.*
Stay you, good gentlemen.—Look you pale,
    mistress?—
Do you perceive the gastness of her eye?—
Nay, if you stare, we shall hear more
    anon.—

Behold her well; I pray you, look upon her:
Do you see, gentlemen? nay, guiltiness will
    speak
Though tongues were out of use.

*Enter* EMILIA.

*Emil.* 'Las, what's the matter? what's the
    matter, husband?
*Iago.* Cassio hath here been set on in the
    dark
By Roderigo, and fellows that are 'scap'd:
He's almost slain, and Roderigo dead.
*Emil.* Alas, good gentleman! alas, good
    Cassio!              [thee, Emilia,
*Iago.* This is the fruit of whoring.—Pr'y-
Go know of Cassio where he supp'd to-
    night.—
What, do you shake at that?
*Bian.* He supp'd at my house; but I there-
    fore shake not.
*Iago.* O, did he so? I charge you, go with
    me.
*Emil.* Fie, fie upon thee, strumpet!
*Bian.* I am no strumpet; but of life as
    honest
As you that thus abuse me.
*Emil.*              As I! foh! fie upon thee!
*Iago.* Kind gentlemen, let's go see poor
    Cassio dress'd.—
Come, mistress, you must tell's another
    tale.—
Emilia, run you to the citadel,
And tell my lord and lady what hath
    happ'd.—
Will you go on afore?—[*Aside.*] This is the
    night
That either makes me or fordoes me quite.
                              [*Exeunt.*

SCENE II.—CYPRUS. *A Bedchamber in the
Castle:* DESDEMONA *in bed asleep; a light
burning.*

*Enter* OTHELLO.

*Oth.* It is the cause, it is the cause, my
    soul,—
Let me not name it to you, you chaste
    stars!—
It is the cause.—Yet I'll not shed her blood;
Nor scar that whiter skin of hers than snow,
And smooth as monumental alabaster.
                    [*Takes off his sword.*
Yet she must die, else she'll betray more
    men.
Put out the light, and then put out the light:
If I quench thee, thou flaming minister,
I can again thy former light restore,    [light,
Should I repent me:—but once put out thy
Thou cunning'st pattern of excelling nature,
I know not where is that Promethean heat
That can thy light relume. When I have
    pluck'd thy rose,
I cannot give it vital growth again,

It needs must wither:—I'll smell it on the
    tree.—             [*Kissing her.*
O balmy breath, that dost almost persuade
Justice to break her sword!—One more, one
    more.—              [thee,
Be thus when thou art dead, and I will kill
And love thee after.—One more, and that's
    the last:
So sweet was ne'er so fatal. I must weep,
But they are cruel tears: this sorrow's heav-
    enly;
It strikes where it doth love.—She wakes.
*Des.* Who's there? Othello?
*Oth.*                        Ay, Desdemona.
*Des.* Will you come to bed, my lord?
*Oth.* Have you pray'd to-night, Desde-
    mon?
*Des.*                        Ay, my lord.
*Oth.* If you bethink yourself of any crime
Unreconcil'd as yet to heaven and grace,
Solicit for it straight.              [by that?
*Des.* Alack, my lord, what may you mean
*Oth.* Well, do it, and be brief; I will walk
    by:
I would not kill thy unprepared spirit;
No,—heaven forfend!—I would not kill thy
    soul.
*Des.* Talk you of killing?
*Oth.*                        Ay, I do.
*Des.*                        Then heaven
Have mercy on me!
*Oth.*              Amen, with all my heart!
*Des.* If you say so, I hope you will not
    kill me.
*Oth.* Hum!                        [then
*Des.* And yet I fear you; for you are fatal
When your eyes roll so: why I should fear I
    know not,              [fear.
Since guiltiness I know not; but yet I feel I
*Oth.* Think on thy sins.
*Des.*              They are loves I bear to you.
*Oth.* Ay, and for that thou diest.
*Des.* That death's unnatural that kills for
    loving.—
Alas, why gnaw you so your nether lip?
Some bloody passion shakes your very
    frame:
These are portents; but yet I hope, I hope,
They do not point on me.
*Oth.*              Peace, and be still!
*Des.* I will so. What's the matter?
*Oth.* That handkerchief which I so lov'd
    and gave thee
Thou gav'st to Cassio.
*Des.*              No, by my life and soul!
Send for the man and ask him.
*Oth.*              Sweet soul, take heed,
Take heed of perjury; thou'rt on thy death-
    bed.
*Des.* Ay, but not yet to die.
*Oth.*                        Yes, presently.
Therefore confess thee freely of thy sin;
For to deny each article with oath

Cannot remove nor choke the strong conception
That I do groan withal. Thou art to die.
   *Des.* Then, Lord have mercy on me!
   *Oth.*                       I say, amen.
   *Des.* And have you mercy too!—I never
did
Offend you in my life; never lov'd Cassio
But with such general warranty of heaven
As I might love: I never gave him token.
   *Oth.* By heaven, I saw my handkerchief
in's hand.
O perjur'd woman! thou dost stone my heart,
And mak'st me call what I intend to do
A murder, which I thought a sacrifice:
I saw the handkerchief.
   *Des.*            He found it, then;
I never gave it him:—send for him hither;
Let him confess a truth.
   *Oth.*            He hath confess'd.
   *Des.* What, my lord?
   *Oth.* That he hath us'd thee.
   *Des.*               How? unlawfully?
   *Oth.*                       Ay.
   *Des.* He will not say so.
   *Oth.*           No, his mouth is stopp'd;
Honest Iago hath ta'en order for't.
   *Des.* O, my fear interprets!—What, is he
dead?
   *Oth.* Had all his hairs been lives, my great
revenge
Had stomach for them all.
   *Des.* Alas, he is betray'd, and I undone!
   *Oth.* Out, strumpet! Weep'st thou for him
to my face?
   *Des.* O, banish me, my lord, but kill me
not!
   *Oth.* Down, strumpet!
   *Des.* Kill me to-morrow; let me live to-
night!
   *Oth.* Nay, if you strive,—
   *Des.* But half an hour!
   *Oth.* Being done, there is no pause.
   *Des.* But while I say one prayer!
   *Oth.* It is too late.       [*Smothers her.*
   *Emil.* [*Within.*] My lord, my lord! what,
ho! my lord, my lord!
   *Oth.* What noise is this?—not dead? not
yet quite dead?
I that am cruel am yet merciful;
I would not have thee linger in thy pain:—
So, so.                         [lord!
   *Emil.* [*Within.*] What, ho! my lord, my
   *Oth.*                  Who's there?
   *Emil.* [*Within.*] O, good my lord, I would
speak a word with you!     [dead.—
   *Oth.* Yes:—'tis Emilia:—by and by.—She's
'Tis like she comes to speak of Cassio's death;
The noise was high.—Ha! no more moving?
Still as the grave.—Shall she come in?—
Were't good?—               [do?
I think she stirs again: no.—What's best to
If she come in she'll sure speak to my wife:

My wife! my wife! what wife? I have no
wife.
O, insupportable! O heavy hour!
Methinks it should be now a huge eclipse
Of sun and moon, and that the affrighted
globe
Should yawn at alteration.
   *Emil.* [*Within.*]         I do beseech you
That I may speak with you, O, good my
lord!
   *Oth.* I had forgot thee: O, come in,
Emilia:
Soft,—by and by:—let me the curtains
draw.—
Where art thou?        [*Unlocks the door.*

*Enter* EMILIA.

      What's the matter with thee now?
   *Emil.* O, my good lord, yonder's foul mur-
ders done!
   *Oth.* What, now?
   *Emil.* But now, my lord.
   *Oth.* It is the very error of the moon;
She comes more nearer earth than she was
wont,
And makes men mad.
   *Emil.* Cassio, my lord, hath kill'd a young
Venetian
Call'd Roderigo.
   *Oth.*           Roderigo kill'd!
And Cassio kill'd!
   *Emil.*        No, Cassio is not kill'd.
   *Oth.* Not Cassio kill'd! then murder's out
of tune,
And sweet revenge grows harsh.
   *Des.* O, falsely, falsely murder'd!
   *Emil.*        Alas, what cry is that?
   *Oth.* That! what?           [voice.—
   *Emil.* Out and alas! that was my lady's
Help! help, ho! help!—O lady, speak again!
Sweet Desdemona! O sweet mistress, speak!
   *Des.* A guiltless death I die.
   *Emil.* O, who hath done this deed?
   *Des.* Nobody; I myself. Farewell:
Commend me to my kind lord: O, farewell!
                           [*Dies.*
   *Oth.* Why, how should she be murder'd?
   *Emil.*          Alas, who knows?
   *Oth.* You heard her say herself it was not
I.
   *Emil.* She said so: I must needs report the
truth.
   *Oth.* She's like a liar, gone to burning hell:
'Twas I that kill'd her.
   *Emil.*        O, the more angel she,
And you the blacker devil!
   *Oth.* She turn'd to folly, and she was a
whore.
   *Emil.* Thou dost belie her, and thou art a
devil.
   *Oth.* She was false as water.
   *Emil.*        Thou art rash as fire, to say
That she was false: O, she was heavenly true.

*Oth.* Cassio did tup her; ask thy husband else.

O, I were damn'd beneath all depth in hell,
But that I did proceed upon just grounds
To this extremity. Thy husband knew it all.

*Emil.* My husband!

*Oth.* Thy husband.

*Emil.* That she was false to wedlock?

*Oth.* Ay, with Cassio. Nay, had she been true,
If heaven would make me such another world
Of one entire and perfect chrysolite,
I'd not have sold her for it.

*Emil.* My husband!

*Oth.*        Ay, 'twas he that told me first:
An honest man he is, and hates the slime
That sticks on filthy deeds.

*Emil.*        My husband!

*Oth.* What needs this iterance, woman? I say thy husband.

*Emil.* O mistress, villany hath made mocks with love!—
My husband say that she was false!

*Oth.*        He, woman;
I say thy husband: dost understand the word?
My friend, thy husband, honest, honest Iago.

*Emil.* If he say so, may his pernicious soul
Rot half a grain a day! he lies to the heart:
She was too fond of her most filthy bargain.

*Oth.* Ha!

*Emil.* Do thy worst:
This deed of thine is no more worthy heaven
Than thou wast worthy her.

*Oth.*        Peace, you were best.

*Emil.* Thou hast not half that power to do me harm
As I have to be hurt. O gull! O dolt!
As ignorant as dirt! thou hast done a deed,—
I care not for thy sword; I'll make thee known,
Though I lost twenty lives.—Help! help, ho! help!     [murder!
The Moor hath kill'd my mistress! murder!

*Enter* MONTANO, GRATIANO, *and* IAGO.

*Mon.* What is the matter?—How now, general!

*Emil.* O, are you come, Iago? you have done well,
That men must lay their murders on your neck.

*Gra.* What is the matter?     [man:

*Emil.* Disprove this villain, if thou be'st a
[He says thou told'st him that his wife was false:
I know thou didst not, thou'rt not such a villain:
Speak, for my heart is full.     [no more

*Iago.* I told him what I thought; and told
Than what he found himself was apt and true.

*Emil.* But did you ever tell him she was false?

*Iago.* I did.

*Emil.* You told a lie; an odious, damned lie;
Upon my soul, a lie; a wicked lie:—
She false with Cassio!—Did you say with Cassio?

*Iago.* With Cassio, mistress. Go to, charm your tongue.

*Emil.* I will not charm my tongue; I am bound to speak:
My mistress here lies murder'd in her bed,—

*All.* O heavens forfend!

*Emil.* And your reports have set the murder on.     [indeed.

*Oth.* Nay, stare not, masters: it is true,

*Gra.* 'Tis a strange truth.

*Mon.* O monstrous act!

*Emil.*        Villany, villany, villany!—
I think upon't,—I think,—I smell't;—O villany!—     [grief:—
I thought so then;—I'll kill myself for
O villany, villany!

*Iago.* What, are you mad? I charge you, get you home.     [speak:

*Emil.* Good gentlemen, let me have leave to
'Tis proper I obey him, but not now.—
Perchance, Iago, I will ne'er go home.

*Oth.* O! O! O!     [*Hanging over his wife.*

*Emil.*        Nay, lay thee down and roar;
For thou hast kill'd the sweetest innocent
That e'er did lift up eye.

*Oth.*        O, she was foul!—
    [*Rising.*
I scarce did know you, uncle: there lies your niece,
Whose breath, indeed, these hands have newly stopp'd:
I know this act shows horrible and grim.

*Gra.* Poor Desdemona! I am glad thy father's dead:
Thy match was mortal to him, and pure grief
Shore his old thread in twain: did he live now,
This sight would make him do a desperate turn,
Yea, curse his better angel from his side,
And fall to reprobance.

*Oth.* 'Tis pitiful; but yet Iago knows
That she with Cassio hath the act of shame
A thousand times committed; Cassio confess'd it:
And she did gratify his amorous works
With that recognizance and pledge of love
Which I first gave her; I saw it in his hand:
It was a handkerchief, an antique token
My father gave my mother.

*Emil.* O heaven! O heavenly powers!

*Iago.* Come, hold your peace.

*Emil.*        'Twill out, 'twill out:—I peace!
No, I will speak as liberal as the north:
Let heaven and men and devils, let them all,

All, all, cry shame against me, yet I'll speak.
*Iago.* Be wise, and get you home.
*Emil.*            I will not.
           [IAGO *offers to stab his wife.*
*Gra.*            Fie!
Your sword upon a woman?
*Emil.* O thou dull Moor! that handker-
chief thou speak'st of.
I found by fortune, and did give my hus-
band;
For often, with a solemn earnestness,—
More than, indeed, belong'd to such a trifle,—
He begg'd of me to steal it.
*Iago.*            Villanous whore!
*Emil.* She give it Cassio! no, alas, I found
it,
And I did give't my husband.
*Iago.*            Filth, thou liest!
*Emil.* By heaven, I do not, I do not, gentle-
men.—
O murderous coxcomb! what should such a
fool
Do with so good a wife?
     [IAGO *stabs* EMILIA, *and then runs out.*
*Oth.*       Are there no stones in heaven
But what serve for the thunder?—Precious
villain!
*Gra.* The woman falls; sure he hath kill'd
his wife.
*Emil.* Ay, ay:—O, lay me by my mistress'
side.
*Gra.* He's gone, but his wife's kill'd.
*Mon.* 'Tis a notorious villain. Take you
this weapon,
Which I have here recover'd from the Moor:
Come, guard the door without: let him not
pass,
But kill him rather. I'll after that same vil-
lain,
For 'tis a damned slave.
           [*Exeunt* MON. *and* GRA.
*Oth.*       I am not valiant neither,
But every puny whipster gets my sword:—
But why should honour outlive honesty?
Let it go all.
*Emil.*      What did thy song bode, lady?
Hark, canst thou hear me? I will play the
swan,
And die in music:—*Willow, willow, willow.*—
           [*Sings.*
Moor, she was chaste; she lov'd thee, cruel
Moor;
So come my soul to bliss, as I speak true;
So speaking as I think, I die,—I die. [*Dies.*
*Oth.* I have another weapon in this cham-
ber;
It is a sword of Spain, the ice-brook's tem-
per:—
O, here it is.—Uncle, I must come forth.
*Gra.* [*Within.*] If thou attempt it, it will
cost thee dear:
Thou hast no weapon, and perforce must
suffer,

*Oth.* Look in upon me, then, and speak
with me,
Or, naked as I am, I will assault thee.

*Re-enter* GRATIANO.

*Gra.* What is the matter?
*Oth.*            Behold, I have a weapon;
A better never did itself sustain
Upon a soldier's thigh: I have seen the day
That, with this little arm and this good
sword,
I have made my way through more impedi-
ments
Than twenty times your stop:—but, O vain
boast!
Who can control his fate? 'tis not so now.—
Be not afraid though you do see me wea-
pon'd;
Here is my journey's end, here is my butt,
And very sea-mark of my utmost sail.
Do you go back dismay'd? 'tis a lost fear;
Man but a rush against Othello's breast,
And he retires:—where should Othello go?—
Now, how dost thou look now? O ill-starr'd
wench!
Pale as thy smock! when we shall meet at
compt,
This look of thine will hurl my soul from
heaven,
And fiends will snatch at it. Cold, cold, my
girl!
Even like thy chastity.—
O cursed, cursed slave!—Whip me, ye devils,
From the possession of this heavenly sight!
Blow me about in winds! roast me in sul-
phur!
Wash me in steep-down gulfs of liquid fire!—
O Desdemon! dead, Desdemon! dead! O!

*Enter* LODOVICO, MONTANO, CASSIO, *carried
in a chair, and* Officers, *with* IAGO *prisoner.*

*Lod.* Where is this rash and most unfortu-
nate man?
*Oth.* That's he that was Othello;—here I
am.
*Lod.* Where is that viper? bring the villain
forth.
*Oth.* I look down towards his feet,—but
that's a fable.—
If that thou be'st a devil, I cannot kill thee.
           [*Wounds* IAGO.
*Lod.* Wrench his sword from him.
*Iago.*        I bleed, sir; but not kill'd.
*Oth.* I am not sorry neither: I'd have thee
live;
For, in my sense, 'tis happiness to die.
*Lod.* O thou Othello, that wert once so
good,
Fall'n in the practice of a damned slave,
What shall be said to thee?
*Oth.*          Why, anything:
An honourable murderer, if you will;

For naught I did in hate, but all in honour.

*Lod.* This wretch hath part confess'd his
    villany:
Did you and he consent in Cassio's death?

*Oth.* Ay.

*Cas.* Dear general, I never gave you cause.

*Oth.* I do believe it, and I ask your pardon.
Will you, I pray, demand that demi-devil
Why he hath thus ensnar'd my soul and
    body?

*Iago.* Demand me nothing: what you
    know, you know:
From this time forth I never will speak word.

*Lod.* What, not to pray?

*Gra.*　　　　Torments will ope your lips.

*Oth.* Well, thou dost best.

*Lod.* Sir, you shall understand what hath
    befall'n,
Which, as I think, you know not. Here is a
    letter
Found in the pocket of the slain Roderigo;
And here another: the one of them imports
The death of Cassio to be undertook
By Roderigo.

*Oth.* O villain!

*Cas.*　　　Most heathenish and most gross.

*Lod.* Now here's another discontented
    paper,
Found in his pocket too; and this, it seems,
Roderigo meant to have sent this damned
    villain;
But that, belike, Iago in the interim
Came in and satisfied him.

*Oth.*　　　　O the pernicious caitiff!—
How came you, Cassio, by that handkerchief
That was my wife's?

*Cas.*　　　　I found it in my chamber:
And he himself confess'd but even now
That there he dropp'd it for a special purpose
Which wrought to his desire.

*Oth.*　　　　　　O fool! fool! fool!

*Cas.* There is besides in Roderigo's letter,—
How he upbraids Iago that he made him
Brave me upon the watch; whereon it came
That I was cast: and even but now he spake,
After long seeming dead,—Iago hurt him,
Iago set him on.

*Lod.* You must forsake this room, and go
    with us:
Your power and your command is taken off,
And Cassio rules in Cyprus. For this slave,—

If there be any cunning cruelty
That can torment him much and hold him
    long,
It shall be his. You shall close prisoner rest
Till that the nature of your fault be known
To the Venetian state.—Come, bring away.

*Oth.* Soft you; a word or two before you
    go.
I have done the state some service, and they
    know's;—
No more of that.—I pray you, in your letters,
When you shall these unlucky deeds relate,
Speak of me as I am; nothing extenuate,
Nor set down aught in malice: then must you
    speak
Of one that lov'd not wisely, but too well;
Of one not easily jealous, but, being wrought,
Perplex'd in the extreme; of one whose hand,
Like the base Júdean, threw a pearl away
Richer than all his tribe; of one whose sub-
    du'd eyes,
Albeit unused to the melting mood,
Drop tears as fast as the Arabian trees
Their medicinal gum. Set you down this;
And say, besides,—that in Allepo once,
Where a malignant and a turban'd Turk
Beat a Venetian and traduc'd the state,
I took by the throat the circumcised dog,
And smote him—thus.　　　　[*Stabs himself.*

*Lod.* O bloody period!

*Gra.*　　　　All that's spoke is marr'd.

*Oth.* I kiss'd thee ere I kill'd thee:—no way
    but this,　　[*Falling upon* DESDEMONA.
Killing myself, to die upon a kiss.　　[*Dies.*

*Cas.* This did I fear, but thought he had no
    weapon;
For he was great of heart.

*Lod.* [*To* IAGO.]　　O Spartan dog,
More fell than anguish, hunger, or the sea!
Look on the tragic loading of this bed;
This is thy work:—the object poisons sight;
Let it be hid.—Gratiano, keep the house,
And seize upon the fortunes of the Moor,
For they succeed on you.—To you, lord
    governor,
Remains the censure of this hellish villain;
The time, the place, the torture,—O, enforce
    it!
Myself will straight aboard; and to the state
This heavy act with heavy heart relate.
　　　　　　　　　　　[*Exeunt.*

# VENUS AND ADONIS

'Vilia miretur vulgus, mihi flavus Apollo
Pocula Castalia plena ministret aqua.'—OVID.

---

TO THE

## RIGHT HONOURABLE HENRY WRIOTHESLY,

### EARL OF SOUTHAMPTON, AND BARON OF TITCHFIELD.

RIGHT HONOURABLE,
I KNOW not how I shall offend in dedicating my unpolished lines to your lordship, nor how the world will censure me for choosing so strong a prop to support so weak a burthen: only if your honour seem but pleased, I account myself highly praised, and vow to take advantage of all idle hours till I have honoured you with some graver labour. But if the first heir of my invention prove deformed, I shall be sorry it had so noble a godfather, and never after ear so barren a land, for fear it yield me still so bad a harvest. I leave it to your honourable survey, and your honour to your heart's content; which I wish may always answer your own wish, and the world's hopeful expectation.
Your Honour's in all duty,

WILLIAM SHAKESPEARE.

EVEN as the sun with purple-colour'd face
Had ta'en his last leave of the weeping morn,
Rose-cheek'd Adonis hied him to the chase;
Hunting .he lov'd, but love he laugh'd to scorn;
    Sick-thoughted Venus makes amain unto him
    And like a bold-fac'd suitor 'gins to woo him.

'Thrice fairer than myself,' thus she began,
'The field's chief flower, sweet above compare,
Stain to all nymphs, more lovely than a man,
More white and red than doves or roses are;
    Nature that made thee, with herself at strife,
    Saith that the world hath ending with thy life.

'Vouchsafe, thou wonder, to alight thy steed,
And rein his proud head to the saddle-bow;
If thou wilt deign this favour, for thy meed
A thousand honey-secrets shalt thou know:
    Here come and sit, where never serpent hisses,
    And being set I'll smother thee with kisses;

'And yet not cloy thy lips with loath'd satiety,
But rather famish them amid their plenty,
Making them red and pale with fresh variety,
Ten kisses short as one, one long as twenty:
    A summer's day will seem an hour but short,
    Being wasted in such time-beguiling sport.'

With this she seizeth on his sweating palm,

The precedent of pith and livelihood,
And, trembling in her passion, calls it balm,
Earth's sovereign salve to do a goddess good:
    Being so enrag'd, desire doth lend her force,
    Courageously to pluck him from his horse.

Over one arm the lusty courser's rein,
Under her other was the tender boy,
Who blush'd and pouted in a full disdain,
With leaden appetite, unapt to toy;
    She red and hot as coals of glowing fire,
    He red for shame, but frosty in desire.

The studded bridle on a ragged bough
Nimbly she fastens; (O how quick is love!)
The steed is stalled up, and even now
To tie the rider she begins to prove:
    Backward she push'd him, as she would be thrust,
    And govern'd him in strength, though not in lust.

So soon was she along, as he was down,
Each leaning on their elbows and their hips:
Now doth she stroke his cheek, now doth he frown,
And 'gins to chide, but soon she stops his lips;
    And kissing speaks, with lustful language broken,
    'If thou wilt chide, thy lips shall never open.'

He burns with bashful shame; she with her tears
Doth quench the maiden burning of his cheeks:

Then with her windy sighs, and golden hairs,
To fan and blow them dry again she seeks:
He saith she is immodest, blames her 'miss;
What follows more she murders with a kiss.

Even as an empty eagle, sharp by fast,
Tires with her beak on feathers, flesh, and
bone,
Shaking her wings, devouring all in haste,
Till either gorge be stuff'd, or prey be gone;
Even so she kiss'd his brow, his cheek, his
chin,
And where she ends she doth anew begin.

Forc'd to content, but never to obey,
Panting he lies, and breatheth in her face;
She feedeth on the steam, as on a prey,
And calls it heavenly moisture, air of grace,
Wishing her cheeks were gardens full of
flowers,
So they were dew'd with such distilling
showers.

Look how a bird lies tangled in a net,
So fastened in her arms Adonis lies;
Pure shame and aw'd resistance made him
fret,
Which bred more beauty in his angry eyes;
Rain added to a river that is rank,
Perforce will force it overflow the bank.

Still she entreats, and prettily entreats,
For to a pretty ear she tunes her tale;
Still is he sullen, still he low'rs and frets,
'Twixt crimson shame, and anger ashy pale;
Being red, she loves him best; and being
white,
Her best is better'd with a more delight.

Look how he can, she cannot choose but love;
And by her fair immortal hand she swears
From his soft bosom never to remove,
Till he take truce with her contending tears,
Which long have rain'd, making her cheeks
all wet;
And one sweet kiss shall pay this countless
debt.

Upon this promise did he raise his chin,
Like a dive-dapper peering through a wave,
Who, being look'd on, ducks as quickly in;
So offers he to give what she did crave; .
But when her lips were ready for his pay,
He winks, and turns his lips another way.

Never did passenger in summer's heat
More thirst for drink, than she for this good
turn:
Her help she sees, but help she cannot get;
She bathes in water, yet her fire must burn:
'O, pity,' 'gan she cry, 'flint-hearted boy!
'Tis but a kiss I beg; why art thou coy?

'I have been woo'd, as I entreat thee now,
Even by the stern and direful god of war,
Whose sinewy neck in battle ne'er did bow,
Who conquers where he comes, in every jar;
Yet hath he been my captive and my slave,
And begg'd for that which thou unask'd
shalt have.

'Over my altars hath he hung his lance,
His batter'd shield, his uncontrolled crest,
And for my sake hath learn'd to sport and
dance,
To toy, to wanton, dally, smile, and jest;
Scorning his churlish drum and ensign red.
Making my arms his field, his tent my bed.

'Thus he that overrul'd I oversway'd,
Leading him prisoner in a red-rose chain:
Strong-temper'd steel his stronger strength
obey'd,
Yet was he servile to my coy disdain.
O, be not proud, nor brag not of thy might,
For mastering her that foil'd the god of
fight!

'Touch but my lips with those fair lips of
thine,
(Though mine be not so fair, yet are they
red.)
The kiss shall be thine own as well as mine:—
What seest thou in the ground? hold up thy
head;
Look in mine eyeballs, there thy beauty
lies:
Then why not lips on lips, since eyes in
eyes?

'Art thou asham'd to kiss? then wink again,
And I will wink, so shall the day seem night:
Love keeps his revels where there are but
twain;
Be bold to play, our sport is not in sight:
These blue-vein'd violets whereon we lean
Never can blab, nor know not what we
mean.

'The tender spring upon thy tempting lip
Shows thee unripe; yet mayst thou well be
tasted;
Make use of time, let not advantage slip;
Beauty within itself should not be wasted:
Fair flowers that are not gather'd in their
prime
Rot and consume themselves in little time.

'Were I hard-favour'd, foul, or wrinkled-old,
Ill-nurtur'd, crooked, churlish, harsh in voice,
O'er-worn, despised, rheumatic, and cold,
Thick-sighted, barren, lean, and lacking juice,
Then mightst thou pause, for then I were
not for thee;
But having no defects, why dost abhor me?

'Thou canst not see one wrinkle in my brow;
Mine eyes are grey, and bright, and quick in
  turning;
My beauty as the spring doth yearly grow,
My flesh is soft and plump, my marrow burn-
  ing;
  My smooth moist hand, were it with thy
    hand felt,
  Would in thy palm dissolve, or seem to
    melt.

'Bid me discourse, I will enchant thine ear,
Or, like a fairy, trip upon the green,
Or, like a nymph, with long dishevell'd hair,
Dance on the sands, and yet no footing seen:
  Love is a spirit all compact of fire,
  Not gross to sink, but light, and will aspire.

'Witness this primrose bank whereon I lie!
These forceless flowers like sturdy trees sup-
  port me;
Two strengthless doves will draw me through
  the sky,
From morn to night, even where I list to
  sport me:
  Is love so light, sweet boy, and may it be
  That thou shouldst think it heavy unto
    thee?

'Is thine own heart to thine own face affect-
  ed?
Can thy right hand seize love upon thy left?
Then woo thyself, be of thyself rejected,
Steal thine own freedom, and complain on
  theft.
  Narcissus so himself himself forsook,
  And died to kiss his shadow in the brook.

'Torches are made to light, jewels to wear,
Dainties to taste, fresh beauty for the use,
Herbs for their smell, and sappy plants to
  bear;
Things growing to themselves are growth's
  abuse:
  Seed spring from seeds, and beauty breed-
    eth beauty,
  Thou wast begot,—to get it is thy duty.

'Upon the earth's increase why shouldst thou
  feed,
Unless the earth with thy increase be fed?
By law of Nature thou are bound to breed,
That thine may live, when thou thyself art
  dead;
  And so in spite of death thou dost survive,
  In that thy likeness still is left alive.'

By this the love-sick queen began to sweat,
For, where they lay, the shadow had forsook
  them,
And Titan, 'tired in the mid-day heat,
With burning eye did hotly overlook them;
  Wishing Adonis had his team to guide,
  So he were like him, and by Venus' side.

And now Adonis, with a lazy spright,
And with a heavy, dark, disliking eye,
His lowering brows o'erwhelming his fair
  sight,
Like misty vapours when they blot the sky,
  Souring his cheeks, cries, 'Fie, no more of
    love!
  The sun doth burn my face; I must re-
    move.'

'Ah me,' quoth Venus, 'young, and so unkind!
What bare excuses mak'st thou to begone!
I'll sigh celestial breath, whose gentle wind
Shall cool the heat of this descending sun;
  I'll make a shadow for thee of my hairs;
  If they burn too, I'll quench them with my
    tears.

'The sun that shines from heaven shines but
  warm,
And lo, I lie between that sun and thee:
The heat I have from thence doth little harm,
Thine eye darts forth the fire that burneth
  me:
  And were I not immortal, life were done,
  Between this heavenly and earthly sun.

'Art thou obdurate, flinty, hard as steel,
Nay, more than flint, for stone at rain relent-
  eth?
Art thou a woman's son, and canst not feel
What 'tis to love? how want of love torment-
  eth?
  O had thy mother borne so hard a mind,
  She had not brought forth thee, but died
    unkind.

'What am I, that thou shouldst contemn me
  this?
Or what great danger dwells upon my suit?
What were thy lips the worse for one poor
  kiss?
Speak, fair; but speak fair words, or else be
  mute:
  Give me one kiss, I'll give it thee again,
  And one for interest, if thou wilt have
    twain.

'Fie, lifeless picture, cold and senseless stone,
Well-painted idol, image dull and dead,
Statue contenting but the eye alone,
Thing like a man, but of no woman bred;
  Thou art no man, though of a man's com-
    plexion,
  For men will kiss even by their own direc-
    tion.'

This said, impatience chokes her pleading
  tongue,
And swelling passion doth provoke a pause;
Red cheeks and fiery eyes blaze forth her
  wrong;
Being judge in love, she cannot right her
  cause:

And now she weeps, and now she fain
   would speak,
And now her sobs do her intendments
   break.

Sometimes she shakes her head, and then his
   hand,
Now gazeth she on him, now on the ground;
Sometimes her arms infold him like a band;
She would, he will not in her arms be bound;
   And when from thence he struggles to be
      gone,
   She locks her lily fingers one in one.

'Fondling,' she saith, 'since I have hemm'd
   thee here,
Within the circuit of this ivory pale,
I'll be a park, and thou shalt be my deer;
Feed where thou wilt, on mountain or in
   dale:
   Graze on my lips; and if those hills be dry,
   Stray lower, where the pleasant fountains
      lie.

'Within this limit is relief enough,
Sweet bottom-grass, and high delightful plain,
Round rising hillocks, brakes obscure and
   rough,
To shelter thee from tempest and from rain;
   Then be my deer, since I am such a park;
   No dog shall rouse thee, tho' a thousand
      bark.'

At this Adonis smiles as in disdain,
That in each cheek appears a pretty dimple:
Love made those hollows, if himself were
   slain,
He might be buried in a tomb so simple;
   Foreknowing well if there he came to lie,
   Why there Love liv'd and there he could
      not die.

These lovely caves, these round enchanting
   pits,
Open'd their mouths to swallow Venus' lik-
   ing:
Being mad before, how doth she now for
   wits?
Struck dead at first, what needs a second
   striking?
   Poor queen of love, in thine own law for-
      lorn,                          [scorn!
   To love a cheek that smiles at thee in

Now which way shall she turn? what shall
   she say?
Her words are done, her woes the more in-
   creasing,
The time is spent, her object will away,
And from her twining arms doth urge releas-
   ing:
   'Pity'—she cries,—'some favour—some re-
      morse—'
Away he springs, and hasteth to his horse.

But lo, from forth a copse that neighbours
   by,
A breeding jennet, lusty, young, and proud,
Adonis' trampling courser doth espy,
And forth she rushes, snorts, and neighs
   aloud:
   The strong-neck'd steed, being tied unto a
      tree,
   Breaketh his rein, and to her straight goes
      he.

Imperiously he leaps, he neighs, he bounds,
And now his woven girths he breaks asunder;
The bearing earth with his hard hoof he
   wounds,
Whose hollow womb resounds like heaven's
   thunder;
   The iron bit he crushes 'tween his teeth,
   Controlling what he was controlled with.

His ears up-prick'd; his braided hanging
   mane
Upon his compass'd crest now stand on end;
His nostrils drink the air, and forth again,
As from a furnace, vapours doth he send:
   His eye, which scornfully glisters like fire,
   Shows his hot courage and his high desire.

Sometimes he trots, as if he told the steps,
With gentle majesty, and modest pride;
Anon he rears upright, curvets, and leaps,
As who should say, lo! thus my strength is
   tried;
   And this I do to captivate the eye
   Of the fair breeder that is standing by.

What recketh he his rider's angry stir,
His flattering 'holla,' or his 'Stand, I say'?
What cares he now for curb, or pricking
   spur?
For rich caparisons, or trapping gay?
   He sees his love, and nothing else he sees,
   Nor nothing else with his proud sight
      agrees.

Look, when a painter would surpass the life,
In limning out a well-porportion'd steed,
His art with nature's workmanship at strife,
As if the dead the living should exceed;
   So did this horse excel a common one,
   In shape, in courage, colour, pace, and bone.

Round-hoof'd, short-jointed, fetlocks shag
   and long,
Broad breast, full eye, small head, and nostril
   wide,
High crest, short ears, straight legs, and pass-
   ing strong,
Thin mane, thick tail, broad buttock, tender
   hide:
   Look what a horse should have, he did not
      lack,
   Save a proud rider on so proud a back.

Sometime he scuds far off, and there he
stares;
Anon he starts at stirring of a feather;
To bid the wind a base he now prepares,
And whe'r he run, or fly, they knew not
whether;
  For thro' his mane and tail the high wind
  sings,
  Fanning the hairs, who wave like feather'd
  wings.

He looks upon his love and neighs unto her;
She answers him as if she knew his mind:
Being proud, as females are, to see him woo
her,
She puts on outward strangeness, seems un-
kind;
  Spurns at his love, and scorns the heat he
  feels,
  Beating his kind embracements with her
  heels.

Then, like a melancholy malecontent,
He vails his tail, that, like a falling plume,
Cool shadow to his melting buttock lent;
He stamps, and bites the poor flies in his
fume:
  His love, perceiving how he is enrag'd,
  Grew kinder, and his fury was assuag'd.

His testy master goeth about to take him;
When lo, the unback'd breeder, full of fear,
Jealous of catching, swiftly doth forsake him,
With her the horse, and left Adonis there:
  As they were mad unto the wood they hie
  them,
  Out-stripping crows that strive to over-fly
  them.

All swoln with chasing, down Adonis sits,
Banning his boisterous and unruly beast;
And now the happy season once more fits,
That love-sick Love by pleading may be
blest;
  For lovers say the heart hath treble wrong,
  When it is barr'd the aidance of the tongue.

An oven that is stopp'd, or river stay'd,
Burneth more hotly, swelleth with more rage:
So of concealed sorrow may be said;
Free vent of words love's fire doth assuage;
  But when the heart's attorney once is mute,
  The client breaks, as desperate in his suit.

He sees her coming, and begins to glow,
Even as a dying coal revives with wind,
And with his bonnet hides his angry brow;
Looks on the dull earth with disturbed mind,
  Taking no notice that she is so nigh,
  For all askaunce he holds her in his eye.
O what a sight it was, wistly to view

How she came stealing to the wayward boy!
To note the fighting conflict of her hue!
How white and red each other did destroy!
  But now her cheek was pale, and by and by
  It flash'd forth fire, as lightning from the
  sky.

Now was she just before him as he sat,
And like a lowly lover down she kneels;
With one fair hand she heaveth up his hat,
Her other tender hand his fair cheek feels:
  His tenderer cheek receives her soft hand's
  print
  As apt as new-fallen snow takes any dint.

O what a war of looks was then between
them!
Her eyes, petitioners, to his eyes suing:
His eyes saw her eyes as they had not seen
them;
  Her eyes woo'd still, his eyes disdain'd the
  wooing:
  And all this dumb play had his acts made
  plain
  With tears, which, chorus-like, her eyes did
  rain.

Full gently now she takes him by the hand,
A lily prison'd in a gaol of snow,
Or ivory in an alabaster band;
So white a friend engirts so white a foe:
  This beauteous combat, wilful and unwill-
  ing,
  Show'd like two silver doves that sit a-bill-
  ing.

Once more the engine of her thoughts began:
'O fairest mover on this mortal round,
Would thou wert as I am, and I a man,
My heart all whole as thine, thy heart my
wound;
  For one sweet look thy help I would assure
  thee,
  Though nothing but my body's bane would
  cure thee.'

'Give me my hand,' saith he, 'why dost thou
feel it?'
'Give me my heart,' saith she, 'and thou shalt
have it;
O give it me lest thy hard heart do steel it,
And being steel'd, soft sighs can never grave
it;
  Then love's deep groans I never shall regard,
  Because Adonis' heart hath made mine
  hard.'

'For shame,' he cries, 'let go, and let me go;
My day's delight is past, my horse is gone,
And 'tis your fault I am bereft him so;
I pray you hence, and leave me here alone:

For all my mind, my thought, my busy
    care,
Is how to get my palfrey from the mare.'

Thus she replies: 'Thy palfrey, as he should,
Welcomes the warm approach of sweet desire.
Affection is a coal that must be cool'd;
Else, suffer'd, it will set the heart on fire:
    The sea hath bounds, but deep desire hath
      none,
    Therefore no marvel though thy horse be
      gone.

'How like a jade he stood, tied to the tree,
Servilely master'd with a leathern rein!
But when he saw his love, his youth's fair fee,
He held such petty bondage in disdain;
    Throwing the base thong from his bending
      crest,
    Enfranchising his mouth, his back, his
      breast.

'Who sees his true love in her naked bed,
Teaching the sheets a whiter hue than white,
But, when his glutton eye so full hath fed,
His other agents aim at like delight?
    Who is so faint that dare not be so bold
    To touch the fire, the weather being cold?

'Let me excuse thy courser, gentle boy;
And learn of him, I heartily beseech thee,
To take advantage on presented joy;
Though I were dumb, yet his proceedings
    teach thee.
    O learn to love; the lesson is but plain,
    And, once made perfect, never lost again.'

'I know not love,' quoth he, 'nor will not
    know it,
Unless it be a boar, and then I chase it:
'Tis much to borrow, and I will not owe it;
My love to love is love but to disgrace it;
    For I have heard it is a life in death,
    That laughs, and weeps, and all but with a
      breath.

'Who wears a garment shapeless and un-
    finish'd?
Who plucks the bud before one leaf put
    forth?
If springing things be any jot diminish'd,
They wither in their prime, prove nothing
    worth:
    The colt that's back'd and burthen'd being
      young
    Loseth his pride, and never. waxeth strong.

'You hurt my hand with wringing; let us
    part,
And leave this idle theme, this bootless chat:
Remove your siege from my unyielding
    heart;
To love's alarm it will not ope the gate.

Dismiss your vows, your feigned tears,
    your flattery;
For where a heart is hard, they make no
    battery.'

'What! canst thou talk,' quoth she, 'hast thou
    a tongue?
O would thou hadst not, or I had no hearing!
Thy mermaid's voice hath done me double
    wrong;
I had my load before, now press'd with bear-
    ing:
    Melodious discord, heavenly tune harsh
      sounding,
    Ear's deep-sweet music, and heart's deep-
      sore wounding.

'Had I no eyes, but ears, my ears would love
That inward beauty and invisible:
Or, were I deaf, thy outward parts would
    move
Each part in me that were but sensible:
    Though neither eyes nor ears, to hear nor
      see,
    Yet should I be in love, by touching thee.

'Say that the sense of feeling were bereft me,
And that I could not see, nor hear, nor touch,
And nothing but the very smell were left me,
Yet would my love to thee be still as much;
    For from the still'tory of thy face excelling
    Comes breath perfum'd, that breedeth love
      by smelling.

'But O, what banquet wert thou to the taste,
Being nurse and feeder of the other four,
Would they not wish the feast might ever
    last,
And bid Suspicion double-lock the door?
    Lest Jealousy, that sour unwelcome guest,
    Should, by his stealing in, disturb the
      feast.'

Once more the ruby-colour'd portal open'd,
Which to his speech did honey passage yield;
Like a red morn, that ever yet betoken'd
Wreck to the seaman, tempest to the field,
    Sorrow to shepherds, woe unto the birds,
    Gusts and foul flaws to herdmen and to
      herds.

This ill presage advisedly she marketh:
Even as the wind is hush'd before it raineth,
Or as the wolf doth grin before it barketh,
Or as the berry breaks before it staineth,
    Or like the deadly bullet of a gun,
    His meaning struck her ere his words
      begun.

And at his look she flatly falleth down,
For looks kill love, and love by looks re-
    viveth:
A smile recures the wounding of a frown,

But blessed bankrupt, that by love so
    thriveth!
  The silly boy, believing she is dead, [red;
  Claps her pale cheek, till clapping makes it

And all-amaz'd brake off his late intent,
For sharply he did think to reprehend her,
Which cunning love did wittily prevent:
Fair fall the wit that can so well defend her!
  For on the grass she lies as she were slain,
  Till his breath breatheth life in her again.

He wrings her nose, he strikes her on the
    cheeks,
He bends her fingers, holds her pulses hard;
He chafes her lips, a thousand ways he seeks
To mend the hurt that his unkindness
    marr'd;
  He kisses her; and she, by her good will,
  Will never rise so he will kiss her still.

The night of sorrow now is turn'd to day:
Her two blue windows faintly she upheaveth,
Like the fair sun, when in his fresh array
He cheers the morn, and all the world re-
    lieveth:
  And as the bright sun glorifies the sky,
  So is her face illumin'd with her eye:

Whose beams upon his hairless face are fix'd,
As if from thence they borrow'd all their
    shine.
Were never four such lamps together mix'd,
Had not his clouded with his brows' repine;
  But hers, which thro' the crystal tears gave
    light,
  Shone like the moon in water seen by night.

'O, where am I?' quoth she, 'in earth or
    heaven,
Or in the ocean drench'd, or in the fire?
What hour is this? or morn, or weary even?
Do I delight to die, or life desire?
  But now I liv'd, and life was death's
    annoy;
  But now I died, and death was lively joy.

'O thou didst kill me;—kill me once again:
Thy eyes' shrewd tutor, that hard heart of
    thine,
Hath taught them scornful tricks, and such
    disdain          [mine;
That they have murder'd this poor heart of
  And these mine eyes, true leaders to their
    queen,
  But for thy piteous lips no more had seen.

'Long may they kiss each other, for this cure!
O never let their crimson liveries wear!
And as they last, their verdure still endure,
To drive infection from the dangerous year!
  That the star-gazers, having writ on death,
  May say the plague is banished by thy
    breath.

'Pure lips, sweet seals in my soft lip im-
    printed,
What bargains may I make, still to be seal-
    ing?
To sell myself I can be well contented,
So thou wilt buy, and pay, and use good
    dealing;
  Which purchase if thou make, for fear of
    slips,
  Set thy seal-manual on my wax-red lips.

'A thousand kisses buys my heart from me;
And pay them at thy leisure, one by one.
What is ten hundred touches unto thee?
Are they not quickly told, and quickly gone?
  Say, for non-payment that the debt should
    double,
  Is twenty hundred kisses such a trouble?'

'Fair queen,' quoth he, 'if any love you owe
    me,
Measure my strangeness with my unripe
    years;
Before I know myself seek not to know me;
No fisher but the ungrown fry forbears:
  The mellow plum doth fall, the green sticks
    fast,
  Or being early pluck'd is sour to taste.

'Look, the world's comforter, with weary
    gait,
His day's hot task hath ended in the west:
The owl, night's herald, shrieks,—'tis very
    late;
The sheep are gone to fold, birds to their
    nest;
  And coal-black clouds that shadow
    heaven's light
  Do summon us to part, and bid good night.

'Now let me say "good night," and so say
    you;
If you will say so, you shall have a kiss.'
'Good night,' quoth she; and, ere he says
    'adieu,'
The honey fee of parting tender'd is:
  Her arms do lend his neck a sweet em-
    brace;
  Incorporate then they seem; face grows to
    face.

Till, breathless, he disjoin'd, and backward
    drew
The heavenly moisture, that sweet coral
    mouth,
Whose precious taste her thirsty lips well
    knew,
Whereon they surfeit, yet complain on
    drouth:
  He with her plenty press'd, she faint with
    dearth,
  (Their lips together glued,) fall to the
    earth.

Now quick Desire hath caught the yielding
     prey,
And glutton-like she feeds, yet never filleth;
Her lips are conquerors, his lips obey,
Paying what ransom the insulter willeth;
     Whose vulture thought doth pitch the price
       so high,
     That she will draw his lips' rich treasure
       dry.

And having felt the sweetness of the spoil,
With blindfold fury she begins to forage;
Her face doth reek and smoke, her blood
     doth boil,
And careless lust stirs up a desperate cour-
     age;
     Planting oblivion, beating reason back,
     Forgetting shame's pure blush, and hon-
       our's wrack.

Hot, faint, and weary, with her hard em-
     bracing,
Like a wild bird being tam'd with too much
     handling,
Or as the fleet-foot roe that's tir'd with
     chasing,
Or like the froward infant still'd with
     dandling,
     He now obeys, and now no more resisteth,
     While she takes all she can, not all she
       listeth.

What wax so frozen but dissolves with tem-
     pering,
And yields at last to every light impression?
Things out of hope are compass'd oft with
     venturing,
Chiefly in love, whose leave exceeds commis-
     sion:
     Affection faints not like a pale-fac'd cow-
       ard,
     But then wooes best when most his choice
       is froward.

When he did frown, O had she then gave
     over,
Such nectar from his lips she had not suck'd.
Foul words and frowns must not repel a
     lover;
What though the rose have prickles, yet 'tis
     pluck'd:
     Were beauty under twenty locks kept fast,
     Yet love breaks through, and picks them
       all at last.

For pity now she can no more detain him;
The poor fool prays her that he may depart:
She is resolv'd no longer to restrain him;
Bids him farewell, and look well to her heart,
     The which, by Cupid's bow she doth pro-
       test,
     He carries thence incaged in his breast.

'Sweet boy,' she says, 'this night I'll waste in
     sorrow,
For my sick heart commands mine eyes to
     watch.
Tell me, love's master, shall we meet to-
     morrow?
Say, shall we? shall we? wilt thou make the
     match?'
     He tells her, no; to-morrow he intends
     To hunt the boar with certain of his
       friends.

'The boar!' quoth she, whereat a sudden pale,
Like lawn being spread upon the blushing
     rose,
Usurps her cheeks; she trembles at his tale,
And on his neck her yoking arms she throws:
     She sinketh down, still hanging by his
       neck,
     He on her belly falls, she on her back.

Now is she in the very lists of love,
Her champion mounted for the hot encoun-
     ter:
All is imaginary she doth prove,
He will not manage her, although he mount
     her;
     That worse than Tantalus' is her annoy,
     To clip Elysium, and to lack her joy.

Even as poor birds, deceiv'd with painted
     grapes,
Do surfeit by the eye, and pine the maw,
Even so she languisheth in her mishaps,
As those poor birds that helpless berries saw:
     The warm effects which she in him finds
       missing,
     She seeks to kindle with continual kissing.

But all in vain; good queen, it will not be:
She hath assay'd as much as may be prov'd;
Her pleading hath deserv'd a greater fee;
She's Love, she loves, and yet she is not
     lov'd.
     'Fie, fie,' he says, 'you crush me; let me
       go;
     You have no reason to withhold me so.'

'Thou hadst been gone,' quoth she, 'sweet
     boy, ere this,        [the boar.
But that thou told'st me thou wouldst hunt
O be advis'd! thou know'st not what it is
With javelin's point a churlish swine to gore,
     Whose tushes never sheath'd he whetteth
       still,
     Like to a mortal butcher, bent to kill.

'On his bow-back he hath a battle set
Of bristly pikes, that ever threat his foes;
His eyes like glowworms shine when he doth
     fret:
His snout digs sepulchres where'er he goes;

Being mov'd, he strikes whate'er is in his way,
And whom he strikes his cruel tushes slay.

'His brawny sides, with hairy bristles arm'd,
Are better proof than thy spear's point can enter;
His short thick neck cannot be easily harm'd;
Being ireful on the lion he will venture:
  The thorny brambles and embracing bushes,
  As fearful of him, part; through whom he rushes.

'Alas, he nought esteems that face of thine,
To which Love's eyes pay tributary gazes;
Nor thy soft hands, sweet lips, and crystal eyne,
Whose full perfection all the world amazes;
  But having thee at vantage, (wondrous dread!)
  Would root these beauties as he roots the mead.

'O, let him keep his loathsome cabin still!
Beauty hath nought to do with such foul fiends:
Come not within his danger by thy will:
They that thrive well take counsel of their friends.
  When thou didst name the boar, not to dissemble,
  I fear'd thy fortune, and my joints did [tremble.

'Didst thou not mark my face? Was it not white?
Saw'st thou not signs of fear lurk in mine eye?
Grew I not faint? And fell I not downright?
Within my bosom, whereon thou dost lie,
  My boding heart pants, beats, and takes no rest,
  But, like an earthquake, shakes thee on my breast.

'For where Love reigns, disturbing Jealousy
Doth call himself Affection's sentinel;
Gives false alarms, suggesteth mutiny,
And in a peaceful hour doth cry, "kill, kill;"
  Distempering gentle Love in his desire,
  As air and water do abate the fire.

'This sour informer, this bate-breeding spy,
This canker that eats up love's tender spring,
This carry-tale, dissentious Jealousy,
That sometime true news, sometime false doth bring,
  Knocks at my heart, and whispers in mine ear,
  That if I love thee I thy death should fear:

'And, more than so, presenteth to mine eye
The picture of an angry-chafing boar,

Under whose sharp fangs on his back doth lie
An image like thyself, all stain'd with gore;
  Whose blood upon the fresh flowers being shed
  Doth make them droop with grief, and hang the head.

'What should I do, seeing thee so indeed,
That tremble at the imagination?
The thought of it doth make my faint heart bleed,
And fear doth teach it divination:
  I prophesy thy death, my living sorrow,
  If thou encounter with the boar to-morrow.

'But if thou needs will hunt, be rul'd by me;
Uncouple at the timorous flying hare,
Or at the fox, which lives by subtilty,
Or at the roe, which no encounter dare:
  Pursue these fearful creatures o'er the downs,
  And on thy well-breath'd horse keep with thy hounds.

'And when thou hast on foot the purblind hare,
Mark the poor wretch, to overshoot his troubles,
How he outruns the wind, and with what care
He cranks and crosses, with a thousand doubles:
  The many musits through the which he goes
  Are like a labyrinth to amaze his foes.

'Sometime he runs among a flock of sheep,
To make the cunning hounds mistake their smell,
And sometime where earth-delving conies keep,
To stop the loud pursuers in their yell;
  And sometime sorteth with a herd of deer;
  Danger deviseth shifts; wit waits on fear:

'For there his smell with others being mingled,
The hot scent-snuffing hounds are driven to doubt,
Ceasing their clamorous cry till they have singled
With much ado the cold fault cleanly out;
  Then do they spend their mouths: Echo replies,
  As if another chase were in the skies.

'By this, poor Wat, far off upon a hill,
Stands on his hinder legs with listening ear
To hearken if his foes pursue him still;
Anon their loud alarums he doth hear;

And now his grief may be compared well
To one sore sick that hears the passing
    bell.

'Then shalt thou see the dew-bedabbled
    wretch
Turn, and return, indenting with the way;
Each envious briar his weary legs doth
    scratch,
Each shadow makes him stop, each murmur
    stay:
    For misery is trodden on by many,
    And being low never reliev'd by any.

'Lie quietly, and hear a little more;
Nay, do not struggle, for thou shalt not rise:
To make thee hate the hunting of the boar,
Unlike myself thou hear'st me moralize,
    Applying this to that, and so to so;
    For love can comment upon every woe.

'Where did I leave?'—'No matter where,'
    quoth he;
'Leave me, and then the story aptly ends:
The night is spent.'—'Why, what of that?'
    quoth she.
'I am,' quoth he, 'expected of my friends;
And now 'tis dark, and going I shall fall.'
    'In night,' quoth she, 'desire sees best of
    all.

'But if thou fall, O then imagine this,
The earth in love with thee thy footing
    trips,
And all is but to rob thee of a kiss. [thy lips
    Rich preys make true men thieves: so do
    Make modest Dian cloudy and forlorn,
    Lest she should steal a kiss, and die for-
    sworn.

'Now of this dark night I perceive the rea-
    son:
Cynthia for shame obscures her silver shine,
Till forging nature be condemn'd of treason,
For stealing moulds from heaven that were
    divine,            [despite,
    Wherein she fram'd thee in high heaven's
    To shame the sun by day, and her by night.

'And therefore hath she brib'd the Destinies,
To cross the curious workmanship of nature,
To mingle beauty with infirmities,
And pure perfection with impure defeature;
    Making it subject to the tyranny
    Of mad mischances and much misery;

'As burning fevers, agues pale and faint,
Life-poisoning pestilence, and frenzies wood,
The marrow-eating sickness, whose attaint
Disorder breeds by heating of the blood:
    Surfeits, imposthumes, grief, and damn'd
    despair,
    Swear Nature's death for framing thee so
    fair.

'And not the least of all these maladies,
But in one minute's fight brings beauty
    under:
Both favour, savour, hue, and qualities,
Whereat the impartial gazer late did won-
    der,
    Are on the sudden wasted, thaw'd and
    done,           [sun.
    As mountain-snow melts with the midday

'Therefore, despite of fruitless chastity,
Love-lacking vestals, and self-loving nuns,
That on the earth would breed a scarcity
And barren dearth of daughters and of sons,
    Be prodigal: the lamp that burns by night
    Dries up his oil to lend the world his light.

'What is thy body but a swallowing grave,
Seeming to bury that posterity     [have,
Which by the rights of time thou needs must
If thou destroy them not in dark obscurity?
    If so, the world will hold thee in disdain,
    Sith in thy pride so fair a hope is slain.

'So in thyself thyself art made away;
A mischief worse than civil home-bred strife,
Or theirs whose desperate hands themselves
    do slay
Or butcher-sire, that reaves his son of life.
    Foul cankering rust the hidden treasure
    frets,
    But gold that's put to use more gold be-
    gets.'

'Nay, then,' quoth Adon, 'you will fall again
Into your idle over-handled theme;
The kiss I gave you is bestow'd in vain,
And all in vain you strive against the stream;
    For by this black-fac'd night, desire's foul
    nurse,           [worse.
    Your treatise makes me like you worse and

'If love have lent you twenty thousand
    tongues,
And every tongue more moving than your
    own,
Bewitching like the wanton mermaid's songs,
Yet from mine ear the tempting tune is
    blown;
    For know, my heart stands armed in mine
    ear,
    And will not let a false sound enter there;

'Lest the deceiving harmony should run
Into the quiet closure of my breast;
And then my little heart were quite undone,
In his bedchamber to be barr'd of rest.
    No, lady, no; my heart longs not to groan,
    But soundly sleeps, while now it sleeps
    alone.

'What have you urg'd that I cannot reprove?
The path is smooth that leadeth on to dan-
    ger;

I hate not love, but your device in love,
That lends embracements unto every strang-
　　er.
　　You do it for increase; O strange excuse!
　　When reason is the bawd to lust's abuse.

'Call it not love, for love to heaven is fled,
Since sweating lust on earth usurp'd his
　　name;
Under whose simple semblance he hath fed
Upon fresh beauty, blotting it with blame;
　　Which the hot tyrant stains, and soon be-
　　reaves,
　　As caterpillars do the tender leaves.

'Love comforteth like sunshine after rain,
But lust's effect is tempest after sun;
Love's gentle spring doth always fresh remain,
Lust's winter comes ere summer half be done.
　　Love surfeits not; lust like a glutton dies:
　　Love is all truth; lust full of forged lies.

'More I could tell, but more I dare not say;
The text is old, the orator too green.
Therefore, in sadness, now I will away;
My face is full of shame, my heart of teen;
　　Mine ears that to your wanton talk at-
　　tended,
　　Do burn themselves for having so offended.'

With this he breaketh from the sweet embrace
Of those fair arms which bound him to her
　　breast,
And homeward through the dark laund runs
　　apace;
Leaves Love upon her back deeply distress'd.
　　Look how a bright star shooteth from the
　　sky,
　　So glides he in the night from Venus' eye;

Which after him she darts, as one on shore
Gazing upon a late-embarked friend,
Till the wild waves will have him seen no
　　more,
Whose ridges with the meeting clouds con-
　　tend;
　　So did the merciless and pitchy night
　　Fold in the object that did feed her sight.

Whereat amaz'd, as one that unaware
Hath dropp'd a precious jewel in the flood,
Or 'stonish'd as night-wanderers often are,
Their light blown out in some mistrustful
　　wood;
　　Even so confounded in the dark she lay,
　　Having lost the fair discovery of her way.

And now she beats her heart, whereat it
　　groans,
That all the neighbour-caves, as seeming
　　troubled,
Make verbal repetition of her moans;
Passion on passion deeply is redoubled:

'Ah me!' she cries, and twenty times, 'woe,
　　woe!'
And twenty echoes twenty times cry so.

She, marking them, begins a wailing note,
And sings extemp'rally a woeful ditty;
How love makes young men thrall, and old
　　men dote;
How love is wise in folly, foolish-witty:
　　Her heavy anthem still concludes in woe,
　　And still the choir of echoes answer so.

Her song was tedious, and outwore the night,
For lovers' hours are long, though seeming
　　short:
If pleas'd themselves, others, they think, de-
　　light
In such like circumstance, with such like
　　sport:
　　Their copious stories, oftentimes begun,
　　End without audience, and are never done.

For who hath she to spend the night withal,
But idle sounds resembling parasites,
Like shrill-tongued tapsters answering every
　　call,
Soothing the humour of fantastic wits?
　　She says, ''tis so:' they answer all, ''tis so;'
　　And would say after her, if she said 'no.'

Lo! here the gentle lark, weary of rest,
From his moist cabinet mounts up on high,
And wakes the morning, from whose silver
　　breast
The sun ariseth in his majesty;
　　Who doth the world so gloriously behold,
　　The cedar-tops and hills seem burnish'd
　　gold.

Venus salutes him with this fair good-mor-
　　row:
'O thou clear god, and patron of all light,
From whom each lamp and shining star doth
　　borrow
The beauteous influence that makes him
　　bright,
　　There lives a son, that suck'd an earthly
　　mother,
　　May lend thee light, as thou dost lend to
　　other.'

This said, she hasteth to a myrtle grove,
Musing the morning is so much o'erworn,
And yet she hears no tidings of her love:
She hearkens for his hounds, and for his
　　horn:
　　Anon she hears them chant it lustily,
　　And all in haste she coasteth to the cry.

And as she runs, the bushes in the way
Some catch her by the neck, some kiss her
　　face,
Some twine about her thigh to make her stay;

She wildly breaketh from their strict embrace,
Like a milch doe, whose swelling dugs do
    ache,
Hasting to feed her fawn, hid in some
    brake.

By this she hears the hounds are at a bay,
Whereat she starts, like one that spies an
    adder
Wreath'd up in fatal folds, just in his way,
The fear whereof doth make him shake and
    shudder;
    Even so the timorous yelping of the hounds
    Appals her senses, and her spright con-
        founds.

For now she knows it is no gentle chase,
But the blunt boar, rough bear, or lion proud,
Because the cry remaineth in one place,
Where fearfully the dogs exclaim aloud:
    Finding their enemy to be so curst,
    They all strain court'sy who shall cope him
        first.

This dismal cry rings sadly in her ear,
Through which it enters to surprise her heart,
Who, overcome by doubt and bloodless fear,
With cold-pale weakness numbs each feeling
    part:
    Like soldiers, when their captain once doth
        yield,
    They basely fly, and dare not stay the field.

Thus stands she in a trembling ecstasy;
Till, cheering up her senses sore-dismay'd,
She tells them 'tis a causeless fantasy,
And childish error that they are afraid;
    Bids them leave quaking, bids them fear no
        more;—
    And with that word she spied the hunted
        boar;

Whose frothy mouth, bepainted all with red,
Like milk and blood being mingled ·both to-
    gether,
A second fear through all her sinews spread,
Which madly hurries her she knows not
    whither:
    This way she runs, and now she will no
        further,                            [ther.
    But back retires, to rate the boar for mur-

A thousand spleens bear her a thousand
    ways;
She treads the path that she untreads again;
Her more than haste is mated with delays,
Like the proceedings of a drunken brain,
    Full of respect, yet nought at all respecting
    In hand with all things, nought at all effect-
        ing.

Here kennell'd in a brake she finds a hound,
And asks the weary caitiff for his master;
And, there another licking of his wound,

'Gainst venom'd sores the only sovereign
    plaster;
    And here she meets another sadly scowling,
    To whom she speaks, and he replies with
        howling.

When he hath ceas'd his ill-resounding noise,
Another flap-mouth'd mourner, black and
    grim,
Against the welkin volleys out his voice;
Another and another answer him,
    Clapping their proud tails to the ground
        below,
    Shaking their scratch'd ears, bleeding as
        they go.

Look, how the world's poor people are
    amaz'd
At apparitions, signs, and prodigies,
Whereon with fearful eyes they long have
    gaz'd,
Infusing them with dreadful prophecies:
    So she at these sad signs draws up her
        breath,
    And, sighing it again, exclaims on Death.

'Hard-favour'd tyrant, ugly, meagre, lean,
Hateful divorce of love,' (thus chides she
    Death,)
'Grim-grinning ghost, earth's worm, what
    dost thou mean
To stifle beauty, and to steal his breath,
    Who when he liv'd, his breath and beauty
        set
    Gloss on the rose, smell to the violet?

'If he be dead,—O no, it cannot be,
Seeing his beauty, thou shouldst strike at it—
O yes, it may; thou hast no eyes to see,
But hatefully at random dost thou hit.
    Thy mark is feeble age; but thy false dart
    Mistakes that aim, and cleaves an infant's
        heart.

'Hadst thou but bid beware, then he had
    spoke,
And hearing him thy power had lost his
    power.
The Destinies will curse thee for this stroke;
They bid thee crop a weed, thou pluck'st a
    flower:
    Love's golden arrow at him should have
        fled,                                [dead.
    And not Death's ebon dart, to strike him

'Dost thou drink tears, that thou provok'st
    such weeping?
What may a heavy groan advantage thee?
Why hast thou cast into eternal sleeping
Those eyes that taught all other eyes to see?
    Now Nature cares not for thy mortal
        vigour,
    Since her best work is ruin'd with thy
        rigour.'

Here overcome, as one full of despair,
She vail'd her eyelids, who, like sluices,
    stopp'd
The crystal tide that from her two cheeks
    fair
In the sweet channel of her bosom dropp'd;
    But through the floodgates breaks the sil-
        ver rain,                    [again.
    And with his strong course opens them

O how her eyes and tears did lend and bor-
    row!
Her eyes seen in the tears, tears in her eye;
Both crystals, where they view'd each other's
    sorrow,
Sorrow, that friendly sighs sought still to
    dry;
    But like a stormy day, now wind, now
        rain,
    Sighs dry her cheeks, tears make them
        wet again.

Variable passions throng her constant woe,
As striving who should best become her
    grief;
All entertain'd, each passion labours so
That every present sorrow seemeth chief,
    But none is best; then join they all to-
        gether,
    Like many clouds consulting for foul
        weather.

By this, far off she hears some huntsmen
    hollo:
A nurse's song ne'er pleas'd her babe so
    well:
The dire imagination she did follow
This sound of hope doth labour to expel;
    For now reviving joy bids her rejoice,
    And flatters her it is Adonis' voice.

Whereat her tears began to turn their tide,
Being prison'd in her eye, like pearls in glass;
Yet sometimes falls an orient drop beside,
Which her cheek melts, as scorning it should
    pass,
    To wash the foul face of the sluttish
        ground,
    Who is but drunken when she seemeth
        drown'd.

O hard-believing love, how strange it seems
Not to believe, and yet too credulous!
Thy weal and woe are both of them ex-
    tremes,
Despair and hope make thee ridiculous:
    The one doth flatter thee in thoughts un-
        likely,
    In likely thoughts the other kills thee
        quickly.

Now she unweaves the web that she hath
    wrought;
Adonis lives, and Death is not to blame;

It was not she that called him all-to naught:
Now she adds honours to his hateful name;
    She clepes him king of graves, and grave
        for kings,
    Imperious supreme of all mortal things.

'No, no,' quoth she, 'sweet Death, I did but
    jest;
Yet pardon me, I felt a kind of fear,
When as I met the boar, that bloody beast,
Which knows no pity, but is still severe;
    Then, gentle shadow (truth I must con-
        fess),
    I rail'd on thee, fearing my love's decease.

''Tis not my fault: the boar provok'd my
    tongue;
Be wreak'd on him, invisible commander;
'Tis he, foul creature, that hath done thee
    wrong;
I did but act, he's author of thy slander:
    Grief hath two tongues, and never woman
        yet
    Could rule them both, without ten wo-
        men's wit.'

Thus, hoping that Adonis is alive,
Her rash suspect she doth extenuate;
And that his beauty may the better thrive,
With Death she humbly doth insinuate;
    Tells him of trophies, statues, tombs; and
        stories
    His victories, his triumphs, and his glories.

'O Jove,' quoth she, 'how much a fool was I
To be of such a weak and silly mind,
To wail his death who lives, and must not
    die,
Till mutual overthrow of mortal kind!
    For he being dead, with him is beauty
        slain,
    And, beauty dead, black chaos comes
        again.

'Fie, fie, fond love, thou art so full of fear
As one with treasure laden, hemm'd with
    thieves,
Trifles, unwitnessed with eye or ear,
Thy coward heart with false bethinking
    grieves.'
    Even at this word she hears a merry horn,
    Whereat she leaps that was but late for-
        lorn.

As falcon to the lure away she flies;
The grass stoops not, she treads on it so
    light;
And in her haste unfortunately spies
The foul boar's conquest on her fair delight;
    Which seen, her eyes, as murder'd with the
        view,
    Like stars asham'd of day, themselves
        withdrew.

Or, as the snail, whose tender horns being hit,
Shrinks backward in his shelly cave with pain,
And there, all smother'd up, in shade doth sit,
Long after fearing to creep forth again;
  So, at his bloody view, her eyes are fled
  Into the deep dark cabins of her head;

Where they resign their office and their light
To the disposing of her troubled brain;
Who bids them still consort with ugly night,
And never wound the heart with looks again;
  Who, like a king perplexed in his throne,
  By their suggestion gives a deadly groan.

Whereat each tributary subject quakes:
As when the wind, imprison'd in the ground,
Struggling for passage, earth's foundation shakes,
Which with cold terror doth men's minds confound,
  The mutiny each part doth so surprise,
  That from their dark beds once more leap her eyes;

And, being open'd, threw unwilling light
Upon the wide wound that the boar had trench'd
In his soft flank; whose wonted lily white
With purple tears, that his wound wept, was drench'd:
  No flower was nigh, no grass, herb, leaf, or weed, [to bleed.
  But stole his blood, and seem'd with him

This solemn sympathy poor Venus noteth;
Over one shoulder doth she hang her head;
Dumbly she passions, franticly she doteth;
She thinks he could not die, he is not dead.
  Her voice is stopp'd, her joints forget to bow;
  Her eyes are mad that they have wept till now.

Upon his hurt she looks so steadfastly,
That her sight dazzling makes the wound seem three;
And then she reprehends her mangling eye
That makes more gashes where no breach should be:
  His face seems twain, each several limb is doubled; [troubled.
  For oft the eye mistakes, the brain being

'My tongue cannot express my grief for one,
And yet,' quoth she, 'behold two Adons dead!
My sighs are blown away, my salt tears gone,

Mine eyes are turn'd to fire, my heart to lead;
  Heavy heart's lead melt at mine eyes' red fire!
  So shall I die by drops of hot desire.

'Alas, poor world, what treasure hast thou lost!
What face remains alive that's worth the viewing? [boast
Whose tongue is music now? what canst thou
Of things long since, or anything ensuing?
  The flowers are sweet, their colours fresh and trim;
  But true-sweet beauty liv'd and died with him.

'Bonnet nor veil henceforth no creature wear!
Nor sun nor wind will ever strive to kiss you:
Having no fair to lose, you need not fear;
The sun doth scorn you, and the wind doth hiss you:
  But when Adonis liv'd, sun and sharp air
  Lurk'd like two thieves to rob him of his fair;

'And therefore would he put his bonnet on,
Under whose brim the gaudy sun would peep;
The wind would blow it off, and, being gone,
Play with his locks; then would Adonis weep:
  And straight, in pity of his tender years,
  They both would strive who first should dry his tears.

'To see his face the lion walk'd along
Behind some hedge, because he would not fear him:
To recreate himself, when he hath sung,
The tiger would be tame and gently hear him:
  If he had spoke the wolf would leave his prey,
  And never fright the silly lamb that day.

'When he beheld his shadow in the brook,
The fishes spread on it their golden gills;
When he was by, the birds such pleasure took
That some would sing, some other in their bills
  Would bring him mulberries, and ripe-red cherries; [berries.
  He fed them with his sight, they him with

'But this foul, grim, and urchin-snouted boar,
Whose downward eye still looketh for a grave,

Ne'er saw the beauteous livery that he wore;
Witness the entertainment that he gave;
  If he did see his face, why then I know
He thought to kiss him, and hath kill'd
  him so.

' 'Tis true, 'tis true; thus was Adonis slain;
He ran upon the boar with his sharp
  spear,
Who did not whet his teeth at him again,
But by a kiss thought to persuade him
  there;
  And nuzzling in his flank the loving swine
  Sheath'd, unaware, the tusk in his soft
  groin.

'Had I been tooth'd like him, I must con-
  fess,
With kissing him I should have kill'd him
  first;
But he is dead, and never did he bless
My youth with his; the more am I accurst.'
  With this she falleth in the place she stood,
  And stains her face with his congealed
  blood.

She looks upon his lips, and they are pale;
She takes him by the hand, and that is
  cold;
She whispers in his ears a heavy tale,
As if they heard the woeful words she told:
  She lifts the coffer-lids that close his eyes,
  Where, lo! two lamps, burnt out, in dark-
  ness lies:

Two glasses where herself herself beheld
A thousand times, and now no more reflect;
Their virtue lost, wherein they late ex-
  cell'd,
And every beauty robb'd of his effect:
  'Wonder of time,' quoth she, 'this is my
  spite,
  That you being dead the day should yet
  be light.

'Since thou art dead, lo! here I prophesy,
Sorrow on love hereafter shall attend;
It shall be waited on with jealousy,
Find sweet beginning but unsavoury end;
  Ne'er settled equally, but high or low;
  That all love's pleasure shall not match
  his woe.

'It shall be fickle, false, and full of fraud;
Bud and be blasted in a breathing while;
The bottom poison, and the top o'erstraw'd
With sweets that shall the truest sight be-
  guile:
  The strongest body shall it make most
  weak,
  Strike the wise dumb, and teach the fool
  to speak.

'It shall be sparing, and too full of riot,
Teaching decrepit age to tread the measures;
The staring ruffian shall it keep in quiet,
Pluck down the rich, enrich the poor with
  treasures:
  It shall be raging mad, and silly mild,
  Make the young old, the old become a
  child.

'It shall suspect where is no cause of fear;
It shall not fear where it should most mis-
  trust;
It shall be merciful, and too severe,
And most deceiving when it seems most
  just;
  Perverse it shall be where it shows most
  toward,
  Put fear to valour, courage to the coward.

'It shall be cause of war and dire events,
And set dissension 'twixt the son and sire;
Subject and servile to all discontents,
As dry combustious matter is to fire;
  Sith in his prime death doth my love de-
  stroy,
  They that love best their love shall not
  enjoy.'

By this, the boy that by her side lay kill'd
Was melted like a vapour from her sight,
And in his blood that on the ground lay
  spill'd,
A purple flower sprung up, chequer'd with
  white,
  Resembling well his pale cheeks, and the
  blood
  Which in round drops upon their white-
  ness stood.

She bows her head, the new-sprung flower
  to smell,
Comparing it to her Adonis' breath;
And says, within her bosom it shall dwell,
Since he himself is reft from her by death:
  She crops the stalk, and in the breach
  appears
  Green dropping sap, which she compares
  to tears.

'Poor flower,' quoth she, 'this was thy
  father's guise,
(Sweet issue of a more sweet-smelling sire,)
For every little grief to wet his eyes:
To grow unto himself was his desire,
  And so 'tis thine; but know, it is as good
  To wither in my breast as in his blood.

'Here was thy father's bed, here in my breast;
Thou art the next of blood, and 'tis thy
  right:
Lo! in this hollow cradle take thy rest,
My throbbing heart shall rock thee day and
  night:

There shall not be one minute in an hour
Wherein I will not kiss my sweet love's
   flower.'

Thus weary of the world, away she hies,
And yokes her silver doves; by whose swift
   aid

Their mistress, mounted, through the empty
   skies
In her light chariot quickly is convey'd,
   Holding their course to Paphos, where
   their queen
   Means to immure herself, and not be
   seen.

# THE RAPE OF LUCRECE

TO THE

## RIGHT HONOURABLE HENRY WRIOTHESLY,

EARL OF SOUTHAMPTON, AND BARON OF TITCHFIELD.

THE love I dedicate to your Lordship is without end; whereof this pamphlet, without beginning, is but a superfluous moiety. The warrant I have of your honourable disposition,
not the worth of my untutored lines, makes it assured of acceptance. What I have done
is yours, what I have to do is yours; being part in all I have, devoted yours. Were my
worth greater my duty would show greater: meantime, as it is, it is bound to your Lordship, to whom I wish long life, still lengthened with all happiness,

Your Lordship's in all duty,

WILLIAM SHAKESPEARE.

## THE ARGUMENT.

LUCIUS TARQUINIUS (for his excessive pride surnamed Superbus), after he had caused his
own father-in-law, Servius Tullius, to be cruelly murdered, and, contrary to the Roman
laws and customs, not requiring or staying for the people's suffrages, had possessed himself of the kingdom, went, accompanied with his sons and other noblemen of Rome, to
besiege Ardea. During which siege, the principal men of the army meeting one evening
at the tent of Sextus Tarquinius, the king's son, in their discourses after supper, every
one commended the virtues of his own wife; among whom, Collatinus extolled the incomparable chastity of his wife Lucretia. In that pleasant humour they all posted to
Rome; and intending by their secret and sudden arrival to make trial of that which every
one had before avouched, only Collatinus finds his wife (though it were late in the night)
spinning amongst her maids: the other ladies were all found dancing and revelling, or in
several disports. Whereupon the noblemen yielded Collatinus the victory, and his wife
the fame. At that time Sextus Tarquinius, being inflamed with Lucrece's beauty, yet
smothering his passions for the present, departed with the rest back to the camp; from
whence he shortly after privily withdrew himself, and was (according to his estate) royally
entertained and lodged by Lucrece at Collatium. The same night he treacherously
stealeth into her chamber, violently ravished her, and early in the morning speedeth
away. Lucrece, in this lamentable plight, hastily despatcheth messengers, one to Rome
for her father, another to the camp for Collatine. They came, the one accompanied with
Junius Brutus, the other with Publius Valerius; and, finding Lucrece attired in mourning
habit, demanded the cause of her sorrow. She, first taking an oath of them for her revenge, revealed the actor and whole manner of his dealing, and withal suddenly stabbed
herself. Which done, with one consent they all vowed to root out the whole hated family
of the Tarquins; and, bearing the dead body to Rome, Brutus acquainted the people with
the doer and manner of the vile deed, with a bitter invective against the tyranny of the
king; wherewith the people were so moved, that with one consent and a general acclamation the Tarquins were all exiled, and the state government changed from kings to consuls.

---

FROM the besieged Ardea all in post,
Borne by the trustless wings of false desire,
Lust-breathed Tarquin leaves the Roman host,
And to Collatium bears the lightless fire
Which, in pale embers hid, lurks to aspire,
    And girdle with embracing flames the waist
    Of Collatine's fair love, Lucrece the chaste.

Haply that name of chaste unhapp'ly set
This bateless edge on his keen appetite;

When Collatine unwisely did not let
To praise the clear unmatched red and white
Which triumph'd in that sky of his delight,
    Where mortal stars, as bright as heaven's beauties,
    With pure aspects did him peculiar duties.

For he the night before, in Tarquin's tent,
Unlock'd the treasure of his happy state,
What priceless wealth the heavens had him lent
In the possession of his beauteous mate;

Reckoning his fortune at such high-proud
   rate,
  That kings might be espoused to more
   fame,
  But king nor peer to such a peerless dame.

O happiness enjoy'd but of a few!
And, if possess'd, as soon decay'd and done
As is the morning's silver-melting dew
Against the golden splendour of the sun!
An expir'd date, cancell'd ere well begun:
  Honour and beauty, in the owner's arms,
  Are weakly fortress'd from a world of
   harms.

Beauty itself doth of itself persuade
The eyes of men without an orator;
What needeth then apologies be made
To set forth that which is so singular?
Or why is Collatine the publisher
  Of that rich jewel he should keep unknown
  From thievish ears, because it is his own?

Perchance his boast of Lucrece's sovereignty
Suggested this proud issue of a king;
For by our ears our hearts oft tainted be:
Perchance that envy of so rich a thing,
Braving compare, disdainfully did sting
  His high-pitch'd thoughts, that meaner
   men should vaunt,
  That golden hap which their superiors
   want.

But some untimely thought did instigate
His all-too-timeless speed, if none of those:
His honour, his affairs, his friends, his state,
Neglected all, with swift intent he goes
To quench the coal which in his liver glows.
  O rash false heat, wrapp'd in repentant
   cold,
  Thy hasty spring still blasts, and ne'er
   grows old!

When at Collatium this false lord arriv'd,
Well was he welcom'd by the Roman dame,
Within whose face beauty and virtue striv'd
Which of them both should underprop her
   fame:
When virtue bragg'd, beauty would blush
   for shame;
  When beauty boasted blushes, in despite
  Virtue would stain that or with silver
   white.

But beauty, in that white intituled,
From Venus' doves doth challenge that fair
   field:
Then virtue claims from beauty beauty's
   red,
Which virtue gave the golden age, to gild
Their silver cheeks, and call'd it then their
   shield;
  Teaching them thus to use it in the fight,—

When shame assail'd, the red should fence
   the white.

This heraldry in Lucrece' face was seen,
Argued by beauty's red, and virtue's white:
Of either's colour was the other queen,
Proving from world's minority their right:
Yet their ambition makes them still to fight;
  The sovereignty of either being so great,
  That oft they interchange each other's
   seat.

This silent war of lilies and of roses
Which Tarquin view'd in her fair face's field,
In their pure ranks his traitor eye encloses;
Where, lest between them both it should be
   kill'd,
The coward captive vanquished doth yield
  To those two armies that would let him
   go,
  Rather than triumph in so false a foe.

Now thinks he that her husband's shallow
   tongue
(The niggard prodigal that prais'd her so)
In that high task hath done her beauty
   wrong,
Which far exceeds his barren skill to show:
Therefore that praise which Collatine doth
   owe,
  Enchanted Tarquin answers with surmise,
  In silent wonder of still-gazing eyes.

This earthly saint, adored by this devil,
Little suspecteth the false worshipper;
For unstain'd thoughts do seldom dream on
   evil;
Birds never lim'd no secret bushes fear:
So guiltless she securely gives good cheer
  And reverend welcome to her princely
   guest,
  Whose inward ill no outward harm ex-
   press'd:

For that he colour'd with his high estate,
Hiding base sin in plaits of majesty;
That nothing in him seem'd inordinate,
Save sometime too much wonder of his eye,
Which, having all, all could not satisfy;
  But, poorly rich, so wanteth in his store
  That cloy'd with much he pineth still for
   more.

But she, that never cop'd with stranger eyes,
Could pick no meaning from their parling
   looks,
Nor read the subtle-shining secrecies
Writ in the glassy margents of such books:
She touch'd no unknown baits, nor fear'd no
   hooks;
  Nor could she moralize his wanton sight,
  More than his eyes were open'd to the
   light.

He stories to her ears her husband's fame,
Won in the fields of fruitful Italy;
And decks with praises Collatine's high name,
Made glorious by his manly chivalry,
With bruised arms and wreaths of victory;
  Her joy with heav'd-up hand she doth express,
    And, wordless, so greets heaven for his success.

Far from the purpose of his coming thither
He makes excuses for his being there.
No cloudy show of stormy blustering weather
Doth yet in his fair welkin once appear;
Till sable Night, mother of Dread and Fear,
  Upon the world dim darkness doth display,
    And in her vaulty prison stows the day.

For then is Tarquin brought unto his bed,
Intending weariness with heavy spright;
For, after supper, long he questioned
With modest Lucrece, and wore out the night:
Now leaden slumber with life's strength doth fight;
  And every one to rest themselves betake,
    Save thieves, and cares, and troubled minds, that wake.

As one of which doth Tarquin lie revolving
The sundry dangers of his will's obtaining;
Yet ever to obtain his will resolving,
Though weak-built hopes persuade him to abstaining;
Despair to gain doth traffic oft for gaining;
  And when great treasure is the meed propos'd,
    Though death be adjunct, there's no death suppos'd.

Those that much covet are with gain so fond
That what they have not, that which they possess
They scatter and unloose it from their bond,
And so, by hoping more, they have but less;
Or, gaining more, the profit of excess
  Is but to surfeit, and such griefs sustain,
    That they prove bankrupt in this poor-rich gain.

The aim of all is but to nurse the life
With honour, wealth, and ease, in waning age;
And in this aim there is such thwarting strife,
That one for all, or all for one we gage;
As life for honour in fell battles' rage;
  Honour for wealth; and oft that wealth doth cost
    The death of all, and all together lost.

So that in vent'ring ill we leave to be
The things we are, for that which we expect;
And this ambitious foul infirmity,
In having much, torments us with defect
Of that we have: so then we do neglect
  The thing we have, and, all for want of wit,
    Make something nothing, by augmenting it.

Such hazard now must doting Tarquin make,
Pawning his honour to obtain his lust;
And for himself himself he must forsake:
Then where is truth if there be no self-trust?
When shall he think to find a stranger just,
  When he himself himself confounds, betrays
    To slanderous tongues, and wretched hateful days?

Now stole upon the time the dead of night,
When heavy sleep had clos'd up mortal eyes;
No comfortable star did lend his light,
No noise but owls' and wolves' death-boding cries;
Now serves the season that they may surprise
  The silly lambs; pure thoughts are dead and still,
    While lust and murder wake to stain and kill.

And now this lustful lord leap'd from his bed,
Throwing his mantle rudely o'er his arm;
Is madly toss'd between desire and dread;
Th' one sweetly flatters, th' other feareth harm;
But honest Fear, bewitch'd with lusts's foul charm,
  Doth too too oft betake him to retire,
    Beaten away by brain-sick rude Desire.

His falchion on a flint he softly smiteth,
That from the cold stone sparks of fire do fly,
Whereat a waxen torch forthwith he lighteth,
Which must be lode-star to his lustful eye:
And to the flame thus speaks advisedly:
  'As from this cold flint I enforc'd this fire,
    So Lucrece must I force to my desire.'

Here pale with fear he doth premeditate
The dangers of his loathsome enterprise,
And in his inward mind he doth debate
What following sorrow may on this arise;
Then looking scornfully, he doth despise
  His naked armour of still-slaughter'd lust,
    And justly thus controls his thoughts unjust:

'Fair torch, burn out thy light, and lend it not
To darken her whose light excelleth thine!

And die, unhallow'd thoughts, before you
 blot
With your uncleanness that which is divine!
Offer pure incense to so pure a shrine:
 Let fair humanity abhor the deed
 That spots and stains love's modest snow-
  white weed.

'O shame to knighthood and to shining
 arms!
O foul dishonour to my household's grave!
O impious act, including all foul harms!
A martial man to be soft fancy's slave;
 True valour still a true respect should have;
 Then my digression is so vile, so base,
 That it will live engraven in my face.

'Yea, though I die, the scandal will survive,
And be an eyesore in my golden coat;
Some loathsome dash the herald will con-
 trive,
To cipher me how fondly I did dote;
 That my posterity, sham'd with the note,
 Shall curse my bones, and hold it for no
  sin
 To wish that I their father had not been.

'What win I if I gain the thing I seek?
A dream, a breath, a froth of fleeting joy:
Who buys a minute's mirth to wail a week?
Or sells eternity to get a toy?
 For one sweet grape who will the vine de-
  stroy?
 Or what fond beggar, but to touch the
  crown,
 Would with the sceptre straight be
  strucken down?

'If Collatinus dream of my intent,
Will he not wake, and in a desperate rage
Post hither, this vile purpose to prevent?
This siege that hath engirt his marriage,
 This blur to youth, this sorrow to the sage,
 This dying virtue, this surviving shame,
 Whose crime will bear an ever-during
  blame?

'O what excuse can my invention make
When thou shalt charge me with so black a
 deed?
Will not my tongue be mute, my frail joints
 shake?
Mine eyes forego their light, my false heart
 bleed?
 The guilt being great, the fear doth still
  exceed;
 And extreme fear can neither fight nor fly,
 But, coward-like, with trembling terror
  die.

'Had Collatinus kill'd my son or sire,
Or lain in ambush to betray my life,

Or were he not my dear friend, this desire
Might have excuse to work upon his wife;
As in revenge or quittal of such strife:
 But as he is my kinsman, my dear friend,
 The shame and fault finds no excuse nor
  end.

'Shameful it is;—ay, if the fact be known:
Hateful it is;—there is no hate in loving;
I'll beg her love;—but she is not her own:
The worst is but denial, and reproving:
 My will is strong, past reason's weak re-
  moving.
 Who fears a sentence or an old man's saw
 Shall by a painted cloth be kept in awe.'

Thus, graceless, holds he disputation
'Tween frozen conscience and hot-burning
 will,
And with good thoughts makes dispensation,
Urging the worser sense for vantage still;
 Which in a moment doth confound and kill
 All pure effects, and doth so far proceed,
 That what is vile shows like a virtuous
  deed.

Quoth he, 'She took me kindly by the hand,
And gaz'd for tidings in my eager eyes,
Fearing some hard news from the warlike
 band
Where her beloved Collatinus lies.
 O how her fear did make her colour rise!
 First red as roses that on lawn we lay,
 Then white as lawn, the roses took away.

'And how her hand, in my hand being
 lock'd,
Forc'd it to tremble with her loyal fear;
Which struck her sad, and then it faster
 rock'd,
Until her husband's welfare she did hear;
 Whereat she smiled with so sweet a cheer,
 That had Narcissus seen her as she stood,
 Self-love had never drown'd him in the
  flood.

'Why hunt I then for colour or excuses?
All orators are dumb when beauty pleadeth;
Poor wretches have remorse in poor abuses;
Love thrives not in the heart that shadows
 dreadeth:
 Affection is my captain, and he leadeth;
 And when his gaudy banner is display'd,
 The coward fights, and will not be dis-
  may'd.

'Then, childish fear, avaunt! debating, die!
Respect and reason wait on wrinkled age!
My heart shall never countermand mine
 eye;
Sad pause and deep regard beseem the sage;
My part is youth and beats these from the
 stage.

Desire my pilot is, beauty my prize;
Then who fears sinking where such treasure lies?'

As corn o'ergrown by weeds, so heedful fear
Is almost chok'd by unresisted lust.
Away he steals with opening, listening ear,
Full of foul hope, and full of fond mistrust;
Both which, as servitors to the unjust,
  So cross him with their opposite persuasion,
    That now he vows a league, and now invasion.

Within his thought her heavenly image sits,
And in the selfsame seat sits Collatine:
That eye which looks on her confounds his wits;
That eye which him beholds, as more divine,
Unto a view so false will not incline;
  But with a pure appeal seeks to the heart,
    Which once corrupted takes the worser part;

And therein heartens up his servile powers,
Who, flatter'd by their leader's jocund show,
Stuff up his lust, as minutes fill up hours;
And as their captain, so their pride doth grow,
Paying more slavish tribute than they owe.
  By reprobate desire thus madly led,
    The Roman lord marcheth to Lucrece' bed.

The locks between her chamber and his will,
Each one by him enforc'd retires his ward;
But as they open they all rate his ill,
Which drives the creeping thief to some regard,
  The threshold grates the door to have him heard;
    Night-wand'ring weasels shriek to see him there;
    They fright him, yet he still pursues his fear.

As each unwilling portal yields him way,
Through little vents and crannies of the place
The wind wars with his torch, to make him stay,
And blows the smoke of it into his face,
Extinguishing his conduct in this case;
  But his hot heart, which fond desire doth scorch,
    Puffs forth another wind that fires the torch:

And being lighted, by the light he spies
Lucretia's glove, wherein her needle sticks;
He takes it from the rushes where it lies,
And griping it, the neeld his finger pricks:
  As who should say this glove to wanton tricks

Is not inur'd; return again in haste;
  Thou seest our mistress' ornaments are chaste.

But all these poor forbiddings could not stay him;
He in the worst sense construes their denial:
The doors, the wind, the glove that did delay him,
He takes for accidental things of trial;
Or as those bars which stop the hourly dial,
  Who with a lingering stay his course doth let,
    Till every minute pays the hour his debt.

'So, so,' quoth he, 'these lets attend the time,
Like little frosts that sometime threat the spring,
To add a more rejoicing to the prime,
And give the sneaped birds more cause to sing.
Pain pays the income of each precious thing:
  Huge rocks, high winds, strong pirates, shelves and sands,
    The merchant fears, ere rich at home he lands.'

Now is he come unto the chamber door
That shuts him from the heaven of his thought,
Which with a yielding latch, and with no more,
Hath barr'd him from the blessed thing he sought.
So from himself impiety hath wrought,
  That for his prey to pray he doth begin,
    As if the heaven should countenance his sin.

But in the midst of his unfruitful prayer,
Having solicited the eternal power,
That his foul thoughts might compass his fair fair,
That they would stand auspicious to the hour,
Even there he starts:—quoth he, 'I must deflower;
  The powers to whom I pray abhor this [fact.
    How can they then assist me in the act?

'Then Love and Fortune be my gods, my guide!
My will is back'd with resolution: [tried,
Thoughts are but dreams till their effects be
The blackest sin is clear'd with absolution;
Against love's fire fear's frost hath dissolution.
  The eye of heaven is out, and misty night
    Covers the shame that follows sweet delight.'

This said, his guilty hand pluck'd up the latch,
And with his knee the door he opens wide:

The dove sleeps fast that this night-owl will
  catch;
Thus treason works ere traitors be espied.
Who sees the lurking serpent steps aside;
  But she, sound sleeping, fearing no such
    thing,
  Lies at the mercy of his mortal sting.

Into the chamber wickedly he stalks,
And gazeth on her yet unstained bed.
The curtains being close, about he walks,
Rolling his greedy eyeballs in his head:
By their high treason is his heart misled;
  Which gives the watchword to his hand
    full soon,
  To draw the cloud that hides the silver
    moon.

Look, as the fair and fiery-pointed sun,
Rushing from forth a cloud, bereaves our
  sight;
Even so, the curtain drawn, his eyes begun
To wink, being blinded with a greater light:
Whether it is that she reflects so bright,
  That dazzleth them, or else some shame
    supposed;                [enclosed.
  But blind they are, and keep themselves

O, had they in that darksome prison died,
Then had they seen the period of their ill!
Then Collatine again by Lucrece' side
In his clear bed might have reposed still:
But they must ope, this blessed league to
  kill;
  And holy-thoughted Lucrece to their sight
  Must sell her joy, her life, her world's
    delight.

Her lily hand her rosy cheek lies under,
Cozening the pillow of a lawful kiss;
Who therefore angry, seems to part in sun-
  der,
Swelling on either side to want his bliss;
Between whose hills her head entombed is:
  Where, like a virtuous monument, she
    lies,
  To be admir'd of lewd unhallow'd eyes.

Without the bed her other fair hand was,
On the green coverlet; whose perfect white
Show'd like an April daisy on the grass,
With pearly sweat, resembling dew of night.
Her eyes, like marigolds, had sheath'd their
  light,
  And canopied in darkness sweetly lay,
  Till they might open to adorn the day.

Her hair, like golden threads, play'd with
  her breath;
O modest wantons! wanton modesty!
Showing life's triumph in the map of death,
And death's dim look in life's mortality:

Each in her sleep themselves so beautify,
  As if between them twain there were no
    strife,
  But that life liv'd in death, and death in
    life.

Her breasts, like ivory globes circled with
  blue,
A pair of maiden worlds unconquered,
Save of their lord no bearing yoke they
  knew,
And him by oath they truly honoured.
These worlds in Tarquin new ambition bred:
  Who like a foul usurper went about
  From this fair throne to heave the owner
    out.

What could he see but mightily he noted?
What did he note but strongly he desir'd?
What he beheld on that he firmly doted,
And in his will his wilful eye he tir'd.
With more than admiration he admir'd
  Her azure veins, her alabaster skin,
  Her coral lips, her snow-white dimpled
    chin.

As the grim lion fawneth o'er his prey,
Sharp hunger by the conquest satisfied,
So o'er this sleeping soul doth Tarquin stay,
His rage of lust by gazing qualified;
Slack'd, not suppress'd; for standing by her
  side,
  His eye, which late this mutiny restrains,
  Unto a greater uproar tempts his veins:

And they, like straggling slaves for pillage
  fighting,
Obdurate vassals, fell exploits effecting,
In bloody death and ravishment delighting,
Nor children's tears, nor mother's groans re-
  specting,
Swell in their pride, the onset still expecting:
  Anon his beating heart, alarum striking,
  Gives the hot charge, and bids them do
    their liking.

His drumming heart cheers up his burning
  eye,
His eye commends the leading to his hand;
His hand, as proud of such a dignity, [stand
Smoking with pride, march'd on to make his
On her bare breast, the heart of all her land;
  Whose ranks of blue veins, as his hand did
    scale,
  Left their round turrets destitute and pale.

They, mustering to the quiet cabinet
Where their dear governess and lady lies,
Do tell her she is dreadfully beset,
And fright her with confusion of their cries:
She, much amaz'd, breaks ope her lock'd-up
  eyes,
  Who, peeping forth this tumult to behold.

Are by his flaming torch dimm'd and controll'd.

Imagine her as one in dead of night
From forth dull sleep by dreadful fancy
   waking,
That thinks she hath beheld some ghastly
   sprite,
Whose grim aspect sets every joint a shak-
   ing;
What terror 'tis! but she, is worser taking,
  From sleep disturbed, heedfully doth view
  The sight which makes supposed terror
    true.

Wrapp'd and confounded in a thousand
   fears,
Like to a new-kill'd bird she trembling lies;
She dares not look; yet, winking, there ap-
   pears
Quick-shifting antics, ugly in her eyes:
Such shadows are the weak brain's forger-
   ies:
  Who, angry that the eyes fly from their
    lights,
  In darkness daunts them with more dread-
    ful sights.

His hand, that yet remains upon her breast,
(Rude ram, to batter such an ivory wall!)
May feel her heart, poor citizen, distress'd,
Wounding itself to death, rise up and fall,
Beating her bulk, that his hand shakes
   withal.
  This moves in him more rage, and lesser
    pity,
  To make.the breach, and enter this sweet
    city.

First, like a trumpet, doth his tongue begin
To sound a parley to his heartless foe,
Who o'er the white sheet peers her whiter
   chin,
The reason of this rash alarm to know,
Which he by dumb demeanour seeks to
   show;
  But she with vehement prayers urgeth still
  Under what colour he commits this ill.

Thus he replies: 'The colour in thy face
(That even for anger makes the lily pale,
And the red rose blush at her own disgrace)
Shall plead for me, and tell my loving tale:
Under that colour am I come to scale
  Thy never-conquer'd fort: the fault is
    thine,
  For those thine eyes betray thee unto mine.

'Thus I forestall thee, if thou mean to chide:
Thy beauty hath ensnar'd thee to this night,
Where thou with patience must my will
   abide,
My will that marks thee for my earth's
   delight,

Which I to conquer sought with all my
   might;
But as reproof and reason beat it dead,
By thy bright beauty was it newly bred.

'I see what crosses my attempt will bring;
I know what thorns the growing rose de-
   fends;
I think the honey guarded with a sting:
All this, beforehand, counsel comprehends:
But will is deaf, and hears no heedful
   friends;
  Only he hath an eye to gaze on beauty
  And dotes on what he looks, 'gainst law or
    duty.

'I have debated, even in my soul,
What wrong, what shame, what sorrow I
   shall breed;
But nothing can Affection's course control,
Or stop the headlong fury of his speed.
I know repentant tears ensue the deed,
  Reproach, disdain, and deadly enmity;
  Yet strive I to embrace mine infamy.'

This said, he shakes aloft his Roman blade,
Which, like a falcon towering in the skies,
Coucheth the fowl below with his wing's
   shade,
Whose crooked beak threats if he mount he
   dies:
So under his insulting falchion lies
  Harmless Lucretia, marking what he tells
  With trembling fear, as fowl hear falcon's
    bells.

'Lucrece,' quoth he, 'this night I must enjoy
   thee:
If thou deny, then force must work my way
For in thy bed I purpose to destroy thee;
That done, some worthless slave of thine I'll
   slay,
To kill thine honour with thy life's decay;
  And in thy dead arms do I mean to place
    him,
  Swearing I slew him, seeing thee embrace
    him.

'So thy surviving husband shall remain
The scornful mark of every open eye;
Thy kinsmen hang their heads at this dis-
   dain,
Thy issue blurr'd with nameless bastardy:
And thou, the author of their obloquy,
  Shall have thy trespass cited up in rhymes,
  And sung by children in succeeding times.

'But if thou yield I rest thy secret friend:
The fault unknown is as a thought unacted;
A little harm, done to a great good end,
For lawful policy remains enacted.
The poisonous simple sometimes is com-
   pacted

In a pure compound; being so applied,
His venom in effect is purified.

'Then, for thy husband and thy children's
    sake,
Tender my suit: bequeath not to their lot
The shame that from them no device can
    take,
The blemish that will never be forgot;
Worse than a slavish wipe, or birth-hour's
    blot:
  For marks descried in men's nativity
  Are nature's faults, not their own infamy.'

Here with a cockatrice' dead-killing eye
He rouseth up himself, and makes a pause;
While she, the picture of pure piety,
Like a white hind under the grype's sharp
    claws,
Pleads in a wilderness, where are no laws,
  To the rough beast that knows no gentle
    right,
  Nor aught obeys but his foul appetite:

But when a black-fac'd cloud the world doth
    threat,
In his dim mist the aspiring mountains hid-
    ing,
From earth's dark womb some gentle gust
    doth get,
Which blows these pitchy vapours from their
    biding,
Hindering their present fall by this divid-
    ing;
  So his unhallow'd haste her words delays,
  And moody Pluto winks while Orpheus
    plays.

Yet, foul night-waking cat, he doth but
    dally,
While in his holdfast foot the weak mouse
    panteth;
Her sad behaviour feeds his vulture folly,
A swallowing gulf that even in plenty want-
    eth:
His ear her prayers admits, but his heart
    granteth
  No penetrable entrance to her plaining:
  Tears harden lust, though marble wear
    with raining.

Her pity-pleading eyes are sadly fix'd
In the remorseless wrinkles of his face; .
Her modest eloquence with sighs is mix'd,
Which to her oratory adds more grace.
She puts the period often from his place,
  And 'midst the sentence so her accent
    breaks,
  That twice she doth begin ere once she
    speaks.

She conjures him by high almighty Jove,
By knighthood, gentry, and sweet friend-
    ship's oath,

By her untimely tears, her husband's love,
By holy human law, and common troth,
By heaven and earth, and all the power of
    both,
  That to his borrow'd bed he make retire,
  And stoop to honour, not to foul desire.

Quoth she, 'Reward not hospitality. [tended;
With such black payment as thou hast pre-
Mud not the fountain that gave drink to
    thee;
Mar not the thing that cannot be amended;
End thy ill aim, before thy shoot be ended:
  He is no woodman that doth bend his bow
  To strike a poor unseasonable doe.

'My husband is thy friend, for his sake
    spare me;
Thyself art mighty, for thine own sake leave
    me;
Myself a weakling, do not then ensnare me;
Thou look'st not like deceit; do not deceive
    me;
My sighs, like whirlwinds, labour hence to
    heave thee.
  If ever man were mov'd with woman's
    moans,
  Be moved with my tears, my sighs, my
    groans:

'All which together, like a troubled ocean,
Beat at thy rocky and wreck-threatening
    heart;
To soften it with their continual motion;
For stones dissolv'd to water do convert.
O, if no harder than a stone thou art,
  Melt at my tears, and be compassionate!
  Soft pity enters at an iron gate.

'In Tarquin's likeness I did entertain thee;
Hast thou put on his shape to do him
    shame?
To all the host of heaven I complain me,
Thou wrong'st his honour, wound'st his
    princely name.
Thou art not what thou seem'st; and if the
    same,
  Thou seem'st not what thou art, a god, a
    king;
  For kings like gods should govern every-
    thing.

'How will thy shame be seeded in thine age,
When thus thy vices bud before thy spring!
If in thy hope thou dar'st do such outrage,
What dar'st thou not when once thou art a
    king!
O be remember'd, no outrageous thing
  From vassal actors can be wip'd away;
  Then kings' misdeeds cannot be hid in
    clay.

'This deed will make thee only lov'd for
    fear,

But happy monarchs still are fear'd for love:
With foul offenders thou perforce must bear,
When they in thee the like offences prove:
If but for fear of this thy will remove;
  For princes are the glass, the school, the book,                                    [look.
    Where subjects' eyes do learn, do read, do

'And wilt thou be the school where Lust shall learn?
Must he in thee read lectures of such shame:
Wilt thou be glass, wherein it shall discern
Authority for sin, warrant for blame,
  To privilege dishonour in thy name?
    Thou back'st reproach against long-lived laud,
    And mak'st fair reputation but a bawd.

'Hast thou command? by him that gave it thee,
From a pure heart command thy rebel will:
Draw not thy sword to guard iniquity,
For it was lent thee all that brood to kill.
  Thy princely office how canst thou fulfil,
    When, pattern'd by thy fault, foul Sin may say,                                    [way?
      He learn'd to sin, and thou didst teach the

'Think but how vile a spectacle it were
To view thy present trespass in another.
Men's faults do seldom to themselves appear;
  Their own transgressions partially they smother:
This guilt would seem death-worthy in thy brother,
    O how are they wrapp'd in with infamies,
    That from their own misdeeds askaunce their eyes!

'To thee, to thee, my heav'd-up hands appeal,
Not to seducing lust, thy rash relier;
I sue for exil'd majesty's repeal;
Let him return and flattering thoughts retire:
  His true respect will 'prison false desire,
    And wipe the dim mist from thy doting eyne,                                    [mine.'
    That thou shalt see thy state, and pity

'Have done,' quoth he; 'my uncontrolled tide
Turns not, but swells the higher by this let.
Small lights are soon blown out, huge fires abide,
And with the wind in greater fury fret:
  The petty streams that pay a daily debt
    To their salt sovereign, with their fresh falls' haste,
    Add to his flow, but alter not his taste.'

'Thou art,' quoth she, 'a sea, a sovereign king;
And lo, there falls into thy boundless flood

Black lust, dishonour, shame, misgoverning,
Who seek to stain the ocean of thy blood.
If all these petty ills shall charge thy good,
  Thy sea within a puddle's womb is hears'd,
  And not the puddle in thy sea dispers'd.

'So shall these slaves be king, and thou their slave;
Thou nobly base, they basely dignified;
Thou their fair life, and they thy fouler grave;
Thou loathed in their shame, they in thy pride:
  The lesser things should not the greater hide;
    The cedar stoops not to the base shrub's foot,
    But low shrubs wither at the cedar's root.

'So let thy thoughts, low vassals to thy state'—
'No more,' quoth he; 'by heaven, I will not hear thee:
Yield to my love; if not, enforced hate,
Instead of love's coy touch, shall rudely tear thee;
  That done, despitefully I mean to bear thee
    Unto the base bed of some rascal groom,
    To be thy partner in this shameful doom.'

This said, he sets the foot upon the light,
For light and lust are deadly enemies;
Shame folded up in blind concealing night,
When most unseen, then most doth tyrannize.
  The wolf hath seiz'd his prey, the poor lamb cries
    Till with her own white fleece her voice controll'd
    Entombs her outcry in her lips' sweet fold:

For with the nightly linen that she wears
He pens her piteous clamours in her head;
Cooling his hot face in the chastest tears
That ever modest eyes with sorrow shed.
  O, that prone lust should stain so pure a bed!
    The spots whereof could weeping purify,
    Her tears should drop on them perpetually.

But she hath lost a dearer thing than life,
And he hath won what he would lose again.
This forced league doth force a further strife,
This momentary joy breeds months of pain,
This hot desire converts to cold disdain:
  Pure Chastity is rifled of her store,
  And Lust, the thief, far poorer than before.

Look, as the full-fed hound or gorged hawk,
Unapt for tender smell or speedy flight,
Make slow pursuit, or altogether balk
The prey wherein by nature they delight;
  So surfeit-taking Tarquin fares this night:
    His taste delicious, in digestion souring,
    Devours his will that liv'd by foul devouring.

O deeper sin than bottomless conceit
Can comprehend in still imagination!
Drunken desire must vomit his receipt,
Ere he can see his own abomination.
While lust is in his pride no exclamation
  Can curb his heat, or rein his rash desire,
  Till, like a jade, self-will himself doth tire.

And then with lank and lean discolour'd
    cheek,
With heavy eye, knit brow, and strengthless
    pace,
Feeble desire, all recreant, poor, and meek,
Like to a bankrupt beggar wails his case:
The flesh being proud, desire doth fight with
    grace,
  For there it revels; and when that decays,
  The guilty rebel for remission prays.

So fares it with this faultful lord of Rome,
Who this accomplishment so hotly chas'd;
For now against himself he sounds his doom,
That through the length of times he stands
    disgrac'd:
Besides, his soul's fair temple is defac'd;
  To whose weak ruins muster troops of
    cares,
  To ask the spotted princess how she fares.

She says, her subjects with foul insurrection
Have batter'd down her consecrated wall,
And by their mortal fault brought in subjec-
    tion
Her immortality, and make her thrall
To living death, and pain perpetual;
  Which in her prescience she controlled still,
  But her foresight could not forestall their
    will.

Even in this thought through the dark night
    he stealeth,
A captive victor that hath lost in gain;
Bearing away the wound that nothing
    healeth,
The scar that will, despite of cure, remain,
Leaving his spoil perplex'd in greater pain.
  She bears the load of lust he left behind,
  And he the burthen of a guilty mind.

He like a thievish dog creeps sadly thence;
She like a wearied lamb lies panting there;
He scowls, and hates himself for his offence;
She, desperate, with her nails her flesh doth
    tear;
He faintly flies, sweating with guilty fear;
  She stays, exclaiming on the direful night;
  He runs, and chides his vanish'd, loath'd
    delight.

He thence departs a heavy convertite;
She there remains a hopeless castaway:
He in his speed looks for the morning light;
She prays she never may behold the day;

'For day,' quoth she, 'night's scapes doth
    open lay;
  And my true eyes have never practis'd how
  To cloak offences with a cunning brow.

'They think not but that every eye can see
The same disgrace which they themselves
    behold;
And therefore would they still in darkness be,
To have their unseen sin remain untold;
For they their guilt with weeping will un-
    fold,
  And grave, like water, that doth eat in
    steel,
  Upon my cheeks what helpless shame I
    feel.'

Here she exclaims against repose and rest,
And bids her eyes hereafter still be blind.
She wakes her heart by beating on her breast,
And bids it leap from thence, where it may
    find
Some purer chest, to close so pure a mind.
  Frantic with grief thus breathes she forth
    her spite
  Against the unseen secrecy of night:

'O comfort-killing night, image of hell!
Dim register and notary of shame!
Black stage for tragedies and murders fell!
Vast sin-concealing chaos! nurse of blame!
Blind muffled bawd! dark harbour for de-
    fame!
  Grim cave of death, whispering conspira-
    tor,
  With close-tongued treason and the rav-
    isher!

'O hateful, vaporous, and foggy night,
Since thou art guilty of my cureless crime,
Muster thy mists to meet the eastern light,
Make war against proportion'd course of
    time!
Or if thou wilt permit the sun to climb
  His wonted height, yet ere he go to bed,
  Knit poisonous clouds about his golden
    head.

'With rotten damps ravish the morning air;
Let their exhal'd unwholesome breaths make
    sick
The life of purity, the supreme fair,
Ere he arrive his weary noontide prick;
And let thy misty vapours march so thick,
  That in their smoky ranks his smother'd
    light,
  May set at noon, and make perpetual
    night.

'Were Tarquin night (as he is but night's
    child),
The silver-shining queen he would distain;
Her twinkling handmaids too, by him defil'd,

Through night's black bosom should not peep
    again;
So should I have copartners in my pain:
    And fellowship in woe doth woe assuage,
    As palmers' chat makes short their pil-
        grimage.

'Where now I have no one to blush with me,
To cross their arms, and hang their heads
    with mine,
To mask their brows, and hide their infamy;
But I alone alone must sit and pine,
Seasoning the earth with showers of silver
    brine,
    Mingling my talk with tears, my grief with
        groans,
    Poor wasting monuments of lasting moans.

'O night, thou furnace of foul-reeking smoke,
Let not the jealous day behold that face
Which underneath thy black all-hiding cloak
Immodestly lies martyr'd with disgrace!
Keep still possession of thy gloomy place,
    That all the faults which in thy reign are
        made,
    May likewise be sepulchred in thy shade!

'Make me not object to the tell-tale day!
The light will show, character'd in my brow,
The story of sweet chastity's decay,
The impious breach of holy wedlock vow:
Yea, the illiterate, that know not how
    To 'cipher what is writ in learned books,
    Will quote my loathsome trespass in my
        looks.

'The nurse, to still her child, will tell my
    story,
And fright her crying babe with Tarquin's
    name;
The orator, to deck his oratory,
Will couple my reproach to Tarquin's shame:
Feast-finding minstrels, tuning my defame,
    Will tie the hearers to attend each line,
    How Tarquin wronged me, I Collatine.

'Let my good name, that senseless reputation,
For Collatine's dear love be kept unspotted:
If that be made a theme for disputation,
The branches of another root are rotted,
And undeserv'd reproach to him allotted,
    That is as clear from this attaint of mine,
    As I, ere this, was pure to Collatine.

'O unseen shame! invisible disgrace!
O unfelt sore! crest-wounding, private scar!
Reproach is stamp'd in Collatinus' face,
And Tarquin's eye may read the mot afar,
How he in peace is wounded, not in war.
    Alas, how many bear such shameful blows,
    Which not themselves but he that gives
        them knows!

'If, Collatine, thine honour lay in me,
From me by strong assault it is bereft.
My honey lost, and I, a drone-like bee,
Have no perfection of my summer left,
But robb'd and ransack'd by injurious theft:
    In thy weak hive a wandering wasp hath
        crept,        [kept.
    And suck'd the honey which thy chaste bee

'Yet am I guilty of thy honour's wrack,—
Yet for thy honour did I entertain him;
Coming from thee, I could not put him back,
For it had been dishonour to disdain him:
Besides of weariness he did complain him,
    And talk'd of virtue:—O, unlook'd for evil,
    When virtue is profan'd in such a devil!

'Why should the worm intrude the maiden
    bud?
Or hateful cuckoos hatch in sparrows' nests?
Or toads infect fair founts with venom
    mud?
Or tyrant folly lurk in gentle breasts?
Or kings be breakers of their own behests?
    But no perfection is so absolute,
    That some impurity doth not pollute.

'The aged man that coffers up his gold
Is plagued with cramps, and gouts, and pain-
    ful fits,
And scarce hath eyes his treasure to behold,
But like still-pining Tantalus he sits,
And useless barns the harvest of his wits;
    Having no other pleasure of his gain
    But torment that it cannot cure his pain.

'So then he hath it, when he cannot use it,
And leaves it to be master'd by his young;
Who in their pride do presently abuse it:
Their father was too weak, and they too
    strong,
To hold their cursed-blessed fortune long,
    The sweets we wish for turn to loathed
        sours,
    Even in the moment that we call them
        ours.

'Unruly blasts wait on the tender spring;
Unwholesome weeds take root with precious
    flowers;
The adder hisses where the sweet birds sing;
What virtue breeds iniquity devours:
We have no good that we can say is ours,
    But ill-annexed Opportunity
    Or kills his life, or else his quality.

'O Opportunity! thy guilt is great:
'Tis thou that execut'st the traitor's treason;
Thou sett'st the wolf where he the lamb
    may get;
Whoever plots the sin, thou 'point'st the sea-
    son;

'Tis thou that spurn'st at right, at law, at
    reason;
And in thy shady cell, where none may
    spy him,
    Sits Sin, to seize the souls that wander by
    him.

'Thou mak'st the vestal violate her oath;
Thou blow'st the fire when temperance is
    thaw'd;
Thou smother'st honesty, thou murther'st
    troth;
Thou foul abettor! thou notorious bawd!
Thou plantest scandal, and displacest laud:
    Thou ravisher, thou traitor, thou false
    thief,
    Thy honey turns to gall, thy joy to grief!

'Thy secret pleasure turns to open shame,
Thy private feasting to a public fast;
Thy smoothing titles to a ragged name;
Thy sugar'd tongue to bitter wormwood
    taste:
Thy violent vanities can never last.
    How comes it then, vile Opportunity,
    Being so bad, such numbers seek for thee?

'When wilt thou be the humble suppliant's
    friend,
And bring him where his suit may be ob-
    tain'd?
When wilt thou sort an hour great strifes to
    end?
Or free that soul which wretchedness hath
    chain'd?
Give physic to the sick, ease to the pain'd?
    The poor, lame, blind, halt, creep, cry out
    for thee;
    But they ne'er meet with Opportunity.

'The patient dies while the physician sleeps;
The orphan pines while the oppressor feeds;
Justice is feasting while the widow weeps;
Advice is sporting while infection breeds;
Thou grant'st no time for charitable deeds:
    Wrath, envy, treason, rape, and murder's
    rages,
    Thy heinous hours wait on them as their
    pages.

'When truth and virtue have to do with thee,
A thousand crosses keep them from thy aid;
They buy thy help: but Sin ne'er gives a fee,
He gratis comes; and thou art well appay'd
As well to hear as grant what he hath said.
    My Collatine would else have come to me
    When Tarquin did, but he was stay'd by
    thee.

'Guilty thou art of murder and of theft;
Guilty of perjury and subornation;
Guilty of treason, forgery, and shift;
Guilty of incest, that abomination:

An accessary by thine inclination
    To all sins past, and all that are to come,
    From the creation to the general doom.

'Mis-shapen Time, copesmate of ugly night,
Swift subtle post, carrier of grisly care,
Eater of youth, false slave to false delight,
Base watch of woes, sin's packhorse, virtue's
    snare;
Thou nursest all, and murtherest all that are.
    O hear me then, injurious, shifting Time!
    Be guilty of my death, since of my crime.

'Why hath thy servant, Opportunity,
Betray'd the hours thou gav'st me to repose?
Cancell'd my fortunes and enchained me
To endless date of never-ending woes?
Time's office is to fine the hate of foes;
    To eat up errors by opinion bred,
    Not spend the dowry of a lawful bed.

'Time's glory is to calm contending kings,
To unmask falsehood, and bring truth to
    light,
To stamp the seal of time in aged things,
To wake the morn, and sentinel the night,
To wrong the wronger till he render right;
    To ruinate proud buildings with thy hours,
    And smear with dust their glittering golden
    towers:

'To fill with worm-holes stately monuments,
To feed oblivion with decay of things,
To blot old books, and alter their contents,
To pluck the quills from ancient ravens'
    wings,
To dry the old oak's sap, and cherish springs;
    To spoil antiquities of hammer'd steel,
    And turn the giddy round of Fortune's
    wheel;

'To show the beldame daughters of her
    daughter,
To make the child a man, the man a child,
To slay the tiger that doth live by slaughter,
To tame the unicorn and lion wild,
To mock the subtle, in themselves beguil'd;
    To cheer the ploughman with increaseful
    crops,
    And waste huge stones with little water-
    drops.

'Why work'st thou mischief in thy pilgrim-
    age,
Unless thou couldst return to make amends?
One poor retiring minute in an age
Would purchase thee a thousand thousand
    friends,
Lending him wit that to bad debtors lends:
    O, this dread night, wouldst thou one hour
    come back,
    I could prevent this storm, and shun thy
    wrack!

'Thou ceaseless lackey to eternity,
With some mischance cross Tarquin in his
    flight:
Devise extremes beyond extremity,
To make him curse this cursed crimeful
    night:
Let ghastly shadows his lewd eyes affright,
    And the dire thought of his committed evil
    Shape every bush a hideous shapeless devil.

'Disturb his hours of rest with restless
    trances,
Afflict him in his bed with bedrid groans;
Let there bechance him pitiful mischances,
To make him moan, but pity not his moans:
Stone him with harden'd hearts, harder than
    stones;
    And let mild women to him lose their
    mildness,
    Wilder to him than tigers in their wildness.

'Let him have time to tear his curled hair,
Let him have time against himself to rave,
Let him have time of Time's help to despair,
Let him have time to live a loathed slave,
Let him have time a beggar's orts to crave;
    And time to see one that by alms doth live
    Disdain to him disdained scraps to give.

'Let him have time to see his friends his foes,
And merry fools to mock at him resort;
Let him have time to mark how slow time
    goes
In time of sorrow, and how swift and short
His time of folly and his time of sport:
    And ever let his unrecalling crime
    Have time to wail the abusing of his time.

'O Time, thou tutor both to good and bad,
Teach me to curse him that thou taught'st
    this ill!
At his own shadow let the thief run mad!
Himself himself seek every hour to kill!
Such wretched hands such wretched blood
    should spill;
    For who so base would such an office have
    As slanderous death's-man to so base a
    slave?

'The baser is he, coming from a king,
To shame his hope with deeds degenerate.
The mightier man, the mightier is the thing
That makes him honour'd, or begets him
    hate;
For greatest scandal waits on greatest state.
    The moon being clouded presently is miss'd,
    But little stars may hide them when they
    list.

'The crow may bathe his coal-black wings in
    mire,
And unperceiv'd fly with the filth away,
But if the like the snow-white swan desire,

The stain upon his silver down will stay.
Poor grooms are sightless night, kings glorious
    day.
    Gnats are unnoted wheresoe'er they fly,
    But eagles gaz'd upon with every eye.

'Out, idle words, servants to shallow fools!
Unprofitable sounds, weak arbitrators!
Busy yourselves in skill-contending schools,
Debate where leisure serves with dull de-
    baters;
To trembling clients be you mediators:
    For me, I force not argument a straw,
    Since that my case is past the help of law.

'In vain I rail at Opportunity,
At Time, at Tarquin, and uncheerful night;
In vain I cavil with my infamy,
In vain I spurn at my confirm'd despite:
This helpless smoke of words doth me no
    right.
    The remedy indeed to do me good,
    Is to let forth my foul, defiled blood.

'Poor hand, why quiver'st thou at this de-
    cree?
Honour thyself to rid me of this shame;
For if I die my honour lives in thee,
But if I live thou liv'st in my defame:
Since thou couldst not defend thy loyal dame,
    And was afear'd to scratch her wicked foe,
    Kill both thyself and her for yielding so.'

This said, from her betumbled couch she
    starteth,
To find some desperate instrument of death:
But this no-slaughter-house no tool im-
    parteth,
To make more vent for passage of her breath,
Which thronging through her lips so van-
    isheth
    As smoke from Ætna, that in air consumes,
    Or that which from discharged cannon
    fumes.

'In vain,' quoth she, 'I live, and seek in vain
Some happy mean to end a hapless life.
I fear'd by Tarquin's falchion to be slain,
Yet for the self-same purpose seek a knife:
But when I fear'd I was a loyal wife;
    So am I now:—O no, that cannot be;
    Or that true type hath Tarquin rifled me.

'O! that is gone for which I sought to live,
And therefore now I need not fear to die.
To clear this spot by death, at least I give
A badge of fame to slander's livery;
A dying life to living infamy;
    Poor helpless help, the treasure stolen away,
    To burn the guiltless casket where it lay!

'Well, well, dear Collatine, thou shalt not
    know

The stained taste of violated troth;
I will not wrong thy true affection so
To flatter thee with an infringed oath;
This bastard graff shall never come to
　　growth:
　　He shall not boast who did thy stock pol-
　　　lute
　　That thou art doting father of his fruit.

'Nor shall he smile at thee in secret thought,
Nor laugh with his companions at thy state;
But thou shalt know thy interest was not
　　bought
Basely with gold, but stolen from forth thy
　　gate.
For me, I am the mistress of my fate,
　　And with my trespass never will dispense,
　　Till life to death acquit my forc'd offence.

'I will not poison thee with my attaint,
Nor fold my fault in cleanly-coin'd excuses;
My sable ground of sin I will not paint,
To hide the truth of this false night's abuses:
My tongue shall utter all; mine eyes like
　　sluices,
　　As from a mountain-spring that feeds a
　　　dale,
　　Shall gush pure streams to purge my im-
　　　pure tale.'

By this, lamenting Philomel had ended
The well-tun'd warble of her nightly sorrow,
And solemn night with slow-sad gait de-
　　scended
To ugly hell; when lo, the blushing morrow
Lends light to all fair eyes that light will
　　borrow:
　　But cloudy Lucrece shames herself to see
　　And therefore still in night would clois-
　　　ter'd be.

Revealing day through every cranny spies,
And seems to point her out where she sits
　　weeping,
To whom she sobbing speaks: 'O eye of eyes,
Why pryest thou through my window? leave
　　thy peeping;
Mock with thy tickling beams eyes that are
　　sleeping:
　　Brand not my forehead with thy piercing
　　　light,
　　For day hath nought to do what's done by
　　　night.'

Thus cavils she with everything she sees:
True grief is fond and testy as a child,
Who wayward once, his mood with nought
　　agrees.
Old woes, not infant sorrows, bear them mild;
Continuance tames the one; the other wild,
　　Like an unpractis'd swimmer plunging still
　　With too much labour drowns for want of
　　　skill.

So she, deep-drenched in a sea of care,
Holds disputation with each thing she views,
And to herself all sorrow doth compare;
No object but her passion's strength renews;
And as one shifts, another straight ensues:
　　Sometime her grief is dumb and hath no
　　　words;
　　Sometime 'tis mad, and too much talk af-
　　　　　　　　　　　　　　　　　　　[fords.

The little birds that tune their morning's joy
Make her moans mad with their sweet mel-
　　ody.
For mirth doth search the bottom of annoy;
Sad souls are slain in merry company:
Grief best is pleas'd with grief's society:
　　True sorrow then is feelingly suffic'd
　　When with like semblance it is sym-
　　　pathiz'd.

'Tis double death to drown in ken of shore;
He ten times pines that pines beholding food;
To see the salve doth make the wound ache
　　more;
Great grief grieves most at that would do it
　　good;
Deep woes roll forward like a gentle flood,
　　Who, being stopp'd, the bounding banks
　　　o'erflows:
　　Grief dallied with nor law nor limit knows.

'You mocking birds,' quoth she, 'your tunes
　　entomb
Within　　your　　hollow-swelling　　feather'd
　　breasts,
And in my hearing be you mute and dumb!
(My restless discord loves no stops nor rests;
A woeful hostess brooks not merry guests:)
　　Relish your nimble notes to pleasing ears;
　　Distress like dumps when time is kept with
　　　tears.

'Come, Philomel, that sing'st of ravishment,
Make thy sad grove in my dishevell'd hair.
As the dank earth weeps at thy languishment,
So I at each sad strain will strain a tear,
And with deep groans the diapason bear:
　　For burthen-wise I'll hum on Tarquin still,
　　While thou on Tereus descant'st better
　　　skill.

'And whiles against a thorn thou bear'st thy
　　part,
To keep thy sharp woes waking, wretched I,
To imitate thee well, against my heart
Will fix a sharp knife, to affright mine eye;
Who, if it wink, shall thereon fall and die.
　　These means, as frets upon an instrument,
　　Shall tune our heartstrings to true lan-
　　　guishment.

'And for, poor bird, thou sing'st not in the
　　day,
As shaming any eye should thee behold,

Some dark deep desert, seated from the way,
That knows nor parching heat nor freezing
  cold,
We will find out; and there we will unfold
  To creatures stern sad tunes, to change
    their kinds:
  Since men prove beasts, let beasts bear
    gentle minds.'

As the poor frighted deer, that stands at gaze,
Wildly determining which way to fly,
Or one encompass'd with a winding maze,
That cannot tread the way out readily;
So with herself is she in mutiny,
  To live or die which of the twain were
    better,
  When life is sham'd, and Death reproach's
    debtor.

'To kill myself,' quoth she, 'alack! what were
  it,
But with my body my poor soul's pollution?
They that lose half with greater patience
  bear it
Than they whose whole is swallow'd in con-
  fusion.
That mother tries a merciless conclusion
  Who, having two sweet babes, when death
    takes one,
  Will slay the other, and be nurse to none.

'My body or my soul, which was the dearer?
When the one pure, the other made divine.
Whose love of either to myself was nearer?
When both were kept for heaven and Colla-
  tine.
Ah, me! the bark peel'd from the lofty pine,
  His leaves will wither, and his sap decay;
  So must my soul, her bark being peel'd
    away.

'Her house is sack'd, her quiet interrupted,
Her mansion batter'd by the enemy;
Her sacred temple spotted, spoil'd, corrupted,
Grossly engirt with daring infamy:
Then let it not be call'd impiety
  If in this blemish'd fort I make some hole
  Through which I may convey this troubled
    soul.

'Yet die I will not till my Collatine
Have heard the cause of my untimely death;
That he may vow, in that sad hour of mine,
Revenge on him that made me stop my
  breath.
My stained blood to Tarquin I'll bequeath,
  Which by him tainted shall for him be
    spent,
  And as his due writ in my testament.

'My honour I'll bequeath unto the knife
That wounds my body so dishonoured.
'Tis honour to deprive dishonour'd life;

The one will live, the other being dead:
So of shame's ashes shall my fame be bred;
  For in my death I murther shameful
    scorn:
  My shame so dead, mine honour is new-
    born.

'Dear lord of that dear jewel I have lost,
What legacy shall I bequeath to thee?
My resolution, Love, shall be thy boast,
By whose example thou reveng'd mayst be.
How Tarquin must be used, read it in me:
  Myself, thy friend, will kill myself, thy
    foe;
  And, for my sake, serve thou false Tar-
    quin so.

'This brief abridgment of my will I make:
My soul and body to the skies and ground;
My resolution, husband, do thou take;
Mine honour be the knife's that makes my
  wound;
My shame be his that did my fame con-
  found;
  And all my fame that lives disbursed be
  To those that live, and think no shame of
    me.

'Thou, Collatine, shalt oversee this will;
How was I overseen that thou shalt see it!
My blood shall wash the slander of mine ill;
My life's foul deed my life's fair end shall
  free it.
Faint not, faint heart, but stoutly say, "so
  be it."
  Yield to my hand; my hand shall conquer
    thee;
  Thou dead, both die, and both shall vic-
    tors be.

This plot of death when sadly she had laid,
And wip'd the brinish pearl from her bright
  eyes,
With untun'd tongue she hoarsely call'd her
  maid,
Whose swift obedience to her mistress hies;
For fleet-wing'd duty with thought's feathers
  flies.
  Poor Lucrece' cheeks unto her maid seem
    so
  As winter meads when sun doth melt their
    snow.

Her mistress she doth give demure good-
  morrow,
With soft-slow tongue, true mark of modesty,
And sorts a sad look to her lady's sorrow,
(For why? her face wore sorrow's livery,)
But durst not ask of her audaciously
  Why her two suns were cloud-eclipsed so,
  Nor why her fair cheeks over-wash'd with
    woe.

But as the earth doth weep, the sun being set,
Each flower moisten'd like a melting eye;
Even so the maid with swelling drops 'gan wet
Her circled eyne, enforc'd by sympathy
Of those fair suns, set in her mistress' sky,
  Who in a salt-wav'd ocean quench their light,
  Which makes the maid weep like the dewy night.

A pretty while these pretty creatures stand,
Like ivory conduits coral cisterns filling:
One justly weeps; the other takes in hand
No cause, but company, of her drops spilling:
Their gentle sex to weep are often willing;
  Grieving themselves to guess at others' smarts,
  And then they drown their eyes, or break their hearts.

For men have marble, women waxen minds,
And therefore are they form'd as marble will;
The weak oppress'd, the impression of strange kinds
Is form'd in them by force, by fraud, or skill:
Then call them not the authors of their ill,
  No more than wax shall be accounted evil,
  Wherein is stamp'd the semblance of a devil.

Their smoothness, like a goodly champaign plain,
Lays open all the little worms that creep;
In men, as in a rough-grown grove, remain
Cave-keeping evils that obscurely sleep:
Through crystal walls each little mote will peep:
  Though men can cover crimes with bold stern looks,
  Poor women's faces are their own faults' books.

No man inveigh against the wither'd flower,
But chide rough winter that the flower hath kill'd!
Not that devour'd, but that which doth devour
Is worthy blame. O, let it not be hild
Poor women's faults that they are so fulfill'd
  With men's abuses! those proud lords, to blame,
  Make weak-made women tenants to their shame.

The precedent whereof in Lucrece view,
Assail'd by night with circumstances strong
Of present death, and shame that might ensue
By that her death, to do her husband wrong:
Such danger to resistance did belong,
  That dying fear through all her body spread;
  And who cannot abuse a body dead?

By this, mild Patience bid fair Lucrece speak
To the poor counterfeit of her complaining:
'My girl,' quoth she, 'on what occasion break
Those tears from thee, that down thy cheeks are raining?
If thou dost weep for grief of my sustaining,
  Know, gentle wench, it small avails my mood:
  If tears could help, mine own would do me good.

'But tell me, girl, when went'—(and there she stay'd
Till after a deep groan) 'Tarquin from hence?'
Madam, ere I was up,' replied the maid,
'The more to blame my sluggard negligence:
Yet with the fault I thus far can dispense;
  Myself was stirring ere the break of day,
  And, ere I rose, was Tarquin gone away.

'But, lady, if your maid may be so bold,
She would request to know your heaviness.'
'O peace!' quoth Lucrece; 'if it should be told,
The repetition cannot make it less;
For more it is than I can well express:
  And that deep torture may be call'd a hell,
  When more is felt than one hath power to tell.

'Go, get me hither paper, ink, and pen—
Yet save that labour, for I have them here.
What should I say?—One of my husband's men
Bid thou be ready, by and by, to bear
A letter to my lord, my love, my dear;
  Bid him with speed prepare to carry it:
  The cause craves haste, and it will soon be writ.'

Her maid is gone, and she prepares to write,
First hovering o'er the paper with her quill:
Conceit and grief an eager combat fight;
What wit sets down is blotted straight with will;
This is too curious-good, this blunt and ill:
  Much like a press of people at a door,
  Throng her inventions, which shall be before.

At last she thus begins:—'Thou worthy lord
Of that unworthy wife that greeteth thee,
Health to thy person! next vouchsafe to afford
(If ever, love, thy Lucrece thou wilt see)
Some present speed to come and visit me:

So I commend me from our house in grief;
My woes are tedious, though my words
are brief.'

Here folds she up the tenor of her woe,
Her certain sorrow writ uncertainly.
By this short schedule Collatine may know
Her grief, but not her grief's true quality;
She dares not thereof make discovery,
 Lest he should hold it her own gross abuse,
 Ere she with blood had stain'd her stain'd
  excuse.

Besides, the life and feeling of her passion
She hoards, to spend when he is by to hear
  her;
When sighs, and groans, and tears may grace
  the fashion
Of her disgrace, the better so to clear her
From that suspicion which the world might
  bear her
 To shun this blot, she would not blot the
  letter    [better.
 With words, till action might become them

To see sad sights moves more than hear them
  told;
For then the eye interprets to the ear
The heavy motion that it doth behold,
When every part a part of woe doth bear.
'Tis but a part of sorrow that we hear:
 Deep sounds make lesser noise than shal-
  low fords,    [of words.
 And sorrow ebbs, being blown with wind

Her letter now is seal'd, and on it writ,
'At Ardea to my lord with more than haste;'
The post attends, and she delivers it,
Charging the sour-fac'd groom to hie as fast
As lagging fowls before the northern blast.
 Speed more than speed but dull and slow
  she deems:
 Extremity still urgeth such extremes.

The homely villain court'sies to her low;
And blushing on her, with a steadfast eye
Receives the scroll, without or yea or no,
And forth with bashful innocence doth hie.
But they whose guilt within their bosoms lie
 Imagine every eye beholds their blame;
 For Lucrece thought he blush'd to see her
  shame;

When, silly groom! God wot, it was defect
Of spirit, life, and bold audacity.
Such harmless creatures have a true respect
To talk in deeds, while others saucily
Promise more speed, but do it leisurely:
 Even so, this pattern of the worn-out age
 Pawn'd honest looks, but laid no words to
  gage.

His kindled duty kindled her mistrust,
That two red fires in both their faces blaz'd;

She thought he blush'd as knowing Tarquin's
  lust,
And, blushing with him, wistly on him gaz'd;
Her earnest eye did make him more amaz'd:
 The more she saw the blood his cheeks
  replenish,    [blemish.
 The more she thought he spied in her some

But long she thinks till he return again,
And yet the duteous vassal scarce is gone.
The weary time she cannot entertain,
For now 'tis stale to sigh, to weep, and
  groan:
So woe hath wearied woe, moan tired moan,
 That she her plaints a little while doth
  stay,
 Pausing for means to mourn some newer
  way.

At last she calls to mind where hangs a piece
Of skilful painting, made for Priam's Troy;
Before the which is drawn the power of
  Greece,
For Helen's rape the city to destroy,
Threat'ning cloud-kissing Ilion with annoy;
 Which the conceited painter drew so
  proud,
 As heaven (it seem'd) to kiss the turrets
  bow'd.

A thousand lamentable objects there,
In scorn of Nature, Art gave lifeless life:
Many a dry drop seem'd a weeping tear,
Shed for the slaughter'd husband by the
  wife:
The red blood reek'd to show the painter's
  strife;
 And dying eyes gleam'd forth their ashy
  lights,
 Like dying coals burnt out in tedious
  nights.

There might you see the labouring pioneer
Begrim'd with sweat, and smeared all with
 • dust;
And from the towers of Troy there would
  appear
The very eyes of men through loopholes
  thrust,
Gazing upon the Greeks with little lust:
 Such sweet observance in this work was
  had,
 That one might see those far-off eyes look
  sad.

In great commanders grace and majesty
You might behold, triumphing in their faces;
In youth, quick bearing and dexterity;
And here and there the painter interlaces
Pale cowards, marching on with trembling
  paces;
 Which heartless peasants did so well re-
  semble,

That one would swear he saw them quake
   and tremble.

In Ajax and Ulysses, O what art
Of physiognomy might one behold!
The face of either 'cipher'd either's heart;
Their face their manners most expressly told:
In Ajax' eyes blunt rage and rigour roll'd;
   But the mild glance that sly Ulysses lent
   Show'd deep regard and smiling govern-
     ment.

There pleading might you see grave Nestor
   stand,
As't were encouraging the Greeks to fight;
Making such sober action with his hand
That it beguil'd attention, charm'd the
   sight:
In speech, it seem'd, his beard all silver
   white
   Wagg'd up and down, and from his lips
     did fly
   Thin winding breath, which purl'd up to
     the sky.

About him were a press of gaping faces,
Which seem'd to swallow up his sound ad-
   vice;
All jointly listening, but with several graces,
As if some mermaid did their ears entice;
Some high, some low, the painter was so
   nice:
   The scalps of many, almost hid behind,
   To jump up higher seem'd to mock the
     mind.

Here one man's hand lean'd on another's
   head,
His nose being shadow'd by his neighbour's
   ear;
Here one being throng'd bears back, all
   boll'n and red;
Another smother'd seems to pelt and swear;
And in their rage such signs of rage they
   bear,
   As, but for loss of Nestor's golden words,
   It seem'd they would debate with angry
     swords.

For much imaginary work was there;
Conceit deceitful, so compact, so kind,
That for Achilles' image stood his spear,
Grip'd in an armed hand; himself, behind,
Was left unseen, save to the eye of mind:
   A hand, a foot, a face, a leg, a head,
   Stood for the whole to be imagined.

And from the walls of strong-besieged Troy
When their brave hope, bold Hector,
   march'd to field,
Stood many Trojan mothers, sharing joy
To see their youthful sons bright weapons
   wield;

And to their hope they such odd action
   yield,
   That through their light joy seemed to
     appear
   (Like bright things stain'd) a kind of
     heavy fear.

And, from the strond of Dardan where they
   fought,
To Simois' reedy banks, the red blood ran,
Whose waves to imitate the battle sought
With swelling ridges; and their ranks began
To break upon the galled shore, and then
   Retire again, till meeting greater ranks
   They join, and shoot their foam at Simois'
     banks.

To this well-painted piece is Lucrece come,
To find a face where all distress is stell'd.
Many she sees where cares have carved
   some,
But none where all distress and dolour
   dwell'd,
Till she despairing Hecuba beheld,
   Staring on Priam's wounds with her old
     eyes,
   Which bleeding under Pyrrhus' proud foot
     lies.

In her the painter had anatomiz'd
Time's ruin, beauty's wrack, and grim care's
   reign;
Her cheeks with chaps and wrinkles were
   disguis'd;
Of what she was no semblance did remain:
Her blue blood, chang'd to black in every
   vein,
   Wanting the spring that those shrunk
     pipes had fed,
   Show'd life imprison'd in a body dead.

On this sad shadow Lucrece spends her eyes,
And shapes her sorrow to the beldame's
   woes,
Who nothing wants to answer her but cries,
And bitter words to ban her cruel foes:
The painter was no god to lend her those;
   And therefore Lucrece swears he did her
     wrong,
   To give her so much grief, and not a
     tongue.

'Poor instrument,' quoth she, 'without a
   sound,
I'll tune thy woes with my lamenting tongue:
And drop sweet balm in Priam's painted
   wound,
And rail on Pyrrhus that hath done him
   wrong,
And with my tears quench Troy that burns
   so long;
   And with my knife scratch out the angry
     eyes
   Of all the Greeks that are thine enemies.

'Show me the strumpet that began this stir,
That with my nails her beauty I may tear.
Thy heat of lust, fond Paris, did incur
This load of wrath that burning Troy doth
    bear;
Thy eye kindled the fire that burneth here:
    And here in Troy, for trespass of thine
        eye,
    The sire, the son, the dame, and daugh-
        ter, die.

'Why should the private pleasure of some
    one
Become the public plague of many mo?
Let sin, alone committed, light alone
Upon his head that hath transgressed so.
Let guiltless souls be freed from guilty woe:
    For one's offence why should so many
        fall,
    To plague a private sin in general?

'Lo, here weeps Hecuba, here Priam dies,
Here manly Hector· faints, here Troilus
    swounds;
Here friend by friend in bloody channel lies,
And friend to friend gives unadvised wounds,
And one man's lust these many lives con-
    founds:
    Had doting Priam check'd his son's de-
        sire,
    Troy had been bright with fame, and not
        with fire.

Here feelingly she weeps Troy's painted
    woes:
For sorrow, like a heavy-hanging bell,
Once set on ringing, with his own weight
    goes;
Then little strength rings out the doleful
    knell:
So Lucrece set a-work sad tales doth tell
    To pencill'd pensiveness and colour'd sor-
        row;
    She lends them words, and she their looks
        doth borrow.

She throws her eyes about the painting
    round,
And whom she finds forlorn she doth la-
    ment:
At last she sees a wretched image bound,
That piteous looks to Phrygian shepherds
    lent;
His face, though full of cares, yet show'd
    content:
    Onward to Troy with the blunt swains he
        goes,
    So mild that Patience seem'd to scorn his
        woes.

In him the painter labour'd with his skill
To hide deceit, and give the harmless show
An humble gait, calm looks, eyes wailing
    still,

A brow unbent, that seem'd to welcome
    woe;
Cheeks neither red nor pale, but mingled so
    That blushing red no guilty instance gave,
    Nor ashy pale the fear that false hearts
        have.

But, like a constant and confirmed devil,
He entertain'd a show so seeming just,
And therein so ensconc'd his secret evil,
That jealousy itself could not mistrust
False-creeping craft and perjury should
    thrust
    Into so bright a day such black-fac'd
        storms,
    Or blot with hell-born sin such saint-like
        forms.

The well-skill'd workman this mild image
    drew
For perjur'd Sinon, whose enchanting story
The credulous old Priam after slew; [glory
Whose words, like wildfire, burnt the shining
Of rich-built Ilion, that the skies were sorry,
    And little stars shot from their fixed
        places,
    When their glass fell wherein they view'd
        their faces.

This picture she advisedly perus'd,
And chid the painter for his wondrous skill;
Saying, some shape in Sinon's was abus'd,
So fair a form lodg'd not a mind so ill;
And still on him she gaz'd, and gazing still,
    Such signs of truth in his plain face she
        spied,
    That she concludes the picture was belied.

'It cannot be,' quoth she, 'that so much
    guile'—
(She would have said) 'can lurk in such a
    look;'
But Tarquin's shape came in her mind the
    while,
And from her tongue 'can lurk' from 'can-
    not' took;
'It cannot be' she in that sense forsook,
    And turn'd it thus: 'It cannot be, I find,
    But such a face should bear a wicked
        mind:

'For even as subtle Sinon here is painted,
So sober-sad, so weary, and so mild,
(As if with grief or travail he had fainted,)
To me came Tarquin armed; so beguil'd
With outward honesty, but yet defil'd
    With inward vice: as Priam him did cher-
        ish,
    So did I Tarquin; so my Troy did perish.

'Look, look, how listening Priam wets his
    eyes,
To see those borrow'd tears that Sinon
    sheds.

Priam, why art thou old, and yet not wise?
For every tear he falls a Trojan bleeds;
His eye drops fire, no water thence pro-
ceeds;
  Those round clear pearls of his that move
  thy pity
  Are balls of quenchless fire to burn thy
  city.

'Such devils steal effects from lightless hell;
For Sinon in his fire doth quake with cold,
And in that cold hot-burning fire doth
dwell;
These contraries such unity do hold
Only to flatter fools, and make them bold;
  So Priam's trust false Sinon's tears doth
  flatter,
  That he finds means to burn his Troy with
  water.'

Here, all enrag'd, such passion her assails,
That patience is quite beaten from her
breast.
She tears the senseless Sinon with her nails,
Comparing him to that unhappy guest
Whose deed hath made herself herself de-
test;
  At last she smilingly with this gives o'er;
  'Fool! fool!' quoth she, 'his wounds will
  not be sore.'

Thus ebbs and flows the current of her sorrow,
And time doth weary time with her complaining.
She looks for night, and then she longs for
morrow,
And both she thinks too long with her remaining:
Short time seems long in sorrow's sharp sustaining.
  Though woe be heavy, yet it seldom
  sleeps;
  And they that watch see time how slow
  it creeps.

Which all this time hath overslipp'd her
thought,
That she with painted images hath spent;
Being from the feeling of her own grief
brought
By deep surmise of others' detriment;
Losing her woes in shows of discontent.
  It easeth some, though none it ever cur'd,
  To think their dolour others have en-
  dur'd.

But now the mindful messenger, come back,
Brings home his lord and other company;
Who finds his Lucrece clad in mourning
black;
And round about her tear-distained eye
Blue circles stream'd, like rainbows in the
sky.

These water-galls in her dim element
Foretell new storms to those already spent.

Which when her sad-beholding husband saw,
Amazedly in her sad face he stares:
Her eyes, though sod in tears, look'd red and
raw,
Her lively colour kill'd with deadly cares.
He hath no power to ask her how she fares,
  But stood like old acquaintance in a
  trance,
  Met far from home, wondering each
  other's chance.

At last he takes her by the bloodless hand,
And thus begins: 'What uncouth ill event
Hath thee befallen, that thou dost trembling
stand?
Sweet love, what spite hath thy fair colour
spent?
Why art thou thus attir'd in discontent?
  Unmask, dear dear, this moody heaviness,
  And tell thy grief, that we may give re-
  dress.'

Three times with sighs she gives her sorrow
fire,
Ere once she can discharge one word of woe:
At length address'd to answer his desire,
She modestly prepares to let them know
Her honour is ta'en prisoner by the foe;
  While Collatine and his consorted lords
  With sad attention long to hear her words.

And now this pale swan in her watery nest
Begins the sad dirge of her certain ending:
'Few words,' quoth she, 'shall fit the tres-
pass best,
Where no excuse can give the fault amend-
ing:
In me more woes than words are now de-
pending;                                    [long,
  And my laments would be drawn out too
  To tell them all with one poor tired
  tongue.

'Then be this all the task it hath to say:--
Dear husband, in the interest of thy bed
A stranger came, and on that pillow lay
Where thou wast wont to rest thy weary
head;
And what wrong else may be imagined
  By foul enforcement might be done to me,
  From that, alas! thy Lucrece is not free.

'For in the dreadful dead of dark midnight,
With shining falchion in my chamber came
A creeping creature, with a flaming light,
And softly cried, Awake, thou Roman dame,
And entertain my love; else lasting shame
  On thee and thine this night I will inflict,
  If thou my love's desire do contradict.

'For some hard-favour'd groom of thine,
    quoth he,
Unless thou yoke thy liking to my will,
I'll murder straight, and then I'll slaughter
    thee,
And swear I found you where you did fulfil
The loathsome act of lust, and so did kill
    The lechers in their deed: this act will be
    My fame, and thy perpetual infamy.

'With this I did begin to start and cry,
And then against my heart he set his sword,
Swearing, unless I took all patiently,
I should not live to speak another word:
So should my shame still rest upon record,
    And never be forgot in mighty Rome
    The adulterate death of Lucrece and her
        groom.

'Mine enemy was strong, my poor self weak,
And far the weaker with so strong a fear:
My bloody judge forbade my tongue to
    speak;
No rightful plea might plead for justice
    there:
His scarlet lust came evidence to swear
    That my poor beauty had purloin'd his
        eyes,
    And when the judge is robb'd, the prisoner
        dies.

'O teach me how to make mine own excuse!
Or, at the least, this refuge let me find;
Though my gross blood be stain'd with this
    abuse,
Immaculate and spotless is my mind;
That was not forc'd; that never was inclin'd
    To accessary yieldings, but still pure
    Doth in her poison'd closet yet endure.'

Lo here, the hopeless merchant of this loss,
With head declin'd, and voice damm'd up
    with woe,
With sad-set eyes, and wretched arms across,
From lips new-waxen pale begins to blow
The grief away that stops his answer so:
    But wretched as he is he strives in vain;
    What he breathes out his breath drinks up
        again.

As through an arch the violent roaring tide
Outruns the eye that doth behold his haste;
Yet in the eddy boundeth in his pride
Back to the strait that forc'd him on so fast;
In rage sent out, recall'd in rage, being past:
    Even so he sighs, his sorrows make a saw,
    To push grief on, and back the same grief
        draw.

Which speechless woe of his poor she at-
    tendeth,
And his untimely frenzy thus awaketh:
'Dear lord, thy sorrow to my sorrow lendeth

Another power; no flood by raining slaketh.
My woe too sensible thy passion maketh
    More feeling-painful: let it then suffice
    To drown one woe, one pair of weeping
        eyes.

'And for my sake, when I might charm thee
    so,
For she that was thy Lucrece,—now attend
    me;
Be suddenly revenged on my foe, [fend me
Thine, mine, his own; suppose thou dost de-
From what is past: the help that thou shalt
    lend me
    Comes all too late, yet let the traitor die;
    For sparing justice feeds iniquity.

'But ere I name him, you, fair lords,' quoth
    she,
(Speaking to those that came with Colla-
    tine)
'Shall plight your honourable faiths to me,
With swift pursuit to venge this wrong of
    mine;
For 'tis a meritorious fair design
    To chase injustice with revengeful arms:
    Knights, by their oaths, should right poor
        ladies' harms.'

At this request, with noble disposition
Each present lord began to promise aid,
As bound in knighthood to her imposition,
Longing to hear the hateful foe bewray'd.
But she, that yet her sad task hath not said,
    The protestation stops. 'O speak,' quoth
        she,                                [me?
    'How may this forced stain be wip'd from

'What is the quality of mine offence,
Being constrain'd with dreadful circum-
    stance?
May my pure mind with the foul act dis-
    pense,
My low-declined honour to advance?
May any terms acquit me from this chance?
    The poison'd fountain clears itself again;
    And why not I from this compelled stain?'

With this, they all at once began to say,
Her body's stain her mind untainted clears;
While with a joyless smile she turns away
The face, that map which deep impression
    bears
Of hard misfortune, carv'd in it with tears.
    'No, no,' quoth she, 'no dame, hereafter
        living,
    By my excuse shall claim excuse's giving.'

Here with a sigh, as if her heart would break,
She throws forth Tarquin's name: 'He, he,'
    she says,                              [not speak;
But more than 'he' her poor tongue could
Till after many accents and delays,

Untimely breathings, sick and short assays,
She utters this: 'He, he, fair lords, 'tis he,
That guides this hand to give this wound
  to me.'

Even here she sheathed in her harmless
    breast
A harmful knife, that thence her soul un-
    sheath'd:
That blow did bail it from the deep unrest
Of that polluted prison where it breath'd:
Her contrite sighs unto the clouds bequeath'd
  Her winged sprite, and through her
    wounds doth fly
  Life's lasting date from cancell'd destiny.

Stone-still, astonish'd with this deadly deed,
Stood Collatine and all his lordly crew;
Till Lucrece' father that beholds her bleed,
Himself on her self-slaughter'd body threw;
And from the purple fountain Brutus drew
  The murderous knife, and as it left the
    place,
  Her blood, in poor revenge, held it in
    chase;

And bubbling from her breast, it doth
    divide
In two slow rivers, that the crimson blood
Circles her body in on every side,
Who like a late-sack'd island vastly stood
Bare and unpeopled, in this fearful flood:
  Some of her blood still pure and red re-
    main'd,
  And some look'd black, and that false
    Tarquin stain'd.

About the mourning and congealed face
Of that black blood a watery rigol goes,
Which seems to weep upon the tainted
    place:
And ever since, as pitying Lucrece' woes,
Corrupted blood some watery token shows;
  And blood untainted still doth red abide,
  Blushing at that which is so putrefied.

'Daughter, dear daughter,' old Lucretius
    cries,
'That life was mine which thou hast here
    depriv'd.
If in the child the father's image lies,
Where shall I live now Lucrece is unliv'd?
Thou wast not to this end from me deriv'd.
  If children predecease progenitors,
  We are their offspring, and they none of
    ours.

'Poor broken glass, I often did behold
In thy sweet semblance my old age new
    born;
But now that fair fresh mirror, dim and old,
Shows me a barebon'd death by time out-
    worn;

O, from thy cheeks my image thou hast
    torn!
And shiver'd all the beauty of my glass,
That I no more can see what once I was.

'O time, cease thou thy course, and last no
    longer,
If they surcease to be that should survive.
Shall rotten death make conquest of the
    stronger,
And leave the faltering feeble souls alive?
The old bees die, the young possess their
    hive:
  Then live, sweet Lucrece, live again, and
    see
  Thy father die, and not thy father thee!'

By this starts Collatine as from a dream,
And bids Lucretius give his sorrow place;
And then in key-cold Lucrece' bleeding
    stream
He falls, and bathes the pale fear in his face,
And counterfeits to die with her a space;
  Till manly shame bids him possess his
    breath,
  And live, to be revenged on her death.

The deep vexation of his inward soul
Hath serv'd a dumb arrest upon his tongue;
Who, mad that sorrow should his use con-
    trol,
Or keep him from heart-easing words so
    long,
Begins to talk; but through his lips do
    throng
  Weak words, so thick come, in his poor
    heart's aid,
  That no man could distinguish what he
    said.

Yet sometime Tarquin was pronounced
    plain,
But through his teeth, as if the name he tore.
This windy tempest, till it blow up rain,
Held back his sorrow's tide, to make it
    more;
At last it rains, and busy winds give o'er:
  Then son and father weep with equal
    strife,
  Who should weep most for daughter or
    for wife.

The one doth call her his, the other his,
Yet neither may possess the claim they lay,
The father says, 'She's mine,' 'O, mine she
    is,'
Replies her husband: 'do not take away
My sorrow's interest; let no mourner say
  He weeps for her, for she was only mine,
  And only must be wail'd by Collatine.'

'O,' quoth Lucretius, 'I did give that life
Which she too early and too late hath
    spill'd.'

'Woe, woe,' quoth Collatine, 'she was my
    wife,
I ow'd her, and 'tis mine that she hath
    kill'd.'
'My daughter!' and 'My wife!' with clam-
    ours fill'd
    The dispers'd air, who, holding Lucrece'
      life,
    Answer'd their cries, 'My daughter!' and
      'My wife!'

Brutus, who pluck'd the knife from Lucrece'
    side,
Seeing such emulation in their woe,
Began to clothe his wit in state and pride,
Burying in Lucrece' wound his folly's show.
He with the Romans was esteemed so
    As silly jeering idiots are with kings,
    For sportive words, and uttering foolish
      things.

But now he throws that shallow habit by,
Wherein deep policy did him disguise;
And arm'd his long-hid wits advisedly,
To check the tears in Collatinus' eyes.
'Thou wronged lord of Rome,' quoth he,
    'arise;
    Let my unsounded self, suppos'd a fool,
    Now set thy long-experienc'd wit to
      school.

'Why, Collatine, is woe the cure for woe?
Do wounds help wounds, or grief help griev-
    ous deeds?
Is it revenge to give thyself a blow,
For his foul act by whom thy fair wife
    bleeds?
Such childish humour from weak minds pro-
    ceeds:
    Thy wretched wife mistook the matter so,
    To slay herself, that should have slain her
      foe.

'Courageous Roman, do not steep thy heart

In such relenting dew of lamentations,
But kneel with me, and help to bear thy
    part,
To rouse our Roman gods with invocations,
That they will suffer these abominations,
    (Since Rome herself in them doth stand
      disgrac'd,)
    By our strong arms from forth her fair
      streets chas'd.

'Now by the Capitol that we adore,
And by this chaste blood so unjustly stain'd,
By heaven's fair sun that breeds the fat
    earth's store,
By all our country rights in Rome main-
    tain'd,
And by chaste Lucrece' soul that late com-
    plain'd
    Her wrongs to us, and by this bloody
      knife,
    We will revenge the death of this true
      wife.'

This said, he struck his hand upon his breast,
And kiss'd the fatal knife to end his vow;
And to his protestation urg'd the rest,
Who, wondering at him, did his words al-
    low;
Then jointly to the ground their knees they
    bow;
    And that deep vow which Brutus made
      before,
    He doth again repeat, and that they swore.

When they had sworn to this advised doom,
They did conclude to bear dead Lucrece
    thence;
To show her bleeding body thorough Rome,
And so to publish Tarquin's foul offence:
Which being done with speedy diligence,
    The Romans plausibly did give consent
    To Tarquin's everlasting banishment.

# SONNETS

TO . THE . ONLIE . BEGETTER . OF
THESE . INSUING . SONNETS .
MR. W. H. ALL . HAPPINESSE .
AND . THAT . ETERNITIE .
PROMISED .

BY .

OUR . EVER - LIVING . POET .
WISHETH .
THE . WELL - WISHING .
ADVENTURER . IN .
SETTING .
FORTH .

T. T.

### I.

FROM fairest creatures we desire increase,
That thereby beauty's rose might never die,
But as the riper should by time decrease,
His tender heir might bear his memory:
But thou, contracted to thine own bright
eyes,
Feed'st thy light's flame with self-substantial
fuel,
Making a famine where abundance lies,
Thyself thy foe, to thy sweet self too cruel.
Thou that art now the world's fresh orna-
ment,
And only herald to the gaudy spring,
Within thine own bud buriest thy content,
And, tender churl, mak'st waste in niggard-
ing.
   Pity the world, or else this glutton be,
   To eat the world's due, by the grave and
   thee.

### II.

When forty winters shall besiege thy brow,
And dig deep trenches in thy beauty's field,
Thy youth's proud livery, so gaz'd on now,
Will be a tatter'd weed, of small worth
held:
Then being ask'd where all thy beauty lies,
Where all the treasure of thy lusty days;
To say, within thine own deep sunken eyes,
Were an all-eating shame and thriftless
praise.
How much more praise deserv'd thy beauty's
use,
If thou couldst answer—'This fair child of
mine

Shall sum my count, and make my old excuse—'
Proving his beauty by succession thine!
   This were to be new-made when thou art
   old,
   And see thy blood warm when thou
   feel'st it cold.

### III.

Look in thy glass, and tell the face thou
viewest,
Now is the time that face should form an-
other;
Whose fresh repair if now thou not renew-
est,
Thou dost beguile the world, unbless some
mother.
For where is she so fair whose unear'd womb
Disdains the tillage of thy husbandry?
Or who is he so fond will be the tomb
Of his self-love, to stop posterity?
Thou art thy mother's glass, and she in thee
Calls back the lovely April of her prime:
So thou through windows of thine age shalt
see,
Despite of wrinkles, this thy golden time.
   But if thou live, remember'd not to be,
   Die single, and thine image dies with thee.

### IV.

Unthrifty loveliness, why dost thou spend
Upon thyself thy beauty's legacy?
Nature's bequest gives nothing, but doth
lend,
And, being frank, she lends to those are free.

[1191]

Then, beauteous niggard, why dost thou
    abuse
The bounteous largess given thee to give?
Profitless usurer, why dost thou use
So great a sum of sums, yet canst not live?
For having traffic with thyself alone,
Thou of thyself thy sweet self dost deceive.
Then how, when nature calls thee to be
    gone,
What acceptable audit canst thou leave?
    The unus'd beauty must be tomb'd with
      thee,
    Which, used, lives th' executor to be.

### v.

Those hours that with gentle work did
    frame
The lovely gaze where every eye doth dwell,
Will play the tyrants to the very same,
And that unfair which fairly doth excel;
For never-resting time leads summer on
To hideous winter, and confounds him
    there;
Sap check'd with frost, and lusty leaves
    quite gone,
Beauty o'ersnow'd, and bareness every-
    where:
Then, were not summer's distillation left,
A liquid prisoner pent in walls of glass,
Beauty's effect with beauty were bereft,
Nor it, nor no remembrance what it was.
    But flowers distill'd, though they with
      winter meet,      [lives sweet.
    Leese but their show; their substance still

### vi.

Then let not winter's ragged hand deface
In thee thy summer, ere thou be distill'd:
Make sweet some phial; treasure thou some
    place
With beauty's treasure, ere it be self-kill'd.
That use is not forbidden usury,
Which happies those that pay the willing
    loan;
That's for thyself to breed another thee,
Or ten times happier, be it ten for one;
Ten times thyself were happier than thou
    art,
If ten of thine ten times refigur'd thee:
Then what could Death do if thou shouldst
    depart,
Leaving thee living in posterity?
    Be not self-will'd, for thou art much too
      fair
    To be Death's conquest and make worms
      thine heir.

### vii.

Lo, in the orient when the gracious light
Lifts up his burning head, each under eye
Doth homage to his new-appearing sight,
Serving with looks his sacred majesty;

And having climb'd the steep-up heavenly
    hill,
Resembling strong youth in his middle age,
Yet mortal looks adore his beauty still,
Attending on his golden pilgrimage;
But when from high-most pitch, with weary
    car,
Like feeble age, he reeleth from the day,
The eyes, 'fore duteous, now converted are
From his low tract, and look another way:
    So thou, thyself, outgoing in thy noon,
    Unlook'd on diest, unless thou get a son.

### viii.

Music to hear, why hear'st thou music
    sadly?
Sweets with sweets war not, joy delights in
    joy,
Why lov'st thou that which thou receiv'st
    not gladly?
Or else receiv'st with pleasure thine annoy?
If the true concord of well-tuned sounds
By unions married, do offend thine ear,
They do but sweetly chide thee, who con-
    founds
In singleness the parts that thou shouldst
    bear.
Mark how one string, sweet husband to an-
    other,
Strikes each in each by mutual ordering;
Resembling sire and child and happy
    mother,
Who, all in one, one pleasing note do sing:
    Whose speechless song, being many, seem-
      ing one,
    Sings this to thee, 'thou single wilt prove
      none.'

### ix.

Is it for fear to wet a widow's eye
That thou consum'st thyself in single life?
Ah! if thou issueless shalt hap to die,
The world will wail thee, like a makeless
    wife:
The world will be thy widow, and still weep
That thou no form of thee hast left behind,
When every private widow well may keep,
By children's eyes, her husband's shape in
    mind.
Look, what an unthrift in the world doth
    spend
Shifts but his place, for still the world enjoys
    it:
But beauty's waste hath in the world an end,
And kept unus'd, the user so destroys it.
    No love toward others in that bosom sits,
    That on himself such murderous shame
      commits.

### x.

For shame! deny that thou bear'st love to
    any,
Who for thyself art so unprovident.

Grant if thou wilt thou art belov'd of many,
But that thou none lov'st is most evident;
For thou art so possess'd with murderous
    hate,
That 'gainst thyself thou stick'st not to con-
    spire,
Seeking that beauteous roof to ruinate,
Which to repair should be thy chief desire.
O change thy thought, that I may change
    my mind!
Shall hate be fairer lodg'd than gentle love?
Be, as thy presence is, gracious and kind,
Or to thyself, at least, kind-hearted prove;
  Make thee another self, for love of me,
  That beauty still may live in thine or thee.

### XI.

As fast as thou shalt wane, so fast thou
    grow'st
In one of thine, from that which thou de-
    partest.
And that fresh blood which youngly thou
    bestow'st,
Thou mayst call thine, when thou from
    youth convertest.
Herein lives wisdom, beauty, and increase:
Without this folly, age, and cold decay.
If all were minded so the times should cease,
And threescore years would make the world
    away.
Let those whom Nature hath not made for
    store,
Harsh, featureless, and rude, barrenly perish:
Look whom she best endow'd, she gave the
    more;        [bounty cherish;
Which bounteous gift thou shouldst in
    She carv'd thee for her seal, and meant
    thereby
    Thou shouldst print more, nor let that
    copy die.

### XII.

When I do count the clock that tells the
    time,
And see the brave day sunk in hideous
    night;
When I behold the violet past prime,
And sable curls, all silver'd o'er with white;
When lofty trees I see barren of leaves,
Which erst from heat did canopy the herd,
And summer's green all girded up in sheaves,
Borne on the bier with white and bristly
    beard;
Then of thy beauty do I question make,
That thou among the wastes of time must
    go,
Since sweets and beauties do themselves for-
    sake,
And die as fast as they see others grow;
  And nothing 'gainst Time's scythe can
    make defence     [thee hence.
  Save breed, to brave him when he takes

### XIII.

O that you were yourself: but, love, you are
No longer yours than you yourself here live:
Against this coming end you should prepare,
And your sweet semblance to some other
    give.
So should that beauty which you hold in
    lease
Find no determination: then you were
Yourself again, after yourself's decease,
When your sweet issue your sweet form
    should bear.
Who lets so fair a house fall to decay,
Which husbandry in honour might uphold
Against the stormy gusts of winter's day,
And barren rage of death's eternal cold?
  O! none but unthrifts:—Dear my love,
    you know
  You had a father; let your son say so.

### XIV.

Not from the stars do I my judgment pluck;
And yet methinks I have astronomy,
But not to tell of good or evil luck,
Of plagues, of dearths, or season's quality:
Nor can I fortune to brief minutes tell,
Pointing to each his thunder, rain, and wind,
Or say with princes if it shall go well,
By oft predict that I in heaven find:
But from thine eyes my knowledge I derive,
And (constant stars) in them I read such
    art,
As truth and beauty shall together thrive,
If from thyself to store thou wouldst con-
    vert:
  Or else of thee this I prognosticate,
  Thy end is truth's and beauty's doom and
    date.

### XV.

When I consider every thing that grows
Holds in perfection but a little moment,
That this huge state presenteth nought but
    shows
Whereon the stars in secret influence com-
    ment;
When I perceive that men as plants increase,
Cheered and check'd even by the self-same
    sky;
Vaunt in their youthful sap, at height de-
    crease,
And wear their brave state out of memory;
Then the conceit of this inconstant stay
Sets you most rich in youth before my
    sight,
Where wasteful time debateth with decay,
To change your day of youth to sullied
    night;
  And, all in war with Time, for love of
    you,
  As he takes from you, I engraft you new.

## XVI.

But wherefore do not you a mightier way
Make war upon this bloody tyrant, Time?
And fortify yourself in your decay
With means more blessed than my barren
    rhyme?
Now stand you on the top of happy hours;
And many maiden gardens, yet unset,
With virtuous wish would bear your living
    flowers,
Much liker than your painted counterfeit:
So should the lines of life that life repair,
Which this, Time's pencil, or my pupil pen,
Neither in inward worth, nor outward fair,
Can make you live yourself in eyes of men.
  To give away yourself keeps yourself still;
  And you must live, drawn by your own
    sweet skill.

## XVII.

Who will believe my verse in time to come,
If it were fill'd with your most high deserts?
Though yet, Heaven knows, it is but as a
    tomb
Which hides your life, and shows not half
    your parts.
If I could write the beauty of your eyes,
And in fresh numbers number all your
    graces,
The age to come would say, this poet lies,
Such heavenly touches ne'er touch'd earthly
    faces.
So should my papers, yellow'd with their
    age,
Be scorn'd, like old men of less truth than
    tongue;
And your true rights be term'd a poet's rage,
And stretched metre of an antique song:
  But were some child of yours alive that
    time,                          [rhyme.
  You should live twice;—in it, and in my

## XVIII.

Shall I compare thee to a summer's day?
Thou art more lovely and more temperate:
Rough winds do shake the darling buds of
    May,                           [date:
And summer's lease hath all too short a
Sometime too hot the eye of heaven shines,
And often is his gold complexion dimm'd;
And every fair from fair sometime declines,
By chance, or nature's changing course, un-
    trimm'd;
But thy eternal summer shall not fade,
Nor lose possession of that fair thou owest;
Nor shall Death brag thou wander'st in his
    shade,
When in eternal lines to time thou growest;
  So long as men can breathe, or eyes can
    see,
  So long lives this, and this gives life to
    thee

## XIX.

Devouring Time, blunt thou the lion's paws,
And make the earth devour her own sweet
    brood;
Pluck the keen teeth from the fierce tiger's
    jaws,
And burn the long-liv'd phœnix in her blood;
Make glad and sorry seasons, as thou fleets,
And do whate'er thou wilt, swift-footed
    Time,
To the wide world, and all her fading
    sweets;
But I forbid thee one most heinous crime:
O carve not with thy hours my love's fair
    brow,
Nor draw no lines there with thine antique
    pen;
Him in thy course untainted do allow,
For beauty's pattern to succeeding men.
  Yet, do thy worst, old Time: despite thy
    wrong,
  My love shall in my verse ever live young.

## XX.

A woman's face, with nature's own hand
    painted,
Hast thou, the master-mistress of my pas-
    sion;
A woman's gentle heart, but not acquainted
With shifting change, as is false woman's
    fashion;
An eye more bright than theirs, less false in
    rolling,
Gilding the object whereupon it gazeth;
A man in hue, all hues in his controlling,
Which steals men's eyes, and women's souls
    amazeth.
And for a woman wert thou first created;
Till Nature, as she wrought thee, fell a-dot-
    ing,
And by addition me of thee defeated,
By adding one thing to my purpose nothing.
  But since she prick'd thee out for women's
    pleasure,
  Mine be thy love, and thy love's use their
    treasure.

## XXI.

So is it not with me as with that muse,
Stirr'd by a painted beauty to his verse,
Who heaven itself for ornament doth use,
And every fair with his fair doth rehearse;
Making a couplement of proud compare,
With sun and moon, with earth and sea's
    rich gems,                      [rare
With April's first-born flowers, and all things
That heaven's air in this huge rondure hems.
O let me, true in love, but truly write,
And then believe me, my love is as fair
As any mother's child, though not so bright
As those gold candles fix'd in heaven's air:

Let them say more that like of hearsay
    well;
I will not praise, that purpose not to sell.

### XXII.

My glass shall not persuade me I am old,
So long as youth and thou are of one date;
But when in thee time's furrows I behold,
Then look I death my days should expiate.
For all that beauty that doth cover thee
Is but the seemly raiment of my heart,
Which in thy breast doth live, as thine in
    me;
How can I then be elder than thou art?
O therefore, love, be of thyself so wary,
As I not for myself but for thee will;
Bearing thy heart, which I will keep so chary
As tender nurse her babe from faring ill.
    Presume not on thy heart when mine is
      slain;
      Thou gav'st me thine, not tc give back
      again.

### XXIII.

As an unperfect actor on the stage,
Who with his fear is put besides his part
Or some fierce thing replete with too much
    rage,
Whose strength's abundance weakens his own
    heart;
So I, for fear of trust, forget to say
The perfect ceremony of love's rite,
And in mine own love's strength seem to de-
    cay,
O'ercharg'd with burthen of mine own love's
    might.
O let my books be, then, the eloquence
And dumb presagers of my speaking breast;
Who plead for love, and look for recom-
    pense
More than that tongue that more hath more
    express'd.
    O learn to read what silent love hath writ:
    To hear with eyes belongs to love's fine
    wit.

### XXIV.

Mine eye hath play'd the painter, and hath
    stell'd
Thy beauty's form in table of my heart;
My body is the frame wherein 'tis held,
And perspective it is best painter's art.
For through the painter must you see his
    skill,
To find where your true image pictur'd lies,
Which in my bosom's shop is hanging still,
That hath his windows glazed with thine
    eyes.
Now see what good turns eyes for eyes have
    done:
Mine eyes have drawn thy shape, and thine
    for me      [the sun
Are windows to my breast, where-through

Delights to peep, to gaze therein on thee;
    Yet eyes this cunning want to grace their
      art,
    They draw but what they see, know not
      the heart.

### XXV.

Let those who are in favour with their stars,
Of public honour and proud titles boast,
Whilst I, whom fortune of such triumph
    bars,
Unlook'd for joy in that I honour most.
Great princes' favourites their fair leaves
    spread
But as the marigold at the sun's eye;
And in themselves their pride lies buried,
For at a frown they in their glory die.
The painful warrior famoused for fight,
After a thousand victories once foil'd,
Is from the book of honour razed quite,
And all the rest forgot for which he toil'd:
    Then happy I, that love and am belov'd
    Where I may not remove, nor be remov'd.

### XXVI.

Lord of my love, to whom in vassalage
Thy merit hath my duty strongly knit,
To thee I send this written embassage,
To witness duty, not to show my wit.
Duty so great, which wit so poor as mine
May make seem bare, in wanting words to
    show it;
But that I hope some good conceit of thine
In thy soul's thought, all naked, will bestow
    it:
Till whatsoever star that guides by moving,
Points on me graciously with fair aspect,
And puts apparel on my tatter'd loving,
To show me worthy of thy sweet respect:
    Then may I dare to boast how I do love
      thee,
    Till then, not show my head where thou
      mayst prove me.

### XXVII.

Weary with toil, I haste me to my bed,
The dear repose for limbs with travel tir'd;
But then begins a journey in my head,
To work my mind, when body's work's ex-
    pir'd:
For then my thoughts (from far where I
    abide)
Intend a zealous pilgrimage to thee,
And keep my drooping eyelids open wide,
Looking on darkness which the blind do see:
Save that my soul's imaginary sight
Presents thy shadow to my sightless view,
Which, like a jewel hung in ghastly night,
Makes black night beauteous, and her old
    face new.
    Lo, thus, by day my limbs, by night my
      mind
    For thee, and for myself, no quiet find.

### XXVIII.

How can I then return in happy plight,
That am debarr'd the benefit of rest?
When day's oppression is not eas'd by night,
But day by night and night by day op-
press'd?
And each, though enemies to either's reign,
Do in consent shake hands to torture me,
The one by toil, the other to complain
How far I toil, still farther off from thee.
I tell the day, to please him, thou art bright,
And dost him grace when clouds do blot the
heaven:
So flatter I the swart-complexion'd night;
When sparkling stars twire not, thou gild'st
the even.
　But day both daily draw my sorrows
longer,
　And night doth nightly make grief's
strength seem stronger.

### XXIX.

When in disgrace with fortune and men's
eyes,
I all alone beweep my outcast state,　[cries,
And trouble deaf Heaven with my bootless
And look upon myself, and curse my fate,
Wishing me like to one more rich in hope,
Featur'd like him, like him with friends pos-
sess'd,
Desiring this man's art, and that man's scope,
With what I most enjoy contented least;
Yet in these thoughts myself almost despising,
Haply I think on thee,—and then my state
(Like to the lark at break of day arising
From sullen earth) sings hymns at heaven's
gate;
　For thy sweet love remember'd such
wealth brings,
　That then I scorn to change my state with
kings.

### XXX.

When to the sessions of sweet silent thought
I summon up remembrance of things past,
I sigh the lack of many a thing I sought,
And with old woes new wail my dear times'
waste:
Then can I drown an eye, unus'd to flow,
For precious friends hid in death's dateless
night.
And weep afresh love's long-since cancell'd
woe,
And moan the expense of many a vanish'd
sight.
Then can I grieve at grievances foregone,
And heavily from woe to woe tell o'er
The sad account of fore-bemoaned moan,
Which I new pay as if not paid before.
　But if the while I think on thee, dear
friend,
　All losses are restor'd, and sorrows end.

### XXXI.

Thy bosom is endeared with all hearts,
Which I by lacking have supposed dead;
And there reigns love and all love's loving
parts,
And all those friends which I thought buried.
How many a holy and obsequious tear
Hath dear religious love stolen- from mine
eye,
As interest of the dead, which now appear
But things remov'd, that hidden in thee lie!
Thou art the grave where buried love doth
live,
Hung with the trophies of my lovers gone,
Who all their parts of, me to thee did give;
That due of many now is thine alone:
　Their images I lov'd I view in thee,
　And thou (all they) hast all the all of me.

### XXXII.

If thou survive my well-contented day,
When that churl Death my bones with dust
shall cover,
And shalt by fortune once more re-survey
These poor rude lines of thy deceased lover,
Compare them with the bettering of the
time;
And though they be outstripp'd by every pen,
Reserve them for my love, not for their
rhyme,
Exceeded by the height of happier men.
O then vouchsafe me but this loving
thought!
'Had my friend's muse grown with this
growing age,
A dearer birth than this his love had brought,
To march in ranks of better equipage:
　But since he died, and poets better prove,
　Theirs for their style I'll read, his for his
love.'

### XXXIII.

Full many a glorious morning have I seen
Flatter the mountain-tops with sovereign eye,
Kissing with golden face the meadows green,
Gilding pale streams with heavenly alchymy;
Anon permit the basest clouds to ride
With ugly rack on his celestial face,
And from the forlorn world his visage hide,
Stealing unseen to west with this disgrace:
Even so my sun one early morn did shine
With all triumphant splendour on my brow;
But out! alack! he was but one hour mine,
The region cloud hath mask'd him from me
now.
　Yet him for this my love no whit dis-
daineth;
　Suns of the world may stain, when heav-
en's sun staineth.

### XXXIV.

Why didst thou promise such a beauteous
day,

And make me travel forth without my cloak,
To let base clouds o'ertake me in my way,
Hiding thy bravery in their rotten smoke?
'Tis not enough that through the cloud thou
    break,
To dry the rain on my storm-beaten face,
For no man well of such a salve can speak,
That heals the wound, and cures not the dis-
    grace:
Nor can thy shame give physic to my grief;
Though thou repent, yet I have still the loss:
The offender's sorrow lends but weak relief
To him that bears the strong offence's cross,
    Ah! but those tears are pearl which thy
        love sheds,
    And they are rich, and ransom all ill deeds.

### XXXV.

No more be griev'd at that which thou hast
    done:
Roses have thorns, and silver fountains mud,
Clouds and eclipses stain both moon and sun,
And loathsome canker lives in sweetest bud.
All men make faults, and even I in this,
Authorising thy trespass with compare,
Myself corrupting, salving thy amiss,
Excusing thy sins more than thy sins are:
For to thy sensual fault I bring in sense,
(Thy adverse party is thy advocate,)
And 'gainst myself a lawful plea commence:
    Such civil war is in my love and hate,
        That I an accessary needs must be
        To that sweet thief which sourly robs
            from me.

### XXXVI.

Let me confess that we two must be twain,
Although our undivided loves are one:
So shall those blots that do with me remain,
Without thy help, by me be borne alone.
In our two loves there is but one respect,
Though in our lives a separable spite,
Which though it alter not love's sole effect,
Yet doth it steal sweet hours from love's
    delight.
I may not evermore acknowledge thee,
Lest my bewailed guilt should do thee
    shame;
Nor thou with public kindness honour me,
Unless thou take that honour from thy
    name:
    But do not so; I love thee in such sort,
    As, thou being mine, mine is thy good re-
        port.

### XXXVII.

As a decrepit father takes delight
To see his active child do deeds of youth,
So I, made lame by fortune's dearest spite,
Take all my comfort of thy worth and
    truth;
For whether beauty, birth, or wealth, or wit,
Or any of these all, or all, or more,

Entitled in thy parts do crowned sit,
I make my love engrafted to this store:
So then I am not lame, poor, nor despis'd,
Whilst that this shadow dost such substance
    give,
That I in thy abundance am suffic'd,
And by a part of all thy glory live.
    Look, what is best, that best I wish in
        thee;
    This wish I have; then ten times happy
        me!

### XXXVIII.

How can my muse want subject to invent,
While thou dost breathe, that pour'st into
    my verse
Thine own sweet argument, too excellent
For every vulgar paper to rehearse?
O, give thyself the thanks, if aught in me
Worthy perusal stand against thy sight;
For who's so dumb that cannot write to thee,
When thou thyself dost give invention light?
Be thou the tenth muse, ten times more in
    worth
Than those old nine which rhymers invocate;
And he that calls on thee, let him bring forth
Eternal numbers to outlive long date.
    If my slight muse do please these curious
        days,                              [praise.
    The pain be mine, but thine shall be the

### XXXIX.

O, how thy worth with manners may I sing,
When thou art all the better part of me?
What can mine own praise to mine own self
    bring?
And what is 't but mine own, when I praise
    thee?
Even for this let us divided live,
And our dear love lose name of single one,
That by this separation I may give
That due to thee, which thou deserv'st alone.
O absence, what a torment wouldst thou
    prove,
Were it not thy sour leisure gave sweet leave
To entertain the time with thoughts of love,
(Which time and thoughts so sweetly doth
    deceive,)
    And that thou teachest how to make one
        twain,
    By praising him here, who doth hence re-
        main!

### XL.

Take all my loves, my love, yea, take them
    all;
What hast thou then more than thou hadst
    before?
No love, my love, that thou mayst true love
    call;
All mine was thine, before thou hadst this
    more.
Then if for my love thou my love receivest,

I cannot blame thee for my love thou usest;
But yet be blam'd, if thou thyself deceivest
By wilful taste of what thyself refusest.
I do forgive thy robbery, gentle thief,
Although thou steal thee all my property;
And yet, love knows, it is a greater grief
To bear love's wrong, than hate's known injury.
 Lascivious grace, in whom all ill well shows,
  Kill me with spites; yet we must not be foes.

### XLI.

Those pretty wrongs that liberty commits
When I am sometime absent from thy heart,
Thy beauty and thy years full well befits,
For still temptation follows where thou art.
Gentle thou art, and therefore to be won,
Beauteous thou art, therefore to be assail'd;
And when a woman wooes, what woman's son
Will sourly leave her till she have prevail'd?
Ah me! but yet thou mightst my seat forbear,
And chide thy beauty and thy straying youth,
Who lead thee in their riot even there
Where thou art forc'd to break a twofold truth;
 Hers, by thy beauty tempting her to thee,
 Thine, by thy beauty being false to me.

### XLII.

That thou hast her, it is not all my grief,
And yet it may be said I lov'd her dearly;
That she hath thee, is of my wailing chief,
A loss in love that touches me more nearly.
Loving offenders, thus I will excuse ye:—
Thou dost love her, because thou knew'st I love her;
And for my sake even so doth she abuse me,
Suffering my friend for my sake to approve her.
If I lose thee, my loss is my love's gain,
And, losing her, my friend hath found that loss;
Both find each other, and I lose both twain,
And both for my sake lay on me this cross:
 But here's the joy; my friend and I are one;
  Sweet flattery! then she loves but me alone.

### XLIII.

When most I wink, then do mine eyes best see,
For all the day they view things unrespected;
But when I sleep, in dreams they look on thee,
And, darkly bright, are bright in dark directed;

Then thou whose shadow shadows doth make bright,
How would thy shadow's form form happy show
To the clear day with thy much clearer light,
When to unseeing eyes thy shade shines so!
How would (I say) mine eyes be blessed made
By looking on thee in the living day,
When in dead night thy fair imperfect shade
Through heavy sleep on sightless eyes doth stay?
 All days are nights to see, till I see thee,
 And nights, bright days, when dreams do show thee me.

### XLIV.

If the dull substance of my flesh were thought,
Injurious distance should not stop my way;
For then, despite of space, I would be brought
From limits far remote, where thou dost stay.
No matter then, although my foot did stand
Upon the farthest earth remov'd from thee,
For nimble thought can jump both sea and land,
As soon as think the place where he would be.
But ah! thought kills me, that I am not thought,
To leap large lengths of miles when thou art gone,
But that, so much of earth and water wrought,
I must attend time's leisure with my moan;
 Receiving nought by elements so slow
 But heavy tears, badges of either's woe:

### XLV.

The other two, slight air and purging fire,
Are both with thee, wherever I abide;
The first my thought, the other my desire,
These present-absent with swift motion slide.
For when these quicker elements are gone
In tender embassy of love to thee,
My life, being made of four, with two alone
Sinks down to death, oppress'd with melancholy;
Until life's composition be recur'd
By those swift messengers return'd from thee,
Who even but now come back again, assur'd
Of thy fair health, recounting it to me:
 This told, I joy; but then no longer glad,
 I send them back again, and straight grow sad.

### XLVI.

Mine eye and heart are at a mortal war,
How to divide the conquest of thy sight;
Mine eye my heart thy picture's sight would bar,
My heart mine eye the freedom of that right.

My heart doth plead that thou in him dost
lie,
(A closet never pierc'd with crystal eyes,)
But the defendant doth that plea deny,
And says in him thy fair appearance lies.
To 'cide this title is impannelled
A quest of thoughts, all tenants to the heart;
And by their verdict is determined
The clear eye's moiety, and the dear heart's
part:
  As thus; mine eye's due is thine outward
  part,
  And my heart's right thine inward love of
  heart.

### XLVII.

Betwixt mine eye and heart a league is took,
And each doth good turns now unto the
other:
When that mine eye is famish'd for a look,
Or heart in love with sighs himself doth
smother,
With my love's picture then my eye doth
feast,
And to the painted banquet bids my heart;
Another time mine eye is my heart's guest,
And in his thoughts of love doth share a
part:
So, either by thy picture or my love,
Thyself away art present still with me;
For thou not farther than my thoughts canst
move,
And I am still with them, and they with
thee;
  Or if they sleep, thy picture in my sight
  Awakes my heart to heart's and eye's de-
  light.

### XLVIII.

How careful was I when I took my way,
Each trifle under truest bars to thrust,
That, to my use, it might unused stay
From hands of falsehood, in sure wards of
trust!
But thou, to whom my jewels trifles are,
Most worthy comfort, now my greatest
grief,
Thou, best of dearest, and mine only care,
Art left the prey of every vulgar thief.
Thee have I not lock'd up in any chest,
Save where thou art not, though I feel thou
art,
Within the gentle closure of my breast,
From whence at pleasure thou mayst come
and part;
  And even thence thou wilt be stolen I fear,
  For truth proves thievish for a prize so
  dear.

### XLIX.

Against that time, if ever that time come,
When I shall see thee frown on my defects,
Whenas thy love hath cast his utmost sum,
Call'd to that audit by advis'd respects;
Against that time, when thou shalt strangely
pass,
And scarcely greet me with that sun, thine
eye,
When love, converted from the thing it was,
Shall reasons find of settled gravity;
Against that time do I ensconce me here
Within the knowledge of mine own desert,
And this my hand against myself uprear,
To guard the lawful reasons on thy part:
  To leave poor me thou hast the strength of
  laws,
  Since, why to love, I can allege no cause.

### L.

How heavy do I journey on the way,
When what I seek—my weary travel's end—
Doth teach that ease and that repose to say,
'Thus far the miles are measur'd from thy
friend!'
The beast that bears me, tired with my woe,
Plods dully on, to bear that weight in me,
As if by some instinct the wretch did know
His rider lov'd not speed, being made from
thee:
The bloody spur cannot provoke him on
That sometimes anger thrusts into his hide,
Which heavily he answers with a groan,
More sharp to me than spurring to his side;
  For that same groan doth put this in my
  mind,
  My grief lies onward, and my joy behind.

### LI.

Thus can my love excuse the slow offence
Of my dull bearer, when from thee I speed:
From where thou art why should I haste me
thence?
Till I return, of posting is no need.
O what excuse will my poor beast then find,
When swift extremity can seem but slow?
Then should I spur, though mounted on the
wind;
In winged speed no motion shall I know:
Then can no horse with my desire keep pace;
Therefore desire, of perfect'st love being
made,
Shall neigh (no dull flesh) in his fiery race;
But love, for love, thus shall excuse my jade;
  Since from thee going he went wilful slow,
  Towards thee I'll run, and give him leave
  to go.

### LII.

So am I as the rich, whose blessed key
Can bring him to his sweet up-locked treas-
ure,
The which he will not every hour survey,
For blunting the fine point of seldom pleas-
ure.
Therefore are feasts so solemn and so rare,
Since seldom coming, in the long year set,

Like stones of worth they thinly placed are,
Or captain jewels in the carcanet.
So is the time that keeps you, as my chest,
Or as the wardrobe which the robe doth hide,
To make some special instant special-blest,
By new unfolding his imprison'd pride.
  Blessed are you, whose worthiness gives
    scope,
  Being had, to triumph, being lack'd, to
    hope.

### LIII.

What is your substance, whereof are you
    made,
That millions of strange shadows on you
    tend?
Since every one hath, every one, one's shade,
And you, but one, can every shadow lend.
Describe Adonis, and the counterfeit
Is poorly imitated after you;
On Helen's cheek all art of beauty set,
And you in Grecian tires are painted new;
Speak of the spring, and foison of the year;
The one doth shadow of your beauty show,
The other as your bounty doth appear,
And you in every blessed shape we know.
  In all external grace you have some part,
  But you like none, none you, for constant
    heart.

### LIV.

O how much more doth beauty beauteous
    seem,
By that sweet ornament which truth doth
    give!
The rose looks fair, but fairer we it deem
For that sweet odour which doth in it live.
The canker-blooms have full as deep a dye
As the perfumed tincture of the roses,
Hang on such thorns, and play as wantonly
When summer's breath their masked buds
    discloses:
But, for their virtue only is their show,
They live unwoo'd, and unrespected fade;
Die to themselves. Sweet roses do not so;
Of their sweet deaths are sweetest odours
    made:
  And so of you, beauteous and lovely
    youth,
  When that shall fade, by verse distils your
    truth.

### LV.

Not marble, nor the gilded monuments
Of princes, shall outlive this powerful rhyme;
But you shall shine more bright in these
    contents
Than unswept stone, besmear'd with sluttish
    time.
When wasteful war shall statues overturn,
And broils root out the work of masonry,
Nor Mars his sword nor war's quick fire
    shall burn

The living record of your memory.
'Gainst death and all-oblivious enmity
Shall you pace forth; your praise shall still
    find room,
Even in the eyes of all posterity
That wear this world out to the ending
    doom.
  So, till the judgment that yourself arise,
  You live in this, and dwell in lovers' eyes.

### LVI.

Sweet love, renew thy force; be it not said,
Thy edge should blunter be than appetite,
Which but to-day by feeding is allay'd,
To-morrow sharpen'd in his former might:
So, love, be thou; although to-day thou fill
Thy hungry eyes, even till they wink with
    fulness,
To-morrow see again, and do not kill
The spirit of love with a perpetual dulness.
Let this sad interim like the ocean be
Which parts the shore, where two contract-
    ed-new
Come daily to the banks, that, when they see
Return of love, more blest may be the view;
  Or call it winter, which, being full of care,
  Makes summer's welcome thrice more
    wish'd, more rare.

### LVII.

Being your slave, what should I do but tend
Upon the hours and times of your desire?
I have no precious time at all to spend,
Nor services to do, till you require.
Nor dare I chide the world-without-end
    hour,
Whilst I, my sovereign, watch the clock for
    you,
Nor think the bitterness of absence sour,
When you have bid your servant once adieu;
Nor dare I question with my jealous thought
Where you may be, or your affairs suppose,
But, like a sad slave, stay and think of
    nought,
Save, where you are how happy you make
    those:
  So true a fool is love, that in your will
  (Though you do anything) he thinks no
    ill.

### LVIII.

That God forbid, that made me first your
    slave,
I should in thought control your times of
    pleasure,
Or at your hand the account of hours to
    crave,
Being your vassal, bound to stay your lei-
    sure!
O, let me suffer (being at your beck)
The imprison'd absence of your liberty,
And patience, tame to sufferance, bide each
    check

Without accusing you of injury.
Be where you list; your charter is so strong,
That you yourself may privilege your time:
Do what you will, to you it doth belong
Yourself to pardon of self-doing crime.
  I am to wait, though waiting so be hell;
  Not blame your pleasure, be it ill or well.

### LIX.

If there be nothing new, but that which is
Hath been before, how are our brains be-
    guil'd,
Which labouring for invention bear amiss
The second burthen of a former child!
O, that record could with a backward look,
Even of five hundred courses of the sun,
Show me your image in some antique book,
Since mind at first in character was done!
That I might see what the old world could
    say
To this composed wonder of your frame;
Whether we are mended, or whe'r better
    they,
Or whether revolution be the same.
  O! sure I am, the wits of former days
  To subjects worse have given admiring
    praise.

### LX.

Like as the waves make towards the pebbled
    shore,
So do our minutes hasten to their end;
Each changing place with that which goes
    before.
In sequent toil all forwards do contend.
Nativity, once in the main of light,
Crawls to maturity, wherewith being
    crown'd,
Crooked eclipses 'gainst his glory fight,
And Time, that gave, doth now his gift con-
    found.
Time doth transfix the flourish set on youth,
And delves the parallels in beauty's brow;
Feeds on the rarities of nature's truth,
And nothing stands but for his scythe to
    mow.
  And yet, to times in hope, my verse shall
    stand,
  Praising thy worth, despite his cruel hand.

### LXI.

Is it thy will thy image should keep open
My heavy eyelids to the weary night?
Dost thou desire my slumbers should be
    broken,
While shadows, like to thee, do mock my
    sight?
Is it thy spirit that thou send'st from thee
So far from home, into my deeds to pry;
To find out shames and idle hours in me,
The scope and tenor of thy jealousy?
O no! thy love, though much, is not so
    great;

It is my love that keeps mine eye awake;
Mine own true love that doth my rest defeat,
To play the watchman ever for thy sake:
  For thee watch I, whilst thou dost wake
    elsewhere,
  From me far off, with others all-too-near.

### LXII.

Sin of self-love possesseth all mine eye,
And all my soul, and all my every part;
And for this sin there is no remedy,
It is so grounded inward in my heart.
Methinks no face so gracious is as mine,
No shape so true, no truth of such account,
And for myself mine own worth to define,
As I all other in all worths surmount.
But when my glass shows me myself indeed,
Beated and chopp'd with tann'd antiquity,
Mine own self-love quite contrary I read,
Self so self-loving were iniquity.
  'Tis thee (myself) that for myself I praise,
  Painting my age with beauty of thy days.

### LXIII.

Against my love shall be, as I am now,
With Time's injurious hand crush'd and o'er-
    worn;
When hours have drain'd his blood, and fill'd
    his brow
With lines and wrinkles; when his youthful
    morn
Hath travell'd on to age's steepy night;
And all those beauties, whereof now he's
    king,
Are vanishing or vanish'd out of sight,
Stealing away the treasure of his spring;
For such a time do I now fortify
Against confounding age's cruel knife,
That he shall never cut from memory
My sweet love's beauty, though my lover's
    life.
  His beauty shall in these black lines be
    seen,
  And they shall live, and he in them, still
    green.

### LXIV.

When I have seen by Time's fell hand de-
    fac'd
The rich-proud cost of outworn buried age;
When sometime lofty towers I see down-
    ras'd,
And brass eternal, slave to mortal rage;
When I have seen the hungry ocean gain
Advantage on the kingdom of the shore,
And the firm soil win of the wat'ry main,
Increasing store with loss, and loss with
    store;
When I have seen such interchange of state,
Or state itself confounded to decay;
Ruin hath taught me thus to ruminate—
That Time will come and take my love
    away.

This thought is as a death, which cannot
choose
But weep to have that which it fears to
lose.

### LXV.

Since brass, nor stone, nor earth, nor bound-
less sea,
But sad mortality o'ersways their power,
How with this rage shall beauty hold a plea,
Whose action is no stronger than a flower?
O, how shall summer's honey breath hold
out
Against the wreckful siege of battering days,
When rocks impregnable are not so stout,
Nor gates of steel so strong, but time decays?
O fearful meditation! where, alack!
Shall Time's best jewel from Time's chest lie
hid?
Or what strong hand can hold his swift foot
back?
Or who his spoil of beauty can forbid?
  O none, unless this miracle have might,
  That in black ink my love may still shine
  bright.

### LXVI.

Tir'd with all these, for restful death I cry,—
As, to behold desert a beggar born,
And needy nothing trimm'd in jollity,
And purest faith unhappily forsworn,
And gilded honour shamefully misplac'd,
And maiden virtue rudely strumpeted,
And right perfection wrongfully disgrac'd,
And strength by limping sway disabled,
And art made tongue-tied by authority,
And folly (doctor-like) controlling skill,
And simple truth miscall'd simplicity,
And captive good attending captain ill:
  Tir'd with all these, from these would I be
  gone,
  Save that, to die, I leave my love alone.

### LXVII.

Ah! wherefore with infection should he live,
And with his presence grace impiety,
That sin by him advantage should achieve,
And lace itself with his society?
Why should false painting imitate his cheek,
And steal dead seeing of his living hue?
Why should poor beauty indirectly seek
Roses of shadow, since his rose is true?
Why should he live now Nature bankrupt is,
Beggar'd of blood to blush through lively
veins?
For she hath no exchequer now but his,
And, proud of many, lives upon his gains.
  O, him she stores, to show what wealth
  she had
  In days long since, before these last so bad.

### LXVIII.

Thus is his cheek the map of days outworn,

When beauty liv'd and died as flowers do
now,
Before these bastard signs of fair were born,
Or durst inhabit on a living brow;
Before the golden tresses of the dead,
The right of sepulchres, were shorn away,
To live a second life on second head,
Ere beauty's dead fleece made another gay:
In him those holy antique hours are seen,
Without all ornament, itself, and true,
Making no summer of another's green,
Robbing no old to dress his beauty new;
  And him as for a map doth Nature store,
  To show false Art what beauty was of
  yore.

### LXIX.

Those parts of thee that the world's eye doth
view
Want nothing that the thought of hearts can
mend:
All tongues (the voice of souls) give thee
that due,
Uttering bare truth, even so as foes com-
mend.
Thine outward thus with outward praise is
crown'd;
But those same tongues that give thee so
thine own,
In other accents do this praise confound,
By seeing farther than the eye hath shown.
They look into the beauty of thy mind,
And that, in guess, they measure by thy
deeds;
Then (churls) their thoughts, although their
eyes were kind,
To thy fair flower add the rank smell of
weeds:
  But why thy odour matcheth not thy
  show,
  The solve is this,—that thou dost com-
  mon grow.

### LXX.

That thou art blam'd shall not be thy defect.
For slander's mark was ever yet the fair;
The ornament of beauty is suspect,
A crow that flies in heaven's sweetest air.
So thou be good, slander doth but approve
Thy worth the greater, being woo'd of time;
For canker vice the sweetest buds doth love,
And thou present'st a pure unstained prime.
Thou hast pass'd by the ambush of young
days,
Either not assail'd, or victor being charg'd;
Yet this thy praise cannot be so thy praise,
To tie up envy, evermore enlarg'd:
  If some suspect of ill mask'd not thy show,
  Then thou alone kingdoms of hearts
  shouldst owe:

### LXXI.

No longer mourn for me when I am dead

Than you shall hear the surly sullen bell
Give warning to the world that I am fled
From this vile world, with vilest worms to dwell:
Nay, if you read this line, remember not
The hand that writ it; for I love you so,
That I in your sweet thoughts would be forgot,
If thinking on me then should make you woe.
O, if (I say) you look upon this verse,
When I perhaps compounded am with clay,
Do not so much as my poor name rehearse;
But let your love even with my life decay:
  Lest the wise world should look into your moan,
  And mock you with me after I am gone.

### LXXII.

O, lest the world should task you to recite
What merit liv'd in me, that you should love
After my death,—dear love, forget me quite,
For you in me can nothing worthy prove;
Unless you would devise some virtuous lie,
To do more for me than mine own desert,
And hang more praise upon deceased I
Than niggard truth would willingly impart:
O, lest your true love may seem false in this,
That you for love speak well of me untrue,
My name be buried where my body is,
And live no more to shame nor me nor you.
  For I am sham'd by that which I bring forth,
  And so should you, to love things nothing worth.

### LXXIII.

That time of year thou mayst in me behold
When yellow leaves, or none, or few, do hang
Upon those boughs which shake against the cold,
Bare ruin'd choirs, where late the sweet birds sang.
In me thou seest the twilight of such day
As after sunset fadeth in the west,
Which by and by black night doth take away,
Death's second self, that seals up all in rest.
In me thou seest the glowing of such fire,
That on the ashes of his youth doth lie,
As the death-bed whereon it must expire,
Consum'd with that which it was nourish'd by.
  This thou perceiv'st which makes thy love more strong,
  To love that well which thou must leave ere long:

### LXXIV.

But be contented: when that fell arrest
Without all bail shall carry me away,
My life hath in this line some interest,
Which for memorial still with thee shall stay.

When thou reviewest this, thou dost review
The very part was consecrate to thee.
The earth can have but earth, which is his due;
My spirit is thine, the better part of me:
So then thou hast but lost the dregs of life,
The prey of worms, my body being dead;
The coward conquest of a wretch's knife,
Too base of thee to be remembered.
  The worth of that, is that which it contains,
  And that is this, and this with thee remains.

### LXXV.

So are you to my thoughts, as food to life,
Or as sweet-season'd showers are to the ground,
And for the peace of you I hold such strife
As 'twixt a miser and his wealth is found:
Now proud as an enjoyer, and anon
Doubting the filching age will steal his treasure;
Now counting best to be with you alone,
Then better'd that the world may see my pleasure:
Sometime all full with feasting on your sight,
And by and by clean starved for a look;
Possessing or pursuing no delight,
Save what is had or must from you be took.
  Thus do I pine and surfeit day by day.
  Or gluttoning on all, or all away.

### LXXVI.

Why is my verse so barren of new pride?
So far from variation or quick change?
Why, with the time, do I not glance aside
To new-found methods and to compounds strange?
Why write I still all one, ever the same,
And keep invention in a noted weed,
That every word doth almost tell my name,
Showing their birth, and where they did proceed?
O know, sweet love, I always write of you,
And you and love are still my argument;
So all my best is dressing old words new,
Spending again what is already spent;
  For as the sun is daily new and old,
  So is my love still telling what is told.

### LXXVII.

Thy glass will show thee how thy beauties wear,
Thy dial how thy precious minutes waste;
The vacant leaves thy mind's imprint will bear,
And of this book this learning mayst thou taste.
The wrinkles which thy glass will truly show,
Of mouthed graves will give thee memory;
Thou by thy dial's shady stealth mayst know
Time's thievish progress to eternity.

Look what thy memory cannot contain,
Commit to these waste blanks, and thou
    shalt find
Those children nurs'd, deliver'd from thy
    brain,
To take a new acquaintance of thy mind.
  These offices, so oft as thou wilt look,
  Shall profit thee, and much enrich thy
    book.

### LXXVIII.

So oft have I invok'd thee for my muse,
And found such fair assistance in my verse,
As every alien pen hath got my use,
And under thee their poesy disperse.
Thine eyes, that taught the dumb on high to
    sing,
And heavy ignorance aloft to fly,
Have added feathers to the learned's wing,
And given grace a double majesty.
Yet be most proud of that which I compile,
Whose influence is thine, and born of thee:
In others' works thou dost but mend the
    style,
And arts with thy sweet graces graced be;
  But thou art all my art, and dost advance
  As high as learning my rude ignorance.

### LXXIX.

Whilst I alone did call upon thy aid,
My verse alone had all thy gentle grace;
But now my gracious numbers are decay'd,
And my sick muse doth give another place.
I grant, sweet love, thy lovely argument
Deserves the travail of a worthier pen;
Yet what of thee thy poet doth invent,
He robs thee of, and pays it thee again.
He lends thee virtue, and he stole that
    word
From thy behaviour; beauty doth he give,
And found it in thy cheek; he can afford
No praise to thee but what in thee doth live.
  Then thank him not for that which he
    doth say,
  Since what he owes thee thou thyself dost
    pay.

### LXXX.

O, how faint when I of you do write,
Knowing a better spirit doth use your name,
And in the praise thereof spends all his
    might,
To make me tongue-tied, speaking of your
    fame!
But since your worth (wide as the ocean is)
The humble as the proudest sail doth bear,
My saucy bark, inferior far to his,
On your broad main doth wilfully appear.
Your shallowest help will hold me up afloat,
Whilst he upon your soundless deep doth
    ride;
Or, being wreck'd, I am a worthless boat,
He of tall building, and of goodly pride:

Then if he thrive, and I be cast away,
The worst was this;—my love was my de-
    cay.

### LXXXI.

Or I shall live your epitaph to make,
Or you survive when I in earth am rotten;
From hence your memory death cannot take,
Although in me each part will be forgotten.
Your name from hence immortal life shall
    have,              [die:
Though I, once gone, to all the world must
The earth can yield me but a common grave,
When you entombed in men's eyes shall lie.
Your monument shall be my gentle verse,
Which eyes not yet created shall o'er-read;
And tongues to be, your being shall re-
    hearse,
When all the breathers of this world are
    dead;
  You still shall live (such virtue hath my
    pen)
  Where breath most breathes,—even in the
    mouths of men.

### LXXXII.

I grant thou wert not married to my muse,
And therefore mayst without attaint o'erlook
The dedicated words which writers use
Of their fair subject, blessing every book.
Thou art as fair in knowledge as in hue,
Finding thy worth a limit past my praise;
And therefore art enforc'd to seek anew
Some fresher stamp of the time-bettering
    days.
And do so, love; yet when they have devis'd
What strained touches rhetoric can lend,
Thou truly fair wert truly sympathiz'd
In true plain words, by thy true-telling
    friend,
  And their gross painting might be better
    us'd
  Where cheeks need blood; in thee it is
    abus'd.

### LXXXIII.

I never saw that you did painting need,
And therefore to your fair no painting set.
I found, or thought I found, you did exceed
The barren tender of a poet's debt:
And therefore have I slept in your report
That you yourself, being extant, well might
    show
How far a modern quill doth come too short,
Speaking of worth, what worth in you doth
    grow.
This silence for my sin you did impute,
Which shall be most my glory, being dumb;
For I impair not beauty being mute,
When others would give life, and bring a
    tomb,
  There lives more life in one of your fair eyes
  Than both your poets can in praise devise.

### LXXXIV.

Who is it that says most? which can say
    more
Than this rich praise,—that you alone are
    you?
In whose confine immured is the store
Which should example where your equal
    grew?
Lean penury within that pen doth dwell,
That to his subject lends not some small
    glory;
But he that writes of you, if he can tell
That you are you, so dignifies his story,
Let him but copy what in you is writ,
Not making worse what nature made so
    clear,
And such a counterpart shall fame his wit,
Making his style admired everywhere.
    You to your beauteous blessings add a
        curse,
    Being fond on praise, which makes your
        praises worse.

### LXXXV.

My tongue-tied muse in manners holds her
    still,
While comments of your praise, richly com-
    pil'd,
Reserve their character with golden quill,
And precious phrase by all the muses fil'd.
I think good thoughts, while others write
    good words,
And, like unlettered clerk, still cry 'Amen'
To every hymn that able spirit affords,
In polish'd form of well-refined pen.
Hearing you prais'd, I say, ' 'Tis so, 'tis true,'
And to the most of praise add something
    more;
But that is in my thought, whose love to
    you,
Though words come hindmost, holds his rank
    before.
    Then others for the breath of words re-
        spect,
    Me for my dumb thoughts, speaking in
        effect.

### LXXXVI.

Was it the proud full sail of his great verse,
Bound for the prize of all-too-precious you,
That did my ripe thoughts in my brain in-
    hearse,
Making their tomb the womb wherein they
    grew?
Was it his spirit, by spirits taught to write
Above a mortal pitch, that struck me dead?
No, neither he, nor his compeers by night
Giving him aid, my verse astonished.
He, nor that affable familiar ghost
Which nightly gulls him with intelligence,
As victors, of my silence cannnot boast;
I was not sick of any fear from thence.
But when your countenance fil'd up his
    line,
Then lack'd I matter; that enfeebled mine.

### LXXXVII.

Farewell! thou art too dear for my possess-
    ing,
And like enough thou know'st thy estimate:
The charter of thy worth gives thee releas-
    ing;
My bonds in thee are all determinate.
For how do I hold thee but by thy grant-
    ing?
And for that riches where is my deserving?
The cause of this fair gift in me is wanting,
And so my patent back again is swerving.
Thyself thou gav'st, thy own worth then not
    knowing,
Or me, to whom thou gav'st it, else mistak-
    ing;
So thy great gift, upon misprision growing,
Comes home again, on better judgment mak-
    ing.
    Thus have I had thee, as a dream doth
        flatter,
    In sleep a king, but, waking, no such
        matter.

### LXXXVIII.

When thou shalt be dispos'd to set me light,
And place my merit in the eye of scorn,
Upon thy side against myself I'll fight,
And prove thee virtuous, though thou art
    forsworn:
With mine own weakness being best ac-
    quainted,
Upon thy part I can set down a story
Of faults conceal'd, wherein I am attainted;
That thou, in losing me, shall win much
    glory:
And I by this will be a gainer too;
For bending all my loving thoughts on thee,
The injuries that to myself I do,
Doing thee vantage, double-vantage me.
    Such is my love, to thee I so belong,
    That for thy right myself will bear all
        wrong.

### LXXXIX.

Say that thou didst forsake me for some
    fault,
And I will comment upon that offence:
Speak of my lameness, and I straight will
    halt;
Against thy reasons making no defence.
Thou canst not, love, disgrace me half so ill,
To set a form upon desired change,
As I'll myself disgrace: knowing thy will,
I will acquaintance strangle, and look
    strange;
Be absent from thy walks; and in my
    tongue

Thy sweet-beloved name no more shall
    dwell;
Lest I (too much profane) should do it
    wrong,
And haply of our old acquaintance tell.
    For thee, against myself I'll vow debate,
    For I must ne'er love him whom thou dost
      hate.

### XC.

Then hate me when thou wilt; if ever, now;
Now while the world is bent my deeds to
    cross,
Join with the spite of fortune, make me bow,
And do not drop in for an after-loss:
Ah! do not, when my heart hath scap'd this
    sorrow,
Come in the rearward of a conquer'd woe;
Give not a windy night a rainy morrow,
To linger out a purpos'd overthrow.
If thou wilt leave me, do not leave me last,
When other petty griefs have done their
    spite,
But in the onset come; so shall I taste
At first the very worst of fortune's might;
    And other strains of woe, which now seem
      woe,
    Compar'd with loss of thee will not seem
      so.

### XCI.

Some glory in their birth, some in their skill,
Some in their wealth, some in their body's
    force;
Some in their garments, though new-fangled
    ill;
Some in their hawks and hounds, some in
    their horse;
And every humour hath his adjunct pleasure,
Wherein it finds a joy above the rest;
But these particulars are not my measure,
All these I better in one general best.
Thy love is better than high birth to me,
Richer than wealth, prouder than garments'
    cost,
Of more delight than hawks and horses be;
And, having thee, of all men's pride I boast.
    Wretched in this alone, that thou mayst
      take
    All this away, and me most wretched
      make.

### XCII.

But do thy worst to steal thyself away,
For term of life thou art assured mine;
And life no longer than thy love will stay,
For it depends upon that love of thine.
Then need I not to fear the worst of wrongs,
When in the least of them my life hath end.
I see a better state to me belongs
Than that which on thy humour doth de-
    pend;

Thou canst not vex me with inconstant
    mind,
Since that my life on thy revolt doth lie.
O what a happy title do I find,
Happy to have thy love, happy to die!
    But what's so blessed-fair that fears no
      blot?—
    Thou mayst be false, and yet I know it
      not:

### XCIII.

So shall I live, supposing thou art true,
Like a deceived husband; so love's face
May still seem love to me, though alter'd
    new;
Thy looks with me, thy heart in other place:
For there can live no hatred in thine eye,
Therefore in that I cannot know thy change.
In many's looks the false heart's history
Is writ, in moods and frowns and wrinkles
    strange;
But heaven in thy creation did decree
That in thy face sweet love should ever
    dwell;
Whate'er thy thoughts or thy heart's work-
    ings be,
Thy looks should nothing thence but sweet-
    ness tell.
    How like Eve's apple doth thy beauty
      grow,
    If thy sweet virtue answer not thy show?

### XCIV.

They that have power to hurt and will do
    none,
That do not do the thing they most do show,
Who, moving others, are themselves as stone,
Unmoved, cold, and to temptation slow;
They rightly do inherit Heaven's graces,
And husband nature's riches from expense;
They are the lords and owners of their faces,
Others but stewards of their excellence.
The summer's flower is to the summer sweet
Though to itself it only live and die;
But if that flower with base infection meet,
The basest weed outbraves his dignity:
    For sweetest things turn sourest by their
      deeds:
    Lilies that fester smell far worse than
      weeds.

### XCV.

How sweet and lovely dost thou make the
    shame,
Which, like a canker in the fragrant rose,
Doth spot the beauty of thy budding name!
O, in what sweets dost thou thy sins enclose!
That tongue that tells the story of thy days,
Making lascivious comments on thy sport,
Cannot dispraise but in a kind of praise:
Naming thy name blesses an ill report.
O, what a mansion have those vices got
Which for their habitation chose cut thee!

Where beauty's veil doth cover every blot,
And all things turn to fair, that eyes can see!
  Take heed, dear heart, of this large privi-
    lege;
  The hardest knife ill-used doth lose his
    edge.

### XCVI.

Some say thy fault is youth, some wanton-
    ness;
Some say thy grace is youth and gentle
    sport;
Both grace and faults are lov'd of more and
    less:
Thou mak'st faults graces that to thee resort.
As on the finger of a throned queen
The basest jewel will be well esteem'd;
So are those errors that in thee are seen
To truths translated, and for true things
    deem'd.
How many lambs might the stern wolf be-
    tray,
If like a lamb he could his looks translate!
How many gazers mightst thou lead away,
If thou wouldst use the strength of all thy
    state!
  But do not so; I love thee in such sort,
  As, thou being mine, mine is thy good re-
    port.

### XCVII.

How like a winter hath my absence been.
From thee, the pleasure of the fleeting year!
What freezings have I felt, what dark days
    seen!
What old December's bareness everywhere!
And yet this time remov'd was summer's
    time,
The teeming autumn, big with rich increase,
Bearing the wanton burden of the prime,
Like widow'd wombs after their lords' de-
    cease;
Yet this abundant issue seem'd to me
But hope of orphans, and unfather'd fruit;
For summer and his pleasures wait on thee,
And, thou away, the very birds are mute;
  Or, if they sing, 'tis with so dull a cheer,
  That leaves look pale, dreading the win-
    ter's near.

### XCVIII.

From you have I been absent in the spring.
When proud-pied April, dress'd in all his
    trim,
Hath put a spirit of youth in everything,
That heavy Saturn laugh'd and leap'd with
    him.
Yet nor the lays of birds, nor the sweet smell
Of different flowers in odour and in hue,
Could make me any summer's story tell,
Or from their proud lap pluck them where
    they grew;
Nor did I wonder at the lilies white,

Nor praise the deep vermilion in the rose;
They were but sweet, but figures of delight,
Drawn after you, you pattern of all those.
  Yet seem'd it winter still, and you, away,
  As with your shadow I with these did
    play:

### XCIX.

The forward violet thus did I chide;—
Sweet thief, whence didst thou steal thy
    sweet that smells,
If not from my love's breath? The purple
    pride
Which on thy soft cheek for complexion
    dwells,
In my love's veins thou hast too grossly dy'd,
The lily I condemned for thy hand,
And buds of marjoram had stolen thy hair:
The roses fearfully on thorns did stand,
One blushing shame, another white despair;
A third, nor red nor white, had stolen of
    both,
And to his robbery had annex'd thy breath;
But for his theft, in pride of all his growth
A vengeful canker eat him up to death.
  More flowers I noted, yet I none could see,
  But sweet or colour it had stolen from
    thee.

### C.

Where art thou, Muse, that thou forgett'st
    so long
To speak of that which gives thee all thy
    might?
Spend'st thou thy fury on some worthless
    song,
Darkening thy power, to lend base subjects
    light?
Return, forgetful Muse, and straight redeem
In gentle numbers time so idly spent;
Sing to the ear that doth thy lays esteem,
And gives thy pen both skill and argument.
Rise; resty Muse, my love's sweet face sur-
    vey,
If Time have any wrinkle graven there;
If any, be a satire to decay,
And make Time's spoils despised everywhere.
  Give my love fame faster than Time wastes
    life;
  So thou prevent'st his scythe and crooked
    knife.

### CI.

O truant Muse, what shall be thy amends
For thy neglect of truth in beauty dy'd?
Both truth and beauty on my love depends;
So dost thou too, and therein dignified.
Make answer, Muse: wilt thou not haply say,
'Truth needs no colour with his colour fix'd,
Beauty no pencil, beauty's truth to lay;
But best is best, if never intermix'd?'—
Because he needs no praise, wilt thou be
    dumb?

Excuse not silence so; for it lies in thee
To make him much outlive a gilded tomb,
And to be prais'd of ages yet to be.
  Then do thy office, Muse; I teach thee how
  To make him seem long hence as he shows
    now.

### CII.

My love is strengthen'd, though more weak
    in seeming;
I love not less, though less the show appear;
That love is merchandiz'd whose rich esteem-
    ing
The owner's tongue doth publish everywhere.
Our love was new, and then but in the
    spring,
When I was wont to greet it with my lays;
As Philomel in summer's front doth sing,
And stops her pipe in growth of riper days:
Not that the summer is less pleasant now
Than when her mournful hymns did hush the
    night,
But that wild music burthens every bough,
And sweets grown common lose their dear
    delight.
  Therefore, like her, I sometime hold my
    tongue,
  Because I would not dull you with my
    song.

### CIII.

Alack! what poverty my Muse brings forth,
That having such a scope to show her pride,
The argument, all bare, is of more worth,
Than when it hath my added praise beside.
O blame me not if I no more can write!
Look in your glass, and there appears a face
That over-goes my blunt invention quite,
Dulling my lines, and doing me disgrace.
Were it not sinful, then, striving to mend,
To mar the subject that before was well?
For to no other pass my verses tend,
Than of your graces and your gifts to tell;
  And more, much more, than in my verse
    can sit,
  Your own glass shows you, when you look
    in it.

### CIV.

To me, fair friend, you never can be old,
For as you were when first your eye I eyed,
Such seems your beauty still. Three winters'
    cold
Have from the forests shook three summers'
    pride;
Three beauteous springs to yellow autumn
    turn'd
In process of the seasons have I seen;
Three April perfumes in three hot Junes
    burn'd,
Since first I saw you fresh, which yet are
    green.
Ah! yet doth beauty, like a dial-hand,

Steal from his figure, and no pace perceiv'd;
So your sweet hue, which methinks still doth
    stand,
Hath motion, and mine eye may be deceiv'd.
  For fear of which, hear this, thou age un-
    bred,
  Ere you were born, was beauty's summer
    dead.

### CV.

Let not my love be call'd idolatry,
Nor my beloved as an idol show,
Since all alike my songs and praises be,
To one, of one, still such, and ever so.
Kind is my love to-day, to-morrow kind,
Still constant in a wondrous excellence;
Therefore my verse, to constancy confin'd,
One thing expressing, leaves out difference.
Fair, kind, and true, is all my argument,
Fair, kind, and true, varying to other words;
And in this change is my invention spent,
Three themes in one, which wondrous scope
    affords.
  Fair, kind, and true, have often liv'd alone,
  Which three, till now, never kept seat in
    one.

### CVI.

When in the chronicle of wasted time
I see descriptions of the fairest wights,
And beauty making beautiful old rhyme,
In praise of ladies dead and lovely knights,
Then in the blazon of sweet beauty's best,
Of hand, of foot, of lip, of eye, of brow,
I see their antique pen would have express'd
Even such a beauty as you master now.
So all their praises are but prophecies
Of this our time, all you prefiguring;
And, for they look'd but with divining eyes,
They had not skill enough your worth to
    sing:
  For we, which now behold these present
    days,
  Have eyes to wonder, but lack tongues to
    praise.

### CVII.

Not mine own fears, nor the prophetic soul
Of the wide world dreaming on things to
    come,
Can yet the lease of my true love control,
Suppos'd as forfeit to a confin'd doom.
The mortal moon hath her eclipse endur'd,
And the sad augurs mock their own presage;
Incertainties now crown themselves assur'd,
And peace proclaims olives of endless age.
Now with the drops of this most balmy time
My love looks fresh, and Death to me sub-
    scribes,
Since spite of him I'll live in this poor rhyme,
While he insults o'er dull and speechless
    tribes.

And thou in this shalt find thy monument,
When tyrants' crests and tombs of brass
   are spent.

### CVIII.

What's in the brain that ink may character,
Which hath not figur'd to thee my true
   spirit?
What's new to speak, what new to register,
That may express my love, or thy dear
   merit?
Nothing, sweet boy; but yet, like prayers di-
   vine,
I must each day say o'er the very same;
Counting no old thing old, thou mine, I
   thine.
Even as when first I hallow'd thy fair name.
So that eternal love in love's fresh case
Weighs not the dust and injury of age,
Nor gives to necessary wrinkles place,
But makes antiquity for aye his page;
   Finding the first conceit of love there bred,
   Where time and outward form would show
      it dead.

### CIX.

O, never say that I was false of heart,
Though absence seem'd my flame to qualify!
As easy might I from myself depart,
As from my soul, where in thy breast doth
   lie:
That is my home of love: if I have rang'd,
Like him that travels, I return again;
Just to the time, not with the time ex-
   chang'd,—
So that myself bring water for my stain.
Never believe, though in my nature reign'd
All frailties that besiege all kinds of blood,
That it could so preposterously be stain'd,
To leave for nothing all thy sum of good;
   For nothing this wide universe I call,
   Save thou, my rose; in it thou art my all.

### CX.

Alas, 'tis true, I have gone here and there,
And made myself a motley to the view,
Gor'd mine own thoughts, sold cheap what is
   most dear,
Made old offences of affections new.
Most true it is, that I have look'd on truth
Askance and strangely; but, by all above,
These blenches gave my heart another youth,
And worst essays prov'd thee my best of
   love.
Now all is done, save what shall have no
   end:
Mine appetite I never more will grind
On newer proof, to try an older friend,
A God in love, to whom I am confined.
   Then give me welcome, next my heaven the
     best,            [breast.
   Even to thy pure and most most loving

### CXI.

O, for my sake do you with Fortune chide,
The guilty goddess of my harmful deeds,
That did not better for my life provide,
Than public means, which public manners
   breeds.
Thence comes it that my name receives a
   brand,
And almost thence my nature is subdued
To what it works in, like the dyer's hand:
Pity me then, and wish I were renew'd;
Whilst, like a willing patient, I will drink
Potions of eysell, 'gainst my strong infection;
No bitterness that I will bitter think,
Nor double penance, to correct correction.
   Pity me then, dear friend, and I assure ye,
   Even that your pity is enough to cure me.

### CXII.

Your love and pity doth the impression fill
Which vulgar scandal stamp'd upon my
   brow;
For what care I who calls me well or ill,
So you o'ergreen my bad, my good allow?
You are my all-the-world, and I must strive
To know my shames and praises from your
   tongue;
None else to me, nor I to none alive,
That my steel'd sense or changes, right or
   wrong.
In so profound abysm I throw all care
Of other's voices, that my adder's sense
To critic and to flatterer stopped are.
Mark how with my neglect I do dispense;—
   You are so strongly in my purpose bred,
   That all the world besides methinks are
      dead.

### CXIII.

Since I left you, mine eye is in my mind;
And that which governs me to go about
Doth part his function, and is partly blind,
Seems seeing, but effectually is out;
For it no form delivers to the heart
Of bird, of flower, or shape, which it doth
   latch;
Of his quick objects hath the mind no part,
Nor his own vision holds what it doth catch;
For if it see the rud'st or gentlest sight,
The most sweet favour, or deformed'st crea-
   ture,
The mountain or the sea, the day or night,
The crow, or dove, it shapes them to your
   feature.
   Incapable of more, replete with you,
   My most true mind thus maketh mine
      untrue.

### CXIV.

Or whether doth my mind being crown'd
   with you,
Drink up the monarch's plague, this flattery,

Or whether shall I say mine eye saith true;
And that your love taught it this alchymy,
To make of monsters and things indigest
Such cherubins as your sweet self resemble,
Creating every bad a perfect best,
As fast as objects to his beams assemble?
O, 'tis the first; 'tis flattery in my seeing,
And my great mind most kingly drinks it up:
Mine eye well knows what with his gust is 'greeing,
And to his palate doth prepare the cup:
  If it be poison'd, 'tis the lesser sin
  That mine eye loves it, and doth first begin.

### CXV.

Those lines that I before have writ, do lie;
Even those that said I could not love you dearer;
Yet then my judgment knew no reason why
My most full flame should afterwards burn clearer.
But reckoning time, whose million'd accidents
Creep in 'twixt vows, and change decrees of kings,
Tan sacred beauty, blunt the sharp'st intents,
Divert strong minds to the course of altering things;
Alas! why, fearing of Time's tyranny,
Might I not then say, 'Now I love you best,'
When I was certain o'er incertainty,
Crowning the present, doubting of the rest?
  Love is a babe; then might I not say so,
  To give full growth to that which still doth grow?

### CXVI.

Let me not to the marriage of true minds
Admit impediments. Love is not love
Which alters when it alteration finds,
Or bends with the remover to remove:
O no; it is an ever-fixed mark,
That looks on tempests, and is never shaken;
It is the star to every wandering bark,
Whose worth's unknown, although his height be taken.
Love's not Time's fool, though rosy lips and cheeks
Within his bending sickle's compass come;
Love alters not with his brief hours and weeks,
But bears it out even to the edge of doom.
  If this be error, and upon me prov'd,
  I never writ, nor no man ever lov'd.

### CXVII.

Accuse me thus; that I have scanted all
Wherein I should your great deserts repay;
Forgot upon your dearest love to call,

Whereto all bonds do tie me day by day;
That I have frequent been with unknown minds,
And given to time your own dear-purchas'd right;
That I have hoisted sail to all the winds
Which should transport me farthest from your sight.
Book both my wilfulness and errors down,
And on just proof surmise accumulate,
Bring me within the level of your frown,
But shoot not at me in your waken'd hate:
  Since my appeal says, I did strive to prove
  The constancy and virtue of your love.

### CXVIII.

Like as, to make our appetites more keen,
With eager compounds we our palate urge;
As, to prevent our maladies unseen,
We sicken to shun sickness, when we purge;
Even so, being full of your ne'er-cloying sweetness,
To bitter sauces did I frame my feeding,
And, sick of welfare, found a kind of meetness
To be diseas'd, ere that there was true needing.
Thus policy in love, to anticipate
The ills that were not, grew to faults assured,
And brought to medicine a healthful state,
Which, rank of goodness, would by ill be cured.
  But thence I learn, and find the lesson true,
  Drugs poison him that so fell sick of you.

### CXIX.

What potions have I drunk of Siren tears,
Distill'd from limbecs foul as hell within,
Applying fears to hopes, and hopes to fears,
Still losing when I saw myself to win!
What wretched errors hath my heart committed,
Whilst it hath thought itself so blessed never!
How have mine eyes out of their spheres been fitted,
In the distraction of this madding fever!
O benefit of ill! now I find true
That better is by evil still made better;
And ruin'd love, when it is built anew,
Grows fairer than at first, more strong, far greater.
  So I return rebuk'd to my content,
  And gain by ill thrice more than I have spent.

### CXX.

That you were once unkind, befriends me now,
And for that sorrow, which I then did feel,
Needs must I under my transgression bow,

Unless my nerves were brass or hammer'd
  steel.
For if you were by my unkindness shaken,
As I by yours, you have pass'd a hell of
  time;
And I, a tyrant, have no leisure taken
To weigh how once I suffer'd in your crime.
O that our night of woe might have remem-
  ber'd
My deepest sense, how hard true sorrow
  hits,
And soon to you, as you to me, then ten-
  der'd
The humble salve which wounded bosoms
  fits!
    But that your trespass now becomes a
      fee;
    Mine ransoms yours, and yours must ran-
      som me.

### CXXI.

'Tis better to be vile than vile esteem'd,
When not to be receives reproach of being,
And the just pleasure lost, which is so
  deem'd
Not by our feeling, but by others' seeing.
For why should others' false adulterate eyes
Give salutation to my sportive blood?
Or on my frailties why are frailer spies,
Which in their wills count bad what I think
  good?
No.—I am that I am; and they that level
At my abuses, reckon up their own:
I may be straight, though they themselves
  be bevel;
By their rank thoughts my deeds must not
  be shown;
    Unless this general evil they maintain,—
    All men are bad, and in their badness
      reign.

### CXXII.

Thy gift, thy tables, are within my brain
Full character'd with lasting memory
Which shall above that idle rank remain,
Beyond all date, even to eternity:
Or at the least so long as brain and heart
Have faculty by nature to subsist;
Till each to raz'd oblivion yield his part
Of thee, thy record never can be miss'd.
That poor retention could not so much hold,
Nor need I tallies thy dear love to score;
Therefore to give them from me was I bold,
To trust those tables that receive thee more:
    To keep an adjunct to remember thee,
    Were to import forgetfulness in me.

### CXXIII.

No! Time, thou shalt not boast that I do
  change:
Thy pyramids built up with newer might
To me are nothing novel, nothing strange;
They are but dressings of a former sight.

Our dates are brief, and therefore we admire
What thou dost foist upon us that is old;
And rather make them born to our desire,
Than think that we before have heard them
  told.
Thy registers and thee I both defy,
Not wondering at the present nor the past;
For thy records and what we see do lie,
Made more or less by thy continual haste:
    This I do vow, and this shall ever be,
    I will be true, despite thy scythe and thee.

### CXXIV.

If my dear love were but the child of state,
It might for Fortune's bastard be unfath-
  er'd,
As subject to Time's love, or to Time's hate,
Weeds among weeds, or flowers with flowers
  gather'd.
No, it was builded far from accident;
It suffers not in smiling pomp, nor falls
Under the blow of thralled discontent,
Whereto the inviting time our fashion calls:
It fears not policy, that heretic,
Which works on leases of short-number'd
  hours,
But all alone stands hugely politic,
That it nor grows with heat, nor drowns
  with showers.
    To this I witness call the fools of time,
    Which die for goodness, who have liv'd
      for crime.

### CXXV.

Were it aught to me I bore the canopy,
With my extern the outward honouring,
Or laid great bases for eternity,
Which prove more short than waste or ruin-
  ing?
Have I not seen dwellers on form and favour
Lose all, and more, by paying too much
  rent,
For compound sweet foregoing simple
  savour,
Pitiful thrivers, in their gazing spent?
No;—let me be obsequious in thy heart,
And take thou my oblation, poor but free,
Which is not mix'd with seconds, knows no
  art,
But mutual render, only me for thee.
    Hence, thou suborn'd informer! a true
      soul,
    When most impeach'd, stands least in thy
      control.

### CXXVI.

O thou, my lovely boy, who in thy power
Dost hold Time's fickle glass, his sickle,
  hour;
Who hast by waning grown, and therein
  show'st
Thy lovers withering, as thy sweet self
  grow'st!

If Nature, sovereign mistress over wrack,
As thou goest onwards, still will pluck thee
back,
She keeps thee to this purpose, that her skill
May time disgrace, and wretched minutes
kill.
Yet fear her, O thou minion of her pleasure;
She may detain, but not still keep her treas-
ure:
  Her audit, though delay'd, answer'd must
  be,
  And her quietus is to render thee.

### CXXVII.

In the old age black was not counted fair,
Or if it were, it bore not beauty's name;
But now is black beauty's successive heir,
And beauty slander'd with a bastard shame:
For since each hand hath put on nature's
power,
Fairing the foul with art's false borrow'd
face,
Sweet beauty hath no name, no holy hour,
But is profan'd, if not lives in disgrace.
Therefore my mistress' eyes are raven black,
Her eyes so suited; and they mourners seem
At such, who, not born fair, no beauty lack,
Slandering creation with a false esteem:
  Yet so they mourn, becoming of their
  woe,
  That every tongue says, beauty should
  look so.

### CXXVIII.

How oft, when thou, my music, music
play'st,
Upon that blessed wood whose motion
sounds
With thy sweet fingers, when thou gently
sway'st
The wiry concord that mine ear confounds,
Do I envy those jacks, that nimble leap
To kiss the tender inward of thy hand,
Whilst my poor lips, which should that har-
vest reap,
At the wood's boldness by thee blushing
stand!
To be so tickled, they would change their
state
And situation with those dancing chips,
O'er whom thy fingers walk with gentle
gait,
Making dead wood more bless'd than living
lips.
  Since saucy jacks so happy are in this,
  Give them thy fingers, me thy lips to kiss.

### CXXIX.

The expense of spirit in a waste of shame
Is lust in action; and till action, lust
Is perjur'd, murderous, bloody, full of
blame,
Savage, extreme, rude, cruel, not to trust;

Enjoy'd no sooner, but despised straight;
Past reason hunted; and no sooner had,
Past reason hated, as a swallow'd bait,
On purpose laid to make the taker mad:
Mad in pursuit, and in possession so;
Had, having, and in quest to have, extreme;
A bliss in proof,—and prov'd, a very woe;
Before, a joy propos'd; behind, a dream:
  All this the world well knows; yet none
  knows well
  To shun the heaven that leads men to this
  hell.

### CXXX.

My mistress' eyes are nothing like the sun;
Coral is far more red than her lips' red:
If snow be white, why then her breasts are
dun;
If hairs be wires, black wires grow on her
head.
I have seen roses damask'd, red and white,
But no such roses see I in her cheeks;
And in some perfumes is there more delight
Than in the breath that from my mistress
reeks.
I love to hear her speak,—yet well I know
That music hath a far more pleasing sound;
I grant I never saw a goddess go,—
My mistress when she walks, treads on the
ground;
  And yet, by heaven, I think my love as
  rare
  As any she belied with false compare.

### CXXXI.

Thou art as tyrannous, so as thou art,
As those whose beauties proudly make them
cruel;
For well thou know'st to my dear doting
heart
Thou art the fairest and most precious
jewel,
Yet, in good faith, some say that thee be-
hold,
Thy face hath not the power to make love
groan:
To say they err, I dare not be so bold,
Although I swear it to myself alone,
And, to be sure that is not false I swear,
A thousand groans, but thinking on thy
face,
One on another's neck, do witness bear
Thy black is fairest in my judgment's place.
  In nothing art thou black, save in thy
  deeds,
  And thence this slander, as I think, pro-
  ceeds.

### CXXXII.

Thine eyes I love, and they, as pitying me,
Knowing thy heart torments me with dis-
dain,
Have put on black, and loving mourners be,

Looking with pretty ruth upon my pain.
And truly not the morning sun of heaven
Better becomes the grey cheeks of the east,
Nor that full star that ushers in the even
Doth half that glory to the sober west,
As those two mourning eyes become thy
face:
O, let it then as well beseem thy heart
To mourn for me, since mourning doth thee
grace,
And suit thy pity like in every part.
   Then will I swear beauty herself is black,
   And all they foul that thy complexion lack.

### CXXXIII.

Beshrew that heart that makes my heart to
groan       [me!
For that deep wound it gives my friend and
Is't not enough to torture me alone,
But slave to slavery my sweet'st friend must
be?
Me from myself thy cruel eye hath taken,
And my next self thou harder hast en-
gross'd;
Of him, myself, and thee, I am forsaken;
A torment thrice three-fold thus to be
cross'd.
Prison my heart in thy steel bosom's ward,
But then my friend's heart let my poor
heart bail;
Who e'er keeps me, let my heart be his
guard;
Thou canst not then use rigour in my goal:
   And yet thou wilt; for I, being pent in
thee
   Perforce am thine, and all that is in me.

### CXXXIV.

So now I have confess'd that he is thine,
And I myself am mortgag'd to thy will;
Myself I'll forfeit, so that other mine
Thou wilt restore, to be my comfort still:
But thou wilt not, nor he will not be free,
For thou art covetous, and he is kind;
He learn'd but, surety-like, to write for me,
Under that bond that him as fast doth bind.
The statute of thy beauty thou wilt take,
Thou usurer, that putt'st forth all to use,
And sue a friend, came debtor for my sake;
So him I lose through my unkind abuse.
   Him have I lost; thou hast both him and
me;
   He pays the whole, and yet am I not free.

### CXXXV.

Whoever hath her wish, thou hast thy will,
And will to boot, and will in over-plus;
More than enough am I that vex thee still,
To thy sweet will making addition thus.
Wilt thou, whose will is large and spacious,
Not once vouchsafe to hide my will in thine?
Shall will in others seem right gracious,
And in my will no fair acceptance shine?

The sea, all water, yet receives rain still,
And in abundance addeth to his store;
So thou, being rich in will, add to thy will
One will of mine, to make thy large will
more.
   Let no unkind, no fair beseechers kill;
   Think all but one, and me in that one
*Will.*

### CXXXVI.

If thy soul check thee that I come so near,
Swear to thy blind soul that I was thy
*Will,*
And will, thy soul knows, is admitted there;
Thus far for love, my love-suit, sweet, fulfil.
*Will* will fulfil the treasure of thy love,
Ay, fill it full with wills, and my will one,
In things of great receipt with ease we
prove;
Among a number one is reckon'd none.
Then in the number let me pass untold,
Though in thy stores' account I one must
be;
For nothing hold me, so it please thee hold
That nothing me, a something sweet to thee;
   Make but my name thy love, and love
that still,       [*Will.*
   And then thou lov'st me,—for my name is

### CXXXVII.

Thou blind fool, Love, what dost thou to
mine eyes,
That they behold, and see not what they
see?
They know what beauty is, see where it
lies,
Yet what the best is, take the worst to be.
If eyes, corrupt by over-partial looks,
Be anchor'd in the bay where all men ride,
Why of eyes' falsehood hast thou forged
hooks,
Whereto the judgment of my heart is tied?
Why should my heart think that a several
plot,
Which my heart knows the wide world's
common place?
Or mine eyes, seeing this, say this is not,
To put fair truth upon so foul a face?
   In things right true my heart and eyes
have err'd,       [transferr'd.
   And to this false plague are they now

### CXXXVIII.

When my love swears that she is made of
truth,
I do believe her, though I know she lies;
That she might think me some untutor'd
youth,
Unlearned in the world's false subtleties.
Thus vainly thinking that she thinks me
young,
Although she knows my days are past the
best,

Simply I credit her false-speaking tongue;
On both sides thus is simple truth supprest,
But wherefore says she not she is unjust?
And wherefore say not I that I am old?
O, love's best habit is in seeming trust,
And age in love loves not to have years
    told:
  Therefore I lie with her, and she with me,
  And in our faults by lies we flatter'd be.

### CXXXIX.

O, call not me to justify the wrong
That thy unkindness lays upon my heart;
Wound me not with thine eye, but with thy
    tongue;
Use power with power, and slay me not by
    art.
Tell me thou lov'st elsewhere; but in my
    sight,
Dear heart, forbear to glance thine eye
    aside.
What need'st thou wound with cunning,
    when thy might
Is more than my o'erpress'd defence can
    'bide?
Let me excuse thee: ah! my love well knows
Her pretty looks have been mine enemies;
And therefore from my face she turns my
    foes,
That they elsewhere might dart their in-
    juries:
  Yet do not so: but since I am near slain,
  Kill me outright with looks, and rid my
    pain.

### CXL.

Be wise as thou art cruel; do not press
My tongue-tied patience with too much
    disdain;
Lest sorrow lend me words, and words ex-
    press
The manner of my pity-wanting pain.
If I might teach thee wit, better it were,
Though not to love, yet, love, to tell me so;
(As testy sick men, when their deaths be
    near,
No news but health from their physicians
    know;)
For, if I should despair, I should grow mad,
And in my madness might speak ill of thee:
Now this ill-wresting world is grown so
    bad,
Mad slanderers by mad ears believed be.
  That I may not be so, nor thou belied,
  Bear thine eyes straight, though thy proud
    heart go wide.

### CXLI.

In faith I do not love thee with mine eyes,
For they in thee a thousand errors note;
But 'tis my heart that loves what they de-
    spise,
Who in despite of view is pleased to dote.

Nor are mine ears with thy tongue's tune
    delighted;
Nor tender feeling, to base touches prone,
Nor taste nor smell, desire to be invited
To any sensual feast with thee alone:
But my five wits, nor my five senses can
Dissuade one foolish heart from serving thee
Who leaves unsway'd the likeness of a man,
Thy proud heart's slave and vassal wretch
    to be:
  Only my plague thus far I count my gain.
  That she that makes me sin, awards me
    pain.

### CXLII.

Love is my sin, and thy dear virtue hate,
Hate of my sin, grounded on sinful loving:
O, but with mine compare thou thine own
    state,
And thou shalt find it merits not reproving;
Or, if it do, not from those lips of thine,
That have profan'd their scarlet ornaments,
And seal'd false bonds of love as oft as
    mine;
Robb'd others' beds' revenues of their rents.
Be it lawful I love thee, as thou lov'st those
Whom thine eyes woo as mine importune
    thee:
Root pity in thy heart, that, when it grows,
Thy pity may deserve to pitied be.
  If thou dost seek to have what thou dost
    hide,
  By self-example mayst thou be denied!

### CXLIII.

Lo, as a careful housewife runs to catch
One of her feather'd creatures broke away,
Sets down her babe, and makes all swift
    despatch
In pursuit of the thing she would have
    stay;
Whilst her neglected child holds her in
    chace,
Cries to catch her whose busy care is bent
To follow that which flies before her face,
Not prizing her poor infant's discontent;
So runn'st thou after that which flies from
    thee,
Whilst I thy babe chase thee afar behind;
But if thou catch thy hope, turn back to
    me,
And play the mother's part, kiss me, be
    kind:
  So will I pray that thou mayst have thy
    _Will_,
  If thou turn back, and my loud crying
    still.

### CXLIV.

Two loves I have of comfort and despair,
Which like two spirits do suggest me still;
The better angel is a man right fair,
The worser spirit a woman, colour'd ill.

To win me soon to hell, my female evil
Tempteth my better angel from my side,
And would corrupt my saint to be a devil,
Wooing his purity with her foul pride.
And whether that my angel be turn'd fiend,
Suspect I may, yet not directly tell;
But, being both from me, both to each
   friend,
I guess one angel in another's hell.
   Yet this shall I ne'er know, but live in
     doubt,
   Till my bad angel fire my good one out.

### CXLV.

Those lips that Love's own hand did make
Breath'd forth the sound that said, 'I hate,'
To me that languish'd for her sake:
But when she saw my woeful state,
Straight in her heart did mercy come,
Chiding that tongue, that ever sweet
Was used in giving gentle doom;
And taught it thus anew to greet:
'I hate' she alter'd with an end,
That follow'd it as gentle day
Doth follow night, who like a fiend
From heaven to hell is flown away.
   'I hate' from hate away she threw,
   And sav'd my life, saying—'not you.'

### CXLVI.

Poor soul, the centre of my sinful earth,
Fool'd by these rebel powers that thee ar-
   ray,
Why dost thou pine within, and suffer
   dearth,
Painting thy outward walls so costly gay?
Why so large cost, having so short a lease,
Dost thou upon thy fading mansion spend?
Shall worms, inheritors of this excess,
Eat up thy charge? Is this thy body's end?
Then, soul, live thou upon thy servant's
   loss,
And let that pine to aggravate thy store;
Buy terms divine in selling hours of dross;
Within be fed, without be rich no more:
   So shalt thou feed on Death, that feeds on
     men,        [ing then.
   And, Death once dead, there's no more dy-

### CXLVII.

My love is as a fever, longing still
For that which longer nurseth the disease;
Feeding on that which doth preserve the ill,
The uncertain sickly appetite to please.
My reason, the physician to my love,
Angry that his prescriptions are not kept,
Hath left me, and I desperate now approve
Desire is death, which physic did except.
Past cure I am, now reason is past care,
And frantic mad with evermore unrest;
My thoughts and my discourse as mad men's
   are,
At random from the truth vainly express'd;

For I have sworn thee fair, and thought
   thee bright,
Who art as black as hell, as dark as night.

### CXLVIII.

O me! what eyes hath love put in my head,
Which have no correspondence with true
   sight!
Or, if they have, where is my judgment
   fled,
That censures falsely what they see aright?
If that be fair whereon my false eyes dote,
What means the world to say it is not so?
If it be not, then love doth well denote
Love's eye is not so true as all men's: no,
How can it? O how can Love's eye be true,
That is so vex'd with watching and with
   tears?
No marvel then though I mistake my view;
The sun itself sees not till heaven clears.
   O cunning Love! with tears thou keep'st
     me blind,
   Lest eyes well-seeing thy foul faults should
     find.

### CXLIX.

Canst thou, O cruel! say I love thee not,
When I, against myself, with thee partake?
Do I not think on thee, when I forgot
Am of myself, all tyrant, for thy sake?
Who hateth thee that I do call my friend?
On whom frown'st thou that I do fawn
   upon?
Nay if thou low'rst on me, do I not spend
Revenge upon myself with present moan?
What merit do I in myself respect,
That is so proud thy service to despise,
When all my best doth worship thy defect,
Commanded by the motion of thine eyes?
   But, love, hate on, for now I know thy
     mind;
   Those that can see thou lov'st, and I am
     blind.

### CL.

O, from what power hast thou this power-
   ful might,
With insufficiency my heart to sway?
To make me give the lie to my true sight,
And swear that brightness doth not grace
   the day?
Whence hast thou this becoming of things
   ill,
That in the very refuse of thy deeds
There is such strength and warrantise of
   skill,
That in my mind, thy worst all best ex-
   ceeds?
Who taught thee how to make me love thee
   more,
The more I hear and see just cause of hate?
O, though I love what others do abhor,

With others thou shouldst not abhor my
    state;
  If thy unworthiness rais'd love in me,
  More worthy I to be belov'd of thee.

### CLI.

Love is too young to know what conscience
  is:
Yet who knows not, conscience is born of
  love?
Then, gentle cheater, urge not my amiss,
Lest guilty of my faults thy sweet self prove.
For thou betraying me, I do betray
My nobler part to my gross body's trea-
  son;
My soul doth tell my body that he may
Triumph in love; flesh stays no farther
  reason;
But, rising at thy name, doth point out thee
As his triumphant prize. Proud of this
  pride,
He is contented thy poor drudge to be,
To stand in thy affairs, fall by thy side,
  No want of conscience hold it that I call
  Her—love, for whose dear love I rise and
    fall.

### CLII.

In loving thee thou know'st I am forsworn,
But thou art twice forsworn, to me love
  swearing;
In act thy bed-vow broke, and new faith
  torn,
In vowing new hate after new love bearing.
But why of two oaths' breach do I accuse
  thee,
When I break twenty? I am perjur'd most;
For all my vows are oaths but to misuse
  thee,
And all my honest faith in thee is lost:
For I have sworn deep oaths of thy deep
  kindness,
Oaths of thy love, thy truth, thy constancy;
And, to enlighten thee, gave eyes to blind-
  ness,

Or made them swear against the thing they
  see;
  For I have sworn thee fair: more per-
    jur'd I,
  To swear, against the truth, so foul a lie!

### CLIII.

Cupid lay by his brand, and fell asleep:
A maid of Dian's this advantage found,
And his love-kindling fire did quickly steep
In a cold valley-fountain of that ground;
Which borrow'd from this holy fire of love
A dateless lively heat, still to endure,
And grew a seething bath, which yet men
  prove
Against strange maladies a sovereign cure.
But at my mistress' eye Love's brand new-
  fir'd,
The boy for trial needs would touch my
  breast;
I, sick withal, the help of bath desir'd,
And thither hied, a sad distemper'd guest,
  But found no cure: the bath for my help
    lies
  Where Cupid got new fire,—my mistress'
    eyes.

### CLIV.

The little love-god, lying once asleep
Laid by his side his heart-inflaming brand,
Whilst many nymphs that vow'd chaste life
  to keep
Came tripping by; but in her maiden hand
The fairest votary took up that fire
Which many legions of true hearts had
  warm'd:
And so the general of hot desire
Was sleeping by a virgin hand disarm'd.
This brand she quenched in a cool well by,
Which from Love's fire took heat perpetual,
Growing a bath and healthful remedy
For men diseas'd; but I, my mistress' thrall,
  Came there for cure, and this by that I
    prove,
  Love's fire heats water, water cools not
    love.

# A LOVER'S COMPLAINT

FROM off a hill whose concave womb re-
worded
A plaintful story from a sistering vale,
My spirits to attend this double voice ac-
corded,
And down I laid to list the sad-tun'd tale;
Ere long espied a fickle maid full pale,
Tearing of papers, breaking rings a-twain,
Storming her world with sorrow's wind and
rain.

Upon her head a platted hive of straw,
Which fortified her visage from the sun,
Whereon the thought might think sometime
it saw
The carcase of a beauty spent and done.
Time had not scythed all that youth begun,
Nor youth all quit; but, spite of Heaven's
fell rage,                          [age.
Some beauty peep'd through lattice of sear'd

Oft did she heave her napkin to her eyne,
Which on it had conceited characters,
Laund'ring the silken figures in the brine
That season'd woe had pelleted in tears,
And often reading what contents it bears;
As often shrieking undistinguish'd woe,
In clamours of all size, both high and low.

Sometimes her levell'd eyes their carriage
ride;
As they did battery to the spheres intend;
Sometimes diverted their poor balls are tied
To th' orbed earth: sometimes they do ex-
tend
Their view right on; anon their gazes lend
To every place at once, and nowhere fix'd,
The mind and sight distractedly commix'd.

Her hair, nor loose, nor tied in formal plat,
Proclaim'd in her a careless hand of pride;
For some, untuck'd, descended her sheav'd
hat,
Hanging her pale and pined cheek beside;
Some in her threaden fillet still did bide,
And, true to bondage, would not break from
thence,
Though slackly braided in loose negligence.

A thousand favours from a maund she drew
Of amber, crystal, and of bedded jet,
Which one by one she in a river threw,
Upon whose weeping margent she was set;
Like usury, applying wet to wet,
Or monarch's hands, that let not bounty fall
Where want cries 'some,' but where excess
begs all.

Of folded schedules had she many a one,
Which she perus'd, sigh'd, tore, and gave the
flood;
Crack'd many a ring of posied gold and
bone,
Bidding them find their sepulchres in mud;
Found yet mo letters sadly penn'd in blood,
With sleided silk feat and affectedly
Enswath'd, and seal'd to curious secresy.

These often bath'd she in her fluxive eyes,
And often kiss'd, and often gave to tear;
Cried, 'O false blood, thou register of lies,
What unapproved witness dost thou bear!
Ink would have seem'd more black and
damned here!'
This said, in top of rage the lines she rents,
Big discontent so breaking their contents.

A reverend man that graz'd his cattle nigh,
Sometime a blusterer, that the ruffle knew
Of court, of city, and had let go by
The swiftest hours, observed as they flew,
Towards this afflicted fancy fastly drew;
And, privileg'd by age, desires to know
In brief, the grounds and motives of her
woe.

So slides he down upon his grained bat,
And comely-distant sits he by her side;
When he again desires her, being sat,
Her grievance with his hearing to divide:
If that from him there may be aught ap-
plied
Which may her suffering ecstasy assuage,
'Tis promis'd in the charity of age.

'Father,' she says, 'though in me you behold
The injury of many a blasting hour,
Let it not tell your judgment I am old;
Not age, but sorrow, over me hath power:
I might as yet have been a spreading
flower,
Fresh to myself, if I had self-applied
Love to myself, and to no love beside.

'But woe is me! too early I attended
A youthful suit (it was to gain my grace)
Of one by nature's outwards so commended,
That maiden's eyes stuck over all his face:
Love lack'd a dwelling, and made him her
place;

And when in his fair parts she did abide,
She was new lodg'd, and newly deified.

'His browny locks did hang in crooked
curls;
And every light occasion of the wind
Upon his lips their silken parcels hurls.
What's sweet to do, to do will aptly find:
Each eye that saw him did enchant the
mind;
For on his visage was in little drawn,
What largeness thinks in paradise was sawn.

'Small show of man was yet upon his chin;
His phœnix down began but to appear,
Like unshorn velvet, on that termless skin,
Whose bare out-bragg'd the web it seem'd
to wear;
Yet show'd his visage by that cost more
dear;
And nice affections wavering stood in doubt
If best 'twere as it was, or best without.

'His qualities were beauteous as his form,
For maiden-tongued he was, and thereof
free;
Yet, if men mov'd him, was he such a storm
As oft 'twixt May and April is to see,
When winds breathe sweet, unruly though
they be.
His rudeness so with his authoriz'd youth
Did livery falseness in a pride of truth.

'Well could he ride, and often men would
say
That horse his mettle from his rider takes:
Proud of subjection, noble by the sway,
What rounds, what bounds, what course,
what stop he makes!
And controversy hence a question takes,
Whether the horse by him became his deed,
Or he his manage by the well-doing steed.

'But quickly on this side the verdict went;
His real habitude gave life and grace
To appertainings and to ornament,
Accomplish'd in himself, not in his case:
All aids, themselves made fairer by their
place,
Can for additions; yet their purpos'd trim
Piec'd not his grace, but were all grac'd by
him.

'So on the tip of his subduing tongue
All kind of arguments and question deep,
All replication prompt, and reason strong,
For his advantage still did wake and sleep:
To make the weeper laugh, the laugher
weep,
He had the dialect and different skill,
Catching all passions in his craft of will;

'That he did in the general bosom reign

Of young, of old; and sexes both enchanted,
To dwell with him in thoughts, or to re-
main
In personal duty, following where he
haunted:
Consents bewitch'd, ere he desire, have
granted;
And dialogued for him what he would say,
Ask'd their own wills, and made their wills
obey.

'Many there were that did his picture get,
To serve their eyes, and in it put their mind;
Like fools that in the imagination set
The goodly objects which abroad they find
Of lands and mansions, theirs in thought
assign'd;
And labouring in mo pleasures to bestow
them,
Than the true gouty landlord which doth
owe them:

'So many have, that never touch'd his hand,
Sweetly suppos'd them mistress of his heart.
My woeful self, that did in freedom stand,
And was my own fee-simple, (not in part,)
What with his heart in youth, and youth in
art,
Threw my affections in his charmed power,
Reserv'd the stalk, and gave him all my
flower.

'Yet did I not, as some my equals did,
Demand of him, nor being desired yielded;
Finding myself in honour so forbid,
With safest distance I mine honour shielded:
Experience for me many bulwarks builded
Of proofs new-bleeding, which remain'd the
foil
Of this false jewel, and his amorous spoil.

'But ah! who ever shunn'd by precedent
The destin'd ill she must herself assay?
Or forc'd examples, 'gainst her own content,
To put the by-pass'd perils in her way?
Counsel may stop a while what will not
stay;
For when we rage, advice is often seen
By blunting us to make our wits more
keen.

'Nor gives it satisfaction to our blood,
That we must curb it upon others' proof,
To be forbid the sweets that seem so good,
For fear of harms that preach in our be-
hoof.
O appetite, from judgment stand aloof!
The one a palate hath that needs will taste,
Though reason weep, and cry It is thy last.

'For further I could say, This man's untrue,
And knew the patterns of his foul beguiling;

Heard where his plants in others' orchards
grew,
Saw how deceits were gilded in his smiling;
Knew vows were ever brokers to defiling;
Thought characters and words, merely but
art,
And bastards of his foul adulterate heart.

'And long upon these terms I held my city,
Till thus he 'gan besiege me: Gentle maid,
Have of my suffering youth some feeling
pity
And be not of my holy vows afraid:
That's to you sworn, to none was ever said;
For feasts of love I have been call'd unto,
Till now did ne'er invite, nor never vow.

'All my offences that abroad you see
Are errors of the blood, none of the mind;
Love made them not; with acture they may
be,
Where neither party is nor true nor kind:
They sought their shame that so their shame
did find;
And so much less of shame in me remains,
By how much of me their reproach con-
tains.

'Among the many that mine eyes have seen,
Not one whose flame my heart so much as
warm'd,
On my affection put to the smallest teen,
Or any of my leisures ever charm'd:
Harm have I done to them, but ne'er was
harm'd;
Kept hearts in liveries, but mine own was
free,
And reign'd, commanding in his monarchy.

'Look here what tributes wounded fancies
sent me,
Of paled pearls, and rubies red as blood;
Figuring that they their passions likewise
lent me
Of grief and blushes, aptly understood
In bloodless white and the encrimson'd
mood;
Effects of terror and dear modesty,
Encamp'd in hearts, but fighting outwardly.

'And lo! behold the talents of their hair,
With twisted metal amorously impleach'd,
I have receiv'd from many a several fair,
(Their kind acceptance weepingly be-
seech'd,)
With the annexions of fair gems enrich'd,
And deep-brain'd sonnets that did amplify
Each stone's dear nature, worth, and
quality.

'The diamond, why 'twas beautiful and hard,
Whereto his invis'd properties did tend;
The deep-green emerald, in whose fresh re-
gard

Weak sights their sickly radiance do amend;
The heaven-hued sapphire and the opal blend
With objects manifold; each several stone,
With wit well blazon'd, smil'd or made some
moan.

'Lo! all these trophies of affections hot,
Of pensiv'd and subdued desires the tender,
Nature hath charg'd me that I hoard them
not,
But yield them up where I myself must ren-
der,
That is, to you, my origin and ender:
For these, of force, must your oblations be,
Since I their altar, you enpatron me.

'O then advance of yours that phraseless
hand,
Whose white bears down the airy scale of
praise;
Take all these similes to your own command,
Hallow'd with sighs that burning lungs did
raise;
What me your minister, for you obeys,
Works under you; and to your audit comes
Their distract parcels in combined sums.

'Lo! this device was sent me from a nun,
Or sister sanctified of holiest note;
Which late her noble suit in court did shun,
Whose rarest havings made the blossoms
dote;
For she was sought by spirits of richest coat,
But kept cold distance, and did thence re-
move,
To spend her living in eternal love.

'But O, my sweet, what labour is 't to leave
The thing we have not, mastering what not
strives?
Paling the place which did no form receive,
Playing patient sports in unconstrained
gyves:
She that her fame so to herself contrives,
The scars of battle 'scapeth by the flight,
And makes her absence valiant, not her
might.

'O pardon me, in that my boast is true;
The accident which brought me to her eye,
Upon the moment did her force subdue,
And now she would the caged cloister fly:
Religious love put out religion's eye:
Not to be tempted, would she be immur'd,
And now, to tempt all, liberty procur'd.

'How mighty then you are, O hear me tell!
The broken bosoms that to me belong
Have emptied all their fountains in my well,
And mine I pour your ocean all among:
I strong o'er them, and you o'er me being
strong,
Must for your victory us all congest,
As compound love to physic your cold breast.

'My parts had power to charm a sacred nun,
Who, disciplin'd and dieted in grace,
Believ'd her eyes when they to assail begun,
All vows and consecrations giving place.
O most potential love! vow, bond, nor space,
In thee hath neither sting, knot, nor confine,
For thou art all, and all things else are thine.

'When thou impressest, what are precepts
 worth
Of stale example? When thou wilt inflame,
How coldly those impediments stand forth,
Of wealth, of filial fear, law, kindred, fame!
Love's arms are peace, 'gainst rule, 'gainst
 sense, 'gainst shame,
And sweetens, in the suffering pangs it bears,
The aloes of all forces, shocks, and fears.

'Now all these hearts that do on mine de-
 pend,
Feeling it break, with bleeding groans they
 pine,
And supplicant their sighs to you extend,
To leave the battery that you make 'gainst
 mine,
Lending soft audience to my sweet design,
And credent soul to that strong-bonded oath,
That shall prefer and undertake my troth.

'This said, his watery eyes he did dismount,
Whose sights till then were levell'd on my
 face;
Each cheek a river running from a fount
With brinish current downward flow'd apace:
O how the channel to the stream gave grace!
Who, glaz'd with crystal, gate the glowing
 roses
That flame through water which their hue
 encloses.

'O father, what a hell of witchcraft lies
In the small orb of one particular tear!
But with the inundation of the eyes
What rocky heart to water will not wear?
What breast so cold that is not warmed
 here?
O cleft effect! cold modesty, hot wrath,

Both fire from hence and chill extincture
 hath!

'For lo! his passion, but an art of craft,
Even there resolv'd my reason into tears;
There my white stole of chastity I daff'd,
Shook off my sober guards, and civil fears;
Appear to him, as he to me appears,  [bore,
All melting; though our drops this difference
His poison'd me, and mine did him restore.

'In him a plenitude of subtle matter,
Applied to cautels, all strange forms receives,
Of burning blushes or of weeping water,
Or swooning paleness ; and he takes and
 leaves,
In either's aptness, as it best deceives,
To blush at speeches rank, to weep at woes,
Or to turn white and swoon at tragic shows;

'That not a heart which in his level came
Could scape the hail of his all-hurting aim,
Showing fair nature is both kind and tame;
And, veil'd in them, did win whom he would
 maim:
Against the thing he sought he would ex-
 claim;
When he most burn'd in heart-wish'd luxury,
He preach'd pure maid, and prais'd cold
 chastity.

'Thus merely with the garment of a Grace
The naked and concealed fiend he cover'd,
That the unexperienc'd gave the tempter
 place,
Which, like a cherubin, above them hover'd.
Who, young and simple, would not be so
 lover'd?
Ah me! I fell; and yet do question make
What I should do again for such a sake.

'O, that infected moisture of his eye,
O, that false fire which in his cheek so
 glow'd,
O, that forc'd thunder from his heart did fly,
O, that sad breath his spongy lungs bestow'd,
O, all that borrow'd motion, seeming ow'd,
Would yet again betray the fore-betray'd,
And new pervert a reconciled maid!'

# THE PASSIONATE PILGRIM

### I.

Did not the heavenly rhetoric of thine eye,
'Gainst whom the world could not hold argument,
Persuade my heart to this false perjury?
Vows for thee broke deserve not punishment.
A woman I forswore; but I will prove,
Thou being a goddess, I forswore not thee:
My vow was earthly, thou a heavenly love;
Thy grace being gain'd cures all disgrace in me.
My vow was breath, and breath a vapour is;
Then, thou fair sun, that on this earth doth shine,
Exhale this vapour vow; in thee it is:
If broken, then it is no fault of mine.
  If by me broke, what fool is not so wise
  To lose an oath, to win a paradise?

### II.

Sweet Cytherea, sitting by a brook
With young Adonis, lovely, fresh, and green,
Did court the lad with many a lovely look,
Such looks as none could look but beauty's queen.
She told him stories to delight his ear;
She show'd him favours to allure his eye;
To win his heart, she touch'd him here and there:
Touches so soft still conquer chastity.
But whether unripe years did want conceit,
Or he refus'd to take her figur'd proffer,
The tender nibbler would not touch the bait,
But smile and jest at every gentle offer:
  Then fell she on her back, fair queen, and toward;
  He rose and ran away; ah, fool too froward!

### III.

If love make me forsworn, how shall I swear to love?
O never faith could hold, if not to beauty vow'd:
Though to myself forsworn, to thee I'll constant prove;      [osiers bow'd.
Those thoughts, to me like oaks, to thee like
Study his bias leaves, and makes his book      [comprehend.
  thine eyes,
Where all those pleasures live that art can
If knowledge be the mark, to know thee shall suffice;      [commend;
Well learned is that tongue that well can thee
All ignorant that soul that sees thee without wonder;

Which is to me some praise, that I thy parts admire:
Thine eye Jove's lightning seems, thy voice his dreadful thunder,
Which (not to anger bent) is music and sweet fire.
Celestial as thou art, O do not love that wrong,
To sing the heavens' praise with such an earthly tongue.

### IV.

Scarce had the sun dried up the dewy morn,
And scarce the herd gone to the hedge for shade,
When Cytherea, all in love forlorn,
A longing tarriance for Adonis made,
Under an osier growing by a brook,
A brook where Adon used to cool his spleen.
Hot was the day; she hotter that did look
For his approach, that often there had been.
Anon he comes, and throws his mantle by,
And stood stark naked on the brook's green brim;
That sun look'd on the world with glorious eye,
Yet not so wistly as this queen on him:
  He, spying her, bounc'd in, whereas he stood;
  O Jove, quoth she, why was not I a flood?

### V.

Fair is my love, but not so fair as fickle;
Mild as a dove, but neither true nor trusty;
Brighter than glass, and yet, as glass is, brittle;
Softer than wax, and yet, as iron, rusty:
  A lily pale, with damask die to grace her,
  None fairer, nor none falser to deface her.

Her lips to mine how often hath she join'd,
Between each kiss her oaths of true love swearing!
How many tales to please me hath she coin'd,
Dreading my love, the loss thereof still fearing!
  Yet in the midst of all her pure protestings,
  Her faith, her oaths, her tears, and all were jestings.

She burn'd with love, as straw with fire flameth,
She burn'd out love, as soon as straw out burneth;      [framing,
She fram'd the love, and yet she foil'd the
She bade love last, and yet she fell a turning.

[1221]

Was this a lover, or a lecher whether?
Bad in the best, though excellent in neither.

### VI.

If music and sweet poetry agree,
As they must needs, the sister and the
brother,
Then must the love be great 'twixt thee and
me,
Because thou lov'st the one, and I the other.
Dowland to thee is dear, whose heavenly
touch
Upon the lute doth ravish human sense;
Spencer to me, whose deep conceit is such,
As, passing all conceit, needs no defence.
Thou lov'st to hear the sweet melodious
sound
That Phœbus' lute, the queen of music,
makes;
And I in deep delight am chiefly drown'd,
Whenas himself to singing he betakes.
  One god is god of both, as poets feign;
  One knight loves both, and both in thee
    remain.

### VII.

Fair was the morn, when the fair queen of
love,
* * * * * * *
Paler for sorrow than her milk-white dove,
For Adon's sake, a youngster proud and
wild;
Her stand she takes upon a steep-up hill:
Anon Adonis comes with horn and hounds;
She, silly queen, with more than love's good
will,
Forbade the boy he should not pass those
grounds;
Once, quoth she, did I see a fair sweet youth
Here in these brakes deep-wounded with a
boar,
Deep in the thigh, a spectacle of ruth!
See in my thigh, quoth she, here was the
sore:
  She showed hers; he saw more wounds
    than one,
  And blushing fled, and left her all alone.

### VIII.

Sweet rose, fair flower, untimely pluck'd,
soon vaded,
Pluck'd in the bud, and vaded in the spring!
Bright orient pearl, alack! too timely shaded!
Fair creature, kill'd too soon by death's sharp
sting!
  Like a green plum that hangs upon a tree,
  And falls, through wind, before the fall
    should be.

I weep for thee, and yet no cause I have;
For why? thou left'st me nothing in thy will.
And yet thou left'st me more than I did
crave;

For why? I craved nothing of thee still:
O yes, dear friend, I pardon crave of thee;
Thy discontent thou didst bequeath to me.

### IX.

Venus, with Adonis sitting by her,
Under a myrtle shade, began to woo him:
She told the youngling how god Mars did
try her,
And as he fell to her, she fell to him.
Even thus, quoth she, the warlike god em-
brac'd me;
And then she clipp'd Adonis in her arms:
Even thus, quoth she, the warlike god un-
lac'd me;
As if the boy should use like loving charms.
Even thus, quoth she, he seized on my lips,
And with her lips on his did act the seizure;
And as she fetched breath, away he skips,
And would not take her meaning nor her
pleasure.
  Ah! that I had my lady at this bay,
  To kiss and clip me till I run away!

### X.

Crabbed age and youth
  Cannot live together;
Youth is full of pleasance,
  Age is full of care:
Youth like summer morn,
  Age like winter weather;
Youth like summer brave,
  Age like winter bare.
Youth is full of sport,
Age's breath is short,
  Youth is nimble, age is lame:
Youth is hot and bold,
Age is weak and cold;
  Youth is wild, and age is tame.
Age, I do abhor thee,
Youth, I do adore thee;
  O, my love, my love is young!
Age, I do defy thee;
O sweet shepherd, hie thee,
  For methinks thou stay'st too long.

### XI.

Beauty is but a vain and doubtful good,
A shining gloss, that vadeth suddenly;
A flower that dies, when first it 'gins to bud;
A brittle glass, that's broken presently:
  A doubtful good, a gloss, a glass, a flower,
  Lost, vaded, broken, dead within an hour.

And as goods lost are seld or never found,
As vaded gloss no rubbing will refresh,
As flowers dead lie wither'd on the ground,
As broken glass no cement can redress,
  So beauty, blemish'd once, for ever's lost,
  In spite of physic, painting, pain, and cost.

### XII.

Good night, good rest. Ah! neither be my
share:

She bade good night, that kept my rest
   away;
And daff'd me to a cabin hang'd with care,
To descant on the doubts of my decay.
  Farewell, quoth she, and come again to-
    morrow;
  Farewell I could not, for I supp'd with
    sorrow.

Yet at my parting sweetly did she smile,
In scorn or friendship, nill I construe
   whether:
'T may be, she joy'd to jest at my exile,
'T may be, again to make me wander
   thither:
  *Wander,* a word for shadows like myself,
  As take the pain, but cannot pluck the pelf.

### XIII.

Lord, how mine eyes throw gazes to the east!
My heart doth charge the watch; the morning rise

Doth cite each moving sense from idle rest.
Not daring trust the office of mine eyes,
  While Philomela sits and sings, I sit and
    mark,
  And wish her lays were tuned like the lark;

For she doth welcome daylight with her ditty,
And drives away dark dismal-dreaming night:
The night so pack'd, I post unto my pretty;
Heart hath his hope, and eyes their wished
   sight;          [sorrow;
  Sorrow chang'd to solace, solace mix'd with
  For why? she sigh'd, and bade me come
    tomorrow.

Were I with her, the night would post too
   soon;
But now are minutes added to the hours;
To spite me now, each minute seems a moon;
Yet not for me, shine sun to succour flowers!
  Pack night, peep day; good day, of night
    now borrow;      [tomorrow.
  Short, night, to-night, and length thyself

# SONNETS TO SUNDRY NOTES OF MUSIC

It was a lording's daughter, the fairest one
    of three,     [be.
That liked of her master as well as well might
Till looking on an Englishman, the fairest
    that eye could see,
  Her fancy fell a turning.
Long was the combat doubtful, that love with
    love did fight,     [knight;
To leave the master loveless, or kill the gallant
To put in practice either, alas it was a spite
  Unto the silly damsel.     [pain,
But one must be refused, more mickle was the
That nothing could be used, to turn them
    both to gain,     [ed with disdain:
For of the two the trusty knight was wound-
  Alas, she could not help it!     [of the day,
Thus art, with arms contending, was victor
Which by a gift of learning did bear the maid
    away;
Then lullaby, the learned man hath got the
    lady gay;
  For now my song is ended.

## II.

On a day (alack the day!),
Love, whose month was ever May,
Spied a blossom passing fair,
Playing in the wanton air:
Through the velvet leaves the wind,
All unseen, 'gan passage find;
That the lover, sick to death,
Wish'd himself the heaven's breath.
Air, quoth he, thy cheeks may blow;
Air, would I might triumph so!
But, alas, my hand hath sworn
Ne'er to pluck thee from thy thorn:
Vow, alack, for youth unmeet,
Youth, so apt to pluck a sweet,
Thou for whom Jove would swear
Juno but an Ethiope were;
And deny himself for Jove,
Turning mortal for thy love.

## III.

My flocks feed not,
My ewes breed not,
My rams speed not,
  All is amiss:
Love is dying,
Faith's defying,
Heart's denying,
  Causer of this.
All my merry jigs are quite forgot,

All my lady's love is lost, God wot:
Where her faith was firmly fix'd in love,
There a nay is plac'd without remove.
One silly cross
Wrought all my loss;
  O frowning Fortune, cursed, fickle dame!
For now I see,
Inconstancy
  More in women than in men remain.

In black mourn I,
All fears scorn I,
Love hath forlorn me,
  Living in thrall:
Heart is bleeding,
All help needing,
(O cruel speeding!)
  Fraughted with gall.
My shepherd's pipe can sound no deal,
My wether's bell rings doleful knell;
My curtail dog, that wont to have play'd,
Plays not at all, but seems afraid;
With sighs so deep,
Procures to weep,
  In howling-wise, to see my doleful plight.
How sighs resound
Through heartless ground,     [fight!
  Like a thousand vanquish'd men in bloody

Clear wells spring not,
Sweet birds sing not,
Green plants bring not
  Forth; they die:
Herds stand weeping,
Flocks all sleeping,
Nymphs back peeping
  Fearfully.
All our pleasure known to us poor swains,
All our merry meetings on the plains,
All our evening sport from us is fled,
All our love is lost, for Love is dead.
Farewell, sweet lass,
Thy like ne'er was     [moan:
  For a sweet content, the cause of all my
Poor Coridon
Must live alone,
  Other help for him I see that there is none.

## IV.

Whenas thine eye hath chose the dame,
And stall'd the deer that thou shouldst
    strike,
Let reason rule things worthy blame,

As well as fancy, partial might:
Take counsel of some wiser head,
Neither too young, nor yet unwed.

And when thou com'st thy tale to tell,
Smooth not thy tongue with filed talk,
Lest she some subtle practice smell;
(A cripple soon can find a halt:)
But plainly say thou lov'st her well,
And set her person forth to sell.

What though her frowning brows be bent,
Her cloudy looks will calm ere night;
And then too late she will repent,
That thus dissembled her delight;
And twice desire, ere it be day,
That which with scorn she put away.

What though she strive to try her
strength,
And ban and brawl, and say thee nay,
Her feeble force will yield at length,
When craft hath taught her thus to say:
'Had women been so strong as men,
In faith you had not had it then.'

And to her will frame all thy ways;
Spare not to spend,—and chiefly there
Where thy desert may merit praise,
By ringing in thy lady's ear:
The strongest castle, tower, and town,
The golden bullet beats it down.

Serve always with assured trust,
And in thy suit be humble, true;
Unless thy lady prove unjust,
Press never thou to choose anew:
When time shall serve, be thou not
slack
To proffer, though she put thee back.

The wiles and guiles that women work,
Dissembled with an outward show,
The tricks and toys that in them lurk,
The cock that treads them shall not
know.
Have you not heard it said full oft,
A woman's nay doth stand for
nought?

Think women still to strive with men,
To sin, and never for to saint:
There is no heaven, by holy then,
When time with age shall them attaint.
Were kisses all the joys in bed,
One woman would another wed.

But soft; enough,—too much I fear,
Lest that my mistress hear my song;
She'll not stick to round me i' th' ear,
To teach my tongue to be so long:
Yet will she blush, here be it said,
To hear her secrets so bewray'd.

## V.

Live with me, and be my love,
And we will all the pleasures prove
That hills and valleys, dales and fields,
And all the craggy mountains yields.

There will we sit upon the rocks,
And see the shepherds feed their flocks.
By shallow rivers, by whose falls
Melodious birds sing madrigals.

There will I make thee a bed of roses,
With a thousand fragrant posies,
A cap of flowers and a kirtle
Embroider'd all with leaves of myrtle.

A belt of straw and ivy buds,
With coral clasps and amber studs;
And if these pleasures may thee move,
Then live with me, and be my love.

### LOVE'S ANSWER

If that the world and love were young,
And truth in every shepherd's tongue,
These pretty pleasures might me move
To live with thee and be thy love.

## VI.

As it fell upon a day,
In the merry month of May,
Sitting in a pleasant shade
With a grove of myrtles made,
Beasts did leap, and birds did sing,
Trees did grow, and plants did spring:
Everything did banish moan,
Save the nightingale alone:
She, poor bird, as all forlorn,
Lean'd her breast up-till a thorn,
And there sung the dolefull'st ditty
That to hear it was great pity:
Fie, fie, fie, now would she cry,
Teru, Teru, by and by:
That to hear her so complain,
Scarce I could from tears refrain;
For her griefs so lively shown,
Made me think upon mine own.
Ah thought I, thou mourn'st in vain;
None take pity on thy pain:
Senseless trees, they cannot hear thee;
Ruthless bears, they will not cheer thee.
King Pandion, he is dead;
All thy friends are lapp'd in lead;
All thy fellow-birds do sing,
Careless of thy sorrowing.
Even so, poor bird, like thee,
None alive will pity me.
Whilst as fickle fortune smil'd,
Thou and I were both beguil'd.
Every one that flatters thee
Is no friend in misery.
Words are easy like the wind;
Faithful friends are hard to find.

Every man will be thy friend,
Whilst thou hast wherewith to spend;
But if store of crowns be scant,
No man will supply thy want.
If that one be prodigal,
Bountiful they will him call:
And with such-like flattering
'Pity but he were a king.'
If he be addict to vice,
Quickly him they will entice;
If to women he be bent,
They have him at commandement;

But if fortune once do frown,
Then farewell his great renown:
They that fawn'd on him before,
Use his company no more.
He that is thy friend indeed,
He will help thee in thy need;
If thou sorrow, he will weep;
If thou wake, he cannot sleep:
Thus of every grief in heart
He with thee doth bear a part.
These are certain signs to know
Faithful friend from flattering foe.

# THE PHŒNIX AND THE TURTLE

LET the bird of loudest lay,
On the sole Arabian tree,
Herald sad and trumpet be,
To whose sound chaste wings obey.

But thou, shrieking harbinger,
Foul pre-currer of the fiend,
Augur of the fever's end,
To this troop come thou not near.

From this session interdict
Every fowl of tyrant wing,
Save the eagle, feather'd king:
Keep the obsequy so strict.

Let the priest in surplice white,
That defunctive music can,
Be the death-divining swan,
Lest the requiem lack his right.

And thou, treble-dated crow,
That thy sable-gender mak'st
With the breath thou giv'st and tak'st,
'Mongst our mourners shalt thou go.

Here the anthem doth commence:
Love and constancy is dead;
Phœnix and the turtle fled
In a mutual flame from hence.

So they lov'd, as love in twain
Had the essence but in one;
Two distincts, division none:
Number there in love was slain.

Hearts remote, yet not asunder;
Distance, and no space was seen
'Twixt the turtle and his queen;
But in them it were a wonder.

So between them love did shine,
That the turtle saw his right
Flaming in the phœnix' sight:
Either was the other's mine.

Property was thus appall'd,
That the self was not the same;
Single nature's double name
Neither two nor one was call'd.

Reason, in itself confounded,
Saw division grow together;
To themselves yet either-neither,
Simple were so well compounded

That it cried how true a twain
Seemeth this concordant one!
Love hath reason, reason none
If what parts can so remain.

Whereupon it made this threne
To the phœnix and the dove,
Co-supremes and stars of love;
As chorus to their tragic scene.

## THRENOS.

Beauty, truth, and rarity,
Grace in all simplicity,
Here enclos'd in cinders lie.

Death is now the phœnix' nest;
And the turtle's loyal breast
To eternity doth rest,

Leaving no posterity:—
'Twas not their infirmity,
It was married chastity.

Truth may seem, but cannot be:
Beauty brag, but 'tis not she;
Truth and beauty buried be.

To this urn let those repair
That are either true or fair;
For these dead birds sigh a prayer.